The Ultimate Yankees Companion

EDITED BY

Gary Gillette & Pete Palmer

Greg Spira, MANAGING EDITOR

Matthew Silverman & Cecilia Tan, ASSOCIATE EDITORS

Stuart Shea & Doug White, CONTRIBUTING WRITERS

Maple Street Press
Hingham, Massachusetts

© 2008 24–7 Baseball. All rights reserved.

No portion of this publication may be reproduced in any way, stored in any type of retrieval device, or transmitted by any method or media, electronic or mechanical, including, but not limited to, photocopy, recording, or scanning, without prior permission in writing from the publisher.

Maple Street Press LLC is in no way affiliated with the New York Yankees, Major League Baseball, or any minor league affiliates. The opinions expressed in this book are those of the authors and not necessarily those of Maple Street Press.

Cover design: Garrett Cullen

Front cover photos, left to right: Focus on Sport/Getty Images, Diamond Images/Getty Images, Mark Rucker/Transcendental Graphics, Getty Images

Interior design and layout: Jeremy C. Ellis (*wonkdevelopment.com*)

Gary Gillette and Pete Palmer. The Ultimate Yankees Companion
ISBN 978-1-934186-00-8

Library of Congress Control Number: 2007940079

All product names and brand names mentioned in this book are trademarks or service marks of their respective companies. Any omission or misuse (of any kind) of service marks or trademarks should not be regarded as intent to infringe upon the property of others. The publisher respects all marks used by companies, manufacturers, and developers as a means to distinguish their products.

Maple Street Press LLC
11 Leavitt Street
Hingham, MA 02043
www.maplestreetpress.com

Printed in Canada
07 7 6 5 4 3 2 First Edition

Dedication

This encyclopedia is dedicated to a titan, Joe Torre, and to a temple, Yankee Stadium. One has now departed from the Bronx, the other soon will be replaced. Both were integral to the Yankees' success and they will be fondly remembered by the citizens of the Yankees' empire.

Acknowledgments

Our sincere thanks for their help in various and sundry ways go to Alex Belth, Jennifer Boudinot, Sean Forman, Jay Jaffe, Richard Johnson, Nathaniel Marunas, Tom Ruane, Sean Lahman, Rod Nelson, and Glenn Stout. And a special tip of our baseball caps to Dennis Skiotis.

Our gratitude also to the publisher of Maple Street Press, Jim Walsh, who made our task easier in so many ways (despite his occasional tendency to bleed carmine). And to Jeremy C. Ellis, who cheerfully designed and composed the book in a New York minute.

Finally, a snappy salute to the spice of our lives—they who also serve by doing a helluva lot more than sitting and waiting. Vicki Gillette, Beth Statz Palmer, Debbie Silverman, Cecilia Garibay, and Anita White have gone above and beyond the call of duty on the home front yet again.

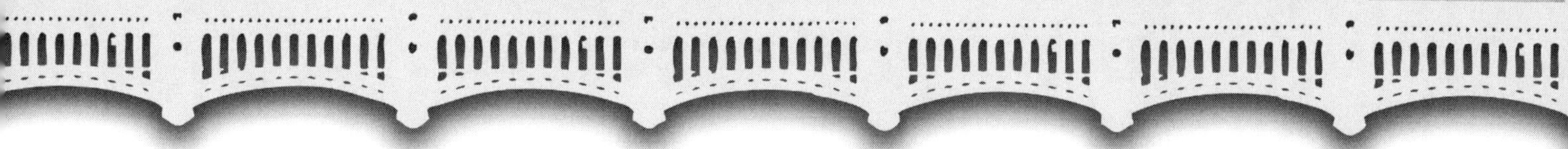

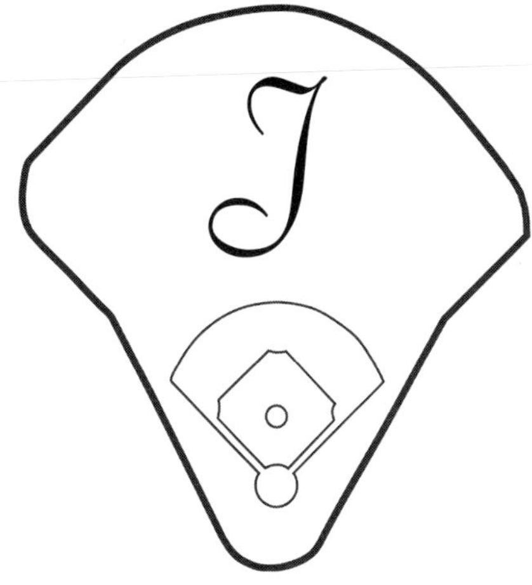

Introduction

Westward the course of empire takes its way;
The four first acts already past,
A fifth shall close the drama with the day.
—George Berkeley, eighteenth-century Anglican bishop,
On the Prospect of Planting Arts and Learing in America

Welcome to the new *Ultimate Yankees Companion.* We start with a quotation that seems—aside from its first word—appropos for the state of the Yankees' empire after the exit of Joe Torre at the end of the fifth great Yankees' dynasty. Berkeley's observation may not be well known to twenty-first century Americans, but its adaptation by a native philosopher certainly is: Henry David Thoreau's "Westward the star of empire takes its way."

While Larry Lucchino and the Yankees' bitter rivals in Boston have tried to paint the Yankees in recent years as an evil empire, that distinction is ultimately without merit. For better and for worse, the grandest empire that the National Pastime has ever seen started in New York in the 1920s with the acquisition of Babe Ruth and the construction of Yankee Stadium; it has survived and prospered for more than eight decades now. Untold millions of fans worldwide love their Yankees and, if their opponents hate them, what difference does it make? Furthermore, Lucchino's comments can't be taken seriously when the Red Sox are busy emulating the Yankees' methods as well as their success.

The Lineup

We have tried our best in this book to put together as complete a history of the Yankees as possible at an affordable price, packing as much information as we could into 400 pages. That's no easy task when your subject has won 26 world championships and appeared in 47 postseasons, playing in an astounding 65 series in October, ranging from the one-time divisional playoffs in the strike-marred 1981 season to 39 Fall Classics.

The *Ultimate Yankees Companion* was modeled after our successful *ESPN Baseball Encyclopedia*, published by Barnes & Noble Publishing/Sterling since 2004, and our *Ultimate Red Sox Companion*, published earlier in 2007.

Leading off is, naturally enough, a section covering the long and rich history of the Yankees, followed by rundowns of the 100 greatest games in franchise history, then by biographies of the 40 greatest Yankees.

At the heart of the order—as well as well as at the core of any baseball encyclopedia—are the player and manager registers. Our batter and pitcher registers include year-by-year statistics for every player that has appeared in a regular-season game in a New York uniform since the club's inaugural season in 1903. If a player spent a large portion of his career in pinstripes, we also show his year-by-year stats with other clubs.

Along with sections such as All-Stars, single-season and career leaders, and complete Yankees rosters for every season, the *Companion* features a 70-page, in-depth postseason section with composite box scores for each October series played by the Yankees, as well line scores and summaries for each postseason game.

Rounding out the *Ultimate Yankees Companion* lineup is a variety of special features that are either unique or are not included in other baseball encyclopedias:

- American League standings and league leaders for every year since 1903;
- Postseason batter and pitcher registers;
- World Series and postseason leaders;

- Our selections for the Yankees All-Time Teams;
- Box scores and summaries of every All-Star Game played at Yankee Stadium;
- A list of Yankees owners and general managers;
- A complete list of all Yankees radio and TV broadcasters for each season, including Spanish-language broadcasters;
- Yankees' minor league farm clubs;
- A selection of the best and worst trades and free agent signings in New York history;
- A comprehensive section on the many awards won and honors bestowed on Yankees players;
- A look at Great Performances by the heroes from the Bronx over the years;
- Home & Away breakdowns for the greatest Yankees' batters and pitchers, showing how playing at Yankee Stadium affected their statistics;
- A roster showing every coach who has pulled on a Yankees' uniform;
- A detailed look at the history of classic Yankee Stadium; and finally
- Year-by-year park effects.

Because an encyclopedia is first and foremost a historical record, this book was written and edited as much as possible from a neutral viewpoint. Readers looking for material about the Yankees will find plenty of that between these covers, but those looking for overt bias toward the home team will be disappointed.

Standards

One of the most precious aspects of the history of our National Pastime is its well-documented history and its treasure-trove of statistics. And a critical factor in keeping baseball fans fascinated with that long history is the incredibly high standards of accuracy in most of that historical documentation and in those uncounted millions of baseball statistics.

We go to enormous lengths to ensure that our scholarship is the best in the field, and we are constantly working on filling in gaps in our knowledge. We also benefit from being active participants in a generous community of like-minded historians and researchers—many of them members of the Society for American Baseball Research (www.SABR.org).

Accuracy

Despite the widespread belief that historical baseball statistics were graven in stone and handed down from the top of Mount Macmillan, the more prosaic truth is that all databases covering more than a century of history are going to have errors in them. We try to be realistic about this, recognizing the limits of our knowledge while not ignoring opportunities to vet and improve our data.

Every statistic and piece of information in this book is accurate to the best of our knowledge. We understand, however, that we are not infallible and that mistakes unfortunately creep into all reference works. If you find a mistake, including omissions of relevant information, please don't hesitate to contact us.

If you want to see a detailed discussion about how baseball statistics are researched and why they can change over time, please check out the introduction to our *ESPN Baseball Encyclopedia*.

Feedback

If you have any questions, comments, or suggestions—including criticism—for us, you can find a feedback form on the Maple Street Press web site at MapleStreetPress.com/feedback.

—Gary Gillette, October 2007

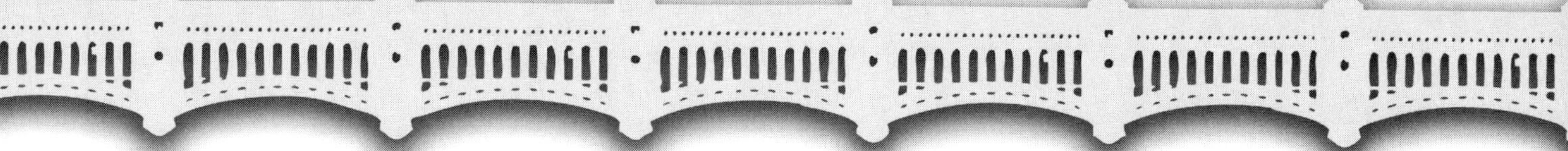

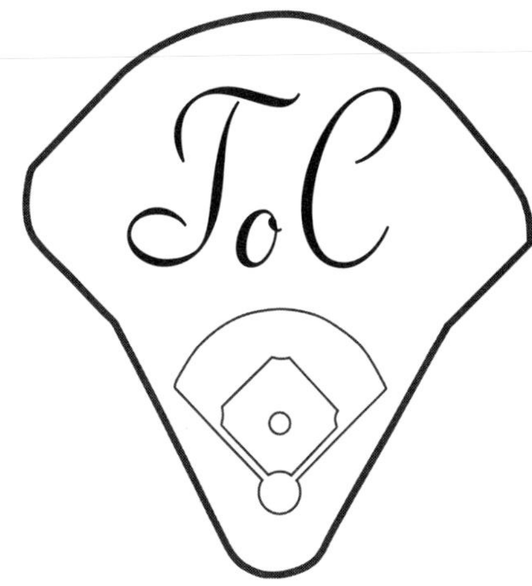

Table of Contents

The Ultimate Yankees Companion

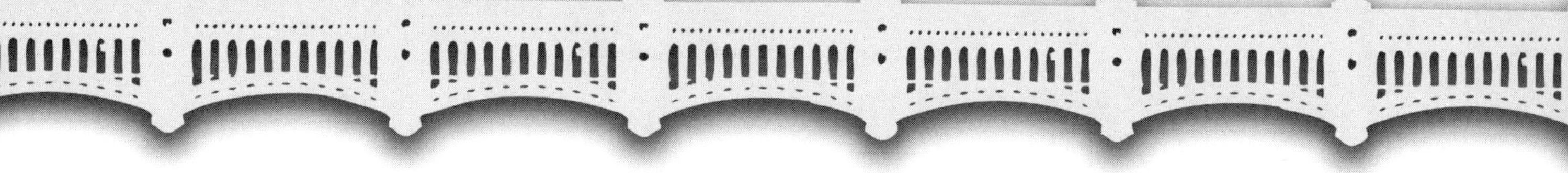

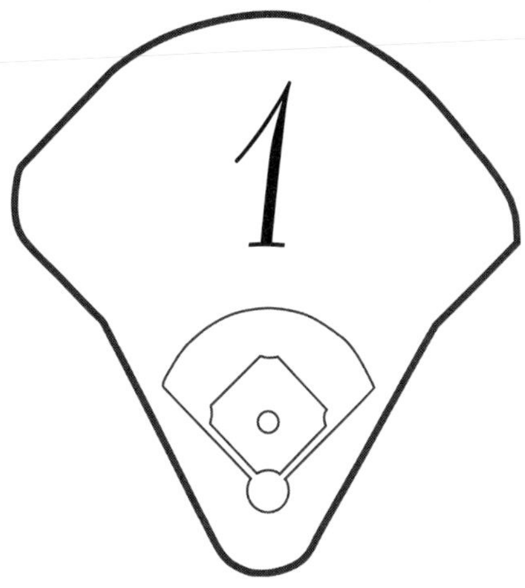

Glory Galore: The History of the Yankees

There is one consistent theme that runs throughout the history of the New York Yankees, post-1919 and the acquistion of George Herman Ruth: winning. Unquestionably the greatest franchise ever to field a team in a competitive major North American sports league—the National Hockey League is neither major any longer, nor was it truly competitive during most of the years when Montreal was winning its championships—the Yankees are as emblematic of American sports as U.S. Steel, General Motors, or Microsoft ever were emblematic of American business. Or as emblematic as Coca-Cola, McDonalds, and Hollywood are of American culture.

Boasting a total of 26 world championships and 39 American League pennants (see the table at the end of this essay), New York has dominated the National Pastime for most of the past century. Even when the Yankees are in a downturn, they remain the team to beat as well as the standard by which other baseball clubs are judged.

The history of the New York Yankees is that of a franchise placed in the commerce and media capital of the country in 1903, becoming the jewel in the newly formed American League's crown. League founder and president Ban Johnson knew that the AL could not be considered on a par with the 27-year-old National League unless the junior league fielded a winning team in New York City, the home of the NL Giants.

The Giants, who hadn't won an NL pennant in 14 years, had finished last in 1902 and next-to-last the year before. Under new manager John McGraw, however, the Giants immediately became the dominant team in the NL as well as the richest team in the game—that is, of course, until the rise of the Yankees in the 1920s. The Giants had one of the most durable arms in history in Joe "Iron Man" McGinnity. The Giants also had a 22-year-old, college-educated hurler named Christy Mathewson, whose precision, durability, and popularity would make him one of the most revered pitchers in the game's history.

On The Hilltop

The story of the Yankees actually begins in Maryland, with the longest-running manager in New York baseball history, John McGraw, guiding an original American League franchise called the Baltimore Orioles. (The 1901–02 AL Orioles shouldn't be confused with the National League Orioles who won three NL pennants in the 1890s, the last with McGraw serving as player-manager, before the NL contracted them after the 1899 season. Nor should they be confused with the minor league Orioles of the International League from 1903–1953. Nor today's American League Orioles of Frank & Brooks Robinson and Cal Ripken Jr. fame. The contemporary Birds started their existence in Milwaukee in 1901 and relocated from St. Louis in 1954.)

The original AL Orioles played in Baltimore in 1901 and 1902 before Johnson converted them into New York's franchise. After skullduggery between Giants owner Andrew Freedman (who secretly bought shares in the team), Reds owner John Brush (who would purchase the Giants from Freedman), and McGraw (who would be rewarded by Brush with the Giants' managerial job) left the Orioles with no manager and too few players to field a team, Johnson took control of the sabotaged club and stocked it with replacements from other AL teams. After the predictably bad finish, the destitute franchise was purchased for $18,000 by Frank Farrell and Bill Devery, questionable characters with influential ties to New York's Tammany Hall political machine. With Johnson's blessing, Farrell and Devery set up shop in Manhattan where they could take on McGraw and Freedman directly—and where they would be the instruments of Johnson's revenge against Brush, McGraw, and the NL. Freedman used his political influence to block them at every turn, including making it difficult for them to purchase land to build a ballpark. Ultimately, though, to stop salary escalation and the AL's continuing raids on NL talent, the National League was forced to call a truce. Part of the price for peace was that the NL's obstruction of the new AL franchise in Manhattan be stopped. Thus, the franchise's new home ended up on a stony hilltop some 13 blocks from the Giants' ballpark in northern Manhattan.

The New York Americans (in the parlance of the day) made their debut in Washington on April 22, 1903, losing their first game, 3–1. They went 3–4 on their season-opening road trip before playing their first home game on April 30, this time beating Washington, 6–2. Their hastily built American League Park had a plain wooden grandstand on an uneven and rocky field. Its situation on the highest spot in Manhattan led to its being dubbed "Hilltop Park," and the team was quickly nicknamed the "Hilltoppers" or "Highlanders" by sportswriters. Before the first year was out, headline writers had come to prefer the moniker "Yankees" because it was shorter, though the team itself wouldn't adopt the name officially until 1912.

Under pitcher-manager Clark Griffith, whom Johnson had pried from Chicago owner Charles Comiskey's grip under the argument it was "for the good of the league," the 1903 team won 22 games more than the hapless Orioles had the year before. Johnson also oversaw the addition of Wee Willie Keeler and other talent, as the determined powerbroker tried to insure that Devery and Farrell would field a winning team. The 1904 squad was 20 games better still, in large part due to Jack Chesbro. In 1903 Chesbro had defected from Pittsburgh and posted his third straight 20-win season. He was twice as good the next year, setting all-time AL marks with 51 starts, 48 complete games, and 41 wins—yet the steel-armed right-hander is best remembered for a game he lost! On the final day of the year, with New York in position to win the pennant with a doubleheader sweep of Boston at Hilltop Park, Chesbro's ninth-inning wild pitch brought in the go-ahead run. That was the closest New York got to a World Series for 17 years (even then, they weren't that close to a Fall Classic since the NL-champion Giants refused to play Boston, so there was no World Series in '04).

The Giants' attitude toward their AL neighbors varied from hatred to disregard as the NL club dominated its league and the city's sporting attention for the next decade and a half. Their AL rivals finished at .500 or better in just three of the next 11 years, although they were in first place in September 1906 before falling off and being passed by the White Sox.

As time passed and the American League was grudgingly accepted by the senior circuit, previously unthinkable things happened. A fire at the Polo Grounds in 1911 forced the Giants to play 28 games at Hilltop Park. They won 20 before returning to the refurbished Polo Grounds and winning the NL pennant. Then, when the Highlanders' lease ran out at Hilltop Park the next year, the Giants took their neighbors in as tenants for a handsome fee.

In the Land of Giants

The 1912 club donned pinstripes for the first time, and the '13 team officially became known as the Yankees, shedding their old nicknames with their old ballpark. The roster now included noteworthy names like Hal Chase, Roger Peckinpaugh, and Ray Caldwell as well as Cubs legend Frank Chance (who came on board to manage in New York at the end of his playing career), but they went 54–97 that year.

The Yankees would have only one (marginal) winning season from 1913–18, and the Giants outdrew them each of the first seven seasons they shared accommodations. The difference in their drawing power, however, was smaller than one might expect because of Federal League competition and the reduced attendance during World War I. It was during this fallow period that McGraw introduced brewing magnate and former U.S. Congressman Jacob Ruppert to wealthy engineer Captain Tillinghast L'Hommedieu Huston and suggested that they buy the Yankees. The pair purchased the fifth-place club for $460,000 in 1915.

In 1919, the Yankees' fortunes began to change. When the war ended and prosperity returned, fans flocked to the Polo Grounds regardless of who was playing. They didn't mind seeing a Yankees team that had Wally Pipp and Home Run Baker at the corners, plus 20-game winner Bob Shawkey on the mound. The 1919 Yankees under Miller Huggins finished closer to first than McGraw's Giants at 80–59 and drew over 600,000 fans, by far the highest in franchise history. That was also the year Ruppert instigated the first real threat to league president Ban Johnson by suing to overturn the suspension on Carl Mays after the star pitcher had jumped from Boston to New York. Mays had been on a downward slide with Boston, racking up a 5–11 record in the first half of the season there. Ruppert secured a restraining order to hold the suspension in abeyance, and the cantankerous Mays went 9–3 with a 1.65 ERA in the second half for the Yankees. The situation fractured the league's comity and eventually led to Johnson's ouster and a change in the way the game was run. Ironically, Ruppert had hired Huggins as manager at the suggestion of Johnson and against the wishes of Huston. That rift eventually led to the dissolution of the Ruppert-Huston partnership. Ruppert's interests always came first, and what really interested him was a winner.

Boston owner Harry Frazee sided with Ruppert regarding Mays since he wound up making $40,000 out of the sale. And when Frazee needed money to pay off the notes called in by the previous owner of the Red Sox, he had an attentive trading partner in New York. Babe Ruth had hit an unheard of 29 home runs—13 more than the previous AL record—in his first year as an everyday player with Boston in 1919. Ruth was difficult to control and wanted more money than Frazee was willing to offer. The Yankees worked out an agreement that paid Frazee $100,000, plus another $10,000 in interest. Furthermore, the Yankees helped Frazee secure a $300,000 loan, which meant that the Yankees essentially held a mortgage on Fenway Park. These cordial relations between the Yankees and Red Sox led to Waite Hoyt, Everett Scott, Joe Bush, Sad Sam Jones, Joe Dugan, George Pipgras, and Herb Pennock, among others, ultimately heading to New York. Frazee then let Ed Barrow leave to run the Yankees. Barrow stripped more parts from Boston, culminating in Red Ruffing going to New York in 1930 for Cedric Durst and $50,000.

While the fleecing of Boston continued to occur for years to come, the change in New York's fortune was instantaneous after Ruth's acquisition. "The Sultan of Swat" hit 54 home runs his first year with the Yankees in 1920. He also had compiled eye-popping totals of 150 walks, 158 runs, and 137 RBIs while batting .376, slugging .847, and posting a .532 on-base percentage. The Yankees drew 1.2 million fans, the first team to crack that mark in the history of the game. The Giants outdrew everyone else with an attendance of 929,000, but Ruth and the Yankees were the talk of the town as well as the country, even if the team barely missed winning the pennant by finishing in third place, three games in back of Cleveland. The Yankees were also involved in baseball's most tragic on-field incident when Mays, who threw hard from a submarine delivery, hit the Indians' star shortstop Ray Chapman in the head with a pitch at the Polo Grounds. The popular shortstop died the following day, the only major leaguer to ever die as a result of on-field incident.

The fans kept coming in 1921 as Ruth set a new major league home run record for the third straight year. His 59 homers helped the Yankees beat out the Indians for the pennant by 4½ games. And what team did they face in their first World Series? The New York Giants, of course. In the inaugural New York-New York World Series, the Yankees won three of the first five games before the Giants took the last three games against their tenants in the last best-of-nine World Series staged. The clubs met again the next year, this time in a best-of-seven contest, with the Giants winning four straight close games, plus one tie. It was the last one-stadium World Series in New York, as the Giants wanted their tenants to leave the Polo Grounds and the Yankees were ready to build their own house.

The House That Ruth—AND Ruppert—Built

The Giants had hoped the Yankees would wind up in Yonkers or some other locale far from Coogan's Bluff; instead, they landed just across the Harlem River in the Bronx. At new 70,000-seat Yankee Stadium, it seemed a day's walk from home plate to distant left-center field, 490 feet away. Right field, however, had a nicely reachable porch for Ruth and the legions of left-handed hitters who would follow him. Ruth cracked the inaugural home run at the $2.5 million ballpark, collecting 19 for the year and 41 all told. He would hit 259 of his 714 career home runs in the magnificent structure that was aptly dubbed "The House That Ruth Built." (Mickey Mantle later topped that figure with 266 home runs at the Stadium.)

The Giants and Yankees once more squared off in the World Series. Giants outfielder Casey Stengel won the opening game with an inside-the-park home run (the first postseason homer at Yankee Stadium), and the Giants took two of the first three. But the Yankees rallied, winning the last three. Ruth homered in Game 6 and the Yankees scored five runs in the eighth, capped by a single by Bob Meusel, to win their first world championship—at the Polo Grounds, of all places.

The Yankees returned to the World Series in 1926, facing the St. Louis Cardinals. Ruth became the first player to hit three homers in a Series game, but he was caught stealing to end Game 7. Tony Lazzeri gained lasting infamy that afternoon by fanning with the bases-loaded against ageless Grover Cleveland Alexander, who'd started and defeated the Yankees the previous day and came out of the bullpen while supposedly still feeling the effects of his celebrations. That bitter taste was quickly washed away the next year in a season of both success and excess.

The 1927 Yankees rolled up 110 wins—setting an AL record that would last until 1954—and led the major leagues in nearly every category, including a .307 team batting average and a 3.20 team ERA. Ruth, now making $70,000 per year, broke his own home run record by hitting No. 60 in the last series of the season. It was not a one-man show, though. Lou Gehrig, signed by the Yankees out of Columbia University, had taken over for a woozy Wally Pipp one afternoon in 1925 and never left the lineup. Gehrig's 175 RBIs in 1927 have since been surpassed by only two hitters (aside from Gehrig himself in 1931). Ruth, Gehrig (47) and Lazzeri (18) gave the '27 Yankees the top three in home runs; Earle Combs gave New York a trifecta among league leaders in runs and total bases. New York had the top four pitchers in winning percentage (Waite Hoyt, Urban Shocker, Wilcy Moore, and Herb Pennock) as well as the top three in ERA, with Moore's 2.28 the lowest. The Pirates were effectively beaten just watching the Yankees take batting practice before Game 1 of the World Series, as the Pirates held a lead for only two innings in the four games. The Cardinals were swept almost as easily in 1928, with the Yankees outscoring them 27–10 while exacting revenge against Alexander.

For 1929, Yankees players were given numbers on their jerseys so opposing fans could keep track of exactly who was circling the bases. New York wasn't the first team to try it, but they made it stick. Within a few years every team would be wearing them. The 1929 season ended an era for the team, as manager Huggins, who had skippered the club for 12 years, died in September of an infection then commonly called "blood poisoning."

In 1932, the Yankees erected a monument to Huggins in center field, the first of many that would be ultimately gathered into "Monument Park." That year, under the leadership of the next great-Yankees' skipper, "Marse Joe" McCarthy, the Yankees were back at their dominating best, cruising past the three-time pennant-winning Athletics by 13 games. The Yankees won 17 more games than their opponent in the World Series, the Cubs.

A running rhubarb between the teams culminated in Babe Ruth pointing—or not, depending on the source—at center field in the fifth inning of Game 3. Ruth then blasted a drive to center, leading to decades of speculation whether he called his shot. Ruth changed his story more than once, making it one of baseball's most debated mysteries as well as one of its most memorable home runs. It was Ruth's 15th and final World Series homer over 36 Series games with the Yankees while he led the club to a stunning 12-game winning streak in the World Series. (The Yankees' dynasty of the late 1990s would exceed that with 14.)

The Pride of the Yankees

Meanwhile, Gehrig couldn't buy a headline. He'd become the first American Leaguer to hit four homers in a game the same day McGraw retired in '32, then hit .529 in the sweep of Chicago—and yet "The Bambino" still overshadowed "The Iron Horse," as Ruth had done throughout his career. McCarthy was likewise overlooked as he became the first manager to claim a pennant in both leagues when his Yankees beat the club that had fired him for barely missing the 1930 pennant. But everything became a mere footnote compared to the controversy generated by the "called shot."

Ruth's heroics were certainly winding down, but the aging titan could still rise to the occasion, as in 1933 when he hit the first home run in the inaugural All-Star Game. At the very end of the season, he even earned his final win as a pitcher, beating the Red Sox 6–5 in a complete game in which he also hit a home run. The next year, Triple Crown winner Gehrig broke Ruth's record for grand slams, but Ruth reached 700 home runs and 2,000 walks, marks that stood unchallenged for decades. Following the 1934 season, Ruppert gave the 40-year-old Ruth his unconditional release, not demanding a cent in recompense from Ruth's next employer. Ruth wanted very much to manage, but was unable to dislodge McCarthy from the job in New York. The Boston Braves expressed interest in the dissatisfied slugger, offering him a job as part-time player and assistant that would supposedly lead to greater responsibility. It was a cynical ploy to take advantage of Ruth's desire to manage, as Boston just wanted his box office draw. Ruth did not last two full months with the Braves before retiring from baseball for good. He never got a chance to manage, the one thing that George Herman Ruth never achieved in the game.

The Yankees rolled on without Ruth. In 1936 Gehrig batted .354, smacked 49 home runs, drove in 152, and scored 167. With rookie Joe DiMaggio tying teammate Red Rolfe for the league lead with 15 triples, with Frankie Crosetti scoring 137, and with slugger Bill Dickey hitting .362 (the highest in AL history for a catcher), the Yankees finished only two shy of their 1931 record of 1,067 runs. Murderers Row blew through the Giants in 1936 and again in '37 for the franchise's sixth world championship, breaking the mark held by the Red Sox and Athletics. And the Yankees were just getting started.

McCarthy's powerhouse club faced the Cubs in '38 and came away with another sweep. This time, however, they did it with pitching and timely hitting. Slick-fielding rookie second baseman Joe Gordon batted .400 in the Series as Red Ruffing won twice. The following year, though, the Yankees were shaken by the unexpected frailty of the seemingly immoveable object in the middle of their lineup.

"Larrupin' Lou" Gehrig had been slowing down—or more accurately, playing more like an average major leaguer than the best first basemen in a league filled with great first sackers. After 2,130 consecutive games—823 games more than his former teammate Everett Scott's record—"The Iron Horse" took a seat and Babe Dahlgren replaced him at first base. The 36-year-old was diagnosed with ALS (amyotrophic lateral sclerosis), forever after known as "Lou Gehrig's Disease." On July 4, 1939, the Yankees retired his number, the first player so honored. Gehrig was inducted into the Hall of Fame that same year as well. He died in 1941, but his moving "luckiest man on the face of the earth" speech lives on, as does Gary Cooper's stirring portrayal in the revered film, *The Pride of the Yankees.*

Joltin' Joe, 56, and The War

Joe DiMaggio was a full-fledged star by 1939 and a leader of the Yankees. He homered in the first All-Star game at Yankee Stadium, won the first of two consecutive batting titles, and earned the first of his three American League MVP Awards. The Yankees' lineup was plenty potent, paced by Red Rolfe, the league leader in runs, hits, and doubles. Yet the Yankees hit just .206 in the World Series. No matter, New York's pitching, the only staff in the AL with an ERA under 4.00, held the Reds to .203 and 1.22 earned runs per game. The result was the Yankees' fourth straight world championship—a first—and the club's fifth sweep in seven World Series going back to 1927. After a year off (the 1940 Yankees finished two games out), they were back for more.

The '41 Yankees cruised to the pennant yet again, but there was plenty of excitement during the season. It began innocently enough with a single by DiMaggio against the White Sox on May 15, soon growing into a notable hitting streak. A couple of controversial scoring decisions kept the streak going, and DiMaggio extended it to 38 games with a double in his last at bat against Eldon Auker of the St. Louis Browns on June 26. He passed Ty Cobb (40) and George Sisler's AL mark (41) during a June 29 doubleheader against Washington. DiMaggio then tied Wee Willie Keeler's 1897 mark of 44 games on July 1 against the Red Sox. He broke the record the next day with a home run at Yankee Stadium against Boston's Dick Newsome.

With the tribute song by Les Brown playing across the country, "Joltin' Joe" hit in 11 more games until he faced the Indians on July 16. DiMaggio was twice robbed by third baseman Ken Keltner, while shortstop Lou Boudreau took a tough hop and turned it into a double play to end the game and the streak at 56 games. DiMaggio then proceeded to hit in another 16 straight games after that. The streak, the song, the 17-game lead over Boston in the standings, and the five DiMaggio RBIs that kept Ted Williams from winning the Triple Crown helped the Yankee Clipper claim the MVP despite "The Splendid Splinter's" famous .406 batting mark that season.

The '41 World Series featured the first Brooklyn-New York championship match-up. The first three games were one-run affairs; the Dodgers were poised for a 4–3 win to even the Series in Game 4. Brooklyn hurler Hugh Casey struck out Tommy Henrich to seemingly end the game, but catcher Mickey Owen couldn't handle the pitch. Given new life, the Yankees scored four runs with two outs as Charlie Keller doubled in the tying and lead runs and Joe Gordon knocked in two more for good measure. Tiny Bonham threw a four-hitter the next day, giving the Yankees their ninth world championship and fifth in six years.

In 1942, with world war heavy on everyone's minds, the Yankees looked to be on their way to another World Series triumph after taking the opening game. Yet the Cardinals, the last team to beat the Yankees in a World Series (eight world championships ago in 1926), surprised everyone by winning the next four games. When the teams met again in '43, the Yankees were missing DiMaggio and Phil Rizzuto (to military service) as well as Rolfe (whose age and health led him to take over as coach at Yale). With veteran Frankie Crosetti resuming a starting role at shortstop, rookie Billy Johnson at third, and with Dickey still hanging tough at age 36, the Yankees knocked off the Cardinals in five games. Spud Chandler, a 20–4 pitcher with a 1.64 ERA over the regular season, beat St. Louis twice, twirling a shutout in the clincher.

The Yankees threatened during the 1944 season, but their 83 wins were the fewest by the club since 1925. They had lost more players to the military and had to dig deeper to find replacements. Nick Etten was the only holdover on the infield, and the pitching staff clearly missed Chandler and Marius Russo. The '45 club won just 81 games despite a superior season from Snuffy Stirnweiss, who won the batting title at .309

while leading the diluted AL in on-base percentage, slugging, runs, hits, triples, stolen bases, and total bases. Etten was tops with 111 RBIs, 18 more than anyone else in the loop.

The Roaring Redhead

Since Colonel Ruppert's death in 1939, his estate had run the Yankees. Barrow—who had advised Frazee not to sell Ruth when he managed the Red Sox, then picked Boston clean after he joined the Yankees' front office—now cautioned against Larry MacPhail taking over the club. Even the powerful Barrow couldn't stop fate, however. MacPhail used $2.8 million from Del Webb and Dan Topping to purchase the franchise, its minor league clubs, and the ballpark. It was a good time to buy: in January 1945, the U.S. was still fighting the Battle of the Bulge and the war in the Pacific was far from resolved. Before World War II the team had been worth about $7 million, but Ruppert's family needed to pay estate taxes. Considering that Ruppert had paid $1.5 million in 1923 just to buy out Huston, the trio of Webb, Topping, and MacPhail got a steal. In 1946, the first full season after the war ended, the new owners presided over the first team in history to surpass two million in attendance, more than three times the gate the year before the team was sold.

There were other changes as well. McCarthy was fired 35 games into '46. Dickey was named player-manager, then Johnny Neun finished out the season. Bucky Harris—with 20 seasons as a big-league manager under his belt, including a world championship at age 27 as Washington's player-manager—came to New York. The Yankees played their first night game in the Bronx and got back to the business of winning.

New York cruised to the pennant and took on the Dodgers in the '47 October Classic. The Yankees won the first two at home before losing the next game at Ebbets Field by one run. Yankees starter Bill Bevens had a no-hitter with one out left in Game 4, but pinch hitter Cookie Lavagetto broke his heart by doubling home the tying and winning runs. Although the Yankees regained the Series lead, Brooklyn tied the Series again thanks to Al Gionfriddo's remarkable catch off of DiMaggio's bat to snuff a rally. Brooklyn had the early lead in Game 7, but Joe Page—the heir to "Fireman" Johnny Murphy in the Yankees' bullpen—allowed just one hit over the last five innings to hand New York another crown.

In the bedlam of the championship clubhouse, Larry MacPhail resigned. He acted impetuously, as he often did while changing managers four times in four years for the best team in the game, but Topping and Webb quickly accepted. While MacPhail later regretted the move, the Yankees' owners didn't. They quickly brought in George Weiss, who put together the most outstanding championship run of them all.

Casey at the Helm

Weiss replaced Harris with Casey Stengel after the 1949 season. The announcement was made amid howls from the press. They questioned Stengel's age (58), his lack of success in two previous big-league managerial stops, and his reputation as a clown. "The Old Perfessor" could be charming or comic, but he could also be callous and tough. In the end, Stengel got results with the Yankees.

That a heel injury kept DiMaggio out of the lineup until almost July was a blessing in disguise as it allowed the new skipper to put his stamp on the team without bucking for the veteran's approval. Stengel moved players to different positions to eke out the best chance to win each day—his later attempt to move DiMaggio to first base in 1950 caused a rift between them that never healed—and the manager wasn't afraid to go against "the book." Stengel showed what he could do in that first season when the undermanned New Yorkers stayed with the power-laden Red Sox till the final weekend. With the Yankees having to win both games of a two-game set with Boston at the Stadium in order to snatch the pennant from their rivals, New York did just that, as Vic Raschi won his 21st game on the final day to give the Yankees the pennant. Raschi won the clinching game of the World Series against Brooklyn, too.

Detroit, Boston, and Cleveland all contended for the 1950 AL pennant, but the Yankees held off all comers. They swept the "Whiz Kids" Phillies despite seeing just 30 total hits in the Series. New York racked up a 0.73 ERA behind Raschi, Allie Reynolds, Tom Ferrick (winning Game 3 in relief of Ed Lopat), and 21-year-old rookie Whitey Ford. "The Chairman of the Board" would set the mark for highest winning percentage in the 20th century at .690 (236–106), a record he might have improved on had he not missed the 1951 and 1952 seasons because of military duty. (Pedro Martinez now holds the career winning percentage record.)

The Yankees won the next two World Series without Ford, both against local competition. "The Shot Heard 'Round the World" echoed no further in 1951 after the Yankees rallied to defeat the Giants. Although the '51 Series would see DiMaggio's final appearance, "The Yankee Clipper" would continue to be a national icon with his marriage to Marilyn Monroe. With DiMaggio's retirement, it was time for a new Yankees superstar to enter the scene. Young Mickey Mantle was signed as a shortstop but, with Phil Rizzuto holding a lock on that position in the Bronx, the speedy kid from Oklahoma was converted to the outfield. In Game 2 of the '51 Series, Mantle tripped on an exposed drain cover, tearing up a knee and missing the rest of the games, but he'd had his first taste of October glory. Allie Reynolds, who earlier had become the first pitcher in history to throw two no-hitters in the same year, won Game 3. Lopat and Raschi won the last two.

Glory Days: Mickey, Yogi, Whitey, Billy, and Scooter

The next year Mantle took over in center field, playing there almost exclusively until late in his career. "The Mick" anchored a tremendous lineup that included catcher Yogi Berra, Rizzuto at shortstop, Gil McDougald at third base, and veterans Gene Woodling and Hank Bauer flanking him in the outfield. Closest to Mantle's elbow were Ford and Billy Martin, painting the town in pinstripes every time they had a chance. Yet every Yankees player seemed able to come through at crucial moments.

The trio of Reynolds, Lopat, and Raschi starred again in the '52 World Series, but it was no easy task to beat the Dodgers. The teams were even through four games before Johnny Sain, pitching six innings of relief for New York, allowed the tying and go-ahead runs in an eleven-inning contest at Yankee Stadium. Carl Furillo preserved the 6–5 win for Brooklyn with a leaping catch of a Johnny Mize drive in the 11th, robbing him of a homer. Reynolds turned into the hero. Over a four-day span, he managed a shutout, a save, and another win in relief to deliver the title. Mantle broke a tie in the sixth inning of Game 7 with the first of his record 18 career Series homers, and Martin saved the game in the seventh with the signature defensive play of his career. With two out and the bases loaded, all runners were in motion. Jackie Robinson hit a pop fly in the infield that would have meant at least two runs had it fallen in. Martin, sensing that both the catcher and first baseman had lost the ball, made a daring dash across the infield to snare the ball off his shoetops along the first base line.

The scrappy Martin's October heroics continued the following year. In the 1953 Fall Classic against Brooklyn—the third time that the two rivals had met in five years—Martin batted .500, hit as many homers and drove in one more run than Mantle. Martin's homer tied Game 2 in the eighth; Mantle's blast later in the inning gave the Yankees the lead. Ford seemed to have the Dodgers beaten in Game 6, but Reynolds couldn't hold the lead for one of the rare times in his October career, as the Dodgers tied it in the ninth with a two-run homer. Martin singled in the winning run in the bottom of the inning to make the Yankees the first—and only team—to win five straight world championships.

The hex the Yanks had on the Dodgers finally broke in 1955 when "Dem Bums" from Brooklyn finally outlasted the lordly Yankees. The next season, Mantle copped the Triple Crown as well as the first of his three AL MVPs, but '56 will always belong to Don Larsen. The erratic right-hander had been knocked out in the second inning of his first start in the Series in Brooklyn, but he followed that with the only perfect game in postseason history. Although Brooklyn evened the Series the next day, the Yankees won Game 7 as Johnny Kucks hurled a shutout and Berra, Moose Skowron, and Elston Howard all homered. Howard was a rookie catcher turned left fielder, playing in his only game of the Series because of a hunch by Stengel. What made Howard different wasn't his talent—he was yet another in a line of versatile Yankees who could hit—it was his color.

Howard was the first African-American to play for the Yankees, making them the 13th team to integrate (only the Phillies, Tigers, and Red Sox were slower to throw off the shackles of prejudice). The Dodgers, famously, and the Giants had broken the color barrier in the 1940s. The National League was much quicker to accept that black players were capable of playing in the majors, and ignoring that vast, untapped talent pool would play a role in the erosion of the Yankees in the next decade. For the time being, however, the Yankees' express rolled on, unimpeded.

A Night at the Copa

In May 1957, a soiree for Billy Martin's 29th birthday degenerated into an incident that ended his days with the Yankees. Six players were involved in a fight at New York's famous Copacabana club. While the six Yankees present were all fined, Martin received a one-way ticket to Kansas City a few weeks later. Martin had played for Stengel in the Pacific Coast League, he would run through a wall for his manager or his team, and he loved being one of the Yankees. But Stengel could neither control Martin after hours nor keep him in pinstripes any longer.

Although Hank Bauer was later suspected of throwing the punch that broke a deli owner's nose at the New York nightspot (no witness would finger a Yankee), Bauer remained with the club through 1959. Bauer was a war hero who came through at key spots in big games. He holds a still-standing record streak of hitting in 17 straight World Series games, and the veteran famously straightened out newcomers who might not understand that everyone in the clubhouse counted on annual World Series checks.

The checks kept coming, but the Yankees only received the loser's share in 1957 when the upstart Milwaukee Braves beat New York behind sinkerballer/spitballer and former Yankees minor leaguer Lew Burdette. In 1958 the Yankees suddenly found themselves as the only team left in New York after both the Dodgers and Giants abandoned the Big Apple for the Golden West. New York saw a rematch with the Braves again in October, and Stengel was in danger of losing his job when the Yankees fell behind Milwaukee three games to one. In vintage Yankees fashion, however, a new hero stepped to the fore to save the day for the Bombers. "Bullet Bob" Turley pitched a shutout in Game 5, saved Game 6 by getting the final out in the bottom of the 10th, and then won Game 7 with 6⅔ innings of shutout relief, bailing Larsen out of a jam. The Yankees broke a 2–2 tie in the eighth inning with a two-out rally as Howard singled in the go-ahead run and Skowron clubbed a three-run homer off Burdette. Bauer, playing in his ninth and final Fall Classic, hit four homers and drove in eight. Stengel was now 7–2 in the World Series since 1948, so he was back in the Yankees' dugout in '59.

Stengel always had plenty to work with. GM Weiss would add seemingly worn-out parts like Enos Slaughter and Johnny Mize, and Stengel managed to get a few more miles out of them. By the end of the decade, Weiss had secured an unexpected source of talent: the Kansas City Athletics. Kansas City had theoretically ceased being a Yankees farm team after the Philadelphia Athletics had relocated there in 1955, but a series of strange and corrupt dealings enabled New York to prop up its dynasty for several more years. K.C. owner Arnold Johnson (a former owner of Yankee Stadium) and Weiss established a shuttle between New York and Kansas City that sent Roger Maris, Bobby Shantz, Hector Lopez, Clete Boyer, Art Ditmar, and Ralph Terry to the Yankees over the course of five years. In return the A's got a few young players, plenty of old ones, and cast-offs like Billy Martin: the fans quickly lost enthusiasm in Kansas City as the losses piled up.

After placing third in 1959, the Yankees overtook the Orioles down the stretch in 1960. MVP Maris and his runner-up Mantle dominated most offensive categories. The Yankees also boasted the best pitching staff and the top bullpen in the majors. They dominated the Pirates in the World Series, too. New York hit 88 points higher than Pittsburgh, posted a 3.54 ERA to Pittsburgh's 7.11, and outscored the Bucs by a whopping 55–27. The only problem was that in between thrashings of 16–3, 10–0, and 12–0, the underdogs from the Steel City beat the Yankees in three close contests. In the final two innings of Game 7, the Yankees took a three-run lead, saw the Pirates rally to go ahead by two, then rallied to tie the game with two runs in the top of the ninth. In the bottom of the ninth, second baseman Bill Mazeroski homered over the left field wall at Forbes Field to send Pittsburgh into a frenzy... and usher out the door the men whose decisions had made the Yankees the game's most formidable franchise.

No. 61, 1961, and Beyond

After the shock of their defeat in the 1960 World Series, the Yankees retired Stengel and Weiss against their wishes. Stengel had guided the club to 10 World Series appearances in 12 years and captured as many world championships (seven) as Joe McCarthy had in 16 years. Weiss had been the architect of the dominant Yankees' minor league system in the 1930s, integrating it seamlessly at the major league level when he was promoted. The pair would have far less success getting the expansion New York Mets off the ground after the NL expansion club sprouted up in Queens in place of the long-gone Giants and Dodgers. Repeating their success at Yankee Stadium would prove difficult, especially when the old parts started to wear down.

Roger Maris wasn't a New York-kind of guy. He admittedly liked Kansas City better, and New York was Mickey Mantle's town. Yet Maris, Mantle, and the Yankees combined for an unforgettable 1961. The schedule was expanded to 162 games for the first time as the first expansion teams in league history—the Washington Senators and the Los Angeles Angels—joined the AL. The Minnesota Twins, ne the Washington Senators, started play. In fact, the new Twins shut out the Yankees in the first game of the year. That was an anomaly, to say the least.

The Yankees, under rookie manager Ralph Houk, mashed 240 home runs. Six players hit at least 20 homers. Maris and Mantle, the "M&M boys," were off the charts. While there would be much ado later about the length of the schedule when Maris was chasing Babe Ruth's 1927 record of 60, the lefty swinger didn't hit his first homer until game no. 11. He quickly made up for lost time, though, and had blasted 27 by June 22. Mantle actually led the chase on July 25, but Maris hit four home runs in a doubleheader and took the lead, 40–38. They stayed neck-and-neck till August 16, when Maris was ahead, 48–45. Mantle hit his 54th and final home run on September 23 before illness—worsened by a quack doctor recommended by announcer Mel Allen—ended his pursuit. By then, his teammate was looking for no. 60, which he hit on September 26 against Baltimore's Jack Fisher. He broke the hallowed mark on the last day of the season with a fourth-inning blast off of Boston's Tracy Stallard.

The Yankees, meanwhile, had run up 109 wins, one victory shy of the record set by Ruth & Company in the year that the Babe had hit 60. Ford, no longer subject to Stengel's whims and hunches that often had him going five or more days between starts, went 25–4 while pitching in regular rotation. The star southpaw also beat the Reds twice in the World Series even though Mantle and Maris combined to hit .120 with one home run in the five-game triumph. Their less-famous teammates, however, picked the M&M boys up by hitting .278 and scoring 27 runs as New York limited Cincinnati to a .206 BA and 13 runs.

The Yankees didn't set any records in 1962, and they even finished 10 home runs behind Detroit with 199. Mantle, who had finished second to Maris the previous two years in the MVP race, won it for the third time. Ford finally allowed a run in October, ending a streak of 32 consecutive scoreless Series innings that had broken another of Ruth's records, this one set as the Red Sox ace in the 1910s. Ford won his record 10th, and final, World Series game. It again came down to Ralph Terry, who'd given up the devastating walk-off home run to Mazeroski in 1960. This time Willie McCovey hit a bullet with the winning runs in scoring position and two outs in Game 7. Bobby Richardson, who'd been the first World Series MVP to come from a losing team in 1960, caught the screaming line drive and the Yankees were again world champs. Terry earned the MVP for the '62 Series. No one foresaw it at the time, of course, but after winning 20 World Series in the previous 40 seasons, the Yankees would go without another championship until 1977.

The pennants continued for a while, though. The Yankees won 104 games in '63 and faced the well-armed Dodgers of Sandy Koufax and Don Drysdale, now of Los Angeles. The historic franchise that had lost a heartbreaking six of seven times to the Yankees when it occupied Brooklyn marched through New York in four games, stifling the Bombers on four measly runs.

Berra, a three-time MVP, converted from player to manager for the 1964 season, with Houk moving up to general manager. Berra had been "one of the guys," known for his malapropisms as much as for his major contributions to a record 10 world championships and 14 pennants as a player. His authority was challenged during the so-called "harmonica incident" with Phil Linz aboard the team bus after a sweep in Chicago had left them 4½ games behind the White Sox on August 20 (the deficit reached 5½ games on August 22). Rookie manager Berra made a stand, the team responded, and the Yankees went on to beat the White Sox for the pennant, pushed along by rookie sinkerball specialist Mel Stottlemyre and the last outstanding years from Jim Bouton, 25, and Whitey Ford, 35.

The Cardinals, who endured an even more furious finish to take the pennant, battled the Yankees tooth and nail in the fifth World Series meeting between the two storied franchises. Mantle homered in the bottom of the ninth to win Game 3 for Bouton. The Brothers Boyer—Ken (Cardinals) and Clete (Yankees)—each hit grand slams during the Series, and Mantle and Maris homered in Game 6 as New York evened the Series. St. Louis held on to win the next day, though. Again, a pennant just wasn't enough. Berra was fired after two decades with the Yankees; in a surprising move, Johnny Keane, who had managed the Cardinals to their victory over New York, took his place.

The End of the Greatest Dynasty in Baseball History

In 1965 the Yankees did not win a pennant for the first time since 1959. The players who had been groomed under Stengel and consummate career Yankees like Houk and Berra did not respond to Keane's NL strategies or attitudes. Worse, their talent was thin with too many old players on the roster. The next year marked two years without a pennant, something that hadn't happened since 1946, as the Yankees finished 10th for the only time in their history and saw their lowest attendance since World War II. CBS, which had bought the team for $11.2 million in 1964, was left holding the bag as the franchise's deteriorating farm system, slowness to sign African-American and Latino players, and the improvement of the AL competition caught up with the Yankees. The amateur player draft, initiated in 1965, helped level the field a little more. Now the worst teams would get first crack at the best players and the Yankees' monetary advantage would be partially nullified.

Horace Clarke, who accumulated many at bats, singles, and outs as a career .256 hitter, would be the poster boy for this era, the leanest since the 1910s. However, compared to cities that had gone multiple decades without any success, New York didn't receive much sympathy from around the game. Mantle was about the only big draw the team had left, and he retired after the 1968 season with 536 home runs and after passing Jimmie Foxx for second on the all-time home run list. The Mick's powerful swing that resulted in so many home runs had also left him the all-time strikeout leader at 1,710. His 1,733 walks, on the other hand, were better than anyone at that time except Ruth and Williams. Mantle's four straight sub-.300 seasons at the end of his career, however, left his overall average at .298 in the record books.

The amateur draft did not garner many first-rate first-round picks by the Yankees, but one pick that worked out just fine was an Ohio catcher out of Kent State: Thurman Munson. Munson was drafted in 1968, debuted at Yankee Stadium a year later, and earned the AL Rookie of the Year award in 1970. Other talented players soon surrounded him.

Roy White, a graceful left fielder who was adept at reaching base, scored 109 runs in '70, the most by a Yankees player since the M&M Boys crossed home plate 132 times apiece as they chased the Babe. Bobby Murcer provided power in center field, hitting 20 or more homers for five straight years, and the '70 Yankees climbed back to the 90-win mark for the first time in six years. By then, however, the Orioles had emerged as the power in the newly formed American League East division. Under Hall of Fame manager Earl Weaver, Baltimore won five of the first six East division titles, usually by runaway margins.

New Owner, New Rules, New Home

The American League's stilted offense (despite the lowered mound), weak attendance, and overall drabness—with the exception of Charlie Finley's colorful A's—led to the creation of the designated hitter in 1973. Yankees sophomore Ron Blomberg was the first DH written onto a lineup card in history (although Jim Ray Hart actually served almost twice as many times in that role as Blomberg in the inaugural year of the 10-man lineup).

Blomberg wasn't the only new face around the Stadium, though. Ohio shipbuilder George Steinbrenner led a group of investors in purchasing the team for $10 million from CBS. A driven man with a football mentality, Steinbrenner soon gained a reputation among both players and fans as a blowhard who didn't understand baseball. "The Boss" was an improvement, though, over the muddled corporate ownership that had been indifferent to the Yankees' success, or lack thereof.

As if a major rule change and a change of ownership were not enough, it was now time for a new home as well. Fifty years earlier the Yankees had been the last American League team to build its own concrete and steel ballpark; now they wanted to refurbish the Stadium completely. It had undergone a $600,000 facelift in 1946 but, by 1972, the Yankees were threatening to move to New Jersey if the city did not renovate the landmark in the South Bronx. The city originally budgeted $24 million, but it wound up costing about $100 million. At the ceremony for the final game at the original Yankee Stadium on September 28, 1973, Mrs. Babe Ruth was given home plate and Mrs. Lou Gehrig was handed first base. The foul poles and the lights went to Osaka, Japan. The Yankees themselves took up temporary residence in Queens.

For the next two years, the team occupied Shea Stadium, which became quite crowded. With the Yankees and NFL Giants both turned out of their home, they joined the Mets and NFL Jets for 173 games at the superstadium in Flushing in 1975. For all the complaining about the experience afterward, the Yankees actually had the best record of anyone at Shea that year and compiled a two-year record of 90–69 in their temporary quarters. Much of that time, they managed without Steinbrenner, who'd made an illegal campaign contribution to President Richard Nixon and was suspended by Commissioner Bowie Kuhn. The Yankees also made due without their first choice as manager. New York tried to hire Dick Williams, who had resigned after winning consecutive World Series with the A's, but he was still under contract to Oakland. The Yankees hired Bill Virdon instead, and Virdon had the honor of being the first manager fired in the Steinbrenner regime, with Billy Martin taking his place in August 1975.

The Yankees put together a solid team during their time at Shea, signing the first modern free agent in Catfish Hunter and making wise deals for Bobby Bonds, Oscar Gamble, non-brothers Rudy and Carlos May, and engineered an all-out heist from Pittsburgh that netted them Willie Randolph, Dock Ellis, and Ken Brett for Doc Medich. GM Gabe Paul flipped Bonds after a 30–30 year at Shea to the Angels for pitcher Ed Figueroa and the speedy Mickey Rivers. And this came on top of shrewd moves earlier in the decade to pick up young corner infielders Chris Chambliss and Graig Nettles, outfielder Lou Piniella, catcher Rick Dempsey, and relievers Dick Tidrow and Sparky Lyle. The only noticeable name dispatched in any of those deals was Fritz Peterson, whose claim to fame rests on his swapping of wives, kids, and even pets with teammate Mike Kekich during spring training in 1973. With all these new faces, the Yankees headed back to their newly refurbished home.

The Bronx Zoo

Yankee Stadium *was* different. The signature copper frieze that ringed the upper tier of the stadium was gone, echoed only by a facsimile along the outfield scoreboard, which blocked the view of the field from the No. 4 subway line platform. The seating capacity had been reduced by some 11,000 seats. The three original monuments in left field (to Huggins, Gehrig, and Ruth were in a new section in left center that was now out of play, called "Monument Park." The capacious area known as "Death Valley" no longer existed, as the left-center fence had been moved in about 70 feet (with 30 more feet to be chopped off in the future). Nevertheless, the Yankees had returned to the Bronx, and so did their fans.

The Yankees drew two million fans for the first time since 1950. You could tell it was going be their year when an umpire wiped out a game-winning grand slam by Don Money in Milwaukee because time had been called. The do-over turned into a fly ball, and the Yankees notched the first of their 97 wins. GM Gabe Paul made a bold move at the trading deadline, sending Rick Dempsey, Tippy Martinez, Rudy May, and Scott McGregor to the Orioles in a 10-player swap that brought the Yankees two-fifths of their rotation—Ken Holtzman and Doyle Alexander—plus reliever Grant Jackson. Their staff allowed the fewest hits and runs and the team cruised to the postseason for the first time in a dozen years.

The Yankees and Royals waited a week to play the first ALCS for either team, and it was worth the wait. The teams split the first four games, with the deciding fifth game just as hotly contested. New York had a seemingly safe 6–3 lead in the eighth, but Grant Jackson allowed a three-run homer to batting champion George Brett to tie the game. With the game knotted in the bottom of the ninth, Chambliss hit a high drive that just cleared the fence in right-center. So many fans poured onto the field that Chambliss couldn't even touch all the bases in the mob scene. The exhilarating win left the Yankees drained; they were stunned in the World Series by the "Big Red Machine." Cincinnati swept the Series in four, though Munson, who would be voted AL MVP, batted .529 in the sweep.

Steinbrenner had helped usher in the free agency era by signing Hunter when the A's didn't live up to the terms of his contract in 1974. Two years later "The Boss" was at the front of the line at the new buffet table known as the free agent draft. The Yankees signed two NL stars, Don Gullet and Jimmy Wynn, but the coup of that first crop was right fielder Reggie Jackson. The slugger had been at the heart of five straight division champions in Oakland, earning MVP awards in 1973 for both the regular season and the World Series. A's owner Charlie O. Finley traded him to Baltimore in 1976 to get something for him before he left; he likewise tried to sell Vida Blue to the Yankees, but Commissioner Kuhn vetoed the deal. The outspoken Jackson immediately rubbed teammates, especially Munson, the wrong way by saying in a national magazine that he was the "straw that stirs the drink." But he did give the lineup a new dimension as the latest in a long line of superstar outfielders at Yankee Stadium. The contentious and chaotic spirit of the '77 team earned them the nickname "the Bronx Zoo." Jackson feuded with Billy Martin, nearly getting into a fight in the dugout at Fenway Park on national television. The egotistic star and the tormented manager forged an uneasy peace, and Jackson finished with 32 homers and 110 RBIs, 49 coming in the final 50 games down the stretch. Nettles hit a career-high 37 home runs and won a Gold Glove. The pitching was the difference, however, in a tight race with the powerful Red Sox's bats and the steady all-around Orioles. Lyle became the first AL reliever to win the Cy Young Award, saving 26 and earning 13 wins, more than starters Hunter and Holtzman combined. Southpaw Ron Guidry won 16 after fighting his way into the rotation (the Yankees initially considered him too slight of build to make it as a starting pitcher).

To make up for their embarrassing sweep in the previous year's World Series, the Yankees would first need to survive a rematch with K.C. Going into the final two games, the Royals needed just one in Kansas City to take the pennant. Lyle won both, coming in to Game 4 in the fourth inning and finishing the 6–4 win. In the deciding game, Martin benched Jackson, who later delivered a key pinch-hit RBI single. Going into the ninth down by a run, Mickey Rivers tied the game and Willie Randolph gave the Yankees the lead. The Royals failed to solve Lyle again, and the Yankees won another tough pennant.

The Bronx Is Burning

Their opponent in the Series would be Tommy Lasorda's Dodgers. Thanks to strong pitching by Guidry and Mike Torrez, New York took three of the first four, but the Dodgers won Game 5 to send the Series back to New York. On a perfect night on a perfect stage, Reggie homered three times, tying Ruth's October feat and forever becoming known as "Mr. October." The three home runs came off three different pitchers, and on three consecutive swings. If one counts the homer Jackson hit at the end of Game 5, he actually hit four homers on four swings off four pitchers. The Dodgers were unable to overcome the deficit, and the Yankees were world champions.

Repeating in 1978 would prove much harder than in past eras. The Red Sox jumped out to a huge early lead while the Yankees feuded, falling 14 games back at one point. Pressed by Jackson on one side and Steinbrenner on the other, the emotionally volatile Martin resigned and unflappable Bob Lemon took over. Aided by a newspaper strike that provided no daily platform for the clubhouse melodrama, the team concentrated on playing ball and took advantage of a poor streak by the Red Sox. The Yankees pulled even with the Sox in the "Boston Massacre," a four-game sweep at Fenway Park without a single close contest. However, the Red Sox rallied and caught New York on the last day of the season when Cleveland's Rick Waits beat the Yankees, setting up only the second one-game playoff in AL history.

The previous playoff of this type had been played in 1948, when the Red Sox lost to the Indians. They were determined not to meet that fate again. The Yankees went into Boston and started the pitcher of the year, Ron Guidry (25–3, 1.74 ERA) on two days rest. Facing him would be former Yankees' starter Mike Torrez. The Red Sox led in the seventh, 2–0, when ninth-place hitter Bucky Dent came to the plate. Dent had hit only .140 in the previous 20 games, but Lemon felt he couldn't pinch hit for him as the Yanks had no utility player available who could handle shortstop. Dent lifted a fly ball off Torrez into the net atop the Green Monster at Fenway Park to give New York a 3–2 lead. Rich Gossage went the last 2⅔ innings, surviving threats in each inning to win the game and the division title. The Yankees blew through the Royals in four games in the ALCS, but then ran into trouble in Los Angeles.

The Dodgers won the first two games at Dodger Stadium, with rookie Bob Welch fanning Jackson in a classic power-versus-power confrontation in Game 2. Game 3 belonged to Nettles: the smooth-fielding third baseman made three spectacular stops that saved runs and turned the momentum in the Series around. Jackson's famous hip flinch turned a Dodgers double play into a game-tying rally in the eighth inning of Game 4 as the Yankees evened the Series. They cruised from there for their 22nd championship; playoff hero Dent earned the MVP award for the Series by hitting .417 with seven RBIs.

Tragedy and Transition

The '79 season was both bizarre and tragic. Lyle, who'd been supplanted as the club's top reliever by Gossage, came out with *The Bronx Zoo*, a book detailing inside scenes in the clubhouse. He was traded to Texas, bringing top pitching prospect Dave Righetti in a 10-player deal. The Yankees imported veteran pitchers Tommy John, Luis Tiant, and Jim Kaat, among others. They meanwhile lost Gossage for half the year after a bathroom fight with teammate Cliff Johnson (subsequently traded). They brought back old Yankees Bobby Murcer and Oscar Gamble, shipping out Mickey Rivers. Adding a touch of melodrama, Martin—whom the Yankees had announced in 1978 would be returning as manager in 1980—replaced Lemon a year early when Lemon suffered a personal tragedy (his son was killed in a traffic accident). But nothing prepared anyone for the tragedy of August 1, when Thurman Munson crashed his personal jet while practicing take-offs and landings on an off day in Ohio. The Yankees' captain, 32, was killed in the crash and the team and many other baseball dignitaries flew to Ohio for the funeral. The Yanks rallied to win an emotional game against the Orioles that night in which Murcer, who had been a close friend of Munson's and who had delivered a eulogy earlier in the day, drove in all runs in the game, including the game-winner in the bottom of the ninth. Despite Guidry's 2.78 ERA and John's 21 wins, the Yankees slumped and the Orioles went on to represent the AL in the World Series.

The 1980 Yankees won 103 times under rookie manager Dick Howser, the most wins by the club since '63. Following a three-game sweep by the overdue Royals in the ALCS, Steinbrenner wanted Howser to fire third base coach Mike Ferraro because Randolph had been waved home and thrown out on a pivotal play in Game 2. Howser stood by his friend and everybody was canned. Former Yankees shortstop Gene "Stick" Michael took over during the tumultuous strike season, but he was sent packing even though he secured the first-half playoff slot in the convoluted strike-year postseason format. Lemon returned and the Yankees squeezed by the Brewers in the first divisional playoffs ever, then bested Billy Martin's A's in the ALCS. Just as the year before, the Yankees ran into a familiar postseason foe whose turn had finally come. The Dodgers took the World Series in six games, winning the last four as reliever George Frazier suffered through a record-tying three losses.

After '81, the team deteriorated. Steinbrenner's acquisitive nature pushed his front office to constantly trade young players while stockpiling expensive veteran "names" whose best days were behind them. Martin returned to manage in 1983, his "Billy Ball" style precipitating the infamous "Pine Tar" game against the Royals. Steinbrenner then rifled through a plethora of managers, including former Yankees outfielder Lou Piniella, Bucky Dent, and Yogi Berra, making an astounding 12 changes over eight chaotic seasons. The dysfunctional behavior resulted in a last-place finish in 1990. The previous Christmas, Billy Martin, fired four times by Steinbrenner, had been killed in a traffic accident in upstate New York. Steinbrenner was banned from baseball for life for paying small-time gambler Howie Spira to find incriminating information on Dave Winfield, whom the Boss had signed to a 10-year contract and quickly dubbed "Mr. May" because of his late-season struggles.

The club had two marquee players during the turmoil. Righetti threw a no-hitter as a starter and should have anchored the rotation in the Bronx for years to come. However, after trading Gossage for spiteful reasons—Steinbrenner was upset over Nettles' tell-all book *Balls* and insisted that both Nettles and his best friend Gossage be shipped out—the team needed a star pitcher to take over as the closer. Righetti complied, setting the major league save record with 46 in 1986 and eventually becoming the Yankees' all-time saves leader with 224 (later surpassed by Mariano Rivera). Nine-time Gold Glove first baseman Don Mattingly won a race against teammate Winfield for the batting title in 1984, then won the 1985 AL MVP, and in 1987 tied the major league record with homers in 10 consecutive games. "Donnie Baseball" set another mark with six grand slams. With Steinbrenner's influence muted by his expulsion from the game (he still kept a hand in the management of the Yankees, but in a much more low-key way), now-GM Gene Michael let players develop while drafting wisely. Bernie Williams, Roberto Kelly, Mike Stanley, Randy Velarde, Gerald Williams, Pat Kelly, Scott Kamieniecki, and Bob Wickman weren't all destined to become stars, but if a team kept trading away its young players, how would it ever know what it had? Minor league manager Buck Showalter took over in the Bronx. By 1994 Steinbrenner had been reinstated—one of Fay Vincent's last acts before being forced out as commissioner—and the Yankees were finally ready to make strides once more.

A Whole New Ballgame

The 1994 Yankees won 70 of 113 games—the best record in the AL and more wins than the 1990 club nadir in 49 fewer games—but the August strike that year led to cancellation of the postseason. The long layoff before the delayed 1995 season opening didn't slow them down much, though. The Red Sox were hotter but, with a hot finish the Yankees put themselves in position to be the first Wild Card winner in AL history. They then played the first Division Series, winning the first two games in the Bronx, the second coming on a 15th-inning walk-off home run by Jim Leyritz. Seattle won the next two in the Kingdome but, in the deciding game, the Yankees had the lead in the eighth inning with trade-deadline acquisition David Cone pitching. The Mariners tied it on a walk with the bases full. Showalter didn't trust his bullpen, including his closer John Wetteland (who had served up a grand slam earlier in the series), so starter Jack McDowell was brought in to pitch with a one-run lead in the 11th inning. Edgar Martinez hit a two-run, game-winning double on McDowell's last pitch with the Yankees.

It was also Showalter's last game in pinstripes. Steinbrenner chose a controversial replacement: Joe Torre. Called "Clueless Joe" in the New York press, the former Mets manager had appeared in the postseason only once in 14 years while managing the Mets, Braves, and Cardinals. The fact that he had never managed an AL team was also an issue. What Torre inherited was an extremely talented team with a new first baseman, Tino Martinez (replacing the retired Mattingly); third baseman Wade Boggs; outfielders Tim Raines, Bernie Williams, and Paul O'Neill; and veteran backstop Joe Girardi. He also was blessed with a stellar pitching staff led by Cone, Jimmy Key, and a 24-year-old, 21-game winner named Andy Pettitte. To keep things lively, there were two rehab projects that paid off: Dwight Gooden, who pitched a no-hitter, and Darryl Strawberry, who hit his 300th home run. The biggest addition, though, was a highly touted first-round draft choice who would become AL Rookie of the Year: Derek Jeter.

After snaring their first AL East title in 15 years, the Yankees took on Texas in the Division Series. New York lost the first game, then started a relentless skein of nine postseason victories against the Rangers. In the ALCS against Baltimore, the Yankees were down by a run in the eighth inning of the opening game when Jeter hit a fly ball to deep right field that a fan interfered with. The umpire mistakenly ruled it a home run, and the Yankees went on to win the game on Williams' homer three innings later. New York went on to beat Baltimore in five games.

The World Series began with a Braves barrage. Atlanta outscored New York, 16–1, while beating the Yankees twice in the Bronx. After the Yankees won Game 3, they went on an historic tear and did not lose a World Series game again until 2000. The crucial blow in the Series came the next night on a game-tying, three-run home run by Leyritz off fireballing reliever Mark Wohlers in the eighth inning. When the games turned close, the Yankees unleashed their fearsome double-barreled bullpen tandem of young Mariano Rivera and veteran John Wetteland. Rivera set up three of Wetteland's four saves, with Wetteland named Series MVP after his last appearance on the mound for the Yankees while nailing down Game 6.

Rivera shifted to the closer's role in 1997; after some struggles in the early going, the lithe right-hander with the golden arm was spectacular for the rest of the season. He endured his first postseason failure, however, allowing a game-tying home run to Sandy Alomar in Game 4 of the Division Series in Cleveland. Yet Rivera would convert his next 23 straight postseason save opportunities, including eight in the Fall Classic.

1927 . . . 1939 . . . 1961 . . . 1998

The 1998 Yankees took their place among the all-time greats, winning 114 times to set AL and club victory records, although the 1954 Indians (.721) and 1927 Yankees (.714) exceeded their .704 winning percentage in shorter schedules. Williams took the batting title on the last day of the season, and the Yankees excelled at team play—as opposed to individual achievements, David Wells and his perfect game notwithstanding. The Yankees lost twice to the Indians and trailed in the ALCS, but Cuban refugee Orlando Hernandez stymied the Tribe in Game 4 and the Yankees went on to win the pennant. They rolled through San Diego in the World Series in four straight. Oakland discard Scott Brosius, a prime example of the club's veteran role-player mentality, won the Series MVP award by homering in consecutive innings with the Yankees trailing in Game 3.

With their roster largely intact from the previous year, the Yankees breezed through the '99 season, enjoying a perfect game from Cone before having to face the novel obstacle of nemesis Boston in the postseason. This first-ever Yankees-Red Sox confrontation in the postseason typically went New York's way, even though the Yankees had to rally late to win the first two games. Roger Clemens, now wearing Yankees pinstripes after a blockbuster deal with Toronto, faltered in his first season with the club and was hit hard at Fenway Park. The Yanks, however, piled on runs in late innings against the sloppy Sox the next two nights to take the LCS in five games. The Braves presented no more of a problem in the World Series than the Padres had the previous year. Even a 5–0 Atlanta lead in Game 3 turned into a Yankees win on a pair of late homers by Chad Curtis and Chuck Knoblauch, the latter on a liner that ticked off Brian Jordan's glove for a homer. Clemens redeemed himself by winning the clinching game the next night.

The Yankees wheezed to the gate in 2000. Their 87–74 mark was the fewest wins ever for a Yankees postseason club over a full season, leading to much skepticism about their postseason chances and much griping about the team being "too old." They faced a young, hot Oakland team in a tight, five-game Division Series, flying across the country without an off day to win Game 5 in Oakland despite a shaky start from Pettitte and a infield pratfall by Luis Sojo. That win broke the tension, and the Yankees seemed to regaine their aura of invincibility again. The Mariners won the first game of the ALCS and were enjoying a 1–0 lead in Game 2 when the Yankees erupted to score seven times in the eighth inning. In Game 4, Clemens fanned 15 while shutting out the Marines in Seattle, allowing his only hit of the game in the seventh inning. David Justice earned MVP honors with a crucial three-run homer in the clinching Game 6. The Yankees then set their sights on their crosstown rivals, the Mets.

Interleague play had brought the Mets and Yankees onto each other's schedules in recent years. After a first-game loss, the Yankees had gone 11–6 against the Mets since 1997, including a July 8, 2000 two-stadium doubleheader that featured a Clemens purpose pitch off Mike Piazza's helmet. When they met again in Game 2 of the World Series—the night after a Paul O'Neill walk fueled a comeback that helped the Bronxers steal the opener—Clemens tossed a broken bat in Piazza's direction as he ran to first base. Nothing much happened, except that Clemens pitched superbly and the Yankees had a two-game lead. After the Mets took Game 3, Jeter led off Game 4 with a homer and the Yankees won by a run. They broke a ninth-inning tie on a Luis Sojo single off a tiring Al Leiter the next night, and Rivera wrapped up another championship. The Yankees had taken the first October Subway Series in 44 years and had run their record to 11–3 against local nines in the World Series.

Beyond September 11

A year later, in the wake of the attacks of September 11, 2001, baseball became a balm for both the city's and the country's grief. With all eyes focused on Gotham, the Yankees played some of their most inspiring ball. Down two games to none against Oakland in the Division Series, Jeter dashed across the infield to grab an errant relay throw, flipping the ball behind him to nail an astonished Jeremy Giambi at the plate and protect a 1–0 lead. Veteran scribes in the press box as well as millions of fans in the stands and watching on television almost didn't believe their eyes until the TV replays confirmed what had just happened. The energized Yankees took the Division Series and turned to face Seattle again, where the Mariners had just broken the 114-win mark set by the '98 Yankees. When ex-Yankees player and manager Lou Piniella insisted that the Mariners would bring the ALCS back to Safeco Field after losing the first two games there, Alfonso Soriano, Bernie Williams, and Company made sure they did not. The Mariners bombed the Bombers in the Bronx in Game 3, but the Yanks took Games 4 and 5 behind Clemens, Rivera, and Pettitte.

Despite hitting just .183 against Arizona, the Yankees had some remarkable October moments with their bats. Tino Martinez was the hero in Game 4 with a game-tying homer in the ninth, and Jeter won it with a homer the next inning, earning the moniker "Mr. November" (because the weeklong suspension of the season in the wake of 9/11 had pushed the Series into November for the first time). In Game 5 Scott Brosius did the same thing against the same Diamondbacks reliever, Byung-Hyun Kim. Soriano knocked in the game-winner in the 12th, scoring the embattled Knoblauch (who was pinch-running). Back in Arizona, though, the Diamondbacks pounded Pettitte and everyone that followed him in Game 6. The Yankees knocked Curt Schilling out of the game the following night on a Soriano homer leading off the eighth that gave New York a 2–1 lead. With Rivera on the mound, it looked like the Yankees were on the verge of their fifth world championship in the past six seasons. But in a stunning change of fortune, a poor throw by the Rivera himself set up the winning rally in the ninth, Rivera's second inning of work. A bloop hit over the drawn in infield was all it took to snuff the Yankees' hopes. In the end, the home team won every game in the 2001 World Series.

After beloved Paul O'Neill retired, a new era was ushered in with the acquisition of free agent slugger Jason Giambi, whose services had grown too expensive for Oakland. He joined veteran hurler Mike Mussina, the big free agent pickup of the previous year, as the faces of the "new look" Yankees. After New York had won 103 games in the regular season, though, the scrappy underdog Angels stunned them in the 2002 Division Series, booting them quickly out of October.

The next year the Yankees said good-bye to Clemens—or so they thought at the time—as he won his 300th game and notched his 4,000th strikeout on the same night. "The Rocket" received warm applause everywhere he went after proclaiming 2003 would be his final year. He was outstanding against the Twins in a four-game victory in the Division Series. Clemens was also superb in a heated ALCS Game 3 at Fenway that featured Pedro Martinez throwing hard-charging Yankees bench coach Don Zimmer to the ground during a brawl, plus a later incident in which a Fenway Park employee incited the Yankees' bullpen to violence. Clemens wasn't as sharp in Game 7 at the Stadium as the Red Sox took an early lead. Mussina came on in relief—his first-ever appearance out of the bullpen—and kept New York in the game. Meanwhile, Boston manager Grady Little stayed with his ace Martinez a few batters too long as Jeter started a rally and Jorge Posada's double tied the game. Midseason acquisition Aaron Boone homered off knuckleballer Tim Wakefield in the eleventh inning for the pennant.

After the gut-wrenching drama of the LCS, the Yankees faltered against the upstart Marlins in the World Series. After splitting the opening pair of games in the Bronx, the far more experienced Yanks won Game 3 behind Mussina and Rivera, putting them in the catbird seat. However, Florida parried to take the last three games behind Series MVP Josh Beckett, who threw a shutout to win the first World Series clincher by a visiting team at Yankee Stadium since the Dodgers in 1981.

Alex Rodriguez, the reigning MVP and the consensus best player in the game, came to the Yankees in a landmark trade before the 2004 season began. With team captain Jeter firmly ensconced at shortstop, A-Rod willingly moved to third base, an open position after Boone had injured his leg playing basketball in the off-season. New York opened the season with two games at the Tokyo Dome in Japan. The Yankees won the division once more despite just one complete game all season (Mussina) as Tom Gordon's stellar setup work and Rivera's club-record 53 saves enabled the starters to work shorter games. The Yankees homered and walked more frequently than any team in the league, even though Giambi, their best player in both categories, was out for half the season. Gary Sheffield's punishing bat and his screeching line drives fit in perfectly, as Hideki Matsui hit 31 homers and knocked in 108 in his second season after coming over from Japan.

The Yankees ran on all cylinders as they buzzed through the Twins in four games in the Division Series, although it took some doing to get through Game 4. Ruben Sierra hit a three-run home run in the eighth to tie the game, then New York won in the 11th when Rodriguez doubled, stole third, and scored on a wild pitch.

The Reverse of "The Curse"

The Yankees pummeled the Red Sox through the first three games of the ALCS, but a fatigued Rivera couldn't hold the lead in two potential clinching games. From there the Yankees couldn't hold back the Red Sox or avoid the effects of 100 years of reverse mojo since Jack Chesbro's pitch had gotten away in 1904. The triumphal Red Sox became the first team ever to come back from a 3–0 deficit in a seven-game series, an historic moment made all the sweeter by their doing it against the Yankees. Boston then went on to sweep the Cardinals in the World Series while New York watched the October Classic on TV for only the third time since 1996.

In 2005, it was back to business as usual. The Yankees-Red Sox rivalry remained on full alert, with the Yankees holding the upper hand in most matters. Rodriguez hit a key home run against Curt Schilling in the pitcher's first game back from his injury in 2005 when Boston manager Terry Francona opted to bring Schilling in from the bullpen as if he were a closer. Although Boston led in the East Division standings for much of the season, the Yankees clinched the division title in Boston on the penultimate day of the season. Unfortunately for the Yankees, the Angels once again handed them an early ticket home, keyed by the Game 3 difficulties of Yankees starter Randy Johnson. A-Rod took home AL MVP honors.

The 2006 season brought a new chapter in the supercharged Boston-New York rivalry. Again the Red Sox led the division for much of the season, but rainouts and rescheduling brought the Yankees to Fenway for a five-game weekend series that would feature two doubleheaders. The Yankees swept all five, including an inspiring performance by late-season pickup Cory Lidle, who bested David Wells in a tight, 2-1 contest. After winning their division, the Yankees were heavy favorites to steamroll Wild Card Detroit. But the pitching-rich Tigers stunned fans around the Yankees' empire, beating the confident Yankees in three straight games after losing the opener at the Stadium. After another Yankees exit from the postseason in the first round, it was little consolation that Jeter narrowly missed winning both AL MVP and the batting title.

The Last Hurrah of the Torre-Jeter-Rivera Dynasty

After another quick exit from postseason play in '07, the New York club has come to a crossroads. Although the Yanks made a valiant attempt to catch AL East leader Boston in the second half—including a 21–9 finish—the Bombers fell short by two games. Worse, as the Wild Card, New York then succumbed to Cleveland in four games in the Division Series, with ace Chien-Ming Wang losing both the opener and the deciding game. The embarrassing Division Series loss cost Torre his job, ending an era in the Bronx. The manager turned down a contract with postseason incentive clauses and a pay cut of more than $2 million, bringing an end to his 12-season tenure that had seen the Yankees reach the postseason every year, win the pennant six times, and capture four world championships.

The best news of 2006 and 2007 was the emergence of the Yankees' young talent. Right-hander Wang won 19 games in both 2006 and in 2007. Young position players Robinson Cano and Melky Cabrera put the lie to criticisms that the Yankees had gone back to their old ways of always trading away prospects for aging stars. Cano was right behind Jeter in the 2006 batting race, and in 2007 Cabrera took the center field starting job away from superstar Johnny Damon. A slew of injuries meant that the Yankees saw a club-record eight different rookies make their debuts as starting pitchers in 2007, including promising appearances by Phil Hughes, Jeff Karstens, Darrell Rasner, Matt DeSalvo. The emergence of fireballing sensation Joba Chamberlain in a relief role added further to the confidence of the team and the fans that the future is bright, despite the recent disappointments in October.

While Steinbrenner has remained surprisingly mum in the past few years, the organization is counting that these young pitchers will emerge as advertised. There is no doubt that the Yankees have the wherewithal to remain at the top of the food chain, thanks mostly to their unmatched ability to generate income. From 2005–07, the club topped four million in attendance annually at premium ticket prices, and the final season for Yankee Stadium in 2008 will see the first All-Star Game in the Bronx in 32 years. The luxurious new stadium, opening in 2009, will be an even bigger cash cow. All of this is topped by the incredibly profitable YES Network, the Yankees' own regional sports television network that has pushed the value of the team to an estimated billion dollars or more.

The Yankees are regularly scheduled October programming, as 26 world championships, 39 American League pennants, 47 postseason appearances, and 65 postseason series will attest. While it hasn't gone as well in the past six years as expected, the Yankees averaged 98 wins each year from 1996–2007. Joe Torre's name certainly belongs with Huggins, McCarthy, and Stengel among the greatest Yankees managers. And while the bar has been set quite high by Ruth, Gehrig, DiMaggio, Mantle, Berra, and Ford, current Yankees Derek Jeter and Mariano Rivera fit right in with any all-time team of Bronx Bombers.

Over 105 years of glory galore, the Yankees' tradition has remained as constant as their uniforms.

New York Yankees (1903–2007) Team History in Brief

ERA	1903-20	1921-45	1946-68	1969-93	1994-2007
World Championships	0	10	10	2	4
AL Pennants	0	14	15	4	6
Division Series Won	—	—	—	—	6
Division Titles (two-division era)	—	—	—	5	—
Division Titles (three-division era)	—	—	—	—	11
Wild Card Berths	—	—	—	—	3
Second-Place Finishes	3	6	1	5	3
Third-Place Finishes	2	3	3	3	0
Fourth-Place Finishes	3	1	0	6	0
Fifth-Place Finishes	3	0	1	5	0
Sixth-Place Finishes	4	0	1	0	—
Seventh-Place Finishes	1	1	0	1	—
Eighth-Place Finishes	2	0	0	—	—
Ninth-Place Finishes	—	—	1	—	—
Tenth-Place Finishes	—	—	1	—	—
Contending Finishes (5 GB or less)	3	3	1	4	2
Last-Place Finishes	2	0	1	1	0
Years at .600 or Better	2	16	15	6	6
Years at .500 or Better	9	24	20	18	14
Years at .400 or Worse	3	0	0	0	0

Composite Won-Lost Record (Pct.): 9,265–7,009 (.569)

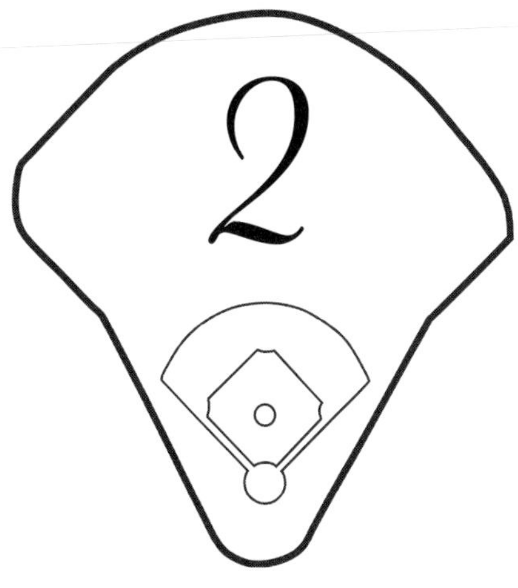

The 100 Greatest Games in Yankees History

1. October 8, 1956   Yankees 2, Dodgers 0

Unheralded Don Larsen manages a singular postseason achievement. He throws a perfect game—the only no-hitter in postseason history—against the Dodgers in Game 5. Larsen, who was knocked out of Game 2 in the second inning, fans Dale Mitchell to finish the ninth and finds Yogi Berra in his arms. Perfect!

2. October 2, 1978   Yankees 5, Red Sox 4 at Fenway Park

The Red Sox won the coin flip, but the Yankees, with a 48–20 record since Bob Lemon took over, won everything else—except the final game of the regular season, thus necessitating the one-game playoff for the division title. The Red Sox take the early lead, but Bucky Dent's pop fly catches the net over the Green Monster for a 3–2 lead in the seventh against Mike Torrez, who had clinched the world championship for the Yankees a year earlier. Thurman Munson doubles in a run later in the inning and Reggie Jackson adds a long home run in the eighth inning. Rich Gossage allows two runs in the bottom of the eighth, but he gets Carl Yastrzemski to pop up to Graig Nettles with runners on the corners to end this fight to the finish at Fenway.

3. October 1, 1932   Yankees 7, Cubs 5 at Wrigley Field

Babe Ruth, the focus of razzing from the Cubs bench, steps up to the plate in the fifth inning of Game 3 of the World Series with the score tied 4–4. Ruth, already with a homer in the game, pauses to point toward center field—or not point, or point at the pitcher, or counts off strikes, depending on the story—but there is no doubt where the 0–2 pitch from Charlie Root goes. His long home run to center field spawns one of the game's greatest legends. Lou Gehrig follows by hitting his second home run of the game. The Yankees win behind George Pipgras, who sets a record by striking out five times in a World Series game (he fans only one on the mound). New York finishes the sweep the next day.

4. October 1, 1961   Yankees 1, Red Sox 0

Roger Maris breaks the single-season home run record with his 61st homer on the final day of the new 162-game season. Amid controversy and anguish, he beats the mark of the beloved Babe Ruth with a home run to right off Tracy Stallard in the fourth inning in front of 23,154. It is also the only run of the game and gives the Yankees their 109th win of the year, the most by the franchise since Babe's Bombers won 110 in 1927, the year he hit 60 in a 154-game season.

5. July 17, 1941   Yankees 6, Indians 5 at Municipal Stadium

Joe DiMaggio's record hitting streak ends at 56 games in front of more than 60,000 fans in Cleveland. Pitchers Al Smith and Jim Bagby hold Joltin' Joe hitless, while third baseman Ken Keltner makes two unbelievable plays to end the streak that has captivated the country. DiMaggio had reached 56 the previous day by going 3-for-4 at Cleveland's League Park. He'll hit in 16 straight games after the streak ends. If not for Keltner, the streak could have been 73 games.

6. June 1, 1925   Senators 5, Yankees 3

Lou Gehrig begins the consecutive game streak that will pass Everett Scott's mark and reach 2,130. It begins with a pinch-hitting assignment for Pee Wee Wanninger, who replaced Scott in the Yankees lineup. When Wally Pipp complains of a headache the next day, Gehrig gets the start and he will not miss another game until a fatal illness in 1939 forces him to retire.

7. September 30, 1927 Yankees 4, Senators 2

With first base open, Babe Ruth hits his 60th home run off Tom Zachary to break a 2–2 in the eighth. Ruth's 17 home runs in September are also a record, the highest monthly total until Rudy York cranks 18 in August 1937. Walter Johnson appears in the 934th game in his remarkable 21-year career. Pinch hitting for Zachary, Johnson flies out to Ruth.

8. October 18, 1977 Yankees 8, Dodgers 4

In one of the greatest displays of showmanship in the game's history, Reggie Jackson delivers three times. His trio of home runs off three different pitchers makes "Mr. October" a legend. Mike Torrez goes all the way to give the Yankees their first world championship since 1962.

9. October 14, 1976 Yankees 7, Royals 6

An inning after George Brett ties the game with a home run, Chris Chambliss homers in the bottom of the ninth inning to give the Yankees their first pennant in 12 years. Fans swarm the field and Chambliss can't even get around the bases before home plate is taken away.

10. October 23, 1996 Yankees 8, Braves 6 at Atlanta–Fulton County Stadium

The Braves take a 6–0 lead after five innings, but the Yankees strike for three runs in the sixth. Jim Leyritz, who did not start the game, comes up in the eighth with two on—thanks to a missed double play—and lifts a home run off Mark Wohlers to tie the game. More sloppy play by the Braves leads to two runs in the 10th inning. The Series is tied and everything goes the Yankees' way.

11. October 16, 2003 Yankees 6, Red Sox 5

It seems like the Red Sox just might break their curse as Boston takes a 5–2 lead into the bottom of the eighth inning with ace Pedro Martinez on the mound in Game 7 of the ALCS. In a much-debated decision, manager Grady Little leaves Martinez in and he allows the game-tying double to Jorge Posada. Unlikely hero Aaron Boone wins it with a home run off Tim Wakefield in the 11th inning. Little will be fired for leaving in Pedro for too long.

12. October 13, 1960 Pirates 10, Yankees 9 at Forbes Field

Bill Mazeroski homers in the bottom of the ninth off Ralph Terry to send Pittsburgh into euphoria. The Yankees had led in the eighth, 7–4, only to blow the lead and then rally for two runs in the top of the ninth to tie it. Bobby Richardson is the first MVP from a losing team as the Yankees doubled Pittsburgh's scoring output but lost the Series. Casey Stengel will be "retired" after the season despite winning seven world championships since 1949.

13. October 5, 1941 Yankees 7, Dodgers 4 at Ebbets Field

The Dodgers are one strike away from evening the World Series in Game 4. They get the strike, but catcher Mickey Owen can't handle it. Tommy Henrich reaches base, goes to second on Joe DiMaggio's hit, and both men score on Charlie Keller's double. The Yankees go on to score four runs off hard-luck Hugh Casey, who loses his second straight game in relief. The Yankees will win the first New York-Brooklyn Series the next day.

14. October 5, 1953 Yankees 4, Dodgers 3

The Yankees claim their record fifth straight world championship, and third in that span against Brooklyn. The Dodgers give it all they have. Carl Furillo's two-run home run in the top of the ninth ties the game, but Billy Martin's run-scoring single in the bottom of the inning wins it.

15. July 4, 1939 Senators 3, Yankees 2

Lou Gehrig's number 4 is retired on Lou Gehrig Appreciation Day, becoming the first uniform number ever retired. His career abruptly ended due to amyotrophic lateral sclerosis, forever after known as Lou Gehrig's disease, Gehrig doesn't leave a dry eye in the house as his speech begins, "Today I consider myself the luckiest man on the face of the earth."

16. October 21, 2000 Yankees 4, Mets 3

The first World Series between two New York teams since 1956 starts with a doozy. Timo Perez's hesitation on the bases proves costly for the Mets and Paul O'Neill's leadoff walk in the ninth is bigger still. The Yankees tie it in the ninth and win it in the 12th on a single by former Met Jose Vizcaino. It is the Yankees' 13th straight World Series game victory, breaking the mark set by the Yankees of 1927, 1928, and 1932.

17. October 9, 1996 Yankees 5, Orioles 4

With the Yankees trailing by a run in Game 1 of the ALCS, Derek Jeter's fly to right is touched by young fan Jeffrey Maier while right fielder Tony Tarasco waits to catch it. It is ruled a home run despite howls from the Orioles and anyone with a TV set. Bernie Williams wins the game with a home run in the 11th inning, the kid is deemed a hero, and the Yankees will go on to beat Baltimore.

18. August 6, 1979 Yankees 5, Orioles 4

The day of Thurman Munson's funeral, his longtime friend Bobby Murcer rallies the Yankees from a 4–0 deficit in the seventh inning. His two-out, three-run homer makes it a one-run game and his two-run double in the bottom of the ninth wins the game on ABC's *Monday Night Baseball*. The Yankees had flown from Ohio for the funeral service for the team captain earlier in the day. Munson, 32, died piloting his plane.

19. May 17, 1998 Yankees 4, Twins 0

David Wells tosses a perfect game. It is just the eighth perfect game in the American League, including Don Larsen's 1956 World Series gem, and it is the first by a Yankee since Larsen. Wells later intimates he was out late the night before and was hung over, but the pitcher, far from perfect in terms of behavior, is indeed perfect on the mound.

20. April 18, 1923 Yankees 4, Red Sox 1

Babe Ruth homers in the first game at Yankee Stadium and he does it against his former team, the Red Sox. Bob Shawkey throws the first pitch and gets the first win. The Yankees open their new stadium by sweeping Boston in a four-game series and cruise to the pennant.

21. July 24, 1983 Royals 5, Yankees 4

"The Pine Tar Game." Moments after George Brett hits a two-out, two-run, ninth-inning home run off Rich Gossage to erase a one-run lead, Yankees manager Billy Martin marches out of the dugout to argue that Brett's bat has more than the legal limit of pine tar on it. Brett is called out, the game is over, and the Royals third baseman goes ballistic. The American League office overrules the umpires and the last four outs are ordered completed on August 18. Martin, furious, puts pitcher Ron Guidry in center field and lefty Don Mattingly at second base. Kansas City's Dan Quisenberry retires the side in order in the only inning played that day at Yankee Stadium. The conclusion lasts 12 minutes before 1,245 curiosity seekers.

22. October 15, 1962 Yankees 1, Giants 0 at Candlestick Park

Tony Kubek's double-play grounder brings in the only run of the game, but the lead is in jeopardy in the bottom of the ninth. After Matty Alou bunts for a hit, Ralph Terry fans the next two. Willie Mays lashes a double but Alou has to stop at third. Terry, who allowed Bill Mazeroski's famous home run to end the 1960 World Series, gets Willie McCovey to hit a blistering liner right at Bobby Richardson. It is the last Yankees' world championship for 15 years. The Yankees beat the Giants in the World Series for the fifth consecutive time since their one-time landlords forced them out of the Polo Grounds in 1922.

23. October 6, 1926 Yankees 9, Cardinals 5 at Sportsman's Park

Babe Ruth becomes the first player to hit three home runs in a World Series game. His first two homers in Game 4 come against Flint Rhem; both sail over the right field roof at Sportsman's Park. His third, against Hi Bell, travels over the center field bleachers, a shot described as the longest ball ever hit at the park. Ruth walks his other two times up and scores four times. While Waite Hoyt is peppered for 14 hits, he strands 10 and goes the distance. The Yankees will also win Game 5 to leave St. Louis with the Series lead, but they will be denied their second world championship.

24. October 31, 2001 Yankees 4, Diamondbacks 3

With two outs in the ninth inning and Arizona up by two runs, Tino Martinez launches a two-run home run to tie the game. Derek Jeter homers in the 11th inning, also off Byung-Hyun Kim. As it occurs in the wee hours after Halloween—baseball's schedule was delayed by the September terrorist attacks in New York—Jeter is quickly proclaimed "Mr. November." The Yankees rally off Kim in the ninth and win in extra innings the next night as well. The home team will win each game in this Series.

25. October 2, 1949 Yankees 5, Red Sox 3

The Red Sox come to New York needing to win one of the final two games of the year to take the pennant. The Yankees win both. After rallying from four runs down to take the opener, New York explodes for four runs in the eighth in the second game. Vic Raschi holds off Red Sox rally in the ninth to win the club's 16th pennant since 1921. They'll soon win their 12th World Series.

26. October 10, 1926 Cardinals 3, Yankees 2

Grover Cleveland Alexander comes out of the bullpen and fans Tony Lazzeri with the bases loaded in the seventh inning, in one of the most famous strikeouts in World Series history. The Cardinals win their first world championship when Babe Ruth is thrown out by Cards catcher Bob O'Farrell in the ninth, the only time a World Series has ended on a caught stealing. The Yankees are 1–3 in World Series play.

27. June 3, 1932 Yankees 20, Athletics 13 at Shibe Park

Lou Gehrig hits four home runs, the first American League player to do so and the first by any major leaguer since 1896. Tony Lazzeri also hits for the cycle at Shibe Park. The Iron Horse's big day, the only time a Yankee has hit four homers, is overshadowed in the papers by John McGraw's resignation as manager of the Giants after 30 years.

28. October 5, 1955 Dodgers 2, Yankees 0

Sadness in the Bronx results in jubilation in Brooklyn, finally. Gil Hodges drives in the game's only two runs against Tommy Byrne and Sandy Amoros makes a game-saving catch on Yogi Berra and turns it into a double play. Johnny Podres throws the Game 7 shutout and becomes a Brooklyn folk hero as the Dodgers finally beat the Yankees on their sixth try.

29. October 10, 1964 Yankees 2, Cardinals 1

Mickey Mantle homers off reliever Barney Schultz's first pitch in the ninth inning to win Game 3 of the World Series. It is Mantle's 16th career World Series home run, pushing him past Babe Ruth for the all-time lead. Mantle will hit two more homers in what will be his 12th and last World Series. Jim Bouton, whose only blemish was a run set up by Mantle's error, gets the win to give the Yankees the lead in the series.

30. October 13, 1978 Yankees 5, Dodgers 1

Friday the 13th is bad luck for the Dodgers. With the Dodgers leading the World Series two games to none, third baseman Graig Nettles puts on a display of diving thievery. Ron Guidry allows 15 baserunners, but only one scores as Nettles saves the day and Guidry goes all the way.

31. October 7, 1952 Yankees 4, Dodgers 2

With the bases loaded, one out, and the Yankees holding a 4–2 lead in the bottom of the seventh inning of Game 7, New York summons lefty Bob Kuzava to make his first appearance of the World Series. He strikes out Andy Pafko, but Jackie Robinson hits a short popup that Billy Martin catches in a dead sprint. Kuzava does not allow a hit the rest of the way as the Yankees dispatch Brooklyn in the World Series for the fourth time.

32. October 26, 1996 Yankees 3, Braves 2

The Yankees, who lost the first two games at home to start the World Series, win their first world championship since 1977 by taking the last four games. Joe Girardi's RBI-triple in the fourth inning off Greg Maddux is the turning point. Mark Lemke pops up John Wetteland's final pitch as a Yankee to end Game 6 and the Series.

33. October 3, 1947 Dodgers 3, Yankees 2 at Ebbets Field

No pitcher has ever been wilder in a World Series game, and through 1947, no one has ever been unhittable for so long. Yankee Bill Bevens leads the Dodgers, 2–1, in the bottom of the ninth inning and is one out from the first Series no-hitter. Bevens walks his 10th man of the game, an intentional pass to Pete Reiser, to get to Eddie Stanky with two men on. Pinch hitter Cookie Lavagetto lines a double off the wall in right to break up Bevens's bid, win the game, and even the Series. The Yankees win in seven games.

34. July 18, 1999 Yankees 2, Expos 0

With an audience of Don Larsen and Yogi Berra—the battery for the 1956 World Series perfecto—David Cone hurls a perfect game at Yankee Stadium. It is the first no-hitter in interleague play.

35. October 26, 2000 Yankees 4, Mets 2 at Shea Stadium

Luis Sojo bounces a ball past Al Leiter to snap a 2–2 tie in the ninth inning of Game 5 of the World Series. Mariano Rivera retires Mike Piazza with a man on in the ninth on a long fly and the Yankees celebrate their 26th world championship. Derek Jeter is named World Series MVP in the first October Subway Series since 1956.

36. June 29, 1941 Yankees 7, Senators 5 at Griffith Stadium

After Joe DiMaggio ties George Sisler's 1922 record by singling off Dutch Leonard in the first game, he goes after the record in the nightcap. Walt Masterson holds him until the seventh inning, when he singles to set the American League record for the longest hitting streak in New York's doubleheader sweep at Griffith Stadium. He has 14 more games in him.

37. October 5, 1947 Dodgers 8, Yankees 6

With the Dodgers up by three runs in the sixth inning of the sixth game, Joe DiMaggio launches a 415-foot blast to left that Al Gionfriddo turns into a dazzling one-handed catch against the bullpen in front of 74,000. As Red Barber exclaims, "Oh Doctor!" The Yanks will win the World Series the next day; Gionfriddo never plays another game in the big leagues.

38. June 13, 2003 Yankees 5, Cardinals 2

Roger Clemens produces a baseball first when he notches his 300th win and 4,000th strikeout on the same night. He fans Cardinal Edgar Renteria to join Nolan Ryan and Steve Carlton in the 4K club. He pitches 6⅔ to win No. 300 on his fourth try.

39. October 9, 1977 Yankees 5, Royals 3 at Royals Stadium

For the second straight year, the Yankees win the pennant in their last at bat in the deciding game of the ALCS. The Royals, who needed to win either of the last two games in the series at home, lead 3–1 in the eighth inning of Game 5, but Reggie Jackson's pinch-hit single makes it a one-run game. Dennis Leonard, who pitched a complete game two days earlier, allows the first two Yankees to reach base in the ninth. Mickey Rivers ties the game with a single against Larry Gura. Mark Littell, who allowed Chris Chambliss's pennant-clinching home run in 1976, surrenders the tiebreaking sacrifice fly to Willie Randolph. Sparky Lyle gets Freddie Patek to hit in a double play to end the series in Kansas City.

40. October 13, 2001 Yankees 1, A's 0 at Network Associates Coliseum

With the Yankees trailing two games to none but leading by a run in the seventh inning of Game 3 of the Division Series, the Yankees pull off a play for the ages on Terrence Long's double to right with two down. The relay is wild, but shortstop Derek Jeter ranges to the first base line, snags the throw, and flips it to Jorge Posada, who tags out Jeremy Giambi standing up. The Yankees hold on to win, 1–0, with Jeremy Giambi making the last out, and will take the series and later the pennant.

41. July 4, 1983 Yankees 4, Red Sox 0

Dave Righetti throws an Independence Day no-hitter. Rags fans Wade Boggs, who will win the first of his five batting titles in 1983, to end the game. It is just the fifth no-hitter in franchise history and the first since Allie Reynolds's second no-no of 1951.

42. October 22, 2000 Yankees 6, Mets 5

Harkening back to a beanball incident in July, a tension-filled at bat between Roger Clemens and Mike Piazza turns surreal in the first inning. Clemens hurls a shard of a broken bat at Piazza. When order is restored, Clemens retires Piazza and the Mets go meekly until the ninth, when their comeback winds up one run short.

43. November 4, 2001 Diamondbacks 3, Yankees 2 at Bank One Ballpark

Alfonso Soriano homers in the eighth to snap a 1–1 tie between Roger Clemens and Curt Schilling. One day after throwing 100 pitches in Game 6, Randy Johnson pitches 1⅓ innings in relief for Arizona. Mariano Rivera, makes a throwing error to put the tying and winning runs on base with nobody out in the bottom of the ninth. Tony Womack ties the game with a double and, with the infield in, Luis Gonzalez's bloop results in the first Yankees' loss in five World Series dating back 20 years. Johnson, who will also win the Cy Young Award, becomes the first pitcher to win three games in one World Series since Mickey Lolich in 1968. The Yankees hit just .183, the lowest average for a team in a seven- or eight-game Series. They are outscored 37–14 by Arizona but still come within an inning of the title.

44. July 13, 1934 Yankees 4, Tigers 2 at Navin Field

Babe Ruth, who the previous winter had put off a meeting with Frank Navin to discuss the Babe's managing the Tigers, makes history in Detroit anyway. Ruth, already the only player with 400, 500, or 600 career home runs, starts another new club with his 700th shot. The Yankees beat Detroit, 4–2, to nudge into first place ahead of player–manager Mickey Cochrane's Tigers. Lou Gehrig has to leave the game with a lumbago seizure, but he will keep his consecutive game streak going by batting first listed as the shortstop and then leaving the game.

45. October 14, 1978 Yankees 4, Dodgers 3
Reggie Jackson's hip spurs a rally. With the Dodgers about to turn a sure double play in the sixth inning, Jackson, already out on the play, stands his ground and lets the ball glance off his hip. It allows a run to score and the Yankees tie the game in the eighth inning and win in the 10th to even the Series.

46. October 10, 1923 Giants 5, Yankees 4
The first World Series game is played at Yankee Stadium. Like the 13 previous Series games played the past two years between the Yankees and Giants, the National League club (9–3–1 in the 1921 and 1922 Series) wins. Starters Mule Watson for the Giants and Waite Hoyt of the Yankees are knocked out by the third inning and neither will pitch again in the Series. Casey Stengel of the Giants hits the first Series home run at the Stadium, an inside-the-park job that breaks a tie in the ninth. The Yankees will win the last three games of the Series and clinch their first world championship at their old home, the Polo Grounds, in six games.

47. October 20, 2004 Red Sox 10, Yankees 3
After coming so close so many times and blowing so many leads against the Yankees at big moments, this time the Red Sox turn the tables on the Yankees. New York led three games to none, but Boston won the next three to tie the ALCS. After David Ortiz homers in the first inning, Johnny Damon knocks a grand slam in the second and collects a two-run blast two innings later. The Red Sox are the first team to rally from three games down in baseball history.

48. October 8, 1961 Yankees 7, Reds 0 at Crosley Field
An ankle injury forces Whitey Ford to leave Game 4 in the sixth inning, but he leaves with a 4–0 lead and a World Series record of 32 consecutive scoreless innings. Elio Chacon's groundout to end the third inning breaks Babe Ruth's coveted mark of 29⅔ innings set as a Red Sox southpaw. Jim Coates preserves the shutout and the Yankees will finish off the Reds the next day. Ford's record will finally end in Game 1 of the 1962 World Series in San Francisco at 33⅔ innings.

49. August 16, 1920 Indians 4, Yankees 3
Yankees submarine pitcher Carl Mays throws the first, and only, fatal pitch in major league history. Cleveland shortstop Ray Chapman, known for crowding the plate, is carried off the Polo Grounds and dies in the hospital the next day. His death will lead to the discarding of old baseballs during games. Mays, surly and already disliked by both teammates and foes, will pitch another five years and amass 208 wins. Yet he will never get more than a handful of votes for the Hall of Fame.

50. September 4, 1993 Yankees 4, Indians 0
Jim Abbott tosses a no-hitter at Yankee Stadium. Abbot, born without a right hand, proves to be inspirational as well as a masterful pitcher when everything falls into place. He strikes out three and walks five. Carlos Baerga grounds out to shortstop Randy Velarde to end it.

51. October 26, 1999 Yankees 6, Braves 5
Atlanta takes a 5–1 lead in the fourth inning, but the Yankees claw back. Chuck Knoblauch's drive tips off Brian Jordan's glove for a game-tying two-run home run in the eighth. Chad Curtis hits his second home run of the night to win it in the 10th inning. The Yankees will sweep the Series the next night behind Roger Clemens.

52. October 8, 1927 Yankees 4, Pirates 3
Babe Ruth slugs his second home run of the World Series—the only two homers in the Series—but the Yankees sweep the Pirates on a wild pitch by reliever Johnny Miljus with the bases loaded and two outs in the ninth inning of Game 4. Wilcy Moore, who held off the Pirates in relief in a one-run game in Game 1, tosses a complete game to cap the sweep.

53. October 10, 1951 Yankees 4, Giants 3
The Giants' magic runs out. Their ninth-inning rally—unlike in the famous playoff against Brooklyn—comes up a run short in Game 6 at Yankee Stadium. Sal Yvars, who years later will be fingered as the lead sign-stealer in an intricate scheme at the Polo Grounds during the Giants' miraculous late-season run, lines out as a pinch hitter against reliever Bob Kuzava to end the World Series. Hank Bauer's bases-clearing triple in the sixth is the decisive blow. Joe DiMaggio doubles in his final at bat in the major leagues.

54. October 17, 1978 Yankees 7, Dodgers 2 at Dodger Stadium
Catfish Hunter allows a home run to Davey Lopes to lead off Game 6 for the Dodgers, but he allows just five more hits and pitches into the eighth. Rich Gossage finishes up for the Yankees' second consecutive world championship. Brian Doyle and Series MVP Bucky Dent each have three hits and bat a combined .425 in the Series.

55. May 14, 1996 Yankees 2, Mariners 0
Dwight Gooden, who did not pitch in the majors in 1995 and was suspended for drugs, tosses a no-hitter at Yankee Stadium. The longtime Met resurfaces across town and has a comeback season at 31, a dozen years after he burst on the scene as a teen.

56. October 21, 1998 Yankees 9, Padres 6
The Padres, in admitted awe playing at Yankee Stadium for the first time, take a 5–2 lead into the seventh, but Chuck Knoblauch hits a three-run homer to tie it. Tino Martinez breaks the tie with a grand slam later in the inning and the Yankees roll to a sweep of San Diego.

57. April 15, 1976 Yankees 11, Twins 4
Yankee Stadium reopens with a Yankees win. Minnesota's Dan Ford hits the first home run in the newer and friendly ballpark for hitters, but the Yankees score plenty of runs late to make a winner of Dick Tidrow. The Yankees will keep on winning and take their first pennant since 1964.

58. September 28, 1951 Yankees 8, Red Sox 0
Allie Reynolds throws his second no hitter of the year. His first was July 12 in Cleveland. The Superchief starts a season-ending five-game sweep against the Red Sox in which pennant-winning New York outscores Boston, 29–4.

59. September 20, 1961 Yankees 4, Orioles 2 at Memorial Stadium
Roger Maris homers off Baltimore's Milt Pappas in New York's 154th game of the season, but it leaves him at 59 home runs. Hardheaded commissioner Ford Frick mandated that Maris must break the home run record in the same number of games as Ruth played. Maris will break the record in game 162. No asterisk is placed in the record books to distinguish the two feats, but the undue stress by the press and the commissioner takes its toll on the Yankees slugger.

60. September 26, 1961 Yankees 3, Orioles 2
Nearly a week after hitting his 59th home run, Roger Maris ties Babe Ruth's 1927 record with number 60 against Baltimore's Jack Fisher. A crowd of just 8,000 sees the historic event on a Tuesday in the Bronx.

61. May 1, 1920 Yankees 6, Red Sox 0
Big game, big bang by the Big Babe. His first home run as a Yankee clears the roof at the Polo Grounds in the first series between the Red Sox and Yankees in New York since Ruth was sold by Boston. The Yankees will double their attendance, becoming the first American League team to draw one million. They will outdraw their landlord for the first time since they moved into the Polo Grounds in 1913.

62. October 14, 2000 Yankees 5, Mariners 0 at Safeco Field
Roger Clemens is nearly unhittable at Safeco Field. He allows just an Al Martin double off Tino Martinez's glove in the seventh inning while striking out 15 Mariners and walking two in a complete game. Derek Jeter breaks up a scoreless Game 4 in the fifth inning with a three-run home run. The Yankees will take the pennant in six games.

63. October 17, 2004 Red Sox 6, Yankees 4 at Fenway Park
Leading three games to none and up by a run in the ninth inning with Mariano Rivera on the mound, pinch runner Dave Roberts steals second and then scores on Bill Mueller's single up the middle. David Ortiz gives the Red Sox the win with a home run off Paul Quantrill in the 12th inning. Everything goes Boston's way in their unprecedented series comeback.

64. October 9, 1938 Yankees 8, Cubs 3
The Yankees complete a sweep of the Cubs for their third straight world championship. New York breaks open a close game with four runs in the eighth inning to back Red Ruffing.

65. June 13, 1948 Yankees 5, Indians 3
Babe Ruth's number 3 is retired at Yankee Stadium to celebrate the 25th anniversary of Yankee Stadium. It is Ruth's last appearance at Yankee Stadium and he addresses the crowd in a raspy voice, leaning on a bat, wearing his old number.

66. October 7, 1904 Highlanders 3, Americans 2
Jack Chesbro wins his 41st game of the season, a number unequaled in American League history (Chicago's Ed Walsh will win 40 in 1908). The win gives the Highlanders a half-game lead over Boston. Chesbro will pitch in two doubleheaders over the next three days—giving him another unmatched AL record with 51 starts—and lose both as Boston takes the pennant.

67. July 18, 1987 Rangers 7, Yankees 2 at Arlington Stadium
Don Mattingly homers for the eighth straight game to tie Dale Long's major league record. Claudell Washington follows with another home run. Mattingly collects 10 homers during the streak. He will hit 30 for the year and set a major league mark with six grand slams in one season.

68. June 16, 1978 Yankees 4, Angels 0
Ron Guidry sets a franchise record by fanning 18 Angels at Yankee Stadium. He has a chance to tie the major league mark, but Ron Jackson grounds out to end the game. Guidry is now 11–0 and he'll reach 13 before finally losing on July 7 in Milwaukee. Guidry will go 25–3 and also lead the American League with nine shutouts and a 1.74 ERA; his 248 strikeouts will be second to Nolan Ryan.

69. April 11, 1912 Red Sox 5, Highlanders 3
Pinstripes first appear on New York's uniforms, creating the franchise's signature look. The team will be forgettable in this, their final year at Hilltop Park. New York will lose 102 times, the second and final time the franchise reaches three-digit losses.

70. April 18, 1929 Yankees 7, Red Sox 3
The Yankees take the field for the first time wearing numbers. The defending champions, who are presented diamond-studded watches by Judge Landis on Opening Day, are numbered according to lineup spots: Earle Combs 1, Mark Koenig 2, Babe Ruth 3, Lou Gehrig 4, Bob Meusel 5, Tony Lazzeri 6, Leo Durocher 7, and Johnny Grabowski 8. Pitcher George Pipgras (14) gets the win and Fred Heimach (17) closes out the game. Babe Ruth, married the previous day, doffs his cap to his new bride rounding second base after a homer against Red Ruffing.

71. May 15, 1941 White Sox 13, Yankees 1
It begins. Chicago murders the Yankees and Joe DiMaggio's single against Ed Smith isn't even worth noting at the time, but the Yankee Clipper will get at least one hit in each of the next 56 games to establish one of the most cherished records in baseball.

72. October 10, 1962 Yankees 5, Giants 2
The Giants and Yankees, in their seventh World Series but first since the continental shift to San Francisco, are tied in the eighth inning of Game 5. Tom Tresh hits a three-run home run off Jack Sanford and the Yankees take a one-game lead in the Series for the third time. Ralph Terry goes the distance. He'll do it again in Game 7 to earn Series MVP.

73. October 4, 1995 Yankees 7, Mariners 5
The Yankees, who blew a lead in the top of the seventh, rally in the bottom of the inning to tie Game 2 of the Division Series. Ken Griffey homers in the 12th for the lead, but the Yankees tie it once more. Finally, in the 15th inning, Jim Leyritz collects the first of many dramatic postseason home runs to send everyone home and give the Yankees a two-game lead in the series.

74. October 11, 2003 Yankees 4, Red Sox 3 at Fenway Park

Don Zimmer, the 72-year-old coach for the Yankees, charges at Pedro Martinez during an exchange between benches. Pedro brushes Zim aside and onto the ground. Yankees right fielder Karim Garcia later hops the wall during a bullpen fracas with a Boston groundskeeper. Mariano Rivera preserves the bizarre win.

75. June 16, 1997 Mets 5, Yankees 0

After 35 years sharing the same city, plus two years sharing the same stadium, the Yankees and Mets finally play a real game. Unsung Dave Mlicki throws a shutout for the Mets in front of 56,198 at Yankee Stadium.

76. October 5, 1921 Yankees 3, Giants 0

The Yankees and Giants play the first all-New York World Series. It is the first one-city World Series since 1906 and the first between two teams sharing the same park. Landlord and tenant will alternate home and away for each of the eight games in the best-of-nine Series. Yankee Carl Mays kicks off the Series with a shutout of the "home" Giants.

77. October 1, 1941 Yankees 3, Dodgers 2

The first of seven World Series between New York and Brooklyn—plus four more after they move to Los Angeles—starts the way many will end. The Yankees win a close game as Red Ruffing goes the distance and Joe Gordon homers at Yankee Stadium.

78. September 25, 1998 Yankees 6, Devil Rays 1

The Yankees set a new American League record for wins, eclipsing Cleveland's 1954 mark of 111. With their last four games against a first-year expansion club with the league's worst record, the Yankees will increase the mark to 114. The mark will last three years.

79. October 24, 1996 Yankees 1, Braves 0 at Atlanta–Fulton County Stadium

The Yankees score Game 5's only run, an unearned run in the fourth inning on Cecil Fielder's double, and Andy Pettitte makes it stand up until he leaves in the ninth. With the tying and go-ahead runs on base, Luis Polonia hits a deep drive against John Wetteland that gimpy Paul O'Neill fetches at the wall in the last game at Atlanta–Fulton County Stadium. The Yankees take a three games to two lead with the World Series heading back to New York.

80. August 13, 1995 Yankees 4, Indians 1

The same day that Mickey Mantle dies of cancer, Yankee Stadium holds an impromptu memorial. It begins with future Yankees center fielder Kenny Lofton, wearing number 7 for Cleveland, lining out to current Yankees center fielder Bernie Williams. Paul O'Neill homers in the first inning with Williams aboard and newcomer David Cone makes it stand up in front of 45,866. A monument for Mantle will be unveiled at Yankee Stadium in 1996.

81. June 8, 1967 Yankees 3, White Sox 1

Mickey Mantle Day honors the Yankees great, who is not in uniform for the first season since 1951. His number 7, first worn by Leo Durocher, is retired. Mantle is given a plaque in center field, as is Joe DiMaggio, which comes as a surprise to the Yankee Clipper and the 60,096 at Yankee Stadium.

82. July 29, 1978 Yankees 7, Twins 3

Just four days after being fired and replaced by Bob Lemon, the fans go wild as the Yankees announce at Old Timers Day that Martin will return as manager in 1980 and Lemon will become general manager. The switch will be made a year early—even after Lemon leads the Yankees to a miraculous comeback in '78—and both will return in a seemingly endless game of managerial musical chairs.

83. October 13, 1999 Yankees 4, Red Sox 3

After nearly a century of battling tooth and nail, the Yankees and Red Sox finally play a postseason game. Predictably, the Yankees win a close game. The Yankees tie it when Scott Brosius knocks the ball out of Jason Varitek's grasp in the seventh and win it in the 10th on a home run by Bernie Williams.

84. July 11, 1939 AL 3, NL 1

The All-Star Game comes to Yankee Stadium for the first time. Red Ruffing is one of six Yankees to start the game and Joe DiMaggio homers, but Bob Feller has the most memorable day. The 20-year-old pitches 3⅔ innings of shutout ball to finish the game, beginning with a double play after coming into a bases-loaded jam in the sixth.

85. October 10, 1904 Americans 3, Highlanders 2

A battle to the death for the pennant between the Boston Americans and New York Highlanders hinges on a season-ending doubleheader in New York. The game is tied in the top of the ninth when 41-game winner Jack Chesbro's wild pitch brings in the winning run. Boston takes the pennant for the second straight year, but there is no World Series because the New York Giants refuse to play. It will take an entire century for Boston to again beat New York in a winner-take-all contest for the American League pennant.

86. October 1, 2005 Yankees 8, Red Sox 4 at Fenway Park

After the Red Sox claimed first place for much of the season, the Yankees take the division title on the penultimate day of the season at Fenway. The Yankees score five times off Tim Wakefield in the first two innings and win behind Randy Johnson. Although Boston will also make the postseason, the ALCS will be without the Yankees and Red Sox for the first time since 2002.

87. October 8, 1995 Mariners 6, Yankees 5 at the Kingdome

After winning the opening two games of baseball's first best-of-five Division Series, the Yankees are locked in a do-or-die Game 5. Down 4–2 in the eighth, the Mariners tie the game and then bring in Randy Johnson, who'd pitched seven innings for a victory just two nights earlier. Johnson allows a run in the 12th, but in the bottom of the inning, Edgar Martinez ends the series with a double off Jack McDowell to plate Joey Cora and Ken Griffey Jr.

88. July 1, 2004 Yankees 5, Red Sox 4

The Yankees, who were swept in New York by the Red Sox the first time they visited, cap off a sweep punctuated by Derek Jeter's spectacular dive into the stands with two men on in the 12th inning. Jeter comes out of the game because of the impact and the Yankees fall behind in the 13th, but the Yankees rally for two in the bottom of the inning after two are out and none on.

89. October 7, 1950 Yankees 5, Phillies 2

So much for the "Whiz Kids." The Yankees complete a sweep of the Phillies despite hitting just .222. The Yanks knock out Bob Miller in the first inning and rookie Whitey Ford earns the first of his 10 World Series wins in the first of his 22 Fall Classic starts. Allie Reynolds gets the last out.

90. July 1, 1990 White Sox 4, Yankees 0 at Comiskey Park

Exactly 80 years after Comiskey Park opened, the Yankees take part in an extraordinary moment in the ballpark's final season. Yankee Andy Hawkins allows no hits and has two outs and nobody on in a scoreless game in the bottom of the eighth, but Mike Blowers misplays Sammy Sosa's grounder for an error, and Hawkins then walks two to load the bases. Outfielders Jim Leyritz and Jesse Barfield drop successive fly balls and four runs cross the plate. Hawkins becomes the first pitcher to throw a no-hitter and lose since Ken Johnson in 1964. Yet even the no-hitter, which would have been the last one at Comiskey, is later taken away from Hawkins when a records clarification requires all pitchers throwing no-hitters to go at least nine innings. Thanks to his teammates, Hawkins doesn't get the chance to go nine.

91. October 13, 1996 Yankees 6, Orioles 4 at Camden Yards

The Yankees take the ALCS in five games. Jim Leyritz, Cecil Fielder, and Darryl Strawberry all homer during a six-run third inning at Camden Yards. Andy Pettitte gets the win and John Wetteland picks up the final out to give the Yankees their first pennant since 1981. New York wins all three games at Camden Yards, twice holding the Orioles to four hits or less, while the Birds allow 10 home runs in five games. Yankees manager Joe Torre reaches the World Series for the first time in 4,272 games as a player and manager.

92. October 12, 1960 Yankees 12, Pirates 0 at Forbes Field

Whitey Ford shuts out the Pirates for the second time, evening the World Series. Game 6 marks the third time in the Series that New York has scored in double figures. Bobby Richardson drives in three runs with two triples to set a World Series record with 12 RBIs. Four Yankees will have at least 10 hits in the Series—Roberto Clemente will lead Pittsburgh with nine—and the Pirates head into Game 7 having been outscored by a margin of 46–17.

93. April 22, 1903 Senators 3, Highlanders 1 at American League Park (Washington)

After relocating from Baltimore, the New York Highlanders play their first game, a 3–1 loss at Washington. Jack Chesbro starts and loses the first game played by New York's American League club. Clark Griffith is manager.

94. October 1, 2005 Yankees 8, Red Sox 4 at Fenway Park

After the Red Sox claimed first place for much of the season, the Yankees take the division title on the penultimate day of the season at Fenway. The Yankees score five times off Tim Wakefield in the first two innings and win behind Randy Johnson. Although Boston will also make the postseason, the ALCS will be without the Yankees and Red Sox for the first time since 2002.

95. July 19, 1977 NL 7, AL 5

Joe Morgan homers to lead off the game and Jim Palmer is torched for four runs in the opening inning, including a Greg Luzinski home run. Don Sutton is named MVP and Dodgers teammate Steve Garvey adds a home run.

96. April 30, 1903 Highlanders 6, Senators 2

In their first home game in New York, the Highlanders defeat Washington in the inaugural game at American League Park, later known as Hilltop Park for its high perch in the city. Players dress at the hotel because the locker rooms are unfinished, as is the grand stand. Jack Chesbro picks up the win.

97. August 21, 2006 Yankees 2, Red Sox 1 at Fenway Park

The Yankees complete a five-game sweep of the Red Sox at Fenway Park, essentially wrapping up the AL East. It is the first five-game sweep by the Yankees over the Red Sox since the end of the 1951 season, Joe DiMaggio's final regular season games and the end of Mickey Mantle's rookie year. Former Yankee David Wells pitches well for Boston, but the Yankees snap a tie in the eighth inning. It is reminiscent of 1978's Boston Massacre, only this time an extra game is added and the Yankees outscore Boston, 49–26.

98. September 30, 1973 Tigers 8, Yankees 5

The original Yankee Stadium hosts its last game as John Hiller gets Mike Hegan to fly out to Mickey Stanley to end the 1973 season. The place will be completely refurbished, with obstructing poles and the famous frieze removed. The Yankees will play the next two years at Shea Stadium.

99. April 24, 1917 Yankees 2, Red Sox 1 at Fenway Park

The first no-hitter by a Yankee comes at Fenway Park. George Mogridge tops the Red Sox.

100. August 27, 1938 Yankees 13, Indians 0

Monte Pearson tosses the first no-hitter at Yankee Stadium. He does it against his former team.

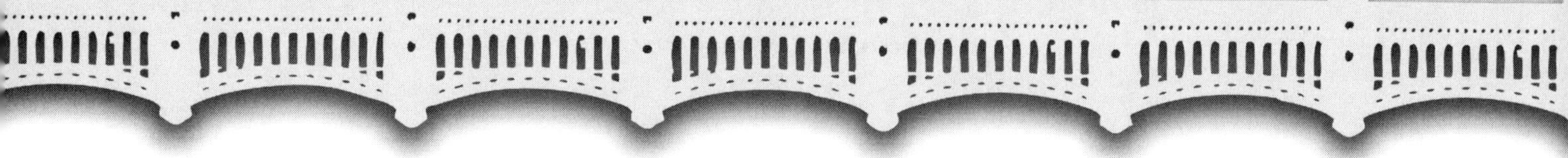

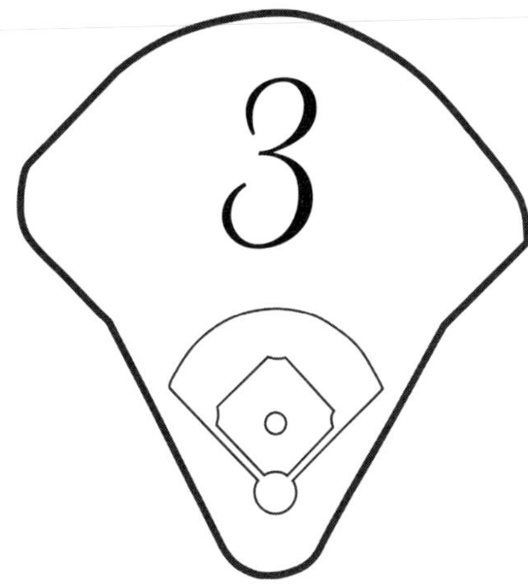

Biographies of the Greatest Yankees

More than 1,400 players and managers have suited up for the New York Yankees since they first took the field in 1903. There obviously isn't room to tell the stories of every one of them, however, so we've narrowed down the field to choose the 40 Yankees who were most integral to the history of the team.

Selecting only 40 Yankees to be profiled was not an easy process. Some choices were no-brainers—for example, everyone inducted into the Hall of Fame with a Yankees cap made our list. The four managers who led the Yankees to most of their postseason appearances also made the cut. But not every choice was so easy.

We tried to ensure that most Yankees teams were represented on this list, but some of history's more forgettable New York teams, such as the 1913 edition, didn't feature a single player who even came close to making our 40-man roster. Most of the 20 players that have played the most games in a Yankees uniform are profiled in the following pages, but three such players—Roy White (No. 6), Frankie Crosetti (No. 12), and Wally Pipp (No. 17)—didn't make the cut. On the other hand, Catfish Hunter, who only appeared in 137 games with the Yankees but was the first free agent signed by George Steinbrenner, is included. Steinbrenner himself, who has now sat atop the organization for a record 34 years, was the only owner we had room for on this list.

Some readers might be surprised that their favorite Yankees' hero isn't profiled in this chapter. That's inevitable when you produce this type of list, especially when dealing with a franchise like the Yankees, who have provided their fans with an almost endless parade of stars over a long and storied history. There can be no doubt, however, that the roster of biographies included in this section is of world-championship caliber.

The roll call:

- Barrow, Ed
- Berra, Yogi
- Chesbro, Jack
- Clemens, Roger
- Combs, Earle
- Dickey, Bill
- DiMaggio, Joe
- Ford, Whitey
- Gehrig, Lou
- Gomez, Lefty
- Guidry, Ron
- Howard, Elston
- Hoyt, Waite
- Huggins, Miller
- Hunter, Catfish
- Jackson, Reggie
- Jeter, Derek
- Lazzeri, Tony
- Mantle, Mickey
- Maris, Roger
- Martin, Billy
- Mattingly, Don
- McCarthy, Joe
- Munson, Thurman
- Nettles, Graig
- O'Neill, Paul
- Pennock, Herb
- Pettitte, Andy
- Posada, Jorge
- Randolph, Willie
- Reynolds, Allie
- Rivera, Mariano
- Rizzuto, Phil
- Ruffing, Red
- Ruth, Babe
- Steinbrenner, George
- Stengel, Casey
- Torre, Joe
- Williams, Bernie
- Winfield, Dave

Ed Barrow

Casual fans recall that Babe Ruth moved from Boston to New York in 1920, launching the Yankees into the ranks of winners while the Red Sox fell back in the dust. But another key piece moved the very next year—Edward Grant Barrow, a man whose influence on the Yankees' success went beyond even Ruth's.

Barrow never played baseball professionally, but he had served as manager and executive for various minor league franchises and had a stint as manager of the Detroit Tigers in 1903–04. After serving a long tenure as president of the Eastern League, Barrow came to the Red Sox in 1918 and managed the club to a World Series win, their last of the century.

While there, Barrow recognized the value in Babe Ruth's bat, converting him to the outfield so that he could hit every day he didn't pitch. After following Ruth to the Yankees to take the post of general manager, Barrow proceeded to continue stocking the New York club with Boston's best talents—which Sox owner Harry Frazee was only too happy to sell.

Four more players from the 1918 championship club followed, and Barrow handpicked three more in the following years. Barrow also built up a Yankee farm system in the days when such things didn't really exist, helping to discover such talents as Lou Gehrig, Tony Lazzeri, Joe DiMaggio, and Yogi Berra. From 1920 through 1945, Barrow was the architect behind "Murderer's Row," and the incredible teams of 1927 and 1936–39. New York won 14 pennants and 10 World Series championships during his tenure.

Barrow was elected to the National Baseball Hall of Fame in Cooperstown, New York, in 1953, just three months before he passed away at age 85.

Yogi Berra

Yogi Berra may be most famous for his malapropisms ("Nobody goes there anymore; it's too popular"), but when you're talking about winning ballplayers, he takes a back seat to no one.

He holds a major league record in being part of 10 world championship clubs, plus appearing in four other World Series his team *didn't* win. As a manager, he is best remembered for being fired after winning the 1964 AL title and getting unceremoniously dumped by George Steinbrenner just 16 games into the 1985 season. Still, Yogi remains the only man to pilot both the Mets and Yankees to the World Series.

Yogi is on the short list of most famous Yankees, yet the Missouri-born catcher came to New York after neither his hometown Browns or Cardinals would cough up a $500 bonus in 1942. Amazingly enough, neither St. Louis team would give Yogi as much as they gave childhood pal Joe Garagiola. While the New York Giants and Brooklyn Dodgers both tried to get Berra later, the Yankees wisely held on to him.

Eventually, Berra survived combat in World War II, a tour through the Yankees' stocked minor league system, and two years as a spare catcher/outfielder before emerging as the linchpin for a baseball dynasty.

He was a three-time American League Most Valuable Player, an All-Star for 15 consecutive years, and enjoyed three streaks of four straight World Series appearances. Yogi swung at anything, but never struck out more than 38 times in a season, making contact and hitting for average and power. Maligned for his defense when he first came up, he is nonetheless the only man to catch a perfect game in the World Series and was the first backstop to go an entire season without an error. Despite frequent comments about Yogi's lack of smarts, manager Casey Stengel, who (wrongfully) received a few such barbs himself, called Berra his "assistant manager."

And although it is unlikely that anyone will ever surpass his 75 games or 71 hits in World Series competition, Yogi's sayings will last longer than the after taste of his most famous endorsement, Yoo-Hoo chocolate drink. Yogi never took himself too seriously. After all, "It ain't the heat, it's the humility."

Jack Chesbro

In 1903, the American League invaded New York City. Former National League star "Happy Jack" Chesbro took the hill on Opening Day for the Big Apple's new team at newly built Hilltop Park. Chesbro had topped the NL in winning percentage in 1901 (21–10) and 1902 (28–6) and, more importantly, had led the Pittsburgh Pirates to two pennants. He jumped ship to the upstart American League at the behest of league president Ban Johnson, who considered a winning franchise in New York key to the new organization's legitimacy.

In 1903, Chesbro's impressive spitball led him to a 21–15 mark, but the team (variously nicknamed the Hilltoppers, Highlanders, and Yankees by the newspapers) did not contend. In 1904, though, Chesbro set the "modern" record for wins, with 41, and took his team to the brink of a pennant, only to throw it away—literally.

"Happy Jack" pitched 48 complete games in 51 starts, went 41–12, and in 454⅔ innings fanned 239 and posted a 1.82 ERA. Chesbro faced down powerhouse Boston multiple times that season, including besting Cy Young 8–2 on Opening Day, and defeated them twice in a five-day stretch at the Huntington Avenue Grounds in September. The very end of the season found the two teams neck and neck, with five final games crammed into three days. In addition, a scheduling glitch (Columbia University's football team had rented Hilltop Park for a day) meant the teams would play one game in New York, then a doubleheader in Boston, then a doubleheader in New York.

Chesbro pitched the first of those five and won 3–2. New York needed to win two of the remaining four games to clinch the pennant. Manager Clark Griffith planned to leave Chesbro at home to rest up for the finale, but Jack begged to pitch in Boston. He did, but unravelled badly and Boston won both games. They returned to New York and, after a day off (Sunday baseball being outlawed at the time), Chesbro took the hill for the fourth time in eight days.

He pitched a good game, with the score 2–2 going into the ninth. A botched grounder, a sacrifice bunt, and a groundout gave Boston a runner on third with two out. Chesbro went to 0–2 on the next batter, then tried to throw his best spitball of the day. Perhaps he did; catcher Red Kleinow missed the ball and the run scored, giving Boston the pennant.

Despite suffering the ignominy of throwing a pennant-losing wild pitch, Chesbro was popular. He remained with the franchise until 1909, when a trade sent the native of North Adams, Massachusetts to Boston, where he started only one game before retiring.

After Chesbro died in 1931, his widow fought unsuccessfully for years to have the scoring decision on the pitch changed from "wild pitch" to "passed ball." John Dwight Chesbro was elected to the Hall of Fame in 1946.

Roger Clemens

It's hard to imagine now that in the 1980s Dwight Gooden was considered by most fans and many pundits to be a greater pitcher than Roger Clemens. It's even harder to imagine now just why and how Clemens left Boston after the 1996 season in one of the greatest miscalculations in baseball history.

In addition to his record seven Cy Young Awards, Clemens enjoys a distinction that practically no one knows about. Through 1999, Clemens had won 247 games and lost 134; a .648 percentage while pitching for teams with a combined winning percentage of .522. The .126 differential is the greatest pitcher-team differential in history for any hurler with 100 or more wins.

Clemens won his first Cy Young in 1986 with a spectacular 24–4 season that also earned him an AL MVP trophy. He followed that by skipping training camp in a contract dispute, limping out of the gate to post a 4–6 record by June, and then smashing through the league the rest of the year to finish 20–9 and earn his second Cy. Despite some shoulder problems, he put together a 21–6 season with a major-league low 1.93 ERA in 1990, yet he didn't win his third Cy Young until the next season—when he had a lesser 18–10 mark. From 1993 through 1996, "The Rocket" won only 50 games due to a combination of injuries and poor support. Famously described by Sox GM Dan Duquette as being in the "twilight of his career," Clemens went to Toronto in 1997 as a free agent. With the Blue Jays, Clemens' "twilight" looked pretty good: he won the pitching Triple Crown two years running and walked away with his fourth and fifth Cy Young trophies, even though the Jays were a mediocre team. Despite his success, Clemens forced the Jays to trade him, setting the stage for him to join the great New York teams of the late 1990s.

In 1986 Clemens set the major league record for strikeouts in a game at 20, then repeated the feat 10 years later when he was supposedly washed up. He passed 3,000 Ks in 1998. Then, in 1999, Clemens was selected by the panel for Major League Baseball's "All Century Team" as one of the 100 greatest players ever as well as chosen by the fans as one of the six greatest pitchers of all-time.

That might have been enough for an ordinary superstar, but Clemens was far from finished. After 15 seasons, the dominant right-hander earned a coveted World Series ring in 1999 while pitching New York's Series-clinching game against Atlanta, remarking that he finally "felt what it was like to be a Yankee." Both he and the Yankees repeated as world champions in 2000. Following a rigorous workout program during both the offseason and the regular season, Clemens went 20–3 in 2001 with a historic winning streak that earned him his sixth Cy Young. In 2002 he passed the 300-win plateau, notching his 3,500th strikeout in the same game.

"The Rocket" supposedly retired after that season, but he was quickly lured out of retirement when his friend and former Yankees teammate Andy Pettitte persuaded Clemens to join him in their hometown Houston Astros' rotation. After two seasons there, including a seventh Cy Young award and some truly heroic postseason pitching that helped vault Houston into its first World Series in 2005, Clemens went into semi-retirement. That didn't last long, though, as he re-emerged in mid season to join Houston in 2006, then did a repeat and rejoined the Yankees in the middle of 2007. Clemens is second to Nolan Ryan on the all-time strikeout record with 4,672.

Earle Combs

Follow the history books backward through the Yankees' great center fielders, from Bernie Williams through Mickey Mantle and Joe DiMaggio, and you eventually arrive at Earle Combs, the leadoff man for the 1927 "Murderer's Row" Yankees.

Playing for the Yankees from 1924–35, he batted in front of and shared the outfield with Babe Ruth nearly his entire career. But he was a counterpoint to the larger-than-life Bambino, quiet when Ruth was loud, clean-living when Ruth caroused.

Combs, who hailed from Pebworth, Kentucky, cut his teeth in the Pine Mountain League. In 1923, he hit .380 at Louisville to become the hottest prospect in the American Association. It cost the Yankees 50 grand to land his contract. The team considered Combs the ideal replacement for underachieving centerfielder Whitey Witt.

Unfortunately, injuries bookended Combs' career. Early in 1924, he broke his leg at Yankee Stadium and only appeared in 24 games, allowing Witt to hang on for one more year. Combs finally took the job in 1925, hitting .342 and racking up 203 hits in 150 games. Thereafter he was never short of a stellar player, his lifetime average coming in at .325 (and his OBP at .397).

"The Kentucky Colonel," as he was known, had his best year in 1927, helping the Yankees to a decisive world championship. An offensive force in every category, he knocked out 231 hits, scored 137 runs, and batted .356. He cracked the AL's top ten in batting, slugging, and on-base percentage. Combs was forced to retire in 1935, a year after fracturing his skull crashing into the outfield wall at Sportsman's Park in St. Louis. That injury, and another to his throwing arm resulting from a second collision with teammate Red Rolfe, shelved Combs for good.

Bill Dickey

Bill Dickey was the heart and soul of the Yankees throughout the 1930s and into the 40s. He played his entire 17- year career in the Bronx, and a left-handed power swing allowed him to hit 135 of his 202 career home runs at home. Dickey also used a rifle of a right arm to shut down enemy baserunners. In addition, he was a quiet influence, steadying his pitchers and sharing a room on the road with the other quiet Yankee, Lou Gehrig. But Dickey could show a fiery streak on the field; he was once fined and suspended for breaking outfielder Carl Reynolds' jaw with one punch after a collision at the plate.

After a brief 1928 call-up, Dickey became the team's starting catcher in 1929, locking up the position with a .324 batting average and .979 fielding percentage. In 1931, he became the first catcher to go an entire season without a passed ball. The following year, the Yankees reached the World Series, where Dickey batted .438 in the four-game sweep of Chicago. From 1933–46 he made 11 All-Star appearances, solidifying his reputation as the pre-eminent catcher of his era.

He and the Yankees hit their stride at the same time; from 1936–39 Dickey topped 20 home runs and 100 RBIs each year, while New York won four consecutive World Series. Though his production slipped a bit in 1940, Dickey bounced back with some good years before losing the 1944 and 1945 seasons to military service. He returned in 1946 as a player—taking a young Yogi Berra under his wing—but moved to the bench midway through the season, taking the place of fired manager Joe McCarthy.

Dickey still holds the record for catching the most World Series games (38), and the Yankees won seven of the eight world championships in which he participated. He also set a record for catching 100 or more games in 13 straight seasons. Dickey returned to the Yankees in 1949 to continue his tutelage of Berra, which transformed the youngster into a premier defensive catcher.

A paucity of funny, salacious, or otherwise unusual anecdotes about Dickey lends credence to the idea that he is among the most colorlessly efficient of all the great Yankees: businesslike, very successful, and somewhat drab in retrospect. But "color" aside, his talent was undeniable. Dickey gained entry to the Baseball Hall of Fame in 1954, and the Yankees retired the No. 8 worn by him (as well as Berra) in 1972 when the student joined his mentor in Cooperstown. Dickey passed away in 1993 at age 86.

Joe DiMaggio

The revered Yankee Clipper has been the face of the Yankees' franchise for nearly 70 years. Even now, close to a decade after his death and more than a half century since he last appeared in pinstripes, Joe DiMaggio remains the standard bearer against which all Yankees greats are judged.

DiMaggio's carefully cultivated image—both during his playing days and in retirement—led to the public viewing him completely differently from any other superstar on the planet. He wasn't perfect, yet Simon & Garfunkel held him up as the model of a bygone era, and Ernest Hemingway made DiMaggio the idol of heroic fisherman Santiago in *The Old Man And The Sea*. Joltin' Joe hobnobbed with Frank Sinatra, married the most revered Hollywood starlet in history, and insisted that he always be announced last at Old Timers festivities at Yankee Stadium.

After starring in his home state Pacific Coast League, DiMaggio hit the ground running, batting .323 in his rookie year in 1936. He finished second in MVP voting the next season after hitting 46 home runs, driving in 167, and scoring 151 runs—all career highs. DiMaggio was named MVP for the first time in 1939, then won the award a second time in 1941 over Ted Williams, even though the Boston superstar finished with a .406 batting average. Joe D. won the coveted award thanks to his 56-game hitting streak and a Yankees pennant that saw the Bronx Bombers finish 17 games ahead of Williams' Red Sox.

Like most ballplayers in their prime in the early 1940s, DiMaggio missed significant time while serving in the military during World War II. He sat out three full seasons (1943–45), then struggled in his first year back, failing to hit .300 for the first time in his career. In 1947, however, the Yankee Clipper was back to his old self, claiming his third MVP award—though it was not without controversy, as Williams won the Triple Crown while pacing the AL in batting average, home runs, RBIs, walks, runs, on-base percentage and slugging percentage. The Yankees, however, won the pennant, and DiMaggio was named MVP by one point, 202–201. Much was (and still is) made of the fact that one of the 24 voters left Williams completely off the ballot, yet three writers inexplicably also failed to list DiMaggio as one of the league's top 10 players. Athletics shortstop Eddie Joost, a .206 hitter that season, received two surprising first-place votes—nearly equaling Williams' total of three—and allegations later surfaced of wagers being placed by the voters with bookies, further complicating the issue.

DiMaggio retired following the 1951 season after hitting a career low .263. His wait for enshrinement in Cooperstown was the shortest possible, as he was elected to baseball's Hall of Fame in 1955.

Whitey Ford

Whitey Ford was the biggest of the big-game pitchers. During his 16 years with the Yankees, Ford set World Series records with ten wins, 146 innings, and 94 strikeouts, and tossed an amazing 32 consecutive scoreless innings.

More than that, in a way Ford *was* the archetype of the Yankees. Unlike the country-fried Mickey Mantle, the New York-born Ford was big city all the way. The star pitcher for the best baseball team in the world was comfortable in crowds, unflappable on the mound, and star material in the Cadillac-and-Marilyn 1950s—when Fun City saw itself (and was seen by others) as the center of the known universe.

Ford was almost two separate pitchers. With nobody on base, he lined up nearly straight-up to the hitter and used a full, protracted wind-up to explode toward the plate. Confusing hitters with the motion of his arms and legs, Ford's delivery made him look faster than he was. With runners on base, Ford came quickly out of a much more straightforward no-windup delivery, quickly taking care of business. Rarely would he give in to a hitter; he wasn't afraid of walking opponents, although his base on balls rate improved over time, especially in 1963 when the strike zone was expanded. As a result, Ford held opponents to a lifetime .235 batting average and allowed just 228 homers in 3,170⅓ career innings.

Ford began his big league career in 1950, going 9–1 in 12 starts and eight relief appearances; this dream season culminated in his winning the clinching game of the World Series. Unfortunately, Ford then missed the next two seasons while serving in the Army. He returned to big league duty in 1953 and won 18 games, the first of four straight seasons in which he posted at least 16 victories.

Ford's best seasons came in the 1960s, as he racked up bigger numbers once Casey Stengel—who staggered Ford's starts in order to save him for key opponents—was fired. Given more games to pitch, Ford took advantage. He went 25–4 in 1961 to win the Cy Young award, and he was 24–7 in 1963, finishing third in AL MVP voting. He won five straight World Series starts (two outings each in 1960 and 1961, and Game 1 of the '62 Fall Classic).

Elston Howard, the Yankees' superb backstop, dubbed Ford "The Chairman of the Board" because of the way Ford managed his fielders, moving them around to match opposing hitters. Drinking partner Mickey Mantle, on the other hand, gave Ford the nickname "Slick" because of Whitey's fondness for whiskey.

Beset by arm problems, Ford retired in 1967 after going 4–9 in his last two seasons. His career winning percentage of .690 (236–106) was the best compiled since 1901 (until surpassed by Pedro Martinez almost a half-century later), though it didn't come without some controversy. Ford admitted to scuffing the baseball, though he was adamant that he only cheated near the end of his career. Enough sportswriters felt uncertain about making him a first-ballot Hall of Famer that Ford had to wait until his second year of eligibility to pass through the portals at Cooperstown in 1974.

Lou Gehrig

Called "The Iron Horse" largely because of his durability, in point of fact he was also one of the strongest players of his day. Immaculately toned and slope-shouldered, the lefty-hitting Gehrig stepped into the pitch and used his whip-like swing to produced fearsome line drives and moon-shot homers. He also had terrific plate discipline, drawing 100 or more walks an amazing 11 times. Four times Gehrig paced the AL in on-base percentage; twice, he led the loop in slugging. Though not fast, he was aggressive on the basepaths but was a very poor percentage base stealer. Lacking flexibility, Gehrig played a mediocre, at best, first base—but his booming offense more than made up for it.

Baseball diehards are already familiar with the story of how Lou Gehrig broke into the Yankees starting lineup, replacing an ailing Wally Pipp at first. But what many do not know is that Gehrig could have started his consecutive games streak 18 months earlier, when skipper Miller Huggins wanted to insert Gehrig for the injured Pipp in the 1923 World Series. Though Gehrig's entry into the Yankees' starting lineup was eventually delayed because Giants manager John McGraw refused to let the Yankees put Gehrig on their postseason roster, Larrupin' Lou's place among the baseball immortals could not be put off for long.

Gehrig became New York's starting first baseman early in 1925, and it didn't take long for him to become Ruth's near equal at the plate. He hit .373 with 46 homers in 1927, and would hit for a *higher* average in two of the next three seasons. Despite his thunderous bat, Gehrig never struck out more than 84 times a season. In fact, in 1931 when he led the league in runs, hits, RBIs, total bases, and home runs, he fanned just 56 times.

By the mid-1930s Gehrig was arguably the best player in the game. He won the Triple Crown in 1934 and led the AL in nearly every offensive category two years later, though he finished fourth in batting, 44 points behind Luke Appling. Unfortunately, the Iron Horse would have only one more good season before his skills began to deteriorate. After hitting .351 with 37 homers and 159 RBI in 1937, Gehrig slipped badly the next season, already starting to feel the effects of ALS, the disease that would kill him, and failed to hit .300 for the first time since his rookie campaign.

Gehrig started the first eight games in 1938, but took himself out in the middle of the eighth game, and never took the field again. His official retirement ceremony, when he proclaimed himself "the luckiest man on the face of the earth," took place three months later. The Hall of Fame suspended its five-year waiting period and allowed Gehrig in right away, which was a sound decision since Gehrig was dead in less than two years.

Lefty Gomez

While not as consistent as fellow Yankees ace Red Ruffing, Lefty Gomez had several better individual seasons for the Bronx Bombers and was funnier, too.

Gomez broke in with New York in 1930, then won 21 or more games three of his first four full years in pinstripes. His 1934 campaign, when he topped the AL in wins (26–5), innings, and strikeouts, earned him a third place finish in MVP voting. Unfortunately, he enjoyed just one more truly great season.

In 1935 Gomez dropped to 12–15—the only full year in which he failed to win more than he lost—which marked the beginning of a steady decline. He reached the 20-game mark just once more, and only one time posted a sub-3.00 ERA. Both of those landmarks came during a fine 1937 season in which he again led the junior circuit in wins, ERA, and strikeouts.

Gomez was known, especially among his teammates, for his quick wit and self-deprecating humor. He claimed Jimmie Foxx had "muscles in his hair," and held up a World Series game to admire an airplane flying overhead.

Arm problems had begun to take a toll. "Goofy" made only five starts in 1940, and the Yankees cut ties with him after just 13 appearances in 1942. He tried briefly to stick with the Washington Senators the next season, but hung up the spikes after only one game.

Upon retiring from baseball, he filled out a job application with the Wilson sporting goods company. When asked the question, "Why did you leave your last job?" he wrote, "I couldn't get anybody out."

It was no joke when the veteran's committee selected him for induction into the Hall of Fame in 1972. While Gomez was at times a great performer, his career as a regular was relatively short (only 10 years with 20 or more starts). His election to the Hall owes much to two factors: his pitching in New York for a series of great teams, and his career as a celebrated dinner speaker, which kept his funny anecdotes and stories in circulation. Certainly Gomez had a top-flight fastball; he led the AL in strikeouts three times, wins and percentage twice, and twice posted the league's best ERA. Despite that, Gomez' 189 career victories are fairly short for a Hall of Famer.

Ron Guidry

"Louisiana Lightning" Ron Guidry, a star Yankees lefty for many years, will forever be remembered for his incredible 1978 campaign, which saw him lead the league in most of the big pitching categories. He even set a big league record.

The model of consistency in an otherwise turbulent year in the Bronx, he won his first 13 decisions, including 10 straight starts from May 5 to June 22. On June 17, he fanned 18 Angels to set an all-time Yankees single-game record, a mark he still holds. Guidry finished the year 25–3, which set a record for winning percentage (.893) for a 20-game winner. He led the AL with a 1.74 ERA—more than half a run better than runner-up Jon Matlack—and nine shutouts, also allowing the fewest hits per nine innings.

Guidry, who hailed from Lafayette, Louisiana, was an avid hunter and fisherman, traits which earned him another nickname, "Gator." An early-career banishment to the bullpen turned out well when Guidry used the time to learn the slider from Sparky Lyle. Once he perfected that pitch, Guidry seemingly became a great pitcher overnight. The Yankees moved him into the starting rotation for good in late May of '77, and he went 11–3 over his final 15 starts.

While Guidry was hardly a flash in the pan, he never did come close to duplicating his magic 1978 season. He won 16 or more games six times and crossed the 20-win threshold three times. In a nine-year stretch between 1977–85, he won more games than any other big league hurler and posted an ERA lower than the league average in 10 of 11 seasons. If the Yankees had more players like him during the 1980s, Guidry might be even better remembered today. The team was mediocre, though, and arm problems forced him to retire in 1988 after making just 10 starts.

From 1990 on, Guidry served the Yankees as a spring training instructor, then in 2006 took over as the team's pitching coach. He worked with many young pitchers who came to the Bronx for the first time.

Elston Howard

Frank "Teannie" Edwards, a former Negro League ballplayer, discovered Elston Howard on the sandlots of St. Louis. When Jackie Robinson made his major league debut in 1947, Howard was 18 years old, working in a grocer's, finishing high school—and playing semi-pro ball for Teannie. Although various Big Ten schools pursued young Elston, waving athletic scholarships, his mother Emmeline agreed to let him join the Kansas City Monarchs for $500 a month. While with the Monarchs, Howard played for Buck O'Neil and roomed with Ernie Banks.

Legendary Yankees scout Tom Greenwade bought Howard from the Monarchs in 1950. Despite Elston's talent, though, it took the Yankees five years to bring him to the big leagues. Mitigating factors for this included Howard's compulsory military service and the fact that the Yankees had three catchers in the bigs: Yogi Berra, Ralph Houk, and Charlie Silvera.

Rather than send him back down in 1954, the Yankees arranged for Howard to play for the Toronto Maple Leafs in the International League. Canada was more welcoming to black players than many other destinations and Howard won the league's MVP Award, hitting .331 with 22 homers and 108 RBI.

During spring training 1955, Casey Stengel batted Howard cleanup, prompting Arthur Daley to write in the *New York Times*, "He seems certain to be the first Negro to make the Yankees. . . . They've waited for one to come along who [is] 'the Yankee type.'" Daley was presumably referring to Elston's quiet demeanor, but his talent and versatility made him an instant contributor. He hit .290 in 97 games, with another five hits in the World Series, including a home run in his first World Series at bat.

In the next five seasons, Stengel relentlessly platooned Howard, using him behind the plate in tandem with Berra and also in the outfield. Howard always wanted more time behind the plate. In 1958, Elston was a World Series hero. With the Yankees down 3–1 in the Series, he started in left despite having dental work that day and made a game-saving catch in the outfield, turning the entire Series around. The New York chapter of the Baseball Writers Association of America named him the outstanding player in the Series.

After the heartbreaking loss to Pittsburgh in the 1960 Series, and subsequent firing of Stengel, Howard was promoted to everyday catcher by new manager Ralph Houk—the same man whose roster slot Howard took in 1955. A new batting stance also helped Howard to a career year, hitting .348 with 21 home runs in 129 games. The Yankees won the World Series handily, then captured the flag again in 1962. In 1963, he became the first African-American to win American League MVP honors, leading the Yankees to the Series again, though the Koufax-Drysdale Dodgers kept them in check.

1964 was the dynasty's last hurrah, with Howard reaching career highs in games (150) and hits (172) and making his eighth consecutive All-Star team. He made his final All-Star appearance in 1965, and after that, injuries limited his effectiveness. His career ended with the 1967–68 Boston Red Sox.

Howard coached for the Yankees but never reached his goal of becoming a major league manager. He died in 1980 as a result of Myocarditis, a condition in which the Coxsackie virus attacked his cardiac muscles.

Waite Hoyt

One of several players to be tagged with the nickname "Schoolboy," Waite Hoyt described himself as a "fastball pitcher." The Giants signed Hoyt when he was only a 15-year-old high school sophomore. After throwing batting practice for them, then spending a couple of years in the minors, Hoyt pitched one game for the Giants in 1918, then sporadically for Boston in 1919–20, and finally joined the mass exodus of Red Sox players to New York in 1921, where he went 19–13 with a 3.09 ERA.

That October he became one of the first members of the Yankees postseason pantheon, starting three games, pitching all 27 innings, and not allowing an earned run. Unfortunately, after winning his first two starts, he lost the series clincher 1–0 on an error. Nonetheless he was the ace of the decade for the Yankees, starting 28 or more games every year until 1929—his final year with New York—when he was 10–9 in 25 starts. Like most good pitchers of the time, Hoyt came out of the bullpen to save some games as well. He never walked more than 81 men in a season, and combined with southpaw Herb Pennock for a great righty-lefty tandem in the rotation.

Hoyt continued to excel in October, posting a career ERA of 1.83 in seven World Series, six with the Yankees (of which they won three) and one with the Philadelphia Athletics in 1931, which they lost. After leaving the Yankees at age 30, Hoyt bounced around several teams, then landed with Pittsburgh from 1933–1937.

But there was more to Hoyt than his fastball. In the off-season, he worked both in vaudeville and for a funeral home, earning him the nickname the "Merry Mortician." He was among the first former players to become a baseball broadcaster and was renowned in Cincinnati, where he was heard from 1941 through 1965, for his "rain delay" stories, many of which featured former teammate Babe Ruth. He was elected to the Hall of Fame in 1969 and passed away in 1984 after a heart attack.

Miller Huggins

Nicknamed the "Mighty Mite" for his small stature and fierce play, Miller Huggins was a switch-hitting second baseman from Cincinnati who went on to be one of baseball's most prominent managers.

Upon finishing his law degree at University of Cincinnati, Huggins, 24, broke in with the Reds in 1904. In 1909 he was traded to the Cardinals, and by 1913 had become the moribund club's player-manager.

Huggins, a fine, scrappy, defensive-minded second baseman, also led the league in walks (by a wide margin) four times, and could be counted on for an on-base percentage around .400, though nobody measured it at the time. During the 1916 season he quit playing and concentrated on the managerial side, but the Cardinals franchise was sold in 1918 and the new owners replaced Huggins with Branch Rickey. Ban Johnson, ever watchful for ways to take talent out of the National League and into the American, urged Yankees owner Colonel Jacob Ruppert to hire Huggins.

In 1918, his first year as Yankee manager, the team finished 60–63—though not great, this was better than the club's finish the previous year—and they reached third in 1919 at 80–59. In 1920, Ruth and other superior weapons arrived, and so did winning; the Bronx Bombers captured 95 games to finish just below the Indians and White Sox. They would win AL titles the next three years, but as Ruth went, so did the club. In spring 1925 Ruth arrived overweight and, in Huggins' eyes, more interested in carousing than in playing ball. His first homer didn't come until two months into the season.

By August, Huggins was fed up. He suspended Ruth and fined him $5,000. The Babe's resulting obscenity-laced tirade ensured he wouldn't play again until he apologized. He was out nine days, and the Yankees ended that season in seventh place, going 69–85. Ruth—as well as several other players—got the message: Huggins was about winning. The Yankees returned to first place for the next three seasons and Huggins was credited with creating the first truly serious-minded, win-or-nothing Yankees: 1927's Murderers Row.

Huggins fell ill partway through the 1929 season with erysipelas, a severe skin infection, which manifested as a carbuncle under his right eye. Unable to fight off the spread of the infection in the age before antibiotics, he died September 25 at St. Francis Hospital. At the time the Yankees received news of his passing, they were at Fenway Park, beating the Sox 7–3. The Yankees then coughed up seven runs, but managed to battle back and win 11–10. Two days later, the AL cancelled all games in honor of Huggins' funeral in Cincinnati.

In Huggins' 12 seasons with the Yankees, the team compiled a 1,023–724 record, amassing a .707 winning percentage. His was the first monument erected in 1932 in Yankee Stadium's deep center field, which would later become Monument Park.

Catfish Hunter

Jim "Catfish" Hunter may be most famous for his pioneering free agency, his nickname, or his bushy mustache, which is something of a shame. After all, Hunter won 20 or more games for five consecutive seasons, and had a hand in winning five World Series titles in seven years.

Hunter's career began with the Kansas City Athletics, who had signed him to a big-money deal out of high school. Given the nickname "Catfish" by attention-desperate owner Charlie Finley, the kid debuted with the A's in 1965 and threw a perfect game in Oakland in 1968, though it was only in 1970 that he became a winning pitcher.

Pitching for bad teams, he had amassed a 55–64 career mark before going 18–14 in 1970, and after that there was no looking back. He won 21 each of the next three seasons for the Athletics before he went 25–12 in 1974, which set him up to be baseball's first big-money free agent. Finley's failure to send Hunter a contracted insurance payment meant that the pitcher's contract was declared void following the '74 season.

As the staff ace for a team that had won three straight World Series, Hunter received contract offers from more than half the teams in baseball. Some proposals went as high as $4 million, an astronomical sum in those days, and Catfish eventually chose the Yankees.

His best year in pinstripes was his first, 1975, when he finished 23–14 with 30 complete games and seven shutouts. Unfortunately, this was his final dominant campaign. Perhaps worn out from a heavy workload, Hunter dropped to 17–15 the next season, and was only a part-time starter during the Yankees championship runs of 1977–78.

Hunter retired after going 2–9 with a 5.31 ERA in 1979, settled down in his native North Carolina, and was elected to the Hall of Fame in 1987. Hunter died in 1999, a year after being diagnosed with ALS, the same incurable disease which claimed the life of another Yankees great: Lou Gehrig.

Reggie Jackson

There may never be another player who could thrive in New York's media frenzy as well as Reggie Jackson.

Despite his arrogance, penchant for strikeouts, and fights with management, there is little doubt that Reggie Jackson indeed was the "straw that stirs the drink," as he claimed to be for the late-1970s Yankees.

Jackson, who originally went to college on a football scholarship and only auditioned for the baseball squad on a bet, nevertheless was the Athletics' first-round pick in 1966. He broke in the next season, becoming a regular in 1968 in Oakland after the club moved to the coast.

He was one of the key players of the Athletics' 1972–74 dynasty, winning MVP honors in 1973. He played the 1976 campaign in Baltimore, after Athletics owner Charlie Finley conducted a first-rate fire sale, then signed with the Yankees the following season.

Jackson's bat—and ability to take the fierce media glare off his teammates—was a big reason that the Yankees captured back-to-back World Series titles in 1977–78. Jackson was able to perform at a high level, leading the reformed Bronx Bombers with a .550 slugging average and 100 runs in '77, despite a famed dugout brawl with skipper Billy Martin. He earned the moniker "Mr. October" by clubbing three home runs on three consecutive pitches in Game 6 of the '77 Series, easily one of the most impressive individual performances in World Series history.

Jackson again led the Yanks in slugging and RBI in 1978, and survived more feuding with Martin, who called Jackson a "liar" and owner George Steinbrenner a "convict" in the same sentence. Despite the distractions—or perhaps because of them, as Martin's mouth got him fired—the Yankees rallied from 14 ½ games behind the Red Sox to claim the AL East crown, then bested the Dodgers in the Series.

After failing to win a title over the next three years, the Yankees allowed Jackson to walk as a free agent, ending his stormy run in the Bronx after five seasons. Jackson finished his career back out west, enjoying five years with the Angels and one final go-round with the Athletics in 1987. He topped the AL in homers four times, ending up with 563 for his career. His 14 All-Star appearances and five finishes in the AL MVP top five voting also speak to his ability, and Jackson was inducted into the Hall of Fame in 1993—the first year he was eligible.

Derek Jeter

Derek Jeter was fated to play shortstop for the Yankees.

Though he grew up in Michigan, he was born in New Jersey, spending summers there with grandparents who loved the Yankees. His father had been an all-glove, no-hit shortstop in college, and when Jeter declared as a child that his dream was to play shortstop for the New York Yankees, his parents encouraged him—not just with words, but with a plan. Young Derek took ground balls on the field behind their house every day in the summer, and practiced his inside-out swing in the garage hundreds of times a day.

This diligence paid off as the Yankees drafted him in the first round (sixth overall) in 1992. Four years later he gained the starting job when Tony Fernandez suffered an injury, and he started hot, hitting a home run and tracking down tricky pops on Opening Day with aplomb.

He never slowed down, taking Rookie of the Year honors, just the first of many accolades. Jeter has perennially been at or near the top of AL lists in hits and runs. In 2000 he was voted MVP of both the All-Star Game and the World Series, the first player to win both honors in the same season. In 2006 he narrowly missed winning the batting title and the league MVP award.

One thing that endears Jeter to his fans is that he seems unconcerned with personal achievements and keeps his focus on winning. The result? A highlight reel of iconic moments. Against the Red Sox on July 1, 2004, with two men on in the 12th inning, Trot Nixon hit a pop fly into the no man's land between short, third, and left. Jeter raced full-out to glove the ball in fair territory, then flew over the camera pit and into the stands. He emerged with his chin bleeding and his cheek bruised, but made the out. Then there was the classic play in the clinching Game 5 of the 2001 ALDS, in which Jeter ended an Oakland rally by racing to the wall to snare a popup headed for the crowd, then went tumbling into the camera pit. The Stadium shook with chants of his name for the next half-inning.

The crowning play, though, came earlier that series with the Yankees facing elimination. Jeter snared a throw that had missed both cutoff men and shovelled it to Jorge Posada in time to swipe-tag Jeremy Giambi at the plate. What was Jeter even *doing* in that section of the field? Answer: Whatever it took to win.

He has also hit some of the most memorable home runs in Yankees postseason history, including a disputed "non-homer" in the 1996 ALCS which was actually hauled in by young fan Jeffrey Maier; the "Mr. November" walk-off homer served up by Arizona Diamondbacks closer Byung-Hyun Kim in 2001; and a leadoff four-bagger in the 2000 "Subway Series" against the Mets on the first pitch thrown after the Yankees had their 14-game World Series win streak snapped.

But highlight films aside, it's Jeter's day-in day-out consistency that has cemented his image in the fans' eyes as a classic Yankees leader and superstar.

Tony Lazzeri

Tony Lazzeri was one of the great San Francisco Italian-Americans to play for the Yankees (Joe DiMaggio being another, of course), earning the nickname "Poosh 'Em Up Tony" for his home-run-hitting prowess. In 1925, while playing in the minors for Salt Lake City, where the air was thin, Lazzeri was the first player at any level of organized baseball to hit more than 60 homers, predating Babe Ruth by two seasons.

Lazzeri joined the Yankees in 1926. It took a while for him to shake the reputation for choking in the clutch; he was stuck with that label after fanning with the bases loaded by a reportedly hung-over Grover Cleveland Alexander, in the seventh inning of Game 7 of that year's World Series.

Happily, Lazzeri had plenty of opportunities to prove his worth. The Yankees won their next five World Series appearances (1927, 1928, 1932, 1936, and 1937), and Tony hit homers in each of those last three series. His regular-season numbers show a story of offensive consistency, beginning with 114 RBI as a rookie and encompassing a career high average of .354 in 1929. He notched seven seasons with over 100 RBI and five seasons batting .300 or higher, providing an offensive edge at second base—a position that most other teams of the time stocked with defensive players. Indeed, Lazzeri was a below average defender.

Selected to the very first All-Star team in 1933, on May 24, 1936 Lazzeri recorded 11 RBIs in a game to set the AL record and also became the first player to hit two grand slams in a single game. Of course, Lazzeri, like other players of the era, benefited from great hitting conditions, but he still comes out with an Adjusted OPS of 122 over his career.

Lazzeri was also the instigator of the famous "mush ball" prank in 1937, his final year as a Yankee. On September 29, a late-season date so lacking in significance that both managers took the day off, Lazzeri swapped the real ball for one doctored (made soft and mushy) as "Indian Bob" Johnson was at the plate for Philadelphia. Pitcher Kemp Wicker grooved the ball and Johnson took a mighty cut, only to have the ball fall dead and foul.

The umpires ruled "no pitch," and Lazzeri never faced disciplinary action from the league, possibly because within a month he had joined the Chicago Cubs. After one season, he moved to Brooklyn for 1939 to play first base, but after just a handful of games he joined the Giants for a last hurrah. He went on to manage in the minor leagues, but left that behind in 1943 and opened a tavern in San Francisco.

Throughout his playing days, Lazzeri was known to suffer from epilepsy, but as general manager Ed Barrow said at the time, "As long as he doesn't take fits between three and six in the afternoon, that's good enough for me." Lazzeri never did suffer a seizure while on the field, but may have in 1946. At age 42, he was found dead in his home, possibly from a fall during a seizure. He was elected to the Hall of Fame in 1991.

Mickey Mantle

How much more could Mickey Mantle have accomplished had he taken better care of himself? It's staggering to think that 536 home runs, a career .298 batting average, a Triple Crown, and three MVP awards weren't all that he could have done.

Mantle's baseball ability was his ticket out of the lead and zinc mines of rural Oklahoma, where his father and grandfather had earned their livings. Groomed by his dad, Mutt, to be a switch-hitter at an early age, Mantle never had much trouble hitting the ball, leading Yankees skipper Casey Stengel to later remark that the Mick "should lead the league in everything."

Mantle joined the Yankees for the first time on Opening Day, 1951, at just 19 and with only two years of professional experience, and that in the low minors. He struggled badly and was sent down to Kansas City. He was still slumping there when his father came by and told his son, "Sure, I can get you a job working in the mines." Suddenly young Mantle was motivated and regained his swing, clubbing 11 home runs and driving in 50 in only 40 games in Triple-A, earning him a promotion back to the Bronx in August.

In Game 2 of that year's World Series, however, Mantle stumbled over a drain cover in Yankee Stadium's outfield and suffered a knee injury which kept him out of the rest of the Series and hampered him the rest of his career.

The speedy Mantle took over center field for Joe DiMaggio in 1952—for which some Yankee fans never forgave him. But a matchless combination of speed, power, grit, baseball smarts, strike-zone judgment, and defensive ability made Mantle an All-Star every year except his rookie campaign, and earned him an astounding nine top-five finishes in MVP voting. He was also the best hitter of the third great Yankees

dynasty. During Mantle's 18-year tenure, the Bronx Bombers won seven World Series titles and 12 AL pennants in a stretch of 14 seasons.

Mantle died in 1995, but the great irony was the cause of his death. After years of hard drinking, both during his playing days and in retirement, and a subsequent liver transplant, Mantle cleaned up his act, only to succumb to cancer a short while later. Mantle had always assumed he'd contract Hodgkin's Disease, which had killed an uncle (at age 32), his father (at age 39), and his grandfather (age 40). As a result of those untimely deaths, Mantle said late in life, only half jokingly, "If I knew I was going to live this long, I would have taken better care of myself."

Roger Maris

When talking about Roger Maris and his place in baseball history, the one fact that seemingly gets lost in all the controversy is that there was never going to be an asterisk.

When it appeared that Maris (or Mickey Mantle) would break Babe Ruth's single season home run record of 60, commissioner Ford Frick said that unless one of them topped 60 home runs in 154 games or less (the length of season when Ruth played), there would be two listings in the record book—one for the shorter season and one for the current length.

Maris came to the Yankees in a preseason trade before the 1960 campaign, and was an instant success, winning the league's MVP award in each of his first two seasons in New York. Despite that, the fickle Yankee supporters never embraced Maris, claiming he wasn't a "true Yankee." A goodly number also openly rooted against him in 1961, wanting Mantle to break Ruth's storied record instead.

Maris obviously couldn't handle the pressure of playing in the Big Apple's spotlight, and his career took a nosedive beginning in 1962. Injuries limited him to half a season or less in 1963 and '65, and the Yankees dumped him on St. Louis after the '66 campaign for Charley Smith, a career .239 hitting third baseman.

Maris had a couple of great seasons, but obviously did not have a Hall of Fame career. He played only 12 seasons and appeared in less than 130 games in seven of them. He hit more than 30 home runs and drove in 100 or more only three seasons each, and concluded his career with two mediocre seasons with the Cardinals.

Billy Martin

It's not a stretch to say that the mercurial Martin lived and died as a Yankee. At the time when his pickup truck skidded off an icy road in upstate New York, rumors had Martin in the running for a sixth tour of duty at the Yankees helm (having been fired and rehired four previous times by George Steinbrenner and having resigned once). His grave is a just bloop hit away from Babe Ruth's at the Gates of Heaven cemetery in Westchester. Finally, an inscription on the gravestone reads "#1 Forever," after the number Martin wore as a Yankee.

He was born Alfred Emanuel Martin in Berkeley, California in 1928. Called "Belli," for '"beautiful boy," by his Italian grandmother, the nickname that stuck was "Billy." Another nickname he carried was "Casey's boy," as he'd played for Casey Stengel with the Oakland Oaks in 1948 and followed him to the majors in 1950. Stengel loved the scrappy, combative Martin, and the two developed a father-son relationship. Martin's heads-up play to save Game 7 of the 1952 World Series, dashing across the infield to catch a pop fly that first sacker Joe Collins lost in the sun, gave him a reputation as an October performer—as did his 12 hits in the 1953 Series, a record for a six-game set. His .500 batting average in that world championship tied a record and led to series MVP honors.

But Martin's combative ways led to his exile after the infamous incident at his 29th birthday party at the Copacabana club, even though he himself may not have been involved in the fisticuffs. He did not return to pinstripes until being hired as manager in 1975, the next year leading the Yankees to their first World Series appearance since 1964. Martin's well-publicized feuds with superstar Reggie Jackson and owner George Steinbrenner were tabloid fodder for years. One memorable Martin quote about the two eventually led to his resignation in 1978: "The two of them deserve each other. One's a born liar, the other's convicted."

Martin's relationship with Steinbrenner was never less than contentious, and yet the men forged a bond that resulted in his numerous rehirings and subsequent firings.

The Copacabana incident presaged a lifetime of altercations on the field and off, involving arguments and fistfights with opponents, his own players and teammates, and even total strangers. When he channeled his aggression into managing, it was known as "Billyball," in which his baserunners and interpretations of the rulebook were equally tenacious. His grave contains another inscription, the words of Martin himself, which serve as fitting words: "I may not have been the greatest Yankee to put on the uniform but I was the proudest."

Don Mattingly

He has been called the greatest Yankees' player never to play in a World Series; the late Hall of Famer Kirby Puckett dubbed him "Donnie Baseball." The best and brightest homegrown Yankee since Thurman Munson, Don Mattingly led and starred for a team that otherwise had little to draw fans to the ballpark.

A versatile left-handed hitter with a line-drive stroke, Mattingly showed patience with two strikes and learned to pull the inside pitch into the Stadium's short porch. Originally drafted as an outfielder, the Yankees shoehorned him in at first base after calling him up in 1982–83. The Yankees of that era viewed their talented prospects as bargaining chips in trades rather than as solutions to problems—but Mattingly was an exception.

From the time he took the first base starting job (in 1984) through 1989—his All-Star seasons—he was one of the league's dominant players at the plate and in the field. He finished his career with nine Gold Gloves and racked up achievements that put him in the company of some of the game's greatest players.

The 1984 season ended with Mattingly and teammate Dave Winfield grappling neck-and-neck for the batting title, Mattingly pulling it out on the final day by going 4-for-5. His .343 ending average was the highest by a Yankees lefty since Lou Gehrig, and the first batting title for a Yankee since Mickey Mantle won the 1956 Triple Crown. Donnie followed up this performance with the AL MVP Award in 1985, racking up 145 RBI, the most by a lefthander since Ted Williams' 159 in 1949. In '86 he batted .352 (second to Wade Boggs' .357) and led the league in hits, slugging, OPS, doubles, extra-base hits, and total bases. He was one of the three toughest men to strike out in the league.

The following season he hit 10 home runs in eight games, the only man to hit that many in such a short span of time and tied Dale Long's 1956 mark by homering in eight straight. That year he also set a record by clubbing six grand slams—coincidentally the only six of his career.

But toward the end of that 1987 season he suffered his first back injury, reportedly while goofing around with pitcher Bob Shirley in the clubhouse. His offensive production, especially his power, dipped after that, though Mattingly maintained much of his skill.

But the back pain became chronic, and Mattingly was forced to experiment with various stances and swings just to stay pain-free and in the lineup. By 1995 he was just about ready to give up, but the Yankees' run for the first-ever AL wild card berth inspired him. In his only postseason appearance, the ALDS against Seattle, Mattingly batted .417 and slugged .708. After the Yankees heartbreaking fifth game, Mattingly retired rather than struggle any longer. His No. 23 was also retired in 1997.

Mattingly himself soon began attending spring training as a special instructor, and in 2003, with his own sons on the verge of being drafted into organized baseball, Mattingly took the job as Yankees hitting coach. In 2007 he became Joe Torre's bench coach, taking on more responsibility in the dugout and in the organization.

Joe McCarthy

One of baseball's most storied managers, McCarthy ran the Cubs, Yankees, and Red Sox over a 24-year span. He never played in the major leagues, but his 2,125 wins at the helm rank him seventh on the all-time list and his winning percentage (.615) is the best ever.

He came to the Yankees after leading the Cubs to a pennant in 1929 and then a second-place finish in 1930. In McCarthy's first year in pinstripes, 1931, he immediately had to rein in the boisterous Babe Ruth, who had openly campaigned for the managerial seat.

And it wasn't just Ruth. The discipline that Miller Huggins had famously instituted in the Bronx had gone by the boards after the Hug's passing in 1929, and "Marse Joe" was forced to find new ways to spur his veteran club. He began by instituting a dress code; he also insisted that players arrive at the park clean-shaven. While his charges grumbled at first, the new work ethic paid off in wins. The following year, 1932, McCarthy led the Yankees to a World Series sweep against his former employers, making him the first manager to win pennants in both leagues.

As Joe Torre would be years later, McCarthy was accused of being a "push-button" manager simply because his teams were so talented, but also like Torre, his ability to handle a clubhouse of fractious veterans should not be underestimated. He was one of the first managers to separate his pitchers into starters and relievers and applied his mental acuity to every aspect of the game. He was also known for *never* arguing with umpires, saying that he could not do his job of managing if he'd been tossed. McCarthy famously wrote to his players, "Try not to find too much fault with the umpires. You cannot expect them to be as perfect as you are."

McCarthy's concept was that a team should score more runs in the ninth inning than any other, and the dynastic club that captured four consecutive World Series from 1936–39 was known for its "late-inning lightning." Under his leadership, the Yankees became World Champions seven times, and McCarthy's squat, square-jawed figure was a perennial fixture in the center of the dugout until after the retirement of front office leader Ed Barrow.

The Yankees' next GM, mercurial Larry "The Roaring Redhead" McPhail, did not mix well with McCarthy. Given McCarthy's strict rules for his players' conduct (no eating in the dugout, everyone expected at breakfast by 8:30 a.m. in jacket and tie when on the road), it was ironic that McCarthy himself had developed a drinking problem. After McCarthy got into a shouting match with relief ace Joe Page on a team flight in 1945, MacPhail forced him to resign.

McCarthy landed with the Red Sox, and led them to within one game of the pennant in both 1948 and 1949; much questioned was his controversial choice of journeyman Denny Galehouse to start the one-game playoff against Cleveland in 1948 rather than aces Mel Parnell or Ellis Kinder. In the loss to the Yankees on the final day of 1949, he passed the torch to the next great Yankees' manager, Casey Stengel. The Red Sox retained McCarthy for 1950, but fired him when, drunk, he missed the Father's Day game. After leaving baseball, McCarthy was elected to the Hall of Fame in 1957 and lived to be 90 years old, passing in 1978.

Thurman Munson

Still referred to as "The Captain" by Yankees fans of the 1970s, Thurman Munson was the Yankees' best player in the fallow years of 1970–74, then played a key role in their return to greatness in 1976.

The Yankees drafted him in the first round (fourth overall) in 1968, and after only 100 games in the minors named him starting catcher for the 1970 season. The tough kid stumbled a bit at first, but manager Ralph Houk stuck with him, and he ended up batting .302 and winning the Rookie of the Year award. The following year, Munson earned the first of seven All-Star nominations, and from 1975–78 he topped .300 with 100 RBIs every year.

He won the AL MVP in 1976, making him the only Yankee to have captured both the MVP and ROY. In addition, that season the club made him the first team captain since Lou Gehrig. Widely considered a great defensive catcher, Munson had a quick release on the throw to second, and his reputation for playing hurt endeared him to the Bronx faithful. But it was his October play that truly vaulted him into the ranks of great Yankees.

In his first World Series, 1976, Munson batted .529 and at one point reeled off six consecutive hits, going 4-for-4 in the final game of the Series, though the Yankees as a whole were flat and drained from the ALCS against Kansas City. In six postseason series, totalling 30 games, Munson averaged a .357 mark. Like Reggie Jackson, with whom he famously clashed, Munson was at his best when the games were biggest.

His life was cut short in August 1979 when the jet plane he was piloting crashed at a small airport near his home in Canton, Ohio. Munson had wanted to learn to fly so he could more easily visit his family during the baseball season, and had been practicing take-offs and landings on an off-day. Stunned teammates, and other baseball dignitaries including Joe Torre, at the time managing the Mets, flew to Ohio for the memorial service then back to New York for a game against the Baltimore Orioles.

Bobby Murcer, a close friend who had delivered a eulogy that day, got the game-winning walk-off hit and all the RBI in a 5–4 win, but the team as a whole slumped after that, ending their postseason hopes. Munson's No. 15 was retired immediately and his locker has stood empty in the Stadium clubhouse ever since.

Graig Nettles

This Southern California native, oddly nicknamed "Puff," played baseball at San Diego State and came up through the Minnesota Twins' system. With Harmon Killebrew ensconced at third for the Twins, Nettles shifted to the outfield but, after a trade to Cleveland in 1970, he moved to third to stay. He became a Yankee in 1973 and struggled a bit, hitting a career-low .234 but drawing 78 walks for a .334 OBP and slugging 22 homers.

As Nettles improved, so did the Yankees. In 1975 he earned an All-Star nod, and the following season he led the league with 32 home runs and 63 extra-base hits while the club reached postseason play for the first time since 1964. He took home Gold Gloves in 1977 and 1978, was the MVP of the 1981 ALCS, and totalled six All-Star selections.

On the field, Nettles may be best remembered for his eye-popping defensive work in the 1978 World Series. Down 0–2 in the Series, the Yankees *had* to have Game 3 to have any chance of survival. Nettles made four hit-robbing plays behind Ron Guidry and turned the tide of the series; the Yankees captured four in a row to win the championship.

Off the field, he is remembered for his wit, famously remarking about reliever Sparky Lyle—who won the Cy Young Award in 1977 but the next year had to fight for a role with newly acquired fireballer Rich "Goose" Gossage—that he "went from Cy Young to sayonara."

His wit may have ultimately cost him (and best friend Gossage) their jobs in pinstripes. Named team captain in 1982, the first to carry that title since the death of Thurman Munson, Nettles soon published a tell-all book entitled *Balls* in the mold of Lyle's *The Bronx Zoo*. Although the tone of the book is light, Nettles spent time (when not recounting an amusing anecdote or thrilling victory) criticizing owner George Steinbrenner. To retaliate, Steinbrenner had Nettles and Gossage packed off to San Diego in early 1984, only to see them make key contributions in getting the Padres to their first World Series that very same year.

At the time of his retirement, Nettles' 319 homers topped the all-time list for AL third basemen. He hung on in the majors for 22 years (six times being the oldest player in his league), then joined the short-lived, over-35 Senior Professional Baseball Association in Florida, where he played with his brother Jim who had also been a major leaguer but never a teammate. In 1991 he took a coaching job with the Yankees, and even now returns to pinstripes from time to time as a special instructor. When new Yankee Alex Rodriguez moved from shortstop to third base, Nettles came in to work with him for several weeks.

Paul O'Neill

When Paul O'Neill, born and bred in Ohio, found out he'd been traded from his hometown Cincinnati Reds (with whom he'd won a World Series) to the New York Yankees, he thought it was the worst thing that had happened in his career. As it turned out, it was one of the *best* things, both for him and the Yankees, who gained a fiery clubhouse presence and a steady bat in the lineup.

When O'Neill was coming through the Reds' system, scouts pegged him as a contact hitter who rarely gave away an at bat. But in Cincinnati, manager Lou Piniella clashed with O'Neill, trying to transform him into a home-run threat.

The Yankees preferred his line-drive stroke, and after never hitting above .276 in six seasons with the Reds, O'Neill in his first season as a Yankee raised his average to .311. In 1994 he had a career year, hitting .359 to capture the AL batting title. It was the only year of his career where he would walk more than he struck out, but over the next seven years in pinstripes, O'Neill's average never dipped below .285.

After the retirement of Don Mattingly after the 1995 season, O'Neill became the Yankees' *de facto* captain, epitomizing the roster's can-do, blue-collar attitude. Known for playing hurt and for smashing the water cooler in the dugout after striking out, O'Neill strove for perfection in a humbling profession. He was often seen practicing his batting stroke while in right field, but maintained a reputation as a strong defensive player. Many fans recall his catch of the final out in Game 5 of the 1996 World Series as one of his defining moments. Snaring the ball at the wall after a long run, O'Neill smacked both hands against the padding as if to say, "Take that, Atlanta."

His father Chick, a minor league player and O'Neill's hero, passed away on the morning of Game 4 of the 1999 World Series—the clincher—and Paul was in right field that night. He broke down in tears during the Yankees' on-field celebration as teammates surrounded him, protecting him from prying cameras as the grief he had held in for nine innings poured out.

"Paulie" could be cool under pressure, too, especially at the plate. His 10-pitch at bat against Armando Benitez in Game 1 of the 2000 World Series opened the door to a blown save and a Yankees win. The other time New York fans saw O'Neill cry on the field came during the 2001 World Series, when the outfielder was appearing in what turned out to be his final game at the stadium. As he took his position in right, fans took up a chant of his name, until the entire assemblage of 56,000-plus were chanting it as one.

It was an emotionally raw time for New York, with the attack on the World Trade Center not even two months old, and the outpouring of love for one of its adopted sons made O'Neill wipe his eyes repeatedly and tip his cap. He did retire after the World Series loss to the Arizona Diamondbacks, and many consider his leaving to mark the end of an era.

Herb Pennock

As a teen phenom in the minors, Herb Pennock threw a no-hitter in 1911. His catcher was Earle Mack, who recommended that his father Connie take a look at the young pitcher. But though Pennock went 11–4 in his first full year in the big leagues, that didn't convince Connie Mack that the 18-year-old was worth protecting, and the Red Sox took him off waivers.

Pennock had trouble getting a chance to start because he didn't throw hard, and in addition experienced control problems early in his career. Relying on a mixture of overhand and three-quarters delivery curveballs, he used a screwball as a change of pace. He was a stringy kid at 160 pounds and six feet tall, as well.

In his first year and a half with the Sox, he appeared in only 14 games, then missed Boston's 1918 World Series triumph because he served in the military during World War I. The Sox slipped into the cellar after that, and although Pennock pitched well in 1922 he went 10–17 for a team that finished dead last, 33 games behind the Yankees.

The Yankees sent the Sox three marginal players and $50,000 to get him, and Pennock immediately racked up the highest winning percentage in the league in his first season in New York, going 19–6 (.760). He topped the .700 mark three more times in his career and in 1924 was 21–9 with a 2.83 ERA and fanned a career-high 101 batters. From 1923–27, he won 115 games, twirling for Yankees teams that won four pennants and three World Series titles. In ten Fall Classic games, Pennock came through with a 5–0 career mark and a 1.95 ERA.

Pennock spent 11 years pitching in the Bronx before returning to Boston in 1934 to work out of the bullpen for one final season. He spent some years coaching, then took the position of general manager back in Philadelphia. He was elected to the Hall of Fame in 1948 by the baseball writers only a few weeks after his sudden death. Pennock had suffered a cerebral hemorrhage at the winter meetings.

Andy Pettitte

Andrew Eugene Pettitte, born in Louisiana, grew up in Texas. He aspired to pitching from a very early age and was labeled a mound prodigy by the time he reached high school—this is fortunate, since his hitting was never stellar.

Drafted by the Yankees, he chose to put in a year of school, then signed with the organization as a free agent in 1991. He rose steadily through the minors and in 1995 made a few appearances out of the bullpen before earning his first start on April 29. He went on to make 25 more starts, going 12–9 with a 4.17 ERA overall and earning third-place in the Rookie of the Year voting. Pettitte went 5–1 in September, helping the Yankees to their first playoff berth in over a decade.

He got the Opening Day nod in 1996 and went on to win 21 games, making him the Yankees' first 20-game winner since another lefty from Louisiana, Ron Guidry, in 1985. He finished second in the Cy Young voting and received an All-Star nod. From then on, he was never anything less than a horse, racking up season after stellar season. From 1996–1998, Pettitte won more games than any AL Pitcher, capturing 55 (John Smoltz outpaced him by one at 56). From 1996–2000, his 88 wins were bested only by Pedro Martinez and Greg Maddux, each with 90. All this came despite the front office's hesitations about him; he was almost dealt in early 1999. This became one of the best trades never made, as Pettitte continued sawing off bats with his dominating cut fastball and inducing ground balls at a league-leading rate.

And every October he was even better, enjoying a streak of nine straight postseason starts ending in Yankees victories from 1998–2000. In the 2001 World Series, though, he was hit hard, and suspicions flew that he had been tipping his pitches. That off-season, he began working out with Texas neighbor Roger Clemens, forging a lasting friendship which added a few miles per hour to Pettitte's fastball, thanks to increased leg and trunk strength. In 2003, Pettitte won 21 games again, but the Yankees let him walk away to pitch for his hometown Houston Astros.

Pettitte's signing for Drayton McLane led Roger Clemens, who had announced his retirement, to join Houston's rotation as well. An unfortunate injury shelved him in 2004, but in 2005 he notched 222 innings for the Astros and the lowest ERA of his career, 2.39. It looked like Pettitte (and Clemens) would retire in an Astros uniform.

But in 2006, at an off-season celebration for the 10th anniversary of the 1996 Yankees, Pettitte reunited with old teammates who encouraged him to return to New York. Shortly thereafter, he signed a one-year deal to put the pinstripes back on, giving the team a much-needed replacement for lefty Randy Johnson, who had been considered a bust. Pettitte lived up to expectations, suffering from low run support early in the season but re-establishing himself as a big-game stopper who could halt a losing streak. In addition, Pettitte's return to New York led Roger Clemens to come back for another term in the Bronx as well. While Pettitte may not accompany Roger into the Hall of Fame, he will always be remembered as one of the Yankees' great pitchers.

Jorge Posada

When people talk about the late 20th-century Yankees dynasty, Jorge Posada's name must be prominent among the "home grown" players forming the club's backbone. While Bernie Williams, Andy Pettitte, and Derek Jeter were critical to the Yankees' success, it would be folly to forget the powerful, switch-hitting catcher.

Posada grew up in Puerto Rico in a baseball family that included his father Jorge Sr., a major league scout, and his uncle Leo, a minor-league hitting instructor for the Dodgers. Drafted as a second baseman in 1990, Jorge converted to catching in his second year in the minor leagues because his coaches deemed him both slow of foot and quick of mind.

Posada and Jeter reached Yankee Stadium the same time, 1995, and became fast friends. Jeter became the everyday shortstop in 1996, but the Yankees spent a bit more time working Posada into a starting role. Splitting catching duties with veteran mentor Joe Girardi, Posada avoided the wear and tear on his legs that many young catchers face.

He struggled a bit early on, at one point being sent by the Yankees to have his eyes examined because his strikeout rate spiked in early 2000. But earning Joe Torre's confidence—which led to more playing time—fixed what ailed him, and from 2000, Posada was behind the plate nearly every day. His lock on the position was such that during Posada's tenure, the Yankees have run through a long string of backup catchers (Anyone remember that Alberto Castillo was a Yankee? Chris Turner? Sal Fasano? Kelly Stinnett? Todd Greene? Joe Oliver?), with only John Flaherty lasting more than one season in the position.

Posada's combination of patience and power from both sides of the plate put him in an elite class of hitters, and producing so well while handling a diverse pitching staff and throwing out runners at an All-Star clip ranked him only behind Ivan Rodriguez among AL catchers. The Yankee backstop won four consecutive Silver Slugger awards from 2000–03.

The advantage of putting Posada's bat in the lineup was almost equal to having two first basemen, a luxury few other teams sported. From 2000–06, Posada batted in 603 runs, significantly outpacing Ivan Rodriguez (476), and homered 159 times as a catcher, tying him with Mike Piazza's output over that same time span.

That edge was the difference in Game 3 of the 2001 ALDS, in which the Yankees were on the verge of being swept. Mike Mussina faced Barry Zito in a pitcher's duel that the Yankees won 1–0 thanks to a Posada home run and a sweep tag that Posada applied to a non-sliding Jeremy Giambi at the tail end of what has become known as "The Play" by Jeter.

In postseason play, Posada has produced when it has counted; he has a .358 on-base percentage in postseason action, drawing 55 walks in his first 300 at bats. Posada's clutch double off Pedro Martinez in the epic Game 7 of the 2003 ALCS (the "Aaron Boone" game) was key to the comeback.

His charitable efforts have garnered him most of baseball's philanthropy awards as well, including the Thurman Munson award, the "You Gotta Have Heart" award, and others. The Jorge Posada Foundation helps families with children suffering from craniosynostis.

Enjoying another excellent campaign in 2007, Posada remains key to the Yankees' success. His career totals continue to climb up the Yankees all-time lists, putting him in the company of Yogi Berra and Bill Dickey.

Willie Randolph

Randolph, born in South Carolina, was raised almost from infancy in Brooklyn's Brownsville section. Although he spent most of his big-league time in New York, playing 13 seasons with the Yankees and one with the Mets, Randolph initially reached the majors at age 20 in 1975 for a 30-game stint with Pittsburgh.

The Yankees liberated him following that season in a one-sided deal that also brought New York Ken Brett and Dock Ellis and sent only Doc Medich to Pittsburgh in return. Perhaps the Bucs didn't know what they were giving away. In Randolph's first year as a Yankee he was an All-Star, hitting .267 but playing a stellar second base and stealing 37 bases. It was the first of five All-Star turns while in pinstripes (he'd add one more in 1989 as a Dodger).

During his time in pinstripes Willie Randolph served as a model of consistency, holding the lock on the second base position while 32 shortstops came and went, batting leadoff much of the time. Randolph was considered a clubhouse leader as well, earning co-captain (with Ron Guidry) honors in 1986. The only two players to have held the position of captain since then? Don Mattingly and Derek Jeter.

In 1980 Randolph tallied 119 walks, the most by a Yankee since Mickey Mantle's 122 in 1962, and his on-base percentage ranked second in the league at .429. In 1987, his .411 OBP was fourth best in the AL and Randolph was the hardest man in the league to strike out (1 K per 18 AB). Injuries slowed him in 1988, though, and he departed via free agency to the Dodgers.

At the time of his departure, he had worked his way on to many all-time Yankee lists, and by the time he returned as a Yankees' coach in 1993, Randolph still ranked second only to Rickey Henderson in stolen bases (251). Only Don Mattingly had leapfrogged him in at bats, runs, hits and games played.

He served as the Bombers' third base coach for 10 straight seasons, pre-dating Joe Torre's arrival by three years, and often expressed a desire to manage someday. Many teams interviewed Randolph over the years, but none tendered an offer. Randolph was occasionally advised to spend a year managing in the minors, but opted to stay in the big leagues . . . and in 2004 Joe Torre made him the Yankees' bench coach.

A year later, the crosstown Mets tapped him to manage, and Don Mattingly moved to Torre's elbow on the bench. Randolph's popularity in New York, and his winning pedigree, made him a natural candidate for the Mets' job despite his lack of managerial experience. He led them to a winning record for the first time since 2001 in 2005, his first year on the job, and followed that in 2006 with an NL East division title. Expect the Yankees to retire his No. 30 in the future.

Allie Reynolds

"Superchief" to his teammates but "Wahoo" in the unenlightened print media of the day (due to his one-quarter Creek Indian heritage), Allie Reynolds was part of the Yankees' "Big Three" of the 1950s. Reynolds, whose fastball was estimated at 100 mph in the days before the radar gun, joined junkballing lefty Eddie Lopat and another fast hurler, Vic Raschi, in a formidable rotation.

Reynolds excelled from the start, despite mediocre control, playing several years for the Cleveland Indians. But in New York he became most dominant. The Yankees traded for him in 1947, when he was 30, dealing the Tribe star second baseman Joe Gordon. As the *New York Times* reported in Reynolds' obituary, Cleveland wanted Gordon so badly they said they'd give up any pitcher but Bob Feller. Joe DiMaggio advised Larry MacPhail to take Reynolds because "he can buzz his hard one by me any time he has a mind to."

Manager Casey Stengel often used the big fireballer out of the bullpen, allowing him to notch 49 saves to go with 182 career wins (36 of those earned in relief). And like all great Yankees, he excelled in the postseason, throwing a gutsy two-hit 1–0 win against the Dodgers in the 1949 World Series. In 15 total Series appearances, Reynolds amassed a 7–2 record, a 2.79 ERA, and four saves; in each of his six World Series relief appearances, he earned either a save or a win—three of those in Series clinchers.

His biggest claim to fame, though, may be in being the first AL pitcher to notch two no-hit games in a season. Johnny Vander Meer had done so for the Reds in 1938 in back-to-back starts. Reynolds' two no-nos, in 1951, came against the Yankees' two biggest pennant rivals, the Indians and Red Sox. On July 12, Reynolds bested Bob Feller in a 1–0 game; Feller himself gave up only four hits, one of which was a home run to Gene Woodling.

Then on September 28, Reynolds tossed a gem over Boston that clinched a tie for first place. With two outs in the ninth, Ted Williams popped up, but catcher Yogi Berra dropped the ball. Reynolds and Berra came back with the same pitch and got the same result; this time, Yogi squeezed it. This was Reynolds' seventh shutout of the year.

In 1952, he paced the league with 160 strikeouts and a 2.06 ERA, finishing 20–8. He finished second in the AL MVP voting. When all was said and done, he had six World Series rings with the Yankees and six All-Star selections, five as a Yankee. He was forced to retire after the 1954 season because of a back injury he sustained when the Yankees' team bus crashed on the way back from Philadelphia.

Reynolds went on to head up the revived American Association, and in 1989 the Yankees dedicated a plaque to him in Monument Park, though they did not retire his No. 22. He passed away in 1994.

Mariano Rivera

As befits any player of legendary status, there are tales about Mariano Rivera—some of them are actually true. One story is that when he was signed, he was playing shortstop for a sandlot team in Panama City. His team needed a pitcher, he filled in, and a Yankees scout who happened to be watching the game signed him on the spot. Actually, Herb Raybourn had to convince the Yankees to sign Rivera, but he eventually did land the young player—who had not been a pitcher prior to that—for $3,000.

As a starter in the minor leagues, Rivera was known to throw only one pitch: a rising fastball right around 90 mph. While coaches tried, and failed, to teach him either an effective breaking ball or a change of speed, Rivera's fastball got great results. Despite losing time in 1992 and 1993 because of arm surgery, Rivera posted a 30–18 record, a 2.34 ERA, and 421 strikeouts and 106 walks in 495⅔ innings in the minors.

After reaching the majors in 1995, Rivera was soon converted to relief. Mariano was Joe Torre's secret weapon in 1996, shortening games to six innings once the "Mo and Wett Show" would take over; Rivera was closer to John Wetteland's primary setup man. In 107⅔ innings, Rivera fanned 130, a Yankees record for a relief pitcher, and allowed only one home run.

Another tale that is told about The Great Mariano is that his signature pitch, the cut fastball, didn't even come to him until he was already anointed as the closer. In 1997, while his famous four-seam fastball was hitting 95 on the radar gun, he was supposedly playing catch with fellow Panamanian Ramiro Mendoza in the outfield one day when he discovered the late-breaking "cutting" action. Others say that Torre encouraged pitching coach Mel Stottlemyre to teach him the pitch after Rivera blew three of his first six save opportunities. Rivera soon went on a tear, ending the year with a 1.88 ERA. Soon, the Yankee Stadium scoreboard operators assigned him Metallica's "Enter Sandman."

Yet another legend concerning Rivera tells that blowing the save in Game 4 of the 1997 ALDS (allowing a home run to Sandy Alomar Jr.) hardened Rivera to the task of closer, providing a trial by fire which tempered him to withstand the doubts and pressure that came with the job over the following decade.

Rivera proceeded to become the best closer baseball has ever seen, as well as his generation's quintessential October player. His lifetime regular-season ERA through the 2006 season was a minuscule 2.28, while his ERA in 112⅓ postseason innings pitched was just *0.80*! He won Rolaids Relief Man Awards in 1999, 2001, 2004, and 2005, but more important for Yankees fans, took 1999 World Series MVP honors and the 2003 ALCS MVP trophy.

How does Rivera fit into the Yankee canon? Well, he broke Whitey Ford's postseason scoreless innings streak and pushed it to 34⅓ innings . . . a record that Ford took from Babe Ruth himself.

Phil Rizzuto

"The Scooter" was beloved by three generations of Yankees fans, first as the defensive anchor of New York's dynasty in the 1940s and '50s, then as a longtime radio and television broadcaster.

Rizzuto's career got off to a slow start. After only two seasons in the big leagues, he entered the Navy during World War II. Always a fine defensive player, he had four so-so offensive years after the war, then exploded in 1950. That year, Rizzuto was the league's Most Valuable Player, as his .324 average helped the Yankees escape a furious threat by the Tigers for the AL flag.

It really was a career year for the diminutive Rizzuto, who had hit better than .284 only one other time in his career. His .418 on-base percentage was 67 points higher than his career mark, and his .439 slugging average 41 points better than his next highest mark—and 84 points over his career percentage.

Rizzuto, a scrappy player with smarts, never came close to duplicating his MVP numbers, and after several more solid seasons, was released in a controversial move late in the 1956 campaign. He immediately moved into the Yankees' radio booth, and continued calling games for the club for 40 years.

His 1994 election to the Hall of Fame caused much controversy. Scooter's supporters saw him as an equal to Dodgers shortstop Pee Wee Reese, who had gained entrance to Cooperstown in 1984. Some detractors felt Reese was far superior, while others believed that neither was worthy and that two wrongs didn't make a right. Ultimately, the addition of Reese, Yankees teammate Yogi Berra, and fellow broadcaster Bill White to the Veteran's Committee led to Rizzuto's induction.

Red Ruffing

As a teenager, he played outfield for the company team managed by his father, but a mine accident left him minus four toes on one foot. Ruffing then switched to pitching and by the time he was 19, found himself on an even worse team than Nokomis Mining Company—the 1924 Boston Red Sox.

From 1924 through 1930, Boston consistently ranked at or near the bottom of the AL, because they couldn't hit or pitch. Ruffing led the AL in losses in both 1928 (10–25) and 1929 (9–22), which only proved he was too good to take out of the rotation. In fact, in 1928 his Adjusted ERA was actually nine percent better than league average.

Red flags should have gone off in the Red Sox front office when the powerful Yankees said, "Sure, we'll take him." Then as now, smart organizations don't trade for table scraps; instead, they raid the weaker clubs for undervalued players.

New York acquired Ruffing in the middle of the 1930 campaign and turned him into an instant winner. He was 0–3 with a 6.38 ERA before the trade, but 15–5 the rest of the way for the Yankees, in the middle of a three-year rebuilding plan after winning six pennants in eight years during the '20s. Over the next 15 years, Ruffing racked up a 231–124 record, and from 1936–39 won 20 or more games each year for a franchise that many call the most dominating of all time.

Six times, Joe McCarthy gave the ball to Ruffing to pitch Game 1 of the World Series, and the hurler went 5–1. His overall World Series record was 7–2, topped only by Whitey Ford for most wins by a Yankees pitcher. Known for a fastball with good movement and a sharply breaking curve, Ruffing was also one of the early masters of the slider. He was elected to the Hall of Fame in 1967 by the Veterans Committee.

Babe Ruth

His life and career are the stuff of legends. A near-orphan who became king of the newly minted twentieth century media-celebrity world, Ruth, a true folk hero, eclipses even Johnny Appleseed and Paul Bunyan in the American psyche. But he was real—a great ballplayer whose accomplishments do not defy measurement. In fact, they inspired greater efforts to quantify his feats. Long before Mickey Mantle's 1953 tape-measure home run, newspapers would regularly run the estimated distance of Ruth's blasts, often including diagrams or photos with arrows tracking the flight of the ball, as if without this proof, the feat might not be believed.

That he was the most storied slugger on baseball's most storied team is not a matter for debate, and yet he started out as a left-handed pitcher on the old minor-league Baltimore Orioles. Jack Dunn sold the big kid to the Red Sox, where he would dominate both from the mound and in the headlines. He won 18 games in 1915, his first full season with Boston, and the next year, 1916, topped the AL with a 1.75 ERA, nine shutouts and 5.7 Pitcher Wins. Ruth played no small part in the Sox' five-game World Series win over Brooklyn, tossing a complete 14-inning 2–1 win.

But no examination of the numbers explains how Ruth captivated the attention in every situation. The following season he did the seemingly impossible—overshadowed a teammate who threw a perfect game. Ernie Shore, who had come to the Sox with Ruth from Baltimore, took over on the hill when Ruth was ejected from a 1917 game after walking the first batter, which led to an altercation with plate umpire Brick Owens. Shore pitched nine perfect innings of relief. The *Boston Herald*'s headline the next day ran in large type: "Ruth Assaults Umpire Owens." Below it, in much smaller letters, "Shore Twirls Record Game."

Shore was dealt to the Yankees in 1918, and Ruth famously followed him in 1920, after having ensured that the Sox beat the Cubs in the 1918 World Series by pitching two games, winning both, and giving up only two runs total. By the time of the trade, BoSox manager/architect Ed Barrow had already begun playing Ruth in the outfield on his non-pitching days in order to maximize his offense. Once in New York, Ruth rarely picked up a ball. (Though of course when he did, it spawned another legend. His final pitching performance came at age 38, when a rotund Ruth earned a complete game win against none other than Boston.)

Ruth's arrival neatly dovetails with the rise of the Yankees as a great team. He and Lou Gehrig proved the two biggest threats of New York's "Murderer's Row" offense, and the Babe's legendary home run feats thrilled fans all over the country. Of course, many old Deadball Era ballplayers and sportswriters disliked the home-run focus that the big man brought to bear, but it can be argued that in the wake of the 1919–20 "Black Sox" scandal, Ruth's feats helped baseball not just survive a tough time, but thrive by doing what was necessary—shunning the old ways and making room for the new.

Some of Ruth's antics were partly a creation of the press—such as the "called shot" in the 1932 World Series, which is still hotly debated—while others, like multiple occasions on which he hit home runs for sick children, are well documented. What can't be disputed are 715 home runs, a .326 World Series batting average (.744 slugging), leading the league in slugging and OPS 13 times and homers 12 times from 1918–31, and topping the league in walks on nine occasions. That he won the 1923 MVP Award seems almost a mere footnote.

Several more pages could be filled with statistical analyses and eye-popping numbers, discussions of his powerful uppercut swing, legends of his childhood, reactions from those who felt either that he had saved the game or destroyed it, or explorations of his infamous personal life, but in the end it may be enough to say that no player has ever dominated baseball like the Babe. He was an inaugural inductee to the Baseball Hall of Fame.

George Steinbrenner

The Yankees' long history includes many infamous owners and executives, but none changed the game of baseball as much as George Steinbrenner.

Heading a team of investors who bought the club from CBS in 1973 for a reported $8.7 million, Steinbrenner initially promised "absentee ownership." As he told the *New York Times*, "I'll stick to building ships."

Biographies

But Steinbrenner, nicknamed "The Boss" for his uncompromising, dictatorial management style, could not resist becoming more involved in the running of the franchise. Though the Ohio-born magnate initially knew little about baseball, his passion for winning fueled his incipient free-spending and micro-managing styles. Long before Donald Trump, Steinbrenner owned the catch phrase "You're Fired," (parodied by Steinbrenner himself in Miller Lite ads from the 1970s) rifling through 20 managers in his first 23 years as owner, canning Billy Martin five times, and changing general managers 11 times in 30 years.

Steinbrenner's conflicts were not limited to the front office. He feuded with players, including (or perhaps especially) his biggest stars Reggie Jackson and Dave Winfield, as well as the Yankees' devoted fan base. After letting Jackson walk away instead of re-signing him, Steinbrenner was greeted at the Stadium with chants of "Steinbrenner Sucks!" when Jackson returned with another team and homered.

But King George's reign finally found both stability and a formula for winning baseball with the addition of Brian Cashman to the front office and Joe Torre to the managerial job. Cashman came into the organization as an intern and worked his way up to assistant GM under Bob Watson as the Yankees put together their postseason runs in 1995–97. The 30-year-old Cashman took over as GM in 1998 and still holds the post. The last decade has been the most successful era of the Steinbrenner ownership, with the Yankees capturing the AL East annually from 1996–2006 and notching four world championships.

To be sure, Steinbrenner has had his share of petty rages, backstabbing, and run-ins with both the law and baseball's commissioners. He was suspended from major league baseball for making illegal contributions to Richard Nixon's re-election campaign, then later "voluntarily" stepped aside before being formally punished for hiring gambler Howie Spira to dig up damaging "dirt" on Winfield. But "The Boss" has also been a significant philanthropist. Some of his causes have a connection to baseball or to the Yankees, as when he paid for the funerals of several children killed in a Bronx house fire, or made out a huge check to the Jimmy Fund during a Red Sox fundraising telethon broadcast. Others include endowments to the alma maters of his children and grandchildren.

As Steinbrenner has mellowed and the team has enjoyed a long run of success, many fans have embraced him as one of their own—a passionate man who loves the Yankees and loves winning. But Steinbrenner has been more than just a rooter with a large wallet. Known for being the first owner to embrace and utilize free agency as a means to build a championship club, Steinbrenner has been a shrewd innovator in other ways. His Yankees became the first team to sign a cable television deal in 1979; he later signed a very lucrative long-term deal with the MSG Network that lasted throughout the 1990s.

When the relationship with MSG and Cablevision went sour due to a huge difference in opinion over the value of renewing the contract for the Yankees' TV rights, Steinbrenner pushed for the creation of the his own regional sports network (RSN). YES (Yankees Entertainment & Sports) Network, the Yankees' own RSN, debuted in 2002. YES has been hugely successful, and *Forbes* magazine estimates that under Steinbrenner's leadership, the value of the Yankees has risen from $10 million to $1.2 billion.

Casey Stengel

His baffling manner of speaking had some listeners convinced he was a genius . . . others, including many sportswriters, felt that he was a buffoon. Casey Stengel was a bit of both, depending on what a situation warranted.

One afternoon in Brooklyn during his playing days, he hid a live bird under his hat that flew out when he tipped his cap to the fans. Testifying in front of Congress in support of baseball's antitrust exemption in 1958, Stengel went on for an hour without seeming to ever finish a sentence, much less make a clear point.

But then there were those seven world championships he won as a Yankees manager; his reintroduction of platooning; and his discovery and nurturing of young players who became stars. Those qualities, and others, made him the greatest skipper ever to wear pinstripes.

He played in the big leagues from 1912–25, serving five years with Brooklyn, and then two to three more for the Pittsburgh Pirates, Philadelphia Phillies, New York Giants, and Boston Braves. During his time with the Giants, he learned all about managing from John McGraw. After his playing days were over, he managed the Toledo Mud Hens, then served as field general for the Dodgers (1934–36) and the Braves from 1938–43, during which he racked up a winning percentage of only .394.

He returned to skippering in the minors, enjoying great success with the Oakland Oaks. On coming to the Yankees in 1949, he shocked all by winning a tight race with Boston, then taking the world title.

Over 12 seasons he led the team to a .623 winning percentage, 10 pennants, and seven world championships (including five consecutive). He had many star players to work with, but Stengel also became the master of eking the most from a lineup of role players through platooning and innovative use of his bullpen. He had also come to recognize, from his time in the bushes (and from his own playing career) that good players were trapped in the minors or on the benches of other teams because of their weaknesses; Stengel often pried such players loose and used them judiciously for their *strengths*.

In 1960, sabermetric "Pythagorean" analysis predicted that the Yankees should have won only 89 games; they won 97 and the pennant. He held back ace pitcher Whitey Ford to face specific teams, never setting a regular rotation. As a result, Ford only once exceeded 30 starts in a year under Stengel and didn't win 20 games in a season until after Stengel departed, though he clearly had the skills to do so.

One of Stengel's most baffling, and debated, decisions was to set up the rotation such that Ford only made two starts in the 1960 Series. Had Ford started Game 1, he would have almost certainly pitched Games 4 and 7 as well. Instead, the Yankees could not hold the Pirates in Game 7 and a fatigued Ralph Terry gave up a historic walk-off homer to Bill Mazeroski. Stengel was fired summarily. On receiving the news of his dismissal, he is reported to have said, "I'll never make the mistake of being seventy again."

It was an ignominious, and regrettable, end to a career that saw him bring glory to Yankee Stadium and thousands of great quotes to sportswriters all over the country who had finally come to respect his managerial genius.

Just two years later, 'Ol Case came back to New York as the first manager of the newly created Metropolitans, where the clowning side of his personality fit right in with the slapstick of a major league club that went 40–120. He managed the lovable-loser Mets until the summer of 1965, when a broken hip forced him into retirement at age 75.

Joe Torre

Joe Torre grew up playing ball with his older brothers Frank and Rocco on the sandlots of Brooklyn. A hotheaded youngster with a less-than-ideal father, Torre took Frank's advice—that the fastest way to the major leagues was as a catcher. Frank was drafted by the Braves in 1951, and made the bigs in 1956. Joe followed him to Milwaukee late in 1960, and began racking up new accolades seemingly every season.

In 1961, Joe finished second in Rookie of the Year voting, but only became a regular in 1963, making the All-Star team for the first of five straight seasons while splitting time between catching and manning first base. In 1964, he garnered enough votes to finish fifth in NL MVP voting. The following season he won the Gold Glove (at catcher) and socked 27 home runs.

Prior to the 1969 campaign he was dealt to the Cardinals for former MVP Orlando Cepeda, whom Torre replaced at first base. He transferred back behind the plate after St. Louis dealt Tim McCarver, but shifted again—this time to third base—when Mike Shannon suffered a career-ending illness.

The time away from the rigors of catching was good for his offense. He topped 100 RBIs in 1969, 1970, and 1971, and in the third of those seasons put together a truly outstanding performance. He captured MVP honors, by leading the league with a .363 average, 137 RBIs, 230 hits, and 352 total bases, and also slugged 24 homers.

After that, it was all downhill, at least on the field. Torre's speed and power soon diminished, and he landed with the Mets. During the 1977 season, he took over as manager, and 18 days later retired as a player with a career .297 batting average.

At the time, Torre was far from the unflappable, green-tea-drinking sage he appears to be with the Yankees. Known for his temper, he argued often with umpires and was not known as a top strategist. After being fired by the Mets, he had a stint managing the Braves to a division title, spent some time as a broadcaster for the Angels, and then had a largely unsuccessful run as manager of the Cardinals.

Unexpectedly, Torre found himself considered for the managerial job in the Bronx. He was a hometown boy, popular in New York, and former manager Buck Showalter was being forced to take the fall for the Yankees' first-round elimination from the 1995 playoffs. Despite this, media skeptics labelled Torre "Clueless Joe."

Torre, however, proved the right fit not only for the mix of veterans and rookies on the Yankees' roster, but also with owner George Steinbrenner. Torre's demeanor had mellowed considerably since his days with the Mets, and experience had taught him how to deal with bullies, prima donnas, and the media. In 1996, his inaugural, he led the Yankees to their first World Series in 16 years despite earlier in the year having set a record for playing and managing the most games (over 4,000) without reaching the World Series.

Under his leadership, the Yankees made the postseason every year from 1996 through 2006, won four World Series in five years, and lost two other world championships. Twice he was named Manager of the Year. Midway through the 2007 season, Torre surpassed Casey Stengel on the Yankees' managerial win list, and also moved into eighth place in victories among all managers.

The 2007 season was Torre's 12th consecutive campaign managing the Yankees; it tied him with Stengel for the club's longest uninterrupted tenure in the position. He was, notably, the only manager in the Steinbrenner era to last more than four years running, until the Yankees' third consecutive loss in the Division Series cost him his job in the New York dugout.

Bernie Williams

In 1983, Bernabe Figueroa Williams, a skinny high school track star in Puerto Rico, probably thought his future lay in classical guitar. Two years later, the Yankees thought differently, hiding Williams away from other teams' scouts by stashing him at a baseball camp in Connecticut the summer before his 17th birthday. They then signed him as a non-drafted free agent.

He got to the majors in 1991, but had a tough baptism as some veterans treated the Bambi-eyed 22-year-old harshly. Don Mattingly took him under his wing, though, and by 1993, Williams showed flashes of the player he would become, racking up in his first full season a 21-game hitting streak during which he batted .361. He batted .325 off left-handed pitchers and .268 overall. His mark climbed to .289 in 1994, then Williams batted.307 in 1995 with 18 homers and 82 RBI. In the ill-fated Division Series against Seattle, Williams excelled, batting .429 and becoming the first player in history to homer from both sides of the plate in a postseason game.

His rise continued in a 1996 breakout season, as he began to fulfill the scouting reports that predicted he would hit for power from both sides of the plate. A weak arm was Bernie's only flaw. With Mattingly retired, and a new core of other farm-raised Yankees—Derek Jeter, Mariano Rivera, Jorge Posada, and Andy Pettitte—taking on roles with the big club, Williams stumbled early in the season, then blossomed while the Yankees grew into a championship team. In the '96 ALDS and ALCS, he batted .471 with five homers and 11 RBIs and won the ALCS MVP Award. That one of those homers was a walk-off in the 11th inning to nail down ALCS Game 1 only brightened the heroic aura beginning to surround him.

It was the beginning of an October resumé to rival those of Yogi Berra, Babe Ruth, and Mickey Mantle. During his run, Williams played at a Hall of Fame caliber, racking up four Gold Gloves, five All-Star selections, and the 1998 AL batting title. Williams found himself a cornerstone of a long-standing dynasty that captured four championships in five years and lost two more. In 2002 he recorded 11 consecutive hits, one short of the record. Upon retiring, Bernie held many MLB records for postseason offense, including most career postseason home runs (22), most doubles (29), and most RBIs (80). He was second to Jeter (85) in most runs scored (83).

He also racked up many unforgettable, uniquely Bernie moments, such as an incident in 1999 against Oakland in which he took ball three, thought it was ball four, and headed toward first. The umpire called him back and, thoroughly chagrined, Williams dug into the batter's box again—and delivered a grand slam on the next pitch.

Who else would borrow an umbrella from the fans in the Yankee Stadium outfield to wait out a brief rain delay while leaning against the outfield fence? At the end of each World Series win, when most eyes were on the celebration near pitcher's mound, anyone who glanced Bernie's way would have seen him drop to one knee in humble thanks before running to join the fray.

In the end, after a 16-year career, Bernie Williams retired in pinstripes, having never played for another team or organization, not even in the minor leagues.

Dave Winfield

Despite being born on October 3, 1951, Dave Winfield was ridiculed by Yankees' owner George Steinbrenner with the nickname "Mr. May." Steinbrenner reflected the opinion of some fans who felt that Winfield's job, as a superstar free-agent signing, was to replace "Mr. October" Reggie Jackson. Winfield's performance in the 1981 World Series, his first year as a Yankee, was found lacking, and Steinbrenner never forgot nor forgave.

It was a shocking experience for a three-sport athlete who had his pick of which professional sport to pursue. He chose baseball, and on being drafted by the San Diego Padres in 1973 came directly to the major leagues without any service time in the minors. He spent seven seasons with the Padres—quickly becoming their best player ever—showing all five tools as well as excellent performance, before climbing on to the biggest sports stage in the world, Yankee Stadium.

Winfield had come to the Yankees by signing a 10-year, $23 million deal, then the largest contract in baseball history. Over the span of his tenure in the Bronx, which ended with a trade in 1989, Winfield was without a doubt one of the best players in the game, but like Reggie had personality conflicts with Steinbrenner.

Winfield was the first active player to establish a charity foundation, and his contract stipulated that the Yankees were to pay part of Winfield's salary directly to the cause. Yet the Yankees withheld payments, claiming impropriety in fund use, and waged various court battles over the issue. Steinbrenner, to retaliate, hired a two-bit henchman to dig up dirt on Winfield and ended up himself expelled from baseball (later, Commissioner Fay Vincent reinstated Big George).

Despite the controversies, Winfield rebounded in 1982, hitting 37 homers and making the All-Star team, which he would then do every year he remained a Yankee. In 1984, he batted .340, but was edged out for the batting crown on the final day of the season by his own teammate, young Don Mattingly. "Mr. May" also won five Gold Gloves in the Bronx.

But one superstar does not a whole team make, and the Yankees as a whole were mired in mediocrity. After leaving the Yankees, Winfield enjoyed happier days with his hometown Minnesota Twins, the California Angels, the Cleveland Indians, and the Toronto Blue Jays, with whom he finally won a World Series in 1992. Winfield had the Series-winning hit in the 11th inning of Game 6, changing his nickname from "Mr. May" into "Mr. Jay."

As his career wound down, Winfield mostly filled the role of designated hitter, and in 1994, at age 42, was playing in Cleveland. The Indians traded him back to Minnesota for a player to be named, but the strike cut the season short. Since Winfield never played a game for the Twins that season and the player to be named was never claimed, the Twins instead discharged their half of the deal by taking Cleveland's executives to a fancy meal—making Winfield probably the only player to be traded for a dinner.

After finishing his career with 3,110 hits, 465 homers, and 223 steals, he gained admission to the Hall of Fame in 2001—on his first ballot.

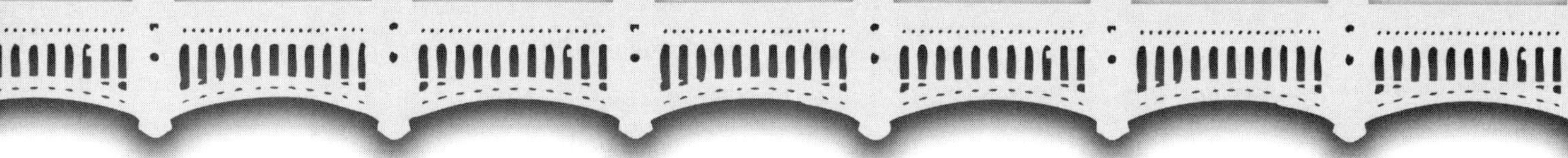

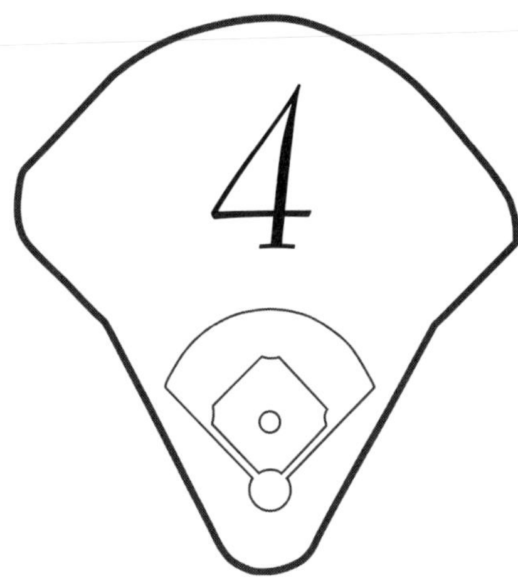

Yankees Batters

SINCE THE ACQUISITION OF BABE Ruth in 1920, the New York Yankees have been known primarily for their great hitting. To be sure, Hall of Fame pitchers such as Whitey Ford, Lefty Gomez, and Red Ruffing have trod the sod at Yankee Stadium in front of cheering throngs, and occasionally a pitcher like Ron Guidry has briefly become the face of the franchise, but the Yankees didn't earn the name the Bronx Bombers because their pitchers hurled bombs at batters.

In the years before Jacob Ruppert took the Babe off Harry Frazee's hands, the Yankees—who were known as the Highlanders through 1912—showed little of the offensive prowess that would later come to embody the franchise. In fact, the Yankees' offense during the first two decades of the century didn't even feature many offensive players fans could follow year-to-year; only two players played in at least 1,000 games for the New York franchise in its first two decades, less than that of any other AL franchise during the period. And no everyday player who spent the majority of his career with the Yankees pre-Ruth would ever be enshrined in the Baseball Hall of Fame.

Once Ruth came on the scene, however, the Yankees would produce great hitters almost by the bundle. Among those great hitters were four who would become legends:

- *George Herman Ruth* The Babe would not only rewrite the record books, he would reinvent the way the sport was played. In his first season as a Yankee, he out-homered every other team in the league. When the Sultan of Swat finished his career in 1935, six times as many home runs were being hit per game as in 1918, the year Ruth first became an everyday player. No athlete would ever dominate an American sport the way Ruth did baseball at his peak.
- *Henry Louis Gehrig* The Iron Horse could never be as big as the Babe, but the record he set for most consecutive games played helped make him the most admired player in baseball history. Today, he is still widely considered the greatest first baseman of all time, he still holds the career record for the most grand slam home runs with 23, and his farewell speech—in which he declared himself "the luckiest man on the face of the earth"—is the best known and most highly regarded speech ever given by a sports figure.
- *Joseph Paul DiMaggio* The Yankee Clipper was baseball's great leading man. His numbers speak volumes, especially his 56-game hitting streak in the summer of 1941, which is considered by many to be the most improbable accomplishment in sports history and one that no player has gotten within a dozen games of since. He is the only baseball player ever voted to the All-Star Game every year of his career. No baseball player has ever been a bigger celebrity and his name remains a cultural touchstone even today.
- *Mickey Charles Mantle* Ruth was larger-than-life, Gehrig was practically a saint, and DiMaggio was an American idol, but the Mick was the All-American. Mantle's power was legendary, and he is widely credited with having launched the longest home runs ever hit. The Mick had two of the most dominant seasons in baseball history—in successive years, no less—in 1956 and 1957. Yet Mantle was not put on a pedestal the way Ruth, Gehrig, and DiMaggio had been and, for much of his career, Mantle had a love-hate relationship with New York fans. In the end, though, the same humanity that made Mantle the target of fan ire in the early days of his career resulted in a fan base that felt a stronger connection with Mantle than with any previous or later Yankee, and that connection did not end with Mantle's death.

The pantheon of great Yankees hitters extends far beyond the four legends, of course. In this register you'll also find the feats of such players as:

- *Yogi Berra* Perhaps now better known for his witticisms, Berra was a three-time MVP and hit at least 20 home runs in 11 different seasons.
- *Earle Combs* Led the league in triples in three different years and finished among the top six in runs seven different seasons.
- *Bill Dickey* Yogi's predecessor behind the plate, Dickey hit .300 in 10 different seasons and finished with a lifetime batting average of .313.
- *Rickey Henderson* Led the AL in runs in both 1985 and 1986 and his 326 steals as a Yankee are by far the club record even though he spent just four full seasons in pinstripes.
- *Tommy Henrich* Finished in the top 10 in the AL in slugging four times in the 1940s.
- *Reggie Jackson* The straw that stirred the drink slugged over .500 in three of his five seasons with the Yankees.
- *Derek Jeter* The slick shortstop and marquee leader has hit at least .290 with double-figure home runs in 11 different seasons with the Yankees.
- *Roger Maris* Hit 61 home runs in 1961 and led the AL in RBIs in both 1960 and 1961 while winning the league MVP both years.
- *Don Mattingly* The best hitter in baseball in the mid-1980s, he led the AL in doubles three consecutive years and remains one of the most popular Yankees.
- *Bob Meusel* Led the AL in home runs and RBIs in 1925 and finished among the top 10 in slugging seven different seasons.
- *Paul O'Neill* Hit .300 six times and posted 100 RBIs four times as a Yankee.
- *Wally Pipp* Finished among the top 10 in the AL in triples six times, home runs six times, and RBIs four times as a Yankee.
- *Jorge Posada* The switch-hitting catcher has finished among the top 10 in the AL in on-base percentage four different seasons.
- *Alex Rodriguez* Has led the AL in runs, home runs, and slugging in two of his four seasons as a Yankee.
- *Roy White* Led the AL in runs in 1976 and finished third in 1968 and 1970.
- *Bernie Williams* Scored 1,366 runs in 16 seasons with the Yankees.

The batter register offers a mix of traditional statistics and analytical statistics for perusal. Traditional stats like at bats, runs, home runs, runs batted in, and batting average are familiar to every kid who has ever read the back of a bubblegum card. Analytical stats like OPS (On-Base Plus Slugging), Adjusted OPS, and Batter-Fielder Wins offer the opportunity to evaluate a player in the context of his ballpark, his league, and his era—as well as making reasonable cross-era comparisons possible.

Biographical Information

There is a wealth of biographical information in a single line atop each player entry. The biographical information answers questions about a player's life away from the batter's box: What year was he born? How long did he live? How tall was he? Was he ever a manager, and for how long? Did he serve the military during his career as a player? Has he been inducted into the Hall of Fame? The biographical line goes beyond the statistics to fill in a more complete picture of each player.

Every player in this register has (at least) a last name and a debut date. If a Latino player has a matronymic name, it is placed in parentheses—for example ***Sanchez, Rey*** *Rey Francisco (Guadalupe)*. Well-known nicknames are included in quotes in the biographical line; if a nickname is what the player was primarily known by during his career, it will be part of his listed name—such as ***Berra, Yogi*** *Lawrence Peter*. Other features and abbreviations for biographical information follow.

B (mm.dd.yyyy) is the date and place of birth.
D (mm.dd.yyyy) is the date and place of death, if death has occurred.

The side of the plate a player bats from is expressed **BR** (bats right), **BL** (bats left), or **BB** (bats both sides). The arm the player throws with is expressed **TR** (throws right), or **TL** (throws left). Likewise, if a player changes from switch-hitting to hitting from one side during his career, the side of the plate he bats from exclusively and the length of that change are presented in parentheses.

Height is shown by feet followed by inches. Weight is expressed in pounds using **#**.

Debuts are marked **d**—note the lower-case letter so as not to be confused with the abbreviation for death—followed by the date the player made his first major league appearance. The debut year is the first year listed in his entry in the register, so it is not repeated in the biographical line.

Besides the basic pieces of information for players available on the biographical line, there are a few other designations for players whose career, family, or duty proved noteworthy.

Mil indicates military service in the army, navy, air force, or marines;
NG indicates National Guard service (two weeks to one month) during the Vietnam War.
Mer indicates merchant marine;
Def indicates defense plant work.

The seasons missed—including partial seasons—are listed after the abbreviations for duty. Since the founding of the Yankees in 1903, four wars involving the U.S. have caused some major leaguers to miss time for military duty (dates include post-war service):

- World War I, 1917–19
- World War II, 1941–46
- Korean War, 1951–59
- Vietnam War, 1962–72

If the player spent time as a coach, manager, or umpire, this is indicated by the following abbreviations:

C Coach
M Manager
U Umpire

A select few players who have reached the Hall of Fame are identified by **HF** and followed by the year of induction.

If the player had a close family member in the major leagues, the relative's relationship is identified by the codes listed below. The relative's first name is given; the last name is included if it is different than the player's.

b brother
twb twin brother
f father

s son
gf grandfather
gs grandson
ggf great grandfather
ggs great grandson

Defensive games in outfield positions (**LF-CF-RF**) are included at the end of the biographical data if there is not enough room to place it in the position career line.

▲ at the end of the biographical information indicates that the player is also listed in the pitcher register. A player whose primary position was not pitcher must have pitched at least 9 innings to appear in the Pitching Register.

Statistical information

Symbols in the first two columns:

† before the team name means he participated in Postseason Play that year;
★ after team name means he participated in All-Star game;
☆ after team name means he was selected to All-Star team but did not play;
✳ after team name means he was selected to All-Star team but replaced due to injury.

The columns that appear in the player register after **Year**:

TM Team. Each team is identified by a three-letter code that is usually the first three letters of the city, state, or area where the team is located.
L League. The leagues in this book include the National League (N), the American League (A), the Federal League (F), and the American Association (AA).
G Games. The number of games is boldfaced if the player appeared in every one of his team's games in a given year.
AB At Bats
R Runs
H Hits
2B Doubles
3B Triples
HR Home Runs
RBI Runs Batted In.
BB Bases on Balls. Walks.
IB Intentional Base on Balls. These have been counted as a distinct category since 1955
HBP Hit-by-Pitch.
SO Strikeouts. Strikeouts are not available for most players before 1913
AVG Batting Average. Hits divided by at bats.
OBP On-Base Percentage. The official current definition of OBP is (Hits plus Bases on Balls plus Hit-by-Pitches) divided by (At Bats plus Bases on Balls plus Hit-by-Pitches plus Sacrifice Flies). This volume uses that definition from 1954 on, but sacrifice fly data is not available in previous years, so it is not used in calculating the statistic in earlier years.
SLG Slugging Percentage. Total bases divided by at bats.
OPS On-Base plus Slugging. The sum of on-base percentage and slugging percentage
AOPS Adjusted On-Base plus Slugging. On-base percentage and slugging average are added and normalized for the context of the offensive level of the league and the player's home park(s) and then converted to a scale in which 0 is average.
SB Stolen Bases.
CS Caught Stealing. This data has only been recorded for all major league players since 1951, though the totals for all Yankees' players are available from 1920 on.
SB Stolen Base Percentage.
G/Pos Games at Position. Positions are listed left to right by decreasing number of games. There are several different variations in this category.
***** before the position indicates that the player fielded the position in the great majority (100 since 1901) of his team's games during the season or for at least 1,000 games during his career
/ Any positions listed after the slash indicate that it was fielded by the player in less than 10 games that season or 100 games during his career.

Positions are identified by easily recognizable one-letter abbreviations:

P Pitcher
1 First Base
2 Second Base
3 Third Base
S Shortstop
O Outfield
D Designated Hitter.

Positions are followed by a dash and the number of games the player played at that position during the season or career. The positions are separated by commas except when there is a slash. If the player spent only one game at that position, the one-letter abbreviation is used without a dash or number. If the player spent only one game at multiple positions, no comma is placed between the abbreviations for those positions.

Outfield is officially counted as only one position, but if the player spent time playing at least two of the three outfield positions, a breakdown of the games in left, center, and right is presented in that order, separated by dashes, in parentheses. If the outfielder only played one outfield position, that position will be identified (**LF**, **CF**, or **RF**) after the number of outfield games played. If a breakdown of the games in left, center, and right is needed in the career line, but there is not enough room, that information will be added to the end of the biographical data and the primary outfield position played will be identified by **L**, **C**, or **R** following the number of games played in the outfield.

DL Disabled List. This shows the number of days spent on the disabled list for each year indicated since the DL was instituted in 1941. This column does not include time spent on the DL before or after the season, but this carryover explains why some players will have DL stints shorter than the 15-day minimum. If a player spent the entire season on the disabled list, the information is given in brackets in his biographical line with the team and time indicated. Rafael Santana, for instance, was the club's regular shortstop in 1988, then spent all season (182 days) on the disabled list without playing a game in '89 *[DL 1989 NY A 182]*.

BFW Batter-Fielder Wins. The sum of a player's batting wins, basestealing wins, and fielding wins, this figure indicates how many games the player won or lost for his team compared to an average player.

For any missing data, such as CS or SO, the career total is underlined if it is a partial figure.

Batters

YEAR	TM LG	G	AB	R	H	2B	3B	HR	RBI	BB	IB	HP	SO	AVG	OBP	SLG	OPS	AOPS	SB	CS	SB%	GAMES AT POSITION	DL	BFW
ABREU, BOBBY BOB KELLY B3.11.1974 MARACAY, ARAGUA, VENEZ BL/TR/6'0"/(160–210) d9.1																								
2006	†NY A	58	209	37	69	16	0	7	42	33	1	1	52	.330	.419	.507	.926	+37	10	2	83	O57(0/1/57)/D	0	1.5
2007	†NY A	158	605	123	171	40	5	16	101	84	0	3	115	.283	.369	.445	.814	+13	25	8	76	O157R/D	0	0.7
Total	12	1643	5881	1074	1766	415	49	221	984	1087	95	28	1296	.300	.408	.500	.908	+36	296	92	76	O1605(16/21/1583),D11	37	30.1
Team	2	216	814	160	240	56	5	23	143	117	1	4	167	.295	.382	.461	.843	+19	35	10	78	O214(0/1/57),D2	0	2.2
/150	1	150	565	111	167	39	3	16	99	81	1	3	116	.295	.382	.461	.843	+19	24	7	77	O149(0/1/40)/D	0	1.5
ADAMS, SPENCER SPENCER DEWEY B6.21.1898 LAYTON UT D11.24.1970 SALT LAKE CITY UT BL/TR/5'9"/158 d5.8																								
1926	†NY A	28	25	7	3	1	0	0	1	3	—	0	7	.120	.214	.160	.374	-101	1	0	100	2b4/3b		0.2
Total	4	180	395	61	101	16	5	0	38	38	—	2	50	.256	.324	.322	.646	-34	5	10	33	2b84,3b32,S14	—	-2.1
AGUAYO, LUIS LUIS (MURIEL) B3.13.1959 VEGA BAJA, PR BR/TR/5'9"/(173–195) d4.19																								
1988	NY A	50	140	12	35	4	0	3	8	7	1	1	33	.250	.289	.343	.632	-23	0	2	0	3b33,2b13,S6	0	-1.2
Total	10	568	1104	142	260	43	10	37	109	94	12	20	220	.236	.304	.393	.697	-10	7	5	58	S259,2b147,3b97,D2	124	-1.4
ALDRETE, MIKE MICHAEL PETER B1.29.1961 CARMEL CA BL/TL/5'11"/(180–185) DR 1983 SFN 7/174 d5.28 C3 COL STANFORD																								
1996	†NY A	32	68	11	17	5	0	3	12	9	0	0	15	.250	.338	.456	.794	-2	0	1	0	O9(6/0/4),1b8/PD	28	-0.3
Total	10	930	2147	277	565	104	9	41	271	314	29	5	381	.263	.356	.377	.733	+4	19	18	51	O409(278/24/135),1b286,D31/P	44	-1.0
ALEXANDER, WALT WALTER ERNEST B3.5.1891 ATLANTA GA D12.29.1978 FORT WORTH TX BR/TR/5'10.5"/165 d6.21																								
1912	StL A	37	97	5	17	4	0	0	5	8	—	1	—	.175	.245	.216	.461	-66	1	3	25	C37	—	-0.9
1913	StL A	43	110	6	15	2	1	0	7	4	—	1	36	.136	.174	.173	.347	-98	1	—	—	C43	—	-0.9
1915	StL A	1	1	0	0	0	0	0	0	0	—	0	0	.000	.000	.000	.000	-199	0	—	—	/C	—	0.0
1915	NY A	25	68	7	17	4	0	1	5	13	—	0	16	.250	.370	.353	.723	+17	2	1	67	C24	—	1.0
1915	Year	26	69	7	17	4	0	1	5	13	—	0	16	.246	.366	.348	.714	+14	2	1	67	C25	—	1.0
1916	NY A	36	78	8	20	6	1	0	3	13	—	2	20	.256	.376	.359	.735	+18	0	—	—	C27	—	0.7
1917	NY A	20	51	1	7	2	1	0	4	4	—	0	11	.137	.200	.216	.416	-73	1	—	—	C20	—	-0.3
Total	5	162	405	26	76	18	3	1	24	42	—	4	83	.188	.271	.254	.525	-44	5	4	100	C152	—	-0.4
Team	3	81	197	16	44	12	2	1	12	30	—	2	47	.223	.332	.320	.652	-4	3	1	100	C71	—	1.4
ALLEN, BERNIE BERNARD KEITH B4.16.1939 E.LIVERPOOL OH BL/TR/6'0"/(175–186) d4.10 COL PURDUE																								
1972	NY A	84	220	26	50	9	0	9	21	23	4	0	42	.227	.296	.391	.687	+7	0	1	0	3b44,2b20	0	0.3
1973	NY A	17	57	5	13	3	0	0	4	5	1	0	5	.228	.290	.281	.571	-37	0	0	0	2b13,D2	0	-0.2
Total	12	1139	3404	357	815	140	21	73	351	370	52	8	424	.239	.314	.357	.671	-10	13	16	45	2b914,3b109,D2	105	0.7
Team	2	101	277	31	63	12	0	9	25	28	5	0	47	.227	.294	.368	.662	-2	0	1	0	3b44,2b33,D2	0	0.1
/150	3	150	411	46	94	18	0	13	37	42	7	0	70	.227	.294	.368	.662	-2	0	1	0	3b65,2b49,D3	0	0.1
ALMONTE, ERICK ERICK R. B2.1.1978 SANTO DOMINGO, D.R. BR/TR/6'2"/180 d9.4																								
2001	NY A	8	4	0	2	1	0	0	0	0	0	0	1	.500	.500	.750	1.250	+121	2	0	100	S4,D3	0	0.2
2003	NY A	31	100	17	26	6	0	1	11	8	0	1	24	.260	.321	.350	.671	-22	1	0	100	S31	0	-0.7
Total	2	39	104	17	28	7	0	1	11	8	0	1	25	.269	.327	.365	.692	-16	3	0	100	S35,D3	0	-0.5
ALOMAR, SANDY SANTOS SR. (CONDE) B10.19.1943 SALINAS, PR BB/TR (BR 1964P, 65–66)/5'9"/(140–170) d9.15 C13 s–ROBERTO s–SANDY OF(5/0/3)																								
1974	NY A	76	279	35	75	8	0	1	27	14	0	0	25	.269	.302	.308	.610	-23	6	4	60	2b76	0	-1.5
1975	NY A	151	489	61	117	18	4	2	39	26	0	0	58	.239	.277	.305	.582	-35	28	6	82	2b150/S	0	-1.5
1976	†NY A	67	163	20	39	4	0	1	10	13	0	0	12	.239	.295	.282	.577	-30	12	7	63	2b38,S6,3b3/1brfD	0	-0.7
Total	15	1481	4760	558	1168	126	19	13	282	302	17	3	482	.245	.290	.288	.578	-32	227	80	74	2b1156,S197,3b43,D39,1b14,O8L	100	-9.2
Team	3	294	931	116	231	30	4	4	76	53	0	0	95	.248	.288	.302	.590	-31	46	17	73	2b264,S7,3b3/1rfD	0	-3.7
/150	2	150	475	59	118	15	2	2	39	27	0	0	48	.248	.288	.302	.590	-31	23	9	72	2b135,S4,3b2/1rfD	0	-1.9
ALOU, FELIPE FELIPE ROJAS (B FELIPE ROJAS (ALOU)) B5.12.1935 HAINA, D.R. BR/TR/6'0"/(190–205) d6.8 M14/C5 B–JESUS B–MATTY s–MOISES OF(434/484/736)																								
1971	NY A	131	461	52	133	20	6	8	69	32	3	2	24	.289	.334	.410	.744	+16	5	5	50	O80(7/20/56),1b42	0	-1.2
1972	NY A	120	324	33	90	18	1	6	37	22	1	2	27	.278	.326	.395	.721	+17	1	0	100	1b95,O15R	0	0.6
1973	NY A	93	280	25	66	12	0	4	27	9	5	0	25	.236	.256	.321	.577	-36	0	1	0	1b67,O22(1/1/21)	0	-2.3
Total	17	2082	7339	985	2101	359	49	206	852	423	67	57	706	.286	.328	.433	.761	+14	107	67	61	O1531R,1b468,3b5,S2	31	1.7
Team	3	344	1065	110	289	50	7	18	133	63	9	4	76	.271	.311	.382	.693	+3	6	6	50	1b204,O117(7/41/77)	0	-2.9
/150	1	150	464	48	126	22	3	8	58	27	4	2	33	.271	.311	.382	.693	+3	3	3	50	1b89,O51(3/18/34)	0	-1.3
ALOU, MATTY MATEO ROJAS (B MATEO ROJAS (ALOU)) B12.22.1938 HAINA, D.R. BL/TL/5'9"/160 d9.26 B–FELIPE B–JESUS																								
1973	NY A	123	497	59	147	22	1	2	28	30	0	3	43	.296	.338	.356	.694	-2	5	2	71	O85R,1b40/D	0	-1.4
Total	15	1667	5789	780	1777	236	50	31	427	311	38	36	377	.307	.345	.381	.726	+4	156	80	66	O1312(197/844/302),1b168/DP	36	-6.2
/150	1	150	606	72	179	27	1	2	34	37	0	4	52	.296	.338	.356	.694	-2	6	2	75	O104R,1b49/D	0	-1.7
ALSTON, DELL WENDELL B9.22.1952 VALHALLA NY BL/TR/6'0"/(174–175) d5.17 COL CONCORDIA (NY)																								
1977	NY A	22	40	10	13	4	0	1	4	3	0	0	4	.325	.364	.500	.864	+36	3	3	50	D10,O2R	0	0.2
1978	NY A	3	3	0	0	0	0	0	0	0	0	0	2	.000	.000	.000	.000	-199	0	0	0	/H	0	-0.1
Total	4	189	332	48	79	7	4	3	35	28	3	2	44	.238	.297	.310	.607	-29	20	21	49	O108(52/4/54),D26,1b9	0	-2.5
Team	2	25	43	10	13	4	0	1	4	3	0	0	6	.302	.340	.465	.805	+21	3	3	50	D10,O2R	0	0.1
AMARO, RUBEN RUBEN SR. (MORA) B1.6.1936 NUEVA LAREDO, TAMAULIPAS, MEXICO BR/TR/5'11"/(165–175) d6.29 C6 s–RUBEN																								
1966	NY A	14	23	0	5	0	0	0	3	0	0	0	2	.217	.217	.217	.434	-74	0	0	0	S14	133	0.1
1967	NY A	130	417	31	93	12	0	1	17	43	4	1	49	.223	.297	.259	.556	-32	3	2	60	S123,3b3,1b2	0	0.2
1968	NY A	47	41	3	5	1	0	0	0	9	0	0	6	.122	.280	.146	.426	-67	0	0	0	S23,1b22	0	-0.7
Total	11	940	2155	211	505	75	13	8	156	227	24	10	280	.234	.309	.292	.601	-30	11	14	44	S705,1b169,3b53,2b20/lf	133	-4.2
Team	3	191	481	34	103	13	0	1	20	52	4	1	57	.214	.292	.247	.539	-37	3	2	60	S160,1b24,3b3	133	-0.4
/150	2	150	378	27	81	10	0	1	16	41	3	1	45	.214	.292	.247	.539	-37	2	2	50	S126,1b19,3b2	104	-0.3
ANDERSON, JOHN JOHN JOSEPH "HONEST JOHN" B12.14.1873 SARPSBORG, NORWAY D7.23.1949 WORCESTER MA BB/TR/6'2"/180 d9.8																								
1904	NY A	143	558	62	155	27	12	3	82	23	—	6	—	.278	.313	.385	.698	+15	20	—	—	O112(46/52/13),1b33	—	0.2
1905	NY A	32	99	12	23	3	1	0	14	8	—	1	—	.232	.296	.283	.579	-25	9	—	—	O22(1/19/2),1b3	—	-0.5
Total	14	1636	6345	871	1843	328	124	50	978	310	—	53	55	.290	.329	.405	.734	+14	338	—	—	O1010(561/229/219),1b599/3b	—	1.9
Team	2	175	657	74	178	30	13	3	96	31	—	7	0	.271	.310	.370	.680	+9	29	—	—	O134(47/71/15),1b36	—	-0.3
/150	2	150	563	63	153	26	11	3	82	27	—	6	0	.271	.310	.370	.680	+9	25	—	—	O115(40/61/13),1b31	—	-0.3
ARAGON, ANGEL ANGEL (VALDES) "PETE" B8.2.1890 HAVANA, CUBA D1.24.1952 NEW YORK NY BR/TR/5'5"/150 d8.20 s–JACK																								
1914	NY A	6	7	1	1	0	0	0	0	1	—	1	2	.143	.333	.143	.476	-56	0	—	—	/cf	—	0.0
1916	NY A	12	24	1	5	0	0	0	3	2	—	0	2	.208	.269	.208	.477	-57	2	—	—	3b8,O2(1/0/1)	—	-0.1
1917	NY A	14	45	2	3	1	0	0	2	2	—	0	2	.067	.106	.089	.195	-140	0	—	—	O6(4/2/0),3b4,S2	—	-0.9
Total	3	32	76	4	9	1	0	0	5	5	—	1	6	.118	.183	.132	.315	-104	2	—	—	3b12,O9(5/3/1),S2	—	-1.0
ARIAS, ALEX ALEJANDRO B11.20.1967 NEW YORK NY BR/TR/6'3"/(185–202) DR 1987 CHIN 3/62 d5.12																								
2002	NY A	6	7	0	0	0	0	0	0	1	0	0	2	.000	.125	.000	.125	-163	0	0	0	3b4/S	0	-0.2
Total	11	775	1773	203	470	84	6	18	196	181	14	23	211	.265	.338	.350	.688	-19	10	5	67	S321,3b193,2b53,1b18	33	-6.9
ASHFORD, TUCKER THOMAS STEVEN B12.4.1954 MEMPHIS TN BR/TR/6'1"/(185–195) DR 1974 SDN*1/2 d9.21 COL U. OF MISSISSIPPI																								
1981	NY A	3	0	0	0	0	0	0	0	0	0	0	0	+	+	+	.000	-100	0	0	0	2b2	0	-0.1
Total	7	222	510	42	111	31	1	6	55	47	6	1	75	.218	.282	.318	.600	-31	5	3	63	3b143,2b37,1b14,S12/C	0	-4.3

Batters

YEAR	TM LG	G	AB	R	H	2B	3B	HR	RBI	BB	IB	HP	SO	AVG	OBP	SLG	OPS	AOPS	SB	CS	SB%	GAMES AT POSITION	DL	BFW
Austin, Jimmy James Philip "Pepper" B12.8.1879 Swansea, Wales D3.6.1965 Laguna Beach CA BB/TR/5'7.5"/155 d4.19 M3/C18																								
1909	NY A	136	437	37	101	11	5	1	39	32	—	1	—	.231	.285	.286	.571	-20	30	—	—	3b111,S23/2b	—	0.7
1910	NY A	133	432	46	94	11	4	2	36	47	—	7	—	.218	.305	.275	.580	-23	22	—	—	3b133	—	-0.4
Total	18	1580	5388	661	1328	174	76	13	390	592	—	44	363	.246	.326	.314	.640	-10	244	61	100	3b1431,S100,2b9	—	1.8
Team	2	269	869	83	195	22	9	3	75	79	—	8	0	.224	.295	.281	.576	-22	52	—	—	3b244,S23/2	—	0.3
/150	1	150	485	46	109	12	5	2	42	44	—	4	0	.224	.295	.281	.576	-22	29	—	—	3b136,S13/2	—	0.2
Autry, Chick Martin Gordon B3.5.1903 Martindale TX D1.26.1950 Savannah GA BR/TR/6'0"/180 d4.20																								
1924	NY A	2	0	1	0	0	0	0	0	0	—	1	0	+	1.000	+	1.000	+72	0	0	0	C2	—	0.0
Total	6	120	277	21	68	17	3	2	33	7	—	2	29	.245	.269	.350	.619	-41	0	0	0	C96	—	-1.1
Azocar, Oscar Oscar Gregorio (Azocar) B2.21.1965 Soro, Sucre, Venez BL/TL/6'1"/(170–195) d7.17																								
1990	NY A	65	214	18	53	8	0	5	19	2	0	1	15	.248	.257	.355	.612	-31	7	0	100	O57(47/0/12)/D	0	-1.0
Total	3	202	439	38	99	16	0	5	36	12	2	2	36	.226	.248	.296	.544	-48	10	0	100	O107(90/0/19)/1bD	0	-3.3
Babe, Loren Loren Rolland "Bee Bee" B1.11.1928 Pisgah IA D2.14.1984 Omaha NE BL/TR/5'10"/180 d8.19 C4																								
1952	NY A	12	21	1	2	1	0	0	0	4	—	0	4	.095	.240	.143	.383	-91	1	0	100	3b9	0	-0.1
1953	NY A	5	18	2	6	1	0	2	6	0	—	0	2	.333	.333	.722	1.055	+85	0	0	0	3b5	0	0.3
Total	2	120	382	37	85	18	2	2	26	39	—	2	26	.223	.298	.296	.594	-41	1	1	50	3b107/S	0	-1.9
Team	2	17	39	3	8	2	0	2	6	4	—	0	6	.205	.279	.410	.689	-17	1	0	100	3b14	0	0.2
Bailey, Bill Harry Lewis B11.19.1881 Shawnee OH D10.27.1967 Seattle WA BL/TR/5'10.5"/170 d4.21																								
1911	NY A	5	9	1	1	0	0	0	0	0	—	0	—	.111	.111	.111	.222	-136	0	—	—	O2/3b	—	-0.1
Baker, Frank Frank Watts B10.29.1946 Meridian MS BL/TR/6'2"/(178–185) d8.9 Col Southern Mississippi																								
1970	NY A	35	117	6	27	4	1	0	11	14	0	2	26	.231	.323	.282	.605	-29	1	2	33	S35	0	0.5
1971	NY A	43	79	9	11	2	0	0	2	16	3	0	22	.139	.281	.165	.446	-69	3	0	100	S38	0	0.1
1973	†Bal A	44	63	10	12	1	2	1	11	7	0	0	7	.190	.268	.317	.585	-35	0	0	0	S32,2b7/1b3b	0	-0.3
1974	†Bal A	24	29	3	5	1	0	0	0	3	0	0	5	.172	.250	.207	.457	-67	0	0	0	S17,2b3/3b	0	-0.4
Total	4	146	288	28	55	8	3	1	24	40	3	2	60	.191	.292	.250	.542	-44	4	2	67	S122,2b10,3b2/1b	0	-0.1
Team	2	78	196	15	38	6	1	0	13	30	3	2	48	.194	.306	.235	.541	-46	4	2	67	S73	0	0.6
Baker, Frank John Franklin "Home Run" B3.13.1886 Trappe MD D6.28.1963 Trappe MD BL/TR/5'11"/173 d9.21 HF1955																								
1908	Phi A	9	31	5	9	3	0	0	2	0	—	0	—	.290	.290	.387	.677	+12	0	—	—	3b9	—	0.2
1909	Phi A	148	541	73	165	27	**19**	4	85	26	—	5	—	.305	.343	.447	.790	+46	20	—	—	3b146	—	2.2
1910	†Phi A	146	561	83	159	25	15	2	74	34	—	4	—	.283	.329	.392	.721	+27	21	—	—	3b146	—	2.3
1911	†Phi A	148	592	96	198	42	14	**11**	115	40	—	2	—	.334	.379	.508	.887	+49	38	—	—	3b148	—	3.5
1912	Phi A	149	577	116	200	40	21	**10**	**130**	50	—	6	—	.347	.404	.541	.945	+76	40	26	61	3b149	—	6.5
1913	†Phi A	149	564	116	190	34	9	**12**	**117**	63	—	10	31	.337	.413	.493	.906	+69	34	—	—	3b149	—	6.6
1914	†Phi A	150	570	84	182	23	10	**9**	89	53	—	3	37	.319	.380	.442	.822	+53	19	20	49	3b149	—	5.0
1916	NY A	100	360	46	97	23	2	10	52	36	—	5	30	.269	.344	.428	.772	+29	15	—	—	3b96	—	1.7
1917	NY A	146	553	57	156	24	2	6	71	48	—	5	27	.282	.345	.365	.710	+16	18	—	—	3b146	—	2.6
1918	NY A	**126**	504	65	154	24	5	6	62	38	—	2	13	.306	.357	.409	.766	+28	8	—	—	3b126	—	2.9
1919	NY A	**141**	567	70	166	22	1	10	83	44	—	2	18	.293	.346	.388	.734	+5	13	—	—	3b141	—	0.3
1921	†NY A	94	330	46	97	16	2	9	71	26	—	4	12	.294	.353	.436	.789	-2	8	5	62	3b83	—	0.8
1922	†NY A	69	234	30	65	12	3	7	36	15	—	2	14	.278	.327	.444	.771	-3	1	3	25	3b60	—	-0.9
Total	13	1575	5984	887	1838	315	103	96	987	473	—	50	182	.307	.363	.442	.805	+36	235	54	100	3b1548	—	33.7
Team	6	676	2548	314	735	121	15	48	375	207	—	20	114	.288	.347	.404	.751	+14	63	8	100	3b652	—	7.4
/150	1	150	565	70	163	27	3	11	83	46	—	4	25	.288	.347	.404	.751	+14	14	2	100	3b145	—	1.6
Balboni, Steve Stephen Charles B1.16.1957 Brockton MA BR/TR/6'3"/(225–250) Dr 1978 NYA 2/52 d4.22 Col Eckerd																								
1981	NY A	4	7	2	2	1	1	0	2	1	0	0	4	.286	.375	.714	1.089	+110	0	0	0	1b3/D	0	0.1
1982	NY A	33	107	8	20	2	1	2	4	6	0	0	34	.187	.228	.280	.508	-60	0	0	0	1b26,D5	0	-1.1
1983	NY A	32	86	8	20	2	0	5	17	8	0	0	23	.233	.295	.430	.725	+1	0	0	0	1b23,D4	0	-0.2
1989	NY A	110	300	33	71	12	2	17	59	25	5	3	67	.237	.296	.460	.756	+13	0	0	0	D82,1b20	0	0.0
1990	NY A	116	266	24	51	6	0	17	34	35	2	3	91	.192	.291	.406	.697	-7	0	0	0	D72,1b28	0	-1.1
Total	11	960	3120	351	714	127	11	181	495	273	21	19	856	.229	.293	.451	.744	+0	1	2	33	1b630,D281	0	-7.5
Team	5	295	766	75	164	23	4	41	116	75	7	6	219	.214	.286	.415	.701	-4	0	0	0	D164,1b100	0	-2.3
/150	3	150	389	38	83	12	2	21	59	38	4	3	111	.214	.286	.415	.701	-4	0	0	0	D83,1b51	0	-1.2
Ball, Neal Cornelius B4.22.1881 Grand Haven MI D10.15.1957 Bridgeport CT BR/TR/5'7"/145 d9.12																								
1907	NY A	15	44	5	9	1	1	0	4	1	—	0	—	.205	.222	.273	.495	-47	1	—	—	S11,2b5	—	-0.6
1908	NY A	132	446	35	110	16	2	0	38	21	—	2	—	.247	.284	.291	.575	-14	32	—	—	S130/2b	—	-1.1
1909	NY A	8	29	5	6	1	1	0	3	3	—	0	—	.207	.281	.310	.591	-14	2	—	—	2b8	—	-0.4
Total	7	502	1613	163	404	56	17	4	151	99	—	4	13	.250	.295	.314	.609	-17	92	5	100	S271,2b179,3b21,O6(0/5/1)	—	-5.6
Team	3	155	519	45	125	18	4	0	45	25	—	2	0	.241	.279	.291	.570	-17	35	—	—	S141,2b14	—	-2.1
/150	3	150	502	44	121	17	4	0	44	24	—	2	0	.241	.279	.291	.570	-17	34	—	—	S136,2b14	—	-2.0
Barfield, Jesse Jesse Lee B10.29.1959 Joliet IL BR/TR/6'1"/(170–206) Dr 1977 TorA 9/233 d9.3 C3 s–Josh																								
1989	NY A	129	441	71	106	19	1	18	56	82	6	2	122	.240	.360	.410	.770	+18	5	3	63	O129(0/18/120)	0	1.8
1990	NY A	153	476	69	117	21	2	25	78	82	4	5	150	.246	.359	.456	.815	+26	4	3	57	O151(0/4/151)	0	2.1
1991	NY A	84	284	37	64	12	0	17	48	36	6	0	80	.225	.312	.447	.759	+7	1	0	100	O81(1/0/81)	70	0.8
1992	NY A	30	95	8	13	2	0	2	7	9	2	0	27	.137	.210	.221	.431	-79	1	1	50	O30R	133	-1.2
Total	12	1428	4759	715	1219	216	30	241	716	551	49	34	1234	.256	.335	.466	.801	+16	66	47	58	O1387(3/87/1340),D16	218	13.8
Team	4	396	1296	185	300	54	3	62	189	209	18	7	379	.231	.339	.421	.760	+12	11	7	61	O391(0/22/352)	203	3.5
/150	2	150	491	70	114	20	1	23	72	79	7	3	144	.231	.339	.421	.760	+12	4	3	57	O148(0/8/133)	77	1.3
Barker, Ray Raymond Herrell "Buddy" B3.12.1936 Martinsburg WV BL/TR/6'0"/(192–200) d9.13																								
1960	Bal A	5	6	0	0	0	0	0	0	0	0	0	3	.000	.000	.000	.000	-199	0	0	0	/lf	0	-0.2
1965	Cle A	11	6	0	0	0	0	0	0	2	1	0	2	.000	.250	.000	.250	-122	0	0	0	1b3	0	-0.1
1965	NY A	98	205	21	52	11	0	7	31	20	5	3	46	.254	.326	.410	.736	+9	1	0	100	1b61,3b3	0	0.6
1965	Year	109	211	21	52	11	0	7	31	22	6	3	48	.246	.324	.398	.722	+5	1	0	100	1b64,3b3	0	0.5
1966	NY A	61	75	11	14	5	0	3	13	4	0	0	20	.187	.225	.373	.598	-28	0	0	0	1b47	0	0.0
1967	NY A	17	26	2	2	0	0	0	0	3	0	0	5	.077	.172	.077	.249	-125	0	0	0	1b13	0	-0.4
Total	4	192	318	34	68	16	0	10	44	29	6	3	76	.214	.283	.358	.641	-16	1	0	100	1b124,3b3/lf	0	-0.1
Team	3	176	306	34	68	16	0	10	44	27	5	3	71	.222	.289	.373	.662	-11	1	0	100	1b121,3b3	0	0.2
/150	3	150	261	29	58	14	0	9	38	23	4	3	61	.222	.289	.373	.662	-11	1	0	100	1b103,3b3	0	0.2
Barnes, Honey John Francis B1.31.1900 Fulton NY D6.18.1981 Lockport NY BL/TR/5'10"/175 d4.20 Col Colgate																								
1926	NY A	1	0	0	0	0	0	0	0	1	—	0	0	+	1.000	+	1.000	+79	0	0	0	/C	—	0.0
Barney, Ed Edmund J. B1.23.1890 Amery WI D10.4.1967 Rice Lake WI BL/TR/5'10.5"/178 d7.22																								
1915	NY A	11	36	1	7	0	0	0	8	3	—	0	6	.194	.256	.194	.450	-65	2	1	67	O10(3/7/0)	—	-0.4
Total	2	88	272	33	61	5	2	0	22	37	—	3	33	.224	.324	.257	.581	-22	17	4	100	O76(26/49/1)	—	-0.7
Basak, Chris Christopher Joseph B12.6.1978 North Platte NE BR/TR/6'2"/190 Dr 2000 NYN 6/185 d6.9 Col Illinois																								
2007	NY A	5	1	0	0	0	0	0	0	0	0	0	0	.000	.000	.000	.000	-199	0	0	0	3b3/S	0	-0.1

YEAR	TM LG	G	AB	R	H	2B	3B	HR	RBI	BB	IB	HP	SO	AVG	OBP	SLG	OPS	AOPS	SB	CS	SB%	GAMES AT POSITION	DL	BFW
BATTEN, GEORGE GEORGE BURNETT B10.7.1891 HADDONFIELD NJ D8.4.1972 NEW PORT RICHEY FL BR/TR/5'11"/165 D9.28																								
1912	NY A	1	3	0	0	0	0	0	0	0	—	0	—	.000	.000	.000	.000	-194	0	—	—	/2b	—	-0.1
BAUER, HANK HENRY ALBERT B7.31.1922 E.ST.LOUIS IL D2.9.2007 LENEXA KS BR/TR/6'0"/(185–192) D9.6 M8/C1																								
1948	NY A	19	50	6	9	1	1	1	9	6	—	0	13	.180	.268	.300	.568	-49	1	0	100	O14(8/0/7)	0	-0.4
1949	†NY A	103	301	56	82	6	6	10	45	37	—	1	42	.272	.354	.432	.786	+7	2	2	50	O95(21/25/60)	0	-0.1
1950	†NY A	113	415	72	133	16	2	13	70	35	—	5	41	.320	.380	.463	.843	+18	2	3	40	O110(36/0/82)	0	0.7
1951	†NY A	118	348	53	103	19	3	10	54	42	—	1	39	.296	.373	.454	.827	+28	5	2	71	O107(51/1/62)	0	1.1
1952	†NY A★	141	553	86	162	31	6	17	74	50	—	3	61	.293	.355	.463	.818	+34	6	7	46	O139(18/0/122)	0	1.5
1953	†NY A★	133	437	77	133	20	6	10	57	59	—	6	45	.304	.394	.446	.840	+31	2	3	40	O126(3/1/124)	0	1.8
1954	NY A★	114	377	73	111	16	5	12	54	40	—	0	42	.294	.360	.459	.819	+28	4	4	50	O108(8/0/104)	0	0.7
1955	†NY A	139	492	97	137	20	5	20	53	56	1	8	65	.278	.360	.461	.821	+22	8	4	67	O133(5/0/131)/C	0	1.5
1956	†NY A	147	539	96	130	18	7	26	84	59	3	2	72	.241	.316	.445	.761	+3	4	2	67	O146(7/0/143)	0	-1.1
1957	†NY A	137	479	70	124	22	**9**	18	65	42	4	4	64	.259	.321	.455	.776	+12	7	2	78	O135(3/0/134)	0	-0.4
1958	†NY A	128	452	62	121	22	6	12	50	32	1	1	56	.268	.316	.423	.739	+6	3	2	60	O123(2/0/121)	0	-0.9
1959	NY A	114	341	44	81	20	0	9	39	33	1	2	54	.238	.307	.375	.682	-10	4	2	67	O111(4/0/108)	0	-1.6
1960	KC A	95	255	30	70	15	0	3	31	21	1	1	36	.275	.326	.369	.695	-11	1	0	100	O67R	0	-1.1
1961	KC A	43	106	11	28	3	1	3	18	9	0	0	8	.264	.319	.396	.715	-11	1	0	100	O35(11/2/27),M	0	-0.5
Total	14	1544	5145	833	1424	229	57	164	703	521	11	34	638	.277	.346	.439	.785	+14	50	33	60	O1449(177/29/1292)/C	0	1.2
Team	12	1406	4784	792	1326	211	56	158	654	491	10	33	594	.277	.347	.444	.791	+16	48	33	59	O1347(54/346/427)/C	0	2.8
/150	1	150	510	84	141	23	6	17	70	52	1	4	63	.277	.347	.444	.791	+16	5	4	56	O144(6/37/46)/C	0	0.3
BAUMANN, PADDY CHARLES JOHN B12.20.1885 INDIANAPOLIS IN D11.20.1969 INDIANAPOLIS IN BR/TR/5'9"/160 D8.10																								
1911	Det A	26	94	8	24	2	4	0	11	6	—	1	—	.255	.307	.362	.669	-18	1	—	—	2b23,O3R	—	0.1
1912	Det A	16	42	3	11	1	0	0	7	6	—	0	—	.262	.354	.286	.640	-14	4	3	57	3b6,2b5,O2(1/1/0)	—	-0.3
1913	Det A	50	191	31	57	7	4	1	22	16	—	0	18	.298	.353	.393	.746	+20	4	—	—	2b49	—	-0.1
1914	Det A	3	11	1	0	0	0	0	0	2	—	0	1	.000	.154	.000	.154	-152	0	—	—	2b3	—	-0.3
1915	NY A	76	219	30	64	13	1	2	28	28	—	3	32	.292	.380	.388	.768	+30	9	10	47	2b43,3b19/cf	—	1.0
1916	NY A	79	237	35	68	5	3	1	25	19	—	5	16	.287	.352	.346	.698	+8	10	—	—	O28(12/1/15),3b26,2b9	—	-0.4
1917	NY A	49	110	10	24	2	1	0	8	4	—	0	9	.218	.246	.255	.501	-48	2	—	—	2b18,O7(4/1/2)/3b	—	-1.5
Total	7	299	904	118	248	30	13	4	101	81	—	9	76	.274	.340	.350	.690	+3	30	13	100	2b150,3b52,O41(17/4/20)	—	-1.5
Team	3	204	566	75	156	20	5	3	61	51	—	8	57	.276	.344	.345	.689	+7	21	10	100	2b70,3b46,O36(0/4/3)	—	-0.9
/150	2	150	416	55	115	15	4	2	45	38	—	6	42	.276	.344	.345	.689	+7	15	7	100	2b51,3b34,O26(0/3/2)	—	-0.7
BAYLOR, DON DON EDWARD B6.28.1949 AUSTIN TX BR/TR/6'1"/(190–210) DR 1967 BALA 2/39 D9.18 M9/C7																								
1983	NY A	144	534	82	162	33	3	21	85	40	11	13	53	.303	.361	.494	.855	+38	17	7	71	D136,O5(2/0/4)/1b	0	2.5
1984	NY A	134	493	84	129	29	1	27	89	38	6	**23**	68	.262	.341	.489	.830	+31	1	1	50	D127,O5(1/0/4)	0	1.7
1985	NY A	142	477	70	110	24	1	23	91	52	6	**24**	90	.231	.330	.430	.760	+10	0	4	0	D140	0	0.2
Total	19	2292	8198	1236	2135	366	28	338	1276	805	91	267	1069	.260	.342	.436	.778	+18	285	120	70	D1285,O822(623/37/195),1b148	46	10.2
Team	3	420	1504	236	401	86	5	71	265	130	23	60	211	.267	.344	.472	.816	+27	18	12	60	D403,O10(3/0/8)/1	0	4.4
/150	1	150	537	84	143	31	2	25	95	46	8	21	75	.267	.344	.472	.816	+27	6	4	60	D144,O4(1/0/3)/1	0	1.6
BECK, ZINN ZINN BERTRAM B9.30.1885 STEUBENVILLE OH D3.19.1981 W.PALM BEACH FL BR/TR/5'10.5"/160 D9.14																								
1918	NY A	11	8	0	0	0	0	0	1	0	—	0	1	.000	.000	.000	.000	-198	0	—	—	1b5/3b	—	-0.2
Total	5	290	902	75	204	32	16	3	73	58	—	8	95	.226	.279	.307	.586	-24	21	10	100	3b242,S25,1b6,2b3	—	-2.3
BELL, RUDY JOHN (B RUDOLPH FRED BAERWALD) B1.1.1881 WAUSAU WI D7.28.1955 ALBUQUERQUE NM BR/TR/5'8.5"/158 D9.16																								
1907	NY A	17	52	4	11	2	1	0	3	3	—	1	—	.212	.268	.288	.556	-28	4	—	—	O17(12/0/5)	—	-0.4
BELLA, ZEKE JOHN B8.23.1930 GREENWICH CT BR/TL/5'11"/(180–185) D9.11																								
1957	NY A	5	10	0	1	0	0	0	0	1	0	0	2	.100	.182	.100	.282	-121	0	0	0	O4(1/0/3)	0	-0.1
Total	2	52	92	10	18	2	1	1	9	10	0	1	16	.196	.282	.272	.554	-48	0	0	0	O29(12/0/17)/1b	0	-0.7
BELLHORN, MARK MARK CHRISTIAN B8.23.1974 BOSTON MA BB/TR/6'1"/(190–209) DR 1995 OAKA 2/35 D6.10 COL AUBURN OF(1/3/4)																								
2005	†NY A	9	17	2	2	0	0	1	2	3	0	0	3	.118	.250	.294	.544	-56	0	0	0	3b4,2b2,S2	0	0.1
Total	10	731	2107	324	484	113	13	69	246	346	6	17	723	.230	.341	.394	.735	-10	30	13	70	2b350,3b221,1b41,S31,D11,O8R	72	-0.9
BELLINGER, CLAY CLAYTON DANIEL B11.18.1968 ONEONTA NY BR/TR/6'3"/(195–215) DR 1989 SFN 2/44 D4.9 COL ROLLINS OF(32/36/7)																								
1999	†NY A	32	45	12	9	2	0	1	2	1	0	0	10	.200	.217	.311	.528	-67	1	0	100	3b16,1b8,O2L/2bSD	0	-0.4
2000	†NY A	98	184	33	38	8	2	6	21	17	1	5	48	.207	.288	.370	.658	-33	5	0	100	O46(17/26/5),2b21,3b18,1b10,S6	0	-0.8
2001	†NY A	51	81	12	13	1	1	5	12	4	0	1	23	.160	.207	.383	.590	-49	1	2	33	O25(13/10/2),3b17,1b6,S2	0	-0.4
2002	Ana A	2	1	0	0	0	0	0	0	0	0	0	1	.000	.000	.000	.000	-199	0	0	0	1b2	0	0.0
Total	4	183	311	57	60	11	3	12	35	22	1	6	82	.193	.257	.363	.620	-42	7	2	78	O73C,3b51,1b26,2b22,S9,D4	0	-1.6
Team	3	181	310	57	60	11	3	12	35	22	1	6	81	.194	.258	.365	.623	-42	7	2	78	O73(22/6/6),3b51,1b24,2b22,S9/D	0	-1.6
/150	2	150	257	47	50	9	2	10	29	18	1	5	67	.194	.258	.365	.623	-42	6	2	75	O60(18/5/5),3b42,1b20,2b18,S7/D	0	-1.3
BENGOUGH, BENNY BERNARD OLIVER B7.27.1898 NIAGARA FALLS NY D12.22.1968 PHILADELPHIA PA BR/TR/5'7.5"/168 D5.18 C19 COL NIAGARA																								
1923	NY A	19	53	1	7	2	0	0	3	4	—	0	2	.132	.193	.170	.363	-104	0	0	0	C19	—	-0.7
1924	NY A	11	16	4	5	1	1	0	3	2	—	0	0	.313	.389	.500	.889	+28	0	0	0	C11	—	0.3
1925	NY A	95	283	17	73	14	2	0	23	19	—	0	9	.258	.305	.322	.627	-40	0	2	0	C94	—	-0.7
1926	NY A	36	84	9	32	6	0	0	14	7	—	1	4	.381	.435	.452	.887	+34	1	0	100	C35	—	1.1
1927	†NY A	31	85	6	21	3	3	0	10	4	—	0	4	.247	.281	.353	.634	-34	0	3	0	C30	—	0.3
1928	†NY A	58	161	12	43	3	1	0	9	7	—	1	8	.267	.302	.298	.600	-40	0	0	0	C58	—	-0.3
1929	NY A	23	62	5	12	2	1	0	7	0	—	0	2	.194	.194	.258	.452	-84	0	0	0	C23	—	-1.0
1930	NY A	44	102	10	24	4	2	0	12	3	—	0	8	.235	.257	.314	.571	-54	1	0	100	C44	—	-0.2
1931	StL A	40	140	6	35	4	1	0	12	4	—	0	4	.250	.271	.293	.564	-54	0	3	0	C37	—	-0.8
1932	StL A	54	139	13	35	7	1	0	15	12	—	0	4	.252	.311	.317	.628	-40	0	1	0	C47	—	-0.1
Total	10	411	1125	83	287	46	12	0	108	62	—	2	45	.255	.295	.317	.612	-41	2	9	18	C398	—	-2.1
Team	8	317	846	64	217	35	10	0	81	46	—	2	37	.257	.296	.322	.618	-39	2	5	29	C314	—	-1.2
/150	4	150	400	30	103	17	5	0	38	22	—	1	18	.257	.296	.322	.618	-39	1	2	33	C149	—	-0.6
BENIQUEZ, JUAN JUAN JOSE (TORRES) B5.13.1950 SAN SEBASTIAN, PR BR/TR/5'11"/(148–175) D9.4 OF(295/735/184)																								
1979	NY A	62	142	19	36	6	1	4	17	9	0	2	17	.254	.299	.394	.693	-11	3	3	50	O60(18/38/4),3b3	60	-0.3
Total	17	1500	4651	610	1274	190	30	79	476	349	11	31	551	.274	.327	.379	.706	-5	104	76	58	O1155C,D111,1b68,3b49,S43/2b	270	-10.5
BERBERET, LOU LOUIS JOSEPH B11.20.1929 LONG BEACH CA D4.6.2004 LAS VEGAS NV BL/TR/5'11"/(200–212) D9.17 COL SANTA CLARA																								
1954	NY A	5	5	1	2	0	0	0	3	1	—	0	1	.400	.500	.400	.900	+54	0	0	0	C3	0	0.1
1955	NY A	2	5	1	2	0	0	0	2	1	0	0	0	.400	.500	.400	.900	+47	0	0	0	/C	0	0.1
Total	7	448	1224	118	281	34	10	31	153	200	20	7	195	.230	.337	.350	.687	-14	2	3	40	C367	0	-1.4
Team	2	7	10	2	4	0	0	0	5	2	0	0	1	.400	.500	.400	.900	+51	0	0	0	C4	0	0.2
BERGMAN, DAVE DAVID BRUCE B6.6.1953 EVANSTON IL BL/TL/6'1.5"/(180–195) DR 1974 NYA 2/36 D8.26 COL ILLINOIS ST.																								
1975	NY A	7	17	0	0	0	0	0	0	2	0	0	4	.000	.105	.000	.105	-169	0	0	0	O6R	0	-0.4
1977	NY A	5	4	1	1	0	0	0	1	0	0	0	0	.250	.200	.250	.450	-63	0	0	0	O3(1/1/1),1b2	0	0.0
Total	17	1349	2679	312	690	100	16	54	289	380	36	7	347	.258	.348	.367	.715	+2	19	14	58	1b866,D133,O106(88/1/18)	52	-2.2
Team	2	12	21	1	1	0	0	0	1	2	0	0	4	.048	.125	.048	.173	-151	0	0	0	O9(1/1/7),1b2	0	-0.4

Batters

YEAR	TM LG	G	AB	R	H	2B	3B	HR	RBI	BB	IB	HP	SO	AVG	OBP	SLG	OPS	AOPS	SB	CS	SB%	GAMES AT POSITION	DL	BFW
Bernhardt, Juan — Juan Ramon (Coradin) B8.31.1953 San Pedro de Macoris, D.R. BR/TR/5'11"/175 d7.10																								
1976	NY A	10	21	1	4	1	0	0	1	0	0	0	4	.190	.190	.238	.428	-75	0	0	0	O4(1/0/3)/3bD	0	-0.3
Total	4	154	492	46	117	19	2	9	43	14	1	3	40	.238	.261	.339	.600	-35	3	4	43	D58,3b44,1b33,O4(1/0/3)	15	-3.1
Berra, Dale — Dale Anthony B12.13.1956 Ridgewood NJ BR/TR/6'0"/(180–190) Dr 1975 PitN 1/20 d8.22 f–Yogi																								
1985	NY A	48	109	8	25	5	1	1	8	7	0	0	20	.229	.276	.321	.597	-36	1	1	50	3b41,S6	0	-0.4
1986	NY A	42	108	10	25	7	0	2	13	9	0	1	14	.231	.294	.352	.646	-24	0	0	0	S19,3b18,D4	0	-0.2
Total	11	853	2553	236	603	109	9	49	278	210	57	12	422	.236	.294	.344	.638	-24	32	17	65	S591,3b247,2b25,D4	15	-4.3
Team	2	90	217	18	50	12	1	3	21	16	0	1	34	.230	.285	.336	.621	-30	1	1	50	3b59,S25,D4	0	-0.6
Berra, Yogi — Lawrence Peter B5.12.1925 St.Louis MO BL/TR/5'8"/(183–194) d9.22 M7/C20 HF1972 s–Dale																								
1946	NY A	7	22	3	8	1	0	2	4	1	—	0	1	.364	.391	.682	1.073	+93	0	0	0	C6	0	0.4
1947	†NY A	83	293	41	82	15	3	11	54	13	—	0	12	.280	.310	.464	.774	+15	0	1	0	C51,O24(12/0/12)	0	0.0
1948	NY A☆	125	469	70	143	24	10	14	98	25	—	1	24	.305	.341	.488	.829	+20	3	3	50	C71,O50R	0	0.8
1949	†NY A★	116	415	59	115	20	2	20	91	22	—	6	25	.277	.323	.480	.803	+11	2	1	67	C109	0	1.7
1950	†NY A★	151	597	116	192	30	6	28	124	55	—	4	12	.322	.383	.533	.916	+36	4	2	67	C148	0	3.8
1951	†NY A★	141	547	92	161	19	4	27	88	44	—	3	20	.294	.350	.492	.842	+31	5	4	56	C141	0	3.5
1952	†NY A★	142	534	97	146	17	1	30	98	66	—	4	24	.273	.358	.478	.836	+39	2	3	40	C140	0	3.5
1953	†NY A★	137	503	80	149	23	5	27	108	50	—	3	32	.296	.363	.523	.886	+42	0	3	0	C133	0	3.8
1954	NY A★	151	584	88	179	28	6	22	125	56	—	4	29	.307	.367	.488	.855	+39	0	1	0	C149/3b	0	4.4
1955	†NY A★	147	541	84	147	20	3	27	108	60	6	7	20	.272	.349	.470	.819	+21	1	0	100	C145	0	2.5
1956	†NY A★	140	521	93	155	29	2	30	105	65	7	5	29	.298	.378	.534	.912	+44	3	2	60	C135/lf	0	4.3
1957	†NY A★	134	482	74	121	14	2	24	82	57	10	1	24	.251	.329	.438	.767	+10	1	2	33	C121,O6(5/0/1)	0	2.3
1958	†NY A★	122	433	60	115	17	3	22	90	35	5	2	35	.266	.319	.471	.790	+20	3	0	100	C88,O21R,1b2	0	2.5
1959	NY A★	131	472	64	134	25	1	19	69	43	5	4	38	.284	.347	.462	.809	+25	1	2	33	C116,O7(1/0/6)	0	3.3
1960	†NY A★	120	359	46	99	14	1	15	62	38	6	3	23	.276	.347	.446	.793	+20	2	1	67	C63,O36(20/0/17)	0	0.8
1961	†NY A★	119	395	62	107	11	0	22	61	35	4	2	28	.271	.330	.466	.796	+17	2	0	100	O87(81/0/8),C15	0	0.8
1962	†NY A★	86	232	25	52	8	0	10	35	24	4	2	18	.224	.297	.388	.685	-13	0	1	0	C31,O28L	0	0.0
1963	†NY A	64	147	20	43	6	0	8	28	15	2	1	17	.293	.360	.497	.857	+39	1	0	100	C35	0	1.8
1965	NY N	4	9	1	2	0	0	0	0	0	0	0	3	.222	.222	.222	.444	-73	0	0	0	C2	0	0.0
Total	19	2120	7555	1175	2150	321	49	358	1430	704	49	52	414	.285	.348	.482	.830	+26	30	26	54	C1699,O260(148/0/115),1b2/3b	0	40.2
Team	18	2116	7546	1174	2148	321	49	358	1430	704	49	52	411	.285	.348	.483	.831	+27	30	26	54	C1697,O260(46/0/13),1b2/3	0	40.2
/150	1	150	535	83	152	23	3	25	101	50	3	4	29	.285	.348	.483	.831	+27	2	2	50	C120,O18(3/0/1)/13	0	2.8
Betemit, Wilson — Wilson B11.2.1981 Santo Domingo, D.R. BB/TR/6'2"/(155–230) d9.18																								
2007	NY A	37	84	11	19	4	0	4	24	6	0	0	33	.226	.278	.417	.695	-21	0	0	0	1b14,3b14,S8,2b2/lf	0	-0.5
Total	5	409	909	121	236	47	4	36	126	102	10	1	258	.260	.332	.439	.771	-3	5	5	50	3b216,S65,1b14,2b14,O2(1/0/1)/D	0	-2.1
Beville, Monte — Henry Monte B2.24.1875 Dublin IN D1.24.1955 Grand Rapids MI BL/TR/5'11"/180 d4.24																								
1903	NY A	82	258	23	50	14	1	0	29	16	—	4	—	.194	.252	.256	.508	-51	4	—	—	C75,1b3	—	-1.6
1904	NY A	9	22	2	6	2	0	0	2	2	—	0	—	.273	.333	.364	.697	+15	0	—	—	1b4,C3	—	-0.1
1904	Det A	54	174	14	36	5	1	0	13	8	—	2	—	.207	.250	.247	.497	-41	2	—	—	C30,1b24	—	-1.1
1904	Year	63	196	16	42	7	1	0	15	10	—	2	—	.214	.260	.260	.520	-34	2	—	—	C33,1b28	—	-1.2
Total	2	145	454	39	92	21	2	0	44	26	—	6	—	.203	.255	.258	.513	-44	6	—	—	C108,1b31	—	-2.8
Team	2	91	280	25	56	16	1	0	31	18	—	4	0	.200	.258	.264	.522	-46	4	—	—	C78,1b7	—	-1.7
Bladt, Rick — Richard Alan B12.9.1946 Santa Cruz CA BR/TR/6'1"/160 d6.15 Col Foothill (CA) JC																								
1969	Chi N	10	13	1	2	0	0	0	1	0	0	0	5	.154	.154	.154	.308	-112	0	0	0	O7(2/5/1)	0	-0.1
1975	NY A	52	117	13	26	3	1	1	11	11	0	1	8	.222	.292	.291	.583	-34	6	2	75	O51C	0	-0.4
Total	2	62	130	14	28	3	1	1	12	11	0	1	13	.215	.280	.277	.557	-42	6	2	75	O58(2/56/1)	0	-0.5
Blair, Paul — Paul L D B2.1.1944 Cushing OK BR/TR (BB 1971p)/6'0"/(168–177) d9.9 OF(31/1801/58)																								
1977	†NY A	83	164	20	43	4	3	4	25	9	1	2	16	.262	.303	.396	.699	-9	3	2	60	O79(6/42/33)/D	0	-0.5
1978	†NY A	75	125	10	22	5	0	2	13	9	0	0	17	.176	.231	.264	.495	-60	1	1	50	O64(1/49/16),2b5,S4,3b3	0	-1.4
1979	NY A	2	5	0	1	0	0	0	0	0	0	0	1	.200	.200	.200	.400	-92	0	0	0	O2(0/1/1)	0	0.0
1980	NY A	12	2	2	0	0	0	0	0	0	0	0	0	.000	.000	.000	.000	-199	0	0	0	O12(6/1/6)	0	0.0
Total	17	1947	6042	776	1513	282	55	134	620	449	23	23	877	.250	.302	.382	.684	-4	171	93	65	O1878C,2b5,3b5,S4,D4/1b	21	-5.6
Team	4	172	296	32	66	9	3	6	38	18	1	2	34	.223	.270	.334	.604	-33	4	3	57	O157(8/98/56),2b5,S4,3b3/D	0	-1.9
/150	3	150	258	28	58	8	3	5	33	16	1	2	30	.223	.270	.334	.604	-33	3	3	50	O137(7/85/49),2b4,S3,3b3/D	0	-1.7
Blair, Walter — Walter Allen "Heavy" B10.13.1883 Landrus PA D8.20.1948 Lewisburg PA BR/TR/6'0"/185 d9.17 M1 Col Bucknell																								
1907	NY A	7	22	1	4	0	0	0	1	2	—	0	—	.182	.250	.182	.432	-65	0	—	—	C7	—	0.0
1908	NY A	76	211	9	40	5	1	1	13	11	—	2	—	.190	.237	.237	.474	-47	4	—	—	C60,O9(2/0/7),1b3	—	-2.1
1909	NY A	42	110	5	23	2	2	0	11	7	—	2	—	.209	.269	.264	.533	-32	2	—	—	C42	—	-0.7
1910	NY A	6	22	2	5	0	1	0	2	0	—	0	—	.227	.227	.318	.545	-33	0	—	—	C6	—	-0.2
1911	NY A	85	222	18	43	9	2	0	26	16	—	3	—	.194	.257	.252	.509	-60	2	—	—	C84/1b	—	-1.0
1914	Buf F	128	378	22	92	11	2	0	33	32	—	1	64	.243	.304	.283	.587	-41	6	—	—	C128	—	-0.6
1915	Buf F	98	290	23	65	15	3	2	20	18	—	2	32	.224	.274	.317	.591	-35	4	—	—	C97,M	—	-1.4
Total	7	442	1255	80	272	42	11	3	106	86	—	10	96	.217	.272	.275	.547	-44	18	—	—	C424,O9(2/0/7),1b4	—	-6.0
Team	5	216	587	35	115	16	6	1	53	36	—	7	0	.196	.251	.249	.500	-49	8	—	—	C199,O9(2/0/7),1b4	—	-4.0
/150	3	150	408	24	80	11	4	1	37	25	—	5	0	.196	.251	.249	.500	-49	6	—	—	C138,O6(1/0/5),1b3	—	-2.8
Blanchard, Johnny — John Edwin B2.26.1933 Minneapolis MN BL/TR/6'1"/(195–204) d9.25																								
1955	NY A	1	3	0	0	0	0	0	0	1	0	0	0	.000	.250	.000	.250	-129	0	0	0	/C	0	0.0
1959	NY A	49	59	6	10	1	0	2	4	7	0	0	12	.169	.258	.288	.546	-49	0	0	0	C12,O8(1/0/7)/1b	0	-0.6
1960	†NY A	53	99	8	24	3	1	4	14	6	1	1	17	.242	.292	.414	.706	-6	0	0	0	C28	32	0.5
1961	†NY A	93	243	38	74	10	1	21	54	27	9	4	28	.305	.382	.613	.995	+70	1	0	100	C48,O15(8/0/7)	0	2.4
1962	†NY A	93	246	33	57	7	0	13	39	28	0	1	32	.232	.309	.419	.728	-2	0	0	0	O47(15/0/32),C15,1b2	0	-1.1
1963	†NY A	76	218	22	49	4	0	16	45	26	3	0	30	.225	.305	.463	.768	+14	0	0	0	O64(22/0/42)	0	-0.7
1964	†NY A	77	161	18	41	8	0	7	28	24	4	0	24	.255	.344	.435	.779	+15	1	0	100	C25,O14(6/0/8),1b3	0	-0.1
1965	NY A	12	34	1	5	1	0	1	3	7	2	0	3	.147	.286	.265	.551	-40	0	0	0	C12	0	-0.2
1965	KC A	52	120	10	24	2	0	2	11	8	1	1	16	.200	.250	.267	.517	-51	0	0	0	O20(1/0/19),C14	0	-1.4
1965	Year	64	154	11	29	3	0	3	14	15	3	1	19	.188	.259	.266	.525	-48	0	0	0	C26,O20(1/0/19)	0	-1.6
1965	Mil N	10	10	1	1	0	0	1	2	2	0	0	1	.100	.250	.400	.650	-21	0	0	0	/lf	0	-0.1
1965	Major	74	164	12	30	3	0	4	16	17	3	1	20	.183	4.264	.274	4.538	-48	0	0	0	—	0	-1.7
Total	8	516	1193	137	285	36	2	67	200	136	20	7	163	.239	.317	.441	.758	+9	2	0	100	O169(54/0/115),C155,1b6	32	-1.3
Team	8	454	1063	126	260	34	2	64	187	126	19	6	146	.245	.325	.461	.786	+16	2	0	100	O148(24/8/22),C140,1b6	32	0.2
/150	3	150	351	42	86	11	1	21	62	42	6	2	48	.245	.325	.461	.786	+16	1	0	100	O49(8/3/7),C46,1b2	11	0.1
Blefary, Curt — Curtis Le Roy B7.5.1943 Brooklyn NY D1.28.2001 Pompano Beach FL BL/TR/6'2"/(195–210) d4.14 Col Wagner OF(323/0/232)																								
1970	NY A	99	269	34	57	6	0	9	37	43	3	3	37	.212	.324	.335	.659	-13	1	3	25	O79R,1b6	0	-1.9
1971	NY A	21	36	4	7	1	0	1	2	3	0	0	5	.194	.256	.306	.562	-39	0	0	0	O6R,1b4	0	-0.3
Total	8	974	2947	394	699	104	20	112	382	456	47	29	444	.237	.342	.400	.742	+15	24	24	50	O544L,1b253,C66,3b8,2b3	0	1.4
Team	2	120	305	38	64	7	0	10	39	46	3	3	42	.210	.317	.331	.648	-16	1	3	25	O85R,1b10	0	-2.2
/150	3	150	381	48	80	9	0	13	49	58	4	4	53	.210	.317	.331	.648	-16	1	4	20	O106R,1b13	0	-2.8
Blomberg, Ron — Ronald Mark "Boomer" B8.23.1948 Atlanta GA BL/TR/6'1"/(185–205) Dr 1967 NYA 1/1 d9.10 [DL 1977 NY A 180]																								
1969	NY A	4	6	0	3	0	0	0	0	1	0	0	0	.500	.571	.500	1.071	+109	0	0	0	O2L	0	0.1
1971	NY A	64	199	30	64	6	2	7	31	14	3	0	23	.322	.363	.477	.840	+44	2	4	33	O57R	0	0.3

Batters

YEAR	TM LG	G	AB	R	H	2B	3B	HR	RBI	BB	IB	HP	SO	AVG	OBP	SLG	OPS	AOPS	SB	CS	SB%	GAMES AT POSITION	DL	BFW
1972	NY A	107	299	36	80	22	1	14	49	38	4	3	26	.268	.355	.488	.843	+53	0	2	0	1b95	0	0.6
1973	NY A	100	301	45	99	13	1	12	57	34	4	0	25	.329	.395	.498	.893	+54	2	0	100	D55,1b41	0	1.9
1974	NY A	90	264	39	82	11	2	10	48	29	2	2	33	.311	.375	.481	.856	+49	2	1	67	D58,O19(2/0/17)	0	1.6
1975	NY A	34	106	18	27	8	2	4	17	13	1	0	10	.255	.336	.481	.817	+30	0	0	0	D27/rf	106	0.3
1976	NY A	1	2	0	0	0	0	0	0	0	0	0	0	.000	.000	.000	.000	-199	0	0	0	/D	148	-0.1
1978	Chi A	61	156	16	36	7	0	5	22	11	2	0	17	.231	.280	.372	.652	-19	0	0	0	D36,1b7	0	-0.7
Total	8	461	1333	184	391	67	8	52	224	140	16	5	134	.293	.360	.473	.833	+40	6	7	46	D177,1b143,O79(4/0/75)	434	4.0
Team	7	400	1177	168	355	60	8	47	202	129	14	5	117	.302	.370	.486	.856	+49	6	7	46	D141,1b136,O79L	434	4.7
/150	3	150	441	63	133	23	3	18	76	48	5	2	44	.302	.370	.486	[illegible]	[illegible]	[illegible]	[illegible]	[illegible]	D53,1b51,Olf	163	1.8
BLOWERS, MIKE MICHAEL ROY B4.24.1965 WURZBURG, WEST GERMANY BR/TR/6'2"/(190–210) DR 1986 MONN 10/252 D9.1 COL WASHINGTON																								
1989	NY A	13	38	2	10	0	0	0	3	3	0	0	13	.263	.317	.263	.580	-34	0	0	0	3b13	0	-0.5
1990	NY A	48	144	16	27	4	0	5	21	12	1	1	50	.188	.255	.319	.574	-41	1	0	100	3b45,D2	0	-2.0
1991	NY A	15	35	3	7	0	0	1	1	4	0	0	3	.200	.282	.286	.568	-43	0	0	0	3b14	0	-0.5
Total	11	761	2300	290	591	116	8	78	365	248	10	6	610	.257	.329	.416	.745	-4	7	8	47	3b616,1b108,O22(16/0/6),D18/SC	74	-6.5
Team	3	76	217	21	44	4	0	6	25	19	1	1	66	.203	.270	.304	.574	-40	1	0	100	3b72,D2	0	-3.0
BOCKMAN, EDDIE JOSEPH EDWARD B7.26.1920 SANTA ANA CA BR/TR/5'9"/175 D9.11																								
1946	NY A	4	12	2	1	1	0	0	0	1	—	0	4	.083	.154	.167	.321	-110	0	0	0	3b4	0	-0.1
Total	4	199	474	54	109	16	4	11	56	46	—	1	87	.230	.299	.350	.649	-26	5	0	100	3b135,2b10/lfS	0	0.0
BODIE, PING FRANK STEPHAN (B FRANCESCO STEPHANO PEZZOLO) B10.8.1887 SAN FRANCISCO CA D12.17.1961 SAN FRANCISCO CA BR/TR/5'8"/195 D4.22																								
1911	Chi A	145	551	75	159	27	13	4	97	49	—	1	—	.289	.348	.407	.755	+14	14	—	—	O128(0/107/21),2b16	—	-0.2
1912	Chi A	138	472	58	139	24	7	5	72	43	—	4	—	.294	.358	.407	.765	+23	12	13	48	O130(8/72/50)	—	-0.6
1913	Chi A	127	406	39	107	14	8	8	48	35	—	2	57	.264	.325	.397	.722	+12	5	—	—	O119(43/76/0)	—	-0.8
1914	Chi A	107	327	21	75	9	5	3	29	21	—	1	35	.229	.278	.315	.593	-21	12	11	52	O95(2/92/1)	—	-2.2
1917	Phi A	148	557	51	162	28	11	7	74	53	—	3	40	.291	.356	.418	.774	+38	13	—	—	O145L/1b	—	2.8
1918	NY A	91	324	36	83	12	6	3	46	27	—	3	24	.256	.319	.358	.677	+2	6	—	—	O90L	—	-0.1
1919	NY A	134	475	45	132	27	8	6	59	36	—	4	46	.278	.334	.406	.740	+7	15	—	—	O134(0/129/5)	—	-1.8
1920	NY A	129	471	63	139	26	12	7	79	40	—	0	30	.295	.350	.446	.796	+6	6	14	30	O129C	—	-2.1
1921	NY A	31	87	5	15	2	2	0	12	8	—	0	8	.172	.242	.241	.483	-77	0	1	0	O25(5/20/0)	—	-1.4
Total	9	1050	3670	393	1011	169	72	43	516	312	—	18	240	.275	.335	.396	.731	+10	83	39	100	O995(293/625/77),2b16/1b	—	-6.4
Team	4	385	1357	149	369	67	28	16	196	111	—	7	108	.272	.330	.398	.728	+0	27	15	100	O378(110/12/12)	—	-5.4
/150	2	150	529	58	144	26	11	6	76	43	—	3	42	.272	.330	.398	.728	+0	11	6	100	O147(43/5/5)	—	-2.1
BOEHMER, LEN LEONARD JOSEPH STEPHEN B6.28.1941 FLINT HILL MO BR/TR/6'1"/192 D6.18 COL ST. LOUIS																								
1967	Cin N	2	3	0	0	0	0	0	0	0	0	0	0	.000	.000	.000	.000	-190	0	0	0	/2b	0	-0.1
1969	NY A	45	108	5	19	4	0	0	7	8	2	0	10	.176	.233	.213	.446	-74	0	1	0	1b21,3b8/2bS	0	-1.2
1971	NY A	3	5	0	0	0	0	0	0	0	0	0	0	.000	.000	.000	.000	-199	0	0	0	/3b	0	-0.2
Total	3	50	116	5	19	4	0	0	7	8	2	0	10	.164	.218	.198	.416	-82	0	1	0	1b21,3b9,2b2/S	0	-1.5
Team	2	48	113	5	19	4	0	0	7	8	2	0	10	.168	.223	.204	.427	-79	0	1	0	1b21,3b9/2S	0	-1.4
BOGGS, WADE WADE ANTHONY B6.15.1958 OMAHA NE BL/TR/6'2"/(185–197) DR 1976 BOSA 7/166 D4.10 C1 HF2005																								
1993	NY A★	143	560	83	169	26	1	2	59	74	4	0	49	.302	.378	.363	.741	+4	0	1	0	3b134,D8	0	2.8
1994	NY A★	97	366	61	125	19	1	11	55	61	3	1	29	.342	.433	.489	.922	+43	2	1	67	3b93,1b4	0	3.3
1995	†NY A★	126	460	76	149	22	4	5	63	74	5	0	50	.324	.412	.422	.834	+20	1	1	50	3b117,1b9	0	1.5
1996	†NY A★	132	501	80	156	29	2	2	41	67	7	0	32	.311	.389	.389	.778	-1	1	2	33	3b123,D4	0	-0.1
1997	†NY A	104	353	55	103	23	1	4	28	48	3	0	38	.292	.373	.397	.770	+3	0	1	0	3b76,D19/P	0	0.4
Total	18	2440	9180	1513	3010	578	61	118	1014	1412	18	23	745	.328	.415	.443	.858	+29	24	35	41	3b2215,D107,1b67,P2/lf	67	50.5
Team	5	602	2240	355	702	119	9	24	246	324	22	1	198	.313	.396	.407	.803	+13	4	6	40	3b543,D31,1b13/P	0	7.9
/150	1	150	558	88	175	30	2	6	61	81	5	0	49	.313	.396	.407	.803	+13	1	1	50	3b135,D8,1b3/P	0	2.0
BOLLWEG, DON DONALD RAYMOND B2.12.1921 WHEATON IL D5.26.1996 WHEATON IL BL/TL/6'1"/190 D9.28																								
1950	StL N	4	11	1	2	0	0	0	1	1	—	0	1	.182	.250	.182	.432	-85	0	—	—	1b4	0	-0.2
1951	StL N	6	9	1	1	1	0	0	2	0	—	0	1	.111	.111	.222	.333	-113	0	0	0	1b2	0	-0.2
1953	†NY A	70	155	24	46	6	4	6	24	21	—	1	31	.297	.384	.503	.887	+43	1	0	100	1b43	0	0.4
1954	Phi A	103	268	35	60	15	3	5	24	35	—	3	33	.224	.319	.358	.677	-15	1	0	100	1b71	0	-0.7
1955	KC A	12	9	1	1	0	0	0	2	3	2	0	2	.111	.333	.111	.444	-77	0	0	0	1b3	0	-0.1
Total	5	195	452	62	110	22	7	11	53	60	2	4	68	.243	.337	.396	.733	+0	2	0	100	1b123	0	-0.8
BONDS, BOBBY BOBBY LEE B3.15.1946 RIVERSIDE CA D8.23.2003 SAN CARLOS CA BR/TR/6'1"/(188–198) D6.25 C8 S–BARRY COL RIVERSIDE (CA) CC																								
1975	NY A★	145	529	93	143	26	3	32	85	89	8	3	137	.270	.375	.512	.887	+51	30	17	64	O129(1/44/90),D12	0	3.8
Total	14	1849	7043	1258	1886	302	66	332	1024	914	75	53	1757	.268	.353	.471	.824	+29	461	169	73	O1736(65/285/1472),D81	154	27.2
/150	1	150	547	96	148	27	3	33	88	92	8	3	142	.270	.375	.512	.887	+51	31	18	63	O133(1/46/93),D12	0	3.9
BONILLA, JUAN JUAN GUILLERMO B2.12.1955 SANTURCE, PR BR/TR/5'9"/170 D4.9 COL FLORIDA ST.																								
1985	NY A	8	16	0	2	1	0	0	2	0	0	0	3	.125	.125	.188	.313	-116	0	0	0	2b7	0	-0.2
1987	NY A	23	55	6	14	3	0	1	3	5	0	0	6	.255	.317	.364	.681	-20	0	0	0	2b22/3bD	0	-0.3
Total	6	429	1462	145	375	50	9	7	101	116	16	9	108	.256	.314	.317	.631	-21	7	10	41	2b390,3b34,D3	124	-5.0
Team	2	31	71	6	16	4	0	1	5	5	0	0	9	.225	.276	.324	.600	-40	0	0	0	2b29/3D	0	-0.5
BOONE, AARON AARON JOHN B3.9.1973 LAMESA CA BR/TR/6'2"/(190–200) DR 1994 CINN 3/72 D6.20 B–BRET F–BOB GF–RAY COL USC [DL 2004 CLE A 100]																								
2003	†NY A	54	189	31	48	13	0	6	31	11	0	3	30	.254	.302	.418	.720	-11	8	0	100	3b54	0	0.3
Total	10	1038	3626	496	961	203	16	120	527	285	19	77	653	.265	.329	.429	.758	-5	107	29	79	3b934,1b48,S30,2b22,D2	342	1.4
BOONE, LUTE LUTE JOSEPH "DANNY" B5.6.1890 PITTSBURGH PA D7.29.1982 PITTSBURGH PA BR/TR/5'9"/160 D9.9																								
1913	NY A	6	12	3	4	0	0	0	1	3	—	0	1	.333	.467	.333	.800	+34	0	—	—	S4	—	0.0
1914	NY A	106	370	34	82	8	2	0	21	31	—	2	41	.222	.285	.254	.539	-37	10	18	36	2b90,3b9/rf	—	-0.2
1915	NY A	130	431	44	88	12	2	5	43	41	—	8	53	.204	.285	.276	.561	-32	14	17	45	2b115,S11,3b4	—	0.3
1916	NY A	46	124	14	23	4	0	1	8	8	—	3	10	.185	.252	.242	.494	-53	7	—	—	3b25,S12,2b8	—	-0.4
1918	Pit N	27	91	7	18	3	0	0	3	8	—	0	6	.198	.263	.231	.494	-51	1	—	—	S26/2b	—	-0.8
Total	5	315	1028	102	215	27	4	6	76	91	—	13	111	.209	.282	.261	.543	-37	32	35	100	2b214,S53,3b38/rf	—	-1.1
Team	4	288	937	95	197	24	4	6	73	83	—	13	105	.210	.283	.264	.547	-36	31	35	100	2b213,3b38,S27/rf	—	-0.3
/150	2	150	488	49	103	13	2	3	38	43	—	7	55	.210	.283	.264	.547	-36	16	18	100	2b111,3b20,S14/rf	—	-0.2
BORDAGARAY, FRENCHY STANLEY GEORGE B1.3.1910 COALINGA CA D4.13.2000 VENTURA CA BR/TR/5'7.5"/175 D4.17 COL CAL ST.–FRESNO																								
1941	†NY A	36	73	10	19	1	0	0	4	6	—	1	8	.260	.325	.274	.599	-39	1	0	100	O19(6/0/13)	0	-0.5
Total	11	930	2632	410	745	120	28	14	270	173	—	16	186	.283	.331	.366	.697	-9	66	2	100	O450(111/170/171),3b240,2b13	0	-7.9
BORTON, BABE WILLIAM BAKER B8.14.1888 MARION IL D7.29.1954 BERKELEY CA BL/TL/6'0"/178 D9.2																								
1913	NY A	33	108	8	14	2	0	0	11	18	—	1	19	.130	.260	.148	.408	-80	1	—	—	1b33	—	-0.8
Total	4	317	940	139	254	31	17	4	136	160	—	9	101	.270	.381	.352	.733	+8	21	7	100	1b270	—	-0.9
BOSTON, DARYL DARYL LAMONT B1.4.1963 CINCINNATI OH BL/TL/6'3"/(185–210) DR 1981 CHIA 1/7 D5.13																								
1994	NY A	52	77	11	14	2	0	4	14	6	0	1	20	.182	.250	.364	.614	-42	0	1	0	O16(7/7/2),D9	0	-0.6
Total	11	1058	2629	378	655	131	22	83	278	237	23	8	469	.249	.312	.410	.722	-6	98	50	66	O847(276/499/94),D35	0	-4.0

Boyer, Clete Cletis Leroy B2.9.1937 Cassville MO D6.4.2007 Atlanta GA BR/TR/6'0"/(165–188) d6.5 C10 b-Cloyd b-Ken

YEAR	TM LG	G	AB	R	H	2B	3B	HR	RBI	BB	IB	HP	SO	AVG	OBP	SLG	OPS	AOPS	SB	CS	SB%	GAMES AT POSITION	DL	BFW
1955	KC A	47	79	3	19	1	0	0	6	3	0	0	17	.241	.268	.253	.521	-60	0	0	0	S12,3b11,2b10	0	-0.4
1956	KC A	67	129	15	28	3	1	1	4	11	1	1	24	.217	.284	.279	.563	-51	1	1	50	2b51,3b7	0	0.3
1957	KC A	10	0	0	0	0	0	0	0	0	0	0	0	+	+	+	.000	-100	0	0	0	/2b3b	0	0.0
1959	NY A	47	114	4	20	2	0	0	3	6	2	0	23	.175	.215	.193	.408	86	1	0	100	S26,3b16	0	-1.0
1960	†NY A	124	393	54	95	20	1	14	46	23	1	3	85	.242	.285	.405	.690	-10	2	3	40	3b99,S33	0	1.8
1961	†NY A	148	504	61	113	19	5	11	55	63	4	2	83	.224	.308	.347	.655	-20	1	3	25	3b141,S12/rf	0	1.3
1962	†NY A	158	566	85	154	24	1	18	68	51	8	3	106	.272	.331	.413	.744	+4	3	2	60	3b157	0	3.6
1963	†NY A	152	557	59	140	20	3	12	54	33	11	2	91	.251	.295	.363	.658	-16	4	2	67	3b141,S9/2b	0	1.0
1964	†NY A	147	510	43	111	10	5	8	52	36	11	1	93	.218	.269	.304	.573	-41	6	1	86	3b123,S21	0	-2.0
1965	NY A	148	514	69	129	23	6	18	58	39	10	2	79	.251	.304	.424	.728	+6	4	1	80	3b147,S2	0	2.5
1966	NY A	144	500	59	120	22	4	14	57	46	4	2	48	.240	.303	.384	.687	+1	6	0	100	3b85,S59	0	2.8
1967	Atl N	154	572	63	140	18	3	26	96	39	3	2	81	.245	.292	.423	.715	+5	6	3	67	3b150,S6	0	0.8
1968	Atl N	71	273	19	62	7	2	4	17	16	3	2	32	.227	.275	.311	.586	-25	2	0	100	3b69	25	-0.6
1969	†Atl N	144	496	57	124	16	1	14	57	55	6	4	87	.250	.328	.371	.699	-5	3	7	30	3b141	0	0.1
1970	Atl N	134	475	44	117	14	1	16	62	41	8	1	71	.246	.305	.381	.686	-21	2	5	29	3b126,S5	0	-0.6
1971	Atl N	30	98	10	24	1	0	6	19	8	2	0	11	.245	.299	.439	.738	+1	0	0	0	3b25/S	0	0.1
Total	16	1725	5780	645	1396	200	33	162	654	470	74	25	931	.242	.299	.372	.671	-13	41	28	59	3b1439,S186,2b63/rf	25	9.7
Team	8	1068	3658	434	882	140	25	95	393	297	51	15	608	.241	.298	.371	.669	-13	27	12	69	3b909,S162/2rf	0	10.0
/150	1	150	514	61	124	20	4	13	55	42	7	2	85	.241	.298	.371	.669	-13	4	2	67	3b128,S23/2OfL	0	1.4

Bradley, Scott Scott William B3.22.1960 Glen Ridge NJ BL/TR/5'11"/(175–185) Dr 1981 NYA 3/64 d9.9 Col North Carolina

YEAR	TM LG	G	AB	R	H	2B	3B	HR	RBI	BB	IB	HP	SO	AVG	OBP	SLG	OPS	AOPS	SB	CS	SB%	GAMES AT POSITION	DL	BFW
1984	NY A	9	21	3	6	1	0	0	2	1	0	0	1	.286	.318	.333	.651	-17	0	0	0	O5L,C3	0	-0.1
1985	NY A	19	49	4	8	2	1	0	1	1	0	1	5	.163	.196	.245	.441	-80	0	0	0	C3,D9	54	-0.7
Total	9	604	1648	149	424	75	6	18	184	104	14	11	110	.257	.302	.343	.645	-24	3	6	33	C433,D42,3b20,O13(7/0/6),1b6	54	-4.6
Team	2	28	70	7	14	3	1	0	3	2	0	1	6	.200	.233	.271	.504	-61	0	0	0	D9,C6,O5L	54	-0.8

Bragg, Darren Darren William B9.7.1969 Waterbury CT BL/TR/5'9"/180 Dr 1991 SeaA 22/578 d4.12 Col Georgia Tech

YEAR	TM LG	G	AB	R	H	2B	3B	HR	RBI	BB	IB	HP	SO	AVG	OBP	SLG	OPS	AOPS	SB	CS	SB%	GAMES AT POSITION	DL	BFW
2001	NY A	5	4	1	1	1	0	0	0	0	0	0	1	.250	.250	.500	.750	-10	0	0	0	O3R	0	0.0
Total	11	916	2461	341	627	145	14	46	260	304	17	25	570	.255	.340	.381	.721	-16	56	24	70	O762(205/280/352),D12/3b	62	-5.2

Brant, Marshall Marshall Lee B9.17.1955 Garberville CA BR/TR/6'5"/185 Dr 1975 NYN*4/73 d10.1 Col Sonoma St.

YEAR	TM LG	G	AB	R	H	2B	3B	HR	RBI	BB	IB	HP	SO	AVG	OBP	SLG	OPS	AOPS	SB	CS	SB%	GAMES AT POSITION	DL	BFW
1980	NY A	3	6	0	0	0	0	0	0	0	0	0	3	.000	.000	.000	.000	-199	0	0	0	1b2/D	0	-0.2
1983	Oak A	5	14	2	2	0	0	0	2	0	0	0	3	.143	.143	.143	.286	-122	0	0	0	1b3/D	0	-0.4
Total	2	8	20	2	2	0	0	0	2	0	0	0	6	.100	.100	.100	.200	-147	0	0	0	1b5,D2	0	-0.6

Brickell, Fritz Fritz Darrell B3.19.1935 Wichita KS D10.15.1965 Wichita KS BR/TR/5'5.5"/(157–160) d4.30 f-Fred

YEAR	TM LG	G	AB	R	H	2B	3B	HR	RBI	BB	IB	HP	SO	AVG	OBP	SLG	OPS	AOPS	SB	CS	SB%	GAMES AT POSITION	DL	BFW
1958	NY A	2	0	0	0	0	0	0	0	0	0	0	0	+	+	+	.000	-100	0	0	0	2b2	0	0.0
1959	NY A	18	39	4	10	1	0	1	4	1	0	0	10	.256	.275	.359	.634	-25	0	0	0	S15,2b3	0	-0.3
1961	LA A	21	49	3	6	0	0	0	3	6	0	0	9	.122	.218	.122	.340	-106	0	0	0	S17	0	-0.7
Total	3	41	88	7	16	1	0	1	7	7	0	0	19	.182	.242	.227	.469	-74	0	0	0	S32,2b5	0	-1.0
Team	2	20	39	4	10	1	0	1	4	1	0	0	10	.256	.275	.359	.634	-25	0	0	0	S15,2b5	0	-0.3

Brideweser, Jim James Ehrenfeld B2.13.1927 Lancaster OH D8.25.1989 El Toro CA BR/TR/6'0"/165 d9.29 Col USC

YEAR	TM LG	G	AB	R	H	2B	3B	HR	RBI	BB	IB	HP	SO	AVG	OBP	SLG	OPS	AOPS	SB	CS	SB%	GAMES AT POSITION	DL	BFW
1951	NY A	2	8	1	3	0	0	0	0	0	—	0	1	.375	.375	.375	.750	+7	0	0	0	S2	0	0.0
1952	NY A	42	38	12	10	0	0	0	2	3	—	0	5	.263	.317	.263	.580	-33	0	0	0	S22,2b4/3b	0	-0.1
1953	NY A	7	3	3	3	0	1	0	3	1	—	0	0	1.000	1.000	1.667	2.667	+531	0	0	0	S3	0	0.2
Total	7	329	620	79	156	22	6	1	50	63	4	2	78	.252	.322	.311	.633	-25	6	2	75	S217,2b57,3b11	0	-0.8
Team	3	51	49	16	16	0	1	0	5	4	—	0	6	.327	.377	.367	.744	+16	0	0	0	S27,2b4/3	0	0.1

Bright, Harry Harry James B9.22.1929 Kansas City MO D3.13.2000 Sacramento CA BR/TR/6'0"/(184–190) d7.25

YEAR	TM LG	G	AB	R	H	2B	3B	HR	RBI	BB	IB	HP	SO	AVG	OBP	SLG	OPS	AOPS	SB	CS	SB%	GAMES AT POSITION	DL	BFW
1963	†NY A	60	157	15	37	7	0	7	23	13	1	1	31	.236	.297	.414	.711	-2	0	0	0	1b35,3b12	0	-0.7
1964	NY A	4	5	0	1	0	0	0	0	1	0	0	1	.200	.333	.200	.533	-48	0	0	0	1b2	0	-0.1
Total	8	336	839	99	214	31	4	32	126	65	2	3	133	.255	.309	.416	.725	-4	2	3	40	1b137,3b63,C11,O4(3/0/1),2b2	0	-1.5
Team	2	64	162	15	38	7	0	7	23	14	1	1	32	.235	.298	.407	.705	-4	0	0	0	1b37,3b12	0	-0.8

Brinkman, Ed Edwin Albert B12.8.1941 Cincinnati OH BR/TR/6'0"/170 d9.6 C8 b-Chuck Col Cincinnati

YEAR	TM LG	G	AB	R	H	2B	3B	HR	RBI	BB	IB	HP	SO	AVG	OBP	SLG	OPS	AOPS	SB	CS	SB%	GAMES AT POSITION	DL	BFW
1975	NY A	44	63	2	11	4	1	0	2	3	0	1	6	.175	.224	.270	.494	-61	0	0	0	S39,2b3,3b3	0	-0.9
Total	15	1845	6045	550	1355	201	38	60	461	444	44	40	845	.224	.280	.300	.580	-35	30	35	46	S1795,3b19,2b5/lf	0	-6.5

Brookens, Tom Thomas Dale B8.10.1953 Chambersburg PA BR/TR/5'10"/170 Dr 1975 DetA*1/4 d7.10 Col Mansfield OF(0/2/6)

YEAR	TM LG	G	AB	R	H	2B	3B	HR	RBI	BB	IB	HP	SO	AVG	OBP	SLG	OPS	AOPS	SB	CS	SB%	GAMES AT POSITION	DL	BFW
1989	NY A	66	168	14	38	6	0	4	14	11	1	0	27	.226	.272	.333	.605	-29	1	3	25	3b51,S7,2b5,O3R,D3	39	-1.3
Total	12	1336	3865	477	950	175	40	71	431	281	12	14	605	.246	.296	.367	.663	-18	86	60	59	3b1065,2b162,S119,D23,O7R,1b2/C	70	-8.2

Brosius, Scott Scott David B8.15.1966 Hillsboro OR BR/TR/6'1"/(185–202) Dr 1987 OakA 20/511 d8.7 Col Linfield OF(37/68/74)

YEAR	TM LG	G	AB	R	H	2B	3B	HR	RBI	BB	IB	HP	SO	AVG	OBP	SLG	OPS	AOPS	SB	CS	SB%	GAMES AT POSITION	DL	BFW
1991	Oak A	36	68	9	16	5	0	2	4	3	0	0	11	.235	.268	.397	.665	-14	3	1	75	2b18,O13(5/0/10),3b7/D	0	-0.2
1992	Oak A	38	87	13	19	2	0	4	13	3	1	2	13	.218	.258	.379	.637	-19	3	0	100	O20(4/0/19),3b12,1b3/SD	45	-0.6
1993	Oak A	70	213	26	53	10	1	6	25	14	0	1	37	.249	.296	.390	.686	-12	6	0	100	O46(8/34/6),1b11,3b10,S6,D2	0	-0.5
1994	Oak A	96	324	31	77	14	1	14	49	24	0	2	57	.238	.289	.417	.706	-13	2	6	25	3b93,O7(2/2/4)/1b	18	-0.4
1995	Oak A	123	389	69	102	19	2	17	46	41	0	8	67	.262	.342	.452	.794	+11	4	2	67	3b60,O49(8/22/22),1b18,2b3,S3,D2	0	0.2
1996	Oak A	114	428	73	130	25	0	22	71	59	4	7	85	.304	.393	.516	.909	+30	7	2	78	3b109,1b10,O4(3/2/0)	51	3.3
1997	Oak A	129	479	59	97	20	1	11	41	34	1	4	102	.203	.259	.317	.576	-50	9	4	69	3b107,S30,O22(6/6/11)	22	-1.8
1998	†NY A★	152	530	86	159	34	0	19	98	52	1	10	97	.300	.371	.472	.843	+23	11	8	58	3b150,1b3/rf	0	2.7
1999	†NY A	133	473	64	117	26	1	17	71	39	2	6	74	.247	.307	.414	.721	-15	9	3	75	3b132/D	15	-0.7
2000	†NY A	135	470	57	108	20	0	16	64	45	1	2	73	.230	.299	.374	.673	-30	0	3	0	3b134,1b2,O2(1/0/1)/D	20	-2.4
2001	†NY A	120	428	57	123	25	2	13	49	34	2	5	83	.287	.343	.446	.789	+6	3	1	75	3b120,O2C	36	0.6
Total	11	1146	3889	544	1001	200	8	141	531	348	12	47	699	.257	.323	.422	.745	-6	57	30	66	3b934,O166R,1b48,S40,2b21,D8	207	0.2
Team	4	540	1901	264	507	105	3	65	282	170	6	23	327	.267	.331	.428	.759	-3	23	15	61	3b536,1b5,O5(1/1/1),D2	71	0.2
/150	1	150	528	73	141	29	1	18	78	47	2	6	91	.267	.331	.428	.759	-3	6	4	60	3b149/1OfLD	20	0.1

Brower, Bob Robert Richard B1.10.1960 Jamaica NY BR/TR/5'11"/190 d9.3 Col Duke

YEAR	TM LG	G	AB	R	H	2B	3B	HR	RBI	BB	IB	HP	SO	AVG	OBP	SLG	OPS	AOPS	SB	CS	SB%	GAMES AT POSITION	DL	BFW
1989	NY A	26	69	9	16	3	0	2	3	6	0	0	11	.232	.293	.362	.655	-16	3	1	75	O25(1/9/15)/D	13	0.2
Total	4	256	582	104	141	21	3	17	60	69	0	0	118	.242	.322	.376	.698	-12	29	17	63	O207(88/110/26),D22	36	-1.7

Brown, Bobby Robert William "Doc" B10.25.1924 Seattle WA BL/TR/6'1"/180 d9.22 Mil 1952–54 Col Tulane

YEAR	TM LG	G	AB	R	H	2B	3B	HR	RBI	BB	IB	HP	SO	AVG	OBP	SLG	OPS	AOPS	SB	CS	SB%	GAMES AT POSITION	DL	BFW
1946	NY A	7	24	1	8	1	0	0	1	4	—	0	0	.333	.429	.375	.804	+24	0	0	0	S5,3b2	0	0.0
1947	†NY A	69	150	21	45	6	1	1	18	21	—	1	9	.300	.390	.373	.763	+14	0	2	0	3b27,S11,O3(0/2/1)	0	-0.4
1948	NY A	113	363	62	109	19	5	3	48	48	—	1	16	.300	.383	.405	.788	+11	0	1	0	3b41,S26,2b17,O4(3/0/1)	0	-0.4
1949	†NY A	104	343	61	97	14	4	6	61	38	—	3	18	.283	.359	.399	.758	+1	4	3	57	3b86,O3(1/0/2)	0	-0.4
1950	†NY A	95	277	33	74	4	2	4	37	39	—	1	18	.267	.360	.339	.699	-18	3	1	75	3b82	0	-1.0
1951	†NY A	103	313	44	84	15	2	6	51	47	—	3	18	.268	.369	.387	.756	+8	1	1	50	3b90	0	-0.1
1952	NY A	29	89	6	22	2	0	1	14	9	—	1	6	.247	.323	.303	.626	-20	1	1	50	3b24	0	-0.1
1954	NY A	28	60	5	13	1	0	1	7	8	—	0	3	.217	.304	.283	.587	-35	0	1	0	3b17	0	-0.3
Total	8	548	1619	233	452	62	14	22	237	214	—	10	88	.279	.367	.376	.743	+0	9	10	47	3b369,S42,2b17,O10(4/2/4)	0	-2.7
/150	2	150	443	64	124	17	4	6	65	59	—	3	24	.279	.367	.376	.743	+0	2	3	40	3b101,S11,2b5,O3(1/1/1)	0	-0.7

Brown, Bobby Rogers Lee B5.24.1954 Norfolk VA BB/TR (BL 1979)/6'1"/(198–231) Dr 1972 BalA 11/264 d4.5

YEAR	TM LG	G	AB	R	H	2B	3B	HR	RBI	BB	IB	HP	SO	AVG	OBP	SLG	OPS	AOPS	SB	CS	SB%	GAMES AT POSITION	DL	BFW
1979	Tor A	4	10	1	0	0	0	0	0	2	0	0	1	.000	.167	.000	.167	-150	0	0	0	O4(2/0/2)	0	-0.2
1979	NY A	30	68	7	17	3	1	0	3	2	0	0	17	.250	.271	.324	.595	-39	2	1	67	O27(7/20/0)/D	0	-0.5

YEAR	TM LG	G	AB	R	H	2B	3B	HR	RBI	BB	IB	HP	SO	AVG	OBP	SLG	OPS	AOPS	SB	CS	SB%	GAMES AT POSITION	DL	BFW
1979	Year	34	78	8	17	3	1	0	3	4	0	0	18	.218	.256	.282	.538	-54	2	1	67	O31(9/20/2)/D	0	-0.7
1980	†NY A	137	412	65	107	12	5	14	47	29	4	0	82	.260	.306	.415	.721	-2	27	8	77	O131(28/81/25)/D	0	0.0
1981	†NY A	31	62	5	14	1	0	0	6	5	0	0	15	.226	.279	.242	.521	-47	4	2	67	O29(6/11/14),D2	0	-0.2
1982	Sea A	79	245	29	59	7	1	4	17	17	2	0	32	.241	.288	.327	.615	-33	28	6	82	O68(51/14/4),D3	21	-0.8
1983	SD N	57	225	40	60	5	3	5	22	23	0	0	38	.267	.333	.382	.715	+1	27	9	75	O54(52/4/0)	0	-0.4
1984	†SD N	85	171	28	43	7	2	3	29	11	0	0	33	.251	.292	.368	.660	-15	16	4	80	O53(27/13/16)	0	-0.2
1985	SD N	79	84	8	13	3	0	0	6	5	0	0	20	.155	.200	.190	.390	-90	6	4	60	O28(9/9/12)	0	-1.1
Total	7	502	1277	183	313	38	12	26	130	94	6	0	238	.245	.295	.355	.650	-20	110	34	76	O394(182/152/73),D7	21	-3.4
Team	3	198	542	77	138	16	6	14	55	36	4	0	114	.255	.299	.384	.683	-12	33	11	75	O187(35/112/11),D4	0	-0.7
/150	2	150	411	58	105	12	5	11	42	27	3	0	86	.255	.299	.384	.683	-12	25	8	76	O142(27/85/8),D3	0	0.6
BRYAN, BILLY William Ronald B12.4.1938 Morgan GA BL/TR/6'4"/(200–215) d9.12																								
1966	NY A	27	69	5	15	2	0	4	5	5	0	0	19	.217	.270	.420	.690	-1	0	0	0	C14,1b3	0	0.0
1967	NY A	16	12	1	2	0	0	1	2	5	0	0	3	.167	.412	.417	.829	+51	0	0	0	/C	0	0.1
Total	8	374	968	86	209	32	9	41	125	91	13	3	283	.216	.284	.395	.679	-9	0	1	0	C274,1b6	0	-2.2
Team	2	43	81	6	17	2	0	5	7	10	0	0	22	.210	.297	.420	.717	+9	0	0	0	C15,1b3	0	0.1
BUHNER, JAY Jay Campbell B8.13.1964 Louisville KY BR/TR/6'3"/(205–222) Dr 1984 PitN*S2/36 d9.11 Col McLennan (TX) CC																								
1987	NY A	7	22	0	5	2	0	0	1	1	0	0	6	.227	.261	.318	.579	-47	0	0	0	O7(2/3/2)	0	-0.2
1988	NY A	25	69	8	13	0	0	3	13	3	0	3	25	.188	.250	.319	.569	-41	0	0	0	O22(3/16/3)	0	-0.3
Total	15	1472	5013	798	1273	233	19	310	965	792	41	56	1406	.254	.359	.494	.853	+23	6	24	20	O1397(17/30/1356),D44/1b	496	8.7
Team	2	32	91	8	18	2	0	3	14	4	0	3	31	.198	.253	.319	.572	-42	0	0	0	O29(5/19/2)	0	-0.5
BURNS, GEORGE George Henry "Tioga George" B1.31.1893 Niles OH D1.7.1978 Kirkland WA BR/TR/6'1.5"/180 d4.14																								
1928	NY A	4	4	1	2	0	0	0	0	0	—	0	1	.500	.500	.500	1.000	+69	0	0	0	1b2	—	0.0
1929	NY A	9	9	0	0	0	0	0	0	0	—	0	4	.000	.000	.000	.000	-199	0	0	0	/H	—	-0.3
Total	16	1866	6573	901	2018	444	72	72	951	363	—	110	433	.307	.354	.429	.783	+12	154	63	100	1b1671,O50(1/0/49)	—	2.2
Team	2	13	13	1	2	0	0	0	0	0	—	0	5	.154	.154	.154	.308	-117	0	0	0	1b2	—	-0.3
BURR, ALEX Alexander Thomson B11.1.1893 Chicago IL D10.12.1918 Cazaux, France BR/TR/6'3.5"/190 d4.21 Col Williams																								
1914	NY A	1	0	0	0	0	0	0	0	0	—	0	0	+	+	+	.000	-100	0	—	—	/cf	—	0.0
BUSH, HOMER Homer Giles B11.12.1972 East St.Louis IL BR/TR/5'11"/(175–185) Dr 1991 SDN 7/185 d8.16 [DL 1996 SD N 133]																								
1997	NY A	10	11	2	4	0	0	0	3	0	0	0	0	.364	.364	.364	.728	-9	0	0	0	2b8/D	0	0.1
1998	†NY A	45	71	17	27	3	0	1	5	5	0	0	19	.380	.421	.465	.886	+36	6	3	67	2b24,D12,3b3,S2	0	0.1
2004	NY A	9	7	2	0	0	0	0	0	0	0	1	2	.000	.125	.000	.125	-163	1	0	100	2b4,D2	0	-0.2
Total	7	409	1274	176	363	50	5	11	115	57	1	20	238	.285	.324	.358	.682	-25	65	20	76	2b332,S24,D16,3b3	321	0.8
Team	3	64	89	21	31	3	0	1	8	5	0	1	21	.348	.389	.416	.805	+14	7	3	70	2b36,D15,3b3,S2	0	0.0
BUZAS, JOE Joseph John B10.2.1919 Alpha NJ D3.19.2003 Salt Lake City UT BR/TR/6'1"/180 d4.17 Col Bucknell																								
1945	NY A	30	65	8	17	2	1	0	6	2	—	0	5	.262	.284	.323	.607	-27	2	0	100	S12	0	-0.4
BYRD, SAMMY Samuel Dewey "Babe Ruth's Legs" B10.15.1906 Bremen GA D5.11.1981 Mesa AZ BR/TR/5'10.5"/175 d5.11																								
1929	NY A	62	170	32	53	12	0	5	28	28	—	0	18	.312	.409	.471	.880	+35	1	4	20	O54(6/16/32)	—	0.8
1930	NY A	92	218	46	62	12	2	6	31	30	—	0	18	.284	.371	.440	.811	+10	5	1	83	O85(47/12/26)	—	0.1
1931	NY A	115	248	51	67	18	2	3	32	29	—	1	26	.270	.349	.395	.744	+1	5	0	100	O88(26/34/34)	—	-0.1
1932	†NY A	105	209	49	62	12	1	8	30	30	—	0	20	.297	.385	.478	.863	+29	1	2	33	O91(11/70/11)	—	0.6
1933	NY A	85	107	26	30	6	1	2	11	15	—	0	12	.280	.369	.411	.780	+13	0	1	0	O71(23/15/35)	—	0.3
1934	NY A	106	191	32	47	8	0	3	23	18	—	2	22	.246	.318	.335	.653	-27	1	2	33	O104(34/13/59)	—	-0.5
1935	Cin N	121	416	51	109	25	4	9	52	37	—	0	51	.262	.322	.406	.728	-3	4	—	—	O115(39/76/0)	—	-0.7
1936	Cin N	59	141	17	35	8	0	2	13	11	—	0	11	.248	.303	.348	.651	-20	0	—	—	O37(15/22/0)	—	-0.4
Total	8	745	1700	304	465	101	10	38	220	198	—	3	178	.274	.350	.412	.762	+4	17	10	100	O645(201/258/197)	—	0.1
Team	6	565	1143	236	321	68	6	27	155	150	—	3	116	.281	.366	.422	.788	+10	13	10	57	O493(89/192/164)	—	1.2
/150	2	150	303	63	85	18	2	7	41	40	—	1	31	.281	.366	.422	.788	+10	3	3	50	O131(24/51/44)	—	0.3
CABRERA, MELKY Melky B8.11.1984 Santo Domingo, D.R. BB/TL/5'11"/170 d7.7																								
2005	NY A	6	19	1	4	0	0	0	0	0	0	0	2	.211	.211	.211	.422	-87	0	0	0	O6C	0	-0.4
2006	†NY A	130	460	75	129	26	2	7	50	56	3	2	59	.280	.360	.391	.751	-7	12	5	71	O127(116/4/8)	0	-0.4
2007	†NY A	150	545	66	149	24	8	8	73	43	0	5	68	.273	.327	.391	.718	-11	13	5	72	O147(18/131/5)	0	0.1
Total	3	286	1024	142	282	50	10	15	123	99	3	7	129	.275	.340	.388	.728	-11	25	10	71	O280(134/141/13)	0	-0.7
/150	2	150	537	74	148	26	5	8	65	52	2	4	68	.275	.340	.388	.728	-11	13	5	72	O147(70/74/7)	0	-0.4
CAIRO, MIGUEL Miguel Jesus B5.4.1974 Anaco, Anzoategui, Venez BR/TR/6'1"/(160–210) d4.17 OF(54/0/12)																								
2004	†NY A	122	360	48	105	17	5	6	42	18	1	14	49	.292	.346	.417	.763	-1	11	3	79	2b113,3b8,S3/1b	0	0.1
2006	NY A	81	222	28	53	12	3	0	30	13	0	1	31	.239	.280	.320	.600	-45	13	1	93	2b45,1b16,S14,3b8/lfD	36	-0.7
2007	NY A	54	107	12	27	7	0	0	10	8	1	1	19	.252	.308	.318	.626	-35	8	1	89	1b22,S16,3b7,2b3,O3L,D3	0	-0.5
Total	12	1092	3095	392	826	150	27	27	295	186	8	47	360	.267	.315	.359	.674	-25	123	34	78	2b717,3b103,O65L,1b57,S50,D14	132	-5.0
Team	3	257	689	88	185	36	8	6	82	39	2	16	99	.269	.319	.370	.689	-20	32	5	86	2b161,1b39,S33,3b23,lf,D4	36	-1.1
/150	2	150	402	51	108	21	5	4	48	23	1	9	58	.269	.319	.370	.689	-20	19	3	86	2b94,1b23,S19,3b13,lf,D2	21	-0.6
CALDWELL, RAY Raymond Benjamin "Rube","Sum" B4.26.1888 Corydon PA D8.17.1967 Salamanca NY BL/TR/6'2"/190 d9.9 ▲																								
1910	NY A	6	6	0	0	0	0	0	0	0	—	0	—	.000	.000	.000	.000	-195	0	—	—	P6	—	0.0
1911	NY A	59	147	14	40	4	1	0	17	11	—	0	—	.272	.323	.313	.636	-27	5	—	—	P41,O11(5/0/5)	—	-0.3
1912	NY A	44	76	18	18	1	2	0	6	5	—	0	—	.237	.284	.303	.587	-36	4	1	80	P30/lf	—	0.0
1913	NY A	59	97	10	28	3	2	0	11	3	—	0	15	.289	.310	.361	.671	-4	3	—	—	P27,O3(0/1/2)	—	-0.1
1914	NY A	59	113	9	22	4	0	0	10	7	—	1	24	.195	.248	.230	.478	-56	2	1	67	P31,1b6	—	-0.5
1915	NY A	72	144	27	35	4	1	4	20	9	—	0	32	.243	.288	.368	.656	-4	4	3	57	P36	—	0.0
1916	NY A	45	93	6	19	2	0	0	4	2	—	0	17	.204	.221	.226	.447	-66	1	—	—	P21,O2	—	0.0
1917	NY A	63	124	12	32	6	1	2	12	16	—	0	16	.258	.343	.371	.714	+17	2	—	—	P32,O8(0/5/3)	—	-0.1
1918	NY A	65	151	14	44	10	0	1	18	13	—	1	23	.291	.352	.377	.729	+17	2	—	—	P24,O19(2/12/5)	—	-0.1
1919	Bos A	33	48	5	13	1	1	0	4	0	—	0	9	.271	.271	.333	.604	-27	0	—	—	P18,O2L	—	-0.1
1919	Cle A	6	23	4	8	4	0	0	2	0	—	0	4	.348	.348	.522	.870	+34	0	—	—	P6	—	0.0
1919	Year	39	71	9	21	5	1	0	6	0	—	0	13	.296	.296	.394	.690	-3	0	—	—	P24,O2L	—	-0.1
1920	†Cle A	41	89	17	19	3	0	0	7	10	—	1	13	.213	.300	.247	.547	-55	0	2	0	P34	—	0.0
1921	Cle A	38	53	2	11	4	0	1	3	2	—	0	5	.208	.236	.340	.576	-55	0	0	0	P37	—	0.0
Total	12	590	1164	138	289	46	8	8	114	78	—	3	158	.248	.297	.322	.619	-22	23	7	100	P343,O46(11/18/15),1b6	—	-1.2
Team	9	472	951	110	238	34	7	7	98	66	—	2	127	.250	.300	.323	.623	-17	23	5	100	P248,O44(7/10/15),1b6	—	-1.1
/150	3	150	302	35	76	11	2	2	31	21	—	1	40	.250	.300	.323	.623	-17	7	2	100	P79,O14(2/3/5),1b2	—	-0.3
CALLISON, JOHNNY John Wesley B3.12.1939 Qualls OK D10.12.2006 Abington PA BL/TR/5'10"/(170–180) d9.9																								
1972	NY A	92	275	28	71	10	0	9	34	18	1	0	34	.258	.299	.393	.692	+8	3	0	100	O74R	0	-0.4
1973	NY A	45	136	10	24	4	0	1	10	4	0	0	24	.176	.197	.228	.425	-79	1	1	50	O32R,D10	0	-2.0
Total	16	1886	6652	926	1757	321	89	226	840	650	73	41	1064	.264	.331	.441	.772	+14	74	51	59	O1777(189/26/1586),D10	52	10.5
Team	2	137	411	38	95	14	0	10	44	22	1	0	58	.231	.266	.338	.604	-20	4	1	80	O106R,D10	0	-2.4
/150	2	150	450	42	104	15	0	11	48	24	1	0	64	.231	.266	.338	.604	-20	4	1	80	O116R,D11	0	-2.6
CAMP, HOWIE Howard Lee "Red" B7.1.1893 Hopeful AL D5.8.1960 Eastaboga AL BL/TR/5'9"/169 d9.19 Mil 1918																								
1917	NY A	5	21	3	6	1	0	0	0	1	—	0	2	.286	.318	.333	.651	-2	0	—	—	O5(0/4/1)	—	0.0

YEAR	TM LG	G	AB	R	H	2B	3B	HR	RBI	BB	IB	HP	SO	AVG	OBP	SLG	OPS	AOPS	SB	CS	SB%	GAMES AT POSITION	DL	BFW
Campaneris, Bert Dagoberto (Blanco) "Campy"(b Dagoberto Campaneria (Blanco)) B3.9.1942 Pueblo Nuevo, Cuba BR/TR/5'10"/(155–160) d7.23 OF(68/2/1)																								
1983	NY A	60	143	19	46	5	0	0	11	8	0	0	9	.322	.355	.357	.712	+0	6	7	46	2b32,3b24	15	-0.2
Total	19	2328	8684	1181	2249	313	86	79	646	618	15	64	1142	.259	.311	.342	.653	-11	649	199	77	S2097,3b76,O69L,2b36,D8/1bCP	68	13.4
Cannizaro, Andy Andrew Lee B12.19.1978 New Orleans LA BR/TR/5'10"/170 Dr 2001 NYA 7/215 d9.5 Col Tulane																								
2006	NY A	13	8	5	2	0	0	1	1	1	0	0	1	.250	.333	.625	.958	+38	0	0	0	S10,2b2,3b2	0	-0.2
Cano, Robinson Robinson Jose (Mercedes) B10.22.1982 San Pedro de Macoris, D.R. BL/TR/6'0"/(170–190) d5.3 f–Jose																								
2005	†NY A	132	522	78	155	34	4	14	62	16	1	3	68	.297	.320	.458	.778	+5	1	3	25	2b131	0	1.2
2006	†NY A∗	122	482	62	165	41	1	15	78	18	3	2	54	.342	.365	.525	.890	+25	5	2	71	2b118,D4	43	2.1
2007	†NY A	160	617	93	189	41	7	19	97	39	5	8	85	.306	.353	.488	.841	+18	4	5	44	2b159	0	3.1
Total	3	414	1621	233	509	116	12	48	237	73	9	13	207	.314	.346	.489	.835	+16	10	10	50	2b408,D4	43	6.4
/150	1	150	587	84	184	42	4	17	86	26	3	5	75	.314	.346	.489	.835	+16	4	4	50	2b148/D	16	2.3
Canseco, Jose Jose (Capas) B7.2.1964 Havana, Cuba BR/TR/6'4"/(195–240) Dr 1982 OakA 15/392 d9.2 twb–Ozzie																								
2000	†NY A	37	111	16	27	3	0	6	19	23	1	0	37	.243	.365	.432	.797	+5	0	0	0	D26,O5(4/0/1)	0	-0.1
Total	17	1887	7057	1186	1877	340	14	462	1407	906	63	84	1942	.266	.353	.515	.868	+32	200	88	69	O1011(356/1/679),D834/P	483	23.3
Carey, Andy Andrew Arthur (b Andrew Arthur Hexem) B10.18.1931 Oakland CA BR/TR/6'1"/(185–198) d5.2 Col St. Marys (CA)																								
1952	NY A	16	40	6	6	0	0	0	1	3	—	0	10	.150	.209	.150	.359	-99	0	0	0	3b14/S	0	-0.7
1953	NY A	51	81	14	26	5	0	4	8	9	—	0	12	.321	.389	.531	.920	+52	2	1	67	3b40,S2/2b	0	1.1
1954	NY A	122	411	60	124	14	6	8	65	43	—	7	38	.302	.373	.423	.796	+23	5	5	50	3b120	0	2.5
1955	†NY A	135	510	73	131	19	**11**	7	47	44	6	1	51	.257	.313	.378	.691	-12	3	3	50	3b135	0	-0.2
1956	†NY A	132	422	54	100	18	2	7	50	45	4	2	53	.237	.310	.339	.649	-25	9	6	60	3b131	0	-1.9
1957	†NY A	85	247	30	63	6	5	6	33	15	3	5	42	.255	.309	.393	.702	-8	2	2	50	3b81	0	-0.5
1958	†NY A	102	315	39	90	19	4	12	45	34	4	6	43	.286	.363	.486	.849	+37	1	2	33	3b99	0	2.4
1959	NY A	41	101	11	26	1	0	3	9	7	0	0	17	.257	.306	.356	.662	-16	1	1	50	3b34	70	-0.4
1960	NY A	4	3	1	1	0	0	0	1	0	0	0	1	.333	.333	.333	.666	-14	0	0	0	3b2/lf	0	0.0
1960	KC A	102	343	30	80	14	4	12	53	26	0	1	52	.233	.287	.402	.689	-16	0	0	0	3b91	0	-0.7
1960	Year	106	346	31	81	14	4	12	54	26	0	1	53	.234	.287	.402	.689	-15	0	0	0	3b93/lf	0	-0.7
1961	KC A	39	123	20	30	6	2	3	11	15	0	2	23	.244	.336	.398	.734	-6	0	0	0	3b39	0	-0.4
1961	Chi A	56	143	21	38	12	3	0	14	11	0	2	24	.266	.323	.392	.715	-7	0	1	0	3b54	0	-1.2
1961	Year	95	266	41	68	18	5	3	25	26	0	4	47	.256	.329	.395	.724	-7	0	1	0	3b93	0	-1.6
1962	LA N	53	111	12	26	5	1	2	13	16	1	1	23	.234	.333	.351	.684	-10	0	0	0	3b42	0	-0.4
Total	11	938	2850	371	741	119	38	64	350	268	18	27	389	.260	.327	.396	.723	-3	23	21	52	3b882,S3/lf2b	70	-0.4
Team	9	688	2130	288	567	82	28	47	259	200	17	21	267	.266	.332	.397	.729	+1	23	20	53	3b656,S3/2lf	70	2.3
/150	2	150	464	63	124	18	6	10	56	44	4	5	58	.266	.332	.397	.729	+1	5	4	56	3b143/S2OfL	15	0.5
Carlyle, Roy Roy Edward "Dizzy" B12.10.1900 Buford GA D11.22.1956 Norcross GA BL/TR/6'2.5"/195 d4.16 b–Cleo Col Oglethorpe																								
1926	NY A	35	62	3	20	5	1	0	11	4	—	1	9	.323	.373	.435	.808	+12	0	0	0	O15R	—	0.0
Total	2	174	504	61	157	31	6	9	76	24	—	4	56	.312	.348	.450	.798	+5	1	1	50	O120(43/0/77)	—	-1.7
Carmel, Duke Leon James B4.23.1937 New York NY BL/TL/6'3"/(197–202) d9.10																								
1965	NY A	6	8	0	0	0	0	0	0	0	0	0	5	.000	.000	.000	.000	-199	0	0	0	1b2	0	-0.2
Total	4	124	227	22	48	7	3	4	23	27	2	0	60	.211	.294	.322	.616	-27	3	4	43	O70(28/35/12),1b23	0	-1.2
Carroll, Tom Thomas Edward B9.17.1936 Jamaica NY BR/TR/6'3"/(186–190) d5.7 Mil 1958 Col Notre Dame																								
1955	†NY A	14	6	3	2	0	0	0	0	0	0	0	2	.333	.333	.333	.666	-19	0	0	0	S4	0	0.1
1956	NY A	36	17	11	6	0	0	0	0	1	0	0	3	.353	.389	.353	.742	+0	1	0	100	3b11/S	0	0.3
1959	KC A	14	7	1	1	0	0	0	1	0	0	0	1	.143	.143	.143	.286	-121	0	0	0	S9,3b3	0	0.0
Total	3	64	30	15	9	0	0	0	1	1	0	0	6	.300	.323	.300	.623	-31	1	0	100	3b14,S14	0	0.4
Team	2	50	23	14	8	0	0	0	0	1	0	0	5	.348	.375	.348	.723	-5	1	0	100	3b11,S5	0	0.4
Castillo, Alberto Alberto Terrero B2.10.1970 San Juan de la Maguana, D.R. BR/TR/6'0"/(184–215) d5.28																								
2002	NY A	15	37	3	5	1	1	0	4	1	0	0	12	.135	.158	.216	.374	-102	0	0	0	C14	0	-0.2
Total	12	418	1026	98	226	39	2	12	101	103	1	7	219	.220	.293	.297	.590	-46	3	6	33	C409/D	30	0.7
Cater, Danny Danny Anderson B2.25.1940 Austin TX BR/TR/5'11.5"/(170–198) d4.14 OF(293/2/16)																								
1970	NY A	155	582	64	175	26	5	6	76	34	6	2	44	.301	.340	.393	.733	+7	4	2	67	1b131,3b42,O7R	0	-1.0
1971	NY A	121	428	39	118	16	5	4	50	19	4	2	25	.276	.308	.364	.672	-5	0	3	0	1b78,3b52	0	-0.1
Total	12	1289	4451	491	1229	191	29	66	519	254	33	22	406	.276	.316	.377	.693	+1	26	30	46	1b731,O308L,3b225,D17,2b5	40	-9.2
Team	2	276	1010	103	293	42	10	10	126	53	10	4	69	.290	.326	.381	.707	+2	4	5	44	1b209,3b94,O7R	0	-1.1
/150	1	150	549	56	159	23	5	5	68	29	5	2	38	.290	.326	.381	.707	+2	2	3	40	1b114,3b51,O4R	0	-0.6
Cerone, Rick Richard Aldo B5.19.1954 Newark NJ BR/TR/5'11"/(184–195) Dr 1975 CleA 1/7 d8.17 Col Seton Hall																								
1975	Cle A	7	12	1	3	1	0	0	0	1	0	0	0	.250	.308	.333	.641	-19	0	0	0	C7	0	-0.1
1976	Cle A	7	16	1	2	0	0	0	1	0	0	0	2	.125	.125	.125	.250	-127	0	0	0	C6/D	0	-0.3
1977	Tor A	31	100	7	20	4	0	1	10	6	0	0	12	.200	.245	.270	.515	-60	0	0	0	C31	0	-0.6
1978	Tor A	88	282	25	63	8	2	3	20	23	0	1	32	.223	.284	.298	.582	-37	0	3	0	C84,D2	0	-1.1
1979	Tor A	136	469	47	112	27	4	7	61	37	1	1	40	.239	.294	.358	.652	-25	1	4	20	C136	0	-0.9
1980	†NY A	147	519	70	144	30	4	14	85	32	2	6	56	.277	.321	.432	.753	+8	1	3	25	C147	0	2.8
1981	†NY A	71	234	23	57	13	2	2	21	12	0	0	24	.244	.276	.342	.618	-21	0	2	0	C69	35	-0.8
1982	NY A	89	300	29	68	10	0	5	28	19	1	1	27	.227	.271	.310	.581	-39	0	2	0	C89	64	-2.4
1983	NY A	80	246	18	54	7	0	2	22	15	1	1	29	.220	.267	.272	.539	-50	0	0	0	C78/3b	0	-1.9
1984	NY A	38	120	8	25	3	0	2	13	9	0	1	15	.208	.269	.283	.552	-45	1	0	100	C38	59	-0.7
1985	Atl N	96	282	15	61	9	0	3	25	29	1	1	25	.216	.288	.280	.568	-43	0	3	0	C91	15	-2.0
1986	Mil A	68	216	22	56	14	0	4	18	15	0	1	28	.259	.304	.380	.684	-16	1	1	50	C68	0	0.2
1987	NY A	113	284	28	69	12	1	4	23	30	0	4	46	.243	.320	.335	.655	-24	0	1	0	C111,P2,1b2	0	0.2
1988	Bos A	84	264	31	71	13	1	3	27	20	0	3	32	.269	.326	.360	.686	-12	0	0	0	C83/D	0	-0.2
1989	Bos A	102	296	28	72	16	1	4	48	34	1	2	40	.243	.320	.345	.665	-16	0	0	0	C97/rfD	0	-0.3
1990	NY A	49	139	12	42	6	0	2	11	5	0	0	13	.302	.324	.388	.712	-2	0	0	0	C35/2bD	64	0.3
1991	NY N	90	227	18	62	13	0	2	16	30	2	1	24	.273	.360	.357	.717	+3	1	1	50	C81	0	0.8
1992	Mon N	33	63	10	17	4	0	1	7	3	0	1	5	.270	.313	.381	.694	-4	1	2	33	C28	0	-0.1
Total	18	1329	4069	393	998	190	15	59	436	320	9	24	450	.245	.301	.343	.644	-22	6	22	21	C1279,D11,1b2,P2/2brf3b	237	-7.1
Team	7	587	1842	188	459	81	7	31	203	122	4	13	210	.249	.297	.351	.648	-20	2	8	20	C567,P2,1b2/23D	222	-2.5
/150	2	150	471	48	117	21	2	8	52	31	1	3	54	.249	.297	.351	.648	-20	1	2	33	C145/P123D	57	-0.6
Cerv, Bob Robert Henry B5.5.1926 Weston NE BR/TR/6'0"/(202–226) d8.1 Col Nebraska																								
1951	NY A	12	28	4	6	1	0	0	2	4	—	0	6	.214	.313	.250	.563	-45	0	0	0	O9R	0	-0.3
1952	NY A	36	87	11	21	3	2	1	8	9	—	0	22	.241	.313	.356	.669	-9	0	1	0	O27(15/12/0)	0	-0.3
1953	NY A	8	6	0	0	0	0	0	0	1	—	0	1	.000	.143	.000	.143	-161	0	0	0	/H	0	-0.1
1954	NY A	56	100	14	26	6	0	5	13	11	—	0	17	.260	.330	.470	.800	+22	0	2	0	O24L	0	-0.1
1955	†NY A	55	85	17	29	4	2	3	22	7	0	3	16	.341	.411	.541	.952	+57	4	0	100	O20(13/7/1)	0	0.6
1956	†NY A	54	115	16	35	5	6	3	25	18	0	0	13	.304	.396	.530	.926	+48	0	1	0	O44(29/16/1)	0	0.7
1957	KC A	124	345	35	94	11	2	11	44	20	1	1	57	.272	.312	.420	.732	-3	1	1	50	O89(40/35/22)	0	-1.0
1958	KC A★	141	515	93	157	20	7	38	104	50	10	5	82	.305	.371	.592	.963	+58	3	3	50	O136L	0	4.4
1959	KC A	125	463	61	132	22	4	20	87	35	5	3	87	.285	.332	.479	.811	+20	3	2	60	O119L	0	0.7
1960	KC A	23	78	14	20	1	1	6	12	10	1	0	17	.256	.337	.526	.863	+30	0	0	0	O21L	0	0.4
1960	†NY A	87	216	32	54	11	1	8	28	30	2	3	36	.250	.349	.421	.770	+14	0	0	0	O51(50/1/1),1b3	0	0.6

Batters

YEAR	TM LG	G	AB	R	H	2B	3B	HR	RBI	BB	IB	HP	SO	AVG	OBP	SLG	OPS	AOPS	SB	CS	SB%	GAMES AT POSITION	DL	BFW
1960	Year	110	294	46	74	12	2	14	40	40	3	3	53	.252	.346	.449	.795	+19	0	0	0	O72(71/1/1),1b3	0	1.0
1961	LA A	18	57	3	9	3	0	2	6	1	0	0	8	.158	.169	.316	.485	-75	0	0	0	O15L	0	-1.0
1961	NY A	57	118	17	32	5	1	6	20	12	0	1	17	.271	.344	.483	.827	+25	1	0	100	O30(28/2/0),1b3	0	0.5
1961	Year	75	175	20	41	8	1	8	26	13	0	1	25	.234	.289	.429	.718	-9	1	0	100	O45(43/2/0),1b3	0	-0.5
1962	NY A	14	17	1	2	1	0	0	0	2	0	1	3	.118	.250	.176	.426	-82	0	0	0	O3(1/0/2)	0	-0.2
1962	Hou N	19	31	2	7	0	0	2	3	2	0	0	10	.226	.273	.419	.692	-11	0	0	0	O6L	0	-0.2
1962	Major	33	48	3	9	1	0	2	3	4	0	1	13	.188	.264	.333	.597	-69	0	0	0	—	0	-0.4
Total	12	829	2261	320	624	96	26	105	374	212	19	17	392	.276	.340	.481	.821	+22	12	10	55	O594(497/72/36),1b6	0	4.7
Team	9	379	772	112	205	36	12	26	118	94	2	8	131	.266	.350	.444	.794	+18	5	4	56	O208(61/18/27),1b6	0	1.4
/150	4	150	306	44	81	14	5	10	47	37	1	3	52	.266	.350	.444	.794	+18	2	2	50	O82(24/7/11),1b2	0	0.6

Chambliss, Chris Carroll Christopher B12.26.1948 Dayton OH BL/TR/6'1"/(195–225) Dr 1970 CleA*1/1 d5.28 NG 1972 C12 Col UCLA

YEAR	TM LG	G	AB	R	H	2B	3B	HR	RBI	BB	IB	HP	SO	AVG	OBP	SLG	OPS	AOPS	SB	CS	SB%	GAMES AT POSITION	DL	BFW
1971	Cle A	111	415	49	114	20	4	9	48	40	1	2	83	.275	.341	.407	.748	+2	2	0	100	1b108	0	-1.4
1972	Cle A	121	466	51	136	27	2	6	44	26	2	0	63	.292	.327	.397	.724	+11	3	4	43	1b119	0	-1.4
1973	Cle A	155	572	70	156	30	2	11	53	58	8	3	76	.273	.342	.390	.732	+4	4	8	33	1b154	0	-0.7
1974	Cle A	17	67	8	22	4	0	0	7	5	1	0	5	.328	.375	.388	.763	+21	0	1	0	1b17	0	-0.3
1974	NY A	110	400	38	97	16	3	6	43	23	1	0	43	.243	.282	.343	.625	-20	0	0	0	1b106	0	-1.5
1974	Year	127	467	46	119	20	3	6	50	28	2	0	48	.255	.296	.349	.645	-14	0	1	0	1b123	0	-1.8
1975	NY A	150	562	66	171	38	4	9	72	29	9	1	50	.304	.336	.434	.770	+18	0	1	0	1b147	0	0.4
1976	†NY A★	156	641	79	188	32	6	17	96	27	1	3	80	.293	.323	.441	.764	+24	1	0	100	1b155/D	0	0.1
1977	†NY A	157	600	90	172	32	6	17	90	45	5	2	73	.287	.336	.445	.781	+12	4	0	100	1b157	0	-0.3
1978	†NY A	162	625	81	171	26	3	12	90	41	3	5	60	.274	.321	.382	.703	-1	2	1	67	1b155,D7	0	-0.7
1979	NY A	149	554	61	155	27	3	18	63	34	4	5	53	.280	.324	.437	.761	+6	3	2	60	1b134,D16	0	-0.3
1980	Atl N	158	602	83	170	37	2	18	72	49	6	4	73	.282	.338	.440	.778	+15	7	3	70	1b158	0	0.1
1981	Atl N	**107**	404	44	110	25	2	8	51	44	10	1	41	.272	.343	.403	.746	+12	4	1	80	1b107	0	0.7
1982	†Atl N	157	534	57	144	25	2	20	86	57	13	0	57	.270	.337	.436	.773	+13	7	3	70	1b151	0	1.2
1983	Atl N	131	447	59	125	24	3	20	78	63	15	0	68	.280	.366	.481	.847	+25	2	7	22	1b126	15	0.7
1984	Atl N	135	389	47	100	14	0	9	44	58	12	1	54	.257	.350	.362	.712	-5	1	2	33	1b109	0	-0.9
1985	Atl N	101	170	16	40	7	0	3	21	18	4	0	22	.235	.307	.329	.636	-26	0	0	0	1b39	0	-0.7
1986	Atl N	97	122	13	38	8	0	2	14	15	4	0	24	.311	.384	.426	.810	+19	0	2	0	1b20	0	0.0
1988	NY A	1	1	0	0	0	0	0	0	0	0	0	1	.000	.000	.000	.000	-199	0	0	0	/H	0	0.0
Total	17	2175	7571	912	2109	392	42	185	972	632	99	27	926	.279	.334	.415	.749	+8	40	35	53	1b1962,D24	15	-5.0
Team	7	885	3383	415	954	171	25	79	454	199	23	16	360	.282	.322	.417	.739	+8	10	4	71	1b854,D24	0	-2.3
/150	1	150	573	70	162	29	4	13	77	34	4	3	61	.282	.322	.417	.739	+8	2	1	67	1b145,D4	0	-0.4

Chance, Frank Frank Leroy "Husk","The Peerless Leader" B9.9.1876 Fresno CA D9.15.1924 Los Angeles CA BR/TR/6'0"/190 d4.29 M11 HF1946

YEAR	TM LG	G	AB	R	H	2B	3B	HR	RBI	BB	IB	HP	SO	AVG	OBP	SLG	OPS	AOPS	SB	CS	SB%	GAMES AT POSITION	DL	BFW
1913	NY A	12	24	3	5	0	0	0	6	8	—	0	1	.208	.406	.208	.614	-19	1	—	—	1b7,M	—	0.0
1914	NY A	1	0	0	0	0	0	0	0	0	—	0	0	+	+	+	.000	-100	0	—	—	/1bM	—	0.0
Total	17	1288	4299	798	1274	200	79	20	596	556	—	137	29	.296	.394	.394	.788	+35	403	—	—	1b997,C187,O73(6/2/65)	—	22.6
Team	2	13	24	3	5	0	0	0	6	8	—	0	1	.208	.406	.208	.614	-19	1	—	—	1b7,M2	—	0.0

Channell, Les Lester Clark "Goat","Gint" B3.3.1886 Crestline OH D5.8.1954 Denver CO BL/TL/6'0"/180 d5.11

YEAR	TM LG	G	AB	R	H	2B	3B	HR	RBI	BB	IB	HP	SO	AVG	OBP	SLG	OPS	AOPS	SB	CS	SB%	GAMES AT POSITION	DL	BFW
1910	NY A	6	19	3	6	0	0	0	3	2	—	0	—	.316	.381	.316	.697	+12	2	—	—	O6L	—	0.0
1914	NY A	1	1	0	1	1	0	0	0	0	—	0	0	1.000	1.000	2.000	3.000	+703	0	—	—	/H	—	0.1
Total	2	7	20	3	7	1	0	0	3	2	—	0	0	.350	.409	.400	.809	+45	2	—	—	O6L	—	0.1

Chapman, Ben William Benjamin B12.25.1908 Nashville TN D7.7.1993 Hoover AL BR/TR/6'0"/190 d4.15 M4/C1 OF(404/583/541) ▲

YEAR	TM LG	G	AB	R	H	2B	3B	HR	RBI	BB	IB	HP	SO	AVG	OBP	SLG	OPS	AOPS	SB	CS	SB%	GAMES AT POSITION	DL	BFW
1930	NY A	138	513	74	162	31	10	10	81	43	—	2	58	.316	.371	.474	.845	+18	14	6	70	3b91,2b45	—	1.1
1931	NY A	149	600	120	189	28	11	17	122	75	—	5	77	.315	.396	.483	.879	+38	**61**	23	73	O137(90/0/50),2b11	—	3.4
1932	†NY A	151	581	101	174	41	15	10	107	71	—	5	55	.299	.381	.473	.854	+26	**38**	18	68	O150(81/0/86)	—	1.9
1933	NY A★	147	565	112	176	36	4	9	98	72	—	4	45	.312	.393	.437	.830	+27	**27**	18	60	O147(76/0/77)	—	2.9
1934	NY A★	149	588	82	181	21	**13**	5	86	67	—	3	68	.308	.381	.413	.794	+13	26	16	62	O149(41/87/23)	—	0.9
1935	NY A★	140	553	118	160	38	8	8	74	61	—	1	39	.289	.361	.430	.791	+10	17	10	63	O138C	—	1.7
1936	NY A	36	139	19	37	14	3	1	21	15	—	0	20	.266	.338	.432	.770	-8	1	2	33	O36C	—	-0.2
1936	Was A★	97	401	91	133	36	7	4	60	69	—	1	18	.332	.431	.486	.917	+33	19	7	73	O97C	—	2.1
1936	Year	133	540	110	170	50	10	5	81	84	—	1	38	.315	.408	.472	.880	+23	20	9	69	O133C	—	1.9
1937	Was A	35	130	23	34	7	1	0	12	26	—	0	7	.262	.385	.331	.716	-14	8	0	100	O32C	—	-0.2
1937	Bos A	113	423	76	130	23	11	7	57	57	—	1	35	.307	.391	.463	.854	+10	27	12	69	O112(2/10/100)/S	—	0.6
1937	Year	148	553	99	164	30	12	7	69	83	—	1	42	.297	.389	.432	.821	+5	**35**	12	74	O144(2/42/100)/S	—	0.4
1938	Bos A	127	480	92	163	40	8	6	80	65	—	0	33	.340	.418	.494	.912	+22	13	6	68	O126(1/0/125)/3b	—	1.6
1939	Cle A	149	545	101	158	31	9	6	82	87	—	2	30	.290	.390	.413	.803	+9	18	6	75	O146(2/137/9)	—	0.3
1940	Cle A	143	548	82	157	40	6	4	50	78	—	2	45	.286	.377	.403	.780	+5	13	7	65	O140(62/18/62)	—	0.2
1941	Was A	28	110	9	28	6	0	1	10	10	—	0	6	.255	.317	.336	.653	-24	2	2	50	O26L	0	-0.4
1941	Chi A	57	190	26	43	9	1	2	19	19	—	0	14	.226	.297	.316	.613	-37	2	2	50	O49(21/22/7)	0	-1.2
1941	Year	85	300	35	71	15	1	3	29	29	—	0	20	.237	.304	.323	.627	-32	4	4	50	O75(47/22/7)	0	-1.6
1944	Bro N	20	38	11	14	4	0	0	11	5	—	0	4	.368	.442	.474	.916	+61	1	—	—	P11	0	0.0
1945	Bro N	13	22	2	3	0	0	0	3	2	—	0	1	.136	.208	.136	.344	-103	0	—	—	P10	0	0.0
1945	Phi N	24	51	4	16	2	0	0	4	2	—	0	1	.314	.340	.353	.693	-5	0	—	—	O10(2/6/2),3b4,P3,M	0	-0.2
1945	Year	37	73	6	19	2	0	0	7	4	—	0	2	.260	.299	.288	.587	-35	0	—	—	P13,O10(2/6/2),3b4	0	-0.2
1946	Phi N	1	1	1	0	0	0	0	0	0	—	0	0	.000	.000	.000	.000	-199	0	—	—	/PM	0	0.0
Total	15	1717	6478	1144	1958	407	107	90	977	824	—	26	556	.302	.383	.440	.823	+15	287	13	100	O1495C,3b96,2b56,P25/S	0	14.5
Team	7	910	3539	626	1079	209	64	60	589	404	—	20	362	.305	.379	.451	.830	+21	184	93	66	O757(288/87/215),3b91,2b56	—	11.7
/150	1	150	583	103	178	34	11	10	97	67	—	3	60	.305	.379	.451	.830	+21	30	15	67	O125(47/14/35),3b15,2b9	—	1.9

Chartak, Mike Michael George "Shotgun" B4.28.1916 Brooklyn NY D7.25.1967 Cedar Rapids IA BL/TL/6'2"/180 d9.13

YEAR	TM LG	G	AB	R	H	2B	3B	HR	RBI	BB	IB	HP	SO	AVG	OBP	SLG	OPS	AOPS	SB	CS	SB%	GAMES AT POSITION	DL	BFW
1940	NY A	11	15	2	2	1	0	0	3	5	—	0	5	.133	.350	.200	.550	-51	0	0	0	O3R	—	-0.1
1942	NY A	5	5	0	0	0	0	0	0	0	—	0	0	.000	.000	.000	.000	-199	0	0	0	/H	0	-0.1
Total	4	256	765	96	186	34	7	21	98	104	—	4	112	.243	.337	.388	.725	+5	4	7	36	O175(4/0/171),1b30	0	-0.3
Team	2	16	20	2	2	1	0	0	3	5	—	0	5	.100	.280	.150	.430	-81	0	0	0	O3R	0	-0.2

Chase, Hal Harold Homer "Prince Hal" B2.13.1883 Los Gatos CA D5.18.1947 Colusa CA BR/TL/6'0"/175 d4.14 M2 Col Santa Clara OF(23/26/1)

YEAR	TM LG	G	AB	R	H	2B	3B	HR	RBI	BB	IB	HP	SO	AVG	OBP	SLG	OPS	AOPS	SB	CS	SB%	GAMES AT POSITION	DL	BFW
1905	NY A	128	465	60	116	16	6	3	49	15	—	3	—	.249	.277	.329	.606	-17	22	—	—	1b124,S2/2b	—	-2.4
1906	NY A	151	597	84	193	23	10	0	76	13	—	3	—	.323	.341	.395	.736	+18	28	—	—	1b150/2b	—	0.6
1907	NY A	125	498	72	143	23	3	2	68	19	—	1	—	.287	.315	.357	.672	+6	32	—	—	1b121,O4L	—	0.0
1908	NY A	106	405	50	104	11	3	1	36	15	—	1	—	.257	.285	.306	.591	-9	27	—	—	1b98,2b3,O3L/3bP	—	-1.2
1909	NY A	118	474	60	134	17	3	4	63	20	—	4	—	.283	.317	.357	.674	+12	25	—	—	1b118/S	—	0.1
1910	NY A	130	524	67	152	20	5	3	73	16	—	1	—	.290	.312	.365	.677	+6	40	—	—	1b130,M	—	-0.6
1911	NY A	133	527	82	166	32	7	3	62	21	—	1	—	.315	.342	.419	.761	+5	36	—	—	1b124,O7C,2b2,M	—	-0.3
1912	NY A	131	522	61	143	21	9	4	58	17	—	2	—	.274	.299	.372	.671	-14	33	22	60	1b122,2b7	—	-1.7
1913	NY A	39	146	15	31	2	4	0	9	11	—	0	13	.212	.268	.281	.549	-40	5	—	—	1b29,2b5,O5C	—	-1.4
1913	Chi A	102	384	49	110	11	10	2	39	16	—	3	41	.286	.320	.383	.703	+7	9	—	—	1b102	—	-0.1
1913	Year	141	530	64	141	13	14	2	48	27	—	3	54	.266	.305	.355	.660	-6	14	—	—	1b131,2b5,O5C	—	-1.5
1914	Chi A	58	206	27	55	10	5	0	20	23	—	1	19	.267	.343	.364	.707	+14	9	4	69	1b58	—	0.5
1914	Buf F	75	291	43	101	19	9	3	48	6	—	2	31	.347	.365	.505	.870	+33	10	—	—	1b73	—	0.5
1914	Major	133	497	70	156	29	14	3	68	29	0	3	50	.314	.355	.447	.802	+167	19	4	—	—	—	1.0
1915	Buf F	145	567	85	165	31	10	**17**	89	20	—	1	50	.291	.316	.471	.787	+18	23	—	—	1b143/rf	—	-0.3
1916	Cin N	142	542	66	**184**	29	12	4	82	19	—	1	48	**.339**	.363	.459	.822	+55	22	11	67	1b98,O25(14/14/0),2b16	—	2.8
1917	Cin N	152	602	71	167	28	15	4	86	15	—	1	49	.277	.296	.394	.690	+15	21	—	—	1b151	—	0.0
1918	Cin N	74	259	30	78	12	6	2	38	13	—	2	15	.301	.339	.417	.756	+33	5	—	—	1b67,O2L	—	0.6
1919	NY N	110	408	58	116	17	7	5	45	17	—	3	40	.284	.318	.397	.715	+15	16	—	—	1b107	—	0.2

YEAR	TM LG	G	AB	R	H	2B	3B	HR	RBI	BB	IB	HP	SO	AVG	OBP	SLG	OPS	AOPS	SB	CS	SB%	GAMES AT POSITION	DL	BFW
Total	15	1919	7417	980	2158	322	124	57	941	276	—	30	306	.291	.319	.391	.710	+10	363	37	100	1b1815,O47C,2b35,S3/P3b	—	-2.7
Team	9	1061	4158	551	1182	165	50	20	494	147	—	16	13	.284	.311	.362	.673	+0	248	22	100	1b1016,2b19,O19(7/12/0),S3,M2/P3	—	-6.9
/150	1	150	588	78	167	23	7	3	70	21	—	2	2	.284	.311	.362	.673	+0	35	3	100	1b144,2b3,O3(1/2/0)/SMP3	—	-1.0
CLARK, ALLIE	ALFRED ALOYSIUS B6.16.1923 S.AMBOY NJ BR/TR/5'11"/185 D8.5																							
1947	†NY A	24	67	9	25	5	0	1	14	5	—	0	2	.373	.417	.493	.910	+54	0	0	0	O16(6/0/10)	0	0.4
Total	7	358	1021	131	267	48	4	32	149	72	—	3	70	.262	.312	.410	.722	-8	2	5	29	O242(62/3/178),3b15,1b5	0	-3.5
CLARK, TONY	ANTHONY CHRISTOPHER B6.15.1972 NEWTON KS BB/TR/6'7"/(205–250) DR 1990 DETA 1/2 D9.3																							
2004	†NY A	106	253	37	56	12	0	16	49	26	3	2	92	.221	.297	.458	.755	-7	0	0	0	1b99/D	0	-0.9
Total	13	1415	4315	610	1142	224	11	244	789	485	54	20	1130	.265	.339	.491	.830	+12	6	9	40	1b1164,D92/lf	144	-3.0
/150	1	150	358	52	79	17	0	23	69	37	4	3	130	.221	.297	.458	.755	-7	0	0	0	1b140/D	0	-1.3
CLARK, JACK	JACK ANTHONY B11.10.1955 NEW BRIGHTON PA BR/TR/6'2"/(170–210) DR 1973 SFN 13/294 D9.12 C3 OF(11/23/1014)																							
1988	NY A	150	496	81	120	14	0	27	93	113	6	2	141	.242	.381	.433	.814	+29	3	2	60	D112,O19(5/0/14),1b10	11	1.9
Total	18	1994	6847	1118	1826	332	39	340	1180	1262	12	24	1441	.267	.379	.476	.855	+37	77	61	56	O1039R,1b580,D311,3b4	246	29.6
/150	1	150	496	81	120	14	0	27	93	113	6	2	141	.242	.381	.433	.814	+29	3	2	60	D112,O19(5/0/14),1b10	11	1.9
CLARKE, HORACE	HORACE MEREDITH B6.2.1940 FREDERIKSTED, V.I. BB/TR/5'9"/(170–182) D5.13																							
1965	NY A	51	108	13	28	1	0	1	9	6	0	0	6	.259	.296	.296	.592	-30	2	1	67	3b17,2b7/S	0	-0.3
1966	NY A	96	312	37	83	10	4	6	28	27	4	1	24	.266	.324	.381	.705	+7	5	3	63	S63,2b16,3b4	0	-0.2
1967	NY A	143	588	74	160	17	0	3	29	42	2	0	64	.272	.321	.316	.637	-8	21	4	84	2b140	0	2.8
1968	NY A	148	579	52	133	6	1	2	26	23	0	0	46	.230	.258	.254	.512	-42	20	7	74	2b139	0	1.3
1969	NY A	156	641	82	183	26	7	4	48	53	1	0	41	.285	.339	.367	.706	+1	33	13	72	2b156	0	1.6
1970	NY A	158	686	81	172	24	2	4	46	35	5	2	35	.251	.286	.309	.595	-32	23	7	77	2b157	0	-2.7
1971	NY A	159	625	76	156	23	7	2	41	64	2	2	43	.250	.321	.318	.639	-14	17	7	71	2b156	0	-0.3
1972	NY A	147	547	65	132	20	2	3	37	56	4	4	44	.241	.315	.302	.617	-14	18	6	75	2b143	0	2.0
1973	NY A	148	590	60	155	21	0	2	35	47	0	2	48	.263	.317	.308	.625	-21	11	10	52	2b147	0	0.9
1974	NY A	24	47	3	11	1	0	0	1	4	0	0	5	.234	.294	.255	.549	-40	1	0	100	2b20/D	0	-0.3
1974	SD N	42	90	5	17	1	0	0	4	8	0	0	6	.189	.255	.200	.455	-70	0	0	0	2b21	0	-0.8
1974	Major	66	137	8	28	2	0	0	5	12	0	0	11	.204	.268	.219	.487	-33	1	0	100	—	0	-1.1
Total	10	1272	4813	548	1230	150	23	27	304	365	18	11	362	.256	.308	.313	.621	-18	151	58	72	2b1102,S64,3b21/D	0	4.0
Team	10	1230	4723	543	1213	149	23	27	300	357	18	11	356	.257	.309	.315	.624	-17	151	58	72	2b1081,S64,3b21/D	0	4.8
/150	1	150	576	66	148	18	3	3	37	44	2	1	43	.257	.309	.315	.624	-17	18	7	72	2b132,S8,3b3/D	0	0.6
CLINTON, LOU	LUCIEAN LOUIS B10.13.1937 PONCA CITY OK D12.6.1997 WICHITA KS BR/TR/6'1"/(185–195) D4.22																							
1966	NY A	80	159	18	35	10	2	5	21	16	1	0	27	.220	.288	.403	.691	+1	0	0	0	O63(5/1/57)	0	-0.4
1967	NY A	6	4	1	2	1	0	0	2	1	1	0	1	.500	.600	.750	1.350	+208	0	0	0	/lf	0	0.1
Total	8	691	2153	270	532	112	31	65	269	188	14	7	418	.247	.308	.418	.726	-1	12	7	63	O619(16/2/603)	0	-2.7
Team	2	86	163	19	37	11	2	5	23	17	2	0	28	.227	.297	.411	.708	+7	0	0	0	O64(5/1/57)	0	-0.3
COCKMAN, JIM	JAMES B4.26.1873 GUELPH ON, CAN. D9.28.1947 GUELPH ON, CAN. BR/TR/5'6"/145 D9.28																							
1905	NY A	13	38	5	4	0	0	0	2	4	—	0	—	.105	.190	.105	.295	-105	2	—	—	3b13	—	-0.6
COGGINS, RICH	RICHARD ALLEN B12.7.1950 INDIANAPOLIS IN BL/TL/5'8"/170 DR 1968 BALA 21/475 D8.29																							
1975	NY A	51	107	7	24	1	0	1	6	7	0	0	16	.224	.272	.262	.534	-48	3	3	50	O36(3/25/8),D9	0	-0.7
1976	NY A	7	4	1	1	0	0	0	1	0	0	0	1	.250	.250	.250	.500	-53	1	0	100	O2(0/1/1)/D	0	0.0
Total	5	342	1083	125	287	42	13	12	90	72	5	5	100	.265	.312	.361	.673	-7	50	21	70	O293(20/106/203),D11	45	-2.4
Team	2	58	111	8	25	1	0	1	7	7	0	0	17	.225	.271	.261	.532	-48	4	3	57	O38(3/26/9),D10	0	-0.7
COLAVITO, ROCKY	ROCCO DOMENICO B8.10.1933 NEW YORK NY BR/TR/6'3"/(183–199) D9.10 C6																							
1968	NY A	39	91	13	20	2	2	5	13	14	0	1	17	.220	.330	.451	.781	+39	0	0	0	O28(6/0/22)/P	0	-0.2
Total	14	1841	6503	971	1730	283	21	374	1159	951	58	29	880	.266	.359	.489	.848	+32	19	27	41	O1774(524/0/1285),1b11,P2	0	22.3
COLEMAN, CURT	CURTIS HANCOCK B2.18.1887 SALEM OR D7.1.1980 NEWPORT OR BL/TR/5'11"/180 D4.13 COL OREGON																							
1912	NY A	12	37	8	9	4	0	0	4	7	—	0	—	.243	.364	.351	.715	-1	0	2	0	3b10	—	0.0
COLEMAN, JERRY	GERALD FRANCIS B9.14.1924 SAN JOSE CA BR/TR/6'0"/(167–170) D4.20 MIL 1952–53 M1																							
1949	†NY A	128	447	54	123	21	5	2	42	63	—	2	44	.275	.367	.358	.725	-8	8	6	57	2b122,S4	0	0.7
1950	†NY A★	153	522	69	150	19	6	6	69	67	—	3	38	.287	.372	.381	.753	-4	3	2	60	2b152,S6	0	-0.6
1951	†NY A	121	362	48	90	11	2	3	43	31	—	4	36	.249	.315	.315	.630	-27	6	1	86	2b102,S18	0	-0.2
1952	NY A	11	42	6	17	2	1	0	4	5	—	0	4	.405	.468	.500	.968	+80	0	1	0	2b11	0	0.7
1953	NY A	8	10	1	2	0	0	0	0	0	—	0	2	.200	.200	.200	.400	-91	0	0	0	2b7/S	0	0.0
1954	NY A	107	300	39	65	7	1	3	21	26	—	0	29	.217	.278	.277	.555	-46	3	0	100	2b79,S30/3b	0	0.2
1955	†NY A	43	96	12	22	5	0	0	8	11	0	2	11	.229	.321	.281	.602	-36	0	2	0	S29,2b13/3b	88	-0.4
1956	†NY A	80	183	15	47	5	1	0	18	12	2	1	33	.257	.305	.295	.600	-39	1	2	33	2b41,S24,3b18	0	0.1
1957	†NY A	72	157	23	42	7	2	2	12	20	0	1	21	.268	.354	.376	.730	+1	1	1	50	2b45,3b21,S4	0	0.1
Total	9	723	2119	267	558	77	18	16	217	235	2	13	218	.263	.340	.339	.679	-17	22	15	59	2b572,S116,3b41	88	0.6
/150	2	150	440	55	116	16	4	3	45	49	0	3	45	.263	.340	.339	.679	-17	5	3	63	2b119,S24,3b9	18	0.1
COLEMAN, MICHAEL	MICHAEL DONNELL B8.16.1975 NASHVILLE TN BR/TR/5'11"/(180–225) DR 1994 BOSA 18/495 D9.1 [DL 2000 BOS A 96, 2002 BOS A 25]																							
1997	Bos A	8	24	2	4	1	0	0	2	0	0	0	11	.167	.167	.208	.375	-103	1	0	100	O7C	0	-0.4
1999	Bos A	2	5	1	1	0	0	0	0	1	0	0	0	.200	.333	.200	.533	-61	0	0	0	O2(1/1/0)	0	-0.1
2001	NY A	12	38	5	8	0	0	1	7	0	0	0	15	.211	.205	.289	.494	-70	0	1	0	O9(1/7/3),D3	0	-0.6
Total	3	22	67	8	13	1	0	1	9	1	0	0	26	.194	.203	.254	.457	-81	1	1	50	O18(2/15/3),D3	121	-1.1
COLLINS, DAVE	DAVID S B10.20.1952 RAPID CITY SD BB/TL/5'11"/(170–175) DR 1972 CALA S1/6 D6.7 C9 COL MESA (AZ) CC																							
1982	NY A	111	348	41	88	12	3	3	25	28	3	5	49	.253	.315	.330	.645	-21	13	8	62	O60(20/20/25),1b52/D	0	-1.5
Total	16	1701	4907	667	1335	187	52	32	373	467	16	38	660	.272	.338	.351	.689	-7	395	139	74	O1118(716/204/220),1b125,D104	18	-3.5
/150	1	150	470	55	119	16	4	4	34	38	4	7	66	.253	.315	.330	.645	-21	18	11	62	O81(27/27/34),1b70/D	0	-2.0
COLLINS, JOE	JOSEPH EDWARD (B JOSEPH EDWARD KOLLONIGE) B12.3.1922 SCRANTON PA D8.30.1989 UNION NJ BL/TL/6'0"/(185–192) D9.25																							
1948	NY A	5	5	0	1	1	0	0	2	0	—	0	1	.200	.200	.400	.600	-42	0	0	0	/H	0	0.0
1949	NY A	7	10	2	1	0	0	0	4	6	—	0	2	.100	.438	.100	.538	-54	0	0	0	1b5	0	-0.1
1950	†NY A	108	205	47	48	8	3	8	28	31	—	0	34	.234	.335	.420	.755	-5	5	0	100	1b99,O2R	0	-0.3
1951	†NY A	125	262	52	75	8	5	9	48	34	—	0	23	.286	.368	.458	.826	+27	9	7	56	1b114,O15R	0	1.1
1952	†NY A	122	428	69	120	16	8	18	59	55	—	1	47	.280	.364	.481	.845	+42	4	2	67	1b119	0	1.7
1953	†NY A	127	387	72	104	11	2	17	44	59	—	0	36	.269	.365	.439	.804	+21	2	6	25	1b113,O4R	0	0.5
1954	NY A	130	343	67	93	20	2	12	46	51	—	0	37	.271	.365	.446	.811	+26	2	2	50	1b117	0	1.0
1955	†NY A	105	278	40	65	9	1	13	45	44	2	2	32	.234	.339	.414	.753	+4	0	2	0	1b73,O27R	0	0.4
1956	†NY A	100	262	38	59	5	3	7	43	34	2	1	33	.225	.313	.347	.660	-22	3	1	75	O51(25/7/24),1b43	0	-0.7
1957	†NY A	79	149	17	30	1	0	2	10	24	2	0	18	.201	.310	.248	.558	-44	2	1	67	1b32,O15(2/2/11)	0	-1.1
Total	10	908	2329	404	596	79	24	86	329	338	6	4	263	.256	.350	.421	.771	+12	27	21	56	1b715,O114(27/9/83)	0	2.5
/150	2	150	385	67	98	13	4	14	54	56	0	1	43	.256	.350	.421	.771	+12	4	3	57	1b118,O10(4/1/14)	0	0.4
COLLINS, ORTH	ORTH STEIN "BUCK" B4.27.1880 LAFAYETTE IN D12.13.1949 FT.LAUDERDALE FL BL/TR/6'0"/150 D6.1																							
1904	NY A	5	17	3	6	1	1	0	1	1	—	0	—	.353	.389	.529	.918	+80	0	—	—	O5(0/5/1)	—	0.4
1909	Was A	8	7	0	0	0	0	0	0	0	—	0	—	.000	.000	.000	.000	-199	0	—	—	O2(0/1/1)/P	—	-0.2
Total	2	13	24	3	6	1	1	0	1	1	—	0	—	.250	.280	.375	.655	+4	0	—	—	O7(0/6/2)/P	—	0.2

Batters

YEAR	TM LG	G	AB	R	H	2B	3B	HR	RBI	BB	IB	HP	SO	AVG	OBP	SLG	OPS	AOPS	SB	CS	SB%	GAMES AT POSITION	DL	BFW
Collins, Rip	Robert Joseph B9.18.1909 Pittsburgh PA D4.19.1969 Pittsburgh PA BR/TR/5'11"/176 d4.28																							
1944	NY A	3	3	0	1	0	0	0	0	1	—	0	0	.333	.500	.333	.833	+36	0	0	0	C3	0	0.1
Total	2	50	123	11	26	3	0	1	14	15	—	1	18	.211	.302	.260	.562	-42	4	0	100	C45	0	-0.7
Collins, Pat	Tharon Leslie B9.13.1896 Sweet Sprgs. MO D5.20.1960 Kansas City KS BR/TR/5'9"/178 d9.5																							
1919	StL A	11	21	2	3	1	0	0	1	4	—	0	2	.143	.280	.190	.470	-68	0	—	—	C5	—	-0.2
1920	StL A	23	28	5	6	1	0	0	6	3	—	0	5	.214	.290	.250	.540	-57	0	0	0	C7	—	-0.3
1921	StL A	58	111	9	27	3	0	1	10	16	—	0	17	.243	.339	.297	.636	-40	1	0	100	C31	—	-0.5
1922	StL A	63	127	14	39	6	0	8	23	21	—	0	21	.307	.405	.543	.948	+40	0	1	0	C28,1b5	—	1.2
1923	StL A	85	181	9	32	8	0	3	30	15	—	0	45	.177	.240	.271	.511	-68	0	0	0	C47	—	-1.6
1924	StL A	32	54	9	17	2	0	1	11	11	—	0	14	.315	.431	.407	.838	+10	0	1	0	C20	—	0.1
1926	†NY A	102	290	41	83	11	3	7	35	73	—	2	57	.286	.433	.417	.850	+24	3	2	60	C100	—	2.2
1927	†NY A	92	251	38	69	9	3	7	36	54	—	2	24	.275	.407	.418	.825	+18	0	1	0	C89	—	1.1
1928	†NY A	70	136	18	30	5	0	6	14	35	—	0	16	.221	.380	.390	.770	+6	0	0	0	C70	—	0.2
1929	Bos N	7	5	1	0	0	0	0	2	3	—	0	1	.000	.375	.000	.375	-98	0	—	—	C6	—	0.0
Total	10	543	1204	146	306	46	6	33	168	235	—	4	202	.254	.378	.385	.763	-2	4	5	100	C403,1b5	—	2.2
Team	3	264	677	97	182	25	6	20	85	162	—	4	97	.269	.413	.412	.825	+18	3	3	50	C259	—	3.5
/150	2	150	385	55	103	14	3	11	48	92	—	2	55	.269	.413	.412	.825	+18	2	2	50	C147	—	2.0
Colman, Frank	Frank Lloyd B3.2.1918 London ON, Can. D2.19.1983 London ON, Can. BL/TL/5'11"/188 d9.12																							
1946	NY A	5	15	2	4	0	0	1	5	1	—	0	1	.267	.313	.467	.780	+14	0	0	0	O5R	0	0.0
1947	NY A	22	28	2	3	0	0	2	6	2	—	0	6	.107	.167	.321	.488	-66	0	0	0	O6L	0	-0.3
Total	6	271	571	66	130	25	8	15	106	49	—	2	66	.228	.291	.378	.669	-15	0	0	0	O103(19/0/83),1b30	0	-2.1
Team	2	27	43	4	7	0	0	3	11	3	—	0	7	.163	.217	.372	.589	-38	0	0	0	O11(6/0/5)	0	-0.3
Combs, Earle	Earle Bryan "The Kentucky Colonel" B5.14.1899 Pebworth KY D7.21.1976 Richmond KY BL/TR/6'0"/185 d4.16 C16 HF1970 Col Eastern Kentucky																							
1924	NY A	24	35	10	14	5	0	0	2	4	—	0	2	.400	.462	.543	1.005	+59	0	1	0	O11(5/3/3)	—	0.2
1925	NY A	150	593	117	203	36	13	3	61	65	—	4	43	.342	.411	.462	.873	+23	12	13	48	O150(12/138/0)	—	0.8
1926	†NY A	145	606	113	181	31	12	8	55	47	—	3	23	.299	.352	.429	.781	+5	8	6	57	O145C	—	-0.7
1927	†NY A	152	648	137	**231**	36	**23**	6	64	62	—	2	31	.356	.414	.511	.925	+43	15	6	71	O152C	—	2.8
1928	†NY A	149	626	118	194	33	**21**	7	56	77	—	2	33	.310	.387	.463	.850	+27	11	8	58	O149C	—	1.7
1929	NY A	142	586	119	202	33	15	3	65	69	—	0	32	.345	.414	.468	.882	+35	12	7	63	O141C	—	1.9
1930	NY A	137	532	129	183	30	**22**	7	82	74	—	0	26	.344	.424	.523	.947	+45	16	10	62	O135(60/45/30)	—	2.3
1931	NY A	138	563	120	179	31	13	5	58	68	—	3	34	.318	.394	.446	.840	+28	11	3	79	O129C	—	1.3
1932	†NY A	144	591	143	190	32	10	9	65	81	—	2	16	.321	.405	.455	.860	+29	3	9	25	O139(42/115/1)	—	1.1
1933	NY A	122	417	86	125	22	16	5	64	47	—	1	19	.300	.372	.465	.837	+28	6	4	60	O104(23/80/2)	—	0.7
1934	NY A	63	251	47	80	13	5	2	25	40	—	0	9	.319	.412	.434	.846	+27	3	1	75	O62(12/51/0)	—	0.7
1935	NY A	89	298	47	84	7	4	3	35	36	—	0	10	.282	.359	.362	.721	-8	1	3	25	O70(57/13/1)	—	-0.8
Total	12	1455	5746	1186	1866	309	154	58	632	670	—	17	278	.325	.397	.462	.859	+27	98	71	58	O1387(211/1161/37)	—	12.0
/150	1	150	592	122	192	32	16	6	65	69	—	2	29	.325	.397	.462	.859	+27	10	7	59	O14(22/120/4)	0	1.2
Connelly, Tom	Thomas Martin B10.20.1897 Chicago IL D2.18.1941 Hines IL BL/TR/5'11.5"/165 d9.24																							
1920	NY A	1	1	0	0	0	0	0	0	0	—	0	0	.000	.000	.000	.000	-197	0	0	0	/H	—	0.0
1921	NY A	4	5	0	1	0	0	0	0	1	—	0	0	.200	.333	.200	.533	-62	0	0	0	O3(0/1/2)	—	0.0
Total	2	5	6	0	1	0	0	0	0	1	—	0	0	.167	.286	.167	.453	-82	0	0	0	O3(0/1/2)	—	0.0
Connor, Joe	Joseph Francis B12.8.1874 Waterbury CT D11.8.1957 Waterbury CT BR/TR/6'2"/185 d9.9 b-Roger																							
1905	NY A	8	22	4	5	1	0	0	2	3	—	0	—	.227	.320	.273	.593	-21	1	—	—	C6,1b2	—	0.2
Total	4	92	271	29	54	7	2	1	22	18	—	3	2	.199	.257	.251	.508	-57	8	—	—	C75,O5(0/1/4),3b3,1b2/S2b	—	-1.4
Conroy, Wid	William Edward B4.5.1877 Philadelphia PA D12.6.1959 Mt.Holly NJ BR/TR/5'9"/158 d4.25 C1 OF(224/76/10)																							
1901	Mil A	131	503	74	129	20	6	5	64	36	—	8	—	.256	.316	.350	.666	-11	21	—	—	S118,3b12	—	1.3
1902	Pit N	99	365	55	89	10	6	1	47	24	—	5	—	.244	.299	.312	.611	-14	10	—	—	S95,O3(2/0/1)	—	0.4
1903	NY A	126	503	74	137	23	12	1	45	32	—	5	—	.272	.322	.372	.694	+1	33	—	—	3b123,S4	—	0.7
1904	NY A	140	489	58	119	18	12	1	52	43	—	7	—	.243	.314	.335	.649	+0	30	—	—	3b110,S27,O3C	—	1.2
1905	NY A	101	385	55	105	19	11	2	25	32	—	0	—	.273	.329	.395	.724	+16	25	—	—	3b48,O25(20/3/2),S17,1b10,2b3	—	0.7
1906	NY A	148	567	67	139	17	10	4	54	47	—	0	—	.245	.303	.332	.635	-11	32	—	—	O97(37/66/0),S49,3b2	—	-1.4
1907	NY A	140	530	58	124	12	11	3	51	30	—	3	—	.234	.279	.315	.594	-17	41	—	—	O100L,S38	—	-1.0
1908	NY A	141	531	44	126	22	3	1	39	14	—	1	—	.237	.258	.296	.554	-21	23	—	—	3b119,2b12,O10(5/1/4)	—	0.3
1909	Was A	139	488	44	119	13	4	1	20	37	—	1	—	.244	.298	.293	.591	-9	24	—	—	3b120,2b13,O5(2/3/0)/S	—	0.1
1910	Was A	103	351	36	89	11	3	1	27	30	—	1	—	.254	.314	.311	.625	+0	11	—	—	3b46,O46(44/0/2),2b5	—	0.0
1911	Was A	106	349	40	81	11	4	2	28	20	—	4	—	.232	.282	.304	.586	-36	12	—	—	3b85,O15(14/0/1)/2b	—	-0.9
Total	11	1374	5061	605	1257	176	82	22	452	345	—	35	—	.248	.301	.329	.630	-9	262	—	—	3b665,S349,O304L,2b34,1b10	—	1.4
Team	6	796	3005	356	750	111	59	12	266	198	—	16	0	.250	.300	.338	.638	-6	184	—	—	3b402,O235(20/70/66),S135,2b15,1b10	—	0.5
/150	1	150	566	67	141	21	11	2	50	37	—	3	0	.250	.300	.338	.638	-6	35	—	—	3b76,O44(4/13/12),S25,2b3,1b2	—	0.1
Cook, Doc	Luther Almus B6.24.1886 Whitt TX D6.30.1973 Lawrenceburg TN BL/TR/6'0"/170 d8.7 Col Vanderbilt																							
1913	NY A	20	72	9	19	2	1	0	1	10	—	2	4	.264	.369	.319	.688	+1	1	—	—	O20(0/13/7)	—	-0.1
1914	NY A	132	470	59	133	11	3	1	40	44	—	9	60	.283	.356	.326	.682	+5	26	32	45	O127(1/10/116)	—	-1.2
1915	NY A	132	476	70	129	16	5	2	33	62	—	8	43	.271	.364	.338	.702	+11	29	18	62	O131R	—	0.1
1916	NY A	4	10	0	1	0	0	0	1	0	—	0	2	.100	.100	.100	.200	-139	0	—	—	O3R	—	-0.2
Total	4	288	1028	138	282	29	9	3	75	116	—	19	109	.274	.359	.329	.688	+6	56	50	100	O281(1/23/257)	—	-1.4
/150	2	150	535	72	147	15	5	2	39	60	—	10	57	.274	.359	.329	.688	+6	29	0	100	O146(1/12/134)	0	-0.7
Cooke, Dusty	Allen Lindsey B6.23.1907 Swepsonville NC D11.21.1987 Raleigh NC BL/TR/6'1"/205 d4.15 M1/C5																							
1930	NY A	92	216	43	55	12	3	6	29	32	—	1	61	.255	.353	.421	.774	+0	4	6	40	O73(21/28/24)	—	-0.3
1931	NY A	27	39	10	13	1	0	1	6	8	—	0	11	.333	.447	.436	.883	+41	4	1	80	O11(7/0/6)	—	0.3
1932	NY A	3	0	1	0	0	0	0	0	1	—	0	0	+	1.000	+	1.000	+91	0	0	0	/H	—	0.0
Total	8	608	1745	324	489	109	28	24	229	290	—	5	276	.280	.384	.416	.800	+6	32	25	100	O470(161/148/199)	—	-0.7
Team	3	122	255	54	68	13	3	7	35	41	—	1	72	.267	.370	.424	.794	+7	8	7	53	O84(28/28/30)	—	0.0
/150	4	150	314	66	84	16	4	9	43	50	—	1	89	.267	.370	.424	.794	+7	10	9	53	O103(34/34/37)	—	0.0
Coomer, Ron	Ronald Bryan B11.18.1966 Crest Hill IL BR/TR/5'11"/(195–225) Dr 1987 OakA 14/355 d8.1 Col Taft (CA) JC																							
2002	†NY A	55	148	14	39	7	0	3	17	6	1	0	23	.264	.290	.372	.662	-25	0	0	0	3b26,D15,1b11	0	-1.1
Total	9	911	3019	333	827	151	8	92	449	177	14	9	429	.274	.313	.421	.734	-14	13	7	65	1b408,3b391,D63,O35R	48	-9.4
Cooney, Johnny	John Walter B3.18.1901 Cranston RI D7.8.1986 Sarasota FL BR/TL/5'10"/165 d4.19 M1/C21 f-Jimmy b-Jimmy ▲																							
1944	NY A	10	8	1	1	0	0	0	1	1	—	0	0	.125	.222	.125	.347	-99	0	0	0	O2L	0	-0.1
Total	20	1172	3372	408	965	130	26	2	219	208	—	6	107	.286	.329	.342	.671	-13	30	5	100	O794(37/633/133),P159,1b93	0	-6.1
Cooney, Phil	Philip Clarence (b Philip Clarence Cohen) B9.14.1882 New York NY D10.6.1957 New York NY BL/TR/5'8"/155 d9.27																							
1905	NY A	1	3	0	0	0	0	0	0	0	—	0	—	.000	.000	.000	.000	-190	0	—	—	/3b	—	-0.1
Costello, Dan	Daniel Francis "Dashing Dan" B9.9.1891 Jessup PA D3.26.1936 Pittsburgh PA BL/TR/6'0.5"/185 d7.2 Col Mount St. Marys																							
1913	NY A	2	2	1	1	0	0	0	0	0	—	0	0	.500	.500	.500	1.000	+92	0	—	—	/H	—	0.0
Total	4	154	350	35	85	6	4	0	24	21	—	0	62	.243	.286	.283	.569	-27	12	1	100	O83(38/13/32)/1b	—	-2.1

YEAR	TM LG	G	AB	R	H	2B	3B	HR	RBI	BB	IB	HP	SO	AVG	OBP	SLG	OPS	AOPS	SB	CS	SB%	GAMES AT POSITION	DL	BFW
Cotto, Henry	Henry B1.5.1961 New York NY BR/TR/6'2"/(178–180) d4.5																						
1985	NY A	34	56	4	17	1	0	1	6	3	0	0	12	.304	.339	.375	.714	-3	1	1	50	O30(14/20/1)	41	0.0
1986	NY A	35	80	11	17	3	0	1	6	2	0	0	17	.213	.229	.287	.516	-59	3	0	100	O29(11/19/0)/D	0	-0.6
1987	NY A	68	149	21	35	10	0	5	20	6	0	1	35	.235	.269	.403	.672	-25	4	2	67	O57(15/41/2)	0	-0.7
Total	10	884	2178	296	569	87	9	44	210	107	10	16	352	.261	.299	.370	.669	-17	130	26	83	O760(322/355/133),D32	106	-3.2
Team	3	137	285	36	69	14	0	7	32	11	0	1	64	.242	.272	.365	.637	-30	8	3	73	O116(40/80/3)/D	41	-1.3
/150	3	150	312	39	76	15	0	8	35	12	0	1	70	.242	.272	.365	.637	-30	9	3	75	O127(44/88/3)/D	45	-1.4
Courtney, Clint	Clinton Dawson "Scrap Iron" B3.16.1927 Hall Summit LA D6.16.1975 Rochester NY BL/TR/5'8"/180 d9.29 C1																						
1951	NY A	1	2	0	0	0	0	0	0	0	—	1	1	.000	.333	.000	.333	-105	0	0	0	/C	0	0.0
Total	11	946	2796	260	750	126	17	38	313	264	22	46	143	.268	.339	.366	.705	-6	3	16	16	C802	30	-3.3
Courtney, Ernie	Edward Ernest B1.20.1875 Des Moines IA D2.29.1920 Buffalo NY BL/TR/5'8"/168 d4.17 OF(40/1/6)																						
1903	NY A	25	79	7	21	3	3	1	8	7	—	2	—	.266	.341	.418	.759	+19	1	—	—	S19,2b4/1b	—	0.3
Total	6	558	1921	226	471	52	17	5	200	188	—	25	—	.245	.321	.298	.619	-9	35	—	—	3b362,1b75,O46L,S36,2b11	—	-5.3
Cowan, Billy	Billy Rolland B8.28.1938 Calhoun City MS BR/TR/6'0"/170 d9.9 Col Utah																						
1969	NY A	32	48	5	8	0	0	1	3	3	0	0	9	.167	.216	.229	.445	-75	0	0	0	O14(8/4/2)	0	-0.6
Total	8	493	1190	131	281	44	8	40	125	50	10	4	297	.236	.269	.387	.656	-17	17	8	68	O329(78/210/41),1b25,3b3,2b3/S	0	-6.5
Cox, Bobby	Robert Joseph B5.21.1941 Tulsa OK BR/TR/5'11"/(180–190) d4.14 M26/C1																						
1968	NY A	135	437	33	100	15	1	7	41	41	7	5	85	.229	.300	.316	.616	-10	3	2	60	3b132	0	-1.2
1969	NY A	85	191	17	41	7	1	2	17	34	7	1	41	.215	.332	.293	.625	-20	0	1	0	3b56,2b6	0	0.2
Total	2	220	628	50	141	22	2	9	58	75	14	6	126	.225	.310	.309	.619	-13	3	3	50	3b188,2b6	0	-1.0
/150	1	150	428	34	96	15	1	6	40	51	10	4	86	.225	.310	.309	.619	-13	2	2	50	3b128,2b4	0	-0.7
Cree, Birdie	William Franklin B10.23.1882 Khedive PA D11.8.1942 Sunbury PA BR/TR/5'6"/150 d9.17 Col Penn St.																						
1908	NY A	21	78	5	21	0	2	0	4	7	—	2	—	.269	.345	.321	.666	+15	1	—	—	O21C	—	0.2
1909	NY A	104	343	48	90	6	3	2	27	30	—	9	—	.262	.338	.315	.653	+5	10	—	—	O79(24/32/25),S6,2b4/3b	—	-0.1
1910	NY A	134	467	58	134	19	16	4	73	40	—	8	—	.287	.353	.422	.775	+35	28	—	—	O134(49/85/0)	—	0.4
1911	NY A	137	520	90	181	30	22	4	88	56	—	3	—	.348	.415	.513	.928	+49	48	—	—	O132(122/7/3),S4,2b2	—	2.4
1912	NY A	50	190	25	63	11	6	0	22	20	—	5	—	.332	.409	.453	.862	+38	12	19	39	O50L	—	0.7
1913	NY A	145	534	51	145	25	6	1	63	50	—	4	51	.272	.338	.346	.684	+0	22	—	—	O144L	—	-1.0
1914	NY A	77	275	45	85	18	5	0	40	30	—	6	24	.309	.389	.411	.800	+41	4	9	31	O76C	—	1.2
1915	NY A	74	196	23	42	8	2	0	15	36	—	6	22	.214	.353	.276	.629	-12	7	8	47	O53(0/37/16)	—	-0.9
Total	8	742	2603	345	761	117	62	11	332	269	—	43	97	.292	.368	.398	.766	+24	132	36	100	O689(389/258/44),S10,2b6/3b	—	2.9
/150	2	150	526	70	154	24	13	2	67	54	—	9	0	.292	.368	.398	.766	+24	27	0	100	O139(79/52/9),S2/23	0	0.6
Criger, Lou	Louis B2.3.1872 Elkhart IN D5.14.1934 Tucson AZ BR/TR/5'10"/165 d9.21																						
1910	NY A	27	69	3	13	2	0	0	4	10	—	0	—	.188	.291	.217	.508	-44	0	—	—	C27	—	-0.1
Total	16	1012	3202	337	709	86	50	11	342	309	—	23	0	.221	.295	.290	.585	-28	58	—	—	C984,1b10/lf3b	—	11.9
Crompton, Herb	Herbert Bryan "Workhorse" B11.7.1911 Taylor Ridge IL D8.5.1963 Moline IL BR/TR/6'0"/185 d4.26																						
1937	Was A	2	3	0	1	0	0	0	0	0	—	0	0	.333	.333	.333	.666	-28	0	0	0	C2	—	0.0
1945	NY A	36	99	6	19	3	0	0	12	2	—	0	7	.192	.208	.222	.430	-76	0	0	0	C33	0	-1.0
Total	2	38	102	6	20	3	0	0	12	2	—	0	7	.196	.212	.225	.437	-75	0	0	0	C35	0	-1.0
Crosby, Bubba	Richard Stephen B8.11.1976 Houston TX BL/TL/5'11"/(180–185) Dr 1998 LAN 1/23 d5.29 Col Rice																						
2003	LA N	9	12	0	1	0	0	0	1	0	0	0	3	.083	.083	.083	.166	-158	0	0	0	/lf	0	-0.3
2004	†NY A	55	53	8	8	2	0	2	7	2	0	1	13	.151	.196	.302	.498	-73	2	0	100	O45(11/12/25),D2	0	-0.7
2005	†NY A	76	98	15	27	0	1	1	6	4	0	0	14	.276	.304	.327	.631	-32	4	1	80	O67(4/41/23),D4	0	-0.1
2006	NY A	65	87	9	18	3	1	1	6	4	0	2	21	.207	.258	.299	.557	-57	3	1	75	O62(10/24/31)/D	27	-0.8
Total	4	205	250	32	54	5	2	4	20	10	0	3	51	.216	.255	.300	.555	-55	9	2	82	O175(26/77/79),D7	27	-1.9
Team	3	196	238	32	53	5	2	4	19	10	0	3	48	.223	.263	.311	.574	-50	9	2	82	O174(15/77/79),D7	27	-1.6
/150	2	150	182	24	41	4	2	3	15	8	0	2	37	.223	.263	.311	.574	-50	7	2	78	O133(11/59/60),D5	21	-1.2
Crosetti, Frankie	Frank Peter Joseph "Crow" B10.4.1910 San Francisco CA D2.11.2002 Stockton CA BR/TR/5'10"/165 d4.12 Def 1944 C25																						
1932	†NY A	116	398	47	96	20	9	5	57	51	—	5	51	.241	.335	.374	.709	-12	3	2	60	S84,3b33/2b	—	-0.5
1933	NY A	136	451	71	114	20	5	9	60	55	—	2	40	.253	.337	.379	.716	-5	4	1	80	S133	—	-0.1
1934	NY A	138	554	85	147	22	10	11	67	61	—	**5**	58	.265	.344	.401	.745	-2	5	6	45	S119,3b23/2b	—	-0.5
1935	NY A	87	305	49	78	17	6	8	50	41	—	4	27	.256	.351	.430	.781	+7	3	1	75	S87	—	0.2
1936	†NY A★	151	632	137	182	35	7	15	78	90	—	**12**	83	.288	.387	.437	.824	+7	18	7	72	S151	—	0.8
1937	†NY A	149	611	127	143	29	5	11	49	86	—	**12**	105	.234	.340	.352	.692	-26	13	7	65	S147	—	-1.1
1938	†NY A	**157**	631	113	166	35	3	9	55	106	—	**15**	97	.263	.382	.371	.753	-10	**27**	12	69	S157	—	2.4
1939	†NY A☆	**152**	656	109	153	25	5	10	56	65	—	**13**	81	.233	.315	.332	.647	-33	11	7	61	S152	—	-1.2
1940	NY A	145	546	84	106	23	4	4	31	72	—	**10**	77	.194	.299	.273	.572	-48	14	8	64	S145	—	-3.9
1941	NY A	50	148	13	33	2	2	1	22	18	—	3	14	.223	.320	.284	.604	-39	0	2	0	S32,3b13	0	-0.1
1942	†NY A	74	285	50	69	5	5	4	23	31	—	**9**	31	.242	.335	.337	.672	-9	1	1	50	3b62,S8,2b2	0	-0.1
1943	†NY A	95	348	36	81	8	1	2	20	36	—	7	47	.233	.317	.279	.596	-26	4	4	50	S90	0	-0.4
1944	NY A	55	197	20	47	4	2	5	30	11	—	6	21	.239	.299	.355	.654	-16	3	0	100	S55	0	-0.5
1945	NY A	130	441	57	105	12	0	4	48	59	—	**10**	65	.238	.341	.293	.634	-19	7	1	88	S126	0	-0.3
1946	NY A	28	59	4	17	3	0	0	3	8	—	1	2	.288	.382	.339	.721	+1	0	3	0	S24	0	0.6
1947	NY A	3	1	0	0	0	0	0	0	0	—	0	0	.000	.000	.000	.000	-199	0	0	0	/2bS	0	-0.1
1948	NY A	17	14	4	4	0	1	0	0	2	—	0	0	.286	.375	.429	.804	+15	0	0	0	2b6,S5	0	0.0
Total	17	1683	6277	1006	1541	260	65	98	649	792	—	114	799	.245	.341	.354	.695	-16	113	62	65	S1516,3b131,2b11	0	-4.8
/150	2	150	559	90	137	23	6	9	58	71	—	10	71	.245	.341	.354	.695	-16	10	6	63	S13,3b12/2	0	-0.4
Cruz, Jose	Jose (Dilan) B8.8.1947 Arroyo, PR BL/TL/6'0"/(170–185) d9.19 C11 b–Tommy b–Hector s–Jose [DL 1969 StL N 34]																						
1988	NY A	38	80	9	16	2	0	1	7	8	1	0	8	.200	.273	.262	.535	-49	0	1	0	D12,O8(4/0/4)	21	-0.7
Total	19	2353	7917	1036	2251	391	94	165	1077	898	14	7	1031	.284	.354	.420	.774	+21	317	136	70	O2156(1411/284/474),D12,1b3	67	20.5
Cruz, Ivan	Luis Ivan B5.3.1968 Fajardo, PR BL/TL/6'3"/(210–225) Dr 1989 DetA 28/733 d7.18 Col Jacksonville																						
1997	NY A	11	20	0	5	1	0	0	3	2	0	0	4	.250	.318	.300	.618	-37	0	0	0	1b3/lfD	0	-0.1
Total	4	41	55	5	15	1	0	2	8	3	0	0	17	.273	.310	.400	.710	-18	0	0	0	1b12,D4,O2(1/0/1)	92	-0.2
Cullenbine, Roy	Roy Joseph B10.18.1913 Nashville TN D5.28.1991 Mt.Clemens MI BB/TR/6'1"/190 d4.19																						
1942	†NY A	21	77	16	28	7	0	2	17	18	—	0	2	.364	.484	.532	1.016	+90	0	1	0	O19R/1b	0	1.0
Total	10	1181	3879	627	1072	209	32	110	599	853	—	11	399	.276	.408	.432	.840	+32	26	20	100	O843(236/12/600),1b208,3b31	0	18.8
Cullop, Nick	Henry Nicholas "Tomato Face"(b Heinrich Nicholas Kolop) B10.16.1900 St.Louis MO D12.8.1978 Westerville OH BR/TR/6'0"/200 d4.14																						
1926	NY A	2	2	0	1	0	0	0	0	0	—	0	1	.500	.500	.500	1.000	+64	0	0	0	/H	—	0.0
Total	5	173	490	49	122	29	12	11	67	40	—	2	128	.249	.308	.424	.732	-4	1	4	100	O124(90/24/12),1b2/P	—	-0.8
Curry, Jim	James L. B3.10.1886 Camden NJ D8.2.1938 Grenloch NJ BR/TR/5'11"/160 d10.2																						
1909	Phi A	1	4	1	1	0	0	0	0	0	—	0	—	.250	.250	.250	.500	-43	0	—	—	/2b	—	-0.1
1911	NY A	4	11	3	2	0	0	0	0	1	—	0	—	.182	.250	.182	.432	-80	0	—	—	2b4	—	-0.3
1918	Det A	5	20	1	5	1	0	0	0	0	—	1	0	.250	.286	.300	.586	-20	0	—	—	2b5	—	-0.2
Total	3	10	35	5	8	1	0	0	0	1	—	1	0	.229	.270	.257	.527	-44	0	—	—	2b10	—	-0.6

YEAR	TM LG	G	AB	R	H	2B	3B	HR	RBI	BB	IB	HP	SO	AVG	OBP	SLG	OPS	AOPS	SB	CS	SB%	GAMES AT POSITION	DL	BFW
Curtis, Chad Chad David B11.6.1968 Marion IN BR/TR/5'10"/(175–185) Dr 1989 CalA 45/1157 d4.8 Col Grand Canyon																								
1997	†NY A	93	320	51	93	21	1	12	50	36	1	5	49	.291	.362	.475	.837	+20	12	6	67	O92(53/43/5)	0	0.4
1998	†NY A	151	456	79	111	21	1	10	56	75	3	7	80	.243	.355	.360	.715	-8	21	5	81	O148(100/45/9),D2	0	0.1
1999	†NY A	96	195	37	51	6	0	5	24	43	0	3	35	.262	.398	.369	.767	+0	8	4	67	O81(72/6/3),D14	0	-0.4
Total	10	1204	4017	648	1061	195	16	101	461	510	11	40	676	.264	.349	.396	.745	-5	212	98	68	O1141(385/686/122),D35,2b3	124	-1.1
Team	3	340	971	167	255	48	2	27	130	154	4	15	164	.263	.366	.400	.766	+3	41	15	73	O321(153/94/8),D16	0	0.1
/150	1	150	428	74	113	21	1	12	57	68	2	7	72	.263	.366	.400	.766	+3	18	7	72	O142(68/41/4),D7	0	0.0
Curtis, Fred Frederick Marion B10.30.1880 Beaver Lake MI D4.5.1939 Minneapolis MN BR/TR/6'1"/? d7.21																								
1905	NY A	2	9	0	2	1	0	0	2	1	—	0	—	.222	.300	.333	.633	-10	1	—	—	1b2	—	0.0
Dahlgren, Babe Ellsworth Tenney B6.15.1912 San Francisco CA D9.4.1996 Arcadia CA BR/TR/6'0"/190 d4.16 C1																								
1937	NY A	1	1	0	0	0	0	0	0	0	—	0	0	.000	.000	.000	.000	-199	0	0	0	/H	—	0.0
1938	NY A	27	43	8	8	1	0	0	1	1	—	0	7	.186	.205	.209	.414	-96	0	0	0	3b8,1b6	—	-0.8
1939	†NY A	144	531	71	125	18	6	15	89	57	—	2	54	.235	.312	.377	.689	-24	2	3	40	1b144	—	-4.0
1940	NY A	**155**	568	51	150	24	4	12	73	46	—	5	54	.264	.325	.384	.709	-14	1	1	50	1b155	—	-3.7
Total	12	1137	4045	470	1056	174	37	82	569	390	—	22	401	.261	.329	.383	.712	-8	18	11	100	1b1030,3b48,S25/C	0	-16.1
Team	4	327	1143	130	283	43	10	27	163	104	—	7	115	.248	.314	.374	.688	-22	3	4	43	1b305,3b8	—	-8.5
/150	2	150	524	60	130	20	5	12	75	48	—	3	53	.248	.314	.374	.688	-22	1	2	33	1b140,3b4	—	-3.9
Daley, Tom Thomas Francis "Pete" B11.13.1884 DuBois PA D12.2.1934 Los Angeles CA BL/TR/5'5"/168 d8.29																								
1908	Cin N	14	46	5	5	0	0	0	1	3	—	2	—	.109	.196	.109	.305	-102	1	—	—	O13R	—	-0.6
1913	Phi A	62	141	13	36	2	1	0	11	13	—	2	28	.255	.327	.284	.611	-19	4	—	—	O39C	—	-0.6
1914	Phi A	28	86	17	22	1	3	0	7	12	—	0	14	.256	.347	.337	.684	+10	4	7	36	O24(15/10/0)	—	0.0
1914	NY A	69	191	36	48	6	4	0	9	38	—	1	13	.251	.378	.325	.703	+12	8	8	50	O58(28/29/0)	—	0.5
1914	Year	97	277	53	70	7	7	0	16	50	—	1	27	.253	.369	.329	.698	+11	12	15	44	O82(43/39/0)	—	0.5
1915	NY A	10	8	2	2	0	0	0	1	2	—	0	2	.250	.400	.250	.650	-5	1	—	—	O2(1/0/1)	—	0.1
Total	4	183	472	73	113	9	8	0	29	68	—	5	57	.239	.341	.292	.633	-8	18	15	100	O136(44/77/14)	—	-0.6
Team	2	79	199	38	50	6	4	0	10	40	—	1	15	.251	.379	.322	.701	+11	9	8	100	O60(29/29/1)	—	0.6
Damon, Johnny Johnny David B11.5.1973 Fort Riley KS BL/TL/6'2"/(175–205) Dr 1992 KCA 1/35 d8.12																								
2006	†NY A	149	593	115	169	35	5	24	80	67	1	4	85	.285	.359	.482	.841	+14	25	10	71	O131C,D16/1b	0	0.9
2007	†NY A	141	533	93	144	27	2	12	63	66	1	2	79	.270	.351	.396	.747	-4	27	3	90	O81(32/48/1),D48,1b5	0	0.1
Total	13	1845	7303	1281	2102	388	87	166	843	731	34	38	868	.288	.353	.433	.786	+1	333	88	79	O1714(360/1260/147),D103,1b6	0	2.7
Team	2	290	1126	208	313	62	7	36	143	133	2	6	164	.278	.355	.441	.796	+5	52	13	80	O212(32/179/48),D64,1b6	0	1.0
/150	1	150	582	108	162	32	4	19	74	69	1	3	85	.278	.355	.441	.796	+5	27	7	79	O110(17/93/25),D33,1b3	0	0.5
Daniels, Bert Bernard Elmer B10.31.1882 Danville IL D6.6.1958 Cedar Grove NJ BR/TR/5'10"/170 d6.25 Col Bucknell																								
1910	NY A	95	356	68	90	13	8	1	17	41	—	**16**	—	.253	.356	.343	.699	+12	41	—	—	O85(79/6/0),3b6,1b4	—	0.1
1911	NY A	131	462	74	132	16	9	2	31	48	—	18	—	.286	.375	.372	.747	+12	40	—	—	O120(8/86/26)	—	-1.0
1912	NY A	135	496	72	136	25	11	2	41	51	—	**18**	—	.274	.363	.381	.744	+6	37	20	65	O131(92/0/39)	—	0.3
1913	NY A	94	320	52	69	13	5	0	22	44	—	**18**	36	.216	.343	.287	.630	-15	27	—	—	O87R	—	-0.7
1914	Cin N	71	269	29	59	9	7	0	19	19	—	2	40	.219	.276	.305	.581	-30	14	—	—	O71(11/26/38)	—	-1.9
Total	5	526	1903	295	486	76	40	5	130	203	—	72	76	.255	.349	.345	.694	-2	159	20	100	O494(190/118/190),3b6,1b4	—	-3.2
Team	4	455	1634	266	427	67	33	5	111	184	—	70	36	.261	.361	.352	.713	+2	145	20	100	O423(87/92/3),3b6,1b4	—	-1.3
/150	1	150	539	88	141	22	11	2	37	61	—	23	12	.261	.361	.352	.713	+2	48	7	100	O139(29/30/1),3b2/1	—	-0.4
Davis, Lefty Alphonzo De Ford B2.4.1875 Nashville TN D2.4.1919 Collins NY BL/TL/5'10"/170 d4.18																								
1903	NY A	104	372	54	88	10	0	0	25	43	—	2	—	.237	.319	.263	.582	-28	11	—	—	O102(95/1/6)/S	—	-2.6
Total	4	348	1296	232	338	32	19	3	110	167	—	6	—	.261	.348	.322	.670	-2	65	—	—	O341(107/72/162)/S2b	—	-2.3
/150	1	150	537	78	127	14	0	0	36	62	—	3	0	.237	.319	.263	.582	-28	16	—	—	O147(137/1/9)/S	—	-3.8
Davis, Chili Charles Theodore B1.17.1960 Kingston, Jamaica BB/TR/6'3"/(195–240) Dr 1977 SFN 11/270 d4.10																								
1998	†NY A	35	103	11	30	7	0	3	9	14	1	0	18	.291	.373	.447	.820	+18	0	1	0	D34	136	0.1
1999	†NY A	146	476	59	128	25	1	19	78	73	7	2	100	.269	.366	.445	.811	+8	4	1	80	D132	0	0.1
Total	19	2436	8673	1240	2380	424	30	350	1372	1194	18	15	1698	.274	.360	.451	.811	+20	142	98	59	O1184(231/538/481),D1161/P1b	200	15.3
Team	2	181	579	70	158	32	1	22	87	87	8	2	118	.273	.367	.446	.813	+10	4	2	67	D166	136	0.2
/150	2	150	480	58	131	27	1	18	72	72	7	2	98	.273	.367	.446	.813	+10	3	2	60	D138	113	0.2
Davis, Kiddo George Willis B2.12.1902 Bridgeport CT D3.4.1983 Bridgeport CT BR/TR/5'11"/178 d6.15 Col NYU																								
1926	NY A	1	0	0	0	0	0	0	0	0	—	0	0	+	+	+	.000	-100	0	0	0	/rf	—	0.0
Total	8	575	1824	281	515	112	16	19	171	142	—	4	141	.282	.336	.393	.729	-8	32	0	100	O483(31/425/29)	—	-2.2
Davis, Russ Russell Stuart B9.13.1969 Birmingham AL BR/TR/6'0"/(170–200) Dr 1988 NYA 29/755 d7.6 Col Shelton St. (AL) CC																								
1994	NY A	4	14	0	2	0	0	0	1	0	0	0	4	.143	.143	.143	.286	-127	0	0	0	3b4	0	-0.3
1995	†NY A	40	98	14	27	5	2	2	12	10	0	1	26	.276	.349	.429	.778	+2	0	0	0	3b34,1b2,D4	0	-0.2
Total	8	612	1980	261	508	108	6	84	276	146	7	16	503	.257	.310	.444	.754	-7	16	11	59	3b556,D9,1b8,O3L,S2	146	-7.8
Team	2	44	112	14	29	5	2	2	13	10	0	1	30	.259	.325	.393	.718	-13	0	0	0	3b38,D4,1b2	0	-0.5
Dayett, Brian Brian Kelly B1.22.1957 New London CT BR/TR/5'10"/(180–185) Dr 1978 NYA 16/416 d9.11 Col St. Leo																								
1983	NY A	11	29	3	6	0	1	0	5	2	0	0	4	.207	.258	.276	.534	-52	0	0	0	O9L	0	-0.1
1984	NY A	64	127	14	31	8	0	4	23	9	0	1	14	.244	.295	.402	.697	-5	0	0	0	O62(55/0/10)/D	0	-0.2
1985	Chi N	22	26	1	6	0	0	1	4	0	0	1	6	.231	.259	.346	.605	-38	0	0	0	O10L	109	-0.2
1986	Chi N	24	67	7	18	4	0	4	11	6	0	0	10	.269	.316	.507	.823	+18	0	1	0	O24(15/1/12)	0	-0.1
1987	Chi N	97	177	20	49	14	1	5	25	20	0	0	37	.277	.348	.452	.800	+6	0	0	0	O78(68/0/12)	0	-0.2
Total	5	218	426	45	110	26	2	14	68	37	0	2	71	.258	.316	.427	.743	-1	0	1	0	O183(158/1/34)/D	109	-0.8
Team	2	75	156	17	37	8	1	4	28	11	0	1	18	.237	.288	.378	.666	-14	0	0	0	O71L/D	0	-0.3
Deidel, Jim James Lawrence B6.6.1949 Denver CO BR/TR/6'2"/195 d5.31																								
1974	NY A	2	2	0	0	0	0	0	0	0	0	0	0	.000	.000	.000	.000	-199	0	0	0	C2	0	0.0
DeJesus, Ivan Ivan (Alvarez) B1.9.1953 Santurce, PR BR/TR/5'11"/(160–185) d9.13																								
1986	NY A	7	4	1	0	0	0	0	0	1	0	0	1	.000	.200	.000	.200	-140	0	0	0	S7	0	-0.2
Total	15	1371	4602	595	1167	175	48	21	324	466	48	16	664	.254	.323	.326	.649	-24	194	88	69	S1303,3b34	0	4.6
Delahanty, Frank Frank George "Pudgie" B12.29.1882 Cleveland OH D7.22.1966 Cleveland OH BR/TR/5'9"/160 d8.23 b–Ed b–Jim b–Joe b–Tom																								
1905	NY A	9	27	0	6	1	0	0	2	1	—	0	—	.222	.250	.259	.509	-45	0	—	—	1b5,O3L	—	-0.3
1906	NY A	92	307	37	73	11	8	2	41	16	—	3	—	.238	.282	.345	.627	-13	11	—	—	O86L	—	-0.9
1907	Cle A	15	52	3	9	0	1	0	4	4	—	0	—	.173	.232	.212	.444	-59	2	—	—	O15(9/0/6)	—	-0.5
1908	NY A	37	125	12	32	1	2	0	10	10	—	1	—	.256	.316	.296	.612	-2	9	—	—	O36L	—	-0.3
1914	Buf F	79	274	29	55	4	7	2	27	23	—	1	19	.201	.265	.288	.553	-50	21	—	—	O78L	—	-3.4
1914	Pit F	41	159	25	38	4	4	1	7	11	—	2	11	.239	.297	.333	.630	-28	7	—	—	O36(13/1/23),2b4	—	-1.3
1914	Year	120	433	54	93	8	11	3	34	34	—	3	30	.215	.277	.305	.582	-42	28	—	—	O114(91/1/23),2b4	—	-4.7
1915	Pit F	14	42	3	10	1	0	0	3	1	—	0	0	.238	.256	.262	.518	-54	0	—	—	O11L	—	-0.3
Total	6	287	986	109	223	22	22	5	94	66	—	7	30	.226	.280	.308	.588	-30	50	—	—	O265(236/1/29),1b5,2b4	—	-7.0
Team	3	138	459	49	111	13	10	2	53	27	—	4	0	.242	.290	.327	.617	-12	20	—	—	O125L,1b5	—	-1.5
/150	3	150	499	53	121	14	11	2	58	29	—	4	0	.242	.290	.327	.617	-12	22	—	—	O136L,1b5	—	-1.6

Batters

YEAR	TM LG	G	AB	R	H	2B	3B	HR	RBI	BB	IB	HP	SO	AVG	OBP	SLG	OPS	AOPS	SB	CS	SB%	GAMES AT POSITION	DL	BFW
DELGADO, WILSON Wilson (Duran) B7.15.1972 San Cristobal, D.R. BB/TR/5'11"/(155–165) d9.24																								
2000	NY A	31	45	6	11	1	0	1	4	5	0	0	9	.244	.314	.333	.647	-33	1	0	100	2b14,S11,3b5	0	-0.4
Total	9	253	542	59	136	15	2	5	43	47	3	4	108	.251	.314	.314	.628	-36	5	1	83	S129,2b66,3b31	0	-2.0
DELGRECO, BOBBY Robert George B4.7.1933 Pittsburgh PA BR/TR/5'11"/(175–190) d4.16																								
1957	NY A	8	7	3	3	0	0	0	0	2	0	0	2	.429	.556	.429	.985	+75	1	0	100	O6C	0	0.0
1958	NY A	12	5	1	1	0	0	0	0	1	0	0	1	.200	.333	.200	.533	-48	0	1	0	O12(11/1/0)	0	-0.1
Total	9	731	1982	271	454	95	11	42	169	271	7	32	372	.229	.330	.352	.682	-16	16	15	52	O665(74/588/16),3b6/2b	0	-4.4
Team	2	20	12	4	4	0	0	0	0	3	0	0	3	.333	.467	.333	.800	+26	1	1	50	O18(11/6/0)	0	-0.1
DELLUCCI, DAVID David Michael B10.31.1973 Baton Rouge LA BL/TL/5'10"/(180–198) Dr 1995 BalA 10/276 d6.3 Col U. of Mississippi																								
2003	†NY A	21	51	8	9	1	0	1	4	4	0	2	13	.176	.263	.255	.518	-62	3	0	100	O18(2/1/16),D2	30	-0.4
Total	11	964	2472	385	644	118	33	90	348	293	18	32	619	.261	.344	.444	.788	+1	38	23	62	O626(373/63/230),D92	216	-2.6
DELSING, JIM James Henry B11.13.1925 Rudolph WI D5.4.2006 Chesterfield MO BL/TR/5'10"/175 d4.21																								
1949	NY A	9	20	5	7	1	0	1	3	1	—	0	2	.350	.381	.550	.931	+45	0	0	0	O5C	0	0.0
1950	NY A	12	10	2	4	0	0	0	2	2	—	0	0	.400	.500	.400	.900	+37	0	0	0	/H	0	0.1
Total	10	822	2461	322	627	112	21	40	286	299	2	19	251	.255	.339	.366	.705	-9	15	23	39	O698(284/383/39)	0	-6.0
Team	2	21	30	7	11	1	0	1	5	3	—	0	2	.367	.424	.500	.924	+42	0	0	0	O5C	0	0.1
DEMAESTRI, JOE Joseph Paul "Oats" B12.9.1928 San Francisco CA BR/TR/6'0"/(174–180) d4.19																								
1960	†NY A	49	35	8	8	1	0	0	2	0	0	0	9	.229	.229	.257	.486	-67	0	0	0	2b19,S17	0	-0.3
1961	NY A	30	41	1	6	0	0	0	2	0	0	0	13	.146	.146	.146	.292	-123	0	0	0	S18,2b5,3b4	0	-0.4
Total	11	1121	3441	322	813	114	23	49	281	168	13	17	511	.236	.274	.325	.599	-38	15	19	44	S1029,2b39,3b14	0	-15.2
Team	2	79	76	9	14	1	0	0	4	0	0	0	22	.184	.184	.197	.381	-97	0	0	0	S35,2b24,3b4	0	-0.7
DEMMITT, RAY Charles Raymond B2.2.1884 Illiopolis IL D2.19.1956 Glen Ellyn IL BL/TR/5'8"/170 d4.12 Col Illinois																								
1909	NY A	123	427	68	105	12	12	4	30	55	—	6	—	.246	.340	.358	.698	+20	16	—	—	O109(0/70/39)	—	0.3
Total	7	498	1631	205	419	61	33	8	165	172	—	17	120	.257	.334	.349	.683	+8	42	20	100	O439(128/74/238)	—	-1.4
/150	1	150	521	83	128	15	15	5	37	67	—	7	0	.246	.340	.358	.698	+20	20	—	—	O133(0/85/48)	—	0.4
DEMPSEY, RICK John Rikard B9.13.1949 Fayetteville TN BR/TR (BB 1982p)/6'0"/(178–195) Dr 1967 MinA 12/237 d9.23 C7																								
1973	NY A	6	11	0	2	0	0	0	0	1	0	0	3	.182	.250	.182	.432	-76	0	0	0	C5	0	-0.4
1974	NY A	43	109	12	26	3	0	2	12	8	0	0	7	.239	.288	.321	.609	-23	1	0	100	C31,O2(1/0/1)/D	0	0.4
1975	NY A	71	145	18	38	8	0	1	11	21	1	0	15	.262	.353	.338	.691	-2	0	0	0	C19,D18,O8(1/0/7)/3b	0	0.2
1976	NY A	21	42	1	5	0	0	0	2	5	0	0	4	.119	.213	.119	.332	-101	0	0	0	C9,O4R	0	-0.3
Total	24	1766	4692	525	1093	223	12	96	471	592	13	18	736	.233	.319	.347	.666	-13	20	19	51	C1633,O23(6/0/17),D22,1b3,P2/3b	111	7.0
Team	4	141	307	31	71	11	0	3	25	35	1	0	29	.231	.308	.296	.604	-25	1	0	100	C64,D19,O14(2/0/8)/3	0	-0.1
/150	4	150	327	33	76	12	0	3	27	37	1	0	31	.231	.308	.296	.604	-25	1	0	100	C68,D20,O15(2/0/9)/3	0	-0.1
DENT, BUCKY Russell Earl (b Russell Earl O'Dey) B11.25.1951 Savannah GA BR/TR/5'11"/(170–190) Dr 1970 ChiA S1/6 d6.1 M2/C13 Col Miami–Dade North (FL) CC																								
1973	Chi A	40	117	17	29	2	0	0	10	10	0	1	18	.248	.308	.265	.573	-38	2	3	40	S36,2b3/3b	0	0.4
1974	Chi A	154	496	55	136	15	3	5	45	28	0	3	48	.274	.316	.347	.663	-12	3	4	43	S154	0	1.6
1975	Chi A★	157	602	52	159	29	4	3	58	36	3	0	48	.264	.301	.341	.642	-19	2	4	33	S157	0	2.1
1976	Chi A	158	562	44	138	18	4	2	52	43	3	2	45	.246	.300	.302	.602	-23	3	5	38	S158	0	-0.4
1977	†NY A	158	477	54	118	18	4	8	49	39	0	1	28	.247	.300	.352	.652	-21	1	1	50	S158	0	-0.8
1978	†NY A	123	379	40	92	11	1	5	40	23	1	2	24	.243	.286	.317	.603	-28	3	1	75	S123	22	-0.7
1979	NY A	141	431	47	99	14	2	2	32	37	1	1	30	.230	.287	.285	.572	-43	0	0	0	S141	0	2.0
1980	†NY A★	141	489	57	128	26	2	5	52	48	1	2	37	.262	.327	.354	.681	-11	0	3	0	S141	15	1.9
1981	NY A★	73	227	20	54	11	0	7	27	19	0	2	17	.238	.300	.379	.679	-4	0	1	0	S73	35	0.4
1982	NY A	59	160	11	27	1	1	0	9	8	0	0	11	.169	.207	.188	.395	-90	0	0	0	S58	0	-0.9
1982	Tex A	46	146	16	32	9	0	1	14	13	0	0	10	.219	.280	.301	.581	-37	0	0	0	S45	0	-0.2
1982	Year	105	306	27	59	10	1	1	23	21	0	0	21	.193	.242	.242	.484	-65	0	0	0	S103	0	-1.1
1983	Tex A	131	417	36	99	15	2	2	34	23	0	1	31	.237	.278	.297	.575	-41	3	7	30	S129/D	0	-2.4
1984	KC A	11	9	2	3	0	0	0	1	1	0	0	2	.333	.400	.333	.733	+4	0	0	0	S9,3b2	0	-0.3
Total	12	1392	4512	451	1114	169	23	40	423	328	9	15	349	.247	.297	.321	.618	-26	17	29	37	S1382,3b3,2b3/D	72	2.7
Team	6	695	2163	229	518	81	10	27	209	174	3	8	147	.239	.295	.324	.619	-27	4	6	40	S694	72	1.9
/150	1	150	467	49	112	17	2	6	45	38	1	2	32	.239	.295	.324	.619	-27	1	1	50	S150	16	0.4
DERRICK, CLAUD Claud Lester "Deek" B6.11.1886 Burton GA D7.15.1974 Clayton GA BR/TR/6'0"/175 d9.8 Col Georgia																								
1913	NY A	23	65	7	19	1	0	1	7	5	—	1	8	.292	.352	.354	.706	+6	2	—	—	S17,3b4/2b	—	0.0
Total	5	113	326	35	79	6	4	1	33	22	—	4	21	.242	.298	.294	.592	-28	13	4	100	S72,2b22,3b6,1b3	—	-1.5
DERRY, RUSS Alva Russell B10.7.1916 Princeton MO D10.26.2004 Kansas City MO BL/TR/6'1"/180 d7.4																								
1944	NY A	38	114	14	29	3	0	4	14	20	—	0	19	.254	.366	.386	.752	+11	1	0	100	O28(16/0/12)	0	-0.1
1945	NY A	78	253	37	57	6	2	13	45	31	—	1	49	.225	.312	.419	.731	+7	1	0	100	O68(10/44/15)	0	-0.2
1946	Phi A	69	184	17	38	8	5	0	14	27	—	1	54	.207	.311	.304	.615	-27	0	0	0	O50(45/2/5)	0	-0.6
1949	StL N	2	2	0	0	0	0	0	0	0	—	0	2	.000	.000	.000	.000	-196	0	—	—	/H	0	-0.1
Total	4	187	553	68	124	17	7	17	73	78	—	2	124	.224	.322	.373	.695	-5	2	0	100	O146(71/46/32)	0	-1.0
Team	2	116	367	51	86	9	2	17	59	51	—	1	68	.234	.329	.409	.738	+8	2	0	100	O96(26/44/13)	0	-0.3
/150	3	150	475	66	111	12	3	22	76	66	—	1	88	.234	.329	.409	.738	+8	3	0	100	O124(34/57/17)	0	-0.4
DESTRADE, ORESTES Orestes (Cucuas) B5.8.1962 Santiago de Cuba, Cuba BB/TR/6'4"/(210–230) d9.11 Col Florida JC																								
1987	NY A	9	19	5	5	0	0	0	1	5	0	0	5	.263	.417	.263	.680	-14	0	0	0	1b3,D2	0	0.0
Total	4	237	765	80	184	25	3	26	106	87	9	5	184	.241	.319	.383	.702	-17	1	2	33	1b200,D2	0	-4.9
DEVORMER, AL Albert E. B8.19.1891 Grand Rapids MI D8.29.1966 Grand Rapids MI BR/TR/6'0.5"/175 d8.4																								
1921	†NY A	22	49	6	17	4	0	0	7	2	—	0	4	.347	.373	.429	.802	+2	2	0	100	C17	—	0.1
1922	NY A	24	59	8	12	4	1	0	11	1	—	0	6	.203	.217	.305	.522	-66	0	0	0	C17/1b	—	-0.6
Total	5	196	477	50	123	20	5	2	57	20	—	3	46	.258	.292	.333	.625	-35	7	0	100	C149,1b6/rf	—	-2.3
Team	2	46	108	14	29	8	1	0	18	3	—	0	10	.269	.288	.361	.649	-35	2	0	100	C34/1	—	-0.5
DICKEY, BILL William Malcolm B6.6.1907 Bastrop LA D11.12.1993 Little Rock AR BL/TR/6'1.5"/185 d8.15 Mil 1944–45 M1/C10 HF1954 b–George																								
1928	NY A	10	15	1	3	1	1	0	2	0	—	0	2	.200	.200	.400	.600	-44	0	0	0	C6	—	-0.2
1929	NY A	130	447	60	145	30	6	10	65	14	—	1	16	.324	.346	.485	.831	+20	4	6	40	C127	—	1.8
1930	NY A	109	366	55	124	25	7	5	65	21	—	0	14	.339	.375	.486	.861	+22	7	1	88	C101	—	0.8
1931	NY A	130	477	65	156	17	10	6	78	39	—	0	20	.327	.378	.442	.820	+22	2	1	67	C125	—	2.0
1932	†NY A	108	423	66	131	20	4	15	84	34	—	0	13	.310	.361	.482	.843	+23	2	4	33	C108	—	1.6
1933	NY A☆	130	478	58	152	24	8	14	97	47	—	2	14	.318	.381	.490	.871	+38	3	4	43	C127	—	3.5
1934	NY A★	104	395	56	127	24	4	12	72	38	—	2	18	.322	.384	.494	.878	+34	0	3	0	C104	—	2.3
1935	NY A	120	448	54	125	26	6	14	81	35	—	6	11	.279	.339	.458	.797	+11	1	1	50	C118	—	1.4
1936	†NY A★	112	423	99	153	26	8	22	107	46	—	3	16	.362	.428	.617	1.045	+61	0	2	0	C107	—	4.2
1937	†NY A★	140	530	87	176	35	2	29	133	73	—	4	22	.332	.417	.570	.987	+45	3	2	60	C137	—	5.6
1938	†NY A★	132	454	84	142	27	4	27	115	75	—	2	22	.313	.412	.568	.980	+44	3	0	100	C126	—	4.1
1939	†NY A★	128	480	98	145	23	3	24	105	77	—	4	37	.302	.403	.512	.915	+35	5	0	100	C126	—	4.5
1940	NY A★	106	372	45	92	11	1	9	54	48	—	2	32	.247	.336	.355	.691	-17	0	3	0	C102	—	-0.2
1941	†NY A★	109	348	35	99	15	5	7	71	45	—	3	17	.284	.371	.417	.788	+10	2	1	67	C104	0	1.3
1942	†NY A✳	82	268	28	79	13	1	2	37	26	—	1	11	.295	.359	.373	.732	+8	2	2	50	C80	0	1.4
1943	†NY A☆	85	242	29	85	18	2	4	33	41	—	0	12	.351	.445	.492	.937	+73	2	1	67	C71	0	3.4

Batters

YEAR	TM LG	G	AB	R	H	2B	3B	HR	RBI	BB	IB	HP	SO	AVG	OBP	SLG	OPS	AOPS	SB	CS	SB%	GAMES AT POSITION	DL	BFW
1946	NY A★	54	134	10	35	8	0	2	10	19	—	1	12	.261	.357	.366	.723	+1	0	1	0	C39,M	0	1.0
Total	17	1789	6300	930	1969	343	72	202	1209	678	—	31	289	.313	.382	.486	.868	+28	36	32	53	C1708	0	38.5
/150	1	150	528	78	165	29	6	17	101	57	—	3	24	.313	.382	.486	.868	+28	3	3	50	C14	0	3.2
DiMaggio, Joe	Joseph Paul "Joltin'Joe","The Yankee Clipper" B11.25.1914 Martinez CA D3.8.1999 Hollywood FL BR/TR/6'2"/193 d5.3 Mil 1943–45 C2 HF1955 b–Dom b–Vince																							
1936	†NY A★	138	637	132	206	44	**15**	29	125	24	—	4	39	.323	.352	.576	.928	+30	4	0	100	O138(66/55/18)	—	2.2
1937	†NY A★	151	621	**151**	215	35	15	**46**	167	64	—	5	37	.346	.412	**.673**	1.085	+68	3	0	100	O150C	—	5.7
1938	†NY A★	145	599	129	194	32	13	32	140	59	—	2	21	.324	.386	.581	.967	+40	6	1	86	O145C	—	2.6
1939	†NY A★	120	462	108	176	32	6	30	126	52	—	4	20	**.381**	.448	.671	1.119	+106	3	0	100	O117C	—	**5.5**
1940	NY A★	132	508	93	179	28	9	31	133	61	—	3	30	**.352**	.425	.626	1.051	+76	1	2	33	O130C	—	**4.5**
1941	†NY A★	139	541	122	193	43	11	30	**125**	76	—	4	13	.357	.440	.643	1.083	+86	4	2	67	O139C	0	6.6
1942	†NY A★	**154**	610	123	186	29	13	21	114	68	—	2	36	.305	.376	.498	.874	+48	4	2	67	O154C	0	3.1
1946	NY A☆	132	503	81	146	20	8	25	95	59	—	2	24	.290	.367	.511	.878	+42	1	0	100	O131(3/128/0)	0	2.6
1947	†NY A★	141	534	97	168	31	10	20	97	64	—	3	32	.315	.391	.522	.913	+54	3	0	100	O139C	0	2.2
1948	NY A★	153	594	110	190	26	11	**39**	**155**	67	—	**8**	30	.320	.396	.598	.994	+64	1	1	50	O152C	0	4.5
1949	†NY A★	76	272	58	94	14	6	14	67	55	—	2	18	.346	.459	.596	1.055	+78	0	1	0	O76C	0	2.5
1950	†NY A★	139	525	114	158	33	10	32	122	80	—	1	33	.301	.394	**.585**	.979	+52	0	0	0	O137C/1b	0	3.0
1951	†NY A☆	116	415	72	109	22	4	12	71	61	—	6	36	.263	.365	.422	.787	+17	0	0	0	O113C	0	0.8
Total	13	1736	6821	1390	2214	389	131	361	1537	790	—	46	369	.325	.398	.579	.977	+56	30	9	77	O1721(69/1635/18)/1b	0	45.8
/150	1	150	589	120	191	34	11	31	133	68	—	4	32	.325	.398	.579	.977	+56	3	1	75	O15(6/141/2)/1	0	4.0
Dineen, Kerry	Kerry Michael B7.1.1952 Englewood NJ BL/TL/5'11"/165 Dr 1973 NYA 4/85 d6.14 Col San Diego																							
1975	NY A	7	22	3	8	1	0	0	1	2	0	0	1	.364	.417	.409	.826	+35	0	0	0	O7C	0	0.1
1976	NY A	4	7	0	2	0	0	0	1	1	0	0	2	.286	.375	.286	.661	-4	1	1	50	O4(0/2/2)	0	0.0
1978	Phi N	5	8	0	2	1	0	0	0	1	0	0	0	.250	.333	.375	.708	-4	0	0	0	/lf	0	0.0
Total	3	16	37	3	12	2	0	0	2	4	0	0	3	.324	.390	.378	.768	+19	1	1	50	O12(1/9/2)	0	0.1
Team	2	11	29	3	10	1	0	0	2	3	0	0	3	.345	.406	.379	.785	+25	1	1	50	O11(0/9/2)	0	0.1
Dolan, Cozy	Albert J. (b James Alberts) B12.23.1889 Chicago IL D12.10.1958 Chicago IL BR/TR/5'10"/160 d8.15 C3 OF(126/48/33)																							
1911	NY A	19	69	19	21	1	2	0	6	8	—	1	—	.304	.385	.377	.762	+6	12	—	—	3b19	—	0.0
1912	NY A	18	60	15	12	1	3	0	11	5	—	1	—	.200	.273	.317	.590	-36	5	3	63	3b17	—	-0.7
Total	7	379	1187	210	299	43	21	6	111	121	—	13	156	.252	.328	.339	.667	-5	102	25	100	O206L,3b116,S10,2b9/1b	—	-4.7
Team	2	37	129	34	33	2	5	0	17	13	—	2	0	.256	.333	.349	.682	-13	17	3	100	3b36	—	-0.7
Donovan, Mike	Michael Berchman B10.18.1881 Brooklyn NY D2.3.1938 New York NY BR/TR/5'8"/155 d5.29																							
1904	Cle A	2	2	0	0	0	0	0	0	0	—	0	—	.000	.000	.000	.000	-199	0	—	—	/S	—	-0.1
1908	NY A	5	19	2	5	1	0	0	2	0	—	0	—	.263	.263	.316	.579	-13	0	—	—	3b5	—	0.1
Total	2	7	21	2	5	1	0	0	2	0	—	0	—	.238	.238	.286	.524	-31	0	—	—	3b5/S	—	0.0
Donovan, Bill	William Edward "Wild Bill" B10.13.1876 Lawrence MA D12.9.1923 Forsyth NY BR/TR/5'11"/190 d4.22 M4/C1 ▲																							
1915	NY A	10	12	1	1	0	0	0	0	1	—	0	6	.083	.154	.083	.237	-129	0	—	—	P9,M	—	0.0
1916	NY A	1	0	0	0	0	0	0	0	0	—	0	0	+	+	+	.000	-100	0	—	—	/PM	—	0.0
Total	18	459	1302	142	251	30	11	7	93	77	—	6	6	.193	.241	.249	.490	-51	36	—	—	P378,O37(15/8/14),1b18,2b8,S3	—	-1.8
Team	2	11	12	1	1	0	0	0	0	1	—	0	6	.083	.154	.083	.237	-129	0	—	—	P9,M2	—	0.0
Dorsett, Brian	Brian Richard B4.9.1961 Terre Haute IN BR/TR/6'3"/(215–222) Dr 1983 OakA 10/241 d9.8 Col Indiana St. [DL 1988 Cle A 64]																							
1989	NY A	8	22	3	8	1	0	0	4	1	0	0	3	.364	.391	.409	.800	+27	0	0	0	C8	0	0.1
1990	NY A	14	35	2	5	2	0	0	0	2	0	0	4	.143	.189	.200	.389	-91	0	0	0	C9,D5	0	-0.6
Total	8	163	411	38	92	15	0	9	51	32	7	2	73	.224	.281	.326	.607	-39	0	0	0	C134,1b6,D5	64	-0.9
Team	2	22	57	5	13	3	0	0	4	3	0	0	7	.228	.267	.281	.548	-46	0	0	0	C17,D5	0	-0.5
Dougherty, Patsy	Patrick Henry B10.27.1876 Andover NY D4.30.1940 Bolivar NY BL/TR/6'2"/190 d4.19																							
1904	NY A	106	452	80	128	13	10	6	22	19	—	3	—	.283	.316	.396	.712	+19	11	—	—	O106L	—	-0.6
1905	NY A	116	418	56	110	9	6	3	29	28	—	6	—	.263	.319	.335	.654	-4	17	—	—	O108L/3b	—	-1.2
1906	NY A	12	52	3	10	2	0	0	4	0	—	0	—	.192	.192	.231	.423	-71	0	—	—	O12L	—	-0.3
Total	10	1233	4558	678	1294	138	78	17	413	378	—	54	—	.284	.346	.360	.706	+17	261	—	—	O1181L,3b2	—	-4.8
Team	3	234	922	139	248	24	16	9	55	47	—	9	0	.269	.311	.359	.670	+4	28	—	—	O226L/3	—	-2.1
/150	2	150	591	89	159	15	10	6	35	30	—	6	0	.269	.311	.359	.670	+4	18	—	—	O145L/3	—	-1.3
Dowd, John	John Leo (b John Leo O'Dowd) B1.3.1891 Weymouth MA D1.31.1981 Ft.Lauderdale FL BR/TR/5'8"/170 d7.3 Col Vermont																							
1912	NY A	10	31	1	6	1	0	0	0	6	—	1	—	.194	.342	.226	.568	-40	0	2	0	S10	—	-0.4
Doyle, Brian	Brian Reed B1.26.1955 Glasgow KY BL/TR/5'10"/(160–162) Dr 1972 TexA 4/76 d4.30 b–Denny																							
1978	†NY A	39	52	6	10	0	0	0	0	0	0	0	3	.192	.192	.192	.384	-91	0	3	0	2b29,S7,3b5	0	-0.2
1979	NY A	20	32	2	4	2	0	0	5	3	0	0	1	.125	.200	.188	.388	-95	0	0	0	2b13,3b6	0	-0.6
1980	NY A	34	75	8	13	1	0	1	5	6	0	0	7	.173	.235	.227	.462	-73	1	1	50	2b20,S12,3b2	0	-0.6
1981	Oak A	17	40	2	5	0	0	0	3	1	0	0	2	.125	.146	.125	.271	-122	0	1	0	2b17	17	-1.0
Total	4	110	199	18	32	3	0	1	13	10	0	0	13	.161	.201	.191	.392	-90	1	5	17	2b79,S19,3b13	17	-2.4
Team	3	93	159	16	27	3	0	1	10	9	0	0	11	.170	.214	.208	.422	-83	1	4	20	2b62,S19,3b13	0	-1.4
Doyle, Jack	John Joseph "Dirty Jack" B10.25.1869 Killorglin, Ireland D12.31.1958 Holyoke MA BR/TR/5'9"/155 d8.27 M2/U1 Col Fordham OF(13/45/76)																							
1905	NY A	1	3	0	0	0	0	0	0	0	—	0	—	.000	.000	.000	.000	-190	0	—	—	/1b	—	-0.2
Total	17	1569	6055	977	1811	316	64	25	971	440	—	49	132	.299	.351	.385	.736	+6	518	—	—	1b1048,C176,O133R,2b127,S53,3b50	—	2.7
Drescher, Bill	William Clayton "Dutch" B5.23.1921 Congers NY D5.15.1968 Haverstraw NY BL/TR/6'2"/190 d4.19																							
1944	NY A	4	7	0	1	0	0	0	0	0	—	0	0	.143	.143	.143	.286	-118	0	0	0	/C	0	-0.1
1945	NY A	48	126	10	34	3	1	0	15	8	—	0	5	.270	.313	.310	.623	-23	0	2	0	C33	0	-0.9
1946	NY A	5	6	0	2	1	0	0	1	0	—	0	0	.333	.333	.500	.833	+29	0	0	0	C3	0	0.1
Total	3	57	139	10	37	4	1	0	16	8	—	0	5	.266	.306	.309	.615	-25	0	2	0	C37	0	-0.9
Dugan, Joe	Joseph Anthony "Jumping Joe" B5.12.1897 Mahanoy City PA D7.7.1982 Norwood MA BR/TR/5'11"/160 d7.5 Col Holy Cross																							
1917	Phi A	43	134	9	26	8	0	0	16	3	—	3	16	.194	.229	.254	.483	-52	0	—	—	S39,2b2	—	-0.6
1918	Phi A	121	411	26	80	11	3	3	34	16	—	3	55	.195	.230	.258	.488	-53	4	—	—	S86,2b34	—	-0.6
1919	Phi A	104	387	25	105	17	2	1	30	11	—	5	30	.271	.300	.333	.633	-23	9	—	—	S98,2b4,3b2	—	-0.5
1920	Phi A	123	491	65	158	40	5	3	60	19	—	3	51	.322	.351	.442	.793	+8	5	8	38	3b60,S32,2b31	—	1.0
1921	Phi A	119	461	54	136	22	6	10	58	28	—	5	45	.295	.342	.434	.776	-4	5	1	83	3b119	—	-1.7
1922	Bos A	84	341	45	98	22	3	3	38	9	—	1	28	.287	.308	.396	.704	-17	2	3	40	3b64,S21	—	-1.2
1922	†NY A	60	252	44	72	9	1	3	25	13	—	4	21	.286	.331	.365	.696	-21	1	0	100	3b60	—	-1.2
1922	Year	144	593	89	170	31	4	6	63	22	—	5	49	.287	.318	.383	.701	-19	3	3	50	3b124,S21	—	-2.4
1923	†NY A	146	644	111	182	30	7	7	67	25	—	2	41	.283	.311	.384	.695	-19	4	2	67	3b146	—	-2.4
1924	NY A	148	610	105	184	31	7	3	56	31	—	5	33	.302	.341	.390	.731	-12	1	2	33	3b148,2b2	—	-1.5
1925	NY A	102	404	50	118	19	4	0	31	19	—	4	20	.292	.330	.359	.689	-24	2	4	33	3b96	—	-0.5
1926	†NY A	123	434	39	125	19	5	1	64	25	—	1	16	.288	.328	.362	.690	-19	2	4	33	3b122	—	-2.0
1927	†NY A	112	387	44	104	24	3	2	43	27	—	3	37	.269	.321	.362	.683	-21	1	4	20	3b111	—	-2.4
1928	†NY A	94	312	33	86	15	0	6	34	16	—	3	15	.276	.317	.381	.698	-15	1	0	100	3b91/2b	—	-1.7
1929	Bos N	60	125	14	38	10	0	0	15	8	—	0	8	.304	.346	.384	.730	-16	0	—	—	3b24,S5,2b2,O2L	—	-0.7
1931	Det A	8	17	1	4	0	0	0	0	0	—	0	3	.235	.235	.235	.470	-77	0	0	0	3b5	—	-0.2

YEAR	TM LG	G	AB	R	H	2B	3B	HR	RBI	BB	IB	HP	SO	AVG	OBP	SLG	OPS	AOPS	SB	CS	SB%	GAMES AT POSITION	DL	BFW
Total	14	1447	5410	665	1516	277	46	42	571	250	—	42	419	.280	.317	.372	.689	-18	37	28	100	3b1048,S281,2b76,O2L	—	-16.2
Team	7	785	3043	426	871	147	27	22	320	156	—	22	183	.286	.326	.374	.700	-18	12	16	43	3b774,2b3	—	-11.7
/150	1	150	581	81	166	28	5	4	61	30	—	4	35	.286	.326	.374	.700	-18	2	3	40	3b148/2	—	-2.2

DUNCAN, SHELLEY DAVID SHELLEY B9.29.1979 TUCSON AZ BR/TR/6'5"/215 DR 2001 NYA 2/62 d7.20 F–DAVE B–CHRIS COL ARIZONA

YEAR	TM LG	G	AB	R	H	2B	3B	HR	RBI	BB	IB	HP	SO	AVG	OBP	SLG	OPS	AOPS	SB	CS	SB%	GAMES AT POSITION	DL	BFW
2007	†NY A	34	74	16	19	1	0	7	17	8	0	0	20	.257	.329	.554	.883	+26	0	0	0	D14,O12(4/0/8),1b9	0	0.3

DUNCAN, MARIANO MARIANO (NALASCO) B3.13.1963 SAN PEDRO DE MACORIS, D.R. BR/TR (BB 1985–87)/6'0"/(160–200) d4.9 C2 OF(88/2/6)

YEAR	TM LG	G	AB	R	H	2B	3B	HR	RBI	BB	IB	HP	SO	AVG	OBP	SLG	OPS	AOPS	SB	CS	SB%	GAMES AT POSITION	DL	BFW
1996	†NY A	109	400	62	136	34	3	8	56	9	1	1	77	.340	.352	.500	.852	+13	4	3	57	2b104,3b3,O3(2/0/1),D2	18	1.1
1997	NY A	50	172	16	42	8	0	1	13	6	0	0	39	.244	.270	.308	.578	-49	2	1	67	2b41,O6L,D2	0	-0.9
Total	12	1279	4677	619	1247	233	37	87	491	201	12	37	913	.267	.300	.388	.688	-14	174	57	75	2b585,S540,O94L,3b36,1b24,D4	186	-6.2
Team	2	159	572	78	178	42	3	9	69	15	1	1	116	.311	.327	.442	.769	-6	6	4	60	2b145,O9(2/0/1),D4,3b3	18	0.2
/150	2	150	540	74	168	40	3	8	65	14	1	1	109	.311	.327	.442	.769	-6	6	4	60	2b137,O8(2/0/1),D4,3b3	17	0.2

DUROCHER, LEO LEO ERNEST "THE LIP" B7.27.1905 W.SPRINGFIELD MA D10.7.1991 PALM SPRINGS CA BR/TR (BB 1928–29)/5'10"/160 d10.2 M24/C4 HF1994

YEAR	TM LG	G	AB	R	H	2B	3B	HR	RBI	BB	IB	HP	SO	AVG	OBP	SLG	OPS	AOPS	SB	CS	SB%	GAMES AT POSITION	DL	BFW
1925	NY A	2	1	1	0	0	0	0	0	0	—	0	0	.000	.000	.000	.000	-199	0	0	0	/H	—	0.0
1928	†NY A	102	296	46	80	8	6	0	31	22	—	3	52	.270	.327	.338	.665	-23	1	4	20	2b66,S29	—	-0.2
1929	NY A	106	341	53	84	4	5	0	32	34	—	3	33	.246	.320	.287	.607	-38	3	1	75	S93,2b12	—	1.0
Total	17	1637	5350	575	1320	210	56	24	567	377	—	18	480	.247	.299	.320	.619	-34	31	5	100	S1509,2b98/3b	0	-17.1
Team	3	210	638	100	164	12	11	0	63	56	—	6	85	.257	.323	.310	.633	-31	4	5	44	S122,2b78	—	0.8
/150	2	150	456	71	117	9	8	0	45	40	—	4	61	.257	.323	.310	.633	-31	3	4	43	S87,2b56	—	0.6

DURST, CEDRIC CEDRIC MONTGOMERY B8.23.1896 AUSTIN TX D2.16.1971 SAN DIEGO CA BL/TL/5'11"/160 d5.30

YEAR	TM LG	G	AB	R	H	2B	3B	HR	RBI	BB	IB	HP	SO	AVG	OBP	SLG	OPS	AOPS	SB	CS	SB%	GAMES AT POSITION	DL	BFW
1922	StL A	15	12	5	4	1	0	0	0	0	—	0	1	.333	.333	.417	.750	-9	0	0	0	O6(1/4/1)	—	0.0
1923	StL A	45	85	11	18	2	0	5	11	8	—	0	14	.212	.280	.412	.692	-24	0	0	0	O10(4/5/1),1b8	—	-0.7
1926	StL A	80	219	32	52	7	5	3	16	22	—	1	19	.237	.310	.356	.666	-30	0	5	0	O57(5/42/10),1b4	—	-1.3
1927	†NY A	65	129	18	32	4	3	0	25	6	—	0	7	.248	.281	.326	.607	-41	0	3	0	O36(13/6/17),1b2	—	-1.2
1928	†NY A	74	135	18	34	2	1	2	10	7	—	0	9	.252	.289	.326	.615	-37	1	0	100	O33(13/5/15),1b3	—	-0.9
1929	NY A	92	202	32	52	3	3	4	31	15	—	0	25	.257	.309	.361	.670	-23	3	2	60	O72(46/6/20)/1b	—	-0.6
1930	NY A	8	19	0	3	1	0	0	5	0	—	0	1	.158	.158	.211	.369	-108	0	0	0	O6L	—	-0.3
1930	Bos A	102	302	29	74	19	5	1	24	17	—	2	24	.245	.290	.351	.641	-36	3	1	75	O75(46/0/29)	—	-2.3
1930	Year	110	321	29	77	20	5	1	29	17	—	2	25	.240	.282	.343	.625	-40	3	1	75	O81(52/0/29)	—	-2.6
Total	7	481	1103	145	269	39	17	15	122	75	—	3	100	.244	.294	.351	.645	-33	7	11	39	O295(134/68/93),1b18	—	-7.3
Team	4	239	485	68	121	10	7	6	71	28	—	0	42	.249	.290	.336	.626	-35	4	5	44	O147(72/17/52),1b6	—	-3.0
/150	3	150	304	43	76	6	4	4	45	18	—	0	26	.249	.290	.336	.626	-35	3	3	50	O92(45/11/33),1b4	—	-1.9

EASLER, MIKE MICHAEL ANTHONY B11.29.1950 CLEVELAND OH BL/TR/6'1"/(190–196) DR 1969 HOUN 14/312 d9.5 C6

YEAR	TM LG	G	AB	R	H	2B	3B	HR	RBI	BB	IB	HP	SO	AVG	OBP	SLG	OPS	AOPS	SB	CS	SB%	GAMES AT POSITION	DL	BFW
1986	NY A	146	490	64	148	26	2	14	78	49	13	0	87	.302	.362	.449	.811	+21	3	2	60	D129,O11(8/0/3)	0	1.0
1987	NY A	65	167	13	47	6	0	4	21	14	0	1	32	.281	.337	.389	.726	-6	1	0	100	D32,O15(14/0/1)	0	-0.3
Total	14	1151	3677	465	1078	189	25	118	522	321	46	17	696	.293	.349	.454	.803	+17	20	26	43	O538(479/0/82),D433,1b29	37	4.5
Team	2	211	657	77	195	32	2	18	99	63	13	1	119	.297	.356	.434	.790	+14	4	2	67	D161,O26(22/0/3)	0	0.7
/150	1	150	467	55	139	23	1	13	70	45	9	1	85	.297	.356	.434	.790	+14	3	1	75	D114,O18(16/0/2)	0	0.5

EDWARDS, DOC HOWARD RODNEY B12.10.1936 RED JACKET WV BR/TR/6'2"/(200–215) d4.21 M3/C8 COL MIRA COSTA (CA) JC

YEAR	TM LG	G	AB	R	H	2B	3B	HR	RBI	BB	IB	HP	SO	AVG	OBP	SLG	OPS	AOPS	SB	CS	SB%	GAMES AT POSITION	DL	BFW
1965	NY A	45	100	3	19	3	0	1	9	13	6	1	14	.190	.289	.250	.539	-45	1	2	33	C43	0	-0.6
Total	5	317	906	69	216	33	0	15	87	53	17	9	109	.238	.287	.325	.612	-32	1	4	20	C274,1b7	0	-2.7

EENHOORN, ROBERT ROBERT FRANCISCUS B2.9.1968 ROTTERDAM, NETHERLANDS BR/TR/6'3"/185 DR 1990 NYA 2/45 d4.27 COL DAVIDSON

YEAR	TM LG	G	AB	R	H	2B	3B	HR	RBI	BB	IB	HP	SO	AVG	OBP	SLG	OPS	AOPS	SB	CS	SB%	GAMES AT POSITION	DL	BFW
1994	NY A	3	4	1	2	1	0	0	0	0	0	0	0	.500	.500	.750	1.250	+124	0	0	0	S3	0	0.0
1995	NY A	5	14	1	2	1	0	0	2	1	0	0	3	.143	.200	.214	.414	-92	0	0	0	2b3,S2	0	-0.2
1996	NY A	12	14	2	1	0	0	0	2	2	0	0	3	.071	.167	.071	.238	-131	0	0	0	2b10,3b2	0	-0.2
1996	Cal A	6	15	1	4	0	0	0	0	0	0	0	2	.267	.267	.267	.534	-65	0	0	0	S4,2b2	0	-0.2
1996	Year	18	29	3	5	0	0	0	2	2	0	0	5	.172	.212	.172	.384	-97	0	0	0	2b12,S4,3b2	0	-0.4
1997	Ana A	11	20	2	7	1	0	1	6	0	0	0	2	.350	.333	.550	.883	+30	0	0	0	3b5,2b3,S2	0	-0.2
Total	4	37	67	7	16	3	0	1	10	3	0	0	10	.239	.260	.328	.588	-47	0	0	0	2b18,S11,3b7	0	-0.8
Team	3	20	32	4	5	2	0	0	4	3	0	0	6	.156	.216	.219	.435	-85	0	0	0	2b13,S5,3b2	0	-0.4

ELBERFELD, KID NORMAN ARTHUR "THE TABASCO KID" B4.13.1875 POMEROY OH D1.13.1944 CHATTANOOGA TN BR/TR/5'7"/158 d5.30 M1

YEAR	TM LG	G	AB	R	H	2B	3B	HR	RBI	BB	IB	HP	SO	AVG	OBP	SLG	OPS	AOPS	SB	CS	SB%	GAMES AT POSITION	DL	BFW
1898	Phi N	14	38	1	9	4	0	0	7	5	—	7	—	.237	.420	.342	.762	+24	0	—	—	3b14	—	-0.2
1899	Cin N	41	138	23	36	4	2	0	22	15	—	11	—	.261	.378	.319	.697	-10	5	—	—	S24,3b18	—	-0.4
1901	Det A	121	432	76	133	21	11	3	76	57	—	7	—	.308	.397	.428	.825	+23	23	—	—	S121	—	3.5
1902	Det A	130	488	70	127	17	6	1	64	55	—	11	—	.260	.348	.326	.674	-14	19	—	—	S130	—	0.8
1903	Det A	35	132	29	45	5	3	0	19	11	—	5	—	.341	.412	.424	.836	+56	6	—	—	S34/3b	—	1.6
1903	NY A	90	349	49	100	18	5	0	45	22	—	10	—	.287	.346	.367	.713	+7	16	—	—	S90	—	1.1
1903	Year	125	481	78	145	23	8	0	64	33	—	**15**	—	.301	.365	.383	.748	+20	22	—	—	S124/3b	—	2.7
1904	NY A	122	445	55	117	13	5	2	46	37	—	13	—	.263	.337	.328	.665	+6	18	—	—	S122	—	2.2
1905	NY A	111	390	48	102	18	2	0	53	23	—	16	—	.262	.329	.318	.647	-5	18	—	—	S108	—	-0.1
1906	NY A	99	346	59	106	11	5	2	31	30	—	10	—	.306	.378	.384	.762	+26	19	—	—	S98	—	1.5
1907	NY A	120	447	61	121	17	6	0	51	36	—	13	—	.271	.343	.336	.679	+8	22	—	—	S118	—	2.4
1908	NY A	19	56	11	11	3	0	0	5	6	—	5	—	.196	.328	.250	.578	-13	1	—	—	S17,M	—	-0.1
1909	NY A	106	379	47	90	9	5	0	26	28	—	14	—	.237	.314	.288	.602	-11	23	—	—	S61,3b44	—	0.4
1910	Was A	127	455	53	114	9	2	2	42	35	—	13	—	.251	.322	.292	.614	-3	19	—	—	3b113,2b10,S3	—	-0.3
1911	Was A	127	404	58	110	19	4	0	47	65	—	**25**	—	.272	.405	.339	.744	+10	24	—	—	2b68,3b52	—	2.2
1914	Bro N	30	62	7	14	1	0	0	1	2	—	5	4	.226	.304	.242	.546	-38	0	—	—	S18/2b	—	-0.6
Total	14	1292	4561	647	1235	169	56	10	535	427	—	165	4	.271	.355	.339	.694	+5	213	—	—	S944,3b242,2b79	—	14.0
Team	7	667	2412	330	647	89	28	4	257	182	—	81	0	.268	.340	.333	.673	+4	117	—	—	S614,3b44/M	—	7.4
/150	2	150	542	74	146	20	6	1	58	41	—	18	0	.268	.340	.333	.673	+4	26	—	—	S138,3b10/M	—	1.7

ELLIOTT, GENE EUGENE BIRMINGHOUSE B2.8.1889 FAYETTE CO. PA D1.5.1976 HUNTINGDON PA BL/TR/5'7"/150 d4.13

YEAR	TM LG	G	AB	R	H	2B	3B	HR	RBI	BB	IB	HP	SO	AVG	OBP	SLG	OPS	AOPS	SB	CS	SB%	GAMES AT POSITION	DL	BFW
1911	NY A	5	13	1	1	1	0	0	1	2	—	0	—	.077	.200	.154	.354	-101	0	—	—	O2R/3b	—	-0.2

ELLIS, JOHN JOHN CHARLES B8.21.1948 NEW LONDON CT BR/TR/6'2.5"/(210–220) d5.17 COL MITCHELL (CT) JC

YEAR	TM LG	G	AB	R	H	2B	3B	HR	RBI	BB	IB	HP	SO	AVG	OBP	SLG	OPS	AOPS	SB	CS	SB%	GAMES AT POSITION	DL	BFW
1969	NY A	22	62	2	18	4	0	1	8	1	0	1	11	.290	.308	.403	.711	+2	0	2	0	C15	0	-0.3
1970	NY A	78	226	24	56	12	1	7	29	18	0	2	47	.248	.305	.403	.708	-1	0	1	0	1b53,3b5,C2	0	-0.7
1971	NY A	83	238	16	58	12	1	3	34	23	5	6	42	.244	.322	.340	.662	-7	0	0	0	1b65,C2	0	-1.0
1972	NY A	52	136	13	40	5	1	5	25	8	0	0	22	.294	.333	.456	.789	+36	0	0	0	C25,1b8	0	0.8
Total	13	883	2672	259	699	116	13	69	391	190	17	19	403	.262	.312	.392	.704	-1	6	10	38	1b304,C297,D170,3b5	215	-7.0
Team	4	235	662	55	172	33	3	16	96	50	5	9	122	.260	.317	.391	.708	+4	0	3	0	1b126,C44,3b5	0	-1.2
/150	3	150	423	35	110	21	2	10	61	32	3	6	78	.260	.317	.391	.708	+4	0	2	0	1b80,C28,3b3	0	-0.8

ELSTER, KEVIN KEVIN DANIEL B8.3.1964 SAN PEDRO CA BR/TR/6'2"/(180–205) DR 1984 NYN*2/28 d9.2 COL GOLDEN WEST (CA) JC

YEAR	TM LG	G	AB	R	H	2B	3B	HR	RBI	BB	IB	HP	SO	AVG	OBP	SLG	OPS	AOPS	SB	CS	SB%	GAMES AT POSITION	DL	BFW
1994	NY A	7	20	0	0	0	0	0	0	1	0	0	6	.000	.048	.000	.048	-189	0	0	0	S7	36	-0.3
1995	NY A	10	17	1	2	1	0	0	0	1	0	0	5	.118	.167	.176	.343	-111	0	0	0	S10/2b	0	-0.3
Total	13	940	2844	332	648	136	12	88	376	295	39	13	562	.228	.300	.377	.677	-18	14	11	56	S895,3b10,1b5/2b	467	1.0
Team	2	17	37	1	2	1	0	0	0	2	0	0	11	.054	.103	.081	.184	-153	0	0	0	S17/2	36	-0.6

ENGLE, CLYDE ARTHUR CLYDE "HACK" B3.19.1884 DAYTON OH D12.26.1939 BOSTON MA BR/TR/5'10"/190 d4.12 OF(142/111/26)

YEAR	TM LG	G	AB	R	H	2B	3B	HR	RBI	BB	IB	HP	SO	AVG	OBP	SLG	OPS	AOPS	SB	CS	SB%	GAMES AT POSITION	DL	BFW
1909	NY A	135	492	66	137	20	5	3	71	47	—	5	—	.278	.347	.358	.705	+22	18	—	—	O134(119/16/0)	—	2.3
1910	NY A	5	13	0	3	0	0	0	0	2	—	0	—	.231	.333	.231	.564	-27	1	—	—	O3L	—	-0.1

YEAR	TM LG	G	AB	R	H	2B	3B	HR	RBI	BB	IB	HP	SO	AVG	OBP	SLG	OPS	AOPS	SB	CS	SB%	GAMES AT POSITION	DL	BFW
Total	8	836	2822	373	748	101	39	12	318	271	—	25	119	.265	.335	.341	.676	-3	128	16	100	O276L,1b255,3b163,2b81,S9	—	-6.1
Team	2	140	505	66	140	20	5	3	71	49	—	5	0	.277	.346	.354	.700	+21	19	—	—	O137(119/16/0)	—	2.2
/150	2	150	541	71	150	21	5	3	76	53	—	5	0	.277	.346	.354	.700	+21	20	—	—	O147(128/17/0)	—	2.4

ESCALONA, FELIX Felix Eduardo B3.12.1979 Puerto Cabello, Carabobo, Venezuela BR/TR/6'0"/(185–190) d4.4

YEAR	TM LG	G	AB	R	H	2B	3B	HR	RBI	BB	IB	HP	SO	AVG	OBP	SLG	OPS	AOPS	SB	CS	SB%	GAMES AT POSITION	DL	BFW
2004	NY A	5	8	1	0	0	0	0	0	0	0	1	2	.000	.111	.000	.111	-168	0	0	0	S4/3b	0	-0.2
2005	NY A	10	14	0	4	1	0	0	2	1	0	1	4	.286	.375	.357	.732	-3	0	0	0	S5,3b3/1b2b	0	0.1
Total	4	84	206	20	43	11	2	0	13	6	0	9	56	.209	.261	.282	.543	-55	8	2	80	S43,2b27,3b9/1bD	0	-1.1
Team	2	15	22	1	4	1	0	0	2	1	0	2	6	.182	.200	.227	[illegible]	[illegible]	0	0	0	S9,3b4/12	0	-0.1

ESPINO, JUAN Juan (Reyes) B3.16.1956 Bonao, D.R. BR/TR/6'1"/190 d6.25

YEAR	TM LG	G	AB	R	H	2B	3B	HR	RBI	BB	IB	HP	SO	AVG	OBP	SLG	OPS	AOPS	SB	CS	SB%	GAMES AT POSITION	DL	BFW
1982	NY A	3	2	0	0	0	0	0	0	0	0	0	1	.000	.000	.000	.000	-199	0	0	0	C3	0	-0.1
1983	NY A	10	23	1	6	0	0	1	3	1	0	0	5	.261	.280	.391	.671	-11	0	0	0	C10	0	-0.2
1985	NY A	9	11	0	4	0	0	0	0	0	0	0	0	.364	.364	.364	.728	+2	0	0	0	C9	0	0.0
1986	NY A	27	37	1	6	2	0	0	5	2	0	0	9	.162	.200	.216	.416	-85	0	0	0	C27	0	-0.4
Total	4	49	73	2	16	2	0	1	8	3	0	0	15	.219	.244	.288	.532	-53	0	0	0	C49	0	-0.7

ESPINOZA, ALVARO Alvaro Alberto B2.19.1962 Valencia, Carabobo, Venez BR/TR/6'0"/(170–190) d9.14

YEAR	TM LG	G	AB	R	H	2B	3B	HR	RBI	BB	IB	HP	SO	AVG	OBP	SLG	OPS	AOPS	SB	CS	SB%	GAMES AT POSITION	DL	BFW
1984	Min A	1	0	0	0	0	0	0	0	0	0	0	0	+	+	+	.000	-100	0	0	0	/S	0	0.0
1985	Min A	32	57	5	15	2	0	0	9	1	0	1	9	.263	.288	.298	.586	-43	0	1	0	S31	0	-0.1
1986	Min A	37	42	4	9	1	0	0	1	1	0	0	10	.214	.233	.238	.471	-72	0	1	0	2b19,S18	0	-0.4
1988	NY A	3	3	0	0	0	0	0	0	0	0	0	0	.000	.000	.000	.000	-199	0	0	0	2b2/S	0	-0.1
1989	NY A	146	503	51	142	23	1	0	41	14	1	1	60	.282	.301	.332	.633	-21	3	3	50	S146	0	1.4
1990	NY A	150	438	31	98	12	2	2	20	16	0	5	54	.224	.258	.274	.532	-51	1	2	33	S150	0	0.2
1991	NY A	148	480	51	123	23	2	5	33	16	0	2	57	.256	.282	.344	.626	-28	4	1	80	S147,3b2/P	0	1.2
1993	Cle A	129	263	34	73	15	0	4	27	8	0	1	36	.278	.298	.380	.678	-18	2	2	50	3b99,S35,2b2	0	-1.2
1994	Cle A	90	231	27	55	13	0	1	19	6	0	1	33	.238	.258	.307	.565	-55	1	3	25	3b37,S36,2b20,1b3	0	-0.1
1995	†Cle A	66	143	15	36	4	0	2	17	2	0	1	16	.252	.264	.322	.586	-49	0	2	0	2b22,3b22,S19,1b2,D3	0	-1.3
1996	Cle A	59	112	12	25	4	2	4	11	6	0	3	18	.223	.279	.402	.681	-30	1	1	50	3b20,1b18,S16,2b5/D	0	-0.5
1996	NY N	48	134	19	41	7	2	4	16	4	0	0	19	.306	.324	.478	.802	+14	0	2	0	3b38,S7,2b2/1b	0	-0.1
1996	Major	107	246	31	66	11	4	8	27	10	0	3	37	.268	2.305	.443	2.748	+32	1	3	25	—	0	-0.6
1997	Sea A	33	72	3	13	1	0	0	7	2	0	1	12	.181	.213	.194	.407	-93	1	1	50	S17,2b14/3b	15	-0.6
Total	12	942	2478	252	630	105	9	22	201	76	1	16	324	.254	.279	.331	.610	-35	13	19	41	S624,3b219,2b86,1b24,D4/P	15	-1.6
Team	4	447	1424	133	363	58	5	7	94	46	1	8	171	.255	.281	.317	.598	-33	8	6	57	S444,2b2,3b2/P	0	2.7
/150	1	150	478	45	122	19	2	2	32	15	0	3	57	.255	.281	.317	.598	-33	3	2	60	S149/23P	0	0.9

ESTALELLA, BOBBY Robert M B8.23.1974 Hialeah FL BR/TR/6'1"/(195–225) Dr 1992 PhiN 23/641 d9.17 gf-Bobby Col Miami-Dade Kendall (FL) CC

YEAR	TM LG	G	AB	R	H	2B	3B	HR	RBI	BB	IB	HP	SO	AVG	OBP	SLG	OPS	AOPS	SB	CS	SB%	GAMES AT POSITION	DL	BFW
2001	NY A	3	4	1	0	0	0	0	0	1	0	1	2	.000	.333	.000	.333	-101	0	0	0	C3	0	0.0
Total	9	310	904	126	195	49	5	48	147	130	11	7	290	.216	.315	.440	.755	-8	6	2	75	C299,D2	265	0.5

ETTEN, NICK Nicholas Raymond Thomas B9.19.1913 Spring Grove IL D10.18.1990 Hinsdale IL BL/TL/6'2"/198 d9.8 Col Villanova

YEAR	TM LG	G	AB	R	H	2B	3B	HR	RBI	BB	IB	HP	SO	AVG	OBP	SLG	OPS	AOPS	SB	CS	SB%	GAMES AT POSITION	DL	BFW
1938	Phi A	22	81	6	21	6	2	0	11	9	—	0	7	.259	.333	.383	.716	-19	1	0	100	1b22	—	-0.6
1939	Phi A	43	155	20	39	11	2	3	29	16	—	0	11	.252	.322	.406	.728	-13	0	0	0	1b41	—	-0.9
1941	Phi N	151	540	78	168	27	4	14	79	82	—	3	33	.311	.405	.454	.859	+47	9	—	—	1b150	0	2.1
1942	Phi N	139	459	37	121	21	3	8	41	67	—	0	26	.264	.357	.375	.732	+20	3	—	—	1b135	0	0.2
1943	†NY A	154	583	78	158	35	5	14	107	76	—	0	31	.271	.355	.420	.775	+26	3	7	30	1b154	0	-0.3
1944	NY A	**154**	573	88	168	25	4	**22**	91	**97**	—	4	29	.293	.399	.466	.865	+42	4	2	67	1b154	0	3.1
1945	NY A*	**152**	565	77	161	24	4	18	**111**	90	—	4	23	.285	.387	.437	.824	+33	2	3	40	1b152	0	0.8
1946	NY A	108	323	37	75	14	1	9	49	38	—	1	35	.232	.315	.365	.680	-12	0	1	0	1b84	0	-0.9
1947	Phi N	14	41	5	10	4	0	1	8	5	—	0	4	.244	.326	.415	.741	-1	0	—	—	1b11	0	0.1
Total	9	937	3320	426	921	167	25	89	526	480	—	12	199	.277	.371	.423	.794	+25	22	13	100	1b903	0	3.6
Team	4	568	2044	280	562	98	14	63	358	301	—	9	118	.275	.370	.429	.799	+27	9	13	41	1b544	0	2.7
/150	1	150	540	74	148	26	4	17	95	79	—	2	31	.275	.370	.429	.799	+27	2	3	40	1b144	0	0.7

EVANS, BARRY Barry Steven B11.30.1956 Atlanta GA BR/TR/6'1"/180 Dr 1977 SDN 2/34 d9.4 Col West Georgia

YEAR	TM LG	G	AB	R	H	2B	3B	HR	RBI	BB	IB	HP	SO	AVG	OBP	SLG	OPS	AOPS	SB	CS	SB%	GAMES AT POSITION	DL	BFW
1982	NY A	17	31	2	8	3	0	0	2	6	0	1	6	.258	.395	.355	.750	+9	0	0	0	2b8,3b6,S4	0	0.0
Total	5	224	501	40	126	17	3	2	41	41	4	1	62	.251	.304	.309	.613	-23	3	5	38	3b150,2b34,S12,1b11	18	-2.4

FALLON, CHARLIE Charles Augustus B3.7.1881 New York NY D6.10.1960 Kings Park NY BR/TR/5'6"/? d6.30

YEAR	TM LG	G	AB	R	H	2B	3B	HR	RBI	BB	IB	HP	SO	AVG	OBP	SLG	OPS	AOPS	SB	CS	SB%	GAMES AT POSITION	DL	BFW
1905	NY A	1	0	0	0	0	0	0	0	0	—	0	—	+	+	+	.000	-100	0	—	—	/R	—	0.0

FARRELL, DOC Edward Stephen B12.26.1901 Johnson City NY D12.20.1966 Livingston NJ BR/TR/5'8"/160 d6.15 Col Penn

YEAR	TM LG	G	AB	R	H	2B	3B	HR	RBI	BB	IB	HP	SO	AVG	OBP	SLG	OPS	AOPS	SB	CS	SB%	GAMES AT POSITION	DL	BFW
1932	NY A	26	63	4	11	1	1	0	4	2	—	1	8	.175	.212	.222	.434	-87	0	0	0	2b16,S5,1b2/3b	—	-0.8
1933	NY A	44	93	16	25	0	0	0	6	16	—	0	6	.269	.376	.269	.645	-22	0	0	0	S22,2b20	—	-0.4
Total	9	591	1799	181	467	63	8	10	213	109	—	10	120	.260	.306	.320	.626	-34	14	1	100	S376,2b118,3b56,1b3	—	-8.5
Team	2	70	156	20	36	1	1	0	10	18	—	1	14	.231	.314	.250	.564	-47	0	0	0	2b36,S27,1b2/3	—	-1.2

FASANO, SAL Salvatore Frank B8.10.1971 Chicago IL BR/TR/6'2"/(220–245) Dr 1993 KCA 37/1029 d4.3 Col Evansville

YEAR	TM LG	G	AB	R	H	2B	3B	HR	RBI	BB	IB	HP	SO	AVG	OBP	SLG	OPS	AOPS	SB	CS	SB%	GAMES AT POSITION	DL	BFW
2006	NY A	28	49	3	7	4	0	1	5	2	0	3	14	.143	.222	.286	.508	-70	0	0	0	C27/D	0	-0.4
Total	10	412	1063	131	233	45	0	47	134	69	1	44	310	.219	.293	.394	.687	-26	2	3	40	C400,1b6,D6/3b	67	-1.7

FERNANDEZ, FRANK Frank B4.16.1943 Staten Island NY BR/TR/6'1"/(192–195) d9.12 Mil 1967

YEAR	TM LG	G	AB	R	H	2B	3B	HR	RBI	BB	IB	HP	SO	AVG	OBP	SLG	OPS	AOPS	SB	CS	SB%	GAMES AT POSITION	DL	BFW
1967	NY A	9	28	1	6	2	0	1	4	2	0	1	7	.214	.281	.393	.674	+4	1	1	50	C7,O2R	0	0.1
1968	NY A	51	135	15	23	6	1	7	30	35	2	0	50	.170	.341	.385	.726	+24	1	0	100	C45,O4R	0	1.3
1969	NY A	89	229	34	51	6	1	12	29	65	3	3	68	.223	.399	.415	.814	+33	1	3	25	C65,O14R	0	1.7
1970	Oak A	94	252	30	54	5	0	15	44	40	4	2	76	.214	.327	.413	.740	+6	1	0	100	C76/lf	0	0.8
1971	Oak A	2	4	0	0	0	0	0	0	1	0	0	2	.000	.200	.000	.200	-140	0	0	0	C2	24	-0.3
1971	Was A	18	30	0	3	0	0	0	4	4	0	0	10	.100	.194	.100	.294	-112	0	0	0	O6(3/1/2)/C	0	-0.6
1971	Oak A	2	5	1	1	1	0	0	1	0	0	0	1	.200	.200	.400	.600	-32	0	0	0	/C	0	-0.3
1971	Year	22	39	1	4	1	0	0	5	5	0	0	13	.103	.196	.128	.324	-104	0	0	0	O6(3/1/2),C4	0	-1.2
1971	Chi N	17	41	11	7	1	0	4	4	17	0	0	15	.171	.414	.488	.902	+35	0	0	0	C16	0	0.4
1971	Major	39	80	12	11	2	0	4	9	22	0	0	28	.138	2.324	.313	2.636	-50	0	0	0	—	24	-0.8
1972	Chi N	3	3	0	0	0	0	0	0	0	0	0	2	.000	.000	.000	.000	-190	0	0	0	/C	0	-0.1
Total	6	285	727	92	145	21	2	39	116	164	9	6	231	.199	.350	.395	.745	+13	4	4	50	C214,O27(4/1/22)	24	3.0
Team	3	149	392	50	80	14	2	20	63	102	5	4	125	.204	.372	.403	.775	+28	3	4	43	C117,O20R	0	3.1
/150	3	150	395	50	81	14	2	20	63	103	5	4	126	.204	.372	.403	.775	+28	3	4	43	C118,O20R	0	3.1

FERNANDEZ, TONY Octavio Antonio (Castro) (b Octavio Antonio Fernando (Castro)) B6.30.1962 San Pedro de Macoris, D.R. BB/TR/6'2"/(175–195) d9.2 [DL 1996 NY A 182]

YEAR	TM LG	G	AB	R	H	2B	3B	HR	RBI	BB	IB	HP	SO	AVG	OBP	SLG	OPS	AOPS	SB	CS	SB%	GAMES AT POSITION	DL	BFW
1995	†NY A	108	384	57	94	20	2	5	45	42	4	4	40	.245	.322	.346	.668	-24	6	6	50	S103,2b4	18	-1.9
Total	17	2158	7911	1057	2276	414	92	94	844	690	48	64	784	.288	.347	.399	.746	+1	246	138	64	S1573,3b302,2b201,D26	224	20.9
/150	1	150	533	79	131	28	3	7	62	58	6	6	56	.245	.322	.346	.668	-24	8	8	50	S143,2b6	278	-2.6

FERRARO, MIKE Michael Dennis B8.18.1944 Kingston NY BR/TR/5'11"/175 d9.6 M2/C13

YEAR	TM LG	G	AB	R	H	2B	3B	HR	RBI	BB	IB	HP	SO	AVG	OBP	SLG	OPS	AOPS	SB	CS	SB%	GAMES AT POSITION	DL	BFW
1966	NY A	10	28	4	5	0	0	0	0	3	0	1	3	.179	.281	.179	.460	-63	0	0	0	3b10	0	-0.2
1968	NY A	23	87	5	14	0	1	0	1	2	1	0	17	.161	.180	.184	.364	-89	0	0	0	3b22	0	-0.7
Total	4	162	500	28	116	18	2	2	30	23	2	1	61	.232	.265	.288	.553	-33	0	5	0	3b147/S	0	-4.3
Team	2	33	115	9	19	0	1	0	1	5	1	1	20	.165	.207	.183	.390	-82	0	0	0	3b32	0	-0.9

Batters

YEAR	TM LG	G	AB	R	H	2B	3B	HR	RBI	BB	IB	HP	SO	AVG	OBP	SLG	OPS	AOPS	SB	CS	SB%	GAMES AT POSITION	DL	BFW
Ferrell, Wes	Wesley Cheek B2.2.1908 Greensboro NC D12.9.1976 Sarasota FL BR/TR/6'2"/195 d9.9 b-Rick ▲																							
1938	NY A	5	12	1	2	1	0	0	1	1	—	0	4	.167	.231	.250	.481	-80	0	0	0	P5	—	0.0
1939	NY A	3	8	0	1	1	0	0	1	0	—	0	2	.125	.125	.250	.375	-106	0	0	0	P3	—	0.0
Total	15	548	1176	175	329	57	12	38	208	129	—	0	185	.280	.351	.446	.797	-1	2	0	100	P374,O13L	0	0.1
Team	2	8	20	1	3	2	0	0	2	1	—	0	6	.150	.190	.250	.440	-90	0	0	0	P8	—	0.0
Fewster, Chick	Wilson Lloyd B11.10.1895 Baltimore MD D4.16.1945 Baltimore MD BR/TR/5'11"/160 d9.19																							
1917	NY A	11	36	2	8	0	0	0	1	5	—	0	5	.222	.317	.222	.539	-36	1	—	—	2b11	—	-0.1
1918	NY A	5	2	1	1	0	0	0	0	0	—	0	0	.500	.500	.500	1.000	+97	0	—	—	2b2	—	0.0
1919	NY A	81	244	38	69	9	3	1	15	34	—	7	36	.283	.386	.357	.743	+8	8	—	—	O41(0/13/28),S24,2b4,3b2	—	0.8
1920	NY A	21	21	8	6	1	0	0	1	7	—	0	2	.286	.464	.333	.797	+10	0	1	0	S6,2b3	—	0.0
1921	†NY A	66	207	44	58	19	0	1	19	28	—	6	43	.280	.382	.386	.768	-6	4	4	50	O43(7/35/1),2b15	—	-0.2
1922	NY A	44	132	20	32	4	1	1	9	16	—	0	23	.242	.324	.311	.635	-35	2	4	33	O38(35/4/0),2b2	—	-0.8
1922	Bos A	23	83	8	24	4	1	0	9	6	—	1	10	.289	.344	.361	.705	-15	8	3	73	3b23	—	0.2
1922	Year	67	215	28	56	8	2	1	18	22	—	1	33	.260	.332	.330	.662	-28	10	7	59	O38(35/4/0),3b23,2b2	—	-0.6
1923	Bos A	90	284	32	67	10	1	0	15	39	—	3	35	.236	.334	.278	.612	-38	7	14	33	2b49,S37,3b3	—	-2.3
1924	Cle A	101	322	36	86	12	2	0	36	24	—	3	36	.267	.324	.317	.641	-35	12	12	50	2b94,3b5	—	-3.5
1925	Cle A	93	294	39	73	16	1	1	38	36	—	0	25	.248	.330	.320	.650	-35	6	9	40	2b83,3b10/rf	—	-2.4
1926	Bro N	105	337	53	82	16	3	2	24	45	—	5	49	.243	.341	.326	.667	-18	9	—	—	2b103	—	-1.6
1927	Bro N	4	1	1	0	0	0	0	0	0	—	0	0	.000	.000	.000	.000	-199	0	—	—	/H	—	0.0
Total	11	644	1963	282	506	91	12	6	167	240	—	25	264	.258	.346	.326	.672	-23	57	47	100	2b366,O123(42/52/30),S67,3b43	—	-9.9
Team	6	228	642	113	174	33	4	3	45	90	—	13	109	.271	.372	.349	.721	-7	15	9	100	O122(12/52/29),2b37,S30,3b2	—	-0.3
/150	4	150	422	74	114	22	3	2	30	59	—	9	72	.271	.372	.349	.721	-7	10	6	100	O80(8/34/19),2b24,S20/3	—	-0.2
Fielder, Cecil	Cecil Grant B9.21.1963 Los Angeles CA BR/TR/6'3"/(230–261) Dr 1982 KCA S4/67 d7.20 s-Prince Col Nevada–Las Vegas																							
1996	†NY A	53	200	30	52	8	0	13	37	24	4	2	48	.260	.342	.495	.837	+9	0	0	0	D43,1b9	0	-0.1
1997	†NY A	98	361	40	94	15	0	13	61	51	3	7	87	.260	.358	.410	.768	+2	0	0	0	D87,1b8	62	-0.2
Total	13	1470	5157	744	1313	200	7	319	1008	693	76	43	1316	.255	.345	.482	.827	+18	2	6	25	1b905,D535,3b7,2b2/lf	62	6.6
Team	2	151	561	70	146	23	0	26	98	75	7	9	135	.260	.352	.440	.792	+4	0	0	0	D130,1b17	62	-0.3
/150	2	150	557	70	145	23	0	26	97	75	7	9	134	.260	.352	.440	.792	+4	0	0	0	D129,1b17	62	-0.3
Figga, Mike	Michael Anthony B7.31.1970 Tampa FL BR/TR/6'0"/200 Dr 1989 NYA 44/1140 d9.16 Col Central Florida CC [DL 1996 NY A 30]																							
1997	NY A	2	4	0	0	0	0	0	0	0	0	0	3	.000	.000	.000	.000	-199	0	0	0	/CD	0	-0.1
1998	NY A	1	4	1	1	0	0	0	0	0	0	0	1	.250	.250	.250	.500	-68	0	0	0	/C	0	-0.1
1999	NY A	2	0	0	0	0	0	0	0	0	0	0	0	+	+	+	.000	-100	0	0	0	C2	0	0.0
Total	3	46	94	13	20	4	0	1	5	2	0	0	31	.213	.227	.287	.514	-68	0	2	0	C45/D	30	-1.3
Team	3	5	8	1	1	0	0	0	0	0	0	0	4	.125	.125	.125	.250	-134	0	0	0	C3/D	30	-0.2
Fischlin, Mike	Michael Thomas B9.13.1955 Sacramento CA BR/TR/6'1"/165 Dr 1975 NYA 7/163 d9.3 Col Cal St.–Sacramento																							
1986	NY A	71	102	9	21	2	0	0	3	8	0	0	29	.206	.261	.225	.486	-65	0	1	0	S42,2b27	0	-1.1
Total	10	517	941	109	207	29	6	3	68	92	1	5	142	.220	.291	.273	.564	-43	24	13	65	S268,2b191,3b32,1b6,D6/C	0	-3.7
Fisher, Gus	August Harris B10.21.1885 Pottsboro TX D4.8.1972 Portland OR BL/TR/5'10"/175 d4.18																							
1912	NY A	4	10	1	1	0	0	0	0	0	—	0	—	.100	.100	.100	.200	-140	0	—	—	C4	—	-0.1
Total	2	74	213	21	54	6	3	0	12	7	—	5	—	.254	.293	.310	.603	-32	6	—	—	C62/1b	—	-0.2
Fitzgerald, Justin	Justin Howard B6.26.1891 San Mateo CA D1.18.1945 San Mateo CA BL/TR/5'8"/160 d6.20 Col Santa Clara																							
1911	NY A	16	37	6	10	1	0	0	6	4	—	0	—	.270	.341	.297	.638	-26	4	—	—	O9L	—	-0.2
Total	2	82	170	27	49	9	0	0	12	17	—	1	6	.288	.356	.341	.697	+2	7	—	—	O68(43/2/19)	—	-0.5
Flaherty, John	John Timothy B10.21.1967 New York NY BR/TR/6'1"/(195–205) Dr 1988 BosA 25/641 d4.12 Col George Washington																							
2003	†NY A	40	105	16	28	8	0	4	14	4	1	1	19	.267	.297	.457	.754	-3	0	0	0	C40	0	-0.4
2004	NY A	47	127	11	32	9	0	6	16	5	2	1	25	.252	.286	.465	.751	-9	0	2	0	C46	0	0.1
2005	†NY A	47	127	10	21	5	0	2	11	6	0	1	26	.165	.206	.252	.458	-78	0	0	0	C45/1b	0	-0.5
Total	14	1047	3372	319	849	176	3	80	395	175	15	19	514	.252	.290	.377	.667	-27	10	19	34	C1032,D2/1b	25	-13.1
Team	3	134	359	37	81	22	0	12	41	15	3	3	70	.226	.261	.387	.648	-32	0	2	0	C131/1	0	-0.8
/150	3	150	402	41	91	25	0	13	46	17	3	3	78	.226	.261	.387	.648	-32	0	2	0	C147/1	0	-0.9
Foli, Tim	Timothy John B12.8.1950 Culver City CA BR/TR/6'0"/(170–176) Dr 1968 NYN 1/1 d9.11 NG 1971 C10																							
1984	NY A	61	163	8	41	11	0	0	16	2	0	1	16	.252	.265	.319	.584	-37	0	0	0	S28,2b21,3b10,1b2	0	0.1
Total	16	1696	6047	576	1515	241	20	25	501	265	29	35	399	.251	.283	.309	.592	-36	81	55	60	S1524,2b92,3b66,O3(1/2/0),1b2	140	2.6
Foote, Barry	Barry Clifton B2.16.1952 Smithfield NC BR/TR/6'3"/(205–220) Dr 1970 MonN 1/3 d9.14 C3																							
1981	†NY A	40	125	12	26	4	0	6	10	8	0	0	21	.208	.256	.384	.640	-17	0	0	0	C34/1bD	0	0.6
1982	NY A	17	48	4	7	5	0	0	2	1	0	0	11	.146	.160	.250	.410	-88	0	0	0	C17	31	-0.9
Total	10	687	2127	191	489	103	10	57	230	136	29	10	287	.230	.277	.368	.645	-25	10	6	63	C637,D4,1b2,3b2	81	-1.6
Team	2	57	173	16	33	9	0	6	12	9	0	0	32	.191	.230	.347	.577	-36	0	0	0	C51/1D	31	-0.3
Foster, Eddie	Edward Cunningham "Kid" B2.13.1887 Chicago IL D1.15.1937 Washington DC BR/TR/5'6.5"/145 d4.14																							
1910	NY A	30	83	5	11	2	0	0	1	8	—	1	—	.133	.217	.157	.374	-84	2	—	—	S22	—	-1.0
Total	13	1500	5652	732	1490	191	71	6	451	528	—	25	255	.264	.329	.326	.655	-11	195	67	100	3b1161,2b269,S25	—	-9.1
Fournier, Jack	John Frank B9.28.1889 AuSable MI D9.5.1973 Tacoma WA BL/TR/6'0"/195 d4.13																							
1918	NY A	27	100	9	35	6	1	0	12	7	—	0	7	.350	.393	.430	.823	+45	7	—	—	1b27	—	0.2
Total	15	1530	5208	822	1631	252	113	136	859	587	—	89	408	.313	.392	.483	.875	+43	146	96	100	1b1313,O87(53/14/20)/P	—	24.4
Fox, Andy	Andrew Junipero B1.12.1971 Sacramento CA BL/TR/6'4"/(200–205) Dr 1989 NYA 2/45 d4.7 OF(24/10/47)																							
1996	†NY A	113	189	26	37	4	0	3	13	20	0	1	28	.196	.276	.265	.541	-62	11	3	79	2b72,3b31,S9/rfD	0	-1.6
1997	†NY A	22	31	13	7	1	0	0	1	7	0	0	9	.226	.368	.258	.626	-32	2	1	67	3b11,2b5,S2,O2R,D2	0	0.3
Total	9	776	1925	248	461	65	17	30	168	197	21	47	407	.239	.324	.338	.662	-27	74	25	75	S264,2b169,3b135,O78R,1b16,D6	120	-8.2
Team	2	135	220	39	44	5	0	3	14	27	0	1	37	.200	.290	.264	.554	-57	13	4	76	2b77,3b42,S11,rf,D3	0	-1.3
/150	2	150	244	43	49	6	0	3	16	30	0	1	41	.200	.290	.264	.554	-57	14	4	78	2b86,3b47,S12,rf,D3	0	-1.4
French, Ray	Raymond Edward B1.9.1895 Alameda CA D4.3.1978 Alameda CA BR/TR/5'9.5"/158 d9.17																							
1920	NY A	2	2	2	0	0	0	0	1	0	—	0	1	.000	.000	.000	.000	-197	0	0	0	/S	—	-0.1
Total	3	82	187	29	36	6	1	0	19	14	—	1	21	.193	.252	.235	.487	-72	3	1	75	S59,2b3	—	-1.5
Frey, Lonny	Linus Reinhard "Junior" B8.23.1910 St.Louis MO BL/TR (BB 1933–38)/5'10"/160 d8.29 Mil 1944–45																							
1947	†NY A	24	28	10	5	2	0	0	2	10	—	1	1	.179	.410	.250	.660	-13	3	0	100	2b8	0	0.3
1948	NY A	1	0	1	0	0	0	0	0	0	—	0	0	+	+	+	.000	-100	0	0	0	/R	0	0.0
Total	14	1535	5517	848	1482	263	69	61	549	752	—	28	525	.269	.359	.374	.733	+4	105	0	100	2b966,S420,O34(7/15/12),3b22	0	13.6
Team	2	25	28	11	5	2	0	0	2	10	—	1	1	.179	.410	.250	.660	-13	3	0	100	2b8	0	0.3
Fultz, Dave	David Lewis B5.29.1875 Staunton VA D10.29.1959 DeLand FL BR/TR/5'11"/170 d7.1 Col Brown OF(34/510/10)																							
1898	Phi N	19	55	7	10	2	2	0	5	6	—	0	—	.182	.262	.291	.553	-39	1	—	—	O14(8/3/3),2b3/S	—	-0.5
1899	Phi N	2	5	0	2	0	0	0	0	0	—	0	—	.400	.400	.400	.800	+24	1	—	—	/2bS	—	-0.1
1899	Bal N	57	210	31	62	3	2	0	18	13	—	2	—	.295	.342	.329	.671	-20	17	—	—	O31(14/14/3),3b20,2b2/1b	—	-1.4
1899	Year	59	215	31	64	3	2	0	18	13	—	2	—	.298	.343	.330	.673	-19	18	—	—	O31(14/14/3),3b20,2b3/S1b	—	-1.5

YEAR	TM LG	G	AB	R	H	2B	3B	HR	RBI	BB	IB	HP	SO	AVG	OBP	SLG	OPS	AOPS	SB	CS	SB%	GAMES AT POSITION	DL	BFW
1901	Phi A	132	561	95	164	17	9	0	52	32	—	3	—	.292	.334	.355	.689	-13	36	—	—	O106(11/95/0),2b18,S9	—	-2.1
1902	Phi A	129	506	**109**	153	20	5	1	49	62	—	2	—	.302	.381	.368	.749	+4	44	—	—	O114C,2b16	—	-0.9
1903	NY A	79	295	39	66	12	1	0	25	25	—	5	—	.224	.295	.271	.566	-33	29	—	—	O77(1/73/3),3b2	—	-1.7
1904	NY A	97	339	39	93	17	4	2	32	24	—	1	—	.274	.324	.366	.690	+13	17	—	—	O90C	—	0.2
1905	NY A	129	422	49	98	13	3	0	42	39	—	7	—	.232	.308	.277	.585	-23	44	—	—	O122(0/121/1)	—	-2.5
Total	7	644	2393	369	648	84	26	3	223	201	—	20	—	.271	.332	.331	.663	-11	189	—	—	O554C,2b40,3b22,S11/1b	—	-9.0
Team	3	305	1056	127	257	42	8	2	99	88	—	13	0	.243	.309	.304	.613	-14	90	—	—	O289(122/74/4),3b2	—	-4.0
/150	1	150	519	62	126	21	4	1	49	43	—	6	0	.243	.309	.304	.613	-14	44	—	—	O142(60/36/2)/3	—	-2.0
FUNK, LIZ	ELIAS CALVIN B10.28.1904 LACYGNE KS D1.16.1968 NORMAN OK BL/TL/5'8.5"/160 d4.26 COL OKLAHOMA																							
1929	NY A	1	0	0	0	0	0	0	0	0	—	0	0	+	+	+	.000	-100	0	0	0	/R	—	0.0
Total	4	273	976	134	261	47	16	6	105	73	—	5	58	.267	.322	.367	.689	-23	29	21	58	O251(5/244/2)	—	-3.5
GALLAGHER, JOE	JOSEPH EMMETT "MUSCLES" B3.7.1914 BUFFALO NY D2.25.1998 HOUSTON TX BR/TR/6'2"/210 d4.20 MIL 1941–45 COL MANHATTAN																							
1939	NY A	14	41	8	10	0	1	2	9	3	—	1	8	.244	.311	.439	.750	-9	1	0	100	O12R	—	-0.1
Total	2	165	487	73	133	26	5	16	73	26	—	3	76	.273	.314	.446	.760	-7	4	1	100	O114(74/0/40)	—	-1.4
GALLEGO, MIKE	MICHAEL ANTHONY B10.31.1960 WHITTIER CA BR/TR/5'8"/(160–175) DR 1981 OAKA 2/33 d4.11 C4 COL UCLA																							
1992	NY A	53	173	24	44	7	1	3	14	20	0	4	22	.254	.343	.358	.701	-2	0	1	0	2b40,S14	113	0.3
1993	NY A	119	403	63	114	20	1	10	54	50	0	4	65	.283	.364	.412	.776	+12	3	2	60	S55,2b52,3b27/D	15	3.8
1994	NY A	89	306	39	73	17	1	6	41	38	1	4	46	.239	.327	.359	.686	-19	0	1	0	S72,2b26	20	1.2
Total	13	1111	2931	374	700	111	12	42	282	326	5	32	465	.239	.320	.328	.648	-20	24	31	44	2b624,S434,3b137,D3/rf	380	-0.1
Team	3	261	882	126	231	44	3	19	109	108	1	12	133	.262	.347	.383	.730	-2	3	4	43	S141,2b118,3b27/D	148	5.3
/150	2	150	507	72	133	25	2	11	63	62	1	7	76	.262	.347	.383	.730	-2	2	2	50	S81,2b68,3b16/D	85	3.0
GAMBLE, OSCAR	OSCAR CHARLES B12.20.1949 RAMER AL BL/TR/5'11"/(160–187) DR 1968 CHIN 16/363 d8.27																							
1969	Chi N	24	71	6	16	1	1	1	5	10	1	0	12	.225	.321	.310	.631	-31	0	2	0	O24(1/23/0)	0	-0.7
1970	Phi N	88	275	31	72	12	4	1	19	27	3	1	37	.262	.330	.345	.675	-17	5	4	56	O74(0/47/28)	0	-1.0
1971	Phi N	92	280	24	62	11	1	6	23	21	2	1	35	.221	.275	.332	.607	-28	5	2	71	O80(54/1/26)	0	-1.9
1972	Phi N	74	135	17	32	5	2	1	13	19	0	1	16	.237	.331	.326	.657	-14	0	1	0	O35R/1b	0	-0.4
1973	Cle A	113	390	56	104	11	3	20	44	34	1	3	37	.267	.329	.464	.793	+19	3	4	43	D70,O37(2/1/35)	0	0.4
1974	Cle A	135	454	74	132	16	4	19	59	48	10	5	51	.291	.363	.469	.832	+39	5	6	45	D115,O13(12/0/1)	0	1.9
1975	Cle A	121	348	60	91	16	3	15	45	53	4	2	39	.261	.361	.454	.815	+29	11	5	69	O82(81/0/1),D29	0	1.1
1976	†NY A	110	340	43	79	13	1	17	57	38	4	4	38	.232	.317	.426	.743	+17	5	3	63	O104R/D	0	0.4
1977	Chi A	137	408	75	121	22	2	31	83	54	2	6	54	.297	.386	.588	.974	+61	1	2	33	D79,O49(5/7/38)	0	2.7
1978	SD N	126	375	46	103	15	3	7	47	51	11	6	45	.275	.366	.387	.753	+20	1	2	33	O107(39/0/70)	0	0.9
1979	Tex A	64	161	27	54	6	0	8	32	37	11	1	15	.335	.458	.522	.980	+66	2	1	67	D37,O21R	27	1.7
1979	NY A	36	113	21	44	4	1	11	32	13	1	0	13	.389	.452	.735	1.187	+117	0	0	0	O27(25/2/0),D6	0	1.7
1979	Year	100	274	48	98	10	1	19	64	50	12	1	28	.358	.456	.609	1.065	+87	2	1	67	O48(25/2/21),D43	0	3.4
1980	†NY A	78	194	40	54	10	2	14	50	28	4	4	21	.278	.376	.567	.943	+58	2	0	100	O49(36/0/14),D20	40	1.2
1981	†NY A	80	189	24	45	8	0	10	27	35	2	1	23	.238	.357	.439	.796	+31	0	2	0	O43(16/0/27),D33	0	0.7
1982	NY A	108	316	49	86	21	2	18	57	58	2	4	47	.272	.387	.522	.909	+50	6	3	67	D74,O29(1/0/28)	0	2.6
1983	NY A	74	180	26	47	10	2	7	26	25	1	3	23	.261	.361	.456	.817	+27	0	0	0	O32(2/0/30),D21	0	0.5
1984	NY A	54	125	17	23	2	0	10	27	25	0	0	18	.184	.318	.440	.758	+12	1	0	100	D28,O12R	48	0.0
1985	Chi A	70	148	20	30	5	0	4	20	34	3	1	22	.203	.353	.318	.671	-18	0	0	0	D48	0	-0.4
Total	17	1584	4502	656	1195	188	31	200	666	610	62	43	546	.265	.356	.454	.810	+26	47	37	56	O818(274/81/469),D561/1b	115	11.4
Team	7	540	1457	220	378	68	8	87	276	222	14	16	183	.259	.361	.496	.857	+40	14	8	64	O296(25/57/189),D183	88	7.1
/150	2	150	405	61	105	19	2	24	77	62	4	4	51	.259	.361	.496	.857	+40	4	2	67	O82(7/16/53),D51	24	2.0
GANZEL, JOHN	JOHN HENRY B4.7.1874 KALAMAZOO MI D1.14.1959 ORLANDO FL BR/TR/6'0.5"/195 d4.21 M2 b–CHARLIE																							
1898	Pit N	15	45	5	6	0	0	0	2	4	—	1	—	.133	.220	.133	.353	-98	0	—	—	1b12	—	-0.7
1900	Chi N	78	284	29	78	14	4	4	32	10	—	7	—	.275	.316	.394	.710	-1	5	—	—	1b78	—	-0.5
1901	NY N	138	526	42	113	13	3	2	66	20	—	9	—	.215	.256	.262	.518	-48	6	—	—	1b138	—	-3.2
1903	NY A	129	476	62	132	25	7	3	71	30	—	12	—	.277	.336	.378	.714	+7	9	—	—	1b129	—	1.0
1904	NY A	130	465	50	121	16	10	6	48	24	—	9	—	.260	.309	.376	.685	+11	13	—	—	1b118,2b9/S	—	0.2
1907	Cin N	145	531	61	135	20	**16**	2	64	29	—	3	—	.254	.297	.363	.660	+2	9	—	—	1b143	—	-0.3
1908	Cin N	112	388	32	97	16	10	1	53	19	—	2	—	.250	.289	.351	.640	+7	6	—	—	1b108,M	—	-0.3
Total	7	747	2715	281	682	104	50	18	336	136	—	43	—	.251	.298	.346	.644	-7	48	—	—	1b726,2b9/S	—	-3.8
Team	2	259	941	112	253	41	17	9	119	54	—	21	0	.269	.323	.377	.700	+9	22	—	—	1b247,2b9/S	—	1.2
/150	1	150	545	65	147	24	10	5	69	31	—	12	0	.269	.323	.377	.700	+9	13	—	—	1b143,2b5/S	—	0.7
GARBARK, MIKE	NATHANIEL MICHAEL B2.3.1916 HOUSTON TX D8.31.1994 CHARLOTTE NC BR/TR/6'0"/200 d4.18 b–BOB COL VILLANOVA																							
1944	NY A	89	299	23	78	9	4	1	33	25	—	1	27	.261	.320	.328	.648	-18	0	1	0	C85	0	0.4
1945	NY A	60	176	23	38	5	3	1	26	23	—	1	12	.216	.310	.295	.605	-27	0	1	0	C59	0	-0.4
Total	2	149	475	46	116	14	7	2	59	48	—	2	39	.244	.316	.316	.632	-21	0	2	0	C144	0	0.0
/150	2	150	478	46	117	14	7	2	59	48	—	2	39	.244	.316	.316	.632	-21	0	2	0	C145	0	0.0
GARCIA, DAMASO	DAMASO DOMINGO (SANCHEZ) B2.7.1955 MOCA, D.R. BR/TR/6'0"/(155–185) d6.24 [DL 1987 ATL N 148]																							
1978	NY A	18	41	5	8	0	0	0	1	2	0	0	6	.195	.227	.195	.422	-78	1	0	100	2b16,S3	0	-0.5
1979	NY A	11	38	3	10	1	0	0	4	0	0	0	2	.263	.263	.289	.552	-50	2	0	100	S10/3b	0	-0.5
Total	11	1032	3914	490	1108	183	27	36	323	130	11	27	322	.283	.309	.371	.680	-17	203	90	69	2b960,D18,S13,3b2/1b	211	-8.8
Team	2	29	79	8	18	1	0	0	5	2	0	0	8	.228	.244	.241	.485	-65	3	0	100	2b16,S13/3	0	-1.0
GARCIA, KARIM	GUSTAVO KARIM B10.29.1975 CIUDAD OBREGON, SONORA, MEXICO BL/TL/6'0"/(172–210) d9.2																							
2002	NY A	2	5	1	1	0	0	0	0	0	0	0	1	.200	.200	.200	.400	-93	0	0	0	O2(1/0/1)	0	-0.1
2003	†NY A	52	151	17	46	5	0	6	21	9	1	0	32	.305	.342	.457	.799	+10	0	2	0	O50(13/3/37)/D	0	0.3
Total	10	488	1463	180	352	44	13	66	212	81	6	2	330	.241	.279	.424	.703	-19	10	13	43	O424(72/35/341),D13,1b3	71	-6.8
Team	2	54	156	18	47	5	0	6	21	9	1	0	33	.301	.337	.449	.786	+7	0	2	0	O52(14/3/1)/D	0	0.2
GARDNER, EARLE	EARLE MCCLURKIN B1.24.1884 SPARTA IL D3.2.1943 SPARTA IL BR/TR/5'11"/160 d9.18																							
1908	NY A	20	75	7	16	2	0	0	4	1	—	1	—	.213	.234	.240	.474	-47	0	—	—	2b20	—	-0.3
1909	NY A	22	85	12	28	4	0	0	15	3	—	0	—	.329	.352	.376	.728	+29	4	—	—	2b22	—	-0.4
1910	NY A	86	271	36	66	4	2	1	24	21	—	2	—	.244	.303	.284	.587	-21	9	—	—	2b70	—	-0.6
1911	NY A	102	357	36	94	13	2	0	39	20	—	5	—	.263	.312	.311	.623	-31	14	—	—	2b101	—	-1.1
1912	NY A	43	160	14	45	3	1	0	26	5	—	0	—	.281	.303	.313	.616	-28	11	8	58	2b43	—	-1.3
Total	5	273	948	105	249	26	5	1	108	50	—	8	—	.263	.305	.304	.609	-24	38	8	100	2b256	—	-3.7
/150	3	150	521	58	137	14	3	1	59	27	—	4	0	.263	.305	.304	.609	-24	21	0	100	2b141	0	-2.0
GARDNER, BILLY	WILLIAM FREDERICK "SHOTGUN" B7.19.1927 WATERFORD CT BR/TR/6'0"/(170–180) d4.22 M6/C5																							
1961	†NY A	41	99	11	21	5	0	1	2	6	0	3	18	.212	.278	.293	.571	-44	0	0	0	3b33,2b6	0	-0.5
1962	NY A	4	1	1	0	0	0	0	0	0	0	0	1	.000	.000	.000	.000	-199	0	0	0	/2b3b	0	0.0
Total	10	1034	3544	356	841	159	18	41	271	246	18	33	439	.237	.292	.327	.619	-30	19	22	46	2b839,S108,3b92	0	-10.2
Team	2	45	100	12	21	5	0	1	2	6	0	3	19	.210	.275	.290	.565	-45	0	0	0	3b34,2b7	0	-0.5
GAZELLA, MIKE	MICHAEL B10.13.1895 OLYPHANT PA D9.11.1978 ODESSA TX BR/TR/5'7.5"/165 d7.2 COL LAFAYETTE																							
1923	NY A	8	13	2	1	0	0	0	1	2	—	0	3	.077	.200	.077	.277	-125	0	0	0	S4,2b2,3b2	—	-0.3
1926	†NY A	66	168	21	39	6	0	0	20	25	—	1	24	.232	.335	.268	.603	-40	2	2	50	3b45,S11	—	-1.1
1927	NY A	54	115	17	32	8	4	0	9	23	—	1	16	.278	.403	.417	.820	+17	4	1	80	3b44,S6	—	0.0

YEAR	TM LG	G	AB	R	H	2B	3B	HR	RBI	BB	IB	HP	SO	AVG	OBP	SLG	OPS	AOPS	SB	CS	SB%	GAMES AT POSITION	DL	BFW
1928	NY A	32	56	11	13	0	0	0	2	6	—	1	7	.232	.317	.232	.549	-52	2	1	67	3b16,2b4,S3	—	-0.5
Total	4	160	352	51	85	14	4	0	32	56	—	3	50	.241	.350	.304	.654	-27	8	4	67	3b107,S24,2b6	—	-1.9
/150	4	150	330	48	80	13	4	0	30	52	—	3	47	.241	.350	.304	.654	-27	7	4	64	3b100,S22,2b6	0	-1.8

GEDEON, JOE ELMER JOSEPH B12.5.1893 SACRAMENTO CA D5.19.1941 SAN FRANCISCO CA BR/TR/6'0"/167 d5.13

YEAR	TM LG	G	AB	R	H	2B	3B	HR	RBI	BB	IB	HP	SO	AVG	OBP	SLG	OPS	AOPS	SB	CS	SB%	GAMES AT POSITION	DL	BFW
1916	NY A	122	435	50	92	14	4	0	27	40	—	3	61	.211	.282	.262	.544	-38	14	—	—	2b122	—	-3.5
1917	NY A	33	117	15	28	7	0	0	8	7	—	1	13	.239	.288	.299	.587	-22	4	—	—	2b31	—	-0.2
Total	7	584	2109	259	515	82	20	1	171	180	—	25	181	.244	.311	.303	.614	-25	34	3	100	2b549,O19(14/1/4),3b7,S2/P	—	-9.1
Team	2	155	552	65	120	21	4	0	35	47	—	4	74	.217	.283	.270	.553	-35	18	—	—	2b153	—	-3.7
/150	2	150	534	63	116	20	4	0	34	45	—	4	72	.217	.283	.270	.553	-35	17	—	—	2b148	—	-3.6

GEHRIG, LOU HENRY LOUIS "THE IRON HORSE" B6.19.1903 NEW YORK NY D6.2.1941 RIVERDALE NY BL/TL/6'0"/200 d6.15 HF1939 COL COLUMBIA

YEAR	TM LG	G	AB	R	H	2B	3B	HR	RBI	BB	IB	HP	SO	AVG	OBP	SLG	OPS	AOPS	SB	CS	SB%	GAMES AT POSITION	DL	BFW
1923	NY A	13	26	6	11	4	1	1	9	2	—	0	5	.423	.464	.769	1.233	+117	0	0	0	1b9	—	0.3
1924	NY A	10	12	2	6	1	0	0	5	1	—	0	3	.500	.538	.583	1.121	+90	0	0	0	1b2/rf	—	0.2
1925	NY A	126	437	73	129	23	10	20	68	46	—	2	49	.295	.365	.531	.896	+27	6	3	67	1b114,O6(2/0/4)	—	-0.2
1926	†NY A	**155**	572	135	179	47	**20**	16	112	105	—	1	73	.313	.420	.549	.969	+54	6	5	55	1b155	—	2.7
1927	†NY A	**155**	584	149	218	**52**	18	47	**175**	109	—	3	84	.373	.474	.765	1.239	+124	10	8	56	1b155	—	8.4
1928	†NY A	**154**	562	139	210	**47**	13	27	**142**	95	—	4	69	.374	**.467**	.648	1.115	+97	4	11	27	1b154	—	5.9
1929	NY A	**154**	553	127	166	32	10	35	126	122	—	5	68	.300	.431	.584	1.015	+70	4	3	57	1b154	—	4.5
1930	NY A	**154**	581	143	220	42	17	41	**174**	101	—	3	63	.379	.473	.721	1.194	+107	12	14	46	1b153/lf	—	**7.7**
1931	NY A	**155**	619	**163**	**211**	31	15	**46**	**184**	117	—	0	56	.341	.446	.662	1.108	+99	17	12	59	1b154/rf	—	6.0
1932	†NY A	**156**	596	138	208	42	9	34	151	108	—	3	38	.349	.451	.621	1.072	+84	4	11	27	1b156	—	5.1
1933	NY A★	**152**	593	**138**	198	41	12	32	139	92	—	1	42	.334	.424	.605	1.029	+81	9	13	41	1b152	—	4.7
1934	NY A★	**154**	579	128	210	40	6	**49**	**165**	109	—	2	31	**.363**	**.465**	**.706**	1.171	+113	9	5	64	1b153/S	—	**7.9**
1935	NY A★	**149**	535	**125**	176	26	10	30	119	**132**	—	5	38	.329	**.466**	.583	1.049	+80	8	7	53	1b149	—	5.3
1936	†NY A★	**155**	579	**167**	205	37	7	**49**	152	**130**	—	7	46	.354	**.478**	**.696**	1.174	+93	3	4	43	1b155	—	**6.6**
1937	†NY A★	**157**	569	138	200	37	9	37	159	**127**	—	4	49	.351	**.473**	.643	1.116	+77	4	3	57	1b157	—	4.8
1938	†NY A★	**157**	576	115	170	32	6	29	114	107	—	5	75	.295	.410	.523	.933	+33	6	1	86	1b157	—	1.5
1939	NY A✳	8	28	2	4	0	0	0	1	5	—	0	1	.143	.273	.143	.416	-91	0	0	0	1b8	—	-0.5
Total	17	2164	8001	1888	2721	534	163	493	1995	1508	—	45	790	.340	.447	.632	1.079	+82	102	100	50	1b2137,O9(3/0/6)/S	—	70.9
/150	1	150	555	131	189	37	11	34	138	105	—	3	55	.340	.447	.632	1.079	+82	7	7	50	1b15/O/LS	0	4.9

GEREN, BOB ROBERT PETER B9.22.1961 SAN DIEGO CA BR/TR/6'3"/(200–228) DR 1979 SDN 1/24 d5.17 M1/C4

YEAR	TM LG	G	AB	R	H	2B	3B	HR	RBI	BB	IB	HP	SO	AVG	OBP	SLG	OPS	AOPS	SB	CS	SB%	GAMES AT POSITION	DL	BFW
1988	NY A	10	10	0	1	0	0	0	0	2	0	0	3	.100	.250	.100	.350	-98	0	0	0	C10	0	-0.1
1989	NY A	65	205	26	59	5	1	9	27	12	0	1	44	.288	.329	.454	.783	+20	0	0	0	C60,D2	0	1.2
1990	NY A	110	277	21	59	7	0	8	31	13	1	5	73	.213	.259	.325	.584	-38	0	0	0	C107/D	0	-0.9
1991	NY A	64	128	7	28	3	0	2	12	9	0	0	31	.219	.270	.289	.559	-46	0	1	0	C63	0	-0.9
1993	SD N	58	145	8	31	6	0	3	6	13	4	0	28	.214	.278	.317	.595	-41	0	0	0	C49/1b3b	0	-0.5
Total	5	307	765	62	178	21	1	22	76	49	5	6	179	.233	.283	.349	.632	-26	0	1	0	C289,D3/3b1b	0	-1.2
Team	4	249	620	54	147	15	1	19	70	36	1	6	151	.237	.284	.356	.640	-22	0	1	0	C240,D3	0	-0.7
/150	2	150	373	33	89	9	1	11	42	22	1	4	91	.237	.284	.356	.640	-22	0	1	0	C145,D2	0	-0.4

GIAMBI, JASON JASON GILBERT B1.8.1971 W.COVINA CA BL/TR/6'3"/(200–235) DR 1992 OAKA 2/58 d5.8 B-JEREMY COL CAL ST.–LONG BEACH

YEAR	TM LG	G	AB	R	H	2B	3B	HR	RBI	BB	IB	HP	SO	AVG	OBP	SLG	OPS	AOPS	SB	CS	SB%	GAMES AT POSITION	DL	BFW
1995	Oak A	54	176	27	45	7	0	6	25	28	0	3	31	.256	.364	.398	.762	+4	2	1	67	3b30,1b26,D2	0	0.0
1996	Oak A	140	536	84	156	40	1	20	79	51	3	5	95	.291	.355	.481	.836	+11	0	1	0	1b45,O45(44/0/1),3b39,D12	0	0.7
1997	Oak A	142	519	66	152	41	2	20	81	55	3	6	89	.293	.362	.495	.857	+23	0	1	0	O68L,1b51,D25	0	0.7
1998	Oak A	153	562	92	166	28	0	27	110	81	7	5	102	.295	.384	.489	.873	+28	2	2	50	1b146,D7	0	0.2
1999	Oak A	158	575	115	181	36	1	33	123	105	6	7	106	.315	.422	.553	.975	+52	1	1	50	1b142,D15/3b	0	1.9
2000	†Oak A★	152	510	108	170	29	1	43	137	**137**	6	9	96	.333	**.476**	.647	1.123	+85	2	0	100	1b124,D24	0	5.1
2001	†Oak A★	154	520	109	178	**47**	2	38	120	**129**	24	13	83	.342	**.477**	**.660**	1.137	+96	2	0	100	1b136,D17	0	6.4
2002	†NY A★	155	560	120	176	34	1	41	122	109	4	15	112	.314	.435	.598	1.033	+73	2	2	50	1b92,D63	0	4.5
2003	†NY A★	156	535	97	134	25	0	41	107	**129**	9	**21**	140	.250	.412	.527	.939	+48	2	1	67	1b85,D69	0	2.0
2004	NY A★	80	264	33	55	9	0	12	40	47	1	8	62	.208	.342	.379	.721	-11	0	1	0	1b47,D28	65	-1.5
2005	†NY A	139	417	74	113	14	0	32	87	**108**	5	19	109	.271	**.440**	.535	.975	+59	0	0	0	1b78,D60	0	2.4
2006	†NY A	139	446	92	113	25	0	37	113	110	12	16	106	.253	.413	.558	.971	+47	2	0	100	D70,1b68	0	1.8
2007	†NY A	83	254	31	60	8	0	14	39	40	2	8	66	.236	.356	.433	.789	+6	1	0	100	D57,1b18	68	-0.2
Total	13	1705	5874	1048	1699	343	8	364	1183	1129	82	135	1197	.289	.411	.536	.947	+46	16	10	62	1b1058,D449,O113(112/0/1),3b70	133	24.0
Team	6	752	2476	447	651	115	1	177	508	543	33	87	595	.263	.410	.525	.935	+45	7	4	64	1b388,D347	133	9.0
/150	1	150	494	89	130	23	0	35	101	108	7	17	119	.263	.410	.525	.935	+45	1	1	50	1b77,D69	27	1.8

GIBBS, JAKE JERRY DEAN B11.7.1938 GRENADA MS BL/TR/6'0"/(180–188) d9.11 COL U. OF MISSISSIPPI

YEAR	TM LG	G	AB	R	H	2B	3B	HR	RBI	BB	IB	HP	SO	AVG	OBP	SLG	OPS	AOPS	SB	CS	SB%	GAMES AT POSITION	DL	BFW
1962	NY A	2	0	2	0	0	0	0	0	0	0	0	0	+	+	+	.000	-100	0	0	0	/3b	0	0.0
1963	NY A	4	8	1	2	0	0	0	0	0	0	0	1	.250	.250	.250	.500	-59	0	0	0	/C	0	-0.2
1964	NY A	3	6	1	1	0	0	0	0	0	0	0	2	.167	.167	.167	.334	-107	0	0	0	C2	0	-0.1
1965	NY A	37	68	6	15	1	0	2	7	4	0	1	20	.221	.267	.324	.591	-30	0	0	0	C21	0	-0.2
1966	NY A	62	182	19	47	6	0	3	20	19	2	0	16	.258	.327	.341	.668	-4	5	2	71	C54	35	0.9
1967	NY A	116	374	33	87	7	1	4	25	28	1	4	57	.233	.291	.289	.580	-25	7	6	54	C99	0	-0.9
1968	NY A	124	423	31	90	12	3	3	29	27	5	6	68	.213	.270	.277	.547	-32	9	8	53	C121	0	-0.7
1969	NY A	71	219	18	49	9	2	0	18	23	9	0	30	.224	.294	.283	.577	-35	3	4	43	C66	0	0.0
1970	NY A	49	153	23	46	9	2	8	26	7	1	1	14	.301	.331	.542	.873	+44	2	0	100	C44	0	1.2
1971	NY A	70	206	23	45	9	0	5	21	12	1	3	23	.218	.270	.335	.605	-26	2	2	50	C51	0	-1.1
Total	10	538	1639	157	382	53	8	25	146	120	19	15	231	.233	.289	.321	.610	-20	28	22	56	C459/3b	35	-1.1
/150	3	150	457	44	107	15	2	7	41	33	5	4	64	.233	.289	.321	.610	-20	8	6	57	C128/3	10	-0.3

GILHOOLEY, FRANK FRANK PATRICK "FLASH" B6.10.1892 TOLEDO OH D7.11.1959 TOLEDO OH BL/TR/5'8"/155 d9.18 COL ST. JOHNS

YEAR	TM LG	G	AB	R	H	2B	3B	HR	RBI	BB	IB	HP	SO	AVG	OBP	SLG	OPS	AOPS	SB	CS	SB%	GAMES AT POSITION	DL	BFW
1911	StL N	1	0	0	0	0	0	0	0	0	—	0	0	+	+	+	.000	-100	0	—	—	/rf	—	0.0
1912	StL N	13	49	5	11	0	0	0	2	3	—	0	8	.224	.269	.224	.493	-63	0	—	—	O11C	—	-0.6
1913	NY A	24	85	10	29	2	1	0	14	4	—	1	9	.341	.378	.388	.766	+24	6	—	—	O24R	—	0.1
1914	NY A	1	3	0	2	0	0	0	0	1	—	0	0	.667	.750	.667	1.417	+227	0	—	—	/rf	—	0.1
1915	NY A	1	4	0	0	0	0	0	0	0	—	0	1	.000	.000	.000	.000	-199	0	—	—	/rf	—	-0.1
1916	NY A	58	223	40	62	5	3	1	10	37	—	1	17	.278	.383	.341	.724	+15	16	—	—	O57(0/2/55)	—	0.3
1917	NY A	54	165	14	40	6	1	0	8	30	—	1	13	.242	.362	.291	.653	-1	6	—	—	O46R	—	-0.2
1918	NY A	112	427	59	118	13	5	1	23	53	—	1	24	.276	.358	.337	.695	+7	7	—	—	O111(0/4/107)	—	0.0
1919	Bos A	48	112	14	27	4	0	0	1	12	—	0	8	.241	.315	.277	.592	-29	2	—	—	O33(30/2/1)	—	-0.6
Total	9	312	1068	142	289	30	10	2	58	140	—	4	80	.271	.357	.323	.680	+2	37	—	—	O285(30/19/236)	—	-1.0
Team	6	250	907	123	251	26	10	2	55	125	—	4	64	.277	.367	.334	.701	+9	35	—	—	O240(4/10/34)	—	0.2
/150	4	150	544	74	151	16	6	1	33	75	—	2	38	.277	.367	.334	.701	+9	21	—	—	O144(2/6/20)	—	0.1

GIPSON, CHARLES CHARLES WELLS B12.16.1972 ORANGE CA BR/TR/6'2"/(180–195) DR 1991 SEAA 63/1493 d3.31 COL CYPRESS (CA) JC OF(142/62/82)

YEAR	TM LG	G	AB	R	H	2B	3B	HR	RBI	BB	IB	HP	SO	AVG	OBP	SLG	OPS	AOPS	SB	CS	SB%	GAMES AT POSITION	DL	BFW
2003	NY A	18	10	3	2	0	0	0	2	1	0	0	2	.200	.273	.200	.473	-72	2	1	67	O8C,D3	0	-0.1
Total	8	373	321	78	76	15	7	0	30	30	1	5	71	.237	.311	.327	.638	-32	16	11	59	O273L,3b39,D20,S16,2b4	52	-0.7

GIRARDI, JOE JOSEPH ELLIOTT B10.14.1964 PEORIA IL BR/TR/5'11"/(195–200) DR 1986 CHIN 5/116 d4.4 M1/C1 COL NORTHWESTERN

YEAR	TM LG	G	AB	R	H	2B	3B	HR	RBI	BB	IB	HP	SO	AVG	OBP	SLG	OPS	AOPS	SB	CS	SB%	GAMES AT POSITION	DL	BFW
1996	†NY A	124	422	55	124	22	3	2	45	30	1	5	55	.294	.346	.374	.720	-17	13	4	76	C120,D2	0	0.0
1997	†NY A	112	398	38	105	23	1	1	50	26	1	2	53	.264	.311	.334	.645	-31	2	3	40	C111/D	0	0.2
1998	†NY A	78	254	31	70	11	4	3	31	14	1	2	38	.276	.317	.386	.703	-14	2	4	33	C78	0	0.9
1999	†NY A	65	209	23	50	16	1	2	27	10	0	0	26	.239	.271	.354	.625	-40	3	1	75	C65	0	-0.5
Total	15	1277	4127	454	1100	186	26	36	422	279	34	25	607	.267	.315	.350	.665	-29	44	31	59	C1247,D3	343	-8.4
Team	4	379	1283	147	349	72	9	8	153	80	3	9	172	.272	.317	.361	.678	-24	20	12	63	C374,D3	0	0.6
/150	2	150	508	58	138	28	4	3	61	32	1	4	68	.272	.317	.361	.678	-24	8	5	62	C148/D	0	0.2

Batters

Batters

GLEICH, FRANK FRANK ELMER "INCH" B3.7.1894 COLUMBUS OH D3.27.1949 COLUMBUS OH BL/TR/5'11"/175 D9.17

YEAR	TM LG	G	AB	R	H	2B	3B	HR	RBI	BB	IB	HP	SO	AVG	OBP	SLG	OPS	AOPS	SB	CS	SB%	GAMES AT POSITION	DL	BFW
1919	NY A	5	4	0	1	0	0	0	1	1	—	0	0	.250	.400	.250	.650	-16	0	—	—	O4(3/1/0)	—	-0.1
1920	NY A	24	41	6	5	0	0	0	3	6	—	0	10	.122	.234	.122	.356	-104	0	0	0	O15(9/4/2)	—	-0.8
Total	2	29	45	6	6	0	0	0	4	7	—	0	10	.133	.250	.133	.383	-96	0	0	0	O19(12/5/2)	—	-0.9

GLENN, JOE JOSEPH CHARLES "GABBY"(B JOSEPH CHARLES GURZENSKY) B11.19.1908 DICKSON CITY PA D5.6.1985 TUNKHANNOCK PA BR/TR/5'11"/175 D9.15

YEAR	TM LG	G	AB	R	H	2B	3B	HR	RBI	BB	IB	HP	SO	AVG	OBP	SLG	OPS	AOPS	SB	CS	SB%	GAMES AT POSITION	DL	BFW
1932	NY A	6	16	0	2	0	0	0	0	1	—	1	5	.125	.222	.125	.347	-108	0	0	0	C5	—	-0.3
1933	NY A	5	21	1	3	0	0	0	1	0	—	0	3	.143	.143	.143	.286	-126	0	0	0	C5	—	-0.4
1935	NY A	17	43	7	10	4	0	0	6	4	—	0	1	.233	.298	.326	.624	[illegible]	0	0	0	C16	—	-0.1
1936	NY A	44	129	21	35	7	0	1	20	20	—	1	10	.271	.373	.349	.722	-18	1	1	50	C44	—	0.2
1937	NY A	25	53	6	15	2	2	0	4	10	—	0	11	.283	.397	.396	.793	+0	0	0	0	C24	—	0.4
1938	NY A	41	123	10	32	7	2	0	25	10	—	0	14	.260	.316	.350	.666	-33	1	0	100	C40	—	-0.4
1939	StL A	88	286	29	78	13	1	4	29	31	—	0	40	.273	.344	.367	.711	-20	4	4	50	C82	—	-1.6
1940	Bos A	22	47	3	6	1	0	0	4	5	—	0	7	.128	.212	.149	.361	-105	0	0	0	C19	—	-0.8
Total	8	248	718	77	181	34	5	5	89	81	—	2	91	.252	.330	.334	.664	-31	6	5	55	C235	—	-3.0
Team	6	138	385	45	97	20	4	1	56	45	—	2	44	.252	.333	.332	.665	-31	2	1	67	C134	—	-0.6
/150	7	150	418	49	105	22	4	1	61	49	—	2	48	.252	.333	.332	.665	-31	2	1	67	C146	—	-0.7

GONDER, JESSE JESSE LEMAR B1.20.1936 MONTICELLO AR D11.14.2004 OAKLAND CA BL/TR/5'10"/190 D9.23

YEAR	TM LG	G	AB	R	H	2B	3B	HR	RBI	BB	IB	HP	SO	AVG	OBP	SLG	OPS	AOPS	SB	CS	SB%	GAMES AT POSITION	DL	BFW
1960	NY A	7	7	1	2	0	0	1	3	1	0	0	1	.286	.333	.714	1.047	+99	0	0	0	/C	0	0.1
1961	NY A	15	12	2	4	1	0	0	3	3	1	0	1	.333	.467	.417	.884	+46	0	0	0	/H	0	0.1
Total	8	395	876	73	220	28	2	26	94	72	20	6	184	.251	.310	.377	.687	-6	1	2	33	C250	0	-0.4
Team	2	22	19	3	6	1	0	1	6	4	1	0	2	.316	.417	.526	.943	+64	0	0	0	/C	0	0.2

GONZALEZ, ALBERTO ALBERTO RAMON B4.18.1983 MARACAIBO, ZULIA, VENEZUELA BR/TR/5'11"/165 D9.1

YEAR	TM LG	G	AB	R	H	2B	3B	HR	RBI	BB	IB	HP	SO	AVG	OBP	SLG	OPS	AOPS	SB	CS	SB%	GAMES AT POSITION	DL	BFW
2007	NY A	12	14	3	1	0	0	0	1	1	0	0	1	.071	.133	.071	.204	-144	0	1	0	S11/3b	0	-0.3

GONZALEZ, FERNANDO JOSE FERNANDO (QUINONES) B6.19.1950 ARECIBO, PR BR/TR/5'10"/(165–178) D9.15

YEAR	TM LG	G	AB	R	H	2B	3B	HR	RBI	BB	IB	HP	SO	AVG	OBP	SLG	OPS	AOPS	SB	CS	SB%	GAMES AT POSITION	DL	BFW
1974	NY A	51	121	11	26	5	1	1	7	7	0	0	7	.215	.258	.298	.556	-40	0	0	0	2b42,3b7,S3	0	-0.5
Total	6	404	1038	85	244	40	7	17	104	58	20	1	114	.235	.274	.336	.610	-29	8	7	53	2b249,3b64,O16(15/0/1),S5/D	0	-5.0

GONZALEZ, PEDRO PEDRO (OLIVARES) B12.12.1937 SAN PEDRO DE MACORIS, D.R. BR/TR/6'0"/(173–180) D4.11

YEAR	TM LG	G	AB	R	H	2B	3B	HR	RBI	BB	IB	HP	SO	AVG	OBP	SLG	OPS	AOPS	SB	CS	SB%	GAMES AT POSITION	DL	BFW
1963	NY A	14	26	3	5	1	0	0	1	0	0	0	5	.192	.192	.231	.423	-82	0	1	0	2b7	0	-0.5
1964	†NY A	80	112	18	31	8	1	0	5	7	0	2	22	.277	.331	.366	.697	-8	3	4	43	1b31,O20(5/0/15),3b9,2b6	0	-0.1
1965	NY A	7	5	0	2	1	0	0	0	0	0	0	2	.400	.400	.600	1.000	+81	0	0	0	/H	0	0.1
Total	5	407	1084	99	264	39	6	8	70	52	8	8	176	.244	.282	.313	.595	-30	22	20	52	2b293,1b35,O24(5/0/19),3b16,S3	0	-1.4
Team	3	101	143	21	38	10	1	0	6	7	0	2	29	.266	.309	.350	.659	-18	3	5	38	1b31,O20(5/0/15),2b13,3b9	0	-0.5
/150	4	150	212	31	56	15	1	0	9	10	0	3	43	.266	.309	.350	.659	-18	4	7	36	1b46,O30(7/0/22),2b19,3b13	0	-0.7

GOOD, WILBUR WILBUR DAVID "LEFTY" B9.28.1885 PUNXSUTAWNEY PA D12.30.1963 BROOKSVILLE FL BL/TL/5'11.5"/180 D8.18 ▲

YEAR	TM LG	G	AB	R	H	2B	3B	HR	RBI	BB	IB	HP	SO	AVG	OBP	SLG	OPS	AOPS	SB	CS	SB%	GAMES AT POSITION	DL	BFW
1905	NY A	5	8	2	3	0	0	0	0	0	—	0	—	.375	.375	.375	.750	+24	0	—	—	P5	—	0.0
Total	11	749	2364	324	609	84	44	9	187	190	—	36	243	.258	.322	.342	.664	-2	104	19	100	O624(23/154/448),P5	—	-4.7

GORDON, JOE JOSEPH LOWELL "FLASH" B2.18.1915 LOS ANGELES CA D4.14.1978 SACRAMENTO CA BR/TR/5'10"/180 D4.18 MIL 1944–45 M5/C1 COL OREGON

YEAR	TM LG	G	AB	R	H	2B	3B	HR	RBI	BB	IB	HP	SO	AVG	OBP	SLG	OPS	AOPS	SB	CS	SB%	GAMES AT POSITION	DL	BFW
1938	†NY A	127	458	83	117	24	7	25	97	56	—	3	72	.255	.340	.502	.842	+9	11	3	79	2b126	—	3.0
1939	†NY A★	151	567	92	161	32	5	28	111	75	—	2	57	.284	.370	.506	.876	+24	11	10	52	2b151	—	3.3
1940	NY A★	**155**	616	112	173	32	10	30	103	52	—	3	57	.281	.340	.511	.851	+22	18	8	69	2b155	—	3.8
1941	†NY A★	**156**	588	104	162	26	7	24	87	72	—	4	80	.276	.358	.466	.824	+18	10	9	53	2b131,1b30	0	2.7
1942	†NY A★	147	538	88	173	29	4	18	103	79	—	1	95	.322	.409	.491	.900	+56	12	6	67	2b147	0	5.8
1943	†NY A☆	152	543	82	135	28	5	17	69	98	—	2	75	.249	.365	.413	.778	+26	4	7	36	2b152	0	5.6
1946	NY A★	112	376	35	79	15	0	11	47	49	—	4	72	.210	.308	.338	.646	-21	2	5	29	2b108	0	1.3
1947	Cle A★	155	562	89	153	27	6	29	93	62	—	1	49	.272	.346	.496	.842	+36	7	3	70	2b155	0	2.8
1948	†Cle A★	144	550	96	154	21	4	32	124	77	—	3	68	.280	.371	.507	.878	+36	5	2	71	2b144,S2	0	2.5
1949	Cle A★	148	541	74	136	18	3	20	84	83	—	4	33	.251	.355	.407	.762	+3	5	6	45	2b145	0	-0.7
1950	Cle A	119	368	59	87	12	1	19	57	56	—	2	44	.236	.340	.429	.769	-1	4	1	80	2b105	0	-1.3
Total	11	1566	5707	914	1530	264	52	253	975	759	—	29	702	.268	.357	.466	.823	+21	89	60	60	2b1519,1b30,S2	0	28.8
Team	7	1000	3686	596	1000	186	38	153	617	481	—	19	508	.271	.358	.467	.825	+21	68	48	59	2b970,1b30	0	25.5
/150	1	150	553	89	150	28	6	23	93	72	—	3	76	.271	.358	.467	.825	+21	10	7	59	2b146,1b5	0	3.8

GOSSETT, DICK JOHN STAR B8.21.1890 DENNISON OH D10.6.1962 MASSILLON OH BR/TR/5'11"/185 D4.30

YEAR	TM LG	G	AB	R	H	2B	3B	HR	RBI	BB	IB	HP	SO	AVG	OBP	SLG	OPS	AOPS	SB	CS	SB%	GAMES AT POSITION	DL	BFW
1913	NY A	39	105	9	17	2	0	0	9	10	—	3	22	.162	.254	.181	.435	-72	1	—	—	C38	—	-1.4
1914	NY A	10	21	3	3	0	0	0	1	5	—	1	5	.143	.333	.143	.476	-56	0	—	—	C10	—	-0.1
Total	2	49	126	12	20	2	0	0	10	15	—	4	27	.159	.269	.175	.444	-69	1	—	—	C48	—	-1.5

GRABOWSKI, JOHNNY JOHN PATRICK "NIG" B1.7.1900 WARE MA D5.23.1946 ALBANY NY BR/TR/5'10"/185 D7.11

YEAR	TM LG	G	AB	R	H	2B	3B	HR	RBI	BB	IB	HP	SO	AVG	OBP	SLG	OPS	AOPS	SB	CS	SB%	GAMES AT POSITION	DL	BFW
1924	Chi A	20	56	10	14	3	0	0	3	2	—	0	4	.250	.276	.304	.580	-49	0	0	0	C19	—	-0.3
1925	Chi A	21	46	5	14	4	1	0	10	2	—	0	4	.304	.333	.435	.768	-1	0	1	0	C21	—	0.1
1926	Chi A	48	122	6	32	1	1	1	11	4	—	0	15	.262	.286	.311	.597	-42	0	1	0	C38/1b	—	-0.8
1927	†NY A	70	195	29	54	2	4	0	25	20	—	2	15	.277	.350	.328	.678	-21	0	0	0	C68	—	-0.1
1928	NY A	75	202	21	48	7	1	1	21	10	—	0	21	.238	.274	.297	.571	-49	0	0	0	C75	—	-1.0
1929	NY A	22	59	4	12	1	0	0	2	3	—	0	6	.203	.242	.220	.462	-79	1	0	100	C22	—	-0.6
1931	Det A	40	136	9	32	7	1	1	14	6	—	0	19	.235	.268	.324	.592	-47	0	0	0	C39	—	-0.7
Total	7	296	816	84	206	25	8	3	86	47	—	2	84	.252	.295	.314	.609	-40	1	2	33	C282/1b	—	-3.4
Team	3	167	456	54	114	10	5	1	48	33	—	2	42	.250	.303	.300	.603	-40	1	0	100	C165	—	-1.7
/150	3	150	410	49	102	9	4	1	43	30	—	2	38	.250	.303	.300	.603	-40	1	0	100	C148	—	-1.5

GREEN, NICK NICHOLAS ANTHONY B9.10.1978 PENSACOLA FL BR/TR/6'0"/(175–180) DR 1998 ATLN 32/971 D5.15 COL GEORGIA PERIMETER JC [DL 2002 ATL N 23]

YEAR	TM LG	G	AB	R	H	2B	3B	HR	RBI	BB	IB	HP	SO	AVG	OBP	SLG	OPS	AOPS	SB	CS	SB%	GAMES AT POSITION	DL	BFW
2006	NY A	46	75	8	18	5	0	2	4	5	0	1	29	.240	.296	.387	.683	-27	1	1	50	2b19,3b17,S10/1bD	0	-0.1
Total	4	275	703	105	169	35	5	10	59	56	1	16	192	.240	.309	.347	.656	-27	5	7	42	2b191,3b35,S23,O3R,D2/1b	23	-4.0

GREENE, PADDY PATRICK JOSEPH "PATSY"(AKA PATRICK FOLEY IN 1902) B3.20.1875 PROVIDENCE RI D10.20.1934 PROVIDENCE RI BR/TR/5'8"/150 D9.10 COL VILLANOVA

YEAR	TM LG	G	AB	R	H	2B	3B	HR	RBI	BB	IB	HP	SO	AVG	OBP	SLG	OPS	AOPS	SB	CS	SB%	GAMES AT POSITION	DL	BFW
1903	NY A	4	13	1	4	1	0	0	0	0	—	0	—	.308	.308	.385	.693	+0	0	—	—	3b2/S	—	0.1
Total	2	24	81	7	15	2	0	0	1	2	—	1	—	.185	.214	.210	.424	-70	2	—	—	3b22/S	—	-0.7

GREENE, TODD TODD ANTHONY B5.8.1971 AUGUSTA GA BR/TR/5'10"/(200–210) DR 1993 CALA 12/327 D7.30 COL GEORGIA SOUTHERN

YEAR	TM LG	G	AB	R	H	2B	3B	HR	RBI	BB	IB	HP	SO	AVG	OBP	SLG	OPS	AOPS	SB	CS	SB%	GAMES AT POSITION	DL	BFW
2001	†NY A	35	96	9	20	4	0	1	11	3	0	1	21	.208	.240	.281	.521	-64	0	0	0	C34,D2	0	-1.3
Total	11	536	1573	181	397	82	3	71	217	67	8	10	332	.252	.286	.444	.730	-18	5	4	56	C294,D90,O44(19/0/25),1b25	291	-9.1

GRIFFEY, KEN GEORGE KENNETH SR. B4.10.1950 DONORA PA BL/TL/6'0"/(185–210) DR 1969 CINN 29/680 D8.25 C7 S–KEN

YEAR	TM LG	G	AB	R	H	2B	3B	HR	RBI	BB	IB	HP	SO	AVG	OBP	SLG	OPS	AOPS	SB	CS	SB%	GAMES AT POSITION	DL	BFW
1982	NY A	127	484	70	134	23	2	12	54	39	1	0	58	.277	.329	.407	.736	+3	10	4	71	O125(0/26/102)	0	0.1
1983	NY A	118	458	60	140	21	3	11	46	34	3	2	45	.306	.355	.437	.792	+20	6	1	86	1b101,O14(2/12/1),D2	31	0.8
1984	NY A	120	399	44	109	20	1	7	56	29	2	1	32	.273	.321	.381	.702	-3	2	2	50	O82(38/35/9),1b27,D2	0	-0.6
1985	NY A	127	438	68	120	28	4	10	69	41	4	0	51	.274	.331	.425	.756	+9	7	7	50	O110(106/5/1)/1bD	15	0.5
1986	NY A	59	198	33	60	7	0	9	26	15	0	1	24	.303	.349	.475	.824	+24	2	2	50	O51(50/2/1),D2	0	0.6
Total	19	2097	7229	1129	2143	364	77	152	859	719	51	14	898	.296	.359	.431	.790	+18	200	83	71	O1703(532/203/989),1b172,D14	211	9.9
Team	5	551	1977	275	563	99	10	49	251	158	10	4	210	.285	.336	.419	.755	+9	27	16	63	O382(2/79/114),1b129,D7	46	1.4
/150	1	150	538	75	153	27	3	13	68	43	3	1	57	.285	.336	.419	.755	+9	7	4	64	O104(1/22/31),1b35,D2	13	0.4

YEAR	TM LG	G	AB	R	H	2B	3B	HR	RBI	BB	IB	HP	SO	AVG	OBP	SLG	OPS	AOPS	SB	CS	SB%	GAMES AT POSITION	DL	BFW
GRIMES, OSCAR Oscar Ray Jr. B4.13.1915 Minerva OH D5.19.1993 Westlake OH BR/TR/5'11"/178 d9.28 f–Ray																								
1938	Cle A	4	10	2	2	0	1	0	2	2	—	0	0	.200	.333	.400	.733	-15	0	0	0	2b2/1b	—	-0.1
1939	Cle A	119	364	51	98	20	5	4	56	56	—	1	61	.269	.368	.385	.753	-4	8	3	73	2b48,1b43,S37,3b3	—	-0.8
1940	Cle A	11	13	3	0	0	0	0	0	0	—	0	5	.000	.000	.000	.000	-199	0	0	0	1b4/3b	—	-0.3
1941	Cle A	77	244	28	58	9	3	4	24	39	—	1	47	.238	.345	.348	.693	-12	4	0	100	1b62,2b13/3b	0	-1.2
1942	Cle A	51	84	10	15	2	0	0	2	13	—	0	17	.179	.289	.202	.491	-58	3	2	60	2b24,3b8/1bS	0	-0.9
1943	NY A	9	20	4	3	0	0	0	1	3	—	0	7	.150	.261	.150	.411	-79	0	0	0	S3/1b	0	-0.2
1944	NY A	116	387	44	108	17	8	5	46	59	—	2	57	.279	.377	.403	.780	+19	6	0	100	3b97,S20	0	0.4
1945	NY A∗	142	480	64	127	19	7	4	45	97	—	6	73	.265	.395	.358	.753	+14	7	6	54	3b141/1b	0	2.3
1946	NY A	14	39	1	8	1	0	0	4	1	—	0	7	.205	.225	.231	.456	-73	0	1	0	S7,2b5	0	-0.5
1946	Phi A	59	191	28	50	5	0	1	20	27	—	1	29	.262	.356	.304	.660	-14	2	0	100	2b43,3b6,S4	0	-0.9
1946	Year	73	230	29	58	6	0	1	24	28	—	1	36	.252	.336	.291	.627	-24	2	1	67	2b48,S11,3b6	0	-1.4
Total	9	602	1832	235	469	73	24	18	200	297	—	11	303	.256	.363	.352	.715	-2	30	12	71	3b257,2b135,1b113,S72	0	-2.2
Team	4	281	926	113	246	37	15	9	96	160	—	8	144	.266	.379	.367	.746	+11	13	7	65	3b238,S30,2b5,1b2	0	2.0
/150	2	150	494	60	131	20	8	5	51	85	—	4	77	.266	.379	.367	.746	+11	7	4	64	3b127,S16,2b3/1	0	1.1
GUIEL, AARON Aaron Colin B10.5.1972 Vancouver BC, Can. BL/TR/5'10"/(190–200) Dr 1992 AnaA 21/580 d6.22																								
2006	NY A	44	82	16	21	3	0	4	11	7	0	3	20	.256	.337	.439	.776	-3	2	1	67	O27(4/3/21),1b15/D	0	-0.3
Total	5	307	970	151	239	58	0	35	128	83	2	30	218	.246	.322	.414	.736	-12	8	12	40	O260(46/31/186),1b15,D10	65	-2.0
GULDEN, BRAD Bradley Lee B6.10.1956 New Ulm MN BL/TR/5'11"/(175–182) Dr 1975 LAN 17/408 d9.22																								
1979	NY A	40	92	10	15	4	0	0	6	9	0	0	16	.163	.238	.207	.445	-79	0	1	0	C40	0	-0.1
1980	NY A	2	3	1	1	0	0	1	2	0	0	0	0	.333	.333	1.333	1.666	+239	0	0	0	C2	0	0.1
Total	7	182	435	45	87	14	2	5	43	45	4	2	61	.200	.277	.276	.553	-47	2	3	40	C163	0	-1.4
Team	2	42	95	11	16	4	0	1	8	9	0	0	16	.168	.240	.242	.482	-70	0	1	0	C42	0	0.0
HADLEY, KENT Kent William B12.17.1934 Pocatello ID D3.10.2005 Pocatello ID BL/TL/6'3"/190 d9.14 Col USC																								
1960	NY A	55	64	8	13	2	0	4	11	6	0	0	19	.203	.271	.422	.693	-10	0	0	0	1b24	0	-0.3
Total	3	171	363	49	88	13	1	14	50	30	0	1	97	.242	.300	.399	.699	-10	1	2	33	1b121	0	-1.5
HAHN, ED William Edgar B8.27.1875 Nevada OH D11.29.1941 Des Moines IA BL/TR/?/160 d8.31																								
1905	NY A	43	160	32	51	5	0	0	11	25	—	5	—	.319	.426	.350	.776	+32	1	—	—	O43(20/10/13)	—	0.7
1906	NY A	11	22	2	2	1	0	0	1	3	—	2	—	.091	.259	.136	.395	-77	2	—	—	O7(3/4/0)	—	-0.2
Total	6	553	2045	291	484	42	20	1	122	258	—	44	—	.237	.335	.278	.613	-3	61	—	—	O545(96/28/421)	—	-5.6
Team	2	54	182	34	53	6	0	0	12	28	—	7	0	.291	.406	.324	.730	+18	3	—	—	O50(23/14/13)	—	0.5
HAINES, HINKEY Henry Luther B12.23.1898 Red Lion PA D1.9.1979 Sharon Hill PA BR/TR/5'10"/170 d4.20 Col Penn St.																								
1923	†NY A	28	25	9	4	2	0	0	3	4	—	0	5	.160	.276	.240	.516	-64	3	1	75	O14(2/8/4)	—	-0.1
HALAS, GEORGE George Stanley B2.2.1895 Chicago IL D10.31.1983 Chicago IL BB/TR/6'0"/164 d5.6 Col Illinois																								
1919	NY A	12	22	0	2	0	0	0	0	0	—	0	8	.091	.091	.091	.182	-149	0	—	—	O6(0/1/5)	—	-0.5
HALE, BOB Robert Houston B11.7.1933 Sarasota FL BL/TL/5'10"/(190–195) d7.4																								
1961	NY A	11	13	2	2	0	0	1	1	0	0	0	0	.154	.154	.385	.539	-59	0	0	0	1b5	0	-0.1
Total	7	376	626	41	171	29	2	2	89	26	3	3	51	.273	.299	.335	.634	-24	0	4	0	1b120	0	-2.7
HALL, JIMMIE Jimmie Randolph B3.17.1938 Mt.Holly NC BL/TR/6'0"/(175–180) d4.9																								
1969	NY A	80	212	21	50	8	5	3	26	19	1	0	34	.236	.296	.363	.659	-13	8	3	73	O50(9/19/22),1b7	0	-1.3
Total	8	963	2848	387	724	100	24	121	391	287	35	2	529	.254	.321	.434	.755	+12	38	18	68	O806(221/443/217),1b7	0	1.3
HALL, MEL Melvin B9.16.1960 Lyons NY BL/TL/6'1"/(185–223) Dr 1978 ChiN 2/39 d9.3																								
1981	Chi N	10	11	1	1	0	0	1	2	1	0	0	4	.091	.167	.364	.531	-55	0	0	0	O3(1/2/0)	0	-0.2
1982	Chi N	24	80	6	21	3	2	0	4	5	1	2	17	.262	.318	.350	.668	-15	0	1	0	O22(0/21/1)	0	-0.3
1983	Chi N	112	410	60	116	23	5	17	56	42	6	3	101	.283	.352	.488	.840	+25	6	6	50	O112(5/108/0)	46	0.8
1984	Chi N	48	150	25	42	11	3	4	22	12	3	0	23	.280	.329	.473	.802	+15	2	1	67	O46(5/5/40)	0	0.1
1984	Cle A	83	257	43	66	13	1	7	30	35	5	2	55	.257	.344	.397	.741	+4	1	1	50	O69(64/1/6),D9	0	0.1
1984	Major	131	407	68	108	24	4	11	52	47	8	2	78	.265	7.344	.425	7.769	+125	3	2	60	—	0	0.2
1985	Cle A	23	66	7	21	6	0	0	12	8	0	0	12	.318	.387	.409	.796	+20	0	1	0	O15(15/0/1),D5	150	-0.1
1986	Cle A	140	442	68	131	29	2	18	77	33	8	2	65	.296	.346	.493	.839	+28	6	2	75	O126(123/0/14),D7	0	1.1
1987	Cle A	142	485	57	136	21	1	18	76	20	6	1	68	.280	.309	.439	.748	-5	5	4	56	O122L,D14	0	-0.5
1988	Cle A	150	515	69	144	32	4	6	71	28	12	0	50	.280	.312	.392	.704	-6	7	3	70	O141(135/7/3),D6	0	-1.0
1989	NY A	113	361	54	94	9	0	17	58	21	4	0	37	.260	.295	.427	.722	+4	0	0	0	O75(46/0/31),D34	30	-0.3
1990	NY A	113	360	41	93	23	2	12	46	6	2	2	46	.258	.272	.433	.705	-6	0	0	0	D54,O50(36/0/15)	16	-1.3
1991	NY A	141	492	67	140	23	2	19	80	26	6	3	40	.285	.321	.455	.776	+12	0	1	0	O120(62/1/65),D10	0	0.2
1992	NY A	152	583	67	163	36	3	15	81	29	4	1	53	.280	.310	.429	.739	+7	4	2	67	O136(99/0/37),D11	0	0.0
1996	SF N	25	25	3	3	0	0	0	5	1	0	0	4	.120	.148	.120	.268	-127	0	0	0	O4(3/0/1)	0	-0.5
Total	13	1276	4237	568	1171	229	25	134	620	267	57	16	575	.276	.318	.437	.755	+6	31	22	58	O1041(716/145/214),D150	242	-1.9
Team	4	519	1796	229	490	91	7	63	265	82	16	6	176	.273	.303	.437	.740	+5	4	3	57	O381(243/1/148),D109	46	-1.4
/150	1	150	519	66	142	26	2	18	77	24	5	2	51	.273	.303	.437	.740	+5	1	1	50	O110(70/0/43),D32	13	-0.4
HANDIBOE, MIKE Aloysius James "Coalyard Mike" B7.21.1887 Washington DC D1.31.1953 Savannah GA BL/TL/5'10"/155 d9.8																								
1911	NY A	5	15	0	1	0	0	0	0	2	—	0	—	.067	.176	.067	.243	-129	0	—	—	O4(2/0/2)	—	-0.3
HANNAH, TRUCK James Harrison B6.5.1889 Larimore ND D4.27.1982 Fountain Valley CA BR/TR/6'1"/190 d4.15																								
1918	NY A	90	250	24	55	6	0	2	21	51	—	4	25	.220	.361	.268	.629	-12	5	—	—	C88	—	1.2
1919	NY A	75	227	14	54	8	3	1	20	22	—	3	19	.238	.313	.313	.626	-24	0	—	—	C73/1b	—	-0.8
1920	NY A	79	259	24	64	11	1	2	25	24	—	1	35	.247	.313	.320	.633	-34	2	0	100	C78	—	-0.7
Total	3	244	736	62	173	25	4	5	66	97	—	8	79	.235	.331	.300	.631	-24	7	0	100	C239/1b	—	-0.3
/150	2	150	452	38	106	15	2	3	41	60	—	5	49	.235	.331	.300	.631	-24	4	0	100	C147/1	0	-0.2
HANSEN, RON Ronald Lavern B4.5.1938 Oxford NE BR/TR/6'3"/(190–200) d4.15 NG 1962 C9																								
1970	NY A	59	91	13	27	4	0	4	14	19	0	1	9	.297	.420	.473	.893	+53	0	1	0	S15,3b11/2b	25	0.9
1971	NY A	61	145	6	30	3	0	2	20	9	2	0	27	.207	.245	.269	.514	-50	0	0	0	3b30,2b9,S3	0	-1.3
Total	15	1384	4311	446	1007	156	17	106	501	551	49	19	643	.234	.320	.351	.671	-8	9	14	39	S1143,3b86,2b47,1b21	185	15.5
Team	2	120	236	19	57	7	0	6	34	28	2	1	36	.242	.317	.347	.664	-7	0	1	0	3b41,S18,2b10	25	-0.4
/150	3	150	295	24	71	9	0	8	43	35	3	1	45	.242	.317	.347	.664	-7	0	1	0	3b51,S23,2b13	31	-0.5
HANSON, HARRY Harry Francis B1.17.1896 Elgin IL D10.5.1966 Savannah GA BR/TR/5'11"/? d7.14																								
1913	NY A	1	2	0	0	0	0	0	0	0	—	0	0	.000	.000	.000	.000	-199	0	—	—	/C	—	-0.1
HARGRAVE, BUBBLES Eugene Franklin B7.15.1892 New Haven IN D2.23.1969 Cincinnati OH BR/TR/5'10.5"/174 d9.18 b–Pinky																								
1930	NY A	45	108	11	30	7	0	0	12	10	—	0	9	.278	.339	.343	.682	-23	0	0	0	C34	—	-0.5
Total	12	852	2533	314	786	155	58	29	376	217	—	32	166	.310	.372	.452	.824	+19	29	16	100	C747	—	8.8
HARRAH, TOBY Colbert Dale B10.26.1948 Sissonville WV BR/TR/6'0"/(165–190) d9.5 M1/C9																								
1984	NY A	88	253	40	55	9	4	1	26	42	2	2	28	.217	.331	.296	.627	-22	3	0	100	3b74,2b4/rfD	17	-0.5
Total	17	2155	7402	1115	1954	307	40	195	918	1153	51	63	868	.264	.365	.395	.760	+14	238	94	72	3b1099,S813,2b244,D21/rf	118	19.2

YEAR	TM LG	G	AB	R	H	2B	3B	HR	RBI	BB	IB	HP	SO	AVG	OBP	SLG	OPS	AOPS	SB	CS	SB%	GAMES AT POSITION	DL	BFW
Harris, Joe	Joseph "Moon" B5.20.1891 Plum Borough PA D12.10.1959 Renton PA BR/TR/5'9"/170 d6.9 Mil 1918																							
1914	NY A	2	1	0	0	0	0	0	0	3	—	1	1	.000	.800	.000	.800	+43	0	—	—	/1blf	—	0.1
Total	10	970	3035	461	963	201	64	47	517	413	—	31	188	.317	.404	.472	.876	+31	36	16	100	1b522,O319(235/0/84),S4,3b2	—	12.2
Hart, Jim Ray	James Ray B10.30.1941 Hookerton NC BR/TR/5'11"/(185–195) d7.7																							
1973	NY A	114	339	29	86	13	2	13	52	36	7	0	45	.254	.324	.419	.743	+11	0	2	0	D106	0	0.1
1974	NY A	10	19	1	1	0	0	0	0	3	0	0	7	.053	.182	.053	.235	-130	0	0	0	D4	0	-0.4
Total	12	1125	3783	518	1052	148	29	170	578	380	49	28	573	.278	.345	.467	.812	+28	17	17	50	3b683,O264(257/0/7),D110	93	6.1
Team	2	124	358	30	87	13	2	13	52	39	7	0	52	.243	.316	.399	.715	+3	0	2	0	D110	0	-0.3
/150	2	150	433	36	105	16	2	16	63	47	8	0	63	.243	.316	.399	.715	+3	0	2	0	D133	0	-0.4
Hartzell, Roy	Roy Allen B7.6.1881 Golden CO D11.6.1961 Golden CO BL/TR/5'8.5"/155 d4.17 OF(213/32/307)																							
1906	StL A	113	404	43	86	7	0	0	24	19	—	10	—	.213	.266	.230	.496	-42	21	—	—	3b103,S6,2b2	—	-2.2
1907	StL A	60	220	20	52	3	5	0	13	11	—	4	—	.236	.285	.295	.580	-15	7	—	—	3b38,2b12,S2,O2R	—	-0.4
1908	StL A	115	422	41	112	5	6	2	32	19	—	3	—	.265	.302	.320	.622	+1	24	—	—	O82(0/4/78),S18,3b7,2b4	—	-0.7
1909	StL A	152	595	64	161	12	5	0	32	29	—	7	—	.271	.312	.308	.620	+3	14	—	—	O85R,S65/2b	—	0.5
1910	StL A	151	542	52	118	13	5	2	30	49	—	6	—	.218	.290	.271	.561	-19	18	—	—	3b89,S38,O23R	—	-0.2
1911	NY A	144	527	67	156	17	11	3	91	63	—	4	—	.296	.375	.387	.762	+6	22	—	—	3b124,S12,O8(2/0/8)	—	-0.3
1912	NY A	125	416	50	113	10	11	1	38	64	—	1	—	.272	.370	.356	.726	+2	20	12	63	3b56,O56(0/13/43),S10,2b2	—	0.0
1913	NY A	141	490	60	127	18	1	0	38	67	—	4	40	.259	.353	.300	.653	-9	26	—	—	2b81,O31(4/11/16),3b21,S4	—	0.2
1914	NY A	137	481	55	112	15	9	1	32	68	—	6	38	.233	.335	.308	.643	-6	22	25	47	O128(91/3/34),2b5	—	-1.6
1915	NY A	119	387	39	97	11	2	0	60	67	—	3	37	.251	.351	.313	.664	-1	7	19	27	O107(105/0/2),2b5,3b2	—	-1.3
1916	NY A	33	64	12	12	1	0	0	7	9	—	1	3	.188	.297	.203	.500	-51	1	—	—	O20(11/1/16)	—	-0.6
Total	11	1290	4548	503	1146	112	55	12	397	455	—	49	118	.252	.327	.309	.636	-7	182	56	100	O550R,3b440,S155,2b112	—	-6.6
Team	6	699	2365	283	617	72	34	8	266	328	—	19	118	.261	.355	.330	.685	-3	98	56	100	O358(10/49/44),3b203,2b93,S26	—	-3.6
/150	1	150	508	61	132	15	7	2	57	70	—	4	25	.261	.355	.330	.685	-3	21	12	100	O77(2/11/9),3b44,2b20,S6	—	-0.8
Hassett, Buddy	John Aloysius B9.5.1911 New York NY D8.23.1997 Westwood NJ BL/TL/5'11"/180 d4.14 Mil 1943–46 Col Manhattan																							
1942	†NY A	132	538	80	153	16	6	5	48	32	—	0	16	.284	.325	.364	.689	-5	5	5	50	1b132	0	-0.8
Total	7	929	3517	469	1026	130	40	12	343	209	—	11	116	.292	.333	.362	.695	-8	53	5	100	1b747,O114(72/6/39)	0	-7.1
/150	1	150	611	91	174	18	7	6	55	36	—	0	18	.284	.325	.364	.689	-5	6	6	50	1b150	0	-0.9
Hassey, Ron	Ronald William B2.27.1953 Tucson AZ BL/TR/6'2"/(195–200) Dr 1976 CleA 18/422 d4.23 C6 Col Arizona																							
1985	NY A	92	267	31	79	16	1	13	42	28	4	3	21	.296	.369	.509	.878	+40	0	0	0	C69,1b2,D2	0	1.5
1986	NY A	64	191	23	57	14	0	6	29	24	1	2	16	.298	.381	.466	.847	+30	1	1	50	C51,D3	0	0.2
Total	14	1192	3440	348	914	172	7	71	438	385	31	21	378	.266	.340	.382	.722	+0	14	10	58	C946,D96,1b23	124	4.4
Team	2	156	458	54	136	30	1	19	71	52	5	5	37	.297	.374	.491	.865	+36	1	1	50	C120,D5,1b2	0	1.7
/150	2	150	440	52	131	29	1	18	68	50	5	5	36	.297	.374	.491	.865	+36	1	1	50	C115,D5,1b2	0	1.6
Hawks, Chicken	Nelson Louis B2.3.1896 San Francisco CA D5.26.1973 San Rafael CA BL/TL/5'11"/167 d4.14 Col Santa Clara																							
1921	NY A	41	73	16	21	2	3	2	15	5	—	0	12	.288	.333	.479	.812	+3	0	1	0	O15(5/10/0)	—	-0.2
Total	2	146	393	68	124	17	8	7	60	37	—	2	45	.316	.377	.453	.830	+3	3	7	30	1b90,O15(5/10/0)	—	-0.6
Hayes, Charlie	Charles Dewayne B5.29.1965 Hattiesburg MS BR/TR/6'0"/(190–224) Dr 1983 SFN 4/96 d9.11 OF(4/0/1)																							
1992	NY A	142	509	52	131	19	2	18	66	28	0	3	100	.257	.297	.409	.706	-3	3	5	38	3b139,1b4	0	-1.5
1996	†NY A	20	67	7	19	3	0	2	13	1	0	0	12	.284	.294	.418	.712	-23	0	0	0	3b19	0	0.0
1997	†NY A	100	353	39	91	16	0	11	53	40	2	1	66	.258	.332	.397	.729	-9	3	2	60	3b98,2b5	0	-0.8
Total	14	1547	5262	580	1379	251	16	144	740	420	30	21	918	.262	.316	.398	.714	-12	47	31	60	3b1328,1b132,D6,2b6,O5L,S3	19	-9.3
Team	3	262	929	98	241	38	2	31	132	69	2	4	178	.259	.311	.405	.716	-7	6	7	46	3b256,2b5,1b4	0	-2.3
/150	2	150	532	56	138	22	1	18	76	40	1	2	102	.259	.311	.405	.716	-7	3	4	43	3b147,2b3,1b2	0	-1.3
Healy, Fran	Francis Xavier B9.6.1946 Holyoke MA BR/TR/6'5"/210 d9.3 Col American International																							
1976	NY A	46	120	10	32	3	0	0	9	9	0	0	17	.267	.318	.292	.610	-20	3	1	75	C31,D9	0	0.1
1977	NY A	27	67	10	15	5	0	0	7	6	0	0	13	.224	.288	.299	.587	-40	1	0	100	C26	0	-0.5
1978	NY A	1	1	0	0	0	0	0	0	0	0	0	1	.000	.000	.000	.000	-199	0	0	0	/C	0	-0.1
Total	9	470	1326	144	332	60	6	20	141	154	4	2	242	.250	.329	.350	.679	-10	30	17	64	C415,D15	0	-0.7
Team	3	74	188	20	47	8	0	0	16	15	0	0	31	.250	.305	.293	.598	-28	4	1	80	C58,D9	0	-0.5
Heath, Mike	Michael Thomas B2.5.1955 Tampa FL BR/TR/5'11"/(175–200) Dr 1973 NYA 2/37 d6.3 OF(79/1/142)																							
1978	†NY A	33	92	6	21	3	1	0	8	4	0	1	9	.228	.265	.283	.548	-44	0	0	0	C33	0	-0.4
Total	14	1325	4212	462	1061	173	27	86	469	278	24	22	616	.252	.300	.367	.667	-13	54	40	57	C1083,O215R,D40,3b38,1b4,S4/2b	131	-3.5
Heffner, Don	Donald Henry "Jeep" B2.8.1911 Rouzerville PA D8.1.1989 Pasadena CA BR/TR/5'10"/155 d4.17 M1/C8																							
1934	NY A	72	241	29	63	8	3	0	25	25	—	0	18	.261	.331	.320	.651	-27	1	1	50	2b68	—	-1.4
1935	NY A	10	36	3	11	3	1	0	8	4	—	0	1	.306	.375	.444	.819	+18	0	0	0	2b10	—	0.1
1936	NY A	19	48	7	11	2	1	0	6	6	—	0	5	.229	.315	.313	.628	-43	0	0	0	3b8,2b5,S3	—	0.0
1937	NY A	60	201	23	50	6	5	0	21	19	—	0	19	.249	.314	.328	.642	-38	1	4	20	2b38,S13,3b3/1brf	—	-1.6
Total	11	743	2526	275	610	99	19	6	248	270	—	9	218	.241	.317	.303	.620	-39	18	26	41	2b595,S89,3b11,1b7/rf	0	-11.2
Team	4	161	526	62	135	19	10	0	60	54	—	0	43	.257	.326	.331	.657	-30	2	5	29	2b121,S16,3b11/1rf	—	-2.9
/150	4	150	490	58	126	18	9	0	56	50	—	0	40	.257	.326	.331	.657	-30	2	5	29	2b113,S15,3b10/1rf	—	-2.7
Hegan, Mike	James Michael B7.21.1942 Cleveland OH BL/TL/6'1"/(185–195) d9.13 Mil 1967 f-Jim Col Holy Cross																							
1964	†NY A	5	5	0	0	0	0	0	0	1	0	0	2	.000	.167	.000	.167	-148	0	0	0	1b2	0	0.0
1966	NY A	13	39	7	8	0	1	0	2	7	0	0	11	.205	.326	.256	.582	-27	1	1	50	1b13	0	-0.2
1967	NY A	68	118	12	16	4	1	1	3	20	1	1	40	.136	.266	.212	.478	-56	7	1	88	1b54,O10R	0	-1.2
1973	NY A	37	131	12	36	3	2	6	14	7	1	0	34	.275	.309	.466	.775	+19	0	0	0	1b37	0	0.0
1974	NY A	18	53	3	12	2	0	2	9	5	0	2	9	.226	.317	.377	.694	+0	1	1	50	1b17	0	-0.1
Total	12	965	2080	281	504	73	18	53	229	311	19	7	489	.242	.341	.371	.712	+3	28	21	57	1b553,O177(57/1/119),D92	0	-1.1
Team	5	141	346	34	72	9	4	9	28	40	2	3	96	.208	.295	.335	.630	-19	9	3	75	1b123,O10R	0	-1.5
/150	5	150	368	36	77	10	4	10	30	43	2	3	102	.208	.295	.335	.630	-19	10	3	77	1b131,O11R	0	-1.6
Held, Woodie	Woodson George B3.25.1932 Sacramento CA BR/TR/5'11"/(170–185) d9.5 OF(113/276/111)																							
1954	NY A	4	3	2	0	0	0	0	0	2	—	0	1	.000	.400	.000	.400	-83	0	0	0	S4/3b	0	0.0
1957	NY A	1	1	0	0	0	0	0	0	0	0	0	0	.000	.000	.000	.000	-199	0	0	0	/H	0	0.0
Total	14	1390	4019	524	963	150	22	179	559	508	45	56	944	.240	.331	.421	.752	+9	14	11	56	S539,O448C,2b179,3b132	67	7.7
Team	2	5	4	2	0	0	0	0	0	2	0	0	1	.000	.333	.000	.333	-102	0	0	0	S4/3	0	0.0
Hemphill, Charlie	Charles Judson "Eagle Eye" B4.20.1876 Greenville MI D6.22.1953 Detroit MI BL/TL/5'9"/160 d6.27 b-Frank																							
1908	NY A	142	505	62	150	12	9	0	44	59	—	3	—	.297	.374	.356	.730	+36	42	—	—	O142(4/130/8)	—	1.4
1909	NY A	73	181	23	44	5	1	0	10	32	—	0	—	.243	.357	.282	.639	+1	10	—	—	O45(13/32/0)	—	0.1
1910	NY A	102	351	45	84	9	4	0	21	55	—	5	—	.239	.350	.288	.638	-5	19	—	—	O94(0/63/31)	—	-0.8
1911	NY A	69	201	32	57	4	2	1	15	37	—	1	—	.284	.397	.338	.735	-1	9	—	—	O55(0/46/9)	—	-0.6
Total	11	1242	4541	580	1230	117	68	22	421	435	—	17	—	.271	.337	.341	.678	+6	207	—	—	O1175(45/607/525),2b3	—	-6.2
Team	4	386	1238	162	335	30	16	1	90	183	—	9	0	.271	.369	.323	.692	+13	80	—	—	O336(17/271/48)	—	0.1
/150	2	150	481	63	130	12	6	0	35	71	—	3	0	.271	.369	.323	.692	+13	31	—	—	O131(7/105/19)	—	0.0

Batters

YEAR	TM LG	G	AB	R	H	2B	3B	HR	RBI	BB	IB	HP	SO	AVG	OBP	SLG	OPS	AOPS	SB	CS	SB%	GAMES AT POSITION	DL	BFW
Hemsley, Rollie	Ralston Burdett B6.24.1907 Syracuse OH D7.31.1972 Washington DC BR/TR/5'10"/170 d4.19 Mil 1944–45 C3																							
1942	NY A	31	85	12	25	3	1	0	15	5	—	0	9	.294	.333	.353	.686	-5	1	0	100	C29	0	0.3
1943	NY A	62	180	12	43	6	3	2	24	13	—	0	9	.239	.290	.339	.629	-17	0	1	0	C52	0	0.1
1944	NY A★	81	284	23	76	12	5	2	26	9	—	0	13	.268	.290	.366	.656	-16	0	2	0	C76	0	-0.3
Total	19	1593	5047	562	1321	257	72	31	555	357	—	4	395	.262	.311	.360	.671	-26	29	18	100	C1482,O7(6/1/0),1b2	0	-4.0
Team	3	174	549	47	144	21	9	4	65	27	—	0	31	.262	.297	.355	.652	-15	1	3	25	C157	0	0.1
/150	3	150	473	41	124	18	8	3	56	23	—	0	27	.262	.297	.355	.652	-15	1	3	25	C135	0	0.1
Henderson, Rickey	Rickey Henley B12.25.1958 Chicago IL BR/TL/5'10"/(180–195) Dr 1976 OakA 4/96 d6.24 C1																							
1985	NY A★	143	547	**146**	172	28	5	24	72	99	1	3	65	.314	.419	.516	.935	+58	**80**	10	89	O141(6/141/0)/D	14	**6.9**
1986	NY A★	153	608	**130**	160	31	5	28	74	89	2	2	81	.263	.358	.469	.827	+24	**87**	18	83	O146(11/138/0),D5	0	3.6
1987	NY A★	95	358	78	104	17	3	17	37	80	1	2	52	.291	.423	.497	.920	+44	41	8	84	O69(34/39/0),D24	61	3.4
1988	NY A★	140	554	118	169	30	2	6	50	82	1	3	54	.305	.394	.399	.793	+24	**93**	13	88	O136(135/3/0),D3	0	3.8
1989	NY A	65	235	41	58	13	1	3	22	56	0	1	29	.247	.392	.349	.741	+12	25	8	76	O65L	0	1.0
Total	25	3081	10961	2295	3055	510	66	297	1115	2190	61	98	1694	.279	.401	.419	.820	+27	1406	335	81	O2826(2421/448/27),D149	176	70.3
Team	5	596	2302	513	663	119	16	78	255	406	5	11	281	.288	.395	.455	.850	+34	326	57	85	O557(17/321/0),D33	75	18.7
/150	1	150	579	129	167	30	4	20	64	102	1	3	71	.288	.395	.455	.850	+34	82	14	85	O140(4/81/0),D8	19	4.7
Hendrick, Harvey	Harvey "Gink" B11.9.1897 Mason TN D10.29.1941 Covington TN BL/TR/6'2"/190 d4.20 Col Vanderbilt OF(128/21/86)																							
1923	†NY A	37	66	9	18	3	1	3	12	2	—	0	8	.273	.294	.485	.779	+1	3	0	100	O13(11/2/0)	—	-0.1
1924	NY A	40	76	7	20	0	0	1	11	2	—	1	7	.263	.291	.303	.594	-47	1	0	100	O17(15/0/2)	—	-0.6
Total	11	922	2910	434	896	157	46	48	413	239	—	16	243	.308	.364	.443	.807	+13	75	0	100	1b378,O220L,3b118,S4/2b	—	-0.0
Team	2	77	142	16	38	3	1	4	23	4	—	1	15	.268	.293	.387	.680	-25	4	0	100	O30(26/2/2)	—	-0.7
Hendricks, Elrod	Elrod Jerome B12.22.1940 Charlotte Amalie, V.I. D12.21.2005 Glen Burnie MD BL/TR/6'1"/(175–185) d4.13 C28																							
1976	†NY A	26	53	6	12	1	0	3	5	3	0	0	10	.226	.263	.415	.678	-2	0	0	0	C18	0	0.0
1977	NY A	10	11	1	3	1	0	1	5	0	0	0	2	.273	.273	.636	.909	+40	0	0	0	C6	0	0.0
Total	12	711	1888	205	415	66	7	62	230	229	40	12	319	.220	.306	.361	.667	-10	1	5	17	C602,1b8,D3/P	0	-1.2
Team	2	36	64	7	15	2	0	4	10	3	0	0	12	.234	.265	.453	.718	+5	0	0	0	C24	0	0.0
Hendryx, Tim	Timothy Green B1.31.1891 LeRoy IL D8.14.1957 Corpus Christi TX BR/TR/5'9"/170 d9.4																							
1911	Cle A	4	7	0	2	0	0	0	0	0	—	0	—	.286	.286	.286	.572	-41	0	—	—	3b3	—	0.0
1912	Cle A	23	70	9	17	2	4	1	14	8	—	1	—	.243	.329	.429	.758	+13	3	3	50	O22C	—	-0.3
1915	NY A	13	40	4	8	2	0	0	1	4	—	1	2	.200	.289	.250	.539	-39	0	3	0	O12C	—	-0.3
1916	NY A	15	62	10	18	7	1	0	5	8	—	1	6	.290	.380	.435	.815	+42	4	—	—	O15R	—	0.2
1917	NY A	125	393	43	98	14	7	5	44	62	—	5	45	.249	.359	.359	.718	+18	6	—	—	O107(0/30/77)	—	0.6
1918	StL A	88	219	22	61	14	3	0	33	37	—	2	35	.279	.388	.370	.758	+33	5	—	—	O65(28/20/18)	—	0.5
1920	Bos A	99	363	54	119	21	5	0	73	42	—	2	27	.328	.400	.413	.813	+21	7	9	44	O98C	—	-0.8
1921	Bos A	49	137	10	33	8	2	0	22	24	—	2	13	.241	.362	.328	.690	-21	1	1	50	O41(2/2/37)	—	-0.8
Total	8	416	1291	152	356	68	22	6	192	185	—	14	128	.276	.372	.376	.748	+15	26	16	100	O360(30/184/147),3b3	—	-0.9
Team	3	153	495	57	124	23	8	5	50	74	—	7	53	.251	.356	.360	.716	+17	10	3	100	O134(0/42/45)	—	0.5
/150	3	150	485	56	122	23	8	5	49	73	—	7	52	.251	.356	.360	.716	+17	10	3	100	O131(0/41/44)	—	0.5
Henrich, Tommy	Thomas David "The Clutch","Old Reliable" B2.20.1913 Massillon OH BL/TL/6'0"/180 d5.11 Mil 1942–45 C4																							
1937	NY A	67	206	39	66	14	5	8	42	35	—	0	17	.320	.419	.553	.972	+42	4	0	100	O59(30/0/29)	—	1.0
1938	†NY A	131	471	109	127	24	7	22	91	92	—	2	32	.270	.391	.490	.881	+20	6	2	75	O130R	—	0.7
1939	NY A	99	347	64	96	18	4	9	57	51	—	1	23	.277	.371	.429	.800	+6	7	0	100	O88(1/38/50)/1b	—	0.2
1940	NY A	90	293	57	90	28	5	10	53	48	—	2	30	.307	.408	.539	.947	+49	1	2	33	O76(1/24/52),1b2	—	1.9
1941	†NY A	144	538	106	149	27	5	31	85	81	—	5	40	.277	.377	.519	.896	+37	3	1	75	O139(0/19/121)	0	1.7
1942	NY A★	127	483	77	129	30	5	13	67	58	—	5	42	.267	.352	.431	.783	+22	4	4	50	O119R,1b7	0	0.6
1946	NY A	150	565	92	142	25	4	19	83	87	—	**7**	63	.251	.358	.411	.769	+13	5	2	71	O111R,1b41	0	0.7
1947	†NY A★	142	550	109	158	35	**13**	16	98	71	—	3	54	.287	.372	.485	.857	+39	3	2	60	O132(0/8/125),1b6	0	2.7
1948	NY A★	146	588	**138**	181	42	**14**	25	100	76	—	4	42	.308	.391	.554	.945	+51	2	3	40	O102(6/3/96),1b46	0	3.2
1949	†NY A☆	115	411	90	118	20	3	24	85	86	—	5	34	.287	.416	.526	.942	+48	2	2	50	O61R,1b52	0	2.1
1950	NY A★	73	151	20	41	6	8	6	34	27	—	0	6	.272	.382	.536	.918	+37	0	1	0	1b34	0	0.2
Total	11	1284	4603	901	1297	269	73	183	795	712	—	34	383	.282	.382	.491	.873	+32	37	19	66	O1017(38/92/894),1b189	0	15.0
/150	1	150	538	105	152	31	9	21	93	83	—	4	45	.282	.382	.491	.873	+32	4	2	67	1b22,O12(4/11/104)	0	1.8
Henson, Drew	Drew Daniel B2.13.1980 San Diego CA BR/TR/6'5"/222 Dr 1998 NYA 3/97 d9.5																							
2002	NY A	3	1	1	0	0	0	0	0	0	0	0	1	.000	.000	.000	.000	-199	0	0	0	D2	0	0.0
2003	NY A	5	8	2	1	0	0	0	0	0	0	0	2	.125	.125	.125	.250	-134	0	0	0	3b3	0	-0.1
Total	2	8	9	3	1	0	0	0	0	0	0	0	3	.111	.111	.111	.222	-142	0	0	0	3b3,D2	0	-0.1
Hernandez, Leo	Leonardo Jesus B11.6.1959 Santa Lucia, Venezuela BR/TR/5'11"/(170–200) d9.19																							
1986	NY A	7	22	2	5	2	0	1	4	1	0	0	8	.227	.261	.455	.716	-9	0	0	0	3b7/2b	0	-0.1
Total	4	85	248	23	56	8	1	7	30	13	1	0	33	.226	.263	.351	.614	-32	1	0	100	3b71,D8/2b/1b	0	-2.3
Hernandez, Michel	Michel B8.12.1978 LaHabana, Cuba BR/TR/6'0"/210 d9.6																							
2003	NY A	5	4	0	1	0	0	0	0	1	0	0	1	.250	.400	.250	.650	-22	0	0	0	C5	0	0.0
Herrmann, Ed	Edward Martin B8.27.1946 San Diego CA BL/TR/6'1"/(200–210) d9.1 gf–Marty																							
1975	NY A	80	200	16	51	9	2	6	30	16	5	0	23	.255	.309	.410	.719	+3	0	0	0	D35,C24	0	0.8
Total	11	922	2729	247	654	92	4	80	320	260	55	29	361	.240	.310	.364	.674	-10	6	8	43	C817,D37	40	0.4
High, Hugh	Hugh Jenken "Bunny" B10.24.1887 Pottstown PA D11.16.1962 St.Louis MO BL/TL/5'7.5"/155 d4.11 b–Andy b–Charlie																							
1913	Det A	87	183	18	42	6	1	0	16	28	—	1	24	.230	.335	.273	.608	-20	6	—	—	O52(3/43/7)	—	-0.5
1914	Det A	84	184	25	49	5	3	0	17	26	—	2	21	.266	.363	.326	.689	+4	7	6	54	O53(13/39/1)	—	-0.8
1915	NY A	119	427	51	110	19	7	1	43	62	—	3	47	.258	.356	.342	.698	+9	22	13	63	O117(44/71/1)	—	-0.6
1916	NY A	116	377	44	99	13	4	1	28	47	—	3	44	.263	.349	.326	.675	+1	13	—	—	O110(107/2/1)	—	-0.5
1917	NY A	103	365	37	86	11	6	1	19	48	—	3	31	.236	.329	.307	.636	-7	8	—	—	O100(99/1/0)	—	-1.1
1918	NY A	7	10	1	0	0	0	0	0	1	—	0	1	.000	.091	.000	.091	-171	0	—	—	O4(2/1/1)	—	-0.2
Total	6	516	1546	176	386	54	21	3	123	212	—	12	168	.250	.345	.318	.663	-2	56	19	100	O436(268/157/11)	—	-3.7
Team	4	345	1179	133	295	43	17	3	90	158	—	9	123	.250	.343	.323	.666	+0	43	13	100	O331(250/75/3)	—	-2.4
/150	2	150	513	58	128	19	7	1	39	69	—	4	53	.250	.343	.323	.666	+0	19	6	100	O144(109/33/1)	—	-1.0
Hill, Glenallen	Glenallen B3.22.1965 Santa Cruz CA BR/TR/6'2"/(210–230) Dr 1983 TorA 9/219 d7.31 C1																							
2000	†NY A	40	132	22	44	5	0	16	29	9	0	1	33	.333	.378	.735	1.113	+76	0	0	0	D24,O12L	0	1.1
Total	13	1162	3715	528	1005	187	21	186	586	270	13	20	845	.271	.321	.482	.803	+11	96	38	72	O847(336/73/452),D152	203	-1.5
Hill, Jesse	Jesse Terrill B1.20.1907 Yates MO D8.31.1993 Pasadena CA BR/TR/5'9"/165 d4.17 Col USC																							
1935	NY A	107	392	69	115	20	3	4	33	42	—	0	32	.293	.362	.390	.752	+0	14	4	78	O94L	—	-0.2
1936	Was A	85	233	50	71	19	5	0	34	29	—	1	23	.305	.384	.429	.813	+6	11	0	100	O60(54/4/2)	—	0.1
1937	Was A	33	92	24	20	2	1	1	4	13	—	0	16	.217	.314	.293	.607	-43	2	1	67	O21(3/18/0)	—	-0.5
1937	Phi A	70	242	32	71	12	3	1	37	31	—	0	20	.293	.374	.380	.754	-8	16	3	84	O68(3/65/0)	—	-0.4
1937	Year	103	334	56	91	14	4	2	41	44	—	0	36	.272	.357	.356	.713	-18	18	4	82	O89(6/83/0)	—	-0.9
Total	3	295	959	175	277	53	12	6	108	115	—	1	91	.289	.366	.388	.754	-5	43	8	84	O243(154/87/2)	—	-1.0
/150	1	150	550	97	161	28	4	6	46	59	—	0	45	.293	.362	.390	.752	+0	20	6	77	O132L	—	-0.3

YEAR	TM LG	G	AB	R	H	2B	3B	HR	RBI	BB	IB	HP	SO	AVG	OBP	SLG	OPS	AOPS	SB	CS	SB%	GAMES AT POSITION	DL	BFW
Hillis, Mack	Malcolm David B7.23.1901 Cambridge MA D6.16.1961 Cambridge MA BR/TR/5'10"/165 d9.13																							
1924	NY A	1	1	1	0	0	0	0	0	0	—	0	0	.000	.000	.000	.000	-199	0	0	0	/2b	—	0.0
Total	2	12	37	7	9	2	3	1	7	0	—	0	6	.243	.243	.541	.784	-4	1	0	100	2b9/3b	—	-0.1
Hoag, Myril	Myril Oliver B3.9.1908 Davis CA D7.28.1971 High Springs FL BR/TR/5'11"/180 d4.15 Mil 1943																							
1931	NY A	44	28	6	4	2	0	0	3	1	—	0	8	.143	.172	.214	.386	-99	0	0	0	O23(11/2/10)/3b	—	-0.3
1932	†NY A	46	54	18	20	5	0	1	7	7	—	0	13	.370	.443	.519	.962	+56	1	1	50	O35(27/2/9)/1b	—	0.5
1934	NY A	97	251	45	67	8	2	3	34	21	—	0	21	.267	.324	.351	.675	-21	1	3	25	O86(29/17/50)	—	-0.7
1935	NY A	48	110	13	28	4	1	1	13	12	—	0	19	.255	.328	.336	.664	-24	4	2	67	O37(2/3/32)/3b	—	-0.3
1936	NY A	45	156	23	47	9	4	3	34	7	—	3	16	.301	.343	.468	.811	+2	3	1	75	O39(2/26/12)	—	-0.3
1937	†NY A	106	362	48	109	19	8	3	46	33	—	3	33	.301	.364	.423	.787	-3	4	7	36	O99(24/9/70)	—	-1.0
1938	†NY A	85	267	28	74	14	3	0	48	25	—	2	31	.277	.344	.352	.696	-25	4	3	57	O70(31/13/28)	—	-1.4
1939	StL A★	129	482	58	142	23	4	10	75	24	—	1	35	.295	.329	.421	.750	-11	9	5	64	O117(11/49/60)/P	—	-1.5
1940	StL A	76	191	20	50	11	0	3	26	13	—	0	30	.262	.309	.366	.675	-27	2	0	100	O46(1/1/44)	—	-1.0
1941	StL A	1	1	0	0	0	0	0	0	0	—	0	0	.000	.000	.000	.000	-197	0	0	0	/H	0	0.0
1941	Chi A	106	380	30	97	13	3	1	44	27	—	1	29	.255	.306	.313	.619	-35	6	10	38	O99(75/25/0)	0	-3.2
1941	Year	107	381	30	97	13	3	1	44	27	—	1	29	.255	.306	.312	.618	-35	6	10	38	O99(75/25/0)	0	-3.2
1942	Chi A	113	412	47	99	18	2	2	37	36	—	0	21	.240	.301	.308	.609	-27	17	8	68	O112(41/81/0)	0	-1.6
1944	Chi A	17	48	5	11	1	0	0	4	10	—	0	1	.229	.362	.250	.612	-23	1	3	25	O14(0/13/1)	0	-0.2
1944	Cle A	67	277	33	79	9	3	1	27	25	—	1	23	.285	.347	.350	.697	+3	6	4	60	O66C	0	-0.6
1944	Year	84	325	38	90	10	3	1	31	35	—	1	24	.277	.349	.335	.684	-1	7	7	50	O80(0/79/1)	0	-0.8
1945	Cle A	40	128	10	27	5	3	0	3	11	—	1	18	.211	.279	.297	.576	-30	1	2	33	O33(0/27/6),P2	0	-0.7
Total	13	1020	3147	384	854	141	33	28	401	252	—	12	298	.271	.328	.364	.692	-17	59	49	55	O876(254/334/322),P3,3b2/1b	0	-12.3
Team	7	471	1228	181	349	61	18	11	185	106	—	8	141	.284	.345	.390	.735	-12	17	17	50	O389(54/72/211),3b2/1	—	-3.5
/150	2	150	391	58	111	19	6	4	59	34	—	3	45	.284	.345	.390	.735	-12	5	5	50	O124(17/23/67)/31	—	-1.1
Hobson, Butch	Clell Lavern B8.17.1951 Tuscaloosa AL BR/TR/6'1"/(190–193) Dr 1973 BosA 8/185 d9.7 M3 Col Alabama																							
1982	NY A	30	58	2	10	2	0	0	3	1	0	0	14	.172	.183	.207	.390	-92	0	0	0	D15,1b11	19	-0.9
Total	8	738	2556	314	634	107	23	98	397	183	12	5	569	.248	.297	.423	.720	-9	11	9	55	3b651,D67,1b11/2b	49	-10.7
Hoffman, Danny	Daniel John B3.2.1880 Canton CT D3.14.1922 Manchester CT BL/TL/5'9"/175 d4.20																							
1906	NY A	100	320	34	82	10	6	0	23	27	—	2	—	.256	.318	.325	.643	-8	32	—	—	O98C	—	-1.1
1907	NY A	136	517	81	131	10	3	5	46	42	—	13	—	.253	.325	.313	.638	-4	30	—	—	O135C	—	-0.4
Total	9	829	2981	361	762	71	52	14	235	226	—	39	—	.256	.316	.328	.644	+1	185	—	—	O809(77/636/96)/P	—	-3.0
Team	2	236	837	115	213	20	9	5	69	69	—	15	0	.254	.322	.318	.640	-6	62	—	—	O233C	—	-1.5
/150	1	150	532	73	135	13	6	3	44	44	—	10	0	.254	.322	.318	.640	-6	39	—	—	O148C	—	-1.0
Hofman, Solly	Arthur Frederick "Circus Solly" B10.29.1882 St.Louis MO D3.10.1956 St.Louis MO BR/TR/6'0"/160 d7.28 OF(77/557/79)																							
1916	NY A	6	27	0	8	1	1	0	2	1	—	0	1	.296	.321	.407	.728	+16	1	—	—	O6C	—	0.1
Total	14	1194	4072	554	1095	162	60	19	495	421	—	15	171	.269	.340	.352	.692	+2	208	3	100	O702C,2b198,1b187,S63,3b25	—	-5.2
Hofmann, Fred	Fred "Bootnose" B6.10.1894 St.Louis MO D11.19.1964 St.Helena CA BR/TR/5'11.5"/175 d9.26 C13																							
1919	NY A	1	1	0	0	0	0	0	0	0	—	0	0	.000	.000	.000	.000	-199	0	—	—	/C	—	0.0
1920	NY A	15	24	3	7	0	0	0	1	1	—	1	2	.292	.346	.292	.638	-32	0	0	0	C14	—	-0.3
1921	NY A	23	62	7	11	1	1	1	5	5	—	1	13	.177	.250	.274	.524	-67	0	0	0	C18/1b	—	-0.6
1922	NY A	37	91	13	27	5	3	2	10	9	—	0	12	.297	.360	.484	.844	+16	0	0	0	C29	—	0.1
1923	†NY A	72	238	24	69	10	4	3	26	18	—	4	27	.290	.350	.403	.753	-4	2	1	67	C70	—	0.0
1924	NY A	62	166	17	29	6	1	1	11	12	—	2	15	.175	.239	.241	.480	-76	2	1	67	C54	—	-1.4
1925	NY A	3	2	0	0	0	0	0	0	0	—	0	0	.000	.000	.000	.000	-199	0	0	0	/C	—	-0.1
1927	Bos A	87	217	20	59	19	1	0	24	21	—	2	26	.272	.342	.369	.711	-14	2	0	100	C81	—	-0.8
1928	Bos A	78	199	14	45	8	1	0	16	11	—	1	25	.226	.270	.276	.546	-55	0	1	0	C71	—	-1.3
Total	9	378	1000	98	247	49	11	7	93	77	—	11	120	.247	.308	.339	.647	-32	6	3	100	C339/1b	—	-4.4
Team	7	213	584	64	143	22	9	7	53	45	—	8	69	.245	.308	.349	.657	-30	4	2	100	C186/1	—	-2.3
/150	5	150	411	45	101	15	6	5	37	32	—	6	49	.245	.308	.349	.657	-30	3	1	100	C131/1	—	-1.6
Holden, Bill	William Paul B9.7.1889 Birmingham AL D9.14.1971 Pensacola FL BR/TR/6'0"/170 d9.11																							
1913	NY A	18	53	6	16	3	1	0	8	8	—	0	5	.302	.393	.396	.789	+31	0	—	—	O16C	—	0.4
1914	NY A	50	165	12	30	3	2	0	12	16	—	0	26	.182	.254	.224	.478	-56	2	4	33	O45(3/37/6)	—	-1.8
1914	Cin N	11	28	2	6	0	0	0	1	3	—	0	5	.214	.290	.214	.504	-51	0	—	—	O10(7/3/1)	—	-0.2
1914	Major	61	193	14	36	3	2	0	13	19	0	0	31	.187	.259	.223	.482	+2	2	4	—	—	—	-2.0
Total	2	79	246	20	52	6	3	0	21	27	—	0	36	.211	.289	.260	.549	-36	2	4	100	O71(10/56/7)	—	-1.6
Team	2	68	218	18	46	6	3	0	20	24	—	0	31	.211	.289	.266	.555	-34	2	4	100	O61(3/53/37)	—	-1.4
Holmes, Fred	Frederick Clarence B7.1.1878 Chicago IL D2.13.1956 Norwood Park IL BR/TR/5'7"/145 d8.23																							
1903	NY A	1	0	0	0	0	0	0	0	1	—	0	—	+	1.000	+	1.000	+107	0	—	—	/1b	—	0.0
1904	Chi N	1	3	1	1	1	0	0	0	0	—	0	—	.333	.333	.667	1.000	+106	0	—	—	/C	—	0.0
Total	2	2	3	1	1	1	0	0	0	1	—	0	—	.333	.500	.667	1.167	+155	0	—	—	/C1b	—	0.0
Holt, Roger	Roger Boyd B4.8.1956 Daytona Beach FL BB/TR/5'11"/165 Dr 1977 NYA 4/101 d10.4 Col Florida																							
1980	NY A	2	6	0	1	0	0	0	1	1	0	0	2	.167	.286	.167	.453	-72	0	0	0	2b2	0	0.0
Hopp, Johnny	John Leonard "Hippity" B7.18.1916 Hastings NE D6.1.2003 Scottsbluff NE BL/TL/5'10"/175 d9.18 C2																							
1950	†NY A	19	27	9	9	2	1	1	8	8	—	0	1	.333	.486	.593	1.079	+80	0	1	0	1b12,O6L	0	0.3
1951	†NY A	46	63	10	13	1	0	2	4	9	—	0	11	.206	.306	.317	.623	-29	2	0	100	1b25	0	-0.4
1952	NY A	15	25	4	4	0	0	0	2	2	—	1	3	.160	.250	.160	.410	-83	2	0	100	1b12	0	-0.2
Total	14	1393	4260	698	1262	216	74	46	458	464	—	19	378	.296	.368	.414	.782	+13	128	1	100	O717(132/471/127),1b479	0	1.1
Team	3	80	115	23	26	3	1	3	14	19	—	1	15	.226	.341	.348	.689	-12	4	1	80	1b49,O6L	0	-0.3
Horan, Shags	Joseph Patrick B9.6.1895 St.Louis MO D2.13.1969 Torrance CA BR/TR/5'10"/170 d7.14																							
1924	NY A	22	31	4	9	1	0	0	7	1	—	0	5	.290	.313	.323	.636	-36	0	0	0	O14(4/1/9)	—	-0.2
Houk, Ralph	Ralph George "Major" B8.9.1919 Lawrence KS BR/TR/5'11"/(191–193) d4.26 M20/C4																							
1947	†NY A	41	92	7	25	3	1	0	12	11	—	1	5	.272	.356	.326	.682	-9	0	0	0	C41	0	0.1
1948	NY A	14	29	3	8	2	0	0	3	0	—	0	0	.276	.276	.345	.621	-35	0	0	0	C14	0	0.1
1949	NY A	5	7	0	4	0	0	0	1	0	—	0	1	.571	.571	.571	1.142	+103	0	0	0	C5	0	0.0
1950	NY A	10	9	0	1	1	0	0	1	0	—	0	2	.111	.111	.222	.333	-117	0	0	0	C9	0	-0.1
1951	NY A	3	5	0	1	0	0	0	2	0	—	0	1	.200	.200	.200	.400	-91	0	0	0	C3	0	-0.1
1952	†NY A	9	6	0	2	0	0	0	0	1	—	0	0	.333	.429	.333	.762	+21	0	0	0	C9	0	0.1
1953	NY A	8	9	2	2	0	0	0	1	0	—	0	1	.222	.222	.222	.444	-79	0	0	0	C8	0	-0.1
1954	NY A	1	1	0	0	0	0	0	0	0	—	0	0	.000	.000	.000	.000	-199	0	0	0	/H	0	0.0
Total	8	91	158	12	43	6	1	0	20	12	—	1	10	.272	.327	.323	.650	-21	0	0	0	C89	0	0.0
Howard, Elston	Elston Gene B2.23.1929 St.Louis MO D12.14.1980 New York NY BR/TR/6'2"/(196–208) d4.14 C11 Negro Lg 1948–50																							
1955	†NY A	97	279	33	81	8	7	10	43	20	5	1	36	.290	.336	.477	.813	+20	0	0	0	O75(62/0/15),C9	0	0.7
1956	†NY A	98	290	35	76	8	3	5	34	21	6	1	30	.262	.312	.362	.674	-19	0	1	0	O65(62/0/5),C26	0	-1.1
1957	†NY A☆	110	356	33	90	13	4	8	44	16	6	0	43	.253	.283	.379	.662	-19	2	5	29	O71(69/0/2),C32,1b2	0	-2.0
1958	†NY A☆	103	376	45	118	19	5	11	66	22	6	0	60	.314	.348	.479	.827	+31	1	1	50	C67,O24(17/0/8),1b5	0	1.5
1959	NY A☆	125	443	59	121	24	6	18	73	20	4	3	57	.273	.306	.476	.782	+16	0	1	0	1b50,C43,O28(18/0/10)	0	0.2
1960	†NY A★	107	323	29	79	11	3	6	39	28	7	0	43	.245	.298	.353	.651	-18	3	0	100	C91/lf	0	-0.2

Batters

YEAR	TM LG	G	AB	R	H	2B	3B	HR	RBI	BB	IB	HP	SO	AVG	OBP	SLG	OPS	AOPS	SB	CS	SB%	GAMES AT POSITION	DL	BFW
1961	†NY A★	129	446	64	155	17	5	21	77	28	6	3	65	.348	.387	.549	.936	+56	0	3	0	C111,1b9	0	4.5
1962	†NY A★	136	494	63	138	23	5	21	91	31	1	1	76	.279	.318	.474	.792	+15	1	1	50	C129	0	2.2
1963	†NY A★	135	487	75	140	21	6	28	85	35	4	6	68	.287	.342	.528	.870	+41	0	0	0	C132	0	3.4
1964	†NY A★	150	550	63	172	27	3	15	84	48	12	5	73	.313	.371	.455	.826	+27	1	1	50	C146	0	4.2
1965	NY A☆	110	391	38	91	15	1	9	45	24	3	1	65	.233	.278	.345	.623	-23	0	0	0	C95,1b5/lf	32	-0.7
1966	NY A	126	410	38	105	19	2	6	35	37	9	1	65	.256	.317	.356	.673	-3	0	0	0	C100,1b13	0	0.6
1967	NY A	66	199	13	39	6	0	3	17	12	3	2	36	.196	.247	.271	.518	-44	0	0	0	C48/1b	0	-1.0
1967	†Bos A	42	116	9	17	3	0	1	11	9	3	1	24	.147	.211	.198	.409	-79	0	0	0	C41	0	-0.7
1967	Year	108	315	22	56	9	0	4	28	21	6	3	60	.178	.233	.244	.477	-58	0	0	0	C89/1b	0	-1.7
1968	Bos A	71	203	22	49	4	0	5	18	22	7	1	45	.241	.317	.335	.652	-7	1	1	50	C68	0	-0.5
Total	14	1605	5363	619	1471	218	50	167	762	373	82	26	786	.274	.322	.427	.749	+8	9	14	39	C1138,O265(230/0/40),1b85	32	11.1
Team	13	1492	5044	588	1405	211	50	161	733	342	72	24	717	.279	.324	.436	.760	+11	8	13	38	C1029,O265(133/10/40),1b85	32	12.3
/150	1	150	507	59	141	21	5	16	74	34	7	2	72	.279	.324	.436	.760	+11	1	1	50	C103,O27(13/1/4),1b9	3	1.2
HOWARD, MATT Matthew Christopher B9.22.1967 Fall River MA BR/TR/5'10"/170 Dr 1989 LAN 34/890 d5.17 Col Pepperdine																								
1996	NY A	35	54	9	11	1	0	1	9	2	0	0	8	.204	.228	.278	.506	-72	1	0	100	2b30,3b6	0	-1.2
HOWSER, DICK Richard Dalton B5.14.1936 Miami FL D6.17.1987 Kansas City MO BR/TR/5'8"/(154–155) d4.11 M8/C10 Col Florida St.																								
1967	NY A	63	149	18	40	6	0	0	10	25	0	2	15	.268	.381	.309	.690	+10	1	4	20	2b22,3b12,S3	46	-0.1
1968	NY A	85	150	24	23	2	1	0	3	35	0	2	17	.153	.321	.180	.501	-43	0	1	0	2b29,3b2/S	0	0.4
Total	8	789	2483	398	617	90	17	16	165	367	2	13	186	.248	.346	.318	.664	-14	105	34	76	S548,2b94,3b14	92	-1.0
Team	2	148	299	42	63	8	1	0	13	60	0	4	32	.211	.350	.244	.594	-17	1	5	17	2b51,3b14,S4	46	0.3
/150	2	150	303	43	64	8	1	0	13	61	0	4	32	.211	.350	.244	.594	-17	1	5	17	2b52,3b14,S4	47	0.3
HUDLER, REX Rex Allen B9.2.1960 Tempe AZ BR/TR/6'0"/(180–202) Dr 1978 NYA 1/18 d9.9 OF(124/65/64) [DL 1987 Bal A 71]																								
1984	NY A	9	7	2	1	1	0	0	0	1	0	1	5	.143	.333	.286	.619	-24	0	0	0	2b9	0	-0.2
1985	NY A	20	51	4	8	0	1	0	1	1	0	0	9	.157	.173	.196	.369	-99	0	1	0	2b16/1bS	0	-0.3
Total	13	774	1767	261	461	96	10	56	169	77	12	14	325	.261	.296	.422	.718	-9	107	43	71	2b281,O247L,S47,1b38,D15,3b11	225	-2.1
Team	2	29	58	6	9	1	1	0	1	2	0	1	14	.155	.197	.207	.404	-88	0	1	0	2b25/1S	0	-0.5
HUGHES, KEITH Keith Wills B9.12.1963 Bryn Mawr PA BL/TL/6'3"/(205–210) d5.19																								
1987	NY A	4	4	0	0	0	0	0	0	0	0	0	2	.000	.000	.000	.000	-199	0	0	0	/H	0	-0.1
Total	4	93	201	18	41	6	2	2	24	23	1	1	44	.204	.286	.284	.570	-43	1	0	100	O57(19/1/37)/D	0	-1.3
HUMMEL, JOHN John Edwin "Silent John" B4.4.1883 Bloomsburg PA D5.18.1959 Springfield MA BR/TR/5'11"/160 d9.12 Col Bloomsburg OF(145/26/125)																								
1918	NY A	22	61	9	18	1	2	0	4	11	—	1	8	.295	.411	.377	.788	+35	5	—	—	O15(6/7/1),1b3/2b	—	0.0
Total	12	1161	3906	421	991	128	84	29	394	346	—	11	269	.254	.316	.352	.668	+3	119	2	100	2b548,O293L,1b160,S74	—	-2.8
HUMPHREYS, MIKE Michael Butler B4.10.1967 Dallas TX BR/TR/6'0"/(185–195) Dr 1988 SDN 15/370 d7.29 Col Texas Tech																								
1991	NY A	25	40	9	8	0	0	0	3	9	0	0	7	.200	.347	.200	.547	-45	2	0	100	O9(8/0/2),3b6,D7	0	-0.3
1992	NY A	4	10	0	1	0	0	0	0	0	0	0	1	.100	.100	.100	.200	-144	0	0	0	O2L/D	0	-0.1
1993	NY A	25	35	6	6	2	1	1	6	4	0	0	11	.171	.250	.371	.621	-32	2	1	67	O21(11/5/7),D3	0	-0.4
Total	3	54	85	15	15	2	1	1	9	13	0	0	19	.176	.283	.259	.542	-49	4	1	80	O32(21/5/9),D11,3b6	0	-0.8
HUNT, KEN Kenneth Lawrence B7.13.1934 Grand Forks ND D6.8.1997 Gardena CA BR/TR/6'1"/(204–205) d9.10																								
1959	NY A	6	12	2	4	1	0	0	1	0	0	0	3	.333	.308	.417	.725	+8	0	0	0	O5R	0	0.0
1960	NY A	25	22	4	6	2	0	0	1	4	0	1	4	.273	.407	.364	.771	+17	0	0	0	O24(17/5/2)	0	0.0
Total	6	310	782	107	177	42	4	33	111	85	4	5	222	.226	.303	.417	.720	-11	9	4	69	O255(52/151/58),1b3/2b	117	-3.4
Team	2	31	34	6	10	3	0	0	2	4	0	1	7	.294	.375	.382	.757	+14	0	0	0	O29(17/0/5)	0	0.0
HUNTER, BILLY Gordon William B6.4.1928 Punxsutawney PA BR/TR/6'0"/(180–185) d4.14 M2/C14 Col Indiana (PA)																								
1955	NY A	98	255	14	58	7	1	3	20	15	2	0	18	.227	.269	.298	.567	-46	9	2	82	S98	0	-1.0
1956	NY A	39	75	8	21	3	4	0	11	2	0	0	4	.280	.299	.427	.726	-7	0	1	0	S32,3b4	32	0.6
Total	6	630	1875	166	410	58	18	16	144	111	5	8	192	.219	.264	.294	.558	-47	23	12	66	S528,2b72,3b24	32	-8.6
Team	2	137	330	22	79	10	5	3	31	17	2	0	22	.239	.276	.327	.603	-37	9	3	75	S130,3b4	32	-0.4
/150	2	150	361	24	86	11	5	3	34	19	2	0	24	.239	.276	.327	.603	-37	10	3	77	S142,3b4	35	-0.4
HYATT, HAM Robert Hamilton B11.1.1884 Buncombe Co. NC D9.11.1963 Liberty Lake WA BL/TR/6'1"/185 d4.15																								
1918	NY A	53	131	11	30	8	0	2	10	8	—	0	8	.229	.273	.336	.609	-18	1	—	—	O25(21/2/2),1b5	—	-0.5
Total	7	465	925	85	247	36	23	10	146	63	—	10	76	.267	.321	.388	.709	+8	11	3	100	1b124,O80(27/7/49)/C	—	-0.6
INCAVIGLIA, PETE Peter Joseph B4.2.1964 Pebble Beach CA BR/TR/6'1"/(220–235) Dr 1985 MonN 1/8 d4.8 Col Oklahoma St.																								
1997	NY A	5	16	1	4	0	0	0	0	0	0	0	3	.250	.250	.250	.500	-69	0	0	0	D5	0	-0.2
Total	12	1284	4233	546	1043	194	21	206	655	360	21	45	1277	.246	.310	.448	.758	+4	33	26	56	O1021(825/37/189),D150	81	-4.6
JACKLITSCH, FRED Frederick Lawrence B5.24.1876 Brooklyn NY D7.18.1937 Brooklyn NY BR/TR/5'9"/180 d6.6																								
1905	NY A	1	3	1	0	0	0	0	1	1	—	0	—	.000	.250	.000	.250	-117	0	—	—	/C	—	0.0
Total	13	490	1344	160	327	64	12	5	153	201	—	17	100	.243	.349	.320	.669	-5	35	—	—	C397,1b19,2b11,O3(0/2/1),3b2/S	—	2.2
JACKSON, REGGIE Reginald Martinez B5.18.1946 Wyncote PA BL/TL/6'0"/(195–208) Dr 1966 OakA 1/2 d6.9 HF1993 Col Arizona St.																								
1977	†NY A★	146	525	93	150	39	2	32	110	74	4	3	129	.286	.375	.550	.925	+50	17	3	85	O127R,D18	0	3.0
1978	†NY A✳	139	511	82	140	13	5	27	97	58	2	9	133	.274	.356	.477	.833	+35	14	11	56	O104R,D35	0	1.4
1979	NY A★	131	465	78	138	24	2	29	89	65	3	2	107	.297	.382	.544	.926	+50	9	8	53	O125R,D3	24	2.6
1980	†NY A★	143	514	94	154	22	4	**41**	111	83	15	2	122	.300	.398	.597	.995	+72	1	2	33	O94R,D46	0	4.0
1981	†NY A★	94	334	33	79	17	1	15	54	46	2	1	82	.237	.330	.428	.758	+19	0	3	0	O61R,D33	9	0.1
Total	21	2820	9864	1551	2584	463	49	563	1702	1375	16	96	2597	.262	.356	.490	.846	+39	228	115	66	O2102(20/186/1939),D630	48	38.7
Team	5	653	2349	380	661	115	14	144	461	326	26	17	573	.281	.371	.526	.897	+47	41	27	60	O511R,D135	33	11.1
/150	1	150	540	87	152	26	3	33	106	75	6	4	132	.281	.371	.526	.897	+47	9	6	60	O117R,D31	8	2.5
JAMES, DION Dion B11.9.1962 Philadelphia PA BL/TL/6'1"/(170–185) Dr 1980 MilA 1/25 d9.16																								
1992	NY A	67	145	24	38	8	0	3	17	22	0	1	15	.262	.359	.379	.738	+8	1	0	100	O46(8/12/27),D5	0	-0.2
1993	NY A	115	343	62	114	21	2	7	36	31	1	2	31	.332	.390	.466	.856	+33	0	0	0	O103(91/14/1)/1bD	0	0.6
1995	†NY A	85	209	22	60	6	1	2	26	20	2	0	16	.287	.346	.354	.700	-16	4	1	80	O29(23/0/6),D27,1b6	0	-0.8
1996	NY A	6	12	1	2	0	0	0	0	1	0	0	2	.167	.231	.167	.398	-97	1	0	100	O4(3/0/1)/D	0	-0.2
Total	11	917	2708	362	781	142	21	32	266	318	20	11	307	.288	.364	.392	.756	+7	43	38	53	O682(322/242/155),D76,1b52	124	-1.6
Team	4	273	709	109	214	35	3	12	79	74	3	3	64	.302	.368	.410	.778	+11	6	1	86	O182(122/26/35),D34,1b7	0	-0.6
/150	2	150	390	60	118	19	2	7	43	41	2	2	35	.302	.368	.410	.778	+11	3	1	75	O100(67/14/19),D19,1b4	0	-0.3
JAVIER, STAN Stanley Julian Antonio (Negrin) B1.9.1964 San Francisco de Macoris, D.R. BB/TR/6'0"/(180–202) d4.15 f-Julian OF(465/691/492)																								
1984	NY A	7	7	1	1	0	0	0	0	0	0	0	1	.143	.143	.143	.286	-121	0	0	0	O5(0/3/3)	0	-0.2
Total	17	1763	5047	781	1358	225	40	57	503	578	26	25	839	.269	.345	.363	.708	-7	246	51	83	O1513C,1b38,D15,2b3,3b2	167	-1.1
JEFFERSON, STAN Stanley B12.4.1962 New York NY BB/TR/5'11"/(175–180) Dr 1983 NYN 1/20 d9.7 Col Bethune-Cookman																								
1989	NY A	10	12	1	1	0	0	0	1	0	0	0	4	.083	.083	.083	.166	-153	1	1	50	O7(0/2/6)/D	0	-0.3
Total	6	296	832	125	180	25	9	16	67	65	2	7	177	.216	.276	.326	.602	-34	60	20	75	O235(100/142/39),D9	39	-4.4

Batters

YEAR	TM LG	G	AB	R	H	2B	3B	HR	RBI	BB	IB	HP	SO	AVG	OBP	SLG	OPS	AOPS	SB	CS	SB%	GAMES AT POSITION	DL	BFW
JENSEN, JACKIE Jack Eugene B3.9.1927 San Francisco CA D7.14.1982 Charlottesville VA BR/TR/5'11"/190 d4.18 Col California																								
1950	†NY A	45	70	13	12	2	2	1	5	7	—	0	8	.171	.247	.300	.547	-59	4	0	100	O23(17/0/7)	0	-0.7
1951	NY A	56	168	30	50	8	1	8	25	18	—	1	18	.298	.369	.500	.869	+38	8	2	80	O48(21/27/1)	0	0.9
1952	NY A	7	19	3	2	1	1	0	2	4	—	0	4	.105	.261	.263	.524	-51	1	0	100	O5C	0	-0.2
Total	11	1438	5236	810	1463	259	45	199	929	750	28	23	546	.279	.369	.460	.829	+19	143	55	72	O1391(54/153/1207)	0	9.6
Team	3	108	257	46	64	11	4	9	32	29	—	1	30	.249	.328	.428	.756	+5	13	2	87	O76(38/27/7)	0	-0.0
/150	4	150	357	64	89	15	6	12	44	40	—	1	42	.249	.328	.428	.756	+5	18	3	86	O106(53/38/10)	0	-0.0
JETER, DEREK Derek Sanderson B6.26.1974 Pequannock NJ BR/TR/6'3"/(185–195) Dr 1992 NYA 1/6 d5.29																								
1995	NY A	15	48	5	12	4	1	0	7	3	0	0	11	.250	.294	.375	.669	-27	0	0	0	S15	0	-0.5
1996	†NY A	157	582	104	183	25	6	10	78	48	1	9	102	.314	.370	.430	.800	+3	14	7	67	S157	0	1.3
1997	†NY A	159	654	116	190	31	7	10	70	74	0	10	125	.291	.370	.405	.775	+4	23	12	66	S159	0	1.2
1998	†NY A★	149	626	**127**	203	25	8	19	84	57	1	5	119	.324	.384	.481	.865	+29	30	6	83	S148	15	1.8
1999	†NY A★	158	627	134	**219**	37	9	24	102	91	5	12	116	.349	.438	.552	.990	+54	19	8	70	S158	0	3.4
2000	†NY A★	148	593	119	201	31	4	15	73	68	4	12	99	.339	.416	.481	.897	+28	22	4	85	S148	14	0.7
2001	†NY A★	150	614	110	191	35	3	21	74	56	3	10	99	.311	.377	.480	.857	+23	27	3	90	S150	6	1.0
2002	†NY A★	157	644	124	191	26	0	18	75	73	2	7	114	.297	.373	.421	.794	+12	32	3	91	S156/D	0	-0.9
2003	†NY A	119	482	87	156	25	3	10	52	43	2	13	88	.324	.393	.450	.843	+24	11	5	69	S118	42	-0.3
2004	†NY A★	154	643	111	188	44	1	23	78	46	1	14	99	.292	.352	.471	.823	+12	23	4	85	S154	0	2.1
2005	†NY A	159	654	122	202	25	5	19	70	77	3	11	117	.309	.389	.450	.839	+24	14	5	74	S157/D	0	4.5
2006	†NY A★	154	623	118	214	39	3	14	97	69	4	12	102	.343	.417	.483	.900	+30	34	5	87	S150,D5	0	2.6
2007	†NY A★	156	639	102	206	39	4	12	73	56	3	14	100	.322	.388	.452	.840	+19	15	8	65	S155	0	0.4
Total	13	1835	7429	1379	2356	306	54	195	933	761	29	129	1291	.317	.388	.462	.850	+22	264	70	79	S1825,D7	77	17.3
/150	1	150	607	113	193	32	4	16	76	62	2	11	106	.317	.388	.462	.850	+22	22	6	79	S15/D	6	1.4
JIMENEZ, D'ANGELO D'Angelo B12.21.1977 Santo Domingo, D.R. BB/TR/6'0"/(160–215) d9.15 [DL 2000 NY A 142]																								
1999	NY A	7	20	3	8	2	0	0	4	3	0	0	4	.400	.478	.500	.978	+52	0	0	0	3b6/2b	0	0.1
Total	8	641	2159	290	568	105	17	36	228	291	9	6	391	.263	.351	.377	.728	-7	36	22	62	2b414,S114,3b49/P	142	-0.2
JIMENEZ, ELVIO Felix Elvio (Rivera) B1.6.1940 San Pedro de Macoris, D.R. BR/TR/5'9"/170 d10.4 b–Manny																								
1964	NY A	1	6	0	2	0	0	0	0	0	0	0	0	.333	.333	.333	.666	-15	0	0	0	/lf	0	0.0
JOHNSON, ALEX Alexander B12.7.1942 Helena AR BR/TR/6'0"/(200–205) d7.25																								
1974	NY A	10	28	3	6	1	0	1	2	0	0	0	3	.214	.214	.357	.571	-37	0	0	0	/lfD	0	-0.2
1975	NY A	52	119	15	31	5	1	1	15	7	1	0	21	.261	.297	.345	.642	-17	2	3	40	D28,O7(5/0/2)	0	-0.5
Total	13	1322	4623	550	1331	180	33	78	525	244	43	36	626	.288	.326	.392	.718	+5	113	63	64	O1000(937/16/54),D199	97	-5.3
Team	2	62	147	18	37	6	1	2	17	7	1	0	24	.252	.282	.347	.629	-21	2	3	40	D29,O7L	0	-0.7
JOHNSON, CLIFF Clifford B7.22.1947 San Antonio TX BR/TR/6'4"/(212–225) Dr 1966 HouN 5/83 d9.13																								
1977	†NY A	56	142	24	42	8	0	12	31	20	0	6	23	.296	.405	.606	1.011	+72	0	1	0	D25,C15,1b11	0	1.6
1978	†NY A	76	174	20	32	9	1	6	19	30	5	1	32	.184	.307	.351	.658	-14	0	0	0	D39,C22/1b	0	-0.8
1979	NY A	28	64	11	17	6	0	2	6	10	4	0	7	.266	.360	.453	.813	+21	0	0	0	D22,C4	0	0.1
Total	15	1369	3945	539	1016	188	10	196	699	568	53	50	719	.258	.355	.459	.814	+25	9	12	43	D746,1b189,C179,O58(57/0/4)	80	7.4
Team	3	160	380	55	91	23	1	20	56	60	9	7	62	.239	.353	.463	.816	+24	0	1	0	D86,C41,1b12	0	0.9
/150	3	150	356	52	85	22	1	19	52	56	8	7	58	.239	.353	.463	.816	+24	0	1	0	D81,C38,1b11	0	0.8
JOHNSON, DARRELL Darrell Dean B8.25.1928 Horace NE D5.3.2004 Fairfield CA BR/TR/6'1"/(170–180) d4.20 M8/C8																								
1957	NY A	21	46	4	10	1	0	1	8	3	0	1	10	.217	.275	.304	.579	-39	0	0	0	C20	0	-0.3
1958	NY A	5	16	1	4	0	0	0	0	0	0	0	2	.250	.250	.250	.500	-61	0	0	0	C4	0	-0.1
Total	6	134	320	24	75	6	1	2	28	26	1	2	39	.234	.294	.278	.572	-43	1	0	100	C124	0	-1.0
Team	2	26	62	5	14	1	0	1	8	3	0	1	12	.226	.269	.290	.559	-44	0	0	0	C24	0	-0.4
JOHNSON, DERON Deron Roger B7.17.1938 San Diego CA D4.23.1992 Poway CA BR/TR/6'2"/(200–209) d9.20 C13 OF(216/1/32)																								
1960	NY A	6	4	0	2	1	0	0	0	0	0	0	0	.500	.500	.750	1.250	+147	0	0	0	3b5	0	0.0
1961	NY A	13	19	1	2	0	0	0	2	2	0	0	5	.105	.182	.105	.287	-120	0	0	0	3b8	0	-0.2
Total	16	1765	5941	706	1447	247	33	245	923	585	54	20	1318	.244	.311	.420	.731	+2	11	18	38	1b880,3b332,D287,O249L	31	-13.4
Team	2	19	23	1	4	1	0	0	2	2	0	0	5	.174	.231	.217	.448	-77	0	0	0	3b13	0	-0.2
JOHNSON, ERNIE Ernest Rudolph B4.29.1888 Chicago IL D5.1.1952 Monrovia CA BL/TR/5'9"/151 d8.5 s–Don																								
1923	†NY A	19	38	6	17	1	1	1	8	1	—	0	1	.447	.462	.605	1.067	+76	0	0	0	S15/3b	—	0.3
1924	NY A	64	119	24	42	4	8	3	12	11	—	1	7	.353	.412	.597	1.009	+58	1	6	14	2b27,S9,3b2	—	0.7
1925	NY A	76	170	30	48	5	1	5	17	8	—	0	10	.282	.315	.412	.727	-15	6	3	67	2b34,S28,3b2	—	-1.0
Total	10	813	2619	372	697	91	36	19	256	181	—	15	153	.266	.317	.350	.667	-20	114	44	100	S624,2b79,3b32	—	-0.5
Team	3	159	327	60	107	10	10	9	37	20	—	1	18	.327	.368	.502	.870	+23	7	9	44	2b61,S52,3b5	—	0.0
/150	3	150	308	57	101	9	9	8	35	19	—	1	17	.327	.368	.502	.870	+23	7	8	47	2b58,S49,3b5	—	0.0
JOHNSON, LANCE Kenneth Lance B7.6.1963 Cincinnati OH BL/TL/5'11"/(155–165) Dr 1984 StLN 6/139 d7.10 Col South Alabama																								
2000	NY A	18	30	6	9	1	0	0	2	0	0	0	7	.300	.300	.333	.633	-39	2	0	100	O4(2/0/2),D2	0	-0.2
Total	14	1447	5379	767	1565	175	117	34	486	352	29	7	384	.291	.334	.386	.720	-6	327	105	76	O1387(53/1327/21),D8	194	-0.9
JOHNSON, NICK Nicholas Robert B9.19.1978 Sacramento CA BL/TL/6'3"/(224–225) Dr 1996 NYA 3/89 d8.21 [DL 2000 NY A 181, 2007 Was N 182]																								
2001	NY A	23	67	6	13	2	0	2	8	7	0	4	15	.194	.308	.313	.621	-36	0	0	0	1b15,D6	0	-0.5
2002	†NY A	129	378	56	92	15	0	15	58	48	5	12	98	.243	.347	.402	.749	-1	1	3	25	1b78,D50,O2L	25	-0.6
2003	†NY A	96	324	60	92	19	0	14	47	70	4	8	57	.284	.422	.472	.894	+38	5	2	71	1b60,D34	70	1.3
2004	Mon N	73	251	35	63	16	0	7	33	40	2	3	58	.251	.359	.398	.757	-8	6	3	67	1b73	98	-1.0
2005	Was N	131	453	66	131	35	3	15	74	80	8	12	87	.289	.408	.479	.887	+38	3	8	27	1b129	29	2.1
2006	Was N	147	500	100	145	46	0	23	77	110	15	13	99	.290	.428	.520	.948	+49	10	3	77	1b147	0	3.2
Total	6	599	1973	323	536	133	3	76	297	355	34	52	414	.272	.395	.458	.853	+25	25	19	57	1b502,D90,O2L	585	4.5
Team	3	248	769	122	197	36	0	31	113	125	9	24	170	.256	.376	.424	.800	+13	6	5	55	1b153,D90,O2L	276	0.2
/150	2	150	465	74	119	22	0	19	68	76	5	15	103	.256	.376	.424	.800	+13	4	3	57	1b93,D54/lf	167	0.1
JOHNSON, OTIS Otis L. B11.5.1883 Fowler IN D11.9.1915 Johnson City NY BB/TR/5'9"/185 d4.12																								
1911	NY A	71	209	21	49	9	6	3	36	39	—	3	—	.234	.363	.378	.741	+0	12	—	—	S47,2b15,3b3	—	-0.4
JOHNSON, ROY Roy Cleveland B2.23.1903 Pryor OK D9.10.1973 Tacoma WA BL/TR/5'9"/175 d4.18 b–Bob																								
1936	†NY A	63	147	21	39	8	2	1	19	21	—	1	14	.265	.361	.367	.728	-17	3	1	75	O33(28/0/3)	—	-0.5
1937	NY A	12	51	5	15	3	0	0	6	3	—	0	2	.294	.333	.353	.686	-27	1	0	100	O12L	—	-0.4
Total	10	1155	4359	717	1292	275	83	58	556	489	—	12	380	.296	.369	.437	.806	+7	135	81	100	O1066(527/70/483)/3b	—	-1.4
Team	2	75	198	26	54	11	2	1	25	24	—	1	16	.273	.354	.364	.718	-19	4	1	80	O45(28/0/3)	—	-0.9
JOHNSON, BILLY William Russell "Bull" B8.30.1918 Montclair NJ D6.20.2006 Augusta GA BR/TR/5'10"/180 d4.22 Mil 1944–46																								
1943	†NY A	**155**	592	70	166	24	6	5	94	53	—	4	30	.280	.344	.367	.711	+7	3	5	38	3b155	0	2.0
1946	NY A	85	296	51	77	14	5	4	35	31	—	2	42	.260	.334	.382	.716	-2	1	0	100	3b74	0	0.5
1947	†NY A★	132	494	67	141	19	8	10	95	44	—	6	43	.285	.351	.417	.768	+14	1	2	33	3b132	0	-1.1
1948	NY A	127	446	59	131	20	6	12	64	41	—	4	30	.294	.358	.446	.804	+14	0	0	0	3b118	0	0.9
1949	†NY A	113	329	48	82	11	3	8	56	48	—	2	44	.249	.348	.374	.722	-9	1	0	100	3b81,1b21/2b	0	-0.8
1950	†NY A	108	327	44	85	16	2	6	40	42	—	1	30	.260	.346	.376	.722	-13	1	0	100	3b100,1b5	0	-0.9
1951	NY A	15	40	5	12	3	0	0	4	7	—	0	0	.300	.404	.375	.779	+16	0	1	0	3b13	0	-0.1

Batters

YEAR	TM LG	G	AB	R	H	2B	3B	HR	RBI	BB	IB	HP	SO	AVG	OBP	SLG	OPS	AOPS	SB	CS	SB%	GAMES AT POSITION	DL	BFW
1951	StL N	124	442	52	116	23	1	14	64	46	—	6	49	.262	.340	.414	.754	+1	5	3	63	3b124	0	1.0
1951	Major	139	482	57	128	26	1	14	68	53	0	6	49	.266	.346	.411	.756	+155	5	4	56	—	0	0.9
1952	StL N	94	282	23	71	10	2	2	34	34	—	3	21	.252	.339	.323	.662	-16	1	0	100	3b89	0	-0.2
1953	StL N	11	5	0	1	1	0	0	1	1	—	0	1	.200	.333	.400	.733	-10	0	0	0	3b11	0	0.1
Total	9	964	3253	419	882	141	33	61	487	347	—	28	290	.271	.346	.391	.737	+2	13	11	54	3b897,1b26/2b	0	1.4
Team	7	735	2524	344	694	107	30	45	388	266	—	19	219	.275	.349	.395	.744	+4	7	8	47	3b673,1b26/2	0	0.5
/150	1	150	515	70	142	22	6	9	79	54	—	4	45	.275	.349	.395	.744	+4	1	2	33	3b137,1b5/2	0	0.1

Johnson, Russ William Russell B2.22.1973 Baton Rouge LA BR/TR/5'10"/180 Dr 1994 HouN S1/30 d4.8 Col Louisiana St.

YEAR	TM LG	G	AB	R	H	2B	3B	HR	RBI	BB	IB	HP	SO	AVG	OBP	SLG	OPS	AOPS	SB	CS	SB%	GAMES AT POSITION	DL	BFW
2005	NY A	22	18	5	4	2	0	0	0	1	0	1	4	.222	.300	.333	.633	-31	0	0	0	3b8,1b7,O3R/2bD	0	-0.3
Total	7	364	836	117	221	46	2	14	97	105	1	5	173	.264	.348	.374	.722	-11	16	10	62	3b179,2b75,S26,D10,1b7,O3R	88	-0.8

Johnstone, Jay John William B11.20.1945 Manchester CT BL/TR/6'1"/(175–190) d7.30 OF(258/521/572)

YEAR	TM LG	G	AB	R	H	2B	3B	HR	RBI	BB	IB	HP	SO	AVG	OBP	SLG	OPS	AOPS	SB	CS	SB%	GAMES AT POSITION	DL	BFW
1978	†NY A	36	65	6	17	0	0	1	6	4	0	3	10	.262	.329	.308	.637	-17	0	1	0	O22(8/0/14),D5	0	-0.3
1979	NY A	23	48	7	10	1	0	1	7	2	0	0	7	.208	.240	.292	.532	-57	1	0	100	O19(14/4/1),D3	0	-0.4
Total	20	1748	4703	578	1254	215	38	102	531	429	61	22	632	.267	.329	.394	.723	+2	50	54	48	O1308R,1b57,D12,2b2	166	-3.5
Team	2	59	113	13	27	1	0	2	13	6	0	3	17	.239	.293	.301	.594	-33	1	1	50	O41(22/4/15),D8	0	-0.7

Jones, Darryl Darryl Lee B6.5.1951 Meadville PA BR/TR/5'10"/175 Dr 1972 NYA 5/110 d6.6 b-Lynn Col Westminster (PA)

YEAR	TM LG	G	AB	R	H	2B	3B	HR	RBI	BB	IB	HP	SO	AVG	OBP	SLG	OPS	AOPS	SB	CS	SB%	GAMES AT POSITION	DL	BFW
1979	NY A	18	47	6	12	5	1	0	6	2	0	0	7	.255	.286	.404	.690	-15	0	0	0	D15,O2(1/0/1)	0	-0.2

Jones, Ruppert Ruppert Sanderson B3.12.1955 Dallas TX BL/TL/5'10"/(170–189) Dr 1973 KCA 3/57 d8.1

YEAR	TM LG	G	AB	R	H	2B	3B	HR	RBI	BB	IB	HP	SO	AVG	OBP	SLG	OPS	AOPS	SB	CS	SB%	GAMES AT POSITION	DL	BFW
1980	NY A	83	328	38	73	11	3	9	42	34	3	3	50	.223	.299	.357	.656	-19	18	8	69	O82C	85	-0.7
Total	12	1331	4415	643	1103	215	38	147	579	534	38	12	817	.250	.330	.416	.746	+6	143	84	63	O1205(174/917/157),D55,1b5	134	4.8

Jordan, Tim Timothy Joseph B2.14.1879 New York NY D9.13.1949 Bronx NY BL/TL/6'1"/170 d8.10

YEAR	TM LG	G	AB	R	H	2B	3B	HR	RBI	BB	IB	HP	SO	AVG	OBP	SLG	OPS	AOPS	SB	CS	SB%	GAMES AT POSITION	DL	BFW
1903	NY A	2	8	2	1	0	0	0	0	0	—	0	—	.125	.125	.125	.250	-123	0	—	—	1b2	—	-0.2
Total	7	540	1813	220	474	74	24	32	232	254	—	9	2	.261	.355	.382	.737	+39	48	—	—	1b518	—	4.4

Jorgens, Art Arndt Ludwig B5.18.1905 Modum, Norway D3.1.1980 Evanston IL BR/TR/5'9"/160 d4.26 b-Orville

YEAR	TM LG	G	AB	R	H	2B	3B	HR	RBI	BB	IB	HP	SO	AVG	OBP	SLG	OPS	AOPS	SB	CS	SB%	GAMES AT POSITION	DL	BFW
1929	NY A	18	34	6	11	3	0	0	4	6	—	0	7	.324	.425	.412	.837	+25	0	4	0	C15	—	0.1
1930	NY A	16	30	7	11	3	0	0	1	2	—	0	4	.367	.406	.467	.873	+26	0	0	0	C16	—	0.1
1931	NY A	46	100	12	27	1	2	0	14	9	—	0	3	.270	.330	.320	.650	-24	0	1	0	C40	—	-0.5
1932	NY A	56	151	13	33	7	1	2	19	14	—	0	11	.219	.285	.318	.603	-41	0	0	0	C56	—	-0.8
1933	NY A	21	50	9	11	3	0	2	13	12	—	0	3	.220	.371	.400	.771	+11	1	0	100	C19	—	0.4
1934	NY A	58	183	14	38	6	1	0	20	23	—	0	24	.208	.296	.251	.547	-55	2	0	100	C56	—	-0.8
1935	NY A	36	84	6	20	2	0	0	8	12	—	0	10	.238	.333	.262	.595	-41	0	0	0	C33	—	0.1
1936	NY A	31	66	5	18	3	1	0	5	2	—	0	3	.273	.294	.348	.642	-40	0	0	0	C30	—	-0.1
1937	NY A	13	23	3	3	1	0	0	3	2	—	0	5	.130	.200	.174	.374	-105	0	0	0	C11	—	-0.3
1938	NY A	9	17	3	4	2	0	0	2	3	—	0	3	.235	.350	.353	.703	-23	0	0	0	C8	—	0.0
1939	NY A	3	0	1	0	0	0	0	0	0	—	0	0	+	+	+	.000	-100	0	0	0	C2	—	0.0
Total	11	307	738	79	176	31	5	4	89	85	—	0	73	.238	.317	.310	.627	-34	3	5	38	C286	—	-1.8
/150	5	150	361	39	86	15	2	2	43	42	—	0	36	.238	.317	.310	.627	-34	1	2	33	C140	0	-0.9

Jose, Felix Domingo Felix Andujar (b Domingo Felix Andujar (Jose)) B5.2.1965 Santo Domingo, D.R. BB/TR/6'1"/(184–221) d9.2

YEAR	TM LG	G	AB	R	H	2B	3B	HR	RBI	BB	IB	HP	SO	AVG	OBP	SLG	OPS	AOPS	SB	CS	SB%	GAMES AT POSITION	DL	BFW
2000	NY A	20	29	4	7	0	0	1	5	2	0	0	9	.241	.281	.345	.626	-39	0	1	0	O14(6/0/8),D2	29	-0.3
Total	11	747	2527	322	708	135	14	54	324	203	28	9	507	.280	.334	.409	.743	+2	102	57	64	O689(39/36/629),D11	64	-2.2

Justice, David David Christopher B4.14.1966 Cincinnati OH BL/TL/6'3"/(195–200) Dr 1985 AtlN 4/94 d5.24 Col Thomas More

YEAR	TM LG	G	AB	R	H	2B	3B	HR	RBI	BB	IB	HP	SO	AVG	OBP	SLG	OPS	AOPS	SB	CS	SB%	GAMES AT POSITION	DL	BFW
2000	†NY A	78	275	43	84	17	0	20	60	39	1	1	42	.305	.391	.585	.976	+45	1	0	100	O60(43/1/25),D18	0	2.0
2001	†NY A	111	381	58	92	16	1	18	51	54	5	0	83	.241	.333	.430	.763	-1	1	2	33	D85,O25(16/0/11)	46	-0.2
Total	14	1610	5625	929	1571	280	24	305	1017	903	85	18	999	.279	.378	.500	.878	+27	53	46	54	O1141(312/3/842),D378,1b69	311	15.9
Team	2	189	656	101	176	33	1	38	111	93	6	1	125	.268	.358	.495	.853	+18	2	2	50	D103,O85(59/1/36)	46	1.8
/150	2	150	521	80	140	26	1	30	88	74	5	1	99	.268	.358	.495	.853	+18	2	2	50	D82,O67(47/1/29)	37	1.4

Kane, Frank Francis Thomas "Sugar"(aka Frank Thomas Kiley in 1915) B3.9.1895 Whitman MA D12.2.1962 Brockton MA BL/TR/5'11.5"/175 d9.13 Mil 1918

YEAR	TM LG	G	AB	R	H	2B	3B	HR	RBI	BB	IB	HP	SO	AVG	OBP	SLG	OPS	AOPS	SB	CS	SB%	GAMES AT POSITION	DL	BFW
1919	NY A	1	1	0	0	0	0	0	0	0	—	0	0	.000	.000	.000	.000	-199	0	—	—	/H	—	0.0
Total	2	4	11	2	2	0	1	0	2	0	—	0	0	.182	.182	.364	.546	-48	0	—	—	O2L	—	0.0

Karlon, Bill William John "Hank" B1.21.1909 Palmer MA D12.7.1964 Ware MA BR/TR/6'1"/190 d4.28

YEAR	TM LG	G	AB	R	H	2B	3B	HR	RBI	BB	IB	HP	SO	AVG	OBP	SLG	OPS	AOPS	SB	CS	SB%	GAMES AT POSITION	DL	BFW
1930	NY A	2	5	0	0	0	0	0	0	0	—	0	1	.000	.000	.000	.000	-199	0	0	0	/lf	—	-0.2

Kauff, Benny Benjamin Michael B1.5.1890 Pomeroy OH D11.17.1961 Columbus OH BL/TL/5'8"/157 d4.20 Mil 1918

YEAR	TM LG	G	AB	R	H	2B	3B	HR	RBI	BB	IB	HP	SO	AVG	OBP	SLG	OPS	AOPS	SB	CS	SB%	GAMES AT POSITION	DL	BFW
1912	NY A	5	11	4	3	0	0	0	2	3	—	0	—	.273	.429	.273	.702	-4	1	—	—	O4C	—	0.0
Total	8	859	3094	521	961	169	57	49	454	367	—	28	313	.311	.389	.450	.839	+46	234	33	100	O853(36/750/68)	—	10.9

Kearse, Eddie Paul Edward "Truck" B2.23.1916 San Francisco CA D7.15.1968 Eureka CA BR/TR/6'1"/195 d6.13 Mil 1943

YEAR	TM LG	G	AB	R	H	2B	3B	HR	RBI	BB	IB	HP	SO	AVG	OBP	SLG	OPS	AOPS	SB	CS	SB%	GAMES AT POSITION	DL	BFW
1942	NY A	11	26	2	5	0	0	0	2	3	—	0	1	.192	.276	.192	.468	-66	1	0	100	C11	0	0.1

Keeler, Willie William Henry "Wee Willie","Hit 'Em Where They Ain't"(b William Henry O'Kelleher) B3.3.1872 Brooklyn NY D1.1.1923 Brooklyn NY BL/TL/5'4.5"/140 d9.30 HF1939

YEAR	TM LG	G	AB	R	H	2B	3B	HR	RBI	BB	IB	HP	SO	AVG	OBP	SLG	OPS	AOPS	SB	CS	SB%	GAMES AT POSITION	DL	BFW
1892	NY N	14	53	7	17	3	0	0	6	3	—	1	3	.321	.368	.377	.745	+28	5	—	—	3b14	—	0.0
1893	NY N	7	24	5	8	2	1	1	7	5	—	0	1	.333	.448	.625	1.073	+83	3	—	—	O3C,2b2,S2	—	0.0
1893	Bro N	20	80	14	25	1	1	1	9	4	—	1	4	.313	.353	.387	.740	+1	2	—	—	3b12,O8L	—	-0.2
1893	Year	27	104	19	33	3	2	2	16	9	—	1	5	.317	.377	.442	.819	+21	5	—	—	3b12,O11(8/3/0),2b2,S2	—	-0.2
1894	†Bal N	**129**	590	165	219	27	22	5	94	40	—	18	6	.371	.427	.517	.944	+21	32	—	—	O128R/2b	—	1.1
1895	†Bal N	**131**	565	162	213	24	15	4	78	37	—	14	12	.377	.429	.494	.923	+34	47	—	—	O131R	—	2.5
1896	†Bal N	126	544	153	210	22	13	4	82	37	—	7	9	.386	.432	.496	.928	+42	67	—	—	O126(2/0/124)	—	2.5
1897	†Bal N	129	564	145	**239**	27	19	0	74	35	—	7	—	**.424**	.464	.539	1.003	+64	64	—	—	O129R	—	3.7
1898	Bal N	129	561	126	**216**	7	2	1	44	31	—	3	—	**.385**	.420	.410	.830	+36	28	—	—	O128R/3b	—	1.7
1899	Bro N	141	570	**140**	216	12	13	1	61	37	—	9	—	.379	.425	.451	.876	+37	45	—	—	O141R	—	2.0
1900	†Bro N	136	563	106	**204**	13	12	4	68	30	—	7	—	.362	.402	.449	.851	+27	41	—	—	O136R/2b	—	1.6
1901	Bro N	136	595	123	202	18	12	2	43	21	—	7	—	.339	.369	.420	.789	+25	23	—	—	O125R,3b10,2b3	—	0.9
1902	Bro N	133	559	86	186	20	5	0	38	21	—	7	—	.333	.365	.386	.751	+31	19	—	—	O133R	—	1.4
1903	NY A	132	512	95	160	14	7	0	32	32	—	13	—	.313	.368	.367	.735	+14	24	—	—	O128(0/5/123),3b4	—	-0.4
1904	NY A	143	543	78	186	14	8	2	40	35	—	7	—	.343	.390	.409	.799	+46	21	—	—	O142R	—	2.1
1905	NY A	149	560	81	169	14	4	4	38	43	—	5	—	.302	.357	.363	.720	+15	19	—	—	O137(3/0/134),2b12,3b3	—	0.6
1906	NY A	152	592	96	180	8	3	2	33	40	—	5	—	.304	.353	.338	.691	+6	23	—	—	O152(1/0/151)	—	-0.5
1907	NY A	107	423	50	99	5	2	0	17	15	—	3	—	.234	.265	.255	.520	-39	7	—	—	O107R	—	-2.9
1908	NY A	91	323	38	85	3	1	1	14	31	—	5	—	.263	.337	.288	.625	+2	14	—	—	O88(2/0/86)	—	-0.3
1909	NY A	99	360	44	95	7	5	1	32	24	—	10	—	.264	.327	.319	.646	+4	10	—	—	O95R	—	-0.9
1910	NY N	19	10	5	3	0	0	0	0	3	—	0	1	.300	.462	.300	.762	+23	1	—	—	O2(1/1/0)	—	0.1
Total	19	2123	8591	1719	2932	241	145	33	810	524	—	129	36	.341	.388	.415	.803	+25	495	—	—	O2039(17/9/2013),3b44,2b19,S2	—	15.0
Team	7	873	3313	482	974	65	30	10	206	220	—	48	0	.294	.347	.341	.688	+9	118	—	—	O849(7/290/408),2b12,3b7	—	-2.3
/150	1	150	569	83	167	11	5	2	35	38	—	8	0	.294	.347	.341	.688	+9	20	—	—	O146(1/50/70),2b2/3	—	0.4

Keller, Charlie Charles Ernest "King Kong" B9.12.1916 Middletown MD D5.23.1990 Frederick MD BL/TR/5'10"/190 d4.22 Mer 1944–45 C2 b-Hal Col Maryland

YEAR	TM LG	G	AB	R	H	2B	3B	HR	RBI	BB	IB	HP	SO	AVG	OBP	SLG	OPS	AOPS	SB	CS	SB%	GAMES AT POSITION	DL	BFW
1939	†NY A	111	398	87	133	21	6	11	83	81	—	0	49	.334	.447	.500	.947	+44	6	3	67	O105(47/0/58)	—	1.9
1940	NY A★	138	500	102	143	18	15	21	93	**106**	—	0	65	.286	.411	.508	.919	+42	8	2	80	O136(65/0/71)	—	2.3
1941	†NY A★	140	507	102	151	24	10	33	122	102	—	1	65	.298	.416	.580	.996	+63	6	4	60	O137L	0	4.0

YEAR	TM LG	G	AB	R	H	2B	3B	HR	RBI	BB	IB	HP	SO	AVG	OBP	SLG	OPS	AOPS	SB	CS	SB%	GAMES AT POSITION	DL	BFW
1942	†NY A	152	544	106	159	24	9	26	108	114	—	2	61	.292	.417	.513	.930	+64	14	2	88	O152L	0	4.2
1943	†NY A✳	141	512	97	139	15	11	31	86	**106**	—	0	60	.271	.396	.525	.921	+67	7	5	58	O141L	0	4.0
1945	NY A	44	163	26	49	7	4	10	34	31	—	0	21	.301	.412	.577	.989	+78	0	2	0	O44L	0	1.6
1946	NY A★	150	538	98	148	29	10	30	101	113	—	4	101	.275	.405	.533	.938	+58	1	4	20	O149(146/0/3)	0	3.2
1947	NY A✳	45	151	36	36	6	1	13	36	41	—	1	18	.238	.404	.550	.954	+65	0	0	0	O43L	0	1.1
1948	NY A	83	247	41	66	15	2	6	44	41	—	0	25	.267	.372	.417	.789	+11	1	1	50	O66L	0	-0.4
1949	NY A	60	116	17	29	4	1	3	16	25	—	2	15	.250	.392	.379	.771	+4	2	0	100	O31(29/0/2)	0	-0.2
1950	Det A	50	51	7	16	1	3	2	16	13	—	0	6	.314	.453	.569	1.022	+55	0	0	0	O6(1/0/5)	0	0.4
1951	Det A	54	62	6	16	2	0	3	21	11	—	0	12	.258	.370	.435	.805	+17	0	0	0	O8(4/0/4)	0	0.2
1952	NY A	2	1	0	0	0	0	0	0	0	—	0	1	.000	.000	.000	.000	-199	0	0	0	/lf	0	0.0
Total	13	1170	3790	725	1085	166	72	189	760	784	—	10	499	.286	.410	.518	.928	+52	45	23	66	O1019(870/0/140)	0	22.3
Team	11	1066	3677	712	1053	163	69	184	723	760	—	10	481	.286	.410	.518	.928	+53	45	23	66	O1005(259/0/132)	0	21.7
/150	2	150	517	100	148	23	10	26	102	107	—	1	68	.286	.410	.518	.928	+53	6	3	67	O141(36/0/19)	0	3.1
KELLY, PAT PATRICK FRANKLIN B10.14.1967 PHILADELPHIA PA BR/TR/6'0"/(180–182) DR 1988 NYA 9/235 D5.20 COL WEST CHESTER																								
1991	NY A	96	298	35	72	12	4	3	23	15	0	5	52	.242	.287	.339	.626	-27	12	1	92	3b80,2b19	0	-0.6
1992	NY A	106	318	38	72	22	2	7	27	25	1	10	72	.226	.301	.374	.675	-11	8	5	62	2b101/D	16	-0.6
1993	NY A	127	406	49	111	24	1	7	51	24	0	5	68	.273	.317	.389	.706	-7	14	11	56	2b125	0	1.0
1994	NY A	93	286	35	80	21	2	3	41	19	1	5	51	.280	.330	.399	.729	-9	6	5	55	2b93	15	0.5
1995	†NY A	89	270	32	64	12	1	4	29	23	0	5	65	.237	.307	.333	.640	-32	8	3	73	2b87/D	41	-0.2
1996	NY A	13	21	4	3	0	0	0	2	2	0	0	9	.143	.217	.143	.360	-106	0	1	0	2b10,D3	147	-0.2
1997	NY A	67	120	25	29	6	1	2	10	14	1	1	37	.242	.324	.358	.682	-21	8	1	89	2b48,D16	39	-0.1
1998	StL N	53	153	18	33	5	0	4	14	13	0	2	48	.216	.284	.327	.611	-39	5	1	83	2b41,O3L,S2	0	-0.7
1999	Tor A	37	116	17	31	7	0	6	20	10	0	0	20	.267	.318	.483	.801	+1	0	1	0	2b35,D2	0	-0.2
Total	9	681	1988	253	495	109	11	36	217	145	3	33	425	.249	.307	.369	.676	-19	61	29	68	2b559,3b100,D23,O3L,S2	258	-1.1
Team	7	591	1719	218	431	97	11	26	183	122	3	31	354	.251	.309	.365	.674	-18	56	27	67	2b483,3b80,D21	258	-0.2
/150	2	150	436	55	109	25	3	7	46	31	1	8	90	.251	.309	.365	.674	-18	14	7	67	2b123,3b20,D5	65	-0.1
KELLY, ROBERTO ROBERTO CONRADO (GRAY) "BOBBY" B10.1.1964 PANAMA CITY, PAN BR/TR/6'2"/(182–202) D7.29																								
1987	NY A	23	52	12	14	3	0	1	7	5	0	0	15	.269	.328	.385	.713	-10	9	3	75	O17(0/16/1),D2	0	0.0
1988	NY A	38	77	9	19	4	1	1	7	3	0	0	15	.247	.272	.364	.636	-22	5	2	71	O30(1/28/2),D3	64	-0.1
1989	NY A	137	441	65	133	18	3	9	48	41	3	6	89	.302	.369	.417	.786	+22	35	12	74	O137C	17	1.6
1990	NY A	**162**	641	85	183	32	4	15	61	33	0	4	148	.285	.323	.418	.741	+5	42	17	71	O160(11/151/0)/D	0	0.3
1991	NY A	126	486	68	130	22	2	20	69	45	2	5	77	.267	.333	.444	.777	+13	32	9	78	O125(52/73/0)	38	0.5
1992	NY A★	152	580	81	158	31	2	10	66	41	4	4	96	.272	.322	.384	.706	-2	28	5	85	O146(47/99/0)	0	0.2
1993	Cin N★	78	320	44	102	17	3	9	35	17	0	2	43	.319	.354	.475	.829	+20	21	5	81	O77C	82	1.2
1994	Cin N	47	179	29	54	8	0	3	21	11	1	3	35	.302	.351	.397	.748	-5	9	8	53	O47C	0	0.0
1994	Atl N	63	255	44	73	15	3	6	24	24	0	0	36	.286	.345	.439	.784	+0	10	3	77	O63C	0	-0.2
1994	Year	110	434	73	127	23	3	9	45	35	1	3	71	.293	.347	.422	.769	-2	19	11	63	O110C	0	-0.2
1995	Mon N	24	95	11	26	4	0	1	9	7	1	2	14	.274	.337	.347	.684	-22	4	3	57	O24C	0	-0.6
1995	†LA N	112	409	47	114	19	2	6	48	15	5	4	65	.279	.306	.379	.685	-13	15	7	68	O110(61/48/2)	0	-1.8
1995	Year	136	504	58	140	23	2	7	57	22	6	6	79	.278	.312	.373	.685	-15	19	10	66	O134(61/72/2)	0	-2.4
1996	Min A	98	322	41	104	17	4	6	47	23	0	7	53	.323	.375	.457	.832	+9	10	2	83	O93(6/40/54),D2	15	0.2
1997	Min A	75	247	39	71	19	2	5	37	17	0	2	50	.287	.336	.441	.777	+0	7	4	64	O59(1/1/57),D12	15	-0.5
1997	†Sea A	30	121	19	36	7	0	7	22	5	0	1	17	.298	.328	.529	.857	+20	2	1	67	O29(28/1/0)/D	0	0.2
1997	Year	105	368	58	107	26	2	12	59	22	0	3	67	.291	.333	.470	.803	+6	9	5	64	O88(29/2/57),D13	0	-0.3
1998	†Tex A	75	257	48	83	7	3	16	46	8	0	3	46	.323	.349	.560	.909	+25	0	2	0	O71(14/41/31),D2	40	1.1
1999	†Tex A	87	290	41	87	17	1	8	37	21	0	5	57	.300	.355	.448	.803	-2	6	1	86	O85(18/37/37)	0	-0.4
2000	NY A	10	25	4	3	1	0	1	1	1	0	1	6	.120	.185	.280	.465	-84	0	0	0	O10(7/3/0)	165	-0.3
Total	14	1337	4797	687	1390	241	30	124	585	317	16	49	862	.290	.337	.430	.767	+5	235	84	74	O1283(246/886/184),D23	436	1.4
Team	7	648	2302	324	640	111	12	57	259	169	9	20	446	.278	.331	.411	.742	+6	151	48	76	O625(2/280/88),D6	284	2.2
/150	2	150	533	75	148	26	3	13	60	39	2	5	103	.278	.331	.411	.742	+6	35	11	76	O145(0/65/20)/D	66	0.5
KEMP, STEVE STEVEN F B8.7.1954 SAN ANGELO TX BL/TL/6'0"/(190–195) DR 1976 DETA*1/1 D4.7 COL USC																								
1983	NY A	109	373	53	90	17	3	12	49	41	3	2	37	.241	.318	.399	.717	+0	1	0	100	O101(25/0/86),D2	18	-0.3
1984	NY A	94	313	37	91	12	1	7	41	40	0	1	54	.291	.369	.403	.772	+18	4	1	80	O75L,D12	16	0.1
Total	11	1168	4058	581	1128	179	25	130	634	576	25	19	605	.278	.367	.431	.798	+18	39	24	62	O1004(925/0/90),D92/1b	47	4.6
Team	2	203	686	90	181	29	4	19	90	81	3	3	91	.264	.341	.401	.742	+8	5	1	83	O176(25/0/86),D14	34	-0.2
/150	1	150	507	67	134	21	3	14	67	60	2	2	67	.264	.341	.401	.742	+8	4	1	80	O130(18/0/64),D10	25	-0.1
KENNEDY, JOHN JOHN EDWARD B5.29.1941 CHICAGO IL BR/TR/6'0"/185 D9.5																								
1967	NY A	78	179	22	35	4	0	1	17	17	0	1	35	.196	.265	.235	.500	-48	2	1	67	S36,3b34,2b2	0	-1.3
Total	12	856	2110	237	475	77	17	32	185	142	10	25	461	.225	.281	.323	.604	-30	14	10	58	3b455,S226,2b143,D9/1b	65	-10.6
KENNEY, JERRY GERALD T B6.30.1945 ST.LOUIS MO BL/TR/6'1"/(160–170) D9.5 MIL 1968																								
1967	NY A	20	58	4	18	2	0	1	5	10	0	0	8	.310	.412	.397	.809	+45	2	1	67	S18	0	0.3
1969	NY A	130	447	49	115	14	2	2	34	48	2	1	36	.257	.328	.311	.639	-17	25	14	64	3b83,O31C,S10	0	0.5
1970	NY A	140	404	46	78	10	7	4	35	52	2	0	44	.193	.284	.282	.566	-40	20	6	77	3b135,2b2	0	-0.5
1971	NY A	120	325	50	85	10	3	0	20	56	3	1	38	.262	.368	.311	.679	+0	9	8	53	3b109,S5/1b	0	1.2
1972	NY A	50	119	16	25	2	0	0	7	16	2	0	13	.210	.304	.227	.531	-39	3	0	100	S45/3b	0	0.3
1973	Cle A	5	16	0	4	0	1	0	2	2	0	0	0	.250	.316	.375	.691	-3	0	0	0	2b5	0	-0.1
Total	6	465	1369	165	325	38	13	7	103	184	9	2	139	.237	.326	.299	.625	-19	59	29	67	3b328,S78,O31C,2b7/1b	0	1.7
Team	5	460	1353	165	321	38	12	7	101	182	9	2	139	.237	.326	.299	.625	-19	59	29	67	3b328,S78,O31C,2b2/1	0	1.8
/150	2	150	441	54	105	12	4	2	33	59	3	1	45	.237	.326	.299	.625	-19	19	9	68	3b107,S25,O10C/21	0	0.6
KIEFER, STEVE STEVEN GEORGE B10.18.1960 CHICAGO IL BR/TR/6'1"/(175–185) DR 1981 OAKA*1/16 D9.3 B-MARK COL FULLERTON (CA) JC																								
1989	NY A	5	8	0	1	0	0	0	0	0	0	0	5	.125	.125	.125	.250	-130	0	0	0	3b5	16	-0.3
Total	6	105	229	34	44	7	3	7	30	12	0	2	68	.192	.234	.341	.575	-45	2	1	67	3b71,S19,2b8,D5	16	-2.4
KINGMAN, DAVE DAVID ARTHUR "KONG" B12.21.1948 PENDLETON OR BR/TR/6'6"/(210–218) DR 1970 SFN S1/1 D7.30 COL USC OF(508/0/144)																								
1977	NY A	8	24	5	6	2	0	4	7	2	0	1	13	.250	.333	.833	1.166	+107	0	1	0	D6	0	0.3
Total	16	1941	6677	901	1575	240	25	442	1210	608	72	53	1816	.236	.302	.478	.780	+14	85	49	63	O648L,1b603,D434,3b154,P2	111	-1.0
KINGMAN, HARRY HENRY LEES B4.3.1892 TIENTSIN, CHINA D12.27.1982 OAKLAND CA BL/TL/6'1.5"/165 D7.1 COL SPRINGFIELD																								
1914	NY A	4	3	0	0	0	0	0	0	1	—	0	2	.000	.250	.000	.250	-124	0	—	—	/1b	—	-0.1
KITTLE, RON RONALD DALE B1.5.1958 GARY IN BR/TR/6'4"/(200–220) D9.2																								
1986	NY A	30	80	8	19	2	0	4	12	7	1	0	23	.237	.292	.412	.704	-8	2	0	100	D24/lf	0	-0.2
1987	NY A	59	159	21	44	5	0	12	28	10	1	1	36	.277	.318	.535	.853	+23	0	1	0	D49,O2L	40	0.3
Total	10	843	2708	356	648	100	3	176	460	236	20	38	744	.239	.306	.473	.779	+9	16	16	50	O353(348/0/5),D351,1b72	174	-2.9
Team	2	89	239	29	63	7	0	16	40	17	2	1	59	.264	.309	.494	.803	+13	2	1	67	D73,lf	40	0.1
KLEINOW, RED JOHN PETER B7.20.1877 MILWAUKEE WI D10.9.1929 NEW YORK NY BR/TR/5'10"/165 D5.3 COL ST. EDWARDS																								
1904	NY A	68	209	12	43	8	4	0	16	15	—	0	—	.206	.259	.282	.541	-32	4	—	—	C62,3b2/rf	—	-0.7
1905	NY A	88	253	23	56	6	3	1	24	20	—	2	—	.221	.284	.281	.565	-29	7	—	—	C83,1b3	—	-0.5
1906	NY A	96	268	30	59	9	3	0	31	24	—	1	—	.220	.287	.276	.563	-31	8	—	—	C95/1b	—	0.0
1907	NY A	90	269	30	71	6	4	0	26	24	—	1	—	.264	.327	.316	.643	-3	5	—	—	C86/1b	—	0.6
1908	NY A	96	279	16	47	3	2	1	13	22	—	3	—	.168	.237	.204	.441	-57	5	—	—	C89,2b2	—	-2.1
1909	NY A	78	206	24	47	11	4	0	15	25	—	1	—	.228	.315	.320	.635	+0	7	—	—	C77	—	0.5

Batters

YEAR	TM LG	G	AB	R	H	2B	3B	HR	RBI	BB	IB	HP	SO	AVG	OBP	SLG	OPS	AOPS	SB	CS	SB%	GAMES AT POSITION	DL	BFW
1910	NY A	6	12	2	5	0	0	0	2	1	—	0	—	.417	.462	.417	.879	+66	2	—	—	C5	—	0.2
1910	Bos A	50	147	9	22	1	0	1	8	20	—	0	—	.150	.251	.177	.428	-66	3	—	—	C49	—	-0.5
1910	Year	56	159	11	27	1	0	1	10	21	—	0	—	.170	.267	.195	.462	-56	5	—	—	C54	—	-0.3
1911	Bos A	8	14	0	3	0	0	0	0	2	—	0	—	.214	.313	.214	.527	-52	1	—	—	C8	—	0.0
1911	Phi N	4	8	0	1	1	0	0	0	0	—	0	1	.125	.125	.250	.375	-96	0	—	—	C4	—	-0.1
1911	Major	12	22	0	4	1	0	0	0	2	0	0	1	.182	.250	.227	.477	-85	1	0	—	—	—	-0.1
Total	8	584	1665	146	354	45	20	3	135	153	—	8	1	.213	.282	.269	.551	-29	42	—	—	C558,1b5,2b2,3b2/rf	—	-2.6
Team	7	522	1496	137	328	43	20	2	127	131	—	8	0	.219	.286	.279	.565	-25	38	—	—	C497,1b5,2b2,3b2/rf	—	-2.0
/150	2	150	430	39	94	12	6	1	36	38	—	2	0	.219	.286	.279	.565	-25	11	—	—	C143/123OfL	—	-0.6

KLUTTS, MICKEY GENE ELLIS B9.20.1954 MONTEBELLO CA BR/TR/5'11"/(170–189) DR 1972 NYA 4/86 D7.7 [DL 1978 OAK A 21]

YEAR	TM LG	G	AB	R	H	2B	3B	HR	RBI	BB	IB	HP	SO	AVG	OBP	SLG	OPS	AOPS	SB	CS	SB%	GAMES AT POSITION	DL	BFW
1976	NY A	2	3	0	0	0	0	0	0	0	0	0	1	.000	.000	.000	.000	-199	0	0	0	S2	0	-0.1
1977	NY A	5	15	3	4	1	0	1	4	2	0	1	1	.267	.389	.533	.922	+49	0	1	0	3b4/S	24	0.2
1978	NY A	1	2	1	2	1	0	0	0	0	0	1	0	1.000	1.000	1.500	2.500	+505	0	0	0	/3b	27	0.2
Total	8	199	536	49	129	26	1	14	59	34	3	3	101	.241	.289	.371	.660	-17	1	7	13	3b153,S21,2b15,D5	428	-3.5
Team	3	8	20	4	6	2	0	1	4	2	0	2	2	.300	.417	.550	.967	+75	0	1	0	3b5,S3	51	0.3

KNICKERBOCKER, BILL WILLIAM HART B12.29.1911 LOS ANGELES CA D9.8.1963 SEBASTOPOL CA BR/TR/5'11"/170 D4.12

YEAR	TM LG	G	AB	R	H	2B	3B	HR	RBI	BB	IB	HP	SO	AVG	OBP	SLG	OPS	AOPS	SB	CS	SB%	GAMES AT POSITION	DL	BFW
1938	NY A	46	128	15	32	8	3	1	21	11	—	0	10	.250	.309	.383	.692	-27	0	0	0	2b34,S3	—	-0.3
1939	NY A	6	13	2	2	1	0	0	1	0	—	0	0	.154	.154	.231	.385	-103	0	0	0	2b2,S2	—	-0.1
1940	NY A	45	124	17	30	8	1	1	10	14	—	3	8	.242	.333	.347	.680	-20	1	1	50	S19,3b17	—	-0.2
Total	10	907	3418	423	943	198	27	28	368	244	—	9	238	.276	.326	.374	.700	-21	25	46	35	S649,2b211,3b17	0	-8.5
Team	3	97	265	34	64	17	4	2	32	25	—	3	18	.242	.314	.358	.672	-27	1	1	50	2b36,S24,3b17	—	-0.6

KNIGHT, JOHN JOHN WESLEY "SCHOOLBOY" B10.6.1885 PHILADELPHIA PA D12.19.1965 WALNUT CREEK CA BR/TR/6'2.5"/180 D4.14 COL PENN

YEAR	TM LG	G	AB	R	H	2B	3B	HR	RBI	BB	IB	HP	SO	AVG	OBP	SLG	OPS	AOPS	SB	CS	SB%	GAMES AT POSITION	DL	BFW
1905	Phi A	88	325	28	66	12	1	3	29	9	—	1	—	.203	.227	.274	.501	-42	4	—	—	S79,3b4	—	-4.5
1906	Phi A	74	253	29	49	7	2	3	20	19	—	0	—	.194	.250	.273	.523	-38	6	—	—	3b67,2b7	—	-0.8
1907	Phi A	40	139	6	29	7	1	0	12	10	—	2	—	.209	.272	.273	.545	-28	1	—	—	3b40	—	-0.6
1907	Bos A	98	360	31	78	9	3	2	29	19	—	0	—	.217	.256	.275	.531	-30	8	—	—	3b92,2b4	—	-0.8
1907	Year	138	499	37	107	16	4	2	41	29	—	2	—	.214	.260	.275	.535	-29	9	—	—	3b132,2b4	—	-1.4
1909	NY A	116	360	46	85	8	5	0	40	37	—	2	—	.236	.311	.286	.597	-12	15	—	—	S76,1b19,2b17,3b3	—	-0.7
1910	NY A	117	414	58	129	25	4	3	45	34	—	6	—	.312	.372	.413	.785	+38	23	—	—	S79,1b23,2b7,3b4/rf	—	2.1
1911	NY A	132	470	69	126	16	7	3	62	42	—	11	—	.268	.342	.351	.693	-12	18	—	—	S82,1b27,2b21/3b	—	-0.8
1912	Was A	32	93	10	15	2	1	0	9	16	—	0	—	.161	.284	.204	.488	-60	4	2	67	2b27,1b5	—	-1.2
1913	NY A	70	250	24	59	10	0	0	24	25	—	2	27	.236	.310	.276	.586	-28	7	—	—	1b50,2b21	—	-0.1
Total	8	767	2664	301	636	96	24	14	270	211	—	24	27	.239	.300	.309	.609	-16	86	2	100	S316,3b211,1b124,2b104/rf	—	-7.4
Team	4	435	1494	197	399	59	16	6	171	138	—	21	27	.267	.338	.340	.678	-1	63	—	—	S237,1b119,2b66,3b8/rf	—	0.5
/150	1	150	515	68	138	20	6	2	59	48	—	7	9	.267	.338	.340	.678	-1	22	—	—	S82,1b41,2b23,3b3/OfL	—	0.2

KNOBLAUCH, CHUCK EDWARD CHARLES B7.7.1968 HOUSTON TX BR/TR/5'9"/(169–181) DR 1989 MINA 1/25 D4.9 COL TEXAS A&M

YEAR	TM LG	G	AB	R	H	2B	3B	HR	RBI	BB	IB	HP	SO	AVG	OBP	SLG	OPS	AOPS	SB	CS	SB%	GAMES AT POSITION	DL	BFW
1998	†NY A	150	603	117	160	25	4	17	64	76	1	**18**	70	.265	.361	.405	.766	+4	31	12	72	2b149/D	0	1.5
1999	†NY A	150	603	120	176	36	4	18	68	83	0	21	57	.292	.393	.454	.847	+18	28	9	76	2b150	0	1.0
2000	†NY A	102	400	75	113	22	2	5	26	46	0	8	45	.283	.366	.385	.751	-8	15	7	68	2b82,D20	28	-1.2
2001	†NY A	137	521	66	130	20	3	9	44	58	1	14	73	.250	.339	.351	.690	-18	38	9	81	O108L,D24	0	-1.3
Total	12	1632	6366	1132	1839	322	64	98	615	804	22	139	730	.289	.378	.406	.784	+5	407	117	78	2b1381,O183(182/1/0),D51,S13	72	8.0
Team	4	539	2127	378	579	103	13	49	202	263	2	61	245	.272	.366	.402	.768	+0	112	37	75	2b381,O108L,D45	28	0.0
/150	1	150	592	105	161	29	4	14	56	73	1	17	68	.272	.366	.402	.768	+0	31	10	76	2b106,O30L,D13	8	0.0

KOENIG, MARK MARK ANTHONY B7.19.1904 SAN FRANCISCO CA D4.22.1993 WILLOWS CA BB/TR/6'0"/180 D9.8 ▲

YEAR	TM LG	G	AB	R	H	2B	3B	HR	RBI	BB	IB	HP	SO	AVG	OBP	SLG	OPS	AOPS	SB	CS	SB%	GAMES AT POSITION	DL	BFW
1925	NY A	28	110	14	23	6	1	0	4	5	—	0	4	.209	.243	.282	.525	-66	0	1	0	S28	—	-1.0
1926	†NY A	147	617	93	167	26	8	5	62	43	—	1	37	.271	.319	.363	.682	-21	4	3	57	S141	—	-0.4
1927	†NY A	123	526	99	150	20	11	3	62	25	—	2	21	.285	.320	.382	.702	-16	3	2	60	S122	—	1.0
1928	†NY A	132	533	89	170	19	10	4	63	32	—	2	19	.319	.360	.415	.775	+6	3	5	38	S125	—	-0.3
1929	NY A	116	373	44	109	27	5	3	41	23	—	1	17	.292	.335	.416	.751	-1	1	1	50	S61,3b37/2b	—	-0.2
1930	NY A	21	74	9	17	5	0	0	9	6	—	1	5	.230	.296	.297	.593	-47	0	0	0	S19	—	-0.2
1930	Det A	76	267	37	64	9	2	1	16	20	—	1	15	.240	.295	.300	.595	-50	2	0	100	S70,P2,3b2/rf	—	-1.9
1930	Year	97	341	46	81	14	2	1	25	26	—	2	20	.238	.295	.299	.594	-49	2	0	100	S89,P2,3b2/rf	—	-2.1
1931	Det A	106	364	33	92	24	4	1	39	14	—	1	12	.253	.282	.349	.631	-37	8	2	80	2b55,S35,P3	—	-3.1
1932	†Chi N	33	102	15	36	5	1	3	11	3	—	1	5	.353	.377	.510	.887	+37	0	—	—	S31	—	1.4
1933	Chi N	80	218	32	62	12	1	3	25	15	—	0	9	.284	.330	.390	.720	+5	5	—	—	3b37,S26,2b2	—	0.7
1934	Cin N	151	633	60	172	26	6	1	67	15	—	0	24	.272	.289	.336	.625	-32	5	—	—	3b64,S58,2b26,1b4	—	-2.4
1935	NY N	107	396	40	112	12	0	3	37	13	—	0	18	.283	.306	.336	.642	-26	0	—	—	2b64,S21,3b15	—	-1.3
1936	†NY N	42	58	7	16	4	0	1	7	8	—	1	4	.276	.373	.397	.770	+9	0	—	—	S10,2b8,3b3	—	0.1
Total	12	1162	4271	572	1190	195	49	28	443	222	—	11	190	.279	.316	.367	.683	-19	31	14	100	S747,3b158,2b156,P5,1b4/rf	—	-7.6
Team	6	567	2233	348	636	103	35	15	241	134	—	7	103	.285	.327	.382	.709	-13	11	12	48	S496,3b37/2	—	-1.1
/150	2	150	591	92	168	27	9	4	64	35	—	2	27	.285	.327	.382	.709	-13	3	3	50	S131,3b10/2	—	-0.3

KOSCO, ANDY ANDREW JOHN B10.5.1941 YOUNGSTOWN OH BR/TR/6'3"/(200–210) D8.13

YEAR	TM LG	G	AB	R	H	2B	3B	HR	RBI	BB	IB	HP	SO	AVG	OBP	SLG	OPS	AOPS	SB	CS	SB%	GAMES AT POSITION	DL	BFW
1968	NY A	131	466	47	112	19	1	15	59	16	2	3	71	.240	.268	.382	.650	-1	2	2	50	O95(1/0/94),1b28	0	-1.4
Total	10	658	1963	204	464	75	8	73	267	99	18	6	350	.236	.273	.394	.667	-8	5	8	38	O453(136/14/312),1b69,3b20	40	-7.4
/150	1	150	534	54	128	22	1	17	68	18	2	3	81	.240	.268	.382	.650	-1	2	2	50	O109(1/0/108),1b32	0	-1.6

KRUEGER, ERNIE ERNEST GEORGE B12.27.1890 CHICAGO IL D4.22.1976 WAUKEGAN IL BR/TR/5'10.5"/185 D8.4 MIL 1918 COL LAKE FOREST

YEAR	TM LG	G	AB	R	H	2B	3B	HR	RBI	BB	IB	HP	SO	AVG	OBP	SLG	OPS	AOPS	SB	CS	SB%	GAMES AT POSITION	DL	BFW
1915	NY A	10	29	3	5	1	0	0	0	0	—	1	5	.172	.200	.207	.407	-78	0	1	0	C8	—	-0.6
Total	8	318	836	87	220	33	14	11	93	64	—	5	85	.263	.319	.376	.695	-3	12	5	100	C257	—	0.6

KRYHOSKI, DICK RICHARD DAVID B3.24.1925 LEONIA NJ D4.10.2007 BEVERLY HILLS MI BL/TL/6'2"/200 D4.19

YEAR	TM LG	G	AB	R	H	2B	3B	HR	RBI	BB	IB	HP	SO	AVG	OBP	SLG	OPS	AOPS	SB	CS	SB%	GAMES AT POSITION	DL	BFW
1949	NY A	54	177	18	52	10	3	1	27	9	—	2	17	.294	.335	.401	.736	-6	2	4	33	1b51	0	-0.5
Total	7	569	1794	203	475	85	14	45	231	119	0	12	163	.265	.314	.403	.717	-7	5	13	28	1b467	0	-4.4

KUBEK, TONY ANTHONY CHRISTOPHER B10.12.1935 MILWAUKEE WI BL/TR/6'3"/(190–193) D4.20 OF(80/46/31)

YEAR	TM LG	G	AB	R	H	2B	3B	HR	RBI	BB	IB	HP	SO	AVG	OBP	SLG	OPS	AOPS	SB	CS	SB%	GAMES AT POSITION	DL	BFW
1957	†NY A	127	431	56	128	21	3	3	39	24	3	3	48	.297	.335	.381	.716	-2	6	6	50	O50(29/23/0),S41,3b38/2b	0	-0.1
1958	†NY A☆	138	559	66	148	21	1	2	48	25	3	1	57	.265	.295	.317	.612	-28	5	4	56	S134,O3(0/1/2)/1b2b	0	0.9
1959	NY A★	132	512	67	143	25	7	6	51	24	3	2	46	.279	.313	.391	.704	-5	3	3	50	S67,O53(22/15/26),3b17/2b	0	0.8
1960	†NY A	147	568	77	155	25	3	14	62	31	5	3	42	.273	.312	.401	.713	-2	3	0	100	S136,O29(22/6/1)	0	1.4
1961	†NY A★	153	617	84	170	38	6	8	46	27	1	1	60	.276	.306	.395	.701	-9	1	3	25	S145	0	1.9
1962	†NY A	45	169	28	53	6	1	4	17	12	0	0	17	.314	.357	.432	.789	+15	2	1	67	S35,O6L	0	1.4
1963	†NY A	135	557	72	143	21	3	7	44	28	6	2	68	.257	.294	.343	.637	-21	4	2	67	S132/cf	0	0.3
1964	NY A	106	415	46	95	16	3	8	31	26	3	1	55	.229	.275	.340	.615	-31	4	1	80	S99	0	-0.3
1965	NY A	109	339	26	74	5	3	5	35	20	0	0	48	.218	.258	.295	.553	-42	1	3	25	S93,O3(1/0/2)/1b	0	-1.8
Total	9	1092	4167	522	1109	178	30	57	373	217	24	13	441	.266	.303	.364	.667	-15	29	23	56	S882,O145L,3b55,2b3,1b2	0	4.5
/150	1	150	572	72	152	24	4	8	51	30	3	2	61	.266	.303	.364	.667	-15	4	3	57	S121,O20L,3b8/21	0	0.6

LAMAR, BILL WILLIAM HARMONG "GOOD TIME BILL" B3.21.1897 ROCKVILLE MD D5.24.1970 ROCKPORT MA BL/TR/6'1"/185 D9.19 MIL 1918

YEAR	TM LG	G	AB	R	H	2B	3B	HR	RBI	BB	IB	HP	SO	AVG	OBP	SLG	OPS	AOPS	SB	CS	SB%	GAMES AT POSITION	DL	BFW
1917	NY A	11	41	2	10	0	0	0	3	0	—	0	2	.244	.244	.244	.488	-52	1	—	—	O11(10/1/0)	—	-0.5
1918	NY A	28	110	12	25	3	0	0	2	6	—	0	2	.227	.267	.255	.522	-44	2	—	—	O27(8/17/2)	—	-1.3
1919	NY A	11	16	1	3	1	0	0	0	2	—	0	1	.188	.278	.250	.528	-52	1	—	—	O3(0/1/2)/1b	—	-0.2
Total	9	550	2040	303	633	114	23	19	245	86	—	2	78	.310	.339	.417	.756	-6	25	27	100	O494(425/58/11)/1b	—	-8.0
Team	3	50	167	15	38	4	0	0	5	8	—	0	5	.228	.263	.251	.514	-47	4	—	—	O41(18/19/4)/1	—	-2.0

Lanier, Hal Harold Clifton B7.4.1942 Denton NC BR/TR (BB 1967p, 68–70)/6'2"/(180–186) d6.18 M3/C7 f–Max

YEAR	TM LG	G	AB	R	H	2B	3B	HR	RBI	BB	IB	HP	SO	AVG	OBP	SLG	OPS	AOPS	SB	CS	SB%	GAMES AT POSITION	DL	BFW
1972	NY A	60	103	5	22	3	0	0	6	2	0	1	13	.214	.234	.243	.477	-57	1	2	33	3b47,S9,2b3	0	-0.7
1973	NY A	35	86	9	18	3	0	0	5	3	0	1	10	.209	.244	.244	.488	-61	0	0	0	S26,2b8/3b	0	-0.6
Total	10	1196	3703	297	843	111	20	8	273	136	25	4	436	.228	.255	.275	.530	-50	11	11	50	S655,2b430,3b131,1b5	0	-9.1
Team	2	95	189	14	40	6	0	0	11	5	0	2	23	.212	.239	.243	.482	-59	1	2	33	3b48,S35,2b11	0	-1.3

LaPorte, Frank Frank Breyfogle "Pot" B2.6.1880 Uhrichsville OH D9.25.1939 Newcomerstown OH BR/TR/5'8"/175 d9.29

YEAR	TM LG	G	AB	R	H	2B	3B	HR	RBI	BB	IB	HP	SO	AVG	OBP	SLG	OPS	AOPS	SB	CS	SB%	GAMES AT POSITION	DL	BFW
1905	NY A	11	40	4	16	1	0	1	12	1	—	0	—	.400	.415	.500	.915	+70	1	—	—	2b11	—	0.1
1906	NY A	123	454	60	120	23	9	2	54	22	—	1	—	.264	.300	.368	.668	-1	10	—	—	3b114,2b5/lf	—	-0.3
1907	NY A	130	470	56	127	20	11	0	48	27	—	5	—	.270	.317	.360	.677	+7	10	—	—	3b64,O63(14/13/36)/1b	—	-0.5
1908	Bos A	62	156	14	37	1	3	0	15	12	—	1	—	.237	.296	.282	.578	-14	3	—	—	2b27,3b12,O5(0/2/3)	—	0.4
1908	NY A	39	145	7	38	3	4	1	15	8	—	0	—	.262	.301	.359	.660	+13	3	—	—	2b26,O11(3/0/8)	—	-0.1
1908	Year	101	301	21	75	4	7	1	30	20	—	1	—	.249	.298	.319	.617	-2	6	—	—	2b53,O16(3/2/11),3b12	—	0.3
1909	NY A	89	309	35	92	19	3	0	31	18	—	2	—	.298	.340	.379	.719	+26	5	—	—	2b83	—	-0.7
1910	NY A	124	432	43	114	14	6	2	67	33	—	3	—	.264	.321	.338	.659	+0	16	—	—	2b79,O23(17/1/5),3b15	—	-0.5
1911	StL A	136	507	71	159	37	12	2	82	34	—	4	—	.314	.361	.446	.807	+30	4	—	—	2b133,3b3	—	1.8
1912	StL A	80	266	32	83	11	4	1	38	20	—	3	—	.312	.367	.395	.762	+22	7	8	47	2b39,O32R	—	0.7
1912	Was A	40	136	13	42	9	1	0	17	12	—	0	—	.309	.365	.390	.755	+15	3	2	60	2b37	—	0.3
1912	Year	120	402	45	125	20	5	1	55	32	—	3	—	.311	.366	.393	.759	+20	10	10	50	2b76,O32R	—	1.0
1913	Was A	79	242	25	61	5	4	0	18	17	—	3	16	.252	.309	.306	.615	-22	10	—	—	3b46,2b13,O12(4/0/8)	—	-0.3
1914	Ind F	133	505	86	157	27	12	4	**107**	36	—	4	36	.311	.361	.436	.797	+5	15	—	—	2b132	—	0.2
1915	New F	148	550	55	139	28	9	3	56	48	—	1	33	.253	.314	.353	.667	-7	14	—	—	2b146	—	-1.5
Total	11	1194	4212	501	1185	198	78	16	560	288	—	27	85	.281	.331	.377	.708	+7	101	10	100	2b731,3b254,O147(39/16/92)/1b	—	-0.4
Team	6	516	1850	205	507	80	33	6	227	109	—	11	0	.274	.318	.363	.681	+8	45	—	—	2b204,3b193,O98L/1	—	-2.0
/150	2	150	538	60	147	23	10	2	66	32	—	3	0	.274	.318	.363	.681	+8	13	—	—	2b59,3b56,Olf/1	—	-0.6

Lary, Lyn Lynford Hobart "Broadway" B1.28.1906 Armona CA D1.9.1973 Downey CA BR/TR/6'0"/165 d5.11

YEAR	TM LG	G	AB	R	H	2B	3B	HR	RBI	BB	IB	HP	SO	AVG	OBP	SLG	OPS	AOPS	SB	CS	SB%	GAMES AT POSITION	DL	BFW
1929	NY A	80	236	48	73	9	2	5	26	24	—	3	15	.309	.380	.428	.808	+15	4	1	80	3b55,S14,2b2	—	1.2
1930	NY A	117	464	93	134	20	8	3	52	45	—	4	40	.289	.357	.386	.743	-8	14	2	88	S113	—	0.5
1931	NY A	**155**	610	100	171	35	9	10	107	88	—	6	54	.280	.376	.416	.792	+15	13	10	57	S155	—	2.9
1932	NY A	91	280	56	65	14	4	3	39	52	—	3	28	.232	.358	.343	.701	-13	9	3	75	S80,1b5,2b2,3b2/lf	—	0.2
1933	NY A	52	127	25	28	3	3	0	13	28	—	0	17	.220	.361	.291	.652	-21	2	1	67	3b28,S16,1b3/lf	—	-0.1
1934	NY A	1	0	0	0	0	0	0	0	1	—	0	0	+	1.000	+	1.000	+89	0	0	0	/1b	—	0.0
1934	Bos A	129	419	58	101	20	4	2	54	66	—	0	51	.241	.344	.322	.666	-32	12	5	71	S129	—	-1.4
1934	Year	130	419	58	101	20	4	2	54	67	—	0	51	.241	.346	.322	.668	-32	12	5	71	S129/1b	—	-1.4
1935	Was A	39	103	8	20	4	0	0	7	12	—	0	10	.194	.278	.233	.511	-65	3	0	100	S30	—	-1.0
1935	StL A	93	371	78	107	25	7	2	35	64	—	2	43	.288	.396	.410	.806	+4	25	4	86	S93	—	2.4
1935	Year	132	474	86	127	29	7	2	42	76	—	2	53	.268	.371	.371	.742	-10	28	4	88	S123	—	1.4
1936	StL A	**155**	619	112	179	30	6	2	52	117	—	2	54	.289	.404	.367	.771	-11	**37**	9	80	S155	—	0.8
1937	Cle A	**156**	644	110	187	46	7	8	77	88	—	3	64	.290	.378	.421	.799	+0	18	8	69	S156	—	2.1
1938	Cle A	141	568	94	152	36	4	3	51	88	—	0	65	.268	.366	.361	.727	-16	23	6	79	S141	—	0.0
1939	Cle A	3	2	0	0	0	0	0	0	0	—	0	1	.000	.000	.000	.000	-199	0	0	0	S2	—	-0.1
1939	Bro N	29	31	7	5	1	1	0	1	12	—	1	6	.161	.409	.258	.667	-20	1	—	—	S12,3b7	—	0.0
1939	StL N	34	75	11	14	3	0	0	9	16	—	0	15	.187	.330	.227	.557	-51	1	—	—	S30,3b3	—	-0.7
1939	Year	63	106	18	19	4	1	0	10	28	—	1	21	.179	.356	.236	.592	-41	2	—	—	S42,3b10	—	-0.7
1939	Major	66	108	18	19	4	1	0	10	28	0	1	22	.176	.350	.231	.582	+159	2	0	—	—	—	-0.8
1940	StL A	27	54	5	3	1	1	0	3	4	—	1	7	.056	.136	.111	.247	-135	0	0	0	S12/2b	—	-1.0
Total	12	1302	4603	805	1239	247	56	38	526	705	—	25	470	.269	.369	.372	.741	-10	162	49	100	S1138,3b95,1b9,2b5,O2L	—	5.8
Team	6	496	1717	322	471	81	26	21	237	238	—	16	154	.274	.368	.388	.756	+1	42	17	71	S378,3b85,1b9,2b4,O2L	—	4.7
/150	2	150	519	97	142	24	8	6	72	72	—	5	47	.274	.368	.388	.756	+1	13	5	72	S114,3b26,1b3/2lf	—	1.4

Latham, Chris Christopher Joseph B5.26.1973 Coeur D'Alene ID BB/TR/6'0"/(185–198) Dr 1991 LAN 11/299 d4.12

YEAR	TM LG	G	AB	R	H	2B	3B	HR	RBI	BB	IB	HP	SO	AVG	OBP	SLG	OPS	AOPS	SB	CS	SB%	GAMES AT POSITION	DL	BFW
2003	NY A	4	2	3	2	0	0	0	0	0	0	0	0	1.000	1.000	1.000	2.000	+336	1	0	100	O2(0/1/1)	0	0.1
Total	5	110	213	34	43	5	1	3	19	23	1	1	85	.202	.280	.277	.557	-54	9	3	75	O89(34/31/27)	0	-1.7

Lawton, Marcus Marcus Dwayne B8.18.1965 Gulfport MS BB/TR/6'1"/160 Dr 1983 NYN 6/136 d8.11 b–Matt

YEAR	TM LG	G	AB	R	H	2B	3B	HR	RBI	BB	IB	HP	SO	AVG	OBP	SLG	OPS	AOPS	SB	CS	SB%	GAMES AT POSITION	DL	BFW
1989	NY A	10	14	1	3	0	0	0	0	0	0	0	3	.214	.214	.214	.428	-79	1	0	100	O8(7/0/1)/D	0	-0.2

Lawton, Matt Matthew B11.30.1971 Gulfport MS BL/TR/5'10"/(186–200) Dr 1991 MinA 13/336 d9.5 b–Marcus Col Mississippi Gulf Coast CC

YEAR	TM LG	G	AB	R	H	2B	3B	HR	RBI	BB	IB	HP	SO	AVG	OBP	SLG	OPS	AOPS	SB	CS	SB%	GAMES AT POSITION	DL	BFW
2005	NY A	21	48	6	6	0	0	2	4	7	0	2	8	.125	.263	.250	.513	-62	1	0	100	O19(8/0/12)	0	-0.6
Total	12	1334	4763	756	1273	267	17	138	631	681	34	94	613	.267	.368	.417	.785	+2	165	66	71	O1244(385/115/794),D53	140	1.7

Layden, Gene Eugene Francis B3.14.1894 Pittsburgh PA D12.12.1984 Pittsburgh PA BL/TL/5'10"/160 d7.29

YEAR	TM LG	G	AB	R	H	2B	3B	HR	RBI	BB	IB	HP	SO	AVG	OBP	SLG	OPS	AOPS	SB	CS	SB%	GAMES AT POSITION	DL	BFW
1915	NY A	3	7	2	2	0	0	0	0	0	—	0	1	.286	.286	.286	.572	-29	0	1	0	O2C	—	-0.1

Lazzeri, Tony Anthony Michael "Poosh 'Em Up Tony" B12.6.1903 San Francisco CA D8.6.1946 San Francisco CA BR/TR/5'11.5"/170 d4.13 C1 HF1991

YEAR	TM LG	G	AB	R	H	2B	3B	HR	RBI	BB	IB	HP	SO	AVG	OBP	SLG	OPS	AOPS	SB	CS	SB%	GAMES AT POSITION	DL	BFW
1926	†NY A	**155**	589	79	162	28	14	18	114	54	—	2	96	.275	.338	.462	.800	+9	16	7	70	2b149,S5/3b	—	-0.8
1927	†NY A	153	570	92	176	29	8	18	102	69	—	0	82	.309	.383	.482	.865	+27	22	14	61	2b113,S38,3b9	—	3.5
1928	†NY A	116	404	62	134	30	11	10	82	43	—	1	50	.332	.397	.535	.932	+48	15	5	75	2b110	—	2.4
1929	NY A	147	545	101	193	37	11	18	106	68	—	4	45	.354	.429	.561	.990	+64	9	10	47	2b147	—	5.2
1930	NY A	143	571	109	173	34	15	9	121	60	—	3	62	.303	.372	.462	.834	+15	4	4	50	2b77,3b60,S8/1blf	—	2.0
1931	NY A	135	484	67	129	27	7	8	83	79	—	1	80	.267	.371	.401	.772	+9	18	9	67	2b90,3b39	—	1.2
1932	†NY A	142	510	79	153	28	16	15	113	82	—	2	64	.300	.399	.506	.905	+40	11	11	50	2b134,3b5	—	3.9
1933	NY A☆	139	523	94	154	22	12	18	104	73	—	2	62	.294	.383	.486	.869	+37	15	7	68	2b138	—	2.4
1934	NY A	123	438	59	117	24	6	14	67	71	—	0	64	.267	.369	.445	.814	+17	11	1	92	2b92,3b30	—	0.5
1935	NY A	130	477	72	130	18	6	13	83	63	—	3	75	.273	.361	.417	.778	+7	11	5	69	2b118,S9	—	-0.7
1936	†NY A	150	537	82	154	29	6	14	109	97	—	1	65	.287	.397	.441	.838	+10	8	5	62	2b148,S2	—	-1.4
1937	†NY A	126	446	56	109	21	3	14	70	71	—	0	76	.244	.348	.399	.747	-13	7	1	88	2b125	—	-0.8
1938	†Chi N	54	120	21	32	5	0	5	23	22	—	0	30	.267	.380	.433	.813	+20	0	—	—	S25,3b7,2b4/lf	—	0.1
1939	Bro N	14	39	6	11	2	0	3	6	10	—	2	7	.282	.451	.564	1.015	+65	1	—	—	2b11,3b2	—	0.4
1939	NY N	13	44	7	13	0	0	1	8	7	—	0	6	.295	.392	.364	.756	+3	0	—	—	3b13	—	-0.1
1939	Year	27	83	13	24	2	0	4	14	17	—	2	13	.289	.422	.458	.880	+33	1	—	—	3b15,2b11	—	0.3
Total	14	1740	6297	986	1840	334	115	178	1191	869	—	21	864	.292	.380	.467	.847	+22	148	79	100	2b1456,3b166,S87,O2L/1b	—	17.8
Team	12	1659	6094	952	1784	327	115	169	1154	830	—	19	821	.293	.379	.467	.846	+23	147	79	65	2b1441,3b144,S62/1lf	—	17.4
/150	1	150	551	86	161	30	10	15	104	75	—	2	74	.293	.379	.467	.846	+23	13	7	65	2b130,3b13,S6/1OfL	—	1.6

Ledee, Ricky Ricardo Alberto B11.22.1973 Ponce, PR BL/TL/6'1"/(160–225) Dr 1990 NYA 16/435 d6.14

YEAR	TM LG	G	AB	R	H	2B	3B	HR	RBI	BB	IB	HP	SO	AVG	OBP	SLG	OPS	AOPS	SB	CS	SB%	GAMES AT POSITION	DL	BFW
1998	†NY A	42	79	13	19	5	2	1	12	7	0	0	29	.241	.299	.392	.691	-18	3	1	75	O42(36/3/4)	0	-0.1
1999	†NY A	88	250	45	69	13	5	9	40	28	5	0	73	.276	.346	.476	.822	+9	4	3	57	O77(69/6/3),D5	0	0.0
2000	NY A	62	191	23	46	11	1	7	31	26	2	1	39	.241	.332	.419	.751	-9	7	3	70	O49(46/4/1),D10	0	-0.5
Total	10	855	2030	290	494	120	17	63	318	244	18	10	495	.243	.325	.412	.737	-9	29	15	66	O566(315/124/156),D19	194	-5.1
Team	3	192	520	81	134	29	8	17	83	61	7	1	141	.258	.334	.442	.776	-2	14	7	67	O168(151/13/8),D15	0	-0.6
/150	2	150	406	63	105	23	6	13	65	48	5	1	110	.258	.334	.442	.776	-2	11	5	69	O131(118/10/6),D12	0	-0.5

Lee, Travis Travis Reynolds B5.26.1975 San Diego CA BL/TL/6'3"/(210–225) d3.31 Col San Diego St.

YEAR	TM LG	G	AB	R	H	2B	3B	HR	RBI	BB	IB	HP	SO	AVG	OBP	SLG	OPS	AOPS	SB	CS	SB%	GAMES AT POSITION	DL	BFW
2004	NY A	7	19	1	2	1	0	0	2	1	1	0	3	.105	.150	.158	.308	-120	0	0	0	1b6	174	-0.3
Total	9	1099	3740	476	958	191	16	115	488	457	35	9	704	.256	.337	.408	.745	-5	59	20	75	1b1018,O67(10/2/56),D2	262	-10.5

Lefebvre, Joe Joseph Henry B2.22.1956 Concord NH BL/TR/5'10"/(170–180) Dr 1977 NYA 3/75 d5.22 C6 Col Eckerd [DL 1985 Phi N 182]

YEAR	TM LG	G	AB	R	H	2B	3B	HR	RBI	BB	IB	HP	SO	AVG	OBP	SLG	OPS	AOPS	SB	CS	SB%	GAMES AT POSITION	DL	BFW
1980	†NY A	74	150	26	34	1	1	8	21	27	3	0	30	.227	.345	.407	.752	+7	0	0	0	O71(20/3/52)	0	-0.4
Total	6	447	1091	139	281	52	13	31	130	139	22	8	204	.258	.344	.414	.758	+15	11	9	55	O321(76/7/254),3b53,C8	287	0.4

Leja, Frank Frank John B2.7.1936 Holyoke MA D5.3.1991 Boston MA BL/TL/6'4"/205 d5.1

YEAR	TM LG	G	AB	R	H	2B	3B	HR	RBI	BB	IB	HP	SO	AVG	OBP	SLG	OPS	AOPS	SB	CS	SB%	GAMES AT POSITION	DL	BFW
1954	NY A	12	5	2	1	0	0	0	0	0	—	0	1	.200	.200	.200	.400	-90	0	0	0	1b6	0	-0.1
1955	NY A	7	2	1	0	0	0	0	0	0	0	0	1	.000	.000	.000	.000	-199	0	0	0	1b2	0	-0.1
1962	LA A	7	16	0	0	0	0	0	0	1	0	0	6	.000	.059	.000	.059	-185	0	0	0	1b4	0	-0.5
Total	3	26	23	3	1	0	0	0	0	1	0	0	8	.043	.083	.043	.126	-167	0	0	0	1b12	0	-0.7
Team	2	19	7	3	1	0	0	0	0	0	0	0	2	.143	.143	.143	.286	-121	0	0	0	1b8	0	-0.2

Lelivelt, Jack John Frank B11.14.1885 Chicago IL D1.20.1941 Seattle WA BL/TL/5'11.5"/175 d6.24 b-Bill

YEAR	TM LG	G	AB	R	H	2B	3B	HR	RBI	BB	IB	HP	SO	AVG	OBP	SLG	OPS	AOPS	SB	CS	SB%	GAMES AT POSITION	DL	BFW
1912	NY A	36	149	12	54	6	7	2	23	4	—	1	—	.362	.383	.537	.920	+53	7	8	47	O36C	—	0.3
1913	NY A	18	28	2	6	0	1	0	4	2	—	0	2	.214	.267	.286	.553	-39	1	—	—	O5C	—	-0.2
Total	6	384	1154	114	347	43	22	2	126	89	—	5	15	.301	.353	.381	.734	+24	46	11	100	O281(157/88/35),1b15	—	2.5
Team	2	54	177	14	60	6	8	2	27	6	—	1	2	.339	.364	.497	.861	+38	8	8	100	O41C	—	0.1

Leon, Eddie Eduardo Antonio B8.11.1946 Tucson AZ BR/TR/6'0"/(170–175) Dr 1967 CleA S2/35 d9.9 Col Arizona

YEAR	TM LG	G	AB	R	H	2B	3B	HR	RBI	BB	IB	HP	SO	AVG	OBP	SLG	OPS	AOPS	SB	CS	SB%	GAMES AT POSITION	DL	BFW
1975	NY A	1	0	0	0	0	0	0	0	0	0	0	0	+	+	+	.000	-100	0	0	0	/S	0	0.0
Total	8	601	1862	165	440	51	10	24	159	156	11	7	358	.236	.296	.313	.609	-31	7	16	30	S296,2b294,3b3/D	0	-1.8

Levy, Ed Edward Clarence (b Edward Clarence Whitner) B10.28.1916 Birmingham AL BR/TR/6'5.5"/190 d4.16 Col Rollins

YEAR	TM LG	G	AB	R	H	2B	3B	HR	RBI	BB	IB	HP	SO	AVG	OBP	SLG	OPS	AOPS	SB	CS	SB%	GAMES AT POSITION	DL	BFW
1940	Phi N	1	1	0	0	0	0	0	0	0	—	0	0	.000	.000	.000	.000	-199	0	—	—	/H	—	0.0
1942	NY A	13	41	5	5	0	0	0	3	4	—	0	5	.122	.200	.122	.322	-109	1	0	100	1b13	0	-0.6
1944	NY A	40	153	12	37	11	2	4	29	6	—	0	19	.242	.270	.418	.688	-8	1	1	50	O36L	0	-0.7
Total	3	54	195	17	42	11	2	4	32	10	—	0	24	.215	.254	.354	.608	-30	2	1	100	O36L,1b13	0	-1.3
Team	2	53	194	17	42	11	2	4	32	10	—	0	24	.216	.255	.356	.611	-30	2	1	67	O36L,1b13	0	-1.3

Lewis, Duffy George Edward B4.18.1888 San Francisco CA D6.17.1979 Salem NH BR/TR/5'10.5"/165 d4.16 Mil 1918 C5 Col St. Marys (CA)

YEAR	TM LG	G	AB	R	H	2B	3B	HR	RBI	BB	IB	HP	SO	AVG	OBP	SLG	OPS	AOPS	SB	CS	SB%	GAMES AT POSITION	DL	BFW
1919	NY A	**141**	559	67	152	23	4	7	89	17	—	0	42	.272	.293	.365	.658	-16	8	—	—	O141L	—	-3.1
1920	NY A	107	365	34	99	8	1	4	61	24	—	2	32	.271	.320	.332	.652	-30	2	8	20	O99(98/0/1)	—	-2.3
Total	11	1459	5351	612	1518	289	68	38	793	352	—	40	353	.284	.333	.384	.717	+8	113	66	100	O1432(1415/15/2)/3bP	—	-2.2
Team	2	248	924	101	251	31	5	11	150	41	—	2	74	.272	.304	.352	.656	-22	10	8	100	O240L	—	-5.4
/150	1	150	559	61	152	19	3	7	91	25	—	1	45	.272	.304	.352	.656	-22	6	5	100	O145L	—	-3.3

Leyritz, Jim James Joseph B12.27.1963 Lakewood OH BR/TR/6'0"/(190–220) d6.8 Col Kentucky OF(25/0/30)

YEAR	TM LG	G	AB	R	H	2B	3B	HR	RBI	BB	IB	HP	SO	AVG	OBP	SLG	OPS	AOPS	SB	CS	SB%	GAMES AT POSITION	DL	BFW
1990	NY A	92	303	28	78	13	1	5	25	27	1	7	51	.257	.331	.356	.687	-8	2	3	40	3b69,O14(10/0/4),C11	0	-1.7
1991	NY A	32	77	8	14	3	0	0	4	13	0	0	15	.182	.300	.221	.521	-54	0	1	0	3b18,C5,1b3/D	0	-1.0
1992	NY A	63	144	17	37	6	0	7	26	14	1	6	22	.257	.341	.444	.785	+21	0	1	0	D31,C18,1b2,3b2,O2R/2b	0	0.6
1993	NY A	95	259	43	80	14	0	14	53	37	3	8	59	.309	.410	.525	.935	+54	0	0	0	1b29,O28(6/0/23),D21,C12	0	1.5
1994	NY A	75	249	47	66	12	0	17	58	35	1	6	61	.265	.365	.518	.883	+30	0	0	0	C37,D25,1b10	0	1.0
1995	†NY A	77	264	37	71	12	0	7	37	37	2	8	73	.269	.374	.394	.768	+1	1	1	50	C46,1b18,D15	0	-0.2
1996	†NY A	88	265	23	70	10	0	7	40	30	3	9	68	.264	.355	.381	.736	-13	2	0	100	C55,3b13,D12,1b5,O3L,2b2	0	-0.3
1997	Ana A	84	294	47	81	7	0	11	50	37	2	3	56	.276	.357	.412	.769	+1	1	1	50	C58,1b15,D13	0	0.7
1997	Tex A	37	85	11	24	4	0	0	14	23	0	3	22	.282	.446	.329	.775	+1	1	0	100	C11,1b9,D9	0	0.0
1997	Year	121	379	58	105	11	0	11	64	60	2	6	78	.277	.379	.393	.772	+1	2	1	67	C69,1b24,D22	0	0.7
1998	Bos A	52	129	17	37	6	0	8	24	21	1	2	34	.287	.385	.519	.904	+32	0	0	0	D39/C1b	0	0.5
1998	†SD N	62	143	17	38	10	0	4	18	21	0	7	40	.266	.384	.420	.804	+20	0	0	0	C24,1b20/3blf	0	0.5
1998	Major	114	272	34	75	16	0	12	42	42	1	9	74	.276	5.390	.467	5.857	+61	0	0	0	—	0	1.0
1999	SD N	50	134	17	32	5	0	8	21	15	1	4	37	.239	.331	.455	.786	+5	0	0	0	C24,1b19/3b	37	0.1
1999	†NY A	31	66	8	15	4	1	0	5	13	1	0	17	.227	.354	.318	.672	-25	0	0	0	D14,1b9/C3b	0	-0.2
1999	Major	81	200	25	47	9	1	8	26	28	2	4	54	.235	1.341	.410	1.751	+22	0	0	0	—	37	-0.1
2000	NY A	24	55	2	12	0	0	1	4	7	0	1	14	.218	.317	.273	.590	-48	0	0	0	D15,C2/1b	0	-0.5
2000	LA N	41	60	3	12	1	0	1	8	7	0	1	12	.200	.294	.267	.561	-55	0	0	0	1b8,O6(5/0/1),C3	0	-0.7
2000	Major	65	115	5	24	1	0	2	12	14	0	2	26	.209	.305	.270	.575	-35	0	0	0	—	0	-1.2
Total	11	903	2527	325	667	107	2	90	387	337	16	65	581	.264	.362	.415	.777	+6	7	7	50	C308,D195,1b149,3b105,O54R,2b3	37	0.3
Team	9	577	1682	213	443	74	2	58	252	213	12	45	380	.263	.359	.413	.772	+6	5	6	45	C187,D134,3b103,1b77,O47(10/23/27),2b3	0	-0.8
/150	2	150	437	55	115	19	1	15	66	55	3	12	99	.263	.359	.413	.772	+6	1	2	33	C49,D35,3b27,1b20,O12(3/6/7)/2	0	-0.2

Lindell, Johnny John Harlan B8.30.1916 Greeley CO D8.27.1985 Newport Beach CA BR/TR/6'4.5"/(217–220) d4.18 Mil 1945 ▲

YEAR	TM LG	G	AB	R	H	2B	3B	HR	RBI	BB	IB	HP	SO	AVG	OBP	SLG	OPS	AOPS	SB	CS	SB%	GAMES AT POSITION	DL	BFW
1941	NY A	1	1	0	0	0	0	0	0	0	—	0	0	.000	.000	.000	.000	-199	0	0	0	/H	0	0.0
1942	NY A	27	24	1	6	1	0	0	4	0	—	0	5	.250	.250	.292	.542	-47	0	0	0	P23	0	0.0
1943	†NY A☆	122	441	53	108	17	**12**	4	51	51	—	4	55	.245	.329	.365	.694	+2	2	5	29	O122(3/55/66)	0	-0.9
1944	NY A	149	594	91	178	33	**16**	18	103	44	—	3	56	.300	.351	.500	.851	+37	5	4	56	O149(2/148/0)	0	2.5
1945	NY A	41	159	26	45	6	3	1	20	17	—	3	10	.283	.363	.377	.740	+10	2	1	67	O41C	0	0.0
1946	NY A	102	332	41	86	10	5	10	40	32	—	2	47	.259	.328	.410	.738	+4	4	1	80	O74(5/31/39),1b14	0	-0.3
1947	†NY A	127	476	66	131	18	7	11	67	32	—	1	70	.275	.322	.412	.734	+4	1	2	33	O118(102/10/11)	0	-0.4
1948	NY A	88	309	58	98	17	2	13	55	35	—	0	50	.317	.387	.511	.898	+39	0	0	0	O79(72/1/7)	0	1.2
1949	†NY A	78	211	33	51	10	0	6	27	35	—	0	27	.242	.350	.374	.724	-8	3	0	100	O65(63/3/1)	0	-0.6
1950	NY A	7	21	2	4	0	0	0	2	4	—	0	2	.190	.320	.190	.510	-66	0	0	0	O6L	0	-0.3
1950	StL N	36	113	16	21	5	2	5	16	15	—	1	24	.186	.287	.398	.685	-26	0	—	—	O33(29/4/0)	0	-0.8
1950	Major	43	134	18	25	5	2	5	18	19	0	1	26	.187	.292	.366	.658	-4	0	0	—	—	0	-1.1
1953	Pit N	58	91	11	26	6	1	4	15	16	—	2	15	.286	.404	.505	.909	+36	0	0	0	P27,1b2	0	0.1
1953	Phi N	11	18	3	7	1	0	0	2	6	—	0	2	.389	.542	.444	.986	+62	0	0	0	P5,O2R	0	0.0
1953	Year	69	109	14	33	7	1	4	17	22	—	2	17	.303	.429	.495	.924	+41	0	0	0	P32,1b2,O2R	0	0.1
1954	Phi N	7	5	0	1	0	0	0	2	2	—	0	3	.200	.429	.200	.629	-30	0	0	0	/H	0	0.0
Total	12	854	2795	401	762	124	48	72	404	289	—	16	366	.273	.344	.429	.773	+13	17	13	100	O689(282/293/126),P55,1b16	0	0.5
Team	10	742	2568	371	707	112	45	63	369	250	—	13	322	.275	.343	.428	.771	+14	17	13	57	O654(8/256/124),P23,1b14	0	1.2
/150	2	150	519	75	143	23	9	13	75	51	—	3	65	.275	.343	.428	.771	+14	3	3	50	O132(2/52/25),P5,1b3	0	0.2

Linz, Phil Philip Francis B6.4.1939 Baltimore MD BR/TR/6'1"/(170–180) d4.13

YEAR	TM LG	G	AB	R	H	2B	3B	HR	RBI	BB	IB	HP	SO	AVG	OBP	SLG	OPS	AOPS	SB	CS	SB%	GAMES AT POSITION	DL	BFW
1962	NY A	71	129	28	37	8	0	1	14	6	2	0	17	.287	.316	.372	.688	-12	6	2	75	S21,3b8,2b5,O2R	0	-0.7
1963	†NY A	72	186	22	50	9	0	2	12	15	0	2	18	.269	.328	.349	.677	-9	1	6	14	S22,3b13,O12(2/5/5),2b6	0	-0.2
1964	†NY A	112	368	63	92	21	3	5	25	43	2	2	61	.250	.332	.364	.696	-8	3	4	43	S55,3b41,2b5,O3(1/2/0)	0	0.9
1965	NY A	99	285	37	59	12	1	2	16	30	1	0	33	.207	.281	.277	.558	-40	2	1	67	S71,3b4,O4R/2b	0	-0.6
1966	Phi N	40	70	4	14	3	0	0	6	2	0	0	14	.200	.222	.243	.465	-71	0	0	0	3b14,S6,2b3	0	-1.1
1967	Phi N	23	18	4	4	2	0	1	5	2	0	0	1	.222	.300	.500	.800	+24	0	0	0	S7/3b	0	-0.2
1967	NY N	24	58	8	12	2	0	0	1	4	0	1	10	.207	.270	.241	.511	-52	0	0	0	2b11,S8/3blf	0	-0.5
1967	Year	47	76	12	16	4	0	1	6	6	0	1	11	.211	.277	.303	.580	-34	0	0	0	S15,2b11,3b2/lf	0	-0.7
1968	NY N	78	258	19	54	7	0	0	17	10	0	2	41	.209	.243	.236	.479	-55	1	0	100	2b71	0	-2.7
Total	7	519	1372	185	322	64	4	11	96	112	5	7	195	.235	.295	.311	.606	-28	13	13	50	S190,2b102,3b82,O22(4/7/11)	0	-5.1
Team	4	354	968	150	238	50	4	10	67	94	5	4	129	.246	.314	.337	.651	-18	12	13	48	S169,3b66,O21(2/5/7),2b17	0	0.6
/150	2	150	410	64	101	21	2	4	28	40	2	2	55	.246	.314	.337	.651	-18	5	6	45	S72,3b28,O9(1/2/3),2b7	0	-0.3

Little, Bryan Richard Bryan "Twig" B10.8.1959 Houston TX BB/TR/5'10"/(155–160) Dr 1980 MonN 9/229 d7.29 C3 Col Texas A&M

YEAR	TM LG	G	AB	R	H	2B	3B	HR	RBI	BB	IB	HP	SO	AVG	OBP	SLG	OPS	AOPS	SB	CS	SB%	GAMES AT POSITION	DL	BFW
1986	NY A	14	41	3	8	1	0	0	0	2	0	0	7	.195	.233	.220	.453	-76	0	0	0	2b14	0	0.1
Total	5	327	922	126	226	37	5	3	77	120	1	6	79	.245	.333	.306	.639	-21	8	10	44	2b238,S86,3b3	0	-2.6

YEAR	TM LG	G	AB	R	H	2B	3B	HR	RBI	BB	IB	HP	SO	AVG	OBP	SLG	OPS	AOPS	SB	CS	SB%	GAMES AT POSITION	DL	BFW
LITTLE, JACK William Arthur B3.12.1891 Mart TX D7.27.1961 Dallas TX BR/TR/5'11"/175 d7.2 Col Baylor																								
1912	NY A	3	12	2	3	0	0	0	0	1	—	1	—	.250	.357	.250	.607	-30	2	—	—	O3C	—	0.0
LOCKLEAR, GENE Gene B7.19.1949 Lumberton NC BL/TR/5'10"/165 d4.5																								
1976	NY A	13	32	2	7	1	0	0	1	2	0	0	7	.219	.265	.250	.515	-49	0	0	0	O3L,D6	0	-0.3
1977	NY A	1	5	1	3	0	0	0	2	0	0	0	0	.600	.600	.600	1.200	+130	0	0	0	/lf	0	0.1
Total	5	292	595	76	163	24	4	9	66	55	6	2	87	.274	.335	.373	.708	+5	13	7	65	O120(111/0/10),D6	0	-0.2
Team	2	14	37	3	10	1	0	0	3	2	0	0	7	.270	.308	.297	.605	-26	0	0	0	D6,O4L	0	-0.2
LOFTON, KENNY Kenneth B5.31.1967 E.Chicago IN BL/TL/6'0"/(180–190) Dr 1988 HouN 17/428 d9.14 Col Arizona																								
2004	†NY A	83	276	51	76	10	7	3	18	31	1	1	27	.275	.346	.395	.741	-6	7	3	70	O74(0/65/10),D4	30	0.2
Total	17	2103	8120	1528	2428	383	116	130	781	945	43	32	1016	.299	.372	.423	.795	+6	622	160	80	O2041(50/1984/10),D12	175	17.3
LOLLAR, SHERM John Sherman B8.23.1924 Durham AR D9.24.1977 Springfield MO BR/TR/6'1"/(180–195) d4.20 C5 Col Pittsburg St. (KS)																								
1947	†NY A	11	32	4	7	0	1	1	6	1	—	0	5	.219	.242	.375	.617	-29	0	1	0	C9	0	-0.1
1948	NY A	22	38	0	8	0	0	0	4	1	—	0	6	.211	.231	.211	.442	-82	0	0	0	C10	0	-0.4
Total	18	1752	5351	623	1415	244	14	155	808	671	49	115	453	.264	.357	.402	.759	+4	20	10	67	C1571,1b27/3b	34	13.0
Team	2	33	70	4	15	0	1	1	10	2	—	0	11	.214	.236	.286	.522	-58	0	1	0	C19	0	-0.5
LOMBARDI, PHIL Phillip Arden B2.20.1963 Abilene TX BR/TR/6'2"/(200–205) Dr 1981 NYA 3/77 d4.26																								
1986	NY A	20	36	6	10	3	0	2	6	4	0	1	7	.278	.366	.528	.894	+40	0	0	0	O8L,C3	0	0.2
1987	NY A	5	8	0	1	0	0	0	0	0	0	0	2	.125	.125	.125	.250	-134	0	0	0	C3	0	-0.1
1989	NY N	18	48	4	11	1	0	1	3	5	0	0	8	.229	.302	.313	.616	-21	0	0	0	C16/1b	0	-0.3
Total	3	43	92	10	22	4	0	3	9	9	0	1	17	.239	.314	.380	.694	-5	0	0	0	C22,O8L/1b	0	-0.2
Team	2	25	44	6	11	3	0	2	6	4	0	1	9	.250	.327	.455	.782	+12	0	0	0	O8L,C6	0	0.1
LONG, HERMAN Herman C. "Germany","Flying Dutchman" B4.13.1866 Chicago IL D9.17.1909 Denver CO BL/TR/5'8.5"/160 d4.17																								
1903	NY A	22	80	6	15	3	0	0	8	2	—	0	—	.188	.207	.225	.432	-72	3	—	—	S22	—	-1.1
Total	16	1875	7678	1456	2129	342	97	91	1055	612	—	57	262	.277	.335	.383	.718	-7	537	—	—	S1795,2b65,O19(18/1/0),1b2/3b	—	2.4
LONG, DALE Richard Dale B2.6.1926 Springfield MO D1.27.1991 Palm Coast FL BL/TL/6'4"/(210–215) d4.21 C1																								
1960	†NY A	26	41	6	15	3	1	3	10	5	1	0	6	.366	.435	.707	1.142	+116	0	0	0	1b11	0	0.5
1962	†NY A	41	94	12	28	4	0	4	17	18	0	0	9	.298	.404	.468	.872	+40	1	0	100	1b31	0	0.6
1963	NY A	14	15	1	3	0	0	0	0	1	0	0	3	.200	.250	.200	.450	-72	0	0	0	1b2	0	-0.2
Total	10	1013	3020	384	805	135	33	132	467	353	39	7	460	.267	.341	.464	.805	+16	10	3	77	1b819,C2/lf	0	0.7
Team	3	81	150	19	46	7	1	7	27	24	1	0	18	.307	.398	.507	.905	+50	1	0	100	1b44	0	0.9
LONG, TERRENCE Terrence Deon B2.29.1976 Montgomery AL BL/TL/6'1"/(190–200) Dr 1994 NYN 1/20 d4.14																								
2006	NY A	12	36	6	6	1	0	0	2	4	0	0	8	.167	.250	.194	.444	-83	0	0	0	O10(2/2/7)/D	0	-0.4
Total	8	890	3068	428	824	166	21	69	376	227	23	7	460	.269	.318	.404	.722	-11	27	15	64	O816(303/409/135),D7	0	-9.5
LOPEZ, ART Arturo (Rodriguez) B5.8.1937 Mayaguez, PR BL/TL/5'9"/170 d4.12 Col New Jersey City																								
1965	NY A	38	49	5	7	0	0	0	0	1	0	0	6	.143	.160	.143	.303	-113	0	0	0	O16(3/0/14)	0	-0.9
LOPEZ, HECTOR Hector Headley (Swainson) B7.9.1929 Colon, Pan BR/TR/5'11"/(168–182) d5.12 OF(477/21/172)																								
1955	KC A	128	483	50	140	15	2	15	68	33	1	3	58	.290	.337	.422	.759	+3	1	4	20	3b93,2b36	0	1.1
1956	KC A	151	561	91	153	27	3	18	69	63	3	3	73	.273	.347	.428	.775	+4	4	5	44	3b121,O20C,2b8,S4	0	0.4
1957	KC A	121	391	51	115	19	4	11	35	41	5	0	66	.294	.357	.448	.805	+18	1	6	14	3b111,2b4,O3(2/0/1)	0	1.3
1958	KC A	151	564	84	147	28	4	17	73	49	2	2	61	.261	.317	.415	.732	-1	2	2	50	2b96,3b55/Slf	0	1.4
1959	KC A	35	135	22	38	10	3	6	24	8	0	1	23	.281	.324	.533	.857	+29	1	0	100	2b33	0	-0.2
1959	NY A	112	406	60	115	16	2	16	69	28	1	6	54	.283	.336	.451	.787	+19	3	1	75	3b76,O35L	0	0.4
1959	Year	147	541	82	153	26	5	22	93	36	1	7	77	.283	.333	.471	.804	+22	4	1	80	3b76,O35L,2b33	0	0.2
1960	†NY A	131	408	66	116	14	6	9	42	46	0	4	64	.284	.361	.414	.775	+16	1	1	50	O106(93/0/17),2b5/3b	0	0.5
1961	†NY A	93	243	27	54	7	2	3	22	24	1	1	38	.222	.292	.305	.597	-36	1	0	100	O72(65/0/9)	0	-1.3
1962	†NY A	106	335	45	92	19	1	6	48	33	2	0	53	.275	.338	.391	.729	-1	0	1	0	O84(64/0/21)/2b3b	0	-0.3
1963	†NY A	130	433	54	108	13	4	14	52	35	5	0	71	.249	.304	.395	.699	-5	1	2	33	O124(104/0/21)/2b	0	-1.4
1964	†NY A	127	285	34	74	9	3	10	34	24	2	1	54	.260	.317	.418	.735	+1	1	1	50	O103(80/1/31)/3b	0	-0.7
1965	NY A	111	283	25	74	12	2	7	39	26	2	1	61	.261	.322	.392	.714	+4	0	0	0	O75(20/0/55),1b2	0	-1.0
1966	NY A	54	117	14	25	4	1	4	16	8	0	1	20	.214	.268	.368	.636	-16	0	0	0	O29(13/0/17)	0	-0.7
Total	12	1450	4644	623	1251	193	37	136	591	418	24	23	696	.269	.330	.415	.745	+4	16	23	41	O652L,3b459,2b184,S5,1b2	0	-0.5
Team	8	864	2510	325	658	94	21	69	322	224	13	14	415	.262	.324	.399	.723	+1	7	6	54	O628(225/86/86),3b79,2b7,1b2	0	-4.5
/150	1	150	436	56	114	16	4	12	56	39	2	2	72	.262	.324	.399	.723	+1	1	1	50	O109(39/15/15),3b14/21	0	-0.8
LOUDEN, BALDY William P. B8.27.1883 Pittsburgh PA D12.8.1935 Piedmont WV BR/TR/5'11"/175 d9.13																								
1907	NY A	4	9	4	1	0	0	0	0	2	—	0	—	.111	.273	.111	.384	-79	1	—	—	3b3	—	-0.1
Total	6	603	1942	267	507	61	22	12	202	254	—	30	162	.261	.355	.334	.689	-2	111	20	100	2b313,S176,3b74,O5(0/1/4)	—	4.2
LOVULLO, TOREY Salvatore Anthony B7.25.1965 Santa Monica CA BB/TR/6'0"/(180–185) Dr 1987 DetA 5/131 d9.10 Col UCLA OF(1/0/2)																								
1991	NY A	22	51	0	9	2	0	0	2	5	1	0	7	.176	.250	.216	.466	-70	0	0	0	3b22	0	-0.4
Total	8	303	737	80	165	35	1	15	60	80	3	3	121	.224	.301	.335	.636	-31	9	8	53	2b133,1b67,3b67,S10,D6,O3R	0	-3.1
LOWELL, MIKE Michael Averett B2.24.1974 San Juan, PR BR/TR/6'4"/(193–212) Dr 1995 NYA 20/562 d9.13 Col Florida International																								
1998	NY A	8	15	1	4	0	0	0	0	0	0	0	1	.267	.267	.267	.534	-59	0	0	0	3b7	0	-0.2
Total	10	1296	4731	636	1323	325	6	184	778	454	37	46	661	.280	.344	.468	.812	+11	26	11	70	3b1253,2b8,D5	97	10.7
LUCADELLO, JOHNNY John B2.22.1919 Thurber TX D10.30.2001 San Antonio TX BB/TR/5'11"/160 d9.24 Mil 1942–45																								
1947	NY A	12	12	0	1	0	0	0	0	1	—	0	5	.083	.154	.083	.237	-133	0	0	0	2b5	0	-0.3
Total	6	239	686	95	181	36	7	5	60	93	—	2	56	.264	.353	.359	.712	-12	6	3	67	2b117,3b49,S12/lf	0	-2.4
LUEBBE, ROY Roy John B9.17.1900 Parkersburg IA D8.21.1985 Papillion NE BB/TR/6'0"/175 d8.22																								
1925	NY A	8	15	1	0	0	0	0	3	2	—	0	6	.000	.118	.000	.118	-169	0	0	0	C8	—	-0.3
LUKE, MATT Matthew Clifford B2.26.1971 Long Beach CA BL/TL/6'5"/220 Dr 1992 NYA 8/214 d4.3 Col California																								
1996	NY A	1	0	1	0	0	0	0	0	0	0	0	0	+	+	+	.000	-100	0	0	0	/R	0	0.0
Total	3	123	269	39	65	12	1	15	40	19	2	1	70	.242	.293	.461	.754	-2	2	1	67	O69(51/0/18),1b22	69	-2.3
LUMPE, JERRY Jerry Dean B6.2.1933 Lincoln MO BL/TR/6'2"/(179–190) d4.17 C1																								
1956	NY A	20	62	12	16	3	0	0	4	5	2	0	11	.258	.313	.306	.619	-34	1	1	50	S17/3b	0	0.0
1957	†NY A	40	103	15	35	6	2	0	11	9	0	0	13	.340	.389	.437	.826	+28	2	2	50	3b30,S6	0	0.2
1958	†NY A	81	232	34	59	8	4	3	32	23	2	1	21	.254	.319	.362	.681	-8	1	2	33	3b65,S5	0	0.2
1959	NY A	18	45	2	10	0	0	0	2	6	5	0	7	.222	.314	.222	.536	-48	0	0	0	3b12,S4/2b	0	-0.2
Total	12	1371	4912	620	1314	190	52	47	454	428	21	8	411	.268	.325	.356	.681	-13	20	15	57	2b1100,3b118,S105	0	1.6
Team	4	159	442	63	120	17	6	3	49	43	9	1	52	.271	.334	.357	.691	-7	4	5	44	3b108,S32/2	0	0.2
/150	4	150	417	59	113	16	6	3	46	41	8	1	49	.271	.334	.357	.691	-7	4	5	44	3b102,S30/2	0	0.2
LUSADER, SCOTT Scott Edward B9.30.1964 Chicago IL BL/TR/5'10"/165 Dr 1985 DetA 6/158 d9.1 Col Florida																								
1991	NY A	11	7	2	1	0	0	0	1	1	0	0	3	.143	.250	.143	.393	-88	0	1	0	O4(1/3/0)/D	47	-0.1
Total	5	135	260	41	64	9	1	5	36	28	1	0	43	.246	.313	.346	.659	-14	4	1	80	O105(25/21/69),D11	79	-1.2

YEAR	TM LG	G	AB	R	H	2B	3B	HR	RBI	BB	IB	HP	SO	AVG	OBP	SLG	OPS	AOPS	SB	CS	SB%	GAMES AT POSITION	DL	BFW
Lyttle, Jim	James Lawrence B5.20.1946 Hamilton OH BL/TR/6'0"/(178–186) Dr 1966 NYA 1/10 d5.17 Col Florida St.																							
1969	NY A	28	83	7	15	4	0	0	4	4	0	0	19	.181	.218	.229	.447	-74	1	2	33	O28C	0	-0.9
1970	NY A	87	126	20	39	7	1	3	14	10	1	0	26	.310	.355	.452	.807	+28	3	6	33	O70(2/4/64)	0	0.2
1971	NY A	49	86	7	17	5	0	1	7	8	2	1	18	.198	.271	.291	.562	-37	0	2	0	O29(3/6/20)	0	-0.7
1972	Chi A	44	82	8	19	5	2	0	5	1	0	0	28	.232	.241	.341	.582	-30	0	1	0	O21(0/16/5)	9	-0.6
1973	Mon N	49	116	12	30	5	1	4	19	9	2	0	14	.259	.305	.422	.727	-2	0	2	0	O36(29/7/0)	0	0.1
1974	Mon N	25	9	1	3	0	0	0	2	1	1	0	3	.333	.364	.333	.697	+1	0	0	0	O18(14/5/0)	0	0.0
1975	Mon N	44	55	7	15	4	0	0	6	13	3	0	6	.273	.406	.345	.751	+6	0	1	0	O16(5/8/3)	0	0.0
1976	Mon N	42	85	6	23	4	1	1	8	7	1	0	13	.271	.326	.376	.702	-6	0	0	0	O29(12/0/20)	0	0.0
1976	LA N	23	68	3	15	3	0	0	5	8	4	0	12	.221	.303	.265	.568	-37	0	1	0	O18(1/17/1)	0	0.0
1976	Year	65	153	9	38	7	1	1	13	15	5	0	25	.248	.315	.327	.642	-20	0	1	0	O47(13/17/21)	0	0.0
Total	8	391	710	71	176	37	5	9	70	61	14	1	139	.248	.305	.352	.657	-15	4	15	21	O265(66/91/113)	9	-1.9
Team	3	164	295	34	71	16	1	4	25	22	3	1	63	.241	.293	.342	.635	-19	4	10	29	O127(2/32/0)	0	-1.4
/150	3	150	270	31	65	15	1	4	23	20	3	1	58	.241	.293	.342	.635	-19	4	9	31	O116(2/29/0)	0	-1.3
Maas, Kevin	Kevin Christian B1.20.1965 Castro Valley CA BL/TL/6'3"/(203–209) Dr 1986 NYA 22/572 d6.29 Col California																							
1990	NY A	79	254	42	64	9	0	21	41	43	10	3	76	.252	.367	.535	.902	+48	1	2	33	1b57,D18	0	1.0
1991	NY A	148	500	69	110	14	1	23	63	83	3	4	128	.220	.333	.390	.723	-1	5	1	83	D109,1b36	0	-0.6
1992	NY A	98	286	35	71	12	0	11	35	25	4	0	63	.248	.305	.406	.711	-1	3	1	75	D62,1b22	0	-0.7
1993	NY A	59	151	20	31	4	0	9	25	24	2	1	32	.205	.316	.411	.727	-3	1	1	50	D31,1b17	0	-0.5
1995	Min A	22	57	5	11	4	0	1	5	7	2	0	11	.193	.281	.316	.597	-45	0	0	0	D12,1b8	16	-0.6
Total	5	406	1248	171	287	43	1	65	169	182	21	8	310	.230	.329	.422	.751	+7	10	5	67	D232,1b140	16	-1.4
Team	4	384	1191	166	276	39	1	64	164	175	19	8	299	.232	.332	.427	.759	+9	10	5	67	D220,1b132	0	-0.8
/150	2	150	465	65	108	15	0	25	64	68	7	3	117	.232	.332	.427	.759	+9	4	2	67	D86,1b52	0	-0.3
Mack, Ray	Raymond James (b Raymond James Mlckovsky) B8.31.1916 Cleveland OH D5.7.1969 Bucyrus OH BR/TR/6'0"/200 d9.9 Mil 1945 Col Case Western Reserve																							
1947	NY A	1	0	0	0	0	0	0	0	0	—	0	0	+	+	+	.000	-100	0	0	0	/R	0	0.0
Total	9	791	2707	273	629	113	24	34	278	261	—	6	365	.232	.301	.330	.631	-24	35	17	100	2b788/3b	0	-5.3
Madden, Tommy	Thomas Joseph B7.31.1883 Philadelphia PA D7.26.1930 Philadelphia PA BL/TL/5'11"/160 d9.10																							
1910	NY A	1	1	0	0	0	0	0	0	0	—	0	—	.000	.000	.000	.000	-195	0	—	—	/H	—	0.0
Total	2	5	16	1	4	0	0	0	0	1	—	0	—	.250	.294	.250	.544	-29	0	—	—	O4L	—	-0.1
Maddox, Elliott	Elliott B12.21.1947 East Orange NJ BR/TR/5'11"/(180–185) Dr 1968 DetA S1/20 d4.7 Col Michigan OF(77/472/189)																							
1974	NY A	137	466	75	141	26	2	3	45	69	4	4	48	.303	.395	.386	.781	+27	6	5	55	O135(1/112/25),2b2/3b	0	2.7
1975	NY A	55	218	36	67	10	3	1	23	21	0	7	24	.307	.382	.394	.776	+22	9	3	75	O55C/2b	107	1.1
1976	†NY A	18	46	4	10	2	0	0	3	4	1	0	3	.217	.275	.261	.536	-41	0	1	0	O13(0/6/7),D2	138	-0.3
Total	11	1029	2843	360	742	121	16	18	234	409	21	34	358	.261	.358	.334	.692	-1	60	54	53	O719C,3b230,S19,2b4,1b3,D3	401	3.5
Team	3	210	730	115	218	38	5	4	71	94	5	11	75	.299	.384	.381	.765	+21	15	9	63	O203(1/112/25),2b3,D2/3	245	3.5
/150	2	150	521	82	156	27	4	3	51	67	4	8	54	.299	.384	.381	.765	+21	11	6	65	O145(1/80/18),2b2/D3	175	2.5
Magee, Lee	Leo Christopher (b Leopold Christopher Hoernschemeyer) B6.4.1889 Cincinnati OH D3.14.1966 Columbus OH BB/TR/5'11"/165 d7.4 M1 OF(230/285/8)																							
1916	NY A	131	510	57	131	18	4	3	45	50	—	1	31	.257	.324	.325	.649	-7	29	25	54	O128(21/107/0),2b2	—	-1.8
1917	NY A	51	173	17	38	4	1	0	8	13	—	1	18	.220	.278	.254	.532	-38	3	—	—	O50(2/48/0)	—	-1.7
Total	9	1015	3741	467	1031	133	54	12	277	265	—	9	208	.276	.325	.350	.675	-2	186	51	100	O519C,2b349,1b58,3b42,S19	—	-4.0
Team	2	182	683	74	169	22	5	3	53	63	—	2	49	.247	.312	.307	.619	-15	32	25	100	O178(23/155/0),2b2	—	-3.5
/150	2	150	563	61	139	18	4	2	44	52	—	2	40	.247	.312	.307	.619	-15	26	21	100	O147(19/128/0),2b2	—	-2.9
Magner, Stubby	Edmund Burke B2.10.1888 Kalamazoo MI D9.6.1956 Chillicothe OH BR/TR/5'3"/135 d7.12 Col Cornell																							
1911	NY A	13	33	3	7	0	0	0	4	4	—	0	—	.212	.297	.212	.509	-60	1	—	—	S6,2b5	—	-0.2
Maisel, Fritz	Frederick Charles "Flash" B12.23.1889 Catonsville MD D4.22.1967 Baltimore MD BR/TR/5'7.5"/170 d8.11 b–George																							
1913	NY A	51	187	33	48	4	3	0	12	34	—	0	20	.257	.371	.310	.681	-1	25	—	—	3b51	—	0.1
1914	NY A	150	548	78	131	23	9	2	47	76	—	2	69	.239	.334	.325	.659	-2	**74**	17	81	3b148	—	-0.2
1915	NY A	135	530	77	149	16	6	4	46	48	—	1	35	.281	.342	.357	.699	+9	51	12	81	3b134	—	0.7
1916	NY A	53	158	18	36	5	0	0	7	20	—	1	18	.228	.318	.259	.577	-28	4	—	—	O26C,3b11,2b4	—	-1.0
1917	NY A	113	404	46	80	4	4	0	20	36	—	2	18	.198	.267	.228	.495	-49	29	—	—	2b100,3b7	—	-2.8
1918	StL A	90	284	43	66	4	2	0	16	46	—	1	17	.232	.341	.261	.602	-16	11	—	—	3b79/rf	—	-0.5
Total	6	592	2111	295	510	56	24	6	148	260	—	7	177	.242	.327	.299	.626	-12	194	29	100	3b430,2b104,O27(0/26/1)	—	-3.7
Team	5	502	1827	252	444	52	22	6	132	214	—	6	160	.243	.324	.305	.629	-11	183	29	100	3b351,2b104,O26C	—	-3.2
/150	1	150	546	75	133	16	7	2	39	64	—	2	48	.243	.324	.305	.629	-11	55	9	100	3b105,2b31,O8C	—	-1.0
Majeski, Hank	Henry "Heeney" B12.13.1916 Staten Island NY D8.9.1991 Staten Island NY BR/TR/5'9"/180 d5.17 Mil 1943–45																							
1946	NY A	8	12	1	1	0	1	0	0	0	—	0	3	.083	.083	.250	.333	-109	0	0	0	3b2	0	-0.3
Total	13	1069	3421	404	956	181	27	57	501	299	1	27	260	.279	.342	.398	.740	+0	10	11	100	3b861,2b48,S12/lf	0	4.0
Maloney, Pat	Patrick William B1.19.1888 Grosvenor Dale CT D6.27.1979 Pawtucket RI BR/TR/6'0"/150 d6.19																							
1912	NY A	25	79	9	17	1	0	0	4	6	—	1	—	.215	.279	.228	.507	-57	3	2	60	O20C	—	-0.9
Mantle, Mickey	Mickey Charles "The Commerce Comet" B10.20.1931 Spavinaw OK D8.13.1995 Dallas TX BB/TR/5'11"/(175–201) d4.17 C1 HF1974 OF(129/1745/146)																							
1951	†NY A	96	341	61	91	11	5	13	65	43	—	0	74	.267	.349	.443	.792	+17	8	7	53	O86(0/3/85)	0	-0.1
1952	†NY A☆	142	549	94	171	37	7	23	87	75	—	0	111	.311	.394	.530	.924	+66	4	1	80	O141(0/121/20)/3b	0	3.9
1953	†NY A★	127	461	105	136	24	3	21	92	79	—	0	90	.295	.398	.497	.895	+45	8	4	67	O121(0/116/4)/S	0	2.3
1954	NY A★	146	543	**129**	163	17	12	27	102	102	—	0	107	.300	.408	.525	.933	+60	5	2	71	O144(0/143/1),S4/2b	0	3.8
1955	†NY A★	147	517	121	158	25	**11**	**37**	99	**113**	6	3	97	.306	**.431**	**.611**	1.042	+81	8	1	89	O145C,S2	0	**5.5**
1956	†NY A★	150	533	**132**	188	22	5	**52**	**130**	112	6	2	99	**.353**	.464	**.705**	1.169	+113	10	1	91	O144C	0	**8.1**
1957	†NY A★	144	474	**121**	173	28	6	34	94	**146**	23	0	75	.365	.512	.665	1.177	+123	16	3	84	O139C	0	**8.0**
1958	†NY A★	150	519	**127**	158	21	1	**42**	97	**129**	**13**	2	120	.304	.443	.592	1.035	+89	18	3	86	O150C	0	**5.5**
1959	NY A★	144	541	104	154	23	4	31	75	93	6	2	126	.285	.390	.514	.904	+52	21	3	88	O143C	0	3.6
1960	†NY A★	153	527	**119**	145	17	6	**40**	94	111	6	1	125	.275	.399	.558	.957	+66	14	3	82	O150C	0	3.6
1961	†NY A★	153	514	**132**	163	16	6	54	128	**126**	9	0	112	.317	.448	**.687**	1.135	+110	12	1	92	O150C	0	7.5
1962	†NY A★	123	377	96	121	15	1	30	89	**122**	9	1	78	.321	**.486**	**.605**	1.091	+98	9	0	100	O117(0/94/23)	0	**5.0**
1963	†NY A✳	65	172	40	54	8	0	15	35	40	4	0	32	.314	.441	.622	1.063	+97	2	1	67	O52C	35	2.2
1964	†NY A★	143	465	92	141	25	2	35	111	99	**18**	0	102	.303	**.423**	.591	1.014	+77	6	3	67	O132(17/102/13)	0	3.4
1965	NY A✳	122	361	44	92	12	1	19	46	73	7	0	76	.255	.379	.452	.831	+36	4	1	80	O108L	0	1.5
1966	NY A	108	333	40	96	12	1	23	56	57	5	0	76	.288	.389	.538	.927	+71	1	1	50	O97(4/93/0)	0	2.4
1967	NY A★	144	440	63	108	17	0	22	55	107	7	1	113	.245	.391	.434	.825	+50	1	1	50	1b131	0	3.3
1968	NY A★	144	435	57	103	14	1	18	54	106	7	1	97	.237	.385	.398	.783	+43	6	2	75	1b131	0	2.3
Total	18	2401	8102	1677	2415	344	72	536	1509	1733	1	13	1710	.298	.421	.557	.978	+73	153	38	80	O2019C,1b262,S7/2b3b	35	71.8
/150	1	150	506	105	151	21	4	33	94	108	0	1	107	.298	.421	.557	.978	+73	10	2	83	1b16,O13C/S23	2	4.5
Manto, Jeff	Jeffrey Paul B8.23.1964 Bristol PA BR/TR/6'3"/210 Dr 1985 CalA 14/355 d6.7 C2 Col Temple																							
1999	NY A	6	8	0	1	0	0	0	0	2	0	0	4	.125	.300	.125	.425	-86	0	0	0	1b3/3b	0	-0.1
Total	9	289	713	97	164	36	2	31	97	97	1	9	182	.230	.329	.415	.744	-7	3	6	33	3b165,1b72,D21,2b5,S5,C5,O4L	49	-2.0
Mapes, Cliff	Clifford Franklin B3.13.1922 Sutherland NE D12.5.1996 Pryor OK BL/TR/6'3"/205 d4.20																							
1948	NY A	53	88	19	22	11	1	1	12	6	—	0	13	.250	.298	.432	.730	-6	1	1	50	O21(9/6/6)	0	0.1
1949	†NY A	111	304	56	75	13	3	7	38	58	—	1	50	.247	.369	.378	.747	-2	6	0	100	O108(4/58/49)	0	0.5
1950	†NY A	108	356	60	88	14	6	12	61	47	—	2	61	.247	.338	.421	.759	-4	1	6	14	O102(4/21/80)	0	-1.1

YEAR	TM LG	G	AB	R	H	2B	3B	HR	RBI	BB	IB	HP	SO	AVG	OBP	SLG	OPS	AOPS	SB	CS	SB%	GAMES AT POSITION	DL	BFW
1951	NY A	45	51	6	11	3	1	2	8	4	—	0	14	.216	.273	.431	.704	-8	0	0	0	O34(2/3/29)	0	-0.1
1951	StL A	56	201	32	55	7	2	7	30	26	—	1	33	.274	.360	.433	.793	+10	0	1	0	O53(15/12/31)	0	0.0
1951	Year	101	252	38	66	10	3	9	38	30	—	1	47	.262	.343	.433	.776	+9	0	1	0	O87(17/15/60)	0	-0.1
1952	Det A	86	193	26	38	7	0	9	23	27	—	0	42	.197	.295	.373	.668	-16	0	1	0	O63(5/18/43)	0	-0.9
Total	5	459	1193	199	289	55	13	38	172	168	—	4	213	.242	.338	.406	.744	-3	8	9	47	O381(39/118/238)	0	-1.5
Team	4	317	799	141	196	41	11	22	119	115	—	3	138	.245	.342	.407	.749	-4	8	7	53	O265(13/95/37)	0	-0.6
/150	2	150	378	67	93	19	5	10	56	54	—	1	65	.245	.342	.407	.749	-4	4	3	57	O125(6/45/18)	0	-0.3

MARIS, ROGER Roger Eugene (b Roger Eugene Maras) B9.10.1934 Hibbing MN D12.14.1985 Houston TX BL/TR/6'0"/(185–204) d4.16

YEAR	TM LG	G	AB	R	H	2B	3B	HR	RBI	BB	IB	HP	SO	AVG	OBP	SLG	OPS	AOPS	SB	CS	SB%	GAMES AT POSITION	DL	BFW
1957	Cle A	116	358	61	84	9	5	14	51	60	5	1	79	.235	.344	.405	.749	+6	8	4	67	O112(26/87/8)	0	0.5
1958	Cle A	51	182	26	41	5	1	9	27	17	2	0	33	.225	.287	.412	.699	-6	4	2	67	O47(0/27/23)	0	0.0
1958	KC A	99	401	61	99	14	3	19	53	28	1	2	52	.247	.298	.439	.737	-1	0	0	0	O99(0/21/90)	0	-1.0
1958	Year	150	583	87	140	19	4	28	80	45	3	2	85	.240	.294	.431	.725	-3	4	2	67	O146(0/48/113)	0	-1.0
1959	KC A★	122	433	69	118	21	7	16	72	58	5	3	53	.273	.359	.464	.823	+23	2	1	67	O117(0/6/113)	31	1.4
1960	†NY A★	136	499	98	141	18	7	39	**112**	70	4	3	65	.283	.371	**.581**	.952	+64	2	2	50	O131(0/7/128)	0	3.7
1961	†NY A★	161	590	**132**	159	16	4	**61**	**142**	94	0	7	67	.269	.372	.620	.992	+70	0	0	0	O160(0/11/156)	0	3.1
1962	†NY A★	157	590	92	151	34	1	33	100	87	11	6	78	.256	.356	.485	.841	+28	1	0	100	O154(0/64/103)	0	1.1
1963	†NY A	90	312	53	84	14	1	23	53	35	3	2	40	.269	.346	.542	.888	+46	1	0	100	O86(0/1/86)	0	1.7
1964	†NY A	141	513	86	144	12	2	26	71	62	1	6	78	.281	.364	.464	.828	+27	3	0	100	O137(0/32/105)	0	0.6
1965	NY A	46	155	22	37	7	0	8	27	29	1	0	29	.239	.357	.439	.796	+26	0	0	0	O43R	0	0.0
1966	NY A	119	348	37	81	9	2	13	43	36	3	3	60	.233	.307	.382	.689	+1	0	0	0	O95(0/1/94)	0	-1.4
1967	†StL N	125	410	64	107	18	7	9	55	52	3	4	61	.261	.346	.405	.751	+17	0	0	0	O118(0/2/118)	0	0.5
1968	†StL N	100	310	25	79	18	2	5	45	24	3	1	38	.255	.307	.374	.681	-10	0	0	0	O04R	0	0.1
Total	12	1463	5101	826	1325	195	42	275	851	652	42	38	733	.260	.345	.476	.821	+28	21	9	70	O1383(26/259/1151)	31	10.3
Team	7	850	3007	520	797	110	17	203	548	413	23	27	417	.265	.357	.515	.872	+41	7	2	78	O806(0/116/247)	0	8.8
/150	1	150	531	92	141	19	3	36	97	73	4	5	74	.265	.357	.515	.872	+41	1	0	100	O142(0/20/44)	0	1.6

MARSANS, ARMANDO Armando B10.3.1887 Matanzas, Cuba D9.3.1960 Havana, Cuba BR/TR/5'10"/157 d7.4 OF(51/459/71)

YEAR	TM LG	G	AB	R	H	2B	3B	HR	RBI	BB	IB	HP	SO	AVG	OBP	SLG	OPS	AOPS	SB	CS	SB%	GAMES AT POSITION	DL	BFW
1917	NY A	25	88	10	20	4	0	0	15	8	—	0	3	.227	.292	.273	.565	-28	6	—	—	O25C	—	-0.3
1918	NY A	37	123	13	29	5	1	0	9	5	—	0	3	.236	.266	.293	.559	-33	3	—	—	O36(0/28/8)	—	-1.3
Total	8	655	2273	267	612	67	19	2	221	173	—	16	117	.269	.325	.318	.643	-12	171	37	100	O575C,1b29,2b8,3b8,S3	—	-8.9
Team	2	62	211	23	49	9	1	0	24	13	—	0	6	.232	.277	.284	.561	-31	9	—	—	O61(0/53/28)	—	-1.6

MARTIN, BILLY Alfred Manuel B5.16.1928 Berkeley CA D12.25.1989 Johnson City NY BR/TR/5'11.5"/(165–175) d4.18 Mil 1954–55 M16/C4

YEAR	TM LG	G	AB	R	H	2B	3B	HR	RBI	BB	IB	HP	SO	AVG	OBP	SLG	OPS	AOPS	SB	CS	SB%	GAMES AT POSITION	DL	BFW
1950	NY A	34	36	10	9	1	0	1	8	3	—	0	3	.250	.308	.361	.669	-27	0	0	0	2b22/3b	0	-0.3
1951	†NY A	51	58	10	15	1	2	0	2	4	—	2	9	.259	.328	.345	.673	-15	0	1	0	2b23,S6,3b2/cf	0	0.8
1952	†NY A	109	363	32	97	13	3	3	33	22	—	8	31	.267	.323	.344	.667	-9	3	6	33	2b107	0	1.8
1953	†NY A	149	587	72	151	24	6	15	75	43	—	6	56	.257	.314	.395	.709	-6	6	7	46	2b146,S18	0	0.4
1955	†NY A	20	70	8	21	2	0	1	9	7	1	0	9	.300	.354	.371	.725	+0	1	2	33	2b17,S3	0	0.3
1956	†NY A★	121	458	76	121	24	5	9	49	30	0	3	56	.264	.310	.397	.707	-10	7	3	70	2b105,3b16	0	-0.7
1957	NY A	43	145	12	35	5	2	1	12	3	0	1	14	.241	.257	.324	.581	-40	2	1	67	2b26,3b13	0	-0.6
1957	KC A	73	265	33	68	9	3	9	27	12	0	3	20	.257	.295	.415	.710	-9	7	1	88	2b52,3b20,S2	0	-1.4
1957	Year	116	410	45	103	14	5	10	39	15	0	4	34	.251	.282	.383	.665	-20	9	2	82	2b78,3b33,S2	0	-2.0
1958	Det A	131	498	56	127	19	1	7	42	16	0	3	62	.255	.279	.339	.618	-35	5	3	63	S88,3b41	0	-3.1
1959	Cle A	73	242	37	63	7	0	9	24	8	2	3	18	.260	.290	.401	.691	-8	0	2	0	2b67,3b4	30	-1.3
1960	Cin N	103	317	34	78	17	1	3	16	27	5	0	34	.246	.304	.334	.638	-26	0	1	0	2b97	0	-1.9
1961	Mil N	6	6	1	0	0	0	0	0	0	0	0	1	.000	.000	.000	.000	-199	0	0	0	/H	0	-0.2
1961	Min A	108	374	44	92	15	5	6	36	13	0	3	42	.246	.275	.361	.636	-35	3	2	60	2b105/S	0	-1.9
1961	Major	114	380	45	92	15	5	6	36	13	0	3	43	.242	3.273	.355	3.628	-828	3	2	60	—	0	-2.1
Total	11	1021	3419	425	877	137	28	64	333	188	8	32	355	.257	.300	.369	.669	-19	34	29	54	2b767,S118,3b97/cf	30	-8.1
Team	7	527	1717	220	449	70	18	30	188	112	1	20	178	.262	.312	.376	.688	-11	19	20	49	2b446,3b32,S27/cf	0	1.7
/150	2	150	489	63	128	20	5	9	54	32	0	6	51	.262	.312	.376	.688	-11	5	6	45	2b127,3b9,S8/OfL	0	0.5

MARTIN, HERSH Hershel Ray B9.19.1909 Birmingham AL D11.17.1980 Cuba MO BB/TR/6'2"/190 d4.23

YEAR	TM LG	G	AB	R	H	2B	3B	HR	RBI	BB	IB	HP	SO	AVG	OBP	SLG	OPS	AOPS	SB	CS	SB%	GAMES AT POSITION	DL	BFW
1944	NY A	85	328	49	99	12	4	9	47	34	—	2	26	.302	.371	.445	.816	+28	5	2	71	O80(78/2/0)	0	0.8
1945	NY A	117	408	53	109	18	6	7	53	65	—	0	31	.267	.368	.392	.760	+15	4	1	80	O102(97/3/2)	0	0.6
Total	6	607	2257	331	643	135	29	28	215	253	—	7	207	.285	.359	.408	.767	+9	33	3	100	O555(187/348/21)	0	1.6
Team	2	202	736	102	208	30	10	16	100	99	—	2	57	.283	.369	.416	.785	+21	9	3	75	O182(175/5/2)	0	1.4
/150	1	150	547	76	154	22	7	12	74	74	—	1	42	.283	.369	.416	.785	+21	7	2	78	O135(130/4/1)	0	1.0

MARTIN, JACK John Christopher B4.19.1887 Plainfield NJ D7.4.1980 Plainfield NJ BR/TR/5'9"/159 d4.25

YEAR	TM LG	G	AB	R	H	2B	3B	HR	RBI	BB	IB	HP	SO	AVG	OBP	SLG	OPS	AOPS	SB	CS	SB%	GAMES AT POSITION	DL	BFW
1912	NY A	71	231	30	52	6	1	0	17	37	—	6	—	.225	.347	.260	.607	-30	14	16	47	S65,3b4/2b	—	-0.6
1914	Bos N	33	85	10	18	2	0	0	5	6	—	0	7	.212	.264	.235	.499	-51	0	—	—	3b26/1b2b	—	-0.5
1914	Phi N	83	292	26	74	5	3	0	21	27	—	1	29	.253	.319	.291	.610	-23	6	—	—	S83	—	-0.6
1914	Year	116	377	36	92	7	3	0	26	33	—	1	36	.244	.307	.279	.586	-29	6	—	—	S83,3b26/1b2b	—	-1.1
Total	2	187	608	66	144	13	4	0	43	70	—	7	36	.237	.323	.271	.594	-29	20	16	100	S148,3b30,2b2/1b	—	-1.7

MARTINEZ, TINO Constantino B12.7.1967 Tampa FL BL/TR/6'2"/(205–230) Dr 1988 SeaA 1/14 d8.20 Col Tampa

YEAR	TM LG	G	AB	R	H	2B	3B	HR	RBI	BB	IB	HP	SO	AVG	OBP	SLG	OPS	AOPS	SB	CS	SB%	GAMES AT POSITION	DL	BFW
1990	Sea A	24	68	4	15	4	0	0	5	9	0	0	9	.221	.308	.279	.587	-34	0	0	0	1b23	0	-0.4
1991	Sea A	36	112	11	23	2	0	4	9	11	0	0	24	.205	.272	.330	.602	-33	0	0	0	1b29,D5	0	-0.6
1992	Sea A	136	460	53	118	19	2	16	66	42	9	2	77	.257	.316	.411	.727	+3	2	1	67	1b78,D47	0	-0.3
1993	Sea A	109	408	48	108	25	1	17	60	45	9	5	56	.265	.343	.456	.799	+11	0	3	0	1b103,D6	55	-0.6
1994	Sea A	97	329	42	86	21	0	20	61	29	2	1	52	.261	.320	.508	.828	+7	1	2	33	1b82,D8	0	-0.4
1995	†Sea A★	141	519	92	152	35	3	31	111	62	15	4	91	.293	.369	.551	.920	+35	0	0	0	1b139/D	0	1.7
1996	†NY A	155	595	82	174	28	0	25	117	68	4	2	85	.292	.364	.466	.830	+9	2	1	67	1b151,D3	0	-0.6
1997	†NY A★	158	594	96	176	31	2	44	141	75	14	3	75	.296	.371	.577	.948	+46	3	1	75	1b150,D9	0	3.2
1998	†NY A	142	531	92	149	33	1	28	123	61	3	6	83	.281	.355	.505	.860	+27	2	1	67	1b142	0	1.0
1999	†NY A	159	589	95	155	27	2	28	105	69	7	3	86	.263	.341	.458	.799	+4	3	4	43	1b158	0	-0.4
2000	†NY A	155	569	69	147	37	4	16	91	52	9	8	74	.258	.328	.422	.750	-10	4	1	80	1b154	0	-2.1
2001	†NY A	154	589	89	165	24	2	34	113	42	2	2	89	.280	.329	.501	.830	+14	1	2	33	1b149,D3	0	0.1
2002	†StL N	150	511	63	134	25	1	21	75	58	9	2	71	.262	.337	.438	.775	+2	3	2	60	1b149	0	-1.3
2003	StL N	138	476	66	130	25	2	15	69	53	7	9	71	.273	.352	.429	.781	+5	1	1	50	1b126,D5	0	-0.7
2004	TB A	138	458	63	120	20	1	23	76	66	9	9	72	.262	.362	.461	.823	+16	3	1	75	1b114,D19	0	0.1
2005	†NY A	131	303	43	73	9	0	17	49	38	3	3	54	.241	.328	.439	.767	+3	2	0	100	1b122/D	0	-0.9
Total	16	2023	7111	1008	1925	365	21	339	1271	780	10	59	1069	.271	.344	.471	.815	+12	27	20	57	1b1869,D107	55	-2.2
Team	7	1054	3770	566	1039	189	11	192	739	405	42	27	546	.276	.347	.484	.831	+14	17	10	63	1b1026,D16	0	0.3
/150	1	150	537	81	148	27	2	27	105	58	6	4	78	.276	.347	.484	.831	+14	2	1	67	1b146,D2	0	0.0

MASON, JIM James Percy B8.14.1950 Mobile AL BL/TR/6'2"/(170–190) Dr 1968 TexA 2/28 d9.26

YEAR	TM LG	G	AB	R	H	2B	3B	HR	RBI	BB	IB	HP	SO	AVG	OBP	SLG	OPS	AOPS	SB	CS	SB%	GAMES AT POSITION	DL	BFW
1971	Was A	3	9	0	3	0	0	0	0	1	0	0	3	.333	.400	.333	.733	+15	0	0	0	S3	0	0.2
1972	Tex A	46	147	10	29	3	0	0	10	9	0	1	39	.197	.247	.218	.465	-59	0	0	0	S32,3b10	0	-1.7
1973	Tex A	92	238	23	49	7	2	3	19	23	0	0	48	.206	.273	.290	.563	-38	0	1	0	S74,2b19/3b	0	-0.6
1974	NY A	152	440	41	110	18	6	5	37	35	1	0	87	.250	.302	.352	.654	-10	1	2	33	S152	0	1.0
1975	NY A	94	223	17	34	3	2	2	16	22	0	0	49	.152	.228	.211	.439	-75	0	2	0	S93/2b	0	-1.7
1976	†NY A	93	217	17	39	7	1	1	14	9	0	0	37	.180	.210	.235	.445	-69	0	0	0	S93	0	-0.6
1977	Tor A	22	79	10	13	3	0	0	2	7	0	0	10	.165	.233	.203	.436	-80	1	1	50	S22	0	-0.9
1977	Tex A	36	55	9	12	3	0	1	7	6	0	0	10	.218	.290	.327	.617	-32	0	0	0	S32/3bD	0	0.1
1977	Year	58	134	19	25	6	0	1	9	13	0	0	20	.187	.257	.254	.511	-60	1	1	50	S54/3bD	0	-0.8
1978	Tex A	55	105	10	20	4	0	0	3	5	0	0	17	.190	.227	.229	.456	-72	0	0	0	S42,3b11/2bD	0	-1.2
1979	Mon N	40	71	3	13	5	1	0	6	7	1	0	16	.183	.256	.282	.538	-53	0	2	0	S33,3b6	0	-0.9

YEAR	TM LG	G	AB	R	H	2B	3B	HR	RBI	BB	IB	HP	SO	AVG	OBP	SLG	OPS	AOPS	SB	CS	SB%	GAMES AT POSITION	DL	BFW
Total	9	633	1584	140	322	53	12	12	114	124	2	1	316	.203	.259	.275	.534	-46	2	8	20	S576,3b29,2b21,D2	0	-6.3
Team	3	339	880	75	183	28	9	8	67	66	1	0	173	.208	.261	.287	.548	-41	1	4	20	S338/2	0	-1.3
/150	1	150	389	33	81	12	4	4	30	29	0	0	77	.208	.261	.287	.548	-41	0	2	0	S150/2	0	-0.6
Mata, Victor	Victor Jose (Abreu) B6.17.1961 Santiago, D.R. BR/TR/6'1"/165 d7.22																							
1984	NY A	30	70	8	23	5	0	1	6	0	0	1	12	.329	.333	.443	.776	+18	1	1	50	O28(2/21/8)	0	-0.1
1985	NY A	6	7	1	1	0	0	0	0	0	0	0	0	.143	.143	.143	.286	-122	0	0	0	O3(1/1/2)	0	-0.2
Total	2	36	77	9	24	5	0	1	6	0	0	1	12	.312	.316	.416	.732	+5	1	1	50	O31(3/22/10)	0	-0.3
Matsui, Hideki	Hideki "Godzilla" B6.12.1974 Ishikawa, Japan BL/TR/6'1"/(210–230) d3.31																							
2003	†NY A★	**163**	623	82	179	42	1	16	106	63	5	3	86	.287	.353	.435	.788	+9	2	2	50	O159(118/46/0),D4	0	0.4
2004	†NY A★	**162**	584	109	174	34	2	31	108	88	2	3	103	.298	.390	.522	.912	+36	3	0	100	O160(160/3/0)	0	2.5
2005	†NY A	**162**	629	108	192	45	3	23	116	63	7	3	78	.305	.367	.496	.863	+29	2	2	50	O142(115/28/4),D19	0	1.9
2006	†NY A	51	172	32	52	9	0	8	29	27	2	0	23	.302	.393	.494	.887	+26	1	0	100	O36L,D13	123	0.8
2007	†NY A	143	547	100	156	28	4	25	103	73	2	3	73	.285	.367	.488	.855	+23	4	2	67	O112L,D32	15	0.9
Total	5	681	2555	431	753	158	10	103	462	314	18	12	363	.295	.371	.485	.856	+24	12	6	67	O609(541/77/4),D68	138	6.5
/150	1	150	563	95	166	35	2	23	102	69	4	3	80	.295	.371	.485	.856	+24	3	1	75	O134(119/17/1),D15	30	1.4
Mattingly, Don	Donald Arthur "Donnie Baseball" B4.20.1961 Evansville IN BL/TL/6'0"/(175–200) Dr 1979 NYA 19/493 d9.8 C4																							
1982	NY A	7	12	0	2	0	0	0	1	0	0	0	1	.167	.154	.167	.321	-108	0	0	0	O6(5/0/1)/1b	0	0.0
1983	NY A	91	279	34	79	15	4	4	32	21	5	1	31	.283	.333	.409	.742	+7	0	0	0	O48(13/1/39),1b42/2b	0	-0.7
1984	NY A★	153	603	91	**207**	**44**	2	23	110	41	8	1	33	**.343**	.381	.537	.918	+58	1	1	50	1b133,O19(13/1/6)	0	5.3
1985	NY A★	159	652	107	211	**48**	3	35	**145**	56	13	2	41	.324	.371	.567	.938	+58	2	2	50	1b159	0	3.0
1986	NY A★	**162**	677	117	**238**	**53**	2	31	113	53	11	1	35	.352	.394	**.573**	.967	+62	0	0	0	1b160,3b3/D	0	4.5
1987	NY A★	141	569	93	186	38	2	30	115	51	13	1	38	.327	.378	.559	.937	+46	1	4	20	1b140/D	15	2.6
1988	NY A★	144	599	94	186	37	0	18	88	41	14	3	29	.311	.353	.462	.815	+28	1	0	100	1b143/lfD	18	1.1
1989	NY A★	158	631	79	191	37	2	23	113	51	18	1	30	.303	.351	.477	.828	+34	3	0	100	1b145,D17/rf	0	1.3
1990	NY A	102	394	40	101	16	0	5	42	28	13	3	20	.256	.308	.335	.643	-20	1	0	100	1b89,D13/lf	47	-1.0
1991	NY A	152	587	64	169	35	0	9	68	46	11	4	42	.288	.339	.394	.733	+3	2	0	100	1b127,D22	0	-0.9
1992	NY A	157	640	89	184	40	0	14	86	39	7	1	43	.287	.327	.416	.743	+8	3	0	100	1b143,D15	0	0.2
1993	NY A	134	530	78	154	27	2	17	86	61	9	2	42	.291	.364	.445	.809	+20	0	0	0	1b130,D5	27	0.5
1994	NY A	97	372	62	113	20	1	6	51	60	7	0	24	.304	.397	.411	.808	+14	0	0	0	1b97	15	0.7
1995	†NY A	128	458	59	132	32	2	7	49	40	7	1	35	.288	.341	.413	.754	-3	0	2	0	1b125/D	0	-1.2
Total	14	1785	7003	1007	2153	442	20	222	1099	588	13	21	444	.307	.358	.471	.829	+27	14	9	61	1b1634,D76,O76(33/2/47),3b3/2b	122	15.4
/150	1	150	588	85	181	37	2	19	92	49	0	2	37	.307	.358	.471	.829	+27	1	1	50	1b14,O6(3/0/4),D6/32	10	1.3
May, Carlos	Carlos B5.17.1948 Birmingham AL BL/TR/6'0"/215 Dr 1966 ChiA 1/18 d9.6 b–Lee																							
1976	†NY A	87	288	38	80	11	2	3	40	34	2	5	32	.278	.358	.361	.719	+13	1	1	50	D71,O7L/1b	0	0.4
1977	NY A	65	181	21	41	7	1	2	16	17	4	1	24	.227	.292	.309	.601	-34	0	0	0	D53,O4(2/0/2)	0	-1.1
Total	10	1165	4120	545	1127	172	23	90	536	512	63	45	565	.274	.357	.392	.749	+11	85	53	62	O677(653/0/26),D242,1b211	17	-0.1
Team	2	152	469	59	121	18	3	5	56	51	6	6	56	.258	.333	.341	.674	-5	1	1	50	D124,O11L/1	0	-0.7
/150	2	150	463	58	119	18	3	5	55	50	6	6	55	.258	.333	.341	.674	-5	1	1	50	D122,O11L/1	0	-0.7
Mayberry, John	John Claiborn B2.18.1949 Detroit MI BL/TL/6'3"/(215–239) Dr 1967 HouN 1/6 d9.10 C2																							
1982	NY A	69	215	20	45	7	0	8	27	28	2	5	38	.209	.313	.353	.666	-16	0	0	0	1b63,D4	0	-1.0
Total	15	1620	5447	733	1379	211	19	255	879	881	10	55	810	.253	.360	.439	.799	+22	20	17	54	1b1478,D96	0	1.8
Mazzilli, Lee	Lee Louis B3.25.1955 New York NY BB/TR/6'1"/(180–195) Dr 1973 NYN 1/14 d9.7 M2/C5																							
1982	NY A	37	128	20	34	2	0	6	17	15	0	1	15	.266	.347	.422	.769	+12	2	3	40	1b23,O2L,D9	0	-0.2
Total	14	1475	4124	571	1068	191	24	93	460	642	41	20	627	.259	.359	.385	.744	+8	197	90	69	O868(201/647/30),1b215,D52	55	3.2
McCarthy, Joe	Joseph Nicodemus B12.25.1881 Syracuse NY D1.12.1937 Syracuse NY BR/TR d9.27 Col Niagara																							
1905	NY A	1	2	0	0	0	0	0	0	0	—	0	—	.000	.000	.000	.000	-190	0	—	—	/C	—	-0.1
Total	2	16	39	3	9	2	0	0	2	2	—	0	—	.231	.268	.282	.550	-26	0	—	—	C16	—	-0.2
McCauley, Pat	Patrick F. B6.10.1870 Ware MA D1.17.1917 Hoboken NJ TR/5'10.5"/156 d9.5																							
1903	NY A	6	19	0	1	0	0	0	1	0	—	0	—	.053	.053	.053	.106	-164	0	—	—	C6	—	-0.5
Total	3	37	119	14	23	3	0	3	12	7	—	1	9	.193	.244	.294	.538	-56	3	—	—	C35/rf	—	-0.9
McClure, Larry	Lawrence Ledwith B10.8.1884 Wayne WV D9.1.1949 Huntington WV BR/TR/5'6.5"/130 d7.26 Col West Virginia																							
1910	NY A	1	1	0	0	0	0	0	0	0	—	0	—	.000	.000	.000	.000	-195	0	—	—	/lf	—	0.0
McConnell, George	George Neely "Slats" B9.16.1877 Shelbyville TN D5.10.1964 Chattanooga TN BR/TR/6'3"/190 d4.13 ▲																							
1909	NY A	13	43	4	9	0	1	0	5	1	—	0	—	.209	.227	.256	.483	-48	1	—	—	1b11,P2	—	-0.2
1912	NY A	42	91	11	27	4	2	0	8	4	—	1	—	.297	.333	.385	.718	-1	0	—	—	P23,1b2	—	0.2
1913	NY A	39	67	4	12	2	0	0	2	0	—	0	11	.179	.179	.209	.388	-87	0	—	—	P35/1b	—	0.2
1914	Chi N	1	2	0	0	0	0	0	0	0	—	0	1	.000	.000	.000	.000	-199	0	—	—	/P	—	0.0
1915	Chi F	53	125	14	31	6	2	1	18	0	—	1	16	.248	.254	.352	.606	-26	2	—	—	P44	—	0.0
1916	Chi N	28	57	2	9	0	0	0	0	2	—	1	4	.158	.200	.158	.358	-90	0	—	—	P28	—	0.0
Total	6	176	385	35	88	12	5	1	33	7	—	3	32	.229	.248	.294	.542	-43	3	—	—	P133,1b14	—	0.2
Team	3	94	201	19	48	6	3	0	15	5	—	1	11	.239	.261	.299	.560	-39	1	—	—	P60,1b14	—	0.2
McDermott, Mickey	Maurice Joseph "Maury" B8.29.1929 Poughkeepsie NY D8.7.2003 Phoenix AZ BL/TL/6'2"/(170–190) d4.24 C1 ▲																							
1956	†NY A	46	52	4	11	0	0	1	4	8	0	0	13	.212	.317	.269	.586	-42	0	0	0	P23	0	0.0
Total	12	443	619	71	156	29	2	9	74	52	2	2	112	.252	.312	.349	.661	-24	1	2	33	P291,1b2	0	0.0
McDonald, Dave	David Bruce B5.20.1943 New Albany IN BL/TR/6'3"/(215–227) d9.15 Col Nebraska																							
1969	NY A	9	23	0	5	1	0	0	2	2	0	0	5	.217	.280	.261	.541	-46	0	1	0	1b7	0	-0.3
Total	2	33	62	3	9	3	0	1	6	6	0	0	19	.145	.214	.242	.456	-70	0	1	0	1b15/lf	0	-0.9
McDonald, Donzell	Donzell B2.20.1975 Long Beach CA BB/TR/5'11"/180 Dr 1995 NYA 22/618 d4.19 b–Darnell Col Yavapai (AZ) JC																							
2001	NY A	5	3	0	1	0	0	0	0	0	0	0	2	.333	.333	.333	.666	-24	0	0	0	O3(1/2/0)	0	0.0
Total	2	15	25	3	5	2	0	0	1	4	0	0	7	.200	.300	.280	.580	-47	1	0	100	O10(8/2/0)	0	-0.3
McDougald, Gil	Gilbert James B5.19.1928 San Francisco CA BR/TR/6'1"/(175–180) d4.20 Col San Francisco																							
1951	†NY A	131	402	72	123	23	4	14	63	56	—	4	54	.306	.396	.488	.884	+43	14	5	74	3b82,2b55	0	2.1
1952	†NY A★	152	555	65	146	16	5	11	78	57	—	4	73	.263	.336	.369	.705	+2	6	5	55	3b117,2b38	0	1.9
1953	†NY A	141	541	82	154	27	7	10	83	60	—	5	65	.285	.361	.416	.777	+13	3	4	43	3b136,2b26	0	1.7
1954	NY A	126	394	66	102	22	2	12	48	62	—	5	64	.259	.364	.416	.780	+18	3	4	43	2b92,3b35	0	2.8
1955	†NY A	141	533	79	152	10	8	13	53	65	2	2	77	.285	.361	.407	.768	+9	6	4	60	2b126,3b17	0	3.7
1956	†NY A☆	120	438	79	136	13	3	13	56	68	1	3	59	.311	.405	.443	.848	+28	3	8	27	S92,2b31,3b5	0	3.5
1957	†NY A★	141	539	87	156	25	**9**	13	62	59	1	4	71	.289	.362	.442	.804	+21	2	5	29	S121,2b21,3b7	0	5.3
1958	†NY A★	138	503	69	126	19	1	14	65	59	1	3	75	.250	.329	.376	.705	-2	6	2	75	2b115,S19	0	1.3
1959	NY A★	127	434	44	109	16	8	4	34	35	3	3	40	.251	.309	.353	.662	-15	0	3	0	2b53,S52,3b25	0	0.4
1960	†NY A	119	337	54	87	16	4	8	34	38	0	3	45	.258	.337	.401	.738	+5	2	4	33	3b84,2b42	0	1.5
Total	10	1336	4676	697	1291	187	51	112	576	559	8	36	623	.276	.356	.410	.766	+12	45	44	51	2b599,3b508,S284	0	24.2
/150	1	150	525	78	145	21	6	13	65	63	0	4	70	.276	.356	.410	.766	+12	5	5	50	2b67,3b57,S32	0	2.7

YEAR	TM LG	G	AB	R	H	2B	3B	HR	RBI	BB	IB	HP	SO	AVG	OBP	SLG	OPS	AOPS	SB	CS	SB%	GAMES AT POSITION	DL	BFW
McFarland, Herm Hermas Walter B3.11.1870 Des Moines IA D9.21.1935 Richmond VA BL/TR/5'6"/150 d4.21																								
1903	NY A	103	362	41	88	16	9	5	45	46	—	3	—	.243	.333	.378	.711	+6	13	—	—	O103(39/58/7)	—	-0.5
Total	5	352	1278	204	340	61	28	13	167	175	—	17	14	.266	.362	.388	.750	+10	64	—	—	O348(189/140/22)/C	—	0.5
/150	1	150	527	60	128	23	13	7	66	67	—	4	0	.243	.333	.378	.711	+6	19	—	—	O150(57/84/10)	—	-0.7
McGuire, Deacon James Thomas B11.18.1863 Youngstown OH D10.31.1936 Duck Lake MI BR/TR/6'1"/185 d6.21 M6/C6																								
1904	NY A	101	322	17	67	12	2	0	20	27	—	3	—	.208	.276	.258	.534	-34	2	—	—	C97/1b	—	0.5
1905	NY A	72	228	9	50	7	2	0	33	18	—	5	—	.219	.291	.268	.559	-31	3	—	—	C71	—	-0.3
1906	NY A	51	144	11	43	5	0	0	14	12	—	3	—	.299	.365	.333	.698	+8	3	—	—	C49/1b	—	0.7
1907	NY A	1	1	0	0	0	0	0	0	0	—	0	—	.000	.000	.000	.000	-193	0	—	—	/C	—	0.0
Total	26	1782	6295	770	1750	300	79	45	840	515	—	84	215	.278	.341	.372	.713	+1	118	—	—	C1612,1b94,O33(4/4/25),3b5,S4/P	—	4.8
Team	4	225	695	37	160	24	4	0	67	57	—	11	0	.230	.299	.276	.575	-24	8	—	—	C218,1b2	—	0.9
/150	3	150	463	25	107	16	3	0	45	38	—	7	0	.230	.299	.276	.575	-24	5	—	—	C145/1	—	0.6
McIlveen, Irish Henry Cooke B7.27.1880 Belfast, Ireland D10.18.1960 Lorain OH BL/TL/5'11.5"/180 d7.4 Col Penn St.																								
1906	Pit N	5	5	1	2	0	0	0	0	0	—	0	—	.400	.400	.400	.800	+43	0	—	—	P2	—	0.0
1908	NY A	44	169	17	36	3	3	0	8	14	—	1	—	.213	.277	.266	.543	-24	6	—	—	O44(13/1/30)	—	-0.8
1909	NY A	4	3	0	0	0	0	0	0	1	—	0	—	.000	.250	.000	.250	-120	0	—	—	/H	—	0.0
Total	3	53	177	18	38	3	3	0	8	15	—	1	—	.215	.280	.266	.546	-24	6	—	—	O44(13/1/30),P2	—	-0.8
Team	2	48	172	17	36	3	3	0	8	15	—	1	0	.209	.277	.262	.539	-26	6	—	—	O44(13/1/30)	—	-0.8
McIntosh, Tim Timothy Allen B3.21.1965 Minneapolis MN BR/TR/5'11"/195 Dr 1986 MilA 3/61 d9.3 Col Minnesota																								
1996	NY A	3	3	0	0	0	0	0	0	0	0	0	0	.000	.000	.000	.000	-199	0	0	0	/C1b3b	0	-0.1
Total	5	71	117	12	21	5	0	2	10	3	0	2	22	.179	.211	.274	.485	-66	1	3	25	C25,O21(15/0/7),1b9,D5/3b	15	-1.2
McKechnie, Bill William Boyd "Deacon" B8.7.1886 Wilkinsburg PA D10.29.1965 Bradenton FL BB/TR/5'10"/160 d9.8 M25/C7 HF1962																								
1913	NY A	45	112	7	15	0	0	0	8	8	—	1	17	.134	.198	.134	.332	-102	2	—	—	2b28,S7,3b2	—	-1.1
Total	11	846	2843	319	713	86	33	8	240	190	—	15	199	.251	.301	.313	.614	-24	127	4	100	3b553,2b117,1b64,S60,O2(0/1/1)	—	-7.8
McKinney, Rich Charles Richard B11.22.1946 Piqua OH BR/TR/5'11"/185 Dr 1968 ChiA 1/14 d6.26 Col Ohio U. OF(6/0/27)																								
1972	NY A	37	121	10	26	2	0	1	7	7	0	0	13	.215	.258	.256	.514	-46	1	0	100	3b33	0	-1.0
Total	7	341	886	79	199	28	2	20	100	77	1	3	124	.225	.286	.328	.614	-27	4	3	57	3b85,2b80,1b33,O33R,D26,S11	0	-4.8
McManus, Frank Francis E. B9.21.1875 Lawrence MA D9.1.1923 Syracuse NY TR/5'7"/150 d9.14																								
1904	NY A	4	7	0	0	0	0	0	0	0	—	0	—	.000	.000	.000	.000	-196	0	—	—	C4	—	-0.2
Total	3	14	35	3	8	1	0	0	2	2	—	0	—	.229	.270	.257	.527	-50	3	—	—	C14	—	-0.2
McMillan, Norm Norman Alexis "Bub" B10.5.1895 Latta SC D9.28.1969 Marion SC BR/TR/6'0"/175 d4.12 Col Clemson OF(0/15/12)																								
1922	†NY A	33	78	7	20	1	2	0	11	6	—	0	10	.256	.310	.321	.631	-37	4	1	80	O26(0/15/12),3b5	—	-0.8
Total	5	413	1356	157	353	74	16	6	147	95	—	10	133	.260	.313	.352	.665	-31	36	10	100	3b229,2b90,S35,O26C,1b2	—	-3.8
McMillan, Tommy Thomas Law "Rebel" B4.18.1888 Pittston PA D7.15.1966 Orlando FL BR/TR/5'5"/130 d8.19 Col Georgia Tech																								
1912	NY A	41	149	24	34	2	0	0	12	15	—	1	—	.228	.303	.242	.545	-47	18	10	64	S41	—	-0.9
Total	4	297	991	73	207	21	4	0	54	81	—	7	33	.209	.273	.238	.511	-44	45	10	100	S280,O14C,2b2/3b	—	-6.5
McNally, Mike Michael Joseph "Minooka Mike" B9.13.1893 Minooka PA D5.29.1965 Bethlehem PA BR/TR/5'11"/150 d4.21 Mil 1918																								
1915	Bos A	23	53	7	8	0	1	0	0	3	—	0	7	.151	.196	.189	.385	-84	0	2	0	3b18,2b5	—	-0.8
1916	†Bos A	87	135	28	23	0	0	0	9	10	—	0	19	.170	.228	.170	.398	-80	9	—	—	2b35,3b14,S7/cf	—	-1.2
1917	Bos A	42	50	9	15	1	0	0	2	6	—	0	3	.300	.375	.320	.695	+13	3	—	—	3b14,S9,2b6	—	0.5
1919	Bos A	33	42	10	11	4	0	0	6	1	—	0	2	.262	.279	.357	.636	-17	4	—	—	S11,3b11,2b3	—	0.5
1920	Bos A	93	312	42	80	5	1	0	23	31	—	1	24	.256	.326	.279	.605	-36	13	10	57	2b76,S8,1b6	—	-2.2
1921	†NY A	71	215	36	56	4	2	1	24	14	—	0	15	.260	.306	.312	.618	-44	5	6	45	3b49,2b16	—	0.1
1922	†NY A	52	143	20	36	2	2	0	18	16	—	1	14	.252	.331	.294	.625	-37	3	0	100	3b34,2b9,S4/1b	—	-0.7
1923	NY A	30	38	5	8	0	0	0	1	3	—	0	4	.211	.268	.211	.479	-73	2	0	100	S13,3b7,2b5	—	-0.4
1924	NY A	49	69	11	17	0	0	0	2	7	—	0	5	.246	.316	.246	.562	-54	1	1	50	2b25,3b13,S6	—	0.0
1925	Was A	12	21	1	3	0	0	0	0	1	—	0	4	.143	.182	.143	.325	-117	0	0	0	3b7,S2/2b	—	-0.4
Total	10	492	1078	169	257	16	6	1	85	92	—	2	97	.238	.299	.267	.566	-46	40	19	100	2b181,3b167,S60,1b7/cf	—	-4.6
Team	4	202	465	72	117	6	4	1	45	40	—	1	38	.252	.312	.288	.600	-46	11	7	61	3b103,2b55,S23/1	—	-1.0
/150	3	150	345	53	87	4	3	1	33	30	—	1	28	.252	.312	.288	.600	-46	8	5	62	3b76,2b41,S17/1	—	-0.7
McQuinn, George George Hartley B5.29.1910 Arlington VA D12.24.1978 Alexandria VA BL/TL/5'11"/165 d4.14																								
1947	†NY A★	144	517	84	157	24	3	13	80	78	—	0	66	.304	.395	.437	.832	+32	0	2	0	1b142	0	1.8
1948	NY A★	94	302	33	75	11	4	11	41	40	—	0	38	.248	.336	.421	.757	+2	0	2	0	1b90	0	-0.5
Total	12	1550	5747	832	1588	315	64	135	794	712	—	8	634	.276	.357	.424	.781	+9	32	31	100	1b1529	0	-0.3
Team	2	238	819	117	232	35	7	24	121	118	—	0	104	.283	.374	.431	.805	+21	0	4	0	1b232	0	1.3
/150	1	150	516	74	146	22	4	15	76	74	—	0	66	.283	.374	.431	.805	+21	0	3	0	1b146	0	0.8
Meacham, Bob Robert Andrew B8.25.1960 Los Angeles CA BB/TR (BR 1987–88)/6'1"/(175–180) Dr 1981 StLN 1/8 d6.30 C2 Col San Diego St.																								
1983	NY A	22	51	5	12	2	0	0	4	4	0	1	10	.235	.304	.275	.579	-38	8	0	100	S18,3b4	0	0.5
1984	NY A	99	360	62	91	13	4	2	25	32	0	3	70	.253	.312	.328	.640	-18	9	5	64	S96,2b2	0	-1.1
1985	NY A	156	481	70	105	16	2	1	47	54	1	5	102	.218	.302	.266	.568	-41	25	7	78	S155	0	-2.7
1986	NY A	56	161	19	36	7	1	0	10	17	0	3	39	.224	.309	.280	.589	-38	3	6	33	S56	0	-0.8
1987	NY A	77	203	28	55	11	1	5	21	19	0	6	33	.271	.349	.409	.758	+1	6	5	55	S56,2b25/D	15	0.1
1988	NY A	47	115	18	25	9	0	0	7	14	0	2	22	.217	.308	.296	.604	-28	7	1	88	S24,2b21,3b5	81	-0.8
Total	6	457	1371	202	324	58	8	8	114	140	1	20	276	.236	.313	.308	.621	-27	58	24	71	S405,2b48,3b9/D	96	-4.8
/150	2	150	450	66	106	19	3	3	37	46	0	7	91	.236	.313	.308	.621	-27	19	8	70	S133,2b16,3b3/D	32	-1.6
Meara, Charlie Charles Edward "Goggy" B4.16.1891 New York NY D2.8.1962 Bronx NY BL/TR/5'10"/160 d6.1 Col Manhattan																								
1914	NY A	4	7	2	2	0	0	0	1	2	—	0	2	.286	.444	.286	.730	+20	0	1	0	O3(0/2/2)	—	0.0
Melvin, Bob Robert Paul B10.28.1961 Palo Alto CA BR/TR/6'4"/(205–210) Dr 1981 DetA*S1/2 d5.25 M5/C4 Col California																								
1994	NY A	9	14	2	4	0	0	1	3	0	0	0	3	.286	.286	.500	.786	+1	0	0	0	C4,1b4/D	29	-0.1
Total	10	692	1955	174	456	85	6	35	212	98	10	1	396	.233	.268	.337	.605	-32	4	13	24	C627,D24,1b11/3b	74	-7.7
Merkle, Fred Frederick Charles (b Carl Frederick Rudolf Merkle) B12.20.1888 Watertown WI D3.2.1956 Daytona Beach FL BR/TR/6'1"/190 d9.21 C2																								
1925	NY A	7	13	4	5	1	0	0	1	1	—	0	1	.385	.429	.462	.891	+28	1	0	100	1b5	—	0.0
1926	NY A	1	2	0	0	0	0	0	0	0	—	0	0	.000	.000	.000	.000	-199	0	0	0	/1b	—	-0.1
Total	16	1638	5782	720	1580	290	81	61	733	454	—	44	583	.273	.331	.383	.714	+9	272	38	100	1b1547,O46(11/29/8),2b3/3b	—	1.5
Team	2	8	15	4	5	1	0	0	1	1	—	0	1	.333	.375	.400	.775	+0	1	0	100	1b6	—	-0.1
Metheny, Bud Arthur Beauregard B6.1.1915 St.Louis MO D1.2.2003 Virginia Beach VA BL/TL/5'11"/190 d4.27 Col William and Mary																								
1943	†NY A	103	360	51	94	18	2	9	36	39	—	0	34	.261	.333	.397	.730	+13	2	3	40	O91R	0	-1.1
1944	NY A	137	518	72	124	16	1	14	67	56	—	2	57	.239	.316	.355	.671	-11	5	5	50	O132(11/0/121)	0	-2.5
1945	NY A	133	509	64	126	18	2	8	53	54	—	4	31	.248	.325	.338	.663	-12	5	2	71	O128R	0	-2.2
1946	NY A	3	3	0	0	0	0	0	0	0	—	0	0	.000	.000	.000	.000	-199	0	0	0	/H	0	-0.1
Total	4	376	1390	187	344	52	5	31	156	149	—	6	122	.247	.323	.359	.682	-6	12	10	55	O351(11/0/340)	0	-5.9
/150	2	150	555	75	137	21	2	12	62	59	—	2	49	.247	.323	.359	.682	-6	5	4	56	O140(4/0/136)	0	-2.4

YEAR	TM LG	G	AB	R	H	2B	3B	HR	RBI	BB	IB	HP	SO	AVG	OBP	SLG	OPS	AOPS	SB	CS	SB%	GAMES AT POSITION	DL	BFW
MEULENS, HENSLEY	HENSLEY FILEMON ACASIO "BAM-BAM" B6.23.1967 WILLEMSTAD, CURACAO BR/TR/6'3"/(190–217) d8.23																							
1989	NY A	8	28	2	5	0	0	0	1	2	0	0	8	.179	.233	.179	.412	-82	0	1	0	3b8	0	-0.2
1990	NY A	23	83	12	20	7	0	3	10	9	0	3	25	.241	.337	.434	.771	+13	1	0	100	O23L	0	0.3
1991	NY A	96	288	37	64	8	1	6	29	18	1	4	97	.222	.276	.319	.595	-36	3	0	100	O73(61/0/13),D13,1b7	0	-1.5
1992	NY A	2	5	1	3	0	0	1	1	1	0	0	0	.600	.667	1.200	1.867	+314	0	0	0	3b2	0	0.2
1993	NY A	30	53	8	9	1	1	2	5	8	0	0	19	.170	.279	.340	.619	-33	0	1	0	O24(22/0/1),1b3/3b	0	-0.5
1997	Mon N	16	24	6	7	1	0	2	6	4	0	0	10	.292	.379	.583	.962	+53	0	1	0	O8L,1b3	0	0.0
1998	Ari N	7	15	1	1	0	0	1	1	0	0	0	6	.067	.067	.267	.334	-118	0	0	0	O4R	0	-0.2
Total	7	182	496	67	109	17	2	15	53	42	1	7	165	.220	.288	.353	.641	-24	4	3	57	O132(114/0/18),1b13,D13,3b11	0	-1.9
Team	5	159	457	60	101	16	2	12	46	38	1	7	149	.221	.290	.344	.634	-25	4	2	67	O120(84/1/1),D13,3b11,1b10	0	-1.7
/150	5	150	431	57	95	15	2	11	43	36	1	7	141	.221	.290	.344	.634	-25	4	2	67	O113(79/1/1),D12,3b10,1b9	0	-1.6
MEUSEL, BOB	ROBERT WILLIAM "LONG BOB" B7.19.1896 SAN JOSE CA D11.28.1977 DOWNEY CA BR/TR/6'3"/190 d4.14 b–IRISH																							
1920	NY A	119	460	75	151	40	7	11	83	20	—	2	72	.328	.359	.517	.876	+26	4	4	50	O64(16/0/48),3b45,1b2	—	0.4
1921	†NY A	149	598	104	190	40	16	24	135	34	—	2	88	.318	.356	.559	.915	+28	17	6	74	O147(10/0/137)	—	1.3
1922	†NY A	121	473	61	151	26	11	16	84	40	—	3	58	.319	.376	.522	.898	+29	13	8	62	O121(47/1/74)	—	1.1
1923	†NY A	132	460	59	144	29	10	9	91	31	—	2	52	.313	.359	.478	.837	+17	13	15	46	O121(78/0/43)	—	-0.3
1924	NY A	143	579	93	188	40	11	12	120	32	—	5	43	.325	.365	.494	.859	+20	26	14	65	O143(93/2/49),3b2	—	0.1
1925	NY A	**156**	624	101	181	34	12	**33**	**138**	54	—	1	55	.290	.348	.542	.890	+25	13	14	48	O131(86/0/46),3b27	—	0.1
1926	†NY A	108	413	73	130	22	3	12	81	37	—	1	32	.315	.373	.470	.843	+21	16	17	48	O107(68/1/38)	—	-0.5
1927	†NY A	135	516	75	174	47	9	8	103	45	—	2	58	.337	.393	.510	.903	+37	24	10	71	O131(83/0/48)	—	1.5
1928	†NY A	131	518	77	154	45	5	11	113	39	—	2	56	.297	.349	.467	.816	+16	6	9	40	O131(87/0/44)	—	0.1
1929	NY A	100	391	46	102	15	3	10	57	17	—	0	42	.261	.292	.391	.683	-21	2	5	29	O96(56/0/40)	—	-2.0
1930	Cin N	113	443	62	128	30	8	10	62	26	—	1	63	.289	.330	.460	.790	-7	9	—	—	O112(70/39/4)	—	-1.4
Total	11	1407	5475	826	1693	368	95	156	1067	375	—	21	619	.309	.356	.497	.853	+19	143	10	100	O1304(694/43/571),3b74,1b2	—	0.4
Team	10	1294	5032	764	1565	338	87	146	1005	349	—	20	556	.311	.358	.500	.858	+21	134	102	57	O1192(26/4/95),3b74,1b2	—	1.8
/150	1	150	583	89	181	39	10	17	116	40	—	2	64	.311	.358	.500	.858	+21	16	12	57	O138(3/0/11),3b9/1	—	0.2
MICHAEL, GENE	EUGENE RICHARD "STICK" B6.2.1938 KENT OH BB/TR/6'2"/(182–185) d7.15 M4/C8 COL KENT ST.																							
1966	Pit N	30	33	9	5	2	1	0	2	0	0	0	7	.152	.152	.273	.425	-85	0	0	0	S8,2b2/3b	0	-0.3
1967	LA N	98	223	20	45	3	1	0	7	11	0	2	30	.202	.246	.224	.470	-61	1	3	25	S83	0	-2.5
1968	NY A	61	116	8	23	3	0	1	8	2	0	1	23	.198	.218	.250	.468	-57	3	2	60	S43/P	0	-1.2
1969	NY A	119	412	41	112	24	4	2	31	43	1	1	56	.272	.341	.364	.705	+1	7	4	64	S118	0	1.6
1970	NY A	134	435	42	93	10	1	2	38	50	5	0	93	.214	.292	.255	.547	-45	3	1	75	S123,3b4,2b3	0	-1.3
1971	NY A	139	456	36	102	15	0	3	35	48	8	3	64	.224	.299	.276	.575	-32	3	3	50	S136	0	2.2
1972	NY A	126	391	29	91	7	4	1	32	32	4	1	45	.233	.290	.279	.569	-28	4	2	67	S121	0	2.7
1973	NY A	129	418	30	94	11	1	3	47	26	0	0	51	.225	.270	.278	.548	-44	1	3	25	S129	0	-0.1
1974	NY A	81	177	19	46	9	0	0	13	14	0	0	24	.260	.313	.311	.624	-19	0	0	0	2b45,S39,3b2	0	0.3
1975	Det A	56	145	15	31	2	0	3	13	8	0	0	28	.214	.253	.290	.543	-49	0	0	0	S44,2b7,3b4	0	-0.5
Total	10	973	2806	249	642	86	12	15	226	234	18	8	421	.229	.288	.284	.572	-34	22	18	55	S844,2b57,3b11/P	0	0.9
Team	7	789	2405	205	561	79	10	12	204	215	18	6	356	.233	.296	.289	.585	-30	21	15	58	S709,2b48,3b6/P	0	4.2
/150	1	150	457	39	107	15	2	2	39	41	3	1	68	.233	.296	.289	.585	-30	4	3	57	S135,2b9/3P	0	0.8
MIDKIFF, EZRA	EZRA MILLINGTON "SALT ROCK" B11.13.1882 SALT ROCK WV D3.20.1957 HUNTINGTON WV BL/TR/5'10"/180 d10.5																							
1909	Cin N	1	2	0	0	0	0	0	0	0	—	0	—	.000	.000	.000	.000	-199	0	—	—	/3b	—	-0.1
1912	NY A	21	86	9	21	1	0	0	9	7	—	0	—	.244	.301	.256	.557	-44	4	4	50	3b21	—	-0.3
1913	NY A	83	284	22	56	9	1	0	14	12	—	1	33	.197	.232	.236	.468	-63	9	—	—	3b76,S4,2b2	—	-0.8
Total	3	105	372	31	77	10	1	0	23	19	—	1	33	.207	.247	.239	.486	-59	13	4	100	3b98,S4,2b2	—	-1.2
Team	2	104	370	31	77	10	1	0	23	19	—	1	33	.208	.249	.241	.490	-58	13	4	100	3b97,S4,2b2	—	-1.1
/150	3	150	534	45	111	14	1	0	33	27	—	1	48	.208	.249	.241	.490	-58	19	6	100	3b140,S6,2b3	—	-1.6
MIENTKIEWICZ, DOUG	DOUGLAS ANDREW B6.19.1974 TOLEDO OH BL/TR/6'2"/(193–205) DR 1995 MINA 5/128 d9.18 COL FLORIDA ST.																							
2007	†NY A	72	166	26	46	12	0	5	24	16	0	3	23	.277	.349	.440	.789	+5	0	0	0	1b70	90	-0.6
Total	10	942	3009	385	814	201	9	64	372	393	31	38	438	.271	.358	.407	.765	-2	14	15	48	1b918,O3R,D3,2b2/3b	217	-10.3
MILBOURNE, LARRY	LAWRENCE WILLIAM B2.14.1951 PORT NORRIS NJ BB/TR/6'0"/(153–165) d4.6 [DL 1985 SEA A 106]																							
1981	†NY A	61	163	24	51	7	2	1	12	9	2	1	14	.313	.351	.399	.750	+17	2	0	100	S39,2b14,3b3,D3	0	0.6
1982	NY A	14	27	2	4	1	0	0	0	1	0	0	4	.148	.179	.185	.364	-100	0	1	0	S9,2b3,3b3	0	-0.5
1983	NY A	31	70	5	14	4	0	0	2	5	0	1	10	.200	.263	.257	.520	-55	1	1	50	2b19,S6,3b4	0	-0.2
Total	11	989	2448	290	623	71	24	11	184	133	10	9	176	.254	.293	.317	.610	-30	41	33	55	2b471,S280,3b112,D29,O4L	121	-8.3
Team	3	106	260	31	69	12	2	1	14	15	2	2	28	.265	.309	.338	.647	-15	3	2	60	S54,2b36,3b10,D3	0	-0.1
/150	4	150	368	44	98	17	3	1	20	21	3	3	40	.265	.309	.338	.647	-15	4	3	57	S76,2b51,3b14,D4	0	-0.1
MILLER, ELMER	ELMER B7.28.1890 SANDUSKY OH D11.28.1944 BELOIT WI BR/TR/6'0"/175 d4.26																							
1912	StL N	12	37	5	7	1	0	0	3	4	—	0	9	.189	.268	.216	.484	-66	1	—	—	O11(4/3/4)	—	-0.3
1915	NY A	26	83	4	12	1	0	0	3	4	—	1	14	.145	.193	.157	.350	-95	0	—	—	O26(0/20/6)	—	-1.5
1916	NY A	43	152	12	34	3	2	1	18	11	—	1	18	.224	.280	.289	.569	-30	8	—	—	O42(18/9/15)	—	-0.5
1917	NY A	114	379	43	95	11	3	3	35	40	—	**9**	44	.251	.336	.319	.655	-1	11	—	—	O112(33/53/26)	—	-1.0
1918	NY A	67	202	18	49	9	2	1	22	19	—	3	17	.243	.317	.322	.639	-9	4	—	—	O62(3/53/6)	—	-0.5
1921	†NY A	56	242	41	72	9	8	4	36	19	—	3	16	.298	.356	.450	.806	+2	2	2	50	O56C	—	-0.4
1922	NY A	51	172	31	46	7	2	3	18	11	—	0	12	.267	.311	.384	.695	-21	2	3	40	O51(7/41/3)	—	-0.8
1922	Bos A	44	147	16	28	2	3	4	16	5	—	1	10	.190	.222	.327	.549	-58	3	1	75	O35(2/33/0)	—	-1.6
1922	Year	95	319	47	74	9	5	7	34	16	—	1	22	.232	.271	.357	.628	-38	5	4	56	O86(9/74/3)	—	-2.4
Total	7	413	1414	170	343	43	20	16	151	113	—	18	140	.243	.307	.335	.642	-20	31	6	100	O395(67/268/60)	—	-6.6
Team	6	357	1230	149	308	40	17	12	132	104	—	17	121	.250	.317	.340	.657	-14	27	5	100	O349(24/128/65)	—	-4.7
/150	3	150	517	63	129	17	7	5	55	44	—	7	51	.250	.317	.340	.657	-14	11	2	100	O147(10/54/27)	—	-2.0
MILLER, JOHN	JOHN ALLEN B3.14.1944 ALHAMBRA CA BR/TR/5'11"/(175–195) d9.11																							
1966	NY A	6	23	1	2	0	0	1	2	0	0	0	9	.087	.087	.217	.304	-116	0	0	0	1b3,O3L	0	-0.6
Total	2	32	61	4	10	1	0	2	3	2	0	0	18	.164	.190	.279	.469	-67	0	0	0	O9L,1b8,3b2/2b	0	-1.1
MILLS, BUSTER	COLONEL BUSTER "BUS" B9.16.1908 RANGER TX D12.1.1991 ARLINGTON TX BR/TR/5'11.5"/195 d4.18 MIL 1943–45 M1/C7 COL OKLAHOMA																							
1940	NY A	34	63	10	25	3	3	1	15	7	—	0	5	.397	.457	.587	1.044	+76	0	0	0	O14(12/0/2)	—	0.5
Total	7	415	1379	200	396	62	19	14	163	131	—	15	137	.287	.355	.390	.745	-9	23	21	100	O341(255/76/12)	0	-3.5
MILOSEVICH, MIKE	MICHAEL "MOLLIE" B1.13.1915 ZEIGLER IL D2.3.1966 E.CHICAGO IN BR/TR/5'10.5"/172 d4.30																							
1944	NY A	94	312	27	77	11	4	0	32	30	—	0	37	.247	.313	.308	.621	-25	1	2	33	S91	0	0.1
1945	NY A	30	69	5	15	2	0	0	7	6	—	1	6	.217	.289	.246	.535	-46	0	0	0	S22/2b	0	-0.3
Total	2	124	381	32	92	13	4	0	39	36	—	1	43	.241	.309	.297	.606	-29	1	2	33	S113/2b	0	-0.2
/150	2	150	461	39	111	16	5	0	47	44	—	1	52	.241	.309	.297	.606	-29	1	2	33	S137/2	0	-0.2
MIRANDA, WILLY	GUILLERMO (PEREZ) B5.24.1926 VELASCO, CUBA D9.7.1996 BALTIMORE MD BB/TR/5'9.5"/(150–160) d5.6																							
1953	NY A	48	58	12	13	0	0	1	5	5	—	0	10	.224	.286	.276	.562	-46	1	1	50	S45	0	0.6
1954	NY A	92	116	12	29	4	2	1	12	10	—	0	10	.250	.300	.345	.645	-18	0	3	0	S88,2b4/3b	0	0.8
Total	9	824	1914	176	423	50	14	6	132	165	11	2	250	.221	.282	.271	.553	-46	13	16	45	S768,3b23,2b12/1b	0	-4.1
Team	2	140	174	24	42	4	2	2	17	15	—	0	20	.241	.295	.322	.617	-27	1	4	20	S133,2b4/3	0	1.4
/150	2	150	186	26	45	4	2	2	18	16	—	0	21	.241	.295	.322	.617	-27	1	4	20	S143,2b4/3	0	1.5

YEAR	TM LG	G	AB	R	H	2B	3B	HR	RBI	BB	IB	HP	SO	AVG	OBP	SLG	OPS	AOPS	SB	CS	SB%	GAMES AT POSITION	DL	BFW
MITCHELL, FRED	Frederick Francis (b Frederick Francis Yapp) B6.5.1878 Cambridge MA D10.13.1970 Newton MA BR/TR/5'9.5"/185 d4.27 M7/C3 OF(1/2/0) ▲																							
1901	Bos A	20	44	5	7	0	2	0	4	2	—	0	—	.159	.196	.250	.446	-77	0	—	—	P17,2b2/S	—	-0.1
1902	Bos A	1	1	0	0	0	0	0	0	0	—	0	—	.000	.000	.000	.000	-197	0	—	—	/P	—	0.0
1902	Phi A	20	48	7	9	1	1	0	3	1	—	0	—	.188	.204	.250	.454	-76	1	—	—	P18/cf	—	0.1
1902	Year	21	49	7	9	1	1	0	3	1	—	0	—	.184	.200	.245	.445	-78	1	—	—	P19/cf	—	0.1
1903	Phi N	29	95	11	19	4	0	0	10	0	—	0	—	.200	.200	.242	.442	-73	0	—	—	P28	—	0.0
1904	Phi N	25	82	9	17	3	1	0	3	5	—	0	—	.207	.253	.268	.521	-37	1	—	—	P13,1b9,3b2/cf	—	0.0
1904	Bro N	8	24	3	7	1	1	0	6	1	—	1	—	.292	.346	.417	.763	+39	0	—	—	P8	—	0.0
1904	Year	33	106	12	24	4	2	0	9	6	—	1	—	.226	.274	.302	.576	-20	1	—	—	P21,1b9,3b2/cf	—	0.0
1905	Bro N	27	79	4	15	0	0	0	8	4	—	1	—	.190	.238	.190	.428	-70	0	[illegible]	[illegible]	[illegible]	—	-0.0
1910	NY A	68	196	16	45	7	2	0	18	9	—	3	—	.230	.274	.286	.560	-29	6	—	—	C62	—	-1.2
1913	Bos N	4	3	0	1	0	0	0	0	0	—	0	2	.333	.333	.333	.666	-11	0	—	—	/H	—	0.0
Total	7	202	572	55	120	16	7	0	52	22	—	5	2	.210	.245	.262	.507	-48	8	—	—	P97,C62,1b16,3b6,O3C,S2,2b2	—	-1.8
MITCHELL, JOHNNY	John Franklin B8.9.1894 Detroit MI D11.4.1965 Birmingham MI BB/TR/5'8"/155 d5.21																							
1921	NY A	13	42	4	11	1	0	0	2	4	—	0	4	.262	.326	.286	.612	-44	1	0	100	S7,2b5	—	-0.6
1922	NY A	4	4	1	0	0	0	0	0	0	—	0	1	.000	.000	.000	.000	-198	0	0	0	S4	—	-0.1
Total	5	329	1175	152	288	38	8	2	63	119	—	5	81	.245	.317	.296	.613	-38	14	14	50	S310,2b10	—	-3.6
Team	2	17	46	5	11	1	0	0	2	4	—	0	5	.239	.300	.261	.561	-56	1	0	100	S11,2b5	—	-0.7
MITCHELL, BOBBY	Robert Vance B10.22.1943 Norristown PA BR/TR/6'4"/(185–190) d7.5																							
1970	NY A	10	22	1	5	2	0	0	4	2	0	1	3	.227	.320	.318	.638	-20	0	2	0	O7(0/2/5)	0	0.0
Total	5	273	609	86	143	29	6	21	91	56	4	2	168	.235	.299	.406	.705	-1	14	15	48	O144(94/11/39),D83	0	-1.1
MIZE, JOHNNY	John Robert "The Big Cat" B1.7.1913 Demorest GA D6.2.1993 Demorest GA BL/TR/6'2"/(205–223) d4.16 Mil 1943–45 C1 HF1981 Col Piedmont																							
1949	†NY A	13	23	4	6	1	0	1	2	4	—	1	2	.261	.393	.435	.828	+19	0	0	0	1b6	0	0.0
1950	†NY A	90	274	43	76	12	0	25	72	29	—	2	24	.277	.351	.595	.946	+43	0	1	0	1b72	0	0.9
1951	†NY A	113	332	37	86	14	1	10	49	36	—	4	24	.259	.339	.398	.737	+2	1	0	100	1b93	0	-0.4
1952	†NY A	78	137	9	36	9	0	4	29	11	—	2	15	.263	.327	.416	.743	+12	0	0	0	1b27	0	0.2
1953	†NY A★	81	104	6	26	3	0	4	27	12	—	2	17	.250	.339	.394	.733	+1	0	0	0	1b15	0	-0.1
Total	15	1884	6443	1118	2011	367	83	359	1337	856	—	52	524	.312	.397	.562	.959	+57	28	1	100	1b1667,O8R	0	37.7
Team	5	375	870	99	230	39	1	44	179	92	—	11	82	.264	.342	.463	.805	+17	1	1	50	1b213	0	0.6
/150	2	150	348	40	92	16	0	18	72	37	—	4	33	.264	.342	.463	.805	+17	0	0	0	1b85	0	0.2
MOLE, FENTON	Fenton Le Roy "Muscles" B6.14.1925 San Leandro CA BL/TL/6'1.5"/200 d9.1																							
1949	NY A	10	27	2	5	2	1	0	2	3	—	0	5	.185	.267	.333	.600	-42	0	0	0	1b8	0	-0.1
MOLINA, JOSE	Jose Benjamin (Matta) B6.3.1975 Bayamon, PR BR/TR/6'1"/(195–245) Dr 1993 ChiN 14/390 d9.6 b–Bengie b–Yadier																							
2007	NY A	29	66	9	21	5	0	1	9	2	0	0	13	.318	.333	.439	.772	+2	0	0	0	C29	0	0.9
Total	8	402	1043	104	253	55	2	16	107	48	1	7	238	.243	.279	.345	.624	-36	9	4	69	C387,1b9,D5	42	2.5
MONDESI, RAUL	Raul Ramon (Avelino) B3.12.1971 San Cristobal, D.R. BR/TR/5'11"/(200–230) d7.19																							
2002	†NY A	71	270	39	65	18	0	11	43	28	2	2	46	.241	.315	.430	.745	-3	6	4	60	O70(0/11/59)/D	0	-1.0
2003	NY A	98	361	56	93	23	3	16	49	38	6	2	66	.258	.330	.471	.801	+10	17	7	71	O97R/D	0	0.4
Total	13	1525	5814	909	1589	319	49	271	860	475	50	41	1130	.273	.331	.485	.816	+13	229	92	71	O1502(34/160/1325),D16	108	5.2
Team	2	169	631	95	158	41	3	27	92	66	8	4	112	.250	.323	.453	.776	+4	23	11	68	O167(0/11/59),D2	0	-0.6
/150	2	150	560	84	140	36	3	24	82	59	7	4	99	.250	.323	.453	.776	+4	20	10	67	O148(0/10/52),D2	0	-0.5
MOORE, ARCHIE	Archie Francis B8.30.1941 Upper Darby PA BL/TL/6'2"/190 d4.20 Col Springfield																							
1964	NY A	31	23	4	4	2	0	0	1	2	0	0	9	.174	.240	.261	.501	-61	0	0	0	O8(0/5/3),1b7	0	-0.2
1965	NY A	9	17	1	7	2	0	1	4	4	1	0	4	.412	.524	.706	1.230	+148	0	0	0	O5(1/0/5)	0	0.4
Total	2	40	40	5	11	4	0	1	5	6	1	0	13	.275	.370	.450	.820	+28	0	0	0	O13(1/5/8),1b7	0	0.2
MOREHART, RAY	Raymond Anderson B12.2.1899 Terrell TX D1.13.1989 Dallas TX BL/TR/5'9"/157 d8.9 Col Austin																							
1924	Chi A	31	100	10	20	4	2	0	8	17	—	0	7	.200	.316	.280	.596	-44	3	1	75	S27,2b2	—	-1.2
1926	Chi A	73	192	27	61	10	3	0	21	11	—	1	15	.318	.358	.401	.759	+1	3	11	21	2b48	—	-0.7
1927	NY A	73	195	45	50	7	2	1	20	29	—	0	18	.256	.353	.328	.681	-20	4	4	50	2b53	—	-0.3
Total	3	177	487	82	131	21	7	1	49	57	—	1	40	.269	.347	.347	.694	-17	10	16	38	2b103,S27	—	-2.2
MORENO, OMAR	Omar Renan (Quintero) B10.24.1952 Puerto Armuelles, Pan BL/TL/6'2"/(170–188) d9.6																							
1983	NY A	48	152	17	38	9	1	1	17	8	0	0	31	.250	.287	.342	.629	-25	7	3	70	O48C	0	-0.7
1984	NY A	117	355	37	92	12	6	4	38	18	1	1	48	.259	.294	.361	.655	-16	20	11	65	O108C/D	0	-1.1
1985	NY A	34	66	12	13	4	1	1	4	1	0	0	16	.197	.209	.333	.542	-54	1	1	50	O26(3/19/4)/D	0	-0.2
Total	12	1382	4992	699	1257	171	87	37	386	387	41	17	885	.252	.306	.343	.649	-22	487	182	73	O1323(22/1221/83),D2	0	-10.4
Team	3	199	573	66	143	25	8	6	59	27	1	1	95	.250	.283	.353	.636	-23	28	15	65	O182(0/49/1),D2	0	-2.0
/150	2	150	432	50	108	19	6	5	44	20	1	1	72	.250	.283	.353	.636	-23	21	11	66	O137(0/37/1),D2	0	-1.5
MORIARTY, GEORGE	George Joseph B7.7.1885 Chicago IL D4.8.1964 Miami FL BR/TR/6'0"/185 d9.27 M2/U22 b–Bill																							
1906	NY A	65	197	22	46	7	7	0	23	17	—	1	—	.234	.298	.340	.638	-10	8	—	—	3b39,O15(14/2/0),1b5/2b	—	-0.3
1907	NY A	126	437	51	121	16	5	0	43	25	—	3	—	.277	.320	.336	.656	+1	28	—	—	3b91,1b22,O9(1/4/3),2b8/S	—	-0.7
1908	NY A	101	348	25	82	12	1	0	27	11	—	5	—	.236	.269	.276	.545	-24	22	—	—	1b52,3b28,O10(8/0/2),2b4	—	-0.4
Total	13	1075	3671	372	920	147	32	5	376	234	—	44	59	.251	.303	.312	.615	-16	251	25	100	3b796,1b180,O44(30/9/5),2b14/S	—	-5.4
Team	3	292	982	98	249	35	13	0	93	53	—	9	0	.254	.298	.316	.614	-10	58	—	—	3b158,1b79,O34(16/6/6),2b13/S	—	-1.4
/150	2	150	504	50	128	18	7	0	48	27	—	5	0	.254	.298	.316	.614	-10	30	—	—	3b81,1b41,O17(8/3/3),2b7/S	—	-0.7
MORONKO, JEFF	Jeffrey Robert B8.17.1959 Houston TX BR/TR/6'2"/190 Dr 1980 CleA 6/140 d9.1 Col Texas Wesleyan																							
1984	Cle A	7	19	1	3	1	0	0	3	3	0	0	5	.158	.273	.211	.484	-65	0	0	0	3b6/D	0	-0.2
1987	NY A	7	11	0	1	0	0	0	0	0	0	1	2	.091	.167	.091	.258	-129	0	0	0	3b3,S2,O2(1/0/1)	0	-0.2
Total	2	14	30	1	4	1	0	0	3	3	0	1	7	.133	.235	.167	.402	-88	0	0	0	3b9,O2(1/0/1),S2/D	0	-0.4
MORRIS, HAL	William Harold B4.9.1965 Fort Rucker AL BL/TL/6'4"/(195–215) Dr 1986 NYA 8/210 d7.29 Col Michigan																							
1988	NY A	15	20	1	2	0	0	0	0	0	0	0	9	.100	.100	.100	.200	-144	0	0	0	O4(3/0/2)/D	0	-0.4
1989	NY A	15	18	2	5	0	0	0	4	1	0	0	4	.278	.316	.278	.594	-31	0	0	0	O5(2/0/3),1b2/D	0	-0.1
Total	13	1246	3998	535	1216	246	21	76	513	356	55	22	548	.304	.361	.433	.794	+10	45	24	65	1b982,O61(56/0/6),D43	261	0.6
Team	2	30	38	3	7	0	0	0	4	1	0	0	13	.184	.205	.184	.389	-89	0	0	0	O9(5/0/5),1b2,D2	0	-0.5
MOSCHITTO, ROSS	Rosaire Allen B2.15.1945 Fresno CA BR/TR/6'2"/(175–177) d4.15 Mil 1966 Col Fresno (CA) City																							
1965	NY A	96	27	12	5	0	0	1	3	0	0	0	12	.185	.179	.296	.475	-65	0	0	0	O89(10/55/24)	0	-0.4
1967	NY A	14	9	1	1	0	0	0	0	1	0	0	2	.111	.200	.111	.311	-106	0	0	0	O8(2/4/2)	0	-0.1
Total	2	110	36	13	6	0	0	1	3	1	0	0	14	.167	.184	.250	.434	-75	0	0	0	O97(12/59/26)	0	-0.5
/150	3	150	49	18	8	0	0	1	4	1	0	0	19	.167	.184	.250	.434	-75	0	0	0	O132(16/80/35)	0	-0.7
MOSES, JERRY	Gerald Braheen B8.9.1946 Yazoo City MS BR/TR/6'3"/(205–215) d5.9																							
1973	NY A	21	59	5	15	2	0	0	3	2	0	0	6	.254	.270	.288	.558	-39	0	0	0	C17/D	0	0.2
Total	9	386	1072	89	269	48	8	25	109	63	19	8	184	.251	.295	.381	.676	-11	1	4	20	C328,1b4,D2,O2(1/0/1)	23	-0.7

YEAR	TM LG	G	AB	R	H	2B	3B	HR	RBI	BB	IB	HP	SO	AVG	OBP	SLG	OPS	AOPS	SB	CS	SB%	GAMES AT POSITION	DL	BFW
Mullen, Charlie Charles George B3.15.1889 Seattle WA D6.6.1963 Seattle WA BR/TR/5'10.5"/155 d5.18																								
1910	Chi A	41	123	15	24	2	1	0	13	4	—	0	—	.195	.220	.228	.448	-58	4	—	—	1b37,O2R	—	-0.9
1911	Chi A	20	59	7	12	2	1	0	5	5	—	0	—	.203	.266	.271	.537	-49	1	—	—	1b20	—	-0.4
1914	NY A	93	323	33	84	8	0	0	44	33	—	2	55	.260	.332	.285	.617	-14	11	17	39	1b93	—	-0.9
1915	NY A	40	90	11	24	1	0	0	7	10	—	0	12	.267	.340	.278	.618	-15	5	2	71	1b27	—	-0.1
1916	NY A	59	146	11	39	9	1	0	18	9	—	0	13	.267	.310	.342	.652	-6	7	—	—	2b20,1b17,O6(1/2/3)	—	-0.7
Total	5	253	741	77	183	22	3	0	87	61	—	2	80	.247	.306	.285	.591	-22	28	19	100	1b194,2b20,O8(1/2/5)	—	-3.0
Team	3	192	559	55	147	18	1	0	69	52	—	2	80	.263	.328	.299	.627	-12	23	19	100	1b137,2b20,O6(1/2/3)	—	-1.7
/150	2	150	437	43	115	14	1	0	54	41	—	2	63	.263	.328	.299	.627	-12	18	15	100	1b107,2b16,O5(1/2/2)	—	-1.3
Mumphrey, Jerry Jerry Wayne B9.9.1952 Tyler TX BB/TR/6'2"/(175–200) Dr 1971 StLN 4/79 d9.10																								
1981	†NY A	80	319	44	98	11	5	6	32	24	1	0	27	.307	.354	.429	.783	+27	14	9	61	O79C	0	1.3
1982	NY A	123	477	76	143	24	10	9	68	50	4	0	66	.300	.364	.449	.813	+24	11	3	79	O123C	42	1.6
1983	NY A	83	267	41	70	11	4	7	36	28	2	0	33	.262	.327	.412	.739	+7	2	3	40	O83C	0	0.7
Total	15	1585	4993	660	1442	217	55	70	575	478	49	4	688	.289	.349	.396	.745	+8	174	80	69	O1386(317/935/212)	58	3.9
Team	3	286	1063	161	311	46	19	22	136	102	7	0	126	.293	.351	.434	.785	+21	27	15	64	O285C	42	3.6
/150	2	150	558	84	163	24	10	12	71	53	4	0	66	.293	.351	.434	.785	+21	14	8	64	O149C	22	1.9
Munson, Thurman Thurman Lee B6.7.1947 Akron OH D8.2.1979 Canton OH BR/TR/5'11"/(190–195) Dr 1968 NYA 1/4 d8.8 Col Kent St.																								
1969	NY A	26	86	6	22	1	2	1	9	10	1	0	10	.256	.330	.349	.679	-6	0	1	0	C25	0	0.1
1970	NY A	132	453	59	137	25	4	6	53	57	6	7	56	.302	.386	.415	.801	+27	5	7	42	C125	0	3.9
1971	NY A★	125	451	71	113	15	4	10	42	52	1	7	65	.251	.335	.368	.703	+5	6	5	55	C117/rf	0	1.7
1972	NY A	140	511	54	143	16	3	7	46	47	5	3	58	.280	.343	.364	.707	+13	6	7	46	C132	0	2.0
1973	NY A★	147	519	80	156	29	4	20	74	48	4	4	64	.301	.362	.487	.849	+41	4	6	40	C142/D	0	4.9
1974	NY A★	144	517	64	135	19	2	13	60	44	12	1	66	.261	.316	.381	.697	+2	2	0	100	C137,D4	0	1.4
1975	NY A★	157	597	83	190	24	3	12	102	45	8	6	52	.318	.366	.429	.795	+27	3	2	60	C130,D22,1b2,O2(1/0/1)/3b	0	4.5
1976	†NY A★	152	616	79	186	27	1	17	105	29	6	9	38	.302	.337	.432	.769	+26	14	11	56	C121,D21,O11(2/0/9)	0	2.5
1977	†NY A★	149	595	85	183	28	5	18	100	39	8	2	55	.308	.351	.462	.813	+21	5	6	45	C136,D10	0	2.3
1978	†NY A✳	154	617	73	183	27	1	6	71	35	6	3	70	.297	.332	.373	.705	+1	2	3	40	C125,D14,O13R	0	1.3
1979	NY A	97	382	42	110	18	3	3	39	32	2	0	37	.288	.340	.374	.714	-5	1	2	33	C88,1b3,D5	0	0.4
Total	11	1423	5344	696	1558	229	32	113	701	438	59	42	571	.292	.346	.410	.756	+16	48	50	49	C1278,D77,O27(3/0/24),1b5/3b	0	25.0
/150	1	150	563	73	164	24	3	12	74	46	6	4	60	.292	.346	.410	.756	+16	5	5	50	C13,D8,O3R/13	0	2.6
Murcer, Bobby Bobby Ray B5.20.1946 Oklahoma City OK BL/TR/5'11"/(165–185) d9.8 Mil 1967–68 OF(56/789/839)																								
1965	NY A	11	37	2	9	0	1	1	4	5	0	0	12	.243	.333	.378	.711	+2	0	0	0	S11	0	0.8
1966	NY A	21	69	3	12	1	1	0	5	4	0	0	5	.174	.219	.217	.436	-73	2	2	50	S18	0	-0.9
1969	NY A	152	564	82	146	24	4	26	82	50	2	3	103	.259	.319	.454	.773	+19	7	5	58	O118(0/27/99),3b31	0	0.0
1970	NY A	159	581	95	146	23	3	23	78	87	5	2	100	.251	.348	.420	.768	+17	15	10	60	O155C	0	0.6
1971	NY A★	146	529	94	175	25	6	25	94	91	13	0	60	.331	**.427**	.543	.970	+82	14	8	64	O143C	0	4.5
1972	NY A★	153	585	**102**	171	30	7	33	96	63	7	2	67	.292	.361	.537	.898	+69	11	9	55	O151C	0	4.3
1973	NY A★	160	616	83	187	29	2	22	95	50	6	3	67	.304	.357	.464	.821	+33	6	7	46	O160C	0	1.5
1974	NY A★	156	606	69	166	25	4	10	88	57	10	2	59	.274	.332	.378	.710	+7	14	5	74	O156(0/59/101)	0	-0.5
1975	SF N★	147	526	80	157	29	4	11	91	91	6	2	45	.298	.396	.432	.828	+27	9	5	64	O144(0/2/143)	0	0.7
1976	SF N	147	533	73	138	20	2	23	90	84	10	4	78	.259	.362	.433	.795	+22	12	7	63	O146R	0	0.5
1977	Chi N	154	554	90	147	18	3	27	89	80	13	3	77	.265	.355	.455	.810	+6	16	7	70	O150R/2bS	0	-1.4
1978	Chi N	146	499	66	140	22	6	9	64	80	15	0	57	.281	.376	.403	.779	+6	14	5	74	O138(0/33/121)	0	-1.4
1979	Chi N	58	190	22	49	4	1	7	22	36	2	1	20	.258	.374	.400	.774	+2	2	3	40	O54R	0	0.0
1979	NY A	74	264	42	72	12	0	8	33	25	2	2	32	.273	.339	.409	.748	+3	1	1	50	O70(12/59/7)	0	-0.2
1979	Major	132	454	64	121	16	1	15	55	61	4	3	52	.267	4.357	.405	4.762	+159	3	4	43	—	0	-0.2
1980	†NY A	100	297	41	80	9	1	13	57	34	2	2	28	.269	.339	.438	.777	+16	2	0	100	O59(44/0/18),D33	0	0.0
1981	†NY A	50	117	14	31	6	0	6	24	12	1	0	15	.265	.331	.470	.801	+31	0	0	0	D33	0	0.4
1982	NY A	65	141	12	32	6	0	7	30	12	2	1	15	.227	.288	.418	.706	-6	2	1	67	D47	0	-0.3
1983	NY A	9	22	2	4	2	0	1	1	1	0	0	1	.182	.217	.409	.626	-30	0	0	0	D5	0	-0.1
Total	17	1908	6730	972	1862	285	45	252	1043	862	96	27	841	.277	.357	.445	.802	+24	127	75	63	O1644R,D118,3b31,S30/2b	0	8.5
Team	13	1256	4428	641	1231	192	29	175	687	491	50	17	564	.278	.349	.453	.802	+30	74	48	61	O1012(0/145/159),D118,3b31,S29	0	10.1
/150	2	150	529	77	147	23	3	21	82	59	6	2	67	.278	.349	.453	.802	+30	9	6	60	O121(0/17/19),D14,3b4,S3	0	1.2
Murray, Larry Larry B4.1.1953 Chicago IL BB/TR/5'11"/(179–180) Dr 1971 NYA 5/115 d9.7																								
1974	NY A	6	1	1	0	0	0	0	0	0	0	0	0	.000	.000	.000	.000	-199	0	1	0	O3(1/1/2)	0	-0.1
1975	NY A	6	1	1	0	0	0	0	0	0	0	0	0	.000	.000	.000	.000	-199	0	0	0	O4(2/1/1)	0	0.0
1976	NY A	8	10	2	1	0	0	0	2	1	0	0	2	.100	.182	.100	.282	-116	2	0	100	O7(0/6/1)	0	-0.1
Total	6	226	412	49	73	16	4	3	31	49	3	0	74	.177	.264	.257	.521	-56	20	10	67	O188(59/56/84),2b3,D3/S	0	-2.9
Team	3	20	12	4	1	0	0	0	2	1	0	0	2	.083	.154	.083	.237	-129	2	1	67	O14(3/8/4)	0	-0.2
Narron, Jerry Jerry Austin B1.15.1956 Goldsboro NC BL/TR/6'3"/(190–205) Dr 1974 NYA 6/132 d4.13 M5/C12																								
1979	NY A	61	123	17	21	3	1	4	18	9	0	0	26	.171	.226	.309	.535	-56	0	0	0	C56/D	0	-1.2
Total	8	392	840	64	177	23	2	21	96	67	8	4	127	.211	.270	.318	.588	-38	0	0	0	C311,D12,1b8	0	-6.3
Navarro, Dioner Dioner Favian (Vivas) B2.9.1984 Caracas, Distrito Capital, Venezuela BB/TR/5'10"/(190–215) d9.7																								
2004	NY A	5	7	2	3	0	0	0	1	0	0	0	0	.429	.429	.429	.858	+25	0	0	0	C4	0	0.0
Total	4	255	839	97	207	37	2	18	87	84	10	4	139	.247	.316	.360	.676	-22	5	2	71	C244	41	-0.8
Nettles, Graig Graig B8.20.1944 San Diego CA BL/TR/6'0"/(180–189) Dr 1965 MinA 4/74 d9.6 C2 b–Jim Col San Diego St. OF(58/2/13)																								
1967	Min A	3	3	0	1	1	0	0	0	0	0	0	0	.333	.333	.667	1.000	+75	0	0	0	/H	0	0.0
1968	Min A	22	76	13	17	2	1	5	8	7	1	1	20	.224	.298	.474	.772	+24	0	0	0	O16(2/1/13),3b5,1b3	0	0.1
1969	†Min A	96	225	27	50	9	2	7	26	32	1	1	47	.222	.319	.373	.692	-9	1	2	33	O54(53/1/0),3b21	0	-0.4
1970	Cle A	157	549	81	129	13	1	26	62	81	3	3	77	.235	.336	.404	.740	-1	3	1	75	3b154,O3L	0	2.6
1971	Cle A	158	598	78	156	18	1	28	86	82	6	3	56	.261	.350	.435	.785	+11	7	4	64	3b158	0	**5.9**
1972	Cle A	150	557	65	141	28	0	17	70	57	5	4	50	.253	.325	.395	.720	+10	2	3	40	3b150	0	1.6
1973	NY A	160	552	65	129	18	0	22	81	78	3	7	76	.234	.334	.386	.720	+5	0	0	0	3b157,D2	0	3.7
1974	NY A	155	566	74	139	21	1	22	75	59	8	3	75	.246	.316	.403	.719	+8	1	0	100	3b154/S	0	2.6
1975	NY A★	157	581	71	155	24	4	21	91	51	3	2	88	.267	.322	.430	.752	+14	1	3	25	3b157	0	2.0
1976	†NY A	158	583	88	148	29	2	**32**	93	62	6	4	94	.254	.327	.475	.802	+34	11	6	65	3b158/S	0	4.2
1977	†NY A★	158	589	99	150	23	4	37	107	68	8	3	79	.255	.333	.496	.829	+24	2	5	29	3b156/D	0	1.0
1978	†NY A★	159	587	81	162	23	2	27	93	59	6	6	69	.276	.343	.460	.803	+28	1	1	50	3b159,S2	0	1.4
1979	NY A★	145	521	71	132	15	1	20	73	59	6	0	53	.253	.325	.401	.726	-3	1	2	33	3b144	0	0.2
1980	†NY A★	89	324	52	79	14	0	16	45	42	5	1	42	.244	.331	.435	.766	+10	0	0	0	3b88/S	67	-0.4
1981	†NY A	103	349	46	85	7	1	15	46	47	4	1	49	.244	.333	.398	.731	+12	0	2	0	3b97,D4	0	0.7
1982	NY A	122	405	47	94	11	2	18	55	51	4	1	49	.232	.317	.402	.719	-2	1	5	17	3b113,D3	21	-0.6
1983	NY A	129	462	56	123	17	3	20	75	51	2	3	65	.266	.341	.446	.787	+19	0	1	0	3b126/D	0	0.1
1984	†SD N	124	395	56	90	11	1	20	65	58	4	5	55	.228	.329	.413	.742	+8	0	0	0	3b119	0	-0.8
1985	SD N★	137	440	66	115	23	1	15	61	72	5	0	59	.261	.363	.420	.783	+20	0	0	0	3b130	0	0.4
1986	SD N	126	354	36	77	9	0	10	55	41	8	2	62	.218	.300	.379	.679	-12	0	1	0	3b114	0	-1.2
1987	Atl N	112	177	16	37	8	1	5	33	22	4	0	25	.209	.294	.350	.644	-32	1	0	100	3b40,1b6	0	-0.0
1988	Mon N	80	93	5	16	4	0	1	14	9	2	0	19	.172	.240	.247	.487	-60	0	0	0	3b12,1b5	0	-1.0
Total	22	2700	8986	1193	2225	328	28	390	1314	1088	94	50	1209	.248	.329	.421	.750	+10	32	36	47	3b2412,O73L,1b14,D11,S5	88	21.2
Team	11	1535	5519	750	1396	202	20	250	834	627	55	31	739	.253	.329	.433	.762	+14	18	25	42	3b1509,D11,S5	88	14.9
/150	1	150	539	73	136	20	2	24	81	61	5	3	72	.253	.329	.433	.762	+14	2	2	50	3b147/DS	9	1.5

YEAR	TM LG	G	AB	R	H	2B	3B	HR	RBI	BB	IB	HP	SO	AVG	OBP	SLG	OPS	AOPS	SB	CS	SB%	GAMES AT POSITION	DL	BFW
NIARHOS, GUS CONSTANTINE GREGORY B12.6.1920 BIRMINGHAM AL D12.29.2004 HARRISONBURG VA BR/TR/6'0"/165 D6.9 C3																								
1946	NY A	37	40	11	9	1	1	0	2	11	—	0	2	.225	.392	.300	.692	-6	1	0	100	C29	0	0.5
1948	NY A	83	228	41	61	12	2	0	19	52	—	0	15	.268	.404	.338	.742	-1	1	3	25	C82	0	1.2
1949	†NY A	32	43	7	12	2	1	0	6	13	—	1	8	.279	.456	.372	.828	+20	0	0	0	C30	0	0.6
1950	NY A	1	0	0	0	0	0	0	0	0	—	0	0	+	+	+	.000	-100	0	0	0	/R	0	0.0
1950	Chi A	41	105	17	34	4	0	0	16	14	—	1	6	.324	.408	.362	.770	+1	0	0	0	C36	0	0.7
1950	Year	42	105	17	34	4	0	0	16	14	—	1	6	.324	.408	.362	.770	+1	0	0	0	C36	0	0.7
1951	Chi A	66	168	27	43	6	0	1	10	47	—	0	9	.256	.410	.310	.720	+1	4	3	57	C59	42	1.0
1952	Bos A	29	58	4	6	0	0	0	4	12	—	1	9	.103	.268	.103	.371	-94	0	0	0	C25	0	0.2
1953	Bos A	16	35	6	7	1	1	0	2	4	—	1	4	.200	.300	.286	.586	-44	0	1	0	C16	0	0.0
1954	Phi N	3	5	0	1	0	0	0	0	0	—	0	1	.200	.200	.200	.400	-95	0	0	0	C3	0	0.0
1955	Phi N	7	9	1	1	0	0	0	0	0	0	0	2	.111	.111	.111	.222	-142	0	0	0	C7	0	-0.1
Total	9	315	691	114	174	26	5	1	59	153	0	4	56	.252	.390	.308	.698	-11	6	7	46	C287	42	3.7
Team	4	153	311	59	82	15	4	0	27	76	—	1	25	.264	.410	.338	.748	+1	2	3	40	C141	0	2.3
/150	4	150	305	58	80	15	4	0	26	75	—	1	25	.264	.410	.338	.748	+1	2	3	40	C138	0	2.3
NIEVES, WILBERT WILBERT B9.25.1977 SAN JUAN, PR BR/TR/5'11"/190 DR 1995 SDN 47/1286 D7.21 B–MELVIN																								
2002	SD N	28	72	2	13	3	1	0	3	4	4	0	15	.181	.224	.250	.474	-73	1	0	100	C27	0	-0.7
2005	NY A	3	4	0	0	0	0	0	0	0	0	0	1	.000	.000	.000	.000	-199	0	0	0	C3	0	0.0
2006	NY A	6	6	0	0	0	0	0	0	0	0	0	1	.000	.000	.000	.000	-198	0	0	0	C6	0	-0.1
2007	NY A	26	61	6	10	4	0	0	8	2	0	0	9	.164	.190	.230	.420	-90	0	0	0	C25/1b	0	-1.2
Total	4	63	143	8	23	7	1	0	11	6	4	0	26	.161	.195	.224	.419	-90	1	0	100	C61/1b	0	-2.0
Team	3	35	71	6	10	4	0	0	8	2	0	0	11	.141	.164	.197	.361	-105	0	0	0	C34/1	0	-1.3
NILES, HARRY HERBERT CLYDE B9.10.1880 BUCHANAN MI D4.18.1953 STURGIS MI BR/TR/5'8"/175 D4.24																								
1908	NY A	95	361	43	90	14	6	4	24	25	—	4	—	.249	.305	.355	.660	+13	18	—	—	2b85,O7(1/1/5)	—	-1.4
Total	5	608	2270	279	561	58	24	12	152	163	—	30	—	.247	.306	.310	.616	-5	107	—	—	O298(95/19/184),2b214,3b52,S18	—	-4.5
NIXON, OTIS OTIS JUNIOR B1.9.1959 COLUMBUS CO. NC BB/TR/6'2"/180 DR 1979 NYA S1/3 D9.9 B–DONELL COL LOUISBURG (NC) JC																								
1983	NY A	13	14	2	2	0	0	0	0	1	0	0	5	.143	.200	.143	.343	-104	2	0	100	O9(0/4/5)	0	-0.1
Total	17	1709	5115	878	1379	142	27	11	318	585	10	5	694	.270	.343	.314	.657	-24	620	186	77	O1527(357/1136/72),D19/S	79	-8.2
NOKES, MATT MATTHEW DODGE B10.31.1963 SAN DIEGO CA BL/TR/6'1"/(185–210) DR 1981 SFN 20/503 D9.3																								
1985	SF N	19	53	3	11	2	0	2	5	1	0	1	9	.208	.236	.358	.594	-33	0	0	0	C14	0	-0.4
1986	Det A	7	24	2	8	1	0	1	2	1	1	0	1	.333	.360	.500	.860	+31	0	0	0	C7	0	0.2
1987	†Det A★	135	461	69	133	14	2	32	87	35	2	6	70	.289	.345	.536	.881	+34	2	1	67	C109,D19,O3(3/0/1),3b2	0	1.8
1988	Det A	122	382	53	96	18	0	16	53	34	3	1	58	.251	.313	.424	.737	+8	0	1	0	C110,D4	0	1.4
1989	Det A	87	268	15	67	10	0	9	39	17	1	2	37	.250	.298	.388	.686	-6	1	0	100	C51,D33	45	-0.5
1990	Det A	44	111	12	30	5	1	3	8	4	3	2	14	.270	.305	.414	.719	-1	0	0	0	D24,C19	0	-0.5
1990	NY A	92	240	21	57	4	0	8	32	20	3	4	33	.237	.307	.354	.661	-16	2	2	50	C46,D30,O2R	0	-0.9
1990	Year	136	351	33	87	9	1	11	40	24	6	6	47	.248	.306	.373	.679	-12	2	2	50	C65,D54,O2R	0	-1.4
1991	NY A	135	456	52	122	20	0	24	77	25	5	5	49	.268	.308	.469	.777	+12	3	2	60	C130,D3	0	0.3
1992	NY A	121	384	42	86	9	1	22	59	37	11	3	62	.224	.293	.424	.717	+0	0	1	0	C111	0	-1.0
1993	NY A	76	217	25	54	8	0	10	35	16	2	2	31	.249	.303	.424	.727	-3	0	0	0	C56,D11	16	-0.9
1994	NY A	28	79	11	23	3	0	7	19	5	0	0	16	.291	.329	.595	.924	+38	0	0	0	C17,1b4,D5	64	0.3
1995	Bal A	26	49	4	6	1	0	2	6	4	0	0	11	.122	.185	.265	.450	-84	0	0	0	C16,D2	0	-0.5
1995	Col N	10	11	1	2	1	0	0	0	1	1	0	4	.182	.250	.273	.523	-71	0	0	0	C3	35	-0.1
1995	Major	36	60	5	8	2	0	2	6	5	1	0	15	.133	1.200	.267	1.467	-73	0	0	0	—	35	-0.6
Total	11	902	2735	310	695	96	4	136	422	200	32	26	395	.254	.308	.441	.749	+6	8	7	53	C689,D131,O5(3/0/3),1b4,3b2	160	-0.8
Team	5	452	1376	151	342	44	1	71	222	103	21	14	191	.249	.304	.437	.741	+3	5	5	50	C360,D49,1b4,O2R	80	-2.2
/150	2	150	457	50	113	15	0	24	74	34	7	5	63	.249	.304	.437	.741	+3	2	2	50	C119,D16/1rf	27	-0.7
NOREN, IRV IRVING ARNOLD B11.29.1924 JAMESTOWN NY BL/TL/6'0"/(190–198) D4.18 C5 COL PASADENA (CA) CITY																								
1950	Was A	138	542	80	160	27	10	14	98	67	—	2	77	.295	.375	.459	.834	+18	5	2	71	O121C,1b17	0	1.8
1951	Was A	129	509	82	142	33	5	8	86	51	—	0	35	.279	.345	.411	.756	+5	10	7	59	O126C	0	1.2
1952	Was A	12	49	4	12	3	1	0	2	6	—	0	3	.245	.327	.347	.674	-9	1	0	100	O12C	0	0.1
1952	†NY A	93	272	36	64	13	2	5	21	26	—	6	34	.235	.316	.353	.669	-9	4	2	67	O60(18/18/25),1b19	0	-0.9
1952	Year	105	321	40	76	16	3	5	23	32	—	6	37	.237	.318	.352	.670	-9	5	2	71	O72(18/30/25),1b19	0	-0.8
1953	†NY A	109	345	55	92	12	6	6	46	42	—	2	39	.267	.350	.388	.738	+3	3	3	50	O96(21/44/38)	0	0.0
1954	NY A★	125	426	70	136	21	6	12	66	43	—	1	38	.319	.377	.481	.858	+40	4	6	40	O116(55/23/49)/1b	0	1.7
1955	†NY A	132	371	49	94	19	1	8	59	43	5	3	33	.253	.331	.375	.706	-8	5	2	71	O126(117/10/3)	0	-0.6
1956	NY A	29	37	4	8	1	0	0	6	12	2	0	7	.216	.408	.243	.651	-22	0	0	0	O10(4/0/6)/1b	77	-0.1
1957	KC A	81	160	8	34	8	0	2	16	11	2	1	19	.213	.267	.300	.567	-46	0	0	0	1b25,O6R	0	-1.3
1957	StL N	17	30	3	11	4	1	1	10	4	2	0	6	.367	.429	.667	1.096	+89	0	1	0	O8(1/0/7)	0	0.2
1957	Major	98	190	11	45	12	1	3	26	15	4	1	25	.237	1.296	.358	1.654	-35	0	1	0	—	0	-1.1
1958	StL N	117	178	24	47	9	1	4	22	13	2	4	21	.264	.327	.393	.720	-13	0	1	0	O77(59/14/10)	0	-0.8
1959	StL N	8	8	0	1	1	0	0	0	0	0	0	2	.125	.125	.250	.375	-103	0	0	0	O2L/1b	0	-0.1
1959	Chi N	65	156	27	50	6	2	4	19	13	1	3	24	.321	.384	.462	.846	+25	2	0	100	O40(16/6/18)/1b	0	0.9
1959	Year	73	164	27	51	7	2	4	19	13	1	3	26	.311	.372	.451	.823	+18	2	0	100	O42(18/6/18),1b2	0	0.8
1960	Chi N	12	11	0	1	0	0	0	1	3	0	0	4	.091	.286	.091	.377	-91	0	0	0	/1brf	0	-0.2
1960	LA N	26	25	1	5	0	0	1	1	1	0	0	8	.200	.231	.320	.551	-54	0	0	0	/H	0	-0.2
1960	Year	38	36	1	6	0	0	1	2	4	0	0	12	.167	.250	.250	.500	-64	0	0	0	/1brf	0	-0.4
Total	11	1093	3119	443	857	157	35	65	453	335	14	22	350	.275	.348	.410	.758	+6	34	24	59	O801(293/374/163),1b66	77	1.7
Team	5	488	1451	214	394	66	15	31	198	166	7	12	151	.272	.348	.402	.750	+8	16	13	55	O408(215/95/121),1b21	77	0.1
/150	2	150	446	66	121	20	5	10	61	51	2	4	46	.272	.348	.402	.750	+8	5	4	56	O125(66/29/37),1b6	24	0.0
NUNAMAKER, LES LESLIE GRANT B1.25.1889 AURORA NE D11.14.1938 HASTINGS NE BR/TR/6'2"/190 D4.28																								
1911	Bos A	62	183	18	47	4	3	0	19	12	—	0	—	.257	.303	.311	.614	-28	1	—	—	C59	—	0.1
1912	Bos A	35	103	15	26	5	2	0	6	6	—	3	—	.252	.313	.340	.653	-18	2	2	50	C35	—	-0.1
1913	Bos A	29	65	9	14	5	2	0	9	8	—	1	8	.215	.311	.354	.665	-8	2	—	—	C27	—	0.3
1914	Bos A	5	5	0	1	0	0	0	0	1	—	0	0	.200	.333	.200	.533	-39	0	—	—	C3/1b	—	0.0
1914	NY A	87	257	19	68	10	3	2	29	22	—	2	34	.265	.327	.350	.677	+4	11	9	55	C70,1b5	—	1.0
1914	Year	92	262	19	69	10	3	2	29	23	—	2	34	.263	.328	.347	.675	+3	11	9	55	C73,1b6	—	1.0
1915	NY A	87	249	24	56	6	3	0	17	23	—	1	24	.225	.293	.273	.566	-30	3	2	60	C77,1b2	—	-0.8
1916	NY A	91	260	25	77	14	7	0	28	34	—	1	21	.296	.380	.404	.784	+33	4	—	—	C79	—	2.1
1917	NY A	104	310	22	81	9	2	0	33	21	—	1	25	.261	.310	.303	.613	-14	5	—	—	C91	—	0.5
1918	StL A	85	274	22	71	9	2	0	22	28	—	5	16	.259	.339	.307	.646	-2	6	—	—	C81/1brf	—	0.4
1919	Cle A	26	56	6	14	1	1	0	7	2	—	0	6	.250	.276	.304	.580	-41	0	—	—	C16	—	-0.5
1920	†Cle A	34	54	10	18	3	3	0	14	4	—	0	5	.333	.379	.500	.879	+28	1	0	100	C17,1b6	—	0.4
1921	Cle A	46	131	16	47	7	2	0	25	11	—	0	8	.359	.408	.443	.851	+15	1	1	50	C46	—	0.7
1922	Cle A	25	43	8	13	2	0	0	7	4	—	0	3	.302	.362	.349	.711	-15	0	0	0	C13	—	-0.3
Total	12	716	1990	194	533	75	30	2	216	176	—	14	150	.268	.332	.339	.671	-5	36	14	100	C614,1b15/rf	—	3.8
Team	4	369	1076	90	282	39	15	2	107	100	—	5	104	.262	.328	.332	.660	-2	23	11	100	C317,1b7	—	2.8
/150	2	150	437	37	115	16	6	1	43	41	—	2	42	.262	.328	.332	.660	-2	9	4	100	C129,1b3	—	1.1

Batters

YEAR	TM LG	G	AB	R	H	2B	3B	HR	RBI	BB	IB	HP	SO	AVG	OBP	SLG	OPS	AOPS	SB	CS	SB%	GAMES AT POSITION	DL	BFW
Oates, Johnny Johnny Lane B1.21.1946 Sylva NC D12.24.2004 Richmond VA BL/TR/5'11"/(185–190) Dr 1967 BalA*S1/10 d9.17 Mil 1970 M11/C7 Col VPI																								
1980	NY A	39	64	6	12	3	0	1	3	2	0	1	3	.188	.224	.281	.505	-62	1	2	33	C39	0	-0.8
1981	NY A	10	26	4	5	1	0	0	0	2	0	0	0	.192	.250	.231	.481	-60	0	0	0	C10	0	-0.4
Total	11	593	1637	146	410	56	2	14	126	141	38	2	149	.250	.309	.313	.622	-28	11	19	37	C533	95	-2.4
Team	2	49	90	10	17	4	0	1	3	4	0	1	3	.189	.232	.267	.499	-61	1	2	33	C49	0	-1.2
O'Berry, Mike Preston Michael B4.20.1954 Birmingham AL BR/TR/6'2"/(190–195) Dr 1975 BosA 22/516 d4.8 Col South Alabama																								
1984	NY A	13	32	3	8	2	0	0	5	2	0	0	2	.250	.294	.313	.607	-30	0	0	0	C12/3b	0	-0.1
Total	7	197	376	38	72	10	1	3	27	43	0	1	77	.191	.274	.247	.521	-54	1	0	100	C196/3b	0	-2.8
O'Connor, Jack John Joseph "Rowdy Jack","Peach Pie" B6.2.1869 St.Louis MO D11.14.1937 St.Louis MO BR/TR/5'10"/170 d4.20 M1 OF(42/113/217)																								
1903	NY A	64	212	13	43	4	1	0	12	8	—	1	—	.203	.235	.231	.466	-62	4	—	—	C63/1b	—	-0.9
Total	21	1452	5383	714	1418	201	66	19	738	302	—	35	152	.263	.307	.336	.643	-21	219	—	—	C861,O372R,1b208,S8,2b6,3b2	—	-5.6
O'Connor, Paddy Patrick Francis B8.4.1879 Co. Kerry, Ireland D8.17.1950 Springfield MA BR/TR/5'8"/168 d4.17 C4																								
1918	NY A	1	3	0	1	0	0	0	0	0	—	0	1	.333	.333	.333	.666	-1	0	—	—	/C	—	0.0
Total	6	108	267	17	60	11	1	0	21	17	—	2	34	.225	.276	.273	.549	-43	4	—	—	C82/3b	—	-0.9
Odom, Heinie Herman Boyd B10.13.1900 Rusk TX D8.31.1970 Rusk TX BB/TR/6'0"/170 d4.22 Col Texas																								
1925	NY A	1	1	0	1	0	0	0	0	0	—	0	0	1.000	1.000	1.000	2.000	+316	0	0	0	/3b	—	0.1
O'Doul, Lefty Francis Joseph B3.4.1897 San Francisco CA D12.7.1969 San Francisco CA BL/TL/6'0"/180 d4.29 ▲																								
1919	NY A	19	16	2	4	0	0	0	1	1	—	0	2	.250	.294	.250	.544	-47	1	—	—	P3/rf	—	-0.1
1920	NY A	13	12	2	2	1	0	0	1	1	—	0	1	.167	.231	.250	.481	-74	0	0	0	P2/cf	—	-0.1
1922	NY A	8	9	0	3	1	0	0	4	0	—	0	2	.333	.333	.444	.777	-1	0	0	0	P6	—	0.0
Total	11	970	3264	624	1140	175	41	113	542	333	—	23	122	.349	.413	.532	.945	+42	36	0	100	O804(744/1/59),P34	—	12.6
Team	3	40	37	4	9	2	0	0	6	2	—	0	5	.243	.282	.297	.579	-45	1	0	100	P11,O2(0/1/1)	—	-0.2
Office, Rowland Rowland Johnie B10.25.1952 Sacramento CA BL/TL/6'0"/(165–170) Dr 1970 AtlN 4/94 d8.5																								
1983	NY A	2	2	0	0	0	0	0	1	0	0	0	0	.000	.000	.000	.000	-199	0	0	0	O2C	0	-0.1
Total	11	899	2413	259	626	101	11	32	242	189	15	16	311	.259	.315	.350	.665	-20	27	30	47	O771(7/687/80)/1b	145	-11.7
Oldring, Rube Reuben Henry B5.30.1884 New York NY D9.9.1961 Bridgeton NJ BR/TR/5'10"/186 d10.2 OF(455/627/48)																								
1905	NY A	8	30	2	9	0	1	1	6	2	—	0	—	.300	.344	.467	.811	+40	4	—	—	S8	—	0.5
1916	NY A	43	158	17	37	8	0	1	12	12	—	0	13	.234	.288	.304	.592	-24	6	—	—	O43(0/2/41)	—	-1.1
Total	13	1239	4690	616	1268	205	76	27	471	206	—	45	125	.270	.307	.364	.671	+3	197	36	100	O1130C,3b59,S16,2b4,1b2	—	-10.2
Team	2	51	188	19	46	8	1	2	18	14	—	0	13	.245	.297	.330	.627	-14	10	—	—	O43(0/2/41),S8	—	-0.6
Olerud, John John Garrett B8.5.1968 Seattle WA BL/TL/6'5"/(205–225) Dr 1989 TorA 3/79 d9.3 Col Washington St.																								
2004	†NY A	49	164	16	46	7	0	4	26	21	1	2	20	.280	.367	.396	.763	+0	0	0	0	1b47	0	-0.5
Total	17	2234	7592	1139	2239	500	13	255	1230	1275	15	88	1016	.295	.398	.465	.863	+29	11	14	44	1b2053,D133	16	24.5
Oliver, Joe Joseph Melton B7.24.1965 Memphis TN BR/TR/6'3"/(210–220) Dr 1983 CinN 2/41 d7.15																								
2001	NY A	12	36	3	9	1	0	1	2	1	0	0	12	.250	.263	.361	.624	-36	0	0	0	C12	0	0.0
Total	13	1076	3367	320	831	174	3	102	476	248	52	15	637	.247	.299	.391	.690	-18	13	13	50	C1033,1b25,D7,O4(2/0/2)	154	-2.5
Oliver, Nate Nathaniel "Peewee" B12.13.1940 St.Petersburg FL BR/TR/5'10"/160 d4.9																								
1969	NY A	1	1	0	0	0	0	0	0	0	0	0	0	.000	.000	.000	.000	-199	0	0	0	/H	0	0.0
Total	7	410	954	107	216	24	5	2	45	72	8	5	172	.226	.283	.268	.551	-38	17	15	53	2b291,S50,3b2/lf	77	-4.1
Oliver, Bob Robert Lee B2.8.1943 Shreveport LA BR/TR/6'2"/(205–215) d9.10 s–Darren Col American River (CA) CC OF(15/48/165)																								
1975	NY A	18	38	3	5	1	0	0	1	1	0	0	9	.132	.154	.158	.312	-112	0	0	0	1b8/3bD	0	-0.7
Total	8	847	2914	293	745	102	19	94	419	156	26	19	562	.256	.295	.400	.695	+0	17	14	55	1b423,O224R,3b152,D17	0	-8.3
O'Neill, Paul Paul Andrew B2.25.1963 Columbus OH BL/TL/6'4"/(200–215) Dr 1981 CinN 4/93 d9.3																								
1985	Cin N	5	12	1	4	1	0	0	1	0	0	0	2	.333	.333	.417	.750	+3	0	0	0	O2L	0	0.1
1986	Cin N	3	2	0	0	0	0	0	0	1	0	0	1	.000	.333	.000	.333	-100	0	0	0	/H	0	0.0
1987	Cin N	84	160	24	41	14	1	7	28	18	1	0	29	.256	.331	.488	.819	+9	2	1	67	O42(14/10/22),1b2/P	0	0.1
1988	Cin N	145	485	58	122	25	3	16	73	38	5	2	65	.252	.306	.414	.720	+2	8	6	57	O118(0/8/114),1b21	0	-0.4
1989	Cin N	117	428	49	118	24	2	15	74	46	8	2	64	.276	.346	.446	.792	+22	20	5	80	O115(0/4/115)	42	1.2
1990	†Cin N	145	503	59	136	28	0	16	78	53	13	2	103	.270	.339	.421	.760	+5	13	11	54	O141(0/1/141)	0	0.2
1991	Cin N★	152	532	71	136	36	0	28	91	73	14	1	107	.256	.346	.481	.827	+25	12	7	63	O150R	0	2.4
1992	Cin N	148	496	59	122	19	1	14	66	77	15	2	85	.246	.346	.373	.719	+2	6	3	67	O143R	0	0.9
1993	NY A	141	498	71	155	34	1	20	75	44	5	2	69	.311	.367	.504	.871	+36	2	4	33	O138(46/0/103),D2	0	1.0
1994	NY A★	103	368	68	132	25	1	21	83	72	13	0	56	**.359**	.460	.603	1.063	+79	5	4	56	O99(12/0/90),D4	0	4.0
1995	†NY A★	127	460	82	138	30	4	22	96	71	8	1	76	.300	.387	.526	.913	+38	1	2	33	O121(25/0/107),D4	16	1.5
1996	†NY A	150	546	89	165	35	1	19	91	102	8	4	76	.302	.411	.474	.885	+24	0	1	0	O146R/1bD	0	2.0
1997	†NY A★	149	553	89	179	42	0	21	117	75	8	0	92	.324	.399	.514	.913	+39	10	7	59	O146R,1b2,D2	0	2.5
1998	†NY A★	152	602	95	191	40	2	24	116	57	2	2	103	.317	.372	.510	.882	+34	15	1	94	O150R/D	0	2.5
1999	†NY A	153	597	70	170	39	4	19	110	66	1	2	89	.285	.353	.459	.812	+8	11	9	55	O151R	0	0.1
2000	†NY A	142	566	79	160	26	0	18	100	51	2	0	90	.283	.336	.424	.760	-6	14	9	61	O140R,D2	0	-0.7
2001	†NY A	137	510	77	136	33	1	21	70	48	4	2	59	.267	.330	.459	.789	+5	22	3	88	O130R,D6	0	-0.8
Total	17	2053	7318	1041	2105	451	21	281	1269	892	10	22	1166	.288	.363	.470	.833	+21	141	73	66	O1932(99/23/1848),1b26,D24/P	58	16.6
Team	9	1254	4700	720	1426	304	14	185	858	586	51	13	710	.303	.377	.492	.869	+27	80	40	67	O1221(63/0/301),D22,1b3	16	12.1
/150	1	150	562	86	171	36	2	22	103	70	6	2	85	.303	.377	.492	.869	+27	10	5	67	O146(8/0/36),D3/1	2	1.4
O'Neill, Steve Stephen Francis B7.6.1891 Minooka PA D1.26.1962 Cleveland OH BR/TR/5'10"/165 d9.18 M14/C4 b–Jim b–Jack b–Mike																								
1925	NY A	35	91	7	26	5	0	1	13	10	—	1	3	.286	.363	.374	.737	-11	0	0	0	C31	—	0.2
Total	17	1590	4795	448	1259	248	34	13	537	592	—	43	383	.263	.349	.337	.686	-12	30	26	100	C1532/1b	—	8.5
O'Rourke, Queenie James Stephen B12.26.1883 Bridgeport CT D12.22.1955 Sparrows Point MD BR/TR/5'7"/150 d8.15 f–Jim Col Holy Cross																								
1908	NY A	34	108	5	25	1	0	0	3	4	—	0	—	.231	.259	.241	.500	-38	4	—	—	O14L,S11,2b4,3b3	—	-0.9
Orth, Al Albert Lewis "Smiling Al","The Curveless Wonder" B9.5.1872 Tipton IN D10.8.1948 Lynchburg VA BL/TR/6'0"/200 d8.15 U6 Col DePauw ▲																								
1895	Phi N	11	45	8	16	4	0	1	13	1	—	0	6	.356	.370	.511	.881	+25	0	—	—	P11	—	0.0
1896	Phi N	25	82	12	21	3	3	1	13	3	—	0	11	.256	.282	.402	.684	-20	2	—	—	P25	—	0.0
1897	Phi N	53	152	26	50	7	4	1	17	3	—	0	—	.329	.342	.447	.789	+10	5	—	—	P36,O6(3/3/0)	—	0.0
1898	Phi N	39	123	17	36	6	4	1	14	3	—	0	—	.293	.310	.431	.741	+17	1	—	—	P32/rf	—	0.0
1899	Phi N	22	62	5	13	3	1	1	5	1	—	0	—	.210	.222	.339	.561	-45	2	—	—	P21/lf	—	-0.2
1900	Phi N	39	129	6	40	4	1	1	21	2	—	1	—	.310	.326	.380	.706	-5	2	—	—	P33,O3C	—	0.0
1901	Phi N	41	128	14	36	6	0	1	15	3	—	1	—	.281	.303	.352	.655	-12	3	—	—	P35,O4C	—	0.1
1902	Was A	56	175	20	38	3	2	2	10	9	—	0	—	.217	.255	.291	.546	-49	2	—	—	P38,O13(1/4/8)/1bS	—	-0.3
1903	Was A	55	102	19	40	0	7	0	11	4	—	1	—	.302	.323	.444	.767	+26	3	—	—	P36,S7,O4(2/0/2),1b2	—	-0.1
1904	Was A	31	102	7	22	3	1	0	11	1	—	2	—	.216	.238	.265	.503	-40	2	—	—	O18(12/6/0),P10	—	-0.8
1904	NY A	24	64	6	19	1	1	0	7	0	—	1	—	.297	.308	.344	.652	+1	2	—	—	P20,O2(0/1/1)	—	0.0
1904	Year	55	166	13	41	4	2	0	18	1	—	3	—	.247	.265	.295	.560	-24	4	—	—	P30,O20(12/7/1)	—	-0.8
1905	NY A	55	131	13	24	3	1	1	8	4	—	1	—	.183	.213	.244	.457	-60	2	—	—	P40/1brf	—	-0.1
1906	NY A	47	135	12	37	2	2	1	17	6	—	0	—	.274	.305	.341	.646	-7	2	—	—	P45/rf	—	0.0

YEAR	TM LG	G	AB	R	H	2B	3B	HR	RBI	BB	IB	HP	SO	AVG	OBP	SLG	OPS	AOPS	SB	CS	SB%	GAMES AT POSITION	DL	BFW
1907	NY A	44	105	11	34	6	0	1	13	4	—	1	—	.324	.355	.410	.765	+33	1	—	—	P36/lf	—	0.1
1908	NY A	38	69	4	20	1	2	0	4	2	—	0	—	.290	.310	.362	.672	+17	0	—	—	P21	—	0.0
1909	NY A	22	34	3	9	0	1	0	5	5	—	0	—	.265	.359	.324	.683	+15	1	—	—	2b6/P	—	-0.1
Total	15	602	1698	183	464	61	30	12	184	51	—	8	17	.273	.298	.366	.664	-9	30	—	—	P440,O55(20/21/14),S8,2b6,1b4	—	-1.4
Team	6	230	538	49	143	13	7	3	54	21	—	3	0	.266	.297	.333	.630	-7	8	—	—	P163,2b6,O5(0/1/1)/1	—	-0.1
/150	4	150	351	32	93	8	5	2	35	14	—	2	0	.266	.297	.333	.630	-7	5	—	—	P106,2b4,O3(0/1/1)/1	—	-0.1

OSTEEN, CHAMP JAMES CHAMPLIN B2.24.1877 HENDERSONVILLE NC D12.14.1962 GREENVILLE SC BL/TR/5'8"/150 d9.18 COL ERSKINE

YEAR	TM LG	G	AB	R	H	2B	3B	HR	RBI	BB	IB	HP	SO	AVG	OBP	SLG	OPS	AOPS	SB	CS	SB%	GAMES AT POSITION	DL	BFW
1903	Was A	10	40	4	8	0	2	0	1	2	—	1	—	.200	.256	.300	.556	-35	0	—	—	S10	—	-0.1
1904	NY A	28	107	15	21	1	4	2	9	1	—	2	—	.196	.218	.336	.554	-29	0	—	—	3b17,S8,1b4	—	-0.5
1908	StL N	29	112	2	22	4	0	0	11	0	—	1	—	.196	.204	.232	.436	-59	0	—	—	S17,3b12	—	-1.4
1909	StL N	16	45	6	9	1	0	0	7	7	—	0	—	.200	.308	.222	.530	-31	1	—	—	S16	—	-0.6
Total	4	83	304	27	60	6	6	2	31	10	—	4	—	.197	.233	.276	.509	-40	1	—	—	S51,3b29,1b4	—	-2.6

OTIS, BILL PAUL FRANKLIN B12.24.1889 SCITUATE MA D12.15.1990 DULUTH MN BL/TR/5'10.5"/150 d7.4 COL WILLIAMS

YEAR	TM LG	G	AB	R	H	2B	3B	HR	RBI	BB	IB	HP	SO	AVG	OBP	SLG	OPS	AOPS	SB	CS	SB%	GAMES AT POSITION	DL	BFW
1912	NY A	4	17	1	1	0	0	0	2	3	—	0	—	.059	.200	.059	.259	-124	0	1	0	O4C	—	-0.4

OWEN, SPIKE SPIKE DEE B4.19.1961 CLEBURNE TX BB/TR/5'10"/(160–170) DR 1982 SEAA 1/6 d6.25 B-DAVE COL TEXAS

YEAR	TM LG	G	AB	R	H	2B	3B	HR	RBI	BB	IB	HP	SO	AVG	OBP	SLG	OPS	AOPS	SB	CS	SB%	GAMES AT POSITION	DL	BFW
1993	NY A	103	334	41	78	16	2	2	20	29	2	0	30	.234	.294	.311	.605	-35	3	2	60	S96,D2	0	-0.5
Total	13	1544	4930	587	1211	215	59	46	439	569	57	15	519	.246	.324	.341	.665	-17	82	62	57	S1373,3b99,2b17,D11,1b4	73	5.7
/150	1	150	486	60	114	23	3	3	29	42	3	0	44	.234	.294	.311	.605	-35	4	3	57	S140,D3	0	-0.7

PADDOCK, DEL DELMAR HAROLD B6.8.1887 VOLGA SD D2.6.1962 REMER MN BL/TR/5'9"/165 d4.14

YEAR	TM LG	G	AB	R	H	2B	3B	HR	RBI	BB	IB	HP	SO	AVG	OBP	SLG	OPS	AOPS	SB	CS	SB%	GAMES AT POSITION	DL	BFW
1912	Chi A	1	1	0	0	0	0	0	0	0	—	0	—	.000	.000	.000	.000	-199	0	—	—	/H	—	0.0
1912	NY A	46	156	26	45	5	3	1	14	23	—	4	—	.288	.393	.378	.771	+14	9	8	53	3b41,2b2/rf	—	-0.1
1912	Year	47	157	26	45	5	3	1	14	23	—	4	—	.287	.391	.376	.767	+13	9	8	53	3b41,2b2/rf	—	-0.1

PAGLIARULO, MIKE MICHAEL TIMOTHY B3.15.1960 MEDFORD MA BL/TR/6'2"/(195–201) DR 1981 NYA 6/155 d7.7 COL MIAMI

YEAR	TM LG	G	AB	R	H	2B	3B	HR	RBI	BB	IB	HP	SO	AVG	OBP	SLG	OPS	AOPS	SB	CS	SB%	GAMES AT POSITION	DL	BFW
1984	NY A	67	201	24	48	15	3	7	34	15	0	0	46	.239	.288	.448	.736	+5	0	0	0	3b67	0	-0.2
1985	NY A	138	380	55	91	16	2	19	62	45	4	4	86	.239	.324	.442	.766	+10	0	0	0	3b134	0	-1.4
1986	NY A	149	504	71	120	24	3	28	71	54	10	4	120	.238	.316	.464	.780	+10	4	1	80	3b143,S2	0	0.1
1987	NY A	150	522	76	122	26	3	32	87	53	9	2	111	.234	.305	.479	.784	+5	1	3	25	3b147/1b	0	-0.3
1988	NY A	125	444	46	96	20	1	15	67	37	9	2	104	.216	.276	.367	.643	-20	1	0	100	3b124	17	-1.8
1989	NY A	74	223	19	44	10	0	4	16	19	0	2	43	.197	.266	.296	.562	-41	1	1	50	3b69/D	0	-1.4
1989	SD N	50	148	12	29	7	0	3	14	18	4	1	39	.196	.287	.304	.591	-31	2	0	100	3b49	0	-1.0
1989	Major	124	371	31	73	17	0	7	30	37	4	3	82	.197	.275	.299	.574	+102	3	1	75	—	0	-2.4
1990	SD N	128	398	29	101	23	2	7	38	39	3	3	66	.254	.322	.374	.696	-9	1	3	25	3b116	0	-1.1
1991	†Min A	121	365	38	102	20	0	6	36	21	3	3	55	.279	.322	.384	.706	-9	1	2	33	3b118/2b	0	0.9
1992	Min A	42	105	10	21	4	0	0	9	1	0	1	17	.200	.213	.238	.451	-74	1	0	100	3b37/D	100	-0.8
1993	Min A	83	253	31	74	16	4	3	23	18	2	5	34	.292	.350	.423	.773	+6	6	6	50	3b79	0	0.1
1993	Bal A	33	117	24	38	9	0	6	21	8	0	1	15	.325	.373	.556	.929	+39	0	0	0	3b28,1b4	0	0.5
1993	Year	116	370	55	112	25	4	9	44	26	2	6	49	.303	.357	.465	.822	+17	6	6	50	3b107,1b4	0	0.6
1995	Tex A	86	241	27	56	16	0	4	27	15	2	1	49	.232	.277	.349	.626	-40	0	0	0	3b68,1b11	16	-0.8
Total	11	1246	3901	462	942	206	18	134	505	343	46	29	785	.241	.306	.407	.713	-7	18	16	53	3b1179,1b16,D2,S2/2b	133	-7.2
Team	6	703	2274	291	521	111	12	105	337	223	32	14	510	.229	.300	.427	.727	-2	7	5	58	3b684,S2/1D	17	-5.0
/150	1	150	485	62	111	24	3	22	72	48	7	3	109	.229	.300	.427	.727	-2	1	1	50	3b146/S1D	4	-1.1

PASCHAL, BEN BENJAMIN EDWIN B10.13.1895 ENTERPRISE AL D11.10.1974 CHARLOTTE NC BR/TR/5'11"/185 d8.16

YEAR	TM LG	G	AB	R	H	2B	3B	HR	RBI	BB	IB	HP	SO	AVG	OBP	SLG	OPS	AOPS	SB	CS	SB%	GAMES AT POSITION	DL	BFW
1915	Cle A	9	9	0	1	0	0	0	0	0	—	0	3	.111	.111	.111	.222	-133	0	—	—	/H	—	-0.2
1920	Bos A	9	28	5	10	0	0	0	5	5	—	0	2	.357	.455	.357	.812	+22	1	0	100	O7R	—	0.1
1924	NY A	4	12	2	3	1	0	0	3	1	—	0	0	.250	.308	.333	.641	-35	0	0	0	O4C	—	0.0
1925	NY A	89	247	49	89	16	5	12	56	22	—	2	29	.360	.417	.611	1.028	+61	14	9	61	O66(16/14/36)	—	1.5
1926	†NY A	96	258	46	74	12	3	7	32	26	—	1	35	.287	.354	.438	.792	+8	7	6	54	O74(12/17/47)	—	-0.2
1927	NY A	50	82	16	26	9	2	2	16	4	—	0	10	.317	.349	.549	.898	+34	0	2	0	O27(11/4/12)	—	0.2
1928	†NY A	65	79	12	25	6	1	1	15	8	—	0	11	.316	.379	.456	.835	+22	1	0	100	O25(16/1/8)	—	0.2
1929	NY A	42	72	13	15	3	0	2	11	6	—	0	3	.208	.269	.333	.602	-42	1	2	33	O20(12/4/4)	—	-0.5
Total	8	364	787	143	243	47	11	24	138	72	—	3	93	.309	.369	.488	.857	+23	24	19	100	O223(67/44/114)	—	1.1
Team	6	346	750	138	232	47	11	24	133	67	—	3	88	.309	.368	.497	.865	+24	23	19	55	O216(49/92/88)	—	1.2
/150	3	150	325	60	101	20	5	10	58	29	—	1	38	.309	.368	.497	.865	+24	10	8	56	O94(21/40/38)	—	0.5

PASQUA, DAN DANIEL ANTHONY B10.17.1961 YONKERS NY BL/TL/6'0"/(203–218) DR 1982 NYA 3/76 d5.30 COL WILLIAM PATERSON

YEAR	TM LG	G	AB	R	H	2B	3B	HR	RBI	BB	IB	HP	SO	AVG	OBP	SLG	OPS	AOPS	SB	CS	SB%	GAMES AT POSITION	DL	BFW
1985	NY A	60	148	17	31	3	1	9	25	16	4	1	38	.209	.289	.426	.715	-5	0	0	0	O37(31/0/6),D14	0	0.0
1986	NY A	102	280	44	82	17	0	16	45	47	3	3	78	.293	.399	.525	.924	+50	2	0	100	O81(71/0/12),1b5,D3	0	1.7
1987	NY A	113	318	42	74	7	1	17	42	40	3	1	99	.233	.319	.421	.740	-5	0	2	0	O74(61/0/14),D20,1b12	0	-0.7
Total	10	905	2620	341	638	129	15	117	390	335	29	15	642	.244	.330	.438	.768	+12	7	10	41	O595(322/0/289),1b147,D116	218	1.8
Team	3	275	746	103	187	27	2	42	112	103	10	5	215	.251	.344	.461	.805	+16	2	2	50	O192(102/0/7),D37,1b17	0	1.0
/150	2	150	407	56	102	15	1	23	61	56	5	3	117	.251	.344	.461	.805	+16	1	1	50	O105(56/0/4),D20,1b9	0	0.5

PATTERSON, MIKE MICHAEL LEE B1.26.1958 SANTA MONICA CA BL/TR/5'10"/(170–190) d4.15

YEAR	TM LG	G	AB	R	H	2B	3B	HR	RBI	BB	IB	HP	SO	AVG	OBP	SLG	OPS	AOPS	SB	CS	SB%	GAMES AT POSITION	DL	BFW
1981	Oak A	12	23	4	8	1	1	0	1	2	1	0	5	.348	.400	.478	.878	+58	0	1	0	O5(2/0/3),D2	0	0.1
1981	NY A	4	9	2	2	0	2	0	0	0	0	0	0	.222	.222	.667	.889	+49	0	0	0	O4(3/0/1)	0	0.0
1981	Year	16	32	6	10	1	3	0	1	2	1	0	5	.313	.353	.531	.884	+56	0	1	0	O9(5/0/4),D2	0	0.1
1982	NY A	11	16	3	3	1	0	1	1	2	0	0	6	.188	.278	.438	.716	-6	1	0	100	O9(2/7/0)/D	0	-0.2
Total	2	27	48	9	13	2	3	1	2	4	1	0	11	.271	.327	.500	.827	+34	1	1	50	O18(7/7/4),D3	0	-0.1
Team	2	15	25	5	5	1	2	1	1	2	0	0	6	.200	.259	.520	.779	+12	1	0	100	O13(5/7/1)/D	0	-0.2

PECKINPAUGH, ROGER ROGER THORPE B2.5.1891 WOOSTER OH D11.17.1977 CLEVELAND OH BR/TR/5'10.5"/165 d9.15 M8

YEAR	TM LG	G	AB	R	H	2B	3B	HR	RBI	BB	IB	HP	SO	AVG	OBP	SLG	OPS	AOPS	SB	CS	SB%	GAMES AT POSITION	DL	BFW
1910	Cle A	15	45	1	9	0	0	0	6	1	—	1	—	.200	.234	.200	.434	-64	3	—	—	S14	—	-0.9
1912	Cle A	70	236	18	50	4	1	1	22	16	—	0	—	.212	.262	.250	.512	-55	11	4	73	S68	—	-1.4
1913	Cle A	1	0	1	0	0	0	0	0	0	—	0	0	+	+	+	.000	-100	0	—	—	/H	—	0.0
1913	NY A	95	340	35	91	10	7	1	32	24	—	0	47	.268	.316	.347	.663	-6	19	—	—	S93	—	-0.1
1913	Year	96	340	36	91	10	7	1	32	24	—	0	47	.268	.316	.347	.663	-6	19	—	—	S93	—	-0.1
1914	NY A	**157**	570	55	127	14	6	3	51	51	—	1	73	.223	.288	.284	.572	-28	38	17	69	S157,M	—	-0.2
1915	NY A	142	540	67	119	18	7	5	44	49	—	3	72	.220	.289	.307	.596	-21	19	12	61	S142	—	0.0
1916	NY A	145	552	65	141	22	8	4	58	62	—	1	50	.255	.332	.346	.678	+1	18	—	—	S145	—	1.2
1917	NY A	148	543	63	141	24	7	0	41	64	—	2	46	.260	.340	.330	.670	+3	17	—	—	S148	—	2.3
1918	NY A	122	446	59	103	15	3	0	43	43	—	3	41	.231	.303	.278	.581	-26	12	—	—	S122	—	1.9
1919	NY A	122	453	89	138	20	2	7	33	59	—	4	37	.305	.390	.404	.794	+22	10	—	—	S121	—	5.1
1920	NY A	139	534	109	144	26	6	8	54	72	—	0	47	.270	.356	.386	.742	-7	8	12	40	S137	—	1.1
1921	†NY A	149	577	128	166	25	7	8	71	84	—	2	44	.288	.380	.397	.777	-4	2	2	50	S149	—	1.1
1922	Was A	147	520	62	132	14	4	2	48	55	—	3	36	.254	.329	.308	.637	-30	11	6	65	S147	—	1.2
1923	Was A	154	568	73	150	18	4	2	62	64	—	1	30	.264	.340	.320	.660	-22	10	8	56	S154	—	2.0
1924	†Was A	155	523	72	142	20	5	2	73	72	—	0	45	.272	.360	.340	.700	-16	9	6	60	S155	—	1.5
1925	†Was A	126	422	67	124	16	4	4	64	49	—	0	23	.294	.367	.379	.746	-9	13	4	76	S124/1b	—	-0.4
1926	Was A	57	147	19	35	4	1	1	14	28	—	0	12	.238	.360	.299	.659	-25	3	0	100	S46/1b	—	-0.1
1927	Chi A	68	217	23	64	6	3	0	23	21	—	1	6	.295	.360	.350	.710	-13	2	3	40	S60	—	0.1
Total	17	2012	7233	1006	1876	256	75	48	739	814	—	22	609	.259	.336	.335	.671	-13	205	74	100	S1982,1b2	—	14.4
Team	9	1219	4555	670	1170	174	53	36	427	508	—	16	457	.257	.334	.342	.676	-7	143	43	100	S1214/M	—	12.4
/150	1	150	561	82	144	21	7	4	53	63	—	2	56	.257	.334	.342	.676	-7	18	5	100	S149/M	—	1.5

Batters

YEAR	TM LG	G	AB	R	H	2B	3B	HR	RBI	BB	IB	HP	SO	AVG	OBP	SLG	OPS	AOPS	SB	CS	SB%	GAMES AT POSITION	DL	BFW
Pepitone, Joe Joseph Anthony "Pepi" B10.9.1940 Brooklyn NY BL/TL/6'2"/(170–200) d4.10 C1																								
1962	NY A	63	138	14	33	3	2	7	17	3	0	0	21	.239	.255	.442	.697	-14	1	1	50	O32(14/7/13),1b16	0	-0.9
1963	†NY A★	157	580	79	157	16	3	27	89	23	2	7	63	.271	.304	.448	.752	+9	3	5	38	1b143,O16(0/7/9)	0	-0.1
1964	†NY A★	160	613	71	154	12	3	28	100	24	7	3	63	.251	.281	.418	.699	-10	2	1	67	1b155,O30(0/28/3)	0	-1.6
1965	NY A★	143	531	51	131	18	3	18	62	43	11	2	59	.247	.305	.394	.699	-2	4	2	67	1b115,O41(2/3/36)	0	-1.1
1966	NY A	152	585	85	149	21	4	31	83	29	6	2	58	.255	.290	.463	.753	+18	4	3	57	1b119,O55(0/49/9)	0	1.2
1967	NY A	133	501	45	126	18	3	13	64	34	4	3	62	.251	.301	.377	.678	+4	1	3	25	O123C,1b6	0	-1.2
1968	NY A	108	380	41	93	9	3	15	56	37	9	1	45	.245	.311	.403	.714	+20	8	2	80	O92(4/88/0),1b12	22	-0.6
1969	NY A	135	513	49	124	16	3	27	70	30	11	1	42	.242	.284	.442	.726	+4	8	6	57	1b132	0	-1.7
1970	Hou N	75	279	44	70	9	5	14	35	18	9	1	28	.251	.298	.470	.768	+7	5	2	71	1b50,O28(15/3/13)	0	-0.5
1970	Chi N	56	213	38	57	9	2	12	44	15	2	0	15	.268	.313	.498	.811	+2	0	2	0	O56C,1b13	0	-0.3
1970	Year	131	492	82	127	18	7	26	79	33	11	1	43	.258	.304	.482	.786	+4	5	4	56	O84(15/59/13),1b63	0	-0.8
1971	Chi N	115	427	50	131	19	4	16	61	24	8	4	41	.307	.347	.482	.829	+16	1	2	33	1b95,O23(1/22/0)	15	-0.3
1972	Chi N	66	214	23	56	5	0	8	21	13	4	3	22	.262	.309	.397	.706	-9	1	2	33	1b66	0	-1.0
1973	Chi N	31	112	16	30	3	0	3	18	8	0	1	6	.268	.320	.375	.695	-14	3	1	75	1b28	0	-0.5
1973	Atl N	3	11	0	4	0	0	0	1	1	0	0	1	.364	.417	.364	.781	+10	0	0	0	1b3	0	-0.1
1973	Year	34	123	16	34	3	0	3	19	9	0	1	7	.276	.328	.374	.702	-12	3	1	75	1b31	0	-0.6
Total	12	1397	5097	606	1315	158	35	219	721	302	73	28	526	.258	.301	.432	.733	+5	41	32	56	1b953,O496(36/386/83)	37	-8.7
Team	8	1051	3841	435	967	113	24	166	541	223	50	19	413	.252	.294	.423	.717	+5	31	23	57	1b698,O389(42/150/34)	22	-6.0
/150	1	150	548	62	138	16	3	24	77	32	7	3	59	.252	.294	.423	.717	+5	4	3	57	1b100,O56(6/21/5)	3	-0.9
Perez, Marty Martin Roman B2.28.1946 Visalia CA BR/TR/5'11"/160 d9.9																								
1977	NY A	1	4	0	2	0	0	0	0	0	0	0	1	.500	.500	.500	1.000	+75	0	0	0	/3b	0	0.1
Total	10	931	3131	313	771	108	22	22	241	245	10	10	369	.246	.301	.316	.617	-30	11	17	39	S465,2b434,3b34	32	-11.3
Perez, Robert Robert Alexander (Jimenez) B6.4.1969 Ciudad Bolivar, Bolivar, Venez BR/TR/6'3"/(190–230) d7.20																								
2001	NY A	6	15	1	4	1	0	0	0	1	0	0	7	.267	.313	.333	.646	-30	0	1	0	O5(0/3/2)/D	0	-0.1
Total	6	221	497	49	126	19	1	8	44	11	0	2	74	.254	.271	.344	.615	-42	3	1	75	O175(114/3/65),D10	22	-3.6
Perkins, Cy Ralph Foster B2.27.1896 Gloucester MA D10.2.1963 Philadelphia PA BR/TR/5'10.5"/158 d9.25 M1/C15																								
1931	NY A	16	47	3	12	1	0	0	7	1	—	1	4	.255	.286	.277	.563	-49	0	0	0	C16	—	-0.5
Total	17	1171	3604	329	933	175	35	30	409	301	—	15	221	.259	.319	.352	.671	-25	18	34	100	C1111,S8,1b2/3b2b	—	-3.1
Phelps, Josh Joshua Lee B5.12.1978 Anchorage AK BR/TR/6'3"/(215–225) Dr 1996 TorA 10/279 d6.13																								
2007	NY A	36	80	8	21	2	0	2	12	6	0	2	19	.262	.330	.363	.693	-19	0	0	0	1b29/CD	0	-0.5
Total	7	446	1360	194	371	73	6	64	243	114	6	36	386	.273	.344	.476	.820	+10	2	2	50	D307,1b82,C12	18	-0.7
Phelps, Ken Kenneth Allen B8.6.1954 Seattle WA BL/TL/6'1"/(200–209) Dr 1976 KCA 15/354 d9.20 Col Arizona St.																								
1988	NY A	45	107	17	24	5	0	10	22	19	3	0	26	.224	.339	.551	.890	+46	0	0	0	D24/1b	0	0.6
1989	NY A	86	185	26	46	3	0	7	29	27	2	0	47	.249	.340	.378	.718	+4	0	0	0	D55,1b8	0	-0.2
Total	11	761	1854	308	443	64	7	123	313	390	28	21	449	.239	.374	.480	.854	+31	10	7	59	D467,1b131	41	6.4
Team	2	131	292	43	70	8	0	17	51	46	5	0	73	.240	.339	.442	.781	+20	0	0	0	D79,1b9	0	0.4
/150	2	150	334	49	80	9	0	19	58	53	6	0	84	.240	.339	.442	.781	+20	0	0	0	D90,1b10	0	0.5
Phillips, Eddie Edward David B2.17.1901 Worcester MA D1.26.1968 Buffalo NY BR/TR/6'0"/178 d5.4 Col Boston College																								
1932	NY A	9	31	4	9	1	0	2	4	2	—	0	3	.290	.333	.516	.849	+23	1	0	100	C9	—	0.2
Total	6	312	997	82	236	54	6	14	126	104	—	5	115	.237	.312	.345	.657	-28	3	1	100	C298	—	-4.4
Phillips, Andy George Andrew B4.6.1977 Tuscaloosa AL BR/TR/6'0"/(205–210) Dr 1999 NYA 7/231 d9.14 Col Alabama																								
2004	NY A	5	8	1	2	0	0	1	2	0	0	0	1	.250	.250	.625	.875	+17	0	0	0	3b4	0	0.0
2005	NY A	27	40	7	6	4	0	1	4	1	0	0	13	.150	.171	.325	.496	-72	0	0	0	1b19/3blfD	0	-0.6
2006	†NY A	110	246	30	59	11	3	7	29	15	0	0	56	.240	.281	.394	.675	-29	3	2	60	1b94,3b10/2bD	15	-2.1
2007	NY A	61	185	27	54	7	1	2	25	12	0	2	26	.292	.338	.373	.711	-13	0	3	0	1b57,3b9/2b	27	-1.0
Total	4	203	479	65	121	22	4	11	60	28	0	2	96	.253	.294	.384	.678	-25	3	5	38	1b170,3b24,D10,2b2/lf	42	-3.7
/150	3	150	354	48	89	16	3	8	44	21	0	1	71	.253	.294	.384	.678	-25	2	4	33	1b126,3b18,D7/2lf	31	-2.7
Phillips, Jack Jack Dorn "Stretch" B9.6.1921 Clarence NY BR/TR/6'4"/(190–193) d8.22 Col Clarkson																								
1947	†NY A	16	36	5	10	0	1	1	2	3	—	0	5	.278	.333	.417	.750	+9	0	0	0	1b10	0	-0.2
1948	NY A	1	2	0	0	0	0	0	0	0	—	0	1	.000	.000	.000	.000	-199	0	0	0	/1b	0	-0.1
1949	NY A	45	91	16	28	4	1	1	10	12	—	0	9	.308	.388	.407	.795	+10	1	0	100	1b38	0	-0.2
Total	9	343	892	111	252	42	16	9	101	85	0	0	86	.283	.344	.396	.740	-5	5	3	100	1b264,3b11/lf2bP	0	-2.4
Team	3	62	129	21	38	4	2	2	12	15	—	0	15	.295	.368	.403	.771	+7	1	0	100	1b49	0	-0.5
Piniella, Lou Louis Victor B8.28.1943 Tampa FL BR/TR/6'2"/(182–200) d9.4 M20/C2 Col Tampa																								
1964	Bal A	4	1	0	0	0	0	0	0	0	0	0	0	.000	.000	.000	.000	-199	0	0	0	/H	0	0.0
1968	Cle A	6	5	1	0	0	0	0	1	0	0	0	0	.000	.000	.000	.000	-199	0	0	0	O2L	0	-0.2
1969	KC A	135	493	43	139	21	6	11	68	33	2	3	56	.282	.325	.416	.741	+6	2	4	33	O129(126/3/0)	0	0.4
1970	KC A	144	542	54	163	24	5	11	88	35	6	2	42	.301	.342	.424	.766	+11	3	6	33	O139L/1b	0	-0.4
1971	KC A	126	448	43	125	21	5	3	51	21	4	2	43	.279	.311	.368	.679	-7	5	3	63	O115L	34	-1.5
1972	KC A★	151	574	65	179	**33**	4	11	72	34	9	8	59	.312	.356	.441	.797	+38	7	2	78	O150L	0	1.8
1973	KC A	144	513	53	128	28	1	9	69	30	7	2	65	.250	.291	.361	.652	-23	5	7	42	O128L,D9	0	-3.2
1974	NY A	140	518	71	158	26	0	9	70	32	7	2	58	.305	.341	.407	.748	+18	1	8	11	O130(99/0/34)/1bD	0	1.1
1975	NY A	74	199	7	39	4	1	0	22	16	3	3	22	.196	.262	.226	.488	-59	0	0	0	O46(15/0/31),D12	19	-2.0
1976	†NY A	100	327	36	92	16	6	3	38	18	8	2	34	.281	.322	.394	.716	+10	0	1	0	O49(10/0/39),D38	0	0.1
1977	†NY A	103	339	47	112	19	3	12	45	20	3	1	31	.330	.365	.510	.875	+38	2	2	50	O51(24/0/27),D43/1b	0	0.9
1978	†NY A	130	472	67	148	34	5	6	69	34	8	2	36	.314	.361	.445	.806	+28	3	1	75	O103(78/2/25),D23	0	1.1
1979	NY A	130	461	49	137	22	2	11	69	17	6	2	31	.297	.320	.425	.745	+2	3	2	60	O112(84/0/29),D16	0	-0.5
1980	†NY A	116	321	39	92	18	0	2	27	29	5	0	20	.287	.343	.361	.704	-5	0	2	0	O104(102/1/1),D7	0	-0.6
1981	†NY A	60	159	16	44	9	0	5	18	13	4	0	9	.277	.331	.428	.759	+19	0	1	0	O36(11/0/25),D19	15	0.4
1982	NY A	102	261	33	80	17	1	6	37	18	6	1	18	.307	.352	.448	.800	+20	0	1	0	D55,O40(13/0/27)	0	0.4
1983	NY A	53	148	19	43	9	1	2	16	11	3	1	12	.291	.344	.405	.749	+9	1	1	50	O43(15/0/28)/D	18	-0.1
1984	NY A	29	86	8	26	4	1	1	6	7	1	0	5	.302	.355	.407	.762	+14	0	0	0	O24(15/0/9),D2	0	0.1
Total	18	1747	5867	651	1705	305	41	102	766	368	82	31	541	.291	.333	.409	.742	+8	32	41	44	O1401(1126/6/275),D231,1b3	86	-2.2
Team	11	1037	3291	392	971	178	20	57	417	215	54	14	276	.295	.338	.413	.751	+11	10	19	34	O738(466/3/275),D217,1b2	52	0.9
/150	2	150	476	57	140	26	3	8	60	31	8	2	40	.295	.338	.413	.751	+11	1	3	25	O107(67/0/40),D31/1	8	0.1
Pipp, Wally Walter Clement B2.17.1893 Chicago IL D1.11.1965 Grand Rapids MI BL/TL/6'1"/180 d6.29 Mil 1918 Col Catholic America																								
1913	Det A	12	31	3	5	0	3	0	5	2	—	1	6	.161	.235	.355	.590	-27	0	—	—	1b10	—	-0.2
1915	NY A	136	479	59	118	20	13	4	60	66	—	1	81	.246	.339	.367	.706	+12	18	7	72	1b134	—	0.8
1916	NY A	151	545	70	143	20	14	**12**	93	54	—	2	82	.262	.331	.417	.748	+22	16	—	—	1b148	—	1.4
1917	NY A	**155**	587	82	143	29	12	**9**	70	60	—	6	66	.244	.320	.380	.700	+12	11	—	—	1b155	—	0.8
1918	NY A	91	349	48	106	15	9	2	44	22	—	0	34	.304	.345	.415	.760	+27	11	—	—	1b91	—	0.8
1919	NY A	138	523	74	144	23	10	7	50	39	—	4	42	.275	.330	.398	.728	+3	9	—	—	1b138	—	-0.3
1920	NY A	153	610	109	171	30	14	11	76	48	—	6	54	.280	.339	.430	.760	-1	4	10	29	1b153	—	-0.9
1921	†NY A	**153**	588	96	174	35	9	8	97	45	—	1	28	.296	.347	.427	.774	-6	17	10	63	1b153	—	2.0
1922	†NY A	152	577	96	190	32	10	9	90	56	—	4	32	.329	.392	.466	.858	+20	7	12	37	1b152	—	-0.1
1923	†NY A	144	569	79	173	19	8	6	108	36	—	6	28	.304	.352	.397	.749	-5	6	13	32	1b144	—	-2.2
1924	NY A	**153**	589	88	174	30	**19**	9	114	51	—	0	36	.295	.352	.457	.809	+8	12	5	71	1b153	—	-0.5
1925	NY A	62	178	19	41	6	3	3	24	13	—	1	12	.230	.286	.348	.634	-39	3	3	50	1b47	—	-1.0

YEAR	TM LG	G	AB	R	H	2B	3B	HR	RBI	BB	IB	HP	SO	AVG	OBP	SLG	OPS	AOPS	SB	CS	SB%	GAMES AT POSITION	DL	BFW
1926	Cin N	155	574	72	167	22	15	6	99	49	—	5	26	.291	.352	.413	.765	+8	8	—	—	1b155	—	-0.3
1927	Cin N	122	443	49	115	19	6	2	41	32	—	0	11	.260	.309	.343	.652	-23	2	—	—	1b114	—	-2.2
1928	Cin N	95	272	30	77	11	3	2	26	23	—	1	13	.283	.341	.368	.709	-13	1	—	—	1b72	—	-0.8
Total	15	1872	6914	974	1941	311	148	90	997	596	—	38	551	.281	.341	.408	.749	+4	125	60	100	1b1819	—	-6.7
Team	11	1488	5594	820	1577	259	121	80	826	490	—	31	495	.282	.343	.414	.757	+7	114	60	100	1b1468	—	-3.2
/150	1	150	564	83	159	26	12	8	83	49	—	3	50	.282	.343	.414	.757	+7	11	6	100	1b148	—	-0.3
PISONI, JIM	JAMES PETER B8.14.1929 ST.LOUIS MO D2.4.2007 DALLAS TX BR/TR/5'10"/(169–172) d9.25																							
1953	StL A	3	12	1	1	0	0	1	1	0	—	0	5	.083	.083	.333	.416	-92	0	0	0	O3(0/2/1)	0	-0.2
1956	KC A	10	30	4	8	0	0	2	5	2	0	0	8	.267	.303	.467	.770	+3	0	0	0	O9L	0	0.3
1957	KC A	44	97	14	23	2	2	3	12	10	1	2	17	.237	.318	.392	.710	-8	0	0	0	O44(0/44/1)	0	-0.1
1959	Mil N	9	24	4	4	1	0	0	0	2	0	0	6	.167	.231	.208	.439	-80	0	0	0	O9(2/8/0)	0	-0.3
1959	NY A	17	17	2	3	0	1	0	1	1	0	0	9	.176	.222	.294	.516	-58	0	0	0	O15(9/3/3)	0	-0.1
1959	Major	26	41	6	7	1	1	0	1	3	0	0	15	.171	.227	.244	.471	-79	0	0	0	—	0	-0.4
1960	NY A	20	9	1	1	0	0	0	1	1	0	0	2	.111	.200	.111	.311	-114	0	0	0	O18(12/6/0)	0	-0.2
Total	5	103	189	26	40	3	3	6	20	16	1	2	47	.212	.278	.354	.632	-29	0	0	0	O98(32/63/5)	0	-0.6
Team	2	37	26	3	4	0	1	0	2	2	0	0	11	.154	.214	.231	.445	-78	0	0	0	O33(21/9/3)	0	-0.3
POLONIA, LUIS	LUIS ANDREW (ALMONTE) B10.12.1963 SANTIAGO, D.R. BL/TL/5'8"/(150–160) d4.24																							
1989	NY A	66	227	39	71	11	2	2	29	16	1	2	29	.313	.359	.405	.764	+17	9	4	69	O53L,D9	0	0.8
1990	NY A	11	22	2	7	0	0	0	3	0	0	0	1	.318	.304	.318	.622	-22	1	0	100	D4	0	-0.1
1994	NY A	95	350	62	109	21	6	1	36	37	1	4	30	.311	.383	.414	.797	+10	20	12	63	O84L,D2	0	0.2
1995	NY A	67	238	37	62	9	3	2	15	25	1	0	29	.261	.326	.349	.675	-22	10	4	71	O64L/D	0	-0.3
2000	†NY A	37	77	11	22	4	0	1	5	7	0	0	7	.286	.341	.377	.718	-16	4	2	67	O28(22/0/6),D7	0	-0.4
Total	12	1379	4840	728	1417	189	70	36	405	369	23	15	543	.293	.342	.383	.725	-4	321	145	69	O1055(927/87/54),D214	0	-4.5
Team	5	276	914	151	271	45	11	6	88	85	3	6	102	.296	.357	.389	.746	+0	44	22	67	O229L,D23	0	0.2
/150	3	150	497	82	147	24	6	3	48	46	2	3	55	.296	.357	.389	.746	+0	24	12	67	O124L,D13	0	0.1
POSADA, JORGE	JORGE RAFAEL (VILLETA) B8.17.1971 SANTURCE, PR BB/TR/6'2"/205 DR 1990 NYA 24/646 d9.4 COL CALHOUN (AL) CC																							
1995	†NY A	1	0	0	0	0	0	0	0	0	0	0	0	+	+	+	.000	-100	0	0	0	/C	0	0.0
1996	NY A	8	14	1	1	0	0	0	0	1	0	0	6	.071	.133	.071	.204	-146	0	0	0	C4,D3	0	-0.3
1997	†NY A	60	188	29	47	12	0	6	25	30	2	3	33	.250	.359	.410	.769	+2	1	2	33	C60	0	-0.1
1998	†NY A	111	358	56	96	23	0	17	63	47	7	0	92	.268	.350	.475	.825	+18	0	1	0	C99/1bD	0	1.9
1999	†NY A	112	379	50	93	19	2	12	57	53	2	3	91	.245	.341	.401	.742	-10	1	0	100	C109/1bD	0	0.2
2000	†NY A★	151	505	92	145	35	1	28	86	107	10	8	151	.287	.417	.527	.944	+39	2	2	50	C142,1b12,D4	0	4.3
2001	†NY A★	138	484	59	134	28	1	22	95	62	10	6	132	.277	.363	.475	.838	+18	2	6	25	C131,1b2,D6	0	1.7
2002	†NY A★	143	511	79	137	40	1	20	99	81	9	3	143	.268	.370	.468	.838	+22	1	0	100	C138,D5	0	3.1
2003	†NY A★	142	481	83	135	24	0	30	101	93	6	10	110	.281	.405	.518	.923	+44	2	4	33	C137,D2	0	5.1
2004	†NY A	137	449	72	122	31	0	21	81	88	5	9	92	.272	.400	.481	.881	+29	1	3	25	C134	0	2.8
2005	†NY A	142	474	67	124	23	0	19	71	66	5	2	94	.262	.352	.430	.782	+8	1	0	100	C133,D3	0	0.9
2006	†NY A	143	465	65	129	27	2	23	93	64	1	11	97	.277	.374	.492	.866	+21	3	0	100	C134/1bD	0	3.3
2007	†NY A★	144	506	91	171	42	1	20	90	74	7	6	98	.338	.426	.543	.969	+52	2	0	100	C138/1bD	0	4.1
Total	13	1432	4814	744	1334	304	8	218	861	766	64	61	1139	.277	.381	.479	.860	+24	16	18	47	C1360,D37,1b18	0	27.0
/150	1	150	504	78	140	32	1	23	90	80	7	6	119	.277	.381	.479	.860	+24	2	2	50	C14,D4,1b2	0	2.8
POSE, SCOTT	SCOTT VERNON B2.11.1967 DAVENPORT IA BL/TR/5'11"/(165–190) DR 1989 CINN 34/888 d4.5 COL ARKANSAS																							
1997	†NY A	54	87	19	19	2	1	0	5	9	0	0	11	.218	.292	.264	.556	-53	3	1	75	O45(28/3/17),D5	0	-0.8
Total	4	202	313	52	75	7	1	0	21	38	1	0	50	.240	.321	.268	.589	-47	9	6	60	O91(55/14/30),D27	0	-2.5
POWELL, JAKE	ALVIN JACOB B7.15.1908 SILVER SPRING MD D11.4.1948 WASHINGTON DC BR/TR/5'11.5"/180 d8.3																							
1930	Was A	3	4	1	0	0	0	0	0	0	—	0	1	.000	.000	.000	.000	-199	0	0	0	O2(1/0/1)	—	-0.1
1934	Was A	9	35	6	10	2	0	0	1	4	—	0	2	.286	.359	.343	.702	-15	1	1	50	O9C	—	0.0
1935	Was A	139	551	88	172	26	10	6	98	37	—	4	37	.312	.360	.428	.788	+7	15	7	68	O136(0/136/1),2b2	—	-0.1
1936	Was A	53	210	40	62	11	5	1	30	18	—	2	21	.295	.357	.410	.767	-6	10	4	71	O53C	—	-0.7
1936	†NY A	87	328	62	99	13	3	7	48	33	—	0	30	.302	.366	.424	.790	-2	16	7	70	O84(42/42/0)	—	-0.3
1936	Year	140	538	102	161	24	8	8	78	51	—	2	51	.299	.362	.418	.780	-4	26	11	70	O137(42/95/0)	—	-1.0
1937	†NY A	97	365	54	96	22	3	3	45	25	—	2	36	.263	.314	.364	.678	-30	7	5	58	O94L	—	-2.3
1938	†NY A	45	164	27	42	12	1	2	20	15	—	2	20	.256	.326	.378	.704	-24	3	1	75	O43(37/1/6)	—	-1.0
1939	NY A	31	86	12	21	4	1	1	9	3	—	0	8	.244	.270	.349	.619	-42	1	2	33	O23(19/2/3)	—	-0.6
1940	NY A	12	27	3	5	0	0	0	2	1	—	0	4	.185	.214	.185	.399	-95	0	0	0	O7(3/2/2)	—	-0.3
1943	Was A	37	132	14	35	10	2	0	20	5	—	1	13	.265	.297	.371	.668	-1	3	5	38	O33(25/8/0)	0	-0.2
1944	Was A	96	367	29	88	9	1	1	37	16	—	0	26	.240	.272	.278	.550	-40	7	2	78	O90(58/0/32)/3b	0	-2.7
1945	Was A	31	98	4	19	2	0	0	3	8	—	0	8	.194	.255	.214	.469	-60	1	1	50	O27(21/0/6)	0	-1.1
1945	Phi N	48	173	13	40	5	0	1	14	8	—	0	13	.231	.265	.277	.542	-48	1	—	—	O44(4/5/35)	0	-1.4
1945	Major	79	271	17	59	7	0	1	17	16	0	0	21	.218	.261	.255	.516	+48	2	1	—	—	0	-2.5
Total	11	688	2540	353	689	116	26	22	327	173	—	11	219	.271	.320	.363	.683	-19	65	35	100	O645(304/258/86),2b2/3b	0	-10.8
Team	5	272	970	158	263	51	8	13	124	77	—	4	98	.271	.327	.380	.707	-22	27	15	64	O251(43/51/8)	—	-4.5
/150	3	150	535	87	145	28	4	7	68	42	—	2	54	.271	.327	.380	.707	-22	15	8	65	O138(24/28/4)	—	-2.5
POWERS, DOC	MICHAEL RILEY B9.22.1870 PITTSFIELD MA D4.26.1909 PHILADELPHIA PA BR/TR d6.12 COL NOTRE DAME																							
1905	NY A	11	33	3	6	1	0	0	2	1	—	0	—	.182	.206	.212	.418	-71	0	—	—	1b7,C4	—	-0.3
Total	11	647	2088	183	450	72	13	4	199	72	—	18	—	.216	.248	.268	.516	-49	27	—	—	C594,1b37,O2(1/0/1)	—	-7.5
PRATT, DEL	DERRILL BURNHAM B1.10.1888 WALHALLA SC D9.30.1977 TEXAS CITY TX BR/TR/5'11"/175 d4.11 COL ALABAMA OF(3/3/8)																							
1918	NY A	**126**	477	65	131	19	7	2	55	35	—	2	26	.275	.327	.356	.683	+4	12	—	—	2b126	—	1.5
1919	NY A	140	527	69	154	27	7	4	56	36	—	4	24	.292	.342	.393	.735	+5	22	—	—	2b140	—	3.1
1920	NY A	**154**	574	84	180	37	8	4	97	50	—	3	24	.314	.372	.427	.799	+7	12	10	55	2b154	—	2.1
Total	13	1836	6826	856	1996	392	117	43	968	513	—	37	360	.292	.345	.403	.748	+12	247	13	100	2b1688,1b79,S22,3b17,O14R	—	22.0
Team	3	420	1578	218	465	83	22	10	208	121	—	9	74	.295	.349	.394	.743	+5	46	10	100	2b420	—	6.7
/150	1	150	564	78	166	30	8	4	74	43	—	3	26	.295	.349	.394	.743	+5	16	4	100	2b150	—	2.4
PRIDDY, JERRY	GERALD EDWARD B11.9.1919 LOS ANGELES CA D3.3.1980 N.HOLLYWOOD CA BR/TR/5'11.5"/(180–186) d4.17 MIL 1944–45																							
1941	NY A	56	174	18	37	7	0	1	26	18	—	1	16	.213	.290	.270	.560	-50	4	2	67	2b31,3b14,1b10	0	-0.5
1942	†NY A	59	189	23	53	9	2	2	28	31	—	1	27	.280	.385	.381	.766	+18	0	1	0	3b35,1b11,2b8,S3	0	0.9
Total	11	1296	4720	612	1252	232	46	61	541	624	—	13	639	.265	.353	.373	.726	-3	44	44	50	2b1179,3b52,1b32,S19	74	11.7
Team	2	115	363	41	90	16	2	3	54	49	—	2	43	.248	.341	.328	.669	-14	4	3	57	3b49,2b39,1b21,S3	0	0.4
/150	3	150	473	53	117	21	3	4	70	64	—	3	56	.248	.341	.328	.669	-14	5	4	56	3b64,2b51,1b27,S4	0	0.5
PRIDE, CURTIS	CURTIS JOHN B12.17.1968 WASHINGTON DC BL/TR/6'0"/(195–210) DR 1986 NYN 10/258 d9.14																							
2003	NY A	4	12	1	1	0	0	1	1	0	0	0	2	.083	.083	.333	.416	-97	0	0	0	O3(1/0/2)	0	-0.2
Total	11	421	796	132	199	39	12	20	82	85	2	7	211	.250	.327	.405	.732	-12	29	14	67	O205(167/6/37),D68	147	-2.0
PRIEST, JOHNNY	JOHN GOODING B6.23.1891 ST.JOSEPH MO D11.4.1979 WASHINGTON DC BR/TR/5'11"/170 d5.30																							
1911	NY A	8	21	2	3	0	0	0	2	2	—	1	—	.143	.250	.143	.393	-90	3	—	—	2b5,3b2	—	-0.5
1912	NY A	2	2	1	1	0	0	0	1	0	—	0	—	.500	.500	.500	1.000	+76	0	—	—	/H	—	0.0
Total	2	10	23	3	4	0	0	0	3	2	—	1	—	.174	.269	.174	.443	-77	3	—	—	2b5,3b2	—	-0.5

Batters

YEAR	TM LG	G	AB	R	H	2B	3B	HR	RBI	BB	IB	HP	SO	AVG	OBP	SLG	OPS	AOPS	SB	CS	SB%	GAMES AT POSITION	DL	BFW
Quirk, Jamie	James Patrick B10.22.1954 Whittier CA BL/TR/6'4"/(185–200) Dr 1972 KCA 1/18 d9.4 C15 OF(24/0/8)																							
1989	NY A	13	24	0	2	0	0	0	0	3	0	0	5	.083	.185	.083	.268	-122	0	1	0	C6/SD	0	-0.4
Total	18	984	2266	193	544	100	7	43	247	177	17	18	435	.240	.298	.347	.645	-22	5	16	24	C525,3b118,D88,1b43,O32L,S22/2b	59	-2.6
Raines, Tim	Timothy Sr. "Rock" B9.16.1959 Sanford FL BB/TR/5'8"/(165–195) Dr 1977 MonN 5/106 d9.11 C3 s–Tim																							
1996	†NY A	59	201	45	57	10	0	9	33	34	1	1	29	.284	.383	.468	.851	+16	10	1	91	O50L,D2	96	0.3
1997	†NY A	74	271	56	87	20	2	4	38	41	0	0	34	.321	.403	.454	.857	+26	8	5	62	O57L,D13	81	0.4
1998	†NY A	109	321	53	93	13	1	5	47	55	1	3	49	.290	.395	.383	.778	+9	8	3	73	D56,O47L	0	0.1
Total	23	2502	8872	1571	2605	430	113	170	980	1330	14	42	966	.294	.385	.425	.810	+23	808	146	85	O2123(1965/165/1),D131,2b53	436	38.2
Team	3	242	793	154	237	43	3	18	118	130	2	4	112	.299	.395	.429	.824	+17	26	9	74	O154L,D71	177	0.8
/150	2	150	492	95	147	27	2	11	73	81	1	2	69	.299	.395	.429	.824	+17	16	6	73	O95L,D44	110	0.5
Ramos, Domingo	Domingo Antonio (De Ramos) B3.29.1958 Santiago, D.R. BR/TR/5'10"/(154–170) d9.8																							
1978	NY A	1	0	0	0	0	0	0	0	0	0	0	0	+	+	+	.000	-100	0	0	0	/S	0	0.0
Total	11	507	1086	109	261	34	2	8	85	92	5	7	138	.240	.302	.297	.599	-36	6	9	40	S201,3b174,2b67,1b24,D7/lf	0	-4.0
Ramos, John	John Joseph B8.6.1965 Tampa FL BR/TR/6'0"/190 Dr 1986 NYA 5/132 d9.18 Col Stanford [DL 1992 NY A 90]																							
1991	NY A	10	26	4	8	1	0	0	3	1	0	0	3	.308	.310	.346	.656	-12	0	0	0	C5,D4	0	-0.2
Ramos, Bobby	Roberto B11.5.1955 Havana, Cuba BR/TR/5'11"/(190–208) Dr 1974 MonN 7/153 d9.26 C5																							
1982	NY A	4	11	1	1	0	0	1	2	0	0	0	3	.091	.091	.364	.455	-82	0	0	0	C4	0	-0.1
Total	6	103	232	20	44	7	1	4	17	22	2	1	38	.190	.262	.280	.542	-48	0	0	0	C96	0	-1.1
Randle, Len	Leonard Shenoff B2.12.1949 Long Beach CA BB/TR (BR 1971)/5'10"/(169–175) Dr 1970 TexA S1/10 d6.16 Col Arizona St. OF(62/85/6)																							
1979	NY A	20	39	2	7	0	0	0	3	3	0	0	2	.179	.238	.179	.417	-85	0	0	0	O11(4/7/0),D2	0	-0.4
Total	12	1138	3950	488	1016	145	40	27	322	372	27	15	505	.257	.321	.335	.656	-14	156	112	58	3b521,2b437,O149C,D21,S10/C	0	-2.4
Randolph, Willie	Willie Larry B7.6.1954 Holly Hill SC BR/TR/5'11"/(161–170) Dr 1972 PitN 7/167 d7.29 M3/C11																							
1975	†Pit N	30	61	9	10	1	0	0	3	7	1	0	6	.164	.246	.180	.426	-79	1	0	100	2b14/3b	0	-0.4
1976	†NY A✳	125	430	59	115	15	4	1	40	58	5	3	39	.267	.356	.328	.684	+2	37	12	76	2b124	0	2.9
1977	†NY A★	147	551	91	151	28	11	4	40	64	1	1	53	.274	.347	.387	.734	+1	13	6	68	2b147	0	2.4
1978	NY A	134	499	87	139	18	6	3	42	82	1	4	51	.279	.381	.357	.738	+12	36	7	84	2b134	21	2.8
1979	NY A	153	574	98	155	15	13	5	61	95	5	3	39	.270	.374	.368	.742	+3	33	12	73	2b153	0	3.3
1980	†NY A★	138	513	99	151	23	7	7	46	**119**	4	2	45	.294	.427	.407	.834	+32	30	5	86	2b138	0	5.0
1981	†NY A★	93	357	59	83	14	3	2	24	57	0	0	24	.232	.336	.305	.641	-12	14	5	74	2b93	0	1.2
1982	NY A	144	553	85	155	21	4	3	36	75	3	3	35	.280	.368	.349	.717	+0	16	9	64	2b142/D	0	2.2
1983	NY A	104	420	73	117	21	1	2	38	53	0	1	32	.279	.361	.348	.709	-1	12	4	75	2b104	38	2.3
1984	NY A	142	564	86	162	24	2	2	31	86	4	0	42	.287	.377	.348	.725	+7	10	6	63	2b142	0	3.9
1985	NY A	143	497	75	137	21	2	5	40	85	3	4	39	.276	.382	.356	.738	+7	16	9	64	2b143	0	2.2
1986	NY A	141	492	76	136	15	2	5	50	94	0	3	49	.276	.393	.346	.739	+4	15	2	88	2b139/D	0	2.1
1987	NY A★	120	449	96	137	24	2	7	67	82	1	2	25	.305	.411	.414	.825	+22	11	1	92	2b119/D	30	3.4
1988	NY A	110	404	43	93	20	1	2	34	55	2	2	39	.230	.322	.300	.622	-24	8	4	67	2b110	40	0.7
1989	LA N★	145	549	62	155	18	0	2	36	71	2	4	51	.282	.366	.326	.692	+1	7	6	54	2b140	0	0.3
1990	LA N	26	96	15	26	4	0	1	9	13	0	1	9	.271	.364	.344	.708	-2	1	0	100	2b26	0	0.1
1990	†Oak A	93	292	37	75	9	3	1	21	32	1	1	25	.257	.331	.318	.649	-14	6	1	86	2b84,D6	17	-1.0
1990	Major	119	388	52	101	13	3	2	30	45	1	2	34	.260	1.340	.325	1.665	+110	7	1	88	—	17	-0.9
1991	Mil A	124	431	60	141	14	3	0	54	75	3	0	38	.327	.424	.374	.798	+26	4	2	67	2b121,D2	0	3.2
1992	NY N	90	286	29	72	11	1	2	15	40	1	4	34	.252	.352	.318	.670	-8	1	3	25	2b79	50	-0.6
Total	18	2202	8018	1239	2210	316	65	54	687	1243	37	38	675	.276	.373	.351	.724	+4	271	94	74	2b2152,D11/3b	196	36.0
Team	13	1694	6303	1027	1731	259	58	48	549	1005	29	28	512	.275	.374	.357	.731	+5	251	82	75	2b1688,D3	129	34.4
/150	1	150	558	91	153	23	5	4	49	89	3	2	45	.275	.374	.357	.731	+5	22	7	76	2b149/D	11	3.0
Reed, Jack	John Burwell B2.2.1933 Silver City MS BR/TR/6'0"/(175–185) d4.23 Col U. of Mississippi																							
1961	†NY A	28	13	4	2	0	0	0	1	1	0	0	1	.154	.214	.154	.368	-100	0	0	0	O27(12/14/1)	0	-0.3
1962	NY A	88	43	17	13	2	1	1	4	4	1	0	7	.302	.362	.465	.827	+25	2	1	67	O75(20/39/16)	0	0.0
1963	NY A	106	73	18	15	3	1	0	1	9	0	0	14	.205	.293	.274	.567	-40	5	1	83	O89(14/30/46)	0	-0.3
Total	3	222	129	39	30	5	2	1	6	14	1	0	22	.233	.308	.326	.634	-24	7	2	78	O191(46/83/63)	0	-0.6
/150	2	150	87	26	20	3	1	1	4	9	1	0	15	.233	.308	.326	.634	-24	5	1	83	O129(31/56/43)	0	-0.4
Reese, Jimmie	James Herman (b James Herman Soloman) B10.1.1901 New York NY D7.13.1994 Santa Ana CA BL/TR/5'11.5"/165 d4.19 C22																							
1930	NY A	77	188	44	65	14	2	3	18	11	—	0	8	.346	.382	.489	.871	+25	1	1	50	2b48,3b5	—	0.3
1931	NY A	65	245	41	59	10	2	3	26	17	—	1	10	.241	.293	.335	.628	-32	2	3	40	2b61	—	-0.7
1932	StL N	90	309	38	82	15	0	2	26	20	—	2	19	.265	.314	.333	.647	-28	4	—	—	2b77	—	0.4
Total	3	232	742	123	206	39	4	8	70	48	—	3	37	.278	.324	.373	.697	-16	7	4	100	2b186,3b5	—	0.0
Team	2	142	433	85	124	24	4	6	44	28	—	1	18	.286	.331	.402	.733	-7	3	4	43	2b109,3b5	—	-0.4
/150	2	150	457	90	131	25	4	6	46	30	—	1	19	.286	.331	.402	.733	-7	3	4	43	2b115,3b5	—	-0.4
Reese, Kevin	Kevin Patrick B3.11.1978 San Diego CA BL/TL/5'11"/195 Dr 2000 SDN 27/799 d6.26 Col San Diego																							
2005	NY A	2	1	0	0	0	0	0	0	1	0	0	1	.000	.500	.000	.500	-50	0	0	0	O2(1/1/0)	0	0.0
2006	NY A	10	12	2	5	0	0	0	1	1	0	1	1	.417	.500	.417	.917	+39	1	0	100	O4(2/0/2),D2	0	0.0
Total	2	12	13	2	5	0	0	0	1	2	0	1	2	.385	.500	.385	.885	+32	1	0	100	O6(3/1/2),D2	0	0.0
Renna, Bill	William Beneditto "Big Bill" B10.14.1924 Hanford CA BR/TR/6'3"/(218–230) d4.14 Col Santa Clara																							
1953	NY A	61	121	19	38	6	3	2	13	13	—	1	31	.314	.385	.463	.848	+33	0	1	0	O40(32/5/3)	0	0.2
Total	6	370	918	123	219	36	10	28	119	99	1	6	166	.239	.315	.391	.706	-9	2	7	22	O277(81/6/192)	0	-2.3
Rensa, Tony	George Anthony "Pug" B9.29.1901 Parsons PA D1.4.1987 Wilkes-Barre PA BR/TR/5'10"/180 d5.5																							
1933	NY A	8	29	4	9	2	1	0	3	1	—	0	3	.310	.333	.448	.781	+12	0	1	0	C8	—	0.0
Total	6	200	514	71	134	26	5	7	65	57	—	3	54	.261	.338	.372	.710	-26	5	2	100	C185	—	-1.3
Repoz, Roger	Roger Allen B8.3.1940 Bellingham WA BL/TL/6'3"/(175–195) d9.11 Col Western Washington																							
1964	NY A	11	1	1	0	0	0	0	0	1	0	0	1	.000	.500	.000	.500	-48	0	0	0	O9R	0	-0.1
1965	NY A	79	218	34	48	7	4	12	28	25	4	0	57	.220	.298	.454	.752	+12	1	1	50	O69(0/65/7)	0	-0.3
1966	NY A	37	43	4	15	4	1	0	9	4	0	0	8	.349	.396	.488	.884	+61	0	0	0	O30(0/28/5)	0	0.0
Total	9	831	2145	257	480	73	19	82	260	280	27	10	499	.224	.314	.390	.704	+5	26	25	51	O623(54/357/242),1b107	0	-2.8
Team	3	127	262	39	63	11	5	12	37	30	4	0	66	.240	.315	.458	.773	+19	1	1	50	O108(28/6/15)	0	-0.4
/150	4	150	309	46	74	13	6	14	44	35	5	0	78	.240	.315	.458	.773	+19	1	1	50	O128(33/7/18)	0	-0.5
Revering, Dave	David Alvin B2.12.1953 Roseville CA BL/TR/6'4"/205 Dr 1971 CinN 7/170 d4.8																							
1981	†NY A	45	119	8	28	4	1	2	7	11	5	0	20	.235	.300	.336	.636	-16	0	1	0	1b44	0	0.0
1982	NY A	14	40	2	6	2	0	0	2	3	2	0	4	.150	.205	.200	.405	-87	0	0	0	1b13/D	0	-0.7
Total	5	557	1032	206	486	83	16	62	234	148	26	2	240	.265	.318	.430	.748	+9	2	10	17	1b454,D78	15	-0.6
Team	2	59	159	10	34	6	1	2	9	14	7	0	24	.214	.276	.302	.578	-34	0	1	0	1b57/D	0	-0.7
Reynolds, Bill	William Dee B8.14.1884 Eastland TX D6.5.1924 Carnegie OK BR/TR/6'0"/185 d9.15																							
1913	NY A	5	5	0	0	0	0	0	0	0	—	0	1	.000	.000	.000	.000	-199	0	—	—	C5	—	-0.1
1914	NY A	4	5	0	2	0	0	0	0	0	—	0	3	.400	.400	.400	.800	+41	0	—	—	/C	—	0.1
Total	2	9	10	0	2	0	0	0	0	0	—	0	4	.200	.200	.200	.400	-81	0	—	—	C6	—	0.0

Batters

YEAR	TM LG	G	AB	R	H	2B	3B	HR	RBI	BB	IB	HP	SO	AVG	OBP	SLG	OPS	AOPS	SB	CS	SB%	GAMES AT POSITION	DL	BFW
Rice, Harry	Harry Francis B11.22.1901 Ware Station IL D1.1.1971 Portland OR BL/TR/5'9"/185 d4.18 OF(28/465/421)																							
1930	NY A	100	346	62	103	17	5	7	74	31	—	3	21	.298	.361	.436	.797	+6	3	3	50	O87(4/83/0),1b6/3b	—	0.1
Total	10	1034	3740	620	1118	186	63	48	506	376	—	32	194	.299	.368	.421	.789	+4	59	55	100	O911C,3b38,1b11,2b9,S4/C	—	-1.5
/150	2	150	519	93	155	26	8	11	111	47	—	5	32	.298	.361	.436	.797	+6	5	5	50	O131(6/125/0),1b9,3b2	—	0.1
Richardson, Nolen	Clifford Nolen B1.18.1903 Chattanooga TN D9.25.1951 Athens GA BR/TR/6'1.5"/170 d4.16 Col Georgia																							
1935	NY A	12	46	3	10	1	1	0	5	3	—	0	1	.217	.265	.283	.548	-56	0	0	0	S12	—	-0.8
Total	6	168	473	39	117	19	5	0	45	23	—	0	22	.247	.282	.309	.591	-45	8	4	100	3b103,S65	—	-2.6
Richardson, Bobby	Robert Clinton B8.19.1935 Sumter SC BR/TR/5'9"/(160–173) d8.5																							
1955	NY A	11	26	2	4	0	0	0	3	2	0	0	0	.154	.214	.154	.368	-100	1	1	50	2b6,S4	0	-0.7
1956	NY A	5	7	1	1	0	0	0	0	0	0	0	1	.143	.143	.143	.286	-125	0	0	0	2b5	0	-0.1
1957	†NY A☆	97	305	36	78	11	1	0	19	9	3	0	26	.256	.274	.298	.572	-42	1	3	25	2b93	0	-1.2
1958	†NY A	73	182	18	45	6	2	0	14	8	0	0	5	.247	.276	.302	.578	-38	1	3	25	2b51,3b13,S2	0	-0.5
1959	NY A☆	134	469	53	141	18	6	2	33	26	3	0	20	.301	.335	.377	.712	-1	5	5	50	2b109,S14,3b12	0	0.5
1960	†NY A	150	460	45	116	12	3	1	26	35	6	0	19	.252	.303	.298	.601	-32	6	6	50	2b141,3b11	0	-2.7
1961	†NY A	162	662	80	173	17	5	3	49	30	1	2	23	.261	.295	.316	.611	-33	9	7	56	2b161	0	-2.4
1962	†NY A★	161	692	99	**209**	38	5	8	59	37	1	1	24	.302	.337	.406	.743	+3	11	9	55	2b161	0	1.2
1963	†NY A★	151	630	72	167	20	6	3	48	25	0	2	22	.265	.294	.330	.624	-24	15	1	94	2b150	0	0.7
1964	†NY A★	159	679	90	181	25	4	4	50	28	1	0	36	.267	.294	.333	.627	-27	11	2	85	2b157/S	0	-2.4
1965	NY A★	160	664	76	164	28	2	6	47	37	4	1	39	.247	.287	.322	.609	-26	7	5	58	2b158	0	-1.0
1966	NY A★	149	610	71	153	21	3	7	42	25	1	1	28	.251	.280	.330	.610	-22	6	6	50	2b147,3b2	0	-0.1
Total	12	1412	5386	643	1432	196	37	34	390	262	20	7	243	.266	.299	.335	.634	-23	73	48	60	2b1339,3b38,S21	0	-8.7
/150	1	150	572	68	152	21	4	4	41	28	2	1	26	.266	.299	.335	.634	-23	8	5	62	2b14,3b4,S2	0	-0.9
Rickey, Branch	Wesley Branch "The Mahatma" B12.20.1881 Flat OH D12.9.1965 Columbia MO BL/TR/5'9"/175 d6.16 M10 HF1967 Col Ohio Wesleyan																							
1905	StL A	1	3	0	0	0	0	0	0	0	—	0	—	.000	.000	.000	.000	-199	0	—	—	/C	—	-0.1
1906	StL A	65	201	22	57	7	3	3	24	16	—	3	—	.284	.345	.393	.738	+37	4	—	—	C55/rf	—	0.8
1907	NY A	52	137	16	25	1	3	0	15	11	—	2	—	.182	.253	.234	.487	-49	4	—	—	O22(20/1/1),C11,1b9	—	-1.4
1914	StL A	2	2	0	0	0	0	0	0	0	—	0	1	.000	.000	.000	.000	-199	0	—	—	/HM	—	-0.1
Total	4	120	343	38	82	8	6	3	39	27	—	5	1	.239	.304	.324	.628	-3	8	—	—	C67,O23(20/1/2),1b9	—	-0.8
Rivera, Juan	Juan Luis B7.3.1978 Guarenas, Miranda, Venez BR/TR/6'2"/(170–225) d9.4																							
2001	NY A	3	4	0	0	0	0	0	0	0	0	0	0	.000	.000	.000	.000	-199	0	0	0	O3(0/1/2)	0	-0.2
2002	†NY A	28	83	9	22	5	0	1	6	6	0	0	10	.265	.311	.361	.672	-20	1	1	50	O28(15/0/15)	72	-0.3
2003	†NY A	57	173	22	46	14	0	7	26	10	1	0	27	.266	.304	.468	.772	+1	0	0	0	O56(34/0/22)	0	-0.2
Total	7	466	1492	193	434	88	2	60	233	107	8	8	189	.291	.340	.473	.813	+10	8	16	33	O394(150/38/221),D51	247	1.1
Team	3	88	260	31	68	19	0	8	32	16	1	0	37	.262	.302	.427	.729	-9	1	1	50	O87(15/1/2)	72	-0.7
Rivera, Ruben	Ruben (Moreno) B11.14.1973 Chorrera, Pan BR/TR/6'3"/(200–208) d9.3 [DL 1997 NY A 59]																							
1995	NY A	5	1	0	0	0	0	0	0	0	0	0	1	.000	.000	.000	.000	-199	0	0	0	O4L	0	0.0
1996	†NY A	46	88	17	25	6	1	2	16	13	0	2	26	.284	.381	.443	.824	+10	6	2	75	O45(13/14/19)	0	0.5
Total	9	662	1586	237	343	67	11	64	203	185	4	29	510	.216	.307	.393	.700	-19	50	20	71	O615(52/455/123),D2	156	-2.5
Team	2	51	89	17	25	6	1	2	16	13	0	2	27	.281	.377	.438	.815	+8	6	2	75	O49(17/19/19)	59	0.5
Rivers, Mickey	John Milton B10.31.1948 Miami FL BL/TL/5'10"/(160–165) Dr 1969 AtlN S2/40 d8.4 Mil 1971 Col Miami–Dade North (FL) CC																							
1970	Cal A	17	25	6	8	2	0	0	3	3	0	1	5	.320	.414	.400	.814	+29	1	0	100	O5R	0	0.1
1971	Cal A	79	268	31	71	12	2	1	12	19	1	1	38	.265	.316	.336	.652	-9	13	1	93	O76(4/61/18)	0	-0.5
1972	Cal A	58	159	18	34	6	2	0	7	8	1	1	26	.214	.256	.277	.533	-38	4	3	57	O48(6/38/7)	0	-1.0
1973	Cal A	30	129	26	45	6	4	0	16	8	0	1	11	.349	.391	.457	.848	+49	8	3	73	O29C	0	0.2
1974	Cal A	118	466	69	133	19	**11**	3	31	39	0	1	47	.285	.341	.393	.734	+17	30	13	70	O116C	43	1.2
1975	Cal A	155	616	70	175	17	**13**	1	53	43	5	2	42	.284	.331	.359	.690	+2	**70**	14	83	O152(27/125/0)/D	0	0.6
1976	†NY A★	137	590	95	184	31	8	8	67	13	0	3	51	.312	.327	.432	.759	+23	43	7	86	O136C	0	1.6
1977	†NY A	138	565	79	184	18	5	12	69	18	4	4	45	.326	.350	.439	.789	+14	22	14	61	O136C/D	0	1.4
1978	†NY A	141	559	78	148	25	8	11	48	29	3	3	51	.265	.302	.397	.699	-2	25	5	83	O138C	15	0.3
1979	NY A	74	286	37	82	18	5	3	25	13	2	1	21	.287	.315	.416	.731	-2	3	7	30	O69C/D	20	-1.1
1979	Tex A	58	247	35	74	9	3	6	25	9	0	1	18	.300	.323	.433	.756	+4	7	2	78	O57C	0	0.1
1979	Year	132	533	72	156	27	8	9	50	22	2	2	39	.293	.319	.424	.743	+1	10	9	53	O126C/D	0	-1.0
1980	Tex A	147	630	96	210	32	6	7	60	20	1	1	34	.333	.353	.437	.790	+19	18	7	72	O141C,D4	0	1.7
1981	Tex A	99	399	62	114	21	2	3	26	24	2	1	31	.286	.327	.371	.698	+6	9	5	64	O97C	0	0.1
1982	Tex A	19	68	6	16	1	1	1	4	0	0	0	7	.235	.232	.324	.556	-46	0	0	0	D16	146	-0.5
1983	Tex A	96	309	37	88	17	0	1	20	11	0	1	21	.285	.309	.350	.659	-18	9	4	69	D53,O23(15/0/8)	0	-0.9
1984	Tex A	102	313	40	94	13	1	4	33	9	1	0	23	.300	.320	.387	.707	-9	5	5	50	D48,O30(26/2/2)	0	-0.7
Total	15	1468	5629	785	1660	247	71	61	499	266	20	22	471	.295	.327	.397	.724	+6	267	90	75	O1253(78/1145/40),D124	224	2.6
Team	4	490	2000	289	598	92	26	34	209	73	9	11	168	.299	.324	.422	.746	+10	93	33	74	O479C,D2	35	2.2
/150	1	150	612	88	183	28	8	10	64	22	3	3	51	.299	.324	.422	.746	+10	28	10	74	O147C/D	11	0.7
Rizzuto, Phil	Philip Francis "Scooter" (b Fiero Francis Rizzuto) B9.25.1917 Brooklyn NY D8.13.2007 West Orange NJ BR/TR/5'6"/160 d4.14 Mil 1943–45 HF1994																							
1941	†NY A	133	515	65	158	20	9	3	46	27	—	1	36	.307	.343	.398	.741	-3	14	5	74	S128	0	2.4
1942	†NY A☆	144	553	79	157	24	7	4	68	44	—	6	40	.284	.343	.374	.717	+4	22	6	79	S144	0	4.6
1946	NY A	126	471	53	121	17	1	2	38	34	—	6	39	.257	.315	.310	.625	-26	14	7	67	S125	0	0.9
1947	†NY A	153	549	78	150	26	9	2	60	57	—	**8**	31	.273	.350	.364	.714	+0	11	6	65	S151	0	2.8
1948	NY A	128	464	65	117	13	2	6	50	60	—	2	24	.252	.340	.328	.668	-21	6	5	55	S128	0	-1.8
1949	†NY A	153	614	110	169	22	7	5	65	72	—	1	34	.275	.362	.350	.710	-12	18	6	75	S152	0	0.3
1950	†NY A★	**155**	617	125	200	36	7	7	66	92	—	7	39	.324	.418	.439	.857	+23	12	8	60	S155	0	**4.0**
1951	†NY A★	144	540	87	148	21	6	2	43	58	—	5	27	.274	.350	.346	.696	-8	18	3	86	S144	0	1.7
1952	†NY A★	152	578	89	147	24	10	2	43	67	—	5	42	.254	.337	.341	.678	-5	17	6	74	S152	0	2.9
1953	†NY A★	134	413	54	112	21	3	2	54	71	—	4	39	.271	.383	.351	.734	+3	4	3	57	S133	0	1.9
1954	NY A	127	307	47	60	11	0	2	15	41	—	1	23	.195	.291	.251	.542	-49	3	2	60	S126/2b	0	-0.6
1955	†NY A	81	143	19	37	4	1	1	9	22	1	3	18	.259	.369	.322	.691	-12	7	1	88	S79/2b	0	-0.4
1956	NY A	31	52	6	12	0	0	0	6	6	0	0	6	.231	.310	.231	.541	-54	3	0	100	S30	0	0.0
Total	13	1661	5816	877	1588	239	62	38	563	651	1	49	398	.273	.351	.355	.706	-7	149	58	72	S1647,2b2	0	18.7
/150	1	150	525	79	143	22	6	3	51	59	0	4	36	.273	.351	.355	.706	-7	13	5	72	S15/2	0	1.7
Roach, Roxey	Wilbur Charles B11.28.1882 Anita PA D12.26.1947 Bay City MI BR/TR/5'11"/160 d5.2																							
1910	NY A	70	220	27	47	9	2	0	20	29	—	3	—	.214	.313	.273	.586	-21	15	—	—	S58,O9L	—	-0.7
1911	NY A	13	40	4	10	2	1	0	2	6	—	0	—	.250	.348	.350	.698	-11	0	—	—	S8,2b5	—	-0.1
1912	Was A	2	2	1	1	0	0	1	1	0	—	0	—	.500	.500	2.000	2.500	+500	0	—	—	S2	—	0.1
1915	Buf F	92	346	35	93	20	3	2	31	17	—	0	34	.269	.303	.361	.664	-15	11	—	—	S92	—	1.1
Total	4	177	608	67	151	31	6	3	54	52	—	3	34	.248	.311	.334	.645	-15	26	—	—	S160,O9L,2b5	—	0.4
Team	2	83	260	31	57	11	3	0	22	35	—	3	0	.219	.319	.285	.604	-19	15	—	—	S66,O9L,2b5	—	-0.8
Robertson, Andre	Andre Levett B10.2.1957 Orange TX BR/TR/5'10"/(155–162) Dr 1979 TorA 4/81 d9.3 Col Texas																							
1981	†NY A	10	19	1	5	1	0	0	0	0	0	0	3	.263	.263	.316	.579	-33	1	1	50	S8,2b3	0	0.0
1982	NY A	44	118	16	26	5	0	2	9	8	0	0	19	.220	.270	.314	.584	-40	0	0	0	S27,2b15,3b2	0	0.0
1983	NY A	98	322	37	80	16	3	1	22	8	0	3	54	.248	.271	.326	.597	-34	2	4	33	S78,2b29	46	0.2
1984	NY A	52	140	10	30	5	1	0	6	4	0	0	20	.214	.236	.264	.500	-60	0	1	0	S49,2b6	0	-0.5

YEAR	TM LG	G	AB	R	H	2B	3B	HR	RBI	BB	IB	HP	SO	AVG	OBP	SLG	OPS	AOPS	SB	CS	SB%	GAMES AT POSITION	DL	BFW
1985	NY A	50	125	16	41	5	0	2	17	6	0	1	24	.328	.358	.416	.774	+15	1	2	33	3b33,S14,2b2	51	-0.4
Total	5	254	724	80	182	32	4	5	54	26	0	4	120	.251	.279	.327	.606	-31	4	8	33	S176,2b55,3b35	97	-0.7
/150	3	150	428	47	107	19	2	3	32	15	0	2	71	.251	.279	.327	.606	-31	2	5	29	S104,2b32,3b21	57	-0.4

Robertson, Gene Eugene Edward B12.25.1898 St.Louis MO D10.21.1981 Fallon NV BL/TR/5'7"/152 d7.4 Col St. Louis

YEAR	TM LG	G	AB	R	H	2B	3B	HR	RBI	BB	IB	HP	SO	AVG	OBP	SLG	OPS	AOPS	SB	CS	SB%	GAMES AT POSITION	DL	BFW
1928	†NY A	83	251	29	73	9	0	1	36	14	—	0	6	.291	.328	.339	.667	-22	2	4	33	3b70,2b3	—	-1.6
1929	NY A	90	309	45	92	15	6	0	35	28	—	1	6	.298	.358	.385	.743	-2	3	3	50	3b77	—	-0.7
Total	9	656	2200	311	615	100	23	20	249	205	—	10	79	.280	.344	.373	.717	-17	29	22	100	3b571,S20,2b10	—	-7.4
Team	2	173	560	74	165	24	6	1	71	42	—	1	12	.295	.345	.364	.709	-11	5	7	42	3b147,2b3	—	-2.3
/150	2	150	486	64	143	21	5	1	62	36	—	1	10	.295	.345	.364	.709	-11	4	6	40	3b127,2b3	—	-2.0

Robinson, Aaron Aaron Andrew B6.23.1915 Lancaster SC D3.9.1966 Lancaster SC BL/TR/6'2"/205 d5.6 Mil 1943–45

YEAR	TM LG	G	AB	R	H	2B	3B	HR	RBI	BB	IB	HP	SO	AVG	OBP	SLG	OPS	AOPS	SB	CS	SB%	GAMES AT POSITION	DL	BFW
1943	NY A	1	1	0	0	0	0	0	0	0	—	0	1	.000	.000	.000	.000	-199	0	0	0	/H	0	0.0
1945	NY A	50	160	19	45	6	1	8	24	21	—	1	23	.281	.368	.481	.849	+39	0	0	0	C45	0	0.7
1946	NY A	100	330	32	98	17	2	16	64	48	—	1	39	.297	.388	.506	.894	+46	0	1	0	C95	0	2.4
1947	†NY A☆	82	252	23	68	11	5	5	36	40	—	0	26	.270	.370	.413	.783	+19	0	1	0	C74	0	1.0
1948	Chi A	98	326	47	82	14	2	8	39	46	—	0	30	.252	.344	.380	.724	-4	0	1	0	C92	0	-0.3
1949	Det A	110	331	38	89	12	0	13	56	73	—	1	21	.269	.402	.423	.825	+18	0	2	0	C108	0	1.3
1950	Det A	107	283	37	64	7	0	9	37	75	—	0	35	.226	.388	.346	.734	-14	0	1	0	C103	0	0.2
1951	Det A	36	82	3	17	6	0	0	9	17	—	0	9	.207	.343	.280	.623	-30	0	0	0	C35	0	-0.3
1951	Bos A	26	74	9	15	1	1	2	7	17	—	0	10	.203	.352	.324	.676	-24	0	0	0	C25	0	-0.1
1951	Year	62	156	12	32	7	1	2	16	34	—	0	19	.205	.347	.301	.648	-27	0	0	0	C60	0	-0.4
Total	8	610	1839	208	478	74	11	61	272	337	—	3	194	.260	.375	.412	.787	+12	0	6	0	C577	0	4.9
Team	4	233	743	74	211	34	8	29	124	109	—	2	89	.284	.377	.468	.845	+35	0	2	0	C214	0	4.1
/150	3	150	478	48	136	22	5	19	80	70	—	1	57	.284	.377	.468	.845	+35	0	1	0	C138	0	2.6

Robinson, Bruce Bruce Philip B4.16.1954 LaJolla CA BL/TR/6'1"/(194–195) Dr 1975 OakA 1/21 d8.19 b–Dave Col Stanford [DL 1981 NY A 151]

YEAR	TM LG	G	AB	R	H	2B	3B	HR	RBI	BB	IB	HP	SO	AVG	OBP	SLG	OPS	AOPS	SB	CS	SB%	GAMES AT POSITION	DL	BFW
1979	NY A	6	12	0	2	0	0	0	2	1	0	0	0	.167	.231	.167	.398	-91	0	0	0	C6	0	0.0
1980	NY A	4	5	0	0	0	0	0	0	0	0	0	4	.000	.000	.000	.000	-199	0	0	0	C3	0	-0.1
Total	3	38	101	5	23	3	1	0	10	4	0	0	12	.228	.257	.277	.534	-49	0	0	0	C37	151	0.4
Team	2	10	17	0	2	0	0	0	2	1	0	0	4	.118	.167	.118	.285	-121	0	0	0	C9	151	-0.1

Robinson, Eddie William Edward B12.15.1920 Paris TX BL/TR/6'2.5"/(205–215) d9.9 Mil 1943–45 C3 Col Paris (TX) JC

YEAR	TM LG	G	AB	R	H	2B	3B	HR	RBI	BB	IB	HP	SO	AVG	OBP	SLG	OPS	AOPS	SB	CS	SB%	GAMES AT POSITION	DL	BFW
1954	NY A	85	142	11	37	9	0	3	27	19	—	0	21	.261	.344	.387	.731	+5	0	0	0	1b29	0	0.1
1955	†NY A	88	173	25	36	1	0	16	42	36	7	5	26	.208	.358	.491	.849	+29	0	0	0	1b46	0	0.2
1956	NY A	26	54	7	12	1	0	5	11	5	1	3	3	.222	.323	.519	.842	+23	0	1	0	1b14	0	0.0
Total	13	1315	4282	546	1146	172	24	172	723	521	10	50	359	.268	.353	.440	.793	+13	10	12	45	1b1126	0	-2.1
Team	3	199	369	43	85	11	0	24	80	60	8	8	50	.230	.348	.455	.803	+19	0	1	0	1b89	0	0.3
/150	2	150	278	32	64	8	0	18	60	45	6	6	38	.230	.348	.455	.803	+19	0	1	0	1b67	0	0.2

Robinson, Bill William Henry B6.26.1943 McKeesport PA D7.29.2007 Las Vegas NV BR/TR/6'3"/(175–200) d9.20 C10

YEAR	TM LG	G	AB	R	H	2B	3B	HR	RBI	BB	IB	HP	SO	AVG	OBP	SLG	OPS	AOPS	SB	CS	SB%	GAMES AT POSITION	DL	BFW
1967	NY A	116	342	31	67	6	1	7	29	28	4	2	56	.196	.259	.281	.540	-38	2	2	50	O102(20/33/53)	0	-2.7
1968	NY A	107	342	34	82	16	7	6	40	26	3	2	54	.240	.294	.380	.674	+8	7	6	54	O98(6/51/44)	0	-0.9
1969	NY A	87	222	23	38	11	2	3	21	16	3	0	39	.171	.226	.279	.505	-58	3	1	75	O62(17/19/29)/1b	0	-2.3
Total	16	1472	4364	536	1127	229	29	166	641	263	49	16	820	.258	.300	.438	.738	+3	71	49	59	O1059(479/280/364),1b201,3b103	169	-8.1
Team	3	310	906	88	187	33	10	16	90	70	10	4	149	.206	.264	.318	.582	-25	12	9	57	O262(33/103/126)/1	0	-5.9
/150	1	150	438	43	90	16	5	8	44	34	5	2	72	.206	.264	.318	.582	-25	6	4	60	O127(16/50/61)/1	0	-2.9

Rodriguez, Alex Alexander Emmanuel "A-Rod" B7.27.1975 New York NY BR/TR/6'3"/(190–225) Dr 1993 SeaA 1/1 d7.8

YEAR	TM LG	G	AB	R	H	2B	3B	HR	RBI	BB	IB	HP	SO	AVG	OBP	SLG	OPS	AOPS	SB	CS	SB%	GAMES AT POSITION	DL	BFW
2004	†NY A★	155	601	112	172	24	2	36	106	80	6	10	131	.286	.375	.512	.887	+29	28	4	88	3b155,S2	0	2.9
2005	†NY A★	**162**	605	**124**	194	29	1	**48**	130	91	8	16	139	.321	.421	**.610**	1.031	+71	21	6	78	3b161,S3/D	0	**6.0**
2006	†NY A★	154	572	113	166	26	1	35	121	90	8	8	139	.290	.392	.523	.915	+32	15	4	79	3b151,D3	0	1.2
2007	†NY A★	158	583	**143**	183	31	0	**54**	**156**	95	11	21	120	.314	.422	**.645**	1.067	+75	24	4	86	3b154,D4	0	5.2
Total	14	1904	7350	1501	2250	395	26	518	1503	915	70	127	1524	.306	.389	.578	.967	+47	265	64	81	S1272,3b621,D13	82	57.4
Team	4	629	2361	492	715	110	4	173	513	356	33	55	529	.303	.403	.573	.976	+52	88	18	83	3b621,D8,S5	0	15.3
/150	1	150	563	117	171	26	1	41	122	85	8	13	126	.303	.403	.573	.976	+52	21	4	84	3b148,D2/S	0	3.6

Rodriguez, Aurelio Aurelio (Ituarte) B12.28.1947 Cananea, Sonora, Mexico D9.23.2000 Detroit MI BR/TR/5'10"/(175–180) d9.1

YEAR	TM LG	G	AB	R	H	2B	3B	HR	RBI	BB	IB	HP	SO	AVG	OBP	SLG	OPS	AOPS	SB	CS	SB%	GAMES AT POSITION	DL	BFW
1980	†NY A	52	164	14	36	6	1	3	14	7	1	0	35	.220	.251	.323	.574	-43	0	0	0	3b49,2b6	0	-2.2
1981	†NY A	27	52	4	18	2	0	2	8	2	0	0	10	.346	.370	.500	.870	+50	0	0	0	3b20,2b3/1bD	0	0.5
Total	17	2017	6611	612	1570	287	46	124	648	324	37	27	943	.237	.275	.351	.626	-25	35	31	53	3b1983,S16,2b14,D2,1b2	95	-12.6
Team	2	79	216	18	54	8	1	5	22	9	1	0	45	.250	.280	.366	.646	-21	0	0	0	3b69,2b9/1D	0	-1.7

Rodriguez, Carlos Carlos (Marquez) B11.1.1967 Mexico City, Distrito Federal, Mexico BB/TR/5'9"/160 d6.16

YEAR	TM LG	G	AB	R	H	2B	3B	HR	RBI	BB	IB	HP	SO	AVG	OBP	SLG	OPS	AOPS	SB	CS	SB%	GAMES AT POSITION	DL	BFW
1991	NY A	15	37	1	7	0	0	0	2	1	0	0	2	.189	.211	.189	.400	-89	0	0	0	S11,2b3	0	-0.3
Total	3	85	241	21	67	16	1	1	20	14	0	1	17	.278	.320	.365	.685	-25	1	0	100	S49,2b30,3b5	0	-0.3

Rodriguez, Edwin Edwin (Morales) B8.14.1960 Ponce, PR BR/TR/5'11"/175 d9.28

YEAR	TM LG	G	AB	R	H	2B	3B	HR	RBI	BB	IB	HP	SO	AVG	OBP	SLG	OPS	AOPS	SB	CS	SB%	GAMES AT POSITION	DL	BFW
1982	NY A	3	9	2	3	0	0	0	1	1	0	0	1	.333	.400	.333	.733	+5	0	0	0	2b3	0	0.2
Total	3	11	22	3	5	1	0	0	1	2	0	0	4	.227	.292	.273	.565	-42	0	0	0	2b8,S2/3b	0	-0.1

Rodriguez, Ellie Eliseo (Delgado) B5.24.1946 Fajardo, PR BR/TR/5'11"/(175–185) d5.26 [DL 1977 LA N 26]

YEAR	TM LG	G	AB	R	H	2B	3B	HR	RBI	BB	IB	HP	SO	AVG	OBP	SLG	OPS	AOPS	SB	CS	SB%	GAMES AT POSITION	DL	BFW
1968	NY A	9	24	1	5	0	0	0	1	3	0	0	3	.208	.296	.208	.504	-43	0	0	0	C9	0	-0.2
Total	9	775	2173	220	533	76	6	16	203	332	29	55	291	.245	.356	.308	.664	-6	17	18	49	C737,D15	72	3.2

Rodriguez, Henry Henry Anderson (Lorenzo) B11.8.1967 Santo Domingo, D.R. BL/TL/6'1"/(180–225) d7.5

YEAR	TM LG	G	AB	R	H	2B	3B	HR	RBI	BB	IB	HP	SO	AVG	OBP	SLG	OPS	AOPS	SB	CS	SB%	GAMES AT POSITION	DL	BFW
2001	NY A	5	8	0	0	0	0	0	0	0	0	0	6	.000	.000	.000	.000	-199	0	0	0	/D	52	-0.2
Total	11	950	3031	389	784	176	9	160	523	276	33	11	803	.259	.321	.481	.802	+7	10	14	42	O765(680/0/95),1b96,D8	142	-2.2

Roenicke, Gary Gary Steven B12.5.1954 Covina CA BR/TR/6'3"/(198–203) Dr 1973 MonN 1/8 d6.8 b–Ron

YEAR	TM LG	G	AB	R	H	2B	3B	HR	RBI	BB	IB	HP	SO	AVG	OBP	SLG	OPS	AOPS	SB	CS	SB%	GAMES AT POSITION	DL	BFW
1986	NY A	69	136	11	36	5	0	3	18	27	0	1	30	.265	.388	.368	.756	+8	1	1	50	O37(33/3/2),D15,3b3,1b2	0	0.0
Total	12	1064	2708	367	670	135	4	121	410	406	16	41	428	.247	.351	.434	.785	+17	16	20	44	O918(693/113/236),D36,1b29,3b5	35	4.5

Roettger, Oscar Oscar Frederick Louis "Okkie" B2.19.1900 St.Louis MO D7.4.1986 St.Louis MO BR/TR/6'0"/170 d7.7 b–Wally ▲

YEAR	TM LG	G	AB	R	H	2B	3B	HR	RBI	BB	IB	HP	SO	AVG	OBP	SLG	OPS	AOPS	SB	CS	SB%	GAMES AT POSITION	DL	BFW
1923	NY A	5	2	0	0	0	0	0	0	0	—	0	0	.000	.000	.000	.000	-198	0	0	0	P5	—	0.0
1924	NY A	1	0	0	0	0	0	0	0	0	—	0	0	+	+	+	.000	-100	0	0	0	/P	—	0.0
Total	4	37	66	7	14	1	0	0	6	6	—	1	5	.212	.288	.227	.515	-66	0	0	0	1b15,P6/rf	—	-0.9
Team	2	6	2	0	0	0	0	0	0	0	—	0	0	.000	.000	.000	.000	-198	0	0	0	P6	—	0.0

Rogers, Jay Jay Lewis B8.3.1888 Sandusky NY D7.1.1964 Carlisle NY BR/TR/5'11.5"/178 d5.22

YEAR	TM LG	G	AB	R	H	2B	3B	HR	RBI	BB	IB	HP	SO	AVG	OBP	SLG	OPS	AOPS	SB	CS	SB%	GAMES AT POSITION	DL	BFW
1914	NY A	5	8	0	0	0	0	0	0	0	—	0	4	.000	.000	.000	.000	-199	0	—	—	C4	—	-0.2

Rolfe, Red Robert Abial B10.17.1908 Penacook NH D7.8.1969 Gilford NH BL/TR/5'11.5"/170 d6.29 M4/C1 Col Dartmouth

YEAR	TM LG	G	AB	R	H	2B	3B	HR	RBI	BB	IB	HP	SO	AVG	OBP	SLG	OPS	AOPS	SB	CS	SB%	GAMES AT POSITION	DL	BFW
1931	NY A	1	0	0	0	0	0	0	0	0	—	0	0	+	+	+	.000	-100	0	0	0	/S	—	0.0
1934	NY A	89	279	54	80	13	2	0	18	26	—	0	16	.287	.348	.348	.696	-14	2	3	40	S46,3b26	—	-0.5
1935	NY A	**149**	639	108	192	33	9	5	67	57	—	3	39	.300	.361	.404	.765	+3	7	3	70	3b136,S17	—	0.2
1936	†NY A	135	568	116	181	39	**15**	10	70	68	—	1	38	.319	.392	.493	.885	+21	3	0	100	3b133	—	2.2
1937	†NY A★	154	648	143	179	34	10	4	62	90	—	1	53	.276	.365	.378	.743	-13	4	2	67	3b154	—	-0.2
1938	†NY A☆	151	631	132	196	36	8	10	80	74	—	3	44	.311	.386	.441	.827	+7	13	1	93	3b151	—	0.9

YEAR	TM LG	G	AB	R	H	2B	3B	HR	RBI	BB	IB	HP	SO	AVG	OBP	SLG	OPS	AOPS	SB	CS	SB%	GAMES AT POSITION	DL	BFW
1939	†NY A★	**152**	648	**139**	**213**	**46**	10	14	80	81	—	1	41	.329	.404	.495	.899	+31	7	6	54	3b152	—	2.0
1940	NY A✶	139	588	102	147	26	6	10	53	50	—	2	48	.250	.311	.366	.677	-22	4	2	67	3b138	—	-1.5
1941	†NY A	136	561	106	148	22	5	8	42	57	—	0	38	.264	.332	.364	.696	-15	3	2	60	3b134	0	-1.5
1942	†NY A	69	265	42	58	8	2	8	25	23	—	0	18	.219	.281	.355	.636	-20	1	1	50	3b60	0	-0.2
Total	10	1175	4827	942	1394	257	67	69	497	526	—	10	335	.289	.360	.413	.773	+0	44	20	69	3b1084,S64	0	1.4
/150	1	150	616	120	178	33	9	9	63	67	—	1	43	.289	.360	.413	.773	+0	6	3	67	3b14,S8	0	0.2
ROSAR, BUDDY WARREN VINCENT B7.3.1914 BUFFALO NY D3.13.1994 ROCHESTER NY BR/TR/5'9"/190 d4.29 DEF 1944–45																								
1939	NY A	43	105	18	29	6	1	0	12	13	—	0	10	.276	.356	.343	.699	-19	4	0	100	C35	—	0.3
1940	NY A	73	228	34	68	11	3	4	37	19	—	2	11	.298	.357	.425	.782	+6	7	1	88	C63	—	0.8
1941	†NY A	67	209	25	60	17	2	1	36	22	—	0	10	.287	.355	.402	.757	+1	0	0	0	C60	0	0.5
1942	†NY A☆	69	209	18	48	10	0	2	34	17	—	0	20	.230	.288	.306	.594	-32	1	2	33	C58	0	0.0
Total	13	988	3198	335	836	147	15	18	367	315	—	10	161	.261	.330	.334	.664	-16	17	18	49	C934	0	2.4
Team	4	252	751	95	205	43	6	7	119	71	—	2	51	.273	.337	.374	.711	-9	12	3	80	C216	0	1.6
/150	2	150	447	57	122	26	4	4	71	42	—	1	30	.273	.337	.374	.711	-9	7	2	78	C129	0	1.0
ROSENTHAL, LARRY LAWRENCE JOHN B5.21.1910 ST.PAUL MN D3.4.1992 WOODBURY MN BL/TL/6'0.5"/190 d6.20																								
1944	NY A	36	101	9	20	3	0	0	9	19	—	0	15	.198	.325	.228	.553	-43	1	0	100	O26(10/5/11)	0	-0.5
Total	8	579	1483	240	390	75	25	22	189	251	—	1	195	.263	.370	.392	.762	-4	13	9	59	O410(109/177/131)/1b	0	-1.5
ROTH, BRAGGO ROBERT FRANK B8.28.1892 BURLINGTON WI D9.11.1936 CHICAGO IL BR/TR/5'7.5"/170 d9.1 B–FRANK																								
1921	NY A	43	152	29	43	9	2	2	10	19	—	2	20	.283	.370	.408	.778	-1	1	2	33	O37(3/17/17)	—	-0.7
Total	8	811	2831	427	804	138	73	30	422	335	—	35	389	.284	.367	.416	.783	+22	190	41	100	O727(42/135/550),3b35	—	1.4
ROYSTER, JERRY JERON KENNIS B10.18.1952 SACRAMENTO CA BR/TR/6'0"/(160–170) d8.14 M1/C4 OF(123/21/9)																								
1987	NY A	18	42	1	15	2	0	0	4	4	0	0	4	.357	.413	.405	.818	+19	2	1	67	3b13/2bSlf	0	0.2
Total	16	1428	4208	552	1049	165	33	40	352	411	20	11	534	.249	.315	.333	.648	-24	189	95	67	3b634,2b416,S187,O153L,D4	21	-3.5
RUEL, MUDDY HEROLD DOMINIC B2.20.1896 ST.LOUIS MO D11.13.1963 PALO ALTO CA BR/TR/5'9"/150 d5.29 MIL 1918 M1/C14																								
1917	NY A	6	17	1	2	0	0	0	1	2	—	0	2	.118	.211	.118	.329	-100	1	—	—	C6	—	-0.2
1918	NY A	3	6	0	2	0	0	0	0	2	—	0	1	.333	.500	.333	.833	+48	1	—	—	C2	—	0.1
1919	NY A	79	233	18	56	6	0	0	31	34	—	1	26	.240	.340	.266	.606	-29	4	—	—	C79	—	-0.2
1920	NY A	82	261	30	70	14	1	1	15	15	—	1	18	.268	.310	.341	.651	-30	4	2	67	C80	—	-0.2
Total	19	1468	4514	494	1242	187	29	4	534	606	—	29	238	.275	.365	.332	.697	-16	61	60	100	C1410,1b3	—	7.0
Team	4	170	517	49	130	20	1	1	47	53	—	2	47	.251	.323	.300	.623	-31	10	2	100	C167	—	-0.5
/150	4	150	456	43	115	18	1	1	41	47	—	2	41	.251	.323	.300	.623	-31	9	2	100	C147	—	-0.4
RUETHER, DUTCH WALTER HENRY B9.13.1893 ALAMEDA CA D5.16.1970 PHOENIX AZ BL/TL/6'1.5"/180 d4.13 MIL 1918 ▲																								
1926	†NY A	13	21	2	2	0	0	0	0	0	—	1	1	.095	.136	.095	.231	-139	0	0	0	P5	—	0.0
1927	NY A	35	80	7	21	3	0	1	10	8	—	0	15	.262	.330	.338	.668	-24	0	0	0	P27	—	0.0
Total	11	488	969	83	250	30	12	7	111	77	—	2	129	.258	.314	.335	.649	-24	3	1	100	P309,1b8	—	-0.1
Team	2	48	101	9	23	3	0	1	10	8	—	1	16	.228	.291	.287	.578	-47	0	0	0	P32	—	0.0
RUFFING, RED CHARLES HERBERT B5.3.1905 GRANVILLE IL D2.17.1986 MAYFIELD HTS. OH BR/TR/6'1.5"/205 d5.31 MIL 1943–45 C1 HF1967 ▲																								
1924	Bos A	8	7	0	1	0	1	0	0	0	—	0	1	.143	.143	.429	.572	-56	0	0	0	P8	—	0.0
1925	Bos A	37	79	6	17	4	2	0	11	1	—	1	22	.215	.235	.316	.551	-61	0	0	0	P37	—	0.0
1926	Bos A	37	51	8	10	1	0	1	5	2	—	0	12	.196	.226	.275	.501	-69	0	1	0	P37	—	0.0
1927	Bos A	29	55	5	14	3	1	0	4	0	—	1	6	.255	.268	.345	.613	-41	0	0	0	P26	—	0.0
1928	Bos A	60	121	12	38	13	1	2	19	3	—	0	12	.314	.331	.488	.819	+15	0	0	0	P42	—	0.0
1929	Bos A	60	114	9	35	9	0	2	17	2	—	1	13	.307	.325	.439	.764	-3	0	0	0	P35,O2L	—	-0.1
1930	Bos A	6	11	2	3	2	0	0	1	0	—	0	1	.273	.273	.455	.728	-16	0	0	0	P4	—	0.0
1930	NY A	52	99	15	37	6	2	4	21	7	—	0	7	.374	.415	.596	1.011	+60	0	0	0	P34	—	0.0
1930	Year	58	110	17	40	8	2	4	22	7	—	0	8	.364	.402	.582	.984	+53	0	0	0	P38	—	0.0
1931	NY A	48	109	14	36	8	1	3	12	1	—	0	13	.330	.336	.505	.841	+25	0	0	0	P37/rf	—	-0.1
1932	†NY A	55	124	20	38	6	1	3	19	6	—	0	10	.306	.338	.444	.782	+6	0	0	0	P35	—	0.0
1933	NY A	55	115	10	29	3	1	2	13	7	—	0	15	.252	.295	.348	.643	-26	0	0	0	P35	—	0.0
1934	NY A★	45	113	11	28	3	0	2	13	3	—	1	17	.248	.274	.327	.601	-42	0	0	0	P36	—	0.0
1935	NY A	50	109	13	37	10	0	2	18	3	—	1	9	.339	.363	.486	.849	+25	0	0	0	P30	—	0.0
1936	†NY A	53	127	14	37	5	0	5	22	11	—	0	12	.291	.348	.449	.797	-1	0	0	0	P33	—	0.0
1937	†NY A	54	129	11	26	3	0	1	10	13	—	0	24	.202	.275	.248	.523	-68	0	0	0	P31	—	0.0
1938	†NY A☆	45	107	12	24	4	1	3	17	17	—	0	21	.224	.331	.364	.695	-26	0	0	0	P31	—	0.0
1939	†NY A★	44	114	12	35	1	0	1	20	7	—	0	18	.307	.347	.342	.689	-22	1	0	100	P28	—	0.0
1940	NY A★	33	89	8	11	4	0	1	7	3	—	0	9	.124	.152	.202	.354	-109	0	0	0	P30	—	0.0
1941	†NY A☆	38	89	10	27	8	1	2	22	4	—	0	12	.303	.333	.483	.816	+15	0	0	0	P23	0	0.0
1942	†NY A☆	30	80	8	20	4	0	1	13	5	—	1	13	.250	.302	.338	.640	-19	0	0	0	P24	0	0.0
1945	NY A	21	46	4	10	0	1	1	5	0	—	0	8	.217	.217	.326	.543	-46	0	0	0	P11	0	0.0
1946	NY A	8	25	1	3	1	0	0	1	1	—	0	8	.120	.154	.160	.314	-112	0	0	0	P8	73	0.0
1947	Chi A	14	24	2	5	0	0	0	3	1	—	0	3	.208	.240	.208	.448	-74	0	0	0	P9	65	0.0
Total	22	882	1937	207	521	98	13	36	273	97	—	6	266	.269	.306	.389	.695	-19	1	1	50	P624,O3(2/0/1)	138	-0.2
Team	15	631	1475	163	398	66	8	31	213	88	—	3	196	.270	.312	.388	.700	-17	1	0	100	P426/rf	73	-0.1
/150	4	150	351	39	95	16	2	7	51	21	—	1	47	.270	.312	.388	.700	-17	0	0	0	P101/OfL	17	-0.0
RUTH, BABE GEORGE HERMAN "THE BAMBINO","THE SULTAN OF SWAT" B2.6.1895 BALTIMORE MD D8.16.1948 NEW YORK NY BL/TL/6'2"/215 d7.11 C1 HF1936 ▲																								
1914	Bos A	5	10	1	2	1	0	0	2	0	—	0	4	.200	.200	.300	.500	-50	0	—	—	P4	—	0.0
1915	†Bos A	42	92	16	29	10	1	4	21	9	—	0	23	.315	.376	.576	.952	+91	0	—	—	P32	—	0.0
1916	†Bos A	67	136	18	37	5	3	3	15	10	—	0	23	.272	.322	.419	.741	+22	0	—	—	P44	—	0.0
1917	Bos A	52	123	14	40	6	3	2	12	12	—	0	18	.325	.385	.472	.857	+63	0	—	—	P41	—	0.0
1918	†Bos A	95	317	50	95	26	11	**11**	66	58	—	2	58	.300	.411	**.555**	.966	+95	6	—	—	O59(47/12/0),P20,1b13	—	2.7
1919	Bos A	130	432	**103**	139	34	12	**29**	**114**	101	—	6	58	.322	**.456**	**.657**	1.113	+124	7	—	—	O111L,P17,1b5	—	**7.3**
1920	NY A	142	458	**158**	172	36	9	**54**	**137**	**150**	—	3	80	.376	**.532**	**.847**	1.379	+152	14	14	50	O141(36/20/85),1b2/P	—	**9.3**
1921	†NY A	152	540	**177**	204	44	16	**59**	**171**	**145**	—	4	81	.378	**.512**	**.846**	1.358	+136	17	13	57	O152(134/18/0),P2,1b2	—	**9.4**
1922	†NY A	110	406	94	128	24	8	35	99	84	—	1	80	.315	.434	**.672**	1.106	+81	2	5	29	O110(71/0/40)/1b	—	3.5
1923	†NY A	**152**	522	**151**	205	45	13	**41**	**131**	**170**	—	4	93	.393	**.545**	**.764**	1.309	+138	17	21	45	O148(68/7/73),1b4	—	**10.1**
1924	NY A	**153**	529	**143**	200	39	7	**46**	121	**142**	—	4	81	**.378**	**.513**	**.739**	1.252	+121	9	13	41	O152(50/7/99)	—	**8.4**
1925	NY A	98	359	61	104	12	2	25	66	59	—	2	68	.290	.393	.543	.936	+38	2	4	33	O98(33/0/66)	—	1.5
1926	†NY A	152	495	**139**	184	30	5	**47**	**146**	**144**	—	3	76	.372	**.516**	**.737**	1.253	+128	11	9	55	O149(82/0/68),1b2	—	**8.5**
1927	†NY A	151	540	**158**	192	29	8	**60**	164	**137**	—	0	89	.356	**.486**	**.772**	1.258	+129	7	6	54	O151(56/0/95)	—	**8.8**
1928	†NY A	**154**	536	**163**	173	29	8	**54**	**142**	**137**	—	3	87	.323	.463	**.709**	1.172	+111	4	5	44	O154(55/0/99)	—	**7.1**
1929	NY A	135	499	121	172	26	6	**46**	154	72	—	3	60	.345	.430	**.697**	1.127	+99	5	3	63	O133(55/0/78)	—	**5.4**
1930	NY A	145	518	150	186	28	9	**49**	153	**136**	—	1	61	.359	**.493**	**.732**	1.225	+116	10	10	50	O144(53/0/91)/P	—	7.6
1931	NY A	145	534	149	199	31	3	**46**	**163**	**128**	—	1	51	.373	**.495**	**.700**	1.195	+123	5	4	56	O142(51/0/91)/1b	—	**8.1**
1932	†NY A	133	457	120	156	13	5	41	137	**130**	—	2	62	.341	**.489**	.661	1.150	+106	2	2	50	O128(44/0/87)/1b	—	6.5
1933	NY A★	137	459	97	138	21	3	34	103	**114**	—	2	90	.301	.442	.582	1.024	+80	4	5	44	O132(55/0/78)/P1b	—	4.7
1934	NY A★	125	365	78	105	17	4	22	84	104	—	2	63	.288	.448	.537	.985	+64	1	3	25	O111(34/0/77)	—	3.0
1935	Bos N	28	72	13	13	0	0	6	12	20	—	0	24	.181	.359	.431	.790	+21	0	—	—	O26(22/0/4)	—	0.1
Total	22	2503	8399	2174	2873	506	136	714	2213	2062	—	43	1330	.342	.474	.690	1.164	+109	123	11	100	O2241(1057/64/1131),P163,1b32	—	112.0
Team	15	2084	7217	1959	2518	424	106	659	1971	1852	—	35	1122	.349	.484	.711	1.195	+112	110	117	48	O2045(402/186/705),1b14,P5	—	101.9
/150	1	150	519	141	181	31	8	47	142	133	—	3	81	.349	.484	.711	1.195	+112	8	8	50	O147(29/13/51)/1P	—	7.3

Batters

RYAN, BLONDY
John Collins B1.4.1906 Lynn MA D11.28.1959 Swampscott MA BR/TR/6'1"/178 d7.13 Col Holy Cross

YEAR	TM LG	G	AB	R	H	2B	3B	HR	RBI	BB	IB	HP	SO	AVG	OBP	SLG	OPS	AOPS	SB	CS	SB%	GAMES AT POSITION	DL	BFW
1935	NY A	30	105	12	25	1	3	0	11	3	—	0	10	.238	.259	.305	.564	-52	0	0	0	S30	—	-1.2
Total	6	386	1330	127	318	36	13	8	133	57	—	2	184	.239	.271	.304	.575	-43	6	0	100	S264,3b93,2b33	—	-3.7

SAKATA, LENN
Lenn Haruki B6.8.1954 Honolulu HI BR/TR/5'9"/(160–174) Dr 1975 MilA*S1/10 d7.21 Col Gonzaga

YEAR	TM LG	G	AB	R	H	2B	3B	HR	RBI	BB	IB	HP	SO	AVG	OBP	SLG	OPS	AOPS	SB	CS	SB%	GAMES AT POSITION	DL	BFW
1987	NY A	19	45	5	12	0	1	2	4	2	0	1	4	.267	.313	.444	.757	-2	0	1	0	3b12,2b6	64	-0.1
Total	11	565	1289	163	296	46	4	25	109	97	5	8	158	.230	.286	.330	.616	-29	30	17	64	2b431,S102,3b12,D4/lfC	82	-3.5

SALAS, MARK
Mark Bruce B3.8.1961 Montebello CA BL/TR/6'0"/(180–205) Dr 1979 StLN 18/448 d6.19

YEAR	TM LG	G	AB	R	H	2B	3B	HR	RBI	BB	IB	HP	SO	AVG	OBP	SLG	OPS	AOPS	SB	CS	SB%	GAMES AT POSITION	DL	BFW
1987	NY A	50	115	13	23	4	0	3	12	10	0	3	17	.200	.279	.313	.592	-42	0	0	0	C41/lfD	0	-0.5
Total	8	509	1292	142	319	49	10	38	143	89	13	12	163	.247	.300	.389	.689	-14	3	3	50	C385,D47,1b5,O4(3/0/1)/3b	24	-1.5

SALTZGAVER, JACK
Otto Hamlin B1.23.1903 Croton IA D2.1.1978 Keokuk IA BL/TR/5'11"/165 d4.12

YEAR	TM LG	G	AB	R	H	2B	3B	HR	RBI	BB	IB	HP	SO	AVG	OBP	SLG	OPS	AOPS	SB	CS	SB%	GAMES AT POSITION	DL	BFW
1932	NY A	20	47	10	6	2	1	0	5	10	—	0	10	.128	.281	.213	.494	-69	1	1	50	2b16	—	-0.6
1934	NY A	94	350	64	95	8	1	6	36	48	—	0	28	.271	.359	.351	.710	-10	8	1	89	3b84,1b4	—	-1.1
1935	NY A	61	149	17	39	6	0	3	18	23	—	2	12	.262	.368	.362	.730	-5	0	2	0	2b25,3b18,1b6	—	-0.8
1936	NY A	34	90	14	19	5	0	1	13	13	—	0	18	.211	.311	.300	.611	-47	0	0	0	3b16,2b6,1b4	—	-0.8
1937	NY A	17	11	6	2	0	0	0	0	3	—	0	4	.182	.357	.182	.539	-60	0	0	0	1b4	—	-0.1
1945	Pit N	52	117	20	38	5	3	0	10	8	—	0	8	.325	.368	.419	.787	+14	0	—	—	2b31/3b	0	0.2
Total	6	278	764	131	199	26	5	10	82	105	—	2	80	.260	.351	.347	.698	-15	9	4	100	3b119,2b78,1b18	0	-3.2
Team	5	226	647	111	161	21	2	10	72	97	—	2	72	.249	.349	.334	.683	-19	9	4	69	3b118,2b47,1b18	—	-3.4
/150	3	150	429	74	107	14	1	7	48	64	—	1	48	.249	.349	.334	.683	-19	6	3	67	3b78,2b31,1b12	—	-2.3

SAMPLE, BILL
William Amos B4.2.1955 Roanoke VA BR/TR/5'9"/175 Dr 1976 TexA 10/228 d9.2 Col James Madison

YEAR	TM LG	G	AB	R	H	2B	3B	HR	RBI	BB	IB	HP	SO	AVG	OBP	SLG	OPS	AOPS	SB	CS	SB%	GAMES AT POSITION	DL	BFW
1985	NY A	59	139	18	40	5	0	1	15	9	0	2	10	.288	.336	.345	.681	-10	2	1	67	O55(51/4/0)	0	-0.4
Total	9	826	2516	371	684	127	9	46	230	195	8	28	230	.272	.329	.384	.713	-3	98	31	76	O711(532/99/97),D19/2b	27	-3.4

SANCHEZ, CELERINO
Celerino (Perez) B2.3.1944 El Guayabal, Veracruz, Mexico D5.1.1992 Leon, Guanajuato, Mexico BR/TR/5'11"/160 d6.13

YEAR	TM LG	G	AB	R	H	2B	3B	HR	RBI	BB	IB	HP	SO	AVG	OBP	SLG	OPS	AOPS	SB	CS	SB%	GAMES AT POSITION	DL	BFW
1972	NY A	71	250	18	62	8	3	0	22	12	1	4	30	.248	.292	.304	.596	-20	0	0	0	3b68	0	-0.6
1973	NY A	34	64	12	14	3	0	1	9	2	0	0	12	.219	.239	.313	.552	-43	1	1	50	3b11,D11,S2,O2R	0	-0.5
Total	2	105	314	30	76	11	3	1	31	14	1	4	42	.242	.281	.306	.587	-25	1	1	50	3b79,D11,O2R,S2	0	-1.1
/150	3	150	449	43	109	16	4	1	44	20	1	6	60	.242	.281	.306	.587	-25	1	1	50	3b113,D16,S3,O3R	0	-1.6

SANCHEZ, REY
Rey Francisco (Guadalupe) B10.5.1967 Rio Piedras, PR BR/TR/5'9"/(165–175) Dr 1986 TexA 13/319 d9.8

YEAR	TM LG	G	AB	R	H	2B	3B	HR	RBI	BB	IB	HP	SO	AVG	OBP	SLG	OPS	AOPS	SB	CS	SB%	GAMES AT POSITION	DL	BFW
1997	†NY A	38	138	21	43	12	0	1	15	5	0	1	21	.312	.338	.420	.758	-2	0	4	0	2b37,S6	0	0.2
2005	NY A	23	43	7	12	1	0	0	2	2	0	1	3	.279	.326	.302	.628	-31	0	1	0	S10,2b9/3bD	115	0.1
Total	15	1490	4850	549	1317	193	32	15	389	229	29	40	508	.272	.308	.334	.642	-32	55	32	63	S984,2b480,3b19,D2	290	3.2
Team	2	61	181	28	55	13	0	1	17	7	0	2	24	.304	.335	.392	.727	-9	0	5	0	2b46,S16/3D	115	0.3

SANDERS, DEION
Deion Luwynn B8.9.1967 Ft.Myers FL BL/TL/6'1"/(195–196) Dr 1988 NYA 30/781 d5.31 Col Florida St. [DL 2000 Cin N 59]

YEAR	TM LG	G	AB	R	H	2B	3B	HR	RBI	BB	IB	HP	SO	AVG	OBP	SLG	OPS	AOPS	SB	CS	SB%	GAMES AT POSITION	DL	BFW
1989	NY A	14	47	7	11	2	0	2	7	3	1	0	8	.234	.280	.404	.684	-9	1	0	100	O14(3/11/0)	0	-0.1
1990	NY A	57	133	24	21	2	2	3	9	13	0	1	27	.158	.236	.271	.507	-58	8	2	80	O42(29/15/0),D4	0	-1.4
Total	9	641	2123	308	558	72	43	39	168	159	7	21	352	.263	.319	.392	.711	-12	186	63	75	O540(139/403/11),D6	119	-3.6
Team	2	71	180	31	32	4	2	5	16	16	1	1	35	.178	.247	.306	.553	-46	9	2	82	O56(32/26/0),D4	0	-1.5

SANDS, CHARLIE
Charles Duane B12.17.1947 Newport News VA BL/TR/6'2"/(200–215) Dr 1965 BalA 11/380 d6.21

YEAR	TM LG	G	AB	R	H	2B	3B	HR	RBI	BB	IB	HP	SO	AVG	OBP	SLG	OPS	AOPS	SB	CS	SB%	GAMES AT POSITION	DL	BFW
1967	NY A	1	1	0	0	0	0	0	0	0	0	0	1	.000	.000	.000	.000	-199	0	0	0	/H	0	0.0
Total	6	93	145	15	31	6	1	6	23	36	4	1	35	.214	.372	.393	.765	+25	0	0	0	D22,C18	64	0.2

SANTANA, RAFAEL
Rafael Francisco (De La Cruz) B1.31.1958 LaRomana, D.R. BR/TR/6'1"/(160–165) d4.5 C2 [DL 1989 NY A 182]

YEAR	TM LG	G	AB	R	H	2B	3B	HR	RBI	BB	IB	HP	SO	AVG	OBP	SLG	OPS	AOPS	SB	CS	SB%	GAMES AT POSITION	DL	BFW
1988	NY A	148	480	50	115	12	1	4	38	33	0	1	61	.240	.289	.294	.583	-36	1	2	33	S148	0	-2.8
Total	7	668	2021	188	497	74	5	13	156	138	34	5	234	.246	.295	.307	.602	-32	3	7	30	S639,2b10,3b4	197	-5.2
/150	1	150	486	51	117	12	1	4	39	33	0	1	62	.240	.289	.294	.583	-36	1	2	33	S150	184	-2.8

SARDINHA, BRONSON
Bronson B4.6.1983 Honolulu HI BL/TR/6'1"/220 Dr 2001 NYA 1/34 d9.15

YEAR	TM LG	G	AB	R	H	2B	3B	HR	RBI	BB	IB	HP	SO	AVG	OBP	SLG	OPS	AOPS	SB	CS	SB%	GAMES AT POSITION	DL	BFW
2007	†NY A	10	9	6	3	0	0	0	2	2	0	0	1	.333	.417	.333	.750	+11	0	0	0	O5(1/0/4)/3b	0	-0.1

SAVAGE, DON
Donald Anthony B3.5.1919 Bloomfield NJ D12.25.1961 Montclair NJ BR/TR/6'0"/180 d4.18 Col Rutgers

YEAR	TM LG	G	AB	R	H	2B	3B	HR	RBI	BB	IB	HP	SO	AVG	OBP	SLG	OPS	AOPS	SB	CS	SB%	GAMES AT POSITION	DL	BFW
1944	NY A	71	239	31	63	7	5	4	24	20	—	1	41	.264	.323	.385	.708	-2	1	1	50	3b60	0	-1.0
1945	NY A	34	58	5	13	1	0	0	3	3	—	0	14	.224	.262	.241	.503	-56	1	0	100	3b14,O2L	0	-0.4
Total	2	105	297	36	76	8	5	4	27	23	—	1	55	.256	.312	.357	.669	-12	2	1	67	3b74,O2L	0	-1.4
/150	3	150	424	51	109	11	7	6	39	33	—	1	79	.256	.312	.357	.669	-12	3	1	75	3b106,O3L	0	-2.0

SAX, STEVE
Stephen Louis B1.29.1960 Sacramento CA BR/TR/5'11"/(175–189) Dr 1978 LAN 9/229 d8.18 b-Dave

YEAR	TM LG	G	AB	R	H	2B	3B	HR	RBI	BB	IB	HP	SO	AVG	OBP	SLG	OPS	AOPS	SB	CS	SB%	GAMES AT POSITION	DL	BFW
1989	NY A★	158	651	88	205	26	3	5	63	52	2	1	44	.315	.364	.387	.751	+13	43	17	72	2b158	0	2.1
1990	NY A★	155	615	70	160	24	2	4	42	49	3	4	46	.260	.316	.325	.641	-20	43	9	83	2b154	0	-1.3
1991	NY A	158	652	85	198	38	2	10	56	41	2	3	38	.304	.345	.414	.759	+9	31	11	74	2b149,3b5,D4	0	1.3
Total	14	1769	6940	913	1949	278	47	54	550	556	47	24	584	.281	.335	.358	.693	-5	444	178	71	2b1679,O33(27/0/6),D26,3b7	110	1.5
Team	3	471	1918	243	563	88	7	19	161	142	7	8	128	.294	.342	.376	.718	+1	117	37	76	2b461,3b5,D4	0	2.1
/150	1	150	611	77	179	28	2	6	51	45	2	3	41	.294	.342	.376	.718	+1	37	12	76	2b147,3b2/D	0	0.7

SCHAEFER, GERMANY
William Herman B2.4.1876 Chicago IL D5.16.1919 Saranac Lake NY BR/TR/5'9"/175 d10.5 C1 OF(18/13/46)

YEAR	TM LG	G	AB	R	H	2B	3B	HR	RBI	BB	IB	HP	SO	AVG	OBP	SLG	OPS	AOPS	SB	CS	SB%	GAMES AT POSITION	DL	BFW
1916	NY A	1	1	0	0	0	0	0	0	0	—	0	0	.000	.000	.000	.000	-198	0	—	—	/O	—	0.0
Total	15	1150	3784	495	972	117	48	9	308	333	—	13	28	.257	.319	.320	.639	-4	201	7	100	2b588,1b145,3b133,S97,O78R,P2	—	-1.5

SCHALK, ROY
Le Roy John B11.9.1908 Chicago IL D3.11.1990 Gainesville TX BR/TR/5'10"/168 d9.17 Mil 1943

YEAR	TM LG	G	AB	R	H	2B	3B	HR	RBI	BB	IB	HP	SO	AVG	OBP	SLG	OPS	AOPS	SB	CS	SB%	GAMES AT POSITION	DL	BFW
1932	NY A	3	12	3	3	1	0	0	0	2	—	0	2	.250	.357	.333	.690	-16	0	0	0	2b3	—	-0.1
Total	3	282	1112	100	259	38	5	2	109	79	—	2	95	.233	.285	.281	.566	-36	8	10	44	2b278,S5	0	-4.1

SCHANG, WALLY
Walter Henry B8.22.1889 S.Wales NY D3.6.1965 St.Louis MO BB/TR/5'10"/180 d5.9 C3 b-Bobby

YEAR	TM LG	G	AB	R	H	2B	3B	HR	RBI	BB	IB	HP	SO	AVG	OBP	SLG	OPS	AOPS	SB	CS	SB%	GAMES AT POSITION	DL	BFW
1921	†NY A	134	424	77	134	30	5	6	55	78	—	5	35	.316	.428	.453	.881	+22	7	4	64	C132	—	2.3
1922	†NY A	124	408	46	130	21	7	1	53	53	—	6	36	.319	.405	.412	.817	+11	12	6	67	C119	—	1.9
1923	†NY A	84	272	39	75	8	2	2	29	27	—	9	17	.276	.360	.342	.702	-16	5	2	71	C81	—	-0.5
1924	NY A	114	356	46	104	19	7	5	52	48	—	4	43	.292	.382	.427	.809	+9	2	6	25	C108	—	1.0
1925	NY A	73	167	17	40	8	1	2	24	17	—	0	9	.240	.310	.335	.645	-35	2	1	67	C58	—	-0.4
Total	19	1842	5307	769	1506	264	90	59	710	849	—	107	573	.284	.393	.401	.794	+17	121	49	100	C1435,O167(97/65/5),3b60/S	—	20.4
Team	5	529	1627	225	483	86	22	16	213	223	—	24	140	.297	.390	.406	.796	+5	28	19	60	C498	—	4.3
/150	1	150	461	64	137	24	6	5	60	63	—	7	40	.297	.390	.406	.796	+5	8	5	62	C141	—	1.2

SCHMIDT, BUTCH
Charles John "Butcher Boy" B7.19.1886 Baltimore MD D9.4.1952 Baltimore MD BL/TL/6'1.5"/200 d5.11

YEAR	TM LG	G	AB	R	H	2B	3B	HR	RBI	BB	IB	HP	SO	AVG	OBP	SLG	OPS	AOPS	SB	CS	SB%	GAMES AT POSITION	DL	BFW
1909	NY A	1	2	0	0	0	0	0	0	0	—	0	—	.000	.000	.000	.000	-199	0	—	—	/P	—	0.0
Total	4	297	1075	119	292	45	18	4	145	81	—	21	119	.272	.335	.358	.693	+9	18	10	100	1b296/P	—	0.1

SCHMIDT, BOB
Robert Benjamin B4.22.1933 St.Louis MO BR/TR/6'2"/(190–205) d4.16

YEAR	TM LG	G	AB	R	H	2B	3B	HR	RBI	BB	IB	HP	SO	AVG	OBP	SLG	OPS	AOPS	SB	CS	SB%	GAMES AT POSITION	DL	BFW
1965	NY A	20	40	4	10	1	0	1	3	3	1	0	8	.250	.302	.350	.652	-15	0	0	0	C20	0	0.0
Total	7	454	1305	133	317	55	4	39	150	100	17	5	199	.243	.297	.381	.678	-16	0	6	0	C444	0	-2.1

YEAR	TM LG	G	AB	R	H	2B	3B	HR	RBI	BB	IB	HP	SO	AVG	OBP	SLG	OPS	AOPS	SB	CS	SB%	GAMES AT POSITION	DL	BFW
SCHOFIELD, DICK	JOHN RICHARD "DUCKY" B1.7.1935 SPRINGFIELD IL BB/TR/5'9"/(155–170) D7.3 S–DICK GS–JAYSON WERTH																							
1966	NY A	25	58	5	9	2	0	0	2	9	0	0	8	.155	.265	.190	.455	-64	0	0	0	S19	0	-0.2
Total	19	1321	3083	394	699	113	20	21	211	390	18	26	526	.227	.317	.297	.614	-27	12	29	29	S660,2b159,3b95,O11(5/0/7)	0	0.7
SCHULT, ART	ARTHUR WILLIAM "DUTCH" B6.20.1928 BROOKLYN NY BR/TR/6'4"/(210–220) D5.17 COL GEORGETOWN																							
1953	NY A	7	0	3	0	0	0	0	0	0	—	0	0	+	+	+	.000	-100	0	0	0	/R	0	0.0
Total	5	164	421	58	111	24	0	6	56	23	1	4	50	.264	.306	.363	.669	-19	0	1	0	1b59,O56(36/1/23)	0	2.1
SCHWERT, PI	PIUS LOUIS B11.22.1892 ANGOLA NY D3.11.1941 WASHINGTON DC BR/TR/5'10.5"/160 D8.20 COL PENN																							
1914	NY A	3	6	0	0	0	0	0	0	2	—	0	3	.000	.250	.000	.250	-124	0	—	—	C3	—	0.0
1915	NY A	9	18	6	5	3	0	0	6	1	—	0	6	.278	.316	.444	.760	+28	0	—	—	C9	—	0.1
Total	2	12	24	6	5	3	0	0	6	3	—	0	9	.208	.296	.333	.629	-11	0	—	—	C12	—	0.1
SCOTT, GEORGE	GEORGE CHARLES "BOOMER" B3.23.1944 GREENVILLE MS BR/TR/6'2"/(205–225) D4.12																							
1979	NY A	16	44	9	14	3	1	1	6	2	0	0	7	.318	.340	.500	.840	+28	1	0	100	D15/1b	0	0.1
Total	14	2034	7433	957	1992	306	60	271	1051	699	85	53	1418	.268	.333	.435	.768	+13	69	57	55	1b1773,3b219,D46	30	-6.3
SCOTT, EVERETT	LEWIS EVERETT "DEACON" B11.19.1892 BLUFFTON IN D11.2.1960 FORT WAYNE IN BR/TR/5'8"/148 D4.14																							
1922	†NY A	**154**	557	64	150	23	5	3	45	23	—	5	22	.269	.304	.345	.649	-33	2	3	40	S154	—	0.5
1923	†NY A	**152**	533	48	131	16	4	6	60	13	—	2	19	.246	.266	.325	.591	-46	1	3	25	S152	—	-3.6
1924	NY A	**153**	548	56	137	12	6	4	64	21	—	0	15	.250	.278	.316	.594	-47	3	7	30	S153	—	-1.6
1925	NY A	22	60	3	13	0	0	0	4	2	—	0	2	.217	.242	.217	.459	-83	0	1	0	S18	—	-0.4
Total	13	1654	5837	552	1455	208	58	20	551	243	—	18	282	.249	.281	.315	.596	-35	69	60	100	S1643,3b3/2b	—	-7.2
Team	4	481	1698	171	431	51	15	13	173	59	—	7	58	.254	.282	.324	.606	-43	6	14	30	S477	—	-5.1
/150	1	150	530	53	134	16	5	4	54	18	—	2	18	.254	.282	.324	.606	-43	2	4	33	S149	—	-1.6
SCOTT, RODNEY	RODNEY DARRELL B10.16.1953 INDIANAPOLIS IN BB/TR (BR 1975)/6'0"/(155–160) DR 1972 KCA 11/258 D4.11 OF(0/10/1)																							
1982	NY A	10	26	5	5	0	0	0	0	4	0	0	2	.192	.300	.192	.492	-61	2	0	100	S6,2b4	0	-0.1
Total	8	690	2132	316	504	43	26	3	150	281	2	10	291	.236	.326	.285	.611	-30	205	62	77	2b443,S153,3b64,D23,O11C	0	-7.4
SEABOL, SCOTT	SCOTT ANTHONY B5.17.1975 MCKEESPORT PA BR/TR/6'4"/200 DR 1996 NYA 88/1718 D4.8 COL WEST VIRGINIA [DL 1998 NY A 28]																							
2001	NY A	1	1	0	0	0	0	0	0	0	0	0	0	.000	.000	.000	.000	-199	0	0	0	/D	0	0.0
Total	2	60	106	11	23	5	0	1	10	8	0	0	23	.217	.270	.292	.562	-53	0	0	0	3b20,2b8,1b5,O4(2/0/2),D4	28	-0.5
SEARS, KEN	KENNETH EUGENE "ZIGGY" B7.6.1917 STREATOR IL D7.17.1968 BRIDGEPORT TX BL/TR/6'1"/200 D5.2 MIL 1944–45 COL ALABAMA																							
1943	NY A	60	187	22	52	7	0	2	22	11	—	3	18	.278	.328	.348	.676	-3	1	3	25	C50	0	0.4
1946	StL A	7	15	1	5	0	0	0	1	3	—	0	0	.333	.444	.333	.777	+14	0	0	0	C4	0	-0.1
Total	2	67	202	23	57	7	0	2	23	14	—	3	18	.282	.338	.347	.685	-1	1	3	25	C54	0	0.3
SEEDS, BOB	IRA ROBERT "SUITCASE BOB" B2.24.1907 RINGGOLD TX D10.28.1993 ERICK OK BR/TR/6'0"/180 D4.19																							
1936	†NY A	13	42	12	11	1	0	4	10	5	—	0	3	.262	.340	.571	.911	+26	3	1	75	O9(1/0/8),3b3	—	0.1
Total	9	615	1937	268	537	77	21	28	233	160	—	10	190	.277	.336	.382	.718	-11	14	15	100	O472(194/160/131),1b43,3b3	—	-7.2
SEGRIST, KAL	KAL HILL B4.14.1931 GREENVILLE TX BR/TR/6'0"/180 D7.16 COL TEXAS																							
1952	NY A	13	23	3	1	0	0	0	1	3	—	0	1	.043	.154	.043	.197	-146	0	0	0	2b11/3b	0	-0.4
1955	Bal A	7	9	1	3	0	0	0	0	2	0	0	0	.333	.455	.333	.788	+23	0	0	0	3b3/1b2b	0	0.1
Total	2	20	32	4	4	0	0	0	1	5	0	0	1	.125	.243	.125	.368	-96	0	0	0	2b12,3b4/1b	0	-0.3
SEGUIGNOL, FERNANDO	FERNANDO ALFREDO B1.19.1975 BOCAS DEL TORO, PAN BB/TR/6'5"/(190–230) D9.5																							
2003	NY A	5	7	0	1	0	0	0	0	1	0	0	3	.143	.250	.143	.393	-92	0	0	0	1b3/D	0	0.0
Total	5	178	366	42	91	23	0	17	40	20	2	11	114	.249	.303	.451	.754	-9	0	1	0	1b70,O60(38/0/25),D2	58	-1.3
SELKIRK, GEORGE	GEORGE ALEXANDER "TWINKLETOES" B1.4.1908 HUNTSVILLE ON, CAN. D1.19.1987 FT.LAUDERDALE FL BL/TR/6'1"/182 D8.12 MIL 1943–45																							
1934	NY A	46	176	23	55	7	1	5	38	15	—	1	17	.313	.370	.449	.819	+18	1	1	50	O46(43/0/7)	—	0.3
1935	NY A	128	491	64	153	29	12	11	94	44	—	3	36	.312	.372	.487	.859	+28	2	7	22	O127R	—	1.3
1936	†NY A★	137	493	93	152	28	9	18	107	94	—	1	60	.308	.420	.511	.931	+33	13	7	65	O135(18/0/118)	—	2.0
1937	†NY A	78	256	49	84	13	5	18	68	34	—	2	24	.328	.411	.629	1.040	+57	8	2	80	O69R	—	2.0
1938	†NY A	99	335	58	85	12	5	10	62	68	—	3	52	.254	.384	.409	.793	-1	9	4	69	O95L	—	-0.6
1939	†NY A★	128	418	103	128	17	4	21	101	103	—	8	49	.306	.452	.517	.969	+49	12	5	71	O124(86/0/38)	—	2.6
1940	NY A	118	379	68	102	17	5	19	71	84	—	3	43	.269	.406	.491	.897	+37	3	6	33	O111(79/2/31)	—	1.5
1941	†NY A	70	164	30	36	5	0	6	25	28	—	2	30	.220	.340	.360	.700	-14	1	0	100	O47(19/0/28)	0	-0.5
1942	†NY A	42	78	15	15	3	0	0	10	16	—	0	8	.192	.330	.231	.561	-40	0	0	0	O19R	0	-0.5
Total	9	846	2790	503	810	131	41	108	576	486	—	23	319	.290	.400	.483	.883	+28	49	32	60	O773(340/2/437)	0	8.1
/150	2	150	495	89	144	23	7	19	102	86	—	4	57	.290	.400	.483	.883	+28	9	6	60	O137(60/0/77)	0	1.4
SEPKOWSKI, TED	THEODORE WALTER (B THEODORE WALTER SCZEPKOWSKI) B11.9.1923 BALTIMORE MD D3.8.2002 SEVERNA PARK MD BL/TR/5'11"/190 D9.9 MIL 1944–45																							
1947	NY A	2	0	1	0	0	0	0	0	0	—	0	0	+	+	+	.000	-100	0	1	0	/R	0	0.0
Total	3	19	26	3	6	2	0	0	1	1	—	0	4	.231	.259	.308	.567	-39	0	1	0	3b2,2b2/rf	0	-0.3
SEVEREID, HANK	HENRY LEVAI B6.1.1891 STORY CITY IA D12.17.1968 SAN ANTONIO TX BR/TR/6'0"/175 D5.15 MIL 1918																							
1926	†NY A	41	127	13	34	8	1	0	13	13	—	0	4	.268	.336	.346	.682	-21	1	1	50	C40	—	-0.3
Total	15	1390	4312	408	1245	204	42	17	539	331	—	19	169	.289	.342	.367	.709	-9	35	19	100	C1225,1b9,O7(6/1/0)/3b	—	-1.7
SEWELL, JOE	JOSEPH WHEELER B10.9.1898 TITUS AL D3.6.1990 MOBILE AL BL/TR/5'6.5"/155 D9.10 C2 HF1977 B–LUKE B–TOMMY COL ALABAMA																							
1931	NY A	130	484	102	146	22	1	6	64	61	—	9	8	.302	.390	.388	.778	+11	1	1	50	3b121/2b	—	0.9
1932	†NY A	125	503	95	137	21	3	11	68	56	—	3	3	.272	.349	.392	.741	-4	0	2	0	3b123	—	0.2
1933	NY A	135	524	87	143	18	1	2	54	71	—	1	4	.273	.361	.323	.684	-13	2	2	50	3b131	—	0.1
Total	14	1903	7132	1141	2226	436	68	49	1055	842	—	80	114	.312	.391	.413	.804	+9	74	72	51	S1216,3b643,2b16	—	35.2
Team	3	390	1511	284	426	61	5	19	186	188	—	13	15	.282	.366	.367	.733	-2	3	5	38	3b375/2	—	1.2
/150	1	150	581	109	164	23	2	7	72	72	—	5	6	.282	.366	.367	.733	-2	1	2	33	3b144/2	—	0.5
SHANKS, HOWIE	HOWARD SAMUEL "HANK" B7.21.1890 CHICAGO IL D7.30.1941 MONACA PA BR/TR/5'11"/170 D5.9 C5 OF(603/55/44)																							
1925	NY A	66	155	15	40	3	1	1	18	20	—	0	15	.258	.343	.310	.653	-32	1	0	100	3b26,2b21,O4(3/0/1)	—	-0.9
Total	14	1665	5699	604	1440	211	96	25	620	415	—	37	443	.253	.308	.337	.645	-18	185	81	100	O702L,3b485,S235,2b159,1b25	—	-16.7
SHANTZ, BILLY	WILMER EBERT B7.31.1927 POTTSTOWN PA D12.13.1993 LAUDERHILL FL BR/TR/6'1"/160 D4.13 B–BOBBY																							
1960	NY A	1	0	0	0	0	0	0	0	0	0	0	0	+	+	+	.000	-100	0	0	0	/C	0	0.0
Total	3	131	381	31	98	13	4	2	29	28	1	0	37	.257	.307	.328	.635	-28	0	0	0	C130	0	-2.7
SHEFFIELD, GARY	GARY ANTONIAN B11.18.1968 TAMPA FL BR/TR/5'11"/(190–215) DR 1986 MILA 1/6 D9.3 OF(435/0/1142)																							
2004	†NY A★	154	573	117	166	30	1	36	121	92	7	11	83	.290	.393	.534	.927	+40	5	6	45	O136R,D18,3b2	0	2.7
2005	†NY A★	154	584	104	170	27	0	34	123	78	7	8	76	.291	.379	.512	.891	+36	10	2	83	O131R,D23	0	2.1
2006	†NY A	39	151	22	45	5	0	6	25	13	2	1	16	.298	.355	.450	.805	+5	5	1	83	O21R,1b9,D9	129	0.0
Total	20	2362	8531	1540	2521	438	25	480	1576	1377	12	128	1042	.296	.397	.522	.919	+44	242	101	71	O1572R,3b468,D190,S94,1b9	438	44.0
Team	3	347	1308	243	381	62	1	76	269	183	16	20	175	.291	.383	.515	.898	+34	20	9	69	O288R,D50,1b9,3b2	129	4.8
/150	1	150	565	105	165	27	0	33	116	79	7	9	76	.291	.383	.515	.898	+34	9	4	69	O124R,D22,1b4/3	56	2.1

YEAR	TM LG	G	AB	R	H	2B	3B	HR	RBI	BB	IB	HP	SO	AVG	OBP	SLG	OPS	AOPS	SB	CS	SB%	GAMES AT POSITION	DL	BFW
Shelton, Skeeter	Andrew Kemper B6.29.1888 Huntington WV D1.9.1954 Huntington WV BR/TR/5'11"/175 d8.25 Col West Virginia																							
1915	NY A	10	40	1	1	0	0	0	0	2	—	0	10	.025	.071	.025	.096	-171	0	—	—	O10C	—	-1.0
Sheridan, Pat	Patrick Arthur B12.4.1957 Ann Arbor MI BL/TR/6'3"/(175–195) Dr 1979 KCA 3/73 d9.16 Col Eastern Michigan																							
1991	NY A	62	113	13	23	3	0	4	7	13	1	0	30	.204	.286	.336	.622	-29	1	1	50	O34(3/6/26),D2	0	-0.5
Total	9	876	2419	319	611	91	21	51	257	236	19	6	501	.253	.319	.371	.690	-10	86	35	71	O779(162/173/481),D19	44	-5.3
Sherrill, Dennis	Dennis Lee B3.3.1956 Miami FL BR/TR/6'0"/165 Dr 1974 NYA 1/12 d9.4																							
1978	NY A	2	1	1	0	0	0	0	0	0	0	0	1	.000	.000	.000	.000	-199	0	0	0	/3bD	0	-0.1
1980	NY A	3	4	0	1	0	0	0	0	0	0	0	1	.250	.250	.250	.500	-62	0	0	0	S2/2b	0	-0.1
Total	2	5	5	1	1	0	0	0	0	0	0	0	2	.200	.200	.200	.400	-89	0	0	0	S2/2bD3b	0	-0.2
Shopay, Tom	Thomas Michael B2.21.1945 Bristol CT BL/TR/5'9.5"/160 Dr 1965 NYA 16/633 d9.17 Col Dean (MA) JC																							
1967	NY A	8	27	2	8	1	0	2	6	1	1	0	5	.296	.310	.556	.866	+61	2	0	100	O7L	0	0.2
1969	NY A	28	48	2	4	0	1	0	0	2	1	0	10	.083	.120	.125	.245	-133	0	1	0	O11(7/0/5)	0	-1.0
Total	7	253	309	40	62	7	1	3	20	26	3	0	51	.201	.262	.259	.521	-51	11	5	69	O110(53/36/37),D5,C2	43	-2.1
Team	2	36	75	4	12	1	1	2	6	3	2	0	15	.160	.190	.280	.470	-63	2	1	67	O18L	0	-0.8
Siebern, Norm	Norman Leroy B7.26.1933 St.Louis MO BL/TR/6'3"/(200–205) d6.15																							
1956	†NY A	54	162	27	33	1	4	4	21	19	0	0	38	.204	.286	.333	.619	-34	1	1	50	O51L	0	-1.4
1958	†NY A	134	460	79	138	19	5	14	55	66	3	1	87	.300	.388	.454	.842	+36	5	8	38	O133(127/11/0)	0	1.8
1959	NY A	120	380	52	103	17	0	11	53	41	2	2	71	.271	.341	.403	.744	+8	3	1	75	O93(82/5/9),1b2	0	-0.4
Total	12	1406	4481	662	1217	206	38	132	636	708	47	10	748	.272	.369	.423	.792	+17	18	25	42	1b827,O420(402/16/11)	0	5.8
Team	3	308	1002	158	274	37	9	29	129	126	5	3	196	.273	.354	.415	.769	+14	9	10	47	O277(178/5/9),1b2	0	-0.0
/150	1	150	488	77	133	18	4	14	63	61	2	1	95	.273	.354	.415	.769	+14	4	5	44	O135(87/2/4)/1	0	-0.0
Sierra, Ruben	Ruben Angel (Garcia) B10.6.1965 Rio Piedras, PR BB/TR/6'1"/(175–220) d6.1																							
1995	†NY A	56	215	33	56	15	0	7	44	22	2	0	34	.260	.322	.428	.750	-4	1	0	100	D46,O10R	0	-0.3
1996	NY A	96	360	39	93	17	1	11	52	40	11	0	58	.258	.327	.403	.730	-15	1	3	25	D61,O33(32/0/1)	0	-1.1
2003	†NY A	63	174	19	48	8	1	6	31	13	2	0	20	.276	.323	.437	.760	+0	1	0	100	D32,O17(6/0/11)	0	-0.3
2004	†NY A	107	307	40	75	12	1	17	65	25	4	0	55	.244	.296	.456	.752	-6	1	0	100	D56,O29(8/0/22)	0	-0.8
2005	†NY A	61	170	14	39	12	0	4	29	9	1	0	41	.229	.265	.371	.636	-32	0	0	0	D30,O18(8/0/10)	73	-1.1
Total	20	2186	8044	1084	2152	428	59	306	1322	610	10	7	1239	.268	.315	.450	.765	+5	142	52	73	O1622(202/31/1425),D453	150	-7.7
Team	5	383	1226	145	311	64	3	45	221	109	20	0	208	.254	.310	.421	.731	-11	4	3	57	D225,O107(40/22/32)	73	-3.6
/150	2	150	480	57	122	25	1	18	87	43	8	0	81	.254	.310	.421	.731	-11	2	1	67	D88,O42(16/9/13)	29	-1.4
Silvera, Charlie	Charles Anthony Ryan "Swede" B10.13.1924 San Francisco CA BR/TR/5'10"/175 d9.29 C6																							
1948	NY A	4	14	1	8	0	1	0	1	0	—	0	1	.571	.571	.714	1.285	+143	0	0	0	C4	0	0.3
1949	†NY A	58	130	8	41	2	0	0	13	18	—	1	5	.315	.403	.331	.734	-5	2	1	67	C51	0	0.5
1950	NY A	18	25	2	4	0	0	0	1	1	—	0	2	.160	.192	.160	.352	-109	0	0	0	C15	0	-0.2
1951	NY A	18	51	5	14	3	0	1	7	5	—	0	3	.275	.339	.392	.731	+1	0	0	0	C18	0	0.2
1952	NY A	20	55	4	18	3	0	0	11	5	—	0	2	.327	.383	.382	.765	+21	0	3	0	C20	0	0.0
1953	NY A	42	82	11	23	3	1	0	12	9	—	0	5	.280	.352	.341	.693	-9	0	1	0	C39/3b	0	0.4
1954	NY A	20	37	1	10	1	0	0	4	3	—	1	2	.270	.341	.297	.638	-21	0	1	0	C18	0	0.2
1955	NY A	14	26	1	5	0	0	0	1	6	0	0	4	.192	.344	.192	.536	-52	0	0	0	C11	0	0.1
1956	NY A	7	9	0	2	0	0	0	0	2	0	0	3	.222	.364	.222	.586	-40	0	0	0	C7	0	-0.1
1957	Chi N	26	53	1	11	3	0	0	2	4	0	0	5	.208	.263	.264	.527	-57	0	0	0	C26	0	-0.5
Total	10	227	482	34	136	15	2	1	52	53	0	2	32	.282	.356	.328	.684	-14	2	6	25	C209/3b	0	0.9
Team	9	201	429	33	125	12	2	1	50	49	0	2	27	.291	.367	.336	.703	-8	2	6	25	C183/3	0	1.4
/150	7	150	320	25	93	9	1	1	37	37	0	1	20	.291	.367	.336	.703	-8	1	4	20	C137/3	0	1.0
Silvestri, Dave	David Joseph B9.29.1967 St.Louis MO BR/TR/6'0"/(180–196) Dr 1988 HouN 2/52 d4.27 Col Missouri																							
1992	NY A	7	13	3	4	0	2	0	1	0	0	0	3	.308	.308	.615	.923	+53	0	0	0	S6	0	0.1
1993	NY A	7	21	4	6	1	0	1	4	5	0	0	3	.286	.423	.476	.899	+45	0	0	0	S4,3b3	0	0.2
1994	NY A	12	18	3	2	0	1	1	2	4	0	0	9	.111	.261	.389	.650	-30	0	1	0	2b9,3b2/S	0	-0.1
1995	NY A	17	21	4	2	0	0	1	4	4	0	1	9	.095	.259	.238	.497	-66	0	0	0	2b7,1b4/SD	17	-0.1
Total	8	181	336	42	68	12	3	6	36	56	6	1	96	.202	.315	.310	.625	-35	4	2	67	3b64,S34,2b23,1b9,O6(5/1/0),D6	17	-1.8
Team	4	43	73	14	14	1	3	3	11	13	0	1	24	.192	.315	.411	.726	-6	0	1	0	2b16,S12,3b5,1b4/D	17	0.1
Silvestri, Ken	Kenneth Joseph "Hawk" B5.3.1916 Chicago IL D3.31.1992 Tallahassee FL BB/TR/6'1"/200 d4.18 Mil 1942–45 M1/C17																							
1941	NY A	17	40	6	10	5	0	1	4	7	—	0	6	.250	.362	.450	.812	+15	0	0	0	C13	0	0.2
1946	NY A	13	21	4	6	1	0	0	1	3	—	0	7	.286	.375	.333	.708	-2	0	0	0	C12	0	0.2
1947	NY A	3	10	0	2	0	0	0	0	2	—	0	2	.200	.333	.200	.533	-49	0	0	0	C3	0	-0.1
Total	8	102	203	26	44	11	1	5	25	31	—	2	41	.217	.326	.355	.681	-22	0	1	0	C62,2b2/S	0	-0.5
Team	3	33	71	10	18	6	0	1	5	12	—	0	15	.254	.361	.380	.741	+1	0	0	0	C28	0	0.3
Simmons, Hack	George Washington B1.29.1885 Brooklyn NY D4.26.1942 Arverne NY BR/TR/5'8"/179 d4.15																							
1910	Det A	42	110	12	25	3	1	0	9	10	—	2	—	.227	.303	.273	.576	-25	1	—	—	1b22,3b7,O2(0/1/1)	—	-0.4
1912	NY A	110	401	45	96	17	2	0	41	33	—	7	—	.239	.308	.292	.600	-32	19	15	56	2b88,1b13,S4	—	-3.3
1914	Bal F	114	352	50	95	16	5	1	38	32	—	6	26	.270	.341	.352	.693	-14	7	—	—	O73(61/0/12),2b26,1b4,S2/3b	—	-1.7
1915	Bal F	39	88	8	18	7	1	1	14	10	—	1	9	.205	.293	.341	.634	-24	1	—	—	2b13,O13L	—	-0.7
Total	4	305	951	115	234	43	9	2	102	85	—	16	35	.246	.318	.317	.635	-24	28	15	100	2b127,O88(74/1/13),1b39,3b8,S6	—	-6.1
/150	1	150	547	61	131	23	3	0	56	45	—	10	0	.239	.308	.292	.600	-32	26	20	57	2b120,1b18,S5	—	-4.5
Simpson, Harry	Harry Leon "Suitcase","Goody" B12.3.1925 Atlanta GA D4.3.1979 Akron OH BL/TR/6'1"/(170–180) d4.21 Negro Lg 1946–48																							
1957	†NY A	75	224	27	56	7	3	7	39	19	0	0	36	.250	.307	.402	.709	-6	1	0	100	O42(16/0/26),1b21	0	-0.7
1958	NY A	24	51	1	11	2	1	0	6	6	0	1	12	.216	.310	.294	.604	-30	0	0	0	O15(8/0/9)	0	-0.3
Total	8	888	2829	343	752	101	41	73	381	271	17	10	429	.266	.331	.408	.739	+2	17	18	49	O579(44/136/415),1b211	0	-7.0
Team	2	99	275	28	67	9	4	7	45	25	0	1	48	.244	.308	.382	.690	-11	1	0	100	O57(24/0/35),1b21	0	-1.0
Simpson, Dick	Richard Charles B7.28.1943 Washington DC BR/TR/6'4"/(170–176) d9.21																							
1969	NY A	6	11	2	3	2	0	0	4	3	0	0	6	.273	.429	.455	.884	+52	0	0	0	O5(3/2/0)	0	0.1
Total	7	288	518	94	107	19	2	15	56	64	5	6	174	.207	.299	.338	.637	-16	10	10	50	O211(31/72/113)	76	-3.9
Sims, Duke	Duane B B6.5.1941 Salt Lake City UT BL/TR/6'2"/(197–209) d9.22																							
1973	NY A	4	9	3	3	0	0	1	1	3	0	0	1	.333	.500	.667	1.167	+131	0	0	0	/CD	0	0.3
1974	NY A	5	15	1	2	1	0	0	2	1	0	0	5	.133	.188	.200	.388	-88	0	0	0	/CD	0	-0.2
Total	11	843	2422	263	580	80	6	100	310	338	34	35	483	.239	.340	.401	.741	+11	6	16	27	C646,1b61,O54(35/0/19),D7	44	6.2
Team	2	9	24	4	5	1	0	1	3	4	0	0	6	.208	.321	.375	.696	+6	0	0	0	D2/C	0	0.1
Skiff, Bill	William Franklin B10.16.1895 New Rochelle NY D12.25.1976 Bronxville NY BR/TR/5'10"/170 d5.17																							
1926	NY A	6	11	0	1	0	0	0	0	0	—	0	1	.091	.091	.091	.182	-153	0	0	0	C6	—	-0.3
Total	2	22	56	7	14	2	0	0	11	0	—	0	5	.250	.250	.286	.536	-60	1	1	50	C19	—	-0.5
Skinner, Camp	Elisha Harrison B6.25.1897 Douglasville GA D8.4.1944 Douglasville GA BL/TR/5'11"/165 d5.2																							
1922	NY A	27	33	1	6	0	0	0	2	0	—	1	4	.182	.206	.182	.388	-98	1	0	100	O4(1/3/0)	—	-0.5
1923	Bos A	7	13	1	3	2	0	0	1	0	—	0	0	.231	.231	.385	.616	-40	0	0	0	O2C	—	-0.1
Total	2	34	46	2	9	2	0	0	3	0	—	1	4	.196	.213	.239	.452	-82	1	0	100	O6(1/5/0)	—	-0.6

SKINNER, JOEL JOEL PATRICK B2.21.1961 LAJOLLA CA BR/TR/6'4"/(198–208) DR 1979 PITN 37/842 D6.12 M1/C7 F–BOB [DL 1992 CLE A 182, 1993 CLE A 182]

YEAR	TM LG	G	AB	R	H	2B	3B	HR	RBI	BB	IB	HP	SO	AVG	OBP	SLG	OPS	AOPS	SB	CS	SB%	GAMES AT POSITION	DL	BFW
1983	Chi A	6	11	2	3	0	0	0	1	0	0	0	1	.273	.273	.273	.546	-51	0	0	0	C6	0	0.1
1984	Chi A	43	80	4	17	2	0	0	3	7	0	0	19	.213	.273	.237	.510	-59	1	0	100	C43	0	-0.1
1985	Chi A	22	44	9	15	4	1	1	5	5	0	0	13	.341	.408	.545	.953	+51	0	0	0	C21	0	0.4
1986	Chi A	60	149	17	30	5	1	4	20	9	0	1	43	.201	.250	.329	.579	-46	1	0	100	C60	0	-1.9
1986	NY A	54	166	6	43	4	0	1	17	7	0	0	40	.259	.287	.301	.588	-39	0	4	0	C54	0	-0.7
1986	Year	114	315	23	73	9	1	5	37	16	0	1	83	.232	.269	.314	.583	-42	1	4	20	C114	0	-2.6
1987	NY A	64	139	9	19	4	0	3	14	8	0	1	46	.107	.187	.230	.417	-89	0	0	0	C64	0	-2.3
1988	NY A	88	251	23	57	15	0	4	23	14	0	0	72	.227	.267	.335	.602	-32	0	0	0	C85,O2(1/0/1)/1b	0	-1.5
1989	Cle A	79	178	10	41	10	0	1	13	9	0	1	42	.230	.271	.303	.574	-40	1	1	50	C79	0	-1.4
1990	Cle A	49	139	16	35	4	1	2	16	7	0	0	44	.252	.288	.338	.626	-26	0	0	0	C49	0	-0.7
1991	Cle A	99	284	23	69	14	0	1	24	14	1	1	67	.243	.279	.303	.582	-39	0	2	0	C99	0	-1.1
Total	9	564	1441	119	329	62	3	17	136	80	1	4	387	.228	.269	.311	.580	-41	3	7	30	C560,O2(1/0/1)/1b	364	-9.2
Team	3	206	556	38	119	23	0	8	54	29	0	1	158	.214	.253	.299	.552	-48	0	4	0	C203,O2(1/0/1)/1	0	-4.5
/150	2	150	405	28	87	17	0	6	39	21	0	1	115	.214	.253	.299	.552	-48	0	3	0	C148/O/(1/0/1)1	0	-3.3

SKIZAS, LOU LOUIS PETER "THE NERVOUS GREEK" B6.2.1932 CHICAGO IL BR/TR/5'11"/(170–175) D4.19

YEAR	TM LG	G	AB	R	H	2B	3B	HR	RBI	BB	IB	HP	SO	AVG	OBP	SLG	OPS	AOPS	SB	CS	SB%	GAMES AT POSITION	DL	BFW
1956	NY A	6	6	0	1	0	0	0	1	0	0	0	2	.167	.167	.167	.334	-112	0	0	0	/H	0	-0.1
Total	4	239	725	80	196	27	4	30	86	50	3	2	37	.270	.317	.443	.760	+2	8	3	73	O161(80/0/89),3b36	0	-0.6

SKOWRON, BILL WILLIAM JOSEPH "MOOSE" B12.18.1930 CHICAGO IL BR/TR/5'11"/(191–200) D4.13 COL PURDUE

YEAR	TM LG	G	AB	R	H	2B	3B	HR	RBI	BB	IB	HP	SO	AVG	OBP	SLG	OPS	AOPS	SB	CS	SB%	GAMES AT POSITION	DL	BFW
1954	NY A	87	215	37	73	12	9	7	41	19	—	1	18	.340	.392	.577	.969	+70	2	1	67	1b61,3b5,2b2	0	1.7
1955	†NY A	108	288	46	92	17	3	12	61	21	4	3	32	.319	.369	.524	.893	+41	1	1	50	1b74,3b3	0	1.0
1956	†NY A	134	464	78	143	21	6	23	90	50	3	6	60	.308	.382	.528	.910	+43	4	4	50	1b120,3b2	0	2.3
1957	†NY A★	122	457	54	139	15	5	17	88	31	6	3	60	.304	.347	.470	.817	+25	3	2	60	1b115	0	1.4
1958	†NY A★	126	465	61	127	22	3	14	73	28	1	4	69	.273	.317	.424	.741	+7	1	1	50	1b118,3b2	0	-0.6
1959	NY A★	74	282	39	84	13	5	15	59	20	0	3	47	.298	.349	.539	.888	+45	1	0	100	1b72	65	1.2
1960	†NY A★	146	538	63	166	34	3	26	91	38	2	2	95	.309	.353	.528	.881	+44	2	3	40	1b142	0	3.1
1961	†NY A☆	150	561	76	150	23	4	28	89	35	9	8	108	.267	.318	.472	.790	+15	0	0	0	1b149	0	0.0
1962	†NY A	140	478	63	129	16	6	23	80	36	4	5	99	.270	.325	.473	.798	+16	0	1	0	1b135	0	-0.5
1963	†LA N	89	237	19	48	8	0	4	19	13	4	3	49	.203	.252	.287	.539	-41	0	1	0	1b66/3b	0	-1.9
1964	Was A	73	262	28	71	10	0	13	41	11	2	3	56	.271	.306	.458	.764	+10	0	0	0	1b66	0	-0.3
1964	Chi A	73	273	19	80	11	3	4	38	19	4	1	36	.293	.337	.399	.736	+8	0	0	0	1b70	0	-0.2
1964	Year	146	535	47	151	21	3	17	79	30	6	4	92	.282	.322	.428	.750	+9	0	0	0	1b136	0	-0.5
1965	Chi A✱	146	559	63	153	24	3	18	78	32	4	5	77	.274	.316	.424	.740	+16	1	3	25	1b145	0	-0.7
1966	Chi A	120	337	27	84	15	2	6	29	26	4	3	45	.249	.308	.359	.667	-2	1	1	50	1b98	0	-0.4
1967	Chi A	8	8	0	0	0	0	0	1	0	0	0	1	.000	.000	.000	.000	-199	0	0	0	/H	0	-0.2
1967	Cal A	62	123	8	27	2	1	1	10	4	1	4	18	.220	.267	.276	.543	-37	0	0	0	1b32	0	-0.9
1967	Year	70	131	8	27	2	1	1	11	4	1	4	19	.206	.252	.260	.512	-47	0	0	0	1b32	0	-1.1
Total	14	1658	5547	681	1566	243	53	211	888	383	48	54	870	.282	.332	.459	.791	+21	16	18	47	1b1463,3b13,2b2	65	5.0
Team	9	1087	3748	517	1103	173	44	165	672	278	29	35	588	.294	.346	.496	.842	+31	14	13	52	1b986,3b12,2b2	65	9.6
/150	1	150	517	71	152	24	6	23	93	38	4	5	81	.294	.346	.496	.842	+31	2	2	50	1b136,3b2/2	9	1.3

SLAUGHT, DON DONALD MARTIN B9.11.1958 LONG BEACH CA BR/TR/6'1"/(185–190) DR 1980 KCA 7/172 D7.6 C1 COL UCLA

YEAR	TM LG	G	AB	R	H	2B	3B	HR	RBI	BB	IB	HP	SO	AVG	OBP	SLG	OPS	AOPS	SB	CS	SB%	GAMES AT POSITION	DL	BFW
1988	NY A	97	322	33	91	25	1	9	43	24	3	3	54	.283	.334	.450	.784	+19	1	0	100	C94/D	36	0.5
1989	NY A	117	350	34	88	21	3	5	38	30	3	5	57	.251	.315	.371	.686	-5	1	1	50	C105,D3	0	0.4
Total	16	1327	4063	415	1151	235	28	77	476	311	28	42	559	.283	.338	.412	.750	+4	18	15	55	C1237,D15/3b	275	4.1
Team	2	214	672	67	179	46	4	14	81	54	6	8	111	.266	.324	.409	.733	+6	2	1	67	C199,D4	36	0.9
/150	1	150	471	47	125	32	3	10	57	38	4	6	78	.266	.324	.409	.733	+6	1	1	50	C139,D3	25	0.6

SLAUGHTER, ENOS ENOS BRADSHER "COUNTRY" B4.27.1916 ROXBORO NC D8.12.2002 DURHAM NC BL/TR/5'9"/(188–195) D4.19 MIL 1943–45 HF1985

YEAR	TM LG	G	AB	R	H	2B	3B	HR	RBI	BB	IB	HP	SO	AVG	OBP	SLG	OPS	AOPS	SB	CS	SB%	GAMES AT POSITION	DL	BFW
1954	NY A	69	125	19	31	4	2	1	19	28	—	0	8	.248	.386	.336	.722	+2	0	2	0	O30(3/0/29)	45	-0.3
1955	NY A	10	9	1	1	0	0	0	1	1	0	0	1	.111	.200	.111	.311	-115	0	0	0	/H	0	-0.2
1956	†NY A	24	83	15	24	4	2	0	4	5	0	0	6	.289	.330	.386	.716	-9	1	1	50	O20(17/0/4)	0	-0.4
1957	†NY A	96	209	24	53	7	1	5	34	40	5	0	19	.254	.369	.368	.737	+5	0	2	0	O64(56/0/9)	0	0.0
1958	†NY A	77	138	21	42	4	1	4	19	21	0	0	16	.304	.396	.435	.831	+33	2	0	100	O35(16/0/20)	0	0.4
1959	NY A	74	99	10	17	2	0	6	21	13	1	0	19	.172	.265	.374	.639	-23	1	0	100	O26(9/0/18)	0	-0.5
Total	19	2380	7946	1247	2383	413	148	169	1304	1018	11	37	538	.300	.382	.453	.835	+22	71	15	100	O2064(513/21/1541)	45	15.1
Team	6	350	663	90	168	21	6	16	98	108	6	0	69	.253	.356	.376	.732	+3	4	5	44	O175(92/0/45)	45	-1.0
/150	3	150	284	39	72	9	3	7	42	46	3	0	30	.253	.356	.376	.732	+3	2	2	50	O75(39/0/19)	19	-0.4

SMALLEY, ROY ROY FREDERICK III B10.25.1952 LOS ANGELES CA BB/TR/6'1"/(180–190) DR 1974 TEXA*1/1 D4.30 F–ROY COL USC

YEAR	TM LG	G	AB	R	H	2B	3B	HR	RBI	BB	IB	HP	SO	AVG	OBP	SLG	OPS	AOPS	SB	CS	SB%	GAMES AT POSITION	DL	BFW
1982	NY A	142	486	55	125	14	2	20	67	68	7	0	100	.257	.346	.418	.764	+11	0	1	0	S89,3b53/2bD	0	0.1
1983	NY A	130	451	70	124	24	1	18	62	58	2	2	68	.275	.357	.452	.809	+26	3	3	50	S91,3b26,1b22	0	1.0
1984	NY A	67	209	17	50	8	1	7	26	15	2	0	35	.239	.286	.388	.674	-11	2	1	67	3b35,S13,1b5,D5	0	-0.6
Total	13	1653	5657	745	1454	244	25	163	694	771	47	14	908	.257	.345	.395	.740	+2	27	34	44	S1069,D272,3b188,2b58,1b34/C	0	16.9
Team	3	339	1146	142	299	46	4	45	155	141	11	2	203	.261	.340	.426	.766	+13	5	5	50	S193,3b114,1b27,D6/2	0	0.5
/150	1	150	507	63	132	20	2	20	69	62	5	1	90	.261	.340	.426	.766	+13	2	2	50	S85,3b50,1b12,D3/2	0	0.2

SMITH, KLONDIKE ARMSTRONG FREDERICK B1.4.1887 LONDON, ENGLAND D11.15.1959 SPRINGFIELD MA BL/TL/5'9"/160 D9.28

YEAR	TM LG	G	AB	R	H	2B	3B	HR	RBI	BB	IB	HP	SO	AVG	OBP	SLG	OPS	AOPS	SB	CS	SB%	GAMES AT POSITION	DL	BFW
1912	NY A	7	27	0	5	1	0	0	0	0	—	0	—	.185	.185	.222	.407	-85	1	—	—	O7(0/5/2)	—	-0.4

SMITH, CHARLEY CHARLES WILLIAM B9.15.1937 CHARLESTON SC D11.29.1994 RENO NV BR/TR/6'0"/(175–177) D9.8

YEAR	TM LG	G	AB	R	H	2B	3B	HR	RBI	BB	IB	HP	SO	AVG	OBP	SLG	OPS	AOPS	SB	CS	SB%	GAMES AT POSITION	DL	BFW
1967	NY A	135	425	38	95	15	3	9	38	32	6	1	110	.224	.278	.336	.614	-16	0	2	0	3b115	0	-0.3
1968	NY A	46	70	2	16	4	1	1	7	5	2	0	18	.229	.280	.357	.637	-5	0	0	0	3b13	32	0.3
Total	10	771	2484	228	594	83	18	69	281	130	19	14	565	.239	.279	.370	.649	-18	7	12	37	3b623,S61,O13L/2b	32	-6.1
Team	2	181	495	40	111	19	4	10	45	37	8	1	128	.224	.279	.339	.618	-14	0	2	0	3b128	32	0.0
/150	2	150	410	33	92	16	3	8	37	31	7	1	106	.224	.279	.339	.618	-14	0	2	0	3b106	27	0.0

SMITH, ELMER ELMER JOHN B9.21.1892 SANDUSKY OH D8.3.1984 COLUMBIA KY BL/TR/5'10"/165 D9.20 MIL 1918

YEAR	TM LG	G	AB	R	H	2B	3B	HR	RBI	BB	IB	HP	SO	AVG	OBP	SLG	OPS	AOPS	SB	CS	SB%	GAMES AT POSITION	DL	BFW
1922	†NY A	21	27	1	5	0	0	1	5	3	—	0	5	.185	.267	.296	.563	-54	0	0	0	O11(2/0/9)	—	-0.2
1923	NY A	70	183	30	56	6	2	7	35	21	—	0	21	.306	.377	.475	.852	+21	3	1	75	O47R	—	0.3
Total	10	1012	3195	469	881	181	62	70	541	319	—	16	359	.276	.344	.437	.781	+12	54	27	100	O870(123/16/732)	—	-1.7
Team	2	91	210	31	61	6	2	8	40	24	—	0	26	.290	.363	.452	.815	+11	3	1	75	O58(2/0/9)	—	0.1

SMITH, KEITH PATRICK KEITH B10.20.1961 LOS ANGELES CA BB/TR/6'1"/(175–185) DR 1979 NYA 15/389 D4.12

YEAR	TM LG	G	AB	R	H	2B	3B	HR	RBI	BB	IB	HP	SO	AVG	OBP	SLG	OPS	AOPS	SB	CS	SB%	GAMES AT POSITION	DL	BFW
1984	NY A	2	4	0	0	0	0	0	0	0	0	1	2	.000	.200	.000	.200	-141	0	0	0	S2	0	0.1
1985	NY A	4	0	1	0	0	0	0	0	0	0	0	0	+	+	+	.000	-100	0	0	0	S3	0	0.0
Total	2	6	4	1	0	0	0	0	0	0	0	1	2	.000	.200	.000	.200	-141	0	0	0	S5	0	0.1

SMITH, JOE SALVATORE JOSEPH (B SALVATORE PERSICO) B12.29.1893 NEW YORK NY D1.12.1974 YONKERS NY BR/TR/5'7"/170 D7.7 COL CALIFORNIA

YEAR	TM LG	G	AB	R	H	2B	3B	HR	RBI	BB	IB	HP	SO	AVG	OBP	SLG	OPS	AOPS	SB	CS	SB%	GAMES AT POSITION	DL	BFW
1913	NY A	14	32	1	5	0	0	0	2	1	—	0	14	.156	.182	.156	.338	-101	1	—	—	C14	—	-0.5

SNOW, J.T. JACK THOMAS B2.26.1968 LONG BEACH CA BL/TL (BB 1992–98)/6'2"/(202–210) DR 1989 NYA 5/129 D9.20 COL ARIZONA

YEAR	TM LG	G	AB	R	H	2B	3B	HR	RBI	BB	IB	HP	SO	AVG	OBP	SLG	OPS	AOPS	SB	CS	SB%	GAMES AT POSITION	DL	BFW
1992	NY A	7	14	1	2	1	0	0	2	5	1	0	5	.143	.368	.214	.582	-33	0	0	0	1b6/D	0	-0.1
Total	15	1715	5641	798	1509	293	19	189	877	760	61	64	1142	.268	.357	.427	.784	+5	20	23	47	1b1656,D2	118	-6.5

Soderholm, Eric Eric Thane B9.24.1948 Cortland NY BR/TR/5'11"/(187–202) Dr 1968 MinA*S1/1 d9.3 Col South Georgia JC [DL 1976 Min A 179, 1981 NY A 180]

YEAR	TM LG	G	AB	R	H	2B	3B	HR	RBI	BB	IB	HP	SO	AVG	OBP	SLG	OPS	AOPS	SB	CS	SB%	GAMES AT POSITION	DL	BFW
1980	†NY A	95	275	38	79	13	1	11	35	27	2	1	25	.287	.353	.462	.815	+23	0	0	0	D51,3b37	0	0.6
Total	9	894	2894	402	764	120	14	102	383	295	15	22	359	.264	.335	.421	.756	+10	18	21	46	3b759,D82,1b2,S2/2b	398	6.2

Sojo, Luis Luis Beltran (Sojo) B1.3.1965 Caracas, Distrito Capital, Venez BR/TR/5'11"/(165–185) d7.14 C2

YEAR	TM LG	G	AB	R	H	2B	3B	HR	RBI	BB	IB	HP	SO	AVG	OBP	SLG	OPS	AOPS	SB	CS	SB%	GAMES AT POSITION	DL	BFW
1996	†NY A	18	40	3	11	2	0	0	5	1	0	0	4	.275	.286	.325	.611	-44	0	0	0	2b14,S4/3b	0	0.0
1997	NY A	77	215	27	66	6	1	2	25	16	0	1	14	.307	.355	.372	.727	-8	3	1	75	2b72,S4,3b3,1b2	45	0.5
1998	†NY A	54	147	16	34	3	1	0	14	4	0	0	15	.231	.250	.265	.515	-64	1	0	100	S20,1b19,2b8,3b6,D2	27	-1.3
1999	†NY A	49	127	20	32	6	0	2	16	4	0	0	17	.252	.275	.346	.621	-42	1	0	100	3b20,2b16,S6,1b4,D2	0	-0.6
2000	†NY A	34	125	19	36	7	1	2	17	6	0	0	6	.288	.321	.408	.729	-16	1	0	100	2b25,3b10,1b7,S2	0	-0.4
2001	†NY A	39	79	5	13	2	0	0	9	4	0	1	12	.165	.214	.190	.404	-92	1	0	100	3b17,1b8,2b7,S5/D	0	-1.0
2003	NY A	3	4	0	0	0	0	0	0	0	0	0	0	.000	.000	.000	.000	-199	0	0	0	/1b2bD	0	-0.1
Total	13	848	2571	300	671	103	12	36	261	124	3	13	198	.261	.297	.352	.649	-29	28	20	58	2b456,S184,3b158,1b41,D12,O12L	129	-3.7
Team	7	274	737	90	192	26	3	6	86	35	0	2	68	.261	.294	.328	.622	-38	7	1	88	2b143,3b57,1b41,S41,D6	72	-2.9
/150	4	150	403	49	105	14	2	3	47	19	0	1	37	.261	.294	.328	.622	-38	4	1	80	2b78,3b31,1b22,S22,D3	39	-1.6

Solaita, Tony Tolia B1.15.1947 Nuuuli, American Samoa D2.10.1990 Tafuna, American Samoa BL/TL/6'0"/(210–215) d9.16

YEAR	TM LG	G	AB	R	H	2B	3B	HR	RBI	BB	IB	HP	SO	AVG	OBP	SLG	OPS	AOPS	SB	CS	SB%	GAMES AT POSITION	DL	BFW
1968	NY A	1	1	0	0	0	0	0	0	0	0	0	1	.000	.000	.000	.000	-199	0	0	0	/1b	0	0.0
Total	7	525	1316	164	336	66	1	50	203	214	18	3	345	.255	.357	.421	.778	+20	2	8	20	1b281,D122/rf	0	3.7

Soriano, Alfonso Alfonso Guilleard B1.7.1976 San Pedro de Macoris, D.R. BR/TR/6'1"/(160–180) d9.14 OF(280/12/0)

YEAR	TM LG	G	AB	R	H	2B	3B	HR	RBI	BB	IB	HP	SO	AVG	OBP	SLG	OPS	AOPS	SB	CS	SB%	GAMES AT POSITION	DL	BFW
1999	NY A	9	8	2	1	0	0	1	1	0	0	0	3	.125	.125	.500	.625	-50	0	1	0	/SD	0	-0.2
2000	NY A	22	50	5	9	3	0	2	3	1	0	0	15	.180	.196	.360	.556	-63	2	0	100	3b10,S9/2bD	0	-0.9
2001	†NY A	158	574	77	154	34	3	18	73	29	0	3	125	.268	.304	.432	.736	-9	43	14	75	2b156,D2	0	-0.8
2002	†NY A★	156	696	**128**	**209**	51	2	39	102	23	1	14	157	.300	.332	.547	.879	+30	**41**	13	76	2b155/D	0	2.6
2003	†NY A★	156	682	114	198	36	5	38	91	38	7	12	130	.290	.338	.525	.863	+25	35	8	81	2b155	0	3.5
2004	Tex A★	145	608	77	170	32	4	28	91	33	4	10	121	.280	.324	.484	.808	+3	18	5	78	2b142,D3	0	1.6
2005	Tex A★	156	637	102	171	43	2	36	104	33	3	7	125	.268	.309	.512	.821	+11	30	2	94	2b153,D2	0	1.0
2006	Was N★	159	647	119	179	41	2	46	95	67	16	9	160	.277	.351	.560	.911	+35	41	17	71	O158L	0	4.4
2007	†Chi N★	135	579	97	173	42	5	33	70	31	4	4	130	.299	.337	.560	.897	+18	19	6	76	O134(122/12/0)/2b	22	2.5
Total	9	1096	4481	721	1264	282	23	241	630	255	35	59	966	.282	.327	.517	.844	+16	229	66	78	2b763,O292L,D15,3b10,S10	22	13.7
Team	5	501	2010	326	571	124	10	98	270	91	8	29	430	.284	.322	.502	.824	+15	121	36	77	2b467,3b10,S9,D5	0	4.2
/150	1	150	602	98	171	37	3	29	81	27	2	9	129	.284	.322	.502	.824	+15	36	11	77	2b140,3b3,S3/D	0	1.3

Souchock, Steve Stephen "Bud" B3.3.1919 Yatesboro PA D7.28.2002 Westland MI BR/TR/6'2.5"/(200–203) d5.25

YEAR	TM LG	G	AB	R	H	2B	3B	HR	RBI	BB	IB	HP	SO	AVG	OBP	SLG	OPS	AOPS	SB	CS	SB%	GAMES AT POSITION	DL	BFW
1946	NY A	47	86	15	26	3	3	2	10	7	—	1	13	.302	.362	.477	.839	+31	0	3	0	1b20	0	-0.1
1948	NY A	44	118	11	24	3	1	3	11	7	—	0	13	.203	.248	.322	.570	-49	3	0	100	1b32	0	-1.1
Total	8	473	1227	163	313	58	20	50	186	88	0	4	164	.255	.307	.457	.764	+6	15	9	63	O243(133/1/114),1b93,3b18/2b	34	-1.4
Team	2	91	204	26	50	6	4	5	21	14	—	1	26	.245	.297	.387	.684	-15	3	3	50	1b52	0	-1.2

Spencer, Jim James Lloyd B7.30.1947 Hanover PA D2.10.2002 Ft.Lauderdale FL BL/TL/6'2"/(190–206) Dr 1965 AnaA 1/11 d9.7 gf–Ben

YEAR	TM LG	G	AB	R	H	2B	3B	HR	RBI	BB	IB	HP	SO	AVG	OBP	SLG	OPS	AOPS	SB	CS	SB%	GAMES AT POSITION	DL	BFW
1978	†NY A	71	150	12	34	9	1	7	24	15	3	0	32	.227	.295	.440	.735	+7	0	1	0	D35,1b15	16	-0.1
1979	NY A	106	295	60	85	15	3	23	53	38	11	0	25	.288	.367	.593	.960	+57	0	2	0	D71,1b26	0	1.8
1980	†NY A	97	259	38	61	9	0	13	43	30	2	1	44	.236	.313	.421	.734	+2	1	0	100	1b75,D15	0	-0.2
1981	NY A	25	63	6	9	2	0	2	4	9	2	0	7	.143	.250	.270	.520	-50	0	0	0	1b25	0	-0.3
Total	15	1553	4908	541	1227	179	27	146	599	407	86	17	582	.250	.307	.387	.694	-2	11	19	37	1b1221,D205,O24L	52	-10.8
Team	4	299	767	116	189	35	4	45	124	92	18	1	108	.246	.325	.478	.803	+20	1	3	25	1b141,D121	16	1.2
/150	2	150	385	58	95	18	2	23	62	46	9	1	54	.246	.325	.478	.803	+20	1	2	33	1b71,D61	8	0.6

Spencer, Shane Michael Shane B2.20.1972 Key West FL BR/TR/5'11"/(210–225) Dr 1990 NYA 28/750 d4.10

YEAR	TM LG	G	AB	R	H	2B	3B	HR	RBI	BB	IB	HP	SO	AVG	OBP	SLG	OPS	AOPS	SB	CS	SB%	GAMES AT POSITION	DL	BFW
1998	†NY A	27	67	18	25	6	0	10	27	5	0	0	12	.373	.411	.910	1.321	+142	0	1	0	O22(9/0/15)/1bD	0	1.1
1999	†NY A	71	205	25	48	8	0	8	20	18	0	2	51	.234	.301	.390	.691	-24	0	4	0	O64(46/0/22),D3	24	-0.8
2000	NY A	73	248	33	70	11	3	9	40	19	0	2	45	.282	.330	.460	.790	+1	1	2	33	O40(33/0/7),D33	81	-0.1
2001	†NY A	80	283	40	73	14	2	10	46	21	0	4	58	.258	.315	.428	.743	-7	4	1	80	O68(44/0/28),D14	28	0.1
2002	†NY A	94	288	32	71	15	2	6	34	31	4	4	62	.247	.324	.375	.699	-13	0	3	0	O91(40/0/55)/D	0	-1.0
2003	Cle A	64	210	23	57	10	0	8	26	18	0	1	52	.271	.328	.433	.761	+0	2	0	100	O43(16/0/30),1b11,D7	0	-0.5
2003	Tex A	55	185	16	42	10	0	4	23	27	0	2	40	.227	.329	.346	.675	-26	0	0	0	O54(50/0/12)/D	0	-0.8
2003	Year	119	395	39	99	20	0	12	49	45	0	3	92	.251	.328	.392	.720	-12	2	0	100	O97(66/0/42),1b11,D8	0	-1.3
2004	NY N	74	185	21	52	10	1	4	26	13	0	2	37	.281	.332	.411	.743	-6	6	0	100	O62(43/6/19)/1b	8	0.1
Total	7	538	1671	208	438	84	8	59	242	152	4	17	357	.262	.326	.428	.754	-4	13	11	54	O444(281/6/188),D63,1b13	141	-1.9
Team	5	345	1091	148	287	54	7	43	167	94	4	12	228	.263	.324	.444	.768	-1	5	11	31	O285(55/0/17),D52/1	133	-0.7
/150	2	150	474	64	125	23	3	19	73	41	2	5	99	.263	.324	.444	.768	-1	2	5	29	O124(24/0/7),D23/1	58	-0.3

Spikes, Charlie Leslie Charles B1.23.1951 Bogalusa LA BR/TR/6'3"/(205–220) Dr 1969 NYA 1/11 d9.1

YEAR	TM LG	G	AB	R	H	2B	3B	HR	RBI	BB	IB	HP	SO	AVG	OBP	SLG	OPS	AOPS	SB	CS	SB%	GAMES AT POSITION	DL	BFW
1972	NY A	14	34	2	5	1	0	0	3	1	0	0	13	.147	.171	.176	.347	-96	0	1	0	O9R	0	-0.5
Total	9	670	2039	240	502	72	12	65	256	154	13	22	388	.246	.304	.389	.693	-4	27	25	52	O533(136/0/398),D32	0	-4.7

Stahl, Jake Garland B4.13.1879 Elkhart IL D9.18.1922 Monrovia CA BR/TR/6'2"/195 d4.20 M4 Col Illinois

YEAR	TM LG	G	AB	R	H	2B	3B	HR	RBI	BB	IB	HP	SO	AVG	OBP	SLG	OPS	AOPS	SB	CS	SB%	GAMES AT POSITION	DL	BFW
1908	NY A	75	274	34	70	18	5	2	42	11	—	8	—	.255	.304	.380	.684	+20	17	—	—	O68(64/4/0),1b6	—	0.7
Total	9	981	3425	405	894	149	87	31	437	221	—	94	1	.261	.323	.382	.705	+20	178	22	100	1b839,O92(65/27/0),C28	—	3.9

Staiger, Roy Roy Joseph B1.6.1950 Tulsa OK BR/TR/6'0"/195 Dr 1970 NYN*S1/24 d9.12 Col Bacone

YEAR	TM LG	G	AB	R	H	2B	3B	HR	RBI	BB	IB	HP	SO	AVG	OBP	SLG	OPS	AOPS	SB	CS	SB%	GAMES AT POSITION	DL	BFW
1979	NY A	4	11	1	3	1	0	0	1	1	0	0	0	.273	.308	.364	.672	-11	0	0	0	3b4	0	0.0
Total	4	152	457	42	104	19	1	4	38	30	6	1	59	.228	.274	.300	.574	-37	4	3	57	3b146,S2	0	-0.9

Stainback, Tuck George Tucker B8.4.1911 Los Angeles CA D11.29.1992 Camarillo CA BR/TR/5'11.5"/175 d4.17

YEAR	TM LG	G	AB	R	H	2B	3B	HR	RBI	BB	IB	HP	SO	AVG	OBP	SLG	OPS	AOPS	SB	CS	SB%	GAMES AT POSITION	DL	BFW
1942	†NY A	15	10	0	2	0	0	0	0	0	—	0	2	.200	.200	.200	.400	-87	0	0	0	O3(2/0/1)	0	-0.1
1943	†NY A	71	231	31	60	11	2	0	10	7	—	1	16	.260	.285	.325	.610	-23	3	3	50	O60(12/43/5)	0	-1.1
1944	NY A	30	78	13	17	3	0	0	5	3	—	0	7	.218	.247	.256	.503	-58	1	0	100	O24(4/4/17)	0	-0.8
1945	NY A	95	327	40	84	12	2	5	32	13	—	2	20	.257	.289	.352	.641	-18	0	4	0	O83(2/72/9)	0	-0.9
Total	13	817	2261	284	585	90	14	17	204	64	—	16	213	.259	.284	.333	.617	-32	27	12	100	O629(182/284/168)/3b	0	-12.8
Team	4	211	646	84	163	26	4	5	47	23	—	3	45	.252	.281	.328	.609	-26	4	7	36	O170(21/56/57)	0	-2.9
/150	3	150	459	60	116	18	3	4	33	16	—	2	32	.252	.281	.328	.609	-26	3	5	38	O121(15/40/41)	0	-2.1

Stankiewicz, Andy Andrew Neal B8.10.1964 Inglewood CA BR/TR/5'9"/165 Dr 1986 NYA 12/314 d4.11 Col Pepperdine

YEAR	TM LG	G	AB	R	H	2B	3B	HR	RBI	BB	IB	HP	SO	AVG	OBP	SLG	OPS	AOPS	SB	CS	SB%	GAMES AT POSITION	DL	BFW
1992	NY A	116	400	52	107	22	2	2	25	38	0	5	42	.268	.338	.348	.686	-7	9	5	64	S81,2b34/D	15	1.5
1993	NY A	16	9	5	0	0	0	0	0	1	0	0	1	.000	.100	.000	.100	-173	0	0	0	2b6,3b4/SD	0	0.0
Total	7	429	844	105	203	45	3	4	59	80	3	11	141	.241	.313	.315	.628	-28	17	9	65	2b157,S140,3b12,D4	126	-1.0
Team	2	132	409	57	107	22	2	2	25	39	0	5	43	.262	.333	.340	.673	-11	9	5	64	S82,2b40,3b4,D2	15	1.5
/150	2	150	465	65	122	25	2	2	28	44	0	6	49	.262	.333	.340	.673	-11	10	6	63	S93,2b45,3b5,D2	17	1.7

Stanley, Fred Frederick Blair B8.13.1947 Farnhamville IA BR/TR (BB 1969–71)/5'10"/(155–170) Dr 1966 HouN 8/143 d9.11 C1

YEAR	TM LG	G	AB	R	H	2B	3B	HR	RBI	BB	IB	HP	SO	AVG	OBP	SLG	OPS	AOPS	SB	CS	SB%	GAMES AT POSITION	DL	BFW
1969	Sea A	17	43	2	12	2	1	0	4	3	0	0	8	.279	.319	.372	.691	-4	1	0	100	S15/2b	0	-0.5
1970	Mil A	6	0	1	0	0	0	0	0	0	0	0	0	+	+	+	.000	-100	0	0	0	2b2	0	0.0
1971	Cle A	60	129	14	29	4	0	2	12	27	3	1	25	.225	.361	.302	.663	-18	1	0	100	S55,2b3	0	0.9
1972	Cle A	6	12	1	2	1	0	0	0	2	0	0	3	.167	.286	.250	.536	-42	0	0	0	S5/2b	0	-0.3
1972	SD N	39	85	15	17	2	0	0	2	12	1	1	19	.200	.306	.224	.530	-43	1	0	100	2b21,S17,3b4	0	-0.2
1972	Major	45	97	16	19	3	0	0	2	14	1	1	22	.196	.304	.227	.530	-44	1	0	100	—	0	-0.5
1973	NY A	26	66	6	14	0	1	1	5	7	0	0	16	.212	.288	.288	.576	-36	0	0	0	S21,2b3	0	0.1

YEAR	TM LG	G	AB	R	H	2B	3B	HR	RBI	BB	IB	HP	SO	AVG	OBP	SLG	OPS	AOPS	SB	CS	SB%	GAMES AT POSITION	DL	BFW
1974	NY A	33	38	2	7	0	0	0	3	3	0	0	2	.184	.244	.184	.428	-75	1	2	33	S19,2b15	0	0.3
1975	NY A	117	252	34	56	5	1	0	15	21	0	1	27	.222	.283	.250	.533	-47	3	1	75	S83,2b33/3b	0	-1.0
1976	†NY A	110	260	32	62	2	2	1	20	34	0	1	29	.238	.329	.273	.602	-22	1	0	100	S110,2b3	0	-2.0
1977	†NY A	48	46	6	12	0	0	1	7	8	0	0	6	.261	.370	.326	.696	-8	1	1	50	S42,3b3,2b2	0	-0.2
1978	†NY A	81	160	14	35	7	0	1	9	25	0	0	31	.219	.324	.281	.605	-27	0	0	0	S71,2b11,3b4	0	-0.7
1979	NY A	57	100	9	20	1	0	2	14	5	0	0	17	.200	.236	.270	.506	-63	0	1	0	S31,3b16,2b8/1blf	0	-0.4
1980	NY A	49	86	13	18	3	0	0	5	5	0	2	5	.209	.266	.244	.510	-58	0	0	0	S19,2b17,3b12	37	0.0
1981	†Oak A	66	145	15	28	4	0	0	7	15	0	0	23	.193	.269	.221	.490	-50	2	0	100	S62,2b6	0	-2.4
1982	Oak A	101	228	33	44	7	0	2	17	29	0	1	32	.193	.287	.250	.537	-49	0	1	0	S98,2b2	0	-2.6
Total	14	816	1650	197	356	38	5	10	120	196	4	7	243	.216	.301	.263	.564	-39	11	6	65	S648,2b128,3b40/lf1b	37	-9.5
Team	8	521	1008	116	224	18	4	6	78	108	0	4	133	.222	.299	.266	.565	-38	6	5	55	S396,2b92,3b36/1lf	37	-4.4
/150	2	150	290	33	64	5	1	2	22	31	0	1	38	.222	.299	.266	.565	-38	2	1	67	S114,2b26,3b10/1OfL	11	-1.3

STANLEY, MIKE ROBERT MICHAEL B6.25.1963 FT.LAUDERDALE FL BR/TR/6'1"/(185–205) DR 1985 TEXA 16/395 D6.24 C1 COL FLORIDA

YEAR	TM LG	G	AB	R	H	2B	3B	HR	RBI	BB	IB	HP	SO	AVG	OBP	SLG	OPS	AOPS	SB	CS	SB%	GAMES AT POSITION	DL	BFW
1992	NY A	68	173	24	43	7	0	8	27	33	0	1	45	.249	.372	.428	.800	+24	0	0	0	C55,1b4,D6	0	0.8
1993	NY A	130	423	70	129	17	1	26	84	57	4	5	85	.305	.389	.534	.923	+51	1	1	50	C122,D2	0	3.3
1994	NY A	82	290	54	87	20	0	17	57	39	2	2	56	.300	.384	.545	.929	+42	0	0	0	C72,1b7,D4	15	2.5
1995	†NY A★	118	399	63	107	29	1	18	83	57	1	5	106	.268	.360	.481	.841	+19	1	1	50	C107,D10	0	1.4
1997	†NY A	28	87	16	25	8	0	3	12	15	4	0	22	.287	.388	.483	.871	+28	0	0	0	D16,1b12	0	0.2
Total	15	1467	4222	625	1138	220	7	187	702	652	25	48	929	.270	.370	.458	.828	+17	13	4	76	C751,D321,1b301,3b26,O4L	71	2.9
Team	5	426	1372	227	391	81	2	72	263	201	11	13	314	.285	.377	.504	.881	+35	2	2	50	C356,D38,1b23	15	8.2
/150	2	150	483	80	138	29	1	25	93	71	4	5	111	.285	.377	.504	.881	+35	1	1	50	C125,D13,1b8	5	2.9

STEGMAN, DAVE DAVID WILLIAM B1.30.1954 INGLEWOOD CA BR/TR/5'11"/(185–190) DR 1976 DETA S1/2 D9.4 COL ARIZONA

YEAR	TM LG	G	AB	R	H	2B	3B	HR	RBI	BB	IB	HP	SO	AVG	OBP	SLG	OPS	AOPS	SB	CS	SB%	GAMES AT POSITION	DL	BFW
1982	NY A	2	0	0	0	0	0	0	0	0	0	0	0	+	+	+	.000	-100	0	0	0	/D	0	0.0
Total	6	172	320	39	66	10	2	8	32	31	0	2	55	.206	.277	.325	.602	-36	5	3	63	O151(30/89/40),D6	0	-2.7

STERRETT, DUTCH CHARLES HURLBUT B10.1.1889 MILROY PA D12.9.1965 BALTIMORE MD BR/TR/5'11.5"/165 D6.20 COL PRINCETON

YEAR	TM LG	G	AB	R	H	2B	3B	HR	RBI	BB	IB	HP	SO	AVG	OBP	SLG	OPS	AOPS	SB	CS	SB%	GAMES AT POSITION	DL	BFW
1912	NY A	66	230	30	61	4	7	1	32	11	—	4	—	.265	.310	.357	.667	-15	8	7	53	O37(0/31/6),1b17,C10/2b	—	-1.3
1913	NY A	21	35	0	6	0	0	0	3	1	—	1	5	.171	.216	.171	.387	-86	1	—	—	1b6/C	—	-0.5
Total	2	87	265	30	67	4	7	1	35	12	—	5	5	.253	.298	.332	.630	-23	9	7	100	O37(0/31/6),1b23,C11/2b	—	-1.8

STEWART, BUD EDWARD PERRY B6.15.1916 SACRAMENTO CA D6.21.2000 PALO ALTO CA BL/TR/5'11"/170 D4.19 DEF 1943 MIL 1944–45 COL UCLA

YEAR	TM LG	G	AB	R	H	2B	3B	HR	RBI	BB	IB	HP	SO	AVG	OBP	SLG	OPS	AOPS	SB	CS	SB%	GAMES AT POSITION	DL	BFW
1948	NY A	6	5	1	1	1	0	0	0	0	—	0	0	.200	.200	.400	.600	-42	0	0	0	/H	0	0.0
Total	9	773	2041	288	547	96	32	32	260	252	—	9	157	.268	.351	.393	.744	+2	29	23	100	O535(281/58/222),3b10,2b6	51	-2.9

STINNETT, KELLY KELLY LEE B2.14.1970 LAWTON OK BR/TR/5'11"/(195–235) DR 1989 CLEA 11/281 D4.5 COL SEMINOLE ST. (OK) JC

YEAR	TM LG	G	AB	R	H	2B	3B	HR	RBI	BB	IB	HP	SO	AVG	OBP	SLG	OPS	AOPS	SB	CS	SB%	GAMES AT POSITION	DL	BFW
2006	NY A	34	79	6	18	3	0	1	9	5	1	1	29	.228	.282	.304	.586	-49	0	0	0	C34	0	-0.4
Total	14	734	2033	228	476	91	4	65	230	196	26	42	567	.234	.313	.379	.692	-22	10	5	67	C679,D4	297	-6.6

STIRNWEISS, SNUFFY GEORGE HENRY B10.26.1918 NEW YORK NY D9.15.1958 NEWARK BAY NJ BR/TR/5'8.5"/175 D4.22 COL NORTH CAROLINA

YEAR	TM LG	G	AB	R	H	2B	3B	HR	RBI	BB	IB	HP	SO	AVG	OBP	SLG	OPS	AOPS	SB	CS	SB%	GAMES AT POSITION	DL	BFW
1943	†NY A	83	274	34	60	8	4	1	25	47	—	0	37	.219	.333	.288	.621	-18	11	9	55	S68,2b4	0	-0.2
1944	NY A	**154**	643	**125**	**205**	35	**16**	8	43	73	—	1	87	.319	.389	.460	.849	+37	**55**	11	83	2b154	0	6.8
1945	NY A✱	**152**	632	**107**	**195**	32	**22**	10	64	78	—	1	62	**.309**	.385	**.476**	.861	+43	**33**	17	66	2b152	0	**7.2**
1946	NY A★	129	487	75	122	19	7	0	37	66	—	0	58	.251	.340	.318	.658	-17	18	6	75	3b79,2b46,S4	0	0.1
1947	†NY A	148	571	102	146	18	8	5	41	89	—	2	47	.256	.358	.342	.700	-4	5	3	63	2b148	0	-0.1
1948	NY A	141	515	90	130	20	7	3	32	86	—	1	62	.252	.360	.336	.696	-13	5	4	56	2b141	0	-0.8
1949	†NY A	70	157	29	41	8	2	0	11	29	—	1	20	.261	.380	.338	.718	-10	3	2	60	2b51,3b4	0	0.3
1950	NY A	7	2	0	0	0	0	0	0	0	—	0	0	.000	.000	.000	.000	-199	0	0	0	2b4	0	0.0
1950	StL A	93	326	32	71	16	2	1	24	51	—	0	49	.218	.324	.288	.612	-44	3	3	50	2b62,3b31,S5	0	-3.3
1950	Year	100	328	32	71	16	2	1	24	51	—	0	49	.216	.322	.287	.609	-45	3	3	50	2b66,3b31,S5	0	-3.3
1951	Cle A	50	88	10	19	1	0	1	4	22	—	0	25	.216	.373	.261	.634	-22	1	0	100	2b25,3b2	0	0.5
1952	Cle A	1	0	0	0	0	0	0	0	0	—	0	0	+	+	+	.000	-100	0	0	0	/3b	0	0.0
Total	10	1028	3695	604	989	157	68	29	281	541	—	6	447	.268	.362	.371	.733	+2	134	55	71	2b787,3b117,S77	0	10.5
Team	8	884	3281	562	899	140	66	27	253	468	—	6	373	.274	.365	.382	.747	+8	130	52	71	2b700,3b83,S72	0	13.3
/150	1	150	557	95	153	24	11	5	43	79	—	1	63	.274	.365	.382	.747	+8	22	9	71	2b119,3b14,S12	0	2.3

STRAWBERRY, DARRYL DARRYL EUGENE B3.12.1962 LOS ANGELES CA BL/TL/6'6"/(190–215) DR 1980 NYN 1/1 D5.6 [DL 1994 LA N 52]

YEAR	TM LG	G	AB	R	H	2B	3B	HR	RBI	BB	IB	HP	SO	AVG	OBP	SLG	OPS	AOPS	SB	CS	SB%	GAMES AT POSITION	DL	BFW
1995	†NY A	32	87	15	24	4	1	3	13	10	1	2	22	.276	.364	.448	.812	+11	0	0	0	D15,O11(1/0/10)	0	0.1
1996	†NY A	63	202	35	53	13	0	11	36	31	5	1	55	.262	.359	.490	.849	+13	6	5	55	O34(26/0/8),D26	0	-0.1
1997	NY A	11	29	1	3	1	0	0	2	3	0	0	9	.103	.188	.138	.326	-113	0	0	0	O4L,D4	130	-0.5
1998	NY A	101	295	44	73	11	2	24	57	46	4	3	90	.247	.354	.542	.896	+34	8	7	53	D81,O16L	0	0.7
1999	†NY A	24	49	10	16	5	0	3	6	17	0	0	16	.327	.500	.612	1.112	+85	2	0	100	D17	0	0.7
Total	17	1583	5418	898	1401	256	38	335	1000	816	13	38	1352	.259	.357	.505	.862	+38	221	99	69	O1384(54/48/1308),D143	471	22.5
Team	5	231	662	105	169	34	3	41	114	107	10	6	192	.255	.362	.502	.864	+23	16	12	57	D143,O65(27/0/18)	130	0.9
/150	3	150	430	68	110	22	2	27	74	69	6	4	125	.255	.362	.502	.864	+23	10	8	56	D93,O42(18/0/12)	84	0.6

STREET, GABBY CHARLES EVARD "OLD SARGE" B9.30.1882 HUNTSVILLE AL D2.6.1951 JOPLIN MO BR/TR/5'11"/180 D9.13 M6/C2

YEAR	TM LG	G	AB	R	H	2B	3B	HR	RBI	BB	IB	HP	SO	AVG	OBP	SLG	OPS	AOPS	SB	CS	SB%	GAMES AT POSITION	DL	BFW
1912	NY A	29	88	4	16	1	1	0	6	7	—	2	—	.182	.258	.216	.474	-66	1	—	—	C29	—	-0.6
Total	8	504	1501	98	312	44	11	2	105	119	—	16	0	.208	.273	.256	.529	-34	17	—	—	C493	—	1.3

STUMPF, BILL WILLIAM FREDERICK B3.21.1892 BALTIMORE MD D2.14.1966 CROWNSVILLE MD BR/TR/6'0.5"/175 D5.11

YEAR	TM LG	G	AB	R	H	2B	3B	HR	RBI	BB	IB	HP	SO	AVG	OBP	SLG	OPS	AOPS	SB	CS	SB%	GAMES AT POSITION	DL	BFW
1912	NY A	42	129	8	31	0	0	0	10	6	—	1	—	.240	.279	.240	.519	-54	5	2	71	S26,2b8,3b5/1bcf	—	-1.3
1913	NY A	12	29	5	6	1	0	0	1	3	—	0	3	.207	.281	.241	.522	-47	0	—	—	S6,2b4/rf	—	-0.4
Total	2	54	158	13	37	1	0	0	11	9	—	1	3	.234	.280	.241	.521	-53	5	2	100	S32,2b12,3b5,O2(0/1/1)/1b	—	-1.7

STURM, JOHNNY JOHN PETER JOSEPH B1.23.1916 ST.LOUIS MO D10.8.2004 ST.LOUIS MO BL/TL/6'1"/185 D4.14 MIL 1942–45

YEAR	TM LG	G	AB	R	H	2B	3B	HR	RBI	BB	IB	HP	SO	AVG	OBP	SLG	OPS	AOPS	SB	CS	SB%	GAMES AT POSITION	DL	BFW
1941	†NY A	124	524	58	125	17	3	3	36	37	—	3	50	.239	.293	.300	.593	-42	3	5	38	1b124	0	-4.7
/150	1	150	634	70	151	21	4	4	44	45	—	4	60	.239	.293	.300	.593	-42	4	6	40	1b150	0	-5.7

SUDAKIS, BILL WILLIAM PAUL "SUDS" B3.27.1946 JOLIET IL BB/TR/6'1"/(190–195) D9.3

YEAR	TM LG	G	AB	R	H	2B	3B	HR	RBI	BB	IB	HP	SO	AVG	OBP	SLG	OPS	AOPS	SB	CS	SB%	GAMES AT POSITION	DL	BFW
1974	NY A	89	259	26	60	8	0	7	39	25	1	1	48	.232	.296	.344	.640	-14	0	0	0	D39,1b33,3b3/C	0	-0.8
Total	8	530	1548	177	362	56	7	59	214	172	18	7	313	.234	.311	.393	.704	+2	9	6	60	3b217,C83,1b80,D60,O6(1/0/6)	135	0.6

SVEUM, DALE DALE CURTIS B11.23.1963 RICHMOND CA BB/TR/6'3"/(185–212) DR 1982 MILA 1/25 D5.12 C4 [DL 1989 MIL A 182]

YEAR	TM LG	G	AB	R	H	2B	3B	HR	RBI	BB	IB	HP	SO	AVG	OBP	SLG	OPS	AOPS	SB	CS	SB%	GAMES AT POSITION	DL	BFW
1998	NY A	30	58	6	9	0	0	0	3	4	0	0	16	.155	.203	.155	.358	-103	0	0	0	1b21,3b6,D3	0	-1.1
Total	12	862	2526	305	597	125	13	69	340	227	12	6	656	.236	.298	.378	.676	-18	10	18	36	S442,3b217,1b71,2b53,D13,O2L	214	-9.2

SWEENEY, ED EDWARD FRANCIS "JEFF" B7.19.1888 CHICAGO IL D7.4.1947 CHICAGO IL BR/TR/6'1"/200 D5.16 MIL 1918 COL LOYOLA–CHICAGO

YEAR	TM LG	G	AB	R	H	2B	3B	HR	RBI	BB	IB	HP	SO	AVG	OBP	SLG	OPS	AOPS	SB	CS	SB%	GAMES AT POSITION	DL	BFW
1908	NY A	32	82	4	12	2	0	0	2	5	—	0	—	.146	.195	.171	.366	-81	0	—	—	C25/1brf	—	-0.9
1909	NY A	67	176	18	47	3	0	0	21	16	—	0	—	.267	.328	.284	.612	-7	3	—	—	C62,1b3	—	0.4
1910	NY A	78	215	25	43	4	4	0	13	17	—	4	—	.200	.271	.256	.527	-38	12	—	—	C77	—	0.0
1911	NY A	83	229	17	53	6	5	0	18	14	—	8	—	.231	.299	.301	.600	-37	8	—	—	C83	—	-0.8
1912	NY A	110	351	37	94	12	1	0	30	27	—	3	—	.268	.325	.308	.633	-23	6	5	55	C108	—	-0.5
1913	NY A	117	351	35	93	10	2	2	40	37	—	8	41	.265	.348	.322	.670	-4	11	—	—	C112/1bcf	—	0.3
1914	NY A	87	258	25	55	8	1	1	22	35	—	4	30	.213	.316	.264	.580	-25	19	6	76	C78	—	0.5
1915	NY A	53	137	12	26	2	0	0	5	25	—	1	12	.190	.319	.204	.523	-43	3	3	50	C53	—	-0.6
1919	Pit N	17	42	0	4	1	0	0	0	5	—	0	6	.095	.191	.119	.310	-105	1	—	—	C15	—	-0.6

YEAR	TM LG	G	AB	R	H	2B	3B	HR	RBI	BB	IB	HP	SO	AVG	OBP	SLG	OPS	AOPS	SB	CS	SB%	GAMES AT POSITION	DL	BFW
Total	9	644	1841	173	427	48	13	3	151	181	—	28	89	.232	.310	.277	.587	-27	63	14	100	C613,1b5,O2(0/1/1)	—	-2.2
Team	8	627	1799	173	423	47	13	3	151	176	—	28	83	.235	.313	.281	.594	-26	62	14	100	C598,1b5,O2(0/1/1)	—	-1.6
/150	2	150	430	41	101	11	3	1	36	42	—	7	20	.235	.313	.281	.594	-26	15	3	100	C143/1OfL	—	-0.4
Swoboda, Ron Ronald Alan "Rocky" B6.30.1944 Baltimore MD BR/TR/6'2"/(195–215) d4.12 Col Maryland																								
1971	NY A	54	138	17	36	2	1	2	20	27	1	3	35	.261	.391	.333	.724	+13	0	0	0	O47(7/1/39)	0	0.1
1972	NY A	63	113	9	28	8	0	1	12	17	1	0	29	.248	.341	.345	.686	+8	0	1	0	O35(0/5/35),1b2	0	0.0
1973	NY A	35	43	6	5	0	0	1	2	4	0	0	18	.116	.191	.186	.377	-93	0	0	0	O20(0/8/12),D4	0	-0.7
Total	9	928	2581	285	624	87	24	73	344	299	18	21	647	.242	.324	.379	.703	+0	20	14	59	O767(201/57/524),1b22,D4	0	-3.9
Team	3	152	294	32	69	10	1	4	34	48	2	3	82	.235	.345	.316	.661	-3	0	1	0	O102(7/14/86),D4,1b2	0	-0.6
/150	3	150	290	32	68	10	1	4	34	47	2	3	81	.235	.345	.316	.661	-3	0	1	0	O101(7/14/85),D4,1b2	0	-0.6
Tannehill, Jesse Jesse Niles "Powder" B7.14.1874 Dayton KY D9.22.1956 Dayton KY BB/TL (BL 1903)/5'8"/150 d6.17 C1 b–Lee ▲																								
1903	NY A	40	111	18	26	6	2	1	13	8	—	1	—	.234	.292	.351	.643	-13	1	—	—	P32,O5(4/1/0)	—	0.1
Total	15	507	1414	190	361	55	23	5	142	105	—	8	3	.255	.310	.337	.647	-11	19	—	—	P359,O87(28/32/27)	—	-0.2
Tarasco, Tony Anthony Giacinto B12.9.1970 New York NY BL/TR/6'1"/205 Dr 1988 AtlN 15/372 d4.30																								
1999	NY A	14	31	5	5	2	0	0	3	3	0	0	5	.161	.229	.226	.455	-81	1	0	100	O12(9/0/5)	0	-0.5
Total	8	457	1006	151	241	46	5	34	118	106	14	4	171	.240	.313	.397	.710	-16	39	10	80	O325(79/12/245),D10,1b7	19	-2.3
Tartabull, Danny Danilo (Mora) B10.30.1962 San Juan, PR BR/TR/6'1"/(185–210) Dr 1980 CinN 3/71 d9.7 f–Jose OF(15/0/904)																								
1992	NY A	123	421	72	112	19	0	25	85	103	14	0	115	.266	.409	.489	.898	+51	2	2	50	O69(1/0/68),D53	35	2.8
1993	NY A	138	513	87	128	33	2	31	102	92	9	2	156	.250	.363	.503	.866	+35	0	0	0	D88,O50R	21	1.6
1994	NY A	104	399	68	102	24	1	19	67	66	3	1	111	.256	.360	.464	.824	+15	1	1	50	D78,O26R	0	0.2
1995	NY A	59	192	25	43	12	0	6	28	33	1	1	54	.224	.335	.380	.715	-12	0	0	0	D39,O18R	0	-0.5
Total	14	1406	5011	756	1366	289	22	262	925	768	47	17	1362	.273	.368	.496	.864	+33	37	30	55	O916R,D405,2b32,S24,3b5	343	13.1
Team	4	424	1525	252	385	88	3	81	282	294	27	4	436	.252	.372	.473	.845	+29	3	3	50	D258,O163(1/0/68)	56	4.1
/150	1	150	540	89	136	31	1	29	100	104	10	1	154	.252	.372	.473	.845	+29	1	1	50	D91,O58R	20	1.5
Taylor, Zack James Wren B7.27.1898 Yulee FL D9.19.1974 Orlando FL BR/TR/5'11.5"/180 d6.15 M5/C8 Col Rollins																								
1934	NY A	4	7	0	1	0	0	0	0	0	—	0	1	.143	.143	.143	.286	-128	0	0	0	C3	—	-0.1
Total	16	918	2865	258	748	113	28	9	311	161	—	16	192	.261	.304	.329	.633	-32	9	7	100	C856	—	-9.5
Tepedino, Frank Frank Ronald B11.23.1947 Brooklyn NY BL/TL/5'11"/(185–192) Dr 1965 BalA 3/55 d5.12																								
1967	NY A	9	5	0	2	0	0	0	0	1	0	0	1	.400	.500	.400	.900	+75	0	0	0	/1b	0	0.1
1969	NY A	13	39	6	9	0	0	0	4	4	0	0	4	.231	.302	.231	.533	-47	1	0	100	O13R	0	-0.4
1970	NY A	16	19	2	6	2	0	0	2	1	0	0	2	.316	.350	.421	.771	+17	0	1	0	/1blf	0	-0.1
1971	NY A	6	6	0	0	0	0	0	0	0	0	0	0	.000	.000	.000	.000	-199	0	0	0	/lf	0	-0.2
1972	NY A	8	8	0	0	0	0	0	0	0	0	0	1	.000	.000	.000	.000	-199	0	0	0	/H	0	-0.2
Total	8	265	507	50	122	13	1	6	58	33	5	2	61	.241	.288	.306	.594	-35	4	5	44	1b134,O15(2/0/13)	0	-3.6
Team	5	52	77	8	17	2	0	0	6	6	0	0	8	.221	.277	.247	.524	-48	1	1	50	O15R/1	0	-0.8
Tettelbach, Dick Richard Morley "Tut" B6.26.1929 New Haven CT D1.26.1995 E.Harwich MA BR/TR/6'0"/195 d9.25 Col Yale																								
1955	NY A	2	5	0	0	0	0	0	0	0	0	0	0	.000	.000	.000	.000	-199	0	0	0	O2L	0	-0.1
Total	3	29	80	12	12	1	2	1	10	18	0	0	17	.150	.300	.250	.550	-51	0	1	0	O23(22/2/0)	0	-0.6
Thames, Marcus Marcus Markley B3.6.1977 Louisville MS BR/TR/6'2"/(205–220) Dr 1996 NYA 30/899 d6.10 Col East Central (MO) JC																								
2002	NY A	7	13	2	3	1	0	1	2	0	0	0	4	.231	.231	.538	.769	-3	0	0	0	O7(3/0/4)	0	0.0
Total	6	332	975	147	235	52	2	63	169	83	2	10	266	.241	.306	.492	.798	+5	3	4	43	O219(159/0/60),D65,1b33	21	-1.4
Thomas, Ira Ira Felix B1.22.1881 Ballston Spa NY D10.11.1958 Philadelphia PA BR/TR/6'2"/200 d5.18 C6																								
1906	NY A	44	115	12	23	1	2	0	15	8	—	1	—	.200	.258	.243	.501	-48	2	—	—	C42	—	-0.7
1907	NY A	80	208	20	40	5	4	1	24	10	—	3	—	.192	.240	.269	.509	-42	5	—	—	C61,1b2	—	0.0
Total	10	484	1352	124	327	46	17	3	155	82	—	22	8	.242	.296	.308	.604	-18	20	1	100	C450,1b2	—	3.9
Team	2	124	323	32	63	6	6	1	39	18	—	4	0	.195	.246	.260	.506	-44	7	—	—	C103,1b2	—	-0.7
/150	2	150	391	39	76	7	7	1	47	22	—	5	0	.195	.246	.260	.506	-44	8	—	—	C125,1b2	—	-0.8
Thomas, Lee James Leroy B2.5.1936 Peoria IL BL/TR/6'2"/(187–198) d4.22 C2																								
1961	NY A	2	2	0	1	0	0	0	0	0	0	0	0	.500	.500	.500	1.000	+77	0	0	0	/H	0	0.0
Total	8	1027	3324	405	847	111	22	106	428	332	35	32	397	.255	.327	.397	.724	-1	25	11	69	O485(83/20/392),1b425	0	-7.3
Thomasson, Gary Gary Leah B7.29.1951 San Diego CA BL/TL/6'1"/(170–195) Dr 1969 SFN 7/160 d9.5																								
1978	†NY A	55	116	20	32	4	1	3	20	13	0	0	22	.276	.346	.405	.751	+13	0	2	0	O50(24/16/12)/D	0	0.6
Total	9	901	2373	315	591	103	25	61	294	291	29	5	463	.249	.330	.391	.721	-2	50	16	76	O587(182/247/206),1b163/D	34	-2.5
Thompson, Homer Homer Thomas B6.1.1891 Spring City TN D9.12.1957 Atlanta GA BR/TR/5'9"/160 d10.5 b–Tommy Col Georgia																								
1912	NY A	1	0	0	0	0	0	0	0	0	—	0	—	+	+	+	.000	-100	0	—	—	/C	—	0.0
Thompson, Kevin Kevin Deshawn B9.18.1979 Fort Worth TX BR/TR/5'10"/(185–190) Dr 1999 NYA 31/951 d6.3 Col Grayson Co. (TX) JC																								
2006	NY A	19	30	5	9	3	0	1	6	6	0	0	9	.300	.417	.500	.917	+33	2	0	100	O15(3/2/10),D3	0	0.2
2007	NY A	13	21	2	4	3	0	0	2	2	0	0	10	.190	.261	.333	.594	-46	0	0	0	O11(5/1/5),D3	0	-0.1
2007	Oak A	9	14	2	1	0	0	0	1	1	0	0	3	.071	.133	.071	.204	-147	0	0	0	O8(2/5/1)	0	-0.5
2007	Year	22	35	4	5	3	0	0	3	3	0	0	13	.143	.211	.229	.440	-84	0	0	0	O19(7/6/6),D3	0	-0.6
Total	2	41	65	9	14	6	0	1	9	9	0	0	22	.215	.311	.354	.665	-27	2	0	100	O34(10/8/16),D6	0	-0.4
Team	2	32	51	7	13	6	0	1	8	8	0	0	19	.255	.356	.431	.787	+2	2	0	100	O26(8/3/15),D6	0	0.1
Thompson, Ryan Ryan Orlando B11.4.1967 Chestertown MD BR/TR/6'3"/(200–215) Dr 1987 TorA 13/335 d9.1																								
2000	NY A	33	50	12	13	3	0	3	14	5	0	1	12	.260	.339	.500	.839	+10	0	1	0	O31(20/9/6)	0	0.0
Total	9	416	1257	165	305	71	6	52	176	90	12	20	347	.243	.301	.433	.734	-7	9	12	43	O393(68/269/76)	66	-0.6
Thoney, Jack John "Bullet Jack"(b John Thoeny) B12.8.1879 Ft.Thomas KY D10.24.1948 Covington KY BR/TR/5'10"/175 d4.26																								
1904	NY A	36	128	17	24	4	2	0	12	8	—	1	—	.188	.241	.250	.491	-47	9	—	—	3b26,O10C	—	-1.0
Total	6	264	912	112	216	23	12	3	73	36	—	4	—	.237	.269	.298	.567	-25	42	—	—	O164(97/52/15),3b31,2b19,S11	—	-5.1
Throneberry, Marv Marvin Eugene "Marvelous Marv" B9.2.1933 Collierville TN D6.23.1994 Fisherville TN BL/TL/6'0"/(185–197) d9.25 b–Maynard																								
1955	NY A	1	2	1	2	1	0	0	3	0	0	0	0	1.000	.667	1.500	2.167	+474	1	0	100	/1b	0	0.2
1958	†NY A	60	150	30	34	5	2	7	19	19	0	1	40	.227	.316	.427	.743	+7	1	1	50	1b40,O5R	0	-0.2
1959	NY A	80	192	27	46	5	0	8	22	18	1	0	51	.240	.302	.391	.693	-7	0	0	0	1b54,O13(1/0/12)	0	-0.5
Total	7	480	1186	143	281	37	8	53	170	130	7	1	295	.237	.311	.416	.727	-4	3	4	43	1b307,O45(1/0/44)	0	-2.5
Team	3	141	344	58	82	11	2	15	44	37	1	1	91	.238	.311	.413	.724	+2	2	1	67	1b94,O18(1/0/5)	0	-0.5
/150	3	150	366	62	87	12	2	16	47	39	1	1	97	.238	.311	.413	.724	+2	2	1	67	1b100,O19(1/0/5)	0	-0.5
Tiemeyer, Eddie Edward Carl B5.9.1885 Cincinnati OH D9.27.1946 Cincinnati OH BR/TR/5'11.5"/185 d8.19																								
1909	NY A	3	8	1	3	1	0	0	0	1	—	0	—	.375	.444	.500	.944	+97	0	—	—	1b3	—	0.0
Total	3	9	19	5	5	1	0	0	0	3	—	0	—	.263	.364	.316	.680	+10	0	—	—	1b3,3b3/P	—	0.0

Tillman, Bob John Robert B3.24.1937 Nashville TN D6.23.2000 Gallatin TN BR/TR/6'4"/(200–210) d4.15 Col Middle Tennessee

YEAR	TM LG	G	AB	R	H	2B	3B	HR	RBI	BB	IB	HP	SO	AVG	OBP	SLG	OPS	AOPS	SB	CS	SB%	GAMES AT POSITION	DL	BFW
1967	NY A	22	63	5	16	1	0	2	9	7	1	0	17	.254	.324	.365	.689	+9	0	0	0	C15	0	-0.1
Total	9	775	2329	189	540	68	10	79	282	228	33	5	510	.232	.300	.371	.671	-15	1	0	100	C725	0	-8.4

Tolleson, Wayne Jimmy Wayne B11.22.1955 Spartanburg SC BB/TR/5'9"/(160–163) Dr 1978 TexA 8/202 d9.1 Col Western Carolina

YEAR	TM LG	G	AB	R	H	2B	3B	HR	RBI	BB	IB	HP	SO	AVG	OBP	SLG	OPS	AOPS	SB	CS	SB%	GAMES AT POSITION	DL	BFW
1981	Tex A	14	24	6	4	0	0	0	1	1	0	0	5	.167	.200	.167	.367	-93	2	0	100	3b6,S2	0	-0.6
1982	Tex A	38	70	6	8	1	0	0	2	5	0	0	14	.114	.173	.129	.302	-116	1	1	50	S26,3b4/2b	0	-0.8
1983	Tex A	134	470	64	122	13	2	1	20	40	0	2	68	.260	.319	.315	.634	-24	33	10	77	2b112,S26/D	0	-0.9
1984	Tex A	118	338	35	72	9	2	0	9	27	0	3	47	.213	.276	.251	.527	-54	22	4	85	2b109,S7,3b5/cfD	0	-2.5
1985	Tex A	123	323	45	101	9	5	1	18	21	0	0	46	.313	.353	.381	.734	-1	21	12	64	S81,2b29,3b12,D6	0	0.5
1986	Chi A	81	260	39	65	7	3	3	29	38	0	0	43	.250	.342	.335	.677	-17	13	6	68	3b65,S18,O2(1/1/0),D2	0	-1.1
1986	NY A	60	215	22	61	9	2	0	14	14	0	2	33	.284	.332	.344	.676	-15	4	4	50	S56,3b7,2b3	0	1.0
1986	Year	141	475	61	126	16	5	3	43	52	0	2	76	.265	.338	.339	.677	-16	17	10	63	S74,3b72,2b3,O2(1/1/0),D2	0	-0.1
1987	NY A	121	349	48	77	4	0	1	22	43	0	0	72	.221	.306	.241	.547	-52	5	3	63	S119,3b3	15	-1.7
1988	NY A	21	59	8	15	2	0	0	5	8	0	0	12	.254	.338	.288	.626	-21	1	0	100	2b12,3b10/S	144	0.5
1989	NY A	80	140	16	23	5	2	1	9	16	0	1	23	.164	.255	.250	.505	-57	5	1	83	3b28,S28,2b13,D10	13	-0.8
1990	NY A	73	74	12	11	1	1	0	4	6	0	0	21	.149	.210	.189	.399	-87	1	0	100	S45,2b13,3b3,D5	0	0.0
Total	10	863	2322	301	559	60	17	9	133	219	0	8	384	.241	.307	.293	.600	-35	108	41	72	S409,2b292,3b143,D25,O3(1/2/0)	172	-6.3
Team	5	355	837	106	187	21	5	2	54	87	0	3	161	.223	.298	.268	.566	-44	16	8	67	S249,3b51,2b41,D15	172	-1.0
/150	2	150	354	45	79	9	2	1	23	37	0	1	68	.223	.298	.268	.566	-44	7	3	70	S105,3b22,2b17,D6	73	-0.4

Torgeson, Earl Clifford Earl "The Earl of Snohomish" B1.1.1924 Snohomish WA D11.8.1990 Everett WA BL/TL/6'3"/(180–190) d4.15 C1

YEAR	TM LG	G	AB	R	H	2B	3B	HR	RBI	BB	IB	HP	SO	AVG	OBP	SLG	OPS	AOPS	SB	CS	SB%	GAMES AT POSITION	DL	BFW
1961	NY A	22	18	3	2	0	0	0	0	8	0	0	3	.111	.385	.111	.496	-58	0	1	0	1b8	0	-0.2
Total	15	1668	4969	848	1318	215	46	149	740	980	7	8	653	.265	.385	.417	.802	+18	133	39	100	1b1416,O6(2/0/4)	122	7.1

Torres, Rusty Rosendo (Hernandez) B9.30.1948 Aguadilla, PR BB/TR/5'10"/(175–180) Dr 1966 NYA 54/811 d9.20

YEAR	TM LG	G	AB	R	H	2B	3B	HR	RBI	BB	IB	HP	SO	AVG	OBP	SLG	OPS	AOPS	SB	CS	SB%	GAMES AT POSITION	DL	BFW
1971	NY A	9	26	5	10	3	0	2	3	0	0	0	8	.385	.385	.731	1.116	+120	0	1	0	O5(0/1/4)	0	0.4
1972	NY A	80	199	15	42	7	0	3	13	18	3	1	44	.211	.280	.291	.571	-28	0	4	0	O62(1/1/60)	0	-1.6
Total	9	654	1314	159	279	45	5	35	126	164	13	6	246	.212	.301	.334	.635	-18	13	20	39	O573(96/251/240),D8/3b	56	-5.9
Team	2	89	225	20	52	10	0	5	16	18	3	1	52	.231	.291	.342	.633	-12	0	5	0	O67(1/2/10)	0	-1.2

Tovar, Cesar Cesar Leonardo "Pepito"(b Cesar Leonardo Perez (Tovar)) B7.3.1940 Caracas, Distrito Capital, Venez D7.14.1994 Caracas, Distrito Capital, Venez BR/TR/5'9"/(150–155) d4.12 OF(378/471/205)

YEAR	TM LG	G	AB	R	H	2B	3B	HR	RBI	BB	IB	HP	SO	AVG	OBP	SLG	OPS	AOPS	SB	CS	SB%	GAMES AT POSITION	DL	BFW
1976	NY A	13	39	2	6	1	0	0	2	4	1	1	3	.154	.250	.179	.429	-73	0	1	0	D10,2b3	0	-0.3
Total	12	1488	5569	834	1546	253	55	46	435	413	23	88	410	.278	.335	.368	.703	-1	226	108	68	O945C,3b227,2b215,D90,S77/1bCP	106	0.6

Trammell, Bubba Thomas Bubba B11.6.1971 Knoxville TN BR/TR/6'2"/(205–220) Dr 1994 DetA 11/305 d4.1 Col Tennessee

YEAR	TM LG	G	AB	R	H	2B	3B	HR	RBI	BB	IB	HP	SO	AVG	OBP	SLG	OPS	AOPS	SB	CS	SB%	GAMES AT POSITION	DL	BFW
2003	NY A	22	55	4	11	5	0	0	5	6	0	0	10	.200	.279	.291	.570	-49	0	0	0	D15,O3L	0	-0.4
Total	7	584	1798	243	469	96	7	82	285	210	5	10	325	.261	.339	.459	.798	+9	10	10	50	O469(194/0/298),D69	0	-1.2

Tresh, Tom Thomas Michael B9.20.1937 Detroit MI BB/TR/6'0"/(175–192) d9.3 f–Mike Col Central Michigan

YEAR	TM LG	G	AB	R	H	2B	3B	HR	RBI	BB	IB	HP	SO	AVG	OBP	SLG	OPS	AOPS	SB	CS	SB%	GAMES AT POSITION	DL	BFW
1961	NY A	9	8	1	2	0	0	0	0	0	0	0	1	.250	.250	.250	.500	-64	0	0	0	S3	0	0.1
1962	†NY A★	157	622	94	178	26	5	20	93	67	3	8	74	.286	.359	.441	.800	+19	4	8	33	S111,O43L	0	0.8
1963	†NY A★	145	520	91	140	28	5	25	71	83	5	4	79	.269	.371	.487	.858	+40	3	3	50	O144(46/101/0)	0	2.0
1964	†NY A	153	533	75	131	25	5	16	73	73	3	7	110	.246	.342	.402	.744	+5	13	0	100	O146(106/69/6)	0	-0.6
1965	NY A	156	602	94	168	29	6	26	74	59	4	5	92	.279	.348	.477	.825	+33	5	2	71	O154(100/105/18)	0	1.5
1966	NY A	151	537	76	125	12	4	27	68	86	5	6	89	.233	.341	.421	.762	+23	5	4	56	O84(69/18/0),3b64	0	4.2
1967	NY A	130	448	45	98	23	3	14	53	50	0	4	86	.219	.301	.377	.678	+4	1	0	100	O118L	0	-0.6
1968	NY A	152	507	60	99	18	3	11	52	76	8	4	97	.195	.304	.308	.612	-11	10	5	67	S119,O27L	0	2.1
1969	NY A	45	143	13	26	5	2	1	9	17	2	0	23	.182	.269	.266	.535	-48	2	1	67	S41	0	-0.4
1969	Det A	94	331	46	74	13	1	13	37	39	0	2	47	.224	.305	.387	.692	-10	2	2	50	S77,O11(7/0/4)/3b	0	-0.8
1969	Year	139	474	59	100	18	3	14	46	56	2	2	70	.211	.294	.350	.644	-21	4	3	57	S118,O11(7/0/4)/3b	0	-1.2
Total	9	1192	4251	595	1041	179	34	153	530	550	30	40	698	.245	.335	.411	.746	+13	45	25	64	O727(516/293/28),S351,3b65	0	8.3
Team	9	1098	3920	549	967	166	33	140	493	511	30	38	651	.247	.337	.413	.750	+14	43	23	65	O716(253/70/70),S274,3b64	0	9.1
/150	1	150	536	75	132	23	5	19	67	70	4	5	89	.247	.337	.413	.750	+14	6	3	67	O98(35/10/10),S37,3b9	0	1.2

Triandos, Gus Gus B7.30.1930 San Francisco CA BR/TR/6'3"/(205–220) d8.13 Col St. Marys (CA)

YEAR	TM LG	G	AB	R	H	2B	3B	HR	RBI	BB	IB	HP	SO	AVG	OBP	SLG	OPS	AOPS	SB	CS	SB%	GAMES AT POSITION	DL	BFW
1953	NY A	18	51	5	8	2	0	1	6	3	—	0	9	.157	.204	.255	.459	-76	0	0	0	1b12,C5	0	-0.6
1954	NY A	2	1	0	0	0	0	0	0	0	—	0	1	.000	.000	.000	.000	-199	0	0	0	/C	0	0.0
Total	13	1206	3907	389	954	147	6	167	608	440	49	21	636	.244	.322	.413	.735	+3	1	0	100	C992,1b168/3b	68	7.8
Team	2	20	52	5	8	2	0	1	6	3	—	0	10	.154	.200	.250	.450	-78	0	0	0	1b12,C6	0	-0.6

Truesdale, Frank Frank Day B3.31.1884 St.Louis MO D8.27.1943 Albuquerque NM BB/TR/5'8"/145 d4.27

YEAR	TM LG	G	AB	R	H	2B	3B	HR	RBI	BB	IB	HP	SO	AVG	OBP	SLG	OPS	AOPS	SB	CS	SB%	GAMES AT POSITION	DL	BFW
1910	StL A	123	415	39	91	7	2	1	25	48	—	2	—	.219	.303	.253	.556	-21	29	—	—	2b122	—	-1.1
1911	StL A	1	0	1	0	0	0	0	0	0	—	0	—	+	+	+	.000	-100	0	—	—	/R	—	0.0
1914	NY A	77	217	22	46	4	0	0	13	39	—	3	35	.212	.340	.230	.570	-28	11	11	50	2b67,3b4	—	-0.2
1918	Bos A	15	36	6	10	1	0	0	2	4	—	0	5	.278	.350	.306	.656	-1	1	—	—	2b10	—	-0.1
Total	4	216	668	68	147	12	2	1	40	91	—	5	40	.220	.318	.249	.567	-22	41	11	100	2b199,3b4	—	-1.4

Turner, Chris Christopher Wan B3.23.1969 Bowling Green KY BR/TR/6'3"/(190–200) Dr 1991 CalA 7/194 d8.27 Col Western Kentucky

YEAR	TM LG	G	AB	R	H	2B	3B	HR	RBI	BB	IB	HP	SO	AVG	OBP	SLG	OPS	AOPS	SB	CS	SB%	GAMES AT POSITION	DL	BFW
2000	NY A	37	89	9	21	3	0	1	7	10	0	1	21	.236	.320	.303	.623	-40	0	1	0	C36/1b	0	-0.7
Total	8	158	379	49	90	16	2	4	36	36	0	4	89	.237	.307	.322	.629	-37	5	2	71	C149,1b3,O2(1/0/1),D2	100	-1.8

Uhle, George George Ernest "The Bull" B9.18.1898 Cleveland OH D2.26.1985 Lakewood OH BR/TR/6'0"/190 d4.30 C4 ▲

YEAR	TM LG	G	AB	R	H	2B	3B	HR	RBI	BB	IB	HP	SO	AVG	OBP	SLG	OPS	AOPS	SB	CS	SB%	GAMES AT POSITION	DL	BFW
1933	NY A	12	20	1	8	1	0	0	1	4	—	0	2	.400	.500	.450	.950	+63	0	0	0	P12	—	0.0
1934	NY A	10	5	1	3	0	1	0	1	0	—	0	0	.600	.600	1.000	1.600	+229	0	0	0	P10	—	0.0
Total	17	722	1360	172	393	60	21	9	187	98	—	4	112	.289	.339	.384	.723	-14	6	8	100	P513	—	0.0
Team	2	22	25	2	11	1	1	0	2	4	—	0	2	.440	.517	.560	1.077	+92	0	0	0	P22	—	0.0

Unglaub, Bob Robert Alexander B7.31.1881 Baltimore MD D11.29.1916 Baltimore MD BR/TR/5'11"/178 d4.15 M1 Col Maryland

YEAR	TM LG	G	AB	R	H	2B	3B	HR	RBI	BB	IB	HP	SO	AVG	OBP	SLG	OPS	AOPS	SB	CS	SB%	GAMES AT POSITION	DL	BFW
1904	NY A	6	19	2	4	0	0	0	2	0	—	0	—	.211	.211	.211	.422	-68	0	—	—	3b4/S	—	-0.3
Total	6	595	2150	188	554	67	35	5	216	88	—	5	—	.258	.288	.328	.616	-1	66	—	—	1b398,3b70,2b62,O42(8/0/34),S2	—	-1.0

Valo, Elmer Elmer William (b Imrich Vallo) B3.5.1921 Rybnik, Czechoslovakia D7.19.1998 Palmerton PA BL/TR/5'11"/(190–200) d9.22 Mil 1943–45 C2

YEAR	TM LG	G	AB	R	H	2B	3B	HR	RBI	BB	IB	HP	SO	AVG	OBP	SLG	OPS	AOPS	SB	CS	SB%	GAMES AT POSITION	DL	BFW
1960	NY A	8	5	1	0	0	0	0	0	2	0	0	1	.000	.286	.000	.286	-117	0	0	0	O2R	0	-0.1
Total	20	1806	5029	768	1420	228	73	58	601	942	12	38	284	.282	.398	.391	.789	+14	110	79	58	O1329(352/38/952)	0	8.2

Vander Wal, John John Henry B4.29.1966 Grand Rapids MI BL/TL/6'2"/(190–205) Dr 1987 MonN 3/70 d9.6 Col Western Michigan

YEAR	TM LG	G	AB	R	H	2B	3B	HR	RBI	BB	IB	HP	SO	AVG	OBP	SLG	OPS	AOPS	SB	CS	SB%	GAMES AT POSITION	DL	BFW
2002	†NY A	84	219	30	57	17	1	6	20	23	3	0	58	.260	.327	.429	.756	+1	1	1	50	O57(8/0/49),D16,1b6	0	-0.6
Total	14	1372	2751	374	717	170	18	97	430	385	32	8	698	.261	.351	.441	.792	+2	38	20	66	O587(238/2/353),1b178,D32	0	-3.1

Vaughn, Bobby Robert B6.4.1885 Stamford NY D4.11.1965 Seattle WA BR/TR/5'9"/150 d6.12 Col Princeton

YEAR	TM LG	G	AB	R	H	2B	3B	HR	RBI	BB	IB	HP	SO	AVG	OBP	SLG	OPS	AOPS	SB	CS	SB%	GAMES AT POSITION	DL	BFW
1909	NY A	5	14	1	2	0	0	0	0	1	—	0	—	.143	.200	.143	.343	-92	1	—	—	2b4/S	—	-0.5
Total	2	149	535	70	148	19	9	0	32	59	—	3	38	.277	.352	.346	.698	-8	25	—	—	2b131,S13,3b8	—	-2.0

Veach, Bobby Robert Hayes B6.29.1888 St.Charles KY D8.7.1945 Detroit MI BL/TR/5'11"/160 d9.6

YEAR	TM LG	G	AB	R	H	2B	3B	HR	RBI	BB	IB	HP	SO	AVG	OBP	SLG	OPS	AOPS	SB	CS	SB%	GAMES AT POSITION	DL	BFW
1925	NY A	56	116	13	41	10	2	0	15	8	—	1	0	.353	.400	.474	.874	+23	1	4	20	O33(13/0/30)	—	0.3
Total	14	1821	6656	953	2063	393	147	64	1166	571	—	59	367	.310	.370	.442	.812	+27	195	88	100	O1740(1671/14/65)/P	—	17.8

YEAR	TM LG	G	AB	R	H	2B	3B	HR	RBI	BB	IB	HP	SO	AVG	OBP	SLG	OPS	AOPS	SB	CS	SB%	GAMES AT POSITION	DL	BFW
VELARDE, RANDY	RANDY LEE B11.24.1962 MIDLAND TX BR/TR/6'0"/(183–200) DR 1985 CHIA 19/475 D8.20 COL LUBBOCK CHRISTIAN OF(97/4/12)																							
1987	NY A	8	22	1	4	0	0	0	1	0	0	0	6	.182	.182	.182	.364	-103	0	0	0	S8	0	-0.4
1988	NY A	48	115	18	20	6	0	5	12	8	0	2	24	.174	.240	.357	.597	-35	1	1	50	2b24,S14,3b11	0	-0.2
1989	NY A	33	100	12	34	4	2	2	11	7	0	1	14	.340	.389	.480	.869	+45	0	3	0	3b27,S9	20	0.5
1990	NY A	95	229	21	48	6	2	5	19	20	0	1	53	.210	.275	.319	.594	-35	0	3	0	3b74,S15,O5L,2b3,D3	0	-0.3
1991	NY A	80	184	19	45	11	1	1	15	18	0	3	43	.245	.322	.332	.654	-19	3	1	75	3b50,S31,O2L	0	0.8
1992	NY A	121	412	57	112	24	1	7	46	38	1	2	78	.272	.333	.386	.719	+2	7	2	78	S75,3b26,O23(14/2/7),2b3	0	0.6
1993	NY A	85	226	28	68	13	2	7	24	18	2	4	39	.301	.360	.469	.829	+25	2	2	50	O50(48/2/0),S26,3b16/D	54	0.9
1994	NY A	77	280	47	78	16	1	9	34	22	0	4	61	.279	.338	.439	.777	+3	4	2	67	S49,3b27,O7(6/0/1),2b5	0	0.5
1995	†NY A	111	367	60	102	19	1	7	46	55	0	4	64	.278	.375	.392	.767	+2	5	1	83	2b62,S28,O20(20/0/1),3b19	0	0.6
1996	Cal A	136	530	82	151	27	3	14	54	70	0	5	118	.285	.372	.426	.798	+0	7	7	50	2b114,3b28,S7	0	-1.0
1997	Ana A	1	0	0	0	0	0	0	0	0	0	0	0	+	+	+	.000	-100	0	0	0	/R	175	0.0
1998	Ana A	51	188	29	49	13	1	4	26	34	0	1	42	.261	.375	.404	.779	+1	7	2	78	2b51	123	0.1
1999	Ana A	95	376	57	115	15	4	9	48	43	1	4	56	.306	.383	.439	.822	+9	13	4	76	2b95	0	1.6
1999	Oak A	61	255	48	85	10	3	7	28	27	1	2	42	.333	.401	.478	.879	+27	11	4	73	2b61	0	1.0
1999	Year	156	631	105	200	25	7	16	76	70	2	6	98	.317	.390	.455	.845	+16	24	8	75	2b156	0	2.6
2000	†Oak A	122	485	82	135	23	0	12	41	54	0	3	95	.278	.354	.400	.754	-8	9	3	75	2b122	34	2.1
2001	Tex A	78	296	46	88	16	2	9	31	29	0	5	73	.297	.369	.456	.825	+13	4	2	67	2b52,1b9,3b7,O2R,D6	48	0.7
2001	†NY A	15	46	4	7	3	0	0	1	5	0	3	13	.152	.278	.217	.495	-67	2	0	100	3b7,O3(2/0/1)/1bD	0	-0.2
2001	Year	93	342	50	95	19	2	9	32	34	0	8	86	.278	.356	.424	.780	+2	6	2	75	2b52,3b14,D11,1b10,O5(2/0/3)	0	0.5
2002	†Oak A	56	133	22	30	8	0	2	8	15	1	5	32	.226	.325	.331	.656	-24	3	0	100	2b38,1b5/3bD	29	0.2
Total	16	1273	4244	633	1171	214	23	100	445	463	6	49	853	.276	.352	.408	.760	+0	78	37	68	2b630,3b293,S262,O112L,D20,1b15	483	7.5
Team	10	673	1981	267	518	102	10	43	209	191	3	24	395	.261	.332	.388	.720	-4	24	15	62	3b257,S255,O110(21/2/0),2b97,D5/1	74	2.8
/150	2	150	442	60	115	23	2	10	47	43	1	5	88	.261	.332	.388	.720	-4	5	3	63	3b57,S57,O25L,2b22/D1	16	0.6
VELEZ, OTTO	OTONIEL (FRANCESCHI) B11.29.1950 PONCE, PR BR/TR/6'0"/(170–195) D9.4																							
1973	NY A	23	77	9	15	4	0	2	7	15	0	0	24	.195	.326	.325	.651	-14	0	1	0	O23R	0	-0.3
1974	NY A	27	67	9	14	1	1	2	10	15	1	0	24	.209	.345	.343	.688	+2	0	0	0	1b21,O3R,3b2	0	-0.4
1975	NY A	6	8	0	2	0	0	0	1	2	0	0	0	.250	.400	.250	.650	-12	0	0	0	/1bD	0	0.0
1976	†NY A	49	94	11	25	6	0	2	10	23	1	0	26	.266	.410	.394	.804	+37	0	0	0	O24(6/0/19),1b8/3bD	0	0.4
Total	11	637	1802	244	452	87	11	78	272	336	17	11	414	.251	.369	.441	.810	+22	6	10	38	O276(88/0/197),D255,1b41,3b3	69	4.5
Team	4	105	246	29	56	11	1	6	28	55	2	0	74	.228	.366	.354	.720	+10	0	1	0	O50R,1b30,3b3,D2	0	-0.3
/150	6	150	351	41	80	16	1	9	40	79	3	0	106	.228	.366	.354	.720	+10	0	1	0	O71R,1b43,3b4,D3	0	-0.4
VENTO, MIKE	MICHAEL B5.25.1978 ALBUQUERQUE NM BR/TR/6'0"/195 DR 1997 NYA 40/1219 D9.13 COL SAN ANA (CA) JC																							
2005	NY A	2	2	0	0	0	0	0	0	0	0	0	1	.000	.000	.000	.000	-199	0	0	0	O2R	0	0.0
Total	2	11	20	3	5	1	0	0	1	4	1	0	6	.250	.375	.300	.675	-19	0	0	0	O10R	0	0.0
VENTURA, ROBIN	ROBIN MARK B7.14.1967 SANTA MARIA CA BL/TR/6'1"/(185–200) DR 1988 CHIA 1/10 D9.12 COL OKLAHOMA ST.																							
2002	†NY A★	141	465	68	115	17	0	27	93	90	9	2	101	.247	.368	.458	.826	+20	3	1	75	3b137,1b5	0	2.6
2003	NY A	89	283	31	71	13	0	9	42	40	2	0	62	.251	.344	.392	.736	-5	0	0	0	3b80/2bD	0	-0.1
Total	16	2079	7064	1006	1885	338	14	294	1182	1075	13	23	1179	.267	.362	.444	.806	+15	24	38	39	3b1887,1b162,D5/P2bS	128	24.5
Team	2	230	748	99	186	30	0	36	135	130	11	2	163	.249	.359	.433	.792	+11	3	1	75	3b217,1b5/2D	0	2.5
/150	1	150	488	65	121	20	0	23	88	85	7	1	106	.249	.359	.433	.792	+11	2	1	67	3b142,1b3/2D	0	1.6
VERDI, FRANK	FRANK MICHAEL B6.2.1926 BROOKLYN NY BR/TR/5'10.5"/170 D5.10																							
1953	NY A	1	0	0	0	0	0	0	0	0	—	0	0	+	+	+	.000	-100	0	0	0	/S	0	0.0
VICK, SAMMY	SAMUEL BRUCE B4.12.1895 BATESVILLE MS D8.17.1986 MEMPHIS TN BR/TR/5'10.5"/163 D9.20 MIL 1918 COL MILLSAPS																							
1917	NY A	10	36	4	10	3	0	0	2	1	—	0	6	.278	.297	.361	.658	+0	2	—	—	O10R	—	-0.1
1918	NY A	2	3	1	2	0	0	0	1	0	—	0	0	.667	.667	.667	1.334	+196	0	—	—	/rf	—	0.1
1919	NY A	106	407	59	101	15	9	2	27	35	—	0	55	.248	.308	.344	.652	-18	9	—	—	O100R	—	-2.3
1920	NY A	51	118	21	26	7	1	0	11	14	—	2	20	.220	.313	.297	.610	-40	1	1	50	O33(4/1/28)	—	-1.0
1921	Bos A	44	77	5	20	3	1	0	9	1	—	0	10	.260	.269	.325	.594	-48	0	1	0	O14R	—	-0.7
Total	5	213	641	90	159	28	11	2	50	51	—	2	91	.248	.305	.335	.640	-24	12	2	100	O158(4/1/153)	—	-4.0
Team	4	169	564	85	139	25	10	2	41	50	—	2	81	.246	.310	.337	.647	-21	12	1	100	O144(0/1/12)	—	-3.3
/150	4	150	501	75	123	22	9	2	36	44	—	2	72	.246	.310	.337	.647	-21	11	1	100	O128(0/1/11)	—	-2.9
VIZCAINO, JOSE	JOSE LUIS (PIMENTAL) B3.26.1968 SAN CRISTOBAL, D.R. BB/TR/6'1"/(150–190) D9.10																							
2000	†NY A	73	174	23	48	8	1	0	10	12	0	0	28	.276	.319	.333	.652	-32	5	7	42	2b62,3b6,S2,D4	0	-0.9
Total	18	1820	5379	633	1453	204	47	36	480	378	33	16	729	.270	.318	.346	.664	-25	74	62	54	S948,2b434,3b227,1b39,D6/lf	187	-8.9
WAKEFIELD, DICK	RICHARD CUMMINGS B5.6.1921 CHICAGO IL D8.26.1985 REDFORD MI BL/TR/6'4"/210 D6.26 MIL 1944–45 F–HOWARD COL MICHIGAN																							
1950	NY A	3	2	0	1	0	0	0	1	1	—	0	1	.500	.667	.500	1.167	+108	0	0	0	/H	0	0.0
Total	9	638	2132	334	625	102	29	56	315	360	—	3	270	.293	.396	.447	.843	+30	10	17	37	O557(541/0/16)	0	3.6
WALEWANDER, JIM	JAMES B5.2.1962 CHICAGO IL BB/TR/5'10"/(158–160) DR 1983 DETA 9/225 D5.31 COL IOWA ST.																							
1990	NY A	9	5	1	1	1	0	0	1	0	0	0	0	.200	.200	.400	.600	-37	1	1	50	2b2,3b2/SD	0	0.0
Total	4	162	242	50	52	9	1	1	14	24	0	0	33	.215	.284	.273	.557	-43	15	7	68	2b89,D22,3b22,S18	0	-1.3
WALKER, DIXIE	FRED "THE PEOPLE'S CHERCE" B9.24.1910 VILLA RICA GA D5.17.1982 BIRMINGHAM AL BL/TR/6'1"/175 D4.28 C5 B–HARRY F–DIXIE																							
1931	NY A	2	10	1	3	2	0	0	1	0	—	0	4	.300	.300	.500	.800	+13	0	0	0	O2(1/0/1)	—	0.0
1933	NY A	98	328	68	90	15	7	15	51	26	—	1	28	.274	.330	.500	.830	+25	2	2	50	O77(15/60/3)	—	0.6
1934	NY A	17	17	2	2	0	0	0	0	1	—	0	3	.118	.167	.118	.285	-127	0	0	0	/lf	—	-0.3
1935	NY A	8	13	1	2	1	0	0	1	0	—	0	1	.154	.154	.231	.385	-102	0	0	0	O2L	—	-0.2
1936	NY A	6	20	3	7	0	2	1	5	1	—	0	3	.350	.381	.700	1.081	+67	1	1	50	O5C	—	0.1
Total	18	1905	6740	1037	2064	376	96	105	1023	817	—	16	325	.306	.383	.437	.820	+21	59	10	100	O1736(249/312/1204),1b3	0	11.7
Team	5	131	388	75	104	18	9	16	58	28	—	1	39	.268	.319	.485	.804	+16	3	3	50	O87(16/60/61)	—	0.2
/150	6	150	444	86	119	21	10	18	66	32	—	1	45	.268	.319	.485	.804	+16	3	3	50	O100(18/69/70)	—	0.2
WALKER, CURT	WILLIAM CURTIS B7.3.1896 BEEVILLE TX D12.9.1955 BEEVILLE TX BL/TR/5'9.5"/170 D9.17 COL SOUTHWESTERN (TX)																							
1919	NY A	1	1	0	0	0	0	0	0	0	—	0	0	.000	.000	.000	.000	-199	0	—	—	/H	—	0.0
Total	12	1359	4858	718	1475	235	117	64	688	535	—	9	254	.304	.374	.440	.814	+10	96	38	100	O1310(105/95/1120)/1b	—	-2.1
WALSH, JIMMY	JAMES CHARLES B9.22.1885 KALLILA, IRELAND D7.3.1962 SYRACUSE NY BL/TR/5'10.5"/170 D8.26 MIL 1918																							
1914	NY A	43	136	13	26	1	3	1	11	29	—	0	21	.191	.333	.265	.598	-20	6	9	40	O41(37/4/0)	—	-0.7
Total	6	541	1771	235	410	71	31	6	150	249	—	11	204	.232	.330	.317	.647	-4	92	55	100	O492(163/170/166),3b7,1b5/S	—	-3.3
WALSH, JOE	JOSEPH FRANCIS B10.14.1886 MINERSVILLE PA D1.6.1967 BUFFALO NY BR/TR/6'2"/170 D10.8 COL VILLANOVA																							
1910	NY A	1	4	0	2	1	0	0	2	0	—	0	—	.500	.500	.750	1.250	+175	0	—	—	/C	—	0.1
1911	NY A	4	9	2	2	1	0	0	0	0	—	0	—	.222	.222	.333	.555	-49	0	—	—	C4	—	-0.2
Total	2	5	13	2	4	2	0	0	2	0	—	0	—	.308	.308	.462	.770	+14	0	—	—	C5	—	-0.1
WALTERS, ROXY	ALFRED JOHN B11.5.1892 SAN FRANCISCO CA D6.3.1956 ALAMEDA CA BR/TR/5'8.5"/160 D9.16																							
1915	NY A	2	3	0	1	0	0	0	0	0	—	0	0	.333	.333	.333	.666	+0	0	—	—	C2	—	0.1
1916	NY A	66	203	13	54	9	3	0	23	14	—	2	42	.266	.320	.340	.660	-4	2	—	—	C65	—	1.8
1917	NY A	61	171	16	45	2	0	0	14	9	—	1	22	.263	.304	.275	.579	-24	2	—	—	C57	—	0.9
1918	NY A	64	191	18	38	5	1	0	12	9	—	1	18	.199	.239	.236	.475	-58	3	—	—	C50,O9R	—	-1.4

YEAR	TM LG	G	AB	R	H	2B	3B	HR	RBI	BB	IB	HP	SO	AVG	OBP	SLG	OPS	AOPS	SB	CS	SB%	GAMES AT POSITION	DL	BFW
1919	Bos A	48	135	7	26	2	0	0	9	7	—	5	15	.193	.259	.207	.466	-67	1	—	—	C47	—	-0.6
1920	Bos A	88	258	25	51	11	1	0	28	30	—	9	21	.198	.303	.248	.551	-51	2	2	50	C85,1b2	—	-0.8
1921	Bos A	54	169	17	34	4	1	0	14	10	—	2	11	.201	.254	.237	.491	-73	3	0	100	C54	—	-0.4
1922	Bos A	38	98	4	19	2	0	0	6	6	—	0	8	.194	.240	.214	.454	-81	0	0	0	C36	—	-0.7
1923	Bos A	40	104	9	26	4	0	0	5	2	—	0	6	.250	.264	.288	.552	-55	0	2	0	C36/2b	—	-0.4
1924	Cle A	32	74	10	19	2	0	0	5	10	—	0	6	.257	.345	.284	.629	-37	0	1	0	C25,2b7	—	0.0
1925	Cle A	5	20	0	4	0	0	0	0	0	—	0	2	.200	.200	.200	.400	-98	0	0	0	C5	—	-0.2
Total	11	498	1426	119	317	41	6	0	116	97	—	20	151	.222	.281	.259	.540	-49	13	5	100	C462,O9R,2b8,1b2	—	-1.7
Team	4	193	568	47	138	16	4	0	49	32	—	4	82	.243	.288	.285	.573	-28	7	—	—	C174,O9R	—	1.4
/150	3	150	441	37	107	12	3	0	38	25	—	3	64	.243	.288	.285	.573	-28	5	—	—	C135,O7R	—	1.1

WALTON, DANNY DANIEL JAMES "MICKEY" B7.14.1947 LOS ANGELES CA BR/TR (BB 1975–80)/6'0"/(185–200) DR 1965 HOUN 8/192 D4.20

YEAR	TM LG	G	AB	R	H	2B	3B	HR	RBI	BB	IB	HP	SO	AVG	OBP	SLG	OPS	AOPS	SB	CS	SB%	GAMES AT POSITION	DL	BFW
1971	NY A	5	14	1	2	0	0	1	2	0	0	0	7	.143	.143	.357	.500	-60	0	0	0	O4(1/0/3)	0	-0.2
Total	9	297	779	69	174	27	4	28	107	88	6	10	240	.223	.309	.376	.685	-10	4	3	57	O178(172/1/6),D18,1b12,C2,3b2	0	-3.9

WANER, PAUL PAUL GLEE "BIG POISON" B4.16.1903 HARRAH OK D8.29.1965 SARASOTA FL BL/TL/5'8.5"/153 D4.13 MIL 1945 C1 HF1952 B–LLOYD COL EAST CENTRAL

YEAR	TM LG	G	AB	R	H	2B	3B	HR	RBI	BB	IB	HP	SO	AVG	OBP	SLG	OPS	AOPS	SB	CS	SB%	GAMES AT POSITION	DL	BFW
1944	NY A	9	7	1	1	0	0	0	1	2	—	0	1	.143	.333	.143	.476	-63	1	0	100	/H	0	0.0
1945	NY A	1	0	0	0	0	0	0	0	1	—	0	0	+	1.000	+	1.000	+91	0	0	0	/H	0	0.0
Total	20	2549	9459	1627	3152	605	191	113	1309	1091	—	38	376	.333	.404	.473	.877	+33	104	0	100	O2288(18/18/2256),1b73	0	33.8
Team	2	10	7	1	1	0	0	0	1	3	—	0	1	.143	.400	.143	.543	-48	1	0	100	/H	0	0.0

WANNER, JACK CLARENCE CURTIS "JOHNNY" B11.29.1885 GENESEO IL D5.28.1919 GENESEO IL BR/TR/5'11.5"/190 D9.28

YEAR	TM LG	G	AB	R	H	2B	3B	HR	RBI	BB	IB	HP	SO	AVG	OBP	SLG	OPS	AOPS	SB	CS	SB%	GAMES AT POSITION	DL	BFW
1909	NY A	3	8	0	1	0	0	0	0	2	—	0	—	.125	.300	.125	.425	-65	1	—	—	S2	—	-0.2

WANNINGER, PEE-WEE PAUL LOUIS B12.12.1902 BIRMINGHAM AL D3.7.1981 N.AUGUSTA SC BL/TR/5'7"/150 D4.22

YEAR	TM LG	G	AB	R	H	2B	3B	HR	RBI	BB	IB	HP	SO	AVG	OBP	SLG	OPS	AOPS	SB	CS	SB%	GAMES AT POSITION	DL	BFW
1925	NY A	117	403	35	95	13	6	1	22	11	—	0	34	.236	.256	.305	.561	-57	3	5	38	S111,3b3/2b	—	-3.1
1927	Bos A	18	60	4	12	0	0	0	1	6	—	1	2	.200	.284	.200	.484	-72	2	4	33	S15	—	-0.6
1927	Cin N	28	93	14	23	2	2	0	8	6	—	0	7	.247	.293	.312	.605	-36	0	—	—	S28	—	0.1
1927	Major	46	153	18	35	2	2	0	9	12	0	1	9	.229	.289	.268	.557	-11	2	4	—	—	—	-0.5
Total	2	163	556	53	130	15	8	1	31	23	—	1	43	.234	.266	.295	.561	-55	5	9	100	S154,3b3/2b	—	-3.6
/150	1	150	517	45	122	17	8	1	28	14	—	0	44	.236	.256	.305	.561	-57	4	6	40	S142,3b4/2	—	-4.0

WARD, AARON AARON LEE B8.28.1896 BOONEVILLE AR D1.30.1961 NEW ORLEANS LA BR/TR/5'10.5"/160 D8.14 MIL 1918 COL OUACHITA BAPTIST

YEAR	TM LG	G	AB	R	H	2B	3B	HR	RBI	BB	IB	HP	SO	AVG	OBP	SLG	OPS	AOPS	SB	CS	SB%	GAMES AT POSITION	DL	BFW
1917	NY A	8	26	0	3	0	0	0	1	1	—	0	5	.115	.148	.115	.263	-119	0	—	—	S7	—	-0.6
1918	NY A	20	32	2	4	1	0	0	1	2	—	0	7	.125	.176	.156	.332	-100	1	—	—	S12,O4C,2b3	—	-0.1
1919	NY A	27	34	5	7	2	0	0	2	5	—	0	6	.206	.308	.265	.573	-39	0	—	—	1b5,3b3,S2/2b	—	0.0
1920	NY A	127	496	62	127	18	7	11	54	33	—	1	84	.256	.304	.387	.691	-21	7	5	58	3b114,S12	—	0.3
1921	†NY A	**153**	556	77	170	30	10	5	75	42	—	8	68	.306	.363	.423	.786	-2	6	8	43	2b124,3b33	—	1.9
1922	†NY A	**154**	558	69	149	19	5	7	68	45	—	6	64	.267	.328	.357	.685	-23	6	4	60	2b152,3b2	—	-1.4
1923	†NY A	**152**	567	79	161	26	11	10	82	56	—	3	65	.284	.351	.422	.773	+1	8	8	50	2b152	—	1.2
1924	NY A	120	400	42	101	13	10	8	66	40	—	2	45	.253	.324	.395	.719	-15	1	4	20	2b120/S	—	-0.2
1925	NY A	125	439	41	108	22	3	4	38	49	—	3	49	.246	.326	.337	.663	-30	1	4	20	2b113,3b10	—	-2.9
1926	NY A	22	31	5	10	2	0	0	3	2	—	0	6	.323	.364	.387	.751	-3	0	0	0	2b4/3b	—	-0.3
1927	Chi A	145	463	75	125	25	8	5	56	63	—	2	56	.270	.360	.391	.751	-3	6	5	55	2b139,3b6	—	-2.0
1928	Cle A	6	9	0	1	0	0	0	0	1	—	0	2	.111	.200	.111	.311	-116	0	0	0	3b3,S2/2b	—	-0.1
Total	12	1059	3611	457	966	158	54	50	446	339	—	25	457	.268	.335	.383	.718	-15	36	38	100	2b809,3b172,S36,1b5,O4C	—	-4.2
Team	10	908	3139	382	840	133	46	45	390	275	—	23	399	.268	.331	.382	.713	-16	30	33	100	2b669,3b163,S34,1b5,O4C	—	-2.1
/150	2	150	519	63	139	22	8	7	64	45	—	4	66	.268	.331	.382	.713	-16	5	5	100	2b111,3b27,S6/1cf	—	-0.3

WARD, GARY GARY LAMELL B12.6.1953 LOS ANGELES CA BR/TR/6'2"/(202–210) D9.3 C3 S–DARYLE OF(848/181/111)

YEAR	TM LG	G	AB	R	H	2B	3B	HR	RBI	BB	IB	HP	SO	AVG	OBP	SLG	OPS	AOPS	SB	CS	SB%	GAMES AT POSITION	DL	BFW
1987	NY A	146	529	65	131	22	1	16	78	33	2	1	101	.248	.291	.384	.675	-22	9	1	90	O94(69/30/5),D36,1b15	0	-2.0
1988	NY A	91	231	26	52	8	0	4	24	24	4	2	41	.225	.302	.312	.614	-27	0	1	0	O54(17/39/3),1b11,3b2,D9	0	-1.1
1989	NY A	8	17	3	5	1	0	0	1	3	1	0	5	.294	.400	.353	.753	+15	0	0	0	O6R/D	0	-0.1
Total	12	1287	4479	594	1236	196	41	130	597	351	28	13	775	.276	.328	.425	.753	+4	83	30	73	O1094L,D101,1b54,3b2	15	2.4
Team	3	245	777	94	188	31	1	20	103	60	7	3	147	.242	.297	.362	.659	-23	9	2	82	O154(86/69/8),D46,1b26,3b2	0	-3.2
/150	2	150	476	58	115	19	1	12	63	37	4	2	90	.242	.297	.362	.659	-23	6	1	86	O94(53/42/5),D28,1b16/3	0	-2.0

WARD, JOE JOSEPH ALOYSIUS B9.2.1884 PHILADELPHIA PA D8.11.1934 PHILADELPHIA PA TR D4.24

YEAR	TM LG	G	AB	R	H	2B	3B	HR	RBI	BB	IB	HP	SO	AVG	OBP	SLG	OPS	AOPS	SB	CS	SB%	GAMES AT POSITION	DL	BFW
1909	NY A	9	28	3	5	0	0	0	0	1	—	1	—	.179	.233	.179	.412	-70	2	—	—	2b7/1b	—	-0.7
Total	3	166	465	47	110	18	9	0	47	18	—	4	11	.237	.271	.314	.585	-22	12	—	—	2b58,1b38,3b28,S10,O2(1/1/0)	—	-3.1

WARD, PETE PETER THOMAS B7.26.1937 MONTREAL QC, CAN. BL/TR/6'1"/(185–205) D9.21 C1 COL LEWIS & CLARK OF(139/0/54)

YEAR	TM LG	G	AB	R	H	2B	3B	HR	RBI	BB	IB	HP	SO	AVG	OBP	SLG	OPS	AOPS	SB	CS	SB%	GAMES AT POSITION	DL	BFW
1970	NY A	66	77	5	20	2	2	1	18	9	0	0	17	.260	.333	.377	.710	+1	0	0	0	1b13	0	-0.2
Total	9	973	3060	345	776	136	17	98	427	371	41	40	539	.254	.339	.405	.744	+16	20	17	54	3b562,O185L,1b113,2b2/S	47	4.4

WASHINGTON, CLAUDELL CLAUDELL B8.31.1954 LOS ANGELES CA BL/TL/6'0"/(190–195) D7.5

YEAR	TM LG	G	AB	R	H	2B	3B	HR	RBI	BB	IB	HP	SO	AVG	OBP	SLG	OPS	AOPS	SB	CS	SB%	GAMES AT POSITION	DL	BFW
1986	NY A	54	135	19	32	5	0	6	16	7	0	2	33	.237	.285	.407	.692	-14	6	1	86	O39(11/20/9)	0	-0.5
1987	NY A	102	312	42	87	17	0	9	44	27	2	0	54	.279	.336	.420	.756	-1	10	1	91	O72(2/69/1),D13	15	0.1
1988	NY A	126	455	62	140	22	3	11	64	24	2	2	74	.308	.342	.442	.784	+19	15	6	71	O117(13/103/8)	0	1.2
1990	NY A	33	80	4	13	1	1	0	6	2	1	0	17	.162	.181	.200	.381	-93	3	1	75	O21(19/0/4),D2	107	-1.0
Total	17	1912	6787	926	1884	334	69	164	824	468	77	36	1266	.278	.325	.420	.745	+6	312	134	70	O1685(324/320/1101),D77	304	-7.4
Team	4	315	982	127	272	45	4	26	130	60	5	4	178	.277	.320	.410	.730	-1	34	9	79	O249(35/192/22),D15	122	-0.2
/150	2	150	468	60	130	21	2	12	62	29	2	2	85	.277	.320	.410	.730	-1	16	4	80	O119(17/91/10),D7	58	-0.1

WATSON, BOB ROBERT JOSE "BULL" B4.10.1946 LOS ANGELES CA BR/TR/6'2"/(200–210) D9.9 NG 1970–71 C3

YEAR	TM LG	G	AB	R	H	2B	3B	HR	RBI	BB	IB	HP	SO	AVG	OBP	SLG	OPS	AOPS	SB	CS	SB%	GAMES AT POSITION	DL	BFW
1980	†NY A	130	469	62	144	25	3	13	68	48	5	1	56	.307	.368	.456	.824	+28	2	1	67	1b104,D21	0	1.5
1981	†NY A	59	156	15	33	3	3	6	12	24	2	0	17	.212	.317	.385	.702	+2	0	0	0	1b50,D6	23	-0.1
1982	NY A	7	17	3	4	3	0	0	3	3	0	0	0	.235	.350	.412	.762	+10	0	0	0	1b6/D	0	-0.1
Total	19	1832	6185	802	1826	307	41	184	989	653	98	48	796	.295	.364	.447	.811	+30	27	28	49	1b1088,O570(570/0/1),D54,C10	99	11.9
Team	3	196	642	80	181	31	6	19	83	75	7	1	73	.282	.355	.438	.793	+21	2	1	67	1b160,D28	23	1.3
/150	2	150	491	61	139	24	5	15	64	57	5	1	56	.282	.355	.438	.793	+21	2	1	67	1b122,D21	18	1.0

WEATHERLY, ROY CYRIL ROY "STORMY" B2.25.1915 WARREN TX D1.19.1991 WOODVILLE TX BL/TR/5'6.5"/170 D6.27 MIL 1944–45

YEAR	TM LG	G	AB	R	H	2B	3B	HR	RBI	BB	IB	HP	SO	AVG	OBP	SLG	OPS	AOPS	SB	CS	SB%	GAMES AT POSITION	DL	BFW
1943	†NY A	77	280	37	74	8	3	7	28	18	—	1	9	.264	.311	.389	.700	+4	4	7	36	O68C	0	-0.8
1946	NY A	2	2	0	1	0	0	0	0	0	—	0	0	.500	.500	.500	1.000	+78	0	0	0	/H	0	0.0
Total	10	811	2781	415	794	152	44	43	290	180	—	7	170	.286	.331	.418	.749	-1	42	49	100	O676(65/480/137)/3b	0	-4.8
Team	2	79	282	37	75	8	3	7	28	18	—	1	9	.266	.312	.390	.702	+4	4	7	36	O68C	0	-0.8

WERA, JULIE JULIAN VALENTINE B2.9.1902 WINONA MN D12.12.1975 ROCHESTER MN BR/TR/5'8"/164 D4.14

YEAR	TM LG	G	AB	R	H	2B	3B	HR	RBI	BB	IB	HP	SO	AVG	OBP	SLG	OPS	AOPS	SB	CS	SB%	GAMES AT POSITION	DL	BFW
1927	NY A	38	42	7	10	3	0	1	8	1	—	1	5	.238	.273	.381	.654	-30	0	0	0	3b19	—	-0.1
1929	NY A	5	12	1	5	0	0	0	2	1	—	0	1	.417	.462	.417	.879	+37	0	0	0	3b4	—	0.1
Total	2	43	54	8	15	3	0	1	10	2	—	1	6	.278	.316	.389	.705	-15	0	0	0	3b23	—	0.0

WERBER, BILLY WILLIAM MURRAY B6.20.1908 BERWYN MD BR/TR/5'10"/170 D6.25 COL DUKE

YEAR	TM LG	G	AB	R	H	2B	3B	HR	RBI	BB	IB	HP	SO	AVG	OBP	SLG	OPS	AOPS	SB	CS	SB%	GAMES AT POSITION	DL	BFW
1930	NY A	4	14	5	4	0	0	0	2	3	—	0	1	.286	.412	.286	.698	-16	0	0	0	S3/3b	—	0.0
1933	NY A	3	2	0	0	0	0	0	0	0	—	0	0	.000	.000	.000	.000	-199	0	0	0	/3b	—	-0.1
Total	11	1295	5024	875	1363	271	50	78	539	701	—	32	363	.271	.364	.392	.756	-3	215	68	100	3b1143,S96,O48(39/2/7),2b3	0	9.7
Team	2	7	16	5	4	0	0	0	2	3	—	0	1	.250	.368	.250	.618	-35	0	0	0	S3,3b2	—	-0.1

Batters

YEAR	TM LG	G	AB	R	H	2B	3B	HR	RBI	BB	IB	HP	SO	AVG	OBP	SLG	OPS	AOPS	SB	CS	SB%	GAMES AT POSITION	DL	BFW
Werth, Dennis Dennis Dean B12.29.1952 Lincoln IL BR/TR/6'1"/(200–201) Dr 1974 NYA 19/437 d9.17 s–Jayson Col Southern Illinois Edwardsville																								
1979	NY A	3	4	1	1	0	0	0	0	0	0	0	0	.250	.250	.250	.500	-64	0	0	0	/1b	0	0.0
1980	NY A	39	65	15	20	3	0	3	12	12	0	0	19	.308	.416	.492	.908	+50	0	1	0	1b12,O8(3/0/5)/C3bD	0	0.3
1981	NY A	34	55	7	6	1	0	0	1	12	2	0	12	.109	.269	.127	.396	-83	1	0	100	1b19,O8(4/0/4),C3,D4	77	-0.5
1982	KC A	41	15	5	2	0	0	0	2	4	0	0	2	.133	.316	.133	.449	-71	0	0	0	1b35,C2	0	-0.1
Total	4	117	139	28	29	4	0	3	15	28	2	0	33	.209	.341	.302	.643	-18	1	1	50	1b67,O16(7/0/9),D12,C6/3b	77	-0.3
Team	3	76	124	23	27	4	0	3	13	24	2	0	31	.218	.345	.323	.668	-13	1	1	50	1b31,O16(7/0/9),D5,C4/3	77	-0.2
Whitaker, Steve Stephen Edward B5.7.1943 Tacoma WA BL/TR/6'1"/(182–187) d8.23																								
1966	NY A	31	114	15	28	3	2	7	15	9	0	1	24	.246	.306	.491	.797	+30	0	0	0	O31(4/20/10)	0	0.1
1967	NY A	122	441	37	107	12	3	11	50	23	2	3	89	.243	.283	.358	.641	-8	2	5	29	O114(26/12/78)	0	-1.5
1968	NY A	28	60	3	7	2	0	0	3	8	0	0	18	.117	.221	.150	.371	-86	0	1	0	O14(6/7/2)	0	-1.0
1969	Sea A	69	116	15	29	2	1	6	13	12	1	1	29	.250	.323	.440	.763	+13	2	0	100	O39(22/0/18)	0	0.1
1970	SF N	16	27	3	3	1	0	0	4	2	0	0	14	.111	.167	.148	.315	-113	0	0	0	O9L	0	-0.6
Total	5	266	758	73	174	20	6	24	85	54	3	5	174	.230	.283	.367	.650	-9	4	6	40	O207(67/39/108)	0	-2.9
Team	3	181	615	55	142	17	5	18	68	40	2	4	131	.231	.281	.363	.644	-9	2	6	25	O159(30/39/19)	0	-2.4
/150	2	150	510	46	118	14	4	15	56	33	2	3	109	.231	.281	.363	.644	-9	2	5	29	O132(25/32/16)	0	-2.0
White, Rondell Rondell Bernard B2.23.1972 Milledgeville GA BR/TR/6'1"/(205–225) Dr 1990 MonN 1/24 d9.1																								
2002	†NY A	126	455	59	109	21	0	14	62	25	1	8	86	.240	.288	.378	.666	-23	1	2	33	O113(113/1/0),D11	0	-1.7
Total	15	1474	5357	756	1519	296	34	198	768	360	21	88	925	.284	.336	.462	.798	+8	94	47	67	O1246(778/514/0),D165	505	3.5
/150	1	150	542	70	130	25	0	17	74	30	1	10	102	.240	.288	.378	.666	-23	1	2	33	O135(135/1/0),D13	0	-2.0
White, Roy Roy Hilton B12.27.1943 Los Angeles CA BB/TR/5'10"/(165–172) d9.7 NG 1969 C5 OF(1520/63/56)																								
1965	NY A	14	42	7	14	2	0	0	3	4	0	1	7	.333	.404	.381	.785	+25	2	1	67	O10(0/1/9)/2b	0	0.1
1966	NY A	115	316	39	71	13	2	7	20	37	1	1	43	.225	.308	.345	.653	-9	14	7	67	O82(72/12/0),2b2	0	-0.8
1967	NY A	70	214	22	48	8	0	2	18	19	0	1	25	.224	.287	.290	.577	-25	10	4	71	O36(5/0/31),3b17	0	-1.7
1968	NY A	159	577	89	154	20	7	17	62	73	6	3	50	.267	.350	.414	.764	+36	20	11	65	O154(119/25/12)	0	2.2
1969	NY A★	130	448	55	130	30	5	7	74	81	4	1	51	.290	.392	.426	.818	+36	18	10	64	O126L	0	2.6
1970	NY A☆	162	609	109	180	30	6	22	94	95	11	0	66	.296	.387	.473	.860	+43	24	10	71	O161(161/0/1)	0	3.1
1971	NY A	147	524	86	153	22	7	19	84	86	7	7	66	.292	.388	.469	.857	+52	14	7	67	O145L	0	3.8
1972	NY A	**155**	556	76	150	29	0	10	54	**99**	10	5	59	.270	.384	.376	.760	+30	23	7	77	O155L	0	2.5
1973	NY A	**162**	639	88	157	22	3	18	60	78	3	2	81	.246	.329	.374	.703	+0	16	9	64	O162L	0	-1.0
1974	NY A	136	473	68	130	19	8	7	43	67	5	4	44	.275	.367	.393	.760	+21	15	6	71	O67L,D53	0	1.2
1975	NY A	148	556	81	161	32	5	12	59	72	1	2	50	.290	.372	.430	.802	+28	16	15	52	O135L,1b7,D2	0	1.9
1976	†NY A	156	626	**104**	179	29	3	14	65	83	1	0	52	.286	.365	.409	.774	+28	31	13	70	O156(140/21/1)	0	1.9
1977	†NY A	143	519	72	139	25	2	14	52	75	9	0	58	.268	.358	.405	.763	+9	18	11	62	O135(133/1/2),D4	0	0.7
1978	†NY A	103	346	44	93	13	3	8	43	42	7	2	35	.269	.349	.393	.742	+11	10	4	71	O74(73/3/0),D23	15	-0.3
1979	NY A	81	205	24	44	6	0	3	27	23	1	0	21	.215	.290	.288	.578	-41	2	2	50	D29,O27L	0	-1.4
Total	15	1881	6650	964	1803	300	51	160	758	934	66	29	708	.271	.360	.404	.764	+21	233	117	67	O1625L,D111,3b17,1b7,2b3	15	14.8
/150	1	150	530	77	144	24	4	13	60	74	5	2	56	.271	.360	.404	.764	+21	19	9	68	O13L,D9/312	1	1.2
Whiteman, George George "Lucky" B12.23.1882 Peoria IL D2.10.1947 Houston TX BR/TR/5'7"/160 d9.13																								
1913	NY A	11	32	8	11	3	1	0	2	7	—	0	2	.344	.462	.500	.962	+81	2	—	—	O11(4/4/3)	—	0.3
Total	3	86	258	32	70	17	1	1	31	27	—	2	11	.271	.345	.357	.702	+13	11	—	—	O82(71/4/7)	—	-0.5
Whiten, Mark Mark Anthony B11.25.1966 Pensacola FL BB/TR/6'3"/(210–235) Dr 1986 TorA*5/130 d7.12 Col Pensacola (FL) JC																								
1997	NY A	69	215	34	57	11	0	5	24	30	5	2	47	.265	.360	.386	.746	-4	4	2	67	O57(44/0/16),D6	0	-0.4
Total	11	940	3104	465	804	129	20	105	423	378	42	17	712	.259	.341	.415	.756	+1	78	40	66	O867(131/67/696),D19/P	114	0.7
Whitfield, Terry Terry Bertland B1.12.1953 Blythe CA BL/TR/6'1"/(195–200) Dr 1971 NYA 1/19 d9.29																								
1974	NY A	2	5	0	1	0	0	0	0	0	0	0	1	.200	.200	.200	.400	-85	0	0	0	/cf	0	-0.1
1975	NY A	28	81	9	22	1	1	0	7	1	0	0	17	.272	.274	.309	.583	-33	1	0	100	O25(2/0/23)/D	0	-0.4
1976	NY A	1	0	0	0	0	0	0	0	0	0	0	0	+	+	+	.000	-100	0	0	0	/lf	0	0.0
Total	10	730	1913	233	537	93	12	33	179	138	20	10	288	.281	.330	.394	.724	+3	18	24	43	O539(408/32/116)/D	15	-1.9
Team	3	31	86	9	23	1	1	0	7	1	0	0	18	.267	.270	.302	.572	-36	1	0	100	O26(3/1/0)/D	0	-0.5
Wickland, Al Albert B1.27.1888 Chicago IL D3.14.1980 Port Washington WI BL/TL/5'7"/155 d8.21																								
1919	NY A	26	46	2	7	1	0	0	1	2	—	0	10	.152	.188	.174	.362	-98	0	—	—	O15R	—	-0.8
Total	5	444	1468	212	397	58	38	12	144	207	—	9	184	.270	.364	.386	.750	+17	58	4	100	O424(145/25/259)	—	0.2
Widger, Chris Christopher Jon B5.21.1971 Wilmington DE BR/TR/6'3"/(195–220) Dr 1992 SeaA 3/82 d6.23 Col George Mason [DL 2001 Sea A 190]																								
2002	NY A	21	64	4	19	5	0	0	5	2	0	2	9	.297	.338	.375	.713	-10	0	0	0	C21	0	-0.3
Total	10	613	1826	180	435	104	7	55	222	141	7	14	384	.238	.296	.393	.689	-22	10	9	53	C574,D7,O5(2/0/3),1b4/3b	250	-8.0
Wilborn, Ted Thaddeaus Iglehart B12.16.1958 Waco TX BB/TR/6'0"/(165–170) Dr 1976 NYA 4/88 d4.5																								
1980	NY A	8	8	2	2	0	0	0	1	0	0	0	1	.250	.250	.250	.500	-62	0	0	0	O3(1/1/1)	0	0.0
Total	2	30	20	5	2	0	0	0	1	1	0	0	8	.100	.143	.100	.243	-133	0	1	0	O10(5/2/3),D4	0	-0.4
Wilkinson, Ed Edward Henry B6.20.1890 Jacksonville OR D4.9.1918 Tucson AZ BR/TR/6'0"/170 d7.4 Col St. Marys (CA)																								
1911	NY A	10	13	2	3	0	0	0	1	0	—	0	—	.231	.231	.231	.462	-73	0	—	—	O3L/2b	—	-0.2
Williams, Bernie Bernabe (Figueroa) B9.13.1968 San Juan, PR BB/TR/6'2"/(180–205) d7.7																								
1991	NY A	85	320	43	76	19	4	3	34	48	0	1	57	.237	.336	.350	.686	-10	10	5	67	O85C	0	-0.4
1992	NY A	62	261	39	73	14	2	5	26	29	1	1	36	.280	.354	.406	.760	+13	7	6	54	O62(4/55/4)	0	0.8
1993	NY A	139	567	67	152	31	4	12	68	53	4	4	106	.268	.333	.400	.733	-1	9	9	50	O139C	25	-0.4
1994	NY A	108	408	80	118	29	1	12	57	61	2	3	54	.289	.384	.453	.837	+20	16	9	64	O107C	0	1.3
1995	†NY A	144	563	93	173	29	9	18	82	75	1	5	98	.307	.392	.487	.879	+29	8	6	57	O144C	0	3.0
1996	†NY A	143	551	108	168	26	7	29	102	82	8	0	72	.305	.391	.535	.926	+32	17	4	81	O140C,D2	15	2.6
1997	†NY A★	129	509	107	167	35	6	21	100	73	7	1	80	.328	.408	.544	.952	+49	15	8	65	O128C	35	2.5
1998	†NY A✳	128	499	101	169	30	5	26	97	74	9	1	81	**.339**	.422	.575	.997	+64	15	9	63	O123C,D5	37	4.0
1999	†NY A★	158	591	116	202	28	6	25	115	100	**17**	1	95	.342	.435	.536	.971	+49	9	10	47	O155C,D2	0	4.3
2000	†NY A★	141	537	108	165	37	6	30	121	71	11	5	84	.307	.391	.566	.957	+41	13	5	72	O137C,D4	0	3.2
2001	†NY A★	146	540	102	166	38	0	26	94	78	11	6	67	.307	.395	.522	.917	+39	11	5	69	O144C/D	0	3.0
2002	†NY A	154	612	102	204	37	2	19	102	83	7	3	97	.333	.415	.493	.908	+42	8	4	67	O147C,D7	0	2.9
2003	†NY A	119	445	77	117	19	1	15	64	71	8	3	61	.263	.367	.411	.778	+7	5	0	100	O115C,D4	47	0.6
2004	†NY A	148	561	105	147	29	1	22	70	85	5	2	96	.262	.360	.435	.795	+6	1	5	17	O97C,D50	0	-0.2
2005	†NY A	141	485	53	121	19	1	12	64	53	1	1	75	.249	.321	.367	.688	-16	1	2	33	O112C,D23	0	-1.5
2006	†NY A	131	420	65	118	29	0	12	61	33	5	2	53	.281	.332	.436	.768	-4	2	0	100	O89(5/28/58),D31	0	-1.1
Total	16	2076	7869	1366	2336	449	55	287	1257	1069	97	39	1212	.297	.381	.477	.858	+25	147	87	63	O1924(9/1856/62),D129	159	24.6
/150	1	150	569	99	169	32	4	21	91	77	7	3	88	.297	.381	.477	.858	+25	11	6	65	O14(1/134/4),D9	11	1.8
Williams, Gerald Gerald Floyd B8.10.1966 New Orleans LA BR/TR/6'2"/(185–190) Dr 1987 NYA 14/367 d9.15 Col Grambling St.																								
1992	NY A	15	27	7	8	2	0	3	6	0	0	0	3	.296	.296	.704	1.000	+73	2	0	100	O12R	0	0.3
1993	NY A	42	67	11	10	2	3	0	6	1	0	2	14	.149	.183	.269	.452	-79	2	0	100	O37(10/17/12)/D	0	-0.9
1994	NY A	57	86	19	25	8	0	4	13	4	0	0	17	.291	.319	.523	.842	+17	1	3	25	O43(26/8/12),D2	0	-0.2
1995	†NY A	100	182	33	45	18	2	6	28	22	1	1	34	.247	.327	.467	.794	+6	4	2	67	O92(70/2/26),D2	0	0.7
1996	NY A	99	233	37	63	15	4	5	30	15	2	4	39	.270	.319	.433	.752	-10	7	8	47	O92(70/14/10),D2	0	-1.0
2001	NY A	38	47	12	8	1	0	0	2	5	0	1	13	.170	.264	.191	.455	-77	3	1	75	O26(6/11/12),D7	0	-0.5

YEAR	TM LG	G	AB	R	H	2B	3B	HR	RBI	BB	IB	HP	SO	AVG	OBP	SLG	OPS	AOPS	SB	CS	SB%	GAMES AT POSITION	DL	BFW
2002	NY A	33	17	6	0	0	0	0	0	2	0	0	4	.000	.105	.000	.105	-169	2	0	100	O30(7/6/17)	0	-0.4
Total	14	1168	3059	474	780	183	18	85	365	180	8	31	530	.255	.301	.410	.711	-18	106	57	65	O1056(446/453/212),D22	0	-8.3
Team	7	384	659	125	159	46	9	18	85	49	3	8	124	.241	.298	.420	.718	-15	21	14	60	O332(10/41/27),D14	0	-2.0
/150	3	150	257	49	62	18	4	7	33	19	1	3	48	.241	.298	.420	.718	-15	8	5	62	O130(4/16/11),D5	0	-0.8

Williams, Harry Harry Peter B6.23.1890 Omaha NE D12.21.1963 Huntington Park CA BR/TR/6'1.5"/200 d8.7 b–Gus

YEAR	TM LG	G	AB	R	H	2B	3B	HR	RBI	BB	IB	HP	SO	AVG	OBP	SLG	OPS	AOPS	SB	CS	SB%	GAMES AT POSITION	DL	BFW
1913	NY A	27	82	18	21	3	1	1	12	15	—	1	10	.256	.378	.354	.732	+14	6	—	—	1b27	—	0.0
1914	NY A	59	178	9	29	5	2	1	17	26	—	5	26	.163	.287	.230	.517	-44	3	6	33	1b58	—	-2.0
Total	2	86	260	27	50	8	3	2	29	41	—	6	36	.192	.316	.269	.585	-25	9	6	100	1b85	—	-2.0

Williams, Jimmy James Thomas B12.20.1876 St.Louis MO D1.16.1965 St.Petersburg FL BR/TR/5'9"/175 d4.15

YEAR	TM LG	G	AB	R	H	2B	3B	HR	RBI	BB	IB	HP	SO	AVG	OBP	SLG	OPS	AOPS	SB	CS	SB%	GAMES AT POSITION	DL	BFW
1899	Pit N	153	621	126	220	28	**27**	9	116	60	—	6	—	.354	.416	.530	.946	+59	26	—	—	3b153	—	4.7
1900	†Pit N	106	416	73	110	15	11	5	68	32	—	4	—	.264	.323	.389	.712	-5	18	—	—	3b103,S4	—	0.2
1901	Bal A	130	501	113	159	26	**21**	7	96	56	—	2	—	.317	.388	.495	.883	+38	21	—	—	2b130	—	2.2
1902	Bal A	125	498	83	156	27	**21**	8	83	36	—	1	—	.313	.361	.500	.861	+31	14	—	—	2b104,3b19/1b	—	2.0
1903	NY A	132	502	60	134	30	12	3	82	39	—	5	—	.267	.326	.392	.718	+8	9	—	—	2b132	—	2.3
1904	NY A	146	559	62	147	31	7	2	74	38	—	4	—	.263	.314	.354	.668	+6	14	—	—	2b146	—	2.3
1905	NY A	129	470	54	107	20	8	6	62	50	—	3	—	.228	.306	.343	.649	-5	14	—	—	2b129	—	0.2
1906	NY A	139	501	61	139	25	7	3	77	44	—	5	—	.277	.342	.373	.715	+12	8	—	—	2b139	—	2.5
1907	NY A	139	504	53	136	17	11	2	63	35	—	1	—	.270	.319	.359	.678	+7	14	—	—	2b139	—	0.2
1908	StL A	148	539	63	127	20	7	4	53	55	—	3	—	.236	.310	.321	.631	+4	7	—	—	2b148	—	0.9
1909	StL A	110	374	32	73	3	6	0	22	29	—	2	—	.195	.257	.235	.492	-40	6	—	—	2b109	—	-2.1
Total	11	1457	5485	780	1508	242	138	49	796	474	—	36	—	.275	.337	.396	.733	+14	151	—	—	2b1176,3b275,S4/1b	—	15.4
Team	5	685	2536	290	663	123	45	16	358	206	—	18	0	.261	.321	.364	.685	+6	59	—	—	2b685	—	7.5
/150	1	150	555	64	145	27	10	4	78	45	—	4	0	.261	.321	.364	.685	+6	13	—	—	2b150	—	1.6

Williams, Bob Robert Elias B4.27.1884 Monday OH D8.6.1962 Nelsonville OH BR/TR/6'0"/190 d7.3

YEAR	TM LG	G	AB	R	H	2B	3B	HR	RBI	BB	IB	HP	SO	AVG	OBP	SLG	OPS	AOPS	SB	CS	SB%	GAMES AT POSITION	DL	BFW
1911	NY A	20	47	3	9	2	0	0	8	5	—	0	—	.191	.269	.234	.503	-62	1	—	—	C20	—	-0.4
1912	NY A	20	44	7	6	1	0	0	3	9	—	0	—	.136	.283	.159	.442	-74	0	—	—	C20	—	-0.5
1913	NY A	6	19	0	3	0	0	0	0	1	—	0	3	.158	.200	.158	.358	-95	0	—	—	C6	—	-0.3
Total	3	46	110	10	18	3	0	0	11	15	—	0	3	.164	.264	.191	.455	-72	1	—	—	C46	—	-1.2

Williams, Walt Walter Allen "No-Neck" B12.19.1943 Brownwood TX BR/TR/5'6"/(185–195) d4.21 C1 Col San Francisco (CA) City

YEAR	TM LG	G	AB	R	H	2B	3B	HR	RBI	BB	IB	HP	SO	AVG	OBP	SLG	OPS	AOPS	SB	CS	SB%	GAMES AT POSITION	DL	BFW
1974	NY A	43	53	5	6	0	0	0	3	1	0	0	10	.113	.127	.113	.240	-130	1	0	100	O24(13/0/13),D3	0	-1.1
1975	NY A	82	185	27	52	5	1	5	16	8	1	3	23	.281	.320	.400	.720	+4	0	1	0	O31(8/10/14),D17,2b6	0	-0.4
Total	10	842	2373	284	640	106	11	33	173	126	7	18	211	.270	.310	.365	.675	-9	34	19	64	O565(242/13/338),D46,2b6,3b2	40	-5.3
Team	2	125	238	32	58	5	1	5	19	9	1	3	33	.244	.278	.336	.614	-25	1	1	50	O55(21/10/27),D20,2b6	0	-1.5
/150	2	150	286	38	70	6	1	6	23	11	1	4	40	.244	.278	.336	.614	-25	1	1	50	O66(25/12/32),D24,2b7	0	-1.8

Wilson, Archie Archibald Clifton B11.25.1923 Los Angeles CA BR/TR/6'0"/175 d9.18 Col USC

YEAR	TM LG	G	AB	R	H	2B	3B	HR	RBI	BB	IB	HP	SO	AVG	OBP	SLG	OPS	AOPS	SB	CS	SB%	GAMES AT POSITION	DL	BFW
1951	NY A	4	4	0	0	0	0	0	0	0	—	1	0	.000	.200	.000	.200	-144	0	0	0	O2R	0	-0.1
1952	NY A	3	2	0	1	0	0	0	1	0	—	0	0	.500	.500	.500	1.000	+90	0	0	0	/H	0	0.0
Total	2	51	140	9	31	5	3	0	17	7	—	2	14	.221	.268	.300	.568	-42	0	0	0	O39(16/12/11)	0	-1.2
Team	2	7	6	0	1	0	0	0	1	0	—	1	0	.167	.286	.167	.453	-77	0	0	0	O2R	0	-0.1

Wilson, Craig Craig Alan B11.30.1976 Fountain Valley CA BR/TR/6'2"/(217–220) Dr 1995 TorA 2/47 d4.22

YEAR	TM LG	G	AB	R	H	2B	3B	HR	RBI	BB	IB	HP	SO	AVG	OBP	SLG	OPS	AOPS	SB	CS	SB%	GAMES AT POSITION	DL	BFW
2006	NY A	40	104	15	22	4	0	4	8	4	0	1	34	.212	.248	.365	.613	-45	0	0	0	1b35,O2R	0	-1.2
Total	7	698	2010	303	527	100	14	99	292	198	12	90	643	.262	.353	.474	.827	+12	14	7	67	O314(47/0/278),1b282,C40,D10	105	-0.3

Wilson, Enrique Enrique (Martes) B7.27.1973 Santo Domingo, D.R. BB/TR/5'11"/(160–195) d9.24

YEAR	TM LG	G	AB	R	H	2B	3B	HR	RBI	BB	IB	HP	SO	AVG	OBP	SLG	OPS	AOPS	SB	CS	SB%	GAMES AT POSITION	DL	BFW
1997	Cle A	5	15	2	5	0	0	0	1	0	0	0	2	.333	.333	.333	.666	-28	0	0	0	S4/2b	0	0.0
1998	†Cle A	32	90	13	29	6	0	2	12	4	0	1	8	.322	.354	.456	.810	+6	2	4	33	2b22,S10,3b2	72	0.2
1999	†Cle A	113	332	41	87	22	1	2	24	25	1	1	41	.262	.310	.352	.662	-33	5	4	56	3b61,S35,2b21/D	0	-2.5
2000	Cle A	40	117	16	38	9	0	2	12	7	0	0	11	.325	.360	.453	.813	+1	2	1	67	3b12,2b7,S7,D8	14	-0.2
2000	Pit N	40	122	11	32	6	1	3	15	11	2	0	13	.262	.321	.402	.723	-19	0	1	0	3b16,2b11,S8	3	-0.3
2000	Major	80	239	27	70	15	1	5	27	18	2	0	24	.293	2.342	.427	2.769	+28	2	2	50	—	17	-0.5
2001	Pit N	46	129	7	24	3	0	1	8	3	0	0	23	.186	.203	.233	.436	-88	0	3	0	S28,2b10,3b2	0	-1.2
2001	†NY A	48	99	10	24	5	1	1	12	6	0	0	14	.242	.283	.343	.626	-36	0	2	0	S20,3b19,2b7/D	0	-0.1
2001	Major	94	228	17	48	8	1	2	20	9	0	0	37	.211	2.241	.281	2.521	+9	0	5	0	—	0	-1.3
2002	†NY A	60	105	17	19	2	2	2	11	8	0	0	22	.181	.239	.295	.534	-59	1	1	50	3b26,S14,2b7/rfD	0	-0.8
2003	†NY A	63	135	18	31	9	0	3	15	7	0	2	14	.230	.276	.363	.639	-32	3	1	75	S33,3b17,2b10/D	0	-0.8
2004	NY A	93	240	19	51	9	0	6	31	15	0	0	20	.213	.254	.325	.579	-49	1	2	33	2b80,S16	0	-2.0
2005	Chi N	15	22	1	3	2	0	0	0	3	0	0	1	.136	.240	.227	.467	-77	0	0	0	2b5,1b3,S3/3b	0	0.0
Total	9	555	1406	155	343	73	5	22	141	89	3	4	169	.244	.288	.350	.638	-37	14	19	42	2b181,S178,3b156,D13,1b3/rf	89	-7.7
Team	4	264	579	64	125	25	3	12	69	36	0	2	70	.216	.261	.332	.593	-45	5	6	45	2b104,S83,3b62,D3/rf	0	-3.7
/150	2	150	329	36	71	14	2	7	39	20	0	1	40	.216	.261	.332	.593	-45	3	3	50	2b59,S47,3b35,D2/rf	0	-2.1

Wilson, George George Washington "Teddy" B8.30.1925 Cherryville NC D10.29.1974 Gastonia NC BL/TR/6'1.5"/185 d4.15

YEAR	TM LG	G	AB	R	H	2B	3B	HR	RBI	BB	IB	HP	SO	AVG	OBP	SLG	OPS	AOPS	SB	CS	SB%	GAMES AT POSITION	DL	BFW
1956	†NY A	11	12	1	2	0	0	0	0	3	0	0	0	.167	.333	.167	.500	-63	0	0	0	O6(1/0/5)	0	-0.2
Total	3	145	209	15	40	8	0	3	19	14	1	1	32	.191	.246	.273	.519	-59	0	0	0	O36(19/1/16),1b2	0	-2.4

Windhorn, Gordie Gordon Ray B12.19.1933 Watseka IL BR/TR/6'1"/185 d9.10

YEAR	TM LG	G	AB	R	H	2B	3B	HR	RBI	BB	IB	HP	SO	AVG	OBP	SLG	OPS	AOPS	SB	CS	SB%	GAMES AT POSITION	DL	BFW
1959	NY A	7	11	0	0	0	0	0	0	0	0	0	3	.000	.000	.000	.000	-199	0	0	0	O4L	0	-0.4
Total	3	95	108	20	19	9	1	2	8	11	2	0	19	.176	.252	.333	.585	-45	1	2	33	O55(38/6/14)	0	-1.1

Winfield, Dave David Mark B10.3.1951 St.Paul MN BR/TR/6'6"/(220–249) Dr 1973 SDN 1/4 d6.19 HF2001 Col Minnesota OF(466/219/1879) [DL 1989 NY A 182]

YEAR	TM LG	G	AB	R	H	2B	3B	HR	RBI	BB	IB	HP	SO	AVG	OBP	SLG	OPS	AOPS	SB	CS	SB%	GAMES AT POSITION	DL	BFW
1973	SD N	56	141	9	39	4	1	3	12	12	1	0	19	.277	.331	.383	.714	+7	0	0	0	O36(34/2/1)/1b	0	-0.3
1974	SD N	145	498	57	132	18	4	20	75	40	2	1	96	.265	.318	.438	.756	+16	9	7	56	O131(81/25/34)	0	0.7
1975	SD N	143	509	74	136	20	2	15	76	69	14	3	82	.267	.354	.403	.757	+19	23	4	85	O138R	0	1.3
1976	SD N	137	492	81	139	26	4	13	69	65	8	3	78	.283	.366	.431	.797	+37	26	7	79	O134(0/10/127)	0	3.1
1977	SD N★	157	615	104	169	29	7	25	92	58	10	0	75	.275	.335	.467	.802	+25	16	7	70	O156R	0	2.3
1978	SD N★	158	587	88	181	30	5	24	97	55	20	2	81	.308	.367	.499	.866	+52	21	9	70	O154(1/84/112),1b2	0	2.7
1979	SD N★	159	597	97	184	27	10	34	**118**	85	**24**	2	71	.308	.395	.558	.953	+68	15	9	63	O157R	0	5.2
1980	SD N★	162	558	89	154	25	6	20	87	79	14	2	83	.276	.365	.450	.815	+36	23	7	77	O159(0/20/154)	0	2.4
1981	†NY A★	105	388	52	114	25	1	13	68	43	3	1	41	.294	.360	.464	.824	+39	11	1	92	O102(80/23/0)/D	0	1.0
1982	NY A★	140	539	84	151	24	8	37	106	45	7	0	64	.280	.331	.560	.891	+43	5	3	63	O135L,D4	15	2.8
1983	NY A★	152	598	99	169	26	8	32	116	58	2	2	77	.283	.345	.513	.858	+38	15	6	71	O151(122/39/9)	0	1.4
1984	NY A★	141	567	106	193	34	4	19	100	53	9	0	71	.340	.393	.515	.908	+55	6	4	60	O140(1/16/127)	15	3.4
1985	NY A★	155	633	105	174	34	6	26	114	52	8	0	96	.275	.328	.471	.799	+18	19	7	73	O152R,D2	0	1.2
1986	NY A★	154	565	90	148	31	5	24	104	77	9	2	106	.262	.349	.462	.811	+20	6	5	55	O145R,3b2,D6	0	0.8
1987	NY A★	156	575	83	158	22	1	27	97	76	5	0	96	.275	.358	.457	.815	+15	5	6	45	O145R,D8	0	-0.6
1988	NY A★	149	559	96	180	37	2	25	107	69	10	2	88	.322	.398	.530	.928	+58	9	4	69	O141R,D4	0	3.0
1990	NY A	20	61	7	13	3	0	2	6	4	0	1	13	.213	.269	.361	.630	-25	0	0	0	O12L,D7	0	-0.5
1990	Cal A	112	414	63	114	18	2	19	72	48	3	1	68	.275	.348	.466	.814	+29	0	1	0	O108R,D3	0	0.1
1990	Year	132	475	70	127	21	2	21	78	52	3	2	81	.267	.338	.453	.791	+22	0	1	0	O120(12/0/108),D10	0	-0.4
1991	Cal A	150	568	75	149	27	4	28	86	56	4	1	109	.262	.326	.472	.798	+19	7	2	78	O115R,D34	0	0.3
1992	†Tor A	156	583	92	169	33	3	26	108	82	10	1	89	.290	.377	.491	.868	+35	2	3	40	D130,O26R	0	2.3
1993	Min A	143	547	72	148	27	2	21	76	45	2	0	106	.271	.325	.442	.767	+3	2	3	40	D105,O31R,1b5	0	-0.7
1994	Min A	77	294	35	74	15	3	10	43	31	5	0	51	.252	.321	.425	.746	-10	2	1	67	D76/rf	16	-0.8

YEAR	TM LG	G	AB	R	H	2B	3B	HR	RBI	BB	IB	HP	SO	AVG	OBP	SLG	OPS	AOPS	SB	CS	SB%	GAMES AT POSITION	DL	BFW
1995	Cle A	46	115	11	22	5	0	2	4	14	2	1	26	.191	.285	.287	.572	-52	1	0	100	D39	56	-1.0
Total	22	2973	11003	1669	3110	540	88	465	1833	1216	17	25	1686	.283	.353	.475	.828	+30	223	96	70	O2469R,D419,1b8,3b2	284	30.1
Team	9	1172	4485	722	1300	236	35	205	818	477	53	8	652	.290	.356	.495	.851	+34	76	36	68	O1123(82/78/136),D32,3b2	212	12.5
/150	1	150	574	92	166	30	4	26	105	61	7	1	83	.290	.356	.495	.851	+34	10	5	67	O144(10/10/17),D4/3	27	1.6

Witek, Mickey Nicholas Joseph B12.19.1915 Luzerne PA D8.24.1990 Kingston PA BR/TR/5'10"/170 d4.16 Mil 1944–45

YEAR	TM LG	G	AB	R	H	2B	3B	HR	RBI	BB	IB	HP	SO	AVG	OBP	SLG	OPS	AOPS	SB	CS	SB%	GAMES AT POSITION	DL	BFW
1949	NY A	2	1	0	1	0	0	0	0	0	—	0	0	1.000	1.000	1.000	2.000	+330	0	0	0	/H	0	0.0
Total	7	581	2147	239	595	65	9	22	196	148	—	0	84	.277	.324	.347	.671	-10	7	0	100	2b437,S89,3b38	0	4.1

Witt, Whitey Lawton Walter (b Ladislaw Waldemar Wittkowski) B9.28.1895 Orange MA D7.14.1988 Salem Co. NJ BL/TR/5'7"/150 d4.12 Mil 1918 Col Bowdoin

YEAR	TM LG	G	AB	R	H	2B	3B	HR	RBI	BB	IB	HP	SO	AVG	OBP	SLG	OPS	AOPS	SB	CS	SB%	GAMES AT POSITION	DL	BFW
1916	Phi A	143	563	64	138	16	15	2	36	55	—	2	71	.245	.315	.337	.652	+1	19	—	—	S142	—	1.4
1917	Phi A	128	452	62	114	13	4	0	28	65	—	0	45	.252	.346	.299	.645	-2	12	—	—	S111,O7L,3b6	—	1.9
1919	Phi A	122	460	56	123	15	6	0	33	46	—	0	26	.267	.334	.326	.660	-15	11	—	—	O59(40/19/0),2b56,3b2	—	-1.6
1920	Phi A	65	218	29	70	11	3	1	25	27	—	0	16	.321	.396	.413	.809	+13	2	3	40	O50(0/5/45),2b10,S2	—	-0.3
1921	Phi A	154	629	100	198	31	11	4	45	77	—	1	52	.315	.390	.418	.808	+6	16	15	52	O154R	—	-0.8
1922	†NY A	140	528	98	157	11	6	4	40	**89**	—	1	29	.297	.400	.364	.764	-2	5	8	38	O139(0/109/30)	—	-1.3
1923	†NY A	146	596	113	187	18	10	6	56	67	—	3	42	.314	.386	.408	.794	+7	2	7	22	O144C	—	-0.5
1924	NY A	147	600	88	178	26	5	1	36	45	—	0	20	.297	.346	.362	.708	-17	9	7	56	O144C	—	-2.6
1925	NY A	31	40	9	8	2	1	0	0	6	—	0	2	.200	.304	.300	.604	-45	1	1	50	O10(0/9/1)	—	-0.2
1926	Bro N	63	85	13	22	1	1	0	3	12	—	0	6	.259	.351	.294	.645	-24	1	—	—	O22(3/17/2)	—	-0.3
Total	10	1139	4171	632	1195	144	62	18	302	489	—	7	309	.287	.362	.364	.726	-3	78	41	100	O729(50/447/232),S255,2b66,3b8	—	-4.3
Team	4	464	1764	308	530	57	22	11	132	207	—	4	93	.300	.375	.376	.751	-5	17	23	43	O437(4/118/30)	—	-4.6
/150	1	150	570	100	171	18	7	4	43	67	—	1	30	.300	.375	.376	.751	-5	5	7	42	O141(1/38/10)	—	-1.5

Wolter, Harry Harry Meiggs B7.11.1884 Monterey CA D7.6.1970 Palo Alto CA BL/TR/5'10"/175 d5.14 Col Santa Clara ▲

YEAR	TM LG	G	AB	R	H	2B	3B	HR	RBI	BB	IB	HP	SO	AVG	OBP	SLG	OPS	AOPS	SB	CS	SB%	GAMES AT POSITION	DL	BFW
1907	Cin N	4	15	1	2	0	0	0	1	0	—	0	—	.133	.133	.133	.266	-116	0	—	—	O4R	—	-0.3
1907	Pit N	1	1	0	0	0	0	0	0	0	—	0	—	.000	.000	.000	.000	-199	0	—	—	/P	—	0.0
1907	StL N	16	47	4	16	0	0	0	6	3	—	0	—	.340	.380	.340	.720	+30	1	—	—	O9(1/6/2),P3	—	0.3
1907	Year	21	63	5	18	0	0	0	7	3	—	0	—	.286	.318	.286	.604	-9	1	—	—	O13(1/6/6),P4	—	0.0
1909	Bos A	54	121	14	29	2	4	2	10	9	—	0	—	.240	.292	.372	.664	+7	2	—	—	1b17,P11,O9R	—	-0.2
1910	NY A	135	479	84	128	15	9	4	42	66	—	7	—	.267	.364	.361	.725	+20	39	—	—	O129(1/0/128),1b2	—	0.7
1911	NY A	122	434	78	132	17	15	4	36	62	—	4	—	.304	.396	.440	.836	+25	28	—	—	O113(0/7/106),1b2	—	1.4
1912	NY A	12	32	8	11	2	1	0	1	10	—	1	—	.344	.512	.469	.981	+71	5	3	63	O9(0/5/4)	—	0.3
1913	NY A	127	425	53	108	18	6	2	43	80	—	4	50	.254	.377	.339	.716	+9	13	—	—	O121(0/106/15)	—	-0.6
1917	Chi N	117	353	44	88	15	7	0	28	38	—	1	40	.249	.324	.331	.655	-6	7	—	—	O97(3/2/94)/1b	—	-0.6
Total	7	588	1907	286	514	69	42	12	167	268	—	17	90	.270	.365	.369	.734	+14	95	3	100	O491(5/126/362),1b22,P15	—	1.0
Team	4	396	1370	223	379	52	31	10	122	218	—	16	50	.277	.382	.382	.764	+19	85	3	100	O372(107/27/253),1b4	—	1.8
/150	2	150	519	84	144	20	12	4	46	83	—	6	19	.277	.382	.382	.764	+19	32	1	100	O141(41/10/96),1b2	—	0.7

Wolverton, Harry Harry Sterling "Fighting Harry" B12.6.1873 Mt.Vernon OH D2.4.1937 Oakland CA BL/TR/5'11"/205 d9.25 M1 Col Kenyon

YEAR	TM LG	G	AB	R	H	2B	3B	HR	RBI	BB	IB	HP	SO	AVG	OBP	SLG	OPS	AOPS	SB	CS	SB%	GAMES AT POSITION	DL	BFW
1912	NY A	34	50	6	15	1	1	0	4	2	—	1	—	.300	.340	.360	.700	-6	1	—	—	3b8,M	—	-0.2
Total	9	783	3001	346	833	95	53	7	352	166	—	48	—	.278	.326	.352	.678	-4	83	—	—	3b756/S	—	-0.1

Womack, Tony Anthony Darrell B9.25.1969 Chatham VA BL/TR/5'9"/(150–175) Dr 1991 PitN 7/201 d9.10 Col Guilford

YEAR	TM LG	G	AB	R	H	2B	3B	HR	RBI	BB	IB	HP	SO	AVG	OBP	SLG	OPS	AOPS	SB	CS	SB%	GAMES AT POSITION	DL	BFW
2005	†NY A	108	329	46	82	8	1	0	15	12	0	1	49	.249	.276	.280	.556	-51	27	5	84	O66(40/22/4),2b24,D11	0	-1.3
Total	13	1303	4963	739	1353	190	59	36	368	308	9	28	649	.273	.317	.356	.673	-28	363	74	83	2b529,S516,O205(40/40/130),D11	41	-12.9
/150	1	150	457	64	114	11	1	0	21	17	0	1	68	.249	.276	.280	.556	-51	38	7	84	O92(56/31/6),2b33,D15	0	-1.8

Woodling, Gene Eugene Richard B8.16.1922 Akron OH D6.2.2001 Barberton OH BL/TR/5'9.5"/(175–200) d9.23 Mil 1943–45 C4

YEAR	TM LG	G	AB	R	H	2B	3B	HR	RBI	BB	IB	HP	SO	AVG	OBP	SLG	OPS	AOPS	SB	CS	SB%	GAMES AT POSITION	DL	BFW
1943	Cle A	8	25	5	8	2	1	1	5	1	—	0	3	.320	.346	.600	.946	+86	0	0	0	O6(0/1/5)	0	0.2
1946	Cle A	61	133	8	25	1	4	0	9	16	—	1	13	.188	.280	.256	.536	-46	1	2	33	O37(6/31/0)	0	-1.2
1947	Pit N	22	79	7	21	2	2	0	10	7	—	0	5	.266	.326	.342	.668	-25	0	—	—	O21(1/20/0)	0	-0.3
1949	†NY A	112	296	60	80	13	7	5	44	52	—	1	21	.270	.381	.412	.793	+10	2	2	50	O98(82/12/5)	0	-0.3
1950	†NY A	122	449	81	127	20	10	6	60	70	—	1	31	.283	.381	.412	.793	+6	5	3	63	O118(117/2/0)	0	0.8
1951	†NY A	120	420	65	118	15	8	15	71	62	—	0	37	.281	.373	.462	.835	+30	0	4	0	O116(101/17/0)	0	0.7
1952	†NY A	122	408	58	126	19	6	12	63	59	—	1	31	.309	.397	.473	.870	+51	1	4	20	O118(112/6/0)	0	2.6
1953	†NY A	125	395	64	121	26	4	10	58	82	—	3	29	.306	**.429**	.468	.897	+47	2	7	22	O119L	0	2.4
1954	NY A	97	304	33	76	12	5	3	40	53	—	0	35	.250	.358	.352	.710	-1	3	4	43	O89L	0	-0.6
1955	Bal A	47	145	22	32	6	2	3	18	24	4	1	18	.221	.329	.352	.681	-9	1	1	50	O44(26/4/25)	0	-0.5
1955	Cle A	79	259	33	72	15	1	5	35	36	2	3	15	.278	.368	.402	.770	+4	2	4	33	O70(64/0/16)	0	-0.3
1955	Year	126	404	55	104	21	3	8	53	60	6	4	33	.257	.354	.384	.738	+0	3	5	38	O114(90/4/41)	0	-0.8
1956	Cle A	100	317	56	83	17	0	8	38	69	2	3	29	.262	.395	.391	.786	+7	2	6	25	O85(85/0/2)	32	-0.3
1957	Cle A	133	430	74	138	25	2	19	78	64	2	3	35	.321	.408	.521	.929	+55	0	5	0	O113L	0	3.6
1958	Bal A	133	413	57	114	16	1	15	65	66	3	2	49	.276	.378	.429	.807	+28	4	2	67	O116(61/0/68)	0	1.0
1959	Bal A★	140	440	63	132	22	2	14	77	78	4	0	35	.300	.402	.455	.857	+39	1	1	50	O124(85/0/57)	0	1.7
1960	Bal A	140	435	68	123	18	3	11	62	84	7	4	40	.283	.401	.414	.815	+23	3	0	100	O124(124/0/1)	0	1.2
1961	Was A	110	342	39	107	16	4	10	57	50	3	2	24	.313	.403	.471	.874	+35	1	0	100	O90(15/0/77)	0	1.2
1962	Was A	44	107	19	30	4	0	5	16	24	4	2	5	.280	.421	.458	.879	+38	1	0	100	O30(3/0/27)	0	0.2
1962	NY N	81	190	18	52	8	1	5	24	24	3	1	22	.274	.353	.405	.758	+3	0	0	0	O48(27/0/21)	0	-0.3
1962	Major	125	297	37	82	12	1	10	40	48	7	3	27	.276	3.382	.424	3.806	+68	1	0	100	—		-0.1
Total	17	1796	5587	830	1585	257	63	147	830	921	34	28	477	.284	.386	.431	.817	+23	29	45	100	O1566(1230/93/304)	32	11.8
Team	6	698	2272	361	648	105	40	51	336	378	—	6	184	.285	.388	.434	.822	+25	13	24	35	O658(300/37/5)	0	5.6
/150	1	150	488	78	139	23	9	11	72	81	—	1	40	.285	.388	.434	.822	+25	3	5	38	O141(64/8/1)	0	1.2

Woods, Ron Ronald Lawrence B2.1.1943 Hamilton OH BR/TR/5'10"/(165–173) d4.22

YEAR	TM LG	G	AB	R	H	2B	3B	HR	RBI	BB	IB	HP	SO	AVG	OBP	SLG	OPS	AOPS	SB	CS	SB%	GAMES AT POSITION	DL	BFW
1969	NY A	72	171	18	30	5	2	1	7	22	1	1	29	.175	.273	.246	.519	-52	2	0	100	O67(1/66/0)	0	-1.3
1970	NY A	95	225	30	51	5	3	8	27	33	3	0	35	.227	.324	.382	.706	-1	4	2	67	O78(2/9/70)	21	-0.6
1971	NY A	25	32	4	8	1	0	1	2	4	0	0	2	.250	.333	.375	.708	+5	0	0	0	O9(3/0/6)	0	0.0
Total	6	582	1247	162	290	34	12	26	130	175	10	2	171	.233	.326	.342	.668	-13	27	18	60	O454(122/268/95)	21	-3.2
Team	3	192	428	52	89	11	5	10	36	59	4	1	66	.208	.305	.327	.632	-21	6	2	75	O154(6/75/76)	21	-1.9
/150	2	150	334	41	70	9	4	8	28	46	3	1	52	.208	.305	.327	.632	-21	5	2	71	O120(5/59/59)	16	-1.5

Workman, Hank Henry Kilgariff B2.5.1926 Los Angeles CA BL/TR/6'1"/185 d9.4 Col USC

YEAR	TM LG	G	AB	R	H	2B	3B	HR	RBI	BB	IB	HP	SO	AVG	OBP	SLG	OPS	AOPS	SB	CS	SB%	GAMES AT POSITION	DL	BFW
1950	NY A	2	5	1	1	0	0	0	0	0	—	0	1	.200	.200	.200	.400	-97	0	0	0	/1b	0	-0.1

Wuestling, Yats George B10.18.1903 St.Louis MO D4.26.1970 St.Louis MO BR/TR/5'11"/167 d6.15

YEAR	TM LG	G	AB	R	H	2B	3B	HR	RBI	BB	IB	HP	SO	AVG	OBP	SLG	OPS	AOPS	SB	CS	SB%	GAMES AT POSITION	DL	BFW
1930	NY A	25	58	5	11	0	1	0	3	4	—	0	14	.190	.242	.224	.466	-80	0	1	0	S21,3b3	—	-0.4
Total	2	83	217	18	41	4	2	0	19	15	—	1	41	.189	.245	.226	.471	-79	1	4	20	S77,3b4/2b	—	-2.2

Wynegar, Butch Harold Delano B3.14.1956 York PA BB/TR/6'0"/(185–200) Dr 1974 MinA 2/38 d4.9 C4

YEAR	TM LG	G	AB	R	H	2B	3B	HR	RBI	BB	IB	HP	SO	AVG	OBP	SLG	OPS	AOPS	SB	CS	SB%	GAMES AT POSITION	DL	BFW
1976	Min A★	149	534	58	139	21	2	10	69	79	7	2	63	.260	.356	.363	.719	+9	0	0	0	C137,D15	0	0.8
1977	Min A★	144	532	76	139	22	3	10	79	68	5	2	61	.261	.344	.370	.714	-3	2	3	40	C142/3b	0	-0.1
1978	Min A	135	454	36	104	22	1	4	45	47	2	6	42	.229	.307	.308	.615	-28	1	0	100	C131/3b	0	-0.7
1979	Min A	149	504	74	136	20	0	7	57	74	5	2	36	.270	.363	.351	.714	-10	2	2	50	C146,D2	0	0.8
1980	Min A	146	486	61	124	18	3	5	57	63	6	2	36	.255	.339	.335	.674	-19	3	1	75	C142/D	0	0.9
1981	Min A	47	150	11	37	5	0	0	10	17	2	1	9	.247	.322	.280	.602	-28	0	1	0	C37,D9	54	-0.4
1982	Min A	24	86	9	18	4	0	1	8	10	1	0	12	.209	.292	.291	.583	-41	0	0	0	C24	0	-0.6
1982	NY A	63	191	27	56	8	1	3	20	40	1	1	21	.293	.413	.393	.806	+26	0	1	0	C62	38	1.3
1982	Year	87	277	36	74	12	1	4	28	50	2	1	33	.267	.378	.361	.739	+5	0	1	0	C86	0	0.7

YEAR	TM LG	G	AB	R	H	2B	3B	HR	RBI	BB	IB	HP	SO	AVG	OBP	SLG	OPS	AOPS	SB	CS	SB%	GAMES AT POSITION	DL	BFW
1983	NY A	94	301	40	89	18	2	6	42	52	1	1	29	.296	.399	.429	.828	+32	1	1	50	C93	15	1.1
1984	NY A	129	442	48	118	13	1	6	45	65	6	0	35	.267	.360	.342	.702	-1	1	4	20	C126	0	0.5
1985	NY A	102	309	27	69	15	0	5	32	64	2	0	43	.223	.356	.320	.676	-11	0	0	0	C96	15	0.5
1986	NY A	61	194	19	40	4	1	7	29	30	2	0	21	.206	.310	.345	.655	-21	0	0	0	C57	15	-0.1
1987	Cal A	31	92	4	19	2	0	0	5	9	0	0	13	.207	.277	.228	.505	-63	0	0	0	C28/D	114	-0.3
1988	Cal A	27	55	8	14	4	1	1	8	8	1	0	7	.255	.338	.418	.756	+17	0	0	0	C26	130	0.4
Total	13	1301	4330	498	1102	176	15	65	506	626	41	17	428	.255	.348	.347	.695	-7	10	13	43	C1247,D28,3b2	381	4.1
Team	5	449	1437	161	372	58	5	27	168	251	12	2	149	.259	.368	.363	.731	+5	2	6	25	C434	83	3.3
/150	2	150	480	54	124	10	2	9	56	84	4	1	50	.259	.368	.363	.731	+5	1	2	33	C145	28	1.1

WYNN, JIMMY JAMES SHERMAN "THE TOY CANNON" B3.12.1942 HAMILTON OH BR/TR/5'9"/(159–170) D7.10 COL CENTRAL ST. OF(298/1181/355)

YEAR	TM LG	G	AB	R	H	2B	3B	HR	RBI	BB	IB	HP	SO	AVG	OBP	SLG	OPS	AOPS	SB	CS	SB%	GAMES AT POSITION	DL	BFW
1977	NY A	30	77	7	11	2	1	1	3	15	1	0	16	.143	.283	.234	.517	-57	1	0	100	D15,O8(5/0/3)	0	-0.5
Total	15	1920	6653	1105	1665	285	39	291	964	1224	84	27	1427	.250	.366	.436	.802	+29	225	101	69	O1810C,D30,S21,3b2	59	29.6

YEAGER, JOE JOSEPH FRANCIS "LITTLE JOE" B8.28.1875 PHILADELPHIA PA D7.2.1937 DETROIT MI BR/TR/5'10"/160 D4.22 ▲

YEAR	TM LG	G	AB	R	H	2B	3B	HR	RBI	BB	IB	HP	SO	AVG	OBP	SLG	OPS	AOPS	SB	CS	SB%	GAMES AT POSITION	DL	BFW
1905	NY A	115	401	54	107	16	7	0	42	25	—	13	—	.267	.330	.342	.672	+2	8	—	—	3b91,S21	—	0.6
1906	NY A	57	123	20	37	6	1	0	12	13	—	9	—	.301	.407	.366	.773	+29	3	—	—	S22,2b13,3b3	—	0.7
Total	10	574	1853	204	467	77	29	4	201	110	—	51	—	.252	.312	.331	.643	-8	37	—	—	3b295,P94,S83,2b48,O18(10/1/7)	—	1.3
Team	2	172	524	74	144	22	8	0	54	38	—	22	0	.275	.349	.347	.696	+9	11	—	—	3b94,S43,2b13	—	1.3
/150	2	150	457	65	126	19	7	0	47	33	—	19	0	.275	.349	.347	.696	+9	10	—	—	3b82,S38,2b11	—	1.1

YOUNG, RALPH RALPH STUART B9.19.1888 PHILADELPHIA PA D1.24.1965 PHILADELPHIA PA BB/TR/5'5"/165 D4.10 COL WASHINGTON COLLEGE

YEAR	TM LG	G	AB	R	H	2B	3B	HR	RBI	BB	IB	HP	SO	AVG	OBP	SLG	OPS	AOPS	SB	CS	SB%	GAMES AT POSITION	DL	BFW
1913	NY A	7	15	2	1	0	0	0	0	3	—	0	3	.067	.222	.067	.289	-115	2	—	—	S7	—	-0.2
Total	9	1022	3643	480	898	108	30	4	254	495	—	15	235	.247	.339	.296	.635	-21	92	59	100	2b993,S18/3b	—	-11.9

ZALUSKY, JACK JOHN FRANCIS B6.22.1879 MINNEAPOLIS MN D8.11.1935 MINNEAPOLIS MN BR/TR/5'11.5"/172 D9.4

YEAR	TM LG	G	AB	R	H	2B	3B	HR	RBI	BB	IB	HP	SO	AVG	OBP	SLG	OPS	AOPS	SB	CS	SB%	GAMES AT POSITION	DL	BFW
1903	NY A	7	16	2	5	0	0	0	1	1	—	0	—	.313	.353	.313	.666	-5	0	—	—	C6/1b	—	-0.1

ZEBER, GEORGE GEORGE WILLIAM B8.29.1950 ELLWOOD CITY PA BB/TR/5'11"/(180–181) DR 1968 NYA 5/88 D5.7

YEAR	TM LG	G	AB	R	H	2B	3B	HR	RBI	BB	IB	HP	SO	AVG	OBP	SLG	OPS	AOPS	SB	CS	SB%	GAMES AT POSITION	DL	BFW
1977	†NY A	25	65	8	21	3	0	3	10	9	1	0	11	.323	.405	.508	.913	+48	0	0	0	2b21,S2,3b2/D	0	0.5
1978	NY A	3	6	0	0	0	0	0	0	0	0	0	0	.000	.000	.000	.000	-199	0	0	0	/2b	0	-0.3
Total	2	28	71	8	21	3	0	3	10	9	1	0	11	.296	.375	.465	.840	+29	0	0	0	2b22,3b2,S2/D	0	0.2

ZEIDER, ROLLIE ROLLIE HUBERT "BUNIONS" B11.16.1883 AUBURN IN D9.12.1967 GARRETT IN BR/TR/5'10"/162 D4.14 OF(6/1/1)

YEAR	TM LG	G	AB	R	H	2B	3B	HR	RBI	BB	IB	HP	SO	AVG	OBP	SLG	OPS	AOPS	SB	CS	SB%	GAMES AT POSITION	DL	BFW
1913	NY A	50	159	15	37	2	0	0	12	25	—	1	9	.233	.341	.245	.586	-28	3	—	—	S24,2b19,1b4,3b2	—	-1.2
Total	9	941	3210	393	769	89	22	5	253	334	—	22	138	.240	.315	.286	.601	-23	224	28	100	2b335,3b307,S162,1b106,O8L	—	-13.6

ZEILE, TODD TODD EDWARD B9.9.1965 VAN NUYS CA BR/TR/6'1"/(190–205) DR 1986 STLN 2/55 D8.18 COL UCLA

YEAR	TM LG	G	AB	R	H	2B	3B	HR	RBI	BB	IB	HP	SO	AVG	OBP	SLG	OPS	AOPS	SB	CS	SB%	GAMES AT POSITION	DL	BFW
2003	NY A	66	186	29	39	8	0	6	23	24	0	0	36	.210	.294	.349	.643	-28	0	0	0	3b30,1b23,D8	0	-0.7
Total	16	2158	7573	986	2004	397	23	253	1110	945	47	42	1279	.265	.346	.423	.769	+3	53	51	51	3b1498,1b466,C130,D9,O3L,P2	14	-4.0

ZINN, GUY GUY B2.13.1887 HOLBROOK WV D10.6.1949 NUTTER FORT WV BL/TR/5'10.5"/170 D9.11

YEAR	TM LG	G	AB	R	H	2B	3B	HR	RBI	BB	IB	HP	SO	AVG	OBP	SLG	OPS	AOPS	SB	CS	SB%	GAMES AT POSITION	DL	BFW
1911	NY A	9	27	5	4	0	2	0	1	4	—	1	—	.148	.281	.296	.577	-43	0	—	—	O8(2/4/2)	—	-0.2
1912	NY A	106	401	56	105	15	10	6	55	50	—	1	—	.262	.345	.394	.739	+5	17	11	61	O106(13/31/61)	—	-1.3
1913	Bos N	36	138	15	41	8	2	1	15	4	—	1	23	.297	.322	.406	.728	+5	3	4	43	O35(1/34/0)	—	-0.1
1914	Bal F	61	225	30	63	10	6	3	25	16	—	3	26	.280	.336	.418	.754	+1	6	—	—	O57(31/12/14)	—	-1.1
1915	Bal F	102	312	30	84	18	3	5	43	35	—	0	28	.269	.343	.394	.737	+4	2	—	—	O88(63/17/8)	—	-0.8
Total	5	314	1103	136	297	51	23	15	139	109	—	6	77	.269	.338	.398	.736	+3	28	15	100	O294(110/98/85)	—	-3.5
Team	2	115	428	61	109	15	12	6	56	54	—	2	0	.255	.341	.388	.729	+2	17	11	100	O114(15/35/33)	—	-1.5
/150	3	150	558	80	142	20	16	8	73	70	—	3	0	.255	.341	.388	.729	+2	22	14	100	O149(20/46/43)	—	-2.0

ZUVELLA, PAUL PAUL B10.31.1958 SAN MATEO CA BR/TR/6'0"/(172–178) DR 1980 ATLN 15/367 D9.4 C1 COL STANFORD

YEAR	TM LG	G	AB	R	H	2B	3B	HR	RBI	BB	IB	HP	SO	AVG	OBP	SLG	OPS	AOPS	SB	CS	SB%	GAMES AT POSITION	DL	BFW
1986	NY A	21	48	2	4	1	0	0	2	5	0	0	4	.083	.170	.104	.274	-123	0	0	0	S21	0	-0.4
1987	NY A	14	34	2	6	0	0	0	0	0	0	0	4	.176	.176	.176	.352	-106	0	0	0	2b7,S6/3b	0	-0.5
Total	9	209	491	41	109	17	2	2	20	34	1	2	50	.222	.275	.277	.552	-48	2	0	100	S133,2b55,3b13,D3	0	-3.2
Team	2	35	82	4	10	1	0	0	2	5	0	0	8	.122	.172	.134	.306	-116	0	0	0	S27,2b7/3	0	-0.9

Batters

Yankees Batters Home & Away Statistics

The table below shows Yankees batting statistics at home and on the road for a number of prominent players. A player normally does about 10% better at home, based on normalized OPS or earned run average. Yankee Stadium is often thought of as an easy park for left-handed batters because of its short right field foul line. In reality, though, it is a neutral park for lefty swingers and puts right-handers at a great disadvantage. This benefits the Yankees as a team, because they can afford to stock up on left-handed sluggers, but does not benefit the sluggers themselves. That said, there are still some surprises when one looks at the home/road splits for the greatest New York hitters.

Babe Ruth was a terror in the Polo Grounds, where he played from 1920–22. "The Bambino" had incredible slugging percentages of .985 in 1920 and .929 in 1921, both easily the highest of all-time. Ruth's home/away ratio for those two years was 1.35, compared to his 1.04 in Yankee Stadium—well below the 1.10 average. Had Yankee Stadium not been built, the Babe might have bashed 70 or more home runs at the Polo Grounds and still owned the single-season home run record. In the field, Ruth did benefit from the smaller right field at the Stadium. He typically played right in Yankee Stadium and left field in all the other parks except Washington, giving him slightly less ground to cover.

Lou Gehrig, on the other hand, never was able to hit well at home, and his .90 rating is almost as bad as the right-handed Joe DiMaggio at .86. Gehrig batted .350 away from the Bronx, compiling the incredible total of 117 runs batted in on the road in 1930. Showing that he wasn't a fluke, he posted 98 RBIs in road games in two other seasons. His stats are so unusual that they basically look like he was a right-handed hitter. Other righty power hitters for the Bombers that did poorly at home were Joe Gordon (.83) and Elston Howard (.93).

The Yankees' lefty sluggers are pretty much clustered around the 1.10 norm, with no one taking great advantage of their home park. Yogi Berra was at 1.13; Earle Combs, 1.07; Bill Dickey, 1.07; Don Mattingly, 1.13; and Graig Nettles, 1.10. The main difference for Berra and Dickey was that they hit a few more homers at home that would have been doubles on the road. Some, like Gehrig, were well below: Tommy Henrich at .93; Reggie Jackson, .91; and Charlie Keller, 1.00. New York's better righty line-drive hitters were able to achieve an average home park ratio; for example, Derek Jeter is at 1.10 and Willie Randolph finished at 1.11. Switch-hitters were about the same: Mickey Mantle, 1.08; Jorge Posada, 1.10; and Bernie Williams, 1.10. So let's put to rest the idea that Yankee Stadium was a boon to lefties.

YR	G-H	AB	R	H	2B	3B	HR	RBI	BB	HB	AVG	OBP	SLG	OPS	G-A	AB	R	H	2B	3B	HR	RBI	BB	HB	AVG	OBP	SLG	OPS	H/A
Frank Baker LHB																													
1916	42	140	19	44	9	1	6	0	15	3	.314	.392	.521	.914	39	139	24	47	5	3	7	29	13	0	.338	.395	.568	.963	0.91
1917	67	247	26	63	10	1	5	0	22	4	.255	.326	.364	.690	68	277	28	83	10	0	2	0	24	1	.300	.358	.357	.715	0.93
1918	67	268	34	80	10	3	5	0	22	1	.299	.354	.414	.768	49	182	21	51	12	0	0	28	12	2	.280	.332	.346	.678	1.26
1919	73	290	42	83	12	1	8	0	20	1	.286	.334	.417	.752	30	95	6	18	7	0	0	7	2	2	.189	.222	.263	.485	2.09
1921	45	148	25	46	4	2	9	43	14	2	.311	.378	.547	.925	0	0	0	0	0	0	0	0	0	0	.000	.000	.000	.000	0.00
total	294	1093	146	316	45	8	33	43	93	11	.289	.351	.435	.786	186	693	79	199	34	3	9	64	51	5	.287	.340	.384	.724	1.17
Yogi Berra LHB																													
1946	3	9	2	4	0	0	2	3	0	0	.444	.444	1.111	1.556	4	13	1	4	1	0	0	1	1	0	.308	.357	.385	.742	3.13
1947	45	156	21	37	3	2	6	36	6	0	.237	.265	.397	.663	38	137	20	45	12	1	5	18	7	0	.328	.361	.540	.901	0.47
1948	62	229	35	71	8	5	9	52	11	1	.310	.344	.507	.851	63	240	35	72	16	5	5	46	14	0	.300	.339	.471	.809	1.09
1949	67	245	31	65	8	0	14	50	14	4	.265	.316	.469	.785	49	170	28	50	12	2	6	41	8	2	.294	.333	.494	.827	0.90
1950	75	283	59	93	13	4	14	63	34	1	.329	.403	.551	.954	76	314	57	99	17	2	14	61	21	3	.315	.364	.516	.880	1.17
1951	72	258	45	74	8	1	12	41	25	1	.287	.352	.465	.817	69	289	47	87	11	3	15	47	19	2	.301	.348	.516	.864	0.91
1952	71	258	56	73	8	1	18	45	33	4	.283	.373	.531	.904	71	276	41	73	9	0	12	53	33	0	.264	.343	.428	.771	1.33
1953	67	227	34	67	10	3	13	44	32	2	.295	.387	.537	.924	70	276	46	82	13	2	14	64	18	1	.297	.342	.511	.853	1.18
1954	76	278	40	88	10	1	15	65	24	3	.317	.377	.522	.899	75	306	48	91	18	5	7	60	32	1	.297	.366	.458	.823	1.17
1955	74	263	43	81	8	0	20	70	36	0	.308	.391	.567	.958	73	278	41	66	12	3	7	38	24	7	.237	.314	.378	.692	1.75
1956	73	261	45	84	14	2	19	52	31	2	.322	.398	.609	1.007	67	260	48	71	15	0	11	53	34	3	.273	.364	.458	.821	1.43
1957	67	224	32	62	5	2	17	49	30	0	.277	.362	.545	.907	67	258	42	59	9	0	7	33	27	1	.229	.304	.345	.649	1.77
1958	63	209	29	52	2	1	13	48	15	2	.249	.305	.455	.760	59	224	31	63	15	2	9	42	20	0	.281	.340	.487	.827	0.83
1959	64	218	28	57	9	1	10	32	22	1	.261	.332	.450	.781	67	254	36	77	16	0	9	37	21	3	.303	.363	.472	.836	0.87
1960	55	158	22	50	5	1	9	26	17	1	.316	.386	.532	.918	65	201	24	49	9	0	6	36	21	2	.244	.321	.378	.700	1.61
1961	54	176	30	51	4	0	12	29	12	0	.290	.335	.517	.852	65	219	32	56	7	0	10	32	23	2	.256	.332	.425	.757	1.23
1962	48	114	10	16	1	0	4	10	20	1	.140	.274	.254	.528	38	118	15	36	7	0	6	25	4	1	.305	.333	.517	.850	0.31
1963	32	73	7	17	2	0	3	12	7	1	.233	.309	.384	.692	32	74	13	26	4	0	5	16	8	0	.351	.415	.608	1.023	0.38
total	1068	3639	569	1042	118	24	210	727	369	24	.286	.356	.505	.861	1048	3907	605	1106	203	25	148	703	335	28	.283	.344	.461	.806	1.13
Wade Boggs LHB																													
1993	70	271	40	85	13	0	1	24	33	0	.314	.388	.373	.761	73	289	43	84	13	1	1	35	41	0	.291	.379	.353	.732	1.08
1994	50	181	33	65	8	1	6	25	28	0	.359	.445	.514	.959	47	185	28	60	11	0	5	30	33	1	.324	.429	.465	.894	1.14
1995	65	253	51	96	15	2	4	35	40	0	.379	.464	.502	.966	61	207	25	53	7	2	1	28	34	0	.256	.361	.324	.685	1.84
1996	71	273	53	90	17	0	2	25	35	0	.330	.406	.414	.820	61	228	27	66	12	2	0	16	32	0	.289	.377	.360	.737	1.23
1997	48	157	26	45	10	0	0	5	20	0	.287	.367	.350	.718	56	196	29	58	13	1	4	23	28	0	.296	.384	.434	.818	0.76
total	304	1135	203	381	63	3	13	114	156	0	.336	.416	.431	.847	298	1105	152	321	56	6	11	132	168	1	.290	.385	.382	.767	1.21
Earle Combs LHB																													
1924	14	13	2	4	2	0	0	2	3	0	.308	.438	.462	.899	10	22	8	10	3	0	0	0	1	0	.455	.478	.591	1.069	0.70
1925	78	305	57	107	15	8	2	36	31	2	.351	.414	.472	.886	72	288	60	96	21	5	1	25	34	2	.333	.407	.451	.859	1.06
1926	68	281	50	84	10	5	6	29	19	1	.299	.346	.434	.780	77	325	63	97	21	7	2	27	28	2	.298	.358	.425	.782	0.99
1927	76	313	55	112	13	10	5	30	31	1	.358	.417	.511	.929	76	335	82	119	23	13	1	34	31	1	.355	.411	.510	.922	1.02
1928	75	289	56	89	8	12	4	29	43	1	.308	.399	.460	.860	74	337	62	105	25	9	3	27	34	1	.312	.376	.466	.842	1.05
1929	69	281	69	110	20	10	3	37	40	0	.391	.467	.566	1.033	73	305	50	92	13	5	0	28	29	0	.302	.362	.377	.739	1.79
1930	65	244	54	83	13	13	5	40	34	0	.340	.421	.561	.982	72	288	75	100	17	9	2	42	40	0	.347	.427	.490	.916	1.13
1931	68	262	53	78	12	6	4	33	35	2	.298	.385	.435	.820	70	301	67	101	19	7	1	25	33	1	.336	.403	.455	.858	0.91
1932	71	281	68	88	12	7	5	41	43	1	.313	.406	.459	.865	73	310	75	102	20	3	4	24	38	1	.329	.404	.452	.856	1.02
1933	58	182	46	57	8	8	2	23	22	0	.313	.387	.478	.865	64	235	40	68	14	8	3	37	25	1	.289	.360	.455	.815	1.13
1934	24	93	15	27	2	2	1	7	16	0	.290	.394	.387	.782	39	158	32	53	11	3	1	18	24	0	.335	.423	.462	.885	0.77
1935	44	130	21	33	3	1	1	12	16	0	.254	.336	.315	.651	45	168	26	51	4	3	2	23	20	0	.304	.378	.399	.776	0.68
total	710	2674	546	872	118	82	38	319	333	8	.326	.402	.474	.877	745	3072	640	994	191	72	20	310	337	9	.324	.392	.452	.844	1.07

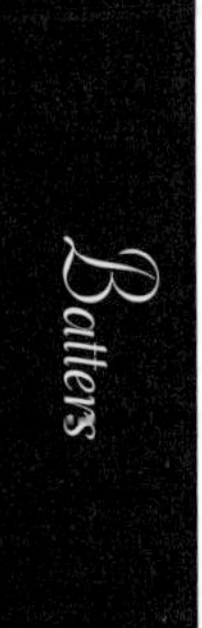

Bill Dickey LHB

YR	G-H	AB	R	H	2B	3B	HR	RBI	BB	HB	AVG	OBP	SLG	OPS	G-A	AB	R	H	2B	3B	HR	RBI	BB	HB	AVG	OBP	SLG	OPS	H/A
1928	7	11	1	3	1	1	0	2	0	0	.273	.273	.545	.818	3	4	0	0	0	0	0	0	0	0	.000	.000	.000	.000	0.00
1929	66	227	30	71	9	4	5	31	6	1	.313	.333	.454	.787	64	220	30	74	21	2	5	34	8	0	.336	.360	.518	.878	0.80
1930	51	158	26	54	11	5	3	40	11	0	.342	.385	.532	.916	58	208	29	70	14	2	2	25	10	0	.337	.367	.452	.819	1.22
1931	67	252	37	79	9	6	4	38	20	0	.313	.364	.444	.808	63	225	28	77	8	4	2	40	19	0	.342	.393	.440	.833	0.94
1932	51	183	35	59	9	1	7	32	19	0	.322	.386	.497	.883	57	240	31	72	11	3	8	52	15	0	.300	.341	.471	.812	1.19
1933	63	213	25	66	9	3	9	45	24	1	.310	.382	.507	.889	67	265	33	86	15	5	5	62	20	1	.325	.381	.475	.856	1.07
1934	55	211	23	56	10	1	6	30	14	1	.265	.311	.400	.722	49	184	33	71	14	3	6	42	24	1	.386	.459	.592	1.052	0.37
1935	58	211	[illegible]	64	12	2	11	35	16	3	.303	.361	.536	.896	62	237	23	61	14	4	3	46	19	3	.257	.320	.388	.709	1.51
1936	51	191	43	67	10	2	14	52	21	1	.351	.418	.644	1.062	61	232	56	86	16	6	8	55	25	2	.371	.436	.595	1.031	1.04
1937	72	270	47	94	13	1	21	85	39	1	.348	.432	.637	1.069	68	260	40	82	22	1	8	48	34	3	.315	.401	.500	.901	1.35
1938	64	213	50	76	9	1	23	83	29	1	.357	.436	.732	1.169	68	241	34	66	18	3	4	32	46	1	.274	.392	.423	.816	1.84
1939	65	217	48	58	5	1	19	49	42	2	.267	.391	.562	.953	63	263	50	87	18	2	5	56	35	2	.331	.413	.471	.885	1.14
1940	57	194	23	45	5	0	5	31	27	0	.232	.326	.335	.661	49	178	22	47	6	1	4	23	21	2	.264	.348	.376	.725	0.83
1941	59	187	15	55	10	2	5	40	25	1	.294	.380	.449	.829	50	161	20	44	5	3	2	31	20	2	.273	.361	.379	.740	1.24
1942	43	140	14	43	4	1	1	16	14	0	.307	.370	.371	.742	39	128	14	36	9	0	1	21	12	1	.281	.348	.375	.723	1.06
1943	46	129	13	44	6	1	2	14	22	0	.341	.437	.450	.887	39	113	16	41	12	1	2	19	19	0	.363	.455	.540	.994	0.79
1946	32	78	6	20	4	0	0	7	12	1	.256	.363	.308	.670	22	56	4	15	4	0	2	3	7	0	.268	.349	.446	.796	0.73
total	907	3085	467	954	136	32	135	630	341	13	.309	.380	.505	.886	882	3215	463	1015	207	40	67	579	337	18	.316	.384	.467	.851	1.07

Joe DiMaggio RHB

YR	G-H	AB	R	H	2B	3B	HR	RBI	BB	HB	AVG	OBP	SLG	OPS	G-A	AB	R	H	2B	3B	HR	RBI	BB	HB	AVG	OBP	SLG	OPS	H/A
1936	67	288	51	90	18	8	8	53	14	2	.313	.349	.514	.863	71	349	81	116	26	7	21	72	10	2	.332	.355	.628	.982	0.80
1937	77	306	83	105	10	8	19	80	42	3	.343	.427	.634	1.061	74	315	68	110	19	7	27	87	22	2	.349	.395	.711	1.106	0.97
1938	74	296	67	104	23	8	15	75	30	0	.351	.411	.635	1.046	71	303	62	90	9	5	17	65	29	2	.297	.362	.528	.890	1.34
1939	64	237	46	83	16	1	12	50	22	2	.350	.410	.578	.988	56	225	62	93	16	5	18	76	30	2	.413	.486	.769	1.255	0.59
1940	63	234	40	84	12	6	16	67	32	1	.359	.438	.667	1.105	69	274	53	95	16	3	15	66	29	2	.347	.413	.591	1.004	1.19
1941	76	292	60	101	21	6	16	69	40	0	.346	.425	.623	1.048	63	249	62	92	22	5	14	56	36	4	.369	.457	.667	1.123	0.86
1942	77	305	51	89	15	6	8	55	29	0	.292	.353	.459	.812	77	305	72	97	14	7	13	59	39	2	.318	.399	.538	.937	0.74
1946	66	254	37	66	8	6	8	35	26	1	.260	.331	.433	.764	66	249	44	80	12	2	17	60	33	1	.321	.403	.590	.993	0.56
1947	70	252	49	77	18	5	9	51	41	1	.306	.405	.524	.929	71	282	48	91	13	5	11	46	23	2	.323	.378	.521	.899	1.08
1948	77	294	54	92	10	8	15	70	30	5	.313	.386	.554	.940	76	300	56	98	16	3	24	85	37	3	.327	.406	.640	1.046	0.82
1949	37	127	25	41	7	3	5	23	28	1	.323	.449	.543	.992	39	145	33	53	7	3	9	44	27	1	.366	.468	.641	1.110	0.81
1950	65	242	48	67	11	6	9	47	35	1	.277	.371	.483	.854	74	283	66	91	22	4	23	75	45	0	.322	.415	.671	1.086	0.61
1951	67	233	37	61	11	2	8	45	29	3	.262	.351	.429	.780	49	182	35	48	11	2	4	26	32	3	.264	.382	.412	.795	0.96
total	880	3360	648	1060	186	73	148	720	398	20	.315	.391	.546	.938	856	3461	742	1154	203	58	213	817	392	26	.333	.405	.610	1.015	0.86

Lou Gehrig LHB

YR	G-H	AB	R	H	2B	3B	HR	RBI	BB	HB	AVG	OBP	SLG	OPS	G-A	AB	R	H	2B	3B	HR	RBI	BB	HB	AVG	OBP	SLG	OPS	H/A
1923	6	4	0	1	1	0	0	2	0	0	.250	.250	.500	.750	7	22	6	10	3	1	1	7	2	0	.455	.500	.818	1.318	0.11
1924	4	6	2	4	0	0	0	2	1	0	.667	.714	.667	1.381	6	6	0	2	1	0	0	3	0	0	.333	.333	.500	.833	2.48
1925	68	237	41	66	14	5	11	42	21	1	.278	.340	.519	.859	58	200	32	63	9	5	9	26	25	1	.315	.394	.545	.939	0.82
1926	75	270	62	81	19	12	4	44	47	1	.300	.406	.504	.909	80	302	73	98	28	8	12	63	58	0	.325	.433	.589	1.023	0.79
1927	77	277	71	96	16	8	24	77	53	2	.347	.455	.722	1.177	78	307	78	122	36	10	23	98	56	1	.397	.492	.805	1.296	0.82
1928	77	262	62	97	26	5	12	66	44	1	.370	.463	.645	1.108	77	300	77	113	21	8	15	76	51	3	.377	.472	.650	1.122	0.97
1929	77	271	60	85	13	7	21	76	59	3	.314	.441	.646	1.087	77	282	67	81	20	2	14	50	63	2	.287	.421	.521	.942	1.29
1930	76	270	59	94	16	10	14	57	48	2	.348	.450	.637	1.087	78	311	84	126	26	7	27	117	53	1	.405	.493	.794	1.287	0.71
1931	77	304	83	92	12	10	24	86	51	0	.303	.403	.645	1.048	78	315	80	119	19	5	22	98	66	0	.378	.486	.679	1.165	0.78
1932	77	289	59	88	13	6	12	60	52	1	.304	.412	.516	.928	79	307	79	120	29	3	22	91	56	2	.391	.488	.720	1.208	0.56
1933	75	281	59	85	12	4	17	69	35	0	.302	.380	.555	.935	77	312	79	113	29	8	15	70	57	1	.362	.462	.651	1.113	0.67
1934	77	290	68	120	20	4	30	98	49	1	.414	.500	.821	1.321	77	289	60	90	20	2	19	67	60	1	.311	.431	.592	1.023	1.55
1935	74	253	45	71	8	5	15	45	64	2	.281	.429	.530	.959	75	282	80	105	18	5	15	74	68	3	.372	.499	.631	1.130	0.70
1936	77	267	81	94	11	1	27	71	69	4	.352	.491	.704	1.195	78	312	86	111	26	6	22	81	61	3	.356	.465	.689	1.155	1.08
1937	79	275	68	104	13	3	24	93	69	1	.378	.504	.709	1.213	78	294	70	96	24	6	13	66	58	3	.327	.442	.582	1.024	1.36
1938	79	287	61	88	12	3	16	58	49	2	.307	.411	.537	.948	78	289	54	82	20	3	13	56	58	3	.284	.409	.509	.917	1.06
1939	5	18	1	3	0	0	0	1	2	0	.167	.250	.167	.417	3	10	1	1	0	0	0	0	3	0	.100	.308	.100	.408	1.48
total	1080	3861	882	1269	206	83	251	947	713	21	.329	.436	.620	1.056	1084	4140	1006	1452	329	79	242	1043	795	24	.351	.458	.644	1.102	0.92

Joe Gordon RHB

YR	G-H	AB	R	H	2B	3B	HR	RBI	BB	HB	AVG	OBP	SLG	OPS	G-A	AB	R	H	2B	3B	HR	RBI	BB	HB	AVG	OBP	SLG	OPS	H/A
1938	59	199	43	49	11	5	13	46	30	2	.246	.351	.548	.898	68	259	40	68	13	2	12	51	26	1	.263	.332	.467	.799	1.23
1939	76	268	36	69	16	3	11	39	30	1	.257	.334	.463	.797	75	299	56	92	16	2	17	72	45	1	.308	.400	.545	.945	0.68
1940	76	298	56	84	15	5	15	50	19	1	.282	.327	.517	.844	79	318	56	89	17	5	15	53	33	2	.280	.351	.506	.858	0.95
1941	78	280	43	70	9	6	8	38	35	2	.250	.338	.411	.748	78	308	61	92	17	1	16	49	37	2	.299	.378	.516	.894	0.69
1942	70	248	34	74	11	1	7	46	36	0	.298	.387	.435	.823	77	290	54	99	18	3	11	57	43	1	.341	.428	.538	.966	0.71
1943	77	274	38	64	10	1	11	35	42	2	.234	.340	.398	.737	75	269	44	71	18	4	6	34	56	0	.264	.391	.428	.818	0.80
1946	53	181	18	39	7	0	4	16	23	3	.215	.314	.320	.634	59	195	17	40	8	0	7	31	26	1	.205	.302	.354	.656	0.95
total	489	1748	268	449	79	21	69	270	215	11	.257	.342	.445	.786	511	1938	328	551	107	17	84	347	266	8	.284	.373	.487	.860	0.83

Tommy Henrich LHB

YR	G-H	AB	R	H	2B	3B	HR	RBI	BB	HB	AVG	OBP	SLG	OPS	G-A	AB	R	H	2B	3B	HR	RBI	BB	HB	AVG	OBP	SLG	OPS	H/A
1937	33	89	18	26	4	2	1	9	20	0	.292	.422	.416	.838	34	117	21	40	10	3	7	33	15	0	.342	.417	.658	1.075	0.64
1938	66	231	69	65	10	3	20	56	47	1	.281	.405	.610	1.015	65	240	40	62	14	4	2	35	45	1	.258	.378	.375	.753	1.70
1939	45	146	23	32	7	0	5	16	19	1	.219	.313	.370	.683	54	201	41	64	11	4	4	41	32	0	.318	.412	.473	.885	0.54
1940	46	155	33	49	15	2	7	32	24	1	.316	.411	.574	.985	44	138	24	41	13	3	3	21	24	1	.297	.405	.500	.905	1.16
1941	76	275	52	78	12	3	15	48	42	3	.284	.384	.513	.897	68	263	54	71	15	2	16	37	39	2	.270	.368	.525	.893	1.02
1942	65	241	42	68	11	3	11	44	33	2	.282	.373	.490	.863	62	242	35	61	19	2	2	23	25	3	.252	.330	.372	.702	1.45
1946	77	278	47	69	12	1	10	47	50	4	.248	.370	.406	.777	73	287	45	73	13	3	9	36	37	3	.254	.346	.415	.760	1.05
1947	68	245	52	69	16	5	4	38	39	2	.282	.385	.437	.821	74	305	57	89	19	8	12	60	32	1	.292	.361	.525	.886	0.90
1948	74	292	69	87	22	8	15	54	37	3	.298	.383	.582	.965	72	296	69	94	20	6	10	46	39	1	.318	.399	.527	.926	1.06
1949	60	205	52	62	8	0	20	55	47	4	.302	.441	.634	1.076	55	206	38	56	12	3	4	30	39	1	.272	.390	.417	.808	1.65
1950	38	81	13	23	6	3	3	14	19	0	.284	.420	.543	.963	35	70	7	18	0	5	3	20	8	0	.257	.333	.529	.862	1.29
total	648	2238	470	628	123	30	111	413	377	21	.281	.389	.511	.900	636	2365	431	669	146	43	72	382	335	13	.283	.375	.472	.847	1.12

Elston Howard RHB

YR	G-H	AB	R	H	2B	3B	HR	RBI	BB	HB	AVG	OBP	SLG	OPS	G-A	AB	R	H	2B	3B	HR	RBI	BB	HB	AVG	OBP	SLG	OPS	H/A
1955	51	131	14	38	2	7	6	28	11	0	.290	.345	.550	.895	46	148	19	43	6	0	4	15	9	1	.291	.335	.412	.748	1.36
1956	51	130	12	32	3	0	2	19	14	0	.246	.319	.315	.635	47	160	23	44	5	3	3	15	7	1	.275	.310	.400	.710	0.82
1957	57	168	11	40	4	2	3	18	9	0	.238	.277	.339	.616	53	188	22	50	9	2	5	26	7	0	.266	.292	.415	.707	0.76
1958	53	175	20	58	10	3	3	27	16	0	.331	.387	.474	.862	50	201	25	60	9	2	8	39	6	0	.299	.319	.483	.801	1.20
1959	63	207	24	49	8	5	5	21	9	1	.237	.272	.396	.668	62	236	35	72	16	1	13	52	11	2	.305	.341	.547	.888	0.52
1960	48	150	11	33	6	2	5	23	16	0	.220	.295	.387	.682	59	173	18	46	5	1	1	16	12	0	.266	.314	.324	.637	1.14
1961	63	211	35	77	9	3	10	38	17	2	.365	.417	.578	0.996	66	235	29	78	8	2	11	39	11	1	.332	.364	.523	.888	1.25
1962	66	218	22	60	16	1	3	31	18	1	.275	.333	.399	.732	70	276	41	78	7	4	18	60	13	0	.283	.315	.533	.847	0.81
1963	66	227	39	62	9	5	10	37	22	5	.273	.350	.489	.839	69	260	36	78	12	1	18	48	13	1	.300	.336	.562	.897	0.91
1964	74	265	24	74	11	3	3	35	22	1	.279	.337	.377	.714	76	285	39	98	16	0	12	49	26	4	.344	.406	.526	.933	0.55
1965	61	203	16	48	8	1	0	22	12	1	.236	.282	.286	.568	49	188	22	43	7	0	9	23	12	0	.229	.275	.410	.685	0.72
1966	60	185	20	61	13	2	1	17	19	1	.330	.395	.438	.833	66	225	18	44	6	0	5	18	18	0	.196	.255	.289	.544	2.06
1967	34	95	6	16	2	0	2	8	6	1	.168	.225	.253	.478	32	104	7	23	4	0	1	9	6	1	.221	.270	.288	.559	0.71
total	747	2365	254	648	101	34	53	324	191	13	.274	.332	.413	.744	745	2679	334	757	110	16	108	409	151	11	.283	.323	.457	.780	0.93

Reggie Jackson LHB

YR	G-H	AB	R	H	2B	3B	HR	RBI	BB	HB	AVG	OBP	SLG	OPS	G-A	AB	R	H	2B	3B	HR	RBI	BB	HB	AVG	OBP	SLG	OPS	H/A
1977	73	247	48	70	17	2	11	42	42	3	.283	.394	.502	.896	73	278	45	80	22	0	21	68	33	0	.288	.363	.594	.957	0.93
1978	71	257	43	74	4	5	17	53	33	4	.288	.378	.541	.918	68	254	39	66	9	0	10	44	25	5	.260	.338	.413	.751	1.43
1979	67	235	39	71	8	1	15	50	32	1	.302	.388	.536	.924	64	230	39	67	16	1	14	39	33	1	.291	.383	.552	.935	0.99

YR	G-H	AB	R	H	2B	3B	HR	RBI	BB	HB	AVG	OBP	SLG	OPS	G-A	AB	R	H	2B	3B	HR	RBI	BB	HB	AVG	OBP	SLG	OPS	H/A
1980	71	256	43	70	3	4	16	46	35	1	.273	.363	.504	.867	72	258	51	84	19	0	25	65	48	1	.326	.433	.690	1.123	0.57
1981	43	145	12	30	1	1	7	22	22	0	.207	.311	.372	.684	51	189	21	49	16	0	8	32	24	1	.259	.346	.471	.817	0.69
total	325	1140	185	315	33	13	66	213	164	9	.276	.372	.502	.873	328	1209	195	346	82	1	78	248	163	8	.286	.375	.549	.924	0.91
DEREK JETER RHB																													
1995	11	36	2	8	3	1	0	5	1	0	.222	.243	.361	.604	4	12	3	4	1	0	0	2	2	0	.333	.429	.417	.845	0.43
1996	79	285	52	86	11	3	3	40	30	3	.302	.374	.393	.767	78	297	52	97	14	3	7	38	18	6	.327	.377	.465	.842	0.84
1997	79	313	61	89	12	3	5	39	38	3	.284	.367	.390	.757	80	341	55	101	19	4	5	31	36	7	.296	.375	.419	.794	0.91
1998	75	312	62	104	14	3	9	37	26	1	.333	.386	.484	.870	74	314	65	99	11	5	10	47	31	4	.315	.384	.478	.862	1.02
1999	81	313	71	103	17	5	15	62	44	6	.329	.421	.559	.981	77	314	63	116	20	4	9	40	47	6	.369	.460	.545	1.005	0.94
2000	76	299	67	101	13	2	8	36	38	5	.338	.421	.475	.896	72	294	52	100	18	2	7	37	30	7	.340	.414	.486	.900	0.99
2001	73	288	63	95	20	1	13	38	28	6	.330	.401	.542	.942	77	326	47	96	15	2	8	36	28	4	.294	.358	.426	.784	1.39
2002	77	297	60	84	14	0	8	31	40	4	.283	.375	.411	.786	80	347	64	107	12	0	10	44	33	3	.308	.373	.429	.803	0.96
2003	63	252	40	80	11	2	7	29	18	6	.317	.377	.460	.837	56	230	47	76	14	1	3	23	25	7	.330	.412	.439	.851	0.96
2004	76	308	58	101	25	1	11	37	24	5	.328	.386	.523	.908	78	335	53	87	19	0	12	41	22	9	.260	.322	.424	.746	1.43
2005	80	322	72	114	14	2	12	34	45	8	.354	.445	.522	.967	79	332	50	88	11	3	7	36	32	3	.265	.335	.380	.715	1.70
2006	76	297	64	105	19	1	8	42	40	4	.354	.437	.505	.942	78	326	54	109	20	2	6	55	29	8	.334	.402	.463	.865	1.18
2007	79	326	55	109	22	1	4	37	28	8	.334	.401	.445	.845	77	313	47	97	17	3	8	36	28	6	.310	.378	.460	.838	1.03
total	925	3648	727	1179	195	25	103	467	400	59	.323	.399	.475	.874	910	3781	652	1177	191	29	92	466	361	70	.311	.382	.450	.832	1.10
CHARLIE KELLER LHB																													
1939	57	180	30	52	11	0	5	30	44	0	.289	.429	.433	.862	54	218	57	81	10	6	6	53	37	0	.372	.463	.555	1.018	0.71
1940	62	220	42	58	5	8	7	37	43	0	.264	.384	.455	.839	76	280	60	85	13	7	14	56	63	0	.304	.431	.550	.981	0.72
1941	68	241	47	71	13	3	17	64	51	1	.295	.420	.585	1.005	72	266	55	80	11	7	16	58	51	0	.301	.413	.575	.988	1.03
1942	77	256	49	66	10	3	13	44	68	2	.258	.417	.473	.890	75	288	57	93	14	6	13	64	46	0	.323	.416	.549	.965	0.86
1943	77	283	53	80	7	6	21	53	47	0	.283	.385	.572	.957	64	229	44	59	8	5	10	33	59	0	.258	.410	.467	.877	1.16
1945	31	113	21	37	5	3	8	28	21	0	.327	.433	.637	1.070	13	50	5	12	2	1	2	6	10	0	.240	.367	.440	.807	1.63
1946	76	265	44	72	17	3	18	52	55	2	.272	.401	.562	.963	74	273	54	76	12	7	12	49	58	2	.278	.408	.505	.914	1.09
1947	20	63	18	18	4	1	8	21	21	0	.286	.464	.762	1.226	25	88	18	18	2	0	5	15	20	1	.205	.358	.398	.756	2.21
1948	40	115	15	31	7	0	3	19	23	0	.270	.391	.409	.800	43	132	26	35	8	2	3	25	18	0	.265	.353	.424	.778	1.07
1949	33	73	12	18	3	0	2	11	15	1	.247	.382	.370	.752	27	43	5	11	1	1	1	5	10	1	.256	.407	.395	.803	0.87
1952	0	0	0	0	0	0	0	0	0	0	.000	.000	.000	.000	2	1	0	0	0	0	0	0	0	0	.000	.000	.000	.000	0.00
total	541	1809	331	503	82	27	102	359	388	6	.278	.407	.522	.930	525	1868	381	550	81	42	82	364	372	4	.294	.413	.514	.927	1.00
TONY LAZZERI RHB																													
1926	75	286	43	77	14	9	9	57	22	1	.269	.324	.476	.799	80	303	36	85	14	5	9	57	32	1	.281	.351	.449	.800	0.98
1927	77	266	52	85	18	4	11	51	40	0	.320	.408	.541	.950	76	304	40	91	11	4	7	51	29	0	.299	.360	.431	.791	1.39
1928	59	195	31	56	10	6	5	30	22	1	.287	.362	.477	.839	57	209	31	78	20	5	5	52	21	0	.373	.430	.589	1.019	0.65
1929	75	281	50	101	13	5	5	39	31	1	.359	.425	.495	.920	72	264	51	92	24	6	13	67	37	3	.348	.434	.633	1.067	0.76
1930	71	269	45	68	12	9	4	58	30	1	.253	.330	.409	.739	72	302	64	105	22	6	5	63	30	2	.348	.410	.510	.920	0.61
1931	63	220	33	59	14	4	4	40	33	0	.268	.364	.423	.786	72	264	34	70	13	3	4	43	46	1	.265	.376	.383	.759	1.07
1932	74	261	48	84	10	12	11	64	43	1	.322	.420	.579	0.998	69	249	31	69	18	4	4	49	39	1	.277	.377	.430	.807	1.46
1933	69	245	43	70	9	7	7	43	36	1	.286	.379	.465	.845	70	278	51	84	13	5	11	61	37	1	.302	.386	.504	.890	0.91
1934	57	199	24	52	6	5	7	27	32	0	.261	.364	.447	.811	66	239	35	65	18	1	7	40	39	0	.272	.374	.444	.818	0.98
1935	67	229	30	65	8	5	6	36	28	2	.284	.367	.441	.808	63	248	42	65	10	1	7	47	35	1	.262	.356	.395	.751	1.15
1936	76	258	40	75	13	4	3	48	47	0	.291	.400	.407	.807	74	279	42	79	16	2	11	61	50	1	.283	.394	.473	.867	0.88
1937	64	216	30	60	12	2	8	35	38	0	.278	.386	.463	.849	62	230	26	49	9	1	6	35	33	0	.213	.312	.339	.651	1.60
total	827	2925	469	852	139	72	80	528	402	8	.291	.378	.470	.848	833	3169	483	932	188	43	89	626	428	11	.294	.380	.465	.845	1.01
MICKEY MANTLE SWB																													
1951	51	174	37	46	2	2	7	33	26	0	.264	.360	.420	.780	45	167	24	45	9	3	6	32	17	0	.269	.337	.467	.804	0.97
1952	69	264	42	77	14	1	11	41	37	0	.292	.379	.477	.856	73	285	52	94	23	6	12	46	38	0	.330	.409	.579	.988	0.75
1953	69	241	50	68	12	3	8	35	42	0	.282	.389	.456	.845	58	220	55	68	12	0	13	57	37	0	.309	.409	.541	.949	0.80
1954	73	267	64	77	4	8	14	51	51	0	.288	.403	.521	.923	73	276	65	86	13	4	13	51	51	0	.312	.419	.529	.948	0.94
1955	75	255	67	86	15	7	19	57	58	2	.337	.463	.675	1.138	72	262	54	72	10	4	18	42	55	1	.275	.403	.550	.952	1.38
1956	77	268	67	99	14	3	27	67	54	1	.369	.477	.746	1.223	73	265	65	89	8	2	25	63	58	1	.336	.457	.664	1.121	1.17
1957	73	230	51	89	13	6	14	44	61	0	.387	.515	.678	1.194	71	244	70	84	15	0	20	50	85	0	.344	.514	.652	1.165	1.04
1958	74	246	65	77	9	0	21	43	73	0	.313	.470	.606	1.076	76	273	62	81	12	1	21	54	56	2	.297	.420	.579	0.999	1.17
1959	73	274	47	84	10	1	18	38	44	1	.307	.404	.547	.952	71	267	57	70	13	3	13	37	49	1	.262	.379	.479	.858	1.21
1960	77	260	58	73	8	2	23	49	51	0	.281	.399	.592	.991	76	267	61	72	9	4	17	45	60	1	.270	.405	.524	.930	1.11
1961	74	230	64	76	8	6	24	59	66	0	.330	.480	.730	1.210	79	284	68	87	8	0	30	69	60	0	.306	.427	.651	1.079	1.24
1962	54	165	39	54	6	0	16	37	48	0	.327	.479	.655	1.133	69	212	57	67	9	1	14	52	74	1	.316	.495	.566	1.061	1.12
1963	30	72	19	23	2	0	8	17	23	0	.319	.484	.681	1.165	35	100	21	31	6	0	7	18	17	0	.310	.410	.580	.990	1.35
1964	72	234	55	78	16	2	16	57	49	0	.333	.449	.624	1.073	71	231	37	63	9	0	19	54	50	0	.273	.402	.558	.961	1.23
1965	67	200	23	47	7	1	9	25	51	0	.235	.390	.415	.805	55	161	21	45	5	0	10	21	22	0	.280	.366	.497	.863	0.90
1966	61	177	20	53	8	1	11	28	35	0	.299	.415	.542	.957	47	156	20	43	4	0	12	28	22	0	.276	.365	.532	.897	1.16
1967	72	209	29	50	9	0	10	31	51	0	.239	.388	.426	.814	72	231	34	58	8	0	12	24	56	1	.251	.399	.442	.841	0.94
1968	71	202	29	53	6	1	10	31	47	1	.262	.404	.450	.854	73	233	28	50	8	0	8	23	59	0	.215	.373	.352	.725	1.36
total	1212	3968	826	1210	163	44	266	743	867	5	.305	.430	.569	0.999	1189	4134	851	1205	181	28	270	766	866	8	.291	.415	.545	.960	1.08
TINO MARTINEZ LHB																													
1996	77	286	38	81	12	0	9	64	33	1	.283	.359	.420	.779	78	309	44	93	16	0	16	53	35	1	.301	.374	.508	.882	0.79
1997	78	280	40	79	12	2	18	63	38	1	.282	.370	.532	.902	80	314	56	97	19	0	26	78	37	2	.309	.385	.618	1.003	0.82
1998	70	259	46	75	18	0	12	61	31	3	.290	.372	.498	.870	72	272	46	74	15	1	16	62	30	3	.272	.351	.511	.862	1.04
1999	80	286	33	65	12	0	7	38	34	1	.227	.312	.343	.654	79	303	62	90	15	2	21	67	35	2	.297	.374	.568	.941	0.44
2000	78	282	36	70	16	2	12	48	26	4	.248	.321	.447	.767	77	287	33	77	21	2	4	43	26	4	.268	.338	.397	.735	1.07
2001	79	298	52	91	14	2	22	66	23	1	.305	.357	.587	.944	75	291	37	74	10	0	12	47	19	1	.254	.302	.412	.715	1.61
2005	65	143	19	41	5	0	9	26	18	3	.287	.378	.510	.889	66	160	24	32	4	0	8	23	20	0	.200	.289	.375	.664	1.67
total	527	1834	264	502	89	6	89	366	203	14	.274	.351	.474	.825	527	1936	302	537	100	5	103	373	202	13	.277	.350	.494	.843	0.96
DON MATTINGLY LHB																													
1982	6	12	0	2	0	0	0	0	0	0	.167	.167	.167	.333	1	0	0	0	0	0	0	1	0	0	.000	.000	.000	.000	0.00
1983	43	134	19	41	11	1	0	17	16	0	.306	.380	.403	.783	48	145	15	38	4	3	4	15	5	1	.262	.291	.414	.705	1.28
1984	73	282	41	90	19	0	12	49	19	0	.319	.362	.514	.876	80	321	50	117	25	2	11	61	22	1	.364	.407	.558	.965	0.81
1985	80	318	56	107	21	1	22	87	24	0	.336	.383	.616	0.999	79	334	51	104	27	2	13	58	32	2	.311	.375	.521	.896	1.20
1986	80	320	54	107	23	0	17	60	28	1	.334	.390	.566	.955	82	357	63	131	30	2	14	53	25	0	.367	.408	.580	.988	0.93
1987	70	283	51	95	14	1	17	56	24	0	.336	.388	.572	.960	71	286	42	91	24	1	13	59	27	1	.318	.379	.545	.924	1.07
1988	74	296	49	87	14	0	11	42	18	2	.294	.339	.453	.791	70	303	45	99	23	0	7	46	23	1	.327	.376	.472	.848	0.86
1989	81	317	48	106	20	0	19	72	26	1	.334	.387	.577	.964	77	314	31	85	17	2	4	41	25	0	.271	.324	.376	.700	1.73
1990	48	183	14	45	4	0	4	20	16	1	.246	.310	.333	.643	54	211	26	56	12	0	1	22	12	2	.265	.311	.336	.648	0.99
1991	71	266	34	81	21	0	7	40	22	1	.305	.360	.462	.822	81	321	30	88	14	0	2	28	24	3	.274	.330	.336	.667	1.46
1992	76	303	51	96	22	0	6	42	27	1	.317	.375	.449	.823	81	337	38	88	18	0	8	44	12	0	.261	.287	.386	.672	1.47
1993	65	241	42	73	15	2	8	40	32	2	.303	.389	.481	.870	69	289	36	81	12	0	9	46	29	0	.280	.346	.415	.761	1.28
1994	46	173	23	51	6	0	3	22	24	0	.295	.381	.382	.762	51	199	39	62	14	1	3	29	36	0	.312	.417	.437	.854	0.79
1995	64	238	30	72	17	1	5	27	15	0	.303	.344	.445	.789	64	220	29	60	15	1	2	22	25	1	.273	.350	.377	.727	1.16
total	877	3366	512	1053	207	6	131	574	291	9	.313	.369	.495	.864	908	3637	495	1100	235	14	91	525	297	12	.302	.357	.450	.807	1.13
THURMAN MUNSON RHB																													
1969	15	49	6	12	1	2	1	8	6	0	.245	.327	.408	.735	11	37	0	10	0	0	0	1	4	0	.270	.341	.270	.612	1.47
1970	70	218	24	61	8	4	1	20	32	4	.280	.382	.367	.749	62	235	35	76	17	0	5	33	25	3	.323	.395	.460	.855	0.76

YR	G-H	AB	R	H	2B	3B	HR	RBI	BB	HB	AVG	OBP	SLG	OPS	G-A	AB	R	H	2B	3B	HR	RBI	BB	HB	AVG	OBP	SLG	OPS	H/A
1971	59	206	29	48	6	1	4	21	20	4	.233	.313	.330	.643	66	245	42	65	9	3	6	21	32	3	.265	.357	.400	.757	0.70
1972	69	235	25	68	9	2	3	24	20	3	.289	.353	.383	.736	71	276	29	75	7	1	4	22	27	0	.272	.337	.348	.684	1.15
1973	71	236	41	73	14	3	7	35	26	3	.309	.385	.483	.868	76	283	39	83	15	1	13	39	22	1	.293	.346	.491	.838	1.09
1974	77	255	36	72	13	0	7	32	28	1	.282	.356	.416	.771	67	262	28	63	6	2	6	28	16	0	.240	.284	.347	.632	1.45
1975	76	287	42	89	13	1	4	43	24	1	.310	.365	.404	.770	81	310	41	101	11	2	8	59	21	5	.326	.378	.452	.830	0.86
1976	75	297	32	83	16	1	5	36	14	3	.279	.318	.391	.709	77	319	47	103	11	0	12	69	15	6	.323	.365	.470	.835	0.70
1977	75	284	42	91	13	3	8	41	20	1	.320	.367	.472	.839	74	311	43	92	15	2	10	59	19	1	.306	[illegible]	.455	.792	1.13
1978	75	299	39	94	16	1	2	33	19	1	.314	.357	.395	.752	70	310	34	89	11	0	4	38	16	2	.280	.318	.352	.671	1.24
1979	46	175	22	60	11	2	0	19	16	0	.343	.398	.429	.826	51	207	20	50	7	1	3	20	16	0	.242	.296	.329	.624	1.65
total	708	2541	338	751	120	20	42	312	225	21	.296	.358	.408	.766	715	2803	358	807	109	12	71	389	213	21	.288	.343	.411	.754	1.04
Graig Nettles LHB																													
1973	79	270	36	65	7	0	12	47	35	3	.241	.334	.400	.734	81	282	29	64	11	0	10	34	43	4	.227	.337	.372	.710	1.07
1974	78	268	29	57	9	0	9	31	31	2	.213	.299	.347	.646	77	298	45	82	12	1	13	44	28	1	.275	.339	.453	.792	0.65
1975	77	278	37	80	12	2	14	54	25	1	.288	.349	.496	.845	80	303	34	75	12	2	7	37	26	1	.248	.309	.370	.679	1.47
1976	80	286	49	78	13	1	18	48	30	3	.273	.348	.514	.862	78	297	39	70	16	1	14	45	32	1	.236	.312	.438	.750	1.29
1977	79	288	45	82	13	3	18	56	32	1	.285	.358	.538	.896	79	301	54	68	10	1	19	51	36	2	.226	.313	.455	.768	1.33
1978	80	289	44	82	10	2	16	52	35	3	.284	.367	.498	.865	79	298	37	80	13	0	11	41	24	3	.268	.329	.423	.752	1.29
1979	73	258	37	67	9	0	11	41	24	0	.260	.323	.422	.745	72	263	34	65	6	1	9	32	35	0	.247	.336	.380	.716	1.07
1980	46	161	34	44	7	0	11	21	20	1	.273	.357	.522	.879	43	163	18	35	7	0	5	24	22	0	.215	.308	.350	.658	1.65
1981	49	162	23	45	3	0	11	30	24	0	.278	.371	.500	.871	54	187	23	40	4	1	4	16	23	1	.214	.303	.310	.613	1.04
1982	67	222	24	47	8	1	10	27	23	0	.212	.286	.392	.678	55	183	20	47	3	1	8	28	28	1	.257	.358	.415	.774	0.74
1983	61	209	25	65	11	1	11	40	21	1	.311	.377	.531	.908	68	253	31	58	6	2	9	29	30	2	.229	.316	.375	.691	1.61
total	769	2691	383	712	102	10	141	453	300	15	.265	.342	.467	.809	766	2828	367	684	100	10	109	381	327	16	.242	.324	.400	.724	1.22
Paul O'Neill LHB																													
1993	73	249	37	81	17	1	8	39	20	2	.325	.380	.498	.878	68	249	34	74	17	0	12	36	24	0	.297	.359	.510	.869	1.04
1994	52	176	32	72	12	1	10	40	28	0	.409	.490	.659	1.149	51	192	36	60	13	0	11	43	44	0	.313	.441	.552	.993	1.31
1995	64	226	44	72	17	3	12	59	44	0	.319	.430	.580	1.009	63	234	38	66	13	1	10	37	27	1	.282	.359	.474	.833	1.42
1996	73	252	44	82	11	1	7	41	53	2	.325	.446	.460	.907	77	294	45	83	24	0	12	50	49	2	.282	.388	.486	.875	1.10
1997	75	263	42	81	19	0	10	53	40	0	.308	.399	.494	.894	74	290	47	98	23	0	11	64	35	0	.338	.409	.531	.940	0.91
1998	77	290	46	94	17	1	10	52	31	0	.324	.389	.493	.883	75	312	49	97	23	1	14	64	26	2	.311	.368	.526	.893	1.00
1999	78	292	31	74	17	2	9	50	43	1	.253	.351	.418	.769	75	305	39	96	22	2	10	60	23	1	.315	.365	.498	.863	0.80
2000	72	279	46	80	15	0	10	51	30	0	.287	.356	.448	.804	70	287	33	80	11	0	8	49	21	0	.279	.328	.401	.729	1.20
2001	68	251	43	73	16	0	13	40	24	1	.291	.355	.510	.865	69	259	34	63	17	1	8	30	24	1	.243	.310	.409	.719	1.39
total	632	2278	365	709	141	9	89	425	313	6	.311	.396	.498	.894	622	2422	355	717	163	5	96	433	273	7	.296	.369	.486	.855	1.10
Jorge Posada SWB																													
1995	1	0	0	0	0	0	0	0	0	0	.000	.000	.000	.000	3	6	0	0	0	0	0	0	1	0	.000	.143	.000	.143	0.00
1996	5	8	1	1	0	0	0	0	0	0	.125	.125	.125	.250	36	110	20	25	5	0	4	16	21	2	.227	.361	.382	.743	-.33
1997	24	78	9	22	7	0	2	9	9	1	.282	.364	.449	.812	58	191	32	49	8	0	11	33	23	0	.257	.336	.471	.808	1.03
1998	53	167	24	47	15	0	6	30	24	0	.281	.372	.479	.851	58	211	24	56	12	2	8	39	20	3	.265	.338	.455	.793	1.15
1999	54	168	26	37	7	0	4	18	33	0	.220	.348	.333	.682	76	255	40	66	17	0	10	30	54	1	.259	.390	.443	.833	0.64
2000	75	250	52	79	18	1	18	56	53	7	.316	.448	.612	1.060	74	268	30	74	15	0	8	42	33	4	.276	.364	.422	.786	1.68
2001	64	216	29	60	13	1	14	53	29	2	.278	.368	.542	.910	73	262	37	70	22	1	8	48	41	0	.267	.366	.450	.817	1.21
2002	70	249	42	67	18	0	12	51	40	3	.269	.377	.486	.863	74	273	45	81	17	0	15	56	49	1	.297	.406	.524	.929	0.86
2003	68	208	38	54	7	0	15	45	44	9	.260	.410	.510	.920	72	244	42	67	23	0	10	45	47	7	.275	.406	.492	.898	1.05
2004	65	205	30	55	8	0	11	36	41	2	.268	.395	.468	.863	72	247	36	65	13	0	8	31	31	2	.263	.350	.413	.763	1.26
2005	70	227	31	59	10	0	11	40	35	0	.260	.359	.449	.808	74	250	36	64	11	2	12	48	33	6	.256	.356	.460	.816	0.98
2006	69	215	29	65	16	0	11	45	31	5	.302	.402	.530	.933	71	247	40	85	27	1	9	49	39	2	.344	.438	.571	1.008	0.85
2007	73	259	51	86	15	0	11	41	35	4	.332	.419	.517	.937	77	313	47	97	17	3	8	36	28	6	.310	.378	.460	.838	1.24
total	691	2250	362	632	134	2	115	424	374	33	.281	.391	.496	.887	818	2877	429	799	187	9	111	473	420	34	.278	.376	.465	.841	1.11
Willie Randolph RHB																													
1976	65	214	26	60	8	3	0	18	30	1	.280	.371	.346	.717	60	216	33	55	7	1	1	22	28	1	.255	.343	.310	.653	1.20
1977	74	255	42	68	11	8	2	20	39	1	.267	.366	.396	.762	73	296	49	83	17	3	2	20	25	0	.280	.336	.378	.715	1.13
1978	66	239	41	67	8	5	2	22	37	2	.280	.381	.381	.762	68	260	46	72	10	1	1	20	45	2	.277	.388	.335	.722	1.12
1979	78	277	48	78	10	6	2	27	55	1	.282	.402	.383	.785	75	297	50	77	5	7	3	34	40	2	.259	.351	.354	.705	1.23
1980	72	269	57	83	13	4	2	19	62	0	.309	.438	.409	.847	66	244	42	68	10	3	5	27	57	2	.279	.419	.406	.825	1.05
1981	45	166	32	39	7	2	1	11	30	0	.235	.352	.319	.671	48	191	27	44	7	1	1	13	27	0	.230	.326	.293	.619	1.17
1982	74	270	43	81	10	4	1	14	45	2	.300	.404	.378	.782	70	283	42	74	11	0	2	22	30	1	.261	.334	.322	.656	1.38
1983	55	221	39	64	8	0	1	22	28	0	.290	.369	.339	.709	49	199	34	53	13	1	1	16	25	1	.266	.351	.357	.708	1.00
1984	72	278	47	76	7	2	1	16	45	0	.273	.375	.324	.698	70	286	39	86	17	0	1	15	41	0	.301	.388	.371	.759	0.84
1985	69	221	32	58	12	1	3	21	45	3	.262	.394	.367	.761	74	276	43	79	9	1	2	19	40	1	.286	.379	.348	.726	1.09
1986	74	241	49	75	9	2	2	24	61	1	.311	.452	.390	.842	67	251	27	61	6	0	3	26	33	2	.243	.336	.303	.638	1.64
1987	68	253	56	74	14	2	3	32	44	1	.292	.399	.399	.799	52	196	40	63	10	0	4	35	38	1	.321	.434	.434	.868	0.84
1988	57	206	21	45	7	0	1	13	29	2	.218	.321	.267	.588	53	198	22	48	13	1	1	21	26	0	.242	.330	.333	.664	0.77
total	869	3110	533	868	124	39	21	259	550	14	.279	.390	.364	.754	825	3193	494	863	135	19	27	290	455	13	.270	.364	.350	.713	1.11
Babe Ruth LHB																													
1920	66	204	77	81	21	6	29	71	61	2	.397	.539	.985	1.525	76	254	81	91	15	3	25	66	87	1	.358	.523	.736	1.260	1.37
1921	78	255	94	103	24	7	32	81	79	0	.404	.545	.929	1.474	74	285	83	101	20	9	27	90	65	4	.354	.480	.772	1.252	1.34
1922	53	195	40	58	7	5	14	45	36	0	.297	.407	.600	1.007	57	211	54	70	17	3	21	54	48	1	.332	.458	.739	1.197	0.70
1923	76	246	74	101	26	7	19	63	92	1	.411	.572	.805	1.377	76	276	78	104	19	6	22	68	78	3	.377	.518	.728	1.246	1.21
1924	78	260	70	99	18	4	24	71	66	2	.381	.509	.758	1.267	75	269	73	101	21	3	22	50	76	2	.375	.516	.721	1.237	1.04
1925	56	203	35	59	8	1	11	34	35	2	.291	.400	.502	.902	42	156	26	45	4	1	14	32	24	0	.288	.383	.596	.979	0.89
1926	75	241	68	88	13	2	23	76	74	1	.365	.516	.722	1.238	77	254	71	96	17	3	24	70	70	2	.378	.515	.752	1.267	0.96
1927	73	253	82	94	10	4	28	70	62	0	.372	.495	.775	1.270	78	287	76	98	19	4	32	94	76	0	.341	.479	.770	1.249	1.04
1928	77	260	76	86	8	4	29	70	59	2	.331	.458	.727	1.185	77	276	87	87	21	4	25	72	76	1	.315	.465	.692	1.157	1.04
1929	60	218	50	72	7	3	21	66	36	1	.330	.427	.679	1.106	75	281	71	100	19	3	25	88	36	2	.356	.433	.712	1.144	0.94
1930	72	244	72	91	13	5	26	75	65	1	.373	.506	.787	1.293	73	274	78	95	15	4	23	78	71	0	.347	.481	.682	1.164	1.21
1931	75	267	72	96	11	0	24	78	63	0	.360	.482	.670	1.152	70	267	77	103	20	3	22	85	65	1	.386	.508	.730	1.238	0.87
1932	72	239	62	78	6	2	19	69	71	1	.326	.482	.607	1.089	61	218	58	78	7	3	22	68	59	1	.358	.496	.720	1.217	0.81
1933	68	214	51	68	9	1	22	56	63	0	.318	.473	.678	1.150	69	245	46	70	12	2	12	47	51	2	.286	.413	.498	.911	1.51
1934	69	190	47	56	11	2	13	50	62	2	.295	.472	.579	1.051	56	175	31	49	6	2	9	34	41	0	.280	.417	.491	.908	1.31
total	1048	3489	970	1230	192	53	334	975	924	15	.353	.490	.725	1.215	1036	3728	990	1288	232	53	325	996	923	20	.345	.478	.698	1.175	1.06
Wally Schang SWB																													
1921	65	207	37	58	11	3	5	26	37	3	.280	.397	.435	.832	69	217	40	76	19	2	1	29	41	2	.350	.458	.470	.928	0.79
1922	72	229	22	74	11	3	0	31	33	5	.323	.419	.397	.817	52	179	24	56	10	4	1	22	20	1	.313	.385	.430	.815	1.01
1923	41	126	15	32	3	1	1	10	14	4	.254	.347	.317	.665	43	146	24	43	5	1	1	19	13	5	.295	.372	.363	.735	0.81
1924	65	185	29	57	10	4	2	25	30	3	.308	.413	.438	.851	49	171	17	47	9	3	3	27	18	1	.275	.347	.415	.763	1.24
1925	38	83	9	19	3	1	0	12	11	0	.229	.319	.289	.608	35	84	8	21	5	0	2	12	6	0	.250	.300	.381	.681	0.82
total	281	830	112	240	38	12	8	104	125	15	.289	.392	.393	.785	248	797	113	243	48	10	8	109	98	9	.305	.387	.420	.807	0.95
Bernie Williams SWB																													
1991	42	159	20	42	10	2	1	19	23	0	.264	.357	.371	.728	43	161	23	34	9	2	2	15	25	1	.211	.321	.329	.650	1.24
1992	33	134	24	39	8	1	3	13	17	1	.291	.375	.433	.808	29	127	15	34	6	1	2	13	12	0	.268	.331	.378	.709	1.28
1993	67	256	26	68	14	2	5	32	28	1	.266	.340	.395	.735	72	311	41	84	17	2	7	36	25	3	.270	.330	.405	.736	1.00
1994	52	184	28	48	12	0	4	20	28	0	.261	.358	.391	.750	56	224	52	70	17	1	8	37	33	3	.313	.408	.504	.912	0.65

YR	G-H	AB	R	H	2B	3B	HR	RBI	BB	HB	AVG	OBP	SLG	OPS	G-A	AB	R	H	2B	3B	HR	RBI	BB	HB	AVG	OBP	SLG	OPS	H/A
1995	73	280	59	92	15	3	7	39	38	3	.329	.414	.479	.893	71	283	34	81	14	6	11	43	37	2	.286	.373	.495	.867	1.08
1996	69	259	53	85	15	3	12	47	44	0	.328	.426	.548	.974	74	292	55	83	11	4	17	55	38	0	.284	.367	.524	.891	1.21
1997	61	240	50	72	16	3	13	43	26	0	.300	.368	.554	.923	68	269	57	95	19	3	8	57	47	1	.353	.451	.535	.986	0.85
1998	69	256	53	91	16	1	14	48	42	0	.355	.446	.590	1.036	59	243	48	78	14	4	12	49	32	1	.321	.402	.560	.962	1.16
1999	80	285	52	96	10	2	11	48	54	0	.337	.442	.502	.944	78	306	64	106	18	4	14	67	46	1	.346	.433	.569	1.002	0.90
2000	67	239	55	74	20	2	15	62	43	5	.310	.425	.598	1.023	74	298	53	91	17	4	15	59	28	0	.305	.365	.540	.905	1.27
2001	80	290	59	91	23	0	14	58	42	4	.314	.408	.538	.946	66	250	43	75	15	0	12	36	36	2	.300	.392	.504	.896	1.11
2002	75	284	51	88	14	0	13	39	45	2	.310	.408	.496	.904	79	328	51	116	23	2	6	63	38	1	.354	.422	.491	.913	0.98
2003	58	198	32	47	5	0	5	22	34	2	.237	.355	.338	.693	61	247	45	70	14	1	10	42	37	1	.283	.379	.470	.849	0.66
2004	77	284	62	75	13	1	13	39	43	1	.264	.363	.454	.817	71	277	43	72	16	0	9	31	42	1	.260	.359	.415	.775	1.10
2005	73	259	33	65	10	1	7	39	23	0	.251	.312	.378	.690	68	226	20	56	9	0	5	25	30	1	.248	.339	.354	.693	0.99
2006	64	200	32	50	14	0	6	29	13	1	.250	.299	.410	.709	67	220	33	68	15	0	6	32	20	1	.309	.369	.459	.828	0.70
total	1040	3807	689	1123	215	21	143	597	543	20	.295	.386	.475	.861	1036	4062	677	1213	234	34	144	660	526	19	.299	.382	.479	.861	1.00
DAVE WINFIELD	RHB																												
1981	50	176	25	46	12	0	4	30	21	1	.261	.343	.398	.741	55	212	27	68	13	1	9	38	22	0	.321	.385	.519	.903	0.66
1982	71	272	38	78	9	4	14	53	17	0	.287	.329	.504	.832	69	267	46	73	15	4	23	53	28	0	.273	.342	.618	.960	0.78
1983	75	284	44	74	15	6	13	62	26	2	.261	.327	.493	.820	77	314	55	95	11	2	19	54	32	0	.303	.367	.532	.899	0.82
1984	66	260	49	86	12	3	9	51	31	0	.331	.402	.504	.906	75	307	57	107	22	1	10	49	22	0	.349	.392	.524	.917	0.99
1985	77	298	56	85	19	1	15	61	27	0	.285	.345	.507	.851	78	335	49	89	15	5	11	53	25	0	.266	.317	.439	.755	1.24
1986	78	279	45	76	15	3	12	56	40	1	.272	.366	.477	.842	76	286	45	72	16	2	12	48	37	1	.252	.340	.448	.787	1.14
1987	76	269	44	76	12	0	11	42	41	0	.283	.377	.450	.827	80	306	39	82	10	1	16	55	35	0	.268	.343	.464	.807	1.07
1988	76	274	52	91	15	0	12	45	34	0	.332	.406	.518	.924	73	285	44	89	22	2	13	62	35	2	.312	.391	.540	.932	1.00
1990	11	33	3	3	2	0	0	0	1	0	.091	.118	.152	.269	9	28	4	10	1	0	2	6	3	1	.357	.438	.607	1.045	-.48
total	580	2145	356	615	111	17	90	400	238	4	.287	.359	.480	.839	592	2340	366	685	125	18	115	418	239	4	.293	.359	.509	.868	0.94

Major League Hitters Developed By the Yankees Since 1975

Though frequently criticized as not being productive enough, the truth about the Yankees' player development system in the past three decades is that too much of the talent New York has produced has ended up playing elsewhere.

Most players developed by any organization were originally drafted or signed by that organization and later made their major league debut with that team. Some players, of course, will be traded to another club while still in the minors, making their ML debut in another uniform (such as Fred McGriff and Willie McGee, two painful examples of the New York front office's previous spendthrift ways). Note that an organization can "gain" or "lose" credit for a player if he was released before ever reaching the high minors (i.e., Double A).

This list shows all 132 players who have played in the majors from 1975–2007 that were produced by the Yankees' organization, with their debut year and team (if not New York). Their career games played with the Yankees and with other teams are also shown through 2007.

PLAYER/DEBUT (TEAM)	G NY/OTHER
Erick Almonte 2001	39/0
Dell Alston 1977	25/164
Joaquin Arias 2006 TEX	0/6
Brad Ausmus 1993 SD	0/1833
Oscar Azocar 1990	65/137
Steve Balboni 1981	295/665
Tom Barrett 1988 PHI	0/54
Dave Bergman 1975	12/1337
Juan Bernhardt 1976	10/144
Ron Blomberg 1969	400/61
Scott Bradley 1984	28/577
Brian Buchanan 2000 MIN	0/346
Melky Cabrera 2005	286/0
Andy Cannizaro 2006	13/0
Robinson Cano 2005	414/0
Bubba Carpenter 2000 COL	0/15
Bernie Castro 2005 BAL	0/66
Pete Dalena 1989 CLE	0/5
Russ Davis 1994	44/568
Brian Dayett 1983	75/143
Orestes Destrade 1987	9/228
Kerry Dineen 1975	11/5
Tom Dodd 1986 BAL	0/8
Robert Eenhoorn 1994	20/17
Jason Ellison 2003 SF	0/335
John Ellis 1969	235/648
Juan Espino 1982	49/0
Carl Everett 1993 FLO	0/1405
Mike Figga 1997	5/41
Jesus Figueroa 1980 CHN	0/115
Mike Fischlin 1977 HOU	71/446
Andy Fox 1996	135/663
Greg Gagne 1983 MIN	0/1798
Damaso Garcia 1978	29/1003
John-Ford Griffin 2005 TOR	0/13
Mario Guerrero 1973 BOS	0/697
Cristian Guzman 1999 MIN	0/1029
Mike Heath 1978	33/1332
Mike Hegan 1964	141/824
Drew Henson 2002	8/0
Michel Hernandez 2003	5/0
Roger Holt 1980	2/0
Rex Hudler 1984	29/772
Garth Iorg 1978 TOR	0/934

PLAYER/DEBUT (TEAM)	G NY/OTHER
Derek Jeter 1995	1835/0
D'Angelo Jimenez 1999	7/653
Brian Johnson 1994 SD	0/471
Deron Johnson 1960	19/1746
Nick Johnson 2001	248/351
Darryl Jones 1979	18/0
Kevin Jordan 1995 PHI	0/560
Pat Kelly 1991	591/90
Mickey Klutts 1976	8/191
Jalal Leach 2001 SF	0/8
Ricky Ledee 1998	192/663
Joe Lefebvre 1980	74/373
Jim Leyritz 1990	577/338
Bill Lindsey 1987 CHA	0/9
Phil Lombardi 1986	25/18
Mike Lowell 1998	8/1288
Matt Luke 1996	1/122
Mitch Lyden 1993 FLO	0/6
Jim Lyttle 1969	164/227
Kevin Maas 1990	384/22
Carlos Martinez 1988 CHA	0/475
Victor Mata 1984	36/0
Hideki Matsui 2003	681/0
Don Mattingly 1982	1785/0
Donzell McDonald 2001	5/10
Willie McGee 1982 STL	0/2201
Fred McGriff 1986 TOR	0/2460
Bob Meacham 1983	457/0
Hensley Meulens 1989	159/23
Orlando Miller 1994 HOU	0/297
Hal Morris 1988	30/1216
Lyle Mouton 1995 CHA	0/328
Thurman Munson 1969	1423/0
Bobby Murcer 1965	1256/652
Larry Murray 1974	20/206
Brian Myrow 2005 LAN	0/31
Jerry Narron 1979	61/331
Dioner Navarro 2004	5/250
Otis Nixon 1983	13/1696
Wayne Nordhagen 1976 CHA	0/521
Sherman Obando 1993 BAL	0/177
Mike Pagliarulo 1984	703/543
Dan Pasqua 1985	275/630
Wily Mo Pena 2002 CIN	0/496

PLAYER/DEBUT (TEAM)	G NY/OTHER
Andy Phillips 2004	203/1
Jorge Posada 1995	1432/0
Domingo Ramos 1978	1/506
John Ramos 1991	10/0
Darren Reed 1990 NYN	0/82
Juan Rivera 2001	88/378
Ruben Rivera 1995	51/611
Andre Robertson 1981	254/0
Carlos Rodriguez 1991	15/70
Edwin Rodriguez 1982	3/8
Ellie Rodriguez 1968	9/766
John Rodriguez 2005 STL	0/158
Charlie Sands 1967	1/92
Deion Sanders 1989	71/570
Rafael Santana 1983 STL	148/520
Dickie Scott 1989 OAK	0/3
Scott Seabol 2001	1/59
Fernando Seguignol 1998 MON	5/173
Dennis Sherrill 1978	5/0
Tom Shopay 1967	36/217
Dave Silvestri 1992	43/138
Keith Smith 1984	6/0
J.T. Snow 1992	7/1708
Tony Solaita 1968	1/524
Alfonso Soriano 1999	501/595
Shane Spencer 1998	345/193
Charlie Spikes 1972	14/656
Andy Stankiewicz 1992	132/297
Pat Tabler 1981 CHN	0/1333
Frank Tepedino 1967	52/213
Marcus Thames 2002	7/325
Kevin Thompson 2006	32/9
Rusty Torres 1971	89/565
Shane Turner 1988 PHI	0/56
Willie Upshaw 1978 TOR	0/1264
Otto Velez 1973	105/538
Mike Vento 2005	2/9
Turner Ward 1990 CLE	0/626
Roy White 1965	1881/0
Bernie Williams 1991	2076/0
Gerald Williams 1992	384/784
Tom Wilson 2001 OAK	0/215
Matt Winters 1989 KC	0/42
George Zeber 1977	28/0

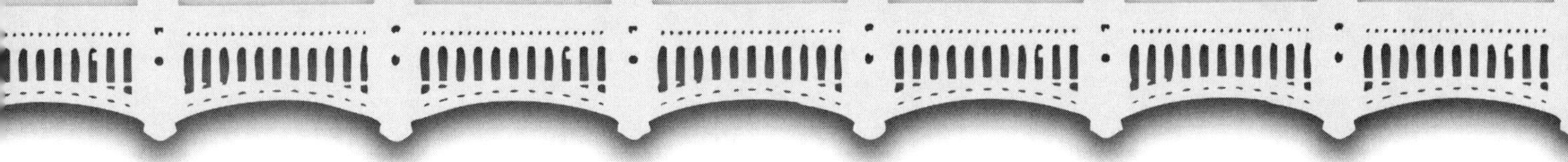

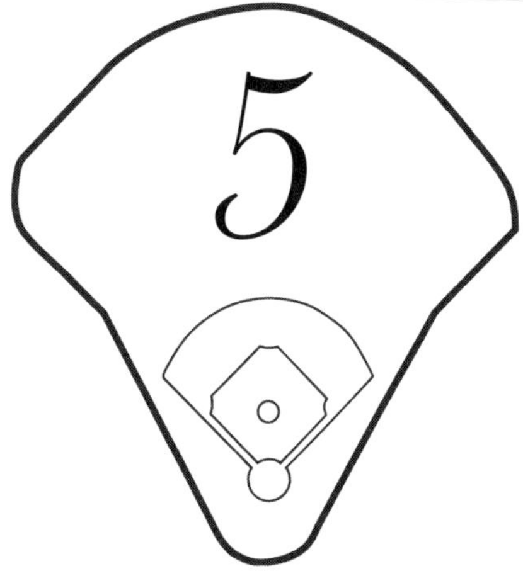

Yankees Pitchers

When people think of the New York Yankees and their long and storied history, the Yankees long tradition of excellent starting pitching is usually not the first thing that comes to mind. Or the second. Or the third. When people think of the Yankees, they think of the *Bronx Bombers*. They think of Murderer's Row. They think of one of the legendary Yankees' sluggers: Babe Ruth, Lou Gehrig, Joe DiMaggio, or Mickey Mantle. They think of Yogi Berra and all the things he may or may not have said on the way to so many Fall Classics. They think of Reggie Jackson and his three home runs on three pitches on one famous October night. They think of Don Mattingly and his hitting excellence. They think of Derek Jeter's athleticism and jaw-dropping clutch plays.

As far as Yankees pitchers are concerned, they really don't come up that often; at least, not until you start digging deeper into the club's history.

The reality of Yankees history, however, is that pitching has always been a key part of the Yankees' formula for success. Most of the great New York teams between the 1930s and 1960s relied just as much on their pitching staffs as on their everyday players. From 1932–1964, the Yankees led the league in ERA 16 times, only one less time than they led the league in runs.

There are logical explanations for why the Yankees' pitching has always had a lower profile than the Yankees' offense. The team has boasted few dominant pitchers over the years; there's never been a Yankees pitcher on the level of Walter Johnson, Christy Mathewson, or Lefty Grove. The only pitcher in pinstripes who belongs in that lofty group is Roger Clemens, and "The Rocket" did not spend the prime of his career in the Bronx. The strength of the Yankees' starting rotation has more often been its depth than its individual brilliance. As a result, the Yankees have never had a pitcher with anywhere near the star wattage of many of their greatest players.

It's not hard to identify the two pitchers in Yankees history that stand out. One is Whitey Ford, whose career 2.75 ERA is the best ERA of any major league starting pitcher since World War II. Ford didn't have the longest career—he threw only 3170⅓ regular season innings, partly because he spent two years in the Army during the Korean War—but his outstanding statistics along with his superlative postseason record clearly place Ford among the top 25 pitchers of all-time.

The other great pitcher in Yankees history is of recent vintage. The remarkable Mariano Rivera has established himself now as the best closer in baseball history, without even factoring in his brilliant postseason accomplishments. No relief pitcher has ever been as consistently excellent as Rivera, currently third in career saves and still going. The Yankees' closer also holds the career lead in postseason saves and World Series saves.

The Yankees have had many other excellent hurlers besides these two titans, but none that truly belong in a conversation about the greatest pitchers in baseball history. Hall of Fame pitchers such as Red Ruffing, Lefty Gomez, Herb Pennock, and Waite Hoyt can be more accurately described as consistently good or excellent rather than great or dominating. The postwar Yankees' dynasty from the late 1940s to the mid-1960s had a number of pitchers who performed similarly (though they did not pitch as many innings for the Yankees), including Vic Raschi, Ed Lopat, Bob Turley, Ralph Terry, and Allie Reynolds. The two most recent Yankees starters of note are Ron Guidry and Andy Pettitte.

The following register includes biographical and statistical information on all those famous pitchers, and many more.

Biographical Information

As evidenced by the name, this section is for pitchers. The separate Batter Register only includes a few pitchers; in order for a pitcher to appear in the Batter Register, he must have at least once played 10 games at a position other than pitcher. Or he must have at least 150 more career games played than games pitched. In order for a batter to appear in the Pitcher Register, he must have at least nine career innings pitched (plus more games at a position other than pitcher).

Pitchers are listed by last name. If a Latin American pitcher has a matronymic name, it is in parentheses, as in *Figueroa, Ed Eduardo (Padilla)*. Commonly used nicknames are also included in the biographical line; if a pitcher was primarily known by his nickname throughout his career, it will be listed as part of his name, as in *Ford, Whitey*. Other features and abbreviations follow.

B10.21.1928 New York, NY is the date of birth and birthplace for "The Chairman of the Board";

D1.14.1970 New York NY is the date and place of death of "Fordham Johnny" Murphy.

The arm a pitcher threw with is expressed **TR** (throws right) and **TL** (throws left). The side of the plate he bats from is listed **BR** (bats right), **BL** (bats left) and **BB** (bats both sides). **TB** is used for a pitcher who throws with both hands during a game. The only pitcher to do so since 1901 was Greg A. Harris, a right-hander who threw with both hands in a game for Montreal at the end of his career in 1995.

Height is shown in feet, followed by inches; weight is given in pounds. Most pitchers since 1950 have a weight *range* listed for their career, as opposed to a single weight. When player weights are given in most other baseball reference books, they show only a single weight for a player's entire career, often using the weight he played at in his first year or two. As is the case with most pitchers, such as Rich Gossage (180–226), there is frequently a substantial difference between waistlines from first career pitch to last. (Who among us weighs the same in middle age as we did 15 years earlier?) Research in this area by the editors—information before 1950 is much harder to come by—assures that these figures are accurate, if not necessarily flattering.

Pitchers selected in the annual amateur/first-year player drafts since 1965 have draft information included in their bio lines. The format is **Dr Year Team/League Round/Ordinal Pick Number**, so Sterling Hitchcock's draft info reads: *Dr 1989 NYA 9/233* (meaning that the 1989 Yankees 9th-round draft pick was the 233rd player taken in that year's June draft). In recent years "sandwich picks" have been awarded at the end of the first three rounds, given to teams as compensation for losing a free agent; they are considered here to be part of the preceding round. For example, Ryan Bradley was taken with the 40th pick in 1998, yet he is still considered a first-rounder *[Dr 1998 NYA 1/48]*.

Debuts are marked **d**—note the lower-case letter so as not to be confused with the abbreviation for death—followed by the date the pitcher made his first major league appearance. The debut year is the first year listed in his entry in the register, so it is not repeated in the biographical line.

Besides the basic pieces of information for pitchers available on the biographical line, there are a few other designations for players whose career, family, or duty proved noteworthy.

Mil indicates military service in the army, navy, air force, or marines;
NG indicates National Guard service (two weeks to one month) during the Vietnam War.
Mer indicates merchant marine;
Def indicates defense plant work.

The seasons missed—including partial seasons—are listed after the abbreviations for duty. In the twentieth century, four wars involving the U.S. have caused some major leaguers to miss time for military duty (years shown can include postwar service):

- World War I, 1917–19
- World War II, 1941–46
- Korean War, 1951–59
- Vietnam War, 1962–72

If the pitcher spent time as a coach, manager, or umpire, this is indicated by the following abbreviations:

C Coach
M Manager
U Umpire

A select few pitchers have reached the Hall of Fame, indicated by **HF** and followed by the year of induction.

If the pitcher had a close family member in the major leagues, the relative's relationship is identified by the codes listed below. The relative's first name is given; the last name is included if it is different than the pitcher's.

b brother
twb twin brother
f father
s son
gf grandfather
gs grandson
ggf great grandfather
ggs great grandson

For pitchers who attended college, this information is on the biographical line following the abbreviation **Col**, so Jim Abbott's school information is shown as: *Col Michigan*.

▲ included at the end of the biographical information means the pitcher is also listed in the Batter Register.

Statistical Information

Every pitcher who appeared in a game for the Yankees from 1903–2007 is included in the Pitcher Register. Every year they pitched for New York is listed here, but the year-by-year annual statistics for other teams are only displayed if they pitched more than one third of their career games for the Yanks. Career statistics for all pitchers who lasted more than one year in the major leagues are listed under **Total**. If they pitched more than one year for New York and pitched for other teams as well, their career statistics with the Yankees are tallied under **Team**. Below that, some pitchers will have a line that reads */180I* or */60G*.

A */180I* line is added to the pitcher's entry if he averaged more than 3 innings per outing and accumulated 120 innings with the team. These lines feature pro-rated statistics that represent a starting pitcher's seasonal average if he were to pitch 180 innings. This seasonal average, among other things, allows pitchers to be compared more easily.

A */60G* line is added to the pitcher's entry if he averaged less than 3 innings per outing and accumulated 40 games with the team. These lines feature pro-rated statistics that represent a reliever's seasonal average if he were to pitch 60 games. This season average provides an easier comparison for relievers.

Symbols included in this section indicate the following:

- **†** before the team name means the pitcher participated in the postseason play that season;
- ★ after the team name means that the pitcher participated in the All-Star Game;
- ☆ after the team name means that the pitcher participated in the All-Star Game but did not play;
- ✳ after the team name means that the pitcher was chosen for the All-Star Game but was replaced due to injury.

Boldface statistics in any category indicates that the pitcher was the league leader or shared the honor.

The columns that appear in the Pitcher Register after Year:

TM Team. Each team is identified with a three-letter. This book provides a list of codes is provided for clubs in the major leagues from 1892 forward.
LG League. The leagues mentioned in this book include the American League (A), the National League (N), and the Federal League, which existed from 1914–15.
W Wins
L Losses
PCT Winning Percentage. This is derived by dividing wins by (wins plus losses).
G Games
GS Games Started
CG Complete Games
ShO Shutouts. Requires that one pitcher get every out in a game without allowing a run to score, earned or unearned, and with no relief help.
QS Quality Starts. A pitcher is considered to have made a quality start if he throws at least the first six innings of a game and allows three runs or less. It is available for starting pitchers from 1957 forward.
SV Saves. In 1969 this became an official statistic. Saves are calculated based on its official definition of the time. Saves before 1969 are based on the number of winning games a relief pitcher finished for his team without getting a win.
BS Blown Saves. Since 1969 this is the number of times a pitcher entered a game in a save situation and allowed the opposing team to tie the game or take the lead. It is not calculated for pitchers before 1969.
QR Quality Relief. This is based on a reliever allowing less than one run for every two innings pitched and taking into account inherited runners. Information is available since 1957.
IP Innings Pitched. Exact innings pitched, including thirds of an inning. One third of an inning is expressed as .1. Two thirds is expressed as .2.
H Hits Allowed
R Runs. This includes unearned runs.
HR Home Runs Allowed
HB Hit Batsmen
BB Bases on balls. Bases on balls (commonly called walks) allowed by a pitcher.
IB Intentional Walks Allowed. Walking an opponent on purpose was first counted as its own category in 1955.
SO Strikeouts
ERA Earned Run Average. This is calculated by dividing earned runs by innings and multiplying by 9.
AERA Adjusted Earned Run Average. AERA is calculated by normalizing ERA for the context of the level of the league and pitcher's home park. The number is converted to a scale where 20 is average and –20 is batting practice.
OAV Opponents Batting Average
OOB Opponents On-Base Percentage
Sup Run Support. This is calculated by dividing the total number of runs scored by the pitcher's team during his starts by pitchers total Games Started. The product is normalized for the offensive level of the league and the pitcher's home park and converted to a scale where 20 is average and –20 should be grounds for suing for lack of support.
DL Disabled List. This shows the number of days spent on the disabled list for each year indicated since the DL was instituted in 1941. This column does not include time spent on the DL before or after the season, but this carryover explains why some players will have DL stints shorter than the 15-day minimum. If a pitcher spent the entire season on the disabled list, the information is given in brackets in his biographical line with the team and time indicated. Mike Jerzembeck, for instance, pitched briefly for New York in 1998, then was disabled for all of the following season *[DL 1999 NY A 182]*.
PW Pitcher Wins. This adds the pitcher's adjusted pitching wins, batting wins, and fielding wins to calculate how many wins the pitcher added to or subtracted from his team compared to what the average pitcher would have done.

Pitchers

YEAR	TM LG	W	L	PCT	G	GS	CG	SHO	QS	SV	BS	QR	IP	H	R	HR	HB	BB	IB	SO	ERA	AERA	OAV	OOB	SUP	DL	PW
ABBOTT, JIM JAMES ANTHONY B9.19.1967 FLINT MI BL/TL/6'3"/(200–210) DR 1988 CALA 1/8 D4.8 COL MICHIGAN																											
1993	NY A	11	14	.440	32	32	4	1	21	0	0	0	214	221	115	22	3	73	4	95	4.37	-4	.271	.332	+3	15	-0.5
1994	NY A	9	8	.529	24	24	2	0	13	0	0	0	160.1	167	88	24	2	64	1	90	4.55	+1	.273	.341	+1	0	0.1
Total	10	87	108	.446	263	254	31	6	143	0	0	6	1674	1779	880	154	32	620	30	888	4.25	+0	.276	.340	-8	42	0.1
Team	2	20	22	.476	56	56	6	1	34	0	—	0	374.1	388	203	46	5	137	5	185	4.45	-2	.272	.336	+2	15	-0.4
/180I	1	10	11	.476	27	27	3	0	16	0	—	0	180	187	98	22	2	66	2	89	4.45	-2	.272	.336	+2	7	-0.2
ABLES, HARRY HARRY TERRELL "HANS" B10.4.1883 TERRELL TX D2.8.1951 SAN ANTONIO TX BR/TL/6'2.5"/200 D9.4 COL SOUTHWESTERN (TX)																											
1911	NY A	0	1	.000	3	2	0	0	—	0	—	—	11	16	15	1	0	7	—	6	9.82	-63	.333	.418	+40	—	-0.6
Total	3	1	5	.167	14	8	4	0	—	0	—	—	71.1	79	51	2	1	30	—	41	4.04	-33	.276	.347	+2	—	-1.5
ACEVEDO, JUAN JUAN CARLOS (LARA) B5.5.1970 CIUDAD JUAREZ, CHIHUAHUA, MEXICO BR/TR/6'2"/(195–243) DR 1992 COLN 14/403 D4.30 COL PARKLAND (IL) JC [DL 1996 NY N 38]																											
2003	NY A	0	3	.000	25	0	0	0	0	6	1	13	25.2	34	24	5	2	10	3	19	7.71	-43	.315	.374	—	0	-1.4
Total	8	28	40	.412	367	34	0	0	11	53	23	229	570	597	316	72	28	226	34	350	4.33	+6	.274	.346	+5	129	1.1
ADKINS, DOC MERLE THERON B8.5.1872 TROY WI D2.21.1934 DURHAM NC BR/TR/5'10.5"/220 D6.24 COL BELOIT																											
1903	NY A	0	0	+	2	1	0	0	—	1	—	—	7	10	8	0	1	5	—	0	7.71	-60	.333	.444	+83	—	-0.2
Total	2	1	1	.500	6	3	1	0	—	1	—	—	27	40	28	2	1	12	—	3	5.00	-31	.342	.408	+4	—	-0.5
ADKINS, STEVE STEVEN THOMAS B10.26.1964 CHICAGO IL BR/TL/6'6"/200 DR 1986 NYA 15/392 D9.12 COL PENN																											
1990	NY A	1	2	.333	5	5	0	0	2	0	0	0	24	19	18	4	0	29	0	14	6.38	-37	.226	.421	+5	0	-0.6
AKER, JACK JACKIE DELANE B7.13.1940 TULARE CA BR/TR/6'2"/(190–202) D5.3 C3 COL SEQUOIAS (CA) [JC]																											
1969	NY A	8	4	.667	38	0	0	0	0	11	4	30	65.2	51	17	4	4	22	5	40	2.06	+71	.217	.294	—	0	2.4
1970	NY A	4	2	.667	41	0	0	0	0	16	4	32	70	57	19	3	4	20	5	36	2.06	+74	.226	.291	—	0	1.4
1971	NY A	4	4	.500	41	0	0	0	0	4	8	29	55.2	48	20	3	0	26	9	24	2.59	+27	.238	.320	—	0	0.6
1972	NY A	0	0	+	4	0	0	0	0	0	0	3	6	5	2	0	1	3	0	1	3.00	+0	.238	.360	—	0	0.0
Total	11	47	45	.511	495	0	0	0	0	123	42	361	746	679	312	63	40	274	68	404	3.28	+5	.247	.322	—	21	4.0
Team	4	16	10	.615	124	0	0	0	0	31	16	94	197.1	161	58	10	9	71	19	101	2.23	+55	.227	.303	—	—	4.4
/60G	2	8	5	.615	60	0	0	0	0	15	8	45	95.1	78	28	5	4	34	9	49	2.24	+55	.227	.303	—	—	2.1
ALEXANDER, DOYLE DOYLE LAFAYETTE B9.4.1950 CORDOVA AL BR/TR/6'3"/(190–205) DR 1968 LAN 9/185 D6.26																											
1976	†NY A	10	5	.667	19	19	5	2	12	0	0	0	136.2	114	54	9	3	39	0	41	3.29	+4	.229	.287	+10	0	0.2
1982	NY A	1	7	.125	16	11	0	0	3	0	0	4	66.2	81	52	14	0	14	2	26	6.08	-34	.298	.329	-30	89	-1.7
1983	NY A	0	2	.000	8	5	0	0	1	0	0	2	28.1	31	21	6	0	7	0	17	6.35	-38	.277	.317	+11	0	-0.5
Total	19	194	174	.527	561	464	98	18	282	3	6	67	3367.2	3376	1541	324	53	978	60	1528	3.76	+3	.261	.314	+3	141	5.4
Team	3	11	14	.440	43	35	5	2	16	0	0	6	231.2	226	127	29	3	60	2	84	4.47	-18	.256	.303	-2	89	-2.0
/180I	2	9	11	.440	33	27	4	2	12	0	0	5	180	176	99	23	2	47	2	65	4.47	-18	.256	.303	-2	69	-1.6
ALLEN, JOHNNY JOHN THOMAS B9.30.1904 LENOIR NC D3.29.1959 ST.PETERSBURG FL BR/TR/6'0"/180 D4.19																											
1932	†NY A	17	4	**.810**	33	21	13	3	—	4	—	—	192	162	86	10	5	76	—	109	3.70	+10	.228	.306	+19	—	0.9
1933	NY A	15	7	.682	25	24	10	1	—	1	—	—	184.2	171	96	9	4	87	—	119	4.39	-11	.242	.328	+31	—	-0.8
1934	NY A	5	2	.714	13	10	4	0	—	0	—	—	71.2	62	30	3	2	32	—	54	2.89	+41	.227	.313	+20	—	0.8
1935	NY A	13	6	.684	23	23	12	2	—	0	—	—	167	149	76	11	4	58	—	113	3.61	+12	**.238**	.307	+33	—	1.2
Total	13	142	75	.654	352	241	109	17	—	18	—	—	1950.1	1849	924	104	38	738	—	1070	3.75	+13	.249	.321	+19	0	9.3
Team	4	50	19	.725	94	78	39	6	—	5	—	—	615.1	544	288	33	15	253	—	395	3.79	+6	.235	.314	+27	—	2.1
/180I	1	15	6	.725	27	23	11	2	—	1	—	—	180	159	84	10	4	74	—	116	3.79	+6	.235	.314	+27	—	0.6
ALLEN, NEIL NEIL PATRICK B1.24.1958 KANSAS CITY KS BR/TR/6'2"/(185–190) DR 1976 NYN 11/253 D4.15																											
1985	NY A	1	0	1.000	17	0	0	0	0	1	0	12	29.1	26	9	1	0	13	0	16	2.76	+46	.234	.315	—	0	0.2
1987	NY A	0	1	.000	8	1	0	0	0	0	0	5	24.2	23	12	2	0	10	1	16	3.65	+22	.242	.314	-38	0	0.1
1988	NY A	5	3	.625	41	2	0	1	0	0	2	24	117.1	121	51	14	2	37	7	61	3.84	+4	.268	.322	-43	36	0.1
Total	11	58	70	.453	434	59	7	6	19	75	27	262	988.1	985	464	73	9	417	68	611	3.88	-1	.264	.336	-6	230	-1.2
Team	3	6	4	.600	66	3	0	1	0	1	2	41	171.1	170	72	17	2	60	8	93	3.62	+12	.259	.320	-41	36	0.4
/60G	3	5	4	.600	60	3	0	1	0	1	2	37	155.2	155	65	15	2	55	7	85	3.63	+12	.259	.320	-41	33	0.4
ALMANZAR, CARLOS CARLOS MANUEL (GIRON) B11.6.1973 SANTIAGO, D.R. BR/TR/6'2"/(166–200) D9.4																											
2001	NY A	0	1	.000	10	0	0	0	0	0	2	6	10.2	14	4	2	0	2	1	6	3.38	+32	.333	.356	—	0	0.1
Total	8	13	13	.500	210	1	0	0	0	0	10	135	239	252	134	35	13	82	12	170	4.82	-5	.271	.335	-57	299	0.7
ANDERSON, JASON JASON ROGER B6.9.1979 DANVILLE IL BL/TR/6'0"/(170–190) DR 2000 NYA 10/308 D3.31 COL ILLINOIS																											
2003	NY A	1	0	1.000	22	0	0	0	0	0	0	14	20.2	23	13	3	2	14	4	9	4.79	-8	.280	.390	—	0	-0.1
2003	NY N	0	0	+	6	0	0	0	0	0	0	4	10.2	10	6	2	1	5	1	7	5.06	-17	.256	.340	—	0	0.0
2003	Major	1	0	1.000	28	0	0	0	0	0	0	18	30	33	19	5	3	19	5	16	4.88	-11	.273	.374	—	0	-0.1
2004	Cle A	0	0	+	1	0	0	0	0	0	0	0	1	1	5	1	0	4	1	1	45.00	-90	.250	.625	—	0	-0.2
2005	NY A	1	0	1.000	3	0	0	0	0	0	0	2	5.2	4	5	0	0	7	1	2	7.94	-46	.200	.407	—	0	-0.3
Total	3	2	0	1.000	32	0	0	0	0	0	0	20	38	38	29	6	3	30	7	19	6.39	-32	.262	.390	—	0	-0.6
Team	2	2	0	1.000	25	0	0	0	0	0	0	16	26.1	27	18	3	2	21	5	11	5.47	-20	.265	.394	—	—	-0.4
ANDERSON, RICK RICHARD LEE B12.25.1953 INGLEWOOD CA D6.23.1989 WILMINGTON CA BR/TR/6'2"/210 DR 1972 NYA*S1/5 D9.18 COL LOS ANGELES VALLEY (CA) JC [DL 1981 SEA A 49]																											
1979	NY A	0	0	+	1	0	0	0	0	0	0	1	2.1	1	1	0	0	4	0	0	3.86	+7	.167	.500	—	0	0.0
Total	2	0	0	+	6	2	0	0	0	0	0	3	12	9	6	1	0	14	2	7	3.75	+11	.220	.418	+50	49	0.0
ANDREWS, IVY IVY PAUL "POISON" B5.6.1907 DORA AL D11.24.1970 BIRMINGHAM AL BR/TR/6'1"/200 D8.15																											
1931	NY A	2	0	1.000	7	3	1	0	—	0	—	—	34.1	36	17	3	0	8	—	10	4.19	-5	.273	.314	+148	—	0.0
1932	NY A	2	1	.667	4	1	1	0	—	0	—	—	24.2	20	8	0	0	9	—	7	1.82	+123	.215	.284	+67	—	0.8
1937	†NY A	3	2	.600	11	5	3	1	—	1	—	—	49	49	19	2	0	17	—	17	3.12	+42	.259	.320	-33	—	0.6
1938	NY A	1	3	.250	19	1	1	0	—	1	—	—	48	51	25	3	0	17	—	13	3.00	+51	.268	.329	-81	—	0.4
Total	8	50	59	.459	249	108	43	2	—	8	—	—	1041	1151	562	59	4	342	—	257	4.14	+15	.279	.335	-11	—	4.4
Team	4	8	6	.571	41	10	6	1	—	2	—	—	156	156	69	8	0	51	—	47	3.12	+38	.258	.316	+27	—	1.8
/180I	5	9	7	.571	47	12	7	1	—	2	—	—	180	180	80	9	0	59	—	54	3.12	+38	.258	.316	+27	—	2.1
APPLETON, PETE PETER WILLIAM "JAKE" (AKA JABLONOWSKI IN 1927–33) B5.20.1904 TERRYVILLE CT D1.18.1974 TRENTON NJ BR/TR/5'11"/180 D9.14 MIL 1943–45 COL MICHIGAN																											
1933	NY A	0	0	+	1	0	0	0	—	0	—	—	2	3	0	0	0	1	—	0	0.00	-100	.375	.444	—	—	0.1
Total	14	57	66	.463	341	73	34	6	—	26	—	—	1141	1187	667	76	26	486	—	420	4.30	+4	.268	.343	-16	0	2.9
ARDIZOIA, RUGGER RINALDO JOSEPH B11.20.1919 OLEGGIO, ITALY BR/TR/5'11"/180 D4.30																											
1947	NY A	0	0	+	1	0	0	0	—	0	—	—	2	4	2	1	0	1	—	0	9.00	-61	.500	.556	—	0	-0.1
ARMSTRONG, MIKE MICHAEL DENNIS B3.7.1954 GLEN COVE NY BR/TR/6'3"/(193–206) DR 1974 CINN*1/24 D8.12 COL MIAMI																											
1984	NY A	3	2	.600	36	0	0	0	0	1	3	25	54.1	47	21	6	0	26	4	43	3.48	+10	.239	.322	—	75	0.3
1985	NY A	0	0	+	9	0	0	0	0	0	0	6	14.2	9	5	4	0	2	0	11	3.07	+32	.173	.204	—	0	0.1
1986	NY A	0	1	.000	7	1	0	0	0	0	0	4	8.2	13	9	4	0	5	1	8	9.35	-56	.351	.429	+76	0	-0.5
Total	8	19	17	.528	197	1	0	0	0	11	8	125	338	300	170	42	6	155	20	221	4.10	-2	.240	.323	+76	75	-0.4
Team	3	3	3	.500	52	1	0	0	0	1	3	35	77.2	69	35	14	0	33	5	62	4.06	-4	.241	.316	+76	75	-0.1
/60G	3	3	3	.500	60	1	0	0	0	1	3	40	89.2	80	40	16	0	38	6	72	4.05	-4	.241	.316	+76	87	-0.1

YEAR	TM LG	W	L	PCT	G	GS	CG	SHO	QS	SV	BS	QR	IP	H	R	HR	HB	BB	IB	SO	ERA	AERA	OAV	OOB	SUP	DL	PW
Arnsberg, Brad Bradley James B8.20.1963 Seattle WA BR/TR/6'4"/(205–215) Dr 1983 NYA S1/9 d9.6 C7 Col Merced (CA) JC [DL 1988 Tex A 150]																											
1986	NY A	0	0	+	2	1	0	0	0	0	0	0	8	13	3	1	0	1	0	3	3.38	+23	.342	.359	+10	0	0.0
1987	NY A	1	3	.250	6	2	0	0	1	0	0	2	19.1	22	12	5	0	13	3	14	5.59	-21	.289	.385	-38	22	-0.3
Total	6	9	6	.600	94	4	0	0	1	6	1	53	158.1	159	85	27	7	85	4	100	4.26	-5	.259	.353	-21	320	0.2
Team	2	1	3	.250	8	3	0	0	1	0	0	2	27.1	35	15	6	0	14	3	17	4.94	-12	.307	.377	-22	22	-0.3
Arroyo, Luis Luis Enrique B2.18.1927 Penuelas, PR BL/TL/5'8"/(175–190) d4.20																											
1955	StL N☆	11	8	.579	35	24	9	1	—	0	—	—	159	162	80	22	2	63	6	68	4.19	-3	.261	.329	-1	0	-0.3
1956	Pit N	3	3	.500	18	2	1	0	—	0	—	—	28.2	36	17	5	0	12	1	17	4.71	-20	.298	.361	+63	0	-0.5
1957	Pit N	3	11	.214	54	10	0	0	3	1	1	25	130.2	151	76	19	7	31	9	101	4.68	-19	.282	.329	-33	0	-1.3
1959	Cin N	1	0	1.000	10	0	0	0	0	0	0	7	13.2	17	11	0	0	11	3	8	3.95	+3	.321	.418	—	0	-0.1
1960	†NY A	5	1	.833	29	0	0	0	0	7	2	22	40.2	30	14	2	0	22	3	29	2.88	+25	.207	.311	—	0	0.7
1961	†NY A☆	15	5	.750	**65**	0	0	0	0	**29**	10	51	119	83	34	5	3	49	8	87	2.19	+69	.199	.284	—	0	**4.4**
1962	NY A	1	3	.250	27	0	0	0	0	7	4	16	33.2	33	20	5	1	17	2	21	4.81	-22	.262	.352	—	34	-0.6
1963	NY A	1	1	.500	6	0	0	0	0	0	1	2	6	12	9	0	0	3	1	5	13.50	-74	.444	.484	—	0	-1.2
Total	8	40	32	.556	244	36	10	1	3	44	18	123	531.1	524	261	58	13	208	33	336	3.93	-2	.256	.326	-3	34	1.1
Team	4	22	10	.688	127	0	0	0	0	43	17	91	199.1	158	77	12	4	91	14	142	3.12	+18	.221	.309	—	34	3.3
/60G	2	10	5	.688	60	0	0	0	0	20	8	43	94.1	75	36	6	2	43	7	67	3.11	+18	.221	.309	—	16	1.6
Assenmacher, Paul Paul Andre B12.10.1960 Detroit MI BL/TL/6'3"/(200–210) d4.12 Col Aquinas																											
1993	NY A	2	2	.500	26	0	0	0	0	0	1	20	17.1	10	6	0	1	9	3	11	3.12	+34	.175	.299	—	0	0.5
Total	14	61	44	.581	884	1	0	0	0	56	59	624	855.2	817	371	73	22	315	78	807	3.53	+18	.252	.320	+11	41	9.0
Ausanio, Joe Joseph John B12.9.1965 Kingston NY BR/TR/6'1"/205 Dr 1988 PitN 11/278 d7.14 Col Jacksonville																											
1994	NY A	2	1	.667	13	0	0	0	0	0	0	7	15.2	16	9	3	0	6	0	15	5.17	-11	.254	.319	—	0	-0.1
1995	NY A	2	0	1.000	28	0	0	0	0	1	2	16	37.2	42	24	9	0	23	0	36	5.73	-19	.286	.378	—	0	-0.2
Total	2	4	1	.800	41	0	0	0	0	1	2	23	53.1	58	33	12	0	29	0	51	5.57	-17	.276	.361	—	0	-0.3
/60G	3	6	1	.800	60	0	0	0	0	1	3	34	78	85	48	18	0	42	0	75	5.57	-17	.276	.361	—	—	-0.4
Bahnsen, Stan Stanley Raymond B12.15.1944 Council Bluffs IA BR/TR/6'2"/(185–198) Dr 1965 NYA 4/68 d9.9 Col Nebraska																											
1966	NY A	1	1	.500	4	3	1	0	1	1	0	1	23	15	9	3	0	7	0	16	3.52	-6	.181	.244	+41	0	0.0
1968	NY A	17	12	.586	37	34	10	1	29	0	0	2	267.1	216	72	14	2	68	6	162	2.05	+42	.221	.271	-3	0	2.4
1969	NY A	9	16	.360	40	33	5	2	15	1	0	6	220.2	222	102	28	0	90	9	130	3.83	-8	.260	.330	-13	0	-0.9
1970	NY A	14	11	.560	36	35	6	2	24	0	0	1	232.2	227	100	23	2	75	4	116	3.33	+7	.256	.312	+2	0	0.6
1971	NY A	14	12	.538	36	34	14	3	23	0	0	1	242	221	99	20	5	72	8	110	3.35	-2	.248	.304	+21	0	0.2
Total	16	146	149	.495	574	327	73	16	186	20	12	175	2529	2440	1127	223	34	924	59	1359	3.60	-3	.255	.321	+0	22	-3.3
Team	5	55	52	.514	153	139	36	8	92	2	0	11	985.2	901	382	88	9	312	27	534	3.10	+7	.244	.302	+3	—	2.3
/180I	1	10	9	.514	28	25	7	1	17	0	0	2	180	165	70	16	2	57	5	98	3.10	+7	.244	.302	+3	—	0.4
Bankhead, Scott Michael Scott B7.31.1963 Raleigh NC BR/TR/5'10"/(175–185) Dr 1984 KCA 1/16 d5.25 Col North Carolina																											
1995	NY A	1	1	.500	20	1	0	0	0	0	0	11	39	44	26	9	0	16	0	20	6.00	-23	.278	.343	+41	0	-0.3
Total	10	57	48	.543	267	110	7	3	56	1	6	103	901	876	451	111	15	289	26	614	4.18	+3	.254	.311	-8	368	1.1
Banks, Willie Willie Anthony B2.27.1969 Jersey City NJ BR/TR/6'1"/(190–202) Dr 1987 MinA 1/3 d7.31																											
1997	NY A	3	0	1.000	5	1	0	0	1	0	1	4	14	9	3	0	1	6	0	8	1.93	+131	.188	.291	-17	0	0.9
1998	NY A	1	1	.500	9	0	0	0	0	0	0	3	14.1	20	16	4	1	12	2	8	10.05	-56	.323	.440	—	0	-1.0
Total	9	33	39	.458	181	84	1	1	33	2	3	59	610.1	632	370	65	15	302	16	428	4.75	-10	.268	.353	-10	0	-4.0
Team	2	4	1	.800	14	1	0	0	1	0	1	7	28.1	29	19	4	2	18	2	16	6.04	-27	.264	.377	-17	—	-0.1
Barber, Steve Stephen David B2.22.1938 Takoma Park MD D2.4.2007 Henderson NV BL/TL/6'0"/(190–200) d4.21																											
1967	NY A	6	9	.400	17	17	3	1	11	0	0	0	97.2	103	47	4	3	54	3	70	4.05	-23	.278	.371	-25	0	-1.2
1968	NY A	6	5	.545	20	19	3	1	15	0	0	0	128.1	127	63	7	3	64	4	87	3.23	-10	.256	.342	+16	0	-0.8
Total	15	121	106	.533	466	272	59	21	161	13	8	131	1999	1818	870	125	42	950	59	1309	3.36	+5	.245	.332	-6	89	3.1
Team	2	12	14	.462	37	36	6	2	26	0	0	0	226	230	110	11	6	118	7	157	3.58	-16	.265	.355	-3	—	-2.0
/180I	2	10	11	.462	29	29	5	2	21	0	0	0	180	183	88	9	5	94	6	125	3.58	-16	.265	.355	-3	—	-1.6
Barger, Cy Eros Bolivar B5.18.1885 Jamestown KY D9.23.1964 Columbia KY BL/TR/6'0"/160 d8.30 Col Transylvania																											
1906	NY A	0	0	+	2	1	0	0	—	1	—	—	5.1	7	8	0	0	3	—	3	10.13	-71	.318	.400	+118	—	-0.2
1907	NY A	0	0	+	1	0	0	0	—	0	—	—	6	10	2	0	1	1	—	0	3.00	-7	.370	.414	—	—	-0.1
Total	7	46	63	.422	151	111	78	5	—	9	—	—	975.2	1010	479	18	28	334	—	297	3.56	-15	.280	.346	-19	—	-4.0
Team	2	0	0	+	3	1	0	0	—	1	—	—	11.1	17	10	0	1	4	—	3	6.35	-55	.347	.407	+118	—	-0.3
Barnes, Frank Frank Samuel "Lefty" B1.9.1900 Dallas TX D9.27.1967 Houston TX BL/TL/6'2.5"/195 d4.18																											
1930	NY A	0	1	.000	2	2	0	0	—	0	—	—	12.1	13	11	0	1	13	—	2	8.03	-46	.283	.450	+30	—	-0.1
Total	2	0	2	.000	6	3	0	0	—	0	—	—	17.1	23	19	0	2	16	—	2	7.79	-45	.324	.461	+6	—	-0.6
Beall, Walter Walter Esau B7.29.1899 Washington DC D1.28.1959 Suitland MD BR/TR/5'10"/178 d9.3																											
1924	NY A	2	0	1.000	4	2	0	0	—	0	—	—	23	19	11	2	0	17	—	18	3.52	+18	.237	.371	+52	—	0.0
1925	NY A	0	1	.000	8	1	0	0	—	0	—	—	11.1	11	17	0	3	19	—	8	12.71	-66	.282	.541	-61	—	-0.8
1926	NY A	2	4	.333	20	9	1	0	—	1	—	—	81.2	71	46	2	6	68	—	56	3.53	+9	.240	.392	+24	—	0.0
1927	NY A	0	0	+	1	0	0	0	—	0	—	—	1	1	1	0	0	0	—	0	9.00	-57	.333	.333	—	—	0.0
1929	Was A	1	0	1.000	3	0	0	0	—	0	—	—	7	8	4	0	0	7	—	3	3.86	+10	.348	.500	—	—	0.0
Total	5	5	5	.500	36	12	1	0	—	1	—	—	124	110	79	4	9	111	—	85	4.43	-10	.249	.410	+20	—	-0.8
Team	4	4	5	.444	33	12	1	0	—	1	—	—	117	102	75	4	9	104	—	82	4.46	-11	.244	.405	+22	—	-0.8
Beam, T.J. Theodore Lester B8.28.1980 Scottsdale AZ BR/TR/6'7"/215 Dr 2002 NYA 10/306 d6.17 Col Mississippi																											
2006	NY A	2	0	1.000	20	0	0	0	0	0	1	7	18	26	17	5	2	6	2	12	8.50	-46	.338	.400	—	0	-0.7
Bean, Colter Randall Colter B1.16.1977 Anniston AL BL/TR/6'6"/255 d4.26 Col Auburn																											
2005	NY A	0	0	+	1	0	0	0	0	0	0	1	2	1	1	0	0	2	0	2	4.50	-4	.143	.333	—	0	0.0
2006	NY A	0	0	+	2	0	0	0	0	0	0	1	2	2	2	0	1	2	0	1	9.00	-49	.333	.500	—	0	0.0
2007	NY A	0	1	.000	3	0	0	0	0	0	0	2	3	5	4	0	0	5	0	2	12.00	-62	.357	.526	—	0	-0.4
Total	3	0	1	.000	6	0	0	0	0	0	0	4	7	8	7	0	1	9	0	5	9.00	-50	.296	.474	—	0	-0.4
Beattie, Jim James Louis B7.4.1954 Hampton VA BR/TR/6'6"/(205–225) Dr 1975 NYA 4/91 d4.25 Col Dartmouth																											
1978	†NY A	6	9	.400	25	22	0	0	11	0	0	3	128	123	60	8	8	51	2	65	3.73	-2	.255	.335	+2	0	-0.1
1979	NY A	3	6	.333	15	13	1	1	5	0	0	0	76	85	45	5	0	41	0	32	5.21	-21	.294	.375	-10	27	-0.7
Total	9	52	87	.374	203	182	31	7	94	1	0	12	1148.2	1174	581	88	29	461	25	660	4.17	-1	.267	.338	-10	259	-0.1
Team	2	9	15	.375	40	35	1	1	16	0	0	3	204	208	105	13	8	92	2	97	4.28	-11	.270	.350	-2	27	-0.8
/180I	2	8	13	.375	35	31	1	1	14	0	0	3	180	184	93	11	7	81	2	86	4.28	-11	.270	.350	-2	24	-0.7
Beck, Rich Richard Henry B1.21.1941 Pasco WA BB/TR/6'3"/190 d9.14 Mil 1966–67 Col Gonzaga																											
1965	NY A	2	1	.667	3	3	1	1	2	0	0	0	21	22	6	1	0	7	1	10	2.14	+59	.275	.333	-23	0	0.4
Beene, Fred Freddy Ray B11.24.1942 Angleton TX BB/TR (BR 1968)/5'9"/(155–160) d9.18 Col Sam Houston St.																											
1968	Bal A	0	0	+	1	0	0	0	0	0	0	0	1	2	1	0	0	1	0	1	9.00	-67	.500	.500	—	0	0.0
1969	Bal A	0	0	+	2	0	0	0	0	0	0	1	2.2	2	0	0	0	1	0	0	0.00	-100	.200	.273	—	0	0.1
1970	Bal A	0	0	+	4	0	0	0	0	0	0	3	6	8	5	1	0	5	4	4	6.00	-39	.320	.433	—	0	-0.1

YEAR	TM LG	W	L	PCT	G	GS	CG	SHO	QS	SV	BS	QR	IP	H	R	HR	HB	BB	IB	SO	ERA	AERA	OAV	OOB	SUP	DL	PW
1972	NY A	1	3	.250	29	1	0	0	0	3	0	22	57.2	55	21	3	1	24	5	37	2.34	+28	.256	.332	+433	0	0.1
1973	NY A	6	0	1.000	19	4	0	0	3	1	0	13	91	67	21	5	1	27	5	49	1.68	+121	.209	.271	+8	0	1.4
1974	NY A	0	0	+	6	0	0	0	0	1	0	4	10	9	4	1	1	2	0	10	2.70	+31	.231	.286	—	0	0.1
1974	Cle A	4	4	.500	32	0	0	0	0	2	3	18	73	68	44	7	1	26	2	35	4.93	-26	.246	.310	—	0	-1.0
1974	Year	4	4	.500	38	0	0	0	0	3	3	22	83	77	48	8	2	28	2	45	4.66	-22	.244	.307	—	0	-0.9
1975	Cle A	1	0	1.000	19	1	0	0	0	1	1	9	46.2	63	42	4	3	25	3	20	6.94	-45	.323	.406	+154	62	-0.8
Total	7	12	7	.632	112	6	0	0	3	8	4	70	288	274	138	21	7	111	19	156	3.63	-2	.253	.331	[illegible]	62	-0.2
Team	3	7	3	.700	54	5	0	0	3	5	0	39	158.2	131	46	0	0	53	10	96	1.99	+73	.228	.295	+93	—	1.6
/60G	3	8	3	.700	60	0	0	0	3	6	0	43	176.1	146	51	10	3	59	11	107	1.98	+73	.228	.295	+93	—	1.8
Beggs, Joe	Joseph Stanley "Fireman" B11.4.1910 Rankin PA D7.19.1983 Indianapolis IN BR/TR/6'1"/182 d4.19 Mil 1944–45 Col Geneva																										
1938	NY A	3	2	.600	14	9	4	0	—	0	—	—	58.1	69	41	7	0	20	—	8	5.40	-16	.299	.355	-5	—	-0.3
Total	9	48	35	.578	238	41	23	4	—	29	—	—	693.2	688	284	39	4	189	—	178	2.96	+22	.265	.316	+1	0	7.1
Benitez, Armando	Armando German B11.3.1972 Ramon Santana, D.R. BR/TR/6'4"/(180–260) d7.28																										
2003	NY A	1	1	.500	9	0	0	0	0	0	0	8	9.1	8	4	0	0	6	1	10	1.93	+128	.235	.350	—	0	0.3
Total	14	40	46	.465	754	0	0	0	0	289	58	566	772.2	541	291	92	16	401	32	937	3.11	+39	.196	.299	—	293	15.1
Bernhardt, Walter	Walter Jacob B5.20.1893 Pleasant Valley Twp. PA D7.26.1958 Watertown NY BR/TR/6'2"/175 d7.16 Col Penn																										
1918	NY A	0	0	+	1	0	0	0	—	0	—	—	0.2	0	0	0	0	0	—	1	0.00	-100	.000	.000	—	—	0.0
Bevens, Bill	Floyd Clifford B10.21.1916 Hubbard OR D10.26.1991 Salem OR BR/TR/6'3.5"/210 d5.12 [DL 1948 NY A 63]																										
1944	NY A	4	1	.800	8	5	3	0	—	0	—	—	43.2	44	18	4	1	13	—	16	2.68	+30	.273	.331	+63	0	0.1
1945	NY A	13	9	.591	29	25	14	2	—	0	—	—	184	174	83	12	1	68	—	76	3.67	-6	.254	.322	+18	0	-0.7
1946	NY A	16	13	.552	31	31	18	3	—	0	—	—	249.2	213	73	11	1	78	—	120	2.23	+54	.232	.293	-12	0	3.2
1947	†NY A	7	13	.350	28	23	11	1	—	0	—	—	165	167	79	13	1	77	—	77	3.82	-7	.264	.345	+4	0	-1.0
Total	4	40	36	.526	96	84	46	6	—	0	—	—	642.1	598	253	40	4	236	—	289	3.08	+13	.250	.318	+6	63	1.6
/180I	1	11	10	.526	27	24	13	2	0	0	0	0	180	168	71	11	1	66	—	81	3.08	+13	.250	.318	+6	18	0.4
Billiard, Harry	Harry Pree "Pree" B11.11.1883 Monroe IN D6.3.1923 Wooster OH BR/TR/6'0"/190 d7.31																										
1908	NY A	0	0	+	6	0	0	0	—	0	—	—	17	15	15	1	5	14	—	10	2.65	-6	.234	.410	—	—	-0.2
Total	3	8	8	.500	52	18	5	0	—	3	—	—	171	164	109	5	15	105	—	62	3.95	-25	.260	.379	+12	—	-1.9
Bird, Doug	James Douglas B3.5.1950 Corona CA BR/TR/6'4"/(180–195) Dr 1969 KCA S3/60 d4.29 Col Mt. San Antonio (CA) JC																										
1980	NY A	3	0	1.000	22	1	0	0	0	1	1	14	50.2	47	16	3	1	14	1	17	2.66	+49	.257	.307	+194	0	0.5
1981	NY A	5	1	.833	17	4	0	0	2	0	1	9	53.1	58	19	5	0	16	3	28	2.70	+34	.280	.326	-32	0	0.6
Total	11	73	60	.549	432	100	8	3	48	60	29	217	1213.2	1273	590	122	22	296	56	680	3.99	-4	.272	.315	-1	21	0.0
Team	2	8	1	.889	39	5	0	0	2	1	2	23	104	105	35	8	1	30	4	45	2.68	+41	.269	.317	+13	—	1.1
Blackwell, Ewell	Ewell "The Whip" B10.23.1922 Fresno CA D10.29.1996 Hendersonville NC BR/TR/6'6"/(185–195) d4.21 Mil 1943–45 Col La Verne																										
1952	†NY A	1	0	1.000	5	2	0	0	—	1	—	—	16	12	2	0	0	12	—	7	0.56	+491	.203	.338	+5	0	0.4
1953	NY A	2	0	1.000	8	4	0	0	—	1	—	—	19.2	17	10	2	1	13	—	11	3.66	+1	.233	.356	+44	0	-0.1
Total	10	82	78	.512	236	169	69	15	—	11	—	—	1321	1150	562	67	44	562	0	839	3.30	+20	.235	.319	-17	0	10.2
Team	2	3	0	1.000	13	6	0	0	—	2	—	—	35.2	29	12	2	1	25	—	18	2.27	+55	.220	.348	+31	—	0.3
Blanco, Gil	Gilbert Henry B12.15.1945 Phoenix AZ BL/TL/6'5"/(205–217) d4.24 Col Phoenix (AZ) JC																										
1965	NY A	1	1	.500	17	1	0	0	0	0	0	13	20.1	16	10	1	1	12	0	14	3.98	-15	.232	.341	-74	0	-0.1
1966	KC A	2	4	.333	11	8	0	0	3	0	0	2	38.1	31	26	3	4	36	1	21	4.70	-28	.237	.415	-16	0	-1.0
Total	2	3	5	.375	28	9	0	0	3	0	0	15	58.2	47	36	4	5	48	1	35	4.45	-24	.235	.391	-22	0	-1.1
Blasingame, Wade	Wade Allen B11.22.1943 Deming NM BL/TL/6'1"/(185–190) d9.17																										
1972	NY A	0	1	.000	12	1	0	0	0	0	0	8	17	14	8	5	1	11	1	7	4.24	-29	.250	.382	-41	0	0.0
Total	10	46	51	.474	222	128	16	2	57	5	4	60	863.2	891	486	75	30	372	32	512	4.52	-23	.271	.348	+15	73	-9.0
Blateric, Steve	Stephen Lawrence B3.20.1944 Denver CO BR/TR/6'3"/200 d9.17 Col Denver																										
1972	NY A	0	0	+	1	0	0	0	0	0	0	1	4	2	0	0	0	0	0	4	0.00	-100	.143	.143	—	0	0.1
Total	3	0	0	+	5	0	0	0	0	0	0	2	11	16	9	2	1	1	0	13	5.73	-42	.333	.353	—	0	-0.1
Blaylock, Gary	Gary Nelson B10.11.1931 Clarkton MO BR/TR/6'0"/198 d4.10 C4																										
1959	StL N	4	5	.444	26	12	3	0	7	0	0	9	100	117	61	14	2	43	3	61	5.13	-17	.298	.366	-19	0	-0.7
1959	NY A	0	1	.000	15	1	0	0	0	0	0	9	25.2	30	13	0	1	15	0	20	3.51	+4	.306	.400	-52	0	0.0
1959	Major	4	6	.400	41	13	3	0	7	0	—	18	125	147	74	14	3	58	3	81	4.80	-13	.299	.373	-22	0	-0.7
Total	1	4	6	.400	41	13	3	0	7	0	0	18	125.2	147	74	14	3	58	3	81	4.80	-14	.300	.373	-20	0	-0.7
Bliss, Elmer	Elmer Ward B3.9.1875 Penfield PA D3.18.1962 Bradford PA BL/TR/6'0"/180 d9.28																										
1903	NY A	1	0	1.000	1	0	0	0	—	0	—	—	7	4	1	0	0	0	—	3	0.00	-100	.167	.167	—	—	0.2
Boehringer, Brian	Brian Edward B1.8.1969 St.Louis MO BB/TR/6'2"/(190–195) Dr 1991 ChiA 4/124 d4.30 Col Nevada–Las Vegas																										
1995	NY A	0	3	.000	7	3	0	0	0	0	1	2	17.2	24	27	5	1	22	1	10	13.75	-66	.320	.475	-26	0	-2.2
1996	†NY A	2	4	.333	15	3	0	0	0	0	1	9	46.1	46	28	6	1	21	2	37	5.44	-9	.260	.337	-25	0	-0.2
1997	†NY A	3	2	.600	34	0	0	0	0	0	3	26	48	39	16	4	0	32	6	53	2.63	+70	.225	.343	—	87	0.9
2001	NY A	0	1	.000	22	0	0	0	0	1	0	16	34.2	35	15	3	3	12	0	33	3.12	+43	.255	.325	—	0	0.2
Total	10	26	32	.448	356	21	0	0	5	3	19	237	534.2	522	280	64	18	274	34	432	4.36	-1	.257	.347	-22	413	-1.7
Team	4	5	10	.333	78	6	0	0	0	1	5	53	146.2	144	86	18	5	87	9	133	4.97	-7	.256	.356	-25	87	-1.3
/60G	3	4	8	.333	60	5	0	0	0	1	4	41	112.2	111	66	14	4	67	7	102	4.98	-7	.256	.356	-25	67	-1.0
Bones, Ricky	Ricardo Ricky B4.7.1969 Salinas, PR BR/TR/6'0"/(175–219) d8.11																										
1996	NY A	0	0	+	4	1	0	0	0	0	0	0	7	14	11	2	1	6	0	4	14.14	-65	.438	.525	-6	0	-0.3
Total	11	63	82	.434	375	164	11	1	77	1	8	134	1278.1	1422	754	167	50	464	34	564	4.85	-5	.283	.346	+3	29	-3.8
Bonham, Tiny	Ernest Edward B8.16.1913 Ione CA D9.15.1949 Pittsburgh PA BR/TR/6'2"/215 d8.5																										
1940	NY A	9	3	.750	12	12	10	3	—	0	—	—	99.1	83	24	4	0	13	—	37	1.90	+112	.224	.250	-24	—	2.8
1941	†NY A	9	6	.600	23	14	7	1	—	2	—	—	126.2	118	44	12	1	31	—	43	2.98	+32	.246	.294	+16	0	1.5
1942	†NY A☆	21	5	**.808**	28	27	**22**	0	—	0	—	—	226	199	65	11	1	24	—	71	2.27	+52	.237	**.259**	+12	0	3.0
1943	†NY A☆	15	8	.652	28	26	17	4	—	1	—	—	225.2	197	63	13	1	52	—	71	2.27	+42	.236	.282	+2	0	2.5
1944	NY A	12	9	.571	26	25	17	1	—	0	—	—	213.2	228	84	14	0	41	—	54	2.99	+16	.273	.307	-2	0	0.6
1945	NY A	8	11	.421	23	23	12	0	—	0	—	—	180.2	186	72	11	1	22	—	42	3.29	+5	.265	.288	-21	0	0.7
1946	NY A	5	8	.385	18	14	6	2	—	3	—	—	104.2	97	47	6	0	23	—	30	3.70	-7	.243	.284	-15	0	-0.3
1947	Pit N	11	8	.579	33	18	7	3	—	3	—	—	149.2	167	67	17	2	35	—	63	3.85	+10	.277	.319	+16	0	0.8
1948	Pit N	6	10	.375	22	20	7	0	—	0	—	—	135.2	145	71	18	3	23	—	42	4.31	-6	.276	.310	-6	0	-0.7
1949	Pit N	7	4	.636	18	14	5	1	—	0	—	—	89	81	43	11	0	23	—	25	4.25	-1	.246	.295	-10	0	-0.1
Total	10	103	72	.589	231	193	110	21	—	9	—	—	1551	1501	580	117	9	287	—	478	3.06	+20	.254	.289	-2	0	10.8
Team	7	79	50	.612	158	141	91	11	—	6	—	—	1176.2	1108	399	71	4	206	—	348	2.73	+29	.248	.282	-3	—	10.8
/180I	1	12	8	.612	24	22	14	2	—	1	—	—	180	169	61	11	1	32	—	53	2.73	+29	.248	.282	-3	—	1.7
Bordi, Rich	Richard Albert B4.18.1959 San Francisco CA BR/TR/6'7"/(210–220) Dr 1980 OakA 3/56 d7.16 Col Cal St.–Fresno																										
1980	Oak A	0	0	+	1	0	0	0	0	0	0	1	2	4	1	0	0	0	0	0	4.50	-15	.400	.400	—	0	0.0
1981	Oak A	0	0	+	2	0	0	0	0	0	0	2	2	1	0	0	0	1	0	0	0.00	-100	.143	.250	—	0	0.0

Pitchers

YEAR	TM LG	W	L	PCT	G	GS	CG	SHO	QS	SV	BS	QR	IP	H	R	HR	HB	BB	IB	SO	ERA	AERA	OAV	OOB	SUP	DL	PW
1982	Sea A	0	2	.000	7	2	0	0	0	0	0	3	13	18	12	4	1	1	0	10	8.31	-48	.310	.333	-26	0	-0.7
1983	Chi N	0	2	.000	11	1	0	0	0	1	0	7	25.1	34	15	2	0	12	1	20	4.97	-23	.321	.390	-77	0	-0.3
1984	Chi N	5	2	.714	31	7	0	0	2	4	0	17	83.1	78	37	11	0	20	4	41	3.46	+13	.242	.284	+36	15	0.1
1985	NY A	6	8	.429	51	3	0	0	3	2	0	31	98	95	41	5	1	29	4	64	3.21	+26	.253	.306	+12	15	1.1
1986	Bal A	6	4	.600	52	1	0	0	0	3	2	32	107	105	56	13	4	41	5	83	4.46	-6	.254	.325	-100	0	-0.2
1987	NY A	3	1	.750	16	1	0	0	0	0	1	6	33	42	28	7	0	12	0	23	7.64	-42	.309	.365	-18	0	-1.1
1988	Oak A	0	1	.000	2	2	0	0	0	0	0	0	7.2	6	6	0	0	5	0	6	4.70	-19	.214	.324	+32	0	-0.2
Total	9	20	20	.500	173	17	0	0	5	10	3	99	371.1	383	196	42	6	121	14	247	4.34	-6	.263	.320	+4	30	-1.3
Team	2	9	9	.500	67	4	0	0	3	2	1	37	131	137	69	12	1	41	4	87	4.33	-4	.268	.322	+5	15	0.0
/60G	2	8	8	.500	60	4	0	0	3	2	1	33	117.1	123	62	11	1	37	4	78	4.33	-4	.268	.322	+5	13	0.0

BOROWSKI, JOE JOSEPH THOMAS B5.4.1971 BAYONNE NJ BR/TR/6'2"/225 DR 1989 CHIA 32/823 D7.9

YEAR	TM LG	W	L	PCT	G	GS	CG	SHO	QS	SV	BS	QR	IP	H	R	HR	HB	BB	IB	SO	ERA	AERA	OAV	OOB	SUP	DL	PW
1997	NY A	0	1	.000	1	0	0	0	0	0	0	0	2	2	2	0	0	4	1	2	9.00	-51	.250	.500	—	0	-0.2
1998	NY A	1	0	1.000	8	0	0	0	0	0	0	7	9.2	11	7	0	0	4	0	7	6.52	-33	.289	.357	—	15	-0.2
Total	11	21	31	.404	405	1	0	0	0	125	29	287	437.2	426	208	49	7	169	30	363	4.05	+7	.254	.323	-12	183	1.2
Team	2	1	1	.500	9	0	0	0	0	0	0	7	11.2	13	9	0	0	8	1	9	6.94	-37	.283	.389	—	15	-0.4

BOROWY, HANK HENRY LUDWIG B5.12.1916 BLOOMFIELD NJ D8.23.2004 BRICK NJ BR/TR/6'0"/175 D4.18 COL FORDHAM

YEAR	TM LG	W	L	PCT	G	GS	CG	SHO	QS	SV	BS	QR	IP	H	R	HR	HB	BB	IB	SO	ERA	AERA	OAV	OOB	SUP	DL	PW
1942	†NY A	15	4	.789	25	21	13	4	—	1	—	—	178.1	157	56	6	0	66	—	85	2.52	+36	.233	.301	+32	0	2.0
1943	†NY A	14	9	.609	29	27	14	3	—	0	—	—	217.1	195	75	11	2	72	—	113	2.82	+14	.241	.305	+6	0	1.6
1944	NY A★	17	12	.586	35	30	19	3	—	2	—	—	252.2	224	93	15	0	88	—	107	2.64	+32	.236	.301	-3	0	2.1
1945	NY A✱	10	5	.667	18	18	7	1	—	0	—	—	132.1	107	61	6	1	58	—	35	3.13	+11	.221	.305	+34	0	0.3
1945	†Chi N	11	2	.846	15	14	11	1	—	1	—	—	122.1	105	33	2	0	47	—	47	**2.13**	+71	.231	.303	+37	0	2.3
1945	Major	21	7	.750	33	32	18	2	—	1	—	—	254	212	94	8	1	105	—	82	2.65	+40	.226	.304	+35	0	2.6
1946	Chi N	12	10	.545	32	28	8	1	—	0	—	—	201	220	96	9	1	61	—	95	3.76	-12	.274	.326	+23	0	-0.9
1947	Chi N	8	12	.400	40	25	7	1	—	2	—	—	183	190	99	19	1	63	—	75	4.38	-10	.267	.328	-10	0	-0.7
1948	Chi N	5	10	.333	39	17	2	1	—	1	—	—	127	156	80	9	0	49	—	50	4.89	-20	.308	.369	-25	0	-1.2
1949	Phi N	12	12	.500	28	28	12	1	—	0	—	—	193.1	188	99	19	0	63	—	43	4.19	-6	.259	.319	+1	0	-0.3
1950	Phi N	0	0	+	3	0	0	0	—	0	—	—	6.1	5	4	0	0	4	—	3	5.68	-29	.250	.375	—	0	-0.1
1950	Pit N	1	3	.250	11	3	0	0	—	0	—	—	25.1	32	19	6	1	9	—	9	6.39	-31	.311	.372	-6	0	-0.7
1950	Year	1	3	.250	14	3	0	0	—	0	—	—	31.2	37	23	6	1	13	—	12	6.25	-31	.301	.372	-5	0	-0.8
1950	Det A	1	1	.500	13	2	1	0	—	0	—	—	32.2	23	15	3	0	16	—	12	3.31	+42	.205	.305	+6	0	0.2
1950	Major	2	4	.333	27	5	1	0	—	0	—	—	63	60	38	9	1	29	—	24	4.76	+6	.255	.340	-1	0	-0.6
1951	Det A	2	2	.500	26	1	0	0	—	0	—	—	45.1	58	39	3	1	27	—	16	6.95	-40	.314	.404	-15	0	-1.1
Total	10	108	82	.568	314	214	94	16	—	7	—	—	1717	1660	769	108	7	623	—	690	3.50	+4	.254	.320	+8	0	3.5
Team	4	56	30	.651	107	96	53	11	—	3	—	—	780.2	683	285	38	3	284	—	340	2.74	+24	.234	.303	+14	—	6.0
/180I	1	13	7	.651	25	22	12	3	—	1	—	—	180	157	66	9	1	65	—	78	2.74	+24	.234	.303	+14	—	1.4

BOUTON, JIM JAMES ALAN B3.8.1939 NEWARK NJ BR/TR/6'0"/(174–185) D4.22 COL WESTERN MICHIGAN

YEAR	TM LG	W	L	PCT	G	GS	CG	SHO	QS	SV	BS	QR	IP	H	R	HR	HB	BB	IB	SO	ERA	AERA	OAV	OOB	SUP	DL	PW
1962	NY A	7	7	.500	36	16	3	1	8	2	0	15	133	124	63	9	0	59	1	71	3.99	-6	.254	.330	+22	0	-0.4
1963	†NY A★	21	7	.750	40	30	12	6	23	1	1	8	249.1	191	79	18	3	87	2	148	2.53	+39	.212	.282	+11	0	2.3
1964	†NY A	18	13	.581	38	**37**	11	4	25	0	0	1	271.1	227	100	32	6	60	4	125	3.02	+20	.225	.272	+10	0	1.4
1965	NY A	4	15	.211	30	25	2	0	9	0	0	3	151.1	158	89	23	5	60	1	97	4.82	-29	.269	.339	-3	0	-2.7
1966	NY A	3	8	.273	24	19	3	0	12	1	0	3	120.1	117	49	13	1	38	5	65	2.69	+23	.257	.313	-9	0	0.3
1967	NY A	1	0	1.000	17	1	0	0	0	0	0	13	44.1	47	31	5	1	18	5	31	4.67	-33	.275	.344	+95	0	-0.6
1968	NY A	1	1	.500	12	3	1	0	2	0	0	5	44	49	20	5	2	9	0	24	3.68	-21	.287	.326	-10	0	-0.2
1969	Sea A	2	1	.667	57	1	0	0	0	1	0	41	92	77	48	12	2	38	4	68	3.91	-7	.219	.298	+70	0	-0.3
1969	Hou N	0	2	.000	16	1	1	0	1	1	0	9	30.2	32	16	1	2	12	1	32	4.11	-13	.267	.343	-50	0	-0.2
1969	Major	2	3	.400	73	2	1	0	1	2	0	50	122	109	64	13	4	50	5	100	3.96	-9	.231	.309	+10	0	-0.5
1970	Hou N	4	6	.400	29	6	1	0	2	0	0	15	73.1	84	53	5	1	33	3	49	5.40	-28	.285	.358	+54	0	-1.5
1978	Atl N	1	3	.250	5	5	0	0	3	0	0	0	29	25	18	4	0	21	1	10	4.97	-19	.234	.357	-33	0	-0.4
Total	10	62	63	.496	304	144	34	11	85	6	1	113	1238.2	1131	566	127	23	435	27	720	3.57	-1	.243	.309	+8	0	-2.3
Team	7	55	51	.519	197	131	32	11	79	4	1	48	1013.2	913	431	105	18	331	18	561	3.36	+4	.241	.303	+7	—	0.1
/180I	1	10	9	.519	35	23	6	2	14	1	0	9	180	162	77	19	3	59	3	100	3.36	+4	.241	.303	+7	—	0.0

BRADLEY, RYAN RYAN J. B10.26.1975 COVINA CA BR/TR/6'4"/226 DR 1997 NYA 1/40 D8.22 COL ARIZONA ST.

YEAR	TM LG	W	L	PCT	G	GS	CG	SHO	QS	SV	BS	QR	IP	H	R	HR	HB	BB	IB	SO	ERA	AERA	OAV	OOB	SUP	DL	PW
1998	NY A	2	1	.667	5	1	0	0	0	0	0	3	12.2	12	9	2	1	9	0	13	5.68	-23	.250	.373	-15	0	-0.4

BRADY, NEAL CORNELIUS JOSEPH B3.4.1897 COVINGTON KY D6.19.1947 FORT MITCHELL KY BR/TR/6'0.5"/197 D9.25 MIL 1918

YEAR	TM LG	W	L	PCT	G	GS	CG	SHO	QS	SV	BS	QR	IP	H	R	HR	HB	BB	IB	SO	ERA	AERA	OAV	OOB	SUP	DL	PW
1915	NY A	0	0	+	2	1	0	0	—	0	—	—	8.2	9	3	0	0	7	—	6	3.12	-6	.281	.410	-1	—	-0.1
1917	NY A	1	0	1.000	2	1	0	0	—	0	—	—	9	6	2	0	0	5	—	4	2.00	+34	.188	.297	-20	—	0.2
Total	3	2	3	.400	24	5	2	0	—	1	—	—	81.1	88	49	4	4	32	—	22	4.20	-9	.278	.351	-6	—	-0.1
Team	2	1	0	1.000	4	2	0	0	—	0	—	—	17.2	15	5	0	0	12	—	10	2.55	+10	.234	.355	-10	—	0.1

BRANCA, RALPH RALPH THEODORE JOSEPH "HAWK" B1.6.1926 MT.VERNON NY BR/TR/6'3"/220 D6.12

YEAR	TM LG	W	L	PCT	G	GS	CG	SHO	QS	SV	BS	QR	IP	H	R	HR	HB	BB	IB	SO	ERA	AERA	OAV	OOB	SUP	DL	PW
1954	NY A	1	0	1.000	5	3	0	0	—	0	—	—	12.2	9	5	0	1	13	—	7	2.84	+21	.209	.390	-23	0	0.1
Total	12	88	68	.564	322	188	71	12	—	19	—	—	1484	1372	702	149	31	663	0	829	3.79	+4	.245	.328	+11	37	2.8

BRANCH, NORM NORMAN DOWNS "RED" B3.22.1915 SPOKANE WA D11.21.1971 NAVASOTA TX BR/TR/6'3"/200 D5.5 MIL 1942–45 COL TEXAS

YEAR	TM LG	W	L	PCT	G	GS	CG	SHO	QS	SV	BS	QR	IP	H	R	HR	HB	BB	IB	SO	ERA	AERA	OAV	OOB	SUP	DL	PW
1941	NY A	5	1	.833	27	0	0	0	—	2	—	—	47	37	16	2	0	26	—	28	2.87	+37	.224	.330	—	0	0.7
1942	NY A	0	1	.000	10	0	0	0	—	2	—	—	15.2	18	15	3	0	16	—	13	6.32	-46	.290	.436	—	0	-0.5
Total	2	5	2	.714	37	0	0	0	—	4	—	—	62.2	55	31	5	0	42	—	41	3.73	+2	.242	.361	—	0	0.2

BRAXTON, GARLAND EDGAR GARLAND B6.10.1900 SNOW CAMP NC D2.25.1966 NORFOLK VA BB/TL/5'11"/152 D5.27

YEAR	TM LG	W	L	PCT	G	GS	CG	SHO	QS	SV	BS	QR	IP	H	R	HR	HB	BB	IB	SO	ERA	AERA	OAV	OOB	SUP	DL	PW
1925	NY A	1	1	.500	3	2	0	0	—	0	—	—	19.1	26	14	1	1	5	—	11	6.52	-35	.338	.386	-31	—	-0.3
1926	NY A	5	1	.833	37	1	0	0	—	2	—	—	67.1	71	28	1	0	19	—	30	2.67	+44	.275	.325	+53	—	0.7
Total	10	50	53	.485	282	71	28	2	—	32	—	—	938	1014	529	38	21	276	—	412	4.13	+1	.278	.332	-12	—	0.4
Team	2	6	2	.750	40	3	0	0	—	2	—	—	86.2	97	42	2	1	24	—	41	3.53	+12	.290	.339	-3	—	0.4
/60G	3	9	3	.750	60	5	0	0	—	3	—	—	130	146	63	3	2	36	—	62	3.53	+12	.290	.339	-3	—	0.6

BRENNAN, DON JAMES DONALD B12.2.1903 AUGUSTA ME D4.26.1953 BOSTON MA BR/TR/6'0"/210 D4.16 COL GEORGETOWN

YEAR	TM LG	W	L	PCT	G	GS	CG	SHO	QS	SV	BS	QR	IP	H	R	HR	HB	BB	IB	SO	ERA	AERA	OAV	OOB	SUP	DL	PW
1933	NY A	5	1	.833	18	10	3	0	—	3	—	—	85	92	56	4	0	47	—	46	4.98	-22	.275	.365	+93	—	-0.6
Total	5	21	12	.636	141	26	7	1	—	19	—	—	397	436	232	14	7	180	—	172	4.19	-6	.281	.358	+42	—	-1.8

BRENNEMAN, JIM JAMES LEROY B2.13.1941 SAN DIEGO CA D3.10.1994 PEARL MS BR/TR/6'2"/180 D7.9 COL MESA ST.

YEAR	TM LG	W	L	PCT	G	GS	CG	SHO	QS	SV	BS	QR	IP	H	R	HR	HB	BB	IB	SO	ERA	AERA	OAV	OOB	SUP	DL	PW
1965	NY A	0	0	+	3	0	0	0	0	0	0	0	2	5	5	1	0	3	0	2	18.00	-81	.455	.571	—	0	-0.2

BRETT, KEN KENNETH ALVEN B9.18.1948 BROOKLYN NY D11.18.2003 SPOKANE WA BL/TL/5'11"/(180–195) DR 1966 BOSA 1/4 D9.27 B–GEORGE

YEAR	TM LG	W	L	PCT	G	GS	CG	SHO	QS	SV	BS	QR	IP	H	R	HR	HB	BB	IB	SO	ERA	AERA	OAV	OOB	SUP	DL	PW
1976	NY A	0	0	+	2	0	0	0	0	1	0	2	2.1	2	0	0	0	0	0	1	0.00	-100	.222	.222	—	0	0.1
Total	14	83	85	.494	349	184	51	8	107	11	3	111	1526.1	1490	734	127	23	562	62	807	3.93	-6	.257	.323	+7	54	0.5

BREUER, MARV MARVIN HOWARD "BABY FACE" B4.29.1914 ROLLA MO D1.17.1991 ROLLA MO BR/TR/6'2"/185 D5.4

YEAR	TM LG	W	L	PCT	G	GS	CG	SHO	QS	SV	BS	QR	IP	H	R	HR	HB	BB	IB	SO	ERA	AERA	OAV	OOB	SUP	DL	PW
1939	NY A	0	0	+	1	0	0	0	—	0	—	—	1	2	1	0	0	1	—	0	9.00	-52	.667	.750	—	—	0.0
1940	NY A	8	9	.471	27	22	10	0	—	0	—	—	164	175	89	20	0	61	—	71	4.55	-11	.267	.329	+23	—	-1.2
1941	†NY A	9	7	.563	26	18	7	1	—	2	—	—	141	131	73	10	2	49	—	77	4.09	-4	.243	.308	-1	0	-0.6
1942	†NY A	8	9	.471	27	19	6	0	—	1	—	—	164.1	157	67	11	1	37	—	72	3.07	+12	.252	.295	-11	0	0.1
1943	NY A	0	1	.000	5	1	0	0	—	0	—	—	14	22	16	0	0	6	—	6	8.36	-61	.349	.406	-21	0	-0.5
Total	5	25	26	.490	86	60	23	1	—	3	—	—	484.1	487	246	41	3	154	—	226	4.03	-6	.258	.315	+5	0	-2.2
/180I	2	9	10	.490	32	22	9	0	0	1	0	0	180	181	91	15	1	57	—	84	4.03	-6	.258	.315	+5	—	-0.8

YEAR	TM LG	W	L	PCT	G	GS	CG	SHO	QS	SV	BS	QR	IP	H	R	HR	HB	BB	IB	SO	ERA	AERA	OAV	OOB	SUP	DL	PW
Brewer, Billy William Robert B4.15.1968 Fort Worth TX BL/TL/6'1"/(175–200) Dr 1990 MonN 28/751 d4.8 Col Dallas Baptist																											
1996	NY A	1	0	1.000	4	0	0	0	0	0	0	2	5.2	7	6	0	0	8	0	8	9.53	-48	.292	.469	—	0	-0.4
Total	7	11	11	.500	203	0	0	0	0	5	12	146	178.2	172	96	26	4	93	7	137	4.79	-1	.255	.345	—	236	0.1
Bridges, Marshall Marshall "Sheriff" B6.2.1931 Jackson MS D9.3.1990 Jackson MS BB/TL (BR 1962–65)/6'1"/(165–190) d6.17																											
1959	StL N	6	3	.667	27	4	1	0	2	1	1	16	76	67	38	10	0	37	8	76	4.26	-1	.240	.324	-5	0	0.1
1960	StL N	2	2	.500	20	1	0	0	0	1	0	12	31.1	33	15	2	1	16	1	27	3.45	+15	.266	.350	-35	0	0.1
1960	Cin N	4	0	1.000	14	0	0	0	0	2	2	12	25.1	14	3	1	0	7	0	26	1.07	+259	.161	.223	—	0	1.4
1960	Year	6	2	.750	34	1	0	0	0	3	2	24	56.2	47	18	3	1	23	1	53	2.38	+67	.223	.300	-33	0	1.5
1961	Cin N	0	1	.000	13	0	0	0	0	0	0	7	20.2	26	19	4	1	11	0	17	7.84	-48	.317	.400	—	0	-0.4
1962	†NY A	8	4	.667	52	0	0	0	0	18	8	40	71.2	49	30	4	0	48	6	66	3.14	+19	.194	.321	—	0	0.8
1963	NY A	2	0	1.000	23	0	0	0	0	1	1	17	33	27	18	2	1	30	2	35	3.82	-8	.237	.392	—	0	-0.1
1964	Was A	0	3	.000	17	0	0	0	0	2	0	9	30	37	22	3	0	17	2	16	5.70	-35	.303	.383	—	0	-0.7
1965	Was A	1	2	.333	40	0	0	0	0	0	1	30	57.1	62	26	3	0	25	4	39	2.67	+30	.268	.340	—	0	0.2
Total	7	23	15	.605	206	5	1	0	2	25	13	143	345.1	315	171	29	3	191	23	302	3.75	+2	.244	.339	-3	0	1.4
Team	2	10	4	.714	75	0	0	0	0	19	9	57	104.2	76	48	6	1	78	8	101	3.35	+10	.207	.344	—	—	0.7
/60G	2	8	3	.714	60	0	0	0	0	15	7	46	83.2	61	38	5	1	62	6	81	3.36	+10	.207	.344	—	—	0.6
Britton, Chris Christopher Daniel B12.16.1982 Hollywood FL BR/TR/6'3"/280 Dr 2001 BalA 8/233 d4.12																											
2007	NY A	0	1	.000	11	0	0	0	0	0	0	10	12.2	9	5	2	0	4	0	5	3.55	+27	.196	.260	—	0	0.1
Total	2	0	3	.000	63	0	0	0	0	1	2	50	66.1	55	27	6	0	21	3	46	3.30	+30	.222	.281	—	0	0.4
Broaca, Johnny John Joseph B10.3.1909 Lawrence MA D5.16.1985 Lawrence MA BR/TR/5'11"/190 d6.2 Col Yale																											
1934	NY A	12	9	.571	26	24	13	1	—	0	—	—	177.1	203	94	9	1	65	—	74	4.16	-2	.284	.344	+20	—	-0.9
1935	NY A	15	7	.682	29	27	14	2	—	0	—	—	201	199	96	16	0	79	—	78	3.58	+13	.254	.323	+33	—	0.5
1936	NY A	12	7	.632	37	27	12	1	—	3	—	—	206	235	110	16	0	66	—	84	4.24	+10	.284	.337	+15	—	0.0
1937	NY A	1	4	.200	7	6	3	0	—	0	—	—	44	58	27	5	0	17	—	9	4.70	-6	.324	.383	-28	—	-0.4
1939	Cle A	4	2	.667	22	2	0	0	—	0	—	—	46	53	39	5	0	28	—	13	4.70	-6	.288	.382	+0	—	-0.9
Total	5	44	29	.603	121	86	42	4	—	3	—	—	674.1	748	366	51	1	255	—	258	4.08	+5	.278	.341	+18	—	-1.7
Team	4	40	27	.597	99	84	42	4	—	3	—	—	628.1	695	327	46	1	227	—	245	4.04	+6	.278	.338	+19	—	-0.8
/180I	1	11	8	.597	28	24	12	1	—	1	—	—	180	199	94	13	0	65	—	70	4.04	+6	.278	.338	+19	—	-0.2
Brockett, Lew Lewis Albert "King" B7.23.1880 Brownsville IL D9.19.1960 Norris City IL BR/TR/5'10.5"/168 d4.25																											
1907	NY A	1	2	.333	8	4	1	0	—	0	—	—	46.1	58	36	1	2	26	—	13	6.22	-55	.309	.398	-27	—	-0.9
1909	NY A	10	8	.556	26	18	10	3	—	1	—	—	170	148	68	3	6	59	—	70	2.12	+19	.245	.318	-6	—	1.1
1911	NY A	2	4	.333	16	8	2	0	—	0	—	—	75.1	73	45	2	5	39	—	25	4.66	-23	.256	.356	-7	—	-0.2
Total	3	13	14	.481	50	30	13	3	—	1	—	—	291.2	279	149	6	13	124	—	108	3.43	-17	.259	.343	-9	—	0.0
/180I	2	8	9	.481	31	19	8	2	0	1	0	0	180	172	92	4	8	77	—	67	3.43	-17	.259	.343	-9	—	0.0
Bronstad, Jim James Warren B6.22.1936 Ft.Worth TX BR/TR/6'3"/(195–196) d6.7																											
1959	NY A	0	3	.000	16	3	0	0	2	2	0	9	29.1	34	19	2	1	13	0	14	5.22	-30	.288	.361	-27	0	-0.6
1963	Was A	1	3	.250	25	0	0	0	0	1	1	19	57.1	66	38	9	1	22	2	22	5.65	-34	.297	.359	—	0	-0.8
1964	Was A	0	1	.000	4	0	0	0	0	0	0	3	7	10	4	0	0	2	0	9	5.14	-28	.345	.387	—	0	-0.1
Total	3	1	7	.125	45	3	0	0	2	3	1	31	93.2	110	61	11	2	37	2	45	5.48	-33	.298	.362	-27	0	-1.5
Brower, Jim James Robert B12.29.1972 Edina MN BR/TR/6'2"/(205–215) Dr 1994 TexA 6/169 d9.5 Col Minnesota																											
2007	NY A	0	0	+	3	0	0	0	0	0	0	0	3.1	8	7	0	1	2	0	1	13.50	-67	.500	.524	—	0	-0.2
Total	9	33	32	.508	354	28	0	0	8	5	10	213	574	596	323	70	28	256	17	397	4.67	-4	.271	.352	+24	0	0.6
Brown, Boardwalk Carroll William B2.20.1889 Woodbury NJ D2.8.1977 Burlington NJ BR/TR/6'1.5"/178 d9.27																											
1914	NY A	6	5	.545	20	14	8	0	—	0	—	—	122.1	123	57	2	1	42	—	57	3.24	-15	.271	.334	+23	—	-0.3
1915	NY A	3	6	.333	19	11	5	0	—	0	—	—	96.2	95	49	4	5	47	—	34	4.10	-28	.275	.370	-34	—	-1.0
Total	5	40	39	.506	133	92	42	6	—	1	—	—	731.1	698	356	15	25	291	—	251	3.47	-17	.262	.340	+26	—	-5.4
Team	2	9	11	.450	39	25	13	0	—	0	—	—	219	218	106	6	6	89	—	91	3.62	-22	.273	.350	-2	—	-1.3
/180I	2	7	9	.450	32	21	11	0	—	0	—	—	180	179	87	5	5	73	—	75	3.62	-22	.273	.350	-2	—	-1.1
Brown, Curt Curtis Steven B1.15.1960 Ft.Lauderdale FL BR/TR/6'5"/(165–175) d6.10 Col Broward (FL) CC																											
1983	Cal A	1	1	.500	10	0	0	0	0	0	0	4	16	25	13	1	0	4	1	7	7.31	-45	.368	.397	—	0	-0.6
1984	NY A	1	1	.500	13	0	0	0	0	0	1	8	16.2	18	5	1	0	4	0	10	2.70	+42	.281	.319	—	0	0.3
1986	Mon N	0	1	.000	6	0	0	0	0	0	0	4	12	15	6	0	0	2	2	4	3.00	+25	.319	.340	—	0	0.0
1987	Mon N	0	1	.000	5	0	0	0	0	0	0	2	7	10	7	2	0	4	1	6	7.71	-45	.333	.412	—	0	-0.3
Total	4	2	4	.333	34	0	0	0	0	0	1	18	51.2	68	31	4	0	14	4	27	4.88	-19	.325	.363	—	0	-0.6
Brown, Hal Hector Harold "Skinny" B12.11.1924 Greensboro NC BR/TR/6'2"/(181–185) d4.19 C1 Col North Carolina																											
1962	NY A	0	1	.000	2	1	0	0	0	0	0	1	6.2	9	10	3	0	2	0	2	6.75	-44	.333	.367	-29	0	-0.5
Total	14	85	92	.480	358	211	47	13	159	11	5	70	1680	1677	781	173	14	389	27	710	3.81	-2	.260	.302	-12	45	0.6
Brown, Kevin James Kevin B3.14.1965 Milledgeville GA BR/TR/6'4"/(188–220) Dr 1986 TexA 1/4 d9.30 Col Georgia Tech																											
2004	†NY A	10	6	.625	22	22	0	0	11	0	0	0	132	132	65	14	3	35	0	83	4.09	+12	.262	.309	+3	50	0.7
2005	NY A	4	7	.364	13	13	0	0	4	0	0	0	73.1	107	57	5	7	19	1	50	6.50	-34	.341	.388	+19	117	-2.1
Total	19	211	144	.594	486	476	72	17	323	0	0	7	3256.1	3079	1357	208	139	901	42	2397	3.28	+28	.249	.306	-3	406	33.7
Team	2	14	13	.519	35	35	0	0	15	0	—	0	205.1	239	122	19	10	54	1	133	4.95	-9	.292	.339	+9	167	-1.4
/180I	2	12	11	.519	31	31	0	0	13	0	—	0	180	210	107	17	9	47	1	117	4.95	-9	.292	.339	+9	146	-1.2
Brown, Jumbo Walter George B4.30.1907 Greene RI D10.2.1966 Freeport NY BR/TR/6'4"/295 d8.26																											
1932	NY A	5	2	.714	19	3	3	1	—	1	—	—	55.2	58	30	1	2	30	—	31	4.53	-10	.270	.364	-30	—	-0.2
1933	NY A	7	5	.583	21	8	1	0	—	0	—	—	74	78	48	3	0	52	—	55	5.23	-26	.269	.380	+45	—	-1.5
1935	NY A	6	5	.545	20	8	3	1	—	0	—	—	87.1	94	41	2	0	37	—	41	3.61	+12	.279	.350	+2	—	0.8
1936	NY A	1	4	.200	20	3	0	0	—	1	—	—	64	93	47	4	0	29	—	19	5.91	-21	.352	.416	+7	—	-0.8
Total	12	33	31	.516	249	23	7	2	—	29	—	—	597.1	619	316	26	5	300	—	301	4.07	-1	.271	.357	+16	0	0.0
Team	4	19	16	.543	80	22	7	2	—	2	—	—	281	323	166	10	2	148	—	146	4.74	-13	.292	.377	+14	—	-1.7
/180I	3	12	10	.543	51	14	4	1	—	1	—	—	180	207	106	6	1	95	—	94	4.74	-13	.292	.377	+14	—	-1.1
Bruney, Brian Brian Anthony B2.17.1982 Astoria OR BR/TR/6'3"/(225–245) Dr 2000 AriN 12/369 d5.8																											
2004	Ari N	3	4	.429	30	0	0	0	0	0	1	23	31.1	20	16	2	1	27	5	34	4.31	+6	.189	.358	—	40	0.2
2005	Ari N	1	3	.250	47	0	0	0	0	12	4	30	46	56	39	6	5	35	2	51	7.43	-40	.299	.421	—	0	-1.7
2006	†NY A	1	1	.500	19	0	0	0	0	0	0	15	20.2	14	2	1	1	15	0	25	0.87	+430	.189	.333	—	0	0.7
2007	NY A	3	2	.600	58	0	0	0	0	0	2	38	50	44	28	5	3	37	2	39	4.68	-4	.243	.370	—	0	-0.1
Total	4	8	10	.444	154	0	0	0	0	12	7	106	148	134	85	14	10	114	9	149	4.93	-8	.245	.380	—	40	-0.9
Team	2	4	3	.571	77	0	0	0	0	0	2	53	70.2	58	30	6	4	52	2	64	3.57	+27	.227	.360	—	—	0.6
/60G	2	3	2	.571	60	0	0	0	0	0	2	41	55	45	23	5	3	41	2	50	3.57	+27	.227	.360	—	—	0.5
Bruske, Jim James Scott B10.7.1964 E.St.Louis IL BR/TR/6'1"/185 Dr 1986 CleA S1/6 d8.25 Col Loyola Marymount																											
1998	NY A	1	0	1.000	3	1	0	0	0	0	0	1	9	9	3	2	0	1	0	3	3.00	+46	.257	.278	+70	0	0.2
Total	5	9	1	.900	105	1	0	0	0	2	2	64	144	154	77	16	8	68	6	95	4.13	-2	.273	.357	+70	92	0.0
Buckles, Jess Jesse Robert "Jim" B5.20.1890 Lordsburg CA D8.2.1975 Westminster CA BL/TL/6'2.5"/205 d9.17																											
1916	NY A	0	0	+	2	0	0	0	—	0	—	—	4	3	2	0	0	1	—	2	2.25	+28	.188	.235	—	—	0.0

YEAR	TM LG	W	L	PCT	G	GS	CG	SHO	QS	SV	BS	QR	IP	H	R	HR	HB	BB	IB	SO	ERA	AERA	OAV	OOB	SUP	DL	PW
Buddie, Mike	Michael Joseph B12.12.1970 Berea OH BR/TR/6'3"/(210–219) Dr 1992 NYA 4/102 d4.6 Col Wake Forest																										
1998	NY A	4	1	.800	24	2	0	0	0	0	0	12	41.2	46	29	5	3	13	1	20	5.62	-22	.284	.346	+49	0	-0.7
1999	NY A	0	0	+	2	0	0	0	0	0	0	1	2	3	1	1	0	0	0	1	4.50	+5	.333	.333	—	0	0.0
Total	5	5	4	.556	87	2	0	0	0	2	2	55	131	137	76	13	8	52	11	76	4.67	-8	.272	.347	+49	20	-0.6
Team	2	4	1	.800	26	2	0	0	0	0	0	13	43.2	49	30	6	3	13	1	21	5.56	-21	.287	.346	+49	—	-0.7
Burbach, Bill	William David B8.22.1947 Dickeyville WI BR/TR/6'4"/(215–222) Dr 1965 NYA 1/19 d4.11																										
1969	NY A	6	8	.429	31	24	2	1	10	0	0	6	140.2	112	68	15	2	102	1	82	3.65	-3	.219	.349	-3	0	-0.5
1970	NY A	0	2	.000	4	4	0	0	0	0	0	0	16.2	23	19	2	1	9	0	10	10.26	-65	.324	.402	+50	0	-1.2
1971	NY A	0	1	.000	2	0	0	0	0	0	0	0	3.1	6	6	0	0	5	2	3	10.80	-70	.400	.524	—	0	-0.7
Total	3	6	11	.353	37	28	2	1	10	0	0	6	160.2	141	93	17	3	116	3	95	4.48	-21	.236	.360	+5	0	-2.4
/180I	3	7	12	.353	41	31	2	1	11	0	0	7	180	158	104	19	3	130	3	106	4.48	-21	.236	.360	+5	—	-2.7
Burdette, Lew	Selva Lewis B11.22.1926 Nitro WV D2.6.2007 Winter Garden FL BR/TR/6'2"/(180–195) d9.26 C2 Col Richmond																										
1950	NY A	0	0	+	2	0	0	0	—	0	—	—	1.1	3	1	0	0	0	—	0	6.75	-36	.500	.500	—	0	0.0
Total	18	203	144	.585	626	373	158	33	278	31	7	129	3067.1	3186	1400	289	56	628	63	1074	3.66	-1	.268	.306	+15	0	3.1
Burke, Tim	Timothy Philip B2.19.1959 Omaha NE BR/TR/6'3"/(200–205) Dr 1980 PitN 2/49 d4.8 Col Nebraska																										
1992	NY A	2	2	.500	23	0	0	0	0	0	0	14	27.2	26	14	2	1	15	4	8	3.25	+21	.250	.350	—	31	0.1
Total	8	49	33	.598	498	2	0	0	1	102	45	359	699.1	624	251	49	21	219	71	444	2.72	+37	.240	.302	-17	89	8.9
Burris, Ray	Bertram Ray B8.22.1950 Idabel OK BR/TR/6'5"/(192–210) Dr 1972 ChiN 17/399 d4.8 C3 Col Southwestern Oklahoma																										
1979	NY A	1	3	.250	15	0	0	0	0	0	2	5	27.2	40	22	5	0	10	1	19	6.18	-33	.342	.388	—	0	-0.9
Total	15	108	134	.446	480	302	47	10	162	4	7	114	2188.2	2310	1133	221	54	764	76	1065	4.17	-6	.274	.335	-5	47	-7.6
Bush, Joe	Leslie Ambrose "Bullet Joe" B11.27.1892 Gull River MN D11.1.1974 Ft.Lauderdale FL BR/TR/5'9"/173 d9.30																										
1922	†NY A	26	7	**.788**	39	30	20	0	—	3	—	—	255.1	240	109	16	1	85	—	92	3.31	+21	.252	.314	+18	—	3.2
1923	†NY A	19	15	.559	37	30	22	3	—	0	—	—	275.2	263	115	7	5	117	—	125	3.43	+15	.260	.340	+3	—	2.6
1924	NY A	17	16	.515	39	31	19	3	—	1	—	—	252	262	117	9	7	109	—	80	3.57	+16	.273	.352	+2	—	3.2
Total	17	196	184	.516	489	370	225	35	—	19	—	—	3087.1	2992	1441	96	63	1263	—	1319	3.51	-1	.260	.336	-2	—	6.7
Team	3	62	38	.620	115	91	61	6	—	4	—	—	783	765	341	32	13	311	—	297	3.44	+17	.262	.336	+8	—	9.0
/180I	1	14	9	.620	26	21	14	1	—	1	—	—	180	176	78	7	3	71	—	68	3.44	+17	.262	.336	+8	—	2.1
Buskey, Tom	Thomas William B2.20.1947 Harrisburg PA D6.7.1998 Harrisburg PA BR/TR/6'3"/(200–228) d8.5 Col North Carolina																										
1973	NY A	0	1	.000	8	0	0	0	0	1	1	4	16.2	18	12	2	1	4	0	8	5.40	-31	.286	.324	—	0	-0.2
1974	NY A	0	1	.000	4	0	0	0	0	1	0	2	5.2	10	4	1	1	3	1	3	6.35	-44	.400	.483	—	0	-0.3
Total	8	21	27	.438	258	0	0	0	0	34	18	163	479.1	479	218	57	9	167	45	212	3.66	+6	.267	.328	—	45	2.9
Team	2	0	2	.000	12	0	0	0	0	2	1	6	22.1	28	16	3	2	7	1	11	5.64	-35	.318	.370	—	—	-0.5
Buxton, Ralph	Ralph Stanley "Buck" B6.7.1914 Rainton SK, Can. D1.6.1988 San Leandro CA BR/TR/5'11.5"/163 d9.11 Mil 1943–45																										
1938	Phi A	0	1	.000	5	0	0	0	—	0	—	—	9.1	12	7	1	0	5	—	9	4.82	+0	.324	.405	—	—	-0.1
1949	NY A	0	1	.000	14	0	0	0	—	2	—	—	26.2	22	13	3	0	16	—	14	4.05	+0	.229	.339	—	0	0.0
Total	2	0	2	.000	19	0	0	0	—	2	—	—	36	34	20	4	0	21	—	23	4.25	+0	.256	.357	—	0	-0.1
Byrd, Harry	Harry Gladwin B2.3.1925 Darlington SC D5.14.1985 Darlington SC BR/TR (BB 1955)/6'1"/188 d4.21																										
1954	NY A	9	7	.563	25	21	5	1	—	0	—	—	132.1	131	56	10	7	43	—	52	2.99	+15	.258	.321	+36	0	0.5
Total	7	46	54	.460	187	108	33	8	0	9	1	26	827.2	890	442	71	41	355	9	381	4.35	-9	.277	.355	-4	0	-3.6
/180I	1	12	10	.563	34	29	7	1	—	0	—	—	180	178	76	14	10	58	—	71	2.99	+15	.258	.321	+36	—	0.7
Byrne, Tommy	Thomas Joseph B12.31.1919 Baltimore MD BL/TL/6'1"/(182–187) d4.27 Mil 1944–45 Col Wake Forest																										
1943	NY A	2	1	.667	11	2	0	0	—	0	—	—	31.2	28	26	1	3	35	—	22	6.54	-51	.248	.437	+5	0	-1.0
1946	NY A	0	1	.000	4	1	0	0	—	0	—	—	9.1	7	8	1	1	8	—	5	5.79	-40	.194	.356	-25	0	-0.2
1947	NY A	0	0	+	4	1	0	0	—	0	—	—	4.1	5	2	0	0	6	—	2	4.15	-15	.294	.478	+125	0	0.0
1948	NY A	8	5	.615	31	11	5	1	—	2	—	—	133.2	79	55	8	9	101	—	93	3.30	+24	.172	.332	+23	0	1.6
1949	†NY A	15	7	.682	32	30	12	3	—	0	—	—	196	125	84	11	13	179	—	129	3.72	+9	**.183**	.362	+40	0	1.0
1950	NY A☆	15	9	.625	31	31	10	2	—	0	—	—	203.1	188	115	23	17	160	—	118	4.74	-9	.245	.387	+40	0	-0.4
1951	NY A	2	1	.667	9	3	0	0	—	0	—	—	21	16	17	0	3	36	—	14	6.86	-44	.213	.482	+24	0	-0.8
1951	StL A	4	10	.286	19	17	7	2	—	0	—	—	122.2	104	56	5	12	114	—	57	3.82	+15	.235	.404	-36	0	1.2
1951	Year	6	11	.353	28	20	7	2	—	0	—	—	143.2	120	73	5	15	150	—	71	4.26	+1	.232	.417	-28	0	0.4
1952	StL A	7	14	.333	29	24	14	0	—	0	—	—	196	182	117	16	10	112	—	91	4.68	-16	.247	.354	-10	0	-1.2
1953	Chi A	2	0	1.000	6	6	0	0	—	0	—	—	16	18	18	0	0	26	—	4	10.13	-60	.295	.506	+58	0	-0.9
1953	Was A	0	5	.000	6	5	2	0	—	0	—	—	33.2	35	17	3	1	22	—	22	4.28	-9	.276	.387	-45	0	-0.2
1953	Year	2	5	.286	12	11	2	0	—	0	—	—	49.2	53	35	3	1	48	—	26	6.16	-36	.282	.430	+13	0	-1.1
1954	NY A	3	2	.600	5	5	4	1	—	0	—	—	40	36	13	1	0	19	—	24	2.70	+27	.240	.325	+49	0	1.0
1955	†NY A	16	5	**.762**	27	22	9	3	—	2	—	—	160	137	69	12	7	87	3	76	3.15	+19	.237	.340	+17	0	1.5
1956	†NY A	7	3	.700	37	8	1	0	—	6	—	—	109.2	108	50	9	2	72	5	52	3.36	+15	.262	.372	+29	0	1.0
1957	†NY A	4	6	.400	30	4	1	0	1	2	1	14	84.2	70	41	8	7	60	2	57	4.36	-18	.227	.363	-13	0	-0.2
Total	13	85	69	.552	281	170	65	12	1	12	1	14	1362	1138	688	98	85	1037	10	766	4.11	-3	.229	.370	+18	0	2.4
Team	11	72	40	.643	221	118	42	10	1	12	1	14	993.2	799	480	74	62	763	10	592	3.93	+0	.222	.366	+31	—	3.5
/180I	2	13	7	.643	40	21	8	2	0	2	0	3	180	145	87	13	11	138	2	107	3.93	+0	.222	.366	+31	—	0.6
Bystrom, Marty	Martin Eugene B7.26.1958 Coral Gables FL BR/TR/6'5"/(200–210) d9.7 Col Miami–Dade Kendall (FL) CC																										
1984	NY A	2	2	.500	7	7	0	0	5	0	0	0	39.1	34	16	3	1	13	1	24	2.97	+29	.230	.296	-23	33	0.3
1985	NY A	3	2	.600	8	8	0	0	3	0	0	0	41	44	29	8	1	19	0	16	5.71	-29	.280	.360	+7	106	-0.8
Total	6	29	26	.527	84	79	4	2	39	0	0	5	435	454	236	28	15	158	9	258	4.26	-13	.268	.333	+7	253	-3.0
Team	2	5	4	.556	15	15	0	0	8	0	—	0	80.1	78	45	11	2	32	1	40	4.37	-10	.256	.329	-7	139	-0.5
Cadaret, Greg	Gregory James B2.27.1962 Detroit MI BL/TL/6'3"/(205–230) Dr 1983 OakA 11/267 d7.5 Col Grand Valley St.																										
1987	Oak A	6	2	.750	29	0	0	0	0	0	1	19	39.2	37	22	6	1	24	1	30	4.54	-8	.252	.356	—	0	-0.2
1988	†Oak A	5	2	.714	58	0	0	0	0	3	1	37	71.2	60	26	2	1	36	1	64	2.89	+32	.226	.317	—	0	0.7
1989	Oak A	0	0	+	26	0	0	0	0	0	1	18	27.2	21	9	0	0	19	3	14	2.28	+63	.214	.336	—	0	0.2
1989	NY A	5	5	.500	20	13	3	1	9	0	1	4	92.1	109	53	7	2	38	1	66	4.58	-15	.298	.364	-5	0	-0.7
1989	Year	5	5	.500	46	13	3	1	9	0	2	22	120	130	62	7	2	57	4	80	4.05	-5	.280	.358	-4	0	-0.5
1990	NY A	5	4	.556	54	6	0	0	2	3	1	37	121.1	120	62	8	1	64	5	80	4.15	-4	.268	.359	-16	0	0.0
1991	NY A	8	6	.571	68	5	0	0	2	3	4	41	121.2	110	52	8	2	59	6	105	3.62	+15	.246	.335	+67	0	0.9
1992	NY A	4	8	.333	46	11	1	1	5	1	2	23	103.2	104	53	12	2	74	7	73	4.25	-7	.267	.385	+7	0	-0.3
1993	Cin N	2	1	.667	34	0	0	0	0	1	0	19	32.2	40	19	3	1	23	5	23	4.96	-19	.305	.413	—	0	-0.3
1993	KC A	1	1	.500	13	0	0	0	0	0	0	9	15.1	14	5	0	1	7	0	2	2.93	+57	.264	.361	—	0	0.3
1993	Major	3	2	.600	47	0	0	0	0	1	0	28	47	54	24	3	2	30	5	25	4.31	+5	.293	.398	—	0	0.0
1994	Tor A	0	1	.000	21	0	0	0	0	0	0	12	20	24	15	4	0	17	2	15	5.85	-17	.289	.410	—	0	-0.1
1994	Det A	1	0	1.000	17	0	0	0	0	2	0	11	20	17	9	0	0	16	3	14	3.60	+37	.227	.363	—	0	0.2
1994	Year	1	1	.500	38	0	0	0	0	2	0	23	40	41	24	4	0	33	5	29	4.72	+4	.259	.387	—	0	0.1
1997	Ana A	0	0	+	15	0	0	0	0	0	0	11	13.2	11	5	1	2	8	2	11	3.29	+40	.220	.350	—	0	0.1
1998	Ana A	1	2	.333	39	0	0	0	0	1	1	27	37	38	17	6	3	15	0	37	4.14	+15	.257	.337	—	0	0.2
1998	Tex A	0	0	+	11	0	0	0	0	0	0	7	7.2	11	4	1	0	3	0	5	4.70	+4	.355	.400	—	0	0.0
1998	Year	1	2	.333	50	0	0	0	0	1	1	34	44.2	49	21	7	3	18	0	42	4.23	+13	.274	.348	—	0	0.2
Total	10	38	32	.543	451	35	4	2	18	14	12	275	724.1	716	351	58	16	403	36	539	3.99	+3	.262	.358	+4	0	1.0
Team	4	22	23	.489	188	35	4	2	18	7	8	105	439	443	220	35	7	235	19	324	4.12	-3	.268	.360	+7	—	-0.1
/60G	1	7	7	.489	60	11	1	1	6	2	3	34	140	141	70	11	2	75	6	103	4.12	-3	.268	.360	+7	—	-0.0

Caldwell, Charlie — Charles William "Chuck" B8.2.1901 Bristol VA D11.1.1957 Princeton NJ BR/TR/5'10"/180 d7.7 Col Princeton

YEAR	TM LG	W	L	PCT	G	GS	CG	SHO	QS	SV	BS	QR	IP	H	R	HR	HB	BB	IB	SO	ERA	AERA	OAV	OOB	SUP	DL	PW
1925	NY A	0	0	+	3	0	0	0	—	0	—	—	2.2	7	6	0	0	3	—	1	16.88	-75	.467	.556	—	—	-0.2

Caldwell, Ray — Raymond Benjamin "Rube","Sum" B4.26.1888 Corydon PA D8.17.1967 Salamanca NY BL/TR/6'2"/190 d9.9 ▲

YEAR	TM LG	W	L	PCT	G	GS	CG	SHO	QS	SV	BS	QR	IP	H	R	HR	HB	BB	IB	SO	ERA	AERA	OAV	OOB	SUP	DL	PW
1910	NY A	1	0	1.000	6	2	1	0	—	1	—	—	19.1	19	8	1	0	9	—	17	3.72	-29	.260	.341	+26	—	-0.2
1911	NY A	14	14	.500	41	26	19	1	—	1	—	—	255	240	115	7	13	79	—	145	3.35	+7	.260	.327	-17	—	1.3
1912	NY A	8	16	.333	30	26	13	3	—	0	—	—	183.1	196	111	1	6	67	—	[illegible]	4.47	-20	.277	.344	-8	—	-1.1
1913	NY A	9	8	.529	27	16	15	2	—	1	—	—	164.1	131	59	5	9	60	—	87	2.41	+24	.221	.303	+13	—	1.7
1914	NY A	18	9	.667	31	23	22	5	—	0	—	—	213	153	53	5	4	51	—	92	1.94	+42	.205	.260	-1	—	3.0
1915	NY A	19	16	.543	36	35	31	3	—	0	—	—	305	266	115	6	5	107	—	130	2.89	+1	.244	.315	+8	—	1.2
1916	NY A	5	12	.294	21	18	14	1	—	0	—	—	165.2	142	62	6	8	65	—	76	2.99	-3	.243	.327	-39	—	0.1
1917	NY A	13	16	.448	32	29	21	1	—	0	—	—	236	199	92	8	6	76	—	102	2.86	-6	.234	.302	-7	—	0.8
1918	NY A	9	8	.529	24	21	14	1	—	1	—	—	176.2	173	69	2	1	62	—	59	3.06	-7	.261	.325	+14	—	0.3
1919	Bos A	7	4	.636	18	12	6	1	—	0	—	—	86.1	92	49	1	3	31	—	23	3.96	-24	.279	.346	+15	—	-1.1
1919	Cle A	5	1	.833	6	6	4	1	—	0	—	—	52.2	33	13	1	2	19	—	24	1.71	+96	.181	.266	+5	—	1.4
1919	Year	12	5	.706	24	18	10	2	—	0	—	—	139	125	62	2	5	50	—	47	3.11	+1	.244	.317	+11	—	0.3
1920	†Cle A	20	10	.667	34	33	20	1	—	0	—	—	237.2	286	135	9	4	63	—	80	3.86	-2	.303	.350	+37	—	-0.7
1921	Cle A	6	6	.500	37	12	4	1	—	4	—	—	147	159	91	7	2	49	—	76	4.90	-13	.275	.333	+44	—	-0.6
Total	12	134	120	.528	343	259	184	21	—	8	—	—	2242	2089	972	59	63	738	—	1006	3.22	-1	.253	.319	+5	—	6.1
Team	9	96	99	.492	248	196	150	17	—	4	—	—	1718.1	1519	684	41	52	576	—	803	3.00	+1	.244	.313	-4	—	7.1
/180I	1	10	10	.492	26	21	16	2	—	0	—	—	180	159	72	4	5	60	—	84	3.00	+1	.244	.313	-4	—	0.7

Campbell, Archie — Archibald Stewart "Iron Man" B10.20.1903 Maplewood NJ D12.22.1989 Sparks NV BR/TR/6'0"/180 d4.21

YEAR	TM LG	W	L	PCT	G	GS	CG	SHO	QS	SV	BS	QR	IP	H	R	HR	HB	BB	IB	SO	ERA	AERA	OAV	OOB	SUP	DL	PW
1928	NY A	0	1	.000	13	1	0	0	—	2	—	—	24	30	22	0	0	11	—	9	5.25	-28	.288	.357	-10	—	-0.4
Total	3	2	6	.250	40	4	1	0	—	6	—	—	86	111	67	3	1	47	—	29	5.86	-23	.315	.398	-47	—	-1.4

Candelaria, John — John Robert "Candy Man" B11.6.1953 New York NY BL/TL (BB 1982p, 83–86 BR 1987–90)/6'7"/(210–250) Dr 1972 PitN 2/47 d6.8

YEAR	TM LG	W	L	PCT	G	GS	CG	SHO	QS	SV	BS	QR	IP	H	R	HR	HB	BB	IB	SO	ERA	AERA	OAV	OOB	SUP	DL	PW
1988	NY A	13	7	.650	25	24	6	2	14	1	0	1	157	150	69	18	2	23	2	121	3.38	+17	.248	.275	+12	0	1.0
1989	NY A	3	3	.500	10	6	1	0	2	0	0	2	49	49	28	8	0	12	1	37	5.14	-24	.258	.299	+1	105	-0.6
Total	19	177	122	.592	600	356	54	13	210	29	17	162	2525.2	2399	1038	245	37	592	63	1673	3.33	+15	.251	.295	+6	415	17.0
Team	2	16	10	.615	35	30	7	2	16	1	0	3	206	199	97	26	2	35	3	158	3.80	+4	.250	.281	+10	105	0.4
/180I	2	14	9	.615	31	26	6	2	14	1	0	3	180	174	85	23	2	31	3	138	3.80	+4	.250	.281	+10	92	0.3

Cantwell, Mike — Michael Joseph B6.15.1894 Washington DC D1.5.1953 Oteen NC BL/TL/5'10"/155 d9.17 b–Tom Col Georgetown

YEAR	TM LG	W	L	PCT	G	GS	CG	SHO	QS	SV	BS	QR	IP	H	R	HR	HB	BB	IB	SO	ERA	AERA	OAV	OOB	SUP	DL	PW
1916	NY A	0	0	+	1	0	0	0	—	0	—	—	2	0	2	0	0	2	—	0	0.00	-100	.000	.333	—	—	0.0
Total	3	1	6	.143	11	4	2	0	—	0	—	—	52.2	61	39	2	5	26	—	14	4.61	-29	.310	.404	+14	—	-1.2

Carroll, Ownie — Owen Thomas B11.11.1902 Kearny NJ D6.8.1975 Orange NJ BR/TR/5'10.5"/165 d6.20 Col Holy Cross

YEAR	TM LG	W	L	PCT	G	GS	CG	SHO	QS	SV	BS	QR	IP	H	R	HR	HB	BB	IB	SO	ERA	AERA	OAV	OOB	SUP	DL	PW
1930	NY A	0	1	.000	10	1	0	0	—	0	—	—	32.2	49	32	2	4	18	—	8	6.61	-35	.374	.464	+40	—	-0.4
Total	9	64	90	.416	248	153	71	2	—	5	—	—	1330.2	1532	808	61	48	486	—	311	4.43	-11	.294	.359	-5	—	-6.6

Carroll, Dick — Richard Thomas "Shadow" B7.21.1884 Cleveland OH D11.22.1945 Cleveland OH BR/TR/6'2"/? d9.25

YEAR	TM LG	W	L	PCT	G	GS	CG	SHO	QS	SV	BS	QR	IP	H	R	HR	HB	BB	IB	SO	ERA	AERA	OAV	OOB	SUP	DL	PW
1909	NY A	0	0	+	2	1	0	0	—	0	—	—	5	7	6	1	0	1	—	1	3.60	-30	.292	.320	+207	—	-0.1

Cary, Chuck — Charles Douglas B3.3.1960 Whittier CA BL/TL/6'4"/(210–216) Dr 1981 DetA 7/172 d8.22 Col California

YEAR	TM LG	W	L	PCT	G	GS	CG	SHO	QS	SV	BS	QR	IP	H	R	HR	HB	BB	IB	SO	ERA	AERA	OAV	OOB	SUP	DL	PW
1985	Det A	0	1	.000	16	0	0	0	0	2	1	12	23.2	16	9	2	2	8	1	22	3.42	+20	.190	.274	—	0	0.1
1986	Det A	1	2	.333	22	0	0	0	0	0	1	16	31.2	33	18	3	0	15	4	21	3.41	+22	.273	.348	—	0	0.0
1987	Atl N	1	1	.500	13	0	0	0	0	1	1	9	16.2	17	7	3	1	4	3	15	3.78	+15	.266	.319	—	0	0.2
1988	Atl N	0	0	+	7	0	0	0	0	0	0	3	8.1	8	6	1	1	4	0	7	6.48	-43	.250	.351	—	129	-0.1
1989	NY A	4	4	.500	22	11	2	0	7	0	0	8	99.1	78	42	13	0	29	6	79	3.26	+19	.209	.266	-1	26	0.3
1990	NY A	6	12	.333	28	27	2	0	15	0	0	1	156.2	155	77	21	1	55	1	134	4.19	-5	.260	.321	-24	36	-0.2
1991	NY A	1	6	.143	10	9	0	0	3	0	0	0	53.1	61	35	6	0	32	2	34	5.91	-29	.285	.378	-24	0	-1.0
1993	Chi A	1	0	1.000	16	0	0	0	0	0	0	10	20.2	22	12	1	3	11	0	10	5.23	-19	.286	.379	—	127	-0.1
Total	8	14	26	.350	134	47	4	0	25	3	3	59	410.1	390	206	50	8	158	17	322	4.17	-3	.250	.319	-19	318	-0.8
Team	3	11	22	.333	60	47	4	0	25	0	0	9	309.1	294	154	40	1	116	9	247	4.19	-5	.249	.315	-19	62	-0.9
/180I	2	6	13	.333	35	27	2	0	15	0	0	5	180	171	90	23	1	68	5	144	4.19	-5	.249	.315	-19	36	-0.5

Casey, Hugh — Hugh Thomas B10.14.1913 Atlanta GA D7.3.1951 Atlanta GA BR/TR/6'1"/207 d4.29 Mil 1943–45

YEAR	TM LG	W	L	PCT	G	GS	CG	SHO	QS	SV	BS	QR	IP	H	R	HR	HB	BB	IB	SO	ERA	AERA	OAV	OOB	SUP	DL	PW
1949	NY A	1	0	1.000	4	0	0	0	—	0	—	—	7.2	11	10	0	0	8	—	5	8.22	-51	.324	.452	—	0	-0.5
Total	9	75	42	.641	343	56	24	3	—	55	—	—	939.2	935	414	58	27	321	—	349	3.45	+10	.260	.325	+5	60	4.9

Castleton, Roy — Royal Eugene B7.26.1885 Salt Lake City UT D6.24.1967 Los Angeles CA BR/TL/5'11"/167 d4.16

YEAR	TM LG	W	L	PCT	G	GS	CG	SHO	QS	SV	BS	QR	IP	H	R	HR	HB	BB	IB	SO	ERA	AERA	OAV	OOB	SUP	DL	PW
1907	NY A	1	1	.500	3	2	1	0	—	0	—	—	16	11	6	1	0	3	—	3	2.81	-1	.196	.237	-40	—	0.0
Total	3	3	4	.429	11	5	3	0	—	0	—	—	43.2	40	17	1	3	15	—	13	2.68	+4	.252	.328	+42	—	0.2

Castro, Bill — William Radhames (Checo) B3.29.1952 Santiago, D.R. BR/TR/5'11"/(170–180) d8.20 C16

YEAR	TM LG	W	L	PCT	G	GS	CG	SHO	QS	SV	BS	QR	IP	H	R	HR	HB	BB	IB	SO	ERA	AERA	OAV	OOB	SUP	DL	PW
1981	NY A	1	1	.500	11	0	0	0	0	0	0	6	19	26	13	2	0	5	1	4	3.79	-5	.329	.369	—	0	-0.2
Total	10	31	26	.544	303	9	0	0	3	45	23	200	546.1	564	245	36	22	145	42	203	3.33	+18	.268	.319	+30	61	4.0

Chacon, Shawn — Shawn Anthony B12.23.1977 Anchorage AK BR/TR/6'3"/(210–220) Dr 1996 ColN 3/86 d4.29

YEAR	TM LG	W	L	PCT	G	GS	CG	SHO	QS	SV	BS	QR	IP	H	R	HR	HB	BB	IB	SO	ERA	AERA	OAV	OOB	SUP	DL	PW
2005	†NY A	7	3	.700	14	12	0	0	9	0	0	1	79	66	26	7	6	30	0	40	2.85	+51	.225	.309	-3	0	1.6
2006	NY A	5	3	.625	17	11	0	0	3	0	0	2	63	77	54	11	5	36	2	35	7.00	-34	.300	.389	+13	25	-1.7
Total	7	43	58	.426	254	119	0	0	56	36	16	79	836.1	828	492	121	64	434	42	566	4.98	-4	.261	.358	-13	148	-3.2
Team	2	12	6	.667	31	23	0	0	12	0	0	3	142	143	80	18	11	66	2	75	4.69	-5	.260	.348	+5	25	-0.1
/180I	3	15	8	.667	39	29	0	0	15	0	0	4	180	181	101	23	14	84	3	95	4.69	-5	.260	.348	+5	32	-0.1

Chamberlain, Joba — Justin L. B9.23.1985 Lincoln NE BR/TR/6'2"/230 Dr 2006 NYA 1/41 d8.7 Col Nebraska

YEAR	TM LG	W	L	PCT	G	GS	CG	SHO	QS	SV	BS	QR	IP	H	R	HR	HB	BB	IB	SO	ERA	AERA	OAV	OOB	SUP	DL	PW
2007	†NY A	2	0	1.000	19	0	0	0	0	1	0	19	24	12	2	1	1	6	0	34	0.38	+1104	.145	.211	—	0	0.8

Chandler, Spud — Spurgeon Ferdinand B9.12.1907 Commerce GA D1.9.1990 S.Pasadena FL BR/TR/6'0"/181 d5.6 Mil 1944–45 C2 Col Georgia

YEAR	TM LG	W	L	PCT	G	GS	CG	SHO	QS	SV	BS	QR	IP	H	R	HR	HB	BB	IB	SO	ERA	AERA	OAV	OOB	SUP	DL	PW
1937	NY A	7	4	.636	12	10	6	2	—	0	—	—	82.1	79	31	8	1	20	—	31	2.84	+56	.253	.300	+29	—	1.7
1938	NY A	14	5	.737	23	23	14	2	—	0	—	—	172	183	86	7	2	47	—	36	4.03	+13	.271	.320	+28	—	1.5
1939	NY A	3	0	1.000	11	0	0	0	—	0	—	—	19	26	7	0	0	9	—	4	2.84	+53	.329	.398	—	—	0.6
1940	NY A	8	7	.533	27	24	6	1	—	0	—	—	172	184	100	12	6	60	—	56	4.60	-12	.275	.341	+41	—	-0.7
1941	†NY A	10	4	.714	28	20	11	4	—	4	—	—	163.2	146	68	5	0	60	—	60	3.19	+23	.239	.307	+20	0	1.2
1942	†NY A★	16	5	.762	24	24	17	3	—	0	—	—	200.2	176	64	13	4	74	—	74	2.38	+45	.237	.309	+38	0	3.0
1943	†NY A☆	**20**	4	**.833**	30	30	**20**	0	—	0	—	—	253	197	62	5	4	54	—	134	**1.64**	+97	.215	**.261**	+10	0	**5.3**
1944	NY A	0	0	+	1	1	0	0	—	0	—	—	6	6	3	1	1	1	—	1	4.50	-23	.300	.364	+44	0	0.0
1945	NY A	2	1	.667	4	4	2	1	—	0	—	—	31	30	16	2	0	7	—	12	4.65	-25	.250	.291	+11	0	-0.2
1946	NY A☆	20	8	.714	34	32	20	6	—	2	—	—	257.1	200	71	7	1	90	—	138	2.10	+64	.218	.288	+19	0	4.5
1947	†NY A☆	9	5	.643	17	16	13	2	—	0	—	—	128	100	41	4	0	41	—	68	2.46	+44	.214	.277	+6	0	2.2
Total	11	109	43	.717	211	184	109	26	—	6	—	—	1485	1327	549	64	19	463	—	614	2.84	+32	.240	.301	+24	0	19.1
/180I	1	13	5	.717	26	22	13	3	0	1	0	0	180	161	67	8	2	56	—	74	2.84	+32	.240	.301	+24	—	2.3

Chapin, Darrin — Darrin John B2.1.1966 Warren OH BR/TR/6'0"/170 Dr 1986 NYA*6/155 d9.21 Col Cleveland St.

YEAR	TM LG	W	L	PCT	G	GS	CG	SHO	QS	SV	BS	QR	IP	H	R	HR	HB	BB	IB	SO	ERA	AERA	OAV	OOB	SUP	DL	PW
1991	NY A	0	1	.000	3	0	0	0	0	0	0	1	5.1	3	3	0	0	6	0	5	5.06	-18	.158	.360	—	0	-0.1
1992	Phi N	0	0	+	1	0	0	0	0	0	0	0	2	2	2	1	0	0	0	1	9.00	-61	.250	.250	—	0	-0.1
Total	2	0	1	.000	4	0	0	0	0	0	0	1	7.1	5	5	1	0	6	0	6	6.14	-35	.185	.333	—	0	-0.2

CHESBRO, JACK JOHN DWIGHT "HAPPY JACK" B6.5.1874 N.ADAMS MA D11.6.1931 CONWAY MA BR/TR/5'9"/180 D7.12 C1 HF1946

YEAR	TM LG	W	L	PCT	G	GS	CG	SHO	QS	SV	BS	QR	IP	H	R	HR	HB	BB	IB	SO	ERA	AERA	OAV	OOB	SUP	DL	PW
1899	Pit N	6	9	.400	19	17	15	0	—	0	—	—	149	165	99	3	11	59	—	28	4.11	-7	.280	.357	-12	—	-0.9
1900	Pit N	15	13	.536	32	26	20	3	—	1	—	—	215.2	220	123	4	12	79	—	56	3.67	-1	.264	.336	+12	—	-0.1
1901	Pit N	21	10	**.677**	36	28	26	0	—	1	—	—	287.2	261	104	4	14	52	—	129	2.38	+37	.240	.284	+8	—	3.3
1902	Pit N	**28**	6	**.824**	35	33	31	0	—	1	—	—	286.1	242	81	1	21	62	—	136	2.17	+26	.229	.285	+47	—	2.3
1903	NY A	21	15	.583	40	36	33	1	—	0	—	—	324.2	300	140	7	9	74	—	147	2.77	+13	.245	.293	-7	—	1.2
1904	NY A	**41**	12	**.774**	**55**	**51**	**48**	6	—	0	—	—	**454.2**	338	128	4	7	88	—	239	1.82	+49	**.208**	.252	+13	—	**6.1**
1905	NY A	19	15	.559	41	38	24	3	—	0	—	—	303.1	262	125	5	6	71	—	156	2.20	+34	.235	.284	-2	—	1.8
1906	NY A	23	17	.575	**49**	**42**	24	4	—	1	—	—	325	314	138	2	10	75	—	152	2.96	+0	.257	.305	+3	—	-0.1
1907	NY A	10	10	.500	30	25	17	1	—	0	—	—	206	192	83	0	6	46	—	78	2.53	+10	.249	.297	-18	—	0.6
1908	NY A	14	20	.412	45	31	20	3	—	1	—	—	288.2	276	134	6	14	67	—	124	2.93	-15	.256	.307	-20	—	-1.6
1909	NY A	0	4	.000	9	4	2	0	—	0	—	—	49.2	70	47	2	3	13	—	17	6.34	-60	.347	.394	-23	—	-1.4
1909	Bos A	0	1	.000	1	1	0	0	—	0	—	—	6	7	4	1	0	4	—	3	4.50	-44	.318	.423	+41	—	-0.2
1909	Year	0	5	.000	10	5	2	0	—	0	—	—	55.2	77	51	3	3	17	—	20	6.14	-59	.344	.398	-11	—	-1.6
Total	11	198	132	.600	392	332	260	35	—	5	—	—	2896.2	2647	1206	39	113	690	—	1265	2.68	+11	.244	.297	+4	—	11.0
Team	7	128	93	.579	269	227	168	18	—	2	—	—	1952	1752	795	26	55	434	—	913	2.58	+9	.242	.290	-3	—	6.6
/180I	1	12	9	.579	25	21	15	2	—	0	—	—	180	162	73	2	5	40	—	84	2.58	+9	.242	.290	-3	—	0.6

CHOATE, RANDY RANDOL DOYLE B9.5.1975 SAN ANTONIO TX BL/TL/6'3"/(180–195) DR 1997 NYA 5/169 D7.1 COL FLORIDA ST.

YEAR	TM LG	W	L	PCT	G	GS	CG	SHO	QS	SV	BS	QR	IP	H	R	HR	HB	BB	IB	SO	ERA	AERA	OAV	OOB	SUP	DL	PW
2000	†NY A	0	1	.000	22	0	0	0	0	0	0	14	17	14	10	3	1	8	0	12	4.76	+0	.215	.307	—	0	0.0
2001	†NY A	3	1	.750	37	0	0	0	0	0	0	28	48.1	34	21	0	9	27	2	35	3.35	+33	.202	.341	—	0	0.4
2002	NY A	0	0	+	18	0	0	0	0	0	0	14	22.1	18	18	1	3	15	0	17	6.04	-28	.217	.356	—	0	-0.3
2003	NY A	0	0	+	5	0	0	0	0	0	0	3	3.2	7	3	0	0	1	0	0	7.36	-40	.467	.500	—	0	-0.1
2004	Ari N	2	4	.333	74	0	0	0	0	0	2	54	50.2	52	26	1	5	28	11	49	4.62	-1	.267	.366	—	0	0.1
2005	Ari N	0	0	+	8	0	0	0	0	0	0	6	7	8	7	0	1	5	1	4	9.00	-51	.276	.400	—	0	-0.1
2006	Ari N	0	1	.000	30	0	0	0	0	0	0	24	16	21	9	0	3	3	0	12	3.94	+19	.304	.360	—	0	0.1
2007	Ari N	0	0	+	2	0	0	0	0	0	0	0	0	3	0	0	0	0	0	0	(0)	-100	1.000	1.000	—	0	0.0
Total	8	5	7	.417	196	0	0	0	0	0	2	143	165	157	94	5	22	87	14	129	4.64	-2	.250	.358	—	0	0.1
Team	4	3	2	.600	82	0	0	0	0	0	0	59	91.1	73	52	4	13	51	2	64	4.43	+1	.221	.345	—	—	-0.0
/60G	3	2	1	.600	60	0	0	0	0	0	0	43	66.2	53	38	3	10	37	1	47	4.45	+1	.221	.345	—	—	-0.0

CHRISTIANSEN, CLAY CLAY C. B6.28.1958 WICHITA KS BR/TR/6'5"/205 DR 1980 NYA 15/386 D5.10 COL KANSAS

YEAR	TM LG	W	L	PCT	G	GS	CG	SHO	QS	SV	BS	QR	IP	H	R	HR	HB	BB	IB	SO	ERA	AERA	OAV	OOB	SUP	DL	PW
1984	NY A	2	4	.333	24	1	0	0	0	2	2	13	38.2	50	28	4	1	12	0	27	6.05	-37	.309	.356	-100	0	-1.4

CICOTTE, AL ALVA WARREN "BOZO" B12.23.1929 MELVINDALE MI D11.29.1982 WESTLAND MI BR/TR/6'3"/(185–190) D4.22

YEAR	TM LG	W	L	PCT	G	GS	CG	SHO	QS	SV	BS	QR	IP	H	R	HR	HB	BB	IB	SO	ERA	AERA	OAV	OOB	SUP	DL	PW
1957	NY A	2	2	.500	20	2	0	0	0	2	0	12	65.1	57	25	5	1	30	1	36	3.03	+18	.237	.324	-50	0	0.2
Total	5	10	13	.435	102	16	0	0	3	4	2	57	260	280	142	30	5	119	7	149	4.36	-10	.284	.361	-17	0	-1.1

CLARK, GEORGE GEORGE MYRON B5.19.1891 SMITHLAND IA D11.14.1940 SIOUX CITY IA BR/TL/6'0"/190 D5.16 COL IOWA ST.

YEAR	TM LG	W	L	PCT	G	GS	CG	SHO	QS	SV	BS	QR	IP	H	R	HR	HB	BB	IB	SO	ERA	AERA	OAV	OOB	SUP	DL	PW
1913	NY A	0	1	.000	11	1	0	0	—	0	—	—	19	22	23	1	3	19	—	5	9.00	-67	.278	.436	-50	—	-0.5

CLARKSON, WALTER WALTER HAMILTON B11.3.1878 CAMBRIDGE MA D10.10.1946 CAMBRIDGE MA BR/TR/5'10"/150 D7.2 B–DAD B–JOHN COL HARVARD

YEAR	TM LG	W	L	PCT	G	GS	CG	SHO	QS	SV	BS	QR	IP	H	R	HR	HB	BB	IB	SO	ERA	AERA	OAV	OOB	SUP	DL	PW
1904	NY A	1	2	.333	13	4	2	0	—	1	—	—	66.1	63	42	3	10	25	—	43	5.02	-46	.251	.343	+5	—	-0.6
1905	NY A	3	3	.500	9	4	3	0	—	0	—	—	46	40	26	1	2	13	—	35	3.91	-25	.235	.297	-28	—	-0.7
1906	NY A	9	4	.692	32	16	9	3	—	0	—	—	151	135	59	6	5	55	—	64	2.32	+28	.242	.316	+6	—	0.4
1907	NY A	1	1	.500	5	2	0	0	—	1	—	—	17.1	19	12	1	2	8	—	3	6.23	-55	.279	.372	+45	—	-0.5
1907	Cle A	4	6	.400	17	10	9	1	—	0	—	—	90.2	77	40	1	3	29	—	32	1.99	+26	.232	.299	-25	—	-0.2
1907	Year	5	7	.417	22	12	9	1	—	1	—	—	108	96	52	2	5	37	—	35	2.67	-4	.240	.312	-12	—	-0.7
1908	Cle A	0	0	+	2	1	0	0	—	0	—	—	3.1	6	4	0	2	2	—	1	10.80	-78	.400	.526	+215	—	-0.1
Total	5	18	16	.529	78	37	23	4	—	2	—	—	374.2	340	183	12	24	132	—	178	3.17	-12	.244	.320	+2	—	-1.7
Team	4	14	10	.583	59	26	14	3	—	2	—	—	280.2	257	139	11	19	101	—	145	3.46	-17	.245	.323	+4	—	-1.4
/180I	3	9	6	.583	38	17	9	2	—	1	—	—	180	165	89	7	12	65	—	93	3.46	-17	.245	.323	+4	—	-0.9

CLAUSSEN, BRANDON BRANDON ALLEN FALKER B5.1.1979 RAPID CITY SD BR/TL/6'2"/200 DR 1998 NYA 34/1027 D6.28 COL HOWARD (TX) JC

YEAR	TM LG	W	L	PCT	G	GS	CG	SHO	QS	SV	BS	QR	IP	H	R	HR	HB	BB	IB	SO	ERA	AERA	OAV	OOB	SUP	DL	PW
2003	NY A	1	0	1.000	1	1	0	0	1	0	0	0	6.1	8	2	1	0	1	0	5	1.42	+209	.296	.321	+89	0	0.3
Total	4	16	27	.372	58	58	0	0	23	0	0	0	316	359	197	48	15	121	8	228	5.04	-13	.286	.353	-4	106	-3.4

CLAY, KEN KENNETH EARL B4.6.1954 LYNCHBURG VA BR/TR/6'3"/(190–195) DR 1972 NYA 2/38 D6.7

YEAR	TM LG	W	L	PCT	G	GS	CG	SHO	QS	SV	BS	QR	IP	H	R	HR	HB	BB	IB	SO	ERA	AERA	OAV	OOB	SUP	DL	PW
1977	†NY A	2	3	.400	21	3	0	0	0	1	1	12	55.2	53	32	6	1	24	3	20	4.37	-9	.251	.329	+28	0	-0.3
1978	†NY A	3	4	.429	28	6	0	0	3	0	0	15	75.2	89	41	3	2	21	3	32	4.28	-15	.291	.338	+31	21	-0.5
1979	NY A	1	7	.125	32	5	0	0	0	2	2	16	78.1	88	49	12	2	25	1	28	5.40	-24	.291	.346	-43	0	-1.0
1980	Tex A	2	3	.400	8	8	0	0	3	0	0	0	43	43	24	4	3	29	2	17	4.60	-16	.256	.373	+9	0	-0.3
1981	Sea A	2	7	.222	22	14	0	0	6	0	0	6	101	116	62	10	3	42	3	32	4.63	-16	.294	.363	-31	66	-0.9
Total	5	10	24	.294	111	36	0	0	12	3	3	49	353.2	389	208	35	11	141	12	129	4.68	-17	.281	.350	-9	87	-3.0
Team	3	6	14	.300	81	14	0	0	3	3	3	43	209.2	230	122	21	5	70	7	80	4.72	-17	.281	.339	+4	21	-1.8
/60G	2	4	10	.300	60	10	0	0	2	2	2	32	155.1	170	90	16	4	52	5	59	4.72	-17	.281	.339	+4	16	-1.3

CLEMENS, ROGER WILLIAM ROGER "ROCKET" B8.4.1962 DAYTON OH BR/TR/6'4"/(205–235) DR 1983 BOSA 1/19 D5.15 COL TEXAS

YEAR	TM LG	W	L	PCT	G	GS	CG	SHO	QS	SV	BS	QR	IP	H	R	HR	HB	BB	IB	SO	ERA	AERA	OAV	OOB	SUP	DL	PW
1999	†NY A	14	10	.583	30	30	1	1	16	0	0	0	187.2	185	101	20	9	90	0	163	4.60	+3	.261	.350	-12	23	0.6
2000	†NY A	13	8	.619	32	32	1	0	21	0	0	0	204.1	184	96	26	10	84	0	188	3.70	+29	.236	.317	-5	16	2.1
2001	†NY A★	20	3	**.870**	33	33	0	0	21	0	0	0	220.1	205	94	19	5	72	1	213	3.51	+26	.246	.309	+23	0	2.2
2002	†NY A	13	6	.684	29	29	0	0	16	0	0	0	180	172	94	18	7	63	6	192	4.35	+0	.250	.317	+16	25	0.2
2003	†NY A★	17	9	.654	33	33	1	1	21	0	0	0	211.2	199	99	24	5	58	1	190	3.91	+12	.247	.299	+7	0	1.4
2007	†NY A	6	6	.500	18	17	0	0	10	0	0	0	99	99	52	9	5	31	0	68	4.18	+8	.261	.323	-3	0	0.3
Total	24	354	184	.658	709	707	118	46	481	0	0	1	4916.2	4185	1885	363	159	1580	63	4672	3.12	+43	.229	.294	-3	202	73.5
Team	6	83	42	.664	175	174	3	2	105	0	0	0	1103	1044	536	116	41	398	8	1014	4.01	+13	.249	.318	+5	64	6.8
/180I	1	14	7	.664	29	28	0	0	17	0	0	0	180	170	87	19	7	65	1	165	4.01	+13	.249	.318	+5	10	1.1

CLEMENTS, PAT PATRICK BRIAN B2.2.1962 MCCLOUD CA BR/TL/6'0"/(175–185) DR 1983 CALA 4/103 D4.9 COL UCLA

YEAR	TM LG	W	L	PCT	G	GS	CG	SHO	QS	SV	BS	QR	IP	H	R	HR	HB	BB	IB	SO	ERA	AERA	OAV	OOB	SUP	DL	PW
1987	NY A	3	3	.500	55	0	0	0	0	7	3	29	80	91	45	4	3	30	2	36	4.95	-10	.299	.364	—	0	-0.2
1988	NY A	0	0	+	6	1	0	0	1	0	1	2	8.1	12	8	1	0	4	0	3	6.48	-39	.343	.390	-31	0	-0.1
Total	8	17	11	.607	288	2	0	0	1	12	14	188	360.1	362	163	17	11	160	27	158	3.77	+6	.272	.351	-32	131	1.0
Team	2	3	3	.500	61	1	0	0	1	7	4	31	88.1	103	53	5	3	34	2	39	5.09	-14	.304	.366	-31	—	-0.3
/60G	2	3	3	.500	60	1	0	0	1	7	4	30	87	101	52	5	3	33	2	38	5.09	-14	.304	.366	-31	—	-0.3

CLEVENGER, TEX TRUMAN EUGENE B7.9.1932 VISALIA CA BR/TR/6'1"/(180–185) D4.18 COL CAL ST.–FRESNO

YEAR	TM LG	W	L	PCT	G	GS	CG	SHO	QS	SV	BS	QR	IP	H	R	HR	HB	BB	IB	SO	ERA	AERA	OAV	OOB	SUP	DL	PW
1961	NY A	1	1	.500	21	0	0	0	0	0	3	13	31.2	35	20	3	1	21	1	14	4.83	-23	.287	.396	—	0	-0.2
1962	NY A	2	0	1.000	21	0	0	0	0	0	0	15	38	36	14	3	1	17	5	11	2.84	+32	.248	.329	—	0	0.1
Total	8	36	37	.493	307	40	6	2	45	30	14	352	694.2	706	370	61	14	298	30	361	4.18	-6	.265	.339	-22	0	-1.6
Team	2	3	1	.750	42	0	0	0	0	0	3	28	69.2	71	34	6	2	38	6	25	3.75	+0	.266	.360	—	—	-0.1
/60G	3	4	1	.750	60	0	0	0	0	0	4	40	99.2	101	49	9	3	54	9	36	3.74	+0	.266	.360	—	—	-0.1

CLIPPARD, TYLER TYLER LEE B2.14.1985 LEXINGTON KY BR/TR/6'4"/170 DR 2003 NYA 9/274 D5.20

YEAR	TM LG	W	L	PCT	G	GS	CG	SHO	QS	SV	BS	QR	IP	H	R	HR	HB	BB	IB	SO	ERA	AERA	OAV	OOB	SUP	DL	PW
2007	NY A	3	1	.750	6	6	0	0	1	0	0	0	27	29	19	6	0	17	1	18	6.33	-29	.271	.371	+82	0	-0.5

CLOSTER, AL ALAN EDWARD B6.15.1943 CREIGHTON NE BL/TL/6'2"/(190–212) D4.19 COL IOWA ST.

YEAR	TM LG	W	L	PCT	G	GS	CG	SHO	QS	SV	BS	QR	IP	H	R	HR	HB	BB	IB	SO	ERA	AERA	OAV	OOB	SUP	DL	PW
1966	Was A	0	0	+	1	0	0	0	0	0	0	0	0.1	1	0	0	0	2	0	0	0.00	-100	.500	.750	—	0	0.0
1971	NY A	2	2	.500	14	1	0	0	0	0	0	8	28.1	33	22	4	2	13	7	22	5.08	-35	.289	.364	-73	0	-1.0
1972	NY A	0	0	+	2	0	0	0	0	0	0	1	2.1	2	3	1	0	4	0	2	11.57	-74	.250	.500	—	0	-0.1

YEAR	TM LG	W	L	PCT	G	GS	CG	SHO	QS	SV	BS	QR	IP	H	R	HR	HB	BB	IB	SO	ERA	AERA	OAV	OOB	SUP	DL	PW
1973	Atl N	0	0	+	4	0	0	0	0	0	1	1	4.1	7	7	1	0	4	1	2	14.54	-73	.389	.500	—	0	-0.2
Total	4	2	2	.500	21	1	0	0	0	0	1	10	35.1	43	32	6	2	23	8	26	6.62	-49	.303	.400	-73	0	-1.3
Team	2	2	2	.500	16	1	0	0	0	0	0	9	30.2	35	25	5	2	17	7	24	5.58	-41	.287	.375	-73	—	-1.1

COAKLEY, ANDY ANDREW JAMES (AKA JACK MCALLISTER IN 1902) B11.20.1882 PROVIDENCE RI D9.27.1963 NEW YORK NY BL/TR/6'0"/165 d9.17 COL HOLY CROSS

YEAR	TM LG	W	L	PCT	G	GS	CG	SHO	QS	SV	BS	QR	IP	H	R	HR	HB	BB	IB	SO	ERA	AERA	OAV	OOB	SUP	DL	PW
1911	NY A	0	1	.000	2	1	1	0	—	0	—	—	11.2	20	13	0	0	2	—	4	5.40	-33	.377	.400	-40	—	-0.2
Total	9	58	59	.496	150	124	87	11	—	3	—	—	1072.1	1021	436	9	26	314	—	428	2.35	+11	.256	.310	+3	—	-0.0

COATES, JIM JAMES ALTON B8.4.1932 FARNHAM VA BR/TR/6'4"/(180–192) d9.21

YEAR	TM LG	W	L	PCT	G	GS	CG	SHO	QS	SV	BS	QR	IP	H	R	HR	HB	BB	IB	SO	ERA	AERA	OAV	OOB	SUP	DL	PW
1956	NY A	0	0	+	2	0	0	0	—	0	—	—	2	1	3	0	1	4	0	0	13.50	-71	.167	.545	—	0	-0.1
1959	NY A	6	1	.857	37	4	2	0	3	3	0	26	100.1	89	39	10	3	36	4	64	2.87	+27	.234	.305	+33	0	0.4
1960	†NY A★	13	3	.813	35	18	6	2	7	1	1	12	149.1	139	78	16	2	66	4	73	4.28	-16	.248	.327	+89	0	-0.8
1961	†NY A	11	5	.688	43	11	4	1	6	5	0	21	141.1	128	60	15	7	53	0	80	3.44	+8	.243	.318	+4	0	0.1
1962	†NY A	7	6	.538	50	6	0	0	2	6	3	29	117.2	119	62	9	5	50	5	67	4.44	-16	.263	.339	+7	0	-1.1
1963	Was A	2	4	.333	20	2	0	0	1	0	1	9	44.1	51	29	4	3	21	4	31	5.28	-30	.297	.377	+44	0	-1.0
1963	Cin N	0	0	+	9	0	0	0	0	0	0	6	16.1	21	10	2	0	7	1	11	5.51	-39	.313	.378	—	0	-0.2
1963	Major	2	4	.333	29	2	0	0	1	0	—	15	60	72	39	6	3	28	5	42	5.34	-32	.301	.377	+44	0	-1.2
1965	Cal A	2	0	1.000	17	0	0	0	0	3	0	12	28	23	13	1	0	16	2	15	3.54	-4	.228	.325	—	0	-0.1
1966	Cal A	1	1	.500	9	4	1	1	2	0	0	4	31.2	32	16	3	0	10	0	16	3.98	-16	.258	.311	+18	0	-0.2
1967	Cal A	1	2	.333	25	1	0	0	0	0	0	17	52.1	47	26	5	4	23	5	39	4.30	-27	.244	.336	-72	0	-0.2
Total	9	43	22	.662	247	46	13	4	21	18	5	136	683.1	650	336	65	25	286	25	396	4.00	-10	.252	.330	+42	0	-3.2
Team	5	37	15	.712	167	39	12	3	18	15	4	88	510.2	476	242	50	18	209	13	284	3.84	-4	.247	.324	+47	—	-1.5
/180I	2	13	5	.712	59	14	4	1	6	5	1	31	180	168	85	18	6	74	5	100	3.84	-4	.247	.324	+47	—	-0.5

COLE, KING LEONARD LESLIE B4.15.1886 TOLEDO IA D1.6.1916 BAY CITY MI BR/TR/6'1"/170 d10.6

YEAR	TM LG	W	L	PCT	G	GS	CG	SHO	QS	SV	BS	QR	IP	H	R	HR	HB	BB	IB	SO	ERA	AERA	OAV	OOB	SUP	DL	PW
1914	NY A	10	9	.526	33	15	8	2	—	0	—	—	141.2	151	63	3	1	51	—	43	3.30	-16	.288	.352	-10	—	-1.5
1915	NY A	2	3	.400	10	6	2	0	—	1	—	—	51	41	27	2	3	22	—	19	3.18	-8	.224	.317	-13	—	-0.4
Total	6	54	27	.667	129	86	47	9	—	2	—	—	730.2	657	309	13	26	331	—	298	3.12	-3	.250	.340	+25	—	-0.3
Team	2	12	12	.500	43	21	10	2	—	1	—	—	192.2	192	90	5	4	73	—	62	3.27	-14	.272	.343	-11	—	-1.9
/180I	2	11	11	.500	40	20	9	2	—	1	—	—	180	179	84	5	4	68	—	58	3.27	-14	.272	.343	-11	—	-1.8

COLEMAN, RIP WALTER GARY B7.31.1931 TROY NY D5.14.2004 WOLFEBORO NH BL/TL/6'2"/185 d8.15 COL SYRACUSE

YEAR	TM LG	W	L	PCT	G	GS	CG	SHO	QS	SV	BS	QR	IP	H	R	HR	HB	BB	IB	SO	ERA	AERA	OAV	OOB	SUP	DL	PW
1955	†NY A	2	1	.667	10	6	0	0	—	1	—	—	29	40	19	2	1	16	0	15	5.28	-29	.331	.413	+35	0	-0.4
1956	NY A	3	5	.375	29	9	0	0	—	2	—	—	88.1	97	42	6	1	42	1	42	3.67	+5	.285	.363	+53	0	-0.1
1957	KC A	0	7	.000	19	6	1	1	5	0	1	20	41	53	32	5	0	25	0	15	5.93	-33	.325	.408	-36	0	-1.5
1959	KC A	2	10	.167	29	11	2	0	5	2	0	20	81	85	46	8	1	34	0	54	4.56	-12	.273	.345	-22	0	-0.8
1959	Bal A	0	0	+	3	0	0	0	0	0	0	3	4	4	0	0	0	2	0	4	0.00	-100	.267	.353	—	0	0.1
1959	Year	2	10	.167	32	11	2	0	5	2	0	23	85	89	46	8	1	36	0	58	4.34	-8	.273	.345	-22	0	-0.7
1960	Bal A	0	2	.000	5	1	0	0	0	0	0	1	4	8	5	0	1	5	1	0	11.25	-66	.444	.583	-54	0	-0.6
Total	5	7	25	.219	95	33	3	1	10	5	1	44	247.1	287	144	21	4	124	2	130	4.58	-15	.296	.376	+4	0	-3.3
Team	2	5	6	.455	39	15	0	0	—	3	—	—	117.1	137	61	8	2	58	1	57	4.07	-6	.297	.376	+46	—	-0.5

COLLINS, RIP HARRY WARREN B2.26.1896 WEATHERFORD TX D5.27.1968 BRYAN TX BR/TR (BB 1920–23)/6'1"/205 d4.19 COL TEXAS A&M

YEAR	TM LG	W	L	PCT	G	GS	CG	SHO	QS	SV	BS	QR	IP	H	R	HR	HB	BB	IB	SO	ERA	AERA	OAV	OOB	SUP	DL	PW
1920	NY A	14	8	.636	36	18	10	2	—	1	—	—	187.1	171	83	6	14	79	—	66	3.22	+19	.247	.337	+9	—	0.9
1921	†NY A	11	5	.688	28	16	7	2	—	0	—	—	137.1	158	103	6	10	78	—	64	5.44	-22	.293	.392	+28	—	-2.0
Total	11	108	82	.568	311	219	84	15	—	5	—	—	1712.1	1795	926	73	81	674	—	569	3.99	+6	.275	.351	+5	—	2.3
Team	2	25	13	.658	64	34	17	4	—	1	—	—	324.2	329	186	12	24	157	—	130	4.16	-4	.267	.361	+18	—	-1.1
/180I	1	14	7	.658	35	19	9	2	—	1	—	—	180	182	103	7	13	87	—	72	4.16	-4	.267	.361	+18	—	-0.6

COLSON, LOYD LOYD ALBERT B11.4.1947 WELLINGTON TX BR/TR/6'1"/195 DR 1967 NYA 28/530 d9.25 COL BACONE

YEAR	TM LG	W	L	PCT	G	GS	CG	SHO	QS	SV	BS	QR	IP	H	R	HR	HB	BB	IB	SO	ERA	AERA	OAV	OOB	SUP	DL	PW
1970	NY A	0	0	+	1	0	0	0	0	0	0	1	2	3	1	0	0	0	0	3	4.50	-21	.333	.333	—	0	0.0

CONE, DAVID DAVID BRIAN B1.2.1963 KANSAS CITY MO BL/TR/6'1"/(180–200) DR 1981 KCA 3/74 d6.8

YEAR	TM LG	W	L	PCT	G	GS	CG	SHO	QS	SV	BS	QR	IP	H	R	HR	HB	BB	IB	SO	ERA	AERA	OAV	OOB	SUP	DL	PW
1995	†NY A	9	2	.818	13	13	1	0	8	0	0	0	99	82	42	12	1	47	0	89	3.82	+21	.223	.312	+28	0	1.0
1996	†NY A	7	2	.778	11	11	1	0	8	0	0	0	72	50	25	3	2	34	0	71	2.88	+72	.198	.293	+26	122	1.8
1997	†NY A★	12	6	.667	29	29	1	0	21	0	0	0	195	155	67	17	4	86	2	222	2.82	+58	.218	.305	-3	33	2.9
1998	†NY A	**20**	7	.741	31	31	3	0	19	0	0	0	207.2	186	89	20	15	59	1	209	3.55	+23	.237	.302	+34	0	2.2
1999	†NY A★	12	9	.571	31	31	1	1	18	0	0	0	193.1	164	84	21	11	90	2	177	3.44	+37	.229	.322	+9	0	2.5
2000	†NY A	4	14	.222	30	29	0	0	10	0	0	0	155	192	124	25	9	82	3	120	6.91	-31	.306	.389	-7	0	-3.2
Total	17	194	126	.606	450	419	56	22	268	1	0	19	2898.2	2504	1222	258	106	1137	42	2668	3.46	+20	.232	.309	+3	310	23.2
Team	6	64	40	.615	145	144	7	1	84	0	0	0	922	829	431	98	42	398	8	888	3.91	+18	.240	.323	+12	155	7.2
/180I	1	12	8	.615	28	28	1	0	16	0	0	0	180	162	84	19	8	78	2	173	3.91	+18	.240	.323	+12	30	1.4

CONTRERAS, JOSE JOSE ARIEL B12.6.1971 LAS MARTINAS, CUBA BR/TR/6'4"/(230–245) d3.31

YEAR	TM LG	W	L	PCT	G	GS	CG	SHO	QS	SV	BS	QR	IP	H	R	HR	HB	BB	IB	SO	ERA	AERA	OAV	OOB	SUP	DL	PW
2003	†NY A	7	2	.778	18	9	0	0	7	0	1	5	71	52	27	4	5	30	1	72	3.30	+33	.202	.297	+7	78	1.0
2004	NY A	8	5	.615	18	18	0	0	8	0	0	0	95.2	93	66	22	6	42	1	82	5.64	-19	.250	.333	+25	0	-1.5
Total	5	58	44	.569	143	132	4	3	66	0	1	7	831	821	467	99	47	306	9	623	4.57	+1	.257	.328	-1	94	-0.9
Team	2	15	7	.682	36	27	0	0	15	0	1	5	166.2	145	93	26	11	72	2	154	4.64	-3	.231	.318	+19	78	-0.5
/180I	2	16	8	.682	39	29	0	0	16	0	1	5	180	157	100	28	12	78	2	166	4.64	-3	.231	.318	+19	84	-0.5

COOK, ANDY ANDREW BERNARD B8.30.1967 MEMPHIS TN BR/TR/6'5"/205 DR 1988 NYA 11/287 d5.9 COL MEMPHIS

YEAR	TM LG	W	L	PCT	G	GS	CG	SHO	QS	SV	BS	QR	IP	H	R	HR	HB	BB	IB	SO	ERA	AERA	OAV	OOB	SUP	DL	PW
1993	NY A	0	1	.000	4	0	0	0	0	0	0	2	5.1	4	3	1	0	7	0	4	5.06	-17	.200	.407	—	0	-0.1

COOPER, DON DONALD JAMES B1.15.1957 NEW YORK NY BR/TR/6'1"/(175–185) DR 1978 NYA 17/442 d4.9 C6 COL NEW YORK TECH

YEAR	TM LG	W	L	PCT	G	GS	CG	SHO	QS	SV	BS	QR	IP	H	R	HR	HB	BB	IB	SO	ERA	AERA	OAV	OOB	SUP	DL	PW
1985	NY A	0	0	+	7	0	0	0	0	0	0	6	10	12	6	2	0	3	0	4	5.40	-25	.300	.341	—	0	-0.1
Total	4	1	6	.143	44	3	0	0	0	0	0	26	85.1	95	55	14	1	46	6	47	5.27	-23	.287	.372	+12	0	-1.0

COOPER, GUY GUY EVANS "REBEL" B1.28.1893 ROME GA D8.2.1951 SANTA MONICA CA BB/TR/6'1"/185 d5.2

YEAR	TM LG	W	L	PCT	G	GS	CG	SHO	QS	SV	BS	QR	IP	H	R	HR	HB	BB	IB	SO	ERA	AERA	OAV	OOB	SUP	DL	PW
1914	NY A	0	0	+	1	0	0	0	—	0	—	—	3	3	3	0	0	2	—	3	9.00	-69	.273	.385	—	—	-0.1
Total	2	1	0	1.000	11	1	0	0	—	0	—	—	27	26	18	1	3	13	—	8	5.33	-49	.280	.385	+142	—	-0.5

COTTRELL, ENSIGN ENSIGN STOVER B8.29.1888 HOOSICK FALLS NY D2.27.1947 SYRACUSE NY BL/TL/5'9.5"/173 d6.21 COL SYRACUSE

YEAR	TM LG	W	L	PCT	G	GS	CG	SHO	QS	SV	BS	QR	IP	H	R	HR	HB	BB	IB	SO	ERA	AERA	OAV	OOB	SUP	DL	PW
1911	Pit N	0	0	+	1	0	0	0	—	0	—	—	1	4	4	0	0	1	—	0	9.00	-62	.667	.714	—	—	-0.1
1912	Chi N	0	0	+	1	0	0	0	—	0	—	—	4	8	4	0	0	1	—	1	9.00	-63	.444	.474	—	—	-0.1
1913	Phi A	1	0	1.000	2	1	1	0	—	0	—	—	10	15	7	0	0	2	—	3	5.40	-49	.333	.362	+168	—	-0.2
1914	Bos N	0	1	.000	1	1	0	0	—	0	—	—	1	2	2	0	0	3	—	1	9.00	-69	.333	.556	-74	—	-0.2
1915	NY A	0	1	.000	7	0	0	0	—	0	—	—	21.1	29	12	2	1	7	—	7	3.38	-13	.330	.385	—	—	-0.2
Total	5	1	2	.333	12	2	1	0	—	0	—	—	37.1	58	29	2	1	14	—	12	4.82	-39	.356	.410	+37	—	-0.8

COVELESKI, STAN STANLEY ANTHONY (B STANISLAUS KOWALEWSKI) B7.13.1889 SHAMOKIN PA D3.20.1984 SOUTH BEND IN BR/TR/5'11"/166 d9.10 HF1969 B–HARRY

YEAR	TM LG	W	L	PCT	G	GS	CG	SHO	QS	SV	BS	QR	IP	H	R	HR	HB	BB	IB	SO	ERA	AERA	OAV	OOB	SUP	DL	PW
1928	NY A	5	1	.833	12	8	2	0	—	0	—	—	58	72	41	5	0	20	—	5	5.74	-34	.323	.379	+58	—	-1.2
Total	14	215	142	.602	450	385	224	38	—	21	—	—	3082	3055	1227	66	30	802	—	981	2.89	+28	.262	.311	+2	—	26.0

COWLEY, JOE JOSEPH ALAN B8.15.1958 LEXINGTON KY BR/TR/6'5"/(207–220) d4.13

YEAR	TM LG	W	L	PCT	G	GS	CG	SHO	QS	SV	BS	QR	IP	H	R	HR	HB	BB	IB	SO	ERA	AERA	OAV	OOB	SUP	DL	PW
1982	Atl N	1	2	.333	17	8	0	0	2	0	0	6	52.1	53	27	6	1	16	2	27	4.47	-18	.265	.321	-4	33	-0.2
1984	NY A	9	2	.818	16	11	3	1	4	0	0	4	83.1	75	34	12	2	31	1	71	3.56	+8	.234	.303	+63	0	0.5
1985	NY A	12	6	.667	30	26	1	0	13	0	0	3	159.2	132	75	29	6	85	2	97	3.95	+3	.224	.327	+16	0	0.3
1986	Chi A	11	11	.500	27	27	4	0	15	0	0	0	162.1	133	81	20	3	83	1	132	3.88	+12	.223	.319	-3	0	0.8
1987	Phi N	0	4	.000	5	4	0	0	0	0	0	0	11.2	21	26	2	2	17	1	5	15.43	-72	.389	.548	-58	0	-2.3

YEAR	TM LG	W	L	PCT	G	GS	CG	SHO	QS	SV	BS	QR	IP	H	R	HR	HB	BB	IB	SO	ERA	AERA	OAV	OOB	SUP	DL	PW
Total	5	33	25	.569	95	76	8	1	34	0	0	13	469.1	414	243	69	14	232	7	332	4.20	-3	.235	.327	+10	33	-0.9
Team	2	21	8	.724	46	37	4	1	17	0	0	7	243	207	109	41	8	116	3	168	3.81	+4	.227	.319	+30	—	0.8
/180I	1	16	6	.724	34	27	3	1	13	0	0	5	180	153	81	30	6	86	2	124	3.81	+4	.227	.319	+30	—	0.6

Cox, Casey Joseph Casey B7.3.1941 Long Beach CA BR/TR/6'5"/(200–215) d4.15 Col Cal St.–Los Angeles

YEAR	TM LG	W	L	PCT	G	GS	CG	SHO	QS	SV	BS	QR	IP	H	R	HR	HB	BB	IB	SO	ERA	AERA	OAV	OOB	SUP	DL	PW
1972	NY A	0	1	.000	5	1	0	0	0	0	0	3	11.2	13	6	0	2	3	1	4	4.63	-35	.289	.353	-100	0	-0.2
1973	NY A	0	0	+	1	0	0	0	0	0	0	0	3	5	3	0	2	1	0	0	6.00	-38	.357	.444	—	0	-0.1
Total	8	39	42	.481	308	59	5	0	29	20	10	188	762	772	377	66	25	234	49	297	3.70	-7	.266	.323	-1	22	-4.4
Team	2	0	1	.000	6	1	0	0	0	0	0	3	14.2	18	9	0	4	4	1	4	4.91	-36	.305	.377	-100	—	-0.3

Cullen, Jack John Patrick B10.6.1939 Newark NJ BR/TR/5'11"/170 d9.9

YEAR	TM LG	W	L	PCT	G	GS	CG	SHO	QS	SV	BS	QR	IP	H	R	HR	HB	BB	IB	SO	ERA	AERA	OAV	OOB	SUP	DL	PW
1962	NY A	0	0	+	2	0	0	0	0	1	0	2	3	2	0	0	0	2	0	2	0.00	-100	.182	.308	—	0	0.1
1965	NY A	3	4	.429	12	9	2	1	5	0	0	3	59	59	22	2	0	21	2	25	3.05	+12	.262	.324	-28	0	0.3
1966	NY A	1	0	1.000	5	0	0	0	0	0	0	2	11.1	11	5	0	0	5	2	7	3.97	-16	.256	.327	—	0	-0.1
Total	3	4	4	.500	19	9	2	1	5	1	0	7	73.1	72	27	2	0	28	4	34	3.07	+11	.258	.324	-28	0	0.3

Cullop, Nick Norman Andrew B9.17.1887 Chilhowie VA D4.15.1961 Tazewell VA BL/TL/5'11.5"/172 d5.20

YEAR	TM LG	W	L	PCT	G	GS	CG	SHO	QS	SV	BS	QR	IP	H	R	HR	HB	BB	IB	SO	ERA	AERA	OAV	OOB	SUP	DL	PW
1916	NY A	13	6	.684	28	22	9	0	—	1	—	—	167	151	60	4	3	32	—	77	2.05	+41	.243	.284	+13	—	0.7
1917	NY A	5	9	.357	30	18	5	2	—	1	—	—	146.1	161	70	2	2	31	—	27	3.32	-19	.307	.348	-12	—	-1.0
Total	6	57	54	.514	174	121	62	9	—	5	—	—	1024	973	424	24	29	259	—	400	2.73	+2	.258	.311	-3	—	-0.6
Team	2	18	15	.545	58	40	14	2	—	2	—	—	313.1	312	130	6	5	63	—	104	2.64	+6	.272	.314	+2	—	-0.3
/180I	1	10	9	.545	33	23	8	1	—	1	—	—	180	179	75	3	3	36	—	60	2.64	+6	.272	.314	+2	—	-0.2

Cumberland, John John Sheldon B5.10.1947 Westbrook ME BR/TL/6'0"/190 d9.27 C7 Col Maine

YEAR	TM LG	W	L	PCT	G	GS	CG	SHO	QS	SV	BS	QR	IP	H	R	HR	HB	BB	IB	SO	ERA	AERA	OAV	OOB	SUP	DL	PW
1968	NY A	0	0	+	1	0	0	0	0	0	0	0	2	3	4	1	0	1	0	1	9.00	-68	.333	.400	—	0	-0.1
1969	NY A	0	0	+	2	0	0	0	0	0	0	1	4	3	2	0	0	4	1	0	4.50	-22	.231	.389	—	0	0.0
1970	NY A	3	4	.429	15	8	1	0	4	0	0	7	64	62	31	9	0	15	3	38	3.94	-9	.252	.292	-22	0	-0.4
Total	6	15	16	.484	110	36	6	2	17	2	2	50	334.1	312	161	46	0	103	12	137	3.82	-9	.246	.301	-2	0	-2.2
Team	3	3	4	.429	18	8	1	0	4	0	0	8	70	68	37	10	0	20	4	39	4.11	-14	.254	.301	-22	—	-0.5

Daley, Bud Leavitt Leo B10.7.1932 Orange CA BL/TL/6'1"/185 d9.10

YEAR	TM LG	W	L	PCT	G	GS	CG	SHO	QS	SV	BS	QR	IP	H	R	HR	HB	BB	IB	SO	ERA	AERA	OAV	OOB	SUP	DL	PW
1961	†NY A	8	9	.471	23	17	7	0	10	0	0	5	129.2	127	63	17	4	51	6	83	3.96	-6	.257	.330	+19	0	-0.6
1962	†NY A	7	5	.583	43	6	0	0	1	4	2	30	105.1	105	47	8	5	21	0	55	3.59	+4	.258	.301	+47	0	0.2
1963	NY A	0	0	+	1	0	0	0	0	1	0	1	1	2	0	0	0	0	0	0	0.00	-100	.667	.500	—	149	0.1
1964	NY A	3	2	.600	13	3	0	0	2	1	1	4	35	37	19	3	4	25	1	16	4.63	-22	.274	.400	+47	0	-0.4
Total	10	60	64	.484	248	116	36	3	80	10	8	102	967.1	998	502	99	60	351	20	549	4.03	-3	.266	.337	+7	149	-1.7
Team	4	18	16	.529	80	26	7	0	13	6	3	40	271	271	129	28	13	97	7	154	3.89	-4	.261	.330	+29	149	-0.7
/180I	3	12	11	.529	53	17	5	0	9	4	2	27	180	180	86	19	9	64	5	102	3.89	-4	.261	.330	+29	99	-0.5

Davidson, Bob Robert Banks B1.6.1963 Bad Kurznach, West Germany BR/TR/6'0"/185 Dr 1984 NYA 24/615 d7.15 Col East Carolina

YEAR	TM LG	W	L	PCT	G	GS	CG	SHO	QS	SV	BS	QR	IP	H	R	HR	HB	BB	IB	SO	ERA	AERA	OAV	OOB	SUP	DL	PW
1989	NY A	0	0	+	1	0	0	0	0	0	0	0	1	1	2	1	0	1	0	0	18.00	-78	.250	.400	—	0	-0.1

Davis, George George Allen "Iron" B3.9.1890 Lancaster NY D6.4.1961 Buffalo NY BB/TR/5'10.5"/175 d7.16 Col Williams

YEAR	TM LG	W	L	PCT	G	GS	CG	SHO	QS	SV	BS	QR	IP	H	R	HR	HB	BB	IB	SO	ERA	AERA	OAV	OOB	SUP	DL	PW
1912	NY A	1	4	.200	10	7	5	0	—	0	—	—	54	61	43	3	3	28	—	22	6.50	-45	.293	.385	+11	—	-1.1
Total	4	7	10	.412	36	22	13	1	—	0	—	—	191	195	118	7	10	78	—	77	4.48	-34	.274	.354	+22	—	-2.4

Davis, Ron Ronald Gene B8.6.1955 Houston TX BR/TR/6'4"/(196–207) Dr 1976 ChiN*3/56 d7.29 Col Blinn (TX) JC

YEAR	TM LG	W	L	PCT	G	GS	CG	SHO	QS	SV	BS	QR	IP	H	R	HR	HB	BB	IB	SO	ERA	AERA	OAV	OOB	SUP	DL	PW
1978	NY A	0	0	+	4	0	0	0	0	0	0	2	2.1	3	4	0	0	3	0	0	11.57	-68	.333	.500	—	0	-0.1
1979	NY A	14	2	.875	44	0	0	0	0	9	10	30	85.1	84	29	5	1	28	9	43	2.85	+45	.262	.320	—	0	2.5
1980	†NY A	9	3	.750	53	0	0	0	0	7	2	39	131	121	50	9	5	32	3	65	2.95	+34	.246	.296	—	0	1.4
1981	†NY A★	4	5	.444	43	0	0	0	0	6	2	34	73	47	22	6	0	25	3	83	2.71	+33	.186	.256	—	0	1.2
Total	11	47	53	.470	481	0	0	0	0	130	43	325	746.2	735	361	82	22	300	56	597	4.05	+2	.260	.332	—	21	2.6
Team	4	27	10	.730	144	0	0	0	0	22	14	105	291.2	255	105	20	6	88	15	191	2.93	+34	.237	.296	—	—	5.0
/60G	2	11	4	.730	60	0	0	0	0	9	6	44	121.2	106	44	8	3	37	6	80	2.93	+34	.237	.296	—	—	2.1

Deering, John John Thomas B6.25.1879 Lynn MA D2.15.1943 Beverly MA BR/TR/6'0"/180 d5.12

YEAR	TM LG	W	L	PCT	G	GS	CG	SHO	QS	SV	BS	QR	IP	H	R	HR	HB	BB	IB	SO	ERA	AERA	OAV	OOB	SUP	DL	PW
1903	Det A	3	4	.429	10	8	5	0	—	0	—	—	60.2	77	38	3	1	24	—	14	3.86	-25	.308	.371	-17	—	-0.5
1903	NY A	4	3	.571	9	7	6	1	—	0	—	—	60	59	33	0	1	18	—	14	3.75	-17	.257	.313	-8	—	-0.7
1903	Year	7	7	.500	19	15	11	1	—	0	—	—	120.2	136	71	3	2	42	—	28	3.80	-21	.283	.344	-13	—	-1.2

DePaula, Jorge Jorge B11.10.1978 Sabana Grande, Monte Plata, D.R BR/TR/6'1"/160 d9.5

YEAR	TM LG	W	L	PCT	G	GS	CG	SHO	QS	SV	BS	QR	IP	H	R	HR	HB	BB	IB	SO	ERA	AERA	OAV	OOB	SUP	DL	PW
2003	NY A	0	0	+	4	1	0	0	1	0	0	2	11.1	3	1	1	1	1	0	7	0.79	+453	.083	.132	-58	0	0.2
2004	NY A	0	1	.000	3	1	0	0	0	0	0	1	9	9	6	2	0	4	0	2	5.00	-8	.281	.342	-40	170	-0.1
2005	NY A	0	0	+	3	0	0	0	0	0	0	2	6.2	8	6	2	0	3	0	3	8.10	-47	.296	.367	—	0	-0.1
Total	3	0	1	.000	10	2	0	0	1	0	0	5	27	20	13	5	1	8	0	12	4.00	+11	.211	.274	-48	170	0.0

DeSalvo, Matt Matthew Thomas B9.11.1980 New Castle PA BR/TR/6'0"/180 d5.7 Col Marietta

YEAR	TM LG	W	L	PCT	G	GS	CG	SHO	QS	SV	BS	QR	IP	H	R	HR	HB	BB	IB	SO	ERA	AERA	OAV	OOB	SUP	DL	PW
2007	NY A	1	3	.250	7	6	0	0	2	0	0	0	27.2	34	20	2	3	18	0	10	6.18	-27	.301	.410	+13	0	-0.6

Deshaies, Jim James Joseph B6.23.1960 Massena NY BL/TL/6'4"/(220–222) Dr 1982 NYA 21/542 d8.7 Col LeMoyne (NY)

YEAR	TM LG	W	L	PCT	G	GS	CG	SHO	QS	SV	BS	QR	IP	H	R	HR	HB	BB	IB	SO	ERA	AERA	OAV	OOB	SUP	DL	PW
1984	NY A	0	1	.000	2	2	0	0	0	0	0	0	7	14	9	1	0	7	0	5	11.57	-67	.438	.525	-6	0	-0.6
Total	12	84	95	.469	257	253	15	6	128	0	0	2	1525	1434	743	179	27	575	39	951	4.14	-9	.251	.320	-5	37	-6.1

DeShong, Jimmie James Brooklyn B11.30.1909 Harrisburg PA D10.16.1993 Lower Paxton Twp. PA BR/TR/5'11"/165 d4.12

YEAR	TM LG	W	L	PCT	G	GS	CG	SHO	QS	SV	BS	QR	IP	H	R	HR	HB	BB	IB	SO	ERA	AERA	OAV	OOB	SUP	DL	PW
1932	Phi A	0	0	+	6	0	0	0	—	0	—	—	10	17	14	3	1	9	—	5	11.70	-61	.378	.491	—	—	-0.4
1934	NY A	6	7	.462	31	12	6	0	—	3	—	—	133.2	126	71	6	2	56	—	40	4.11	-1	.243	.319	+3	—	0.1
1935	NY A	4	1	.800	29	3	0	0	—	3	—	—	69	64	30	6	2	33	—	30	3.26	+24	.242	.331	+21	—	0.4
1936	Was A	18	10	.643	34	31	16	2	—	2	—	—	223.2	255	135	11	3	96	—	59	4.63	+3	.285	.356	+28	—	0.5
1937	Was A	14	15	.483	37	34	20	0	—	1	—	—	264.1	290	161	15	3	124	—	86	4.90	-10	.280	.359	+11	—	-0.8
1938	Was A	5	8	.385	31	14	1	0	—	0	—	—	131.1	160	104	11	1	83	—	41	6.58	-31	.310	.407	+6	—	-2.0
1939	Was A	0	3	.000	7	6	1	0	—	0	—	—	40.2	56	45	7	0	31	—	12	8.63	-50	.337	.442	+28	—	-1.1
Total	7	47	44	.516	175	100	44	2	—	9	—	—	872.2	968	560	59	12	432	—	273	5.08	-13	.281	.363	+17	—	-3.3
Team	2	10	8	.556	60	15	6	0	—	6	—	—	202.2	190	101	12	4	89	—	70	3.82	+6	.243	.323	+7	—	0.5
/180I	2	9	7	.556	53	13	5	0	—	5	—	—	180	169	90	11	4	79	—	62	3.82	+6	.243	.323	+7	—	0.4

Devens, Charlie Charles B1.1.1910 Milton MA D8.13.2003 Scarborough ME BR/TR/6'1"/180 d9.24 Col Harvard

YEAR	TM LG	W	L	PCT	G	GS	CG	SHO	QS	SV	BS	QR	IP	H	R	HR	HB	BB	IB	SO	ERA	AERA	OAV	OOB	SUP	DL	PW
1932	NY A	1	0	1.000	1	1	1	0	—	0	—	—	9	6	2	0	0	7	—	4	2.00	+104	.200	.351	+67	—	0.2
1933	NY A	3	3	.500	14	8	2	0	—	0	—	—	62	59	39	1	0	50	—	23	4.35	-11	.250	.381	+48	—	-0.6
1934	NY A	1	0	1.000	1	1	1	0	—	0	—	—	11	9	3	0	0	5	—	4	1.64	+148	.225	.311	-14	—	0.5
Total	3	5	3	.625	16	10	4	0	—	0	—	—	82	74	44	1	0	62	—	31	3.73	+5	.242	.370	+43	—	0.1

Dickson, Murry Murry Monroe B8.21.1916 Tracy MO D9.21.1989 Kansas City KS BR/TR/5'10.5"/(150–160) d9.30 Mil 1944–45

YEAR	TM LG	W	L	PCT	G	GS	CG	SHO	QS	SV	BS	QR	IP	H	R	HR	HB	BB	IB	SO	ERA	AERA	OAV	OOB	SUP	DL	PW
1958	†NY A	1	2	.333	6	2	0	0	0	1	0	4	20.1	18	17	4	1	12	0	9	5.75	-39	.237	.348	+27	0	-0.8
Total	18	172	181	.487	625	338	149	27	13	23	2	69	3052.1	3029	1431	302	37	1058	18	1281	3.66	+10	.260	.323	-3	33	16.2

Dingman, Craig Craig Allen B3.12.1974 Wichita KS BR/TR/6'4"/(195–230) Dr 1993 NYA 36/1009 d6.30 Col Hutchinson (KS) CC [DL 2006 Det A 182]

YEAR	TM LG	W	L	PCT	G	GS	CG	SHO	QS	SV	BS	QR	IP	H	R	HR	HB	BB	IB	SO	ERA	AERA	OAV	OOB	SUP	DL	PW
2000	NY A	0	0	+	10	0	0	0	0	0	0	6	11	18	8	1	0	3	0	8	6.55	-27	.375	.412	—	0	-0.1
Total	4	4	5	.444	75	0	0	0	0	5	3	47	79.2	92	55	13	7	37	5	50	6.10	-26	.300	.385	—	197	-0.8

Ditmar, Art Arthur John B4.3.1929 Winthrop MA BR/TR/6'2"/(185–197) d4.19

YEAR	TM LG	W	L	PCT	G	GS	CG	SHO	QS	SV	BS	QR	IP	H	R	HR	HB	BB	IB	SO	ERA	AERA	OAV	OOB	SUP	DL	PW
1954	Phi A	1	4	.200	14	5	0	0	—	0	—	—	39.1	50	35	4	1	36	—	14	6.41	-39	.314	.442	+31	0	-1.3
1955	KC A	12	12	.500	35	22	7	1	—	1	—	—	175.1	180	109	23	7	86	5	79	5.03	-17	.270	.358	+7	0	-1.9
1956	KC A	12	22	.353	44	34	14	2	—	1	—	—	254.1	254	141	30	7	108	6	126	4.42	-2	.262	.338	-10	0	-0.8
1957	†NY A	8	3	.727	46	11	0	0	32	6	3	56	127.1	128	55	9	2	35	1	64	3.25	+10	.261	.312	+15	0	0.3
1958	†NY A	9	8	.529	38	13	4	0	32	4	1	56	139.2	124	71	14	5	38	2	52	3.42	+3	.237	.292	+43	0	-0.2
1959	NY A	13	9	.591	38	25	7	1	32	1	0	56	202	156	75	17	8	52	2	96	3.00	+20	.211	.268	+18	0	1.9
1960	†NY A	15	9	.625	34	28	8	1	19	0	0	1	200	195	77	25	1	56	1	65	3.06	+17	.256	.308	+17	0	1.4
1961	NY A	2	3	.400	12	8	1	0	4	0	0	1	54.1	59	33	9	2	14	0	24	4.64	-20	.285	.329	+28	0	-0.7
1961	KC A	0	5	.000	20	5	0	0	2	1	0	9	54	60	34	6	2	23	1	19	5.67	-26	.286	.359	-45	0	-0.6
1961	Year	2	8	.200	32	13	1	0	6	1	0	10	108.1	119	67	15	4	37	1	43	5.15	-23	.285	.344	-4	0	-1.3
1962	KC A	0	2	.000	6	5	0	0	0	0	0	1	21.2	31	19	1	2	13	1	13	6.65	-36	.323	.411	-3	0	-0.5
Total	9	72	77	.483	287	156	41	5	121	14	4	183	1268	1237	649	138	37	461	19	552	3.98	-3	.256	.324	+10	0	-2.4
Team	5	47	32	.595	168	85	20	2	119	11	4	173	723.1	662	311	74	18	195	6	301	3.24	+11	.243	.296	+22	—	2.7
/180I	1	12	8	.595	42	21	5	0	30	3	1	43	180	165	77	18	4	49	1	75	3.24	+11	.243	.296	+22	—	0.7

Dixon, Sonny John Craig B11.5.1924 Charlotte NC BB/TR/6'2.5"/205 d4.20

YEAR	TM LG	W	L	PCT	G	GS	CG	SHO	QS	SV	BS	QR	IP	H	R	HR	HB	BB	IB	SO	ERA	AERA	OAV	OOB	SUP	DL	PW
1956	NY A	0	1	.000	3	0	0	0	—	1	—	—	4.1	5	3	0	0	5	1	1	2.08	+86	.294	.455	—	0	0.0
Total	4	11	18	.379	102	12	4	0	—	9	—	—	263	296	141	25	5	75	1	90	4.17	-7	.284	.334	-12	0	-0.6

Dobson, Pat Patrick Edward B2.12.1942 Depew NY D11.22.2006 Buffalo NY BR/TR/6'3"/190 d5.31 C8

YEAR	TM LG	W	L	PCT	G	GS	CG	SHO	QS	SV	BS	QR	IP	H	R	HR	HB	BB	IB	SO	ERA	AERA	OAV	OOB	SUP	DL	PW
1973	NY A	9	8	.529	22	21	6	1	10	0	0	1	142.1	150	72	22	2	34	8	70	4.17	-11	.266	.309	+19	0	-0.6
1974	NY A	19	15	.559	39	39	12	2	26	0	0	0	281	282	111	23	4	75	5	157	3.07	+15	.262	.311	-10	0	1.7
1975	NY A	11	14	.440	33	30	7	1	15	0	0	2	207.2	205	105	21	1	83	10	129	4.07	-9	.261	.330	-3	0	-0.9
Total	11	122	129	.486	414	279	74	14	169	19	6	94	2120.1	2043	939	197	26	665	76	1301	3.54	+1	.255	.312	-1	0	-0.2
Team	3	39	37	.513	94	90	25	4	51	0	0	3	631	637	288	66	7	192	23	356	3.65	+0	.263	.317	-1	—	0.2
/180I	1	11	11	.513	27	26	7	1	15	0	0	1	180	182	82	19	2	55	7	102	3.65	+0	.263	.317	-1	—	0.1

Donald, Atley Richard Atley "Swampy" B8.19.1910 Morton MS D10.19.1992 West Monroe LA BL/TR/6'1"/186 d4.21 Col Louisiana Tech

YEAR	TM LG	W	L	PCT	G	GS	CG	SHO	QS	SV	BS	QR	IP	H	R	HR	HB	BB	IB	SO	ERA	AERA	OAV	OOB	SUP	DL	PW
1938	NY A	0	1	.000	2	2	0	0	—	0	—	—	12	7	8	0	1	14	—	6	5.25	-14	.175	.400	-22	—	-0.1
1939	NY A	13	3	.813	24	20	11	2	—	1	—	—	153	144	74	12	0	60	—	55	3.71	+18	.247	.317	+38	—	1.0
1940	NY A	8	3	.727	24	11	6	1	—	0	—	—	118.2	113	49	11	2	59	—	60	3.03	+33	.249	.339	+11	—	0.7
1941	†NY A	9	5	.643	22	20	10	0	—	0	—	—	159	141	69	11	3	69	—	71	3.57	+10	.237	.320	+17	0	0.2
1942	†NY A	11	3	.786	20	19	10	1	—	0	—	—	147.2	133	58	6	0	45	—	53	3.11	+11	.239	.296	+44	0	0.2
1943	NY A	6	4	.600	22	15	2	0	—	0	—	—	119.1	134	69	10	0	38	—	57	4.60	-30	.276	.329	+59	0	-1.7
1944	NY A	13	10	.565	30	19	9	0	—	0	—	—	159	173	77	13	2	59	—	48	3.34	+4	.280	.345	+38	0	-0.2
1945	NY A	5	4	.556	9	9	6	2	—	0	—	—	63.2	62	29	3	0	25	—	19	2.97	+17	.248	.316	+26	0	0.1
Total	8	65	33	.663	153	115	54	6	—	1	—	—	932.1	907	433	66	8	369	—	369	3.52	+7	.253	.325	+32	0	0.2
/180I	2	13	6	.663	30	22	10	1	0	0	0	0	180	175	84	13	2	71	—	71	3.52	+7	.253	.325	+32	—	0.0

Donovan, Bill William Edward "Wild Bill" B10.13.1876 Lawrence MA D12.9.1923 Forsyth NY BR/TR/5'11"/190 d4.22 M4/C1 ▲

YEAR	TM LG	W	L	PCT	G	GS	CG	SHO	QS	SV	BS	QR	IP	H	R	HR	HB	BB	IB	SO	ERA	AERA	OAV	OOB	SUP	DL	PW
1915	NY A	0	3	.000	9	1	0	0	—	0	—	—	33.2	35	18	1	1	10	—	17	4.81	-39	.278	.336	-1	—	-0.6
1916	NY A	0	0	+	1	0	0	0	—	0	—	—	1	1	0	0	0	1	—	0	0.00	-100	.250	.400	—	—	0.0
Total	18	185	139	.571	378	327	289	35	—	8	—	—	2964.2	2631	1212	30	90	1059	—	1552	2.69	+6	.239	.310	+8	—	7.2
Team	2	0	3	.000	10	1	0	0	—	0	—	—	34.2	36	18	1	1	11	—	17	4.67	-37	.277	.338	-1	—	-0.6

Dotel, Octavio Octavio Eduardo (Diaz) B11.25.1973 Santo Domingo, D.R. BR/TR/6'0"/(175–210) d6.26

YEAR	TM LG	W	L	PCT	G	GS	CG	SHO	QS	SV	BS	QR	IP	H	R	HR	HB	BB	IB	SO	ERA	AERA	OAV	OOB	SUP	DL	PW
2006	NY A	0	0	+	14	0	0	0	0	0	0	6	10	18	13	2	0	11	1	7	10.80	-57	.383	.492	—	136	-0.3
Total	9	39	32	.549	428	34	0	0	14	82	32	289	641	511	286	80	30	282	24	773	3.76	+21	.218	.306	+8	367	6.7

Dotson, Richard Richard Elliott B1.10.1959 Cincinnati OH BR/TR/6'0"/(185–205) Dr 1977 CalA 1/7 d9.4

YEAR	TM LG	W	L	PCT	G	GS	CG	SHO	QS	SV	BS	QR	IP	H	R	HR	HB	BB	IB	SO	ERA	AERA	OAV	OOB	SUP	DL	PW
1988	NY A	12	9	.571	32	29	4	0	12	0	0	2	171	178	103	27	4	72	3	77	5.00	-21	.266	.338	+30	17	-2.2
1989	NY A	2	5	.286	11	9	1	0	5	0	0	0	51.2	69	33	8	1	17	0	14	5.57	-30	.317	.366	+1	0	-1.0
Total	12	111	113	.496	305	295	55	11	149	0	0	4	1857.1	1884	964	194	40	740	24	973	4.23	-2	.264	.334	+1	149	-1.8
Team	2	14	14	.500	43	38	5	0	17	0	0	2	222.2	247	136	35	5	89	3	91	5.13	-23	.278	.345	+23	17	-3.2
/180I	2	11	11	.500	35	31	4	0	14	0	0	2	180	200	110	28	4	72	2	74	5.13	-23	.278	.345	+23	14	-2.6

Downing, Al Alphonso Erwin B6.28.1941 Trenton NJ BR/TL/5'11"/(177–185) d7.19 Col Rider

YEAR	TM LG	W	L	PCT	G	GS	CG	SHO	QS	SV	BS	QR	IP	H	R	HR	HB	BB	IB	SO	ERA	AERA	OAV	OOB	SUP	DL	PW
1961	NY A	0	1	.000	5	1	0	0	0	0	0	2	9	7	8	0	1	12	0	12	8.00	-54	.212	.426	-52	0	-0.4
1962	NY A	0	0	+	1	0	0	0	0	0	0	1	1	0	0	0	0	0	0	1	0.00	-100	.000	.000	—	0	0.0
1963	†NY A	13	5	.722	24	22	10	4	18	0	0	1	175.2	114	52	7	0	80	1	171	2.56	+37	**.184**	.277	+6	0	1.8
1964	†NY A	13	8	.619	37	35	11	1	20	2	0	2	244	201	104	18	0	120	5	**217**	3.47	+4	.223	.312	+7	0	0.4
1965	NY A	12	14	.462	35	32	8	2	20	0	0	3	212	185	92	16	2	105	2	179	3.40	+0	.237	.326	+4	0	-0.1
1966	NY A	10	11	.476	30	30	1	0	18	0	0	0	200	178	90	23	1	79	3	152	3.56	-6	.235	.307	+9	0	-0.9
1967	NY A★	14	10	.583	31	28	10	4	18	0	0	3	201.2	158	65	13	6	61	1	171	2.63	+19	.217	.281	-12	0	1.7
1968	NY A	3	3	.500	15	12	1	0	5	0	0	3	61.1	54	24	7	1	20	2	40	3.52	-17	.237	.299	-35	31	-0.2
1969	NY A	7	5	.583	30	15	5	1	9	0	0	9	130.2	117	57	12	0	49	6	85	3.38	+4	.240	.306	+12	0	0.0
1970	Oak A	3	3	.500	10	6	1	0	3	0	0	2	41	39	19	5	1	22	0	26	3.95	-11	.252	.346	+22	0	-0.1
1970	Mil A	2	10	.167	17	16	1	0	9	0	0	1	94.1	79	47	8	3	59	2	53	3.34	+13	.232	.346	-42	0	0.0
1970	Year	5	13	.278	27	22	2	0	12	0	0	3	135.1	118	66	13	4	81	2	79	3.52	+5	.238	.346	-26	0	-0.1
1971	LA N	20	9	.690	37	36	12	0	26	0	0	1	262.1	245	93	16	3	84	3	136	2.68	+22	.247	.307	+26	0	1.9
1972	LA N	9	9	.500	31	30	7	4	18	0	0	1	202.2	196	81	13	7	67	2	117	2.98	+13	.254	.317	+16	0	0.9
1973	LA N	9	9	.500	30	28	5	2	18	0	0	2	193	155	87	19	1	68	3	124	3.31	+5	.219	.288	+10	0	0.0
1974	†LA N	5	6	.455	21	16	1	1	7	0	1	4	98.1	94	52	7	3	45	0	63	3.66	-6	.255	.338	+32	0	-0.5
1975	LA N	2	1	.667	22	6	0	0	5	1	2	11	74.2	59	31	6	2	28	1	39	2.89	+18	.215	.292	+3	0	0.1
1976	LA N	1	2	.333	17	3	0	0	3	0	0	10	46.2	43	21	3	0	18	1	30	3.86	-12	.250	.318	-48	0	-0.2
1977	LA N	0	1	.000	12	1	0	0	0	0	0	6	20	22	15	4	0	16	0	23	6.75	-43	.278	.400	+15	21	-0.3
Total	17	123	107	.535	405	317	73	24	197	3	3	62	2268.1	1946	938	177	31	933	32	1639	3.22	+6	.232	.309	+5	52	4.1
Team	9	72	57	.558	208	175	46	12	108	2	0	24	1235.1	1014	492	96	11	526	20	1028	3.23	+5	.224	.304	+1	31	2.3
/180I	1	10	8	.558	30	25	7	2	16	0	0	3	180	148	72	14	2	77	3	150	3.23	+5	.224	.304	+1	5	0.3

Doyle, Slow Joe Judd Bruce B9.15.1881 Clay Center KS D11.21.1947 Tannersville NY BR/TR/5'8"/150 d8.25

YEAR	TM LG	W	L	PCT	G	GS	CG	SHO	QS	SV	BS	QR	IP	H	R	HR	HB	BB	IB	SO	ERA	AERA	OAV	OOB	SUP	DL	PW
1906	NY A	2	1	.667	9	6	3	2	—	0	—	—	45.1	34	15	1	1	13	—	28	2.38	+24	.211	.274	-19	—	0.2
1907	NY A	11	11	.500	29	23	15	1	—	1	—	—	193.2	169	86	2	6	67	—	94	2.65	+5	.237	.308	-8	—	0.0
1908	NY A	1	1	.500	12	4	2	1	—	0	—	—	48	42	24	1	2	14	—	20	2.63	-6	.235	.297	+10	—	-0.1
1909	NY A	8	6	.571	17	15	8	3	—	0	—	—	125.2	103	49	3	2	37	—	57	2.58	-2	.232	.294	+32	—	-0.1
1910	NY A	0	2	.000	3	2	1	0	—	0	—	—	12.1	19	13	0	1	5	—	6	8.03	-67	.365	.431	-62	—	-0.8
1910	Cin N	0	0	+	5	0	0	0	—	0	—	—	11.1	16	19	0	0	11	—	4	6.35	-54	.327	.450	—	—	-0.4
1910	Major	0	2	.000	8	2	1	0	—	0	—	—	23	35	32	0	1	16	—	10	7.23	-61	.347	.441	-62	—	-1.2
Total	5	22	21	.512	75	50	29	7	—	1	—	—	436.1	383	206	7	12	147	—	209	2.85	-5	.240	.308	+1	—	-1.2
Team	5	22	21	.512	70	50	29	7	—	1	—	—	425	367	187	7	12	136	—	205	2.75	-2	.237	.303	+2	—	-0.8
/180I	2	9	9	.512	30	21	12	3	—	0	—	—	180	155	79	3	5	58	—	87	2.75	-2	.237	.303	+2	—	-0.3

Drabek, Doug Douglas Dean B7.25.1962 Victoria TX BR/TR/6'1"/(185–190) Dr 1983 ChiA 11/279 d5.30 Col Houston

YEAR	TM LG	W	L	PCT	G	GS	CG	SHO	QS	SV	BS	QR	IP	H	R	HR	HB	BB	IB	SO	ERA	AERA	OAV	OOB	SUP	DL	PW
1986	NY A	7	8	.467	27	21	0	0	10	0	0	4	131.2	126	64	13	3	50	1	76	4.10	+1	.251	.322	-5	0	0.1
Total	13	155	134	.536	398	387	53	21	236	0	0	7	2535	2448	1141	246	53	704	56	1594	3.73	+2	.255	.308	+5	69	5.3
/180I	1	10	11	.467	37	29	0	0	14	0	0	5	180	172	87	18	4	68	1	104	4.10	+1	.251	.322	+5	—	0.1

YEAR	TM LG	W	L	PCT	G	GS	CG	SHO	QS	SV	BS	QR	IP	H	R	HR	HB	BB	IB	SO	ERA	AERA	OAV	OOB	SUP	DL	PW
Drews, Karl	Karl August B2.22.1920 Staten Island NY D8.15.1963 Dania FL BR/TR/6'4"/198 d9.8																										
1946	NY A	0	1	.000	3	1	0	0	—	0	—	—	6.1	6	6	0	1	6	—	4	8.53	-60	.250	.419	+99	0	-0.5
1947	†NY A	6	6	.500	30	10	0	0	—	1	—	—	91.2	92	57	6	5	55	—	45	4.91	-28	.264	.373	+5	0	-2.1
1948	NY A	2	3	.400	19	2	0	0	—	1	—	—	38	35	17	3	0	31	—	11	3.79	+8	.248	.384	-45	0	0.2
Total	8	44	53	.454	218	107	26	7	—	7	—	—	826.2	913	493	72	35	332	—	322	4.76	-16	.284	.356	-8	0	-6.9
Team	3	8	10	.444	52	13	0	0	—	2	—	—	136	133	80	9	6	92	—	60	4.76	-23	.259	.378	+5	—	-2.4
/60G	3	9	12	.444	60	15	0	0	—	2	—	—	157	153	92	10	7	106	—	69	4.76	-23	.259	.378	+5	—	-2.8
Dubiel, Monk	Walter John B2.12.1918 Hartford CT D10.23.1969 Hartford CT BR/TR/6'0"/(190–196) d4.19																										
1944	NY A	13	13	.500	30	28	19	3	—	0	—	—	232	217	93	12	1	86	—	79	3.38	+3	.248	.316	-7	0	0.5
1945	NY A	10	9	.526	26	20	9	1	—	0	—	—	151.1	157	88	9	0	62	—	45	4.64	-25	.266	.335	+33	0	-1.8
Total	7	45	53	.459	187	97	41	9	—	11	—	—	879.1	854	436	65	4	349	—	289	3.87	-2	.254	.325	+2	0	-0.5
Team	2	23	22	.511	56	48	28	4	—	0	—	—	383.1	374	181	21	1	148	—	124	3.87	-10	.255	.324	+10	—	-1.3
/180I	1	11	10	.511	26	23	13	2	—	0	—	—	180	176	85	10	0	69	—	58	3.87	-10	.255	.324	+10	—	-0.6
Duren, Ryne	Rinold George B2.22.1929 Cazenovia WI BR/TR/6'1"/(194–197) d9.25																										
1954	Bal A	0	0	+	1	0	0	0	—	0	—	—	2	3	3	0	0	1	—	2	9.00	-60	.333	.400	—	0	-0.1
1957	KC A	0	3	.000	14	6	0	0	5	1	0	3	42.2	37	26	4	2	30	1	37	5.27	-25	.236	.359	-47	0	-0.5
1958	†NY A☆	6	4	.600	44	1	0	0	0	**20**	3	65	75.2	40	20	4	7	43	1	87	2.02	+75	.157	.296	-49	0	2.6
1959	NY A★	3	6	.333	41	0	0	0	0	14	7	65	76.2	49	18	6	3	43	2	96	1.88	+94	.181	.300	—	0	2.4
1960	†NY A	3	4	.429	42	1	0	0	0	9	1	28	49	27	29	3	7	49	1	67	4.96	-28	.160	.367	+23	0	-1.3
1961	NY A	0	1	.000	4	0	0	0	0	0	0	2	5	2	3	2	0	4	0	7	5.40	-31	.125	.300	—	0	-0.2
1961	LA A☆	6	12	.333	40	14	1	1	5	2	4	14	99	87	70	13	3	75	1	108	5.18	-13	.233	.361	-10	0	-1.6
1961	Year	6	13	.316	44	14	1	1	5	2	4	16	104	89	73	15	3	79	1	115	5.19	-14	.229	.358	-10	0	-1.8
1962	LA A	2	9	.182	42	3	0	0	0	8	2	23	71.1	53	38	1	6	57	2	74	4.42	-13	.206	.361	+54	0	-0.7
1963	Phi N	6	2	.750	33	7	1	0	5	2	0	17	87.1	65	33	6	5	52	1	84	3.30	-2	.210	.332	+18	0	0.1
1964	Phi N	0	0	+	2	0	0	0	0	0	0	1	3	5	3	0	1	1	0	5	6.00	-42	.357	.438	—	0	-0.1
1964	Cin N	0	2	.000	26	0	0	0	0	1	0	19	43.2	41	17	1	3	15	1	39	2.89	+25	.248	.319	—	0	0.1
1964	Year	0	2	.000	28	0	0	0	0	1	0	20	46.2	46	20	1	4	16	1	44	3.09	+17	.257	.328	—	0	0.0
1965	Phi N	0	0	+	6	0	0	0	0	0	0	4	11	10	7	0	1	4	1	6	3.27	+6	.270	.349	—	0	0.0
1965	Was A	1	1	.500	16	0	0	0	0	0	0	9	23	24	17	0	3	18	4	18	6.65	-48	.286	.421	—	0	-0.6
1965	Major	1	1	.500	22	0	0	0	0	0	—	13	34	34	24	0	4	22	5	24	5.56	-31	.281	.400	—	0	-0.6
Total	10	27	44	.380	311	32	2	1	15	57	17	250	589.1	443	284	40	41	392	15	630	3.83	-2	.209	.341	+0	0	0.1
Team	4	12	15	.444	131	2	0	0	0	43	11	160	206.1	118	70	15	17	139	4	257	2.75	+31	.166	.316	-13	—	3.5
/60G	2	5	7	.444	60	1	0	0	0	20	5	73	94.2	54	32	7	8	64	2	118	2.74	+31	.166	.316	-13	—	1.6
Eastwick, Rawly	Rawlins Jackson B10.24.1950 Camden NJ BR/TR/6'3"/(172–180) Dr 1969 CinN 3/62 d9.12																										
1978	NY A	2	1	.667	8	0	0	0	0	0	0	6	24.2	22	9	2	1	4	0	13	3.28	+11	.232	.270	—	0	0.2
Total	8	28	27	.509	326	1	0	0	0	68	23	232	525.1	519	215	38	8	156	21	295	3.31	+12	.258	.312	+19	21	3.0
Edwards, Foster	Foster Hamilton "Eddie" B9.1.1903 Holstein IA D1.4.1980 Orleans MA BR/TR/6'3"/175 d7.2 Col Dartmouth																										
1930	NY A	0	0	+	2	0	0	0	—	0	—	—	1.2	5	4	0	0	2	—	1	21.60	-80	.500	.583	—	—	-0.1
Total	5	6	9	.400	56	17	4	0	—	0	—	—	170	193	108	4	5	84	—	60	4.76	-21	.292	.377	-16	—	-1.9
Eiland, Dave	David William B7.5.1966 Dade City FL BR/TR/6'3"/(205–210) Dr 1987 NYA 7/185 d8.3 Col South Florida																										
1988	NY A	0	0	+	3	3	0	0	1	0	0	0	12.2	15	9	6	2	4	0	7	6.39	-38	.294	.368	+61	0	-0.1
1989	NY A	1	3	.250	6	6	0	0	2	0	0	0	34.1	44	25	5	2	13	3	11	5.77	-33	.328	.391	+5	0	-0.8
1990	NY A	2	1	.667	5	5	0	0	3	0	0	0	30.1	31	14	2	0	5	0	16	3.56	+12	.254	.283	+46	0	0.1
1991	NY A	2	5	.286	18	13	0	0	2	0	0	3	72.2	87	51	10	3	23	1	18	5.33	-22	.302	.356	-27	45	-1.0
1992	SD N	0	2	.000	7	7	0	0	1	0	0	0	27	33	21	1	0	5	0	10	5.67	-37	.287	.317	+1	105	-0.4
1993	SD N	0	3	.000	10	9	0	0	3	0	0	1	48.1	58	33	5	1	17	1	14	5.21	-21	.297	.353	-6	0	-0.4
1995	NY A	1	1	.500	4	1	0	0	0	0	0	1	10	16	10	1	1	3	1	6	6.30	-27	.348	.392	+61	0	-0.5
1998	TB A	0	1	.000	1	1	0	0	0	0	0	0	2.2	6	6	0	0	3	0	1	20.25	-76	.429	.529	-81	0	-0.6
1999	TB A	4	8	.333	21	15	0	0	6	0	1	4	80.1	98	59	8	3	27	1	53	5.60	-11	.294	.349	-15	30	-0.8
2000	TB A	2	3	.400	17	10	0	0	3	0	0	2	54.2	77	46	8	4	18	0	17	7.24	-32	.326	.381	-18	76	-0.9
Total	10	12	27	.308	92	70	0	0	21	0	1	11	373	465	274	46	16	118	7	153	5.74	-24	.303	.356	-7	256	-5.4
Team	5	6	10	.375	36	28	0	0	8	0	0	4	160	193	109	24	8	48	5	58	5.23	-22	.301	.354	+5	45	-2.3
/180I	6	7	11	.375	41	32	0	0	9	0	0	5	180	217	123	27	9	54	6	65	5.23	-22	.301	.354	+5	51	-2.6
Einertson, Darrell	Darrell Lee B9.4.1972 Rhinelander WI BR/TR/6'2"/190 Dr 1995 NYA 11/310 d4.15 Col Iowa Wesleyan [DL 1999 NY A 104, 2001 NY A 190]																										
2000	NY A	0	0	+	11	0	0	0	0	0	0	8	12.2	16	9	1	0	4	0	3	3.55	+34	.302	.345	—	26	0.0
Ellis, Dock	Dock Phillip B3.11.1945 Los Angeles CA BB/TR/6'3"/(185–203) d6.18																										
1976	†NY A	17	8	.680	32	32	8	1	21	0	0	0	211.2	195	83	14	4	76	1	65	3.19	+7	.247	.312	-4	0	0.5
1977	NY A	1	1	.500	3	3	1	0	2	0	0	0	19.2	18	9	1	0	8	0	5	1.83	+117	.237	.306	-2	0	0.2
Total	12	138	119	.537	345	317	71	14	194	1	0	21	2128	2067	958	140	44	674	66	1136	3.46	+4	.255	.313	+7	21	-0.1
Team	2	18	9	.667	35	35	9	1	23	0	—	0	231.1	213	92	15	4	84	1	70	3.07	+13	.246	.312	-4	—	0.7
/180I	2	14	7	.667	27	27	7	1	18	0	—	0	180	166	72	12	3	65	1	54	3.07	+13	.246	.312	-4	—	0.5
Embree, Alan	Alan Duane B1.23.1970 The Dalles OR BL/TL/6'2"/(185–190) Dr 1989 CleA 5/125 d9.15 [DL 1993 Cle A 124]																										
2005	NY A	1	1	.500	24	0	0	0	0	0	0	11	14.1	20	14	2	1	3	1	8	7.53	-43	.328	.364	—	0	-0.7
Total	14	35	38	.479	776	4	0	0	0	25	24	547	687.2	657	375	84	17	251	28	622	4.52	-3	.252	.318	-13	231	-0.2
Embree, Red	Charles Willard B8.30.1917 ElMonte CA D9.24.1996 Eugene OR BR/TR/6'0"/165 d9.10 Def 1943 Col Citrus (CA) JC																										
1948	NY A	5	3	.625	20	8	4	0	—	0	—	—	76.2	77	37	6	1	30	—	25	3.76	+9	.261	.331	+33	0	0.0
Total	8	31	48	.392	141	90	29	1	—	1	—	—	707	653	334	50	10	330	—	286	3.72	-2	.246	.331	+2	0	-1.1
Enright, Jack	Jackson Percy B11.29.1895 Fort Worth TX D8.18.1975 Pompano Beach FL BR/TR/5'11"/177 d9.26																										
1917	NY A	0	1	.000	1	1	0	0	—	0	—	—	5	5	5	0	0	3	—	1	5.40	-50	.294	.400	-73	—	-0.3
Erdos, Todd	Todd Michael B11.21.1973 Washington PA BR/TR/6'1"/(190–204) Dr 1992 SDN 9/253 d6.8																										
1998	NY A	0	0	+	2	0	0	0	0	0	0	1	2	5	2	0	0	1	1	0	9.00	-51	.500	.545	—	0	-0.1
1999	NY A	0	0	+	4	0	0	0	0	0	0	2	7	5	4	2	0	4	0	4	3.86	+23	.192	.290	—	0	0.0
2000	NY A	0	0	+	14	0	0	0	0	1	0	8	25	31	14	2	1	11	0	18	5.04	-5	.304	.377	—	0	0.0
Total	5	2	0	1.000	63	0	0	0	0	2	1	34	93.2	105	62	12	12	45	3	58	5.57	-20	.283	.372	—	0	-0.8
Team	3	0	0	+	20	0	0	0	0	1	0	11	34	41	20	4	1	16	1	22	5.03	-6	.297	.372	—	—	-0.1
Erickson, Roger	Roger Farrell B8.30.1956 Springfield IL BR/TR/6'3"/(180–199) Dr 1977 MinA 3/67 d4.6 Col New Orleans																										
1982	NY A	4	5	.444	16	11	0	0	5	1	0	4	70.2	86	36	5	0	17	1	37	4.46	-10	.301	.334	-22	28	-0.3
1983	NY A	0	1	.000	5	0	0	0	0	0	0	2	16.2	13	8	1	0	8	1	7	4.32	-9	.213	.304	—	0	0.0
Total	6	35	53	.398	135	117	24	0	65	1	0	11	799.1	868	419	68	14	251	9	365	4.13	-1	.277	.331	-12	75	-0.9
Team	2	4	6	.400	21	11	0	0	5	1	0	6	87.1	99	44	6	0	25	2	44	4.43	-9	.285	.329	-22	28	-0.3
Erickson, Scott	Scott Gavin B2.2.1968 Long Beach CA BR/TR/6'4"/(222–234) Dr 1989 MinA 4/112 d6.25 Col Arizona [DL 2001 Bal A 190, 2003 Bal A 183]																										
2006	NY A	0	0	+	9	0	0	0	0	0	0	4	11.1	13	12	2	3	7	2	2	7.94	-42	.283	.411	—	0	-0.2
Total	15	142	136	.511	389	364	51	17	194	0	0	16	2360.2	2586	1306	228	103	865	32	1252	4.59	-1	.282	.348	+0	601	-0.3

YEAR	TM LG	W	L	PCT	G	GS	CG	SHO	QS	SV	BS	QR	IP	H	R	HR	HB	BB	IB	SO	ERA	AERA	OAV	OOB	SUP	DL	PW
Farnsworth, Kyle	Kyle Lynn B4.14.1976 Wichita KS BR/TR/6'4"/(215–240) Dr 1994 ChN 47/1290 d4.29 Col Abraham Baldwin (GA) JC																										
2006	†NY A	3	6	.333	72	0	0	0	0	6	4	52	66	62	34	8	1	28	3	75	4.36	+6	.243	.318	—	0	0.3
2007	†NY A	2	1	.667	64	0	0	0	0	0	3	44	60	60	35	9	2	27	2	48	4.80	-6	.256	.336	—	0	-0.1
Total	9	28	45	.384	551	26	1	1	7	26	28	386	674.2	634	368	97	17	306	25	677	4.47	-1	.246	.328	+15	70	-3.5
Team	2	5	7	.417	136	0	0	0	0	6	7	96	126	122	69	17	3	55	5	123	4.57	+0	.249	.327	—	—	0.2
/60G	1	2	3	.417	60	0	0	0	0	3	3	42	55.2	54	30	8	1	24	2	54	4.56	+0	.249	.327	—	—	0.1
Farr, Steve	Steven Michael B12.12.1956 LaPlata MD BR/TR/5'11"/(190–206) d6.10 Col American																										
1991	NY A	3	5	.500	60	0	0	0	0	23	6	50	70	57	19	4	5	20	3	60	2.19	+91	.219	.288	—	0	2.9
1992	NY A	2	2	.500	50	0	0	0	0	30	6	42	52	34	10	2	2	19	0	37	1.56	+154	.186	.267	—	18	2.3
1993	NY A	2	2	.500	49	0	0	0	0	25	6	33	47	44	22	8	2	28	4	39	4.21	-1	.253	.356	—	17	0.2
Total	11	48	45	.516	509	28	1	1	11	132	38	352	824.1	751	326	70	32	334	47	668	3.25	+28	.244	.322	-30	88	12.4
Team	3	9	9	.500	159	0	0	0	0	78	18	125	169	135	51	14	9	67	7	136	2.56	+61	.219	.302	—	35	5.4
/60G	1	3	3	.500	60	0	0	0	0	29	7	47	63.2	51	19	5	3	25	3	51	2.56	+61	.219	.302	—	13	2.0
Ferguson, Alex	James Alexander B2.16.1897 Montclair NJ D4.26.1976 Sepulveda CA BR/TR/6'0"/180 d8.16 Mil 1918																										
1918	NY A	0	0	+	1	0	0	0	—	0	—	—	1.2	2	0	0	0	2	—	1	0.00	-100	.333	.500	—	—	0.0
1921	NY A	3	1	.750	17	4	1	0	—	1	—	—	56.1	64	40	4	4	27	—	9	5.91	-28	.296	.385	+18	—	-0.6
1925	NY A	4	2	.667	21	6	0	0	—	1	—	—	54.1	83	57	3	2	42	—	20	7.79	-45	.358	.460	+35	—	-2.1
Total	10	61	85	.418	257	166	62	2	—	10	—	—	1241.2	1455	778	68	45	482	—	397	4.93	-15	.299	.368	-10	—	-12.6
Team	3	7	3	.700	39	10	1	0	—	2	—	—	112.1	149	97	7	6	71	—	30	0.73	-37	.328	.426	+28	—	-2.7
Ferrell, Wes	Wesley Cheek B2.2.1908 Greensboro NC D12.9.1976 Sarasota FL BR/TR/6'2"/195 d9.9 b–Rick ▲																										
1938	NY A	2	2	.500	5	4	1	0	—	0	—	—	30	52	33	6	0	18	—	7	8.10	-44	.388	.461	+21	—	-1.2
1939	NY A	1	2	.333	3	3	1	0	—	0	—	—	19.1	14	10	2	0	17	—	6	4.66	-6	.219	.383	-53	—	0.0
Total	15	193	128	.601	374	323	227	17	—	13	—	—	2623	2845	1382	132	23	1040	—	985	4.04	+17	.275	.343	+2	0	31.1
Team	2	3	4	.429	8	7	2	0	—	0	—	—	49.1	66	43	8	0	35	—	13	6.75	-34	.333	.433	-11	—	-1.2
Ferrick, Tom	Thomas Jerome B1.6.1915 New York NY D10.15.1996 Lima PA BR/TR/6'2.5"/220 d4.19 Mil 1943–45 C12																										
1950	†NY A	8	4	.667	30	0	0	0	—	9	—	—	56.2	49	26	5	0	22	—	20	3.65	+18	.233	.306	—	0	0.8
1951	NY A	1	1	.500	9	0	0	0	—	1	—	—	12	21	12	4	0	7	—	3	7.50	-49	.389	.459	—	0	-0.8
Total	9	40	40	.500	323	7	4	1	—	56	—	—	674	654	306	44	1	227	—	245	3.47	+17	.256	.317	+37	0	5.1
Team	2	9	5	.643	39	0	0	0	—	10	—	—	68.2	70	38	9	0	29	—	23	4.33	-3	.265	.338	—	—	0.0
Figueroa, Ed	Eduardo (Padilla) B10.14.1948 Ciales, PR BR/TR/6'1"/(174–194) d4.9																										
1974	Cal A	2	8	.200	25	12	5	1	8	0	0	8	105.1	119	46	3	4	36	2	49	3.67	-6	.294	.355	-20	0	-0.1
1975	Cal A	16	13	.552	33	32	16	2	23	0	0	0	244.2	213	96	14	5	84	6	139	2.91	+23	.233	.299	+0	0	2.0
1976	†NY A	19	10	.655	34	34	14	4	24	0	0	0	256.2	237	101	13	3	94	0	119	3.02	+13	.246	.312	+32	0	0.8
1977	†NY A	16	11	.593	32	32	12	2	21	0	0	0	239.1	228	102	19	3	75	1	104	3.57	+11	.252	.308	+3	0	1.2
1978	†NY A	20	9	.690	35	35	12	2	26	0	0	0	253	233	96	22	3	77	4	92	2.99	+22	.248	.305	+11	0	2.0
1979	NY A	4	6	.400	16	16	4	1	7	0	0	0	104.2	109	49	6	0	35	1	42	4.13	+0	.275	.333	-2	88	0.1
1980	NY A	3	3	.500	15	9	0	0	1	1	0	3	58	90	47	3	1	24	2	16	6.98	-43	.363	.417	+3	0	-1.6
1980	Tex A	0	7	.000	8	8	0	0	2	0	0	0	39.2	62	29	9	0	12	0	9	5.90	-34	.365	.400	-42	0	-1.3
1980	Year	3	10	.231	23	17	0	0	3	1	0	3	97.2	152	76	12	1	36	2	25	6.54	-40	.364	.410	-18	0	-2.9
1981	Oak A	0	0	+	2	1	0	0	0	0	0	0	8.1	8	5	1	0	6	0	1	5.40	-35	.258	.378	+2	0	-0.1
Total	8	80	67	.544	200	179	63	12	112	1	0	11	1309.2	1299	571	90	19	443	16	571	3.51	+5	.261	.322	+5	88	3.0
Team	5	62	39	.614	132	126	42	9	79	1	0	3	911.2	897	395	63	10	305	8	373	3.53	+6	.260	.319	+12	88	2.5
/180I	1	12	8	.614	26	25	8	2	16	0	0	1	180	177	78	12	2	60	2	74	3.53	+6	.260	.319	+12	17	0.5
Filson, Pete	William Peter B9.28.1958 Darby PA BB/TL/6'2"/(175–195) Dr 1979 NYA 9/233 d5.15 Col Temple																										
1987	NY A	1	0	1.000	7	2	0	0	1	0	0	3	22	26	10	2	1	9	1	10	3.27	+36	.299	.371	-28	0	0.1
Total	7	15	18	.455	148	34	1	0	12	4	3	77	391.2	398	198	51	8	150	13	187	4.18	+2	.260	.327	-17	74	-0.5
Finneran, Happy	Joseph Ignatius "Smokey Joe" B10.29.1890 E.Orange NJ D2.3.1942 Orange NJ BR/TR/5'10.5"/169 d8.20																										
1918	NY A	3	6	.333	23	13	4	0	—	0	—	—	114.1	134	52	7	2	35	—	34	3.78	-25	.305	.359	+23	—	-0.7
Total	5	25	33	.431	109	66	29	3	—	5	—	—	570	568	270	17	18	202	—	168	3.30	-13	.266	.335	-1	—	-3.9
Fisher, Brian	Brian Kevin B3.18.1962 Honolulu HI BR/TR/6'4"/210 Dr 1980 AtlN 2/29 d5.7																										
1985	NY A	4	4	.500	55	0	0	0	0	14	4	46	98.1	77	32	4	0	29	3	85	2.38	+70	.216	.273	—	0	1.8
1986	NY A	9	5	.643	62	0	0	0	0	6	9	37	96.2	105	61	14	1	37	2	67	4.93	-16	.277	.341	—	0	-1.4
1987	Pit N	11	9	.550	37	26	6	3	12	0	0	7	185.1	185	99	27	4	72	7	117	4.52	-8	.262	.332	-1	0	-0.2
1988	Pit N	8	10	.444	33	22	1	1	7	1	1	9	146.1	157	78	13	5	57	4	66	4.61	-25	.277	.345	+15	15	-2.2
1989	Pit N	0	3	.000	9	3	0	0	0	1	0	3	17	25	17	2	0	10	3	8	7.94	-57	.329	.402	-22	101	-1.5
1990	Hou N	0	0	+	4	0	0	0	0	0	0	1	5	9	5	1	0	0	0	1	7.20	-48	.409	.375	—	0	-0.1
1992	Sea A	4	3	.571	22	14	0	0	8	1	0	5	91.1	80	49	9	1	47	2	26	4.53	-12	.234	.326	+14	0	-0.3
Total	7	36	34	.514	222	65	7	4	27	23	14	108	640	638	341	70	11	252	21	370	4.39	-10	.261	.330	+5	116	-3.9
Team	2	13	9	.591	117	0	0	0	0	20	13	83	195	182	93	18	1	66	5	152	3.65	+12	.248	.309	—	—	0.4
/60G	1	7	5	.591	60	0	0	0	0	10	7	43	100	93	48	9	1	34	3	78	3.65	+12	.248	.309	—	—	0.2
Fisher, Ray	Ray Lyle "Pick" B10.4.1887 Middlebury VT D11.3.1982 Ann Arbor MI BR/TR/5'11.5"/180 d7.2 Mil 1918 Col Middlebury																										
1910	NY A	5	3	.625	17	7	3	0	—	1	—	—	92.1	95	41	0	3	18	—	42	2.92	-9	.274	.315	+1	—	-0.3
1911	NY A	10	11	.476	29	22	8	2	—	0	—	—	171.2	178	85	3	5	55	—	99	3.25	+11	.269	.330	-12	—	0.5
1912	NY A	2	8	.200	17	13	5	0	—	0	—	—	90.1	107	70	2	2	32	—	47	5.88	-39	.312	.374	-26	—	-1.9
1913	NY A	12	16	.429	43	31	14	1	—	1	—	—	246.1	244	113	3	9	71	—	92	3.18	-6	.263	.321	-16	—	0.1
1914	NY A	10	12	.455	29	26	17	2	—	1	—	—	209	177	65	2	4	61	—	86	2.28	+21	.241	.303	-22	—	1.2
1915	NY A	18	11	.621	30	28	20	4	—	0	—	—	247.2	219	82	7	5	62	—	97	2.11	+39	.243	.295	+0	—	1.7
1916	NY A	11	8	.579	31	21	9	1	—	2	—	—	179	191	81	4	4	51	—	56	3.17	-9	.285	.339	+13	—	-0.6
1917	NY A	8	9	.471	23	18	12	3	—	0	—	—	144	126	49	3	2	43	—	64	2.19	+23	.243	.304	-11	—	0.9
1919	†Cin N	14	5	.737	26	20	12	5	—	1	—	—	174.1	141	55	4	1	38	—	41	2.17	+28	.226	.271	+36	—	1.9
1920	Cin N	10	11	.476	33	21	10	1	—	1	—	—	201	189	86	5	8	50	—	56	2.73	+11	.249	.302	+13	—	0.6
Total	10	100	94	.515	278	207	110	19	—	7	—	—	1755.2	1667	727	33	43	481	—	680	2.82	+6	.257	.312	-3	—	4.1
Team	8	76	78	.494	219	166	88	13	—	5	—	—	1380.1	1337	586	24	34	393	—	583	2.91	+3	.262	.319	-10	—	1.6
/180I	1	10	10	.494	29	22	11	2	—	1	—	—	180	174	76	3	4	51	—	76	2.91	+3	.262	.319	-10	—	0.2
Fontenot, Ray	Silton Ray B8.8.1957 Lake Charles LA BL/TL/6'0"/175 Dr 1979 TexA 34/815 d6.30 Col McNeese St.																										
1983	NY A	8	2	.800	15	15	3	1	8	0	0	0	97.1	101	41	3	1	25	0	27	3.33	+19	.266	.313	+32	0	0.6
1984	NY A	8	9	.471	35	24	0	0	14	0	0	9	169.1	189	77	8	3	58	4	85	3.61	+6	.290	.349	+0	0	0.3
1985	Chi N	6	10	.375	38	23	0	0	11	0	1	9	154.2	177	86	23	0	45	4	70	4.36	-8	.294	.342	-8	0	-1.0
1986	Chi N	3	5	.375	42	0	0	0	0	2	1	28	56	57	30	5	0	21	3	24	3.86	+6	.266	.332	—	0	-0.1
1986	Min A	0	0	+	15	0	0	0	0	0	0	6	16.1	27	19	3	2	4	0	10	9.92	-56	.360	.407	—	0	-0.4
1986	Major	3	5	.375	57	0	0	0	0	2	1	34	72	84	49	8	2	25	3	34	5.23	-8	.291	.351	—	0	-0.5
Total	4	25	26	.490	145	62	3	1	33	2	2	52	493.2	551	253	42	6	153	11	216	4.03	-2	.287	.340	+4	0	-0.6
Team	2	16	11	.593	50	39	3	1	22	0	0	9	266.2	290	118	11	4	83	4	112	3.51	+10	.281	.336	+12	—	0.9
/180I	1	11	7	.593	34	26	2	1	15	0	0	6	180	196	80	7	3	56	3	76	3.51	+10	.281	.336	+12	—	0.6
Ford, Ben	Benjamin Cooper B8.15.1975 Cedar Rapids IA BR/TR/6'7"/(200–230) Dr 1994 NYA 20/563 d8.20 Col Indian Hills (IA) CC																										
2000	NY A	0	1	.000	4	2	0	0	1	0	0	1	11	14	11	1	3	7	0	5	9.00	-47	.333	.462	-12	0	-0.4
Total	3	1	2	.333	31	2	0	0	1	0	3	16	45	52	40	7	7	20	0	23	7.80	-43	.291	.382	-12	47	-1.0

Pitchers

FORD, WHITEY EDWARD CHARLES "THE CHAIRMAN OF THE BOARD" B10.21.1928 NEW YORK NY BL/TL/5'10"/(175–185) d7.1 MIL 1951–52 C4 HF1974

YEAR	TM LG	W	L	PCT	G	GS	CG	SHO	QS	SV	BS	QR	IP	H	R	HR	HB	BB	IB	SO	ERA	AERA	OAV	OOB	SUP	DL	PW
1950	†NY A	9	1	.900	20	12	7	2	—	1	—	—	112	87	39	7	2	52	—	59	2.81	+53	.216	.309	+31	0	1.5
1953	†NY A	18	6	.750	32	30	11	3	—	0	—	—	207	187	77	13	4	110	—	110	3.00	+23	.245	.344	+51	0	2.5
1954	NY A★	16	8	.667	34	28	11	3	—	1	—	—	210.2	170	72	10	1	101	—	125	2.82	+22	.227	.317	+16	0	2.1
1955	†NY A★	**18**	7	.720	39	33	**18**	5	—	2	—	—	253.2	188	83	20	1	113	7	137	2.63	+43	.208	.296	+19	0	3.4
1956	†NY A★	19	6	**.760**	31	30	18	2	—	1	—	—	225.2	187	70	13	4	84	3	141	**2.47**	+56	.228	.301	+10	0	4.6
1957	†NY A	11	5	.688	24	17	5	0	53	0	1	9	129.1	114	46	10	1	53	3	84	2.57	+39	.237	.313	+32	0	1.6
1958	†NY A☆	14	7	.667	30	29	15	0	53	1	0	9	219.1	174	62	14	3	62	3	145	**2.01**	+76	.217	**.276**	+14	0	**3.9**
1959	NY A★	16	10	.615	35	29	9	2	53	1	2	9	204	194	82	13	1	89	5	114	3.04	+20	.250	.327	+9	0	2.6
1960	†NY A★	12	9	.571	33	29	8	0	15	0	0	3	192.2	168	76	15	1	65	5	85	3.08	+16	.235	.297	+9	0	1.5
1961	†NY A★	**25**	4	**.862**	39	**39**	11	3	26	0	0	0	**283**	242	108	23	1	92	3	209	3.21	+16	.229	.291	+35	0	2.1
1962	†NY A	17	8	.680	38	37	7	0	21	0	0	1	257.2	243	90	22	4	69	1	160	2.90	+29	.246	.296	+7	0	2.7
1963	†NY A	**24**	7	**.774**	38	**37**	13	3	26	1	0	1	**269.1**	240	94	26	2	56	3	189	2.74	+28	.241	.281	+16	0	2.5
1964	†NY A☆	17	6	.739	39	36	12	8	25	1	0	3	244.2	212	67	10	2	57	3	172	2.13	+70	.230	.276	+1	0	3.9
1965	NY A	16	13	.552	37	36	9	2	25	1	0	1	244.1	241	97	22	1	50	2	162	3.24	+5	.258	.296	+0	0	1.0
1966	NY A	2	5	.286	22	9	0	0	5	0	4	9	73	79	33	8	0	24	6	43	2.47	+35	.277	.330	-15	60	0.2
1967	NY A	2	4	.333	7	7	2	1	5	0	0	0	44	40	11	2	0	9	0	21	1.64	+91	.247	.285	-8	0	1.1
Total	16	236	106	.690	498	438	156	45	307	10	7	45	3170.1	2766	1107	228	28	1086	44	1956	2.75	+33	.235	.300	+15	60	37.2
/180I	1	13	6	.690	28	25	9	3	0	1	0	0	180	157	63	13	2	62	0	111	2.75	+33	.235	.300	+15	3	2.1

FORD, RUSS RUSSELL WILLIAM B4.25.1883 BRANDON MB, CAN. D1.24.1960 ROCKINGHAM NC BR/TR/5'11"/175 d4.28 B–GENE

YEAR	TM LG	W	L	PCT	G	GS	CG	SHO	QS	SV	BS	QR	IP	H	R	HR	HB	BB	IB	SO	ERA	AERA	OAV	OOB	SUP	DL	PW
1909	NY A	0	0	+	1	0	0	0	—	0	—	—	3	4	4	0	3	4	—	2	9.00	-72	.333	.579	—	—	-0.1
1910	NY A	26	6	.813	36	33	29	8	—	1	—	—	299.2	194	69	4	8	70	—	209	1.65	+61	.188	.245	+2	—	4.2
1911	NY A	22	11	.667	37	33	26	1	—	0	—	—	281.1	251	119	3	4	76	—	158	2.27	+58	.237	.291	-1	—	3.0
1912	NY A	13	21	.382	36	35	30	0	—	0	—	—	291.2	317	165	11	5	79	—	112	3.55	+1	.280	.329	-8	—	0.6
1913	NY A	12	18	.400	33	28	15	1	—	2	—	—	237	244	101	9	4	58	—	72	2.66	+13	.277	.324	-23	—	0.7
1914	Buf F	21	6	**.778**	35	26	19	5	—	**6**	—	—	247.1	190	63	11	7	41	—	123	1.82	+63	.214	.254	-8	—	3.0
1915	Buf F	5	9	.357	21	15	7	0	—	0	—	—	127.1	140	74	7	3	48	—	34	4.52	-38	.285	.352	+0	—	-1.9
Total	7	99	71	.582	199	170	126	15	—	9	—	—	1487.1	1340	595	45	34	376	—	710	2.59	+21	.244	.296	-6	—	9.5
Team	5	73	56	.566	143	129	100	10	—	3	—	—	1112.2	1010	458	27	24	287	—	553	2.54	+26	.245	.298	-7	—	8.4
/180I	1	12	9	.566	23	21	16	2	—	0	—	—	180	163	74	4	4	46	—	89	2.54	+26	.245	.298	-7	—	1.4

FOSSAS, TONY EMILIO ANTONIO (MOREJON) B9.23.1957 HAVANA, CUBA BL/TL/6'0"/(187–198) DR 1979 TEXA 12/303 d5.15 COL SOUTH FLORIDA

YEAR	TM LG	W	L	PCT	G	GS	CG	SHO	QS	SV	BS	QR	IP	H	R	HR	HB	BB	IB	SO	ERA	AERA	OAV	OOB	SUP	DL	PW
1999	NY A	0	0	+	5	0	0	0	0	0	0	2	1	6	4	1	0	1	1	0	36.00	-87	.667	.700	—	0	-0.2
Total	12	17	24	.415	567	0	0	0	0	7	15	398	415.2	434	211	39	10	180	36	324	3.90	+10	.269	.344	—	0	0.5

FRANCIS, RAY RAY JAMES B3.8.1893 SHERMAN TX D7.6.1934 ATLANTA GA BL/TL/6'1.5"/182 d4.18

YEAR	TM LG	W	L	PCT	G	GS	CG	SHO	QS	SV	BS	QR	IP	H	R	HR	HB	BB	IB	SO	ERA	AERA	OAV	OOB	SUP	DL	PW
1925	NY A	0	0	+	4	0	0	0	—	0	—	—	4.2	5	4	0	1	3	—	1	7.71	-45	.278	.409	—	—	-0.1
Total	3	12	28	.300	82	36	15	2	—	3	—	—	337	409	220	12	12	110	—	96	4.65	-16	.310	.368	-14	—	-3.3

FRANKLIN, WAYNE GARY WAYNE B3.9.1974 WILMINGTON DE BL/TL/6'2"/(195–205) DR 1996 LAN 36/1078 d7.24 COL MARYLAND–BALTIMORE CO.

YEAR	TM LG	W	L	PCT	G	GS	CG	SHO	QS	SV	BS	QR	IP	H	R	HR	HB	BB	IB	SO	ERA	AERA	OAV	OOB	SUP	DL	PW
2005	NY A	0	1	.000	13	0	0	0	0	0	3	9	12.2	11	12	1	1	8	0	10	6.39	-33	.239	.357	—	0	-0.3
Total	7	14	16	.467	143	40	1	1	17	0	4	69	323	332	215	57	18	168	8	216	5.54	-21	.268	.360	+9	20	-3.3

FRAZIER, GEORGE GEORGE ALLEN B10.13.1954 OKLAHOMA CITY OK BR/TR/6'5"/(200–205) DR 1976 MILA 9/196 d5.25 COL OKLAHOMA

YEAR	TM LG	W	L	PCT	G	GS	CG	SHO	QS	SV	BS	QR	IP	H	R	HR	HB	BB	IB	SO	ERA	AERA	OAV	OOB	SUP	DL	PW
1978	StL N	0	3	.000	14	0	0	0	0	0	0	8	22	22	14	2	0	6	2	8	4.09	-13	.250	.292	—	0	-0.3
1979	StL N	2	4	.333	25	0	0	0	0	0	2	19	32.1	35	19	3	1	12	2	14	4.45	-14	.278	.343	—	0	-0.5
1980	StL N	1	4	.200	22	0	0	0	0	3	4	15	23	24	10	2	0	7	3	11	2.74	+37	.273	.326	—	0	0.3
1981	†NY A	0	1	.000	16	0	0	0	0	3	0	13	27.2	26	7	1	0	11	2	17	1.63	+122	.245	.316	—	0	0.3
1982	NY A	4	4	.500	63	0	0	0	0	1	1	42	111.2	103	51	7	5	39	5	69	3.47	+16	.252	.321	—	0	0.4
1983	NY A	4	4	.500	61	0	0	0	0	8	2	44	115.1	94	44	5	3	45	4	78	3.43	+15	.227	.300	—	0	0.7
1984	Cle A	3	2	.600	22	0	0	0	0	1	2	14	44.1	45	19	3	0	14	4	24	3.65	+13	.259	.314	—	0	0.2
1984	†Chi N	6	3	.667	37	0	0	0	0	3	1	25	63.2	53	30	4	1	26	8	58	4.10	-5	.221	.296	—	0	-0.1
1984	Major	9	5	.643	59	0	0	0	0	4	3	39	107	98	49	7	1	40	12	82	3.92	+2	.237	.303	—	0	0.1
1985	Chi N	7	8	.467	51	0	0	0	0	2	2	30	76	88	57	11	3	52	9	46	6.39	-37	.299	.409	—	0	-3.3
1986	Chi N	2	4	.333	35	0	0	0	0	0	0	20	51.2	63	36	5	1	34	4	41	5.40	-25	.310	.407	—	0	-1.0
1986	Min A	1	1	.500	15	0	0	0	0	6	3	10	26.2	23	13	2	0	16	1	25	4.39	-1	.232	.331	—	0	0.1
1986	Major	3	5	.375	50	0	0	0	0	6	3	30	77	86	49	7	1	50	5	66	5.06	-17	.285	.382	—	0	-0.9
1987	†Min A	5	5	.500	54	0	0	0	0	2	5	31	81.1	77	49	9	2	51	4	58	4.98	-7	.258	.359	—	0	-0.4
Total	10	35	43	.449	415	0	0	0	0	29	22	271	675.2	653	349	54	16	313	48	449	4.20	-3	.257	.338	—	0	-3.6
Team	3	8	9	.471	140	0	0	0	0	12	3	99	254.2	223	102	13	8	95	11	164	3.25	+21	.240	.311	—	—	1.4
/60G	1	3	4	.471	60	0	0	0	0	5	1	42	109	96	44	6	3	41	5	70	3.26	+21	.240	.311	—	—	0.6

FREEMAN, MARK MARK PRICE B12.7.1930 MEMPHIS TN D2.21.2006 RANCHO MIRAGE CA BR/TR/6'4"/220 d4.18 COL LOUISIANA ST.

YEAR	TM LG	W	L	PCT	G	GS	CG	SHO	QS	SV	BS	QR	IP	H	R	HR	HB	BB	IB	SO	ERA	AERA	OAV	OOB	SUP	DL	PW
1959	NY A	0	0	+	1	1	0	0	1	0	0	0	7	6	2	0	1	2	0	4	2.57	+42	.240	.310	-52	0	0.0
Total	2	3	3	.500	34	9	1	0	2	1	1	16	87.1	82	59	10	6	38	3	55	5.56	-32	.246	.331	+35	0	-1.3

FRIEND, BOB ROBERT BARTMESS "WARRIOR" B11.24.1930 LAFAYETTE IN BR/TR/6'0"/(190–200) d4.28 COL PURDUE

YEAR	TM LG	W	L	PCT	G	GS	CG	SHO	QS	SV	BS	QR	IP	H	R	HR	HB	BB	IB	SO	ERA	AERA	OAV	OOB	SUP	DL	PW
1966	NY A	1	4	.200	12	8	0	0	3	0	0	2	44.2	61	25	2	0	9	1	22	4.84	-31	.330	.359	-30	0	-0.8
Total	16	197	230	.461	602	497	163	36	351	11	2	18	3611	3772	1652	286	46	894									
1	1734	3.58	+7	.269	.313	-8	0	7.1																			

FRILL, JOHN JOHN EDMOND B4.3.1879 READING PA D9.28.1918 WESTERLY RI BR/TL/5'10.5"/170 d4.16

YEAR	TM LG	W	L	PCT	G	GS	CG	SHO	QS	SV	BS	QR	IP	H	R	HR	HB	BB	IB	SO	ERA	AERA	OAV	OOB	SUP	DL	PW
1910	NY A	2	2	.500	10	5	3	1	—	1	—	—	48.1	55	33	1	1	5	—	27	4.47	-41	.289	.311	+11	—	-0.9
1912	StL A	0	1	.000	3	3	0	0	—	0	—	—	4.1	16	11	1	1	1	—	2	20.77	-84	.571	.600	+63	—	-1.2
1912	Cin N	1	0	1.000	3	2	0	0	—	0	—	—	15	19	11	0	2	1	—	4	6.00	-44	.345	.379	-13	—	-0.2
1912	Major	1	1	.500	6	5	0	0	—	0	—	—	19	35	22	1	3	2	—	6	9.31	-53	.422	.455	+33	—	-1.4
Total	2	3	3	.500	16	10	3	1	—	1	—	—	67.2	90	55	2	4	7	—	33	5.85	-51	.330	.356	+25	—	-2.3

FULTON, BILL WILLIAM DAVID B10.22.1963 PITTSBURGH PA BR/TR/6'3"/195 DR 1983 NYA S2/35 d9.12 COL PENSACOLA (FL) JC

YEAR	TM LG	W	L	PCT	G	GS	CG	SHO	QS	SV	BS	QR	IP	H	R	HR	HB	BB	IB	SO	ERA	AERA	OAV	OOB	SUP	DL	PW
1987	NY A	1	0	1.000	3	0	0	0	0	0	0	1	4.2	9	6	4	1	1	0	2	11.57	-62	.409	.458	—	0	-0.6

GABLER, JOHN JOHN RICHARD "GAB" B10.2.1930 KANSAS CITY MO BB/TR/6'2"/(165–175) d9.18

YEAR	TM LG	W	L	PCT	G	GS	CG	SHO	QS	SV	BS	QR	IP	H	R	HR	HB	BB	IB	SO	ERA	AERA	OAV	OOB	SUP	DL	PW
1959	NY A	1	1	.500	3	1	0	0	1	0	0	2	19.1	21	6	1	1	10	0	11	2.79	+30	.284	.376	-76	0	0.1
1960	NY A	3	3	.500	21	4	0	0	1	1	1	12	52	46	27	2	0	32	1	19	4.15	-14	.242	.348	-14	0	-0.4
1961	Was A	3	8	.273	29	9	0	0	4	4	1	13	92.2	104	61	5	1	37	3	33	4.86	-17	.283	.349	-53	0	-1.0
Total	3	7	12	.368	53	14	0	0	6	5	2	27	164	171	94	8	2	79	4	63	4.39	-13	.271	.352	-44	0	-1.3
Team	2	4	4	.500	24	5	0	0	2	1	1	14	71.1	67	33	3	1	42	1	30	3.79	-5	.254	.356	-26	—	-0.3

GARDNER, ROB RICHARD FRANK B12.19.1944 BINGHAMTON NY BR/TL/6'1"/(165–185) d9.1

YEAR	TM LG	W	L	PCT	G	GS	CG	SHO	QS	SV	BS	QR	IP	H	R	HR	HB	BB	IB	SO	ERA	AERA	OAV	OOB	SUP	DL	PW
1970	NY A	1	0	1.000	1	1	0	0	0	0	0	0	7.1	8	4	2	0	4	0	6	4.91	-27	.276	.364	+50	0	0.0
1971	NY A	0	0	+	2	0	0	0	0	0	0	2	3	3	1	0	0	2	0	2	3.00	+10	.273	.385	—	0	0.0
1972	NY A	8	5	.615	20	14	1	0	10	0	1	2	97	91	43	9	0	28	3	58	3.06	-2	.243	.295	+10	0	-0.6
Total	8	14	18	.438	109	42	4	0	19	2	3	42	331	345	180	35	4	133	8	193	4.35	-22	.269	.338	-6	0	-3.7
Team	3	9	5	.643	23	15	1	0	10	0	1	4	107.1	102	48	11	0	34	3	66	3.19	-5	.246	.303	+13	—	-0.6

GARVIN, NED VIRGIL LEE B1.1.1874 NAVASOTA TX D6.16.1908 FRESNO CA BR/TR/6'3.5"/160 d7.13

YEAR	TM LG	W	L	PCT	G	GS	CG	SHO	QS	SV	BS	QR	IP	H	R	HR	HB	BB	IB	SO	ERA	AERA	OAV	OOB	SUP	DL	PW
1904	NY A	0	1	.000	2	2	0	0	—	0	—	—	12	14	4	0	0	2	—	8	2.25	+21	.292	.320	-47	—	0.0
Total	7	58	97	.374	181	158	134	13	—	3	—	—	1400.2	1320	714	20	71	413	—	612	2.72	+25	.249	.312	-17	—	5.6

Pitchers

YEAR	TM LG	W	L	PCT	G	GS	CG	SHO	QS	SV	BS	QR	IP	H	R	HR	HB	BB	IB	SO	ERA	AERA	OAV	OOB	SUP	DL	PW
Gaston, Milt	Nathaniel Milton B1.27.1896 Ridgefield Park NJ D4.26.1996 Barnstable MA BR/TR (BB 1933)/6'1"/185 d4.20 b–Alex																										
1924	NY A	5	3	.625	29	2	0	0	—	1	—	—	86	92	48	3	6	44	—	24	4.50	-8	.286	.382	-49	—	-0.4
Total	11	97	164	.372	355	269	127	10	—	8	—	—	2105	2338	1277	114	24	836	—	615	4.55	-3	.287	.355	-15	—	-4.1
Gettel, Al	Allen Jones B9.17.1917 Norfolk VA D4.8.2005 Norfolk VA BR/TR/6'3.5"/200 d4.20																										
1945	NY A	9	8	.529	27	17	9	0	—	3	—	—	154.2	141	70	11	7	53	—	67	3.90	-11	.243	.314	-7	0	-0.3
1946	NY A	6	7	.462	26	11	5	2	—	0	—	—	103	89	40	6	2	40	—	54	2.97	+16	.229	.305	-19	0	0.5
Total	7	38	45	.458	184	79	31	5	—	6	—	—	734.1	711	362	72	19	310	0	310	4.28	-12	.255	.334	-4	0	-1.9
Team	2	15	15	.500	53	28	14	2	—	3	—	—	257.2	230	110	17	9	93	—	121	3.53	-2	.237	.310	-12	—	0.2
/180I	1	10	10	.500	37	20	10	1	—	2	—	—	180	161	77	12	6	65	—	85	3.53	-2	.237	.310	-12	—	0.1
Giard, Joe	Joseph Oscar "Peco" B10.7.1898 Ware MA D7.10.1956 Worcester MA BL/TL/5'10.5"/170 d4.18																										
1927	NY A	0	0	+	16	0	0	0	—	0	—	—	27	38	25	1	0	19	—	10	8.00	-52	.352	.449	—	—	-0.5
Total	3	13	15	.464	68	36	11	4	—	0	—	—	277.2	330	202	21	6	173	—	71	5.96	-25	.309	.408	-3	—	-4.0
Gibson, Paul	Paul Marshall B1.4.1960 Southampton NY BR/TL/6'0"/(165–195) Dr 1978 CinN*3/70 d4.8																										
1993	NY A	2	0	1.000	20	0	0	0	0	0	0	15	35.1	31	15	4	0	9	0	25	3.06	+37	.238	.282	—	0	0.2
1994	NY A	1	1	.500	30	0	0	0	0	0	2	20	29	26	17	5	1	17	3	21	4.97	-7	.236	.338	—	22	-0.1
1996	NY A	0	0	+	4	0	0	0	0	0	0	3	4.1	6	3	1	0	0	0	3	6.23	-21	.316	.316	—	0	0.0
Total	8	22	24	.478	319	15	0	0	7	11	15	188	556.2	570	269	55	13	236	43	345	4.07	-3	.267	.341	-17	55	-0.4
Team	3	3	1	.750	54	0	0	0	0	0	2	38	68.2	63	35	10	1	26	3	49	4.06	+9	.243	.309	—	22	0.1
/60G	3	3	1	.750	60	0	0	0	0	0	2	42	76.1	70	39	11	1	29	3	54	4.06	+9	.243	.309	—	24	0.1
Gibson, Sam	Samuel Braxton B8.5.1899 King NC D1.31.1983 High Point NC BL/TR/6'2"/198 d4.19 Col Catawba																										
1930	NY A	0	1	.000	2	2	0	0	—	0	—	—	6	14	11	1	0	6	—	3	15.00	-71	.424	.513	+160	—	-0.8
Total	5	32	38	.457	131	75	33	4	—	5	—	—	588.1	676	352	27	23	249	—	208	4.28	-5	.295	.370	+12	—	-2.0
Glade, Fred	Frederick Monroe "Lucky" B1.25.1876 Dubuque IA D11.21.1934 Grand Island NE BR/TR/6'0"/190 d5.27																										
1908	NY A	0	4	.000	5	5	2	0	—	0	—	—	32	30	18	0	4	14	—	11	4.22	-41	.275	.378	-34	—	-0.7
Total	6	52	68	.433	132	126	107	14	—	2	—	—	1072.2	950	411	11	48	237	—	464	2.62	-3	.240	.291	-9	—	-0.5
Gomez, Lefty	Vernon Louis "Goofy" B11.26.1908 Rodeo CA D2.17.1989 Greenbrae CA BL/TL/6'2"/173 d4.29 Def 1943 HF1972																										
1930	NY A	2	5	.286	15	6	2	0	—	1	—	—	60	66	41	12	1	28	—	22	5.55	-22	.280	.358	+20	—	-0.8
1931	NY A	21	9	.700	40	26	17	1	—	3	—	—	243	206	88	7	4	85	—	150	2.67	+49	.226	.295	+26	—	3.6
1932	†NY A	24	7	.774	37	31	21	1	—	1	—	—	265.1	266	140	23	2	105	—	176	4.21	-3	.259	.329	+45	—	-0.5
1933	NY A★	16	10	.615	35	30	14	4	—	2	—	—	234.2	218	108	16	0	106	—	**163**	3.18	+22	.240	.319	+7	—	1.0
1934	NY A★	**26**	5	**.839**	38	33	**25**	0	—	1	—	—	**281.2**	223	86	12	0	96	—	**158**	**2.33**	+74	**.215**	**.282**	+25	—	5.5
1935	NY A★	12	15	.444	34	30	15	2	—	1	—	—	246	223	104	18	2	86	—	138	3.18	+27	.242	.309	-4	—	1.8
1936	†NY A☆	13	7	.650	31	30	10	0	—	0	—	—	188.2	184	104	6	1	122	—	105	4.39	+6	.254	.362	+17	—	0.2
1937	†NY A★	**21**	11	.656	34	34	25	0	—	0	—	—	278.1	233	88	10	1	93	—	**194**	**2.33**	+91	**.223**	.287	+6	—	**6.8**
1938	†NY A★	18	12	.600	32	32	20	0	—	0	—	—	239	239	110	7	1	99	—	129	3.35	+35	.260	.332	+7	—	3.2
1939	†NY A☆	12	8	.600	26	26	14	2	—	0	—	—	198	173	80	11	3	84	—	102	3.41	+28	.235	.316	+0	—	1.9
1940	NY A	3	3	.500	9	5	0	0	—	0	—	—	27.1	37	20	2	1	18	—	14	6.59	-39	.325	.421	+39	—	-1.4
1941	NY A	15	5	**.750**	23	23	8	2	—	0	—	—	156.1	151	76	10	1	103	—	76	3.74	+5	.250	.360	+28	0	0.1
1942	NY A	6	4	.600	13	13	2	0	—	0	—	—	80	67	42	4	2	65	—	41	4.27	-20	.237	.383	+53	0	-1.0
1943	Was A	0	1	.000	1	1	0	0	—	0	—	—	4.2	4	4	0	0	5	—	0	5.79	-45	.250	.429	-74	0	-0.3
Total	14	189	102	.649	368	320	173	28	—	9	—	—	2503	2290	1091	138	19	1095	—	1468	3.34	+25	.242	.321	+17	0	20.1
Team	13	189	101	.652	367	319	173	12	—	9	—	—	2498.1	2286	1087	138	19	1090	—	1468	3.34	+25	.241	.321	+17	—	20.4
/180I	1	14	7	.652	26	23	12	1	—	1	—	—	180	165	78	10	1	79	—	106	3.34	+25	.241	.321	+17	—	1.5
Good, Wilbur	Wilbur David "Lefty" B9.28.1885 Punxsutawney PA D12.30.1963 Brooksville FL BL/TL/5'11.5"/180 d8.18 ▲																										
1905	NY A	0	2	.000	5	2	0	0	—	0	—	—	19	18	17	1	0	14	—	13	4.74	-38	.250	.372	-76		-0.4
Gooden, Doc	Dwight Eugene "Doctor K" B11.16.1964 Tampa FL BR/TR/6'3"/(190–210) Dr 1982 NYN 1/5 d4.7																										
1996	NY A	11	7	.611	29	29	1	1	12	0	0	0	170.2	169	101	19	9	88	4	126	5.01	-1	.259	.352	-6	0	-0.1
1997	†NY A	9	5	.643	20	19	0	0	8	0	0	1	106.1	116	61	14	7	53	1	66	4.91	-9	.283	.373	+0	70	-0.5
2000	†NY A	4	2	.667	18	5	0	0	2	2	0	8	64.1	66	28	8	0	21	3	31	3.36	+42	.266	.321	+10	0	0.8
Total	16	194	112	.634	430	410	68	24	257	3	0	13	2800.2	2564	1198	210	78	954	42	2293	3.51	+11	.244	.309	+13	386	18.4
Team	3	24	14	.632	67	53	1	1	22	2	0	9	341.1	351	190	41	16	162	8	223	4.67	+2	.268	.353	-2	70	0.2
/180I	2	13	7	.632	35	28	1	1	12	1	0	5	180	185	100	22	8	85	4	118	4.67	+2	.268	.353	-2	37	0.1
Goodwin, Art	Arthur Ingram B2.27.1877 Whiteley Twp. PA D6.19.1943 Franklin Twp. PA TR/5'8"/195 d10.7																										
1905	NY A	0	0	+	1	0	0	0	—	0	—	—	0.1	2	4	0	0	2	—	0	81.00	-96	.667	.800	—	—	-0.1
Gordon, Tom	Thomas B11.18.1967 Sebring FL BR/TR/5'9"/(160–195) Dr 1986 KCA 6/157 d9.8 [DL 2000 Bos A 181]																										
2004	†NY A★	9	4	.692	80	0	0	0	0	4	6	66	89.2	56	23	5	1	23	5	96	2.21	+108	.180	.237	—	0	3.3
2005	†NY A	5	4	.556	79	0	0	0	0	2	7	58	80.2	59	25	8	0	29	4	69	2.57	+68	.203	.272	—	0	1.7
Total	19	133	121	.524	853	203	18	4	110	156	53	487	2076.2	1855	993	173	38	957	56	1902	3.93	+14	.238	.322	+3	565	18.5
Team	2	14	8	.636	159	0	0	0	0	6	13	124	170.1	115	48	13	1	52	9	165	2.38	+87	.191	.254	—	—	5.0
/60G	1	5	3	.636	60	0	0	0	0	2	5	47	64.1	43	18	5	0	20	3	62	2.38	+87	.191	.254	—	—	1.9
Gorman, Tom	Thomas Aloysius B1.4.1925 New York NY D12.26.1992 Valley Stream NY BR/TR/6'1"/(190–200) d7.16																										
1952	†NY A	6	2	.750	12	6	1	1	—	1	—	—	60.2	63	34	8	2	22	—	31	4.60	-28	.272	.340	+27	0	-1.2
1953	†NY A	4	5	.444	40	1	0	0	—	6	—	—	77	65	32	5	6	32	—	38	3.39	+9	.226	.317	-52	0	0.3
1954	NY A	0	0	+	23	0	0	0	—	2	—	—	36.2	30	14	1	1	14	—	31	2.21	+56	.222	.300	—	0	0.1
Total	8	36	36	.500	289	33	5	2	16	42	7	177	689.1	659	332	77	20	239	19	321	3.77	+5	.254	.320	-14	0	0.1
Team	3	10	7	.588	75	7	1	1	—	9	—	—	174.1	158	80	14	9	68	—	100	3.56	-2	.241	.321	+16	—	-0.8
/60G	2	8	6	.588	60	6	1	1	—	7	—	—	139.1	126	64	11	7	54	—	80	3.57	-2	.241	.321	+16	—	-0.6
Gossage, Rich	Richard Michael "Goose" B7.5.1951 Colorado Springs CO BR/TR/6'3"/(180–226) Dr 1970 ChiA 9/204 d4.16																										
1978	†NY A★	10	11	.476	63	0	0	0	0	**27**	10	53	134.1	87	41	9	2	59	8	122	2.01	+82	.187	.277	—	0	4.3
1979	NY A	5	3	.625	36	0	0	0	0	18	3	29	58.1	48	18	5	0	19	4	41	2.62	+57	.227	.291	—	79	1.9
1980	†NY A★	6	2	.750	64	0	0	0	0	**33**	4	52	99	74	29	5	1	37	3	103	2.27	+74	.211	.285	—	0	2.8
1981	†NY A✳	3	2	.600	32	0	0	0	0	20	3	30	46.2	22	6	2	1	14	1	48	0.77	+369	.141	.215	—	0	3.0
1982	NY A☆	4	5	.444	56	0	0	0	0	30	9	47	93	63	23	5	0	28	5	102	2.23	+81	.196	.259	—	0	3.2
1983	NY A	13	5	.722	57	0	0	0	0	22	13	40	87.1	82	27	5	1	25	5	90	2.27	+74	.248	.298	—	0	3.1
1989	NY A	1	0	1.000	11	0	0	0	0	1	0	8	14.1	14	6	0	1	3	1	6	3.77	+3	.275	.327	—	0	0.0
Total	22	124	107	.537	1002	37	16	0	18	310	11	716	1809.1	1497	670	119	47	732	90	1502	3.01	+26	.228	.308	-34	292	29.7
Team	7	42	28	.600	319	0	0	0	0	151	42	259	533	390	150	31	6	185	27	512	2.14	+81	.207	.277	—	79	18.3
/60G	1	8	5	.600	60	0	0	0	0	28	8	49	100.1	73	28	6	1	35	5	96	2.14	+81	.207	.277	—	15	3.4
Gowell, Larry	Lawrence Clyde B5.2.1948 Lewiston ME BR/TR/6'2"/190 Dr 1967 NYA 4/61 d9.21																										
1972	NY A	0	1	.000	2	1	0	0	0	0	0	1	7	3	1	0	0	2	0	7	1.29	+133	.143	.208	-100	0	0.3
Graman, Alex	Alex Joseph B11.17.1977 Huntingburg IN BL/TL/6'4"/210 Dr 1999 NYA 3/111 d4.20 Col Indiana St.																										
2004	NY A	0	0	+	3	2	0	0	0	0	0	1	5	14	11	1	0	2	0	4	19.80	-77	.500	.516	+81	0	-0.4
2005	NY A	0	0	+	2	0	0	0	0	0	0	0	1.1	3	2	1	0	2	1	0	13.50	-68	.429	.556	—	0	-0.1
Total	2	0	0	+	5	2	0	0	0	0	0	1	6.1	17	13	2	0	4	1	4	18.47	-75	.486	.525	+81	0	-0.5

YEAR	TM LG	W	L	PCT	G	GS	CG	SHO	QS	SV	BS	QR	IP	H	R	HR	HB	BB	IB	SO	ERA	AERA	OAV	OOB	SUP	DL	PW
Granger, Wayne	Wayne Allan B3.15.1944 Springfield MA BR/TR/6'2"/(165–170) d6.5 Col Springfield																										
1973	NY A	0	1	.000	7	0	0	0	0	0	0	5	15.1	19	7	1	1	3	1	10	1.76	+111	.279	.319	—	0	0.1
Total	9	35	35	.500	451	0	0	0	0	108	31	313	638.2	632	290	47	22	201	57	303	3.14	+13	.260	.319	—	0	3.1
Gray, Ted	Ted Glenn B12.31.1924 Detroit MI BB/TL (BR 1946)/5'11"/(160–175) d5.15																										
1955	NY A	0	0	+	1	1	0	0	—	0	—	—	3	3	1	0	0	0	0	1	3.00	+25	.300	.273	+90	0	0.0
Total	9	59	74	.444	222	162	50	7	—	4	—	—	1134	1072	624	114	28	595	1	687	4.37	-6	.251	.346	-10	0	-5.5
Grba, Eli	Eli B8.9.1934 Chicago IL BR/TR/6'2"/(204–208) d7.10																										
1959	NY A	2	5	.286	19	6	0	0	3	0	2	7	50.1	52	44	6	0	39	0	23	6.44	-43	.269	.387	+9	0	-2.0
1960	†NY A	6	4	.600	24	9	1	0	4	1	1	12	80.2	65	45	9	2	46	3	32	3.68	-3	.226	.333	-10	0	-0.3
Total	5	28	33	.459	135	75	10	0	34	4	5	40	536.1	513	318	62	12	284	19	255	4.48	-10	.250	.342	+6	0	-2.7
Team	2	8	9	.471	43	15	1	0	7	1	3	19	131	117	89	15	2	85	3	55	4.74	-24	.243	.355	-2	—	-2.3
/180I	3	11	12	.471	59	21	1	0	10	1	4	26	180	161	122	21	3	117	4	76	4.74	-24	.243	.355	-2	—	-3.2
Griffin, Mike	Michael Leroy B6.26.1957 Colusa CA BR/TR/6'5"/(195–210) Dr 1976 TexA 3/60 d9.17																										
1979	NY A	0	0	+	3	0	0	0	0	1	0	2	4.1	5	2	0	0	2	0	5	4.15	-1	.313	.389	—	0	0.0
1980	NY A	2	4	.333	13	9	0	0	1	0	0	2	54	64	36	6	1	23	2	25	4.83	-18	.287	.353	+23	0	-0.7
1981	NY A	0	0	+	2	0	0	0	0	0	0	2	4.1	5	1	0	0	0	0	4	2.08	+74	.278	.278	—	0	0.1
Total	6	7	15	.318	67	24	1	0	5	3	1	27	203.2	235	115	19	4	73	7	101	4.60	-12	.288	.346	-18	0	-1.0
Team	3	2	4	.333	18	9	0	0	1	1	0	6	62.2	74	39	6	1	25	2	34	4.60	-14	.288	.351	+23	—	-0.6
Griffith, Clark	Clark Calvin "The Old Fox" B11.20.1869 Clear Creek MO D10.27.1955 Washington DC BR/TR/5'6.5"/156 d4.11 M20 HF1946																										
1903	NY A	14	11	.560	25	24	22	2	—	0	—	—	213	201	92	3	6	33	—	69	2.70	+16	.249	.283	-24	—	1.0
1904	NY A	7	5	.583	16	11	8	1	—	0	—	—	100.1	91	40	3	4	16	—	36	2.87	-6	.243	.281	+12	—	-0.2
1905	NY A	9	6	.600	25	7	4	2	—	1	—	—	101.2	82	30	1	1	15	—	46	1.68	+74	.223	.255	-24	—	1.8
1906	NY A	2	2	.500	17	2	1	0	—	2	—	—	59.2	58	30	0	4	15	—	16	3.02	-2	.258	.316	+46	—	-0.1
1907	NY A	0	0	+	4	0	0	0	—	0	—	—	8.1	15	16	0	0	6	—	5	8.64	-68	.395	.477	—	—	-0.3
Total	20	237	146	.619	453	372	337	22	—	8	—	—	3385.2	3670	1852	76	171	774	—	955	3.31	+21	.274	.322	+1	—	28.3
Team	5	32	24	.571	87	44	35	5	—	3	—	—	483	447	208	7	15	85	—	172	2.66	+12	.247	.286	-12	—	2.2
/180I	2	12	9	.571	32	16	13	2	—	1	—	—	180	167	78	3	6	32	—	64	2.66	+12	.247	.286	-12	—	0.8
Grim, Bob	Robert Anton B3.8.1930 New York NY D10.23.1996 Shawnee KS BR/TR/6'1"/185 d4.18																										
1954	NY A	20	6	.769	37	20	8	1	—	0	—	—	199	175	78	9	3	85	—	108	3.26	+6	.244	.322	+41	0	0.5
1955	†NY A	7	5	.583	26	11	1	1	—	4	—	—	92.1	81	49	9	3	42	2	63	4.19	-11	.238	.321	+34	47	-0.7
1956	NY A	6	1	.857	26	6	1	0	—	5	—	—	74.2	64	27	3	2	31	0	48	2.77	+39	.235	.317	+23	0	0.8
1957	†NY A★	12	8	.600	46	0	0	0	0	**19**	7	40	72	60	22	5	0	36	5	52	2.63	+37	.239	.330	—	0	2.0
1958	NY A	0	1	.000	11	0	0	0	0	0	1	40	16.1	12	10	3	1	10	0	11	5.51	-36	.211	.338	—	0	-0.2
1958	KC A	7	6	.538	26	14	5	1	13	0	1	24	113.2	118	54	7	3	41	4	54	3.56	+10	.269	.334	-13	0	0.1
1958	Year	7	7	.500	37	14	5	1	13	0	2	64	130	130	64	10	4	51	4	65	3.81	+1	.263	.335	-12	0	-0.1
1959	KC A	6	10	.375	40	9	3	1	13	4	3	24	125.1	124	69	10	3	57	6	65	4.09	-2	.260	.341	+25	0	-0.5
1960	Cle A	0	1	.000	3	0	0	0	0	0	0	0	2.1	6	3	0	0	1	0	2	11.57	-68	.500	.538	—	0	-0.4
1960	Cin N	2	2	.500	26	0	0	0	0	2	0	17	30.1	32	18	3	0	10	2	22	4.45	-14	.274	.321	—	0	-0.4
1960	StL N	1	0	1.000	15	0	0	0	0	0	1	8	20.2	22	7	1	0	9	1	15	3.05	+34	.272	.337	—	0	0.1
1960	Year	3	2	.600	41	0	0	0	0	2	1	25	51	54	25	4	0	19	3	37	3.88	+1	.273	.327	—	0	-0.3
1960	Major	3	3	.500	44	0	0	0	0	2	—	25	52	60	28	4	0	20	3	39	4.22	+2	.286	.339	—	0	-0.7
1962	KC A	0	1	.000	12	0	0	0	0	3	3	7	13	14	9	0	0	8	2	3	6.23	-32	.292	.393	—	0	-0.3
Total	8	61	41	.598	268	60	18	4	26	37	16	160	759.2	708	346	50	15	330	22	443	3.61	+4	.252	.330	+22	47	1.0
Team	5	45	21	.682	146	37	10	2	0	28	8	80	454.1	392	186	29	9	204	7	282	3.35	+7	.239	.323	+36	47	2.4
/180I	2	18	8	.682	58	15	4	1	0	11	3	32	180	155	74	11	4	81	3	112	3.35	+7	.239	.323	+36	19	1.0
Grimes, Burleigh	Burleigh Arland "Ol' Stubblebeard" B8.18.1893 Emerald WI D12.6.1985 Clear Lake WI BR/TR/5'10"/175 d9.10 M2/C1 HF1964																										
1934	NY A	1	2	.333	10	0	0	0	—	1	—	—	18	22	11	0	1	14	—	5	5.50	-26	.319	.440	—	—	-0.3
Total	19	270	212	.560	616	497	314	35	—	18	—	—	4180	4412	2050	148	101	1295	—	1512	3.53	+7	.273	.331	+9	—	18.3
Grimsley, Jason	Jason Alan B8.7.1967 Cleveland TX BR/TR/6'3"/(180–205) Dr 1985 PhiN 10/252 d9.8																										
1999	†NY A	7	2	.778	55	0	0	0	0	1	3	37	75	66	39	7	4	40	5	49	3.60	+31	.231	.330	—	0	0.7
2000	†NY A	3	2	.600	63	4	0	0	0	1	3	37	96.1	100	58	10	5	42	1	53	5.04	-5	.268	.345	+38	0	-0.1
Total	15	42	58	.420	552	72	3	1	27	4	34	317	936.2	954	549	83	47	498	46	622	4.77	-2	.265	.359	-6	212	-0.8
Team	2	10	4	.714	118	4	0	0	0	2	6	74	171.1	166	97	17	9	82	6	102	4.41	+8	.252	.339	+38	—	0.6
/60G	1	5	2	.714	60	2	0	0	0	1	3	38	87	84	49	9	5	42	3	52	4.42	+8	.252	.339	+38	—	0.3
Grissom, Lee	Lee Theo B10.23.1907 Sherman TX D10.4.1998 Corning CA BB/TL (BR 1934, 37)/6'3"/200 d9.2 Mil 1942–45 b-Marv																										
1940	NY A	0	0	+	5	0	0	0	—	0	—	—	4.2	4	0	0	0	2	—	1	0.00	-100	.250	.333	—	—	0.1
Total	8	29	48	.377	162	95	23	6	—	7	—	—	701.2	668	346	35	9	305	—	384	3.89	-3	.250	.329	-12	0	-1.3
Groom, Buddy	Wedsel Gary B7.10.1965 Dallas TX BL/TL/6'2"/(200–208) Dr 1987 ChiA 12/297 d6.20 Col Mary Hardin-Baylor																										
2005	NY A	1	0	1.000	24	0	0	0	0	0	0	17	25.2	32	14	3	3	7	2	13	4.91	-12	.305	.362	—	0	-0.1
Total	14	31	32	.492	786	15	0	0	2	27	31	534	734.2	825	403	73	21	260	36	494	4.64	-1	.285	.345	-15	0	-1.2
Guante, Cecilio	Cecilio (Magallane) B2.1.1960 Villa Mella, D.R. BR/TR/6'3"/(185–205) d5.1																										
1987	NY A	3	2	.600	23	0	0	0	0	1	1	15	44	42	30	8	1	20	0	46	5.73	-23	.247	.323	—	84	-0.7
1988	NY A	5	6	.455	56	0	0	0	0	11	6	36	75	59	25	10	5	22	3	61	2.88	+38	.213	.282	—	0	1.5
Total	9	29	34	.460	363	1	0	0	0	35	25	254	595	512	256	61	27	236	38	503	3.48	+11	.232	.310	-31	145	2.4
Team	2	8	8	.500	79	0	0	0	0	12	7	51	119	101	55	18	6	42	3	107	3.93	+5	.226	.298	—	84	0.8
/60G	2	6	6	.500	60	0	0	0	0	9	5	39	90.1	77	42	14	5	32	2	81	3.93	+5	.226	.298	—	64	0.6
Guetterman, Lee	Arthur Lee B11.22.1958 Chattanooga TN BL/TL/6'8"/(225–235) Dr 1981 SeaA 4/80 d9.12 Col Liberty																										
1984	Sea A	0	0	+	3	0	0	0	0	0	0	1	4.1	9	2	0	0	2	0	2	4.15	-3	.450	.500	—	0	0.0
1986	Sea A	0	4	.000	41	4	1	0	2	0	3	19	76	108	67	7	4	30	3	38	7.34	-42	.347	.406	+12	0	-1.2
1987	Sea A	11	4	.733	25	17	2	1	8	0	0	7	113.1	117	60	13	2	35	2	42	3.81	+24	.267	.320	+6	0	1.0
1988	NY A	1	2	.333	20	2	0	0	0	0	1	12	40.2	49	21	2	1	14	0	15	4.65	-15	.306	.364	-77	0	-0.2
1989	NY A	5	5	.500	70	0	0	0	0	13	0	56	103	98	31	6	0	26	9	51	2.45	+59	.258	.304	—	0	2.0
1990	NY A	11	7	.611	64	0	0	0	0	2	5	47	93	80	37	6	0	26	7	48	3.39	+18	.236	.288	—	15	1.3
1991	NY A	3	4	.429	64	0	0	0	0	6	3	47	88	91	42	6	3	25	5	35	3.68	+13	.268	.320	—	0	0.3
1992	NY A	1	1	.500	15	0	0	0	0	0	0	7	22.2	35	24	5	0	13	3	5	9.53	-59	.354	.421	—	0	-1.0
1992	NY N	3	4	.429	43	0	0	0	0	2	1	27	43.1	57	28	5	1	14	5	15	5.82	-40	.324	.371	—	0	-1.6
1992	Major	4	5	.444	58	0	0	0	0	2	1	34	65	92	52	10	1	27	8	20	7.09	-47	.335	.390	—	0	-2.6
1993	StL N	3	3	.500	40	0	0	0	0	1	3	31	46	41	18	1	2	16	5	19	2.93	+37	.240	.309	—	0	0.6
1995	Sea A	0	0	+	23	0	0	0	0	1	1	9	17	21	13	1	3	11	0	11	6.88	-31	.300	.417	—	0	-0.1
1996	Sea A	0	2	.000	17	0	0	0	0	0	0	13	11	11	8	0	0	10	2	6	4.09	+22	.275	.420	—	0	0.0
Total	11	38	36	.514	425	23	3	1	10	25	17	276	658.1	717	351	52	16	222	41	287	4.33	-4	.282	.340	+11	15	1.1
Team	5	21	19	.525	233	2	0	0	0	21	9	169	347.1	353	155	25	4	104	24	154	3.73	+7	.268	.321	-77	15	2.4
/60G	1	5	5	.525	60	1	0	0	0	5	2	44	89.1	91	40	6	1	27	6	40	3.74	+7	.268	.321	-77	4	0.6
Guidry, Ron	Ronald Ames B8.28.1950 Lafayette LA BL/TL/5'11"/(157–170) Dr 1971 NYA 3/65 d7.27 C2 Col Louisiana–Lafayette [DL 1989 NY A 78]																										
1975	NY A	0	1	.000	10	1	0	0	0	0	0	5	15.2	15	6	0	1	9	0	15	3.45	+8	.259	.362	-5	0	0.0
1976	†NY A	0	0	+	7	0	0	0	0	0	0	3	16	20	12	1	0	4	0	12	5.63	-39	.294	.333	—	0	-0.2
1977	†NY A	16	7	.696	31	25	9	5	18	1	0	5	210.2	174	72	12	0	65	2	176	2.82	+41	.224	.283	+7	0	2.9

YEAR	TM LG	W	L	PCT	G	GS	CG	SHO	QS	SV	BS	QR	IP	H	R	HR	HB	BB	IB	SO	ERA	AERA	OAV	OOB	SUP	DL	PW
1978	†NY A★	**25**	3	**.893**	35	35	16	0	29	0	0	0	273.2	187	61	13	1	72	1	248	**1.74**	+110	**.193**	**.249**	+16	0	**6.4**
1979	NY A★	18	8	.692	33	30	15	2	22	2	0	3	236.1	203	83	20	0	71	0	201	**2.78**	+48	.236	.292	+0	0	3.6
1980	†NY A	17	10	.630	37	29	5	3	16	1	1	6	219.2	215	97	19	1	80	1	166	3.56	+11	.260	.322	+18	0	1.3
1981	†NY A	11	5	.688	23	21	0	0	12	0	0	2	127	100	41	12	1	26	0	104	2.76	+31	.214	**.256**	-2	0	1.7
1982	NY A☆	14	8	.636	34	33	6	1	21	0	0	1	222	216	104	22	1	69	3	162	3.81	+6	.254	.309	+24	0	0.4
1983	NY A✱	21	9	.700	31	31	**21**	3	19	0	0	0	250.1	232	99	26	2	60	3	156	3.42	+16	.244	.288	+5	0	2.1
1984	NY A	10	11	.476	29	28	5	1	13	0	0	1	195.2	223	102	24	2	44	3	127	4.51	-15	.287	.323	+9	18	1.2
1985	NY A	**22**	6	**.786**	34	33	11	2	24	0	0	1	259	243	104	28	0	42	0	143	3.27	+24	.248	.277	+25	0	2.3
1986	NY A	9	12	.429	30	30	5	0	10	0	0	0	192.1	202	94	28	1	38	2	140	3.98	+4	.265	.300	-11	24	0.3
1987	NY A	5	8	.385	22	17	2	0	8	0	0	4	117.2	111	50	14	1	38	3	96	3.67	+21	.248	.307	-14	0	1.0
1988	NY A	2	3	.400	12	10	0	0	2	0	0	2	56	57	28	7	2	15	3	32	4.18	-5	.259	.311	-6	100	-0.1
Total	14	170	91	.651	368	323	95	26	202	4	1	33	2392	2198	953	226	13	633	24	1778	3.29	+20	.244	.292	+8	220	20.5
/180I	1	13	7	.651	28	24	7	2	15	0	0	2	180	165	72	17	1	48	2	134	3.29	+20	.244	.292	+8	17	1.5

GULLETT, DON DONALD EDWARD B1.6.1951 LYNN KY BR/TL/6'0"/(187–190) DR 1969 CINN 1/14 D4.10 C13 [DL 1979 NY A 180, 1980 NY A 180]

YEAR	TM LG	W	L	PCT	G	GS	CG	SHO	QS	SV	BS	QR	IP	H	R	HR	HB	BB	IB	SO	ERA	AERA	OAV	OOB	SUP	DL	PW
1977	†NY A	14	4	.778	22	22	7	1	14	0	0	0	158.1	137	67	14	1	69	1	116	3.58	+11	.232	.312	+31	24	0.8
1978	NY A	4	2	.667	8	8	2	0	5	0	0	0	44.2	46	19	3	1	20	1	28	3.63	+1	.269	.347	+29	98	0.1
Total	9	109	50	.686	266	186	44	14	121	11	6	56	1390	1205	528	115	12	501	42	921	3.11	+14	.233	.301	+23	544	7.8
Team	2	18	6	.750	30	30	9	1	19	0	—	0	203	183	86	17	2	89	2	144	3.59	+9	.240	.320	+30	122	0.9
/180I	2	16	5	.750	27	27	8	1	17	0	—	0	180	162	76	15	2	79	2	128	3.59	+9	.240	.320	+30	108	0.8

GULLICKSON, BILL WILLIAM LEE B2.20.1959 MARSHALL MN BR/TR/6'3"/(198–225) DR 1977 MONN 1/2 D9.26

YEAR	TM LG	W	L	PCT	G	GS	CG	SHO	QS	SV	BS	QR	IP	H	R	HR	HB	BB	IB	SO	ERA	AERA	OAV	OOB	SUP	DL	PW
1987	NY A	4	2	.667	8	8	1	0	3	0	0	0	48	46	29	7	1	11	1	28	4.88	-9	.253	.296	+23	0	-0.3
Total	14	162	136	.544	398	390	54	11	222	0	0	4	2560	2659	1228	282	34	622	82	1279	3.93	-2	.268	.311	+8	74	-2.6

GUMPERT, RANDY RANDALL PENNINGTON B1.23.1918 MONOCACY PA BR/TR/6'3"/205 D6.13 MIL 1943–45 C1

YEAR	TM LG	W	L	PCT	G	GS	CG	SHO	QS	SV	BS	QR	IP	H	R	HR	HB	BB	IB	SO	ERA	AERA	OAV	OOB	SUP	DL	PW
1946	NY A	11	3	.786	33	12	4	0	—	1	—	—	132.2	113	44	8	0	32	—	63	2.31	+50	.229	.276	+51	0	1.2
1947	NY A	4	1	.800	24	6	2	0	—	0	—	—	56.1	71	36	4	0	28	—	25	5.43	-35	.311	.387	+8	0	-1.1
1948	NY A	1	0	1.000	15	0	0	0	—	0	—	—	25	27	10	0	1	6	—	12	2.88	+42	.267	.315	—	0	0.1
Total	10	51	59	.464	261	113	47	6	—	7	—	—	1052.2	1099	548	92	16	346	—	352	4.17	-2	.268	.328	-4	0	-1.6
Team	3	16	4	.800	72	18	6	0	—	1	—	—	214	211	90	12	1	66	—	100	3.20	+11	.257	.313	+37	—	0.2
/60G	3	13	3	.800	60	15	5	0	—	1	—	—	178.1	176	75	10	1	55	—	83	3.20	+11	.257	.313	+37	—	0.2

GURA, LARRY LAWRENCE CYRIL B11.26.1947 JOLIET IL BB/TL (BR 1970–72)/6'1"/(170–185) DR 1969 CHIN 2/40 D4.30 COL ARIZONA ST.

YEAR	TM LG	W	L	PCT	G	GS	CG	SHO	QS	SV	BS	QR	IP	H	R	HR	HB	BB	IB	SO	ERA	AERA	OAV	OOB	SUP	DL	PW
1974	NY A	5	1	.833	8	8	4	2	6	0	0	0	56	54	17	2	0	12	1	17	2.41	+47	.248	.287	+24	0	0.8
1975	NY A	7	8	.467	26	20	5	0	15	0	0	3	151.1	173	65	13	3	41	1	65	3.51	+6	.295	.342	-19	0	0.4
Total	16	126	97	.565	403	261	71	16	156	14	9	93	2047	2020	958	204	46	600	38	801	3.76	+6	.260	.313	+6	22	5.0
Team	2	12	9	.571	34	28	9	2	21	0	0	3	207.1	227	82	15	3	53	2	82	3.21	+14	.282	.327	-7	—	1.2
/180I	2	10	8	.571	30	24	8	2	18	0	0	3	180	197	71	13	3	46	2	71	3.21	+14	.282	.327	-7	—	1.0

HABYAN, JOHN JOHN GABRIEL B1.29.1964 BAY SHORE NY BR/TR/6'2"/(178–198) DR 1982 BALA 3/78 D9.29 [DL 1989 BAL A 67]

YEAR	TM LG	W	L	PCT	G	GS	CG	SHO	QS	SV	BS	QR	IP	H	R	HR	HB	BB	IB	SO	ERA	AERA	OAV	OOB	SUP	DL	PW
1985	Bal A	1	0	1.000	2	0	0	0	0	0	0	2	2.2	3	1	0	0	0	0	2	0.00	-100	.250	.250	—	0	0.2
1986	Bal A	1	3	.250	6	5	0	0	2	0	0	1	26.1	24	17	3	0	18	2	14	4.44	-6	.250	.365	-39	0	-0.3
1987	Bal A	6	7	.462	27	13	0	0	3	1	0	8	116.1	110	67	20	2	40	1	64	4.80	-7	.248	.311	-18	0	-0.4
1988	Bal A	1	0	1.000	7	0	0	0	0	0	0	3	14.2	22	10	2	0	4	0	4	4.30	-8	.355	.382	—	0	-0.1
1990	NY A	0	0	+	6	0	0	0	0	0	1	5	8.2	10	2	0	1	2	0	4	2.08	+92	.294	.351	—	0	0.1
1991	NY A	4	2	.667	66	0	0	0	0	2	2	52	90	73	28	2	2	20	2	70	2.30	+81	.225	.274	—	0	1.1
1992	NY A	5	6	.455	56	0	0	0	0	7	5	40	72.2	84	32	6	2	21	5	44	3.84	+3	.295	.344	—	0	0.3
1993	NY A	2	1	.667	36	0	0	0	0	1	2	26	42.1	45	20	5	0	16	2	29	4.04	+4	.276	.337	—	0	0.1
1993	KC A	0	0	+	12	0	0	0	0	0	0	7	14	14	7	1	0	4	2	10	4.50	+3	.259	.310	—	0	0.0
1993	Year	2	1	.667	48	0	0	0	0	1	2	33	56.1	59	27	6	0	20	4	39	4.15	+3	.272	.331	—	0	0.1
1994	StL N	1	0	1.000	52	0	0	0	0	1	2	36	47.1	50	17	2	0	20	8	46	3.23	+31	.275	.347	—	22	0.3
1995	StL N	3	2	.600	31	0	0	0	0	0	1	24	40.2	32	18	0	1	15	4	35	2.88	+49	.222	.298	—	0	0.5
1995	Cal A	1	2	.333	28	0	0	0	0	0	1	17	32.2	36	16	2	1	12	0	25	4.13	+14	.279	.340	—	0	0.1
1995	Major	4	4	.500	59	0	0	0	0	0	2	41	72	68	34	2	2	27	4	60	3.44	+33	.249	.318	—	0	0.6
1996	Col N	1	1	.500	19	0	0	0	0	0	0	8	24	34	19	4	1	14	1	25	7.13	-27	.347	.430	—	0	-0.3
Total	11	26	24	.520	348	18	0	0	5	12	14	229	532.1	537	254	47	10	186	27	372	3.85	+12	.265	.327	-22	89	1.6
Team	4	11	9	.550	164	0	0	0	0	10	10	123	213.2	212	82	13	5	59	9	147	3.16	+30	.263	.315	—	—	1.6
/60G	1	4	3	.550	60	0	0	0	0	4	4	45	78.1	78	30	5	2	22	3	54	3.15	+30	.263	.315	—	—	0.6

HADLEY, BUMP IRVING DARIUS B7.5.1904 LYNN MA D2.15.1963 LYNN MA BR/TR/5'11"/190 D4.20 COL BROWN

YEAR	TM LG	W	L	PCT	G	GS	CG	SHO	QS	SV	BS	QR	IP	H	R	HR	HB	BB	IB	SO	ERA	AERA	OAV	OOB	SUP	DL	PW
1936	†NY A	14	4	.778	31	17	8	1	—	1	—	—	173.2	194	97	12	1	89	—	74	4.35	+7	.283	.366	+29	—	0.6
1937	†NY A	11	8	.579	29	25	6	0	—	0	—	—	178.1	199	122	16	3	83	—	70	5.30	-16	.281	.358	+27	—	-1.4
1938	NY A	9	8	.529	29	17	8	1	—	1	—	—	167.1	165	79	13	3	66	—	61	3.60	+26	.254	.325	+13	—	1.6
1939	†NY A	12	6	.667	26	18	7	1	—	2	—	—	154	132	62	10	3	85	—	65	2.98	+46	.237	.342	-2	—	2.4
1940	NY A	3	5	.375	25	2	0	0	—	2	—	—	80	88	62	4	1	52	—	39	5.74	-30	.276	.379	-56	—	-1.7
Total	16	161	165	.494	528	355	135	14	—	25	—	—	2945.2	2980	1609	167	63	1442	—	1318	4.24	+5	.263	.350	-3	0	6.7
Team	5	49	31	.613	140	79	29	3	—	6	—	—	753.1	778	422	55	11	375	—	309	4.28	+4	.266	.352	+16	—	1.5
/180I	1	12	7	.612	33	19	7	1	—	1	—	—	180	186	101	13	3	90	—	74	4.28	+4	.266	.352	+16	—	0.4

HAHN, NOODLES FRANK GEORGE B4.29.1879 NASHVILLE TN D2.6.1960 CANDLER NC BL/TL/5'9"/160 D4.18

YEAR	TM LG	W	L	PCT	G	GS	CG	SHO	QS	SV	BS	QR	IP	H	R	HR	HB	BB	IB	SO	ERA	AERA	OAV	OOB	SUP	DL	PW
1906	NY A	3	2	.600	6	6	3	1	—	0	—	—	42	38	22	0	3	6	—	17	3.86	-23	.245	.287	+13	—	-0.3
Total	8	130	94	.580	243	231	212	25	—	0	—	—	2029.1	1916	821	27	52	381	—	917	2.55	+33	.249	.289	-8	—	17.0

HALSEY, BRAD BRADFORD ALEXANDER B2.14.1981 HOUSTON TX BL/TL/6'1"/(180–185) DR 2002 NYA 8/246 D6.19 COL TEXAS

YEAR	TM LG	W	L	PCT	G	GS	CG	SHO	QS	SV	BS	QR	IP	H	R	HR	HB	BB	IB	SO	ERA	AERA	OAV	OOB	SUP	DL	PW
2004	NY A	1	3	.250	8	7	0	0	0	0	0	1	32	41	26	4	2	14	0	25	6.47	-29	.306	.375	+24	0	-0.7
Total	3	14	19	.424	88	40	0	0	14	0	0	32	286.1	340	180	35	16	99	10	160	4.84	-8	.297	.359	+5	0	-2.0

HAMBRIGHT, ROGER ROGER DEE B3.26.1949 SUNNYSIDE WA BR/TR/5'10"/180 DR 1967 NYA 67/955 D7.19

YEAR	TM LG	W	L	PCT	G	GS	CG	SHO	QS	SV	BS	QR	IP	H	R	HR	HB	BB	IB	SO	ERA	AERA	OAV	OOB	SUP	DL	PW
1971	NY A	3	1	.750	18	0	0	0	0	2	0	13	26.2	22	13	5	0	10	2	14	4.39	-25	.224	.294	—	0	-0.4

HAMILTON, STEVE STEVE ABSHER B11.30.1935 COLUMBIA KY D12.2.1997 MOREHEAD KY BL/TL/6'7"/(190–196) D4.23 C1 COL MOREHEAD ST.

YEAR	TM LG	W	L	PCT	G	GS	CG	SHO	QS	SV	BS	QR	IP	H	R	HR	HB	BB	IB	SO	ERA	AERA	OAV	OOB	SUP	DL	PW
1961	Cle A	0	0	+	2	0	0	0	0	0	0	2	3	2	1	0	0	3	0	4	3.00	+31	.200	.385	—	0	0.1
1962	Was A	3	8	.273	41	10	1	0	5	2	5	20	107.1	103	51	10	3	39	5	83	3.77	+7	.248	.317	-12	0	0.2
1963	Was A	0	1	.000	3	0	0	0	0	0	1	1	2	5	3	0	0	2	0	1	13.50	-73	.556	.583	—	0	-0.4
1963	†NY A	5	1	.833	34	0	0	0	0	5	0	25	62.1	49	19	3	1	24	2	63	2.60	+35	.220	.296	—	0	1.0
1963	Year	5	2	.714	37	0	0	0	0	5	1	26	64.1	54	22	3	1	26	2	64	2.94	+20	.233	.309	—	0	0.6
1964	†NY A	7	2	.778	30	3	1	0	2	3	4	16	60.1	55	24	6	0	15	0	49	3.28	+10	.246	.289	+64	0	0.4
1965	NY A	3	1	.750	46	1	0	0	1	5	3	35	58.1	47	12	2	0	16	5	51	1.39	+145	.214	.265	+3	0	1.0
1966	NY A	8	3	.727	44	3	1	1	1	3	0	27	90	69	32	8	3	22	3	57	3.00	+11	.218	.273	-38	0	0.3
1967	NY A	2	4	.333	44	0	0	0	0	4	3	36	62	57	25	7	1	23	4	55	3.48	-10	.250	.320	—	0	-0.2
1968	NY A	2	2	.500	40	0	0	0	0	11	1	30	50.2	37	13	0	1	13	4	42	2.13	+37	.211	.268	—	0	0.7
1969	NY A	3	4	.429	38	0	0	0	0	2	2	30	57	39	22	7	0	21	5	39	3.32	+6	.194	.269	—	0	0.2
1970	NY A	4	3	.571	35	0	0	0	0	3	1	27	45.1	36	16	3	1	16	5	33	2.78	+29	.222	.294	—	0	0.6
1970	Chi A	0	0	+	3	0	0	0	0	0	0	1	3	4	2	0	0	1	0	3	6.00	-35	.333	.385	—	0	0.0
1970	Year	4	3	.571	38	0	0	0	0	3	1	28	48.1	40	18	3	1	17	5	36	2.98	+21	.230	.301	—	0	0.6
1971	†SF N	2	2	.500	39	0	0	0	0	4	3	33	44.2	29	15	4	1	11	6	38	3.02	+13	.186	.238	—	0	0.3
1972	Chi N	1	0	1.000	22	0	0	0	0	0	0	14	17	24	9	1	1	8	3	13	4.76	-20	.333	.398	—	0	-0.1

YEAR	TM LG	W	L	PCT	G	GS	CG	SHO	QS	SV	BS	QR	IP	H	R	HR	HB	BB	IB	SO	ERA	AERA	OAV	OOB	SUP	DL	PW
Total	12	40	31	.563	421	17	3	1	9	42	23	297	663	556	244	51	12	214	42	531	3.05	+15	.229	.293	+6	0	4.1
Team	8	34	20	.630	311	7	2	1	4	36	14	226	486	389	163	36	7	150	28	389	2.78	+21	.222	.284	+12	—	4.0
/60G	2	7	4	.630	60	1	0	0	1	7	3	44	93.2	75	31	7	1	29	5	75	2.78	+21	.222	.284	+12	—	0.8
Hammond, Chris	Christopher Andrew B1.21.1966 Atlanta GA BL/TL/6'1"/(190–210) Dr 1986 CinN*6/148 d7.16 b–Steve Col Alabama–Birmingham																										
2003	†NY A	3	2	.600	62	0	0	0	0	1	3	43	63	65	23	5	2	11	0	45	2.86	+54	.270	.304	—	0	0.7
Total	14	66	62	.516	441	136	5	3	61	3	13	225	1123.2	1163	572	105	31	387	32	712	4.14	+1	.269	.332	-7	316	0.6
/60G	1	3	2	.600	60	0	0	0	0	1	3	42	61	63	22	5	2	11	0	44	2.86	+54	.270	.304	—	—	0.7
Hanley, Jim	James Patrick B10.13.1885 Providence RI D5.1.1961 Elmhurst NY BR/TL/5'11"/165 d7.3 Col Manhattan																										
1913	NY A	0	0	+	1	0	0	0	—	0	—	—	4	5	3	0	0	4	—	2	6.75	-56	.313	.450	—	—	-0.1
Hardin, Jim	James Warren B8.6.1943 Morris Chapel TN D3.9.1991 Key West FL BR/TR/6'0"/(170–176) d6.23 Col Memphis																										
1971	NY A	0	2	.000	12	3	0	0	1	0	0	5	28.1	35	19	3	1	9	3	14	5.08	-35	.313	.366	+27	27	-0.5
Total	6	43	32	.573	164	100	28	7	62	4	3	37	751.2	691	302	70	23	202	23	408	3.18	+5	.244	.299	+11	27	1.1
Harper, Harry	Harry Clayton B4.24.1895 Hackensack NJ D4.23.1963 New York NY BL/TL/6'2"/165 d6.27																										
1921	†NY A	4	3	.571	8	7	4	0	—	0	—	—	52.2	52	23	3	2	25	—	22	3.76	+13	.263	.351	-24	—	0.3
Total	10	57	76	.429	219	171	66	12	—	5	—	—	1256	1100	531	26	40	582	—	623	2.87	+5	.244	.335	-12	—	-1.7
Harris, Greg	Greg Allen B11.2.1955 Lynwood CA BB/TR (TB 1995p)/6'0"/(165–175) d5.20 Col Long Beach (CA) City																										
1994	NY A	0	1	.000	3	0	0	0	0	0	1	1	5	4	5	1	2	3	1	4	5.40	-15	.222	.375	—	0	-0.2
Total	15	74	90	.451	703	98	4	0	39	54	46	442	1467	1329	689	129	54	652	86	1141	3.69	+13	.243	.327	-2	0	8.7
Hawkins, Andy	Melton Andrew B1.21.1960 Waco TX BR/TR/6'3"/(200–223) Dr 1978 SDN 1/5 d7.17																										
1989	NY A	15	15	.500	34	34	5	2	16	0	0	0	208.1	238	127	23	6	76	6	98	4.80	-19	.290	.354	-2	0	-3.0
1990	NY A	5	12	.294	28	26	2	1	9	0	0	1	157.2	156	101	20	2	82	3	74	5.37	-26	.260	.349	-14	0	-2.2
1991	NY A	0	2	.000	4	3	0	0	0	0	0	0	12.2	23	15	5	0	6	0	5	9.95	-58	.383	.439	-12	0	-0.9
Total	10	84	91	.480	280	249	27	10	125	0	0	23	1558.1	1574	815	152	39	612	39	706	4.22	-13	.265	.335	+4	34	-11.1
Team	3	20	29	.408	66	63	7	3	25	0	0	1	378.2	417	243	48	8	164	9	177	5.21	-24	.282	.355	-7	—	-6.1
/180I	1	10	14	.408	31	30	3	1	12	0	0	0	180	198	116	23	4	78	4	84	5.21	-24	.282	.355	-7	—	-2.9
Heaton, Neal	Neal B3.3.1960 South Ozone Park NY BL/TL/6'1"/(195–205) Dr 1981 CleA 2/39 d9.3 Col Miami																										
1993	NY A	1	0	1.000	18	0	0	0	0	0	0	8	27	34	19	6	3	11	1	15	6.00	-30	.301	.375	—	0	-0.2
Total	12	80	96	.455	382	202	22	6	93	10	8	120	1507	1589	804	163	32	524	51	699	4.37	-8	.273	.334	-4	21	-5.8
Heimach, Fred	Frederick Amos "Lefty" B1.27.1901 Camden NJ D6.1.1973 Ft.Myers FL BL/TL/6'0"/175 d10.1																										
1928	NY A	2	3	.400	13	9	5	0	—	0	—	—	68	66	30	3	1	16	—	25	3.31	+14	.250	.295	+43	—	0.1
1929	NY A	11	6	.647	35	10	3	3	—	4	—	—	134.2	141	72	4	3	29	—	26	4.01	-4	.272	.314	+7	—	-0.1
Total	13	62	69	.473	296	127	56	5	—	7	—	—	1288.2	1510	755	64	27	360	—	334	4.46	-10	.296	.346	-4	—	-2.7
Team	2	13	9	.591	48	19	8	3	—	4	—	—	202.2	207	102	7	4	45	—	51	3.77	+1	.265	.308	+24	—	0.0
/180I	2	12	8	.591	43	17	7	3	—	4	—	—	180	184	91	6	4	40	—	45	3.77	+1	.265	.308	+24	—	0.0
Henderson, Bill	William Maxwell B11.4.1901 Pensacola FL D10.6.1966 Pensacola FL BR/TR/6'0"/190 d6.20																										
1930	NY A	0	0	+	3	0	0	0	—	0	—	—	8	7	6	1	0	4	—	2	4.50	-4	.250	.344	—	—	0.0
Henn, Sean	Sean Michael B4.23.1981 Fort Worth TX BR/TL/6'5"/200 Dr 2000 NYA 26/788 d5.4 Col McLennan (TX) JC																										
2005	NY A	0	3	.000	3	3	0	0	0	0	0	0	11.1	18	16	3	0	11	0	3	11.12	-61	.360	.475	+8	0	-1.4
2006	NY A	0	1	.000	4	1	0	0	0	0	0	1	9.1	11	5	2	1	5	0	7	4.82	-4	.297	.386	-59	0	0.0
2007	NY A	2	2	.500	29	1	0	0	0	0	0	15	36.2	44	32	6	3	27	1	28	7.12	-37	.293	.411	+106	0	-1.0
Total	3	2	6	.250	36	5	0	0	0	0	0	16	57.1	73	53	11	4	43	1	38	7.53	-40	.308	.421	+12	0	-2.4
Henry, Bill	William Francis B2.15.1942 Long Beach CA BL/TL/6'3"/195 d9.13 Col Seton Hall																										
1966	NY A	0	0	+	2	0	0	0	0	0	0	2	3	0	0	0	0	2	0	3	0.00	-100	.000	.200	—	0	0.1
Heredia, Felix	Felix (Perez) B6.18.1975 Barahona, Barahona, D.R BL/TL/6'0"/(165–185) d8.9																										
2003	†NY A	0	1	.000	12	0	0	0	0	0	1	11	15	13	5	1	0	5	2	4	1.20	+266	.228	.290	—	0	0.3
2004	†NY A	1	1	.500	47	0	0	0	0	0	1	27	38.2	44	28	5	2	20	0	25	6.28	-27	.278	.365	—	30	-0.3
Total	10	28	19	.596	511	2	0	0	0	6	23	354	458.1	448	259	45	18	232	22	351	4.42	-2	.255	.344	-15	227	-1.0
Team	2	1	2	.333	59	0	0	0	0	0	2	38	53.2	57	33	6	2	25	2	29	4.86	-7	.265	.346	—	30	0.0
/60G	2	1	2	.333	60	0	0	0	0	0	2	39	54.2	58	34	6	2	25	2	29	4.86	-7	.265	.346	—	31	0.0
Hernandez, Adrian	Adrian B3.25.1975 Havana, Cuba BR/TR/6'1"/(180–185) d4.21																										
2001	NY A	0	3	.000	6	3	0	0	1	0	0	3	22	15	10	7	2	10	1	10	3.68	+21	.190	.297	-58	0	0.2
2002	NY A	0	1	.000	2	1	0	0	0	0	0	0	6	10	8	2	0	6	0	9	12.00	-64	.357	.471	-36	0	-0.6
2004	Mil N	0	2	.000	6	1	0	0	0	0	1	1	16	20	18	1	0	14	0	14	8.44	-48	.294	.410	+27	0	-0.8
Total	3	0	6	.000	14	5	0	0	1	0	1	4	44	45	36	10	2	30	1	33	6.55	-33	.257	.370	-37	0	-1.2
Team	2	0	4	.000	8	4	0	0	1	0	0	3	28	25	18	9	2	16	1	19	5.46	-19	.234	.344	-52	—	-0.4
Hernandez, Xavier	Francis Xavier B8.16.1965 Port Arthur TX BL/TR/6'2"/(185–195) Dr 1986 TorA 4/107 d6.4 Col Louisiana–Lafayette																										
1994	NY A	4	4	.500	31	0	0	0	0	6	2	17	40	48	27	7	2	21	3	37	5.85	-21	.300	.384	—	15	-0.9
Total	10	40	35	.533	463	7	0	0	3	35	28	324	671	621	324	67	20	266	36	562	3.90	+2	.244	.318	-61	131	0.4
Hernandez, Orlando	Orlando P. "El Duque" B10.11.1965 Villa Clara, Cuba BR/TR/6'2"/(190–220) d6.3 b–Livan [DL 2003 Mon N 183]																										
1998	†NY A	12	4	.750	21	21	3	1	14	0	0	0	141	113	53	11	6	52	1	131	3.13	+40	.222	.299	+46	0	2.1
1999	†NY A	17	9	.654	33	33	2	1	23	0	0	0	214.1	187	108	24	8	87	2	157	4.12	+15	.233	.311	+5	0	1.6
2000	†NY A	12	13	.480	29	29	3	0	16	0	0	0	195.2	186	104	34	6	51	2	141	4.51	+6	.247	.298	-18	22	0.7
2001	†NY A	4	7	.364	17	16	0	0	5	0	0	1	94.2	90	51	19	5	42	1	77	4.85	-8	.248	.333	-30	87	-0.2
2002	†NY A	8	5	.615	24	22	0	0	13	1	0	2	146	131	63	17	8	36	2	113	3.64	+19	.236	.289	+7	42	1.1
2004	†NY A	8	2	.800	15	15	0	0	7	0	0	0	84.2	73	31	9	5	36	0	84	3.30	+39	.230	.318	+10	103	1.4
2005	†Chi A	9	9	.500	24	22	0	0	10	1	0	2	128.1	137	77	18	12	50	1	91	5.12	-12	.275	.352	-11	50	-0.8
2006	Ari N	2	4	.333	9	9	0	0	3	0	0	0	45.2	52	32	8	4	20	3	52	6.11	-23	.292	.376	+3	0	-0.6
2006	NY N	9	7	.563	20	20	1	0	12	0	0	0	116.2	103	58	14	8	41	2	112	4.09	+7	.236	.310	+2	0	0.5
2006	Year	11	11	.500	29	29	1	0	15	0	0	0	162.1	155	90	22	12	61	5	164	4.66	-4	.252	.329	+3	0	-0.1
2007	NY N	9	5	.643	27	24	0	0	17	0	0	2	147.2	109	64	23	5	64	4	128	3.72	+16	.206	.297	+1	30	1.0
Total	9	90	65	.581	219	211	9	2	120	2	0	7	1314.2	1181	641	177	67	479	18	1086	4.13	+9	.239	.312	+1	517	6.8
Team	6	61	40	.604	139	136	8	2	78	1	0	3	876.1	780	410	114	38	304	8	703	3.96	+15	.236	.306	+3	254	6.7
/180I	1	13	8	.604	29	28	2	0	16	0	0	1	180	160	84	23	8	62	2	144	3.96	+15	.236	.306	+3	52	1.4
Hildebrand, Oral	Oral Clyde B4.7.1907 Indianapolis IN D9.8.1977 Southport IN BR/TR/6'3"/175 d9.8 Col Butler																										
1939	†NY A	10	4	.714	21	15	7	1	—	2	—	—	126.2	102	44	11	1	41	—	50	3.06	+43	.219	.284	+13	—	2.0
1940	NY A	1	1	.500	13	0	0	0	—	0	—	—	19.1	19	7	1	1	14	—	5	1.86	+117	.268	.395	—	—	0.3
Total	10	83	78	.516	258	182	80	9	—	13	—	—	1430.2	1490	781	99	22	623	—	527	4.35	+7	.267	.343	-1	—	4.5
Team	2	11	5	.688	34	15	7	1	—	2	—	—	146	121	51	12	2	55	—	55	2.90	+49	.225	.300	+13	—	2.3
/180I	2	14	6	.688	42	18	9	1	—	2	—	—	180	149	63	15	2	68	—	68	2.90	+49	.225	.300	+13	—	2.8

HILLEGAS, SHAWN Shawn Patrick B8.21.1964 Dos Palos CA BR/TR/6'2"/(208–223) Dr 1984 LAN*S1/4 d8.9 Col Middle Georgia JC

YEAR	TM LG	W	L	PCT	G	GS	CG	SHO	QS	SV	BS	QR	IP	H	R	HR	HB	BB	IB	SO	ERA	AERA	OAV	OOB	SUP	DL	PW
1992	NY A	1	8	.111	21	9	1	1	3	0	0	8	78.1	96	52	12	0	33	1	46	5.51	-28	.306	.369	-28	0	-1.4
Total	7	24	38	.387	181	62	1	1	21	10	2	81	515.1	521	284	54	13	238	16	332	4.61	-15	.264	.344	-7	0	-5.0

HILLER, FRANK Frank Walter "Dutch" B7.13.1920 Irvington NJ D1.10.1987 West Chester PA BR/TR/6'0"/200 d5.25 Col Lafayette

YEAR	TM LG	W	L	PCT	G	GS	CG	SHO	QS	SV	BS	QR	IP	H	R	HR	HB	BB	IB	SO	ERA	AERA	OAV	OOB	SUP	DL	PW
1946	NY A	0	2	.000	3	1	0	0	—	0	—	—	11.1	13	7	2	0	6	—	4	4.76	-28	.295	.380	-25	0	-0.3
1948	NY A	5	2	.714	22	5	1	0	—	0	—	—	62.1	59	29	8	1	30	—	25	4.04	+1	.244	.330	+33	0	0.0
1949	NY A	0	2	.000	4	0	0	0	—	1	—	—	7.2	9	6	0	0	7	—	3	5.87	-31	.290	.421	—	0	-0.2
Total	7	30	32	.484	138	60	22	5	—	4	—	—	533.2	553	288	56	24	158	—	197	4.42	-8	.266	.325	+3	0	-2.0
Team	3	5	6	.455	29	6	1	0	—	1	—	—	81.1	81	41	10	1	43	—	32	4.32	-7	.256	.346	+23	—	-0.2

HINTON, RICH Richard Michael B5.22.1947 Tucson AZ BL/TL/6'2"/(170–185) Dr 1969 ChiA S3/62 d7.17 Col Arizona

YEAR	TM LG	W	L	PCT	G	GS	CG	SHO	QS	SV	BS	QR	IP	H	R	HR	HB	BB	IB	SO	ERA	AERA	OAV	OOB	SUP	DL	PW
1972	NY A	1	0	1.000	7	3	0	0	1	0	0	3	16.2	20	11	2	0	8	2	13	4.86	-38	.299	.364	+58	0	-0.3
Total	6	9	17	.346	116	13	2	0	3	3	7	70	249.2	283	152	23	7	91	12	152	4.87	-22	.289	.350	+3	0	-2.8

HITCHCOCK, STERLING Sterling Alex B4.29.1971 Fayetteville NC BL/TL/6'1"/(192–205) Dr 1989 NYA 9/233 d9.11

YEAR	TM LG	W	L	PCT	G	GS	CG	SHO	QS	SV	BS	QR	IP	H	R	HR	HB	BB	IB	SO	ERA	AERA	OAV	OOB	SUP	DL	PW
1992	NY A	0	2	.000	3	3	0	0	1	0	0	0	13	23	12	2	1	6	0	6	8.31	-52	.377	.441	+23	0	-0.7
1993	NY A	1	2	.333	6	6	0	0	1	0	0	0	31	32	18	4	1	14	1	26	4.65	-10	.271	.348	+17	0	-0.2
1994	NY A	4	1	.800	23	5	1	0	3	2	0	12	49.1	48	24	3	0	29	1	37	4.20	+10	.265	.355	+0	0	0.2
1995	†NY A	11	10	.524	27	27	4	1	15	0	0	0	168.1	155	91	22	5	68	1	121	4.70	-2	.245	.319	-2	0	-0.2
1996	Sea A	13	9	.591	35	35	0	0	15	0	0	0	196.2	245	131	27	7	73	4	132	5.35	-7	.309	.368	+4	0	-1.0
1997	SD N	10	11	.476	32	28	1	0	12	0	0	3	161	172	102	24	4	55	2	106	5.20	-24	.276	.337	+12	27	-2.8
1998	†SD N	9	7	.563	39	27	2	1	16	1	1	10	176.1	169	83	29	9	48	2	158	3.93	+1	.251	.308	+10	0	-0.1
1999	SD N	12	14	.462	33	33	1	0	18	0	0	0	205.2	202	99	29	5	76	6	194	4.11	+4	.254	.320	-5	0	0.4
2000	SD N	1	6	.143	11	11	0	0	4	0	0	0	65.2	69	38	12	5	26	1	61	4.93	-10	.267	.345	-12	127	-0.5
2001	SD N	2	1	.667	3	3	0	0	2	0	0	0	19	22	9	1	1	3	0	15	3.32	+25	.275	.310	+86	94	0.2
2001	†NY A	4	4	.500	10	9	1	0	4	0	0	1	51.1	67	37	5	2	18	0	28	6.49	-32	.315	.367	+20	0	-1.3
2001	Major	6	5	.545	13	12	1	0	6	0	0	1	70	89	46	6	3	21	0	43	5.63	-17	.304	.352	+37	94	-1.1
2002	NY A	1	2	.333	20	2	0	0	0	0	0	13	39.1	57	29	4	1	15	3	31	5.49	-21	.326	.380	+39	68	-0.4
2003	NY A	1	3	.250	27	1	0	0	1	0	0	14	49.2	57	33	6	0	18	3	36	5.44	-19	.285	.341	+5	0	-0.4
2003	StL N	5	1	.833	8	6	0	0	2	0	0	2	38	34	17	8	1	14	1	32	3.79	+9	.238	.308	-1	0	0.1
2003	Major	6	4	.600	35	7	0	0	3	0	0	16	87	91	50	14	1	32	4	68	4.72	-7	.265	.327	-0	0	-0.3
2004	SD N	0	3	.000	4	4	0	0	1	0	0	0	21.1	22	15	5	0	8	0	14	6.33	-38	.265	.330	-35	121	-0.7
Total	13	74	76	.493	281	200	10	2	95	3	1	55	1285.2	1374	738	181	42	471	25	997	4.80	-9	.273	.337	+5	437	-7.4
Team	7	22	24	.478	116	53	6	1	25	2	0	40	402	439	244	46	10	168	9	285	5.15	-13	.278	.346	+7	68	-3.0
/180I	3	10	11	.478	52	24	3	0	11	1	0	18	180	197	109	21	4	75	4	128	5.15	-13	.278	.346	+7	30	-1.3

HOFF, CHET Chester Cornelius "Red" B5.8.1891 Ossining NY D9.17.1998 Daytona Beach FL BL/TL/5'9"/162 d9.6

YEAR	TM LG	W	L	PCT	G	GS	CG	SHO	QS	SV	BS	QR	IP	H	R	HR	HB	BB	IB	SO	ERA	AERA	OAV	OOB	SUP	DL	PW
1911	NY A	0	1	.000	5	1	0	0	—	0	—	—	20.2	21	8	0	0	7	—	10	2.18	+65	.262	.322	-20	—	0.2
1912	NY A	0	1	.000	5	1	0	0	—	0	—	—	15.2	20	14	0	0	6	—	14	6.89	-48	.303	.361	-18	—	-0.3
1913	NY A	0	0	+	2	0	0	0	—	0	—	—	3	0	0	0	0	1	—	2	0.00	-100	.000	.111	—	—	0.0
1915	StL A	2	2	.500	11	3	2	0	—	0	—	—	43.2	26	16	0	1	24	—	23	1.24	+132	.169	.285	-24	—	0.4
Total	4	2	4	.333	23	5	2	0	—	0	—	—	83	67	38	0	1	38	—	49	2.49	+27	.218	.305	-22	—	0.3
Team	3	0	2	.000	12	2	0	0	—	0	—	—	39.1	41	22	0	0	14	—	26	3.89	-9	.281	.327	-19	—	-0.1

HOGG, BILL William Johnston "Buffalo Bill" B9.11.1881 Port Huron MI D12.8.1909 New Orleans LA BR/TR/6'0"/200 d4.25

YEAR	TM LG	W	L	PCT	G	GS	CG	SHO	QS	SV	BS	QR	IP	H	R	HR	HB	BB	IB	SO	ERA	AERA	OAV	OOB	SUP	DL	PW
1905	NY A	9	13	.409	39	22	9	3	—	1	—	—	205	178	104	1	13	101	—	125	3.20	-8	.236	.336	-21	—	-1.5
1906	NY A	14	13	.519	28	25	15	3	—	0	—	—	206	171	77	5	12	72	—	107	2.93	+1	.229	.307	-3	—	-0.2
1907	NY A	10	8	.556	25	21	13	0	—	0	—	—	166.2	173	84	3	6	83	—	64	3.08	-9	.270	.359	+1	—	-0.6
1908	NY A	4	16	.200	24	21	6	0	—	0	—	—	152.1	155	89	4	4	63	—	72	3.01	-18	.262	.337	-37	—	-2.1
Total	4	37	50	.425	116	89	43	6	—	1	—	—	730	677	354	13	35	319	—	368	3.06	-8	.248	.334	-14	—	-4.4
/180I	1	9	12	.425	29	22	11	1	0	0	0	0	180	167	87	3	9	79	—	91	3.06	-8	.248	.334	-14	—	-1.1

HOGUE, BOBBY Robert Clinton B4.5.1921 Miami FL D12.22.1987 Miami FL BR/TR/5'10"/195 d4.24

YEAR	TM LG	W	L	PCT	G	GS	CG	SHO	QS	SV	BS	QR	IP	H	R	HR	HB	BB	IB	SO	ERA	AERA	OAV	OOB	SUP	DL	PW
1951	†NY A	1	0	1.000	7	0	0	0	—	0	—	—	7.1	4	0	0	0	3	—	2	0.00	-100	.174	.269	—	0	0.4
1952	NY A	3	5	.375	27	0	0	0	—	4	—	—	47.1	52	30	6	1	25	—	12	5.32	-38	.294	.384	—	0	-1.8
Total	5	18	16	.529	172	3	0	0	—	17	—	—	326.2	336	154	25	9	142	—	108	3.97	-4	.271	.350	+1	0	-0.9
Team	2	4	5	.444	34	0	0	0	—	4	—	—	54.2	56	30	6	1	28	—	14	4.61	-26	.280	.371	—	—	-1.4

HOLCOMBE, KEN Kenneth Edward B8.23.1918 Burnsville NC BR/TR/5'11.5"/169 d4.27

YEAR	TM LG	W	L	PCT	G	GS	CG	SHO	QS	SV	BS	QR	IP	H	R	HR	HB	BB	IB	SO	ERA	AERA	OAV	OOB	SUP	DL	PW
1945	NY A	3	3	.500	23	2	0	0	—	0	—	—	55.1	43	19	2	0	27	—	20	1.79	+94	.226	.323	-26	0	0.7
Total	6	18	32	.360	99	48	18	2	—	2	—	—	375	377	196	25	3	170	—	118	3.98	+1	.265	.345	-23	0	-0.3

HOLLAND, AL Alfred Willis B8.16.1952 Roanoke VA BR/TL/5'11"/(200–213) d9.5 Col North Carolina A&T

YEAR	TM LG	W	L	PCT	G	GS	CG	SHO	QS	SV	BS	QR	IP	H	R	HR	HB	BB	IB	SO	ERA	AERA	OAV	OOB	SUP	DL	PW
1986	NY A	1	0	1.000	25	1	0	0	0	0	1	19	40.2	44	29	5	0	9	2	37	5.09	-19	.268	.301	+163	15	-0.3
1987	NY A	0	0	+	3	0	0	0	0	0	0	0	6.1	9	10	1	0	9	0	5	14.21	-69	.321	.486	—	56	-0.3
Total	10	34	30	.531	384	11	0	0	5	78	25	276	646	548	241	55	5	232	54	513	2.98	+22	.227	.293	+16	120	6.7
Team	2	1	0	1.000	28	1	0	0	0	0	1	19	47	53	39	6	0	18	2	42	6.32	-34	.276	.333	+163	71	-0.6

HOLLOWAY, KEN Kenneth Eugene (b Kenneth Eugene Hollaway) B8.8.1897 Barwick GA D9.25.1968 Thomasville GA BR/TR/6'0"/185 d8.27 Col Georgia

YEAR	TM LG	W	L	PCT	G	GS	CG	SHO	QS	SV	BS	QR	IP	H	R	HR	HB	BB	IB	SO	ERA	AERA	OAV	OOB	SUP	DL	PW
1930	NY A	0	0	+	16	0	0	0	—	0	—	—	34.1	52	23	3	0	8	—	11	5.24	-18	.374	.408	—	—	-0.2
Total	9	64	52	.552	285	110	43	4	—	18	—	—	1160	1370	684	50	37	397	—	293	4.40	-5	.303	.364	+1	—	-3.8

HOLMES, DARREN Darren Lee B4.25.1966 Asheville NC BR/TR/6'0"/(199–203) Dr 1984 LAN 16/415 d9.1

YEAR	TM LG	W	L	PCT	G	GS	CG	SHO	QS	SV	BS	QR	IP	H	R	HR	HB	BB	IB	SO	ERA	AERA	OAV	OOB	SUP	DL	PW
1998	NY A	0	3	.000	34	0	0	0	0	2	1	23	51.1	53	19	4	2	14	3	31	3.33	+32	.270	.321	—	36	0.4
Total	13	35	33	.515	557	6	0	0	3	59	32	395	680	709	348	63	15	256	36	581	4.25	+9	.269	.334	+49	229	4.3

HOLTZMAN, KEN Kenneth Dale B11.3.1945 St.Louis MO BR/TL/6'2"/(175–198) Dr 1965 ChiN 4/61 d9.4 Mil 1967 Col Illinois

YEAR	TM LG	W	L	PCT	G	GS	CG	SHO	QS	SV	BS	QR	IP	H	R	HR	HB	BB	IB	SO	ERA	AERA	OAV	OOB	SUP	DL	PW
1976	NY A	9	7	.563	21	21	10	2	16	0	0	0	149	165	74	14	0	35	0	41	4.17	-18	.283	.322	+14	0	-1.1
1977	NY A	2	3	.400	18	11	0	0	3	0	0	3	71.2	105	55	7	1	24	2	14	5.78	-31	.362	.410	+20	0	-0.9
1978	NY A	1	0	1.000	5	3	0	0	0	0	0	2	17.2	21	8	2	0	9	0	3	4.08	-10	.313	.395	+15	0	0.0
Total	15	174	150	.537	451	410	127	31	253	3	2	23	2867.1	2787	1273	249	49	910	70	1601	3.49	+5	.255	.313	+8	21	6.2
Team	3	12	10	.545	44	35	10	2	19	0	0	5	238.1	291	137	23	1	68	2	58	4.64	-23	.310	.355	+16	—	-2.0
/180I	2	9	8	.545	33	26	8	2	14	0	0	4	180	220	103	17	1	51	2	44	4.64	-23	.310	.355	+16	—	-1.5

HONEYCUTT, RICK Frederick Wayne B6.29.1954 Chattanooga TN BL/TL/5'11"/(185–195) Dr 1976 PitN 17/405 d8.24 C2 Col Tennessee

YEAR	TM LG	W	L	PCT	G	GS	CG	SHO	QS	SV	BS	QR	IP	H	R	HR	HB	BB	IB	SO	ERA	AERA	OAV	OOB	SUP	DL	PW
1995	NY A	0	0	+	3	0	0	0	0	0	0	1	1	2	3	1	0	1	0	0	27.00	-83	.400	.500	—	0	-0.1
Total	21	109	143	.433	797	268	47	11	137	38	27	389	2160	2183	1034	185	50	657	81	1038	3.72	+4	.264	.320	-12	315	3.6

HOOD, DON Donald Harris B10.16.1949 Florence SC BL/TL/6'2"/(180–190) Dr 1969 BalA 1/17 d7.16

YEAR	TM LG	W	L	PCT	G	GS	CG	SHO	QS	SV	BS	QR	IP	H	R	HR	HB	BB	IB	SO	ERA	AERA	OAV	OOB	SUP	DL	PW
1979	NY A	3	1	.750	27	6	0	0	1	1	0	11	67.1	62	24	3	2	30	1	22	3.07	+34	.252	.333	+32	0	0.5
Total	10	34	35	.493	297	72	6	1	33	6	7	147	848.1	840	412	57	19	364	32	374	3.79	+2	.263	.339	-2	21	-0.7

HOOD, WALLY Wallace James Jr. B9.24.1925 Los Angeles CA D6.16.2001 Glendale CA BR/TR/6'1"/190 d9.23 f–Wally Col USC

YEAR	TM LG	W	L	PCT	G	GS	CG	SHO	QS	SV	BS	QR	IP	H	R	HR	HB	BB	IB	SO	ERA	AERA	OAV	OOB	SUP	DL	PW
1949	NY A	0	0	+	2	0	0	0	—	0	—	—	2.1	0	0	0	0	1	—	2	0.00	-100	.000	.143	—	0	0.1

HOWE, STEVE STEVEN ROY B3.10.1958 PONTIAC MI D4.28.2006 COACHELLA CA BL/TL/6'1"/(180–198) DR 1979 LAN 1/16 D4.11 COL MICHIGAN

YEAR	TM LG	W	L	PCT	G	GS	CG	SHO	QS	SV	BS	QR	IP	H	R	HR	HB	BB	IB	SO	ERA	AERA	OAV	OOB	SUP	DL	PW
1980	LA N	7	9	.438	59	0	0	0	0	17	9	45	84.2	83	33	1	2	22	10	39	2.66	+31	.256	.305	—	0	1.2
1981	†LA N	5	3	.625	41	0	0	0	0	8	2	29	54	51	17	2	0	18	7	32	2.50	+32	.254	.309	—	0	0.8
1982	LA N★	7	5	.583	66	0	0	0	0	13	9	53	99.1	87	27	3	0	17	11	49	2.08	+67	.240	.272	—	0	2.1
1983	LA N	4	7	.364	46	0	0	0	0	18	5	34	68.2	55	15	2	1	12	7	52	1.44	+150	.217	.253	—	32	3.4
1985	LA N	1	1	.500	19	0	0	0	0	3	0	13	22	30	17	2	1	5	2	11	4.91	-29	.319	.353	—	0	-0.5
1985	Min A	2	3	.400	13	0	0	0	0	0	3	4	19	28	16	1	0	7	2	10	6.16	-28	.333	.372	—	0	-0.8
1985	Major	3	4	.429	32	0	0	0	0	3	3	17	41	58	33	3	1	12	4	21	5.49	-29	.326	.362	—	0	-1.3
1987	Tex A	3	3	.500	24	0	0	0	0	1	2	15	31.1	33	15	2	3	8	1	19	4.31	+5	.280	.341	—	0	0.3
1991	NY A	3	1	.750	37	0	0	0	0	3	0	29	48.1	39	12	1	3	7	2	34	1.68	+149	.222	.262	—	22	1.1
1992	NY A	3	0	1.000	20	0	0	0	0	6	1	15	22	9	7	1	0	3	1	12	2.45	+61	.122	.154	—	0	0.6
1993	NY A	3	5	.375	51	0	0	0	0	4	3	37	50.2	58	31	7	3	10	4	19	4.97	-16	.297	.338	—	29	-0.7
1994	NY A	3	0	1.000	40	0	0	0	0	15	4	30	40	28	8	2	0	7	1	18	1.80	+156	.194	.232	—	18	1.8
1995	†NY A	6	3	.667	56	0	0	0	0	2	1	36	49	66	29	7	4	17	3	28	4.96	-7	.324	.383	—	0	-0.3
1996	NY A	0	1	.000	25	0	0	0	0	1	1	14	17	19	12	1	1	6	3	5	6.35	-22	.284	.351	—	0	-0.1
Total	12	47	41	.534	497	0	0	0	0	91	40	354	606	586	239	32	18	139	54	328	3.03	+29	.255	.300	—	101	8.9
Team	6	18	10	.643	229	0	0	0	0	31	10	161	227	219	99	19	11	50	14	116	3.57	+23	.255	.302	—	69	2.4
/60G	2	5	3	.643	60	0	0	0	0	8	3	42	59.1	57	26	5	3	13	4	30	3.58	+23	.255	.302	—	18	0.6

HOWELL, HARRY HARRY TAYLOR B11.14.1876 NJ D5.22.1956 SPOKANE WA BR/TR/5'9"/? D10.10 U1

YEAR	TM LG	W	L	PCT	G	GS	CG	SHO	QS	SV	BS	QR	IP	H	R	HR	HB	BB	IB	SO	ERA	AERA	OAV	OOB	SUP	DL	PW
1903	NY A	9	6	.600	25	15	13	0	—	0	—	—	155.2	140	79	4	6	44	—	62	3.53	-11	.240	.300	+19	—	-0.1
Total	13	131	146	.473	340	282	244	20	—	6	—	—	2567.2	2435	1158	27	97	677	—	986	2.74	+8	.252	.307	-2	—	12.5
/180I	1	10	7	.600	29	17	15	0	—	0	—	—	180	162	91	5	7	51	—	72	3.53	-11	.240	.300	+19	—	-0.1

HOWELL, JAY JAY CANFIELD B11.26.1955 MIAMI FL BR/TR/6'3"/(200–220) DR 1976 CINN 31/668 D8.10 COL COLORADO

YEAR	TM LG	W	L	PCT	G	GS	CG	SHO	QS	SV	BS	QR	IP	H	R	HR	HB	BB	IB	SO	ERA	AERA	OAV	OOB	SUP	DL	PW
1982	NY A	2	3	.400	6	6	0	0	1	0	0	0	28	42	25	1	0	13	0	21	7.71	-48	.341	.399	+47	0	-1.5
1983	NY A	1	5	.167	19	12	2	0	4	0	0	3	82	89	53	7	3	35	0	61	5.38	-27	.275	.346	-2	30	-0.8
1984	NY A	9	4	.692	61	1	0	0	0	7	2	39	103.2	86	33	5	0	34	3	109	2.69	+42	.223	.284	+89	0	1.9
Total	15	58	53	.523	568	21	2	0	5	155	49	399	844.2	782	335	57	19	291	38	666	3.34	+15	.246	.310	+26	204	10.5
Team	3	12	12	.500	86	19	2	0	5	7	2	42	213.2	217	111	13	3	82	3	191	4.38	-11	.261	.325	+18	30	-0.4
/60G	2	8	8	.500	60	13	1	0	3	5	1	29	149	151	77	9	2	57	2	133	4.38	-11	.261	.325	+18	21	-0.3

HOYT, WAITE WAITE CHARLES "SCHOOLBOY" B9.9.1899 BROOKLYN NY D8.25.1984 CINCINNATI OH BR/TR/6'0"/180 D7.24 HF1969

YEAR	TM LG	W	L	PCT	G	GS	CG	SHO	QS	SV	BS	QR	IP	H	R	HR	HB	BB	IB	SO	ERA	AERA	OAV	OOB	SUP	DL	PW
1918	NY N	0	0	+	1	0	0	0	—	0	—	—	1	0	0	0	0	0	—	2	0.00	-100	.000	.000	—	—	0.0
1919	Bos A	4	6	.400	13	11	6	1	—	0	—	—	105.1	99	42	1	0	22	—	28	3.25	-7	.262	.303	-17	—	-0.3
1920	Bos A	6	6	.500	22	11	6	2	—	1	—	—	121.1	123	72	2	1	47	—	45	4.38	-17	.270	.339	+3	—	-1.3
1921	†NY A	19	13	.594	43	32	21	1	—	3	—	—	282.1	301	121	3	5	81	—	102	3.09	+37	.276	.329	+2	—	3.3
1922	†NY A	19	12	.613	37	31	17	3	—	0	—	—	265	271	114	13	9	76	—	95	3.43	+17	.269	.326	-6	—	2.0
1923	†NY A	17	9	.654	37	28	19	1	—	1	—	—	238.2	227	97	9	4	66	—	60	3.02	+31	.253	.307	-9	—	1.8
1924	NY A	18	13	.581	46	32	14	2	—	4	—	—	247	295	117	8	3	76	—	71	3.79	+10	.300	.352	-4	—	0.7
1925	NY A	11	14	.440	46	30	17	1	—	6	—	—	243	283	124	14	1	78	—	86	4.00	+7	.292	.346	-5	—	1.3
1926	†NY A	16	12	.571	40	28	12	1	—	4	—	—	217.2	224	112	4	2	62	—	79	3.85	+0	.264	.316	+15	—	-0.1
1927	†NY A	**22**	7	**.759**	36	32	23	3	—	1	—	—	256.1	242	90	10	4	54	—	86	2.63	+46	.251	.294	+45	—	3.8
1928	†NY A	23	7	.767	42	31	19	3	—	**8**	—	—	273	279	118	16	1	60	—	67	3.36	+12	.272	.313	+46	—	1.6
1929	NY A	10	9	.526	30	25	12	0	—	1	—	—	201.2	219	115	9	3	69	—	57	4.24	-9	.279	.339	+34	—	-0.7
1930	NY A	2	2	.500	8	7	2	0	—	0	—	—	47.2	64	27	7	0	9	—	10	4.53	-5	.317	.346	+37	—	-0.2
1930	Det A	9	8	.529	26	20	8	1	—	4	—	—	135.2	176	89	7	2	47	—	25	4.78	+0	.313	.368	-19	—	-0.5
1930	Year	11	10	.524	34	27	10	1	—	4	—	—	183.1	240	116	14	2	56	—	35	4.71	-1	.314	.363	-5	—	-0.7
1931	Det A	3	8	.273	16	12	5	0	—	0	—	—	92	124	70	2	2	32	—	10	5.87	-22	.319	.374	-29	—	-1.4
1931	†Phi A	10	5	.667	16	14	9	2	—	0	—	—	111	130	60	9	0	37	—	30	4.22	+7	.298	.353	+9	—	0.7
1931	Year	13	13	.500	32	26	14	2	—	0	—	—	203	254	130	11	2	69	—	40	4.97	-9	.308	.363	-9	—	-0.7
1932	Bro N	1	3	.250	8	4	0	0	—	1	—	—	26.2	38	27	3	0	12	—	7	7.76	-51	.342	.407	-39	—	-1.6
1932	NY N	5	7	.417	18	12	3	0	—	0	—	—	97.1	103	43	6	5	25	—	29	3.42	+9	.275	.328	-17	—	0.3
1932	Year	6	10	.375	26	16	3	0	—	1	—	—	124	141	70	9	5	37	—	36	4.35	-14	.290	.347	-23	—	-1.3
1933	Pit N	5	7	.417	36	8	4	1	—	4	—	—	117	118	45	3	1	19	—	44	2.92	+14	.262	.293	-34	—	0.6
1934	Pit N	15	6	.714	48	17	8	3	—	5	—	—	190.2	184	75	6	2	43	—	105	2.93	+41	.252	.296	-5	—	2.3
1935	Pit N	7	11	.389	39	11	5	0	—	6	—	—	164	187	72	8	1	27	—	63	3.40	+21	.285	.315	-25	—	1.7
1936	Pit N	7	5	.583	22	9	6	0	—	1	—	—	116.2	115	44	5	3	20	—	37	2.70	+50	.255	.291	-19	—	1.5
1937	Pit N	1	2	.333	11	0	0	0	—	2	—	—	28	31	14	3	0	6	—	21	4.50	-14	.270	.306	—	—	-0.2
1937	Bro N	7	7	.500	27	19	10	1	—	0	—	—	167	180	83	5	0	30	—	44	3.23	+25	.270	.301	-7	—	0.6
1937	Year	8	9	.471	38	19	10	1	—	2	—	—	195	211	97	8	0	36	—	65	3.42	+17	.270	.302	-6	—	0.4
1938	Bro N	0	3	.000	6	1	0	0	—	0	—	—	16.1	24	9	1	0	5	—	3	4.96	-21	.333	.377	-57	—	-0.2
Total	21	237	182	.566	674	425	226	26	—	52	—	—	3762.1	4037	1780	154	49	1003	—	1206	3.59	+12	.276	.325	+4	—	15.7
Team	10	157	98	.616	365	276	156	15	—	28	—	—	2272.1	2405	1035	93	32	631	—	713	3.48	+15	.274	.325	+14	—	13.5
/180I	1	12	8	.616	29	22	12	1	—	2	—	—	180	191	82	7	3	50	—	56	3.48	+15	.274	.325	+14	—	1.1

HUDSON, CHARLES CHARLES LYNN B3.16.1959 ENNIS TX BB/TR (BR 1983, 84P)/6'3"/185 DR 1981 PHIN 12/305 D5.31 COL PRAIRIE VIEW A&M

YEAR	TM LG	W	L	PCT	G	GS	CG	SHO	QS	SV	BS	QR	IP	H	R	HR	HB	BB	IB	SO	ERA	AERA	OAV	OOB	SUP	DL	PW
1987	NY A	11	7	.611	35	16	6	2	7	0	0	15	154.2	137	63	19	3	57	1	100	3.61	+23	.239	.308	+9	0	1.6
1988	NY A	6	6	.500	28	12	1	0	6	2	0	13	106.1	93	53	9	4	36	4	58	4.49	-11	.235	.301	+17	34	-0.4
Total	7	50	60	.455	208	140	14	3	72	2	0	48	1007.2	997	518	110	12	361	26	580	4.14	-7	.258	.321	+7	86	-3.7
Team	2	17	13	.567	63	28	7	2	13	2	0	28	261	230	116	28	7	93	5	158	3.97	+7	.237	.305	+12	34	1.2
/180I	1	12	9	.567	43	19	5	1	9	1	0	19	180	159	80	19	5	64	3	109	3.97	+7	.237	.305	+12	23	0.8

HUGHES, PHILIP PHILIP JOSEPH B6.24.1986 MISSION VIEJO CA BR/TR/6'5"/220 DR 2004 NYA 1/23 D4.26

YEAR	TM LG	W	L	PCT	G	GS	CG	SHO	QS	SV	BS	QR	IP	H	R	HR	HB	BB	IB	SO	ERA	AERA	OAV	OOB	SUP	DL	PW
2007	†NY A	5	3	.625	13	13	0	0	5	0	0	0	72.2	64	39	8	2	29	0	58	4.46	+1	.235	.313	+39	94	0.0

HUGHES, TOM THOMAS JAMES "LONG TOM" B11.29.1878 CHICAGO IL D2.8.1956 CHICAGO IL BR/TR/6'1"/175 D9.7 B–ED

YEAR	TM LG	W	L	PCT	G	GS	CG	SHO	QS	SV	BS	QR	IP	H	R	HR	HB	BB	IB	SO	ERA	AERA	OAV	OOB	SUP	DL	PW
1904	NY A	7	11	.389	19	18	12	1	—	0	—	—	136.1	141	72	3	5	48	—	75	3.70	-27	.268	.334	+5	—	-1.7
Total	13	132	174	.431	399	313	227	25	—	15	—	—	2644	2610	1292	52	102	853	—	1368	3.09	-7	.260	.324	-1	—	-6.4
/180I	1	9	15	.389	25	24	16	1	—	0	—	—	180	186	95	4	7	63	—	99	3.70	-27	.268	.334	+5	—	-2.2

HUGHES, TOM THOMAS L. "SALIDA TOM" B1.28.1884 COAL CREEK CO D11.1.1961 LOS ANGELES CA BR/TR/6'2"/175 D9.18

YEAR	TM LG	W	L	PCT	G	GS	CG	SHO	QS	SV	BS	QR	IP	H	R	HR	HB	BB	IB	SO	ERA	AERA	OAV	OOB	SUP	DL	PW
1906	NY A	1	0	1.000	3	1	1	0	—	0	—	—	15	11	8	2	0	1	—	5	4.20	-29	.208	.222	+21	—	-0.1
1907	NY A	2	0	1.000	4	3	2	0	—	0	—	—	27	16	10	0	2	11	—	10	2.67	+5	.174	.276	+21	—	0.0
1909	NY A	7	8	.467	24	15	9	2	—	2	—	—	118.2	109	42	3	4	37	—	69	2.65	-5	.249	.313	+4	—	0.2
1910	NY A	7	9	.438	23	15	11	0	—	1	—	—	151.2	153	77	2	3	37	—	64	3.50	-24	.271	.320	-11	—	-1.3
1914	Bos N	2	0	1.000	2	2	1	0	—	0	—	—	17	14	7	0	0	4	—	11	2.65	+4	.226	.273	+56	—	-0.1
1915	Bos N	16	14	.533	**50**	25	17	4	—	**9**	—	—	280.1	208	88	4	11	58	—	171	2.12	+22	.213	.265	-28	—	1.3
1916	Bos N	16	3	**.842**	40	13	7	1	—	5	—	—	161	121	46	2	8	51	—	97	2.35	+6	.215	.290	+23	—	1.0
1917	Bos N	5	3	.625	11	8	6	2	—	0	—	—	74	54	21	1	3	30	—	40	1.95	+31	.216	.307	+18	—	0.2
1918	Bos N	0	2	.000	3	3	1	0	—	0	—	—	18.1	17	10	1	0	6	—	9	3.44	-22	.250	.311	-34	—	0.0
Total	9	56	39	.589	160	85	55	9	—	17	—	—	863	703	309	15	31	235	—	476	2.56	+2	.229	.291	-3	—	1.2
Team	4	17	17	.500	54	34	23	2	—	3	—	—	312.1	289	137	7	9	86	—	148	3.14	-16	.252	.309	-1	—	-1.2
/180I	2	10	10	.500	31	20	13	1	—	2	—	—	180	167	79	4	5	50	—	85	3.14	-16	.252	.309	-1	—	-0.7

HUNTER, CATFISH JAMES AUGUSTUS "JIM" B4.8.1946 HERTFORD NC D9.9.1999 HERTFORD NC BR/TR/6'0"/(190–202) D5.13 HF1987

YEAR	TM LG	W	L	PCT	G	GS	CG	SHO	QS	SV	BS	QR	IP	H	R	HR	HB	BB	IB	SO	ERA	AERA	OAV	OOB	SUP	DL	PW
1975	NY A★	**23**	14	.622	39	39	**30**	7	32	0	0	0	**328**	248	107	25	5	83	4	177	2.58	+44	**.208**	**.261**	+10	0	4.4
1976	†NY A★	17	15	.531	36	36	21	2	25	0	0	0	298.2	268	126	28	3	68	5	173	3.53	-3	.241	.283	+16	0	-0.3
1977	†NY A	9	9	.500	22	22	8	1	10	0	0	0	143.1	137	83	29	3	47	3	52	4.71	-16	.250	.310	+27	21	-1.4

YEAR	TM LG	W	L	PCT	G	GS	CG	SHO	QS	SV	BS	QR	IP	H	R	HR	HB	BB	IB	SO	ERA	AERA	OAV	OOB	SUP	DL	PW
1978	†NY A	12	6	.667	21	20	5	1	12	0	0	0	118	98	49	16	1	35	0	56	3.58	+2	.226	.283	+19	44	0.4
1979	NY A	2	9	.182	19	19	1	0	7	0	0	0	105	128	68	15	1	34	0	34	5.31	-22	.312	.361	-13	0	-1.3
Total	15	224	166	.574	500	476	181	42	311	1	0	17	3449.1	2958	1380	374	49	954	57	2012	3.26	+4	.231	.285	+12	101	9.8
Team	5	63	53	.543	137	136	65	11	86	0	0	0	993	879	433	113	13	267	12	492	3.58	+3	.238	.289	+12	65	1.8
/180I	1	11	10	.543	25	25	12	2	16	0	0	0	180	159	78	20	2	48	2	89	3.58	+3	.238	.289	+12	12	0.3

Hutton, Mark Mark Steven B2.6.1970 South Adelaide, South Australia, Australia BR/TR/6'6"/(225–240) d7.23

YEAR	TM LG	W	L	PCT	G	GS	CG	SHO	QS	SV	BS	QR	IP	H	R	HR	HB	BB	IB	SO	ERA	AERA	OAV	OOB	SUP	DL	PW
1993	NY A	1	1	.500	7	4	0	0	1	0	0	1	22	24	17	2	1	17	0	12	5.73	-27	.293	.412	+37	0	-0.4
1994	NY A	0	0	+	2	0	0	0	0	0	0	1	3.2	4	3	0	0	0	0	1	4.91	-6	.250	.250	—	0	0.0
1996	NY A	0	2	.000	12	2	0	0	0	0	0	0	30.1	32	19	3	1	18	1	25	5.04	[illegible]	.269	.364	-63	44	-0.1
Total	5	9	7	.563	84	18	0	0	7	0	3	42	189.2	203	110	23	12	96	4	111	4.75	-9	.279	.368	-10	81	-0.2
Team	3	1	3	.250	21	6	0	0	1	0	0	8	56	60	39	5	2	35	1	38	5.30	-13	.276	.376	+4	44	-0.5

Igawa, Kei Kei B7.13.1979 Oarai, Japan BL/TL/6'1"/210 d4.7

YEAR	TM LG	W	L	PCT	G	GS	CG	SHO	QS	SV	BS	QR	IP	H	R	HR	HB	BB	IB	SO	ERA	AERA	OAV	OOB	SUP	DL	PW
2007	NY A	2	3	.400	14	12	0	0	1	0	0	1	67.2	76	48	15	4	37	1	53	6.25	-28	.279	.374	+29	0	-0.8

Irabu, Hideki Hideki B5.5.1969 Hyogo, Japan BR/TR/6'4"/(240–250) d7.10

YEAR	TM LG	W	L	PCT	G	GS	CG	SHO	QS	SV	BS	QR	IP	H	R	HR	HB	BB	IB	SO	ERA	AERA	OAV	OOB	SUP	DL	PW
1997	NY A	5	4	.556	13	9	0	0	2	0	0	2	53.1	69	47	15	1	20	0	56	7.09	-37	.311	.367	+44	0	-2.2
1998	NY A	13	9	.591	29	28	2	1	17	0	0	0	173	148	79	27	9	76	1	126	4.06	+8	.233	.321	+5	0	0.8
1999	†NY A	11	7	.611	32	27	2	1	14	0	0	4	169.1	180	98	26	6	46	0	133	4.84	-2	.267	.317	+44	0	-0.2
2000	Mon N	2	5	.286	11	11	0	0	6	0	0	0	54.2	77	45	9	1	14	0	42	7.24	-35	.339	.377	+8	124	-1.4
2001	Mon N	0	2	.000	3	3	0	0	1	0	0	0	16.2	22	9	3	0	3	0	18	4.86	-11	.314	.338	-64	139	-0.1
2002	Tex A	3	8	.273	38	2	0	0	0	16	4	28	47	51	30	11	1	16	2	30	5.74	-17	.279	.337	-32	79	-0.7
Total	6	34	35	.493	126	80	4	2	40	16	4	34	514	547	308	91	10	175	3	405	5.16	-11	.272	.333	+20	342	-3.8
Team	3	29	20	.592	74	64	4	2	33	0	0	6	395.2	397	224	68	16	142	1	315	4.80	-5	.259	.326	+27	—	-1.6
/180I	1	13	9	.592	34	29	2	1	15	0	0	3	180	181	102	31	7	65	0	143	4.80	-5	.259	.326	+27	—	-0.7

Jackson, Grant Grant Dwight "Buck" B9.28.1942 Fostoria OH BB/TL (BL 1971–79)/6'0"/(180–204) d9.3 C4 Col Bowling Green

YEAR	TM LG	W	L	PCT	G	GS	CG	SHO	QS	SV	BS	QR	IP	H	R	HR	HB	BB	IB	SO	ERA	AERA	OAV	OOB	SUP	DL	PW
1976	†NY A	6	0	1.000	21	2	1	1	2	1	0	16	58.2	38	11	1	1	16	0	25	1.69	+102	.186	.244	+106	0	1.2
Total	18	86	75	.534	692	83	16	5	43	79	30	420	1358.2	1272	589	109	21	511	71	889	3.46	+5	.251	.318	-15	0	4.3

James, Johnny John Phillip B7.23.1933 Bonners Ferry ID BL/TR/5'10"/160 d9.6 Col USC

YEAR	TM LG	W	L	PCT	G	GS	CG	SHO	QS	SV	BS	QR	IP	H	R	HR	HB	BB	IB	SO	ERA	AERA	OAV	OOB	SUP	DL	PW
1958	NY A	0	0	+	1	0	0	0	0	0	0	1	3	2	0	0	0	4	0	1	0.00	-100	.250	.500	—	0	0.1
1960	NY A	5	1	.833	28	0	0	0	0	2	2	20	43.1	38	22	3	3	26	2	29	4.36	-18	.248	.362	—	0	-0.4
1961	NY A	0	0	+	1	0	0	0	0	0	0	1	1.1	1	0	0	0	0	0	2	0.00	-100	.250	.250	—	0	0.0
1961	LA A	0	2	.000	36	3	0	0	1	0	0	22	71.1	66	44	12	2	54	1	41	5.30	-15	.246	.375	-15	0	-0.3
1961	Year	0	2	.000	37	3	0	0	1	0	0	23	72.2	67	44	12	2	54	1	43	5.20	-14	.246	.374	-15	0	-0.3
Total	3	5	3	.625	66	3	0	0	1	2	2	44	119	107	66	15	5	84	3	73	4.76	-13	.247	.373	-7	0	-0.6
Team	3	5	1	.833	30	0	0	0	0	2	2	22	47.2	41	22	3	3	30	2	32	3.97	-10	.248	.368	—	—	-0.3

Jean, Domingo Domingo (Luisa) B1.9.1969 San Pedro de Macoris, D.R. BR/TR/6'2"/175 d8.8

YEAR	TM LG	W	L	PCT	G	GS	CG	SHO	QS	SV	BS	QR	IP	H	R	HR	HB	BB	IB	SO	ERA	AERA	OAV	OOB	SUP	DL	PW
1993	NY A	1	1	.500	10	6	0	0	3	0	0	1	40.1	37	20	7	0	19	1	20	4.46	-6	.237	.318	+6	0	0.0

Jerzembeck, Mike Michael Joseph B5.18.1972 Queens NY BR/TR/6'1"/185 Dr 1993 NYA 5/141 d8.8 Col North Carolina [DL 1999 NY A 182]

YEAR	TM LG	W	L	PCT	G	GS	CG	SHO	QS	SV	BS	QR	IP	H	R	HR	HB	BB	IB	SO	ERA	AERA	OAV	OOB	SUP	DL	PW
1998	NY A	0	1	.000	3	2	0	0	0	0	0	1	6.1	9	9	2	0	4	0	1	12.79	-66	.346	.419	+27	0	-0.7

Jodie, Brett Brett Paul B3.25.1977 Columbia SC BR/TR/6'4"/208 Dr 1998 NYA 6/187 d7.20 Col South Carolina

YEAR	TM LG	W	L	PCT	G	GS	CG	SHO	QS	SV	BS	QR	IP	H	R	HR	HB	BB	IB	SO	ERA	AERA	OAV	OOB	SUP	DL	PW
2001	NY A	0	1	.000	1	1	0	0	0	0	0	0	2	7	6	3	0	1	0	0	27.00	-84	.583	.615	-17	0	-0.7
Total	1	0	2	.000	8	3	0	0	0	0	0	2	25.1	26	18	10	0	13	1	13	6.39	-35	.274	.361	-56	0	-0.8

John, Tommy Thomas Edward B5.22.1943 Terre Haute IN BR/TL/6'3"/(180–203) d9.6 [DL 1975 LA N 175]

YEAR	TM LG	W	L	PCT	G	GS	CG	SHO	QS	SV	BS	QR	IP	H	R	HR	HB	BB	IB	SO	ERA	AERA	OAV	OOB	SUP	DL	PW
1979	NY A☆	21	9	.700	37	36	17	3	29	0	0	1	276.1	268	109	9	4	65	1	111	2.96	+39	.260	.305	+5	0	3.3
1980	†NY A★	22	9	.710	36	36	16	0	24	0	0	0	265.1	270	115	13	6	56	1	78	3.43	+16	.268	.309	+19	0	1.8
1981	†NY A	9	8	.529	20	20	7	0	14	0	0	0	140.1	135	50	10	3	39	2	50	2.63	+37	.256	.309	-8	65	1.7
1982	NY A	10	10	.500	30	26	9	2	17	0	0	3	186.2	190	84	11	3	34	1	54	3.66	+10	.266	.299	+2	0	0.9
1986	NY A	5	3	.625	13	10	1	0	6	0	0	2	70.2	73	27	8	2	15	1	28	2.93	+41	.275	.316	-6	60	1.0
1987	NY A	13	6	.684	33	33	3	1	19	0	0	0	187.2	212	95	12	6	47	7	63	4.03	+10	.288	.335	+20	0	0.5
1988	NY A	9	8	.529	35	32	0	0	17	0	0	2	176.1	221	96	11	6	46	4	81	4.49	-12	.308	.354	+11	0	-0.8
1989	NY A	2	7	.222	10	10	0	0	4	0	0	0	63.2	87	45	6	3	22	2	18	5.80	-33	.336	.392	-28	0	-1.5
Total	26	288	231	.555	760	700	162	46	443	4	0	44	4710.1	4783	2017	302	98	1259	10	2245	3.34	+11	.265	.315	+2	444	20.4
Team	8	91	60	.603	214	203	53	6	130	0	0	8	1367	1456	621	80	33	324	19	483	3.59	+13	.277	.321	+7	125	6.9
/180I	1	12	8	.603	28	27	7	1	17	0	0	1	180	192	82	11	4	43	3	64	3.59	+13	.277	.321	+7	16	0.9

Johnson, Don Donald Roy B11.12.1926 Portland OR BR/TR/6'3"/(190–200) d4.20

YEAR	TM LG	W	L	PCT	G	GS	CG	SHO	QS	SV	BS	QR	IP	H	R	HR	HB	BB	IB	SO	ERA	AERA	OAV	OOB	SUP	DL	PW
1947	NY A	4	3	.571	15	8	2	0	—	0	—	—	54.1	57	26	2	1	23	—	16	3.64	-3	.270	.345	+28	0	-0.4
1950	NY A	1	0	1.000	8	0	0	0	—	0	—	—	18	35	21	2	0	12	—	9	10.00	-57	.398	.470	—	0	-0.6
Total	7	27	38	.415	198	70	17	5	0	12	0	11	631	712	371	55	11	285	3	262	4.78	-16	.288	.363	-7	0	-4.7
Team	2	5	3	.625	23	8	2	0	—	0	—	—	72.1	92	47	4	1	35	—	25	5.23	-29	.308	.382	+28	—	-1.0

Johnson, Hank Henry Ward B5.21.1906 Bradenton FL D8.20.1982 Bradenton FL BR/TR (BB 1933)/5'11.5"/175 d4.17

YEAR	TM LG	W	L	PCT	G	GS	CG	SHO	QS	SV	BS	QR	IP	H	R	HR	HB	BB	IB	SO	ERA	AERA	OAV	OOB	SUP	DL	PW
1925	NY A	1	3	.250	24	4	2	1	—	0	—	—	67	88	58	3	8	37	—	25	6.85	-38	.319	.414	-1	—	-1.0
1926	NY A	0	0	+	1	0	0	0	—	1	—	—	1	2	2	0	0	2	—	0	18.00	-79	.400	.571	—	—	-0.2
1928	NY A	14	9	.609	31	22	10	1	—	0	—	—	199	188	107	16	12	104	—	110	4.30	-12	.250	.351	+22	—	-0.9
1929	NY A	3	3	.500	12	8	2	0	—	0	—	—	42.2	37	28	5	0	39	—	24	5.06	-24	.237	.390	+23	—	-0.8
1930	NY A	14	11	.560	44	15	7	1	—	2	—	—	175.1	177	112	12	2	104	—	115	4.67	-8	.265	.366	+30	—	-0.5
1931	NY A	13	8	.619	40	23	8	0	—	4	—	—	196.1	176	114	13	1	102	—	106	4.72	-16	.234	.326	+45	—	-1.5
1932	NY A	2	2	.500	5	4	2	0	—	0	—	—	31.1	34	18	7	0	15	—	27	4.88	-17	.266	.343	+31	—	-0.2
1933	Bos A	8	6	.571	25	21	7	0	—	1	—	—	155.1	156	84	13	3	74	—	65	4.06	+8	.263	.348	-7	—	0.7
1934	Bos A	6	8	.429	31	14	7	1	—	1	—	—	124.1	162	95	12	5	53	—	66	5.36	-10	.316	.385	-8	—	-0.9
1935	Bos A	2	1	.667	13	2	0	0	—	1	—	—	31	41	21	3	0	14	—	14	5.52	-14	.331	.399	+19	—	-0.3
1936	Phi A	0	2	.000	3	3	0	0	—	0	—	—	11.2	16	16	4	1	10	—	6	7.71	-34	.296	.415	-25	—	-0.7
1939	Cin N	0	3	.000	20	0	0	0	—	1	—	—	31.1	30	10	1	0	13	—	10	2.01	+91	.268	.344	—	—	0.5
Total	12	63	56	.529	249	116	45	4	—	11	—	—	1066.1	1107	665	89	32	567	—	568	4.75	-12	.268	.361	+16	—	-5.8
Team	7	47	36	.566	157	76	31	3	—	7	—	—	712.2	702	439	56	23	403	—	407	4.84	-17	.256	.357	+30	—	-5.1
/180I	2	12	9	.566	40	19	8	1	—	2	—	—	180	177	111	14	6	102	—	103	4.84	-17	.256	.357	+30	—	-1.3

Johnson, Johnny John Clifford "Swede" B9.29.1914 Belmore OH D6.26.1991 Iron Mountain MI BL/TL/6'0"/182 d4.19 Col Eastern Michigan [DL 1946 Chi A 119]

YEAR	TM LG	W	L	PCT	G	GS	CG	SHO	QS	SV	BS	QR	IP	H	R	HR	HB	BB	IB	SO	ERA	AERA	OAV	OOB	SUP	DL	PW
1944	NY A	0	2	.000	22	1	0	0	—	3	—	—	26.2	25	14	0	1	24	—	11	4.05	-14	.243	.391	-76	0	-0.1
1945	Chi A	3	0	1.000	29	0	0	0	—	4	—	—	69.2	85	39	2	1	35	—	38	4.26	-22	.306	.385	—	0	-0.2
Total	2	3	2	.600	51	1	0	0	—	7	—	—	96.1	110	53	2	2	59	—	49	4.20	-20	.289	.387	-76	119	-0.3

Johnson, Ken Kenneth Travis B6.16.1933 W.Palm Beach FL BR/TR/6'4"/(200–222) d9.13

YEAR	TM LG	W	L	PCT	G	GS	CG	SHO	QS	SV	BS	QR	IP	H	R	HR	HB	BB	IB	SO	ERA	AERA	OAV	OOB	SUP	DL	PW
1969	NY A	1	2	.333	12	0	0	0	0	0	0	9	26	19	11	1	0	11	2	21	3.46	+2	.202	.286	—	0	0.1
Total	13	91	106	.462	334	231	50	7	145	9	8	68	1737.1	1670	778	157	56	413	56	1042	3.46	+1	.253	.301	-8	0	-0.5

Johnson, Randy Randall David "The Big Unit" B9.10.1963 Walnut Creek CA BR/TL/6'10"/(225–232) Dr 1985 MonN 2/36 d9.15 Col USC

YEAR	TM LG	W	L	PCT	G	GS	CG	SHO	QS	SV	BS	QR	IP	H	R	HR	HB	BB	IB	SO	ERA	AERA	OAV	OOB	SUP	DL	PW
2005	†NY A	17	8	.680	34	34	4	0	22	0	0	0	225.2	207	102	32	12	47	2	211	3.79	+14	.243	.291	+21	0	1.3
2006	†NY A	17	11	.607	33	33	2	0	16	0	0	0	205	194	125	28	10	60	1	172	5.00	-8	.250	.309	+29	0	-1.1

YEAR	TM LG	W	L	PCT	G	GS	CG	SHO	QS	SV	BS	QR	IP	H	R	HR	HB	BB	IB	SO	ERA	AERA	OAV	OOB	SUP	DL	PW
Total	20	284	150	.654	566	556	98	37	389	2	1	8	3855.1	3065	1556	368	182	1422	29	4616	3.22	+39	.218	.296	-1	366	49.2
Team	2	34	19	.642	67	67	6	0	38	0	—	0	430.2	401	227	60	22	107	3	383	4.37	+2	.246	.300	+25	—	0.2
/180I	1	14	8	.642	28	28	3	0	16	0	—	0	180	168	95	25	9	45	1	160	4.37	+2	.246	.300	+25	—	0.1
Johnson, Jeff William Jeffrey B8.4.1966 Durham NC BR/TL/6'3"/(200–206) Dr 1988 NYA 6/157 d6.5 Col North Carolina–Charlotte																											
1991	NY A	6	11	.353	23	23	0	0	9	0	0	0	127	156	89	15	6	33	1	62	5.95	-30	.305	.351	-10	0	-2.6
1992	NY A	2	3	.400	13	8	0	0	3	0	0	3	52.2	71	44	4	2	23	0	14	6.66	-41	.329	.395	+4	0	-1.4
1993	NY A	0	2	.000	2	2	0	0	0	0	0	0	2.2	12	10	1	0	2	0	0	30.38	-86	.600	.636	-56	0	-1.2
Total	3	8	16	.333	38	33	0	0	12	0	0	3	182.1	239	143	20	8	58	1	76	6.52	-37	.320	.372	-10	0	-5.2
/180I	3	8	16	.333	38	33	0	0	12	0	0	3	180	236	141	20	8	57	1	75	6.52	-37	.320	.372	-10	—	-5.1
Jones, Gary Gareth Howell B6.12.1945 Huntington Park CA BL/TL/6'0"/(185–191) d9.25 b-Steve Col Whittier																											
1970	NY A	0	0	+	2	0	0	0	0	0	0	2	2	3	0	0	0	1	0	2	0.00	-100	.375	.444	—	0	0.0
1971	NY A	0	0	+	12	0	0	0	0	0	0	7	14	19	14	1	0	7	1	10	9.00	-63	.317	.382	—	0	-0.5
Total	2	0	0	+	14	0	0	0	0	0	0	9	16	22	14	1	0	8	1	12	7.88	-58	.324	.390	—	0	-0.5
Jones, Jimmy James Condia B4.20.1964 Dallas TX BR/TR/6'2"/(175–191) Dr 1982 SDN 1/3 d9.21																											
1989	NY A	2	1	.667	11	6	0	0	3	0	0	2	48	56	29	7	2	16	1	25	5.25	-26	.293	.352	+67	0	-0.3
1990	NY A	1	2	.333	17	7	0	0	0	0	0	7	50	72	42	8	1	23	0	25	6.30	-37	.344	.405	+4	0	-0.8
Total	8	43	39	.524	153	118	7	3	55	0	0	21	755	809	431	72	19	239	12	376	4.46	-18	.275	.331	+10	117	-6.0
Team	2	3	3	.500	28	13	0	0	3	0	0	9	98	128	71	15	3	39	1	50	5.79	-32	.320	.380	+33	—	-1.1
Jones, Sam Samuel Pond "Sad Sam" B7.26.1892 Woodsfield OH D7.6.1966 Barnesville OH BR/TR/6'0"/170 d6.13																											
1922	†NY A	13	13	.500	45	28	20	0	—	**8**	—	—	260	270	132	16	3	76	—	81	3.67	+9	.275	.329	-3	—	1.4
1923	†NY A	21	8	.724	39	27	18	3	—	4	—	—	243	239	114	11	6	69	—	68	3.63	+9	.257	.312	+36	—	0.9
1924	NY A	9	6	.600	36	21	8	3	—	3	—	—	178.2	187	85	6	1	76	—	53	3.63	+15	.276	.350	-18	—	0.7
1925	NY A	15	21	.417	43	31	14	1	—	2	—	—	246.2	267	147	14	3	104	—	92	4.63	-8	.281	.354	-16	—	-1.5
1926	†NY A	9	8	.529	39	23	6	1	—	5	—	—	161	186	104	6	4	80	—	69	4.98	-23	.298	.381	+24	—	-1.9
Total	22	229	217	.513	647	487	250	36	—	31	—	—	3883	4084	2008	152	69	1396	—	1223	3.84	+4	.274	.339	+0	—	7.2
Team	5	67	56	.545	202	130	66	8	—	22	—	—	1089.1	1149	582	53	17	405	—	363	4.06	+0	.276	.343	+4	—	-0.4
/180I	1	11	9	.545	33	21	11	1	—	4	—	—	180	190	96	9	3	67	—	60	4.06	+0	.276	.343	+4	—	-0.1
Juden, Jeff Jeffrey Daniel B1.19.1971 Salem MA BR/TR/6'8"/(245–265) Dr 1989 HouN 1/12 d9.15																											
1999	NY A	0	1	.000	2	1	0	0	0	0	0	1	5.2	5	9	1	1	3	0	9	1.59	+198	.200	.310	-61	0	-0.2
Total	8	27	32	.458	147	76	6	0	33	0	0	47	533	510	325	73	34	247	6	441	4.81	-11	.253	.341	-1	0	-4.6
Jurewicz, Mike Michael Allen B9.20.1945 Buffalo NY BB/TL/6'3"/205 d9.7																											
1965	NY A	0	0	+	2	0	0	0	0	0	0	0	2.1	5	2	0	0	1	0	2	7.71	-56	.417	.462	—	0	-0.1
Kaat, Jim James Lee B11.7.1938 Zeeland MI BL/TL/6'4"/(195–227) d8.2 C2 Col Hope																											
1979	NY A	2	3	.400	40	1	0	0	0	2	2	27	58.1	64	29	4	2	14	2	23	3.86	+7	.287	.329	+10	0	0.0
1980	NY A	0	1	.000	4	0	0	0	0	0	0	2	5	8	5	0	0	4	2	1	7.20	-45	.381	.462	—	0	-0.3
Total	25	283	237	.544	898	625	180	31	379	18	16	177	4530.1	4620	2038	395	122	1083	11	2461	3.45	+7	.264	.309	+5	104	16.4
Team	2	2	4	.333	44	1	0	0	0	2	2	29	63.1	72	34	4	2	18	4	24	4.12	+0	.295	.342	+10	—	-0.3
/60G	3	3	5	.333	60	1	0	0	0	3	3	40	86.1	98	46	5	3	25	5	33	4.12	+0	.295	.342	+10	—	-0.4
Kamieniecki, Scott Scott Andrew B4.19.1964 Mt.Clemens MI BR/TR/6'0"/(195–200) Dr 1986 NYA 14/366 d6.18 Col Michigan																											
1991	NY A	4	4	.500	9	9	0	0	7	0	0	0	55.1	54	24	8	3	22	1	34	3.90	+7	.256	.333	-20	65	0.4
1992	NY A	6	14	.300	28	28	4	0	14	0	0	0	188	193	100	13	5	74	9	88	4.36	-9	.269	.340	+3	23	-0.9
1993	NY A	10	7	.588	30	20	2	0	12	1	0	4	154.1	163	73	17	3	59	7	72	4.08	+3	.277	.343	-2	0	0.4
1994	NY A	8	6	.571	22	16	1	0	9	0	0	4	117.1	115	53	13	3	59	5	71	3.76	+22	.261	.350	+34	0	1.2
1995	†NY A	7	6	.538	17	16	1	0	6	0	0	1	89.2	83	43	8	3	49	1	43	4.01	+15	.246	.346	-1	70	0.7
1996	NY A	1	2	.333	7	5	0	0	0	0	1	1	22.2	36	30	6	2	19	1	15	11.12	-55	.364	.475	+35	84	-1.5
1997	†Bal A	10	6	.625	30	30	0	0	17	0	0	0	179.1	179	83	20	4	67	2	109	4.01	+10	.261	.328	-1	0	0.8
1998	Bal A	2	6	.250	12	11	0	0	3	0	0	1	54.2	67	41	7	4	26	0	25	6.75	-33	.313	.394	-28	117	-1.5
1999	Bal A	2	4	.333	43	3	0	0	0	2	0	30	56.1	52	32	4	4	29	2	39	4.95	-5	.250	.348	-14	33	0.0
2000	Cle A	1	3	.250	26	0	0	0	0	0	0	16	33.1	42	22	6	1	20	5	29	5.67	-12	.311	.404	—	0	-0.2
2000	Atl N	2	1	.667	26	0	0	0	0	2	0	19	24.2	22	18	3	0	22	1	17	5.47	-18	.239	.386	—	0	-0.4
2000	Major	3	4	.429	52	0	0	0	0	2	0	35	57	64	40	9	1	42	6	46	5.59	-15	.282	.396	—	0	-0.6
Total	10	53	59	.473	250	138	8	0	68	5	1	76	975.2	1006	519	105	32	446	34	542	4.52	-3	.270	.351	+1	392	-1.0
Team	6	36	39	.480	113	94	8	0	48	1	1	10	627.1	644	323	65	19	282	24	323	4.33	-1	.269	.349	+6	242	0.3
/180I	2	10	11	.480	32	27	2	0	14	0	0	3	180	185	93	19	5	81	7	93	4.33	-1	.269	.349	+6	69	0.1
Kammeyer, Bob Robert Lynn B12.2.1950 Kansas City KS D1.27.2003 Sacramento CA BR/TR/6'4"/210 Dr 1972 NYA 21/492 d7.3 Col Stanford																											
1978	NY A	0	0	+	7	0	0	0	0	0	0	5	21.2	24	15	1	2	6	0	11	5.82	-37	.276	.327	—	0	-0.2
1979	NY A	0	0	+	1	0	0	0	0	0	0	0	0	7	8	2	1	0	0	0	(8)	-100	1.000	1.000	—	0	-0.6
Total	2	0	0	+	8	0	0	0	0	0	0	5	21.2	31	23	3	3	6	0	11	9.14	-60	.330	.377	—	0	-0.8
Karpel, Herb Herbert "Lefty" B12.27.1917 Brooklyn NY D1.24.1995 San Diego CA BL/TL/5'9.5"/180 d4.19																											
1946	NY A	0	0	+	2	0	0	0	—	0	—	—	1.2	4	2	0	0	0	—	0	10.80	-68	.500	.500	—	0	-0.1
Karsay, Steve Stefan Andrew B3.24.1972 Flushing NY BR/TR/6'3"/(185–215) Dr 1990 TorA 1/22 d8.17 [DL 1995 Oak A 160, 2003 NY A 183]																											
2002	†NY A	6	4	.600	78	0	0	0	0	12	4	55	88.1	87	33	7	2	30	14	65	3.26	+33	.258	.320	—	0	1.5
2004	NY A	0	0	+	7	0	0	0	0	0	0	4	6.2	5	3	2	0	2	0	4	2.70	+70	.217	.259	—	155	0.0
2005	NY A	0	0	+	6	0	0	0	0	0	0	4	6	10	5	0	0	2	1	5	6.00	-28	.385	.414	—	0	-0.1
Total	11	32	39	.451	357	40	1	0	18	41	19	224	603.1	636	289	59	23	199	38	458	4.01	+15	.272	.332	-9	712	5.3
Team	3	6	4	.600	91	0	0	0	0	12	4	63	101	102	41	9	2	34	15	74	3.39	+28	.264	.322	—	155	1.4
/60G	2	4	3	.600	60	0	0	0	0	8	3	42	66.2	67	27	6	1	22	10	49	3.38	+28	.264	.322	—	102	0.9
Karstens, Jeff Jeffrey Wayne B9.24.1982 San Diego CA BR/TR/6'3"/175 Dr 2003 NYA 19/574 d8.22 Col Texas Tech																											
2006	NY A	2	1	.667	8	6	0	0	4	0	0	2	42.2	40	20	6	1	11	2	16	3.80	+22	.242	.291	+19	0	0.2
2007	NY A	1	4	.200	7	3	0	0	0	0	0	2	14.2	27	21	4	0	9	0	5	11.05	-59	.397	.462	-45	114	-1.9
Total	2	3	5	.375	15	9	0	0	4	0	0	4	57.1	67	41	10	1	20	2	21	5.65	-19	.288	.342	-2	114	-1.7
Kaufman, Curt Curt Gerrard B7.19.1957 Omaha NE BR/TR/6'2"/175 d9.10 Col Iowa St.																											
1982	NY A	1	0	1.000	7	0	0	0	0	0	0	4	8.2	9	5	2	0	6	1	1	5.19	-22	.265	.375	—	0	-0.1
1983	NY A	0	0	+	4	0	0	0	0	0	0	2	8.2	10	3	0	0	4	0	8	3.12	+27	.303	.359	—	0	0.0
Total	3	3	3	.500	40	1	0	0	0	1	0	25	86.1	87	45	15	0	30	5	50	4.48	-11	.260	.316	+36	0	-0.3
Team	2	1	0	1.000	11	0	0	0	0	0	0	6	17.1	19	8	2	0	10	1	9	4.15	-4	.284	.367	—	—	-0.1
Keating, Ray Raymond Herbert B7.21.1893 Bridgeport CT D12.28.1963 Sacramento CA BR/TR/5'11"/185 d9.12 Col Niagara																											
1912	NY A	0	3	.000	6	5	3	0	—	0	—	—	35.2	36	27	0	1	18	—	21	5.80	-38	.265	.355	+19	—	-0.3
1913	NY A	6	12	.333	28	21	9	2	—	0	—	—	151.1	147	77	3	2	51	—	83	3.21	-7	.256	.318	-20	—	-1.0
1914	NY A	8	11	.421	34	25	14	0	—	0	—	—	210	198	94	1	5	67	—	109	2.96	-7	.253	.316	+2	—	-0.5
1915	NY A	3	6	.333	11	10	8	1	—	0	—	—	79.1	66	41	3	3	45	—	37	3.63	-19	.228	.337	+9	—	-0.7
1916	NY A	5	6	.455	14	11	6	0	—	0	—	—	91	91	42	4	2	37	—	35	3.07	-6	.272	.349	+16	—	-0.1
1918	NY A	2	2	.500	15	6	1	0	—	0	—	—	48.1	39	27	0	2	30	—	16	3.91	-28	.238	.362	-16	—	-0.5
1919	Bos N	7	11	.389	22	14	9	1	—	0	—	—	136	129	61	2	2	45	—	48	2.98	-4	.261	.325	-22	—	-0.5

YEAR	TM LG	W	L	PCT	G	GS	CG	SHO	QS	SV	BS	QR	IP	H	R	HR	HB	BB	IB	SO	ERA	AERA	OAV	OOB	SUP	DL	PW
Total	7	31	51	.378	130	92	50	4	—	0	—	—	751.2	706	369	13	17	293	—	349	3.29	-12	.254	.329	-3	—	-3.6
Team	6	24	40	.375	108	78	41	3	—	0	—	—	615.2	577	308	11	15	248	—	301	3.36	-13	.253	.330	-1	—	-3.1
/180I	2	7	12	.375	32	23	12	1	—	0	—	—	180	169	90	3	4	73	—	88	3.36	-13	.253	.330	-1	—	-0.9

Keefe, Bobby Robert Francis B6.16.1882 Folsom CA D12.6.1964 Sacramento CA BR/TR/5'11"/155 d4.15 Col Santa Clara

YEAR	TM LG	W	L	PCT	G	GS	CG	SHO	QS	SV	BS	QR	IP	H	R	HR	HB	BB	IB	SO	ERA	AERA	OAV	OOB	SUP	DL	PW
1907	NY A	3	5	.375	19	3	0	0	—	3	—	—	57.2	60	18	1	1	20	—	20	2.50	+12	.270	.333	-68	—	0.4
Total	3	16	21	.432	75	35	15	0	—	8	—	—	360.2	334	158	8	8	129	—	154	3.14	+3	.248	.317	-14	—	1.0

Keisler, Randy Randy Dean B2.24.1976 Richards TX BL/TL/6'3"/190 Dr 1998 NYA 2/67 d9.10 Col Louisiana St. [DL 2002 NY A 183]

YEAR	TM LG	W	L	PCT	G	GS	CG	SHO	QS	SV	BS	QR	IP	H	R	HR	HB	BB	IB	SO	ERA	AERA	OAV	OOB	SUP	DL	PW
2000	NY A	1	0	1.000	4	1	0	0	0	0	0	0	10.2	16	14	1	0	8	0	6	11.81	-60	.364	.462	+18	0	-0.6
2001	NY A	1	2	.333	10	10	0	0	3	0	0	0	50.2	52	36	12	0	34	0	36	6.22	-29	.259	.364	+42	0	-0.5
Total	6	4	4	.500	55	20	0	0	4	0	0	19	150.2	174	121	32	2	84	3	100	6.63	-34	.286	.372	+30	208	-2.3
Team	2	2	2	.500	14	11	0	0	3	0	0	0	61.1	68	50	13	0	42	0	42	7.19	-37	.278	.382	+40	—	-1.1

Kekich, Mike Michael Dennis B4.2.1945 San Diego CA BR/TL/6'1"/(196–206) d6.9

YEAR	TM LG	W	L	PCT	G	GS	CG	SHO	QS	SV	BS	QR	IP	H	R	HR	HB	BB	IB	SO	ERA	AERA	OAV	OOB	SUP	DL	PW
1965	LA N	0	1	.000	5	1	0	0	0	0	0	2	10.1	10	12	2	0	13	0	9	9.58	-66	.263	.451	-20	0	-0.7
1968	LA N	2	10	.167	25	20	1	1	9	0	0	4	115	116	54	9	1	46	0	84	3.91	-29	.267	.336	-22	0	-1.6
1969	NY A	4	6	.400	28	13	1	0	6	1	0	10	105	91	58	11	2	49	5	66	4.54	-22	.236	.323	-28	0	-1.2
1970	NY A	6	3	.667	26	14	1	0	6	0	0	7	98.2	103	59	12	1	55	3	63	4.83	-26	.267	.358	+9	22	-1.3
1971	NY A	10	9	.526	37	24	3	0	11	0	0	7	170.1	167	89	13	4	82	11	93	4.07	-19	.257	.341	+16	0	-1.6
1972	NY A	10	13	.435	29	28	2	0	16	0	0	1	175.1	172	77	13	4	76	5	78	3.70	-19	.263	.343	+6	0	-1.7
1973	NY A	1	1	.500	5	4	0	0	1	0	0	0	14.2	20	15	1	2	14	0	4	9.20	-60	.351	.486	+44	0	-0.9
1973	Cle A	1	4	.200	16	6	0	0	0	0	0	5	50	73	47	6	0	35	0	26	7.02	-44	.349	.437	-17	0	-1.6
1973	Year	2	5	.286	21	10	0	0	1	0	0	5	64.2	93	62	7	2	49	0	30	7.52	-48	.350	.449	+5	0	-2.5
1975	Tex A	0	0	+	23	0	0	0	0	2	2	13	31.1	33	16	2	0	21	2	19	3.73	+1	.282	.388	—	0	0.0
1977	Sea A	5	4	.556	41	2	0	0	0	3	1	22	90	90	58	11	3	51	3	55	5.60	-26	.265	.363	-78	24	-1.2
Total	9	39	51	.433	235	112	8	1	49	6	3	71	860.2	875	485	80	17	442	29	497	4.59	-27	.268	.355	-6	46	-11.8
Team	5	31	32	.492	125	83	7	0	40	1	0	25	564	553	298	50	13	276	24	304	4.31	-23	.259	.346	+6	22	-6.7
/180I	2	10	10	.492	40	26	2	0	13	0	0	8	180	176	95	16	4	88	8	97	4.31	-23	.259	.346	+6	7	-2.1

Kennedy, Ian Ian Patrick B12.19.1984 Huntington Beach CA BR/TR/6'0"/190 Dr 2006 NYA 1/21 d9.1 Col USC

YEAR	TM LG	W	L	PCT	G	GS	CG	SHO	QS	SV	BS	QR	IP	H	R	HR	HB	BB	IB	SO	ERA	AERA	OAV	OOB	SUP	DL	PW
2007	NY A	1	0	1.000	3	3	0	0	2	0	0	0	19	13	6	1	0	9	0	15	1.89	+138	.191	.286	-11	0	0.2

Keough, Matt Matthew Lon B7.3.1955 Pomona CA BR/TR/6'3"/(175–190) Dr 1973 OakA 7/167 d9.3 f–Marty

YEAR	TM LG	W	L	PCT	G	GS	CG	SHO	QS	SV	BS	QR	IP	H	R	HR	HB	BB	IB	SO	ERA	AERA	OAV	OOB	SUP	DL	PW
1983	NY A	3	4	.429	12	12	0	0	4	0	0	0	55.2	59	42	12	2	20	0	26	5.17	-24	.266	.331	+25	0	-1.2
Total	9	58	84	.408	215	175	53	7	92	0	2	24	1190	1190	631	132	27	510	14	590	4.17	-8	.262	.338	-8	0	-5.2

Key, Jimmy James Edward B4.22.1961 Huntsville AL BR/TL/6'1"/(185–190) Dr 1982 TorA 3/56 d4.6 Col Clemson

YEAR	TM LG	W	L	PCT	G	GS	CG	SHO	QS	SV	BS	QR	IP	H	R	HR	HB	BB	IB	SO	ERA	AERA	OAV	OOB	SUP	DL	PW
1993	NY A★	18	6	**.750**	34	34	4	2	26	0	0	0	236.2	219	84	26	1	43	1	173	3.00	+39	.246	.279	+27	0	3.1
1994	NY A★	**17**	4	.810	25	**25**	1	0	18	0	0	0	168	177	68	10	3	52	0	97	3.27	+41	.273	.329	+34	0	2.9
1995	NY A	1	2	.333	5	5	0	0	2	0	0	0	30.1	40	20	3	0	6	1	14	5.64	-18	.323	.351	+29	138	-0.3
1996	†NY A	12	11	.522	30	30	0	0	13	0	0	0	169.1	171	93	21	2	58	1	116	4.68	+6	.266	.326	-5	30	0.7
Total	15	186	117	.614	470	389	34	13	241	10	8	53	2591.2	2518	1104	254	38	668	29	1538	3.51	+22	.255	.303	+5	356	23.3
Team	4	48	23	.676	94	94	5	2	59	0	—	0	604.1	607	265	60	6	159	3	400	3.68	+23	.263	.310	+19	168	6.4
/180I	1	14	7	.676	28	28	1	1	18	0	—	0	180	181	79	18	2	47	1	119	3.68	+23	.263	.310	+19	50	1.9

Kipp, Fred Fred Leo B10.1.1931 Piqua KS BL/TL/6'4"/(180–200) d9.10 Col Emporia St.

YEAR	TM LG	W	L	PCT	G	GS	CG	SHO	QS	SV	BS	QR	IP	H	R	HR	HB	BB	IB	SO	ERA	AERA	OAV	OOB	SUP	DL	PW
1960	NY A	0	1	.000	4	0	0	0	0	0	0	3	4.1	4	3	0	0	0	0	2	6.23	-43	.250	.250	—	0	-0.2
Total	4	6	7	.462	47	9	0	0	10	0	0	47	113.1	119	67	18	1	48	8	64	5.08	-20	.274	.346	-20	0	-0.9

Kitson, Frank Frank R. B9.11.1869 Hopkins MI D4.14.1930 Allegan MI BL/TR/5'11"/165 d5.19

YEAR	TM LG	W	L	PCT	G	GS	CG	SHO	QS	SV	BS	QR	IP	H	R	HR	HB	BB	IB	SO	ERA	AERA	OAV	OOB	SUP	DL	PW
1907	NY A	4	0	1.000	12	4	3	0	—	0	—	—	61	75	31	0	4	17	—	14	3.10	-10	.305	.360	+63	—	-0.1
Total	10	129	118	.522	304	250	211	19	—	7	—	—	2221.2	2331	1087	52	81	491	—	731	3.18	-1	.270	.315	+0	—	2.3

Kleinhans, Ted Theodore Otto (b Traugott Otto Kleinhans) B4.8.1899 Deer Park WI D7.24.1985 Redington Beach FL BR/TL/6'0"/170 d4.20

YEAR	TM LG	W	L	PCT	G	GS	CG	SHO	QS	SV	BS	QR	IP	H	R	HR	HB	BB	IB	SO	ERA	AERA	OAV	OOB	SUP	DL	PW
1934	Phi N	0	0	+	5	0	0	0	—	0	—	—	6	11	8	1	0	3	—	2	9.00	-48	.379	.438	—	—	-0.1
1934	Cin N	2	6	.250	24	9	0	0	—	0	—	—	80	107	63	2	1	38	—	23	5.74	-29	.321	.392	-39	—	-1.3
1934	Year	2	6	.250	29	9	0	0	—	0	—	—	86	118	71	3	1	41	—	25	5.97	-31	.326	.396	-40	—	-1.4
1936	NY A	1	1	.500	19	0	0	0	—	1	—	—	29.1	36	25	0	0	23	—	10	5.83	-20	.300	.413	—	—	-0.4
1937	Cin N	1	2	.333	7	3	1	0	—	0	—	—	27.1	29	13	1	1	12	—	13	2.30	+62	.271	.350	-15	—	0.2
1938	Cin N	0	0	+	1	0	0	0	—	0	—	—	1	2	1	0	0	0	—	0	9.00	-59	.400	.400	—	—	0.0
Total	4	4	9	.308	56	12	1	0	—	1	—	—	143.2	185	110	4	2	76	—	48	5.26	-21	.311	.391	-36	—	-1.6

Klepfer, Ed Edward Lloyd "Big Ed" B3.17.1888 Summerville PA D8.9.1950 Tulsa OK BR/TR/6'0"/185 d7.4 Mil 1918 Col Penn St.

YEAR	TM LG	W	L	PCT	G	GS	CG	SHO	QS	SV	BS	QR	IP	H	R	HR	HB	BB	IB	SO	ERA	AERA	OAV	OOB	SUP	DL	PW
1911	NY A	0	0	+	2	0	0	0	—	0	—	—	4	5	3	0	0	2	—	4	6.75	-47	.250	.318	—	—	-0.1
1913	NY A	0	1	.000	8	1	0	0	—	0	—	—	24.2	38	22	2	2	12	—	10	7.66	-61	.376	.452	-100	—	-0.5
Total	6	22	17	.564	98	50	16	1	—	3	—	—	447.2	457	204	3	6	137	—	165	2.81	+4	.273	.330	-5	—	-0.7
Team	2	0	1	.000	10	1	0	0	—	0	—	—	28.2	43	25	2	2	14	—	14	7.53	-59	.355	.431	-100	—	-0.6

Klimkowski, Ron Ronald Bernard B3.1.1944 Jersey City NJ BR/TR/6'2"/(186–195) d9.15 Col Morehead St.

YEAR	TM LG	W	L	PCT	G	GS	CG	SHO	QS	SV	BS	QR	IP	H	R	HR	HB	BB	IB	SO	ERA	AERA	OAV	OOB	SUP	DL	PW
1969	NY A	0	0	+	3	1	0	0	1	0	0	2	14	6	1	0	0	5	1	3	0.64	+448	.130	.212	-100	0	0.2
1970	NY A	6	7	.462	45	3	1	1	1	1	1	33	98.1	80	36	7	3	33	7	40	2.65	+35	.223	.293	+33	0	1.0
1971	Oak A	2	2	.500	26	0	0	0	0	2	0	19	45.1	37	19	3	1	23	8	25	3.38	-1	.220	.316	—	0	0.1
1972	NY A	0	3	.000	16	2	0	0	1	1	0	12	31.1	32	15	3	1	15	7	11	4.02	-26	.271	.356	-70	0	-0.4
Total	4	8	12	.400	90	6	1	1	3	4	1	66	189	155	71	13	5	76	23	79	2.90	+18	.224	.304	-22	0	0.9
Team	3	6	10	.375	64	6	1	1	3	2	1	47	143.2	118	52	10	4	53	15	54	2.76	+25	.226	.300	-23	—	0.8
/60G	3	6	9	.375	60	6	1	1	3	2	1	44	134.2	111	49	9	4	50	14	51	2.76	+25	.226	.300	-23	—	0.8

Kline, Steve Steven Jack B10.6.1947 Wenatchee WA BR/TR/6'3"/(196–205) Dr 1966 NYA 7/130 d7.10 [DL 1975 Cle A 175]

YEAR	TM LG	W	L	PCT	G	GS	CG	SHO	QS	SV	BS	QR	IP	H	R	HR	HB	BB	IB	SO	ERA	AERA	OAV	OOB	SUP	DL	PW
1970	NY A	6	6	.500	16	15	5	0	9	0	0	1	100.1	99	42	8	0	24	3	49	3.41	+5	.254	.296	-12	0	0.5
1971	NY A	12	13	.480	31	30	15	1	22	0	0	0	222.1	206	87	21	0	37	7	81	2.96	+11	.244	.275	-5	0	0.9
1972	NY A	16	9	.640	32	32	11	4	22	0	0	0	236.1	210	79	11	10	44	6	58	2.40	+25	.237	.279	+1	0	1.2
1973	NY A	4	7	.364	14	13	2	1	5	0	0	1	74	76	39	5	1	31	3	19	4.01	-8	.270	.342	-15	92	-0.4
1974	NY A	2	2	.500	4	4	0	0	2	0	0	0	26	26	12	3	1	5	0	6	3.46	+2	.263	.305	-1	0	0.0
1974	Cle A	3	8	.273	16	11	1	0	4	0	0	2	71	70	44	9	4	31	2	17	5.07	-28	.266	.350	-36	46	-1.4
1974	Year	5	10	.333	20	15	1	0	6	0	0	2	97	96	56	12	5	36	2	23	4.64	-22	.265	.338	-27	0	-1.4
1977	Atl N	0	0	+	16	0	0	0	0	1	0	9	20.1	21	15	4	0	12	3	10	6.64	-33	.259	.355	—	0	-0.2
Total	6	43	45	.489	129	105	34	6	64	1	0	13	750.1	708	318	61	16	184	24	240	3.26	+3	.249	.297	-9	313	0.6
Team	5	40	37	.519	97	94	33	6	60	0	0	2	659	617	259	48	12	141	19	213	2.96	+11	.247	.289	-5	92	2.2
/180I	1	11	10	.519	26	26	9	2	16	0	0	1	180	169	71	13	3	39	5	58	2.96	+11	.247	.289	-5	25	0.6

Knight, Brandon Brandon Michael B10.1.1975 Oxnard CA BL/TR/6'0"/170 Dr 1995 TexA 14/374 d6.5 Col Ventura (CA) JC

YEAR	TM LG	W	L	PCT	G	GS	CG	SHO	QS	SV	BS	QR	IP	H	R	HR	HB	BB	IB	SO	ERA	AERA	OAV	OOB	SUP	DL	PW
2001	NY A	0	0	+	4	0	0	0	0	0	0	0	10.2	18	12	5	0	3	0	7	10.13	-56	.367	.404	—	0	-0.3
2002	NY A	0	0	+	7	0	0	0	0	0	0	4	8.2	11	12	2	0	5	0	7	11.42	-62	.306	.390	—	0	-0.3
Total	2	0	0	+	11	0	0	0	0	0	0	4	19.1	29	24	7	0	8	0	14	10.71	-59	.341	.398	—	0	-0.6

Konstanty, Jim Casimir James B3.2.1917 Strykersville NY D6.11.1976 Oneonta NY BR/TR/6'1.5"/(195–202) d6.18 Mil 1945 Col Syracuse

YEAR	TM LG	W	L	PCT	G	GS	CG	SHO	QS	SV	BS	QR	IP	H	R	HR	HB	BB	IB	SO	ERA	AERA	OAV	OOB	SUP	DL	PW
1954	NY A	1	1	.500	9	0	0	0	—	2	—	—	18.1	11	2	0	0	6	—	3	0.98	+250	.183	.254	—	0	0.7
1955	NY A	7	2	.778	45	0	0	0	—	11	—	—	73.2	68	28	5	0	24	2	19	2.32	+61	.247	.305	—	0	1.4

YEAR	TM LG	W	L	PCT	G	GS	CG	SHO	QS	SV	BS	QR	IP	H	R	HR	HB	BB	IB	SO	ERA	AERA	OAV	OOB	SUP	DL	PW
1956	NY A	0	0	+	8	0	0	0	—	2	—	—	11	15	6	3	0	6	0	6	4.91	-21	.319	.396	—	0	-0.1
Total	11	66	48	.579	433	36	14	2	—	74	—	—	945.2	957	420	88	5	269	3	268	3.46	+12	.268	.319	+12	0	6.6
Team	3	8	3	.727	62	0	0	0	—	15	—	—	103	94	36	8	0	36	2	28	2.36	+57	.246	.308	—	—	2.0
/60G	3	8	3	.727	60	0	0	0	—	15	—	—	99.2	91	35	8	0	35	2	27	2.36	+57	.246	.308	—	—	1.9

Kraly, Steve Steve Charles "Lefty" B4.18.1929 Whiting IN BL/TL/5'10"/152 d8.9

YEAR	TM LG	W	L	PCT	G	GS	CG	SHO	QS	SV	BS	QR	IP	H	R	HR	HB	BB	IB	SO	ERA	AERA	OAV	OOB	SUP	DL	PW
1953	NY A	0	2	.000	5	3	0	0	—	1	—	—	25	19	10	2	2	16	—	8	3.24	+14	.209	.339	-60	0	0.0

Kramer, Jack John Henry B1.5.1918 New Orleans LA D5.18.1995 Metairie LA BR/TR/6'2"/190 d4.25 Def 1942

YEAR	TM LG	W	L	PCT	G	GS	CG	SHO	QS	SV	BS	QR	IP	H	R	HR	HB	BB	IB	SO	ERA	AERA	OAV	OOB	SUP	DL	PW
1951	NY A	1	3	.250	19	3	0	0	—	0	—	—	40.2	46	27	1	0	21	—	15	4.65	-18	.280	.362	+62	0	-0.6
Total	12	95	103	.480	322	215	88	14	—	7	—	—	1637.1	1761	895	92	10	682	—	613	4.24	-4	.276	.347	+7	0	-3.8

Kucks, Johnny John Charles B7.27.1933 Hoboken NJ BR/TR/6'3"/(170–190) d4.17

YEAR	TM LG	W	L	PCT	G	GS	CG	SHO	QS	SV	BS	QR	IP	H	R	HR	HB	BB	IB	SO	ERA	AERA	OAV	OOB	SUP	DL	PW
1955	†NY A	8	7	.533	29	13	3	1	—	0	—	—	126.2	122	54	8	2	44	6	49	3.41	+10	.252	.315	+11	0	0.2
1956	†NY A☆	18	9	.667	34	31	12	3	—	0	—	—	224.1	223	113	19	10	72	0	67	3.85	+0	.261	.323	+27	0	-0.3
1957	†NY A	8	10	.444	37	23	4	1	23	2	1	26	179.1	169	82	13	8	59	2	78	3.56	+1	.251	.316	+23	0	0.0
1958	†NY A	8	8	.500	34	15	4	1	23	4	0	26	126	132	67	14	6	39	2	46	3.93	-10	.269	.328	+22	0	-0.9
1959	NY A	0	1	.000	9	1	0	0	23	0	0	26	16.2	21	16	5	0	9	0	9	8.64	-58	.323	.405	-3	0	-0.5
1959	KC A	8	11	.421	33	23	6	1	12	1	0	9	151.1	163	76	10	12	42	0	51	3.87	+4	.278	.336	-25	0	0.0
1959	Year	8	12	.400	42	24	6	1	35	1	0	35	168	184	92	15	12	51	0	60	4.34	-9	.282	.343	-24	0	-0.5
1960	KC A	4	10	.286	31	17	1	0	6	0	0	8	114	140	85	22	1	43	2	38	6.00	-34	.306	.361	-21	0	-2.7
Total	6	54	56	.491	207	123	30	7	87	7	1	95	938.1	970	493	91	39	308	12	338	4.10	-8	.269	.330	+7	0	-4.2
Team	5	42	35	.545	143	83	23	6	69	6	1	78	673	667	332	59	26	223	10	249	3.82	-3	.260	.323	+22	—	-1.5
/180I	1	11	9	.545	38	22	6	2	18	2	0	21	180	178	89	16	7	60	3	67	3.82	-3	.260	.323	+22	—	-0.4

Kunkel, Bill William Gustave James B7.7.1936 Hoboken NJ D5.4.1985 Red Bank NJ BR/TR/6'1"/(165–187) d4.15 U17 s–Jeff

YEAR	TM LG	W	L	PCT	G	GS	CG	SHO	QS	SV	BS	QR	IP	H	R	HR	HB	BB	IB	SO	ERA	AERA	OAV	OOB	SUP	DL	PW
1963	NY A	3	2	.600	22	0	0	0	0	0	1	15	46.1	42	15	3	0	13	3	31	2.72	+29	.239	.289	—	0	0.5
Total	3	6	6	.500	89	2	0	0	0	4	4	55	142.2	153	80	17	0	49	5	83	4.29	-8	.272	.327	-100	0	-0.3

Kuzava, Bob Robert Leroy "Sarge" B5.28.1923 Wyandotte MI BB/TL/6'2"/204 d9.21

YEAR	TM LG	W	L	PCT	G	GS	CG	SHO	QS	SV	BS	QR	IP	H	R	HR	HB	BB	IB	SO	ERA	AERA	OAV	OOB	SUP	DL	PW
1946	Cle A	1	0	1.000	2	2	0	0	—	0	—	—	12	9	7	0	1	11	—	4	3.00	+10	.191	.356	+55	0	0.0
1947	Cle A	1	1	.500	4	4	1	1	—	0	—	—	21.2	22	10	1	1	9	—	9	4.15	-16	.265	.344	+8	0	-0.1
1949	Chi A	10	6	.625	29	18	9	1	—	0	—	—	156.2	139	76	6	1	91	—	83	4.02	+4	.240	.344	+1	0	-0.4
1950	Chi A	1	3	.250	10	7	1	0	—	0	—	—	44.1	43	28	5	0	27	—	21	5.68	-21	.257	.361	+12	0	-0.4
1950	Was A	8	7	.533	22	22	8	1	—	0	—	—	155	156	80	8	1	75	—	84	3.95	+14	.263	.346	-14	0	0.5
1950	Year	9	10	.474	32	29	9	1	—	0	—	—	199.1	199	108	13	1	102	—	105	4.33	+4	.261	.350	-8	0	0.1
1951	Was A	3	3	.500	8	8	3	0	—	0	—	—	52.1	57	34	5	2	28	—	22	5.50	-26	.284	.377	+0	0	-0.7
1951	†NY A	8	4	.667	23	8	4	1	—	5	—	—	82.1	76	27	5	1	27	—	50	2.40	+59	.241	.303	+13	0	1.9
1951	Year	11	7	.611	31	16	7	1	—	5	—	—	134.2	133	61	10	3	55	—	72	3.61	+9	.258	.333	+7	0	1.2
1952	†NY A	8	8	.500	28	12	6	1	—	3	—	—	133	115	53	7	1	63	—	67	3.45	-4	.240	.329	+12	0	-0.1
1953	†NY A	6	5	.545	33	6	2	2	—	4	—	—	92.1	92	35	9	0	34	—	48	3.31	+11	.264	.330	-20	0	0.5
1954	NY A	1	3	.250	20	3	0	0	—	1	—	—	39.2	46	30	3	0	18	—	22	5.45	-37	.297	.366	+3	0	-1.1
1954	Bal A	1	3	.250	4	4	0	0	—	0	—	—	23.2	30	11	0	0	11	—	15	4.18	-14	.323	.387	-38	0	-0.3
1954	Year	2	6	.250	24	7	0	0	—	1	—	—	63.1	76	41	3	0	29	—	37	4.97	-30	.306	.374	-21	0	-1.4
1955	Bal A	0	1	.000	6	1	0	0	—	0	—	—	12.1	10	7	0	0	4	1	5	3.65	+5	.222	.280	-100	0	-0.1
1955	Phi N	1	0	1.000	17	4	0	0	—	0	—	—	32.1	47	26	5	0	12	1	13	7.24	-45	.333	.386	+18	0	-0.5
1955	Major	1	1	.500	23	5	0	0	—	0	—	—	44	57	33	5	0	16	2	18	6.25	-31	.306	.360	-6	0	-0.6
1957	Pit N	0	0	+	4	0	0	0	0	0	0	2	2	3	2	0	0	3	0	1	9.00	-58	.333	.500	—	0	-0.1
1957	StL N	0	0	+	3	0	0	0	0	0	0	2	2.1	4	1	0	0	2	0	2	3.86	+3	.364	.462	—	0	0.0
1957	Year	0	0	+	7	0	0	0	0	0	0	4	4.1	7	3	0	0	5	0	3	6.23	-38	.350	.480	—	0	-0.1
Total	10	49	44	.527	213	99	34	7	0	13	0	4	862	849	427	54	8	415	2	446	4.05	-3	.260	.344	+0	0	-0.9
Team	4	23	20	.535	104	29	12	4	—	13	—	—	347.1	329	145	24	2	142	—	187	3.39	+5	.254	.328	+5	—	1.2
/180I	2	12	10	.535	54	15	6	2	—	7	—	—	180	170	75	12	1	74	—	97	3.39	+5	.254	.328	+5	—	0.6

Lake, Joe Joseph Henry B1.6.1881 Brooklyn NY D6.30.1950 Brooklyn NY BR/TR/6'0"/185 d4.21

YEAR	TM LG	W	L	PCT	G	GS	CG	SHO	QS	SV	BS	QR	IP	H	R	HR	HB	BB	IB	SO	ERA	AERA	OAV	OOB	SUP	DL	PW
1908	NY A	9	22	.290	38	27	19	2	—	0	—	—	269.1	252	157	6	6	77	—	118	3.17	-22	.242	.298	-21	—	-3.0
1909	NY A	14	11	.560	31	26	17	3	—	1	—	—	215.1	180	81	2	5	59	—	117	1.88	+35	.225	.283	+7	—	1.7
1910	StL A	11	17	.393	35	29	24	1	—	2	—	—	261.1	243	116	2	1	77	—	141	2.20	+12	.248	.304	-22	—	0.6
1911	StL A	10	15	.400	30	25	14	2	—	0	—	—	215.1	245	115	3	4	40	—	69	3.30	+2	.282	.316	-17	—	0.6
1912	StL A	1	7	.125	11	6	4	0	—	0	—	—	57	70	41	0	1	16	—	28	4.42	-25	.314	.363	-26	—	-1.0
1912	Det A	9	11	.450	26	14	11	0	—	1	—	—	162.2	190	94	3	3	39	—	86	3.10	+5	.296	.340	-24	—	-0.7
1912	Year	10	18	.357	37	20	15	0	—	1	—	—	219.2	260	135	3	4	55	—	114	3.44	-5	.301	.346	-24	—	-1.7
1913	Det A	8	7	.533	28	12	6	0	—	1	—	—	137	149	67	3	0	24	—	35	3.28	-11	.279	.310	+4	—	0.1
Total	6	62	90	.408	199	139	95	8	—	5	—	—	1318	1329	671	19	20	332	—	594	2.85	-1	.261	.309	-14	—	-1.7
Team	2	23	33	.411	69	53	36	5	—	1	—	—	484.2	432	238	8	11	136	—	235	2.60	-4	.235	.292	-7	—	-1.3
/180I	1	9	12	.411	26	20	13	2	—	0	—	—	180	160	88	3	4	51	—	87	2.60	-4	.235	.292	-7	—	-0.5

LaPoint, Dave David Jeffrey B7.29.1959 Glens Falls NY BL/TL/6'3"/(205–231) Dr 1977 MilA 10/237 d9.10

YEAR	TM LG	W	L	PCT	G	GS	CG	SHO	QS	SV	BS	QR	IP	H	R	HR	HB	BB	IB	SO	ERA	AERA	OAV	OOB	SUP	DL	PW
1989	NY A	6	9	.400	20	20	0	0	7	0	0	0	113.2	146	73	12	2	45	4	51	5.62	-31	.310	.370	+0	77	-2.3
1990	NY A	7	10	.412	28	27	2	0	12	0	0	1	157.2	180	84	11	1	57	3	67	4.11	-3	.292	.347	-12	0	-0.4
Total	12	80	86	.482	294	227	11	4	129	1	1	46	1486.2	1598	748	117	17	559	47	802	4.02	-6	.277	.340	+0	92	-5.8
Team	2	13	19	.406	48	47	2	0	19	0	0	1	271.1	326	157	23	3	102	7	118	4.74	-17	.300	.357	-7	77	-2.7
/180I	1	9	13	.406	32	31	1	0	13	0	0	1	180	216	104	15	2	68	5	78	4.74	-17	.300	.357	-7	51	-1.8

LaRoche, Dave David Eugene B5.14.1948 Colorado Springs CO BL/TL/6'2"/(185–200) Dr 1967 AnaA*S5/86 d5.11 C5 s–Adam s–Andy Col Nevada–Las Vegas

YEAR	TM LG	W	L	PCT	G	GS	CG	SHO	QS	SV	BS	QR	IP	H	R	HR	HB	BB	IB	SO	ERA	AERA	OAV	OOB	SUP	DL	PW
1981	†NY A	4	1	.800	26	1	0	0	0	0	2	18	47	38	16	3	1	16	1	24	2.49	+45	.229	.291	+24	0	0.5
1982	NY A	4	2	.667	25	0	0	0	0	0	0	17	50	54	19	4	1	11	2	31	3.42	+18	.273	.313	—	0	0.4
1983	NY A	0	0	+	1	0	0	0	0	0	0	0	1	2	2	1	0	0	0	0	18.00	-78	.400	.400	—	0	-0.1
Total	14	65	58	.528	647	15	1	0	3	126	41	446	1049.1	919	448	94	29	459	81	819	3.53	+6	.239	.322	+0	12	4.4
Team	3	8	3	.727	52	1	0	0	0	0	2	35	98	94	37	8	2	27	3	55	3.12	+23	.255	.304	+24	—	0.8
/60G	3	9	3	.727	60	1	0	0	0	0	2	40	113	108	43	9	2	31	3	63	3.12	+23	.255	.304	+24	—	0.9

Larsen, Don Don James B8.7.1929 Michigan City IN BR/TR/6'4"/(215–227) d4.18

YEAR	TM LG	W	L	PCT	G	GS	CG	SHO	QS	SV	BS	QR	IP	H	R	HR	HB	BB	IB	SO	ERA	AERA	OAV	OOB	SUP	DL	PW
1955	†NY A	9	2	.818	19	13	5	1	—	2	—	—	97	81	38	8	2	51	3	44	3.06	+22	.229	.328	+39	0	1.0
1956	†NY A	11	5	.688	38	20	6	1	—	1	—	—	179.2	133	72	19	7	96	0	107	3.26	+19	.204	.312	+31	0	1.7
1957	†NY A	10	4	.714	27	20	4	1	29	0	1	9	139.2	113	68	12	0	87	0	81	3.74	-4	.220	.332	+33	0	0.2
1958	†NY A	9	6	.600	19	19	5	3	29	0	0	9	114.1	100	43	4	4	52	3	55	3.07	+15	.233	.320	+34	0	1.8
1959	NY A	6	7	.462	25	18	3	1	29	0	0	9	124.2	122	65	14	2	76	2	69	4.33	-16	.260	.361	+47	0	-0.4
Total	14	81	91	.471	412	171	44	11	98	23	7	157	1548	1442	728	130	26	725	35	849	3.78	-1	.247	.331	+9	0	4.5
Team	5	45	24	.652	128	90	23	7	87	3	1	27	655.1	549	286	57	15	362	8	356	3.50	+5	.227	.330	+36	—	4.3
/180I	1	12	7	.652	35	25	6	2	24	1	0	7	180	151	79	16	4	99	2	98	3.50	+5	.227	.330	+36	—	1.2

Leary, Tim Timothy James B12.23.1958 Santa Monica CA BR/TR/6'3"/(190–220) Dr 1979 NYN 1/2 d4.12 Col UCLA

YEAR	TM LG	W	L	PCT	G	GS	CG	SHO	QS	SV	BS	QR	IP	H	R	HR	HB	BB	IB	SO	ERA	AERA	OAV	OOB	SUP	DL	PW
1990	NY A	9	19	.321	31	31	6	1	19	0	0	0	208	202	105	18	7	78	1	138	4.11	-3	.257	.328	-30	0	-0.2
1991	NY A	4	10	.286	28	18	1	0	4	0	0	5	120.2	150	89	20	4	57	1	83	6.49	-36	.312	.388	+5	0	-2.8
1992	NY A	5	6	.455	18	15	2	0	6	0	0	2	97	84	62	9	4	57	2	34	5.57	-29	.245	.354	-3	0	-1.6
Total	13	78	105	.426	292	224	25	9	107	1	2	42	1491.1	1570	792	147	52	535	45	888	4.36	-10	.273	.338	-12	122	-5.3
Team	3	18	35	.340	77	64	9	1	29	0	0	7	425.2	436	256	47	15	192	4	255	5.12	-21	.271	.352	-14	—	-4.6
/180I	1	8	15	.340	33	27	4	0	12	0	0	3	180	184	108	20	6	81	2	108	5.12	-21	.271	.352	-14	—	-1.9

Pitchers

Leiter, Al Alois Terry B10.23.1965 Toms River NJ BL/TL/6'3"/(200–220) Dr 1984 NYA 2/50 d9.15 b–Mark

YEAR	TM LG	W	L	PCT	G	GS	CG	SHO	QS	SV	BS	QR	IP	H	R	HR	HB	BB	IB	SO	ERA	AERA	OAV	OOB	SUP	DL	PW
1987	NY A	2	2	.500	4	4	0	0	1	0	0	0	22.2	24	16	2	0	15	0	28	6.35	-30	.273	.379	-28	0	-0.6
1988	NY A	4	4	.500	14	14	0	0	3	0	0	0	57.1	49	27	7	5	33	0	60	3.92	+1	.231	.348	+2	34	0.1
1989	NY A	1	2	.333	4	4	0	0	1	0	0	0	26.2	23	20	1	2	21	0	22	6.08	-36	.235	.377	-1	0	-0.6
2005	†NY A	4	5	.444	16	10	0	0	3	0	0	4	62.1	66	42	4	6	38	0	45	5.49	-22	.268	.375	+5	0	-1.1
Total	19	162	132	.551	419	382	16	10	217	2	1	24	2391	2152	1101	198	117	1163	53	1974	3.80	+12	.242	.336	-8	499	11.2
Team	4	11	13	.458	38	32	0	0	8	0	0	4	169	162	105	14	13	107	0	155	5.17	-20	.252	.367	-1	34	-2.2
/180I	4	12	14	.458	40	34	0	0	9	0	0	4	180	173	112	15	14	114	0	165	5.17	-20	.252	.367	-1	36	-2.3

Leiter, Mark Mark Edward B4.13.1963 Joliet IL BR/TR/6'3"/(210–220) Dr 1983 BalA*4/103 d7.24 b–Al Col Ramapo

YEAR	TM LG	W	L	PCT	G	GS	CG	SHO	QS	SV	BS	QR	IP	H	R	HR	HB	BB	IB	SO	ERA	AERA	OAV	OOB	SUP	DL	PW
1990	NY A	1	1	.500	8	3	0	0	1	0	0	2	26.1	33	20	5	2	9	0	21	6.84	-42	.314	.376	+29	0	-0.4
Total	11	65	73	.471	335	149	15	1	69	26	15	129	1184.1	1205	664	155	75	424	43	892	4.57	-7	.265	.334	+6	383	-4.8

LeRoy, Louis Louis Paul "Chief" B2.18.1879 Omro WI D10.10.1944 Shawano WI BR/TR/5'10"/180 d9.22

YEAR	TM LG	W	L	PCT	G	GS	CG	SHO	QS	SV	BS	QR	IP	H	R	HR	HB	BB	IB	SO	ERA	AERA	OAV	OOB	SUP	DL	PW
1905	NY A	1	1	.500	3	3	2	0	—	0	—	—	24	26	14	2	1	1	—	8	3.75	-22	.277	.292	+13	—	-0.2
1906	NY A	2	0	1.000	11	2	1	0	—	1	—	—	44.2	33	19	0	2	12	—	28	2.22	+34	.209	.273	+70	—	0.1
1910	Bos A	0	0	+	1	0	0	0	—	0	—	—	4	7	9	1	0	2	—	3	11.25	-77	.389	.450	—	—	-0.2
Total	3	3	1	.750	15	5	3	0	—	1	—	—	72.2	66	42	3	3	15	—	39	3.22	-9	.244	.292	+36	—	-0.3
Team	2	3	1	.750	14	5	3	0	—	1	—	—	68.2	59	33	2	3	13	—	36	2.75	+7	.234	.280	+36	—	-0.1

Lewis, Jim James Martin B10.12.1955 Miami FL BR/TR/6'3"/190 d9.12 Col South Carolina

YEAR	TM LG	W	L	PCT	G	GS	CG	SHO	QS	SV	BS	QR	IP	H	R	HR	HB	BB	IB	SO	ERA	AERA	OAV	OOB	SUP	DL	PW
1982	NY A	0	0	+	1	0	0	0	0	0	0	0	0.2	3	7	0	0	3	0	0	54.00	-93	.500	.667	—	0	-0.2
Total	4	0	1	.000	11	1	0	0	0	0	0	4	25.2	45	31	7	3	12	0	9	8.77	-51	.391	.462	-35	0	-0.9

Ley, Terry Terrence Richard B2.21.1947 Portland OR BL/TL/6'0"/180 Dr 1967 NYA*S3/60 d8.20 Col Oregon

YEAR	TM LG	W	L	PCT	G	GS	CG	SHO	QS	SV	BS	QR	IP	H	R	HR	HB	BB	IB	SO	ERA	AERA	OAV	OOB	SUP	DL	PW
1971	NY A	0	0	+	6	0	0	0	0	0	0	4	9	9	9	1	2	9	2	7	5.00	-34	.257	.426	—	0	-0.2

Lidle, Cory Cory Fulton B3.22.1972 Hollywood CA D10.11.2006 New York NY BR/TR/5'11"/(180–190) d5.8 [DL 1998 Ari N 181]

YEAR	TM LG	W	L	PCT	G	GS	CG	SHO	QS	SV	BS	QR	IP	H	R	HR	HB	BB	IB	SO	ERA	AERA	OAV	OOB	SUP	DL	PW
2006	†NY A	4	3	.571	10	9	0	0	5	0	0	0	45.1	49	26	11	3	19	1	32	5.16	-11	.272	.351	+9	0	-0.1
Total	9	82	72	.532	277	199	11	5	96	2	1	53	1322.2	1400	738	159	54	356	34	838	4.57	-1	.272	.324	+3	399	-1.3

Lieber, Jon Jonathan Ray B4.2.1970 Council Bluffs IA BL/TR/6'2"/(220–235) Dr 1992 KCA 2/44 d5.15 Col South Alabama [DL 2003 NY A 183]

YEAR	TM LG	W	L	PCT	G	GS	CG	SHO	QS	SV	BS	QR	IP	H	R	HR	HB	BB	IB	SO	ERA	AERA	OAV	OOB	SUP	DL	PW
2004	†NY A	14	8	.636	27	27	0	0	16	0	0	0	176.2	216	95	20	2	18	2	102	4.33	+6	.300	.316	+24	32	0.3
Total	13	129	121	.516	375	326	25	5	179	2	4	28	2151.1	2329	1134	275	47	416	48	1526	4.28	+3	.275	.310	+1	462	1.1
/180I	1	14	8	.636	28	28	0	0	16	0	—	0	180	220	97	20	2	18	2	104	4.33	+6	.300	.316	+24	33	0.3

Lilly, Ted Theodore Roosevelt B1.4.1976 Lomita CA BL/TL/6'0"/(180–190) Dr 1996 LAN 23/688 d5.14 Col Fresno (CA) City

YEAR	TM LG	W	L	PCT	G	GS	CG	SHO	QS	SV	BS	QR	IP	H	R	HR	HB	BB	IB	SO	ERA	AERA	OAV	OOB	SUP	DL	PW
2000	NY A	0	0	+	7	0	0	0	0	0	0	4	8	8	6	1	0	5	0	11	5.63	-15	.235	.333	—	49	0.0
2001	NY A	5	6	.455	26	21	0	0	7	0	0	4	120.2	126	81	20	7	51	1	112	5.37	-17	.267	.344	+6	0	-1.0
2002	NY A	3	6	.333	16	11	2	1	6	0	0	4	76.2	57	31	10	5	24	3	59	3.40	+27	.202	.274	-46	0	0.9
Total	9	74	66	.529	219	194	4	2	91	0	0	15	1143	1089	602	172	37	437	18	973	4.46	+4	.248	.319	-6	148	2.8
Team	3	8	12	.400	49	32	2	1	13	0	0	12	205.1	191	118	31	12	80	4	182	4.65	-5	.242	.319	-12	49	-0.1
/180I	3	7	11	.400	43	28	2	1	11	0	0	11	180	167	103	27	11	70	4	160	4.65	-5	.242	.319	-12	43	-0.1

Lindblad, Paul Paul Aaron B8.9.1941 Chanute KS D1.1.2006 Arlington TX BL/TL/6'1"/(185–195) d9.15

YEAR	TM LG	W	L	PCT	G	GS	CG	SHO	QS	SV	BS	QR	IP	H	R	HR	HB	BB	IB	SO	ERA	AERA	OAV	OOB	SUP	DL	PW
1978	†NY A	0	0	+	7	1	0	0	0	0	0	5	18.1	21	9	4	0	8	0	9	4.42	-17	.284	.354	-2	0	0.0
Total	14	68	63	.519	655	32	1	1	14	64	33	450	1213.2	1157	510	112	26	384	88	671	3.29	+4	.253	.312	-14	19	2.6

Lindell, Johnny John Harlan B8.30.1916 Greeley CO D8.27.1985 Newport Beach CA BR/TR/6'4.5"/(217–220) d4.18.1941 Mil 1945 ▲

YEAR	TM LG	W	L	PCT	G	GS	CG	SHO	QS	SV	BS	QR	IP	H	R	HR	HB	BB	IB	SO	ERA	AERA	OAV	OOB	SUP	DL	PW
1942	NY A	2	1	.667	23	2	0	0	—	1	—	—	52.2	52	25	3	1	22	—	28	3.76	-8	.254	.329	-1	0	0.0
1953	Pit N	5	16	.238	27	23	13	1	—	0	—	—	175.2	173	106	17	6	116	—	102	4.71	-5	.262	.377	-24	0	1.0
1953	Phi N	1	1	.500	5	3	2	0	—	0	—	—	23.1	22	16	0	0	23	—	16	4.24	-1	.259	.417	-15	0	0.1
1953	Year	6	17	.261	32	26	15	1	—	0	—	—	199	195	122	17	6	139	—	118	4.66	-5	.261	.382	-23	0	1.1
Total	2	8	18	.308	55	28	15	1	—	1	—	—	251.2	247	147	20	7	161	—	146	4.47	-5	.260	.371	-19	0	1.1

Llewellyn, Clem Clement Manly "Lew" B8.1.1895 Dobson NC D11.27.1969 Concord NC BL/TR/6'3.5"/195 d6.18 Col North Carolina

YEAR	TM LG	W	L	PCT	G	GS	CG	SHO	QS	SV	BS	QR	IP	H	R	HR	HB	BB	IB	SO	ERA	AERA	OAV	OOB	SUP	DL	PW
1922	NY A	0	0	+	1	0	0	0	—	0	—	—	1	1	0	0	0	0	—	0	0.00	-100	.250	.250	—	—	0.0

Lloyd, Graeme Graeme John B4.9.1967 Geelong, Victoria, Australia BL/TL/6'7"/(215–234) d4.11 [DL 2000 Mon N 181]

YEAR	TM LG	W	L	PCT	G	GS	CG	SHO	QS	SV	BS	QR	IP	H	R	HR	HB	BB	IB	SO	ERA	AERA	OAV	OOB	SUP	DL	PW
1996	†NY A	0	2	.000	13	0	0	0	0	0	2	6	5.2	12	11	1	0	5	1	6	17.47	-72	.429	.486	—	0	-1.3
1997	†NY A	1	1	.500	46	0	0	0	0	1	0	35	49	55	24	6	1	20	7	26	3.31	+35	.293	.355	—	0	0.2
1998	†NY A	3	0	1.000	50	0	0	0	0	0	2	39	37.2	26	10	3	2	6	2	20	1.67	+162	.191	.234	—	15	0.7
Total	10	30	36	.455	568	0	0	0	0	17	28	396	533	560	274	51	23	161	36	304	4.04	+14	.271	.327	—	258	0.9
Team	3	4	3	.571	109	0	0	0	0	1	4	80	92.1	93	45	10	3	31	10	52	3.51	+27	.264	.322	—	15	-0.4
/60G	2	2	2	.571	60	0	0	0	0	1	2	44	50.2	51	25	6	2	17	6	29	3.52	+27	.264	.322	—	8	-0.2

Loaiza, Esteban Esteban Antonio (Veyna) B12.31.1971 Tijuana, Baja California, Mexico BR/TR/6'3"/(190–230) d4.29

YEAR	TM LG	W	L	PCT	G	GS	CG	SHO	QS	SV	BS	QR	IP	H	R	HR	HB	BB	IB	SO	ERA	AERA	OAV	OOB	SUP	DL	PW
2004	†NY A	1	2	.333	10	6	0	0	0	0	0	0	42.1	61	43	9	2	26	2	34	8.50	-46	.337	.416	+7	0	-1.0
Total	13	125	112	.527	367	330	14	6	179	1	1	23	2072	2325	1153	255	74	599	39	1372	4.64	-2	.285	.336	-1	281	0.1

Lollar, Tim William Timothy B3.17.1956 Poplar Bluff MO BL/TL/6'3"/(195–204) Dr 1978 NYA 4/104 d6.28 Col Arkansas

YEAR	TM LG	W	L	PCT	G	GS	CG	SHO	QS	SV	BS	QR	IP	H	R	HR	HB	BB	IB	SO	ERA	AERA	OAV	OOB	SUP	DL	PW
1980	NY A	1	0	1.000	14	1	0	0	1	2	0	9	32.1	33	14	3	0	20	2	13	3.34	+19	.280	.379	-55	0	0.1
Total	7	47	52	.475	199	131	9	4	67	4	1	40	906	841	459	93	17	480	21	600	4.27	-14	.249	.343	+0	0	-2.9

Lopat, Ed Edmund Walter (b Edmund Walter Lopatynski) B6.21.1918 New York NY D6.15.1992 Darien CT BL/TL/5'10"/(182–185) d4.30 M2/C3

YEAR	TM LG	W	L	PCT	G	GS	CG	SHO	QS	SV	BS	QR	IP	H	R	HR	HB	BB	IB	SO	ERA	AERA	OAV	OOB	SUP	DL	PW
1944	Chi A	11	10	.524	27	25	13	1	—	0	—	—	210	217	96	12	2	59	—	75	3.26	+5	.265	.316	-2	0	1.0
1945	Chi A	10	13	.435	26	24	17	1	—	1	—	—	199.1	226	101	8	6	56	—	74	4.11	-19	.285	.336	+9	0	-1.2
1946	Chi A	13	13	.500	29	29	20	2	—	0	—	—	231	216	80	18	1	48	—	89	2.73	+25	.248	.288	+9	0	3.2
1947	Chi A	16	13	.552	31	31	22	3	—	0	—	—	252.2	241	88	17	2	73	—	109	2.81	+30	.253	.307	-9	0	2.9
1948	NY A	17	11	.607	33	31	13	3	—	0	—	—	226.2	246	106	16	2	66	—	83	3.65	+12	.284	.336	+10	0	1.0
1949	†NY A	15	10	.600	31	30	14	4	—	1	—	—	215.1	222	93	19	5	69	—	70	3.26	+24	.269	.330	-2	0	2.6
1950	†NY A	18	8	.692	35	32	15	3	—	1	—	—	236.1	244	110	19	4	65	—	72	3.47	+24	.266	.317	+24	0	2.5
1951	†NY A★	21	9	.700	31	31	20	4	—	0	—	—	234.2	209	86	12	3	71	—	93	2.91	+31	.239	**.298**	-1	0	3.3
1952	†NY A	10	5	.667	20	19	10	2	—	0	—	—	149.1	127	47	11	4	53	—	56	2.53	+31	.234	.307	+19	0	1.6
1953	†NY A	16	4	**.800**	25	24	9	3	—	0	—	—	178.1	169	58	13	4	32	—	50	**2.42**	+52	.250	.288	+26	0	2.9
1954	NY A	12	4	.750	26	23	7	0	—	0	—	—	170	189	74	14	6	33	—	54	3.55	-3	.288	.326	+17	0	-0.7
1955	NY A	4	8	.333	16	12	3	1	—	0	—	—	86.2	101	45	12	1	16	3	24	3.74	+0	.294	.327	-17	0	-0.4
1955	Bal A	3	4	.429	10	7	1	0	—	0	—	—	49	57	24	8	3	9	2	10	4.22	-10	.294	.332	-27	0	-0.1
1955	Year	7	12	.368	26	19	4	1	—	0	—	—	135.2	158	69	20	4	25	5	34	3.91	-4	.294	.329	-21	0	-0.5
Total	12	166	112	.597	340	318	164	27	—	3	—	—	2439.1	2464	1008	179	43	650	5	859	3.21	+16	.264	.315	+7	0	18.6
Team	8	113	59	.657	217	202	91	20	—	2	—	—	1497.1	1507	619	116	29	405	3	502	3.19	+21	.264	.316	+11	—	12.8
/180I	1	14	7	.657	26	24	11	2	—	0	—	—	180	181	74	14	3	49	0	60	3.19	+21	.264	.316	+11	—	1.5

Love, Slim Edward Haughton B8.1.1890 Love MS D11.30.1942 Memphis TN BL/TL/6'7"/195 d9.8

YEAR	TM LG	W	L	PCT	G	GS	CG	SHO	QS	SV	BS	QR	IP	H	R	HR	HB	BB	IB	SO	ERA	AERA	OAV	OOB	SUP	DL	PW
1913	Was A	1	0	1.000	5	1	0	0	—	1	—	—	16.2	14	5	0	0	6	—	5	1.62	+82	.233	.303	-50	—	0.1
1916	NY A	2	0	1.000	20	1	0	0	—	0	—	—	47.2	46	29	2	0	23	—	21	4.91	-41	.274	.361	-21	—	-0.7
1917	NY A	6	5	.545	33	9	2	0	—	1	—	—	130.1	115	50	0	1	57	—	82	2.35	+14	.251	.335	-29	—	0.0
1918	NY A	13	12	.520	38	29	13	1	—	1	—	—	228.2	207	92	3	10	116	—	95	3.07	-8	.253	.353	-9	—	-0.5

YEAR	TM LG	W	L	PCT	G	GS	CG	SHO	QS	SV	BS	QR	IP	H	R	HR	HB	BB	IB	SO	ERA	AERA	OAV	OOB	SUP	DL	PW
1919	Det A	6	4	.600	22	8	4	0	—	1	—	—	89.2	92	40	3	6	40	—	46	3.01	+6	.275	.363	-14	—	0.0
1920	Det A	0	0	+	1	0	0	0	—	0	—	—	4.1	6	4	0	0	4	—	2	8.31	-55	.375	.500	—	—	-0.1
Total	6	28	21	.571	119	48	19	1	—	4	—	—	517.1	480	220	8	17	246	—	251	3.04	-6	.259	.351	-15	—	-1.2
Team	3	21	17	.553	91	39	15	1	—	2	—	—	406.2	368	171	5	11	196	—	198	3.05	-9	.255	.348	-14	—	-1.2
/180I	1	9	8	.553	40	17	7	0	—	1	—	—	180	163	76	2	5	87	—	88	3.05	-9	.255	.348	-14	—	-0.5
Lyle, Sparky Albert Walter B7.22.1944 DuBois PA BL/TL/6'1"/(182–198) d7.4																											
1967	Bos A	1	2	.333	27	0	0	0	0	5	1	25	43.1	33	13	3	2	14	1	42	2.28	+53	.213	.283	—	0	0.5
1968	Bos A	6	1	.857	49	0	0	0	0	11	8	35	65.2	67	25	6	0	14	2	52	2.74	+15	.261	.298	—	0	0.2
1969	Bos A	8	3	.727	71	0	0	0	0	17	9	49	102.2	91	33	8	1	48	4	93	2.54	+50	.240	.323	—	0	2.0
1970	Bos A	1	7	.125	63	0	0	0	0	20	10	43	67.1	62	37	5	1	34	5	51	3.88	+3	.244	.334	—	0	-0.3
1971	Bos A	6	4	.600	50	0	0	0	0	16	4	36	52.1	41	16	5	0	23	2	37	2.75	+35	.228	.311	—	0	1.5
1972	NY A	9	5	.643	59	0	0	0	0	**35**	7	50	107.2	84	25	3	0	29	7	75	1.92	+56	.216	.268	—	0	3.1
1973	NY A★	5	9	.357	51	0	0	0	0	27	6	39	82.1	66	30	4	0	18	2	63	2.51	+48	.216	.258	—	0	2.0
1974	NY A	9	3	.750	66	0	0	0	0	15	7	49	114	93	30	6	1	43	7	89	1.66	+114	.226	.297	—	0	2.9
1975	NY A	5	7	.417	49	0	0	0	0	6	6	32	89.1	94	34	1	2	36	5	65	3.12	+19	.275	.345	—	0	0.9
1976	†NY A☆	7	8	.467	64	0	0	0	0	**23**	8	51	103.2	82	33	5	0	42	7	61	2.26	+51	.225	.302	—	0	2.3
1977	†NY A★	13	5	.722	**72**	0	0	0	0	26	8	54	137	131	41	7	2	33	6	68	2.17	+83	.257	.302	—	0	4.3
1978	†NY A	9	3	.750	59	0	0	0	0	9	2	42	111.2	116	46	6	4	33	8	33	3.47	+5	.278	.332	—	0	0.5
1979	Tex A	5	8	.385	67	0	0	0	0	13	7	49	95	78	37	9	0	28	6	48	3.13	+33	.226	.283	—	0	1.6
1980	Tex A	3	2	.600	49	0	0	0	0	8	4	26	80.2	97	47	9	0	28	6	43	4.69	-17	.306	.359	—	0	-0.5
1980	Phi N	0	0	+	10	0	0	0	0	2	1	8	14	11	5	0	0	6	1	6	1.93	+98	.220	.293	—	0	0.1
1980	Major	3	2	.600	59	0	0	0	0	10	5	34	94	108	52	9	0	34	7	49	4.28	+0	.294	.350	—	0	-0.4
1981	†Phi N	9	6	.600	48	0	0	0	0	2	2	34	75	85	40	4	1	33	9	29	4.44	-18	.301	.372	—	0	-1.0
1982	Phi N	3	3	.500	34	0	0	0	0	2	5	18	36.2	50	23	3	0	12	3	12	5.15	-28	.327	.373	—	0	-0.8
1982	Chi A	0	0	+	11	0	0	0	0	1	0	8	12	11	4	0	0	7	0	6	3.00	+36	.262	.360	—	0	0.1
1982	Major	3	3	.500	45	0	0	0	0	3	5	26	48	61	27	3	0	19	3	18	4.62	-12	.313	.370	—	0	-0.7
Total	16	99	76	.566	899	0	0	0	0	238	95	648	1390.1	1292	519	84	14	481	81	873	2.88	+28	.251	.313	—	0	19.4
Team	7	57	40	.588	420	0	0	0	0	141	44	317	745.2	666	239	32	9	234	42	454	2.41	+48	.243	.302	—	—	16.0
/60G	1	8	6	.588	60	0	0	0	0	20	6	45	106.2	95	34	5	1	33	6	65	2.41	+48	.243	.302	—	—	2.3
Lyons, Al Albert Harold B7.18.1918 St.Joseph MO D12.20.1965 Inglewood CA BR/TR/6'2"/195 d4.19 Mil 1944–45																											
1944	NY A	0	0	+	11	0	0	0	—	0	—	—	39.2	43	22	2	2	24	—	14	4.54	-23	.291	.397	—	0	0.0
1946	NY A	0	1	.000	2	1	0	0	—	0	—	—	8.1	11	5	0	1	6	—	4	5.40	-36	.314	.429	-1	0	-0.2
1947	NY A	1	0	1.000	6	0	0	0	—	0	—	—	11	18	11	2	0	9	—	7	9.00	-61	.367	.466	—	0	-0.3
1947	Pit N	1	2	.333	13	0	0	0	—	0	—	—	28.1	36	24	4	1	12	—	16	7.31	-42	.300	.368	—	0	-0.6
1947	Major	2	2	.500	19	0	0	0	—	0	—	—	39	54	35	6	1	21	—	23	7.78	-47	.320	.398	—	0	-0.9
1948	Bos N	1	0	1.000	7	0	0	0	—	0	—	—	12.2	17	11	1	0	8	—	5	7.82	-51	.309	.397	—	0	-0.3
Total	4	3	3	.500	39	1	0	0	—	0	—	—	100	125	73	9	4	59	—	46	6.30	-41	.307	.400	-1	0	-1.4
Team	3	1	1	.500	19	1	0	0	—	0	—	—	59	72	38	4	3	39	—	25	5.49	-36	.310	.416	-1	—	-0.5
Maas, Duke Duane Fredrick B1.31.1929 Utica MI D12.7.1976 Mt.Clemens MI BR/TR/5'10"/(165–176) d4.21																											
1955	Det A	5	6	.455	18	16	5	2	—	0	—	—	86.2	91	52	7	2	50	3	42	4.88	-21	.271	.366	+17	0	-1.1
1956	Det A	0	7	.000	26	7	0	0	—	0	—	—	63.1	81	51	9	6	32	3	34	6.54	-37	.313	.398	-14	0	-1.6
1957	Det A	10	14	.417	45	26	8	2	18	6	0	15	219.1	210	92	23	4	65	7	116	3.28	+18	.252	.307	-15	0	0.9
1958	KC A	4	5	.444	10	7	3	1	5	1	1	2	55.1	49	25	3	1	13	0	19	3.90	+0	.241	.290	-38	0	0.2
1958	†NY A	7	3	.700	22	13	2	1	15	0	0	19	101.1	93	51	9	2	36	0	50	3.82	-8	.242	.308	+45	0	-0.6
1958	Year	11	8	.579	32	20	5	2	20	1	1	21	156.2	142	76	12	3	49	0	69	3.85	-5	.242	.302	+14	0	-0.4
1959	NY A	14	8	.636	38	21	3	1	15	4	0	19	138	149	82	14	2	53	1	67	4.43	-18	.278	.342	+14	0	-2.2
1960	†NY A	5	1	.833	35	1	0	0	0	4	1	24	70.1	70	44	6	1	35	2	28	4.09	-13	.265	.346	-75	0	-0.7
1961	NY A	0	0	+	1	0	0	0	0	0	0	0	0.1	2	2	0	0	0	0	0	54.00	-93	1.000	1.000	—	0	-0.1
Total	7	45	44	.506	195	91	21	7	53	15	2	79	734.2	745	399	71	18	284	16	356	4.19	-10	.264	.333	+3	0	-5.2
Team	4	26	12	.684	96	35	5	2	30	8	1	62	310	314	179	29	5	124	3	145	4.21	-15	.265	.333	+23	—	-3.6
/180I	2	15	7	.684	56	20	3	1	17	5	1	36	180	182	104	17	3	72	2	84	4.21	-15	.265	.333	+23	—	-2.1
MacDonald, Rob Robert Joseph B4.27.1965 East Orange NJ BL/TL/6'3"/(200–208) Dr 1987 TorA 19/491 d8.14 Col Rutgers																											
1995	NY A	1	1	.500	33	0	0	0	0	0	1	20	46.1	50	25	7	1	22	0	41	4.86	-5	.282	.365	—	0	0.0
Total	6	8	9	.471	197	0	0	0	0	3	8	133	234.1	234	120	26	3	107	12	142	4.34	-1	.264	.342	—	0	0.2
MacFayden, Danny Daniel Knowles "Deacon Danny" B6.10.1905 N.Truro MA D8.26.1972 Brunswick ME BR/TR/5'11"/170 d8.25																											
1932	NY A	7	5	.583	17	15	9	0	—	1	—	—	121.1	137	69	11	2	37	—	33	3.93	+4	.281	.334	+38	—	-0.4
1933	NY A	3	2	.600	25	6	2	0	—	0	—	—	90.1	120	62	8	2	37	—	28	5.88	-34	.319	.383	+31	—	-1.3
1934	NY A	4	3	.571	22	11	4	0	—	0	—	—	96	110	57	5	2	31	—	41	4.50	-10	.288	.345	+48	—	-0.6
Total	17	132	159	.454	465	333	158	18	—	9	—	—	2706	2981	1394	112	64	872	—	797	3.96	+1	.281	.340	-10	0	-0.4
Team	3	14	10	.583	64	32	15	0	—	1	—	—	307.2	367	188	24	6	105	—	102	4.68	-14	.295	.353	+40	—	-2.3
/180I	2	8	6	.583	37	19	9	0	—	1	—	—	180	215	110	14	4	61	—	60	4.68	-14	.295	.353	+40	—	-1.3
Madison, Dave David Pledger B2.1.1921 Brooksville MS D12.8.1985 Macon MS BR/TR/6'3"/(188–190) d9.26 Mil 1951 Col Louisiana St.																											
1950	NY A	0	0	+	1	0	0	0	—	0	—	—	3	3	2	1	0	1	—	1	6.00	-28	.273	.333	—	0	0.0
Total	3	8	7	.533	74	6	0	0	—	0	—	—	158	173	117	16	8	103	—	70	5.70	-30	.282	.392	+7	0	-3.2
Maglie, Sal Salvatore Anthony "The Barber" B4.26.1917 Niagara Falls NY D12.28.1992 Niagara Falls NY BR/TR/6'2"/(180–190) d8.9 C6 Col Niagara																											
1957	NY A	2	0	1.000	6	3	1	1	5	3	0	5	26	22	6	1	1	7	0	9	1.73	+107	.227	.283	+0	0	0.6
1958	NY A	1	1	.500	7	3	0	0	5	0	0	5	23.1	27	12	3	0	9	2	7	4.63	-24	.300	.364	-7	0	-0.1
Total	10	119	62	.657	303	232	93	25	24	14	0	12	1723	1591	684	169	44	562	8	862	3.15	+27	.245	.309	+4	0	13.8
Team	2	3	1	.750	13	6	1	1	10	3	0	10	49.1	49	18	4	1	16	2	16	3.10	+15	.262	.322	-3	—	0.5
Magnuson, Jim James Robert B8.18.1946 Marinette WI D5.30.1991 Green Bay WI BR/TL/6'2"/190 Dr 1966 ChiA 3/58 d6.28 Col Wisconsin–Oshkosh																											
1973	NY A	0	1	.000	8	0	0	0	0	0	0	5	27.1	38	17	2	0	9	1	9	4.28	-13	.342	.382	—	0	-0.1
Total	3	2	7	.222	36	10	0	0	3	0	0	17	102	113	63	9	3	41	2	40	4.59	-18	.286	.354	-12	0	-1.1
Makosky, Frank Frank B1.20.1910 Boonton NJ D1.10.1987 Stroudsburg PA BR/TR/6'1"/185 d4.30																											
1937	NY A	5	2	.714	26	1	1	0	—	3	—	—	58	64	42	6	0	24	—	27	4.97	-10	.277	.345	-41	—	-0.4
Malone, Pat Perce Leigh B9.25.1902 Altoona PA D5.13.1943 Altoona PA BL/TR (BB 1935–37)/6'0"/200 d4.12 Col Juniata																											
1935	NY A	3	5	.375	29	2	0	0	—	3	—	—	56.1	53	45	7	1	33	—	25	5.43	-25	.252	.357	+93	—	-1.7
1936	†NY A	12	4	.750	35	9	5	0	—	**9**	—	—	134.2	144	60	4	4	60	—	72	3.81	+22	.273	.352	+60	—	1.6
1937	NY A	4	4	.500	28	9	3	0	—	6	—	—	92	109	65	5	4	35	—	49	5.48	-19	.291	.357	+46	—	-1.4
Total	10	134	92	.593	357	219	115	15	—	26	—	—	1915	1934	936	103	45	705	—	1024	3.74	+11	.262	.330	+15	—	7.4
Team	3	19	13	.594	92	20	8	0	—	18	—	—	283	306	170	16	9	128	—	146	4.67	-4	.275	.354	+57	—	-1.5
/180I	2	12	8	.594	59	13	5	0	—	11	—	—	180	195	108	10	6	81	—	93	4.67	-4	.275	.354	+57	—	-1.0
Mamaux, Al Albert Leon B5.30.1894 Pittsburgh PA D12.31.1962 Santa Monica CA BR/TR/6'0.5"/168 d9.23 Mil 1918 Col Duquesne																											
1924	NY A	1	1	.500	14	2	0	0	—	0	—	—	38	44	28	2	1	20	—	12	5.68	-27	.308	.396	+123	—	-0.5
Total	12	76	67	.531	254	137	78	15	—	10	—	—	1293	1138	541	22	35	511	—	625	2.90	+4	.245	.325	+0	—	1.4
Manning, Rube Walter S. B4.29.1883 Chambersburg PA D4.23.1930 Williamsport PA BR/TR/6'0"/180 d9.25																											
1907	NY A	0	1	.000	1	1	1	0	—	0	—	—	9	8	3	0	1	3	—	3	3.00	-7	.242	.324	-76	—	0.0
1908	NY A	13	16	.448	41	26	19	2	—	1	—	—	245	228	114	4	18	86	—	113	2.94	-16	.256	.334	-23	—	-1.3

YEAR	TM LG	W	L	PCT	G	GS	CG	SHO	QS	SV	BS	QR	IP	H	R	HR	HB	BB	IB	SO	ERA	AERA	OAV	OOB	SUP	DL	PW
1909	NY A	7	11	.389	26	21	11	2	—	1	—	—	173	167	76	2	9	48	—	71	3.17	-20	.265	.326	+2	—	-0.8
1910	NY A	2	4	.333	16	9	4	0	—	0	—	—	75	80	43	4	4	25	—	25	3.72	-29	.283	.349	+23	—	-0.7
Total	4	22	32	.407	84	57	35	4	—	2	—	—	502	483	236	10	32	162	—	212	3.14	-19	.263	.333	-7	—	-2.8
/180I	1	8	11	.407	30	20	13	1	0	1	0	0	180	173	85	4	11	58	—	76	3.14	-19	.263	.333	-7	—	-1.0
Manzanillo, Josias Josias (Adams) B10.16.1967 San Pedro de Macoris, D.R. BR/TR/6'0"/(190–205) d10.5 b–Ravelo																											
1995	NY A	0	0	+	11	0	0	0	0	0	0	8	17.1	19	4	1	2	9	2	11	2.08	+123	.279	.380	—	88	0.3
Total	11	13	15	.464	267	1	0	0	0	6	17	176	342	330	198	46	18	153	20	300	4.71	-7	.255	.338	-15	240	-3.7
Markle, Cliff Clifford Monroe B5.3.1894 Dravosburg PA D5.24.1974 Temple City CA BR/TR/5'9"/165 d9.18																											
1915	NY A	2	0	1.000	3	2	2	0	—	0	—	—	23	15	3	1	0	6	—	12	0.39	+650	.185	.241	+24	—	0.5
1916	NY A	4	3	.571	11	7	3	1	—	0	—	—	45.2	41	26	0	4	31	—	14	4.53	-36	.256	.390	+38	—	-1.2
1921	Cin N	2	6	.250	10	6	5	0	—	0	—	—	67	75	36	0	0	20	—	23	3.76	-5	.291	.342	-31	—	-0.4
1922	Cin N	4	5	.444	25	3	2	1	—	0	—	—	75.2	75	41	3	0	33	—	34	3.81	+5	.268	.345	-5	—	0.1
1924	NY A	0	3	.000	7	3	0	0	—	0	—	—	23.1	29	26	5	0	20	—	7	8.87	-53	.333	.458	-5	—	-1.4
Total	5	12	17	.414	56	21	12	2	—	0	—	—	234.2	235	132	9	4	110	—	90	4.10	-13	.271	.356	-1	—	-2.4
Team	3	6	6	.500	21	12	5	1	—	0	—	—	92	85	55	6	4	57	—	33	4.60	-30	.259	.375	+25	—	-2.1
Marquis, Jim James Milburn B11.18.1900 Yoakum TX D8.5.1992 Jackson CA BR/TR/5'11"/174 d8.8																											
1925	NY A	0	0	+	2	0	0	0	—	0	—	—	7.1	12	8	1	0	6	—	0	9.82	-57	.414	.514	—	—	-0.2
Marshall, Cuddles Clarence Westly B4.28.1925 Bellingham WA BR/TR/6'3"/200 d4.24 Col Western Washington																											
1946	NY A	3	4	.429	23	11	1	0	—	0	—	—	81	96	49	4	0	56	—	32	5.33	-35	.308	.413	+38	0	-1.2
1948	NY A	0	0	+	1	0	0	0	—	0	—	—	1	0	0	0	0	3	—	0	0.00	-100	.000	.500	—	0	0.0
1949	NY A	3	0	1.000	21	2	0	0	—	3	—	—	49.1	48	31	3	2	48	—	13	5.11	-21	.259	.417	+0	0	-0.4
1950	StL A	1	3	.250	28	2	0	0	—	1	—	—	53.2	72	52	1	1	51	—	24	7.88	-37	.321	.449	+18	0	-1.0
Total	4	7	7	.500	73	15	1	0	—	4	—	—	185	216	132	8	3	158	—	69	5.98	-33	.298	.426	+21	0	-2.6
Team	3	6	4	.600	45	13	1	0	—	3	—	—	131.1	144	80	7	2	107	—	45	5.21	-29	.290	.415	+32	—	-1.6
/60G	4	8	5	.600	60	17	1	0	—	4	—	—	175	192	107	9	3	143	—	60	5.21	-29	.290	.415	+32	—	-2.1
Marsonek, Sam Samuel R. B7.10.1978 Tampa FL BR/TR/6'6"/225 Dr 1996 TexA 1/24 d7.11																											
2004	NY A	0	0	+	1	0	0	0	0	0	0	1	1.1	2	0	0	0	0	0	0	0.00	-100	.333	.333	—	81	0.0
Martinez, Tippy Felix Anthony B5.31.1950 LaJunta CO BL/TL/5'10"/(170–180) d8.9 Col Colorado St. [DL 1987 Bal A 59]																											
1974	NY A	0	0	+	10	0	0	0	0	0	0	7	12.2	14	7	0	1	9	2	10	4.26	-17	.286	.400	—	0	-0.1
1975	NY A	1	2	.333	23	2	0	0	1	8	0	14	37	27	15	2	1	32	3	20	2.68	+39	.208	.364	-64	0	0.4
1976	NY A	2	0	1.000	11	0	0	0	0	2	0	9	28	18	6	1	0	14	0	14	1.93	+77	.191	.296	—	0	0.5
Total	14	55	42	.567	546	2	0	0	11	15	40	379	834	732	357	53	8	425	57	632	3.45	+12	.242	.333	-64	219	7.9
Team	3	3	2	.600	44	2	0	0	1	10	0	30	77.2	59	28	3	2	55	5	44	2.67	+34	.216	.348	-64	—	0.8
/60G	4	4	3	.600	60	3	0	0	1	14	0	41	106	80	38	4	3	75	7	60	2.66	+34	.216	.348	-64	—	1.1
May, Darrell Darrell Kevin B6.13.1972 San Bernardino CA BL/TL/6'2"/(170–185) Dr 1992 AtlN 46/1293 d9.10 Col Sacramento (CA) City																											
2005	NY A	0	1	.000	2	1	0	0	0	0	0	0	7	14	13	4	0	3	0	3	16.71	-74	.400	.447	+51	0	-0.9
Total	7	26	43	.377	161	97	7	3	38	0	3	39	660.2	746	411	123	6	212	11	414	5.16	-9	.283	.334	-6	47	-3.9
May, Rudy Rudolph B7.18.1944 Coffeyville KS BL/TL/6'3"/(195–205) d4.18 Mer 1970 [DL 1984 NY A 182]																											
1965	Cal A	4	9	.308	30	19	2	1	12	0	0	8	124	111	59	7	4	78	1	76	3.92	-13	.245	.359	-29	0	-0.4
1969	Cal A	10	13	.435	43	25	4	0	13	2	0	14	180.1	142	81	20	3	66	5	133	3.44	+2	.220	.295	-24	0	-0.2
1970	Cal A	7	13	.350	38	34	2	2	18	0	0	3	208.2	190	102	20	3	81	7	164	4.01	-10	.245	.318	-29	0	-1.0
1971	Cal A	11	12	.478	32	31	7	2	21	0	1	0	208.1	160	74	12	2	87	6	156	3.02	+7	.213	.296	-23	23	0.9
1972	Cal A	12	11	.522	35	30	10	3	20	1	0	4	205.1	162	79	15	0	82	6	169	2.94	+0	.215	.292	-19	0	-0.4
1973	Cal A	7	17	.292	34	28	10	4	14	0	2	3	185	177	101	20	3	80	9	134	4.38	-18	.254	.330	+7	0	-1.8
1974	Cal A	0	1	.000	18	3	0	0	0	2	0	13	27	29	24	2	1	10	0	12	7.00	-50	.274	.331	+35	0	-0.5
1974	NY A	8	4	.667	17	15	8	2	10	0	0	1	114.1	75	36	5	4	48	0	90	2.28	+55	.188	.280	+29	21	1.5
1974	Year	8	5	.615	35	18	8	2	10	2	0	14	141.1	104	60	7	5	58	0	102	3.18	+11	.206	.290	+30	0	1.0
1975	NY A	14	12	.538	32	31	13	1	18	0	0	1	212	179	87	9	2	99	2	145	3.06	+21	.231	.317	+7	0	1.5
1976	NY A	4	3	.571	11	11	2	1	5	0	0	0	68	49	32	5	1	28	2	38	3.57	-4	.206	.291	+40	0	-0.2
1976	Bal A	11	7	.611	24	21	5	1	14	0	1	2	152.1	156	73	11	0	42	3	71	3.78	-13	.267	.314	+23	0	-1.1
1976	Year	15	10	.600	35	32	7	2	19	0	1	2	220.1	205	105	16	1	70	5	109	3.72	-10	.249	.307	+29	0	-1.3
1977	Bal A	18	14	.563	37	37	11	4	24	0	0	0	251.2	243	114	25	5	78	2	105	3.61	+6	.255	.313	+5	0	0.4
1978	Mon N	8	10	.444	27	23	4	1	11	0	0	3	144	141	73	15	6	42	1	87	3.88	-8	.255	.313	+25	43	-0.8
1979	Mon N	10	3	.769	33	7	2	1	3	0	1	22	93.2	88	30	4	4	31	4	67	2.31	+61	.255	.320	-12	0	1.8
1980	†NY A	15	5	.750	41	17	3	1	13	3	2	19	175.1	144	56	14	0	39	2	133	**2.46**	+61	.224	**.268**	-6	13	3.2
1981	†NY A	6	11	.353	27	22	4	0	13	1	0	4	147.2	137	71	10	2	41	0	79	4.14	-13	.246	.298	-5	0	-0.6
1982	NY A	6	6	.500	41	6	0	0	3	3	3	25	106	109	43	4	1	14	5	85	2.89	+40	.267	.289	-13	23	1.3
1983	NY A	1	5	.167	15	0	0	0	0	0	2	7	18.1	22	15	1	1	12	1	16	6.87	-43	.293	.398	—	76	-1.1
Total	16	152	156	.494	535	360	87	24	212	12	12	129	2622	2314	1150	199	42	958	56	1760	3.46	+3	.238	.308	-4	381	2.5
Team	7	54	46	.540	184	102	30	5	62	7	7	57	841.2	715	340	48	11	281	12	586	3.12	+20	.231	.295	+8	133	5.6
/180I	1	12	10	.540	39	22	6	1	13	1	1	12	180	153	73	10	2	60	3	125	3.12	+20	.231	.295	+8	28	1.2
Mays, Carl Carl William "Sub" B11.12.1891 Liberty KY D4.4.1971 El Cajon CA BL/TR/5'11.5"/195 d4.15																											
1915	Bos A	6	5	.545	38	6	2	0	—	**7**	—	—	131.2	119	54	0	5	21	—	65	2.60	+7	.244	.282	+18	—	0.4
1916	†Bos A	18	13	.581	44	24	14	2	—	3	—	—	245	208	79	3	9	74	—	76	2.39	+16	.234	.299	-3	—	2.8
1917	Bos A	22	9	.710	35	33	27	2	—	0	—	—	289	230	81	1	14	74	—	91	1.74	+48	.221	.282	+8	—	4.0
1918	†Bos A	21	13	.618	35	33	**30**	0	—	0	—	—	293.1	230	94	2	11	81	—	114	2.21	+21	.221	.284	+19	—	3.7
1919	Bos A	5	11	.313	21	16	14	2	—	2	—	—	146	131	57	2	5	40	—	53	2.47	+23	.247	.306	-22	—	0.6
1919	NY A	9	3	.750	13	13	12	1	—	0	—	—	120	96	34	3	5	37	—	54	1.65	+93	.216	.283	+28	—	2.3
1919	Year	14	14	.500	34	29	26	3	—	2	—	—	266	227	91	5	10	77	—	107	2.10	+48	.233	.295	+1	—	2.9
1920	NY A	26	11	.703	45	37	26	0	—	2	—	—	312	310	127	13	7	84	—	92	3.06	+25	.263	.316	+33	—	3.5
1921	†NY A	**27**	9	**.750**	**49**	38	30	1	—	**7**	—	—	**336.2**	332	145	11	9	76	—	70	3.05	+39	.257	.303	+52	—	5.4
1922	†NY A	13	14	.481	34	29	21	1	—	2	—	—	240	257	111	12	7	50	—	41	3.60	+11	.285	.327	+10	—	1.5
1923	NY A	5	2	.714	23	7	2	0	—	0	—	—	81.1	119	59	8	4	32	—	16	6.20	-36	.357	.420	+38	—	-1.2
1924	Cin N	20	9	.690	37	27	15	2	—	0	—	—	226	238	97	3	4	36	—	63	3.15	+20	.270	.302	+7	—	3.0
1925	Cin N	3	5	.375	12	5	3	0	—	2	—	—	51.2	60	22	0	2	13	—	10	3.31	+24	.294	.342	-34	—	0.9
1926	Cin N	19	12	.613	39	33	**24**	3	—	1	—	—	281	286	112	3	4	53	—	58	3.14	+18	.269	.306	+14	—	2.9
1927	Cin N	3	7	.300	14	9	6	0	—	0	—	—	82	89	39	1	1	10	—	17	3.51	+8	.276	.300	-48	—	1.0
1928	Cin N	4	1	.800	14	6	4	1	—	1	—	—	62.2	67	33	3	0	22	—	10	3.88	+2	.275	.335	+19	—	0.1
1929	NY N	7	2	.778	37	8	1	0	—	4	—	—	123	140	67	8	2	31	—	32	4.32	+6	.287	.333	+19	—	0.8
Total	15	208	126	.623	490	324	231	29	—	31	—	—	3021.1	2912	1211	73	89	734	—	862	2.92	+19	.257	.307	+17	—	31.7
Team	5	80	39	.672	164	124	91	3	—	11	—	—	1090	1114	476	47	32	279	—	273	3.25	+21	.268	.319	+33	—	11.5
/180I	1	13	6	.672	27	20	15	0	—	2	—	—	180	184	79	8	5	46	—	45	3.25	+21	.268	.319	+33	—	1.9
McCall, Larry Larry Stephen B9.8.1952 Asheville NC BL/TR/6'2"/182 d9.10 C1																											
1977	NY A	0	1	.000	2	0	0	0	0	0	0	0	6	12	7	1	0	1	0	0	7.50	-47	.375	.394	—	0	-0.4
1978	NY A	1	1	.500	5	1	0	0	0	0	0	2	16	20	10	2	1	6	0	7	5.63	-35	.323	.391	-51	0	-0.3
1979	Tex A	1	0	1.000	2	1	0	0	1	0	0	0	8.1	7	2	0	0	3	0	3	2.16	+92	.226	.286	-13	0	0.2
Total	3	2	2	.500	9	2	0	0	1	0	0	2	30.1	39	19	3	1	10	0	10	5.04	-24	.312	.365	-30	0	-0.5
Team	2	1	2	.333	7	1	0	0	0	0	0	2	22	32	17	3	1	7	0	7	6.14	-39	.340	.392	-51	—	-0.7

Pitchers

YEAR	TM LG	W	L	PCT	G	GS	CG	SHO	QS	SV	BS	QR	IP	H	R	HR	HB	BB	IB	SO	ERA	AERA	OAV	OOB	SUP	DL	PW
McConnell, George	George Neely "Slats" B9.16.1877 Shelbyville TN D5.10.1964 Chattanooga TN BR/TR/6'3"/190 d4.13 ▲																										
1909	NY A	0	1	.000	2	1	0	0	—	0	—	—	4	3	2	0	0	3	—	4	2.25	+12	.231	.375	-72	—	0.0
1912	NY A	8	12	.400	23	20	19	0	—	0	—	—	176.2	172	96	3	4	52	—	91	2.75	+31	.269	.328	-35	—	1.6
1913	NY A	4	15	.211	35	20	8	0	—	3	—	—	180	162	90	2	7	60	—	72	3.20	-6	.247	.317	-17	—	-0.4
1914	Chi N	0	1	.000	1	1	0	0	—	0	—	—	7	3	1	0	0	3	—	3	1.29	+116	.125	.222	-100	—	0.2
1915	Chi F	**25**	10	**.714**	44	35	23	4	—	1	—	—	303	262	103	8	8	89	—	151	2.20	+14	.232	.292	+24	—	1.7
1916	Chi N	4	12	.250	28	21	8	1	—	0	—	—	171.1	137	66	8	5	35	—	82	2.57	+13	.223	.271	-35	—	0.4
Total	6	41	51	.446	133	98	58	5	—	4	—	—	842	739	358	21	24	242	—	403	2.60	+12	.240	.301	-14	—	3.5
Team	3	12	28	.300	60	41	27	0	—	3	—	—	360.2	337	188	5	11	115	—	167	2.97	+10	.258	.323	-27	—	1.2
/180I	1	6	14	.300	30	20	13	0	—	1	—	—	180	168	94	2	5	57	—	83	2.97	+10	.258	.323	-27	—	0.6
McCormick, Mike	Michael Francis B9.29.1938 Pasadena CA BL/TL/6'2"/(185–200) d9.3																										
1970	NY A	2	0	1.000	9	4	0	0	0	0	0	4	20.2	26	15	2	0	13	1	12	6.10	-41	.295	.386	+25	0	-0.5
Total	16	134	128	.511	484	333	91	23	224	12	10	123	2380.1	2281	1100	256	24	795	10	1321	3.73	-5	.251	.312	+7	0	-1.6
McCullers, Lance	Lance Graye B3.8.1964 Tampa FL BB/TR/6'1"/(185–218) Dr 1982 PhiN 2/41 d8.12																										
1989	NY A	4	3	.571	52	1	0	0	0	3	3	31	84.2	83	46	9	3	37	4	82	4.57	-15	.255	.332	-53	0	-0.5
1990	NY A	1	0	1.000	11	0	0	0	0	0	1	7	15	14	8	2	0	6	2	11	3.60	+11	.241	.308	—	15	0.0
Total	7	28	31	.475	306	9	0	0	4	39	27	209	526.1	427	219	47	10	252	42	442	3.25	+15	.223	.315	-12	92	3.2
Team	2	5	3	.625	63	1	0	0	0	3	4	38	99.2	97	54	11	3	43	6	93	4.42	-12	.253	.329	-53	15	-0.5
/60G	2	5	3	.625	60	1	0	0	0	3	4	36	95	92	51	10	3	41	6	89	4.42	-12	.253	.329	-53	14	-0.5
McDaniel, Lindy	Lyndall Dale B12.13.1935 Hollis OK BR/TR/6'3"/(182–196) d9.2 b–Von Col Oklahoma																										
1968	NY A	4	1	.800	24	0	0	0	0	10	3	20	51.1	30	10	5	1	12	3	43	1.75	+66	.166	.221	—	0	1.1
1969	NY A	5	6	.455	51	0	0	0	0	5	4	35	83.2	84	37	4	0	23	6	60	3.55	-1	.261	.305	—	0	0.0
1970	NY A	9	5	.643	62	0	0	0	0	29	6	54	111.2	88	29	7	0	23	5	81	2.01	+77	.217	.258	—	0	**3.5**
1971	NY A	5	10	.333	44	0	0	0	0	4	7	25	69.2	82	41	12	0	24	6	39	5.04	-35	.296	.350	—	0	-2.6
1972	NY A	3	1	.750	37	0	0	0	0	0	0	26	68	54	23	4	0	25	5	47	2.25	+33	.217	.287	—	0	0.5
1973	NY A	12	6	.667	47	3	1	0	2	10	4	33	160.1	148	54	11	1	49	9	93	2.86	+30	.250	.304	-52	0	2.3
Total	21	141	119	.542	987	74	18	2	82	172	73	716	2139.1	2099	934	172	15	623	13	1361	3.45	+9	.258	.309	+7	29	13.0
Team	6	38	29	.567	265	3	1	0	2	58	24	193	544.2	486	194	43	2	156	34	363	2.89	+19	.240	.292	-52	—	4.8
/60G	1	9	7	.567	60	1	0	0	0	13	5	44	123.1	110	44	10	0	35	8	82	2.89	+19	.240	.292	-52	—	1.1
McDermott, Mickey	Maurice Joseph "Maury" B8.29.1929 Poughkeepsie NY D8.7.2003 Phoenix AZ BL/TL/6'2"/(170–190) d4.24 C1 ▲																										
1956	†NY A	2	6	.250	23	9	1	0	—	0	—	—	87	85	46	10	0	47	2	38	4.24	-9	.261	.350	-8	0	-0.1
Total	12	69	69	.500	291	156	54	11	0	14	3	33	1316.2	1161	655	86	28	838	8	757	3.91	+5	.240	.354	+2	0	8.4
McDevitt, Danny	Daniel Eugene B11.18.1932 New York NY BL/TL/5'10"/(164–175) d6.17 Col St. Bonaventure																										
1961	NY A	1	2	.333	8	2	0	0	0	1	0	5	13	18	11	2	1	8	0	8	7.62	-51	.353	.443	-17	0	-1.0
Total	6	21	27	.438	155	60	13	4	40	7	5	78	456	461	266	42	32	264	12	303	4.40	-6	.265	.370	-3	0	-3.1
McDonald, Jim	Jimmie Le Roy "Hot Rod" B5.17.1927 Grants Pass OR BR/TR (BB 1950–51)/5'10.5"/(185–192) d7.27																										
1950	Bos A	1	0	1.000	9	0	0	0	—	0	—	—	19	23	9	1	1	10	—	5	3.79	+29	.329	.420	—	0	0.2
1951	StL A	4	7	.364	16	11	5	0	—	1	—	—	84	84	48	5	2	46	—	28	4.07	+8	.260	.356	-19	0	0.1
1952	NY A	3	4	.429	26	5	1	0	—	0	—	—	69.1	71	31	1	2	40	—	20	3.50	-5	.268	.368	+31	0	0.4
1953	†NY A	9	7	.563	27	18	6	2	—	0	—	—	129.2	128	64	4	1	39	—	43	3.82	-3	.260	.316	+22	0	-0.5
1954	NY A	4	1	.800	16	10	3	1	—	0	—	—	71	54	28	3	1	45	—	20	3.17	+8	.213	.332	+59	60	0.4
1955	Bal A	3	5	.375	21	8	0	0	—	0	—	—	51.2	76	48	5	0	30	1	20	7.14	-47	.345	.421	-16	0	-2.5
1956	Chi A	0	2	.000	8	3	0	0	—	0	—	—	18.2	29	18	2	1	7	0	10	8.68	-53	.377	.425	-64	0	-0.8
1957	Chi A	0	1	.000	10	0	0	0	0	0	0	8	22.1	18	8	2	0	10	1	12	2.01	+85	.234	.315	—	0	0.2
1958	Chi A	0	0	+	3	0	0	0	0	0	0	8	2.1	6	8	1	0	4	0	0	19.29	-81	.429	.556	—	0	-0.3
Total	9	24	27	.471	136	55	15	3	0	1	0	16	468	489	262	24	8	231	2	158	4.27	-11	.273	.357	+9	60	-2.8
Team	3	16	12	.571	69	33	10	3	—	0	—	—	270	253	123	8	4	124	—	83	3.57	-1	.250	.334	+35	60	0.3
/180I	2	11	8	.571	46	22	7	2	—	0	—	—	180	169	82	5	3	83	—	55	3.57	-1	.250	.334	+35	40	0.2
McDowell, Jack	Jack Burns B1.16.1966 Van Nuys CA BR/TR/6'5"/(179–190) Dr 1987 ChiA 1/5 d9.15 Col Stanford																										
1995	†NY A	15	10	.600	30	30	**8**	2	21	0	0	0	217.2	211	106	25	5	78	1	157	3.93	+18	.254	.320	-1	0	1.4
Total	12	127	87	.593	277	275	62	13	175	0	0	2	1889	1854	874	173	48	606	29	1311	3.85	+11	.257	.317	+1	365	10.2
/180I	1	12	8	.600	25	25	7	2	17	0	—	0	180	174	88	21	4	65	1	130	3.93	+18	.254	.320	-1	—	1.2
McDowell, Sam	Samuel Edward Thomas "Sudden Sam" B9.21.1942 Pittsburgh PA BL/TL/6'5"/(190–220) d9.15																										
1973	NY A	5	8	.385	16	15	2	1	9	0	0	1	95.2	73	47	4	0	64	2	75	3.95	-6	.212	.332	-18	0	-0.2
1974	NY A	1	6	.143	13	7	0	0	2	0	0	3	48	42	27	6	0	41	2	33	4.69	-24	.236	.379	-36	68	-0.8
Total	15	141	134	.513	425	346	103	23	217	14	3	57	2492.1	1948	999	164	59	1312	74	2453	3.17	+13	.215	.317	-9	89	9.9
Team	2	6	14	.300	29	22	2	1	11	0	0	4	143.2	115	74	10	0	105	4	108	4.20	-13	.220	.348	-24	68	-1.0
/180I	3	8	18	.300	36	28	3	1	14	0	0	5	180	144	93	13	0	132	5	135	4.20	-13	.220	.348	-24	85	-1.3
McEvoy, Lou	Louis Anthony B5.30.1902 Williamsburg KS D12.17.1953 Webster Groves MO BR/TR/6'2.5"/203 d4.28																										
1930	NY A	1	3	.250	28	1	0	0	—	3	—	—	52.1	64	51	4	2	29	—	14	6.71	-36	.288	.375	-80	—	-1.4
1931	NY A	0	0	+	6	0	0	0	—	1	—	—	12.1	19	17	1	1	12	—	3	12.41	-68	.358	.485	—	—	-0.6
Total	2	1	3	.250	34	1	0	0	—	4	—	—	64.2	83	68	5	3	41	—	17	7.79	-46	.302	.398	-80	—	-2.0
McGaffigan, Andy	Andrew Joseph B10.25.1956 W.Palm Beach FL BR/TR/6'3"/(190–200) Dr 1978 NYA 6/156 d9.22 Col Florida Southern																										
1981	NY A	0	0	+	2	0	0	0	0	0	0	2	7	5	3	1	0	3	0	2	2.57	+41	.200	.267	—	0	0.0
Total	11	38	33	.535	363	62	3	1	28	24	12	224	833.1	773	351	55	16	294	38	610	3.38	+11	.247	.312	-2	32	2.1
McGlothen, Lynn	Lynn Everatt B3.27.1950 Monroe LA D8.14.1984 Dubach LA BL/TR/6'2"/(182–215) Dr 1968 BosA 3/60 d6.25																										
1982	NY A	0	0	+	4	0	0	0	0	0	0	2	5	9	6	1	0	2	0	2	10.80	-63	.375	.423	—	21	-0.2
Total	11	86	93	.480	318	201	41	13	112	2	6	71	1497.2	1553	735	127	25	572	63	939	3.98	-5	.270	.336	-7	42	-3.0
McGraw, Bob	Robert Emmett B4.10.1895 LaVeta CO D6.2.1978 Boise ID BR/TR/6'2"/160 d9.25 Mil 1918–19 Col Georgetown																										
1917	NY A	0	1	.000	2	2	1	0	—	0	—	—	11	9	5	0	0	3	—	3	0.82	+228	.257	.316	-33	—	0.0
1918	NY A	0	1	.000	1	1	0	0	—	0	—	—	0	0	4	0	0	4	—	0	(4)	-100	+	1.000	+7	—	-0.3
1919	NY A	1	0	1.000	6	0	0	0	—	0	—	—	16.1	11	6	1	1	10	—	3	3.31	-3	.216	.355	—	—	0.0
1920	NY A	0	0	+	15	0	0	0	—	0	—	—	27	24	18	1	1	20	—	11	4.67	-18	.240	.372	—	—	-0.3
Total	9	26	38	.406	168	47	17	1	—	6	—	—	579.1	675	393	31	11	265	—	164	5.00	-19	.303	.380	+1	—	-6.9
Team	4	1	2	.333	24	3	1	0	—	0	—	—	54.1	44	33	2	2	37	—	17	4.14	-18	.237	.369	-20	—	-0.6
McHale, Marty	Martin Joseph B10.30.1886 Stoneham MA D5.7.1979 Hempstead NY BR/TR/5'11.5"/174 d9.28 Col Maine																										
1910	Bos A	0	2	.000	2	2	1	0	—	0	—	—	13.2	15	8	0	1	6	—	14	4.61	-45	.259	.338	+5	—	-0.4
1911	Bos A	0	0	+	4	1	0	0	—	0	—	—	9.1	19	12	1	1	3	—	3	9.64	-66	.475	.523	+98	—	-0.3
1913	NY A	2	4	.333	7	6	4	1	—	0	—	—	48.2	49	21	1	1	10	—	11	2.96	+1	.268	.309	-46	—	-0.1
1914	NY A	6	16	.273	31	23	12	0	—	1	—	—	191	195	82	3	4	33	—	75	2.97	-7	.268	.303	-27	—	-0.6
1915	NY A	3	7	.300	13	11	6	0	—	0	—	—	78.1	86	45	1	0	19	—	25	4.25	-31	.277	.318	+2	—	-1.2
1916	Bos A	0	1	.000	2	1	0	0	—	0	—	—	6	7	7	0	1	4	—	1	3.00	-8	.280	.400	-100	—	-0.3
1916	Cle A	0	0	+	5	0	0	0	—	0	—	—	11.1	10	7	1	0	6	—	2	5.56	-46	.270	.372	—	—	-0.2
1916	Year	0	1	.000	7	1	0	0	—	0	—	—	17.1	17	14	1	1	10	—	3	4.67	-37	.274	.384	-100	—	-0.5

YEAR	TM LG	W	L	PCT	G	GS	CG	SHO	QS	SV	BS	QR	IP	H	R	HR	HB	BB	IB	SO	ERA	AERA	OAV	OOB	SUP	DL	PW
Total	6	11	30	.268	64	44	23	1	—	1	—	—	358.1	381	182	7	8	81	—	131	3.57	-20	.276	.320	-19	—	-3.1
Team	3	11	27	.289	51	40	22	1	—	1	—	—	318	330	148	5	5	62	—	111	3.28	-14	.270	.308	-22	—	-1.9
/180I	2	6	15	.289	29	23	12	1	—	1	—	—	180	187	84	3	3	35	—	63	3.28	-14	.270	.308	-22	—	-1.1

McQuaid, Herb Herbert George B3.29.1899 San Francisco CA D4.4.1966 Richmond CA BR/TR/6'2"/185 d6.22

YEAR	TM LG	W	L	PCT	G	GS	CG	SHO	QS	SV	BS	QR	IP	H	R	HR	HB	BB	IB	SO	ERA	AERA	OAV	OOB	SUP	DL	PW
1923	Cin N	1	0	1.000	12	1	0	0	—	0	—	—	34.1	31	11	0	3	10	—	9	2.36	+64	.238	.308	+6	—	0.2
1926	NY A	1	0	1.000	17	1	0	0	—	0	—	—	38.1	48	34	5	2	13	—	6	6.10	-37	.329	.391	-13	—	-0.6
Total	2	2	0	1.000	29	2	0	0	—	0	—	—	72.2	79	45	5	5	23	—	15	4.33	-11	.286	.352	-3	—	-0.4

Mecir, Jim James Jason B5.16.1970 Bayside NY BB/TR/6'1"/(195–230) Dr 1991 SeaA 3/84 d9.4 Col Eckerd

YEAR	TM LG	W	L	PCT	G	GS	CG	SHO	QS	SV	BS	QR	IP	H	R	HR	HB	BB	IB	SO	ERA	AERA	OAV	OOB	SUP	DL	PW
1996	NY A	1	1	.500	26	0	0	0	0	0	0	15	40.1	42	24	6	0	23	4	38	5.13	-3	.275	.361	—	0	0.0
1997	NY A	0	4	.000	25	0	0	0	0	0	1	14	33.2	36	23	5	2	10	1	25	5.88	-24	.279	.338	—	0	-0.5
Total	11	29	35	.453	474	0	0	0	0	12	34	344	527	482	240	41	23	225	28	450	3.77	+23	.244	.326	—	275	5.9
Team	2	1	5	.167	51	0	0	0	0	0	1	29	74	78	47	11	2	33	5	63	5.47	-14	.277	.351	—	—	-0.5
/60G	2	1	6	.167	60	0	0	0	0	0	1	34	87	92	55	13	2	39	6	74	5.48	-14	.277	.351	—	—	-0.6

Medich, Doc George Francis B12.9.1948 Aliquippa PA BR/TR/6'5"/(225–227) Dr 1970 NYA 30/700 d9.5 Col Pittsburgh

YEAR	TM LG	W	L	PCT	G	GS	CG	SHO	QS	SV	BS	QR	IP	H	R	HR	HB	BB	IB	SO	ERA	AERA	OAV	OOB	SUP	DL	PW
1972	NY A	0	0	+	1	1	0	0	0	0	0	0	0	2	2	0	0	2	0	0	(2)	-100	1.000	1.000	+107	0	-0.2
1973	NY A	14	9	.609	34	32	11	3	20	0	0	1	235	217	84	20	3	74	6	145	2.95	+26	.241	.299	+5	0	2.0
1974	NY A	19	15	.559	38	38	17	4	24	0	0	0	279.2	275	122	24	8	91	8	154	3.60	-2	.259	.321	+7	0	0.1
1975	NY A	16	16	.500	38	37	15	2	24	0	0	1	272.1	271	115	25	1	72	5	132	3.50	+6	.264	.309	+5	0	0.8
1976	Pit N	8	11	.421	29	26	3	0	15	0	0	3	179	193	80	10	2	48	9	86	3.52	+0	.281	.326	-18	0	-0.1
1977	Oak A	10	6	.625	26	25	1	0	10	0	0	1	147.2	155	89	19	3	49	3	74	4.69	-14	.265	.322	+18	0	-1.1
1977	Sea A	2	0	1.000	3	3	1	0	1	0	0	0	22.1	26	9	1	2	4	0	3	3.63	+14	.286	.327	+45	0	0.1
1977	Year	12	6	.667	29	28	2	0	11	0	0	1	170	181	98	20	5	53	3	77	4.55	-11	.268	.323	+20	0	-1.0
1977	NY N	0	1	.000	1	1	0	0	1	0	0	0	7	6	3	0	0	1	0	3	3.86	-2	.261	.280	-53	0	0.0
1977	Major	12	7	.632	30	29	2	0	12	0	0	1	176	187	101	20	5	54	3	80	4.53	-10	.268	.321	+18	0	-1.0
1978	Tex A	9	8	.529	28	22	6	2	12	2	0	5	171	166	78	10	3	52	2	71	3.74	+0	.255	.311	+2	0	0.2
1979	Tex A	10	7	.588	29	19	4	1	12	0	1	5	149	156	78	9	4	49	3	58	4.17	+0	.269	.328	+12	0	0.0
1980	Tex A	14	11	.560	34	32	6	0	17	0	0	2	204.1	230	104	13	3	56	1	91	3.92	-1	.285	.333	+20	0	-0.2
1981	Tex A	10	6	.625	20	20	4	0	11	0	0	0	143.1	136	51	8	2	33	5	65	3.08	+13	.252	.296	+19	0	0.9
1982	Tex A	7	11	.389	21	21	2	0	10	0	0	0	122.2	146	73	8	3	61	5	37	5.06	-23	.307	.383	-17	0	-2.0
1982	†Mil A	5	4	.556	10	10	1	0	6	0	0	0	63	57	37	4	1	32	1	36	5.00	-23	.242	.332	+7	0	-1.0
1982	Year	12	15	.444	31	31	3	0	16	0	0	0	185.2	203	110	12	4	93	6	73	5.04	-23	.286	.366	-10	0	-3.0
Total	11	124	105	.541	312	287	71	16	163	2	1	18	1996.1	2036	925	151	35	624	48	955	3.78	-1	.266	.321	+6	0	-0.5
Team	4	49	40	.551	111	108	43	9	68	0	0	2	787	765	323	69	12	239	19	431	3.40	+8	.256	.311	+7	—	2.7
/180I	1	11	9	.551	25	25	10	2	16	0	0	0	180	175	74	16	3	55	4	99	3.40	+8	.256	.311	+7	—	0.6

Mendoza, Ramiro Ramiro B6.15.1972 Los Santos, Pan BR/TR/6'2"/(154–195) d5.25

YEAR	TM LG	W	L	PCT	G	GS	CG	SHO	QS	SV	BS	QR	IP	H	R	HR	HB	BB	IB	SO	ERA	AERA	OAV	OOB	SUP	DL	PW
1996	NY A	4	5	.444	12	11	0	0	3	0	0	1	53	80	43	5	4	10	1	34	6.79	-27	.343	.379	-25	0	-1.4
1997	†NY A	8	6	.571	39	15	0	0	7	2	2	18	133.2	157	67	15	5	28	2	82	4.24	+5	.292	.330	+28	0	0.5
1998	†NY A	10	2	.833	41	14	1	1	7	1	3	18	130.1	131	50	9	9	30	6	56	3.25	+35	.264	.314	+41	0	1.5
1999	†NY A	9	9	.500	53	6	0	0	3	3	3	31	123.2	141	68	13	3	27	3	80	4.29	+10	.284	.323	-18	0	0.7
2000	NY A	7	4	.636	14	9	1	1	5	0	1	4	65.2	66	32	9	4	20	1	30	4.25	+12	.260	.321	+40	95	0.6
2001	†NY A	8	4	.667	56	2	0	0	0	6	2	41	100.2	89	44	9	2	23	3	70	3.75	+18	.241	.287	+36	9	1.0
2002	†NY A	8	4	.667	62	0	0	0	0	4	4	44	91.2	102	43	8	2	16	2	61	3.44	+26	.275	.305	—	8	1.0
2003	Bos A	3	5	.375	37	5	0	0	0	0	1	19	66.2	98	51	10	5	20	4	36	6.75	-31	.349	.397	+31	53	-1.3
2004	†Bos A	2	1	.667	27	0	0	0	0	0	0	20	30.2	25	12	3	1	7	1	13	3.52	+39	.225	.277	—	98	0.4
2005	NY A	0	0	+	1	0	0	0	0	0	0	0	1	2	2	1	0	0	0	1	18.00	-76	.400	.400	—	0	-0.1
Total	10	59	40	.596	342	62	2	2	25	16	16	196	797	891	412	82	35	181	23	463	4.30	+6	.283	.326	+20	263	2.9
Team	8	54	34	.614	278	57	2	2	25	16	15	157	699.2	768	349	69	29	154	18	414	4.10	+11	.278	.320	+18	112	3.8
/60G	2	12	7	.614	60	12	0	0	5	3	3	34	151	166	75	15	6	33	4	89	4.10	+11	.278	.320	+18	24	0.8

Messersmith, Andy John Alexander B8.6.1945 Toms River NJ BR/TR/6'1"/(195–200) Dr 1966 AnaA S1/12 d7.4 Col California

YEAR	TM LG	W	L	PCT	G	GS	CG	SHO	QS	SV	BS	QR	IP	H	R	HR	HB	BB	IB	SO	ERA	AERA	OAV	OOB	SUP	DL	PW
1978	NY A	0	3	.000	6	5	0	0	1	0	0	0	22.1	24	21	7	1	15	0	16	5.64	-35	.267	.377	-7	119	-0.9
Total	12	130	99	.568	344	295	98	27	206	15	0	41	2230.1	1719	812	174	40	831	44	1625	2.86	+21	.212	.287	+1	313	17.6

Metcalf, Tom Thomas John B7.16.1940 Amherst WI BR/TR/6'2.5"/175 d8.4 Col Northwestern

YEAR	TM LG	W	L	PCT	G	GS	CG	SHO	QS	SV	BS	QR	IP	H	R	HR	HB	BB	IB	SO	ERA	AERA	OAV	OOB	SUP	DL	PW
1963	NY A	1	0	1.000	8	0	0	0	0	0	0	7	13	12	4	1	0	3	1	3	2.77	+27	.250	.294	—	0	0.1

Meyer, Bob Robert Bernard B8.4.1939 Toledo OH BR/TL/6'2"/(185–195) d4.20 Col Toledo

YEAR	TM LG	W	L	PCT	G	GS	CG	SHO	QS	SV	BS	QR	IP	H	R	HR	HB	BB	IB	SO	ERA	AERA	OAV	OOB	SUP	DL	PW
1964	NY A	0	3	.000	7	1	0	0	0	0	0	5	18.1	16	12	1	0	12	0	12	4.91	-26	.235	.350	-100	0	-0.5
Total	3	2	12	.143	38	18	3	0	7	0	0	14	129.1	132	72	11	3	80	0	92	4.38	-16	.273	.376	-8	108	-1.4

Miceli, Dan Daniel B9.9.1970 Newark NJ BR/TR/6'0"/(205–225) d9.9

YEAR	TM LG	W	L	PCT	G	GS	CG	SHO	QS	SV	BS	QR	IP	H	R	HR	HB	BB	IB	SO	ERA	AERA	OAV	OOB	SUP	DL	PW
2003	NY A	0	0	+	7	0	0	0	0	1	0	3	4.2	4	3	2	0	3	0	1	5.79	-24	.211	.318	—	0	0.0
Total	14	43	52	.453	631	9	0	0	0	39	39	417	700.2	684	383	93	20	310	47	632	4.48	-2	.256	.334	-13	220	-1.6

Mikkelsen, Pete Peter James B10.25.1939 Staten Island NY D11.29.2006 Mabton WA BR/TR/6'2"/(210–220) d4.17

YEAR	TM LG	W	L	PCT	G	GS	CG	SHO	QS	SV	BS	QR	IP	H	R	HR	HB	BB	IB	SO	ERA	AERA	OAV	OOB	SUP	DL	PW
1964	†NY A	7	4	.636	50	0	0	0	0	12	4	34	86	79	35	3	4	41	5	63	3.56	+2	.247	.338	—	0	0.2
1965	NY A	4	9	.308	41	3	0	0	1	1	4	29	82.1	78	40	10	3	36	9	69	3.28	+4	.249	.332	-91	0	-0.2
Total	9	45	40	.529	364	3	0	0	1	49	27	254	653.1	576	288	59	30	250	52	436	3.38	+3	.237	.315	-91	49	0.5
Team	2	11	13	.458	91	3	0	0	1	13	8	63	168.1	157	75	13	7	77	14	132	3.42	+3	.248	.335	-91	—	0.0
/60G	1	7	9	.458	60	2	0	0	1	9	5	42	111	104	49	9	5	51	9	87	3.42	+3	.248	.335	-91	—	0.0

Militello, Sam Sam Salvatore B11.26.1969 Tampa FL BR/TR/6'3"/(195–200) Dr 1990 NYA 6/165 d8.9 Col Tampa

YEAR	TM LG	W	L	PCT	G	GS	CG	SHO	QS	SV	BS	QR	IP	H	R	HR	HB	BB	IB	SO	ERA	AERA	OAV	OOB	SUP	DL	PW
1992	NY A	3	3	.500	9	9	0	0	6	0	0	0	60	43	24	6	2	32	1	42	3.45	+15	.195	.302	+0	0	0.3
1993	NY A	1	1	.500	3	2	0	0	0	0	0	1	9.1	10	8	1	2	7	1	5	6.75	-38	.270	.413	+10	0	-0.5
Total	2	4	4	.500	12	11	0	0	6	0	0	1	69.1	53	32	7	4	39	2	47	3.89	+2	.205	.319	+2	0	-0.2

Miller, Bill William Paul "Lefty","Hooks" B7.26.1927 Minersville PA D7.1.2003 Lititz PA BL/TL/6'0"/175 d4.20

YEAR	TM LG	W	L	PCT	G	GS	CG	SHO	QS	SV	BS	QR	IP	H	R	HR	HB	BB	IB	SO	ERA	AERA	OAV	OOB	SUP	DL	PW
1952	NY A	4	6	.400	21	13	5	2	—	0	—	—	88	78	43	5	2	49	—	45	3.48	-4	.241	.345	+25	0	-0.3
1953	NY A	2	1	.667	13	3	0	0	—	1	—	—	34	46	19	3	1	19	—	17	4.76	-23	.324	.407	+12	0	-0.3
1954	NY A	0	1	.000	2	1	0	0	—	0	—	—	5.2	9	4	0	0	1	—	6	6.35	-46	.375	.385	-49	0	-0.3
1955	Bal A	0	1	.000	5	1	0	0	—	0	—	—	4	3	6	0	0	10	1	4	13.50	-72	.200	.520	+63	0	-0.7
Total	4	6	9	.400	41	18	5	2	—	1	—	—	131.2	136	72	8	3	79	1	72	4.24	-19	.270	.371	+21	0	-1.6
Team	3	6	8	.429	36	17	5	2	—	1	—	—	127.2	133	66	8	3	69	—	68	3.95	-13	.271	.365	+18	—	-0.9
/180I	4	8	11	.429	51	24	7	3	—	1	—	—	180	188	93	11	4	97	—	96	3.95	-13	.271	.365	+18	—	-1.3

Mills, Alan Alan Bernard B10.18.1966 Lakeland FL BR/TR/6'1"/(190–195) Dr 1986 CalA S1/8 d4.14 Col Tuskegee

YEAR	TM LG	W	L	PCT	G	GS	CG	SHO	QS	SV	BS	QR	IP	H	R	HR	HB	BB	IB	SO	ERA	AERA	OAV	OOB	SUP	DL	PW
1990	NY A	1	5	.167	36	0	0	0	0	0	2	25	41.2	48	21	4	1	33	6	24	4.10	-3	.298	.418	—	0	0.0
1991	NY A	1	1	.500	6	2	0	0	0	0	0	3	16.1	16	9	1	0	8	0	11	4.41	-5	.254	.333	-56	0	0.0
Total	12	39	32	.549	474	5	0	0	0	15	22	321	636	577	306	83	21	395	46	456	4.12	+9	.245	.356	-26	233	2.5
Team	2	2	6	.250	42	2	0	0	0	0	2	28	58	64	30	5	1	41	6	35	4.19	-3	.286	.396	-56	—	0.0
/60G	3	3	9	.250	60	3	0	0	0	0	3	40	83	91	43	7	1	59	9	50	4.18	-3	.286	.396	-56	—	0.0

Mirabella, Paul Paul Thomas B3.20.1954 Belleville NJ BL/TL/6'2"/(185–196) Dr 1976 TexA*S1/21 d7.28 Col Montclair St.

YEAR	TM LG	W	L	PCT	G	GS	CG	SHO	QS	SV	BS	QR	IP	H	R	HR	HB	BB	IB	SO	ERA	AERA	OAV	OOB	SUP	DL	PW
1979	NY A	0	4	.000	10	1	0	0	0	0	0	5	14.1	16	15	3	1	10	1	4	8.79	-53	.276	.391	-34	0	-1.4
Total	13	19	29	.396	298	33	3	1	6	13	10	169	499.2	526	284	43	13	239	29	258	4.45	-8	.272	.352	-6	132	-2.7

Mmahat, Kevin Kevin Paul B11.9.1964 Memphis TN BL/TL/6'5"/220 Dr 1987 TexA 31/805 d9.9 Col Tulane

YEAR	TM LG	W	L	PCT	G	GS	CG	SHO	QS	SV	BS	QR	IP	H	R	HR	HB	BB	IB	SO	ERA	AERA	OAV	OOB	SUP	DL	PW
1989	NY A	0	2	.000	4	2	0	0	0	0	0	0	7.2	13	12	2	1	8	0	3	12.91	-70	.406	.500	-19	0	-1.3

Mogridge, George George Anthony B2.18.1889 Rochester NY D3.4.1962 Rochester NY BL/TL/6'2"/165 d8.17

YEAR	TM LG	W	L	PCT	G	GS	CG	SHO	QS	SV	BS	QR	IP	H	R	HR	HB	BB	IB	SO	ERA	AERA	OAV	OOB	SUP	DL	PW
1911	Chi A	0	2	.000	4	1	0	0	—	0	—	—	12.2	12	10	1	0	1	—	5	4.97	-35	.255	.271	+79	—	-0.3
1912	Chi A	3	4	.429	17	8	2	0	—	3	—	—	64.2	69	32	2	1	15	—	31	4.04	-21	.264	.307	-22	—	-0.5
1915	NY A	2	3	.400	6	5	3	1	—	0	—	—	41	33	11	0	3	11	—	11	1.76	+67	.219	.285	-11	—	0.5
1916	NY A	6	12	.333	30	21	10	2	—	0	—	—	194.2	174	71	3	7	45	—	66	2.31	+25	.252	.305	-28	—	1.0
1917	NY A	9	11	.450	29	25	15	1	—	0	—	—	196.1	185	82	5	9	39	—	46	2.98	-10	.255	.301	-6	—	-0.6
1918	NY A	16	13	.552	**45**	19	13	1	—	**7**	—	—	239.1	232	78	6	8	43	—	62	2.18	+30	.263	.304	+25	—	2.0
1919	NY A	10	9	.526	35	18	13	3	—	0	—	—	169	159	68	6	7	46	—	58	2.77	+15	.250	.307	+0	—	0.7
1920	NY A	5	9	.357	26	15	7	0	—	1	—	—	125.1	146	83	4	3	36	—	35	4.31	-11	.287	.338	+3	—	-1.0
1921	Was A	18	14	.563	38	36	21	4	—	0	—	—	288	301	119	12	7	66	—	101	3.00	+37	.269	.313	-25	—	3.0
1922	Was A	18	13	.581	34	32	18	3	—	0	—	—	251.2	300	120	12	11	72	—	61	3.58	+8	.304	.358	-3	—	1.4
1923	Was A	13	13	.500	33	30	17	3	—	1	—	—	211	228	90	10	3	56	—	62	3.11	+21	.285	.334	+5	—	2.0
1924	†Was A	16	11	.593	30	30	13	2	—	0	—	—	213	217	97	2	7	61	—	48	3.76	+7	.270	.327	-14	—	1.0
1925	Was A	3	4	.429	10	8	3	0	—	0	—	—	53	58	27	2	4	18	—	12	4.08	+4	.291	.362	-3	—	0.0
1925	StL A	1	1	.500	2	2	1	0	—	0	—	—	15.1	17	10	2	1	5	—	8	5.87	-20	.279	.343	-1	—	-0.1
1925	Year	4	5	.444	12	10	4	0	—	0	—	—	68.1	75	37	4	5	23	—	20	4.48	-3	.288	.358	-3	—	-0.1
1926	Bos N	6	10	.375	39	10	2	0	—	3	—	—	142	173	82	6	3	36	—	46	4.50	-21	.311	.356	+20	—	-1.6
1927	Bos N	6	4	.600	20	1	0	0	—	5	—	—	48.2	48	23	4	2	15	—	26	3.70	+0	.257	.319	-77	—	0.1
Total	15	132	133	.498	398	261	138	20	—	20	—	—	2265.2	2352	1003	77	76	565	—	678	3.23	+9	.273	.323	-5	—	7.6
Team	6	48	57	.457	171	103	61	8	—	8	—	—	965.2	929	393	24	37	220	—	278	2.73	+10	.259	.308	-3	—	2.6
/180I	1	9	11	.457	32	19	11	1	—	1	—	—	180	173	73	4	7	41	—	52	2.73	+10	.259	.308	-3	—	0.5

Mohorcic, Dale Dale Robert B1.25.1956 Cleveland OH BR/TR/6'3"/220 d5.31 Col Cleveland St.

YEAR	TM LG	W	L	PCT	G	GS	CG	SHO	QS	SV	BS	QR	IP	H	R	HR	HB	BB	IB	SO	ERA	AERA	OAV	OOB	SUP	DL	PW
1988	NY A	2	2	.500	13	0	0	0	0	1	2	8	22.2	21	7	1	3	9	2	19	2.78	+43	.239	.327	—	0	0.5
1989	NY A	2	1	.667	32	0	0	0	0	2	3	18	57.2	65	41	8	6	18	3	24	4.99	-22	.286	.352	—	0	-0.5
Total	5	16	21	.432	254	0	0	0	0	33	22	168	363.2	378	163	37	21	99	25	174	3.49	+19	.272	.327	—	38	3.3
Team	2	4	3	.571	45	0	0	0	0	3	5	26	80.1	86	48	9	9	27	5	43	4.37	-10	.273	.345	—	—	0.0
/60G	3	5	4	.571	60	0	0	0	0	4	7	35	107	115	64	12	12	36	7	57	4.37	-10	.273	.345	—	—	0.0

Monbouquette, Bill William Charles B8.11.1936 Medford MA BR/TR/5'11"/(190–195) d7.18 C3

YEAR	TM LG	W	L	PCT	G	GS	CG	SHO	QS	SV	BS	QR	IP	H	R	HR	HB	BB	IB	SO	ERA	AERA	OAV	OOB	SUP	DL	PW
1967	NY A	6	5	.545	33	10	2	1	9	1	1	15	133.1	122	39	6	4	17	7	53	2.36	+32	.246	.274	-14	0	1.0
1968	NY A	5	7	.417	17	11	2	0	6	0	0	3	89.1	92	47	7	3	13	2	32	4.43	-34	.264	.293	-2	0	-1.7
Total	11	114	112	.504	343	263	78	18	171	3	3	64	1961.1	1995	910	211	20	462	44	1122	3.68	+4	.263	.305	-3	0	-0.3
Team	2	11	12	.478	50	21	4	1	15	1	1	18	222.2	214	86	13	7	30	9	85	3.19	-5	.254	.282	-8	—	-0.7
/180I	2	9	10	.478	40	17	3	1	12	1	1	15	180	173	70	11	6	24	7	69	3.19	-5	.254	.282	-8	—	-0.6

Monroe, Ed Edward Oliver "Peck" B2.22.1895 Louisville KY D4.29.1969 Louisville KY BR/TR/6'5"/187 d5.29 Mil 1918

YEAR	TM LG	W	L	PCT	G	GS	CG	SHO	QS	SV	BS	QR	IP	H	R	HR	HB	BB	IB	SO	ERA	AERA	OAV	OOB	SUP	DL	PW
1917	NY A	1	0	1.000	9	1	1	0	—	1	—	—	28.2	35	15	1	2	6	—	12	3.45	-22	.310	.355	+34	—	-0.2
1918	NY A	0	0	+	1	0	0	0	—	0	—	—	2	1	2	0	0	2	—	1	4.50	-37	.143	.333	—	—	0.0
Total	2	1	0	1.000	10	1	1	0	—	1	—	—	30.2	36	17	1	2	8	—	13	3.52	-23	.300	.354	+34	—	-0.2

Monroe, Zach Zachary Charles B7.8.1931 Peoria IL BR/TR/6'0"/198 d6.27 Col Bradley

YEAR	TM LG	W	L	PCT	G	GS	CG	SHO	QS	SV	BS	QR	IP	H	R	HR	HB	BB	IB	SO	ERA	AERA	OAV	OOB	SUP	DL	PW
1958	†NY A	4	2	.667	21	6	1	0	3	1	1	13	58	57	29	8	0	27	1	18	3.26	+8	.263	.344	+99	0	-0.1
1959	NY A	0	0	+	3	0	0	0	3	0	1	13	3.1	3	2	2	0	2	0	1	5.40	-33	.231	.333	—	0	0.0
Total	2	4	2	.667	24	6	1	0	6	1	2	26	61.1	60	31	10	0	29	1	19	3.38	+5	.261	.344	+99	0	-0.1

Montefusco, John John Joseph "Count" B5.25.1950 Long Branch NJ BR/TR/6'1"/(180–192) d9.3 Col Brookdale (NJ) CC

YEAR	TM LG	W	L	PCT	G	GS	CG	SHO	QS	SV	BS	QR	IP	H	R	HR	HB	BB	IB	SO	ERA	AERA	OAV	OOB	SUP	DL	PW
1983	NY A	5	0	1.000	6	6	0	0	4	0	0	0	38	39	14	3	1	10	0	15	3.32	+19	.271	.318	+7	0	0.4
1984	NY A	5	3	.625	11	11	0	0	5	0	0	0	55.1	55	26	5	1	13	2	23	3.58	+7	.253	.295	+3	109	0.1
1985	NY A	0	0	+	3	1	0	0	0	0	0	1	7	12	8	3	0	2	0	2	10.29	-61	.387	.412	+125	166	-0.2
1986	NY A	0	0	+	4	0	0	0	0	0	1	2	12.1	9	3	2	0	5	0	3	2.19	+89	.200	.280	—	157	0.2
Total	13	90	83	.520	298	244	32	11	139	5	3	42	1652.1	1604	728	135	29	513	57	1081	3.54	+3	.255	.311	-5	558	1.1
Team	4	10	3	.769	24	18	0	0	9	0	1	3	112.2	115	51	13	2	30	2	43	3.75	+4	.263	.309	+11	432	0.5

Monteleone, Rich Richard B3.22.1963 Tampa FL BR/TR/6'2"/(205–236) Dr 1982 DetA 1/20 d4.15 C4

YEAR	TM LG	W	L	PCT	G	GS	CG	SHO	QS	SV	BS	QR	IP	H	R	HR	HB	BB	IB	SO	ERA	AERA	OAV	OOB	SUP	DL	PW
1987	Sea A	0	0	+	3	0	0	0	0	0	0	2	7	10	5	2	1	4	0	2	6.43	-26	.345	.441	—	0	0.0
1988	Cal A	0	0	+	3	0	0	0	0	0	0	2	4.1	4	0	0	1	1	1	3	0.00	-100	.222	.300	—	0	0.1
1989	Cal A	2	2	.500	24	0	0	0	0	0	2	16	39.2	39	15	3	1	13	1	27	3.18	+21	.255	.314	—	0	0.3
1990	NY A	0	1	.000	5	0	0	0	0	0	0	4	7.1	8	5	0	0	2	0	8	6.14	-35	.276	.323	—	0	-0.2
1991	NY A	3	1	.750	26	0	0	0	0	0	0	17	47	42	27	5	0	19	3	34	3.64	+15	.236	.307	—	0	0.0
1992	NY A	7	3	.700	47	0	0	0	0	0	2	31	92.2	82	35	7	0	27	3	62	3.30	+20	.235	.289	—	0	0.7
1993	NY A	7	4	.636	42	0	0	0	0	0	1	24	85.2	85	52	14	0	35	10	50	4.94	-15	.262	.329	—	0	-0.9
1994	SF N	4	3	.571	39	0	0	0	0	0	1	26	45.1	43	18	6	0	13	2	16	3.18	+28	.253	.299	—	32	0.5
1995	Cal A	1	0	1.000	9	0	0	0	0	0	1	7	9	8	2	1	0	3	0	5	2.00	+136	.267	.314	—	0	0.3
1996	Cal A	0	3	.000	12	0	0	0	0	0	0	5	15.1	23	11	5	1	2	0	5	5.87	-14	.348	.377	—	52	-0.2
Total	10	24	17	.585	210	0	0	0	0	0	7	134	353.1	344	170	43	4	119	20	212	3.87	+6	.255	.314	—	84	0.6
Team	4	17	9	.654	120	0	0	0	0	0	3	76	232.2	217	119	26	0	83	16	154	4.06	+1	.247	.309	—	—	-0.4
/60G	2	9	5	.654	60	0	0	0	0	0	2	38	116.1	109	60	13	0	42	8	77	4.06	+1	.247	.309	—	—	-0.2

Moore, Earl Earl Alonzo "Big Ebbie","Crossfire" B7.29.1879 Pickerington OH D11.28.1961 Columbus OH BR/TR/6'0"/195 d4.25

YEAR	TM LG	W	L	PCT	G	GS	CG	SHO	QS	SV	BS	QR	IP	H	R	HR	HB	BB	IB	SO	ERA	AERA	OAV	OOB	SUP	DL	PW
1907	NY A	2	6	.250	12	9	3	0	—	1	—	—	64	72	49	1	4	30	—	28	3.94	-29	.286	.371	-3	—	-1.1
Total	14	163	154	.514	388	326	230	34	—	6	—	—	2776	2474	1231	57	106	1108	—	1403	2.78	+10	.241	.321	+0	—	3.2

Moore, Wilcy William Wilcy "Cy" B5.20.1897 Bonita TX D3.29.1963 Hollis OK BR/TR/6'0"/195 d4.14

YEAR	TM LG	W	L	PCT	G	GS	CG	SHO	QS	SV	BS	QR	IP	H	R	HR	HB	BB	IB	SO	ERA	AERA	OAV	OOB	SUP	DL	PW
1927	†NY A	19	7	.731	50	12	6	1	—	**13**	—	—	213	185	68	3	1	59	—	75	**2.28**	+69	**.234**	**.289**	+19	—	4.5
1928	NY A	4	4	.500	35	2	0	0	—	2	—	—	60.1	71	44	4	0	31	—	18	4.18	-10	.286	.366	+103	—	-0.9
1929	NY A	6	4	.600	41	0	0	0	—	8	—	—	61	64	36	4	0	19	—	21	4.13	-7	.268	.322	—	—	-0.6
1931	Bos A	11	13	.458	53	15	8	1	—	**10**	—	—	185.1	195	88	7	1	55	—	37	3.88	+11	.269	.322	-36	—	1.3
1932	Bos A	4	10	.286	37	2	0	0	—	4	—	—	84.1	98	59	5	1	42	—	28	5.23	-14	.284	.363	-72	—	-1.1
1932	†NY A	2	0	1.000	10	1	0	0	—	4	—	—	25	27	8	1	0	6	—	8	2.52	+62	.273	.314	-16	—	0.4
1932	Year	6	10	.375	47	3	0	0	—	8	—	—	109.1	125	67	6	1	48	—	36	4.61	-5	.282	.353	-55	—	-0.7
1933	NY A	5	6	.455	35	0	0	0	—	8	—	—	62	92	53	1	0	20	—	17	5.52	-30	.333	.378	—	—	-2.9
Total	6	51	44	.537	261	32	14	2	—	49	—	—	691	732	356	25	3	232	—	204	3.70	+10	.269	.327	-9	—	0.7
Team	5	36	21	.632	171	15	6	1	—	35	—	—	421.1	439	209	13	1	135	—	139	3.31	+17	.266	.322	+28	—	0.5
/60G	2	13	7	.632	60	5	2	0	—	12	—	—	148	154	73	5	0	47	—	49	3.31	+17	.266	.322	+28	—	0.2

Morgan, Mike Michael Thomas B10.8.1959 Tulare CA BR/TR/6'2"/(185–226) Dr 1978 OakA 1/4 d6.11

YEAR	TM LG	W	L	PCT	G	GS	CG	SHO	QS	SV	BS	QR	IP	H	R	HR	HB	BB	IB	SO	ERA	AERA	OAV	OOB	SUP	DL	PW
1982	NY A	7	11	.389	30	23	2	0	10	0	0	5	150.1	167	77	15	2	67	5	71	4.37	-8	.285	.358	-11	0	-0.4
Total	22	141	186	.431	597	411	46	10	209	8	5	135	2772.1	2943	1431	270	73	938	77	1403	4.23	-2	.276	.337	-8	729	-4.6
/180I	1	8	13	.389	36	28	2	0	12	0	0	6	180	200	92	18	2	80	6	85	4.37	-8	.285	.358	-11	—	-0.5

Morgan, Tom Tom Stephen "Plowboy" B5.20.1930 ElMonte CA D1.13.1987 Anaheim CA BR/TR/6'2"/(190–200) d4.20 Mil 1952–53 C8

YEAR	TM LG	W	L	PCT	G	GS	CG	SHO	QS	SV	BS	QR	IP	H	R	HR	HB	BB	IB	SO	ERA	AERA	OAV	OOB	SUP	DL	PW
1951	†NY A	9	3	.750	27	16	4	2	—	2	—	—	124.2	119	56	11	3	36	—	57	3.68	+4	.253	.310	+1	0	0.6
1952	NY A	5	4	.556	16	12	2	1	—	2	—	—	93.2	86	34	8	4	33	—	35	3.07	+8	.252	.325	+55	0	0.6
1954	NY A	11	5	.688	32	17	7	4	—	1	—	—	143	149	58	8	5	40	—	34	3.34	+3	.274	.327	+33	0	0.4
1955	†NY A	7	3	.700	40	1	0	0	—	10	—	—	72	72	29	3	5	24	4	17	3.25	+15	.267	.337	+19	0	0.9

YEAR	TM LG	W	L	PCT	G	GS	CG	SHO	QS	SV	BS	QR	IP	H	R	HR	HB	BB	IB	SO	ERA	AERA	OAV	OOB	SUP	DL	PW
1956	†NY A	6	7	.462	41	0	0	0	—	11	—	—	71.1	74	41	2	3	27	4	20	4.16	-7	.284	.347	—	0	-0.8
1957	KC A	9	7	.563	46	13	5	0	5	7	2	21	143.2	160	76	19	3	61	9	32	4.64	-15	.299	.370	-10	0	-0.9
1958	Det A	2	5	.286	39	1	0	0	0	1	2	59	62.2	70	28	7	1	4	0	32	3.16	+28	.286	.299	+11	0	0.4
1959	Det A	1	4	.200	46	1	0	0	0	9	3	59	92.2	94	48	11	6	18	3	39	3.98	+2	.265	.308	-13	0	0.4
1960	Det A	3	2	.600	22	0	0	0	0	1	2	16	29	33	17	6	0	10	1	12	4.66	-15	.295	.347	—	0	-0.3
1960	Was A	1	3	.250	14	0	0	0	0	0	0	7	24	36	15	6	1	5	3	11	3.75	+4	.343	.375	—	0	-0.2
1960	Year	4	5	.444	36	0	0	0	0	1	2	23	53	69	32	12	1	15	4	23	4.25	-8	.318	.360	—	0	-0.5
1961	LA A	8	2	.800	59	0	0	0	0	10	5	49	91.2	74	31	7	5	17	3	39	2.36	+91	.224	.269	—	0	2.2
1962	LA A	5	2	.714	48	0	0	0	0	9	4	36	58.2	53	23	6	1	19	6	29	2.91	+32	.247	.304		0	0.7
1963	LA A	0	0	+	13	0	0	0	0	1	0	6	16.1	20	11	1	3	6	1	7	5.51	-38	.313	.392	—	0	-0.2
Total	12	67	47	.588	443	61	18	7	5	64	18	253	1023.1	1040	467	95	40	300	34	364	3.61	+6	.270	.326	+12	0	3.8
Team	5	38	22	.633	156	46	13	7	—	26	—	—	504.2	500	218	32	20	160	8	163	3.48	+4	.265	.327	+27	—	1.7
/180I	2	14	8	.633	56	16	5	2	—	9	—	—	180	178	78	11	7	57	3	58	3.48	+4	.265	.327	+27	—	0.6

MULHOLLAND, TERRY TERENCE JOHN B3.9.1963 UNIONTOWN PA BR/TL/6'3"/(200–225) DR 1984 SFN 1/24 D6.8 COL MARIETTA

YEAR	TM LG	W	L	PCT	G	GS	CG	SHO	QS	SV	BS	QR	IP	H	R	HR	HB	BB	IB	SO	ERA	AERA	OAV	OOB	SUP	DL	PW
1994	NY A	6	7	.462	24	19	2	0	6	0	0	4	120.2	150	94	24	3	37	1	72	6.49	-29	.303	.353	+35	0	-2.3
Total	20	124	142	.466	685	332	46	10	180	5	9	235	2575.2	2833	1396	293	70	681	65	1325	4.41	-6	.281	.328	-2	273	-9.2
/180I	1	9	10	.462	36	28	3	0	9	0	0	6	180	224	140	36	4	55	1	107	6.49	-29	.303	.353	+35	—	-3.4

MUNCRIEF, BOB ROBERT CLEVELAND B1.28.1916 MADILL OK D2.6.1996 DUNCANVILLE TX BR/TR/6'2"/190 D9.30

YEAR	TM LG	W	L	PCT	G	GS	CG	SHO	QS	SV	BS	QR	IP	H	R	HR	HB	BB	IB	SO	ERA	AERA	OAV	OOB	SUP	DL	PW
1951	NY A	0	0	+	2	0	0	0	—	0	—	—	3	5	3	0	0	4	—	2	9.00	-57	.417	.563	—	0	-0.1
Total	12	80	82	.494	288	165	67	11	—	9	—	—	1401.1	1503	669	106	15	392	—	525	3.80	+0	.275	.325	-2	0	-1.9

MUNOZ, BOBBY ROBERTO (BOBBY) B3.3.1968 RIO PIEDRAS, PR BR/TR/6'7"/(237–259) DR 1988 NYA 15/391 D5.29 COL PALM BEACH (FL) CC

YEAR	TM LG	W	L	PCT	G	GS	CG	SHO	QS	SV	BS	QR	IP	H	R	HR	HB	BB	IB	SO	ERA	AERA	OAV	OOB	SUP	DL	PW
1993	NY A	3	3	.500	38	0	0	0	0	0	2	26	45.2	48	27	1	0	26	5	33	5.32	-21	.270	.357	—	0	-0.6
1994	Phi N	7	5	.583	21	14	1	0	10	1	1	3	104.1	101	40	8	1	35	0	59	2.67	+60	.252	.310	-10	0	1.9
1995	Phi N	0	2	.000	3	3	0	0	1	0	0	0	15.2	15	13	2	3	9	0	6	5.74	-27	.268	.386	-43	148	-0.4
1996	Phi N	0	3	.000	6	6	0	0	1	0	0	0	25.1	42	28	5	1	7	1	8	7.82	-45	.375	.413	-30	159	-1.1
1997	Phi N	1	5	.167	8	7	0	0	1	0	0	0	33.1	47	35	4	2	15	1	20	8.91	-53	.338	.403	-25	0	-2.2
1998	Bal A	0	0	+	9	1	0	0	0	0	0	3	12	18	13	4	1	6	0	6	9.75	-53	.383	.439	+63	0	-0.3
2001	Mon N	0	4	.000	15	7	0	0	3	0	0	6	42	53	25	6	2	21	1	21	5.14	-16	.321	.404	-54	0	-0.4
Total	7	11	22	.333	100	38	1	0	16	1	3	38	278.1	324	181	30	10	119	8	153	5.17	-17	.295	.364	-24	307	-3.1

MURPHY, JOHNNY JOHN JOSEPH "GRANDMA" "FIREMAN","FORDHAM JOHNNY" B7.14.1908 NEW YORK NY D1.14.1970 NEW YORK NY BR/TR/6'2"/190 D5.19 DEF 1944–45 COL FORDHAM

YEAR	TM LG	W	L	PCT	G	GS	CG	SHO	QS	SV	BS	QR	IP	H	R	HR	HB	BB	IB	SO	ERA	AERA	OAV	OOB	SUP	DL	PW
1932	NY A	0	0	+	2	0	0	0	—	0	—	—	3.1	7	6	0	0	3	—	2	16.20	-75	.438	.526	—	—	-0.2
1934	NY A	14	10	.583	40	20	10	0	—	4	—	—	207.2	193	79	11	0	76	—	70	3.12	+30	.250	.317	-6	—	2.5
1935	NY A	10	5	.667	40	8	4	0	—	5	—	—	117	110	67	7	0	55	—	28	4.08	-1	.243	.325	+23	—	-0.1
1936	†NY A	9	3	.750	27	5	2	0	—	5	—	—	88	90	38	5	1	36	—	34	3.38	+38	.262	.334	+89	—	2.0
1937	†NY A☆	13	4	.765	39	4	0	0	—	10	—	—	110	121	59	7	1	50	—	36	4.17	+7	.277	.352	+57	—	0.9
1938	†NY A☆	8	2	.800	32	2	1	0	—	**11**	—	—	91.1	90	47	5	1	41	—	43	4.24	+7	.256	.336	-13	—	0.4
1939	†NY A☆	3	6	.333	38	0	0	0	—	**19**	—	—	61.1	57	33	2	0	28	—	30	4.40	-1	.252	.335	—	—	0.1
1940	NY A	8	4	.667	35	1	0	0	—	9	—	—	63.1	58	27	5	0	15	—	23	3.69	+9	.247	.292	+9	—	0.7
1941	†NY A	8	3	.727	35	0	0	0	—	**15**	—	—	77.1	68	20	1	0	40	—	29	1.98	+99	.237	.330	—	0	2.9
1942	NY A	4	10	.286	31	0	0	0	—	**11**	—	—	58	66	27	2	2	23	—	24	3.41	+1	.293	.364	—	0	-0.1
1943	†NY A	12	4	.750	37	0	0	0	—	8	—	—	68	44	22	2	0	30	—	31	2.51	+28	.183	.273	—	0	1.0
1946	NY A	4	2	.667	27	0	0	0	—	7	—	—	45	40	22	4	0	19	—	19	3.40	+2	.240	.317	—	0	-0.1
1947	Bos A	0	0	+	32	0	0	0	—	3	—	—	54.2	41	17	1	0	28	—	9	2.80	+39	.206	.304	—	0	0.5
Total	13	93	53	.637	415	40	17	0	—	107	—	—	1045	985	464	52	5	444	—	378	3.50	+17	.249	.326	+23	0	10.5
Team	12	93	53	.637	383	40	17	0	—	104	—	—	990.1	944	447	51	5	416	—	369	3.54	+16	.251	.327	+18	—	10.0
/60G	2	15	8	.637	60	6	3	0	—	16	—	—	155	148	70	8	1	65	—	58	3.54	+16	.251	.327	+18	—	1.6

MURPHY, ROB ROBERT ALBERT B5.26.1960 MIAMI FL BL/TL/6'2"/(200–215) DR 1981 CINN*S1/3 D9.13 COL FLORIDA

YEAR	TM LG	W	L	PCT	G	GS	CG	SHO	QS	SV	BS	QR	IP	H	R	HR	HB	BB	IB	SO	ERA	AERA	OAV	OOB	SUP	DL	PW
1994	NY A	0	0	+	3	0	0	0	0	0	0	1	1.2	3	3	2	0	0	0	0	16.20	-72	.375	.375	—	0	-0.1
Total	11	32	38	.457	597	0	0	0	0	30	25	413	623.1	598	277	54	5	247	41	520	3.64	+9	.254	.324	—	19	2.1

MURRAY, DALE DALE ALBERT B2.2.1950 CUERO TX BR/TR/6'4"/(200–205) DR 1970 MONN 18/418 D7.7 COL BLINN (TX) JC

YEAR	TM LG	W	L	PCT	G	GS	CG	SHO	QS	SV	BS	QR	IP	H	R	HR	HB	BB	IB	SO	ERA	AERA	OAV	OOB	SUP	DL	PW
1983	NY A	2	4	.333	40	0	0	0	0	1	2	22	94.1	113	56	5	1	22	4	45	4.48	-12	.297	.333	—	0	-0.4
1984	NY A	1	2	.333	19	0	0	0	0	0	1	14	23.2	30	15	2	2	5	0	13	4.94	-22	.306	.352	—	96	-0.4
1985	NY A	0	0	+	3	0	0	0	0	0	0	2	2	4	3	0	0	0	0	0	13.50	-70	.400	.400	—	0	-0.1
Total	12	53	50	.515	518	1	0	0	0	60	42	356	902.1	976	448	40	14	329	80	400	3.85	+1	.282	.343	+239	132	-0.2
Team	3	3	6	.333	62	0	0	0	0	1	3	38	120	147	74	7	3	27	4	58	4.72	-17	.301	.338	—	96	-0.9
/60G	3	3	6	.333	60	0	0	0	0	1	3	37	116	142	72	7	3	26	4	56	4.73	-17	.301	.338	—	93	-0.9

MURRAY, GEORGE GEORGE KING "SMILER" B9.23.1898 CHARLOTTE NC D10.18.1955 MEMPHIS TN BR/TR/6'2"/200 D5.8 COL NORTH CAROLINA ST.

YEAR	TM LG	W	L	PCT	G	GS	CG	SHO	QS	SV	BS	QR	IP	H	R	HR	HB	BB	IB	SO	ERA	AERA	OAV	OOB	SUP	DL	PW
1922	NY A	3	2	.600	22	2	0	0	—	0	—	—	56.2	53	27	0	1	26	—	14	3.97	+1	.255	.340	-15	—	0.2
Total	6	19	26	.422	110	42	10	0	—	0	—	—	416.1	450	282	17	23	199	—	114	5.38	-24	.288	.376	-10	—	-5.5

MUSSINA, MIKE MICHAEL COLE B12.8.1968 WILLIAMSPORT PA BL/TR/6'1"/(180–190) DR 1990 BALA 1/20 D8.4 COL STANFORD

YEAR	TM LG	W	L	PCT	G	GS	CG	SHO	QS	SV	BS	QR	IP	H	R	HR	HB	BB	IB	SO	ERA	AERA	OAV	OOB	SUP	DL	PW
1991	Bal A	4	5	.444	12	12	2	0	9	0	0	0	87.2	77	31	7	1	21	0	52	2.87	+38	.239	.286	-4	0	1.0
1992	Bal A★	18	5	**.783**	32	32	8	4	26	0	0	0	241	212	70	16	2	48	2	130	2.54	+60	.239	**.278**	+0	0	3.8
1993	Bal A☆	14	6	.700	25	25	3	2	14	0	0	0	167.2	163	84	20	3	44	2	117	4.46	+1	.256	.306	+19	29	0.3
1994	Bal A★	16	5	.762	24	24	3	0	18	0	0	0	176.1	163	63	19	1	42	1	99	3.06	+65	.248	.291	-5	0	4.0
1995	Bal A	**19**	9	.679	32	32	7	0	21	0	0	0	221.2	187	86	24	1	50	4	158	3.29	+45	.226	.270	-9	0	4.1
1996	†Bal A	19	11	.633	36	**36**	4	1	18	0	0	0	243.1	264	137	31	3	69	0	204	4.81	+3	.275	.325	+24	0	0.5
1997	†Bal A☆	15	8	.652	33	33	4	1	25	0	0	0	224.2	197	87	27	3	54	3	218	3.20	+38	.234	.282	+9	0	2.8
1998	Bal A	13	10	.565	29	29	4	2	18	0	0	0	206.1	189	85	22	4	41	3	175	3.49	+30	.242	.282	+1	38	2.5
1999	Bal A★	18	7	.720	31	31	4	0	17	0	0	0	203.1	207	88	16	1	52	0	172	3.50	+34	.268	.312	+29	0	3.2
2000	Bal A	11	15	.423	34	34	6	1	22	0	0	0	**237.2**	236	105	28	3	46	0	210	3.79	+24	.255	.291	-34	0	2.4
2001	†NY A	17	11	.607	34	34	4	3	24	0	0	0	228.2	202	87	20	4	42	2	214	3.15	+41	.237	**.274**	-14	0	3.7
2002	†NY A	18	10	.643	33	33	2	2	18	0	0	0	215.2	208	103	27	5	48	1	182	4.05	+7	.253	.296	+25	0	1.3
2003	†NY A	17	8	.680	31	31	2	1	20	0	0	0	214.2	192	86	21	3	40	4	195	3.40	+29	.238	.275	-7	0	2.8
2004	†NY A	12	9	.571	27	27	1	0	13	0	0	0	164.2	178	91	22	2	40	1	132	4.59	+0	.276	.318	+10	42	0.0
2005	†NY A	13	8	.619	30	30	2	2	16	0	0	0	179.2	199	93	23	7	47	0	142	4.41	-2	.283	.333	+17	0	-0.1
2006	†NY A	15	7	.682	32	32	1	0	23	0	0	0	197.1	184	88	22	5	35	1	172	3.51	+31	.241	.279	+15	15	2.1
2007	†NY A	11	10	.524	28	27	0	0	13	0	0	0	152	188	90	14	4	35	2	91	5.15	-12	.311	.349	+18	21	-1.0
Total	17	250	144	.635	503	502	57	23	315	0	0	0	3362.1	3246	1474	359	52	754	26	2663	3.70	+23	.253	.296	+6	145	33.4
Team	7	103	63	.620	215	214	12	8	127	0	0	0	1352.2	1351	638	149	30	287	11	1128	3.95	+13	.260	.301	+9	78	8.8
/180I	1	14	8	.620	29	28	2	1	17	0	0	0	180	180	85	20	4	38	1	150	3.95	+13	.260	.301	+9	10	1.2

MYERS, MIKE MICHAEL STANLEY B6.26.1969 ARLINGTON HEIGHTS IL BL/TL/6'4"/(197–225) DR 1990 SFN 4/122 D4.25 COL IOWA ST. [DL 1994 FLA N 60]

YEAR	TM LG	W	L	PCT	G	GS	CG	SHO	QS	SV	BS	QR	IP	H	R	HR	HB	BB	IB	SO	ERA	AERA	OAV	OOB	SUP	DL	PW
2006	†NY A	1	2	.333	62	0	0	0	0	0	1	49	30.2	29	14	3	3	10	1	22	3.23	+43	.244	.318	—	0	0.3
2007	NY A	3	0	1.000	55	0	0	0	0	0	2	39	40.2	38	14	3	2	16	0	21	2.66	+70	.247	.322	—	0	0.6
Total	13	25	24	.510	883	0	0	0	0	14	27	636	541.2	525	278	58	43	256	33	429	4.29	+12	.257	.349	—	60	2.3
Team	2	4	2	.667	117	0	0	0	0	0	3	88	71.1	67	28	6	5	26	1	43	2.90	+57	.245	.320	—	—	0.9
/60G	1	2	1	.667	60	0	0	0	0	0	2	45	36.2	34	14	3	3	13	1	22	2.90	+57	.245	.320	—	—	0.5

NAULTY, DAN DANIEL DONOVAN B1.6.1970 LOS ANGELES CA BR/TR/6'6"/(211–224) DR 1992 MINA 14/402 D4.2 COL CAL ST.–FULLERTON

YEAR	TM LG	W	L	PCT	G	GS	CG	SHO	QS	SV	BS	QR	IP	H	R	HR	HB	BB	IB	SO	ERA	AERA	OAV	OOB	SUP	DL	PW
1999	NY A	1	0	1.000	33	0	0	0	0	0	0	26	49.1	40	24	8	4	22	0	25	4.38	+8	.225	.322	—	0	0.2
Total	4	5	5	.500	130	0	0	0	0	5	8	93	160.2	137	86	24	4	77	4	119	4.54	+7	.231	.321	—	232	0.6

YEAR	TM LG	W	L	PCT	G	GS	CG	SHO	QS	SV	BS	QR	IP	H	R	HR	HB	BB	IB	SO	ERA	AERA	OAV	OOB	SUP	DL	PW
NEAGLE, DENNY	DENNIS EDWARD B9.13.1968 GAMBRILLS MD BL/TL/6'2"/(200–225) DR 1989 MINA 3/85 D7.27 COL MINNESOTA [DL 2004 COL N 183]																										
2000	†NY A	7	7	.500	16	15	1	0	6	0	0	0	91.1	99	61	16	2	31	1	58	5.81	-18	.278	.335	+14	0	-1.2
Total	13	124	92	.574	392	286	20	7	163	3	2	76	1890.1	1887	948	250	53	594	44	1415	4.24	+5	.260	.319	+3	449	4.8
NEKOLA, BOTS	FRANCIS JOSEPH B12.10.1906 NEW YORK NY D3.11.1987 ROCKVILLE MD BL/TL/5'11.5"/175 D7.19 COL HOLY CROSS																										
1929	NY A	0	0	+	9	1	0	0	—	0	—	—	18.2	21	10	0	0	15	—	2	4.34	-11	.296	.419	+141	—	0.1
1933	Det A	0	0	+	2	0	0	0	—	0	—	—	1.1	4	4	1	0	1	—	0	27.00	-84	.500	.556	—	—	-0.1
Total	2	0	0	+	11	1	0	0	—	0	—	—	20	25	14	1	0	16	—	2	5.85	-34	.316	.432	+141	—	0.0
NELSON, JEFF	JEFFREY ALLAN B11.17.1966 BALTIMORE MD BR/TR/6'8"/(225–235) DR 1984 LAN 22/569 D4.16 COL CATONSVILLE (MD) CC																										
1992	Sea A	1	7	.125	66	0	0	0	0	6	8	46	81	71	34	7	6	44	12	46	3.44	+16	.245	.353	—	0	0.5
1993	Sea A	5	3	.625	71	0	0	0	0	1	10	44	60	57	30	5	8	34	10	61	4.35	+3	.258	.371	—	0	0.2
1994	Sea A	0	0	+	28	0	0	0	0	0	0	18	42.1	35	18	3	8	20	4	44	2.76	+78	.226	.342	—	0	0.4
1995	†Sea A	7	3	.700	62	0	0	0	0	2	2	51	78.2	58	21	4	6	27	5	96	2.17	+119	.209	.291	—	0	2.6
1996	†NY A	4	4	.500	73	0	0	0	0	2	2	47	74.1	75	38	6	2	36	1	91	4.36	+14	.262	.348	—	0	0.5
1997	†NY A	3	7	.300	77	0	0	0	0	2	6	57	78.2	53	32	7	4	37	12	81	2.86	+56	.191	.294	—	0	1.5
1998	†NY A	5	3	.625	45	0	0	0	0	3	3	32	40.1	44	18	1	8	22	4	35	3.79	+15	.278	.387	—	71	0.5
1999	†NY A	2	1	.667	39	0	0	0	0	1	1	24	30.1	27	14	2	3	22	2	35	4.15	+14	.245	.380	—	86	0.3
2000	†NY A	8	4	.667	73	0	0	0	0	0	4	55	69.2	44	24	2	2	45	1	71	2.45	+95	.183	.314	—	0	2.4
2001	†Sea A★	4	3	.571	69	0	0	0	0	4	1	57	65.1	30	21	3	6	44	1	88	2.76	+55	.136	.295	—	0	1.2
2002	Sea A	3	2	.600	41	0	0	0	0	2	2	28	45.2	36	20	4	3	27	3	55	3.94	+9	.221	.335	—	52	0.3
2003	Sea A	3	2	.600	46	0	0	0	0	7	4	32	37.2	34	16	3	2	14	1	47	3.35	+29	.248	.323	—	0	0.5
2003	†NY A	1	0	1.000	24	0	0	0	0	1	2	15	17.2	17	9	1	2	10	2	21	4.58	-4	.246	.358	—	0	0.0
2003	Year	4	2	.667	70	0	0	0	0	8	6	47	55.1	51	25	4	4	24	3	68	3.74	+16	.248	.335	—	0	0.5
2004	Tex A	1	2	.333	29	0	0	0	0	1	0	19	23.2	17	16	3	0	19	0	22	5.32	-7	.207	.353	—	105	-0.2
2005	Sea A	1	3	.250	49	0	0	0	0	1	3	32	36.2	32	17	3	4	22	0	34	3.93	+6	.237	.358	—	0	0.1
2006	Chi A	0	1	.000	6	0	0	0	0	0	1	3	2.2	3	1	1	0	5	1	2	3.38	+40	.300	.533	—	120	0.1
Total	15	48	45	.516	798	0	0	0	0	33	49	560	784.2	633	329	55	64	428	59	829	3.41	+33	.224	.336	—	434	10.9
Team	6	23	19	.548	331	0	0	0	0	9	18	230	311	260	135	19	21	172	22	334	3.47	+34	.228	.337	—	157	5.2
/60G	1	4	3	.548	60	0	0	0	0	2	3	42	56.1	47	24	3	4	31	4	61	3.48	+34	.228	.337	—	28	0.9
NELSON, LUKE	LUTHER MARTIN B12.4.1893 CABLE IL D11.14.1985 MOLINE IL BR/TR/6'0"/180 D5.25																										
1919	NY A	3	0	1.000	9	1	0	0	—	0	—	—	24.1	22	9	1	1	11	—	11	2.96	+8	.244	.333	+146	—	0.1
NELSON, GENE	WAYLAND EUGENE B12.3.1960 TAMPA FL BR/TR/6'0"/(174–180) DR 1978 TEXA 30/690 D5.4																										
1981	NY A	3	1	.750	8	7	0	0	3	0	0	1	39.1	40	24	5	1	23	1	16	4.81	-25	.261	.358	+38	24	-0.5
Total	13	53	64	.453	493	68	6	1	26	28	26	283	1080	1061	537	117	33	418	32	655	4.13	-1	.258	.328	-8	79	0.3
NEUER, TEX	JOHN S. B6.8.1877 FREMONT OH D1.14.1966 NORTHUMBERLAND PA TL D8.28																										
1907	NY A	4	2	.667	7	6	6	3	—	0	—	—	54	40	21	1	0	19	—	22	2.17	+29	.208	.280	+33	—	0.1
NEVEL, ERNIE	ERNIE WYRE B8.17.1918 CHARLESTON MO D7.10.1988 SPRINGFIELD MO BR/TR/6'1"/(190–200) D9.26																										
1950	NY A	0	1	.000	3	1	0	0	—	0	—	—	6.1	10	7	0	0	6	—	3	9.95	-57	.345	.457	-37	0	-0.5
1951	NY A	0	0	+	1	0	0	0	—	1	—	—	4	1	0	0	0	1	—	1	0.00	-100	.083	.154	—	0	0.1
Total	3	0	1	.000	14	1	0	0	—	1	—	—	20.2	27	14	0	0	8	—	9	6.10	-31	.329	.389	-37	0	-0.5
Team	2	0	1	.000	4	1	0	0	—	1	—	—	10.1	11	7	0	0	7	—	4	6.10	-33	.268	.375	-37	—	-0.4
NEWKIRK, FLOYD	FLOYD ELMO "THREE-FINGER" B7.16.1908 NORRIS CITY IL D4.15.1976 CLAYTON MO BR/TR/5'11"/178 D8.21 B–JOEL COL ILLINOIS COLLEGE																										
1934	NY A	0	0	+	1	0	0	0	—	0	—	—	1	1	0	0	0	1	—	0	0.00	-100	.333	.500	—	—	0.0
NEWSOM, BOBO	LOUIS NORMAN "BUCK" B8.11.1907 HARTSVILLE SC D12.7.1962 ORLANDO FL BR/TR/6'2"/(195–220) D9.11																										
1947	†NY A	7	5	.583	17	15	6	2	—	0	—	—	115.2	109	38	8	2	30	—	42	2.80	+26	.250	.301	+27	0	0.6
Total	20	211	222	.487	600	483	246	31	—	21	—	—	3759.1	3769	1908	206	61	1732	—	2082	3.98	+7	.261	.342	-11	0	5.3
NEWTON, DOC	EUSTACE JAMES B10.26.1877 INDIANAPOLIS IN D5.14.1931 MEMPHIS TN BL/TL/6'0"/185 D4.27																										
1900	Cin N	9	15	.375	36	27	22	1	—	0	—	—	235.2	255	146	4	12	100	—	89	4.12	-11	.275	.354	-26	—	-1.2
1901	Cin N	4	13	.235	20	18	17	0	—	0	—	—	168.1	190	117	6	14	59	—	65	4.12	-22	.282	.353	-10	—	-2.2
1901	Bro N	6	5	.545	13	12	9	0	—	0	—	—	105	110	42	1	7	30	—	45	2.83	+19	.268	.328	+7	—	0.8
1901	Year	10	18	.357	33	30	26	0	—	0	—	—	273.1	300	159	7	21	89	—	110	3.62	-10	.277	.343	-3	—	-1.4
1902	Bro N	15	14	.517	31	28	26	4	—	2	—	—	264.1	208	95	2	11	87	—	107	2.42	+14	**.217**	.289	-3	—	1.0
1905	NY A	2	2	.500	11	7	2	0	—	0	—	—	59.2	61	23	1	2	24	—	15	2.11	+39	.266	.341	+7	—	0.1
1906	NY A	7	5	.583	21	15	6	2	—	0	—	—	125	118	53	3	7	33	—	52	3.17	-6	.252	.311	-6	—	-0.1
1907	NY A	7	10	.412	19	15	10	0	—	0	—	—	133	132	66	0	7	31	—	70	3.18	-12	.261	.313	-5	—	-0.6
1908	NY A	4	5	.444	23	13	6	1	—	1	—	—	88.1	78	52	0	7	41	—	49	2.95	-16	.242	.341	+34	—	-0.8
1909	NY A	0	3	.000	4	4	1	0	—	0	—	—	22.1	27	17	0	3	11	—	11	2.82	-10	.300	.394	-37	—	-0.3
Total	8	54	72	.429	178	139	99	8	—	3	—	—	1201.2	1179	611	17	70	416	—	503	3.22	-4	.257	.328	-7	—	-3.3
Team	5	20	25	.444	78	54	25	3	—	1	—	—	428.1	416	211	4	26	140	—	197	2.96	-6	.258	.327	+3	—	-1.7
/180I	2	8	11	.444	33	23	11	1	—	0	—	—	180	175	89	2	11	59	—	83	2.96	-6	.258	.327	+3	—	-0.7
NIEKRO, JOE	JOSEPH FRANKLIN B11.7.1944 MARTINS FERRY OH BR/TR/6'1"/(185–195) DR 1966 CHIN S3/43 D4.16 B–PHIL S–LANCE COL WEST LIBERTY ST.																										
1985	NY A	2	1	.667	3	3	0	0	0	0	0	0	12.1	14	8	3	0	8	0	4	5.84	-31	.280	.379	+42	0	-0.4
1986	NY A	9	10	.474	25	25	0	0	10	0	0	0	125.2	139	84	15	1	63	3	59	4.87	-15	.275	.356	+9	18	-1.8
1987	NY A	3	4	.429	8	8	1	0	5	0	0	0	50.2	40	25	4	4	19	0	30	3.55	+25	.215	.300	-31	0	0.4
Total	22	221	204	.520	702	500	107	29	293	16	12	145	3584.1	3466	1620	276	65	1262	71	1747	3.59	-2	.255	.319	+6	43	-4.3
Team	3	14	15	.483	36	36	1	0	15	0	—	0	188.2	193	117	22	5	90	3	93	4.58	-8	.260	.344	+3	18	-1.8
/180I	3	13	14	.483	34	34	1	0	14	0	—	0	180	184	112	21	5	86	3	89	4.58	-8	.260	.344	+3	17	-1.7
NIEKRO, PHIL	PHILIP HENRY B4.1.1939 BLAINE OH BR/TR/6'1"/(180–195) D4.15 HF1997 B–JOE																										
1984	NY A☆	16	8	.667	32	31	5	1	22	0	0	1	215.2	219	85	15	3	76	0	136	3.09	+24	.267	.327	+24	0	1.8
1985	NY A	16	12	.571	33	33	7	1	18	0	0	0	220	203	110	29	2	120	1	149	4.09	-1	.245	.341	+6	0	-0.1
Total	24	318	274	.537	864	716	245	45	481	29	8	110	5404	5044	2337	482	123	1809	86	3342	3.35	+15	.247	.311	-3	16	29.1
Team	2	32	20	.615	65	64	12	2	40	0	0	1	435.2	422	195	44	5	196	1	285	3.59	+10	.256	.334	+15	—	1.7
/180I	1	13	8	.615	27	26	5	1	17	0	0	0	180	174	81	18	2	81	0	118	3.59	+10	.256	.334	+15	—	0.7
NIELSEN, JERRY	GERALD ARTHUR B8.5.1966 SACRAMENTO CA BL/TL/6'3"/185 DR 1988 NYA 18/469 D7.12 COL FLORIDA ST.																										
1992	NY A	1	0	1.000	20	0	0	0	0	0	0	15	19.2	17	10	1	0	18	2	12	4.58	-14	.243	.393	—	0	0.0
1993	Cal A	0	0	+	10	0	0	0	0	0	0	4	12.1	18	13	1	1	4	0	8	8.03	-43	.340	.377	—	0	-0.2
Total	2	1	0	1.000	30	0	0	0	0	0	0	19	32	35	23	2	1	22	2	20	5.91	-29	.285	.387	—	0	-0.2
NIELSEN, SCOTT	JEFFREY SCOTT B12.18.1958 SALT LAKE CITY UT BR/TR/6'1"/190 DR 1983 SEAA 6/139 D7.7 COL BRIGHAM YOUNG																										
1986	NY A	4	4	.500	10	9	2	2	6	0	0	1	56	66	29	12	2	12	0	20	4.02	+3	.299	.340	+29	0	0.0
1987	Chi A	3	5	.375	19	7	1	1	3	2	0	4	66.1	83	48	9	1	25	1	23	6.24	-26	.307	.366	+27	0	-1.2
1988	NY A	1	2	.333	7	2	0	0	0	0	0	3	19.2	27	16	5	0	13	2	4	6.86	-42	.333	.426	+26	0	-0.8
1989	NY A	1	0	1.000	2	0	0	0	0	0	0	1	0.2	2	1	0	0	1	0	0	13.50	-71	.500	.600	—	0	-0.1
Total	4	9	11	.450	38	18	3	3	9	2	0	9	142.2	178	94	26	3	51	3	47	5.49	-21	.309	.367	+27	0	-2.1
Team	3	6	6	.500	19	11	2	2	6	0	0	5	76.1	95	46	17	2	26	2	24	4.83	-15	.310	.368	+28	—	-0.9

YEAR	TM LG	W	L	PCT	G	GS	CG	SHO	QS	SV	BS	QR	IP	H	R	HR	HB	BB	IB	SO	ERA	AERA	OAV	OOB	SUP	DL	PW
Nitkowski, C. J. Christopher John B3.9.1973 Suffern NY BL/TL/6'3"/(190–210) Dr 1994 CinN 1/9 d6.3 Col St. Johns																											
2004	NY A	1	1	.500	19	0	0	0	0	0	0	12	13	18	11	1	4	6	0	10	7.62	-40	.327	.431	—	0	-0.5
Total	10	18	32	.360	336	44	0	0	7	3	11	184	479	519	318	57	36	263	21	347	5.37	-13	.279	.375	-1	18	-3.3
Nottebart, Don Donald Edward B1.23.1936 West Newton MA D10.4.2007 Cypress TX BR/TR/6'1"/(190–208) d7.1																											
1969	NY A	0	0	+	4	0	0	0	0	0	0	3	6	6	3	1	1	0	0	5	4.50	-22	.261	.292	—	0	0.0
Total	9	36	51	.414	296	89	16	2	48	21	6	140	928.1	902	443	69	18	283	29	525	3.65	-4	.256	.312	-5	0	-3.0
O'Connor, Andy Andrew James B9.14.1884 Roxbury MA D9.26.1980 Norwood MA BR/TR/6'0"/160 d10.6																											
1908	NY A	0	1	.000	1	1	1	0	—	0	—	—	8	15	11	0	3	7	—	5	10.13	-76	.429	.556	-17	—	-0.6
O'Doul, Lefty Francis Joseph B3.4.1897 San Francisco CA D12.7.1969 San Francisco CA BL/TL/6'0"/180 d4.29 ▲																											
1919	NY A	0	0	+	3	0	0	0	—	0	—	—	5	7	6	0	0	4	—	2	3.60	-11	.304	.407	—	—	-0.1
1920	NY A	0	0	+	2	0	0	0	—	0	—	—	3.2	4	2	0	1	2	—	2	4.91	-22	.286	.412	—	—	0.0
1922	NY A	0	0	+	6	0	0	0	—	0	—	—	16	24	13	0	0	12	—	5	3.38	+19	.353	.450	—	—	0.0
Total	4	1	1	.500	34	1	0	0	—	0	—	—	77.2	104	71	2	5	49	—	19	4.87	-17	.335	.434	+21	—	-0.8
Team	3	0	0	+	11	0	0	0	—	0	—	—	24.2	35	21	0	1	18	—	9	3.65	+5	.333	.435	—	—	-0.1
Ohlendorf, Ross Curtis Ross B8.8.1982 Austin TX BR/TR/6'4"/235 Dr 2004 AriN 4/116 d9.11 Col Princeton																											
2007	†NY A	0	0	+	6	0	0	0	0	0	0	4	6.1	5	2	1	0	2	0	9	2.84	+59	.208	.269	—	0	0.1
Ojeda, Bob Robert Michael B12.17.1957 Los Angeles CA BL/TL/6'1"/(185–195) d7.13 Col Sequoias (CA) [JC]																											
1994	NY A	0	0	+	2	2	0	0	0	0	0	0	3	11	8	1	0	6	0	3	24.00	-81	.611	.680	+20	0	-0.3
Total	15	115	98	.540	351	291	41	16	165	1	2	50	1884.1	1833	856	145	24	676	48	1128	3.65	+4	.257	.321	+1	274	4.7
Orosco, Jesse Jesse Russell B4.21.1957 Santa Barbara CA BR/TL/6'2"/(174–205) Dr 1978 MinA*2/41 d4.5 Col Santa Barbara (CA) City																											
2003	NY A	0	0	+	15	0	0	0	0	0	1	11	4.1	4	6	0	0	6	3	4	10.38	-58	.250	.435	—	0	-0.1
Total	24	87	80	.521	1252	4	0	0	0	144	76	934	1295.1	1055	512	113	34	581	86	1179	3.16	+26	.223	.309	-3	195	18.9
Orth, Al Albert Lewis "Smiling Al","The Curveless Wonder" B9.5.1872 Tipton IN D10.8.1948 Lynchburg VA BL/TR/6'0"/200 d8.15 U6 Col DePauw ▲																											
1895	Phi N	8	1	.889	11	10	9	0	—	1	—	—	88	103	50	0	2	22	—	25	3.89	+23	.288	.332	+59	—	1.0
1896	Phi N	15	10	.600	25	23	19	0	—	0	—	—	196	244	128	10	3	46	—	23	4.41	-2	.302	.342	+3	—	0.2
1897	Phi N	14	19	.424	36	34	29	2	—	0	—	—	282.1	349	194	12	6	82	—	64	4.62	-9	.301	.350	+4	—	-0.4
1898	Phi N	15	13	.536	32	28	25	1	—	0	—	—	250	290	131	2	8	53	—	52	3.02	+14	.288	.329	+22	—	1.7
1899	Phi N	14	3	.824	21	15	13	3	—	1	—	—	144.2	149	67	0	3	19	—	35	**2.49**	+48	.266	.294	+5	—	1.6
1900	Phi N	14	14	.500	33	30	24	2	—	1	—	—	262	302	145	4	13	60	—	68	3.78	-4	.288	.335	+5	—	0.5
1901	Phi N	20	12	.625	35	33	30	0	—	1	—	—	281.2	250	101	3	8	32	—	92	2.27	+50	.237	**.264**	-5	—	**4.4**
1902	Was A	19	18	.514	38	37	36	1	—	0	—	—	324	367	181	18	9	40	—	76	3.97	-7	.286	.312	+1	—	-0.3
1903	Was A	10	22	.313	36	32	30	2	—	**2**	—	—	279.2	326	174	8	7	62	—	88	4.34	-28	.290	.331	-25	—	-2.4
1904	Was A	3	4	.429	10	7	7	0	—	0	—	—	73.2	88	49	2	3	15	—	23	4.76	-44	.297	.338	+34	—	-1.3
1904	NY A	11	6	.647	20	18	11	2	—	0	—	—	137.2	122	47	0	3	19	—	47	2.68	+1	.238	.270	-2	—	0.8
1904	Year	14	10	.583	30	25	18	2	—	0	—	—	211.1	210	96	2	6	34	—	70	3.41	-21	.260	.295	+8	—	-0.5
1905	NY A	18	16	.529	40	37	26	6	—	0	—	—	305.1	273	122	8	7	61	—	121	2.86	+3	.241	.284	-1	—	0.6
1906	NY A	**27**	17	.614	45	39	**36**	3	—	0	—	—	**338.2**	317	115	2	1	66	—	133	2.34	+27	.251	.289	-10	—	3.4
1907	NY A	14	21	.400	36	33	21	2	—	0	—	—	248.2	244	134	2	6	53	—	78	2.61	+7	.259	.303	-2	—	0.5
1908	NY A	2	13	.133	21	17	8	1	—	0	—	—	139.1	134	62	4	4	30	—	22	3.42	-28	.255	.300	-7	—	-0.5
1909	NY A	0	0	+	1	1	0	0	—	0	—	—	3	6	4	0	0	1	—	1	12.00	-79	.429	.467	+151	—	-0.1
Total	15	204	189	.519	440	394	324	31	—	6	—	—	3354.2	3564	1704	75	83	661	—	948	3.37	+1	.272	.311	+1	—	9.7
Team	6	72	73	.497	163	145	102	14	—	0	—	—	1172.2	1096	484	16	21	230	—	402	2.72	+4	.250	.290	-3	—	4.7
/180I	1	11	11	.497	25	22	16	2	—	0	—	—	180	168	74	2	3	35	—	62	2.72	+4	.250	.290	-3	—	0.7
Osborne, Donovan Donovan Alan B6.21.1969 Roseville CA BB/TL/6'2"/(195–210) Dr 1990 StLN 1/13 d4.9 Col Nevada–Las Vegas [DL 1994 StL N 131]																											
2004	NY A	2	0	1.000	9	2	0	0	0	0	0	4	17.2	25	16	3	2	5	0	10	7.13	-36	.347	.405	+41	0	-0.5
Total	9	49	46	.516	163	140	4	2	84	0	0	14	873.2	895	442	100	18	246	19	558	4.03	+0	.266	.317	-8	668	0.0
Ostrowski, Joe Joseph Paul "Professor","Specs" B11.15.1916 W.Wyoming PA D1.3.2003 Wilkes–Barre PA BL/TL/6'0"/180 d7.18 Col Scranton																											
1948	StL A	4	6	.400	26	9	3	0	—	3	—	—	78.1	108	54	6	0	17	—	20	5.97	-24	.333	.367	-30	0	-1.0
1949	StL A	8	8	.500	40	13	4	0	—	2	—	—	141	185	94	16	0	27	—	34	4.79	-5	.307	.337	+3	0	-0.4
1950	StL A	2	4	.333	9	7	2	0	—	0	—	—	57.1	57	22	2	0	7	—	15	2.51	+97	.251	.274	-32	0	1.4
1950	NY A	1	1	.500	21	4	1	0	—	3	—	—	43.2	50	26	11	0	15	—	15	5.15	-17	.294	.351	+47	0	-0.2
1950	Year	3	5	.375	30	11	3	0	—	3	—	—	101	107	48	13	0	22	—	30	3.65	+28	.270	.308	-5	0	1.2
1951	†NY A	6	4	.600	34	3	2	0	—	5	—	—	95.1	103	44	4	1	18	—	30	3.49	+10	.279	.314	+109	0	0.1
1952	NY A	2	2	.500	20	1	0	0	—	2	—	—	40	56	31	5	1	14	—	17	5.62	-41	.327	.382	+5	0	-1.4
Total	5	23	25	.479	150	37	12	0	—	15	—	—	455.2	559	271	44	2	98	—	131	4.54	-5	.300	.336	+4	0	-1.5
Team	3	9	7	.563	75	8	3	0	—	10	—	—	179	209	101	20	2	47	—	62	4.37	-13	.294	.339	+65	—	-1.5
/60G	2	7	6	.563	60	6	2	0	—	8	—	—	143.1	167	81	16	2	38	—	50	4.37	-13	.294	.339	+65	—	-1.2
Osuna, Antonio Antonio Pedro B4.12.1973 Guasave, Sinaloa, Mexico BR/TR/5'11"/(160–225) d4.25																											
2003	NY A	2	5	.286	48	0	0	0	0	0	1	29	50.2	58	22	3	2	20	3	47	3.73	+18	.282	.348	—	49	0.5
Total	11	36	29	.554	411	0	0	0	0	21	22	292	488.2	432	217	44	17	209	27	501	3.68	+12	.238	.320	—	749	5.1
/60G	1	3	6	.286	60	0	0	0	0	0	1	36	63.1	73	28	4	3	25	4	59	3.73	+18	.282	.348	—	61	0.6
Overmire, Stubby Frank W. B5.16.1919 Moline MI D3.3.1977 Lakeland FL BR/TL/5'7"/170 d4.25 C4 Col Western Michigan																											
1951	NY A	1	1	.500	15	4	1	0	—	0	—	—	44.2	50	27	2	2	18	—	14	4.63	-17	.287	.361	+33	0	-0.2
Total	10	58	67	.464	266	137	50	11	—	10	—	—	1130.2	1259	569	56	11	325	—	301	3.96	-2	.280	.330	-6	0	-1.1
Pacella, John John Lewis B9.15.1956 Brooklyn NY BR/TR/6'3"/(180–195) Dr 1974 NYN 4/89 d9.15																											
1982	NY A	0	1	.000	3	1	0	0	0	0	0	0	10	13	8	0	1	9	1	2	7.20	-44	.342	.451	-77	0	-0.3
Total	6	4	10	.286	74	21	0	0	7	3	1	33	191.2	206	135	21	3	133	5	116	5.73	-32	.282	.391	-4	24	-2.8
Padilla, Juan Juan Miguel B2.17.1977 Rio Piedras, PR BR/TR/6'0"/200 Dr 1998 MinA 24/709 d7.16 Col Jacksonville [DL 2007 NY N 182]																											
2004	NY A	0	0	+	6	0	0	0	0	0	0	3	11.1	16	5	1	0	4	0	5	3.97	+16	.348	.400	—	0	0.1
Total	2	4	1	.800	42	0	0	0	0	1	1	30	62	63	29	7	3	25	2	34	4.06	+5	.259	.336	—	182	0.7
Pagan, Dave David Percy B9.15.1949 Nipawin SK, Can. BR/TR/6'2"/175 d7.1																											
1973	NY A	0	0	+	4	1	0	0	0	0	0	3	12.2	16	4	1	0	1	0	9	2.84	+31	.320	.333	+165	0	0.1
1974	NY A	1	3	.250	16	6	1	0	1	0	0	5	49.1	49	29	1	0	28	0	39	5.11	-31	.265	.362	+12	0	-0.6
1975	NY A	0	0	+	13	0	0	0	0	1	0	9	31	30	16	2	2	13	5	18	4.06	-9	.256	.336	—	0	-0.1
1976	NY A	1	1	.500	7	2	1	0	1	0	0	4	23.2	18	7	0	0	4	0	13	2.28	+50	.222	.253	-23	0	0.2
1976	Bal A	1	4	.200	20	5	0	0	2	1	1	7	46.2	54	33	2	1	23	1	34	5.98	-45	.298	.370	+7	0	-1.5
1976	Year	2	5	.286	27	7	1	0	3	1	1	11	70.1	72	40	2	1	27	1	47	4.73	-30	.275	.336	-2	0	-1.3
1977	Sea A	1	1	.500	24	4	1	1	1	2	1	8	66	86	52	3	2	26	2	30	6.14	-32	.323	.383	+8	0	-0.8
1977	Pit N	0	0	+	1	0	0	0	0	0	0	1	3	1	0	0	0	0	0	4	0.00	-100	.100	.100	—	0	0.1
1977	Major	1	1	.500	25	4	1	1	1	2	1	9	69	87	52	3	2	26	2	34	5.87	-35	.315	.373	+8	0	-0.7
Total	5	4	9	.308	85	18	3	1	5	4	2	37	232.1	254	141	9	5	95	8	147	4.96	-26	.285	.353	+12	0	-2.6
Team	4	2	4	.333	40	9	2	0	2	1	0	21	116.2	113	56	4	2	46	5	79	4.01	-11	.261	.332	+21	—	-0.4
/60G	6	3	6	.333	60	14	3	0	3	2	0	32	175	170	84	6	3	69	8	119	4.01	-11	.261	.332	+21	—	-0.6

Page, Joe Joseph Francis "Fireman" B10.28.1917 Cherry Valley PA D4.21.1980 Latrobe PA BL/TL/6'2"/205 d4.19

YEAR	TM LG	W	L	PCT	G	GS	CG	SHO	QS	SV	BS	QR	IP	H	R	HR	HB	BB	IB	SO	ERA	AERA	OAV	OOB	SUP	DL	PW
1944	NY A☆	5	7	.417	19	16	4	0	—	0	—	—	102.2	100	65	3	3	52	—	63	4.56	-24	.258	.351	-3	0	-1.5
1945	NY A	6	3	.667	20	9	4	0	—	0	—	—	102	95	43	1	0	46	—	50	2.82	+23	.246	.326	+39	0	0.4
1946	NY A	9	8	.529	31	17	6	1	—	3	—	—	136	126	66	7	4	72	—	77	3.57	-3	.252	.351	+42	0	-0.5
1947	†NY A★	14	8	.636	56	2	0	0	—	**17**	—	—	141.1	105	41	5	1	72	—	116	2.48	+42	.208	.308	+63	0	3.3
1948	NY A☆	7	8	.467	**55**	1	0	0	—	16	—	—	107.2	116	59	6	1	66	—	77	4.26	-4	.275	.374	+143	0	-0.2
1949	†NY A	13	8	.619	**60**	0	0	0	—	**27**	—	—	135.1	103	44	8	5	75	—	99	2.59	+56	.215	.328	—	0	4.0
1950	NY A	3	7	.300	37	0	0	0	—	13	—	—	55.1	66	34	8	0	31	—	33	5.04	-15	.295	.380	—	0	-0.9
1954	Pit N	0	0	+	7	0	0	0	—	0	—	—	9.2	16	17	4	1	7	—	4	11.17	-63	.364	.462	—	0	-0.4
Total	8	57	49	.538	285	45	14	1	—	76	—	—	790	727	369	42	15	421	—	519	3.53	+6	.247	.344	+24	0	4.2
Team	7	57	49	.538	278	45	14	1	—	76	—	—	780.1	711	352	38	14	414	—	515	3.44	+9	.245	.342	+29	—	4.6
/60G	2	12	11	.538	60	10	3	0	—	16	—	—	168.1	153	76	8	3	89	—	111	3.44	+9	.245	.342	+29	—	1.0

Pall, Donn Donn Steven B1.11.1962 Chicago IL BR/TR/6'1"/(179–185) Dr 1985 ChiA 23/579 d8.1 Col Illinois

YEAR	TM LG	W	L	PCT	G	GS	CG	SHO	QS	SV	BS	QR	IP	H	R	HR	HB	BB	IB	SO	ERA	AERA	OAV	OOB	SUP	DL	PW
1994	NY A	1	2	.333	26	0	0	0	0	0	0	16	35	43	18	3	1	9	0	21	3.60	+28	.295	.338	—	0	0.2
Total	10	24	23	.511	328	0	0	0	0	10	9	213	505.1	519	231	52	21	139	29	278	3.63	+10	.268	.322	—	14	1.8

Parker, Christian Christian Michael B7.3.1975 Albuquerque NM BR/TR/6'1"/200 Dr 1996 MonN 4/100 d4.6 Col Notre Dame [DL 2002 NY A 183]

YEAR	TM LG	W	L	PCT	G	GS	CG	SHO	QS	SV	BS	QR	IP	H	R	HR	HB	BB	IB	SO	ERA	AERA	OAV	OOB	SUP	DL	PW
2001	NY A	0	1	.000	1	1	0	0	0	0	0	0	3	8	7	2	0	1	0	1	21.00	-79	.471	.500	-17	184	-0.7

Parker, Clay James Clayton B12.19.1962 Columbia LA BR/TR/6'1"/(175–185) Dr 1985 SeaA 15/373 d9.14 Col Louisiana St.

YEAR	TM LG	W	L	PCT	G	GS	CG	SHO	QS	SV	BS	QR	IP	H	R	HR	HB	BB	IB	SO	ERA	AERA	OAV	OOB	SUP	DL	PW
1987	Sea A	0	0	+	3	1	0	0	0	0	0	0	7.2	15	10	2	1	4	0	8	10.57	-55	.405	.465	-4	0	-0.2
1989	NY A	4	5	.444	22	17	2	0	8	0	0	5	120	123	53	12	2	31	3	53	3.68	+6	.264	.311	-7	21	0.3
1990	NY A	1	1	.500	5	2	0	0	1	0	0	2	22	19	11	5	0	7	1	20	4.50	-11	.229	.286	+25	0	-0.1
1990	Det A	2	2	.500	24	1	0	0	0	0	0	16	51	45	18	6	1	25	5	20	3.18	+25	.242	.332	-31	0	0.4
1990	Year	3	3	.500	29	3	0	0	1	0	0	18	73	64	29	11	1	32	6	40	3.58	+11	.238	.318	+7	0	0.3
1992	Sea A	0	2	.000	8	6	0	0	1	0	0	1	33.1	47	28	6	2	11	0	20	7.56	-47	.338	.390	+18	118	-0.6
Total	4	7	10	.412	62	27	2	0	10	0	0	24	234	249	120	31	6	78	9	121	4.42	-10	.273	.332	+0	139	-0.2
Team	2	5	6	.455	27	19	2	0	9	0	0	7	142	142	64	17	2	38	4	73	3.80	+3	.259	.307	-4	21	0.2
/180I	3	6	8	.455	34	24	3	0	11	0	0	9	180	180	81	22	3	48	5	93	3.80	+3	.259	.307	-4	27	0.3

Patterson, Gil Gilbert Thomas B9.5.1955 Philadelphia PA BR/TR/6'1"/185 Dr 1975 NYA S1/7 d4.19 C4 Col Miami–Dade Kendall (FL) CC

YEAR	TM LG	W	L	PCT	G	GS	CG	SHO	QS	SV	BS	QR	IP	H	R	HR	HB	BB	IB	SO	ERA	AERA	OAV	OOB	SUP	DL	PW
1977	NY A	1	2	.333	10	6	0	0	1	1	0	3	33.1	38	20	3	3	20	1	29	5.40	-27	.290	.396	+10	0	-0.4

Patterson, Jeff Jeffrey Simmons B10.1.1968 Anaheim CA BR/TR/6'2"/200 Dr 1988 PhiN 58/1353 d4.30 Col Cypress (CA) JC

YEAR	TM LG	W	L	PCT	G	GS	CG	SHO	QS	SV	BS	QR	IP	H	R	HR	HB	BB	IB	SO	ERA	AERA	OAV	OOB	SUP	DL	PW
1995	NY A	0	0	+	3	0	0	0	0	0	0	2	3.1	3	1	1	0	3	0	3	2.70	+71	.231	.375	—	0	0.0

Pavano, Carl Carl Anthony B1.8.1976 New Britain CT BR/TR/6'5"/(225–240) Dr 1994 BosA 13/355 d5.23 [DL 2006 NY A 182]

YEAR	TM LG	W	L	PCT	G	GS	CG	SHO	QS	SV	BS	QR	IP	H	R	HR	HB	BB	IB	SO	ERA	AERA	OAV	OOB	SUP	DL	PW
2005	NY A	4	6	.400	17	17	1	1	8	0	0	0	100	129	66	17	8	18	1	56	4.77	-10	.315	.354	+11	97	-0.9
2007	NY A	1	0	1.000	2	2	0	0	1	0	0	0	11.1	12	7	1	0	2	0	4	4.76	-5	.273	.304	+75	173	0.0
Total	9	62	64	.492	186	168	6	4	98	0	0	12	1049	1126	549	113	58	291	36	677	4.27	-1	.276	.330	-3	747	-0.7
Team	2	5	6	.455	19	19	1	1	9	0	—	0	111.1	141	73	18	8	20	1	60	4.77	-9	.311	.349	+18	270	-0.9

Pavlas, Dave David Lee B8.12.1962 Frankfurt, West Germany BR/TR/6'7"/(180–205) d8.21 Col Rice

YEAR	TM LG	W	L	PCT	G	GS	CG	SHO	QS	SV	BS	QR	IP	H	R	HR	HB	BB	IB	SO	ERA	AERA	OAV	OOB	SUP	DL	PW
1990	Chi N	2	0	1.000	13	0	0	0	0	0	0	10	21.1	23	7	2	0	6	2	12	2.11	+94	.271	.312	—	0	0.3
1991	Chi N	0	0	+	1	0	0	0	0	0	0	0	1	3	2	1	0	0	0	0	18.00	-78	.750	.750	—	0	-0.1
1995	NY A	0	0	+	4	0	0	0	0	0	0	3	5.2	8	2	0	0	0	0	3	3.18	+46	.333	.333	—	0	0.0
1996	NY A	0	0	+	16	0	0	0	0	1	0	11	23	23	7	0	1	7	2	18	2.35	+111	.264	.326	—	0	0.3
Total	4	2	0	1.000	34	0	0	0	0	1	0	24	51	57	18	3	1	13	4	33	2.65	+72	.285	.329	—	0	0.5
Team	2	0	0	+	20	0	0	0	0	1	0	14	28.2	31	9	0	1	7	2	21	2.51	+95	.279	.328	—	—	0.3

Pearson, Monte Montgomery Marcellus "Hoot" B9.2.1909 Oakland CA D1.27.1978 Fresno CA BR/TR/6'0"/175 d4.22 Col California [DL 1942 Cin N 140]

YEAR	TM LG	W	L	PCT	G	GS	CG	SHO	QS	SV	BS	QR	IP	H	R	HR	HB	BB	IB	SO	ERA	AERA	OAV	OOB	SUP	DL	PW
1932	Cle A	0	0	+	8	0	0	0	—	0	—	—	8	10	9	1	0	11	—	5	10.13	-53	.323	.500	—	—	-0.1
1933	Cle A	10	5	.667	19	16	10	0	—	0	—	—	135.1	111	45	5	0	55	—	54	**2.33**	+91	.221	.297	-2	—	3.1
1934	Cle A	18	13	.581	39	33	19	0	—	2	—	—	254.2	257	144	16	1	130	—	140	4.52	+1	.260	.346	+6	—	0.9
1935	Cle A	8	13	.381	30	24	10	1	—	0	—	—	181.2	199	117	9	0	103	—	90	4.90	-8	.279	.371	-9	—	-0.8
1936	†NY A☆	19	7	**.731**	33	31	15	1	—	1	—	—	223	191	99	13	3	135	—	118	3.71	+25	**.233**	.343	+52	—	3.3
1937	†NY A	9	3	.750	22	20	7	1	—	1	—	—	144.2	145	60	6	1	64	—	71	3.17	+40	.261	.339	+21	—	1.6
1938	†NY A	16	7	.696	28	27	17	1	—	1	—	—	202	198	107	12	0	113	—	98	3.97	+14	.258	.354	+33	—	1.3
1939	†NY A	12	5	.706	22	20	8	0	—	0	—	—	146.1	151	77	9	1	70	—	76	4.49	-3	.272	.354	+58	—	0.6
1940	NY A☆	7	5	.583	16	16	7	1	—	0	—	—	109.2	108	48	8	0	44	—	43	3.69	+9	.262	.333	+8	—	0.6
1941	Cin N	1	3	.250	7	4	1	0	—	0	—	—	24.1	22	15	3	0	15	—	8	5.18	-31	.242	.349	-29	0	-0.6
Total	10	100	61	.621	224	191	94	5	—	4	—	—	1429.2	1392	721	82	6	740	—	703	4.00	+12	.256	.346	+21	140	9.9
Team	5	63	27	.700	121	114	54	4	—	2	—	—	825.2	793	391	48	5	426	—	406	3.82	+17	.255	.346	+37	—	7.4
/180I	1	14	6	.700	26	25	12	1	—	0	—	—	180	173	85	10	1	93	—	89	3.82	+17	.255	.346	+37	—	1.6

Peek, Steve Stephen George B7.30.1914 Springfield MA D9.20.1991 Syracuse NY BB/TR/6'2"/195 d4.16 Mil 1942–45 Col St. Lawrence

YEAR	TM LG	W	L	PCT	G	GS	CG	SHO	QS	SV	BS	QR	IP	H	R	HR	HB	BB	IB	SO	ERA	AERA	OAV	OOB	SUP	DL	PW
1941	NY A	4	2	.667	17	8	2	0	—	0	—	—	80	85	48	6	0	39	—	18	5.06	-22	.276	.357	+21	0	-0.8

Pena, Hipolito Hipolito (Concepcion) B1.30.1964 Fantino, D.R. BL/TL/6'3"/165 d9.1

YEAR	TM LG	W	L	PCT	G	GS	CG	SHO	QS	SV	BS	QR	IP	H	R	HR	HB	BB	IB	SO	ERA	AERA	OAV	OOB	SUP	DL	PW
1986	Pit N	0	3	.000	10	1	0	0	0	1	0	6	8.1	7	10	3	1	3	1	6	8.64	-55	.206	.289	-100	0	-0.9
1987	Pit N	0	3	.000	16	1	0	0	0	1	0	11	25.2	16	14	2	0	26	3	16	4.56	-9	.184	.372	-78	0	-0.1
1988	NY A	1	1	.500	16	0	0	0	0	0	0	11	14.1	10	8	1	0	9	1	10	3.14	+26	.192	.306	—	0	0.0
Total	3	1	7	.125	42	2	0	0	0	2	0	28	48.1	33	32	6	1	38	5	32	4.84	-16	.191	.338	-89	0	-1.0

Pennock, Herb Herbert Jefferis "The Knight of Kennett Square" B2.10.1894 Kennett Square PA D1.30.1948 New York NY BB/TL/6'0"/160 d5.14 Mil 1918 C4 HF1948

YEAR	TM LG	W	L	PCT	G	GS	CG	SHO	QS	SV	BS	QR	IP	H	R	HR	HB	BB	IB	SO	ERA	AERA	OAV	OOB	SUP	DL	PW
1912	Phi A	1	2	.333	17	2	1	0	—	2	—	—	50	48	31	1	3	30	—	38	4.50	-32	.262	.375	+20	—	-0.5
1913	Phi A	2	1	.667	14	3	1	0	—	0	—	—	33.1	30	24	4	0	22	—	17	5.13	-46	.242	.356	+123	—	-0.8
1914	†Phi A	11	4	.733	28	14	8	3	—	3	—	—	151.2	136	56	1	2	65	—	90	2.79	-6	.248	.330	+40	—	-0.1
1915	Phi A	3	6	.333	11	8	3	1	—	1	—	—	44	46	34	2	2	29	—	24	5.32	-45	.266	.377	-19	—	-1.9
1915	Bos A	0	0	+	5	1	0	0	—	0	—	—	14	23	16	0	0	10	—	7	9.64	-71	.390	.478	+162	—	-0.5
1915	Year	3	6	.333	16	9	3	1	—	1	—	—	58	69	50	2	2	39	—	31	6.36	-55	.297	.403	+1	—	-2.4
1916	Bos A	0	2	.000	9	2	0	0	—	1	—	—	26.2	23	11	0	1	8	—	12	3.04	-9	.245	.311	-73	—	-0.1
1917	Bos A	5	5	.500	24	5	4	1	—	1	—	—	100.2	90	49	2	3	23	—	35	3.31	-22	.243	.292	+17	—	-0.7
1919	Bos A	16	8	.667	32	26	16	5	—	0	—	—	219	223	78	2	3	48	—	70	2.71	+11	.274	.316	+20	—	1.0
1920	Bos A	16	13	.552	37	31	19	4	—	2	—	—	242.1	244	108	9	4	61	—	68	3.68	-1	.264	.312	-3	—	0.6
1921	Bos A	13	14	.481	32	31	15	1	—	0	—	—	222.2	268	121	7	2	59	—	91	4.04	+5	.307	.352	-21	—	0.5
1922	Bos A	10	17	.370	32	26	15	1	—	1	—	—	202	230	108	7	1	74	—	59	4.32	-5	.297	.359	-28	—	-0.5
1923	†NY A	19	6	**.760**	35	27	21	1	—	3	—	—	238.1	235	86	11	2	68	—	93	3.13	+26	.261	.314	+21	—	2.4
1924	NY A	21	9	.700	40	34	25	4	—	3	—	—	286.1	302	104	13	1	64	—	101	2.83	+47	.273	.314	+7	—	3.8
1925	NY A	16	17	.485	47	31	21	2	—	2	—	—	**277**	267	117	11	2	71	—	88	2.96	+44	.254	**.303**	-16	—	3.3
1926	†NY A	23	11	.676	40	33	19	1	—	2	—	—	266.1	294	133	11	4	43	—	78	3.62	+7	.282	**.313**	+19	—	1.0
1927	†NY A	19	8	.704	34	26	18	1	—	2	—	—	209.2	225	89	5	2	48	—	51	3.00	+28	.283	.325	+34	—	2.1
1928	NY A	17	6	.739	28	24	18	0	—	3	—	—	211	215	71	2	0	40	—	53	2.56	+47	.267	.302	+14	—	3.1
1929	NY A	9	11	.450	27	23	8	1	—	2	—	—	157.1	205	101	11	3	28	—	49	4.92	-22	.318	.349	+8	—	-2.1
1930	NY A	11	7	.611	25	19	11	1	—	0	—	—	156.1	194	95	8	0	20	—	46	4.32	+0	.301	.322	+37	—	-0.5
1931	NY A	11	6	.647	25	25	12	1	—	0	—	—	189.1	247	96	7	1	30	—	65	4.28	-7	.315	.342	+47	—	-0.2
1932	†NY A	9	5	.643	22	21	9	1	—	0	—	—	146.2	191	94	8	0	38	—	54	4.60	-11	.310	.350	+43	—	-1.0
1933	NY A	7	4	.636	23	5	2	1	—	4	—	—	65	96	46	4	0	21	—	22	5.54	-30	.342	.387	+80	—	-1.9

YEAR	TM LG	W	L	PCT	G	GS	CG	SHO	QS	SV	BS	QR	IP	H	R	HR	HB	BB	IB	SO	ERA	AERA	OAV	OOB	SUP	DL	PW
1934	Bos A	2	0	1.000	30	2	1	0	—	1	—	—	62	68	31	2	0	16	—	16	3.05	+58	.276	.321	+63	—	0.3
Total	22	241	162	.598	617	419	247	35	—	33	—	—	3571.2	3900	1699	128	36	916	—	1227	3.60	+6	.282	.328	+13	—	7.3
Team	11	162	90	.643	346	268	164	14	—	21	—	—	2203.1	2471	1032	91	15	471	—	700	3.54	+13	.285	.323	+21	—	10.0
/180I	1	13	7	.643	28	22	13	1	—	2	—	—	180	202	84	7	1	38	—	57	3.54	+13	.285	.323	+21	—	0.8

PEREZ, MELIDO MELIDO TURPEN GROSS (B MELIDO TURPEN GROSS (PEREZ)) B2.15.1966 SAN CRISTOBAL, D.R. BR/TR/6'4"/(180–210) D9.4 B–PASCUAL B–CARLOS [DL 1996 NY A 182]

YEAR	TM LG	W	L	PCT	G	GS	CG	SHO	QS	SV	BS	QR	IP	H	R	HR	HB	BB	IB	SO	ERA	AERA	OAV	OOB	SUP	DL	PW
1987	KC A	1	1	.500	3	3	0	0	1	0	0	0	10.1	18	12	2	0	5	0	5	7.84	-41	.375	.434	+26	0	-0.7
1988	Chi A	12	10	.545	32	32	3	1	19	0	0	0	197	186	105	26	2	72	0	138	3.79	+6	.248	.313	-1	0	-0.1
1989	Chi A	11	14	.440	31	31	2	0	15	0	0	0	183.1	187	106	23	3	90	0	141	5.01	-23	.264	.348	-4	0	-2.5
1990	Chi A	13	14	.481	35	35	3	3	19	0	0	0	197	177	111	14	2	86	1	161	4.61	-17	.241	.320	+2	0	-2.2
1991	Chi A	8	7	.533	49	8	0	0	2	1	4	29	135.2	111	49	15	1	52	0	128	3.12	+28	.224	.299	-14	0	1.5
1992	NY A	13	16	.448	33	33	10	1	25	0	0	0	247.2	212	94	16	5	93	5	218	2.87	+38	.235	.308	-11	0	2.9
1993	NY A	6	14	.300	25	25	0	0	10	0	0	0	163	173	103	22	1	64	5	148	5.19	-19	.267	.333	-26	13	-2.0
1994	NY A	9	4	.692	22	22	1	0	15	0	0	0	151.1	134	74	16	3	58	5	109	4.10	+12	.238	.311	+0	0	0.6
1995	NY A	5	5	.500	13	12	1	0	8	0	0	1	69.1	70	46	10	1	31	2	44	5.58	-17	.261	.337	+29	69	-1.0
Total	9	78	85	.479	243	201	20	5	114	1	4	30	1354.2	1268	700	144	18	551	21	1092	4.17	-2	.248	.321	-4	264	-3.5
Team	4	33	39	.458	93	92	12	1	58	0	0	1	631.1	589	317	64	10	246	17	519	4.06	+5	.247	.319	-7	82	0.5
/180I	1	9	11	.458	27	26	3	0	17	0	0	0	180	168	90	18	3	70	5	148	4.06	+5	.247	.319	-7	23	0.1

PEREZ, PASCUAL PASCUAL GROSS (B PASCUAL GROSS (PEREZ)) B5.17.1957 SAN CRISTOBAL, D.R. BR/TR/6'2"/(162–183) D5.7 B–MELIDO B–CARLOS

YEAR	TM LG	W	L	PCT	G	GS	CG	SHO	QS	SV	BS	QR	IP	H	R	HR	HB	BB	IB	SO	ERA	AERA	OAV	OOB	SUP	DL	PW
1990	NY A	1	2	.333	3	3	0	0	1	0	0	0	14	8	3	0	0	3	0	12	1.29	+211	.163	.212	-62	161	0.8
1991	NY A	2	4	.333	14	14	0	0	7	0	0	0	73.2	68	26	7	0	24	1	41	3.18	+31	.250	.311	-17	112	0.7
Total	11	67	68	.496	207	193	21	4	118	0	1	10	1244.1	1167	541	107	25	344	63	822	3.44	+11	.249	.302	-6	407	4.0
Team	2	3	6	.333	17	17	0	0	8	0	—	0	87.2	76	29	7	0	27	1	53	2.87	+44	.237	.296	-25	273	1.5

PERKINS, CECIL CECIL BOYCE B12.1.1940 BALTIMORE MD BR/TR/6'0"/175 D7.5 COL SHEPHERD

YEAR	TM LG	W	L	PCT	G	GS	CG	SHO	QS	SV	BS	QR	IP	H	R	HR	HB	BB	IB	SO	ERA	AERA	OAV	OOB	SUP	DL	PW
1967	NY A	0	1	.000	2	1	0	0	0	0	0	1	5	6	5	1	0	2	0	1	9.00	-65	.316	.381	+11	0	-0.5

PERRY, GAYLORD GAYLORD JACKSON B9.15.1938 WILLIAMSTON NC BR/TR/6'4"/(205–220) D4.14 HF1991 B–JIM

YEAR	TM LG	W	L	PCT	G	GS	CG	SHO	QS	SV	BS	QR	IP	H	R	HR	HB	BB	IB	SO	ERA	AERA	OAV	OOB	SUP	DL	PW
1980	NY A	4	4	.500	10	8	0	0	4	0	0	0	50.2	65	33	2	1	18	0	28	4.44	-11	.320	.372	-10	0	-0.7
Total	22	314	265	.542	777	690	303	53	482	11	5	61	5350	4938	2128	399	108	1379	16	3534	3.11	+17	.245	.296	-4	15	32.9

PETERSON, FRITZ FRITZ FRED (B FRED INGELS PETERSON) B2.8.1942 CHICAGO IL BB/TL/6'0"/(185–207) D4.15 COL NORTHERN ILLINOIS

YEAR	TM LG	W	L	PCT	G	GS	CG	SHO	QS	SV	BS	QR	IP	H	R	HR	HB	BB	IB	SO	ERA	AERA	OAV	OOB	SUP	DL	PW
1966	NY A	12	11	.522	34	32	11	2	17	0	0	2	215	196	89	15	3	40	6	96	3.31	+1	.241	.277	+10	0	0.6
1967	NY A	8	14	.364	36	30	6	1	17	0	0	5	181.1	179	88	11	3	43	9	102	3.47	-10	.256	.301	-22	0	-1.0
1968	NY A	12	11	.522	36	27	6	2	23	0	0	8	212.1	187	72	13	4	29	9	115	2.63	+11	.241	.270	+0	0	0.8
1969	NY A	17	16	.515	37	37	16	4	24	0	0	0	272	228	95	15	3	43	11	150	2.55	+38	.229	.261	-26	0	3.4
1970	NY A★	20	11	.645	39	37	8	2	26	0	0	2	260.1	247	102	24	3	40	6	127	2.90	+23	.248	**.279**	+11	0	2.8
1971	NY A	15	13	.536	37	35	16	4	30	1	0	2	274	269	106	25	4	42	7	139	3.05	+8	.258	.287	+1	0	0.6
1972	NY A	17	15	.531	35	35	12	3	27	0	0	0	250.1	270	98	17	5	44	5	100	3.24	-8	.276	.309	+21	0	-0.2
1973	NY A	8	15	.348	31	31	6	0	14	0	0	0	184.1	207	93	18	7	49	10	59	3.95	-6	.286	.336	-27	0	-0.6
1974	NY A	0	0	+	3	1	0	0	0	0	0	2	7.2	13	4	1	0	2	1	5	4.70	-24	.361	.395	+49	0	0.0
1974	Cle A	9	14	.391	29	29	3	0	13	0	0	0	152.2	187	89	16	4	37	7	52	4.36	-17	.305	.346	-3	0	-1.9
1974	Year	9	14	.391	32	30	3	0	13	0	0	2	160.1	200	93	17	4	39	8	57	4.38	-17	.308	.349	-1	0	-1.9
1975	Cle A	14	8	.636	25	25	6	2	14	0	0	0	146.1	154	73	15	6	40	4	47	3.94	-3	.275	.330	+23	28	-0.2
1976	Cle A	0	3	.000	9	9	0	0	3	0	0	0	47	59	31	3	0	10	0	19	5.55	-37	.309	.342	+28	0	-0.6
1976	Tex A	1	0	1.000	4	2	0	0	2	0	1	0	15	21	7	0	0	7	0	4	3.60	+0	.344	.412	+22	68	0.0
1976	Year	1	3	.250	13	11	0	0	5	0	1	0	62	80	38	3	0	17	0	23	5.08	-30	.317	.359	+27	0	-0.6
Total	11	133	131	.504	355	330	90	20	210	1	1	21	2218.1	2217	947	173	42	426	75	1015	3.30	+2	.261	.298	+0	96	3.7
Team	9	109	106	.507	288	265	81	18	178	1	0	21	1857.1	1796	747	139	32	332	64	893	3.10	+7	.254	.289	-3	—	6.4
/180I	1	11	10	.507	28	26	8	2	17	0	0	2	180	174	72	13	3	32	6	87	3.10	+7	.254	.289	-3	—	0.6

PETTITTE, ANDY ANDREW EUGENE B6.15.1972 BATON ROUGE LA BL/TL/6'5"/(225–235) D4.29 COL SAN JACINTO NORTH (TX) JC

YEAR	TM LG	W	L	PCT	G	GS	CG	SHO	QS	SV	BS	QR	IP	H	R	HR	HB	BB	IB	SO	ERA	AERA	OAV	OOB	SUP	DL	PW
1995	†NY A	12	9	.571	31	26	3	0	16	0	0	3	175	183	86	15	1	63	3	114	4.17	+11	.272	.333	-9	0	0.9
1996	†NY A☆	**21**	8	.724	35	34	2	0	19	0	0	1	221	229	105	23	3	72	2	162	3.87	+28	.271	.330	+2	0	2.8
1997	†NY A	18	7	.720	35	**35**	4	1	24	0	0	0	240.1	233	86	7	3	65	0	166	2.88	+54	.256	.307	+28	0	4.1
1998	†NY A	16	11	.593	33	32	5	0	16	0	0	1	216.1	226	110	20	6	87	1	146	4.24	+3	.274	.344	+2	0	0.3
1999	†NY A	14	11	.560	31	31	0	0	16	0	0	0	191.2	216	105	20	3	89	3	121	4.70	+1	.289	.364	+9	12	0.5
2000	†NY A	19	9	.679	32	32	3	1	17	0	0	0	204.2	219	111	17	4	80	4	125	4.35	+10	.271	.338	+30	17	1.0
2001	†NY A★	15	10	.600	31	31	2	0	21	0	0	0	200.2	224	103	14	6	41	3	164	3.99	+11	.281	.319	+9	15	0.9
2002	†NY A	13	5	.722	22	22	3	1	11	0	0	0	134.2	144	58	6	4	32	2	97	3.27	+32	.272	.317	+17	59	2.0
2003	†NY A	21	8	.724	33	33	1	0	20	0	0	0	208.1	227	109	21	1	50	3	180	4.02	+9	.272	.312	+39	0	0.7
2004	Hou N	6	4	.600	15	15	0	0	4	0	0	0	83	71	37	8	0	31	2	79	3.90	+12	.226	.296	-25	102	0.7
2005	†Hou N	17	9	.654	33	33	0	0	27	0	0	0	222.1	188	66	17	3	41	0	171	2.39	+77	.230	.268	+0	0	4.8
2006	Hou N	14	13	.519	36	**35**	2	1	20	0	0	0	214.1	238	114	27	2	70	9	178	4.20	+6	.284	.339	-8	0	0.6
2007	†NY A	15	9	.625	36	**34**	0	0	23	0	0	2	215.1	238	106	16	1	69	1	141	4.05	+11	.286	.338	+21	0	1.0
Total	13	201	113	.640	403	393	25	4	234	0	0	7	2527.2	2636	1196	211	37	790	33	1844	3.83	+18	.270	.325	+10	205	20.3
Team	10	164	87	.653	319	310	23	3	183	0	0	7	2008	2139	979	159	32	648	22	1416	3.95	+16	.274	.330	+15	103	14.2
/180I	1	15	8	.653	29	28	2	0	16	0	0	1	180	192	88	14	3	58	2	127	3.95	+16	.274	.330	+15	9	1.3

PIEH, CY EDWIN JOHN B9.29.1886 WAUNAKEE WI D9.12.1945 JACKSONVILLE FL BR/TR/6'2"/190 D9.6

YEAR	TM LG	W	L	PCT	G	GS	CG	SHO	QS	SV	BS	QR	IP	H	R	HR	HB	BB	IB	SO	ERA	AERA	OAV	OOB	SUP	DL	PW
1913	NY A	1	0	1.000	4	0	0	0	—	0	—	—	10.1	10	8	0	0	7	—	6	4.35	-31	.256	.370	—	—	-0.1
1914	NY A	3	4	.429	18	4	1	0	—	0	—	—	62.1	68	41	6	0	29	—	24	5.05	-45	.289	.367	-14	—	-1.6
1915	NY A	4	5	.444	21	8	3	2	—	0	—	—	94	78	40	2	5	39	—	46	2.87	+2	.234	.324	-25	—	-0.4
Total	3	8	9	.471	43	12	4	2	—	0	—	—	166.2	156	89	8	5	75	—	76	3.78	-24	.257	.344	-22	—	-2.1
/180I	3	9	10	.471	46	13	4	2	0	0	0	0	180	168	96	9	5	81	—	82	3.78	-24	.257	.344	-22	—	-2.3

PIERCY, BILL WILLIAM BENTON "WILD BILL" B5.2.1896 ELMONTE CA D8.28.1951 LONG BEACH CA BR/TR/6'1"/185 D10.3

YEAR	TM LG	W	L	PCT	G	GS	CG	SHO	QS	SV	BS	QR	IP	H	R	HR	HB	BB	IB	SO	ERA	AERA	OAV	OOB	SUP	DL	PW
1917	NY A	0	1	.000	1	1	1	0	—	0	—	—	9	9	3	0	0	2	—	4	3.00	-10	.257	.297	-73	—	0.0
1921	†NY A	5	4	.556	14	10	5	1	—	0	—	—	81.2	82	40	4	7	28	—	35	2.98	+42	.263	.337	-3	—	0.9
Total	6	27	43	.386	116	70	28	2	—	0	—	—	610.2	676	364	16	43	268	—	165	4.26	-3	.292	.376	-12	—	-1.1
Team	2	5	5	.500	15	11	6	1	—	0	—	—	90.2	91	43	4	7	30	—	39	2.98	+37	.262	.333	-9	—	0.9

PILLETTE, DUANE DUANE XAVIER "DEE" B7.24.1922 DETROIT MI BR/TR/6'3"/(195–205) D7.19 F–HERMAN COL SANTA CLARA

YEAR	TM LG	W	L	PCT	G	GS	CG	SHO	QS	SV	BS	QR	IP	H	R	HR	HB	BB	IB	SO	ERA	AERA	OAV	OOB	SUP	DL	PW
1949	NY A	2	4	.333	12	3	2	0	—	0	—	—	37.1	43	20	6	0	19	—	9	4.34	-7	.299	.380	-11	0	-0.2
1950	NY A	0	0	+	4	0	0	0	—	0	—	—	7	9	3	0	0	3	—	4	1.29	+234	.321	.387	—	0	0.1
Total	8	38	66	.365	188	119	34	4	—	2	—	—	904	985	498	67	17	391	5	305	4.40	-7	.277	.351	-22	51	-3.0
Team	2	2	4	.333	16	3	2	0	—	0	—	—	44.1	52	23	6	0	22	—	13	3.86	+6	.302	.381	-11	—	-0.1

PIPGRAS, GEORGE GEORGE WILLIAM B12.20.1899 IDA GROVE IA D10.19.1986 GAINESVILLE FL BR/TR/6'1.5"/185 D6.9 U9 B–ED

YEAR	TM LG	W	L	PCT	G	GS	CG	SHO	QS	SV	BS	QR	IP	H	R	HR	HB	BB	IB	SO	ERA	AERA	OAV	OOB	SUP	DL	PW
1923	NY A	1	3	.250	8	2	2	0	—	0	—	—	33.1	34	22	2	1	25	—	12	5.94	-34	.276	.403	-16	—	-0.7
1924	NY A	0	1	.000	9	1	0	0	—	1	—	—	15.1	20	18	0	4	18	—	4	9.98	-58	.351	.532	+1	—	-0.6
1927	†NY A	10	3	.769	29	21	9	1	—	0	—	—	166.1	148	81	2	1	77	—	81	4.11	-6	.247	.334	+56	—	0.1
1928	†NY A	**24**	13	.649	46	**38**	22	4	—	3	—	—	**300.2**	314	132	4	3	103	—	139	3.38	+11	.272	.333	+27	—	1.1
1929	NY A	18	12	.600	39	33	13	3	—	0	—	—	225.1	229	132	16	5	95	—	125	4.23	-9	.264	.340	+29	—	-1.8
1930	NY A	15	15	.500	44	30	15	0	—	4	—	—	221	230	133	9	8	70	—	111	4.11	+5	.263	.324	+43	—	-0.3
1931	NY A	7	6	.538	36	14	6	1	—	3	—	—	137.2	134	73	8	2	58	—	59	3.79	+5	.251	.327	-1	—	-0.6
1932	†NY A	16	9	.640	32	27	14	2	—	0	—	—	219	235	120	15	6	87	—	111	4.19	-3	.269	.340	+30	—	-0.4
1933	NY A	2	2	.500	4	4	3	0	—	0	—	—	33	32	13	1	0	12	—	14	3.27	+19	.252	.317	-1	—	0.3

Pitchers

YEAR	TM LG	W	L	PCT	G	GS	CG	SHO	QS	SV	BS	QR	IP	H	R	HR	HB	BB	IB	SO	ERA	AERA	OAV	OOB	SUP	DL	PW
1933	Bos A	9	8	.529	22	17	9	2	—	1	—	—	128.1	140	65	5	2	45	—	56	4.07	+8	.276	.337	+2	—	0.5
1933	Year	11	10	.524	26	21	12	2	—	1	—	—	161.1	172	78	6	2	57	—	70	3.90	+10	.271	.333	+1	—	0.8
1934	Bos A	0	0	+	2	1	0	0	—	0	—	—	3.1	4	3	1	0	3	—	0	8.10	-41	.308	.438	+9	—	0.0
1935	Bos A	0	1	.000	5	1	0	0	—	0	—	—	5	9	9	3	1	5	—	2	14.40	-67	.391	.517	-63	—	-0.8
Total	11	102	73	.583	276	189	93	16	—	12	—	—	1488.1	1529	801	66	33	598	—	714	4.09	-2	.266	.339	+27	—	-3.2
Team	9	93	64	.592	247	170	84	11	—	11	—	—	1351.2	1376	724	57	30	545	—	656	4.04	-2	.264	.337	+31	—	-2.9
/180I	1	12	9	.592	33	23	11	1	—	1	—	—	180	183	96	8	4	73	—	87	4.04	-2	.264	.337	+31	—	-0.4

PLUNK, ERIC Eric Vaughn B9.3.1963 Wilmington CA BR/TR/6'5"/(210–224) Dr 1981 NYA 4/103 d5.12

YEAR	TM LG	W	L	PCT	G	GS	CG	SHO	QS	SV	BS	QR	IP	H	R	HR	HB	BB	IB	SO	ERA	AERA	OAV	OOB	SUP	DL	PW
1989	NY A	7	5	.583	27	7	0	0	2	0	0	10	75.2	65	36	9	0	52	2	61	3.69	+6	.237	.355	+16	0	0.1
1990	NY A	6	3	.667	47	0	0	0	0	0	1	32	72.2	58	27	6	2	43	4	67	2.72	+47	.225	.340	—	0	1.1
1991	NY A	2	5	.286	43	8	0	0	3	0	0	21	111.2	128	69	18	1	62	1	103	4.76	-12	.286	.371	-31	0	-0.6
Total	14	72	58	.554	714	41	0	0	17	35	35	458	1151	1009	537	122	32	647	45	1081	3.82	+12	.236	.339	-12	15	6.7
Team	3	15	13	.536	117	15	0	0	5	0	1	63	260	251	132	33	3	157	7	231	3.88	+4	.256	.358	-9	—	0.6
/60G	2	8	7	.536	60	8	0	0	3	0	1	32	133.1	129	68	17	2	81	4	118	3.88	+4	.256	.358	-9	—	0.3

POLLEY, DALE Ezra Dale B8.9.1965 Georgetown KY BR/TL/6'0"/185 d6.23 Col Kentucky St.

YEAR	TM LG	W	L	PCT	G	GS	CG	SHO	QS	SV	BS	QR	IP	H	R	HR	HB	BB	IB	SO	ERA	AERA	OAV	OOB	SUP	DL	PW
1996	NY A	1	3	.250	32	0	0	0	0	0	0	20	21.2	23	20	5	3	11	1	14	7.89	-37	.264	.363	—	0	-1.1

PONSON, SIDNEY Sidney Alton B11.2.1976 Noord, Aruba BR/TR/6'2"/(200–265) d4.19

YEAR	TM LG	W	L	PCT	G	GS	CG	SHO	QS	SV	BS	QR	IP	H	R	HR	HB	BB	IB	SO	ERA	AERA	OAV	OOB	SUP	DL	PW
2006	NY A	0	1	.000	5	3	0	0	0	0	0	1	16.1	26	20	3	0	7	0	15	10.47	-56	.351	.407	+63	0	-0.5
Total	10	82	101	.448	259	245	28	4	117	1	1	7	1566	1755	912	203	36	536	16	941	4.94	-8	.285	.344	+2	91	-6.3

PORTERFIELD, BOB Erwin Coolidge B8.10.1923 Newport VA D4.28.1980 Sealy TX BR/TR/6'0"/(187–190) d8.8

YEAR	TM LG	W	L	PCT	G	GS	CG	SHO	QS	SV	BS	QR	IP	H	R	HR	HB	BB	IB	SO	ERA	AERA	OAV	OOB	SUP	DL	PW
1948	NY A	5	3	.625	16	12	2	1	—	0	—	—	78	85	42	5	0	34	—	30	4.50	-9	.273	.345	+38	0	-0.3
1949	NY A	2	5	.286	12	8	3	0	—	0	—	—	57.2	53	26	3	1	29	—	25	4.06	+0	.251	.344	-3	0	0.0
1950	NY A	1	1	.500	10	2	0	0	—	1	—	—	19.2	28	19	2	0	8	—	9	8.69	-51	.341	.400	-16	42	-0.8
1951	NY A	0	0	+	2	0	0	0	—	0	—	—	3	5	6	0	0	3	—	2	15.00	-74	.385	.500	—	0	-0.2
Total	12	87	97	.473	318	193	92	23	14	8	3	159	1567.2	1571	732	113	14	552	20	572	3.79	+2	.263	.326	-4	42	4.2
Team	4	8	9	.471	40	22	5	1	—	1	—	—	158.1	171	93	10	1	74	—	66	5.06	-19	.277	.355	+18	42	-1.3
/180I	5	9	10	.471	45	25	6	1	—	1	—	—	180	194	106	11	1	84	—	75	5.06	-19	.277	.355	+18	48	-1.5

POWELL, JACK John Joseph "Red" B7.9.1874 Bloomington IL D10.17.1944 Chicago IL BR/TR/5'11"/195 d6.23

YEAR	TM LG	W	L	PCT	G	GS	CG	SHO	QS	SV	BS	QR	IP	H	R	HR	HB	BB	IB	SO	ERA	AERA	OAV	OOB	SUP	DL	PW
1904	NY A	23	19	.548	47	45	38	3	—	0	—	—	390.1	340	154	15	10	92	—	202	2.44	+11	.235	.286	-10	—	0.1
1905	NY A	8	13	.381	37	23	13	1	—	1	—	—	203	214	107	4	6	57	—	84	3.50	-16	.272	.326	-5	—	-1.4
Total	16	245	254	.491	578	516	422	46	—	15	—	—	4389	4319	1991	110	120	1021	—	1621	2.97	+6	.258	.305	-6	—	8.0
Team	2	31	32	.492	84	68	51	4	—	1	—	—	593.1	554	261	19	16	149	—	286	2.81	-1	.248	.300	-8	—	-1.3
/180I	1	9	10	.492	25	21	15	1	—	0	—	—	180	168	79	6	5	45	—	87	2.81	-1	.248	.300	-8	—	-0.4

PRINZ, BRET Bret Randolph B6.15.1977 Chicago Heights IL BR/TR/6'3"/(185–215) Dr 1998 AriN 18/553 d4.22 Col Phoenix (AZ) JC

YEAR	TM LG	W	L	PCT	G	GS	CG	SHO	QS	SV	BS	QR	IP	H	R	HR	HB	BB	IB	SO	ERA	AERA	OAV	OOB	SUP	DL	PW
2003	NY A	0	0	+	2	0	0	0	0	0	0	0	2	6	4	1	0	3	1	2	18.00	-76	.500	.600	—	0	-0.1
2004	NY A	1	0	1.000	26	0	0	0	0	0	0	17	28.1	28	17	5	1	14	0	22	5.08	-10	.259	.347	—	0	-0.1
Total	6	5	4	.556	102	0	0	0	0	9	5	65	92	99	52	13	3	50	5	64	4.89	-6	.277	.367	—	257	0.3
Team	2	1	0	1.000	28	0	0	0	0	0	0	17	30.1	34	21	6	1	17	1	24	5.93	-23	.283	.374	—	—	-0.2

PROCTOR, SCOTT Scott Christopher B1.2.1977 Stuart FL BR/TR/6'1"/(195–200) Dr 1998 LAN 5/156 d4.20 Col Florida St.

YEAR	TM LG	W	L	PCT	G	GS	CG	SHO	QS	SV	BS	QR	IP	H	R	HR	HB	BB	IB	SO	ERA	AERA	OAV	OOB	SUP	DL	PW
2004	NY A	2	1	.667	26	0	0	0	0	0	0	13	25	29	18	5	0	14	0	21	5.40	-15	.284	.364	—	0	-0.3
2005	†NY A	1	0	1.000	29	1	0	0	0	0	0	15	44.2	46	32	10	2	17	4	36	6.04	-29	.257	.327	+94	0	-0.4
2006	†NY A	6	4	.600	**83**	0	0	0	0	1	7	61	102.1	89	41	12	2	33	6	89	3.52	+31	.232	.292	—	0	1.1
2007	NY A	2	5	.286	52	0	0	0	0	0	4	38	54.1	53	27	8	3	29	3	37	3.81	+19	.257	.348	—	0	0.3
2007	LA N	3	0	1.000	31	0	0	0	0	0	2	23	32	25	14	4	3	15	1	27	3.38	+33	.216	.319	—	0	0.3
2007	Major	5	5	.500	83	0	0	0	0	0	6	61	86	78	41	12	6	44	4	64	3.65	+24	.242	.338	—	0	0.6
Total	4	14	10	.583	221	1	0	0	0	1	13	150	258.1	242	132	39	10	108	14	210	4.18	+8	.245	.321	+94	0	1.0
Team	4	11	10	.524	190	1	0	0	0	1	11	127	226.1	217	118	35	7	93	13	183	4.29	+5	.249	.322	+94	—	0.7
/60G	1	3	3	.524	60	0	0	0	0	0	3	40	71.1	69	37	11	2	29	4	58	4.30	+5	.249	.322	—	—	0.2

PULIDO, ALFONSO Alfonso (Manzo) B1.23.1957 Tierra Blanca, Veracruz, Mexico BL/TL/5'11"/(170–175) d9.5

YEAR	TM LG	W	L	PCT	G	GS	CG	SHO	QS	SV	BS	QR	IP	H	R	HR	HB	BB	IB	SO	ERA	AERA	OAV	OOB	SUP	DL	PW
1983	Pit N	0	0	+	1	1	0	0	0	0	0	0	2	4	3	2	0	1	0	1	9.00	-58	.400	.455	+42	0	-0.1
1984	Pit N	0	0	+	1	0	0	0	0	0	0	0	2	3	2	0	0	1	0	2	9.00	-60	.333	.400	—	0	-0.1
1986	NY A	1	1	.500	10	3	0	0	0	1	0	4	30.2	38	17	8	0	9	0	13	4.70	-12	.306	.351	+24	0	-0.1
Total	3	1	1	.500	12	4	0	0	0	1	0	4	34.2	45	22	10	0	11	0	16	5.19	-21	.315	.361	+27	0	-0.3

PUTTMANN, AMBROSE Ambrose Nicholas "Putty","Brose" B9.9.1880 Cincinnati OH D6.21.1936 Jamaica NY TL/6'4"/185 d9.4

YEAR	TM LG	W	L	PCT	G	GS	CG	SHO	QS	SV	BS	QR	IP	H	R	HR	HB	BB	IB	SO	ERA	AERA	OAV	OOB	SUP	DL	PW
1903	NY A	2	0	1.000	3	2	1	0	—	0	—	—	19	16	9	0	1	4	—	8	0.95	+230	.229	.280	+106	—	0.3
1904	NY A	2	0	1.000	9	3	2	1	—	0	—	—	49.1	40	21	0	0	17	—	26	2.74	-1	.222	.289	+5	—	0.2
1905	NY A	2	7	.222	17	9	5	1	—	1	—	—	86.1	79	50	2	5	37	—	39	4.27	-31	.245	.332	-4	—	-0.7
1906	StL N	2	2	.500	4	4	0	0	—	0	—	—	18.2	23	13	2	2	9	—	12	5.30	-50	.303	.391	+39	—	-0.9
Total	4	8	9	.471	33	18	8	2	—	1	—	—	173.1	158	93	4	8	67	—	85	3.58	-20	.244	.322	+19	—	-1.1
Team	3	6	7	.462	29	14	8	2	—	1	—	—	154.2	135	80	2	6	58	—	73	3.38	-14	.236	.313	+14	—	-0.2
/180I	3	7	8	.462	34	16	9	2	—	1	—	—	180	157	93	2	7	68	—	85	3.38	-14	.236	.313	+14	—	-0.2

QUANTRILL, PAUL Paul John B11.3.1968 London ON, Can. BL/TR/6'1"/(175–200) Dr 1989 BosA 6/163 d7.20 Col Wisconsin–Madison

YEAR	TM LG	W	L	PCT	G	GS	CG	SHO	QS	SV	BS	QR	IP	H	R	HR	HB	BB	IB	SO	ERA	AERA	OAV	OOB	SUP	DL	PW
2004	†NY A	7	3	.700	**86**	0	0	0	0	1	4	54	95.1	124	54	5	4	20	9	37	4.72	-3	.316	.352	—	0	-0.2
2005	NY A	1	0	1.000	22	0	0	0	0	0	1	12	32	48	24	5	2	7	2	11	6.75	-36	.361	.383	—	0	-0.4
Total	14	68	78	.466	841	64	1	1	22	21	46	567	1255.2	1442	601	112	45	336	68	725	3.83	+18	.292	.339	-17	71	9.5
Team	2	8	3	.727	108	0	0	0	0	1	5	66	127.1	172	78	10	6	27	11	48	5.23	-14	.328	.360	—	—	-0.6
/60G	1	4	2	.727	60	0	0	0	0	1	3	37	70.2	96	43	6	3	15	6	27	5.24	-14	.328	.360	—	—	-0.3

QUEEN, MEL Melvin Joseph B3.4.1918 Maxwell PA D4.4.1982 Fort Smith AR BR/TR/6'0.5"/(200–204) d4.18 Mil 1945–46 f–Mel

YEAR	TM LG	W	L	PCT	G	GS	CG	SHO	QS	SV	BS	QR	IP	H	R	HR	HB	BB	IB	SO	ERA	AERA	OAV	OOB	SUP	DL	PW
1942	NY A	1	0	1.000	4	0	0	0	—	0	—	—	5.2	6	0	0	2	3	—	0	0.00	-100	.300	.440	—	0	0.4
1944	NY A	6	3	.667	10	10	4	1	—	0	—	—	81.2	68	32	7	1	34	—	30	3.31	+5	.227	.308	+25	0	0.2
1946	NY A	1	1	.500	14	3	1	0	—	0	—	—	30.1	40	28	2	0	21	—	26	6.53	-47	.315	.412	+16	0	-0.8
1947	NY A	0	0	+	5	0	0	0	—	0	—	—	6.2	9	7	2	1	4	—	2	9.45	-63	.321	.424	—	0	-0.2
Total	8	27	40	.403	146	77	15	3	—	1	—	—	556.2	567	354	68	11	329	—	328	5.09	-20	.262	.362	+0	0	-7.6
Team	4	8	4	.667	33	13	5	1	—	0	—	—	124.1	123	67	11	4	62	—	58	4.27	-19	.259	.350	+23	—	-0.4
/180I	6	12	6	.667	48	19	7	1	—	0	—	—	180	178	97	16	6	90	—	84	4.27	-19	.259	.350	+23	—	-0.6

QUICK, EDDIE Edward B12.1881 Baltimore MD D6.19.1913 Rocky Ford CO TR/5'11"/? d9.28

YEAR	TM LG	W	L	PCT	G	GS	CG	SHO	QS	SV	BS	QR	IP	H	R	HR	HB	BB	IB	SO	ERA	AERA	OAV	OOB	SUP	DL	PW
1903	NY A	0	0	+	1	1	0	0	—	0	—	—	2	5	5	0	0	1	—	0	9.00	-65	.455	.500	+60	—	-0.1

QUINN, JACK John Picus (b Joannes Pajkos) B7.1.1883 Stefurov, Austria–Hungary (now Slovakia) D4.17.1946 Pottsville PA BR/TR/6'0"/196 d4.15

YEAR	TM LG	W	L	PCT	G	GS	CG	SHO	QS	SV	BS	QR	IP	H	R	HR	HB	BB	IB	SO	ERA	AERA	OAV	OOB	SUP	DL	PW
1909	NY A	9	5	.643	23	11	8	0	—	1	—	—	118.2	110	45	1	4	24	—	36	1.97	+28	.252	.297	+19	—	0.8
1910	NY A	18	12	.600	35	31	20	0	—	0	—	—	235.2	214	88	2	6	58	—	82	2.37	+12	.247	.299	+2	—	1.6
1911	NY A	8	10	.444	40	16	7	0	—	2	—	—	174.2	203	111	2	4	41	—	71	3.76	-4	.297	.341	-26	—	-0.6
1912	NY A	5	7	.417	18	11	7	0	—	0	—	—	102.2	139	89	4	4	23	—	47	5.79	-38	.325	.365	-16	—	-2.1
1919	NY A	15	14	.517	38	31	18	4	—	0	—	—	266	242	96	8	6	65	—	97	2.61	+23	.244	.295	-1	—	2.0
1920	NY A	18	10	.643	41	32	17	2	—	3	—	—	253.1	271	110	8	2	48	—	101	3.20	+19	.273	.308	+5	—	1.4
1921	†NY A	8	7	.533	33	13	6	0	—	0	—	—	119	158	61	2	5	32	—	44	3.78	+12	.327	.375	-3	—	0.8

YEAR	TM LG	W	L	PCT	G	GS	CG	SHO	QS	SV	BS	QR	IP	H	R	HR	HB	BB	IB	SO	ERA	AERA	OAV	OOB	SUP	DL	PW
Total	23	247	218	.531	756	443	243	28	—	57	—	—	3920.1	4238	1837	102	91	860	—	1329	3.29	+13	.280	.323	-5	—	19.4
Team	7	81	65	.555	228	145	83	6	—	6	—	—	1270	1337	600	27	31	291	—	478	3.15	+6	.274	.319	-2	—	3.9
/180I	1	11	9	.555	32	21	12	1	—	1	—	—	180	189	85	4	4	41	—	68	3.15	+6	.274	.319	-2	—	0.6
Rajsich, Dave David Christopher B9.28.1951 Youngstown OH BL/TL/6'5"/(175–180) d7.2 b–Gary Col Arizona																											
1978	NY A	0	0	+	4	2	0	0	0	0	0	2	13.1	16	6	0	0	6	0	9	4.05	-10	.320	.379	+23	0	0.0
Total	3	3	4	.429	55	6	0	0	1	2	0	26	115.1	128	65	14	3	46	0	76	4.60	-13	.284	.350	-25	0	-0.4
Ramirez, Edwar Edwar Emilio B3.28.1981 San Juan P R BR/TR/6'3"/160 d7.0																											
2007	NY A	1	1	.500	21	0	0	0	0	1	2	10	21	24	19	6	3	14	2	31	8.14	-45	.286	.402	—	0	-0.7
Ramos, Pedro Pedro (Guerra) "Pete" B4.28.1935 Pinar Del Rio, Cuba BB/TR (BR 1955–59)/6'0"/(175–189) d4.11																											
1964	NY A	1	0	1.000	13	0	0	0	0	8	0	12	21.2	13	3	1	0	0	0	21	1.25	+191	.183	.176	—	0	0.6
1965	NY A	5	5	.500	65	0	0	0	0	19	2	48	92.1	80	34	7	1	27	9	68	2.92	+16	.237	.294	—	0	0.6
1966	NY A	3	9	.250	52	1	0	0	0	13	3	36	89.2	98	43	10	1	18	4	58	3.61	-8	.283	.317	-47	0	-0.7
Total	15	117	160	.422	582	268	73	13	227	55	12	197	2355.2	2364	1210	316	68	724	76	1305	4.08	-5	.261	.318	-4	0	-7.3
Team	3	9	14	.391	130	1	0	0	0	40	5	96	203.2	191	80	18	2	45	13	147	3.05	+11	.253	.294	-47	—	0.5
/60G	1	4	6	.391	60	0	0	0	0	18	2	44	94	88	37	8	1	21	6	68	3.05	+11	.253	.294	—	—	0.2
Raschi, Vic Victor John Angelo B3.28.1919 W.Springfield MA D10.14.1988 Groveland NY BR/TR/6'1"/(185–210) d9.23 Col William and Mary																											
1946	NY A	2	0	1.000	2	2	2	0	—	0	—	—	16	14	7	0	0	5	—	11	3.94	-12	.230	.288	+37	0	0.0
1947	†NY A	7	2	.778	15	14	6	1	—	0	—	—	104.2	89	47	11	1	38	—	51	3.87	-0	.220	.296	+39	0	-0.1
1948	NY A★	19	8	.704	36	31	10	0	—	1	—	—	222.2	208	103	15	3	74	—	124	3.84	+6	.247	.310	+34	0	1.0
1949	†NY A★	21	10	.677	38	**37**	21	3	—	0	—	—	274.2	247	120	16	6	138	—	124	3.34	+21	.241	.334	+23	0	2.1
1950	†NY A★	21	8	**.724**	33	32	17	2	—	1	—	—	256.2	232	120	19	3	116	—	155	4.00	+7	.243	.327	+16	0	1.1
1951	†NY A	21	10	.677	35	**34**	15	4	—	0	—	—	258.1	233	110	20	5	103	—	**164**	3.27	+17	.242	.319	+23	0	1.4
1952	†NY A★	16	6	.727	31	31	13	4	—	0	—	—	223	174	78	12	6	91	—	127	2.78	+19	.216	.300	+13	0	1.6
1953	†NY A	13	6	.684	28	26	7	4	—	1	—	—	181	150	74	11	1	55	—	76	3.33	+11	.224	**.283**	+35	0	0.5
1954	StL N	8	9	.471	30	29	6	2	—	0	—	—	179	182	99	24	0	71	—	73	4.73	-13	.268	.335	+5	0	-0.9
1955	StL N	0	1	.000	1	1	0	0	—	0	—	—	1.2	5	4	0	0	1	1	1	21.60	-81	.556	.545	-12	0	-0.5
1955	KC A	4	6	.400	20	18	1	0	—	0	—	—	101.1	132	66	10	1	35	4	38	5.42	-23	.312	.364	-20	0	-1.1
1955	Major	4	7	.364	21	19	1	0	—	0	—	—	102	137	70	10	1	36	5	39	5.68	-24	.317	.368	-20	0	-1.6
Total	10	132	66	.667	269	255	106	26	—	3	—	—	1819	1666	828	138	26	727	5	944	3.72	+5	.244	.319	+19	0	5.1
Team	8	120	50	.706	218	207	99	24	—	3	—	—	1537	1347	659	104	25	620	—	832	3.47	+11	.236	.313	+25	—	7.6
/180I	1	14	6	.706	26	24	12	3	—	0	—	—	180	158	77	12	3	73	—	97	3.47	+11	.236	.313	+25	—	0.9
Rasmussen, Dennis Dennis Lee B4.18.1959 Los Angeles CA BL/TL/6'7"/(223–240) Dr 1980 CalA 1/17 d9.16 gf–Bill Brubaker Col Creighton																											
1983	SD N	0	0	+	4	1	0	0	1	0	0	3	13.2	10	5	1	0	8	0	13	1.98	+78	.200	.310	+1	0	0.1
1984	NY A	9	6	.600	24	24	1	0	10	0	0	0	147.2	127	79	16	4	60	0	110	4.57	-16	.234	.312	+29	0	-1.0
1985	NY A	3	5	.375	22	16	2	0	7	0	0	3	101.2	97	56	10	1	42	1	63	3.98	+2	.255	.327	+4	0	-0.1
1986	NY A	18	6	.750	31	31	3	1	20	0	0	0	202	160	91	28	2	74	0	131	3.88	+7	.217	.289	+28	0	0.9
1987	NY A	9	7	.563	26	25	2	0	12	0	0	1	146	145	78	31	4	55	1	89	4.75	-7	.260	.328	+20	0	-0.3
1987	Cin N	4	1	.800	7	7	0	0	5	0	0	0	45.1	39	22	5	1	12	0	39	3.97	+6	.229	.283	+19	0	0.1
1987	Major	13	8	.619	33	32	2	0	17	0	0	1	191	184	100	36	5	67	1	128	4.56	-4	.253	.318	+20	0	-0.2
1988	Cin N	2	6	.250	11	11	1	1	4	0	0	0	56.1	68	36	8	2	22	4	27	5.75	-38	.300	.364	-10	0	-1.4
1988	SD N	14	4	.778	20	20	6	0	18	0	0	0	148.1	131	48	9	2	36	0	85	2.55	+33	.238	.286	+29	0	2.1
1988	Year	16	10	.615	31	31	7	1	22	0	0	0	204.2	199	84	17	4	58	4	112	3.43	+1	.256	.309	+15	0	0.7
1989	SD N	10	10	.500	33	33	1	0	16	0	0	0	183.2	190	100	18	3	72	6	87	4.26	-18	.270	.335	-1	0	-1.5
1990	SD N	11	15	.423	32	32	3	1	13	0	0	0	187.2	217	110	28	3	62	4	86	4.51	-15	.292	.348	+10	0	-1.4
1991	SD N	6	13	.316	24	24	1	1	15	0	0	0	146.2	155	74	12	2	49	3	75	3.74	+2	.271	.328	-17	47	0.0
1992	Chi N	0	0	+	3	1	0	0	0	0	0	1	5	7	6	2	1	2	1	0	10.80	-66	.350	.417	+0	19	-0.2
1992	KC A	4	1	.800	5	5	1	1	4	0	0	0	37.2	25	7	0	0	6	0	12	1.43	+185	.197	.233	-37	0	1.6
1992	Major	4	1	.800	8	6	1	1	4	0	0	1	42	32	13	2	1	8	1	12	2.53	+156	.218	.261	-31	19	1.4
1993	KC A	1	2	.333	9	4	0	0	1	0	0	4	29	40	25	4	1	14	1	12	7.45	-38	.328	.399	+25	60	-0.7
1995	KC A	0	1	.000	5	1	0	0	0	0	0	2	10	13	10	3	0	8	2	6	9.00	-47	.302	.412	-3	0	-0.4
Total	12	91	77	.542	256	235	21	5	126	0	0	14	1460.2	1424	747	175	26	522	23	835	4.15	-6	.257	.321	+11	126	-2.2
Team	4	39	24	.619	103	96	8	1	49	0	0	4	597.1	529	304	85	11	231	2	393	4.28	-4	.239	.311	+22	—	-0.5
/180I	1	12	7	.619	31	29	2	0	15	0	0	1	180	159	92	26	3	70	1	118	4.28	-4	.239	.311	+22	—	-0.2
Rasner, Darrell Darrell Wayne B1.13.1981 Carson City NV BR/TR/6'3"/210 Dr 2002 MonN 2/46 d9.6 Col Nevada–Reno																											
2005	Was N	0	1	.000	5	1	0	0	0	0	0	4	7.1	5	3	0	2	2	1	4	3.68	+12	.192	.300	-54	0	0.0
2006	NY A	3	1	.750	6	3	0	0	2	0	0	2	20.1	18	10	2	1	5	0	11	4.43	+4	.237	.293	+22	83	0.1
2007	NY A	1	3	.250	6	6	0	0	0	0	0	0	24.2	29	14	4	2	8	0	11	4.01	+12	.290	.351	-4	133	0.0
Total	3	4	5	.444	17	10	0	0	2	0	0	6	52.1	52	27	6	5	15	1	26	4.13	+9	.257	.323	+0	216	0.1
Team	2	4	4	.500	12	9	0	0	2	0	0	2	45	47	24	6	3	13	0	22	4.20	+9	.267	.326	+5	216	0.1
Rawley, Shane Shane William B7.27.1955 Racine WI BR/TL/6'0"/(155–185) Dr 1974 MonN S2/29 d4.6 Col Indian Hills (IA) CC																											
1982	NY A	11	10	.524	47	17	3	0	9	3	1	20	164	165	79	10	2	54	5	111	4.06	-1	.267	.324	-3	0	0.2
1983	NY A	14	14	.500	34	33	13	2	18	1	0	1	238.1	246	111	19	3	79	1	124	3.78	+5	.269	.327	-4	0	0.5
1984	NY A	2	3	.400	11	10	0	0	2	0	0	1	42	46	33	0	0	27	0	24	6.21	-38	.272	.372	-22	15	-1.2
Total	12	111	118	.485	469	230	41	7	119	40	23	157	1871.1	1934	917	153	28	734	64	991	4.02	-2	.271	.338	+0	174	0.1
Team	3	27	27	.500	92	60	16	2	29	4	1	22	444.1	457	223	29	5	160	6	259	4.11	-3	.269	.331	-7	15	-0.5
/180I	1	11	11	.500	37	24	6	1	12	2	0	9	180	185	90	12	2	65	2	105	4.11	-3	.269	.331	-7	6	-0.2
Reardon, Jeff Jeffrey James B10.1.1955 Dalton MA BR/TR/6'1"/(190–205) d8.25 Col Massachusetts																											
1994	NY A	1	0	1.000	11	0	0	0	0	2	1	5	9.2	17	9	3	0	3	0	4	8.38	-45	.386	.426	—	0	-0.5
Total	16	73	77	.487	880	0	0	0	0	367	10	651	1132.1	1000	426	109	27	358	65	877	3.16	+22	.236	.297	—	44	13.9
Redding, Tim Timothy James B2.12.1978 Rochester NY BR/TR/6'0"/(180–200) Dr 1997 HouN 20/610 d6.24 Col Monroe (NY) CC																											
2005	NY A	0	1	.000	1	1	0	0	0	0	0	0	1	4	6	0	0	4	0	2	54.00	-92	.571	.727	-78	0	-0.7
Total	6	24	40	.375	116	94	0	0	35	0	0	17	520.1	572	321	69	21	222	15	356	4.91	-11	.281	.355	-10	44	-4.5
Reniff, Hal Harold Eugene "Porky" B7.2.1938 Warren OH D9.7.2004 Ontario CA BR/TR/6'0"/(205–215) d6.8																											
1961	NY A	2	0	1.000	25	0	0	0	0	2	0	23	45.1	31	14	1	0	31	3	21	2.58	+44	.197	.330	—	0	0.2
1962	NY A	0	0	+	2	0	0	0	0	0	0	0	3.2	6	3	0	1	5	1	1	7.36	-49	.400	.545	—	0	-0.1
1963	†NY A	4	3	.571	48	0	0	0	0	18	4	36	89.1	63	31	3	2	42	5	56	2.62	+34	.202	.300	—	0	1.0
1964	†NY A	6	4	.600	41	0	0	0	0	9	1	30	69.1	47	26	3	0	30	4	38	3.12	+16	.199	.287	—	0	0.6
1965	NY A	3	4	.429	51	0	0	0	0	3	0	35	85.1	74	40	4	5	48	7	74	3.80	-10	.232	.340	—	0	-0.3
1966	NY A	3	7	.300	56	0	0	0	0	9	3	38	95.1	80	37	2	5	49	8	79	3.21	+4	.229	.330	—	0	0.3
1967	NY A	0	2	.000	24	0	0	0	0	0	2	15	40	40	22	0	3	14	2	24	4.27	-27	.256	.328	—	0	-0.3
1967	NY N	3	3	.500	29	0	0	0	0	4	1	19	43	42	20	1	1	23	4	21	3.35	+1	.266	.361	—	0	-0.2
1967	Major	3	5	.375	53	0	0	0	0	4	—	34	83	82	42	1	4	37	6	45	3.80	-12	.261	.345	—	0	-0.5
Total	7	21	23	.477	276	0	0	0	0	45	11	196	471.1	383	193	14	17	242	34	314	3.27	+6	.225	.326	—	0	1.2
Team	7	18	20	.474	247	0	0	0	0	41	10	177	428.1	341	173	13	16	219	30	293	3.26	+6	.221	.322	—	—	1.4
/60G	2	4	5	.474	60	0	0	0	0	10	2	43	104	83	42	3	4	53	7	71	3.26	+6	.221	.322	—	—	0.3
Reuschel, Rick Rickey Eugene B5.16.1949 Quincy IL BR/TR/6'3"/(210–250) Dr 1970 ChiN 3/67 d6.19 b–Paul Col Western Illinois [DL 1982 NY A 182, 1983 NY A 66]																											
1981	†NY A	4	4	.500	12	11	3	0	7	0	0	1	70.2	75	24	4	1	10	0	22	2.67	+35	.280	.306	+4	0	0.8
Total	19	214	191	.528	557	529	102	26	348	5	1	16	3548.1	3588	1494	221	88	935	11	2015	3.37	+15	.264	.313	-6	459	23.2

Pitchers

YEAR	TM LG	W	L	PCT	G	GS	CG	SHO	QS	SV	BS	QR	IP	H	R	HR	HB	BB	IB	SO	ERA	AERA	OAV	OOB	SUP	DL	PW
Reyes, Al	Rafael Alberto B4.10.1971 San Cristobal, D.R. BR/TR/6'1"/(193–210) d4.27																										
2003	NY A	0	0	+	13	0	0	0	0	0	1	9	17	13	7	1	0	9	1	9	3.18	+38	.203	.301	—	0	0.1
Total	12	21	14	.600	358	2	0	0	0	32	13	257	406	319	178	51	24	185	12	403	3.79	+18	.215	.310	+53	135	2.3
Reynolds, Allie	Allie Pierce "Superchief" B2.10.1917 Bethany OK D12.26.1994 Oklahoma City OK BR/TR/6'0"/195 d9.17 Col Oklahoma St.																										
1942	Cle A	0	0	+	2	0	0	0	—	0	—	—	5	5	1	0	0	4	—	2	0.00	-100	.250	.375	—	0	0.0
1943	Cle A	11	12	.478	34	21	11	3	—	3	—	—	198.2	140	72	3	7	109	—	**151**	2.99	+4	**.202**	.316	+12	0	0.5
1944	Cle A	11	8	.579	28	21	5	1	—	1	—	—	158	141	63	2	4	91	—	84	3.30	+0	.240	.346	+2	0	-0.1
1945	Cle A✱	18	12	.600	44	30	16	2	—	4	—	—	247.1	227	102	7	5	130	—	112	3.20	+1	.247	.343	+8	0	-0.7
1946	Cle A	11	15	.423	31	28	9	3	—	0	—	—	183.1	180	93	10	1	108	—	107	3.88	-15	.259	.359	-4	0	-1.7
1947	†NY A	19	8	**.704**	34	30	17	4	—	2	—	—	241.2	207	94	23	4	123	—	129	3.20	+10	.227	.322	+53	0	0.7
1948	NY A	16	7	.696	39	31	11	1	—	3	—	—	236.1	240	108	17	4	111	—	101	3.77	+8	.268	.351	+29	0	0.7
1949	†NY A☆	17	6	.739	35	31	4	2	—	1	—	—	213.2	200	102	15	4	123	—	105	4.00	+1	.250	.353	+26	0	0.8
1950	†NY A★	16	12	.571	35	29	14	2	—	2	—	—	240.2	215	108	12	8	138	—	160	3.74	+15	.242	.349	+22	0	1.7
1951	†NY A	17	8	.680	40	26	16	0	—	7	—	—	221	171	84	12	5	100	—	126	3.05	+25	**.213**	.304	+40	0	2.2
1952	†NY A☆	20	8	.714	35	29	24	0	—	6	—	—	244.1	194	70	10	7	97	—	**160**	**2.06**	+61	.218	.300	+18	0	4.1
1953	†NY A★	13	7	.650	41	15	5	1	—	13	—	—	145	140	64	9	5	61	—	86	3.41	+8	.253	.333	+6	0	0.5
1954	NY A✱	13	4	.765	36	18	5	4	—	7	—	—	157.1	133	65	13	3	66	—	100	3.32	+4	.233	.314	+85	0	0.2
Total	13	182	107	.630	434	309	137	36	—	49	—	—	2492.1	2193	1026	133	57	1261	—	1423	3.30	+10	.238	.333	+25	0	8.9
Team	8	131	60	.686	295	209	96	14	—	41	—	—	1700	1500	695	111	40	819	—	967	3.30	+15	.238	.329	+34	—	10.9
/180I	1	14	6	.686	31	22	10	1	—	4	—	—	180	159	74	12	4	87	—	102	3.30	+15	.238	.329	+34	—	1.2
Rhoden, Rick	Richard Alan B5.16.1953 Boynton Beach FL BR/TR/6'3"/(190–203) Dr 1971 LAN 1/20 d7.5																										
1987	NY A	16	10	.615	30	29	4	0	15	0	0	1	181.2	184	84	22	3	61	5	107	3.86	+15	.268	.327	-17	0	1.4
1988	NY A	12	12	.500	30	30	5	1	16	0	0	0	197	206	107	20	8	56	4	94	4.29	-8	.269	.322	+0	22	-1.1
Total	16	151	125	.547	413	380	69	17	233	1	1	24	2593.2	2606	1143	198	39	801	62	1419	3.59	+4	.264	.319	-1	243	9.4
Team	2	28	22	.560	60	59	9	1	31	0	0	1	378.2	390	191	42	11	117	9	201	4.09	+3	.268	.324	-8	22	0.3
/180I	1	13	10	.560	29	28	4	0	15	0	0	0	180	185	91	20	5	56	4	96	4.09	+3	.268	.324	-8	10	0.1
Rhodes, Gordon	John Gordon "Dusty" B8.11.1907 Winnemucca NV D3.22.1960 Long Beach CA BR/TR/6'0"/187 d4.29																										
1929	NY A	0	4	.000	10	4	0	0	—	0	—	—	42.2	57	32	3	2	16	—	13	4.85	-20	.333	.397	-18	—	-0.5
1930	NY A	0	0	+	3	0	0	0	—	0	—	—	2	3	3	0	0	4	—	1	9.00	-52	.500	.700	—	—	-0.1
1931	NY A	6	3	.667	18	11	4	0	—	0	—	—	87	82	49	3	0	52	—	36	3.41	+16	.235	.334	+47	—	0.1
1932	NY A	1	2	.333	10	2	1	0	—	0	—	—	24	25	22	0	0	21	—	15	7.88	-48	.275	.411	+130	—	-0.9
Total	8	43	74	.368	200	135	47	1	—	5	—	—	1048.2	1196	676	74	10	477	—	356	4.85	-5	.286	.361	-5	—	-3.5
Team	4	7	9	.438	41	17	5	0	—	0	—	—	155.2	167	106	6	2	93	—	65	4.57	-13	.271	.368	+41	—	-1.4
/180I	5	8	10	.438	47	20	6	0	—	0	—	—	180	193	123	7	2	108	—	75	4.57	-13	.271	.368	+41	—	-1.6
Righetti, Dave	David Allan B11.28.1958 San Jose CA BL/TL/6'3"/(175–220) Dr 1977 TexA*1/9 d9.16 C8 Col San Jose (CA) City																										
1979	NY A	0	1	.000	3	3	0	0	1	0	0	0	17.1	10	7	2	0	10	0	13	3.63	+13	.182	.303	-27	0	0.1
1981	†NY A	8	4	.667	15	15	2	0	13	0	0	0	105.1	75	25	1	0	38	0	89	2.05	+76	.196	.268	-4	0	2.2
1982	NY A	11	10	.524	33	27	4	0	16	1	0	5	183	155	88	11	6	108	4	163	3.79	+7	.229	.338	-6	0	0.3
1983	NY A	14	8	.636	31	31	7	2	21	0	0	0	217	194	96	12	2	67	2	169	3.44	+15	.237	.296	+19	0	1.0
1984	NY A	5	6	.455	64	0	0	0	0	31	9	54	96.1	79	29	5	0	37	7	90	2.34	+64	.223	.293	—	15	2.7
1985	NY A	12	7	.632	74	0	0	0	0	29	10	56	107	96	36	5	0	45	3	92	2.78	+46	.241	.316	—	0	3.2
1986	NY A★	8	8	.500	74	0	0	0	0	**46**	10	61	106.2	88	31	4	2	35	7	83	2.45	+69	.226	.291	—	0	4.2
1987	NY A★	8	6	.571	60	0	0	0	0	31	13	45	95	95	45	9	2	44	4	77	3.51	+27	.262	.341	—	0	1.4
1988	NY A	5	4	.556	60	0	0	0	0	25	9	43	87	86	35	5	1	37	2	70	3.52	+13	.257	.332	—	0	0.7
1989	NY A	2	6	.250	55	0	0	0	0	25	9	45	69	73	32	3	1	26	6	51	3.00	+30	.277	.341	—	0	0.7
1990	NY A	1	1	.500	53	0	0	0	0	36	3	41	53	48	24	8	2	26	2	43	3.57	+12	.234	.325	—	0	0.2
1991	SF N	2	7	.222	61	0	0	0	0	24	5	43	71.2	64	29	4	3	28	6	51	3.39	+6	.240	.317	—	0	0.3
1992	SF N	2	7	.222	54	4	0	0	1	3	2	38	78.1	79	47	4	0	36	5	47	5.06	-34	.269	.344	-25	0	-1.8
1993	SF N	1	1	.500	51	0	0	0	0	1	2	36	47.1	58	31	11	1	17	0	31	5.70	-31	.305	.365	—	0	-0.4
1994	Oak A	0	0	+	7	0	0	0	0	0	1	2	7	13	13	3	1	9	0	4	16.71	-73	.419	.548	—	0	-0.4
1994	Tor A	0	1	.000	13	0	0	0	0	0	1	8	13.1	9	10	2	0	10	0	10	6.75	-28	.188	.322	—	0	-0.1
1994	Year	0	1	.000	20	0	0	0	0	0	2	10	20.1	22	23	5	1	19	0	14	10.18	-53	.278	.416	—	0	-0.5
1995	Chi A	3	2	.600	10	9	0	0	2	0	0	1	49.1	65	24	6	0	18	0	29	4.20	+7	.325	.377	+13	0	0.2
Total	16	82	79	.509	718	89	13	2	54	252	74	478	1403.2	1287	602	95	21	591	48	1112	3.46	+14	.244	.321	+3	15	14.5
Team	11	74	61	.548	522	76	13	2	51	224	63	350	1136.2	999	448	65	16	473	37	940	3.11	+28	.236	.313	+4	15	16.7
/60G	1	9	7	.548	60	9	1	0	6	26	7	40	130.2	115	51	7	2	54	4	108	3.11	+28	.236	.313	+4	2	1.9
Rijo, Jose	Jose Antonio (Abreu) B5.13.1965 San Cristobal, D.R. BR/TR/6'2"/(160–215) d4.5 [DL 1997 Cin N 181]																										
1984	NY A	2	8	.200	24	5	0	0	2	2	1	12	62.1	74	40	5	1	33	1	47	4.76	-20	.298	.382	-39	0	-1.2
Total	14	116	91	.560	376	269	22	4	170	3	6	71	1880	1710	772	147	28	663	34	1606	3.24	+21	.243	.308	-1	450	13.9
Rios, Danny	Daniel B11.11.1972 Madrid, Spain BR/TR/6'2"/192 d5.30 Col Miami																										
1997	NY A	0	0	+	2	0	0	0	0	0	0	0	2.1	9	5	3	1	2	0	1	19.29	-77	.563	.632	—	0	-0.2
Total	2	0	1	.000	7	0	0	0	0	0	0	3	9.2	18	14	4	2	8	0	7	9.31	-49	.391	.491	—	0	-0.5
Rivera, Mariano	Mariano B11.29.1969 Panama City, Pan BR/TR/6'2"/(168–195) d5.23																										
1995	†NY A	5	3	.625	19	10	0	0	3	0	1	6	67	71	43	11	2	30	0	51	5.51	-16	.266	.342	+5	0	-0.6
1996	†NY A	8	3	.727	61	0	0	0	0	5	3	51	107.2	73	25	1	2	34	3	130	2.09	+137	.189	.258	—	0	3.3
1997	†NY A★	6	4	.600	66	0	0	0	0	43	9	54	71.2	65	17	5	0	20	6	68	1.88	+136	.237	.285	—	0	4.1
1998	†NY A	3	0	1.000	54	0	0	0	0	36	5	45	61.1	48	13	3	1	17	1	36	1.91	+130	.215	.270	—	18	2.6
1999	†NY A✱	4	3	.571	66	0	0	0	0	**45**	4	58	69	43	15	2	3	18	3	52	1.83	+159	.176	.239	—	0	4.5
2000	†NY A★	7	4	.636	66	0	0	0	0	36	5	52	75.2	58	26	4	0	25	3	58	2.85	+67	.208	.271	—	0	3.2
2001	†NY A✱	4	6	.400	71	0	0	0	0	**50**	7	59	80.2	61	24	5	1	12	2	83	2.34	+90	.209	.242	—	0	3.8
2002	†NY A★	1	4	.200	45	0	0	0	0	28	4	34	46	35	16	3	2	11	2	41	2.74	+58	.203	.259	—	67	1.6
2003	†NY A	5	2	.714	64	0	0	0	0	40	6	50	70.2	61	15	3	4	10	1	63	1.66	+165	.235	.272	—	30	4.3
2004	†NY A★	4	2	.667	74	0	0	0	0	**53**	4	65	78.2	65	17	3	5	20	3	66	1.94	+136	.225	.287	—	0	4.9
2005	†NY A★	7	4	.636	71	0	0	0	0	43	4	64	78.1	50	18	2	4	18	0	80	1.38	+212	.177	.235	—	0	**4.9**
2006	†NY A★	5	5	.500	63	0	0	0	0	34	3	52	75	61	16	3	5	11	4	55	1.80	+157	.223	.264	—	0	**4.7**
2007	†NY A	3	4	.429	67	0	0	0	0	30	4	51	71.1	68	25	4	6	12	2	74	3.15	+43	.247	.293	—	0	1.9
Total	13	62	44	.585	787	10	0	0	3	443	59	641	953	759	270	49	35	238	30	857	2.35	+94	.216	.271	+5	115	43.2
/60G	1	5	3	.585	60	1	0	0	0	34	4	49	72.2	58	21	4	3	18	2	65	2.35	+94	.216	.271	+5	9	3.3
Roberts, Dale	Dale "Mountain Man" B4.12.1942 Owenton KY BR/TL/6'4"/180 d9.9																										
1967	NY A	0	0	+	2	0	0	0	0	0	0	0	2	3	2	0	2	2	1	0	9.00	-65	.429	.636	—	0	-0.1
Robinson, Jeff	Jeffrey Daniel B12.13.1960 Santa Ana CA BR/TR/6'4"/200 Dr 1983 SFN 2/44 d4.7 Col Cal St.–Fullerton																										
1990	NY A	3	6	.333	54	4	1	0	3	0	2	34	88.2	82	35	8	1	34	3	43	3.45	+16	.248	.319	-26	0	0.7
Total	9	46	57	.447	454	62	2	1	22	39	23	270	901.1	880	433	75	18	349	53	629	3.79	-4	.258	.327	-6	0	-1.7
/60G	1	3	7	.333	60	4	1	0	3	0	2	38	98.2	91	39	9	1	38	3	48	3.45	+16	.248	.319	-26	—	0.8
Robinson, Hank	John Henry "Rube" (b John Henry Roberson) B8.16.1887 Floyd AR D7.3.1965 N.Little Rock AR BR/TL/5'11.5"/160 d9.2																										
1918	NY A	2	4	.333	11	3	1	0	—	0	—	—	48	47	21	0	3	16	—	14	3.00	-6	.269	.340	-29	—	-0.4
Total	6	42	37	.532	150	72	32	3	—	2	—	—	701.1	646	269	7	32	159	—	238	2.53	+18	.253	.305	-1	—	3.2

YEAR	TM LG	W	L	PCT	G	GS	CG	SHO	QS	SV	BS	QR	IP	H	R	HR	HB	BB	IB	SO	ERA	AERA	OAV	OOB	SUP	DL	PW
RODRIGUEZ, FELIX	FELIX ANTONIO B9.9.1972 MONTE CRISTI, D.R. BR/TR/6'1"/(180–210) D5.13																										
2005	NY A	0	0	+	34	0	0	0	0	0	0	20	32.1	33	18	2	2	20	0	18	5.01	-14	.264	.374	—	73	-0.1
Total	11	38	26	.594	563	1	0	0	0	11	23	396	586.1	526	256	50	32	283	19	512	3.71	+14	.240	.333	+51	235	5.4
ROETTGER, OSCAR	OSCAR FREDERICK LOUIS "OKKIE" B2.19.1900 ST.LOUIS MO D7.4.1986 ST.LOUIS MO BR/TR/6'0"/170 D7.7 B–WALLY ▲																										
1923	NY A	0	0	+	5	0	0	0	—	1	—	—	11.2	16	15	3	1	12	—	7	8.49	-54	.340	.483	—	—	-0.4
1924	NY A	0	0	+	1	0	0	0	—	0	—	—	0	1	0	0	0	2	—	0	(0)	-100	1.000	1.000	—	—	0.0
Total	2	0	0	+	6	0	0	0	—	1	—	—	11.2	17	15	3	1	14	—	7	8.49	-54	.354	.508	—	—	-0.4
ROGERS, KENNY	KENNETH SCOTT B11.10.1964 SAVANNAH GA BL/TL/6'1"/(190–217) DR 1982 TEXA 39/816 D4.6																										
1996	†NY A	12	8	.600	30	30	2	1	13	0	0	0	179	179	97	16	8	83	2	92	4.68	+6	.261	.346	+6	0	0.7
1997	NY A	6	7	.462	31	22	1	0	4	0	0	7	145	161	100	18	7	62	1	78	5.65	-21	.280	.354	+30	0	-1.3
Total	19	210	143	.595	732	444	36	9	237	28	16	209	3129	3245	1621	317	118	1104	50	1886	4.19	+10	.268	.333	+8	199	15.6
Team	2	18	15	.545	61	52	3	1	17	0	0	7	324	340	197	34	15	145	3	170	5.11	-8	.270	.350	+16	—	-0.6
/180I	1	10	8	.545	34	29	2	1	9	0	0	4	180	189	109	19	8	81	2	94	5.11	-8	.270	.350	+16	—	-0.3
ROGERS, TOM	THOMAS ANDREW "SHOTGUN" B2.12.1892 SPARTA TN D3.7.1936 NASHVILLE TN BR/TR/6'0.5"/180 D4.14																										
1921	†NY A	0	1	.000	5	0	0	0	—	1	—	—	11	12	9	1	1	9	—	0	7.36	-42	.300	.440	—	—	-0.2
Total	4	15	30	.333	83	42	21	1	—	3	—	—	414.2	431	221	15	10	162	—	94	3.95	-25	.282	.354	-14	—	-3.5
ROLAND, JIM	JAMES IVAN B12.14.1942 FRANKLIN NC BR/TL/6'3"/(185–200) D9.20																										
1972	NY A	0	1	.000	16	0	0	0	0	0	0	12	25	27	14	3	1	16	1	13	5.04	-41	.287	.396	—	0	-0.3
Total	10	19	17	.528	216	29	6	1	14	9	1	127	450.1	357	185	34	19	229	22	272	3.22	+6	.218	.319	+12	95	0.5
ROSER, STEVE	EMERSON COREY B1.25.1918 ROME NY D2.8.2002 UTICA NY BR/TR/6'4"/220 D5.5 COL CLARKSON																										
1944	NY A	4	3	.571	16	6	1	0	—	1	—	—	84	80	39	3	0	34	—	34	3.86	-10	.256	.329	-4	0	-0.4
1945	NY A	0	0	+	11	0	0	0	—	0	—	—	27	27	15	1	0	8	—	11	3.67	-6	.262	.315	—	0	-0.1
1946	NY A	1	1	.500	4	1	0	0	—	0	—	—	3.1	7	6	0	0	4	—	1	16.20	-79	.438	.550	+24	0	-0.8
1946	Bos N	1	1	.500	14	1	0	0	—	1	—	—	35	33	15	1	0	18	—	18	3.60	-5	.250	.340	-25	0	-0.1
1946	Major	2	2	.500	18	2	0	0	—	1	—	—	38	40	21	1	0	22	—	19	4.70	-11	.270	.365	-1	0	-0.9
Total	3	6	5	.545	45	8	1	0	—	2	—	—	149.1	147	75	5	0	64	—	64	4.04	-14	.261	.336	-3	0	-1.4
Team	3	5	4	.556	31	7	1	0	—	1	—	—	114.1	114	60	4	0	46	—	46	4.17	-17	.264	.335	+0	—	-1.3
RUETHER, DUTCH	WALTER HENRY B9.13.1893 ALAMEDA CA D5.16.1970 PHOENIX AZ BL/TL/6'1.5"/180 D4.13 MIL 1918 ▲																										
1926	†NY A	2	3	.400	5	5	1	0	—	0	—	—	36	32	14	0	1	18	—	8	3.50	+10	.248	.345	-21	—	0.1
1927	NY A	13	6	.684	27	26	12	3	—	0	—	—	184	202	88	8	7	52	—	45	3.38	+14	.287	.343	+32	—	1.2
Total	11	137	95	.591	309	272	155	18	—	8	—	—	2124.2	2244	989	54	66	739	—	708	3.50	+4	.277	.342	+9	—	10.2
Team	2	15	9	.625	32	31	13	3	—	0	—	—	220	234	102	8	8	70	—	53	3.40	+14	.281	.343	+23	—	1.3
/180I	2	12	7	.625	26	25	11	2	—	0	—	—	180	191	83	7	7	57	—	43	3.40	+14	.281	.343	+23	—	1.1
RUFFING, RED	CHARLES HERBERT B5.3.1905 GRANVILLE IL D2.17.1986 MAYFIELD HTS. OH BR/TR/6'1.5"/205 D5.31 MIL 1943–45 C1 HF1967 ▲																										
1924	Bos A	0	0	+	8	2	0	0	—	0	—	—	23	29	17	0	3	9	—	10	6.65	-34	.333	.414	+35	—	-0.2
1925	Bos A	9	18	.333	37	27	13	3	—	1	—	—	217.1	253	135	10	2	75	—	64	5.01	-9	.299	.357	-12	—	-0.5
1926	Bos A	6	15	.286	37	22	6	0	—	2	—	—	166	169	96	4	5	68	—	58	4.39	-7	.274	.351	-31	—	-0.8
1927	Bos A	5	13	.278	26	18	10	0	—	2	—	—	158.1	160	94	7	4	87	—	77	4.66	-9	.277	.375	-28	—	-0.4
1928	Bos A	10	25	.286	42	34	**25**	1	—	2	—	—	289.1	303	147	8	10	96	—	118	3.89	+6	.275	.339	-29	—	1.8
1929	Bos A	9	22	.290	35	32	18	1	—	1	—	—	244.1	280	162	17	2	118	—	109	4.86	-12	.297	.376	-24	—	-1.1
1930	Bos A	0	3	.000	4	3	1	0	—	0	—	—	24	32	19	1	1	6	—	14	6.38	-28	.323	.368	-44	—	-0.4
1930	NY A	15	5	.750	34	25	12	2	—	1	—	—	197.2	200	106	10	2	62	—	117	4.14	+4	.260	.317	+30	—	1.9
1930	Year	15	8	.652	38	28	13	2	—	1	—	—	221.2	232	125	11	3	68	—	131	4.38	-1	.268	.323	+22	—	1.5
1931	NY A	16	14	.533	37	30	19	1	—	2	—	—	237	240	130	11	6	87	—	132	4.41	-10	.256	.323	+43	—	-0.1
1932	†NY A	18	7	.720	35	29	22	3	—	2	—	—	259	219	102	16	3	115	—	**190**	3.09	+32	**.226**	.311	+29	—	4.0
1933	NY A	9	14	.391	35	28	18	0	—	3	—	—	235	230	118	7	4	93	—	122	3.91	-1	.258	.330	+11	—	0.7
1934	NY A★	19	11	.633	36	31	19	5	—	0	—	—	256.1	232	134	18	1	104	—	149	3.93	+3	.236	.310	+22	—	0.7
1935	NY A	16	11	.593	30	29	19	2	—	0	—	—	222	201	88	17	1	76	—	81	3.12	+30	.239	.303	+3	—	4.2
1936	†NY A	20	12	.625	33	33	25	3	—	0	—	—	271	274	133	22	3	90	—	102	3.85	+21	.263	.323	+19	—	3.9
1937	†NY A	20	7	.741	31	31	22	4	—	0	—	—	256.1	242	101	17	1	68	—	131	2.98	+49	.247	.296	+37	—	4.0
1938	†NY A☆	**21**	7	**.750**	31	31	22	3	—	0	—	—	247.1	246	104	16	0	82	—	127	3.31	+37	.258	.317	+27	—	**4.5**
1939	†NY A★	21	7	.750	28	28	22	0	—	0	—	—	233.1	211	88	15	2	75	—	95	2.93	+49	.240	.301	+52	—	4.8
1940	NY A★	15	12	.556	30	30	20	3	—	0	—	—	226	218	98	24	3	76	—	97	3.38	+19	.252	.314	-1	—	1.3
1941	†NY A☆	15	6	.714	23	23	13	2	—	0	—	—	185.2	177	87	13	1	54	—	60	3.54	+11	.252	.306	+36	0	1.7
1942	†NY A☆	14	7	.667	24	24	16	4	—	0	—	—	193.2	183	72	10	3	41	—	80	3.21	+7	.250	.292	+42	0	1.5
1945	NY A	7	3	.700	11	11	8	1	—	0	—	—	87.1	85	32	2	1	20	—	24	2.89	+20	.251	.294	+32	0	0.6
1946	NY A	5	1	.833	8	8	4	2	—	0	—	—	61	37	13	2	0	23	—	19	1.77	+95	.171	.251	+2	73	1.0
1947	Chi A	3	5	.375	9	9	1	0	—	0	—	—	53	63	39	7	0	16	—	11	6.11	-40	.290	.339	+18	65	-1.7
Total	22	273	225	.548	624	538	335	45	—	16	—	—	4344	4284	2115	254	58	1541	—	1987	3.80	+9	.258	.323	+12	138	31.4
Team	15	231	124	.651	426	391	261	35	—	8	—	—	3168.2	2995	1406	200	31	1066	—	1526	3.47	+19	.248	.310	+26	73	34.7
/180I	1	13	7	.651	24	22	15	2	—	0	—	—	180	170	80	11	2	61	—	87	3.47	+19	.248	.310	+26	4	2.0
RUSSELL, ALLAN	ALLAN "RUBBERARM" B7.31.1893 BALTIMORE MD D10.20.1972 BALTIMORE MD BB/TR/5'11"/165 D9.13 B–LEFTY																										
1915	NY A	1	2	.333	5	3	1	0	—	0	—	—	27	21	10	1	1	21	—	21	2.67	+10	.228	.377	-50	—	0.1
1916	NY A	6	10	.375	34	19	8	1	—	6	—	—	171.1	138	83	8	7	75	—	104	3.20	-10	.232	.324	-16	—	-1.1
1917	NY A	7	8	.467	25	10	6	0	—	2	—	—	104.1	89	42	2	7	39	—	55	2.24	+20	.236	.319	-28	—	0.7
1918	NY A	7	11	.389	27	18	7	2	—	4	—	—	141	139	68	6	5	73	—	54	3.26	-13	.267	.363	-10	—	-1.3
1919	NY A	5	5	.500	23	9	4	1	—	1	—	—	90.2	89	48	5	2	32	—	50	3.47	-8	.251	.317	-15	—	-0.4
Total	11	70	76	.479	345	112	54	5	—	42	—	—	1394.1	1382	693	58	44	610	—	603	3.52	-1	.269	.351	-20	—	-2.4
Team	5	26	36	.419	114	59	26	4	—	13	—	—	534.1	476	251	22	22	240	—	284	3.05	-5	.245	.335	-18	—	-2.0
/180I	2	9	12	.419	38	20	9	1	—	4	—	—	180	160	85	7	7	81	—	96	3.05	-5	.245	.335	-18	—	-0.7
RUSSO, MARIUS	MARIUS UGO "LEFTY" B7.19.1914 BROOKLYN NY D3.26.2005 FORT MYERS FL BR/TL/6'1"/190 D6.6 MIL 1944–45 COL LONG ISLAND–BROOKLYN																										
1939	NY A	8	3	.727	21	11	9	2	—	2	—	—	116	86	37	6	1	41	—	55	2.41	+81	.210	.283	+31	—	2.4
1940	NY A	14	8	.636	30	24	15	0	—	1	—	—	189.1	181	79	17	1	55	—	87	3.28	+23	.249	.303	+33	—	2.1
1941	†NY A☆	14	10	.583	28	27	17	3	—	1	—	—	209.2	195	85	8	1	87	—	105	3.09	+27	.247	.322	+8	0	2.4
1942	NY A	4	1	.800	9	5	2	0	—	0	—	—	45.1	41	15	2	1	14	—	15	2.78	+24	.244	.306	+54	0	0.5
1943	†NY A	5	10	.333	24	14	5	1	—	1	—	—	101.2	89	53	7	2	45	—	42	3.72	-13	.235	.319	-8	0	-0.9
1946	NY A	0	2	.000	8	3	0	0	—	0	—	—	18.2	26	9	1	0	11	—	7	4.34	-20	.333	.416	-59	0	-0.2
Total	6	45	34	.570	120	84	48	6	—	5	—	—	680.2	618	278	41	6	253	—	311	3.13	+24	.242	.312	+16	0	6.3
/180I	2	12	9	.570	32	22	13	2	0	1	0	0	180	163	74	11	2	67	—	82	3.13	+24	.242	.312	+16	—	1.7
RUTH, BABE	GEORGE HERMAN "THE BAMBINO","THE SULTAN OF SWAT" B2.6.1895 BALTIMORE MD D8.16.1948 NEW YORK NY BL/TL/6'2"/215 D7.11 C1 HF1936 ▲																										
1920	NY A	1	0	1.000	1	1	0	0	—	0	—	—	4	3	4	0	0	2	—	0	4.50	-15	.200	.294	+191	—	-0.1
1921	†NY A	2	0	1.000	2	1	0	0	—	0	—	—	9	14	10	1	0	9	—	2	9.00	-53	.350	.469	+156	—	-0.6
1930	NY A	1	0	1.000	1	1	1	0	—	0	—	—	9	11	3	0	0	2	—	3	3.00	+43	.306	.342	+80	—	0.3
1933	NY A★	1	0	1.000	1	1	1	0	—	0	—	—	9	12	5	0	0	3	—	0	5.00	-22	.308	.357	+31	—	0.0
Total	10	94	46	.671	163	148	107	17	—	4	—	—	1221.1	974	400	10	29	441	—	488	2.28	+22	.221	.297	+17	—	17.0
Team	4	5	0	1.000	5	4	2	0	—	0	—	—	31	40	22	1	0	16	—	5	5.52	-26	.308	.384	+115	—	-0.4

YEAR	TM LG	W	L	PCT	G	GS	CG	SHO	QS	SV	BS	QR	IP	H	R	HR	HB	BB	IB	SO	ERA	AERA	OAV	OOB	SUP	DL	PW
RYAN, ROSY	WILFRED PATRICK DOLAN B3.15.1898 WORCESTER MA D12.10.1980 SCOTTSDALE AZ BL/TR/6'0"/185 d9.7 COL HOLY CROSS																										
1928	NY A	0	0	+	3	0	0	0	—	0	—	—	6	17	11	1	0	1	—	5	16.50	-77	.486	.500	—	—	-0.4
Total	10	52	47	.525	248	75	29	1	—	19	—	—	881	941	486	33	11	278	—	315	4.14	-9	.277	.333	+21	—	-1.9
SAIN, JOHNNY	JOHN FRANKLIN B9.25.1917 HAVANA AR D11.7.2006 DOWNERS GROVE IL BR/TR/6'2"/(185–200) d4.24 MIL 1942–45 C17																										
1951	†NY A	2	1	.667	7	4	1	0	—	1	—	—	37	41	17	5	0	8	—	21	4.14	-7	.281	.318	+10	0	0.1
1952	†NY A	11	6	.647	35	16	8	0	—	7	—	—	148.1	149	70	15	2	38	—	57	3.46	-4	.261	.310	+44	0	0.1
1953	†NY A☆	14	7	.667	40	19	10	1	—	9	—	—	189	189	68	16	3	45	—	84	3.00	+23	.262	.308	+36	0	2.4
1954	NY A	6	6	.500	45	0	0	0	—	**22**	—	—	77	66	27	11	0	15	—	33	3.16	+9	.229	.266	—	0	1.1
1955	NY A	0	0	+	3	0	0	0	—	0	—	—	5.1	6	4	4	0	1	0	5	6.75	-45	.300	.333	—	0	-0.1
Total	11	139	116	.545	412	245	140	16	—	51	—	—	2125.2	2145	947	180	30	619	4	910	3.49	+6	.261	.315	+11	0	11.2
Team	5	33	20	.623	130	39	19	1	—	39	—	—	456.2	451	186	51	5	107	0	200	3.31	+7	.258	.303	+37	—	3.6
/180I	2	13	8	.623	51	15	7	0	—	15	—	—	180	178	73	20	2	42	0	79	3.31	+7	.258	.303	+37	—	1.4
SANDERS, ROY	ROY LEE "SIMON" B6.10.1894 PITTSBURG KS D7.8.1963 LOUISVILLE KY BR/TR/6'0"/185 d8.6																										
1918	NY A	0	2	.000	6	2	0	0	—	0	—	—	25.2	28	15	0	2	16	—	8	4.21	-33	.301	.414	-73	—	-0.5
1920	StL A	1	1	.500	8	1	0	0	—	0	—	—	17.1	20	10	1	1	17	—	2	5.19	-25	.313	.463	+143	—	-0.2
Total	2	1	3	.250	14	3	0	0	—	0	—	—	43	48	25	1	3	33	—	10	4.60	-29	.306	.435	+10	—	-0.7
SANDERSON, SCOTT	SCOTT DOUGLAS B7.22.1956 DEARBORN MI BR/TR/6'5"/(192–200) DR 1977 MONN 3/54 d8.6 COL VANDERBILT																										
1991	NY A☆	16	10	.615	34	34	2	2	16	0	0	0	208	200	95	22	3	29	0	130	3.81	+9	.252	.279	+1	0	0.8
1992	NY A	12	11	.522	33	33	2	1	17	0	0	0	193.1	220	116	28	4	64	5	104	4.93	-20	.286	.340	+18	0	-2.3
Total	19	163	143	.533	472	407	43	14	196	5	4	51	2561.2	2590	1209	297	43	625	51	1611	3.84	+3	.263	.307	+1	470	-0.2
Team	2	28	21	.571	67	67	4	3	33	0	—	0	401.1	420	211	50	7	93	5	234	4.35	-7	.269	.310	+9	—	-1.5
/180I	1	13	9	.571	30	30	2	1	15	0	—	0	180	188	95	22	3	42	2	105	4.35	-7	.269	.310	+9	—	-0.7
SANFORD, FRED	JOHN FREDERICK B8.9.1919 GARFIELD UT BB/TR (BR 1948)/6'1"/200 d5.5 MIL 1944–45																										
1943	StL A	0	0	+	3	0	0	0	—	0	—	—	9.1	7	2	0	0	4	—	2	1.93	+72	.219	.306	—	0	0.1
1946	StL A	2	1	.667	3	3	2	2	—	0	—	—	22	19	7	0	0	9	—	8	2.05	+82	.235	.311	-54	0	0.6
1947	StL A	7	16	.304	34	23	9	0	—	4	—	—	186.2	186	89	17	0	76	—	62	3.71	+4	.261	.332	-34	0	0.2
1948	StL A	12	21	.364	42	33	9	1	—	2	—	—	227	250	123	19	2	91	—	79	4.64	-2	.279	.347	-27	0	0.0
1949	NY A	7	3	.700	29	11	3	0	—	0	—	—	95.1	100	53	9	0	57	—	51	3.87	+5	.270	.367	+15	0	-0.4
1950	NY A	5	4	.556	26	12	2	0	—	0	—	—	112.2	103	60	9	1	79	—	54	4.55	-6	.252	.374	+3	0	0.0
1951	NY A	0	3	.000	11	2	0	0	—	0	—	—	26.2	15	11	2	0	25	—	10	3.71	+3	.169	.351	-42	0	0.1
1951	Was A	2	3	.400	7	7	0	0	—	0	—	—	37	51	27	5	0	27	—	12	6.57	-38	.329	.429	+15	0	-1.1
1951	StL A	2	4	.333	9	7	1	0	—	0	—	—	27.1	37	33	6	0	23	—	7	10.21	-57	.308	.420	+36	0	-2.6
1951	Year	4	10	.286	27	16	1	0	—	0	—	—	91	103	71	13	0	75	—	29	6.82	-40	.283	.405	+20	0	-3.6
Total	7	37	55	.402	164	98	26	3	—	6	—	—	744	768	405	67	3	391	—	285	4.45	-6	.268	.357	-13	0	-3.1
Team	3	12	10	.545	66	25	5	0	—	0	—	—	234.2	218	124	20	1	161	—	115	4.18	-1	.251	.369	+5	—	-0.3
/180I	2	9	8	.545	51	19	4	0	—	0	—	—	180	167	95	15	1	123	—	88	4.18	-1	.251	.369	+5	—	-0.2
SAWYER, RICK	RICHARD CLYDE B4.7.1948 BAKERSFIELD CA BR/TR/6'2"/200 DR 1968 CLEA*S3/45 d4.28 COL BAKERSFIELD (CA) JC																										
1974	NY A	0	0	+	1	0	0	0	0	0	0	0	1.2	2	3	0	0	1	0	1	16.20	-78	.500	.600	—	0	-0.1
1975	NY A	0	0	+	4	0	0	0	0	0	0	4	6	7	4	0	0	2	0	3	3.00	+24	.304	.360	—	0	0.0
Total	4	12	9	.571	74	20	4	2	9	0	0	32	200.1	229	108	17	8	96	19	82	4.49	-23	.299	.380	+21	0	-1.9
Team	2	0	0	+	5	0	0	0	0	0	0	4	7.2	9	7	0	0	3	0	4	5.87	-37	.333	.400	—	—	-0.1
SCARBOROUGH, RAY	RAY WILSON (B RAE WILSON SCARBOROUGH) B7.23.1917 MT.GILEAD NC D7.1.1982 MOUNT OLIVE NC BR/TR/6'0"/(178–185) d6.26 MIL 1943–45 C1 COL WAKE FOREST																										
1952	†NY A	5	1	.833	9	4	1	0	—	0	—	—	34	27	11	4	1	15	—	13	2.91	+14	.223	.314	+64	0	0.6
1953	NY A	2	2	.500	25	1	0	0	—	2	—	—	54.2	52	23	4	4	26	—	20	3.29	+12	.250	.345	+44	0	0.2
Total	10	80	85	.485	318	168	59	9	—	14	—	—	1428.2	1487	755	89	44	611	—	564	4.13	-3	.267	.344	-4	0	-2.0
Team	2	7	3	.700	34	5	1	0	—	2	—	—	88.2	79	34	8	5	41	—	33	3.15	+13	.240	.333	+60	—	0.8
SCHAEFFER, HARRY	HARRY EDWARD "LEFTY" B6.23.1924 READING PA BL/TL/6'2.5"/175 d7.28 COL EAST STROUDSBURG																										
1952	NY A	0	1	.000	5	2	0	0	—	0	—	—	17	18	14	2	0	18	—	15	5.29	-37	.265	.419	-21	0	-0.3
SCHALLOCK, ART	ARTHUR LAWRENCE B4.25.1924 MILL VALLEY CA BL/TL/5'9"/(156–160) d7.16 COL MARIN (CA) CC																										
1951	NY A	3	1	.750	11	6	1	0	—	0	—	—	46.1	50	20	3	1	20	—	19	3.88	-1	.272	.346	+43	0	0.2
1952	NY A	0	0	+	2	0	0	0	—	0	—	—	2	3	2	0	0	2	—	1	9.00	-63	.375	.500	—	0	-0.1
1953	†NY A	0	0	+	7	1	0	0	—	1	—	—	21.1	30	12	2	1	15	—	13	2.95	+25	.345	.447	+44	0	0.0
1954	NY A	0	1	.000	6	1	1	0	—	0	—	—	17.1	20	10	3	1	11	—	9	4.15	-17	.282	.386	-74	0	-0.2
1955	NY A	0	0	+	2	0	0	0	—	0	—	—	3	4	2	1	0	1	0	2	6.00	-38	.333	.385	—	0	0.0
1955	Bal A	3	5	.375	30	6	1	0	—	0	—	—	80.1	92	52	2	2	42	3	33	4.15	-8	.294	.378	-42	0	-0.7
1955	Year	3	5	.375	32	6	1	0	—	0	—	—	83.1	96	54	3	2	43	3	35	4.21	-10	.295	.378	-42	0	-0.7
Total	5	6	7	.462	58	14	3	0	—	1	—	—	170.1	199	98	11	5	91	3	77	4.02	-6	.295	.381	+0	0	-0.8
Team	5	3	2	.600	28	8	2	0	—	1	—	—	90	107	46	9	3	49	0	44	3.90	-5	.296	.384	+29	—	-0.1
SCHMITZ, JOHNNY	JOHN ALBERT "BEAR TRACKS" B11.27.1920 WAUSAU WI BR/TL/6'0"/(168–170) d9.6 MIL 1943–45																										
1952	NY A	1	1	.500	5	2	1	0	—	1	—	—	15	15	7	0	1	9	—	3	3.60	-8	.263	.373	+5	0	0.1
1953	NY A	0	0	+	3	0	0	0	—	0	—	—	4.1	2	1	1	0	3	—	0	2.08	+78	.143	.294	—	0	0.1
Total	13	93	114	.449	366	235	86	16	—	19	—	—	1812.2	1766	841	97	35	757	5	746	3.55	+7	.258	.335	-9	0	6.0
Team	2	1	1	.500	8	2	1	0	—	1	—	—	19.1	17	8	1	1	12	—	3	3.26	+4	.239	.357	+5	—	0.2
SCHNEIDER, PETE	PETER JOSEPH B8.20.1895 LOS ANGELES CA D6.1.1957 LOS ANGELES CA BR/TR/6'1"/194 d6.20																										
1919	NY A	0	1	.000	7	4	0	0	—	0	—	—	29	19	14	1	3	22	—	11	3.41	-6	.192	.355	-8	—	-0.2
Total	6	59	86	.407	207	157	84	10	—	4	—	—	1274	1199	541	16	52	498	—	487	2.66	+2	.257	.336	-11	—	0.5
SCHREIBER, PAUL	PAUL FREDERICK "VON" B10.8.1902 JACKSONVILLE FL D1.28.1982 SARASOTA FL BR/TR/6'2"/180 d9.2 C13																										
1945	NY A	0	0	+	2	0	0	0	—	0	—	—	4.1	4	2	0	0	2	—	1	4.15	-17	.267	.353	—	0	0.0
Total	3	0	0	+	12	0	0	0	—	1	—	—	20.1	22	11	1	2	10	—	5	3.98	-4	.286	.382	—	0	-0.1
SCHULZ, AL	ALBERT CHRISTOPHER B5.12.1889 TOLEDO OH D12.13.1931 GALLIPOLIS OH BR/TL/6'0"/182 d9.25																										
1912	NY A	1	1	.500	3	1	1	0	—	0	—	—	16.1	11	8	0	0	11	—	8	2.20	+63	.183	.310	-100	—	0.2
1913	NY A	7	14	.333	38	22	9	0	—	0	—	—	193	197	110	4	5	69	—	77	3.73	-20	.269	.336	-8	—	-1.7
1914	NY A	1	3	.250	6	4	1	0	—	0	—	—	28.1	27	17	0	2	10	—	18	4.76	-42	.237	.310	-21	—	-0.7
Total	5	47	63	.427	160	110	56	5	—	4	—	—	933.1	867	440	19	20	409	—	445	3.32	-15	.254	.338	-9	—	-6.6
Team	3	9	18	.333	47	27	11	0	—	0	—	—	237.2	235	135	4	7	90	—	103	3.75	-20	.259	.331	-13	—	-2.2
/180I	2	7	14	.333	36	20	8	0	—	0	—	—	180	178	102	3	5	68	—	78	3.75	-20	.259	.331	-13	—	-1.7
SCHULZE, DON	DONALD ARTHUR B9.27.1962 ROSELLE IL BR/TR/6'3"/(215–230) DR 1980 CHIN 1/11 d9.13																										
1989	NY A	1	1	.500	2	2	0	0	1	0	0	0	11	12	5	1	1	5	0	5	4.09	-5	.300	.375	-30	0	0.0
Total	6	15	25	.375	76	59	4	0	22	0	0	7	338.2	422	231	40	12	105	2	144	5.47	-26	.306	.357	+12	41	-5.5
SCURRY, ROD	RODNEY GRANT B3.17.1956 SACRAMENTO CA D11.5.1992 RENO NV BL/TL/6'2"/(180–195) DR 1974 PITN 1/11 d4.17																										
1985	NY A	1	0	1.000	5	0	0	0	0	1	0	4	12.2	5	4	2	0	10	1	17	2.84	+42	.125	.300	—	0	0.2
1986	NY A	1	2	.333	31	0	0	0	0	2	1	15	39.1	38	18	1	2	22	1	36	3.66	+13	.252	.354	—	73	0.2
Total	8	19	32	.373	332	7	0	0	4	39	19	205	460.2	384	190	31	19	274	29	431	3.24	+16	.227	.339	-55	131	1.9
Team	2	2	2	.500	36	0	0	0	0	3	1	19	52	43	22	3	2	32	2	53	3.46	+19	.225	.342	—	73	0.4

Pitchers

YEAR	TM LG	W	L	PCT	G	GS	CG	SHO	QS	SV	BS	QR	IP	H	R	HR	HB	BB	IB	SO	ERA	AERA	OAV	OOB	SUP	DL	PW
SHANTZ, BOBBY ROBERT CLAYTON B9.26.1925 POTTSTOWN PA BR/TL/5'6"/(138–154) d5.1 b–BILLY																											
1957	†NY A☆	11	5	.688	30	21	9	1	29	5	0	41	173	157	58	15	6	40	1	72	**2.45**	+47	.248	.296	+16	0	2.7
1958	NY A	7	6	.538	33	13	3	0	29	0	2	41	126	127	52	8	2	35	7	80	3.36	+5	.262	.312	-12	0	0.8
1959	NY A	7	3	.700	33	4	2	2	29	3	0	41	94.2	64	33	4	0	33	5	66	2.38	+53	.189	.260	-15	0	1.6
1960	†NY A	5	4	.556	42	0	0	0	0	11	4	28	67.2	57	24	5	2	24	4	54	2.79	+28	.235	.302	—	0	1.0
Total	16	119	99	.546	537	171	78	15	93	48	16	271	1935.2	1795	817	151	41	643	53	1072	3.38	+19	.248	.312	-3	95	18.7
Team	4	30	18	.625	138	38	14	3	87	19	6	151	461.1	405	167	32	10	132	17	272	2.73	+31	.238	.294	+3	—	6.1
/180I	2	12	7	.625	54	15	5	1	34	7	2	59	180	158	65	12	4	52	7	100	2.73	+31	.238	.294	+3	—	2.4
SHAWKEY, BOB JAMES ROBERT B12.4.1890 SIGEL PA D12.31.1980 SYRACUSE NY BR/TR/5'11"/168 d7.16 MIL 1918 M1/C1 COL SLIPPERY ROCK																											
1913	Phi A	6	5	.545	18	15	8	1	—	0	—	—	111.1	92	41	2	3	50	—	52	2.34	+18	.221	.309	+16	—	0.2
1914	†Phi A	15	8	.652	38	31	18	5	—	2	—	—	237	223	88	4	2	75	—	89	2.73	-4	.262	.323	+22	—	-0.2
1915	Phi A	6	6	.500	17	13	7	1	—	0	—	—	100	103	57	3	1	38	—	56	4.05	-28	.278	.346	+23	—	-1.2
1915	NY A	4	7	.364	16	9	5	1	—	0	—	—	85.2	78	38	2	2	35	—	31	3.26	-10	.265	.347	-39	—	-0.2
1915	Year	10	13	.435	33	22	12	2	—	0	—	—	185.2	181	95	5	3	73	—	87	3.68	-20	.272	.347	-3	—	-1.4
1916	NY A	24	14	.632	53	27	21	4	—	**8**	—	—	276.2	204	78	4	6	81	—	122	2.21	+31	.209	.273	+2	—	3.4
1917	NY A	13	15	.464	32	26	16	2	—	0	—	—	236.1	207	81	2	6	72	—	97	2.44	+10	.243	.306	-1	—	1.2
1918	NY A	1	1	.500	3	2	1	1	—	0	—	—	16	7	2	0	0	10	—	3	1.13	+151	.143	.288	+7	—	0.7
1919	NY A	20	11	.645	41	27	22	3	—	**5**	—	—	261.1	218	94	7	5	92	—	122	2.72	+17	.231	.303	+4	—	1.8
1920	NY A	20	13	.606	38	31	20	5	—	2	—	—	267.2	246	88	10	1	85	—	126	**2.45**	+56	.248	.308	-2	—	4.6
1921	†NY A	18	12	.600	38	31	18	3	—	2	—	—	245	245	131	15	7	86	—	126	4.08	+4	.263	.329	+25	—	0.8
1922	†NY A	20	12	.625	39	34	22	3	—	1	—	—	299.2	286	112	16	0	98	—	130	2.91	+38	.256	.316	+3	—	3.3
1923	†NY A	16	11	.593	36	31	17	1	—	1	—	—	258.2	232	114	17	4	102	—	125	3.51	+12	**.246**	.322	+15	—	0.8
1924	NY A	16	11	.593	38	25	10	1	—	0	—	—	207.2	226	107	11	3	74	—	114	4.12	+1	.286	.350	+33	—	0.8
1925	NY A	6	14	.300	33	19	9	1	—	0	—	—	186	209	101	12	5	67	—	81	4.11	+4	.294	.359	-41	—	-0.3
1926	†NY A	8	7	.533	29	10	3	1	—	3	—	—	104.1	102	49	8	2	37	—	63	3.62	+6	.263	.330	+25	—	0.6
1927	NY A	2	3	.400	19	2	0	0	—	4	—	—	43.2	44	19	1	1	16	—	23	2.89	+34	.262	.330	+30	—	0.4
Total	15	195	150	.565	488	333	197	33	—	28	—	—	2937	2722	1200	114	48	1018	—	1360	3.09	+14	.252	.319	+8	—	16.7
Team	13	168	131	.562	415	274	164	26	—	26	—	—	2488.2	2304	1014	105	42	855	—	1163	3.12	+17	.252	.318	+5	—	17.9
/180I	1	12	9	.562	30	20	12	2	—	2	—	—	180	167	73	8	3	62	—	84	3.12	+17	.252	.318	+5	—	1.3
SHEA, SPEC FRANCIS JOSEPH "THE NAUGATUCK NUGGETT" (B FRANCIS JOSEPH O'SHEA) B10.2.1920 NAUGATUCK CT D7.19.2002 NEW HAVEN CT BR/TR/6'0"/195 d4.19																											
1947	†NY A★	14	5	.737	27	23	13	3	—	1	—	—	178.2	127	63	10	4	89	—	89	3.07	+15	**.200**	.303	+28	0	1.2
1948	NY A	9	10	.474	28	22	8	3	—	1	—	—	155.2	117	66	10	2	87	—	71	3.41	+20	**.208**	.316	+5	0	1.2
1949	NY A	1	1	.500	20	3	0	0	—	1	—	—	52.1	48	36	5	0	43	—	22	5.33	-24	.250	.387	-19	0	-0.3
1951	NY A	5	5	.500	25	11	2	2	—	0	—	—	95.2	112	59	11	4	50	—	38	4.33	-12	.300	.389	+35	0	-0.7
1952	Was A	11	7	.611	22	21	12	2	—	0	—	—	169	144	62	6	2	92	—	65	2.93	+21	.231	.331	+4	0	1.5
1953	Was A	12	7	.632	23	23	11	1	—	0	—	—	164.2	151	82	11	4	75	—	38	3.94	-1	.244	.329	+20	0	-0.3
1954	Was A	2	9	.182	23	11	1	0	—	0	—	—	71.1	97	54	9	2	34	—	22	6.18	-42	.340	.412	+8	0	-2.9
1955	Was A	2	2	.500	27	4	1	1	—	2	—	—	56.1	53	31	4	1	27	0	16	3.99	-4	.251	.335	-7	0	0.0
Total	8	56	46	.549	195	118	48	12	—	5	—	—	943.2	849	453	66	19	497	0	361	3.80	-1	.243	.339	+14	0	-0.3
Team	4	29	21	.580	100	59	23	8	—	3	—	—	482.1	404	224	36	10	269	—	220	3.68	+4	.229	.335	+18	—	1.4
/180I	1	11	8	.580	37	22	9	3	—	1	—	—	180	151	84	13	4	100	—	82	3.68	+4	.229	.335	+18	—	0.5
SHEALY, AL ALBERT BERLEY B5.24.1900 CHAPIN SC D3.7.1967 HAGERSTOWN MD BR/TR/5'11"/175 d4.13 COL NEWBERRY																											
1928	NY A	8	6	.571	23	12	3	0	—	2	—	—	96	124	64	4	1	42	—	39	5.06	-26	.308	.375	+28	—	-1.7
1930	Chi N	0	0	+	24	0	0	0	—	0	—	—	27	37	24	2	0	14	—	14	8.00	-39	.327	.402	—	—	-0.2
Total	2	8	6	.571	47	12	3	0	—	2	—	—	123	161	88	6	1	56	—	53	5.71	-30	.313	.381	+28	—	-1.9
SHEARS, GEORGE GEORGE PENFIELD B4.13.1890 MARSHALL MO D11.12.1978 LOVELAND CO BR/TL/6'3"/180 d4.24																											
1912	NY A	0	0	+	4	0	0	0	—	0	—	—	15	24	18	0	0	11	—	9	5.40	-33	.364	.455	—	—	-0.2
SHEEHAN, TOM THOMAS CLANCY B3.31.1894 GRAND RIDGE IL D10.29.1982 CHILLICOTHE OH BR/TR/6'2.5"/190 d7.14 M1/C5																											
1921	NY A	1	0	1.000	12	1	0	0	—	1	—	—	33	43	23	1	1	19	—	7	5.45	-22	.326	.414	+117	—	0.0
Total	6	17	39	.304	146	50	26	3	—	5	—	—	607	677	359	14	7	242	—	169	4.00	-14	.294	.362	-18	—	-3.3
SHELDON, ROLLIE ROLAND FRANK B12.17.1936 PUTNAM CT BR/TR/6'4"/(190–201) d4.23 COL CONNECTICUT																											
1961	NY A	11	5	.688	35	21	6	2	13	0	0	9	162.2	149	70	17	2	55	2	84	3.60	+3	.246	.310	+12	0	0.1
1962	NY A	7	8	.467	34	16	2	0	7	1	0	10	118	136	78	12	1	28	3	54	5.49	-32	.289	.324	+15	0	-2.6
1964	†NY A	5	2	.714	19	12	3	0	6	1	0	5	102.1	92	43	18	1	18	2	57	3.61	+0	.243	.276	+29	0	-0.1
1965	NY A	0	0	+	3	0	0	0	0	0	0	2	6.1	5	1	0	0	1	0	7	1.42	+140	.238	.261	—	0	0.1
1965	KC A	10	8	.556	32	29	4	1	16	0	0	3	186.2	180	86	22	7	56	3	105	3.95	-12	.251	.311	-4	0	-1.0
1965	Year	10	8	.556	35	29	4	1	16	0	0	5	193	185	87	22	7	57	3	112	3.87	-10	.251	.310	-4	0	-0.9
1966	KC A	4	7	.364	14	13	1	1	7	0	0	0	69	73	31	3	1	26	3	26	3.13	+9	.275	.337	-18	0	-0.1
1966	Bos A	1	6	.143	23	10	1	0	5	0	0	7	79.2	106	49	15	2	23	4	38	4.97	-23	.320	.367	-24	0	-0.8
1966	Year	5	13	.278	37	23	2	1	12	0	0	7	148.2	179	80	18	3	49	7	64	4.12	-12	.300	.353	-22	0	-0.9
Total	5	38	36	.514	160	101	17	4	54	2	0	36	724.2	741	358	87	14	207	17	371	4.09	-11	.266	.317	+2	0	-4.4
Team	4	23	15	.605	91	49	11	2	26	2	0	26	389.1	382	192	47	4	102	7	202	4.14	-11	.259	.305	+17	—	-2.5
/180I	2	11	7	.605	42	23	5	1	12	1	0	12	180	177	89	22	2	47	3	93	4.14	-11	.259	.305	+17	—	-1.2
SHERID, ROY ROYDEN RICHARD B1.25.1907 NORRISTOWN PA D2.28.1982 PARKER FORD PA BR/TR/6'2"/185 d5.11 COL ALBRIGHT																											
1929	NY A	6	6	.500	33	15	9	0	—	1	—	—	154.2	165	81	6	5	55	—	51	3.61	+7	.277	.343	+20	—	0.0
1930	NY A	12	13	.480	37	21	8	0	—	4	—	—	184	214	122	13	5	87	—	59	5.23	-18	.289	.368	+31	—	-2.5
1931	NY A	5	5	.500	17	8	3	0	—	2	—	—	74.1	94	52	4	3	24	—	39	5.69	-30	.306	.362	+49	—	-1.5
Total	3	23	24	.489	87	44	20	0	—	7	—	—	413	473	255	23	13	166	—	149	4.71	-13	.288	.358	+31	—	-4.0
/180I	1	10	10	.489	38	19	9	0	0	3	0	0	180	206	111	10	6	72	—	65	4.71	-13	.288	.358	+31	—	-1.7
SHIELDS, BEN BENJAMIN COWAN "BIG BEN","LEFTY" B6.17.1903 HUNTERSVILLE NC D1.24.1982 WOODRUFF SC BR/TL (BB 1930–31)/6'1.5"/195 d4.17																											
1924	NY A	0	0	+	2	0	0	0	—	0	—	—	2	6	6	0	0	2	—	3	27.00	-85	.545	.615	—	—	-0.2
1925	NY A	3	0	1.000	4	2	2	0	—	0	—	—	24	24	13	2	2	12	—	5	4.88	-13	.267	.365	+28	—	-0.2
1930	Bos A	0	0	+	3	0	0	0	—	0	—	—	10	16	11	0	0	6	—	1	9.00	-49	.400	.478	—	—	-0.2
1931	Phi N	1	0	1.000	4	0	0	0	—	0	—	—	5.1	9	9	1	0	7	—	0	15.19	-72	.391	.533	—	—	-0.8
Total	4	4	0	1.000	13	2	2	0	—	0	—	—	41.1	55	39	3	2	27	—	9	8.27	-47	.335	.435	+28	—	-1.4
Team	2	3	0	1.000	6	2	2	0	—	0	—	—	26	30	19	2	2	14	—	8	6.58	-35	.297	.393	+28	—	-0.4
SHIELDS, STEVE STEPHEN MACK B11.30.1958 GADSDEN AL BR/TR/6'5"/(220–230) DR 1977 BOSA 10/247 d6.1																											
1985	Atl N	1	2	.333	23	6	0	0	3	0	0	9	68	86	46	9	1	32	6	29	5.16	-25	.320	.390	-8	0	-0.6
1986	Atl N	0	0	+	6	0	0	0	0	0	0	2	12.2	13	10	4	0	7	0	6	7.11	-44	.271	.364	—	0	-0.2
1986	KC A	0	0	+	3	0	0	0	0	0	1	2	8.2	3	3	1	0	4	1	2	2.08	+106	.111	.212	—	0	0.1
1986	Major	0	0	+	9	0	0	0	0	0	1	4	20	16	13	5	0	11	1	8	5.06	+17	.213	.307	—	0	-0.1
1987	Sea A	2	0	1.000	20	0	0	0	0	3	1	9	30	43	25	7	0	12	1	22	6.60	-28	.333	.382	—	30	-0.5
1988	NY A	5	5	.500	39	0	0	0	0	0	2	22	82.1	96	44	8	2	30	4	55	4.37	-9	.298	.360	—	0	-0.4
1989	Min A	0	1	.000	11	0	0	0	0	0	1	4	17.1	28	18	3	0	6	1	12	7.79	-47	.354	.400	—	104	-0.4
Total	5	8	8	.500	102	6	0	0	3	3	5	48	219	269	146	32	3	91	13	126	5.26	-23	.308	.371	-8	134	-2.0
SHIRLEY, BOB ROBERT CHARLES B6.25.1954 CUSHING OK BR/TL/5'11"/(180–185) DR 1976 SDN*S1/8 d4.10 COL OKLAHOMA																											
1977	SD N	12	18	.400	39	35	1	0	18	0	0	3	214	215	107	22	4	100	14	146	3.70	-3	.259	.339	-8	0	-0.9
1978	SD N	8	11	.421	50	20	2	0	10	5	2	25	166	164	75	10	3	61	11	102	3.69	-9	.262	.328	+2	0	-0.5
1979	SD N	8	16	.333	49	25	4	1	16	0	1	20	205	196	89	15	6	59	8	117	3.38	+4	.257	.313	+6	0	0.2

Pitchers

YEAR	TM LG	W	L	PCT	G	GS	CG	SHO	QS	SV	BS	QR	IP	H	R	HR	HB	BB	IB	SO	ERA	AERA	OAV	OOB	SUP	DL	PW
1980	SD N	11	12	.478	59	12	3	0	5	7	3	38	137	143	58	12	0	54	15	67	3.55	-4	.276	.341	-6	0	-0.3
1981	StL N	6	4	.600	28	11	1	0	5	1	0	11	79.1	78	42	6	1	34	3	36	4.08	-11	.260	.335	+12	0	-0.8
1982	Cin N	8	13	.381	41	20	1	0	11	0	0	14	152.2	138	74	17	3	73	13	89	3.60	+2	.248	.335	-36	0	-0.2
1983	NY A	5	8	.385	25	17	1	1	6	0	0	4	108	122	71	10	0	36	3	53	5.08	-22	.293	.345	+6	0	-1.6
1984	NY A	3	3	.500	41	7	1	0	3	0	1	28	114.1	119	47	8	0	38	2	48	3.38	+13	.274	.331	-23	0	0.3
1985	NY A	5	5	.500	48	8	2	0	5	2	2	26	109	103	34	5	0	26	2	55	2.64	+53	.251	.293	-10	0	1.6
1986	NY A	0	4	.000	39	6	0	0	2	3	0	23	105.1	108	60	13	3	40	1	64	5.04	-18	.271	.336	-52	0	-0.3
1987	NY A	1	0	1.000	12	1	0	0	0	0	0	5	34	36	20	4	0	16	0	12	4.50	-1	.277	.342	-18	0	-0.1
1987	KC A	0	0	+	3	0	0	0	0	0	0	1	7.1	10	12	5	0	6	0	1	14.73	-69	.323	.432	—	0	-0.3
1987	Year	1	0	1.000	15	1	0	0	0	0	0	6	41.1	46	32	9	0	22	0	13	6.31	-29	.286	.360	-18	0	-0.4
Total	11	67	94	.416	434	162	16	2	81	18	9	198	1432	1432	689	127	20	543	72	790	3.82	-3	.264	.331	-9	0	-2.9
Team	5	14	20	.412	165	39	4	1	16	5	3	86	470.2	488	232	40	3	156	8	232	4.05	-1	.273	.328	-12	—	-0.1
/60G	2	5	7	.412	60	14	1	0	6	2	1	31	171	177	84	15	1	57	3	84	4.06	-1	.273	.328	-12	—	-0.0

SHOCKER, URBAN Urban James (b Urbain Jacques Shockcor) B9.22.1890 Cleveland OH D9.9.1928 Denver CO BR/TR/5'10"/170 d4.24 Mil 1918

YEAR	TM LG	W	L	PCT	G	GS	CG	SHO	QS	SV	BS	QR	IP	H	R	HR	HB	BB	IB	SO	ERA	AERA	OAV	OOB	SUP	DL	PW
1916	NY A	4	3	.571	12	9	4	1	—	0	—	—	82.1	67	25	2	6	32	—	43	2.62	+10	.230	.319	+2	—	0.5
1917	NY A	8	5	.615	26	13	7	0	—	1	—	—	145	124	59	5	0	46	—	68	2.61	+3	.241	.303	+9	—	0.0
1918	StL A	6	5	.545	14	9	7	0	—	2	—	—	94.2	69	26	0	1	40	—	33	1.81	+52	.209	.296	-39	—	1.8
1919	StL A	13	11	.542	30	25	14	5	—	0	—	—	211	193	75	6	4	55	—	86	2.69	+23	.244	.296	-17	—	1.7
1920	StL A	20	10	.667	38	28	22	5	—	**5**	—	—	245.2	224	97	10	4	70	—	107	2.71	+45	.248	.305	-2	—	3.7
1921	StL A	**27**	12	.692	47	38	30	4	—	4	—	—	326.2	345	151	21	6	86	—	132	3.55	+26	.270	.319	+5	—	4.2
1922	StL A	24	17	.585	48	38	29	2	—	3	—	—	348	365	141	22	4	57	—	**149**	2.97	+39	.272	.304	-3	—	**4.9**
1923	StL A	20	12	.625	43	35	24	3	—	5	—	—	277.1	292	122	12	3	49	—	109	3.41	+22	.272	**.306**	-7	—	2.6
1924	StL A	16	13	.552	40	33	17	4	—	1	—	—	246.1	270	128	11	3	52	—	88	4.20	+7	.277	.315	+5	—	1.5
1925	NY A	12	12	.500	41	30	15	2	—	2	—	—	244.1	278	108	17	3	58	—	74	3.65	+17	.294	.336	+4	—	2.1
1926	†NY A	19	11	.633	41	32	18	0	—	2	—	—	258.1	272	113	13	2	71	—	59	3.38	+14	.269	.318	+17	—	1.7
1927	NY A	18	6	.750	31	27	13	2	—	0	—	—	200	207	86	8	1	41	—	35	2.84	+36	.268	.306	+27	—	2.3
1928	NY A	0	0	+	1	0	0	0	—	0	—	—	2	3	0	0	0	0	—	0	0.00	-100	.429	.429	—	—	0.0
Total	13	187	117	.615	412	317	200	28	—	25	—	—	2681.2	2709	1131	127	37	657	—	983	3.17	+24	.265	.311	+3	—	27.0
Team	6	61	37	.622	152	111	57	5	—	5	—	—	932	951	391	45	12	248	—	279	3.14	+18	.268	.318	+14	—	6.6
/180I	1	12	7	.622	29	21	11	1	—	1	—	—	180	184	76	9	2	48	—	54	3.14	+18	.268	.318	+14	—	1.3

SHORE, ERNIE Ernest Grady B3.24.1891 East Bend NC D9.24.1980 Winston-Salem NC BR/TR/6'4"/220 d6.20 Mil 1918 Col Guilford

YEAR	TM LG	W	L	PCT	G	GS	CG	SHO	QS	SV	BS	QR	IP	H	R	HR	HB	BB	IB	SO	ERA	AERA	OAV	OOB	SUP	DL	PW
1919	NY A	5	8	.385	20	13	3	0	—	0	—	—	95	105	50	4	1	44	—	24	4.17	-23	.288	.366	-30	—	-1.2
1920	NY A	2	2	.500	14	5	2	0	—	1	—	—	44.1	61	31	1	1	21	—	12	4.87	-22	.333	.405	+12	—	-0.4
Total	7	65	43	.602	160	121	56	9	—	5	—	—	979.1	906	370	12	27	270	—	309	2.47	+13	.247	.304	-9	—	2.4
Team	2	7	10	.412	34	18	5	0	—	1	—	—	139.1	166	81	5	2	65	—	36	4.39	-23	.303	.379	-18	—	-1.6
/180I	3	9	13	.412	44	23	6	0	—	1	—	—	180	214	105	6	3	84	—	47	4.39	-23	.303	.379	-18	—	-2.1

SHORT, BILL William Ross B11.27.1937 Kingston NY BL/TL/5'9"/(170–180) d4.23

YEAR	TM LG	W	L	PCT	G	GS	CG	SHO	QS	SV	BS	QR	IP	H	R	HR	HB	BB	IB	SO	ERA	AERA	OAV	OOB	SUP	DL	PW
1960	NY A	3	5	.375	10	10	2	0	4	0	0	0	47	49	25	5	1	30	1	14	4.79	-25	.282	.390	+3	0	-0.7
Total	6	5	11	.313	73	16	3	1	7	2	1	38	131.1	130	75	8	3	64	2	71	4.73	-28	.262	.346	-15	0	-1.7

SLAGLE, ROGER Roger Lee B11.4.1953 Wichita KS BR/TR/6'3"/190 Dr 1976 NYA S1/19 d9.7 Col Kansas

YEAR	TM LG	W	L	PCT	G	GS	CG	SHO	QS	SV	BS	QR	IP	H	R	HR	HB	BB	IB	SO	ERA	AERA	OAV	OOB	SUP	DL	PW
1979	NY A	0	0	+	1	0	0	0	0	0	0	1	2	0	0	0	0	0	0	2	0.00	-100	.000	.000	—	0	0.0

SMALL, AARON Aaron James B11.23.1971 Oxnard CA BR/TR/6'5"/(200–235) Dr 1989 TorA 22/575 d6.11

YEAR	TM LG	W	L	PCT	G	GS	CG	SHO	QS	SV	BS	QR	IP	H	R	HR	HB	BB	IB	SO	ERA	AERA	OAV	OOB	SUP	DL	PW
2005	†NY A	10	0	1.000	15	9	1	1	5	0	1	4	76	71	27	4	5	24	0	37	3.20	+35	.250	.317	+55	0	1.2
2006	NY A	0	3	.000	11	3	0	0	0	0	0	4	27.2	42	29	9	1	12	1	12	8.46	-45	.341	.401	+22	29	-1.1
Total	9	25	13	.658	172	15	1	1	5	4	5	98	321.2	380	202	37	14	137	12	170	5.20	-13	.297	.368	+33	29	-1.1
Team	2	10	3	.769	26	12	1	1	5	0	1	8	103.2	113	56	13	6	36	1	49	4.60	-5	.278	.343	+47	29	0.1

SMALLWOOD, WALT Walter Clayton B4.24.1893 Dayton MD D4.29.1967 Baltimore MD BR/TR/6'2"/190 d9.19 Mil 1918–19

YEAR	TM LG	W	L	PCT	G	GS	CG	SHO	QS	SV	BS	QR	IP	H	R	HR	HB	BB	IB	SO	ERA	AERA	OAV	OOB	SUP	DL	PW
1917	NY A	0	0	+	2	0	0	0	—	0	—	—	2	1	0	0	0	1	—	1	0.00	-100	.167	.286	—	—	0.0
1919	NY A	0	0	+	6	0	0	0	—	0	—	—	21.2	20	12	1	2	9	—	6	4.98	-36	.263	.356	—	—	-0.3
Total	2	0	0	+	8	0	0	0	—	0	—	—	23.2	21	12	1	2	10	—	7	4.56	-31	.256	.351	—	—	-0.3

SMITH, LEE Lee Arthur B12.4.1957 Shreveport LA BR/TR/6'6"/(220–269) Dr 1975 ChiN 2/28 d9.1

YEAR	TM LG	W	L	PCT	G	GS	CG	SHO	QS	SV	BS	QR	IP	H	R	HR	HB	BB	IB	SO	ERA	AERA	OAV	OOB	SUP	DL	PW
1993	NY A	0	0	+	8	0	0	0	0	3	0	8	8	4	0	0	0	5	1	11	0.00	-100	.148	.273	—	0	0.2
Total	18	71	92	.436	1022	6	0	0	3	478	10	764	1289.1	1133	475	89	10	486	10	1251	3.03	+33	.237	.306	-25	35	22.9

SMITH, MATT Matthew Joel B6.15.1979 Las Vegas NV BL/TL/6'5"/225 Dr 2000 NYA 4/128 d4.14 Col Oklahoma St.

YEAR	TM LG	W	L	PCT	G	GS	CG	SHO	QS	SV	BS	QR	IP	H	R	HR	HB	BB	IB	SO	ERA	AERA	OAV	OOB	SUP	DL	PW
2006	NY A	0	0	+	12	0	0	0	0	0	0	11	12	4	0	0	0	8	1	9	0.00	-100	.105	.261	—	0	0.3
2006	Phi N	0	1	.000	14	0	0	0	0	0	0	13	8.2	3	2	0	0	4	0	12	2.08	+122	.111	.226	—	0	0.2
2006	Major	0	1	.000	26	0	0	0	0	0	0	24	20	7	2	0	0	12	1	21	0.87	-7	.108	.247	—	0	0.5
2007	Phi N	0	0	+	9	0	0	0	0	0	0	5	4	4	5	0	0	11	1	1	11.25	-60	.250	.556	—	0	-0.1
Total	2	0	1	.000	35	0	0	0	0	0	0	29	24.2	11	7	0	0	23	2	22	2.55	+80	.136	.327	—	0	0.4

SMYTHE, HARRY William Henry B10.24.1904 Augusta GA D8.28.1980 Augusta GA BL/TL/5'10.5"/179 d7.21

YEAR	TM LG	W	L	PCT	G	GS	CG	SHO	QS	SV	BS	QR	IP	H	R	HR	HB	BB	IB	SO	ERA	AERA	OAV	OOB	SUP	DL	PW
1934	NY A	0	2	.000	8	0	0	0	—	1	—	—	15	24	16	1	0	8	—	7	7.80	-48	.381	.451	—	—	-0.8
Total	3	5	12	.294	60	12	2	0	—	4	—	—	154.2	232	142	10	5	62	—	33	6.40	-22	.349	.408	+14	—	-2.1

SPRINGER, RUSS Russell Paul B11.7.1968 Alexandria LA BR/TR/6'4"/(195–215) Dr 1989 NYA 7/181 d4.17 Col Louisiana St.

YEAR	TM LG	W	L	PCT	G	GS	CG	SHO	QS	SV	BS	QR	IP	H	R	HR	HB	BB	IB	SO	ERA	AERA	OAV	OOB	SUP	DL	PW
1992	NY A	0	0	+	14	0	0	0	0	0	0	7	16	18	11	0	1	10	0	12	6.19	-36	.281	.387	—	0	-0.2
Total	15	33	40	.452	594	27	1	0	5	8	21	391	747.1	715	416	108	33	314	30	671	4.70	-6	.250	.329	+4	402	-1.9

STAFFORD, BILL William Charles B8.13.1939 Catskill NY D9.19.2001 Wayne MI BR/TR/6'2"/(185–198) d8.17

YEAR	TM LG	W	L	PCT	G	GS	CG	SHO	QS	SV	BS	QR	IP	H	R	HR	HB	BB	IB	SO	ERA	AERA	OAV	OOB	SUP	DL	PW
1960	†NY A	3	1	.750	11	8	2	1	6	0	0	2	60	50	17	3	1	18	0	36	2.25	+59	.226	.286	-20	0	0.4
1961	†NY A	14	9	.609	36	25	8	3	18	2	1	6	195	168	65	13	5	59	4	101	2.68	+39	.232	.294	+20	0	2.8
1962	†NY A	14	9	.609	35	33	7	2	19	0	0	1	213.1	188	95	23	4	77	6	109	3.67	+2	.233	.301	+30	0	0.5
1963	NY A	4	8	.333	28	14	0	0	5	3	1	9	89.2	104	64	16	3	42	3	52	6.02	-42	.287	.363	+17	0	-2.9
1964	NY A	5	0	1.000	31	1	0	0	0	4	1	20	60.2	50	19	4	2	22	7	39	2.67	+36	.231	.308	+170	0	0.6
1965	NY A	3	8	.273	22	15	1	0	9	0	0	5	111.1	93	45	16	2	31	4	71	3.56	-4	.229	.284	-11	32	-0.3
1966	KC A	0	4	.000	9	8	0	0	2	0	0	1	39.2	42	28	2	2	12	1	31	4.99	-32	.273	.327	-32	0	-0.9
1967	KC A	0	1	.000	14	0	0	0	0	0	0	10	16	12	4	0	0	9	2	10	1.69	+89	.214	.323	—	0	0.1
Total	8	43	40	.518	186	104	18	6	59	9	3	54	785.2	707	337	77	19	270	27	449	3.52	+3	.240	.306	+13	32	0.3
Team	6	43	35	.551	163	96	18	6	57	9	3	43	730	653	305	75	17	249	24	408	3.48	+5	.239	.305	+16	32	1.1
/180I	1	11	9	.551	40	24	4	1	14	2	1	11	180	161	75	18	4	61	6	101	3.48	+5	.239	.305	+16	8	0.3

STALEY, GERRY Gerald Lee B8.21.1920 Brush Prairie WA BR/TR/6'0"/(185–195) d4.20

YEAR	TM LG	W	L	PCT	G	GS	CG	SHO	QS	SV	BS	QR	IP	H	R	HR	HB	BB	IB	SO	ERA	AERA	OAV	OOB	SUP	DL	PW
1955	NY A	0	0	+	2	0	0	0	—	0	—	—	2	5	5	1	0	1	0	0	13.50	-72	.417	.462	—	0	-0.1
1956	NY A	0	0	+	1	0	0	0	—	0	—	—	0.1	4	4	0	0	0	0	1	108.00	-96	.800	.800	—	0	-0.2
Total	15	134	111	.547	640	186	58	9	0	61	27	441	1981.2	2070	946	186	63	529	37	727	3.70	+8	.270	.321	+1	0	6.2
Team	2	0	0	+	3	0	0	0	—	0	—	—	2.1	9	9	1	0	1	0	1	27.00	-86	.529	.556	—	—	-0.3

STANCEU, CHARLEY Charles B1.9.1916 Canton OH D4.3.1969 Canton OH BR/TR/6'2"/190 d4.16 Mil 1942–45

YEAR	TM LG	W	L	PCT	G	GS	CG	SHO	QS	SV	BS	QR	IP	H	R	HR	HB	BB	IB	SO	ERA	AERA	OAV	OOB	SUP	DL	PW
1941	NY A	3	3	.500	22	2	0	0	—	0	—	—	48	58	41	3	1	35	—	21	5.63	-30	.296	.405	-23	0	-1.5
1946	NY A	0	0	+	3	0	0	0	—	0	—	—	4	6	4	0	0	5	—	3	9.00	-62	.316	.458	—	0	-0.1
1946	Phi N	2	4	.333	14	11	1	0	—	0	—	—	70.1	71	35	4	0	39	—	23	4.22	-19	.270	.364	-21	0	-0.6

YEAR	TM LG	W	L	PCT	G	GS	CG	SHO	QS	SV	BS	QR	IP	H	R	HR	HB	BB	IB	SO	ERA	AERA	OAV	OOB	SUP	DL	PW
1946	Major	2	4	.333	17	11	1	0	—	0	—	—	74	77	39	4	0	44	—	26	4.48	-21	.273	.371	-21	0	-0.7
Total	2	5	7	.417	39	13	1	0	—	0	—	—	122.1	135	80	7	1	79	—	47	4.93	-26	.282	.385	-24	0	-2.2
Team	2	3	3	.500	25	2	0	0	—	0	—	—	52	64	45	3	1	40	—	24	5.88	-34	.298	.410	-23	—	-1.6

STANTON, MIKE WILLIAM MICHAEL B6.2.1967 HOUSTON TX BL/TL/6'1"/(190–215) DR 1987 ATLN 13/324 D8.24 COL SOUTHWESTERN (TX)

YEAR	TM LG	W	L	PCT	G	GS	CG	SHO	QS	SV	BS	QR	IP	H	R	HR	HB	BB	IB	SO	ERA	AERA	OAV	OOB	SUP	DL	PW
1989	Atl N	0	1	.000	20	0	0	0	0	7	1	18	24	17	4	0	0	8	1	27	1.50	+144	.207	.278	—	0	0.5
1990	Atl N	0	3	.000	7	0	0	0	0	2	1	2	7	16	16	1	1	4	2	7	18.00	-78	.444	.512	—	160	-1.8
1991	†Atl N	5	5	.500	74	0	0	0	0	7	3	54	78	62	27	6	1	21	0	54	2.88	+34	.217	.273	—	0	1.5
1992	†Atl N	5	4	.556	65	0	0	0	0	8	3	45	63.2	59	32	6	2	20	2	44	4.10	-11	.247	.308	—	0	-0.4
1993	†Atl N	4	6	.400	63	0	0	0	0	27	6	45	52	51	35	4	0	29	7	43	4.67	-13	.255	.346	—	0	-1.2
1994	Atl N	3	1	.750	49	0	0	0	0	3	1	34	45.2	41	18	2	3	26	3	35	3.55	+22	.248	.359	—	0	0.5
1995	Atl N	1	1	.500	26	0	0	0	0	1	1	16	19.1	31	14	3	1	6	2	13	5.59	-23	.369	.413	—	0	-0.3
1995	†Bos A	1	0	1.000	22	0	0	0	0	0	1	18	21	17	9	3	0	8	0	10	3.00	+62	.224	.298	—	0	0.2
1995	Major	2	1	.667	48	0	0	0	0	1	2	34	40	48	23	6	1	14	2	23	4.24	+21	.300	.358	—	0	-0.1
1996	Bos A	4	3	.571	59	0	0	0	0	1	4	38	56.1	58	24	9	0	23	4	46	3.83	+33	.275	.343	—	0	1.0
1996	†Tex A	0	1	.000	22	0	0	0	0	0	1	16	22.1	20	8	2	0	4	1	14	3.22	+63	.241	.276	—	0	0.2
1996	Year	4	4	.500	81	0	0	0	0	1	5	54	78.2	78	32	11	0	27	5	60	3.66	+41	.265	.325	—	0	1.2
1997	†NY A	6	1	.857	64	0	0	0	0	3	2	48	66.2	50	19	3	3	34	2	70	2.57	+74	.205	.310	—	0	1.5
1998	†NY A	4	1	.800	67	0	0	0	0	6	4	43	79	71	51	13	4	26	1	69	5.47	-20	.239	.307	—	0	-0.7
1999	†NY A	2	2	.500	73	1	0	0	0	0	5	52	62.1	71	30	5	1	18	4	59	4.33	+9	.289	.337	+18	0	0.2
2000	†NY A	2	3	.400	69	0	0	0	0	0	4	49	68	68	32	5	2	24	2	75	4.10	+16	.263	.325	—	0	0.4
2001	†NY A★	9	4	.692	76	0	0	0	0	0	1	51	80.1	80	25	4	1	20	0	70	2.58	+72	.263	.332	—	0	2.4
2002	†NY A	7	1	.875	79	0	0	0	0	6	3	57	78	73	29	4	0	28	3	44	3.00	+44	.256	.316	—	0	1.2
2003	NY N	2	7	.222	50	0	0	0	0	5	2	35	45.1	37	25	6	2	19	4	34	4.57	-8	.219	.301	—	46	-0.4
2004	NY N	2	6	.250	83	0	0	0	0	0	6	60	77	70	32	6	2	33	6	58	3.16	+36	.237	.317	—	0	0.9
2005	NY A	1	2	.333	28	0	0	0	0	0	0	17	14	17	11	1	0	6	0	12	7.07	-39	.298	.359	—	0	-0.7
2005	Was N	2	1	.667	30	0	0	0	0	0	1	23	27.2	31	13	2	0	9	4	14	3.58	+15	.292	.348	—	0	0.2
2005	Bos A	0	0	+	1	0	0	0	0	0	0	1	1	1	0	0	0	0	0	1	0.00	-100	.333	.333	—	0	0.0
2005	Major	3	3	.500	59	0	0	0	0	0	1	41	42	49	24	3	0	15	4	27	4.64	-5	.295	.352	—	0	-0.5
2006	Was N	3	5	.375	56	0	0	0	0	0	3	38	44.1	47	22	1	1	21	11	30	4.47	-3	.278	.356	—	0	0.0
2006	SF N	4	2	.667	26	0	0	0	0	8	3	19	23.1	23	8	1	1	6	0	18	3.09	+44	.267	.319	—	0	0.7
2006	Year	7	7	.500	82	0	0	0	0	8	6	57	67.2	70	30	2	2	27	11	48	3.99	+10	.275	.344	—	0	0.7
2007	Cin N	1	3	.250	69	0	0	0	0	0	3	46	57.2	75	39	6	5	18	2	40	5.93	-22	.315	.374	—	18	-0.5
Total	19	68	63	.519	1178	1	0	0	0	84	59	825	1114	1086	523	93	33	420	76	895	3.92	+12	.257	.327	+18	224	5.4
Team	7	31	14	.689	456	1	0	0	0	15	19	317	448.1	430	197	35	14	165	21	407	3.77	+19	.254	.322	+18	—	4.3
/60G	1	4	2	.689	60	0	0	0	0	2	3	42	59	57	26	5	2	22	3	54	3.77	+19	.254	.322	—	—	0.6

STARR, DICK RICHARD EUGENE B3.2.1921 KITTANNING PA BR/TR/6'3"/190 D9.5

YEAR	TM LG	W	L	PCT	G	GS	CG	SHO	QS	SV	BS	QR	IP	H	R	HR	HB	BB	IB	SO	ERA	AERA	OAV	OOB	SUP	DL	PW
1947	NY A	1	0	1.000	4	1	1	0	—	0	—	—	12.1	12	4	1	0	8	—	1	1.46	+142	.250	.357	+100	0	0.2
1948	NY A	0	0	+	1	0	0	0	—	0	—	—	2	0	1	0	0	2	—	2	4.50	-9	.000	.250	—	0	0.0
Total	5	12	24	.333	93	45	7	2	—	2	—	—	344.2	390	230	40	10	198	—	120	5.25	-14	.286	.381	-2	0	-3.1
Team	2	1	0	1.000	5	1	1	0	—	0	—	—	14.1	12	5	1	0	10	—	3	1.88	+92	.250	.344	+100	—	0.2

STINE, LEE LEE ELBERT B11.17.1913 STILLWATER OK D5.6.2005 HEMET CA BR/TR/5'11"/185 D4.17

YEAR	TM LG	W	L	PCT	G	GS	CG	SHO	QS	SV	BS	QR	IP	H	R	HR	HB	BB	IB	SO	ERA	AERA	OAV	OOB	SUP	DL	PW
1938	NY A	0	0	+	4	0	0	0	—	0	—	—	8.2	9	1	0	0	1	—	4	1.04	+337	.333	.357	—	—	0.2
Total	4	3	8	.273	49	13	5	1	—	2	—	—	143.1	179	92	9	9	55	—	39	5.09	-22	.315	.384	+7	—	-1.0

STODDARD, TIM TIMOTHY PAUL B1.24.1953 E.CHICAGO IN BR/TR/6'7"/(235–253) DR 1975 CHIA*S2/44 D9.7 COL NORTH CAROLINA ST.

YEAR	TM LG	W	L	PCT	G	GS	CG	SHO	QS	SV	BS	QR	IP	H	R	HR	HB	BB	IB	SO	ERA	AERA	OAV	OOB	SUP	DL	PW
1986	NY A	4	1	.800	24	0	0	0	0	0	1	16	49.1	41	23	6	0	23	3	34	3.83	+8	.232	.317	—	0	0.2
1987	NY A	4	3	.571	57	0	0	0	0	8	1	41	92.2	83	38	13	0	30	2	78	3.50	+27	.235	.293	—	9	0.8
1988	NY A	2	2	.500	28	0	0	0	0	3	0	16	55	62	41	5	2	27	1	33	6.38	-38	.286	.361	—	21	-1.0
Total	13	41	35	.539	485	0	0	0	0	76	26	317	729.2	680	343	72	10	356	45	582	3.95	+1	.250	.335	—	129	0.9
Team	3	10	6	.625	109	0	0	0	0	11	2	73	197	186	102	24	2	80	6	145	4.39	-4	.249	.319	—	30	0.0
/60G	2	6	3	.625	60	0	0	0	0	6	1	40	108.1	102	56	13	1	44	3	80	4.39	-4	.249	.319	—	17	0.0

STOTTLEMYRE, MEL MELVIN LEON SR. B11.13.1941 HAZLETON MO BR/TR/6'2"/(170–192) D8.12 C22 S–MEL S–TODD COL YAKIMA VALLEY (WA) CC

YEAR	TM LG	W	L	PCT	G	GS	CG	SHO	QS	SV	BS	QR	IP	H	R	HR	HB	BB	IB	SO	ERA	AERA	OAV	OOB	SUP	DL	PW
1964	†NY A	9	3	.750	13	12	5	2	11	0	0	1	96	77	26	3	2	35	3	49	2.06	+76	.219	.294	+13	0	2.3
1965	NY A☆	20	9	.690	37	37	**18**	4	29	0	0	0	**291**	250	99	18	7	88	3	155	2.63	+29	.233	.294	+9	0	2.8
1966	NY A★	12	20	.375	37	35	9	3	20	1	0	1	251	239	116	18	1	82	7	146	3.80	-13	.253	.311	-2	0	-1.1
1967	NY A	15	15	.500	36	36	10	4	24	0	0	0	255	235	96	20	2	88	11	151	2.96	+5	.248	.311	-4	0	0.6
1968	NY A★	21	12	.636	36	36	19	6	28	0	0	0	278.2	243	86	21	3	65	7	140	2.45	+19	.234	.280	+8	0	2.3
1969	NY A★	20	14	.588	39	39	**24**	3	31	0	0	0	303	267	105	19	6	97	11	113	2.82	+25	.239	.301	-9	0	3.8
1970	NY A★	15	13	.536	37	37	14	0	28	0	0	0	271	262	110	23	6	84	8	126	3.09	+16	.255	.313	+4	0	2.4
1971	NY A	16	12	.571	35	35	19	7	24	0	0	0	269.2	234	100	16	4	69	6	132	2.87	+15	.233	.284	+13	0	1.7
1972	NY A	14	18	.438	36	36	9	7	26	0	0	0	260	250	99	13	4	85	13	110	3.22	-7	.254	.314	-11	0	0.0
1973	NY A	16	16	.500	38	38	19	4	26	0	0	0	273	259	112	13	5	79	3	95	3.07	+21	.253	.307	-6	0	2.1
1974	NY A	6	7	.462	16	15	6	0	9	0	0	0	113	119	54	7	4	37	3	40	3.58	-1	.272	.333	-17	91	-0.2
Total	11	164	139	.541	360	356	152	40	256	1	0	2	2661.1	2435	1003	171	44	809	75	1257	2.97	+13	.245	.303	+0	91	16.7
/180I	1	11	9	.541	24	24	10	3	17	0	0	0	180	165	68	12	3	55	5	85	2.97	+13	.245	.303	+0	6	1.1

STOWE, HAL HAROLD RUDOLPH B8.29.1937 GASTONIA NC BL/TL/6'0"/170 D9.30 COL CLEMSON

YEAR	TM LG	W	L	PCT	G	GS	CG	SHO	QS	SV	BS	QR	IP	H	R	HR	HB	BB	IB	SO	ERA	AERA	OAV	OOB	SUP	DL	PW
1960	NY A	0	0	+	1	0	0	0	0	0	0	0	1	0	1	0	0	1	0	0	9.00	-60	.000	.333	—	0	0.0

STUART, MARLIN MARLIN HENRY B8.8.1918 PARAGOULD AR D6.16.1994 PARAGOULD AR BL/TR/6'2"/185 D4.26

YEAR	TM LG	W	L	PCT	G	GS	CG	SHO	QS	SV	BS	QR	IP	H	R	HR	HB	BB	IB	SO	ERA	AERA	OAV	OOB	SUP	DL	PW
1954	NY A	3	0	1.000	10	0	0	0	—	1	—	—	18.1	28	12	0	0	12	—	2	5.40	-36	.350	.435	—	0	-0.6
Total	6	23	17	.575	196	31	7	0	—	15	—	—	485.2	544	300	37	14	256	—	185	4.65	-13	.289	.378	+4	0	-3.1

STURDIVANT, TOM THOMAS VIRGIL "SNAKE" B4.28.1930 GORDON KS BL/TR/6'1"/(170–186) D4.14

YEAR	TM LG	W	L	PCT	G	GS	CG	SHO	QS	SV	BS	QR	IP	H	R	HR	HB	BB	IB	SO	ERA	AERA	OAV	OOB	SUP	DL	PW
1955	†NY A	1	3	.250	33	1	0	0	—	0	—	—	68.1	48	24	6	2	42	1	48	3.16	+18	.203	.329	-76	0	0.2
1956	†NY A	16	8	.667	32	17	6	2	—	5	—	—	158.1	134	63	15	4	52	4	110	3.30	+17	.224	.291	+41	0	2.0
1957	†NY A	16	6	**.727**	28	28	7	2	27	0	0	9	201.2	170	65	14	4	80	2	118	2.54	+41	.232	.309	+6	0	2.6
1958	NY A	3	6	.333	15	10	0	0	27	0	0	9	70.2	77	37	6	3	38	0	41	4.20	-16	.274	.364	-1	30	-0.6
1959	NY A	0	2	.000	7	3	0	0	27	0	0	9	25.1	20	16	4	0	9	0	16	4.97	-27	.222	.290	-52	0	-0.3
1959	KC A	2	6	.250	36	3	0	0	0	5	3	24	71.2	70	45	9	6	34	4	57	4.65	-14	.258	.347	-5	0	-0.8
1959	Year	2	8	.200	43	6	0	0	27	5	3	33	97	90	61	13	6	43	4	73	4.73	-17	.249	.333	-29	0	-1.1
1960	Bos A	3	3	.500	40	3	0	0	1	1	2	18	101.1	106	58	16	2	45	5	67	4.97	-19	.279	.353	-6	0	-0.5
1961	Was A	2	6	.250	15	10	1	1	4	0	0	4	80	67	42	6	3	40	3	39	4.61	-13	.233	.328	-10	0	-0.4
1961	Pit N	5	2	.714	13	11	6	1	9	1	0	2	85.2	81	29	6	1	17	3	45	2.84	+41	.249	.288	+21	0	0.9
1961	Major	7	8	.467	28	21	7	2	13	1	—	6	165	148	71	12	4	57	6	84	3.69	+15	.241	.308	+6	0	0.5
1962	Pit N	9	5	.643	49	12	2	1	7	2	0	24	125.1	120	62	12	3	39	11	76	3.73	+5	.260	.318	-13	0	0.2
1963	Pit N	0	0	+	3	0	0	0	0	0	0	1	8.1	8	6	1	0	4	0	6	6.48	-49	.267	.353	—	0	-0.1
1963	Det A	1	2	.333	28	0	0	0	0	2	1	21	55	43	26	7	1	24	2	36	3.76	-1	.221	.304	—	0	-0.1
1963	KC A	1	2	.333	17	3	0	0	2	0	1	12	53	47	24	3	1	17	2	26	3.74	+4	.237	.300	-1	0	-0.1
1963	Year	2	4	.333	45	3	0	0	2	2	2	34	108	90	50	10	2	41	4	62	3.75	+2	.229	.302	+1	0	-0.2
1963	Major	2	4	.333	48	3	0	0	2	2	—	34	116	98	56	11	2	45	4	68	3.95	-2	.232	.305	-1	0	-0.3
1964	KC A	0	0	+	3	0	0	0	0	0	0	2	3.2	4	4	0	2	1	0	1	9.82	-61	.308	.438	—	0	-0.1
1964	NY N	0	0	+	16	0	0	0	0	1	1	8	28.2	34	20	2	2	7	0	18	5.97	-40	.306	.347	—	0	-0.4
1964	Major	0	0	+	19	0	0	0	0	1	—	10	31	38	24	2	4	8	0	19	6.40	-42	.306	.357	—	0	-0.5

Pitchers

YEAR	TM LG	W	L	PCT	G	GS	CG	SHO	QS	SV	BS	QR	IP	H	R	HR	HB	BB	IB	SO	ERA	AERA	OAV	OOB	SUP	DL	PW
Total	10	59	51	.536	335	101	22	7	104	17	8	143	1137	1029	521	107	34	449	37	704	3.74	+2	.244	.319	+5	30	2.5
Team	5	36	25	.590	115	59	13	4	81	5	0	27	524.1	449	205	45	13	221	7	333	3.19	+16	.232	.313	+11	30	3.9
/180I	2	12	9	.590	39	20	4	1	28	2	0	9	180	154	70	15	4	76	2	114	3.19	+16	.232	.313	+11	10	1.3

STURTZE, TANYON TANYON JAMES B10.12.1970 WORCESTER MA BR/TR/6'5"/(200–225) DR 1990 OAKA 23/636 D5.3 COL QUINSIGAMOND (MA) CC [DL 2007 ATL N 143]

YEAR	TM LG	W	L	PCT	G	GS	CG	SHO	QS	SV	BS	QR	IP	H	R	HR	HB	BB	IB	SO	ERA	AERA	OAV	OOB	SUP	DL	PW
1995	Chi N	0	0	+	2	0	0	0	0	0	0	0	2	2	2	1	0	1	0	0	9.00	-54	.250	.333	—	0	-0.1
1996	Chi N	1	0	1.000	6	0	0	0	0	0	0	2	11	16	11	3	0	5	0	7	9.00	-51	.348	.412	—	0	-0.4
1997	Tex A	1	1	.500	9	5	0	0	0	0	0	2	32.2	45	30	6	0	18	0	18	8.27	-41	.338	.406	+17	0	-0.6
1999	Chi A	0	0	+	1	1	0	0	1	0	0	0	6	4	0	0	0	2	0	2	0.00	-100	.200	.273	-81	0	0.2
2000	Chi A	1	2	.333	10	1	0	0	0	0	0	1	15.2	25	23	4	2	15	0	6	12.06	-58	.379	.494	-63	0	-1.7
2000	TB A	4	0	1.000	19	5	0	0	3	0	0	11	52.2	47	16	4	1	14	1	38	2.56	+91	.236	.290	+26	35	0.9
2000	Year	5	2	.714	29	6	0	0	3	0	0	12	68.1	72	39	8	3	29	1	44	4.74	+4	.272	.348	+11	0	-0.8
2001	TB A	11	12	.478	39	27	0	0	15	1	2	8	195.1	200	98	23	9	79	0	110	4.42	+2	.271	.345	-3	0	0.6
2002	TB A	4	18	.182	33	33	4	0	12	0	0	0	224	271	141	33	9	89	2	137	5.18	-13	.302	.369	-24	0	-1.5
2003	Tor A	7	6	.538	40	8	0	0	3	0	0	20	89.1	107	67	14	7	43	3	54	5.94	-20	.296	.380	+9	0	-1.5
2004	†NY A	6	2	.750	28	3	0	0	1	1	0	15	77.1	75	49	9	6	33	2	56	5.47	-16	.254	.340	+54	0	-0.6
2005	†NY A	5	3	.625	64	1	0	0	0	1	5	44	78	76	43	10	6	27	1	45	4.73	-9	.257	.329	+180	18	-0.2
2006	NY A	0	0	+	18	0	0	0	0	0	0	9	10.2	17	10	3	1	6	0	6	7.59	-39	.354	.429	—	140	-0.2
Total	11	40	44	.476	269	84	4	0	35	3	7	112	794.2	885	490	110	41	332	9	479	5.21	-12	.285	.359	-4	336	-5.1
Team	3	11	5	.688	110	4	0	0	1	2	5	68	166	168	102	22	13	66	3	107	5.26	-15	.263	.342	+86	158	-1.0
/60G	2	6	3	.688	60	2	0	0	1	1	3	37	90.2	92	56	12	7	36	2	58	5.25	-15	.263	.342	+86	86	-0.5

SUNDRA, STEVE STEPHEN RICHARD "SMOKEY" B3.27.1910 LUXOR PA D3.23.1952 CLEVELAND OH BR/TR (BB 1936–40)/6'2"/190 D4.17 MIL 1944–45

YEAR	TM LG	W	L	PCT	G	GS	CG	SHO	QS	SV	BS	QR	IP	H	R	HR	HB	BB	IB	SO	ERA	AERA	OAV	OOB	SUP	DL	PW
1936	NY A	0	0	+	1	0	0	0	—	0	—	—	2	2	0	0	0	2	—	1	0.00	-100	.286	.444	—	—	0.0
1938	NY A	6	4	.600	25	8	3	0	—	0	—	—	93.2	107	61	7	0	43	—	33	4.80	-6	.291	.365	+41	—	-0.2
1939	†NY A	11	1	.917	24	11	8	1	—	0	—	—	120.2	110	43	7	0	56	—	27	2.76	+58	.240	.323	+62	—	2.3
1940	NY A	4	6	.400	27	8	2	0	—	2	—	—	99.1	121	68	11	1	42	—	26	5.53	-27	.299	.366	+1	—	-1.6
1941	Was A	9	13	.409	28	23	11	0	—	0	—	—	168.1	203	108	11	1	61	—	50	5.29	-24	.294	.352	+5	0	-2.0
1942	Was A	1	3	.250	6	4	2	0	—	0	—	—	33.2	43	24	1	1	15	—	5	5.61	-35	.305	.376	-1	0	-0.7
1942	StL A	8	3	.727	20	13	6	0	—	0	—	—	110.2	122	56	2	0	29	—	26	3.82	-3	.275	.319	+38	0	0.1
1942	Year	9	6	.600	26	17	8	0	—	0	—	—	144.1	165	80	3	1	44	—	31	4.24	-13	.282	.333	+29	0	-0.6
1943	StL A	15	11	.577	32	29	13	3	—	0	—	—	208	212	89	10	0	66	—	44	3.25	+3	.266	.322	+4	0	0.2
1944	StL A	2	0	1.000	3	3	2	0	—	0	—	—	19	15	3	1	0	4	—	1	1.42	+153	.211	.253	-15	0	0.5
1946	StL A	0	0	+	2	0	0	0	—	0	—	—	4	9	9	0	0	3	—	1	11.25	-67	.409	.480	—	0	-0.2
Total	9	56	41	.577	168	99	47	4	—	2	—	—	859.1	944	461	50	3	321	—	214	4.17	-6	.277	.340	+16	0	-1.6
Team	4	21	11	.656	77	27	13	1	—	2	—	—	315.2	340	172	25	1	143	—	87	4.22	+2	.275	.350	+38	—	0.5
/180I	2	12	6	.656	44	15	7	1	—	1	—	—	180	194	98	14	1	82	—	50	4.22	+2	.275	.350	+38	—	0.3

TALBOT, FRED FREDERICK LEALAND "BUBBY" B6.28.1941 WASHINGTON DC BR/TR/6'2"/(195–212) D9.28

YEAR	TM LG	W	L	PCT	G	GS	CG	SHO	QS	SV	BS	QR	IP	H	R	HR	HB	BB	IB	SO	ERA	AERA	OAV	OOB	SUP	DL	PW
1963	Chi A	0	0	+	1	0	0	0	0	0	0	1	3	2	1	0	0	4	0	2	3.00	+17	.222	.462	—	0	0.0
1964	Chi A	4	5	.444	17	12	3	2	5	0	0	4	75.1	83	31	7	4	20	0	34	3.70	-7	.288	.340	-1	0	0.2
1965	KC A	10	12	.455	39	33	2	1	15	0	0	4	198	188	96	25	6	86	3	117	4.14	-16	.251	.330	-1	0	-0.9
1966	KC A	4	4	.500	11	11	0	0	5	0	0	0	67.2	65	39	6	2	28	6	37	4.79	-29	.248	.324	-22	0	-1.0
1966	NY A	7	7	.500	23	19	3	0	10	0	0	4	124.1	123	59	16	3	45	3	48	4.13	-19	.262	.329	+17	0	-0.8
1966	Year	11	11	.500	34	30	3	0	15	0	0	4	192	188	98	22	5	73	9	85	4.36	-23	.257	.327	+3	0	-1.8
1967	NY A	6	8	.429	29	22	2	0	10	0	0	4	138.2	132	78	20	6	54	5	61	4.22	-26	.252	.325	+11	0	-1.3
1968	NY A	1	9	.100	29	11	1	0	3	0	2	15	99	89	47	6	2	42	6	67	3.36	-13	.241	.319	-37	0	-0.6
1969	NY A	0	0	+	8	0	0	0	0	0	1	4	12.1	13	9	1	0	6	2	7	5.11	-31	.283	.352	—	0	-0.1
1969	Sea A	5	8	.385	25	16	1	1	6	0	0	5	114.2	125	58	12	4	41	6	67	4.16	-12	.278	.342	+0	0	-0.4
1969	Oak A	1	2	.333	12	2	0	0	0	1	0	6	19	22	11	2	0	7	0	9	5.21	-34	.297	.358	+41	0	-0.5
1969	Year	6	10	.375	45	18	1	1	6	1	1	15	146	160	78	15	4	54	8	83	4.38	-18	.281	.345	+5	0	-1.0
1970	Oak A	0	1	.000	1	0	0	0	0	0	0	0	1.2	2	2	1	0	1	0	0	10.80	-67	.286	.375	—	0	-0.2
Total	8	38	56	.404	195	126	12	4	54	1	3	47	853.2	844	431	96	27	334	31	449	4.12	-19	.260	.331	+0	0	-5.6
Team	4	14	24	.368	89	52	6	0	23	0	3	27	374.1	357	193	43	11	147	16	183	3.99	-21	.254	.326	+3	—	-2.8
/180I	2	7	12	.368	43	25	3	0	11	0	1	13	180	172	93	21	5	71	8	88	3.99	-21	.254	.326	+3	—	-1.3

TAMULIS, VITO VITAUTIS CASIMIRUS B7.11.1911 CAMBRIDGE MA D5.5.1974 NASHVILLE TN BL/TL/5'9"/170 D9.25

YEAR	TM LG	W	L	PCT	G	GS	CG	SHO	QS	SV	BS	QR	IP	H	R	HR	HB	BB	IB	SO	ERA	AERA	OAV	OOB	SUP	DL	PW
1934	NY A	1	0	1.000	1	1	1	1	—	0	—	—	9	7	0	0	0	1	—	5	0.00	-100	.219	.242	+7	—	0.6
1935	NY A	10	5	.667	30	19	9	3	—	1	—	—	160.2	178	80	7	2	55	—	57	4.09	-1	.280	.339	+29	—	0.5
Total	6	40	28	.588	170	70	31	6	—	10	—	—	691.2	758	340	37	16	202	—	294	3.97	+1	.278	.331	+9	0	0.3
Team	2	11	5	.688	31	20	10	4	—	1	—	—	169.2	185	80	7	2	56	—	62	3.87	+5	.277	.335	+28	—	1.1
/180I	2	12	5	.687	33	21	11	4	—	1	—	—	180	196	85	7	2	59	—	66	3.87	+5	.277	.335	+28	—	1.2

TANANA, FRANK FRANK DARYL B7.3.1953 DETROIT MI BL/TL/6'3"/(185–200) DR 1971 CALA 1/13 D9.9

YEAR	TM LG	W	L	PCT	G	GS	CG	SHO	QS	SV	BS	QR	IP	H	R	HR	HB	BB	IB	SO	ERA	AERA	OAV	OOB	SUP	DL	PW
1993	NY A	0	2	.000	3	3	0	0	3	0	0	0	19.2	18	10	2	0	7	1	12	3.20	+31	.222	.284	-5	0	0.1
Total	21	240	236	.504	638	616	143	34	380	1	1	16	4188.1	4063	1910	448	129	1255	11	2773	3.66	+6	.254	.312	+1	57	12.8

TANNEHILL, JESSE JESSE NILES "POWDER" B7.14.1874 DAYTON KY D9.22.1956 DAYTON KY BB/TL (BL 1903)/5'8"/150 D6.17 C1 B–LEE ▲

YEAR	TM LG	W	L	PCT	G	GS	CG	SHO	QS	SV	BS	QR	IP	H	R	HR	HB	BB	IB	SO	ERA	AERA	OAV	OOB	SUP	DL	PW
1903	NY A	15	15	.500	32	31	22	2	—	0	—	—	239.2	258	123	3	10	34	—	106	3.27	-4	.274	.307	+7	—	0.2
Total	15	197	117	.627	359	321	264	34	—	7	—	—	2759.1	2794	1199	40	130	478	—	944	2.80	+14	.263	.303	+9	—	20.2
/180I	1	11	11	.500	24	23	17	2	—	0	—	—	180	194	92	2	8	26	—	80	3.27	-4	.274	.307	+7	—	0.2

TAYLOR, WADE WADE ERIC B10.19.1965 MOBILE AL BR/TR/6'1"/185 D6.2 COL MIAMI

YEAR	TM LG	W	L	PCT	G	GS	CG	SHO	QS	SV	BS	QR	IP	H	R	HR	HB	BB	IB	SO	ERA	AERA	OAV	OOB	SUP	DL	PW
1991	NY A	7	12	.368	23	22	0	0	9	0	0	0	116.1	144	85	13	7	53	0	72	6.27	-34	.314	.388	-9	0	-3.4

TERRELL, WALT CHARLES WALTER B5.11.1958 JEFFERSONVILLE IN BL/TR/6'2"/(205–215) DR 1980 TEXA 33/764 D9.18 COL MOREHEAD ST.

YEAR	TM LG	W	L	PCT	G	GS	CG	SHO	QS	SV	BS	QR	IP	H	R	HR	HB	BB	IB	SO	ERA	AERA	OAV	OOB	SUP	DL	PW
1989	NY A	6	5	.545	13	13	1	1	5	0	0	0	83	102	52	9	2	24	0	30	5.20	-25	.307	.356	+22	0	-1.3
Total	11	111	124	.472	321	294	56	14	164	0	1	17	1986.2	2090	1031	187	37	748	60	929	4.22	-6	.274	.339	+2	26	-6.1

TERRY, RALPH RALPH WILLARD B1.9.1936 BIG CABIN OK BR/TR/6'3"/(182–195) D8.6

YEAR	TM LG	W	L	PCT	G	GS	CG	SHO	QS	SV	BS	QR	IP	H	R	HR	HB	BB	IB	SO	ERA	AERA	OAV	OOB	SUP	DL	PW
1956	NY A	1	2	.333	3	3	0	0	—	0	—	—	13.1	17	15	2	0	11	0	8	9.45	-59	.347	.459	+0	0	-1.3
1957	NY A	1	1	.500	7	2	1	1	11	0	0	9	20.2	18	7	1	0	8	1	7	3.05	+18	.240	.310	+0	0	0.2
1957	KC A	4	11	.267	21	19	3	1	31	0	1	6	130.2	119	63	15	4	47	2	80	3.38	+17	.239	.309	-29	0	0.3
1957	Year	5	12	.294	28	21	4	2	42	0	1	15	151.1	137	70	16	4	55	3	87	3.33	+17	.239	.309	-26	0	0.5
1958	KC A	11	13	.458	40	33	8	3	29	2	1	6	216.2	217	111	29	2	61	4	134	4.24	-8	.262	.313	+14	0	-0.9
1959	KC A	2	4	.333	9	7	2	0	29	0	0	6	46.1	56	29	9	1	19	1	35	5.24	-24	.308	.374	+13	0	-0.6
1959	NY A	3	7	.300	24	16	5	1	11	0	0	9	127.1	130	55	7	2	30	5	55	3.39	+7	.270	.312	-14	0	0.0
1959	Year	5	11	.313	33	23	7	1	40	0	0	15	173.2	186	84	16	3	49	6	90	3.89	-4	.281	.329	-5	0	-0.6
1960	†NY A	10	8	.556	35	23	7	3	15	1	0	5	166.2	149	78	15	4	52	3	92	3.40	+5	.237	.299	-4	0	-0.1
1961	†NY A	16	3	.842	31	27	9	2	16	0	0	2	188.1	162	74	19	1	42	0	86	3.15	+18	.232	.275	+27	0	1.3
1962	†NY A☆	**23**	12	.657	43	**39**	14	3	25	2	1	2	**298.2**	257	123	40	3	57	1	176	3.19	+17	.231	.268	+27	0	1.8
1963	†NY A	17	15	.531	40	**37**	**18**	3	26	1	1	2	268	246	103	29	4	39	1	114	3.22	+9	.242	**.271**	+3	0	0.5
1964	†NY A	7	11	.389	27	14	2	1	7	4	0	8	115	130	60	20	1	31	3	77	4.54	-20	.283	.326	+3	0	-1.4
1965	Cle A	11	6	.647	30	26	6	2	14	0	0	2	165.2	154	77	22	1	23	3	84	3.69	-6	.242	.268	+16	0	-0.3
1966	KC A	1	5	.167	15	10	0	0	3	0	0	4	64	65	35	7	1	15	3	33	3.80	-11	.263	.305	+1	24	-0.3
1966	NY N	0	1	.000	11	1	0	0	0	1	1	7	24.2	27	14	1	0	11	1	14	4.74	-23	.293	.369	+21	0	-0.2
1966	Major	1	6	.143	26	11	0	0	3	1	—	11	88	92	49	8	1	26	4	47	4.06	-14	.271	.322	+3	24	-0.5
1967	NY N	0	0	+	2	0	0	0	0	0	0	2	3.1	1	0	0	0	0	0	5	0.00	-100	.091	.091	—	0	0.1

YEAR	TM LG	W	L	PCT	G	GS	CG	SHO	QS	SV	BS	QR	IP	H	R	HR	HB	BB	IB	SO	ERA	AERA	OAV	OOB	SUP	DL	PW
Total	12	107	99	.519	338	257	75	20	217	11	5	70	1849.1	1748	844	216	24	446	28	1000	3.62	+2	.249	.294	+8	24	-0.9
Team	8	78	59	.569	210	161	56	14	111	8	2	37	1198	1109	515	133	15	270	14	615	3.44	+6	.245	.288	+10	—	1.0
/180I	1	12	9	.569	32	24	8	2	17	1	0	6	180	167	77	20	2	41	2	92	3.44	+6	.245	.288	+10	—	0.2
TESSMER, JAY	JAY WELDON B12.26.1971 MEADVILLE PA BR/TR/6'3"/190 DR 1995 NYA 19/534 D8.27 COL MIAMI																										
1998	NY A	1	0	1.000	7	0	0	0	0	0	0	7	8.2	4	3	1	0	4	0	6	3.12	+41	.143	.242	—	0	0.1
1999	NY A	0	0	+	6	0	0	0	0	0	0	3	6.2	16	11	1	1	4	2	3	14.85	-68	.444	.512	—	0	-0.3
2000	NY A	0	0	+	7	0	0	0	0	0	0	4	6.2	9	6	3	0	1	1	5	6.75	-29	.300	.323	—	0	-0.1
2002	NY A	0	0	+	2	0	0	0	0	0	0	1	1.1	0	1	0	0	2	0	0	6.75	36	.000	.333		0	0.0
Total	4	1	0	1.000	22	0	0	0	0	0	0	15	23.1	29	21	5	1	11	3	14	7.71	-41	.296	.369	—	0	-0.3
TEWKSBURY, BOB	ROBERT ALAN B11.30.1960 CONCORD NH BR/TR/6'4"/(180–208) DR 1981 NYA 19/493 D4.11 COL ST. LEO																										
1986	NY A	9	5	.643	23	20	2	0	13	0	0	2	130.1	144	58	8	5	31	0	49	3.31	+25	.282	.325	+10	0	1.1
1987	NY A	1	4	.200	8	6	0	0	1	0	0	1	33.1	47	26	5	1	7	0	12	6.75	-34	.338	.374	-7	0	-1.0
Total	13	110	102	.519	302	277	31	7	160	1	1	15	1807	2043	884	142	41	292	22	812	3.92	+5	.287	.316	-2	211	2.9
Team	2	10	9	.526	31	26	2	0	14	0	0	3	163.2	191	84	13	6	38	0	61	4.01	+5	.294	.335	+6	—	0.1
/180I	2	11	10	.526	34	29	2	0	15	0	0	3	180	210	92	14	7	42	0	67	4.01	+5	.294	.335	+6	—	0.1
THOMAS, MYLES	MYLES LEWIS B10.22.1897 STATE COLLEGE PA D12.12.1963 TOLEDO OH BR/TR/5'9.5"/170 D4.18 COL PENN ST.																										
1926	†NY A	6	6	.500	33	13	3	0	—	0	—	—	140.1	140	79	6	3	65	—	38	4.23	-9	.271	.356	+36	—	-0.7
1927	NY A	7	4	.636	21	9	1	0	—	0	—	—	88.2	111	58	4	1	43	—	25	4.87	-21	.322	.398	+30	—	-1.0
1928	NY A	1	0	1.000	12	1	0	0	—	0	—	—	31.2	33	19	3	0	9	—	10	3.41	+10	.277	.328	+35	—	0.0
1929	NY A	0	2	.000	5	1	0	0	—	0	—	—	15	27	21	1	0	9	—	3	10.80	-64	.409	.480	-13	—	-1.2
1929	Was A	7	8	.467	22	14	7	0	—	2	—	—	125.1	139	72	3	0	48	—	33	3.52	+21	.288	.352	-1	—	0.6
1929	Year	7	10	.412	27	15	7	0	—	2	—	—	140.1	166	93	4	0	57	—	36	4.30	-2	.302	.368	-1	—	-0.6
1930	Was A	2	2	.500	12	2	0	0	—	0	—	—	33.2	49	35	3	0	15	—	12	8.29	-45	.358	.421	-44	—	-1.4
Total	5	23	22	.511	105	40	11	0	—	2	—	—	434.2	499	284	20	4	189	—	121	4.64	-13	.299	.372	+16	—	-3.7
Team	4	14	12	.538	71	24	4	0	—	0	—	—	275.2	311	177	14	4	126	—	76	4.70	-18	.297	.375	+32	—	-2.9
/180I	3	9	8	.538	46	16	3	0	—	0	—	—	180	203	116	9	3	82	—	50	4.70	-18	.297	.375	+32	—	-1.9
THOMAS, STAN	STANLEY BROWN B7.11.1949 RUMFORD ME BR/TR/6'2"/185 DR 1971 TEXA 27/616 D7.5 COL NEW HAVEN																										
1977	NY A	1	0	1.000	3	0	0	0	0	0	0	2	6.1	7	7	0	0	4	0	1	7.11	-44	.280	.367	—	0	-0.4
Total	4	11	14	.440	111	17	3	0	6	9	3	67	265.1	263	135	16	10	110	12	123	3.70	+1	.261	.338	+1	22	-0.5
THOMPSON, TOMMY	THOMAS CARL B11.7.1889 SPRING CITY TN D1.16.1963 LAJOLLA CA BR/TR/5'9.5"/170 D6.5 B–HOMER COL GEORGIA																										
1912	NY A	0	2	.000	7	2	1	0	—	0	—	—	32.2	43	32	0	3	13	—	15	6.06	-41	.341	.415	-18	—	-0.5
THORMAHLEN, HANK	HERBERT EHLER "LEFTY" B7.5.1896 JERSEY CITY NJ D2.6.1955 LOS ANGELES CA BL/TL/6'0"/180 D9.29																										
1917	NY A	0	1	.000	1	1	0	0	—	0	—	—	8	9	3	0	1	4	—	5	2.25	+19	.281	.378	-73	—	0.0
1918	NY A	7	3	.700	16	12	5	2	—	0	—	—	112.2	85	39	1	6	52	—	22	2.48	+14	.217	.318	+18	—	0.0
1919	NY A	12	8	.600	30	25	13	2	—	1	—	—	188.2	155	69	10	4	61	—	62	2.62	+22	.228	.295	+3	—	1.1
1920	NY A	9	6	.600	29	15	6	0	—	1	—	—	143.1	178	86	5	2	43	—	35	4.14	-8	.312	.362	+16	—	-0.5
1921	Bos A	1	7	.125	23	9	3	0	—	0	—	—	96.1	101	56	3	6	34	—	17	4.48	-6	.277	.349	-43	—	-0.3
1925	Bro N	0	3	.000	5	2	0	0	—	0	—	—	16	22	14	0	2	9	—	7	3.94	+6	.333	.429	-39	—	-0.2
Total	6	29	28	.509	104	64	27	4	—	2	—	—	565	550	267	19	21	203	—	148	3.33	+5	.261	.332	-2	—	0.1
Team	4	28	18	.609	76	53	24	4	—	2	—	—	452.2	427	197	16	13	160	—	124	3.06	+8	.255	.324	+9	—	0.6
/180I	2	11	7	.609	30	21	10	2	—	1	—	—	180	170	78	6	5	64	—	49	3.06	+8	.255	.324	+9	—	0.2
THURMAN, MIKE	MICHAEL RICHARD B7.22.1973 CORVALLIS OR BR/TR/6'5"/(210–215) DR 1994 MONN S1/31 D9.2 COL OREGON ST.																										
2002	NY A	1	0	1.000	12	2	0	0	1	0	1	6	33	45	21	2	1	12	1	23	5.18	-16	.328	.387	+146	0	-0.2
Total	6	26	36	.419	105	87	0	0	34	0	1	12	493.2	537	311	59	21	190	18	296	5.05	-13	.278	.346	-3	127	-5.1
TIANT, LUIS	LUIS CLEMENTE (VEGA) B11.23.1940 MARIANAO, CUBA BR/TR/5'11"/(180–205) D7.19																										
1979	NY A	13	8	.619	30	30	5	1	17	0	0	0	195.2	190	94	22	0	53	1	104	3.91	+5	.251	.299	+17	0	0.4
1980	NY A	8	9	.471	25	25	3	0	10	0	0	0	136.1	139	79	10	1	50	3	84	4.89	-19	.265	.326	+8	22	-1.3
Total	19	229	172	.571	573	484	187	49	298	15	6	66	3486.1	3075	1400	346	49	1104	53	2416	3.30	+14	.236	.297	+5	98	21.6
Team	2	21	17	.553	55	55	8	1	27	0	—	0	332	329	173	32	1	103	4	188	4.31	-6	.257	.310	+13	22	-0.9
/180I	1	11	9	.553	30	30	4	1	15	0	—	0	180	178	94	17	1	56	2	102	4.31	-6	.257	.310	+13	12	-0.5
TIDROW, DICK	RICHARD WILLIAM B5.14.1947 SAN FRANCISCO CA BR/TR/6'4"/(210–215) DR 1967 CLEA*S4/76 D4.18 COL CHABOT (CA) JC																										
1972	Cle A	14	15	.483	39	34	10	3	22	0	0	4	237.1	200	83	21	6	70	13	123	2.77	+18	.230	.289	-19	0	0.9
1973	Cle A	14	16	.467	42	40	13	2	19	0	0	2	274.2	289	150	31	8	95	10	138	4.42	-11	.270	.332	-5	0	-1.5
1974	Cle A	1	3	.250	4	4	0	0	0	0	0	0	19	21	17	4	2	13	1	8	7.11	-49	.276	.387	-15	0	-1.2
1974	NY A	11	9	.550	33	25	5	0	14	1	0	6	190.2	205	99	14	4	53	7	100	3.87	-8	.279	.327	+17	0	-0.9
1974	Year	12	12	.500	37	29	5	0	14	1	0	6	209.2	226	116	18	6	66	8	108	4.16	-15	.279	.333	+13	0	-2.1
1975	NY A	6	3	.667	37	0	0	0	0	5	4	25	69.1	65	27	5	3	31	6	38	3.12	+19	.256	.341	—	53	0.6
1976	†NY A	4	5	.444	47	2	0	0	2	10	3	34	92.1	80	29	5	1	24	1	65	2.63	+30	.233	.282	+119	0	1.0
1977	†NY A	11	4	.733	49	7	0	0	6	5	2	29	151	143	57	20	2	41	11	83	3.16	+26	.250	.300	+62	0	1.4
1978	†NY A	7	11	.389	31	25	4	0	15	0	0	4	185.1	191	87	13	5	53	3	73	3.84	-5	.267	.320	-1	0	-0.4
1979	NY A	2	1	.667	14	0	0	0	0	2	1	8	22.2	38	20	5	0	4	0	7	7.94	-48	.409	.424	—	0	-1.1
1979	Chi N	11	5	.688	63	0	0	0	0	4	1	45	102.2	86	35	5	2	42	11	68	2.72	+53	.231	.310	—	0	2.4
1979	Major	13	6	.684	77	0	0	0	0	6	2	53	124	124	55	10	2	46	11	75	3.66	+35	.267	.332	—	0	1.3
1980	Chi N	6	5	.545	**84**	0	0	0	0	6	6	59	116	97	44	10	5	53	16	97	2.79	+42	.229	.319	—	0	1.2
1981	Chi N	3	10	.231	51	0	0	0	0	9	4	30	74.2	73	45	6	1	30	15	39	5.06	-26	.256	.328	—	0	-1.8
1982	Chi N	8	3	.727	65	0	0	0	0	6	1	48	103.2	106	45	6	3	29	10	62	3.39	+12	.265	.318	—	0	0.3
1983	†Chi A	2	4	.333	50	1	0	0	0	7	2	27	91.2	86	50	13	1	34	8	66	4.22	+0	.242	.308	+8	0	0.0
1984	NY N	0	0	+	11	0	0	0	0	0	0	4	15.2	25	19	5	0	7	0	8	9.19	-61	.357	.410	—	0	-0.5
Total	13	100	94	.515	620	138	32	5	78	55	24	325	1746.2	1705	807	163	43	579	11	975	3.68	+2	.257	.318	-1	53	0.4
Team	6	41	33	.554	211	59	9	0	37	23	10	106	711.1	722	319	62	15	206	28	366	3.61	+2	.266	.319	+18	53	0.6
/180I	2	10	8	.554	53	15	2	0	9	6	3	27	180	183	81	16	4	52	7	93	3.61	+2	.266	.319	+18	13	0.2
TIEFENAUER, BOBBY	BOBBY GENE B10.10.1929 DESLOGE MO D6.13.2000 DESLOGE MO BR/TR/6'2"/(185–188) D7.14 C1 [DL 1959 CLE A 172]																										
1965	NY A	1	1	.500	10	0	0	0	0	2	0	7	20.1	19	10	3	1	5	1	15	3.54	-4	.253	.301	—	0	-0.1
Total	10	9	25	.265	179	0	0	0	0	23	7	104	316	312	161	29	12	87	15	204	3.84	-6	.260	.314	—	172	-1.9
TIFT, RAY	RAYMOND FRANK B6.21.1884 FITCHBURG MA D3.29.1945 VERONA NJ TL/5'10.5"/155 D8.7 COL BROWN																										
1907	NY A	0	0	+	4	1	0	0	—	0	—	—	19	33	14	0	0	4	—	6	4.74	-41	.384	.411	+45	—	-0.3
TILLOTSON, THAD	THADDEUS ASA B12.20.1940 MERCED CA BR/TR/6'2.5"/195 D4.14 COL FRESNO (CA) CITY																										
1967	NY A	3	9	.250	43	5	1	0	2	2	0	30	98.1	99	52	9	2	39	3	62	4.03	-22	.261	.331	-44	0	-1.3
1968	NY A	1	0	1.000	7	0	0	0	0	0	0	4	10.1	11	6	0	0	7	2	1	4.35	-33	.282	.383	—	0	-0.2
Total	2	4	9	.308	50	5	1	0	2	2	0	34	108.2	110	58	9	2	46	5	63	4.06	-23	.263	.336	-44	0	-1.5
/60G	2	5	11	.308	60	6	1	0	2	2	0	41	130.1	132	70	11	2	55	6	76	4.06	-23	.263	.336	-44	—	-1.8
TIPPLE, DAN	DANIEL E. "BIG DAN","RUSTY" B2.13.1890 ROCKFORD IL D3.26.1960 OMAHA NE BR/TR/6'0"/176 D9.18																										
1915	NY A	1	1	.500	3	2	2	0	—	0	—	—	19	14	6	1	0	11	—	14	0.95	+210	.203	.313	-1	—	0.1

Pitchers

TORREZ, MIKE MICHAEL AUGUSTINE B8.28.1946 TOPEKA KS BR/TR/6'5"/210 D9.10

YEAR	TM LG	W	L	PCT	G	GS	CG	SHO	QS	SV	BS	QR	IP	H	R	HR	HB	BB	IB	SO	ERA	AERA	OAV	OOB	SUP	DL	PW
1977	†NY A	14	12	.538	31	31	15	2	16	0	0	0	217	212	99	20	6	75	1	90	3.82	+4	.259	.324	+10	0	0.5
Total	18	185	160	.536	494	458	117	15	245	0	0	20	3043.2	3043	1501	223	59	1371	84	1404	3.96	-2	.264	.343	+8	0	-2.2
/180I	1	12	10	.538	26	26	12	2	13	0	—	0	180	176	82	17	5	62	1	75	3.82	+4	.259	.324	+10	—	0.4

TROUT, STEVE STEVEN RUSSELL B7.30.1957 DETROIT MI BL/TL/6'4"/(189–195) DR 1976 CHIA 1/8 D7.1 F–DIZZY

YEAR	TM LG	W	L	PCT	G	GS	CG	SHO	QS	SV	BS	QR	IP	H	R	HR	HB	BB	IB	SO	ERA	AERA	OAV	OOB	SUP	DL	PW
1987	NY A	0	4	.000	14	9	0	0	1	0	0	2	46.1	51	36	4	1	37	0	27	6.60	-33	.274	.397	-15	0	-0.8
Total	12	88	92	.489	301	236	32	9	100	4	6	40	1501.1	1665	791	90	33	578	48	656	4.18	-4	.286	.351	+3	139	-3.9

TRUCKS, VIRGIL VIRGIL OLIVER "FIRE" B4.26.1917 BIRMINGHAM AL BR/TR/5'11"/(190–210) D9.27 MIL 1944–45 C1

YEAR	TM LG	W	L	PCT	G	GS	CG	SHO	QS	SV	BS	QR	IP	H	R	HR	HB	BB	IB	SO	ERA	AERA	OAV	OOB	SUP	DL	PW
1958	NY A	2	1	.667	25	0	0	0	0	1	0	15	39.2	40	24	1	2	24	0	26	4.54	-22	.265	.359	—	0	-0.4
Total	17	177	135	.567	517	328	124	33	7	30	5	92	2682.1	2416	1124	188	47	1088	19	1534	3.39	+17	.240	.316	+1	0	16.8

TURLEY, BOB ROBERT LEE "BULLET BOB" B9.19.1930 TROY IL BR/TR/6'2"/(214–218) D9.29 MIL 1952–53 C1

YEAR	TM LG	W	L	PCT	G	GS	CG	SHO	QS	SV	BS	QR	IP	H	R	HR	HB	BB	IB	SO	ERA	AERA	OAV	OOB	SUP	DL	PW
1951	StL A	0	1	.000	1	1	0	0	—	0	—	—	7.1	11	6	0	0	3	—	5	7.36	-40	.355	.412	-39	0	-0.2
1953	StL A	2	6	.250	10	7	3	1	—	0	—	—	60.1	39	24	4	2	44	—	61	3.28	+28	.184	.329	-61	0	0.9
1954	Bal A☆	14	15	.483	35	35	14	0	—	0	—	—	247.1	178	106	7	7	181	—	**185**	3.46	+4	**.203**	.340	-18	0	0.2
1955	†NY A☆	17	13	.567	36	34	13	6	—	1	—	—	246.2	168	92	16	7	177	4	210	3.06	+22	**.193**	.331	+18	0	2.4
1956	†NY A	8	4	.667	27	21	5	1	—	1	—	—	132	138	76	13	4	103	0	91	5.05	-23	.273	.398	+52	0	-1.3
1957	†NY A	13	6	.684	32	23	9	4	50	3	1	14	176.1	120	59	17	9	85	1	152	2.71	+33	**.194**	.298	+15	0	1.8
1958	†NY A★	**21**	7	**.750**	33	31	**19**	6	50	1	0	14	245.1	178	82	24	8	128	2	168	2.97	+19	**.206**	.311	+28	0	2.2
1959	NY A	8	11	.421	33	22	7	3	50	0	1	14	154.1	141	80	15	3	83	3	111	4.32	-16	.245	.338	-10	0	-1.3
1960	†NY A	9	3	.750	34	24	4	1	13	5	1	9	173.1	138	67	14	5	87	3	87	3.27	+10	.222	.319	+39	0	0.2
1961	NY A	3	5	.375	15	12	1	0	4	0	0	2	72	74	47	11	4	51	0	48	5.75	-35	.269	.390	+3	33	-1.6
1962	NY A	3	3	.500	24	8	0	0	3	1	0	14	69	68	45	8	4	47	2	42	4.57	-18	.263	.379	+10	0	-0.9
1963	LA A	2	7	.222	19	12	3	2	7	0	1	5	87.1	71	41	5	2	51	6	70	3.30	+4	.222	.331	-27	0	0.0
1963	Bos A	1	4	.200	11	7	0	0	1	0	0	3	41.1	42	28	6	1	28	0	35	6.10	-38	.256	.366	-23	0	-1.0
1963	Year	3	11	.214	30	19	3	2	8	0	1	8	128.2	113	69	11	3	79	6	105	4.20	-16	.233	.343	-25	0	-1.0
Total	12	101	85	.543	310	237	78	24	178	12	4	75	1712.2	1366	753	140	56	1068	21	1265	3.64	+1	.220	.337	+9	33	1.4
Team	8	82	52	.612	234	175	58	21	170	12	3	67	1269	1025	548	118	44	761	15	909	3.62	+1	.223	.336	+21	33	1.5
/180I	1	12	7	.612	33	25	8	3	24	2	0	10	180	145	78	17	6	108	2	129	3.62	+1	.223	.336	+21	5	0.2

TURNER, JIM JAMES RILEY "MILKMAN JIM" B8.6.1903 ANTIOCH TN D11.29.1998 NASHVILLE TN BL/TR/6'0"/185 D4.30 C24

YEAR	TM LG	W	L	PCT	G	GS	CG	SHO	QS	SV	BS	QR	IP	H	R	HR	HB	BB	IB	SO	ERA	AERA	OAV	OOB	SUP	DL	PW
1937	Bos N	20	11	.645	33	30	**24**	0	—	1	—	—	256.2	228	80	13	0	52	—	69	**2.38**	+50	.235	**.274**	+0	—	**4.8**
1938	Bos N☆	14	18	.438	35	34	22	3	—	0	—	—	268	267	123	21	5	54	—	71	3.46	-1	.259	.299	-13	—	0.5
1939	Bos N	4	11	.267	25	22	9	0	—	0	—	—	157.2	181	83	10	4	51	—	50	4.28	-14	.293	.351	-4	—	-0.4
1940	†Cin N	14	7	.667	24	23	11	0	—	0	—	—	187	187	70	9	0	32	—	53	2.89	+31	.264	.296	-5	—	2.1
1941	Cin N	6	4	.600	23	10	3	0	—	0	—	—	113	120	49	5	1	24	—	34	3.11	+16	.277	.317	+16	0	0.4
1942	Cin N	0	0	+	3	0	0	0	—	0	—	—	3.1	5	5	1	0	3	—	0	10.80	-70	.333	.444	—	0	-0.1
1942	†NY A	1	1	.500	5	0	0	0	—	1	—	—	7	4	1	0	0	1	—	2	1.29	+168	.167	.200	—	0	0.4
1942	Major	1	1	.500	8	0	0	0	—	1	—	—	10	9	6	1	0	4	—	2	4.35	+91	.231	.302	—	0	0.3
1943	NY A	3	0	1.000	18	0	0	0	—	1	—	—	43.1	44	22	1	0	13	—	15	3.53	-9	.260	.313	—	0	-0.3
1944	NY A	4	4	.500	35	0	0	0	—	7	—	—	41.2	42	23	3	0	22	—	13	3.46	+1	.264	.354	—	0	-0.3
1945	NY A	3	4	.429	30	0	0	0	—	**10**	—	—	54.1	45	26	4	0	31	—	22	3.64	-5	.225	.329	—	0	-0.3
Total	9	69	60	.535	231	119	69	8	—	20	—	—	1132	1123	482	67	10	283	—	329	3.22	+11	.260	.307	-4	0	6.8
Team	4	11	9	.550	88	0	0	0	—	19	—	—	146.1	135	72	8	0	67	—	52	3.44	-1	.245	.326	—	—	-0.5
/60G	3	8	6	.550	60	0	0	0	—	13	—	—	99.2	92	49	5	0	46	—	35	3.45	-1	.245	.326	—	—	-0.3

UHLE, GEORGE GEORGE ERNEST "THE BULL" B9.18.1898 CLEVELAND OH D2.26.1985 LAKEWOOD OH BR/TR/6'0"/190 D4.30 C4 ▲

YEAR	TM LG	W	L	PCT	G	GS	CG	SHO	QS	SV	BS	QR	IP	H	R	HR	HB	BB	IB	SO	ERA	AERA	OAV	OOB	SUP	DL	PW
1933	NY A	6	1	.857	12	6	4	0	—	0	—	—	61	63	42	4	3	20	—	26	5.16	-25	.257	.321	+79	—	-0.6
1934	NY A	2	4	.333	10	2	0	0	—	0	—	—	16.1	30	19	3	0	7	—	10	9.92	-59	.400	.451	+7	—	-1.7
Total	17	200	166	.546	513	368	232	21	—	25	—	—	3119.2	3417	1635	119	113	966	—	1135	3.99	+5	.281	.340	+6	—	15.9
Team	2	8	5	.615	22	8	4	0	—	0	—	—	77.1	93	61	7	3	27	—	36	6.17	-36	.291	.351	+61	—	-2.3

UNDERWOOD, TOM THOMAS GERALD B12.22.1953 KOKOMO IN BR/TL/5'11"/(170–185) DR 1972 PHIN 2/27 D8.19 B–PAT

YEAR	TM LG	W	L	PCT	G	GS	CG	SHO	QS	SV	BS	QR	IP	H	R	HR	HB	BB	IB	SO	ERA	AERA	OAV	OOB	SUP	DL	PW
1980	†NY A	13	9	.591	38	27	2	2	10	2	1	7	187	163	85	15	4	66	4	116	3.66	+8	.237	.306	+26	0	0.8
1981	NY A	1	4	.200	9	6	0	0	3	0	0	2	32.2	32	17	2	0	13	1	29	4.41	-18	.262	.333	-13	0	-0.4
Total	11	86	87	.497	379	203	35	6	107	18	11	118	1586	1554	772	130	28	662	38	948	3.89	+1	.259	.333	-3	0	-1.2
Team	2	14	13	.519	47	33	2	2	13	2	1	9	219.2	195	102	17	4	79	5	145	3.77	+4	.241	.310	+19	—	0.4
/180I	2	11	11	.519	39	27	2	2	11	2	1	7	180	160	84	14	3	65	4	119	3.77	+4	.241	.310	+19	—	0.3

UPSHAW, CECIL CECIL LEE B10.22.1942 SPEARSVILLE LA D2.7.1995 LAWRENCEVILLE GA BR/TR/6'6"/185 D10.1 COL CENTENARY LOUISIANA [DL 1970 ATL N 165]

YEAR	TM LG	W	L	PCT	G	GS	CG	SHO	QS	SV	BS	QR	IP	H	R	HR	HB	BB	IB	SO	ERA	AERA	OAV	OOB	SUP	DL	PW
1974	NY A	1	5	.167	36	0	0	0	0	6	3	27	59.2	53	25	1	3	24	3	27	3.02	+18	.254	.339	—	0	0.4
Total	9	34	36	.486	348	0	0	0	0	86	26	244	563	545	220	37	20	177	50	323	3.13	+12	.258	.320	—	187	3.7

VAN ATTA, RUSS RUSSELL "SHERIFF" B6.21.1906 AUGUSTA NJ D10.10.1986 ANDOVER NJ BL/TL/6'0"/184 D4.25 COL PENN ST.

YEAR	TM LG	W	L	PCT	G	GS	CG	SHO	QS	SV	BS	QR	IP	H	R	HR	HB	BB	IB	SO	ERA	AERA	OAV	OOB	SUP	DL	PW
1933	NY A	12	4	.750	26	22	10	2	—	1	—	—	157	160	81	8	1	63	—	76	4.18	-7	.262	.332	+49	—	0.0
1934	NY A	3	5	.375	28	9	0	0	—	0	—	—	88	107	69	3	2	46	—	39	6.34	-36	.307	.390	+0	—	-1.6
1935	NY A	0	0	+	5	0	0	0	—	0	—	—	4.2	5	5	0	0	4	—	3	3.86	+5	.263	.391	—	—	-0.1
Total	7	33	41	.446	207	76	17	3	—	6	—	—	712.1	838	498	39	10	368	—	339	5.60	-18	.293	.376	-5	—	-5.2
Team	3	15	9	.625	59	31	10	2	—	1	—	—	249.2	272	155	11	3	113	—	118	4.94	-20	.278	.354	+35	—	-1.7
/180I	2	11	6	.625	43	22	7	1	—	1	—	—	180	196	112	8	2	81	—	85	4.94	-20	.278	.354	+35	—	-1.2

VANCE, DAZZY CLARENCE ARTHUR B3.4.1891 ORIENT IA D2.16.1961 HOMOSASSA SPRINGS FL BR/TR/6'2"/200 D4.16 HF1955

YEAR	TM LG	W	L	PCT	G	GS	CG	SHO	QS	SV	BS	QR	IP	H	R	HR	HB	BB	IB	SO	ERA	AERA	OAV	OOB	SUP	DL	PW
1915	NY A	0	3	.000	8	3	1	0	—	0	—	—	28	23	14	1	2	16	—	18	3.54	-17	.232	.350	-59	—	0.0
1918	NY A	0	0	+	2	0	0	0	—	0	—	—	2.1	9	5	0	0	2	—	0	15.43	-82	.692	.733	—	—	-0.2
Total	16	197	140	.585	442	349	216	29	—	11	—	—	2966.2	2809	1246	132	77	840	—	2045	3.24	+25	.251	.308	-8	—	29.2
Team	2	0	3	.000	10	3	1	0	—	0	—	—	30.1	32	19	1	2	18	—	18	4.45	-34	.286	.394	-59	—	-0.2

VANCE, JOE JOSEPH ALBERT "SANDY" B9.16.1905 DEVINE TX D7.4.1978 SAN ANTONIO TX BR/TR/6'1.5"/190 D4.18 COL TEXAS ST.

YEAR	TM LG	W	L	PCT	G	GS	CG	SHO	QS	SV	BS	QR	IP	H	R	HR	HB	BB	IB	SO	ERA	AERA	OAV	OOB	SUP	DL	PW
1937	NY A	1	0	1.000	2	2	0	0	—	0	—	—	15	11	5	2	0	9	—	3	3.00	+48	.204	.317	-12	—	0.1
1938	NY A	0	0	+	3	1	0	0	—	0	—	—	11.1	20	9	2	0	4	—	2	7.15	-37	.408	.453	+36	—	0.1
Total	3	3	2	.600	15	3	0	0	—	0	—	—	57.1	67	40	5	0	34	—	17	5.81	-21	.298	.390	+2	—	-0.5
Team	2	1	0	1.000	5	3	0	0	—	0	—	—	26.1	31	14	4	0	13	—	5	4.78	-6	.301	.379	+4	—	0.2

VAUGHN, HIPPO JAMES LESLIE B4.9.1888 WEATHERFORD TX D5.29.1966 CHICAGO IL BB/TL/6'4"/215 D6.19

YEAR	TM LG	W	L	PCT	G	GS	CG	SHO	QS	SV	BS	QR	IP	H	R	HR	HB	BB	IB	SO	ERA	AERA	OAV	OOB	SUP	DL	PW
1908	NY A	0	0	+	2	0	0	0	—	0	—	—	2.1	1	1	0	0	4	—	2	3.86	-36	.167	.500	—	—	0.0
1910	NY A	13	11	.542	30	25	18	5	—	1	—	—	221.2	190	76	1	10	58	—	107	1.83	+46	.237	.297	-2	—	1.3
1911	NY A	8	10	.444	26	19	10	0	—	0	—	—	145.2	158	92	2	7	54	—	74	4.39	-18	.284	.354	+0	—	-1.2
1912	NY A	2	8	.200	15	10	5	1	—	0	—	—	63	66	48	1	1	37	—	46	5.14	-30	.264	.361	+9	—	-1.4
Total	13	178	137	.565	390	332	214	41	—	5	—	—	2730	2461	1039	39	85	817	—	1416	2.49	+20	.244	.306	-2	—	16.3
Team	4	23	29	.442	73	54	33	6	—	1	—	—	432.2	415	217	4	18	153	—	229	3.18	-2	.257	.328	+1	—	-1.3
/180I	2	10	12	.442	30	22	14	2	—	0	—	—	180	173	90	2	7	64	—	95	3.18	-2	.257	.328	+1	—	-0.5

VAZQUEZ, JAVIER JAVIER CARLOS B6.25.1976 PONCE, PR BR/TR/6'2"/(180–215) DR 1994 MONN 5/140 D4.3

YEAR	TM LG	W	L	PCT	G	GS	CG	SHO	QS	SV	BS	QR	IP	H	R	HR	HB	BB	IB	SO	ERA	AERA	OAV	OOB	SUP	DL	PW
2004	†NY A★	14	10	.583	32	32	0	0	16	0	0	0	198	195	114	33	11	60	3	150	4.91	-6	.255	.315	-9	0	-0.4
Total	10	115	113	.504	322	320	22	7	172	0	0	1	2062.1	2056	1056	275	69	543	42	1815	4.28	+5	.258	.310	-9	0	7.8
/180I	1	13	9	.583	29	29	0	0	15	0	—	0	180	177	104	30	10	55	3	136	4.91	-6	.255	.315	-9	—	-0.4

Pitchers

Pitchers

VERAS, JOSE JOSE ENGER B10.20.1980 SANTO DOMINGO, D.R. BR/TR/6'5"/230 d8.5

YEAR	TM LG	W	L	PCT	G	GS	CG	SHO	QS	SV	BS	QR	IP	H	R	HR	HB	BB	IB	SO	ERA	AERA	OAV	OOB	SUP	DL	PW
2006	NY A	0	0	+	12	0	0	0	0	1	0	8	11	8	5	2	0	5	0	6	4.09	+13	.211	.302	—	0	0.0
2007	†NY A	0	0	+	9	0	0	0	0	2	0	7	9.1	6	6	0	0	7	1	7	5.79	-22	.176	.317	—	135	-0.1
Total	2	0	0	+	21	0	0	0	0	3	0	15	20.1	14	11	2	0	12	1	13	4.87	-6	.194	.310	—	135	-0.1

VERBANIC, JOE JOSEPH MICHAEL B4.24.1943 WASHINGTON PA BR/TR/6'0"/175 d7.20 [DL 1969 NY A 124]

YEAR	TM LG	W	L	PCT	G	GS	CG	SHO	QS	SV	BS	QR	IP	H	R	HR	HB	BB	IB	SO	ERA	AERA	OAV	OOB	SUP	DL	PW
1966	Phi N	1	1	.500	17	0	0	0	0	0	0	11	14	12	9	2	0	10	3	7	5.14	-30	.226	.344	—	0	-0.3
1967	NY A	4	3	.571	28	6	1	1	5	2	0	17	80.1	74	27	6	2	21	3	39	2.80	+12	.249	.300	-21	0	0.4
1968	NY A	6	7	.462	40	11	2	1	4	4	4	23	97	104	36	6	6	41	8	40	3.15	-8	.284	.363	+3	0	-0.2
1970	NY A	1	0	1.000	7	0	0	0	0	0	0	4	15.2	20	9	1	1	12	0	8	4.60	-22	.323	.440	—	0	0.0
Total	4	12	11	.522	92	17	3	2	9	6	4	55	207	210	81	15	9	84	14	94	3.26	-5	.270	.345	-9	124	-0.1
Team	3	11	10	.524	75	17	3	2	9	6	4	44	193	198	72	13	9	74	11	87	3.12	-2	.273	.345	-5	—	0.2
/60G	2	9	8	.524	60	14	2	2	7	5	3	35	154.1	158	58	10	7	59	9	70	3.13	-2	.273	.345	-5	—	0.2

VILLONE, RON RONALD THOMAS B1.16.1970 ENGLEWOOD NJ BL/TL/6'3"/(235–245) DR 1992 SEAA 1/14 d4.28 COL MASSACHUSETTS

YEAR	TM LG	W	L	PCT	G	GS	CG	SHO	QS	SV	BS	QR	IP	H	R	HR	HB	BB	IB	SO	ERA	AERA	OAV	OOB	SUP	DL	PW
2006	†NY A	3	3	.500	70	0	0	0	0	0	1	50	80.1	75	48	9	4	51	9	72	5.04	-8	.250	.362	—	0	-0.1
2007	†NY A	0	0	+	37	0	0	0	0	0	1	26	42.1	36	20	5	3	18	3	25	4.25	+6	.234	.324	—	15	0.1
Total	13	55	57	.491	580	93	2	0	36	6	19	326	1069.1	1016	613	126	64	571	33	842	4.76	-4	.253	.352	+1	49	-3.4
Team	2	3	3	.500	107	0	0	0	0	0	2	76	122.2	111	68	14	7	69	12	97	4.77	-4	.244	.350	—	15	0.0
/60G	1	2	2	.500	60	0	0	0	0	0	1	43	68.2	62	38	8	4	39	7	54	4.78	-4	.244	.350	—	8	0.0

VIZCAINO, LUIS LUIS (ARIAS) B8.6.1974 BANI, D.R. BR/TR/5'11"/(169–185) d7.23

YEAR	TM LG	W	L	PCT	G	GS	CG	SHO	QS	SV	BS	QR	IP	H	R	HR	HB	BB	IB	SO	ERA	AERA	OAV	OOB	SUP	DL	PW
2007	†NY A	8	2	.800	77	0	0	0	0	0	3	56	75.1	66	37	6	2	43	11	62	4.30	+5	.235	.334	—	0	0.3
Total	9	33	25	.569	485	0	0	0	0	7	19	347	485.1	437	238	67	15	206	34	431	4.25	+5	.240	.319	—	0	2.4
/60G	1	6	2	.800	60	0	0	0	0	0	2	44	58.2	51	29	5	2	34	9	48	4.30	+5	.235	.334	—	—	0.2

WADE, JAKE JACOB FIELDS "WHISTLING JAKE" B4.1.1912 MOREHEAD CITY NC D2.1.2006 WILDWOOD NC BL/TL/6'2"/175 d4.22 MIL 1945 B–BEN COL NORTH CAROLINA ST.

YEAR	TM LG	W	L	PCT	G	GS	CG	SHO	QS	SV	BS	QR	IP	H	R	HR	HB	BB	IB	SO	ERA	AERA	OAV	OOB	SUP	DL	PW
1946	NY A	2	1	.667	13	1	0	0	—	1	—	—	35.1	33	9	2	1	14	—	22	2.29	+51	.250	.327	-100	0	0.5
Total	8	27	40	.403	171	71	20	3	—	3	—	—	668.1	690	421	42	9	440	—	291	5.00	-16	.269	.378	-11	0	-4.7

WALLACE, MIKE MICHAEL SHERMAN B2.3.1951 GASTONIA NC BL/TL/6'2"/(185–204) DR 1969 PHIN 4/76 d6.27

YEAR	TM LG	W	L	PCT	G	GS	CG	SHO	QS	SV	BS	QR	IP	H	R	HR	HB	BB	IB	SO	ERA	AERA	OAV	OOB	SUP	DL	PW
1974	NY A	6	0	1.000	23	1	0	0	1	0	0	17	52.1	42	18	3	0	35	3	34	2.41	+47	.222	.339	-25	0	0.6
1975	NY A	0	0	+	3	0	0	0	0	0	0	0	4.1	11	7	1	0	1	0	2	14.54	-74	.458	.480	—	0	-0.2
Total	5	11	3	.786	117	4	1	0	2	3	3	70	181.2	188	90	9	0	107	11	105	3.91	-6	.273	.367	+20	0	0.0
Team	2	6	0	1.000	26	1	0	0	1	0	0	17	56.2	53	25	4	0	36	3	36	3.34	+7	.249	.353	-25	—	0.4

WANG, CHIEN-MING CHIEN-MING B3.31.1980 TAINAN CITY, TAIWAN BR/TR/6'3"/(200–220) d4.30 COL TAIPEI COLLEGE OF PE

YEAR	TM LG	W	L	PCT	G	GS	CG	SHO	QS	SV	BS	QR	IP	H	R	HR	HB	BB	IB	SO	ERA	AERA	OAV	OOB	SUP	DL	PW
2005	†NY A	8	5	.615	18	17	0	0	12	0	0	1	116.1	113	58	9	6	32	3	47	4.02	+7	.256	.313	-6	59	0.5
2006	†NY A	**19**	6	.760	34	33	2	1	18	1	0	1	218	233	92	12	2	52	4	76	3.63	+27	.277	.320	+14	0	2.7
2007	†NY A	19	7	.731	30	30	1	0	20	0	0	0	199.1	199	84	9	8	59	1	104	3.70	+22	.265	.324	+33	23	2.4
Total	3	46	18	.719	82	80	3	1	50	1	0	2	533.2	545	234	30	16	143	8	227	3.74	+20	.268	.320	+17	82	5.6
/180I	1	16	6	.719	28	27	1	0	17	0	0	1	180	184	79	10	5	48	3	77	3.74	+20	.268	.320	+17	28	1.9

WARHOP, JACK JOHN MILTON "CHIEF","CRAB" (B JOHN MILTON WAUHOP) B7.4.1884 HINTON WV D10.4.1960 FREEPORT IL BR/TR/5'9.5"/168 d9.19

YEAR	TM LG	W	L	PCT	G	GS	CG	SHO	QS	SV	BS	QR	IP	H	R	HR	HB	BB	IB	SO	ERA	AERA	OAV	OOB	SUP	DL	PW
1908	NY A	1	2	.333	5	4	3	0	—	0	—	—	36.1	40	19	0	4	8	—	11	4.46	-44	.292	.349	-38	—	-0.5
1909	NY A	13	15	.464	36	23	21	3	—	2	—	—	243.1	197	84	2	26	81	—	95	2.40	+5	.233	.319	+1	—	0.6
1910	NY A	14	14	.500	37	27	20	0	—	2	—	—	243	219	108	1	18	79	—	75	3.00	-11	.246	.320	+4	—	-1.2
1911	NY A	12	13	.480	31	25	17	1	—	0	—	—	209.2	239	118	6	15	44	—	71	4.16	-14	.286	.333	-15	—	-1.3
1912	NY A	10	19	.345	39	22	16	0	—	3	—	—	258	256	121	3	16	59	—	110	2.86	+26	.266	.319	-36	—	1.6
1913	NY A	4	5	.444	15	7	1	0	—	0	—	—	62.1	69	42	1	12	33	—	11	3.75	-20	.297	.412	+13	—	-1.1
1914	NY A	8	15	.348	37	23	15	0	—	0	—	—	216.2	182	75	8	11	44	—	56	2.37	+17	.235	.286	-17	—	0.7
1915	NY A	7	9	.438	21	19	12	0	—	0	—	—	143.1	164	74	7	12	52	—	34	3.96	-26	.309	.384	+3	—	-1.7
Total	8	69	92	.429	221	150	105	4	—	7	—	—	1412.2	1366	641	28	114	400	—	463	3.12	-4	.262	.328	-11	—	-2.9
/180I	1	9	12	.429	28	19	13	1	0	1	0	0	180	174	82	4	15	51	—	59	3.12	-4	.262	.328	-11	—	-0.4

WASHBURN, GEORGE GEORGE EDWARD B10.6.1914 SOLON ME D1.5.1979 BATON ROUGE LA BL/TR/6'1"/175 d5.4

YEAR	TM LG	W	L	PCT	G	GS	CG	SHO	QS	SV	BS	QR	IP	H	R	HR	HB	BB	IB	SO	ERA	AERA	OAV	OOB	SUP	DL	PW
1941	NY A	0	1	.000	1	1	0	0	—	0	—	—	2	2	4	0	0	5	—	1	13.50	-71	.286	.583	-78	0	-0.4

WASLEWSKI, GARY GARY LEE B7.21.1941 MERIDEN CT BR/TR/6'4"/(190–195) d6.11 COL CONNECTICUT

YEAR	TM LG	W	L	PCT	G	GS	CG	SHO	QS	SV	BS	QR	IP	H	R	HR	HB	BB	IB	SO	ERA	AERA	OAV	OOB	SUP	DL	PW
1970	NY A	2	2	.500	26	5	0	0	1	0	0	15	55	42	20	4	4	27	4	27	3.11	+15	.219	.323	-30	0	0.2
1971	NY A	0	1	.000	24	0	0	0	0	1	0	17	35.2	28	15	2	1	16	2	17	3.28	+0	.214	.302	—	57	0.0
Total	6	11	26	.297	152	42	5	1	20	5	1	79	410.1	368	184	32	21	197	31	229	3.44	+1	.243	.336	-23	57	-0.5
Team	2	2	3	.400	50	5	0	0	1	1	0	32	90.2	70	35	6	5	43	6	44	3.18	+9	.217	.315	-30	57	0.2
/60G	2	2	4	.400	60	6	0	0	1	1	0	38	108.2	84	42	7	6	52	7	53	3.18	+9	.217	.315	-30	68	0.2

WATSON, ALLEN ALLEN KENNETH B11.18.1970 JAMAICA NY BL/TL/6'3"/(190–212) DR 1991 STLN 1/21 d7.8 COL NEW YORK TECH [DL 2001 NY A 190]

YEAR	TM LG	W	L	PCT	G	GS	CG	SHO	QS	SV	BS	QR	IP	H	R	HR	HB	BB	IB	SO	ERA	AERA	OAV	OOB	SUP	DL	PW
1999	†NY A	4	0	1.000	21	0	0	0	0	0	1	16	34.1	30	8	3	0	10	0	30	2.10	+125	.236	.292	—	0	1.1
2000	NY A	0	0	+	17	0	0	0	0	0	0	7	22	30	25	6	2	18	0	20	10.23	-53	.330	.442	—	118	-0.6
Total	8	51	55	.481	206	137	3	0	57	1	2	41	892	979	547	139	35	351	7	589	5.03	-13	.283	.352	-1	412	-5.0
Team	2	4	0	1.000	38	0	0	0	0	0	1	23	56.1	60	33	9	2	28	0	50	5.27	-10	.275	.360	—	118	0.5

WEATHERS, DAVID JOHN DAVID B9.25.1969 LAWRENCEBURG TN BR/TR/6'3"/(205–233) DR 1988 TORA 3/82 d8.2 COL MOTLOW ST. (TN) CC

YEAR	TM LG	W	L	PCT	G	GS	CG	SHO	QS	SV	BS	QR	IP	H	R	HR	HB	BB	IB	SO	ERA	AERA	OAV	OOB	SUP	DL	PW
1996	†NY A	0	2	.000	11	4	0	0	0	0	0	7	17.1	23	19	1	2	14	1	13	9.35	-47	.315	.433	+54	0	-0.8
1997	NY A	0	1	.000	10	0	0	0	0	0	1	6	9	15	10	1	0	7	0	4	10.00	-55	.375	.468	—	0	-0.5
Total	17	65	76	.461	824	69	0	0	27	74	46	539	1245	1303	655	117	52	546	68	893	4.32	+1	.273	.352	+3	36	1.0
Team	2	0	3	.000	21	4	0	0	0	0	1	13	26.1	38	29	2	2	21	1	17	9.57	-50	.336	.445	+54	—	-1.3

WEAVER, JIM JAMES DEMENT "BIG JIM" B11.25.1903 OBION CO. TN D12.12.1983 LAKELAND FL BR/TR/6'6"/230 d8.27 COL WESTERN KENTUCKY

YEAR	TM LG	W	L	PCT	G	GS	CG	SHO	QS	SV	BS	QR	IP	H	R	HR	HB	BB	IB	SO	ERA	AERA	OAV	OOB	SUP	DL	PW
1931	NY A	2	1	.667	17	5	2	0	—	0	—	—	57.2	66	37	1	1	29	—	28	5.31	-25	.280	.361	+156	—	-0.6
Total	8	57	36	.613	189	108	38	7	—	3	—	—	893.1	891	455	38	10	336	—	449	3.88	+2	.258	.326	+12	—	-0.5

WEAVER, JEFF JEFFREY CHARLES B8.22.1976 NORTHRIDGE CA BR/TR/6'5"/200 DR 1998 DETA 1/14 d4.14 B–JERED COL CAL ST.–FRESNO

YEAR	TM LG	W	L	PCT	G	GS	CG	SHO	QS	SV	BS	QR	IP	H	R	HR	HB	BB	IB	SO	ERA	AERA	OAV	OOB	SUP	DL	PW
2002	†NY A	5	3	.625	15	8	0	0	4	2	0	6	78	81	38	12	3	15	3	57	4.04	+7	.260	.300	+34	0	0.3
2003	†NY A	7	9	.438	32	24	0	0	9	0	0	2	159.1	211	113	16	11	47	2	93	5.99	-27	.320	.371	+4	0	-2.4
Total	9	93	114	.449	284	267	16	7	143	2	0	9	1714.2	1862	959	215	118	463	30	1124	4.72	-6	.277	.332	-4	29	-3.8
Team	2	12	12	.500	47	32	0	0	13	2	0	8	237.1	292	151	28	14	62	5	150	5.35	-18	.301	.349	+12	—	-2.1
/180I	2	9	9	.500	36	24	0	0	10	2	0	6	180	221	115	21	11	47	4	114	5.35	-18	.301	.349	+12	—	-1.6

WEHRMEISTER, DAVE DAVID THOMAS B11.9.1952 BERWYN IL BR/TR/6'4"/195 DR 1973 SDN*1/3 d4.16 COL TRUMAN ST.

YEAR	TM LG	W	L	PCT	G	GS	CG	SHO	QS	SV	BS	QR	IP	H	R	HR	HB	BB	IB	SO	ERA	AERA	OAV	OOB	SUP	DL	PW
1981	NY A	0	0	+	5	0	0	0	0	0	0	2	7	6	4	0	0	7	2	7	5.14	-30	.240	.394	—	0	0.0
Total	6	4	9	.308	76	10	0	0	3	2	2	33	157.2	175	106	14	7	84	10	96	5.65	-34	.284	.373	+20	0	-2.8

WEINERT, LEFTY PHILLIP WALTER B4.21.1902 PHILADELPHIA PA D4.17.1973 ROCKLEDGE FL BL/TL/6'1"/195 d9.24

YEAR	TM LG	W	L	PCT	G	GS	CG	SHO	QS	SV	BS	QR	IP	H	R	HR	HB	BB	IB	SO	ERA	AERA	OAV	OOB	SUP	DL	PW
1931	NY A	2	2	.500	17	0	0	0	—	0	—	—	24.2	31	19	2	5	19	—	24	6.20	-36	.316	.451	—	—	-0.9
Total	9	18	33	.353	131	49	19	0	—	2	—	—	437	528	315	26	21	222	—	160	4.59	-3	.308	.393	-15	—	-2.3

WELLS, DAVID David Lee "Boomer" B5.20.1963 Torrance CA BL/TL/6'4"/(225–250) Dr 1982 TorA 2/30 d6.30

YEAR	TM LG	W	L	PCT	G	GS	CG	SHO	QS	SV	BS	QR	IP	H	R	HR	HB	BB	IB	SO	ERA	AERA	OAV	OOB	SUP	DL	PW
1997	†NY A	16	10	.615	32	32	5	2	18	0	0	0	218	239	109	24	6	45	0	156	4.21	+6	.278	.317	-5	0	0.8
1998	†NY A★	18	4	**.818**	30	30	8	0	20	0	0	0	214.1	195	86	29	1	29	0	163	3.49	+26	.239	**.265**	+42	0	2.1
2002	†NY A	19	7	.731	31	31	2	1	20	0	0	0	206.1	210	100	21	5	45	2	137	3.75	+16	.259	.300	+38	0	1.2
2003	†NY A	15	7	.682	31	30	4	1	16	0	0	1	213	242	101	24	8	20	0	101	4.14	+6	.286	.306	+20	0	0.9
Total	21	239	157	.604	660	489	54	12	273	13	13	118	3439	3635	1702	407	83	719	65	2201	4.13	+8	.271	.310	+10	332	12.5
Team	4	68	28	.708	124	123	19	4	74	0	0	1	851.2	886	396	98	20	139	2	557	3.90	+13	.266	.297	+23	—	5.0
/180I	1	14	6	.708	26	26	4	1	16	0	0	0	180	187	84	21	4	29	0	118	3.90	+13	.266	.297	+23	—	1.1

WELLS, ED Edwin Lee "Satchelfoot" B6.7.1900 Ashland OH D5.1.1986 Montgomery AL BL/TL/6'1.5"/183 d6.16 Col Bethany

YEAR	TM LG	W	L	PCT	G	GS	CG	SHO	QS	SV	BS	QR	IP	H	R	HR	HB	BB	IB	SO	ERA	AERA	OAV	OOB	SUP	DL	PW
1923	Det A	0	0	+	7	0	0	0	—	0	—	—	10	11	6	0	0	6	—	6	5.40	-28	.306	.405	—	—	-0.1
1924	Det A	6	8	.429	29	15	5	0	—	4	—	—	102	117	58	2	1	42	—	33	4.06	+1	.291	.360	-21	—	0.0
1925	Det A	6	9	.400	35	14	5	0	—	2	—	—	134.1	190	106	8	2	62	—	45	6.23	-31	.345	.413	+3	—	-2.4
1926	Det A	12	10	.545	36	26	9	0	—	0	—	—	178	201	101	7	2	76	—	58	4.15	-2	.297	.370	+14	—	-0.4
1927	Det A	0	1	.000	8	1	0	0	—	1	—	—	20	28	16	3	0	5	—	5	6.75	-38	.333	.371	-60	—	-0.2
1929	NY A	13	9	.591	31	23	10	3	—	0	—	—	193.1	179	102	19	1	81	—	78	4.33	-11	.248	.324	+56	—	-0.7
1930	NY A	12	3	.800	27	21	7	0	—	0	—	—	150.2	185	101	11	4	49	—	46	5.20	-17	.302	.358	+51	—	-1.2
1931	NY A	9	5	.643	27	10	6	0	—	2	—	—	116.2	130	68	7	1	37	—	34	4.32	-8	.286	.341	+94	—	-0.7
1932	NY A	3	3	.500	22	0	0	0	—	2	—	—	31.2	38	19	1	0	12	—	13	4.26	-4	.302	.362	—	—	-0.3
1933	StL A	6	14	.300	36	22	10	0	—	1	—	—	203.2	230	113	13	1	63	—	58	4.20	+11	.278	.330	-5	—	0.4
1934	StL A	1	7	.125	33	8	2	0	—	1	—	—	92	108	60	7	0	35	—	27	4.79	+4	.292	.353	-11	—	0.0
Total	11	68	69	.496	291	140	54	7	—	13	—	—	1232.1	1417	750	78	12	468	—	403	4.65	-9	.291	.355	+21	—	-5.6
Team	4	37	20	.649	107	54	23	3	—	4	—	—	492.1	532	290	38	6	179	—	171	4.59	-12	.278	.341	+61	—	-2.9
/180I	1	14	7	.649	39	20	8	1	—	1	—	—	180	195	106	14	2	65	—	63	4.59	-12	.278	.341	+61	—	-1.1

WENSLOFF, BUTCH Charles William B12.3.1915 Sausalito CA D2.18.2001 San Rafael CA BR/TR/5'11"/185 d5.2 Def 1944

YEAR	TM LG	W	L	PCT	G	GS	CG	SHO	QS	SV	BS	QR	IP	H	R	HR	HB	BB	IB	SO	ERA	AERA	OAV	OOB	SUP	DL	PW
1943	NY A	13	11	.542	29	27	18	1	—	1	—	—	223.1	179	80	7	1	70	—	105	2.54	+27	.219	.282	-4	0	1.5
1947	†NY A	3	1	.750	11	5	1	0	—	0	—	—	51.2	41	17	3	0	22	—	18	2.61	+35	.217	.299	+55	0	0.4
1948	Cle A	0	1	.000	1	0	0	0	—	0	—	—	1.2	2	2	1	0	3	—	2	10.80	-62	.286	.500	—	0	-0.2
Total	3	16	13	.552	41	32	19	1	—	1	—	—	276.2	222	99	11	1	95	—	125	2.60	+26	.219	.287	+5	0	1.7
Team	2	16	12	.571	40	32	19	1	—	1	—	—	275	220	97	10	1	92	—	123	2.55	+28	.219	.285	+5	—	1.9
/180I	1	10	8	.571	26	21	12	1	—	1	—	—	180	144	63	7	1	60	—	81	2.55	+28	.219	.285	+5	—	1.2

WESTBROOK, JAKE Jacob Cauthen B9.29.1977 Athens GA BR/TR/6'3"/(185–215) Dr 1996 ColN 1/21 d6.17 [DL 2000 Cle A 30]

YEAR	TM LG	W	L	PCT	G	GS	CG	SHO	QS	SV	BS	QR	IP	H	R	HR	HB	BB	IB	SO	ERA	AERA	OAV	OOB	SUP	DL	PW
2000	NY A	0	2	.000	3	2	0	0	0	0	0	1	6.2	15	10	1	0	4	1	1	13.50	-65	.469	.500	+8	0	-1.0
Total	8	62	62	.500	195	155	11	3	80	0	2	26	1035.2	1118	553	88	39	321	22	564	4.35	+2	.278	.335	+4	219	1.2

WETTELAND, JOHN John Karl B8.21.1966 San Mateo CA BR/TR/6'2"/(195–215) Dr 1985 LAN*S2/39 d5.31 C1 Col San Mateo (CA) [JC]

YEAR	TM LG	W	L	PCT	G	GS	CG	SHO	QS	SV	BS	QR	IP	H	R	HR	HB	BB	IB	SO	ERA	AERA	OAV	OOB	SUP	DL	PW
1995	†NY A	1	5	.167	60	0	0	0	0	31	6	47	61.1	40	22	6	0	14	2	66	2.93	+58	.185	.233	—	0	1.9
1996	†NY A☆	2	3	.400	62	0	0	0	0	**43**	4	49	63.2	54	23	9	0	21	4	69	2.83	+75	.224	.284	—	24	2.6
Total	12	48	45	.516	618	17	0	0	5	330	63	462	765	616	287	73	16	252	30	804	2.93	+48	.218	.284	-14	58	21.0
Team	2	3	8	.273	122	0	0	0	0	74	10	96	125	94	45	15	0	35	6	135	2.88	+66	.206	.260	—	24	4.5
/60G	1	1	4	.273	60	0	0	0	0	36	5	47	61.1	46	22	7	0	17	3	66	2.89	+66	.206	.260	—	12	2.2

WEVER, STEFAN Stefan Matthew B4.22.1958 Marburg, West Germany BR/TR/6'8"/245 Dr 1979 NYA 6/155 d9.17 Col California–Santa Barbara

YEAR	TM LG	W	L	PCT	G	GS	CG	SHO	QS	SV	BS	QR	IP	H	R	HR	HB	BB	IB	SO	ERA	AERA	OAV	OOB	SUP	DL	PW
1982	NY A	0	1	.000	1	1	0	0	0	0	0	0	2.2	6	9	1	0	3	0	2	27.00	-85	.429	.500	-100	0	-0.9

WHITE, GABE Gabriel Allen B11.20.1971 Sebring FL BL/TL/6'2"/(200–205) Dr 1990 MonN 1/28 d5.27 [DL 1996 Cin N 13]

YEAR	TM LG	W	L	PCT	G	GS	CG	SHO	QS	SV	BS	QR	IP	H	R	HR	HB	BB	IB	SO	ERA	AERA	OAV	OOB	SUP	DL	PW
2003	†NY A	2	1	.667	12	0	0	0	0	0	1	10	12.1	8	7	2	1	2	1	6	4.38	+0	.182	.229	—	26	0.0
2004	NY A	0	1	.000	24	0	0	0	0	0	2	12	20.2	33	19	2	2	7	4	8	8.27	-44	.355	.408	—	0	-0.4
Total	11	34	26	.567	472	15	0	0	5	17	18	313	570.2	556	293	96	16	141	26	454	4.51	+4	.254	.301	-14	130	2.6
Team	2	2	2	.500	36	0	0	0	0	0	3	22	33	41	26	4	3	9	5	14	6.82	-34	.299	.351	—	26	-0.4

WHITEHURST, WALLY Walter Richard B4.11.1964 Shreveport LA BR/TR/6'3"/(180–200) Dr 1985 OakA 3/65 d7.17 Col New Orleans

YEAR	TM LG	W	L	PCT	G	GS	CG	SHO	QS	SV	BS	QR	IP	H	R	HR	HB	BB	IB	SO	ERA	AERA	OAV	OOB	SUP	DL	PW
1996	NY A	1	1	.500	2	2	0	0	1	0	0	0	8	11	6	1	0	2	0	1	6.75	-27	.324	.361	-25	0	-0.2
Total	7	20	37	.351	163	66	0	0	21	3	3	69	487.2	525	236	43	12	130	19	313	4.02	-5	.277	.325	-14	167	-1.3

WHITSON, ED Eddie Lee B5.19.1955 Johnson City TN BR/TR/6'3"/(190–202) Dr 1974 PitN 6/131 d9.4 [DL 1992 SD N 182]

YEAR	TM LG	W	L	PCT	G	GS	CG	SHO	QS	SV	BS	QR	IP	H	R	HR	HB	BB	IB	SO	ERA	AERA	OAV	OOB	SUP	DL	PW
1985	NY A	10	8	.556	30	30	2	2	12	0	0	0	158.2	201	100	19	2	43	0	89	4.88	-17	.309	.350	+33	0	-1.7
1986	NY A	5	2	.714	14	4	0	0	1	0	0	3	37	54	37	5	0	23	1	27	7.54	-45	.335	.412	+54	21	-2.3
Total	15	126	123	.506	452	333	35	12	186	8	3	69	2240	2240	1045	211	29	698	54	1266	3.79	-3	.261	.316	+1	358	-4.4
Team	2	15	10	.600	44	34	2	2	13	0	0	3	195.2	255	137	24	2	66	1	116	5.38	-25	.314	.363	+35	21	-4.0
/180I	2	14	9	.600	40	31	2	2	12	0	0	3	180	235	126	22	2	61	1	107	5.38	-25	.314	.363	+35	19	-3.7

WICKER, KEMP Kemp Caswell (b Kemp Caswell Whicker) B8.13.1906 Kernersville NC D6.11.1973 Kernersville NC BR/TL/5'11"/182 d8.14 Col North Carolina St.

YEAR	TM LG	W	L	PCT	G	GS	CG	SHO	QS	SV	BS	QR	IP	H	R	HR	HB	BB	IB	SO	ERA	AERA	OAV	OOB	SUP	DL	PW
1936	NY A	1	2	.333	7	0	0	0	—	0	—	—	20	31	18	2	0	11	—	5	7.65	-39	.356	.429	—	—	-0.8
1937	†NY A	7	3	.700	16	10	6	1	—	0	—	—	88	107	52	8	0	26	—	14	4.40	+1	.296	.343	+53	—	-0.4
1938	NY A	1	0	1.000	1	0	0	0	—	0	—	—	1	0	0	0	0	1	—	0	0.00	-100	.000	.250	—	—	0.1
1941	Bro N	1	2	.333	16	2	0	0	—	1	—	—	32	30	14	3	0	14	—	8	3.66	+0	.252	.331	-19	0	0.1
Total	4	10	7	.588	40	12	6	1	—	1	—	—	141	168	84	13	0	52	—	27	4.66	-8	.294	.353	+43	0	-1.0
Team	3	9	5	.643	24	10	6	1	—	0	—	—	109	138	70	10	0	38	—	19	4.95	-9	.308	.359	+53	—	-1.1

WICKMAN, BOB Robert Joe B2.6.1969 Green Bay WI BR/TR/6'1"/(207–242) Dr 1990 ChiA 2/44 d8.24 Col Wisconsin–Whitewater [DL 2003 Cle A 183]

YEAR	TM LG	W	L	PCT	G	GS	CG	SHO	QS	SV	BS	QR	IP	H	R	HR	HB	BB	IB	SO	ERA	AERA	OAV	OOB	SUP	DL	PW
1992	NY A	6	1	.857	8	8	0	0	5	0	0	0	50.1	51	25	2	2	20	0	21	4.11	-4	.273	.344	+44	0	-0.1
1993	NY A	14	4	.778	41	19	1	1	7	4	4	15	140	156	82	13	5	69	7	70	4.63	-10	.284	.368	+60	0	-1.0
1994	NY A	5	4	.556	**53**	0	0	0	0	6	4	39	70	54	26	3	1	27	3	56	3.09	+49	.213	.287	—	0	1.5
1995	†NY A	2	4	.333	63	1	0	0	0	1	9	44	80	77	38	6	5	33	3	51	4.05	+14	.253	.335	-20	0	0.4
1996	NY A	4	1	.800	58	0	0	0	0	0	3	36	79	94	41	7	5	34	1	61	4.67	+6	.299	.373	—	0	0.3
Total	15	63	61	.508	835	28	1	1	12	267	68	605	1059	1051	469	80	38	432	45	785	3.57	+26	.260	.335	+41	361	15.4
Team	5	31	14	.689	223	28	1	1	12	11	20	134	419.1	432	212	31	18	183	14	259	4.21	+6	.269	.347	+53	—	1.1
/60G	1	8	4	.689	60	8	0	0	3	3	5	36	112.2	116	57	8	5	49	4	70	4.21	+6	.269	.347	+53	—	0.3

WIESLER, BOB Robert George B8.13.1930 St.Louis MO BB/TL/6'2"/195 d8.3 Mil 1951–52

YEAR	TM LG	W	L	PCT	G	GS	CG	SHO	QS	SV	BS	QR	IP	H	R	HR	HB	BB	IB	SO	ERA	AERA	OAV	OOB	SUP	DL	PW
1951	NY A	0	2	.000	4	3	0	0	—	0	—	—	9.1	13	15	0	0	11	—	3	13.50	-72	.361	.511	-46	0	-1.6
1954	NY A	3	2	.600	6	5	0	0	—	0	—	—	30.1	28	15	0	0	30	—	25	4.15	-17	.259	.420	-3	0	-0.3
1955	NY A	0	2	.000	16	7	0	0	—	0	—	—	53	39	27	1	1	49	0	22	3.91	-4	.212	.380	+5	0	-0.1
1956	Was A	3	12	.200	37	21	3	0	—	0	—	—	123	141	98	11	3	112	1	49	6.44	-33	.300	.435	-12	0	-3.0
1957	Was A	1	1	.500	3	2	1	0	1	0	0	2	16.1	15	8	2	1	11	0	9	4.41	-12	.250	.375	+26	0	0.0
1958	Was A	0	0	+	4	0	0	0	1	0	0	2	9.1	14	8	2	1	5	0	5	6.75	-44	.359	.435	—	0	-0.2
Total	6	7	19	.269	70	38	4	0	2	0	0	4	241.1	250	171	16	6	218	1	113	5.74	-30	.279	.421	-8	0	-5.2
Team	3	3	6	.333	26	15	0	0	—	0	—	—	92.2	80	57	1	1	90	0	50	4.95	-26	.244	.408	-8	—	-2.0

WIGHT, BILL William Robert "Lefty" B4.12.1922 Rio Vista CA D5.17.2007 Mount Shasta CA BL/TL/6'1"/(180–190) d4.17

YEAR	TM LG	W	L	PCT	G	GS	CG	SHO	QS	SV	BS	QR	IP	H	R	HR	HB	BB	IB	SO	ERA	AERA	OAV	OOB	SUP	DL	PW
1946	NY A	2	2	.500	14	4	1	0	—	0	—	—	40.1	44	22	1	1	30	—	11	4.46	-23	.289	.410	+24	0	-0.5
1947	NY A	1	0	1.000	1	1	1	0	—	0	—	—	9	8	3	0	0	2	—	3	1.00	+253	.242	.286	+25	0	0.2
Total	12	77	99	.438	347	198	66	15	12	8	0	27	1563	1656	791	74	14	714	7	574	3.95	+3	.277	.354	-16	0	-0.2
Team	2	3	2	.600	15	5	2	0	—	0	—	—	49.1	52	25	1	1	32	—	14	3.83	-9	.281	.390	+24	—	-0.3

YEAR	TM LG	W	L	PCT	G	GS	CG	SHO	QS	SV	BS	QR	IP	H	R	HR	HB	BB	IB	SO	ERA	AERA	OAV	OOB	SUP	DL	PW
Williams, Stan	Stanley Wilson B9.14.1936 Enfield NH BR/TR/6'5"/(200–230) d5.17 C14																										
1963	†NY A	9	8	.529	29	21	6	1	12	0	0	6	146	137	59	7	6	57	1	98	3.21	+10	.249	.325	+26	0	0.4
1964	NY A	1	5	.167	21	10	1	0	4	0	0	9	82	76	39	7	0	38	2	54	3.84	-6	.248	.329	-9	0	-0.2
Total	14	109	94	.537	482	208	42	11	128	43	19	215	1764.1	1527	785	160	71	748	62	1305	3.48	+8	.232	.315	+1	0	4.3
Team	2	10	13	.435	50	31	7	1	16	0	0	15	228	213	98	14	6	95	3	152	3.43	+3	.249	.326	+15	—	0.2
/180I	2	8	10	.435	39	24	6	1	13	0	0	12	180	168	77	11	5	75	2	120	3.43	+3	.249	.326	+15	—	0.2
Williams, Todd	Todd Michael B2.13.1971 Syracuse NY BR/TR/6'3"/(185–220) Dr 1990 LAN 54/1333 d4.29 Col Onondaga (NY) CC																										
2001	NY A	1	0	1.000	10	0	0	0	0	0	0	9	15.1	22	9	1	2	9	2	13	4.70	-5	.324	.402	—	61	0.0
Total	8	12	14	.462	227	0	0	0	0	2	8	161	232.2	260	125	23	14	87	11	116	4.33	+3	.285	.353	—	88	-0.0
Wilson, Kris	Kristopher Kyle B8.6.1976 Washington DC BR/TR/6'4"/(220–225) Dr 1997 KCA 9/271 d7.28 Col Georgia Tech																										
2006	NY A	0	0	+	5	1	0	0	0	0	0	2	8.1	14	8	4	0	4	0	6	8.64	-47	.368	.429	+2	0	-0.2
Total	5	14	9	.609	95	20	0	0	6	1	4	44	243.1	305	169	53	15	68	6	142	5.44	-9	.306	.356	-14	56	-1.6
Wilson, Pete	Peter Alex B10.9.1885 Springfield MA D6.5.1957 St.Petersburg FL TL d9.15																										
1908	NY A	3	3	.500	6	6	4	1	—	0	—	—	39	27	16	0	1	33	—	28	3.46	-28	.191	.349	-45	—	-0.4
1909	NY A	6	5	.545	14	13	7	1	—	0	—	—	93.2	82	55	2	4	43	—	44	3.17	-20	.230	.320	+14	—	-1.1
Total	2	9	8	.529	20	19	11	2	—	0	—	—	132.2	109	71	2	5	76	—	72	3.26	-23	.219	.329	-6	—	-1.5
/180I	3	12	11	.529	27	26	15	3	0	0	0	0	180	148	96	3	7	103	—	98	3.26	-23	.219	.329	-6	—	-2.0
Wiltse, Snake	Lewis De Witt B12.5.1871 Bouckville NY D8.25.1928 Harrisburg PA BR/TL d5.5 b–Hooks																										
1903	NY A	0	3	.000	4	3	2	0	—	1	—	—	25	35	17	1	1	6	—	6	5.40	-42	.330	.372	-54	—	-0.5
Total	3	29	31	.483	68	62	54	2	—	2	—	—	537.1	674	362	15	26	146	—	121	4.59	-20	.305	.356	+13	—	-2.8
Witasick, Jay	Gerald Alphonse B8.28.1972 Baltimore MD BR/TR/6'4"/(205–250) Dr 1993 StLN 2/58 d7.7 Col Maryland–Baltimore Co.																										
2001	†NY A	3	0	1.000	32	0	0	0	0	0	1	21	40.1	47	27	5	2	18	1	53	4.69	-5	.283	.356	—	0	-0.2
Total	12	32	41	.438	405	56	3	1	19	5	15	244	731.1	775	429	97	35	364	29	645	4.64	-2	.272	.359	+12	341	-2.0
Witt, Mike	Michael Atwater B7.20.1960 Fullerton CA BR/TR/6'7"/(185–203) Dr 1978 CalA 4/92 d4.11 [DL 1992 NY A 182]																										
1990	NY A	5	6	.455	16	16	2	1	8	0	0	0	96.2	87	53	8	4	34	2	60	4.47	-11	.240	.308	-13	59	-0.5
1991	NY A	0	1	.000	2	2	0	0	0	0	0	0	5.1	8	7	1	0	1	0	0	10.13	-59	.320	.346	-12	175	-0.5
1993	NY A	3	2	.600	9	9	0	0	3	0	0	0	41	39	26	7	3	22	0	30	5.27	-21	.248	.352	+22	144	-0.5
Total	12	117	116	.502	341	299	72	11	174	6	5	32	2108.1	2066	1012	183	55	713	40	1373	3.83	+5	.257	.320	-1	560	3.0
Team	3	8	9	.471	27	27	2	1	11	0	—	0	143	134	86	16	7	57	2	90	4.91	-17	.246	.322	-1	378	-1.5
/180I	4	10	11	.471	34	34	3	1	14	0	—	0	180	169	108	20	9	72	3	113	4.91	-17	.246	.322	-1	476	-1.9
Wohlers, Mark	Mark Edward B1.23.1970 Holyoke MA BR/TR/6'4"/207 Dr 1988 AtlN 8/190 d8.17 [DL 1999 Cin N 171, 2003 Cle A 183]																										
2001	†NY A	1	0	1.000	31	0	0	0	0	0	0	20	35.2	33	20	3	1	18	0	33	4.54	-2	.241	.329	—	0	0.0
Total	12	39	29	.574	533	0	0	0	0	119	26	384	553.1	490	273	37	13	272	30	557	3.97	+8	.238	.328	—	413	4.2
Wolfe, Barney	Wilbert Otto B1.9.1876 Independence (now Allenport) PA D2.27.1953 N.Charleroi PA BR/TR/6'1"/? d4.24																										
1903	NY A	6	9	.400	20	16	12	1	—	0	—	—	148.1	143	66	1	6	26	—	48	2.97	+5	.253	.293	-11	—	-0.2
1904	NY A	0	3	.000	7	3	2	0	—	0	—	—	33.2	31	18	1	2	4	—	8	3.21	-15	.246	.280	-56	—	-0.3
1904	Was A	6	10	.375	17	16	13	2	—	0	—	—	126.2	131	64	0	11	22	—	44	3.27	-19	.268	.314	-18	—	-1.3
1904	Year	6	13	.316	24	19	15	2	—	0	—	—	160.1	162	82	1	13	26	—	52	3.26	-18	.263	.307	-24	—	-1.6
1905	Was A	9	14	.391	28	23	17	1	—	1	—	—	182	162	76	1	8	37	—	52	2.57	+3	.240	.287	-34	—	-0.2
1906	Was A	0	3	.000	4	3	2	0	—	0	—	—	20	17	11	0	2	10	—	8	4.05	-35	.233	.341	-45	—	-0.3
Total	4	21	39	.350	76	61	46	4	—	1	—	—	510.2	484	235	3	29	99	—	160	2.96	-6	.251	.298	-25	—	-2.3
Team	2	6	12	.333	27	19	14	1	—	0	—	—	182	174	84	2	8	30	—	56	3.02	+1	.252	.291	-18	—	-0.5
/180I	2	6	12	.333	27	19	14	1	—	0	—	—	180	172	83	2	8	30	—	55	3.02	+1	.252	.291	-18	—	-0.5
Womack, Dooley	Horace Guy B8.25.1939 Columbia SC BL/TR/6'0"/170 d4.14																										
1966	NY A	7	3	.700	42	1	0	0	0	4	1	32	75	52	25	6	3	23	3	50	2.64	+26	.198	.270	-47	0	1.0
1967	NY A	5	6	.455	65	0	0	0	0	18	2	48	97	80	33	6	3	35	14	57	2.41	+30	.230	.300	—	0	1.4
1968	NY A	3	7	.300	45	0	0	0	0	2	2	34	61.2	53	23	6	1	29	9	27	3.21	-9	.244	.335	—	0	0.0
1969	Hou N	2	1	.667	30	0	0	0	0	0	1	18	51.1	49	21	1	3	20	5	32	3.51	+1	.259	.338	—	0	0.2
1969	Sea A	2	1	.667	9	0	0	0	0	0	0	5	14.1	15	4	0	0	3	2	8	2.51	+45	.273	.310	—	0	0.4
1969	Major	4	2	.667	39	0	0	0	0	0	1	23	65	64	25	1	3	23	7	40	3.29	+11	.262	.332	—	0	0.6
1970	Oak A	0	0	+	2	0	0	0	0	0	0	0	3	4	5	2	0	1	0	3	15.00	-76	.308	.357	—	0	-0.2
Total	5	19	18	.514	193	1	0	0	0	24	6	137	302.1	253	111	21	10	111	33	177	2.95	+10	.233	.308	-47	0	2.8
Team	3	15	16	.484	152	1	0	0	0	24	5	114	233.2	185	81	18	7	87	26	134	2.70	+16	.223	.300	-47	—	2.4
/60G	1	6	6	.484	60	0	0	0	0	9	2	45	92.1	73	32	7	3	34	10	53	2.69	+16	.223	.300	—	—	0.9
Woodson, Dick	Richard Lee B3.30.1945 Oelwein IA BR/TR/6'5"/(190–207) d4.8																										
1974	NY A	1	2	.333	8	3	0	0	1	0	0	2	28	34	19	6	1	12	2	12	5.79	-39	.301	.370	-25	0	-0.6
Total	5	34	32	.515	137	76	15	5	46	2	2	36	589	522	263	55	9	253	10	315	3.47	+2	.236	.316	+0	21	0.1
Wright, Jaret	Jaret Samuel B12.29.1975 Anaheim CA BR/TR/6'2"/230 Dr 1994 CleA 1/10 d6.24 f–Clyde																										
2005	NY A	5	5	.500	13	13	0	0	3	0	0	0	63.2	81	51	8	6	32	1	34	6.08	-29	.313	.394	+39	113	-1.9
2006	†NY A	11	7	.611	30	27	0	0	10	0	0	2	140.1	157	76	10	7	57	0	84	4.49	+3	.283	.355	+10	0	0.2
Total	11	68	60	.531	226	171	2	2	74	2	3	30	972.2	1046	599	99	45	467	13	694	5.09	-9	.277	.360	+13	661	-7.4
Team	2	16	12	.571	43	40	0	0	13	0	0	2	204	238	127	18	13	89	1	118	4.99	-9	.292	.368	+19	113	-1.7
/180I	2	14	11	.571	38	35	0	0	11	0	0	2	180	210	112	16	11	79	1	104	4.99	-9	.292	.368	+19	100	-1.5
Wright, Ken	Kenneth Warren B9.4.1946 Pensacola FL BR/TR/6'2"/(210–220) d4.10																										
1974	NY A	0	0	+	3	0	0	0	0	0	0	1	5.2	5	2	0	0	7	0	2	3.18	+12	.227	.414	—	0	0.0
Total	5	11	15	.423	113	24	2	1	9	8	3	52	236	195	127	14	11	180	1	181	4.54	-18	.230	.369	-17	42	-2.5
Wright, Chase	Sebern Chase B2.8.1983 Wichita Falls TX BL/TL/6'2"/205 Dr 2001 NYA 3/95 d4.17																										
2007	NY A	2	0	1.000	3	2	0	0	0	0	0	1	10	12	8	5	2	6	0	8	7.20	-37	.293	.408	+65	0	-0.4
Wyatt, John	John Thomas B4.19.1935 Chicago IL D4.6.1998 Omaha NE BR/TR/5'11.5"/(195–205) d9.8																										
1968	NY A	0	2	.000	7	0	0	0	0	0	1	4	8.1	7	3	1	0	9	0	6	2.16	+35	.219	.381	—	0	0.1
Total	9	42	44	.488	435	9	0	0	4	103	28	300	687.1	600	290	72	23	346	39	540	3.47	+8	.237	.331	+1	0	2.6
Yarnall, Ed	Harvey Edward B12.4.1975 Lima PA BL/TL/6'3"/234 Dr 1996 NYN 3/78 d7.15 Col Louisiana St.																										
1999	NY A	1	0	1.000	5	2	0	0	1	0	0	3	17	17	8	1	0	10	0	13	3.71	+28	.254	.351	+68	0	0.1
2000	NY A	0	0	+	2	1	0	0	0	0	0	1	3	5	5	1	1	3	0	1	15.00	-68	.417	.563	+155	0	-0.2
Total	2	1	0	1.000	7	3	0	0	1	0	0	4	20	22	13	2	1	13	0	14	5.40	-12	.278	.387	+97	0	-0.1
York, Jim	James Harlan B8.27.1947 Maywood CA BR/TR/6'3"/200 Dr 1969 KCA 16/381 d9.21 Col UCLA																										
1976	NY A	1	0	1.000	3	0	0	0	0	0	0	1	9.2	14	7	1	1	4	0	6	5.59	-39	.333	.404	—	0	-0.2
Total	7	16	17	.485	174	4	0	0	2	10	6	111	285	290	131	19	12	132	24	194	3.79	-8	.264	.346	+55	0	-0.9
Young, Curt	Curtis Allen B4.16.1960 Saginaw MI BR/TL/6'1"/(175–180) Dr 1981 OakA 4/92 d6.24 C4 Col Central Michigan																										
1992	NY A	3	0	1.000	13	5	0	0	4	0	1	4	43.1	51	21	1	2	10	1	13	3.32	+19	.298	.341	+34	27	0.1
Total	11	69	53	.566	251	162	15	3	76	0	2	55	1107	1133	581	147	33	366	11	536	4.31	-10	.265	.326	+10	235	-4.7

YEAR	TM LG	W	L	PCT	G	GS	CG	SHO	QS	SV	BS	QR	IP	H	R	HR	HB	BB	IB	SO	ERA	AERA	OAV	OOB	SUP	DL	PW
Zachary, Tom Jonathan Thompson Walton (aka Zach Walton in 1918) B5.7.1896 Graham NC D1.24.1969 Burlington NC BL/TL/6'1"/187 d7.11 Mil 1918–19 Col Guilford																											
1928	†NY A	3	3	.500	7	6	3	0	—	1	—	—	45.2	54	26	1	0	15	—	7	3.94	-5	.320	.375	+9	—	-0.2
1929	NY A	12	0	1.000	26	11	7	2	—	2	—	—	119.2	131	43	5	2	30	—	35	2.48	+55	.277	.323	+35	—	1.7
1930	NY A	1	1	.500	3	3	0	0	—	0	—	—	16.2	18	16	0	0	9	—	1	6.48	-34	.269	.355	+26	—	-0.4
Total	19	186	191	.493	533	408	186	24	—	22	—	—	3126.1	3580	1551	119	41	914	—	720	3.73	+6	.294	.345	-5	—	10.6
Team	3	16	4	.800	36	20	10	2	—	3	—	—	182	203	85	6	2	54	—	43	3.21	+21	.286	.339	+26	—	1.1
/180I	3	16	4	.800	36	20	10	2	—	3	—	—	180	201	84	6	2	53	—	43	3.21	+21	.286	.339	+26	—	1.1
Zuber, Bill William Henry "Goober" B3.26.1913 Middle Amana IA D11.2.1982 Cedar Rapids IA BR/TR/6'2"/195 d9.16																											
1943	NY A	8	4	.667	20	13	7	0	—	1	—	—	118	100	54	3	0	74	—	57	3.89	-17	.234	.347	+67	0	-0.5
1944	NY A	5	7	.417	22	13	2	1	—	0	—	—	107	101	54	5	1	54	—	59	4.21	-17	.255	.346	-8	0	-0.9
1945	NY A	5	11	.313	21	14	7	0	—	1	—	—	127	121	50	2	0	56	—	50	3.19	+9	.259	.338	-44	0	0.4
1946	NY A	0	1	.000	3	0	0	0	—	0	—	—	5.2	10	9	2	0	3	—	3	12.71	-73	.385	.448	—	0	-0.9
Total	11	43	42	.506	224	65	23	3	—	6	—	—	786	767	418	35	4	468	—	383	4.28	-13	.260	.362	+3	0	-4.7
Team	4	18	23	.439	66	40	16	1	—	2	—	—	357.2	332	167	12	1	187	—	169	3.88	-13	.252	.346	+4	—	-1.9
/180I	2	9	12	.439	33	20	8	1	—	1	—	—	180	167	84	6	1	94	—	85	3.88	-13	.252	.346	+4	—	-1.0

Yankees Pitchers Home & Away Statistics

The table below shows Yankees pitching statistics at home and on the road for a number of their prominent pitchers. A player normally does about 10% better at home, based on normalized OPS or earned run average. That means that a typical New York pitcher will see a ratio of around .90 between his home ERA and his road ERA.

Yankee Stadium is often thought of as an easy park for left-handed batters because of its short right field foul line. In reality, though, it is a neutral park for lefty swingers and puts right-handers at a great disadvantage. As the introduction to the Yankees' hitters home & away stats describes (at the end of the Batters Register), the idea that Yankee Stadium has been a boon to lefty hitters over the years is a myth.

Yankees pitchers, on the other hand, do gain a substantial advantage at 161st Street and River Avenue. Why? Because most batters are right-handed and the dimensions of the Stadium hurt them badly. Almost all the longlasting Yankees pitchers have an .80 ERA ratio home to road, compared to the norm of .90. Of course, there are always exceptions: the great Mariano Rivera actually has a higher ERA in home games than in away contests.

There seems to be no particular advantage to being left- or right handed when facing hitters at Yankee Stadium. The two pitchers with the largest improvement at home were righty Red Ruffing (home ERA 2.81, road ERA 4.21; a ratio of 67%) and lefty Eddie Lopat (2.60/3.84/68%). Southpaw Whitey Ford, on the other hand, who would seem to have an edge in the Stadium because he would see more right-handed batters, was at .88—almost normal. Ford's road ERA was somewhat lower than expected because Casey Stengel wouldn't let him pitch in Fenway Park.

YR	G-H	GS	CG	SHO	W	L	IP	ERA	G-A	GS	CG	SHO	W	L	IP	ERA	H/A
Spud Chandler RHP																	
1937	7	7	5	2	6	1	60.2	2.52	5	3	1	0	1	3	21.2	3.74	0.67
1938	12	12	7	1	7	2	90.1	3.69	11	11	7	1	7	3	81.2	4.41	0.84
1939	4	0	0	0	0	0	8.2	4.15	7	0	0	0	3	0	10.1	1.74	2.38
1940	14	12	2	1	4	4	93.1	4.24	13	12	4	0	4	3	78.2	5.03	0.84
1941	13	11	9	4	7	2	95.2	1.69	15	9	2	0	3	2	68.0	5.29	0.32
1942	14	14	9	1	9	2	119.0	2.50	10	10	8	2	7	3	81.2	2.20	1.13
1943	15	15	9	1	10	2	124.2	1.66	15	15	11	4	10	2	128.1	1.61	1.03
1944	1	1	0	0	0	0	6.0	4.50	0	0	0	0	0	0	0.0	0.00	0.00
1945	3	3	2	1	2	1	24.0	4.13	1	1	0	0	0	0	7.0	6.43	0.64
1946	15	15	11	1	11	3	125.0	1.73	19	17	9	5	9	5	132.1	2.45	0.71
1947	8	8	6	1	5	3	63.1	3.13	9	8	7	1	4	2	64.2	1.81	1.73
total	106	98	60	13	61	20	810.2	2.62	105	86	49	13	48	23	674.1	3.10	0.85
Roger Clemens RHP																	
1999	17	17	1	1	9	5	113.2	3.56	13	13	0	0	5	5	74.0	6.20	0.57
2000	19	19	1	0	8	4	126.0	3.86	13	13	0	0	5	4	78.1	3.45	1.12
2001	14	14	0	0	10	1	98.2	3.10	19	19	0	0	10	2	121.2	3.85	0.81
2002	15	15	0	0	9	1	101.1	2.84	14	14	0	0	4	5	78.2	6.29	0.45
2003	18	18	0	0	7	7	108.2	5.22	15	15	1	1	10	2	103.0	2.53	2.06
2007	9	9	0	0	4	2	52.0	3.29	9	8	0	0	2	4	47.0	5.17	0.64
total	92	92	2	1	47	20	600.1	3.70	83	82	1	1	36	22	502.2	4.37	0.85
Whitey Ford LHP																	
1950	7	5	2	1	3	0	45.2	2.76	13	7	5	1	6	1	66.1	2.85	0.97
1953	17	16	9	3	8	5	117.0	2.85	15	14	2	0	10	1	90.0	3.20	0.89
1954	18	17	6	1	9	6	124.0	2.90	16	11	5	2	7	2	86.2	2.70	1.08
1955	21	17	13	5	11	3	149.0	1.69	18	16	5	0	7	4	104.2	3.96	0.43
1956	15	15	9	2	9	3	116.1	2.32	16	15	9	0	10	3	109.1	2.63	0.88
1957	11	9	4	0	5	3	70.2	1.91	13	8	1	0	6	2	58.2	3.38	0.57
1958	16	15	6	4	7	3	113.0	2.71	14	14	9	3	7	4	106.1	1.27	2.13
1959	19	16	4	0	8	7	106.1	3.39	16	13	5	2	8	3	97.2	2.67	1.27
1960	17	15	4	3	7	3	96.2	2.51	16	14	4	1	5	6	96.0	3.66	0.69
1961	20	20	7	2	12	2	149.1	2.65	19	19	4	1	13	2	133.2	3.84	0.69
1962	18	18	3	0	9	1	116.0	2.79	20	19	4	0	8	7	141.2	2.99	0.94
1963	21	21	7	1	12	6	145.0	2.86	17	16	6	2	12	1	124.1	2.61	1.10
1964	20	20	7	5	9	3	138.1	1.95	19	16	5	3	8	3	106.1	2.37	0.82
1965	19	19	5	1	10	4	137.1	2.95	18	17	4	1	6	9	107.0	3.62	0.82
1966	12	5	0	0	0	3	43.1	2.70	10	4	0	0	2	2	29.2	2.12	1.27
1967	4	4	1	0	1	2	27.0	2.00	3	3	1	1	1	2	17.0	1.06	1.89
total	255	232	87	28	120	54	1695.0	2.58	243	206	69	17	116	52	1475.1	2.94	0.88

YR	G-H	GS	CG	SHO	W	L	IP	ERA	G-A	GS	CG	SHO	W	L	IP	ERA	H/A
LEFTY GOMEZ LHP																	
1930	6	4	2	0	2	2	31.0	5.81	9	2	0	0	0	3	29.0	5.28	1.10
1931	18	15	11	0	11	5	136.1	2.31	22	11	6	1	10	4	106.2	3.12	0.74
1932	18	16	13	1	13	2	143.1	3.39	19	15	8	0	11	5	122.0	5.16	0.66
1933	16	15	8	2	9	5	122.1	2.21	19	15	6	2	7	5	112.1	4.25	0.52
1934	22	21	17	6	18	2	182.1	2.07	16	12	8	0	8	3	99.1	2.81	0.74
1935	18	17	7	2	6	10	132.0	3.34	16	13	8	0	6	5	114.0	3.00	1.11
1936	17	17	8	0	10	3	122.1	3.46	14	13	2	0	3	4	66.1	6.11	0.57
1937	16	16	12	4	11	1	101.0	2.13	18	18	13	2	10	7	147.1	2.50	0.85
1938	16	16	10	3	11	5	121.0	3.42	16	16	10	1	7	7	118.0	3.28	1.04
1939	13	13	7	1	5	5	103.1	3.22	13	13	7	1	7	3	94.2	3.61	0.89
1940	2	2	0	0	2	0	8.2	6.23	7	3	0	0	1	3	18.2	6.75	0.92
1941	13	13	6	1	10	1	96.0	3.28	10	10	2	1	5	4	60.1	4.48	0.73
1942	4	4	2	0	4	0	29.0	1.24	9	9	0	0	2	4	51.0	6.00	0.21
total	179	169	103	20	112	44	1358.2	2.89	188	150	70	8	77	57	1139.2	3.88	0.74
RON GUIDRY LHP																	
1975	6	1	0	0	0	1	11.2	4.63	4	0	0	0	0	0	4.0	0.00	0.00
1976	6	0	0	0	0	0	14.1	6.28	1	0	0	0	0	0	1.2	0.00	0.00
1977	13	12	5	3	9	2	97.2	2.58	18	13	4	2	7	5	113.0	3.03	0.85
1978	17	17	10	4	12	1	140.2	1.79	18	18	6	5	13	2	133.0	1.69	1.06
1979	18	16	10	2	13	2	133.2	2.22	15	14	5	0	5	6	102.2	3.51	0.93
1980	20	16	2	2	9	7	117.2	3.07	17	13	3	1	8	3	102.0	3.44	1.07
1981	11	11	0	0	6	2	65.0	2.49	12	10	0	0	5	3	62.0	3.05	0.82
1982	17	16	3	0	6	5	113.1	3.57	17	17	3	1	8	3	108.2	4.06	0.88
1983	16	16	13	2	14	2	138.1	2.34	15	15	8	1	7	7	112.0	4.74	0.49
1984	14	13	4	1	8	2	101.1	2.93	15	15	1	0	2	9	94.1	6.20	0.47
1985	17	17	7	0	13	2	137.1	2.82	17	16	4	2	9	4	121.2	3.77	0.75
1986	19	19	4	0	6	8	121.0	4.39	11	11	1	0	3	4	71.1	3.28	1.34
1987	12	8	1	0	2	4	59.1	2.58	10	9	1	0	3	4	58.1	4.78	0.54
1988	3	3	0	0	1	1	17.0	2.65	9	7	0	0	1	2	39.0	4.85	0.55
total	189	165	59	14	99	39	1268.1	2.90	179	158	36	12	71	52	1123.2	3.72	0.78
CATFISH HUNTER RHP																	
1975	19	19	13	3	12	6	164.2	2.46	20	20	17	4	11	8	163.1	2.70	0.91
1976	17	17	10	1	7	8	141.0	3.64	19	19	11	1	10	7	157.2	3.42	1.06
1977	13	13	5	1	6	4	89.1	3.93	9	9	3	0	3	5	53.2	6.04	0.65
1978	13	13	3	1	7	5	80.1	3.47	8	7	2	0	5	1	37.2	3.82	0.91
1979	10	10	0	0	1	4	57.2	3.90	9	9	1	0	1	5	47.1	7.04	0.55
total	72	72	31	6	33	27	533.0	3.33	65	64	34	5	30	26	459.2	3.88	0.86
EDDIE LOPAT LHP																	
1948	17	16	6	2	9	5	119.2	3.16	16	15	7	1	8	6	107.0	4.21	0.75
1949	15	15	9	3	9	5	114.0	2.61	16	15	5	1	6	5	101.1	4.00	0.65
1950	15	15	8	3	9	4	109.0	3.39	20	17	7	0	9	4	127.1	3.53	0.96
1951	16	16	13	3	14	2	134.2	1.94	15	15	7	1	7	7	100.0	4.23	0.46
1952	9	9	5	2	7	2	71.0	2.28	11	10	5	0	3	3	78.1	2.76	0.83
1953	15	14	5	3	9	2	102.0	1.85	10	10	4	0	7	2	76.1	3.18	0.58
1954	12	12	6	0	9	2	96.0	2.81	14	11	1	0	3	2	74.0	4.50	0.63
1955	7	7	3	1	2	4	45.2	2.96	9	5	0	0	2	4	41.0	4.61	0.64
total	106	104	55	17	68	26	792.0	2.60	111	98	36	3	45	33	705.1	3.84	0.68
HERB PENNOCK LHP																	
1923	18	14	9	1	8	4	119.1	3.24	17	13	12	0	11	2	119.0	3.03	1.07
1924	22	19	15	3	11	5	156.1	2.65	18	15	10	1	10	4	130.0	3.05	0.87
1925	23	16	10	2	9	7	147.0	2.33	24	15	11	0	7	10	129.2	3.68	0.63
1926	19	14	9	0	13	3	124.1	2.39	21	19	10	1	10	8	142.0	4.69	0.51
1927	18	14	9	0	10	6	104.1	3.45	16	12	9	1	9	2	105.1	2.56	1.35
1928	14	11	8	5	8	3	97.0	1.95	14	13	10	0	9	3	114.0	3.08	0.63
1929	13	11	4	0	5	3	72.2	5.20	14	12	4	1	4	8	84.2	4.68	1.11
1930	11	10	6	1	5	4	73.0	4.56	14	9	5	0	6	3	83.1	4.10	1.11
1931	14	14	6	0	8	1	106.0	4.33	11	11	6	1	3	5	83.1	4.21	1.03
1932	9	9	4	1	5	2	69.0	3.78	13	12	5	0	4	3	77.2	5.33	0.71
1933	8	2	1	1	2	1	20.0	3.60	15	3	1	0	5	3	45.1	6.35	0.57
total	169	134	81	14	84	39	1089.0	3.21	177	134	83	5	78	51	1114.1	3.87	0.83
ANDY PETTITTE LHP																	
1995	14	13	3	0	8	2	100.0	2.61	17	13	0	0	4	7	75.0	6.24	0.42
1996	17	17	2	0	10	4	120.1	3.22	18	17	0	0	11	4	100.2	4.65	0.69
1997	17	17	2	0	9	4	118.2	2.65	18	18	2	1	9	3	121.2	3.11	0.85
1998	16	15	2	0	9	4	103.2	4.34	17	17	3	0	7	7	112.2	4.15	1.05
1999	16	16	0	0	8	5	102.1	4.22	15	15	0	0	6	6	89.1	5.24	0.81
2000	14	14	2	0	9	2	94.0	3.93	18	18	1	1	10	7	110.2	4.72	0.83
2001	16	16	1	0	10	3	108.1	3.16	15	15	1	0	5	7	92.1	4.97	0.64
2002	10	10	3	1	8	2	67.1	3.48	12	12	0	0	5	3	67.1	3.07	1.13
2003	16	16	1	0	10	4	100.0	3.78	17	17	0	0	11	4	108.1	4.24	0.89
2007	17	16	0	0	8	4	101.1	4.17	19	18	0	0	7	5	114.0	3.95	1.06
total	153	150	16	1	89	34	1016.0	3.53	166	160	7	2	75	53	992.0	4.38	0.81
MARIANO RIVERA RHP																	
1995	9	5	0	0	3	2	31.2	7.11	10	5	0	0	2	1	35.1	4.08	1.74
1996	29	0	0	0	6	2	50.0	1.80	32	0	0	0	2	1	57.2	2.34	0.77
1997	38	0	0	0	4	3	40.0	2.25	28	0	0	0	2	1	31.2	1.42	1.58
1998	32	0	0	0	3	0	36.1	1.24	22	0	0	0	0	0	25.0	2.88	0.43
1999	33	0	0	0	2	2	32.2	2.48	33	0	0	0	2	1	36.1	1.24	2.00
2000	31	0	0	0	4	2	34.1	3.41	35	0	0	0	3	2	41.1	2.40	1.42
2001	36	0	0	0	3	4	41.1	3.48	35	0	0	0	1	2	39.1	1.14	3.05
2002	19	0	0	0	1	2	20.1	2.66	26	0	0	0	0	2	25.2	2.81	0.95
2003	33	0	0	0	3	1	35.1	1.78	31	0	0	0	2	1	35.1	1.53	1.17
2004	39	0	0	0	3	1	43.0	2.30	35	0	0	0	1	1	35.2	1.51	1.52
2005	37	0	0	0	7	4	43.1	2.28	34	0	0	0	0	0	35.0	0.26	8.88
2006	32	0	0	0	1	1	35.2	1.51	31	0	0	0	4	4	39.1	2.06	0.74
2007	31	0	0	0	3	2	33.2	3.21	36	0	0	0	0	2	37.2	3.11	1.03
total	399	5	0	0	43	26	477.2	2.66	388	5	0	0	19	18	475.1	2.04	1.30
RED RUFFING RHP																	
1930	17	11	9	2	10	1	111.2	2.58	17	14	3	0	5	4	86.0	6.17	0.42
1931	20	17	11	1	9	8	137.2	4.05	17	13	8	0	7	6	99.1	4.89	0.83
1932	16	13	11	1	11	3	123.1	2.63	19	16	11	2	7	4	135.2	3.52	0.75

Pitchers

YR	G-H	GS	CG	SHO	W	L	IP	ERA	G-A	GS	CG	SHO	W	L	IP	ERA	H/A
1933	16	13	9	0	4	9	114.0	3.71	19	15	9	0	5	5	121.0	4.09	0.91
1934	16	15	12	4	12	2	131.1	2.60	20	16	7	1	7	9	125.0	5.33	0.49
1935	15	14	11	1	7	7	126.1	2.64	15	15	8	1	9	4	95.2	3.76	0.70
1936	19	19	15	3	12	7	165.0	3.16	14	14	10	0	8	5	106.0	4.92	0.64
1937	16	16	13	2	12	3	142.1	2.66	15	15	9	2	8	4	114.0	3.39	0.78
1938	16	16	14	2	12	3	138.2	2.53	15	15	8	1	9	4	108.2	4.31	0.59
1939	14	14	11	3	10	4	116.1	2.24	14	14	11	2	11	3	117.0	3.62	0.62
1940	14	14	10	3	8	4	111.0	2.03	16	16	10	0	7	8	115.0	4.70	0.43
1941	12	12	7	0	5	5	99.2	3.61	11	11	6	2	10	1	86.0	3.45	1.05
1942	12	12	7	2	7	3	99.0	2.55	12	12	9	2	7	4	94.2	3.90	0.65
1945	6	6	4	0	4	1	47.0	3.06	5	5	4	1	3	2	40.1	2.68	1.14
1946	5	5	3	2	3	1	37.1	1.45	3	3	1	0	2	0	23.2	2.28	0.63
total	214	197	147	26	126	61	1700.2	2.83	212	194	114	14	105	63	1468.0	4.21	0.67

Babe Ruth LHP

YR	G-H	GS	CG	SHO	W	L	IP	ERA	G-A	GS	CG	SHO	W	L	IP	ERA	H/A
1920	1	1	0	0	1	0	4.0	4.50	0	0	0	0	0	0	0.0	0.00	0.00
1921	2	1	0	0	2	0	9.0	9.00	0	0	0	0	0	0	0.0	0.00	0.00
1930	0	0	0	0	0	0	0.0	0.00	1	1	1	0	1	0	9.0	3.00	0.00
1933	1	1	1	0	1	0	9.0	5.00	0	0	0	0	0	0	0.0	0.00	0.00
total	4	3	1	0	4	0	22.0	6.55	1	1	1	0	1	0	9.0	3.00	2.18

Urban Shocker RHP

YR	G-H	GS	CG	SHO	W	L	IP	ERA	G-A	GS	CG	SHO	W	L	IP	ERA	H/A
1916	6	5	2	0	2	1	43.0	2.30	6	4	2	1	2	2	39.1	2.97	0.77
1917	16	8	4	0	5	4	91.0	2.97	10	5	3	0	3	1	54.0	2.00	1.48
1925	22	15	7	1	7	5	125.2	3.58	19	15	8	1	5	7	118.2	3.72	0.96
1926	19	16	10	0	11	4	129.1	3.41	22	16	8	0	8	7	129.0	3.35	1.02
1927	13	11	7	0	9	2	89.2	2.51	18	16	6	2	9	4	110.1	3.10	0.81
1928	1	0	0	0	0	0	2.0	0.00	0	0	0	0	0	0	0.0	0.00	0.00
total	77	55	30	1	34	16	480.2	3.09	75	56	27	4	27	21	451.1	3.19	0.97

Mel Stottlemyre RHP

YR	G-H	GS	CG	SHO	W	L	IP	ERA	G-A	GS	CG	SHO	W	L	IP	ERA	H/A
1964	7	6	2	0	4	2	47.2	2.64	6	6	3	2	5	1	48.1	1.49	1.77
1965	18	18	8	1	9	5	145.0	2.61	19	19	10	3	11	4	146.0	2.65	0.98
1966	18	18	5	2	7	8	131.1	3.15	19	17	4	1	5	12	119.2	4.51	0.70
1967	20	20	5	1	8	8	141.0	2.81	16	16	5	3	7	7	114.0	3.16	0.89
1968	18	18	12	4	11	6	146.1	2.21	18	18	7	2	10	6	132.1	2.72	0.81
1969	20	20	14	1	12	5	167.1	2.37	19	19	10	2	8	9	135.2	3.38	0.70
1970	20	20	7	0	9	8	146.2	2.45	17	17	7	0	6	5	124.1	3.84	0.64
1971	17	17	9	3	8	5	138.0	2.54	18	18	10	4	8	7	131.2	3.21	0.79
1972	17	17	4	4	7	8	124.2	3.18	19	19	5	3	7	10	135.1	3.26	0.97
1973	20	20	10	2	10	7	145.0	2.86	18	18	9	2	6	9	128.0	3.30	0.86
1974	10	9	4	0	4	3	73.2	2.93	6	6	2	0	2	4	39.1	4.81	0.61
total	185	183	80	18	89	65	1406.2	2.68	175	173	72	22	75	74	1254.2	3.29	0.81

Major League Pitchers Developed By the Yankees Since 1975

Though frequently criticized as not being productive enough, the truth about the Yankees' player development system in the past three decades is that too much of the talent New York has produced has ended up playing elsewhere. The Yankees have, however, retained substantially more of their young pitching than their young hitting prospects.

Most players developed by any organization were originally drafted or signed by that organization and later made their major league debut with that team. Some players, of course, were traded to another club while still in the minors, and made their ML debut in another uniform (e.g., Scott McGregor). Note that an organization can "gain" or "lose" credit for a player if he was released before ever reaching the high minors (i.e., Double A).

This list shows all 126 pitchers who have played in the majors from 1975–2007 that were produced by the Yankees' organization, with their debut year and team (if not New York). Their career innings pitched with the Yankees and with other teams are also shown through 2007.

PLAYER/DEBUT (TEAM)	IP NY/OTHER
Steve Adkins 1990	24/0
Jason Anderson 2003	25/11
Rick Anderson 1979	2/9
Tony Armas 1999 MON	0/916
Brad Arnsberg 1986	27/129
Stan Bahnsen 1966	984/1540
Rich Batchelor 1993 STL	0/53
T.J. Beam 2006	18/0
Colter Bean 2005	7/0
Jim Beattie 1978	204/942
Tim Birtsas 1985 OAK	0/327
Paul Boris 1982 MIN	0/49
Jim Bouton 1962	1012/224
Ryan Bradley 1998	12/0
Yhency Brazoban 2004 LAN	0/110
Mike Buddie 1998	43/86
Tom Buskey 1973	21/455
Ben Callahan 1983 OAK	0/9
Amalio Carreno 1991 PHI	0/3
Darrin Chapin 1991	5/2
Randy Choate 2000	90/73
Clay Christiansen 1984	38/0
Mike Christopher 1991 LAN	0/124
Brandon Claussen 2003	6/309
Ken Clay 1977	208/144
Jose Contreras 2003	166/663
Andy Cook 1993	5/0
Don Cooper 1981 MIN	10/74
Ken Crosby 1975 CHN	0/20
Darwin Cubillan 2000 TOR	0/68
Bob Davidson 1989	1/0
Zach Day 2002 MON	0/370
Mike DeJean 1997 COL	0/618
Luis DeLosSantos 2002 TB	0/14
Jim Deshaies 1984	7/1516
Craig Dingman 2000	11/68
Al Downing 1961	1233/1030
Mike Draper 1993 NYN	0/42
Matt Dunbar 1995 FLO	0/7
Logan Easley 1987 PIT	0/38
Dave Eiland 1988	158/211
Darrell Einertson 2000	12/0

PLAYER/DEBUT (TEAM)	IP NY/OTHER
Tom Filer 1982 CHN	0/305
Pete Filson 1982 MIN	22/367
Randy Flores 2002 TEX	0/180
Ben Ford 1998 ARI	11/34
Steve Frey 1989 MON	0/300
Bill Fulton 1987	4/0
Keith Garagozzo 1994 MIN	0/9
Rosman Garcia 2003 TEX	0/52
Alex Graman 2004	6/0
Kenneth William Greer 1993 NYN	0/13
Ron Guidry 1975	2387/0
Brad Halsey 2004	32/254
Sean Henn 2005	56/0
Adrian Hernandez 2001	28/16
Orlando Hernandez 1998	874/436
Sterling Hitchcock 1992	400/881
Chris Howard 1993 CHA	0/45
Lamarr Hoyt 1979 CHA	0/1308
Mark Hutton 1993	55/132
Hideki Irabu 1997	395/117
Marty Janzen 1996 TOR	0/98
Mike Jerzembeck 1998	6/0
Brett Jodie 2001	2/23
Jeff Johnson 1991	181/0
Mark Johnson 2000 DET	0/24
Mike Judd 1997 LAN	0/74
Scott Kamieniecki 1991	625/346
Bob Kammeyer 1978	21/0
Ryan Karp 1995 PHI	0/17
Jeff Karstens 2006	56/0
Curt Kaufman 1982	16/69
Randy Keisler 2000	60/89
Steve Kline 1970	658/91
Frank Lankford 1998 LAN	0/19
Tim Layana 1990 CIN	0/102
Al Leiter 1987	167/2217
Oswaldo Mairena 2000 CHN	0/35
Tippy Martinez 1974	77/754
Andy McGaffigan 1981	7/823
Scott McGregor 1976 BAL	0/2138
Doc Medich 1972	786/1207
Rafael Medina 1998 FLO	0/90

PLAYER/DEBUT (TEAM)	IP NY/OTHER
Ramiro Mendoza 1996	696/96
Sam Militello 1992	69/0
Eric Milton 1998 MIN	0/1556
Kevin Mmahat 1989	7/0
Danny Mota 2000 MIN	0/5
Bobby Munoz 1993	45/231
Jerry Nielsen 1992	19/12
Kirt Ojala 1997 FLO	0/163
Ed Olwine 1986 ATL	0/88
Joe Pactwa 1975 CAL	0/16
Dave Pagan 1973	115/115
Gil Patterson 1977	33/0
Ken Patterson 1988 CHA	0/314
Mike Pazik 1975 MIN	0/46
Fritz Peterson 1966	1855/360
Andy Pettitte 1995	2004/519
Gerry Pirtle 1978 MON	0/25
Eric Plunk 1986 OAK	258/887
Rafael Quirico 1996 PHI	0/1
Dave Rajsich 1978	13/101
Ramon Ramirez 2006 COL	0/84
Stephen Randolph 2003 ARI	0/154
Brian Reith 2001 CIN	0/127
Jose Rijo 1984	62/1815
Danny Rios 1997	2/7
Mariano Rivera 1995	948/0
Jake Robbins 2004 CLE	0/1
Steven Rosenberg 1988 CHA	0/209
Rich Scheid 1992 HOU	0/54
Mickey Scott 1972 BAL	0/171
Matt Smith 2006	12/12
Russell Springer 1992	16/725
Chris Spurling 2003 DET	0/218
Jay Tessmer 1998	21/0
Bob Tewksbury 1986	163/1639
Freddie Toliver 1984 CIN	0/268
Chien-Ming Wang 2005	533/0
Chris Welsh 1981 SD	0/535
Stefan Wever 1982	2/0
Wally Whitehurst 1989 NYN	8/478
Scott Wiggins 2002 TOR	0/2
Dean Wilkins 1989 CHN	0/30

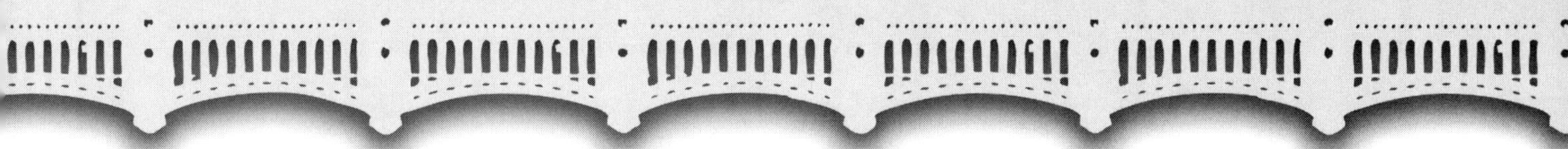

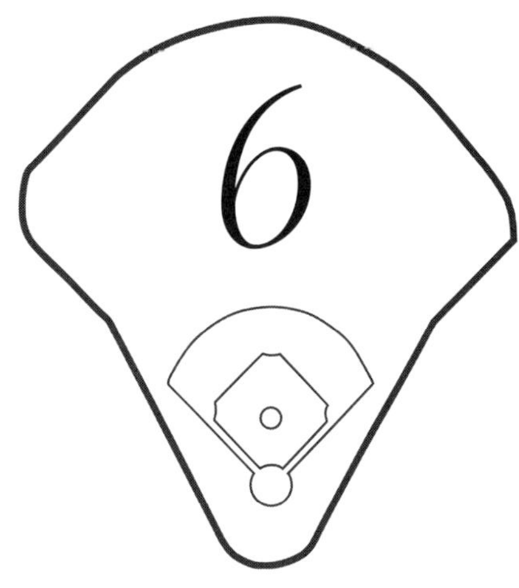

Yankees Managers & Coaches

A TOTAL OF 32 MEN have commanded the Yankees on the field since the franchise was established in 1903. Over the course of 41 managerial stints, five of those 32 have been hired as managers more than once: Yogi Berra, Bob Lemon, Lou Piniella, Gene Michael, and, of course, Billy Martin. Three of those 32 skippers—Art Fletcher, Johnny Neun, and Clyde King—were interim managers only.

Martin's tempestuous relationship with George Steinbrenner is so famous that it has been chronicled in the media in ways ranging from the recent ESPN miniseries *The Bronx Is Burning* to humorous beer commercials. Steinbrenner hired and fired Martin five separate times over a 14-year span, contrasting starkly with the Yankees' longest lasting manager, Joe McCarthy, who held the reigns for more than 15 seasons (from 1931 through May 1946). The team's shortest-lived manager (not counting interim hirings, stints by active players, and strike-shortened terms) was Bucky Dent with a short run at the end of the 1989 season and the beginning of the 1990 season.

From 1918 into the 1960s, the Yankees' managerial job was one of baseball's most stable—once a manager survived his first season. Miller Huggins was hired in 1918 and remained until his death in 1929. Two years later, the Yankees hired McCarthy, who stayed on until his resignation in 1946. Three years later, the Yanks hired Casey Stengel for the 1949 season; Stengel held onto the job until he was fired because of his age after 1960.

Ralph Houk was hired to replace Stengel, moving up to the front office in 1964 after three years in the dugout. After short spells by Yogi Berra and Johnny Keane, however, Houk took back the job and stayed on until 1974, just when new owner Steinbrenner was settling in. Also departing with Houk was the previous stability for the position. "The Boss" would prove to be the most impatient owner in baseball history, hiring and firing managers capriciously. Steinbrenner's first new hire, Bill Virdon, lasted barely more than a year. His second new manager, Martin, would find himself at the center of many controversies, even though his first term in office actually lasted 471 games and would not be surpassed in length by another Yankees manager until the 1990s.

Martin's first firing in mid-1978 came as a result of the most famous words he would ever utter: "They deserve each other. One's a born liar and the other's convicted." Martin's verbal criticism of Reggie Jackson and Steinbrenner (previously convicted of making illegal campaign donations to Richard Nixon) cost him his job, with Bob Lemon replacing him. Later in the season, however, the Yankees announced that Martin would return as manager in 1980, at which time Lemon would be promoted to general manager. Steinbrenner couldn't remain patient for that long, however, and the mercurial owner brought back Martin less than halfway through the '79 season.

After Martin failed to lead the Yankees to another pennant, however, he was once again dismissed. Dick Howser replaced Martin and rode the Yankees to a 103-win season, yet their loss to Kansas City in the 1980 ALCS resulted in Howser's dismissal. Gene Michael was hired as the new Yankees' manager for 1981, but he was replaced by Lemon by the end of the season. Lemon started 1982 in the Yankees' dugout, only to be replaced after several weeks by Michael, the same manager he had succeeded!

This dizzying series of affairs continued for the rest of the decade. Martin was hired again for 1983, but he was let go again after the season. Berra was hired before the '84 season and managed to survive until early 1985, when Martin was brought back again. After getting into a bar brawl with Yankees pitcher Ed Whitson in late September, Martin was once again dismissed. Lou Piniella was hired as manager for 1986 and held the job for two full seasons before moving up to the front office. Martin was hired *again* for 1988, then fired *again* midway through the season after throwing dirt on an umpire and getting into a fight outside a topless bar in Dallas.

Piniella, who had decided in the meantime that he hated working in the front office, returned to the dugout in late June with a long-term deal to keep him there through 1991. Piniella wouldn't even make it to 1989, though, as Dallas Green took the helm. In turn, Green was fired 110 games into the season and replaced by former Yankees shortstop Bucky Dent. Nevertheless, when the Yankees got off to their worst start in 70 years in 1990, Dent became an ex-manager even quicker than Green.

The turmoil caused by Steinbrenner's constant managerial changes clearly were not helping the Yankees on the field. Early in Steinbrenner's reign, many observers thought that there was a method to his madness and that Martin was a great short-term manager who could fire up the team. If one assumes that Martin would have worn the team out over the long haul, Steinbrenner's moves actually made some sense. Eventually, though, it became clear even to "The Boss" that he couldn't solve all the Yankees' problems simply by changing managers. When Stump Merrill was promoted from the New York farm system to replace Dent, everyone knew Merrill wasn't expected to take the club to the World Series, because the team didn't have that kind of talent anymore.

Merrill held the job for a season and a half before being replaced by Buck Showalter. Under Showalter, who lasted longer than any Yankees manager since Houk, the Yankees emerged as a young contender and returned to the newly expanded postseason in 1995. Showalter's intense style caused conflicts with the front office, however, and he was replaced by Joe Torre before 1996.

Under Torre, the Yankees embarked on a remarkable and historic run, winning four World Series in five seasons from 1996–2000. Torre led the Yankees to the postseason for 12 consecutive years, though he failed to win a World Series for the last seven years. Based on his spectacular record in the Bronx, Torre will almost certainly make it into the Hall of Fame as a manager whether he ever manages another big-league game after leaving the Yankees at the end of 2007.

Key to Manager's Register

In this section player-managers are designated with the years they both played *and* managed in bold since many player-managers eventually shifted to managing only.

Each manager's birth date is given. If the birth date is all that is listed beside the manager's name, it signifies that he was also a major league player. If a manager's full name, nickname, birth date and birthplace, etc., are listed, it means that the manager never played in the majors. For those skippers, their primary position as a minor league player is also shown at the end of their biographical info. **DNP** is shown instead of a position if they did not play in either the majors or the minors. Each manager's full career as a big-league skipper is included, showing jobs with other clubs before or after the Yankees.

The Finish column indicates how the team fared under the manager in the eight-team American League (1903–60), 10-team AL (1961–68), six-team AL East division (1969–76), seven-team division (1977–93), or five-team division (1994–present). A **t** in that column indicates a tie in the standings.

In the case of multiple managers for one season, the final position in the standings for each manager is given. In Gene Michael's 1982 entry, for example, *4t-5t-5* in this column indicates that the club was tied for fourth place when he took over, tied for fifth when he was replaced, and finished the year in fifth place. In the Mgr/Yr column for Michael, the *2/3* signifies that his stint was the second of three managers in '82 (in this case, Bob Lemon preceded him and Clyde King finished the season).

Symbols after the finish show if a team that finished first won one or more postseason series. A solid star (★) indicates the team won the World Series. A solid diamond (◆) means the team won the LSC but lost the World Series (1969–present). A hollow star (☆) indicates the team won the Division Series but lost the LCS (1995–present). A cross (†) indicates a wild card team. A solid triangle (▲) shows that the team was tied at the end of the regular season for first place and played a one-game playoff.

The plus minus column (**+/–**) indicates how many games the team won compared to how many the team was projected to win based on its run production. So, in 1997, the Yankees under Joe Torre ended up 4.5 games below their projection based on their runs scored and allowed. The following year, the Yanks played 3.7 games above their projection for Torre.

On the career line, the manager's lifetime seasons as a manager along with his won-lost record and winning percentage are added under **Total**. A manager's record for the Yankees' portion of his career is listed as **Team**. If he did not manage a team other than New York, then his Yankees numbers are merely listed as **Total**. If he managed just one year, there is no career line.

At the end of the Manager's Register is the year-by-year of all Yankees's managers in October, broken out into World Series, League Championship Series, and Division Series.

Yankees Manager Register

BERRA, YOGI B5.12.1925

YEAR	TM LG	W	L	PCT	FINISH	MGR/YR	+/-
1964	NY A	99	63	.611	1		1.7
1972	NY N e	83	73	.532	3		10.6
1973	NY N e	82	79	.509	1◆		-0.7
1974	NY N e	71	91	.438	5		-1.9
1975	NY N e	56	53	.514	3–3*t*	1/2	-0.0
1984	NY A e	87	75	.537	3		-2.0
1985	NY A e	6	10	.375	7–2	1/2	-3.7
Total	7	484	444	.522			4.0
Team	3	192	148	.565			-4.0

CHANCE, FRANK B9.9.1876

YEAR	TM LG	W	L	PCT	FINISH	MGR/YR	+/-
1913	NY A	57	94	.377	7		-3.6
1914	NY A	60	74	.448	7–6*t*	1/2	-5.7
Total	11	946	648	.593			20.4
Team	2	117	168	.411			-9.3

CHASE, HAL B2.13.1883

YEAR	TM LG	W	L	PCT	FINISH	MGR/YR	+/-
1910	NY A	10	4	.714	3–2	2/2	2.3
1911	NY A	76	76	.500	6		3.9
Total	2	86	80	.518			6.2

DENT, BUCKY B11.25.1951

YEAR	TM LG	W	L	PCT	FINISH	MGR/YR	+/-
1989	NY A e	18	22	.450	6–5	2/2	0.3
1990	NY A e	18	31	.367	7–7	1/2	-1.9
Total	2	36	53	.404			-1.6

DICKEY, BILL B6.6.1907

YEAR	TM LG	W	L	PCT	FINISH	MGR/YR	+/-
1946	NY A	57	48	.543	2–3–3	2/3	-5.4

DONOVAN, BILL B10.13.1876

YEAR	TM LG	W	L	PCT	FINISH	MGR/YR	+/-
1915	NY A	69	83	.454	5		-6.6
1916	NY A	80	74	.519	4		1.2
1917	NY A	71	82	.464	6		-1.6
1921	Phi N	25	62	.287	8–8	1/2	-2.3
Total	4	245	301	.449			-9.3
Team	3	220	239	.479			-7.0

ELBERFELD, KID B4.13.1875

YEAR	TM LG	W	L	PCT	FINISH	MGR/YR	+/-
1908	NY A	27	71	.276	6–8	2/2	-4.4

FLETCHER, ART B1.5.1885

YEAR	TM LG	W	L	PCT	FINISH	MGR/YR	+/-
1929	NY A	6	5	.545	2–2	2/2	-0.3
Total	5	237	383	.382			-4.0

GREEN, DALLAS B8.4.1934

YEAR	TM LG	W	L	PCT	FINISH	MGR/YR	+/-
1989	NY A e	56	65	.463	6–5	1/2	2.5
Total	8	454	478	.487			-5.6

GRIFFITH, CLARK B11.20.1869

YEAR	TM LG	W	L	PCT	FINISH	MGR/YR	+/-
1903	NY A	72	62	.537	4		4.4
1904	NY A	92	59	.609	2		8.5
1905	NY A	71	78	.477	6		0.2
1906	NY A	90	61	.596	2		4.0
1907	NY A	70	78	.473	5		2.4
1908	NY A	24	32	.429	6–8	1/2	6.0
Total	20	1491	1367	.522			24.9
Team	6	419	370	.531			25.5

HARRIS, BUCKY B11.8.1896

YEAR	TM LG	W	L	PCT	FINISH	MGR/YR	+/-
1947	NY A	97	57	.630	1★		-2.9
1948	NY A	94	60	.610	3		-4.6
Total	29	2157	2218	.493			-32.5
Team	2	191	117	.620			-7.5

HOUK, RALPH B8.9.1919

YEAR	TM LG	W	L	PCT	FINISH	MGR/YR	+/-
1961	NY A	109	53	.673	1★		6.3
1962	NY A	96	66	.593	1★		1.5
1963	NY A	104	57	.646	1		5.6
1966	NY A	66	73	.475	10–10	2/2	-3.4
1967	NY A	72	90	.444	9		2.2
1968	NY A	83	79	.512	5		1.4
1969	NY A e	80	81	.497	5		2.3
1970	NY A e	93	69	.574	2		4.8
1971	NY A e	82	80	.506	4		0.3
1972	NY A e	79	76	.510	4		-1.9
1973	NY A e	80	82	.494	4		-4.3
1974	Det A e	72	90	.444	6		6.2
1975	Det A e	57	102	.358	6		-0.3
1976	Det A e	74	87	.460	5		4.0
1977	Det A e	74	88	.457	4		-3.3
1978	Det A e	86	76	.531	5		-1.3
1981–1	Bos A e	30	26	.536	5		1.3
1981–2	Bos A e	29	23	.558	2*t*		1.3
1982	Bos A e	89	73	.549	3		4.0
1983	Bos A e	78	84	.481	6		2.0
1984	Bos A e	86	76	.531	4		0.6
Total	20	1619	1531	.514			29.0
Team	11	944	806	.539			14.8

HOWSER, DICK B5.14.1936

YEAR	TM LG	W	L	PCT	FINISH	MGR/YR	+/-
1978	NY A e	0	1	.000	3–4–1★▲	2/3	-0.6
1980	NY A e	103	59	.636	1		6.3
Total	8	507	425	.544			23.4
Team	2	103	60	.632			5.7

HUGGINS, MILLER B3.27.1878

YEAR	TM LG	W	L	PCT	FINISH	MGR/YR	+/-
1913	StL N	51	99	.340	8		-0.5
1914	StL N	81	72	.529	3		2.5
1915	StL N	72	81	.471	6		-3.3
1916	StL N	60	93	.392	7t		0.6
1917	StL N	82	70	.539	3		10.0
1918	NY A	60	63	.488	4		-3.4
1919	NY A	80	59	.576	3		2.7
1920	NY A	95	59	.617	3		-2.3
1921	NY A	98	55	.641	1		-0.4
1922	NY A	94	60	.610	1		2.9
1923	NY A	98	54	.645	1★		2.4
1924	NY A	89	63	.586	2		0.3
1925	NY A	69	85	.448	7		-1.4
1926	NY A	91	63	.591	1		1.3
1927	NY A	110	44	.714	1★		-2.4
1928	NY A	101	53	.656	1★		4.4
1929	NY A	82	61	.573	2–2	1/2	0.0
Total	17	1413	1134	.555			13.5
Team	12	1067	719	.597			4.1

KEANE, JOHNNY JOHN JOSEPH B11.3.1911
MO D1.6.1967 HOUSTON, TX BR/TR/5'10"/165(SS)

YEAR	TM LG	W	L	PCT	FINISH	MGR/YR	+/-
1961	StL N	47	33	.587	6–5	2/2	5.2
1962	StL N	84	78	.519	6		-8.1
1963	StL N	93	69	.574	2		-0.3
1964	StL N	93	69	.574	1★		5.5
1965	NY A	77	85	.475	6		-4.8
1966	NY A	4	16	.200	10–10	1/2	-6.0
Total	6	398	350	.532			-8.5
Team	2	81	101	.445			-10.8

KING, CLYDE B5.23.1924

YEAR	TM LG	W	L	PCT	FINISH	MGR/YR	+/-
1982	NY A e	29	33	.468	5*t*-5	3/3	-1.7
Total	5	234	229	.505			4.1

LEMON, BOB B9.22.1920

YEAR	TM LG	W	L	PCT	FINISH	MGR/YR	+/-
1970	KC A w	46	64	.418	5–4*t*	2/2	-2.3
1971	KC A w	85	76	.528	2		0.4
1972	KC A w	76	78	.494	4		-4.9
1977	Chi A w	90	72	.556	3		2.1
1978	Chi A w	34	40	.459	5–5	1/2	1.6
1978	NY A e	48	20	.706	4–1★▲	3/3	7.3
1979	NY A e	34	31	.523	4–4	1/2	-1.0
1981–2	NY A e	11	14	.440	4–6	2/2	-3.5
1982	NY A e	6	8	.429	4*t*-5	1/3	-0.9
Total	8	430	403	.516			-1.4
Team	3	88	59	.599			5.4

MARTIN, BILLY B5.16.1928

YEAR	TM LG	W	L	PCT	FINISH	MGR/YR	+/-
1969	Min A w	97	65	.599	1		-1.5
1971	Det A e	91	71	.562	2		4.2
1972	Det A e	86	70	.551	1		3.0
1973	Det A e	71	63	.530	3–3	1/2	6.8
1973	Tex A w	9	14	.391	6–6	3/3	0.7
1974	Tex A w	84	76	.525	2		4.8
1975	Tex A w	44	51	.463	4–3	1/2	-2.4
1975	NY A e	30	26	.536	3–3	2/2	-1.5
1976	NY A e	97	62	.610	1◆		1.3
1977	NY A e	100	62	.617	1★		1.1
1978	NY A e	52	42	.553	3–1★▲	1/3	-4.3
1979	NY A e	55	40	.579	4–4	2/2	3.8
1980	Oak A w	83	79	.512	2		-2.6
1981–1	Oak A w	37	23	.617	1☆		3.6
1981–2	Oak A w	27	22	.551	2		3.6
1982	Oak A w	68	94	.420	5		-0.4
1983	NY A e	91	71	.562	3		3.3
1985	NY A e	91	54	.628	7–2	2/2	2.6
1988	NY A e	40	28	.588	2–5	1/2	5.0
Total	16	1253	1013	.553			31.2
Team	8	556	385	.591			11.3

MCCARTHY, JOE JOSEPH VINCENT "MARSE JOE" B4.21.1887
PHILADELPHIA, PA D1.13.1978 BUFFALO, NY BR/TR/5'8.5"/190(2B)

YEAR	TM LG	W	L	PCT	FINISH	MGR/YR	+/-
1926	Chi N	82	72	.532	4		-3.3
1927	Chi N	85	68	.556	4		-0.3
1928	Chi N	91	63	.591	3		3.9
1929	Chi N	98	54	.645	1		1.9
1930	Chi N	86	64	.573	2–2	1/2	0.2
1931	NY A	94	59	.614	2		-9.3
1932	NY A	107	47	.695	1★		4.9
1933	NY A	91	59	.607	2		1.7
1934	NY A	94	60	.610	2		0.4
1935	NY A	89	60	.597	2		-3.4
1936	NY A	102	51	.667	1★		-3.9
1937	NY A	102	52	.662	1★		-3.5
1938	NY A	99	53	.651	1★		-0.5
1939	NY A	106	45	.702	1★		-8.5
1940	NY A	88	66	.571	3		-3.1
1941	NY A	101	53	.656	1★		4.5
1942	NY A	103	51	.669	1		-4.3
1943	NY A	98	56	.636	1★		7.4
1944	NY A	83	71	.539	3		0.1
1945	NY A	81	71	.533	4		-2.2
1946	NY A	22	13	.629	2–3	1/3	1.2
1948	Bos A	96	59	.619	2▲		1.2
1949	Bos A	96	58	.623	2		-2.6
1950	Bos A	31	28	.525	4–3	1/2	-5.9
Total	24	2125	1333	.615			-23.6
Team	16	1460	867	.627			-18.5

MERRILL, STUMP CARL HARRISON B2.25.1944
BRUNSWICK, ME BL/TR/5'8"/190(C)

YEAR	TM LG	W	L	PCT	FINISH	MGR/YR	+/-
1990	NY A e	49	64	.434	7–7	2/2	3.1
1991	NY A e	71	91	.438	5		0.3
Total	2	120	155	.436			3.4

MICHAEL, GENE B6.2.1938

YEAR	TM LG	W	L	PCT	FINISH	MGR/YR	+/-
1982	NY A e	44	42	.512	4*t*-5t-5	2/3	1.4
Total	4	206	200	.507			5.1

NEUN, JOHNNY B10.28.1900

YEAR	TM LG	W	L	PCT	FINISH	MGR/YR	+/-
1946	NY A	8	6	.571	3–3	3/3	-0.3
1947	Cin N	73	81	.474	5		3.3
1948	Cin N	44	56	.440	7–7	1/2	4.8
Total	3	125	143	.466			7.8

PECKINPAUGH, ROGER B2.5.1891

YEAR	TM LG	W	L	PCT	FINISH	MGR/YR	+/-
1914	NY A	10	10	.500	7–6*t*	2/2	0.2
Total	8	500	491	.505			9.5

PINIELLA, LOU B8.28.1943

YEAR	TM LG	W	L	PCT	FINISH	MGR/YR	+/-
1986	NY A e	90	72	.556	2		3.2
1987	NY A e	89	73	.549	4		5.1
1988	NY A e	45	48	.484	2–5	2/2	-2.9
Total	20	1604	1497	.517			-4.8
Team	3	224	193	.537			5.4

SHAWKEY, BOB B12.4.1890

YEAR	TM LG	W	L	PCT	FINISH	MGR/YR	+/-
1930	NY A	86	68	.558	3		-4.8

SHOWALTER, BUCK WILLIAM NATHANIEL B5.23.1956
DEFUNIAK SPRINGS, FL BL/TL/5'9"/195(1B)

YEAR	TM LG	W	L	PCT	FINISH	MGR/YR	+/-
1992	NY A e	76	86	.469	4*t*		-3.7
1993	NY A e	88	74	.543	2		1.2
1994	NY A e	70	43	.619	1		1.0
1995	NY A e	79	65	.549	2✣		1.2
1998	Ari N w	65	97	.401	5		-1.4
1999	Ari N w	100	62	.617	1		-3.3
2000	Ari N w	85	77	.525	3		0.3
2003	Tex A w	71	91	.438	4		2.9
2004	Tex A w	89	73	.549	3		1.8
2005	Tex A w	79	83	.488	3		-2.6
2006	Tex A w	80	82	.494	3		-5.8
Total	11	882	833	.514			-8.4
Team	4	313	268	.539			-0.3

STALLINGS, GEORGE B11.17.1867

YEAR	TM LG	W	L	PCT	FINISH	MGR/YR	+/-
1909	NY A	74	77	.490	5		-1.7
1910	NY A	78	59	.569	3–2	1/2	2.7
Total	13	879	898	.495			-6.6
Team	2	152	136	.528			1.0

STENGEL, CASEY B7.30.1890

YEAR	TM LG	W	L	PCT	FINISH	MGR/YR	+/-
1934	Bro N	71	81	.467	6		-0.6
1935	Bro N	70	83	.458	5		-1.1
1936	Bro N	67	87	.435	7		-1.0
1938	Bos N	77	75	.507	5		7.2
1939	Bos N	63	88	.417	7		-3.3
1940	Bos N	65	87	.428	7		1.2
1941	Bos N	62	92	.403	7		-1.8
1942	Bos N	59	89	.399	7		-1.0
1943	Bos N	47	60	.439	6–6	2/2	5.1
1949	NY A	97	57	.630	1★		1.3
1950	NY A	98	56	.636	1★		0.2
1951	NY A	98	56	.636	1★		3.5
1952	NY A	95	59	.617	1★		0.3
1953	NY A	99	52	.656	1★		-2.0
1954	NY A	103	51	.669	2		1.6
1955	NY A	96	58	.623	1		-0.7
1956	NY A	97	57	.630	1★		-1.8
1957	NY A	98	56	.636	1		1.2
1958	NY A	92	62	.597	1★		-3.6
1959	NY A	79	75	.513	3		-2.1
1960	NY A	97	57	.630	1		8.0
1962	NY N	40	120	.250	10		-8.1
1963	NY N	51	111	.315	10		-0.8

Managers & Coaches

YEAR	TM LG	W	L	PCT	FINISH	MGR/YR	+/-
1964	NY N	53	109	.327	10		-6.4
1965	NY N	31	64	.326	10–10	1/2	-0.1
Total	25	1905	1842	.508			-4.8
Team	12	1149	696	.623			5.9

TORRE, JOE B7.18.1940

YEAR	TM LG	W	L	PCT	FINISH	MGR/YR	+/-
1977	NY N	49	68	.419	6–6	2/2	-3.6
1978	NY N e	66	96	.407	6		-6.2
1979	NY N e	63	99	.389	6		-6.0
1980	NY N e	67	95	.414	5		-4.4
1981–1	NY N e	17	34	.333	5		-1.3
1981–2	NY N e	24	28	.462	4		-1.3
1982	Atl N w	89	73	.549	1		4.3
1983	Atl N w	88	74	.543	2		-3.9
1984	Atl N w	80	82	.494	2t		1.4
1990	StL N e	24	34	.414	6–6	3/3	-1.2
1991	StL N e	84	78	.519	2		2.7
1992	StL N e	83	79	.512	3		-0.9
1993	StL N e	87	75	.537	3		4.6
1994	StL N c	53	61	.465	3t		4.1
1995	StL N c	20	27	.426	4–4	1/2	-0.3
1996	NY A e	92	70	.568	1★		3.1
1997	NY A e	96	66	.593	2✜		-4.5
1998	NY A e	114	48	.704	1★		3.7
1999	NY A e	77	49	.611	1–1★	2/2	1.6
2000	NY A e	87	74	.540	1★		1.2
2001	NY A e	95	65	.594	1◆		6.1
2002	NY A e	103	58	.640	1		3.4
2003	NY A e	101	61	.623	1◆		4.5
2004	NY A e	101	61	.623	1☆		11.8
2005	NY A e	95	67	.586	1		4.9
2006	NY A e	97	65	.599	1		0.9
2007	NY A e	94	68	.580	2✜		-4.5
Total	26	2046	1755	.538			20.5
Team	12	1152	752	.605			32.2

VIRDON, BILL B6.9.1931

YEAR	TM LG	W	L	PCT	FINISH	MGR/YR	+/-
1974	NY A e	89	73	.549	2		2.9
1975	NY A e	53	51	.510	3–3	1/2	-5.4
Total	13	995	921	.519			-4.5
Team	2	142	124	.534			-2.5

WOLVERTON, HARRY B12.6.1873

YEAR	TM LG	W	L	PCT	FINISH	MGR/YR	+/-
1912	NY A	50	102	.329	8		-5.5

ZIMMER, DON B1.17.1931

YEAR	TM LG	W	L	PCT	FINISH	MGR/YR	+/-
1999	NY A e	21	15	.583	1–1	1/2	-0.6
Total	14	906	873	.509			17.4

Yankees Managers in the Postseason

		WS		ALCS		ALDS	
MANAGER	YEAR	W	L	W	L	W	L
Miller Huggins	1921	3	5				
Miller Huggins	1922	0	4				
Miller Huggins	1923	4	2				
Miller Huggins	1926	3	4				
Miller Huggins	1927	4	0				
Miller Huggins	1928	4	0				
Miller Huggins	*total*	*18*	*15*				
Joe McCarthy	1932	4	0				
Joe McCarthy	1936	4	2				
Joe McCarthy	1937	4	1				
Joe McCarthy	1938	4	0				
Joe McCarthy	1939	4	0				
Joe McCarthy	1941	4	1				
Joe McCarthy	1942	1	4				
Joe McCarthy	1943	4	1				
Joe McCarthy	*total*	*29*	*9*				
Bucky Harris	1947	4	3				
Casey Stengel	1949	4	1				
Casey Stengel	1950	4	0				
Casey Stengel	1951	4	2				
Casey Stengel	1952	4	3				
Casey Stengel	1953	4	2				
Casey Stengel	1955	3	4				
Casey Stengel	1956	4	3				
Casey Stengel	1957	3	4				
Casey Stengel	1958	4	3				
Casey Stengel	1960	3	4				
Casey Stengel	*total*	*37*	*26*				

		WS		ALCS		ALDS	
MANAGER	YEAR	W	L	W	L	W	L
Ralph Houk	1961	4	1				
Ralph Houk	1962	4	3				
Ralph Houk	1963	0	4				
Ralph Houk	*total*	*8*	*8*				
Yogi Berra	1964	3	4				
Billy Martin	1976	0	4	3	2		
Billy Martin	1977	4	2	3	2		
Billy Martin	*total*	*4*	*6*	*6*	*4*		
Bob Lemon	1978	4	2	3	1		
Bob Lemon	1981	2	4	3	0		
Bob Lemon	*total*	*6*	*6*	*6*	*1*		
Dick Howser	1980			0	3		
Buck Showalter	1995					2	3
Joe Torre	1996	4	2	4	1	3	1
Joe Torre	1997					2	3
Joe Torre	1998	4	0	4	2	3	0
Joe Torre	1999	4	0	4	1	3	0
Joe Torre	2000	4	1	4	2	3	2
Joe Torre	2001	3	4	4	1	3	2
Joe Torre	2002					1	3
Joe Torre	2003	2	4	4	3	3	1
Joe Torre	2004			3	4	3	1
Joe Torre	2005					2	3
Joe Torre	2006					1	3
Joe Torre	2007					1	3
Joe Torre	*total*	*21*	*11*	*27*	*14*	*28*	*22*

Yankees Coaches

Since baseball was first played it has been apparent that every team needs a leader. Given the permutations that can be made in creating a lineup, a manager is required to lay down the law, if not fill out the lineup card. As the responsibility, accountability, and salaries of major league managers have increased over the years, managers have been helped by an increasing array of assistants and instructors. Delegating responsibility to them, in theory, serves the greater good of the team, even if it is not always good for the manager himself.

Coaches, like many others in the game, have become more specialized over the years. Whereas teams once had a couple of coaches to help out with the pitchers and to coach at first and third, teams now have six coaches on a major league staff: bench, hitting and pitching, first base and third base, and bullpen. The bench coach is the latest power coaching spot, a sounding board for the manager on in-game decisions and, oftentimes, a devil's advocate off the field.

The history of the game is filled with stories of old friends who, as coaches, turn into adversaries and speak poorly of the manager to the front office. While these machinations may lead to the manager's dismissal, it can also often lead to the coach's firing as well. Other times, the front office—reluctant to fire the manager—will fire one or more coaches to appease the fans or the media.

Paradoxically, as the number of coaches has grown in recent years with the addition of bench coaches and bullpen coaches, the ability of many coaches to demand that the ballplayers listen to their advice has declined. On many teams, coaches now have to wait for superstars with enormous, long-term contracts to ask for their help.

Even though big-league coaches are mostly anonymous and frequently underpaid—the annual distributions that coaches receive from the Players Association for their share of licensing revenues are often greater than their salaries—coaching at the major league level is still good work if you can find it.

Coaches in this section are shown with a minus sign if they left during the middle of a season. Likewise, a plus sign is placed next to a coach's name if he is added to the staff after the season begins. Coaches with **+/–** next to their name were both hired and fired in the middle of the same season. Yankees coaches who stepped directly from the coaching box to the manager's chair are not fitted with minus signs because they remained on the coaching staff, even if their promotion came with its own office and had their new position stenciled on the door.

1909
Duke Farrell

1911
Duke Farrell

1914
Tom Daly

1915
Duke Farrell

1916
Duke Farrell
Germany Schaefer

1917
Duke Farrell

1918
Paddy O'Connor

1919
Paddy O'Connor

1920
Paddy O'Connor
Charley O'Leary

1921
Paddy O'Connor -
Charley O'Leary
Frank Roth

1922
Charley O'Leary
Frank Roth

1923
Charley O'Leary

1924
Charley O'Leary

1925
Fred Merkle +
Charley O'Leary
Hooks Wiltse

1926
Fred Merkle
Charley O'Leary

1927
Art Fletcher
Charley O'Leary

1928
Art Fletcher
Charley O'Leary

1929
Art Fletcher
Harry Mathews
Charley O'Leary
Bob Shawkey

1930
Art Fletcher
Charley O'Leary

1931
Jimmy Burke
Art Fletcher

1932
Jimmy Burke
Art Fletcher
Cy Perkins

1933
Jimmy Burke
Art Fletcher
Cy Perkins

1934
Art Fletcher
Johnny Schulte +
Joe Sewell

1935
Art Fletcher
Johnny Schulte
Joe Sewell

1936
Earle Combs
Art Fletcher
Johnny Schulte

1937
Earle Combs
Art Fletcher
Johnny Schulte

1938
Earle Combs
Art Fletcher
Johnny Schulte

1939
Earle Combs
Art Fletcher
Johnny Schulte

1940
Earle Combs
Art Fletcher
Johnny Schulte

1941
Earle Combs
Art Fletcher
Johnny Schulte

1942
Earle Combs
Art Fletcher
Paul Schreiber
Johnny Schulte

1943
Earle Combs
Art Fletcher
Johnny Schulte

1944
Earle Combs
Art Fletcher
Johnny Neun
Johnny Schulte

1945
Art Fletcher
Johnny Neun
Johnny Schulte

1946
Johnny Neun
Red Rolfe
Johnny Schulte

1947
Red Corriden
Frankie Crosetti
Chuck Dressen
Johnny Schulte

1948
Red Corriden
Frankie Crosetti
Chuck Dressen
Johnny Schulte

1949
Frankie Crosetti
Bill Dickey
Jim Turner

1950
Frankie Crosetti
Bill Dickey
Jim Turner

1951
Frankie Crosetti
Bill Dickey
Tommy Henrich
Jim Turner

1952
Frankie Crosetti
Bill Dickey
Jim Turner

1953
Frankie Crosetti
Bill Dickey
Jim Turner

1954
Frankie Crosetti
Bill Dickey
Ralph Houk
Jim Turner

1955
Frankie Crosetti
Bill Dickey
Jim Turner

1956
Frankie Crosetti
Bill Dickey
Jim Turner

1957
Frankie Crosetti
Bill Dickey -
Randy Gumpert +
Charlie Keller +
Jim Turner

1958
Frankie Crosetti
Ralph Houk
Jim Turner

1959
Frankie Crosetti
Ralph Houk
Charlie Keller +/-
Jim Turner

1960
Frankie Crosetti
Bill Dickey
Jim Hegan +
Ralph Houk
Ed Lopat

1961
Frankie Crosetti
Jim Hegan
Wally Moses
Johnny Sain
Earl Torgeson +

1962
Frankie Crosetti
Jim Hegan
Wally Moses
Johnny Sain

1963
Yogi Berra +
Frankie Crosetti
Jim Hegan
Dale Long +
Johnny Sain

1964
Frankie Crosetti
Whitey Ford
Jim Gleeson
Jim Hegan

1965
Vern Benson
Frankie Crosetti
Cot Deal
Jim Hegan

1966
Vern Benson -
Frankie Crosetti
Jim Hegan
Wally Moses +
Jim Turner

1967
Loren Babe
Frankie Crosetti
Jim Hegan
Jim Turner

1968
Frankie Crosetti
Whitey Ford
Jim Hegan
Jim Turner

1969
Jim Hegan
Elston Howard
Dick Howser
Jim Turner

1970
Jim Hegan
Elston Howard
Dick Howser
Mickey Mantle +
Jim Turner

1971
Jim Hegan
Elston Howard
Dick Howser
Jim Turner

1972
Jim Hegan
Elston Howard
Dick Howser
Jim Turner

1973
Jim Hegan
Elston Howard
Dick Howser
Jim Turner

1974
Whitey Ford
Elston Howard
Dick Howser
Mel Wright

1975
Cloyd Boyer +
Whitey Ford -
Elston Howard
Dick Howser
Mel Wright

1976
Yogi Berra
Elston Howard
Dick Howser
Bob Lemon
Gene Michael +

1977
Yogi Berra
Cloyd Boyer
Bobby Cox
Art Fowler +
Elston Howard
Dick Howser
Gene Michael -

1978
Yogi Berra
Art Fowler
Elston Howard
Dick Howser
Clyde King +
Gene Michael

1979
Yogi Berra
Mike Ferraro
Art Fowler
Jim Hegan
Elston Howard
Charley Lau
Tom Morgan -
Jeff Torborg +

1980
Yogi Berra
Mike Ferraro
Jim Hegan
Charley Lau
Jeff Torborg
Stan Williams

1981
Joe Altobelli
Yogi Berra
Mike Ferraro
Clyde King +
Charley Lau
Jeff Torborg
Jerry Walker +
Stan Williams -

1982
Joe Altobelli
Yogi Berra
Sammy Ellis +
Mike Ferraro
Clyde King +/-
Joe Pepitone +
Jeff Torborg
Mickey Vernon
Jerry Walker -
Stan Williams +/-

1983
Yogi Berra
Sammy Ellis +
Art Fowler -
Jeff Torborg
Lee Walls +
Roy White
Don Zimmer

1984
Mark Connor +
Sammy Ellis -
Doug Holmquist +
Jerry McNertney -
Gene Michael
Lou Piniella +
Jeff Torborg
Roy White -

1985
Mark Connor -
Doug Holmquist +
Willie Horton +
Stump Merrill -
Gene Michael
Bill Monbouquette +
Lou Piniella
Jeff Torborg

1986
Joe Altobelli
Mark Connor +
Sammy Ellis -
Stump Merrill
Gene Michael -
Jeff Torborg
Roy White
Don Zimmer +

1987
Mark Connor
Mike Ferraro
Stump Merrill
Jeff Torborg
Jay Ward
Stan Williams

1988
Clete Boyer -
Chris Chambliss -
Mike Ferraro
Art Fowler -
Clyde King +
Gene Michael +
George Mitterwald -
Jeff Torborg
Stan Williams +

1989
Billy Connors
Pat Corrales -
Lee Elia -
Mike Ferraro +
Charlie Fox -
Frank Howard -
Gene Michael +
John Stearns
Champ Summers +

1990
Mark Connor
Billy Connors
Darrell Evans +
Mike Ferraro
Buck Showalter +
Joe Sparks -
Champ Summers -

1991
Mark Connor
Mike Ferraro
Marc Hill
Frank Howard
Graig Nettles
Buck Showalter

1992
Clete Boyer
Tony Cloninger
Mark Connor
Frank Howard
Russ Meyer
Ed Napoleon

1993
Clete Boyer
Tony Cloninger
Mark Connor
Rick Down
Frank Howard
Ed Napoleon

1994
Clete Boyer
Brian Butterfield
Tony Cloninger
Billy Connors
Rick Down
Willie Randolph

1995
Brian Butterfield
Tony Cloninger
Billy Connors
Nardi Contreras +
Rick Down
Willie Randolph

1996
Jose Cardenal
Chris Chambliss
Tony Cloninger
Willie Randolph
Mel Stottlemyre
Don Zimmer

1997
Jose Cardenal
Chris Chambliss
Tony Cloninger
Willie Randolph
Mel Stottlemyre
Don Zimmer

1998
Jose Cardenal
Chris Chambliss
Tony Cloninger
Willie Randolph
Mel Stottlemyre
Don Zimmer

1999
Jose Cardenal
Chris Chambliss
Tony Cloninger
Willie Randolph
Mel Stottlemyre
Don Zimmer

2000
Chris Chambliss
Tony Cloninger
Billy Connors +
Lee Mazzilli
Willie Randolph
Mel Stottlemyre -
Don Zimmer

2001
Tony Cloninger
Gary Denbo
Lee Mazzilli
Willie Randolph
Mel Stottlemyre
Don Zimmer

2002
Rick Down
Lee Mazzilli
Rich Monteleone
Willie Randolph
Mel Stottlemyre
Don Zimmer

2003
Rick Down
Lee Mazzilli
Rich Monteleone
Willie Randolph
Mel Stottlemyre
Don Zimmer

2004
Don Mattingly
Rich Monteleone
Willie Randolph
Luis Sojo
Mel Stottlemyre
Roy White

2005
Joe Girardi
Don Mattingly
Rich Monteleone
Luis Sojo
Mel Stottlemyre
Roy White

2006
Larry Bowa
Ron Guidry
Joe Kerrigan
Don Mattingly
Lee Mazzilli
Tony Pena

2007
Larry Bowa
Ron Guidry
Joe Kerrigan
Kevin Long
Don Mattingly
Tony Pena

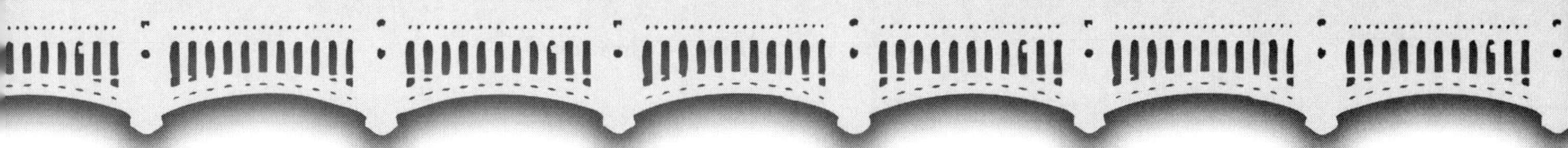

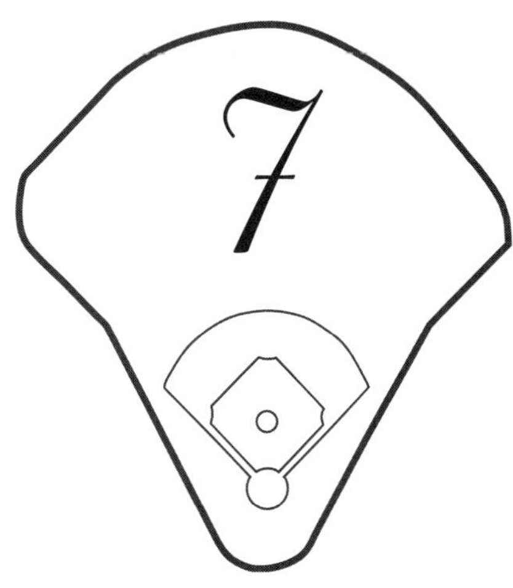

Yankees Executives & Broadcasters

WHILE THERE HAVE BEEN EIGHT other owners or ownership groups in Yankees history, none has had the import or influence of the current owner: George Steinbrenner, colloquially known as "The Boss." *Not* the Tammany Hall insiders Frank Farrell and Bill Devery, who bought the bankrupt franchise from the two-year–old American League and moved it from Baltimore to New York in 1903. *Not* Jacob Rupert, who bought the team with Colonel William Tillinghast in 1915 and who would solely finance the building of Yankee Stadium as well as the club's first dynasty. *Not* Dan Topping and Del Webb, who oversaw the club's glory days that spanned the post-World War II era to the collapse of the team as a national power in the mid-1960s. *Certainly not* CBS, the clueless network that paid top dollar for a soon-to-be second-division club.

Steinbrenner bought the club for an incredibly low price—the $10 million he paid for the club in 1973 was less than the annual salaries of 11 of his players in 2007—and has reaped tremendous profits. His Yankees are beamed live to Japan and followed around the world. Through his broadcast entity, the YES Network, the Yankees' story can be viewed 24–7: not only the games, but also the Steinbrennerian spin on the team's history, present, and future.

Though his ownership hasn't been free of interruptions, Steinbrenner long ago gained the distinction as the longest-running owner in franchise history. Less than two years after purchasing the Yankees, however, Steinbrenner pleaded guilty to illegal campaign contributions and, as a result, was suspended from the game for two years by Commissioner Bowie Kuhn. That suspension began on November 27, 1974.

Patrick Cunningham (the team's general counsel) and Gabe Paul (the general manager and a minority owner) were left in charge of the franchise. Steinbrenner clearly did not distance himself from the running of the franchise as much as the commissioner's office required, but his suspension nevertheless was cut short as a result of "good behavior" as of March 1, 1975. A decade and a half later, Steinbrenner found himself in deep trouble again after paying Howard Spira [no relation to the managing editor of this book] $40,000 to supply him with dirt on Dave Winfield, with whom Steinbrenner had been feuding in public and in court. Commissioner Fay Vincent was ready to suspend Steinbrenner again, but "The Boss"—evidently wary of being suspended because it might result in the loss of his position on the U.S. Olympic Committee—volunteered instead to go onto the Permanently Ineligible List. Even before Steinbrenner was placed on the list on October 20, 1990, his deal with Vincent started to turn sour.

Steinbrenner wanted his son Hank to replace him as general partner of the Yankees but Hank, unsure about wanting the job and uncomfortable about the approval process, declined his father's nomination. Steinbrenner then endorsed his associate, Leonard Kleinman, but Vincent decided that Kleinman was not an option because he was still under investigation for his own role in the Spira affair. Finally, Steinbrenner unexpectedly endorsed Robert Nederlander, a member of one of New York's most prominent theatrical families and a minority owner of the Yankees. Nederlander was quickly approved as the new general partner, and Steinbrenner began his exile from baseball.

However, "The Boss" quickly realized that he had made a serious mistake. During his suspension in the mid-1970s, Steinbrenner was still significantly involved in his other businesses. By the 1990s, though, he had made the Yankees his life. In addition, Vincent had taken steps to ensure that Steinbrenner couldn't ignore the rules and interfere with the Yankees' day-to-day operations as he had during his suspension under Kuhn. Very quickly lawsuits began flying around and Steinbrenner started sniping publicly about mistakes being made by the new Yankees' management. By the end of 1991, Nederlander had had enough and stepped down as managing partner. Steinbrenner nominated Daniel McCarthy to replace Nederlander, but McCarthy had been involved in a lawsuit against baseball and as a result and was not approved by the commissioner's office. The Yankees went months without a permanent general partner before Steinbrenner nominated his son-in-law, Joseph Molloy, who was quickly approved by major league owners on April 8, 1992.

By this time, Steinbrenner apparently realized that his attempts to get back into baseball were getting him nowhere, so he switched tactics and became far more conciliatory. Vincent told Steinbrenner that he'd be given an opportunity to get back into the game if he got rid of all the lawsuits that had been initiated by various parties at "The Boss's" behest. That proved easier said than done, but Steinbrenner eventually coaxed—and paid—all his erstwhile allies to drop their legal proceedings. On July 24, 1992, Fay Vincent announced that Steinbrenner would be allowed to return to baseball 30 months after he had left. So on March 1, 1993, Steinbrenner was finally reinstated. By then, the other owners had forced out Vincent, and Milwaukee Brewers owner Bud Selig was acting as commissioner.

Though Steinbrenner clearly took back full control of the Yankees at the end of his second suspension, he has never reclaimed the title of general partner. Another of George's sons-in-law, Steve Swindal, was made a general partner in the mid-1990s. Steinbrenner's son Hal has also been appointed a general partner and, since Swindal divorced Steinbrenner's daughter, it is Hal who has emerged as the general partner representing the Yankees.

Meanwhile, the Yankees' corporate structure has undergone major changes as a result of a 1999 merger with the New Jersey Nets, forming YankeeNets. Five years later, the 2004 sale of the Nets left the Yankees and the YES Network to form Yankee Global Enterprises. Steinbrenner remains today in charge of the Yankees through this parent company. Nevertheless, with "The Boss" aging and somewhat withdrawn from the public eye, and with no official succession plan, it is not clear how long the Steinbrenner family will keep control of the Yankees.

FRANK J. FARRELL AND WILLIAM S. "BILL" DEVERY
$18,000 JANUARY 9, 1903–JANUARY 29, 1915

Farrell owned 75 percent of the club

Two unscrupulous Tammany Hall figures who were both incompetent and corrupt, they bought the remains of the Baltimore Orioles franchise and moved it to New York

COL. JACOB "JAKE" RUPPERT JR. AND COL. TILLINGHAST L'HOMMEDIEU HUSTON
$460,000 JANUARY 29, 1915–MAY 21, 1922

After Huston enlisted in the war effort in early 1917, Ruppert assumed control of the club and never gave it up

COL. JACOB "JAKE" RUPPERT JR.
$1.5 MILLION MAY 21, 1922–JANUARY 13, 1939

JACOB RUPPERT ESTATE (HELEN HOLLERAN, RUTH MCGUIRE, AND HELEN WEYANT)
JANUARY 13, 1939–FEBRUARY 21, 1945

Four trustees had to unanimously approve any sale: Edward G. Barrow, George E. Ruppert, H. Garrison Silleck Jr. and Byron Clark Jr.

DAN TOPPING, DEL WEBB, AND LARRY MACPHAIL
$2.8 MILLION FEBRUARY 21, 1945–OCTOBER 1947

$2.5 million for Rupert's 86.9 percent of the club and $300,000 for Barrow's 10 percent

George E. Ruppert, Jacob's brother, held on to 3.1 percent of the team

DAN TOPPING AND DEL WEBB
OCTOBER 1947–NOVEMBER 2, 1964

Reportedly paid $1.5 million to buy out MacPhail

COLUMBIA BROADCASTING SYSTEM
$11.2 MILLION FOR 80% NOVEMBER 2, 1964–JANUARY 3, 1973

At time of sale, Webb and Topping each held on to 10 percent of the club. Webb sold out to CBS on March 1, 1965 for $1.2 million. Topping held on to his 10 percent until CBS bought him out for a similar amount on September 19; 1966; Topping had stayed on as team President until then as well

Michael Burke was CBS's liaison to baseball after Dan Topping stepped down

GEORGE STEINBRENNER
$10 MILLION JANUARY 3, 1973–

Through their investment firm Henry Crown and Company, Chicago's Crown family is by far the second biggest shareholder in the Yankees with 12%

There are conflicting reports whether Michael Burke was a co-general partner during the first four months of Steinbrenner's reign

Yankees General Managers

The first general manager in baseball history was the Yankee's Ed Barrow. Barrow was hired in 1920 as the club's business manager but, while Barrow did handle a lot of financial matters for the Yankees, his main contribution to the franchise was his astute handling of player personnel. Before Barrow, such matters had typically been taken care of by the team's owner—who often had little knowledge of the game—or the team's on-field manager—who had to balance the requirements of two different jobs that often required two different mindsets.

Barrow turned out to be the final piece of a dynastic puzzle for Jacob Ruppert's Yankees. Ruppert had hired his manager, Miller Huggins, several years earlier, and had just recently acquired the superstar player he needed from the Red Sox in Babe Ruth. Barrow was a shrewd judge of talent and, in the years following his arrival, made numerous trades that would boost the Yankees' fortunes for years to come. Many of Barrow's early trades now appear to be steals for the Yankees, but few saw them that way when they were made.

Barrow ran the Yankees for 25 years until Larry MacPhail purchased the club along with Dan Topping and Del Webb and installed himself as the general manager. MacPhail successfully put the Yankees back together after World War II, resulting in a World Series victory in 1947. Nevertheless, MacPhail's problems with alcohol and his erratic behavior led to a quick exit after that world championship. His replacement was George Weiss, who had been in line to succeed Barrow before the club was sold.

Under Weiss, the Yankees achieved their greatest success, dominating the National Pastime in the 1950s and early 1960s like no team before or since. Weiss was pushed out after the 1960 season, however, supposedly because he had reached 65 years of age, which had suddenly became the Yankees' official retirement age. In reality, the owners wanted new blood, so they hired longtime baseball executive Roy Hamey to replace Weiss.

When Weiss left, it was hard to imagine that the Yankees' blueprint wouldn't continue to keep the team on top of the league for decades to come. In reality, several issues had surfaced while Weiss was GM—problems that would hurt the team badly in the following decade. For one thing, the Yankees didn't embrace integration quickly. They escaped the consequences of their prejudice for 15 years or so while many of the other AL clubs also dragged their feet. By the mid-1960s, though, the Yankees had fallen behind other American League franchises in integrating as well, allowing the league to become competitive again.

Meanwhile, co-owners Dan Topping and Del Webb had focused more on maximizing the Yankees' profit than securing the Yankees' future. As a result, when Topping and Webb sold out to CBS in 1964, they sold a franchise that was in far worse shape than the team's recent records had indicated.

After Hamey retired in 1963, manager Ralph Houk stepped up to the front office to become the new GM. The Yankees won the World Series in Houk's first season as GM, but he soon found himself in charge of an organization that was in deep decline. Unable to right the ship from the front office, Houk resigned in May 1966 to return to the dugout. Lee MacPhail, son of the former Yankees' co-owner/GM, was brought in to replace Houk in the fall of that year. MacPhail was never quite able to return the club to October glory, but he did turn the Yankees organization in the right direction. He remained as general manager until he became the president of the American League at the end of 1974.

Enter George Steinbrenner as the new owner in 1974. Despite his famous declaration, "I won't be active in the day-to-day operations of the club at all. I can't spread myself so thin. I've got enough headaches with my shipping company," the job of Yankees general managers would never be the same thereafter.

Steinbrenner's first hire as GM, Gabe Paul, actually was given a significant amount of latitude and was able to make many deals that played an important role in rebuilding the Yankees. But once Paul left to become president of the Cleveland Indians in 1978, things changed dramatically. Over the next 13 years, GMs in the Bronx would come and go at a rate the staid old game had never seen before. At some times, there were two official general managers while, at other times, there didn't seem to be anyone with real authority. General managers saw their influence in the organization rise and fall unpredictably, depending on Steinbrenner's moods and the Yankees' daily fortunes. Sometimes the identity of the person in charge of the organization seemed to change on a day-to-day basis. It could be argued that "The Boss" was really his own general manager the whole time, but the situation wasn't quite that simple.

In 1990, Steinbrenner agreed to remove himself from the day-to-day operations of the Yankees after baseball Commissioner Fay Vincent threatened to suspend him for two years as a result of Steinbrenner paying someone to dig up dirt on Dave Winfield. Gene Michael was appointed as the new GM just before Steinbrenner began his exile. As a result of Steinbrenner's absence, Michael had the opportunity to run the club as he thought it should be run; so, instead of having to constantly implement short-term fixes in order to appease "The Boss", Michael was able to build for the long term. Impatient as always, Steinbrenner made it clear that he was displeased with what Michael was doing because the results on the field initially weren't improving, but this time Steinbrenner did not have the power to change GMs.

Steinbrenner soon realized that his self-imposed sentence had been a mistake, but no one in Major League Baseball was particularly sympathetic. It took several years for Steinbrenner to convince Commissioner Fay Vincent that he should be allowed to return to the Yankees. After Steinbrenner's return, he offered to keep Michael as the GM only with a major pay cut, so Michael turned down the offer and took a scouting job. Many people in the Yankees' organization today credit Michael more than anyone else for the team's resounding success over the past decade, and so Michael retains quite a bit of influence in the organization despite no longer being in the public eye.

Michael's successor was Bob Watson, who stayed for several years until he retired for health reasons. Brian Cashman replaced Watson, becoming the youngest GM in baseball history to that point. Though Cashman quickly earned a high level of respect around the game as a result of his knowledge and hard work, he was not given the typical authority handed to most general managers for most of his first decade on the job. With Steinbrenner back in the saddle and quick to interfere, Cashman found himself barely consulted on some major personnel decisions—oftentimes these moves seemed to be decided by Steinbrenner's staff in Tampa and not by the Yankees' front office in New York.

In 2005, however, Cashman's leverage increased greatly when his contract was set to expire. The much sought-after young executive made it clear that he would be open to offers from other clubs if the Yankees didn't accede to his demands, and Cashman was able to extract from Steinbrenner a contractual commitment finally giving Cashman the autonomy of a traditional GM.

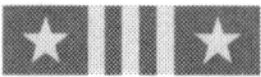

ED BARROW

EDWARD GRANT BARROW MAY 5, 1920–FEBUARY 21, 1945 TSN: 1937, 1941

Originally hired as business manager, but became the majors' first true general manager; generally given the most credit for building the Yankees into baseball's dominant franchise

Reason for Leaving: New owners brought in their own general manager in Larry MacPahil; Barrow was appointed the head of the board of directors

LARRY MACPHAIL

LELAND STANFORD MACPHAIL SR. FEBUARY 21, 1945–OCTOBER 6, 1947

Modernized the Yankees and Yankee Stadium

Reason for Leaving: A drunk MacPhail unexpectedly announced his resignation while celebrating the Yankees' World Series victory immediately after the deciding game; Topping and Webb were only too happy to accept the controversial and somewhat out-of-control MacPhail's resignation

GEORGE WEISS

GEORGE MARTIN WEISS OCTOBER 7, 1947–NOVEMBER 15, 1960 TSN: 1950–52, 1960

Joined the Yankees organization in 1932; served as MacPhail's assistant; president of the Mets from 1962–66.

Reason for Leaving: Was pushed aside to advisory position because he hit team age limit of 65

ROY HAMEY

H. ROY HAMEY NOVEMBER 3, 1960–OCTOBER 22, 1963

Hamey started working in the Yankees organization in 1934; left twice to become the GM of other teams (first the Pirates and later the Phillies), but returned to the Yankees after he lost those jobs; later briefly ran the Seattle Pilots

Reason for Leaving: Stepped down for health reasons and moved to advisory position

RALPH HOUK

RALPH GEORGE "MAJOR" HOUK OCTOBER 22, 1963–MAY 6, 1966

Manged the Yankees through 1973 and later managed the Tigers for 5 years and the Red Sox for 4 years

Reason for Leaving: Returned to field manager; request to continue with both jobs was turned down

DAN TOPPING JR.

DANIEL R. TOPPING JR. MAY 7, 1966–OCTOBER 13, 1966

Figurehead, though his father had tried to groom him for more; Houk was still making most player personnel decisions during Jr's term as GM

Reason for Leaving: Team president's son only took on role until a new permanent GM could be found

LEE MACPHAIL

LELAND STANFORD MACPHAIL JR. OCTOBER 13, 1966–DECEMBER 31, 1974

Larry's son, Andy's father

Reason for Leaving: Became president of the American League

TAL SMITH

TALBOT M. SMITH JANUARY 1, 1974–AUGUST 7, 1975

Was hired away from Houston after a decade as executive; protégé of Gabe Paul

Reason for Leaving: Left to become GM of the Astros

GABE PAUL

GABRIEL H. PAUL JANUARY 1, 1974–JANUARY 1, 1978 TSN: 1974

Top executive in Reds, Colt 45s, Yankees and Indians front offices for almost four decades; was minority owner in Yankees while GM

Reason for Leaving: Left to return home to Cleveland and become GM of the Indians

AL ROSEN

ALBERT LEONARD "FLIP" ROSEN JANUARY 1, 1978–JULY 19, 1979

The "Hebrew Hammer" was probably the best player to ever serve as Yankees GM (though Bob Watson is close); went on to spend 12 years as the GM of first the Astros and then the Giants; Was already minority owner in Yankees when he was hired by Steinbrenner

Reason for Leaving: Left because his influence had diminished as a result of battles with Billy Martin

CEDRIC TALLIS

JANUARY 1, 1978–NOVEMBER 1, 1979

Served as the GM of the Royals from the team's inception through mid-1974.

Reason for Leaving: Wanted to take a lesser role in organization so he could return home to Kansas City, and was shifted to the position of vice-president of baseball operations. Repeatedly tried to extricate himself from playing an important role with the Yankees but was coaxed into staying on as a stabilizing force until finally leaving permanently on September 23, 1983 to join a group trying to bring major league baseball to Tampa Bay

GENE MICHAEL

EUGENE RICHARD "STICK" MICHAEL NOVEMBER 1, 1979–NOVEMBER 21, 1981

Former player and coach for Yankees

Reason for Leaving: Became Yankees' field manager

BILL BERGESCH

LOUIS WILLIAM BERGESCH NOVEMBER 21, 1981–SEPTEMBER 23, 1983

Original Mets scouting director; returned to baseball as director of scouting for Yankees in 1978 before becoming vice president and assistant GM

Reason for Leaving: Bergesch had never been formally made the general manager; he took on the role by default when Michael became manager; Bergesch's official position with the Yankees did not change when Cook was hired, though Bergesch did leave to become the Reds GM in 1985

MURRAY COOK

GEORGE EARL MURRAY COOK JUNE 20, 1983–APRIL 9, 1984

An affair he had while he was the GM of the Expos with team owner Claude Brochu's wife cost him his job and probably permanently damaged his career; later briefly served as Reds GM but has worked as a scout for the Marlins, Red Sox, and now Tigers

Reason for Leaving: Was reassigned as director of scouting

CLYDE KING

CLYDE EDWARD KING APRIL 9, 1984–OCTOBER 10, 1986

Remains a Yankees adviser

Reason for Leaving: King wanted to spend more time at home in North Carolina, so he took on a reduced role in the organization as a special assistant to Steinbrenner

WOODY WOODWARD

WILLIAM FREDERICK WOODWARD OCTOBER 10, 1986–OCTOBER 19, 1987

Left organization to become Phillies GM for a brief unhappy stint in which he clashed with Phillies owner Bill Giles; served as Mariners GM for a decade

Reason for Leaving: Wanted to find a similar position with a less demanding schedule

LOU PINIELLA

LOUIS VICTOR PINIELLA OCTOBER 19, 1987–MAY 15, 1988

Much-traveled manager (Yankees, Reds, Mariners, Devil Rays) now leading Cubs

Reason for Leaving: Did not like duties of front office job; was hired as Yankees manager weeks later

BOB QUINN SR.

ROBERT E. QUINN SR. JUNE 8, 1988–OCTOBER 13, 1989

Grandfather Bob, father John, and grandson Bob also were or are baseball executives

Reason for Leaving: Unhappy with reduced role after first Thrift and then Bradley were given much of job's authority; became Reds GM

SYD THRIFT

SYDNOR W. THRIFT JR. MARCH 21, 1989–AUGUST 29, 1989

Much-traveled (worked for nine different organizations) baseball executive, self-promoter

Reason for Leaving: Personal reasons

GEORGE BRADLEY

SEPTEMBER 1, 1989–AUGUST 20, 1990

Shared job with Harding Peterson

Reason for Leaving: Demoted and moved from Tampa to New York to work under Michael; left organization on Febuary 6, 1991

HARDING PETERSON

HARDING WILLIAM "PETE" PETERSON OCTOBER 13, 1989–AUGUST 20, 1990

Shared job with George Bradley after spending almost a decade as GM of the Pirates in the late 1970s and the 1980s.

Reason for Leaving: Demoted

GENE MICHAEL

EUGENE RICHARD "STICK" MICHAEL AUGUST 20, 1990–OCTOBER 17, 1995

Built up minor league system during Steinbrenner's second suspension; remains very influential in the organization

Reason for Leaving: Offered salary cut from $550,000 a year to $400,000 a year; took easier job as director of major league scouting for $150,000 a year

BOB WATSON

ROBERT JOSE "BULL" WATSON OCTOBER 24, 1995–FEBUARY 3, 1998

Former player had been GM for Astros

Reason for Leaving: Resigned because of health issues, most notably high blood pressure

BRIAN CASHMAN

FEBUARY 3, 1998–

Has now lasted longer as Yankees GM than anyone since George Weiss, though he did not have full authority to make important decisions until he signed his latest contract in the fall of 2005

Yankees Broadcasting History

Having seen what radio's arrival did to vaudeville, New York's baseball clubs were initially chary about allowing the wireless into their ballparks. Ultimately, the new medium proved too much for even the staid Yankees to resist. After trial broadcasts by Al Helfer in 1937–38, New York hired Senators radio man Arch McDonald to handle their 1939 home games on WABC. "The Old Pine Tree" was assisted by young Melvin Israel—renamed Mel Allen—while Don Dunphy re-created road games from tickertape on WINS.

McDonald soon returned to Washington and Allen took over. Mel's career in the Yankees booth lasted nearly a quarter-century; his genteel, enthusiastic tones conveyed a love of baseball that helped millions of New Yorkers appreciate the National Game in a new way.

Allen saw military service in 1944–45, but returned in '46. The first year after the war saw a huge change, as the Yankees began covering road games live and, in addition, started televising. WPIX, New York's longest-running over-the-air TV partner, showed Yankees games from 1951 all the way through 1998.

In 1954, Red Barber, formerly Brooklyn's voice, joined Allen on the broadcasts. The two—bound by a love for the game but separated by very different styles—worked together until 1964.

The two legends of the air departed just as the Yankees dynasty crumbled, Allen was fired after the '64 series by sponsor Ballantine Beer. Barber was let go in 1966 after noting a low attendance figure for a late-season contest at Yankee Stadium. By then, three new ex-player broadcasters—Jerry Coleman, Phil Rizzuto, and Joe Garagiola—had entered the picture.

Yankees broadcasts quickly became less distinctive as some forgettable professionals and unqualified ex-players manned the booth, but the legendary Rizzuto served the team on its broadcasts from 1957–96, longer than anyone else in the history of the Bronx Bombers.

New team president George Steinbrenner fully embraced the cable TV revolution, with SportsChannel televising a regular schedule starting in 1979. Allen returned triumphantly to the booth, with SportsChannel, for five years in the 1980s. The club added Spanish-language radio broadcasts in 1996, followed by cable TV broadcasts *en Espanol* a year later.

Over the last two decades, ex-player commentators Bobby Murcer, Tom Seaver, Ken Singleton, and Jim Kaat have served the Yanks' broadcasts with distinction. Popular—though polarizing—radio voices John Sterling and Suzyn Waldman and TV broadcaster Michael Kay have also "manned" the broadcast booths in the Bronx in recent seasons. Eventually, Steinbrenner created his own RSN, the Yankees Entertainment & Sports Network in 2002 (YES), and quickly moved most televised games to it.

YEAR	RADIO ANNOUNCERS (STATION)	OVER-THE-AIR TV ANNOUNCERS (STATION)	PAY TV/CABLE ANNOUNCERS (STATION)	SPANISH RADIO/TV ANNOUNCERS (STATION)
1937	Al Helfer (several games as experiment)			
1938	Al Helfer (several games as experiment)			
1939	Arch McDonald, Mel Allen, Garnett Marks (WABC home games), Don Dunphy (WINS road games)			
1940	Mel Allen, J.C. Flippen (WABC)			
1941	[No broadcasts]			
1942	Mel Allen, Connie Desmond (WOR day games, WNEW night games)			
1943	[No broadcasts]			
1944	Don Dunphy, Al Schacht (WINS)			
1945	Bill Slater, Al Helfer (WINS)			
1946	Mel Allen, Russ Hodges (WINS)	Mel Allen, Russ Hodges (WABD)		
1947	Mel Allen, Russ Hodges (WINS)	Bill Slater (WABD)		
1948	Mel Allen, Russ Hodges (WINS)	Mel Allen, Russ Hodges, Bill Slater (WABD)		
1949	Mel Allen, Curt Gowdy (WINS)	Mel Allen, Curt Gowdy (WABD)		
1950	Mel Allen, Curt Gowdy (WINS)	Mel Allen, Curt Gowdy, Dizzy Dean (WABD)		
1951	Mel Allen, Art Gleeson (WINS)	Mel Allen, Art Gleeson, Bill Crowley, Dizzy Dean (WABD/WPIX)		
1952	Mel Allen, Art Gleeson, Bill Crowley, Joe DiMaggio (WINS)	Mel Allen, Art Gleeson, Bill Crowley (WPIX)		
1953	Mel Allen, Jim Woods, Joe E. Brown (WINS)	Mel Allen, Jim Woods, Joe E. Brown (WPIX)		
1954	Mel Allen, Jim Woods, Red Barber (WINS)	Mel Allen, Jim Woods, Red Barber (WPIX)		
1955	Mel Allen, Jim Woods, Red Barber (WINS)	Mel Allen, Jim Woods, Red Barber (WPIX)		
1956	Mel Allen, Jim Woods, Red Barber (WINS)	Mel Allen, Jim Woods, Red Barber (WPIX)		
1957	Mel Allen, Red Barber, Phil Rizzuto (WINS)	Mel Allen, Red Barber, Phil Rizutto (WPIX)		
1958	Mel Allen, Red Barber, Phil Rizzuto (WMGM)	Mel Allen, Red Barber, Phil Rizutto (WPIX)		
1959	Mel Allen, Red Barber, Phil Rizzuto (WMGM)	Mel Allen, Red Barber, Phil Rizutto (WPIX)		
1960	Mel Allen, Red Barber, Phil Rizzuto (WMGM)	Mel Allen, Red Barber, Phil Rizutto (WPIX)		
1961	Mel Allen, Red Barber, Phil Rizzuto (WCBS)	Mel Allen, Red Barber, Phil Rizutto (WPIX)		
1962	Mel Allen, Red Barber, Phil Rizzuto (WCBS)	Mel Allen, Red Barber, Phil Rizutto (WPIX)		
1963	Mel Allen, Red Barber, Phil Rizzuto, Jerry Coleman (WCBS)	Mel Allen, Red Barber, Phil Rizutto, Jerry Coleman (WPIX)		
1964	Mel Allen, Red Barber, Phil Rizzuto, Jerry Coleman (WCBS)	Mel Allen, Red Barber, Phil Rizutto, Jerry Coleman (WPIX)		
1965	Red Barber, Jerry Coleman, Phil Rizzuto, Joe Garagiola (WCBS)	Red Barber, Jerry Coleman, Phil Rizzuto, Joe Garagiola (WPIX)		

YEAR	RADIO ANNOUNCERS (STATION)	OVER-THE-AIR TV ANNOUNCERS (STATION)	PAY TV/CABLE ANNOUNCERS (STATION)	SPANISH RADIO/TV ANNOUNCERS (STATION)
1966	Red Barber, Jerry Coleman, Phil Rizzuto, Joe Garagiola (WCBS)	Red Barber, Jerry Coleman, Phil Rizzuto, Joe Garagiola (WPIX)		
1967	Phil Rizzuto, Jerry Coleman, Joe Garagiola (WHN)	Phil Rizzuto, Jerry Coleman, Joe Garagiola (WPIX)		
1968	Phil Rizzuto, Jerry Coleman, Frank Messer (WHN)	Phil Rizzuto, Jerry Coleman, Frank Messer (WPIX)		
1969	Phil Rizzuto, Jerry Coleman, Frank Messer (WHN)	Phil Rizzuto, Jerry Coleman, Frank Messer, Whitey Ford (WPIX)		
1970	Phil Rizzuto, Frank Messer, Bob Gamere (WHN)	Phil Rizzuto, Frank Messer, Bob Gamere, Whitey Ford (WPIX)		
1971	Phil Rizzuto, Frank Messer, Bill White (WHN)	Phil Rizzuto, Frank Messer, Bill White, Whitey Ford (WPIX)		
1972	Phil Rizzuto, Frank Messer, Bill White (WMCA)	Phil Rizzuto, Frank Messer, Bill White (WPIX)		
1973	Phil Rizzuto, Frank Messer, Bill White (WMCA)	Phil Rizzuto, Frank Messer, Bill White (WPIX)		
1974	Phil Rizzuto, Frank Messer, Bill White (WMCA)	Phil Rizzuto, Frank Messer, Bill White (WPIX)	Dick Stockton (HBO)	
1975	Phil Rizzuto, Frank Messer, Bill White, Dom Valentino (WMCA)	Phil Rizzuto, Frank Messer, Bill White (WPIX)		
1976	Phil Rizzuto, Frank Messer, Bill White (WMCA)	Phil Rizzuto, Frank Messer, Bill White (WPIX)		
1977	Phil Rizzuto, Frank Messer, Bill White, Pam Boucher (WMCA)	Phil Rizzuto, Frank Messer, Bill White (WPIX)		
1978	Phil Rizzuto, Frank Messer, Bill White (WINS)	Phil Rizzuto, Frank Messer, Bill White (WPIX)		
1979	Phil Rizzuto, Frank Messer, Bill White, Fran Healy (WINS)	Phil Rizzuto, Frank Messer, Bill White (WPIX)	Frank Messer, Bill White, Fran Healy (SportsChannel)	
1980	Phil Rizzuto, Frank Messer, Bill White, Fran Healy (WINS)	Phil Rizzuto, Frank Messer, Bill White (WPIX)	Frank Messer, Bill White, Fran Healy (SportsChannel)	
1981	Phil Rizzuto, Frank Messer, Bill White, Fran Healy (WABC)	Phil Rizzuto, Frank Messer, Bill White (WPIX)	Bill White, Fran Healy (SportsChannel)	
1982	Phil Rizzuto, Frank Messer, Bill White (WABC)	Phil Rizzuto, Frank Messer, Bill White, John Gordon (WPIX)	Mel Allen, Phil Rizzuto, Frank Messer, Bill White (SportsChannel)	
1983	Phil Rizzuto, Frank Messer, Bill White (WABC)	Phil Rizzuto, Frank Messer, Bill White, John Gordon (WPIX)	Mel Allen, Fran Healy, Bobby Murcer (SportsChannel)	
1984	Phil Rizzuto, Frank Messer, Bill White, John Gordon, Bobby Murcer (WABC)	Phil Rizzuto, Frank Messer, Bill White, Bobby Murcer (WPIX)	Phil Rizzuto, Frank Messer, Bill White, Bobby Murcer, Mel Allen (SportsChannel)	
1985	Phil Rizzuto, Bill White, Frank Messer, John Gordon (WABC)	Phil Rizzuto, Bill White, Spencer Ross (WPIX)	Phil Rizzuto, Mel Allen, Bill White, Mickey Mantle (SportsChannel)	
1986	Phil Rizzuto, Bill White, Bobby Murcer, Spencer Ross, Billy Martin (WABC)	Phil Rizzuto, Bill White, Jim Kaat (WPIX)	Mel Allen, Mickey Mantle (SportsChannel)	
1987	Hank Greenwald, Tommy Hutton (WABC)	Phil Rizzuto, Bill White, Billy Martin (WPIX)	Ken Harrelson, Spencer Ross (SportsChannel)	
1988	Hank Greenwald, Tommy Hutton (WABC)	Phil Rizzuto, Bill White (WPIX)	Ken Harrelson, Bobby Murcer, Mickey Mantle (SportsChannel)	
1989	John Sterling, Tommy Hutton, Jay Johnstone (WABC)	Phil Rizzuto, Tom Seaver, George Grande (WPIX)	Greg Gumbel, Lou Piniella, Tommy Hutton, Bobby Murcer (MSG)	
1990	John Sterling, Jay Johnstone (WABC)	Phil Rizzuto, Tom Seaver, George Grande (WPIX)	DeWayne Staats, Tony Kubek, Al Trautwig (MSG)	
1991	John Sterling, Joe Angel (WABC)	Phil Rizzuto, Tom Seaver, Bobby Murcer (WPIX)	DeWayne Staats, Tony Kubek, Al Trautwig (MSG)	
1992	John Sterling, Michael Kay (WABC)	Phil Rizzuto, Tom Seaver, Bobby Murcer (WPIX)	DeWayne Staats, Tony Kubek, Al Trautwig (MSG)	
1993	John Sterling, Michael Kay (WABC)	Phil Rizzuto, Tom Seaver, Bobby Murcer (WPIX)	DeWayne Staats, Tony Kubek, Al Trautwig (MSG)	
1994	John Sterling, Michael Kay (WABC)	Phil Rizzuto, Bobby Murcer, Paul Olden (WPIX)	DeWayne Staats, Tony Kubek, Al Trautwig (MSG)	
1995	John Sterling, Michael Kay (WABC)	Phil Rizzuto, Bobby Murcer, Paul Olden (WPIX)	Dave Cohen, Jim Kaat, Al Trautwig, Steve Palermo (MSG)	
1996	John Sterling, Michael Kay (WABC)	Phil Rizzuto, Rick Cerone, Suzyn Waldman, Paul Olden (WPIX)	Dave Cohen, Jim Kaat, Al Trautwig, Steve Palermo (MSG)	Armando Talavera, Roberto Clemente Jr. (WADO/MSG SAP)
1997	John Sterling, Michael Kay (WABC)	Bobby Murcer, Ken Singleton, Rick Cerone, Suzyn Waldman (WPIX)	Jim Kaat, Al Trautwig, Suzyn Waldman, Ken Singleton (MSG)	Armando Talavera, Roberto Clemente Jr., Beto Villa (WADO/MSG SAP)
1998	John Sterling, Michael Kay (WABC)	Bobby Murcer, Tommy John (WPIX)	Jim Kaat, Al Trautwig, Suzyn Waldman, Ken Singleton (MSG)	Armando Talavera, Roberto Clemente Jr., Beto Villa (WADO/MSG SAP)
1999	John Sterling, Michael Kay (WABC)	Bobby Murcer, Tim McCarver (WNYW)	Jim Kaat, Al Trautwig, Suzyn Waldman, Ken Singleton (MSG)	Armando Talavera, Roberto Clemente Jr., Beto Villa (WADO/MSG SAP)
2000	John Sterling, Michael Kay (WABC)	Bobby Murcer, Tim McCarver (WNYW)	Jim Kaat, Al Trautwig, Suzyn Waldman, Ken Singleton (MSG)	Armando Talavera, Roberto Clemente Jr., Beto Villa (WADO/MSG SAP)
2001	John Sterling, Michael Kay (WABC)	Bobby Murcer, Tim McCarver (WNYW)	Jim Kaat, Al Trautwig, Suzyn Waldman, Ken Singleton (MSG)	Armando Talavera, Roberto Clemente Jr., Beto Villa (WADO/MSG SAP)
2002	John Sterling, Charley Steiner (WCBS)	Michael Kay, Jim Kaat, Ken Singleton (WCBS)	Michael Kay, Jim Kaat, Suzyn Waldman, Ken Singleton (YES)	Armando Talavera, Beto Villa (WADO/YES SAP)
2003	John Sterling, Charley Steiner (WCBS)	Michael Kay, Jim Kaat, Ken Singleton (WCBS)	Michael Kay, Jim Kaat, Ken Singleton, Paul O'Neill (YES)	Armando Talavera, Beto Villa (WADO/YES SAP)
2004	John Sterling, Charley Steiner (WCBS)	Michael Kay, Jim Kaat, Ken Singleton,) Bobby Murcer (WCBS	Michael Kay, Jim Kaat, Ken Singleton, Bobby Murcer, Paul O'Neill (YES)	Armando Talavera, Beto Villa (WADO/YES SAP)
2005	John Sterling, Suzyn Waldman (WCBS)	Michael Kay, Jim Kaat (WWOR)	Michael Kay, Jim Kaat, Ken Singleton, Bobby Murcer, Paul O'Neill (YES)	Beto Villa, Francisco Rivera (WKDM/YES SAP)
2006	John Sterling, Suzyn Waldman (WCBS)	Michael Kay, Jim Kaat (WWOR)	Michael Kay, Jim Kaat, Ken Singleton, Bobby Murcer, Paul O'Neill, Al Leiter, John Flaherty (YES)	Beto Villa, Francisco Rivera (WKDM/YES SAP)
2007	John Sterling, Suzyn Waldman (WCBS)	Michael Kay, Ken Singleton (WWOR)	Michael Kay, Ken Singleton, Bobby Murcer, Al Leiter, John Flaherty, David Justice, Paul O'Neill, Joe Girardi (YES)	Beto Villa, Francisco Rivera, Felix DeJesus (WZAA/YES SAP)

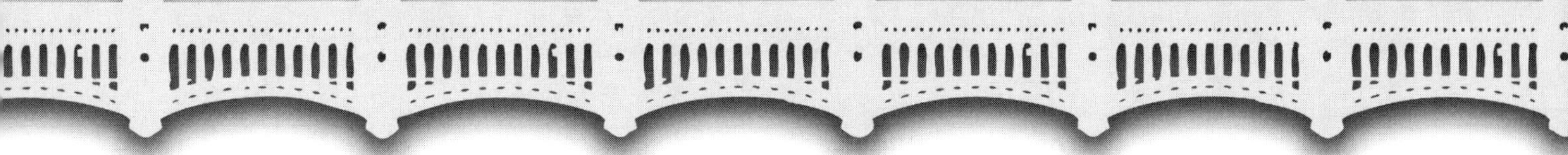

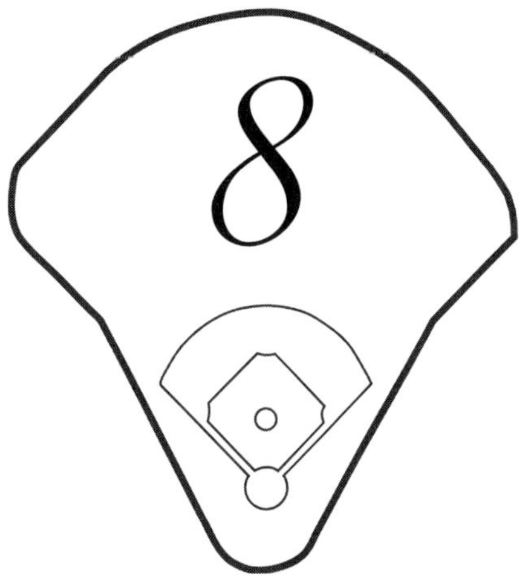

The Historical Record

The emergence of the American League is one of the most significant events in the history of American sport. Ban Johnson's bold venture succeeded in challenging the established National League after three other leagues had tried and failed in the nineteenth century. The AL was the Hatfield to the NL's McCoy in the first years of their shared existence; they quickly formed a cautious alliance when it became apparent that their continued war would do nothing but harm both enterprises.

The World Series as we know it today was the offspring of this union, beginning in 1903 and taking a year off in 1904 when the lordly New York Giants, the NL champions, would not stoop so low as to play Boston, the AL pennant-winner.

In 1902, the Baltimore club, one of the AL's charter members, was utterly destroyed by a cynical series of machinations by then-Orioles' manager John McGraw, aided and abetted by the Reds and the Giants. AL president Johnson and the league took over the bereft franchise to enable it to finish out the season. Johnson, furious at the role McGraw and the Giants had played in the Orioles' destruction, then sold the franchise to New York owners, allowing the AL to compete head-to-head with the senior circuit in the largest and most lucrative market in the country.

Thus were sowed the seeds of the greatest franchise that the National Pastime has ever seen: the New York Yankees. At first called the Highlanders, the New York Americans saw little success until the acquisition of Babe Ruth in 1920 and became the foundation of the Yankees' first dynasty.

The American League has seen several non-New York dynasties in its century-plus of existence, but no other club has come close to matching the repeated and prolonged dominance of the Yankees:

- The first Yankees' dynasty started in 1921, lasting eight years and claiming six AL pennants and three world championships;
- The second Bronx dynasty lasted from 1936–43 as the Bombers won an astonishing six World Series and seven pennants, failing to reach the Fall Classic only in 1940;
- The third New York dynasty was the biggest and best of all: from 1947–64, the Yankees won 15 pennants in 18 years, besting the NL champions 10 times, including a remarkable stretch from 1947–53 when New York won the World Series every year save in 1948;
- After an unaccustomed drought, the Yanks returned to dominance from 1976–81 with a fourth dynasty, copping four pennants and two world championships;
- Finally, after 14 years on the outside, the Bombers returned to glory in the mid-1990s, winning four World Series from 1996–2000 and going to the postseason for 13 consecutive years, starting in 1995.

The Historical Record tracks everything that has happened in the AL during the regular season from the Yankees' inception through 2007. At the top of each page in the Historical Record are the final standings for the league for a given season, along with team batting, baserunning, pitching, and fielding statistics. The wild card team for every season since 1995 is in bold.

Below the standings and team statistics are individual league-leaders in 35 categories of batting, pitching, and fielding stats. Each category lists the top five players (unless multiple tied players would lengthen the list past the top five). Among the batting and pitching leaders, the minimums for qualifying as a league leader for any average or rate statistics are normally the same as qualifying for the batting or ERA titles. However, the minimum for qualifying as a league leader in Base Runners per 9 Innings was deliberately set low enough to include relief pitchers (60 innings pitched). This was in contrast to other pitching leaders like Opponents' Average and Opponents OBP, for which relief pitchers would typically not qualify. The relief pitching categories (starting with Games and ending with Relief Ranking) have been grouped together for ease of comparison.

The lists below show all abbreviations used in the Historical Record section. Those that have not been defined elsewhere are explained here. Further information about the statistics, formulas, and computations shown in the Historical Record section can be found in the Glossary at the end of the encyclopedia.

W Wins
L Losses
T Ties. Ties occur only if the game has completed five or more full innings, the game was tied after the last full inning, and no further runs have scored.
PCT Winning Percentage. Calculated by dividing the number of wins by the number of wins and losses.
GB Games Behind. The number of games each club finished behind first place.
R Runs
OR Opponent Runs
HR Home Runs
AVG Batting Average. Hits divided by at bats.
OBP On-Base Percentage. Hits plus walks plus hit by pitch divided by at bats plus walks plus hit by pitch plus sacrifice flies.
SLG Slugging Average. Total bases divided by at bats.
OPS On-Base Plus Slugging Average. This figure is multiplied by 1000, so .400 plus .500 is 900.
AOPS Adjusted On-Base Plus Slugging Average. On-base percentage and slugging average are added and normalized for the context of the offensive level of the league and the team's home park and converted to a scale in which 100 is average. It is expressed here as the number above or below average, so 116 is written as +16 and 84 is written as -16.
PF Hitters' Park Factor. This measures how the team's home park affects offense; it is used to adjust the team's raw offensive performance to account for the team's home park. This also includes a correction for not having to face your own pitchers; it is used in AOPS and ABR.
SB Stolen Bases
CG Complete Games
HR Home Runs Allowed
BB Bases on Balls Allowed
SO Strikeouts
BR/9 Baserunners Allowed Per 9 Innings
ERA Earned Run Average. Calculated by dividing earned runs by innings pitched and multiplying by 9.
AERA Adjusted Earned Run Average. Calculated by normalizing ERA for the context of offensive level of the league and the team's home park and converting to a scale in which 100 is average. It is expressed here as the number above or below average, so 110 is written as +10 and 90 is written as -10.
OAV Opponents' Batting Average: Hits allowed divided by opponent at bats.
OOB Opponents' On-Base Percentage. Hits plus walks plus hit by pitch divided by at bats plus walks plus hit by pitch plus sacrifice flies.
FW Fielding Wins. Number of wins the team achieved through its fielding compared to the average team in context of the league offensive level and the team's home park.
PW Pitching Wins. Number of wins the team achieved through its pitching compared to the average team in context of the league offensive level and the team's home park.
BW Batting Wins. Number of wins the team achieved through its hitting compared to the average team in context of the league offensive level and the team's home park.
BSW Basestealing Wins. Number of wins the team achieved through its basestealing compared to the average team in context of the league offensive level and the team's home park.
DIF Differential. Measures the difference between how many games the team was projected to win based on its hitting, pitching, fielding, and baserunning, and how many games the team actually won. It is measured the same way as teams measure how many games they are behind in the standings.

Leaderboards

Not shown among team statistics.

Batter-Fielder Wins The sum of a player's batting wins, basestealing wins, and fielding wins, this figure indicates how many games the player won or lost for his team compared to the average player.

Adjusted Batter Runs Batter runs are adjusted to the home park and the league average offensive level but ignore the offensive contributions of pitchers.

Hits

Doubles

Triples

Total Bases Calculated by adding singles plus 2x doubles plus 3x triples plus 4x home runs.

Runs Batted In

Stolen Bases

Basestealing Runs The number of runs added by a team's basestealing attempts.

Fielding Runs Infield and Outfield Measures the difference between how many games the player saves or loses for his team in the field compared to an average fielder. The formula takes into account putouts, assists, double plays, and errors. Defensive innings are based on play-by-play from 1969 forward; they are estimated for previous years.

Wins

Fewest Bases on Balls Per Game

Games

Saves The save became an official statistic in 1969. Saves are calculated based on the official definition of saves at the time. Saves before 1969 are based on how many times a relief pitcher finished a victory for his team without getting a win.

Base Runners Per 9 Innings

Historical Record

Adjusted Relief Runns How many runs the pitcher allowed to score compared to the average pitcher in the context of the league offensive level and the pitcher's home park(s). Relief pitchers are those who average less than 3 innings per appearance.

Relief Ranking Calculated by putting Adjusted Relief Runs into context by the importance of the relief innings pitched; takes into account the number of saves and decisions assigned to the pitcher.

Innings Pitched

Adjusted Starter Runs How many runs the pitcher allowed to score compared to the average pitcher in the context of the league offensive level and the pitcher's home park(s). Starting pitchers are those who average at least 3 innings per appearance.

Pitcher Wins Individual pitcher wins are calculated by adding up pitching, batting, fielding, and basestealing wins; this is different from team pitching wins.

1903 American League

TEAM	W	L	T	PCT	GB	R	OR	HR	AVG	OBP	SLG	OPS	AOPS	PF	SB	CG	HR	BB	SO	BR/9	ERA	AERA	OAV	OOB	FW	PW	BW	BSW	DIF
Bos	91	47	3	.659		**708**	**504**	**48**	**.272**	.313	**.392**	**705**	111	105	141	123	23	269	579	**10.4**	**2.57**	**118**	**.242**	**.288**	2.3	**6.5**	5.7		7.5
Phi	75	60	2	.556	14.5	597	519	32	.264	.309	.363	672	102	105	157	112	20	315	**728**	11.3	2.98	103	.246	.305	**3.2**	1.0	1.3		1.9
Cle	77	63	0	.550	15	639	579	31	.265	.308	.373	681	**112**	98	175	**125**	**16**	271	521	10.6	2.73	105	.247	.293	-3.2	1.9	**6.5**		1.8
NY	72	62	2	.537	17	579	573	18	.249	.309	.330	639	92	106	160	111	19	245	463	10.9	3.08	101	.255	.299	.0	.5	-3.7		8.2
Det	65	71	1	.478	25	567	539	12	.268	**.318**	.351	669	110	97	128	123	19	336	554	11.5	2.75	106	.256	.310	-.9	2.2	5.7		-10.0
StL	65	74	0	.468	26.5	500	525	12	.244	.290	.317	607	90	97	101	124	26	**237**	511	11.0	2.77	105	.260	.300	.2	2.0	-5.6		-1.0
Chi	60	77	1	.438	30.5	516	613	14	.247	.301	.314	615	94	96	**180**	114	23	287	391	11.5	3.02	93	.260	.309	-1.8	-3.1	-2.2		-1.4
Was	43	94	0	.314	47.5	437	691	17	.231	.277	.311	588	80	102	131	122	38	306	452	12.4	3.82	82	.277	.325	.8	-9.2	-11.3		-5.7
Total	554					34543		184	.255	.303	.344	648			1173	954				11.2	2.96		.255	.303					

Batter-Fielder Wins
Lajoie-Cle 8.1
Williams-NY 2.3
Ganzel-NY 1.0
Conroy-NY .7

Batting Average
Lajoie-Cle .344
Keeler-NY .313
Ganzel-NY .277
Conroy-NY .272

On-Base Percentage
Barrett-Det .407
Keeler-NY .368
Ganzel-NY .336
Williams-NY .326

Slugging Average
Lajoie-Cle .518
Williams-NY .392
McFarland-NY .378
Ganzel-NY .378

On-Base Plus Slugging
Lajoie-Cle 896
Keeler-NY 735
Williams-NY 718
Ganzel-NY 714

Adjusted OPS
Lajoie-Cle 170
Keeler-NY 114
Williams-NY 108
Ganzel-NY 107

Adjusted Batter Runs
Lajoie-Cle 40.6
Keeler-NY 9.6
Williams-NY 5.3
Ganzel-NY 5.0

Runs
Dougherty-Bos 107
Keeler-NY 95
Conroy-NY 74
Ganzel-NY 62

Hits
Dougherty-Bos 195
Keeler-NY 160
Conroy-NY 137
Williams-NY 134

Doubles
Seybold-Phi 45
Williams-NY 30
Ganzel-NY 25
Conroy-NY 23

Triples
Crawford-Det 25
Williams-NY 12
Conroy-NY 12
McFarland-NY 9

Home Runs
Freeman-Bos 13
McFarland-NY 5
Williams-NY 3
Ganzel-NY 3

Total Bases
Freeman-Bos 281
Williams-NY 197
Keeler-NY 188
Conroy-NY 187

Runs Batted In
Freeman-Bos 104
Williams-NY 82
Ganzel-NY 71
2 players tied 45

Stolen Bases
Bay-Cle 45
Conroy-NY 33
Fultz-NY 29
Keeler-NY 24

Base Stealing Runs

Fielding Runs-Infield
Lajoie-Cle 39.1
Williams-NY 15.5
Ganzel-NY 6.8
Conroy-NY 3.2

Fielding Runs-Outfield
Lush-Det 12.8

Wins
Young-Bos 28
Chesbro-NY 21
Tannehill-NY 15
Griffith-NY 14

Winning Pct.
Young-Bos .757
Chesbro-NY .583
Tannehill-NY .500

Complete Games
3 players tied 34
Chesbro-NY 33
Tannehill-NY 22
Griffith-NY 22

Strikeouts
Waddell-Phi 302
Chesbro-NY 147
Tannehill-NY 106
Griffith-NY 69

Fewest BB/Game
Young-Bos .97
Tannehill-NY 1.28
Griffith-NY 1.39
Wolfe-NY 1.58

Games
Plank-Phi 43
Chesbro-NY 40
Tannehill-NY 32
2 players tied 25

Saves
5 players tied 2
Wiltse-NY 1
Adkins-NY 1

Base Runners/9
Joss-Cle 8.82
Griffith-NY 10.14
Chesbro-NY 10.62
Wolfe-NY 10.62

Adjusted Relief Runs

Relief Ranking

Innings Pitched
Young-Bos 341.2
Chesbro-NY 324.2
Tannehill-NY 239.2
Griffith-NY 213.0

Opponents' Avg.
Moore-Cle .217
Howell-NY .240
Chesbro-NY .245
Griffith-NY .249

Opponents' OBP
Joss-Cle .256
Griffith-NY .283
Chesbro-NY .293
Wolfe-NY .293

Earned Run Average
Moore-Cle 1.74
Griffith-NY 2.70
Chesbro-NY 2.77
Wolfe-NY 2.97

Adjusted ERA
Moore-Cle 164
Griffith-NY 115
Chesbro-NY 113
Wolfe-NY 105

Adjusted Starter Runs
Young-Bos 34.0
Chesbro-NY 11.8
Griffith-NY 8.4
Wolfe-NY 3.1

Pitcher Wins
Young-Bos 4.8
Chesbro-NY 1.2
Griffith-NY 1.0
Puttmann-NY .3

1904 American League

TEAM	W	L	T	PCT	GB	R	OR	HR	AVG	OBP	SLG	OPS	AOPS	PF	SB	CG	HR	BB	SO	BR/9	ERA	AERA	OAV	OOB	FW	PW	BW	BSW	DIF
Bos	95	59	3	.617		608	**466**	26	.247	.301	.340	641	102	106	101	**148**	31	**233**	612	**9.4**	**2.12**	**126**	.233	**.270**	1.6	**9.4**	1.0		6.0
NY	92	59	4	.609	1.5	598	526	27	.259	**.308**	.347	655	107	105	163	123	29	311	684	10.0	2.57	106	.232	.282	-.8	2.3	4.6		10.4
Chi	89	65	2	.578	6	600	482	14	.242	.300	.316	616	104	96	**216**	134	13	303	550	9.8	2.30	107	**.229**	.279	**1.7**	2.7	3.2		4.4
Cle	86	65	3	.570	7.5	**647**	482	27	**.260**	**.308**	**.354**	**662**	**116**	99	178	141	**10**	285	627	10.6	2.22	114	.249	.294	.4	5.4	**9.6**		-4.9
Phi	81	70	4	.536	12.5	557	503	**31**	.249	.298	.336	634	101	105	137	136	13	366	**887**	10.4	2.35	114	.230	.291	.8	5.4	.1		-.8
StL	65	87	4	.428	29	481	604	10	.239	.291	.294	585	96	94	150	135	25	333	577	11.0	2.83	88	.251	.303	-.2	-6.5	-2.1		-2.2
Det	62	90	10	.408	32	505	627	11	.231	.282	.292	574	90	97	112	143	16	433	556	11.6	2.77	92	.250	.314	.0	-4.0	-6.8		-3.2
Was	38	113	6	.252	55.5	437	743	10	.227	.275	.288	563	84	98	150	137	19	347	533	12.5	3.62	73	.279	.330	-3.1	-15.9	-9.8		-8.6
Total	626					34433		156	.244	.295	.321	616			1207	097				10.7	2.60		.244	.295					

Batter-Fielder Wins
Lajoie-Cle 7.4
Williams-NY 2.3
Elberfeld-NY 2.2
Keeler-NY 2.1

Batting Average
Lajoie-Cle .376
Keeler-NY .343
Anderson-NY .278
Fultz-NY .274

On-Base Percentage
Lajoie-Cle .413
Keeler-NY .390
Elberfeld-NY .337
2 players tied .314

Slugging Average
Lajoie-Cle .546
Keeler-NY .409
Anderson-NY .385
Ganzel-NY .376

On-Base Plus Slugging
Lajoie-Cle 959
Keeler-NY 799
Anderson-NY 699
Ganzel-NY 686

Adjusted OPS
Lajoie-Cle 204
Keeler-NY 146
Anderson-NY 115
Ganzel-NY 111

Adjusted Batter Runs
Lajoie-Cle 64.3
Keeler-NY 28.4
Anderson-NY 8.3
Chesbro-NY 5.7

Runs
Dougherty-Bos-NY 113
Williams-NY 62
Anderson-NY 62
Conroy-NY 58

Hits
Lajoie-Cle 208
Keeler-NY 186
Anderson-NY 155
Williams-NY 147

Doubles
Lajoie-Cle 49
Williams-NY 31
Anderson-NY 27
Conroy-NY 18

Triples
3 players tied 19
Conroy-NY 12
Anderson-NY 12
Ganzel-NY 10

Home Runs
Davis-Phi 10
Ganzel-NY 6
Anderson-NY 3

Total Bases
Lajoie-Cle 302
Keeler-NY 222
Anderson-NY 215
Williams-NY 198

Runs Batted In
Lajoie-Cle 102
Anderson-NY 82
Williams-NY 74
Conroy-NY 52

Stolen Bases
Flick-Cle 38
Bay-Cle 38
Conroy-NY 30
Keeler-NY 21

Base Stealing Runs

Fielding Runs-Infield
Tannehill-Chi 27.3
Williams-NY 14.5
Elberfeld-NY 11.3
Conroy-NY 6.5

Fielding Runs-Outfield
McIntyre-Det 12.4

Wins
Chesbro-NY 41
Powell-NY 23
Griffith-NY 7
Puttmann-NY 2

Winning Pct.
Chesbro-NY .774
Powell-NY .548

Complete Games
Chesbro-NY 48
Powell-NY 38
Griffith-NY 8
2 players tied 2

Strikeouts
Waddell-Phi 349
Chesbro-NY 239
Powell-NY 202
Clarkson-NY 43

Fewest BB/Game
Young-Bos .69
Chesbro-NY 1.74
Powell-NY 2.12

Games
Chesbro-NY 55
Powell-NY 47
Griffith-NY 16
Clarkson-NY 13

Saves
Patten-Was 3
Clarkson-NY 1

Base Runners/9
Young-Bos 8.53
Chesbro-NY 8.57
Griffith-NY 9.96
Powell-NY 10.19

Adjusted Relief Runs

Relief Ranking

Innings Pitched
Chesbro-NY 454.2
Powell-NY 390.1
Griffith-NY 100.1
Clarkson-NY 66.1

Opponents' Avg.
Chesbro-NY .208
Powell-NY .236

Opponents' OBP
Young-Bos .251
Chesbro-NY .252
Powell-NY .286

Earned Run Average
Joss-Cle 1.59
Chesbro-NY 1.82
Powell-NY 2.44

Adjusted ERA
Waddell-Phi 165
Chesbro-NY 149
Powell-NY 111

Adjusted Starter Runs
Chesbro-NY 41.2
Powell-NY 6.6
Garvin-NY .6

Pitcher Wins
Chesbro-NY 6.1
Puttmann-NY .2
Powell-NY .0
Garvin-NY .0

1905 American League

TEAM	W	L	T	PCT	GB	R	OR	HR	AVG	OBP	SLG	OPS	AOPS	PF	SB	CG	HR	BB	SO	BR/9	ERA	AERA	OAV	OOB	FW	PW	BW	BSW	DIF
Phi	92	56	4	.622		**623**	488	24	**.255**	**.310**	**.338**	**648**	**109**	102	190	117	21	409	**895**	10.5	2.19	121	.227	.294	.3	7.5	**5.9**		4.3
Chi	92	60	6	.605	2	612	**451**	11	.237	.305	.304	609	103	96	194	131	**11**	329	613	**9.6**	**1.99**	**124**	**.226**	**.277**	**4.1**	**8.6**	3.1		.2
Det	79	74	1	.516	15.5	512	604	13	.243	.302	.311	613	99	101	129	124	**11**	474	578	11.7	2.83	96	.246	.318	.4	-2.0	-.3		4.4
Bos	78	74	1	.513	16	579	565	**29**	.234	.305	.311	616	100	101	131	124	33	**292**	652	10.2	2.84	95	.238	.286	-1.6	-2.2	.8		5.1
Cle	76	78	1	.494	19	564	587	18	**.255**	.301	.334	635	106	101	188	**140**	23	334	555	10.9	2.85	92	.245	.299	2.8	-3.5	2.6		-2.9
NY	71	78	3	.477	21.5	586	621	23	.248	.307	.319	626	93	111	**200**	88	26	396	642	11.1	2.93	100	.246	.307	-1.5	-.2	-3.8		2.1
Was	64	87	3	.424	29.5	559	623	22	.224	.274	.302	576	92	96	169	118	12	385	539	11.2	2.87	92	.247	.308	-3.0	-4.0	-5.7		1.1
StL	54	99	3	.353	40.5	512	608	16	.232	.288	.289	577	93	95	144	134	19	389	633	11.0	2.74	93	.243	.304	-1.3	-3.7	-4.1		-13.4
Total	617					34547		156	.241	.299	.314	613			1345	976				10.8	2.65		.241	.299					

Batter-Fielder Wins
Davis-Chi 4.4
Hahn-NY .7
Conroy-NY .7
2 players tied .6

Batting Average
Flick-Cle .308
Keeler-NY .302
Conroy-NY .273
Yeager-NY .267

On-Base Percentage
Hartsel-Phi .409
Keeler-NY .357
Fultz-NY .308
Williams-NY .306

Slugging Average
Flick-Cle .462
Conroy-NY .395
Keeler-NY .363
Williams-NY .343

On-Base Plus Slugging
Flick-Cle 845
Keeler-NY 719
Williams-NY 648
Chase-NY 606

Adjusted OPS
Flick-Cle 165
Keeler-NY 115
Williams-NY 95
Chase-NY 83

Adjusted Batter Runs
Flick-Cle 37.7
Keeler-NY 9.6
Hahn-NY 8.0
Conroy-NY 6.2

Runs
Davis-Phi 93
Keeler-NY 81
Chase-NY 60
Dougherty-NY 56

Hits
Stone-StL 187
Keeler-NY 169
Chase-NY 116
Dougherty-NY 110

Doubles
Davis-Phi 47
Williams-NY 20
Conroy-NY 19
Elberfeld-NY 18

Triples
Flick-Cle 18
Conroy-NY 11
Williams-NY 8
Yeager-NY 7

Home Runs
Davis-Phi 8
Williams-NY 6
Keeler-NY 4
2 players tied 3

Total Bases
Stone-StL 259
Keeler-NY 203
Williams-NY 161
Chase-NY 153

Runs Batted In
Davis-Phi 83
Williams-NY 62
Elberfeld-NY 53
Chase-NY 49

Stolen Bases
Hoffman-Phi 46
Fultz-NY 44
Conroy-NY 25
Chase-NY 22

Base Stealing Runs

Fielding Runs-Infield
Cassidy-Was 34.8
Williams-NY 2.9
Yeager-NY 1.0

Fielding Runs-Outfield
McIntyre-Det 17.8
Keeler-NY 3.7

Wins
Waddell-Phi 27
Chesbro-NY 19
Orth-NY 18
2 players tied 9

Winning Pct.
Waddell-Phi .730
Chesbro-NY .559
Orth-NY .529

Complete Games
3 players tied 35
Orth-NY 26
Chesbro-NY 24
Hogg-NY 9

Strikeouts
Waddell-Phi 287
Chesbro-NY 156
Hogg-NY 125
Orth-NY 121

Fewest BB/Game
Young-Bos .84
Orth-NY 1.80
Chesbro-NY 2.11
Hogg-NY 4.43

Games
Waddell-Phi 46
Chesbro-NY 41
Orth-NY 40
Hogg-NY 39

Saves
Buchanan-StL 2
Puttmann-NY 1
Hogg-NY 1
Griffith-NY 1

Base Runners/9
Young-Bos 8.03
Griffith-NY 8.68
Orth-NY 10.05
Chesbro-NY 10.06

Adjusted Relief Runs

Relief Ranking

Innings Pitched
Mullin-Det 347.2
Orth-NY 305.1
Chesbro-NY 303.1
Hogg-NY 205.0

Opponents' Avg.
Waddell-Phi .200
Chesbro-NY .235
Hogg-NY .236
Orth-NY .241

Opponents' OBP
Young-Bos .241
Orth-NY .284
Chesbro-NY .285
Hogg-NY .336

Earned Run Average
Waddell-Phi 1.48
Chesbro-NY 2.20
Orth-NY 2.86
Hogg-NY 3.20

Adjusted ERA
Waddell-Phi 179
Chesbro-NY 133
Orth-NY 102
Hogg-NY 91

Adjusted Starter Runs
Waddell-Phi 40.1
Chesbro-NY 15.7
Griffith-NY 11.7
Orth-NY 6.8

Pitcher Wins
Waddell-Phi 4.5
Chesbro-NY 1.8
Griffith-NY 1.8
Orth-NY .6

1906 American League

TEAM	W	L	T	PCT	GB	R	OR	HR	AVG	OBP	SLG	OPS	AOPS	PF	SB	CG	HR	BB	SO	BR/9	ERA	AERA	OAV	OOB	FW	PW	BW	BSW	DIF
Chi	93	58	3	.616		570	**460**	7	.230	.301	.286	587	91	97	216	117	11	**255**	543	**9.8**	2.13	119	.239	**.280**	1.8	7.3	-3.4		11.8
NY	90	61	4	.596	3	640	543	17	.266	.316	.339	655	101	110	192	99	21	351	605	10.8	2.78	107	.246	.301	.1	2.7	-.1		11.7
Cle	89	64	4	.582	5	**663**	481	12	**.279**	**.325**	**.357**	**682**	**121**	99	203	**133**	16	365	530	10.3	**2.09**	**125**	.232	.289	**3.8**	**9.6**	**13.6**		-14.5
Phi	78	67	4	.538	12	561	539	**32**	.247	.308	.330	638	102	103	165	107	**9**	425	**749**	11.0	2.60	105	.236	.305	-.2	1.8	1.9		2.1
StL	76	73	5	.510	16	560	499	20	.247	.304	.312	616	102	96	221	**133**	14	314	558	10.0	2.23	116	**.230**	.284	-1.1	6.2	2.0		-5.5
Det	71	78	2	.477	21	518	598	10	.242	.295	.306	601	91	103	206	128	14	389	469	12.4	3.06	90	.272	.330	.4	-4.6	-5.6		6.3
Was	55	95	1	.367	37.5	519	665	26	.238	.289	.309	598	97	95	**233**	115	15	451	558	12.4	3.25	81	.265	.331	-.8	-10.2	-2.3		-6.7
Bos	49	105	1	.318	45.5	463	706	13	.237	.284	.304	588	89	100	99	124	37	285	549	11.0	3.41	81	.262	.306	-3.9	-11.3	-7.5		-5.3
Total	613					34494		137	.249	.303	.318	621			1535	956				11.0	2.69		.249	.303					

Batter-Fielder Wins
Lajoie-Cle 7.6
Williams-NY 2.5
Elberfeld-NY 1.5
2 players tied .7

Batting Average
Stone-StL .358
Chase-NY .323
Elberfeld-NY .306
Keeler-NY .304

On-Base Percentage
Stone-StL .417
Keeler-NY .353
Williams-NY .342
Chase-NY .341

Slugging Average
Stone-StL .501
Chase-NY .395
Elberfeld-NY .384
Williams-NY .373

On-Base Plus Slugging
Stone-StL 918
Chase-NY 736
Williams-NY 715
Keeler-NY 691

Adjusted OPS
Stone-StL 195
Chase-NY 118
Williams-NY 112
Keeler-NY 106

Adjusted Batter Runs
Stone-StL 63.3
Elberfeld-NY 11.6
Chase-NY 10.0
Williams-NY 8.0

Runs
Flick-Cle 98
Keeler-NY 96
Chase-NY 84
Conroy-NY 67

Hits
Lajoie-Cle 214
Chase-NY 193
Keeler-NY 180
2 players tied 139

Doubles
Lajoie-Cle 48
Williams-NY 25
LaPorte-NY 23
Chase-NY 23

Triples
Flick-Cle 22
Conroy-NY 10
Chase-NY 10
LaPorte-NY 9

Home Runs
Davis-Phi 12
Conroy-NY 4
Williams-NY 3

Total Bases
Stone-StL 291
Chase-NY 236
Keeler-NY 200
Conroy-NY 188

Runs Batted In
Davis-Phi 96
Williams-NY 77
Chase-NY 76
2 players tied 54

Stolen Bases
Flick-Cle 39
Anderson-Was 39
Conroy-NY 32
Chase-NY 28

Base Stealing Runs

Fielding Runs-Infield
Tannehill-Chi 32.4
Williams-NY 13.9

Fielding Runs-Outfield
Niles-StL 13.7
LaPorte-NY 1.0
Conroy-NY .7

Wins
Orth-NY 27
Chesbro-NY 23
Hogg-NY 14
Clarkson-NY 9

Winning Pct.
Plank-Phi .760
Orth-NY .614
Chesbro-NY .575

Complete Games
Orth-NY 36
Chesbro-NY 24
Hogg-NY 15
Clarkson-NY 9

Strikeouts
Waddell-Phi 196
Chesbro-NY 152
Orth-NY 133
Hogg-NY 107

Fewest BB/Game
Young-Bos .78
Orth-NY 1.75
Chesbro-NY 2.08
Hogg-NY 3.15

Games
Chesbro-NY 49
Orth-NY 45
Clarkson-NY 32
Hogg-NY 28

Saves
Hess-Cle 3
Bender-Phi 3
Griffith-NY 2
3 players tied 1

Base Runners/9
White-Chi 8.33
Orth-NY 10.20
Chesbro-NY 11.05
Hogg-NY 11.14

Adjusted Relief Runs

Relief Ranking

Innings Pitched
Orth-NY 338.2
Chesbro-NY 325.0
Hogg-NY 206.0
Clarkson-NY 151.0

Opponents' Avg.
Pelty-StL .206
Hogg-NY .229
Orth-NY .251
Chesbro-NY .257

Opponents' OBP
White-Chi .249
Orth-NY .289
Chesbro-NY .305
Hogg-NY .307

Earned Run Average
White-Chi 1.52
Orth-NY 2.34
Hogg-NY 2.93
Chesbro-NY 2.96

Adjusted ERA
White-Chi 167
Orth-NY 127
Hogg-NY 101
Chesbro-NY 100

Adjusted Starter Runs
Rhoads-Cle 28.5
Orth-NY 21.0
Clarkson-NY 6.8
Hogg-NY 4.2

Pitcher Wins
White-Chi 3.9
Orth-NY 3.4
Clarkson-NY .4
Doyle-NY .2

1907 American League

TEAM	W	L	T	PCT	GB	R	OR	HR	AVG	OBP	SLG	OPS	AOPS	PF	SB	CG	HR	BB	SO	BR/9	ERA	AERA	OAV	OOB	FW	PW	BW	BSW	DIF
Det	92	58	3	.613		**693**	531	11	**.266**	**.313**	**.335**	**648**	**108**	104	196	120	**8**	380	512	11.2	2.33	**112**	.251	.309	1.0	**4.3**	4.4		7.3
Phi	88	57	5	.607	1.5	584	511	**22**	.255	.311	.329	640	106	102	137	106	13	378	**789**	10.3	2.35	111	**.226**	.290	.4	4.1	**4.7**		6.3
Chi	87	64	6	.576	5.5	588	**474**	5	.238	.302	.283	585	95	97	175	112	13	**305**	604	10.3	**2.22**	108	.245	.290	**3.4**	3.1	-1.8		6.8
Cle	85	67	6	.559	8	531	525	11	.241	.295	.310	605	97	101	193	127	**8**	362	513	10.8	2.26	111	.244	.300	1.3	4.0	-1.8		5.5
NY	70	78	4	.473	21	605	667	15	.249	.299	.315	614	93	108	206	93	13	428	511	12.2	3.03	92	.262	.325	-4.4	-3.5	-4.6		8.5
StL	69	83	3	.454	24	541	555	10	.253	.308	.313	621	103	100	144	**129**	17	352	463	10.8	2.61	96	.245	.300	.8	-1.8	2.1		-8.1
Bos	59	90	6	.396	32.5	466	558	18	.234	.281	.292	573	89	99	125	100	22	337	517	**10.2**	2.45	105	.236	**.288**	.2	2.0	-8.2		-9.5
Was	49	102	0	.325	43.5	506	691	12	.243	.304	.299	603	105	92	**223**	106	10	344	570	11.8	3.11	78	.268	.320	-2.4	-12.3	4.1		-15.9
Total	617					34514		104	.247	.302	.309	611			1399	893				10.9	2.54		.247	.302					

Batter-Fielder Wins
Lajoie-Cle 7.0
Elberfeld-NY 2.4
Kleinow-NY............. .6
Williams-NY............ .2

Batting Average
Cobb-Det .... .350
Chase-NY .... .287
Moriarty-NY .... .277
Elberfeld-NY .... .271

On-Base Percentage
Hartsel-Phi............ .405
Elberfeld-NY .... .343
Hoffman-NY.......... .325
Williams-NY.......... .319

Slugging Average
Cobb-Det .... .468
LaPorte-NY .... .360
Williams-NY.......... .359
Chase-NY............. .357

On-Base Plus Slugging
Cobb-Det 848
Elberfeld-NY 678
Williams-NY........... 678
LaPorte-NY............ 676

Adjusted OPS
Cobb-Det 164
Elberfeld-NY 108
Williams-NY........... 107
LaPorte-NY............ 107

Adjusted Batter Runs
Cobb-Det 40.4
Elberfeld-NY 5.3
Orth-NY 3.7
Williams-NY............ 3.0

Runs
Crawford-Det 102
Hoffman-NY............ 81
Chase-NY................ 72
Elberfeld-NY 61

Hits
Cobb-Det 212
Chase-NY............. 143
Williams-NY.......... 136
Hoffman-NY.......... 131

Doubles
Davis-Phi 35
Chase-NY................ 23
LaPorte-NY............. 20
2 players tied 17

Triples
Flick-Cle.................. 18
Williams-NY.............11
LaPorte-NY..............11
Conroy-NY................11

Home Runs
Davis-Phi 8
Hoffman-NY.............. 5
Conroy-NY................. 3
2 players tied 2

Total Bases
Cobb-Det 283
Williams-NY.......... 181
Chase-NY............. 178
LaPorte-NY........... 169

Runs Batted In
Cobb-Det 119
Chase-NY................ 68
Williams-NY............ 63
2 players tied 51

Stolen Bases
Cobb-Det 53
Conroy-NY.............. 41
Chase-NY................ 32
Hoffman-NY............ 30

Base Stealing Runs

Fielding Runs-Infield
Lajoie-Cle 44.9
Elberfeld-NY 12.8
Conroy-NY............. 3.1

Fielding Runs-Outfield
D.Jones-Det.......... 12.8
Conroy-NY............. 4.9
Hoffman-NY........... 4.3
Chase-NY.............. 1.2

Wins
White-Chi................ 27
Joss-Cle.................. 27
Orth-NY 14
Doyle-NY 11

Winning Pct.
Donovan-Det .... .862

Complete Games
Walsh-Chi 37
Orth-NY 21
Chesbro-NY............ 17
Doyle-NY 15

Strikeouts
Waddell-Phi 232
Doyle-NY 94
Orth-NY.................. 78
Chesbro-NY............ 78

Fewest BB/Game
White-Chi............. 1.18
Orth-NY 1.92
Chesbro-NY.......... 2.01
Doyle-NY 3.11

Games
Walsh-Chi 56
Orth-NY 36
Chesbro-NY............ 30
Doyle-NY 29

Saves
3 players tied 4
Keefe-NY................... 3
Doyle-NY 1

Base Runners/9
Young-Bos 9.02
Chesbro-NY......... 10.66
Orth-NY 10.97
Doyle-NY 11.25

Adjusted Relief Runs

Relief Ranking

Innings Pitched
Walsh-Chi........... 422.1
Orth-NY 248.2
Chesbro-NY........ 206.0
Doyle-NY 193.2

Opponents' Avg.
Dygert-Phi............ .214
Doyle-NY .... .237
Chesbro-NY.......... .250
Orth-NY .... .259

Opponents' OBP
Young-Bos .... .263
Chesbro-NY.......... .297
Orth-NY .... .303
Doyle-NY .... .308

Earned Run Average
Walsh-Chi............. 1.60
Chesbro-NY.......... 2.53
Orth-NY 2.61
Doyle-NY 2.65

Adjusted ERA
Walsh-Chi 150
Chesbro-NY...........110
Orth-NY 107
Doyle-NY 105

Adjusted Starter Runs
Walsh-Chi 32.8
Chesbro-NY........... 6.3
Keefe-NY............... 3.5
Neuer-NY............... 2.9

Pitcher Wins
Walsh-Chi 4.6
Chesbro-NY.............. .6
Orth-NY 5
Keefe-NY.................. .4

1908 American League

TEAM	W	L	T	PCT	GB	R	OR	HR	AVG	OBP	SLG	OPS	AOPS	PF	SB	CG	HR	BB	SO	BR/9	ERA	AERA	OAV	OOB	FW	PW	BW	BSW	DIF
Det	90	63	1	.588		**647**	547	19	**.263**	**.312**	**.347**	**659**	**115**	104	165	**119**	12	318	553	11.1	2.40	100	.255	.306	-2.1	.2	**8.8**		6.6
Cle	90	64	3	.584	0.5	569	**459**	18	.239	.297	.309	606	103	100	177	108	16	328	548	9.7	**2.02**	**118**	.229	.280	1.6	**6.4**	1.7		3.3
Chi	88	64	4	.579	1.5	537	470	3	.224	.298	.271	569	91	98	209	107	11	**284**	623	**9.4**	2.22	104	**.225**	**.269**	**3.2**	1.6	-3.1		10.3
StL	83	69	3	.546	6.5	544	483	20	.245	.296	.310	606	102	101	126	107	**7**	387	607	10.3	2.15	111	.230	.294	2.7	4.1	1.3		-1.1
Bos	75	79	1	.487	15.5	564	513	14	.245	.295	.312	607	100	103	156	102	18	364	624	10.5	2.28	108	.238	.295	-1.4	3.0	-.9		-2.6
Phi	68	85	4	.444	22	486	562	**21**	.223	.281	.292	573	86	107	116	102	10	410	**741**	10.6	2.56	100	.235	.298	.6	-.5	-8.4		-.2
Was	67	85	3	.441	22.5	479	539	8	.235	.293	.296	589	106	92	170	106	16	348	649	10.5	2.34	97	.241	.294	.1	-1.5	3.4		-11.0
NY	51	103	1	.331	39.5	460	713	13	.236	.283	.291	574	91	101	**231**	90	26	458	585	12.0	3.16	78	.252	.322	-4.1	-11.6	-5.8		-4.4
Total	622					34286		116	.239	.294	.304	598			1350	841				10.5	2.39		.239	.294					

Batter-Fielder Wins
Lajoie-Cle 8.0
Hemphill-NY 1.4
Conroy-NY............... .3
Cree-NY 2

Batting Average
Cobb-Det .... .324
Hemphill-NY .... .297
Chase-NY .... .257
Ball-NY .... .247

On-Base Percentage
Gessler-Bos.......... .394
Hemphill-NY .... .374
Ball-NY .... .284
Conroy-NY............ .258

Slugging Average
Cobb-Det .... .475
Hemphill-NY .... .356
Chase-NY............. .306
Conroy-NY............ .296

On-Base Plus Slugging
Cobb-Det 842
Hemphill-NY 730
Ball-NY 575
Conroy-NY............. 554

Adjusted OPS
Cobb-Det 166
Hemphill-NY 136
Ball-NY 86
Conroy-NY............... 79

Adjusted Batter Runs
Cobb-Det 40.0
Hemphill-NY 22.2
Orth-NY 4.7
Keeler-NY............... 2.1

Runs
McIntyre-Det.......... 105
Hemphill-NY 62
Chase-NY................ 50
Conroy-NY............... 44

Hits
Cobb-Det 188
Hemphill-NY 150
Conroy-NY............ 126
Ball-NY 110

Doubles
Cobb-Det 36
Conroy-NY.............. 22
Ball-NY 16
2 players tied 12

Triples
Cobb-Det 20
Hemphill-NY 9
3 players tied 3

Home Runs
Crawford-Det 7
6 players tied 1

Total Bases
Cobb-Det 276
Hemphill-NY 180
Conroy-NY............ 157
Ball-NY 130

Runs Batted In
Cobb-Det 108
Hemphill-NY 44
Conroy-NY............... 39
Ball-NY 38

Stolen Bases
Dougherty-Chi 47
Hemphill-NY 42
Ball-NY 32
Chase-NY................ 27

Base Stealing Runs

Fielding Runs-Infield
Lajoie-Cle 46.8
Conroy-NY............ 13.9

Fielding Runs-Outfield
McIntyre-Det......... 16.4
Conroy-NY................ .0

Wins
Walsh-Chi 40
Chesbro-NY............ 14
Manning-NY............ 13
Lake-NY.................... 9

Winning Pct.
Walsh-Chi .... .727

Complete Games
Walsh-Chi 42
Chesbro-NY............ 20
Manning-NY............ 19
Lake-NY.................. 19

Strikeouts
Walsh-Chi 269
Chesbro-NY........... 124
Lake-NY..................118
Manning-NY...........113

Fewest BB/Game
Joss-Cle.................. .83
Chesbro-NY.......... 2.09
Lake-NY 2.57
Manning-NY.......... 3.16

Games
Walsh-Chi 66
Chesbro-NY............ 45
Manning-NY............ 41
Lake-NY.................. 38

Saves
Walsh-Chi 6
Newton-NY 1
Manning-NY............... 1
Chesbro-NY............... 1

Base Runners/9
Joss-Cle................ 7.31
Orth-NY 10.85
Chesbro-NY.........11.13
Lake-NY...............11.19

Adjusted Relief Runs

Relief Ranking

Innings Pitched
Walsh-Chi........... 464.0
Chesbro-NY........ 288.2
Lake-NY.............. 269.1
Manning-NY........ 245.0

Opponents' Avg.
Joss-Cle................ .197
Lake-NY .... .242
Chesbro-NY.......... .256
Manning-NY.......... .256

Opponents' OBP
Joss-Cle................ .218
Lake-NY .... .298
Chesbro-NY.......... .307
Manning-NY.......... .334

Earned Run Average
Joss-Cle 1.16
Chesbro-NY.......... 2.93
Manning-NY.......... 2.94
Lake-NY................ 3.17

Adjusted ERA
Joss-Cle................. 205
Chesbro-NY............. 84
Manning-NY............. 84
Lake-NY................... 78

Adjusted Starter Runs
Walsh-Chi 42.7

Pitcher Wins
Walsh-Chi 6.8
Chase-NY.................. .0

Historical Record

1909 American League

TEAM	W	L	T	PCT	GB	R	OR	HR	AVG	OBP	SLG	OPS	AOPS	PF	SB	CG	HR	BB	SO	BR/9	ERA	AERA	OAV	OOB	FW	PW	BW	BSW	DIF
Det	98	54	6	.645		**666**	493	19	**.267**	**.325**	.342	**667**	113	104	**280**	**117**	16	359	528	10.6	2.26	111	.238	.293	.4	4.4	8.5		8.7
Phi	95	58	0	.621	3.5	605	**411**	**21**	.256	.321	**.343**	664	**115**	102	201	110	9	386	**728**	**9.9**	**1.93**	**124**	**.217**	**.282**	1.8	**8.4**	**9.1**		-.8
Bos	88	63	1	.583	9.5	601	549	20	.263	.321	.333	654	112	102	215	75	18	384	555	10.9	2.59	96	.243	.303	-1.3	-1.7	6.8		8.7
Chi	78	74	7	.513	20	492	464	4	.221	.291	.275	566	89	96	211	115	**8**	**340**	669	**9.9**	2.05	114	.229	.283	**2.4**	5.3	-5.8		.0
NY	74	77	2	.490	23.5	589	587	16	.248	.313	.311	624	103	101	187	94	21	422	597	11.4	2.65	95	.248	.316	-3.6	-2.4	2.4		2.1
Cle	71	82	2	.464	27.5	493	532	10	.241	.288	.313	601	92	104	173	110	9	348	568	10.6	2.40	106	.250	.307	-.0	2.3	-5.7		-2.0
StL	61	89	4	.407	36	441	575	10	.232	.287	.279	566	91	93	136	105	16	383	620	11.4	2.88	84	.261	.319	.5	-8.4	-5.5		-.6
Was	42	110	4	.276	56	380	656	9	.223	.276	.275	551	84	-95	136	99	12	424	653	11.6	3.04	80	.248	.312	-.0	-11.1	-10.0		-12.8
Total	620					34267		109	.244	.303	.309	612			1539	825				10.8	2.47		.244	.303					

Batter-Fielder Wins
Cobb-Det 6.0
Engle-NY 2.3
Austin-NY .7
Kleinow-NY .5

Batting Average
Cobb-Det .377
Chase-NY .283
Engle-NY .278
Keeler-NY .264

On-Base Percentage
Cobb-Det .431
Engle-NY .347
Demmitt-NY .340
Chase-NY .317

Slugging Average
Cobb-Det .517
Demmitt-NY .358
Engle-NY .358
Chase-NY .357

On-Base Plus Slugging
Cobb-Det 947
Engle-NY 705
Demmitt-NY 698
Chase-NY 674

Adjusted OPS
Cobb-Det 190
Engle-NY 122
Demmitt-NY 120
Chase-NY 112

Adjusted Batter Runs
Cobb-Det 59.2
Engle-NY 13.4
Demmitt-NY 10.7
LaPorte-NY 9.0

Runs
Cobb-Det 116
Demmitt-NY 68
Engle-NY 66
Chase-NY 60

Hits
Cobb-Det 216
Engle-NY 137
Chase-NY 134
Demmitt-NY 105

Doubles
Crawford-Det 35
Engle-NY 20
LaPorte-NY 19
Chase-NY 17

Triples
Baker-Phi 19
Demmitt-NY 12

Home Runs
Cobb-Det 9
Demmitt-NY 4
Chase-NY 4
Engle-NY 3

Total Bases
Cobb-Det 296
Engle-NY 176
Chase-NY 169
Demmitt-NY 153

Runs Batted In
Cobb-Det 107
Engle-NY 71
Chase-NY 63
Knight-NY 40

Stolen Bases
Cobb-Det 76
Austin-NY 30
Chase-NY 25
Elberfeld-NY 23

Base Stealing Runs

Fielding Runs-Infield
Lajoie-Cle 23.3
Austin-NY 13.0
Elberfeld-NY 4.3

Fielding Runs-Outfield
Speaker-Bos 18.5
Engle-NY 14.9

Wins
Mullin-Det 29
Lake-NY 14
Warhop-NY 13
Brockett-NY 10

Winning Pct.
Mullin-Det .784

Complete Games
Smith-Chi 37
Warhop-NY 21
Lake-NY 17
Manning-NY 11

Strikeouts
Smith-Chi 177
Lake-NY 117
Warhop-NY 95
Manning-NY 71

Fewest BB/Game
Joss-Cle 1.15
Lake-NY 2.47
Manning-NY 2.50
Warhop-NY 3.00

Games
Smith-Chi 51
Warhop-NY 36
Lake-NY 31
2 players tied 26

Saves
Arellanes-Bos 8
Warhop-NY 2
Hughes-NY 2

Base Runners/9
Walsh-Chi 8.60
Doyle-NY 10.17
Lake-NY 10.20
Quinn-NY 10.47

Adjusted Relief Runs

Relief Ranking

Innings Pitched
Smith-Chi 365.0
Warhop-NY 243.1
Lake-NY 215.1
Manning-NY 173.0

Opponents' Avg.
Morgan-Bos-Phi .202
Lake-NY .225
Warhop-NY .233
Brockett-NY .245

Opponents' OBP
Walsh-Chi .253
Lake-NY .283
Brockett-NY .318
Warhop-NY .319

Earned Run Average
Krause-Phi 1.39
Lake-NY 1.88
Brockett-NY 2.12
Warhop-NY 2.40

Adjusted ERA
Krause-Phi 172
Lake-NY 134
Brockett-NY 119
Warhop-NY 105

Adjusted Starter Runs
Walsh-Chi 24.9
Lake-NY 10.3
Warhop-NY 7.2
Quinn-NY 4.9

Pitcher Wins
Walsh-Chi 4.1
Smith-Chi 4.1
Lake-NY 1.7
Brockett-NY 1.1

1910 American League

TEAM	W	L	T	PCT	GB	R	OR	HR	AVG	OBP	SLG	OPS	AOPS	PF	SB	CG	HR	BB	SO	BR/9	ERA	AERA	OAV	OOB	FW	PW	BW	BSW	DIF
Phi	102	48	5	.680		674	**442**	19	**.266**	.326	**.355**	**681**	**120**	99	207	**123**	**8**	450	**789**	10.2	**1.79**	**133**	**.221**	.292	**3.9**	**10.8**	**12.3**		.0
NY	88	63	5	.583	14.5	626	557	20	.248	.320	.322	642	101	106	**288**	110	16	**364**	654	10.7	2.61	102	.243	.300	.2	.6	1.2		10.5
Det	86	68	1	.558	18	**679**	584	28	.261	**.329**	.344	673	110	107	249	108	34	460	532	11.6	2.82	93	.248	.319	-.0	-2.9	6.3		5.6
Bos	81	72	5	.529	22.5	641	564	**43**	.259	.323	.351	674	114	102	194	100	30	414	670	10.7	2.45	104	.235	.297	-1.1	1.6	8.7		-4.6
Cle	71	81	9	.467	32	548	657	9	.244	.296	.308	604	94	101	189	92	10	488	617	11.9	2.88	90	.261	.330	3.4	-5.4	-5.1		2.2
Chi	68	85	3	.444	35.5	457	479	7	.211	.275	.261	536	76	-96	183	103	16	381	785	**9.8**	2.03	118	.222	**.281**	-1.7	6.6	-15.1		1.8
Was	66	85	6	.437	36.5	501	551	9	.236	.309	.289	598	98	95	192	119	19	375	674	10.8	2.46	101	.244	.304	1.8	.6	-.4		-11.4
StL	47	107	4	.305	57	451	743	12	.218	.281	.274	555	84	-94	169	101	14	532	557	12.6	3.09	80	.265	.341	-6.3	-10.8	-10.0		-2.9
Total	628					34577		147	.243	.308	.313	621			1671	856				11.0	2.52		.243	.308					

Batter-Fielder Wins
Lajoie-Cle 8.9
Knight-NY 2.1
Wolter-NY .7
Cree-NY .4

Batting Average
Cobb-Det .383
Knight-NY .312
Chase-NY .290
Cree-NY .287

On-Base Percentage
Cobb-Det .456
Wolter-NY .364
Cree-NY .353
LaPorte-NY .321

Slugging Average
Cobb-Det .551
Cree-NY .422
Knight-NY .413
Chase-NY .365

On-Base Plus Slugging
Cobb-Det 1008
Cree-NY 775
Wolter-NY 725
Chase-NY 677

Adjusted OPS
Cobb-Det 202
Cree-NY 135
Wolter-NY 120
Chase-NY 106

Adjusted Batter Runs
Lajoie-Cle 69.3
Knight-NY 18.7
Cree-NY 17.6
Wolter-NY 13.5

Runs
Cobb-Det 106
Wolter-NY 84
Daniels-NY 68
Chase-NY 67

Hits
Lajoie-Cle 227
Chase-NY 152
Cree-NY 134
Knight-NY 129

Doubles
Lajoie-Cle 51
Knight-NY 25
Chase-NY 20
Cree-NY 19

Triples
Crawford-Det 19
Cree-NY 16
Wolter-NY 9
Daniels-NY 8

Home Runs
Stahl-Bos 10
Wolter-NY 4
Cree-NY 4
2 players tied 3

Total Bases
Lajoie-Cle 304
Cree-NY 197
Chase-NY 191
Wolter-NY 173

Runs Batted In
Crawford-Det 120
Cree-NY 73
Chase-NY 73
LaPorte-NY 67

Stolen Bases
Collins-Phi 81
Daniels-NY 41
Chase-NY 40
Wolter-NY 39

Base Stealing Runs

Fielding Runs-Infield
McBride-Was 32.8
Austin-NY 3.2

Fielding Runs-Outfield
Lewis-Bos 11.5

Wins
Coombs-Phi 31
Ford-NY 26
Quinn-NY 18
Warhop-NY 14

Winning Pct.
Bender-Phi .821
Ford-NY .813
Quinn-NY .600

Complete Games
Johnson-Was 38
Ford-NY 29
Warhop-NY 20
Quinn-NY 20

Strikeouts
Johnson-Was 313
Ford-NY 209
Vaughn-NY 107
Quinn-NY 82

Fewest BB/Game
Walsh-Chi 1.49
Young-Cle 1.49
Ford-NY 2.10
Quinn-NY 2.21

Games
3 players tied 45
Warhop-NY 37
Ford-NY 36
Quinn-NY 35

Saves
Walsh-Chi 5
Warhop-NY 2

Base Runners/9
Walsh-Chi 7.47
Ford-NY 8.17
Vaughn-NY 10.48
Quinn-NY 10.62

Adjusted Relief Runs

Relief Ranking

Innings Pitched
Johnson-Was 370.0
Ford-NY 299.2
Warhop-NY 243.0
Quinn-NY 235.2

Opponents' Avg.
Walsh-Chi .187
Ford-NY .188
Vaughn-NY .237
Warhop-NY .246

Opponents' OBP
Walsh-Chi .226
Ford-NY .245
Vaughn-NY .297
Quinn-NY .299

Earned Run Average
Walsh-Chi 1.27
Ford-NY 1.65
Vaughn-NY 1.83
Quinn-NY 2.37

Adjusted ERA
Walsh-Chi 189
Ford-NY 161
Vaughn-NY 145
Quinn-NY 112

Adjusted Starter Runs
Coombs-Phi 46.6
Ford-NY 33.9
Vaughn-NY 14.4
Quinn-NY 6.1

Pitcher Wins
Walsh-Chi 6.3
Ford-NY 4.2
Quinn-NY 1.6
Vaughn-NY 1.3

1911 American League

TEAM	W	L	T	PCT	GB	R	OR	HR	AVG	OBP	SLG	OPS	AOPS	PF	SB	CG	HR	BB	SO	BR/9	ERA	AERA	OAV	OOB	FW	PW	BW	BSW	DIF
Phi	101	50	1	.669		**861**	**602**	**35**	**.296**	**.357**	**.398**	**755**	**119**	98	226	97	**17**	487	739	12.5	3.01	105	.264	.338	**4.9**	2.2	**12.2**		6.3
Det	89	65	0	.578	13.5	831	777	30	.292	.355	.388	743	108	105	**276**	**108**	28	460	538	13.3	3.73	93	.283	.348	-.9	-4.2	5.2		12.0
Cle	80	73	3	.523	22	693	712	20	.282	.333	.369	702	101	101	209	93	**17**	552	675	12.9	3.36	101	.267	.345	.3	.7	-.7		3.2
Chi	77	74	3	.510	24	718	624	20	.269	.325	.350	675	97	97	201	85	22	**384**	**752**	**11.5**	2.97	108	**.255**	**.310**	3.4	3.8	-2.8		-2.9
Bos	78	75	0	.510	24	680	643	**35**	.275	.350	.363	713	106	99	190	87	21	473	711	12.2	**2.74**	**119**	.262	.332	-1.4	**7.9**	4.8		-9.8
NY	76	76	1	.500	25.5	684	723	25	.272	.344	.362	706	97	107	269	90	26	406	667	12.3	3.54	101	.270	.329	-1.7	.9	-2.1		2.9
Was	64	90	0	.416	38.5	624	765	16	.258	.330	.320	650	89	98	215	106	39	410	628	12.8	3.52	93	.277	.334	-.0	-3.7	-6.2		-3.0
StL	45	107	0	.296	56.5	567	812	17	.239	.307	.311	618	81	96	125	92	28	463	383	13.4	3.86	87	.278	.342	-3.8	-7.2	-11.9		-8.1
Total	614					35658		198	.273	.338	.358	696			1711	758				12.6	3.34		.273	.338					

Batter-Fielder Wins
Cobb-Det 6.6
Cree-NY 2.4
Wolter-NY 1.4
Brockett-NY............ .0

Batting Average
Cobb-Det .... .420
Cree-NY................ .348
Chase-NY .... .315
Wolter-NY .... .304

On-Base Percentage
Jackson-Cle.......... .468
Cree-NY................ .415
Wolter-NY .... .396
2 players tied .... .375

Slugging Average
Cobb-Det .... .621
Cree-NY................ .513
Wolter-NY .... .440
Chase-NY .... .419

On-Base Plus Slugging
Cobb-Det 1088
Cree-NY................ 928
Wolter-NY 836
Hartzell-NY 763

Adjusted OPS
Cobb-Det 193
Cree-NY 149
Wolter-NY 125
Hartzell-NY 106

Adjusted Batter Runs
Cobb-Det 71.7
Cree-NY................ 33.1
Wolter-NY 15.4
Hartzell-NY 5.0

Runs
Cobb-Det 147
Cree-NY.................. 90
Chase-NY 82
Wolter-NY 78

Hits
Cobb-Det 248
Cree-NY................ 181
Chase-NY 166
Hartzell-NY 156

Doubles
Cobb-Det 47
Chase-NY 32
Cree-NY.................. 30
2 players tied 17

Triples
Cobb-Det 24
Cree-NY.................. 22
Wolter-NY 15
Hartzell-NY 11

Home Runs
Baker-Phi..................11
Wolter-NY 4
Cree-NY.................... 4

Total Bases
Cobb-Det 367
Cree-NY................ 267
Chase-NY 221
Hartzell-NY 204

Runs Batted In
Cobb-Det 127
Hartzell-NY 91
Cree-NY.................. 88
2 players tied 62

Stolen Bases
Cobb-Det 83
Cree-NY.................. 48
Daniels-NY 40
Chase-NY 36

Base Stealing Runs

Fielding Runs-Infield
Tannehill-Chi......... 36.3
Gardner-NY 2.6

Fielding Runs-Outfield
Hogan-Phi-StL 12.6
Wolter-NY 4.7
Hartzell-NY 6

Wins
Coombs-Phi............ 28
Ford-NY.................. 22
Caldwell-NY............ 14
Warhop-NY.............. 12

Winning Pct.
Bender-Phi............ .773
Ford-NY .... .667

Complete Games
Johnson-Was.......... 36
Ford-NY.................. 26
Caldwell-NY............ 19
Warhop-NY.............. 17

Strikeouts
Walsh-Chi 255
Ford-NY 158
Caldwell-NY.......... 145
Fisher-NY 99

Fewest BB/Game
White-Chi.............. 1.47
Warhop-NY........... 1.89
Quinn-NY..............2.11
Ford-NY 2.43

Games
Walsh-Chi 56
Caldwell-NY............ 41
Quinn-NY................ 40
Ford-NY.................. 37

Saves
3 players tied 4
Quinn-NY................... 2
Caldwell-NY.............. 1

Base Runners/9
Gregg-Cle............ 9.86
Ford-NY............. 10.59
Caldwell-NY.........11.72
Fisher-NY 12.48

Adjusted Relief Runs

Relief Ranking

Innings Pitched
Walsh-Chi........... 368.2
Ford-NY............. 281.1
Caldwell-NY........ 255.0
Warhop-NY......... 209.2

Opponents' Avg.
Gregg-Cle .... .205
Ford-NY................ .237
Caldwell-NY.......... .260
Fisher-NY .... .269

Opponents' OBP
Walsh-Chi .... .280
Ford-NY................ .291
Caldwell-NY.......... .327
Fisher-NY .... .330

Earned Run Average
Gregg-Cle............ 1.80
Ford-NY............... 2.27
Fisher-NY 3.25
Caldwell-NY.......... 3.35

Adjusted ERA
Gregg-Cle............ 189
Ford-NY................ 158
Fisher-NY 110
Caldwell-NY.......... 107

Adjusted Starter Runs
Johnson-Was........ 43.1
Ford-NY............... 30.4
Caldwell-NY.......... 10.8
Fisher-NY 5.6

Pitcher Wins
Wood-Bos............... 5.7
Ford-NY.................. 3.0
Caldwell-NY........... 1.3
Fisher-NY 5

1912 American League

TEAM	W	L	T	PCT	GB	R	OR	HR	AVG	OBP	SLG	OPS	AOPS	PF	SB	CG	HR	BB	SO	BR/9	ERA	AERA	OAV	OOB	FW	PW	BW	BSW	DIF
Bos	105	47	2	.691		**799**	**544**	**29**	.277	**.355**	**.380**	**735**	110	105	185	**108**	18	**385**	712	**11.0**	2.76	124	.248	**.306**	2.4	10.1	7.3		9.2
Was	91	61	2	.599	14	699	581	20	.256	.324	.341	665	94	101	273	98	24	525	**828**	11.8	**2.69**	**125**	**.242**	.320	.7	**10.4**	-3.6		7.6
Phi	90	62	1	.592	15	779	658	22	**.282**	.349	.377	726	**117**	96	258	95	**12**	518	601	12.3	3.32	93	.258	.336	**2.5**	-3.3	**11.1**		3.7
Chi	78	76	4	.506	28	639	648	17	.255	.317	.329	646	93	97	213	85	26	426	698	11.8	3.06	105	.264	.322	1.5	2.7	-5.0		1.8
Cle	75	78	2	.490	30.5	677	681	12	.273	.333	.353	686	98	103	194	94	15	523	622	12.9	3.30	104	.272	.346	1.4	2.0	-1.5		-3.4
Det	69	84	1	.451	36.5	720	777	19	.268	.343	.349	692	106	97	**277**	107	16	521	512	13.3	3.77	87	.277	.350	-1.7	-7.2	5.1		-3.7
StL	53	101	3	.344	53	552	764	19	.248	.315	.320	635	90	96	176	85	17	442	547	12.7	3.71	90	.277	.341	-1.6	-5.5	-6.7		-10.3
NY	50	102	1	.329	55	630	842	18	.259	.329	.334	663	90	106	247	105	28	436	637	13.0	4.13	88	.282	.344	-4.4	-6.6	-7.0		-8.0
Total	619					35495		156	.265	.333	.348	681			1823	777				12.3	3.34		.265	.333					

Batter-Fielder Wins
Speaker-Bos.......... 7.2
Cree-NY 1.1
Lelivelt-NY 4
Wolter-NY 3

Batting Average
Cobb-Det .... .409
Daniels-NY .... .274
Chase-NY .... .274
Hartzell-NY .... .272

On-Base Percentage
Speaker-Bos......... .464
Hartzell-NY .... .370
Daniels-NY .... .363
Chase-NY .... .299

Slugging Average
Cobb-Det .... .584
Zinn-NY .... .394
Daniels-NY .... .381
Chase-NY .... .372

On-Base Plus Slugging
Cobb-Det 1040
Daniels-NY 744
Hartzell-NY 726
Chase-NY 671

Adjusted OPS
Cobb-Det 203
Daniels-NY 106
Hartzell-NY 102
Chase-NY 86

Adjusted Batter Runs
Cobb-Det 71.5
Cree-NY.................. 9.9
Lelivelt-NY 8.5
Daniels-NY 5.3

Runs
Collins-Phi 137
Daniels-NY 72
Chase-NY 61
Zinn-NY 56

Hits
Jackson-Cle........... 226
Cobb-Det 226
Chase-NY 143
Daniels-NY 136

Doubles
Speaker-Bos........... 53
Daniels-NY 25
Chase-NY 21
Simmons-NY 17

Triples
Jackson-Cle............ 26
Hartzell-NY 11
Daniels-NY 11
Zinn-NY 10

Home Runs
Speaker-Bos........... 10
Baker-Phi................ 10
Zinn-NY 6
Chase-NY 4

Total Bases
Jackson-Cle........... 331
Chase-NY 194
Daniels-NY 189
Zinn-NY 158

Runs Batted In
Baker-Phi.............. 130
Chase-NY 58
Zinn-NY 55
2 players tied 41

Stolen Bases
Milan-Was............... 88
Daniels-NY 37
Chase-NY 33
Hartzell-NY 20

Base Stealing Runs

Fielding Runs-Infield
McBride-Was 27.8

Fielding Runs-Outfield
Speaker-Bos......... 16.3
Daniels-NY 3.1
Hartzell-NY 2.3

Wins
Wood-Bos............... 34
Ford-NY.................. 13
Warhop-NY............. 10
2 players tied 8

Winning Pct.
Wood-Bos............. .872

Complete Games
Wood-Bos............... 35
Ford-NY.................. 30
McConnell-NY 19
Warhop-NY............. 16

Strikeouts
Johnson-Was......... 303
Ford-NY..................112
Warhop-NY............110
Caldwell-NY............ 95

Fewest BB/Game
Bender-Phi........... 1.74
Warhop-NY........... 2.06
Ford-NY 2.44
McConnell-NY 2.65

Games
Walsh-Chi 62
Warhop-NY............. 39
Ford-NY.................. 36
Caldwell-NY............ 30

Saves
Walsh-Chi 10
Warhop-NY............... 3

Base Runners/9
Johnson-Was....... 8.56
Warhop-NY..........11.55
McConnell-NY 11.62
Ford-NY............. 12.37

Adjusted Relief Runs

Relief Ranking

Innings Pitched
Walsh-Chi........... 393.0
Ford-NY............. 291.2
Warhop-NY......... 258.0
Caldwell-NY....... 183.1

Opponents' Avg.
Johnson-Was........ .196
Warhop-NY........... .266
McConnell-NY ...... .269
Caldwell-NY.......... .277

Opponents' OBP
Johnson-Was........ .248
Warhop-NY........... .319
McConnell-NY ...... .328
Ford-NY................ .329

Earned Run Average
Johnson-Was........ 1.39
McConnell-NY 2.75
Warhop-NY........... 2.86
Ford-NY............... 3.55

Adjusted ERA
Johnson-Was........ 241
McConnell-NY 131
Warhop-NY........... 126
Ford-NY................ 102

Adjusted Starter Runs
Johnson-Was........ 77.1
Warhop-NY.......... 17.2
McConnell-NY 8.4
Schulz-NY.............. 1.5

Pitcher Wins
Johnson-Was........ 10.6
McConnell-NY 1.6
Warhop-NY............. 1.6
Ford-NY..................... .6

1913 American League

TEAM	W	L	T	PCT	GB	R	OR	HR	AVG	OBP	SLG	OPS	AOPS	PF	SB	CG	HR	BB	SO	BR/9	ERA	AERA	OAV	OOB	FW	PW	BW	BSW	DIF
Phi	96	57	0	.627		**794**	592	**33**	**.280**	**.356**	**.375**	**731**	**124**	98	221	69	24	532	630	11.8	3.19	87	.243	.321	**3.3**	-7.3	**16.7**		6.9
Was	90	64	1	.584	6.5	596	562	19	.252	.317	.326	643	93	102	**287**	78	35	465	**758**	**11.0**	2.73	108	**.233**	.306	.4	3.6	-5.3		14.3
Cle	86	66	3	.566	9.5	633	536	16	.268	.331	.348	679	102	103	191	93	19	502	689	11.8	2.54	119	.251	.324	1.6	7.6	1.4		-.5
Bos	79	71	1	.527	15.5	631	610	17	.268	.336	.364	700	109	103	189	83	**6**	442	710	11.9	2.94	100	.262	.325	1.4	-.3	5.4		-2.5
Chi	78	74	1	.513	17.5	488	**498**	24	.236	.299	.311	610	86	99	156	84	10	**438**	602	**11.0**	**2.33**	**125**	.239	**.305**	.5	**9.5**	-9.8		1.8
Det	66	87	0	.431	30	625	716	24	.265	.336	.355	691	111	99	218	90	13	504	468	12.6	3.38	86	.267	.339	-2.5	-7.6	6.8		-7.2
NY	57	94	2	.377	38	529	668	8	.237	.320	.292	612	85	100	203	75	31	455	530	12.2	3.27	91	.262	.330	-1.9	-4.4	-8.0		-4.2
StL	57	96	2	.373	39	528	642	18	.237	.306	.312	618	90	97	209	**104**	21	454	476	12.2	3.06	96	.269	.335	-2.2	-2.3	-7.0		-7.9
Total	614					34824		159	.256	.325	.336	661			1674	676				11.8	2.93		.256	.325					

Batter-Fielder Wins	Batting Average	On-Base Percentage	Slugging Average	On-Base Plus Slugging	Adjusted OPS	Adjusted Batter Runs
Collins-Phi............ 7.0	Cobb-Det.............. .390	Cobb-Det.............. .467	Jackson-Cle.......... .551	Jackson-Cle.........1011	Cobb-Det.............. 196	Jackson-Cle.......... 63.4
Holden-NY............... .4	Cree-NY................ .272	Wolter-NY............. .377	Cree-NY................ .346	Wolter-NY............. 716	Wolter-NY............. 109	Wolter-NY............... 9.6
Whiteman-NY.......... .3	Sweeney-NY......... .265	Hartzell-NY........... .353	Wolter-NY............. .339	Cree-NY................ 685	Cree-NY................ 100	Whiteman-NY......... 3.8
Sweeney-NY............ .3	Hartzell-NY........... .259	Cree-NY................ .338	Sweeney-NY......... .322	Hartzell-NY........... 653	Hartzell-NY............. 91	Fisher-NY............... 3.3

Runs	Hits	Doubles	Triples	Home Runs	Total Bases	Runs Batted In
Collins-Phi............ 125	Jackson-Cle.......... 197	Jackson-Cle............ 39	Crawford-Det.......... 23	Baker-Phi................ 12	Crawford-Det......... 298	Baker-Phi...............117
Hartzell-NY............. 60	Cree-NY................ 145	Cree-NY.................. 25	Wolter-NY................ 6	Wolter-NY................ 2	Cree-NY................ 185	Cree-NY.................. 63
Wolter-NY............... 53	Hartzell-NY........... 127	Wolter-NY............... 18	Cree-NY.................... 6	Sweeney-NY............. 2	Hartzell-NY........... 147	Wolter-NY............... 43
Daniels-NY............. 52	Wolter-NY............. 108	Hartzell-NY............. 18	Daniels-NY............... 5	4 players tied............ 1	Wolter-NY............. 144	Sweeney-NY........... 40

Stolen Bases	Base Stealing Runs	Fielding Runs-Infield	Fielding Runs-Outfield	Wins	Winning Pct.	Complete Games
Milan-Was............... 75		Weaver-Chi.......... 35.5	Speaker-Bos......... 18.6	Johnson-Was.......... 36	Johnson-Was........ .837	Johnson-Was.......... 29
Daniels-NY............. 27		Hartzell-NY............ 2.5	Hartzell-NY............... .8	Ford-NY.................. 12		Ford-NY.................. 15
Hartzell-NY............. 26				Fisher-NY............... 12		Caldwell-NY............ 15
Maisel-NY............... 25				Caldwell-NY.............. 9		Fisher-NY............... 14

Strikeouts	Fewest BB/Game	Games	Saves	Base Runners/9	Adjusted Relief Runs	Relief Ranking
Johnson-Was......... 243	Johnson-Was.......... .99	Russell-Chi.............. 52	Bender-Phi.............. 13	Johnson-Was........ 7.26		
Fisher-NY................ 92	Ford-NY............... 2.20	Fisher-NY............... 43	McConnell-NY........... 3	Caldwell-NY........ 10.95		
Caldwell-NY............ 87	Fisher-NY............ 2.59	Schulz-NY............... 38	Ford-NY.................... 2	McConnell-NY..... 11.45		
Keating-NY............. 83	McConnell-NY...... 3.00	McConnell-NY......... 35	2 players tied............ 1	Ford-NY...............11.62		

Innings Pitched	Opponents' Avg.	Opponents' OBP	Earned Run Average	Adjusted ERA	Adjusted Starter Runs	Pitcher Wins
Johnson-Was...... 346.0	Johnson-Was........ .190	Johnson-Was........ .220	Johnson-Was........ 1.14	Johnson-Was......... 258	Johnson-Was........ 69.8	Johnson-Was........ 10.9
Fisher-NY........... 246.1	Caldwell-NY.......... .221	Caldwell-NY.......... .303	Caldwell-NY......... 2.41	Caldwell-NY.......... 124	Caldwell-NY......... 10.8	Caldwell-NY............ 1.7
Ford-NY............. 237.0	McConnell-NY...... .247	McConnell-NY...... .317	Ford-NY............... 2.66	Ford-NY.................112	Ford-NY.................. 6.6	Ford-NY.................... .7
Schulz-NY.......... 193.0	Fisher-NY............ .263	Fisher-NY............ .321	Fisher-NY............ 3.18	Fisher-NY............... 94	McHale-NY............... .5	Fisher-NY................. .1

1914 American League

TEAM	W	L	T	PCT	GB	R	OR	HR	AVG	OBP	SLG	OPS	AOPS	PF	SB	CG	HR	BB	SO	BR/9	ERA	AERA	OAV	OOB	FW	PW	BW	BSW	DIF
Phi	99	53	6	.651		**749**	529	**29**	**.272**	**.348**	**.352**	**700**	**123**	96	231	89	18	521	720	11.6	2.78	94	.249	.322	**3.5**	-3.2	**15.7**	-.0	7.1
Bos	91	62	6	.595	8.5	589	**510**	18	.250	.320	.338	658	105	100	177	88	18	393	602	**10.3**	**2.36**	**114**	.236	**.295**	1.8	**5.6**	3.1	-1.0	4.9
Was	81	73	4	.526	19	572	519	18	.244	.313	.320	633	93	104	220	75	20	520	**784**	11.0	2.54	111	**.233**	.311	1.0	4.4	-4.4	.6	2.4
Det	80	73	4	.523	19.5	615	618	25	.258	.336	.344	680	109	103	211	81	17	498	567	11.8	2.86	98	.249	.322	-1.1	-1.1	6.4	**.8**	-1.6
StL	71	82	6	.464	28.5	523	615	17	.243	.306	.319	625	99	96	233	81	20	540	553	12.1	2.85	95	.251	.327	-2.7	-2.5	-2.1	-.0	2.0
NY	70	84	3	.455	30	537	550	12	.229	.315	.287	602	88	100	**251**	**98**	30	**390**	563	10.9	2.81	98	.250	.308	1.9	-1.1	-6.3	.3	-1.7
Chi	70	84	3	.455	30	487	560	19	.239	.302	.311	613	92	99	167	74	15	401	660	10.5	2.48	108	.239	.298	-1.9	3.4	-6.1	-.2	-2.3
Cle	51	102	4	.333	48.5	538	709	10	.245	.310	.312	622	90	104	167	69	**10**	666	688	13.4	3.21	90	.267	.357	-1.9	-5.9	-6.6	-.4	-10.7
Total	631					34610		148	.248	.319	.323	642			1657	655				11.5	2.73		.248	.319					

Batter-Fielder Wins	Batting Average	On-Base Percentage	Slugging Average	On-Base Plus Slugging	Adjusted OPS	Adjusted Batter Runs
Speaker-Bos.......... 7.3	Cobb-Det.............. .368	Collins-Phi............ .452	Cobb-Det.............. .513	Speaker-Bos.......... 926	Collins-Phi............ 179	Collins-Phi............ 57.6
Cree-NY................. 1.2	Cook-NY............... .283	Cook-NY............... .356	Cook-NY............... .326	Cook-NY............... 681	Cook-NY............... 105	Cree-NY............... 15.0
Sweeney-NY............ .5	Maisel-NY............. .239	Hartzell-NY........... .335	Maisel-NY............. .325	Maisel-NY............. 659	Maisel-NY............... 98	Cook-NY.................. 4.2
Gilhooley-NY........... .1	Hartzell-NY........... .233	Maisel-NY............. .334	Hartzell-NY........... .308	Hartzell-NY........... 643	Hartzell-NY............. 94	McHale-NY............. 1.5

Runs	Hits	Doubles	Triples	Home Runs	Total Bases	Runs Batted In
Collins-Phi............ 122	Speaker-Bos.......... 193	Speaker-Bos............ 46	Crawford-Det........... 26	Baker-Phi.................. 9	Speaker-Bos.......... 287	Crawford-Det......... 104
Maisel-NY............... 78	Cook-NY............... 133	Maisel-NY............... 23	Maisel-NY.................. 9	Peckinpaugh-NY........ 3	Maisel-NY............. 178	Peckinpaugh-NY...... 51
Cook-NY.................. 59	Maisel-NY............. 131	Cree-NY.................. 18	Hartzell-NY................ 9	Maisel-NY.................. 2	Peckinpaugh-NY.... 162	Maisel-NY............... 47
2 players tied........... 55	Peckinpaugh-NY.... 127	Hartzell-NY............. 15	Peckinpaugh-NY........ 6		Cook-NY................ 153	Mullen-NY............... 44

Stolen Bases	Base Stealing Runs	Fielding Runs-Infield	Fielding Runs-Outfield	Wins	Winning Pct.	Complete Games
Maisel-NY............... 74	Maisel-NY............ 10.3	Bush-Det.............. 31.8	Speaker-Bos......... 23.0	Johnson-Was........... 28	Bender-Phi............ .850	Johnson-Was.......... 33
Peckinpaugh-NY...... 38	Peckinpaugh-NY..... 2.4	Boone-NY............. 17.7		Caldwell-NY............ 18	Caldwell-NY.......... .667	Caldwell-NY............ 22
Cook-NY.................. 26	Sweeney-NY........... 2.1	Peckinpaugh-NY..... 5.3		Fisher-NY............... 10		Fisher-NY............... 17
Hartzell-NY............. 22				Cole-NY.................. 10		Warhop-NY.............. 15

Strikeouts	Fewest BB/Game	Games	Saves	Base Runners/9	Adjusted Relief Runs	Relief Ranking
Johnson-Was......... 225	McHale-NY........... 1.55	Johnson-Was........... 51	4 players tied............ 4	Leonard-Bos......... 8.29		
Keating-NY............ 109	Warhop-NY........... 1.83	Warhop-NY.............. 37	McHale-NY................ 1	Caldwell-NY.......... 8.79		
Caldwell-NY............ 92	Caldwell-NY.......... 2.15	Keating-NY.............. 34	Fisher-NY.................. 1	Warhop-NY........... 9.84		
Fisher-NY................ 86	Fisher-NY............ 2.63	Cole-NY.................. 33		Fisher-NY........... 10.42		

Innings Pitched	Opponents' Avg.	Opponents' OBP	Earned Run Average	Adjusted ERA	Adjusted Starter Runs	Pitcher Wins
Johnson-Was...... 371.2	Leonard-Bos......... .180	Leonard-Bos......... .246	Leonard-Bos........... .96	Leonard-Bos.......... 279	Johnson-Was........ 45.3	Johnson-Was.......... 7.2
Warhop-NY......... 216.2	Caldwell-NY.......... .205	Caldwell-NY.......... .260	Caldwell-NY......... 1.94	Caldwell-NY.......... 142	Caldwell-NY......... 21.0	Caldwell-NY............ 3.0
Caldwell-NY........ 213.0	Warhop-NY........... .235	Warhop-NY........... .286	Fisher-NY............ 2.28	Fisher-NY............. 121	Fisher-NY.............11.5	Fisher-NY............... 1.2
Keating-NY......... 210.0	Fisher-NY............ .241	2 players tied........ .303	Warhop-NY.......... 2.37	Warhop-NY............116	Warhop-NY............ 7.9	Warhop-NY................ .7

1915 American League

TEAM	W	L	T	PCT	GB	R	OR	HR	AVG	OBP	SLG	OPS	AOPS	PF	SB	CG	HR	BB	SO	BR/9	ERA	AERA	OAV	OOB	FW	PW	BW	BSW	DIF
Bos	101	50	4	.669		669	499	14	.260	.336	.339	675	110	97	118	81	18	446	634	10.7	2.39	116	**.231**	.300	2.5	6.6	7.3	-.9	10.1
Det	100	54	2	.649	2.5	**778**	597	23	**.268**	**.357**	**.358**	**715**	**114**	105	**241**	86	14	492	550	11.5	2.86	106	.243	.316	.5	2.5	**10.4**	.9	8.7
Chi	93	61	1	.604	9.5	717	509	25	.258	.345	.348	693	110	103	233	91	14	**350**	635	**10.4**	2.43	122	.241	**.294**	2.7	8.8	6.6	-.7	-1.4
Was	85	68	2	.556	17	569	**491**	12	.244	.312	.312	624	90	102	186	87	**12**	455	**715**	10.7	**2.31**	**129**	.232	.302	2.2	**10.7**	-6.9	**1.1**	1.4
NY	69	83	2	.454	32.5	584	588	**31**	.233	.317	.305	622	91	100	198	**101**	41	517	559	12.0	3.06	96	.254	.329	**2.9**	-2.1	-4.7	.4	-3.5
StL	63	91	5	.409	39.5	522	680	19	.246	.315	.315	630	98	96	202	76	21	612	566	12.4	3.04	94	.249	.338	-4.3	-3.4	-2.4	-.6	-3.2
Cle	57	95	2	.375	44.5	539	670	20	.240	.312	.317	629	91	102	138	62	18	518	610	12.0	3.13	97	.256	.329	-1.2	-1.4	-5.8	-.5	-10.1
Phi	43	109	2	.283	58.5	545	888	10	.207	.301	.311	616	92	97	127	78	22	827	588	15.0	4.29	68	.278	.388	-5.0	-22.0	-5.9	.4	-.4
Total	621					34923		160	.248	.325	.326	651			1443	662				11.8	2.93		.248	.325					

Batter-Fielder Wins
E.Collins-Chi 6.6
Baumann-NY 1.0
Pipp-NY .8
Maisel-NY .7

Batting Average
Cobb-Det .369
Maisel-NY .281
Cook-NY .271
High-NY .258

On-Base Percentage
Cobb-Det .486
Cook-NY .364
High-NY .356
Maisel-NY .342

Slugging Average
Fournier-Chi .491
Pipp-NY .367
Maisel-NY .357
High-NY .342

On-Base Plus Slugging
Cobb-Det 973
Pipp-NY 706
Cook-NY 703
Maisel-NY 699

Adjusted OPS
Cobb-Det 182
Pipp-NY 112
Cook-NY 111
2 players tied 109

Adjusted Batter Runs
Cobb-Det 66.6
Baumann-NY 9.3
Cook-NY 8.5
Caldwell-NY 8.1

Runs
Cobb-Det 144
Maisel-NY 77
Cook-NY 70
Peckinpaugh-NY 67

Hits
Cobb-Det 208
Maisel-NY 149
Cook-NY 129
Peckinpaugh-NY 119

Doubles
Veach-Det 40
Pipp-NY 20
High-NY 19
Peckinpaugh-NY 18

Triples
Crawford-Det 19
Pipp-NY 13
Peckinpaugh-NY 7
High-NY 7

Home Runs
Roth-Chi-Cle 7
Peckinpaugh-NY 5
Boone-NY 5
3 players tied 4

Total Bases
Cobb-Det 274
Maisel-NY 189
Pipp-NY 176
Peckinpaugh-NY 166

Runs Batted In
Veach-Det 112
Crawford-Det 112
Pipp-NY 60
Hartzell-NY 60

Stolen Bases
Cobb-Det 96
Maisel-NY 51
Cook-NY 29
High-NY 22

Base Stealing Runs
Cobb-Det 7.8
Maisel-NY 7.0
Pipp-NY 1.5
Mullen-NY .4

Fielding Runs-Infield
Boone-NY 20.5
Peckinpaugh-NY 5.4
Pipp-NY 2.3

Fielding Runs-Outfield
Strunk-Phi 11.1

Wins
Johnson-Was 27
Caldwell-NY 19
Fisher-NY 18
Warhop-NY 7

Winning Pct.
Wood-Bos .750
Fisher-NY .621
Caldwell-NY .543

Complete Games
Johnson-Was 35
Caldwell-NY 31
Fisher-NY 20
Warhop-NY 12

Strikeouts
Johnson-Was 203
Caldwell-NY 130
Fisher-NY 97
Pieh-NY 46

Fewest BB/Game
Johnson-Was 1.50
Fisher-NY 2.25
Caldwell-NY 3.16

Games
Faber-Chi 50
Coveleski-Det 50
Caldwell-NY 36
Fisher-NY 30

Saves
Mays-Bos 7
Cole-NY 1

Base Runners/9
Johnson-Was 8.90
Fisher-NY 10.39
Caldwell-NY 11.15
Pieh-NY 11.68

Adjusted Relief Runs

Relief Ranking

Innings Pitched
Johnson-Was 336.2
Caldwell-NY 305.0
Fisher-NY 247.2
Warhop-NY 143.1

Opponents' Avg.
Leonard-Bos .208
Fisher-NY .243
Caldwell-NY .244

Opponents' OBP
Johnson-Was .260
Fisher-NY .295
Caldwell-NY .315

Earned Run Average
Wood-Bos 1.49
Fisher-NY 2.11
Caldwell-NY 2.89
Warhop-NY 3.96

Adjusted ERA
Johnson-Was 191
Fisher-NY 139
Caldwell-NY 101

Adjusted Starter Runs
Johnson-Was 51.1
Fisher-NY 18.8
Markle-NY 5.8
Mogridge-NY 4.9

Pitcher Wins
Johnson-Was 7.4
Fisher-NY 1.7
Caldwell-NY 1.2
2 players tied .5

1916 American League

TEAM	W	L	T	PCT	GB	R	OR	HR	AVG	OBP	SLG	OPS	AOPS	PF	SB	CG	HR	BB	SO	BR/9	ERA	AERA	OAV	OOB	FW	PW	BW	BSW	DIF
Bos	91	63	2	.591		550	**480**	14	.248	.317	.318	635	97	100	129	76	**10**	463	584	11.0	2.48	112	.239	.307	**3.0**	5.0	-2.4		8.4
Chi	89	65	1	.578	2	601	497	17	.251	.319	.339	658	103	101	197	73	14	**405**	644	**10.3**	**2.36**	**117**	**.236**	**.296**	1.5	**7.0**	1.0		2.5
Det	87	67	1	.565	4	**670**	595	17	**.264**	**.337**	**.350**	**687**	**109**	104	190	81	12	578	531	12.1	2.97	96	.248	.333	1.1	-2.0	**6.2**		4.6
NY	80	74	2	.519	11	577	561	**35**	.246	.318	.326	644	98	102	179	84	37	476	616	11.2	2.77	104	.244	.314	.7	1.9	-1.8		2.2
StL	79	75	4	.513	12	588	545	14	.245	.331	.307	638	103	95	**234**	74	15	478	505	11.3	2.58	106	.248	.316	-.9	3.0	3.9		-3.9
Cle	77	77	3	.500	14	630	602	16	.250	.324	.331	655	97	106	160	65	16	467	537	12.0	2.90	103	.264	.328	.0	1.7	-1.3		-.3
Was	76	77	6	.497	14.5	536	543	12	.242	.320	.306	626	95	99	185	85	14	490	**706**	11.3	2.67	104	.244	.314	.2	2.0	-2.7		-.0
Phi	36	117	1	.235	54.5	447	776	19	.242	.303	.313	616	96	95	151	**94**	26	715	575	13.8	3.92	73	.267	.364	-5.5	-17.6	-4.4		-13.0
Total	625					34599		144	.248	.321	.324	645			1425	632				11.6	2.82		.248	.321					

Batter-Fielder Wins
Speaker-Cle 5.7
Nunamaker-NY 2.1
Walters-NY 1.8
Baker-NY 1.7

Batting Average
Speaker-Cle .386
Baker-NY .269
High-NY .263
Pipp-NY .262

On-Base Percentage
Speaker-Cle .470
Peckinpaugh-NY .332
Pipp-NY .331
Magee-NY .324

Slugging Average
Speaker-Cle .502
Baker-NY .428
Pipp-NY .417
Peckinpaugh-NY .346

On-Base Plus Slugging
Speaker-Cle 972
Pipp-NY 748
Peckinpaugh-NY 678
Magee-NY 650

Adjusted OPS
Speaker-Cle 181
Pipp-NY 122
Peckinpaugh-NY 101
Magee-NY 93

Adjusted Batter Runs
Speaker-Cle 59.5
Baker-NY 12.3
Pipp-NY 11.5
Nunamaker-NY 11.0

Runs
Cobb-Det 113
Pipp-NY 70
Peckinpaugh-NY 65
Magee-NY 57

Hits
Speaker-Cle 211
Pipp-NY 143
Peckinpaugh-NY 141
Magee-NY 131

Doubles
Speaker-Cle 41
Graney-Cle 41
Baker-NY 23
Peckinpaugh-NY 22

Triples
Jackson-Chi 21
Pipp-NY 14
Peckinpaugh-NY 8
Nunamaker-NY 7

Home Runs
Pipp-NY 12
Baker-NY 10
Peckinpaugh-NY 4
Magee-NY 3

Total Bases
Jackson-Chi 293
Pipp-NY 227
Peckinpaugh-NY 191
Magee-NY 166

Runs Batted In
Pratt-StL 103
Pipp-NY 93
Peckinpaugh-NY 58
Baker-NY 52

Stolen Bases
Cobb-Det 68
Magee-NY 29
Peckinpaugh-NY 18
2 players tied 16

Base Stealing Runs
Cobb-Det 6.6

Fielding Runs-Infield
Lajoie-Phi 26.7
Pipp-NY 5.1
Magee-NY .6

Fielding Runs-Outfield
Milan-Was 14.1

Wins
Johnson-Was 25
Shawkey-NY 24
Cullop-NY 13
Fisher-NY 11

Winning Pct.
Cicotte-Chi .682
Shawkey-NY .632

Complete Games
Johnson-Was 36
Shawkey-NY 21
Caldwell-NY 14
Mogridge-NY 10

Strikeouts
Johnson-Was 228
Shawkey-NY 122
Russell-NY 104
Cullop-NY 77

Fewest BB/Game
Russell-Chi 1.43
Cullop-NY 1.72
Mogridge-NY 2.08
Fisher-NY 2.56

Games
Davenport-StL 59
Shawkey-NY 53
Russell-NY 34
Fisher-NY 31

Saves
Shawkey-NY 8
Russell-NY 6
Fisher-NY 2
Cullop-NY 1

Base Runners/9
Russell-Chi 8.51
Shawkey-NY 9.47
Cullop-NY 10.02
Mogridge-NY 10.45

Adjusted Relief Runs

Relief Ranking

Innings Pitched
Johnson-Was 369.2
Shawkey-NY 276.2
Mogridge-NY 194.2
Fisher-NY 179.0

Opponents' Avg.
Ruth-Bos .201
Shawkey-NY .209
Russell-NY .232
2 players tied .243

Opponents' OBP
Russell-Chi .254
Shawkey-NY .273
Cullop-NY .284
Mogridge-NY .305

Earned Run Average
Ruth-Bos 1.75
Cullop-NY 2.05
Shawkey-NY 2.21
Mogridge-NY 2.31

Adjusted ERA
Ruth-Bos 158
Cullop-NY 141
Shawkey-NY 130
Mogridge-NY 125

Adjusted Starter Runs
Ruth-Bos 35.1
Shawkey-NY 23.6
Cullop-NY 10.8
Mogridge-NY 9.4

Pitcher Wins
Ruth-Bos 5.7
Shawkey-NY 3.4
Mogridge-NY 1.0
Cullop-NY .7

Historical Record

1917 American League

TEAM	W	L	T	PCT	GB	R	OR	HR	AVG	OBP	SLG	OPS	AOPS	PF	SB	CG	HR	BB	SO	BR/9	ERA	AERA	OAV	OOB	FW	PW	BW	BSW	DIF
Chi	100	54	2	.649		**655**	463	18	.253	**.329**	.326	655	103	102	**219**	78	**10**	**413**	517	10.6	**2.16**	**123**	.238	.298	2.3	**8.5**	2.4		9.8
Bos	90	62	5	.592	9	555	**455**	14	.246	.314	.319	633	100	99	105	**115**	12	**413**	509	**10.5**	2.20	117	**.231**	**.295**	**3.9**	6.9	-.3		3.5
Cle	88	66	2	.571	12	584	543	13	.245	.324	.322	646	96	107	210	73	17	438	451	11.1	2.52	112	.247	.310	-.5	5.0	-1.8		8.3
Det	78	75	1	.510	21.5	639	577	25	**.259**	.328	**.344**	**672**	**111**	100	163	78	12	504	516	11.4	2.56	103	.240	.316	-.1	1.4	**7.2**		-7.1
Was	74	79	4	.484	25.5	544	566	4	.241	.313	.304	617	95	99	166	84	12	537	**637**	11.4	2.75	95	.239	.316	-1.0	-2.2	-3.1		3.9
NY	71	82	2	.464	28.5	524	558	**27**	.239	.310	.308	618	93	101	136	87	28	427	571	11.1	2.66	101	.252	.314	.6	.3	-4.3		-2.1
StL	57	97	1	.370	43	510	687	15	.246	.305	.315	620	98	96	157	66	19	537	429	12.3	3.20	81	.257	.332	-3.4	-11.0	-2.2		-3.3
Phi	55	98	1	.359	44.5	529	691	17	.254	.316	.323	639	101	99	112	80	23	562	516	12.5	3.27	84	.261	.338	-1.4	-8.6	.7		-12.3
Total	622					34540		133	.248	.318	.320	638			1268	661				11.4	2.66		.248	.318					

Batter-Fielder Wins	Batting Average	On-Base Percentage	Slugging Average	On-Base Plus Slugging	Adjusted OPS	Adjusted Batter Runs
Cobb-Det 7.4	Cobb-Det .... .383	Cobb-Det .... .444	Cobb-Det .... .570	Cobb-Det 1014	Cobb-Det 210	Cobb-Det 75.9
Baker-NY 2.6	Baker-NY .... .282	Baker-NY .... .345	Pipp-NY .... .380	Baker-NY 710	Baker-NY 116	Hendryx-NY 10.5
Peckinpaugh-NY ... 2.3	Nunamaker-NY ..... .261	Peckinpaugh-NY.... .340	Baker-NY .... .365	Pipp-NY 700	Pipp-NY 112	Baker-NY 10.4
Walters-NY............... .9	Peckinpaugh-NY.... .260	Pipp-NY .... .320	Hendryx-NY .... .359	Peckinpaugh-NY.... 670	Peckinpaugh-NY.... 103	Pipp-NY 7.4

Runs	Hits	Doubles	Triples	Home Runs	Total Bases	Runs Batted In
Bush-Det.................112	Cobb-Det 225	Cobb-Det 44	Cobb-Det 24	Pipp-NY 9	Cobb-Det 335	Veach-Det............... 103
Pipp-NY 82	Baker-NY 156	Pipp-NY 29	Pipp-NY 12	Baker-NY 6	Pipp-NY 223	Baker-NY 71
Peckinpaugh-NY...... 63	Pipp-NY 143	Peckinpaugh-NY...... 24	Peckinpaugh-NY........ 7	Hendryx-NY 5	Baker-NY 202	Pipp-NY 70
Baker-NY 57	Peckinpaugh-NY.... 141	Baker-NY 24	Hendryx-NY 7	Miller-NY 3	Peckinpaugh-NY.... 179	Hendryx-NY 44

Stolen Bases	Base Stealing Runs	Fielding Runs-Infield	Fielding Runs-Outfield	Wins	Winning Pct.	Complete Games
Cobb-Det 55		Chapman-Cle 23.6	Felsch-Chi 14.6	Cicotte-Chi.............. 28	Russell-Chi .... .750	Ruth-Bos.................. 35
Maisel-NY 29		Baker-NY 9.4	Hendryx-NY 1.7	Shawkey-NY........... 13		Caldwell-NY 21
Baker-NY 18		Peckinpaugh-NY..... 6.8		Caldwell-NY 13		Shawkey-NY 16
Peckinpaugh-NY...... 17		Pipp-NY 4.3		Mogridge-NY 9		Mogridge-NY 15

Strikeouts	Fewest BB/Game	Games	Saves	Base Runners/9	Adjusted Relief Runs	Relief Ranking
Johnson-Was......... 188	Russell-Chi 1.52	Danforth-Chi 50	Danforth-Chi 9	Cicotte-Chi............ 8.28		
Caldwell-NY 102	Mogridge-NY 1.79	Love-NY................... 33	Russell-NY................. 2	Shocker-NY 10.55		
Shawkey-NY 97	Shawkey-NY.......... 2.74	Shawkey-NY........... 32	4 players tied 1	Mogridge-NY 10.68		
Love-NY.................. 82	Caldwell-NY.......... 2.90	Caldwell-NY 32		Fisher-NY 10.69		

Innings Pitched	Opponents' Avg.	Opponents' OBP	Earned Run Average	Adjusted ERA	Adjusted Starter Runs	Pitcher Wins
Cicotte-Chi.......... 346.2	Coveleski-Cle .... .194	Cicotte-Chi............ .248	Cicotte-Chi............ 1.53	Cicotte-Chi............ 173	Cicotte-Chi............ 44.8	Cicotte-Chi............. 5.7
Shawkey-NY....... 236.1	Caldwell-NY.......... .234	Mogridge-NY .... .301	Fisher-NY 2.19	Shawkey-NY..........110	Shawkey-NY........... 8.1	Shawkey-NY........... 1.2
Caldwell-NY........ 236.0	Shawkey-NY.......... .243	Caldwell-NY.......... .302	Shawkey-NY......... 2.44	Caldwell-NY............ 94	Fisher-NY 7.0	Fisher-NY 9
Mogridge-NY 196.1	Mogridge-NY .... .255	Shawkey-NY......... .306	Caldwell-NY.......... 2.86	Mogridge-NY 90	Love-NY.................. 3.1	Caldwell-NY.............. .8

1918 American League

TEAM	W	L	T	PCT	GB	R	OR	HR	AVG	OBP	SLG	OPS	AOPS	PF	SB	CG	HR	BB	SO	BR/9	ERA	AERA	OAV	OOB	FW	PW	BW	BSW	DIF
Bos	75	51	0	.595		474	**380**	15	.249	.322	.327	649	103	98	110	**105**	**9**	380	392	10.8	2.31	116	**.231**	.302	**2.5**	5.5	1.7		2.4
Cle	73	54	2	.575	2.5	**504**	447	9	**.260**	**.344**	**.341**	**685**	102	110	**171**	78	**9**	343	364	11.5	2.64	114	.262	.319	-.7	4.7	2.6		2.9
Was	72	56	2	.563	4	461	412	4	.256	.318	.315	633	98	98	137	75	10	395	**505**	**10.6**	**2.14**	**127**	**.231**	**.298**	-1.8	**9.0**	-1.6		2.3
NY	60	63	3	.488	13.5	493	475	20	.257	.320	.330	650	99	102	92	59	25	463	370	12.5	3.00	94	.261	.340	1.9	-2.6	-.9		.0
StL	58	64	1	.475	15	426	448	5	.259	.331	.320	651	**105**	97	139	67	11	402	346	11.5	2.75	99	.246	.319	-.2	-.2	**3.1**		-5.7
Chi	57	67	0	.460	17	457	446	8	.256	.322	.321	643	98	101	119	76	**9**	**300**	349	11.3	2.73	100	.261	.314	1.2	-.3	-1.2		-4.7
Det	55	71	2	.437	20	476	557	13	.249	.325	.318	643	103	96	123	74	10	437	374	12.4	3.40	78	.263	.335	-1.1	-11.6	2.0		2.7
Phi	52	76	2	.406	24	412	538	**22**	.243	.303	.308	611	88	101	83	80	13	486	277	12.7	3.22	91	.266	.348	-1.9	-4.1	-7.4		1.4
Total	508					23703		96	.254	.323	.322	646			974	614				11.7	2.77		.254	.323					

Batter-Fielder Wins	Batting Average	On-Base Percentage	Slugging Average	On-Base Plus Slugging	Adjusted OPS	Adjusted Batter Runs
T.Cobb-Det............. 4.3	T.Cobb-Det .... .382	T.Cobb-Det .... .440	Ruth-Bos............... .555	T.Cobb-Det 955	T.Cobb-Det 196	T.Cobb-Det 47.7
Baker-NY 2.9	Baker-NY .... .306	Gilhooley-NY .... .358	Pipp-NY .... .415	Baker-NY 765	Baker-NY 128	Baker-NY 15.8
Peckinpaugh-NY ... 1.9	Pipp-NY .... .304	Baker-NY .... .357	Baker-NY .... .409	Gilhooley-NY 695	Gilhooley-NY 107	Pipp-NY 9.1
Pratt-NY 1.5	Gilhooley-NY .... .276	Pratt-NY................ .327	Bodie-NY .... .358	Pratt-NY................. 683	Pratt-NY................. 104	Fournier-NY 5.3

Runs	Hits	Doubles	Triples	Home Runs	Total Bases	Runs Batted In
Chapman-Cle 84	Burns-Phi............... 178	Speaker-Cle............ 33	T.Cobb-Det 14	Walker-Phi 11	Burns-Phi............... 236	Veach-Det................ 78
Pratt-NY.................. 65	Baker-NY 154	Baker-NY 24	Pipp-NY 9	Ruth-Bos....................11	Baker-NY 206	Baker-NY 62
Baker-NY 65	Pratt-NY................. 131	Pratt-NY.................. 19	Pratt-NY...................... 7	Baker-NY 6	Pratt-NY................. 170	Pratt-NY.................. 55
2 players tied 59	Gilhooley-NY 118	2 players tied 15	Bodie-NY 6	Bodie-NY 3	Pipp-NY 145	Bodie-NY 46

Stolen Bases	Base Stealing Runs	Fielding Runs-Infield	Fielding Runs-Outfield	Wins	Winning Pct.	Complete Games
Sisler-StL 45		Peckinpaugh-NY... 22.1	S.Collins-Chi..........11.9	Johnson-Was........... 23	Jones-Bos............. .762	Perry-Phi................. 30
Pratt-NY.................. 12		Pratt-NY................ 10.1	Bodie-NY 3.6	Mogridge-NY 16	Mogridge-NY .... .552	Mays-Bos................. 30
Peckinpaugh-NY...... 12		Baker-NY 7.4	Gilhooley-NY 9	Love-NY................... 13		Caldwell-NY 14
Pipp-NY 11		Pipp-NY 5		Caldwell-NY 9		2 players tied 13

Strikeouts	Fewest BB/Game	Games	Saves	Base Runners/9	Adjusted Relief Runs	Relief Ranking
Johnson-Was......... 162	Cicotte-Chi............ 1.35	Mogridge-NY 45	Mogridge-NY 7	Johnson-Was........ 8.81	Houck-StL............... 3.2	Houck-StL............... 2.6
Love-NY.................. 95	Mogridge-NY 1.62	Love-NY................... 38	Russell-NY................ 4	Mogridge-NY 10.64		
Mogridge-NY 62	Caldwell-NY.......... 3.16	Russell-NY.............. 27	Love-NY...................... 1	Thormahlen-NY ... 11.42		
Caldwell-NY............. 59	Love-NY................ 4.57	Caldwell-NY 24	Caldwell-NY 1	Caldwell-NY........ 12.02		

Innings Pitched	Opponents' Avg.	Opponents' OBP	Earned Run Average	Adjusted ERA	Adjusted Starter Runs	Pitcher Wins
Perry-Phi............. 332.1	Sothoron-StL .... .205	Johnson-Was........ .260	Johnson-Was........ 1.27	Johnson-Was......... 214	Johnson-Was......... 51.4	Johnson-Was.......... 7.6
Mogridge-NY 239.1	Love-NY................ .253	Mogridge-NY .... .304	Mogridge-NY 2.18	Mogridge-NY 129	Mogridge-NY 14.1	Mogridge-NY 2.0
Love-NY............. 228.2	Caldwell-NY.......... .261	Caldwell-NY.......... .325	Caldwell-NY.......... 3.06	Caldwell-NY............ 92	Thormahlen-NY 3.9	Shawkey-NY............. .7
Caldwell-NY........ 176.2	Mogridge-NY .... .263	Love-NY................ .353	Love-NY................ 3.07	Love-NY.................. 92	Shawkey-NY........... 3.1	Caldwell-NY.............. .3

1919 American League

TEAM	W	L	T	PCT	GB	R	OR	HR	AVG	OBP	SLG	OPS	AOPS	PF	SB	CG	HR	BB	SO	BR/9	ERA	AERA	OAV	OOB	FW	PW	BW	BSW	DIF
Chi	88	52	0	.629		**667**	534	25	**.287**	.351	.380	731	111	100	**150**	88	24	**342**	468	11.5	3.04	105	.262	.315	1.6	2.0	7.1		7.2
Cle	84	55	0	.604	3.5	636	537	24	.278	**.354**	**.381**	**735**	107	106	117	79	19	362	432	11.8	2.94	**114**	.264	.321	-.0	5.3	4.7		4.5
NY	80	59	2	.576	7.5	578	**506**	**45**	.267	.326	.356	682	96	101	101	85	47	433	500	**11.3**	**2.82**	113	**.240**	**.309**	.7	**5.7**	-2.6		6.8
Det	80	60	0	.571	8	618	578	23	.283	.346	**.381**	727	**113**	98	121	85	35	436	428	12.4	3.30	97	.266	.333	-.2	-1.5	**8.0**		3.7
StL	67	72	1	.482	20.5	533	567	31	.264	.326	.355	681	95	103	74	78	35	421	415	12.3	3.13	106	.263	.328	-.8	2.4	-3.9		-.2
Bos	66	71	1	.482	20.5	564	552	33	.261	.336	.344	680	103	94	108	**89**	**16**	421	381	12.5	3.31	91	.275	.341	**3.8**	-4.6	2.6		-4.3
Was	56	84	2	.400	32	533	570	24	.260	.325	.339	664	93	99	142	68	20	451	**536**	12.2	3.01	106	.259	.328	-1.4	2.9	-4.6		-10.9
Phi	36	104	0	.257	52	457	742	35	.244	.300	.334	634	82	101	103	72	44	503	417	13.8	4.26	80	.292	.364	-3.5	-11.6	-12.4		-6.5
Total	560					34586		240	.268	.333	.359	692			916	644				12.2	3.22		.268	.333					

Batter-Fielder Wins
Ruth-Bos 7.3
Peckinpaugh-NY ... 5.1
Pratt-NY 3.1
Fewster-NY............. .8

Batting Average
Cobb-Det .... .384
Peckinpaugh-NY... .305
Baker-NY .... .293
Pratt-NY................ .292

On-Base Percentage
Ruth-Bos................ .456
Peckinpaugh-NY... .390
Baker-NY .... .346
Pratt-NY................ .342

Slugging Average
Ruth-Bos................ .657
Bodie-NY .... .406
Peckinpaugh-NY... .404
Pipp-NY .... .398

On-Base Plus Slugging
Ruth-Bos..............1114
Peckinpaugh-NY.... 794
Bodie-NY 740
Pratt-NY................ 735

Adjusted OPS
Ruth-Bos................ 224
Peckinpaugh-NY.... 122
Bodie-NY 107
2 players tied 105

Adjusted Batter Runs
Ruth-Bos............... 76.3
Peckinpaugh-NY... 15.8
Fewster-NY............ 4.8
Baker-NY 3.3

Runs
Ruth-Bos................ 103
Peckinpaugh-NY...... 89
Pipp-NY 74
Baker-NY 70

Hits
Veach-Det............. 191
Cobb-Det 191
Baker-NY 166
Pratt-NY................ 154

Doubles
Veach-Det................ 45
Pratt-NY................... 27
Bodie-NY 27
2 players tied 23

Triples
Veach-Det................ 17
Pipp-NY 10
Vick-NY...................... 9
Bodie-NY 8

Home Runs
Ruth-Bos.................. 29
Baker-NY 10
3 players tied 7

Total Bases
Ruth-Bos................ 284
Baker-NY 220
Pipp-NY 208
Pratt-NY................. 207

Runs Batted In
Ruth-Bos.................114
Lewis-NY 89
Baker-NY 83
Bodie-NY 59

Stolen Bases
E.Collins-Chi........... 33
Pratt-NY................... 22
Bodie-NY 15
Baker-NY 13

Base Stealing Runs

Fielding Runs-Infield
Peckinpaugh-NY... 25.5
Pratt-NY................ 24.6

Fielding Runs-Outfield
Felsch-Chi 17.4

Wins
Cicotte-Chi.............. 29
Shawkey-NY 20
Quinn-NY................. 15
Thormahlen-NY 12

Winning Pct.
Cicotte-Chi.............. .806
Shawkey-NY.......... .645
Quinn-NY .... .517

Complete Games
Cicotte-Chi............... 30
Shawkey-NY 22
Quinn-NY.................. 18
2 players tied 13

Strikeouts
Johnson-Was......... 147
Shawkey-NY.......... 122
Quinn-NY 97
Thormahlen-NY 62

Fewest BB/Game
Cicotte-Chi........... 1.44
Quinn-NY.............. 2.20
Mogridge-NY 2.45
Thormahlen-NY 2.91

Games
Shaw-Was 45
Shawkey-NY 41
Quinn-NY.................. 38
Mogridge-NY 35

Saves
3 players tied 5
Shawkey-NY 5
Thormahlen-NY 1

Base Runners/9
Cicotte-Chi........... 9.01
Thormahlen-NY .. 10.49
Quinn-NY........... 10.59
Shawkey-NY....... 10.85

Adjusted Relief Runs
Phillips-Cle............. 1.1

Relief Ranking
Phillips-Cle................ .9

Innings Pitched
Shaw-Was 306.2
Cicotte-Chi.......... 306.2
Quinn-NY............ 266.0
Shawkey-NY....... 261.1

Opponents' Avg.
Johnson-Was........ .219
Thormahlen-NY .... .228
Shawkey-NY......... .231
Quinn-NY.............. .244

Opponents' OBP
Johnson-Was........ .259
Quinn-NY.............. .295
Thormahlen-NY ..... .295
Shawkey-NY......... .303

Earned Run Average
Johnson-Was........ 1.49
Quinn-NY.............. 2.61
Thormahlen-NY 2.62
Shawkey-NY......... 2.72

Adjusted ERA
Johnson-Was......... 215
Quinn-NY............... 122
Thormahlen-NY 121
Shawkey-NY...........117

Adjusted Starter Runs
Johnson-Was........ 52.4
Quinn-NY.............. 17.7
Shawkey-NY......... 15.8
Thormahlen-NY 12.0

Pitcher Wins
Johnson-Was.......... 6.7
Quinn-NY................ 2.0
Shawkey-NY........... 1.8
Thormahlen-NY 1.1

1920 American League

TEAM	W	L	T	PCT	GB	R	OR	HR	AVG	OBP	SLG	OPS	AOPS	PF	SB	CG	HR	BB	SO	BR/9	ERA	AERA	OAV	OOB	FW	PW	BW	BSW	DIF
Cle	98	56	0	.636		**857**	642	35	.303	**.376**	.417	**793**	**113**	103	73	94	**31**	**401**	466	**12.3**	3.41	111	.276	.331	2.1	5.6	**10.1**	-.5	3.7
Chi	96	58	0	.623	2	794	665	37	.295	.357	.402	759	107	100	109	**109**	45	405	438	**12.3**	3.59	105	.280	.335	1.2	2.3	4.8	.0	10.7
NY	95	59	0	.617	3	838	**629**	**115**	.280	.350	**.426**	776	107	104	64	88	48	420	480	**12.3**	**3.32**	**115**	**.270**	**.328**	1.4	**7.3**	4.6	-.4	5.2
StL	76	77	1	.497	21.5	797	766	50	**.308**	.363	.419	782	110	103	121	84	53	578	444	13.7	4.03	97	.283	.359	-1.2	-2.1	6.8	**.9**	-4.8
Bos	72	81	1	.471	25.5	650	698	22	.269	.342	.350	692	93	96	98	92	39	461	481	12.7	3.82	95	.279	.339	**2.2**	-3.0	-4.0	-.6	.9
Was	68	84	1	.447	29	723	802	36	.291	.351	.386	737	104	97	**160**	81	51	520	418	13.7	4.17	89	.288	.357	-1.3	-6.9	2.4	.5	-2.8
Det	61	93	1	.396	37	652	833	30	.270	.334	.359	693	91	98	76	74	46	561	**483**	13.7	4.04	92	.284	.359	-.9	-5.0	-6.3	.3	-4.0
Phi	48	106	2	.312	50	558	834	44	.252	.305	.338	643	74	-101	50	79	56	461	423	13.8	3.93	102	.302	.362	-3.3	1.1	-19.1	-.2	-7.5
Total	617					35869		369	.284	.347	.387	735			751	701				13.1	3.79		.284	.347					

Batter-Fielder Wins
Ruth-NY 9.3
Pratt-NY 2.1
Peckinpaugh-NY ... 1.1
Meusel-NY 4

Batting Average
Sisler-StL .... .407
Ruth-NY................ .376
Meusel-NY............ .328
Pratt-NY................ .314

On-Base Percentage
Ruth-NY................ .532
Pratt-NY................ .372
Meusel-NY............ .359
Peckinpaugh-NY.... .356

Slugging Average
Ruth-NY................ .847
Meusel-NY............ .517
Bodie-NY .... .446
Pipp-NY .... .430

On-Base Plus Slugging
Ruth-NY............... 1379
Meusel-NY............. 876
Pratt-NY................ 798
Bodie-NY 796

Adjusted OPS
Ruth-NY................. 252
Meusel-NY............. 126
Pratt-NY................. 107
Bodie-NY 106

Adjusted Batter Runs
Ruth-NY...............110.5
Meusel-NY............ 15.0
Pratt-NY.................. 6.6
Bodie-NY 2.6

Runs
Ruth-NY................. 158
Pipp-NY 109
Peckinpaugh-NY.... 109
Pratt-NY................... 84

Hits
Sisler-StL 257
Pratt-NY................ 180
Ruth-NY................ 172
Pipp-NY 171

Doubles
Speaker-Cle............ 50
Meusel-NY.............. 40
Pratt-NY.................. 37
Ruth-NY.................. 36

Triples
Jackson-Chi............ 20
Pipp-NY 14
Bodie-NY 12
Ruth-NY.................... 9

Home Runs
Ruth-NY................... 54
Ward-NY...................11
Pipp-NY 11
Meusel-NY...............11

Total Bases
Sisler-StL 399
Ruth-NY................. 388
Pipp-NY 262
Pratt-NY................. 245

Runs Batted In
Ruth-NY................. 137
Pratt-NY................... 97
Meusel-NY............... 83
Bodie-NY 79

Stolen Bases
Rice-Was 63
Ruth-NY.................... 14
Pratt-NY................... 12
Peckinpaugh-NY........ 8

Base Stealing Runs
Rice-Was 3.4
Hannah-NY 4
Ruel-NY 2

Fielding Runs-Infield
Ward-NY 16.5
Pratt-NY................ 13.4
Peckinpaugh-NY..... 8.2
Pipp-NY 3

Fielding Runs-Outfield
Rice-Was 17.0

Wins
Bagby-Cle................ 31
Mays-NY.................. 26
Shawkey-NY 20
Quinn-NY................. 18

Winning Pct.
Bagby-Cle............. .721
Mays-NY............... .703
Quinn-NY .... .643
Shawkey-NY......... .606

Complete Games
Bagby-Cle................ 30
Mays-NY.................. 26
Shawkey-NY 20
Quinn-NY.................. 17

Strikeouts
Coveleski-Cle 133
Shawkey-NY.......... 126
Quinn-NY 101
Mays-NY 92

Fewest BB/Game
Quinn-NY.............. 1.71
Mays-NY............... 2.42
Shawkey-NY 2.86
Collins-NY............ 3.80

Games
Bagby-Cle................ 48
Mays-NY.................. 45
Quinn-NY.................. 41
Shawkey-NY 38

Saves
Shocker-StL.............. 5
Kerr-Chi 5
Quinn-NY................... 3
2 players tied 2

Base Runners/9
Coveleski-Cle 10.09
Shawkey-NY........11.16
Quinn-NY............11.40
Mays-NY.............11.57

Adjusted Relief Runs

Relief Ranking

Innings Pitched
Bagby-Cle........... 339.2
Mays-NY............ 312.0
Shawkey-NY....... 267.2
Quinn-NY........... 253.1

Opponents' Avg.
Coveleski-Cle .... .243
Collins-NY............ .247
Shawkey-NY......... .248
Mays-NY .... .263

Opponents' OBP
Coveleski-Cle .... .285
Shawkey-NY......... .308
Quinn-NY.............. .308
Mays-NY .... .316

Earned Run Average
Shawkey-NY......... 2.45
Mays-NY............... 3.06
Quinn-NY.............. 3.20
Collins-NY............ 3.22

Adjusted ERA
Shawkey-NY.......... 155
Mays-NY................ 125
Quinn-NY................119
Collins-NY..............118

Adjusted Starter Runs
Coveleski-Cle 44.4
Shawkey-NY......... 41.3
Mays-NY............... 28.0
Quinn-NY.............. 18.1

Pitcher Wins
Coveleski-Cle 5.5
Shawkey-NY........... 4.6
Mays-NY................. 3.5
Quinn-NY................ 1.4

1921 American League

TEAM	W	L	T	PCT	GB	R	OR	HR	AVG	OBP	SLG	OPS	AOPS	PF	SB	CG	HR	BB	SO	BR/9	ERA	AERA	OAV	OOB	FW	PW	BW	BSW	DIF
NY	98	55	0	.641		**948**	708	**134**	.300	.375	**.464**	**839**	**116**	102	89	**92**	51	470	**481**	13.1	**3.82**	**111**	**.277**	**.342**	-.3	**5.9**	11.8	.2	3.9
Cle	94	60	0	.610	4.5	925	712	42	.308	.383	.430	813	111	102	51	81	**43**	**431**	475	**13.0**	3.90	109	.288	.344	.8	5.1	10.0	.2	.8
StL	81	73	0	.526	17.5	835	845	67	.304	.357	.425	782	98	106	91	77	71	556	477	13.9	4.61	97	.288	.360	-.3	-2.0	-2.0	.0	8.2
Was	80	73	1	.523	18	704	738	42	.277	.342	.383	725	95	95	**112**	80	51	442	452	13.3	3.97	104	.291	.349	-.9	2.2	-4.5	**.7**	6.1
Bos	75	79	0	.487	23.5	668	**696**	17	.277	.335	.361	696	84	-97	83	88	53	452	446	13.3	3.98	106	.291	.352	**3.5**	3.6	-10.9	.1	1.8
Det	71	82	1	.464	27	883	852	58	**.316**	**.385**	.433	818	115	99	95	73	71	495	452	14.2	4.40	97	.297	.361	-.8	-1.9	**12.2**	-.5	-14.6
Chi	62	92	0	.403	36.5	683	858	35	.283	.343	.379	722	90	99	94	84	52	549	392	14.4	4.94	86	.303	.372	1.0	-10.2	-7.4	-.6	2.2
Phi	53	100	2	.346	45	657	894	82	.274	.331	.389	720	88	-101	69	75	85	548	431	14.3	4.61	97	.300	.367	-3.1	-2.2	-9.9	.1	-8.4
Total	616					36303		477	.292	.357	.408	765			684	650				13.7	4.28		.292	.357					

Batter-Fielder Wins	Batting Average	On-Base Percentage	Slugging Average	On-Base Plus Slugging	Adjusted OPS	Adjusted Batter Runs
Ruth-NY 9.4	Heilmann-Det .394	Ruth-NY .512	Ruth-NY .846	Ruth-NY 1359	Ruth-NY 236	Ruth-NY 117.7
Schang-NY 2.3	Ruth-NY .378	Schang-NY .428	Meusel-NY .559	Meusel-NY 915	Meusel-NY 128	Meusel-NY 20.0
Ward-NY 1.9	Meusel-NY .318	Peckinpaugh-NY .380	Schang-NY .453	Schang-NY 881	Schang-NY 122	Schang-NY 19.2
Meusel-NY 1.3	Schang-NY .316	Ward-NY .363	Baker-NY .436	Ward-NY 786	Ward-NY 98	Mays-NY 10.8

Runs	Hits	Doubles	Triples	Home Runs	Total Bases	Runs Batted In
Ruth-NY 177	Heilmann-Det 237	Speaker-Cle 52	3 players tied 18	Ruth-NY 59	Ruth-NY 457	Ruth-NY 171
Peckinpaugh-NY 128	Ruth-NY 204	Ruth-NY 44	Ruth-NY 16	Meusel-NY 24	Meusel-NY 334	Meusel-NY 135
Meusel-NY 104	Meusel-NY 190	Meusel-NY 40	Meusel-NY 16	Baker-NY 9	Pipp-NY 251	Pipp-NY 97
Pipp-NY 96	Pipp-NY 174	Pipp-NY 35	Ward-NY 10	2 players tied 8	Ward-NY 235	Ward-NY 75

Stolen Bases	Base Stealing Runs	Fielding Runs-Infield	Fielding Runs-Outfield	Wins	Winning Pct.	Complete Games
Sisler-StL 35	Sisler-StL 3.8	Scott-Bos 41.2	Veach-Det 12.9	Shocker-StL 27	Mays-NY .750	Faber-Chi 32
Ruth-NY 17	Meusel-NY 1.6	Ward-NY 18.8	Meusel-NY 4.2	Mays-NY 27	Shawkey-NY .600	Mays-NY 30
Pipp-NY 17	DeVormer-NY .4			Mays-NY 27	Hoyt-NY .594	Hoyt-NY 21
Meusel-NY 17	2 players tied .2			Hoyt-NY 19		Shawkey-NY 18

Strikeouts	Fewest BB/Game	Games	Saves	Base Runners/9	Adjusted Relief Runs	Relief Ranking
Johnson-Was 143	Hasty-Phi 2.01	Mays-NY 49	Middleton-Det 7	Faber-Chi 10.53		
Shawkey-NY 126	Mays-NY 2.03	Hoyt-NY 43	Mays-NY 7	Mays-NY 11.15		
Hoyt-NY 102	Hoyt-NY 2.58	Shawkey-NY 38	Mays-NY 7	Hoyt-NY 12.34		
Mays-NY 70	Shawkey-NY 3.16	Quinn-NY 33	Hoyt-NY 3	Shawkey-NY 12.42		

Innings Pitched	Opponents' Avg.	Opponents' OBP	Earned Run Average	Adjusted ERA	Adjusted Starter Runs	Pitcher Wins
Mays-NY 336.2	Faber-Chi .242	Faber-Chi .297	Faber-Chi 2.48	Faber-Chi 171	Faber-Chi 64.1	Faber-Chi 6.8
Hoyt-NY 282.1	Mays-NY .257	Mays-NY .303	Mays-NY 3.05	Mays-NY 139	Mays-NY 42.6	Mays-NY 5.4
Shawkey-NY 245.0	Shawkey-NY .263	Hoyt-NY .329	Hoyt-NY 3.09	Hoyt-NY 137	Hoyt-NY 35.3	Hoyt-NY 3.3
Collins-NY 137.1	Hoyt-NY .276	Shawkey-NY .329	Shawkey-NY 4.08	Shawkey-NY 104	Piercy-NY 8.7	Piercy-NY .9

1922 American League

TEAM	W	L	T	PCT	GB	R	OR	HR	AVG	OBP	SLG	OPS	AOPS	PF	SB	CG	HR	BB	SO	BR/9	ERA	AERA	OAV	OOB	FW	PW	BW	BSW	DIF
NY	94	60	0	.610		758	**618**	95	.287	.353	.412	765	103	102	62	**100**	73	423	458	**11.9**	3.39	118	**.268**	**.325**	2.0	8.9	1.7	-.3	4.6
StL	93	61	0	.604	1	**867**	643	98	**.313**	**.372**	**.455**	**827**	**117**	104	**136**	79	71	**419**	**534**	12.1	**3.38**	**122**	**.268**	.327	-.5	**10.9**	**12.4**	**.7**	-7.5
Det	79	75	1	.513	15	828	791	54	.306	**.372**	.415	787	115	97	78	67	62	473	461	13.7	4.27	91	.288	.354	.2	-6.5	11.8	-.0	-3.4
Cle	78	76	1	.506	16	768	817	32	.292	.364	.398	762	104	101	90	76	58	464	489	13.7	4.59	87	.296	.356	-.5	-9.0	4.2	.4	5.9
Chi	77	77	1	.500	17	691	691	45	.278	.343	.373	716	92	100	109	86	57	529	484	13.0	3.94	103	.278	.346	**2.2**	1.5	-4.8	-.0	1.1
Was	69	85	0	.448	25	650	706	45	.268	.334	.367	701	93	95	97	84	49	500	422	13.4	3.81	101	.286	.354	-.2	.6	-5.1	.3	-3.6
Phi	65	89	1	.422	29	705	830	**111**	.270	.331	.402	733	94	103	60	73	107	469	373	13.7	4.59	92	.297	.357	-1.2	-5.0	-5.3	-.6	.2
Bos	61	93	0	.396	33	598	769	45	.263	.316	.357	673	82	-99	64	71	**48**	503	359	13.5	4.30	95	.287	.354	-1.8	-3.0	-14.2	-.4	3.4
Total	618					35865		525	.285	.348	.398	746			696	636				13.1	4.03		.285	.348					

Batter-Fielder Wins	Batting Average	On-Base Percentage	Slugging Average	On-Base Plus Slugging	Adjusted OPS	Adjusted Batter Runs
Sisler-StL 6.3	Sisler-StL .420	Speaker-Cle .474	Ruth-NY .672	Ruth-NY 1106	Ruth-NY 181	Sisler-StL 60.0
Ruth-NY 3.5	Pipp-NY .329	Ruth-NY .434	Meusel-NY .522	Meusel-NY 898	Meusel-NY 129	Ruth-NY 49.2
Schang-NY 1.9	Meusel-NY .319	Schang-NY .405	Pipp-NY .466	Pipp-NY 859	Pipp-NY 120	Meusel-NY 18.4
Meusel-NY 1.1	Schang-NY .319	Witt-NY .400	Schang-NY .412	Schang-NY 816	Schang-NY 111	Pipp-NY 17.8

Runs	Hits	Doubles	Triples	Home Runs	Total Bases	Runs Batted In
Sisler-StL 134	Sisler-StL 246	Speaker-Cle 48	Sisler-StL 18	Williams-StL 39	Williams-StL 367	Williams-StL 155
Witt-NY 98	Pipp-NY 190	Pipp-NY 32	Meusel-NY 11	Ruth-NY 35	Ruth-NY 273	Ruth-NY 99
Pipp-NY 96	Witt-NY 157	Meusel-NY 26	Pipp-NY 10	Meusel-NY 16	Pipp-NY 269	Pipp-NY 90
Ruth-NY 94	Meusel-NY 151	Ruth-NY 24	Ruth-NY 8	Pipp-NY 9	Meusel-NY 247	Meusel-NY 84

Stolen Bases	Base Stealing Runs	Fielding Runs-Infield	Fielding Runs-Outfield	Wins	Winning Pct.	Complete Games
Sisler-StL 51	Sisler-StL 4.6	Harris-Was 31.2	Veach-Det 9.7	Rommel-Phi 27	Bush-NY .788	Faber-Chi 31
Meusel-NY 13	McNally-NY .7	Scott-NY 16.6	Meusel-NY 1.9	Bush-NY 26	Shawkey-NY .625	Shawkey-NY 22
Schang-NY 12	Schang-NY .5	Ward-NY .7		Shawkey-NY 20	Hoyt-NY .613	Mays-NY 21
Pipp-NY 7	McMillan-NY .5			Hoyt-NY 19		2 players tied 20

Strikeouts	Fewest BB/Game	Games	Saves	Base Runners/9	Adjusted Relief Runs	Relief Ranking
Shocker-StL 149	Shocker-StL 1.47	Rommel-Phi 51	Jones-NY 8	Faber-Chi 10.82	Murray-NY 1.2	Murray-NY 1.0
Shawkey-NY 130	Mays-NY 1.88	Jones-NY 45	Bush-NY 3	Bush-NY 11.49		
Hoyt-NY 95	Hoyt-NY 2.58	Shawkey-NY 39	Mays-NY 2	Shawkey-NY 11.53		
Bush-NY 92	Jones-NY 2.63	Bush-NY 39	Shawkey-NY 1	Mays-NY 11.78		

Innings Pitched	Opponents' Avg.	Opponents' OBP	Earned Run Average	Adjusted ERA	Adjusted Starter Runs	Pitcher Wins
Faber-Chi 352.0	Davis-StL .250	Faber-Chi .299	Faber-Chi 2.81	Faber-Chi 144	Faber-Chi 46.6	Shocker-StL 4.9
Shawkey-NY 299.2	Bush-NY .252	Bush-NY .314	Shawkey-NY 2.91	Shawkey-NY 137	Shawkey-NY 37.3	Shawkey-NY 3.3
Hoyt-NY 265.0	Shawkey-NY .256	Shawkey-NY .316	Bush-NY 3.31	Bush-NY 121	Bush-NY 20.2	Bush-NY 3.2
Jones-NY 260.0	Hoyt-NY .269	Hoyt-NY .326	Hoyt-NY 3.43	Hoyt-NY 116	Hoyt-NY 18.9	Hoyt-NY 2.0

1923 American League

TEAM	W	L	T	PCT	GB	R	OR	HR	AVG	OBP	SLG	OPS	AOPS	PF	SB	CG	HR	BB	SO	BR/9	ERA	AERA	OAV	OOB	FW	PW	BW	BSW	DIF
NY	98	54	0	.645		823	**622**	**105**	.291	.357	**.422**	779	108	102	69	**101**	68	491	**506**	**12.3**	**3.62**	**109**	**.263**	**.330**	**3.3**	**4.7**	5.5	-.5	8.9
Det	83	71	1	.539	16	831	741	41	.300	.377	.401	778	113	98	87	61	58	**449**	447	13.1	4.09	94	.283	.345	.0	-3.4	10.7	.3	-1.7
Cle	82	71	0	.536	16.5	**888**	746	59	**.301**	**.381**	.420	**801**	**117**	100	79	77	**36**	465	407	13.2	3.91	101	.285	.346	-1.7	.4	**13.8**	-.4	-6.7
Was	75	78	2	.490	23.5	720	747	26	.274	.346	.367	713	98	95	102	71	56	563	474	14.0	3.98	95	.291	.364	-.9	-3.1	-1.2	.5	3.2
StL	74	78	2	.487	24	688	720	82	.281	.339	.398	737	94	106	64	83	59	528	488	13.2	3.93	106	.275	.348	1.4	3.4	-5.3	.1	-1.6
Phi	69	83	1	.454	29	661	761	53	.271	.333	.370	703	89	101	72	65	68	550	400	13.5	4.08	101	.280	.352	-1.4	.0	-8.2	.0	2.5
Chi	69	85	2	.448	30	692	741	42	.279	.350	.373	723	97	99	**191**	74	49	534	467	13.4	4.05	98	.283	.353	1.1	-1.3	-1.5	**.7**	-7.0
Bos	61	91	2	.401	37	584	809	34	.261	.318	.351	669	81	101	75	77	48	520	412	13.9	4.20	[illegible]	.284	[illegible]	2.0	1.6	11.2	.0	3.1
Total	616					35887		442	.282	.351	.388	739			743	609				13.3	3.98		.282	.351					

Batter-Fielder Wins	Batting Average	On-Base Percentage	Slugging Average	On-Base Plus Slugging	Adjusted OPS	Adjusted Batter Runs
Ruth-NY 10.1	Heilmann-Det .... .403	Ruth-NY .... .545	Ruth-NY .... .764	Ruth-NY 1309	Ruth-NY 238	Ruth-NY 119.2
Ward-NY 1.2	Ruth-NY .... .393	Witt-NY .... .386	Meusel-NY .... .478	Meusel-NY 837	Meusel-NY 117	Meusel-NY 9.1
Gehrig-NY 3	Witt-NY .... .314	Meusel-NY .... .359	Ward-NY .... .422	Witt-NY 794	Witt-NY 107	Witt-NY 6.8
Smith-NY 3	Meusel-NY .... .313	Pipp-NY .... .352	Witt-NY .... .408	Ward-NY 773	Ward-NY 101	Bush-NY 6.8

Runs	Hits	Doubles	Triples	Home Runs	Total Bases	Runs Batted In
Ruth-NY 151	Jamieson-Cle 222	Speaker-Cle 59	Rice-Was 18	Ruth-NY 41	Ruth-NY 399	Ruth-NY 131
Witt-NY 113	Ruth-NY 205	Ruth-NY 45	Goslin-Was 18	Ward-NY 10	Dugan-NY 247	Pipp-NY 108
Dugan-NY 111	Witt-NY 187	Dugan-NY 30	Ruth-NY 13	Meusel-NY 9	Witt-NY 243	Meusel-NY 91
2 players tied 79	Dugan-NY 182	Meusel-NY 29	Ward-NY 11	2 players tied 7	Ward-NY 239	Ward-NY 82

Stolen Bases	Base Stealing Runs	Fielding Runs-Infield	Fielding Runs-Outfield	Wins	Winning Pct.	Complete Games
Collins-Chi 48	Mostil-Chi 3.4	Peckinpaugh-Was 21.8	Mostil-Chi 16.0	Uhle-Cle 26	Pennock-NY .... .760	Uhle-Cle 29
Ruth-NY 17	Hendrick-NY 7	Ward-NY 9.5	Ruth-NY 6.4	Jones-NY 21	Jones-NY .... .724	Bush-NY 22
Meusel-NY 13	McNally-NY 4			Pennock-NY 19	Hoyt-NY .... .654	Pennock-NY 21
Ward-NY 8	Schang-NY 4			Bush-NY 19	Shawkey-NY .... .593	Hoyt-NY 19

Strikeouts	Fewest BB/Game	Games	Saves	Base Runners/9	Adjusted Relief Runs	Relief Ranking
Johnson-Was 130	Shocker-StL 1.59	Rommel-Phi 56	Russell-Was 9	Shocker-StL 11.16		
Shawkey-NY 125	Hoyt-NY 2.49	Jones-NY 39	Jones-NY 4	Hoyt-NY 11.20		
Bush-NY 125	Jones-NY 2.56	Hoyt-NY 37	Pennock-NY 3	Pennock-NY 11.52		
Pennock-NY 93	Pennock-NY 2.57	Bush-NY 37	3 players tied 1	Jones-NY 11.63		

Innings Pitched	Opponents' Avg.	Opponents' OBP	Earned Run Average	Adjusted ERA	Adjusted Starter Runs	Pitcher Wins
Uhle-Cle 357.2	Shawkey-NY .... .246	Shocker-StL .... .306	Coveleski-Cle 2.76	Coveleski-Cle 143	Vangilder-StL 27.8	Uhle-Cle 3.4
Bush-NY 275.2	Hoyt-NY .... .253	Hoyt-NY .... .307	Hoyt-NY 3.02	Hoyt-NY 131	Pennock-NY 24.6	Bush-NY 2.6
Shawkey-NY 258.2	Jones-NY .... .257	Jones-NY .... .312	Pennock-NY 3.13	Pennock-NY 126	Hoyt-NY 21.3	Pennock-NY 2.4
Jones-NY 243.0	Bush-NY .... .260	Pennock-NY .... .314	Bush-NY 3.43	Bush-NY 115	Bush-NY 16.9	Hoyt-NY 1.8

1924 American League

TEAM	W	L	T	PCT	GB	R	OR	HR	AVG	OBP	SLG	OPS	AOPS	PF	SB	CG	HR	BB	SO	BR/9	ERA	AERA	OAV	OOB	FW	PW	BW	BSW	DIF
Was	92	62	2	.597		755	**613**	22	.294	.361	.387	748	101	97	116	74	**34**	505	469	**12.2**	**3.34**	**121**	**.259**	**.330**	1.3	**10.6**	1.3	.1	1.6
NY	89	63	1	.586	2	798	667	**98**	.289	.352	**.426**	**778**	106	100	69	76	59	522	**487**	13.4	3.86	108	.284	.353	**2.0**	4.2	2.5	-.2	4.4
Det	86	68	2	.558	6	**849**	796	35	**.298**	**.373**	.404	777	**108**	98	100	60	55	**467**	441	13.5	4.19	98	.293	.354	.4	-1.1	**6.7**	.0	3.0
StL	74	78	1	.487	17	769	807	67	.295	.356	.408	764	96	106	85	66	68	517	386	13.8	4.57	99	.289	.358	.3	-.8	-3.3	-.5	2.4
Phi	71	81	0	.467	20	685	778	63	.281	.334	.389	723	90	101	77	68	43	597	371	14.4	4.39	98	.292	.368	.5	-1.4	-8.1	-.2	4.2
Cle	67	86	0	.438	24.5	755	814	41	.296	.361	.399	760	100	101	85	**87**	43	503	315	14.3	4.40	97	.300	.365	-1.0	-1.9	.0	**.4**	-7.1
Bos	67	87	3	.435	25	735	806	30	.277	.356	.374	730	94	100	78	73	43	523	414	13.9	4.35	100	.290	.359	-1.0	.2	-3.8	.1	-5.5
Chi	66	87	1	.431	25.5	793	858	41	.288	.365	.382	747	101	97	**137**	76	52	512	360	14.3	4.74	87	.305	.368	-2.4	-9.3	1.9	.3	-1.1
Total	617					36139		397	.290	.357	.397	754			747	580				13.7	4.23		.290	.357					

Batter-Fielder Wins	Batting Average	On-Base Percentage	Slugging Average	On-Base Plus Slugging	Adjusted OPS	Adjusted Batter Runs
Ruth-NY 8.4	Ruth-NY .... .378	Ruth-NY .... .513	Ruth-NY .... .739	Ruth-NY 1252	Ruth-NY 221	Ruth-NY 104.0
Schang-NY 1.0	Meusel-NY .... .325	Meusel-NY .... .365	Meusel-NY .... .494	Meusel-NY 859	Meusel-NY 120	Meusel-NY 14.3
Johnson-NY 7	Dugan-NY .... .302	Pipp-NY .... .352	Pipp-NY .... .457	Pipp-NY 808	Pipp-NY 108	Bush-NY 13.3
Bengough-NY 3	Witt-NY .... .297	Witt-NY .... .346	Schang-NY .... .427	Dugan-NY 731	Dugan-NY 88	Johnson-NY 9.0

Runs	Hits	Doubles	Triples	Home Runs	Total Bases	Runs Batted In
Ruth-NY 143	Rice-Was 216	J.Sewell-Cle 45	Pipp-NY 19	Ruth-NY 46	Ruth-NY 391	Goslin-Was 129
Dugan-NY 105	Ruth-NY 200	Heilmann-Det 45	Meusel-NY 11	Meusel-NY 12	Meusel-NY 286	Ruth-NY 121
Meusel-NY 93	Meusel-NY 188	Meusel-NY 40	Ward-NY 10	Pipp-NY 9	Pipp-NY 269	Meusel-NY 120
2 players tied 88	Dugan-NY 184	Ruth-NY 39	Johnson-NY 8	Ward-NY 8	Dugan-NY 238	Pipp-NY 114

Stolen Bases	Base Stealing Runs	Fielding Runs-Infield	Fielding Runs-Outfield	Wins	Winning Pct.	Complete Games
Collins-Chi 42	Collins-Chi 3.3	J.Sewell-Cle 21.8	Hooper-Chi 10.4	Johnson-Was 23	Johnson-Was .... .767	Thurston-Chi 28
Meusel-NY 26	Pipp-NY 9	Scott-NY 10.3	Ruth-NY 3.1	Pennock-NY 21	Pennock-NY .... .700	Pennock-NY 25
Pipp-NY 12	Meusel-NY 8	Ward-NY 7.9		Hoyt-NY 18	Shawkey-NY .... .593	Bush-NY 19
2 players tied 9	2 players tied 2	Pipp-NY 1.4		Bush-NY 17	Hoyt-NY .... .581	Hoyt-NY 14

Strikeouts	Fewest BB/Game	Games	Saves	Base Runners/9	Adjusted Relief Runs	Relief Ranking
Johnson-Was 158	Smith-Cle 1.53	Marberry-Was 50	Marberry-Was 15	Johnson-Was 10.37	Speece-Was 4.0	Speece-Was 2.0
Shawkey-NY 114	Pennock-NY 2.01	Hoyt-NY 46	Hoyt-NY 4	Pennock-NY 11.54		
Pennock-NY 101	Hoyt-NY 2.77	Pennock-NY 40	Pennock-NY 3	Shawkey-NY 13.13		
Bush-NY 80	Shawkey-NY 3.21	Bush-NY 39	Jones-NY 3	Jones-NY 13.30		

Innings Pitched	Opponents' Avg.	Opponents' OBP	Earned Run Average	Adjusted ERA	Adjusted Starter Runs	Pitcher Wins
Ehmke-Bos 315.0	Johnson-Was .... .224	Johnson-Was .... .284	Johnson-Was 2.72	Baumgartner-Phi ... 149	Johnson-Was 43.8	Johnson-Was 4.9
Pennock-NY 286.1	Pennock-NY .... .273	Pennock-NY .... .314	Pennock-NY 2.83	Pennock-NY 147	Pennock-NY 42.5	Pennock-NY 3.8
Bush-NY 252.0	Bush-NY .... .273	Shawkey-NY .... .350	Bush-NY 3.57	Bush-NY 116	Bush-NY 15.5	Bush-NY 3.2
Hoyt-NY 247.0	Jones-NY .... .276	Jones-NY .... .350	Jones-NY 3.63	Jones-NY 115	Hoyt-NY 11.2	Shawkey-NY 8

1925 American League

TEAM	W	L	T	PCT	GB	R	OR	HR	AVG	OBP	SLG	OPS	AOPS	PF	SB	CG	HR	BB	SO	BR/9	ERA	AERA	OAV	OOB	FW	PW	BW	BSW	DIF
Was	96	55	1	.636		829	**670**	56	.303	.373	.411	784	106	98	**135**	69	49	543	463	**13.3**	**3.70**	114	.278	.351	1.8	7.6	5.1	.4	5.7
Phi	88	64	1	.579	8.5	831	713	76	**.307**	.364	.434	798	101	107	67	61	60	544	**495**	**13.3**	3.87	**120**	**.276**	**.347**	-.6	**10.5**	.0	.0	2.1
StL	82	71	1	.536	15	900	906	**110**	.298	.360	**.439**	**799**	103	105	85	67	99	675	419	15.0	4.92	95	.298	.380	-1.4	-3.4	1.0	-.3	9.6
Det	81	73	2	.526	16.5	**903**	829	50	.302	**.379**	.413	792	**109**	99	97	66	70	556	419	14.2	4.61	94	.296	.366	1.9	-4.4	**7.2**	**.5**	-1.2
Chi	79	75	0	.513	18.5	811	770	38	.284	.370	.385	755	102	95	131	71	69	**489**	374	13.6	4.29	97	.295	.356	.2	-2.1	4.0	.4	-.4
Cle	70	84	1	.455	27.5	782	817	52	.297	.361	.399	760	97	101	90	**93**	**41**	493	345	14.0	4.49	98	.296	.359	-.4	-.8	-1.7	-.0	-4.0
NY	69	85	2	.448	28.5	706	774	**110**	.275	.336	.410	746	96	98	69	80	78	505	492	13.6	4.33	98	.289	.353	**2.7**	-1.0	-4.8	-.4	-4.5
Bos	47	105	0	.309	49.5	639	922	41	.266	.336	.364	700	83	-100	42	68	67	510	310	14.7	4.97	92	.308	.374	-4.2	-5.6	-12.2	-.4	-6.6
Total	616					36401		533	.292	.360	.408	768			716	575				14.0	4.39		.292	.360					

Batter-Fielder Wins
Speaker-Cle 4.3
Ruth-NY 1.5
Paschal-NY 1.5
Combs-NY 8

Batting Average
Heilmann-Det........ .393
Combs-NY............ .342
Gehrig-NY............ .295
Dugan-NY............ .292

On-Base Percentage
Speaker-Cle.......... .479
Combs-NY............ .411
Gehrig-NY............ .365
Meusel-NY............ .348

Slugging Average
Williams-StL.......... .613
Ruth-NY................ .543
Meusel-NY............ .542
Gehrig-NY............ .531

On-Base Plus Slugging
Cobb-Det............ 1066
Gehrig-NY............ 896
Meusel-NY............ 889
Combs-NY............ 873

Adjusted OPS
Cobb-Det............... 171
Gehrig-NY............. 127
Meusel-NY............. 125
Combs-NY............. 123

Adjusted Batter Runs
Heilmann-Det........ 55.5
Combs-NY............ 22.5
Paschal-NY........... 21.7
Ruth-NY................ 20.0

Runs
Mostil-Chi............... 135
Combs-NY.............117
Meusel-NY............ 101
Gehrig-NY............... 73

Hits
Simmons-Phi......... 253
Combs-NY............ 203
Meusel-NY............ 181
Gehrig-NY............ 129

Doubles
McManus-StL.......... 44
Combs-NY.............. 36
Meusel-NY.............. 34
Gehrig-NY.............. 23

Triples
Goslin-Was............. 20
Combs-NY.............. 13
Meusel-NY.............. 12
Gehrig-NY.............. 10

Home Runs
Meusel-NY.............. 33
Ruth-NY................... 25
Gehrig-NY............... 20
Paschal-NY............. 12

Total Bases
Simmons-Phi......... 392
Meusel-NY............ 338
Combs-NY............ 274
Gehrig-NY............ 232

Runs Batted In
Meusel-NY............ 138
Gehrig-NY............... 68
Ruth-NY.................. 66
Combs-NY............... 61

Stolen Bases
Mostil-Chi................ 43
Paschal-NY............. 14
Meusel-NY.............. 13
Combs-NY.............. 12

Base Stealing Runs
Goslin-Was............ 3.1
E.Johnson-NY 3
Gehrig-NY................ .3
3 players tied 2

Fielding Runs-Infield
J.Sewell-Cle.......... 15.8
Dugan-NY.............. 5.6

Fielding Runs-Outfield
Goslin-Was........... 14.3

Wins
Rommel-Phi............ 21
Lyons-Chi............... 21
Pennock-NY 16
Jones-NY................ 15

Winning Pct.
Coveleski-Was...... .800
Pennock-NY .... .485
Jones-NY............. .417

Complete Games
Smith-Cle................ 22
Ehmke-Bos.............. 22
Pennock-NY 21
Hoyt-NY.................. 17

Strikeouts
Grove-Phi 116
Jones-NY................ 92
Pennock-NY 88
Hoyt-NY.................. 86

Fewest BB/Game
Smith-Cle............. 1.82
Shocker-NY 2.14
Pennock-NY 2.31
Hoyt-NY.............. 2.89

Games
Marberry-Was.......... 55
Pennock-NY 47
Hoyt-NY.................. 46
Jones-NY................ 43

Saves
Marberry-Was.......... 15
Hoyt-NY..................... 6
3 players tied 2

Base Runners/9
Pennock-NY 11.05
Shocker-NY 12.49
Hoyt-NY............. 13.41
Shawkey-NY....... 13.60

Adjusted Relief Runs
Marberry-Was......... 5.2

Relief Ranking
Marberry-Was......... 8.9

Innings Pitched
Pennock-NY 277.0
Jones-NY........... 246.2
Shocker-NY 244.1
Hoyt-NY............. 243.0

Opponents' Avg.
Johnson-Was........ .250
Pennock-NY .... .254
Jones-NY............. .281
Hoyt-NY............... .292

Opponents' OBP
Pennock-NY .... .303
Shocker-NY .... .336
Hoyt-NY............... .346
Jones-NY............. .354

Earned Run Average
Coveleski-Was...... 2.84
Pennock-NY 2.96
Shocker-NY 3.65
Hoyt-NY............... 4.00

Adjusted ERA
Coveleski-Was....... 149
Pennock-NY 144
Shocker-NY 117
Hoyt-NY................ 107

Adjusted Starter Runs
Coveleski-Was...... 40.9
Pennock-NY 36.3
Shocker-NY 20.2
Hoyt-NY................. 7.8

Pitcher Wins
Johnson-Was.......... 4.6
Pennock-NY 3.3
Shocker-NY 2.1
Hoyt-NY.................. 1.3

1926 American League

TEAM	W	L	T	PCT	GB	R	OR	HR	AVG	OBP	SLG	OPS	AOPS	PF	SB	CG	HR	BB	SO	BR/9	ERA	AERA	OAV	OOB	FW	PW	BW	BSW	DIF
NY	91	63	1	.591		**847**	713	**121**	.289	**.369**	**.437**	**806**	**119**	98	79	63	56	478	486	12.8	3.86	100	.274	.337	-1.1	-.0	**13.4**	-.0	1.9
Cle	88	66	0	.571	3	738	612	27	.289	.349	.386	735	97	101	88	**96**	49	**450**	381	12.5	3.40	119	.271	.334	1.1	9.7	-1.8	**.8**	1.3
Phi	83	67	0	.553	6	677	**570**	61	.269	.341	.383	724	90	106	56	62	**38**	451	**571**	**12.3**	**3.00**	**139**	**.268**	**.331**	.9	**16.3**	-7.3	.0	-1.9
Was	81	69	2	.540	8	802	761	43	**.292**	.364	.401	765	109	98	117	65	45	566	418	14.0	4.34	89	.287	.361	.2	-7.2	6.4	-.2	6.8
Chi	81	72	2	.529	9.5	730	665	32	.289	.361	.390	751	106	96	**123**	85	47	506	458	12.7	3.74	103	.271	.336	**1.6**	1.6	5.6	.4	-4.7
Det	79	75	3	.513	12	793	830	36	.291	.367	.398	765	105	101	88	57	58	555	469	14.0	4.41	92	.292	.363	.0	-5.1	4.2	-.1	3.0
StL	62	92	1	.403	29	682	845	72	.276	.335	.394	729	92	105	64	64	86	654	337	14.7	4.66	92	.297	.379	-2.6	-5.3	-7.1	-.5	.5
Bos	46	107	1	.301	44.5	562	835	32	.256	.321	.343	664	82	-97	52	53	45	546	336	13.9	4.72	86	.294	.365	-.2	-9.6	-13.6	-.1	-7.1
Total	616					35831		424	.281	.351	.392	743			667	545				13.3	4.02		.281	.351					

Batter-Fielder Wins
Ruth-NY 8.5
Gehrig-NY............. 2.7
Collins-NY 2.2
Bengough-NY........ 1.1

Batting Average
Manush-Det.......... .378
Ruth-NY................ .372
Meusel-NY............ .315
Gehrig-NY............ .313

On-Base Percentage
Ruth-NY................ .516
Gehrig-NY............ .420
Combs-NY............ .352
Lazzeri-NY............ .338

Slugging Average
Ruth-NY................ .737
Gehrig-NY............ .549
Meusel-NY............ .470
Lazzeri-NY............ .462

On-Base Plus Slugging
Ruth-NY.............. 1253
Gehrig-NY............ 969
Lazzeri-NY............ 800
Combs-NY............ 781

Adjusted OPS
Ruth-NY................ 228
Gehrig-NY............. 154
Lazzeri-NY............ 109
Combs-NY............ 105

Adjusted Batter Runs
Ruth-NY............. 102.8
Gehrig-NY............ 47.5
Collins-NY............ 15.2
Meusel-NY.............11.4

Runs
Ruth-NY................ 139
Gehrig-NY............. 135
Combs-NY.............113
Koenig-NY.............. 93

Hits
Rice-Was.............. 216
Burns-Cle.............. 216
Ruth-NY................ 184
Combs-NY............ 181

Doubles
Burns-Cle................ 64
Gehrig-NY.............. 47
Combs-NY.............. 31
Ruth-NY.................. 30

Triples
Gehrig-NY............... 20
Lazzeri-NY............. 14
Combs-NY.............. 12
Koenig-NY................ 8

Home Runs
Ruth-NY................... 47
Lazzeri-NY.............. 18
Gehrig-NY............... 16
Meusel-NY.............. 12

Total Bases
Ruth-NY................ 365
Gehrig-NY............. 314
Lazzeri-NY............ 272
Combs-NY............ 260

Runs Batted In
Ruth-NY................ 146
Lazzeri-NY.............114
Gehrig-NY..............112
Meusel-NY.............. 81

Stolen Bases
Mostil-Chi................ 35
Meusel-NY.............. 16
Lazzeri-NY.............. 16
Ruth-NY...................11

Base Stealing Runs
Mostil-Chi............... 2.8
Lazzeri-NY............. 1.1
3 players tied 2

Fielding Runs-Infield
Rigney-Bos........... 21.1
Koenig-NY 1.9

Fielding Runs-Outfield
Goslin-Was........... 14.1
Ruth-NY.................... .6

Wins
Uhle-Cle.................. 27
Pennock-NY 23
Shocker-NY 19
Hoyt-NY.................. 16

Winning Pct.
Uhle-Cle.................711
Pennock-NY .... .676
Shocker-NY .... .633
Hoyt-NY............... .571

Complete Games
Uhle-Cle.................. 32
Pennock-NY 19
Shocker-NY 18
Hoyt-NY.................. 12

Strikeouts
Grove-Phi 194
Hoyt-NY.................. 79
Pennock-NY 78
Jones-NY................ 69

Fewest BB/Game
Pennock-NY 1.45
Shocker-NY 2.47
Hoyt-NY............... 2.56
Jones-NY............. 4.47

Games
Marberry-Was.......... 64
Shocker-NY 41
Pennock-NY 40
Hoyt-NY.................. 40

Saves
Marberry-Was.......... 22
Jones-NY.................. 5
Hoyt-NY..................... 4
Shawkey-NY 3

Base Runners/9
Russell-Bos 10.93
Pennock-NY 11.52
Hoyt-NY..............11.91
Shocker-NY 12.02

Adjusted Relief Runs
Pate-Phi............... 19.6
Braxton-NY............ 7.6

Relief Ranking
Marberry-Was....... 21.2
Braxton-NY............ 6.6

Innings Pitched
Uhle-Cle............. 318.1
Pennock-NY 266.1
Shocker-NY 258.1
Hoyt-NY............. 217.2

Opponents' Avg.
Thomas-Chi.......... .244
Grove-Phi .... .244
Hoyt-NY............... .264
Shocker-NY .... .269

Opponents' OBP
Pennock-NY .... .313
Hoyt-NY............... .316
Shocker-NY .... .318
Jones-NY............. .381

Earned Run Average
Grove-Phi 2.51
Shocker-NY 3.38
Pennock-NY 3.62
Hoyt-NY............... 3.85

Adjusted ERA
Grove-Phi 166
Shocker-NY 114
Pennock-NY 107
Hoyt-NY................ 100

Adjusted Starter Runs
Uhle-Cle............... 44.6
Shocker-NY 16.1
Pennock-NY 5.9
Shawkey-NY........... 3.6

Pitcher Wins
Uhle-Cle.................. 5.4
Shocker-NY 1.7
Pennock-NY 1.0
Braxton-NY................ .7

1927 American League

TEAM	W	L	T	PCT	GB	R	OR	HR	AVG	OBP	SLG	OPS	AOPS	PF	SB	CG	HR	BB	SO	BR/9	ERA	AERA	OAV	OOB	FW	PW	BW	BSW	DIF
NY	110	44	1	.714		**975**	**599**	**158**	**.307**	**.383**	**.489**	**872**	**135**	97	90	82	42	**409**	431	**11.9**	**3.20**	**120**	**.267**	**.323**	.7	**10.2**	**25.5**	-.2	-3.1
Phi	91	63	1	.591	19	841	726	56	.303	.372	.414	786	103	106	101	65	65	442	**553**	12.6	3.97	107	.278	.338	1.0	4.2	3.3	.0	5.4
Was	85	69	3	.552	25	782	730	29	.287	.351	.386	737	97	99	133	62	53	491	497	12.6	3.97	102	.269	.335	.8	1.3	-1.7	**1.1**	6.4
Det	82	71	3	.536	27.5	845	805	51	.289	.363	.409	772	105	101	**139**	75	52	577	421	14.0	4.14	102	.290	.364	.1	.9	3.3	.5	.7
Chi	70	83	0	.458	39.5	662	708	36	.278	.344	.378	722	94	98	89	**85**	55	440	365	12.7	3.91	103	.283	.342	**1.6**	1.9	-3.3	-.6	-6.0
Cle	66	87	0	.431	43.5	668	766	26	.283	.337	.379	716	90	101	65	72	**37**	508	366	13.9	4.27	98	.295	.361	.2	-1.0	-6.9	-1.0	-1.7
StL	59	94	2	.386	50.5	724	904	55	.276	.338	.380	718	88	103	90	80	79	604	385	14.7	4.95	88	.304	.378	-2.5	-8.3	-8.6	-.2	2.1
Bos	51	103	0	.331	59	597	856	28	.259	.320	.357	677	82	[illegible]	81	63	56	558	381	14.6	4.72	89	.305	.376	-1.4	-7.2	-13.2	.3	-4.5
Total	619					36094		439	.285	.351	.399	751			788	584				13.4	4.14		.285	.351					

Batter-Fielder Wins	Batting Average	On-Base Percentage	Slugging Average	On-Base Plus Slugging	Adjusted OPS	Adjusted Batter Runs
Ruth-NY 8.8	Heilmann-Det .398	Ruth-NY .486	Ruth-NY .772	Ruth-NY 1258	Ruth-NY 229	Gehrig-NY 108.8
Gehrig-NY 8.4	Gehrig-NY .373	Gehrig-NY .474	Gehrig-NY .765	Gehrig-NY 1240	Gehrig-NY 224	Ruth-NY 108.0
Lazzeri-NY 3.5	Combs-NY .356	Combs-NY .414	Combs-NY .511	Combs-NY 925	Combs-NY 143	Combs-NY 40.3
Combs-NY 2.8	Ruth-NY .356	Meusel-NY .393	Meusel-NY .510	Meusel-NY 902	Meusel-NY 137	Meusel-NY 27.9

Runs	Hits	Doubles	Triples	Home Runs	Total Bases	Runs Batted In
Ruth-NY 158	Combs-NY 231	Gehrig-NY 52	Combs-NY 23	Ruth-NY 60	Gehrig-NY 447	Gehrig-NY 175
Gehrig-NY 149	Gehrig-NY 218	Meusel-NY 47	Gehrig-NY 18	Gehrig-NY 47	Ruth-NY 417	Ruth-NY 164
Combs-NY 137	Ruth-NY 192	Combs-NY 36	Koenig-NY 11	Lazzeri-NY 18	Combs-NY 331	Meusel-NY 103
Koenig-NY 99	Lazzeri-NY 176	2 players tied 29	Meusel-NY 9	Meusel-NY 8	Lazzeri-NY 275	Lazzeri-NY 102

Stolen Bases	Base Stealing Runs	Fielding Runs-Infield	Fielding Runs-Outfield	Wins	Winning Pct.	Complete Games
Sisler-StL 27	Sisler-StL 3.5	Gehringer-Det 17.1	Falk-Chi 18.1	Lyons-Chi 22	Hoyt-NY .759	Lyons-Chi 30
Meusel-NY 24	Meusel-NY 1.8	Koenig-NY 12.1	Ruth-NY .6	Hoyt-NY 22	Shocker-NY .750	Hoyt-NY 23
Lazzeri-NY 22	Combs-NY 1.2	Lazzeri-NY 8.2		Hoyt-NY 22	Moore-NY .731	Pennock-NY 18
Combs-NY 15	Gazella-NY .5			2 players tied 19	Pennock-NY .704	Shocker-NY 13

Strikeouts	Fewest BB/Game	Games	Saves	Base Runners/9	Adjusted Relief Runs	Relief Ranking
Grove-Phi 174	Quinn-Phi 1.65	Braxton-Was 58	Moore-NY 13	Moore-NY 10.35	Braxton-Was 18.7	Braxton-Was 24.1
Hoyt-NY 86	Shocker-NY 1.85	Moore-NY 50	Shawkey-NY 4	Hoyt-NY 10.53		
Pipgras-NY 81	Hoyt-NY 1.90	Hoyt-NY 36	Pennock-NY 2	Shocker-NY 11.20		
Moore-NY 75	Pennock-NY 2.06	Pennock-NY 34	Hoyt-NY 1	Pennock-NY 11.80		

Innings Pitched	Opponents' Avg.	Opponents' OBP	Earned Run Average	Adjusted ERA	Adjusted Starter Runs	Pitcher Wins
Thomas-Chi 307.2	Moore-NY .234	Moore-NY .289	Moore-NY 2.28	Moore-NY 169	Thomas-Chi 42.0	Lyons-Chi 4.7
Lyons-Chi 307.2	Pipgras-NY .247	Hoyt-NY .294	Hoyt-NY 2.63	Hoyt-NY 146	Moore-NY 38.8	Moore-NY 4.5
Hoyt-NY 256.1	Hoyt-NY .251	Shocker-NY .306	Shocker-NY 2.84	Shocker-NY 136	Hoyt-NY 37.6	Hoyt-NY 3.8
Moore-NY 213.0	Shocker-NY .268	Pennock-NY .325	Pennock-NY 3.00	Pennock-NY 128	Shocker-NY 20.0	Shocker-NY 2.3

1928 American League

TEAM	W	L	T	PCT	GB	R	OR	HR	AVG	OBP	SLG	OPS	AOPS	PF	SB	CG	HR	BB	SO	BR/9	ERA	AERA	OAV	OOB	FW	PW	BW	BSW	DIF
NY	101	53	0	.656		**894**	685	**133**	**.296**	**.365**	**.450**	**815**	**124**	97	51	82	59	452	487	12.7	3.74	101	.276	.335	-.0	.3	**17.1**	-.4	7.1
Phi	98	55	0	.641	2.5	829	**615**	89	.295	.363	.436	799	112	103	59	81	66	**424**	**607**	**11.8**	**3.36**	**119**	**.259**	**.318**	.6	**9.5**	9.4	-.3	2.3
StL	82	72	0	.532	19	772	742	63	.274	.346	.393	739	97	103	78	80	93	454	456	12.8	4.17	101	.282	.340	.2	.3	-1.8	**.4**	5.9
Was	75	79	1	.487	26	718	705	40	.284	.346	.393	739	101	99	108	77	**40**	466	462	12.5	3.88	103	.272	.335	**1.0**	1.8	.5	**.4**	-5.7
Chi	72	82	1	.468	29	656	725	24	.270	.334	.358	692	88	99	**144**	**88**	66	501	418	13.4	3.98	102	.287	.352	.5	.8	-8.0	**.4**	1.4
Det	68	86	0	.442	33	744	804	62	.279	.340	.401	741	99	102	113	65	58	567	451	13.7	4.32	95	.281	.355	-1.5	-3.2	-1.5	-.0	-2.8
Cle	62	92	1	.403	39	674	830	34	.285	.335	.382	717	93	101	50	71	52	511	416	14.2	4.47	93	.303	.369	-1.6	-4.9	-5.4	-.4	-2.7
Bos	57	96	1	.373	43.5	589	770	38	.264	.319	.361	680	86	-98	97	70	49	452	407	13.2	4.39	93	.288	.349	.9	-4.3	-10.4	.0	-5.8
Total	617					35876		483	.281	.344	.397	741			700	614				13.0	4.04		.281	.344					

Batter-Fielder Wins	Batting Average	On-Base Percentage	Slugging Average	On-Base Plus Slugging	Adjusted OPS	Adjusted Batter Runs
Ruth-NY 7.1	Goslin-Was .379	Gehrig-NY .467	Ruth-NY .709	Ruth-NY 1172	Ruth-NY 211	Ruth-NY 92.1
Gehrig-NY 5.9	Gehrig-NY .374	Ruth-NY .463	Gehrig-NY .648	Gehrig-NY 1115	Gehrig-NY 196	Gehrig-NY 83.3
Lazzeri-NY 2.4	Lazzeri-NY .332	Combs-NY .387	Lazzeri-NY .535	Combs-NY 850	Combs-NY 127	Lazzeri-NY 27.6
Combs-NY 1.7	Ruth-NY .323	Koenig-NY .360	Meusel-NY .467	Meusel-NY 816	Meusel-NY 116	Combs-NY 24.4

Runs	Hits	Doubles	Triples	Home Runs	Total Bases	Runs Batted In
Ruth-NY 163	Manush-StL 241	Manush-StL 47	Combs-NY 21	Ruth-NY 54	Ruth-NY 380	Ruth-NY 142
Gehrig-NY 139	Gehrig-NY 210	Gehrig-NY 47	Gehrig-NY 13	Gehrig-NY 27	Gehrig-NY 364	Gehrig-NY 142
Combs-NY 118	Combs-NY 194	Gehrig-NY 47	Lazzeri-NY 11	Meusel-NY 11	Combs-NY 290	Meusel-NY 113
Koenig-NY 89	Ruth-NY 173	Meusel-NY 45	Koenig-NY 10	Lazzeri-NY 10	Meusel-NY 242	Lazzeri-NY 82

Stolen Bases	Base Stealing Runs	Fielding Runs-Infield	Fielding Runs-Outfield	Wins	Winning Pct.	Complete Games
Myer-Bos 30	Rice-Was 2.5	Gerber-StL-Bos 25.7	Jamieson-Cle 15.9	Pipgras-NY 24	Crowder-StL .808	Ruffing-Bos 25
Lazzeri-NY 15	Goslin-Was 2.5	Durocher-NY 5.2	Meusel-NY 1.8	Hoyt-NY 23	Hoyt-NY .767	Pipgras-NY 22
Combs-NY 11	Lazzeri-NY 1.5		Combs-NY .3	Pennock-NY 17	Pennock-NY .739	Hoyt-NY 19
Meusel-NY 6	3 players tied .2			Johnson-NY 14	Pipgras-NY .649	Pennock-NY 18

Strikeouts	Fewest BB/Game	Games	Saves	Base Runners/9	Adjusted Relief Runs	Relief Ranking
Grove-Phi 183	Rommel-Phi 1.35	Marberry-Was 48	Hoyt-NY 8	Braxton-Was 9.32		
Pipgras-NY 139	Pennock-NY 1.71	Pipgras-NY 46	Pipgras-NY 3	Pennock-NY 10.88		
Johnson-NY 110	Hoyt-NY 1.98	Hoyt-NY 42	Pennock-NY 3	Heimach-NY 10.99		
Hoyt-NY 67	Pipgras-NY 3.08	Moore-NY 35		Hoyt-NY 11.21		

Innings Pitched	Opponents' Avg.	Opponents' OBP	Earned Run Average	Adjusted ERA	Adjusted Starter Runs	Pitcher Wins
Pipgras-NY 300.2	Braxton-Was .222	Braxton-Was .267	Braxton-Was 2.51	Braxton-Was 159	Grove-Phi 40.7	Grove-Phi 4.7
Hoyt-NY 273.0	Johnson-NY .250	Pennock-NY .302	Pennock-NY 2.56	Pennock-NY 147	Pennock-NY 30.6	Pennock-NY 3.1
Pennock-NY 211.0	Pennock-NY .267	Hoyt-NY .313	Hoyt-NY 3.36	Hoyt-NY 112	Pipgras-NY 15.0	Hoyt-NY 1.6
Johnson-NY 199.0	2 players tied .272	Pipgras-NY .333	Pipgras-NY 3.38	Pipgras-NY 111	Hoyt-NY 14.8	Pipgras-NY 1.1

1929 American League

TEAM	W	L	T	PCT	GB	R	OR	HR	AVG	OBP	SLG	OPS	AOPS	PF	SB	CG	HR	BB	SO	BR/9	ERA	AERA	OAV	OOB	FW	PW	BW	BSW	DIF
Phi	104	46	1	.693		901	**615**	122	.296	**.365**	.451	**816**	111	104	63	70	73	487	**573**	**12.4**	**3.44**	**123**	**.264**	**.329**	**2.6**	**11.2**	7.9	.4	6.8
NY	88	66	0	.571	18	899	775	**142**	.295	.364	.450	814	**123**	93	52	64	83	485	484	13.1	4.19	92	.278	.341	.8	-5.4	**16.4**	-.1	-.7
Cle	81	71	0	.533	24	717	736	62	.294	.354	.417	771	100	104	75	80	56	488	389	13.9	4.05	109	.295	.357	-.6	5.1	.0	-.9	1.4
StL	79	73	2	.520	26	733	713	46	.276	.352	.381	733	91	104	70	83	100	**462**	415	12.8	4.08	108	.279	.340	2.2	4.6	-5.5	.3	1.3
Was	71	81	1	.467	34	730	776	48	.276	.347	.375	722	90	101	89	62	**48**	496	494	12.9	4.34	98	.276	.342	-.3	-1.5	-5.8	.3	2.3
Det	70	84	1	.455	36	**926**	928	110	**.299**	.360	**.453**	813	114	100	95	82	73	646	467	15.0	4.96	86	.301	.377	-3.0	-9.8	10.2	-.0	-4.3
Chi	59	93	0	.388	46	627	792	37	.268	.325	.363	688	83	-99	**109**	78	84	505	328	13.4	4.41	97	.284	.351	.0	-2.1	-12.4	**.5**	-3.2
Bos	58	96	1	.377	48	605	803	28	.267	.325	.365	690	85	-98	86	**84**	78	496	416	13.6	4.43	96	.291	.355	-1.6	-2.4	-10.9	-.5	-3.6
Total	613					36138		595	.284	.349	.407	757			639	603				13.4	4.24		.284	.349					

Batter-Fielder Wins
Ruth-NY 5.4
Lazzeri-NY 5.2
Gehrig-NY 4.5
Combs-NY 1.9

Batting Average
Fonseca-Cle .... .369
Lazzeri-NY .... .354
Combs-NY .... .345
Ruth-NY .... .345

On-Base Percentage
Foxx-Phi .... .463
Gehrig-NY .... .431
Ruth-NY .... .430
Lazzeri-NY .... .429

Slugging Average
Ruth-NY .... .697
Gehrig-NY .... .584
Lazzeri-NY .... .561
Dickey-NY .... .485

On-Base Plus Slugging
Ruth-NY 1128
Gehrig-NY 1015
Lazzeri-NY 991
Combs-NY 881

Adjusted OPS
Ruth-NY 199
Gehrig-NY 170
Lazzeri-NY 164
Combs-NY 135

Adjusted Batter Runs
Ruth-NY 72.3
Gehrig-NY 63.0
Lazzeri-NY 53.7
Combs-NY 32.9

Runs
Gehringer-Det 131
Gehrig-NY 127
Ruth-NY 121
Combs-NY 119

Hits
Gehringer-Det 215
Alexander-Det 215
Combs-NY 202
Lazzeri-NY 193

Doubles
3 players tied 45
Lazzeri-NY 37
Combs-NY 33
Gehrig-NY 32

Triples
Gehringer-Det 19
Combs-NY 15
Lazzeri-NY 11
Gehrig-NY 10

Home Runs
Ruth-NY 46
Gehrig-NY 35
Lazzeri-NY 18
2 players tied 10

Total Bases
Simmons-Phi 373
Ruth-NY 348
Gehrig-NY 323
Lazzeri-NY 306

Runs Batted In
Simmons-Phi 157
Ruth-NY 154
Gehrig-NY 126
Lazzeri-NY 106

Stolen Bases
Gehringer-Det 27
Combs-NY 12
Lazzeri-NY 9
Ruth-NY 5

Base Stealing Runs
Gehringer-Det 2.4
Lary-NY 5
Durocher-NY 3
2 players tied 2

Fielding Runs-Infield
Melillo-StL 20.4
Durocher-NY 20.2
Lazzeri-NY 5

Fielding Runs-Outfield
Simmons-Phi 19.6

Wins
Earnshaw-Phi 24
Pipgras-NY 18
Wells-NY 13
Zachary-NY 12

Winning Pct.
Grove-Phi .... .769
Pipgras-NY .... .600

Complete Games
Thomas-Chi 24
Pipgras-NY 13
Hoyt-NY 12
Wells-NY 10

Strikeouts
Grove-Phi 170
Pipgras-NY 125
Wells-NY 78
Hoyt-NY 57

Fewest BB/Game
Russell-Bos 1.58
Pennock-NY 1.60
Hoyt-NY 3.08
Sherid-NY 3.20

Games
Marberry-Was 49
Moore-NY 41
Pipgras-NY 39
Heimach-NY 35

Saves
Marberry-Was 11
Moore-NY 8
Heimach-NY 4
2 players tied 2

Base Runners/9
Marberry-Was 11.07
Heimach-NY 11.56
Wells-NY 12.15
Moore-NY 12.25

Adjusted Relief Runs

Relief Ranking

Innings Pitched
Gray-StL 305.0
Pipgras-NY 225.1
Hoyt-NY 201.2
Wells-NY 193.1

Opponents' Avg.
Earnshaw-Phi .... .241
Wells-NY .... .248
Pipgras-NY .... .264
Sherid-NY .... .277

Opponents' OBP
Marberry-Was .... .308
Wells-NY .... .324
Hoyt-NY .... .339
Pipgras-NY .... .340

Earned Run Average
Grove-Phi 2.81
Sherid-NY 3.61
Pipgras-NY 4.23
Hoyt-NY 4.24

Adjusted ERA
Grove-Phi 150
Sherid-NY 107
Pipgras-NY 91
Hoyt-NY 91

Adjusted Starter Runs
Grove-Phi 42.6
Zachary-NY 18.8
Sherid-NY 2.1

Pitcher Wins
Marberry-Was 4.0
Zachary-NY 1.7
Nekola-NY 1
Sherid-NY 0

1930 American League

TEAM	W	L	T	PCT	GB	R	OR	HR	AVG	OBP	SLG	OPS	AOPS	PF	SB	CG	HR	BB	SO	BR/9	ERA	AERA	OAV	OOB	FW	PW	BW	BSW	DIF
Phi	102	52	0	.662		951	751	125	.294	.369	.452	821	108	104	48	72	84	488	**672**	12.9	4.28	109	.274	.337	**3.0**	5.2	6.0	.0	10.7
Was	94	60	0	.610	8	892	**689**	57	.302	.369	.426	795	106	100	**101**	**78**	**52**	504	524	**12.5**	**3.96**	**116**	**.264**	**.332**	2.3	**8.8**	5.0	.0	.9
NY	86	68	0	.558	16	**1062**	898	**152**	**.309**	**.384**	**.488**	**872**	**131**	96	91	65	93	524	572	13.9	4.88	88	.287	.352	-.7	-8.9	**23.4**	.0	-4.9
Cle	81	73	0	.526	21	890	915	72	.304	.364	.431	795	102	104	51	68	85	528	442	14.6	4.88	99	.305	.368	-2.5	-.8	2.4	-.3	5.2
Det	75	79	0	.487	27	783	833	82	.284	.344	.421	765	96	102	98	68	86	570	574	14.0	4.70	102	.286	.359	.2	1.2	-3.1	-.0	-.2
StL	64	90	0	.416	38	751	886	75	.268	.333	.391	724	85	103	93	68	124	449	470	13.9	5.07	96	.300	.356	.4	-2.6	-10.9	-.2	.3
Chi	62	92	0	.403	40	729	884	63	.276	.328	.391	719	89	-97	74	63	74	**407**	471	13.6	4.71	98	.300	.352	-2.4	-1.4	-8.3	**.4**	-3.3
Bos	52	102	0	.338	50	612	814	47	.264	.313	.365	678	79	-96	42	**78**	75	488	356	13.4	4.68	98	.286	.348	-.0	-1.1	-15.6	-.0	-8.2
Total	616					36670		673	.288	.351	.421	772			598	560				13.6	4.65		.288	.351					

Batter-Fielder Wins
Gehrig-NY 7.7
Ruth-NY 7.6
Combs-NY 2.3
Lazzeri-NY 2.0

Batting Average
Simmons-Phi .... .381
Gehrig-NY .... .379
Ruth-NY .... .359
Combs-NY .... .344

On-Base Percentage
Ruth-NY .... .493
Gehrig-NY .... .473
Combs-NY .... .424
Lazzeri-NY .... .372

Slugging Average
Ruth-NY .... .732
Gehrig-NY .... .721
Combs-NY .... .523
Dickey-NY .... .486

On-Base Plus Slugging
Ruth-NY 1225
Gehrig-NY 1194
Combs-NY 947
Chapman-NY 845

Adjusted OPS
Ruth-NY 216
Gehrig-NY 207
Combs-NY 145
Chapman-NY 118

Adjusted Batter Runs
Ruth-NY 100.0
Gehrig-NY 98.5
Combs-NY 38.2
Lazzeri-NY 13.4

Runs
Simmons-Phi 152
Ruth-NY 150
Gehrig-NY 143
Combs-NY 129

Hits
Hodapp-Cle 225
Gehrig-NY 220
Ruth-NY 186
Combs-NY 183

Doubles
Hodapp-Cle 51
Gehrig-NY 42
Lazzeri-NY 34
Chapman-NY 31

Triples
Combs-NY 22
Gehrig-NY 17
Lazzeri-NY 15
Chapman-NY 10

Home Runs
Ruth-NY 49
Gehrig-NY 41
Chapman-NY 10
Lazzeri-NY 9

Total Bases
Gehrig-NY 419
Ruth-NY 379
Combs-NY 278
Lazzeri-NY 264

Runs Batted In
Gehrig-NY 174
Ruth-NY 153
Lazzeri-NY 121
Combs-NY 82

Stolen Bases
McManus-Det 23
Combs-NY 16
Lary-NY 14
Chapman-NY 14

Base Stealing Runs
Lary-NY 2.4
Dickey-NY 1.2
Chapman-NY 1.0
Byrd-NY 8

Fielding Runs-Infield
Cronin-Was 26.5
Lazzeri-NY 2.3
Gehrig-NY 1.5

Fielding Runs-Outfield
Haas-Phi 7.4

Wins
Grove-Phi 28
Pipgras-NY 15
Johnson-NY 14
2 players tied 12

Winning Pct.
Grove-Phi .... .848
Pipgras-NY .... .500

Complete Games
Lyons-Chi 29
Pipgras-NY 15
Pennock-NY 11
Sherid-NY 8

Strikeouts
Grove-Phi 209
Johnson-NY 115
Pipgras-NY 111
Sherid-NY 59

Fewest BB/Game
Pennock-NY 1.15
Pipgras-NY 2.85
Sherid-NY 4.26
Johnson-NY 5.34

Games
Grove-Phi 50
Pipgras-NY 44
Johnson-NY 44
Sherid-NY 37

Saves
Grove-Phi 9
Sherid-NY 4
Pipgras-NY 4
McEvoy-NY 3

Base Runners/9
Grove-Phi 10.45
Pennock-NY 12.32
Pipgras-NY 12.54
Wells-NY 14.22

Adjusted Relief Runs
Quinn-Phi 2.4

Relief Ranking
Quinn-Phi 4.2

Innings Pitched
Lyons-Chi 297.2
Pipgras-NY 221.0
Sherid-NY 184.0
Johnson-NY 175.1

Opponents' Avg.
Grove-Phi .... .247
Hadley-Was .... .247
Pipgras-NY .... .263
Johnson-NY .... .265

Opponents' OBP
Grove-Phi .... .288
Pennock-NY .... .322
Pipgras-NY .... .324
Johnson-NY .... .366

Earned Run Average
Grove-Phi 2.54
Pipgras-NY 4.11
Pennock-NY 4.32
Johnson-NY 4.67

Adjusted ERA
Grove-Phi 184
Pipgras-NY 105
Pennock-NY 100
Johnson-NY 92

Adjusted Starter Runs
Grove-Phi 65.8
Ruth-NY 1.7
Pipgras-NY 1

Pitcher Wins
Grove-Phi 6.9
Ruth-NY 3

1931 American League

TEAM	W	L	T	PCT	GB	R	OR	HR	AVG	OBP	SLG	OPS	AOPS	PF	SB	CG	HR	BB	SO	BR/9	ERA	AERA	OAV	OOB	FW	PW	BW	BSW	DIF
Phi	107	45	1	.704		858	**626**	118	.287	.355	.435	790	107	106	25	**97**	73	457	574	**11.9**	**3.47**	**130**	**.256**	**.316**	3.2	**14.2**	4.2	-.0	9.5
NY	94	59	2	.614	13.5	**1067**	760	**155**	**.297**	**.383**	**.457**	**840**	**135**	94	**138**	78	67	543	**686**	12.9	4.20	94	.263	.332	1.7	-3.8	**26.5**	**.9**	-7.8
Was	92	62	2	.597	16	843	690	49	.285	.345	.400	745	100	101	72	60	73	498	582	12.6	3.76	114	.264	.327	**3.3**	7.7	.2	-.4	4.2
Cle	78	76	1	.506	30	885	833	71	.296	.363	.419	782	105	106	63	76	64	561	470	14.4	4.63	100	.286	.355	-2.0	-.2	4.5	-.4	-.8
StL	63	91	0	.409	45	721	870	76	.271	.333	.390	723	92	104	73	65	84	**448**	436	13.8	4.76	97	.293	.348	-2.1	-1.6	-6.1	-.9	-3.3
Bos	62	90	1	.408	45	625	800	37	.262	.315	.349	664	85	-95	42	61	**54**	473	365	13.5	4.60	94	.285	.344	.4	-4.2	-11.1	-.3	1.2
Det	61	93	0	.396	47	651	836	43	.268	.330	.371	701	87	103	117	86	79	597	511	14.1	4.59	100	.282	.355	-1.4	-.0	-9.6	.2	-5.1
Chi	56	97	3	.366	51.5	704	939	27	.260	.323	.343	[illegible]	[illegible]	-94	[illegible]	[illegible]	[illegible]	[illegible]	[illegible]	14.6	5.04	85	.287	.358	-2.7	-11.6	-10.3	.9	3.3
Total	618					36354		576	.278	.344	.396	740			624	577				13.5	4.38		.278	.344					

Batter-Fielder Wins
- **Ruth-NY 8.1**
- **Gehrig-NY............. 6.0**
- **Chapman-NY......... 3.4**
- **Lary-NY................. 2.9**

Batting Average
- Simmons-Phi .... .390
- Ruth-NY .... .373
- Gehrig-NY .... .341
- Dickey-NY .... .327

On-Base Percentage
- Ruth-NY .... .495
- Gehrig-NY .... .446
- Chapman-NY .... .396
- Combs-NY .... .394

Slugging Average
- Ruth-NY .... .700
- Gehrig-NY .... .662
- Chapman-NY .... .483
- Combs-NY .... .446

On-Base Plus Slugging
- Ruth-NY 1195
- Gehrig-NY 1108
- Chapman-NY 879
- Combs-NY 840

Adjusted OPS
- Ruth-NY 223
- Gehrig-NY 199
- Chapman-NY 138
- Combs-NY 127

Adjusted Batter Runs
- Ruth-NY 104.4
- Gehrig-NY 91.0
- Chapman-NY 33.6
- Combs-NY 24.1

Runs
- Gehrig-NY 163
- Ruth-NY 149
- Combs-NY 120
- Chapman-NY 120

Hits
- Gehrig-NY 211
- Ruth-NY 199
- Chapman-NY 189
- Combs-NY 179

Doubles
- Webb-Bos 67
- Lary-NY 35
- 3 players tied 31

Triples
- Johnson-Det 19
- Gehrig-NY 15
- Combs-NY 13
- Chapman-NY 11

Home Runs
- Ruth-NY 46
- Gehrig-NY 46
- Chapman-NY 17
- Lary-NY 10

Total Bases
- Gehrig-NY 410
- Ruth-NY 374
- Chapman-NY 290
- Lary-NY 254

Runs Batted In
- Gehrig-NY 184
- Ruth-NY 163
- Chapman-NY 122
- Lary-NY 107

Stolen Bases
- Chapman-NY 61
- Lazzeri-NY 18
- Gehrig-NY 17
- Lary-NY 13

Base Stealing Runs
- Chapman-NY 5.4
- Combs-NY 1.4
- Byrd-NY 1.1
- Lazzeri-NY 8

Fielding Runs-Infield
- Melillo-StL 35.3
- Lary-NY 4.1
- Chapman-NY 5

Fielding Runs-Outfield
- West-Was 13.6
- Chapman-NY 5.3
- Byrd-NY 0

Wins
- Grove-Phi 31
- Gomez-NY 21
- Ruffing-NY 16
- Johnson-NY 13

Winning Pct.
- Grove-Phi .... .886
- Gomez-NY .... .700
- Ruffing-NY .... .533

Complete Games
- Grove-Phi 27
- Ferrell-Cle 27
- Ruffing-NY 19
- Gomez-NY 17

Strikeouts
- Grove-Phi 175
- Gomez-NY 150
- Ruffing-NY 132
- Johnson-NY 106

Fewest BB/Game
- Pennock-NY 1.43
- Gomez-NY 3.15
- Ruffing-NY 3.30
- Johnson-NY 4.68

Games
- Hadley-Was 55
- Johnson-NY 40
- Gomez-NY 40
- Ruffing-NY 37

Saves
- Moore-Bos 10
- Johnson-NY 4
- Pipgras-NY 3
- Gomez-NY 3

Base Runners/9
- Grove-Phi 9.73
- Gomez-NY 10.93
- Ruffing-NY 12.65
- Pipgras-NY 12.68

Adjusted Relief Runs
- Kimsey-StL 7

Relief Ranking
- Kimsey-StL 8

Innings Pitched
- Walberg-Phi 291.0
- Gomez-NY 243.0
- Ruffing-NY 237.0
- Johnson-NY 196.1

Opponents' Avg.
- Hadley-Was .... .218
- Gomez-NY .... .226
- Johnson-NY .... .234
- Ruffing-NY .... .256

Opponents' OBP
- Grove-Phi .... .271
- Gomez-NY .... .295
- Ruffing-NY .... .323
- Johnson-NY .... .326

Earned Run Average
- Grove-Phi 2.06
- Gomez-NY 2.67
- Pennock-NY 4.28
- Ruffing-NY 4.41

Adjusted ERA
- Grove-Phi 218
- Gomez-NY 149
- Pennock-NY 93
- Ruffing-NY 90

Adjusted Starter Runs
- Grove-Phi 73.9
- Gomez-NY 36.5
- Rhodes-NY 7
- Pipgras-NY 0

Pitcher Wins
- Grove-Phi 8.2
- Gomez-NY 3.6
- Rhodes-NY 1
- Andrews-NY 0

Historical Record

1932 American League

TEAM	W	L	T	PCT	GB	R	OR	HR	AVG	OBP	SLG	OPS	AOPS	PF	SB	CG	HR	BB	SO	BR/9	ERA	AERA	OAV	OOB	FW	PW	BW	BSW	DIF
NY	107	47	2	.695		**1002**	724	160	.286	**.376**	.454	**830**	**128**	95	77	**96**	93	561	**780**	**12.8**	**3.98**	102	**.260**	.331	.2	1.6	**21.5**	-.3	7.1
Phi	94	60	0	.610	13	981	752	**172**	**.290**	.366	**.457**	823	115	104	38	95	112	511	595	13.0	4.45	102	.271	.336	**3.8**	1.0	11.0	.3	.9
Was	93	61	0	.604	14	840	**716**	61	.284	.347	.408	755	102	99	70	66	73	526	437	13.0	4.16	104	.271	.337	**3.8**	2.3	1.6	.2	8.2
Cle	87	65	1	.572	19	845	747	78	.285	.357	.413	770	99	107	52	94	**70**	**446**	439	**12.8**	4.12	**115**	.273	**.329**	-.2	**8.3**	-.6	-.4	3.8
Det	76	75	2	.503	29.5	799	787	80	.273	.335	.401	736	92	104	**103**	67	89	592	521	13.5	4.30	109	.269	.346	.0	5.4	-6.1	**.8**	.4
StL	63	91	0	.409	44	736	898	67	.276	.339	.388	727	89	106	69	63	103	574	496	14.3	5.01	97	.290	.359	.0	-2.0	-8.1	-.4	-3.5
Chi	49	102	1	.325	56.5	667	897	36	.267	.327	.360	687	90	-94	89	50	88	580	379	14.4	4.82	90	.287	.359	-4.6	-7.1	-7.2	.2	-7.7
Bos	43	111	0	.279	64	566	915	53	.251	.314	.351	665	80	-97	46	42	79	612	365	14.6	5.02	90	.289	.364	-2.6	-7.3	-14.6	-.3	-9.2
Total	615					36436		707	.277	.346	.404	750			544	573				13.6	4.48		.277	.346					

Batter-Fielder Wins
- **Foxx-Phi 6.7**
- **Ruth-NY 6.5**
- **Gehrig-NY.............. 5.1**
- **Lazzeri-NY 3.9**

Batting Average
- Alexander-Det-Bos ...... .367
- Gehrig-NY .... .349
- Ruth-NY .... .341
- Combs-NY .... .321

On-Base Percentage
- Ruth-NY .... .489
- Gehrig-NY .... .451
- Combs-NY .... .405
- Lazzeri-NY .... .399

Slugging Average
- Foxx-Phi .... .749
- Ruth-NY .... .661
- Gehrig-NY .... .621
- Lazzeri-NY .... .506

On-Base Plus Slugging
- Foxx-Phi 1218
- Ruth-NY 1150
- Gehrig-NY 1072
- Lazzeri-NY 905

Adjusted OPS
- Ruth-NY 206
- Gehrig-NY 184
- Lazzeri-NY 140
- Combs-NY 129

Adjusted Batter Runs
- Foxx-Phi 91.5
- Ruth-NY 80.5
- Gehrig-NY 79.4
- Lazzeri-NY 31.6

Runs
- Foxx-Phi 151
- Combs-NY 143
- Gehrig-NY 138
- Ruth-NY 120

Hits
- Simmons-Phi 216
- Gehrig-NY 208
- Combs-NY 190
- Chapman-NY 174

Doubles
- McNair-Phi 47
- Gehrig-NY 42
- Chapman-NY 41
- Combs-NY 32

Triples
- Cronin-Was 18
- Lazzeri-NY 16
- Chapman-NY 15
- Combs-NY 10

Home Runs
- Foxx-Phi 58
- Ruth-NY 41
- Gehrig-NY 34
- 2 players tied 15

Total Bases
- Foxx-Phi 438
- Gehrig-NY 370
- Ruth-NY 302
- Chapman-NY 275

Runs Batted In
- Foxx-Phi 169
- Gehrig-NY 151
- Ruth-NY 137
- Lazzeri-NY 113

Stolen Bases
- Chapman-NY 38
- Lazzeri-NY 11
- Lary-NY 9
- Gehrig-NY 4

Base Stealing Runs
- Walker-Det 4.5
- Chapman-NY 2.1
- Lary-NY 9
- Phillips-NY 2

Fielding Runs-Infield
- Warstler-Bos 22.8
- Lazzeri-NY 4.3
- Sewell-NY 7

Fielding Runs-Outfield
- Vosmik-Cle 18.9
- Chapman-NY 4.1

Wins
- Crowder-Was 26
- Gomez-NY 24
- Ruffing-NY 18
- Allen-NY 17

Winning Pct.
- Allen-NY .... .810
- Gomez-NY .... .774
- Ruffing-NY .... .720
- Pipgras-NY .... .640

Complete Games
- Grove-Phi 27
- Ruffing-NY 22
- Gomez-NY 21
- Pipgras-NY 14

Strikeouts
- Ruffing-NY 190
- Gomez-NY 176
- Pipgras-NY 111
- Allen-NY 109

Fewest BB/Game
- Brown-Cle 1.71
- Gomez-NY 3.56
- Allen-NY 3.56
- Pipgras-NY 3.58

Games
- Marberry-Was 54
- Gomez-NY 37
- Ruffing-NY 35
- Allen-NY 33

Saves
- Marberry-Was 13
- Allen-NY 4
- Wells-NY 2
- Ruffing-NY 2

Base Runners/9
- Grove-Phi 10.77
- Allen-NY 11.39
- Ruffing-NY 11.71
- Gomez-NY 12.65

Adjusted Relief Runs
- Kimsey-StL-Chi 7.7

Relief Ranking
- Kimsey-StL-Chi 7.2

Innings Pitched
- Crowder-Was 327.0
- Gomez-NY 265.1
- Ruffing-NY 259.0
- Pipgras-NY 219.0

Opponents' Avg.
- Ruffing-NY .... .226
- Allen-NY .... .228
- Gomez-NY .... .259
- Pipgras-NY .... .269

Opponents' OBP
- Grove-Phi .... .292
- Allen-NY .... .306
- Ruffing-NY .... .311
- Gomez-NY .... .329

Earned Run Average
- Grove-Phi 2.84
- Ruffing-NY 3.09
- Allen-NY 3.70
- Pipgras-NY 4.19

Adjusted ERA
- Grove-Phi 159
- Ruffing-NY 132
- Allen-NY 110
- 2 players tied 97

Adjusted Starter Runs
- Grove-Phi 54.0
- Ruffing-NY 31.8
- Allen-NY 11.5
- Devens-NY 2.4

Pitcher Wins
- Grove-Phi 5.9
- Ruffing-NY 4.0
- Allen-NY 9
- Devens-NY 2

1933 American League

TEAM	W	L	T	PCT	GB	R	OR	HR	AVG	OBP	SLG	OPS	AOPS	PF	SB	CG	HR	BB	SO	BR/9	ERA	AERA	OAV	OOB	FW	PW	BW	BSW	DIF
Was	99	53	1	.651		850	**665**	60	**.287**	.353	.402	755	107	99	65	68	64	**452**	447	**12.2**	3.82	109	**.263**	**.322**	**2.6**	5.4	5.2	.0	9.7
NY	91	59	2	.607	7	**927**	768	**144**	.283	**.369**	**.440**	**809**	**129**	94	**76**	70	66	612	**711**	13.6	4.36	89	.267	.344	.4	-7.6	**20.4**	.0	2.8
Phi	79	72	1	.523	19.5	875	853	139	.285	.362	**.440**	802	118	101	34	69	77	644	423	14.6	4.81	89	.283	.361	-1.9	-7.4	12.4	.0	.4
Cle	75	76	0	.497	23.5	654	669	50	.261	.321	.360	681	82	-105	36	**74**	**60**	465	437	12.4	**3.71**	**120**	.264	.325	.9	**10.1**	-12.9	-.2	1.5
Det	75	79	1	.487	25	722	733	57	.269	.329	.380	709	92	102	68	69	84	561	575	12.9	3.95	109	**.263**	.335	-.2	5.3	-6.4	.0	-.8
Chi	67	83	1	.447	31	683	814	43	.272	.342	.360	702	96	96	43	53	85	519	423	13.5	4.45	95	.277	.343	-1.0	-3.1	-1.9	-.3	-1.7
Bos	63	86	0	.423	34.5	700	758	50	.271	.339	.377	716	97	99	58	60	75	591	467	13.6	4.35	101	.271	.348	-2.2	.4	-1.7	**.4**	-8.3
StL	55	96	2	.364	43.5	669	820	64	.253	.322	.360	682	81	-106	72	55	96	531	426	14.0	4.82	97	.289	.354	1.5	-2.2	-13.4	-.0	-6.3
Total	608					36080		607	.273	.342	.390	732			452	518				13.3	4.28		.273	.342					

Batter-Fielder Wins
Foxx-Phi 6.9
Ruth-NY 4.7
Gehrig-NY 4.7
Dickey-NY 3.5

Batting Average
Foxx-Phi .... .356
Gehrig-NY .... .334
Dickey-NY .... .318
Chapman-NY .... .312

On-Base Percentage
Cochrane-Phi .... .459
Ruth-NY .... .442
Gehrig-NY .... .424
Chapman-NY .... .393

Slugging Average
Foxx-Phi .... .703
Gehrig-NY .... .605
Ruth-NY .... .582
Walker-NY .... .500

On-Base Plus Slugging
Foxx-Phi 1153
Gehrig-NY 1030
Ruth-NY 1023
Dickey-NY 871

Adjusted OPS
Foxx-Phi 199
Gehrig-NY 181
Ruth-NY 180
Dickey-NY 138

Adjusted Batter Runs
Foxx-Phi 82.4
Gehrig-NY 70.1
Ruth-NY 58.8
Lazzeri-NY 27.6

Runs
Gehrig-NY 138
Chapman-NY 112
Ruth-NY 97
Lazzeri-NY 94

Hits
Manush-Was 221
Gehrig-NY 198
Chapman-NY 176
Lazzeri-NY 154

Doubles
Cronin-Was 45
Gehrig-NY 41
Chapman-NY 36
Dickey-NY 24

Triples
Manush-Was 17
Combs-NY 16
Lazzeri-NY 12
Gehrig-NY 12

Home Runs
Foxx-Phi 48
Ruth-NY 34
Gehrig-NY 32
Lazzeri-NY 18

Total Bases
Foxx-Phi 403
Gehrig-NY 359
Ruth-NY 267
Lazzeri-NY 254

Runs Batted In
Foxx-Phi 163
Gehrig-NY 139
Lazzeri-NY 104
Ruth-NY 103

Stolen Bases
Chapman-NY 27
Lazzeri-NY 15
Gehrig-NY 9
Combs-NY 6

Base Stealing Runs
Walker-Det 2.6
Lazzeri-NY 9
Crosetti-NY 5
2 players tied 2

Fielding Runs-Infield
Melillo-StL 22.3
Sewell-NY 3.7

Fielding Runs-Outfield
Chapman-NY 14.1
Ruth-NY 7

Wins
Grove-Phi 24
Crowder-Was 24
Gomez-NY 16
Allen-NY 15

Winning Pct.
Grove-Phi .... .750
Allen-NY .... .682
Gomez-NY .... .615

Complete Games
Grove-Phi 21
Ruffing-NY 18
Gomez-NY 14
2 players tied 10

Strikeouts
Gomez-NY 163
Ruffing-NY 122
Allen-NY 119
VanAtta-NY 76

Fewest BB/Game
Brown-Cle 1.65
Ruffing-NY 3.56
VanAtta-NY 3.61
Gomez-NY 4.07

Games
Crowder-Was 52
Ruffing-NY 35
Moore-NY 35
Gomez-NY 35

Saves
Russell-Was 13
Moore-NY 8
Pennock-NY 4
2 players tied 3

Base Runners/9
Heving-Chi 10.83
Gomez-NY 12.43
Ruffing-NY 12.52
Allen-NY 12.77

Adjusted Relief Runs
Russell-Was 19.6

Relief Ranking
Russell-Was 30.3

Innings Pitched
Hadley-StL 316.2
Ruffing-NY 235.0
Gomez-NY 234.2
Allen-NY 184.2

Opponents' Avg.
Bridges-Det .... .226
Gomez-NY .... .240
Allen-NY .... .242
Ruffing-NY .... .258

Opponents' OBP
Marberry-Det .... .302
Gomez-NY .... .319
Allen-NY .... .328
Ruffing-NY .... .330

Earned Run Average
Pearson-Cle 2.33
Gomez-NY 3.18
Ruffing-NY 3.91
VanAtta-NY 4.18

Adjusted ERA
Harder-Cle 151
Gomez-NY 122
Ruffing-NY 99
VanAtta-NY 93

Adjusted Starter Runs
Harder-Cle 35.1
Gomez-NY 14.9

Pitcher Wins
Harder-Cle 4.4
Gomez-NY 1.0
Ruffing-NY 7
3 players tied 0

1934 American League

TEAM	W	L	T	PCT	GB	R	OR	HR	AVG	OBP	SLG	OPS	AOPS	PF	SB	CG	HR	BB	SO	BR/9	ERA	AERA	OAV	OOB	FW	PW	BW	BSW	DIF
Det	101	53	0	.656		**958**	708	74	**.300**	**.376**	.424	**800**	113	100	**125**	74	86	**488**	640	12.9	4.06	108	.273	.335	1.2	4.8	10.9	.6	6.5
NY	94	60	0	.610	7	842	**669**	135	.278	.364	.419	783	**117**	93	71	**83**	71	542	**656**	**12.4**	**3.76**	108	**.254**	**.324**	**1.3**	4.9	**12.4**	-.1	-1.4
Cle	85	69	0	.552	16	814	763	100	.287	.353	.423	776	105	102	52	72	**70**	582	554	13.7	4.28	106	.275	.349	.4	3.7	3.3	-.1	.6
Bos	76	76	1	.500	24	820	775	51	.274	.350	.383	733	90	107	116	68	**70**	543	538	13.8	4.32	**111**	.283	.351	-.5	**6.3**	-7.2	**.7**	.6
Phi	68	82	3	.453	31	764	838	**144**	.280	.343	**.425**	768	108	96	57	68	84	693	480	14.4	5.01	87	.275	.363	-1.0	-9.0	4.3	-.1	-1.2
StL	67	85	2	.441	33	674	800	62	.268	.335	.373	708	82	108	43	50	94	632	499	14.3	4.49	**111**	.283	.361	-.4	**6.3**	-13.0	-.2	-1.7
Was	66	86	3	.434	34	729	806	51	.278	.348	.382	730	99	96	47	61	74	503	412	13.9	4.68	92	.295	.355	1.0	-5.3	-.6	-.5	-4.7
Chi	53	99	1	.349	47	704	946	71	.263	.336	.363	699	84	103	36	72	139	628	506	14.9	5.41	88	.292	.367	-1.6	-8.9	-11.1	-.3	-1.1
Total	615					36305		688	.279	.351	.399	750			547	548				13.8	4.50		.279	.351					

Batter-Fielder Wins
Gehrig-NY 7.9
Ruth-NY 3.0
Dickey-NY 2.3
Chapman-NY 9

Batting Average
Gehrig-NY .... .363
Dickey-NY .... .322
Chapman-NY .... .308
Ruth-NY .... .288

On-Base Percentage
Gehrig-NY .... .465
Chapman-NY .... .381
Lazzeri-NY .... .369
Crosetti-NY .... .344

Slugging Average
Gehrig-NY 706
Ruth-NY .... .537
Dickey-NY .... .494
Lazzeri-NY .... .445

On-Base Plus Slugging
Gehrig-NY 1172
Lazzeri-NY 815
Chapman-NY 795
Crosetti-NY 744

Adjusted OPS
Gehrig-NY 213
Lazzeri-NY 117
Chapman-NY 113
Crosetti-NY 98

Adjusted Batter Runs
Gehrig-NY 100.4
Ruth-NY 41.6
Dickey-NY 19.3
Combs-NY 11.9

Runs
Gehringer-Det 134
Gehrig-NY 128
Crosetti-NY 85
Chapman-NY 82

Hits
Gehringer-Det 214
Gehrig-NY 210
Chapman-NY 181
Crosetti-NY 147

Doubles
Greenberg-Det 63
Gehrig-NY 40
Lazzeri-NY 24
Dickey-NY 24

Triples
Chapman-NY 13
Crosetti-NY 10
Lazzeri-NY 6
Gehrig-NY 6

Home Runs
Gehrig-NY 49
Ruth-NY 22
Lazzeri-NY 14
Dickey-NY 12

Total Bases
Gehrig-NY 409
Chapman-NY 243
Crosetti-NY 222
Ruth-NY 196

Runs Batted In
Gehrig-NY 165
Chapman-NY 86
Ruth-NY 84
Dickey-NY 72

Stolen Bases
Werber-Bos 40
Chapman-NY 26
Lazzeri-NY 11
Gehrig-NY 9

Base Stealing Runs
White-Det 4.1
Lazzeri-NY 2.1
Saltzgaver-NY 1.4
Jorgens-NY 4

Fielding Runs-Infield
Hale-Cle 25.9
Gehrig-NY 1.2

Fielding Runs-Outfield
Johnson-Phi 8.6
Byrd-NY 6.1
Chapman-NY 4.1

Wins
Gomez-NY 26
Ruffing-NY 19
Murphy-NY 14
Broaca-NY 12

Winning Pct.
Gomez-NY .... .839
Ruffing-NY .... .633

Complete Games
Gomez-NY 25
Ruffing-NY 19
Broaca-NY 13
Murphy-NY 10

Strikeouts
Gomez-NY 158
Ruffing-NY 149
Broaca-NY 74
Murphy-NY 70

Fewest BB/Game
W.Ferrell-Bos 2.44
Gomez-NY 3.07
Murphy-NY 3.29
Broaca-NY 3.30

Games
Russell-Was 54
Murphy-NY 40
Gomez-NY 38
Ruffing-NY 36

Saves
Russell-Was 7
Murphy-NY 4
DeShong-NY 3
3 players tied 1

Base Runners/9
Gomez-NY 10.19
Murphy-NY 11.66
Ruffing-NY 11.83
Allen-NY 12.06

Adjusted Relief Runs
Pennock-Bos 8.9

Relief Ranking
Pennock-Bos 4.5
Bean-Cle 4.5

Innings Pitched
Gomez-NY 281.2
Ruffing-NY 256.1
Murphy-NY 207.2
Broaca-NY 177.1

Opponents' Avg.
Gomez-NY .... .215
Ruffing-NY .... .236
Murphy-NY .... .250
Broaca-NY .... .284

Opponents' OBP
Gomez-NY .... .282
Ruffing-NY .... .310
Murphy-NY .... .317
Broaca-NY .... .344

Earned Run Average
Gomez-NY 2.33
Murphy-NY 3.12
Ruffing-NY 3.93
Broaca-NY 4.16

Adjusted ERA
Harder-Cle 174
Gomez-NY 174
Gomez-NY 174
Murphy-NY 130

Adjusted Starter Runs
Gomez-NY 59.3
Murphy-NY 26.3
Allen-NY 8.8
Tamulis-NY 4.5

Pitcher Wins
Harder-Cle 5.7
Gomez-NY 5.5
Murphy-NY 2.5
Allen-NY 8

1935 American League

TEAM	W	L	T	PCT	GB	R	OR	HR	AVG	OBP	SLG	OPS	AOPS	PF	SB	CG	HR	BB	SO	BR/9	ERA	AERA	OAV	OOB	FW	PW	BW	BSW	DIF
Det	93	58	1	.616		**919**	665	106	**.290**	**.366**	**.435**	**801**	**116**	97	70	**87**	78	522	584	13.1	3.82	109	.271	.339	**2.3**	5.3	**12.1**	.1	-2.3
NY	89	60	0	.597	3	818	**632**	104	.280	.358	.416	774	111	94	68	76	91	516	**594**	**12.2**	**3.60**	112	**.251**	**.321**	.8	6.7	8.3	.0	-1.4
Cle	82	71	3	.536	12	776	739	93	.284	.341	.421	762	100	102	63	67	68	**457**	498	12.9	4.15	108	.278	.335	-.3	5.1	-1.0	-.4	2.1
Bos	78	75	1	.510	16	718	732	69	.276	.353	.392	745	92	107	**91**	82	**67**	520	470	13.5	4.05	**117**	.280	.346	-1.4	**9.4**	-5.3	.0	-1.2
Chi	74	78	1	.487	19.5	738	750	74	.275	.348	.382	730	92	103	46	80	105	574	436	13.5	4.38	106	.272	.346	1.3	3.3	-5.4	.1	-1.3
Was	67	86	1	.438	27	823	903	32	.285	.357	.381	738	99	97	54	67	89	613	456	15.1	5.25	82	.302	.374	-.0	-13.7	.5	.0	3.7
StL	65	87	3	.428	28.5	718	930	73	.270	.344	.384	728	90	105	45	42	92	641	435	15.2	5.26	91	.297	.371	-.9	-6.3	-7.4	**.2**	3.4
Phi	58	91	0	.389	34	710	[illegible]	**112**	.270	.311	.406	747	99	99	43	58	73	704	469	15.0	5.12	89	.285	.372	-1.4	-7.8	-1.8	-.2	-5.3
Total	611					36220		663	.280	.351	.402	753			480	559				13.8	4.46		.280	.351					

Batter-Fielder Wins
Foxx-Phi 5.9
Gehrig-NY 5.3
Chapman-NY 1.7
Dickey-NY 1.4

Batting Average
Myer-Was .349
Gehrig-NY .329
Selkirk-NY .312
Rolfe-NY .300

On-Base Percentage
Gehrig-NY .466
Selkirk-NY .372
3 players tied .361

Slugging Average
Foxx-Phi .636
Gehrig-NY .583
Selkirk-NY .487
Dickey-NY .458

On-Base Plus Slugging
Foxx-Phi 1096
Gehrig-NY 1049
Selkirk-NY 859
Dickey-NY 797

Adjusted OPS
Foxx-Phi 182
Gehrig-NY 180
Selkirk-NY 128
Dickey-NY 111

Adjusted Batter Runs
Gehrig-NY 71.7
Selkirk-NY 18.2
Ruffing-NY 13.4
Chapman-NY 8.3

Runs
Gehrig-NY 125
Chapman-NY 118
Rolfe-NY 108
Lazzeri-NY 72

Hits
Vosmik-Cle 216
Rolfe-NY 192
Gehrig-NY 176
Chapman-NY 160

Doubles
Vosmik-Cle 47
Chapman-NY 38
Rolfe-NY 33
Selkirk-NY 29

Triples
Vosmik-Cle 20
Selkirk-NY 12
Gehrig-NY 10
Rolfe-NY 9

Home Runs
Greenberg-Det 36
Foxx-Phi 36
Gehrig-NY 30
Dickey-NY 14

Total Bases
Greenberg-Det 389
Gehrig-NY 312
Rolfe-NY 258
Selkirk-NY 239

Runs Batted In
Greenberg-Det 170
Gehrig-NY 119
Selkirk-NY 94
Lazzeri-NY 83

Stolen Bases
Werber-Bos 29
Chapman-NY 17
Hill-NY 14
Lazzeri-NY 11

Base Stealing Runs
Lary-Was-StL 4.8
Hill-NY 1.7
Lazzeri-NY .7
Rolfe-NY .5

Fielding Runs-Infield
Appling-Chi 24.9
Gehrig-NY .4

Fielding Runs-Outfield
Solters-Bos-StL 13.5
Chapman-NY 13.4
Selkirk-NY 5.0
Hill-NY 1.5

Wins
W.Ferrell-Bos 25
Ruffing-NY 16
Broaca-NY 15
Allen-NY 13

Winning Pct.
Auker-Det .720
Broaca-NY .682
Ruffing-NY .593

Complete Games
W.Ferrell-Bos 31
Ruffing-NY 19
Gomez-NY 15
Broaca-NY 14

Strikeouts
Bridges-Det 163
Gomez-NY 138
Allen-NY 113
Ruffing-NY 81

Fewest BB/Game
Harder-Cle 1.66
Tamulis-NY 3.08
Ruffing-NY 3.08
Allen-NY 3.13

Games
VanAtta-NY-StL 58
Murphy-NY 40
Gomez-NY 34
2 players tied 30

Saves
Knott-StL 7
Murphy-NY 5
Malone-NY 3
DeShong-NY 3

Base Runners/9
Grove-Bos 11.11
Ruffing-NY 11.27
Allen-NY 11.37
Gomez-NY 11.38

Adjusted Relief Runs
L.Brown-Cle 13.7
DeShong-NY 6.5

Relief Ranking
L.Brown-Cle 16.2
DeShong-NY 4.9

Innings Pitched
W.Ferrell-Bos 322.1
Gomez-NY 246.0
Ruffing-NY 222.0
Broaca-NY 201.0

Opponents' Avg.
Allen-NY .238
Ruffing-NY .239
Gomez-NY .242
Broaca-NY .254

Opponents' OBP
Rowe-Det .301
Ruffing-NY .303
Allen-NY .307
Gomez-NY .309

Earned Run Average
Grove-Bos 2.70
Ruffing-NY 3.12
Gomez-NY 3.18
Broaca-NY 3.58

Adjusted ERA
Grove-Bos 176
Ruffing-NY 130
Gomez-NY 127
Broaca-NY 113

Adjusted Starter Runs
Grove-Bos 55.0
Ruffing-NY 26.7
Gomez-NY 25.7
Broaca-NY 11.0

Pitcher Wins
W.Ferrell-Bos 6.8
Ruffing-NY 4.2
Gomez-NY 1.8
Allen-NY 1.2

1936 American League

TEAM	W	L	T	PCT	GB	R	OR	HR	AVG	OBP	SLG	OPS	AOPS	PF	SB	CG	HR	BB	SO	BR/9	ERA	AERA	OAV	OOB	FW	PW	BW	BSW	DIF
NY	102	51	2	.667		**1065**	**731**	**182**	.300	**.381**	**.483**	**864**	**124**	97	77	77	84	663	**624**	13.8	**4.17**	112	**.271**	.351	.8	7.2	**17.9**	.1	-.5
Det	83	71	0	.539	19.5	921	871	94	.300	.377	.431	808	106	100	73	76	100	562	526	14.2	5.00	99	.289	.358	**1.3**	-.6	5.1	-.2	.4
Chi	81	70	2	.536	20	920	873	60	.292	.374	.397	771	94	104	66	**80**	104	578	414	14.5	5.06	103	.293	.363	.4	1.8	-3.4	.2	6.6
Was	82	71	0	.536	20	889	799	62	.295	.365	.414	779	105	94	**104**	78	**73**	588	462	14.0	4.58	104	.279	.353	-.4	2.7	3.7	**.6**	-1.1
Cle	80	74	3	.519	22.5	921	862	123	**.304**	.364	.461	825	109	101	66	74	**73**	607	619	14.5	4.83	104	.289	.362	.0	2.8	5.6	-.5	-5.0
Bos	74	80	1	.481	28.5	775	764	86	.276	.349	.400	749	86	106	55	78	78	**552**	584	**13.6**	4.39	**121**	.277	**.346**	.7	**11.8**	-10.2	-.4	-4.9
StL	57	95	3	.375	44.5	804	1064	79	.279	.356	.403	759	91	103	62	54	115	609	399	16.2	6.24	86	.314	.385	-.6	-10.8	-6.4	.5	-1.6
Phi	53	100	1	.346	49	714	1045	72	.269	.336	.376	712	84	-98	59	68	131	696	405	15.7	6.08	84	.300	.381	-1.9	-12.7	-12.5	-.3	3.9
Total	618					37009		758	.289	.363	.421	784			562	585				14.6	5.04		.289	.363					

Batter-Fielder Wins
Gehrig-NY 6.6
Dickey-NY 4.2
Rolfe-NY 2.2
DiMaggio-NY 2.2

Batting Average
Appling-Chi .388
Dickey-NY .362
Gehrig-NY .354
DiMaggio-NY .323

On-Base Percentage
Gehrig-NY .478
Selkirk-NY .420
Lazzeri-NY .397
Rolfe-NY .392

Slugging Average
Gehrig-NY .696
Dickey-NY .617
DiMaggio-NY .576
Selkirk-NY .511

On-Base Plus Slugging
Gehrig-NY 1174
Selkirk-NY 931
DiMaggio-NY 928
Rolfe-NY 884

Adjusted OPS
Gehrig-NY 193
Selkirk-NY 133
DiMaggio-NY 130
Rolfe-NY 121

Adjusted Batter Runs
Gehrig-NY 90.9
Dickey-NY 39.2
Selkirk-NY 28.8
DiMaggio-NY 22.7

Runs
Gehrig-NY 167
Crosetti-NY 137
DiMaggio-NY 132
Rolfe-NY 116

Hits
Averill-Cle 232
DiMaggio-NY 206
Gehrig-NY 205
Crosetti-NY 182

Doubles
Gehringer-Det 60
DiMaggio-NY 44
Rolfe-NY 39
Gehrig-NY 37

Triples
3 players tied 15
Rolfe-NY 15
DiMaggio-NY 15
Selkirk-NY 9

Home Runs
Gehrig-NY 49
DiMaggio-NY 29
Dickey-NY 22
Selkirk-NY 18

Total Bases
Trosky-Cle 405
Gehrig-NY 403
DiMaggio-NY 367
Rolfe-NY 280

Runs Batted In
Trosky-Cle 162
Gehrig-NY 152
DiMaggio-NY 125
Lazzeri-NY 109

Stolen Bases
Lary-StL 37
Crosetti-NY 18
Selkirk-NY 13
Lazzeri-NY 8

Base Stealing Runs
Lary-StL 5.0
Crosetti-NY 1.5
DiMaggio-NY .9
Rolfe-NY .7

Fielding Runs-Infield
Hale-Cle 16.7
Rolfe-NY 1.4
Gehrig-NY .6

Fielding Runs-Outfield
Solters-StL 12.5
DiMaggio-NY 8.1
Selkirk-NY 1.6

Wins
Bridges-Det 23
Ruffing-NY 20
Pearson-NY 19
Hadley-NY 14

Winning Pct.
Pearson-NY .731
Ruffing-NY .625

Complete Games
W.Ferrell-Bos 28
Ruffing-NY 25
Pearson-NY 15
Broaca-NY 12

Strikeouts
Bridges-Det 175
Pearson-NY 118
Gomez-NY 105
Ruffing-NY 102

Fewest BB/Game
Lyons-Chi 2.23
Broaca-NY 2.88
Ruffing-NY 2.99
Hadley-NY 4.61

Games
VanAtta-StL 52
Broaca-NY 37
Malone-NY 35
2 players tied 33

Saves
Malone-NY 9
Murphy-NY 5
Broaca-NY 3

Base Runners/9
Grove-Bos 10.87
Ruffing-NY 12.19
Murphy-NY 12.99
Broaca-NY 13.15

Adjusted Relief Runs
Brown-Chi 2.9

Relief Ranking
Brown-Chi 2.9

Innings Pitched
W.Ferrell-Bos 301.0
Ruffing-NY 271.0
Pearson-NY 223.0
Broaca-NY 206.0

Opponents' Avg.
Pearson-NY .233
Gomez-NY .254
Ruffing-NY .263
Hadley-NY .283

Opponents' OBP
Grove-Bos .297
Ruffing-NY .323
Broaca-NY .337
Pearson-NY .343

Earned Run Average
Grove-Bos 2.81
Pearson-NY 3.71
Ruffing-NY 3.85
Broaca-NY 4.24

Adjusted ERA
Grove-Bos 189
Pearson-NY 125
Ruffing-NY 121
Broaca-NY 110

Adjusted Starter Runs
Grove-Bos 67.0
Pearson-NY 27.5
Ruffing-NY 25.0
Malone-NY 15.7

Pitcher Wins
Grove-Bos 6.6
Ruffing-NY 3.9
Pearson-NY 3.3
Murphy-NY 2.0

1937 American League

TEAM	W	L	T	PCT	GB	R	OR	HR	AVG	OBP	SLG	OPS	AOPS	PF	SB	CG	HR	BB	SO	BR/9	ERA	AERA	OAV	OOB	FW	PW	BW	BSW	DIF
NY	102	52	3	.662		**979**	**671**	**174**	.283	.369	**.456**	**825**	**113**	101	60	**82**	92	**506**	652	**12.5**	**3.65**	**122**	**.261**	**.325**	.2	**11.7**	**9.8**	.0	3.2
Det	89	65	1	.578	13	935	841	150	**.292**	**.370**	.452	822	111	102	89	70	102	635	485	14.2	4.87	96	.279	.357	**1.4**	-2.8	8.2	**.3**	4.9
Chi	86	68	0	.558	16	780	730	67	.280	.350	.400	750	95	100	70	70	115	532	533	13.2	4.17	110	.273	.341	-.2	6.0	-3.5	**.3**	6.5
Cle	83	71	2	.539	19	817	768	103	.280	.352	.423	775	100	101	78	64	**61**	566	630	14.0	4.39	105	.285	.356	.8	3.0	.0	-.2	2.4
Bos	80	72	2	.526	21	821	775	100	.281	.357	.411	768	96	104	79	74	92	597	**682**	14.0	4.48	106	.279	.352	-.4	3.6	-2.8	-.4	4.1
Was	73	80	5	.477	28.5	757	841	47	.279	.351	.379	730	94	96	61	75	96	671	524	14.1	4.58	97	.275	.357	.3	-2.2	-4.0	.0	2.5
Phi	54	97	3	.358	46.5	699	854	94	.267	.341	.397	738	93	98	**95**	65	105	613	469	14.3	4.85	97	.281	.358	-1.7	-1.8	-4.8	**.3**	-13.5
StL	46	108	2	.299	56	715	1023	71	.285	.348	.399	747	93	101	30	55	143	653	468	16.2	6.00	80	.315	.390	-.0	-15.6	-4.6	-.3	-10.4
Total	622					36503		806	.281	.355	.415	770			562	555				14.1	4.62		.281	.355					

Batter-Fielder Wins
- **Clift-StL 7.4**
- **DiMaggio-NY 5.7**
- **Dickey-NY 5.6**
- **Gehrig-NY 4.8**

Batting Average
- Gehringer-Det .... .371
- Gehrig-NY .... .351
- DiMaggio-NY .... .346
- Dickey-NY .... .332

On-Base Percentage
- Gehrig-NY .... .473
- Dickey-NY .... .417
- DiMaggio-NY .... .412
- Rolfe-NY .... .365

Slugging Average
- DiMaggio-NY .... .673
- Gehrig-NY .... .643
- Dickey-NY .... .570
- Hoag-NY .... .423

On-Base Plus Slugging
- Gehrig-NY 1116
- DiMaggio-NY 1085
- Dickey-NY 987
- Lazzeri-NY 747

Adjusted OPS
- Gehrig-NY 177
- DiMaggio-NY 168
- Dickey-NY 145
- 2 players tied 87

Adjusted Batter Runs
- Gehrig-NY 74.1
- DiMaggio-NY 60.1
- Dickey-NY 37.9
- Selkirk-NY 21.6

Runs
- DiMaggio-NY 151
- Rolfe-NY 143
- Gehrig-NY 138
- Crosetti-NY 127

Hits
- Bell-StL 218
- DiMaggio-NY 215
- Gehrig-NY 200
- Rolfe-NY 179

Doubles
- Bell-StL 51
- Gehrig-NY 37
- DiMaggio-NY 35
- Dickey-NY 35

Triples
- Walker-Chi 16
- Kreevich-Chi 16
- DiMaggio-NY 15
- Rolfe-NY 10

Home Runs
- DiMaggio-NY 46
- Gehrig-NY 37
- Dickey-NY 29
- Selkirk-NY 18

Total Bases
- DiMaggio-NY 418
- Gehrig-NY 366
- Dickey-NY 302
- Rolfe-NY 245

Runs Batted In
- Greenberg-Det 183
- DiMaggio-NY 167
- Gehrig-NY 159
- Dickey-NY 133

Stolen Bases
- Chapman-Was-Bos . 35
- Werber-Phi 35
- Crosetti-NY 13
- Selkirk-NY 8

Base Stealing Runs
- Chapman-Was-Bos 3.5
- Lazzeri-NY 1.2
- Selkirk-NY 1.1
- Henrich-NY 9

Fielding Runs-Infield
- Clift-StL 41.3
- Rolfe-NY 3.1
- Crosetti-NY 2

Fielding Runs-Outfield
- Johnson-Phi 9.6
- DiMaggio-NY 6.0

Wins
- Gomez-NY 21
- Ruffing-NY 20
- Murphy-NY 13
- Hadley-NY 11

Winning Pct.
- Allen-Cle .... .938
- Ruffing-NY .... .741
- Gomez-NY .... .656

Complete Games
- W.Ferrell-Bos-Was 26
- Gomez-NY 25
- Ruffing-NY 22
- Pearson-NY 7

Strikeouts
- Gomez-NY 194
- Ruffing-NY 131
- Pearson-NY 71
- Hadley-NY 70

Fewest BB/Game
- Stratton-Chi 2.02
- Ruffing-NY 2.39
- Gomez-NY 3.01
- Hadley-NY 4.19

Games
- Brown-Chi 53
- Murphy-NY 39
- Gomez-NY 34
- Ruffing-NY 31

Saves
- Brown-Chi 18
- Murphy-NY 10
- Malone-NY 6
- Makosky-NY 3

Base Runners/9
- Stratton-Chi 9.89
- Gomez-NY 10.57
- Ruffing-NY 10.92
- Chandler-NY 10.93

Adjusted Relief Runs
- Brown-Chi 12.0
- Murphy-NY 4.1

Relief Ranking
- Brown-Chi 20.0
- Murphy-NY 6.6

Innings Pitched
- W.Ferrell-Bos-Was ... 281.0
- Gomez-NY 278.1
- Ruffing-NY 256.1
- Hadley-NY 178.1

Opponents' Avg.
- Gomez-NY .... .223
- Ruffing-NY .... .247
- Hadley-NY .... .281

Opponents' OBP
- Stratton-Chi .... .280
- Gomez-NY .... .287
- Ruffing-NY .... .296
- Hadley-NY .... .358

Earned Run Average
- Gomez-NY 2.33
- Ruffing-NY 2.98
- Hadley-NY 5.30

Adjusted ERA
- Stratton-Chi 191
- Gomez-NY 191
- Gomez-NY 191
- Ruffing-NY 149

Adjusted Starter Runs
- Gomez-NY 66.9
- Ruffing-NY 43.2
- Pearson-NY 21.5
- Chandler-NY 15.2

Pitcher Wins
- Gomez-NY 6.8
- Ruffing-NY 4.0
- Chandler-NY 1.7
- Pearson-NY 1.6

1938 American League

TEAM	W	L	T	PCT	GB	R	OR	HR	AVG	OBP	SLG	OPS	AOPS	PF	SB	CG	HR	BB	SO	BR/9	ERA	AERA	OAV	OOB	FW	PW	BW	BSW	DIF
NY	99	53	5	.651		**966**	**710**	**174**	.274	.366	**.446**	**812**	**111**	100	**91**	**91**	**85**	566	567	**13.1**	**3.91**	**116**	**.268**	**.339**	.5	**9.1**	**7.8**	**.8**	4.8
Bos	88	61	1	.591	9.5	902	751	98	**.299**	**.378**	.434	**812**	105	105	55	67	102	**528**	484	13.8	4.46	111	.281	.349	-1.1	6.1	4.6	-.6	4.6
Cle	86	66	1	.566	13	847	782	113	.281	.350	.434	784	104	98	83	68	100	681	**717**	14.1	4.60	101	**.268**	.355	1.2	.6	2.3	.5	5.4
Det	84	70	1	.545	16	862	795	137	.272	.359	.411	770	94	106	76	75	110	608	435	14.4	4.79	104	.287	.361	1.6	2.8	-4.2	.1	6.6
Was	75	76	1	.497	23.5	814	873	85	.293	.362	.416	778	108	93	65	59	92	655	515	14.3	4.94	91	.276	.358	-.5	-6.1	6.7	.0	-.6
Chi	65	83	1	.439	32	709	752	67	.277	.343	.383	726	86	102	56	83	101	550	432	13.8	4.36	112	.279	.350	-1.6	6.9	-9.9	-.2	-4.2
StL	55	97	4	.362	44	755	962	92	.281	.355	.397	752	95	100	51	71	132	737	632	15.7	5.80	86	.295	.382	**1.8**	-10.8	-3.1	-.3	-8.5
Phi	53	99	2	.349	46	726	956	98	.270	.348	.396	744	95	97	65	56	142	599	473	14.9	5.48	88	.292	.365	-1.8	-8.5	-3.4	-.4	-8.9
Total	613					36581		864	.281	.358	.415	773			542	570				14.3	4.79		.281	.358					

Batter-Fielder Wins
- **Foxx-Bos 5.8**
- **Dickey-NY 4.1**
- **Gordon-NY 3.0**
- **DiMaggio-NY 2.6**

Batting Average
- Foxx-Bos .... .349
- DiMaggio-NY .... .324
- Dickey-NY .... .313
- Rolfe-NY .... .311

On-Base Percentage
- Foxx-Bos .... .462
- Dickey-NY .... .412
- Gehrig-NY .... .410
- Henrich-NY .... .391

Slugging Average
- Foxx-Bos .... .704
- DiMaggio-NY .... .581
- Dickey-NY .... .568
- Gehrig-NY .... .523

On-Base Plus Slugging
- Foxx-Bos 1166
- Dickey-NY 981
- DiMaggio-NY 967
- Gehrig-NY 932

Adjusted OPS
- Foxx-Bos 180
- Dickey-NY 144
- DiMaggio-NY 140
- Gehrig-NY 133

Adjusted Batter Runs
- Foxx-Bos 71.9
- DiMaggio-NY 32.9
- Dickey-NY 31.6
- Gehrig-NY 31.5

Runs
- Greenberg-Det 144
- Rolfe-NY 132
- DiMaggio-NY 129
- Gehrig-NY 115

Hits
- Vosmik-Bos 201
- Rolfe-NY 196
- DiMaggio-NY 194
- Gehrig-NY 170

Doubles
- Cronin-Bos 51
- Rolfe-NY 36
- Crosetti-NY 35
- 2 players tied 32

Triples
- Heath-Cle 18
- DiMaggio-NY 13
- Rolfe-NY 8
- 2 players tied 7

Home Runs
- Greenberg-Det 58
- DiMaggio-NY 32
- Gehrig-NY 29
- Dickey-NY 27

Total Bases
- Foxx-Bos 398
- DiMaggio-NY 348
- Gehrig-NY 301
- Rolfe-NY 278

Runs Batted In
- Foxx-Bos 175
- DiMaggio-NY 140
- Dickey-NY 115
- Gehrig-NY 114

Stolen Bases
- Crosetti-NY 27
- Rolfe-NY 13
- Gordon-NY 11
- Selkirk-NY 9

Base Stealing Runs
- Lary-Cle 3.0
- Rolfe-NY 2.5
- Crosetti-NY 1.7
- Gordon-NY 1.4

Fielding Runs-Infield
- Gordon-NY 20.5
- Crosetti-NY 18.4

Fielding Runs-Outfield
- Johnson-Phi 9.6

Wins
- Ruffing-NY 21
- Gomez-NY 18
- Pearson-NY 16
- Chandler-NY 14

Winning Pct.
- Ruffing-NY .... .750
- Pearson-NY .... .696
- Gomez-NY .... .600

Complete Games
- Newsom-StL 31
- Ruffing-NY 22
- Gomez-NY 20
- Pearson-NY 17

Strikeouts
- Feller-Cle 240
- Gomez-NY 129
- Ruffing-NY 127
- Pearson-NY 98

Fewest BB/Game
- Leonard-Was 2.14
- Chandler-NY 2.46
- Ruffing-NY 2.98
- Hadley-NY 3.55

Games
- Humphries-Cle 45
- Murphy-NY 32
- Gomez-NY 32
- Ruffing-NY 31

Saves
- Murphy-NY 11
- Hadley-NY 1
- Andrews-NY 1

Base Runners/9
- Leonard-Was 11.32
- Ruffing-NY 11.94
- Chandler-NY 12.14
- Hadley-NY 12.59

Adjusted Relief Runs
- Murphy-NY 4.9

Relief Ranking
- Murphy-NY 6.1

Innings Pitched
- Newsom-StL 329.2
- Ruffing-NY 247.1
- Gomez-NY 239.0
- Pearson-NY 202.0

Opponents' Avg.
- Feller-Cle .... .220
- Hadley-NY .... .254
- Ruffing-NY .... .258
- Pearson-NY .... .258

Opponents' OBP
- Leonard-Was .... .305
- Ruffing-NY .... .317
- Chandler-NY .... .320
- Hadley-NY .... .325

Earned Run Average
- Grove-Bos 3.08
- Ruffing-NY 3.31
- Gomez-NY 3.35
- Hadley-NY 3.60

Adjusted ERA
- Grove-Bos 160
- Ruffing-NY 137
- Gomez-NY 135
- Hadley-NY 126

Adjusted Starter Runs
- Ruffing-NY 37.1
- Gomez-NY 31.0
- Hadley-NY 18.4
- Pearson-NY 12.7

Pitcher Wins
- Ruffing-NY 4.5
- Gomez-NY 3.2
- Hadley-NY 1.6
- Chandler-NY 1.5

1939 American League

TEAM	W	L	T	PCT	GB	R	OR	HR	AVG	OBP	SLG	OPS	AOPS	PF	SB	CG	HR	BB	SO	BR/9	ERA	AERA	OAV	OOB	FW	PW	BW	BSW	DIF
NY	106	45	1	.702		**967**	**556**	**166**	.287	**.374**	**.451**	**825**	**119**	98	72	**87**	85	567	565	**11.9**	**3.31**	**132**	**.241**	**.319**	**2.9**	**15.3**	**14.0**	.2	-1.9
Bos	89	62	1	.589	17	890	795	124	**.291**	.363	.436	799	106	104	42	52	77	543	539	14.0	4.56	104	.287	.355	.0	2.3	4.5	-.7	7.2
Cle	87	67	0	.565	20.5	797	700	85	.280	.350	.413	763	105	97	72	69	**75**	602	614	13.3	4.08	108	.267	.344	.2	4.7	3.0	-.1	2.1
Chi	85	69	1	.552	22.5	755	737	64	.275	.349	.374	723	89	103	**113**	62	99	**454**	535	12.7	4.31	110	.275	.333	1.0	5.8	-7.6	.3	8.6
Det	81	73	1	.526	26.5	849	762	124	.279	.356	.426	782	99	108	88	64	104	574	**633**	13.3	4.29	114	.268	.341	-.6	7.9	-1.3	**.5**	-2.4
Was	65	87	1	.428	41.5	702	797	44	.278	.346	.379	725	98	93	94	72	**75**	602	521	13.6	4.60	94	.271	.348	-1.1	-3.8	-.6	.3	-5.7
Phi	55	97	1	.362	51.5	711	1022	98	.271	.336	.400	736	96	98	60	50	148	579	397	15.3	5.79	81	.307	.375	-1.4	-14.7	-3.6	.0	-1.4
StL	43	111	2	.279	64.5	733	1035	91	.268	.338	.381	720	88	102	48	56	133	739	516	16.4	6.01	81	.310	.393	-.6	-15.3	-8.8	-.4	-8.8
Total	615					36404		796	.279	.352	.407	759			589	512				13.8	4.62		.279	.352					

Batter-Fielder Wins
DiMaggio-NY 5.5
Dickey-NY 4.5
Gordon-NY 3.3
Selkirk-NY 2.6

Batting Average
DiMaggio-NY .... .381
Rolfe-NY .... .329
Selkirk-NY .... .306
Dickey-NY .... .302

On-Base Percentage
Foxx-Bos .... .464
Selkirk-NY .... .452
DiMaggio-NY .... .448
Keller-NY .... .447

Slugging Average
Foxx-Bos .... .694
DiMaggio-NY .... .671
Selkirk-NY .... .517
Dickey-NY .... .512

On-Base Plus Slugging
Foxx-Bos 1158
DiMaggio-NY 1119
Selkirk-NY 969
Keller-NY 947

Adjusted OPS
DiMaggio-NY 185
Selkirk-NY 149
Keller-NY 144
Dickey-NY 135

Adjusted Batter Runs
Foxx-Bos 62.0
DiMaggio-NY 59.0
Selkirk-NY 37.9
Rolfe-NY 31.9

Runs
Rolfe-NY 139
Crosetti-NY 109
DiMaggio-NY 108
Selkirk-NY 103

Hits
Rolfe-NY 213
DiMaggio-NY 176
Gordon-NY 161
Crosetti-NY 153

Doubles
Rolfe-NY 46
Gordon-NY 32
DiMaggio-NY 32
Crosetti-NY 25

Triples
Lewis-Was 16
Rolfe-NY 10
3 players tied 6

Home Runs
Foxx-Bos 35
DiMaggio-NY 30
Gordon-NY 28
Dickey-NY 24

Total Bases
Williams-Bos 344
Rolfe-NY 321
DiMaggio-NY 310
Gordon-NY 287

Runs Batted In
Williams-Bos 145
DiMaggio-NY 126
Gordon-NY 111
Dickey-NY 105

Stolen Bases
Case-Was 51
Selkirk-NY 12
Gordon-NY 11
Crosetti-NY 11

Base Stealing Runs
Case-Was 5.3
Henrich-NY 1.5
Dickey-NY 1.1
2 players tied 9

Fielding Runs-Infield
Doerr-Bos 26.5
Crosetti-NY 9.8
Gordon-NY 8.1

Fielding Runs-Outfield
Johnson-Phi 9.7
DiMaggio-NY 4.5

Wins
Feller-Cle 24
Ruffing-NY 21
Donald-NY 13
3 players tied 12

Winning Pct.
Grove-Bos .... .789
Ruffing-NY .... .750

Complete Games
Newsom-StL-Det 24
Feller-Cle 24
Ruffing-NY 22
Gomez-NY 14

Strikeouts
Feller-Cle 246
Gomez-NY 102
Ruffing-NY 95
Pearson-NY 76

Fewest BB/Game
Lyons-Chi 1.36
Ruffing-NY 2.89
Donald-NY 3.53
Gomez-NY 3.82

Games
Brown-Chi 61
Murphy-NY 38
Ruffing-NY 28
2 players tied 26

Saves
Murphy-NY 19
Russo-NY 2
Hildebrand-NY 2
Hadley-NY 2

Base Runners/9
Lyons-Chi 9.85
Russo-NY 9.93
Hildebrand-NY 10.23
Ruffing-NY 11.11

Adjusted Relief Runs
Brown-Chi 10.5

Relief Ranking
Brown-Chi 20.4

Innings Pitched
Feller-Cle 296.2
Ruffing-NY 233.1
Gomez-NY 198.0
Hadley-NY 154.0

Opponents' Avg.
Feller-Cle .... .210
Gomez-NY .... .235
Hadley-NY .... .237
Ruffing-NY .... .240

Opponents' OBP
Lyons-Chi .... .276
Ruffing-NY .... .301
Gomez-NY .... .316
Donald-NY .... .317

Earned Run Average
Grove-Bos 2.54
Ruffing-NY 2.93
Hadley-NY 2.98
Gomez-NY 3.41

Adjusted ERA
Grove-Bos 186
Ruffing-NY 149
Hadley-NY 146
Gomez-NY 128

Adjusted Starter Runs
Feller-Cle 54.2
Ruffing-NY 37.8
Russo-NY 25.6
Gomez-NY 24.0

Pitcher Wins
Feller-Cle 6.0
Ruffing-NY 4.8
Russo-NY 2.4
Hadley-NY 2.4

1940 American League

TEAM	W	L	T	PCT	GB	R	OR	HR	AVG	OBP	SLG	OPS	AOPS	PF	SB	CG	HR	BB	SO	BR/9	ERA	AERA	OAV	OOB	FW	PW	BW	BSW	DIF
Det	90	64	1	.584		**888**	717	134	**.286**	**.366**	.442	**808**	105	110	66	59	102	570	**752**	13.2	4.01	**119**	.266	.338	-.7	**9.9**	4.7	.2	-1.2
Cle	89	65	1	.578	1	710	**637**	101	.265	.332	.398	730	98	97	53	72	**86**	512	686	12.2	**3.63**	116	.254	.324	**1.7**	8.8	-2.1	.0	3.5
NY	88	66	1	.571	2	817	671	**155**	.259	.344	.418	762	107	96	59	76	119	511	559	12.6	3.89	104	.261	.328	1.6	2.3	5.5	.1	1.6
Chi	82	72	1	.532	8	735	672	73	.278	.340	.387	727	93	101	52	**83**	111	**480**	574	**11.9**	3.74	118	**.250**	**.313**	-.2	**9.9**	-5.1	-.8	1.2
Bos	82	72	0	.532	8	872	825	145	**.286**	.356	**.449**	805	**110**	104	55	51	124	625	613	14.5	4.89	92	.284	.359	.4	-5.5	**7.2**	-.3	3.2
StL	67	87	2	.435	23	757	882	118	.263	.333	.401	734	94	102	51	64	113	646	439	14.8	5.12	89	.290	.367	1.3	-7.5	-4.7	-.1	1.0
Was	64	90	0	.416	26	665	811	52	.271	.331	.374	705	95	94	**94**	74	93	618	618	14.2	4.59	91	.281	.359	-.7	-6.3	-3.9	**.8**	-2.9
Phi	54	100	0	.351	36	703	932	105	.262	.334	.387	721	95	98	48	72	135	534	488	14.0	5.22	85	.283	.348	-3.1	-10.8	-3.8	.0	-5.4
Total	619					36147		883	.271	.342	.407	750			478	551				13.4	4.38		.271	.342					

Batter-Fielder Wins
DiMaggio-NY 4.5
Gordon-NY 3.8
Keller-NY 2.3
Henrich-NY 1.9

Batting Average
DiMaggio-NY .... .352
Keller-NY .... .286
Gordon-NY .... .281
Dahlgren-NY .... .264

On-Base Percentage
Williams-Bos .... .442
DiMaggio-NY .... .425
Keller-NY 411
Gordon-NY .... .340

Slugging Average
Greenberg-Det ...... .670
DiMaggio-NY .... .626
Gordon-NY 511
Keller-NY .... .508

On-Base Plus Slugging
Greenberg-Det 1103
DiMaggio-NY 1051
Keller-NY 919
Gordon-NY 851

Adjusted OPS
DiMaggio-NY 176
Keller-NY 142
Gordon-NY 122
Dahlgren-NY 86

Adjusted Batter Runs
Greenberg-Det 57.4
DiMaggio-NY 56.3
Keller-NY 34.4
Selkirk-NY 23.9

Runs
Williams-Bos 134
Gordon-NY 112
Rolfe-NY 102
Keller-NY 102

Hits
3 players tied 200
DiMaggio-NY 179
Gordon-NY 173
Dahlgren-NY 150

Doubles
Greenberg-Det 50
Gordon-NY 32
Henrich-NY 28
DiMaggio-NY 28

Triples
McCosky-Det 19
Keller-NY 15
Gordon-NY 10
DiMaggio-NY 9

Home Runs
Greenberg-Det 41
DiMaggio-NY 31
Gordon-NY 30
Keller-NY 21

Total Bases
Greenberg-Det 384
DiMaggio-NY 318
Gordon-NY 315
Keller-NY 254

Runs Batted In
Greenberg-Det 150
DiMaggio-NY 133
Gordon-NY 103
Keller-NY 93

Stolen Bases
Case-Was 35
Gordon-NY 18
Crosetti-NY 14
Keller-NY 8

Base Stealing Runs
Case-Was 4.2
Rosar-NY 1.2
Gordon-NY 1.2
Keller-NY 1.1

Fielding Runs-Infield
Heffner-StL 15.7
Gordon-NY 13.8
Rolfe-NY 2

Fielding Runs-Outfield
Kreevich-Chi 6.9

Wins
Feller-Cle 27
Ruffing-NY 15
Russo-NY 14
Bonham-NY 9

Winning Pct.
Rowe-Det .... .842
Ruffing-NY .... .556

Complete Games
Feller-Cle 31
Ruffing-NY 20
Russo-NY 15
2 players tied 10

Strikeouts
Feller-Cle 261
Ruffing-NY 97
Russo-NY 87
Breuer-NY 71

Fewest BB/Game
Lyons-Chi 1.79
Russo-NY 2.61
Ruffing-NY 3.03
Chandler-NY 3.14

Games
Feller-Cle 43
Murphy-NY 35
Russo-NY 30
Ruffing-NY 30

Saves
Benton-Det 17
Murphy-NY 9
Sundra-NY 2
Hadley-NY 2

Base Runners/9
Bonham-NY 8.70
Murphy-NY 10.37
Russo-NY 11.27
Ruffing-NY 11.83

Adjusted Relief Runs
Eisenstat-Cle 10.6
Murphy-NY 3.7

Relief Ranking
Brown-Chi 10.3
Murphy-NY 7.5

Innings Pitched
Feller-Cle 320.1
Ruffing-NY 226.0
Russo-NY 189.1
Chandler-NY 172.0

Opponents' Avg.
Feller-Cle .... .210
Russo-NY .... .249
Ruffing-NY .... .252
Breuer-NY .... .267

Opponents' OBP
Feller-Cle .... .285
Russo-NY .... .303
Ruffing-NY .... .314
Breuer-NY .... .329

Earned Run Average
Feller-Cle 2.61
Russo-NY 3.28
Ruffing-NY 3.38
Breuer-NY 4.55

Adjusted ERA
Newsom-Det 168
Russo-NY 123
Ruffing-NY 119
Breuer-NY 89

Adjusted Starter Runs
Feller-Cle 61.5
Bonham-NY 25.4
Ruffing-NY 16.8
Russo-NY 16.8

Pitcher Wins
Feller-Cle 6.8
Bonham-NY 2.8
Russo-NY 2.1
Ruffing-NY 1.3

1941 American League

TEAM	W	L	T	PCT	GB	R	OR	HR	AVG	OBP	SLG	OPS	AOPS	PF	SB	CG	HR	BB	SO	BR/9	ERA	AERA	OAV	OOB	FW	PW	BW	BSW	DIF
NY	101	53	2	.656		830	**631**	**151**	.269	.346	.419	765	111	99	51	75	81	598	589	12.4	3.53	112	**.248**	.325	.5	6.4	7.3	.1	9.7
Bos	84	70	1	.545	17	**865**	750	124	**.283**	**.366**	**.430**	**796**	**115**	102	67	70	88	611	574	13.7	4.19	100	.270	.347	.0	-.3	**11.7**	-.2	-4.3
Chi	77	77	2	.500	24	638	649	47	.255	.322	.343	665	84	-99	**91**	**106**	89	**521**	564	**12.1**	**3.52**	**116**	.252	**.320**	-.3	**8.9**	-11.8	.2	3.0
Det	75	79	1	.487	26	686	743	81	.263	.340	.375	715	87	110	43	52	80	645	**697**	13.4	4.18	109	.260	.341	-.7	5.0	-8.9	.1	2.5
Cle	75	79	1	.487	26	677	668	103	.256	.323	.393	716	101	95	63	68	71	660	617	13.4	3.90	101	.259	.344	**1.7**	.7	-.8	-.2	-3.4
Was	70	84	2	.455	31	728	798	52	.272	.331	.376	707	99	95	79	69	**69**	603	544	13.9	4.35	93	.279	.353	-.7	-4.7	-2.4	**.6**	.3
StL	70	84	3	.455	31	765	823	91	.266	.360	.390	750	103	103	50	65	120	549	454	13.8	4.72	91	.283	.350	1.3	-6.0	3.4	-.2	-5.5
Phi	64	90	0	.416	37	713	840	85	.268	.340	.387	727	102	98	27	64	136	557	386	13.8	4.83	87	.279	.348	-1.6	-9.4	.9	-.6	-2.3
Total	622					35902		734	.266	.341	.389	730			471	569				13.3	4.15		.266	.341					

Batter-Fielder Wins
Williams-Bos 8.5
DiMaggio-NY 6.6
Keller-NY 4.0
Gordon-NY 2.7

Batting Average
Williams-Bos .406
DiMaggio-NY .357
Rizzuto-NY .307
Keller-NY .298

On-Base Percentage
Williams-Bos .553
DiMaggio-NY .440
Keller-NY .416
Henrich-NY .377

Slugging Average
Williams-Bos .735
DiMaggio-NY .643
Keller-NY .580
Henrich-NY .519

On-Base Plus Slugging
Williams-Bos 1287
DiMaggio-NY 1083
Keller-NY 996
Henrich-NY 895

Adjusted OPS
Williams-Bos 232
DiMaggio-NY 186
Keller-NY 163
Henrich-NY 137

Adjusted Batter Runs
Williams-Bos 101.7
DiMaggio-NY 67.7
Keller-NY 48.0
Henrich-NY 28.1

Runs
Williams-Bos 135
DiMaggio-NY 122
Rolfe-NY 106
Henrich-NY 106

Hits
Travis-Was 218
DiMaggio-NY 193
Gordon-NY 162
Rizzuto-NY 158

Doubles
Boudreau-Cle 45
DiMaggio-NY 43
Henrich-NY 27
Gordon-NY 26

Triples
Heath-Cle 20
DiMaggio-NY 11
Keller-NY 10
Rizzuto-NY 9

Home Runs
Williams-Bos 37
Keller-NY 33
Henrich-NY 31
DiMaggio-NY 30

Total Bases
DiMaggio-NY 348
Keller-NY 294
Henrich-NY 279
Gordon-NY 274

Runs Batted In
DiMaggio-NY 125
Keller-NY 122
Gordon-NY 87
Henrich-NY 85

Stolen Bases
Case-Was 33
Rizzuto-NY 14
Gordon-NY 10
Keller-NY 6

Base Stealing Runs
Case-Was 4.1
Rizzuto-NY 1.3
Henrich-NY .3
2 players tied .2

Fielding Runs-Infield
Bloodworth-Was 27.2
Rizzuto-NY 19.0
Gordon-NY 8.6

Fielding Runs-Outfield
Case-Was 11.7
S.Chapman-Phi 11.7
DiMaggio-NY 5.8
Keller-NY 2.1

Wins
Feller-Cle 25
Ruffing-NY 15
Gomez-NY 15
Russo-NY 14

Winning Pct.
Gomez-NY .750
Ruffing-NY .714

Complete Games
Lee-Chi 30
Russo-NY 17
Ruffing-NY 13
Chandler-NY 11

Strikeouts
Feller-Cle 260
Russo-NY 105
Breuer-NY 77
Gomez-NY 76

Fewest BB/Game
Lyons-Chi 1.78
Ruffing-NY 2.62
Chandler-NY 3.30
Russo-NY 3.73

Games
Feller-Cle 44
Murphy-NY 35
Russo-NY 28
Chandler-NY 28

Saves
Murphy-NY 15
Chandler-NY 4
3 players tied 2

Base Runners/9
Humphries-Chi 10.55
Bonham-NY 10.66
Ruffing-NY 11.25
Chandler-NY 11.33

Adjusted Relief Runs
Murphy-NY 17.5

Relief Ranking
Murphy-NY 30.1

Innings Pitched
Feller-Cle 343.0
Russo-NY 209.2
Ruffing-NY 185.2
Chandler-NY 163.2

Opponents' Avg.
Benton-Det .221
Donald-NY .237
Chandler-NY .239
Russo-NY .247

Opponents' OBP
Lee-Chi .293
Ruffing-NY .306
Chandler-NY .307
Donald-NY .320

Earned Run Average
Lee-Chi 2.37
Russo-NY 3.09
Chandler-NY 3.19
Ruffing-NY 3.54

Adjusted ERA
Lee-Chi 173
Russo-NY 127
Chandler-NY 123
Ruffing-NY 111

Adjusted Starter Runs
Lee-Chi 56.1
Russo-NY 19.8
Bonham-NY 16.1
Chandler-NY 13.7

Pitcher Wins
Lee-Chi 6.5
Murphy-NY 2.9
Russo-NY 2.4
Ruffing-NY 1.7

1942 American League

TEAM	W	L	T	PCT	GB	R	OR	HR	AVG	OBP	SLG	OPS	AOPS	PF	SB	CG	HR	BB	SO	BR/9	ERA	AERA	OAV	OOB	FW	PW	BW	BSW	DIF
NY	103	51	0	.669		**801**	**507**	**108**	.269	.346	.394	740	**118**	98	69	**88**	71	**431**	558	**11.2**	**2.91**	118	**.244**	**.304**	**2.0**	8.9	**12.5**	.6	1.9
Bos	93	59	0	.612	9	761	594	103	**.276**	**.352**	**.403**	**755**	116	103	68	84	65	553	500	12.1	3.44	108	.247	.322	1.0	4.3	11.2	-.4	.9
StL	82	69	0	.543	19.5	730	637	98	.259	.338	.385	723	109	102	37	68	63	505	488	12.7	3.59	103	.262	.330	.4	1.7	6.0	-.3	-1.4
Cle	75	79	2	.487	28	590	659	50	.253	.320	.345	665	100	94	69	61	61	560	448	12.4	3.59	96	.254	.327	1.0	-2.5	-.7	-.9	1.1
Det	73	81	2	.474	30	589	587	76	.246	.314	.344	658	85	108	39	65	60	598	**671**	12.5	3.13	**126**	.248	.326	-.8	**12.1**	-10.6	-.3	-4.5
Chi	66	82	0	.446	34	538	609	25	.246	.316	.318	634	87	98	**114**	86	74	473	432	12.3	3.58	100	.258	.325	-.1	.3	-7.7	.3	-.9
Was	62	89	0	.411	39.5	653	817	40	.258	.333	.341	674	98	99	98	68	**50**	558	496	13.8	4.58	80	.279	.349	-2.7	-14.2	-.7	**1.4**	2.7
Phi	55	99	0	.357	48	549	801	33	.249	.309	.325	634	86	-99	44	67	89	639	546	13.5	4.45	85	.263	.344	-.6	-10.1	-10.3	-.4	-.6
Total	611					35211		533	.257	.329	.357	686			538	587				12.6	3.66		.257	.329					

Batter-Fielder Wins
Williams-Bos 8.5
Gordon-NY 5.8
Rizzuto-NY 4.6
Keller-NY 4.2

Batting Average
Williams-Bos .356
Gordon-NY .322
DiMaggio-NY .305
Keller-NY .292

On-Base Percentage
Williams-Bos .499
Keller-NY .417
Gordon-NY .409
DiMaggio-NY .376

Slugging Average
Williams-Bos .648
Keller-NY .513
DiMaggio-NY .498
Gordon-NY .491

On-Base Plus Slugging
Williams-Bos 1147
Keller-NY 930
Gordon-NY 900
DiMaggio-NY 875

Adjusted OPS
Williams-Bos 214
Keller-NY 164
Gordon-NY 156
DiMaggio-NY 148

Adjusted Batter Runs
Williams-Bos 89.9
Keller-NY 50.4
Gordon-NY 41.9
DiMaggio-NY 36.6

Runs
Williams-Bos 141
DiMaggio-NY 123
Keller-NY 106
Gordon-NY 88

Hits
Pesky-Bos 205
DiMaggio-NY 186
Gordon-NY 173
Keller-NY 159

Doubles
Kolloway-Chi 40
Henrich-NY 30
Gordon-NY 29
DiMaggio-NY 29

Triples
Spence-Was 15
DiMaggio-NY 13
Keller-NY 9
Rizzuto-NY 7

Home Runs
Williams-Bos 36
Keller-NY 26
DiMaggio-NY 21
Gordon-NY 18

Total Bases
Williams-Bos 338
DiMaggio-NY 304
Keller-NY 279
Gordon-NY 264

Runs Batted In
Williams-Bos 137
DiMaggio-NY 114
Keller-NY 108
Gordon-NY 103

Stolen Bases
Case-Was 44
Rizzuto-NY 22
Keller-NY 14
Gordon-NY 12

Base Stealing Runs
Case-Was 7.6
Rizzuto-NY 2.7
Keller-NY 2.4
Gordon-NY .5

Fielding Runs-Infield
Rizzuto-NY 30.0
Hassett-NY 10.7
Gordon-NY 6.1

Fielding Runs-Outfield
DiMaggio-Bos 13.1
Henrich-NY 1.0

Wins
Hughson-Bos 22
Bonham-NY 21
Chandler-NY 16
Borowy-NY 15

Winning Pct.
Bonham-NY .808
Borowy-NY .789
Chandler-NY .762

Complete Games
Hughson-Bos 22
Bonham-NY 22
Bonham-NY 22
Chandler-NY 17

Strikeouts
Newsom-Was 113
Hughson-Bos 113
Borowy-NY 85
Ruffing-NY 80

Fewest BB/Game
Bonham-NY .96
Ruffing-NY 1.91
Breuer-NY 2.03
Chandler-NY 3.32

Games
Haynes-Chi 40
Murphy-NY 31
Bonham-NY 28
Breuer-NY 27

Saves
Murphy-NY 11
Branch-NY 2

Base Runners/9
Bonham-NY 8.92
Ruffing-NY 10.55
Breuer-NY 10.68
Donald-NY 10.85

Adjusted Relief Runs
Ferrick-Cle 14.5

Relief Ranking
Haynes-Chi 13.3

Innings Pitched
Hughson-Bos 281.0
Bonham-NY 226.0
Chandler-NY 200.2
Ruffing-NY 193.2

Opponents' Avg.
Newhouser-Det .207
Borowy-NY .233
Chandler-NY .237
Bonham-NY .237

Opponents' OBP
Bonham-NY .259
Ruffing-NY .292
Breuer-NY .295
Borowy-NY .301

Earned Run Average
Lyons-Chi 2.10
Bonham-NY 2.27
Chandler-NY 2.38
Borowy-NY 2.52

Adjusted ERA
Lyons-Chi 172
Bonham-NY 152
Chandler-NY 145
Borowy-NY 136

Adjusted Starter Runs
Hughson-Bos 35.0
Bonham-NY 31.3
Chandler-NY 23.6
Borowy-NY 19.8

Pitcher Wins
Lyons-Chi 3.8
Bonham-NY 3.0
Chandler-NY 3.0
Borowy-NY 2.0

1943 American League

TEAM	W	L	T	PCT	GB	R	OR	HR	AVG	OBP	SLG	OPS	AOPS	PF	SB	CG	HR	BB	SO	BR/9	ERA	AERA	OAV	OOB	FW	PW	BW	BSW	DIF
NY	98	56	1	.636		**669**	**542**	**100**	.256	**.337**	**.376**	**713**	**114**	101	46	**83**	60	489	653	**11.0**	**2.93**	110	**.234**	**.301**	.2	5.1	**10.1**	-.9	6.5
Was	84	69	0	.549	13.5	666	595	47	.254	.336	.347	683	110	96	142	61	**48**	540	495	12.0	3.18	101	.246	.318	-1.0	.3	8.0	**1.6**	-1.4
Cle	82	71	0	.536	15.5	600	577	55	.255	.329	.350	679	112	94	47	64	52	606	585	11.9	3.15	99	.239	.322	.3	-.8	8.2	-.8	-1.4
Chi	82	72	1	.532	16	573	594	33	.247	.322	.320	642	94	100	**173**	70	54	501	476	12.1	3.20	104	.255	.324	-.0	2.3	-3.6	1.1	5.3
Det	78	76	1	.506	20	632	560	77	**.261**	.324	.359	683	98	108	40	67	51	549	**706**	11.4	3.00	**117**	**.234**	.308	-.7	**8.2**	-1.7	-.4	-4.4
StL	72	80	1	.474	25	596	604	78	.245	.322	.349	671	100	102	37	64	74	**488**	572	12.4	3.41	97	.263	.327	**.6**	-1.4	.3	-.5	-3.0
Bos	68	84	3	.447	29	563	607	57	.244	.308	.332	640	92	102	86	62	61	615	513	12.6	3.45	96	.257	.335	**.6**	-2.4	-6.3	.0	-.0
Phi	49	105	1	.318	49	497	717	[illegible]	[illegible]	[illegible]	.297	591	78	100	55	73	73	536	503	12.9	4.05	84	.265	.336	.1	-10.6	-15.3	-.0	-2.2
Total	617					34796		473	.249	.322	.341	663			626	544				12.0	3.30		.249	.322					

Batter-Fielder Wins
- **Boudreau-Cle 6.8**
- **Gordon-NY 5.6**
- **Keller-NY 4.0**
- **Dickey-NY 3.4**

Batting Average
- Appling-Chi .328
- Johnson-NY .280
- Keller-NY .271
- Etten-NY .271

On-Base Percentage
- Appling-Chi .419
- Keller-NY .390
- Gordon-NY .365
- Etten-NY .355

Slugging Average
- York-Det .527
- Keller-NY .525
- Etten-NY .420
- Gordon-NY .413

On-Base Plus Slugging
- Keller-NY 922
- Gordon-NY 778
- Etten-NY 775
- Johnson-NY 710

Adjusted OPS
- Keller-NY 167
- Gordon-NY 126
- Etten-NY 126
- Johnson-NY 107

Adjusted Batter Runs
- Keller-NY 45.1
- Dickey-NY 24.8
- Gordon-NY 21.1
- Etten-NY 19.5

Runs
- Case-Was 102
- Keller-NY 97
- Gordon-NY 82
- Etten-NY 78

Hits
- Wakefield-Det 200
- Johnson-NY 166
- Etten-NY 158
- Keller-NY 139

Doubles
- Wakefield-Det 38
- Etten-NY 35
- Gordon-NY 28
- Johnson-NY 24

Triples
- Moses-Chi 12
- Lindell-NY 12
- Lindell-NY 12
- Keller-NY 11

Home Runs
- York-Det 34
- Keller-NY 31
- Gordon-NY 17
- Etten-NY 14

Total Bases
- York-Det 301
- Keller-NY 269
- Etten-NY 245
- Gordon-NY 224

Runs Batted In
- York-Det 118
- Etten-NY 107
- Johnson-NY 94
- Keller-NY 86

Stolen Bases
- Case-Was 61
- Stirnweiss-NY 11
- Keller-NY 7
- 3 players tied 4

Base Stealing Runs
- Case-Was 8.5
- Dickey-NY .0

Fielding Runs-Infield
- Boudreau-Cle 25.1
- Gordon-NY 24.7
- Johnson-NY 13.1

Fielding Runs-Outfield
- Tucker-Chi 9.2
- Keller-NY 1.8

Wins
- Trout-Det 20
- Chandler-NY 20
- Chandler-NY 20
- Bonham-NY 15

Winning Pct.
- Chandler-NY .833
- Bonham-NY .652

Complete Games
- Hughson-Bos 20
- Chandler-NY 20
- Chandler-NY 20
- Wensloff-NY 18

Strikeouts
- Reynolds-Cle 151
- Chandler-NY 134
- Borowy-NY 113
- Wensloff-NY 105

Fewest BB/Game
- Leonard-Was 1.88
- Chandler-NY 1.92
- Bonham-NY 2.07
- Wensloff-NY 2.82

Games
- Brown-Bos 49
- Murphy-NY 37
- Chandler-NY 30
- 2 players tied 29

Saves
- Maltzberger-Chi 14
- Murphy-NY 8

Base Runners/9
- Chandler-NY 9.07
- Murphy-NY 9.79
- Bonham-NY 9.97
- Wensloff-NY 10.07

Adjusted Relief Runs
- Brown-Bos 11.6
- Murphy-NY 5.6

Relief Ranking
- Caster-StL 18.0
- Murphy-NY 11.2

Innings Pitched
- Bagby-Cle 273.0
- Chandler-NY 253.0
- Bonham-NY 225.2
- Wensloff-NY 223.1

Opponents' Avg.
- Reynolds-Cle .202
- Chandler-NY .215
- Wensloff-NY .219
- Bonham-NY .236

Opponents' OBP
- Chandler-NY .261
- Wensloff-NY .282
- Bonham-NY .282
- Borowy-NY .305

Earned Run Average
- Chandler-NY 1.64
- Bonham-NY 2.27
- Wensloff-NY 2.54
- Borowy-NY 2.82

Adjusted ERA
- Chandler-NY 197
- Bonham-NY 141
- Wensloff-NY 127
- Borowy-NY 114

Adjusted Starter Runs
- Chandler-NY 42.1
- Bonham-NY 26.0
- Wensloff-NY 14.7
- Borowy-NY 12.1

Pitcher Wins
- Chandler-NY 5.3
- Bonham-NY 2.5
- Borowy-NY 1.6
- Wensloff-NY 1.5

1944 American League

TEAM	W	L	T	PCT	GB	R	OR	HR	AVG	OBP	SLG	OPS	AOPS	PF	SB	CG	HR	BB	SO	BR/9	ERA	AERA	OAV	OOB	FW	PW	BW	BSW	DIF
StL	89	65	0	.578		684	587	72	.252	.323	.352	675	94	106	44	71	58	469	**581**	12.1	3.17	114	.259	.320	.5	6.6	-3.9	-.2	9.0
Det	88	66	2	.571	1	658	**581**	60	.263	.332	.354	686	97	106	61	**87**	**39**	452	568	11.9	**3.09**	**116**	.257	.318	-.5	**7.6**	-1.3	-.6	5.8
NY	83	71	0	.539	6	674	617	**96**	.264	.333	**.387**	**720**	108	103	91	78	82	532	529	12.3	3.39	103	.257	.326	**1.3**	1.6	5.4	**.9**	-3.2
Bos	77	77	2	.500	12	**739**	676	69	**.270**	**.336**	.380	716	**112**	99	60	58	66	592	524	13.0	3.82	89	.263	.339	.6	-6.9	**9.0**	-.1	-2.6
Phi	72	82	1	.468	17	525	594	36	.257	.314	.327	641	90	99	42	72	58	**390**	534	**11.4**	3.26	107	**.252**	**.307**	.2	3.7	-7.4	-.2	-1.3
Cle	72	82	1	.468	17	643	677	70	.266	.331	.372	703	111	96	48	48	40	621	524	13.2	3.65	90	.265	.344	.9	-6.1	8.2	-.4	-7.6
Chi	71	83	0	.461	18	543	662	23	.247	.307	.320	627	86	99	66	64	68	420	481	12.0	3.58	96	.264	.320	-.2	-2.4	-9.7	-.2	6.5
Was	64	90	0	.416	25	592	664	33	.261	.324	.330	654	97	96	**127**	83	48	475	503	12.4	3.49	93	.264	.327	-2.3	-4.0	-1.6	.7	-5.9
Total	619					35058		459	.260	.325	.353	678			539	561				12.3	3.43		.260	.325					

Batter-Fielder Wins
- **Boudreau-Cle 7.5**
- **Stirnweiss-NY 6.8**
- **Etten-NY 3.1**
- **Lindell-NY 2.5**

Batting Average
- Boudreau-Cle .327
- Stirnweiss-NY .319
- Lindell-NY .300
- Etten-NY .293

On-Base Percentage
- B.Johnson-Bos .431
- Etten-NY .399
- Stirnweiss-NY .389
- Lindell-NY .351

Slugging Average
- Doerr-Bos .528
- B.Johnson-Bos .528
- Lindell-NY .500
- Etten-NY .466

On-Base Plus Slugging
- B.Johnson-Bos 959
- Etten-NY 865
- Lindell-NY 851
- Stirnweiss-NY 849

Adjusted OPS
- B.Johnson-Bos 175
- Etten-NY 142
- Stirnweiss-NY 137
- Lindell-NY 137

Adjusted Batter Runs
- B.Johnson-Bos 56.6
- Etten-NY 34.8
- Stirnweiss-NY 32.0
- Lindell-NY 25.2

Runs
- Stirnweiss-NY 125
- Lindell-NY 91
- Etten-NY 88
- Metheny-NY 72

Hits
- Stirnweiss-NY 205
- Lindell-NY 178
- Etten-NY 168
- Metheny-NY 124

Doubles
- Boudreau-Cle 45
- Stirnweiss-NY 35
- Lindell-NY 33
- Etten-NY 25

Triples
- Stirnweiss-NY 16
- Lindell-NY 16
- Grimes-NY 8
- 3 players tied 5

Home Runs
- Etten-NY 22
- Lindell-NY 18
- Metheny-NY 14
- Martin-NY 9

Total Bases
- Lindell-NY 297
- Stirnweiss-NY 296
- Etten-NY 267
- Metheny-NY 184

Runs Batted In
- Stephens-StL 109
- Lindell-NY 103
- Etten-NY 91
- Metheny-NY 67

Stolen Bases
- Stirnweiss-NY 55
- Grimes-NY 6
- 3 players tied 5

Base Stealing Runs
- Stirnweiss-NY 8.3
- Grimes-NY 1.3
- Crosetti-NY .7
- Martin-NY .4

Fielding Runs-Infield
- Mayo-Det 33.5
- Stirnweiss-NY 18.0
- Etten-NY 3.0

Fielding Runs-Outfield
- Spence-Was 15.4
- Lindell-NY 4.0

Wins
- Newhouser-Det 29
- Borowy-NY 17
- Dubiel-NY 13
- Donald-NY 13

Winning Pct.
- Hughson-Bos .783
- Borowy-NY .586

Complete Games
- Trout-Det 33
- Dubiel-NY 19
- Borowy-NY 19
- Bonham-NY 17

Strikeouts
- Newhouser-Det 187
- Borowy-NY 107
- Dubiel-NY 79
- Page-NY 63

Fewest BB/Game
- Harris-Phi 1.34
- Bonham-NY 1.73
- Borowy-NY 3.13
- 2 players tied 3.34

Games
- Heving-Cle 63
- Turner-NY 35
- Borowy-NY 35
- 2 players tied 30

Saves
- 3 players tied 12
- Turner-NY 7
- Johnson-NY 3
- Borowy-NY 2

Base Runners/9
- Berry-Phi 8.33
- Borowy-NY 11.11
- Bonham-NY 11.33
- Queen-NY 11.35

Adjusted Relief Runs
- Berry-Phi 17.2

Relief Ranking
- Berry-Phi 29.2

Innings Pitched
- Trout-Det 352.1
- Borowy-NY 252.2
- Dubiel-NY 232.0
- Bonham-NY 213.2

Opponents' Avg.
- Gromek-Cle .219
- Borowy-NY .236
- Dubiel-NY .248
- Bonham-NY .273

Opponents' OBP
- Hughson-Bos .267
- Borowy-NY .301
- Bonham-NY .307
- Dubiel-NY .316

Earned Run Average
- Trout-Det 2.12
- Borowy-NY 2.64
- Bonham-NY 2.99
- Donald-NY 3.34

Adjusted ERA
- Trout-Det 168
- Borowy-NY 132
- Bonham-NY 117
- Donald-NY 104

Adjusted Starter Runs
- Trout-Det 53.1
- Borowy-NY 21.1
- Bonham-NY 11.5
- Dubiel-NY 6.8

Pitcher Wins
- Trout-Det 8.2
- Borowy-NY 2.1
- Bonham-NY .6
- Dubiel-NY .5

1945 American League

TEAM	W	L	T	PCT	GB	R	OR	HR	AVG	OBP	SLG	OPS	AOPS	PF	SB	CG	HR	BB	SO	BR/9	ERA	AERA	OAV	OOB	FW	PW	BW	BSW	DIF
Det	88	65	2	.575		633	565	77	.256	.324	.361	685	98	106	60	78	48	538	**588**	12.1	2.99	**118**	.250	.322	.4	**8.4**	-1.7	-.2	4.7
Was	87	67	2	.565	1.5	622	562	27	.258	.330	.334	664	107	92	**110**	82	42	**440**	550	**11.2**	**2.92**	106	**.242**	**.301**	-1.0	3.2	5.0	**.5**	2.2
StL	81	70	3	.536	6	597	**548**	63	.249	.316	.341	657	91	105	25	**91**	59	506	570	11.8	3.14	112	.249	.316	1.2	5.9	-6.0	-.1	4.6
NY	81	71	0	.533	6.5	**676**	606	**93**	.259	**.343**	**.373**	**716**	108	105	64	78	66	485	474	11.8	3.45	100	.250	.316	-.7	.1	**6.3**	.3	-1.0
Cle	73	72	2	.503	11	557	**548**	65	.255	.326	.359	685	**109**	96	19	76	**39**	501	497	12.4	3.31	98	.257	.328	**1.7**	-1.0	5.4	-.3	-5.3
Chi	71	78	1	.477	15	596	633	22	**.262**	.326	.337	663	101	97	78	84	63	448	486	12.7	3.69	90	.270	.332	-1.1	-6.0	.2	.2	3.2
Bos	71	83	3	.461	17.5	599	674	50	.260	.330	.346	676	100	102	72	71	58	656	490	13.4	3.80	90	.264	.348	-.1	-6.4	.0	.2	.3
Phi	52	98	3	.347	34.5	494	638	33	.245	.306	.316	622	86	100	25	65	55	571	531	12.9	3.62	95	.262	.337	-.3	-3.1	-10.3	-.7	-8.7
Total	612					34774		430	.255	.325	.346	671			453	625				12.3	3.36		.255	.325					

Batter-Fielder Wins
Stirnweiss-NY 7.2
Grimes-NY 2.3
Keller-NY 1.6
Etten-NY 8

Batting Average
Stirnweiss-NY .... .309
Etten-NY .... .285
Martin-NY .... .267
Grimes-NY .... .265

On-Base Percentage
Lake-Bos .... .412
Grimes-NY .... .395
Etten-NY .... .387
Stirnweiss-NY .... .385

Slugging Average
Stirnweiss-NY .... .476
Etten-NY .... .437
Martin-NY .... .392
Grimes-NY .... .358

On-Base Plus Slugging
Stirnweiss-NY 862
Etten-NY 824
Martin-NY 760
Grimes-NY 753

Adjusted OPS
Stirnweiss-NY 143
Etten-NY 133
Martin-NY 115
Grimes-NY 114

Adjusted Batter Runs
Stirnweiss-NY 33.9
Etten-NY 26.5
Keller-NY 16.4
Grimes-NY 14.2

Runs
Stirnweiss-NY 107
Etten-NY 77
Metheny-NY 64
Grimes-NY 64

Hits
Stirnweiss-NY 195
Etten-NY 161
Grimes-NY 127
Metheny-NY 126

Doubles
Moses-Chi 35
Stirnweiss-NY 32
Etten-NY 24
Grimes-NY 19

Triples
Stirnweiss-NY 22
Grimes-NY 7
Martin-NY 6
2 players tied 4

Home Runs
Stephens-StL 24
Etten-NY 18
Derry-NY 13
2 players tied 10

Total Bases
Stirnweiss-NY 301
Etten-NY 247
Metheny-NY 172
Grimes-NY 172

Runs Batted In
Etten-NY 111
Stirnweiss-NY 64
Metheny-NY 53
Martin-NY 53

Stolen Bases
Stirnweiss-NY 33
Grimes-NY 7
Crosetti-NY 7
Metheny-NY 5

Base Stealing Runs
Dickshot-Chi 2.9
Stirnweiss-NY 1.3
Crosetti-NY 1.2
Martin-NY 5

Fielding Runs-Infield
Stirnweiss-NY 25.2
Grimes-NY 6.7

Fielding Runs-Outfield
Cullenbine-Cle-Det 9.1
Martin-NY 1.2

Wins
Newhouser-Det 25
Bevens-NY 13
Dubiel-NY 10
Borowy-NY 10

Winning Pct.
Newhouser-Det ..... .735

Complete Games
Newhouser-Det 29
Bevens-NY 14
Bonham-NY 12
2 players tied 9

Strikeouts
Newhouser-Det 212
Bevens-NY 76
Gettel-NY 67
2 players tied 50

Fewest BB/Game
Bonham-NY 1.10
Gettel-NY 3.08
Bevens-NY 3.33

Games
Berry-Phi 52
Turner-NY 30
Bevens-NY 29
Gettel-NY 27

Saves
Turner-NY 10
Gettel-NY 3
Zuber-NY 1

Base Runners/9
Wolff-Was 9.14
Bonham-NY 10.41
Ruffing-NY 10.92
Borowy-NY 11.29

Adjusted Relief Runs
Berry-Phi 15.0
Holcombe-NY 7.4

Relief Ranking
Berry-Phi 16.8
Holcombe-NY 7.2

Innings Pitched
Newhouser-Det ... 313.1
Bevens-NY 184.0
Bonham-NY 180.2
Gettel-NY 154.2

Opponents' Avg.
Newhouser-Det .... .211
Gettel-NY .... .243
Bevens-NY .... .254
Bonham-NY .... .265

Opponents' OBP
Wolff-Was .... .258
Bonham-NY .... .288
Gettel-NY .... .314
Bevens-NY .... .322

Earned Run Average
Newhouser-Det 1.81
Bonham-NY 3.29
Bevens-NY 3.67
Gettel-NY 3.90

Adjusted ERA
Newhouser-Det 194
Bonham-NY 105
Bevens-NY 94
Gettel-NY 89

Adjusted Starter Runs
Newhouser-Det 58.4
Ruffing-NY 5.7
Bonham-NY 5.5
Zuber-NY 4.8

Pitcher Wins
Newhouser-Det 7.6
Bonham-NY 7
Holcombe-NY 7
Ruffing-NY 6

1946 American League

TEAM	W	L	T	PCT	GB	R	OR	HR	AVG	OBP	SLG	OPS	AOPS	PF	SB	CG	HR	BB	SO	BR/9	ERA	AERA	OAV	OOB	FW	PW	BW	BSW	DIF
Bos	104	50	2	.675		**792**	594	109	**.271**	**.356**	**.402**	**758**	**113**	106	45	79	89	501	667	12.1	3.38	108	.254	.319	**1.5**	4.4	**10.5**	.0	10.6
Det	92	62	1	.597	12	704	567	108	.258	.337	.374	711	100	106	65	**94**	97	**497**	**896**	**11.5**	3.22	**114**	**.241**	**.307**	.5	**6.8**	.4	**.4**	6.9
NY	87	67	0	.565	17	684	**547**	**136**	.248	.334	.387	721	107	101	48	68	**66**	552	653	11.9	3.13	110	.243	.319	.7	5.1	4.9	.2	-.9
Was	76	78	1	.494	28	608	706	60	.260	.327	.366	693	106	94	51	71	81	547	537	13.1	3.74	89	.269	.339	-2.8	-6.7	4.4	-.2	4.4
Chi	74	80	1	.481	30	562	595	37	.257	.323	.333	656	94	96	**78**	62	80	508	550	12.1	**3.10**	110	.255	.323	-.7	5.2	-4.6	-.1	-2.8
Cle	68	86	2	.442	36	537	638	79	.245	.313	.356	669	99	94	57	63	84	649	789	12.6	3.62	91	.245	.331	1.0	-5.3	-1.0	-.1	-3.5
StL	66	88	2	.429	38	621	710	84	.251	.313	.356	669	89	105	23	63	73	573	574	13.3	3.95	94	.272	.343	.3	-3.4	-8.6	-.3	1.0
Phi	49	105	1	.318	55	529	680	40	.253	.318	.338	656	91	99	39	61	83	577	562	13.2	3.90	91	.264	.340	-.2	-5.4	-7.0	.2	-15.5
Total	621					35037		653	.256	.328	.364	692			406	561				12.5	3.50		.256	.328					

Batter-Fielder Wins
Williams-Bos 8.1
Keller-NY 3.2
DiMaggio-NY 2.6
Robinson-NY 2.4

Batting Average
Vernon-Was .... .353
DiMaggio-NY .... .290
Keller-NY .... .275
Rizzuto-NY .... .257

On-Base Percentage
Williams-Bos .... .497
Keller-NY .... .405
DiMaggio-NY .... .367
Henrich-NY .... .358

Slugging Average
Williams-Bos .... .667
Keller-NY .... .533
DiMaggio-NY .... .511
Henrich-NY .... .411

On-Base Plus Slugging
Williams-Bos 1164
Keller-NY 938
DiMaggio-NY 878
Henrich-NY 769

Adjusted OPS
Williams-Bos 211
Keller-NY 158
DiMaggio-NY 142
Henrich-NY 113

Adjusted Batter Runs
Williams-Bos 88.3
Keller-NY 45.6
DiMaggio-NY 26.3
Robinson-NY 21.1

Runs
Williams-Bos 142
Keller-NY 98
Henrich-NY 92
DiMaggio-NY 81

Hits
Pesky-Bos 208
Keller-NY 148
DiMaggio-NY 146
Henrich-NY 142

Doubles
Vernon-Was 51
Keller-NY 29
Henrich-NY 25
DiMaggio-NY 20

Triples
Edwards-Cle 16
Keller-NY 10
DiMaggio-NY 8
Stirnweiss-NY 7

Home Runs
Greenberg-Det 44
Keller-NY 30
DiMaggio-NY 25
Henrich-NY 19

Total Bases
Williams-Bos 343
Keller-NY 287
DiMaggio-NY 257
Henrich-NY 232

Runs Batted In
Greenberg-Det 127
Keller-NY 101
DiMaggio-NY 95
Henrich-NY 83

Stolen Bases
Case-Cle 28
Stirnweiss-NY 18
Rizzuto-NY 14
Henrich-NY 5

Base Stealing Runs
Case-Cle 2.3
Stirnweiss-NY 1.9
Rizzuto-NY 6
Lindell-NY 5

Fielding Runs-Infield
Doerr-Bos 27.3
Gordon-NY 18.1
Rizzuto-NY 16.7
Stirnweiss-NY 5.6

Fielding Runs-Outfield
Zarilla-StL 9.6
Henrich-NY 2.3
DiMaggio-NY 2.2

Wins
Newhouser-Det 26
Feller-Cle 26
Chandler-NY 20
Bevens-NY 16

Winning Pct.
Ferriss-Bos .... .806
Chandler-NY .... .714
Bevens-NY .... .552

Complete Games
Feller-Cle 36
Chandler-NY 20
Bevens-NY 18
2 players tied 6

Strikeouts
Feller-Cle 348
Chandler-NY 138
Bevens-NY 120
Page-NY 77

Fewest BB/Game
Hughson-Bos 1.65
Bevens-NY 2.81
Chandler-NY 3.15

Games
Feller-Cle 48
Chandler-NY 34
Gumpert-NY 33
2 players tied 31

Saves
Klinger-Bos 9
Murphy-NY 7
Page-NY 3
Bonham-NY 3

Base Runners/9
Ruffing-NY 8.85
Gumpert-NY 9.84
Chandler-NY 10.18
Bonham-NY 10.32

Adjusted Relief Runs
Caldwell-Chi 12.9

Relief Ranking
Caldwell-Chi 24.4

Innings Pitched
Feller-Cle 371.1
Chandler-NY 257.1
Bevens-NY 249.2
Page-NY 136.0

Opponents' Avg.
Newhouser-Det ..... .201
Chandler-NY .... .218
Bevens-NY .... .232

Opponents' OBP
Newhouser-Det ...... .269
Chandler-NY .... .288
Bevens-NY .... .293

Earned Run Average
Newhouser-Det 1.94
Chandler-NY 2.10
Bevens-NY 2.23

Adjusted ERA
Newhouser-Det 189
Chandler-NY 164
Bevens-NY 154

Adjusted Starter Runs
Newhouser-Det 51.1
Chandler-NY 38.5
Bevens-NY 33.6
Gumpert-NY 15.0

Pitcher Wins
Newhouser-Det 6.4
Chandler-NY 4.5
Bevens-NY 3.2
Gumpert-NY 1.2

1947 American League

TEAM	W	L	T	PCT	GB	R	OR	HR	AVG	OBP	SLG	OPS	AOPS	PF	SB	CG	HR	BB	SO	BR/9	ERA	AERA	OAV	OOB	FW	PW	BW	BSW	DIF
NY	97	57	1	.630		**794**	**568**	**115**	**.271**	.349	**.407**	**756**	**117**	99	27	73	95	628	**691**	**12.2**	**3.39**	104	**.238**	**.323**	1.5	2.4	**12.2**	.2	3.7
Det	85	69	4	.552	12	714	642	103	.258	**.353**	.377	730	106	103	52	**77**	79	**531**	648	12.4	3.57	106	.258	.326	-1.0	3.1	6.3	-.7	.2
Bos	83	71	3	.539	14	720	669	103	.265	.349	.382	731	102	107	41	64	84	575	586	12.8	3.81	102	.261	.335	-.0	1.1	2.2	.0	2.6
Cle	80	74	3	.519	17	687	588	112	.259	.324	.385	709	106	97	29	55	94	628	590	**12.2**	3.44	101	.240	.325	**1.9**	.7	2.7	.2	-2.5
Phi	78	76	2	.506	19	633	614	61	.252	.333	.349	682	94	102	37	70	85	597	493	12.3	3.51	**109**	.247	.326	-.4	**4.7**	-3.6	.0	.3
Chi	70	84	1	.455	27	553	661	53	.256	.321	.342	663	93	96	**91**	47	76	603	522	13.0	3.64	100	.261	.339	-1.2	.3	-5.1	**.4**	-1.5
Was	64	90	0	.416	33	496	675	42	.241	.313	.321	634	84	-97	53	67	**63**	579	551	13.2	3.97	94	.267	.342	-.5	-3.8	-11.1	-.2	2.7
StL	59	95	0	.383	38	564	744	90	.241	.320	.330	650	90	102	69	50	103	604	552	10.4	4.00	90	.272	.318	.0	6.7	7.0	.2	4.4
Total	623					35161		679	.256	.333	.364	698			399	503				12.7	3.71		.256	.333					

Batter-Fielder Wins	Batting Average	On-Base Percentage	Slugging Average	On-Base Plus Slugging	Adjusted OPS	Adjusted Batter Runs
Williams-Bos 7.2	Williams-Bos .... .343	Williams-Bos .... .499	Williams-Bos .... .634	Williams-Bos 1133	Williams-Bos 199	Williams-Bos 82.7
Rizzuto-NY 2.8	DiMaggio-NY .... .315	McQuinn-NY .... .395	DiMaggio-NY .... .522	DiMaggio-NY 913	DiMaggio-NY 154	DiMaggio-NY 38.0
Henrich-NY 2.7	McQuinn-NY .... .304	DiMaggio-NY .... .391	Henrich-NY .... .485	Henrich-NY 857	Henrich-NY 139	Henrich-NY 27.9
DiMaggio-NY 2.2	Henrich-NY .... .287	Henrich-NY .... .372	McQuinn-NY .... .437	McQuinn-NY 832	McQuinn-NY 132	McQuinn-NY 25.0

Runs	Hits	Doubles	Triples	Home Runs	Total Bases	Runs Batted In
Williams-Bos 125	Pesky-Bos 207	Boudreau-Cle 45	Henrich-NY 13	Williams-Bos 32	Williams-Bos 335	Williams-Bos 114
Henrich-NY 109	DiMaggio-NY 168	Henrich-NY 35	DiMaggio-NY 10	DiMaggio-NY 20	DiMaggio-NY 279	Henrich-NY 98
Stirnweiss-NY 102	Henrich-NY 158	DiMaggio-NY 31	Rizzuto-NY 9	Henrich-NY 16	Henrich-NY 267	DiMaggio-NY 97
DiMaggio-NY 97	McQuinn-NY 157	Rizzuto-NY 26	2 players tied 8	2 players tied 13	McQuinn-NY 226	B.Johnson-NY 95

Stolen Bases	Base Stealing Runs	Fielding Runs-Infield	Fielding Runs-Outfield	Wins	Winning Pct.	Complete Games
Dillinger-StL 34	Dillinger-StL 2.9	Doerr-Bos 25.2	DiMaggio-Bos 15.0	Feller-Cle 20	Reynolds-NY .... .704	Newhouser-Det 24
Rizzuto-NY 11	Frey-NY 7	Rizzuto-NY 17.7	Lindell-NY 5.6	Reynolds-NY 19		Reynolds-NY 17
Stirnweiss-NY 5	DiMaggio-NY 7		Henrich-NY 4.6	Shea-NY 14		Shea-NY 13
3 players tied 3	Rizzuto-NY 3			Page-NY 14		Chandler-NY 13

Strikeouts	Fewest BB/Game	Games	Saves	Base Runners/9	Adjusted Relief Runs	Relief Ranking
Feller-Cle 196	Galehouse-StL-Bos 2.48	Klieman-Cle 58	Page-NY 17	Chandler-NY 9.91	Page-NY 18.1	Page-NY 30.3
Reynolds-NY 129	Bevens-NY 4.20	Page-NY 56	Reynolds-NY 2	Raschi-NY 11.01		
Page-NY 116	Shea-NY 4.48	Reynolds-NY 34	Shea-NY 1	Shea-NY 11.08		
Shea-NY 89	Reynolds-NY 4.58	Drews-NY 30	Drews-NY 1	Page-NY 11.33		

Innings Pitched	Opponents' Avg.	Opponents' OBP	Earned Run Average	Adjusted ERA	Adjusted Starter Runs	Pitcher Wins
Feller-Cle 299.0	Shea-NY .... .200	Dobson-Bos .... .299	Haynes-Chi 2.42	Haynes-Chi 151	Feller-Cle 28.7	Newhouser-Det 3.7
Reynolds-NY 241.2	Reynolds-NY .... .227	Shea-NY .... .303	Chandler-NY 2.46	Shea-NY 115	Chandler-NY 14.8	Hutchinson-Det 3.7
Shea-NY 178.2	Bevens-NY .... .264	Reynolds-NY .... .322	Shea-NY 3.07	Reynolds-NY 110	Shea-NY 11.5	Page-NY 3.3
Bevens-NY 165.0		Bevens-NY .... .345	Reynolds-NY 3.20	Bevens-NY 93	Reynolds-NY 9.5	Chandler-NY 2.2

1948 American League

TEAM	W	L	T	PCT	GB	R	OR	HR	AVG	OBP	SLG	OPS	AOPS	PF	SB	CG	HR	BB	SO	BR/9	ERA	AERA	OAV	OOB	FW	PW	BW	BSW	DIF
Cle	97	58	1	.626		840	**568**	**155**	**.282**	.360	.431	**791**	**119**	97	54	66	82	625	593	**12.1**	**3.22**	**126**	**.239**	**.323**	**1.4**	**13.4**	**13.2**	-.1	-8.3
Bos	96	59	0	.619	1	**907**	720	121	.274	**.374**	.409	783	109	105	38	70	83	592	513	13.4	4.26	103	.270	.345	1.2	1.9	7.9	**.4**	7.0
NY	94	60	0	.610	2.5	857	633	139	.278	.356	**.432**	788	116	99	24	62	94	641	654	12.9	3.75	109	.250	.336	.9	5.1	10.4	-.0	.6
Phi	84	70	0	.545	12.5	729	735	68	.260	.353	.362	715	96	100	40	**74**	86	638	486	13.9	4.43	97	.275	.355	1.3	-1.9	-1.8	.0	9.4
Det	78	76	0	.506	18.5	700	726	78	.267	.353	.375	728	96	103	22	60	92	**589**	**678**	12.9	4.15	105	.259	.335	-.9	3.2	-1.9	-.3	1.0
StL	59	94	2	.386	37	671	849	63	.271	.345	.378	723	96	103	63	35	103	737	531	14.9	5.01	91	.281	.371	-1.6	-6.3	-3.8	.0	-5.9
Was	56	97	1	.366	40	578	796	31	.244	.322	.331	653	81	-97	**76**	42	**81**	734	446	14.6	4.65	93	.273	.364	-.9	-4.5	-13.6	.3	-1.8
Chi	51	101	2	.336	44.5	559	814	55	.251	.329	.331	660	84	-97	46	35	89	673	403	14.4	4.89	87	.280	.365	-1.2	-9.2	-11.4	-.3	-2.8
Total	618					35841		710	.266	.349	.382	731			363	444				13.6	4.29		.266	.349					

Batter-Fielder Wins	Batting Average	On-Base Percentage	Slugging Average	On-Base Plus Slugging	Adjusted OPS	Adjusted Batter Runs
Boudreau-Cle 7.1	Williams-Bos .... .369	Williams-Bos .... .497	Williams-Bos .... .615	Williams-Bos 1112	Williams-Bos 185	Williams-Bos 71.5
DiMaggio-NY 4.5	DiMaggio-NY .... .320	DiMaggio-NY .... .396	DiMaggio-NY .... .598	DiMaggio-NY 994	DiMaggio-NY 164	DiMaggio-NY 49.7
Henrich-NY 3.2	Henrich-NY .... .308	Henrich-NY .... .391	Henrich-NY .... .554	Henrich-NY 945	Henrich-NY 151	Henrich-NY 40.8
2 players tied 1.2	Berra-NY .... .305	Stirnweiss-NY .... .360	Berra-NY .... .488	Berra-NY 830	Berra-NY 120	Lindell-NY 16.3

Runs	Hits	Doubles	Triples	Home Runs	Total Bases	Runs Batted In
Henrich-NY 138	Dillinger-StL 207	Williams-Bos 44	Henrich-NY 14	DiMaggio-NY 39	DiMaggio-NY 355	DiMaggio-NY 155
DiMaggio-NY 110	DiMaggio-NY 190	Henrich-NY 42	DiMaggio-NY 11	Henrich-NY 25	Henrich-NY 326	Henrich-NY 100
Stirnweiss-NY 90	Henrich-NY 181	DiMaggio-NY 26	Berra-NY 10	Berra-NY 14	Berra-NY 229	Berra-NY 98
Berra-NY 70	Berra-NY 143	Berra-NY 24	Stirnweiss-NY 7	Lindell-NY 13	Johnson-NY 199	Johnson-NY 64

Stolen Bases	Base Stealing Runs	Fielding Runs-Infield	Fielding Runs-Outfield	Wins	Winning Pct.	Complete Games
Dillinger-StL 28	Dillinger-StL 2.3	Priddy-StL 22.5	Coan-Was 11.9	Newhouser-Det 21	Kramer-Bos .... .783	Lemon-Cle 20
Rizzuto-NY 6	Souchock-NY 7	Johnson-NY 2.5	Henrich-NY 1.8	Raschi-NY 19	Raschi-NY .... .704	Raschi-NY 18
Stirnweiss-NY 5	Bauer-NY 2		DiMaggio-NY 1.4	Lopat-NY 17	Reynolds-NY .... .696	Lopat-NY 13
2 players tied 3			Berra-NY 1.2	Reynolds-NY 16	Lopat-NY .... .607	Reynolds-NY 11

Strikeouts	Fewest BB/Game	Games	Saves	Base Runners/9	Adjusted Relief Runs	Relief Ranking
Feller-Cle 164	Hutchinson-Det 1.95	Page-NY 55	Christopher-Cle 17	Paige-Cle 10.40	Klieman-Cle 13.6	Christopher-Cle 11.6
Raschi-NY 124	Lopat-NY 2.62	Reynolds-NY 39	Page-NY 16	Raschi-NY 11.52	Hiller-NY 1.3	Hiller-NY 1.3
Reynolds-NY 101	Raschi-NY 2.99	Raschi-NY 36	Reynolds-NY 3	Shea-NY 11.91		
Byrne-NY 93	Reynolds-NY 4.23	Lopat-NY 33	Byrne-NY 2	Lopat-NY 12.47		

Innings Pitched	Opponents' Avg.	Opponents' OBP	Earned Run Average	Adjusted ERA	Adjusted Starter Runs	Pitcher Wins
Lemon-Cle 293.2	Shea-NY .... .208	Hutchinson-Det ..... .297	Bearden-Cle 2.43	Bearden-Cle 167	Bearden-Cle 42.9	Lemon-Cle 6.6
Reynolds-NY 236.1	Raschi-NY .... .247	Raschi-NY .... .310	Shea-NY 3.41	Shea-NY 120	Shea-NY 12.1	Byrne-NY 1.6
Lopat-NY 226.2	Reynolds-NY .... .268	Shea-NY .... .316	Lopat-NY 3.65	Lopat-NY 112	Byrne-NY 12.0	Shea-NY 1.2
Raschi-NY 222.2	Lopat-NY .... .284	Lopat-NY .... .336	Reynolds-NY 3.77	Reynolds-NY 108	2 players tied 9.7	2 players tied 1.0

Historical Record

1949 American League

TEAM	W	L	T	PCT	GB	R	OR	HR	AVG	OBP	SLG	OPS	AOPS	PF	SB	CG	HR	BB	SO	BR/9	ERA	AERA	OAV	OOB	FW	PW	BW	BSW	DIF
NY	97	57	1	.630		829	637	115	.269	.362	.400	762	108	100	58	59	98	812	**671**	13.6	3.69	110	**.242**	.351	.0	5.4	5.7	**.5**	8.3
Bos	96	58	1	.623	1	**896**	667	**131**	**.282**	**.381**	**.420**	**801**	**111**	107	43	84	82	661	598	13.5	3.97	110	.262	.347	1.1	5.5	**9.1**	.4	2.9
Cle	89	65	0	.578	8	675	**574**	112	.260	.339	.384	723	99	98	44	65	82	**611**	594	**12.4**	**3.36**	**119**	.247	**.329**	**2.1**	**10.0**	-2.0	-.0	2.1
Det	87	67	1	.565	10	751	655	88	.267	.361	.378	739	102	100	39	70	102	628	631	12.8	3.77	110	.254	.335	.4	5.9	1.8	-.7	2.5
Phi	81	73	0	.526	16	726	725	82	.260	.361	.369	730	104	97	36	**85**	105	758	490	14.1	4.23	97	.263	.360	-.1	-1.8	3.3	.2	2.5
Chi	63	91	0	.409	34	648	737	43	.257	.347	.347	694	93	97	**62**	57	108	693	502	13.7	4.30	97	.264	.353	-.2	-1.8	-4.5	-.3	-7.2
StL	53	101	1	.344	44	667	913	117	.254	.339	.377	716	92	104	38	43	113	685	432	15.4	5.21	87	.294	.377	-1.6	-9.1	-6.6	-.2	-6.4
Was	50	104	0	.325	47	584	868	81	.254	.333	.356	689	90	98	46	44	**79**	779	451	15.0	5.10	84	.276	.373	-1.4	-12.1	-8.0	.2	-5.7
Total	618					35776		769	.263	.353	.379	732			366	507				13.8	4.20		.263	.353					

Batter-Fielder Wins
Williams-Bos 6.4
DiMaggio-NY 2.5
Henrich-NY 2.1
Berra-NY 1.7

Batting Average
Kell-Det .343
Williams-Bos .343
Henrich-NY .287
Berra-NY .277

On-Base Percentage
Williams-Bos .490
Henrich-NY .416
Coleman-NY .367
Rizzuto-NY .352

Slugging Average
Williams-Bos .650
Henrich-NY .526
Berra-NY .480
2 players tied .358

On-Base Plus Slugging
Williams-Bos 1141
Henrich-NY 942
Coleman-NY 725
Rizzuto-NY 711

Adjusted OPS
Williams-Bos 187
Henrich-NY 148
Coleman-NY 92
Rizzuto-NY 88

Adjusted Batter Runs
Williams-Bos 79.9
DiMaggio-NY 32.1
Henrich-NY 30.6
Lopat-NY 7.0

Runs
Williams-Bos 150
Rizzuto-NY 110
Henrich-NY 90
Brown-NY 61

Hits
Mitchell-Cle 203
Rizzuto-NY 169
Coleman-NY 123
Henrich-NY 118

Doubles
Williams-Bos 39
Rizzuto-NY 22
Coleman-NY 21
2 players tied 20

Triples
Mitchell-Cle 23
Woodling-NY 7
Rizzuto-NY 7
2 players tied 6

Home Runs
Williams-Bos 43
Henrich-NY 24
Berra-NY 20
DiMaggio-NY 14

Total Bases
Williams-Bos 368
Rizzuto-NY 220
Henrich-NY 216
Berra-NY 199

Runs Batted In
Williams-Bos 159
Stephens-Bos 159
Berra-NY 91
Henrich-NY 85

Stolen Bases
Dillinger-StL 20
Rizzuto-NY 18
Coleman-NY 8
Mapes-NY 6

Base Stealing Runs
Rizzuto-NY 1.9
Mapes-NY 1.3
Lindell-NY .7
Keller-NY .4

Fielding Runs-Infield
Doerr-Bos 27.1
Coleman-NY 4.6
Rizzuto-NY 3.1

Fielding Runs-Outfield
Valo-Phi 9.4
Mapes-NY 6.4
Bauer-NY 1.0

Wins
Parnell-Bos 25
Raschi-NY 21
Reynolds-NY 17
2 players tied 15

Winning Pct.
Kinder-Bos .793
Reynolds-NY .739
Byrne-NY .682
Raschi-NY .677

Complete Games
Parnell-Bos 27
Raschi-NY 21
Lopat-NY 14
Byrne-NY 12

Strikeouts
Trucks-Det 153
Byrne-NY 129
Raschi-NY 124
Reynolds-NY 105

Fewest BB/Game
Hutchinson-Det 2.48
Lopat-NY 2.88
Raschi-NY 4.52
Reynolds-NY 5.18

Games
Page-NY 60
Raschi-NY 38
Reynolds-NY 35
Byrne-NY 32

Saves
Page-NY 27
Marshall-NY 3
Buxton-NY 2

Base Runners/9
Hutchinson-Det 10.49
Page-NY 12.17
Lopat-NY 12.37
Raschi-NY 12.81

Adjusted Relief Runs
Page-NY 22.7

Relief Ranking
Page-NY 41.9

Innings Pitched
Parnell-Bos 295.1
Raschi-NY 274.2
Lopat-NY 215.1
Reynolds-NY 213.2

Opponents' Avg.
Byrne-NY .183
Raschi-NY .241
Reynolds-NY .250
Lopat-NY .269

Opponents' OBP
Hutchinson-Det .290
Lopat-NY .330
Raschi-NY .334
Reynolds-NY .353

Earned Run Average
Garcia-Cle 2.36
Lopat-NY 3.26
Raschi-NY 3.34
Byrne-NY 3.72

Adjusted ERA
Garcia-Cle 169
Lopat-NY 124
Raschi-NY 121
Byrne-NY 109

Adjusted Starter Runs
Parnell-Bos 49.2
Raschi-NY 20.2
Lopat-NY 17.3
Byrne-NY 10.9

Pitcher Wins
Lemon-Cle 5.6
Page-NY 4.0
Lopat-NY 2.6
Raschi-NY 2.1

1950 American League

TEAM	W	L	T	PCT	GB	R	OR	HR	AVG	OBP	SLG	OPS	AOPS	PF	SB	CG	HR	BB	SO	BR/9	ERA	AERA	OAV	OOB	FW	PW	BW	BSW	DIF
NY	98	56	1	.636		914	691	159	.282	.367	.441	808	**116**	97	41	66	118	708	**712**	13.5	4.15	103	.255	.348	1.3	2.2	**11.0**	.1	6.4
Det	95	59	3	.617	3	837	713	114	.282	.369	.417	786	104	103	23	**72**	141	**553**	576	13.0	4.12	114	.267	.339	1.3	8.1	3.6	-.6	5.7
Bos	94	60	0	.610	4	**1027**	804	161	**.302**	**.385**	**.464**	**849**	112	110	32	66	121	748	630	14.4	4.88	100	.270	.364	**1.7**	.2	9.5	**.3**	5.4
Cle	92	62	1	.597	6	806	**654**	**164**	.269	.358	.422	780	109	97	40	69	120	647	674	**12.8**	**3.75**	**115**	**.248**	**.333**	.7	**8.8**	6.4	-.0	-.8
Was	67	87	1	.435	31	690	813	76	.260	.347	.360	707	91	95	**42**	59	**99**	648	486	14.2	4.66	96	.278	.359	-1.4	-2.3	-5.8	.2	-.7
Chi	60	94	2	.390	38	625	749	93	.260	.333	.364	697	86	-97	19	62	107	734	566	14.0	4.41	102	.263	.356	.2	1.1	-10.6	-.1	-7.6
StL	58	96	0	.377	40	684	916	106	.246	.337	.370	707	84	-104	39	56	129	651	448	15.2	5.20	95	.295	.372	-3.1	-3.3	-11.7	-.2	-.7
Phi	52	102	0	.338	46	670	913	100	.261	.349	.378	727	94	98	**42**	50	138	729	466	15.3	5.49	83	.287	.376	-.8	-13.2	-4.1	.2	-7.1
Total	620					36253		973	.271	.356	.402	759			278	500				14.0	4.58		.271	.356					

Batter-Fielder Wins
Rizzuto-NY 4.0
Berra-NY 3.8
DiMaggio-NY 3.0
Mize-NY .9

Batting Average
Goodman-Bos .354
Rizzuto-NY .324
Berra-NY .322
Bauer-NY .320

On-Base Percentage
Doby-Cle .442
Rizzuto-NY .418
DiMaggio-NY .394
Berra-NY .383

Slugging Average
DiMaggio-NY .585
Berra-NY .533
Bauer-NY .463
Rizzuto-NY .439

On-Base Plus Slugging
Doby-Cle 986
DiMaggio-NY 979
Berra-NY 915
Rizzuto-NY 857

Adjusted OPS
Doby-Cle 156
DiMaggio-NY 152
Berra-NY 136
Rizzuto-NY 123

Adjusted Batter Runs
Doby-Cle 46.9
DiMaggio-NY 39.5
Berra-NY 29.3
Rizzuto-NY 26.1

Runs
DiMaggio-Bos 131
Rizzuto-NY 125
Berra-NY 116
DiMaggio-NY 114

Hits
Kell-Det 218
Rizzuto-NY 200
Berra-NY 192
DiMaggio-NY 158

Doubles
Kell-Det 56
Rizzuto-NY 36
DiMaggio-NY 33
Berra-NY 30

Triples
3 players tied 11
Woodling-NY 10
DiMaggio-NY 10
Henrich-NY 8

Home Runs
Rosen-Cle 37
DiMaggio-NY 32
Berra-NY 28
Mize-NY 25

Total Bases
Dropo-Bos 326
Berra-NY 318
DiMaggio-NY 307
Rizzuto-NY 271

Runs Batted In
Stephens-Bos 144
Dropo-Bos 144
Berra-NY 124
DiMaggio-NY 122

Stolen Bases
DiMaggio-Bos 15
Rizzuto-NY 12
Woodling-NY 5
Collins-NY 5

Base Stealing Runs
DiMaggio-Bos 1.9
Collins-NY 1.1
Jensen-NY .9
Brown-NY .3

Fielding Runs-Infield
Priddy-Det 27.9
Rizzuto-NY 8.2
Collins-NY .3

Fielding Runs-Outfield
Woodling-NY 12.4
Bauer-NY 2.2

Wins
B.Lemon-Cle 23
Raschi-NY 21
Lopat-NY 18
Reynolds-NY 16

Winning Pct.
Raschi-NY .724
Lopat-NY .692
Byrne-NY .625
Reynolds-NY .571

Complete Games
B.Lemon-Cle 22
Garver-StL 22
Raschi-NY 17
Lopat-NY 15

Strikeouts
B.Lemon-Cle 170
Reynolds-NY 160
Raschi-NY 155
Byrne-NY 118

Fewest BB/Game
Hutchinson-Det 1.86
Lopat-NY 2.48
Raschi-NY 4.07
Reynolds-NY 5.16

Games
Harris-Was 53
Page-NY 37
Reynolds-NY 35
Lopat-NY 35

Saves
Harris-Was 15
Page-NY 13
Reynolds-NY 2

Base Runners/9
Gromek-Cle 10.56
Ford-NY 11.33
Lopat-NY 11.92
Raschi-NY 12.31

Adjusted Relief Runs
Judson-Chi 7.8

Relief Ranking
Ferrick-StL-NY 10.6

Innings Pitched
B.Lemon-Cle 288.0
Raschi-NY 256.2
Reynolds-NY 240.2
Lopat-NY 236.1

Opponents' Avg.
Wynn-Cle .212
Reynolds-NY .242
Raschi-NY .243
Byrne-NY .245

Opponents' OBP
Wynn-Cle .305
Lopat-NY .317
Raschi-NY .327
Reynolds-NY .349

Earned Run Average
Wynn-Cle 3.20
Lopat-NY 3.47
Reynolds-NY 3.74
Raschi-NY 4.00

Adjusted ERA
Garver-StL 146
Lopat-NY 124
Reynolds-NY 115
Raschi-NY 107

Adjusted Starter Runs
Garver-StL 39.1
Ford-NY 19.3
Lopat-NY 18.0
Reynolds-NY 16.4

Pitcher Wins
Garver-StL 4.9
Lopat-NY 2.5
Reynolds-NY 1.7
Ford-NY 1.5

1951 American League

TEAM	W	L	T	PCT	GB	R	OR	HR	AVG	OBP	SLG	OPS	AOPS	PF	SB	CG	HR	BB	SO	BR/9	ERA	AERA	OAV	OOB	FW	PW	BW	BSW	DIF
NY	98	56	0	.636		798	621	**140**	.269	.349	**.408**	**757**	**113**	96	78	66	92	562	**664**	12.4	3.56	107	.250	.328	.3	4.3	**8.9**	**.6**	6.9
Cle	93	61	1	.604	5	696	**594**	**140**	.256	.336	.389	725	106	94	52	**76**	**85**	577	642	**12.2**	**3.38**	112	**.245**	**.323**	**.9**	6.7	4.0	.1	4.2
Bos	87	67	0	.565	11	**804**	725	127	.266	**.358**	.392	750	98	110	20	46	99	599	658	13.2	4.14	108	.264	.342	.5	4.5	-.4	-.0	5.5
Chi	81	73	1	.526	17	714	644	86	**.270**	.349	.385	734	105	98	**99**	74	109	**549**	572	**12.2**	3.50	**115**	.252	**.323**	.0	**8.5**	3.7	-.0	-8.1
Det	73	81	0	.474	25	685	741	104	.265	.338	.380	718	99	100	37	51	103	602	597	13.2	4.29	97	.262	.342	-.7	-1.8	-1.8	-.2	.4
Phi	70	84	0	.455	28	736	745	102	.262	.349	.386	735	101	102	47	52	109	569	437	13.4	4.47	96	.272	.347	.8	-2.7	1.8	.0	-6.9
Was	62	92	0	.403	36	672	764	54	.263	.336	.355	691	93	98	45	58	110	630	475	13.7	4.49	91	.269	.348	-.5	-5.8	-4.7	-.0	-3.9
StL	52	102	0	.338	46	611	882	86	.247	.317	.357	674	84	103	35	56	132	801	550	15.5	5.18	85	.282	.379	-1.2	-11.0	-12.0	-.4	-.4
Total	617					35716		839	.262	.342	.381	723			413	479				13.2	4.12		.262	.342					

Batter-Fielder Wins
- **Fain-Phi 4.3**
- **Joost-Phi 4.3**
- **Berra-NY 3.5**
- **McDougald-NY 2.1**

Batting Average
- Fain-Phi .344
- McDougald-NY .306
- Berra-NY .294
- Woodling-NY .281

On-Base Percentage
- Williams-Bos .464
- Woodling-NY .370
- DiMaggio-NY .365
- 2 players tied .350

Slugging Average
- Williams-Bos .556
- Berra-NY .492
- McDougald-NY .488
- Woodling-NY .462

On-Base Plus Slugging
- Williams-Bos 1019
- Berra-NY 842
- Woodling-NY 835
- DiMaggio-NY 787

Adjusted OPS
- Doby-Cle 163
- Berra-NY 131
- Woodling-NY 130
- DiMaggio-NY 117

Adjusted Batter Runs
- Williams-Bos 52.1
- McDougald-NY 25.4
- Berra-NY 19.4
- Woodling-NY 17.0

Runs
- DiMaggio-Bos 113
- Berra-NY 92
- Rizzuto-NY 87
- 2 players tied 72

Hits
- Kell-Det 191
- Berra-NY 161
- Rizzuto-NY 148
- McDougald-NY 123

Doubles
- 3 players tied 36
- McDougald-NY 23
- DiMaggio-NY 22
- Rizzuto-NY 21

Triples
- Minoso-Cle-Chi 14
- Woodling-NY 8
- Rizzuto-NY 6
- 2 players tied 5

Home Runs
- Zernial-Chi-Phi 33
- Berra-NY 27
- Woodling-NY 15
- McDougald-NY 14

Total Bases
- Williams-Bos 295
- Berra-NY 269
- McDougald-NY 196
- Woodling-NY 194

Runs Batted In
- Zernial-Chi-Phi 129
- Berra-NY 88
- Woodling-NY 71
- DiMaggio-NY 71

Stolen Bases
- Minoso-Cle-Chi 31
- Rizzuto-NY 18
- McDougald-NY 14
- Collins-NY 9

Base Stealing Runs
- Minoso-Cle-Chi 3.3
- Rizzuto-NY 2.9
- McDougald-NY 1.3
- Jensen-NY 1.1

Fielding Runs-Infield
- Fain-Phi 16.2
- Rizzuto-NY 11.2
- Coleman-NY 5.7
- Collins-NY 4.8

Fielding Runs-Outfield
- Coan-Was 18.4
- Bauer-NY 2.1
- DiMaggio-NY .7
- Collins-NY .2

Wins
- Feller-Cle 22
- Raschi-NY 21
- Lopat-NY 21
- Reynolds-NY 17

Winning Pct.
- Feller-Cle .733
- Lopat-NY .700
- Reynolds-NY .680
- Raschi-NY .677

Complete Games
- Garver-StL 24
- Lopat-NY 20
- Reynolds-NY 16
- Raschi-NY 15

Strikeouts
- Raschi-NY 164
- Reynolds-NY 126
- Lopat-NY 93
- Morgan-NY 57

Fewest BB/Game
- Hutchinson-Det 1.29
- Lopat-NY 2.72
- Raschi-NY 3.59
- Reynolds-NY 4.07

Games
- Kinder-Bos 63
- Reynolds-NY 40
- Raschi-NY 35
- Ostrowski-NY 34

Saves
- Kinder-Bos 14
- Reynolds-NY 7
- Ostrowski-NY 5
- Morgan-NY 2

Base Runners/9
- Aloma-Chi 10.13
- Lopat-NY 10.85
- Reynolds-NY 11.24
- Morgan-NY 11.41

Adjusted Relief Runs
- Kinder-Bos 24.3
- Ostrowski-NY 3.1

Relief Ranking
- Kinder-Bos 28.4
- Ostrowski-NY 3.3

Innings Pitched
- Wynn-Cle 274.1
- Raschi-NY 258.1
- Lopat-NY 234.2
- Reynolds-NY 221.0

Opponents' Avg.
- Reynolds-NY .213
- Lopat-NY .239
- Raschi-NY .242

Opponents' OBP
- Lopat-NY .298
- Reynolds-NY .304
- Raschi-NY .319

Earned Run Average
- Rogovin-Det-Chi 2.78
- Lopat-NY 2.91
- Reynolds-NY 3.05
- Raschi-NY 3.27

Adjusted ERA
- Rogovin-Det-Chi 146
- Lopat-NY 131
- Reynolds-NY 125
- Raschi-NY 117

Adjusted Starter Runs
- Rogovin-Det-Chi 29.7
- Lopat-NY 26.2
- Reynolds-NY 21.4
- Raschi-NY 16.1

Pitcher Wins
- Parnell-Bos 3.3
- Lopat-NY 3.3
- Lopat-NY 3.3
- Reynolds-NY 2.2

1952 American League

TEAM	W	L	T	PCT	GB	R	OR	HR	AVG	OBP	SLG	OPS	AOPS	PF	SB	CG	HR	BB	SO	BR/9	ERA	AERA	OAV	OOB	FW	PW	BW	BSW	DIF
NY	95	59	0	.617		727	**557**	129	**.267**	.341	.403	744	121	94	52	72	94	581	666	12.1	**3.14**	106	.243	.324	.8	3.2	14.1	.0	-.2
Cle	93	61	1	.604	2	**763**	606	**148**	.262	.342	**.404**	**746**	**122**	94	46	**80**	94	556	671	11.9	3.32	101	.241	**.316**	-.8	.4	**15.3**	-.0	1.2
Chi	81	73	2	.526	14	610	568	80	.252	.327	.348	675	93	101	**61**	53	86	578	**774**	**11.7**	3.25	**112**	**.238**	**.316**	**1.1**	**6.5**	-4.3	**.4**	.2
Phi	79	75	1	.513	16	664	723	89	.253	**.343**	.359	702	96	106	52	73	113	**526**	562	12.8	4.15	95	.263	.333	.0	-2.9	-1.1	-.0	6.0
Was	78	76	3	.506	17	598	608	50	.239	.317	.326	643	88	97	48	75	**78**	577	574	12.7	3.37	105	.258	.332	.6	3.1	-8.1	.2	5.2
Bos	76	78	0	.494	19	668	658	113	.255	.328	.377	705	96	108	59	53	107	623	624	13.1	3.80	104	.256	.340	-.3	2.0	-3.2	.0	.5
StL	64	90	1	.416	31	604	733	82	.250	.322	.356	678	92	103	30	48	111	598	581	13.0	4.12	95	.260	.339	-.8	-3.1	-5.8	-.1	-3.1
Det	50	104	2	.325	45	557	738	103	.243	.318	.352	670	92	101	27	51	111	591	702	13.0	4.25	90	.262	.338	-.6	-6.8	-6.1	-.4	-13.1
Total	621					35191		794	.253	.330	.365	695			375	505				12.5	3.67		.253	.330					

Batter-Fielder Wins
- **Fain-Phi 4.5**
- **Mantle-NY 3.9**
- **Berra-NY 3.5**
- **Rizzuto-NY 2.9**

Batting Average
- Fain-Phi .327
- Mantle-NY .311
- Woodling-NY .309
- Bauer-NY .293

On-Base Percentage
- Fain-Phi .438
- Mantle-NY .394
- Collins-NY .364
- Berra-NY .358

Slugging Average
- Doby-Cle .541
- Mantle-NY .530
- Collins-NY .481
- Berra-NY .478

On-Base Plus Slugging
- Mantle-NY 924
- Collins-NY 845
- Berra-NY 835
- Bauer-NY 818

Adjusted OPS
- Doby-Cle 166
- Mantle-NY 166
- Mantle-NY 166
- Collins-NY 142

Adjusted Batter Runs
- Mantle-NY 48.4
- Woodling-NY 28.7
- Berra-NY 26.4
- Bauer-NY 23.4

Runs
- Doby-Cle 104
- Berra-NY 97
- Mantle-NY 94
- Rizzuto-NY 89

Hits
- Fox-Chi 192
- Mantle-NY 171
- Bauer-NY 162
- Rizzuto-NY 147

Doubles
- Fain-Phi 43
- Mantle-NY 37
- Bauer-NY 31
- Rizzuto-NY 24

Triples
- Avila-Cle 11
- Rizzuto-NY 10
- Collins-NY 8
- Mantle-NY 7

Home Runs
- Doby-Cle 32
- Berra-NY 30
- Mantle-NY 23
- Collins-NY 18

Total Bases
- Rosen-Cle 297
- Mantle-NY 291
- Bauer-NY 256
- Berra-NY 255

Runs Batted In
- Rosen-Cle 105
- Berra-NY 98
- Mantle-NY 87
- McDougald-NY 78

Stolen Bases
- Minoso-Chi 22
- Rizzuto-NY 17
- McDougald-NY 6
- Bauer-NY 6

Base Stealing Runs
- Jensen-NY-Was 1.9
- Rizzuto-NY 1.6
- Mantle-NY .5
- 2 players tied .2

Fielding Runs-Infield
- Goodman-Bos 23.0
- Rizzuto-NY 21.4
- Martin-NY 18.3
- McDougald-NY 16.2

Fielding Runs-Outfield
- Philley-Phi 6.9
- Woodling-NY 5.9

Wins
- Shantz-Phi 24
- Reynolds-NY 20
- Raschi-NY 16
- Sain-NY 11

Winning Pct.
- Shantz-Phi .774
- Raschi-NY .727
- Reynolds-NY .714

Complete Games
- Lemon-Cle 28
- Reynolds-NY 24
- Raschi-NY 13
- Lopat-NY 10

Strikeouts
- Reynolds-NY 160
- Raschi-NY 127
- Kuzava-NY 67
- Sain-NY 57

Fewest BB/Game
- Shantz-Phi 2.03
- Reynolds-NY 3.57
- Raschi-NY 3.67

Games
- Kennedy-Chi 47
- Sain-NY 35
- Reynolds-NY 35
- Raschi-NY 31

Saves
- Dorish-Chi 11
- Sain-NY 7
- Reynolds-NY 6
- Kuzava-NY 3

Base Runners/9
- Shantz-Phi 9.56
- Raschi-NY 10.94
- Reynolds-NY 10.98
- Lopat-NY 11.09

Adjusted Relief Runs
- Dorish-Chi 11.9

Relief Ranking
- Dorish-Chi 17.3

Innings Pitched
- Lemon-Cle 309.2
- Reynolds-NY 244.1
- Raschi-NY 223.0
- Lopat-NY 149.1

Opponents' Avg.
- Lemon-Cle .208
- Raschi-NY .216
- Reynolds-NY .218

Opponents' OBP
- Shantz-Phi .272
- Reynolds-NY .300
- Raschi-NY .300

Earned Run Average
- Reynolds-NY 2.06
- Raschi-NY 2.78

Adjusted ERA
- Reynolds-NY 161
- Raschi-NY 119

Adjusted Starter Runs
- Shantz-Phi 42.7
- Reynolds-NY 35.3
- Raschi-NY 15.6
- Lopat-NY 15.2

Pitcher Wins
- Shantz-Phi 5.1
- Reynolds-NY 4.1
- Lopat-NY 1.6
- Raschi-NY 1.6

Historical Record

1953 American League

TEAM	W	L	T	PCT	GB	R	OR	HR	AVG	OBP	SLG	OPS	AOPS	PF	SB	CG	HR	BB	SO	BR/9	ERA	AERA	OAV	OOB	FW	PW	BW	BSW	DIF
NY	99	52	0	.656		**801**	**547**	139	**.273**	**.359**	**.417**	**776**	**120**	97	34	50	94	500	604	**12.1**	**3.20**	115	.251	**.321**	.3	8.0	**14.4**	-.4	1.1
Cle	92	62	1	.597	8.5	770	627	**160**	.270	.349	.410	759	114	97	33	**81**	**92**	519	586	12.2	3.64	103	.253	.325	.4	1.7	9.8	.1	2.9
Chi	89	65	2	.578	11.5	716	592	74	.258	.341	.364	705	93	103	**73**	57	113	583	**714**	12.2	3.41	**118**	**.246**	.324	.6	**9.5**	-3.7	.1	5.5
Bos	84	69	0	.549	16	656	632	101	.264	.332	.384	716	94	105	33	41	**92**	584	642	12.7	3.58	**118**	.254	.331	-.9	9.1	-4.3	-.4	3.9
Was	76	76	0	.500	23.5	687	614	69	.263	.343	.368	711	100	98	65	76	112	**478**	515	12.2	3.66	106	.258	.324	**.7**	3.6	1.2	**.6**	-6.1
Det	60	94	4	.390	40.5	695	923	108	.266	.331	.387	718	100	99	30	50	154	585	645	14.4	5.25	77	.291	.363	.1	-18.3	-.1	-.2	1.5
Phi	59	95	3	.383	41.5	632	799	116	.256	.321	.372	693	89	104	41	51	121	594	566	13.6	4.67	92	.271	.349	-.0	-5.6	-8.7	.5	-4.2
StL	54	100	0	.351	46.5	555	778	112	.249	.317	.363	680	87	102	17	28	101	626	639	13.8	4.48	94	.273	.351	-1.0	-4.0	-9.6	-.4	-8.0
Total	618					35512		879	.262	.337	.383	720			326	434				12.9	3.99		.262	.337					

Batter-Fielder Wins
Rosen-Cle............. 7.4
Berra-NY................ 3.8
Woodling-NY......... 2.4
Mantle-NY............. 2.3

Batting Average
Vernon-Was.......... .337
Bauer-NY.............. .304
Berra-NY............... .296
Mantle-NY............. .295

On-Base Percentage
Woodling-NY .... .429
Mantle-NY............. .398
Bauer-NY.............. .394
Rizzuto-NY........... .383

Slugging Average
Rosen-Cle............. .613
Berra-NY............... .523
Mantle-NY............. .497
Bauer-NY.............. .446

On-Base Plus Slugging
Rosen-Cle........... 1034
Woodling-NY 898
Mantle-NY............. 895
Berra-NY............... 886

Adjusted OPS
Rosen-Cle............. 181
Woodling-NY 147
Mantle-NY............. 145
Berra-NY............... 142

Adjusted Batter Runs
Rosen-Cle............ 68.0
Woodling-NY 31.7
Mantle-NY............ 31.4
Berra-NY.............. 27.0

Runs
Rosen-Cle...............115
Mantle-NY............. 105
McDougald-NY 82
Berra-NY.................. 80

Hits
Kuenn-Det 209
McDougald-NY 154
Martin-NY 151
Berra-NY............... 149

Doubles
Vernon-Was............ 43
McDougald-NY 27
Woodling-NY 26
2 players tied 24

Triples
Rivera-Chi............... 16
McDougald-NY 7
3 players tied 6

Home Runs
Rosen-Cle............... 43
Berra-NY................. 27
Mantle-NY............... 21
Collins-NY............... 17

Total Bases
Rosen-Cle............. 367
Berra-NY............... 263
Martin-NY 232
Mantle-NY............. 229

Runs Batted In
Rosen-Cle............. 145
Berra-NY............... 108
Mantle-NY................ 92
McDougald-NY 83

Stolen Bases
Minoso-Chi 25
Mantle-NY................. 8
Martin-NY 6
Rizzuto-NY 4

Base Stealing Runs
Michaels-Phi........... 1.5
Coan-Was.............. 1.5
Mantle-NY................. .4
Bollweg-NY............... .2

Fielding Runs-Infield
Strickland-Cle 21.0
McDougald-NY 7.0
Rizzuto-NY 2.8
Martin-NY 2.4

Fielding Runs-Outfield
Busby-Was 12.9
Noren-NY............... 3.0
Bauer-NY............... 2.7
Woodling-NY 1.3

Wins
Porterfield-Was........ 22
Ford-NY................... 18
Lopat-NY 16
Sain-NY................... 14

Winning Pct.
Lopat-NY .... .800
Ford-NY............... .750

Complete Games
Porterfield-Was........ 24
Ford-NY....................11
Sain-NY 10
Lopat-NY 9

Strikeouts
Pierce-Chi............. 186
Ford-NY..................110
Reynolds-NY 86
Sain-NY 84

Fewest BB/Game
Lopat-NY 1.61
Sain-NY 2.14
Raschi-NY 2.73
Ford-NY................ 4.78

Games
Kinder-Bos.............. 69
Reynolds-NY 41
Sain-NY 40
Gorman-NY 40

Saves
Kinder-Bos.............. 27
Reynolds-NY 13
Sain-NY 9
Gorman-NY 6

Base Runners/9
Raschi-NY 10.24
Lopat-NY 10.35
Sain-NY................11.29
McDonald-NY 11.66

Adjusted Relief Runs
Kinder-Bos............ 24.7
Kuzava-NY 5.9
Gorman-NY 3.2

Relief Ranking
Kinder-Bos............ 47.3
Kuzava-NY 6.9
Gorman-NY 3.9

Innings Pitched
B.Lemon-Cle....... 286.2
Ford-NY............. 207.0
Sain-NY 189.0
Raschi-NY 181.0

Opponents' Avg.
Pierce-Chi............ .218
Raschi-NY .... .224
Ford-NY............... .245
Lopat-NY .... .250

Opponents' OBP
Raschi-NY .... .283
Lopat-NY .... .288
Sain-NY .... .308
Ford-NY............... .344

Earned Run Average
Lopat-NY 2.42
Sain-NY 3.00
Ford-NY............... 3.00
Raschi-NY 3.33

Adjusted ERA
Lopat-NY 152
Sain-NY 123
Ford-NY................ 123
Raschi-NY 111

Adjusted Starter Runs
Pierce-Chi............ 37.8
Lopat-NY 25.5
Ford-NY............... 17.7
Sain-NY 17.3

Pitcher Wins
Kinder-Bos............. 5.2
Lopat-NY 2.9
Ford-NY................ 2.5
Sain-NY 2.4

1954 American League

TEAM	W	L	T	PCT	GB	R	OR	HR	AVG	OBP	SLG	OPS	AOPS	PF	SB	CG	HR	BB	SO	BR/9	ERA	AERA	OAV	OOB	FW	PW	BW	BSW	DIF
Cle	111	43	2	.721		746	**504**	**156**	.262	.341	.403	744	108	102	30	**77**	89	**486**	678	**10.9**	**2.78**	**132**	**.232**	**.297**	.7	**14.7**	6.7	-.2	12.1
NY	103	51	1	.669	8	**805**	563	133	**.268**	**.348**	**.408**	**756**	**118**	97	34	51	86	552	655	12.2	3.26	105	.251	.325	.8	3.0	**13.5**	-.4	9.1
Chi	94	60	1	.610	17	711	521	94	.267	.347	.379	726	103	103	**98**	60	94	517	701	11.6	3.05	122	.244	.312	**1.8**	10.8	3.1	**.4**	.9
Bos	69	85	2	.448	42	700	728	123	.266	.345	.395	740	98	111	51	41	118	612	**707**	13.3	4.01	102	.265	.341	-2.0	1.4	.3	**.4**	-8.2
Det	68	86	1	.442	43	584	664	90	.258	.322	.367	689	97	98	48	58	138	506	603	12.5	3.81	97	.261	.328	.6	-1.9	-2.6	-.2	-4.9
Was	66	88	1	.429	45	632	680	81	.246	.325	.355	680	97	95	37	69	79	573	562	13.0	3.84	93	.265	.338	.2	-4.8	-1.2	**.4**	-5.6
Bal	54	100	0	.351	57	483	668	52	.251	.313	.338	651	91	-93	30	58	**78**	688	668	13.0	3.88	92	.250	.338	-.4	-4.9	-6.6	-.1	-11.0
Phi	51	103	2	.331	60	542	875	94	.236	.305	.342	647	83	-100	30	49	141	685	555	14.7	5.18	75	.285	.366	-1.6	-19.1	-12.5	-.1	7.3
Total	621					35203		823	.257	.331	.373	704			358	463				12.6	3.72		.257	.331					

Batter-Fielder Wins
Williams-Bos......... 5.1
Berra-NY................ 4.4
Mantle-NY............. 3.8
McDougald-NY...... 2.8

Batting Average
Avila-Cle .... .341
Noren-NY.............. .319
Berra-NY............... .307
Carey-NY.............. .302

On-Base Percentage
Williams-Bos......... .513
Mantle-NY............. .408
Noren-NY.............. .377
Berra-NY............... .367

Slugging Average
Minoso-Chi .... .535
Mantle-NY............. .525
Berra-NY............... .488
Noren-NY.............. .481

On-Base Plus Slugging
Williams-Bos.........1148
Mantle-NY............. 933
Noren-NY.............. 859
Berra-NY............... 855

Adjusted OPS
Williams-Bos.......... 193
Mantle-NY............. 160
Noren-NY.............. 140
Berra-NY............... 139

Adjusted Batter Runs
Williams-Bos......... 60.7
Mantle-NY............ 46.9
Berra-NY.............. 29.2
Noren-NY............. 22.9

Runs
Mantle-NY............. 129
Berra-NY................. 88
Bauer-NY................ 73
Noren-NY................ 70

Hits
Kuenn-Det 201
Fox-Chi.................. 201
Berra-NY............... 179
Mantle-NY............. 163

Doubles
Vernon-Was............ 33
Berra-NY................. 28
McDougald-NY 22
Noren-NY................. 21

Triples
Minoso-Chi 18
Mantle-NY............... 12
Skowron-NY 9
3 players tied 6

Home Runs
Doby-Cle.................. 32
Mantle-NY............... 27
Berra-NY................. 22

Total Bases
Minoso-Chi 304
Mantle-NY............. 285
Berra-NY............... 285
Noren-NY.............. 205

Runs Batted In
Doby-Cle............... 126
Berra-NY............... 125
Mantle-NY............. 102
Noren-NY................. 66

Stolen Bases
Jensen-Bos............. 22
Mantle-NY.................. 5
Carey-NY................... 5
2 players tied 4

Base Stealing Runs
Busby-Was 3.0
Coleman-NY 7
Mantle-NY................. .4
Skowron-NY 0

Fielding Runs-Infield
Coleman-NY......... 14.6
Carey-NY.............. 12.5
McDougald-NY 10.2
Rizzuto-NY 5.7

Fielding Runs-Outfield
Diering-Bal............. 9.8
Noren-NY.................. .5

Wins
Wynn-Cle................. 23
Lemon-Cle............... 23
Grim-NY.................. 20
Ford-NY.................. 16

Winning Pct.
Consuegra-Chi ...... .842
Grim-NY............... .769
Ford-NY............... .667

Complete Games
Porterfield-Was........ 21
Lemon-Cle............... 21
Ford-NY....................11
Grim-NY..................... 8

Strikeouts
Turley-Bal 185
Ford-NY................. 125
Grim-NY................. 108
Reynolds-NY 100

Fewest BB/Game
Lopat-NY 1.75
Reynolds-NY 3.78
Grim-NY................ 3.84
Ford-NY................ 4.31

Games
Dixon-Was-Phi......... 54
Sain-NY 45
Grim-NY.................. 37
Reynolds-NY 36

Saves
Sain-NY 22
Reynolds-NY 7
Konstanty-NY 2
Gorman-NY 2

Base Runners/9
Mossi-Cle.............. 9.29
Sain-NY 9.47
Reynolds-NY 11.56
Ford-NY 11.62

Adjusted Relief Runs
Mossi-Cle............. 18.6
Sain-NY 4.2

Relief Ranking
Mossi-Cle............. 15.8
Sain-NY 8.5

Innings Pitched
Wynn-Cle............ 270.2
Ford-NY............. 210.2
Grim-NY............. 199.0
Lopat-NY 170.0

Opponents' Avg.
Turley-Bal .... .203
Ford-NY................ .227
Reynolds-NY .... .233
Grim-NY................ .244

Opponents' OBP
Garcia-Cle .... .282
Reynolds-NY .... .314
Ford-NY................ .317
Grim-NY................ .322

Earned Run Average
Garcia-Cle 2.64
Ford-NY............... 2.82
Grim-NY............... 3.26
Reynolds-NY 3.32

Adjusted ERA
Garcia-Cle 139
Ford-NY................ 122
Grim-NY................ 106
Reynolds-NY 104

Adjusted Starter Runs
Garcia-Cle 31.0
Ford-NY............... 16.8
Grim-NY................. 5.8
Byrd-NY................. 4.0

Pitcher Wins
Gromek-Det............ 3.7
Lemon-Cle.............. 3.7
Ford-NY.................. 2.1
Sain-NY 1.1

1955 American League

TEAM	W	L	T	PCT	GB	R	OR	HR	AVG	OBP	SLG	OPS	AOPS	PF	SB	CG	HR	BB	SO	BR/9	ERA	AERA	OAV	OOB	FW	PW	BW	BSW	DIF
NY	96	58	0	.623		762	569	**175**	.260	.340	**.418**	**758**	**112**	98	55	52	108	688	731	12.3	**3.23**	116	**.232**	.326	.5	8.2	**8.2**	.5	1.6
Cle	93	61	0	.604	3	698	601	148	.257	.349	.394	743	102	104	28	45	111	558	**877**	12.1	3.39	**118**	.245	.319	**1.7**	**9.2**	3.6	.0	1.5
Chi	91	63	1	.591	5	725	**557**	116	**.268**	.344	.388	732	100	103	**69**	55	111	**497**	720	**11.9**	3.37	117	.251	**.317**	1.5	8.9	1.2	.1	2.2
Bos	84	70	0	.545	12	755	652	137	.264	**.351**	.402	753	100	109	43	44	128	582	674	12.7	3.72	115	.253	.329	.0	8.1	1.8	**.6**	-3.5
Det	79	75	0	.513	17	**775**	658	130	.266	.345	.394	739	107	98	41	**66**	126	517	629	12.6	3.79	101	.261	.328	-.2	.8	6.6	.3	-5.6
KC	63	91	1	.409	33	638	911	121	.261	.322	.382	704	94	101	22	29	175	707	572	14.6	5.35	78	.278	.363	-.5	-17.2	-5.1	-.6	9.5
Bal	57	97	2	.370	39	540	754	54	.240	.314	.320	634	83	-93	34	35	103	625	595	13.4	4.21	91	.266	.344	-1.7	-6.4	-12.3	-.7	1.1
Was	53	101	0	.344	43	598	789	80	.248	.322	.351	673	82	96	25	37	**99**	634	607	14.2	4.62	83	.279	.359	-1.0	-12.4	-5.6	-.4	-4.5
Total	618					35491		961	.258	.336	.381	717			317	363				13.0	3.96		.258	.336					

Batter-Fielder Wins
- **Mantle-NY 5.5**
- **McDougald-NY 3.7**
- **Berra-NY 2.5**
- **Bauer-NY 1.5**

Batting Average
- Kaline-Det .340
- Mantle-NY .306
- McDougald-NY .285
- Bauer-NY .278

On-Base Percentage
- Mantle-NY .431
- McDougald-NY .361
- Bauer-NY .360
- Berra-NY .349

Slugging Average
- Mantle-NY .611
- Berra-NY .470
- Bauer-NY .461
- McDougald-NY .407

On-Base Plus Slugging
- Mantle-NY 1042
- Bauer-NY 821
- Berra-NY 819
- McDougald-NY 768

Adjusted OPS
- Mantle-NY 181
- Bauer-NY 122
- Berra-NY 121
- McDougald-NY 109

Adjusted Batter Runs
- Mantle-NY 62.2
- Skowron-NY 15.3
- Berra-NY 14.5
- Bauer-NY 14.4

Runs
- Smith-Cle 123
- Mantle-NY 121
- Bauer-NY 97
- Berra-NY 84

Hits
- Kaline-Det 200
- Mantle-NY 158
- McDougald-NY 152
- Berra-NY 147

Doubles
- Kuenn-Det 38
- Mantle-NY 25
- Berra-NY 20
- Bauer-NY 20

Triples
- Mantle-NY 11
- Carey-NY 11
- McDougald-NY 8
- Howard-NY 7

Home Runs
- Mantle-NY 37
- Berra-NY 27
- Bauer-NY 20
- Robinson-NY 16

Total Bases
- Kaline-Det 321
- Mantle-NY 316
- Berra-NY 254
- Bauer-NY 227

Runs Batted In
- Jensen-Bos 116
- Boone-Det 116
- Berra-NY 108
- Mantle-NY 99

Stolen Bases
- Rivera-Chi 25
- Hunter-NY 9
- Mantle-NY 8
- Bauer-NY 8

Base Stealing Runs
- Torgeson-Det 2.0
- Mantle-NY 1.4
- Hunter-NY 1.3
- Rizzuto-NY 1.2

Fielding Runs-Infield
- Fox-Chi 31.1
- McDougald-NY 22.3
- Carey-NY 10.2
- Collins-NY 5.2

Fielding Runs-Outfield
- Rivera-Chi 11.4
- Bauer-NY 5.1
- Noren-NY 4.1
- Collins-NY 1.4

Wins
- 3 players tied 18
- Ford-NY 18
- Turley-NY 17
- Byrne-NY 16

Winning Pct.
- Byrne-NY .762
- Ford-NY .720
- Turley-NY .567

Complete Games
- Ford-NY 18
- Turley-NY 13
- Byrne-NY 9
- Larsen-NY 5

Strikeouts
- Score-Cle 245
- Turley-NY 210
- Ford-NY 137
- Byrne-NY 76

Fewest BB/Game
- Gromek-Det 1.84
- Ford-NY 4.01
- Byrne-NY 4.89
- Turley-NY 6.46

Games
- Narleski-Cle 60
- Konstanty-NY 45
- Morgan-NY 40
- Ford-NY 39

Saves
- Narleski-Cle 19
- Konstanty-NY 11
- Morgan-NY 10
- Grim-NY 4

Base Runners/9
- Kinder-Bos 9.85
- Ford-NY 10.71
- Konstanty-NY 11.24
- Kucks-NY 11.94

Adjusted Relief Runs
- Consuegra-Chi 17.5
- Konstanty-NY 9.5
- Sturdivant-NY 6.4
- Morgan-NY 4.6

Relief Ranking
- Kinder-Bos 21.0
- Konstanty-NY 13.7
- Morgan-NY 7.2
- Sturdivant-NY 3.4

Innings Pitched
- F.Sullivan-Bos 260.0
- Ford-NY 253.2
- Turley-NY 246.2
- Byrne-NY 160.0

Opponents' Avg.
- Turley-NY .193
- Ford-NY .208
- Byrne-NY .237

Opponents' OBP
- Pierce-Chi .277
- Ford-NY .296
- Turley-NY .331
- Byrne-NY .340

Earned Run Average
- Pierce-Chi 1.97
- Ford-NY 2.63
- Turley-NY 3.06
- Byrne-NY 3.15

Adjusted ERA
- Pierce-Chi 201
- Ford-NY 143
- Turley-NY 122
- Byrne-NY 119

Adjusted Starter Runs
- Pierce-Chi 44.7
- Ford-NY 34.4
- Turley-NY 21.9
- Byrne-NY 9.2

Pitcher Wins
- Pierce-Chi 5.3
- Ford-NY 3.4
- Turley-NY 2.4
- Byrne-NY 1.5

1956 American League

TEAM	W	L	T	PCT	GB	R	OR	HR	AVG	OBP	SLG	OPS	AOPS	PF	SB	CG	HR	BB	SO	BR/9	ERA	AERA	OAV	OOB	FW	PW	BW	BSW	DIF
NY	97	57	0	.630		**857**	631	**190**	.270	.347	**.434**	**781**	**115**	97	51	50	114	652	732	12.9	3.63	107	.249	.335	.6	3.9	**10.3**	-.0	5.3
Cle	88	66	1	.571	9	712	**581**	153	.244	.335	.381	716	92	102	40	**67**	116	564	**845**	**11.9**	**3.32**	**127**	**.238**	**.314**	1.0	**13.1**	-4.8	-.0	1.7
Chi	85	69	0	.552	12	776	634	128	.267	.349	.397	746	101	101	**70**	65	118	**524**	722	12.3	3.73	110	.255	.324	**1.3**	5.8	2.0	**.5**	-1.6
Bos	84	70	1	.545	13	780	751	139	.275	**.362**	.419	**781**	100	112	28	50	130	668	712	13.3	4.17	111	.254	.340	-1.2	6.3	1.4	.1	.4
Det	82	72	1	.532	15	789	699	150	**.279**	.356	.420	776	110	100	43	62	140	655	788	13.6	4.06	101	.264	.348	.4	.9	8.0	.1	-4.5
Bal	69	85	0	.448	28	571	705	91	.244	.320	.350	670	89	-92	39	38	**99**	547	715	12.8	4.20	93	.263	.334	.5	-4.4	-7.6	-.4	4.0
Was	59	95	1	.383	38	652	924	112	.250	.341	.377	718	95	100	37	36	171	730	663	15.1	5.33	81	.287	.373	-1.3	-14.4	-2.6	-.2	.6
KC	52	102	0	.338	45	619	831	112	.252	.315	.370	685	86	-100	40	30	187	679	636	14.1	4.86	89	.271	.357	-1.1	-7.6	-11.1	-.0	-5.2
Total	618					35756		1075	.260	.341	.394	735			348	398				13.2	4.16		.260	.341					

Batter-Fielder Wins
- **Mantle-NY 8.1**
- **Berra-NY 4.3**
- **McDougald-NY 3.5**
- **Skowron-NY 2.3**

Batting Average
- Mantle-NY .353
- McDougald-NY .311
- Skowron-NY .308
- Berra-NY .298

On-Base Percentage
- Williams-Bos .479
- Mantle-NY .464
- McDougald-NY .405
- Skowron-NY .382

Slugging Average
- Mantle-NY .705
- Berra-NY .534
- Skowron-NY .528
- Bauer-NY .445

On-Base Plus Slugging
- Mantle-NY 1169
- Berra-NY 911
- Skowron-NY 910
- McDougald-NY 848

Adjusted OPS
- Mantle-NY 213
- Berra-NY 144
- Skowron-NY 143
- McDougald-NY 128

Adjusted Batter Runs
- Mantle-NY 90.0
- Berra-NY 32.2
- Skowron-NY 27.3
- McDougald-NY 20.3

Runs
- Mantle-NY 132
- Bauer-NY 96
- Berra-NY 93
- McDougald-NY 79

Hits
- Kuenn-Det 196
- Mantle-NY 188
- Berra-NY 155
- Skowron-NY 143

Doubles
- Piersall-Bos 40
- Berra-NY 29
- Martin-NY 24
- Mantle-NY 22

Triples
- 4 players tied 11
- Bauer-NY 7
- Skowron-NY 6
- Cerv-NY 6

Home Runs
- Mantle-NY 52
- Berra-NY 30
- Bauer-NY 26
- Skowron-NY 23

Total Bases
- Mantle-NY 376
- Berra-NY 278
- Skowron-NY 245
- Bauer-NY 240

Runs Batted In
- Mantle-NY 130
- Berra-NY 105
- Skowron-NY 90
- Bauer-NY 84

Stolen Bases
- Aparicio-Chi 21
- Mantle-NY 10
- Carey-NY 9
- Martin-NY 7

Base Stealing Runs
- Aparicio-Chi 3.2
- Mantle-NY 1.9
- Rizzuto-NY .7
- Martin-NY .5

Fielding Runs-Infield
- McDougald-NY 8.8
- Skowron-NY 4.0

Fielding Runs-Outfield
- Kaline-Det 12.2
- Berra-NY 1.1
- Mantle-NY .1

Wins
- Lary-Det 21
- Ford-NY 19
- Kucks-NY 18
- Sturdivant-NY 16

Winning Pct.
- Ford-NY .760
- Sturdivant-NY .667
- Kucks-NY .667

Complete Games
- Pierce-Chi 21
- Lemon-Cle 21
- Ford-NY 18
- Kucks-NY 12

Strikeouts
- Score-Cle 263
- Ford-NY 141
- Sturdivant-NY 110
- Larsen-NY 107

Fewest BB/Game
- Stobbs-Was 2.03
- Kucks-NY 2.89
- Sturdivant-NY 2.96
- Ford-NY 3.35

Games
- Zuverink-Bal 62
- Morgan-NY 41
- Larsen-NY 38
- Byrne-NY 37

Saves
- Zuverink-Bal 16
- Morgan-NY 11
- Byrne-NY 6
- 2 players tied 5

Base Runners/9
- Score-Cle 10.58
- Sturdivant-NY 10.80
- Ford-NY 10.97
- Grim-NY 11.69

Adjusted Relief Runs
- Narleski-Cle 17.7
- Grim-NY 9.3
- Byrne-NY 4.9

Relief Ranking
- Narleski-Cle 16.1
- Grim-NY 9.3
- Byrne-NY 4.6

Innings Pitched
- Lary-Det 294.0
- Ford-NY 225.2
- Kucks-NY 224.1
- Larsen-NY 179.2

Opponents' Avg.
- Score-Cle .186
- Larsen-NY .204
- Sturdivant-NY .224
- Ford-NY .228

Opponents' OBP
- Donovan-Chi .290
- Score-Cle .290
- Sturdivant-NY .291
- Ford-NY .301

Earned Run Average
- Ford-NY 2.47
- Larsen-NY 3.26
- Sturdivant-NY 3.30
- Kucks-NY 3.85

Adjusted ERA
- Score-Cle 166
- Ford-NY 156
- Larsen-NY 119
- Sturdivant-NY 117

Adjusted Starter Runs
- Wynn-Cle 46.3
- Ford-NY 37.7
- Larsen-NY 13.9
- Sturdivant-NY 12.1

Pitcher Wins
- Wynn-Cle 5.1
- Ford-NY 4.6
- Sturdivant-NY 2.0
- Larsen-NY 1.7

1957 American League

TEAM	W	L	T	PCT	GB	R	OR	HR	AVG	OBP	SLG	OPS	AOPS	PF	SB	CG	HR	BB	SO	BR/9	ERA	AERA	OAV	OOB	FW	PW	BW	BSW	DIF
NY	98	56	0	.636		**723**	**534**	145	**.268**	.339	**.409**	**748**	**112**	98	49	41	110	580	**810**	11.7	**3.00**	**120**	**.234**	.315	.2	**9.9**	**9.0**	.0	1.8
Chi	90	64	1	.584	8	707	566	106	.260	**.345**	.375	720	102	101	**109**	**59**	124	**470**	665	11.6	3.35	112	.248	.311	**1.1**	6.4	3.9	**.9**	.6
Bos	82	72	0	.532	16	721	668	153	.262	.341	.405	746	104	106	29	55	116	498	692	12.6	3.88	103	.264	.329	-1.2	1.7	4.1	.2	.2
Det	78	76	0	.506	20	614	614	116	.257	.323	.378	701	95	103	36	52	147	505	756	11.9	3.56	108	.250	.318	.3	4.8	-3.5	-.6	.0
Bal	76	76	2	.500	21	597	588	87	.252	.318	.353	671	95	94	57	44	**95**	493	767	**11.5**	3.46	104	.243	**.310**	.8	2.2	-3.0	.3	-.3
Cle	76	77	0	.497	21.5	682	722	140	.252	.329	.382	711	101	99	40	46	130	618	807	13.3	4.06	92	.261	.340	-1.4	-5.6	1.9	-.5	5.1
KC	59	94	1	.386	38.5	563	710	**166**	.244	.295	.394	689	91	102	35	26	153	565	626	12.7	4.19	94	.260	.333	.1	-3.5	-7.5	.1	-6.7
Was	55	99	0	.357	43	603	808	111	.244	.316	.363	679	92	99	13	31	149	580	691	13.7	4.85	80	.278	.349	-.0	-14.7	-5.0	-.7	-1.6
Total	616					35210		1024	.255	.326	.382	708			368	354				12.4	3.79		.255	.326					

Batter-Fielder Wins
Mantle-NY 8.0
McDougald-NY 5.3
Berra-NY 2.3
Skowron-NY 1.4

Batting Average
Williams-Bos .388
Mantle-NY .365
Skowron-NY .304
McDougald-NY .289

On-Base Percentage
Williams-Bos .526
Mantle-NY .512
McDougald-NY .362
Skowron-NY .347

Slugging Average
Williams-Bos .731
Mantle-NY .665
Skowron-NY .470
Bauer-NY .455

On-Base Plus Slugging
Williams-Bos 1257
Mantle-NY 1177
Skowron-NY 818
McDougald-NY 804

Adjusted OPS
Williams-Bos 227
Mantle-NY 223
Skowron-NY 125
McDougald-NY 121

Adjusted Batter Runs
Mantle-NY 94.0
McDougald-NY 15.6
Skowron-NY 13.6
Bauer-NY 5.9

Runs
Mantle-NY 121
McDougald-NY 87
Berra-NY 74
Bauer-NY 70

Hits
Fox-Chi 196
Mantle-NY 173
McDougald-NY 156
Skowron-NY 139

Doubles
Minoso-Chi 36
Gardner-Bal 36
Mantle-NY 28
McDougald-NY 25

Triples
3 players tied 9
McDougald-NY 9
Bauer-NY 9
Mantle-NY 6

Home Runs
Sievers-Was 42
Mantle-NY 34
Berra-NY 24
Bauer-NY 18

Total Bases
Sievers-Was 331
Mantle-NY 315
McDougald-NY 238
Bauer-NY 218

Runs Batted In
Sievers-Was 114
Mantle-NY 94
Skowron-NY 88
Berra-NY 82

Stolen Bases
Aparicio-Chi 28
Mantle-NY 16
Bauer-NY 7
Kubek-NY 6

Base Stealing Runs
Aparicio-Chi 3.4
Mantle-NY 2.5
Bauer-NY .8
DelGreco-NY .2

Fielding Runs-Infield
Bridges-Was 27.7
McDougald-NY 26.4
Skowron-NY 6.4
Kubek-NY 2.5

Fielding Runs-Outfield
Maxwell-Det 10.1

Wins
Pierce-Chi 20
Bunning-Det 20
Sturdivant-NY 16
Turley-NY 13

Winning Pct.
Sturdivant-NY .727

Complete Games
Pierce-Chi 16
Donovan-Chi 16
Turley-NY 9
Shantz-NY 9

Strikeouts
Wynn-Cle 184
Turley-NY 152
Sturdivant-NY 118
Ford-NY 84

Fewest BB/Game
F.Sullivan-Bos 1.80
Shantz-NY 2.08
Kucks-NY 2.96
Sturdivant-NY 3.57

Games
Zuverink-Bal 56
Grim-NY 46
Ditmar-NY 46
Kucks-NY 37

Saves
Grim-NY 19
Ditmar-NY 6
Shantz-NY 5
2 players tied 3

Base Runners/9
O'Dell-Bal 9.68
Shantz-NY 10.56
Turley-NY 10.92
Sturdivant-NY 11.34

Adjusted Relief Runs
Staley-Chi 19.4
Grim-NY 9.1
Ditmar-NY 4.0

Relief Ranking
Zuverink-Bal 19.1
Grim-NY 18.2
Ditmar-NY 3.6

Innings Pitched
Bunning-Det 267.1
Sturdivant-NY 201.2
Kucks-NY 179.1
Turley-NY 176.1

Opponents' Avg.
Turley-NY .194
Sturdivant-NY .232
Shantz-NY .248
Kucks-NY .251

Opponents' OBP
F.Sullivan-Bos .273
Shantz-NY .296
Turley-NY .298
Sturdivant-NY .309

Earned Run Average
Shantz-NY 2.45
Sturdivant-NY 2.54
Turley-NY 2.71
Kucks-NY 3.56

Adjusted ERA
Shantz-NY 147
Sturdivant-NY 141
Turley-NY 133
Kucks-NY 101

Adjusted Starter Runs
F.Sullivan-Bos 34.5
Sturdivant-NY 24.9
Shantz-NY 21.3
Turley-NY 19.1

Pitcher Wins
F.Sullivan-Bos 3.5
Shantz-NY 2.7
Sturdivant-NY 2.6
Grim-NY 2.0

1958 American League

TEAM	W	L	T	PCT	GB	R	OR	HR	AVG	OBP	SLG	OPS	AOPS	PF	SB	CG	HR	BB	SO	BR/9	ERA	AERA	OAV	OOB	FW	PW	BW	BSW	DIF
NY	92	62	1	.597		**759**	577	**164**	**.268**	.336	**.416**	**752**	**116**	96	48	53	116	557	796	11.8	**3.22**	110	**.235**	.313	-.1	5.3	**12.1**	.2	-2.4
Chi	82	72	1	.532	10	634	615	101	.257	.327	.367	694	99	98	**101**	55	152	515	751	11.8	3.61	101	.250	.317	.7	.5	-.1	**1.4**	2.5
Bos	79	75	1	.513	13	697	691	155	.256	**.338**	.400	738	102	107	29	44	121	521	695	12.7	3.92	102	.264	.332	-1.1	1.3	2.9	.2	-1.3
Cle	77	76	0	.503	14.5	694	635	161	.258	.325	.403	728	108	98	50	51	123	604	766	12.5	3.73	98	.249	.328	-1.5	-1.3	5.8	-.4	-2.0
Det	77	77	0	.500	15	659	606	109	.266	.326	.389	715	95	107	48	**59**	133	437	**797**	11.8	3.59	**112**	.252	.314	**1.1**	**6.4**	-2.5	.2	-5.2
Bal	74	79	1	.484	17.5	521	**575**	108	.241	.308	.350	658	91	95	33	55	**106**	**403**	749	**11.3**	3.40	106	.249	**.306**	.6	3.3	-5.7	-.3	-.5
KC	73	81	2	.474	19	642	713	138	.247	.307	.381	688	92	102	22	42	150	467	721	12.2	4.15	94	.262	.323	.1	-3.7	-5.6	-.6	5.8
Was	61	93	2	.396	31	553	747	121	.240	.307	.357	664	90	98	22	28	156	558	762	13.3	4.53	84	.272	.341	.5	-11.2	-7.3	-.8	2.8
Total	619					35159		1057	.254	.322	.383	705			353	387				12.2	3.77		.254	.322					

Batter-Fielder Wins
Mantle-NY 5.5
Berra-NY 2.5
Carey-NY 2.4
Siebern-NY 1.8

Batting Average
Williams-Bos .328
Mantle-NY .304
Siebern-NY .300
Skowron-NY .273

On-Base Percentage
Williams-Bos .458
Mantle-NY .443
Siebern-NY .388
McDougald-NY .329

Slugging Average
Colavito-Cle .620
Mantle-NY .592
Siebern-NY .454
Skowron-NY .424

On-Base Plus Slugging
Williams-Bos 1042
Mantle-NY 1035
Siebern-NY 842
Skowron-NY 740

Adjusted OPS
Mantle-NY 189
Siebern-NY 136
Skowron-NY 107
Bauer-NY 106

Adjusted Batter Runs
Mantle-NY 71.2
Siebern-NY 24.6
Carey-NY 16.4
Howard-NY 14.3

Runs
Mantle-NY 127
Siebern-NY 79
McDougald-NY 69
Kubek-NY 66

Hits
Fox-Chi 187
Mantle-NY 158
Kubek-NY 148
Siebern-NY 138

Doubles
Kuenn-Det 39
Skowron-NY 22
Bauer-NY 22
2 players tied 21

Triples
Power-KC-Cle 10
Bauer-NY 6
Siebern-NY 5
Howard-NY 5

Home Runs
Mantle-NY 42
Berra-NY 22
3 players tied 14

Total Bases
Mantle-NY 307
Siebern-NY 209
Berra-NY 204
Skowron-NY 197

Runs Batted In
Jensen-Bos 122
Mantle-NY 97
Berra-NY 90
Skowron-NY 73

Stolen Bases
Aparicio-Chi 29
Mantle-NY 18
McDougald-NY 6
2 players tied 5

Base Stealing Runs
Aparicio-Chi 4.3
Mantle-NY 2.9
Berra-NY .7
McDougald-NY .6

Fielding Runs-Infield
Kubek-NY 21.2
Carey-NY 7.5
McDougald-NY 2.8

Fielding Runs-Outfield
Kaline-Det 20.4
Siebern-NY 2.5
Howard-NY 1.6
Berra-NY 1.4

Wins
Turley-NY 21
Ford-NY 14
Larsen-NY 9
Ditmar-NY 9

Winning Pct.
Turley-NY .750

Complete Games
3 players tied 19
Turley-NY 19
Ford-NY 15
Larsen-NY 5

Strikeouts
Wynn-Chi 179
Turley-NY 168
Ford-NY 145
Duren-NY 87

Fewest BB/Game
Donovan-Chi 1.92
Ford-NY 2.54
Turley-NY 4.70

Games
Clevenger-Was 55
Duren-NY 44
Ditmar-NY 38
Kucks-NY 34

Saves
Duren-NY 20
Kucks-NY 4
Ditmar-NY 4

Base Runners/9
Wilhelm-Cle-Bal 9.76
Ford-NY 9.81
Duren-NY 10.70
Ditmar-NY 10.76

Adjusted Relief Runs
Hyde-Was 21.3
Duren-NY 13.5

Relief Ranking
Hyde-Was 32.6
Duren-NY 24.1

Innings Pitched
Lary-Det 260.1
Turley-NY 245.1
Ford-NY 219.1
Ditmar-NY 139.2

Opponents' Avg.
Turley-NY .206
Ford-NY .217

Opponents' OBP
Ford-NY .276
Turley-NY .311

Earned Run Average
Ford-NY 2.01
Turley-NY 2.97

Adjusted ERA
Ford-NY 176
Turley-NY 119

Adjusted Starter Runs
Ford-NY 37.4
Turley-NY 22.1
Larsen-NY 7.5
Shantz-NY 4.0

Pitcher Wins
Ford-NY 3.9
Duren-NY 2.6
Turley-NY 2.2
Larsen-NY 1.8

1959 American League

TEAM	W	L	T	PCT	GB	R	OR	HR	AVG	OBP	SLG	OPS	AOPS	PF	SB	CG	HR	BB	SO	BR/9	ERA	AERA	OAV	OOB	FW	PW	BW	BSW	DIF
Chi	94	60	2	.610		669	**588**	97	.250	.327	.364	691	96	99	**113**	44	129	525	761	11.7	**3.29**	**114**	.242	**.311**	.6	**7.7**	-1.0	**.5**	9.2
Cle	89	65	0	.578	5	**745**	646	**167**	**.263**	.321	**.408**	729	**109**	96	33	**58**	148	635	799	12.3	3.75	98	**.239**	.323	.7	-1.0	**6.0**	-.6	7.0
NY	79	75	1	.513	15	687	647	153	.260	.319	.402	721	107	97	45	38	120	594	**836**	12.2	3.60	101	.244	.322	.5	.7	4.2	.0	-3.5
Det	76	78	0	.494	18	713	732	160	.258	**.335**	.400	**735**	102	105	34	53	177	**432**	829	11.9	4.20	97	.254	.315	**.9**	-2.0	2.0	.0	-2.0
Bos	75	79	0	.487	19	726	696	125	.256	**.335**	.385	720	98	105	68	38	135	589	724	13.2	4.17	97	.266	.341	.5	-1.6	.9	**.5**	-2.3
Bal	74	80	1	.481	20	551	621	109	.238	.310	.345	655	87	98	36	45	**111**	476	735	**11.5**	3.56	106	.246	**.311**	-.4	3.5	-8.6	-.1	2.5
KC	66	88	0	.429	28	681	760	117	**.263**	.326	.390	716	100	102	34	44	148	492	703	13.2	4.35	92	.274	.338	-1.2	-5.2	.4	-.2	-4.8
Was	63	91	0	.409	31	619	701	163	.237	.308	.379	687	93	100	51	46	123	467	694	12.3	4.01	98	.259	.321	-1.4	-1.4	-4.3	-.2	-0.7
Total	618					35391		1091	.253	.323	.384	707			414	366				12.3	3.86		.253	.323					

Batter-Fielder Wins
Runnels-Bos 3.9
Mantle-NY 3.6
Berra-NY 3.3
Skowron-NY 1.2

Batting Average
Kuenn-Det .... .353
Richardson-NY ..... .301
Mantle-NY .... .285
Berra-NY .... .284

On-Base Percentage
Yost-Det .... .435
Mantle-NY .... .390
Berra-NY .... .347
Richardson-NY ...... .335

Slugging Average
Kaline-Det .... .530
Mantle-NY .... .514
Berra-NY .... .462
Kubek-NY .... .391

On-Base Plus Slugging
Kaline-Det 940
Mantle-NY 904
Berra-NY 809
Richardson-NY 713

Adjusted OPS
Mantle-NY 152
Berra-NY 125
Richardson-NY 99
Kubek-NY 95

Adjusted Batter Runs
Mantle-NY 40.7
Skowron-NY 15.9
Berra-NY 15.6
Ford-NY 7.1

Runs
Yost-Det 115
Mantle-NY 104
Kubek-NY 67
Berra-NY 64

Hits
Kuenn-Det 198
Mantle-NY 154
Kubek-NY 143
Richardson-NY 141

Doubles
Kuenn-Det 42
Kubek-NY 25
Berra-NY 25
Howard-NY 24

Triples
Allison-Was 9
McDougald-NY 8
Kubek-NY 7
2 players tied 6

Home Runs
Killebrew-Was 42
Colavito-Cle 42
Mantle-NY 31
Berra-NY 19

Total Bases
Colavito-Cle 301
Mantle-NY 278
Berra-NY 218
Howard-NY 211

Runs Batted In
Jensen-Bos 112
Mantle-NY 75
Howard-NY 73
Berra-NY 69

Stolen Bases
Aparicio-Chi 56
Mantle-NY 21
Richardson-NY 5
Bauer-NY 4

Base Stealing Runs
Aparicio-Chi 7.8
Mantle-NY 3.6
Siebern-NY 3

Fielding Runs-Infield
Gardner-Bal 21.8
Kubek-NY 13.3
McDougald-NY 7.3
Siebern-NY 3

Fielding Runs-Outfield
Jensen-Bos 10.5
Berra-NY 0

Wins
Wynn-Chi 22
Ford-NY 16
Maas-NY 14
Ditmar-NY 13

Winning Pct.
Shaw-Chi .... .750
Ford-NY .... .615

Complete Games
Pascual-Was 17
Ford-NY 9
Turley-NY 7
Ditmar-NY 7

Strikeouts
Bunning-Det 201
Ford-NY 114
Turley-NY 111
2 players tied 96

Fewest BB/Game
Brown-Bal 1.76
Ditmar-NY 2.32
Ford-NY 3.93
Turley-NY 4.84

Games
Staley-Chi 67
Duren-NY 41
Maas-NY 38
Ditmar-NY 38

Saves
Lown-Chi 15
Duren-NY 14
Maas-NY 4
2 players tied 3

Base Runners/9
Shantz-NY 9.22
Ditmar-NY 9.62
Duren-NY 11.15
Coates-NY 11.48

Adjusted Relief Runs
Staley-Chi 17.2
Duren-NY 16.2
Shantz-NY 12.2
Coates-NY 8.2

Relief Ranking
Duren-NY 23.7
Shantz-NY 12.5
Coates-NY 5.7

Innings Pitched
Wynn-Chi 255.2
Ford-NY 204.0
Ditmar-NY 202.0
Turley-NY 154.1

Opponents' Avg.
Score-Cle .... .210
Ditmar-NY .... .211
Turley-NY .... .245
Ford-NY .... .250

Opponents' OBP
Ditmar-NY .... .268
Ford-NY .... .327
Turley-NY .... .338

Earned Run Average
Wilhelm-Bal 2.19
Ditmar-NY 2.90
Ford-NY 3.04
Turley-NY 4.32

Adjusted ERA
Wilhelm-Bal 173
Ditmar-NY 126
Ford-NY 120
Turley-NY 84

Adjusted Starter Runs
Wilhelm-Bal 39.8
Ditmar-NY 17.9
Ford-NY 13.4
Gabler-NY 2.4

Pitcher Wins
Pascual-Was 4.7
Ford-NY 2.6
Duren-NY 2.4
Ditmar-NY 1.9

1960 American League

TEAM	W	L	T	PCT	GB	R	OR	HR	AVG	OBP	SLG	OPS	AOPS	PF	SB	CG	HR	BB	SO	BR/9	ERA	AERA	OAV	OOB	FW	PW	BW	BSW	DIF
NY	97	57	1	.630		**746**	627	**193**	.260	.329	**.426**	**755**	**115**	94	37	38	123	609	712	12.0	**3.52**	102	**.238**	.320	.2	1.1	**10.7**	-.1	8.1
Bal	89	65	0	.578	8	682	**606**	123	.253	.332	.377	709	99	99	37	**48**	**117**	552	785	**11.8**	**3.52**	108	.241	.317	**1.4**	4.6	.2	-.1	6.0
Chi	87	67	0	.565	10	741	617	112	**.270**	**.345**	.396	741	107	99	**122**	42	127	533	695	12.3	3.60	105	.258	.326	**1.4**	2.8	6.8	**.9**	-1.8
Cle	76	78	0	.494	21	667	693	127	.267	.325	.388	713	101	97	58	32	161	636	771	12.8	3.95	95	.252	.334	.2	-3.4	.9	.3	1.1
Was	73	81	0	.474	24	672	696	147	.244	.324	.384	708	98	99	52	34	130	538	775	12.6	3.77	103	.260	.329	-2.1	1.8	-1.2	-.5	-1.9
Det	71	83	0	.461	26	633	644	150	.239	.324	.375	699	93	103	66	40	141	**474**	**824**	11.9	3.64	**109**	.251	**.316**	-.5	**5.0**	-5.0	.2	-5.7
Bos	65	89	0	.422	32	658	775	124	.261	.333	.389	722	98	104	34	34	127	580	767	13.6	4.62	87	.273	.346	-.6	-8.5	-.5	-.3	-2.0
KC	58	96	1	.377	39	615	756	110	.249	.316	.366	682	89	101	16	44	160	525	664	13.1	4.38	91	.271	.339	.3	-6.0	-7.5	-.1	-5.7
Total	617					35414		1086	.255	.328	.388	716			422	312				12.5	3.87		.255	.328					

Batter-Fielder Wins
Aparicio-Chi 3.9
Maris-NY 3.7
Mantle-NY 3.6
Skowron-NY 3.1

Batting Average
Runnels-Bos .... .320
Skowron-NY .... .309
Maris-NY .... .283
Mantle-NY .... .275

On-Base Percentage
Yost-Det .... .414
Mantle-NY .... .399
Maris-NY .... .371
Skowron-NY .... .353

Slugging Average
Maris-NY .... .581
Mantle-NY .... .558
Skowron-NY .... .528
Kubek-NY .... .401

On-Base Plus Slugging
Mantle-NY 957
Maris-NY 952
Skowron-NY 881
Kubek-NY 713

Adjusted OPS
Mantle-NY 166
Maris-NY 164
Skowron-NY 144
Kubek-NY 97

Adjusted Batter Runs
Mantle-NY 51.4
Maris-NY 42.4
Skowron-NY 30.5
Berra-NY 9.7

Runs
Mantle-NY 119
Maris-NY 98
Kubek-NY 77
Lopez-NY 66

Hits
Minoso-Chi 184
Skowron-NY 166
Kubek-NY 155
Mantle-NY 145

Doubles
Francona-Cle 36
Skowron-NY 34
Kubek-NY 25
Boyer-NY 20

Triples
Fox-Chi 10
Maris-NY 7
Mantle-NY 6
Lopez-NY 6

Home Runs
Mantle-NY 40
Maris-NY 39
Skowron-NY 26
Berra-NY 15

Total Bases
Mantle-NY 294
Maris-NY 290
Skowron-NY 284
Kubek-NY 228

Runs Batted In
Maris-NY 112
Mantle-NY 94
Skowron-NY 91
2 players tied 62

Stolen Bases
Aparicio-Chi 51
Mantle-NY 14
Richardson-NY 6
2 players tied 3

Base Stealing Runs
Aparicio-Chi 8.4
Mantle-NY 2.0
Kubek-NY 7
Howard-NY 7

Fielding Runs-Infield
Aparicio-Chi 33.5
Boyer-NY 24.0
McDougald-NY 12.3
Skowron-NY 9.5

Fielding Runs-Outfield
Piersall-Cle 8.6
Lopez-NY 3.5

Wins
Perry-Cle 18
Estrada-Bal 18
Ditmar-NY 15
Coates-NY 13

Winning Pct.
Perry-Cle .... .643
Ditmar-NY .... .625

Complete Games
Lary-Det 15
Ford-NY 8
Ditmar-NY 8
Terry-NY 7

Strikeouts
Bunning-Det 201
Terry-NY 92
Turley-NY 87
Ford-NY 85

Fewest BB/Game
Brown-Bal 1.25
Ditmar-NY 2.52
Terry-NY 2.81
Ford-NY 3.04

Games
Fornieles-Bos 70
B.Shantz-NY 42
Duren-NY 42
3 players tied 35

Saves
Klippstein-Cle 14
Fornieles-Bos 14
B.Shantz-NY 11
Duren-NY 9

Base Runners/9
Staley-Chi 9.52
Stafford-NY 10.35
Ford-NY 10.93
B.Shantz-NY 11.04

Adjusted Relief Runs
Staley-Chi 15.4
B.Shantz-NY 6.5

Relief Ranking
Staley-Chi 28.2
B.Shantz-NY 10.1

Innings Pitched
Lary-Det 274.1
Ditmar-NY 200.0
Ford-NY 192.2
Turley-NY 173.1

Opponents' Avg.
Estrada-Bal .... .218
Turley-NY .... .222
Ford-NY .... .235
Terry-NY .... .237

Opponents' OBP
Brown-Bal .... .283
Ford-NY .... .297
Terry-NY .... .299
Ditmar-NY .... .308

Earned Run Average
Baumann-Chi 2.67
Ditmar-NY 3.06
Ford-NY 3.08
Turley-NY 3.27

Adjusted ERA
Bunning-Det 142
Ditmar-NY 117
Ford-NY 116
Turley-NY 109

Adjusted Starter Runs
Bunning-Det 30.6
Ditmar-NY 13.0
Ford-NY 11.4
Stafford-NY 9.7

Pitcher Wins
Staley-Chi 3.2
Ford-NY 1.5
Ditmar-NY 1.4
B.Shantz-NY 1.0

1961 American League

TEAM	W	L	T	PCT	GB	R	OR	HR	AVG	OBP	SLG	OPS	AOPS	PF	SB	CG	HR	BB	SO	BR/9	ERA	AERA	OAV	OOB	FW	PW	BW	BSW	DIF
NY	109	53	1	.673		827	612	**240**	.263	.330	**.442**	**772**	**118**	95	28	47	137	542	866	**11.5**	3.46	107	.239	.311	**1.6**	4.5	**12.3**	-.2	9.8
Det	101	61	1	.623	8	**841**	671	180	**.266**	**.347**	.421	768	108	103	98	**62**	170	**469**	836	11.7	3.55	116	.252	.311	.3	8.7	7.2	**.7**	3.0
Bal	95	67	1	.586	14	691	**588**	149	.254	.326	.390	716	101	97	39	54	**109**	617	926	**11.5**	**3.22**	**120**	**.227**	**.308**	1.4	**10.7**	1.0	-.4	1.3
Chi	86	76	1	.531	23	765	726	138	.265	.335	.395	730	103	98	**100**	39	158	498	814	12.4	4.06	97	.268	.326	1.4	-2.3	2.8	.6	2.5
Cle	78	83	0	.484	30.5	737	752	150	**.266**	.326	.406	732	104	97	34	35	178	599	801	12.8	4.15	95	.258	.331	.6	-3.4	3.0	.2	-2.9
Bos	76	86	1	.469	33	729	792	112	.254	.334	.374	708	94	102	56	35	167	679	831	13.5	4.29	97	.266	.345	.4	-1.9	-3.6	-.2	.2
Min	70	90	1	.438	38	707	778	167	.250	.326	.397	723	94	106	47	49	163	570	914	12.8	4.28	99	.256	.329	-1.4	-.6	-4.3	-.7	-3.0
LA	70	91	1	.435	38.5	744	784	189	.245	.331	.398	729	91	111	37	25	180	713	**973**	13.4	4.31	105	.254	.341	-2.4	2.8	-6.0	-.4	-4.4
Was	61	100	0	.379	47.5	618	776	119	.244	.315	.367	682	89	99	81	39	131	586	666	12.8	4.23	95	.260	.333	-.4	-3.4	-7.3	-.0	-8.3
KC	61	100	1	.379	47.5	683	863	90	.247	.320	.354	674	84	102	58	32	141	629	703	14.0	4.74	88	.275	.351	-1.4	-8.4	-10.1	.3	.2
Total	811					47342		1534	.256	.329	.395	724			578	417				12.6	4.02		.256	.329					

Batter-Fielder Wins
Cash-Det............... 7.6
Mantle-NY............. 7.5
Howard-NY........... 4.5
Maris-NY............... 3.1

Batting Average
Cash-Det.............. .361
Mantle-NY............ .317
Kubek-NY............. .276
Maris-NY............... .269

On-Base Percentage
Cash-Det.............. .487
Mantle-NY............ .448
Maris-NY............... .372
Skowron-NY......... .318

Slugging Average
Mantle-NY............ .687
Maris-NY............... .620
Skowron-NY......... .472
Kubek-NY............. .395

On-Base Plus Slugging
Cash-Det.............1148
Mantle-NY............1135
Maris-NY............... 993
Skowron-NY......... 790

Adjusted OPS
Mantle-NY............. 210
Maris-NY.............. 170
Skowron-NY...........115
Kubek-NY............... 91

Adjusted Batter Runs
Mantle-NY............ 85.6
Maris-NY.............. 56.8
Howard-NY........... 33.1
Blanchard-NY....... 23.4

Runs
Maris-NY............... 132
Mantle-NY............. 132
Kubek-NY............... 84
Richardson-NY........ 80

Hits
Cash-Det............... 193
Richardson-NY...... 173
Kubek-NY............. 170
Mantle-NY............. 163

Doubles
Kaline-Det............... 41
Kubek-NY................ 38
Skowron-NY........... 23
Boyer-NY................. 19

Triples
Wood-Det............... 14
Mantle-NY................. 6
Kubek-NY.................. 6
3 players tied............ 5

Home Runs
Maris-NY................. 61
Mantle-NY............... 54
Skowron-NY........... 28
Berra-NY................. 22

Total Bases
Maris-NY............... 366
Mantle-NY............. 353
Skowron-NY.......... 265
Howard-NY........... 245

Runs Batted In
Maris-NY............... 142
Mantle-NY............. 128
Skowron-NY........... 89
Howard-NY............. 77

Stolen Bases
Aparicio-Chi............ 53
Mantle-NY............... 12
Richardson-NY......... 9
Berra-NY................... 2

Base Stealing Runs
Aparicio-Chi........... 7.1
Mantle-NY.............. 2.3
Berra-NY.................... .4
2 players tied............ .2

Fielding Runs-Infield
Boyer-NY............. 28.5
Kubek-NY............ 17.9
Skowron-NY........... 1.1

Fielding Runs-Outfield
Kaline-Det............ 13.5

Wins
Ford-NY.................. 25
Terry-NY................. 16
Arroyo-NY............... 15
Stafford-NY............. 14

Winning Pct.
Ford-NY............... .862
Terry-NY............... .842
Arroyo-NY............ .750

Complete Games
Lary-Det.................. 22
Ford-NY...................11
Terry-NY..................... 9
Stafford-NY.............. 8

Strikeouts
Pascual-Min.......... 221
Ford-NY................ 209
Stafford-NY........... 101
Arroyo-NY............... 87

Fewest BB/Game
Mossi-Det............ 1.76
Terry-NY.............. 2.01
Stafford-NY.......... 2.72
Ford-NY............... 2.93

Games
Arroyo-NY............... 65
Coates-NY.............. 43
Ford-NY.................. 39
Stafford-NY............. 36

Saves
Arroyo-NY............... 29
Coates-NY................ 5
Stafford-NY............... 2
Reniff-NY................... 2

Base Runners/9
Donovan-Was....... 9.39
Terry-NY.............. 9.80
Arroyo-NY.......... 10.21
Ford-NY............. 10.65

Adjusted Relief Runs
Arroyo-NY............ 20.7

Relief Ranking
Arroyo-NY............ 41.5

Innings Pitched
Ford-NY............. 283.0
Stafford-NY......... 195.0
Terry-NY............ 188.1
Sheldon-NY........ 162.2

Opponents' Avg.
Estrada-Bal........... .207
Ford-NY................ .229
Stafford-NY........... .232
Terry-NY............... .232

Opponents' OBP
Donovan-Was....... .267
Terry-NY.............. .275
Ford-NY................ .291
Stafford-NY.......... .294

Earned Run Average
Donovan-Was....... 2.40
Stafford-NY.......... 2.68
Terry-NY.............. 3.15
Ford-NY............... 3.21

Adjusted ERA
Donovan-Was........ 167
Stafford-NY........... 139
Terry-NY.................118
Ford-NY..................116

Adjusted Starter Runs
Hoeft-Bal.............. 28.2
Stafford-NY.......... 23.7
Ford-NY............... 18.6
Terry-NY.............. 12.0

Pitcher Wins
Arroyo-NY.............. 4.4
Stafford-NY............ 2.8
Ford-NY................. 2.1
Terry-NY................ 1.3

1962 American League

TEAM	W	L	T	PCT	GB	R	OR	HR	AVG	OBP	SLG	OPS	AOPS	PF	SB	CG	HR	BB	SO	BR/9	ERA	AERA	OAV	OOB	FW	PW	BW	BSW	DIF
NY	96	66	0	.593		**817**	680	199	**.267**	.337	**.426**	**763**	**115**	97	42	33	146	499	838	**11.6**	3.70	101	**.247**	**.310**	.4	.8	**11.7**	-.3	2.5
Min	91	71	1	.562	5	798	713	185	.260	**.338**	.412	750	104	104	33	**53**	166	**493**	**948**	11.9	3.89	105	.253	.317	.5	3.0	3.9	-.2	2.8
LA	86	76	0	.531	10	718	706	137	.250	.325	.380	705	99	97	46	23	**118**	616	858	12.8	3.70	104	.253	.330	-2.2	2.7	.1	-.1	4.5
Det	85	76	0	.528	10.5	758	692	**209**	.248	.330	.411	741	101	104	69	46	169	503	873	12.4	3.81	**107**	.259	.321	-1.1	**4.1**	1.5	.6	-.6
Chi	85	77	0	.525	11	707	**658**	92	.257	.334	.372	706	96	100	76	50	123	537	821	12.0	3.73	105	.251	.317	**1.6**	2.9	-.7	.0	.1
Cle	80	82	0	.494	16	682	745	180	.245	.312	.388	700	97	97	35	45	174	594	780	12.7	4.14	94	.258	.331	-.1	-4.4	-2.7	-.0	6.2
Bal	77	85	0	.475	19	652	680	156	.248	.314	.387	701	100	94	45	32	147	549	898	12.0	**3.69**	100	.249	.318	.9	.1	.2	-.3	-4.9
Bos	76	84	0	.475	19	707	756	146	.258	.324	.403	727	98	103	39	34	159	632	923	13.1	4.22	98	.258	.337	.3	-1.4	-1.2	-.5	-1.1
KC	72	90	0	.444	24	745	837	116	.263	.332	.386	718	95	105	76	32	199	655	825	13.5	4.79	88	.263	.343	.3	-8.5	-3.1	**.7**	1.7
Was	60	101	1	.373	35.5	599	716	132	.250	.308	.373	681	90	99	**99**	38	151	593	771	12.5	4.04	100	.256	.328	-.1	-.1	-8.0	.0	-12.3
Total	809					47183		1552	.255	.325	.394	719			560	386				12.4	3.97		.255	.325					

Batter-Fielder Wins
Mantle-NY............. 5.0
Boyer-NY.............. 3.6
Howard-NY........... 2.2
Kubek-NY............. 1.4

Batting Average
Runnels-Bos......... .326
Mantle-NY............ .321
Richardson-NY...... .302
Tresh-NY............. .286

On-Base Percentage
Mantle-NY............ .486
Tresh-NY.............. .359
Maris-NY............... .356
Richardson-NY...... .337

Slugging Average
Mantle-NY............ .605
Maris-NY............... .485
Howard-NY........... .474
Skowron-NY......... .473

On-Base Plus Slugging
Mantle-NY........... 1091
Maris-NY............... 840
Tresh-NY............... 800
Skowron-NY.......... 798

Adjusted OPS
Mantle-NY............. 198
Maris-NY.............. 128
Tresh-NY................119
Skowron-NY...........116

Adjusted Batter Runs
Mantle-NY............ 62.9
Maris-NY.............. 24.8
Tresh-NY.............. 17.0
Skowron-NY........... 8.2

Runs
Pearson-LA.............115
Richardson-NY........ 99
Mantle-NY............... 96
Tresh-NY................ 94

Hits
Richardson-NY...... 209
Tresh-NY.............. 178
Boyer-NY.............. 154
Maris-NY............... 151

Doubles
Robinson-Chi.......... 45
Richardson-NY........ 38
Maris-NY................. 34
Tresh-NY................. 26

Triples
Cimoli-KC................ 15
Skowron-NY............. 6
3 players tied............ 5

Home Runs
Killebrew-Min.......... 48
Maris-NY................. 33
Mantle-NY............... 30
Skowron-NY........... 23

Total Bases
Colavito-Det.......... 309
Maris-NY.............. 286
Richardson-NY...... 281
Tresh-NY.............. 274

Runs Batted In
Killebrew-Min......... 126
Maris-NY............... 100
Tresh-NY................. 93
Howard-NY............. 91

Stolen Bases
Aparicio-Chi............ 31
Richardson-NY.........11
Mantle-NY................. 9
Linz-NY..................... 6

Base Stealing Runs
Wood-Det............... 4.2
Mantle-NY.............. 2.0
Linz-NY...................... .6
2 players tied............ .2

Fielding Runs-Infield
Versalles-Min........ 34.9
Boyer-NY............. 34.3

Fielding Runs-Outfield
Colavito-Det......... 12.4

Wins
Terry-NY.................. 23
Ford-NY................... 17
Stafford-NY............. 14
Bridges-NY............... 8

Winning Pct.
Herbert-Chi........... .690
Ford-NY............... .680
Terry-NY.............. .657

Complete Games
Pascual-Min............ 18
Terry-NY.................. 14
Stafford-NY.............. 7
Ford-NY..................... 7

Strikeouts
Pascual-Min.......... 206
Terry-NY............... 176
Ford-NY................ 160
Stafford-NY........... 109

Fewest BB/Game
Donovan-Cle......... 1.69
Terry-NY.............. 1.72
Ford-NY............... 2.41
Stafford-NY.......... 3.25

Games
Radatz-Bos............. 62
Bridges-NY............. 52
Coates-NY.............. 50
2 players tied.......... 43

Saves
Radatz-Bos............. 24
Bridges-NY............. 18
Arroyo-NY................. 7
Coates-NY................. 6

Base Runners/9
Hall-Bal................. 9.20
Terry-NY.............. 9.55
Ford-NY..............11.04
Daley-NY.............11.19

Adjusted Relief Runs
Radatz-Bos.......... 26.4
Bridges-NY............ 4.2
Daley-NY................ 2.1

Relief Ranking
Radatz-Bos.......... 39.8
Bridges-NY............ 8.5
Daley-NY................ 2.3

Innings Pitched
Terry-NY............ 298.2
Ford-NY.............. 257.2
Stafford-NY........ 213.1
Bouton-NY.......... 133.0

Opponents' Avg.
Aguirre-Det........... .205
Terry-NY............... .231
Stafford-NY........... .233
Ford-NY................ .246

Opponents' OBP
Aguirre-Det........... .267
Terry-NY............... .268
Ford-NY................ .296
Stafford-NY........... .301

Earned Run Average
Aguirre-Det.......... 2.21
Ford-NY............... 2.90
Terry-NY.............. 3.19
Stafford-NY.......... 3.67

Adjusted ERA
Aguirre-Det........... 184
Ford-NY................ 129
Terry-NY.................117
Stafford-NY........... 102

Adjusted Starter Runs
Aguirre-Det.......... 40.6
Ford-NY............... 27.3
Terry-NY.............. 17.6
Stafford-NY............ 3.3

Pitcher Wins
Radatz-Bos............. 3.9
Ford-NY.................. 2.7
Terry-NY................. 1.8
Bridges-NY................ .8

1963 American League

TEAM	W	L	T	PCT	GB	R	OR	HR	AVG	OBP	SLG	OPS	AOPS	PF	SB	CG	HR	BB	SO	BR/9	ERA	AERA	OAV	OOB	FW	PW	BW	BSW	DIF
NY	104	57	0	.646		714	547	188	.252	.309	.403	712	105	99	42	**59**	115	476	965	**10.8**	3.07	114	**.232**	**.295**	1.4	7.7	3.3	-.3	11.5
Chi	94	68	0	.580	10.5	683	**544**	114	.250	.323	.365	688	101	98	64	49	**100**	**440**	932	10.9	**2.97**	**118**	.239	.297	.3	**9.5**	1.8	.1	1.4
Min	91	70	0	.565	13	**767**	602	**225**	**.255**	.325	**.430**	**755**	**115**	102	32	58	162	459	941	11.2	3.28	111	.242	.302	-.5	6.1	**10.8**	-.0	-5.8
Bal	86	76	0	.531	18.5	644	621	146	.249	.310	.380	690	103	96	**97**	35	137	507	913	11.7	3.45	101	.248	.314	**2.1**	.4	1.9	**.7**	-.0
Det	79	83	0	.488	25.5	700	703	148	.252	**.327**	.382	709	102	103	73	42	195	477	930	11.9	3.90	96	.253	.315	1.3	-2.6	2.2	.2	-3.1
Cle	79	83	0	.488	25.5	635	702	169	.239	.301	.381	682	97	99	59	40	176	478	**1018**	11.6	3.79	95	.249	.309	-.4	-2.9	-2.1	-.3	3.7
Bos	76	85	0	.472	28	666	704	171	.252	.312	.400	712	102	103	27	29	152	539	1009	12.0	3.97	95	.248	.316	-.0	-3.0	1.3	-.3	-2.4
KC	73	89	0	.451	31.5	615	704	95	.247	.313	.353	666	88	106	47	35	156	540	887	12.4	3.92	100	.256	.324	.5	-.3	-7.7	-.2	-.3
LA	70	91	0	.435	34	597	660	95	.250	.309	.354	663	97	94	43	30	120	578	889	12.0	3.52	97	.242	.318	-1.0	-1.0	1.7	.1	6.0
Was	56	106	0	.346	48.5	578	812	138	.227	.293	.351	644	86	100	68	29	176	537	744	12.8	4.42	84	.266	.331	-2.6	-11.7	-10.1	.2	-.9
Total	808					46599		1489	.247	.312	.380	692			552	406				11.7	3.63		.247	.312					

Batter-Fielder Wins
- **Yastrzemski-Bos... 4.2**
- **Howard-NY 3.4**
- **Mantle-NY 2.2**
- **Tresh-NY 2.0**

Batting Average
- Yastrzemski-Bos... .321
- Howard-NY .... .287
- Pepitone-NY .... .271
- Tresh-NY .... .269

On-Base Percentage
- Yastrzemski-Bos.... .418
- Tresh-NY .... .371
- Howard-NY .... .342
- Pepitone-NY .... .304

Slugging Average
- Killebrew-Min .... .555
- Howard-NY .... .528
- Tresh-NY .... .487
- Pepitone-NY .... .448

On-Base Plus Slugging
- Allison-Min 911
- Howard-NY 869
- Tresh-NY 857
- Pepitone-NY 752

Adjusted OPS
- Allison-Min 150
- Howard-NY 141
- Tresh-NY 140
- Pepitone-NY 109

Adjusted Batter Runs
- Yastrzemski-Bos... 40.7
- Tresh-NY 30.6
- Howard-NY 24.0
- Mantle-NY............. 24.5

Runs
- Allison-Min 99
- Tresh-NY 91
- Pepitone-NY 79
- Howard-NY 75

Hits
- Yastrzemski-Bos.... 183
- Richardson-NY 167
- Pepitone-NY 157
- Kubek-NY 143

Doubles
- Yastrzemski-Bos...... 40
- Tresh-NY 28
- Kubek-NY 21
- Howard-NY 21

Triples
- Versalles-Min 13
- Richardson-NY 6
- Howard-NY 6
- Tresh-NY 5

Home Runs
- Killebrew-Min 45
- Howard-NY 28
- Pepitone-NY 27
- Tresh-NY 25

Total Bases
- Stuart-Bos 319
- Pepitone-NY 260
- Howard-NY 257
- Tresh-NY 253

Runs Batted In
- Stuart-Bos...............118
- Pepitone-NY 89
- Howard-NY 85
- Tresh-NY 71

Stolen Bases
- Aparicio-Bal 40
- Richardson-NY 15
- Reed-NY 5
- 2 players tied 4

Base Stealing Runs
- Aparicio-Bal 6.7
- Richardson-NY 3.0
- Reed-NY 8
- 2 players tied 2

Fielding Runs-Infield
- Hansen-Chi.......... 27.5
- Boyer-NY 21.9
- Richardson-NY 12.9
- Kubek-NY 8.4

Fielding Runs-Outfield
- Hall-Min 10.5

Wins
- Ford-NY 24
- Bouton-NY 21
- Terry-NY 17
- Downing-NY 13

Winning Pct.
- Ford-NY .... .774
- Bouton-NY .... .750
- Terry-NY .... .531

Complete Games
- Terry-NY 18
- Ford-NY 13
- Bouton-NY 12
- Downing-NY 10

Strikeouts
- Pascual-Min 202
- Ford-NY 189
- Downing-NY 171
- Bouton-NY 148

Fewest BB/Game
- Donovan-Cle 1.22
- Terry-NY 1.31
- Ford-NY 1.87
- Bouton-NY 3.14

Games
- S.Miller-Bal 71
- Reniff-NY 48
- Terry-NY 40
- Bouton-NY 40

Saves
- S.Miller-Bal 27
- Reniff-NY 18
- Stafford-NY 3

Base Runners/9
- Dailey-Min............. 8.20
- Terry-NY 9.71
- Downing-NY 9.94
- Ford-NY 9.96

Adjusted Relief Runs
- Radatz-Bos 26.0
- Reniff-NY 8.1

Relief Ranking
- Radatz-Bos 48.1
- Reniff-NY 9.4

Innings Pitched
- Ford-NY 269.1
- Terry-NY 268.0
- Bouton-NY 249.1
- Downing-NY 175.2

Opponents' Avg.
- Downing-NY .... .184
- Bouton-NY .... .212
- Ford-NY .... .241
- Terry-NY .... .242

Opponents' OBP
- Terry-NY .... .271
- Downing-NY .... .277
- Ford-NY .... .281
- Bouton-NY .... .282

Earned Run Average
- Peters-Chi............ 2.33
- Bouton-NY 2.53
- Downing-NY 2.56
- Ford-NY 2.74

Adjusted ERA
- Peters-Chi............. 150
- Bouton-NY 139
- Downing-NY 137
- Ford-NY 128

Adjusted Starter Runs
- Peters-Chi............ 33.6
- Bouton-NY 27.5
- Ford-NY 22.3
- Downing-NY 20.7

Pitcher Wins
- Radatz-Bos............ 5.0
- Ford-NY 2.5
- Bouton-NY 2.3
- Downing-NY 1.8

1964 American League

TEAM	W	L	T	PCT	GB	R	OR	HR	AVG	OBP	SLG	OPS	AOPS	PF	SB	CG	HR	BB	SO	BR/9	ERA	AERA	OAV	OOB	FW	PW	BW	BSW	DIF
NY	99	63	2	.611		730	577	162	.253	.317	.387	704	100	102	54	46	129	504	989	11.0	3.15	115	.234	.299	1.1	8.2	.1	**.5**	8.1
Chi	98	64	0	.605	1	642	**501**	106	.247	.320	.353	673	97	97	75	44	124	**401**	955	**10.1**	**2.72**	**127**	**.226**	**.282**	.2	**13.1**	-1.6	.2	5.0
Bal	97	65	1	.599	2	679	567	162	.248	.316	.387	703	101	100	78	44	129	456	939	11.0	3.16	113	.239	.300	**1.9**	7.2	2.1	.3	4.6
Det	85	77	1	.525	14	699	678	157	.253	.319	.395	714	102	102	60	35	164	536	993	12.0	3.84	95	.244	.316	1.0	-3.0	2.4	.3	3.4
LA	82	80	0	.506	17	544	551	102	.242	.304	.344	648	95	90	49	30	**100**	530	965	11.5	2.91	113	.236	.309	-.7	7.0	-3.3	-.5	-1.6
Min	79	83	1	.488	20	**737**	678	**221**	.252	**.322**	**.427**	**749**	**113**	101	46	**47**	181	545	1099	11.8	3.58	100	.243	.312	-1.1	.1	**9.9**	.0	-11.0
Cle	79	83	2	.488	20	689	693	164	.247	.312	.380	692	99	99	**79**	37	154	565	**1162**	12.3	3.75	96	.255	.324	.6	-2.6	-.3	-.1	.5
Bos	72	90	0	.444	27	688	793	186	**.258**	**.322**	.416	738	106	105	18	21	178	571	1094	13.1	4.50	86	.266	.336	-.7	-10.0	4.7	-.4	-2.7
Was	62	100	0	.383	37	578	733	125	.231	.299	.348	647	86	100	47	27	172	505	794	12.2	3.98	93	.259	.322	-.0	-4.6	-9.7	-.1	-4.5
KC	57	105	1	.352	42	621	836	166	.239	.311	.379	690	95	103	34	18	220	614	966	13.5	4.71	81	.269	.344	-1.9	-14.3	-3.4	-.1	-4.3
Total	814					46607		1551	.247	.315	.382	696			540	349				11.8	3.63		.247	.315					

Batter-Fielder Wins
- **Fregosi-LA............. 5.6**
- **Howard-NY 4.2**
- **Mantle-NY............. 3.4**
- **Linz-NY 9**

Batting Average
- Oliva-Min .... .323
- Howard-NY .... .313
- Mantle-NY............. .303
- Maris-NY............... .281

On-Base Percentage
- Mantle-NY............. .423
- Howard-NY .... .371
- Maris-NY............... .364
- Tresh-NY .... .342

Slugging Average
- Powell-Bal............. .606
- Mantle-NY............. .591
- Maris-NY............... .464
- Howard-NY .... .455

On-Base Plus Slugging
- Mantle-NY........... 1015
- Maris-NY............... 828
- Howard-NY 825
- Tresh-NY 743

Adjusted OPS
- Mantle-NY............. 177
- Howard-NY 127
- Maris-NY............... 127
- Tresh-NY 105

Adjusted Batter Runs
- Mantle-NY............ 52.9
- Howard-NY 20.8
- Maris-NY.............. 19.1
- Tresh-NY 5.5

Runs
- Oliva-Min 109
- Mantle-NY................ 92
- Richardson-NY 90
- Maris-NY.................. 86

Hits
- Oliva-Min 217
- Richardson-NY 181
- Howard-NY 172
- Pepitone-NY 154

Doubles
- Oliva-Min 43
- Howard-NY 27
- 3 players tied 25

Triples
- Versalles-Min 10
- Rollins-Min............... 10
- Tresh-NY 5
- Boyer-NY 5

Home Runs
- Killebrew-Min 49
- Mantle-NY................ 35
- Pepitone-NY 28
- Maris-NY.................. 26

Total Bases
- Oliva-Min 374
- Mantle-NY............. 275
- Pepitone-NY 256
- Howard-NY 250

Runs Batted In
- B.Robinson-Bal.......118
- Mantle-NY...............111
- Pepitone-NY 100
- Howard-NY 84

Stolen Bases
- Aparicio-Bal 57
- Tresh-NY 13
- Richardson-NY 11
- 2 players tied 6

Base Stealing Runs
- Aparicio-Bal 6.6
- Tresh-NY 2.9
- Richardson-NY 1.7
- Boyer-NY 1.0

Fielding Runs-Infield
- Knoop-LA............. 37.9
- Boyer-NY 8.3
- Pepitone-NY 7.1

Fielding Runs-Outfield
- Yastrzemski-Bos... 19.5

Wins
- Peters-Chi................ 20
- Chance-LA............... 20
- Bouton-NY 18
- Ford-NY 17

Winning Pct.
- Bunker-Bal............ .792
- Ford-NY .... .739
- Bouton-NY .... .581

Complete Games
- Chance-LA............... 15
- Ford-NY 12
- Downing-NY 11
- Bouton-NY 11

Strikeouts
- Downing-NY 217
- Ford-NY 172
- Bouton-NY 125
- Terry-NY 77

Fewest BB/Game
- Monbouquette-Bos 1.54
- Bouton-NY 1.99
- Ford-NY 2.10
- Downing-NY 4.43

Games
- Wyatt-KC 81
- Mikkelsen-NY 50
- Reniff-NY 41
- Ford-NY 39

Saves
- Radatz-Bos.............. 29
- Mikkelsen-NY 12
- Reniff-NY 9
- 2 players tied 4

Base Runners/9
- Hall-Bal 7.60
- Bouton-NY 9.72
- Sheldon-NY 9.76
- Ford-NY 9.97

Adjusted Relief Runs
- B.Lee-LA............... 27.9
- Stafford-NY 6.7
- Reniff-NY 4.0
- Hamilton-NY 2.3

Relief Ranking
- Radatz-Bos 46.7
- Reniff-NY 6.2
- Stafford-NY 5.9
- Hamilton-NY 3.3

Innings Pitched
- Chance-LA.......... 278.1
- Bouton-NY 271.1
- Ford-NY 244.2
- Downing-NY 244.0

Opponents' Avg.
- Horlen-Chi .... .190
- Downing-NY .... .223
- Bouton-NY .... .225
- Ford-NY .... .230

Opponents' OBP
- Horlen-Chi .... .248
- Bouton-NY .... .272
- Ford-NY .... .276
- Downing-NY .... .312

Earned Run Average
- Chance-LA............ 1.65
- Ford-NY 2.13
- Bouton-NY 3.02
- Downing-NY 3.47

Adjusted ERA
- Chance-LA............. 199
- Ford-NY 170
- Bouton-NY 120
- Downing-NY 104

Adjusted Starter Runs
- Chance-LA............ 57.7
- Ford-NY 38.8
- Bouton-NY 17.9
- Stottlemyre-NY 15.8

Pitcher Wins
- Chance-LA.............. 5.6
- Ford-NY 3.9
- Stottlemyre-NY 2.3
- Bouton-NY 1.4

1965 American League

TEAM	W	L	T	PCT	GB	R	OR	HR	AVG	OBP	SLG	OPS	AOPS	PF	SB	CG	HR	BB	SO	BR/9	ERA	AERA	OAV	OOB	FW	PW	BW	BSW	DIF
Min	102	60	0	.630		**774**	600	150	**.254**	.324	.399	723	**107**	104	92	32	166	503	934	11.2	3.14	113	.235	.301	-2.3	7.0	6.0	**.6**	9.6
Chi	95	67	0	.586	7	647	**555**	125	.246	.315	.364	679	105	94	50	21	122	**460**	946	**10.6**	2.99	107	**.231**	**.292**	.6	3.7	4.6	-.4	5.6
Bal	94	68	0	.580	8	641	578	125	.238	.307	.363	670	94	102	67	32	120	510	939	11.0	**2.98**	**116**	.233	.300	.6	**8.4**	-3.4	.0	7.3
Det	89	73	0	.549	13	680	602	162	.238	.312	.374	686	100	101	57	**45**	137	509	1069	11.4	3.35	104	.237	.306	1.3	2.1	.4	-.5	4.7
Cle	87	75	0	.537	15	663	613	156	.250	.315	.379	694	102	101	109	41	129	500	**1156**	11.0	3.30	106	.232	.298	**1.4**	3.2	2.2	.5	-1.3
NY	77	85	0	.475	25	611	604	149	.235	.299	.364	663	95	99	35	41	126	511	1001	11.6	3.28	104	.245	.311	-.0	2.1	-4.3	-.2	-1.6
Cal	75	87	0	.463	27	527	569	92	.239	.297	.341	638	89	98	107	39	**91**	563	847	11.5	3.17	107	.237	.312	.8	3.9	-7.5	.0	-3.4
Was	70	92	0	.432	32	591	721	136	.228	.304	.350	654	93	99	30	21	160	633	867	12.8	3.93	88	.254	.334	-.4	-7.7	-4.2	-.3	1.6
Bos	62	100	0	.383	40	669	791	**165**	.251	**.327**	**.400**	**727**	**107**	106	47	33	158	543	993	12.6	4.24	88	.260	.327	-1.6	-8.1	**6.1**	-.1	-15.2
KC	59	103	0	.364	43	585	755	110	.240	.309	.358	667	97	99	**110**	18	161	574	882	12.6	4.24	82	.256	.329	-.2	-12.6	-2.0	.3	-7.5
Total	810					46388		1370	.242	.311	.369	680			704	323				11.6	3.46		.242	.311					

Batter-Fielder Wins
Buford-Chi **5.3**
Boyer-NY **2.5**
Tresh-NY **1.5**
Mantle-NY **1.5**

Batting Average
Oliva-Min .... .321
Tresh-NY .... .279
Boyer-NY .... .251
2 players tied .... .247

On-Base Percentage
Yastrzemski-Bos .... .395
Tresh-NY .... .348
Pepitone-NY .... .305
Boyer-NY .... .304

Slugging Average
Yastrzemski-Bos .... .536
Tresh-NY .... .477
Boyer-NY .... .424
Pepitone-NY .... .394

On-Base Plus Slugging
Yastrzemski-Bos 932
Tresh-NY 825
Boyer-NY 728
Pepitone-NY 699

Adjusted OPS
Yastrzemski-Bos 154
Tresh-NY 133
Boyer-NY 106
Pepitone-NY 98

Adjusted Batter Runs
Yastrzemski-Bos ... 38.1
Tresh-NY 25.3
Mantle-NY 20.0
Maris-NY 6.3

Runs
Versalles-Min 126
Tresh-NY 94
Richardson-NY 76
Boyer-NY 69

Hits
Oliva-Min 185
Tresh-NY 168
Richardson-NY 164
Pepitone-NY 131

Doubles
Yastrzemski-Bos 45
Versalles-Min 45
Tresh-NY 29
Richardson-NY 28

Triples
Versalles-Min 12
Campaneris-KC 12
Tresh-NY 6
Boyer-NY 6

Home Runs
Conigliaro-Bos 32
Tresh-NY 26
Mantle-NY 19
2 players tied 18

Total Bases
Versalles-Min 308
Tresh-NY 287
Boyer-NY 218
Richardson-NY 214

Runs Batted In
Colavito-Cle 108
Tresh-NY 74
Pepitone-NY 62
Boyer-NY 58

Stolen Bases
Campaneris-KC 51
Richardson-NY 7
Tresh-NY 5
3 players tied 4

Base Stealing Runs
Campaneris-KC 4.6
Mantle-NY 5
Boyer-NY 5
Tresh-NY 4

Fielding Runs-Infield
Knoop-Cal 22.9
Boyer-NY 21.4
Pepitone-NY 1.5
Richardson-NY 1.0

Fielding Runs-Outfield
Conigliaro-Bos 9.0

Wins
Grant-Min 21
Stottlemyre-NY 20
Ford-NY 16
Downing-NY 12

Winning Pct.
Grant-Min .... .750
Stottlemyre-NY ...... .690
Ford-NY .... .552

Complete Games
Stottlemyre-NY 18
Ford-NY 9
Downing-NY 8
2 players tied 2

Strikeouts
McDowell-Cle 325
Downing-NY 179
Ford-NY 162
Stottlemyre-NY 155

Fewest BB/Game
Terry-Cle 1.25
Ford-NY 1.84
Stottlemyre-NY 2.72
Downing-NY 4.46

Games
Fisher-Chi 82
Ramos-NY 65
Reniff-NY 51
Hamilton-NY 46

Saves
Kline-Was 29
Ramos-NY 19
Hamilton-NY 5
Reniff-NY 3

Base Runners/9
Wilhelm-Chi 7.63
Stafford-NY 10.19
Ramos-NY 10.53
Stottlemyre-NY ... 10.67

Adjusted Relief Runs
Wilhelm-Chi 23.3
Hamilton-NY 12.5
Ramos-NY 5.0

Relief Ranking
S.Miller-Bal 44.3
Hamilton-NY 9.8
Ramos-NY 6.9

Innings Pitched
Stottlemyre-NY ... 291.0
Ford-NY 244.1
Downing-NY 212.0
Bouton-NY 151.1

Opponents' Avg.
McDowell-Cle .... .185
Stottlemyre-NY ..... .233
Downing-NY .... .237
Ford-NY .... .258

Opponents' OBP
Siebert-Cle .... .259
Fisher-Chi .... .259
Stottlemyre-NY ..... .294
Ford-NY .... .296

Earned Run Average
McDowell-Cle 2.18
Stottlemyre-NY 2.63
Ford-NY 3.24
Downing-NY 3.40

Adjusted ERA
McDowell-Cle 160
Stottlemyre-NY 129
Ford-NY 105
Downing-NY 100

Adjusted Starter Runs
McDowell-Cle 37.5
Stottlemyre-NY 24.3
Ford-NY 5.8
Beck-NY 2.8

Pitcher Wins
S.Miller-Bal 4.9
Stottlemyre-NY 2.8
Hamilton-NY 1.0
Ford-NY 1.0

1966 American League

TEAM	W	L	T	PCT	GB	R	OR	HR	AVG	OBP	SLG	OPS	AOPS	PF	SB	CG	HR	BB	SO	BR/9	ERA	AERA	OAV	OOB	FW	PW	BW	BSW	DIF
Bal	97	63	0	.606		**755**	601	175	**.258**	**.324**	**.409**	**733**	**118**	98	55	23	127	514	1070	11.1	3.32	100	.233	.301	**1.3**	.2	**14.0**	-.4	1.9
Min	89	73	0	.549	9	663	581	144	.249	.316	.382	698	100	106	67	**52**	139	**392**	1015	10.4	3.13	115	.232	.286	.0	7.6	1.2	-.0	-.8
Det	88	74	0	.543	10	719	698	**179**	.251	.321	.406	727	111	102	41	36	185	520	1026	11.9	3.85	90	.247	.315	1.1	-6.3	9.5	-.4	3.2
Chi	83	79	1	.512	15	574	**517**	87	.231	.297	.331	628	92	93	**153**	38	**101**	403	896	**10.2**	**2.68**	**118**	**.226**	**.282**	-1.1	**9.2**	-4.8	.6	-1.9
Cle	81	81	0	.500	17	574	586	155	.237	.297	.360	657	94	100	53	49	129	489	**1111**	10.9	3.23	107	.232	.297	.0	3.8	-4.4	-.4	1.0
Cal	80	82	0	.494	18	604	643	122	.232	.303	.354	657	98	97	80	31	136	511	836	11.8	3.56	94	.251	.317	.2	-3.7	-1.5	-.2	4.1
KC	74	86	0	.463	23	564	648	70	.236	.294	.337	631	90	97	132	19	106	630	854	12.2	3.56	96	.241	.323	-.0	-2.7	-7.3	**1.2**	2.9
Was	71	88	0	.447	25.5	557	659	126	.234	.295	.355	650	93	99	53	25	154	448	866	11.1	3.70	93	.242	.302	-.3	-4.1	-4.9	-.2	1.0
Bos	72	90	0	.444	26	655	731	145	.240	.310	.376	686	93	110	35	32	164	577	977	12.4	3.92	97	.253	.325	-.9	-1.7	-3.9	-.2	-2.3
NY	70	89	1	.440	26.5	611	612	162	.235	.299	.374	673	103	96	49	29	124	443	842	11.3	3.41	97	.248	.306	-.3	-1.6	1.7	.0	-9.4
Total	806					46276		1365	.240	.306	.369	674			718	334				11.3	3.44		.240	.306					

Batter-Fielder Wins
F.Robinson-Bal **6.3**
Tresh-NY **4.2**
Boyer-NY **2.8**
Mantle-NY **2.4**

Batting Average
F.Robinson-Bal ...... .316
Pepitone-NY .... .255
Richardson-NY ...... .251
Boyer-NY .... .240

On-Base Percentage
F.Robinson-Bal ...... .410
Tresh-NY .... .341
Boyer-NY .... .303
Pepitone-NY .... .290

Slugging Average
F.Robinson-Bal ...... .637
Pepitone-NY .... .463
Tresh-NY .... .421
Boyer-NY .... .384

On-Base Plus Slugging
F.Robinson-Bal 1047
Tresh-NY 762
Pepitone-NY 753
Boyer-NY 687

Adjusted OPS
F.Robinson-Bal 200
Tresh-NY 123
Pepitone-NY 118
Boyer-NY 101

Adjusted Batter Runs
F.Robinson-Bal 78.0
Mantle-NY 32.0
Tresh-NY 17.9
Pepitone-NY 9.6

Runs
F.Robinson-Bal 122
Pepitone-NY 85
Tresh-NY 76
Richardson-NY 71

Hits
Oliva-Min 191
Richardson-NY 153
Pepitone-NY 149
Tresh-NY 125

Doubles
Yastrzemski-Bos 39
Boyer-NY 22
Richardson-NY 21
Pepitone-NY 21

Triples
Knoop-Cal 11
4 players tied 4

Home Runs
F.Robinson-Bal 49
Pepitone-NY 31
Tresh-NY 27
Mantle-NY 23

Total Bases
F.Robinson-Bal 367
Pepitone-NY 271
Tresh-NY 226
Richardson-NY 201

Runs Batted In
F.Robinson-Bal 122
Pepitone-NY 83
Tresh-NY 68
Boyer-NY 57

Stolen Bases
Campaneris-KC 52
White-NY 14
Richardson-NY 6
Boyer-NY 6

Base Stealing Runs
Campaneris-KC 7.9
Boyer-NY 1.3
White-NY 6
Gibbs-NY 4

Fielding Runs-Infield
Knoop-Cal 21.8
Boyer-NY 20.0
Pepitone-NY 8.8
Richardson-NY 7.1

Fielding Runs-Outfield
Northrup-Det 10.1

Wins
Kaat-Min 25
Stottlemyre-NY 12
Peterson-NY 12
Downing-NY 10

Winning Pct.
Siebert-Cle .... .667

Complete Games
Kaat-Min 19
Peterson-NY 11
Stottlemyre-NY 9
Bouton-NY 3

Strikeouts
McDowell-Cle 225
Downing-NY 152
Stottlemyre-NY 146
Peterson-NY 96

Fewest BB/Game
Kaat-Min 1.62
Peterson-NY 1.67
Stottlemyre-NY 2.94
Downing-NY 3.56

Games
Fisher-Chi-Bal 67
Reniff-NY 56
Ramos-NY 52
Hamilton-NY 44

Saves
Aker-KC 32
Ramos-NY 13
Reniff-NY 9
Womack-NY 4

Base Runners/9
Wilhelm-Chi 7.52
Womack-NY 9.36
Hamilton-NY 9.40
Peterson-NY 10.00

Adjusted Relief Runs
Aker-KC 18.6
Womack-NY 5.9
Hamilton-NY 4.4
Reniff-NY 2.1

Relief Ranking
Aker-KC 28.2
Womack-NY 7.8
Hamilton-NY 5.1
Reniff-NY 2.3

Innings Pitched
Kaat-Min 304.2
Stottlemyre-NY ... 251.0
Peterson-NY 215.0
Downing-NY 200.0

Opponents' Avg.
McDowell-Cle .... .188
Downing-NY .... .235
Peterson-NY .... .241
Stottlemyre-NY ..... .253

Opponents' OBP
Peters-Chi .... .260
Peterson-NY .... .277
Downing-NY .... .307
Stottlemyre-NY .... .311

Earned Run Average
Peters-Chi 1.98
Peterson-NY 3.31
Downing-NY 3.56
Stottlemyre-NY 3.80

Adjusted ERA
Peters-Chi 160
Peterson-NY 101
Downing-NY 94
Stottlemyre-NY 87

Adjusted Starter Runs
Peters-Chi 28.9
Bouton-NY 5.1
Ford-NY 2.6
Peterson-NY 9

Pitcher Wins
Peters-Chi 4.0
Womack-NY 1.0
Peterson-NY 6
3 players tied 3

1967 American League

TEAM	W	L	T	PCT	GB	R	OR	HR	AVG	OBP	SLG	OPS	AOPS	PF	SB	CG	HR	BB	SO	BR/9	ERA	AERA	OAV	OOB	FW	PW	BW	BSW	DIF
Bos	92	70	0	.568		**722**	614	**158**	**.255**	.321	**.395**	**716**	109	108	68	41	142	477	1010	11.3	3.36	104	.239	.304	-.6	2.1	7.3	-.5	2.7
Min	91	71	2	.562	1	671	590	131	.240	.309	.369	678	98	108	55	**58**	115	**396**	1089	10.9	3.14	110	.243	.296	.1	5.4	-.4	.0	4.8
Det	91	71	1	.562	1	683	587	152	.243	**.325**	.376	701	**111**	103	37	46	151	472	1038	10.8	3.32	98	.230	.295	.0	-1.0	**9.3**	.3	1.4
Chi	89	73	0	.549	3	531	**491**	89	.225	.291	.320	611	90	96	124	36	**87**	465	927	**10.4**	**2.45**	**127**	**.219**	**.287**	-.3	**12.4**	-6.8	.0	2.8
Cal	84	77	0	.522	7.5	567	587	114	.238	.301	.349	650	102	96	40	19	118	525	892	11.4	3.19	98	.237	.308	**1.3**	-.9	.8	-.3	2.6
Was	76	85	0	.472	15.5	550	637	115	.223	.288	.326	614	91	96	53	24	113	495	878	11.4	3.38	93	.242	.307	-.8	-4.1	-6.8	.0	7.1
Bal	76	85	0	.472	15.5	654	592	138	.240	.310	.372	682	109	99	54	29	116	566	1034	11.2	3.32	95	.228	.304	.5	-3.1	6.7	.0	-8.7
Cle	75	87	0	.463	17	559	613	131	.235	.299	.359	658	97	101	53	49	120	559	**1189**	11.3	3.25	101	.231	.305	1.0	.3	-2.2	-1.0	-4.1
NY	72	90	1	.444	20	522	621	100	.225	.296	.317	613	90	96	63	37	110	480	898	11.5	3.24	97	.249	.310	-1.3	-2.1	-6.1	.3	.2
KC	62	99	0	.385	29.5	533	660	69	.233	.296	.330	626	94	97	**132**	26	125	558	990	11.7	3.68	87	.238	.313	-.0	-8.8	-4.1	**1.0**	-6.6
Total	810					45992		1197	.236	.303	.351	654			679	365				11.2	3.23		.236	.303					

BATTER-FIELDER WINS
Yastrzemski-Bos ... 6.9
Mantle-NY ... 3.3
Clarke-NY ... 2.8
Kenney-NY 3

BATTING AVERAGE
Yastrzemski-Bos ... .326
Clarke-NY ... .272
Pepitone-NY ... .251
Mantle-NY ... .245

ON-BASE PERCENTAGE
Yastrzemski-Bos ... .418
Mantle-NY ... .391
Clarke-NY ... .321
2 players tied ... .301

SLUGGING AVERAGE
Yastrzemski-Bos ... .622
Mantle-NY ... .434
Pepitone-NY ... .377
Tresh-NY ... .377

ON-BASE PLUS SLUGGING
Yastrzemski-Bos .. 1040
Mantle-NY ... 825
Tresh-NY ... 678
Pepitone-NY ... 678

ADJUSTED OPS
Yastrzemski-Bos ... 189
F.Robinson-Bal ... 189
Mantle-NY ... 150
2 players tied ... 104

ADJUSTED BATTER RUNS
Yastrzemski-Bos ... 67.2
Mantle-NY ... 34.0
Kenney-NY ... 3.9
Howser-NY ... 3.7

RUNS
Yastrzemski-Bos ... 112
Clarke-NY ... 74
Mantle-NY ... 63
2 players tied ... 45

HITS
Yastrzemski-Bos ... 189
Clarke-NY ... 160
Pepitone-NY ... 126
Mantle-NY ... 108

DOUBLES
Oliva-Min ... 34
Tresh-NY ... 23
Pepitone-NY ... 18
2 players tied ... 17

TRIPLES
Blair-Bal ... 12
5 players tied ... 3

HOME RUNS
Yastrzemski-Bos ... 44
Killebrew-Min ... 44
Mantle-NY ... 22
Tresh-NY ... 14

TOTAL BASES
Yastrzemski-Bos ... 360
Mantle-NY ... 191
Pepitone-NY ... 189
Clarke-NY ... 186

RUNS BATTED IN
Yastrzemski-Bos ... 121
Pepitone-NY ... 64
Mantle-NY ... 55
Tresh-NY ... 53

STOLEN BASES
Campaneris-KC ... 55
Clarke-NY ... 21
White-NY ... 10
2 players tied ... 7

BASE STEALING RUNS
Campaneris-KC ... 6.5
Clarke-NY ... 3.2
Hegan-NY ... 1.2
White-NY 8

FIELDING RUNS-INFIELD
B.Robinson-Bal ... 32.1
Clarke-NY ... 16.3
Smith-NY ... 7.8
Amaro-NY ... 7.5

FIELDING RUNS-OUTFIELD
Blair-Bal ... 9.1
Whitaker-NY ... 1.5

WINS
Wilson-Det ... 22
Lonborg-Bos ... 22
Stottlemyre-NY ... 15
Downing-NY ... 14

WINNING PCT.
Horlen-Chi ... .731
Stottlemyre-NY ... .500

COMPLETE GAMES
Chance-Min ... 18
Stottlemyre-NY ... 10
Downing-NY ... 10
Peterson-NY ... 6

STRIKEOUTS
Lonborg-Bos ... 246
Downing-NY ... 171
Stottlemyre-NY ... 151
Peterson-NY ... 102

FEWEST BB/GAME
Merritt-Min ... 1.19
Peterson-NY ... 2.13
Downing-NY ... 2.72
Stottlemyre-NY ... 3.11

GAMES
Locker-Chi ... 77
Womack-NY ... 65
Hamilton-NY ... 44
Tillotson-NY ... 43

SAVES
Rojas-Cal ... 27
Womack-NY ... 18
Hamilton-NY ... 4
2 players tied ... 2

BASE RUNNERS/9
Horlen-Chi ... 8.72
Downing-NY ... 10.04
Verbanic-NY ... 10.87
Womack-NY ... 10.95

ADJUSTED RELIEF RUNS
Wilhelm-Chi ... 16.1
Womack-NY ... 6.8
Verbanic-NY ... 4.0

RELIEF RANKING
Wilhelm-Chi ... 22.4
Womack-NY ... 9.5
Verbanic-NY ... 3.3

INNINGS PITCHED
Chance-Min ... 283.2
Stottlemyre-NY ... 255.0
Downing-NY ... 201.2
Peterson-NY ... 181.1

OPPONENTS' AVG.
Peters-Chi ... .199
Downing-NY ... .217
Stottlemyre-NY ... .248
Peterson-NY ... .256

OPPONENTS' OBP
Horlen-Chi ... .253
Downing-NY ... .281
Peterson-NY ... .301
Stottlemyre-NY ... .311

EARNED RUN AVERAGE
Horlen-Chi ... 2.06
Downing-NY ... 2.63
Stottlemyre-NY ... 2.96
Peterson-NY ... 3.47

ADJUSTED ERA
Horlen-Chi ... 151
Downing-NY ... 119
Stottlemyre-NY ... 105
Peterson-NY ... 90

ADJUSTED STARTER RUNS
Horlen-Chi ... 33.5
Downing-NY ... 13.1
Ford-NY ... 6.8
Stottlemyre-NY ... 5.6

PITCHER WINS
Horlen-Chi ... 3.8
Downing-NY ... 1.7
Womack-NY ... 1.4
Ford-NY ... 1.1

1968 American League

TEAM	W	L	T	PCT	GB	R	OR	HR	AVG	OBP	SLG	OPS	AOPS	PF	SB	CG	HR	BB	SO	BR/9	ERA	AERA	OAV	OOB	FW	PW	BW	BSW	DIF
Det	103	59	2	.636		**671**	**492**	**185**	.235	.307	**.385**	**692**	**113**	103	26	**59**	129	486	1115	**10.3**	2.71	111	.217	**.284**	**2.0**	5.6	**9.6**	-.7	5.4
Bal	91	71	0	.562	12	579	497	133	.225	.304	.352	656	105	100	78	53	101	502	1044	**10.3**	**2.66**	110	.212	.285	1.0	4.9	5.3	.5	-1.8
Cle	86	75	1	.534	16.5	516	504	75	.234	.293	.327	620	96	98	115	48	98	540	**1157**	**10.3**	**2.66**	**112**	**.206**	.285	.6	**5.8**	-2.9	.3	1.6
Bos	86	76	0	.531	17	614	611	125	.236	**.313**	.352	665	102	106	76	55	115	523	972	11.7	3.33	95	.241	.312	.6	-3.1	3.6	-.7	4.7
NY	83	79	2	.512	20	536	531	109	.214	.292	.318	610	94	97	90	45	99	424	831	10.8	2.79	104	.240	.297	.0	2.3	-3.6	.0	3.2
Oak	82	80	1	.506	21	569	544	94	**.240**	.304	.343	647	107	96	**147**	45	124	505	997	10.9	2.94	96	.227	.295	-.4	-2.4	5.0	**1.1**	-2.3
Min	79	83	0	.488	24	562	546	105	.237	.299	.350	649	98	106	98	46	**92**	**414**	996	10.5	2.89	107	.229	.288	-2.0	3.3	-1.1	.2	-2.4
Cal	67	95	0	.414	36	498	615	83	.227	.291	.318	609	94	97	62	29	131	519	869	11.2	3.43	85	.233	.303	-.2	-9.6	-4.2	-.6	.7
Chi	67	95	0	.414	36	463	527	71	.228	.284	.311	595	86	101	90	20	97	451	834	11.1	2.75	110	.236	.301	-.8	5.2	-10.4	.0	-8.0
Was	65	96	0	.404	37.5	524	665	124	.224	.287	.336	623	98	97	29	26	118	517	826	12.3	3.64	80	.258	.325	-.7	-13.5	-1.9	-.2	.8
Total	812					45532		1104	.230	.297	.339	637			811	426				10.9	2.98		.230	.297					

BATTER-FIELDER WINS
Yastrzemski-Bos ... 6.3
Mantle-NY ... 2.3
White-NY ... 2.2
Tresh-NY ... 2.1

BATTING AVERAGE
Yastrzemski-Bos ... .301
White-NY ... .267
Mantle-NY ... .237
Clarke-NY ... .230

ON-BASE PERCENTAGE
Yastrzemski-Bos ... .426
Mantle-NY ... .385
White-NY ... .350
Tresh-NY ... .304

SLUGGING AVERAGE
F.Howard-Was ... .552
White-NY ... .414
Mantle-NY ... .398
Tresh-NY ... .308

ON-BASE PLUS SLUGGING
Yastrzemski-Bos ... 922
Mantle-NY ... 782
White-NY ... 764
Tresh-NY ... 612

ADJUSTED OPS
F.Howard-Was ... 173
Mantle-NY ... 143
White-NY ... 136
Tresh-NY ... 89

ADJUSTED BATTER RUNS
Yastrzemski-Bos ... 53.1
Mantle-NY ... 29.0
White-NY ... 25.7
Pepitone-NY ... 7.7

RUNS
McAuliffe-Det ... 95
White-NY ... 89
Tresh-NY ... 60
Mantle-NY ... 57

HITS
Campaneris-Oak ... 177
White-NY ... 154
Clarke-NY ... 133
Kosco-NY ... 112

DOUBLES
Smith-Bos ... 37
White-NY ... 20
Kosco-NY ... 19
Tresh-NY ... 18

TRIPLES
Fregosi-Cal ... 13
White-NY ... 7
Robinson-NY ... 7
4 players tied ... 3

HOME RUNS
F.Howard-Was ... 44
Mantle-NY ... 18
White-NY ... 17
2 players tied ... 15

TOTAL BASES
F.Howard-Was ... 330
White-NY ... 239
Kosco-NY ... 178
Mantle-NY ... 173

RUNS BATTED IN
Harrelson-Bos ... 109
White-NY ... 62
Kosco-NY ... 59
Pepitone-NY ... 56

STOLEN BASES
Campaneris-Oak ... 62
White-NY ... 20
Clarke-NY ... 20
Tresh-NY ... 10

BASE STEALING RUNS
Campaneris-Oak ... 5.9
Clarke-NY ... 2.0
Pepitone-NY ... 1.1
2 players tied 6

FIELDING RUNS-INFIELD
Clarke-NY ... 29.0
Tresh-NY ... 15.8

FIELDING RUNS-OUTFIELD
Yastrzemski-Bos ... 11.2
White-NY ... 1.6

WINS
McLain-Det ... 31
Stottlemyre-NY ... 21
Bahnsen-NY ... 17
Peterson-NY ... 12

WINNING PCT.
McLain-Det ... .838
Stottlemyre-NY ... .636
Bahnsen-NY ... .586

COMPLETE GAMES
McLain-Det ... 28
Stottlemyre-NY ... 19
Bahnsen-NY ... 10
Peterson-NY ... 6

STRIKEOUTS
McDowell-Cle ... 283
Bahnsen-NY ... 162
Stottlemyre-NY ... 140
Peterson-NY ... 115

FEWEST BB/GAME
Peterson-NY ... 1.23
Stottlemyre-NY ... 2.10
Bahnsen-NY ... 2.29

GAMES
Wood-Chi ... 88
Womack-NY ... 45
Verbanic-NY ... 40
Hamilton-NY ... 40

SAVES
Worthington-Min ... 18
Hamilton-NY ... 11
McDaniel-NY ... 10
Verbanic-NY ... 4

BASE RUNNERS/9
McNally-Bal ... 7.91
Peterson-NY ... 9.32
Bahnsen-NY ... 9.63
Stottlemyre-NY ... 10.04

ADJUSTED RELIEF RUNS
Wood-Chi ... 20.0

RELIEF RANKING
Wood-Chi ... 32.9

INNINGS PITCHED
McLain-Det ... 336.0
Stottlemyre-NY ... 278.2
Bahnsen-NY ... 267.1
Peterson-NY ... 212.1

OPPONENTS' AVG.
Tiant-Cle ... .168
Bahnsen-NY ... .221
Stottlemyre-NY ... .234
Peterson-NY ... .241

OPPONENTS' OBP
McNally-Bal ... .232
Peterson-NY ... .270
Bahnsen-NY ... .271
Stottlemyre-NY ... .280

EARNED RUN AVERAGE
Tiant-Cle ... 1.60
Bahnsen-NY ... 2.05
Stottlemyre-NY ... 2.45
Peterson-NY ... 2.63

ADJUSTED ERA
Tiant-Cle ... 185
Bahnsen-NY ... 142
Stottlemyre-NY ... 119
Peterson-NY ... 111

ADJUSTED STARTER RUNS
Tiant-Cle ... 39.7
Bahnsen-NY ... 25.8
Stottlemyre-NY ... 15.7
Peterson-NY ... 7.0

PITCHER WINS
Tiant-Cle ... 4.4
McLain-Det ... 4.4
Bahnsen-NY ... 2.4
Stottlemyre-NY ... 2.3

1969 American League

TEAM	W	L	T	PCT	GB	R	OR	HR	AVG	OBP	SLG	OPS	AOPS	PF	SB	CG	HR	BB	SO	BR/9	ERA	AERA	OAV	OOB	FW	PW	BW	BSW	DIF
East																													
Bal	109	53	0	.673		779	**517**	175	.265	**.343**	.414	**757**	**117**	101	82	50	**117**	**498**	897	**10.5**	**2.83**	**127**	**.223**	**.290**	**2.2**	**13.1**	**13.7**	-.0	-1.0
Det	90	72	0	.556	19	701	601	182	.242	.316	.387	703	99	104	35	**55**	128	586	**1032**	11.6	3.31	113	.232	.310	.5	7.2	-1.0	-.5	2.7
Bos	87	75	0	.537	22	743	736	**197**	.251	.333	**.415**	748	110	105	41	30	155	685	935	13.2	3.92	97	.256	.341	-1.0	-1.7	8.2	-1.0	1.5
Was	86	76	0	.531	23	694	644	148	.251	.330	.378	708	110	95	52	28	135	656	835	12.4	3.49	100	.244	.328	-.0	.2	7.8	-.6	-2.4
NY	80	81	1	.497	28.5	562	587	94	.235	.308	.344	652	91	97	119	53	118	522	801	11.2	3.23	109	.236	.304	.5	4.9	-5.6	-.2	-.1
Cle	62	99	0	.385	46.5	573	717	119	.237	.307	.345	652	85	103	85	35	134	681	1000	12.9	3.94	96	.248	.335	-.4	-2.3	-10.0	.4	-6.2
West																													
Min	97	65	0	.599		**790**	618	163	**.268**	.340	.408	748	113	103	115	41	119	524	906	11.7	3.24	112	.246	.313	-.6	6.9	10.5	-.1	-.7
Oak	88	74	0	.543	9	740	678	148	.249	.329	.376	705	108	96	100	42	163	586	887	12.0	3.71	93	.245	.320	.2	-5.0	6.4	.6	4.8
Cal	71	91	1	.438	26	528	652	88	.230	.300	.319	619	83	-96	54	25	126	517	885	11.7	3.54	99	.242	.313	.2	-.8	-12.5	-.5	3.5
KC	69	93	1	.426	28	586	688	98	.240	.309	.338	647	86	101	129	42	136	560	894	11.9	3.72	99	.246	.316	-1.0	-.4	-9.9	.2	-.9
Chi	68	94	0	.420	29	625	723	112	.247	.320	.357	677	92	105	54	29	146	564	810	12.9	4.21	91	.267	.337	1.0	-5.8	-5.6	.2	-2.8
Sea	64	98	1	.395	33	639	799	125	.234	.316	.346	662	92	99	**167**	21	172	653	963	13.5	4.35	84	.264	.343	-1.5	-12.1	-5.1	**1.4**	.3
Total	973					57960		1649	.246	.321	.369	690			1033	451				12.1	3.62		.246	.321					

Batter-Fielder Wins
Petrocelli-Bos 7.6
White-NY................ 2.6
Fernandez-NY 1.7
2 players tied......... 1.6

Batting Average
Carew-Min .... .332
White-NY .... .290
Clarke-NY .... .285
Murcer-NY .... .259

On-Base Percentage
Killebrew-Min .... .427
White-NY .... .392
Clarke-NY .... .339
Kenney-NY .... .328

Slugging Average
Jackson-Oak......... .608
Murcer-NY .... .454
Pepitone-NY .... .442
White-NY .... .426

On-Base Plus Slugging
Jackson-Oak........ 1018
White-NY 818
Murcer-NY 773
Pepitone-NY 726

Adjusted OPS
Jackson-Oak.......... 189
White-NY 136
Murcer-NY 119
Pepitone-NY 104

Adjusted Batter Runs
Jackson-Oak......... 69.6
White-NY 26.1
Fernandez-NY 14.0
Murcer-NY 11.7

Runs
Jackson-Oak.......... 123
Murcer-NY 82
Clarke-NY 82
White-NY 55

Hits
Oliva-Min 197
Clarke-NY 183
Murcer-NY 146
White-NY 130

Doubles
Oliva-Min 39
White-NY 30
Clarke-NY 26
2 players tied 24

Triples
Unser-Was................ 8
Clarke-NY 7
White-NY 5
2 players tied 4

Home Runs
Killebrew-Min 49
Pepitone-NY 27
Murcer-NY 26
Fernandez-NY 12

Total Bases
Howard-Was.......... 340
Murcer-NY 256
Clarke-NY 235
Pepitone-NY 227

Runs Batted In
Killebrew-Min 140
Murcer-NY 82
White-NY 74
Pepitone-NY 70

Stolen Bases
Harper-Sea 73
Clarke-NY 33
Kenney-NY 25
White-NY 18

Base Stealing Runs
Campaneris-Oak .. 10.8
Clarke-NY 2.7
Kenney-NY 6
White-NY 5

Fielding Runs-Infield
Knoop-Cal-Chi...... 32.5
Aparicio-Chi.......... 32.5
Clarke-NY 2.4
Michael-NY 3

Fielding Runs-Outfield
Blair-Bal 11.7
White-NY 5.7

Wins
McLain-Det 24
Stottlemyre-NY 20
Peterson-NY 17
Bahnsen-NY 9

Winning Pct.
Palmer-Bal............ .800
Stottlemyre-NY ...... .588
Peterson-NY .... .515

Complete Games
Stottlemyre-NY 24
Peterson-NY 16
Downing-NY 5
Bahnsen-NY 5

Strikeouts
McDowell-Cle 279
Peterson-NY.......... 150
Bahnsen-NY 130
Stottlemyre-NY 113

Fewest BB/Game
Peterson-NY 1.42
Stottlemyre-NY 2.88
Bahnsen-NY 3.67

Games
Wood-Chi................. 76
McDaniel-NY 51
Bahnsen-NY 40
Stottlemyre-NY 39

Saves
Perranoski-Min 31
McDaniel-NY 5
Hamilton-NY 2
2 players tied 1

Base Runners/9
Hall-Bal 8.09
Peterson-NY 9.07
Stottlemyre-NY ... 10.99
Downing-NY 11.43

Adjusted Relief Runs
K.Tatum-Cal.......... 22.2
Hamilton-NY 2.2

Relief Ranking
Perranoski-Min 40.7
Hamilton-NY 2.6

Innings Pitched
McLain-Det 325.0
Stottlemyre-NY ... 303.0
Peterson-NY 272.0
Bahnsen-NY 220.2

Opponents' Avg.
Messersmith-Cal... .190
Peterson-NY .... .229
Stottlemyre-NY ..... .239
Bahnsen-NY .... .260

Opponents' OBP
Cuellar-Bal............ .260
Bosman-Was .... .260
Peterson-NY .... .261
Stottlemyre-NY ..... .301

Earned Run Average
Bosman-Was 2.19
Peterson-NY 2.55
Stottlemyre-NY 2.82
Bahnsen-NY 3.83

Adjusted ERA
Bosman-Was 160
Peterson-NY 138
Stottlemyre-NY 125
Bahnsen-NY 92

Adjusted Starter Runs
McLain-Det 37.2
Peterson-NY 26.9
Stottlemyre-NY 25.6
Klimkowski-NY........ 4.7

Pitcher Wins
Perranoski-Min 4.3
Stottlemyre-NY 3.8
Peterson-NY 3.4
2 players tied 2

1970 American League

TEAM	W	L	T	PCT	GB	R	OR	HR	AVG	OBP	SLG	OPS	AOPS	PF	SB	CG	HR	BB	SO	BR/9	ERA	AERA	OAV	OOB	FW	PW	BW	BSW	DIF
East																													
Bal	108	54	0	.667		**792**	**574**	179	.257	**.344**	.401	745	**110**	102	84	**60**	139	469	941	**11.0**	**3.15**	**117**	.240	**.300**	**1.1**	**9.1**	**9.5**	.6	6.7
NY	93	69	1	.574	15	680	612	111	.251	.324	.365	689	100	96	105	36	**130**	**451**	777	11.4	3.24	110	.249	.306	.4	5.8	1.2	.3	4.3
Bos	87	75	0	.537	21	786	722	**203**	**.262**	.335	**.428**	**763**	109	107	50	38	156	594	1003	12.6	3.87	103	.251	.327	-1.2	1.8	7.5	-.6	-1.5
Det	79	83	0	.488	29	666	731	148	.238	.322	.374	696	97	101	29	33	153	623	1045	13.1	4.09	92	.260	.336	.2	-5.4	-.9	-.4	4.5
Cle	76	86	0	.469	32	649	675	183	.249	.314	.394	708	96	105	25	34	163	689	**1076**	12.8	3.91	102	.247	.335	.2	1.6	-3.1	-.7	-2.9
Was	70	92	0	.432	38	626	689	138	.238	.321	.358	679	97	96	72	20	139	611	823	12.4	3.80	95	.252	.328	**1.1**	-3.3	-.6	.2	-8.4
West																													
Min	98	64	0	.605		744	605	153	**.262**	.327	.403	730	105	102	57	26	**130**	486	940	11.5	3.23	114	.244	.308	.7	7.9	4.0	-.6	4.9
Oak	89	73	0	.549	9	678	593	171	.249	.325	.392	717	107	97	**131**	33	134	542	858	11.4	3.30	107	**.234**	.307	-.3	3.9	5.4	.6	-1.6
Cal	86	76	0	.531	12	631	630	114	.251	.309	.363	672	94	97	69	21	154	559	922	11.6	3.48	104	.237	.312	.5	2.4	-5.1	**.7**	6.5
Mil	65	97	1	.401	33	613	751	126	.242	.319	.358	677	93	100	91	31	146	587	895	12.6	4.21	90	.255	.330	.0	-7.1	-4.3	-.6	-4.2
KC	65	97	0	.401	33	611	705	97	.244	.309	.348	657	87	100	97	30	138	641	915	12.4	3.78	99	.247	.328	-.9	-.8	-9.6	.4	-5.0
Chi	56	106	0	.346	42	633	822	123	.253	.315	.362	677	90	104	53	20	164	556	762	13.6	4.54	85	.280	.347	-1.7	-10.5	-7.6	.0	-5.3
Total	973					58109		1746	.250	.322	.379	701			863	382				12.2	3.71		.250	.322					

Batter-Fielder Wins
Harper-Mil............. 5.6
Munson-NY............ 3.9
White-NY............... 3.1
Gibbs-NY 1.2

Batting Average
Johnson-Cal .... .329
Yastrzemski-Bos..... .329
Munson-NY........... .302
Cater-NY............... .301

On-Base Percentage
Yastrzemski-Bos... .452
White-NY .... .387
Munson-NY............ .386
Murcer-NY .... .348

Slugging Average
Yastrzemski-Bos.... .592
White-NY .... .473
Murcer-NY .... .420
Munson-NY........... .415

On-Base Plus Slugging
Yastrzemski-Bos.. 1044
White-NY 860
Munson-NY............ 801
Murcer-NY 768

Adjusted OPS
Yastrzemski-Bos.... 174
White-NY 143
Munson-NY............ 127
Murcer-NY 117

Adjusted Batter Runs
Yastrzemski-Bos... 64.5
White-NY 38.6
Munson-NY........... 19.5
Murcer-NY 14.3

Runs
Yastrzemski-Bos.... 125
White-NY 109
Murcer-NY 95
Clarke-NY 81

Hits
Oliva-Min 204
White-NY 180
Cater-NY............... 175
Clarke-NY 172

Doubles
3 players tied 36
White-NY 30
Cater-NY................. 26
Munson-NY.............. 25

Triples
Tovar-Min................. 13
Kenney-NY 7
White-NY 6
Cater-NY................... 5

Home Runs
Howard-Was............ 44
Murcer-NY 23
White-NY 22
Blefary-NY 9

Total Bases
Yastrzemski-Bos.... 335
White-NY 288
Murcer-NY 244
Cater-NY............... 229

Runs Batted In
Howard-Was.......... 126
White-NY 94
Murcer-NY 78
Cater-NY.................. 76

Stolen Bases
Campaneris-Oak 42
White-NY 24
Clarke-NY 23
Kenney-NY 20

Base Stealing Runs
Otis-KC 6.6
Clarke-NY 2.6
Kenney-NY 2.3
White-NY 1.8

Fielding Runs-Infield
Brinkman-Was 31.4
Kenney-NY 16.2

Fielding Runs-Outfield
Oliva-Min 13.3
White-NY 3

Wins
3 players tied 24
Peterson-NY 20
Stottlemyre-NY 15
Bahnsen-NY 14

Winning Pct.
Cuellar-Bal............ .750
Peterson-NY .... .645
Stottlemyre-NY ..... .536

Complete Games
Cuellar-Bal.............. 21
Stottlemyre-NY 14
Peterson-NY 8
Bahnsen-NY 6

Strikeouts
McDowell-Cle 304
Peterson-NY.......... 127
Stottlemyre-NY 126
Bahnsen-NY 116

Fewest BB/Game
Peterson-NY 1.38
Stottlemyre-NY 2.79
Bahnsen-NY 2.90

Games
Wood-Chi................ 77
McDaniel-NY 62
Klimkowski-NY......... 45
Aker-NY 41

Saves
Perranoski-Min 34
McDaniel-NY 29
Aker-NY 16
Klimkowski-NY........... 1

Base Runners/9
Hall-Bal 8.36
McDaniel-NY 8.95
Peterson-NY 10.03
Aker-NY 10.41

Adjusted Relief Runs
Grant-Oak............ 25.6
McDaniel-NY 20.0
Aker-NY 12.0
Klimkowski-NY........ 9.3

Relief Ranking
McDaniel-NY 32.4
Aker-NY 14.4
Klimkowski-NY........11.2
Waslewski-NY......... 2.5

Innings Pitched
Palmer-Bal........... 305.0
McDowell-Cle 305.0
Stottlemyre-NY ... 271.0
Peterson-NY 260.1

Opponents' Avg.
Messersmith-Cal.... .205
Peterson-NY .... .248
Stottlemyre-NY ..... .255
Bahnsen-NY .... .256

Opponents' OBP
Peterson-NY .... .279
Bahnsen-NY .... .312
Stottlemyre-NY ..... .313

Earned Run Average
Segui-Oak............. 2.56
Peterson-NY 2.90
Stottlemyre-NY 3.09
Bahnsen-NY 3.33

Adjusted ERA
Segui-Oak.............. 138
Peterson-NY 123
Stottlemyre-NY 116
Bahnsen-NY 107

Adjusted Starter Runs
Palmer-Bal............ 35.0
Peterson-NY 17.8
Stottlemyre-NY 13.9
Bahnsen-NY 6.2

Pitcher Wins
McDaniel-NY 3.5
Peterson-NY 2.8
Stottlemyre-NY 2.4
Aker-NY 1.4

Historical Record

1971 American League

TEAM	W	L	T	PCT	GB	R	OR	HR	AVG	OBP	SLG	OPS	AOPS	PF	SB	CG	HR	BB	SO	BR/9	ERA	AERA	OAV	OOB	FW	PW	BW	BSW	DIF
East																													
Bal	101	57	0	.639		**742**	**530**	158	**.261**	**.347**	.398	**745**	**117**	101	66	**71**	125	**416**	793	**10.8**	**2.99**	**114**	.239	**.295**	.7	7.1	**14.2**	.1	-.0
Det	91	71	0	.562	12	701	645	**179**	.254	.325	**.405**	730	108	104	35	53	126	609	**1000**	12.3	3.63	100	.247	.325	**1.2**	-.3	6.2	-.7	3.6
Bos	85	77	0	.525	18	691	667	161	.252	.322	.397	719	102	107	51	44	136	535	871	12.5	3.80	98	.259	.327	.6	-1.4	2.6	-.0	2.3
NY	82	80	0	.506	21	648	641	97	.254	.328	.360	688	107	95	75	67	126	423	707	11.3	3.43	96	.252	.306	.1	-2.8	5.8	-.3	-1.8
Was	63	96	0	.396	38.5	537	660	86	.230	.307	.326	633	90	95	68	30	132	554	762	12.5	3.70	91	.258	.331	-1.0	-5.7	-6.6	-.0	-3.2
Cle	60	102	0	.370	43	543	747	109	.238	.300	.342	642	80	110	57	21	154	770	937	13.6	4.28	90	.252	.348	.6	-6.3	-14.1	.0	-1.2
West																													
Oak	101	60	0	.627		691	564	160	.252	.321	.384	705	108	98	80	57	131	501	999	**10.8**	3.05	109	**.228**	.296	.5	4.9	5.8	-.0	9.3
KC	85	76	0	.528	16	603	566	80	.250	.313	.353	666	96	99	**130**	34	**84**	496	775	11.6	3.25	106	.247	.314	-.4	3.2	-2.5	**1.4**	2.7
Chi	79	83	0	.488	22.5	617	597	138	.250	.325	.373	698	101	103	83	46	100	468	976	11.4	3.12	**114**	.247	.307	-1.9	**7.3**	1.7	-.4	-8.7
Cal	76	86	0	.469	25.5	511	576	96	.231	.290	.329	619	87	-93	72	39	101	607	904	11.5	3.10	105	.230	.310	-.2	2.7	-10.2	.4	2.3
Min	74	86	0	.463	26.5	654	670	116	.260	.323	.372	695	100	103	66	43	139	529	895	12.4	3.81	93	.257	.326	.4	-4.6	1.0	-.0	-2.7
Mil	69	92	0	.429	32	534	609	104	.229	.304	.329	633	86	99	82	32	130	569	795	12.1	3.38	103	.247	.321	-.7	1.7	-9.1	-.0	-3.3
Total	966					47472		1484	.247	.317	.364	681			865	537				11.9	3.46		.247	.317					

Batter-Fielder Wins	Batting Average	On-Base Percentage	Slugging Average	On-Base Plus Slugging	Adjusted OPS	Adjusted Batter Runs
Nettles-Cle 5.9	Oliva-Min .337	Murcer-NY .427	Oliva-Min .546	Murcer-NY 969	Murcer-NY 182	Murcer-NY 60.5
Murcer-NY 4.5	Murcer-NY .331	White-NY .388	Murcer-NY .543	White-NY 857	White-NY 152	White-NY 39.2
White-NY 3.8	White-NY .292	Munson-NY .335	White-NY .469	Munson-NY 703	Munson-NY 105	Blomberg-NY 10.4
Michael-NY 2.2	Munson-NY .251	Clarke-NY .321	Munson-NY .368	Clarke-NY 639	Clarke-NY 86	Swoboda-NY 4.0

Runs	Hits	Doubles	Triples	Home Runs	Total Bases	Runs Batted In
Buford-Bal 99	Tovar-Min 204	Smith-Bos 33	Patek-KC 11	Melton-Chi 33	Smith-Bos 302	Killebrew-Min 119
Murcer-NY 94	Murcer-NY 175	Murcer-NY 25	White-NY 7	Murcer-NY 25	Murcer-NY 287	Murcer-NY 94
White-NY 86	Clarke-NY 156	Clarke-NY 23	Clarke-NY 7	White-NY 19	White-NY 246	White-NY 84
Clarke-NY 76	White-NY 153	White-NY 22	Murcer-NY 6	Munson-NY 10	Clarke-NY 199	Cater-NY 50

Stolen Bases	Base Stealing Runs	Fielding Runs-Infield	Fielding Runs-Outfield	Wins	Winning Pct.	Complete Games
Otis-KC 52	Otis-KC 8.6	Nettles-Cle 46.1	Tovar-Min 14.1	Lolich-Det 25	McNally-Bal .808	Lolich-Det 29
Clarke-NY 17	Clarke-NY 1.3	Michael-NY 24.6	White-NY 4.5	Stottlemyre-NY 16	Stottlemyre-NY .571	Stottlemyre-NY 19
White-NY 14	Baker-NY .7	Cater-NY 10.2		Peterson-NY 15	Peterson-NY .536	Peterson-NY 16
Murcer-NY 14	White-NY .6	Kenney-NY 9.8		Bahnsen-NY 14		Kline-NY 15

Strikeouts	Fewest BB/Game	Games	Saves	Base Runners/9	Adjusted Relief Runs	Relief Ranking
Lolich-Det 308	Peterson-NY 1.38	Sanders-Mil 83	Sanders-Mil 31	Blue-Oak 8.68	Sanders-Mil 22.9	Sanders-Mil 40.5
Peterson-NY 139	Kline-NY 1.50	McDaniel-NY 44	McDaniel-NY 4	Kline-NY 9.84	Aker-NY 3.9	Aker-NY 5.6
Stottlemyre-NY 132	Stottlemyre-NY 2.30	Aker-NY 41	Aker-NY 4	Stottlemyre-NY 10.25		
Bahnsen-NY 110	Bahnsen-NY 2.68	2 players tied 37	Hambright-NY 2	Peterson-NY 10.35		

Innings Pitched	Opponents' Avg.	Opponents' OBP	Earned Run Average	Adjusted ERA	Adjusted Starter Runs	Pitcher Wins
Lolich-Det 376.0	Blue-Oak .189	Blue-Oak .251	Blue-Oak 1.82	Wood-Chi 186	Wood-Chi 55.1	Wood-Chi 5.7
Peterson-NY 274.0	Stottlemyre-NY .233	Kline-NY .275	Stottlemyre-NY 2.87	Stottlemyre-NY 115	Stottlemyre-NY 12.8	Stottlemyre-NY 1.7
Stottlemyre-NY 269.2	Kline-NY .244	Stottlemyre-NY .284	Kline-NY 2.96	Kline-NY 111	Peterson-NY 8.0	Kline-NY .9
Bahnsen-NY 242.0	Bahnsen-NY .248	Peterson-NY .287	Peterson-NY 3.05	Peterson-NY 108	Kline-NY 7.4	2 players tied .6

1972 American League

TEAM	W	L	T	PCT	GB	R	OR	HR	AVG	OBP	SLG	OPS	AOPS	PF	SB	CG	HR	BB	SO	BR/9	ERA	AERA	OAV	OOB	FW	PW	BW	BSW	DIF
East																													
Det	86	70	0	.551		558	514	122	.237	.305	.356	661	99	104	17	46	101	465	952	11.2	2.96	107	.236	.304	**1.9**	3.4	-.2	-.4	3.3
Bos	85	70	0	.548	0.5	**640**	620	124	.248	.318	**.376**	**694**	107	106	66	48	101	512	918	12.1	3.47	93	.251	.321	-.0	-4.0	5.8	**.5**	5.3
Bal	80	74	0	.519	5	519	**430**	100	.229	.302	.339	641	93	104	78	**62**	**85**	**395**	788	**10.0**	**2.53**	**123**	.224	**.282**	1.6	**9.8**	-3.5	.4	-5.2
NY	79	76	0	.510	6.5	557	527	103	.249	.316	.357	673	109	98	71	35	87	419	625	11.5	3.05	98	.252	.310	-.3	-1.1	6.8	.1	-4.0
Cle	72	84	0	.462	14	472	519	91	.234	.293	.330	623	88	104	49	47	123	534	846	11.5	2.92	111	.237	.311	.8	5.6	-8.2	-.9	-3.3
Mil	65	91	0	.417	21	493	595	88	.235	.302	.328	630	96	98	64	37	116	486	740	11.7	3.45	88	.247	.312	-.5	-7.0	-3.1	-.7	-1.7
West																													
Oak	93	62	0	.600		604	457	**134**	.240	.306	.366	672	**111**	95	87	42	96	418	862	10.2	2.58	110	.226	.284	-.0	5.1	7.5	.2	2.7
Chi	87	67	0	.565	5.5	566	538	108	.238	.310	.346	656	100	102	100	36	94	431	936	11.2	3.12	100	.245	.305	-.4	-.1	.3	**.5**	9.7
Min	77	77	0	.500	15.5	537	535	93	.244	.310	.344	654	96	105	53	37	105	444	838	10.7	2.84	113	.230	.294	-1.8	6.1	-2.0	-.3	-2.0
KC	76	78	0	.494	16.5	580	545	78	**.255**	**.327**	.353	680	110	100	85	44	**85**	405	801	11.3	3.24	94	.251	.307	.7	-3.6	**8.1**	.4	-6.5
Cal	75	80	0	.484	18	454	533	78	.242	.293	.330	623	96	95	57	57	90	620	**1000**	11.5	3.06	96	**.222**	.310	.8	-2.5	-3.8	.0	2.9
Tex	54	100	0	.351	38.5	461	628	56	.217	.290	.290	580	82	-97	**126**	11	92	613	868	12.6	3.53	86	.246	.329	-2.2	-8.5	-11.5	.2	-1.0
Total	929					56441		1175	.239	.306	.343	649			853	502				11.3	3.06		.239	.306					

Batter-Fielder Wins	Batting Average	On-Base Percentage	Slugging Average	On-Base Plus Slugging	Adjusted OPS	Adjusted Batter Runs
D.Allen-Chi 5.8	Carew-Min .318	D.Allen-Chi .420	D.Allen-Chi .603	D.Allen-Chi 1023	D.Allen-Chi 198	D.Allen-Chi 65.1
Murcer-NY 4.3	Murcer-NY .292	White-NY .384	Murcer-NY .537	Murcer-NY 898	Murcer-NY 169	Murcer-NY 47.7
Michael-NY 2.7	Munson-NY .280	Murcer-NY .361	White-NY .376	White-NY 760	White-NY 130	White-NY 26.7
White-NY 2.5	White-NY .270	Munson-NY .343	Munson-NY .364	Munson-NY 707	Munson-NY 113	Blomberg-NY 20.0

Runs	Hits	Doubles	Triples	Home Runs	Total Bases	Runs Batted In
Murcer-NY 102	Rudi-Oak 181	Piniella-KC 33	Rudi-Oak 9	D.Allen-Chi 37	Murcer-NY 314	D.Allen-Chi 113
White-NY 76	Murcer-NY 171	Murcer-NY 30	Fisk-Bos 9	Murcer-NY 33	White-NY 209	Murcer-NY 96
Clarke-NY 65	White-NY 150	White-NY 29	Murcer-NY 7	Blomberg-NY 14	Munson-NY 186	White-NY 54
Munson-NY 54	Munson-NY 143	Blomberg-NY 22	Michael-NY 4	White-NY 10	Clarke-NY 165	Blomberg-NY 49

Stolen Bases	Base Stealing Runs	Fielding Runs-Infield	Fielding Runs-Outfield	Wins	Winning Pct.	Complete Games
Campaneris-Oak 52	Campaneris-Oak 6.5	Patek-KC 37.7	Berry-Cal 8.0	Wood-Chi 24	Hunter-Oak .750	Perry-Cle 29
White-NY 23	White-NY 2.6	Michael-NY 24.0	White-NY 1.9	Perry-Cle 24	Kline-NY .640	Peterson-NY 12
Clarke-NY 18	Clarke-NY 1.9	Clarke-NY 15.3		Peterson-NY 17	Peterson-NY .531	Kline-NY 11
Murcer-NY 11	2 players tied .7			Kline-NY 16		Stottlemyre-NY 9

Strikeouts	Fewest BB/Game	Games	Saves	Base Runners/9	Adjusted Relief Runs	Relief Ranking
Ryan-Cal 329	Peterson-NY 1.58	Lindblad-Tex 66	Lyle-NY 35	Nelson-KC 7.89	Lyle-NY 13.6	Lyle-NY 25.9
Stottlemyre-NY 110	Kline-NY 1.68	Lyle-NY 59	Beene-NY 3	Lyle-NY 9.45	McDaniel-NY 4.1	McDaniel-NY 2.1
Peterson-NY 100	Stottlemyre-NY 2.94	McDaniel-NY 37	Klimkowski-NY 1	Kline-NY 10.05	Beene-NY 2.5	Beene-NY 1.8
Kekich-NY 78	Kekich-NY 3.90	Stottlemyre-NY 36		McDaniel-NY 10.46		

Innings Pitched	Opponents' Avg.	Opponents' OBP	Earned Run Average	Adjusted ERA	Adjusted Starter Runs	Pitcher Wins
Wood-Chi 376.2	Ryan-Cal .171	Nelson-KC .234	Tiant-Bos 1.91	Perry-Cle 170	Perry-Cle 49.2	Perry-Cle 6.8
Stottlemyre-NY 260.0	Kline-NY .237	Kline-NY .279	Kline-NY 2.40	Tiant-Bos 170	Kline-NY 12.5	Lyle-NY 3.1
Peterson-NY 250.1	Stottlemyre-NY .254	Peterson-NY .309	Stottlemyre-NY 3.22	Kline-NY 125	Gowell-NY 1.4	Kline-NY 1.2
Kline-NY 236.1	Kekich-NY .263	Stottlemyre-NY .314	Peterson-NY 3.24	Stottlemyre-NY 93		McDaniel-NY .5

1973 American League

TEAM	W	L	T	PCT	GB	R	OR	HR	AVG	OBP	SLG	OPS	AOPS	PF	SB	CG	HR	BB	SO	BR/9	ERA	AERA	OAV	OOB	FW	PW	BW	BSW	DIF
East																													
Bal	97	65	0	.599		754	**561**	119	.266	**.345**	.389	734	105	101	**146**	67	124	475	715	**11.0**	**3.07**	**123**	**.240**	**.302**	1.3	**11.9**	6.0	**1.0**	-4.2
Bos	89	73	0	.549	8	738	647	147	.267	.338	**.401**	**739**	101	106	114	67	158	499	808	12.2	3.65	110	.259	.323	.8	5.8	1.7	.9	-1.3
Det	85	77	0	.525	12	642	674	157	.254	.320	.390	710	93	107	28	39	154	493	911	12.4	3.90	105	.265	.326	**1.7**	3.0	-5.2	-.4	5.0
NY	80	82	0	.494	17	641	610	131	.261	.322	.378	700	99	98	47	47	109	**457**	708	11.7	3.34	111	.254	.313	-.8	6.0	-1.0	-.5	-4.7
Mil	74	88	0	.457	23	708	731	145	.253	.325	.388	713	101	99	110	50	119	623	671	13.2	3.98	95	.265	.340	-.2	-3.0	1.1	.0	-5.1
Cle	71	91	0	.438	26	680	826	**158**	.256	.315	.387	702	95	102	60	55	172	602	883	13.4	4.58	86	.271	.343	.2	-10.2	-4.5	-1.1	5.7
West																													
Oak	94	68	0	.580		**758**	615	147	.260	.333	.389	722	**108**	96	128	46	143	494	797	11.3	3.29	108	.241	.305	.3	4.8	**6.4**	.8	.7
KC	88	74	0	.543	6	755	752	114	.261	.339	.381	720	95	108	105	40	114	617	790	13.5	4.19	98	.273	.346	-1.4	-1.3	-1.8	-.1	11.7
Min	81	81	0	.500	13	738	692	120	**.270**	.342	.393	735	102	104	87	48	115	519	879	12.4	3.77	105	.259	.324	.2	3.1	2.7	.3	-6.2
Cal	79	83	0	.488	15	629	657	93	.253	.318	.348	666	93	93	59	**72**	**104**	614	**1010**	12.4	3.53	101	.246	.324	-.8	.8	-4.4	-.3	2.7
Chi	77	85	0	.475	17	652	705	111	.256	.324	.372	696	93	104	83	48	110	574	848	13.0	3.86	102	.266	.336	-.1	1.3	-5.2	-.7	.7
Tex	57	105	0	.352	37	619	844	110	.255	.318	.361	679	94	96	91	35	130	680	831	14.1	4.64	81	.273	.353	-1.1	-14.6	-4.3	.0	-4.1
Total	972					58314		1552	.259	.328	.381	710			1058	614				12.5	3.82		.259	.328					

Batter-Fielder Wins
Carew-Min 5.8
Munson-NY 4.9
Nettles-NY 3.7
Blomberg-NY 1.9

Batting Average
Carew-Min .350
Murcer-NY .304
Munson-NY .301
M.Alou-NY .296

On-Base Percentage
Mayberry-KC .417
Munson-NY .362
Murcer-NY .357
M.Alou-NY .338

Slugging Average
Jackson-Oak .531
Munson-NY .487
Murcer-NY .464
Nettles-NY .386

On-Base Plus Slugging
Jackson-Oak 914
Munson-NY 849
Murcer-NY 821
Nettles-NY 720

Adjusted OPS
Jackson-Oak 164
Munson-NY 141
Murcer-NY 133
Nettles-NY 105

Adjusted Batter Runs
Jackson-Oak 46.9
Munson-NY 27.8
Murcer-NY 26.1
Blomberg-NY 22.0

Runs
Jackson-Oak 99
White-NY 88
Murcer-NY 83
Munson-NY 80

Hits
Carew-Min 203
Murcer-NY 187
White-NY 157
Munson-NY 156

Doubles
Garcia-Mil 32
Bando-Oak 32
Murcer-NY 29
Munson-NY 29

Triples
Carew-Min 11
Bumbry-Bal 11
Munson-NY 4
White-NY 3

Home Runs
Jackson-Oak 32
Nettles-NY 22
Murcer-NY 22
Munson-NY 20

Total Bases
3 players tied 295
Murcer-NY 286
Munson-NY 253
White-NY 239

Runs Batted In
Jackson-Oak 117
Murcer-NY 95
Nettles-NY 81
Munson-NY 74

Stolen Bases
Harper-Bos 54
White-NY 16
Clarke-NY 11
Murcer-NY 6

Base Stealing Runs
Harper-Bos 7.0
Blomberg-NY .4
M.Alou-NY .4
White-NY .4

Fielding Runs-Infield
Patek-KC 39.8
Nettles-NY 32.7
Clarke-NY 16.2
Michael-NY 10.7

Fielding Runs-Outfield
North-Oak 15.4

Wins
Wood-Chi 24
Stottlemyre-NY 16
Medich-NY 14
McDaniel-NY 12

Winning Pct.
Hunter-Oak .808
Stottlemyre-NY .500

Complete Games
Perry-Cle 29
Stottlemyre-NY 19
Medich-NY 11
2 players tied 6

Strikeouts
Ryan-Cal 383
Medich-NY 145
Stottlemyre-NY 95
McDaniel-NY 93

Fewest BB/Game
Kaat-Min-Chi 1.73
Peterson-NY 2.39
Stottlemyre-NY 2.60
Medich-NY 2.83

Games
Hiller-Det 65
Lyle-NY 51
McDaniel-NY 47
Stottlemyre-NY 38

Saves
Hiller-Det 38
Lyle-NY 27
McDaniel-NY 10
2 players tied 1

Base Runners/9
Jackson-Bal 8.74
Lyle-NY 9.18
Beene-NY 9.40
McDaniel-NY 11.11

Adjusted Relief Runs
Hiller-Det 34.8
Lyle-NY 9.7

Relief Ranking
Hiller-Det 61.1
Lyle-NY 19.4

Innings Pitched
Wood-Chi 359.1
Stottlemyre-NY 273.0
Medich-NY 235.0
Peterson-NY 184.1

Opponents' Avg.
Bibby-Tex .192
Medich-NY .241
Stottlemyre-NY .253
Peterson-NY .286

Opponents' OBP
Tiant-Bos .278
Medich-NY .299
Stottlemyre-NY .307
Peterson-NY .336

Earned Run Average
Palmer-Bal 2.40
Medich-NY 2.95
Stottlemyre-NY 3.07
Peterson-NY 3.95

Adjusted ERA
Blyleven-Min 158
Medich-NY 126
Stottlemyre-NY 121
Peterson-NY 94

Adjusted Starter Runs
Blyleven-Min 48.2
Medich-NY 22.6
Beene-NY 20.5
Stottlemyre-NY 18.0

Pitcher Wins
Hiller-Det 6.7
McDaniel-NY 2.3
Stottlemyre-NY 2.1
2 players tied 2.0

1974 American League

TEAM	W	L	T	PCT	GB	R	OR	HR	AVG	OBP	SLG	OPS	AOPS	PF	SB	CG	HR	BB	SO	BR/9	ERA	AERA	OAV	OOB	FW	PW	BW	BSW	DIF
East																													
Bal	91	71	0	.562		659	612	116	.256	.322	.370	692	101	98	145	57	101	480	701	11.6	3.27	106	.253	.314	1.0	3.7	1.7	**1.2**	2.5
NY	89	73	0	.549	2	671	623	101	.263	.324	.368	692	100	99	53	53	104	528	829	12.1	3.31	107	.256	.323	.2	4.0	.8	-.2	3.1
Bos	84	78	0	.519	7	**696**	661	109	.264	.333	.377	710	97	107	104	**71**	126	463	751	12.1	3.72	103	.262	.320	.0	1.9	-.5	.3	1.3
Cle	77	85	0	.475	14	662	694	131	.255	.311	.370	681	96	99	79	45	138	479	650	12.0	3.80	96	.260	.320	-.0	-2.8	-3.6	-.7	3.1
Mil	76	86	0	.469	15	647	660	120	.244	.309	.369	678	94	100	106	43	126	493	621	12.3	3.76	97	.266	.326	**1.1**	-2.1	-4.2	-.4	.6
Det	72	90	0	.444	19	620	768	131	.247	.303	.366	669	89	104	67	54	148	621	869	13.0	4.16	92	.262	.338	-.7	-5.4	-9.3	.0	6.4
West																													
Oak	90	72	0	.556		689	**551**	132	.247	.321	.373	694	105	94	**164**	49	**90**	**430**	755	**11.1**	**2.95**	**113**	**.246**	**.302**	.3	**7.0**	4.4	.4	-3.0
Tex	84	76	1	.525	5	690	698	99	**.272**	**.336**	.377	713	**108**	98	113	62	126	449	871	12.0	3.82	94	.260	.318	-1.1	-4.1	**6.1**	-.4	3.4
Min	82	80	1	.506	8	673	669	111	**.272**	**.336**	.378	714	102	103	74	43	115	513	934	12.3	3.64	102	.260	.325	-.3	1.5	2.1	.0	-2.3
Chi	80	80	3	.500	9	684	721	**135**	.268	.330	**.389**	**719**	103	103	64	55	103	548	826	12.7	3.94	95	.263	.332	-.0	-3.1	3.3	-.5	.3
KC	77	85	0	.475	13	667	662	89	.259	.327	.364	691	94	106	146	54	91	482	731	12.2	3.51	109	.263	.322	-.4	4.9	-3.9	.6	-5.2
Cal	68	94	1	.420	22	618	657	95	.254	.321	.356	677	100	95	119	64	101	649	**986**	12.7	3.52	98	.248	.332	-.0	-.9	.4	-.2	-12.3
Total	973					57976		1369	.258	.323	.371	694			1234	650				12.2	3.62		.258	.323					

Batter-Fielder Wins
Carew-Min 6.9
Maddox-NY 2.7
Nettles-NY 2.6
Blomberg-NY 1.6

Batting Average
Carew-Min .364
Piniella-NY .305
Maddox-NY .303
White-NY .275

On-Base Percentage
Carew-Min .433
Maddox-NY .395
White-NY .367
Piniella-NY .341

Slugging Average
D.Allen-Chi .563
Piniella-NY .407
Nettles-NY .403
White-NY .393

On-Base Plus Slugging
D.Allen-Chi 938
Maddox-NY 781
White-NY 761
Piniella-NY 748

Adjusted OPS
Jackson-Oak 170
Maddox-NY 127
White-NY 121
Piniella-NY 118

Adjusted Batter Runs
Burroughs-Tex 50.0
Maddox-NY 21.0
Blomberg-NY 16.8
White-NY 14.8

Runs
Yastrzemski-Bos 93
Maddox-NY 75
Nettles-NY 74
Piniella-NY 71

Hits
Carew-Min 218
Murcer-NY 166
Piniella-NY 158
Maddox-NY 141

Doubles
Rudi-Oak 39
Piniella-NY 26
Maddox-NY 26
Murcer-NY 25

Triples
Rivers-Cal 11
White-NY 8
Mason-NY 6
Murcer-NY 4

Home Runs
D.Allen-Chi 32
Nettles-NY 22
Munson-NY 13
2 players tied 10

Total Bases
Rudi-Oak 287
Murcer-NY 229
Nettles-NY 228
Piniella-NY 211

Runs Batted In
Burroughs-Tex 118
Murcer-NY 88
Nettles-NY 75
Piniella-NY 70

Stolen Bases
North-Oak 54
White-NY 15
Murcer-NY 14
Maddox-NY 6

Base Stealing Runs
Jackson-Oak 3.8
Murcer-NY 1.3
White-NY 1.2
Munson-NY .4

Fielding Runs-Infield
Nettles-NY 20.3
Mason-NY .4

Fielding Runs-Outfield
Evans-Bos 11.6
Maddox-NY 10.0
Piniella-NY 9.3

Wins
Jenkins-Tex 25
Hunter-Oak 25
Medich-NY 19
Dobson-NY 19

Winning Pct.
Cuellar-Bal .688
Medich-NY .559
Dobson-NY .559

Complete Games
Jenkins-Tex 29
Medich-NY 17
Dobson-NY 12
Stottlemyre-NY 6

Strikeouts
Ryan-Cal 367
Dobson-NY 157
Medich-NY 154
Lyle-NY 89

Fewest BB/Game
Jenkins-Tex 1.23
Dobson-NY 2.40
Medich-NY 2.93

Games
Fingers-Oak 76
Lyle-NY 66
Dobson-NY 39
Medich-NY 38

Saves
Forster-Chi 24
Lyle-NY 15

Base Runners/9
Hunter-Oak 8.99
Lyle-NY 10.82
Dobson-NY 11.56
Medich-NY 12.04

Adjusted Relief Runs
Murphy-Mil 24.2
Lyle-NY 22.0

Relief Ranking
Murphy-Mil 44.3
Lyle-NY 27.3

Innings Pitched
Ryan-Cal 332.2
Dobson-NY 281.0
Medich-NY 279.2
Lyle-NY 114.0

Opponents' Avg.
Ryan-Cal .190
Medich-NY .259
Dobson-NY .262

Opponents' OBP
Hunter-Oak .258
Dobson-NY .311
Medich-NY .321

Earned Run Average
Hunter-Oak 2.49
Dobson-NY 3.07
Medich-NY 3.60

Adjusted ERA
G.Perry-Cle 145
Dobson-NY 115
Medich-NY 98

Adjusted Starter Runs
G.Perry-Cle 41.9
Dobson-NY 15.3
Gura-NY 7.4
Medich-NY 1.7

Pitcher Wins
Murphy-Mil 5.0
Lyle-NY 2.9
Dobson-NY 1.7
Gura-NY .8

1975 American League

TEAM	W	L	T	PCT	GB	R	OR	HR	AVG	OBP	SLG	OPS	AOPS	PF	SB	CG	HR	BB	SO	BR/9	ERA	AERA	OAV	OOB	FW	PW	BW	BSW	DIF
East																													
Bos	95	65	0	.594		**796**	709	134	**.275**	**.344**	**.417**	**761**	105	108	66	62	145	**490**	720	12.4	3.98	102	.265	.325	.9	1.1	**5.1**	-.7	8.6
Bal	90	69	0	.566	4.5	682	**553**	124	.252	.326	.373	699	103	94	104	**70**	110	500	717	**11.1**	**3.17**	112	.242	**.306**	**2.6**	6.4	2.9	.3	-1.7
NY	83	77	0	.519	12	681	588	110	.264	.325	.382	707	100	99	102	**70**	104	502	809	11.7	3.29	**113**	.249	.314	1.1	**6.8**	.4	.0	-5.4
Cle	79	80	0	.497	15.5	688	703	**153**	.261	.327	.392	719	102	100	106	37	136	599	800	12.7	3.84	99	.258	.333	1.1	-.7	1.4	-.9	-1.4
Mil	68	94	0	.420	28	675	792	146	.250	.320	.389	709	99	101	65	36	133	624	643	13.7	4.34	89	.271	.348	-1.4	-7.9	-.5	-.9	-2.3
Det	57	102	0	.358	37.5	570	786	125	.249	.301	.366	667	84	-104	63	52	137	533	787	13.3	4.27	94	.275	.340	-1.1	-3.7	-12.7	-.7	-4.3
West																													
Oak	98	64	0	.605		758	606	151	.254	.333	.391	724	**106**	98	183	36	**102**	523	784	11.4	3.27	111	**.236**	**.306**	.7	6.3	**5.1**	**1.1**	3.7
KC	91	71	0	.562	7	710	649	118	.261	.333	.394	727	102	103	155	52	108	498	815	12.0	3.47	111	.258	.320	.0	6.2	2.5	.7	.5
Tex	79	83	0	.488	19	714	733	134	.256	.330	.371	701	99	99	102	60	123	518	792	12.4	3.86	97	.261	.327	-2.0	-1.6	-.2	.0	1.8
Min	76	83	0	.478	20.5	724	736	121	.271	.341	.386	727	104	101	81	57	137	617	846	12.9	4.05	94	.257	.335	-.9	-3.7	4.1	.0	-3.0
Chi	75	86	0	.466	22.5	655	703	94	.255	.331	.358	689	94	101	101	34	107	655	799	13.5	3.93	99	.268	.347	.9	-.8	-3.3	.2	-2.5
Cal	72	89	0	.447	25.5	628	723	55	.246	.322	.328	650	90	-93	**220**	59	123	613	**975**	12.6	3.89	92	.253	.330	-1.6	-5.5	-5.8	1.0	3.5
Total	963					58281		1465	.258	.328	.379	707			1348	625				12.5	3.78		.258	.328					

Batter-Fielder Wins
- **Harrah-Tex............ 6.9**
- **Munson-NY........... 4.5**
- **Bonds-NY............. 3.8**
- **Nettles-NY............ 2.0**

Batting Average
- Carew-Min............ .359
- Munson-NY............ .318
- Chambliss-NY....... .304
- White-NY.............. .290

On-Base Percentage
- Carew-Min............ .421
- Bonds-NY............ .375
- White-NY.............. .372
- Munson-NY........... .366

Slugging Average
- Lynn-Bos.............. .566
- Bonds-NY............ .512
- Chambliss-NY....... .434
- 2 players tied........ .430

On-Base Plus Slugging
- Lynn-Bos.............. 967
- Bonds-NY............ 888
- White-NY.............. 802
- Munson-NY........... 795

Adjusted OPS
- Mayberry-KC......... 167
- Bonds-NY............ 151
- White-NY.............. 128
- Munson-NY........... 127

Adjusted Batter Runs
- Mayberry-KC........ 55.3
- Bonds-NY............ 37.5
- White-NY.............. 22.3
- Munson-NY........... 21.0

Runs
- Lynn-Bos.............. 103
- Bonds-NY.............. 93
- Munson-NY............ 83
- White-NY................ 81

Hits
- Brett-KC................ 195
- Munson-NY........... 190
- Chambliss-NY....... 171
- White-NY.............. 161

Doubles
- Lynn-Bos................ 47
- Chambliss-NY......... 38
- White-NY................ 32
- Bonds-NY............... 26

Triples
- Rivers-Cal............... 13
- Brett-KC................. 13
- White-NY.................. 5
- 3 players tied............ 4

Home Runs
- Scott-Mil................ 36
- Jackson-Oak........... 36
- Bonds-NY............... 32
- Nettles-NY.............. 21

Total Bases
- Scott-Mil.............. 318
- Bonds-NY............ 271
- Munson-NY.......... 256
- Nettles-NY........... 250

Runs Batted In
- Scott-Mil.............. 109
- Munson-NY.......... 102
- Nettles-NY.............. 91
- Bonds-NY............... 85

Stolen Bases
- Rivers-Cal............... 70
- Bonds-NY............... 30
- Alomar-NY.............. 28
- White-NY................ 16

Base Stealing Runs
- Rivers-Cal............ 10.5
- Alomar-NY............. 4.1
- Maddox-NY............... .9
- Bonds-NY................. .7

Fielding Runs-Infield
- Belanger-Bal......... 29.5
- Nettles-NY........... 12.5
- Chambliss-NY......... 3.6

Fielding Runs-Outfield
- Evans-Bos............ 18.7
- White-NY............... 8.1
- Bonds-NY.............. 5.3

Wins
- Palmer-Bal.............. 23
- Hunter-NY.............. 23
- Hunter-NY.............. 23
- Medich-NY.............. 16

Winning Pct.
- Torrez-Bal............ .690
- Hunter-NY............ .622
- Medich-NY........... .500

Complete Games
- Hunter-NY.............. 30
- Medich-NY.............. 15
- May-NY.................. 13
- Dobson-NY................ 7

Strikeouts
- Tanana-Cal........... 269
- Hunter-NY............ 177
- May-NY................ 145
- Medich-NY........... 132

Fewest BB/Game
- Jenkins-Tex.......... 1.87
- Hunter-NY............ 2.28
- Medich-NY........... 2.38
- Dobson-NY........... 3.60

Games
- Fingers-Oak............ 75
- Lyle-NY.................. 49
- Hunter-NY.............. 39
- Medich-NY.............. 38

Saves
- Gossage-Chi........... 26
- Martinez-NY.............. 8
- Lyle-NY..................... 6
- Tidrow-NY.................. 5

Base Runners/9
- Hunter-NY............ 9.22
- Medich-NY..........11.37
- May-NY................11.89
- Dobson-NY.......... 12.52

Adjusted Relief Runs
- Gossage-Chi......... 31.4
- Lyle-NY................. 6.4
- Tidrow-NY............. 4.7

Relief Ranking
- Gossage-Chi......... 46.9
- Lyle-NY................. 8.7
- Tidrow-NY............. 6.3

Innings Pitched
- Hunter-NY.......... 328.0
- Medich-NY.......... 272.1
- May-NY.............. 212.0
- Dobson-NY......... 207.2

Opponents' Avg.
- Hunter-NY............ .208
- May-NY................ .231
- Dobson-NY.......... .261
- Medich-NY........... .264

Opponents' OBP
- Hunter-NY............ .261
- Medich-NY........... .309
- May-NY................ .317
- Dobson-NY.......... .330

Earned Run Average
- Palmer-Bal........... 2.09
- Hunter-NY............ 2.58
- May-NY................ 3.06
- Medich-NY........... 3.50

Adjusted ERA
- Palmer-Bal............ 170
- Hunter-NY............ 144
- May-NY................ 121
- Medich-NY........... 106

Adjusted Starter Runs
- Palmer-Bal........... 53.0
- Hunter-NY............ 41.7
- May-NY................ 13.2
- Medich-NY............. 8.6

Pitcher Wins
- Palmer-Bal............. 5.7
- Hunter-NY.............. 4.4
- May-NY.................. 1.5
- Lyle-NY..................... .9

1976 American League

TEAM	W	L	T	PCT	GB	R	OR	HR	AVG	OBP	SLG	OPS	AOPS	PF	SB	CG	HR	BB	SO	BR/9	ERA	AERA	OAV	OOB	FW	PW	BW	BSW	DIF
East																													
NY	97	62	0	.610		730	**575**	120	.269	.328	.389	717	**110**	100	163	62	97	448	674	**10.9**	**3.19**	107	**.241**	**.298**	.9	3.9	**7.3**	.8	4.6
Bal	88	74	0	.543	10.5	619	598	119	.243	.310	.358	668	101	95	150	59	**80**	489	678	11.7	3.32	99	.255	.315	**1.5**	-.4	.2	.7	5.1
Bos	83	79	0	.512	15.5	716	660	**134**	.263	.324	**.402**	**726**	100	112	95	49	109	**409**	673	12.0	3.52	**110**	.267	.318	.2	**5.5**	.5	-1.0	-3.2
Cle	81	78	0	.509	16	615	615	85	.263	.321	.359	680	100	99	75	30	**80**	533	928	12.1	3.47	101	.255	.324	1.2	.7	.0	-1.5	1.0
Det	74	87	0	.460	24	609	709	101	.257	.315	.365	680	95	104	107	55	101	550	738	12.6	3.87	96	.263	.331	-1.4	-2.3	-3.6	-.3	1.2
Mil	66	95	0	.410	32	570	655	88	.246	.311	.340	651	93	98	62	45	99	567	677	12.6	3.64	96	.260	.331	-.5	-2.2	-5.2	-1.5	-5.1
West																													
KC	90	72	0	.556		713	611	65	.269	.327	.371	698	103	101	218	41	83	493	735	11.5	3.21	109	.247	.309	.3	5.1	3.6	.6	-.6
Oak	87	74	0	.540	2.5	686	598	113	.246	.323	.361	684	104	96	**341**	39	96	415	711	11.5	3.26	103	.255	.308	-.0	1.9	4.5	**2.8**	-2.6
Min	85	77	0	.525	5	**743**	704	81	**.274**	**.341**	.375	716	108	102	146	29	89	610	762	12.8	3.69	97	.259	.335	-1.6	-2.1	7.0	.0	.7
Tex	76	86	0	.469	14	616	652	80	.250	.321	.341	662	92	102	87	63	106	461	773	12.0	3.45	104	.262	.320	-.7	2.2	-4.6	-.3	-1.7
Cal	76	86	0	.469	14	550	631	63	.235	.306	.318	624	88	-94	126	**64**	95	553	**992**	11.7	3.36	100	**.241**	.313	-.3	-.2	-7.3	-.6	3.5
Chi	64	97	0	.398	25.5	586	745	73	.255	.314	.349	663	93	101	120	54	87	600	802	13.0	4.25	84	.266	.338	.7	-11.6	-4.5	.2	-1.5
Total	967					57753		1122	.256	.320	.361	681			1690	590				12.0	3.52		.256	.320					

Batter-Fielder Wins
- **Grich-Bal.............. 4.8**
- **Nettles-NY............ 4.2**
- **Randolph-NY......... 2.9**
- **Munson-NY........... 2.5**

Batting Average
- Brett-KC................ .333
- Rivers-NY............. .312
- Munson-NY........... .302
- Chambliss-NY....... .293

On-Base Percentage
- McRae-KC............ .407
- White-NY.............. .365
- Randolph-NY........ .356
- Munson-NY........... .337

Slugging Average
- R.Jackson-Bal...... .502
- Nettles-NY........... .475
- Chambliss-NY....... .441
- 2 players tied........ .432

On-Base Plus Slugging
- McRae-KC............ 868
- Nettles-NY........... 802
- White-NY.............. 774
- Munson-NY........... 769

Adjusted OPS
- R.Jackson-Bal....... 157
- Nettles-NY........... 134
- White-NY.............. 128
- Munson-NY........... 126

Adjusted Batter Runs
- McRae-KC........... 39.5
- White-NY............. 24.9
- Nettles-NY........... 23.9
- Munson-NY........... 18.5

Runs
- White-NY.............. 104
- Rivers-NY............... 95
- Nettles-NY.............. 88
- 2 players tied.......... 79

Hits
- Brett-KC................ 215
- Chambliss-NY....... 188
- Munson-NY........... 186
- Rivers-NY............. 184

Doubles
- Otis-KC................... 40
- Chambliss-NY......... 32
- Rivers-NY............... 31
- 2 players tied.......... 29

Triples
- Brett-KC.................. 14
- Rivers-NY.................. 8
- Piniella-NY................ 6
- Chambliss-NY........... 6

Home Runs
- Nettles-NY.............. 32
- Munson-NY............. 17
- Gamble-NY.............. 17
- Chambliss-NY......... 17

Total Bases
- Brett-KC............... 298
- Chambliss-NY....... 283
- Nettles-NY........... 277
- Munson-NY.......... 266

Runs Batted In
- L.May-Bal............. 109
- Munson-NY.......... 105
- Chambliss-NY......... 96
- Nettles-NY.............. 93

Stolen Bases
- North-Oak............... 75
- Rivers-NY............... 43
- Randolph-NY.......... 37
- White-NY................ 31

Base Stealing Runs
- Campaneris-Oak.... 7.7
- Rivers-NY.............. 7.0
- Randolph-NY......... 3.9
- White-NY............... 2.3

Fielding Runs-Infield
- Remy-Cal............. 19.2
- Nettles-NY........... 16.9
- Randolph-NY........11.2

Fielding Runs-Outfield
- Beniquez-Tex........ 12.9

Wins
- Palmer-Bal.............. 22
- Figueroa-NY........... 19
- Hunter-NY.............. 17
- Ellis-NY.................. 17

Winning Pct.
- Campbell-Min....... .773
- Ellis-NY............... .680
- Figueroa-NY......... .655
- Hunter-NY............ .531

Complete Games
- Fidrych-Det............ 24
- Hunter-NY.............. 21
- Figueroa-NY........... 14
- Ellis-NY.................... 8

Strikeouts
- Ryan-Cal............... 327
- Hunter-NY............ 173
- Figueroa-NY...........119
- 2 players tied.......... 65

Fewest BB/Game
- Bird-KC................ 1.41
- Hunter-NY............ 2.05
- Ellis-NY............... 3.23
- Figueroa-NY......... 3.30

Games
- Campbell-Min.......... 78
- Lyle-NY.................. 64
- Tidrow-NY.............. 47
- Hunter-NY.............. 36

Saves
- Lyle-NY................... 23
- Tidrow-NY.............. 10

Base Runners/9
- Tanana-Cal........... 9.18
- Hunter-NY.......... 10.22
- Tidrow-NY.......... 10.23
- Lyle-NY.............. 10.77

Adjusted Relief Runs
- Littell-KC............. 17.4
- Lyle-NY.................11.9
- Tidrow-NY............. 8.8

Relief Ranking
- Hiller-Det............. 29.5
- Lyle-NY................ 21.5
- Tidrow-NY.............. 9.9

Innings Pitched
- Palmer-Bal.......... 315.0
- Hunter-NY.......... 298.2
- Figueroa-NY....... 256.2
- Ellis-NY...............211.2

Opponents' Avg.
- Ryan-Cal.............. .195
- Hunter-NY............ .241
- Figueroa-NY......... .246
- Ellis-NY................ .247

Opponents' OBP
- Tanana-Cal.......... .261
- Hunter-NY........... .283
- Ellis-NY............... .312
- Figueroa-NY......... .312

Earned Run Average
- Fidrych-Det.......... 2.34
- Figueroa-NY........ 3.02
- Ellis-NY............... 3.19
- Hunter-NY........... 3.53

Adjusted ERA
- Fidrych-Det.......... 159
- Figueroa-NY..........113
- Ellis-NY................ 107
- Hunter-NY.............. 97

Adjusted Starter Runs
- Fidrych-Det.......... 36.1
- Figueroa-NY.......... 9.4
- Ellis-NY................ 5.8

Pitcher Wins
- Fidrych-Det............ 4.5
- Lyle-NY.................. 2.3
- Tidrow-NY.............. 1.0
- Figueroa-NY............ .8

1977 American League

TEAM	W	L	T	PCT	GB	R	OR	HR	AVG	OBP	SLG	OPS	AOPS	PF	SB	CG	HR	BB	SO	BR/9	ERA	AERA	OAV	OOB	FW	PW	BW	BSW	DIF
East																													
NY	100	62	0	.617		831	**651**	184	.281	.344	.444	788	**114**	99	93	52	139	486	758	11.8	3.61	110	.254	**.315**	.6	5.7	**11.0**	.1	1.6
Bal	97	64	0	.602	2.5	719	653	148	.261	.329	.393	722	102	94	90	**65**	124	494	737	12.0	3.74	102	.260	.322	**2.0**	1.4	2.0	.2	10.9
Bos	97	64	0	.602	2.5	859	712	**213**	.281	.345	**.465**	**810**	106	111	66	40	158	**378**	758	12.3	4.11	109	.278	.325	.5	5.2	5.6	-.2	5.4
Det	74	88	0	.457	26	714	751	166	.264	.318	.410	728	92	105	60	44	162	470	784	12.5	4.13	104	.271	.327	.0	2.6	-6.3	-.3	-3.1
Cle	71	90	0	.441	28.5	676	739	100	.269	.334	.380	714	97	97	87	45	136	550	876	12.5	4.10	97	.261	.329	.7	-1.9	-1.2	-1.1	-6.0
Mil	67	95	0	.414	33	639	765	125	.258	.314	.389	703	90	100	85	38	136	566	719	13.0	4.32	95	.268	.337	.2	-3.6	-7.5	-.5	-2.7
Tor	54	107	0	.335	45.5	605	822	100	.252	.316	.365	681	84	-101	65	40	152	623	771	13.7	4.57	93	.278	.350	-1.2	-5.1	-11.4	-.5	-8.3
West																													
KC	102	60	0	.630		822	**651**	146	.277	.340	.436	776	109	101	170	41	**110**	499	850	11.8	**3.52**	**114**	**.251**	**.315**	.3	**8.1**	7.5	.7	4.3
Tex	94	68	0	.580	8	767	657	135	.270	.342	.405	747	102	101	154	49	134	471	864	**11.7**	3.56	**114**	.255	**.315**	1.5	8.0	2.8	.4	.3
Chi	90	72	0	.556	12	844	771	192	.278	.344	.444	788	113	100	42	34	136	516	842	13.2	4.25	96	.277	.339	-.9	-2.9	10.7	-.6	2.6
Min	84	77	0	.522	17.5	**867**	776	123	**.282**	**.348**	.417	765	108	99	105	35	151	507	737	13.0	4.36	91	.278	.340	-.0	-6.3	8.1	.0	1.6
Cal	74	88	0	.457	28	675	695	131	.255	.324	.386	710	96	97	159	53	136	572	**965**	12.5	3.72	105	.256	.330	-.2	3.3	-2.2	.4	-8.3
Sea	64	98	0	.395	38	624	855	133	.256	.312	.381	693	88	100	110	18	194	578	785	13.5	4.83	86	.272	.344	-.2	-10.8	-9.0	.1	3.0
Oak	63	98	0	.391	38.5	605	749	117	.240	.308	.352	660	80	-99	**176**	32	145	560	788	12.8	4.04	100	.265	.333	-2.7	-.3	-14.1	**.8**	-1.2
Total	1131					50247		2013	.266	.330	.405	735			1462	586				12.6	4.06		.266	.330					

Batter-Fielder Wins
Carew-Min 6.5
Jackson-NY 3.0
Randolph-NY 2.4
Munson-NY 2.3

Batting Average
Carew-Min .... .388
Rivers-NY .... .326
Munson-NY .... .308
Chambliss-NY .... .287

On-Base Percentage
Carew-Min .... .449
Jackson-NY .... .375
White-NY .... .358
Munson-NY .... .351

Slugging Average
Rice-Bos .... .593
Jackson-NY .... .550
Nettles-NY .... .496
Munson-NY .... .462

On-Base Plus Slugging
Carew-Min 1019
Jackson-NY 925
Nettles-NY 829
Munson-NY 813

Adjusted OPS
Carew-Min 178
Jackson-NY 150
Nettles-NY 124
Munson-NY 121

Adjusted Batter Runs
Carew-Min 69.3
Jackson-NY 38.1
Nettles-NY 18.0
Piniella-NY 16.9

Runs
Carew-Min 128
Nettles-NY 99
Jackson-NY 93
Randolph-NY 91

Hits
Carew-Min 239
Rivers-NY 184
Munson-NY 183
Chambliss-NY 172

Doubles
McRae-KC 54
Jackson-NY 39
Chambliss-NY 32
2 players tied 28

Triples
Carew-Min 16
Randolph-NY 11
Chambliss-NY 6
2 players tied 5

Home Runs
Rice-Bos 39
Nettles-NY 37
Jackson-NY 32
Munson-NY 18

Total Bases
Rice-Bos 382
Nettles-NY 292
Jackson-NY 289
Munson-NY 275

Runs Batted In
Hisle-Min 119
Jackson-NY 110
Nettles-NY 107
Munson-NY 100

Stolen Bases
Patek-KC 53
Rivers-NY 22
White-NY 18
Jackson-NY 17

Base Stealing Runs
Page-Oak 7.5
Jackson-NY 2.7
Chambliss-NY 9
Randolph-NY 8

Fielding Runs-Infield
Campaneris-Tex ... 26.1
Randolph-NY 13.7

Fielding Runs-Outfield
Lemon-Chi 23.1
Rivers-NY 6.5
White-NY 3.9

Wins
3 players tied 20
Guidry-NY 16
Figueroa-NY 16
Gullett-NY 14

Winning Pct.
Splittorff-KC .... .727
Guidry-NY .... .696
Figueroa-NY .... .593

Complete Games
Ryan-Cal 22
Palmer-Bal 22
Figueroa-NY 12
Guidry-NY 9

Strikeouts
Ryan-Cal 341
Guidry-NY 176
Gullett-NY 116
Figueroa-NY 104

Fewest BB/Game
Rozema-Det 1.40
Guidry-NY 2.78
Figueroa-NY 2.82

Games
Lyle-NY 72
Tidrow-NY 49
Figueroa-NY 32
Guidry-NY 31

Saves
Campbell-Bos 31
Lyle-NY 26
Tidrow-NY 5
3 players tied 1

Base Runners/9
Foucault-Det 9.81
Guidry-NY 10.21
Lyle-NY 10.91
Tidrow-NY 11.09

Adjusted Relief Runs
Lyle-NY 26.2

Relief Ranking
Campbell-Bos 42.7
Lyle-NY 42.1

Innings Pitched
Palmer-Bal 319.0
Figueroa-NY 239.1
Guidry-NY 210.2
Gullett-NY 158.1

Opponents' Avg.
Ryan-Cal .... .193
Guidry-NY .... .224
Figueroa-NY .... .252

Opponents' OBP
Eckersley-Cle .... .276
Guidry-NY .... .283
Figueroa-NY .... .308

Earned Run Average
Tanana-Cal 2.54
Guidry-NY 2.82
Figueroa-NY 3.57

Adjusted ERA
Tanana-Cal 155
Guidry-NY 141
Figueroa-NY 111

Adjusted Starter Runs
Tanana-Cal 41.8
Guidry-NY 28.3
Tidrow-NY 14.9
Figueroa-NY 12.6

Pitcher Wins
Campbell-Bos 4.5
Lyle-NY 4.3
Guidry-NY 2.9
Tidrow-NY 1.4

1978 American League

TEAM	W	L	T	PCT	GB	R	OR	HR	AVG	OBP	SLG	OPS	AOPS	PF	SB	CG	HR	BB	SO	BR/9	ERA	AERA	OAV	OOB	FW	PW	BW	BSW	DIF
East																													
NY	100	63	0	.613		735	**582**	125	.267	.329	.388	717	103	98	98	39	111	478	817	**11.3**	**3.18**	115	**.243**	**.306**	1.5	8.0	2.7	.6	5.6
Bos	99	64	0	.607	1	796	657	172	.267	.336	.424	760	101	110	74	57	137	464	706	12.4	3.54	**116**	.270	.327	-.3	**8.8**	2.4	-.3	7.0
Mil	93	69	0	.574	6.5	**804**	650	**173**	**.276**	**.339**	**.432**	**771**	**114**	101	95	62	109	**398**	577	11.8	3.65	104	.262	.313	-.6	2.1	**11.4**	.1	-1.0
Bal	90	71	0	.559	9	659	633	154	.258	.326	.396	722	108	94	75	**65**	107	509	754	11.7	3.56	99	.251	.316	**1.6**	-.8	6.5	-.6	2.8
Det	86	76	0	.531	13.5	714	653	129	.271	**.339**	.392	731	102	103	90	60	135	503	684	12.2	3.64	107	.263	.325	1.2	3.9	2.3	.6	-3.0
Cle	69	90	0	.434	29	639	694	106	.261	.323	.379	702	98	99	64	36	**100**	568	739	12.7	3.97	95	.261	.332	.8	-3.2	-1.5	-.9	-5.6
Tor	59	102	0	.366	40	590	775	98	.250	.308	.359	667	85	102	28	35	149	614	758	13.6	4.54	87	.279	.351	.4	-9.3	-11.1	-1.3	-.2
West																													
KC	92	70	0	.568		743	634	98	.268	.329	.399	728	101	103	**216**	53	108	478	657	11.6	3.44	111	.251	.313	-.6	6.1	1.6	**1.8**	2.1
Tex	87	75	0	.537	5	692	632	132	.253	.332	.381	713	99	101	196	54	108	421	776	11.6	3.36	111	.259	.312	-.8	6.4	.8	1.0	-1.5
Cal	87	75	0	.537	5	691	666	108	.259	.330	.370	700	99	97	86	44	125	599	**892**	12.4	3.65	99	.253	.327	.2	-.5	.9	-.6	6.0
Min	73	89	0	.451	19	666	678	82	.267	**.339**	.375	714	99	103	99	48	102	520	703	12.5	3.69	104	.266	.330	-.4	2.2	.5	.1	-10.4
Chi	71	90	0	.441	20.5	634	731	106	.264	.317	.379	696	94	101	83	38	128	586	710	12.8	4.21	90	.259	.334	-.0	-6.8	-4.6	-.7	2.7
Oak	69	93	0	.426	23	532	690	100	.245	.303	.351	654	87	-95	144	26	106	582	750	12.6	3.62	101	.259	.330	-2.3	.4	-9.7	-1.0	.6
Sea	56	104	0	.350	35	614	834	97	.248	.314	.359	673	89	100	123	28	155	567	630	13.6	4.67	82	.280	.348	-.2	-13.4	-7.5	1.0	-3.9
Total	1131					69509		1680	.261	.326	.385	711			1471	645				12.4	3.76		.261	.326					

Batter-Fielder Wins
Smalley-Min 5.1
Randolph-NY 2.8
Nettles-NY 1.4
Jackson-NY 1.4

Batting Average
Carew-Min .... .333
Piniella-NY .... .314
Munson-NY .... .297
Randolph-NY .... .279

On-Base Percentage
Carew-Min .... .411
Randolph-NY .... .381
Piniella-NY .... .361
Jackson-NY .... .356

Slugging Average
Rice-Bos .... .600
Jackson-NY .... .477
Nettles-NY .... .460
Piniella-NY .... .445

On-Base Plus Slugging
Rice-Bos 970
Jackson-NY 834
Piniella-NY 806
Nettles-NY 803

Adjusted OPS
Singleton-Bal 154
Jackson-NY 135
Piniella-NY 128
Nettles-NY 128

Adjusted Batter Runs
Rice-Bos 44.5
Jackson-NY 23.4
Nettles-NY 20.9
Piniella-NY 17.7

Runs
LeFlore-Det 126
Randolph-NY 87
Jackson-NY 82
2 players tied 81

Hits
Rice-Bos 213
Munson-NY 183
Chambliss-NY 171
Nettles-NY 162

Doubles
Brett-KC 45
Piniella-NY 34
Munson-NY 27
Chambliss-NY 26

Triples
Rice-Bos 15
Rivers-NY 8
Randolph-NY 6
2 players tied 5

Home Runs
Rice-Bos 46
Nettles-NY 27
Jackson-NY 27
Chambliss-NY 12

Total Bases
Rice-Bos 406
Nettles-NY 270
Jackson-NY 244
Chambliss-NY 239

Runs Batted In
Rice-Bos 139
Jackson-NY 97
Nettles-NY 93
Chambliss-NY 90

Stolen Bases
LeFlore-Det 68
Randolph-NY 36
Rivers-NY 25
Jackson-NY 14

Base Stealing Runs
Cruz-Sea 9.5
Randolph-NY 5.5
Rivers-NY 3.8
White-NY 8

Fielding Runs-Infield
Belanger-Bal 30.3
Chambliss-NY 4.3
Randolph-NY 3.3

Fielding Runs-Outfield
Bosetti-Tor 14.4
Rivers-NY 4.3

Wins
Guidry-NY 25
Figueroa-NY 20
Hunter-NY 12
Gossage-NY 10

Winning Pct.
Guidry-NY .... .893
Figueroa-NY .... .690

Complete Games
Caldwell-Mil 23
Guidry-NY 16
Figueroa-NY 12
Hunter-NY 5

Strikeouts
Ryan-Cal 260
Guidry-NY 248
Gossage-NY 122
Figueroa-NY 92

Fewest BB/Game
Jenkins-Tex 1.48
Guidry-NY 2.37
Tidrow-NY 2.57
Figueroa-NY 2.74

Games
Lacey-Oak 74
Gossage-NY 63
Lyle-NY 59
2 players tied 35

Saves
Gossage-NY 27
Lyle-NY 9

Base Runners/9
Guidry-NY 8.55
Gossage-NY 9.92
Hunter-NY 10.22
Figueroa-NY 11.13

Adjusted Relief Runs
Gossage-NY 22.1
Lyle-NY 3.6

Relief Ranking
Gossage-NY 41.1
Lyle-NY 4.1

Innings Pitched
Palmer-Bal 296.0
Guidry-NY 273.2
Figueroa-NY 253.0
Tidrow-NY 185.1

Opponents' Avg.
Guidry-NY .... .193
Figueroa-NY .... .248
Tidrow-NY .... .267

Opponents' OBP
Guidry-NY .... .249
Figueroa-NY .... .305
Tidrow-NY .... .320

Earned Run Average
Guidry-NY 1.74
Figueroa-NY 2.99
Tidrow-NY 3.84

Adjusted ERA
Guidry-NY 210
Figueroa-NY 122
Tidrow-NY 95

Adjusted Starter Runs
Guidry-NY 59.6
Figueroa-NY 18.9
Hunter-NY 2.8
Gullett-NY 8

Pitcher Wins
Guidry-NY 6.4
Gossage-NY 4.3
Figueroa-NY 2.0
Lyle-NY 5

1979 American League

TEAM	W	L	T	PCT	GB	R	OR	HR	AVG	OBP	SLG	OPS	AOPS	PF	SB	CG	HR	BB	SO	BR/9	ERA	AERA	OAV	OOB	FW	PW	BW	BSW	DIF
East																													
Bal	102	57	0	.642		757	**582**	181	.261	.336	.419	755	106	97	99	52	133	467	786	**11.0**	**3.26**	**124**	**.241**	**.301**	.8	**12.6**	5.5	.2	3.5
Mil	95	66	0	.590	8	807	722	185	.280	.345	.448	793	**112**	100	100	**61**	162	**381**	580	12.3	4.03	104	.279	.324	.7	2.4	9.4	.0	1.9
Bos	91	69	0	.569	11.5	841	711	**194**	**.283**	.344	**.456**	**800**	108	106	60	47	133	463	731	12.5	4.03	110	.270	.328	-.2	6.1	6.5	-.5	-1.0
NY	89	71	0	.556	13.5	734	672	150	.266	.328	.406	734	99	98	65	43	123	455	731	12.0	3.83	107	.268	.323	1.0	4.4	-1.1	-.5	5.2
Det	85	76	0	.528	18	770	738	164	.269	.339	.415	754	99	103	176	25	167	547	802	12.8	4.27	102	.265	.335	**1.1**	1.0	-.0	.6	1.9
Cle	81	80	0	.503	22	760	805	138	.258	.340	.384	724	95	100	143	28	138	570	781	13.2	4.57	94	.272	.339	.3	-4.4	-2.1	-.3	7.0
Tor	53	109	0	.327	50.5	613	862	95	.251	.311	[illegible]	674	[illegible]	101	75	44	165	594	613	13.8	4.82	91	.281	.353	-1.0	-6.5	-14.6	-.6	-5.2
West																													
Cal	88	74	0	.543		**866**	768	164	.282	**.351**	.429	780	**112**	97	100	46	131	573	**820**	13.0	4.34	94	.267	.336	.3	-4.3	**10.7**	.0	.2
KC	85	77	0	.525	3	851	816	116	.282	.343	.422	765	103	102	**207**	42	165	536	640	12.7	4.45	96	.267	.331	-.3	-3.0	3.1	**1.6**	2.6
Tex	83	79	0	.512	5	750	698	140	.278	.334	.409	743	100	99	79	26	135	532	773	12.1	3.86	107	.253	.321	.6	4.3	.5	-.3	-3.1
Min	82	80	0	.506	6	764	725	112	.278	.341	.402	743	96	104	66	31	128	452	721	12.8	4.13	106	.285	.338	.4	3.8	-2.4	-.4	-.4
Chi	73	87	0	.456	14	730	748	127	.275	.333	.410	743	99	100	97	28	**114**	618	675	12.9	4.10	104	.256	.334	-1.9	2.1	-.5	-.3	-6.5
Sea	67	95	0	.414	21	711	820	132	.269	.331	.404	735	95	102	126	37	165	571	736	13.6	4.58	95	.281	.348	.0	-3.2	-3.3	.7	-8.2
Oak	54	108	0	.333	34	573	860	108	.239	.302	.346	648	78	-95	104	41	147	654	726	14.5	4.75	85	.288	.363	-1.9	-11.4	-16.3	-.4	2.9
Total	1128					60527		2006	.270	.334	.408	743			1497	551				12.8	4.22		.270	.334					

Batter-Fielder Wins
Smalley-Min............ 5.6
Randolph-NY......... 3.3
Jackson-NY........... 2.6
Dent-NY................. 2.0

Batting Average
Lynn-Bos .... .333
Jackson-NY .... .297
Chambliss-NY....... .280
Randolph-NY .... .270

On-Base Percentage
Lynn-Bos .... .423
Jackson-NY .... .382
Randolph-NY .... .374
Nettles-NY .... .325

Slugging Average
Lynn-Bos .... .637
Jackson-NY .... .544
Chambliss-NY....... .437
Nettles-NY .... .401

On-Base Plus Slugging
Lynn-Bos 1059
Jackson-NY 926
Chambliss-NY........ 761
Randolph-NY......... 741

Adjusted OPS
Lynn-Bos 173
Jackson-NY 150
Chambliss-NY........ 106
Randolph-NY......... 103

Adjusted Batter Runs
Lynn-Bos 57.1
Jackson-NY 33.4
Spencer-NY 23.0
Randolph-NY.......... 5.8

Runs
Baylor-Cal............. 120
Randolph-NY........... 98
Jackson-NY 78
Nettles-NY 71

Hits
Brett-KC................ 212
Randolph-NY........ 155
Chambliss-NY........ 155
Jackson-NY 138

Doubles
Lemon-Chi.............. 44
Cooper-Mil.............. 44
Chambliss-NY......... 27
Jackson-NY 24

Triples
Brett-KC.................. 20
Randolph-NY........... 13
3 players tied 3

Home Runs
Thomas-Mil............. 45
Jackson-NY 29
Spencer-NY 23
Nettles-NY 20

Total Bases
Rice-Bos............... 369
Jackson-NY 253
Chambliss-NY........ 242
Randolph-NY..........211

Runs Batted In
Baylor-Cal............. 139
Jackson-NY 89
Nettles-NY 73
Piniella-NY.............. 69

Stolen Bases
Wilson-KC................ 83
Randolph-NY........... 33
Jackson-NY 9
3 players tied 3

Base Stealing Runs
Wilson-KC............. 14.1
Randolph-NY.......... 3.1
Garcia-NY................. .4
Johnstone-NY............ .2

Fielding Runs-Infield
Smalley-Min.......... 32.6
Dent-NY............... 31.8
Randolph-NY........ 16.5
Nettles-NY 7.0

Fielding Runs-Outfield
Wilson-KC............ 13.1
Piniella-NY................ .7
Jackson-NY 6

Wins
Flanagan-Bal.......... 23
John-NY................... 21
Guidry-NY................ 18
Davis-NY................. 14

Winning Pct.
Caldwell-Mil .... .727
John-NY................ .700
Guidry-NY............ .692

Complete Games
D.Martinez-Bal......... 18
John-NY................... 17
Guidry-NY................ 15
Tiant-NY..................... 5

Strikeouts
Ryan-Cal............... 223
Guidry-NY............. 201
John-NY................. 111
Tiant-NY................ 104

Fewest BB/Game
McGregor-Bal 1.19
John-NY............... 2.12
Tiant-NY.............. 2.44
Guidry-NY............ 2.70

Games
Marshall-Min........... 90
Davis-NY 44
Kaat-NY................... 40
John-NY................... 37

Saves
Marshall-Min........... 32
Gossage-NY 18
Davis-NY 9

Base Runners/9
McGregor-Bal 9.79
Guidry-NY........... 10.43
John-NY.............. 10.98
Tiant-NY..............11.18

Adjusted Relief Runs
Kern-Tex 38.7
Davis-NY 12.7
Gossage-NY 10.3
Kaat-NY.................. 1.0

Relief Ranking
Kern-Tex 61.5
Davis-NY 24.4
Gossage-NY 19.8
Kaat-NY..................... .9

Innings Pitched
D.Martinez-Bal.... 292.1
John-NY.............. 276.1
Guidry-NY........... 236.1
Tiant-NY.............. 195.2

Opponents' Avg.
Ryan-Cal.............. .212
Guidry-NY............ .236
Tiant-NY............... .251
John-NY................ .260

Opponents' OBP
McGregor-Bal .... .273
Guidry-NY............ .292
Tiant-NY............... .299
John-NY................ .305

Earned Run Average
Guidry-NY............. 2.78
John-NY............... 2.96
Tiant-NY............... 3.91

Adjusted ERA
Eckersley-Bos........ 149
Guidry-NY.............. 148
John-NY................ 139
Tiant-NY................ 105

Adjusted Starter Runs
Eckersley-Bos....... 38.9
Guidry-NY............ 34.8
John-NY............... 32.1
Tiant-NY................. 4.3

Pitcher Wins
Kern-Tex 6.3
Guidry-NY................ 3.6
John-NY................... 3.3
Davis-NY 2.5

1980 American League

TEAM	W	L	T	PCT	GB	R	OR	HR	AVG	OBP	SLG	OPS	AOPS	PF	SB	CG	HR	BB	SO	BR/9	ERA	AERA	OAV	OOB	FW	PW	BW	BSW	DIF
East																													
NY	103	59	0	.636		820	662	189	.267	.343	.425	768	111	99	86	29	**102**	463	845	11.8	3.58	110	.259	.316	.0	6.1	9.4	.3	6.3
Bal	100	62	0	.617	3	805	**640**	156	.273	.342	.413	755	108	99	111	42	134	507	789	12.1	3.64	109	.261	.323	**2.4**	5.2	6.7	.7	3.9
Mil	86	76	0	.531	17	811	682	**203**	.275	.329	**.448**	**777**	**114**	98	131	48	137	**420**	575	12.3	3.71	105	.273	.323	-.5	3.3	**10.0**	.6	-8.3
Bos	83	77	0	.519	19	757	767	162	.283	.340	.436	776	105	105	79	30	129	481	696	12.9	4.38	97	.279	.337	-.7	-1.8	4.7	-.2	1.1
Det	84	78	1	.519	19	**830**	757	143	.273	.348	.409	757	104	103	75	40	152	558	741	12.8	4.25	97	.267	.334	.3	-2.1	4.6	-1.0	1.2
Cle	79	81	0	.494	23	738	807	89	.277	**.350**	.381	731	99	101	118	35	137	552	843	13.3	4.68	88	.275	.341	1.8	-8.6	1.9	.3	3.7
Tor	67	95	0	.414	36	624	762	126	.251	.309	.383	692	85	104	67	39	135	635	705	13.4	4.19	103	.274	.348	.3	1.8	-12.0	-1.3	-2.8
West																													
KC	97	65	0	.599		809	694	115	**.286**	.345	.413	758	105	102	**185**	37	129	465	614	12.2	3.83	106	.267	.323	-.2	3.4	5.0	**2.2**	5.5
Oak	83	79	0	.512	14	686	642	137	.259	.322	.385	707	99	94	175	**94**	142	521	769	**11.6**	**3.46**	110	**.244**	**.310**	.5	5.9	-1.2	.6	-3.8
Min	77	84	0	.478	19.5	670	724	99	.265	.319	.381	700	85	107	62	35	120	468	744	12.4	3.93	**111**	.272	.328	-.6	**6.4**	-11.1	-.5	2.4
Tex	76	85	2	.472	20.5	756	752	124	.284	.339	.405	744	106	97	91	35	119	519	**890**	13.1	4.02	96	.277	.339	-.5	-2.4	5.2	-.0	-6.8
Chi	70	90	2	.438	26	587	722	91	.259	.311	.370	681	86	-100	68	32	108	563	724	12.8	3.92	103	.263	.333	-1.9	2.1	-10.4	-.7	.9
Cal	65	95	0	.406	31	698	797	106	.265	.332	.378	710	95	99	91	22	141	529	725	13.3	4.52	87	.278	.342	.1	-9.2	-2.2	-.5	-3.2
Sea	59	103	1	.364	38	610	793	104	.248	.308	.356	664	80	-102	116	31	159	540	703	13.2	4.38	95	.278	.341	-.6	-3.5	-14.8	.0	-3.2
Total	1132					50201		1844	.269	.331	.399	731			1455	549				12.7	4.03		.269	.331					

Batter-Fielder Wins
G.Brett-KC............. 6.5
Randolph-NY.......... 5.0
Jackson-NY........... 4.0
Cerone-NY............. 2.8

Batting Average
G.Brett-KC............ .390
Watson-NY .... .307
Jackson-NY .... .300
Randolph-NY .... .294

On-Base Percentage
G.Brett-KC............ .454
Randolph-NY......... .427
Jackson-NY .... .398
Watson-NY .... .368

Slugging Average
G.Brett-KC............ .664
Jackson-NY .... .597
Watson-NY .... .456
Cerone-NY............ .432

On-Base Plus Slugging
G.Brett-KC...........1118
Jackson-NY 995
Randolph-NY......... 834
Watson-NY 825

Adjusted OPS
G.Brett-KC............ 201
Jackson-NY 172
Randolph-NY......... 132
Watson-NY 128

Adjusted Batter Runs
G.Brett-KC........... 64.0
Jackson-NY 51.6
Randolph-NY........ 31.7
Watson-NY 18.6

Runs
Wilson-KC............. 133
Randolph-NY........... 99
Jackson-NY 94
Cerone-NY............... 70

Hits
Wilson-KC............. 230
Jackson-NY 154
Randolph-NY......... 151
2 players tied 144

Doubles
Yount-Mil................. 49
Cerone-NY............... 30
Dent-NY.................. 26
Watson-NY 25

Triples
Wilson-KC................ 15
Griffin-Tor................ 15
Randolph-NY............. 7
Brown-NY 5

Home Runs
Oglivie-Mil............... 41
Jackson-NY 41
Jackson-NY 41
Nettles-NY 16

Total Bases
Cooper-Mil 335
Jackson-NY 307
Cerone-NY............ 224
Watson-NY 214

Runs Batted In
Cooper-Mil 122
Jackson-NY 111
Cerone-NY............... 85
Watson-NY 68

Stolen Bases
Henderson-Oak 100
Randolph-NY........... 30
Brown-NY 27
Jones-NY................. 18

Base Stealing Runs
Wilson-KC............. 13.9
Randolph-NY.......... 4.8
Brown-NY 3.1
Jones-NY................. 1.2

Fielding Runs-Infield
Burleson-Bos........ 31.2
Dent-NY................11.8
Randolph-NY.......... 7.1

Fielding Runs-Outfield
Wilson-KC............. 13.9
Henderson-Oak 13.9
Brown-NY 2.6

Wins
Stone-Bal................ 25
John-NY................... 22
Guidry-NY................ 17
May-NY.................... 15

Winning Pct.
Stone-Bal.............. .781
May-NY................ .750
John-NY................ .710
Guidry-NY............ .630

Complete Games
Langford-Oak.......... 28
John-NY................... 16
Guidry-NY.................. 5
2 players tied 3

Strikeouts
Barker-Cle 187
Guidry-NY............. 166
May-NY.................. 133
Underwood-NY.......116

Fewest BB/Game
Matlack-Tex 1.84
John-NY................ 1.90
May-NY................. 2.00
Underwood-NY..... 3.18

Games
Quisenberry-KC....... 75
Gossage-NY 64
Davis-NY 53
May-NY.................... 41

Saves
Quisenberry-KC....... 33
Gossage-NY 33
Gossage-NY 33
Davis-NY 7

Base Runners/9
May-NY................. 9.39
Gossage-NY....... 10.18
Davis-NY 10.85
Underwood-NY....11.21

Adjusted Relief Runs
Corbett-Min........... 34.8
Gossage-NY 18.7
Davis-NY 14.4

Relief Ranking
Corbett-Min........... 45.2
Gossage-NY 27.4
Davis-NY 13.6

Innings Pitched
Langford-Oak...... 290.0
John-NY.............. 265.1
Guidry-NY........... 219.2
Underwood-NY... 187.0

Opponents' Avg.
Norris-Oak .... .209
May-NY................ .224
Underwood-NY...... .237
Guidry-NY............ .260

Opponents' OBP
May-NY................ .268
Underwood-NY ...... .306
John-NY................ .309
Guidry-NY............ .322

Earned Run Average
May-NY................ 2.46
John-NY............... 3.43
Guidry-NY............ 3.56
Underwood-NY..... 3.66

Adjusted ERA
May-NY.................. 161
John-NY.................116
Guidry-NY..............111
Underwood-NY...... 108

Adjusted Starter Runs
Norris-Oak 43.8
May-NY................ 29.1
John-NY............... 15.9
Guidry-NY............ 10.6

Pitcher Wins
Corbett-Min............ 4.8
Norris-Oak 4.8
May-NY................... 3.2
Gossage-NY 2.8

1981 American League

TEAM	W	L	T	PCT	GB	R	OR	HR	AVG	OBP	SLG	OPS	AOPS	PF	SB	CG	HR	BB	SO	BR/9	ERA	AERA	OAV	OOB	FW	PW	BW	BSW	DIF
East *Split Season: First-half Winner NY (34–22); Second-half Winner MIL (31–22)*																													
Mil	62	47	0	.569		493	459	96	.257	.313	.391	704	106	96	39	25	83	347	489	12.3	3.70	99	.260	.326	.8	-.6	2.8	-.4	3.9
Bal	59	46	0	.562	1	429	437	88	.251	.329	.379	708	104	100	41	16	64	287	606	**10.7**	**2.90**	**125**	**.235**	**.293**	.7	**8.0**	3.7	-.0	-6.8
NY	59	48	0	.551	2	421	**343**	100	.252	.325	.391	716	106	99	47	33	83	373	476	11.5	3.53	107	.236	.310	**1.0**	2.7	-.2	-.0	2.0
Det	60	49	0	.550	2	427	404	65	.256	.331	.368	699	97	104	61	19	90	354	536	12.4	3.81	103	.262	.328	-.4	1.2	3.7	-.5	1.0
Bos	59	49	0	.546	2.5	**519**	481	90	**.275**	**.340**	**.399**	**739**	105	107	32	33	67	311	569	12.7	3.88	95	.274	.330	-.4	-2.1	-.9	1.3	2.6
Cle	52	51	0	.505	7	431	442	39	.263	.327	.351	678	96	99	**119**	20	72	377	451	12.5	3.81	104	.252	.326	-1.3	1.5	-13.0	-.6	-2.6
Tor	37	69	0	.349	23.5	329	466	61	.226	.286	.330	616	73	-106	66														
West *Split Season: First-half Winner OAK (37–23); Second-half Winner KC (30–23)*																													
Oak	64	45	0	.587		458	403	**104**	.247	.312	.379	691	102	96	98	23	67	322	488	11.4	3.40	102	.243	.308	.7	.8	2.9	-.5	.5
Tex	57	48	0	.543	5	452	389	49	.270	.326	.369	695	105	95	46	20	73	336	529	12.0	3.47	104	.252	.319	-.3	1.6	4.9	.4	-5.6
Chi	54	52	0	.509	8.5	476	423	76	.272	.335	.387	722	**110**	99	86	24	75	273	404	11.7	3.56	101	.260	.313	.5	.5	1.8	.3	-4.6
KC	50	53	0	.485	11	397	405	61	.267	.325	.383	708	103	100	100	27	81	323	426	12.1	3.70	99	.261	.321	-.9	-.3	2.3	-.3	-4.9
Cal	51	59	0	.464	13.5	476	453	97	.256	.330	.380	710	103	101	44	10	76	360	478	12.8	4.23	92	.271	.334	-.3	-3.9	-4.0	.5	-2.8
Sea	44	65	1	.404	20	426	521	89	.251	.314	.368	682	92	105	100	13	79	376	500	13.0	3.98	99	.272	.338	-.6	-.3	-11.5	-.3	-.8
Min	41	68	1	.376	23	378	486	47	.240	.293	.338	631	76	106	34	**334**				12.1	3.66		.256	.321					
Total	750					36112		1062	.256	.321	.373	693			913	549				12.7	4.03		.269	.331					

Batter-Fielder Wins
- **Grich-Cal 5.2**
- **Mumphrey-NY 1.3**
- **Randolph-NY......... 1.2**
- **Winfield-NY 1.0**

Batting Average
- Lansford-Bos .... .336
- Mumphrey-NY ...... .307
- Winfield-NY........... .294
- Nettles-NY .... .244

On-Base Percentage
- Hargrove-Cle .... .424
- Winfield-NY........... .360
- Mumphrey-NY ...... .354
- Randolph-NY .... .336

Slugging Average
- Grich-Cal .... .543
- Winfield-NY........... .464
- Mumphrey-NY ...... .429
- Jackson-NY .... .428

On-Base Plus Slugging
- Evans-Bos 937
- Winfield-NY............ 824
- Mumphrey-NY 783
- Jackson-NY 758

Adjusted OPS
- Grich-Cal 162
- Winfield-NY............ 139
- Mumphrey-NY 127
- Jackson-NY 119

Adjusted Batter Runs
- Evans-Bos 35.1
- Winfield-NY........... 20.4
- Mumphrey-NY 10.1
- Gamble-NY.............. 8.6

Runs
- Henderson-Oak 89
- Randolph-NY........... 59
- Winfield-NY............. 52
- Nettles-NY 46

Hits
- Henderson-Oak 135
- Winfield-NY.............114
- Mumphrey-NY 98
- Nettles-NY 85

Doubles
- Cooper-Mil............... 35
- Winfield-NY.............. 25
- Jackson-NY 17
- Randolph-NY........... 14

Triples
- Castino-Min 9
- Mumphrey-NY 5
- Watson-NY 3
- Randolph-NY............ 3

Home Runs
- 4 players tied 22
- Nettles-NY 15
- Jackson-NY 15
- Winfield-NY............. 13

Total Bases
- Evans-Bos 215
- Winfield-NY............ 180
- Jackson-NY 143
- Nettles-NY 139

Runs Batted In
- Murray-Bal............... 78
- Winfield-NY.............. 68
- Jackson-NY 54
- Nettles-NY 46

Stolen Bases
- Henderson-Oak 56
- Randolph-NY........... 14
- Mumphrey-NY 14
- Winfield-NY..............11

Base Stealing Runs
- Cruz-Sea 6.7
- Winfield-NY............. 2.1
- Randolph-NY........... 1.3
- Milbourne-NY........... .4

Fielding Runs-Infield
- Bell-Tex................. 34.3
- Randolph-NY 9.0
- Nettles-NY 3.6

Fielding Runs-Outfield
- Wilson-KC............. 17.6
- Mumphrey-NY 3.2

Wins
- 4 players tied 14
- Guidry-NY.................11
- John-NY..................... 9
- Righetti-NY 8

Winning Pct.
- Vuckovich-Mil .... .778
- Guidry-NY............. .688

Complete Games
- Langford-Oak........... 18
- John-NY...................... 7
- May-NY....................... 4
- Reuschel-NY 3

Strikeouts
- Barker-Cle 127
- Guidry-NY.............. 104
- Righetti-NY 89
- Davis-NY 83

Fewest BB/Game
- Honeycutt-Tex....... 1.20
- Guidry-NY............. 1.84
- May-NY................. 2.50
- John-NY................ 2.50

Games
- Corbett-Min.............. 54
- Davis-NY 43
- Gossage-NY 32
- May-NY.................... 27

Saves
- Fingers-Mil............... 28
- Gossage-NY 20
- Davis-NY 6
- Frazier-NY 3

Base Runners/9
- Fingers-Mil............. 7.96
- Davis-NY 8.88
- Guidry-NY.............. 9.00
- Righetti-NY 9.66

Adjusted Relief Runs
- Fingers-Mil........... 22.6
- Gossage-NY 14.3
- Davis-NY 8.7
- LaRoche-NY 5.3

Relief Ranking
- Fingers-Mil........... 41.4
- Gossage-NY 27.3
- Davis-NY 11.2
- LaRoche-NY 5.1

Innings Pitched
- Leonard-KC 201.2
- May-NY............... 147.2
- John-NY.............. 140.1
- Guidry-NY........... 127.0

Opponents' Avg.
- McCatty-Oak...........211
- Guidry-NY............. .214
- May-NY................. .246
- John-NY................ .256

Opponents' OBP
- Guidry-NY............ .256
- May-NY................. .298
- John-NY................ .309

Earned Run Average
- McCatty-Oak......... 2.33
- John-NY................ 2.63
- Guidry-NY............ 2.76
- May-NY................. 4.14

Adjusted ERA
- Stewart-Bal 157
- John-NY................. 137
- Guidry-NY............. 131
- May-NY................... 87

Adjusted Starter Runs
- McCatty-Oak......... 27.1
- Righetti-NY 19.5
- John-NY............... 13.8
- Guidry-NY............ 13.5

Pitcher Wins
- Fingers-Mil............. 4.6
- Gossage-NY 3.0
- Righetti-NY 2.2
- 2 players tied 1.7

1982 American League

TEAM	W	L	T	PCT	GB	R	OR	HR	AVG	OBP	SLG	OPS	AOPS	PF	SB	CG	HR	BB	SO	BR/9	ERA	AERA	OAV	OOB	FW	PW	BW	BSW	DIF
East																													
Mil	95	67	1	.586		**891**	717	**216**	.279	.335	**.455**	**790**	**120**	95	84	34	152	511	717	12.5	3.98	96	.270	.330	.1	-2.6	**15.4**	-.2	1.3
Bal	94	68	1	.580	1	774	687	179	.266	.341	.419	760	108	99	49	38	147	488	719	**12.0**	3.99	102	.257	**.317**	**1.4**	1.1	7.7	-.5	3.3
Bos	89	73	0	.549	6	753	713	136	.274	.340	.407	747	98	106	42	23	155	478	816	12.8	4.03	108	.276	.334	.3	4.7	-.2	-.6	3.8
Det	83	79	0	.512	12	729	685	177	.266	.324	.418	742	101	101	93	**45**	172	554	740	12.1	**3.80**	107	**.251**	.321	.5	4.5	.9	-.5	-3.4
NY	79	83	0	.488	16	709	716	161	.256	.328	.398	726	99	99	69	24	113	491	939	12.2	3.99	101	.264	.323	-.0	.5	.5	-.3	-2.6
Tor	78	84	0	.481	17	651	701	106	.262	.314	.383	697	83	109	118	41	147	493	776	12.1	3.95	**114**	.257	.319	-.5	**8.0**	-12.4	-.4	2.3
Cle	78	84	0	.481	17	683	748	109	.262	.341	.373	714	96	101	151	31	122	589	882	12.5	4.11	101	.257	.327	.2	.6	-1.5	.7	-3.0
West																													
Cal	93	69	0	.574		814	**670**	186	.274	**.347**	.433	780	112	101	55	40	124	482	728	**12.0**	3.82	107	.259	.321	1.0	4.3	10.4	-.8	-2.9
KC	90	72	0	.556	3	784	717	132	**.285**	.337	.428	765	107	101	133	16	163	471	650	12.2	4.08	100	.262	.320	-.0	-.1	6.2	1.0	1.9
Chi	87	75	0	.537	6	786	710	136	.273	.337	.413	750	104	101	136	30	**99**	**460**	753	12.4	3.87	105	.270	.326	-1.5	3.2	4.0	.8	-.5
Sea	76	86	0	.469	17	651	712	130	.254	.311	.381	692	86	104	131	23	173	547	**1002**	12.2	3.88	110	.256	.324	-.7	6.2	-10.7	-.2	.4
Oak	68	94	0	.420	25	691	819	149	.236	.309	.367	676	88	-97	**232**	42	177	648	697	13.5	4.54	87	.268	.343	-1.8	-10.0	-8.7	**1.9**	5.6
Tex	64	98	0	.395	29	590	749	115	.249	.308	.359	667	86	-96	63	32	128	483	690	13.1	4.28	91	.280	.339	.3	-6.8	-10.5	-.4	.4
Min	60	102	0	.370	33	657	819	148	.257	.316	.396	712	91	103	38	26	208	643	812	13.4	4.72	90	.269	.344	1.0	-7.0	-6.7	-.5	-7.8
Total	1135					60163		2080	.264	.328	.402	730			1394	445				12.5	4.07		.264	.328					

Batter-Fielder Wins
- **Yount-Mil 7.1**
- **Winfield-NY 2.8**
- **Gamble-NY 2.6**
- **Randolph-NY......... 2.2**

Batting Average
- Wilson-KC............. .332
- Mumphrey-NY .... .300
- Randolph-NY......... .280
- Winfield-NY........... .280

On-Base Percentage
- Evans-Bos .... .402
- Randolph-NY......... .368
- Mumphrey-NY ...... .364
- Winfield-NY........... .331

Slugging Average
- Yount-Mil............... .578
- Winfield-NY........... .560
- Mumphrey-NY ...... .449
- Griffey-NY .... .407

On-Base Plus Slugging
- Yount-Mil................ 957
- Winfield-NY............ 891
- Mumphrey-NY 813
- Griffey-NY 736

Adjusted OPS
- Yount-Mil................ 168
- Winfield-NY............ 143
- Mumphrey-NY 124
- Griffey-NY.............. 103

Adjusted Batter Runs
- Yount-Mil............... 58.1
- Winfield-NY........... 28.5
- Gamble-NY........... 24.4
- Mumphrey-NY 16.0

Runs
- Molitor-Mil............. 136
- Randolph-NY........... 85
- Winfield-NY............. 84
- Mumphrey-NY 76

Hits
- Yount-Mil................ 210
- Randolph-NY.......... 155
- Winfield-NY............ 151
- Mumphrey-NY 143

Doubles
- Yount-Mil................. 46
- McRae-KC............... 46
- Winfield-NY.............. 24
- Mumphrey-NY 24

Triples
- Wilson-KC................ 15
- Mumphrey-NY 10
- Winfield-NY................ 8
- Randolph-NY............. 4

Home Runs
- Thomas-Mil.............. 39
- R.Jackson-Cal 39
- Winfield-NY.............. 37
- 2 players tied 18

Total Bases
- Yount-Mil................ 367
- Winfield-NY............ 302
- Mumphrey-NY 214
- Griffey-NY.............. 197

Runs Batted In
- McRae-KC 133
- Winfield-NY............ 106
- Mumphrey-NY 68
- Gamble-NY.............. 57

Stolen Bases
- Henderson-Oak 130
- Randolph-NY........... 16
- Collins-NY................ 13
- Mumphrey-NY 11

Base Stealing Runs
- Henderson-Oak 13.9
- Mumphrey-NY 1.4
- Griffey-NY 8
- 2 players tied 4

Fielding Runs-Infield
- Bell-Tex................. 37.7
- Randolph-NY.........11.1

Fielding Runs-Outfield
- Brunansky-Min.........11.3
- Winfield-NY............. 6.1
- Griffey-NY 4.4
- Mumphrey-NY 3

Wins
- Hoyt-Chi.................. 19
- Guidry-NY................ 14
- Righetti-NY 11
- Rawley-NY................11

Winning Pct.
- Vuckovich-Mil .... .750
- Palmer-Bal............ .750

Complete Games
- Stieb-Tor 19
- Guidry-NY.................. 6
- Righetti-NY 4
- Rawley-NY.................. 3

Strikeouts
- Bannister-Sea........ 209
- Righetti-NY 163
- Guidry-NY.............. 162
- Rawley-NY.............. 111

Fewest BB/Game
- John-NY-Cal 1.58
- Guidry-NY............. 2.80
- Rawley-NY............ 2.96
- Righetti-NY 5.31

Games
- VandeBerg-Sea 78
- Frazier-NY 63
- Gossage-NY 56
- Rawley-NY............... 47

Saves
- Quisenberry-KC....... 35
- Gossage-NY 30
- Rawley-NY................. 3
- May-NY...................... 3

Base Runners/9
- Gossage-NY 8.81
- May-NY................ 10.53
- Guidry-NY............11.59
- Frazier-NY 11.85

Adjusted Relief Runs
- Stanley-Bos 23.5
- Gossage-NY 20.0
- May-NY..................11.2
- Frazier-NY 5.5

Relief Ranking
- Spillner-Cle 42.0
- Gossage-NY 31.7
- May-NY.................. 12.1
- Frazier-NY 3.7

Innings Pitched
- Stieb-Tor 288.1
- Guidry-NY........... 222.0
- Righetti-NY 183.0
- Rawley-NY.......... 164.0

Opponents' Avg.
- Sutcliffe-Cle .... .226
- Righetti-NY .... .229
- Guidry-NY............. .254
- Rawley-NY............ .267

Opponents' OBP
- Palmer-Bal............ .286
- Guidry-NY............. .309
- Rawley-NY............ .324
- Righetti-NY .... .338

Earned Run Average
- Sutcliffe-Cle 2.96
- Righetti-NY 3.79
- Guidry-NY............ 3.81
- Rawley-NY........... 4.06

Adjusted ERA
- Stanley-Bos 140
- Sutcliffe-Cle 140
- Righetti-NY 107
- Guidry-NY............. 106

Adjusted Starter Runs
- Stieb-Tor 36.2
- Guidry-NY.............. 5.5
- Righetti-NY 3.7
- Rawley-NY................ .8

Pitcher Wins
- 3 players tied 4.2
- Gossage-NY 3.2
- May-NY.................... 1.3
- 3 players tied 4

1983 American League

TEAM	W	L	T	PCT	GB	R	OR	HR	AVG	OBP	SLG	OPS	AOPS	PF	SB	CG	HR	BB	SO	BR/9	ERA	AERA	OAV	OOB	FW	PW	BW	BSW	DIF
East																													
Bal	98	64	0	.605		799	652	**168**	.269	**.340**	.421	761	109	99	61	36	130	452	774	11.9	3.63	110	.261	.316	.5	6.0	8.5	-.3	2.3
Det	92	70	0	.568	6	789	679	156	.274	.335	.427	762	110	98	93	42	170	522	875	11.6	3.80	103	**.242**	.309	.3	2.2	8.6	-.3	.2
NY	91	71	0	.562	7	770	703	153	.273	.337	.416	753	109	97	84	**47**	116	455	892	11.9	3.86	102	.260	.315	-.5	1.3	7.7	-.1	1.6
Tor	89	73	0	.549	9	795	726	167	**.277**	.338	**.436**	**774**	104	107	131	43	145	517	835	12.4	4.12	105	.259	.325	.9	3.2	3.7	-.1	.4
Mil	87	75	0	.537	11	764	708	132	**.277**	.333	.418	751	**113**	93	101	35	133	491	689	12.6	4.02	94	.270	.329	**1.0**	-4.3	**10.0**	-.0	-.6
Bos	78	84	0	.481	20	724	775	142	.270	.335	.409	744	97	108	30	29	158	493	767	13.0	4.34	101	.279	.337	.0	.6	-1.7	-.7	-1.2
Cle	70	92	0	.432	28	704	785	86	.265	.328	.369	707	90	104	109	34	120	529	794	13.1	4.43	96	.275	.339	.5	-2.6	-4.8	-.6	-3.5
West																													
Chi	99	63	0	.611		**800**	650	157	.262	.329	.413	742	99	104	165	35	128	**447**	877	**11.4**	3.67	115	.248	**.307**	.6	8.4	-.4	1.4	8.1
KC	79	83	1	.488	20	696	767	109	.271	.320	.397	717	95	101	182	19	133	471	593	12.7	4.25	96	.274	.330	-1.9	-2.5	-3.9	**1.9**	4.4
Tex	77	85	1	.475	22	639	**609**	106	.255	.310	.366	676	86	-99	119	43	**97**	471	826	11.7	**3.31**	**122**	.252	.313	**1.0**	**11.9**	-10.4	-.0	-6.5
Oak	74	88	0	.457	25	708	782	121	.262	.326	.381	707	99	95	**235**	22	135	626	719	13.1	4.34	89	.263	.337	-1.5	-8.0	.4	1.2	.9
Cal	70	92	0	.432	29	722	779	154	.260	.322	.393	715	96	100	41	39	130	496	668	13.2	4.31	94	.284	.341	-1.3	-4.6	-2.8	-1.0	-1.3
Min	70	92	0	.432	29	709	822	141	.261	.319	.401	720	93	104	44	20	163	580	748	13.6	4.66	91	.280	.348	.5	-6.0	-5.1	-.5	.0
Sea	60	102	0	.370	39	558	740	111	.240	.301	.360	661	78	-104	144	25	145	544	**910**	12.9	4.12	104	.268	.337	-.3	2.3	-15.9	-.1	-7.0
Total	1135					60177		1903	.266	.328	.401	728			1539	469				12.5	4.06		.266	.328					

Batter-Fielder Wins
- **Ripken-Bal 7.0**
- **Baylor-NY 2.5**
- **Randolph-NY 2.3**
- **Winfield-NY 1.4**

Batting Average
- Boggs-Bos .... .361
- Baylor-NY .... .303
- Winfield-NY .... .283
- Smalley-NY .... .275

On-Base Percentage
- Boggs-Bos .... .444
- Baylor-NY .... .361
- Smalley-NY .... .357
- Winfield-NY .... .345

Slugging Average
- Brett-KC .... .563
- Winfield-NY .... .513
- Baylor-NY .... .494
- Smalley-NY .... .452

On-Base Plus Slugging
- Brett-KC 947
- Winfield-NY 868
- Baylor-NY 856
- Smalley-NY 810

Adjusted OPS
- Murray-Bal 157
- Baylor-NY 138
- Winfield-NY 138
- Smalley-NY 126

Adjusted Batter Runs
- Murray-Bal 47.6
- Winfield-NY 28.8
- Baylor-NY 28.3
- Smalley-NY 17.2

Runs
- Ripken-Bal 121
- Winfield-NY 99
- Baylor-NY 82
- Randolph-NY 73

Hits
- Ripken-Bal 211
- Winfield-NY 169
- Baylor-NY 162
- Griffey-NY 140

Doubles
- Ripken-Bal 47
- Baylor-NY 33
- Winfield-NY 26
- Smalley-NY 24

Triples
- Yount-Mil 10
- Winfield-NY 8
- Mumphrey-NY 4
- Mattingly-NY 4

Home Runs
- Rice-Bos 39
- Winfield-NY 32
- Baylor-NY 21
- Nettles-NY 20

Total Bases
- Rice-Bos 344
- Winfield-NY 307
- Baylor-NY 264
- Nettles-NY 206

Runs Batted In
- Rice-Bos 126
- Cooper-Mil 126
- Winfield-NY 116
- Baylor-NY 85

Stolen Bases
- Henderson-Oak 108
- Baylor-NY 17
- Winfield-NY 15
- Randolph-NY 12

Base Stealing Runs
- Henderson-Oak 17.1
- Meacham-NY 1.8
- Baylor-NY 1.3
- 2 players tied 1.2

Fielding Runs-Infield
- T.Cruz-Sea-Bal 24.2

Fielding Runs-Outfield
- Ward-Min 18.5

Wins
- Hoyt-Chi 24
- Guidry-NY 21
- Righetti-NY 14
- Rawley-NY 14

Winning Pct.
- Dotson-Chi .... .759
- Guidry-NY .... .700

Complete Games
- Guidry-NY 21
- Rawley-NY 13
- Righetti-NY 7
- Fontenot-NY 3

Strikeouts
- Morris-Det 232
- Righetti-NY 169
- Guidry-NY 156
- Rawley-NY 124

Fewest BB/Game
- Hoyt-Chi 1.07
- Guidry-NY 2.16
- Righetti-NY 2.78
- Rawley-NY 2.98

Games
- Quisenberry-KC 69
- Frazier-NY 61
- Gossage-NY 57
- Murray-NY 40

Saves
- Quisenberry-KC 45
- Gossage-NY 22
- Frazier-NY 8
- 2 players tied 1

Base Runners/9
- Quisenberry-KC 8.35
- Guidry-NY 10.57
- Righetti-NY 10.91
- Frazier-NY 11.08

Adjusted Relief Runs
- Quisenberry-KC 32.7
- Gossage-NY 15.7
- Frazier-NY 9.1

Relief Ranking
- Quisenberry-KC 38.4
- Gossage-NY 31.4
- Frazier-NY 7.0

Innings Pitched
- Morris-Det 293.2
- Guidry-NY 250.1
- Rawley-NY 238.1
- Righetti-NY 217.0

Opponents' Avg.
- Boddicker-Bal .... .216
- Righetti-NY .... .237
- Guidry-NY .... .244
- Rawley-NY .... .269

Opponents' OBP
- Hoyt-Chi .... .260
- Guidry-NY .... .288
- Righetti-NY .... .296
- Rawley-NY .... .327

Earned Run Average
- Honeycutt-Tex 2.42
- Guidry-NY 3.42
- Righetti-NY 3.44
- Rawley-NY 3.78

Adjusted ERA
- Honeycutt-Tex 167
- Guidry-NY 116
- Righetti-NY 115
- Rawley-NY 104

Adjusted Starter Runs
- Stieb-Tor 37.1
- Guidry-NY 18.5
- Righetti-NY 11.0
- Fontenot-NY 6.5

Pitcher Wins
- Quisenberry-KC 4.0
- Gossage-NY 3.1
- Guidry-NY 2.1
- Righetti-NY 1.0

1984 American League

TEAM	W	L	T	PCT	GB	R	OR	HR	AVG	OBP	SLG	OPS	AOPS	PF	SB	CG	HR	BB	SO	BR/9	ERA	AERA	OAV	OOB	FW	PW	BW	BSW	DIF
East																													
Det	104	58	0	.642		**829**	**643**	**187**	.271	**.342**	.432	774	**113**	100	106	19	130	489	914	**11.5**	**3.49**	**113**	**.246**	**.308**	.3	**7.6**	**10.7**	-.2	4.6
Tor	89	73	1	.549	15	750	696	143	.273	.331	.421	752	102	104	**193**	34	140	528	875	12.3	3.86	107	.257	.323	.6	4.2	2.1	**1.7**	-.6
NY	87	75	0	.537	17	758	679	130	.276	.339	.404	743	109	97	62	15	**120**	518	**992**	12.4	3.78	101	.264	.325	-.5	.9	7.7	-.2	-1.9
Bos	86	76	0	.531	18	810	764	181	**.283**	.341	**.441**	**782**	110	105	38	40	141	517	927	12.9	4.18	100	.270	.332	-.6	.3	7.3	-.2	-1.8
Bal	85	77	0	.525	19	681	667	160	.252	.328	.391	719	100	98	51	**48**	137	512	714	12.1	3.71	105	.256	.320	.5	3.2	1.0	-.3	-.4
Cle	75	87	1	.463	29	761	766	123	.265	.335	.384	719	96	102	126	21	141	545	803	12.8	4.26	97	.269	.332	-.7	-2.2	-1.1	-.1	-1.9
Mil	67	94	0	.416	36.5	641	734	96	.262	.317	.370	687	92	97	52	13	137	480	785	12.8	4.06	96	.274	.331	-.3	-2.8	-5.4	-1.1	-3.9
West																													
KC	84	78	0	.519		673	686	117	.268	.317	.399	716	96	101	106	18	136	**433**	724	11.8	3.92	103	.258	.312	.0	1.9	-3.3	-.1	4.4
Cal	81	81	0	.500	3	696	697	150	.249	.319	.381	700	93	100	80	36	143	474	754	12.5	3.96	101	.271	.328	.2	.5	-4.6	-.2	4.1
Min	81	81	0	.500	3	673	675	114	.265	.318	.385	703	88	105	39	32	159	463	713	12.1	3.85	110	.260	.319	**.7**	5.7	-7.8	-.4	1.8
Oak	77	85	0	.475	7	738	796	158	.259	.327	.404	731	107	94	145	15	155	592	695	13.7	4.48	84	.278	.348	-.8	-12.1	6.8	.8	1.2
Sea	74	88	0	.457	10	682	774	129	.258	.324	.384	708	96	99	116	26	138	619	972	13.5	4.31	93	.270	.345	.2	-4.7	-2.7	.2	.0
Chi	74	88	0	.457	10	679	736	172	.247	.314	.395	709	90	105	109	43	155	483	840	12.0	4.13	101	.256	.317	.6	.6	-7.1	.5	-1.5
Tex	69	92	0	.429	14.5	656	714	120	.261	.313	.377	690	87	104	81	38	148	518	863	12.5	3.91	107	.260	.325	-.4	3.9	-10.2	-.2	-4.7
Total	1134					60027		1980	.264	.326	.398	724			1304	398				12.5	3.99		.264	.326					

Batter-Fielder Wins
- **Ripken-Bal 9.4**
- **Mattingly-NY 5.3**
- **Randolph-NY 3.9**
- **Winfield-NY 3.4**

Batting Average
- Mattingly-NY .... .343
- Winfield-NY .... .340
- Randolph-NY .... .287
- Wynegar-NY .... .267

On-Base Percentage
- Murray-Bal .... .410
- Winfield-NY .... .393
- Mattingly-NY .... .381
- Randolph-NY .... .377

Slugging Average
- Baines-Chi .... .541
- Mattingly-NY .... .537
- Winfield-NY .... .515
- Baylor-NY .... .489

On-Base Plus Slugging
- Evans-Bos 920
- Mattingly-NY 918
- Winfield-NY 908
- Baylor-NY 830

Adjusted OPS
- Mattingly-NY 158
- Winfield-NY 155
- Baylor-NY 131
- Randolph-NY 107

Adjusted Batter Runs
- Murray-Bal 50.3
- Mattingly-NY 46.7
- Winfield-NY 43.1
- Baylor-NY 21.3

Runs
- Evans-Bos 121
- Winfield-NY 106
- Mattingly-NY 91
- Randolph-NY 86

Hits
- Mattingly-NY 207
- Winfield-NY 193
- Randolph-NY 162
- Baylor-NY 129

Doubles
- Mattingly-NY 44
- Winfield-NY 34
- Baylor-NY 29
- Randolph-NY 24

Triples
- Moseby-Tor 15
- Collins-Tor 15
- Moreno-NY 6
- 3 players tied 4

Home Runs
- Armas-Bos 43
- Baylor-NY 27
- Mattingly-NY 23
- Winfield-NY 19

Total Bases
- Armas-Bos 339
- Mattingly-NY 324
- Winfield-NY 292
- Baylor-NY 241

Runs Batted In
- Armas-Bos 123
- Mattingly-NY 110
- Winfield-NY 100
- Baylor-NY 89

Stolen Bases
- Henderson-Oak 66
- Moreno-NY 20
- Randolph-NY 10
- Meacham-NY 9

Base Stealing Runs
- Wilson-KC 8.6
- Harrah-NY 7
- Moreno-NY 6
- Kemp-NY 5

Fielding Runs-Infield
- Ripken-Bal 39.3
- Randolph-NY 21.5
- Mattingly-NY 15.3

Fielding Runs-Outfield
- Vukovich-Cle 18.8

Wins
- Boddicker-Bal 20
- Niekro-NY 16
- Guidry-NY 10
- 4 players tied 9

Winning Pct.
- Alexander-Tor .... .739
- Niekro-NY .... .667

Complete Games
- Hough-Tex 17
- Niekro-NY 5
- Guidry-NY 5
- Cowley-NY 3

Strikeouts
- Langston-Sea 204
- Niekro-NY 136
- Guidry-NY 127
- Rasmussen-NY 110

Fewest BB/Game
- Hoyt-Chi 1.64
- Guidry-NY 2.02
- Fontenot-NY 3.08
- Niekro-NY 3.17

Games
- Hernandez-Det 80
- Righetti-NY 64
- Howell-NY 61
- Shirley-NY 41

Saves
- Quisenberry-KC 44
- Righetti-NY 31
- Howell-NY 7
- 3 players tied 2

Base Runners/9
- Hernandez-Det 8.72
- Howell-NY 10.42
- Righetti-NY 10.84
- Rasmussen-NY ... 11.64

Adjusted Relief Runs
- Hernandez-Det 33.8
- Righetti-NY 16.0
- Howell-NY 14.2
- Shirley-NY 6.1

Relief Ranking
- Hernandez-Det 41.3
- Righetti-NY 26.7
- Howell-NY 18.0
- Shirley-NY 3.0

Innings Pitched
- Stieb-Tor 267.0
- Niekro-NY 215.2
- Guidry-NY 195.2
- Fontenot-NY 169.1

Opponents' Avg.
- Stieb-Tor .... .221
- Niekro-NY .... .267
- Guidry-NY .... .287
- Fontenot-NY .... .290

Opponents' OBP
- Black-KC .... .283
- Guidry-NY .... .323
- Niekro-NY .... .327
- Fontenot-NY .... .349

Earned Run Average
- Boddicker-Bal 2.79
- Niekro-NY 3.09
- Fontenot-NY 3.61
- Guidry-NY 4.51

Adjusted ERA
- Stieb-Tor 146
- Niekro-NY 124
- Fontenot-NY 106
- Guidry-NY 85

Adjusted Starter Runs
- Stieb-Tor 39.9
- Niekro-NY 16.9
- Cowley-NY 3.7
- Fontenot-NY 3.2

Pitcher Wins
- Hernandez-Det 4.3
- Righetti-NY 2.7
- Howell-NY 1.9
- Niekro-NY 1.8

1985 American League

TEAM	W	L	T	PCT	GB	R	OR	HR	AVG	OBP	SLG	OPS	AOPS	PF	SB	CG	HR	BB	SO	BR/9	ERA	AERA	OAV	OOB	FW	PW	BW	BSW	DIF
East																													
Tor	99	62	0	.615		759	**588**	158	.269	.331	.425	756	102	103	144	18	147	484	823	**11.3**	**3.31**	**128**	.243	**.306**	.2	**14.5**	2.2	.0	1.6
NY	97	64	0	.602	2	**839**	660	176	.267	.344	.425	769	**111**	98	**155**	25	157	518	907	11.9	3.69	110	.251	.316	.2	5.8	**9.9**	**1.1**	-.5
Det	84	77	0	.522	15	729	688	202	.253	.318	.424	742	101	100	75	31	141	556	943	11.7	3.78	109	**.240**	.311	-.8	5.2	.9	-.3	-1.5
Bal	83	78	0	.516	16	818	764	**214**	.263	.336	**.430**	766	110	98	69	32	160	568	793	13.1	4.38	93	.270	.338	-.0	-5.0	8.1	-.5	-.0
Bos	81	81	1	.500	18.5	800	720	162	**.282**	**.347**	.429	**776**	106	104	66	35	130	540	913	12.7	4.06	106	.265	.331	-.8	4.0	6.2	.0	-9.4
Mil	71	90	0	.441	28	690	802	101	.263	.319	.379	698	90	100	69	34	175	499	777	12.8	4.39	96	.271	.331	-.7	-3.1	-6.9	-.2	1.4
Cle	60	102	0	.370	39.5	729	861	116	.265	.324	.385	709	93	100	132	24	170	547	702	13.6	4.91	85	.281	.346	-.6	-11.7	-4.1	-.1	-4.5
West																													
KC	91	71	0	.562		687	639	154	.252	.313	.401	714	93	101	128	27	**103**	463	846	11.9	3.49	120	.257	.315	.1	11.0	-5.3	.6	3.6
Cal	90	72	0	.556	1	732	703	153	.251	.333	.386	719	96	100	106	22	171	514	767	12.3	3.91	105	.263	.326	1.0	3.5	-1.6	.0	6.1
Chi	85	77	1	.525	6	736	720	146	.253	.315	.392	707	88	105	108	20	161	569	**1023**	12.5	4.07	107	.256	.327	**1.1**	4.3	-8.4	-.1	7.2
Min	77	85	0	.475	14	705	782	141	.264	.326	.407	733	93	106	68	**41**	164	**462**	767	12.4	4.48	99	.268	.326	.5	-.8	-4.3	-.5	1.0
Oak	77	85	0	.475	14	757	787	155	.264	.325	.401	726	104	93	117	10	172	607	785	12.9	4.41	88	.259	.331	-.6	-9.1	3.6	.0	2.1
Sea	74	88	0	.457	17	719	818	171	.255	.326	.412	738	99	101	94	23	154	637	868	13.4	4.68	90	.265	.343	.4	-6.9	.2	.3	-1.0
Tex	62	99	0	.385	28.5	617	785	129	.253	.322	.381	703	90	102	130	18	173	501	863	12.9	4.56	93	.269	.331	.5	-4.5	-6.9	-.3	-7.2
Total	1132					60317		2178	.261	.327	.406	733			1461	360				12.5	4.15		.261	.327					

Batter-Fielder Wins
- **Henderson-NY....... 6.9**
- **Mattingly-NY.......... 3.0**
- **Randolph-NY......... 2.2**
- **Hassey-NY............ 1.5**

Batting Average
- Boggs-Bos............ .368
- Mattingly-NY......... .324
- Henderson-NY...... .314
- Randolph-NY........ .276

On-Base Percentage
- Boggs-Bos............ .450
- Henderson-NY...... .419
- Randolph-NY........ .382
- Mattingly-NY......... .371

Slugging Average
- Brett-KC................ .585
- Mattingly-NY......... .567
- Henderson-NY...... .516
- Winfield-NY.......... .471

On-Base Plus Slugging
- Brett-KC............... 1022
- Mattingly-NY.......... 939
- Henderson-NY....... 934
- Winfield-NY............ 799

Adjusted OPS
- Brett-KC................. 177
- Henderson-NY....... 158
- Mattingly-NY.......... 158
- Winfield-NY............118

Adjusted Batter Runs
- Brett-KC................ 64.4
- Mattingly-NY......... 51.3
- Henderson-NY...... 48.8
- Hassey-NY............ 15.0

Runs
- Henderson-NY....... 146
- Mattingly-NY.......... 107
- Winfield-NY............ 105
- Randolph-NY........... 75

Hits
- Boggs-Bos............. 240
- Mattingly-NY...........211
- Winfield-NY............ 174
- Henderson-NY....... 172

Doubles
- Mattingly-NY........... 48
- Winfield-NY............. 34
- Henderson-NY......... 28
- Griffey-NY............... 28

Triples
- Wilson-KC................ 21
- Winfield-NY................ 6
- Henderson-NY........... 5
- Griffey-NY.................. 4

Home Runs
- Evans-Det................ 40
- Mattingly-NY............ 35
- Winfield-NY.............. 26
- Henderson-NY.......... 24

Total Bases
- Mattingly-NY.......... 370
- Winfield-NY............ 298
- Henderson-NY....... 282
- Baylor-NY.............. 205

Runs Batted In
- Mattingly-NY.......... 145
- Winfield-NY............114
- Baylor-NY................ 91
- Henderson-NY.......... 72

Stolen Bases
- Henderson-NY......... 80
- Meacham-NY........... 25
- Winfield-NY............. 19
- Randolph-NY........... 16

Base Stealing Runs
- Henderson-NY...... 14.1
- Meacham-NY.......... 3.0
- Winfield-NY............. 1.7
- Randolph-NY............ .4

Fielding Runs-Infield
- Buckner-Bos......... 25.4
- Randolph-NY.......... 5.2

Fielding Runs-Outfield
- Barfield-Tor........... 15.1
- Henderson-NY...... 10.0
- Griffey-NY.............. 4.7
- Winfield-NY............ 4.1

Wins
- Guidry-NY................ 22
- P.Niekro-NY............ 16
- Righetti-NY............. 12
- Cowley-NY............... 12

Winning Pct.
- Guidry-NY............. .786
- P.Niekro-NY.......... .571

Complete Games
- Blyleven-Cle-Min..... 24
- Guidry-NY.................11
- P.Niekro-NY.............. 7
- 3 players tied............. 2

Strikeouts
- Blyleven-Cle-Min ... 206
- P.Niekro-NY........... 149
- Guidry-NY.............. 143
- Cowley-NY............... 97

Fewest BB/Game
- Haas-Mil............... 1.39
- Guidry-NY............. 1.46
- P.Niekro-NY.......... 4.91

Games
- Quisenberry-KC....... 84
- Righetti-NY.............. 74
- Fisher-NY................ 55
- Bordi-NY.................. 51

Saves
- Quisenberry-KC....... 37
- Righetti-NY.............. 29
- Fisher-NY................ 14
- 3 players tied............. 2

Base Runners/9
- Ontiveros-Oak...... 7.96
- Fisher-NY............. 9.70
- Guidry-NY............. 9.90
- Shirley-NY.......... 10.65

Adjusted Relief Runs
- James-Chi............ 24.8
- Shirley-NY............ 18.3
- Fisher-NY............. 17.3
- Righetti-NY........... 15.9

Relief Ranking
- Moore-Cal............. 47.1
- Righetti-NY........... 31.8
- Fisher-NY............. 17.5
- Shirley-NY............ 15.7

Innings Pitched
- Blyleven-Cle-Min 293.2
- Guidry-NY........... 259.0
- P.Niekro-NY........ 220.0
- Cowley-NY.......... 159.2

Opponents' Avg.
- Stieb-Tor............... .213
- P.Niekro-NY.......... .245
- Guidry-NY............. .248

Opponents' OBP
- Saberhagen-KC.... .271
- Guidry-NY............. .277
- P.Niekro-NY.......... .341

Earned Run Average
- Stieb-Tor.............. 2.48
- Guidry-NY............. 3.27
- P.Niekro-NY.......... 4.09

Adjusted ERA
- Stieb-Tor................ 171
- Guidry-NY.............. 124
- P.Niekro-NY............ 99

Adjusted Starter Runs
- Stieb-Tor.............. 47.1
- Guidry-NY............ 23.5
- Cowley-NY............. 3.3

Pitcher Wins
- Stieb-Tor................. 4.9
- Righetti-NY............. 3.2
- Guidry-NY............... 2.3
- Fisher-NY............... 1.8

1986 American League

TEAM	W	L	T	PCT	GB	R	OR	HR	AVG	OBP	SLG	OPS	AOPS	PF	SB	CG	HR	BB	SO	BR/9	ERA	AERA	OAV	OOB	FW	PW	BW	BSW	DIF
East																													
Bos	95	66	0	.590		794	696	144	.271	.346	.415	761	105	101	41	36	167	**474**	1033	12.4	3.93	107	.266	.325	-.2	4.0	6.1	-.7	5.2
NY	90	72	0	.556	5.5	797	738	188	.271	**.347**	**.430**	**777**	**111**	99	139	13	175	492	878	12.3	4.11	100	.263	.323	.0	.3	**9.6**	**1.0**	-1.9
Det	87	75	0	.537	8.5	798	714	**198**	.263	.338	.424	762	106	100	138	33	183	571	880	12.3	4.02	103	.251	.323	1.1	2.2	5.0	.6	-2.9
Tor	86	76	1	.531	9.5	809	733	181	.269	.329	.427	756	101	103	110	16	164	487	1002	12.2	4.08	104	.261	.322	**1.7**	2.6	.9	.0	-.0
Cle	84	78	1	.519	11.5	**831**	841	157	**.284**	.337	**.430**	767	109	99	**141**	31	167	605	744	13.7	4.58	91	.273	.346	-1.7	-6.3	6.6	.8	3.7
Mil	77	84	0	.478	18	667	734	127	.255	.321	.385	706	88	103	100	29	158	494	952	12.6	4.01	108	.267	.328	-1.2	5.1	-8.1	.0	.5
Bal	73	89	0	.451	22.5	708	760	169	.258	.327	.395	722	96	99	64	17	177	535	954	12.6	4.30	97	.263	.328	-.5	-2.3	-2.0	-.2	-3.1
West																													
Cal	92	70	0	.568		786	684	167	.255	.338	.404	742	102	99	109	29	153	478	955	**11.5**	3.84	107	.248	**.309**	1.2	4.6	3.0	.5	1.6
Tex	87	75	0	.537	5	771	743	184	.267	.331	.428	759	102	103	103	15	145	736	**1059**	13.2	4.11	105	.249	.340	.3	3.2	1.4	-1.1	2.2
KC	76	86	0	.469	16	654	**673**	137	.252	.313	.390	703	88	102	97	24	**121**	479	888	12.1	**3.82**	**112**	.258	.319	.2	**6.8**	-9.1	.0	-3.0
Oak	76	86	0	.469	16	731	760	163	.252	.322	.390	712	100	93	139	22	166	667	937	12.8	4.31	90	**.247**	.330	-.5	-7.1	.3	.5	1.8
Chi	72	90	0	.444	20	644	699	121	.247	.310	.363	673	79	-104	115	18	143	561	895	12.2	3.93	110	.251	.323	.6	6.1	-14.8	.2	-1.0
Min	71	91	0	.438	21	741	839	196	.261	.325	.428	753	100	103	81	**39**	200	503	937	13.4	4.77	91	.281	.342	.5	-6.6	-.2	-.8	-3.0
Sea	67	95	0	.414	25	718	835	158	.253	.326	.399	725	95	101	93	33	171	585	944	13.9	4.65	92	.283	.353	-1.7	-6.1	-3.6	-1.0	-1.6
Total	1134					60449		2290	.262	.330	.408	737			1470	355				12.7	4.18		.262	.330					

Batter-Fielder Wins
- **Boggs-Bos 5.4**
- **Mattingly-NY.......... 4.5**
- **Henderson-NY....... 3.6**
- **Randolph-NY......... 2.1**

Batting Average
- Boggs-Bos............ .357
- Mattingly-NY......... .352
- Easler-NY............. .302
- Randolph-NY........ .276

On-Base Percentage
- Boggs-Bos............ .453
- Mattingly-NY......... .394
- Randolph-NY........ .393
- Easler-NY............. .362

Slugging Average
- Mattingly-NY......... .573
- Henderson-NY...... .469
- Pagliarulo-NY....... .464
- Winfield-NY.......... .462

On-Base Plus Slugging
- Mattingly-NY.......... 967
- Henderson-NY....... 827
- Winfield-NY............811
- Easler-NY...............811

Adjusted OPS
- Mattingly-NY.......... 162
- Henderson-NY....... 124
- Easler-NY.............. 121
- Winfield-NY............ 120

Adjusted Batter Runs
- Mattingly-NY......... 58.2
- Pasqua-NY........... 21.5
- Henderson-NY...... 21.5
- Winfield-NY.......... 16.8

Runs
- Henderson-NY....... 130
- Mattingly-NY...........117
- Winfield-NY.............. 90
- Randolph-NY........... 76

Hits
- Mattingly-NY.......... 238
- Henderson-NY....... 160
- Winfield-NY............ 148
- Easler-NY.............. 148

Doubles
- Mattingly-NY........... 53
- Winfield-NY............. 31
- Henderson-NY......... 31
- Easler-NY................ 26

Triples
- Butler-Cle................ 14
- Winfield-NY................ 5
- Henderson-NY........... 5
- Pagliarulo-NY............ 3

Home Runs
- Barfield-Tor............. 40
- Mattingly-NY............ 31
- Pagliarulo-NY.......... 28
- Henderson-NY......... 28

Total Bases
- Mattingly-NY.......... 388
- Henderson-NY....... 285
- Winfield-NY............ 261
- Pagliarulo-NY........ 234

Runs Batted In
- Carter-Cle.............. 121
- Mattingly-NY...........113
- Winfield-NY............ 104
- Easler-NY................ 78

Stolen Bases
- Henderson-NY......... 87
- Randolph-NY........... 15
- Winfield-NY................ 6
- Washington-NY.......... 6

Base Stealing Runs
- Henderson-NY...... 12.8
- Randolph-NY.......... 2.6
- Washington-NY....... 1.0
- Cotto-NY................... .7

Fielding Runs-Infield
- Owen-Sea-Bos..... 35.8
- Randolph-NY.......... 2.8

Fielding Runs-Outfield
- Barfield-Tor........... 16.0
- Henderson-NY........ 3.8

Wins
- Clemens-Bos.......... 24
- Rasmussen-NY 18
- 5 players tied 9

Winning Pct.
- Clemens-Bos........ .857
- Rasmussen-NY ..... .750

Complete Games
- Candiotti-Cle............ 17
- Guidry-NY.................. 5
- Rasmussen-NY 3
- 2 players tied 2

Strikeouts
- Langston-Sea........ 245
- Guidry-NY............. 140
- Rasmussen-NY 131
- Righetti-NY.............. 83

Fewest BB/Game
- Guidry-NY............. 1.78
- Rasmussen-NY 3.30

Games
- Williams-Tex 80
- Righetti-NY.............. 74
- Fisher-NY................ 62
- Shirley-NY............... 39

Saves
- Righetti-NY.............. 46
- Fisher-NY.................. 6
- Shirley-NY................. 3
- Scurry-NY.................. 2

Base Runners/9
- Clemens-Bos.......... 8.86
- Rasmussen-NY .. 10.51
- Righetti-NY......... 10.55
- Guidry-NY...........11.28

Adjusted Relief Runs
- Eichhorn-Tor......... 43.9
- Righetti-NY........... 20.9

Relief Ranking
- Eichhorn-Tor......... 55.7
- Righetti-NY........... 41.9

Innings Pitched
- Blyleven-Min....... 271.2
- Rasmussen-NY .. 202.0
- Guidry-NY........... 192.1
- Drabek-NY.......... 131.2

Opponents' Avg.
- Clemens-Bos........ .195
- Rasmussen-NY ..... .217
- Guidry-NY............. .265

Opponents' OBP
- Clemens-Bos........ .252
- Rasmussen-NY ..... .289
- Guidry-NY............. .300

Earned Run Average
- Clemens-Bos........ 2.48
- Rasmussen-NY 3.88
- Guidry-NY............ 3.98

Adjusted ERA
- Clemens-Bos......... 169
- Rasmussen-NY 107
- Guidry-NY.............. 104

Adjusted Starter Runs
- Clemens-Bos........ 48.8
- Tewksbury-NY...... 10.1
- John-NY................. 9.0
- Rasmussen-NY...... 8.8

Pitcher Wins
- Eichhorn-Tor........... 5.8
- Righetti-NY............. 4.2
- Tewksbury-NY........ 1.1
- John-NY................. 1.0

1987 American League

TEAM	W	L	T	PCT	GB	R	OR	HR	AVG	OBP	SLG	OPS	AOPS	PF	SB	CG	HR	BB	SO	BR/9	ERA	AERA	OAV	OOB	FW	PW	BW	BSW	DIF
East																													
Det	98	64	0	.605		**896**	735	**225**	.272	.349	**.451**	**800**	**114**	96	106	33	180	563	976	12.5	4.02	106	.256	.325	.1	3.6	**12.5**	-.2	1.0
Tor	96	66	0	.593	2	845	**655**	215	.269	.336	.446	782	103	102	126	18	158	567	1064	**11.8**	**3.74**	**121**	**.244**	**.316**	.8	**11.7**	2.2	.2	.1
Mil	91	71	0	.562	7	862	817	163	.276	.346	.428	774	101	103	**176**	28	169	529	1039	12.9	4.62	99	.271	.333	-1.3	-.5	1.4	**.5**	9.9
NY	89	73	0	.549	9	788	758	196	.262	.336	.418	754	99	99	105	19	179	542	900	12.8	4.36	101	.266	.332	1.3	1.0	.0	.0	5.6
Bos	78	84	0	.481	20	842	825	174	**.278**	**.352**	.430	782	103	103	77	**47**	190	517	1034	13.4	4.77	95	.282	.344	.8	-3.2	3.8	-.7	-3.7
Bal	67	95	0	.414	31	729	880	211	.258	.322	.418	740	96	98	69	17	226	547	870	13.3	5.01	88	.276	.341	.8	-9.0	-3.1	-.9	-1.9
Cle	61	101	0	.377	37	742	957	187	.263	.324	.422	746	95	101	140	24	219	606	849	14.1	5.28	86	.278	.351	-1.8	-10.8	-4.1	.4	-3.7
West																													
Min	85	77	0	.525		786	806	196	.261	.328	.430	758	95	104	113	16	210	564	990	13.1	4.63	100	.266	.337	**1.6**	.0	-3.4	-.6	6.4
KC	83	79	0	.512	2	715	691	168	.262	.328	.412	740	91	103	125	44	**128**	548	923	12.7	3.86	119	.261	.330	-.5	10.6	-5.9	.4	-2.6
Oak	81	81	0	.500	4	806	789	199	.260	.333	.428	761	107	94	140	18	176	531	1042	12.5	4.32	96	.258	.324	-1.1	-2.9	5.7	.1	-1.8
Sea	78	84	0	.481	7	760	801	161	.272	.335	.428	763	95	105	174	39	199	**497**	919	12.8	4.49	105	.272	.332	.1	3.4	-2.9	**.5**	-4.2
Chi	77	85	0	.475	8	748	746	173	.258	.319	.415	734	90	103	138	29	189	537	792	12.5	4.30	107	.259	.327	.5	4.7	-7.3	.4	-2.2
Tex	75	87	0	.463	10	823	849	194	.266	.333	.430	763	99	101	120	20	199	760	**1103**	13.7	4.63	97	.253	.347	-1.7	-2.0	.4	-.6	-2.1
Cal	75	87	0	.463	10	770	803	172	.252	.326	.401	727	94	97	125	20	212	504	941	12.5	4.38	99	.264	.327	.4	-1.0	-3.8	.4	-1.9
Total	1134					61112		2634	.265	.333	.425	759			1734	372				12.9	4.46		.265	.333					

Batter-Fielder Wins
- **Boggs-Bos 6.5**
- **Randolph-NY 3.4**
- **Henderson-NY 3.4**
- **Mattingly-NY 2.6**

Batting Average
- Boggs-Bos .363
- Mattingly-NY .327
- Randolph-NY .305
- Winfield-NY .275

On-Base Percentage
- Boggs-Bos .461
- Randolph-NY .411
- Mattingly-NY .378
- Winfield-NY .358

Slugging Average
- McGwire-Oak .618
- Mattingly-NY .559
- Pagliarulo-NY .479
- Winfield-NY .457

On-Base Plus Slugging
- Boggs-Bos 1049
- Mattingly-NY 937
- Randolph-NY 825
- Winfield-NY 815

Adjusted OPS
- Boggs-Bos 172
- Mattingly-NY 146
- Randolph-NY 122
- Winfield-NY 115

Adjusted Batter Runs
- Boggs-Bos 64.5
- Mattingly-NY 38.2
- Henderson-NY 27.0
- Randolph-NY 19.3

Runs
- Molitor-Mil 114
- Randolph-NY 96
- Mattingly-NY 93
- Winfield-NY 83

Hits
- Seitzer-KC 207
- Puckett-Min 207
- Mattingly-NY 186
- Winfield-NY 158

Doubles
- Molitor-Mil 41
- Mattingly-NY 38
- Pagliarulo-NY 26
- Randolph-NY 24

Triples
- Wilson-KC 15
- Pagliarulo-NY 3
- Henderson-NY 3
- 2 players tied 2

Home Runs
- McGwire-Oak 49
- Pagliarulo-NY 32
- Mattingly-NY 30
- Winfield-NY 27

Total Bases
- Bell-Tor 369
- Mattingly-NY 318
- Winfield-NY 263
- Pagliarulo-NY 250

Runs Batted In
- Bell-Tor 134
- Mattingly-NY 115
- Winfield-NY 97
- Pagliarulo-NY 87

Stolen Bases
- Reynolds-Sea 60
- Henderson-NY 41
- Randolph-NY 11
- Washington-NY 10

Base Stealing Runs
- Wilson-KC 9.1
- Henderson-NY 6.2
- Randolph-NY 2.1
- Washington-NY 1.9

Fielding Runs-Infield
- Barrett-Bos 32.6
- Randolph-NY 8.5

Fielding Runs-Outfield
- White-Cal 17.6

Wins
- Stewart-Oak 20
- Clemens-Bos 20
- Rhoden-NY 16
- John-NY 13

Winning Pct.
- Clemens-Bos .690
- Rhoden-NY .615

Complete Games
- Clemens-Bos 18
- Hudson-NY 6
- Rhoden-NY 4
- John-NY 3

Strikeouts
- Langston-Sea 262
- Rhoden-NY 107
- Hudson-NY 100
- Guidry-NY 96

Fewest BB/Game
- Long-Chi 1.49
- John-NY 2.25
- Rhoden-NY 3.02

Games
- Eichhorn-Tor 89
- Righetti-NY 60
- Stoddard-NY 57
- Clements-NY 55

Saves
- Henke-Tor 34
- Righetti-NY 31
- Stoddard-NY 8
- Clements-NY 7

Base Runners/9
- Henke-Tor 8.33
- Stoddard-NY 10.97
- Hudson-NY 11.46
- Guidry-NY 11.47

Adjusted Relief Runs
- Henke-Tor 21.6
- Stoddard-NY 10.1
- Righetti-NY 7.4

Relief Ranking
- Henke-Tor 29.2
- Righetti-NY 14.9
- Stoddard-NY 8.7

Innings Pitched
- Hough-Tex 285.1
- John-NY 187.2
- Rhoden-NY 181.2
- Hudson-NY 154.2

Opponents' Avg.
- Key-Tor .221
- Rhoden-NY .268
- John-NY .288

Opponents' OBP
- Key-Tor .272
- Rhoden-NY .327
- John-NY .335

Earned Run Average
- Key-Tor 2.76
- Rhoden-NY 3.86
- John-NY 4.03

Adjusted ERA
- Key-Tor 164
- Rhoden-NY 115
- John-NY 110

Adjusted Starter Runs
- Clemens-Bos 49.2
- Hudson-NY 16.0
- Rhoden-NY 11.5
- Guidry-NY 10.8

Pitcher Wins
- Clemens-Bos 4.5
- Viola-Min 4.5
- Hudson-NY 1.6
- 2 players tied 1.4

1988 American League

TEAM	W	L	T	PCT	GB	R	OR	HR	AVG	OBP	SLG	OPS	AOPS	PF	SB	CG	HR	BB	SO	BR/9	ERA	AERA	OAV	OOB	FW	PW	BW	BSW	DIF
East																													
Bos	89	73	0	.549		**813**	689	124	**.283**	**.357**	.420	**777**	**112**	105	65	26	143	493	**1085**	12.3	3.97	104	.259	.322	1.6	2.3	**10.9**	-.5	-6.4
Det	88	74	0	.543	1	703	658	143	.250	.324	.378	702	99	97	87	34	150	497	890	11.8	3.71	103	.248	.312	.6	2.1	.3	-.3	4.2
Tor	87	75	0	.537	2	763	680	**158**	.268	.332	.419	751	108	101	107	16	143	528	904	12.4	3.80	104	.256	.326	.6	2.6	6.3	.5	-3.9
Mil	87	75	0	.537	2	682	**616**	113	.257	.314	.375	689	91	101	**159**	30	125	**437**	832	**11.2**	3.45	**116**	.248	**.303**	-.0	**8.9**	-6.6	1.0	2.7
NY	85	76	0	.528	3.5	772	748	148	.263	.333	.395	728	103	100	146	16	157	487	861	12.7	4.26	93	.267	.328	-.9	-4.9	4.0	**1.2**	5.0
Cle	78	84	0	.481	11	666	731	134	.261	.314	.387	701	92	103	97	35	120	442	812	12.4	4.16	99	.270	.326	-.3	-.5	-5.8	-.3	3.8
Bal	54	107	0	.335	34.5	550	789	137	.238	.305	.359	664	87	-98	69	20	153	523	709	13.2	4.54	87	.274	.340	.0	-9.8	-9.2	-.7	-6.8
West																													
Oak	104	58	0	.642		800	620	156	.263	.336	.399	735	108	97	129	22	116	553	983	11.8	**3.44**	110	.247	.316	.9	6.3	7.7	.2	7.9
Min	91	71	0	.562	13	759	672	151	.274	.340	**.421**	761	109	103	107	18	146	453	897	12.3	3.93	104	.266	.325	**2.1**	2.3	7.4	-.6	-1.2
KC	84	77	0	.522	19.5	704	648	121	.259	.321	.391	712	97	101	137	29	**102**	465	886	12.1	3.65	109	.258	.318	-.3	5.5	-1.8	.5	-.3
Cal	75	87	0	.463	29	714	771	124	.261	.321	.385	706	99	98	86	26	135	568	817	13.1	4.32	90	.270	.338	-.9	-7.4	-.2	-.6	3.0
Chi	71	90	0	.441	32.5	631	757	132	.244	.303	.370	673	87	100	98	11	138	533	754	12.7	4.12	97	.266	.331	-2.1	-2.0	-9.6	-.2	4.3
Tex	70	91	0	.435	33.5	637	735	112	.252	.320	.368	688	90	103	130	**41**	129	654	912	12.6	4.05	101	**.244**	.329	-.7	.7	-6.8	.2	-4.0
Sea	68	93	0	.422	35.5	664	744	148	.257	.317	.398	715	95	105	95	28	144	558	981	12.5	4.15	101	.256	.327	-.2	.3	-3.7	-.7	-8.2
Total	1131					69858		1901	.259	.324	.391	715			1512	352				12.4	3.97		.259	.324					

Batter-Fielder Wins
- **Boggs-Bos 6.4**
- **Henderson-NY 3.8**
- **Winfield-NY 3.0**
- **Clark-NY 1.9**

Batting Average
- Boggs-Bos .366
- Winfield-NY .322
- Mattingly-NY .311
- Henderson-NY .305

On-Base Percentage
- Boggs-Bos .476
- Winfield-NY .398
- Henderson-NY .394
- Clark-NY .381

Slugging Average
- Canseco-Oak .569
- Winfield-NY .530
- Mattingly-NY .462
- Clark-NY .433

On-Base Plus Slugging
- Boggs-Bos 965
- Winfield-NY 927
- Mattingly-NY 816
- Clark-NY 815

Adjusted OPS
- Canseco-Oak 171
- Winfield-NY 158
- Clark-NY 129
- Mattingly-NY 128

Adjusted Batter Runs
- Boggs-Bos 62.2
- Winfield-NY 45.3
- Clark-NY 24.3
- Henderson-NY 22.7

Runs
- Boggs-Bos 128
- Henderson-NY 118
- Winfield-NY 96
- Mattingly-NY 94

Hits
- Puckett-Min 234
- Mattingly-NY 186
- Winfield-NY 180
- Henderson-NY 169

Doubles
- Boggs-Bos 45
- Winfield-NY 37
- Mattingly-NY 37
- Henderson-NY 30

Triples
- 3 players tied 11
- Washington-NY 3
- Winfield-NY 2
- Henderson-NY 2

Home Runs
- Canseco-Oak 42
- Clark-NY 27
- Winfield-NY 25
- Mattingly-NY 18

Total Bases
- Puckett-Min 358
- Winfield-NY 296
- Mattingly-NY 277
- Henderson-NY 221

Runs Batted In
- Canseco-Oak 124
- Winfield-NY 107
- Clark-NY 93
- Mattingly-NY 88

Stolen Bases
- Henderson-NY 93
- Washington-NY 15
- Winfield-NY 9
- Randolph-NY 8

Base Stealing Runs
- Henderson-NY 15.9
- Washington-NY 1.2
- Meacham-NY 1.2
- Winfield-NY .6

Fielding Runs-Infield
- Guillen-Chi 40.8
- Randolph-NY 13.9

Fielding Runs-Outfield
- Barfield-Tor 13.1
- Henderson-NY 4.0
- Washington-NY 1.9

Wins
- Viola-Min 24
- Candelaria-NY 13
- Rhoden-NY 12
- Dotson-NY 12

Winning Pct.
- Viola-Min .774

Complete Games
- Stewart-Oak 14
- Clemens-Bos 14
- Candelaria-NY 6
- Rhoden-NY 5

Strikeouts
- Clemens-Bos 291
- Candelaria-NY 121
- Rhoden-NY 94
- John-NY 81

Fewest BB/Game
- Anderson-Min 1.65
- John-NY 2.35
- Rhoden-NY 2.56
- Dotson-NY 3.79

Games
- Crim-Mil 70
- Righetti-NY 60
- Allen-NY 41
- Shields-NY 39

Saves
- Eckersley-Oak 45
- Righetti-NY 25
- Stoddard-NY 3
- Hudson-NY 2

Base Runners/9
- Eckersley-Oak 7.93
- Candelaria-NY 10.03
- Hudson-NY 11.26
- Allen-NY 12.27

Adjusted Relief Runs
- Henneman-Det 19.7
- Righetti-NY 5.3
- Allen-NY 3.3

Relief Ranking
- Henneman-Det 37.7
- Righetti-NY 7.6
- Allen-NY 2.0

Innings Pitched
- Stewart-Oak 275.2
- Rhoden-NY 197.0
- John-NY 176.1
- Dotson-NY 171.0

Opponents' Avg.
- Robinson-Det .197
- Dotson-NY .266
- Rhoden-NY .269
- John-NY .308

Opponents' OBP
- Higuera-Mil .263
- Rhoden-NY .322
- Dotson-NY .338
- John-NY .354

Earned Run Average
- Anderson-Min 2.45
- Higuera-Mil 2.45
- Rhoden-NY 4.29
- John-NY 4.49

Adjusted ERA
- Anderson-Min 167
- Rhoden-NY 92
- John-NY 88
- Dotson-NY 79

Adjusted Starter Runs
- Higuera-Mil 40.2
- Candelaria-NY 8.0
- Leiter-NY .3

Pitcher Wins
- Viola-Min 4.7
- Candelaria-NY 1.0
- Righetti-NY .7
- Allen-NY .1

1989 American League

TEAM	W	L	T	PCT	GB	R	OR	HR	AVG	OBP	SLG	OPS	AOPS	PF	SB	CG	HR	BB	SO	BR/9	ERA	AERA	OAV	OOB	FW	PW	BW	BSW	DIF
East																													
Tor	89	73	0	.549		731	651	142	.260	.323	.398	721	103	99	144	12	99	478	849	11.8	3.58	106	.255	.317	-.1	3.5	3.0	.4	1.3
Bal	87	75	0	.537	2	708	686	129	.252	.326	.379	705	101	97	118	16	134	486	676	12.6	4.00	95	.272	.331	**2.3**	-3.2	1.3	.0	5.5
Bos	83	79	0	.512	6	**774**	735	108	**.277**	**.351**	**.403**	**754**	**105**	106	56	14	131	548	1054	12.5	4.01	102	.261	.328	-.1	1.5	**6.4**	-.7	-5.1
Mil	81	81	0	.500	8	707	679	126	.259	.318	.382	700	97	99	**165**	16	129	457	812	12.2	3.80	101	.265	.321	-1.8	.8	-1.9	.8	2.1
NY	74	87	0	.460	14.5	698	792	130	.269	.331	.391	722	104	99	137	15	150	521	787	13.4	4.50	86	.281	.344	.1	-10.0	3.1	.2	.0
Cle	73	89	0	.451	16	604	654	127	.245	.310	.365	675	88	102	74	23	107	**452**	844	11.8	3.65	109	.257	.313	.4	5.2	-8.8	-.9	-4.0
Det	59	103	0	.364	30	617	816	116	.242	.318	.351	669	90	98	103	24	150	652	831	13.9	4.53	84	.274	.352	-.3	-11.6	-6.3	-.2	-3.6
West																													
Oak	99	63	0	.611		712	**576**	127	.261	.331	.381	712	103	97	157	17	103	510	930	**11.3**	**3.09**	**120**	**.238**	**.305**	-.2	**10.4**	3.6	.8	3.4
KC	92	70	0	.568	7	690	635	101	.261	.329	.373	702	97	100	154	27	**86**	455	978	11.7	3.55	109	.257	.314	.7	5.3	-.9	**.9**	5.0
Cal	91	71	0	.562	8	669	578	**145**	.256	.311	.386	697	97	98	89	**32**	113	465	897	11.6	3.28	116	.253	.312	1.7	9.1	-3.3	-.0	2.5
Tex	83	79	0	.512	16	695	714	122	.263	.326	.394	720	100	102	101	26	119	654	**1112**	12.4	3.91	102	.239	.324	-.6	1.1	.5	-.2	1.2
Min	80	82	0	.494	19	740	738	117	.276	.334	.402	736	99	107	111	19	139	500	851	12.8	4.28	97	.269	.332	1.1	-2.1	.8	-.0	-.7
Sea	73	89	0	.451	26	694	728	134	.257	.320	.384	704	95	103	81	15	114	560	897	12.7	4.00	101	.259	.330	-1.1	.5	-3.8	-.8	-2.9
Chi	69	92	0	.429	29.5	693	750	94	.271	.328	.383	711	102	98	97	9	144	539	778	12.9	4.23	91	.269	.335	-1.6	-6.4	1.7	-.4	-4.8
Total	1133					69732		1718	.261	.326	.384	709			1587	265				12.4	3.88		.261	.326					

Batter-Fielder Wins
R.Henderson-NY-Oak ... 4.6
Sax-NY 2.1
Kelly-NY 1.6
Espinoza-NY 1.4

Batting Average
Puckett-Min .... .339
Sax-NY .... .315
Mattingly-NY .... .303
Espinoza-NY .... .282

On-Base Percentage
Boggs-Bos .... .430
Sax-NY .... .364
Mattingly-NY .... .351
Espinoza-NY .... .301

Slugging Average
Sierra-Tex .... .543
Mattingly-NY .... .477
Sax-NY .... .387
Espinoza-NY .... .332

On-Base Plus Slugging
McGriff-Tor 924
Mattingly-NY 828
Sax-NY 751
Espinoza-NY 633

Adjusted OPS
McGriff-Tor 161
Mattingly-NY 134
Sax-NY 113
Espinoza-NY 79

Adjusted Batter Runs
McGriff-Tor 50.1
Mattingly-NY 27.2
Kelly-NY 13.4
Sax-NY 12.0

Runs
R.Henderson-NY-Oak ... 113
Boggs-Bos 113
Sax-NY 88
Mattingly-NY 79

Hits
Puckett-Min 215
Sax-NY 205
Mattingly-NY 191
Espinoza-NY 142

Doubles
Boggs-Bos 51
Mattingly-NY 37
Sax-NY 26
Espinoza-NY 23

Triples
Sierra-Tex 14
Slaught-NY 3
Sax-NY 3
Kelly-NY 3

Home Runs
McGriff-Tor 36
Mattingly-NY 23
Hall-NY 17
Balboni-NY 17

Total Bases
Sierra-Tex 344
Mattingly-NY 301
Sax-NY 252
Kelly-NY 184

Runs Batted In
Sierra-Tex 119
Mattingly-NY 113
Sax-NY 63
Balboni-NY 59

Stolen Bases
R.Henderson-NY-Oak 77
Sax-NY 43
Kelly-NY 35
Tolleson-NY 5

Base Stealing Runs
R.Henderson-NY-Oak . 12.0
Sax-NY 3.5
Kelly-NY 3.5
Tolleson-NY 8

Fielding Runs-Infield
Reynolds-Sea 24.6
Espinoza-NY 18.5
Sax-NY 1.2

Fielding Runs-Outfield
Snyder-Cle 12.9

Wins
Saberhagen-KC 23
Hawkins-NY 15
Terrell-NY 6
LaPoint-NY 6

Winning Pct.
Saberhagen-KC ..... .793
Hawkins-NY .... .500

Complete Games
Saberhagen-KC 12
Hawkins-NY 5
Parker-NY 2
Cary-NY 2

Strikeouts
Ryan-Tex 301
Hawkins-NY 98
McCullers-NY 82
Cary-NY 79

Fewest BB/Game
Key-Tor 1.13
Hawkins-NY 3.28

Games
Crim-Mil 76
Guetterman-NY 70
Righetti-NY 55
McCullers-NY 52

Saves
Russell-Tex 38
Righetti-NY 25
Guetterman-NY 13
McCullers-NY 3

Base Runners/9
Saberhagen-KC 8.71
Cary-NY 9.69
Guetterman-NY .. 10.83
Parker-NY 11.70

Adjusted Relief Runs
Montgomery-KC ... 25.5
Guetterman-NY 16.6
Righetti-NY 3.9

Relief Ranking
Montgomery-KC ... 33.7
Guetterman-NY 18.2
Righetti-NY 6.6

Innings Pitched
Saberhagen-KC .. 262.1
Hawkins-NY 208.1
Parker-NY 120.0
LaPoint-NY 113.2

Opponents' Avg.
Ryan-Tex .... .187
Hawkins-NY .... .290

Opponents' OBP
Saberhagen-KC .... .251
Hawkins-NY .... .354

Earned Run Average
Saberhagen-KC 2.16
Hawkins-NY 4.80

Adjusted ERA
Saberhagen-KC 179
Hawkins-NY 81

Adjusted Starter Runs
Saberhagen-KC 48.4
Cary-NY 6.1
Parker-NY 3.5
Schulze-NY 0

Pitcher Wins
Saberhagen-KC 5.3
Guetterman-NY 2.0
Righetti-NY 7
2 players tied 3

1990 American League

TEAM	W	L	T	PCT	GB	R	OR	HR	AVG	OBP	SLG	OPS	AOPS	PF	SB	CG	HR	BB	SO	BR/9	ERA	AERA	OAV	OOB	FW	PW	BW	BSW	DIF
East																													
Bos	88	74	0	.543		699	664	106	**.272**	**.344**	.395	739	101	105	53	15	**92**	519	997	12.5	3.72	110	.261	.327	-.2	5.7	2.4	-1.1	.2
Tor	86	76	0	.531	2	**767**	661	167	.265	.328	**.419**	**747**	105	102	111	6	143	**445**	892	11.9	3.84	103	.260	.317	**2.0**	1.8	3.9	.2	-2.9
Det	79	83	0	.488	9	750	754	**172**	.259	.337	.409	746	**107**	101	82	15	154	661	856	13.3	4.39	90	.259	.341	-.7	-6.6	5.5	-.6	.4
Cle	77	85	0	.475	11	732	737	110	.267	.324	.391	715	99	100	107	12	163	518	860	12.9	4.26	92	.270	.334	.2	-5.4	-.6	.0	1.7
Bal	76	85	0	.472	11.5	669	698	132	.245	.330	.370	700	98	97	94	10	161	537	776	12.5	4.04	94	.264	.328	1.6	-3.9	-.2	-.2	-1.8
Mil	74	88	0	.457	14	732	760	128	.256	.320	.384	704	96	100	**164**	23	121	469	771	12.9	4.08	95	.275	.331	-1.8	-3.4	-2.3	.7	-.2
NY	67	95	0	.414	21	603	749	147	.241	.300	.366	666	84	-101	119	15	144	618	909	12.9	4.21	95	.261	.336	-.4	-3.7	-12.1	.6	1.6
West																													
Oak	103	59	0	.636		733	**570**	164	.254	.336	.391	727	**107**	96	141	18	123	494	831	**11.2**	**3.18**	**117**	**.238**	**.302**	**2.0**	**9.5**	**5.9**	**.8**	3.9
Chi	94	68	0	.580	9	682	633	106	.258	.320	.379	699	97	98	140	17	106	548	914	11.8	3.61	106	.244	.316	-.3	3.8	-2.4	-.5	12.5
Tex	83	79	0	.512	20	676	696	110	.259	.331	.376	707	97	100	115	**25**	113	623	997	12.5	3.83	102	.248	.327	-.8	1.5	-1.3	.5	2.1
Cal	80	82	0	.494	23	690	706	147	.260	.329	.391	720	103	98	69	21	106	544	944	12.8	3.79	101	.267	.334	-1.4	.6	2.1	-.4	-2.0
Sea	77	85	0	.475	26	640	680	107	.259	.333	.373	706	96	101	105	21	120	606	**1064**	12.3	3.69	107	.243	.321	-.6	4.5	-1.4	.0	-6.5
KC	75	86	0	.466	27.5	707	709	100	.267	.328	.395	723	102	99	107	18	116	560	1006	13.0	3.93	98	.264	.334	-.2	-1.3	2.5	-.2	-6.3
Min	74	88	0	.457	29	666	729	100	.265	.324	.385	709	91	106	96	13	134	489	872	12.7	4.12	101	.273	.332	1.1	.4	-5.8	-.1	-2.6
Total	1133					69746		1796	.259	.327	.388	715			1503	229				12.5	3.91		.259	.327					

Batter-Fielder Wins
R.Henderson-Oak . 7.7
Barfield-NY 2.1
Maas-NY 1.0
3 players tied 3

Batting Average
Brett-KC .... .329
Kelly-NY .... .285
Sax-NY .... .260
Barfield-NY .... .246

On-Base Percentage
R.Henderson-Oak .439
Barfield-NY .... .359
Kelly-NY .... .323
Sax-NY .... .316

Slugging Average
Fielder-Det .... .592
Barfield-NY .... .456
Kelly-NY .... .418
Sax-NY .... .325

On-Base Plus Slugging
R.Henderson-Oak 1016
Barfield-NY 815
Kelly-NY 741
Sax-NY 641

Adjusted OPS
R.Henderson-Oak.. 189
Barfield-NY 126
Kelly-NY 105
Sax-NY 80

Adjusted Batter Runs
R.Henderson-Oak 64.2
Barfield-NY 18.6
Maas-NY 16.6
Kelly-NY 2.5

Runs
R.Henderson-Oak ... 119
Kelly-NY 85
Sax-NY 70
Barfield-NY 69

Hits
Palmeiro-Tex 191
Kelly-NY 183
Sax-NY 160
Barfield-NY 117

Doubles
J.Reed-Bos 45
Brett-KC 45
Kelly-NY 32
Sax-NY 24

Triples
Fernandez-Tor 17
Kelly-NY 4

Home Runs
Fielder-Det 51
Barfield-NY 25
Maas-NY 21
Balboni-NY 17

Total Bases
Fielder-Det 339
Kelly-NY 268
Barfield-NY 217
Sax-NY 200

Runs Batted In
Fielder-Det 132
Barfield-NY 78
Kelly-NY 61
Hall-NY 46

Stolen Bases
R.Henderson-Oak 65
Sax-NY 43
Kelly-NY 42
Sanders-NY 8

Base Stealing Runs
R.Henderson-Oak 10.8
Sax-NY 6.3
Kelly-NY 3.3
Azocar-NY 1.5

Fielding Runs-Infield
Espinoza-NY 22.9

Fielding Runs-Outfield
Orsulak-Bal 8.9
Barfield-NY 6.7

Wins
Welch-Oak 27
Guetterman-NY 11
Leary-NY 9
LaPoint-NY 7

Winning Pct.
Welch-Oak .... .818

Complete Games
Stewart-Oak 11
Morris-Det 11
Leary-NY 6
3 players tied 2

Strikeouts
Ryan-Tex 232
Leary-NY 138
Cary-NY 134
Cadaret-NY 80

Fewest BB/Game
Anderson-Min 1.86
Leary-NY 3.38

Games
Thigpen-Chi 77
Guetterman-NY 64
Robinson-NY 54
Cadaret-NY 54

Saves
Thigpen-Chi 57
Righetti-NY 36
Cadaret-NY 3
Guetterman-NY 2

Base Runners/9
Eckersley-Oak 5.52
Guetterman-NY .. 10.26
Robinson-NY 11.88
Cary-NY 12.12

Adjusted Relief Runs
Farr-KC 26.9
Plunk-NY 8.8
Guetterman-NY 6.9
Robinson-NY 6.4

Relief Ranking
Eckersley-Oak 44.7
Guetterman-NY 12.2
Plunk-NY 9.9
Robinson-NY 5.8

Innings Pitched
Stewart-Oak 267.0
Leary-NY 208.0
LaPoint-NY 157.2
Hawkins-NY 157.2

Opponents' Avg.
Ryan-Tex .... .188
Leary-NY .... .257

Opponents' OBP
Ryan-Tex .... .267
Leary-NY .... .328

Earned Run Average
Clemens-Bos 1.93
Leary-NY 4.11

Adjusted ERA
Clemens-Bos 212
Leary-NY 97

Adjusted Starter Runs
Clemens-Bos 50.6
Perez-NY 3.8
Eiland-NY 1.1

Pitcher Wins
Clemens-Bos 6.2
Guetterman-NY 1.3
Plunk-NY 1.1
Perez-NY 8

1991 American League

TEAM	W	L	T	PCT	GB	R	OR	HR	AVG	OBP	SLG	OPS	AOPS	PF	SB	CG	HR	BB	SO	BR/9	ERA	AERA	OAV	OOB	FW	PW	BW	BSW	DIF
East																													
Tor	91	71	0	.562		684	**622**	133	.257	.322	.400	722	94	104	148	10	121	523	971	**11.5**	**3.50**	**120**	**.238**	**.307**	-.6	**11.3**	-3.3	**1.0**	1.6
Det	84	78	0	.519	7	817	794	**209**	.247	.333	.416	749	104	102	109	18	148	593	739	13.6	4.51	93	.280	.348	.7	-5.3	3.7	.4	3.5
Bos	84	78	0	.519	7	731	712	126	.269	.340	.401	741	99	106	59	15	147	530	999	12.3	4.01	108	.257	.323	.0	4.7	.7	-.5	-1.9
Mil	83	79	0	.512	8	799	744	116	.271	.336	.396	732	104	98	106	23	147	527	859	12.7	4.14	96	.266	.332	-.0	-2.6	3.6	-.4	1.5
NY	71	91	0	.438	20	674	777	147	.256	.316	.387	703	92	101	109	3	152	506	936	12.8	4.42	94	.271	.334	-.9	-4.1	-5.4	.7	-.2
Bal	67	95	0	.414	24	686	796	170	.254	.319	.401	720	102	96	50	8	147	504	868	12.8	4.59	86	.273	.333	**1.4**	-10.4	.9	-.5	-5.4
Cle	57	105	0	.352	34	576	759	79	.254	.313	.350	663	82	-101	84	22	110	**441**	862	12.7	4.23	98	.276	.329	-1.8	-1.0	-12.7	-.6	-7.9
West																													
Min	95	67	0	.586		776	652	140	**.280**	**.344**	.420	764	105	105	107	21	139	488	876	11.9	3.69	116	.255	.317	1.2	8.9	4.5	-.4	-.2
Chi	87	75	0	.537	8	758	681	139	.262	.336	.391	727	102	98	134	**28**	154	601	923	11.8	3.79	105	.239	.315	.0	3.4	2.5	-.0	.0
Tex	85	77	0	.525	10	**829**	814	177	.270	.341	**.424**	**765**	**112**	98	102	9	151	662	**1022**	13.3	4.47	91	.262	.341	-1.0	-7.0	**10.1**	.0	1.8
Oak	84	78	0	.519	11	760	776	159	.248	.331	.389	720	103	95	**151**	14	155	655	892	13.3	4.57	84	.260	.342	.5	-12.4	4.0	.7	10.2
Sea	83	79	0	.512	12	702	674	126	.255	.328	.383	711	96	100	97	10	136	628	1003	12.7	3.79	109	.253	.332	.3	5.6	-2.2	.2	-1.9
KC	82	80	0	.506	13	727	722	117	.264	.328	.394	722	98	101	119	17	**105**	529	1004	12.6	3.92	106	.261	.327	-.5	3.5	-1.0	-.2	-.8
Cal	81	81	0	.500	14	653	649	115	.255	.314	.374	688	89	100	94	18	141	543	990	12.1	3.69	112	.250	.321	.8	6.8	-8.2	-.3	.9
Total	1134					50172		1953	.260	.329	.395	724			1469	216				12.6	4.09		.260	.329					

Batter-Fielder Wins
C.Ripken-Bal 8.5
Sax-NY 1.3
Espinoza-NY 1.2
2 players tied 8

Batting Average
Franco-Tex .... .341
Sax-NY .... .304
Mattingly-NY .... .288
Hall-NY .... .285

On-Base Percentage
Thomas-Chi .... .453
Sax-NY .... .345
Mattingly-NY .... .339
2 players tied .... .333

Slugging Average
Tartabull-KC .... .593
Hall-NY .... .455
R.Kelly-NY .... .444
Sax-NY .... .414

On-Base Plus Slugging
Thomas-Chi 1006
R.Kelly-NY 777
Hall-NY 776
Sax-NY 759

Adjusted OPS
Thomas-Chi 181
R.Kelly-NY 113
Hall-NY 112
Sax-NY 109

Adjusted Batter Runs
Thomas-Chi 71.1
R.Kelly-NY 7.9
Sax-NY 7.8
Hall-NY 6.2

Runs
Molitor-Mil 133
Sax-NY 85
Maas-NY 69
R.Kelly-NY 68

Hits
Molitor-Mil 216
Sax-NY 198
Mattingly-NY 169
Hall-NY 140

Doubles
Palmeiro-Tex 49
Sax-NY 38
Mattingly-NY 35
2 players tied 23

Triples
Molitor-Mil 13
Johnson-Chi 13
Williams-NY 4
P.Kelly-NY 4

Home Runs
Fielder-Det 44
Canseco-Oak 44
Nokes-NY 24
Maas-NY 23

Total Bases
C.Ripken-Bal 368
Sax-NY 270
Mattingly-NY 231
Hall-NY 224

Runs Batted In
Fielder-Det 133
Hall-NY 80
Nokes-NY 77
R.Kelly-NY 69

Stolen Bases
R.Henderson-Oak 58
R.Kelly-NY 32
Sax-NY 31
P.Kelly-NY 12

Base Stealing Runs
Alomar-Tor 7.8
R.Kelly-NY 3.9
Sax-NY 3.0
P.Kelly-NY 2.3

Fielding Runs-Infield
Sojo-Cal 26.6
Espinoza-NY 21.0

Fielding Runs-Outfield
Orsulak-Bal 17.2
Hall-NY 2

Wins
Gullickson-Det 20
Erickson-Min 20
Sanderson-NY 16
Cadaret-NY 8

Winning Pct.
Erickson-Min .... .714
Sanderson-NY .... .615

Complete Games
McDowell-Chi 15
Sanderson-NY 2
Leary-NY 1

Strikeouts
Clemens-Bos 241
Sanderson-NY 130
Cadaret-NY 105
Plunk-NY 103

Fewest BB/Game
Swindell-Cle 1.17
Sanderson-NY 1.25

Games
D.Ward-Tor 81
Cadaret-NY 68
Habyan-NY 66
Guetterman-NY 64

Saves
Harvey-Cal 46
Farr-NY 23
Guetterman-NY 6
2 players tied 3

Base Runners/9
Gray-Bos 7.30
Habyan-NY 9.50
Sanderson-NY 10.04
Farr-NY 10.54

Adjusted Relief Runs
Frohwirth-Bal 22.0
Habyan-NY 17.1
Farr-NY 15.0
Cadaret-NY 7.9

Relief Ranking
Harvey-Cal 32.8
Farr-NY 27.4
Habyan-NY 10.9
Cadaret-NY 8.5

Innings Pitched
Clemens-Bos 271.1
Sanderson-NY 208.0
Johnson-NY 127.0
Cadaret-NY 121.2

Opponents' Avg.
Ryan-Tex .... .172
Sanderson-NY ...... .252

Opponents' OBP
Ryan-Tex .... .263
Sanderson-NY ...... .279

Earned Run Average
Clemens-Bos 2.62
Sanderson-NY 3.81

Adjusted ERA
Clemens-Bos 165
Sanderson-NY 109

Adjusted Starter Runs
Clemens-Bos 46.5
Perez-NY 9.1
Sanderson-NY 8.7
Kamieniecki-NY 2.6

Pitcher Wins
Clemens-Bos 4.7
Farr-NY 2.9
Habyan-NY 1.1
Howe-NY 1.1

1992 American League

TEAM	W	L	T	PCT	GB	R	OR	HR	AVG	OBP	SLG	OPS	AOPS	PF	SB	CG	HR	BB	SO	BR/9	ERA	AERA	OAV	OOB	FW	PW	BW	BSW	DIF
East																													
Tor	96	66	0	.593		780	682	163	.263	.333	**.414**	**747**	103	105	129	18	124	541	954	12.1	3.91	105	.248	.318	1.4	3.0	2.7	1.0	6.9
Mil	92	70	0	.568	4	740	**604**	82	.268	.330	.375	705	98	99	**256**	19	127	**435**	793	**11.3**	**3.43**	113	**.246**	**.305**	**1.6**	7.2	-.1	**1.1**	1.2
Bal	89	73	0	.549	7	705	656	148	.259	.340	.398	738	103	103	89	20	124	518	846	12.1	3.79	107	.256	.322	1.4	4.4	3.3	-.2	-.8
NY	76	86	0	.469	20	733	746	163	.261	.328	.406	734	104	100	78	20	129	612	851	13.0	4.21	94	.263	.338	.2	-4.3	3.7	-.1	-4.5
Cle	76	86	0	.469	20	674	746	127	.266	.323	.383	706	98	99	144	13	159	566	890	12.9	4.11	96	.268	.336	-1.3	-3.0	-1.9	.3	.9
Det	75	87	0	.463	21	**791**	794	**182**	.256	.337	.407	744	106	101	66	10	155	564	693	13.3	4.60	87	.277	.343	.1	-9.8	5.5	-.6	-1.2
Bos	73	89	0	.451	23	599	669	84	.246	.321	.347	668	81	107	44	22	107	535	943	12.3	3.58	**118**	.255	.323	-1.2	**10.0**	-12.7	-1.3	-2.9
West																													
Oak	96	66	0	.593		745	672	142	.258	**.346**	.386	732	**110**	95	143	8	129	601	843	12.7	3.73	101	.256	.331	-.4	.7	**9.5**	.6	4.6
Min	90	72	0	.556	6	747	653	104	**.277**	.341	.391	732	101	104	123	16	121	479	923	11.8	3.70	110	.254	.316	1.3	5.9	1.9	-.4	.3
Chi	86	76	0	.531	10	738	690	110	.261	.336	.383	719	102	99	160	21	123	550	810	12.3	3.82	101	.252	.323	-.6	.9	2.6	1.0	1.0
Tex	77	85	0	.475	19	682	753	159	.250	.321	.393	714	102	97	81	19	113	598	**1034**	13.0	4.09	93	.264	.337	-2.0	-4.6	1.7	-.3	1.2
KC	72	90	0	.444	24	610	667	75	.256	.315	.364	679	87	103	131	9	**106**	512	834	12.3	3.81	107	.259	.323	-.2	4.2	-9.6	-.1	-3.3
Cal	72	90	0	.444	24	579	671	88	.243	.301	.338	639	78	-101	160	**26**	130	532	888	12.6	3.84	104	.264	.331	-.9	2.7	-16.7	-.5	6.4
Sea	64	98	0	.395	32	679	799	149	.263	.323	.402	725	101	101	100	21	129	661	894	13.6	4.55	88	.266	.348	.3	-8.9	.5	-.2	-8.8
Total	1134					69802		1776	.259	.328	.385	713			1704	242				12.5	3.94		.259	.328					

Batter-Fielder Wins
Ventura-Chi 5.1
Tartabull-NY 2.8
Stankiewicz-NY 1.5
2 players tied 8

Batting Average
E.Martinez-Sea ..... .343
Mattingly-NY .... .287
Hall-NY .... .280
R.Kelly-NY .... .272

On-Base Percentage
Thomas-Chi .... .439
Tartabull-NY .... .409
Mattingly-NY .... .327
R.Kelly-NY .... .322

Slugging Average
McGwire-Oak .... .585
Tartabull-NY .... .489
Hall-NY .... .429
Mattingly-NY .... .416

On-Base Plus Slugging
Thomas-Chi 975
Tartabull-NY 898
Mattingly-NY 742
Hall-NY 739

Adjusted OPS
McGwire-Oak 178
Tartabull-NY 151
Mattingly-NY 108
Hall-NY 107

Adjusted Batter Runs
Thomas-Chi 66.4
Tartabull-NY 34.2
Stanley-NY 6.6
Mattingly-NY 5.4

Runs
Phillips-Det 114
Mattingly-NY 89
R.Kelly-NY 81
Tartabull-NY 72

Hits
Puckett-Min 210
Mattingly-NY 184
Hall-NY 163
R.Kelly-NY 158

Doubles
Thomas-Chi 46
E.Martinez-Sea 46
Mattingly-NY 40
Hall-NY 36

Triples
Johnson-Chi 12
Hall-NY 3

Home Runs
Gonzalez-Tex 43
Tartabull-NY 25
Nokes-NY 22
Hayes-NY 18

Total Bases
Puckett-Min 313
Mattingly-NY 266
Hall-NY 250
R.Kelly-NY 223

Runs Batted In
Fielder-Det 124
Mattingly-NY 86
Tartabull-NY 85
Hall-NY 81

Stolen Bases
Lofton-Cle 66
R.Kelly-NY 28
Stankiewicz-NY 9
P.Kelly-NY 8

Base Stealing Runs
Lofton-Cle 10.3
R.Kelly-NY 4.4
Velarde-NY 8
Mattingly-NY 7

Fielding Runs-Infield
Reed-Bos 30.4
Stankiewicz-NY 10.9
Mattingly-NY 6.1

Fielding Runs-Outfield
Raines-Chi 9.6
R.Kelly-NY 1.8
Hall-NY 1.4

Wins
Morris-Tor 21
Brown-Tex 21
Perez-NY 13
Sanderson-NY 12

Winning Pct.
Mussina-Bal .... .783

Complete Games
McDowell-Chi 13
Perez-NY 10
Kamieniecki-NY 4
Sanderson-NY 2

Strikeouts
Johnson-Sea 241
Perez-NY 218
Sanderson-NY 104
Kamieniecki-NY 88

Fewest BB/Game
Bosio-Mil 1.71
Sanderson-NY 2.98
Perez-NY 3.38
Kamieniecki-NY 3.54

Games
Rogers-Tex 81
Habyan-NY 56
Farr-NY 50
Monteleone-NY 47

Saves
Eckersley-Oak 51
Farr-NY 30
Habyan-NY 7
Howe-NY 6

Base Runners/9
Eckersley-Oak 8.32
Monteleone-NY ... 10.59
Perez-NY 11.27
Militello-NY 11.55

Adjusted Relief Runs
D.Ward-Tor 22.0
Monteleone-NY 7.7
Habyan-NY 1.8

Relief Ranking
Eckersley-Oak 35.7
Monteleone-NY 7.5
Habyan-NY 2.8

Innings Pitched
Brown-Tex 265.2
Perez-NY 247.2
Sanderson-NY 193.1
Kamieniecki-NY .. 188.0

Opponents' Avg.
Johnson-Sea .... .206
Perez-NY .... .235
Kamieniecki-NY ..... .269
Sanderson-NY ...... .286

Opponents' OBP
Mussina-Bal .... .278
Clemens-Bos .... .278
Perez-NY .... .308
2 players tied .... .340

Earned Run Average
Clemens-Bos 2.41
Perez-NY 2.87
Kamieniecki-NY 4.36
Sanderson-NY 4.93

Adjusted ERA
Clemens-Bos 177
Perez-NY 138
Kamieniecki-NY 91
Sanderson-NY 80

Adjusted Starter Runs
Clemens-Bos 45.1
Perez-NY 26.4
Militello-NY 3.9

Pitcher Wins
Clemens-Bos 5.3
Perez-NY 2.9
Farr-NY 2.3
Monteleone-NY 7

1993 American League

TEAM	W	L	T	PCT	GB	R	OR	HR	AVG	OBP	SLG	OPS	AOPS	PF	SB	CG	HR	BB	SO	BR/9	ERA	AERA	OAV	OOB	FW	PW	BW	BSW	DIF
East																													
Tor	95	67	0	.586		847	742	159	**.279**	.350	**.436**	786	108	102	**170**	11	134	620	1023	13.1	4.21	104	.261	.336	.5	2.4	7.1	**1.7**	2.3
NY	88	74	0	.543	7	821	761	178	**.279**	.353	.435	788	**113**	97	39	11	170	552	899	12.8	4.35	96	.266	.333	.6	-2.8	11.7	-.6	-1.8
Bal	85	77	0	.525	10	786	745	157	.267	.346	.413	759	98	105	73	21	153	579	900	12.8	4.31	105	.261	.333	.9	2.9	.2	-.5	.6
Det	85	77	0	.525	10	**899**	837	178	.275	**.362**	.434	**796**	**113**	100	104	11	188	542	828	13.4	4.65	93	.276	.342	-1.0	-4.8	**12.0**	-.2	-2.0
Bos	80	82	0	.494	15	686	698	114	.264	.330	.395	725	88	106	73	9	127	552	997	**12.3**	3.77	**122**	**.252**	**.322**	-.4	**12.5**	-8.0	.0	-5.1
Cle	76	86	0	.469	19	790	813	141	.275	.335	.409	744	99	100	159	7	182	591	888	13.8	4.58	95	.281	.351	-1.9	-3.2	-.9	1.3	-.3
Mil	69	93	0	.426	26	733	792	125	.258	.328	.378	706	90	99	138	**26**	153	522	810	13.0	4.45	97	.271	.336	-.9	-2.3	-7.1	-.4	-1.2
West																													
Chi	94	68	0	.580		776	**664**	162	.265	.338	.411	749	102	98	106	16	125	566	974	12.4	**3.70**	114	.255	.328	.2	8.1	1.9	.0	2.8
Tex	86	76	0	.531	8	835	751	**181**	.267	.329	.431	760	105	97	113	20	144	562	957	13.0	4.28	98	.267	.337	-1.0	-1.6	3.9	-.2	3.8
KC	84	78	0	.519	10	675	694	125	.263	.320	.397	717	85	107	100	16	**105**	571	985	12.4	4.04	114	.254	.327	1.0	8.2	-10.9	-.6	5.3
Sea	82	80	0	.506	12	734	731	161	.260	.339	.406	745	97	102	91	22	135	605	**1083**	13.0	4.20	106	.259	.337	**1.5**	3.9	-1.2	-.6	-2.5
Cal	71	91	0	.438	23	684	770	114	.260	.331	.380	711	88	103	169	**26**	153	550	843	13.1	4.34	104	.270	.339	-.3	2.7	-8.3	-.0	-4.1
Min	71	91	0	.438	23	693	830	121	.264	.327	.385	712	90	101	83	5	148	**514**	901	13.4	4.71	93	.283	.344	.9	-4.8	-7.7	-.4	2.0
Oak	68	94	0	.420	26	715	846	158	.254	.330	.394	724	99	95	131	8	157	680	864	14.1	4.90	84	.276	.356	.2	-12.7	-.3	.5	-.7
Total	1134					60674		2074	.267	.337	.408	745			1549	209				13.0	4.32		.267	.337					

Batter-Fielder Wins	Batting Average	On-Base Percentage	Slugging Average	On-Base Plus Slugging	Adjusted OPS	Adjusted Batter Runs
Olerud-Tor 5.7	Olerud-Tor .363	Olerud-Tor .473	Gonzalez-Tex .632	Olerud-Tor 1072	Olerud-Tor 184	Olerud-Tor 75.0
Gallego-NY 3.8	O'Neill-NY .311	Boggs-NY .378	O'Neill-NY .504	O'Neill-NY 871	O'Neill-NY 136	Stanley-NY 31.0
Stanley-NY 3.3	Boggs-NY .302	O'Neill-NY .367	Tartabull-NY .503	Tartabull-NY 866	Tartabull-NY 135	Tartabull-NY 26.7
Boggs-NY 2.8	Mattingly-NY .291	Mattingly-NY .364	Mattingly-NY .445	Mattingly-NY 809	Mattingly-NY 120	O'Neill-NY 24.9

Runs	Hits	Doubles	Triples	Home Runs	Total Bases	Runs Batted In
Palmeiro-Tex 124	Molitor-Tor 211	Olerud-Tor 54	Johnson-Chi 14	Gonzalez-Tex 46	Griffey-Sea 359	Belle-Cle 129
Tartabull-NY 87	Boggs-NY 169	O'Neill-NY 34	B.Williams-NY 4	Tartabull-NY 31	Tartabull-NY 258	Tartabull-NY 102
Boggs-NY 83	O'Neill-NY 155	Tartabull-NY 33	G.Williams-NY 3	Stanley-NY 26	O'Neill-NY 251	Mattingly-NY 86
Mattingly-NY 78	Mattingly-NY 154	B.Williams-NY 31		O'Neill-NY 20	Mattingly-NY 236	Stanley-NY 84

Stolen Bases	Base Stealing Runs	Fielding Runs-Infield	Fielding Runs-Outfield	Wins	Winning Pct.	Complete Games
Lofton-Cle 70	Lofton-Cle 10.5	Gallego-NY 26.2	Kirby-Cle 14.1	McDowell-Chi 22	Key-NY .750	Finley-Cal 13
Kelly-NY 14	G.Williams-NY .4	Boggs-NY 21.3		Key-NY 18		Key-NY 4
B.Williams-NY 9	Humphreys-NY .0	Kelly-NY 10.5		Wickman-NY 14		Abbott-NY 4
2 players tied 3		Mattingly-NY 1.0		Abbott-NY 11		Kamieniecki-NY 2

Strikeouts	Fewest BB/Game	Games	Saves	Base Runners/9	Adjusted Relief Runs	Relief Ranking
Johnson-Sea 308	Key-NY 1.64	Harris-Bos 80	D.Ward-Tor 45	Montgomery-KC 9.27	Montgomery-KC 22.1	Montgomery-KC 44.2
Key-NY 173	Abbott-NY 3.07	Howe-NY 51	Montgomery-KC 45	Key-NY 10.00		
Perez-NY 148	Perez-NY 3.53	Farr-NY 49	Farr-NY 25	Abbott-NY 12.49		
Abbott-NY 95		Monteleone-NY 42	2 players tied 4	Monteleone-NY 12.61		

Innings Pitched	Opponents' Avg.	Opponents' OBP	Earned Run Average	Adjusted ERA	Adjusted Starter Runs	Pitcher Wins
Eldred-Mil 258.0	Johnson-Sea .203	Darwin-Bos .272	Appier-KC 2.56	Appier-KC 180	Appier-KC 50.6	Appier-KC 5.1
Key-NY 236.2	Key-NY .246	Key-NY .279	Key-NY 3.00	Key-NY 139	Key-NY 33.2	Key-NY 3.1
Abbott-NY 214.0	Perez-NY .267	Abbott-NY .332	Abbott-NY 4.37	Abbott-NY 96	Kamieniecki-NY 3.5	Assenmacher-NY .5
Perez-NY 163.0	Abbott-NY .271	Perez-NY .333	Perez-NY 5.19	Perez-NY 81	Tanana-NY 1.1	Kamieniecki-NY .4

1994 American League

TEAM	W	L	T	PCT	GB	R	OR	HR	AVG	OBP	SLG	OPS	AOPS	PF	SB	CG	HR	BB	SO	BR/9	ERA	AERA	OAV	OOB	FW	PW	BW	BSW	DIF
East																													
NY	70	43	0	.619		670	534	139	**.290**	**.374**	.462	**836**	**118**	97	55	8	120	398	656	12.9	4.34	106	.267	.335	.1	2.8	**11.8**	-.6	-.6
Bal	63	49	0	.563	6.5	589	**497**	139	.272	.349	.438	787	96	106	69	13	131	**351**	666	12.5	4.31	117	.263	.327	**1.5**	7.2	-1.8	**.6**	-.4
Tor	55	60	0	.478	16	566	579	115	.269	.336	.424	760	93	101	79	13	127	482	**832**	13.8	4.70	104	.266	.348	.2	1.8	-3.5	.3	-1.2
Bos	54	61	0	.470	17	552	621	120	.263	.334	.421	755	89	105	81	6	120	450	729	13.9	4.93	102	.276	.351	.2	1.0	-5.8	.0	1.1
Det	53	62	0	.461	18	652	671	161	.265	.352	.454	806	105	101	46	15	148	449	560	14.3	5.38	91	.282	.356	.1	-4.7	3.2	-.6	-2.6
Central																													
Chi	67	46	0	.593		633	498	121	.287	.366	.444	810	109	99	77	13	115	377	754	**12.1**	**3.96**	118	**.250**	**.317**	.2	7.8	5.8	.2	-3.5
Cle	66	47	0	.584	1	**679**	562	**167**	**.290**	.351	**.484**	835	111	101	131	**17**	**94**	404	666	13.6	4.36	109	.275	.346	-.4	4.1	6.3	**.6**	-1.1
KC	64	51	0	.557	4	574	532	100	.269	.335	.419	754	89	105	**140**	5	95	392	717	12.6	4.23	**119**	.260	.328	.2	**7.9**	-6.1	.4	4.0
Min	53	60	0	.469	14	594	688	103	.276	.340	.427	767	95	101	94	6	153	388	602	14.5	5.68	87	.299	.361	.4	-7.6	-2.1	.5	5.3
Mil	53	62	0	.461	15	547	586	99	.263	.335	.408	743	86	105	59	11	127	421	577	13.2	4.62	110	.269	.340	-.0	4.5	-7.3	-.5	-1.2
West																													
Tex	52	62	0	.456		613	697	124	.280	.353	.436	789	101	101	82	10	157	394	683	14.1	5.45	89	.288	.351	-1.4	-6.5	1.1	.0	1.6
Oak	51	63	0	.447	1	549	589	113	.260	.330	.399	729	94	92	91	12	128	510	732	13.7	4.80	93	.257	.347	-.3	-3.5	-2.5	.0	.2
Sea	49	63	0	.438	2	569	616	153	.269	.335	.451	786	98	102	48	13	109	486	763	14.3	4.99	99	.274	.357	-.8	-.7	-1.4	-.2	-3.9
Cal	47	68	0	.409	5.5	543	660	120	.264	.334	.409	743	88	102	65	11	150	436	682	14.3	5.42	91	.287	.360	.5	-5.3	-6.0	-.9	1.2
Total	797					48330		1774	.273	.345	.434	779			1117	153				13.5	4.80		.273	.345					

Batter-Fielder Wins	Batting Average	On-Base Percentage	Slugging Average	On-Base Plus Slugging	Adjusted OPS	Adjusted Batter Runs
Thomas-Chi 5.2	O'Neill-NY .359	Thomas-Chi .487	Thomas-Chi .729	Thomas-Chi 1217	Thomas-Chi 212	Thomas-Chi 75.4
O'Neill-NY 4.0	Boggs-NY .342	O'Neill-NY .460	O'Neill-NY .603	O'Neill-NY 1064	O'Neill-NY 179	O'Neill-NY 47.9
Boggs-NY 3.3	Polonia-NY .311	Boggs-NY .433	Boggs-NY .489	Boggs-NY 922	Boggs-NY 143	Boggs-NY 27.5
Stanley-NY 2.4	Mattingly-NY .304	Mattingly-NY .397	Tartabull-NY .464	B.Williams-NY 837	B.Williams-NY 119	Stanley-NY 18.8

Runs	Hits	Doubles	Triples	Home Runs	Total Bases	Runs Batted In
Thomas-Chi 106	Lofton-Cle 160	Knoblauch-Min 45	L.Johnson-Chi 14	Griffey-Sea 40	Belle-Cle 294	Puckett-Min 112
B.Williams-NY 80	O'Neill-NY 132	B.Williams-NY 29	Polonia-NY 6	O'Neill-NY 21	O'Neill-NY 222	O'Neill-NY 83
Tartabull-NY 68	Boggs-NY 125	O'Neill-NY 25	Kelly-NY 2	Tartabull-NY 19	B.Williams-NY 185	Tartabull-NY 67
O'Neill-NY 68	B.Williams-NY 118	Tartabull-NY 24		3 players tied 17	Tartabull-NY 185	Leyritz-NY 58

Stolen Bases	Base Stealing Runs	Fielding Runs-Infield	Fielding Runs-Outfield	Wins	Winning Pct.	Complete Games
Lofton-Cle 60	Lofton-Cle 9.0	Valentin-Mil 21.3	Edmonds-Cal 8.3	Key-NY 17	Bere-Chi .857	Johnson-Sea 9
Polonia-NY 20	B.Williams-NY .4	Gallego-NY 15.7	O'Neill-NY .7	Perez-NY 9	Key-NY .810	Mulholland-NY 2
B.Williams-NY 16	Polonia-NY .2	Boggs-NY 8.6		Abbott-NY 9		Abbott-NY 2
Kelly-NY 6	Velarde-NY .2	Mattingly-NY 5.3		Kamieniecki-NY 8		

Strikeouts	Fewest BB/Game	Games	Saves	Base Runners/9	Adjusted Relief Runs	Relief Ranking
Johnson-Sea 204	Gubicza-KC 1.80	Wickman-NY 53	L.Smith-Bal 33	Ontiveros-Oak 9.75	Eichhorn-Bal 21.2	Eichhorn-Bal 30.1
Perez-NY 109	Mulholland-NY 2.76	Howe-NY 40	Howe-NY 15	Wickman-NY 10.54	Howe-NY 13.3	Howe-NY 18.8
Key-NY 97	Key-NY 2.79	Hernandez-NY 31	Wickman-NY 6	Perez-NY 11.60	Wickman-NY 12.3	Wickman-NY 16.3
Abbott-NY 90	Perez-NY 3.45	Gibson-NY 30	Hernandez-NY 6	Key-NY 12.43	Hitchcock-NY 2.8	Hitchcock-NY 2.8

Innings Pitched	Opponents' Avg.	Opponents' OBP	Earned Run Average	Adjusted ERA	Adjusted Starter Runs	Pitcher Wins
Finley-Cal 183.1	Clemens-Bos .203	Ontiveros-Oak .271	Ontiveros-Oak 2.65	Clemens-Bos 177	Cone-KC 38.7	Cone-KC 4.3
Key-NY 168.0	Perez-NY .238	Perez-NY .311	Key-NY 3.27	Key-NY 141	Key-NY 25.1	Key-NY 2.9
Abbott-NY 160.1	Kamieniecki-NY .261	Key-NY .329	Kamieniecki-NY 3.76	Kamieniecki-NY 122	Kamieniecki-NY 11.6	Howe-NY 1.8
Perez-NY 151.1	2 players tied .273	Abbott-NY .341	Perez-NY 4.10	Perez-NY 112	Perez-NY 9.2	Wickman-NY 1.5

Historical Record

1995 American League

TEAM	W	L	T	PCT	GB	R	OR	HR	AVG	OBP	SLG	OPS	AOPS	PF	SB	CG	HR	BB	SO	BR/9	ERA	AERA	OAV	OOB	FW	PW	BW	BSW	DIF
East																													
Bos	86	58	0	.597		791	698	175	.280	.357	.455	812	106	103	99	7	**127**	476	888	12.9	4.39	110	.268	.334	-1.2	6.0	5.2	-.0	4.1
NY	79	65	1	.549	7	749	688	122	.276	.357	.420	777	102	99	50	18	159	535	908	13.0	4.56	101	.261	.334	**1.4**	.8	3.6	-.5	1.7
Bal	71	73	0	.493	15	704	640	173	.262	.342	.428	770	97	102	92	**19**	149	523	930	12.3	4.31	111	**.245**	.322	**1.4**	6.0	-1.6	-.2	-6.6
Det	60	84	0	.417	26	654	844	159	.247	.327	.404	731	89	100	73	5	170	536	729	14.8	5.49	88	.296	.365	-.4	-8.9	-7.5	-.3	5.2
Tor	56	88	0	.389	30	642	777	140	.260	.328	.409	737	90	100	75	16	145	654	894	14.2	4.88	97	.267	.356	.0	-1.8	-6.7	**.4**	-8.1
Central																													
Cle	100	44	0	.694		**840**	**607**	**207**	**.291**	**.361**	**.479**	**840**	**114**	102	**132**	10	135	**445**	926	**12.1**	**3.83**	**123**	.255	**.320**	-.2	**12.0**	**10.1**	**.4**	5.7
KC	70	74	0	.486	30	629	691	119	.260	.328	.396	724	85	102	120	11	142	503	763	13.0	4.49	107	.268	.338	.4	4.0	-9.8	.2	3.1
Chi	68	76	1	.472	32	755	758	146	.280	.354	.431	785	107	96	110	12	164	617	892	14.2	4.85	92	.275	.356	-.5	-5.4	6.1	**.4**	-4.6
Mil	65	79	0	.451	35	740	747	128	.266	.336	.409	745	88	106	105	7	146	603	699	14.3	4.82	104	.280	.360	-.4	2.3	-8.4	.3	-.8
Min	56	88	0	.389	44	703	889	120	.279	.346	.419	765	97	101	105	7	210	533	790	14.3	5.76	83	.287	.356	-.1	-12.4	-1.4	-.3	-1.8
West																													
Sea	79	66	0	.545		796	708	182	.276	.350	.448	798	105	101	110	9	149	591	**1068**	13.8	4.50	106	.268	.347	-.3	3.6	3.6	**.4**	-.7
Cal	78	67	0	.538	1	801	697	186	.277	.352	.448	800	107	99	58	8	163	486	901	12.9	4.52	104	.265	.333	.2	2.5	5.5	-.7	-2.1
Tex	74	70	0	.514	4.5	691	720	138	.265	.338	.410	748	90	103	90	14	152	514	838	13.6	4.66	104	.278	.346	.0	2.3	-6.1	-.3	6.1
Oak	67	77	0	.465	11.5	730	761	169	.264	.341	.420	761	102	95	112	8	153	556	890	13.6	4.93	92	.269	.347	-.2	-5.6	2.0	.3	-1.4
Total	1010					50225		2164	.270	.344	.427	771			1331	151				13.5	4.71		.270	.344					

Batter-Fielder Wins	Batting Average	On-Base Percentage	Slugging Average	On-Base Plus Slugging	Adjusted OPS	Adjusted Batter Runs
E.Martinez-Sea 5.8	E.Martinez-Sea .356	E.Martinez-Sea .479	Belle-Cle .690	E.Martinez-Sea 1107	E.Martinez-Sea 184	E.Martinez-Sea 73.1
B.Williams-NY 3.0	Boggs-NY .324	Boggs-NY .412	O'Neill-NY .526	O'Neill-NY 913	O'Neill-NY 138	O'Neill-NY 27.5
O'Neill-NY 1.5	B.Williams-NY .307	B.Williams-NY .392	B.Williams-NY .487	B.Williams-NY 878	B.Williams-NY 129	B.Williams-NY 25.1
Boggs-NY 1.5	O'Neill-NY .300	O'Neill-NY .387	Stanley-NY .481	Stanley-NY 841	Boggs-NY 120	Boggs-NY 17.7

Runs	Hits	Doubles	Triples	Home Runs	Total Bases	Runs Batted In
E.Martinez-Sea 121	Johnson-Chi 186	E.Martinez-Sea 52	Lofton-Cle 13	Belle-Cle 50	Belle-Cle 377	Vaughn-Bos 126
Belle-Cle 121	B.Williams-NY 173	Belle-Cle 52	B.Williams-NY 9	O'Neill-NY 22	B.Williams-NY 274	Belle-Cle 126
B.Williams-NY 93	Boggs-NY 149	Mattingly-NY 32	O'Neill-NY 4	B.Williams-NY 18	O'Neill-NY 242	O'Neill-NY 96
O'Neill-NY 82	O'Neill-NY 138	O'Neill-NY 30	Boggs-NY 4	Stanley-NY 18	Boggs-NY 194	Stanley-NY 83

Stolen Bases	Base Stealing Runs	Fielding Runs-Infield	Fielding Runs-Outfield	Wins	Winning Pct.	Complete Games
Lofton-Cle 54	Johnson-Chi 6.7	Fryman-Det 27.3	Cordova-Min 13.8	Mussina-Bal 19	Johnson-Sea .900	McDowell-NY 8
Polonia-NY 10	Polonia-NY .8	Mattingly-NY .1	B.Williams-NY 5.3	McDowell-NY 15	McDowell-NY .600	Hitchcock-NY 4
B.Williams-NY 8	Velarde-NY .8			Pettitte-NY 12		Pettitte-NY 3
Kelly-NY 8	Kelly-NY .7			Hitchcock-NY 11		3 players tied 1

Strikeouts	Fewest BB/Game	Games	Saves	Base Runners/9	Adjusted Relief Runs	Relief Ranking
Johnson-Sea 294	Mussina-Bal 2.03	Orosco-Bal 65	Mesa-Cle 46	Percival-Cal 7.78	Mesa-Cle 25.5	Mesa-Cle 44.5
McDowell-NY 157	McDowell-NY 3.23	Wickman-NY 63	Wetteland-NY 31	Wetteland-NY 7.92	Wetteland-NY 11.4	Wetteland-NY 20.6
Hitchcock-NY 121	Pettitte-NY 3.24	Wetteland-NY 60	Howe-NY 2	McDowell-NY 12.16	Wickman-NY 5.3	Wickman-NY 3.7
Pettitte-NY 114	Hitchcock-NY 3.64	Howe-NY 56	3 players tied 1	Hitchcock-NY 12.19		

Innings Pitched	Opponents' Avg.	Opponents' OBP	Earned Run Average	Adjusted ERA	Adjusted Starter Runs	Pitcher Wins
Cone-Tor-NY 229.1	Johnson-Sea .201	Johnson-Sea .266	Johnson-Sea 2.48	Johnson-Sea 193	Johnson-Sea 53.9	Johnson-Sea 4.6
Pettitte-NY 175.0	Hitchcock-NY .245	Hitchcock-NY .319	McDowell-NY 3.93	McDowell-NY 118	McDowell-NY 14.6	Wetteland-NY 1.9
Hitchcock-NY 168.1	McDowell-NY .254	McDowell-NY .320	Pettitte-NY 4.17	Pettitte-NY 111	Pettitte-NY 9.0	McDowell-NY 1.4
Kamieniecki-NY 89.2	Pettitte-NY .272	Pettitte-NY .333	Hitchcock-NY 4.70	Hitchcock-NY 98	Kamieniecki-NY 5.9	Pettitte-NY .9

1996 American League

TEAM	W	L	T	PCT	GB	R	OR	HR	AVG	OBP	SLG	OPS	AOPS	PF	SB	CG	HR	BB	SO	BR/9	ERA	AERA	OAV	OOB	FW	PW	BW	BSW	DIF
East																													
NY	92	70	0	.568		871	787	162	.288	.360	.436	796	100	100	96	6	**143**	610	1139	13.3	4.65	106	**.265**	.341	1.2	4.4	1.7	-.2	3.9
Bal	88	74	1	.543	4	949	903	**257**	.274	.350	.472	822	106	99	76	13	209	597	1047	13.7	5.14	96	.280	.349	.9	-3.0	5.2	-.4	4.2
Bos	85	77	0	.525	7	928	921	209	.283	.359	.457	816	102	102	91	17	185	722	**1165**	14.7	4.98	102	.279	.360	-1.2	1.5	2.9	-.2	1.0
Tor	74	88	0	.457	18	766	809	177	.259	.331	.420	751	89	-99	116	**19**	187	610	1033	13.2	4.57	110	.266	.340	.2	6.4	-8.8	.5	-5.2
Det	53	109	0	.327	39	783	1103	204	.256	.323	.420	743	86	-100	87	10	241	784	957	16.1	6.38	80	.296	.384	-1.4	-18.4	-11.6	-.5	3.8
Central																													
Cle	99	62	0	.615		952	**769**	218	**.293**	**.369**	.475	844	111	100	160	13	173	484	1033	**12.7**	**4.34**	**113**	.271	**.331**	-.7	8.2	10.6	**1.0**	-.6
Chi	85	77	0	.525	14.5	898	794	195	.281	.360	.447	807	107	96	105	7	174	616	1039	13.4	4.52	105	.270	.343	.2	3.6	6.9	.2	-7.0
Mil	80	82	0	.494	19.5	894	899	178	.279	.353	.441	794	95	104	101	6	213	635	846	14.1	5.14	101	.278	.354	-1.2	.7	-3.1	-.2	2.7
Min	78	84	0	.481	21.5	877	900	118	.288	.357	.425	782	95	102	143	13	233	581	959	13.6	5.28	97	.277	.346	1.1	-2.1	-2.5	.5	-.0
KC	75	86	0	.466	24	746	786	123	.267	.332	.398	730	83	-100	**195**	17	176	**460**	926	12.9	4.55	110	.277	.335	.0	6.8	-12.6	.5	-.4
West																													
Tex	90	72	1	.556		928	799	221	.284	.358	.469	827	101	106	83	**19**	168	582	976	13.6	4.65	**113**	.278	.347	**1.5**	**8.4**	1.2	.2	-2.2
Sea	85	76	0	.528	4.5	**993**	895	245	.287	.366	**.484**	**850**	**112**	100	90	4	216	605	1000	14.0	5.21	95	.279	.353	.1	-3.6	**10.9**	-.0	-2.9
Oak	78	84	0	.481	12	861	900	243	.265	.344	.452	796	100	99	58	7	205	644	884	14.4	5.20	96	.287	.362	.6	-3.5	.2	-.5	.3
Cal	70	91	0	.435	19.5	762	943	192	.276	.339	.431	770	92	101	53	12	219	662	1052	14.3	5.30	95	.275	.357	-.9	-3.6	-6.9	-.8	1.8
Total	1133					52208		2742	.277	.350	.445	795			1454	163				13.9	4.99		.277	.350					

Batter-Fielder Wins	Batting Average	On-Base Percentage	Slugging Average	On-Base Plus Slugging	Adjusted OPS	Adjusted Batter Runs
Alomar-Bal 6.1	Rodriguez-Sea .358	McGwire-Oak .467	McGwire-Oak .730	McGwire-Oak 1198	McGwire-Oak 199	F.Thomas-Chi 71.5
B.Williams-NY 2.6	Jeter-NY .314	O'Neill-NY .411	B.Williams-NY .535	B.Williams-NY 926	B.Williams-NY 132	B.Williams-NY 28.0
O'Neill-NY 2.0	Boggs-NY .311	B.Williams-NY .391	O'Neill-NY .474	O'Neill-NY 885	O'Neill-NY 124	O'Neill-NY 25.9
Jeter-NY 1.3	B.Williams-NY .305	Boggs-NY .389	Martinez-NY .466	Martinez-NY 830	Martinez-NY 109	Martinez-NY 8.2

Runs	Hits	Doubles	Triples	Home Runs	Total Bases	Runs Batted In
Rodriguez-Sea 141	Molitor-Min 225	Rodriguez-Sea 54	Knoblauch-Min 14	McGwire-Oak 52	Rodriguez-Sea 379	Belle-Cle 148
B.Williams-NY 108	Jeter-NY 183	O'Neill-NY 35	B.Williams-NY 7	B.Williams-NY 29	B.Williams-NY 295	Martinez-NY 117
Jeter-NY 104	Martinez-NY 174	Duncan-NY 34	Jeter-NY 6	Martinez-NY 25	Martinez-NY 277	B.Williams-NY 102
O'Neill-NY 89	B.Williams-NY 168	Boggs-NY 29	3 players tied 3	O'Neill-NY 19	O'Neill-NY 259	O'Neill-NY 91

Stolen Bases	Base Stealing Runs	Fielding Runs-Infield	Fielding Runs-Outfield	Wins	Winning Pct.	Complete Games
Lofton-Cle 75	Lofton-Cle 10.6	Gonzalez-Tor 28.4	Becker-Min 17.2	Pettitte-NY 21	Nagy-Cle .773	Hentgen-Tor 10
B.Williams-NY 17	B.Williams-NY 2.3	Duncan-NY .8	O'Neill-NY 3.3	Rogers-NY 12	Pettitte-NY .724	Rogers-NY 2
Jeter-NY 14	Raines-NY 1.9			Key-NY 12		Pettitte-NY 2
Girardi-NY 13	Girardi-NY 1.5			Gooden-NY 11		2 players tied 1

Strikeouts	Fewest BB/Game	Games	Saves	Base Runners/9	Adjusted Relief Runs	Relief Ranking
Clemens-Bos 257	Haney-KC 2.01	Myers-Det 83	Wetteland-NY 43	Percival-Cal 8.64	M.Rivera-NY 35.3	Hernandez-Chi 54.7
Pettitte-NY 162	Pettitte-NY 2.93	Guardado-Min 83	M.Rivera-NY 5	M.Rivera-NY 9.11	Wetteland-NY 14.3	M.Rivera-NY 35.5
M.Rivera-NY 130	Key-NY 3.08	Nelson-NY 73	Nelson-NY 2	Wetteland-NY 10.60	Nelson-NY 5.0	Wetteland-NY 28.5
Gooden-NY 126	Rogers-NY 4.17	Wetteland-NY 62	3 players tied 1	Cone-NY 10.75		Nelson-NY 5.1

Innings Pitched	Opponents' Avg.	Opponents' OBP	Earned Run Average	Adjusted ERA	Adjusted Starter Runs	Pitcher Wins
Hentgen-Tor 265.2	Guzman-Tor .228	Guzman-Tor .289	Guzman-Tor 2.93	Guzman-Tor 171	Hentgen-Tor 52.7	Hentgen-Tor 5.2
Pettitte-NY 221.0	Gooden-NY .259	Key-NY .326	Pettitte-NY 3.87	Pettitte-NY 128	Pettitte-NY 24.7	M.Rivera-NY 3.3
Rogers-NY 179.0	Rogers-NY .261	Pettitte-NY .330	Rogers-NY 4.68	Rogers-NY 106	Cone-NY 16.5	Pettitte-NY 2.8
Gooden-NY 170.2	Key-NY .266	Rogers-NY .346	Key-NY 4.68	Key-NY 106	Rogers-NY 6.2	Wetteland-NY 2.6

1997 American League

TEAM	W	L	T	PCT	GB	R	OR	HR	AVG	OBP	SLG	OPS	AOPS	PF	SB	CG	HR	BB	SO	BR/9	ERA	AERA	OAV	OOB	FW	PW	BW	BSW	DIF
East																													
Bal	98	64	0	.605		812	**681**	196	.268	.341	.429	770	103	97	63	8	164	563	1139	**12.3**	3.91	113	**.253**	**.323**	.8	7.9	2.9	-.0	5.4
NY	96	66	0	.593	2	891	688	161	.287	**.362**	.436	798	108	99	99	11	**144**	532	1165	12.5	**3.84**	116	.260	.327	.5	9.7	8.9	-.4	-3.7
Det	79	83	0	.488	19	784	790	176	.258	.332	.415	747	94	100	**161**	13	178	552	982	12.9	4.56	101	.266	.334	**1.1**	.8	-4.2	.4	-.1
Bos	78	84	0	.481	20	851	857	185	**.291**	.352	.463	815	109	102	68	7	149	611	987	13.9	4.85	96	.277	.351	-1.3	-3.0	7.7	-.7	-5.7
Tor	76	86	0	.469	22	654	694	147	.244	.310	.389	699	81	-100	134	**19**	167	497	1150	12.4	3.92	**117**	.263	.326	1.0	**10.1**	-14.8	.6	-1.9
Central																													
Cle	86	75	0	.534		868	815	220	.286	.358	.467	825	109	104	118	4	181	575	1036	13.6	4.73	99	.276	.347	.3	-.5	8.2	-.0	-2.5
Chi	80	81	0	.497	6	779	833	158	.273	.341	.417	758	100	97	106	6	175	575	961	13.4	4.73	93	.271	.340	-.9	-5.1	1.0	-.0	4.6
Mil	78	83	0	.484	8	681	742	135	.260	.325	.398	723	87	101	103	6	177	542	1016	12.7	4.22	110	.261	.333	-.5	6.0	-9.6	-.2	1.9
Min	68	94	0	.420	18.5	772	861	132	.270	.333	.409	742	91	102	151	10	187	**495**	908	13.3	5.00	93	.283	.342	.6	-4.9	-6.6	**.9**	-3.0
KC	67	94	0	.416	19	747	820	158	.264	.333	.407	740	89	103	130	11	186	531	961	13.2	4.70	101	.274	.340	**1.1**	.6	-8.0	.0	-7.3
West																													
Sea	90	72	0	.556		**925**	833	**264**	.280	.355	**.485**	**840**	**117**	100	89	9	192	598	**1207**	13.5	4.78	95	.267	.342	-.8	-3.9	**13.9**	.0	-.3
Ana	84	78	0	.519	6	829	794	161	.272	.346	.416	762	98	100	126	9	202	605	1050	13.4	4.52	102	.269	.343	-.6	1.3	-.6	-.2	3.1
Tex	77	85	0	.475	13	807	823	187	.274	.334	.438	772	94	107	72	8	169	541	925	13.7	4.69	103	.283	.347	-.5	2.3	-5.1	-.2	-.4
Oak	65	97	0	.401	25	764	946	197	.260	.339	.423	762	98	100	71	2	197	642	953	15.2	5.48	84	.301	.372	-.6	-13.5	-1.1	-.2	-.6
Total	1132					51164		2477	.271	.340	.428	768			1491	123				13.3	4.56		.271	.340					

Batter-Fielder Wins	Batting Average	On-Base Percentage	Slugging Average	On-Base Plus Slugging	Adjusted OPS	Adjusted Batter Runs
Griffey-Sea 6.0	F.Thomas-Chi .347	F.Thomas-Chi .456	Griffey-Sea .646	F.Thomas-Chi 1067	F.Thomas-Chi 183	F.Thomas-Chi 71.9
Martinez-NY 3.2	Williams-NY .328	E.Martinez-Sea .456	Martinez-NY .577	Williams-NY 952	Williams-NY 149	Martinez-NY 39.6
Williams-NY 2.5	O'Neill-NY .324	Williams-NY .408	Williams-NY .544	Martinez-NY 948	Martinez-NY 146	Williams-NY 38.8
O'Neill-NY 2.5	Martinez-NY .296	O'Neill-NY .399	O'Neill-NY .514	O'Neill-NY 912	O'Neill-NY 139	O'Neill-NY 34.6

Runs	Hits	Doubles	Triples	Home Runs	Total Bases	Runs Batted In
Griffey-Sea 125	Garciaparra-Bos 209	Valentin-Bos 47	Garciaparra-Bos 11	Griffey-Sea 56	Griffey-Sea 393	Griffey-Sea 147
Jeter-NY 116	Jeter-NY 190	O'Neill-NY 42	Jeter-NY 7	Martinez-NY 44	Martinez-NY 343	Martinez-NY 141
Williams-NY 107	O'Neill-NY 179	Williams-NY 35	Williams-NY 6	Williams-NY 21	O'Neill-NY 284	O'Neill-NY 117
Martinez-NY 96	Martinez-NY 176	2 players tied 31	2 players tied 2	O'Neill-NY 21	Williams-NY 277	Williams-NY 100

Stolen Bases	Base Stealing Runs	Fielding Runs-Infield	Fielding Runs-Outfield	Wins	Winning Pct.	Complete Games
Hunter-Det 74	Knoblauch-Min 10.1	Cirillo-Mil 24.0	Cameron-Chi 13.0	Clemens-Tor 21	Johnson-Sea .833	Hentgen-Tor 9
Jeter-NY 23	Kelly-NY 1.4	Martinez-NY 7.1		Pettitte-NY 18	Pettitte-NY .720	Clemens-Tor 9
Williams-NY 15	Jeter-NY .9			Wells-NY 16	Wells-NY .615	Wells-NY 5
O'Neill-NY 10	Williams-NY .5			Cone-NY 12		Pettitte-NY 4

Strikeouts	Fewest BB/Game	Games	Saves	Base Runners/9	Adjusted Relief Runs	Relief Ranking
Clemens-Tor 292	Burkett-Tex 1.43	Myers-Det 88	Myers-Bal 45	Jones-Mil 8.29	Quantrill-Tor 23.9	Jones-Mil 46.0
Cone-NY 222	Wells-NY 1.86	Nelson-NY 77	Rivera-NY 43	Rivera-NY 10.67	Rivera-NY 20.8	Rivera-NY 41.5
Pettitte-NY 166	Pettitte-NY 2.43	Rivera-NY 66	Stanton-NY 3	Nelson-NY 10.75	Stanton-NY 15.2	Stanton-NY 15.6
Wells-NY 156	Cone-NY 3.97	Stanton-NY 64	2 players tied 2	Pettitte-NY 11.27	Nelson-NY 12.2	Nelson-NY 14.5

Innings Pitched	Opponents' Avg.	Opponents' OBP	Earned Run Average	Adjusted ERA	Adjusted Starter Runs	Pitcher Wins
Hentgen-Tor 264.0	Johnson-Sea .194	Clemens-Tor .273	Clemens-Tor 2.05	Clemens-Tor 224	Clemens-Tor 74.8	Clemens-Tor 7.9
Clemens-Tor 264.0	Cone-NY .218	Cone-NY .305	Cone-NY 2.82	Cone-NY 158	Pettitte-NY 42.3	Pettitte-NY 4.1
Pettitte-NY 240.1	Pettitte-NY .256	Pettitte-NY .307	Pettitte-NY 2.88	Pettitte-NY 154	Cone-NY 36.4	Rivera-NY 4.1
Wells-NY 218.0	Wells-NY .278	Wells-NY .317	Wells-NY 4.21	Wells-NY 106	Wells-NY 7.4	Cone-NY 2.9

1998 American League

TEAM	W	L	T	PCT	GB	R	OR	HR	AVG	OBP	SLG	OPS	AOPS	PF	SB	CG	HR	BB	SO	BR/9	ERA	AERA	OAV	OOB	FW	PW	BW	BSW	DIF
East																													
NY	114	48	0	.704		**965**	**656**	207	.288	**.364**	.460	**824**	**118**	96	153	**22**	**156**	466	1080	**11.7**	**3.82**	**114**	**.247**	**.312**	.9	**9.0**	**15.7**	**.4**	7.0
Bos	92	70	0	.568	22	876	729	205	.280	.348	.463	811	107	102	72	5	168	504	1025	12.3	4.18	113	.255	.321	.5	8.0	5.7	-.5	-2.6
Tor	88	74	1	.543	26	816	768	221	.266	.340	.448	788	103	100	**184**	10	169	587	1154	12.7	4.28	109	.256	.329	-.6	5.7	2.6	**.4**	-1.1
Bal	79	83	0	.488	35	817	785	214	.273	.347	.447	794	107	98	86	16	169	535	1065	13.1	4.74	96	.272	.338	**1.8**	-3.0	5.9	-.5	-6.2
TB	63	99	0	.389	51	620	751	111	.261	.321	.385	706	81	-103	120	7	171	643	1008	13.4	4.35	110	.261	.345	1.1	6.4	-14.8	-.6	-10.1
Central																													
Cle	89	73	0	.549		850	779	198	.272	.347	.448	795	101	104	143	9	171	563	1037	13.5	4.44	107	.274	.344	.2	4.9	2.3	.2	.4
Chi	80	82	1	.494	9	861	931	198	.271	.339	.444	783	104	98	127	8	211	580	911	13.8	5.22	88	.278	.348	-1.4	-10.0	2.9	**.4**	7.0
KC	72	89	0	.447	16.5	714	899	134	.263	.324	.399	723	84	-104	135	6	196	568	999	13.9	5.15	94	.281	.350	-.7	-4.3	-12.1	**.4**	8.1
Min	70	92	0	.432	19	734	818	115	.266	.328	.389	717	84	-103	112	7	180	**457**	952	13.2	4.75	101	.284	.338	.3	.6	-12.2	-.1	.4
Det	65	97	0	.401	24	722	863	165	.264	.323	.415	738	89	101	122	9	185	595	947	13.6	4.93	96	.277	.348	-.0	-2.7	-8.4	-.2	-4.6
West																													
Tex	88	74	0	.543		940	871	201	**.289**	.357	.462	819	105	106	82	10	164	519	994	13.8	4.99	98	.285	.346	-.4	-1.5	5.3	-.5	4.1
Ana	85	77	0	.525	3	787	783	147	.272	.335	.415	750	92	102	93	3	164	630	1091	13.5	4.49	106	.267	.344	.4	3.7	-5.4	-.2	5.5
Sea	76	85	0	.472	11.5	859	855	**234**	.276	.345	**.468**	813	108	101	115	17	196	528	**1156**	13.4	4.93	95	.273	.340	-.7	-3.9	6.7	**.4**	-7.1
Oak	74	88	0	.457	14	804	866	149	.257	.338	.397	735	92	99	131	12	179	529	922	13.4	4.81	96	.276	.342	-1.5	-2.8	-5.1	**.4**	2.0
Total	1134					51365		2499	.271	.340	.432	771			1675	141				13.2	4.65		.271	.340					

Batter-Fielder Wins	Batting Average	On-Base Percentage	Slugging Average	On-Base Plus Slugging	Adjusted OPS	Adjusted Batter Runs
Belle-Chi 5.8	Williams-NY .339	Martinez-Sea .429	Belle-Chi .655	Belle-Chi 1055	Belle-Chi 173	Belle-Chi 66.9
Williams-NY 4.0	Jeter-NY .324	Williams-NY .422	Williams-NY .575	Williams-NY 997	Williams-NY 164	Williams-NY 49.5
Brosius-NY 2.7	O'Neill-NY .317	Jeter-NY .384	O'Neill-NY .510	O'Neill-NY 882	O'Neill-NY 134	O'Neill-NY 30.4
O'Neill-NY 2.5	Brosius-NY .300	O'Neill-NY .372	Martinez-NY .505	Jeter-NY 864	Jeter-NY 129	Jeter-NY 26.4

Runs	Hits	Doubles	Triples	Home Runs	Total Bases	Runs Batted In
Jeter-NY 127	Rodriguez-Sea 213	Gonzalez-Tex 50	Offerman-KC 13	Griffey-Sea 56	Belle-Chi 399	Gonzalez-Tex 157
Knoblauch-NY 117	Jeter-NY 203	O'Neill-NY 40	Jeter-NY 8	Martinez-NY 28	O'Neill-NY 307	Martinez-NY 123
Williams-NY 101	O'Neill-NY 191	Brosius-NY 34	Williams-NY 5	Williams-NY 26	Jeter-NY 301	O'Neill-NY 116
O'Neill-NY 95	Williams-NY 169	Martinez-NY 33	2 players tied 4	2 players tied 24	Williams-NY 287	Brosius-NY 98

Stolen Bases	Base Stealing Runs	Fielding Runs-Infield	Fielding Runs-Outfield	Wins	Winning Pct.	Complete Games
Henderson-Oak 66	Henderson-Oak 10.0	Easley-Det 25.7	Lawton-Min 14.3	3 players tied 20	Wells-NY .818	Erickson-Bal 11
Knoblauch-NY 31	Jeter-NY 4.5	Brosius-NY 9.3	Curtis-NY 4.3	Cone-NY 20	Cone-NY .741	Wells-NY 8
Jeter-NY 30	O'Neill-NY 3.0	Martinez-NY 1.2	O'Neill-NY .8	Wells-NY 18	Pettitte-NY .593	Pettitte-NY 5
Curtis-NY 21	Curtis-NY 2.9	Knoblauch-NY .8		Pettitte-NY 16		2 players tied 3

Strikeouts	Fewest BB/Game	Games	Saves	Base Runners/9	Adjusted Relief Runs	Relief Ranking
Clemens-Tor 271	Wells-NY 1.22	Runyan-Det 88	Gordon-Bos 46	Jackson-Cle 8.44	Jackson-Cle 22.8	Gordon-Bos 36.8
Cone-NY 209	Cone-NY 2.56	Stanton-NY 67	Rivera-NY 36	Wells-NY 9.45	Rivera-NY 18.3	Rivera-NY 26.7
Wells-NY 163	Pettitte-NY 3.62	Rivera-NY 54	Stanton-NY 6	Rivera-NY 9.68		
Pettitte-NY 146	Irabu-NY 3.95	Lloyd-NY 50	Nelson-NY 3	Hernandez-NY 10.91		

Innings Pitched	Opponents' Avg.	Opponents' OBP	Earned Run Average	Adjusted ERA	Adjusted Starter Runs	Pitcher Wins
Erickson-Bal 251.1	Clemens-Tor .197	Wells-NY .265	Clemens-Tor 2.65	Clemens-Tor 176	Clemens-Tor 51.5	Clemens-Tor 5.2
Pettitte-NY 216.1	Irabu-NY .233	Cone-NY .302	Wells-NY 3.49	Wells-NY 126	Wells-NY 23.6	Rivera-NY 2.6
Wells-NY 214.1	Cone-NY .237	Irabu-NY .321	Cone-NY 3.55	Cone-NY 123	Hernandez-NY 20.3	Cone-NY 2.2
Cone-NY 207.2	Wells-NY .239	Pettitte-NY .344	Irabu-NY 4.06	Irabu-NY 108	Cone-NY 19.2	2 players tied 2.1

1999 American League

TEAM	W	L	T	PCT	GB	R	OR	HR	AVG	OBP	SLG	OPS	AOPS	PF	SB	CG	HR	BB	SO	BR/9	ERA	AERA	OAV	OOB	FW	PW	BW	BSW	DIF
East																													
NY	98	64	0	.605		900	731	193	.282	.366	.453	819	**110**	99	104	6	**158**	581	1111	12.8	4.13	114	.255	.330	.2	8.8	**9.1**	-.3	-.8
Bos	94	68	0	.580	4	836	**718**	176	.278	.350	.448	798	99	103	67	6	160	**469**	**1131**	**12.0**	**4.00**	**124**	**.253**	**.315**	-.6	**14.0**	.0	-.4	.1
Tor	84	78	0	.519	14	883	862	212	.280	.352	.457	809	103	102	119	14	191	575	1009	13.8	4.92	100	.280	.349	.4	-.2	3.2	.3	-.8
Bal	78	84	0	.481	20	851	815	203	.279	.353	.447	800	107	97	107	**17**	198	647	982	13.6	4.77	98	.269	.348	**1.3**	-1.2	6.0	.1	-9.2
TB	69	93	0	.426	29	772	913	145	.274	.343	.411	754	91	102	73	6	172	695	1055	14.9	5.06	98	.286	.370	-1.1	1.6	7.1	.0	-1.7
Central																													
Cle	97	65	0	.599		**1009**	860	209	.289	**.373**	.467	**840**	107	105	**147**	3	197	634	1120	13.6	4.89	104	.268	.346	.4	2.6	7.9	**.9**	4.2
Chi	75	86	1	.466	21.5	777	870	162	.277	.337	.429	766	92	102	110	6	210	596	968	14.2	4.92	100	.282	.353	-1.1	.0	-6.0	.1	1.4
Det	69	92	0	.429	27.5	747	882	212	.261	.326	.443	769	93	102	108	4	209	583	976	13.8	5.17	96	.276	.349	.4	-2.8	-6.6	-.6	-1.9
KC	64	97	0	.398	32.5	856	921	151	.282	.348	.433	781	94	104	127	11	202	643	831	14.7	5.35	95	.288	.365	-.6	-3.9	-4.0	.8	-8.8
Min	63	97	1	.394	33	686	845	105	.264	.328	.384	712	77	-105	118	13	208	487	927	13.3	5.00	103	.283	.341	1.1	2.2	-17.1	-.0	-3.2
West																													
Tex	95	67	0	.586		945	859	230	**.293**	.361	**.479**	**840**	106	106	111	6	186	509	979	13.6	5.07	102	.286	.346	-.2	1.2	5.4	.0	7.6
Oak	87	75	0	.537	8	893	846	235	.259	.355	.446	801	106	97	70	6	160	569	967	13.5	4.69	101	.274	.344	-.4	.4	6.0	-.3	.4
Sea	79	83	0	.488	16	859	905	**244**	.269	.343	.455	798	103	99	130	7	191	684	980	14.9	5.24	91	.287	.368	.0	-6.9	2.0	.7	2.2
Ana	70	92	0	.432	25	711	826	158	.256	.322	.395	717	82	-100	71	4	177	624	877	13.5	4.79	102	.269	.346	.4	1.2	-14.2	-.5	2.0
Total	1132					51725		2635	.275	.347	.439	786			1462	109				13.7	4.86		.275	.347					

Batter-Fielder Wins
R.Alomar-Cle......... 5.1
Williams-NY........... 4.3
Jeter-NY................. 3.4
Knoblauch-NY....... 1.0

Batting Average
Garciaparra-Bos ... .357
Jeter-NY .... .349
Williams-NY.......... .342
Knoblauch-NY ...... .292

On-Base Percentage
Martinez-Sea .... .447
Jeter-NY .... .438
Williams-NY.......... .435
Knoblauch-NY ...... .393

Slugging Average
M.Ramirez-Cle...... .663
Jeter-NY .... .552
Williams-NY.......... .536
O'Neill-NY............. .459

On-Base Plus Slugging
M.Ramirez-Cle......1105
Jeter-NY 989
Williams-NY........... 971
Knoblauch-NY 848

Adjusted OPS
M.Ramirez-Cle....... 170
Jeter-NY 154
Williams-NY........... 149
Knoblauch-NY 118

Adjusted Batter Runs
M.Ramirez-Cle...... 59.1
Jeter-NY 55.5
Williams-NY.......... 48.4
Knoblauch-NY 20.5

Runs
R.Alomar-Cle......... 138
Jeter-NY 134
Knoblauch-NY 120
Williams-NY............116

Hits
Jeter-NY 219
Williams-NY........... 202
Knoblauch-NY 176
O'Neill-NY............. 170

Doubles
Green-Tor 45
O'Neill-NY............... 39
Jeter-NY 37
Knoblauch-NY 36

Triples
Offerman-Bos 11
Jeter-NY 9
Williams-NY............... 6
Ledee-NY 5

Home Runs
Griffey-Sea 48
Martinez-NY............. 28
Williams-NY............. 25
Jeter-NY 24

Total Bases
Green-Tor 361
Jeter-NY 346
Williams-NY........... 317
2 players tied 274

Runs Batted In
M.Ramirez-Cle....... 165
Williams-NY............115
O'Neill-NY...............110
Martinez-NY............ 105

Stolen Bases
Hunter-Det-Sea 44
Knoblauch-NY 28
Jeter-NY 19
O'Neill-NY.................11

Base Stealing Runs
Hunter-Det-Sea 6.9
Knoblauch-NY 3.0
Jeter-NY 1.4
Brosius-NY 9

Fielding Runs-Infield
Bordick-Bal 35.1
Martinez-NY............ 7.4
Brosius-NY 3.5

Fielding Runs-Outfield
Dye-KC 14.3
O'Neill-NY............... 1.3

Wins
P.Martinez-Bos 23
Hernandez-NY......... 17
Pettitte-NY 14
Clemens-NY 14

Winning Pct.
P.Martinez-Bos ...... .852
Hernandez-NY...... .654

Complete Games
D.Wells-Tor 7
Irabu-NY 2
Hernandez-NY........... 2
2 players tied 1

Strikeouts
P.Martinez-Bos 313
Cone-NY................ 177
Clemens-NY 163
Hernandez-NY....... 157

Fewest BB/Game
Heredia-Oak 1.53
Irabu-NY 2.44
Hernandez-NY...... 3.65
Pettitte-NY 4.18

Games
Wells-Min................. 76
Groom-Oak.............. 76
Stanton-NY.............. 73
Rivera-NY 66

Saves
Rivera-NY................ 45
Mendoza-NY............. 3
Nelson-NY 1
Grimsley-NY 1

Base Runners/9
Zimmerman-Tex.... 7.70
Rivera-NY............ 8.35
Hernandez-NY.....11.84
Irabu-NY 12.33

Adjusted Relief Runs
Foulke-Chi 31.7
Rivera-NY............. 23.1
Grimsley-NY 6.8
Mendoza-NY........... 4.6

Relief Ranking
Rivera-NY 46.2
Grimsley-NY 7.6
Mendoza-NY............ 6.3
Stanton-NY.............. 2.4

Innings Pitched
D.Wells-Tor 231.2
Hernandez-NY.... 214.1
Cone-NY............. 193.1
Pettitte-NY 191.2

Opponents' Avg.
P.Martinez-Bos ..... .205
Cone-NY............... .229
Hernandez-NY...... .233
Clemens-NY .... .261

Opponents' OBP
P.Martinez-Bos ...... .248
Hernandez-NY........311
Irabu-NY .... .317
Cone-NY............... .322

Earned Run Average
P.Martinez-Bos 2.07
Cone-NY............... 3.44
Hernandez-NY...... 4.12
Clemens-NY 4.60

Adjusted ERA
P.Martinez-Bos 241
Cone-NY................ 137
Hernandez-NY........115
Clemens-NY 103

Adjusted Starter Runs
P.Martinez-Bos 67.2
Cone-NY............... 27.1
Hernandez-NY...... 14.9
Clemens-NY 4.7

Pitcher Wins
P.Martinez-Bos 8.1
Rivera-NY............... 4.5
Cone-NY.................. 2.5
Hernandez-NY........ 1.6

2000 American League

TEAM	W	L	T	PCT	GB	R	OR	HR	AVG	OBP	SLG	OPS	AOPS	PF	SB	CG	HR	BB	SO	BR/9	ERA	AERA	OAV	OOB	FW	PW	BW	BSW	DIF
East																													
NY	87	74	0	.540		871	814	205	.277	.354	.450	804	103	99	99	9	177	577	1040	13.2	4.76	100	.263	.336	.2	.0	3.7	-.0	2.6
Bos	85	77	0	.525	2.5	792	**745**	167	.267	.341	.423	764	89	103	43	7	173	498	1121	**12.3**	**4.23**	**118**	**.257**	**.322**	.2	**11.3**	-7.5	-.6	.6
Tor	83	79	0	.512	4.5	861	908	**244**	.275	.341	.469	810	100	103	89	**15**	195	560	978	14.0	5.14	98	.285	.354	.7	-1.6	-.7	.2	3.4
Bal	74	88	0	.457	13.5	794	913	184	.272	.341	.435	776	100	95	**126**	14	202	665	1017	14.1	5.37	87	.275	.352	-.2	-10.4	.4	-.0	3.2
TB	69	92	0	.429	18	733	842	162	.257	.329	.399	728	85	-99	90	10	198	533	955	13.5	4.86	101	.277	.345	-.4	.4	-11.9	-.2	.6
Central																													
Chi	95	67	0	.586		**978**	839	216	.286	.356	.470	826	103	104	119	5	195	614	1037	13.5	4.66	108	.270	.346	-1.2	5.6	3.4	.5	5.7
Cle	90	72	0	.556	5	950	816	221	**.288**	**.367**	.470	**837**	106	104	113	6	173	666	**1213**	13.8	4.84	103	.270	.350	**2.4**	2.4	**6.6**	.7	-3.0
Det	79	83	0	.488	16	823	827	177	.275	.343	.438	781	97	99	83	6	177	**496**	978	13.3	4.71	104	.280	.340	.5	2.7	-2.0	-.0	-3.1
KC	77	85	0	.475	18	879	930	150	**.288**	.348	.425	773	90	106	121	10	239	693	927	14.5	5.48	95	.282	.362	.6	-3.7	-7.4	**.8**	5.7
Min	69	93	0	.426	26	748	880	116	.270	.337	.407	744	82	107	90	6	212	516	1042	13.7	5.14	102	.287	.347	.6	1.5	-13.5	-.2	-.5
West																													
Oak	91	70	0	.565		947	813	239	.270	.360	.458	818	**107**	99	40	7	**158**	615	963	13.8	4.58	106	.274	.348	-1.3	3.9	6.5	-.2	1.5
Sea	91	71	0	.562	0.5	907	780	198	.269	.361	.442	803	104	98	122	4	167	634	998	13.2	4.49	107	.262	.339	.8	4.7	5.1	.1	-.7
Ana	82	80	0	.506	9.5	864	869	236	.280	.352	**.472**	824	104	103	93	5	228	662	846	13.9	5.00	103	.273	.351	-1.2	2.1	3.1	-.3	-2.6
Tex	71	91	0	.438	20.5	848	974	173	.283	.352	.446	798	100	101	69	3	202	661	918	15.2	5.52	92	.294	.369	-1.3	-6.1	.0	-.6	-2.0
Total	1132					61995		2688	.276	.349	.443	792			1297	107				13.7	4.91		.276	.349					

Batter-Fielder Wins
A.Rodriguez-Sea... 6.6
Posada-NY............. 4.3
Williams-NY........... 3.2
Hill-NY.................... 1.1

Batting Average
Garciaparra-Bos ... .372
Jeter-NY .... .339
Williams-NY.......... .307
Posada-NY .... .287

On-Base Percentage
J.Giambi-Oak......... .476
Posada-NY .... .417
Jeter-NY .... .416
Williams-NY.......... .391

Slugging Average
M.Ramirez-Cle...... .697
Williams-NY.......... .566
Posada-NY .... .527
Jeter-NY .... .481

On-Base Plus Slugging
M.Ramirez-Cle......1154
Williams-NY........... 957
Posada-NY 943
Jeter-NY 896

Adjusted OPS
J.Giambi-Oak......... 185
Williams-NY........... 141
Posada-NY 139
Jeter-NY 128

Adjusted Batter Runs
Delgado-Tor.......... 76.7
Posada-NY 36.1
Williams-NY.......... 34.3
Jeter-NY 29.0

Runs
Damon-KC............. 136
Jeter-NY 119
Williams-NY........... 108
Posada-NY 92

Hits
Erstad-Ana............ 240
Jeter-NY 201
Williams-NY........... 165
O'Neill-NY............. 160

Doubles
Delgado-Tor 57
Williams-NY............. 37
Martinez-NY............. 37
Posada-NY 35

Triples
Guzman-Min 20
Williams-NY............... 6
Martinez-NY............... 4
Jeter-NY 4

Home Runs
Glaus-Ana............... 47
Williams-NY............. 30
Posada-NY 28
O'Neill-NY................ 18

Total Bases
Delgado-Tor 378
Williams-NY........... 304
Jeter-NY 285
Posada-NY 266

Runs Batted In
Martinez-Sea 145
Williams-NY........... 121
O'Neill-NY............. 100
Martinez-NY............. 91

Stolen Bases
Damon-KC............... 46
Jeter-NY 22
Knoblauch-NY 15
O'Neill-NY................ 14

Base Stealing Runs
R.Alomar-Cle 7.2
Jeter-NY 3.4
Williams-NY............ 1.1
Bellinger-NY 1.1

Fielding Runs-Infield
Velarde-Oak.......... 22.0

Fielding Runs-Outfield
Martinez-TB-Tx-Tor 11.5
O'Neill-NY................ 4.4

Wins
D.Wells-Tor 20
Hudson-Oak 20
Pettitte-NY 19
Clemens-NY 13

Winning Pct.
Hudson-Oak .... .769
Pettitte-NY .... .679

Complete Games
D.Wells-Tor 9
Pettitte-NY 3
Hernandez-NY........... 3
3 players tied 1

Strikeouts
P.Martinez-Bos 284
Clemens-NY 188
Hernandez-NY....... 141
Pettitte-NY 125

Fewest BB/Game
D.Wells-Tor........... 1.21
Hernandez-NY...... 2.35
Pettitte-NY 3.52
Clemens-NY 3.70

Games
Wunsch-Chi............. 83
Nelson-NY 73
Stanton-NY.............. 69
Rivera-NY 66

Saves
Lowe-Bos................. 42
Jones-Det 42
Rivera-NY................ 36
2 players tied 1

Base Runners/9
P.Martinez-Bos 7.22
Rivera-NY............. 9.87
Hernandez-NY.....11.18
Nelson-NY...........11.76

Adjusted Relief Runs
Lowe-Bos.............. 25.0
Nelson-NY............ 16.9
Rivera-NY............. 16.6
Stanton-NY............. 5.9

Relief Ranking
Lowe-Bos.............. 41.3
Rivera-NY............. 33.2
Nelson-NY 26.1
Stanton-NY.............. 3.9

Innings Pitched
Mussina-Bal........ 237.2
Pettitte-NY 204.2
Clemens-NY 204.1
Hernandez-NY.... 195.2

Opponents' Avg.
P.Martinez-Bos ..... .167
Clemens-NY .... .236
Hernandez-NY...... .247
Pettitte-NY .... .271

Opponents' OBP
P.Martinez-Bos ...... .213
Hernandez-NY...... .298
Clemens-NY .... .317
Pettitte-NY .... .338

Earned Run Average
P.Martinez-Bos 1.74
Clemens-NY 3.70
Pettitte-NY 4.35
Hernandez-NY...... 4.51

Adjusted ERA
P.Martinez-Bos 288
Clemens-NY 129
Pettitte-NY 110
Hernandez-NY....... 106

Adjusted Starter Runs
P.Martinez-Bos 78.3
Clemens-NY 22.7
Pettitte-NY 8.0
Hernandez-NY........ 6.9

Pitcher Wins
P.Martinez-Bos 8.4
Rivera-NY............... 3.2
Nelson-NY 2.4
Clemens-NY 2.1

2001 American League

TEAM	W	L	T	PCT	GB	R	OR	HR	AVG	OBP	SLG	OPS	AOPS	PF	SB	CG	HR	BB	SO	BR/9	ERA	AERA	OAV	OOB	FW	PW	BW	BSW	DIF
East																													
NY	95	65	1	.594		804	713	203	.267	.334	.435	769	100	101	161	7	158	465	**1266**	12.1	4.02	110	.257	.318	.3	6.4	.4	.8	7.2
Bos	82	79	0	.509	13.5	772	745	198	.266	.334	.439	773	102	100	46	3	**146**	544	1259	12.7	4.15	107	.254	.329	.0	4.4	1.8	-1.1	-3.7
Tor	80	82	0	.494	16	767	753	195	.263	.325	.430	755	95	102	156	7	165	490	1041	13.0	4.28	107	.275	.339	1.0	4.5	-4.0	.6	-3.1
Bal	63	98	1	.391	32.5	687	829	136	.248	.319	.380	699	89	-95	133	10	194	528	938	13.2	4.67	92	.269	.337	-.6	-5.8	-8.3	.2	-2.9
TB	62	100	0	.383	34	672	887	121	.258	.320	.388	708	87	-98	115	1	207	569	1030	13.6	4.94	91	.273	.345	-1.4	-6.6	-9.6	-.2	-1.2
Central																													
Cle	91	71	0	.562		897	821	212	.278	.350	.458	808	107	104	79	3	148	573	1218	13.3	4.64	99	.270	.341	.4	-.9	6.2	-.6	4.8
Min	85	77	0	.525	6	771	766	164	.272	.337	.433	770	96	106	146	12	192	445	965	12.5	4.51	103	.268	.325	.4	2.3	-2.4	.0	3.7
Chi	83	79	0	.512	8	798	795	214	.268	.334	.451	785	99	106	123	8	181	500	921	12.9	4.55	102	.266	.334	-.2	1.4	-.6	-.3	1.7
Det	66	96	0	.407	25	724	876	139	.260	.320	.409	729	93	98	133	**16**	180	553	859	14.2	5.01	88	.288	.357	-1.0	-9.1	-5.3	-.1	.4
KC	65	97	0	.401	26	729	858	152	.266	.318	.409	727	82	110	100	5	209	576	911	13.6	4.87	102	.276	.348	-.2	1.1	-14.1	-.2	-2.7
West																													
Sea	116	46	0	.716		**927**	**627**	169	**.288**	**.360**	.445	805	**117**	95	**174**	8	160	465	1051	**11.2**	**3.54**	120	**.236**	**.301**	**1.8**	11.7	**15.7**	**1.4**	4.4
Oak	102	60	0	.630	14	884	645	199	.264	.345	.439	784	104	101	68	13	153	**440**	1117	11.5	3.59	**127**	.249	.308	-.6	**14.8**	5.5	-.4	1.8
Ana	75	87	0	.463	41	691	730	158	.261	.327	.405	732	90	102	116	6	168	525	947	12.8	4.20	111	.263	.331	.7	6.5	-7.0	-.2	-6.0
Tex	73	89	0	.451	43	890	968	**246**	.275	.344	**.471**	**815**	109	103	97	4	222	596	951	14.6	5.71	83	.293	.362	.0	-13.6	7.9	.0	-2.4
Total	1133					51013		2506	.267	.334	.428	762			1647	103				12.9	4.47		.267	.334					

Batter-Fielder Wins
A.Rodriguez-Tex ... 6.9
B.Williams-NY 3.0
Posada-NY............ 1.7
Jeter-NY................ 1.0

Batting Average
Suzuki-Sea .... .350
Jeter-NY .... .311
B.Williams-NY....... .307
Martinez-NY.......... .280

On-Base Percentage
J.Giambi-Oak........ .477
B.Williams-NY....... .395
Jeter-NY .... .377
Posada-NY .... .363

Slugging Average
J.Giambi-Oak........ .660
B.Williams-NY....... .522
Martinez-NY.......... .501
Jeter-NY .... .480

On-Base Plus Slugging
J.Giambi-Oak........1137
B.Williams-NY........ 917
Jeter-NY 858
Posada-NY 838

Adjusted OPS
J.Giambi-Oak......... 196
B.Williams-NY........ 139
Jeter-NY 123
Posada-NY 118

Adjusted Batter Runs
J.Giambi-Oak........ 84.2
B.Williams-NY....... 34.1
Jeter-NY 21.6
Posada-NY 14.1

Runs
A.Rodriguez-Tex.... 133
Jeter-NY 110
B.Williams-NY........ 102
Martinez-NY............ 89

Hits
Suzuki-Sea 242
Jeter-NY 191
B.Williams-NY........ 166
Martinez-NY........... 165

Doubles
J.Giambi-Oak.......... 47
B.Williams-NY......... 38
Jeter-NY 35
Soriano-NY 34

Triples
Guzman-Min 14
Soriano-NY 3
Knoblauch-NY 3
Jeter-NY 3

Home Runs
A.Rodriguez-Tex...... 52
Martinez-NY............ 34
B.Williams-NY......... 26
Posada-NY 22

Total Bases
A.Rodriguez-Tex.... 393
Martinez-NY........... 295
Jeter-NY 295
B.Williams-NY........ 282

Runs Batted In
Boone-Sea............. 141
Martinez-NY............113
Posada-NY 95
B.Williams-NY.......... 94

Stolen Bases
Suzuki-Sea 56
Soriano-NY 43
Knoblauch-NY 38
Jeter-NY 27

Base Stealing Runs
Suzuki-Sea 7.4
Knoblauch-NY 5.2
Jeter-NY 4.9
Soriano-NY 4.6

Fielding Runs-Infield
Gonzalez-Tor 33.3
Martinez-NY............ 5.0
Brosius-NY 1.8

Fielding Runs-Outfield
Hunter-Min............ 18.6

Wins
Mulder-Oak.............. 21
Clemens-NY 20
Mussina-NY 17
Pettitte-NY 15

Winning Pct.
Clemens-NY .... .870
Mussina-NY .... .607
Pettitte-NY .... .600

Complete Games
Sparks-Det................. 8
Mussina-NY 4
Pettitte-NY 2
Hitchcock-NY............. 1

Strikeouts
Nomo-Bos............. 220
Mussina-NY........... 214
Clemens-NY 213
Pettitte-NY 164

Fewest BB/Game
Radke-Min 1.04
Mussina-NY.......... 1.65
Pettitte-NY 1.84
Clemens-NY 2.94

Games
Quantrill-Tor............. 80
Stanton-NY 76
M.Rivera-NY 71
Mendoza-NY........... 56

Saves
M.Rivera-NY 50
Mendoza-NY 6
Boehringer-NY 1

Base Runners/9
Rhodes-Sea.......... 7.81
M.Rivera-NY 8.26
Mussina-NY 9.76
Mendoza-NY....... 10.19

Adjusted Relief Runs
Foulke-Chi 21.0
M.Rivera-NY.......... 18.5
Stanton-NY 16.9
Mendoza-NY 8.7

Relief Ranking
Foulke-Chi 42.0
M.Rivera-NY 37.0
Stanton-NY 24.6
Mendoza-NY 10.2

Innings Pitched
Garcia-Sea 238.2
Mussina-NY 228.2
Clemens-NY 220.1
Pettitte-NY 200.2

Opponents' Avg.
Garcia-Sea .... .225
Mussina-NY .... .237
Clemens-NY .... .246
Pettitte-NY .... .281

Opponents' OBP
Mussina-NY .... .274
Clemens-NY .... .309
Pettitte-NY .... .319

Earned Run Average
Garcia-Sea 3.05
Mussina-NY 3.15
Clemens-NY 3.51
Pettitte-NY 3.99

Adjusted ERA
Mays-Min............... 148
Mussina-NY 141
Clemens-NY 126
Pettitte-NY 111

Adjusted Starter Runs
Mays-Min.............. 37.6
Mussina-NY 33.4
Clemens-NY 23.0
Pettitte-NY 7.5

Pitcher Wins
Mays-Min................ 4.4
M.Rivera-NY 3.8
Mussina-NY 3.7
Stanton-NY 2.4

2002 American League

TEAM	W	L	T	PCT	GB	R	OR	HR	AVG	OBP	SLG	OPS	AOPS	PF	SB	CG	HR	BB	SO	BR/9	ERA	AERA	OAV	OOB	FW	PW	BW	BSW	DIF
East																													
NY	103	58	0	.640		**897**	697	223	.275	**.354**	**.455**	**809**	**114**	99	100	9	144	**403**	1135	11.7	3.87	112	.256	.309	-1.2	7.2	**12.7**	.4	3.4
Bos	93	69	0	.574	10.5	859	665	177	.277	.345	.444	789	106	102	80	5	146	430	**1157**	**11.5**	3.75	119	**.246**	**.308**	.2	11.0	6.1	.3	-5.5
Tor	78	84	0	.481	25.5	813	828	187	.261	.327	.430	757	95	104	71	6	177	590	991	13.5	4.80	96	.269	.344	.0	-2.8	-2.8	.4	2.2
Bal	67	95	0	.414	36.5	667	773	165	.246	.309	.403	712	93	95	110	8	208	549	967	13.0	4.46	97	.266	.336	.9	-2.0	-5.9	.2	-7.2
TB	55	106	0	.342	48	673	918	133	.253	.314	.390	704	88	-98	102	**12**	215	620	925	14.3	5.29	85	.279	.357	-1.2	-11.8	-9.4	.2	-3.3
Central																													
Min	94	67	0	.584		768	712	167	.272	.332	.437	769	99	103	79	8	184	439	1026	12.1	4.12	108	.261	.318	**1.9**	5.2	.0	-.9	7.3
Chi	81	81	0	.500	13.5	856	798	217	.268	.338	.449	787	103	104	75	7	190	528	945	12.7	4.53	99	.260	.330	.6	-.5	3.0	.1	-3.2
Cle	74	88	0	.457	20.5	739	837	192	.249	.321	.412	733	91	102	52	9	142	603	1058	13.7	4.91	90	.274	.348	-.4	-7.3	-6.2	-.7	7.5
KC	62	100	0	.383	32.5	737	891	140	.256	.323	.398	721	81	113	**140**	**12**	212	572	909	13.8	5.21	96	.281	.349	-1.4	-3.2	-14.1	.3	-.6
Det	55	106	0	.342	39	575	864	124	.248	.300	.379	679	82	-96	65	11	163	463	794	13.5	4.92	89	.285	.343	-2.1	-8.5	-13.6	-.6	-.8
West																													
Oak	103	59	0	.636		800	654	205	.261	.339	.432	771	104	99	46	9	**135**	474	1021	11.9	**3.68**	**122**	.252	.315	.3	**12.3**	3.9	-.2	5.6
Ana	99	63	0	.611	4	851	**644**	152	**.282**	.341	.433	774	106	98	117	7	169	509	999	11.8	3.69	121	.247	.314	1.2	12.2	5.6	.3	-1.3
Sea	93	69	0	.574	10	814	699	152	.275	.350	.419	769	108	97	137	8	178	441	1063	11.9	4.07	106	.257	.315	1.1	3.7	7.5	**.5**	-.8
Tex	72	90	0	.444	31	843	882	**230**	.269	.338	**.455**	793	106	103	62	4	194	669	1030	14.2	5.15	93	.272	.355	.5	-5.4	5.1	-.3	-8.9
Total	1132					60892		2464	.264	.331	.424	755			1236	115				12.8	4.46		.264	.331					

Batter-Fielder Wins
A.Rodriguez-Tex ... 7.4
Giambi-NY 4.5
Posada-NY............ 3.1
B.Williams-NY 2.9

Batting Average
Ramirez-Bos......... .349
B.Williams-NY....... .333
Giambi-NY .... .314
Soriano-NY .... .300

On-Base Percentage
Ramirez-Bos......... .450
Giambi-NY .... .435
B.Williams-NY....... .415
Jeter-NY .... .373

Slugging Average
Thome-Cle............ .677
Giambi-NY .... .598
Soriano-NY .... .547
B.Williams-NY....... .493

On-Base Plus Slugging
Thome-Cle............1122
Giambi-NY 1034
B.Williams-NY........ 908
Soriano-NY 880

Adjusted OPS
Thome-Cle............. 190
Giambi-NY 173
B.Williams-NY........ 142
Soriano-NY 130

Adjusted Batter Runs
Thome-Cle............ 68.3
Giambi-NY 65.8
B.Williams-NY....... 40.5
Soriano-NY 27.8

Runs
Soriano-NY 128
Jeter-NY 124
Giambi-NY 120
B.Williams-NY........ 102

Hits
Soriano-NY 209
B.Williams-NY........ 204
Jeter-NY 191
Giambi-NY 176

Doubles
Garciaparra-Bos 56
Anderson-Ana.......... 56
Soriano-NY 51
Posada-NY 40

Triples
Damon-Bos...............11
4 players tied 2

Home Runs
A.Rodriguez-Tex...... 57
Giambi-NY 41
Soriano-NY 39
Ventura-NY 27

Total Bases
A.Rodriguez-Tex.... 389
Soriano-NY 381
Giambi-NY 335
B.Williams-NY........ 302

Runs Batted In
A.Rodriguez-Tex.... 142
Giambi-NY 122
B.Williams-NY........ 102
Soriano-NY 102

Stolen Bases
Soriano-NY 41
Jeter-NY 32
B.Williams-NY............ 8
Ventura-NY 3

Base Stealing Runs
Jeter-NY 6.0
Soriano-NY 4.5
G.Williams-NY 4
B.Williams-NY........... .4

Fielding Runs-Infield
Bordick-Bal 26.2
Ventura-NY 10.5

Fielding Runs-Outfield
Erstad-Ana........... 19.4
White-NY 3.8

Wins
Zito-Oak.................. 23
Wells-NY................. 19
Mussina-NY 18
2 players tied 13

Winning Pct.
Martinez-Bos .... .833
Wells-NY............... .731
Mussina-NY .... .643

Complete Games
Byrd-KC 7
Pettitte-NY 3
Wells-NY.................... 2
Mussina-NY............... 2

Strikeouts
Martinez-Bos 239
Clemens-NY 192
Mussina-NY 182
Wells-NY................ 137

Fewest BB/Game
Reed-Min 1.24
Wells-NY.............. 1.96
Mussina-NY.......... 2.00
Clemens-NY 3.15

Games
Koch-Oak................ 84
Stanton-NY 79
Karsay-NY 78
Mendoza-NY........... 62

Saves
Guardado-Min.......... 45
M.Rivera-NY 28
Karsay-NY 12
Stanton-NY 6

Base Runners/9
Rhodes-Sea.......... 7.49
O.Hernandez-NY 10.79
Mussina-NY 10.89
Wells-NY..............11.34

Adjusted Relief Runs
Romero-Min........... 23.8
Karsay-NY 12.0
Stanton-NY 11.9
Mendoza-NY 7.5

Relief Ranking
Percival-Ana 32.9
Karsay-NY 15.2
Stanton-NY 12.6
Mendoza-NY 9.4

Innings Pitched
Halladay-Tor 239.1
Mussina-NY 215.2
Wells-NY............. 206.1
Clemens-NY 180.0

Opponents' Avg.
Martinez-Bos .... .198
Clemens-NY .... .250
Mussina-NY .... .253
Wells-NY............... .259

Opponents' OBP
Martinez-Bos .... .254
Mussina-NY .... .296
Wells-NY............... .300
Clemens-NY .... .317

Earned Run Average
Martinez-Bos 2.26
Wells-NY............... 3.75
Mussina-NY 4.05
Clemens-NY 4.35

Adjusted ERA
Martinez-Bos 198
Wells-NY.................115
Mussina-NY 107
Clemens-NY 100

Adjusted Starter Runs
Lowe-Bos.............. 48.2
Pettitte-NY 14.7
O.Hernandez-NY .. 12.8
Wells-NY................11.7

Pitcher Wins
Lowe-Bos................ 6.2
Pettitte-NY 2.0
M.Rivera-NY 1.6
Karsay-NY 1.5

2003 American League

TEAM	W	L	T	PCT	GB	R	OR	HR	AVG	OBP	SLG	OPS	AOPS	PF	SB	CG	HR	BB	SO	BR/9	ERA	AERA	OAV	OOB	FW	PW	BW	BSW	DIF
East																													
NY	101	61	1	.623		877	716	230	.271	.356	.453	809	113	99	98	8	145	**375**	1119	11.9	4.02	109	.265	.314	-.4	5.9	12.3	.3	1.9
Bos	95	67	0	.586	6	**961**	809	238	**.289**	**.360**	**.491**	**851**	**117**	104	88	5	153	488	**1141**	12.7	4.48	104	.263	.327	-.4	2.7	**15.1**	.0	-3.4
Tor	86	76	0	.531	15	894	826	190	.279	.349	.455	804	106	104	37	14	184	485	984	13.2	4.69	101	.276	.337	-.7	.8	6.1	-.7	-.5
Bal	71	91	1	.438	30	743	820	152	.268	.323	.405	728	92	99	89	9	198	526	981	13.6	4.76	97	.278	.346	.0	-2.5	-6.6	.0	-1.0
TB	63	99	0	.389	38	715	852	137	.265	.320	.404	724	92	98	**142**	7	196	639	877	13.7	4.93	93	.264	.347	.1	-5.3	-6.4	1.0	-7.5
Central																													
Min	90	72	0	.556		801	758	155	.277	.341	.431	772	98	104	94	7	187	402	997	12.2	4.41	102	.268	.319	1.0	1.3	.0	-.1	6.8
Chi	86	76	0	.531	4	791	715	220	.263	.331	.446	777	99	104	77	12	162	518	1056	12.2	4.17	110	.253	.321	.7	6.3	-.6	.0	-1.5
KC	83	79	0	.512	7	836	867	162	.274	.336	.427	763	94	107	120	7	190	566	865	13.8	5.05	95	.279	.348	-.1	-3.4	-4.2	.5	9.3
Cle	68	94	0	.420	22	699	778	158	.254	.316	.401	717	88	100	86	5	179	501	943	12.6	4.21	105	.264	.329	-1.2	3.4	-9.0	-.8	-5.5
Det	43	119	0	.265	47	591	928	153	.240	.300	.375	675	81	-96	98	3	195	557	764	13.9	5.30	83	.286	.352	-1.8	-14.6	-15.4	-.6	-5.5
West																													
Oak	96	66	0	.593		768	643	176	.254	.327	.417	744	95	101	48	**16**	**140**	499	1018	11.8	**3.63**	**126**	**.246**	.314	-.0	**14.4**	-3.5	-.0	4.3
Sea	93	69	0	.574	3	795	**637**	139	.271	.344	.410	754	103	95	108	8	173	466	1001	**11.6**	3.76	115	.247	**.311**	**2.3**	9.1	4.2	.4	-4.0
Ana	77	85	0	.475	19	736	743	150	.268	.330	.413	743	99	96	129	5	190	486	980	12.6	4.28	102	.261	.327	.0	1.5	-.6	.0	-5.0
Tex	71	91	0	.438	25	826	969	**239**	.266	.330	.454	784	97	107	65	4	208	603	1009	14.4	5.67	88	.288	.360	.6	-9.9	-1.9	-.0	1.2
Total	1135					61033		2499	.267	.333	.428	761			1279	110				12.9	4.52		.267	.333					

Batter-Fielder Wins	Batting Average	On-Base Percentage	Slugging Average	On-Base Plus Slugging	Adjusted OPS	Adjusted Batter Runs
Rodriguez-Tex....... 6.7	Mueller-Bos .... .326	Ramirez-Bos.......... .427	Rodriguez-Tex ...... .600	Delgado-Tor 1019	Delgado-Tor........... 160	Delgado-Tor.......... 55.6
Posada-NY............ 6.1	Jeter-NY .... .324	Giambi-NY............ .412	Giambi-NY............ .527	Giambi-NY............ 939	Giambi-NY............. 148	Giambi-NY............ 45.0
Soriano-NY........... 3.5	Soriano-NY........... .290	Posada-NY .... .405	Soriano-NY........... .525	Posada-NY 922	Posada-NY 144	Posada-NY 35.1
Giambi-NY 1.9	Matsui-NY............. .287	Jeter-NY .... .393	Posada-NY .... .518	Soriano-NY............ 863	Soriano-NY............ 125	Johnson-NY........... 22.6

Runs	Hits	Doubles	Triples	Home Runs	Total Bases	Runs Batted In
Rodriguez-Tex 124	Wells-Tor................ 215	Wells-Tor................. 49	Guzman-Min............ 14	Rodriguez-Tex 47	Wells-Tor.................. 373	Delgado-Tor........... 145
Soriano-NY.............114	Soriano-NY............ 198	Anderson-Ana.......... 49	Soriano-NY............... 5	Giambi-NY............... 41	Soriano-NY............ 358	Giambi-NY............. 107
Giambi-NY.................. 97	Matsui-NY.............. 179	Matsui-NY................ 42	Mondesi-NY............... 3	Soriano-NY.............. 38	Giambi-NY.............. 282	Matsui-NY.............. 106
Jeter-NY 87	Jeter-NY 156	Soriano-NY.............. 36	Jeter-NY 3	Posada-NY 30	Matsui-NY............... 271	Posada-NY 101

Stolen Bases	Base Stealing Runs	Fielding Runs-Infield	Fielding Runs-Outfield	Wins	Winning Pct.	Complete Games
Crawford-TB 55	Crawford-TB 8.6	Hudson-Tor 44.6	Cameron-Sea 16.2	Halladay-Tor 22	Halladay-Tor .... .759	3 players tied 9
Soriano-NY.............. 35	Soriano-NY............ 4.9	Soriano-NY............ 2.9		Pettitte-NY............... 21	Pettitte-NY .... .724	Wells-NY.................... 4
Mondesi-NY.............. 17	Boone-NY 1.8			Mussina-NY.............. 17	Wells-NY................ .682	Mussina-NY................ 2
Jeter-NY 11	Mondesi-NY............ 1.3			Clemens-NY 17	Mussina-NY.......... .680	2 players tied 1

Strikeouts	Fewest BB/Game	Games	Saves	Base Runners/9	Adjusted Relief Runs	Relief Ranking
Loaiza-Chi 207	Wells-NY................. .85	Miller-Tor.................. 79	Foulke-Oak.............. 43	Foulke-Oak........... 8.72	Marte-Chi.............. 25.9	Foulke-Oak........... 48.0
Mussina-NY........... 195	Mussina-NY.......... 1.68	M.Rivera-NY............ 64	M.Rivera-NY............ 40	M.Rivera-NY......... 9.55	M.Rivera-NY......... 21.8	M.Rivera-NY......... 42.6
Clemens-NY........... 190	Pettitte-NY........... 2.16	Hammond-NY........... 62	Hammond-NY............ 1	Mussina-NY........... 9.85	Hammond-NY....... 10.6	Hammond-NY......... 7.9
Pettitte-NY............. 180	Clemens-NY 2.47	Osuna-NY................ 48		Contreras-NY.......11.03		

Innings Pitched	Opponents' Avg.	Opponents' OBP	Earned Run Average	Adjusted ERA	Adjusted Starter Runs	Pitcher Wins
Halladay-Tor 266.0	Martinez-Bos .... .215	Martinez-Bos .... .272	Martinez-Bos 2.22	Martinez-Bos 210	Martinez-Bos 48.8	Loaiza-Chi 5.5
Mussina-NY........ 214.2	Mussina-NY.......... .238	Mussina-NY.......... .275	Mussina-NY.......... 3.40	Mussina-NY........... 129	Mussina-NY.......... 25.7	M.Rivera-NY............ 4.3
Wells-NY............ 213.0	Clemens-NY......... .247	Clemens-NY .... .299	Clemens-NY 3.91	Clemens-NY 112	Clemens-NY 12.4	Mussina-NY............ 2.8
Clemens-NY 211.2	Pettitte-NY .... .272	Wells-NY............... .306	Pettitte-NY 4.02	Pettitte-NY 109	Contreras-NY.......... 9.6	Clemens-NY 1.4

2004 American League

TEAM	W	L	T	PCT	GB	R	OR	HR	AVG	OBP	SLG	OPS	AOPS	PF	SB	CG	HR	BB	SO	BR/9	ERA	AERA	OAV	OOB	FW	PW	BW	BSW	DIF
East																													
NY	101	61	0	.623		897	808	**242**	.268	.353	.458	811	109	100	84	1	182	445	1058	12.7	4.69	98	.271	.328	.6	-1.5	8.8	.2	12.0
Bos	98	64	0	.605	3	**949**	768	222	**.282**	**.360**	**.472**	**832**	109	106	68	4	**159**	447	1132	**12.2**	4.18	**117**	**.255**	**.318**	-.5	**10.1**	8.5	-.1	-1.0
Bal	78	84	0	.481	23	842	830	169	.281	.345	.432	777	102	99	101	8	**159**	687	1090	13.8	4.70	99	.264	.348	-.0	-.7	2.8	.2	-5.4
TB	70	91	0	.435	30.5	714	842	145	.258	.320	.405	725	90	98	132	3	192	580	923	13.5	4.81	97	.265	.342	-.6	-2.2	-7.7	.8	-.8
Tor	67	94	0	.416	33.5	719	823	145	.260	.328	.403	731	84	106	58	6	181	608	956	13.8	4.91	100	.273	.348	1.0	-.3	-11.0	-.3	-2.9
Central																													
Min	92	70	0	.568		780	**715**	191	.266	.332	.431	763	95	103	116	4	167	**431**	1123	**12.2**	**4.03**	115	.267	.323	.5	9.2	-3.9	.3	4.9
Chi	83	79	0	.512	9	865	831	**242**	.268	.333	.457	790	100	103	78	8	224	527	1013	13.1	4.91	96	.272	.338	.5	-3.2	.0	-.6	5.2
Cle	80	82	0	.494	12	858	857	184	.276	.351	.444	795	**110**	96	94	8	201	579	1115	13.5	4.81	90	.271	.342	.2	-7.7	**9.3**	-.4	-2.3
Det	72	90	0	.444	20	827	844	201	.272	.337	.449	786	107	96	86	7	190	530	995	13.3	4.93	91	.275	.340	-2.0	-7.1	5.2	-.4	-4.7
KC	58	104	0	.358	34	720	905	150	.259	.322	.397	719	86	-100	67	6	208	518	887	14.0	5.15	90	.290	.352	-1.3	-7.4	-10.2	-.7	-3.5
West																													
Ana	92	70	0	.568		836	734	162	**.282**	.341	.429	770	103	96	**143**	2	170	502	**1164**	12.5	4.28	104	.263	.326	**1.1**	2.8	2.9	**.9**	3.2
Oak	91	71	0	.562	1	793	742	189	.270	.343	.433	776	102	99	47	**10**	164	544	1034	12.7	4.17	111	.262	.332	**1.1**	6.9	2.5	-.2	-.3
Tex	89	73	0	.549	3	860	794	227	.266	.329	.457	786	98	104	69	5	182	547	979	13.5	4.53	109	.273	.344	-.5	5.7	-1.0	-.2	4.1
Sea	63	99	0	.389	29	698	823	136	.270	.331	.396	727	94	95	110	7	212	575	1036	13.2	4.76	94	.265	.338	.4	-4.7	-4.7	.4	-9.4
Total	1133					61358		2605	.270	.338	.433	771			1253	79				13.1	4.63		.270	.338					

Batter-Fielder Wins	Batting Average	On-Base Percentage	Slugging Average	On-Base Plus Slugging	Adjusted OPS	Adjusted Batter Runs
Tejada-Bal............. 6.6	Suzuki-Sea .... .372	Mora-Bal............... .419	Ramirez-Bos......... .613	Ramirez-Bos........ 1009	Hafner-Cle 162	Guerrero-Ana........ 54.3
Rodriguez-NY........ 2.9	Matsui-NY............. .298	Posada-NY .... .400	Sheffield-NY .... .534	Sheffield-NY 927	Sheffield-NY 140	Sheffield-NY 36.8
Posada-NY............ 2.8	Jeter-NY .... .292	Sheffield-NY .... .393	Matsui-NY............. .522	Matsui-NY.............. 912	Matsui-NY.............. 136	Matsui-NY............. 33.2
Sheffield-NY 2.7	Sheffield-NY .... .290	Matsui-NY............. .390	Rodriguez-NY....... .512	Rodriguez-NY........ 888	2 players tied 129	Rodriguez-NY....... 27.1

Runs	Hits	Doubles	Triples	Home Runs	Total Bases	Runs Batted In
Guerrero-Ana......... 124	Suzuki-Sea 262	Roberts-Bal............. 50	Crawford-TB 19	Ramirez-Bos............ 43	Guerrero-Ana.......... 366	Tejada-Bal.............. 150
Sheffield-NY 117	Jeter-NY 188	Jeter-NY.................. 44	Lofton-NY.................. 7	Sheffield-NY............ 36	Rodriguez-NY........ 308	Sheffield-NY 121
Rodriguez-NY 112	Matsui-NY............. 174	Matsui-NY................ 34	Cairo-NY.................... 5	Rodriguez-NY 36	Sheffield-NY 306	Matsui-NY.............. 108
Jeter-NY 111	Rodriguez-NY 172	Posada-NY 31	2 players tied 2	Matsui-NY................ 31	Matsui-NY.............. 305	Rodriguez-NY........ 106

Stolen Bases	Base Stealing Runs	Fielding Runs-Infield	Fielding Runs-Outfield	Wins	Winning Pct.	Complete Games
Crawford-TB 59	Crawford-TB 7.7	Hudson-Tor........... 33.2	Baldelli-TB 10.0	Schilling-Bos............ 21	Schilling-Bos......... .778	3 players tied 5
Rodriguez-NY.......... 28	Rodriguez-NY......... 4.8		Sheffield-NY 1.1	Vazquez-NY............. 14		Mussina-NY................ 1
Jeter-NY 23	Jeter-NY 3.7			Lieber-NY 14		
Cairo-NY...................11	Cairo-NY................. 1.4			Mussina-NY.............. 12		

Strikeouts	Fewest BB/Game	Games	Saves	Base Runners/9	Adjusted Relief Runs	Relief Ranking
Santana-Min 265	Lieber-NY .... .92	Quantrill-NY............. 86	Rivera-NY................. 53	Gordon-NY 8.03	Gordon-NY 24.3	Rivera-NY............. 47.4
Vazquez-NY........... 150	Mussina-NY.......... 2.19	Gordon-NY 80	Gordon-NY 4	Rivera-NY........... 10.30	Rivera-NY............. 24.0	Gordon-NY 33.8
Mussina-NY........... 132	Vazquez-NY.......... 2.73	Rivera-NY................ 74	Sturtze-NY.................. 1	Brown-NY 11.59		
Lieber-NY 102		Heredia-NY.............. 47	Quantrill-NY............... 1	2 players tied 12.02		

Innings Pitched	Opponents' Avg.	Opponents' OBP	Earned Run Average	Adjusted ERA	Adjusted Starter Runs	Pitcher Wins
Buehrle-Chi......... 245.1	Santana-Min .... .192	Santana-Min .... .249	Santana-Min 2.61	Santana-Min 178	Santana-Min 51.9	Santana-Min 5.6
Vazquez-NY........ 198.0	Vazquez-NY.......... .255	Vazquez-NY.......... .315	Lieber-NY 4.33	Lieber-NY 106	Hernandez-NY...... 13.4	Rivera-NY............... 4.9
Lieber-NY 176.2	Mussina-NY.......... .276	Lieber-NY .... .316	Mussina-NY.......... 4.59	Mussina-NY........... 100	Brown-NY 7.2	Gordon-NY 3.3
Mussina-NY........ 164.2	Lieber-NY .... .300	Mussina-NY.......... .318	Vazquez-NY.......... 4.91	Vazquez-NY............ 94	Lieber-NY 3.5	Hernandez-NY........ 1.4

2005 American League

TEAM	W	L	T	PCT	GB	R	OR	HR	AVG	OBP	SLG	OPS	AOPS	PF	SB	CG	HR	BB	SO	BR/9	ERA	AERA	OAV	OOB	FW	PW	BW	BSW	DIF
East																													
NY	95	67	0	.586		886	789	229	.276	.355	.450	805	**114**	99	84	8	164	463	985	12.8	4.52	95	.269	.332	.5	-3.6	**11.9**	.3	4.9
Bos	95	67	0	.586		**910**	805	199	**.281**	**.357**	.454	**811**	109	104	45	6	164	440	959	13.1	4.74	96	.276	.335	-.4	-3.1	9.8	-.0	7.8
Tor	80	82	0	.494	15	775	705	136	.265	.331	.407	738	90	105	72	**9**	185	444	958	12.4	4.06	113	.264	.324	.5	7.6	-5.9	-.2	-3.0
Bal	74	88	0	.457	21	729	800	189	.269	.327	.434	761	101	100	83	2	180	580	1052	13.2	4.56	96	.263	.336	-.3	-2.6	.9	-.1	-4.8
TB	67	95	0	.414	28	750	936	157	.274	.329	.425	754	101	98	151	1	194	615	949	14.2	5.39	81	.280	.355	-1.5	-15.1	.9	**.9**	.8
Central																													
Chi	99	63	0	.611		741	645	200	.262	.322	.425	747	93	104	137	**9**	167	459	1040	11.6	**3.61**	**125**	.249	.310	.6	**13.7**	-4.8	.0	8.4
Cle	93	69	0	.574	6	790	**642**	207	.271	.334	.453	787	111	97	62	6	157	413	1050	**11.3**	**3.61**	115	.247	**.302**	-.2	8.9	9.2	-.5	-5.3
Min	83	79	0	.512	16	688	662	134	.259	.323	.391	714	88	102	102	**9**	169	**348**	965	11.4	3.71	118	.261	.307	.0	10.3	-8.9	.0	.5
Det	71	91	0	.438	28	723	787	168	.272	.321	.428	749	99	98	66	7	193	461	907	12.6	4.51	95	.272	.330	-.5	-3.8	-.8	-.1	-4.8
KC	56	106	0	.346	43	701	935	126	.263	.320	.396	716	92	97	53	4	178	580	924	14.6	5.49	80	.291	.362	-1.6	-16.9	-5.2	-.6	-.7
West																													
LA	95	67	0	.586		761	643	147	.270	.325	.409	734	97	97	**161**	7	158	443	**1126**	11.7	3.68	116	.254	.312	1.1	9.5	-2.5	.8	5.1
Oak	88	74	0	.543	7	772	658	155	.262	.330	.407	737	96	99	31	**9**	**154**	504	1075	11.7	3.69	119	**.241**	.311	1.0	10.5	-2.1	-.7	-1.7
Tex	79	83	0	.488	16	865	858	**260**	.267	.329	**.468**	797	106	103	67	2	159	522	932	13.6	4.96	92	.279	.343	-.4	-6.2	4.9	.3	-.6
Sea	69	93	0	.426	26	699	751	130	.256	.317	.391	708	94	93	102	6	179	496	892	12.8	4.49	93	.268	.332	**1.2**	-5.2	-4.2	-.0	-3.7
Total	1134					60790		2437	.268	.330	.424	755			1216	85				12.6	4.35		.268	.330					

Batter-Fielder Wins
A.Rodriguez-NY 6.0
Jeter-NY 4.5
Giambi-NY 2.4
Sheffield-NY 2.1

Batting Average
M.Young-Tex......... .331
A.Rodriguez-NY.... .321
Jeter-NY .... .309
Matsui-NY............. .305

On-Base Percentage
Giambi-NY............ .440
A.Rodriguez-NY.... .421
Jeter-NY .... .389
Sheffield-NY .... .379

Slugging Average
A.Rodriguez-NY.... .610
Giambi-NY............ .535
Sheffield-NY .... .512
Matsui-NY............. .496

On-Base Plus Slugging
A.Rodriguez-NY... 1031
Giambi-NY............ 975
Sheffield-NY 891
Matsui-NY.............. 863

Adjusted OPS
A.Rodriguez-NY..... 171
Giambi-NY............. 159
Sheffield-NY 136
Matsui-NY.............. 129

Adjusted Batter Runs
A.Rodriguez-NY.... 65.5
Giambi-NY............ 43.4
Sheffield-NY 31.9
Matsui-NY.............. 27.3

Runs
A.Rodriguez-NY..... 124
Jeter-NY 122
Matsui-NY.............. 108
Sheffield-NY 104

Hits
M.Young-Tex.......... 221
Jeter-NY 202
A.Rodriguez-NY..... 194
Matsui-NY.............. 192

Doubles
Tejada-Bal............... 50
Matsui-NY............... 45
Cano-NY.................. 34
A.Rodriguez-NY....... 29

Triples
Crawford-TB 15
Jeter-NY 5
Cano-NY.................... 4
Matsui-NY.................. 3

Home Runs
A.Rodriguez-NY....... 48
Sheffield-NY 34
Giambi-NY............... 32
Matsui-NY................ 23

Total Bases
Teixeira-Tex 370
A.Rodriguez-NY..... 369
Matsui-NY.............. 312
Sheffield-NY 299

Runs Batted In
Ortiz-Bos................ 148
A.Rodriguez-NY..... 130
Sheffield-NY 123
Matsui-NY...............116

Stolen Bases
Figgins-LA............... 62
Womack-NY 27
A.Rodriguez-NY....... 21
Jeter-NY 14

Base Stealing Runs
Figgins-Ala............. 7.7
Womack-NY 4.2
A.Rodriguez-NY...... 2.5
Sheffield-NY 1.5

Fielding Runs-Infield
Hudson-Tor........... 28.3
Jeter-NY 9.4
Cano-NY.................. 4.4

Fielding Runs-Outfield
Suzuki-Sea 12.8

Wins
Colon-Ala................. 21
R.Johnson-NY 17
Mussina-NY............. 13
Small-NY 10

Winning Pct.
Lee-Cle................. .783
R.Johnson-NY ...... .680

Complete Games
Halladay-Tor 5
R.Johnson-NY 4
Mussina-NY............... 2
2 players tied 1

Strikeouts
Santana-Min 238
R.Johnson-NY 211
Mussina-NY........... 142
Rivera-NY................ 80

Fewest BB/Game
Silva-Min.................. .43
R.Johnson-NY 1.87
Mussina-NY.......... 2.35

Games
Timlin-Bos................ 81
Gordon-NY 79
Rivera-NY................ 71
Sturtze-NY............... 64

Saves
Wickman-Cle 45
Rodriguez-LA.......... 45
Rivera-NY............... 43
Gordon-NY 2

Base Runners/9
Howry-Cle............. 8.01
Rivera-NY.............. 8.27
Gordon-NY 9.82
R.Johnson-NY 10.61

Adjusted Relief Runs
Rivera-NY............ 23.5
Gordon-NY 16.8

Relief Ranking
Rivera-NY............ 47.1
Gordon-NY 16.6

Innings Pitched
Buehrle-Chi......... 236.2
R.Johnson-NY 225.2
Mussina-NY........ 179.2
Wang-NY 116.1

Opponents' Avg.
Santana-Min .... .210
R.Johnson-NY ...... .243
Mussina-NY .... .283

Opponents' OBP
Santana-Min .... .250
R.Johnson-NY .... .291
Mussina-NY .... .333

Earned Run Average
Millwood-Cle 2.86
R.Johnson-NY 3.79
Mussina-NY.......... 4.41

Adjusted ERA
Santana-Min 152
R.Johnson-NY 113
Mussina-NY............. 98

Adjusted Starter Runs
Santana-Min 40.4
R.Johnson-NY 13.9
Chacon-NY........... 13.6
Small-NY 10.6

Pitcher Wins
Rivera-NY............... 4.9
Gordon-NY 1.7
Chacon-NY.............. 1.6
R.Johnson-NY 1.3

2006 American League

TEAM	W	L	T	PCT	GB	R	OR	HR	AVG	OBP	SLG	OPS	AOPS	PF	SB	CG	HR	BB	SO	BR/9	ERA	AERA	OAV	OOB	FW	PW	BW	BSW	DIF
East																													
NY	97	65	0	.599		**930**	767	210	.285	**.363**	.461	**824**	**+10**	102	139	5	170	496	1019	12.6	4.41	+4	.262	.326	-.4	2.9	**9.5**	**1.0**	3.0
Tor	87	75	0	.537	10	809	754	199	.284	.348	.463	811	+5	103	65	6	185	504	1076	12.7	4.37	+7	.262	.328	-.0	4.4	5.0	-.4	-3.0
Bos	86	76	0	.531	11	820	825	192	.269	.351	.435	786	-3	105	51	3	181	509	1070	13.4	4.83	-1	.278	.343	**2.4**	-.7	-.2	-.4	3.9
Bal	70	92	0	.432	27	768	899	164	.277	.339	.424	763	-3	99	121	5	216	613	1016	14.2	5.35	-13	.284	.357	-.3	-10.6	-1.7	.7	.8
TB	61	101	0	.377	36	689	856	190	.255	.314	.420	734	-10	-97	134	3	180	606	979	14.4	4.96	-7	.286	.358	-1.3	-5.1	-8.3	.4	-5.6
Central																													
Min	96	66	0	.593		801	683	143	**.287**	.347	.425	772	+1	99	101	1	182	**356**	**1164**	**11.8**	3.95	+14	.267	**.312**	1.1	8.4	.9	.0	4.6
Det	95	67	0	.586	1	822	**675**	203	.274	.329	.449	778	+0	99	60	3	160	489	1003	12.2	**3.84**	**+18**	.257	.321	-.6	**10.5**	-1.0	-.8	5.9
Chi	90	72	0	.556	6	868	794	**236**	.280	.342	**.464**	806	+4	102	93	5	200	433	1012	12.6	4.61	+2	.271	.326	.6	1.4	3.3	-.3	4.0
Cle	78	84	0	.481	18	870	782	196	.280	.349	.457	806	+7	100	55	**13**	166	429	948	13.0	4.41	+2	.282	.335	-1.4	1.5	5.9	-.3	-8.6
KC	62	100	0	.383	34	757	971	124	.271	.332	.411	743	-8	99	65	3	213	637	904	14.8	5.65	-17	.292	.367	.0	-14.1	-5.7	-.5	1.2
West																													
Oak	93	69	0	.574		771	727	175	.260	.340	.412	752	-2	96	61	5	162	529	1003	13.1	4.21	+5	.272	.338	1.1	3.4	-.5	-.1	8.1
LA	89	73	0	.549	4	766	732	159	.274	.334	.425	759	-5	100	**148**	5	**158**	471	**1164**	12.0	4.04	+13	**.254**	.316	-1.9	8.0	-3.3	.6	4.6
Tex	80	82	0	.494	13	835	784	183	.278	.338	.446	784	+2	99	53	3	162	496	972	13.3	4.60	+0	.278	.341	.0	.0	2.2	-.4	-2.9
Sea	78	84	0	.481	15	756	792	172	.272	.325	.424	749	-3	95	106	6	183	560	1067	13.1	4.60	-4	.267	.337	.8	-2.8	-2.8	.3	1.6
Total	1134					11262		2546	.275	.339	.437	776			1252	66		7128	4397	13.1	4.56		.275	.339					

Batter-Fielder Wins
Mauer-Min............. 5.1
Posada-NY............ 3.3
Jeter-NY................ 2.6
Cano-NY 2.1

Batting Average
Mauer-Min .... .347
Jeter-NY .... .343
Cano-NY............... .342
Rodriguez-NY....... .290

On-Base Percentage
Ramirez-Bos......... .439
Hafner-Cle .... .439
Jeter-NY .... .417
Giambi-NY............ .413

Slugging Average
Hafner-Cle .... .659
Giambi-NY............ .558
Cano-NY............... .525
Rodriguez-NY....... .523

On-Base Plus Slugging
Hafner-Cle 1097
Giambi-NY............. 971
Rodriguez-NY........ 914
Jeter-NY 900

Adjusted OPS
Hafner-Cle 178
Giambi-NY............. 147
Rodriguez-NY........ 132
Jeter-NY 130

Adjusted Batter Runs
Hafner-Cle 58.0
Giambi-NY............ 36.8
Jeter-NY 32.0
Rodriguez-NY....... 29.6

Runs
Sizemore-Cle......... 134
Jeter-NY 118
Damon-NY.............115
Rodriguez-NY.........113

Hits
Suzuki-Sea 224
Jeter-NY 214
Damon-NY............. 169
Rodriguez-NY........ 166

Doubles
Sizemore-Cle........... 53
Cano-NY.................. 41
Jeter-NY 39
Damon-NY............... 35

Triples
Crawford-TB 16
Damon-NY................. 5
3 players tied 3

Home Runs
Ortiz-Bos.................. 54
Giambi-NY............... 37
Rodriguez-NY........... 35
Damon-NY............... 24

Total Bases
Ortiz-Bos................ 355
Jeter-NY 301
Rodriguez-NY........ 299
Damon-NY............. 286

Runs Batted In
Ortiz-Bos................ 137
Rodriguez-NY......... 121
Giambi-NY.............113
Jeter-NY 97

Stolen Bases
Crawford-TB 58
Jeter-NY 34
Damon-NY............... 25
Rodriguez-NY.......... 15

Base Stealing Runs
Crawford-TB 9.6
Jeter-NY 5.7
Cairo-NY................. 2.5
Damon-NY.............. 2.0

Fielding Runs-Infield
Inge-Det................ 24.7

Fielding Runs-Outfield
Markakis-Bal........... 8.3
Cabrera-NY 2.6

Wins
Santana-Min 19
Wang-NY 19
Johnson-NY............. 17
Mussina-NY............. 15

Winning Pct.
Halladay-Tor .... .762
Wang-NY............... .760
Mussina-NY........... .682
Johnson-NY.......... .607

Complete Games
Sabathia-Cle............. 6
Wang-NY................... 2
Johnson-NY............... 2
Mussina-NY............... 1

Strikeouts
Santana-Min 245
Mussina-NY........... 172
Johnson-NY........... 172
Proctor-NY............... 89

Fewest BB/Game
Schilling-Bos......... 1.24
Mussina-NY.......... 1.60
Wang-NY 2.15
Johnson-NY.......... 2.63

Games
Proctor-NY.............. 83
Farnsworth-NY 72
Villone-NY............... 70
Rivera-NY................ 63

Saves
Rodriguez-LA........... 47
Rivera-NY 34
Farnsworth-NY 6
3 players tied 1

Base Runners/9
Papelbon-Bos........7.11
Rivera-NY............. 9.24
Mussina-NY........ 10.22
Proctor-NY.......... 10.91

Adjusted Relief Runs
Papelbon-Bos....... 27.7
Rivera-NY............ 23.3
Proctor-NY........... 13.4
Farnsworth-NY 2.1

Relief Ranking
Papelbon-Bos....... 47.4
Rivera-NY............ 46.6
Proctor-NY........... 12.0
Farnsworth-NY 2.9

Innings Pitched
Santana-Min 233.2
Wang-NY 218.0
Johnson-NY........ 205.0
Mussina-NY........ 197.1

Opponents' Avg.
Santana-Min .... .216
Mussina-NY .... .241
Johnson-NY .... .250
Wang-NY .... .277

Opponents' OBP
Santana-Min .... .258
Mussina-NY .... .279
Johnson-NY .... .309
Wang-NY .... .320

Earned Run Average
Santana-Min 2.77
Mussina-NY.......... 3.51
Wang-NY 3.63
Johnson-NY.......... 5.00

Adjusted ERA
Santana-Min 163
Mussina-NY............ 132
Wang-NY 127
Johnson-NY............. 92

Adjusted Starter Runs
Santana-Min 45.1
Wang-NY 25.0
Mussina-NY.......... 21.8
Karstens-NY 3.6

Pitcher Wins
Rivera-NY............... 4.7
Wang-NY 2.7
Mussina-NY............ 2.1
Proctor-NY............. 1.1

2007 American League

TEAM	W	L	T	PCT	GB	R	OR	HR	AVG	OBP	SLG	OPS	AOPS	PF	SB	CG	HR	BB	SO	BR/9	ERA	AERA	OAV	OOB	FW	PW	BW	BSW	DIF
East																													
Bos	96	66	0	.593		867	**657**	166	.279	.362	.444	806	+5	106	96	5	151	482	1149	**11.8**	**3.87**	**+23**	**.247**	**.314**	1.2	**13.0**	6.2	.4	-5.7
NY	94	68	0	.580	2	**968**	777	**201**	**.290**	**.366**	**.463**	**829**	**+16**	101	123	1	150	578	1009	13.3	4.49	+0	.268	.340	.7	.2	**13.8**	.4	-2.1
Tor	83	79	0	.512	13	753	699	165	.259	.327	.419	746	-6	102	57	**11**	157	479	1067	11.9	4.00	+15	.251	.315	-.3	9.1	-4.4	-.4	-2.0
Bal	69	93	0	.426	27	756	868	142	.272	.333	.412	745	-6	101	**144**	4	161	696	1087	14.1	5.17	-10	.268	.354	**1.3**	-7.7	3.6	**.0**	2.0
TB	66	96	0	.407	30	782	944	187	.268	.336	.433	769	+4	97	131	2	199	**568**	**1104**	14.4	5.53	-18	.290	.358	-1.3	-14.9	3.2	.3	-2.3
Central																													
Cle	96	66	0	.593		811	704	178	.268	.343	.428	771	-1	103	72	9	146	**410**	1047	12.2	4.05	+14	.268	.322	.4	8.9	.2	-.8	6.3
Det	88	74	0	.543	8	887	797	177	.287	.345	.458	803	+9	101	103	1	174	566	1047	13.3	4.57	-1	.266	.338	-.0	-.4	6.8	.3	.4
Min	79	83	0	.488	17	718	725	118	.264	.330	.391	721	-9	98	112	5	185	420	1094	12.4	4.15	+7	.269	.324	.2	4.3	-6.3	.5	-.7
Chi	72	90	0	.444	24	693	839	190	.246	.318	.404	722	-13	102	78	9	174	499	1015	13.2	4.77	-1	.276	.338	-.7	-.9	-10.2	-.8	3.5
KC	69	93	0	.426	27	706	778	102	.261	.322	.388	710	-16	-102	78	2	168	520	993	13.2	4.48	+6	.276	.339	-.6	4.0	-11.5	-.7	-3.3
West																													
LA	94	68	0	.580		822	731	123	.284	.345	.417	762	-1	101	139	5	151	477	1156	12.6	4.23	+8	.266	.327	-.2	5.0	.5	.2	7.6
Sea	88	74	0	.543	6	794	813	153	.287	.337	.425	762	+5	94	81	6	147	546	1020	13.7	4.73	-9	.281	.349	.6	-6.5	4.0	-.2	9.1
Oak	76	86	0	.469	18	741	758	171	.256	.338	.407	745	+1	94	52	4	**138**	530	1036	12.7	4.28	+0	.263	.329	.6	-.4	3.0	-.5	-7.7
Tex	75	87	0	.463	19	816	844	179	.263	.328	.426	754	-2	99	88	0	155	668	976	14.2	4.75	-5	.274	.356	-1.8	-3.5	-1.6	.2	.8
Total	1134					11114		2252	.271	.338	.423	761			1354	64		7439	4890	13.1	4.50		.271	.338					

Batter-Fielder Wins
- **Pena-TB 5.9**
- **Rodriguez-NY 5.2**
- **Posada-NY 4.1**
- **Cano-NY 3.1**

Batting Average
- Ordonez-Det .... .363
- Posada-NY .... .338
- Jeter-NY .... .322
- Rodriguez-NY .... .314

On-Base Percentage
- Ortiz-Bos .... .445
- Posada-NY .... .426
- Rodriguez-NY .... .422
- Jeter-NY .... .388

Slugging Average
- Rodriguez-NY .... .645
- Posada-NY .... .543
- Matsui-NY .... .488
- Cano-NY .... .488

On-Base Plus Slugging
- Rodriguez-NY 1067
- Posada-NY 970
- Matsui-NY 855
- Cano-NY 841

Adjusted OPS
- Rodriguez-NY 175
- Posada-NY 152
- Matsui-NY 123
- Jeter-NY 119

Adjusted Batter Runs
- Rodriguez-NY 67.4
- Posada-NY 42.4
- Jeter-NY 20.1
- Matsui-NY 18.9

Runs
- Rodriguez-NY 143
- Abreu-NY 123
- Jeter-NY 102
- Matsui-NY 100

Hits
- Suzuki-Sea 238
- Jeter-NY 206
- Cano-NY 189
- Rodriguez-NY 183

Doubles
- Ordonez-Det 54
- Posada-NY 42
- Cano-NY 41
- Abreu-NY 40

Triples
- Granderson-Det 23
- Cabrera-NY 8
- Cano-NY 7
- Abreu-NY 5

Home Runs
- Rodriguez-NY 54
- Matsui-NY 25
- Posada-NY 20
- Cano-NY 19

Total Bases
- Rodriguez-NY 376
- Cano-NY 301
- Jeter-NY 289
- Posada-NY 275

Runs Batted In
- Rodriguez-NY 156
- Matsui-NY 103
- Abreu-NY 101
- Cano-NY 97

Stolen Bases
- Roberts-Bal 50
- Crawford-TB 50
- Damon-NY 27
- Abreu-NY 25

Base Stealing Runs
- Roberts-Bal 8.6
- Damon-NY 4.9
- Rodriguez-NY 3.9
- Abreu-NY 2.7

Fielding Runs-Infield
- Ellis-Oak 24.9
- Cano-NY 10.9

Fielding Runs-Outfield
- Teahen-KC 18.1
- Cabrera-NY 9.1

Wins
- Beckett-Bos 20
- Wang-NY 19
- Pettitte-NY 15
- Mussina-NY 11

Winning Pct.
- Verlander-Det .... .750
- Wang-NY .... .731
- Pettitte-NY .... .625

Complete Games
- Halladay-Tor 7
- Wang-NY 1

Strikeouts
- Kazmir-TB 239
- Pettitte-NY 141
- Wang-NY 104
- Mussina-NY 91

Fewest BB/Game
- Byrd-Cle 1.31
- Wang-NY 2.66
- Pettitte-NY 2.88

Games
- Walker-Bal 81
- Downs-Tor 81
- Vizcaino-NY 77
- Rivera-NY 67

Saves
- Borowski-Cle 45
- Rivera-NY 30
- Veras-NY 2
- 2 players tied 1

Base Runners/9
- Putz-Sea 6.53
- Rivera-NY 10.85
- Hughes-NY 11.77
- Wang-NY 12.01

Adjusted Relief Runs
- Betancourt-Cle 27.6
- Rivera-NY 11.6
- Proctor-NY 3.2
- Vizcaino-NY 2.5

Relief Ranking
- Putz-Sea 47.7
- Rivera-NY 19.4
- Proctor-NY 3.7
- Vizcaino-NY 3.0

Innings Pitched
- Sabathia-Cle 241.0
- Pettitte-NY 215.1
- Wang-NY 199.1
- Mussina-NY 152.0

Opponents' Avg.
- Bedard-Bal .... .212
- Wang-NY .... .265
- Pettitte-NY .... .286

Opponents' OBP
- Santana-Min .... .273
- Wang-NY .... .324
- Pettitte-NY .... .338

Earned Run Average
- Lackey-LA 3.01
- Wang-NY 3.70
- Pettitte-NY 4.05

Adjusted ERA
- Carmona-Cle 152
- Lackey-LA 152
- Wang-NY 122
- Pettitte-NY 111

Adjusted Starter Runs
- Carmona-Cle 36.9
- Wang-NY 19.8
- Pettitte-NY 10.1
- Kennedy-NY 4.7

Pitcher Wins
- Putz-Sea 4.7
- Wang-NY 2.4
- Rivera-NY 1.9
- Pettitte-NY 1.0

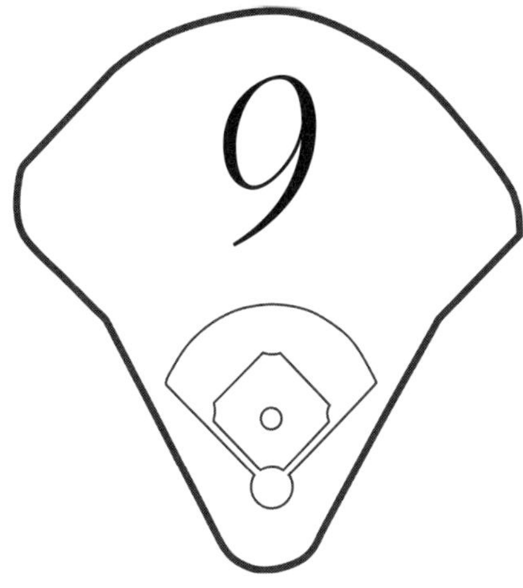

The Postseason

Most major league baseball teams start off the season with their sights set on making it to the postseason. The New York Yankees, on the other hand, start each season confident in the knowledge that they will be playing in the postseason—simply making it to October isn't enough for the Yankees. A season in which the Yankees do not win the World Series is deemed a failure by Yankees ownership as well as the team's media and fans.

This attitude may be considered arrogant by some, but it is not irrational by any means. The Yankees have been by far baseball's most successful franchise since 1921. The Bronx Bombers have gone on to play postseason baseball in 47 of 87 seasons since then. And in those 47 postseason appearances, the Yankees have carried home the world championship 26 times. No other team in the majors has won more than 10 world championships.

The New York franchise in the American League was not always so successful, however. In the franchise's first 18 years, the team known as the Highlanders through 1912 and the Yankees thereafter didn't make it to the Fall Classic at all. Moreover, 13 of the 15 other major league franchises in existence when the first World Series was staged in 1903 made their way to that premier event before the Yankees did.

The Yankees' transformation from also-rans into the dominant team in baseball came after the sale of the team in 1915. Co-owner Jacob Ruppert took a floundering franchise that had been run crookedly and incompetently by previous owners and made numerous upgrades. By 1919, the Yankees had the manager Ruppert wanted in Miller Huggins, and New York finished that season with its best winning percentage since 1912. In 1920, the Yankees acquired the final two major elements in their turnaround with the purchase of Babe Ruth from the Red Sox in January and the hiring of Ed Barrow in May. The acquisition of Ruth transformed not only the Yankees but also the whole sport, while Barrow spent the next 25 years building and running an efficient organization that was designed for winning.

The Yankees won their first AL pennant in 1921 but were beaten by their landlords in the Polo Grounds, the Giants, five games to three with one tie. The Yankees and Giants again met in the World Series in 1922, and this time the Giants swept the Yankees. In 1923, though, things turned out differently, as the Yankees now had their own stadium in the Bronx across the Harlem River from the Polo Grounds. The Yankees again met the Giants in the World Series, and this time Babe Ruth stepped up with a remarkable performance, slugging 1.000 and reaching base more than half the time as he led the Yankees to their first world championship.

The Yankees finished second in 1924 and then stumbled all the way to seventh place in 1925. However, '25 was also the year that longtime Yankees first baseman Wally Pipp was replaced in the lineup by a young slugger named Lou Gehrig. In 1926, the Yankees made it to the World Series again, losing in seven games to the Cardinals. There was no stopping the 1927 Yankees, however—this most famous of all Yankees teams, featuring the legendary Murderer's Row. Called by many the greatest team of all-time, New York ran away with the AL pennant by winning 110 games, then swept the Pirates in the World Series. The 1928 Yankees faced much tougher competition for the AL pennant, but the World Series against the Cardinals that fall was one of the most lopsided in baseball history. The Yankees swept the Series, outscoring the Cardinals 27-to-10 in four games, with Gehrig slugging four homers and Ruth hammering three.

That spelled the end of the Yankees' first dynasty, however. New York would make it back to the World Series only once in the following seven seasons, when they swept the Cubs in 1932—the year that the Babe *might* have called his famous home run at Wrigley Field. During the first few years of this drought, the offense continued to produce but the pitching was, at best, erratic. In the mid-1930s, however, Ruth's age finally caught up with him and it was the offense that slipped.

In 1936, Ruth was gone and one of the most hyped rookies in baseball history, Joe DiMaggio, arrived to quickly prove himself worthy of the build-up. The addition of DiMaggio, combined with another typical Gehrig year, Bill Dickey's career year, and a deep starting rotation, propelled the Yankees to another World Series. There, facing the crosstown rival Giants for the first time since 1923, the Bombers won in six games, marking the start of another Yankees dynasty. The Yankees made it to the World Series in seven of the eight seasons between 1936 and 1943, emerging victorious six times. These Yankee teams were somewhat different from those of the first dynasty, however. While they were great offensive teams—with Joe DiMaggio and Charlie Keller playing starring roles—they had equally great pitching staffs, usually anchored by Lefty Gomez and Red Ruffing. Rather than bombing the opposition into submission, as many of Ruth's great teams did, these teams were just as good at preventing runs as scoring them. In six of these eight seasons, the Yankees led the AL in both ERA and runs.

The Yankees faced five different NL teams in their seven World Series of this era: the Giants, the Cubs, the Cardinals, the Reds and—in the first of many October meetings—the Brooklyn Dodgers. Only in 1942 (when the Yankees lost to the Cardinals in five games) and in 1936 (when the Yankees beat the Giants in six) did the Yankees' opponents win more than one game. New York's world championships of this era were truly team victories, achieved with contributions from many different Yankees, and there were few spectacular performances by individual Yankees. The most valuable Yankees postseason player of this era was undoubtedly pitcher Red Ruffing, who pitched 76⅔ innings in these series while compiling a sub-3.00 ERA and also occasionally rapping a key hit while at bat.

World War II ended the second Yankees dynasty, but only a few years would pass before New York began its third and longest dynasty. Between 1947 and 1964, the Yankees managed to pound their way to an astonishing 15 World Series in 18 years. The Yankees won the first six October Classics that they played in during this era but, as the National League became far more competitive as a result of integration, it defeated the Yankees in five of their nine Series between 1955 and 1964. In the first part of this era, the Yankees successfully transitioned from one offensive core to another. The 1946 Yankees' team featured DiMaggio, Joe Gordon, Snuffy Stirnweiss, Charlie Keller, and Tommy Henrich in major roles and Bill Dickey in a minor one. The only player on that list that also played for the 1952 Yanks was Keller, who had one lone at bat. By the time 1952 arrived, the Yankees' offensive core consisted of Mickey Mantle, Yogi Berra, Hank Bauer, Gene Woodling, and Gil McDougald. The story was similar on the mound, as the only pitcher from the 1946 club that was left by 1952 was Vic Raschi, and Raschi had pitched only 16 major league innings in his debut season in '46.

While the Yankees did more winning during this period, the team's road to victory was usually more difficult than previously. The Yankees won the 1947 AL race by 12 games, but they would never again win an AL pennant by so large a margin, finishing first by a margin of five games or less in 1949, 1950, 1951, 1952, 1955, 1959, 1962, and 1964. New York's World Series victories of this era were similarly tougher than those of the earlier Yankees' dynasties. Only one of the Yankees' 11 world championships in this era came as a sweep, and that was against the all-white 1950 Philadelphia Phillies, playing in the World Series for only the second time in their history. And all but two of the other World Series won by New York went at least six games.

The Yankees' starting pitching was the key to the club's postseason triumphs in this era. Numerous starters—including Bob Turley, Ed Lopat, Vic Raschi, Allie Reynolds, and Ralph Terry—posted strong postseason records. The most valuable Yankees player in these years, however, was undoubtedly Whitey Ford. Between 1950 and 1964, Ford threw 146 innings of World Series ball, posting an ERA of only 2.71, including the 31 consecutive scoreless innings Ford threw primarily in 1960 and 1961. Ford's pitching garnered him many World Series records, many of which may never be seriously challenged.

The Yankees fell apart after 1964, though, failing to return to the postseason until 1976. During those 12 years on the outside, both the Yankees' organization and the game itself had changed dramatically. The Yankees now had an owner in George Steinbrenner with a voracious desire to win. More importantly, Steinbrenner was willing to spend a lot to win—sometimes wisely, sometimes not. Meanwhile, baseball saw the advent of both free agency and a new postseason series, the League Championship Series.

Several trades by Yankees GM Gabe Paul helped strengthen New York enough to earn them their first postseason berth in 12 years in 1976, when the Yanks won their first LCS against the Royals before being swept by Cincinnati's Big Red Machine. Yankees owner George Steinbrenner was very unhappy with the result, so he signed free agent slugger Reggie Jackson that winter to bring additional spark to the team's offense. In a memorable and contentious year, Reggie helped lead the Yankees to a world championship in 1977, blasting three homers in the final game. The Yankees won another World Series (after defeating the Royals in the ALCS for the third consecutive year) in 1978. New York fell short in 1979, but returned to its winning ways in 1980 by capturing the AL East before finally losing a League Championship Series to the Royals. In 1981, the Yankees returned to the postseason for the fifth time in six years, this time forced to win two postseason series (in an ad hoc system set up for that year only because of the midsummer strike) before losing to the Los Angeles Dodgers in six games in the World Series.

The most recent Yankees' dynasty has dealt with a very different postseason structure. With smaller divisions and a Wild Card berth, it is now significantly easier for the better teams to reach the postseason. At the same time, it is much harder for the best team to come away with a world championship since it now requires winning 11 games in three October series. The Yankees have now made it to the postseason for a record 13 years in a row, getting knocked out in the first-round Division Series in six of those 13 years. The Yankees have made it through the Division Series and LCS to the World Series six times, winning four World Series. Only once, in their unprecedented loss to Boston in 2004, did the Yankees make it to the League Championship Series but fail to advance to the World Series.

This Yankees' dynasty has relied on a mix of homegrown talent, free agents, and trades. New York organization products Bernie Williams, Jorge Posada, Derek Jeter, Andy Pettitte, and Mariano Rivera have served as the foundation of this dynasty. But the Yankees have also acquired an enormous amount of talent through trades and free agency: David Cone, David Wells, Roger Clemens, Scott Brosius, Gary Sheffield, Hideki Matsui, Paul O'Neill, Chuck Knoblauch, Johnny Damon, and

Alex Rodriguez. The Yankees have spent more money on talent than any other team for much of the franchise's history, but the Yankees' payroll is now much larger than the average team payroll. Those deep pockets have enabled New York to overcome serious mistakes while ensuring that the Yankees are always in the pennant chase.

Nevertheless, the modern postseason structure is a minefield for any club, no matter how large its budget. The Yankees won four World Series between 1996 and 2000 because they had superior teams as well as because luck was on their side in October. In recent years, with only slightly less talented squads, the Yankees have been unable to convert their talent into another world championship.

This section chronicles every postseason game in the Yankees' long and glorious history. It includes summaries and composite box scores for each series as well as line scores for each game.

Yankees Postseason Award Winners

YEAR	ALCS MVP	TEAM	WORLD SERIES MVP	TEAM	BABE RUTH AWARD	TEAM
1949					Joe Page	Yankees
1950					Jerry Coleman	Yankees
1951					Phil Rizzuto	Yankees
1952					Johnny Mize	Yankees
1953					Billy Martin	Yankees
1955			Johnny Podres	Dodgers	Johnny Podres	Dodgers
1956			Don Larsen	Yankees	Don Larsen	Yankees
1957			Lew Burdette	Brewers	Lew Burdette	Brewers
1958			Bob Turley	Yankees	Elston Howard	Yankees
1961			*Bobby Richardson*	*Yankees*	Bill Mazeroski	Pirates
1962			Whitey Ford	Yankees	Whitey Ford	Yankees
1963			Ralph Terry	Yankees	Ralph Terry	Yankees
1964			Bob Gibson	Cardinals	Bob Gibson	Cardinals
1076			Johnny Bench	Reds	Johnny Bench	Reds
1977			Reggie Jackson	Yankees	Reggie Jackson	Yankees
1978			Bucky Dent	Yankees	Bucky Dent	Yankees
1980	Frank White	Royals				
1981	Graig Nettles	Yankees	Ron Cey & Pedro Guerrero & Steve Yeager	Dodgers	Ron Cey	Dodgers
1996	Bernie Williams	Yankees	John Wetteland	Yankees	Cecil Fielder	Yankees
1998	David Wells	Yankees	Scott Brosius	Yankees		
1999	Orlando Hernandez	Yankees	Mariano Rivera	Yankees		
2000	David Justice	Yankees	Derek Jeter	Yankees		
2001	Alfonso Soriano	Yankees	Randy Johnson & Curt Schilling	Diamondbacks		
2003	Mariano Rivera	Yankees	Josh Beckett	Marlins		
2004	David Ortiz	Red Sox				

Italics indicate player was on the losing team in that series
Babe Ruth Award by New York chapter of Baseball Writers of America first given out in 1949
World Series MVP Award first given out by SPORT magazine in 1955; since 2000, it has been given out by MLB
ALCS MVP Award first given out by American League in 1980
No Division Series MVP Awards have ever been established

Yankees in October List

YEAR	SERIES	WINNING TEAM (LEAGUE)	T	LOSING TEAM (LEAGUE)	T
1921	World Series	New York Giants (NL)	5	New York Yankees (AL)	3
1922	World Series	New York Giants (NL)	4	New York Yankees (AL)	0
1923	World Series	New York Yankees (AL)	4	New York Giants (NL)	2
1926	World Series	St. Louis Cardinals (NL)	4	New York Yankees (AL)	3
1927	World Series	New York Yankees (AL)	4	Pittsburgh Pirates (NL)	0
1928	World Series	New York Yankees (AL)	4	St. Louis Cardinals (NL)	0
1932	World Series	New York Yankees (AL)	4	Chicago Cubs (NL)	0
1936	World Series	New York Yankees (AL)	4	New York Giants (NL)	2
1937	World Series	New York Yankees (AL)	4	New York Giants (NL)	1
1938	World Series	New York Yankees (AL)	4	Chicago Cubs (NL)	0
1939	World Series	New York Yankees (AL)	4	Cincinnati Reds (NL)	0
1941	World Series	New York Yankees (AL)	4	Brooklyn Dodgers (NL)	1
1942	World Series	St. Louis Cardinals (NL)	4	New York Yankees (AL)	1
1943	World Series	New York Yankees (AL)	4	St. Louis Cardinals (NL)	1
1947	World Series	New York Yankees (AL)	4	Brooklyn Dodgers (NL)	3
1949	World Series	New York Yankees (AL)	4	Brooklyn Dodgers (NL)	1
1950	World Series	New York Yankees (AL)	4	Philadelphia Phillies (NL)	0
1951	World Series	New York Yankees (AL)	4	New York Giants (NL)	2
1952	World Series	New York Yankees (AL)	4	Brooklyn Dodgers (NL)	3
1953	World Series	New York Yankees (AL)	4	Brooklyn Dodgers (NL)	2
1955	World Series	Brooklyn Dodgers (NL)	4	New York Yankees (AL)	3
1956	World Series	New York Yankees (AL)	4	Brooklyn Dodgers (NL)	3
1957	World Series	Milwaukee Braves (NL)	4	New York Yankees (AL)	3
1958	World Series	New York Yankees (AL)	4	Milwaukee Braves (NL)	3
1960	World Series	Pittsburgh Pirates (NL)	4	New York Yankees (AL)	3
1961	World Series	New York Yankees (AL)	4	Cincinnati Reds (NL)	1
1962	World Series	New York Yankees (AL)	4	San Francisco Giants (NL)	3
1963	World Series	Los Angeles Dodgers (NL)	4	New York Yankees (AL)	0
1964	World Series	St. Louis Cardinals (NL)	4	New York Yankees (AL)	3
1976	ALCS	New York Yankees (AL)	3	Kansas City Royals (AL)	2
	World Series	Cincinnati Reds (NL)		New York Yankees (AL)	0
1977	ALCS	New York Yankees (AL)	3	Kansas City Royals (AL)	2
	World Series	New York Yankees (AL)	4	Los Angeles Dodgers (NL)	2
1978	ALCS	New York Yankees (AL)	3	Kansas City Royals (AL)	1
	World Series	New York Yankees (AL)	4	Los Angeles Dodgers (NL)	2
1980	ALCS	Kansas City Royals (AL)	3	New York Yankees (AL)	0
1981	Division Series	New York Yankees (AL)	3	Milwaukee Brewers (AL)	2
	ALCS	New York Yankees (AL)	3	Oakland Athletics (AL)	0
	World Series	Los Angeles Dodgers (NL)	4	New York Yankees (AL)	2
1995	Division Series	Seattle Mariners (AL)	3	New York Yankees (AL)	2
1996	Division Series	New York Yankees (AL)	3	Texas Rangers (AL)	1
	ALCS	New York Yankees (AL)	4	Baltimore Orioles (AL)	1
	World Series	New York Yankees (AL)	4	Atlanta Braves (NL)	2
1997	Division Series	Cleveland Indians (AL)	3	New York Yankees (AL)	2
1998	Division Series	New York Yankees (AL)	3	Texas Rangers (AL)	0
	ALCS	New York Yankees (AL)	4	Cleveland Indians (AL)	2
	World Series	New York Yankees (AL)	4	San Diego Padres (NL)	0
1999	Division Series	New York Yankees (AL)	3	Texas Rangers (AL)	0
	ALCS	New York Yankees (AL)	4	Boston Red Sox (AL)	1
	World Series	New York Yankees (AL)	4	Atlanta Braves (NL)	0
2000	Division Series	New York Yankees (AL)	3	Oakland Athletics (AL)	2
	ALCS	New York Yankees (AL)	4	Seattle Mariners (AL)	2
	World Series	New York Yankees (AL)	4	New York Mets (NL)	1
2001	Division Series	New York Yankees (AL)	3	Oakland Athletics (AL)	2
	ALCS	New York Yankees (AL)	4	Seattle Mariners (AL)	1
	World Series	Arizona Diamondbacks (NL)	4	New York Yankees (AL)	3
2002	Division Series	Anaheim Angels (AL)	3	New York Yankees (AL)	1
2003	Division Series	New York Yankees (AL)	3	Minnesota Twins (AL)	1
	ALCS	New York Yankees (AL)	4	Boston Red Sox (AL)	3
	World Series	Florida Marlins (NL)	4	New York Yankees (AL)	2
2004	Division Series	New York Yankees (AL)	3	Minnesota Twins (AL)	1
	ALCS	Boston Red Sox (AL)	4	New York Yankees (AL)	3
2005	Division Series	Los Angeles Angels (AL)	3	New York Yankees (AL)	2
2006	Division Series	Detroit Tigers (AL)	3	New York Yankees (AL)	1
2007	Division Series	Cleveland Indians (AL)	3	New York Yankees (AL)	1

1921 World Series
New York Yankees (3) vs. New York Giants (5)

The Yankees pulled away from Cleveland in the last week of the season to claim the first of their 39 American League pennants.

NY (NL)

PLAYER, POS	G	AB	R	H	2B	3B	HR	RBI	BB	SO	SB	AVG	OBP	SLG
D.Bancroft, ss	8	33	3	5	1	0	0	3	1	5	0	.152	.176	.182
G.Burns, of	8	33	2	11	4	1	0	2	3	5	1	.333	.389	.515
F.Frisch, 3b	8	30	5	9	0	1	0	1	4	3	3	.300	.382	.367
G.Kelly, 1b	8	30	3	7	1	0	0	4	3	10	0	.233	.303	.267
J.Rawlings, 2b	8	30	2	10	3	0	0	4	0	3	0	.333	.333	.433
I.Meusel, of	8	29	4	10	2	1	1	7	2	3	1	.345	.387	.483
R.Youngs, of	8	25	3	7	1	1	0	4	7	2	2	.280	.438	.400
F.Snyder, c	7	22	4	8	1	0	1	3	0	2	0	.364	.364	.409
J.Barnes, p	3	9	3	4	0	0	0	0	0	0	0	.444	.444	.444
A.Nehf, p	3	9	0	0	0	0	0	0	1	3	0	.000	.100	.000
P.Douglas, p	3	7	0	0	0	0	0	0	0	2	0	.000	.000	.000
E.Smith, c	3	7	0	0	0	0	0	0	1	0	0	.000	.125	.000
Totals		264	20	71	13	4	2	28	22	38	7	.269	.328	.348

PITCHER	W	L	ERA	G	GS	SV	IP	H	BB	SO
P.Douglas	2	1	2.08	3	3	0	26.0	20	5	17
A.Nehf	1	2	1.38	3	3	0	26.0	13	13	8
J.Barnes	2	0	1.65	3	0	0	16.1	10	6	18
F.Toney	0	0	23.63	2	2	0	2.2	7	3	1
Totals	5	3	2.54	11	8	0	71.0	50	27	44

NY (AL)

PLAYER, POS	G	AB	R	H	2B	3B	HR	RBI	BB	SO	SB	AVG	OBP	SLG
E.Miller, of	8	31	3	5	1	0	0	2	2	5	0	.161	.212	.194
B.Meusel, of	8	30	3	6	2	0	0	3	2	5	1	.200	.250	.267
R.Peckinpaugh, ss	8	28	2	5	1	0	0	0	4	3	0	.179	.281	.214
W.Pipp, 1b	8	26	1	4	1	0	0	2	2	3	1	.154	.214	.192
A.Ward, 2b	8	26	1	6	0	0	0	4	2	6	0	.231	.286	.231
W.Schang, c	8	21	1	6	1	1	0	1	5	4	0	.286	.423	.429
M.McNally, 3b	7	20	3	4	1	0	0	1	1	3	2	.200	.238	.250
B.Ruth, of	6	16	3	5	0	0	1	4	5	8	2	.313	.476	.313
C.Fewster, of	4	10	3	2	0	0	1	2	3	3	0	.200	.385	.200
W.Hoyt, p	3	9	0	2	0	0	0	1	0	1	0	.222	.222	.222
C.Mays, p	3	9	0	1	0	0	0	0	0	1	0	.111	.111	.111
F.Baker, 3b	4	8	0	2	0	0	0	0	1	0	0	.250	.333	.250
B.Shawkey, p	2	4	2	2	0	0	0	0	0	1	0	.500	.500	.500
J.Quinn, p	1	2	0	0	0	0	0	0	0	1	0	.000	.000	.000
A.DeVormer, c	2	1	0	0	0	0	0	0	0	0	0	.000	.000	.000
Totals		241	22	50	7	1	2	20	27	44	6	.207	.290	.245

PITCHER	W	L	ERA	G	GS	SV	IP	H	BB	SO
W.Hoyt	2	1	0.00	3	3	0	27.0	18	11	18
C.Mays	1	2	1.73	3	3	0	26.0	20	0	9
B.Shawkey	0	1	7.00	2	1	0	9.0	13	6	5
J.Quinn	0	1	9.82	1	0	0	3.2	8	2	2
H.Harper	0	0	20.25	1	1	0	1.1	3	2	1
T.Rogers	0	0	6.75	1	0	0	1.1	3	0	1
B.Piercy	0	0	0.00	1	0	0	1.0	2	0	2
R.Collins	0	0	54.00	1	0	0	0.2	4	1	0
Totals	3	5	3.09	13	8	0	70.0	71	22	38

GAME 1 / OCT. 5

MAYS VS. DOUGLAS, BARNES(9)							30,202
NY-A	100	011	000	3	7	0	
NY-N	000	000	000	0	5	0	

Carl Mays, another Red Sox castoff, tossed a five-hitter to get the Yankees off to a good start in their first-ever World Series game. Mike McNally had two hits and stole home in the fifth to lead the Yanks offensively.

GAME 2 / OCT. 6

NEHF VS. HOYT							34,939
NY-N	000	000	000	0	2	3	
NY-A	000	100	02X	3	3	0	

Another shutout and another steal of home added up to another 3–0 win for the Yankees. This time it was Waite Hoyt on the mound and Bob Meusel stealing home with two outs in the eighth.

GAME 3 / OCT. 7

SHAWKEY, QUINN(3), COLLINS(7), ROGERS(8) VS. TONEY, BARNES(3)							36,509
NY-A	004	000	010	5	8	0	
NY-N	004	000	81X	13	20	0	

The first eight Giants in the seventh reached—on seven hits and a walk—turning a tie game into a rout.

GAME 4 / OCT. 9

DOUGLAS VS. MAYS							36,372
NY-N	000	000	031	4	9	1	
NY-A	000	010	001	2	7	1	

Babe Ruth smacked his first World Series homer in the bottom of the ninth, but the solo blast wasn't enough to rescue the Yanks from a 4–1 hole.

GAME 5 / OCT. 10

HOYT VS. NEHF							35,758
NY-A	001	200	000	3	6	1	
NY-N	100	000	000	1	10	1	

A bunt single by Ruth started what wound up to be the game-winning rally in the fourth inning. Hoyt allowed an unearned run in the bottom of the first, but he scattered eight hits the rest of the way for his second consecutive complete game win.

GAME 6 / OCT. 11

TONEY, BARNES(1) VS. HARPER, SHAWKEY(2), PIERCY(9)							34,283
NY-N	030	401	000	8	13	0	
NY-A	320	000	000	5	7	2	

Jesse Barnes struck out 10 in 8⅓ innings of relief for the Giants, who rallied from two early deficits to even the series.

GAME 7 / OCT. 12

MAYS VS. DOUGLAS							36,503
NY-A	010	000	000	1	8	1	
NY-N	000	100	10X	2	6	0	

The Yankees really could have used Babe Ruth, who didn't start the final three games because of knee and elbow injuries. Their only run, and the last one they'd score in the series, came in the second on a double by Wally Pipp and a single by McNally.

GAME 8 / OCT. 13

NEHF VS. HOYT							25,410
NY-N	100	000	000	1	6	0	
NY-A	000	000	000	0	4	1	

Hoyt was brilliant for the third time, again giving up just a lone unearned run, but Art Nehf was even better, blanking the Yankees on just four hits. The Giants scored the only run of the game in the top of the first when Yankees shortstop Roger Peckinpaugh let a two-out grounder go through his legs.

1922 World Series
New York Yankees (0) vs. New York Giants (4)

It was a rematch of the previous year's World Series, with the Polo Grounds once again hosting every game. After 10 seasons sharing the ballpark, this was the last time the park did double duty for the Giants and Yankees. The Series featured a controversial tie called by darkness despite plenty of sunshine while another game was played in a downpour. John McGraw was pleased to have beaten his soon-to-be former tenants twice in a row and that his pitchers held Babe Ruth to just five singles, one double, and one home run in two World Series. It was to be Mugsy's third and last world championship.

NY (NL)

PLAYER, POS	G	AB	R	H	2B	3B	HR	RBI	BB	SO	SB	AVG	OBP	SLG
I.Meusel, of	5	20	3	5	0	0	1	7	0	1	0	.250	.250	.250
D.Bancroft, ss	5	19	4	4	0	0	0	2	2	1	0	.211	.286	.211
H.Groh, 3b	5	19	4	9	0	1	0	0	2	1	0	.474	.524	.579
G.Kelly, 1b	5	18	0	5	0	0	0	2	0	3	0	.278	.278	.278
F.Frisch, 2b	5	17	3	8	1	0	0	2	1	0	1	.471	.500	.529
R.Youngs, of	5	16	2	6	0	0	0	2	3	1	0	.375	.474	.375
F.Snyder, c	4	15	1	5	0	0	0	0	0	1	0	.333	.333	.333

PLAYER, POS	G	AB	R	H	2B	3B	HR	RBI	BB	SO	SB	AVG	OBP	SLG
B.Cunningham, of	4	10	0	2	0	0	0	2	2	1	0	.200	.333	.200
E.Smith, c	4	7	0	1	0	0	0	0	0	2	0	.143	.143	.143
C.Stengel, of	2	5	0	2	0	0	0	0	0	1	0	.400	.400	.400
J.Barnes, p	1	4	0	0	0	0	0	0	0	1	0	.000	.000	.000
H.McQuillan, p	1	4	1	1	1	0	0	0	0	1	0	.250	.250	.500
J.Scott, p	1	4	0	1	0	0	0	0	0	1	0	.250	.250	.250
A.Nehf, p	2	3	0	0	0	0	0	0	2	0	0	.000	.400	.000
L.King, of	2	1	0	1	0	0	0	1	0	0	0	1.000	1.000	1.000
Totals		162	18	50	2	1	1	18	12	15	1	.309	.356	.333

PITCHER	W	L	ERA	G	GS	SV	IP	H	BB	SO
A.Nehf	1	0	2.25	2	2	0	16.0	11	3	6
J.Barnes	0	0	1.80	1	1	0	10.0	8	2	6
H.McQuillan	1	0	3.00	1	1	0	9.0	8	2	4
J.Scott	1	0	0.00	1	1	0	9.0	4	1	2
R.Ryan	1	0	0.00	1	0	0	2.0	1	0	2
Totals	4	0	1.76	6	5	0	46.0	32	8	20

NY (AL)

PLAYER, POS	G	AB	R	H	2B	3B	HR	RBI	BB	SO	SB	AVG	OBP	SLG
W.Pipp, 1b	5	21	0	6	1	0	0	3	0	2	1	.286	.286	.333
J.Dugan, 3b	5	20	4	5	1	0	0	0	0	1	0	.250	.250	.300
B.Meusel, of	5	20	2	6	1	0	0	2	1	3	1	.300	.333	.350
W.Witt, of	5	18	1	4	1	1	0	0	1	2	0	.222	.263	.389
B.Ruth, of	5	17	1	2	1	0	0	1	2	3	0	.118	.211	.176
W.Schang, c	5	16	0	3	1	0	0	0	0	3	0	.188	.188	.250
E.Scott, ss	5	14	0	2	0	0	0	1	1	0	0	.143	.200	.143
A.Ward, 2b	5	13	3	2	0	0	2	3	3	3	0	.154	.313	.154
J.Bush, p	2	6	0	1	0	0	0	1	0	0	0	.167	.167	.167
B.Shawkey, p	1	4	0	0	0	0	0	0	0	1	0	.000	.000	.000
W.Hoyt, p	2	2	0	1	0	0	0	0	0	0	0	.500	.500	.500
C.Mays, p	1	2	0	0	0	0	0	0	0	0	0	.000	.000	.000
N.McMillan, of	1	2	0	0	0	0	0	0	0	0	0	.000	.000	.000
E.Smith, ph	2	2	0	0	0	0	0	0	0	2	0	.000	.000	.000
F.Baker, ph	1	1	0	0	0	0	0	0	0	0	0	.000	.000	.000
M.McNally, 2b	1	0	0	0	0	0	0	0	0	0	0	.000	.000	.000
Totals		158	11	32	6	1	2	11	8	20	2	.203	.250	.253

PITCHER	W	L	ERA	G	GS	SV	IP	H	BB	SO
J.Bush	0	2	4.80	2	2	0	15.0	21	5	6
B.Shawkey	0	0	2.70	1	1	0	10.0	8	2	4
W.Hoyt	0	1	1.13	2	1	0	8.0	11	2	4
C.Mays	0	1	4.50	1	1	0	8.0	9	2	1
S.Jones	0	0	0.00	2	0	0	2.0	1	1	0
Totals	0	4	3.35	8	5	0	43.0	50	12	15

GAME 1 / OCT. 4

BUSH, HOYT(8) VS. NEHF, RYAN(8) **36,514**

NY-A	000	001	100	2	7	0
NY-N	000	000	03X	3	11	3

The Yankees had a 2–0 lead heading into the bottom of the eighth. The Giants put together four straight singles to start the inning, with Irish Meusel's two-run hit tying the score and driving Joe Bush from the game. Waite Hoyt came in and Ross Youngs brought in the go-ahead run on a long fly. Reliever Rosy Ryan got the win in the only game not completed by a Giants starter.

GAME 2 / OCT. 5

BARNES VS. SHAWKEY **37,020**

NY-N	300	000	000	0	3	8	1
NY-A	100	100	010	0	3	8	0

Jesse Barnes and Bob Shawkey each pitched 10 innings, but the fans wanted more. Umpires George Hildebrand and Bill Klem called the game due to darkness before five o'clock, even though the sun still shone and there was at least a half an hour of light left. Fans littered the field with bottles and cushions, and Commissioner Landis received an earful even though he had no part in the decision. He donated the game's receipts—about $120,000—to military hospitals for disabled veterans.

GAME 3 / OCT. 6

HOYT, JONES(8) VS. J.SCOTT **37,620**

NY-A	000	000	000	0	4	1
NY-N	002	000	10X	3	12	1

The players were angry the next day when Babe Ruth slid hard into diminutive Heinie Groh at third base and harsh words were exchanged. Jack Scott, who'd been released by Cincinnati because of a perceived sore arm, calmed things down with a four-hit shutout.

GAME 4 / OCT. 7

MCQUILLAN VS. MAYS, JONES(9) **36,242**

NY-N	000	040	000	4	9	1
NY-A	200	000	100	3	8	0

The Yankees scored twice in the first and might have done more if not for Giants center fielder Bill Cunningham. He made an excellent catch on a Babe Ruth drive and threw out Wally Pipp trying to stretch a single. Hugh McQuillan allowed just four hits the rest of the way and added a key double during the four-run fifth on a rain-soaked afternoon. It was the last time the Yankees appeared as the home team at the Polo Grounds.

GAME 5 / OCT. 8

BUSH VS. NEHF **38,551**

NY-A	100	010	100	3	5	0
NY-N	020	000	03X	5	10	0

Again the Yankees scored in the first inning—with Babe Ruth laying down a sacrifice—and the teams twice traded the lead. The Yankees were up by a run in the eighth with two outs, two on, and first base open. Joe Bush walked Ross Youngs to pitch to George Kelly, who promptly singled to bring in the tying and lead runs. Art Nehf was on the mound for the clincher for the second straight year.

1923 World Series
New York Yankees (4) vs. New York Giants (2)

This was the year Yankee Stadium opened, making this the only one of the three straight Subway Series that wasn't played entirely at the Polo Grounds. It was also the only one of the three the Yankees won, setting a precedent that forever changed October baseball.

NY (AL)

PLAYER, POS	G	AB	R	H	2B	3B	HR	RBI	BB	SO	SB	AVG	OBP	SLG
B.Meusel, of	6	26	1	7	1	2	0	8	0	3	0	.269	.269	.462
J.Dugan, 3b	6	25	5	7	2	1	1	5	3	0	0	.280	.357	.440
W.Witt, of	6	25	1	6	2	0	0	4	1	1	0	.240	.269	.320
A.Ward, 2b	6	24	4	10	0	0	1	2	1	3	1	.417	.440	.417
W.Schang, c	6	22	3	7	1	0	0	0	1	2	0	.318	.348	.364
E.Scott, ss	6	22	2	7	0	0	0	3	0	1	0	.318	.318	.318
W.Pipp, 1b	6	20	2	5	0	0	0	2	4	1	0	.250	.375	.250
B.Ruth, of-1b	6	19	8	7	1	1	3	3	8	6	0	.368	.556	.526
J.Bush, p	4	7	2	3	1	0	0	1	1	1	0	.429	.500	.571
H.Pennock, p	3	6	0	0	0	0	0	0	0	2	0	.000	.000	.000
B.Shawkey, p	1	3	0	1	0	0	0	1	0	0	0	.333	.333	.333
S.Jones, p	2	2	0	0	0	0	0	0	0	1	0	.000	.000	.000
H.Haines, of	2	1	1	0	0	0	0	0	0	0	0	.000	.000	.000
H.Hendrick, ph	1	1	0	0	0	0	0	0	0	0	0	.000	.000	.000
F.Hofmann, ph	2	1	0	0	0	0	0	0	1	0	0	.000	.500	.000
W.Hoyt, p	1	1	0	0	0	0	0	0	0	1	0	.000	.000	.000
E.Johnson, ss	2	0	1	0	0	0	0	0	0	0	0	.000	.000	.000
Totals		205	30	60	8	4	5	29	20	22	1	.293	.358	.371

PITCHER	W	L	ERA	G	GS	SV	IP	H	BB	SO
H.Pennock	2	0	3.63	3	2	1	17.1	19	1	8
J.Bush	1	1	1.08	3	1	0	16.2	7	4	5
S.Jones	0	1	0.90	2	1	1	10.0	5	2	3
B.Shawkey	1	0	3.52	1	1	0	7.2	12	4	2
W.Hoyt	0	0	15.43	1	1	0	2.1	4	1	0
Totals	4	2	2.83	10	6	2	54.0	47	12	18

NY (NL)

PLAYER, POS	G	AB	R	H	2B	3B	HR	RBI	BB	SO	SB	AVG	OBP	SLG
F.Frisch, 2b	6	25	2	10	0	1	0	1	0	0	0	.400	.400	.480
I.Meusel, of	6	25	3	7	1	1	1	2	0	2	0	.280	.280	.400
D.Bancroft, ss	6	24	1	2	0	0	0	1	1	2	1	.083	.120	.083
R.Youngs, of	6	23	2	8	0	0	1	3	2	0	0	.348	.400	.348
H.Groh, 3b	6	22	3	4	0	1	0	2	3	1	0	.182	.280	.273
G.Kelly, 1b	6	22	1	4	0	0	0	1	1	2	0	.182	.217	.182
F.Snyder, c	5	17	1	2	0	0	1	2	0	2	0	.118	.118	.118
C.Stengel, of	6	12	3	5	0	0	2	4	4	0	0	.417	.563	.417
B.Cunningham, of	4	7	0	1	0	0	0	1	0	1	0	.143	.143	.143
A.Nehf, p	2	6	0	1	0	0	0	0	0	4	0	.167	.167	.167
J.Bentley, p	5	5	0	3	1	0	0	0	0	0	0	.600	.600	.800
H.Gowdy, c	3	4	0	0	0	0	0	0	1	0	0	.000	.200	.000
H.McQuillan, p	2	3	0	0	0	0	0	0	0	1	0	.000	.000	.000

NY (NL) (CONT.)														
PLAYER, POS	G	AB	R	H	2B	3B	HR	RBI	BB	SO	SB	AVG	OBP	SLG
R.Ryan, p	3	2	0	0	0	0	0	0	0	1	0	.000	.000	.000
V.Barnes, p	2	1	0	0	0	0	0	0	0	1	0	.000	.000	.000
T.Jackson, ph	1	1	0	0	0	0	0	0	0	0	0	.000	.000	.000
J.O'Connell, ph	2	1	0	0	0	0	0	0	0	1	0	.000	.000	.000
J.Scott, p	2	1	0	0	0	0	0	0	0	0	0	.000	.000	.000
D.Gearin, pr	1	0	0	0	0	0	0	0	0	0	0	.000	.000	.000
F.Maguire, pr	2	0	1	0	0	0	0	0	0	0	0	.000	.000	.000
Totals		201	17	47	2	3	5	17	12	18	1	.234	.280	.274

PITCHER	W	L	ERA	G	GS	SV	IP	H	BB	SO
A.Nehf	1	1	2.76	2	2	0	16.1	10	6	7
R.Ryan	1	0	0.96	3	0	0	9.1	11	3	3
H.McQuillan	0	1	5.00	2	1	0	9.0	11	4	3
J.Bentley	0	1	9.45	2	1	0	6.2	10	4	1
V.Barnes	0	0	0.00	2	0	0	4.2	4	0	4
J.Scott	0	1	12.00	2	1	0	3.0	9	1	2
C.Jonnard	0	0	0.00	2	0	0	2.0	1	1	1
M.Watson	0	0	13.50	1	1	0	2.0	4	1	1
Totals	2	4	4.25	16	6	0	53.0	60	20	22

GAME 1 / OCT. 10						
WATSON, RYAN(3) VS. HOYT, BUSH(3)						55,307
NY-N	004	000	001	5	8	0
NY-A	120	000	100	4	12	1

Casey Stengel's two-out inside the park home run in the top of the ninth was the first World Series home run at Yankee Stadium and was also a game winner for the Giants.

GAME 2 / OCT. 11						
PENNOCK VS. MCQUILLAN, BENTLEY(4)						40,402
NY-A	010	210	000	4	10	0
NY-N	010	001	000	2	9	2

Babe Ruth hit two solo home runs, including a tape-measure blast in the fourth that towered over the right-field roof at the Polo Grounds, but Herb Pennock's performance in the sixth, when he got out of a no-out, bases-loaded jam with only one run scoring, saved the day for the Yankees.

GAME 3 / OCT. 12						
NEHF VS. JONES, BUSH(9)						62,430
NY-N	000	000	100	1	4	0
NY-A	000	000	000	0	6	1

Casey Stengel's home run in the top of the seventh—a conventional one this time that landed in the right-field bleachers—was the only run of the game. He was later fined $50 for thumbing his nose at the Yankees' dugout as he rounded the bases.

GAME 4 / OCT. 13						
SHAWKEY, PENNOCK(8) VS. J.SCOTT, RYAN(2), MCQUILLAN(2), JONNARD(8), BARNES(9)						46,302
NY-A	061	100	000	8	13	1
NY-N	000	000	031	4	13	1

Maybe Casey Stengel's gesture awakened the Yankees' bats. Whatever the reason, they were back to being the Bronx Bombers. From the second inning on, the Yankees pounded out 22 runs the rest of the Series. Eight scored in this contest without benefit of a long ball. Both teams had 13 hits, but the Giants got most of theirs after it was already 8–0.

GAME 5 / OCT. 14						
BENTLEY, J.SCOTT(2), BARNES(4), JONNARD(8) VS. BUSH						62,817
NY-N	010	000	000	1	3	2
NY-A	340	100	00X	8	14	0

Eight more runs and 14 hits for the Yankees overshadowed the pitching of Bullet Joe Bush. He allowed only three hits—all to Irish Meusel—and two walks in a complete-game victory.

GAME 6 / OCT. 15						
PENNOCK, JONES(8) VS. NEHF, RYAN(8)						34,172
NY-A	100	000	050	6	5	0
NY-N	100	111	000	4	10	1

The Yankees had only two hits through seven innings, but exploded for five runs in the eighth. The first two came on bases loaded walks, and the last three came on a single by Bob Meusel, aided by an error by Giants center fielder Bill Cunningham. Art Nehf, who'd won the other two clinching games for the Giants against the Yankees in 1921 and 1922, lost this one to Herb Pennock.

1926 World Series
New York Yankees (3) vs. St. Louis Cardinals (4)

New York led the American League in both runs and slugging, yet their 10-run outburst in the fourth game was the only time the powerful Yankees scored more than 3 runs in the Series. St. Louis was an inferior offensive club to the Yankees and had never been to the World Series, much less won one before.

STL (NL)														
PLAYER, POS	G	AB	R	H	2B	3B	HR	RBI	BB	SO	SB	AVG	OBP	SLG
J.Bottomley, 1b	7	29	4	10	3	0	0	5	1	2	0	.345	.367	.448
B.Southworth, of	7	29	6	10	1	1	1	4	0	0	1	.345	.345	.448
R.Hornsby, 2b	7	28	2	7	1	0	0	4	2	2	1	.250	.300	.286
L.Bell, 3b	7	27	4	7	1	0	1	6	2	5	0	.259	.310	.296
C.Hafey, of	7	27	2	5	2	0	0	0	0	7	0	.185	.185	.259
T.Thevenow, ss	7	24	5	10	1	0	1	4	0	1	0	.417	.417	.458
B.O'Farrell, c	7	23	2	7	1	0	0	2	2	2	0	.304	.360	.348
W.Holm, of	5	16	1	2	0	0	0	1	1	2	0	.125	.176	.125
T.Douthit, of	4	15	3	4	2	0	0	1	3	2	0	.267	.389	.400
P.Alexander, p	3	7	1	0	0	0	0	0	0	2	0	.000	.000	.000
J.Haines, p	3	5	1	3	0	0	1	2	0	1	0	.600	.600	.600
B.Sherdel, p	2	5	0	0	0	0	0	0	0	2	0	.000	.000	.000
J.Flowers, ph	3	3	0	0	0	0	0	0	0	1	0	.000	.000	.000
F.Rhem, p	1	1	0	0	0	0	0	0	0	1	0	.000	.000	.000
S.Toporcer, ph	1	0	0	0	0	0	0	1	0	0	0	.000	.000	.000
Totals		239	31	65	12	1	4	30	11	30	2	.272	.307	.331

PITCHER	W	L	ERA	G	GS	SV	IP	H	BB	SO
P.Alexander	2	0	1.33	3	2	1	20.1	12	4	17
B.Sherdel	0	2	2.12	2	2	0	17.0	15	8	3
J.Haines	2	0	1.08	3	2	0	16.2	13	9	5
F.Rhem	0	0	6.75	1	1	0	4.0	7	2	4
H.Bell	0	0	9.00	1	0	0	2.0	4	1	1
B.Hallahan	0	0	4.50	1	0	0	2.0	2	3	1
V.Keen	0	0	0.00	1	0	0	1.0	0	0	0
A.Reinhart	0	1	INF	1	0	0	0.0	1	4	0
Totals	4	3	2.71	13	7	1	63.0	54	31	31

NY (AL)														
PLAYER, POS	G	AB	R	H	2B	3B	HR	RBI	BB	SO	SB	AVG	OBP	SLG
M.Koenig, ss	7	32	2	4	1	0	0	2	0	6	0	.125	.125	.156
E.Combs, of	7	28	3	10	2	0	0	2	5	2	0	.357	.455	.429
T.Lazzeri, 2b	7	26	2	5	1	0	0	3	1	6	0	.192	.222	.231
J.Dugan, 3b	7	24	2	8	1	0	0	2	1	1	0	.333	.360	.375
L.Gehrig, 1b	7	23	1	8	2	0	0	4	5	4	0	.348	.464	.435
H.Severeid, c	7	22	1	6	1	0	0	1	1	2	0	.273	.304	.318
B.Meusel, of	7	21	3	5	1	1	0	0	6	1	0	.238	.407	.381
B.Ruth, of	7	20	6	6	0	0	4	5	11	2	1	.300	.548	.300
H.Pennock, p	3	7	1	1	1	0	0	0	0	0	0	.143	.143	.286
W.Hoyt, p	2	6	0	0	0	0	0	0	0	1	0	.000	.000	.000
B.Paschal, ph	5	4	0	1	0	0	0	1	1	2	0	.250	.400	.250
D.Ruether, p	3	4	0	0	0	0	0	0	0	0	0	.000	.000	.000
P.Collins, c	3	2	0	0	0	0	0	0	0	1	0	.000	.000	.000
B.Shawkey, p	3	2	0	0	0	0	0	0	0	1	0	.000	.000	.000
U.Shocker, p	2	2	0	0	0	0	0	0	0	2	0	.000	.000	.000
S.Adams, ph	2	0	0	0	0	0	0	0	0	0	0	.000	.000	.000
M.Gazella, 3b	1	0	0	0	0	0	0	0	0	0	0	.000	.000	.000
Totals		223	21	54	10	1	4	20	31	31	1	.242	.337	.296

PITCHER	W	L	ERA	G	GS	SV	IP	H	BB	SO
H.Pennock	2	0	1.23	3	2	0	22.0	13	4	8
W.Hoyt	1	1	1.20	2	2	0	15.0	19	1	10
B.Shawkey	0	1	5.40	3	1	0	10.0	8	2	7
U.Shocker	0	1	5.87	2	1	0	7.2	13	0	3
D.Ruether	0	1	8.31	1	1	0	4.1	7	2	1
M.Thomas	0	0	3.00	2	0	0	3.0	3	0	0
S.Jones	0	0	9.00	1	0	0	1.0	2	2	1
Totals	3	4	3.14	14	7	0	63.0	65	11	30

GAME 1 / OCT. 2						
SHERDEL, HAINES(8) VS. PENNOCK						61,658
STL	100	000	000	1	3	1
NY	100	001	00X	2	6	0

After giving up a run in the top of the first, Herb Pennock held the Cardinals hitless until the ninth. Lou Gehrig drove in both runs for the Yankees, on a groundout in the first and a single in the sixth.

GAME 2 / OCT. 3						
ALEXANDER VS. SHOCKER, SHAWKEY(8), JONES(9)						**63,600**
STL	002	000	301	6	12	1
NY	020	000	000	2	4	0

Grover Cleveland Alexander gave up three hits and two runs in the second, but was lights out after that. Following Earle Combs' leadoff single in the third, Alexander retired the final 21 Yankees in what was his finest start of his career in the fall classic.

GAME 3 / OCT. 5						
RUETHER, SHAWKEY(5), THOMAS(8) VS. HAINES						**37,708**
NY	000	000	000	0	5	1
STL	000	310	00X	4	8	0

Jesse Haines was even better. He tossed a five-hit shutout and smacked a two-run homer in the fourth inning.

GAME 4 / OCT. 6						
HOYT VS. RHEM, REINHART(5), H.BELL(5), HALLAHAN(7), KEEN(9)						**38,825**
NY	101	142	100	10	14	1
STL	100	300	001	5	14	0

Waite Hoyt went the distance, giving up all 14 hits and all 5 runs. His subpar performance hardly mattered due to Babe Ruth's three-homer barrage, the first such outburst in Series history.

GAME 5 / OCT. 7							
PENNOCK VS. SHERDEL							**39,552**
NY	000	001	001	1	3	9	1
STL	000	100	100	0	2	7	1

On the verge of defeat, the Yankees tied the game in the ninth on a single by little-used Ben Paschal. New York then won it in the 10th on a sacrifice fly by Tony Lazzeri. Lazzeri would not reach base the rest of the Series.

GAME 6 / OCT. 9						
ALEXANDER VS. SHAWKEY, SHOCKER(7), THOMAS(8)						**48,615**
STL	300	010	501	10	13	2
NY	000	100	100	2	8	1

Grover Cleveland Alexander threw another complete game, but he had much more breathing room. Les Bell drove in four and the Cardinals' bats erupted for 10 runs.

GAME 7 / OCT. 10						
HAINES, ALEXANDER(7) VS. HOYT, PENNOCK(7)						**38,093**
STL	000	300	000	3	8	0
NY	001	001	000	2	8	3

The Yankees took the early lead on a solo homer by Babe Ruth, but gave it away by committing two errors in the fourth as the Cardinals plated three unearned runs. New York had a chance to get back into it in the seventh after loading the bases with two outs, but Grover Cleveland Alexander relieved Jesse Haines and struck out Tony Lazzeri to end the threat in one of the most heralded confrontations in history. Alexander retired the Yankees in order in the eighth and got the first two out in the ninth before walking Ruth. The Babe, however, was thrown out trying to steal second by Bob O'Farrell to end the Series.

1927 World Series
New York Yankees (4) vs. Pittsburgh Pirates (0)

The '27 Yankees are often referred to as the best team in baseball history. It's hard to argue that; they won 117 games and finished 19 ahead of the Athletics. New York's adjusted OPS was 37 percent better than league average, scoring 6.29 runs a game, close to a run better than any other AL team. They also allowed nearly a run less than anybody else. The Pirates didn't stand a prayer.

NY (AL)

PLAYER, POS	G	AB	R	H	2B	3B	HR	RBI	BB	SO	SB	AVG	OBP	SLG
M.Koenig, ss	4	18	5	9	2	0	0	2	0	2	0	.500	.500	.611
B.Meusel, of	4	17	1	2	0	0	0	1	1	7	1	.118	.167	.118
E.Combs, of	4	16	6	5	0	0	0	2	1	2	0	.313	.353	.313
J.Dugan, 3b	4	15	2	3	0	0	0	0	0	0	0	.200	.200	.200
T.Lazzeri, 2b	4	15	1	4	1	0	0	2	1	4	0	.267	.313	.333
B.Ruth, of	4	15	4	6	0	0	2	7	2	2	1	.400	.471	.400
L.Gehrig, 1b	4	13	2	4	2	2	0	4	3	3	0	.308	.438	.769
P.Collins, c	2	5	0	3	1	0	0	0	3	0	0	.600	.750	.800
W.Moore, p	2	5	0	1	0	0	0	0	0	3	0	.200	.200	.200
B.Bengough, c	2	4	1	0	0	0	0	0	1	0	0	.000	.200	.000
H.Pennock, p	1	4	1	0	0	0	0	1	0	1	0	.000	.000	.000
W.Hoyt, p	1	3	0	0	0	0	0	0	0	0	0	.000	.000	.000
G.Pipgras, p	1	3	0	1	0	0	0	0	1	1	0	.333	.500	.333
J.Grabowski, c	1	2	0	0	0	0	0	0	0	0	0	.000	.000	.000
C.Durst, ph	1	1	0	0	0	0	0	0	0	0	0	.000	.000	.000
Totals		136	23	38	6	2	2	19	13	25	2	.279	.347	.353

PITCHER	W	L	ERA	G	GS	SV	IP	H	BB	SO
W.Moore	1	0	0.84	2	1	1	10.2	11	2	2
H.Pennock	1	0	1.00	1	1	0	9.0	3	0	1
G.Pipgras	1	0	2.00	1	1	0	9.0	7	1	2
W.Hoyt	1	0	4.91	1	1	0	7.1	8	1	2
Totals	4	0	2.00	5	4	1	36.0	29	4	7

PIT (NL)

PLAYER, POS	G	AB	R	H	2B	3B	HR	RBI	BB	SO	SB	AVG	OBP	SLG
C.Barnhart, of	4	16	0	5	1	0	0	4	0	0	0	.313	.313	.375
J.Harris, 1b	4	15	0	3	0	0	0	1	0	0	0	.200	.200	.200
P.Traynor, 3b	4	15	1	3	1	0	0	0	0	1	0	.200	.200	.267
L.Waner, of	4	15	5	6	1	1	0	0	1	0	0	.400	.438	.600
P.Waner, of	4	15	0	5	1	0	0	3	0	1	0	.333	.333	.400
G.Wright, ss	4	13	1	2	0	0	0	2	0	0	0	.154	.154	.154
G.Grantham, 2b	3	11	0	4	1	0	0	0	1	1	0	.364	.417	.455
E.Smith, c	3	8	0	0	0	0	0	0	0	0	0	.000	.000	.000
J.Gooch, c	3	5	0	0	0	0	0	0	1	1	0	.000	.167	.000
H.Rhyne, 2b	1	4	0	0	0	0	0	0	0	0	0	.000	.000	.000
V.Aldridge, p	1	2	0	0	0	0	0	0	0	0	0	.000	.000	.000
F.Brickell, ph	2	2	1	0	0	0	0	0	0	0	0	.000	.000	.000
R.Kremer, p	1	2	1	1	1	0	0	0	0	1	0	.500	.500	1.000
L.Meadows, p	1	2	0	0	0	0	0	0	0	0	0	.000	.000	.000
J.Miljus, p	2	2	0	0	0	0	0	0	0	2	0	.000	.000	.000
H.Groh, ph	1	1	0	0	0	0	0	0	0	0	0	.000	.000	.000
C.Hill, p	1	1	0	0	0	0	0	0	1	0	0	.000	.500	.000
R.Spencer, c	1	1	0	0	0	0	0	0	0	0	0	.000	.000	.000
E.Yde, pr	1	0	1	0	0	0	0	0	0	0	0	.000	.000	.000
Totals		130	10	29	6	1	0	10	4	7	0	.223	.252	.285

PITCHER	W	L	ERA	G	GS	SV	IP	H	BB	SO
V.Aldridge	0	1	7.36	1	1	0	7.1	10	4	4
J.Miljus	0	1	1.35	2	0	0	6.2	4	4	6
L.Meadows	0	1	9.95	1	1	0	6.1	7	1	6
C.Hill	0	0	4.50	1	1	0	6.0	9	1	6
R.Kremer	0	1	3.60	1	1	0	5.0	5	3	1
M.Cvengros	0	0	3.86	2	0	0	2.1	3	0	2
J.Dawson	0	0	0.00	1	0	0	1.0	0	0	0
Totals	0	4	5.19	9	4	0	34.2	38	13	25

GAME 1 / OCT. 5						
HOYT, MOORE(8) VS. KREMER, MILJUS(6)						**41,467**
NY	103	010	000	5	6	1
PIT	101	010	010	4	9	2

Defensive miscues allowed the Yankees to score four times in the first three innings. Lou Gehrig's RBI triple in the first came after Paul Waner botched the fly ball. (Superior outfielder Kiki Cuyler, meanwhile, sat out the Series for Pittsburgh because of a disagreement with management.) Two more errors made all three runs New York scored in the third unearned.

GAME 2 / OCT. 6						
PIPGRAS VS. ALDRIDGE, CVENGROS(8), DAWSON(9)						**41,634**
NY	003	000	030	6	11	0
PIT	100	000	010	2	7	2

Seven of the nine Yankees starters, including pitcher George Pipgras had at least one hit. New York cruised to a second easy victory at Forbes Field.

GAME 3 / OCT. 7						
MEADOWS, CVENGROS(7) VS. PENNOCK						**60,695**
PIT	000	000	010	1	3	1
NY	200	000	60X	8	9	0

Herb Pennock was perfect through 7⅓ innings, when Pie Traynor got the first hit. Pennock wound up allowing three hits and a run, but the Yankees provided more than enough offense. Babe Ruth's three-run blast in the seventh made it a rout.

GAME 4 / OCT. 8						
HILL, MILJUS(7) VS. MOORE						**57,909**
PIT	100	000	200	3	10	1
NY	100	020	001	4	12	2

The Pirates had a chance to go ahead in the eighth, but reliever Johnny Miljus struck out with two on and two out. He then threw two wild pitches in the ninth, including one with two outs that let Earle Combs score the run that ended the game and clinched the Series for the Yankees.

1928 World Series
New York Yankees (4) vs. St. Louis Cardinals (0)

This World Series was as lopsided, as the 1926 match between the clubs had been entertaining. Even with starter Herb Pennock and outfielder Earle Combs out with injuries, the Yankees still never trailed after the seventh inning. They outscored St. Louis, 27–10. Babe Ruth alone had 10 hits and scored 9 times, while Lou Gehrig drove in a World Series record 9 runs; they combined to hit 7 homers

NY (AL)

PLAYER, POS	G	AB	R	H	2B	3B	HR	RBI	BB	SO	SB	AVG	OBP	SLG
M.Koenig, ss	4	19	1	3	0	0	0	0	0	1	0	.158	.158	.158
B.Ruth, of	4	16	9	10	3	0	3	4	1	2	0	.625	.647	.813
B.Meusel, of	4	15	5	3	1	0	1	3	2	5	2	.200	.294	.267
B.Bengough, c	4	13	1	3	0	0	0	1	1	1	0	.231	.286	.231
T.Lazzeri, 2b	4	12	2	3	1	0	0	0	1	0	2	.250	.308	.333
L.Gehrig, 1b	4	11	5	6	1	0	4	9	6	0	0	.545	.706	.636
B.Paschal, of	3	10	0	2	0	0	0	1	1	0	0	.200	.273	.200
C.Durst, of	4	8	3	3	0	0	1	2	0	1	0	.375	.375	.375
G.Robertson, 3b	3	8	1	1	0	0	0	2	1	0	0	.125	.222	.125
W.Hoyt, p	2	7	0	1	0	0	0	0	0	0	0	.143	.143	.143
J.Dugan, 3b	3	6	0	1	0	0	0	1	0	0	0	.167	.167	.167
T.Zachary, p	1	4	0	0	0	0	0	0	0	1	0	.000	.000	.000
L.Durocher, 2b	4	2	0	0	0	0	0	0	0	1	0	.000	.000	.000
G.Pipgras, p	1	2	0	0	0	0	0	1	0	1	0	.000	.000	.000
P.Collins, c	1	1	0	1	1	0	0	0	0	0	0	1.000	1.000	2.000
E.Combs, ph	1	0	0	0	0	0	0	1	0	0	0	.000	.000	.000
Totals		134	27	37	7	0	9	25	13	13	4	.276	.345	.328

PITCHER	W	L	ERA	G	GS	SV	IP	H	BB	SO
W.Hoyt	2	0	1.50	2	2	0	18.0	14	6	14
G.Pipgras	1	0	2.00	1	1	0	9.0	4	4	8
T.Zachary	1	0	3.00	1	1	0	9.0	9	1	7
Totals	4	0	2.00	4	4	0	36.0	27	11	29

STL (NL)

PLAYER, POS	G	AB	R	H	2B	3B	HR	RBI	BB	SO	SB	AVG	OBP	SLG
A.High, 3b	4	17	1	5	2	0	0	1	1	3	0	.294	.333	.412
C.Hafey, of	4	15	0	3	0	0	0	0	1	4	0	.200	.250	.200
J.Bottomley, 1b	4	14	1	3	0	1	1	3	2	6	0	.214	.313	.357
F.Frisch, 2b	4	13	1	3	0	0	0	1	2	2	2	.231	.333	.231
R.Maranville, ss	4	13	2	4	1	0	0	0	1	1	1	.308	.357	.385
T.Douthit, of	3	11	1	1	0	0	0	1	1	1	0	.091	.167	.091
J.Wilson, c	3	11	1	1	1	0	0	1	0	3	0	.091	.091	.182
G.Harper, of	3	9	1	1	0	0	0	0	2	2	0	.111	.273	.111
E.Orsatti, of	4	7	1	2	1	0	0	0	1	3	0	.286	.375	.429
W.Holm, of	3	6	0	1	0	0	0	1	0	1	0	.167	.167	.167
B.Sherdel, p	2	5	0	0	0	0	0	0	0	2	0	.000	.000	.000
E.Smith, c	1	4	0	3	0	0	0	0	0	0	0	.750	.750	.750
J.Haines, p	1	2	0	0	0	0	0	0	0	0	0	.000	.000	.000
C.Mitchell, p	1	2	0	0	0	0	0	0	0	0	0	.000	.000	.000
P.Alexander, p	2	1	0	0	0	0	0	1	0	0	0	.000	.000	.000
R.Blades, ph	1	1	0	0	0	0	0	0	0	1	0	.000	.000	.000

STL (NL) (CONT.)

PLAYER, POS	G	AB	R	H	2B	3B	HR	RBI	BB	SO	SB	AVG	OBP	SLG
P.Martin, pr	1	0	1	0	0	0	0	0	0	0	0	.000	.000	.000
T.Thevenow, ss	1	0	0	0	0	0	0	0	0	0	0	.000	.000	.000
Totals		131	10	27	5	1	1	9	11	29	3	.206	.273	.260

PITCHER	W	L	ERA	G	GS	SV	IP	H	BB	SO
B.Sherdel	0	2	4.72	2	2	0	13.1	15	3	3
J.Haines	0	1	4.50	1	1	0	6.0	6	3	3
C.Mitchell	0	0	1.59	1	0	0	5.2	2	2	3
P.Alexander	0	1	19.80	2	1	0	5.0	10	4	2
S.Johnson	0	0	4.50	2	0	0	2.0	4	1	1
F.Rhem	0	0	0.00	1	0	0	2.0	0	0	1
Totals	0	4	6.09	9	4	0	34.0	37	13	13

GAME 1 / OCT. 4						
SHERDEL, JOHNSON(8) VS. HOYT						**61,425**
STL	000	000	100	1	3	1
NY	100	200	01X	4	7	0

The Yankees got a quick run in the first on back-to-back doubles by Babe Ruth and Lou Gehrig, and cruised behind the three-hit pitching of Waite Hoyt. Ruth had three hits, including two doubles, and scored twice, while Gehrig and Bob Meusel both drove in two.

GAME 2 / OCT. 5						
ALEXANDER, MITCHELL(3) VS. PIPGRAS						**60,714**
STL	030	000	000	3	4	1
NY	314	000	10X	9	8	2

Lou Gehrig's three-run bomb in the first set the tone for the Yankees, who repaid Grover Cleveland Alexander for his supremacy in the 1926 Series. Alexander wasn't so great, allowing 8 runs in 2⅓ innings. Middle of the order mates Babe Ruth, Gehrig, and Bob Meusel combined for four hits, four RBIs, and six runs scored.

GAME 3 / OCT. 7						
ZACHARY VS. HAINES, JOHNSON(7), RHEM(8)						**39,602**
NY	010	203	100	7	7	2
STL	200	010	000	3	9	3

Four of the New York's seven runs were unearned, including the three they got in the sixth and the single run in the seventh. Their first run also was tainted as Gehrig got an inside-the-park homer in the second inning on center fielder Taylor Douthit's mental mistake.

GAME 4 / OCT. 9						
HOYT VS. SHERDEL, ALEXANDER(7)						**37,331**
NY	000	100	420	7	15	2
STL	001	100	001	3	11	0

Babe Ruth's tremendous solo blast in the fourth was the Yankees' only run through six innings. New York wouldn't be denied a second consecutive World Series sweep, however. The Bronx Bombers blasted four more homers in the seventh and eighth innings and wound up easy winners. Ruth hit three on the day—two that went over the right field roof at Sportsman's Park and another that landed on it—and Lou Gehrig hit his fourth of the Series in the seventh. Ruth, who'd been thrown out to end the '26 Series, made a great running catch to end the '28 sweep.

1932 World Series
New York Yankees (4) vs. Chicago Cubs (0)

New York had two of the greatest players of all time in the lineup, scored 1,000 runs for the third straight year, owned the best record in baseball by 13 games, and won 17 more than the Cubs. All of this added up to a drubbing. This would forever go down in history because of the spectacle of Babe Ruth at home plate in his final World Series perhaps doing something with his hand, but definitely doing something with his bat.

NY (AL)

PLAYER, POS	G	AB	R	H	2B	3B	HR	RBI	BB	SO	SB	AVG	OBP	SLG
B.Chapman, of	4	17	1	5	2	0	0	6	2	4	0	.294	.368	.412
L.Gehrig, 1b	4	17	9	9	1	0	3	8	2	1	0	.529	.579	.588
T.Lazzeri, 2b	4	17	4	5	0	0	2	5	2	1	0	.294	.368	.294
E.Combs, of	4	16	8	6	1	0	1	4	4	3	0	.375	.500	.438
B.Dickey, c	4	16	2	7	0	0	0	4	2	1	0	.438	.500	.438
F.Crosetti, ss	4	15	2	2	1	0	0	0	2	3	0	.133	.235	.200
B.Ruth, of	4	15	6	5	0	0	2	6	4	3	0	.333	.474	.333
J.Sewell, 3b	4	15	4	5	1	0	0	3	4	0	0	.333	.474	.400
G.Pipgras, p	1	5	0	0	0	0	0	0	0	5	0	.000	.000	.000
R.Ruffing, p	2	4	0	0	0	0	0	0	1	1	0	.000	.200	.000
L.Gomez, p	1	3	0	0	0	0	0	0	0	2	0	.000	.000	.000
W.Moore, p	1	3	0	1	0	0	0	0	0	2	0	.333	.333	.333
H.Pennock, p	2	1	0	0	0	0	0	0	0	0	0	.000	.000	.000
S.Byrd, of	1	0	0	0	0	0	0	0	0	0	0	.000	.000	.000
M.Hoag, pr	1	0	1	0	0	0	0	0	0	0	0	.000	.000	.000
Totals		144	37	45	6	0	8	36	23	26	0	.313	.421	.354

PITCHER	W	L	ERA	G	GS	SV	IP	H	BB	SO
L.Gomez	1	0	1.00	1	1	0	9.0	9	1	8
R.Ruffing	1	0	3.00	1	1	0	9.0	10	6	10
G.Pipgras	1	0	4.50	1	1	0	8.0	9	3	1
W.Moore	1	0	0.00	1	0	0	5.1	2	0	1
H.Pennock	0	0	2.25	2	0	2	4.0	2	1	4
J.Allen	0	0	40.50	1	1	0	0.2	5	0	0
Totals	4	0	3.00	7	4	2	36.0	37	11	24

CHI (NL)

PLAYER, POS	G	AB	R	H	2B	3B	HR	RBI	BB	SO	SB	AVG	OBP	SLG
K.Cuyler, of	4	18	2	5	1	1	1	2	0	3	1	.278	.278	.444
B.Herman, 2b	4	18	5	4	1	0	0	1	1	3	0	.222	.263	.278
R.Stephenson, of	4	18	2	8	1	0	0	4	0	0	0	.444	.444	.500
W.English, 3b	4	17	2	3	0	0	0	1	2	2	0	.176	.263	.176
G.Hartnett, c	4	16	2	5	2	0	1	1	1	3	0	.313	.353	.438
C.Grimm, 1b	4	15	2	5	2	0	0	1	2	2	0	.333	.412	.467
B.Jurges, ss	3	11	1	4	1	0	0	1	0	1	2	.364	.364	.455
F.Demaree, of	2	7	1	2	0	0	1	4	1	0	0	.286	.375	.286
J.Moore, of	2	7	1	0	0	0	0	0	2	1	0	.000	.222	.000
M.Koenig, ss	2	4	1	1	0	1	0	1	1	0	0	.250	.400	.750
L.Warneke, p	2	4	0	0	0	0	0	0	0	3	0	.000	.000	.000
R.Hemsley, c	3	3	0	0	0	0	0	0	0	3	0	.000	.000	.000
M.Gudat, ph	2	2	0	0	0	0	0	0	0	1	0	.000	.000	.000
J.May, p	2	2	0	0	0	0	0	0	0	0	0	.000	.000	.000
C.Root, p	1	2	0	0	0	0	0	0	0	1	0	.000	.000	.000
G.Bush, p	2	1	0	0	0	0	0	0	1	0	0	.000	.500	.000
B.Grimes, p	2	1	0	0	0	0	0	0	0	1	0	.000	.000	.000
S.Hack, ph	1	0	0	0	0	0	0	0	0	0	0	.000	.000	.000
Totals		146	19	37	8	2	3	16	11	24	3	.253	.306	.336

PITCHER	W	L	ERA	G	GS	SV	IP	H	BB	SO
L.Warneke	0	1	5.91	2	1	0	10.2	15	5	8
G.Bush	0	1	14.29	2	2	0	5.2	5	6	2
J.May	0	1	11.57	2	0	0	4.2	9	3	4
C.Root	0	1	10.38	1	1	0	4.1	6	3	4
B.Grimes	0	0	23.63	2	0	0	2.2	7	2	0
P.Malone	0	0	0.00	1	0	0	2.2	1	4	4
B.Tinning	0	0	0.00	2	0	0	2.1	0	0	3
B.Smith	0	0	9.00	1	0	0	1.0	2	0	1
Totals	0	4	9.26	13	4	0	34.0	45	23	26

GAME 1 / SEPT. 28

BUSH, GRIMES(6), SMITH(8) VS. RUFFING							41,459
CHI	200	000	220	6	10	1	
NY	000	305	31X	12	8	2	

The Cubs got to Red Ruffing for two in the top of the first inning as Babe Ruth's slip in right field led to both runs. That was Chicago's moment in the sun, however. In the fourth, Ruth singled in a run and Lou Gehrig lined a two-run blast to put New York ahead to stay. The Bronx Bombers added four in the sixth.

GAME 2 / SEPT. 29

WARNEKE VS. GOMEZ							50,709
CHI	101	000	000	2	9	0	
NY	202	010	00X	5	10	1	

Chicago again took advantage of porous Yankees defense to go ahead in the first inning, but the lead lasted even less time than the previous day as Lou Gehrig and Bill Dickey singled in runs in the home first. When the Cubs tied it in the top of the third, Ben Chapman's two-run single in the bottom of the inning put New York ahead to stay.

GAME 3 / OCT. 1

PIPGRAS, PENNOCK(9) VS. ROOT, MALONE(5), MAY(7), TINNING(9)							49,986
NY	301	020	001	7	8	1	
CHI	102	100	001	5	9	4	

The Wrigley Field faithful had been all over Babe Ruth from the start, and really tore into the Babe after he missed a liner in the bottom of the fourth. When Ruth heard a fresh dose of abuse from the Chicago dugout as he came to the plate against Charlie Root in the top of the fifth, finger pointing and arm waving ensued (according to some). Ruth followed by blasting one to the base of the flagpole in center, and the legend of the "Called Shot" was born. Lou Gehrig, a .529 hitter in the Series, followed Ruth's momentous second blast with *his* second home run of the game. Not even an Iron Horse could upstage the Bambino.

GAME 4 / OCT. 2

ALLEN, MOORE(1), PENNOCK(7) VS. BUSH, WARNEKE(1), MAY(4), TINNING(7), GRIMES(9)							49,844
NY	102	002	404	13	19	4	
CHI	400	001	001	6	9	1	

The Cubs again held the early lead, chasing Johnny Allen with four runs in the bottom of the first. Yet the game still wound up lopsided in favor of the Yankees. The Cubs outscored New York in the first inning during the Series, 8–6, but the Yankees outscored them in every other inning, 31–11. The seventh and ninth were the big innings for New York this time. Tony Lazzeri homered twice, one to left and once to right, and the Yankees won their 12th straight World Series game.

1936 World Series
New York Yankees (4) vs. New York Giants (2)

This was the first World Series the Yankees played without Babe Ruth in the lineup, but a new dynasty was beginning. Joe DiMaggio was stellar as a rookie, Lou Gehrig hit 49 homers and drove in 152, the Yankees hit .300 as a team, and finished 19 ½ games ahead of the Tigers. The Giants, who twice beat the Yankees in the 1920s, were in deep trouble this time.

NY (AL)

PLAYER, POS	G	AB	R	H	2B	3B	HR	RBI	BB	SO	SB	AVG	OBP	SLG
F.Crosetti, ss	6	26	5	7	2	0	0	3	3	5	0	.269	.345	.346
J.DiMaggio, of	6	26	3	9	3	0	0	3	1	3	0	.346	.370	.462
B.Dickey, c	6	25	5	3	0	0	1	5	3	4	0	.120	.214	.120
R.Rolfe, 3b	6	25	5	10	0	0	0	4	3	1	0	.400	.464	.400
L.Gehrig, 1b	6	24	5	7	1	0	2	7	3	2	0	.292	.370	.333
G.Selkirk, of	6	24	6	8	0	1	2	3	4	4	0	.333	.429	.417
J.Powell, of	6	22	8	10	1	0	1	5	4	4	1	.455	.538	.500
T.Lazzeri, 2b	6	20	4	5	0	0	1	7	4	4	0	.250	.375	.250
L.Gomez, p	2	8	1	2	0	0	0	3	0	3	0	.250	.250	.250
R.Ruffing, p	3	5	0	0	0	0	0	0	1	2	0	.000	.167	.000
M.Pearson, p	1	4	0	2	1	0	0	0	0	0	0	.500	.500	.750
B.Hadley, p	1	2	0	0	0	0	0	0	0	1	0	.000	.000	.000
J.Murphy, p	1	2	1	1	0	0	0	1	0	1	0	.500	.500	.500
R.Johnson, ph	2	1	0	0	0	0	0	0	0	1	0	.000	.000	.000
P.Malone, p	2	1	0	1	0	0	0	0	0	0	0	1.000	1.000	1.000
B.Seeds, pr	1	0	0	0	0	0	0	0	0	0	0	.000	.000	.000
Totals		215	43	65	8	1	7	41	26	35	1	.302	.380	.349

PITCHER	W	L	ERA	G	GS	SV	IP	H	BB	SO
L.Gomez	2	0	4.70	2	2	0	15.1	14	11	9
R.Ruffing	0	1	5.14	2	2	0	14.0	16	5	12
M.Pearson	1	0	2.00	1	1	0	9.0	7	2	7
B.Hadley	1	0	1.13	1	1	0	8.0	10	1	2
P.Malone	0	1	1.80	2	0	1	5.0	2	1	2
J.Murphy	0	0	3.38	1	0	1	2.2	1	1	1
Totals	4	2	3.50	9	6	2	54.0	50	21	33

NY (NL)

PLAYER, POS	G	AB	R	H	2B	3B	HR	RBI	BB	SO	SB	AVG	OBP	SLG
J.Moore, of	6	28	4	6	2	0	1	1	1	4	0	.214	.241	.286
B.Terry, 1b	6	25	1	6	0	0	0	5	1	4	0	.240	.269	.240
M.Ott, of	6	23	4	7	2	0	1	3	3	1	0	.304	.385	.391
D.Bartell, ss	6	21	5	8	3	0	1	3	4	4	0	.381	.480	.524
T.Jackson, 3b	6	21	1	4	0	0	0	1	1	3	0	.190	.227	.190

NY (NL) (CONT.)

PLAYER, POS	G	AB	R	H	2B	3B	HR	RBI	BB	SO	SB	AVG	OBP	SLG
B.Whitehead, 2b	6	21	1	1	0	0	0	2	1	3	0	.048	.091	.048
G.Mancuso, c	6	19	3	5	2	0	0	1	3	3	0	.263	.364	.368
J.Ripple, of	5	12	2	4	0	0	1	3	3	3	0	.333	.467	.333
C.Hubbell, p	2	6	0	2	0	0	0	1	0	0	0	.333	.333	.333
H.Leiber, of	2	6	0	0	0	0	0	0	2	2	0	.000	.250	.000
F.Fitzsimmons, p	2	4	0	2	0	0	0	0	0	1	0	.500	.500	.500
H.Schumacher, p	2	4	0	0	0	0	0	0	1	0	0	.000	.200	.000
M.Koenig, 2b	3	3	0	1	0	0	0	0	0	1	0	.333	.333	.333
S.Leslie, ph	3	3	0	2	0	0	0	0	0	0	0	.667	.667	.667
S.Castleman, p	1	2	0	1	0	0	0	0	0	0	0	.500	.500	.500
H.Danning, c	2	2	0	0	0	0	0	0	0	1	0	.000	.000	.000
K.Davis, ph	4	2	2	1	0	0	0	0	0	0	0	.500	.500	.500
E.Mayo, 3b	1	1	0	0	0	0	0	0	0	0	0	.000	.000	.000
F.Gabler, p	2	0	0	0	0	0	0	0	1	0	0	.000	1.000	.000
Totals		203	23	50	9	0	4	20	21	33	0	.246	.317	.291

PITCHER	W	L	ERA	G	GS	SV	IP	H	BB	SO
C.Hubbell	1	1	2.25	2	2	0	16.0	15	2	10
H.Schumacher	1	1	5.25	2	2	0	12.0	13	10	11
F.Fitzsimmons	0	2	5.40	2	2	0	11.2	13	2	6
F.Gabler	0	0	7.20	2	0	0	5.0	7	4	0
S.Castleman	0	0	2.08	1	0	0	4.1	3	2	5
H.Gumbert	0	0	36.00	2	0	0	2.0	7	4	2
D.Coffman	0	0	32.40	2	0	0	1.2	5	1	1
A.Smith	0	0	81.00	1	0	0	0.1	2	1	0
Totals	2	4	6.79	14	6	0	53.0	65	26	35

GAME 1 / SEPT. 30

RUFFING VS. HUBBELL — **39,419**

				R	H	E
NY-A	001	000	000	1	7	2
NY-N	000	011	04X	6	9	1

After winning his final 16 decisions of the regular season, Carl Hubbell continued his masterful pitching. He allowed only one run while striking out eight. A four-run eighth by the Giants gave Hubbell breathing room.

GAME 2 / OCT. 2

GOMEZ VS. SCHUMACHER, SMITH(3), COFFMAN(3), GABLER(5), GUMBERT(9) — **43,543**

				R	H	E
NY-A	207	001	206	18	17	0
NY-N	010	300	000	4	6	1

Tony Lazzeri's grand slam in the third highlighted the record 18-run onslaught. The Yankees scored against all five pitchers the Giants ran out to the mound.

GAME 3 / OCT. 3

FITZSIMMONS VS. HADLEY, MALONE(9) — **64,842**

				R	H	E
NY-N	000	010	000	1	11	0
NY-A	010	000	01X	2	4	0

Missed opportunities beat the Giants, who stranded nine runners, including two in each of the fifth, seventh, and eighth innings. The Yankees won it in the eighth on a two-out hit by Frankie Crosetti.

GAME 4 / OCT. 4

HUBBELL, GABLER(8) VS. PEARSON — **66,669**

				R	H	E
NY-N	000	100	010	2	7	1
NY-A	013	000	01X	5	10	1

The Yankees finally got to Carl Hubbell, getting five hits and four runs in the first three innings. Lou Gehrig's two-run homer in the third was the big blow.

GAME 5 / OCT. 5

SCHUMACHER VS. RUFFING, MALONE(7) — **50,024**

					R	H	E
NY-N	300	001	000	1	5	8	3
NY-A	011	002	000	0	4	10	1

Hal Schumacher allowed 10 hits and 6 walks, but the Yankees let him off the hook by hitting into 3 double plays and twice being caught stealing. Bill Terry's sacrifice fly in the 10th brought home Jo-Jo Moore with the go-ahead run. Schumacher escaped trouble again in the bottom of the inning when Bob Seeds, running for Bill Dickey, was caught stealing to end the game.

GAME 6 / OCT. 6

GOMEZ, MURPHY(7) VS. FITZSIMMONS, CASTLEMAN(4), COFFMAN(9), GUMBERT(9) — **38,427**

				R	H	E
NY-A	021	200	017	13	17	2
NY-N	200	010	110	5	9	1

Things seemed to be looking up for the Giants after getting two in the bottom of the first off Lefty Gomez. But the Yankees got those runs right back in the second on a two-run homer by Jake Powell and took the lead for good in the next frame. The Giants still had a chance, trailing by one headed into the top of the ninth, but the Yankees sent 13 men to the plate. Joe DiMaggio had two hits in the inning as the Yankees scored seven to ice the game and the Series.

1937 World Series
New York Yankees (4) vs. New York Giants (1)

Other than a six-run second inning in the fourth game of the World Series, which led to the Giants' only win, the boys from Manhattan were thoroughly outclassed by their counterparts from the Bronx. Aside from that one inning, the Giants scored only six runs the rest of the Series had had no real chances to win any of the other four games.

NY (AL)

PLAYER, POS	G	AB	R	H	2B	3B	HR	RBI	BB	SO	SB	AVG	OBP	SLG
J.DiMaggio, of	5	22	2	6	0	0	1	4	0	3	0	.273	.273	.273
F.Crosetti, ss	5	21	2	1	0	0	0	0	3	2	0	.048	.167	.048
M.Hoag, of	5	20	4	6	1	0	1	2	0	1	0	.300	.300	.350
R.Rolfe, 3b	5	20	3	6	2	1	0	1	3	2	0	.300	.391	.500
B.Dickey, c	5	19	3	4	0	1	0	3	2	2	0	.211	.286	.316
G.Selkirk, of	5	19	5	5	1	0	0	6	2	0	0	.263	.333	.316
L.Gehrig, 1b	5	17	4	5	1	1	1	3	5	4	0	.294	.455	.471
T.Lazzeri, 2b	5	15	3	6	0	1	1	2	3	3	0	.400	.500	.533
L.Gomez, p	2	6	2	1	0	0	0	1	2	1	0	.167	.375	.167
R.Ruffing, p	1	4	0	2	1	0	0	3	0	0	0	.500	.500	.750
M.Pearson, p	1	3	0	0	0	0	0	0	1	1	0	.000	.250	.000
I.Andrews, p	1	2	0	0	0	0	0	0	0	1	0	.000	.000	.000
J.Powell, ph	1	1	0	0	0	0	0	0	0	1	0	.000	.000	.000
Totals		169	28	42	6	4	4	25	21	21	0	.249	.335	.331

PITCHER	W	L	ERA	G	GS	SV	IP	H	BB	SO
L.Gomez	2	0	1.50	2	2	0	18.0	16	2	8
R.Ruffing	1	0	1.00	1	1	0	9.0	7	3	8
M.Pearson	1	0	1.04	1	1	0	8.2	5	2	4
I.Andrews	0	0	3.18	1	0	0	5.2	6	4	1
B.Hadley	0	1	33.75	1	1	0	1.1	6	0	0
K.Wicker	0	0	0.00	1	0	0	1.0	0	0	0
J.Murphy	0	0	0.00	1	0	1	0.1	0	0	0
Totals	4	1	2.45	8	5	1	44.0	40	11	21

NY (NL)

PLAYER, POS	G	AB	R	H	2B	3B	HR	RBI	BB	SO	SB	AVG	OBP	SLG
J.Moore, of	5	23	1	9	1	0	0	1	0	1	0	.391	.391	.435
D.Bartell, ss	5	21	3	5	1	0	0	1	0	3	0	.238	.238	.286
M.Ott, 3b	5	20	1	4	0	0	1	3	1	4	0	.200	.238	.200
J.McCarthy, 1b	5	19	1	4	1	0	0	1	1	2	0	.211	.250	.263
J.Ripple, of	5	17	2	5	0	0	0	0	3	1	0	.294	.400	.294
B.Whitehead, 2b	5	16	1	4	2	0	0	0	2	0	1	.250	.333	.375
H.Danning, c	3	12	0	3	1	0	0	2	0	2	0	.250	.250	.333
H.Leiber, of	3	11	2	4	0	0	0	2	1	1	0	.364	.417	.364
G.Mancuso, c	3	8	0	0	0	0	0	1	0	1	0	.000	.000	.000
L.Chiozza, of	2	7	0	2	0	0	0	0	1	1	0	.286	.375	.286
C.Hubbell, p	2	6	1	0	0	0	0	1	0	0	0	.000	.000	.000
W.Berger, ph	3	3	0	0	0	0	0	0	0	1	0	.000	.000	.000
C.Melton, p	3	2	0	0	0	0	0	0	1	1	0	.000	.333	.000
D.Coffman, p	2	1	0	0	0	0	0	0	0	1	0	.000	.000	.000
S.Leslie, ph	2	1	0	0	0	0	0	0	1	0	0	.000	.500	.000
B.Ryan, ph	1	1	0	0	0	0	0	0	0	1	0	.000	.000	.000
H.Schumacher, p	1	1	0	0	0	0	0	0	0	1	0	.000	.000	.000
Totals		169	12	40	6	0	1	12	11	21	1	.237	.283	.272

PITCHER	W	L	ERA	G	GS	SV	IP	H	BB	SO
C.Hubbell	1	1	3.77	2	2	0	14.1	12	4	7
C.Melton	0	2	4.91	3	2	0	11.0	12	6	7
H.Schumacher	0	1	6.00	1	1	0	6.0	9	4	3
D.Coffman	0	0	4.15	2	0	0	4.1	2	5	1
D.Brennan	0	0	0.00	2	0	0	3.0	1	1	1
A.Smith	0	0	3.00	2	0	0	3.0	2	0	1
H.Gumbert	0	0	27.00	2	0	0	1.1	4	1	1
Totals	1	4	4.81	14	5	0	43.0	42	21	21

GAME 1 / OCT. 6

HUBBELL, GUMBERT(6), COFFMAN(6), SMITH(8) VS. GOMEZ — **60,573**

				R	H	E
NY-N	000	010	000	1	6	2
NY-A	000	007	01X	8	7	0

Five singles, four walks, and two errors led to seven runs in the bottom of the sixth for the Yankees. Lefty Gomez was extremely efficient on the mound, allowing only one run on six hits while striking out just two Giants.

GAME 2 / OCT. 7						
MELTON, GUMBERT(5), COFFMAN(6) VS. RUFFING						**57,675**
NY-N	100	000	000	1	7	0
NY-A	000	024	20X	8	12	0

It took the Yankees a while to get going—they had only one runner in the first three innings—but the end result was the same as in the first game. Red Ruffing was the star all the way around, throwing a complete game and driving in three runs with a single in the fifth and a two-run double in the sixth.

GAME 3 / OCT. 8						
PEARSON, MURPHY(9) VS. SCHUMACHER, MELTON(7), BRENNAN(9)						**37,385**
NY-A	012	110	000	5	9	0
NY-N	000	000	100	1	5	4

The Giants were held to only one run for the third straight day. It could have been worse than a four-run loss for the Giants, but the Yankees left seven runners on in the first four innings.

GAME 4 / OCT. 9						
HADLEY, ANDREWS(2), WICKER(8) VS. HUBBELL						**44,293**
NY-A	101	000	001	3	6	0
NY-N	060	000	10X	7	12	3

The Giants managed only one extra-base hit in the game, a seventh-inning double by Harry Danning that plated an insurance run. The Giants unloaded on Bump Hadley in the second to avoid being swept. Joe DiMaggio, Lou Gehrig and Bill Dickey combined to go 1-for-12 against Carl Hubbell.

GAME 5 / OCT. 10						
GOMEZ VS. MELTON, SMITH(6), BRENNAN(8)						**38,216**
NY-A	011	020	000	4	8	0
NY-N	002	000	000	2	10	0

Solo home runs by Myril Hoag and Joe DiMaggio staked the Yankees to an early lead. After the Giants rallied to tie the game in the third on a two-run blast by Mel Ott, the Yankees came up with the deciding runs in the fifth. Lefty Gomez singled in Tony Lazzeri, who tripled to lead off the frame; Lefty then came home on a two-out double by Lou Gehrig. Gomez went the distance to make the Yankees the first team to win six world championships.

1938 World Series
New York Yankees (4) vs. Chicago Cubs (0)

As was the case in 1932, the Yankees were simply too powerful for the Cubs. With three .300 hitters—plus Lou Gehrig at .295 in his final full season—and five guys belting at least 22 home runs, the Bronx Bombers hit the most homers and scored the most runs in baseball. The Yankees outscored the Cubs in the sweep, 22–9, and Chicago never led by more than one run in any game.

NY (AL)

PLAYER, POS	G	AB	R	H	2B	3B	HR	RBI	BB	SO	SB	AVG	OBP	SLG
R.Rolfe, 3b	4	18	0	3	0	0	0	1	0	3	1	.167	.167	.167
F.Crosetti, ss	4	16	1	4	2	1	1	6	2	4	0	.250	.333	.500
T.Henrich, of	4	16	3	4	1	0	1	1	0	1	0	.250	.250	.313
B.Dickey, c	4	15	2	6	0	0	1	2	1	0	1	.400	.438	.400
J.DiMaggio, of	4	15	4	4	0	0	1	2	1	1	0	.267	.313	.267
J.Gordon, 2b	4	15	3	6	2	0	1	6	1	3	1	.400	.438	.533
L.Gehrig, 1b	4	14	4	4	0	0	0	0	2	3	0	.286	.375	.286
G.Selkirk, of	3	10	0	2	0	0	0	1	2	1	0	.200	.333	.200
R.Ruffing, p	2	6	1	1	0	0	0	1	1	0	0	.167	.286	.167
M.Hoag, of	2	5	3	2	1	0	0	1	0	0	0	.400	.400	.600
M.Pearson, p	1	3	1	1	0	0	0	0	1	0	0	.333	.500	.333
L.Gomez, p	1	2	0	0	0	0	0	0	0	0	0	.000	.000	.000
J.Powell, of	1	0	0	0	0	0	0	0	0	0	0	.000	.000	.000
Totals		135	22	37	6	1	5	21	11	16	3	.274	.333	.333

PITCHER	W	L	ERA	G	GS	SV	IP	H	BB	SO
R.Ruffing	2	0	1.50	2	2	0	18.0	17	2	11
M.Pearson	1	0	1.00	1	1	0	9.0	5	2	9
L.Gomez	1	0	3.86	1	1	0	7.0	9	1	5
J.Murphy	0	0	0.00	1	0	1	2.0	2	1	1
Totals	4	0	1.75	5	4	1	36.0	33	6	26

CHI (NL)

PLAYER, POS	G	AB	R	H	2B	3B	HR	RBI	BB	SO	SB	AVG	OBP	SLG
S.Hack, 3b	4	17	3	8	1	0	0	1	1	2	0	.471	.500	.529
B.Herman, 2b	4	16	1	3	0	0	0	0	1	4	0	.188	.235	.188
R.Collins, 1b	4	15	1	2	0	0	0	0	0	3	0	.133	.133	.133
P.Cavarretta, of	4	13	1	6	1	0	0	0	0	1	0	.462	.462	.538
B.Jurges, ss	4	13	0	3	1	0	0	0	1	3	0	.231	.286	.308
J.Marty, of	3	12	1	6	1	0	1	5	0	2	0	.500	.500	.583
C.Reynolds, of	4	12	0	0	0	0	0	0	1	3	0	.000	.077	.000
G.Hartnett, c	3	11	0	1	0	1	0	0	0	2	0	.091	.091	.273
F.Demaree, of	3	10	1	1	0	0	0	0	1	2	0	.100	.182	.100
K.O'Dea, c	3	5	1	1	0	0	1	2	1	0	0	.200	.333	.200
D.Dean, p	2	3	0	2	0	0	0	0	0	0	0	.667	.667	.667
B.Lee, p	2	3	0	0	0	0	0	0	0	1	0	.000	.000	.000
C.Bryant, p	1	2	0	0	0	0	0	0	0	1	0	.000	.000	.000
A.Galan, ph	2	2	0	0	0	0	0	0	0	1	0	.000	.000	.000
T.Lazzeri, ph	2	2	0	0	0	0	0	0	0	1	0	.000	.000	.000
Totals		136	9	33	4	1	2	8	6	26	0	.243	.275	.287

PITCHER	W	L	ERA	G	GS	SV	IP	H	BB	SO
B.Lee	0	2	2.45	2	2	0	11.0	15	1	8
D.Dean	0	1	6.48	2	1	0	8.1	8	1	2
C.Bryant	0	1	6.75	1	1	0	5.1	6	5	3
L.French	0	0	2.70	3	0	0	3.1	1	1	2
C.Root	0	0	3.00	1	0	0	3.0	3	0	1
J.Russell	0	0	0.00	2	0	0	1.2	1	1	0
V.Page	0	0	13.50	1	0	0	1.1	2	0	0
T.Carleton	0	0	INF	1	0	0	0.0	1	2	0
Totals	0	4	5.03	13	4	0	34.0	37	11	16

GAME 1 / OCT. 5						
RUFFING VS. LEE, RUSSELL(9)						**43,642**
NY	020	000	100	3	12	1
CHI	001	000	000	1	9	1

The opener featured Red Ruffing and Bill Lee, the leaders in wins in each league, but Red ruled the day. Ruffing scattered nine hits and didn't walk anybody. Bill Dickey's RBI single in the sixth—the third of his four hits—proved to be more than enough.

GAME 2 / OCT. 6						
GOMEZ, MURPHY(8) VS. J.DEAN, FRENCH(9)						**42,108**
NY	020	000	022	6	7	2
CHI	102	000	000	3	11	0

This was, realistically, the only chance the Cubs had to win a game in the World Series. Chicago jumped out to an early 1–0 lead and went up 3–2 on Joe Marty's two-run double in the third. Dizzy Dean made that score stand up until two outs in the top of the eighth inning. Frankie Crosetti's two-run blast gave the Yankees the lead and Joe DiMaggio added a two-run homer in the top of the ninth to end any hopes of a Cubs comeback.

GAME 3 / OCT. 8						
BRYANT, RUSSELL(6), FRENCH(7) VS. PEARSON						**55,236**
CHI	000	010	010	2	5	1
NY	000	022	01X	5	7	2

Cubs starter Clay Bryant carried a no-hitter two outs into the bottom of the fifth before rookie second baseman Joe Gordon hit a solo home run to tie the game and erase Chicago's last lead of the Series. Gordon's two-run single the next inning gave the Yankees an insurmountable lead. Monte Pearson cruised for New York, fanning nine.

GAME 4 / OCT. 9						
LEE, ROOT(4), PAGE(7), FRENCH(8), CARLETON(8), J.DEAN(8) VS. RUFFING						59,847
CHI	000	100	020	3	8	1
NY	030	001	04X	8	11	1

The Yankees jumped on the Cubs quickly with three unearned runs in the bottom of the second. Red Ruffing's second complete game wasn't as spectacular as his first, yet it was still enough. It marked the eighth straight time the Yankees had beaten the Cubs in a World Series game, dating to 1932. It was the Yankees' third straight world championship, and seventh overall.

1939 World Series
New York Yankees (4) vs. Cincinnati Reds (0)

Bing. Bang. Boom. The Yankees concluded the most dominant performance in World Series history with their second straight sweep. In the last three fall classics combined, New York lost only one game. They lost three contests total in their streak of four straight titles that began in '36.

NY (AL)

PLAYER, POS	G	AB	R	H	2B	3B	HR	RBI	BB	SO	SB	AVG	OBP	SLG
F.Crosetti, ss	4	16	2	1	0	0	0	1	2	2	0	.063	.167	.063
J.DiMaggio, of	4	16	3	5	0	0	1	3	1	1	0	.313	.353	.313
C.Keller, of	4	16	8	7	1	1	3	6	1	2	0	.438	.471	.625
R.Rolfe, 3b	4	16	2	2	0	0	0	0	0	0	0	.125	.125	.125
B.Dickey, c	4	15	2	4	0	0	2	5	1	2	0	.267	.313	.267
B.Dahlgren, 1b	4	14	2	3	2	0	1	2	0	4	0	.214	.214	.357
J.Gordon, 2b	4	14	1	2	0	0	0	1	0	2	0	.143	.143	.143
G.Selkirk, of	4	12	0	2	1	0	0	0	3	2	0	.167	.333	.250
B.Hadley, p	1	3	0	0	0	0	0	0	0	0	0	.000	.000	.000
R.Ruffing, p	1	3	0	1	0	0	0	0	0	1	0	.333	.333	.333
J.Murphy, p	1	2	0	0	0	0	0	0	0	1	0	.000	.000	.000
M.Pearson, p	1	2	0	0	0	0	0	0	0	1	0	.000	.000	.000
L.Gomez, p	1	1	0	0	0	0	0	0	0	1	0	.000	.000	.000
O.Hildebrand, p	1	1	0	0	0	0	0	0	0	1	0	.000	.000	.000
S.Sundra, p	1	0	0	0	0	0	0	0	1	0	0	.000	1.000	.000
Totals		131	20	27	4	1	7	18	9	20	0	.206	.257	.252

PITCHER	W	L	ERA	G	GS	SV	IP	H	BB	SO
M.Pearson	1	0	0.00	1	1	0	9.0	2	1	8
R.Ruffing	1	0	1.00	1	1	0	9.0	4	1	4
B.Hadley	1	0	2.25	1	0	0	8.0	7	3	2
O.Hildebrand	0	0	0.00	1	1	0	4.0	2	0	3
J.Murphy	1	0	2.70	1	0	0	3.1	5	0	2
S.Sundra	0	0	0.00	1	0	0	2.2	4	1	2
L.Gomez	0	0	9.00	1	1	0	1.0	3	0	1
Totals	4	0	1.22	7	4	0	37.0	27	6	22

CIN (NL)

PLAYER, POS	G	AB	R	H	2B	3B	HR	RBI	BB	SO	SB	AVG	OBP	SLG
L.Frey, 2b	4	17	0	0	0	0	0	0	1	4	0	.000	.056	.000
B.Werber, 3b	4	16	1	4	0	0	0	2	2	0	0	.250	.333	.250
W.Berger, of	4	15	0	0	0	0	0	1	0	4	0	.000	.000	.000
I.Goodman, of	4	15	3	5	1	0	0	1	1	2	1	.333	.375	.400
F.McCormick, 1b	4	15	1	6	1	0	0	1	0	1	0	.400	.400	.467
E.Lombardi, c	4	14	0	3	0	0	0	2	0	1	0	.214	.214	.214
B.Myers, ss	4	12	2	4	0	1	0	0	2	3	0	.333	.429	.500
H.Craft, of	4	11	0	1	0	0	0	0	0	6	0	.091	.091	.091
P.Derringer, p	2	5	0	1	0	0	0	0	0	0	0	.200	.200	.200
A.Simmons, of	1	4	1	1	1	0	0	0	0	0	0	.250	.250	.500
B.Walters, p	2	3	0	0	0	0	0	0	0	0	0	.000	.000	.000
W.Hershberger, c	3	2	0	1	0	0	0	1	0	0	0	.500	.500	.500
N.Bongiovanni, ph	1	1	0	0	0	0	0	0	0	0	0	.000	.000	.000
L.Gamble, ph	1	1	0	0	0	0	0	0	0	1	0	.000	.000	.000
W.Moore, p	1	1	0	0	0	0	0	0	0	0	0	.000	.000	.000
J.Thompson, p	1	1	0	1	0	0	0	0	0	0	0	1.000	1.000	1.000
F.Bordagaray, pr	2	0	0	0	0	0	0	0	0	0	0	.000	.000	.000
Totals		133	8	27	3	1	0	8	6	22	1	.203	.243	.241

PITCHER	W	L	ERA	G	GS	SV	IP	H	BB	SO
P.Derringer	0	1	2.35	2	2	0	15.1	9	3	9
B.Walters	0	2	4.91	2	1	0	11.0	13	1	6
J.Thompson	0	1	13.50	1	1	0	4.2	5	4	3
W.Moore	0	0	0.00	1	0	0	3.0	0	0	2
L.Grissom	0	0	0.00	1	0	0	1.1	0	1	0
Totals	0	4	4.33	7	4	0	35.1	27	9	20

GAME 1 / OCT. 4						
DERRINGER VS. RUFFING						58,541
CIN	000	100	000	1	4	0
NY	000	010	001	2	6	0

This game was tied heading into the bottom of the ninth. Charlie Keller tripled with one out, bringing up Joe DiMaggio with Bill Dickey on deck. Paul Derringer walked DiMaggio intentionally, to no one's surprise, but the Reds elected to pitch to Dickey, rather than walk him and pitch to George Selkirk with the bases loaded. Dickey delivered a single to center, and the Reds lost a golden opportunity.

GAME 2 / OCT. 5						
WALTERS VS. PEARSON						59,791
CIN	000	000	000	0	2	0
NY	003	100	00X	4	9	0

Monte Pearson was spectacular for the Yankees, holding the Reds without a hit until Ernie Lombardi singled with one out in the eighth. Pearson was the only Yankee to win once in each of the four straight world championships.

GAME 3 / OCT. 7						
GOMEZ, HADLEY(2) VS. THOMPSON, GRISSOM(5), MOORE(7)						32,723
NY	202	030	000	7	5	1
CIN	120	000	000	3	10	0

Two-run blasts by Joe DiMaggio in the third and Charlie Keller in the fifth—his second homer of the game—erased an early Cincinnati lead. Bill Dickey also homered in the fifth for New York. The Yankees needed only five hits to score seven times, thanks to early control problems from Cincinnati's Junior Thompson.

GAME 4 / OCT. 8							
HILDEBRAND, SUNDRA(5), MURPHY(7) VS. DERRINGER, WALTERS(8)							32,794
NY	000	000	202	3	7	7	1
CIN	000	000	310	0	4	11	4

Late-inning defensive woes doomed the Reds. The Yankees tied the game in the top of the ninth after shortstop Billy Myers dropped a throw from second baseman Lonny Frey on what might have been a double play. Myers booted another ball in the 10th that opened the gates again for the Yankees. Three runs scored on one play as Ernie Lombardi lay dazed after a collision while Joe DiMaggio raced around the bases during "Lombardi's snooze." The Reds got the first two on in the bottom of the inning, but Johnny Murphy retired Lombardi, Al Simmons, and Wally Berger in order to complete the sweep.

1941 World Series
New York Yankees (4) vs. Brooklyn Dodgers (1)

The Yankees were back in the World Series after placing third in 1940, the lowest the club had finished in a decade. For the first time they took on the Brooklyn Dodgers in the World Series. Brooklyn hadn't played in a Series since 1920, but they would become the Yankees' favorite fall partner. The results were predictable; the games were not.

NY (AL)

PLAYER, POS	G	AB	R	H	2B	3B	HR	RBI	BB	SO	SB	AVG	OBP	SLG
J.Sturm, 1b	5	21	0	6	0	0	0	2	0	2	1	.286	.286	.286
R.Rolfe, 3b	5	20	2	6	0	0	0	0	2	1	0	.300	.364	.300
J.DiMaggio, of	5	19	1	5	0	0	0	1	2	2	0	.263	.333	.263
B.Dickey, c	5	18	3	3	1	0	0	1	3	1	0	.167	.286	.222
T.Henrich, of	5	18	4	3	1	0	1	1	3	3	0	.167	.286	.222
C.Keller, of	5	18	5	7	2	0	0	5	3	1	0	.389	.476	.500
P.Rizzuto, ss	5	18	0	2	0	0	0	0	3	1	1	.111	.238	.111
J.Gordon, 2b	5	14	2	7	1	1	1	5	7	0	0	.500	.667	.714
T.Bonham, p	1	4	0	0	0	0	0	0	0	4	0	.000	.000	.000
M.Russo, p	1	4	0	0	0	0	0	0	0	1	0	.000	.000	.000
R.Ruffing, p	1	3	0	0	0	0	0	0	0	0	0	.000	.000	.000
S.Chandler, p	1	2	0	1	0	0	0	1	0	0	0	.500	.500	.500
A.Donald, p	1	2	0	0	0	0	0	0	0	1	0	.000	.000	.000
J.Murphy, p	2	2	0	0	0	0	0	0	0	1	0	.000	.000	.000
G.Selkirk, ph	2	2	0	1	0	0	0	0	0	0	0	.500	.500	.500
M.Breuer, p	1	1	0	0	0	0	0	0	0	0	0	.000	.000	.000
F.Bordagaray, pr	1	0	0	0	0	0	0	0	0	0	0	.000	.000	.000
B.Rosar, c	1	0	0	0	0	0	0	0	0	0	0	.000	.000	.000
Totals		166	17	41	5	1	2	16	23	18	2	.247	.346	.289

NY (AL) (CONT.)										
PITCHER	W	L	ERA	G	GS	SV	IP	H	BB	SO
T.Bonham	1	0	1.00	1	1	0	9.0	4	2	2
R.Ruffing	1	0	1.00	1	1	0	9.0	6	3	5
M.Russo	1	0	1.00	1	1	0	9.0	4	2	5
J.Murphy	1	0	0.00	2	0	0	6.0	2	1	3
S.Chandler	0	1	3.60	1	1	0	5.0	4	2	2
A.Donald	0	0	9.00	1	1	0	4.0	6	3	2
M.Breuer	0	0	0.00	1	0	0	3.0	3	1	2
Totals	4	1	1.80	8	5	0	45.0	29	14	21

BRO (NL)														
PLAYER, POS	G	AB	R	H	2B	3B	HR	RBI	BB	SO	SB	AVG	OBP	SLG
P.Wee Reese, ss	5	20	1	4	0	0	0	2	0	0	0	.200	.200	.200
P.Reiser, of	5	20	1	4	1	1	1	3	1	6	0	.200	.238	.350
D.Camilli, 1b	5	18	1	3	1	0	0	1	1	6	0	.167	.211	.222
D.Walker, of	5	18	3	4	2	0	0	0	2	1	0	.222	.300	.333
J.Medwick, of	5	17	1	4	1	0	0	0	1	2	0	.235	.278	.294
M.Owen, c	5	12	1	2	0	1	0	2	3	0	0	.167	.333	.333
C.Lavagetto, 3b	3	10	1	1	0	0	0	0	2	0	0	.100	.250	.100
B.Herman, 2b	4	8	0	1	0	0	0	0	2	0	0	.125	.300	.125
L.Riggs, 3b	3	8	0	2	0	0	0	1	1	1	0	.250	.333	.250
P.Coscarart, 2b	3	7	1	0	0	0	0	0	1	2	0	.000	.125	.000
W.Wyatt, p	2	6	1	1	1	0	0	0	0	1	0	.167	.167	.333
J.Wasdell, of	3	5	0	1	1	0	0	2	0	0	0	.200	.200	.400
H.Casey, p	3	2	0	1	0	0	0	0	0	1	0	.500	.500	.500
C.Davis, p	1	2	0	0	0	0	0	0	0	0	0	.000	.000	.000
F.Fitzsimmons, p	1	2	0	0	0	0	0	0	0	0	0	.000	.000	.000
A.Galan, ph	2	2	0	0	0	0	0	0	0	1	0	.000	.000	.000
H.Franks, c	1	1	0	0	0	0	0	0	0	0	0	.000	.000	.000
K.Higbe, p	1	1	0	1	0	0	0	0	0	0	0	1.000	1.000	1.000
Totals		159	11	29	7	2	1	11	14	21	0	.182	.249	.252

PITCHER	W	L	ERA	G	GS	SV	IP	H	BB	SO
W.Wyatt	1	1	2.50	2	2	0	18.0	15	10	14
F.Fitzsimmons	0	0	0.00	1	1	0	7.0	4	3	1
H.Casey	0	2	3.38	3	0	0	5.1	9	2	1
C.Davis	0	1	5.06	1	1	0	5.1	6	3	1
J.Allen	0	0	0.00	3	0	0	3.2	1	3	0
K.Higbe	0	0	7.36	1	1	0	3.2	6	2	1
L.French	0	0	0.00	2	0	0	1.0	0	0	0
Totals	1	4	2.66	13	5	0	44.0	41	23	18

GAME 1 / OCT. 1						
DAVIS, CASEY(6), ALLEN(7) VS. RUFFING						68,540
BRO	000	010	100	2	6	0
NY	010	101	00X	3	6	1

The Yankees won a nail-biter, surviving a ninth-inning rally when Red Ruffing induced Herman Franks to ground into a double play to end the game.

GAME 2 / OCT. 2						
WYATT VS. CHANDLER, MURPHY(6)						66,248
BRO	000	021	000	3	6	2
NY	011	000	000	2	9	1

The Dodgers got what would be their only win in the World Series behind the superb pitching of Whit Wyatt. After allowing single runs in the second and third, Wyatt didn't allow a Yankee past second base the rest of the way.

GAME 3 / OCT. 4						
RUSSO VS. FITZSIMMONS, CASEY(8), FRENCH(8), ALLEN(9)						33,100
NY	000	000	020	2	8	0
BRO	000	000	010	1	4	0

Pee Wee Reese caught a line drive after it ricocheted off Brooklyn starter Freddie Fitzsimmons for the third out of the seventh. The liner, ironically hit by Yankees hurler Marius Russo, broke Fitzsimmons' kneecap and forced him out of the game. The Yankees then got two in the eighth off reliever Hugh Casey to win the game.

GAME 4 / OCT. 5						
DONALD, BREUER(5), MURPHY(8) VS. HIGBE, FRENCH(4), ALLEN(5), CASEY(5)						33,813
NY	100	200	004	7	12	0
BRO	000	220	000	4	9	1

Ahead by a run with two outs in the ninth, the Dodgers would have evened the Series had catcher Mickey Owen only caught strike three from Hugh Casey. But the ball went to the backstop, Tommy Henrich ran to first, the next five Yankees reached base, and Brooklyn wound up one loss away from elimination.

GAME 5 / OCT. 6						
BONHAM VS. WYATT						34,072
NY	020	010	000	3	6	0
BRO	001	000	000	1	4	1

The Yankees got all the runs they would need in the second on a wild pitch by Whit Wyatt and a single by Joe Gordon. Tiny Bonham gave one of those back in the third, but Henrich homered in the fifth to push the margin back to two runs. Bonham allowed only two baserunners, one walk and one single, in the final six innings.

1942 World Series
New York Yankees (1) vs. St. Louis Cardinals (4)

The Yankees won the opening game to run their World Series record to 35–5 since 1926, but the Cardinals weren't intimidated. Despite being huge underdogs, St. Louis rallied behind the pitching of rookie Johnny Beazley, who hurled complete-game victories in the second and fifth games.

STL (NL)														
PLAYER, POS	G	AB	R	H	2B	3B	HR	RBI	BB	SO	SB	AVG	OBP	SLG
W.Cooper, c	5	21	3	6	1	0	0	4	0	1	0	.286	.286	.333
J.Brown, 2b	5	20	2	6	0	0	0	1	3	0	0	.300	.391	.300
E.Slaughter, of	5	19	3	5	1	0	1	2	3	2	0	.263	.364	.316
M.Marion, ss	5	18	2	2	0	1	0	3	1	2	0	.111	.158	.222
S.Musial, of	5	18	2	4	1	0	0	2	4	0	0	.222	.364	.278
J.Hopp, 1b	5	17	3	3	0	0	0	0	1	1	0	.176	.222	.176
T.Moore, of	5	17	2	5	1	0	0	2	2	3	0	.294	.368	.353
W.Kurowski, 3b	5	15	3	4	0	1	1	5	2	3	0	.267	.353	.400
J.Beazley, p	2	7	0	1	0	0	0	0	0	5	0	.143	.143	.143
M.Cooper, p	2	5	1	1	0	0	0	2	0	1	0	.200	.200	.200
E.White, p	1	2	0	0	0	0	0	0	0	0	0	.000	.000	.000
M.Lanier, p	2	1	0	1	0	0	0	1	0	0	0	1.000	1.000	1.000
K.O'Dea, ph	1	1	0	1	0	0	0	1	0	0	0	1.000	1.000	1.000
R.Sanders, ph	2	1	1	0	0	0	0	0	1	0	0	.000	.500	.000
H.Walker, ph	1	1	0	0	0	0	0	0	0	1	0	.000	.000	.000
C.Crespi, pr	1	0	1	0	0	0	0	0	0	0	0	.000	.000	.000
Totals		163	23	39	4	2	2	23	17	19	0	.239	.311	.288

PITCHER	W	L	ERA	G	GS	SV	IP	H	BB	SO
J.Beazley	2	0	2.50	2	2	0	18.0	17	3	6
M.Cooper	0	1	5.54	2	2	0	13.0	17	4	9
E.White	1	0	0.00	1	1	0	9.0	6	0	6
M.Lanier	1	0	0.00	2	0	0	4.0	3	1	1
H.Gumbert	0	0	0.00	2	0	0	0.2	1	0	0
H.Pollet	0	0	0.00	1	0	0	0.1	0	0	0
Totals	4	1	2.60	10	5	0	45.0	44	8	22

NY (AL)														
PLAYER, POS	G	AB	R	H	2B	3B	HR	RBI	BB	SO	SB	AVG	OBP	SLG
J.DiMaggio, of	5	21	3	7	0	0	0	3	0	1	0	.333	.333	.333
J.Gordon, 2b	5	21	1	2	1	0	0	0	0	7	0	.095	.095	.143
P.Rizzuto, ss	5	21	2	8	0	0	1	1	2	1	2	.381	.435	.381
C.Keller, of	5	20	2	4	0	0	2	5	1	3	0	.200	.238	.200
R.Cullenbine, of	5	19	3	5	1	0	0	2	1	2	1	.263	.300	.316
B.Dickey, c	5	19	1	5	0	0	0	0	1	0	0	.263	.300	.263
R.Rolfe, 3b	4	17	5	6	2	0	0	0	1	2	0	.353	.389	.471
J.Priddy, 1b-3b	3	10	0	1	1	0	0	1	1	0	0	.100	.182	.200
B.Hassett, 1b	3	9	1	3	1	0	0	2	0	1	0	.333	.333	.444
R.Ruffing, p	4	9	0	2	0	0	0	0	0	2	0	.222	.222	.222
F.Crosetti, 3b	1	3	0	0	0	0	0	0	0	1	0	.000	.000	.000
T.Bonham, p	2	2	0	0	0	0	0	0	1	0	0	.000	.333	.000
S.Chandler, p	2	2	0	0	0	0	0	0	0	1	0	.000	.000	.000
A.Donald, p	1	2	0	0	0	0	0	0	0	0	0	.000	.000	.000
H.Borowy, p	1	1	0	0	0	0	0	0	0	1	0	.000	.000	.000
B.Rosar, ph	1	1	0	1	0	0	0	0	0	0	0	1.000	1.000	1.000
G.Selkirk, ph	1	1	0	0	0	0	0	0	0	0	0	.000	.000	.000
T.Stainback, pr	2	0	0	0	0	0	0	0	0	0	0	.000	.000	.000
Totals		178	18	44	6	0	3	14	8	22	3	.247	.280	.281

PITCHER	W	L	ERA	G	GS	SV	IP	H	BB	SO
R.Ruffing	1	1	4.08	2	2	0	17.2	14	7	11
T.Bonham	0	1	4.09	2	1	0	11.0	9	3	3
S.Chandler	0	1	1.08	2	1	1	8.1	5	1	3
H.Borowy	0	0	18.00	1	1	0	3.0	6	3	1
A.Donald	0	1	6.00	1	0	0	3.0	3	2	1
J.Turner	0	0	0.00	1	0	0	1.0	0	1	0
M.Breuer	0	0	INF	1	0	0	0.0	2	0	0
Totals	1	4	4.50	10	5	1	44.0	39	17	19

GAME 1 / SEPT. 30						
RUFFING, CHANDLER(9) VS. M.COOPER, GUMBERT(8), LANIER(9)						34,769
NY	000	110	032	7	11	0
STL	000	000	004	4	7	4

This started out as a laugher, with Red Ruffing holding St. Louis hitless until Terry Moore singled with two outs in the eighth. The Cardinals made it interesting, though, getting four in the ninth and then loading the bases with two outs. But rookie Stan Musial hit a grounder to first for the game's final out.

GAME 2 / OCT. 1

BONHAM VS. BEAZLEY						34,255
NY	000	000	030	3	10	2
STL	200	000	11X	4	6	0

It was New York's turn to mount a late-inning rally, tying the game in the eighth on a two-run homer by Charlie Keller. St. Louis scored the winning run in the bottom of that frame when Stan Musial's two-out single plated Enos Slaughter.

GAME 3 / OCT. 2

WHITE VS. CHANDLER, BREUER(9), TURNER(9)						69,123
STL	001	000	001	2	5	1
NY	000	000	000	0	6	1

Ernie White's gem put the Cardinals ahead to stay in the World Series. He allowed just six singles—and no walks—and only one Yankee got past second base.

GAME 4 / OCT. 4

M.COOPER, GUMBERT(6), POLLET(6), LANIER(7) VS. BOROWY, DONALD(4), BONHAM(7)						69,902
STL	000	600	201	9	12	1
NY	100	005	000	6	10	1

St. Louis had only two extra base hits—both doubles—but scored nine times thanks to seven free passes issued by the Yankees. Back-to-back walks leading off the seventh inning led to two runs that put the Cardinals ahead for good.

GAME 5 / OCT. 5

BEAZLEY VS. RUFFING						69,052
STL	000	101	002	4	9	4
NY	100	100	000	2	7	1

This game had a little bit of everything. Phil Rizzuto's homer in the first staked the Yankees to an early lead, but the Cardinals came back with a solo shot by Enos Slaughter and a two-run blast by Whitey Kurowski in the ninth. The Yankees weren't dead, though, putting the first two on in the bottom of the ninth. But Cardinals catcher Walker Cooper picked Joe Gordon off second base, and second baseman Jimmy Gordon made a fine catch on a popup by Jerry Priddy. With the worst over, Beazley retired George Selkirk on an easy grounder to second for the final out.

1943 World Series
New York Yankees (4) vs. St. Louis Cardinals (1)

Though the same teams were playing in the World Series as the year before, it could hardly be characterized as a rematch, since both clubs had lost many players to military duty as World War II raged. Joe DiMaggio wasn't around for the Yankees, and Enos Slaughter and Johnny Beazley, who won 21 games as a rookie in '42 and hurled two complete-game wins in that World Series, didn't play for the Cardinals in '43.

NY (AL)

PLAYER, POS	G	AB	R	H	2B	3B	HR	RBI	BB	SO	SB	AVG	OBP	SLG
B.Johnson, 3b	5	20	3	6	1	1	0	3	0	3	0	.300	.300	.450
N.Etten, 1b	5	19	0	2	0	0	0	2	1	2	0	.105	.150	.105
F.Crosetti, ss	5	18	4	5	0	0	0	1	2	3	1	.278	.350	.278
B.Dickey, c	5	18	1	5	0	0	1	4	2	2	0	.278	.350	.278
C.Keller, of	5	18	3	4	0	1	0	2	2	5	1	.222	.300	.333
J.Gordon, 2b	5	17	2	4	1	0	1	2	3	3	0	.235	.350	.294
T.Stainback, of	5	17	0	3	0	0	0	0	0	2	0	.176	.176	.176
J.Lindell, of	4	9	1	1	0	0	0	0	1	4	0	.111	.200	.111
B.Metheny, of	2	8	0	1	0	0	0	0	0	2	0	.125	.125	.125
S.Chandler, p	2	6	0	1	0	0	0	0	0	2	0	.167	.167	.167
M.Russo, p	1	3	1	2	2	0	0	0	1	1	0	.667	.750	1.333

NY (AL) (CONT.)

PLAYER, POS	G	AB	R	H	2B	3B	HR	RBI	BB	SO	SB	AVG	OBP	SLG
T.Bonham, p	1	2	0	0	0	0	0	0	0	0	0	.000	.000	.000
H.Borowy, p	1	2	1	1	1	0	0	0	0	1	0	.500	.500	1.000
S.Stirnweiss, ph	1	1	1	0	0	0	0	0	0	0	0	.000	.000	.000
R.Weatherly, ph	1	1	0	0	0	0	0	0	0	0	0	.000	.000	.000
Totals		159	17	35	5	2	2	14	12	30	2	.220	.275	.277

PITCHER	W	L	ERA	G	GS	SV	IP	H	BB	SO
S.Chandler	2	0	0.50	2	2	0	18.0	17	3	10
M.Russo	1	0	0.00	1	1	0	9.0	7	1	2
T.Bonham	0	1	4.50	1	1	0	8.0	6	3	9
H.Borowy	1	0	2.25	1	1	0	8.0	6	3	4
J.Murphy	0	0	0.00	2	0	1	2.0	1	1	1
Totals	4	1	1.40	7	5	1	45.0	37	11	26

STL (NL)

PLAYER, POS	G	AB	R	H	2B	3B	HR	RBI	BB	SO	SB	AVG	OBP	SLG
L.Klein, 2b	5	22	0	3	0	0	0	0	1	2	0	.136	.174	.136
W.Kurowski, 3b	5	18	2	4	1	0	0	1	0	3	0	.222	.222	.278
S.Musial, of	5	18	2	5	0	0	0	0	2	2	0	.278	.350	.278
H.Walker, of	5	18	0	3	1	0	0	0	0	2	0	.167	.167	.222
W.Cooper, c	5	17	1	5	0	0	0	0	0	1	0	.294	.294	.294
R.Sanders, 1b	5	17	3	5	0	0	1	2	3	4	0	.294	.400	.294
D.Litwhiler, of	5	15	0	4	1	0	0	2	2	4	0	.267	.353	.333
M.Marion, ss	5	14	1	5	2	0	1	2	3	1	1	.357	.471	.500
M.Cooper, p	2	5	0	0	0	0	0	0	0	3	0	.000	.000	.000
D.Garms, of	2	5	0	0	0	0	0	0	0	2	0	.000	.000	.000
J.Hopp, of	1	4	0	0	0	0	0	0	0	1	0	.000	.000	.000
M.Lanier, p	3	4	0	1	0	0	0	1	0	0	0	.250	.250	.250
A.Brazle, p	1	3	0	0	0	0	0	0	0	1	0	.000	.000	.000
K.O'Dea, c	2	3	0	2	0	0	0	0	0	0	0	.667	.667	.667
F.Demaree, ph	1	1	0	0	0	0	0	0	0	0	0	.000	.000	.000
S.Narron, ph	1	1	0	0	0	0	0	0	0	0	0	.000	.000	.000
E.White, pr	1	0	0	0	0	0	0	0	0	0	0	.000	.000	.000
Totals		165	9	37	5	0	2	8	11	26	1	.224	.273	.255

PITCHER	W	L	ERA	G	GS	SV	IP	H	BB	SO
M.Cooper	1	1	2.81	2	2	0	16.0	11	3	10
M.Lanier	0	1	1.76	3	2	0	15.1	13	3	13
A.Brazle	0	1	3.68	1	1	0	7.1	5	2	4
H.Brecheen	0	1	2.45	3	0	0	3.2	5	3	3
M.Dickson	0	0	0.00	1	0	0	0.2	0	1	0
H.Krist	0	0	INF	1	0	0	0.0	1	0	0
Totals	1	4	2.51	11	5	0	43.0	35	12	30

GAME 1 / OCT. 5

LANIER, BRECHEEN(8) VS. CHANDLER						68,676
STL	010	010	000	2	7	2
NY	000	202	00X	4	8	2

The Yankees scored the go-ahead runs in the sixth, thanks in large part to a crucial wild pitch from St. Louis starter Max Lanier. Spud Chandler went the distance for New York.

GAME 2 / OCT. 6

M.COOPER VS. BONHAM, MURPHY(9)						68,578
STL	001	300	000	4	7	2
NY	000	100	002	3	6	0

Ray Sanders' two-run homer in the fourth was the big blow for the Cardinals, who had to fight off a rally by the Yankees in the ninth. Billy Johnson doubled and Charlie Keller tripled to start the inning, but the next three batters made outs and St. Louis escaped with their only win of the Series.

GAME 3 / OCT. 7

BRAZLE, KRIST(8), BRECHEEN(8) VS. BOROWY, MURPHY(9)						69,990
STL	000	200	000	2	6	4
NY	000	001	05X	6	8	0

Two walks, two errors, and five hits in the eighth turned a one-run St. Louis lead into a 6–2 New York win. A bases-clearing triple by Billy Johnson was the key hit in front of a then-record Series crowd of 69,990.

GAME 4 / OCT. 10

RUSSO VS. LANIER, BRECHEEN(8)						36,196
NY	000	100	010	2	6	2
STL	000	000	100	1	7	1

Yankees starter Marius Russo was nearly unhittable. Two New York errors in the seventh were all that kept him from hurling a shutout.

GAME 5 / OCT. 11

CHANDLER VS. M.COOPER, LANIER(8), DICKSON(9)						33,872
NY	000	002	000	2	7	1
STL	000	000	000	0	10	1

Bill Dickey homered off Mort Cooper in the sixth for the only runs the Yankees would need or get. The Cardinals got 10 hits, but they were all singles as Spud Chandler topped his Game 1 performance. There still was some drama, however, as St. Louis got two of their safeties with one out in the ninth. Chandler took care of things by striking out Lou Klein and getting Debs Garms to ground out to second for the Yankees' 10th world championship.

1947 World Series
New York Yankees (4) vs. Brooklyn Dodgers (3)

The Dodgers hit only one home run, a solo shot by Dixie Walker in the second game, lost the first two contests, were outhit by 52 points, and were outscored by nine runs in the seven games. Yet the Yankees needed all of their experience—and five nearly perfect innings of relief from Joe Page in Game 7—to claim their first championship since 1943.

NY (AL)

PLAYER, POS	G	AB	R	H	2B	3B	HR	RBI	BB	SO	SB	AVG	OBP	SLG
T.Henrich, of	7	31	2	10	2	0	1	5	2	3	0	.323	.364	.387
S.Stirnweiss, 2b	7	27	3	7	0	1	0	3	8	8	0	.259	.429	.333
J.DiMaggio, of	7	26	4	6	0	0	2	5	6	2	0	.231	.375	.231
B.Johnson, 3b	7	26	8	7	0	3	0	2	3	4	0	.269	.345	.500
P.Rizzuto, ss	7	26	3	8	1	0	0	2	4	0	2	.308	.400	.346
G.McQuinn, 1b	7	23	3	3	0	0	0	1	5	8	0	.130	.286	.130
Y.Berra, c-of	6	19	2	3	0	0	1	2	1	2	0	.158	.200	.158
J.Lindell, of	6	18	3	9	3	1	0	7	5	2	0	.500	.609	.778
A.Robinson, c	3	10	2	2	0	0	0	1	2	1	0	.200	.333	.200
S.Shea, p	3	5	0	2	1	0	0	1	0	2	0	.400	.400	.600
B.Bevens, p	2	4	0	0	0	0	0	0	0	2	0	.000	.000	.000
S.Lollar, c	2	4	3	3	2	0	0	1	0	0	0	.750	.750	1.250
J.Page, p	4	4	0	0	0	0	0	0	0	1	0	.000	.000	.000
A.Reynolds, p	2	4	2	2	0	0	0	1	0	0	0	.500	.500	.500
B.Brown, ph	4	3	2	3	2	0	0	3	1	0	0	1.000	1.000	1.667
A.Clark, of	3	2	1	1	0	0	0	1	1	0	0	.500	.667	.500
K.Drews, p	2	2	0	0	0	0	0	0	0	2	0	.000	.000	.000
J.Phillips, 1b	2	2	0	0	0	0	0	0	0	0	0	.000	.000	.000
L.Frey, ph	1	1	0	0	0	0	0	1	0	0	0	.000	.000	.000
R.Houk, ph	1	1	0	1	0	0	0	0	0	0	0	1.000	1.000	1.000
Totals		238	38	67	11	5	4	36	38	37	2	.282	.385	.370

PITCHER	W	L	ERA	G	GS	SV	IP	H	BB	SO
S.Shea	2	0	2.35	3	3	0	15.1	10	8	10
J.Page	1	1	4.15	4	0	1	13.0	12	2	7
B.Bevens	0	1	2.38	2	1	0	11.1	3	11	7
A.Reynolds	1	0	4.76	2	2	0	11.1	15	3	6
K.Drews	0	0	3.00	2	0	0	3.0	2	1	0
B.Newsom	0	1	19.29	2	1	0	2.1	6	2	0
S.Chandler	0	0	9.00	1	0	0	2.0	2	3	1
B.Wensloff	0	0	0.00	1	0	0	2.0	0	0	0
V.Raschi	0	0	6.75	2	0	0	1.1	2	0	1
Totals	4	3	4.09	19	7	1	61.2	52	30	32

BRO (NL)

PLAYER, POS	G	AB	R	H	2B	3B	HR	RBI	BB	SO	SB	AVG	OBP	SLG
B.Edwards, c	7	27	3	6	1	0	0	2	2	7	0	.222	.276	.259
J.Robinson, 1b	7	27	3	7	2	0	0	3	2	4	2	.259	.310	.333
D.Walker, of	7	27	1	6	1	0	1	4	3	1	1	.222	.300	.259
E.Stanky, 2b	7	25	4	6	1	0	0	2	3	2	0	.240	.321	.280
P.Wee Reese, ss	7	23	5	7	1	0	0	4	6	3	3	.304	.448	.348
S.Jorgensen, 3b	7	20	1	4	2	0	0	3	2	4	0	.200	.273	.300
G.Hermanski, of	7	19	4	3	0	1	0	1	3	3	0	.158	.273	.263
C.Furillo, of	6	17	2	6	2	0	0	3	3	0	0	.353	.450	.471
P.Reiser, of	5	8	1	2	0	0	0	0	3	1	0	.250	.455	.250
C.Lavagetto, 3b	5	7	0	1	1	0	0	3	0	2	0	.143	.143	.286
R.Branca, p	3	4	0	0	0	0	0	0	0	1	0	.000	.000	.000
E.Miksis, 2b-of	5	4	1	1	0	0	0	0	0	1	0	.250	.250	.250
A.Gionfriddo, of	4	3	2	0	0	0	0	0	1	0	1	.000	.250	.000
H.Gregg, p	3	3	0	0	0	0	0	0	1	1	0	.000	.250	.000
J.Hatten, p	4	3	1	1	0	0	0	0	0	0	0	.333	.333	.333
V.Lombardi, p	3	3	0	0	0	0	0	0	0	0	0	.000	.000	.000
A.Vaughan, ph	3	2	0	1	1	0	0	0	1	0	0	.500	.667	1.000
R.Barney, p	3	1	0	0	0	0	0	0	0	0	0	.000	.000	.000
B.Bragan, ph	1	1	0	1	1	0	0	1	0	0	0	1.000	1.000	2.000
H.Casey, p	6	1	0	0	0	0	0	0	0	1	0	.000	.000	.000
G.Hodges, ph	1	1	0	0	0	0	0	0	0	1	0	.000	.000	.000
D.Bankhead, pr	1	0	1	0	0	0	0	0	0	0	0	.000	.000	.000
Totals		226	29	52	13	1	1	26	30	32	7	.230	.323	.296

PITCHER	W	L	ERA	G	GS	SV	IP	H	BB	SO
H.Gregg	0	1	3.55	3	1	0	12.2	9	8	10
H.Casey	2	0	0.87	6	0	1	10.1	5	1	3
J.Hatten	0	0	7.00	4	1	0	9.0	12	7	5
R.Branca	1	1	8.64	3	1	0	8.1	12	5	8
R.Barney	0	1	2.70	3	1	0	6.2	4	10	3
V.Lombardi	0	1	12.15	2	2	0	6.2	14	1	5

BRO (NL) (cont.)

PITCHER	W	L	ERA	G	GS	SV	IP	H	BB	SO
H.Behrman	0	0	7.11	5	0	0	6.1	9	5	3
H.Taylor	0	0	INF	1	1	0	0.0	2	1	0
Totals	3	4	5.55	27	7	1	60.0	67	38	37

GAME 1 / SEPT. 30

BRANCA, BEHRMAN(5), CASEY(7) VS. SHEA, PAGE(6) — **73,365**

				R	H	E
BRO	100	001	100	3	6	0
NY	000	050	00X	5	4	0

Brooklyn's Ralph Branca retired the first 12 Yankee hitters, but Joe DiMaggio's leadoff single in the fifth opened the floodgates. The Yankees sent 10 batters to the plate and took a 5–0 lead. That was more than enough for Spec Shea and Joe Page, who combined on a six-hitter.

GAME 2 / OCT. 1

LOMBARDI, GREGG(5), BEHRMAN(7), BARNEY(7) VS. REYNOLDS — **69,865**

				R	H	E
BRO	001	100	001	3	9	2
NY	101	121	40X	10	15	1

The Yankees broke open a tie game by scoring eight times from the fourth through the seventh. Allie Reynolds went the distance in his first World Series appearance.

GAME 3 / OCT. 2

NEWSOM, RASCHI(2), DREWS(3), CHANDLER(4), PAGE(6) VS. HATTEN, BRANCA(5), CASEY(7) — **33,098**

				R	H	E
NY	002	221	100	8	13	0
BRO	061	200	00X	9	13	1

The Dodgers got six in the second but had to fight off a furious Yankees rally. After Yogi Berra connected for the first pinch-hit home run in World Series history to make it 9–8, Hugh Casey came in and tossed the last $2^2/_3$ innings to hold the slim lead. Getting Joe DiMaggio to ground into a double play with two on and no outs in the eighth was the deciding moment.

GAME 4 / OCT. 3

BEVENS VS. TAYLOR, GREGG(1), BEHRMAN(8), CASEY(9) — **33,443**

				R	H	E
NY	100	100	000	2	8	1
BRO	000	010	002	3	1	3

Even though he had walked nine, Yankees starter Bill Bevens had a no-hitter with two outs in the ninth. But pinch runner Al Gionfriddo stole second, pinch hitter Pete Reiser was walked intentionally, and Cookie Lavagetto lined one off the wall in right to bring in the tying and winning runs to even the Series.

GAME 5 / OCT. 4

SHEA VS. BARNEY, HATTEN(5), BEHRMAN(7), CASEY(8) — **34,379**

				R	H	E
NY	000	110	000	2	5	0
BRO	000	001	000	1	4	1

Cookie Lavagetto had a chance to be the hero for the second straight game, but he struck out with the tying run on second. Spec Shea won his second game of the Series, striking out seven and giving up only four hits.

GAME 6 / OCT. 5

LOMBARDI, BRANCA(3), HATTEN(6), CASEY(9) VS. REYNOLDS, DREWS(3), PAGE(5), NEWSOM(6), RASCHI(7), WENSLOFF(8) — **74,065**

				R	H	E
BRO	202	004	000	8	12	1
NY	004	100	001	6	15	2

Al Gionfriddo, just inserted into the game in left field, came up with the biggest play of the World Series. With two outs and two on in an 8–5 game, Gionfriddo robbed Joe DiMaggio, in the immortal words of Red Barber, with "a one-handed catch against the bullpen. Oh, Doctor!" The Yankees also put the tying runs on in the seventh and ninth innings, but couldn't push home the critical runs.

GAME 7 / OCT. 6

GREGG, BEHRMAN(4), HATTEN(6), BARNEY(6), CASEY(7) VS. SHEA, BEVENS(2), PAGE(5) — **71,548**

				R	H	E
BRO	020	000	000	2	7	0
NY	010	201	10X	5	7	0

Bill Bevens, in the last game of his major league career, and Joe Page combined for seven shutout innings in relief after Spec Shea was knocked out in the second inning. While five Brooklyn pitchers silenced New York's big bats—Joe DiMaggio and Yogi Berra went hitless—the bottom of the order came through for the Yankees, getting five of their seven hits, including three safeties by Phil Rizzuto, and scoring four of the five runs.

1949 World Series
New York Yankees (4) vs. Brooklyn Dodgers (1)

The Yankees took the pennant by winning their final two regular-season games to steal the title from the rival Red Sox. Though they lost only one game to Brooklyn in Casey Stengel's first World Series as a manager, the Series was far from a blowout. Two of the first three games were decided in the ninth inning, the first three were one-run affairs, the fourth contest was a two-run game, and even high-scoring Game 5 required Joe Page to come in after a Gil Hodges homer put the Dodgers within shouting distance.

NY (AL)

PLAYER, POS	G	AB	R	H	2B	3B	HR	RBI	BB	SO	SB	AVG	OBP	SLG
J.Coleman, 2b	5	20	0	5	3	0	0	4	0	4	0	.250	.250	.400
T.Henrich, 1b	5	19	4	5	0	0	1	1	3	0	0	.263	.364	.263
J.DiMaggio, of	5	18	2	2	0	0	1	2	3	5	0	.111	.238	.111
P.Rizzuto, ss	5	18	2	3	0	0	0	1	3	1	1	.167	.286	.167
Y.Berra, c	4	16	2	1	0	0	0	1	1	3	0	.063	.118	.063
B.Brown, 3b	4	12	4	6	1	2	0	5	2	2	0	.500	.571	.917
C.Mapes, of	4	10	3	1	1	0	0	2	2	4	0	.100	.250	.200
G.Woodling, of	3	10	4	4	3	0	0	0	3	0	0	.400	.538	.700
B.Johnson, 3b	2	7	0	1	0	0	0	0	0	2	1	.143	.143	.143
J.Lindell, of	2	7	0	1	0	0	0	0	0	2	0	.143	.143	.143
H.Bauer, of	3	6	0	1	0	0	0	0	0	0	0	.167	.167	.167
V.Raschi, p	2	5	0	1	0	0	0	1	1	1	0	.200	.333	.200
J.Page, p	3	4	0	0	0	0	0	0	0	2	0	.000	.000	.000
A.Reynolds, p	2	4	0	2	1	0	0	0	0	1	0	.500	.500	.750
E.Lopat, p	1	3	0	1	1	0	0	1	0	0	0	.333	.333	.667
J.Mize, ph	2	2	0	2	0	0	0	2	0	0	0	1.000	1.000	1.000
C.Silvera, c	1	2	0	0	0	0	0	0	0	0	0	.000	.000	.000
T.Byrne, p	1	1	0	1	0	0	0	0	0	0	0	1.000	1.000	1.000
G.Niarhos, c	1	0	0	0	0	0	0	0	0	0	0	.000	.000	.000
S.Stirnweiss, ph	1	0	0	0	0	0	0	0	0	0	0	.000	.000	.000
Totals		164	21	37	10	2	2	20	18	27	2	.226	.302	.311

PITCHER	W	L	ERA	G	GS	SV	IP	H	BB	SO
V.Raschi	1	1	4.30	2	2	0	14.2	15	5	11
A.Reynolds	1	0	0.00	2	1	1	12.1	2	4	14
J.Page	1	0	2.00	3	0	1	9.0	6	3	8
E.Lopat	1	0	6.35	1	1	0	5.2	9	1	4
T.Byrne	0	0	2.70	1	1	0	3.1	2	2	1
Totals	4	1	2.80	9	5	2	45.0	34	15	38

BRO (NL)

PLAYER, POS	G	AB	R	H	2B	3B	HR	RBI	BB	SO	SB	AVG	OBP	SLG
D.Snider, of	5	21	2	3	1	0	0	0	0	8	0	.143	.143	.190
P.Wee Reese, ss	5	19	2	6	1	0	1	2	1	0	1	.316	.350	.368
G.Hodges, 1b	5	17	2	4	0	0	1	4	1	4	0	.235	.278	.235
J.Robinson, 2b	5	16	2	3	1	0	0	2	4	2	0	.188	.350	.250
R.Campanella, c	5	15	2	4	1	0	1	2	3	1	0	.267	.389	.333
G.Hermanski, of	4	13	1	4	0	1	0	2	3	3	0	.308	.438	.462
S.Jorgensen, 3b	4	11	1	2	2	0	0	0	2	2	0	.182	.308	.364
L.Olmo, of	4	11	2	3	0	0	1	2	0	2	0	.273	.273	.273
C.Furillo, of	3	8	0	1	0	0	0	0	1	0	0	.125	.222	.125
E.Miksis, 3b	3	7	0	2	1	0	0	0	0	1	0	.286	.286	.429
M.Rackley, of	2	5	0	0	0	0	0	0	0	2	0	.000	.000	.000
D.Newcombe, p	2	4	0	0	0	0	0	0	0	3	0	.000	.000	.000
R.Branca, p	1	3	0	0	0	0	0	0	0	3	0	.000	.000	.000
B.Cox, 3b	2	3	0	1	0	0	0	0	0	1	0	.333	.333	.333
P.Roe, p	1	3	0	0	0	0	0	0	0	3	0	.000	.000	.000
T.Brown, ph	2	2	0	0	0	0	0	0	0	1	0	.000	.000	.000
B.Edwards, ph	2	2	0	1	0	0	0	0	0	1	0	.500	.500	.500
J.Banta, p	3	1	0	0	0	0	0	0	0	0	0	.000	.000	.000
D.Whitman, ph	1	1	0	0	0	0	0	0	0	1	0	.000	.000	.000
M.McCormick, of	1	0	0	0	0	0	0	0	0	0	0	.000	.000	.000
Totals		162	14	34	7	1	4	14	15	38	1	.210	.281	.265

PITCHER	W	L	ERA	G	GS	SV	IP	H	BB	SO
D.Newcombe	0	2	3.09	2	2	0	11.2	10	3	11
P.Roe	1	0	0.00	1	1	0	9.0	6	0	3
R.Branca	0	1	4.15	1	1	0	8.2	4	4	6
J.Banta	0	0	3.18	3	0	0	5.2	5	1	4
R.Barney	0	1	16.88	1	1	0	2.2	3	6	2
E.Palica	0	0	0.00	1	0	0	2.0	1	1	1
C.Erskine	0	0	16.20	2	0	0	1.2	3	1	0

BRO (NL) (CONT.)

PITCHER	W	L	ERA	G	GS	SV	IP	H	BB	SO
J.Hatten	0	0	16.20	2	0	0	1.2	4	2	0
P.Minner	0	0	0.00	1	0	0	1.0	1	0	0
Totals	1	4	4.30	14	5	0	44.0	37	18	27

GAME 1 / OCT. 5

NEWCOMBE VS. REYNOLDS							66,224
BRO	000	000	000		0	2	0
NY	000	000	001		1	5	1

Brooklyn rookie Don Newcombe and Allie Reynolds both put up goose eggs through eight innings. The Yankees won the game in the bottom of the ninth when Tommy Henrich clubbed a home run leading off the frame.

GAME 2 / OCT. 6

ROE VS. RASCHI, PAGE(9)							70,053
BRO	010	000	000		1	7	2
NY	000	000	000		0	6	1

Preacher Roe was masterful, giving up only six hits and never allowing a Yankee past second base. A double by Jackie Robinson and a single by Gil Hodges off Vic Raschi plated the game's only run in the second inning.

GAME 3 / OCT. 7

BYRNE, PAGE(4) VS. BRANCA, BANTA(9)							32,788
NY	001	000	003		4	5	0
BRO	000	100	002		3	5	0

The Dodgers were one out away from a victory when the Yankees rallied for three off Brooklyn's Ralph Branca. Johnny Mize's pinch-hit single brought in the tying and go-ahead runs. The Dodgers got two solo home runs in the bottom of the ninth from Luis Olmo and Roy Campanella, but Joe Page, on in relief since the fourth inning, fanned Bruce Edwards to end the game.

GAME 4 / OCT. 8

LOPAT, REYNOLDS(6) VS. NEWCOMBE, HATTEN(4), ERSKINE(6), BANTA(7)							33,934
NY	000	330	000		6	10	0
BRO	000	004	000		4	9	1

Don Newcombe was fine for three innings pitching on two days rest, but he fell apart in the fourth. The Yankees got to him for three runs that inning and scored three more in the fourth off reliever Joe Hatten. Allie Reynolds snuffed Brooklyn's big rally in the sixth and retired all 10 batters he faced.

GAME 5 / OCT. 9

RASCHI, PAGE(7) VS. BARNEY, BANTA(3), ERSKINE(6), HATTEN(6), PALICA(7), MINNER(9)							33,711
NY	203	113	000		10	11	1
BRO	001	001	400		6	11	2

The Yankees cruised to another championship by getting 9 of their 11 hits and all 10 of their runs in the first six innings. The cushion was so big that not even a four-run rally by Brooklyn in the seventh could break their stride en route to a 12th world championship.

1950 World Series
New York Yankees (4) vs. Philadelphia Phillies (0)

Philadelphia's "Whiz Kids" couldn't regain their form in time for the postseason after nearly blowing a seven-game lead over the Dodgers late in September. While they held off Brooklyn for the pennant, the Phillies were outclassed by the far more experienced Yankees in the Series.

NY (AL)

PLAYER, POS	G	AB	R	H	2B	3B	HR	RBI	BB	SO	SB	AVG	OBP	SLG
H.Bauer, of	4	15	0	2	0	0	0	1	0	0	0	.133	.133	.133
Y.Berra, c	4	15	2	3	0	0	1	2	2	1	0	.200	.294	.200

NY (AL) (cont.)														
PLAYER, POS	G	AB	R	H	2B	3B	HR	RBI	BB	SO	SB	AVG	OBP	SLG
J.Mize, 1b	4	15	0	2	0	0	0	0	0	1	0	.133	.133	.133
J.Coleman, 2b	4	14	2	4	1	0	0	3	2	0	0	.286	.375	.357
P.Rizzuto, ss	4	14	1	2	0	0	0	0	3	0	1	.143	.294	.143
G.Woodling, of	4	14	2	6	0	0	0	1	2	0	0	.429	.500	.429
J.DiMaggio, of	4	13	2	4	1	0	1	2	3	1	0	.308	.438	.385
B.Brown, 3b	4	12	2	4	1	1	0	1	0	0	0	.333	.333	.583
B.Johnson, 3b	4	6	0	0	0	0	0	0	0	3	0	.000	.000	.000
C.Mapes, of	1	4	0	0	0	0	0	0	0	1	0	.000	.000	.000
W.Ford, p	1	3	0	0	0	0	0	0	0	2	0	.000	.000	.000
V.Raschi, p	1	3	0	1	0	0	0	0	0	0	0	.333	.333	.333
A.Reynolds, p	2	3	0	1	0	0	0	0	1	2	0	.333	.500	.333
J.Hopp, 1b	3	2	0	0	0	0	0	0	0	0	0	.000	.000	.000
E.Lopat, p	1	2	0	1	0	0	0	0	0	1	0	.500	.500	.500
J.Collins, 1b	1	0	0	0	0	0	0	0	0	0	0	.000	.000	.000
J.Jensen, pr	1	0	0	0	0	0	0	0	0	0	0	.000	.000	.000
Totals		135	11	30	3	1	2	10	13	12	1	.222	.295	.259

PITCHER	W	L	ERA	G	GS	SV	IP	H	BB	SO
A.Reynolds	1	0	0.87	2	1	1	10.1	7	4	7
V.Raschi	1	0	0.00	1	1	0	9.0	2	1	5
W.Ford	1	0	0.00	1	1	0	8.2	7	1	7
E.Lopat	0	0	2.25	1	1	0	8.0	9	0	5
T.Ferrick	1	0	0.00	1	0	0	1.0	1	1	0
Totals	4	0	0.73	6	4	1	37.0	26	7	24

PHI (NL)														
PLAYER, POS	G	AB	R	H	2B	3B	HR	RBI	BB	SO	SB	AVG	OBP	SLG
R.Ashburn, of	4	17	0	3	1	0	0	1	0	4	0	.176	.176	.235
D.Sisler, of	4	17	0	1	0	0	0	1	0	5	0	.059	.059	.059
E.Waitkus, 1b	4	15	0	4	1	0	0	0	2	0	0	.267	.353	.333
D.Ennis, of	4	14	1	2	1	0	0	0	0	1	0	.143	.143	.214
M.Goliat, 2b	4	14	1	3	0	0	0	1	1	2	0	.214	.267	.214
G.Hamner, ss	4	14	1	6	2	1	0	0	1	2	1	.429	.467	.714
W.Jones, 3b	4	14	1	4	1	0	0	0	0	3	0	.286	.286	.357
A.Seminick, c	4	11	0	2	0	0	0	0	1	3	0	.182	.250	.182
J.Konstanty, p	3	4	0	1	0	0	0	0	0	1	0	.250	.250	.250
K.Heintzelman, p	1	2	0	0	0	0	0	0	0	0	0	.000	.000	.000
R.Roberts, p	2	2	0	0	0	0	0	0	0	1	0	.000	.000	.000
D.Whitman, ph	3	2	0	0	0	0	0	0	1	0	0	.000	.333	.000
P.Caballero, ph	3	1	0	0	0	0	0	0	0	1	0	.000	.000	.000
S.Lopata, c	2	1	0	0	0	0	0	0	0	1	0	.000	.000	.000
J.Bloodworth, 2b	1	0	0	0	0	0	0	0	0	0	0	.000	.000	.000
K.Johnson, pr	1	0	1	0	0	0	0	0	0	0	0	.000	.000	.000
J.Mayo, of	3	0	0	0	0	0	0	0	1	0	0	.000	1.000	.000
K.Silvestri, c	1	0	0	0	0	0	0	0	0	0	0	.000	.000	.000
Totals		128	5	26	6	1	0	3	7	24	1	.203	.250	.266

PITCHER	W	L	ERA	G	GS	SV	IP	H	BB	SO
J.Konstanty	0	1	2.40	3	1	0	15.0	9	4	3
R.Roberts	0	1	1.64	2	1	0	11.0	11	3	5
K.Heintzelman	0	0	1.17	1	1	0	7.2	4	6	3
R.Meyer	0	1	5.40	2	0	0	1.2	4	0	1
B.Miller	0	1	27.00	1	1	0	0.1	2	0	0
Totals	0	4	2.27	9	4	0	35.2	30	13	12

GAME 1 / OCT. 4

RASCHI VS. KONSTANTY, MEYER(9)							30,746
NY	000	100	000	1	5	0	
PHI	000	000	000	0	2	1	

Even though he hadn't started a game in more than four seasons, Philadelphia's Jim Konstanty allowed only one run in eight innings. It wasn't enough as Vic Raschi hurled a complete game two-hitter.

GAME 2 / OCT. 5

REYNOLDS VS. ROBERTS								32,660
NY	010	000	000	1	2	10	0	
PHI	000	010	000	0	1	7	0	

Robin Roberts didn't have his best stuff—after all, he was on the mound for the fourth time in nine days—but he kept the Phillies in the game until the 10th, when he served up a leadoff homer to Joe DiMaggio.

GAME 3 / OCT. 6

HEINTZELMAN, KONSTANTY(8), MEYER(9) VS. LOPAT, FERRICK(9)							64,505
PHI	000	001	100	2	10	2	
NY	001	000	011	3	7	0	

Three consecutive walks and an error led to the tying run in the eighth, and the Yankees won it in the bottom of the ninth when Jerry Coleman plated Gene Woodling with a two out single.

GAME 4 / OCT. 7

MILLER, KONSTANTY(1), ROBERTS(8) VS. FORD, REYNOLDS(9)							68,098
PHI	000	000	002	2	7	1	
NY	200	003	00X	5	8	2	

The Yankees took advantage of an error and a wild pitch to score two in the first, and then added three more in the sixth. Allie Reynolds relieved Yankee starter Whitey Ford with two outs and the tying run at the plate and struck out pinch hitter Stan Lopata to secure the sweep.

1951 World Series
New York Yankees (4) vs. New York Giants (2)

While the Giants had all the momentum in the world following Bobby Thompson's "Shot Heard 'Round The World" in their playoff win over Brooklyn and victories in two of the first three World Series games, it ultimately wasn't enough to defeat the powerful Yankees, who won their third straight title, and fourth crown in five seasons.

NY (AL)														
PLAYER, POS	G	AB	R	H	2B	3B	HR	RBI	BB	SO	SB	AVG	OBP	SLG
P.Rizzuto, ss	6	25	5	8	0	0	1	3	2	3	0	.320	.370	.320
Y.Berra, c	6	23	4	6	1	0	0	0	2	1	0	.261	.320	.304
J.DiMaggio, of	6	23	3	6	2	0	1	5	2	4	0	.261	.320	.348
G.McDougald, 3b-2b	6	23	2	6	1	0	1	7	2	2	0	.261	.320	.304
H.Bauer, of	6	18	0	3	0	1	0	3	1	1	0	.167	.211	.278
J.Collins, 1b-of	6	18	2	4	0	0	1	3	2	1	0	.222	.300	.222
G.Woodling, of	6	18	6	3	1	1	1	1	5	3	0	.167	.348	.333
B.Brown, 3b	5	14	1	5	1	0	0	0	2	1	0	.357	.438	.429
J.Coleman, 2b	5	8	2	2	0	0	0	0	1	2	0	.250	.333	.250
E.Lopat, p	2	8	0	1	0	0	0	1	0	2	0	.125	.125	.125
J.Mize, 1b	4	7	2	2	1	0	0	1	2	0	0	.286	.444	.429
A.Reynolds, p	2	6	0	2	0	0	0	1	0	1	0	.333	.333	.333
M.Mantle, of	2	5	1	1	0	0	0	0	2	1	0	.200	.429	.200
V.Raschi, p	2	2	0	0	0	0	0	0	2	1	0	.000	.500	.000
J.Sain, p	1	1	0	0	0	0	0	0	0	0	0	.000	.000	.000
J.Hopp, ph	1	0	0	0	0	0	0	0	1	0	0	.000	1.000	.000
B.Martin, pr	1	0	1	0	0	0	0	0	0	0	0	.000	.000	.000
Totals		199	29	49	7	2	5	25	26	23	0	.246	.336	.302

PITCHER	W	L	ERA	G	GS	SV	IP	H	BB	SO
E.Lopat	2	0	0.50	2	2	0	18.0	10	3	4
A.Reynolds	1	1	4.20	2	2	0	15.0	16	11	8
V.Raschi	1	1	0.87	2	2	0	10.1	12	8	4
B.Hogue	0	0	0.00	2	0	0	2.2	1	0	0
T.Morgan	0	0	0.00	1	0	0	2.0	2	1	3
J.Ostrowski	0	0	0.00	1	0	0	2.0	1	0	1
J.Sain	0	0	9.00	1	0	0	2.0	4	2	2
B.Kuzava	0	0	0.00	1	0	1	1.0	0	0	0
Totals	4	2	1.87	12	6	1	53.0	46	25	22

NY (NL)														
PLAYER, POS	G	AB	R	H	2B	3B	HR	RBI	BB	SO	SB	AVG	OBP	SLG
W.Lockman, 1b	6	25	1	6	2	0	1	4	1	2	0	.240	.269	.320
A.Dark, ss	6	24	5	10	3	0	1	4	2	3	0	.417	.462	.542
M.Irvin, of	6	24	3	11	0	1	0	2	2	1	2	.458	.500	.542
W.Mays, of	6	22	1	4	0	0	0	1	2	2	0	.182	.250	.182
E.Stanky, 2b	6	22	3	3	0	0	0	1	3	2	0	.136	.240	.136
B.Thomson, 3b	6	21	1	5	1	0	0	2	5	0	0	.238	.385	.286
W.Westrum, c	6	17	1	4	1	0	0	0	5	3	0	.235	.409	.294
H.Thompson, of	5	14	3	2	0	0	0	0	5	2	0	.143	.368	.143
D.Koslo, p	2	5	0	0	0	0	0	0	0	2	0	.000	.000	.000
C.Hartung, of	2	4	0	0	0	0	0	0	0	0	0	.000	.000	.000
B.Rigney, ph	4	4	0	1	0	0	0	1	0	1	0	.250	.250	.250
J.Hearn, p	2	3	0	0	0	0	0	0	0	1	0	.000	.000	.000
L.Jansen, p	3	2	0	0	0	0	0	0	0	0	0	.000	.000	.000
J.Lohrke, ph	2	2	0	0	0	0	0	0	0	1	0	.000	.000	.000
R.Noble, c	2	2	0	0	0	0	0	0	0	1	0	.000	.000	.000
S.Maglie, p	1	1	0	0	0	0	0	0	0	1	0	.000	.000	.000
D.Williams, ph	2	1	0	0	0	0	0	0	0	0	0	.000	.000	.000
S.Yvars, ph	1	1	0	0	0	0	0	0	0	0	0	.000	.000	.000
H.Schenz, pr	1	0	0	0	0	0	0	0	0	0	0	.000	.000	.000
Totals		194	18	46	7	1	2	15	25	22	2	.237	.327	.284

PITCHER	W	L	ERA	G	GS	SV	IP	H	BB	SO
D.Koslo	1	1	3.00	2	2	0	15.0	12	7	6
L.Jansen	0	2	6.30	3	2	0	10.0	8	4	6
J.Hearn	1	0	1.04	2	1	0	8.2	5	8	1
S.Maglie	0	1	7.20	1	1	0	5.0	8	2	3
S.Jones	0	0	2.08	2	0	1	4.1	5	1	2
G.Spencer	0	0	18.90	2	0	0	3.1	6	3	0
M.Kennedy	0	0	6.00	2	0	0	3.0	3	1	4
A.Corwin	0	0	0.00	1	0	0	1.2	1	0	1
A.Konikowski	0	0	0.00	1	0	0	1.0	1	0	0
Totals	2	4	4.67	16	6	1	52.0	49	26	23

GAME 1 / OCT. 4

KOSLO VS. REYNOLDS, HOGUE(7), MORGAN(8)							65,673
NY-N	200	003	000	5	10	1	
NY-A	010	000	000	1	7	1	

Monte Irvin's four hits—and thrilling steal of home in the top of the first—sparked the Giants. After scoring in the second, the Yankees managed to get only one more runner as far as second base.

GAME 2 / OCT. 5							
JANSEN, SPENCER(7) VS. LOPAT							66,018
NY-N	000	000	100	1	5	1	
NY-A	110	000	01X	3	6	0	

The Yankees bounced back behind the five-hit pitching of Eddie Lopat. They would play the rest of the series without Mickey Mantle, who suffered a serious knee injury chasing after a fly ball in the fifth inning.

GAME 3 / OCT. 6							
RASCHI, HOGUE(5), OSTROWSKI(7) VS. HEARN, JONES(8)							52,035
NY-A	000	000	011	2	5	2	
NY-N	010	050	00X	6	7	2	

The Giants put this one out of reach with five in the fifth. The big blow was a three-run homer by Whitey Lockman, but the Yankees helped out with two key errors.

GAME 4 / OCT. 8							
REYNOLDS VS. MAGLIE, JONES(6), KENNEDY(9)							49,010
NY-A	010	120	200	6	12	0	
NY-N	100	000	001	2	8	2	

Joe DiMaggio's final home run—a two-run blast in the fifth—gave the Yankees an insurmountable lead. Allie Reynolds gave up single runs in the first and ninth, but threw seven straight shutout frames in between.

GAME 5 / OCT. 9							
LOPAT VS. JANSEN, KENNEDY(4), SPENCER(6), CORWIN(7), KONIKOWSKI(9)							47,530
NY-A	005	202	400	13	12	1	
NY-N	100	000	000	1	5	3	

The powerful Yankee bats overshadowed another fine mound performance by Lopat, who allowed just three hits and a walk after giving up an unearned run in the first.

GAME 6 / OCT. 10							
KOSLO, HEARN(7), JANSEN(8) VS. RASCHI, SAIN(7), KUZAVA(9)							61,711
NY-N	000	010	002	3	11	1	
NY-A	100	003	00X	4	7	0	

The Yankees looked to have it locked up, ahead by three going into the ninth, but they had to fight off a furious rally to win the title. The Giants loaded the bases on three straight singles, forcing Casey Stengel to bring in reliever Bob Kuzava. Two straight sacrifice flies made it 4–3, but Kuzava got Sal Yvars to line out to right to end the Series.

1952 World Series
New York Yankees (4) vs. Brooklyn Dodgers (3)

Though they had won the last three championships, the Yankees hadn't been challenged, losing only four postseason games from 1950–52. The last time the Bronx Bombers were tested was in 1947, when the Dodgers forced a seventh game. This one would also be a classic, with all but one of the games being decided by one or two runs, and would again wind up in heartbreak for Brooklyn fans.

NY (AL)

PLAYER, POS	G	AB	R	H	2B	3B	HR	RBI	BB	SO	SB	AVG	OBP	SLG
M.Mantle, of	7	29	5	10	1	1	2	3	3	4	0	.345	.406	.448
Y.Berra, c	7	28	2	6	1	0	2	3	2	4	0	.214	.267	.250
P.Rizzuto, ss	7	27	2	4	1	0	0	0	5	2	0	.148	.281	.185
G.McDougald, 3b	7	25	5	5	0	0	1	3	5	2	1	.200	.333	.200

NY (AL) (CONT.)

PLAYER, POS	G	AB	R	H	2B	3B	HR	RBI	BB	SO	SB	AVG	OBP	SLG
B.Martin, 2b	7	23	2	5	0	0	1	4	2	2	0	.217	.280	.217
G.Woodling, of	7	23	4	8	1	1	1	1	3	3	0	.348	.423	.478
H.Bauer, of	7	18	2	1	0	0	0	1	4	3	0	.056	.227	.056
J.Mize, 1b	5	15	3	6	1	0	3	6	3	1	0	.400	.500	.467
J.Collins, 1b	6	12	1	0	0	0	0	0	1	3	0	.000	.077	.000
I.Noren, of	4	10	0	3	0	0	0	1	1	3	0	.300	[illegible]	.300
A.Reynolds, p	4	7	0	0	0	0	0	0	0	2	0	.000	.000	.000
V.Raschi, p	3	6	0	1	0	0	0	1	1	2	0	.167	.286	.167
E.Lopat, p	2	3	0	1	0	0	0	1	1	1	0	.333	.500	.333
J.Sain, p	2	3	0	0	0	0	0	0	0	0	0	.000	.000	.000
E.Blackwell, p	1	1	0	0	0	0	0	0	0	0	0	.000	.000	.000
R.Houk, ph	1	1	0	0	0	0	0	0	0	0	0	.000	.000	.000
B.Kuzava, p	1	1	0	0	0	0	0	0	0	0	0	.000	.000	.000
Totals		232	26	50	5	2	10	24	31	32	1	.216	.311	.254

PITCHER	W	L	ERA	G	GS	SV	IP	H	BB	SO
A.Reynolds	2	1	1.77	4	2	1	20.1	12	6	18
V.Raschi	2	0	1.59	3	2	0	17.0	12	8	18
E.Lopat	0	1	4.76	2	2	0	11.1	14	4	3
J.Sain	0	1	3.00	1	0	0	6.0	6	3	3
E.Blackwell	0	0	7.20	1	1	0	5.0	4	3	4
B.Kuzava	0	0	0.00	1	0	1	2.2	0	0	2
R.Scarborough	0	0	9.00	1	0	0	1.0	1	0	1
T.Gorman	0	0	0.00	1	0	0	0.2	1	0	0
Totals	4	3	2.81	14	7	2	64.0	50	24	49

BRO (NL)

PLAYER, POS	G	AB	R	H	2B	3B	HR	RBI	BB	SO	SB	AVG	OBP	SLG
P.Wee Reese, ss	7	29	4	10	0	0	1	4	2	2	1	.345	.387	.345
D.Snider, of	7	29	5	10	2	0	4	8	1	5	1	.345	.367	.414
R.Campanella, c	7	28	0	6	0	0	0	1	1	6	0	.214	.241	.214
B.Cox, 3b	7	27	4	8	2	0	0	0	3	4	0	.296	.367	.370
C.Furillo, of	7	23	1	4	2	0	0	0	3	3	0	.174	.269	.261
J.Robinson, 2b	7	23	4	4	0	0	1	2	7	5	2	.174	.367	.174
G.Hodges, 1b	7	21	1	0	0	0	0	1	5	6	0	.000	.192	.000
A.Pafko, of	7	21	0	4	0	0	0	2	0	4	0	.190	.190	.190
G.Shuba, of	4	10	0	3	1	0	0	0	0	4	0	.300	.300	.400
J.Black, p	3	6	0	0	0	0	0	0	1	6	0	.000	.143	.000
C.Erskine, p	3	6	1	0	0	0	0	0	0	1	0	.000	.000	.000
B.Loes, p	2	3	0	1	0	0	0	0	0	1	1	.333	.333	.333
R.Nelson, ph	4	3	0	0	0	0	0	0	1	2	0	.000	.250	.000
P.Roe, p	3	2	0	0	0	0	0	0	0	0	0	.000	.000	.000
T.Holmes, of	3	1	0	0	0	0	0	0	0	0	0	.000	.000	.000
B.Morgan, 3b	2	1	0	0	0	0	0	0	0	0	0	.000	.000	.000
S.Amoros, ph	1	0	0	0	0	0	0	0	0	0	0	.000	.000	.000
Totals		233	20	50	7	0	6	18	24	49	5	.215	.291	.245

PITCHER	W	L	ERA	G	GS	SV	IP	H	BB	SO
J.Black	1	2	2.53	3	3	0	21.1	15	8	9
C.Erskine	1	1	4.50	3	2	0	18.0	12	10	10
P.Roe	1	0	3.18	3	1	0	11.1	9	6	7
B.Loes	0	1	4.35	2	1	0	10.1	11	5	5
K.Lehman	0	0	0.00	1	0	0	2.0	2	1	0
J.Rutherford	0	0	9.00	1	0	0	1.0	1	1	1
Totals	3	4	3.52	13	7	0	64.0	50	31	32

GAME 1 / OCT. 1							
REYNOLDS, SCARBOROUGH(8) VS. BLACK							34,861
NY	010	000	010	2	6	2	
BRO	010	002	01X	4	6	0	

Joe Black, who spent most of the year as a reliever, got the start for the Dodgers and became the first African-American pitcher to win a World Series game. Jackie Robinson, Duke Snider and Pee Wee Reese all homered for the Dodgers.

GAME 2 / OCT. 2							
RASCHI VS. ERSKINE, LOES(6), LEHMAN(8)							33,792
NY	000	115	000	7	10	0	
BRO	001	000	000	1	3	1	

Billy Martin's three-run blast in the top of the sixth was the big blow for the Yankees, though it was just icing on the cake. Vic Raschi went the distance, giving up only three hits.

GAME 3 / OCT. 3							
ROE VS. LOPAT, GORMAN(9)							66,698
BRO	001	010	012	5	11	0	
NY	010	000	011	3	6	2	

After a double steal, Reese and Robinson both scored on a passed ball, giving the Dodgers two insurance runs in the ninth, which became especially needed after Johnny Mize's solo homer in the bottom of the frame.

GAME 4 / OCT. 4							
BLACK, RUTHERFORD(8) VS. REYNOLDS							71,787
BRO	000	000	000	0	4	1	
NY	000	100	01X	2	4	1	

Black was again masterful, though Allie Reynolds was even better, blanking the Dodgers on four hits. Reynolds was able to get out of trouble in the fifth when Black whiffed on a suicide squeeze attempt, resulting in Andy Pafko getting tagged out at the plate.

GAME 5 / OCT. 5						
ERSKINE VS. BLACKWELL, SAIN(6)						70,536
BRO	010	030	100	01	6	10	0
NY	000	050	000	00	5	5	1

Carl Erskine recovered after giving up five in the fifth, retiring the final 19 Yankee hitters in the game. That allowed Snider to be the hero as he tied the game in the seventh on a two out single and won with a double in the 11th.

GAME 6 / OCT. 6						
RASCHI, REYNOLDS(8) VS. LOES, ROE(9)						30,037
NY	000	000	210	3	9	0
BRO	000	001	010	2	8	1

Snider clubbed two home runs, but the Dodgers got little else off Raschi, who broke a 1–1 tie with a single in the seventh.

GAME 7 / OCT. 7						
LOPAT, REYNOLDS(4), RASCHI(7), KUZAVA(7) VS. BLACK, ROE(6), ERSKINE(8)						33,195
NY	000	111	100	4	10	4
BRO	000	110	000	2	8	1

The key point in the game came in the bottom of the seventh with the Yankees ahead by two. Brooklyn loaded the bases with one out, but Kuzava, relieving Raschi, who started the inning in relief even though he'd gone nine the day before, got both Snider and Robinson on infield popups to end the threat. The Dodgers got only one more runner in the final two innings—Gil Hodges, who reached on an error in the eighth—and the Yankees walked away with another championship.

1953 World Series
New York Yankees (4) vs. Brooklyn Dodgers (2)

The two best teams in baseball in 1953 met in the World Series for the second straight year. Many felt this year's Brooklyn team was the borough's best, though in the end, the Yankees won their fifth straight championship, a record for consecutive titles that hasn't come close to being broken in more than 50 years.

NY (AL)

PLAYER, POS	G	AB	R	H	2B	3B	HR	RBI	BB	SO	SB	AVG	OBP	SLG
J.Collins, 1b	6	24	4	4	1	0	1	2	3	8	0	.167	.259	.208
M.Mantle, of	6	24	3	5	0	0	2	7	3	8	0	.208	.296	.208
B.Martin, 2b	6	24	5	12	1	2	2	8	1	2	1	.500	.520	.708
G.McDougald, 3b	6	24	2	4	0	1	2	4	1	3	0	.167	.200	.250
H.Bauer, of	6	23	6	6	0	1	0	1	2	4	0	.261	.320	.348
Y.Berra, c	6	21	3	9	1	0	1	4	3	3	0	.429	.500	.476
G.Woodling, of	6	20	5	6	0	0	1	3	6	2	0	.300	.462	.300
P.Rizzuto, ss	6	19	4	6	1	0	0	0	3	2	1	.316	.409	.368
W.Ford, p	2	3	0	1	0	0	0	0	0	0	0	.333	.333	.333
E.Lopat, p	1	3	0	0	0	0	0	0	0	2	0	.000	.000	.000
J.Mize, ph	3	3	0	0	0	0	0	0	0	1	0	.000	.000	.000
D.Bollweg, 1b	3	2	0	0	0	0	0	0	0	2	0	.000	.000	.000
J.McDonald, p	1	2	0	1	1	0	0	1	1	1	0	.500	.667	1.000
V.Raschi, p	1	2	0	0	0	0	0	0	0	1	0	.000	.000	.000
A.Reynolds, p	3	2	0	1	0	0	0	0	1	1	0	.500	.667	.500
J.Sain, p	2	2	1	1	1	0	0	2	0	1	0	.500	.500	1.000
T.Gorman, p	1	1	0	0	0	0	0	0	0	1	0	.000	.000	.000
B.Kuzava, p	1	1	0	0	0	0	0	0	0	1	0	.000	.000	.000
I.Noren, ph	2	1	0	0	0	0	0	0	1	0	0	.000	.500	.000
Totals		201	33	56	6	4	9	32	25	43	2	.279	.370	.348

PITCHER	W	L	ERA	G	GS	SV	IP	H	BB	SO
E.Lopat	1	0	2.00	1	1	0	9.0	9	4	3
W.Ford	0	1	4.50	2	2	0	8.0	9	2	7
V.Raschi	0	1	3.38	1	1	0	8.0	9	3	4
A.Reynolds	1	0	6.75	3	1	1	8.0	9	4	9
J.McDonald	1	0	5.87	1	1	0	7.2	12	0	3
J.Sain	1	0	4.76	2	0	0	5.2	8	1	1
T.Gorman	0	0	3.00	1	0	0	3.0	4	0	1
A.Schallock	0	0	4.50	1	0	0	2.0	2	1	1
B.Kuzava	0	0	13.50	1	0	0	0.2	2	0	1
Totals	4	2	4.50	13	6	1	52.0	64	15	30

BRO (NL)

PLAYER, POS	G	AB	R	H	2B	3B	HR	RBI	BB	SO	SB	AVG	OBP	SLG
J.Gilliam, 2b	6	27	4	8	3	0	2	4	0	2	0	.296	.296	.407
J.Robinson, of	6	25	3	8	2	0	0	2	1	0	1	.320	.346	.400
D.Snider, of	6	25	3	8	3	0	1	5	2	6	0	.320	.370	.440
C.Furillo, of	6	24	4	8	2	0	1	4	1	3	0	.333	.360	.417
P.Wee Reese, ss	6	24	0	5	0	1	0	0	4	1	0	.208	.321	.292
B.Cox, 3b	6	23	3	7	3	0	1	6	1	4	0	.304	.333	.435
R.Campanella, c	6	22	6	6	0	0	1	2	2	3	0	.273	.333	.273
G.Hodges, 1b	6	22	3	8	0	0	1	1	3	3	1	.364	.440	.364
C.Erskine, p	3	4	0	1	0	0	0	0	0	1	0	.250	.250	.250
B.Loes, p	1	3	0	2	0	0	0	0	0	0	0	.667	.667	.667
P.Roe, p	1	3	0	0	0	0	0	0	0	2	0	.000	.000	.000
W.Belardi, ph	2	2	0	0	0	0	0	0	0	1	0	.000	.000	.000
C.Labine, p	3	2	0	0	0	0	0	0	0	1	0	.000	.000	.000
D.Williams, ph	3	2	0	1	0	0	0	0	1	1	0	.500	.667	.500
J.Hughes, p	1	1	0	0	0	0	0	0	0	1	0	.000	.000	.000
R.Meyer, p	1	1	0	0	0	0	0	0	0	1	0	.000	.000	.000
B.Morgan, ph	1	1	0	0	0	0	0	0	0	0	0	.000	.000	.000
J.Podres, p	1	1	0	1	0	0	0	0	0	0	0	1.000	1.000	1.000
G.Shuba, ph	2	1	1	1	0	0	1	2	0	0	0	1.000	1.000	1.000
D.Thompson, of	2	0	0	0	0	0	0	0	0	0	0	.000	.000	.000
Totals		213	27	64	13	1	8	26	15	30	2	.300	.352	.371

PITCHER	W	L	ERA	G	GS	SV	IP	H	BB	SO
C.Erskine	1	0	5.79	3	3	0	14.0	14	9	16
B.Loes	1	0	3.38	1	1	0	8.0	8	2	8
P.Roe	0	1	4.50	1	1	0	8.0	5	4	4
C.Labine	0	2	3.60	3	0	1	5.0	10	1	3
R.Meyer	0	0	6.23	1	0	0	4.1	8	4	5
J.Hughes	0	0	2.25	1	0	0	4.0	3	1	3
J.Podres	0	1	3.38	1	1	0	2.2	1	2	0
B.Wade	0	0	15.43	2	0	0	2.1	4	1	2
B.Milliken	0	0	0.00	1	0	0	2.0	2	1	0
J.Black	0	0	9.00	1	0	0	1.0	1	0	2
Totals	2	4	4.91	15	6	1	51.1	56	25	43

GAME 1 / SEPT. 30						
ERSKINE, HUGHES(2), LABINE(6), WADE(8) VS. REYNOLDS, SAIN(6)						69,374
BRO	000	013	100	5	12	2
NY	400	010	13X	9	12	0

Brooklyn's Cark Erskine got bounced in the first inning, though the Dodgers came back to tie the game by the seventh. The rally didn't last long, however, as Joe Collins belted a solo homer in the bottom of the seventh, and the Yankees got three more in the eighth for a four-run win.

GAME 2 / OCT. 1						
ROE VS. LOPAT						66,786
BRO	000	200	000	2	9	1
NY	100	000	12X	4	5	0

The Yankees were trailing headed into the seventh, but home runs by Billy Martin and Mickey Mantle helped give New York a two-game lead.

GAME 3 / OCT. 2						
RASCHI VS. ERSKINE						35,270
NY	000	010	010	2	6	0
BRO	000	011	01X	3	9	0

Although he got only three outs two days before, Erskine hurled one of the greatest World Series performances, striking out a record 14 Yankees.

GAME 4 / OCT. 3						
FORD, GORMAN(2), SAIN(5), SCHALLOCK(7) VS. LOES, LABINE(9)						36,775
NY	000	020	001	3	9	0
BRO	300	102	10X	7	12	0

Brooklyn evened the series, thanks in part to a baserunning blunder in the ninth by Billy Martin. Down 7–2 with two outs in the ninth, Mantle singled in a run. Though stopping at third would have brought the tying run to the plate, Martin inexplicably tried to score from second, and was thrown out easily to end the game.

GAME 5 / OCT. 4						
MCDONALD, KUZAVA(8), REYNOLDS(9) VS. PODRES, MEYER(3), WADE(8), BLACK(9)						36,775
NY	105	000	311	11	11	1
BRO	010	010	041	7	14	1

The Yankees put on a power display, clubbing four home runs, including a grand slam by Mantle in the third and were never seriously challenged.

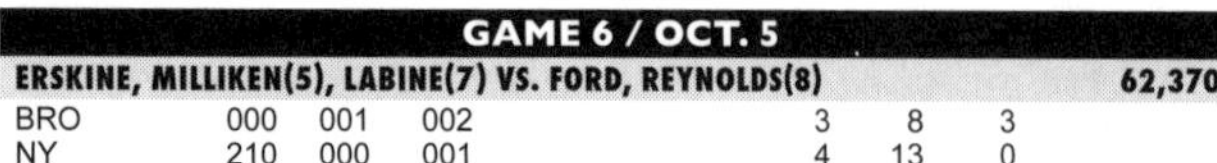

GAME 6 / OCT. 5						
ERSKINE, MILLIKEN(5), LABINE(7) VS. FORD, REYNOLDS(8)						62,370
BRO	000	001	002	3	8	3
NY	210	000	001	4	13	0

The Yankees led from the first until Carl Furillo's two-run shot tied it in the top of the ninth. New York fans didn't suffer long, however. Hank Bauer walked leading off the bottom of the ninth, and Mantle followed with an infield hit. Next up was Martin, the goat in Game 4. He knocked one up the middle that scored Bauer and gave Martin the record for most hits (12) in a six-game series and gave the Yankees yet another title.

1955 World Series
New York Yankees (3) vs. Brooklyn Dodgers (4)

The Yankees and Dodgers were meeting in the Fall Classic for the third time in four years, and the fourth time in seven. This year would be different. Instead of letting a 3-games-to-2 lead get away, as they had done in '52, the Dodgers pulled out a seventh game, giving Brooklyn its only title before the beloved Bums departed for Los Angeles.

BRO (NL)

PLAYER, POS	G	AB	R	H	2B	3B	HR	RBI	BB	SO	SB	AVG	OBP	SLG
R.Campanella, c	7	27	4	7	3	0	2	4	3	3	0	.259	.333	.370
C.Furillo, of	7	27	4	8	1	0	1	3	3	5	0	.296	.367	.333
P.Wee Reese, ss	7	27	5	8	1	0	0	2	3	5	0	.296	.367	.333
D.Snider, of	7	25	5	8	1	0	4	7	2	6	0	.320	.370	.360
J.Gilliam, 2b-of	7	24	2	7	1	0	0	3	8	1	1	.292	.469	.333
G.Hodges, 1b	7	24	2	7	0	0	1	5	3	2	0	.292	.370	.292
J.Robinson, 3b	6	22	5	4	1	1	0	1	2	1	1	.182	.250	.318
S.Amoros, of	5	12	3	4	0	0	1	3	4	4	0	.333	.500	.333
D.Zimmer, 2b	4	9	0	2	0	0	0	2	2	5	0	.222	.364	.222
J.Podres, p	2	7	1	1	0	0	0	0	0	1	0	.143	.143	.143
C.Labine, p	4	4	0	0	0	0	0	0	0	3	0	.000	.000	.000
D.Hoak, 3b	3	3	0	1	0	0	0	0	2	0	0	.333	.600	.333
F.Kellert, ph	3	3	0	1	0	0	0	0	0	0	0	.333	.333	.333
D.Newcombe, p	1	3	0	0	0	0	0	0	0	0	0	.000	.000	.000
R.Meyer, p	1	2	0	0	0	0	0	0	0	1	0	.000	.000	.000
D.Bessent, p	3	1	0	0	0	0	0	0	0	1	0	.000	.000	.000
C.Erskine, p	1	1	0	0	0	0	0	0	0	0	0	.000	.000	.000
B.Loes, p	1	1	0	0	0	0	0	0	0	0	0	.000	.000	.000
G.Shuba, ph	1	1	0	0	0	0	0	0	0	0	0	.000	.000	.000
R.Craig, p	1	0	0	0	0	0	0	0	1	0	0	.000	1.000	.000
Totals		223	31	58	8	1	9	30	33	38	2	.260	.360	.305

PITCHER	W	L	ERA	G	GS	SV	IP	H	BB	SO
J.Podres	2	0	1.00	2	2	0	18.0	15	4	10
C.Labine	1	0	2.89	4	0	1	9.1	6	2	2
R.Craig	1	0	3.00	1	1	0	6.0	4	5	4
R.Meyer	0	0	0.00	1	0	0	5.2	4	2	4
D.Newcombe	0	1	9.53	1	1	0	5.2	8	2	4
B.Loes	0	1	9.82	1	1	0	3.2	7	1	5
D.Bessent	0	0	0.00	3	0	0	3.1	3	1	1
K.Spooner	0	1	13.50	2	1	0	3.1	4	3	6
C.Erskine	0	0	9.00	1	1	0	3.0	3	2	3
E.Roebuck	0	0	0.00	1	0	0	2.0	1	0	0
Totals	4	3	3.75	17	7	1	60.0	55	22	39

NY (AL)

PLAYER, POS	G	AB	R	H	2B	3B	HR	RBI	BB	SO	SB	AVG	OBP	SLG
G.McDougald, 3b	7	27	2	7	0	0	1	1	2	6	0	.259	.310	.259
E.Howard, of	7	26	3	5	0	0	1	3	1	8	0	.192	.222	.192
B.Martin, 2b	7	25	2	8	1	1	0	4	1	5	0	.320	.346	.440
Y.Berra, c	7	24	5	10	1	0	1	2	3	1	0	.417	.481	.458
B.Cerv, of	5	16	1	2	0	0	1	1	0	4	0	.125	.125	.125
I.Noren, of	5	16	0	1	0	0	0	1	1	1	0	.063	.118	.063
P.Rizzuto, ss	7	15	2	4	0	0	0	1	5	1	2	.267	.450	.267
H.Bauer, of	6	14	1	6	0	0	0	1	0	1	0	.429	.429	.429
J.Collins, 1b-of	5	12	6	2	0	0	2	3	6	4	1	.167	.444	.167
B.Skowron, 1b	5	12	2	4	2	0	1	3	0	1	0	.333	.333	.500
M.Mantle, of	3	10	1	2	0	0	1	1	0	2	0	.200	.200	.200
T.Byrne, p	3	6	0	1	0	0	0	2	0	2	0	.167	.167	.167
W.Ford, p	2	6	1	0	0	0	0	0	1	1	0	.000	.143	.000
J.Coleman, ss	3	3	0	0	0	0	0	0	0	1	0	.000	.000	.000
E.Robinson, 1b	4	3	0	2	0	0	0	1	2	1	0	.667	.800	.667
A.Carey, ph	2	2	0	1	0	1	0	1	0	0	0	.500	.500	1.500
B.Grim, p	3	2	0	0	0	0	0	0	0	0	0	.000	.000	.000
D.Larsen, p	1	2	0	0	0	0	0	0	0	0	0	.000	.000	.000
B.Turley, p	3	1	0	0	0	0	0	0	0	0	0	.000	.000	.000
T.Carroll, pr	2	0	0	0	0	0	0	0	0	0	0	.000	.000	.000
Totals		222	26	55	4	2	8	25	22	39	3	.248	.321	.284

NY (AL) (CONT.)

PITCHER	W	L	ERA	G	GS	SV	IP	H	BB	SO
W.Ford	2	0	2.12	2	2	0	17.0	13	8	10
T.Byrne	1	1	1.88	2	2	0	14.1	8	8	8
B.Grim	0	1	4.15	3	1	1	8.2	8	5	8
B.Turley	0	1	8.44	3	1	0	5.1	7	4	7
D.Larsen	0	1	11.25	1	1	0	4.0	5	2	2
T.Morgan	0	0	4.91	2	0	0	3.2	3	3	1
J.Kucks	0	0	6.00	2	0	0	3.0	4	1	1
T.Sturdivant	0	0	6.00	2	0	0	3.0	5	2	0
R.Coleman	0	0	9.00	1	0	0	1.0	5	0	1
Totals	3	4	4.20	18	7	1	60.0	58	33	38

GAME 1 / SEPT. 28						
NEWCOMBE, BESSENT(6), LABINE(8) VS. FORD, GRIM(9)						63,869
BRO	021	000	020	5	10	0
NY	021	102	00X	6	9	1

Joe Collins smacked two home runs—a solo shot in the fourth and a two-run blast in the sixth—lifting the Yankees past Brooklyn, which had more hits but couldn't match New York's power totals.

GAME 2 / SEPT. 29						
LOES, BESSENT(4), SPOONER(5), LABINE(8) VS. BYRNE						64,707
BRO	000	110	000	2	5	2
NY	000	400	00X	4	8	0

The Yankees scored in only one inning, but thanks to a five-hitter by Tommy Byrne, that's all they needed.

GAME 3 / SEPT. 30						
TURLEY, MORGAN(2), KUCKS(5), STURDIVANT(7) VS. PODRES						34,209
NY	020	000	100	3	7	0
BRO	220	200	20X	8	11	1

Brooklyn finally got into the win column behind a complete game win from Johnny Padres. An early two-run homer from Roy Campanella set the tone for the Dodgers.

GAME 4 / OCT. 1						
LARSEN, KUCKS(5), R.COLEMAN(6), MORGAN(7), STURDIVANT(8) VS. ERSKINE, BESSENT(4), LABINE(5)						36,242
NY	110	102	000	5	9	0
BRO	001	330	10X	8	14	0

Brooklyn's big bats came alive as Campanella, Duke Snider and Gil Hodges drove in six of the Dodgers' eight runs with long balls.

GAME 5 / OCT. 2						
GRIM, TURLEY(7) VS. CRAIG, LABINE(7)						36,796
NY	000	100	110	3	6	0
BRO	021	010	01X	5	9	2

Snider walloped two more homers to pace the Dodgers. New York got to within one in the eighth after Yogi Berra led off the inning with a homer, but got only one runner on the rest of the way.

GAME 6 / OCT. 3						
SPOONER, MEYER(1), ROEBUCK(7) VS. FORD						64,022
BRO	000	100	000	1	4	1
NY	500	000	00X	5	8	0

Whitey Ford snapped Brooklyn's winning streak with a four-hitter. Moose Skowron's three-run homer in New York's five-run first was the big blow.

GAME 7 / OCT. 4						
PODRES VS. BYRNE, GRIM(6), TURLEY(8)						62,465
BRO	000	101	000	2	5	0
NY	000	000	000	0	8	1

It can be argued that Brooklyn's only title came because of one play. The Yankees trailed 2–0 in the bottom of the sixth, but had two on with Berra at the plate. Berra knocked one down the left field line that would have tied the game were it not for Sandy Amoros, a defensive replacement for Jim Gilliam. Amoros made a superb running grab of Berra's liner and was able to turn and throw back to the infield for a double play. It ended New York's best threat of the game, and ultimately made the Dodgers world champions for the first time ever.

1956 World Series
New York Yankees (4) vs. Brooklyn Dodgers (3)

It was a mirror image of the previous year's series, with the home team winning every game but the last, when the visitors pitched a shutout. This time, the Yankees came out on top to claim their first title in three years, which at the time was a drought of epic proportions to the storied franchise.

NY (AL)

PLAYER, POS	G	AB	R	H	2B	3B	HR	RBI	BB	SO	SB	AVG	OBP	SLG
H.Bauer, of	7	32	3	9	0	0	1	3	0	5	1	.281	.281	.281
B.Martin, 2b-3b	7	27	5	8	0	0	2	3	1	6	0	.296	.321	.296
Y.Berra, c	7	25	5	9	2	0	3	10	4	1	0	.360	.448	.440
M.Mantle, of	7	24	6	6	1	0	3	4	6	5	1	.250	.400	.292
J.Collins, 1b	6	21	2	5	2	0	0	2	2	3	0	.238	.304	.333
G.McDougald, ss	7	21	0	3	0	0	0	1	3	6	0	.143	.250	.143
E.Slaughter, of	6	20	6	7	0	0	1	4	4	0	0	.350	.458	.350
A.Carey, 3b	7	19	2	3	0	0	0	0	1	6	0	.158	.200	.158
B.Skowron, 1b	3	10	1	1	0	0	1	4	0	3	0	.100	.100	.100
E.Howard, of	1	5	1	2	1	0	1	1	0	0	0	.400	.400	.600
W.Ford, p	2	4	0	0	0	0	0	0	0	3	0	.000	.000	.000
B.Turley, p	3	4	0	0	0	0	0	0	0	1	0	.000	.000	.000
J.Kucks, p	3	3	0	0	0	0	0	0	0	1	0	.000	.000	.000
D.Larsen, p	2	3	1	1	0	0	0	1	0	1	0	.333	.333	.333
T.Sturdivant, p	2	3	0	1	0	0	0	0	0	1	0	.333	.333	.333
J.Coleman, 2b	2	2	0	0	0	0	0	0	0	0	0	.000	.000	.000
T.Byrne, p	2	1	0	0	0	0	0	0	0	0	0	.000	.000	.000
B.Cerv, ph	1	1	0	1	0	0	0	0	0	0	0	1.000	1.000	1.000
M.McDermott, p	1	1	0	1	0	0	0	0	0	0	0	1.000	1.000	1.000
T.Morgan, p	2	1	1	1	0	0	0	0	0	0	0	1.000	1.000	1.000
N.Siebern, ph	1	1	0	0	0	0	0	0	0	0	0	.000	.000	.000
G.Wilson, ph	1	1	0	0	0	0	0	0	0	1	0	.000	.000	.000
Totals		229	33	58	6	0	12	33	21	43	2	.253	.316	.279

PITCHER	W	L	ERA	G	GS	SV	IP	H	BB	SO
W.Ford	1	1	5.25	2	2	0	12.0	14	2	8
J.Kucks	1	0	0.82	3	1	0	11.0	6	3	2
B.Turley	0	1	0.82	3	1	0	11.0	4	8	14
D.Larsen	1	0	0.00	2	2	0	10.2	1	4	7
T.Sturdivant	1	0	2.79	2	1	0	9.2	8	8	9
T.Morgan	0	1	9.00	2	0	0	4.0	6	4	3
M.McDermott	0	0	3.00	1	0	0	3.0	2	3	3
T.Byrne	0	0	0.00	1	0	0	0.1	1	0	1
Totals	4	3	2.48	16	7	0	61.2	42	32	47

BRO (NL)

PLAYER, POS	G	AB	R	H	2B	3B	HR	RBI	BB	SO	SB	AVG	OBP	SLG
P.Wee Reese, ss	7	27	3	6	0	1	0	2	2	6	0	.222	.276	.296
C.Furillo, of	7	25	2	6	2	0	0	1	2	3	0	.240	.296	.320
J.Gilliam, 2b-of	7	24	2	2	0	0	0	2	7	3	1	.083	.290	.083
J.Robinson, 3b	7	24	5	6	1	0	1	2	5	2	0	.250	.379	.292
G.Hodges, 1b	7	23	5	7	2	0	1	8	4	4	0	.304	.407	.391
D.Snider, of	7	23	5	7	1	0	1	4	6	8	0	.304	.448	.348
R.Campanella, c	7	22	2	4	1	0	0	3	3	7	0	.182	.280	.227
S.Amoros, of	6	19	1	1	0	0	0	1	2	4	0	.053	.143	.053
S.Maglie, p	2	5	0	0	0	0	0	0	0	2	0	.000	.000	.000
C.Labine, p	2	4	0	1	1	0	0	0	0	2	0	.250	.250	.500
D.Mitchell, ph	4	4	0	0	0	0	0	0	0	1	0	.000	.000	.000
C.Neal, 2b	1	4	0	0	0	0	0	0	0	1	0	.000	.000	.000
R.Jackson, ph	3	3	0	0	0	0	0	0	0	2	0	.000	.000	.000
D.Bessent, p	2	2	0	1	0	0	0	1	1	1	0	.500	.667	.500
R.Craig, p	2	2	0	1	0	0	0	0	0	0	0	.500	.500	.500
R.Walker, ph	2	2	0	0	0	0	0	0	0	0	0	.000	.000	.000
C.Erskine, p	2	1	0	0	0	0	0	0	0	1	0	.000	.000	.000
D.Newcombe, p	2	1	0	0	0	0	0	0	0	0	0	.000	.000	.000
G.Cimoli, of	1	0	0	0	0	0	0	0	0	0	0	.000	.000	.000
Totals		215	25	42	8	1	3	24	32	47	1	.195	.300	.242

PITCHER	W	L	ERA	G	GS	SV	IP	H	BB	SO
S.Maglie	1	1	2.65	2	2	0	17.0	14	6	15
C.Labine	1	0	0.00	2	1	0	12.0	8	3	7
D.Bessent	1	0	1.80	2	0	0	10.0	8	3	5
R.Craig	0	1	12.00	2	1	0	6.0	10	3	4
C.Erskine	0	1	5.40	2	1	0	5.0	4	2	2
D.Newcombe	0	1	21.21	2	2	0	4.2	11	3	4

BRO (NL) (CONT.)

PITCHER	W	L	ERA	G	GS	SV	IP	H	BB	SO
E.Roebuck	0	0	2.08	3	0	0	4.1	1	0	5
D.Drysdale	0	0	9.00	1	0	0	2.0	2	1	1
Totals	3	4	4.72	16	7	0	61.0	58	21	43

GAME 1 / OCT. 3

FORD, KUCKS(4), MORGAN(6), TURLEY(8) VS. MAGLIE							34,479
NY	200	100	000	3	9	1	
BRO	023	100	00X	6	9	0	

Although neither starter had his best stuff, in the end Brooklyn's Sal Maglie was a little better than Whitey Ford. Gil Hodges' three-run blast with two outs in the bottom of the third was the game's biggest hit.

GAME 2 / OCT. 5

LARSEN, KUCKS(2), BYRNE(2), STURDIVANT(3), MORGAN(3), TURLEY(5), MCDERMOTT(6) VS. NEWCOMBE, ROEBUCK(2), BESSENT(3)							36,217
NY	150	100	001	8	12	2	
BRO	061	220	02X	13	12	0	

Don Larsen gave away an early six-run lead, though it wasn't all his fault, and he certainly wasn't the only Yankee pitcher to struggle. All six runs the Dodgers scored in the second were unearned, thanks to an error by first baseman Joe Collins. Six of Brooklyn's last seven runs were earned, however, and the Dodgers dented the plate off of five of the six Yankee relievers.

GAME 3 / OCT. 6

CRAIG, LABINE(7) VS. FORD							73,977
BRO	010	001	100	3	8	1	
NY	010	003	01X	5	8	1	

Enos Slaughter, a 40-year-old reserve, clubbed a three-run homer in the bottom of the sixth to save the Yankees from what would have been a three-games-to-none hole.

GAME 4 / OCT. 7

ERSKINE, ROEBUCK(5), DRYSDALE(7) VS. STURDIVANT							69,705
BRO	000	100	001	2	6	0	
NY	100	201	20X	6	7	2	

The Dodgers had the leadoff runner on in each of the first six innings, though they could turn that into only one run as New York's Tom Sturdivant worked around six hits and six walks for a complete game victory.

GAME 5 / OCT. 8

MAGLIE VS. LARSEN							64,519
BRO	000	000	000	0	0	0	
NY	000	101	00X	2	5	0	

The Yankees didn't decide on their starting pitcher until the morning of the game, yet Don Larsen turned in the best World Series pitching performance in history with his perfect game. There were only a couple of tough outs, one in the second and one in the fifth. New York needed every bit of Larsen's dominance as they managed only five hits off Maglie.

GAME 6 / OCT. 9

TURLEY VS. LABINE								33,224
NY	000	000	000	0	0	7	0	
BRO	000	000	000	1	1	4	0	

Both teams had chances to score, but neither could get it done through nine. The Yankees had the best shot in the eighth, after a one-out double by Collins and an intentional walk to Mickey Mantle, though Yogi Berra and Slaughter made easy outs. Brooklyn sent the series to a seventh game on a two-out single by Jackie Robinson in the bottom of the 10th.

GAME 7 / OCT. 10						
KUCKS VS. NEWCOMBE, BESSENT(4), CRAIG(7), ROEBUCK(7), ERSKINE(9)						**33,782**
NY	202	100	400	9	10	0
BRO	000	000	000	0	3	1

Berra's two-run blast in the top of the first made it all over but the shouting. Between the mound dominance of Johnny Kucks (a complete game three-hitter) and three more homers (a second one by Berra in the third, followed by shots from Elston Howard and Bill Skowron) the Dodgers never had a chance.

1957 World Series
New York Yankees (3) vs. Milwaukee Braves (4)

After years of winning championships with players who came to the big leagues in other organizations, the Yankees were finally on the losing end of that trick, thanks to Lew Burdette. Burdette, who signed originally with New York in 1947 but was traded to the Braves before the 1951 campaign after appearing in only two games for the Yankees, was the unquestioned MVP of the series. He allowed only two earned runs in three complete game wins, including consecutive route-going shutouts in Games 5 and 7.

MIL (NL)

PLAYER, POS	G	AB	R	H	2B	3B	HR	RBI	BB	SO	SB	AVG	OBP	SLG
H.Aaron, of	7	28	5	11	0	1	3	7	1	6	0	.393	.414	.464
J.Logan, ss	7	27	5	5	1	0	1	2	3	6	0	.185	.267	.222
W.Covington, of	7	24	1	5	1	0	0	1	2	6	1	.208	.269	.250
E.Mathews, 3b	7	22	4	5	3	0	1	4	8	5	0	.227	.433	.364
D.Crandall, c	6	19	1	4	0	0	1	1	1	1	0	.211	.250	.211
R.Schoendienst, 2b	5	18	0	5	1	0	0	2	0	1	0	.278	.278	.333
J.Adcock, 1b	5	15	1	3	0	0	0	2	0	2	0	.200	.200	.200
A.Pafko, of	6	14	1	3	0	0	0	0	0	1	0	.214	.214	.214
B.Hazle, of	4	13	2	2	0	0	0	0	1	2	0	.154	.214	.154
F.Mantilla, 2b	4	10	1	0	0	0	0	0	1	0	0	.000	.091	.000
F.Torre, 1b	7	10	2	3	0	0	2	3	2	0	0	.300	.417	.300
L.Burdette, p	3	8	0	0	0	0	0	0	1	2	0	.000	.111	.000
D.Rice, c	2	6	0	1	0	0	0	0	1	2	0	.167	.286	.167
W.Spahn, p	2	4	0	0	0	0	0	0	1	2	0	.000	.200	.000
N.Jones, ph	3	2	0	0	0	0	0	0	0	0	0	.000	.000	.000
C.Sawatski, ph	2	2	0	0	0	0	0	0	0	2	0	.000	.000	.000
B.Buhl, p	2	1	0	0	0	0	0	0	0	1	0	.000	.000	.000
E.Johnson, p	3	1	0	0	0	0	0	0	0	1	0	.000	.000	.000
J.Pizarro, p	1	1	0	0	0	0	0	0	0	0	0	.000	.000	.000
J.DeMerit, pr	1	0	0	0	0	0	0	0	0	0	0	.000	.000	.000
Totals		225	23	47	6	1	8	22	22	40	1	.209	.288	.244

PITCHER	W	L	ERA	G	GS	SV	IP	H	BB	SO
L.Burdette	3	0	0.67	3	3	0	27.0	21	4	13
W.Spahn	1	1	4.70	2	2	0	15.1	18	2	2
E.Johnson	0	1	1.29	3	0	0	7.0	2	1	8
D.McMahon	0	0	0.00	3	0	0	5.0	3	3	5
B.Buhl	0	1	10.80	2	2	0	3.1	6	6	4
G.Conley	0	0	10.80	1	0	0	1.2	2	1	0
J.Pizarro	0	0	10.80	1	0	0	1.2	3	2	1
B.Trowbridge	0	0	45.00	1	0	0	1.0	2	3	1
Totals	4	3	3.48	16	7	0	62.0	57	22	34

NY (AL)

PLAYER, POS	G	AB	R	H	2B	3B	HR	RBI	BB	SO	SB	AVG	OBP	SLG
H.Bauer, of	7	31	3	8	2	1	2	6	1	6	0	.258	.281	.387
T.Kubek, of-3b	7	28	4	8	0	0	2	4	0	4	0	.286	.286	.286
Y.Berra, c	7	25	5	8	1	0	1	2	4	0	0	.320	.414	.360
G.McDougald, ss	7	24	3	6	0	0	0	2	3	3	1	.250	.333	.250
J.Coleman, 2b	7	22	2	8	2	0	0	2	3	1	0	.364	.440	.455
M.Mantle, of	6	19	3	5	0	0	1	2	3	1	0	.263	.364	.263
J.Lumpe, 3b	6	14	0	4	0	0	0	2	1	1	0	.286	.333	.286
H.Simpson, 1b	5	12	0	1	0	0	0	1	0	4	0	.083	.083	.083
E.Slaughter, of	5	12	2	3	1	0	0	0	3	2	0	.250	.400	.333
E.Howard, 1b	6	11	2	3	0	0	1	3	1	3	0	.273	.333	.273
A.Carey, 3b	2	7	0	2	1	0	0	1	1	0	0	.286	.375	.429
J.Collins, 1b	6	5	0	0	0	0	0	0	0	3	0	.000	.000	.000
W.Ford, p	2	5	0	0	0	0	0	0	0	1	0	.000	.000	.000
B.Skowron, 1b	2	4	0	0	0	0	0	0	0	0	0	.000	.000	.000
B.Turley, p	3	4	0	0	0	0	0	0	0	2	0	.000	.000	.000
T.Byrne, p	2	2	0	1	0	0	0	0	0	1	0	.500	.500	.500
D.Larsen, p	2	2	1	0	0	0	0	0	2	1	0	.000	.500	.000
A.Ditmar, p	2	1	0	0	0	0	0	0	0	1	0	.000	.000	.000
B.Shantz, p	3	1	0	0	0	0	0	0	0	0	0	.000	.000	.000
T.Sturdivant, p	2	1	0	0	0	0	0	0	0	0	0	.000	.000	.000
B.Richardson, 2b	2	0	0	0	0	0	0	0	0	0	0	.000	.000	.000
Totals		230	25	57	7	1	7	25	22	34	1	.248	.313	.287

PITCHER	W	L	ERA	G	GS	SV	IP	H	BB	SO
W.Ford	1	1	1.13	2	2	0	16.0	11	5	7
B.Turley	1	0	2.31	3	2	0	11.2	7	6	12

NY (AL) (CONT.)

PITCHER	W	L	ERA	G	GS	SV	IP	H	BB	SO
D.Larsen	1	1	3.72	2	1	0	9.2	8	5	6
B.Shantz	0	1	4.05	3	1	0	6.2	8	2	7
A.Ditmar	0	0	0.00	2	0	0	6.0	2	0	2
T.Sturdivant	0	0	6.00	2	1	0	6.0	6	1	2
T.Byrne	0	0	5.40	2	0	0	3.1	1	2	1
B.Grim	0	1	7.71	2	0	0	2.1	3	0	2
J.Kucks	0	0	0.00	1	0	0	0.2	1	1	1
Totals	3	4	2.89	19	7	0	62.1	47	22	40

GAME 1 / OCT. 2						
SPAHN, JOHNSON(6), MCMAHON(7) VS. FORD						**69,476**
MIL	000	000	100	1	5	0
NY	000	012	00X	3	9	1

New York's Whitey Ford did a better job pitching out of trouble than Milwaukee's Warren Spahn, though neither great southpaw had his best stuff. Ford settled down after giving up a leadoff double in the seventh, which wound up being the Braves' only run, retiring nine of the last 10 batters.

GAME 2 / OCT. 3						
BURDETTE VS. SHANTZ, DITMAR(4), GRIM(8)						**65,202**
MIL	011	200	000	4	8	0
NY	011	000	000	2	7	2

This was Burdette's first gem, although it didn't start out that way after the Yankees got one in the second on a two-out single by Jerry Coleman and a leadoff homer in the third by Hank Bauer. The Yankees wouldn't score again in the series against Burdette, who limited New York to just four hits the rest of the way.

GAME 3 / OCT. 5						
TURLEY, LARSEN(2) VS. BUHL, PIZARRO(1), CONLEY(3), JOHNSON(5), TROWBRIDGE(7), MCMAHON(8)						**45,804**
NY	302	200	500	12	9	0
MIL	010	020	000	3	8	1

Milwaukee native Tony Kubek belted two home runs in New York's rout. Don Larsen got the win by allowing two runs in $7^1/_3$ innings of relief of Bob Turley, who was yanked after walking two, giving up two hits and a run, and throwing a wild pitch in the second.

GAME 4 / OCT. 6							
STURDIVANT, SHANTZ(5), KUCKS(8), BYRNE(8), GRIM(10) VS. SPAHN							**45,804**
NY	100	000	003	1	5	11	0
MIL	000	400	000	3	7	7	0

Spahn had an easy time until he got two outs in the ninth. Elston Howard followed two straight singles with a three-run blast to tie the game. The Yankees got another run off Spahn in the top of the 10th, but Eddie Mathews took him off the hook with a two-run shot in the bottom of the frame.

GAME 5 / OCT. 7						
FORD, TURLEY(8) VS. BURDETTE						**45,811**
NY	000	000	000	0	7	0
MIL	000	001	00X	1	6	1

Burdette walked none and never gave up more than one hit an inning. New York's only real threat came in the fourth when they had men on first and second (thanks to an error) with one out, but Burdette got Harry Simpson to ground into a double play to end the inning.

GAME 6 / OCT. 9						
BUHL, JOHNSON(3), MCMAHON(8) VS. TURLEY						**61,408**
MIL	000	010	100	2	4	0
NY	002	000	10X	3	7	0

Though the Braves had only four baserunners through seven innings, two of them were solo homers by Joe Torre and Hank Aaron, leaving the game tied, 2–2. Bauer's solo homer in the bottom of the seventh kept the Yankees alive and sent the series to a deciding game.

GAME 7 / OCT. 10							
BURDETTE VS. LARSEN, SHANTZ(3), DITMAR(4), STURDIVANT(6), BYRNE(8)							61,207
MIL	004	000	010	5	9	1	
NY	000	000	000	0	7	3	

Burdette again allowed only seven hits, though he had to earn the win after giving up three singles in the ninth. In the end, Bill Skowron grounded into a force out with the bases loaded and two outs, giving Burdette 24 straight scoreless innings and the Braves their first championship since 1914.

1958 World Series
New York Yankees (4) vs. Milwaukee Braves (3)

The Braves appeared headed toward their second straight world championship, ahead 3-games-to-1 with two games left to play in Milwaukee. However, the Yankees weaved their World Series magic again, breaking open tie contests in the final two games with late-inning runs to giving the club its seventh championship in 10 seasons.

NY (AL)

PLAYER, POS	G	AB	R	H	2B	3B	HR	RBI	BB	SO	SB	AVG	OBP	SLG
H.Bauer, of	7	31	6	10	0	0	4	8	0	5	0	.323	.323	.323
G.McDougald, 2b	7	28	5	9	2	0	2	4	2	4	0	.321	.367	.393
Y.Berra, c	7	27	3	6	3	0	0	2	1	0	0	.222	.250	.333
B.Skowron, 1b	7	27	3	7	0	0	2	7	1	4	0	.259	.286	.259
M.Mantle, of	7	24	4	6	0	1	2	3	7	4	0	.250	.419	.333
T.Kubek, ss	7	21	0	1	0	0	0	1	1	7	0	.048	.091	.048
E.Howard, of	6	18	4	4	0	0	0	2	1	4	1	.222	.263	.222
A.Carey, 3b	5	12	1	1	0	0	0	0	0	3	0	.083	.083	.083
J.Lumpe, 3b-ss	6	12	0	2	0	0	0	0	1	2	0	.167	.231	.167
N.Siebern, of	3	8	1	1	0	0	0	0	3	2	0	.125	.364	.125
B.Richardson, 3b	4	5	0	0	0	0	0	0	0	0	0	.000	.000	.000
B.Turley, p	4	5	0	1	0	0	0	2	0	1	0	.200	.200	.200
W.Ford, p	3	4	1	0	0	0	0	0	2	2	0	.000	.333	.000
R.Duren, p	3	3	0	0	0	0	0	0	0	2	0	.000	.000	.000
E.Slaughter, ph	4	3	1	0	0	0	0	0	1	1	0	.000	.250	.000
D.Larsen, p	2	2	0	0	0	0	0	0	1	0	0	.000	.333	.000
A.Ditmar, p	1	1	0	0	0	0	0	0	0	0	0	.000	.000	.000
J.Kucks, p	2	1	0	1	0	0	0	0	0	0	0	1.000	1.000	1.000
M.Throneberry, ph	1	1	0	0	0	0	0	0	0	1	0	.000	.000	.000
Totals		233	29	49	5	1	10	29	21	42	1	.210	.276	.240

PITCHER	W	L	ERA	G	GS	SV	IP	H	BB	SO
B.Turley	2	1	2.76	4	2	1	16.1	10	7	13
W.Ford	0	1	4.11	3	3	0	15.1	19	5	16
R.Duren	1	1	1.93	3	0	1	9.1	7	6	14
D.Larsen	1	0	0.96	2	2	0	9.1	9	6	9
J.Kucks	0	0	2.08	2	0	0	4.1	4	1	0
M.Dickson	0	0	4.50	2	0	0	4.0	4	0	1
A.Ditmar	0	0	0.00	1	0	0	3.2	2	0	2
Z.Monroe	0	0	27.00	1	0	0	1.0	3	1	1
D.Maas	0	0	81.00	1	0	0	0.1	2	1	0
Totals	4	3	3.39	19	7	2	63.2	60	27	56

MIL (NL)

PLAYER, POS	G	AB	R	H	2B	3B	HR	RBI	BB	SO	SB	AVG	OBP	SLG
R.Schoendienst, 2b	7	30	5	9	3	1	0	0	2	1	0	.300	.344	.467
H.Aaron, of	7	27	3	9	2	0	0	2	4	6	0	.333	.419	.407
W.Covington, of	7	26	2	7	0	0	0	4	2	4	0	.269	.321	.269
D.Crandall, c	7	25	4	6	0	0	1	3	3	10	0	.240	.321	.240
J.Logan, ss	7	25	3	3	2	0	0	2	2	4	0	.120	.185	.200
E.Mathews, 3b	7	25	3	4	2	0	0	3	6	11	1	.160	.323	.240
B.Bruton, of	7	17	2	7	0	0	1	2	5	5	0	.412	.545	.412
F.Torre, 1b	7	17	0	3	0	0	0	1	2	0	0	.176	.263	.176
J.Adcock, 1b	4	13	1	4	0	0	0	0	1	3	0	.308	.357	.308
W.Spahn, p	3	12	0	4	0	0	0	3	0	6	0	.333	.333	.333
L.Burdette, p	3	9	1	1	0	0	1	3	0	3	0	.111	.111	.111
A.Pafko, of	4	9	0	3	1	0	0	1	0	0	0	.333	.333	.444
H.Hanebrink, ph	2	2	0	0	0	0	0	0	0	0	0	.000	.000	.000
B.Rush, p	1	2	0	0	0	0	0	0	0	2	0	.000	.000	.000
C.Wise, ph	2	1	0	0	0	0	0	0	0	1	0	.000	.000	.000
F.Mantilla, ss	4	0	1	0	0	0	0	0	0	0	0	.000	.000	.000
Totals		240	25	60	10	1	3	24	27	56	1	.250	.326	.300

PITCHER	W	L	ERA	G	GS	SV	IP	H	BB	SO
W.Spahn	2	1	2.20	3	3	0	28.2	19	8	18
L.Burdette	1	2	5.64	3	3	0	22.1	22	4	12
B.Rush	0	1	3.00	1	1	0	6.0	3	5	2
D.McMahon	0	0	5.40	3	0	0	3.1	3	3	5
J.Pizarro	0	0	5.40	1	0	0	1.2	2	1	3
C.Willey	0	0	0.00	1	0	0	1.0	0	0	2
Totals	3	4	3.71	12	7	0	63.0	49	21	42

GAME 1 / OCT. 1								
FORD, DUREN(8) VS. SPAHN								46,367
NY	000	120	000	0	3	8	1	
MIL	000	200	010	1	4	10	0	

Warren Spahn went all 10 innings, allowing only two hits after giving up Hank Bauer's two-run homer in the fifth inning. Bill Bruton's two-out single in the bottom of the 10th was the game-winner.

GAME 2 / OCT. 2							
TURLEY, MAAS(1), KUCKS(1), DICKSON(5), MONROE(8) VS. BURDETTE							46,367
NY	100	100	003	5	7	0	
MIL	710	000	23X	13	15	1	

Bruton's leadoff homer in the bottom of the first was only the beginning for the Braves. Before the frame was over, Milwaukee had four more hits and six more runs, the last coming on a three-run homer by starting pitcher Lew Burdette. Three meaningless runs in the ninth was all that kept it from being truly embarrassing.

GAME 3 / OCT. 4							
RUSH, MCMAHON(7) VS. LARSEN, DUREN(8)							71,599
MIL	000	000	000	0	6	0	
NY	000	020	20X	4	4	0	

Bauer drove in all four runs with a two-run single in the fifth and a two-run homer in the seventh. The Braves got six hits and six walks off starter Don Larsen and reliever Ryne Duren, but couldn't get a key hit, leaving two on in the sixth, seventh and eighth innings.

GAME 4 / OCT. 5							
SPAHN VS. FORD, KUCKS(8), DICKSON(9)							71,563
MIL	000	001	110	3	9	0	
NY	000	000	000	0	2	1	

The Yankees got only one man past first base against Spahn, who extended his scoreless streak to 14 innings. Spahn also drove in a run with a single in the seventh.

GAME 5 / OCT. 6							
BURDETTE, PIZARRO(6), WILLEY(8) VS. TURLEY							65,279
MIL	000	000	000	0	5	0	
NY	001	006	00X	7	10	0	

New York came back with a shutout, as Bob Turley limited the Braves to five hits. The Yankees put the game away by sending 10 men to the plate in the sixth. Turley had the final blow in that inning with a two-out, two-run single.

GAME 6 / OCT. 8								
FORD, DITMAR(2), DUREN(6), TURLEY(10) VS. SPAHN, MCMAHON(10)								46,367
NY	100	001	000	2	4	10	1	
MIL	110	000	000	1	3	10	4	

Spahn was forced to pitch into the 10th for the second time in the series, but gave up two runs this time. Gil McDougald led off the inning with a homer, and Bill Skowron singled in the second run off reliever Don McMahon. It proved to be a key run, as the Braves scored one and had runners on first and third with two outs following Joe Adcock's single. Turley then relieved Duren and got Joe Torre to line to second to preserve the win.

GAME 7 / OCT. 9							
LARSEN, TURLEY(3) VS. BURDETTE, MCMAHON(8)							46,367
NY	020	000	040	6	8	0	
MIL	100	001	000	2	5	2	

Turley came to the rescue again for the Yankees. Pitching for the third straight game, he hurled $6^2/_3$ innings in relief of Larsen, who was lifted after putting two on in the third. Turley got out of that inning and allowed only one run the rest of the way, and got the win when the Yankees scored four times in the eighth. Turley, who was the winning pitcher in Games 5 and 7 and saved the sixth contest, was named MVP.

1960 World Series
New York Yankees (3) vs. Pittsburgh Pirates (4)

Unfortunately for the Yankees, three double-digit victories didn't count for any more than the four much closer games Pittsburgh won. So the Yankees, who batted .338, clubbed 10 home runs and outscored the Pirates by 28 runs, wound up on the short end of a 4-games-to-3 outcome. In some ways, it was the beginning of the end of the great Yankee dynasty. Ownership believed 70 year old Casey Stengel, who led the team to seven series titles in 10 years and 10 AL pennants in 12 seasons, was past his prime and dismissed him following the heartbreaking loss.

PIT (NL)

PLAYER, POS	G	AB	R	H	2B	3B	HR	RBI	BB	SO	SB	AVG	OBP	SLG
R.Clemente, of	7	29	1	9	0	0	0	3	0	4	0	.310	.310	.310
B.Virdon, of	7	29	2	7	3	0	0	5	1	3	1	.241	.267	.345
D.Groat, ss	7	28	3	6	2	0	0	2	0	1	0	.214	.214	.286
B.Mazeroski, 2b	7	25	4	8	2	0	2	5	0	3	0	.320	.320	.400
D.Hoak, 3b	7	23	3	5	2	0	0	3	4	1	0	.217	.333	.304
G.Cimoli, of	7	20	4	5	0	0	0	1	2	4	0	.250	.318	.250
D.Stuart, 1b	5	20	0	3	0	0	0	0	0	3	0	.150	.150	.150
S.Burgess, c	5	18	2	6	1	0	0	0	2	1	0	.333	.400	.389
R.Nelson, 1b	4	9	2	3	0	0	1	2	1	1	0	.333	.400	.333
H.Smith, c	3	8	1	3	0	0	1	3	0	0	0	.375	.375	.375
V.Law, p	3	6	1	2	1	0	0	1	0	1	0	.333	.333	.500
B.Skinner, of	2	5	2	1	0	0	0	1	1	0	1	.200	.333	.200
G.Baker, ph	3	3	0	0	0	0	0	0	0	1	0	.000	.000	.000
R.Face, p	4	3	0	0	0	0	0	0	0	2	0	.000	.000	.000
H.Haddix, p	2	3	0	1	0	0	0	0	0	1	0	.333	.333	.333
D.Schofield, ss	3	3	0	1	0	0	0	0	1	0	0	.333	.500	.333
B.Friend, p	3	1	0	0	0	0	0	0	0	0	0	.000	.000	.000
F.Green, p	3	1	0	0	0	0	0	0	0	0	0	.000	.000	.000
J.Christopher, ph	3	0	2	0	0	0	0	0	0	0	0	.000	.000	.000
B.Oldis, c	2	0	0	0	0	0	0	0	0	0	0	.000	.000	.000
Totals		234	27	60	11	0	4	26	12	26	2	.256	.301	.303

PITCHER	W	L	ERA	G	GS	SV	IP	H	BB	SO
V.Law	2	0	3.44	3	3	0	18.1	22	3	8
R.Face	0	0	5.23	4	0	3	10.1	9	2	4
H.Haddix	2	0	2.45	2	1	0	7.1	6	2	6
B.Friend	0	2	13.50	3	2	0	6.0	13	3	7
T.Cheney	0	0	4.50	3	0	0	4.0	4	1	6
F.Green	0	0	22.50	3	0	0	4.0	11	1	3
C.Labine	0	0	13.50	3	0	0	4.0	13	1	2
J.Gibbon	0	0	9.00	2	0	0	3.0	4	1	2
G.Witt	0	0	0.00	3	0	0	2.2	5	2	1
V.Bend Mizell	0	1	15.43	2	1	0	2.1	4	2	1
Totals	4	3	7.11	28	7	3	62.0	91	18	40

NY (AL)

PLAYER, POS	G	AB	R	H	2B	3B	HR	RBI	BB	SO	SB	AVG	OBP	SLG
B.Skowron, 1b	7	32	7	12	2	0	2	6	0	6	0	.375	.375	.438
T.Kubek, ss-of	7	30	6	10	1	0	0	3	2	2	0	.333	.375	.367
R.Maris, of	7	30	6	8	1	0	2	2	2	4	0	.267	.313	.300
B.Richardson, 2b	7	30	8	11	2	2	1	12	1	1	0	.367	.387	.567
M.Mantle, of	7	25	8	10	1	0	3	11	8	9	0	.400	.545	.440
Y.Berra, of-c	7	22	6	7	0	0	1	8	2	0	0	.318	.375	.318
G.McDougald, 3b	6	18	4	5	1	0	0	2	2	3	0	.278	.350	.333
B.Cerv, of	4	14	1	5	0	0	0	0	0	3	0	.357	.357	.357
E.Howard, c	5	13	4	6	1	1	1	4	1	4	0	.462	.500	.692
C.Boyer, 3b-ss	4	12	1	3	2	1	0	1	0	1	0	.250	.250	.583
J.Blanchard, c	5	11	2	5	2	0	0	2	0	0	0	.455	.455	.636
W.Ford, p	2	8	1	2	0	0	0	2	0	2	0	.250	.250	.250
H.Lopez, of	3	7	0	3	0	0	0	0	0	0	0	.429	.429	.429
B.Turley, p	2	4	0	1	0	0	0	1	0	1	0	.250	.250	.250
D.Long, ph	3	3	0	1	0	0	0	0	0	0	0	.333	.333	.333
B.Shantz, p	3	3	0	1	0	0	0	0	0	0	0	.333	.333	.333
J.DeMaestri, ss	4	2	1	1	0	0	0	0	0	1	0	.500	.500	.500
R.Terry, p	2	2	0	0	0	0	0	0	0	1	0	.000	.000	.000
L.Arroyo, p	1	1	0	0	0	0	0	0	0	0	0	.000	.000	.000
J.Coates, p	3	1	0	0	0	0	0	0	0	1	0	.000	.000	.000
B.Stafford, p	2	1	0	0	0	0	0	0	0	1	0	.000	.000	.000
E.Grba, pr	1	0	0	0	0	0	0	0	0	0	0	.000	.000	.000
Totals		269	55	91	13	4	10	54	18	40	0	.338	.384	.416

PITCHER	W	L	ERA	G	GS	SV	IP	H	BB	SO
W.Ford	2	0	0.00	2	2	0	18.0	11	2	8
B.Turley	1	0	4.82	2	2	0	9.1	15	4	0
R.Terry	0	2	5.40	2	1	0	6.2	7	1	5
J.Coates	0	0	5.68	3	0	0	6.1	6	1	3
B.Shantz	0	0	4.26	3	0	1	6.1	4	1	1
B.Stafford	0	0	1.50	2	0	0	6.0	5	1	2
R.Duren	0	0	2.25	2	0	0	4.0	2	1	5
D.Maas	0	0	4.50	1	0	0	2.0	2	0	1
A.Ditmar	0	2	21.60	2	2	0	1.2	6	1	0
L.Arroyo	0	0	13.50	1	0	0	0.2	2	0	1
Totals	3	4	3.54	20	7	1	61.0	60	12	26

GAME 1 / OCT. 5

DITMAR, COATES(1), MAAS(5), DUREN(7) VS. LAW, FACE(8)							36,676
NY	100	100	002	4	13	2	
PIT	300	201	00X	6	8	0	

This game would set the tone for the entire series. The Yankees had more hits and more home runs, but the Pirates turned three hits, a walk, and two stolen bases into three first-inning runs. Pittsburgh did get a two-run homer from Bill Mazeroski in the fourth which provided enough runs to win the game.

GAME 2 / OCT. 6

TURLEY, SHANTZ(9) VS. FRIEND, GREEN(5), LABINE(6), WITT(6), GIBBON(7), CHENEY(9)							37,308
NY	002	127	301	16	19	1	
PIT	000	100	002	3	13	1	

Mickey Mantle tied a series record with five RBIs, which came on two home runs. His first one came in the fifth, which helped break open what was then a close game. The second blast came in the seventh, and merely added to what was then a rout.

GAME 3 / OCT. 8

MIZELL, LABINE(1), GREEN(1), WITT(4), CHENEY(6), GIBBON(8) VS. FORD							70,001
PIT	000	000	000	0	4	0	
NY	600	400	00X	10	16	1	

Bobby Richardson did Mantle one better, knocking in six with a grand slam to cap a six-run first, and a two-run single in the fourth. Even with the offensive explosion in the late 20th and early 21st Centuries, Richardson's six RBI performance has yet to be equaled or surpassed.

GAME 4 / OCT. 9

LAW, FACE(7) VS. TERRY, SHANTZ(7), COATES(8)							67,812
PIT	000	030	000	3	7	0	
NY	000	100	100	2	8	0	

Cy Young winner Vern Law—who also was the winner in the first game—limited the Yankees to one run and provided a key hit in the fifth. His two-out double plated Pittsburgh's first run and extended the inning for leadoff hitter Bill Virdon, who drove in two more with a single.

GAME 5 / OCT. 10

HADDIX, FACE(7) VS. DITMAR, ARROYO(2), STAFFORD(3), DUREN(8)							62,753
PIT	031	000	001	5	10	2	
NY	011	000	000	2	5	2	

This was the only game in the series in which the Pirates outhit the Yankees. More importantly, Pittsburgh took advantage of a key third-inning error by New York third baseman Gil McDougald to score a couple of unearned runs on a two-out double by Mazeroski in the second.

GAME 6 / OCT. 12

FORD VS. FRIEND, CHENEY(3), MIZELL(4), GREEN(6), LABINE(6), WITT(9)							38,580
NY	015	002	220	12	17	1	
PIT	000	000	000	0	7	1	

Another offensive explosion overshadowed a second shutout by Yankees ace southpaw Whitey Ford.

GAME 7 / OCT. 13

TURLEY, STAFFORD(2), SHANTZ(3), COATES(8), TERRY(8) VS. LAW, FACE(6), FRIEND(9), HADDIX(9)							36,683
NY	000	014	022	9	13	1	
PIT	220	000	051	10	11	0	

There were enough memorable moments in this game for an entire series. From Yankee shortstop Tony Kubek taking a bad hop in the neck to 10 total runs in the final two innings (with each team giving away the lead). None, of course, was more important than Mazeroski's game-winning homer in the bottom of the ninth inning. Maz, the only Pirate who didn't hit in the five-run eighth, pulled Ralph Terry's second pitch, a high fastball, over the left field wall to give Pittsburgh the championship. It remains the only time the seventh game of a World Series has been decided with a walk-off home run.

1961 World Series
New York Yankees (4) vs. Cincinnati Reds (1)

The Reds were in the World Series for the first time in 21 years because they were the best of a mediocre National League and were thoroughly dominated by a Yankee squad that won 109 games and was loaded with postseason experience. A strong starting staff, led by 24 game winner Whitey Ford, held Cincinnati to a .206 series average and just 13 runs in five games.

NY (AL)

PLAYER, POS	G	AB	R	H	2B	3B	HR	RBI	BB	SO	SB	AVG	OBP	SLG
B.Richardson, 2b	5	23	2	9	1	0	0	0	0	0	1	.391	.391	.435
T.Kubek, ss	5	22	3	5	0	0	0	1	1	4	0	.227	.261	.227
E.Howard, c	5	20	5	5	3	0	1	1	2	3	0	.250	.318	.400
R.Maris, of	5	19	4	2	1	0	1	2	4	6	0	.105	.261	.158
B.Skowron, 1b	5	17	3	6	0	0	1	5	3	4	0	.353	.450	.353
C.Boyer, 3b	5	15	0	4	2	0	0	3	4	0	0	.267	.421	.400
Y.Berra, of	4	11	2	3	0	0	1	3	5	1	0	.273	.500	.273
J.Blanchard, of	4	10	4	4	1	0	2	3	2	0	0	.400	.500	.500
H.Lopez, of	4	9	3	3	0	1	1	7	2	3	0	.333	.455	.556
M.Mantle, of	2	6	0	1	0	0	0	0	0	2	0	.167	.167	.167
W.Ford, p	2	5	1	0	0	0	0	0	1	0	0	.000	.167	.000
R.Terry, p	2	3	0	0	0	0	0	0	0	1	0	.000	.000	.000
B.Stafford, p	1	2	0	0	0	0	0	0	0	0	0	.000	.000	.000
J.Coates, p	1	1	0	0	0	0	0	0	0	1	0	.000	.000	.000
B.Daley, p	2	1	0	0	0	0	0	1	0	0	0	.000	.000	.000
B.Gardner, ph	1	1	0	0	0	0	0	0	0	0	0	.000	.000	.000
J.Reed, of	3	0	0	0	0	0	0	0	0	0	0	.000	.000	.000
Totals		165	27	42	8	1	7	26	24	25	1	.255	.349	.315

PITCHER	W	L	ERA	G	GS	SV	IP	H	BB	SO
W.Ford	2	0	0.00	2	2	0	14.0	6	1	7
R.Terry	0	1	4.82	2	2	0	9.1	12	2	7
B.Daley	1	0	0.00	2	0	0	7.0	5	0	3
B.Stafford	0	0	2.70	1	1	0	6.2	7	2	5
L.Arroyo	1	0	2.25	2	0	0	4.0	4	2	3
J.Coates	0	0	0.00	1	0	1	4.0	1	1	2
Totals	4	1	1.60	10	5	1	45.0	35	8	27

CIN (NL)

PLAYER, POS	G	AB	R	H	2B	3B	HR	RBI	BB	SO	SB	AVG	OBP	SLG
E.Kasko, ss	5	22	1	7	0	0	0	1	0	2	0	.318	.318	.318
V.Pinson, of	5	22	0	2	1	0	0	0	0	1	0	.091	.091	.136
G.Coleman, 1b	5	20	2	5	0	0	1	2	0	1	0	.250	.250	.250
W.Post, of	5	18	3	6	1	0	1	2	0	1	0	.333	.333	.389
G.Freese, 3b	5	16	0	1	1	0	0	0	3	4	0	.063	.211	.125
F.Robinson, of	5	15	3	3	2	0	1	4	3	4	0	.200	.333	.333
E.Chacon, 2b	4	12	2	3	0	0	0	0	1	2	0	.250	.308	.250
J.Edwards, c	3	11	1	4	2	0	0	2	0	0	0	.364	.364	.545
D.Blasingame, 2b	3	7	1	1	0	0	0	0	0	3	0	.143	.143	.143
D.Gernert, ph	4	4	0	0	0	0	0	0	0	1	0	.000	.000	.000
J.Jay, p	2	4	0	0	0	0	0	0	0	2	0	.000	.000	.000
D.Johnson, c	2	4	0	2	0	0	0	0	0	0	0	.500	.500	.500
G.Bell, ph	3	3	0	0	0	0	0	0	0	0	0	.000	.000	.000
L.Cardenas, ph	3	3	0	1	1	0	0	0	0	1	0	.333	.333	.667
J.Lynch, ph	4	3	0	0	0	0	0	0	1	1	0	.000	.250	.000
J.O'Toole, p	2	3	0	0	0	0	0	0	0	1	0	.000	.000	.000
B.Purkey, p	2	3	0	0	0	0	0	0	0	3	0	.000	.000	.000
J.Zimmerman, c	2	0	0	0	0	0	0	0	0	0	0	.000	.000	.000
Totals		170	13	35	8	0	3	11	8	27	0	.206	.254	.253

PITCHER	W	L	ERA	G	GS	SV	IP	H	BB	SO
J.O'Toole	0	2	3.00	2	2	0	12.0	11	7	4
B.Purkey	0	1	1.64	2	1	0	11.0	6	3	5
J.Jay	1	1	5.59	2	2	0	9.2	8	6	6
J.Brosnan	0	0	7.50	3	0	0	6.0	9	4	5
B.Henry	0	0	19.29	2	0	0	2.1	4	2	3
K.Hunt	0	0	0.00	1	0	0	1.0	0	1	1
K.Johnson	0	0	0.00	1	0	0	0.2	0	0	0
S.Jones	0	0	0.00	1	0	0	0.2	0	0	0
J.Maloney	0	0	27.00	1	0	0	0.2	4	1	1
Totals	1	4	4.91	15	5	0	44.0	42	24	25

GAME 1 / OCT. 4

O'TOOLE, BROSNAN(8) VS. FORD							62,397
CIN	000	000	000	0	2	0	
NY	000	101	00X	2	6	0	

Cincinnati managed only two hits off Ford and got only one runner as far as second base. Jim O'Toole wasn't bad for the Reds, allowing only six hits, though Elston Howard and Bill Skowron each deposited an O'Toole mistake over the fence for the Yankee runs.

GAME 2 / OCT. 5

JAY VS. TERRY, ARROYO(8)							63,083
CIN	000	211	020	6	9	0	
NY	000	200	000	2	4	3	

Cincy's only win came thanks to the right arm of Joey Jay. After giving up two tying runs in the fourth, Jay held the Yankees to only two hits the rest of the way. Gordy Coleman and Johnny Edwards each had two RBIs for the Reds.

GAME 3 / OCT. 7

STAFFORD, DALEY(7), ARROYO(8) VS. PURKEY							32,589
NY	000	000	111	3	6	1	
CIN	001	000	100	2	8	0	

A couple of solo home runs gave New York its second win in the series. Pinch hitter Johnny Blanchard tied the game with a two-out shot in the eighth, and Roger Maris provided the winning run with a leadoff homer in the ninth.

GAME 4 / OCT. 8

FORD, COATES(6) VS. O'TOOLE, BROSNAN(6), HENRY(9)							32,589
NY	000	112	300	7	11	0	
CIN	000	000	000	0	5	1	

Ford continued his dominance of the postseason by hurling five more shutout innings. It could have been more had he not been forced out of the game with an ankle injury after giving up a leadoff single in the sixth. Combined with his complete game shutout in the first game of the series—and the two he threw against the Pirates in 1960—it meant 32 scoreless innings in World Series play, breaking the record previously held by Babe Ruth.

GAME 5 / OCT. 9

TERRY, DALEY(3) VS. JAY, MALONEY(1), K.JOHNSON(2), HENRY(3), JONES(4), PURKEY(5), BROSNAN(7), HUNT(9)							32,589
NY	510	502	000	13	15	1	
CIN	003	020	000	5	11	3	

Frank Robinson hit his first World Series home run, a three-run shot in the third, but by then it was already way too late. Little-used Hector Lopez had a triple and a home run and drove in five for the Yankees, who claimed the championship for first-year skipper Ralph Houk.

1962 World Series
New York Yankees (4) vs. San Francisco Giants (3)

The Giants were in the World Series for the first time since moving west after winning 103 games, the most since 1912. The ending resembled so many other fall classics, though, with the Yankees celebrating another championship. It was the organization's ninth title in 14 years, and 20th overall, so it was likely few expected 15 years to pass before the club claimed another one.

NY (AL)

PLAYER, POS	G	AB	R	H	2B	3B	HR	RBI	BB	SO	SB	AVG	OBP	SLG
T.Kubek, ss	7	29	2	8	1	0	0	1	1	3	0	.276	.300	.310
T.Tresh, of	7	28	5	9	1	0	1	4	1	4	2	.321	.345	.357
B.Richardson, 2b	7	27	3	4	0	0	0	0	3	1	0	.148	.233	.148
M.Mantle, of	7	25	2	3	1	0	0	0	4	5	2	.120	.241	.160

Postseason

NY (AL) (CONT.)

PLAYER, POS	G	AB	R	H	2B	3B	HR	RBI	BB	SO	SB	AVG	OBP	SLG
R.Maris, of	7	23	4	4	1	0	1	5	5	2	0	.174	.321	.217
C.Boyer, 3b	7	22	2	7	1	0	1	4	1	3	0	.318	.348	.364
E.Howard, c	6	21	1	3	1	0	0	1	1	4	0	.143	.182	.190
B.Skowron, 1b	6	18	1	4	0	1	0	1	1	5	0	.222	.263	.333
R.Terry, p	3	8	0	1	0	0	0	0	1	6	0	.125	.222	.125
W.Ford, p	3	7	0	0	0	0	0	0	1	3	0	.000	.125	.000
D.Long, 1b	2	5	0	1	0	0	0	1	0	1	0	.200	.200	.200
B.Stafford, p	1	3	0	0	0	0	0	0	0	1	0	.000	.000	.000
Y.Berra, c	2	2	0	0	0	0	0	0	2	0	0	.000	.500	.000
H.Lopez, ph	2	2	0	0	0	0	0	0	0	0	0	.000	.000	.000
J.Blanchard, ph	1	1	0	0	0	0	0	0	0	1	0	.000	.000	.000
Totals		221	20	44	6	1	3	17	21	39	4	.199	.275	.235

PITCHER	W	L	ERA	G	GS	SV	IP	H	BB	SO
R.Terry	2	1	1.80	3	3	0	25.0	17	2	16
W.Ford	1	1	4.12	3	3	0	19.2	24	4	12
B.Stafford	1	0	2.00	1	1	0	9.0	4	2	5
M.Bridges	0	0	4.91	2	0	0	3.2	4	2	3
J.Coates	0	1	6.75	2	0	0	2.2	1	1	3
B.Daley	0	0	0.00	1	0	0	1.0	1	1	0
Totals	4	3	2.95	12	7	0	61.0	51	12	39

SF (NL)

PLAYER, POS	G	AB	R	H	2B	3B	HR	RBI	BB	SO	SB	AVG	OBP	SLG
W.Mays, of	7	28	3	7	2	0	0	1	1	5	1	.250	.276	.321
F.Alou, of	7	26	2	7	1	1	0	1	1	4	0	.269	.296	.385
C.Hiller, 2b	7	26	4	7	3	0	1	5	3	4	0	.269	.345	.385
J.Davenport, 3b	7	22	1	3	1	0	0	1	4	7	0	.136	.269	.182
O.Cepeda, 1b	5	19	1	3	1	0	0	2	0	4	0	.158	.158	.211
J.Pagan, ss	7	19	2	7	0	0	1	2	0	1	0	.368	.368	.368
W.McCovey, 1b-of	4	15	2	3	0	1	1	1	1	3	0	.200	.250	.333
E.Bailey, c	6	14	1	1	0	0	1	2	0	3	0	.071	.071	.071
T.Haller, c	4	14	1	4	1	0	1	3	0	2	0	.286	.286	.357
M.Alou, of	6	12	2	4	1	0	0	1	0	1	0	.333	.333	.417
H.Kuenn, of	3	12	1	1	0	0	0	0	1	1	0	.083	.154	.083
J.Sanford, p	3	7	0	3	0	0	0	0	0	2	0	.429	.429	.429
B.Pierce, p	2	5	0	0	0	0	0	0	0	1	0	.000	.000	.000
B.O'Dell, p	3	3	0	1	0	0	0	0	0	0	0	.333	.333	.333
J.Marichal, p	1	2	0	0	0	0	0	0	0	1	0	.000	.000	.000
E.Bowman, ss	2	1	1	0	0	0	0	0	0	0	0	.000	.000	.000
J.Orsino, c	1	1	0	0	0	0	0	0	0	0	0	.000	.000	.000
B.Nieman, ph	1	0	0	0	0	0	0	0	1	0	0	.000	1.000	.000
Totals		226	21	51	10	2	5	19	12	39	1	.226	.268	.288

PITCHER	W	L	ERA	G	GS	SV	IP	H	BB	SO
J.Sanford	1	2	1.93	3	3	0	23.1	16	8	19
B.Pierce	1	1	2.40	2	2	0	15.0	8	2	5
B.O'Dell	0	1	4.38	3	1	1	12.1	12	3	9
J.Marichal	0	0	0.00	1	1	0	4.0	2	2	4
B.Bolin	0	0	6.75	2	0	0	2.2	4	2	2
D.Larsen	1	0	3.86	3	0	0	2.1	1	2	0
S.Miller	0	0	0.00	2	0	0	1.1	1	2	0
Totals	3	4	2.66	16	7	1	61.0	44	21	39

GAME 1 / OCT. 4

FORD VS. O'DELL, LARSEN(7), MILLER(9)							43,852
NY	200	000	121	6	11	0	
SF	011	000	000	2	10	0	

Whitey Ford wasn't as good as he'd been in the postseason the previous two years, but that only means he gave up a couple of runs. His scoreless innings streak ended in the second at 33²/₃ innings, and he allowed a second run in the third, but he recovered to blank San Francisco the rest of the way, allowing the Yankees to score four times in the final three innings.

GAME 2 / OCT. 5

TERRY, DALEY(8) VS. SANFORD							43,910
NY	000	000	000	0	3	1	
SF	100	000	10X	2	6	0	

The run the Giants got in the first on an RBI groundout by Felipe Alou was enough because of Jack Sanford's marvelous pitching. Sanford held the Yankees to just three hits and prevented New York from getting a runner to third in the complete game whitewash.

GAME 3 / OCT. 7

PIERCE, LARSEN(7), BOLIN(8) VS. STAFFORD							71,434
SF	000	000	002	2	4	3	
NY	000	000	30X	3	5	1	

It was scoreless until the seventh, when the Giants suddenly decided to stop pitching and fielding. The Yankees got three straight singles to start the inning, and combined those with two errors and a hit batsman to score three times. Ed Bailey hit a two-run homer in the ninth, which would have tied the game had Willie McCovey's error in the seventh (the second miscue of the frame) not allowed the third run to score.

GAME 4 / OCT. 8

MARICHAL, BOLIN(5), LARSEN(6), O'DELL(7) VS. FORD, COATES(7), BRIDGES(7)							66,607
SF	020	000	401	7	9	1	
NY	000	002	001	3	9	1	

Chuck Hiller broke a 2–2 tie in the seventh with a two-out grand slam. The Giants suffered a huge loss, though, as Juan Marichal had to leave the game in the fifth after hurting his hand while trying to bunt. He wouldn't be available for the rest of the series.

GAME 5 / OCT. 10

SANFORD, MILLER(8) VS. TERRY							63,165
SF	001	010	001	3	8	2	
NY	000	101	03X	5	6	0	

It was New York's turn to win a game with a late-inning home run. Tom Tresh's three-run blast in the eighth provided the winning runs for the Yankees.

GAME 6 / OCT. 15

FORD, COATES(5), BRIDGES(8) VS. PIERCE							43,948
NY	000	010	010	2	3	2	
SF	000	320	00X	5	10	1	

Torrential rains forced a three-day postponement before Game 6 and gave the tired Giants some much-needed rest. It paid off in the fourth when San Francisco got to Ford for three runs. The Giants got two more in the fifth, and Billy Pierce's three-hitter made it stand up.

GAME 7 / OCT. 16

TERRY VS. SANFORD, O'DELL(8)							43,948
NY	000	100	000	1	7	0	
SF	000	000	000	0	4	1	

Ralph Terry got a big measure of redemption, becoming the hero two years after giving up a Series-losing homer to Bill Mazeroski in 1960. Since that fateful pitch, Terry had become one of the best pitchers in baseball, winning 23 games in the regular season. Terry was dominating from the start: perfect through five innings, allowing only four hits and no walks. Bill Skowron scored the game's only run in the fifth when he scampered home while the Giants were turning a double play.

1963 World Series
New York Yankees (0) vs. Los Angeles Dodgers (4)

The Yankees averaged nearly 4.5 runs per game as they won 104 games and cruised to their 13th pennant in 15 seasons, besting the White Sox by 10 ½ games. However, the Dodger mound trio of Sandy Koufax, Johnny Podres, and Don Drysdale limited New York to only four runs total in four games and sent the Yankees home for the winter bruised and bloodied.

LA (NL)

PLAYER, POS	G	AB	R	H	2B	3B	HR	RBI	BB	SO	SB	AVG	OBP	SLG
T.Davis, of	4	15	0	6	0	2	0	2	0	2	1	.400	.400	.667
M.Wills, ss	4	15	1	2	0	0	0	0	1	3	1	.133	.188	.133
J.Roseboro, c	4	14	1	2	0	0	1	3	0	4	0	.143	.143	.143
J.Gilliam, 3b	4	13	3	2	0	0	0	0	3	1	0	.154	.313	.154
B.Skowron, 1b	4	13	2	5	0	0	1	3	1	3	0	.385	.429	.385
D.Tracewski, 2b	4	13	1	2	0	0	0	0	1	2	0	.154	.214	.154
W.Davis, of	4	12	2	2	2	0	0	3	0	6	0	.167	.167	.333
F.Howard, of	3	10	2	3	1	0	1	1	0	2	0	.300	.300	.400
S.Koufax, p	2	6	0	0	0	0	0	0	0	2	0	.000	.000	.000
J.Podres, p	1	4	0	1	0	0	0	0	0	0	0	.250	.250	.250

LA (NL) (cont.)

PLAYER, POS	G	AB	R	H	2B	3B	HR	RBI	BB	SO	SB	AVG	OBP	SLG
D.Drysdale, p	1	1	0	0	0	0	0	0	2	0	0	.000	.667	.000
R.Fairly, of	4	1	0	0	0	0	0	0	3	0	0	.000	.750	.000
Totals		117	12	25	3	2	3	12	11	25	2	.214	.281	.274

PITCHER	W	L	ERA	G	GS	SV	IP	H	BB	SO
S.Koufax	2	0	1.50	2	2	0	18.0	12	3	23
D.Drysdale	1	0	0.00	1	1	0	9.0	3	1	9
J.Podres	1	0	1.08	1	1	0	8.1	6	1	4
R.Perranoski	0	0	0.00	1	0	1	0.2	1	0	1
Totals	4	0	1.00	5	4	1	36.0	22	5	37

NY (AL)

PLAYER, POS	G	AB	R	H	2B	3B	HR	RBI	BB	SO	SB	AVG	OBP	SLG
T.Kubek, ss	4	16	1	3	0	0	0	0	0	3	0	.188	.188	.188
E.Howard, c	4	15	0	5	0	0	0	1	0	3	0	.333	.333	.333
M.Mantle, of	4	15	1	2	0	0	1	1	1	5	0	.133	.188	.133
T.Tresh, of	4	15	1	3	0	0	1	2	1	6	0	.200	.250	.200
B.Richardson, 2b	4	14	0	3	1	0	0	0	1	3	0	.214	.267	.286
C.Boyer, 3b	4	13	0	1	0	0	0	0	1	6	0	.077	.143	.077
J.Pepitone, 1b	4	13	0	2	0	0	0	0	1	3	0	.154	.214	.154
H.Lopez, of	3	8	1	2	2	0	0	0	0	1	0	.250	.250	.500
R.Maris, of	2	5	0	0	0	0	0	0	0	1	0	.000	.000	.000
J.Blanchard, of	1	3	0	0	0	0	0	0	0	0	0	.000	.000	.000
W.Ford, p	2	3	0	0	0	0	0	0	0	0	0	.000	.000	.000
P.Linz, ph	3	3	0	1	0	0	0	0	0	1	0	.333	.333	.333
J.Bouton, p	1	2	0	0	0	0	0	0	0	2	0	.000	.000	.000
H.Bright, ph	2	2	0	0	0	0	0	0	0	2	0	.000	.000	.000
Y.Berra, ph	1	1	0	0	0	0	0	0	0	0	0	.000	.000	.000
A.Downing, p	1	1	0	0	0	0	0	0	0	1	0	.000	.000	.000
Totals		129	4	22	3	0	2	4	5	37	0	.171	.207	.194

PITCHER	W	L	ERA	G	GS	SV	IP	H	BB	SO
W.Ford	0	2	4.50	2	2	0	12.0	10	3	8
J.Bouton	0	1	1.29	1	1	0	7.0	4	5	4
A.Downing	0	1	5.40	1	1	0	5.0	7	1	6
H.Reniff	0	0	0.00	3	0	0	3.0	0	1	1
R.Terry	0	0	3.00	1	0	0	3.0	3	1	0
S.Williams	0	0	0.00	1	0	0	3.0	1	0	5
S.Hamilton	0	0	0.00	1	0	0	1.0	0	0	1
Totals	0	4	2.91	10	4	0	34.0	25	11	25

GAME 1 / OCT. 2

KOUFAX VS. FORD, WILLIAMS(6), HAMILTON(9)							69,000
LA	041	000	000	5	9	0	
NY	000	000	020	2	6	0	

Whitey Ford and Sandy Koufax combined to win 49 games during the regular season, but this game wasn't close at all. After retiring the first four Dodgers' hitters, Ford gave up four straight hits, including a three-run homer by John Roseboro. The Dodgers could have put away their bats right then, as Koufax was in the process of striking out 15 Yankee hitters.

GAME 2 / OCT. 3

PODRES, PERRANOSKI(9) VS. DOWNING, TERRY(6), RENIFF(9)							66,455
LA	200	100	010	4	10	1	
NY	000	000	001	1	7	0	

Johnny Podres wasn't as overpowering as Koufax, though he was just as effective. New York managed only a single run in the ninth, which though charged to Podres was scored while reliever Ron Perranoski was on the mound.

GAME 3 / OCT. 5

BOUTON, RENIFF(8) VS. DRYSDALE							55,912
NY	000	000	000	0	3	0	
LA	100	000	00X	1	4	1	

Jim Bouton's wild pitch with two outs in the bottom of the first let Jim Gilliam scamper home from second on a single by Terry Davis. Bouton and Yankee reliever Hal Reniff kept the Dodgers off the scoreboard the rest of the way, but New York couldn't muster anything off Don Drysdale, who retired 12 of the last 13 hitters in the game.

GAME 4 / OCT. 6

FORD, RENIFF(8) VS. KOUFAX							55,912
NY	000	000	100	1	6	1	
LA	000	010	10X	2	2	1	

Los Angeles managed just two hits in the game, and only Frank Howard's solo homer in the fifth resulted in a run, but the Dodgers came out on top thanks to a brutal error by Yankee first baseman Joe Pepitone. His inability to handle a routine throw from third put Jim Gilliam on third with nobody out in the seventh, who then scored the winning run on a sacrifice fly by Willie Davis. The Yankees had a shot in the ninth after Bill Richardson led off with a single and went to second when Elston Howard reached on a two-out error. But Koufax didn't get rattled, he got Hector Lopez to ground to short, and gave the Dodgers a second title in six years since moving to L.A.

1964 World Series
New York Yankees (3) vs. St. Louis Cardinals (4)

The Yankees still had Mickey Mantle and Whitey Ford, but they were a vastly different club than the one that won most of the AL pennants since 1949. The Yankees had only two .300 hitters (Mantle and catcher Elston Howard), only three pitchers with more than nine wins, languished in third place for half the season, and were obviously in decline. The Cardinals, in the series for the first time since '46, were polar opposites: young (average age of less than 28 years) and on the way up.

STL (NL)

PLAYER, POS	G	AB	R	H	2B	3B	HR	RBI	BB	SO	SB	AVG	OBP	SLG
L.Brock, of	7	30	2	9	2	0	1	5	0	3	0	.300	.300	.367
C.Flood, of	7	30	5	6	0	1	0	3	3	1	0	.200	.273	.267
M.Shannon, of	7	28	6	6	0	0	1	2	0	9	1	.214	.214	.214
K.Boyer, 3b	7	27	5	6	1	0	2	6	1	5	0	.222	.250	.259
D.White, 1b	7	27	2	3	1	0	0	2	2	6	1	.111	.172	.148
D.Groat, ss	7	26	3	5	1	1	0	1	4	3	0	.192	.300	.308
T.McCarver, c	7	23	4	11	1	1	1	5	5	1	1	.478	.571	.609
D.Maxvill, 2b	7	20	0	4	1	0	0	1	1	4	0	.200	.238	.250
B.Gibson, p	3	9	1	2	0	0	0	0	0	3	0	.222	.222	.222
C.Simmons, p	2	4	0	2	0	0	0	1	0	1	0	.500	.500	.500
C.Warwick, ph	5	4	2	3	0	0	0	1	1	0	0	.750	.800	.750
C.James, ph	3	3	0	0	0	0	0	0	0	1	0	.000	.000	.000
B.Skinner, ph	4	3	0	2	1	0	0	1	1	0	0	.667	.750	1.000
R.Sadecki, p	2	2	0	1	0	0	0	1	0	1	0	.500	.500	.500
J.Buchek, 2b	4	1	1	1	0	0	0	0	0	0	0	1.000	1.000	1.000
R.Craig, p	2	1	0	0	0	0	0	0	0	0	0	.000	.000	.000
B.Schultz, p	4	1	0	0	0	0	0	0	0	0	0	.000	.000	.000
R.Taylor, p	2	1	0	0	0	0	0	0	0	1	0	.000	.000	.000
J.Javier, 2b	1	0	1	0	0	0	0	0	0	0	0	.000	.000	.000
Totals		240	32	61	8	3	5	29	18	39	3	.254	.306	.313

PITCHER	W	L	ERA	G	GS	SV	IP	H	BB	SO
B.Gibson	2	1	3.00	3	3	0	27.0	23	8	31
C.Simmons	0	1	2.51	2	2	0	14.1	11	3	8
R.Sadecki	1	0	8.53	2	2	0	6.1	12	5	2
R.Craig	1	0	0.00	2	0	0	5.0	2	3	9
R.Taylor	0	0	0.00	2	0	1	4.2	0	1	2
B.Schultz	0	1	18.00	4	0	1	4.0	9	3	1
B.Humphreys	0	0	0.00	1	0	0	1.0	0	0	1
G.Richardson	0	0	40.50	2	0	0	0.2	3	2	0
Totals	4	3	4.29	18	7	2	63.0	60	25	54

NY (AL)

PLAYER, POS	G	AB	R	H	2B	3B	HR	RBI	BB	SO	SB	AVG	OBP	SLG
B.Richardson, 2b	7	32	3	13	2	0	0	3	0	2	1	.406	.406	.469
P.Linz, ss	7	31	5	7	1	0	2	2	2	5	0	.226	.273	.258
R.Maris, of	7	30	4	6	0	0	1	1	1	4	0	.200	.226	.200
J.Pepitone, 1b	7	26	1	4	1	0	1	5	2	3	0	.154	.214	.192
C.Boyer, 3b	7	24	2	5	1	0	1	3	1	5	1	.208	.240	.250
E.Howard, c	7	24	5	7	1	0	0	2	4	6	0	.292	.393	.333
M.Mantle, of	7	24	8	8	2	0	3	8	6	8	0	.333	.467	.417
T.Tresh, of	7	22	4	6	2	0	2	7	6	7	0	.273	.429	.364
M.Stottlemyre, p	3	8	0	1	0	0	0	0	0	6	0	.125	.125	.125
J.Bouton, p	2	7	0	1	0	0	0	1	0	2	0	.143	.143	.143
J.Blanchard, ph	4	4	0	1	1	0	0	0	0	1	0	.250	.250	.500
A.Downing, p	3	2	0	0	0	0	0	0	0	2	0	.000	.000	.000
H.Lopez, of	3	2	0	0	0	0	0	0	0	2	0	.000	.000	.000
W.Ford, p	1	1	0	1	0	0	0	1	2	0	0	1.000	1.000	1.000
P.Gonzalez, 3b	1	1	0	0	0	0	0	0	0	0	0	.000	.000	.000
M.Hegan, ph	3	1	1	0	0	0	0	0	1	1	0	.000	.500	.000
Totals		239	33	60	11	0	10	33	25	54	2	.251	.327	.297

PITCHER	W	L	ERA	G	GS	SV	IP	H	BB	SO
M.Stottlemyre	1	1	3.15	3	3	0	20.0	18	6	12
J.Bouton	2	0	1.56	2	2	0	17.1	15	5	7
A.Downing	0	1	8.22	3	1	0	7.2	9	2	5
W.Ford	0	1	8.44	1	1	0	5.1	8	1	4
P.Mikkelsen	0	1	5.79	4	0	0	4.2	4	2	4
R.Sheldon	0	0	0.00	2	0	0	2.2	0	2	2
S.Hamilton	0	0	4.50	2	0	1	2.0	3	0	2
R.Terry	0	0	0.00	1	0	0	2.0	2	0	3
H.Reniff	0	0	0.00	1	0	0	0.1	2	0	0
Totals	3	4	3.77	19	7	1	62.0	61	18	39

GAME 1 / OCT. 7							
FORD, DOWNING(6), SHELDON(8), MIKKELSEN(9) VS. SADECKI, SCHULTZ(7)							30,805
NY	030	010	010	5	12	2	
STL	110	004	03X	9	12	0	

The Yankees led early, but the Cardinals got back in it when Whitey Ford began to lose strength in his arm. The man with the most World Series wins wound up giving up five runs in less than six innings, and wouldn't pitch again in the series. The four they got in the sixth gave the Cardinals the lead for good, though they added three unearned runs in the eighth thanks to an error and a passed ball.

GAME 2 / OCT. 8							
STOTTLEMYRE VS. GIBSON, SCHULTZ(9), RICHARDSON(9), CRAIG(9)							30,805
NY	000	101	204	8	12	0	
STL	001	000	011	3	7	0	

Rookie Mel Stottlemyre gave up just one run in the first seven innings, which was more than enough time for the Yankees to get all the runs they'd need. The top of the order—the key to the St. Louis attack—combined to go hitless in 15 at bats.

GAME 3 / OCT. 10							
SIMMONS, SCHULTZ(9) VS. BOUTON							67,101
STL	000	010	000	1	6	0	
NY	010	000	001	2	5	2	

Jim Bouton and Curt Simmons each allowed only one run through eight innings. But Simmons was lifted for a pinch hitter in the top of the ninth, and Mantle crushed the first pitch he saw from reliever Barney Schultz in the bottom of the frame for the game-winner.

GAME 4 / OCT. 11							
SADECKI, CRAIG(1), TAYLOR(6) VS. DOWNING, MIKKELSEN(7), TERRY(8)							66,312
STL	000	004	000	4	6	1	
NY	300	000	000	3	6	1	

The Yankees had a 3–0 lead and had forced Cardinals starter Ray Sadecki out of the game after only a third of an inning. However, they managed only two more hits the rest of the way, allowing St. Louis to rally in the sixth behind a grand slam from Ken Boyer. Ron Taylor saved it for Roger Craig and the Cardinals with four hitless innings of relief.

GAME 5 / OCT. 12								
GIBSON VS. STOTTLEMYRE, RENIFF(8), MIKKELSEN(8)								65,633
STL	000	020	000	3	5	10	1	
NY	000	000	002	0	2	6	2	

Dick Groat's error on a ball hit by Mantle leading off the bottom of the ninth prevented Bob Gibson from closing out a win in regulation. However, the Cards needed only one extra frame to win it after a three-run blast by Tim McCarver in the top of the 10th and an easy bottom half of the inning from Gibson, who gave up only a meaningless single in the frame.

GAME 6 / OCT. 14							
BOUTON, HAMILTON(9) VS. SIMMONS, TAYLOR(7), SCHULTZ(8), RICHARDSON(8), HUMPHREYS(9)							30,805
NY	000	012	050	8	10	0	
STL	100	000	011	3	10	1	

The Yankees brought out the heavy lumber to send the series to a deciding seventh game. Joe Pepitone's grand slam in the eighth cinched it for New York, which also got homers from Mantle and Roger Maris.

GAME 7 / OCT. 15							
STOTTLEMYRE, DOWNING(5), SHELDON(5), HAMILTON(7), MIKKELSEN(8) VS. GIBSON							30,346
NY	000	003	002	5	9	2	
STL	000	330	10X	7	10	1	

Neither Gibson nor Stottlemyre were sharp, as each was starting for the third time in eight days. By the time the Yankees finally got to Gibson in the sixth they were already in a deep hole to the Cardinals, who scored six runs in the middle innings almost every conceivable way—a home run, two ground outs, a sacrifice fly, steal of home, and a base hit. Gibson, who allowed a meaningless two-out homer to Phil Linz in the ninth, fanned nine to set a series record with 31 strikeouts.

1976 AL Championship Series
New York Yankees (3) vs. Kansas City Royals (2)

After a dozen years watching five different teams capture the American League pennant—including the Orioles four times, the A's three, and the Red Sox two—the Yankees were finally back in October. The club played in a refurbished Yankee Stadium and for the first time experienced having to win a preliminary series to reach the World Series. The Yankees played a team that hadn't even existed when they'd last hoisted the AL flag in 1964; the Royals were tough and would prove to be a determined, if snake-bitten, foe in the Yankees' path to postseason glory.

NY (E)

PLAYER, POS	G	AB	R	H	2B	3B	HR	RBI	BB	SO	SB	AVG	OBP	SLG
T.Munson, c	5	23	3	10	2	0	0	3	0	1	0	.435	.435	.522
M.Rivers, of	5	23	5	8	0	1	0	0	1	1	0	.348	.375	.435
C.Chambliss, 1b	5	21	5	11	1	1	2	8	0	1	2	.524	.524	.667
G.Nettles, 3b	5	17	2	4	1	0	2	4	3	3	0	.235	.350	.294
W.Randolph, 2b	5	17	0	2	0	0	0	1	3	1	1	.118	.250	.118
R.White, of	5	17	4	5	3	0	0	3	5	1	1	.294	.455	.471
F.Stanley, ss	5	15	1	5	2	0	0	0	2	0	0	.333	.412	.467
L.Piniella, dh	4	11	1	3	1	0	0	0	0	1	0	.273	.273	.364
C.May, dh	3	10	1	2	1	0	0	0	1	4	0	.200	.273	.300
E.Maddox, of	3	9	0	2	1	0	0	1	0	1	0	.222	.222	.333
O.Gamble, of	3	8	1	2	1	0	0	1	1	1	0	.250	.333	.375
S.Alomar, dh	2	1	0	0	0	0	0	0	0	0	0	.000	.000	.000
E.Hendricks, ph	1	1	0	1	0	0	0	0	0	0	0	1.000	1.000	1.000
O.Velez, ph	1	1	0	0	0	0	0	0	0	0	0	.000	.000	.000
R.Guidry, pr	1	0	0	0	0	0	0	0	0	0	0	.000	.000	.000
J.Mason, ss	2	0	0	0	0	0	0	0	0	0	0	.000	.000	.000
Totals		174	23	55	13	2	4	21	16	15	4	.316	.374	.414

PITCHER	W	L	ERA	G	GS	SV	IP	H	BB	SO
E.Figueroa	0	1	5.84	2	2	0	12.1	14	2	5
C.Hunter	1	1	4.50	2	2	0	12.0	10	1	5
D.Ellis	1	0	3.38	1	1	0	8.0	6	2	5
D.Tidrow	1	0	3.68	3	0	0	7.1	6	4	0
G.Jackson	0	0	8.10	2	0	0	3.1	4	1	3
S.Lyle	0	0	0.00	1	0	1	1.0	0	1	0
Totals	3	2	4.70	11	5	1	44.0	40	11	18

KC (W)

PLAYER, POS	G	AB	R	H	2B	3B	HR	RBI	BB	SO	SB	AVG	OBP	SLG
A.Cowens, of	5	21	3	4	0	1	0	0	1	1	2	.190	.227	.286
G.Brett, 3b	5	18	4	8	1	1	1	5	2	1	0	.444	.500	.611
J.Mayberry, 1b	5	18	4	4	0	0	1	3	1	0	0	.222	.263	.222
F.Patek, ss	5	18	2	7	2	0	0	4	0	1	0	.389	.389	.500
H.McRae, dh-of	5	17	2	2	1	1	0	1	1	4	0	.118	.200	.294
T.Poquette, of	5	16	1	3	2	0	0	4	2	3	0	.188	.278	.313
B.Martinez, c	5	15	0	5	0	0	0	4	1	3	0	.333	.375	.333
J.Wohlford, of	5	11	3	2	0	0	0	0	3	1	2	.182	.357	.182
C.Rojas, 2b	4	9	2	3	0	0	0	1	0	0	1	.333	.333	.333
F.White, 2b	4	8	2	1	0	0	0	0	0	1	0	.125	.125	.125
J.Quirk, dh	4	7	1	1	0	1	0	2	0	2	0	.143	.143	.429
D.Nelson, dh	2	2	0	0	0	0	0	0	0	1	0	.000	.000	.000
A.Otis, of	1	1	0	0	0	0	0	0	0	0	0	.000	.000	.000
B.Stinson, c	2	1	0	0	0	0	0	0	0	0	0	.000	.000	.000
J.Wathan, c	1	0	0	0	0	0	0	0	0	0	0	.000	.000	.000
Totals		162	24	40	6	4	2	24	11	18	5	.247	.297	.333

PITCHER	W	L	ERA	G	GS	SV	IP	H	BB	SO
L.Gura	0	1	4.22	2	2	0	10.2	18	1	4
P.Splittorff	1	0	1.93	2	0	0	9.1	7	5	2
A.Hassler	0	1	6.14	2	1	0	7.1	8	6	4
D.Bird	1	0	1.93	1	0	0	4.2	4	0	1
M.Littell	0	1	1.93	3	0	0	4.2	4	1	3
S.Mingori	0	0	2.70	3	0	1	3.1	4	0	1
D.Leonard	0	0	19.29	2	2	0	2.1	9	2	0
T.Hall	0	0	0.00	1	0	0	0.1	1	0	0
M.Pattin	0	0	27.00	2	0	0	0.1	0	1	0
Totals	2	3	4.40	18	5	1	43.0	55	16	15

GAME 1 / OCT. 9						
HUNTER VS. GURA, LITTELL(9)						**41,077**
NY	200	000	002	4	12	0
KC	000	000	010	1	5	2

Catfish Hunter tossed a five-hitter and Roy White drove in two as the Yankees won their first postseason game since 1964.

GAME 2 / OCT. 10						
FIGUEROA, TIDROW(6) VS. LEONARD, SPLITTORFF(3), MINGORI(9)						**41,091**
NY	012	000	000	3	12	5
KC	200	002	03X	7	9	0

Paul Splittorff and Steve Mingori combined for $6^2/_3$ innings of shutout relief, giving the Royals a chance to stage a late comeback. Neither team hit a home run in the two games at Royals Stadium.

GAME 3 / OCT. 12						
HASSLER, PATTIN(6), HALL(6), MINGORI(6), LITTELL(6) VS. ELLIS, LYLE(9)						**56,808**
KC	300	000	000	3	6	0
NY	000	203	00X	5	9	0

Graig Nettles delivered a tie-breaking two-run single in the sixth to lift the Yankees to victory. Dock Ellis was solid on the mound before Sparky Lyle saved it.

GAME 4 / OCT. 13						
GURA, BIRD(3), MINGORI(7) VS. HUNTER, TIDROW(4), JACKSON(7)						**56,355**
KC	030	201	010	7	9	1
NY	020	000	101	4	11	0

Freddie Patek drove in three as the Royals staved off elimination, again using a deep bullpen to compensate for a poor start. Catfish Hunter was hit hard early, and two Graig Nettles homers couldn't spur a comeback.

GAME 5 / OCT. 14						
LEONARD, SPLITTORFF(1), PATTIN(4), HASSLER(5), LITTELL(7) VS. FIGUEROA, JACKSON(8), TIDROW(9)						**56,821**
KC	210	000	030	6	11	1
NY	202	002	001	7	11	1

The Yankees claimed their first AL pennant in 12 seasons, but it certainly wasn't easy. Batting champion George Brett tied the game with a three-run blast in the eighth. The Yankees won when Chris Chambliss smacked a leadoff homer in the bottom of the ninth against Mark Littell, sending so many fans pouring onto the field that Chambliss couldn't even touch all the bases.

1976 World Series
New York Yankees (0) vs. Cincinnati Reds (4)

The Yankees were a good team, though not nearly as good as a Big Red Machine in its prime, which featured three future Hall of Famers (four had Pete Rose not gotten caught betting on baseball). Cincinnati dominated every aspect of the series, outscoring New York 22–8 and limiting the Yankees to only five extra-base hits (for a meager .281 slugging percentage).

CIN (NL)

PLAYER, POS	G	AB	R	H	2B	3B	HR	RBI	BB	SO	SB	AVG	OBP	SLG
K.Griffey, of	4	17	2	1	0	0	0	1	0	1	1	.059	.059	.059
T.Perez, 1b	4	16	1	5	1	0	0	2	1	2	0	.313	.353	.375
P.Rose, 3b	4	16	1	3	1	0	0	1	2	2	0	.188	.278	.250
J.Bench, c	4	15	4	8	1	1	2	6	0	1	0	.533	.533	.733
J.Morgan, 2b	4	15	3	5	1	1	1	2	2	2	2	.333	.412	.533
D.Concepcion, ss	4	14	1	5	1	1	0	3	1	3	1	.357	.400	.571
D.Driessen, dh	4	14	4	5	2	0	1	1	2	0	1	.357	.438	.500
G.Foster, of	4	14	3	6	1	0	0	4	2	3	0	.429	.500	.500
C.Geronimo, of	4	13	3	4	2	0	0	1	2	2	2	.308	.400	.462
Totals		134	22	42	10	3	4	21	12	16	7	.313	.370	.433

CIN (NL) (CONT.)

PITCHER	W	L	ERA	G	GS	SV	IP	H	BB	SO
D.Gullett	1	0	1.23	1	1	0	7.1	5	3	4
G.Nolan	1	0	2.70	1	1	0	6.2	8	1	1
P.Zachry	1	0	2.70	1	1	0	6.2	6	5	6
F.Norman	0	0	4.26	1	1	0	6.1	9	2	2
W.McEnaney	0	0	0.00	2	0	2	4.2	2	1	2
J.Billingham	1	0	0.00	1	0	0	2.2	0	0	1
P.Borbon	0	0	0.00	1	0	0	1.2	0	0	0
Totals	4	0	2.00	8	4	2	36.0	30	12	16

NY (AL)

PLAYER, POS	G	AB	R	H	2B	3B	HR	RBI	BB	SO	SB	AVG	OBP	SLG
M.Rivers, of	4	18	1	3	0	0	0	0	1	2	1	.167	.211	.167
T.Munson, c	4	17	2	9	0	0	0	2	0	1	0	.529	.529	.529
C.Chambliss, 1b	4	16	1	5	1	0	0	1	0	2	0	.313	.313	.375
R.White, of	4	15	0	2	0	0	0	0	3	0	0	.133	.278	.133
W.Randolph, 2b	4	14	1	1	0	0	0	0	1	3	0	.071	.133	.071
G.Nettles, 3b	4	12	0	3	0	0	0	2	3	1	0	.250	.400	.250
C.May, dh	4	9	0	0	0	0	0	0	0	1	0	.000	.000	.000
L.Piniella, of-dh	4	9	1	3	1	0	0	0	0	0	0	.333	.333	.444
O.Gamble, of	3	8	0	1	0	0	0	1	0	0	0	.125	.125	.125
F.Stanley, ss	4	6	1	1	1	0	0	1	3	1	0	.167	.444	.333
E.Maddox, of-dh	2	5	0	1	0	1	0	0	1	2	0	.200	.333	.600
O.Velez, ph	3	3	0	0	0	0	0	0	0	3	0	.000	.000	.000
E.Hendricks, ph	2	2	0	0	0	0	0	0	0	0	0	.000	.000	.000
J.Mason, ss	3	1	1	1	0	0	1	1	0	0	0	1.000	1.000	1.000
Totals		135	8	30	3	1	1	8	12	16	1	.222	.291	.259

PITCHER	W	L	ERA	G	GS	SV	IP	H	BB	SO
C.Hunter	0	1	3.12	1	1	0	8.2	10	4	5
E.Figueroa	0	1	5.63	1	1	0	8.0	6	5	2
D.Alexander	0	1	7.50	1	1	0	6.0	9	2	1
G.Jackson	0	0	4.91	1	0	0	3.2	4	0	3
D.Ellis	0	1	10.80	1	1	0	3.1	7	0	1
S.Lyle	0	0	0.00	2	0	0	2.2	1	0	3
D.Tidrow	0	0	7.71	2	0	0	2.1	5	1	1
Totals	0	4	5.45	9	4	0	34.2	42	12	16

GAME 1 / OCT. 16						
ALEXANDER, LYLE(7) VS. GULLETT, BORBON(8)						**54,826**
NY	010	000	000	1	5	1
CIN	101	001	20X	5	10	1

The Reds also had plenty of pitching to go with their fantastic offensive attack. In the opener, Don Gullett and Pedro Borbon held the Yankees to just five hits. The Reds took the lead in the third on a triple by Dave Concepcion and a sacrifice fly by Pete Rose, then efficiently added insurance runs later.

GAME 2 / OCT. 17						
HUNTER VS. NORMAN, BILLINGHAM(7)						**54,816**
NY	000	100	200	3	9	1
CIN	030	000	001	4	10	0

The first six Reds reached in the third, and could have scored more than their three runs had George Foster not gotten thrown out trying to steal second early in the inning. The Yankees tied it in the seventh on a double by Fred Stanley and an RBI groundout by Thurman Munson, though it was Stanley's error in the ninth that led to the winning run. Stanley's miscue put Ken Griffey on second, and following an intentional walk of Joe Morgan, Tony Perez singled in Griffey with the game-winner.

GAME 3 / OCT. 19						
ZACHRY, MCENANEY(7) VS. ELLIS, JACKSON(4), TIDROW(8)						**56,667**
CIN	030	100	020	6	13	2
NY	000	100	100	2	8	0

The Reds rocked Dock Ellis and Grant Jackson for 11 hits and six runs in seven innings. Three singles, a double, and two stolen bases added up to three runs for Cincinnati in the second. The Reds put the game out of reach in the eighth on consecutive singles by Rose and Griffey, a double by Morgan and a single later in the inning by Foster.

GAME 4 / OCT. 21						
NOLAN, MCENANEY(7) VS. FIGUEROA, TIDROW(9), LYLE(9)						**56,700**
CIN	000	300	004	7	9	2
NY	100	010	000	2	8	0

A two-out double in the first by Chris Chambliss gave the Yankees their only lead of the series, but it was short lived. Johnny Bench smacked two home runs, including a two-run blast in the fourth as the Reds went ahead for good. Bench was the best of a devastating bunch of bats, batting .533 with a double, a triple and the two homers, and was named MVP of the Series.

1977 AL Championship Series
New York Yankees (3) vs. Kansas City Royals (2)

Despite a season in the Bronx worthy of its own soap opera, it looked like the Royals—the best team in baseball during the regular season—would go to the World Series after they won two of the first three LCS games. The Yankees saved up the drama for the end, closing out the series with a big finish.

NY (E)

PLAYER, POS	G	AB	R	H	2B	3B	HR	RBI	BB	SO	SB	AVG	OBP	SLG
M.Rivers, of	5	23	5	9	2	0	0	2	0	2	1	.391	.391	.478
T.Munson, c	5	21	3	6	1	0	1	5	0	2	0	.286	.286	.333
L.Piniella, of-dh	5	21	1	7	3	0	0	2	0	1	0	.333	.333	.476
G.Nettles, 3b	5	20	1	3	0	0	0	1	0	3	0	.150	.150	.150
W.Randolph, 2b	5	18	4	5	1	0	0	2	1	0	0	.278	.316	.333
C.Chambliss, 1b	5	17	0	1	0	0	0	0	3	4	0	.059	.200	.059
R.Jackson, of-dh	5	16	1	2	0	0	0	1	2	2	1	.125	.222	.125
C.Johnson, dh	5	15	2	6	2	0	1	2	1	2	0	.400	.438	.533
B.Dent, ss	5	14	1	3	1	0	0	2	1	0	0	.214	.267	.286
P.Blair, of	3	5	1	2	0	0	0	0	0	0	0	.400	.400	.400
R.White, of-dh	4	5	2	2	2	0	0	0	1	0	0	.400	.500	.800
F.Stanley, ss	2	0	0	0	0	0	0	0	0	0	0	.000	.000	.000
Totals		175	21	46	12	0	2	17	9	16	2	.263	.299	.331

PITCHER	W	L	ERA	G	GS	SV	IP	H	BB	SO
R.Guidry	1	0	3.97	2	2	0	11.1	9	3	8
M.Torrez	0	1	4.09	2	1	0	11.0	11	5	5
S.Lyle	2	0	0.96	4	0	0	9.1	7	0	3
D.Tidrow	0	0	3.86	2	0	0	7.0	6	3	3
E.Figueroa	0	0	10.80	1	1	0	3.1	5	2	3
D.Gullett	0	1	18.00	1	1	0	2.0	4	2	0
Totals	3	2	4.50	12	5	0	44.0	42	15	22

KC (W)

PLAYER, POS	G	AB	R	H	2B	3B	HR	RBI	BB	SO	SB	AVG	OBP	SLG
G.Brett, 3b	5	20	2	6	0	2	0	2	1	0	0	.300	.333	.500
A.Cowens, of	5	19	2	5	0	0	1	5	1	3	0	.263	.300	.263
H.McRae, dh-of	5	18	6	8	3	0	1	2	3	1	0	.444	.524	.611
F.Patek, ss	5	18	4	7	3	1	0	5	1	2	0	.389	.421	.667
F.White, 2b	5	18	1	5	1	0	0	2	0	4	1	.278	.278	.333
A.Otis, of	5	16	1	2	1	0	0	2	2	3	2	.125	.222	.188
D.Porter, c	5	15	3	5	0	0	0	0	3	0	0	.333	.444	.333
J.Mayberry, 1b	4	12	1	2	1	0	1	3	1	2	0	.167	.231	.250
J.Zdeb, of	4	9	0	0	0	0	0	0	0	2	1	.000	.000	.000
T.Poquette, of	2	6	0	1	0	0	0	0	0	0	0	.167	.167	.167
J.Wathan, 1b-c-dh	4	6	0	0	0	0	0	0	0	3	0	.000	.000	.000
C.Rojas, dh	1	4	0	1	0	0	0	0	0	0	1	.250	.250	.250
P.LaCock, 1b	1	1	0	0	0	0	0	0	1	1	0	.000	.500	.000
J.Lahoud, dh	1	1	2	0	0	0	0	0	2	0	0	.000	.667	.000
Totals		163	22	42	9	3	3	21	15	22	5	.258	.320	.350

PITCHER	W	L	ERA	G	GS	SV	IP	H	BB	SO
P.Splittorff	1	0	2.40	2	2	0	15.0	14	3	4
D.Leonard	1	1	3.00	2	1	0	9.0	5	2	4
M.Pattin	0	0	1.50	1	0	0	6.0	6	0	0
A.Hassler	0	1	4.76	1	1	0	5.2	5	0	3
M.Littell	0	0	3.00	2	0	0	3.0	5	3	1
D.Bird	0	0	0.00	3	0	0	2.0	4	0	1
L.Gura	0	1	18.00	2	1	0	2.0	7	1	2
S.Mingori	0	0	0.00	3	0	0	1.1	0	0	1
Totals	2	3	3.27	16	5	0	44.0	46	9	16

GAME 1 / OCT. 5

SPLITTORFF, BIRD(9) VS. GULLETT, TIDROW(3), LYLE(9) — **54,930**

				R	H	E
KC	222	000	010	7	9	0
NY	002	000	000	2	9	0

A pair of two-run homers by Hal McRae and John Mayberry allowed the Royals to score six times in the first three innings. Battered starter Don Gullett did not pitch again in the series.

GAME 2 / OCT. 6

HASSLER, LITTELL(6), MINGORI(8) VS. GUIDRY — **56,230**

				R	H	E
KC	001	001	000	2	3	1
NY	000	023	01X	6	10	1

The Yankees evened the series behind a three-hitter by Ron Guidry. A key two-out error by George Brett in New York's three-run sixth inning helped the Yankees go ahead for good.

GAME 3 / OCT. 7

TORREZ, LYLE(6) VS. LEONARD — **41,285**

				R	H	E
NY	000	010	001	2	4	1
KC	011	012	10X	6	12	1

Dennis Leonard went the distance for the Royals, holding the Yankees to just four hits and two runs, one of which was unearned.

GAME 4 / OCT. 8

FIGUEROA, TIDROW(4), LYLE(4) VS. GURA, PATTIN(3), MINGORI(9), BIRD(9) — **41,135**

				R	H	E
NY	121	100	001	6	13	0
KC	002	200	000	4	8	2

Sparky Lyle's 5 1/3 innings of shutout relief helped the Yankees win what started out as a slugfest.

GAME 5 / OCT. 9

GUIDRY, TORREZ(3), LYLE(8) VS. SPLITTORFF, BIRD(8), MINGORI(8), LEONARD(9), GURA(9), LITTELL(9) — **41,133**

				R	H	E
NY	001	000	013	5	10	0
KC	201	000	000	3	10	1

The Royals appeared headed for their first pennant until New York rallied for four runs in the last two innings. Reggie Jackson, who wasn't even in the starting lineup against lefty Paul Splittorff, singled in a run to start the comeback in the eighth. Mickey Rivers tied the game in the ninth; Willie Randolph gave New York the lead. Royals manager Whitey Herzog tried six pitchers the last two innings yet couldn't get the six outs quick enough. Sparky Lyle won for the second time in as many days.

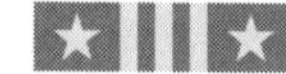

1977 World Series
New York Yankees (4) vs. Los Angeles Dodgers (2)

Reggie Jackson would be forever known as "Mr. October" after belting a series record five home runs, including three in consecutive at bats in the sixth contest. He also hit .450 overall, and obviously was named MVP of the Fall Classic. Los Angeles had four sluggers with at least 30 homers, but in the end, New York had "the straw that stirs the drink," and took home a championship for the first time since 1964.

NY (AL)

PLAYER, POS	G	AB	R	H	2B	3B	HR	RBI	BB	SO	SB	AVG	OBP	SLG
M.Rivers, of	6	27	1	6	2	0	0	1	0	2	1	.222	.222	.296
T.Munson, c	6	25	4	8	2	0	1	3	2	8	0	.320	.370	.400
W.Randolph, 2b	6	25	5	4	2	0	1	1	2	2	0	.160	.222	.240
C.Chambliss, 1b	6	24	4	7	2	0	1	4	0	2	0	.292	.292	.375
L.Piniella, of	6	22	1	6	0	0	0	3	0	3	0	.273	.292	.273
G.Nettles, 3b	6	21	1	4	1	0	0	2	2	3	0	.190	.261	.238
R.Jackson, of	6	20	10	9	1	0	5	8	3	4	0	.450	.522	.500
B.Dent, ss	6	19	0	5	0	0	0	2	2	1	0	.263	.333	.263
M.Torrez, p	2	6	0	0	0	0	0	0	0	4	0	.000	.000	.000
P.Blair, of	4	4	0	1	0	0	0	1	0	0	0	.250	.250	.250
R.Guidry, p	1	2	0	0	0	0	0	0	0	1	0	.000	.000	.000
D.Gullett, p	2	2	0	0	0	0	0	0	0	2	0	.000	.000	.000
S.Lyle, p	2	2	0	0	0	0	0	0	0	2	0	.000	.000	.000
R.White, ph	2	2	0	0	0	0	0	0	0	0	0	.000	.000	.000
G.Zeber, ph	2	2	0	0	0	0	0	0	0	2	0	.000	.000	.000
C.Johnson, c	2	1	0	0	0	0	0	0	0	0	0	.000	.000	.000
D.Tidrow, p	2	1	0	0	0	0	0	0	0	1	0	.000	.000	.000
F.Stanley, ss	1	0	0	0	0	0	0	0	0	0	0	.000	.000	.000
Totals		205	26	50	10	0	8	25	11	37	1	.244	.288	.293

PITCHER	W	L	ERA	G	GS	SV	IP	H	BB	SO
M.Torrez	2	0	2.50	2	2	0	18.0	16	5	15
D.Gullett	0	1	6.39	2	2	0	12.2	13	7	10
R.Guidry	1	0	2.00	1	1	0	9.0	4	3	7
S.Lyle	1	0	1.93	2	0	0	4.2	2	0	2
C.Hunter	0	1	10.38	2	1	0	4.1	6	0	1
K.Clay	0	0	2.45	2	0	0	3.2	2	1	0
D.Tidrow	0	0	4.91	2	0	0	3.2	5	0	1
Totals	4	2	4.02	13	6	0	56.0	48	16	36

LA (NL)													
PLAYER, POS	G	AB	R	H	2B	3B	HR	RBI	BB	SO	SB	AVG	OBP	SLG
B.Russell, ss	6	26	3	4	0	1	0	2	1	3	0	.154	.185	.231
D.Baker, of	6	24	4	7	0	0	1	5	0	2	0	.292	.292	.292
S.Garvey, 1b	6	24	5	9	1	1	1	3	1	4	0	.375	.400	.500
D.Lopes, 2b	6	24	3	4	0	1	1	2	4	3	2	.167	.286	.250
R.Smith, of	6	22	7	6	1	0	3	5	4	3	0	.273	.385	.318
R.Cey, 3b	6	21	2	4	1	0	1	3	3	5	0	.190	.292	.238
S.Yeager, c	6	19	2	6	1	0	2	5	1	1	0	.316	.350	.368
R.Monday, of	4	12	0	2	0	0	0	0	0	3	0	.167	.167	.167
L.Lacy, of	4	7	1	3	0	0	0	2	1	1	0	.429	.500	.429
D.Sutton, p	2	6	0	0	0	0	0	0	1	4	0	.000	.143	.000
G.Burke, of	3	5	0	1	0	0	0	0	0	1	0	.200	.200	.200
B.Hooton, p	2	5	0	0	0	0	0	0	0	2	0	.000	.000	.000
V.Davalillo, ph	3	3	0	1	0	0	0	1	0	0	0	.333	.333	.333
M.Mota, ph	3	3	0	0	0	0	0	0	0	1	0	.000	.000	.000
T.John, p	1	2	0	0	0	0	0	0	0	2	0	.000	.000	.000
R.Rhoden, p	2	2	1	1	1	0	0	0	0	0	0	.500	.500	1.000
E.Goodson, ph	1	1	0	0	0	0	0	0	0	1	0	.000	.000	.000
J.Grote, c	1	1	0	0	0	0	0	0	0	0	0	.000	.000	.000
J.Oates, c	1	1	0	0	0	0	0	0	0	0	0	.000	.000	.000
R.Landestoy, pr	1	0	0	0	0	0	0	0	0	0	0	.000	.000	.000
Totals		208	28	48	5	3	9	28	16	36	2	.231	.289	.284

PITCHER	W	L	ERA	G	GS	SV	IP	H	BB	SO
D.Sutton	1	0	3.94	2	2	0	16.0	17	1	6
B.Hooton	1	1	3.75	2	2	0	12.0	8	2	9
R.Rhoden	0	1	2.57	2	0	0	7.0	4	1	5
T.John	0	1	6.00	1	1	0	6.0	9	3	7
C.Hough	0	0	1.80	2	0	0	5.0	3	0	5
M.Garman	0	0	0.00	2	0	0	4.0	2	1	3
D.Rau	0	1	11.57	2	1	0	2.1	4	0	1
E.Sosa	0	0	11.57	2	0	0	2.1	3	1	1
L.Rautzhan	0	0	0.00	1	0	0	0.1	0	2	0
Totals	2	4	4.09	16	6	0	55.0	50	11	37

GAME 1 / OCT. 11							
SUTTON, RAUTZHAN(8), SOSA(8), GARMAN(9), RHODEN(12) VS. GULLETT, LYLE(9)							56,668
LA	200	000	001	000	3	6	0
NY	100	001	010	001	4	11	0

Paul Blair wasn't supposed to win the game for the Yankees, but he did anyway. Blair, who came into the game as a defensive replacement for Reggie Jackson with New York up a run going into the top of the ninth, initially couldn't get a bunt down following a double and an intentional walk leading off the last of the 12th, but redeemed himself with a game-winning single.

GAME 2 / OCT. 12						
HOOTON VS. HUNTER, TIDROW(3), CLAY(6), LYLE(9)						56,691
LA	212	000	001	6	9	0
NY	000	100	000	1	5	0

Los Angeles scored all six of its runs on long balls—two-run shots by Ron Cey and Reggie Smith, and solo blasts from Steve Garvey and Steve Yeager. New York managed only one run and five hits off Burt Hooton, who went the distance for L.A.

GAME 3 / OCT. 14						
TORREZ VS. JOHN, HOUGH(7)						55,992
NY	300	110	000	5	10	0
LA	003	000	000	3	7	1

Though New York jumped ahead early, the Dodgers tied it in the third on a three-run homer by Dusty Baker. The Yankees came right back, however, getting what would be the winning run in the fourth on a groundout by Mickey Rivers, and an insurance run in the fifth on a single by Chris Chambliss. Mike Torrez allowed only two hits after Baker's blast and retired the last 11 batters in his complete game win.

GAME 4 / OCT. 15						
GUIDRY VS. RAU, RHODEN(2), GARMAN(9)						55,995
NY	030	001	000	4	7	0
LA	002	000	000	2	4	0

Ron Guidry hurled New York's second consecutive complete game win, giving up only two runs and four hits. Jackson hit the first of his five home runs in the sixth, and doubled and scored in the three-run second.

GAME 5 / OCT. 16						
GULLETT, CLAY(5), TIDROW(6), HUNTER(7) VS. SUTTON						55,955
NY	000	000	220	4	9	2
LA	100	432	00X	10	13	0

The Dodgers won in a rout, pelting Don Gullett for eight hits and seven runs in $4^1/_3$ innings. Yeager had a three-run homer in the fourth and drove in four overall to lead the onslaught.

GAME 6 / OCT. 18						
HOOTON, SOSA(4), RAU(5), HOUGH(7) VS. TORREZ						56,407
LA	201	000	001	4	9	0
NY	020	320	01X	8	8	1

Jackson's performance was perhaps the most dominating individual effort in World Series play since Don Larsen's perfect game in 1956. Trailing 3–2 in the bottom of the fourth, Jackson connected off Hooton for a two-run blast that gave the Yankees the lead. He belted another two-run shot the next inning to make it 7–3 and added one in the eighth for show.

1978 AL Championship Series New York Yankees (3) vs. Kansas City Royals (1)

The Yankees had their easiest time yet with the Royals in the ALCS; it was getting there that was the Herculean task. The Yankees rallied from 14 games back in July to catch the Red Sox, pass them in the standings, then finish the season tied with them—only to win the first one-game playoff in franchise history at their rival's ballpark after trailing for six innings. Catching a flight to Kansas City and beating the rested and ready Royals the next night was child's play in comparison.

NY (E)													
PLAYER, POS	G	AB	R	H	2B	3B	HR	RBI	BB	SO	SB	AVG	OBP	SLG
T.Munson, c	4	18	2	5	1	0	1	2	0	0	0	.278	.278	.333
L.Piniella, of	4	17	2	4	0	0	0	0	0	3	0	.235	.235	.235
R.White, of-dh	4	16	5	5	1	0	1	1	1	2	0	.313	.353	.375
C.Chambliss, 1b	4	15	1	6	0	0	0	2	0	4	0	.400	.400	.400
B.Dent, ss	4	15	0	3	0	0	0	4	0	0	0	.200	.200	.200
G.Nettles, 3b	4	15	3	5	0	1	1	2	0	1	0	.333	.333	.467
R.Jackson, dh-of	4	13	5	6	1	0	2	6	3	4	0	.462	.563	.538
M.Rivers, of	4	11	0	5	0	0	0	0	2	0	0	.455	.538	.455
B.Doyle, 2b	3	7	0	2	0	0	0	1	1	1	0	.286	.375	.286
P.Blair, of-2b	4	6	1	0	0	0	0	0	0	1	0	.000	.000	.000
F.Stanley, 2b	2	5	0	1	0	0	0	0	0	2	0	.200	.200	.200
C.Johnson, ph	1	1	0	0	0	0	0	0	0	0	0	.000	.000	.000
G.Thomasson, of	3	1	0	0	0	0	0	0	0	0	0	.000	.000	.000
Totals		140	19	42	3	1	5	18	7	18	0	.300	.333	.336

PITCHER	W	L	ERA	G	GS	SV	IP	H	BB	SO
R.Guidry	1	0	1.13	1	1	0	8.0	7	1	7
C.Hunter	0	0	4.50	1	1	0	6.0	7	3	5
D.Tidrow	0	0	4.76	1	0	0	5.2	8	2	1
J.Beattie	1	0	1.69	1	1	0	5.1	2	5	3
R.Gossage	1	0	4.50	2	0	1	4.0	3	0	3
K.Clay	0	0	0.00	1	0	1	3.2	0	3	2
S.Lyle	0	0	13.50	1	0	0	1.1	3	0	0
E.Figueroa	0	1	27.00	1	1	0	1.0	5	0	0
Totals	3	1	3.86	9	4	2	35.0	35	14	21

KC (W)													
PLAYER, POS	G	AB	R	H	2B	3B	HR	RBI	BB	SO	SB	AVG	OBP	SLG
G.Brett, 3b	4	18	7	7	1	1	3	3	0	1	0	.389	.389	.556
A.Cowens, of	4	15	2	2	0	0	0	1	0	2	0	.133	.133	.133
H.McRae, dh	4	14	0	3	0	0	0	2	2	2	1	.214	.313	.214
A.Otis, of	4	14	2	6	2	0	0	1	3	5	4	.429	.529	.571
D.Porter, c	4	14	1	5	1	0	0	3	2	0	0	.357	.438	.429
F.Patek, ss	4	13	2	1	0	0	1	2	1	4	0	.077	.143	.077
F.White, 2b	4	13	1	3	0	0	0	2	0	0	0	.231	.231	.231
P.LaCock, 1b	4	11	1	4	2	1	0	1	3	1	1	.364	.500	.727
C.Hurdle, of	4	8	1	3	0	1	0	1	2	3	0	.375	.500	.625
S.Braun, of	2	5	0	0	0	0	0	0	1	1	0	.000	.167	.000
W.Wilson, of	3	4	0	1	0	0	0	0	0	2	0	.250	.250	.250
J.Wathan, 1b	1	3	0	0	0	0	0	0	0	0	0	.000	.000	.000
T.Poquette, ph	1	1	0	0	0	0	0	0	0	0	0	.000	.000	.000
Totals		133	17	35	6	3	4	16	14	21	6	.263	.333	.353

PITCHER	W	L	ERA	G	GS	SV	IP	H	BB	SO
D.Leonard	0	2	3.75	2	2	0	12.0	13	2	11
P.Splittorff	0	0	4.91	1	1	0	7.1	9	0	2
L.Gura	1	0	2.84	1	1	0	6.1	8	2	2
S.Mingori	0	0	7.36	1	0	0	3.2	5	3	0
A.Hrabosky	0	0	3.00	3	0	0	3.0	3	0	2

KC (W) (cont.)

PITCHER	W	L	ERA	G	GS	SV	IP	H	BB	SO
D.Bird	0	1	9.00	2	0	0	1.0	2	0	1
M.Pattin	0	0	27.00	1	0	0	0.2	2	0	0
Totals	1	3	4.76	11	4	0	34.0	42	7	18

GAME 1 / OCT. 3

BEATTIE, CLAY(6) VS. LEONARD, MINGORI(5), HRABOSKY(8), BIRD(9)							41,143
NY	011	020	030	7	16	0	
KC	000	001	000	1	2	2	

The Yankees rapped at least two hits in each of the first five innings, cruising to an easy victory behind the two-hit pitching of Jim Beattie and Ken Clay.

GAME 2 / OCT. 4

FIGUEROA, TIDROW(2), LYLE(7) VS. GURA, PATTIN(7), HRABOSKY(8)							41,158
NY	000	000	220	4	12	1	
KC	140	000	32X	10	16	1	

The travel and travails caught up with the Yankees, as Kansas City pummeled Ed Figueroa, Dick Tidrow, and Sparky Lyle. The winning team had 16 hits for the second straight day.

GAME 3 / OCT. 6

SPLITTORFF, BIRD(8), HRABOSKY(8) VS. HUNTER, GOSSAGE(7)							55,535
KC	101	010	020	5	10	1	
NY	010	201	02X	6	10	0	

George Brett hit three homers, with his third putting the Royals ahead in the top of the eighth. Thurman Munson's long two-run shot in the bottom of the inning gave the Yankees the lead in the game and the series.

GAME 4 / OCT. 7

LEONARD VS. GUIDRY, GOSSAGE(9)							56,356
KC	100	000	000	1	7	0	
NY	010	001	00X	2	4	0	

Ron Guidry made solo shots by Graig Nettles and Roy White hold up with eight innings of seven-hit, one-run ball. Rich Gossage retired the side in order in the ninth for the save and the pennant.

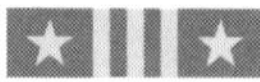

1978 World Series
New York Yankees (4) vs. Los Angeles Dodgers (2)

The Yankees very nearly didn't even make the postseason, much less win a second consecutive championship. Down by 14 ½ games in July, the Yankees roared back and were able to defend their title after Bucky Dent's miraculous home run in the one-game divisional playoff against the Red Sox. The Series was a rematch of the year before, and they again won in six games, though this time they spotted the Dodgers the first two.

NY (AL)

PLAYER, POS	G	AB	R	H	2B	3B	HR	RBI	BB	SO	SB	AVG	OBP	SLG
T.Munson, c	6	25	5	8	3	0	0	7	3	7	1	.320	.393	.440
G.Nettles, 3b	6	25	2	4	0	0	0	1	0	6	0	.160	.160	.160
L.Piniella, of	6	25	3	7	0	0	0	4	0	0	1	.280	.280	.280
B.Dent, ss	6	24	3	10	1	0	0	7	1	2	0	.417	.440	.458
R.White, of	6	24	9	8	0	0	1	4	4	5	2	.333	.429	.333
R.Jackson, dh	6	23	2	9	1	0	2	8	3	7	0	.391	.462	.435
M.Rivers, of	5	18	2	6	0	0	0	1	0	2	1	.333	.333	.333
B.Doyle, 2b	6	16	4	7	1	0	0	2	0	0	0	.438	.438	.500
J.Spencer, 1b	4	12	3	2	0	0	0	0	2	4	0	.167	.286	.167
C.Chambliss, 1b	3	11	1	2	0	0	0	0	1	1	0	.182	.250	.182
P.Blair, of	6	8	2	3	1	0	0	0	1	4	0	.375	.444	.500
F.Stanley, 2b	3	5	0	1	1	0	0	0	1	0	0	.200	.333	.400
G.Thomasson, of	3	4	0	1	0	0	0	0	0	1	0	.250	.250	.250
C.Johnson, ph	2	2	0	0	0	0	0	0	0	1	0	.000	.000	.000
M.Heath, c	1	0	0	0	0	0	0	0	0	0	0	.000	.000	.000
J.Johnstone, of	2	0	0	0	0	0	0	0	0	0	0	.000	.000	.000
Totals		222	36	68	8	0	3	34	16	40	5	.306	.358	.342

NY (AL) (cont.)

PITCHER	W	L	ERA	G	GS	SV	IP	H	BB	SO
C.Hunter	1	1	4.15	2	2	0	13.0	13	1	5
J.Beattie	1	0	2.00	1	1	0	9.0	9	4	8
R.Guidry	1	0	1.00	1	1	0	9.0	8	7	4
E.Figueroa	0	1	8.10	2	2	0	6.2	9	5	2
R.Gossage	1	0	0.00	3	0	0	6.0	1	1	4
D.Tidrow	0	0	1.93	2	0	0	4.2	4	0	5
K.Clay	0	0	11.57	1	0	0	2.1	4	2	2
P.Lindblad	0	0	11.57	1	0	0	2.1	4	0	1
Totals	4	2	3.74	13	6	0	53.0	52	20	31

LA (NL)

PLAYER, POS	G	AB	R	H	2B	3B	HR	RBI	BB	SO	SB	AVG	OBP	SLG
D.Lopes, 2b	6	26	7	8	0	0	3	7	2	1	2	.308	.357	.308
B.Russell, ss	6	26	1	11	2	0	0	2	2	2	1	.423	.464	.500
R.Smith, of	6	25	3	5	0	0	1	5	2	6	0	.200	.259	.200
S.Garvey, 1b	6	24	1	5	1	0	0	0	1	7	1	.208	.240	.250
D.Baker, of	6	21	2	5	0	0	1	1	1	3	0	.238	.273	.238
R.Cey, 3b	6	21	2	6	0	0	1	4	3	3	0	.286	.375	.286
L.Lacy, dh	4	14	0	2	0	0	0	1	1	3	0	.143	.200	.143
R.Monday, of-dh	6	13	2	2	1	0	0	0	4	3	0	.154	.353	.231
S.Yeager, c	5	13	2	3	1	0	0	0	1	2	0	.231	.286	.308
B.North, of	4	8	2	1	1	0	0	2	1	0	1	.125	.222	.250
J.Ferguson, c	2	4	1	2	2	0	0	0	0	1	0	.500	.500	1.000
V.Davalillo, dh	2	3	0	1	0	0	0	0	0	0	0	.333	.333	.333
J.Oates, c	1	1	0	1	0	0	0	0	1	0	0	1.000	1.000	1.000
J.Grote, c	2	0	0	0	0	0	0	0	0	0	0	.000	.000	.000
M.Mota, ph	1	0	0	0	0	0	0	0	1	0	0	.000	1.000	.000
Totals		199	23	52	8	0	6	22	20	31	5	.261	.329	.302

PITCHER	W	L	ERA	G	GS	SV	IP	H	BB	SO
T.John	1	0	3.07	2	2	0	14.2	14	4	6
D.Sutton	0	2	7.50	2	2	0	12.0	17	4	8
B.Hooton	1	1	6.48	2	2	0	8.1	13	3	6
C.Hough	0	0	8.44	2	0	0	5.1	10	2	5
B.Welch	0	1	6.23	3	0	1	4.1	4	2	6
T.Forster	0	0	0.00	3	0	0	4.0	5	1	6
D.Rau	0	0	0.00	1	0	0	2.0	1	0	3
L.Rautzhan	0	0	13.50	2	0	0	2.0	4	0	0
Totals	2	4	5.47	17	6	1	52.2	68	16	40

GAME 1 / OCT. 10

FIGUEROA, CLAY(2), LINDBLAD(5), TIDROW(7) VS. JOHN, FORSTER(8)							55,997
NY	000	000	320	5	9	1	
LA	030	310	31X	11	15	2	

Davey Lopes hit two home runs in the first four innings and the Dodgers clubbed four overall and scored off all four New York pitchers.

GAME 2 / OCT. 11

HUNTER, GOSSAGE(7) VS. HOOTON, FORSTER(7), WELCH(9)							55,982
NY	002	000	100	3	11	0	
LA	000	103	00X	4	7	0	

Los Angeles trailed until the sixth, when they got three on a two-out homer by Ron Cey. The Dodgers didn't get through the ninth without trouble, however. Bob Welch came on with two on and one out to get Thurman Munson to fly out and Reggie Jackson to strike out to preserve the win.

GAME 3 / OCT. 13

SUTTON, RAUTZHAN(7), HOUGH(8) VS. GUIDRY							56,447
LA	001	000	000	1	8	0	
NY	110	000	30X	5	10	1	

Ron Guidry allowed 15 baserunners in nine innings (eight hits and seven walks), but he and third baseman Graig Nettles, who made three fantastic plays in the field, let only one of them touch home plate. The Yankees bunched nine singles, and a solo home run by Roy White, to score their runs.

GAME 4 / OCT. 14

JOHN, FORSTER(8), WELCH(8) VS. FIGUEROA, TIDROW(6), GOSSAGE(9)								56,445
LA	000	030	000	0	3	6	1	
NY	000	002	010	1	4	9	0	

The Yankees had to claw their way back after quickly falling behind three runs. Jackson accounted for both New York runs in the sixth. He singled in a run, then his hip-check of a throw from second on what could have been an inning-ending double play allowed the second one to score. After tying it in the eighth on a two-out single by Munson, the Yankees won it in the 10th when Lou Piniella plated White with a safety to center.

GAME 5 / OCT. 15					
HOOTON, RAUTZHAN(3), HOUGH(4) VS. BEATTIE					**56,448**
LA	101 000 000		2	9	3
NY	004 300 41X		12	18	0

The Yankees set a series record by hitting 16 singles—to go with a couple of doubles—and routed the Dodgers. Most of the damage came off knuckleballer Charlie Hough, who allowed 10 hits in $4^1/_3$ innings of relief.

GAME 6 / OCT. 17					
HUNTER, GOSSAGE(8) VS. SUTTON, WELCH(7), RAU(8)					**55,985**
NY	030 002 200		7	11	0
LA	101 000 000		2	7	1

New York's Nos. 7 and 8 hitters did most of the damage. Denny Doyle and Bucky Dent combined for six hits and five RBIs in the clincher. Doyle also scored twice for the Yankees, who became the first team in World Series history to win four straight games after dropping the first two.

1980 AL Championship Series
New York Yankees (0) vs. Kansas City Royals (3)

After losing to the Yankees in every devastating way possible from 1976 to 1978, the Royals became the first team to bounce the Yankees from the ALCS. This time the breaks and the big hits went Kansas City's way.

KC (W)

PLAYER, POS	G	AB	R	H	2B	3B	HR	RBI	BB	SO	SB	AVG	OBP	SLG
W.Wilson, of	3	13	2	4	2	1	0	4	1	2	0	.308	.357	.615
A.Otis, of	3	12	2	4	1	0	0	0	0	3	2	.333	.333	.417
W.Aikens, 1b	3	11	0	4	0	0	0	2	0	1	0	.364	.364	.364
G.Brett, 3b	3	11	3	3	1	0	2	4	1	0	0	.273	.333	.364
U.L Washington, ss	3	11	1	4	1	0	0	1	2	3	0	.364	.462	.455
F.White, 2b	3	11	3	6	1	0	1	3	0	1	1	.545	.545	.636
H.McRae, dh	3	10	0	2	0	0	0	0	1	3	0	.200	.273	.200
D.Porter, c	3	10	2	1	0	0	0	0	1	0	0	.100	.182	.100
J.Wathan, of	3	6	1	0	0	0	0	0	3	1	0	.000	.333	.000
C.Hurdle, of	3	2	0	0	0	0	0	0	0	1	0	.000	.000	.000
P.LaCock, 1b	1	0	0	0	0	0	0	0	0	0	0	.000	.000	.000
Totals		97	14	28	6	1	3	14	9	15	3	.289	.355	.371

PITCHER	W	L	ERA	G	GS	SV	IP	H	BB	SO
L.Gura	1	0	2.00	1	1	0	9.0	10	1	4
D.Leonard	1	0	2.25	1	1	0	8.0	7	1	8
P.Splittorff	0	0	1.69	1	1	0	5.1	5	2	3
D.Quisenberry	1	0	0.00	2	0	1	4.2	4	2	1
Totals	3	0	1.67	5	3	1	27.0	26	6	16

NY (E)

PLAYER, POS	G	AB	R	H	2B	3B	HR	RBI	BB	SO	SB	AVG	OBP	SLG
W.Randolph, 2b	3	13	0	5	2	0	0	1	1	3	0	.385	.429	.538
R.Cerone, c	3	12	1	4	0	0	1	2	0	1	0	.333	.333	.333
B.Watson, 1b	3	12	0	6	3	1	0	0	0	0	0	.500	.500	.917
B.Dent, ss	3	11	0	2	0	0	0	0	0	1	0	.182	.182	.182
R.Jackson, of	3	11	1	3	1	0	0	0	1	4	0	.273	.333	.364
B.Brown, of	3	10	1	0	0	0	0	0	1	2	0	.000	.091	.000
G.Nettles, 3b	2	6	1	1	0	0	1	1	0	1	0	.167	.167	.167
A.Rodriguez, 3b	2	6	0	2	1	0	0	0	0	0	0	.333	.333	.500
E.Soderholm, dh	2	6	0	1	0	0	0	0	0	0	0	.167	.167	.167
O.Gamble, of-dh	2	5	1	1	0	0	0	0	1	1	0	.200	.333	.200
L.Piniella, of	2	5	1	1	0	0	1	1	2	1	0	.200	.429	.200
B.Murcer, dh	1	4	0	0	0	0	0	0	0	2	0	.000	.000	.000
J.Spencer, ph	1	1	0	0	0	0	0	0	0	0	0	.000	.000	.000
J.Lefebvre, of	1	0	0	0	0	0	0	0	0	0	0	.000	.000	.000
Totals		102	6	26	7	1	3	5	6	16	0	.255	.296	.343

PITCHER	W	L	ERA	G	GS	SV	IP	H	BB	SO
R.May	0	1	3.38	1	1	0	8.0	6	3	4
T.John	0	0	2.70	1	1	0	6.2	8	1	3
R.Davis	0	0	2.25	1	0	0	4.0	3	1	3
R.Guidry	0	1	12.00	1	1	0	3.0	5	4	2
T.Underwood	0	0	0.00	2	0	0	3.0	3	0	3
R.Gossage	0	1	54.00	1	0	0	0.1	3	0	0
Totals	0	3	4.32	7	3	0	25.0	28	9	15

GAME 1 / OCT. 8					
GUIDRY, DAVIS(4), UNDERWOOD(8) VS. GURA					**42,598**
NY	020 000 000		2	10	1
KC	022 000 12X		7	10	0

The Yankees got solo home runs from Rick Cerone and Lou Piniella in the second, but managed little else against Larry Gura. The Royals tied it on Frank White's double in the second and knocked out Ron Guidry in the third.

GAME 2 / OCT. 9					
MAY VS. LEONARD, QUISENBERRY(9)					**42,633**
NY	000 020 000		2	8	0
KC	003 000 00X		3	6	0

The Royals bunched four hits together in the third, including a two-run triple by Willie Wilson and an RBI-double by U.L. Washington. Those three runs held up, but it took some work. Willie Randolph was thrown out at the plate to end the eighth inning, starting a controversy between owner George Steinbrenner, third-base coach Mike Ferraro, and manager Dick Howser that eventually led to a managerial change despite a 103-win season.

GAME 3 / OCT. 10					
SPLITTORFF, QUISENBERRY(6) VS. JOHN, GOSSAGE(7), UNDERWOOD(8)					**56,588**
KC	000 010 300		4	12	1
NY	000 002 000		2	8	0

New York brought in Rich Gossage to protect a one-run lead with two outs and a runner on second in the top of the seventh. Gossage, who hadn't pitched since the regular season ended, had trouble getting the third out, giving up a single to U.L. Washington and a mammoth three-run homer to George Brett. Dan Quisenberry threw the last $3^2/_3$ innings to finally give Kansas City the pennant.

1981 Division Series
New York Yankees (3) vs. Milwaukee Brewers (2)

A two-month strike by the players wiped out a third of the season, and caused the commissioner to implement a first-round playoff before the League Championship Series. The season was split with crowns for both pre- and post-strike division champs. (Ironically, this left the team with the best overall record in baseball, the Cincinnati Reds, on the sidelines, as the Reds finished a close second in both halves.) The Yankees were under .500 in the second half, but qualified for the postseason by winning the first half under Gene Michael, who was fired in September and replaced by Bob Lemon.

NY (E)

PLAYER, POS	G	AB	R	H	2B	3B	HR	RBI	BB	SO	SB	AVG	OBP	SLG
J.Mumphrey, of	5	21	2	2	0	0	0	0	0	1	1	.095	.095	.095
R.Jackson, of	5	20	4	6	0	0	2	4	1	5	0	.300	.333	.300
W.Randolph, 2b	5	20	0	4	0	0	0	1	1	4	0	.200	.238	.200
D.Winfield, of	5	20	2	7	3	0	0	0	1	5	0	.350	.381	.500
L.Milbourne, ss	5	19	4	6	1	0	0	0	0	1	0	.316	.316	.368
R.Cerone, c	5	18	1	6	2	0	1	5	0	2	0	.333	.333	.444
G.Nettles, 3b	5	17	1	1	0	0	0	1	3	1	0	.059	.200	.059
B.Watson, 1b	5	16	2	7	0	0	0	1	1	1	0	.438	.471	.438
L.Piniella, dh	4	10	1	2	1	0	1	3	0	0	0	.200	.200	.300
O.Gamble, dh	4	9	2	5	1	0	2	3	1	2	0	.556	.600	.667
B.Murcer, ph	2	1	0	0	0	0	0	0	1	0	0	.000	.500	.000
B.Brown, pr	1	0	0	0	0	0	0	0	0	0	0	.000	.000	.000
B.Foote, ph	1	0	0	0	0	0	0	0	0	0	0	.000	.000	.000
D.Revering, 1b	2	0	0	0	0	0	0	0	0	0	0	.000	.000	.000
Totals		171	19	46	8	0	6	18	9	22	1	.269	.306	.316

PITCHER	W	L	ERA	G	GS	SV	IP	H	BB	SO
D.Righetti	2	0	1.00	2	1	0	9.0	8	3	13
R.Guidry	0	0	5.40	2	2	0	8.1	11	3	8

NY (E) (CONT.)										
PITCHER	W	L	ERA	G	GS	SV	IP	H	BB	SO
T.John	0	1	6.43	1	1	0	7.0	8	2	0
R.Gossage	0	0	0.00	3	0	3	6.2	3	2	8
R.Davis	1	0	0.00	3	0	0	6.0	1	2	6
R.Reuschel	0	1	3.00	1	1	0	6.0	4	1	3
R.May	0	0	0.00	1	0	0	2.0	1	0	1
Totals	3	2	2.60	13	5	3	45.0	36	13	39

MIL (E)														
PLAYER, POS	G	AB	R	H	2B	3B	HR	RBI	BB	SO	SB	AVG	OBP	SLG
P.Molitor, of	5	20	2	5	0	0	1	1	2	5	0	.250	.318	.250
R.Yount, ss	5	19	4	6	0	1	0	1	2	2	1	.316	.381	.421
C.Cooper, 1b	5	18	1	4	0	0	0	3	1	3	0	.222	.263	.222
B.Oglivie, of	5	18	0	3	1	0	0	1	0	7	0	.167	.167	.222
T.Simmons, c	5	18	1	4	1	0	1	4	2	2	0	.222	.300	.278
G.Thomas, of-dh	5	18	2	2	0	0	1	1	1	9	0	.111	.158	.111
S.Bando, 3b	5	17	1	5	3	0	0	1	2	3	0	.294	.368	.471
J.Gantner, 2b	4	14	1	2	1	0	0	0	0	2	0	.143	.143	.214
C.Moore, of-dh	4	9	0	2	0	0	0	1	1	2	0	.222	.300	.222
R.Howell, dh	4	5	0	2	0	0	0	0	2	2	0	.400	.571	.400
D.Money, 2b-dh	2	3	0	0	0	0	0	0	0	0	0	.000	.000	.000
E.Romero, 2b	1	2	1	1	0	0	0	0	0	1	0	.500	.500	.500
M.Edwards, of	2	1	0	0	0	0	0	0	0	1	0	.000	.000	.000
T.Dusley, dh	1	0	0	0	0	0	0	0	0	0	0	.000	.000	.000
Totals		162	13	36	6	1	3	13	13	39	1	.222	.280	.272

PITCHER	W	L	ERA	G	GS	SV	IP	H	BB	SO
M.Caldwell	0	1	4.32	2	1	0	8.1	9	0	4
M.Haas	0	2	9.45	2	2	0	6.2	13	1	1
R.Lerch	0	0	1.50	1	1	0	6.0	3	4	3
J.Slaton	0	0	3.00	4	0	0	6.0	6	0	2
P.Vuckovich	1	0	0.00	2	1	0	5.1	2	3	4
R.Fingers	1	0	3.86	3	0	1	4.2	7	1	5
B.McClure	0	0	0.00	3	0	0	3.1	4	0	2
D.Bernard	0	0	0.00	2	0	0	2.1	0	0	0
J.Easterly	0	0	6.75	2	0	0	1.1	2	0	1
Totals	2	3	3.48	21	5	1	44.0	46	9	22

GAME 1 / OCT. 7						
GUIDRY, DAVIS(5), GOSSAGE(8) VS. HAAS, BERNARD(4), MCCLURE(5), SLATON(6), FINGERS(8)						35,064
NY	000	400	001	5	13	1
MIL	011	010	000	3	8	3

In the first postseason game in Wisconsin since the Yankees played the Milwaukee Braves in the 1957 and 1958 World Series, New York overcame an early deficit against the Brewers, who were playing their first postseason game as a franchise. The Yankees took the lead for good in the fourth thanks to a two-run homer by Oscar Gamble and a two-run double by Rick Cerone.

GAME 2 / OCT. 8						
RIGHETTI, DAVIS(7), GOSSAGE(7) VS. CALDWELL, SLATON(9)						26,395
NY	000	100	002	3	7	0
MIL	000	000	000	0	7	0

Dave Righetti, Ron Davis, and Rich Gossage combined on a seven-hit shutout. Righetti fanned 10 in his six innings, and Goose whiffed another four in the final $2^1/_3$ innings. The game was still 1–0 in the ninth when Reggie Jackson hit a two-run homer off Mike Caldwell with first base open.

GAME 3 / OCT. 9						
LERCH, FINGERS(7) VS. JOHN, MAY(8)						56,411
MIL	000	000	320	5	9	0
NY	000	100	200	3	8	2

Home runs by Ted Simmons and Paul Molitor highlighted a five-run rally by the Brewers in the seventh and eighth innings to avoid a sweep.

GAME 4 / OCT. 10						
VUCKOVICH, EASTERLY(6), SLATON(7), MCCLURE(8), FINGERS(9) VS. REUSCHEL, DAVIS(7)						52,077
MIL	000	200	000	2	4	2
NY	000	001	000	1	5	0

Rollie Fingers, the fifth pitcher of the night for the Brewers, came on with two outs and nobody on in the ninth, but he made it interesting. He allowed a walk and a single before striking out Rick Cerone to even the series.

GAME 5 / OCT. 11						
HAAS, CALDWELL(4), BERNARD(4), MCCLURE(6), SLATON(7), EASTERLY(8), VUCKOVICH(8) VS. GUIDRY, RIGHETTI(5), GOSSAGE(8)						47,505
MIL	011	000	100	3	8	0
NY	000	400	12X	7	13	0

Dave Righetti won for the second time in the series, hurling three innings in relief of Ron Guidry. Back-to-back homers from Reggie Jackson and Oscar Gamble highlighted New York's four-run fourth. Seven Milwaukee pitchers couldn't contain the Yankees.

1981 AL Championship Series New York Yankees (3) vs. Oakland A's (0)

New York made quick work of the A's and former manager Billy Martin. The Yankees outscored Oakland, 20–4, and dominated every facet of the game. ALCS MVP Graig Nettles and center fielder Jerry Mumphrey, started every game, each batted .500; shortstop Larry Milbourne hit .462 and scored as many times as Oakland did in the sweep.

NY (E)														
PLAYER, POS	G	AB	R	H	2B	3B	HR	RBI	BB	SO	SB	AVG	OBP	SLG
L.Milbourne, ss	3	13	4	6	0	0	0	1	0	0	0	.462	.462	.462
D.Winfield, of	3	13	2	2	1	0	0	2	2	2	1	.154	.267	.231
J.Mumphrey, of	3	12	2	6	1	0	0	0	3	2	0	.500	.600	.583
G.Nettles, 3b	3	12	2	6	2	0	1	9	1	0	0	.500	.538	.667
W.Randolph, 2b	3	12	2	4	0	0	1	2	0	1	0	.333	.333	.333
B.Watson, 1b	3	12	0	3	0	0	0	1	0	1	0	.250	.250	.250
R.Cerone, c	3	10	1	1	0	0	0	0	0	0	0	.100	.100	.100
O.Gamble, dh-of	3	6	2	1	0	0	0	1	5	3	0	.167	.545	.167
L.Piniella, dh-of	3	5	2	3	0	0	1	3	0	0	0	.600	.600	.600
R.Jackson, of	2	4	1	0	0	0	0	1	1	0	1	.000	.200	.000
B.Murcer, dh	1	3	0	1	0	0	0	0	1	1	0	.333	.500	.333
D.Revering, 1b	2	2	0	1	0	0	0	0	0	0	0	.500	.500	.500
B.Brown, of	3	1	2	1	0	0	0	0	0	0	0	1.000	1.000	1.000
B.Foote, c	2	1	0	1	0	0	0	0	0	0	0	1.000	1.000	1.000
A.Robertson, ss	1	1	0	0	0	0	0	0	0	0	0	.000	.000	.000
A.Rodriguez, 3b	1	0	0	0	0	0	0	0	0	0	0	.000	.000	.000
Totals		107	20	36	4	0	3	20	13	10	2	.336	.418	.374

PITCHER	W	L	ERA	G	GS	SV	IP	H	BB	SO
T.John	1	0	1.50	1	1	0	6.0	6	1	3
D.Righetti	1	0	0.00	1	1	0	6.0	4	2	4
G.Frazier	1	0	0.00	1	0	0	5.2	5	1	5
R.Davis	0	0	0.00	2	0	0	3.1	0	2	4
R.May	0	0	8.10	1	1	0	3.1	6	0	5
R.Gossage	0	0	0.00	2	0	1	2.2	1	0	2
Totals	3	0	1.33	8	3	1	27.0	22	6	23

OAK (W)														
PLAYER, POS	G	AB	R	H	2B	3B	HR	RBI	BB	SO	SB	AVG	OBP	SLG
T.Armas, of	3	12	0	2	0	0	0	0	0	5	0	.167	.167	.167
R.Henderson, of	3	11	0	4	2	1	0	1	1	2	2	.364	.417	.727
D.McKay, 2b	3	11	0	3	0	0	0	1	0	2	0	.273	.273	.273
K.Moore, 1b	3	8	0	2	0	0	0	0	0	1	0	.250	.250	.250
D.Murphy, of	3	8	0	2	1	0	0	1	2	3	0	.250	.400	.375
M.Klutts, 3b	3	7	1	3	0	0	0	0	0	1	0	.429	.429	.429
M.Heath, c-of	3	6	1	2	0	0	0	0	0	1	0	.333	.333	.333
C.Johnson, dh	2	6	0	0	0	0	0	0	2	2	0	.000	.250	.000
W.Gross, 3b	3	5	0	0	0	0	0	0	0	0	0	.000	.000	.000
J.Newman, c	2	5	0	0	0	0	0	0	0	2	0	.000	.000	.000
R.Picciolo, ss	2	5	1	1	0	0	0	0	0	2	0	.200	.200	.200
R.Bosetti, of-dh	2	4	1	1	1	0	0	0	0	1	0	.250	.250	.500
K.Drumright, dh	3	4	0	0	0	0	0	0	1	0	0	.000	.200	.000
J.Spencer, 1b	2	3	0	0	0	0	0	0	0	0	0	.000	.000	.000
F.Stanley, ss	2	3	0	1	0	0	0	1	0	1	0	.333	.333	.333
M.Davis, ph	1	1	0	1	0	0	0	0	0	0	0	1.000	1.000	1.000
Totals		99	4	22	4	1	0	4	6	23	2	.222	.267	.283

PITCHER	W	L	ERA	G	GS	SV	IP	H	BB	SO
M.Keough	0	1	1.08	1	1	0	8.1	7	6	4
M.Norris	0	1	3.68	1	1	0	7.1	6	2	4
S.McCatty	0	1	13.50	1	1	0	3.1	6	2	2
J.Jones	0	0	4.50	1	0	0	2.0	2	1	0
B.Owchinko	0	0	5.40	1	0	0	1.2	3	0	0
T.Underwood	0	0	13.50	2	0	0	1.1	4	2	0
D.Beard	0	0	40.50	1	0	0	0.2	5	0	0
B.Kingman	0	0	81.00	1	0	0	0.1	3	0	0
Totals	0	3	6.84	9	3	0	25.0	36	13	10

GAME 1 / OCT. 13						
NORRIS, UNDERWOOD(8) VS. JOHN, DAVIS(7), GOSSAGE(8)						55,740
OAK	000	010	000	1	6	1
NY	300	000	00X	3	7	1

Graig Nettles' bases-clearing double in the first plated the only runs New York would score, but Tommy John, Ron Davis, and Rich Gossage made them hold up by limiting Oakland to three hits over the final six innings.

GAME 2 / OCT. 14						
MCCATTY, BEARD(4), JONES(5), KINGMAN(7), OWCHINKO(7) VS. MAY, FRAZIER(4)						48,497
OAK	001	200	000	3	11	1
NY	100	701	40X	13	19	0

Graig Nettles and Lou Piniella each smacked three-run homers in a rout that saw five Yankees get multiple hits.

GAME 3 / OCT. 15						
RIGHETTI, DAVIS(7), GOSSAGE(9) VS. KEOUGH, UNDERWOOD(9)						47,302
NY	000	001	003	4	10	0
OAK	000	000	000	0	5	2

Graig Nettles hit a bases-clearing double in the ninth, giving him nine RBIs in the three games. Dave Righetti, Ron Davis, and Rich Gossage limited Oakland to five hits.

1981 World Series
New York Yankees (2) vs. Los Angeles Dodgers (4)

The Dodgers repaid a three-year old favor—not to mention a 2–8 World Series record against the Yankees—by coming back to win four straight contests after dropping the first two. The Yankees had done the exact same thing the last time they'd played in 1978.

LA (NL)

PLAYER, POS	G	AB	R	H	2B	3B	HR	RBI	BB	SO	SB	AVG	OBP	SLG
B.Russell, ss	6	25	1	6	0	0	0	2	0	1	1	.240	.240	.240
D.Baker, of	6	24	3	4	0	0	0	1	1	6	0	.167	.200	.167
S.Garvey, 1b	6	24	3	10	1	0	0	0	2	5	0	.417	.462	.458
D.Lopes, 2b	6	22	6	5	1	0	0	2	4	3	4	.227	.346	.273
P.Guerrero, of	6	21	2	7	1	1	2	7	2	6	0	.333	.391	.476
R.Cey, 3b	6	20	3	7	0	0	1	6	3	3	0	.350	.435	.350
S.Yeager, c	6	14	2	4	1	0	2	4	0	2	0	.286	.286	.357
R.Monday, of	5	13	1	3	1	0	0	0	3	6	0	.231	.375	.308
D.Thomas, of-3b-ss	5	7	2	0	0	0	0	1	1	2	0	.000	.125	.000
K.Landreaux, of	5	6	1	1	1	0	0	0	0	2	1	.167	.167	.333
B.Hooton, p	2	4	1	0	0	0	0	0	1	3	0	.000	.200	.000
M.Scioscia, c	3	4	1	1	0	0	0	0	1	0	0	.250	.400	.250
J.Johnstone, ph	3	3	1	2	0	0	1	3	0	0	0	.667	.667	.667
J.Reuss, p	2	3	0	0	0	0	0	0	1	2	0	.000	.250	.000
F.Valenzuela, p	1	3	0	0	0	0	0	0	1	0	0	.000	.250	.000
S.Howe, p	3	2	0	0	0	0	0	0	0	2	0	.000	.000	.000
R.Smith, ph	2	2	0	1	0	0	0	0	0	1	0	.500	.500	.500
S.Sax, 2b	2	1	0	0	0	0	0	0	0	0	0	.000	.000	.000
Totals		198	27	51	6	1	6	26	20	44	6	.258	.332	.298

PITCHER	W	L	ERA	G	GS	SV	IP	H	BB	SO
J.Reuss	1	1	3.86	2	2	0	11.2	10	3	8
B.Hooton	1	1	1.59	2	2	0	11.1	8	9	3
F.Valenzuela	1	0	4.00	1	1	0	9.0	9	7	6
S.Howe	1	0	3.86	3	0	1	7.0	7	1	4
T.Niedenfuer	0	0	0.00	2	0	0	5.0	3	1	0
D.Goltz	0	0	5.40	2	0	0	3.1	4	1	2
T.Forster	0	0	0.00	2	0	0	2.0	1	3	0
D.Stewart	0	0	0.00	2	0	0	1.2	1	2	1
B.Castillo	0	0	9.00	1	0	0	1.0	0	5	0
B.Welch	0	0	INF	1	1	0	0.0	3	1	0
Totals	4	2	3.29	18	6	1	52.0	46	33	24

NY (AL)

PLAYER, POS	G	AB	R	H	2B	3B	HR	RBI	BB	SO	SB	AVG	OBP	SLG
B.Watson, 1b	6	22	2	7	1	0	2	7	3	0	0	.318	.400	.364
D.Winfield, of	6	22	0	1	0	0	0	1	5	4	1	.045	.222	.045
R.Cerone, c	6	21	2	4	1	0	1	3	4	2	0	.190	.320	.238
L.Milbourne, ss	6	20	2	5	2	0	0	3	4	0	0	.250	.375	.350
W.Randolph, 2b	6	18	5	4	1	1	2	3	9	0	1	.222	.481	.389
L.Piniella, of	6	16	2	7	1	0	0	3	0	1	1	.438	.438	.500
J.Mumphrey, of	5	15	2	3	0	0	0	0	3	2	1	.200	.333	.200
R.Jackson, of	3	12	3	4	1	0	1	1	2	3	0	.333	.429	.417
A.Rodriguez, 3b	4	12	1	5	0	0	0	0	1	2	0	.417	.462	.417
G.Nettles, 3b	3	10	1	4	1	0	0	0	1	1	0	.400	.455	.500
O.Gamble, of	3	6	1	2	0	0	0	1	1	0	0	.333	.429	.333
R.Guidry, p	2	5	0	0	0	0	0	0	0	3	0	.000	.000	.000
B.Murcer, ph	4	3	0	0	0	0	0	0	0	0	0	.000	.000	.000
G.Frazier, p	3	2	0	0	0	0	0	0	0	1	0	.000	.000	.000

NY (AL) (CONT.)

PLAYER, POS	G	AB	R	H	2B	3B	HR	RBI	BB	SO	SB	AVG	OBP	SLG
T.John, p	3	2	0	0	0	0	0	0	0	0	0	.000	.000	.000
R.Reuschel, p	2	2	0	0	0	0	0	0	0	1	0	.000	.000	.000
B.Brown, of	4	1	1	0	0	0	0	0	0	1	0	.000	.000	.000
B.Foote, ph	1	1	0	0	0	0	0	0	0	1	0	.000	.000	.000
R.Gossage, p	3	1	0	0	0	0	0	0	0	1	0	.000	.000	.000
R.May, p	3	1	0	0	0	0	0	0	0	0	0	.000	.000	.000
D.Righetti, p	1	1	0	0	0	0	0	0	0	1	0	.000	.000	.000
A.Robertson, pr	1	0	0	0	0	0	0	0	0	0	0	.000	.000	.000
Totals		193	22	46	8	1	6	22	33	24	4	.238	.350	.290

PITCHER	W	L	ERA	G	GS	SV	IP	H	BB	SO
R.Guidry	1	1	1.93	2	2	0	14.0	8	4	15
T.John	1	0	0.69	3	2	0	13.0	11	0	8
R.May	0	0	2.84	3	0	0	6.1	5	1	5
R.Gossage	0	0	0.00	3	0	2	5.0	2	2	5
G.Frazier	0	3	17.18	3	0	0	3.2	9	3	2
R.Reuschel	0	0	4.91	2	1	0	3.2	7	3	2
R.Davis	0	0	23.14	4	0	0	2.1	4	5	4
D.Righetti	0	0	13.50	1	1	0	2.0	5	2	1
D.LaRoche	0	0	0.00	1	0	0	1.0	0	0	2
Totals	2	4	4.24	22	6	2	51.0	51	20	44

GAME 1 / OCT. 20						
REUSS, CASTILLO(3), GOLTZ(4), NIEDENFUER(5), STEWART(8) VS. GUIDRY, DAVIS(8), GOSSAGE(8)						56,470
LA	000	010	020	3	5	0
NY	301	100	00X	5	6	0

Bob Watson's three-run homer in the first put the Yankees ahead early, and Ron Guidry held the Dodgers to one run and four hits through seven. Rich Gossage came on in the eighth to preserve the win, but not before allowing two inherited runners to score.

GAME 2 / OCT. 21						
HOOTON, FORSTER(7), HOWE(8), STEWART(8) VS. JOHN, GOSSAGE(8)						56,505
LA	000	000	000	0	4	2
NY	000	010	02X	3	6	1

Tommy John and Rich Gossage were brilliant on the mound, combining for a four-hit shutout. An unearned run in the fifth was the game's only run until the Yankees sealed it in the bottom of the eighth on a single by Bob Watson and a sacrifice fly by Willie Randolph.

GAME 3 / OCT. 23						
RIGHETTI, FRAZIER(3), MAY(5), DAVIS(8) VS. VALENZUELA						56,236
NY	022	000	000	4	9	0
LA	300	020	00X	5	11	1

The Dodgers began their comeback with a 145-pitch complete game from rookie Fernando Valenzuela at Dodger Stadium. Valenzuela wasn't dominant, allowing nine hits and seven walks, but he was much better after letting New York take the lead in the third. After that he limited the Yankees to just three hits and two unintentional walks over the final six innings. The Dodgers took the lead in the fifth on a double-play ball.

GAME 4 / OCT. 24						
REUSCHEL, MAY(4), DAVIS(5), FRAZIER(5), JOHN(7) VS. WELCH, GOLTZ(1), FORSTER(4), NIEDENFUER(5), HOWE(7)						56,242
NY	211	002	010	7	13	1
LA	002	013	20X	8	14	2

Los Angeles outlasted the Yankees in a sloppy game. Both starting pitchers had hit the showers by the fourth inning, and 8 of the 10 combined hurlers allowed runs to score. Jay Johnstone's pinch-hit two-run blast in the sixth started the comeback. The Dodgers tied the score with an unearned run later in the inning. A sacrifice fly and a high chopper gave the Dodgers the lead in the next inning. An error kept the Yankees alive in the ninth, but Willie Randolph's long fly was tracked down to end the game.

GAME 5 / OCT. 25

GUIDRY, GOSSAGE(8) VS. REUSS							56,115
NY	010	000	000		1	5	0
LA	000	000	20X		2	4	3

Ron Guidry was cruising through six with a 1–0 lead, having allowed only two hits and a pair of walks. The Dodgers got to him in the seventh with back-to-back solo home runs by Pedro Guerrero and Steve Yeager. Jerry Reuss made it stand.

GAME 6 / OCT. 28

HOOTON, HOWE(6) VS. JOHN, FRAZIER(5), DAVIS(6), REUSCHEL(6), MAY(7), LAROCHE(9)							56,513
LA	000	134	010		9	13	1
NY	001	001	000		2	7	2

Los Angeles exploded for eight runs in the middle three innings, with Pedro Guerrero's two-run triple in the fifth the big blow. George Frazier took his third loss of the Series, entering the game after manager Bob Lemon batted for Tommy John in the fourth with the game tied, 1–1. Dodger Steve Howe came into the game with the bases loaded and one out in the sixth and got out of that mess with only one run scoring. He threw three shutout innings to seal L.A.'s first world championship since 1965. It would be the Yankees' last World Series appearance until 1996.

1995 AL Division Series
New York Yankees (2) vs. Seattle Mariners (3)

The Yankees, who finished second in the AL East to Boston, returned to the postseason for the first time in 14 years because they qualified through baseball's new Wild Card format.

SEA (W)

PLAYER, POS	G	AB	R	H	2B	3B	HR	RBI	BB	SO	SB	AVG	OBP	SLG
J.Buhner, of	5	24	2	11	1	0	1	3	2	4	0	.458	.500	.500
V.Coleman, of	5	23	6	5	0	1	1	1	2	4	1	.217	.280	.304
K.Griffey, of	5	23	9	9	0	0	5	7	2	4	1	.391	.444	.391
T.Martinez, 1b	5	22	4	9	1	0	1	5	3	4	0	.409	.480	.455
E.Martinez, dh	5	21	6	12	3	0	2	10	6	2	0	.571	.667	.714
L.Sojo, ss	5	20	0	5	0	0	0	3	0	3	0	.250	.250	.250
J.Cora, 2b	5	19	7	6	1	0	1	1	3	0	1	.316	.409	.368
M.Blowers, 3b-1b	5	18	0	3	0	0	0	1	3	7	0	.167	.286	.167
D.Wilson, c	5	17	0	2	0	0	0	1	2	6	0	.118	.211	.118
D.Strange, 3b	2	4	0	0	0	0	0	1	1	1	0	.000	.200	.000
A.Diaz, of	2	3	0	1	0	0	0	0	1	1	0	.333	.500	.333
C.Widger, c	2	3	0	0	0	0	0	0	0	3	0	.000	.000	.000
F.Fermin, ss-2b	3	1	0	0	0	0	0	0	0	1	0	.000	.000	.000
W.Newson, ph	1	1	0	0	0	0	0	0	0	1	0	.000	.000	.000
A.Rodriguez, ss	1	1	1	0	0	0	0	0	0	0	0	.000	.000	.000
Totals		200	35	63	6	1	11	33	25	41	3	.315	.395	.355

PITCHER	W	L	ERA	G	GS	SV	IP	H	BB	SO
A.Benes	0	0	5.40	2	2	0	11.2	10	9	8
R.Johnson	2	0	2.70	2	1	0	10.0	5	6	16
C.Bosio	0	0	10.57	2	2	0	7.2	10	4	2
N.Charlton	1	0	2.45	4	0	1	7.1	4	3	9
J.Nelson	0	1	3.18	3	0	0	5.2	7	3	7
T.Belcher	0	1	6.23	2	0	0	4.1	4	5	0
B.Risley	0	0	6.00	4	0	1	3.0	2	0	1
B.Wells	0	0	9.00	1	0	0	1.0	2	1	0
B.Ayala	0	0	54.00	2	0	0	0.2	6	1	0
Totals	3	2	5.79	22	5	2	51.1	50	32	43

NY (E)

PLAYER, POS	G	AB	R	H	2B	3B	HR	RBI	BB	SO	SB	AVG	OBP	SLG
D.Mattingly, 1b	5	24	3	10	4	0	1	6	1	5	0	.417	.440	.583
R.Sierra, dh	5	23	2	4	2	0	2	5	2	7	0	.174	.240	.261
T.Fernandez, ss	5	21	0	5	2	0	0	0	2	2	0	.238	.304	.333
B.Williams, of	5	21	8	9	2	0	2	5	7	3	1	.429	.571	.524
W.Boggs, 3b	4	19	4	5	2	0	1	3	3	5	0	.263	.364	.368
P.O'Neill, of	5	18	5	6	0	0	3	6	5	5	0	.333	.478	.333
R.Velarde, 2b-3b-of	5	17	3	3	0	0	0	1	6	4	0	.176	.391	.176
M.Stanley, c	4	16	2	5	0	0	1	3	2	1	0	.313	.389	.313
D.James, of	4	12	0	1	0	0	0	0	1	1	0	.083	.154	.083
J.Leyritz, c	2	7	1	1	0	0	1	2	0	1	0	.143	.143	.143
R.Davis, 3b	2	5	0	1	0	0	0	0	0	2	0	.200	.200	.200
G.Williams, of	5	5	1	0	0	0	0	0	2	3	0	.000	.286	.000
P.Kelly, 2b	5	3	3	0	0	0	0	1	1	3	0	.000	.250	.000
D.Strawberry, ph	2	2	0	0	0	0	0	0	0	1	0	.000	.000	.000
J.Posada, pr	1	0	1	0	0	0	0	0	0	0	0	.000	.000	.000
Totals		193	33	50	12	0	11	32	32	43	1	.259	.370	.321

NY (E) (CONT.)

PITCHER	W	L	ERA	G	GS	SV	IP	H	BB	SO
D.Cone	1	0	4.60	2	2	0	15.2	15	9	14
J.McDowell	0	2	9.00	2	1	0	7.0	8	4	6
A.Pettitte	0	0	5.14	1	1	0	7.0	9	3	0
M.Rivera	1	0	0.00	3	0	0	5.1	3	1	8
S.Kamieniecki	0	0	7.20	1	1	0	5.0	9	4	4
J.Wetteland	0	1	14.54	3	0	0	4.1	8	2	5
B.Wickman	0	0	0.00	3	0	0	3.0	5	0	3
S.Hitchcock	0	0	5.40	2	0	0	1.2	2	2	1
S.Howe	0	0	18.00	2	0	0	1.0	4	0	0
Totals	2	3	5.94	19	5	0	50.0	63	25	41

GAME 1 / OCT. 3

BOSIO, NELSON(6), AYALA(7), RISLEY(7), WELLS(8) VS. CONE, WETTELAND(9)							57,178
SEA	000	101	202		6	9	0
NY	002	002	41X		9	13	0

Ken Griffey Jr. hit two home runs for Seattle. However, a four-run fourth, capped by a two-run homer from Ruben Sierra, gave the Yankees the lead for good.

GAME 2 / OCT. 4

BENES, RISLEY(6), CHARLTON(7), NELSON(11), BELCHER(12) VS. PETTITTE, WICKMAN(8), WETTELAND(9), RIVERA(12)									57,126
SEA	001	001	200	001	000		5	16	2
NY	000	012	100	001	002		7	11	0

The Yankees needed a two-out RBI from Sierra in the 12th just to stay alive. They won it in the 15th, 5 hours and 12 minutes after the first pitch, on a two-run homer by Jim Leyritz.

GAME 3 / OCT. 6

MCDOWELL, HOWE(6), WICKMAN(6), HITCHCOCK(7), RIVERA(7) VS. JOHNSON, RISLEY(8), CHARLTON(8)							57,944
NY	000	100	120		4	6	2
SEA	000	024	10X		7	7	0

Two long balls from Bernie Williams weren't enough, as the Mariners rocked Jack McDowell for five runs in 5 1/3 innings.

GAME 4 / OCT. 7

KAMIENIECKI, HITCHCOCK(6), WICKMAN(7), WETTELAND(8), HOWE(8) VS. BOSIO, NELSON(3), BELCHER(7), CHARLTON(8), AYALA(9), RISLEY(9)							57,180
NY	302	000	012		8	14	1
SEA	004	011	05X		11	16	0

Edgar Martinez drove in seven with a three-run homer in the third and a grand slam in the eighth as Seattle won a slugfest.

GAME 5 / OCT. 8

CONE, RIVERA(8), MCDOWELL(9) VS. BENES, CHARLTON(7), JOHNSON(9)								57,411
NY	000	202	000	01		5	6	0
SEA	001	100	020	02		6	15	0

Randy Velarde's one-out single in the 11th gave the Yankees a brief lead, though the two runners they left on base that inning came back to cost them. Three straight hits off McDowell, including the game-winner on a two-run double by Edgar Martinez, sent the Mariners to the ALCS for the first time in franchise history.

1996 AL Division Series
New York Yankees (3) vs. Texas Rangers (1)

The Yankees weren't a great team in the regular season, winning only 92 games, but they were good enough to claim their first AL East title since 1980 (not counting winning the first half of the strike-shortened 1981 season).

NY (E)

PLAYER, POS	G	AB	R	H	2B	3B	HR	RBI	BB	SO	SB	AVG	OBP	SLG
D.Jeter, ss	4	17	2	7	1	0	0	1	0	2	0	.412	.412	.471
M.Duncan, 2b	4	16	0	5	0	0	0	3	0	4	0	.313	.313	.313
T.Raines, of	4	16	3	4	0	0	0	0	3	1	0	.250	.368	.250

NY (E) (CONT.)

PLAYER, POS	G	AB	R	H	2B	3B	HR	RBI	BB	SO	SB	AVG	OBP	SLG
T.Martinez, 1b	4	15	3	4	2	0	0	0	3	1	0	.267	.389	.400
P.O'Neill, of	4	15	0	2	0	0	0	0	0	2	0	.133	.133	.133
B.Williams, of	4	15	5	7	0	0	3	5	2	1	1	.467	.529	.467
W.Boggs, 3b	3	12	0	1	1	0	0	0	0	2	0	.083	.083	.167
C.Fielder, dh	3	11	2	4	0	0	1	4	1	2	0	.364	.417	.364
J.Girardi, c	4	9	1	2	0	0	0	0	4	1	0	.222	.462	.222
C.Hayes, 3b	3	5	0	1	0	0	0	1	0	0	0	.200	.200	.200
D.Strawberry, dh	2	5	0	0	0	0	0	0	0	2	0	.000	.000	.000
J.Leyritz, c	2	3	0	0	0	0	0	1	0	1	0	.000	.000	.000
R.Rivera, of	2	1	0	0	0	0	0	0	0	1	0	.000	.000	.000
A.Fox, dh	2	0	0	0	0	0	0	0	0	0	0	.000	.000	.000
L.Sojo, 2b	2	0	0	0	0	0	0	0	0	0	0	.000	.000	.000
Totals		140	16	37	4	0	4	15	13	20	1	.264	.335	.293

PITCHER	W	L	ERA	G	GS	SV	IP	H	BB	SO
A.Pettitte	0	0	5.68	1	1	0	6.1	4	6	3
D.Cone	0	1	9.00	1	1	0	6.0	8	2	8
J.Key	0	0	3.60	1	1	0	5.0	5	1	3
D.Weathers	1	0	0.00	2	0	0	5.0	1	0	5
M.Rivera	0	0	0.00	2	0	0	4.2	0	1	1
J.Wetteland	0	0	0.00	3	0	2	4.0	2	4	4
J.Nelson	1	0	0.00	2	0	0	3.2	2	2	5
K.Rogers	0	0	9.00	2	1	0	2.0	5	2	1
B.Boehringer	1	0	6.75	2	0	0	1.1	3	2	0
G.Lloyd	0	0	0.00	2	0	0	1.0	1	0	0
Totals	3	1	3.46	18	4	2	39.0	31	20	30

TEX (W)

PLAYER, POS	G	AB	R	H	2B	3B	HR	RBI	BB	SO	SB	AVG	OBP	SLG
D.Hamilton, of	4	19	0	3	0	0	0	0	0	2	0	.158	.158	.158
D.Palmer, 3b	4	19	3	4	1	0	1	2	0	5	0	.211	.211	.263
W.Clark, 1b	4	16	1	2	0	0	0	0	3	2	0	.125	.263	.125
J.Gonzalez, of	4	16	5	7	0	0	5	9	3	2	0	.438	.526	.438
R.Greer, of	4	16	2	2	0	0	0	0	3	3	0	.125	.263	.125
I.Rodriguez, c	4	16	1	6	1	0	0	2	2	3	0	.375	.444	.438
M.McLemore, 2b	4	15	1	2	0	0	0	2	0	4	0	.133	.133	.133
K.Elster, ss	4	12	2	4	2	0	0	0	3	2	1	.333	.467	.500
M.Tettleton, dh	4	12	1	1	0	0	0	1	5	7	0	.083	.353	.083
W.Newson, ph	2	1	0	0	0	0	0	0	1	0	0	.000	.500	.000
D.Buford, pr	2	0	0	0	0	0	0	0	0	0	0	.000	.000	.000
R.Gonzales, ss	1	0	0	0	0	0	0	0	0	0	0	.000	.000	.000
Totals		142	16	31	4	0	6	16	20	30	1	.218	.315	.246

PITCHER	W	L	ERA	G	GS	SV	IP	H	BB	SO
J.Burkett	1	0	2.00	1	1	0	9.0	10	1	7
D.Oliver	0	1	3.38	1	1	0	8.0	6	2	3
K.Hill	0	0	4.50	1	1	0	6.0	5	3	1
M.Stanton	0	1	2.70	3	0	0	3.1	2	3	3
B.Witt	0	0	8.10	1	1	0	3.1	4	2	3
J.Russell	0	0	3.00	2	0	0	3.0	3	0	1
R.Pavlik	0	1	6.75	1	0	0	2.2	4	0	1
D.Cook	0	0	0.00	2	0	0	1.1	0	1	0
M.Henneman	0	0	0.00	3	0	0	1.0	1	1	1
D.Patterson	0	0	0.00	1	0	0	0.1	1	0	0
E.Vosberg	0	0	INF	1	0	0	0.0	1	0	0
Totals	1	3	3.55	17	4	0	38.0	37	13	20

GAME 1 / OCT. 1

BURKETT VS. CONE, LLOYD(7), WEATHERS(8) — **57,205**

				R	H	E
TEX	000	501	000	6	8	0
NY	100	100	000	2	19	0

A three-run homer from Juan Gonzalez in the fourth inning gave Texas an insurmountable lead. John Burkett went the distance for Texas, coughing up 10 hits but only two runs.

GAME 2 / OCT. 2

HILL, COOK(7), RUSSELL(8), STANTON(10), HENNEMAN(12) VS. PETTITTE, RIVERA(7), WETTELAND(10), LLOYD(12), NELSON(12), ROGERS(12), BOEHRINGER(12) — **57,156**

					R	H	E
TEX	013	000	000	000	4	8	1
NY	010	100	110	001	5	8	0

The Yankees never led until they plated the winning run in the bottom of the 12th when Dean Palmer's throwing error let Derek Jeter scamper home.

GAME 3 / OCT. 4

KEY, NELSON(6), WETTELAND(9) VS. OLIVER, HENNEMAN(9), STANTON(9) — **50,860**

				R	H	E
NY	100	000	002	3	7	1
TEX	000	110	000	2	6	1

New York won with another late-inning rally, scoring two in the ninth. John Wetteland earned the save by striking out Darryl Hamilton with two outs and the tying run on third.

GAME 4 / OCT. 5

ROGERS, BOEHRINGER(3), WEATHERS(4), RIVERA(7), WETTELAND(9) VS. WITT, PATTERSON(4), COOK(4), PAVLIK(5), VOSBERG(7), RUSSELL(7), STANTON(8), HENNEMAN(9) — **50,066**

				R	H	E
NY	000	310	101	6	12	1
TEX	022	000	000	4	9	0

Seven Texas relievers couldn't hold a 4–2 lead. Bernie Williams tied it in the fifth with a solo homer, then scored what would be the winning run in the seventh on a two-out single by Cecil Fielder.

1996 AL Championship Series
New York Yankees (4) vs. Baltimore Orioles (1)

Though the Yankees got a gift victory in the first game, thanks to the overeager hands of 12-year-old Jeffrey Maier, they won three more without controversy to claim their first pennant in 15 years.

NY (E)

PLAYER, POS	G	AB	R	H	2B	3B	HR	RBI	BB	SO	SB	AVG	OBP	SLG
D.Jeter, ss	5	24	5	10	2	0	1	1	0	5	2	.417	.417	.500
T.Martinez, 1b	5	22	3	4	1	0	0	0	0	2	0	.182	.182	.227
B.Williams, of	5	19	6	9	3	0	2	6	5	4	1	.474	.583	.632
C.Fielder, dh	5	18	3	3	0	0	2	8	4	5	0	.167	.318	.167
W.Boggs, 3b	3	15	1	2	0	0	0	0	1	3	0	.133	.188	.133
M.Duncan, 2b	4	15	0	3	2	0	0	0	0	3	0	.200	.200	.333
T.Raines, of	5	15	2	4	1	0	0	0	1	1	0	.267	.313	.333
J.Girardi, c	4	12	1	3	0	1	0	0	1	3	0	.250	.308	.417
D.Strawberry, of	4	12	4	5	0	0	3	5	2	2	0	.417	.500	.417
P.O'Neill, of	4	11	1	3	0	0	1	2	3	2	0	.273	.429	.273
J.Leyritz, c-of	3	8	1	2	0	0	1	2	1	4	0	.250	.333	.250
C.Hayes, 3b-dh	4	7	0	1	0	0	0	0	2	2	0	.143	.333	.143
L.Sojo, 2b	3	5	0	1	0	0	0	0	0	1	0	.200	.200	.200
M.Aldrete, ph	1	0	0	0	0	0	0	0	0	0	0	.000	.000	.000
A.Fox, dh	2	0	0	0	0	0	0	0	0	0	0	.000	.000	.000
Totals		183	27	50	9	1	10	24	20	37	3	.273	.351	.333

PITCHER	W	L	ERA	G	GS	SV	IP	H	BB	SO
A.Pettitte	1	0	3.60	2	2	0	15.0	10	5	7
J.Key	1	0	2.25	1	1	0	8.0	3	1	5
D.Cone	0	0	3.00	1	1	0	6.0	5	5	5
M.Rivera	1	0	0.00	2	0	0	4.0	6	1	5
J.Wetteland	0	0	4.50	4	0	1	4.0	2	1	5
K.Rogers	0	0	12.00	1	1	0	3.0	5	2	3
D.Weathers	1	0	0.00	2	0	0	3.0	3	0	0
J.Nelson	0	1	11.57	2	0	0	2.1	5	0	2
G.Lloyd	0	0	0.00	2	0	0	1.2	0	0	1
Totals	4	1	3.64	17	5	1	47.0	39	15	33

BAL (E)

PLAYER, POS	G	AB	R	H	2B	3B	HR	RBI	BB	SO	SB	AVG	OBP	SLG
R.Alomar, 2b	5	23	2	5	2	0	0	1	0	4	0	.217	.217	.304
T.Zeile, 3b	5	22	3	8	0	0	3	5	2	1	0	.364	.417	.364
B.Anderson, of	5	21	5	4	1	0	1	1	3	5	0	.190	.292	.238
B.Bonilla, of	5	20	1	1	0	0	1	2	1	4	0	.050	.095	.050
C.Ripken, ss	5	20	1	5	1	0	0	0	1	4	0	.250	.286	.300
R.Palmeiro, 1b	5	17	4	4	0	0	2	4	4	4	0	.235	.381	.235
E.Murray, dh	5	15	1	4	0	0	1	2	2	2	0	.267	.353	.267
B.Surhoff, of	5	15	0	4	0	0	0	2	1	2	0	.267	.313	.267
C.Hoiles, c	4	12	1	2	0	0	1	2	1	3	0	.167	.231	.167
M.Parent, c	2	6	0	1	0	0	0	0	0	2	0	.167	.167	.167
M.Devereaux, of	3	2	0	0	0	0	0	0	0	1	0	.000	.000	.000
P.Incaviglia, dh	1	2	1	1	0	0	0	0	0	0	0	.500	.500	.500
T.Tarasco, of	2	1	0	0	0	0	0	0	0	1	0	.000	.000	.000
Totals		176	19	39	4	0	9	19	15	33	0	.222	.283	.244

PITCHER	W	L	ERA	G	GS	SV	IP	H	BB	SO
S.Erickson	0	1	2.38	2	2	0	11.1	14	4	8
M.Mussina	0	1	5.87	1	1	0	7.2	8	2	6
D.Wells	1	0	4.05	1	1	0	6.2	8	3	6
R.Coppinger	0	1	8.44	1	1	0	5.1	6	1	3
R.Myers	0	1	2.25	3	0	0	4.0	4	3	2
A.Benitez	0	0	7.71	3	0	1	2.1	3	3	2
T.Mathews	0	0	0.00	3	0	0	2.1	0	2	3
A.Mills	0	0	3.86	3	0	0	2.1	3	1	3
J.Orosco	0	0	4.50	4	0	0	2.0	2	1	2
A.Lee Rhodes	0	0	0.00	3	0	0	2.0	2	0	2
Totals	1	4	4.11	24	5	1	46.0	50	20	37

GAME 1 / OCT. 9

ERICKSON, OROSCO(7), BENITEZ(7), RHODES(8), MATHEWS(9), MYERS(9) VS. PETTITTE, NELSON(8), WETTELAND(9), RIVERA(10) — **56,495**

					R	H	E
BAL	011	101	000	00	4	11	1
NY	110	000	110	01	5	11	0

Right field umpire Rich Garcia admitted he was wrong to call Derek Jeter's fly ball at the wall in the eighth a home run rather than fan interference. Instead of an out, the controversial hit tied the game, allowing the Yanks to win it in the bottom of the 11th on Bernie Williams leadoff homer.

GAME 2 / OCT. 10

WELLS, MILLS(7), OROSCO(7), MYERS(9), BENITEZ(9) VS. CONE, NELSON(7), LLOYD(8), WEATHERS(9) — **56,432**

				R	H	E
BAL	002	000	210	5	10	0
NY	200	000	100	3	11	1

Rafael Palmeiro clubbed a two-run homer in the seventh to break a 2–2 tie and allow the Orioles to even the series.

GAME 3 / OCT. 11

KEY, WETTELAND(9) VS. MUSSINA, OROSCO(8), MATHEWS(9) — **48,635**

				R	H	E
NY	000	100	040	5	8	0
BAL	200	000	000	2	3	2

Mike Mussina had allowed just four hits and a run after retiring the first two in the eighth, but the veteran righty couldn't finish the inning. New York got two doubles, a single, and a two-run homer by Cecil Fielder to score four times and forge ahead in the LCS.

GAME 4 / OCT. 12

ROGERS, WEATHERS(4), LLOYD(6), RIVERA(7), WETTELAND(9) VS. COPPINGER, RHODES(6), MILLS(7), OROSCO(8), BENITEZ(8), MATHEWS(9) — **48,974**

				R	H	E
NY	210	200	030	8	9	0
BAL	101	200	000	4	11	0

Darryl Strawberry and Williams combined for five hits, five runs, and five RBIs as the Yankees took a commanding lead in the series. Williams homered once and Strawberry went deep twice.

GAME 5 / OCT. 13

PETTITTE, WETTELAND(9) VS. ERICKSON, RHODES(6), MILLS(7), MYERS(8) — **48,718**

				R	H	E
NY	006	000	000	6	11	0
BAL	000	001	012	4	4	1

New York nearly blew a 6–0 lead. Bobby Bonilla homered with two outs and a runner on to draw the Orioles to within two, but John Wetteland got Cal Ripken Jr. to ground out short to end the game.

1996 World Series
New York Yankees (4) vs. Atlanta Braves (2)

Yankees skipper Joe Torre finally made it to the Fall Classic after 4,272 games as a player and manager. His calm demeanor helped New York rally for four straight victories after getting blown out in the first two games.

NY (AL)

PLAYER, POS	G	AB	R	H	2B	3B	HR	RBI	BB	SO	SB	AVG	OBP	SLG
B.Williams, of	6	24	3	4	0	0	1	4	3	6	1	.167	.259	.167
C.Fielder, 1b-dh	6	23	1	9	2	0	0	2	2	2	0	.391	.440	.478
D.Jeter, ss	6	20	5	5	0	0	0	1	4	6	1	.250	.375	.250
M.Duncan, 2b	6	19	1	1	0	0	0	0	0	4	1	.053	.053	.053
C.Hayes, 3b-1b	5	16	2	3	0	0	0	1	1	5	0	.188	.235	.188
D.Strawberry, of	5	16	0	3	0	0	0	1	4	6	0	.188	.350	.188
T.Raines, of	4	14	2	3	0	0	0	0	2	1	0	.214	.313	.214
P.O'Neill, of	5	12	1	2	2	0	0	0	3	2	0	.167	.333	.333
W.Boggs, 3b	4	11	0	3	1	0	0	2	1	0	0	.273	.333	.364
T.Martinez, 1b	6	11	0	1	0	0	0	0	2	5	0	.091	.231	.091
J.Girardi, c	4	10	1	2	0	1	0	1	1	2	0	.200	.273	.400
J.Leyritz, c	4	8	1	3	0	0	1	3	3	2	1	.375	.545	.375
L.Sojo, 2b	5	5	0	3	1	0	0	1	0	0	0	.600	.600	.800
A.Pettitte, p	2	4	0	0	0	0	0	0	0	1	0	.000	.000	.000
D.Cone, p	1	2	0	0	0	0	0	0	0	1	0	.000	.000	.000
M.Aldrete, of	2	1	0	0	0	0	0	0	0	0	0	.000	.000	.000
G.Lloyd, p	4	1	0	0	0	0	0	0	0	0	0	.000	.000	.000
M.Rivera, p	4	1	0	0	0	0	0	0	0	0	0	.000	.000	.000
K.Rogers, p	1	1	0	1	0	0	0	0	0	0	0	1.000	1.000	1.000
A.Fox, 2b-3b	4	0	1	0	0	0	0	0	0	0	0	.000	.000	.000
Totals		199	18	43	6	1	2	16	26	43	4	.216	.310	.256

NY (AL) (CONT.)

PITCHER	W	L	ERA	G	GS	SV	IP	H	BB	SO
J.Key	1	1	3.97	2	2	0	11.1	15	5	1
A.Pettitte	1	1	5.91	2	2	0	10.2	11	4	5
D.Cone	1	0	1.50	1	1	0	6.0	4	4	3
M.Rivera	0	0	1.59	4	0	0	5.2	4	3	4
B.Boehringer	0	0	5.40	2	0	0	5.0	5	0	5
J.Nelson	0	0	0.00	3	0	0	4.1	1	1	5
J.Wetteland	0	0	2.00	5	0	4	4.1	4	1	6
D.Weathers	0	0	3.00	3	0	0	3.0	2	3	3
G.Lloyd	1	0	0.00	4	0	0	2.2	0	0	4
K.Rogers	0	0	22.50	1	1	0	2.0	5	2	0
Totals	4	2	3.93	27	6	4	55.0	51	23	36

ATL (NL)

PLAYER, POS	G	AB	R	H	2B	3B	HR	RBI	BB	SO	SB	AVG	OBP	SLG
M.Grissom, of	6	27	4	12	2	1	0	5	1	2	1	.444	.464	.593
M.Lemke, 2b	6	26	2	6	1	0	0	2	0	3	0	.231	.231	.269
C.Jones, 3b-ss	6	21	3	6	3	0	0	3	4	2	1	.286	.400	.429
J.Lopez, c	6	21	3	4	0	0	0	1	3	4	0	.190	.292	.190
A.Jones, of	6	20	4	8	1	0	2	6	3	6	1	.400	.478	.450
F.McGriff, 1b	6	20	4	6	0	0	2	6	5	4	0	.300	.440	.300
J.Blauser, ss	6	18	2	3	1	0	0	1	1	4	0	.167	.211	.222
J.Dye, of	5	17	0	2	0	0	0	1	1	1	0	.118	.167	.118
R.Klesko, of-1b-dh	5	10	2	1	0	0	0	1	2	4	0	.100	.250	.100
T.Pendleton, dh-3b	4	9	1	2	1	0	0	0	1	1	0	.222	.300	.333
L.Polonia, ph	6	5	0	0	0	0	0	0	1	3	0	.000	.167	.000
J.Smoltz, p	2	2	0	1	0	0	0	0	0	0	0	.500	.500	.500
M.Bielecki, p	2	1	0	0	0	0	0	0	0	1	0	.000	.000	.000
T.Glavine, p	1	1	1	0	0	0	0	0	1	0	0	.000	.500	.000
M.Mordecai, ph	1	1	0	0	0	0	0	0	0	0	0	.000	.000	.000
D.Neagle, p	2	1	0	0	0	0	0	0	0	1	0	.000	.000	.000
E.Perez, c	2	1	0	0	0	0	0	0	0	0	0	.000	.000	.000
R.Belliard, ss	4	0	0	0	0	0	0	0	0	0	0	.000	.000	.000
Totals		201	26	51	9	1	4	26	23	36	3	.254	.333	.308

PITCHER	W	L	ERA	G	GS	SV	IP	H	BB	SO
G.Maddux	1	1	1.72	2	2	0	15.2	14	1	5
J.Smoltz	1	1	0.64	2	2	0	14.0	6	8	14
T.Glavine	0	1	1.29	1	1	0	7.0	4	3	8
D.Neagle	0	0	3.00	2	1	0	6.0	5	4	3
M.Wohlers	0	0	6.23	4	0	0	4.1	7	2	4
M.Bielecki	0	0	0.00	2	0	0	3.0	0	3	6
B.Clontz	0	0	0.00	3	0	0	1.2	1	1	2
G.McMichael	0	0	27.00	2	0	0	1.0	5	0	1
S.Avery	0	1	13.50	1	0	0	0.2	1	3	0
T.Wade	0	0	0.00	2	0	0	0.2	0	1	0
Totals	2	4	2.33	21	6	0	54.0	43	26	43

GAME 1 / OCT. 20

SMOLTZ, MCMICHAEL(7), NEAGLE(8), WADE(9), CLONTZ(9) VS. PETTITTE, BOEHRINGER(3), WEATHERS(6), NELSON(8), WETTELAND(9) — **56,365**

				R	H	E
ATL	026	013	000	12	13	0
NY	000	010	000	1	4	1

Atlanta's John Smoltz took a no-hitter into the fifth as the Braves' bats exploded for 11 hits and 12 runs in the first six innings. Andruw Jones, a callow 19 years old, belted home runs the second and third innings, making him only the second player in history to go deep in his first two World Series at bats.

GAME 2 / OCT. 21

MADDUX, WOHLERS(9) VS. KEY, LLOYD(7), NELSON(7), RIVERA(9) — **56,340**

				R	H	E
ATL	101	011	000	4	10	0
NY	000	000	000	0	7	1

Greg Maddux and Mark Wohlers combined on a seven-hit shutout. Fred McGriff drove in Atlanta's first three runs with two singles and a sac fly.

GAME 3 / OCT. 22

CONE, RIVERA(7), LLOYD(8), WETTELAND(9) VS. GLAVINE, MCMICHAEL(8), CLONTZ(8), BIELECKI(9) — **51,843**

				R	H	E
NY	100	100	030	5	8	1
ATL	000	001	010	2	6	1

Though the Yankees led the whole way, it took a two-run shot by Bernie Williams in the eighth to give New York more than a one-run cushion. Graeme Lloyd and John Wetteland combined to get the final five outs.

GAME 4 / OCT. 23

ROGERS, BOEHRINGER(3), WEATHERS(5), NELSON(6), RIVERA(8), LLOYD(9), WETTELAND(10) VS. NEAGLE, WADE(6), BIELECKI(6), WOHLERS(8), AVERY(10), CLONTZ(10) — **51,881**

					R	H	E
NY	000	003	030	2	8	12	0
ATL	041	010	000	0	6	9	2

The Yankees appeared dead after dropping six runs behind while managing just two hits through five, but shoddy defense did the Braves in. Without a couple of errors and mental mistakes, Atlanta would have been up three games to one. Nonetheless, the Yankees won the game in the 10th on a bases-loaded walk and an error when reliever Brad Clontz failed to cover first on a grounder.

GAME 5 / OCT. 24

PETTITTE, WETTELAND(9) VS. SMOLTZ, WOHLERS(9) — 51,881

				R	H	E
NY	000	100	000	1	4	1
ATL	000	000	000	0	5	1

Starters Andy Pettitte and Smoltz were equally brilliant. The only difference was the run New York scored in the fifth thanks to more bad defense by the Braves. Charlie Hayes began the inning by taking second on an error by Marquis Grissom, who was distracted when right fielder Jermaine Dye cut in front of him as he was trying to make the play. Hayes scored the game's only run one out later on a double by Cecil Fielder.

GAME 6 / OCT. 26

MADDUX, WOHLERS(8) VS. KEY, WEATHERS(6), LLOYD(6), RIVERA(7), WETTELAND(9) — 56,375

				R	H	E
ATL	000	100	001	2	8	0
NY	003	000	00X	3	8	1

A three-run third, capped by a two-out RBI single by Williams, proved to be enough to end New York's 18-year championship drought. Closer Wetteland made it interesting by giving up three singles and a run in the bottom of the ninth before getting Mark Lemke to pop up with the tying run on second.

1997 AL Division Series
New York Yankees (2) vs. Cleveland Indians (3)

The Yankees had the second-best record in the AL, copping the Wild Card berth for the second time in three years after finishing two games behind Baltimore in the AL East.

CLE (C)

PLAYER, POS	G	AB	R	H	2B	3B	HR	RBI	BB	SO	SB	AVG	OBP	SLG
M.Ramirez, of	5	21	2	3	1	0	0	3	0	3	0	.143	.143	.190
S.Alomar, c	5	19	4	6	1	0	2	5	0	2	0	.316	.316	.368
D.Justice, dh	5	19	3	5	2	0	1	2	2	3	0	.263	.333	.368
B.Roberts, of-2b	5	19	1	6	0	0	0	1	2	2	2	.316	.381	.316
O.Vizquel, ss	5	18	3	9	0	0	0	1	2	1	4	.500	.550	.500
M.Grissom, of	5	17	3	4	0	1	0	0	1	2	0	.235	.278	.353
M.Williams, 3b	5	17	4	4	1	0	1	3	3	3	0	.235	.350	.294
J.Thome, 1b	4	15	1	3	0	0	0	1	0	5	0	.200	.200	.200
T.Fernandez, 2b	4	11	0	2	1	0	0	4	0	0	0	.182	.182	.273
B.Giles, of	3	7	0	1	0	0	0	0	0	1	0	.143	.143	.143
K.Seitzer, 1b	1	4	0	0	0	0	0	0	0	0	0	.000	.000	.000
Totals		167	21	43	6	1	4	20	10	22	6	.257	.303	.305

PITCHER	W	L	ERA	G	GS	SV	IP	H	BB	SO
O.Hershiser	0	0	3.97	2	2	0	11.1	14	2	4
J.Wright	2	0	3.97	2	2	0	11.1	11	7	10
C.Ogea	0	0	1.69	1	0	0	5.1	2	0	1
M.Jackson	1	0	0.00	4	0	0	4.1	3	1	5
C.Nagy	0	1	9.82	1	1	0	3.2	2	6	1
P.Assenmacher	0	0	5.40	4	0	0	3.1	2	2	2
J.Mesa	0	0	2.70	2	0	1	3.1	5	1	2
E.Plunk	0	1	27.00	1	0	0	1.1	4	0	1
A.Morman	0	0	INF	1	0	0	0.0	0	1	0
Totals	3	2	4.50	18	5	1	44.0	43	20	26

NY (E)

PLAYER, POS	G	AB	R	H	2B	3B	HR	RBI	BB	SO	SB	AVG	OBP	SLG
D.Jeter, ss	5	21	6	7	1	0	2	2	3	5	1	.333	.417	.381
P.O'Neill, of	5	19	5	8	2	0	2	7	3	0	0	.421	.500	.526
T.Raines, of-dh	5	19	4	4	0	0	1	3	3	1	2	.211	.318	.211
T.Martinez, 1b	5	18	1	4	1	0	1	4	2	4	0	.222	.300	.278
B.Williams, of	5	17	3	2	1	0	0	1	4	3	0	.118	.286	.176
J.Girardi, c	5	15	2	2	0	0	0	0	1	3	0	.133	.188	.133
C.Hayes, 3b-2b	5	15	0	5	0	0	0	1	0	2	0	.333	.333	.333
R.Sanchez, 2b	5	15	1	3	1	0	0	1	1	2	0	.200	.250	.267
C.Fielder, dh	2	8	0	1	0	0	0	1	0	3	0	.125	.125	.125

NY (E) (CONT.)

PLAYER, POS	G	AB	R	H	2B	3B	HR	RBI	BB	SO	SB	AVG	OBP	SLG
W.Boggs, 3b	3	7	1	3	0	0	0	2	0	0	0	.429	.429	.429
C.Curtis, of	4	6	0	1	0	0	0	0	3	1	0	.167	.444	.167
M.Stanley, dh	2	4	1	3	1	0	0	1	0	1	0	.750	.750	1.000
J.Posada, c	2	2	0	0	0	0	0	0	0	1	0	.000	.000	.000
A.Fox, 2b	2	0	0	0	0	0	0	0	0	0	0	.000	.000	.000
S.Pose, pr	1	0	0	0	0	0	0	0	0	0	0	.000	.000	.000
Totals		166	24	43	7	0	6	23	20	26	3	.259	.349	.301

PITCHER	W	L	ERA	G	GS	SV	IP	H	BB	SO
A.Pettitte	0	2	8.49	2	2	0	11.2	15	1	5
D.Wells	1	0	1.00	1	1	0	9.0	5	0	1
D.Gooden	0	0	1.59	1	1	0	5.2	5	3	5
J.Nelson	0	0	0.00	4	0	0	4.0	4	2	0
R.Mendoza	1	1	2.45	2	0	0	3.2	3	0	2
D.Cone	0	0	16.20	1	1	0	3.1	7	2	2
M.Rivera	0	0	4.50	2	0	1	2.0	2	0	1
B.Boehringer	0	0	0.00	1	0	0	1.2	1	1	2
G.Lloyd	0	0	0.00	2	0	0	1.1	0	0	1
M.Stanton	0	0	0.00	3	0	0	1.0	1	1	3
Totals	2	3	4.36	19	5	1	43.1	43	10	22

GAME 1 / SEPT. 30

HERSHISER, MORMAN(5), PLUNK(5), ASSENMACHER(7), JACKSON(7) VS. CONE, MENDOZA(4), STANTON(7), NELSON(7), RIVERA(8) — 57,398

				R	H	E
CLE	500	100	000	6	11	0
NY	010	115	00X	8	11	0

Starter David Cone was awful, but four relievers combined to allow only four hits and no runs in $5^2/_3$ innings. That allowed the Yankees' bats to mount a comeback, capped by back-to-back-to-back homers by Tim Raines, Derek Jeter, and Paul O'Neill in the pivotal five-run sixth inning.

GAME 2 / OCT. 2

WRIGHT, JACKSON(7), ASSENMACHER(7), MESA(8) VS. PETTITTE, BOEHRINGER(6), LLOYD(7), NELSON(9) — 57,360

				R	H	E
CLE	000	520	000	7	11	1
NY	300	000	011	5	7	2

New York posted a trey in the first but managed only two additional hits in the next five innings off 21-year-old wunderkind Jaret Wright. Four straight two-out hits produced five runs in the fourth, giving Cleveland the lead for good.

GAME 3 / OCT. 4

WELLS VS. NAGY, OGEA(4) — 45,274

				R	H	E
NY	101	400	000	6	4	1
CLE	010	000	000	1	5	1

Paul O'Neill's grand slam in the fourth put the Yankees ahead to stay. David Wells went the distance, retiring the final 10 batters while being touched for only three hits after allowing a run in the second inning.

GAME 4 / OCT. 5

GOODEN, LLOYD(6), NELSON(6), STANTON(7), RIVERA(8), MENDOZA(9) VS. HERSHISER, ASSENMACHER(8), JACKSON(8) — 45,231

				R	H	E
NY	200	000	000	2	9	1
CLE	010	000	011	3	9	0

Cleveland evened the series by scoring two runs in the final two frames off Yankees closer Mariano Rivera. A two-out homer by Sandy Alomar Jr. in the eighth tied it, then the Indians won it in the ninth when Marquis Grissom scored from second on Omar Vizquel's smash up the middle, which deflected off Rivera into shallow left field.

GAME 5 / OCT. 6

PETTITTE, NELSON(7), STANTON(8) VS. WRIGHT, JACKSON(6), ASSENMACHER(7), MESA(8) — 45,203

				R	H	E
NY	000	021	000	3	12	0
CLE	003	100	00X	4	7	2

Cleveland's bullpen saved their rookie sensation again. Mike Jackson wriggled out of a jam in the sixth to preserve the Indians' lead, then combined with two teammates to shut out the Yankees over the final three innings.

1998 AL Division Series
New York Yankees (3) vs. Texas Rangers (0)

Texas averaged nearly six runs per game in the regular season yet managed only half that and hit a miserable .141 while being swept by the Yankees.

NY (E)

PLAYER, POS	G	AB	R	H	2B	3B	HR	RBI	BB	SO	SB	AVG	OBP	SLG
C.Knoblauch, 2b	3	11	0	1	0	0	0	0	0	4	0	.091	.091	.091
T.Martinez, 1b	3	11	1	3	2	0	0	0	0	2	0	.273	.273	.455
P.O'Neill, of	3	11	1	4	2	0	1	1	1	1	0	.364	.417	.545
B.Williams, of	3	11	0	0	0	0	0	0	1	4	0	.000	.083	.000
S.Brosius, 3b	3	10	1	4	0	0	1	3	0	3	0	.400	.400	.400
D.Jeter, ss	3	9	0	1	0	0	0	0	2	2	0	.111	.273	.111
J.Girardi, c	2	7	0	3	0	0	0	0	0	1	0	.429	.429	.429
C.Davis, dh	2	6	0	1	0	0	0	0	0	2	0	.167	.167	.167
S.Spencer, of	2	6	3	3	0	0	2	4	0	1	0	.500	.500	.500
T.Raines, dh	2	4	1	1	1	0	0	0	1	1	0	.250	.400	.500
C.Curtis, of	3	3	1	2	1	0	0	0	1	1	1	.667	.750	1.000
J.Posada, c	1	2	1	0	0	0	0	0	1	2	0	.000	.333	.000
H.Bush, dh	1	0	0	0	0	0	0	0	0	0	1	.000	.000	.000
Totals		91	9	23	6	0	4	8	7	24	2	.253	.313	.319

PITCHER	W	L	ERA	G	GS	SV	IP	H	BB	SO
D.Wells	1	0	0.00	1	1	0	8.0	5	1	9
A.Pettitte	1	0	1.29	1	1	0	7.0	3	0	8
D.Cone	1	0	0.00	1	1	0	5.2	2	1	6
M.Rivera	0	0	0.00	3	0	2	3.1	1	1	2
J.Nelson	0	0	0.00	2	0	0	2.2	2	1	2
G.Lloyd	0	0	0.00	1	0	0	0.1	0	0	0
Totals	3	0	0.33	9	3	2	27.0	13	4	27

TEX (W)

PLAYER, POS	G	AB	R	H	2B	3B	HR	RBI	BB	SO	SB	AVG	OBP	SLG
J.Gonzalez, of	3	12	1	1	1	0	0	0	0	3	0	.083	.083	.167
W.Clark, 1b	3	11	0	1	0	0	0	0	1	2	0	.091	.167	.091
R.Greer, of	3	11	0	1	0	0	0	0	1	2	0	.091	.167	.091
M.McLemore, 2b	3	10	0	1	1	0	0	0	2	3	0	.100	.250	.200
I.Rodriguez, c	3	10	0	1	0	0	0	1	0	5	0	.100	.100	.100
R.Clayton, ss	3	9	0	2	0	0	0	0	0	4	0	.222	.222	.222
T.Zeile, 3b	3	9	0	3	0	0	0	0	0	2	0	.333	.333	.333
R.Kelly, of	1	7	0	1	1	0	0	0	0	2	0	.143	.143	.286
M.Simms, dh	2	5	0	1	0	0	0	0	0	2	0	.200	.200	.200
T.Goodwin, of	2	4	0	1	0	0	0	0	0	1	0	.250	.250	.250
L.Stevens, dh	1	3	0	0	0	0	0	0	0	1	0	.000	.000	.000
L.Alicea, ph	1	1	0	0	0	0	0	0	0	0	0	.000	.000	.000
Totals		92	1	13	3	0	0	1	4	27	0	.141	.177	.174

PITCHER	W	L	ERA	G	GS	SV	IP	H	BB	SO
T.Stottlemyre	0	1	2.25	1	1	0	8.0	6	4	8
R.Helling	0	1	4.50	1	1	0	6.0	8	1	9
A.Sele	0	1	6.00	1	1	0	6.0	8	1	4
T.Crabtree	0	0	0.00	2	0	0	4.0	1	0	2
J.Wetteland	0	0	0.00	1	0	0	1.0	0	1	1
Totals	0	3	3.24	6	3	0	25.0	23	7	24

GAME 1 / SEPT. 29

STOTTLEMYRE VS. WELLS, RIVERA(9)							57,362
TEX	000	000	000	0	5	0	
NY	020	000	00X	2	6	0	

David Wells allowed only five hits and a walk in eight shutout innings. The Yankees scratch out two runs in the second, the second of which came when Chad Curtis scored from third as Scott Brosius was caught in a rundown between first and second.

GAME 2 / SEPT. 30

HELLING, CRABTREE(7) VS. PETTITTE, NELSON(8), RIVERA(8)							57,360
TEX	000	010	000	1	5	0	
NY	010	200	00X	3	8	0	

The Rangers finally got on the scoreboard in the fifth, but by that time they were already down by three, thanks to home runs by Brosius and Shane Spencer.

GAME 3 / OCT. 2

CONE, LLOYD(6), NELSON(7), RIVERA(9) VS. SELE, CRABTREE(7), WETTELAND(9)							49,450
NY	000	004	000	4	9	1	
TEX	000	000	000	0	3	1	

Home runs from Spencer and Paul O'Neill plus superb pitching once again carried the day. David Cone and three relievers, necessitated by a three-hour rain delay in the sixth, combined for a three-hit shutout.

1998 AL Championship Series
New York Yankees (3) vs. Cleveland Indians (2)

The Yankees faced the Indians in the postseason for the second time in as many years. This time, New York was the team to rally from a 2 games to 1 deficit, pounding out 18 runs in the final three contests after plating only two in the first two games combined.

NY (E)

PLAYER, POS	G	AB	R	H	2B	3B	HR	RBI	BB	SO	SB	AVG	OBP	SLG
D.Jeter, ss	6	25	3	5	1	1	0	2	2	5	3	.200	.259	.320
C.Knoblauch, 2b	6	25	4	5	1	0	0	0	4	2	0	.200	.310	.240
P.O'Neill, of	6	25	6	7	2	0	1	3	3	4	2	.280	.357	.360
B.Williams, of	6	21	4	8	1	0	0	5	7	4	1	.381	.536	.429
S.Brosius, 3b	6	20	2	6	1	0	1	6	2	4	0	.300	.364	.350
T.Martinez, 1b	6	19	1	2	1	0	0	1	6	8	2	.105	.333	.158
C.Davis, dh	5	14	2	4	1	0	1	5	2	3	0	.286	.375	.357
J.Posada, c	5	11	1	2	0	0	1	2	4	2	0	.182	.400	.182
T.Raines, dh-of	3	10	0	1	0	0	0	1	2	6	0	.100	.250	.100
S.Spencer, of	3	10	1	1	0	0	0	0	1	3	0	.100	.182	.100
J.Girardi, c	3	8	2	2	0	0	0	0	1	0	0	.250	.333	.250
R.Ledee, of-dh	3	5	0	0	0	0	0	0	0	0	0	.000	.000	.000
C.Curtis, of	2	4	0	0	0	0	0	0	1	2	0	.000	.200	.000
H.Bush, dh	2	0	1	0	0	0	0	0	0	0	1	.000	.000	.000
L.Sojo, 1b	1	0	0	0	0	0	0	0	0	0	0	.000	.000	.000
Totals		197	27	43	8	1	4	25	35	42	9	.218	.340	.269

PITCHER	W	L	ERA	G	GS	SV	IP	H	BB	SO
D.Wells	2	0	2.87	2	2	0	15.2	12	2	18
D.Cone	1	0	4.15	2	2	0	13.0	12	6	13
O.Hernandez	1	0	0.00	1	1	0	7.0	3	2	6
M.Rivera	0	0	0.00	4	0	1	5.2	0	1	5
A.Pettitte	0	1	11.57	1	1	0	4.2	8	3	1
R.Mendoza	0	0	0.00	2	0	0	4.1	4	0	1
M.Stanton	0	0	0.00	3	0	0	3.2	2	1	4
J.Nelson	0	1	20.25	3	0	0	1.1	3	1	3
G.Lloyd	0	0	0.00	1	0	0	0.2	1	0	0
Totals	4	2	3.21	19	6	1	56.0	45	16	51

CLE (C)

PLAYER, POS	G	AB	R	H	2B	3B	HR	RBI	BB	SO	SB	AVG	OBP	SLG
K.Lofton, of	6	27	2	5	1	0	1	3	1	7	1	.185	.214	.222
O.Vizquel, ss	6	25	2	11	0	1	0	0	1	3	4	.440	.462	.520
T.Fryman, 3b	6	23	2	4	0	0	0	0	1	5	1	.174	.208	.174
J.Thome, 1b-dh	6	23	4	7	0	0	4	8	1	8	0	.304	.333	.304
M.Ramirez, of	6	21	2	7	1	0	2	4	4	9	0	.333	.440	.381
D.Justice, dh-of	6	19	2	3	0	0	1	2	3	3	0	.158	.273	.158
S.Alomar, c	5	16	1	1	0	0	0	0	0	2	0	.063	.063	.063
E.Wilson, 2b	5	14	2	3	0	0	0	1	1	3	0	.214	.267	.214
B.Giles, of	4	12	0	1	0	0	0	0	1	3	0	.083	.154	.083
J.Cora, 2b	2	7	1	1	0	0	0	0	2	1	0	.143	.333	.143
M.Whiten, of	2	7	2	2	1	0	1	1	1	3	0	.286	.375	.429
R.Sexson, 1b	3	6	0	0	0	0	0	0	0	3	0	.000	.000	.000
E.Diaz, c	5	4	0	0	0	0	0	0	0	1	0	.000	.000	.000
J.Branson, ph	1	1	0	0	0	0	0	0	0	0	0	.000	.000	.000
Totals		205	20	45	3	1	9	19	16	51	6	.220	.292	.244

PITCHER	W	L	ERA	G	GS	SV	IP	H	BB	SO
C.Nagy	0	1	3.72	2	2	0	9.2	13	1	6
B.Colon	1	0	1.00	1	1	0	9.0	4	4	3
C.Ogea	0	1	8.10	2	1	0	6.2	9	5	4
J.Wright	0	1	8.10	2	1	0	6.2	7	8	4
P.Shuey	0	0	0.00	5	0	0	6.1	4	7	7
D.Burba	1	0	3.00	3	0	0	6.0	3	5	8
D.Gooden	0	1	5.79	1	1	0	4.2	3	3	3
P.Assenmacher	0	0	0.00	3	0	0	2.0	0	0	3
S.Reed	0	0	0.00	3	0	0	1.2	0	1	0
J.Poole	0	0	0.00	4	0	0	1.1	0	1	2
M.Jackson	0	0	0.00	1	0	1	1.0	0	0	2
Totals	2	4	3.60	27	6	1	55.0	43	35	42

GAME 1 / OCT. 6

WRIGHT, OGEA(1), POOLE(7), REED(7), SHUEY(8) VS. WELLS, NELSON(9)							57,138
CLE	000	000	002	2	5	0	
NY	500	001	10X	7	11	0	

The Yankees singled 1997 nemesis Jaret Wright out of the game in the first, scoring five times on six safeties and a walk.

GAME 2 / OCT. 7

NAGY, REED(7), POOLE(8), SHUEY(8), ASSENMACHER(10), BURBA(11), JACKSON(12) VS. CONE, RIVERA(9), STANTON(11), NELSON(11), LLOYD(12)								57,128
CLE	000	100	000	003	4	8	1	
NY	000	000	100	000	1	7	1	

A mental mistake by Chuck Knoblauch (arguing with the umpire before time had been called) let Enrique Wilson score

Postseason

from first on a bunt to give Cleveland the go-ahead run in the top of the 12th. It hardly cost the Yankees the game as the Indians scored two more times in the frame.

GAME 3 / OCT. 9							
PETTITTE, MENDOZA(5), STANTON(7) VS. COLON							44,904
NY	100	000	000	1	4	0	
CLE	020	040	00X	6	12	0	

A powerful attack (four home runs, including three in the fifth), combined with a four-hit shutout by Bartolo Colon put Cleveland ahead, albeit briefly, in the series.

GAME 4 / OCT. 10							
HERNANDEZ, STANTON(8), RIVERA(9) VS. GOODEN, POOLE(5), BURBA(6), SHUEY(9)							44,981
NY	100	200	001	4	4	0	
CLE	000	000	000	0	4	3	

The Yankees evened the series with their own four-hit whitewash, this one a combined effort from Orlando Hernandez, Mike Stanton, and Mariano Rivera.

GAME 5 / OCT. 11							
WELLS, NELSON(8), RIVERA(8) VS. OGEA, WRIGHT(2), REED(8), ASSENMACHER(8), SHUEY(9)							44,966
NY	310	100	000	5	6	0	
CLE	200	001	000	3	8	0	

New York led the entire way after scoring three in the first. Rivera earned the save by getting the final five outs, coming on in the eighth with two on and only one out.

GAME 6 / OCT. 13							
NAGY, BURBA(4), POOLE(6), SHUEY(6), ASSENMACHER(8) VS. CONE, MENDOZA(6), RIVERA(9)							57,142
CLE	000	050	000	5	8	3	
NY	213	003	00X	9	11	1	

Scott Brosius' three-run blast in the third gave the Yankees a six-run lead. However, a grand slam by Jim Thome in the fifth brought the Indians to within one run before a throwing error by Omar Vizquel on the first batter of the sixth helped the Yankees put the game away.

1998 World Series
New York Yankees (4) vs. San Diego Padres (0)

San Diego twice took leads into the seventh inning, but tired starters and ineffective relievers cost the Padres any hopes of an upset in the Series. The Yankees, who scored nearly six runs per game in winning 114 regular season contests, plated 14 of their 26 runs in the series in the seventh inning or later.

NY (AL)

PLAYER, POS	G	AB	R	H	2B	3B	HR	RBI	BB	SO	SB	AVG	OBP	SLG
P.O'Neill, of	4	19	3	4	1	0	0	0	1	2	0	.211	.250	.263
S.Brosius, 3b	4	17	3	8	0	0	2	6	0	4	0	.471	.471	.471
D.Jeter, ss	4	17	4	6	0	0	0	1	3	3	0	.353	.450	.353
C.Knoblauch, 2b	4	16	3	6	0	0	1	3	3	2	1	.375	.474	.375
B.Williams, of	4	16	2	1	0	0	1	3	2	5	0	.063	.167	.063
T.Martinez, 1b	4	13	4	5	0	0	1	4	4	2	0	.385	.529	.385
R.Ledee, of	4	10	1	6	3	0	0	4	2	1	0	.600	.667	.900
J.Posada, c	3	9	2	3	0	0	1	2	2	2	0	.333	.455	.333
C.Davis, dh	3	7	3	2	0	0	0	2	3	2	0	.286	.500	.286
J.Girardi, c	2	6	0	0	0	0	0	0	0	2	0	.000	.000	.000
S.Spencer, of	1	3	1	1	1	0	0	0	0	2	0	.333	.333	.667
D.Cone, p	1	2	0	1	0	0	0	0	0	0	0	.500	.500	.500
A.Pettitte, p	1	2	0	0	0	0	0	0	0	2	0	.000	.000	.000
R.Mendoza, p	1	1	0	0	0	0	0	0	0	0	0	.000	.000	.000
M.Rivera, p	3	1	0	0	0	0	0	0	0	0	0	.000	.000	.000
H.Bush, dh	2	0	0	0	0	0	0	0	0	0	0	.000	.000	.000
Totals		139	26	43	5	0	6	25	20	29	1	.309	.400	.345

PITCHER	W	L	ERA	G	GS	SV	IP	H	BB	SO
A.Pettitte	1	0	0.00	1	1	0	7.1	5	3	4
O.Hernandez	1	0	1.29	1	1	0	7.0	6	3	7
D.Wells	1	0	6.43	1	1	0	7.0	7	2	4
D.Cone	0	0	3.00	1	1	0	6.0	2	3	4
M.Rivera	0	0	0.00	3	0	3	4.1	5	0	4

NY (AL) (cont.)

PITCHER	W	L	ERA	G	GS	SV	IP	H	BB	SO
J.Nelson	0	0	0.00	3	0	0	2.1	2	1	4
R.Mendoza	1	0	9.00	1	0	0	1.0	2	0	1
M.Stanton	0	0	27.00	1	0	0	0.2	3	0	1
G.Lloyd	0	0	0.00	1	0	0	0.1	0	0	0
Totals	4	0	2.75	13	4	3	36.0	32	12	29

SD (NL)

PLAYER, POS	G	AB	R	H	2B	3B	HR	RBI	BB	SO	SB	AVG	OBP	SLG
T.Gwynn, of	4	16	2	8	0	0	1	3	1	0	0	.500	.529	.500
G.Vaughn, of-dh	4	15	3	2	0	0	2	4	1	2	0	.133	.188	.133
Q.Veras, 2b	4	15	3	3	2	0	0	1	3	4	0	.200	.333	.333
K.Caminiti, 3b	4	14	1	2	1	0	0	1	2	7	0	.143	.250	.214
S.Finley, of	3	12	0	1	1	0	0	0	0	2	1	.083	.083	.167
C.Gomez, ss	4	11	2	4	0	1	0	0	1	1	0	.364	.417	.545
C.Hernandez, c	4	10	0	2	0	0	0	0	0	3	0	.200	.200	.200
J.Leyritz, 1b-c-dh	4	10	0	0	0	0	0	0	1	4	0	.000	.091	.000
W.Joyner, 1b	3	8	0	0	0	0	0	0	3	1	0	.000	.273	.000
R.Rivera, of	3	5	1	4	2	0	0	1	0	0	0	.800	.800	1.200
J.Vander Wal, of	4	5	0	2	1	0	0	0	0	2	0	.400	.400	.600
G.Myers, c	2	4	0	0	0	0	0	0	0	2	0	.000	.000	.000
M.Sweeney, ph	3	3	0	2	0	0	0	1	0	0	0	.667	.667	.667
K.Brown, p	2	2	0	1	0	0	0	0	0	0	0	.500	.500	.500
S.Hitchcock, p	1	2	1	1	0	0	0	0	0	0	0	.500	.500	.500
A.Sheets, ss	2	2	0	0	0	0	0	0	0	1	0	.000	.000	.000
Totals		134	13	32	7	1	3	11	12	29	1	.239	.301	.306

PITCHER	W	L	ERA	G	GS	SV	IP	H	BB	SO
K.Brown	0	1	4.40	2	2	0	14.1	14	6	13
S.Hitchcock	0	0	1.50	1	1	0	6.0	7	1	7
A.Ashby	0	1	13.50	1	1	0	2.2	10	1	1
D.Wall	0	1	6.75	2	0	0	2.2	3	3	1
B.Boehringer	0	0	9.00	2	0	0	2.0	4	2	3
T.Hoffman	0	1	9.00	1	0	0	2.0	2	1	0
D.Miceli	0	0	0.00	2	0	0	1.2	2	2	1
J.Hamilton	0	0	0.00	1	0	0	1.0	0	1	1
R.Myers	0	0	9.00	3	0	0	1.0	0	1	2
M.Langston	0	0	40.50	1	0	0	0.2	1	2	0
Totals	0	4	5.82	16	4	0	34.0	43	20	29

GAME 1 / OCT. 17							
BROWN, WALL(7), LANGSTON(7), BOEHRINGER(8), R.MYERS(8) VS. WELLS, NELSON(8), RIVERA(8)							56,712
SD	002	030	010	6	8	1	
NY	020	000	70X	9	9	1	

The Padres were up by three runs with one out in the seventh when the wheels fell off. Four hits and three walks later, the Yankees led by four, thanks to a three-run homer by Chuck Knoblauch and a grand salami from Tino Martinez.

GAME 2 / OCT. 18							
ASHBY, BOEHRINGER(3), WALL(5), MICELI(8) VS. HERNANDEZ, STANTON(8), NELSON(8)							56,692
SD	000	010	020	3	10	1	
NY	331	020	00X	9	16	0	

New York continued the onslaught with three unearned runs in the first, then three more in the second, two of which scored on a homer by Bernie Williams. Orlando Hernandez allowed only one run in seven innings in his first World Series start after defecting from Cuba.

GAME 3 / OCT. 20							
CONE, LLOYD(7), MENDOZA(7), RIVERA(9) VS. HITCHCOCK, HAMILTON(7), R.MYERS(8), HOFFMAN(8)							64,667
NY	000	000	230	5	9	1	
SD	000	003	010	4	7	1	

Scott Brosius drove in four of the Yankees' runs in the seventh and eighth innings on two homers, a solo shot in the seventh and a three-run blast in the eighth. Mariano Rivera struggled to get the final five outs, getting nicked for three hits while letting an inherited runner score in the eighth. Rivera finally ended it by striking out Andy Sheets with the tying run on third in the ninth.

GAME 4 / OCT. 21							
PETTITTE, NELSON(8), RIVERA(8) VS. BROWN, MICELI(9), R.MYERS(9)							65,427
NY	000	001	020	3	9	0	
SD	000	000	000	0	7	0	

The Yankees completed the sweep by scratching out three runs—which scored on a groundout, a single, and a sacrifice fly—and getting dominating pitching from Andy Pettitte, Jeff Nelson and Rivera.

1999 AL Division Series
New York Yankees (3) vs. Texas Rangers (0)

The Yankees and Rangers met in the Division Series for the second straight year. The outcome was exactly the same as New York limited impotent Texas to one lone run in 27 innings.

NY (E)

PLAYER, POS	G	AB	R	H	2B	3B	HR	RBI	BB	SO	SB	AVG	OBP	SLG
C.Knoblauch, 2b	3	12	1	2	0	0	0	0	1	3	0	.167	.231	.167
D.Jeter, ss	3	11	3	5	1	1	0	0	2	3	0	.455	.538	.727
R.Ledee, of	3	11	1	3	2	0	0	2	1	5	0	.273	.333	.455
T.Martinez, 1b	3	11	2	2	0	0	0	0	2	2	0	.182	.308	.182
B.Williams, of	3	11	2	4	1	0	1	6	1	2	0	.364	.417	.455
S.Brosius, 3b	3	10	0	1	1	0	0	1	0	0	0	.100	.100	.200
P.O'Neill, of	3	8	2	2	0	0	0	0	1	1	0	.250	.333	.250
J.Girardi, c	2	6	0	0	0	0	0	0	0	1	0	.000	.000	.000
D.Strawberry, dh	2	6	2	2	0	0	1	3	1	0	0	.333	.429	.333
J.Posada, c	1	4	0	1	1	0	0	0	0	0	0	.250	.250	.500
C.Curtis, of	3	3	1	0	0	0	0	0	0	0	0	.000	.000	.000
C.Davis, dh	1	3	0	1	0	0	0	0	0	2	0	.333	.333	.333
J.Leyritz, dh	2	2	0	0	0	0	0	1	1	0	0	.000	.333	.000
C.Bellinger, dh	1	0	0	0	0	0	0	0	0	0	0	.000	.000	.000
Totals		98	14	23	6	1	2	13	10	19	0	.235	.312	.316

PITCHER	W	L	ERA	G	GS	SV	IP	H	BB	SO
O.Hernandez	1	0	0.00	1	1	0	8.0	2	6	4
A.Pettitte	1	0	1.23	1	1	0	7.1	7	0	5
R.Clemens	1	0	0.00	1	1	0	7.0	3	2	2
M.Rivera	0	0	0.00	2	0	2	3.0	1	0	3
J.Nelson	0	0	0.00	3	0	0	1.2	1	1	3
Totals	3	0	0.33	8	3	2	27.0	14	9	17

TEX (W)

PLAYER, POS	G	AB	R	H	2B	3B	HR	RBI	BB	SO	SB	AVG	OBP	SLG
I.Rodriguez, c	3	12	0	3	1	0	0	0	0	2	1	.250	.250	.333
J.Gonzalez, of	3	11	1	2	0	0	1	1	1	3	0	.182	.250	.182
R.Palmeiro, dh	3	11	0	3	0	0	0	0	1	1	0	.273	.333	.273
R.Clayton, ss	3	10	0	0	0	0	0	0	0	1	0	.000	.000	.000
M.McLemore, 2b	3	10	0	1	0	0	0	0	1	3	0	.100	.182	.100
T.Zeile, 3b	3	10	0	1	0	0	0	0	2	1	0	.100	.250	.100
R.Greer, of	3	9	0	1	0	0	0	0	3	1	0	.111	.333	.111
L.Stevens, 1b	3	9	0	1	1	0	0	0	1	2	0	.111	.200	.222
T.Goodwin, of	3	7	0	1	0	0	0	0	0	1	0	.143	.143	.143
R.Kelly, of	1	3	0	1	0	0	0	0	0	2	0	.333	.333	.333
Totals		92	1	14	2	0	1	1	9	17	1	.152	.228	.174

PITCHER	W	L	ERA	G	GS	SV	IP	H	BB	SO
E.Loaiza	0	1	3.86	1	1	0	7.0	5	1	4
R.Helling	0	1	2.84	1	1	0	6.1	5	1	8
A.Sele	0	1	5.40	1	1	0	5.0	6	5	3
T.Crabtree	0	0	5.40	2	0	0	1.2	1	1	1
J.Fassero	0	0	9.00	1	0	0	1.0	2	1	1
D.Patterson	0	0	0.00	1	0	0	1.0	1	0	0
M.Venafro	0	0	0.00	2	0	0	1.0	2	1	0
J.Wetteland	0	0	0.00	1	0	0	1.0	0	0	1
J.Zimmerman	0	0	0.00	1	0	0	1.0	1	0	1
Totals	0	3	3.60	11	3	0	25.0	23	10	19

GAME 1 / OCT. 5

SELE, CRABTREE(6), VENAFRO(6), PATTERSON(7), FASSERO(8) VS. HERNANDEZ, NELSON(9) 57,099

				R	H	E
TEX	000	000	000	0	2	1
NY	010	024	01X	8	10	0

After allowing two hits and three walks in the first three innings, Orlando Hernandez rebounded to hold Texas hitless for the next five. Bernie Williams chipped in with three hits and six RBIs, three coming on a homer in the sixth.

GAME 2 / OCT. 7

HELLING, CRABTREE(7), VENAFRO(8) VS. PETTITTE, NELSON(8), RIVERA(9) 57,485

				R	H	E
TEX	000	100	000	1	7	0
NY	000	010	11X	3	7	2

The Rangers actually led for an inning after a home run in the fourth by Juan Gonzalez. Texas couldn't score after putting runners on second and third with no outs in the fifth, however, as Scott Brosius doubled home the tying run that inning and Ricky Ledee doubled in the winning run in the seventh.

GAME 3 / OCT. 9

CLEMENS, NELSON(8), RIVERA(8) VS. LOAIZA, ZIMMERMAN(8), WETTELAND(9) 50,269

				R	H	E
NY	300	000	000	3	6	0
TEX	000	000	000	0	5	1

A three-run homer in the top of the first effectively ended the series. Though the Yankees wouldn't score the rest of the game, Roger Clemens was masterful, blanking Texas on three hits over seven innings. Jeff Nelson and Mariano Rivera finished off the whitewash for New York.

1999 AL Championship Series
New York Yankees (4) vs. Boston Red Sox (1)

New York and Boston had been bitter rivals ever since Boston sold Babe Ruth to the Yankees, establishing the Bronx Bombers as the preeminent franchise in professional sports. Now, thanks to the Wild Card, they got to meet for the first time in the postseason. Despite this history, the historic LCS failed to live up to expectations, especially for Red Sox rooters, as the Yankees needed only five games to advance to the Fall Classic.

NY (E)

PLAYER, POS	G	AB	R	H	2B	3B	HR	RBI	BB	SO	SB	AVG	OBP	SLG
P.O'Neill, of	5	21	2	6	0	0	0	1	1	5	0	.286	.318	.286
D.Jeter, ss	5	20	3	7	1	0	1	3	2	3	0	.350	.409	.400
B.Williams, of	5	20	3	5	1	0	1	2	2	5	1	.250	.318	.300
T.Martinez, 1b	5	19	3	5	1	0	1	3	2	4	0	.263	.333	.316
S.Brosius, 3b	5	18	3	4	0	1	2	3	1	4	0	.222	.263	.333
C.Knoblauch, 2b	5	18	3	6	1	0	0	1	3	0	1	.333	.429	.389
C.Davis, dh	5	11	0	1	0	0	0	1	3	4	0	.091	.286	.091
J.Posada, c	3	10	1	1	0	0	1	2	1	2	0	.100	.182	.100
S.Spencer, of	3	9	1	1	0	0	0	0	1	6	0	.111	.200	.111
J.Girardi, c	3	8	0	2	0	0	0	0	0	2	0	.250	.250	.250
R.Ledee, of	3	8	2	2	0	0	1	4	1	4	0	.250	.333	.250
C.Curtis, of-dh	3	6	1	0	0	0	0	0	0	2	1	.000	.000	.000
D.Strawberry, dh	3	6	1	2	0	0	1	1	1	2	0	.333	.429	.333
C.Bellinger, dh-ss	3	1	0	0	0	0	0	0	0	1	0	.000	.000	.000
L.Sojo, 2b	2	1	0	0	0	0	0	0	0	0	0	.000	.000	.000
Totals		176	23	42	4	1	8	21	18	44	3	.239	.313	.273

PITCHER	W	L	ERA	G	GS	SV	IP	H	BB	SO
O.Hernandez	1	0	1.80	2	2	0	15.0	12	6	13
A.Pettitte	1	0	2.45	1	1	0	7.1	8	1	5
D.Cone	1	0	2.57	1	1	0	7.0	7	3	9
H.Irabu	0	0	13.50	1	0	0	4.2	13	0	3
M.Rivera	1	0	0.00	3	0	2	4.2	5	0	3
R.Mendoza	0	0	0.00	2	0	1	2.1	0	0	2
R.Clemens	0	1	22.50	1	1	0	2.0	6	2	2
A.Watson	0	0	0.00	3	0	0	1.0	2	2	1
J.Nelson	0	0	0.00	2	0	0	0.2	0	0	0
M.Stanton	0	0	0.00	3	0	0	0.1	1	1	0
Totals	4	1	3.80	19	5	3	45.0	54	15	38

BOS (E)

PLAYER, POS	G	AB	R	H	2B	3B	HR	RBI	BB	SO	SB	AVG	OBP	SLG
J.Offerman, 2b	5	24	4	11	0	1	0	2	1	3	1	.458	.480	.542
J.Valentin, 3b	5	23	3	8	2	0	1	5	2	4	0	.348	.400	.435
N.Garciaparra, ss	5	20	2	8	2	0	2	5	2	2	1	.400	.455	.500
T.O'Leary, of	5	20	2	7	3	0	0	1	2	5	0	.350	.409	.500
J.Varitek, c	5	20	1	4	1	1	1	1	1	4	0	.200	.238	.350
M.Stanley, 1b	5	18	1	4	0	0	0	1	2	4	0	.222	.300	.222
B.Daubach, dh-1b	5	17	2	3	1	0	1	3	1	4	0	.176	.222	.235
D.Lewis, of	5	17	2	2	1	0	0	1	1	3	1	.118	.167	.176
T.Nixon, of	5	14	2	4	2	0	0	0	1	5	0	.286	.333	.429
D.Buford, of	4	5	1	2	0	0	0	0	0	2	1	.400	.400	.400
B.Huskey, dh	4	5	1	1	1	0	0	0	1	1	0	.200	.333	.400
S.Hatteberg, c	3	1	0	0	0	0	0	0	0	1	0	.000	.000	.000
L.Merloni, ph	1	0	0	0	0	0	0	0	1	0	0	.000	1.000	.000
D.Sadler, of-dh	2	0	0	0	0	0	0	0	0	0	0	.000	.000	.000
Totals		184	21	54	13	2	5	19	15	38	4	.293	.350	.386

PITCHER	W	L	ERA	G	GS	SV	IP	H	BB	SO
K.Mercker	0	1	4.70	2	2	0	7.2	12	4	5
P.Martinez	1	0	0.00	1	1	0	7.0	2	2	12
R.Martinez	0	1	4.05	1	1	0	6.2	6	3	5
D.Lowe	0	0	1.42	3	0	0	6.1	6	2	7
B.Saberhagen	0	1	1.50	1	1	0	6.0	5	1	5
R.Cormier	0	0	0.00	4	0	0	3.2	3	3	4
R.Garces	0	0	12.00	2	0	0	3.0	3	1	2
T.Gordon	0	0	13.50	3	0	0	2.0	3	1	3
P.Rapp	0	0	0.00	1	0	0	1.0	0	1	0
R.Beck	0	1	27.00	2	0	0	0.2	2	0	1
Totals	1	4	3.68	20	5	0	44.0	42	18	44

GAME 1 / OCT. 13

MERCKER, GARCES(5), LOWE(7), CORMIER(9), BECK(10) VS. HERNANDEZ, RIVERA(9) 57,181

					R	H	E
BOS	210	000	000	0	3	8	2
NY	020	000	100	1	4	10	1

A leadoff homer by Bernie Williams in the bottom of the 10th capped New York's rally. It was the first lead of the game for the Yankees, who tied it in the seventh on a single by Derek Jeter.

GAME 2 / OCT. 14

R.MARTINEZ, GORDON(7), CORMIER(7) VS. CONE, STANTON(8), NELSON(8), WATSON(8), MENDOZA(8), RIVERA(9) — **57,180**

BOS	000	020	000	2	10	0
NY	000	100	20X	3	7	0

Boston again led into the late innings, only to let the Yankees stage a comeback. This time New York took the lead for good in the seventh on a double by Chuck Knoblauch and a single by Paul O'Neill.

GAME 3 / OCT. 16

CLEMENS, IRABU(3), STANTON(7), WATSON(8) VS. P.MARTINEZ, GORDON(8), RAPP(9) — **33,190**

NY	000	000	010	1	3	3
BOS	222	021	40X	13	21	1

Boston pounded former Sox icon Roger Clemens for six hits and five runs in two innings. The Sox then carpet bombed reliever Hideki Irabu for 13 hits and eight runs in $4^2/_3$ innings.

GAME 4 / OCT. 17

PETTITTE, RIVERA(8) VS. SABERHAGEN, LOWE(7), CORMIER(8), GARCES(8), BECK(9) — **33,586**

NY	010	200	006	9	11	0
BOS	011	000	000	2	10	3

After taking a 2–1 lead in the third, Boston wouldn't put another runner in scoring position until two outs in the bottom of the ninth. By then it hardly mattered, as the Yankees had blown the game open on Ricky Ledee's grand slam in the top of that frame.

GAME 5 / OCT. 18

HERNANDEZ, STANTON(8), NELSON(8), WATSON(8), MENDOZA(8) VS. MERCKER, LOWE(4), CORMIER(7), GORDON(9) — **33,589**

NY	200	000	202	6	11	1
BOS	000	000	010	1	5	2

It was all over but the shouting after only two hitters, when Knoblauch began the game with a single and Jeter followed with a round-tripper. New York padded its lead in the seventh on two unearned runs, thanks to Boston's ninth and 10th errors of the series (an LCS record). Boston had one last chance in the eighth after loading the bases with one out, but Ramiro Mendoza retired Scott Hatteberg and Trot Nixon, then pitched a perfect ninth for the save.

1999 World Series
New York Yankees (4) vs. Atlanta Braves (0)

It was the second straight World Series sweep for New York, the first time a team had accomplished that since the Yankees broomed away the Cubs in 1938 and the Reds in '39. Yankees closer Mariano Rivera was named MVP after winning one game and saving two others.

NY (AL)

PLAYER, POS	G	AB	R	H	2B	3B	HR	RBI	BB	SO	SB	AVG	OBP	SLG
D.Jeter, ss	4	17	4	6	1	0	0	1	1	3	3	.353	.389	.412
S.Brosius, 3b	4	16	2	6	1	0	0	1	0	5	0	.375	.375	.438
C.Knoblauch, 2b	4	16	5	5	1	0	1	3	1	3	1	.313	.353	.375
T.Martinez, 1b	4	15	3	4	0	0	1	5	2	4	0	.267	.353	.267
P.O'Neill, of	4	15	0	3	0	0	0	4	2	2	0	.200	.294	.200
B.Williams, of	4	13	2	3	0	0	0	0	4	2	1	.231	.412	.231
R.Ledee, of	3	10	0	2	1	0	0	1	1	4	0	.200	.273	.300

NY (AL) (CONT.)

PLAYER, POS	G	AB	R	H	2B	3B	HR	RBI	BB	SO	SB	AVG	OBP	SLG
J.Posada, c	2	8	0	2	1	0	0	1	0	3	0	.250	.250	.375
J.Girardi, c	2	7	1	2	0	0	0	0	0	1	0	.286	.286	.286
C.Curtis, of	3	6	3	2	0	0	2	2	0	0	0	.333	.333	.333
D.Cone, p	1	4	0	0	0	0	0	0	0	0	0	.000	.000	.000
C.Davis, dh	1	4	0	0	0	0	0	0	0	2	0	.000	.000	.000
D.Strawberry, dh	2	3	0	1	0	0	0	0	1	2	0	.333	.500	.333
O.Hernandez, p	1	1	0	0	0	0	0	0	0	0	0	.000	.000	.000
J.Leyritz, dh	2	1	1	1	0	0	1	2	1	0	0	1.000	1.000	1.000
R.Mendoza, p	1	1	0	0	0	0	0	0	0	0	0	.000	.000	.000
L.Sojo, 2b	1	0	0	0	0	0	0	0	0	0	0	.000	.000	.000
Totals		137	21	37	5	0	5	20	13	31	5	.270	.333	.307

PITCHER	W	L	ERA	G	GS	SV	IP	H	BB	SO
R.Clemens	1	0	1.17	1	1	0	7.2	4	2	4
D.Cone	1	0	0.00	1	1	0	7.0	1	5	4
O.Hernandez	1	0	1.29	1	1	0	7.0	1	2	10
M.Rivera	1	0	0.00	3	0	2	4.2	3	1	3
A.Pettitte	0	0	12.27	1	1	0	3.2	10	1	1
J.Nelson	0	0	0.00	4	0	0	2.2	2	1	3
J.Grimsley	0	0	0.00	1	0	0	2.1	2	2	0
R.Mendoza	0	0	10.80	1	0	0	1.2	3	1	0
M.Stanton	0	0	0.00	1	0	0	0.1	0	0	1
Totals	4	0	2.19	14	4	2	37.0	26	15	26

ATL (NL)

PLAYER, POS	G	AB	R	H	2B	3B	HR	RBI	BB	SO	SB	AVG	OBP	SLG
G.Williams, of	4	17	2	3	0	1	0	0	0	4	0	.176	.176	.294
B.Boone, 2b	4	13	1	7	4	0	0	3	1	3	0	.538	.571	.846
A.Jones, of	4	13	1	1	0	0	0	0	1	3	0	.077	.143	.077
C.Jones, 3b	4	13	2	3	0	0	1	2	4	2	0	.231	.412	.231
B.Jordan, of	4	13	1	1	0	0	0	1	4	2	0	.077	.294	.077
R.Klesko, 1b	4	12	0	2	0	0	0	0	0	1	0	.167	.167	.167
W.Weiss, ss	3	9	1	2	0	0	0	0	0	1	0	.222	.222	.222
E.Perez, c	3	8	0	1	0	0	0	0	1	3	0	.125	.222	.125
K.Lockhart, 2b-dh	4	7	1	1	0	0	0	0	2	0	0	.143	.333	.143
G.Myers, c	4	6	0	2	0	0	0	1	1	0	0	.333	.429	.333
O.Guillen, ss-dh	3	5	0	0	0	0	0	0	0	1	0	.000	.000	.000
J.Hernandez, ss-dh	2	5	0	1	1	0	0	2	0	2	1	.200	.200	.400
B.Hunter, 1b	2	4	0	1	0	0	0	0	0	1	0	.250	.250	.250
G.Maddux, p	1	2	0	0	0	0	0	0	0	2	0	.000	.000	.000
O.Nixon, of	2	2	0	1	0	0	0	0	0	0	0	.500	.500	.500
J.Fabregas, ph	1	1	0	0	0	0	0	0	0	1	0	.000	.000	.000
H.Battle, ph	1	0	0	0	0	0	0	0	0	0	0	.000	.000	.000
T.Mulholland, p	2	0	0	0	0	0	0	0	1	0	0	.000	1.000	.000
Totals		130	9	26	5	1	1	9	15	26	1	.200	.283	.254

PITCHER	W	L	ERA	G	GS	SV	IP	H	BB	SO
T.Glavine	0	0	5.14	1	1	0	7.0	7	0	3
G.Maddux	0	1	2.57	1	1	0	7.0	5	3	5
J.Smoltz	0	1	3.86	1	1	0	7.0	6	3	11
T.Mulholland	0	0	7.36	2	0	0	3.2	5	1	3
J.Rocker	0	0	0.00	2	0	0	3.0	2	2	4
R.Springer	0	0	0.00	2	0	0	2.1	1	0	1
K.McGlinchy	0	0	0.00	1	0	0	2.0	2	1	2
K.Millwood	0	1	18.00	1	1	0	2.0	8	2	2
M.Remlinger	0	1	9.00	2	0	0	1.0	1	1	0
Totals	0	4	4.37	13	4	0	35.0	37	13	31

GAME 1 / OCT. 23

HERNANDEZ, NELSON(8), STANTON(8), RIVERA(8) VS. MADDUX, ROCKER(8), REMLINGER(9) — **51,342**

NY	000	000	040	4	6	0
ATL	000	100	000	1	2	2

Brian Hunter's misplay on a sacrifice bunt extended New York's seventh inning and allowed the Yankees to score two extra runs in the frame. The Braves had the tying run at the plate with one out in the ninth, but Rivera struck out Brian Jordan and got Greg Myers to pop to third to end it.

GAME 2 / OCT. 24

CONE, MENDOZA(8), NELSON(9) VS. MILLWOOD, MULHOLLAND(3), SPRINGER(6), MCGLINCHY(8) — **51,226**

NY	302	110	000	7	14	1
ATL	000	000	002	2	5	1

Of the 15 hitters Atlanta starter Kevin Millwood faced, 10 reached base, digging the Braves into a deep, early five-run hole. It became a seven-run deficit after Chuck Knoblauch singled in a run in the fifth.

GAME 3 / OCT. 26

GLAVINE, ROCKER(8), REMLINGER(10) VS. PETTITTE, GRIMSLEY(4), NELSON(7), RIVERA(9) — **56,794**

ATL	103	100	000	0	5	14	1
NY	100	010	120	1	6	9	0

Atlanta rocked Andy Pettitte for 10 hits and five runs in the first four innings, but let the Yankees hang close as they stranded eight runners through five. New York tied it in the eighth on Knoblauch's two-run homer off Tom Glavine, then won it in the 10th on a solo shot by Chad Curtis.

GAME 4 / OCT. 27						
SMOLTZ, MULHOLLAND(8), SPRINGER(8) VS. CLEMENS, NELSON(8), RIVERA(8) 56,752						
ATL	000	000	010	1	5	0
NY	003	000	01X	4	8	0

The Braves couldn't get a runner past first base off Roger Clemens until the eighth inning, when a pair of two-out singles put runners on first and second. Jeff Nelson relieved Clemens and allowed a run-scoring single to Bret Boone, but Rivera got Chipper Jones to ground out before retiring the side in order in the ninth for his second save.

2000 AL Division Series
New York Yankees (3) vs. Oakland Athletics (2)

After losing only one game in three postseason series a year earlier, the Yankees were immediately stretched to the brink in their quest to become the first club since the 1972–74 Athletics to win three straight world championships.

NY (E)

PLAYER, POS	G	AB	R	H	2B	3B	HR	RBI	BB	SO	SB	AVG	OBP	SLG
B.Williams, of	5	20	3	5	3	0	0	1	1	4	0	.250	.286	.400
D.Jeter, ss	5	19	1	4	0	0	0	2	2	3	0	.211	.286	.211
T.Martinez, 1b	5	19	2	8	2	0	0	4	1	3	0	.421	.450	.526
P.O'Neill, of	5	19	4	4	1	0	0	0	2	4	0	.211	.286	.263
D.Justice, of	5	18	2	4	0	0	1	1	3	4	0	.222	.333	.222
S.Brosius, 3b	5	17	0	3	1	0	0	1	1	4	0	.176	.222	.235
J.Posada, c	5	17	2	4	2	0	0	1	3	5	0	.235	.350	.353
L.Sojo, 2b	5	16	2	3	2	0	0	5	2	1	0	.188	.278	.313
G.Hill, dh	4	12	1	1	0	0	0	2	1	5	0	.083	.154	.083
C.Knoblauch, dh	3	9	1	3	0	0	0	1	0	2	1	.333	.333	.333
C.Bellinger, of	2	1	0	1	1	0	0	1	0	0	0	1.000	1.000	2.000
L.Polonia, ph	1	1	0	1	0	0	0	0	0	0	0	1.000	1.000	1.000
J.Vizcaino, 2b	1	0	1	0	0	0	0	0	0	0	0	.000	.000	.000
Totals		168	19	41	12	0	1	19	16	35	1	.244	.314	.315

PITCHER	W	L	ERA	G	GS	SV	IP	H	BB	SO
A.Pettitte	1	0	3.97	2	2	0	11.1	15	3	7
R.Clemens	0	2	8.18	2	2	0	11.0	13	8	10
O.Hernandez	1	0	2.45	2	1	0	7.1	5	5	5
M.Rivera	0	0	0.00	3	0	3	5.0	2	0	2
M.Stanton	1	0	2.08	3	0	0	4.1	5	1	3
J.Nelson	0	0	0.00	2	0	0	2.0	0	0	2
D.Gooden	0	0	21.60	1	0	0	1.2	4	1	1
R.Choate	0	0	6.75	1	0	0	1.1	0	1	1
Totals	3	2	4.70	16	5	3	44.0	44	19	31

OAK (W)

PLAYER, POS	G	AB	R	H	2B	3B	HR	RBI	BB	SO	SB	AVG	OBP	SLG
E.Chavez, 3b	5	21	4	7	3	0	0	4	0	5	0	.333	.333	.476
M.Tejada, ss	5	20	5	7	2	0	0	1	2	2	1	.350	.409	.450
R.Velarde, 2b	5	20	2	5	1	0	0	3	2	3	1	.250	.318	.300
T.Long, of	5	19	2	3	0	0	1	1	3	2	0	.158	.273	.158
B.Grieve, of	5	17	1	2	0	0	0	2	3	7	0	.118	.250	.118
R.Hernandez, c	5	16	3	6	2	0	0	3	0	3	0	.375	.375	.500
J.Giambi, 1b	5	14	2	4	0	0	0	1	7	2	1	.286	.524	.286
O.Saenz, dh	4	13	1	3	0	0	1	4	0	2	0	.231	.267	.231
J.Giambi, of-dh	4	9	1	3	0	0	0	1	2	2	0	.333	.455	.333
M.Stairs, of	3	9	0	1	1	0	0	0	0	1	0	.111	.111	.222
A.Piatt, of	3	6	2	1	0	0	0	0	0	1	0	.167	.167	.167
R.Christenson, of	2	2	0	1	0	0	0	1	0	1	0	.500	.500	.500
B.Porter, of	2	1	0	1	0	0	0	1	0	0	0	1.000	1.000	1.000
S.Fasano, c	1	0	0	0	0	0	0	0	0	0	0	.000	.000	.000
F.Menechino, 2b	1	0	0	0	0	0	0	0	0	0	0	.000	.000	.000
Totals		167	23	44	9	0	2	22	19	31	3	.263	.344	.317

PITCHER	W	L	ERA	G	GS	SV	IP	H	BB	SO
K.Appier	0	1	3.48	2	1	0	10.1	10	6	13
T.Hudson	0	1	3.38	1	1	0	8.0	6	4	5
G.Heredia	1	1	12.79	2	2	0	6.1	11	3	3
B.Zito	1	0	1.59	1	1	0	5.2	7	2	5
J.Mecir	0	0	0.00	3	0	0	5.1	1	0	2
M.Magnante	0	0	0.00	2	0	0	3.0	1	0	2
J.Isringhausen	0	0	0.00	2	0	1	2.0	1	0	3
J.Tam	0	0	0.00	3	0	0	2.0	3	1	1
D.Jones	0	0	0.00	2	0	0	1.1	1	0	1
Totals	2	3	3.48	18	5	1	44.0	41	16	35

GAME 1 / OCT. 3						
CLEMENS, STANTON(7), NELSON(8) VS. HEREDIA, TAM(7), MECIR(7), ISRINGHAUSEN(9) 47,360						
NY	020	001	000	3	7	0
OAK	000	031	01X	5	10	2

After managing only one hit through the first four innings, the Athletics scored three in the fifth off Roger Clemens. It could have been a bigger inning had not Jason Giambi grounded into an inning ending double play.

GAME 2 / OCT. 4						
PETTITTE, RIVERA(8) VS. APPIER, MAGNANTE(7), TAM(9), JONES(9) 47,860						
NY	000	003	001	4	8	1
OAK	000	000	000	0	6	1

Andy Pettitte retired 13 straight hitters in the middle innings as he combined with Mariano Rivera on a six-hit shutout.

GAME 3 / OCT. 6						
HUDSON VS. HERNANDEZ, RIVERA(8) 56,606						
OAK	010	010	000	2	4	2
NY	020	100	01X	4	6	1

The Athletics drew first blood, but the Yankees took the lead for good in the second on a single by Derek Jeter. Rivera notched his second save by pitching the final two innings.

GAME 4 / OCT. 7						
ZITO, MECIR(6), MAGNANTE(7), JONES(9) VS. CLEMENS, STANTON(6), CHOATE(7), GOODEN(8) 56,915						
OAK	300	003	014	11	11	0
NY	000	001	000	1	8	0

A three-run homer by Olmedo Saenz in the top of the first jump started the Athletics on a rout of Yankees starter Clemens.

GAME 5 / OCT. 8						
PETTITTE, STANTON(4), NELSON(6), HERNANDEZ(8), RIVERA(8) VS. HEREDIA, TAM(1), APPIER(2), MECIR(6), ISRINGHAUSEN(9) 41,170						
NY	600	100	000	7	12	0
OAK	021	200	000	5	13	0

The Athletics managed to make it a contest even after the Bombers scored six in the first, as Pettitte was strafed for 10 hits in less than four innings. Four relievers saved the day, including Rivera, who allowed only one hit in the final $1^2/_3$ innings.

2000 AL Championship Series
New York Yankees (4) vs. Seattle Mariners (2)

The Yankees averaged more than six runs per contest after getting blanked in the opening game of the LCS. New York won its third straight pennant, and fourth in five years, easily the club's most productive stretch since the early 1960s.

NY (E)

PLAYER, POS	G	AB	R	H	2B	3B	HR	RBI	BB	SO	SB	AVG	OBP	SLG
D.Justice, of	6	26	4	6	2	0	2	8	2	7	0	.231	.286	.308
T.Martinez, 1b	6	25	5	8	2	0	1	1	2	4	0	.320	.370	.400
C.Knoblauch, dh	6	23	3	6	2	0	0	2	3	4	0	.261	.346	.348
L.Sojo, 2b-3b	6	23	1	6	1	0	0	2	2	3	0	.261	.320	.304
B.Williams, of	6	23	5	10	1	0	1	3	2	3	1	.435	.481	.478
D.Jeter, ss	6	22	6	7	0	0	2	5	6	7	1	.318	.464	.318
P.O'Neill, of	6	20	0	5	0	0	0	5	1	2	0	.250	.286	.250
J.Posada, c	6	19	2	3	1	0	0	3	5	5	0	.158	.333	.211
S.Brosius, 3b	6	18	2	4	0	0	0	0	2	3	0	.222	.300	.222
G.Hill, ph	2	2	0	0	0	0	0	0	0	2	0	.000	.000	.000
J.Vizcaino, 2b	4	2	3	2	1	0	0	2	0	0	2	1.000	1.000	1.500
L.Polonia, ph	1	1	0	0	0	0	0	0	0	1	0	.000	.000	.000
C.Bellinger, of	5	0	0	0	0	0	0	0	0	0	0	.000	.000	.000
Totals		204	31	57	10	0	6	31	25	41	4	.279	.365	.328

PITCHER	W	L	ERA	G	GS	SV	IP	H	BB	SO
O.Hernandez	2	0	4.20	2	2	0	15.0	13	8	14
D.Neagle	0	2	4.50	2	2	0	10.0	6	7	7
R.Clemens	1	0	0.00	1	1	0	9.0	1	2	15
A.Pettitte	1	0	2.70	1	1	0	6.2	9	1	2

NY (E) (CONT.)

PITCHER	W	L	ERA	G	GS	SV	IP	H	BB	SO
M.Rivera	0	0	1.93	3	0	1	4.2	4	0	1
J.Nelson	0	0	9.00	3	0	0	3.0	5	0	6
D.Gooden	0	0	0.00	1	0	0	2.1	1	0	1
D.Cone	0	0	0.00	1	0	0	1.0	0	0	0
J.Grimsley	0	0	0.00	2	0	0	1.0	2	3	1
R.Choate	0	0	0.00	1	0	0	0.1	0	0	1
Totals	4	2	3.06	17	6	1	53.0	41	21	48

SEA (W)

PLAYER, POS	G	AB	R	H	2B	3B	HR	RBI	BB	SO	SB	AVG	OBP	SLG
A.Rodriguez, ss	6	22	4	9	2	0	2	5	3	8	1	.409	.480	.500
E.Martinez, dh	6	21	2	5	1	0	1	4	3	5	0	.238	.333	.286
J.Olerud, 1b	6	20	2	7	3	0	1	2	2	2	1	.350	.409	.500
D.Bell, 3b-2b	5	18	0	4	0	0	0	0	0	0	0	.222	.222	.222
M.Cameron, of	6	18	3	2	0	0	0	1	2	7	1	.111	.200	.111
M.McLemore, 2b	5	16	2	4	3	0	0	2	2	1	0	.250	.333	.438
S.Javier, of	4	14	0	1	0	0	0	1	0	4	0	.071	.071	.071
J.Buhner, of	4	11	0	2	0	0	0	0	1	6	0	.182	.250	.182
A.Martin, of	4	11	2	2	2	0	0	0	2	3	0	.182	.308	.364
D.Wilson, c	4	11	0	1	0	0	0	0	1	5	0	.091	.167	.091
R.Henderson, of	3	9	2	2	1	0	0	1	2	2	0	.222	.364	.333
R.Ibanez, of	6	9	0	0	0	0	0	0	0	2	0	.000	.000	.000
J.Oliver, c	4	6	0	1	0	0	0	0	1	1	0	.167	.286	.167
C.Guillen, 3b	2	5	1	1	0	0	1	2	2	2	0	.200	.429	.200
C.Gipson, of	2	0	0	0	0	0	0	0	0	0	0	.000	.000	.000
Totals		191	18	41	12	0	5	18	21	48	3	.215	.292	.277

PITCHER	W	L	ERA	G	GS	SV	IP	H	BB	SO
F.Garcia	2	0	1.54	2	2	0	11.2	10	4	11
J.Halama	0	0	2.89	2	2	0	9.1	10	5	3
A.Sele	0	1	6.00	1	1	0	6.0	9	0	4
P.Abbott	0	1	5.40	1	1	0	5.0	3	3	3
B.Tomko	0	0	7.20	2	0	0	5.0	3	4	4
J.Mesa	0	0	12.46	3	0	0	4.1	5	3	3
J.Paniagua	0	1	4.15	5	0	0	4.1	4	1	4
K.Sasaki	0	0	0.00	2	0	1	2.2	3	1	3
A.Lee Rhodes	0	1	31.50	4	0	0	2.0	8	4	5
R.Ramsay	0	0	0.00	2	0	0	1.2	2	0	1
Totals	2	4	5.37	24	6	1	52.0	57	25	41

GAME 1 / OCT. 10

GARCIA, PANIAGUA(7), RHODES(8), SASAKI(9) VS. NEAGLE, NELSON(6), CHOATE(9), GRIMSLEY(9) — **54,481**

				R	H	E
SEA	000	011	000	2	5	0
NY	000	000	000	0	6	1

Freddy Garcia and three relievers held New York in check with a combined six-hit shutout. Rickey Henderson singled in a run in the fifth and Alex Rodriguez homered in the sixth to account for the only runs of the game.

GAME 2 / OCT. 11

HALAMA, PANIAGUA(7), RHODES(8), MESA(8) VS. HERNANDEZ, RIVERA(9) — **55,317**

				R	H	E
SEA	001	000	000	1	7	2
NY	000	000	07X	7	14	0

Headed into the eighth inning, things looked dire for the Yankees, who hadn't scored in 16 innings in the LCS. That changed with a seven-run eighth, capped by Derek Jeter's two-run homer, making a winner of Orlando Hernandez, who allowed only one run in eight innings.

GAME 3 / OCT. 13

PETTITTE, NELSON(7), RIVERA(8) VS. SELE, TOMKO(7), RAMSAY(9) — **47,827**

				R	H	E
NY	021	001	004	8	13	0
SEA	100	010	000	2	10	1

Consecutive homers in the second inning from Bernie Williams and Tino Martinez set the stage for another Yankees' win, sealed by four runs in the ninth.

GAME 4 / OCT. 14

CLEMENS VS. ABBOTT, RAMSAY(6), MESA(7), PANIAGUA(9) — **47,803**

				R	H	E
NY	000	030	020	5	5	0
SEA	000	000	000	0	1	0

Roger Clemens turned in one of the most dominating October pitching performances ever, striking out 15 and allowing only one hit and two walks. "The Rocket" retired 16 straight hitters between a walk to Alex Rodriguez in the first and Al Martin's leadoff double in the seventh.

GAME 5 / OCT. 15

NEAGLE, NELSON(5), GRIMSLEY(5), GOODEN(5), CONE(8) VS. GARCIA, PANIAGUA(6), RHODES(7), SASAKI(8) — **47,802**

				R	H	E
NY	000	200	000	2	8	0
SEA	100	050	00X	6	8	0

A five-run fifth temporarily saved Seattle from elimination. The inning started with a bunt single and a walk, then saw back-to-back homers from Edgar Martinez and John Olerud.

GAME 6 / OCT. 17

HALAMA, TOMKO(4), PANIAGUA(7), RHODES(7), MESA(7) VS. HERNANDEZ, RIVERA(8) — **56,598**

				R	H	E
SEA	200	200	030	7	10	0
NY	000	300	60X	9	11	0

As in the first game, a big inning doomed Seattle. The Mariners tried three different relievers in New York's six-run seventh, but none could figure out how to cool off the Yankees' big bats. A three-run, upper deck homer by David Justice was the big blow.

2000 World Series
New York Yankees (4) vs. New York Mets (1)

The first subway series since 1956 captivated the five boroughs, but it generated little interest in the provinces. Television ratings were down more than 20 percent from the year before, and overall it was the least-watched Fall Classic ever. Every game took at least three hours and 20 minutes; the first game was the longest Series game ever at four hours, 51 minutes.

NY (AL)

PLAYER, POS	G	AB	R	H	2B	3B	HR	RBI	BB	SO	SB	AVG	OBP	SLG
D.Jeter, ss	5	22	6	9	2	1	2	2	3	8	0	.409	.480	.591
T.Martinez, 1b	5	22	3	8	1	0	0	2	1	4	0	.364	.391	.409
D.Justice, of	5	19	1	3	2	0	0	3	3	2	0	.158	.273	.263
P.O'Neill, of	5	19	2	9	2	2	0	2	3	4	0	.474	.545	.789
J.Posada, c	5	18	2	4	1	0	0	1	5	4	0	.222	.391	.278
B.Williams, of	5	18	2	2	0	0	1	1	5	5	0	.111	.304	.111
J.Vizcaino, 2b	4	17	0	4	0	0	0	1	0	5	0	.235	.235	.235
S.Brosius, 3b	5	13	2	4	0	0	1	3	2	2	0	.308	.444	.308
C.Knoblauch, dh	4	10	1	1	0	0	0	1	2	1	0	.100	.250	.100
L.Sojo, 2b-3b	4	7	0	2	0	0	0	2	1	0	1	.286	.375	.286
G.Hill, dh	3	3	0	0	0	0	0	0	0	0	0	.000	.000	.000
A.Pettitte, p	2	3	0	0	0	0	0	0	0	1	0	.000	.000	.000
O.Hernandez, p	1	2	0	0	0	0	0	0	0	2	0	.000	.000	.000
D.Neagle, p	1	2	0	0	0	0	0	0	0	1	0	.000	.000	.000
L.Polonia, ph	2	2	0	1	0	0	0	0	0	0	0	.500	.500	.500
J.Canseco, ph	1	1	0	0	0	0	0	0	0	1	0	.000	.000	.000
M.Rivera, p	4	1	0	0	0	0	0	0	0	0	0	.000	.000	.000
C.Bellinger, of	4	0	0	0	0	0	0	0	0	0	0	.000	.000	.000
Totals		179	19	47	8	3	4	18	25	40	1	.263	.361	.341

PITCHER	W	L	ERA	G	GS	SV	IP	H	BB	SO
A.Pettitte	0	0	1.98	2	2	0	13.2	16	4	9
R.Clemens	1	0	0.00	1	1	0	8.0	2	0	9
O.Hernandez	0	1	4.91	1	1	0	7.1	9	3	12
M.Rivera	0	0	3.00	4	0	2	6.0	4	1	7
D.Neagle	0	0	3.86	1	1	0	4.2	4	2	3
M.Stanton	2	0	0.00	4	0	0	4.1	0	0	7
J.Nelson	1	0	10.13	3	0	0	2.2	5	1	1
D.Cone	0	0	0.00	1	0	0	0.1	0	0	0
Totals	4	1	2.68	17	5	2	47.0	40	11	48

NY (NL)

PLAYER, POS	G	AB	R	H	2B	3B	HR	RBI	BB	SO	SB	AVG	OBP	SLG
M.Piazza, c	5	22	3	6	2	0	2	4	0	4	0	.273	.273	.364
E.Alfonzo, 2b	5	21	1	3	0	0	0	1	1	5	0	.143	.182	.143
J.Payton, of	5	21	3	7	0	0	1	3	0	5	0	.333	.333	.333
R.Ventura, 3b	5	20	1	3	1	0	1	1	1	5	0	.150	.190	.200
T.Zeile, 1b	5	20	1	8	2	0	0	1	1	5	0	.400	.429	.500
B.Agbayani, of	5	18	2	5	2	0	0	2	3	6	0	.278	.381	.389
T.Perez, of	5	16	1	2	0	0	0	0	1	4	0	.125	.176	.125
K.Abbott, ss	5	8	0	2	1	0	0	0	1	3	0	.250	.333	.375
M.Bordick, ss	4	8	0	1	0	0	0	0	0	3	0	.125	.125	.125
B.Trammell, of	4	5	1	2	0	0	0	3	1	1	0	.400	.500	.400
L.Harris, dh	3	4	1	0	0	0	0	0	1	1	0	.000	.200	.000
D.Hamilton, ph	4	3	0	0	0	0	0	0	0	2	0	.000	.000	.000
B.Jones, p	1	2	0	0	0	0	0	0	0	1	0	.000	.000	.000
A.Leiter, p	2	2	0	0	0	0	0	0	0	0	0	.000	.000	.000
T.Pratt, c	1	2	1	0	0	0	0	0	1	2	0	.000	.333	.000
M.Franco, 1b	1	1	0	0	0	0	0	0	0	1	0	.000	.000	.000
J.McEwing, of	3	1	1	0	0	0	0	0	0	0	0	.000	.000	.000
R.Reed, p	1	1	0	1	0	0	0	0	0	0	0	1.000	1.000	1.000
Totals		175	16	40	8	0	4	15	11	48	0	.229	.286	.274

NY (NL) (CONT.)										
PITCHER	W	L	ERA	G	GS	SV	IP	H	BB	SO
A.Leiter	0	1	2.87	2	2	0	15.2	12	6	16
M.Hampton	0	1	6.00	1	1	0	6.0	8	5	4
R.Reed	0	0	3.00	1	1	0	6.0	6	1	8
B.Jones	0	1	5.40	1	1	0	5.0	4	3	3
G.Rusch	0	0	2.25	3	0	0	4.0	6	2	2
J.Franco	1	0	0.00	4	0	0	3.1	3	0	1
A.Benitez	0	0	3.00	3	0	1	3.0	3	2	2
T.Wendell	0	1	5.40	2	0	0	1.2	3	2	2
R.White	0	0	6.75	1	0	0	1.1	1	1	1
D.Cook	0	0	0.00	3	0	0	0.2	1	3	1
Totals	1	4	3.47	21	5	1	46.2	47	25	40

GAME 1 / OCT. 21						
LEITER, J.FRANCO(8), BENITEZ(9), COOK(10), RUSCH(10), WENDELL(11) VS. PETTITTE, NELSON(7), RIVERA(9), STANTON(11)						55,913
NY-N	000	000	300	000	3	10	0
NY-A	000	002	001	001	4	12	0

The Yankees won the opening game because Timo Perez loafed on a ball he thought was a home run in the top of the sixth. Todd Zeile's two-out drive hit right at the top of the wall but stayed in play, and Perez was thrown out at home by three steps. Absent that run, the Yankees tied the game in the bottom of the ninth on a sac fly by Chuck Knoblauch and won it in the 12th on a two-out single by Jose Vizcaino.

GAME 2 / OCT. 22						
HAMPTON, RUSCH(7), WHITE(7), COOK(8) VS. CLEMENS, NELSON(9), RIVERA(9)						56,059
NY-N	000	000	005	5	7	3
NY-A	210	010	11X	6	12	1

A confrontation between Mike Piazza and Roger Clemens, who feuded during the regular season after Clemens hit Piazza in the head, overshadowed a furious finish. In the top of the first, Piazza broke his bat on a grounder to second. Part of the bat wound up near Clemens, who picked it up and threw it close to Piazza as he was running to first. Both benches emptied, though no punches were thrown. Piazza later hit a two-run homer in the ninth, followed five batters later by a three-run dinger by Jay Payton that brought the Mets to within one run of tying the game. Mariano Rivera finally fanned Kurt Abbott to end the game.

GAME 3 / OCT. 24						
HERNANDEZ, STANTON(8) VS. REED, WENDELL(7), COOK(7), J.FRANCO(8), BENITEZ(9)						55,299
NY-A	001	100	000	2	8	0
NY-N	010	001	02X	4	9	0

The Mets won their only game with two runs in the eighth off gutty veteran Orlando Hernandez. The Yankees were unable to call upon their redoubtable closer, who had pitched a total of three innings in the first two contests.

GAME 4 / OCT. 25						
NEAGLE, CONE(5), NELSON(6), STANTON(7), RIVERA(8) VS. B.J.JONES, RUSCH(6), J.FRANCO(8), BENITEZ(9)						55,290
NY-A	111	000	000	3	8	0
NY-N	002	000	000	2	6	1

Single runs in each of the first three innings were enough for the Yankees. Four pinstriped relievers combined to hold the Mets to just two hits over the final $4^1/_3$ innings, including Rivera, who threw two innings for the second time in the Series to earn the save.

GAME 5 / OCT. 26						
PETTITTE, STANTON(8), RIVERA(9) VS. LEITER, J.FRANCO(9)						55,292
NY-A	010	001	002	4	7	1
NY-N	020	000	000	2	8	1

Through eight innings, Al Leiter allowed only two runs and five hits; he was one out away from a complete game after striking out the first two Yankees' hitters in the ninth, but couldn't finish it. After a walk and a single, Luis Sojo drove in the winning run with a single to left. Jorge Posada was hit by the throw from left fielder Jay Payton as he slid home, and a second run scored as the ball rolled away from the plate.

2001 AL Division Series
New York Yankees (3) vs. Oakland Athletics (2)

Derek Jeter single-handedly kept the Yankees in the series with two spectacular defensive plays in Game 3. On the verge of elimination, Jeter's hustle kept the Athletics from tying the game in the seventh, and the superstar shortstop followed up with a spectacular catch in the eighth.

NY (F)														
PLAYER, POS	G	AB	R	H	2B	3B	HR	RBI	BB	SO	SB	AVG	OBP	SLG
C.Knoblauch, of	5	22	1	6	1	0	0	1	0	0	1	.273	.273	.318
D.Jeter, ss	5	18	2	8	1	0	0	1	1	0	0	.444	.476	.500
T.Martinez, 1b	5	18	1	2	0	0	1	2	1	6	0	.111	.158	.111
J.Posada, c	5	18	3	8	1	0	1	2	2	2	1	.444	.500	.500
A.Soriano, 2b	5	18	2	4	0	0	0	3	1	5	2	.222	.263	.222
B.Williams, of	5	18	4	4	3	0	0	5	3	3	0	.222	.333	.389
S.Brosius, 3b	5	17	0	1	0	0	0	1	0	3	0	.059	.059	.059
D.Justice, of-dh	4	13	3	3	0	1	1	1	2	5	0	.231	.333	.385
P.O'Neill, dh-of	3	11	1	1	1	0	0	0	0	0	0	.091	.091	.182
S.Spencer, of	3	8	1	2	1	0	0	0	1	4	0	.250	.333	.375
R.Velarde, dh	2	5	0	1	0	0	0	0	0	1	0	.200	.200	.200
C.Bellinger, pr	1	0	0	0	0	0	0	0	0	0	0	.000	.000	.000
Totals		166	18	40	8	1	3	16	11	29	4	.241	.302	.301

PITCHER	W	L	ERA	G	GS	SV	IP	H	BB	SO
R.Clemens	0	1	5.40	2	2	0	8.1	9	4	6
M.Mussina	1	0	0.00	1	1	0	7.0	4	1	4
A.Pettitte	0	1	1.42	1	1	0	6.1	7	2	4
O.Hernandez	1	0	3.18	1	1	0	5.2	8	2	5
M.Rivera	0	0	0.00	3	0	2	5.0	4	0	4
M.Stanton	1	0	0.00	3	0	0	4.2	3	0	1
R.Mendoza	0	0	0.00	3	0	0	4.1	2	1	5
S.Hitchcock	0	0	6.00	1	0	0	3.0	5	0	2
J.Witasick	0	0	13.50	1	0	0	0.2	1	1	0
Totals	3	2	2.20	16	5	2	45.0	43	11	31

OAK (W)														
PLAYER, POS	G	AB	R	H	2B	3B	HR	RBI	BB	SO	SB	AVG	OBP	SLG
J.Damon, of	5	22	3	9	2	1	0	0	1	1	2	.409	.435	.591
E.Chavez, 3b	5	21	0	3	1	0	0	0	0	5	0	.143	.143	.190
M.Tejada, ss	5	21	1	6	3	0	0	1	0	3	0	.286	.304	.429
T.Long, of	5	18	3	7	3	0	2	3	1	2	0	.389	.421	.556
J.Giambi, 1b	1	17	2	6	0	0	1	4	4	2	0	.353	.476	.353
J.Dye, of	4	13	0	3	2	0	0	0	2	2	0	.231	.333	.385
J.Giambi, dh	5	13	0	4	1	0	0	2	1	0	1	.308	.357	.385
F.Menechino, 2b	4	12	2	1	0	0	0	0	1	4	0	.083	.154	.083
R.Gant, of-dh	4	11	1	2	0	0	1	1	0	3	0	.182	.182	.182
R.Hernandez, c	5	10	0	0	0	0	0	0	1	4	0	.000	.091	.000
G.Myers, c	3	7	0	1	0	0	0	0	0	3	0	.143	.143	.143
O.Saenz, dh	3	4	0	0	0	0	0	0	0	1	0	.000	.000	.000
F.P. Santangelo, 2b	2	3	0	1	1	0	0	0	0	0	0	.333	.333	.667
E.Byrnes, dh	2	2	0	0	0	0	0	0	0	1	0	.000	.000	.000
Totals		174	12	43	13	1	4	11	11	31	3	.247	.302	.333

PITCHER	W	L	ERA	G	GS	SV	IP	H	BB	SO
M.Mulder	1	1	2.45	2	2	0	11.0	14	2	7
T.Hudson	1	0	0.93	2	1	0	9.2	8	1	5
B.Zito	0	1	1.13	1	1	0	8.0	2	1	6
C.Lidle	0	1	10.80	1	1	0	3.1	5	3	0
J.Mecir	0	0	5.40	2	0	0	3.1	4	0	4
M.Guthrie	0	0	0.00	2	0	0	3.0	0	0	2
J.Isringhausen	0	0	0.00	2	0	2	2.0	1	1	3
M.Magnante	0	0	0.00	1	0	0	1.1	3	1	1
C.Bradford	0	0	0.00	1	0	0	1.0	0	0	1
J.Tam	0	0	18.00	1	0	0	1.0	3	0	0
E.Hiljus	0	0	27.00	1	0	0	0.1	0	2	0
Totals	2	3	2.86	16	5	2	44.0	40	11	29

GAME 1 / OCT. 10						
MULDER, MECIR(7), ISRINGHAUSEN(9) VS. CLEMENS, HITCHCOCK(5), WITASICK(8), STANTON(8)						56,697
OAK	100	100	120	5	10	1
NY	000	010	020	3	10	1

Mark Mulder bested Roger Clemens in the opener as Oakland grabbed an early lead and never trailed. Terrance Long hit two home runs for the Athletics.

GAME 2 / OCT. 11						
HUDSON, ISRINGHAUSEN(9) VS. PETTITTE, MENDOZA(7), RIVERA(9)						56,684
OAK	000	100	001	2	9	0
NY	000	000	000	0	7	1

Andy Pettitte allowed but one run in 6⅓ innings, yet his counterpart Tim Hudson was better, shutting out New York over eight. Jason Isringhausen put the first two batters on base in the ninth, but the A's closer the next three for his second save of the series.

GAME 3 / OCT. 13						
MUSSINA, RIVERA(8) VS. ZITO, GUTHRIE(9)						55,861
NY	000	010	000	1	2	0
OAK	000	000	000	0	6	1

Jeter's jaw-dropping plays overshadowed the fine pitching of Mike Mussina and Mariano Rivera, who blanked Oakland on six hits.

GAME 4 / OCT. 14						
HERNANDEZ, STANTON(6), MENDOZA(8) VS. LIDLE, HILJUS(4), MAGNANTE(4), GUTHRIE(6), BRADFORD(8), TAM(9)						43,681
NY	022	300	002	9	11	1
OAK	002	000	000	2	11	1

Bernie Williams' two-run double in the third took the life out of Oakland. The Bronxers tallied seven times in the first four innings, six off Athletics' starter Cory Lidle.

GAME 5 / OCT. 15						
MULDER, HUDSON(5), MECIR(7) VS. CLEMENS, STANTON(5), MENDOZA(7), RIVERA(8)						56,642
OAK	110	010	000	3	7	3
NY	021	101	00X	5	10	1

New York scored the go-ahead run in the third on an error by Oakland third baseman Eric Chavez. Yankees starter Roger Clemens settled down after being touched for two early runs; "The Rocket" and three relievers limited the Athletics to three hits and a run in the final seven innings.

2001 AL Championship Series
New York Yankees (4) vs. Seattle Mariners (1)

Subtract their 14-run outburst in the fourth game and the Mariners managed to score only eight runs in the rest of the series. Meanwhile, the Yankees had little trouble handling a Seattle club that had won 116 games in the regular season.

NY (E)

PLAYER, POS	G	AB	R	H	2B	3B	HR	RBI	BB	SO	SB	AVG	OBP	SLG
T.Martinez, 1b	5	20	3	5	1	0	1	3	0	4	0	.250	.250	.300
D.Justice, dh	5	18	3	5	1	0	0	4	3	1	0	.278	.381	.333
C.Knoblauch, of	5	18	0	6	1	0	0	3	2	3	0	.333	.400	.389
D.Jeter, ss	5	17	0	2	0	0	0	2	2	2	0	.118	.211	.118
B.Williams, of	5	17	4	4	0	0	3	5	5	4	0	.235	.409	.235
S.Brosius, 3b	5	16	3	3	2	0	0	2	0	6	0	.188	.188	.313
A.Soriano, 2b	5	15	5	6	0	0	1	2	3	3	2	.400	.500	.400
J.Posada, c	5	14	4	3	1	0	0	0	6	7	0	.214	.450	.286
P.O'Neill, of	5	12	2	5	0	0	2	3	1	0	0	.417	.462	.417
S.Spencer, of	5	7	1	2	1	0	0	0	1	1	1	.286	.375	.429
C.Bellinger, of	1	1	0	0	0	0	0	0	0	0	0	.000	.000	.000
T.Greene, c	1	1	0	0	0	0	0	0	0	0	0	.000	.000	.000
L.Sojo, 1b	1	1	0	0	0	0	0	0	0	0	0	.000	.000	.000
R.Velarde, 3b	1	1	0	0	0	0	0	0	0	0	0	.000	.000	.000
E.Wilson, ss	1	1	0	1	0	0	0	0	0	0	0	1.000	1.000	1.000
Totals		159	25	42	7	0	7	24	23	31	3	.264	.364	.308

PITCHER	W	L	ERA	G	GS	SV	IP	H	BB	SO
A.Pettitte	2	0	2.51	2	2	0	14.1	11	2	8
M.Mussina	1	0	3.00	1	1	0	6.0	4	1	3
R.Mendoza	0	0	1.69	3	0	0	5.1	3	2	4
R.Clemens	0	0	0.00	1	1	0	5.0	1	4	7
O.Hernandez	0	1	7.20	1	1	0	5.0	5	5	7
M.Rivera	1	0	1.93	4	0	2	4.2	2	1	3
J.Witasick	0	0	9.00	1	0	0	3.0	6	0	2
M.Stanton	0	0	27.00	2	0	0	1.0	1	2	0
M.Wohlers	0	0	13.50	1	0	0	0.2	3	1	1
Totals	4	1	3.80	16	5	2	45.0	36	18	35

SEA (W)

PLAYER, POS	G	AB	R	H	2B	3B	HR	RBI	BB	SO	SB	AVG	OBP	SLG
E.Martinez, dh	5	20	1	3	1	0	0	0	1	6	0	.150	.190	.200
B.Boone, 2b	5	19	2	6	0	0	2	6	2	2	0	.316	.381	.316
J.Olerud, 1b	5	19	2	4	0	0	1	3	2	4	0	.211	.286	.211

SEA (W) (CONT.)

PLAYER, POS	G	AB	R	H	2B	3B	HR	RBI	BB	SO	SB	AVG	OBP	SLG
I.Suzuki, of	5	18	3	4	1	0	0	1	4	4	2	.222	.364	.278
M.Cameron, of	5	17	3	3	2	0	0	0	4	4	0	.176	.333	.294
D.Bell, 3b	5	16	1	3	0	0	0	4	0	3	0	.188	.188	.188
S.Javier, of	5	14	2	3	0	0	1	2	1	3	1	.214	.267	.214
M.McLemore, ss-1b-of	1	14	1	2	0	1	0	3	2	2	0	.143	.250	.286
D.Wilson, c	4	13	2	2	0	0	0	0	0	1	0	.154	.154	.154
C.Guillen, ss	3	8	1	2	0	0	0	0	0	1	0	.250	.250	.250
J.Buhner, of	3	6	2	2	0	0	1	1	1	3	0	.333	.429	.333
T.Lampkin, c	2	4	0	1	0	0	0	0	1	2	0	.250	.400	.250
A.Martin, ph	2	2	1	1	0	1	0	0	0	0	0	.500	.500	1.500
C.Gipson, of	2	1	1	0	0	0	0	0	0	0	0	.000	.000	.000
Totals		171	22	36	4	2	5	20	18	35	3	.211	.289	.257

PITCHER	W	L	ERA	G	GS	SV	IP	H	BB	SO
A.Sele	0	2	3.60	2	2	0	10.0	11	4	5
F.Garcia	0	1	3.68	1	1	0	7.1	7	4	6
J.Moyer	1	0	2.57	1	1	0	7.0	4	1	5
P.Abbott	0	0	0.00	1	1	0	5.0	0	8	2
J.Paniagua	0	0	12.27	3	0	0	3.2	7	1	1
J.Nelson	0	0	0.00	2	0	0	2.1	1	1	3
J.Halama	0	0	13.50	2	0	0	2.0	3	0	0
J.Pineiro	0	0	4.50	1	0	0	2.0	4	2	5
A.Lee Rhodes	0	0	4.50	2	0	0	2.0	2	0	2
N.Charlton	0	0	0.00	2	0	0	1.2	1	2	2
K.Sasaki	0	1	54.00	1	0	0	0.1	2	0	0
Totals	1	4	4.36	18	5	0	43.1	42	23	31

GAME 1 / OCT. 17						
PETTITTE, RIVERA(9) VS. SELE, CHARLTON(7), PANIAGUA(8)						47,644
NY	010	200	001	4	9	0
SEA	000	010	001	2	4	0

Yankees' closer Mariano Rivera hardly had his best stuff—allowing Ichiro Suzuki to score on two wild pitches after doubling—but he still managed to save the game for Andy Pettitte.

GAME 2 / OCT. 18						
MUSSINA, MENDOZA(7), RIVERA(8) VS. GARCIA, RHODES(8), NELSON(9)						47,791
NY	030	000	000	3	9	1
SEA	000	200	000	2	6	0

Ramiro Mendoza and Rivera combined for three shutout innings in relief of Mike Mussina, with Rivera retiring all five hitters he faced for his second save.

GAME 3 / OCT. 20						
MOYER, PANIAGUA(8), HALAMA(9) VS. HERNANDEZ, STANTON(6), WOHLERS(6), WITASICK(7)						56,517
SEA	000	027	212	14	15	0
NY	200	000	010	3	7	1

Bret Boone drove in five as Seattle, the highest scoring team in the league, finally started hitting the ball. Jamie Moyer collected the *W*, pitching seven strong innings.

GAME 4 / OCT. 21						
ABBOTT, CHARLTON(6), NELSON(6), RHODES(8), SASAKI(9) VS. CLEMENS, MENDOZA(6), RIVERA(9)						56,375
SEA	000	000	010	1	2	0
NY	000	000	012	3	4	0

Two late homers put the Yankees within a win of a fourth straight trip to the Fall Classic. Bernie Williams tied the game in the eighth with a solo shot, and Alfonso Soriano won it with a two-run blast in the bottom of the ninth off Seattle closer Kaz Sasaki.

GAME 5 / OCT. 22						
SELE, HALAMA(5), PINEIRO(6), PANIAGUA(8) VS. PETTITTE, MENDOZA(7), STANTON(8), RIVERA(9)						56,370
SEA	000	000	300	3	9	0
NY	004	104	03X	12	13	1

The Yankees were up by a whopping nine runs before Seattle even got on the scoreboard. New York put away the game in the sixth, scoring four runs on five singles and two walks to claim another AL pennant.

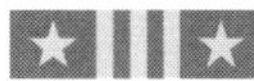

2001 World Series New York Yankees (3) vs. Arizona Diamondbacks (4)

This was an historic World Series for several reasons. First, it concluded in November for the first time after the regular season was delayed a full week by the terrorist attacks of September 11 in New York City. Second, the Diamondbacks won a championship in only their fourth year of existence, the quickest of any expansion team.

ARI (NL)

PLAYER, POS	G	AB	R	H	2B	3B	HR	RBI	BB	SO	SB	AVG	OBP	SLG
T.Womack, ss	7	32	3	8	3	0	0	3	1	7	1	.250	.273	.344
L.Gonzalez, of	7	27	4	7	2	0	1	5	1	11	0	.259	.286	.333
M.Williams, 3b	7	26	3	7	2	0	1	7	0	6	0	.269	.269	.346
C.Counsell, 2b	6	24	1	2	0	0	1	1	0	7	0	.083	.083	.083
R.Sanders, of	6	23	6	7	1	0	0	1	1	7	1	.304	.333	.348
D.Miller, c	6	21	3	4	2	0	0	2	1	11	0	.190	.227	.286
S.Finley, of	7	19	5	7	0	0	1	2	4	5	0	.368	.478	.368
M.Grace, 1b	6	19	1	5	1	0	1	3	4	1	0	.263	.391	.316
D.Bautista, of-dh	5	12	1	7	2	0	0	7	1	1	0	.583	.615	.750
E.Durazo, dh	4	11	0	4	1	0	0	1	3	4	0	.364	.500	.455
J.Bell, 2b	3	7	3	1	0	0	0	1	0	2	0	.143	.143	.143
R.Johnson, p	3	7	2	1	0	0	0	1	0	2	0	.143	.143	.143
C.Schilling, p	3	6	0	0	0	0	0	0	0	5	0	.000	.000	.000
R.Barajas, c	2	5	1	2	0	0	1	1	0	0	0	.400	.400	.400
G.Colbrunn, 1b	1	5	2	2	0	0	0	1	1	1	0	.400	.500	.400
D.Dellucci, of	2	2	0	1	0	0	0	0	0	0	0	.500	.500	.500
M.Cummings, dh	2	0	2	0	0	0	0	0	0	0	0	.000	.000	.000
Totals		246	37	65	14	0	6	36	17	70	2	.264	.327	.321

PITCHER	W	L	ERA	G	GS	SV	IP	H	BB	SO
C.Schilling	1	0	1.69	3	3	0	21.1	12	2	26
R.Johnson	3	0	1.04	3	2	0	17.1	9	3	19
M.Batista	0	0	0.00	2	1	0	8.0	5	5	6
B.Anderson	0	1	3.38	1	1	0	5.1	5	3	1
M.Morgan	0	0	0.00	3	0	0	4.2	1	0	1
B.Kim	0	1	13.50	2	0	0	3.1	6	1	6
G.Swindell	0	0	0.00	3	0	0	2.2	1	1	2
T.Brohawn	0	0	0.00	1	0	0	1.0	1	0	1
B.Witt	0	0	0.00	1	0	0	1.0	0	1	1
A.Lopez	0	1	27.00	1	0	0	0.1	2	0	0
Totals	4	3	1.94	20	7	0	65.0	42	16	63

NY (AL)

PLAYER, POS	G	AB	R	H	2B	3B	HR	RBI	BB	SO	SB	AVG	OBP	SLG
D.Jeter, ss	7	27	3	4	0	0	1	1	0	6	0	.148	.148	.148
A.Soriano, 2b	7	25	1	6	0	0	1	2	0	7	0	.240	.240	.240
S.Brosius, 3b	7	24	1	4	2	0	1	3	0	8	0	.167	.167	.250
B.Williams, of	7	24	2	5	1	0	0	1	4	6	0	.208	.321	.250
J.Posada, c	7	23	2	4	1	0	1	1	3	8	0	.174	.269	.217
T.Martinez, 1b	6	21	1	4	0	0	1	3	2	2	0	.190	.261	.190
S.Spencer, of	7	20	1	4	0	0	1	2	2	6	0	.200	.273	.200
C.Knoblauch, of-dh	6	18	1	1	0	0	0	0	1	2	0	.056	.105	.056
P.O'Neill, of	5	15	1	5	1	0	0	0	2	2	1	.333	.412	.400
D.Justice, of-dh	5	12	0	2	0	0	0	0	1	9	0	.167	.231	.167
A.Pettitte, p	2	3	0	1	0	0	0	0	0	1	0	.333	.333	.333
L.Sojo, 1b	2	3	0	1	0	0	0	1	0	0	0	.333	.333	.333
R.Velarde, 1b	1	3	0	0	0	0	0	0	1	1	0	.000	.250	.000
E.Wilson, ss	2	3	0	0	0	0	0	0	0	0	0	.000	.000	.000
C.Bellinger, of	2	2	0	0	0	0	0	0	0	2	0	.000	.000	.000
R.Clemens, p	2	2	0	0	0	0	0	0	0	1	0	.000	.000	.000
T.Greene, c	1	2	1	1	1	0	0	0	0	0	0	.500	.500	1.000
R.Choate, p	2	1	0	0	0	0	0	0	0	1	0	.000	.000	.000
M.Mussina, p	2	1	0	0	0	0	0	0	0	1	0	.000	.000	.000
Totals		229	14	42	6	0	6	14	16	63	1	.183	.240	.210

PITCHER	W	L	ERA	G	GS	SV	IP	H	BB	SO
R.Clemens	1	0	1.35	2	2	0	13.1	10	4	19
M.Mussina	0	1	4.09	2	2	0	11.0	11	4	14
A.Pettitte	0	2	10.00	2	2	0	9.0	12	2	9
O.Hernandez	0	0	1.42	1	1	0	6.1	4	4	5
M.Rivera	1	1	1.42	4	0	1	6.1	6	1	7
M.Stanton	0	0	3.18	5	0	0	5.2	3	1	3
S.Hitchcock	1	0	0.00	2	0	0	4.0	1	0	6
R.Choate	0	0	2.45	2	0	0	3.2	7	1	2
R.Mendoza	0	0	0.00	2	0	0	2.2	1	0	1
J.Witasick	0	0	54.00	1	0	0	1.1	10	0	4
Totals	3	4	4.26	23	7	1	63.1	65	17	70

GAME 1 / OCT. 27

MUSSINA, CHOATE(4), HITCHCOCK(5), STANTON(8) VS. SCHILLING, MORGAN(8), SWINDELL(9) — 49,646

				R	H	E
NY	100	000	000	1	3	1
ARI	104	400	00X	9	10	0

After spotting the Yanks a run in the top of the first, Curt Schilling allowed only two hits in the next six innings. Shoddy defense took New York out of the game and led to five unearned runs in the third and fourth innings.

GAME 2 / OCT. 28

PETTITTE, STANTON(8) VS. JOHNSON — 49,646

				R	H	E
NY	000	000	000	0	3	0
ARI	010	000	30X	4	5	0

Randy Johnson retired the first 10 Bronx hitters, not being marked for a safety until the fifth. The superstar southpaw allowed only one runner past first base, finishing with a three-hit complete game. A three-run homer by Matt Williams in the seventh put the game out of reach.

GAME 3 / OCT. 30

ANDERSON, MORGAN(6), SWINDELL(7) VS. CLEMENS, RIVERA(8) — 55,820

				R	H	E
ARI	000	100	000	1	3	3
NY	010	001	00X	2	7	1

Another dominating pitching performance; this time, though, it was by the superstar in the pinstriped uniform as Roger Clemens allowed three hits and a run in seven innings. The Yankees scored the winning run in the sixth on a two-out single by Scott Brosius; Mariano Rivera pitched two perfect innings for the save.

GAME 4 / OCT. 31

SCHILLING, KIM(8) VS. HERNANDEZ, STANTON(7), MENDOZA(8), RIVERA(10) — 55,863

					R	H	E
ARI	000	100	020	0	3	6	0
NY	001	000	002	1	4	7	0

New York managed only three hits and a run in seven innings off Schilling, pitching on short rest. The Bombers had little trouble with reliever Byung-Hyun Kim, however, tying the game in the ninth on a homer by Tino Martinez and winning it in the 10th on another long ball by Derek Jeter.

GAME 5 / NOV 1

BATISTA, SWINDELL(8), KIM(9), MORGAN(9), LOPEZ(12) VS. MUSSINA, MENDOZA(9), RIVERA(10), HITCHCOCK(12) — 56,018

					R	H	E
ARI	000	020	000	000	2	8	0
NY	000	000	002	001	3	9	1

The Yankees tied the game in the bottom of the ninth with a two-out long ball for the second straight game. As in the fourth game, Kim was one out away from the save before being smoked for the tying blast. The image of a forlorn Kim crouching at the front edge of the mound with his head down has now become etched in October legend. New York finally won it in the 12th on a single, a sac bunt, and a single by Alfonso Soriano.

GAME 6 / NOV 3

PETTITTE, WITASICK(3), CHOATE(4), STANTON(7) VS. JOHNSON, WITT(8), BROHAWN(9) — 49,707

				R	H	E
NY	000	002	000	2	7	1
ARI	138	300	00X	15	22	0

Arizona didn't need another dominating start from Johnson as the Diamondbacks exploded for 17 hits and 15 runs in the first four innings off Andy Pettitte and Jay Witasick.

GAME 7 / NOV 4

CLEMENS, STANTON(7), RIVERA(8) VS. SCHILLING, BATISTA(8), JOHNSON(8) — 49,589

				R	H	E
NY	000	000	110	2	6	3
ARI	000	001	002	3	11	0

In one of the greatest games in Series history, iron man Schilling held the defending champions to just one hit through six, then was reached for the tying run in the seventh and the go-ahead run in the eighth (on a leadoff homer by Soriano). As he had so often before, Mariano Rivera was called upon to get six outs to save the lead, the game, and the world championship. Initially, the virtually invincible closer looked to be in fine form, striking out the side while allowing only a harmless two-out hit in the eighth. Surprisingly, however, after allowing a leadoff single in the ninth, Rivera couldn't recover from his own throwing error on a bunt, serving up a game-tying double and hitting a batter. Luis Gonzalez won it for Arizona with a broken bat single to center, sending Jay Bell home with the run that terminated the Yankees' string of three consecutive championships. Johnson pitched $1^1/_3$ innings of perfect relief on one day's rest to pick up the win; he and Schilling were named co-MVPs of the Series.

2002 AL Division Series
New York Yankees (1) vs. Anaheim Angels (3)

There wasn't much quality pitching on display in this series, as the Angels won three of four games despite posting a 6.17 team ERA. Every Yankees' hurler aside from Orlando Hernandez and Mariano Rivera was pounded, and Rivera only pitched one inning. Overall, New York compiled an 8.21 ERA, abruptly ending their streak of four AL pennants.

ANA (W)

PLAYER, POS	G	AB	R	H	2B	3B	HR	RBI	BB	SO	SB	AVG	OBP	SLG
D.Erstad, of	4	19	4	8	2	0	0	2	0	1	1	.421	.421	.526
T.Salmon, of	4	19	3	5	1	0	2	7	1	5	0	.263	.300	.316
G.Anderson, of	4	18	5	7	2	0	1	4	1	3	0	.389	.421	.500
D.Eckstein, ss	4	18	2	5	0	0	0	1	0	0	1	.278	.278	.278
T.Glaus, 3b	4	16	4	5	0	0	3	3	1	3	0	.313	.353	.313
B.Molina, c	4	15	0	4	2	0	0	2	0	1	0	.267	.267	.400
S.Spiezio, 1b	4	15	2	6	1	0	1	6	2	1	0	.400	.471	.467
S.Wooten, dh	3	9	4	6	0	0	1	2	0	1	0	.667	.667	.667
A.Kennedy, 2b	4	8	4	4	1	0	1	3	1	2	1	.500	.556	.625
B.Fullmer, dh	3	7	1	2	1	0	0	0	1	1	0	.286	.375	.429
R.Gil, 2b	2	5	1	4	0	0	0	1	0	0	0	.800	.800	.800
C.Figgins, dh	1	0	1	0	0	0	0	0	0	0	1	.000	.000	.000
A.Ochoa, of	3	0	0	0	0	0	0	0	0	0	0	.000	.000	.000
Totals		149	31	56	10	0	9	31	7	18	4	.376	.411	.443

PITCHER	W	L	ERA	G	GS	SV	IP	H	BB	SO
J.Washburn	1	0	3.75	2	2	0	12.0	12	3	4
F.Rodriguez	2	0	3.18	3	0	0	5.2	2	2	8
K.Appier	0	0	5.40	1	1	0	5.0	5	3	3
T.Percival	0	0	5.40	3	0	2	3.1	6	0	4
J.Lackey	0	0	0.00	1	0	0	3.0	3	1	3
D.Ortiz	0	0	20.25	1	1	0	2.2	3	4	1
B.Donnelly	0	0	13.50	3	0	0	2.0	3	1	2
B.Weber	0	1	18.00	2	0	0	1.0	2	2	0
S.Schoeneweis	0	0	27.00	3	0	0	0.1	2	0	0
Totals	3	1	6.17	19	4	2	35.0	38	16	25

NY (E)

PLAYER, POS	G	AB	R	H	2B	3B	HR	RBI	BB	SO	SB	AVG	OBP	SLG
J.Posada, c	4	17	2	4	0	0	1	3	0	3	0	.235	.235	.235
A.Soriano, 2b	4	17	2	2	1	0	1	2	1	4	1	.118	.167	.176
D.Jeter, ss	4	16	6	8	0	0	2	3	2	3	0	.500	.556	.500
B.Williams, of	4	15	4	5	1	0	1	3	3	2	0	.333	.444	.400
J.Giambi, 1b-dh	4	14	5	5	0	0	1	3	4	1	0	.357	.500	.357
R.Ventura, 3b	4	14	1	4	2	0	0	4	1	2	0	.286	.333	.429
R.Mondesi, of	4	12	1	3	0	0	0	1	3	1	0	.250	.400	.250
J.Rivera, of	4	12	2	3	0	0	0	3	1	3	0	.250	.308	.250
N.Johnson, dh-1b	3	11	1	2	0	0	0	1	1	5	0	.182	.250	.182
R.White, dh	1	3	1	1	0	0	1	1	0	0	0	.333	.333	.333
R.Coomer, dh	1	2	0	1	0	0	0	0	0	0	0	.500	.500	.500
J.Vander Wal, of	2	2	0	0	0	0	0	0	0	1	0	.000	.000	.000
S.Spencer, of	1	0	0	0	0	0	0	0	0	0	0	.000	.000	.000
E.Wilson, ph	1	0	0	0	0	0	0	0	0	0	0	.000	.000	.000
Totals		135	25	38	4	0	7	24	16	25	1	.281	.374	.311

PITCHER	W	L	ERA	G	GS	SV	IP	H	BB	SO
O.Hernandez	0	1	2.84	2	0	0	6.1	5	0	7
R.Clemens	0	0	6.35	1	1	0	5.2	8	3	5
D.Wells	0	1	15.43	1	1	0	4.2	10	0	0
M.Mussina	0	0	9.00	1	1	0	4.0	6	0	2
A.Pettitte	0	0	12.00	1	1	0	3.0	8	0	1
S.Karsay	1	0	6.75	4	0	0	2.2	3	0	1
M.Stanton	0	1	10.13	3	0	0	2.2	6	1	1
J.Weaver	0	0	6.75	2	0	0	2.2	4	3	1
R.Mendoza	0	0	13.50	2	0	0	1.1	5	0	0
M.Rivera	0	0	0.00	1	0	1	1.0	1	0	0
Totals	1	3	8.21	18	4	1	34.0	56	7	18

GAME 1 / OCT. 1

WASHBURN, WEBER(8), SCHOENEWEIS(8), DONNELLY(8) VS. CLEMENS, MENDOZA(6), KARSAY(8), RIVERA(9) — **56,710**

				R	H	E
ANA	001	021	010	5	12	0
NY	100	210	04X	8	8	1

The Yankees were four outs away from an opening game loss, but they rallied for four runs in the bottom of the eighth with two out. Bernie Williams' three-run homer was the big blow.

GAME 2 / OCT. 2

APPIER, RODRIGUEZ(6), WEBER(8), DONNELLY(8), PERCIVAL(8) VS. PETTITTE, HERNANDEZ(4), KARSAY(8), STANTON(8), WEAVER(9) — **56,695**

				R	H	E
ANA	121	000	031	8	17	1
NY	001	202	001	6	12	1

This time, it was Anaheim's turn to rally in the eighth. The Angels blasted four home runs, two off starter Andy Pettitte and two off reliever Orlando Hernandez, who was victimized by Garrett Anderson and Troy Glaus solo homers leading off the eighth.

GAME 3 / OCT. 4

MUSSINA, WEAVER(5), STANTON(6), KARSAY(8) VS. ORTIZ, LACKEY(3), SCHOENEWEIS(6), RODRIGUEZ(7), PERCIVAL(9) — **45,072**

				R	H	E
NY	303	000	000	6	6	0
ANA	012	101	13X	9	12	0

New York led 6–1 after three innings before the Angels started chipping it away, scoring in six of their final seven at bats. Tim Salmon had four RBIs, two of which came on a home run in the eighth.

GAME 4 / OCT. 5

WELLS, MENDOZA(5), HERNANDEZ(5), KARSAY(8), STANTON(8) VS. WASHBURN, DONNELLY(6), SCHOENEWEIS(7), RODRIGUEZ(7), PERCIVAL(9) — **45,067**

				R	H	E
NY	010	011	101	5	12	2
ANA	001	080	00X	9	15	1

The series was settled as the Angels battered big-game pitcher David Wells. Anaheim plated eight runs in the fifth (seven off Wells) on eight singles, a double, and a solo home run.

2003 AL Division Series
New York Yankees (3) vs. Minnesota Twins (1)

The Twins were division winners only because the AL Central was so weak that their 90 wins were good enough to top the White Sox by four games. They were quickly disposed of by the Yankees who, with 101 wins, were five games better than anybody else in the AL during the regular season.

NY (E)

PLAYER, POS	G	AB	R	H	2B	3B	HR	RBI	BB	SO	SB	AVG	OBP	SLG
A.Soriano, 2b	4	19	2	7	1	0	0	4	0	6	2	.368	.368	.421
J.Posada, c	4	17	1	3	1	0	0	0	0	6	0	.176	.176	.235
J.Giambi, dh	4	16	1	4	2	0	0	2	2	5	0	.250	.333	.375
A.Boone, 3b	4	15	1	3	1	0	0	0	0	3	1	.200	.200	.267
H.Matsui, of	4	15	2	4	1	0	1	3	2	3	0	.267	.353	.333
B.Williams, of	4	15	3	6	2	0	0	3	2	2	0	.400	.471	.533
D.Jeter, ss	4	14	2	6	0	0	1	1	4	2	1	.429	.556	.429
N.Johnson, 1b	4	13	2	1	1	0	0	2	3	2	0	.077	.250	.154
J.Rivera, of	4	12	2	4	0	0	0	0	1	0	0	.333	.385	.333
R.Sierra, of	1	2	0	0	0	0	0	0	0	0	0	.000	.000	.000
D.Dellucci, ph	1	0	0	0	0	0	0	0	0	0	0	.000	.000	.000
Totals		138	16	38	9	0	2	15	14	29	4	.275	.346	.341

PITCHER	W	L	ERA	G	GS	SV	IP	H	BB	SO
D.Wells	1	0	1.17	1	1	0	7.2	8	0	5
R.Clemens	1	0	1.29	1	1	0	7.0	5	1	6
M.Mussina	0	1	3.86	1	1	0	7.0	7	3	6
A.Pettitte	1	0	1.29	1	1	0	7.0	4	3	10
M.Rivera	0	0	0.00	2	0	2	4.0	0	0	4
F.Heredia	0	0	0.00	1	0	0	2.0	1	1	1
G.White	0	0	0.00	1	0	0	1.1	1	0	1

NY (E) (CONT.)										
PITCHER	W	L	ERA	G	GS	SV	IP	H	BB	SO
J.Nelson	0	0	INF	1	0	0	0.0	0	1	0
Totals	3	1	1.50	9	4	2	36.0	26	9	33

MIN (C)														
PLAYER, POS	G	AB	R	H	2B	3B	HR	RBI	BB	SO	SB	AVG	OBP	SLG
J.Jones, of	4	16	0	2	0	0	0	0	0	5	0	.125	.125	.125
C.Koskie, 3b	4	15	0	3	1	0	0	0	0	5	0	.200	.200	.267
D.Mientkiewicz, 1b	4	15	0	2	0	0	0	0	1	2	0	.133	.188	.133
S.Stewart, of	4	15	0	6	2	0	0	0	2	4	1	.400	.471	.533
T.Hunter, of	4	14	3	6	0	1	1	2	2	2	0	.429	.500	.571
C.Guzman, ss	4	13	1	2	0	0	0	0	1	2	0	.154	.214	.154
A.Pierzynski, c	4	13	1	3	0	0	1	1	2	0	0	.231	.333	.231
L.Rivas, 2b	4	13	0	0	0	0	0	1	0	4	0	.000	.000	.000
M.LeCroy, dh	3	11	1	1	0	0	0	0	1	4	0	.091	.167	.091
M.Cuddyer, ph	1	4	0	1	0	0	0	1	0	3	0	.250	.250	.250
L.Ford, ph	1	1	0	0	0	0	0	0	0	1	0	.000	.000	.000
M.Ryan, ph	1	1	0	0	0	0	0	0	0	1	0	.000	.000	.000
C.Gomez, 2b	1	0	0	0	0	0	0	0	0	0	0	.000	.000	.000
D.Hocking, 2b	1	0	0	0	0	0	0	0	0	0	0	.000	.000	.000
Totals		131	6	26	3	1	2	5	9	33	1	.198	.250	.237

PITCHER	W	L	ERA	G	GS	SV	IP	H	BB	SO
J.Santana	0	1	7.04	2	2	0	7.2	9	3	6
B.Radke	0	1	2.84	1	1	0	6.1	5	2	4
K.Lohse	0	1	5.40	1	1	0	5.0	6	2	5
E.Milton	0	0	0.00	1	0	0	3.1	2	0	2
J.Romero	0	0	0.00	3	0	0	3.1	3	2	1
L.Hawkins	1	0	6.00	3	0	0	3.0	5	0	5
J.Rincon	0	0	0.00	3	0	0	2.1	1	4	1
E.Guardado	0	0	9.00	2	0	1	2.0	5	0	2
K.Rogers	0	0	0.00	1	0	0	1.1	1	1	3
R.Reed	0	0	0.00	1	0	0	0.2	1	0	0
Totals	1	3	3.86	18	4	1	35.0	38	14	29

GAME 1 / SEPT. 30

SANTANA, REED(5), ROMERO(5), HAWKINS(7), GUARDADO(9) VS. MUSSINA, NELSON(8), HEREDIA(8) — 56,292

				R	H	E
MIN	001	002	000	3	8	5
NY	000	000	001	1	9	1

Twins ace Johan Santana was forced out after four innings, but Rick Reed, J.C. Romero, and LaTroy Hawkins held New York scoreless until the ninth. Minny scored twice in the sixth on Torii Hunter's RBI triple, as Hunter scampered home on an E4 on the play.

GAME 2 / OCT. 2

RADKE, HAWKINS(7), ROMERO(7), RINCON(8) VS. PETTITTE, RIVERA(8) — 56,479

				R	H	E
MIN	000	010	000	1	4	1
NY	100	000	30X	4	8	1

Andy Pettitte shut down the Twins on only four hits and a single run for seven innings as the Yanks scored three times in the seventh. Mariano Rivera got the save by retiring all six batters he faced.

GAME 3 / OCT. 4

CLEMENS, RIVERA(8) VS. LOHSE, ROGERS(6), ROMERO(7), RINCON(8) — 55,915

				R	H	E
NY	021	000	000	3	8	1
MIN	001	000	000	1	5	0

Hideki Matsui's two-run homer in the second provided the Yankees with all the runs they needed as Roger Clemens and Rivera nearly duplicated the pitching performance of the previous game.

GAME 4 / OCT. 5

WELLS, WHITE(8) VS. SANTANA, RINCON(4), MILTON(4), HAWKINS(8), GUARDADO(9) — 55,875

				R	H	E
NY	000	600	011	8	13	0
MIN	000	100	000	1	9	1

Santana retired nine of the first 10 Yankees' hitters, but the Twins' ace couldn't survive the fourth. New York doubled three times in the inning, scoring six runs and putting the game far beyond the reach of the Twins, who scored just one run for the third straight game.

2003 AL Championship Series
New York Yankees (4) vs. Boston Red Sox (3)

Even though it was already heated, this series cemented the Yankees-Red Sox rivalry as one of the greatest in all of team sports. Neither team had more than a one-game lead in the LCS, New York scored only one more run than Boston in the series. It took an epic home run in the bottom of the 11th inning of the seventh game to decide the pennant winner.

NY (E)														
PLAYER, POS	G	AB	R	H	2B	3B	HR	RBI	BB	SO	SB	AVG	OBP	SLG
D.Jeter, ss	7	30	3	7	2	0	1	2	2	4	1	.233	.281	.300
A.Soriano, 2b	7	30	0	4	1	0	0	3	1	11	2	.133	.161	.167
J.Posada, c	7	27	5	8	4	0	1	6	3	4	0	.296	.367	.444
J.Giambi, ph	7	26	4	6	0	0	3	3	4	7	0	.231	.333	.231
N.Johnson, 1b	7	26	4	6	1	0	1	3	2	4	0	.231	.286	.269
H.Matsui, of	7	26	3	8	3	0	0	4	1	3	0	.308	.333	.423
B.Williams, of	7	26	5	5	1	0	0	2	4	3	0	.192	.300	.231
A.Boone, 3b	7	17	2	3	0	0	1	2	1	6	1	.176	.222	.176
K.Garcia, of	5	16	1	4	0	0	0	3	2	4	0	.250	.333	.250
E.Wilson, 3b	2	7	0	1	0	0	0	0	0	1	0	.143	.143	.143
D.Dellucci, of	3	3	2	1	0	0	0	0	0	1	1	.333	.333	.333
J.Rivera, of	2	2	0	0	0	0	0	0	0	1	0	.000	.000	.000
R.Sierra, of	3	2	1	1	0	0	1	1	1	0	0	.500	.667	.500
Totals		238	30	54	12	0	8	29	21	49	5	.227	.300	.277

PITCHER	W	L	ERA	G	GS	SV	IP	H	BB	SO
M.Mussina	0	2	4.11	3	2	0	15.1	16	4	17
A.Pettitte	1	0	4.63	2	2	0	11.2	17	4	10
R.Clemens	1	0	5.00	2	2	0	9.0	11	2	8
M.Rivera	1	0	1.13	4	0	2	8.0	5	0	6
D.Wells	1	0	2.35	2	1	0	7.2	5	2	5
J.Contreras	0	1	5.79	4	0	0	4.2	6	2	7
J.Nelson	0	0	6.00	4	0	0	3.0	4	0	3
F.Heredia	0	0	3.38	5	0	0	2.2	0	3	3
G.White	0	0	4.50	2	0	0	2.0	4	0	1
Totals	4	3	3.94	28	7	2	64.0	68	17	60

BOS (E)														
PLAYER, POS	G	AB	R	H	2B	3B	HR	RBI	BB	SO	SB	AVG	OBP	SLG
N.Garciaparra, ss	7	29	2	7	0	1	0	1	2	8	0	.241	.290	.310
K.Millar, 1b	7	29	3	7	0	0	1	3	1	9	0	.241	.267	.241
M.Ramirez, of	7	29	6	9	1	0	2	4	1	4	0	.310	.333	.345
B.Mueller, 3b	7	27	1	6	2	0	0	0	2	7	0	.222	.276	.296
T.Walker, 2b	7	27	5	10	1	1	2	2	1	2	0	.370	.393	.481
D.Ortiz, ph	7	26	4	7	1	0	2	6	3	8	0	.269	.345	.308
T.Nixon, of	7	24	3	8	1	0	3	5	3	7	1	.333	.407	.375
J.Damon, of	5	20	1	4	1	0	0	1	3	3	1	.200	.304	.250
J.Varitek, c	6	20	4	6	2	0	2	3	1	5	0	.300	.333	.400
G.Kapler, of	3	8	0	1	0	0	0	0	0	3	0	.125	.125	.125
D.Mirabelli, c	3	7	0	2	0	0	0	0	0	2	0	.286	.286	.286
D.Jackson, 2b	5	3	0	1	0	0	0	1	0	1	0	.333	.333	.333
D.McCarty, ph	1	1	0	0	0	0	0	0	0	1	0	.000	.000	.000
Totals		250	29	68	9	2	12	26	17	60	2	.272	.326	.324

PITCHER	W	L	ERA	G	GS	SV	IP	H	BB	SO
P.Martinez	0	1	5.65	2	2	0	14.1	16	2	14
D.Lowe	0	2	6.43	2	2	0	14.0	14	7	5
T.Wakefield	2	1	2.57	3	2	0	14.0	8	6	10
M.Timlin	0	0	0.00	5	0	0	5.1	1	2	6
A.Embree	1	0	0.00	5	0	0	4.2	3	0	1
J.Burkett	0	0	7.36	1	1	0	3.2	7	0	1
B.Arroyo	0	0	2.70	3	0	0	3.1	2	2	5
S.Williamson	0	0	3.00	3	0	3	3.0	1	0	6
T.Jones	0	0	0.00	1	0	0	0.1	1	1	1
S.Sauerbeck	0	0	0.00	1	0	0	0.1	1	1	0
Totals	3	4	4.00	26	7	3	63.0	54	21	49

GAME 1 / OCT. 8

WAKEFIELD, EMBREE(7), TIMLIN(8), WILLIAMSON(9) VS. MUSSINA, HEREDIA(6), NELSON(7), WHITE(7), CONTRERAS(9) — 56,281

				R	H	E
BOS	000	220	100	5	13	0
NY	000	000	200	2	3	0

Knuckleballer Tim Wakefield baffled Yankees hitters, allowing only two hits in six innings and enabling Boston to jump out to a 5–0 lead. David Ortiz, Manny Ramirez and Todd Walker all homered off Mike Mussina.

GAME 2 / OCT. 9

LOWE, SAUERBECK(7), ARROYO(8) VS. PETTITTE, CONTRERAS(7), RIVERA(9) — 56,295

				R	H	E
BOS	010	001	000	2	10	1
NY	021	010	20X	6	8	0

Boston got three hits and a walk in the top of the first, but failed to score. Nick Johnson's two-run homer in the bottom of the second allowed the Yankees to take the lead for good and hand Andy Pettitte the win.

GAME 3 / OCT. 11						
CLEMENS, HEREDIA(7), CONTRERAS(7), RIVERA(8) VS. MARTINEZ, TIMLIN(8), EMBREE(9)						34,209
NY	011	200	000	4	7	0
BOS	200	000	100	3	6	0

Tempers flared when Boston ace Pedro Martinez hit a batter in the top of the fourth inning and Roger Clemens followed by throwing one up-and-in to Manny Ramirez. Both benches emptied, resulting in a 13-minute delay that featured 72-year-old Yankee bench coach Don Zimmer charging at Martinez, who won the brawl but lost the game after allowing four runs. Later in the game, a Red Sox employee got in a fight with New York reliever Jeff Nelson and backup outfielder Karim Garcia.

GAME 4 / OCT. 13						
MUSSINA, HEREDIA(7), NELSON(8) VS. WAKEFIELD, TIMLIN(8), WILLIAMSON(9)						34,599
NY	000	010	001	2	6	1
BOS	000	110	10X	3	6	0

The game was delayed a day by rain, giving tempers a chance to calm down before the Red Sox evened the series. Wakefield again flummoxed the Yankees with his flutterball, this time allowing a sole run in seven innings. Scott Williamson struck out the side in the ninth for the save, despite a solo homer by Ruben Sierra.

GAME 5 / OCT. 14						
WELLS, RIVERA(8) VS. LOWE, EMBREE(8), ARROYO(9)						34,619
NY	030	000	010	4	7	1
BOS	000	100	010	2	6	1

Three runs in the second, all scoring on two-out singles, were enough for the Yankees, who got splendid pitching from David Wells. Mariano Rivera was shaky in the eighth but threw a perfect ninth to close out the win.

GAME 6 / OCT. 15						
BURKETT, ARROYO(4), JONES(6), EMBREE(6), TIMLIN(8), WILLIAMSON(9) VS. PETTITTE, CONTRERAS(6), HEREDIA(7), NELSON(8), WHITE(9)						56,277
BOS	004	000	302	9	16	1
NY	100	410	000	6	12	2

Neither starter was effective, with New York's Pettitte lasting only five and Boston's John Burkett failing to make it out of the fourth. Boston won because its quintet of relievers (one run in 5[1]/3 innings) were better than New York's foursome, who were stroked for five runs in four innings.

GAME 7 / OCT. 16							
MARTINEZ, EMBREE(8), TIMLIN(8), WAKEFIELD(9) VS. CLEMENS, MUSSINA(4), HEREDIA(7), NELSON(7), WELLS(7), RIVERA(8)							56,279
BOS	030	100	010	00	5	11	0
NY	000	010	130	01	6	11	1

Boston fans were feeling confident with Martinez on the mound holding a 4–0 lead, but their ace ran out of gas in the eighth, allowing the three tying runs on a pair of doubles by Hideki Matsui and Jorge Posada. Neither team had a legitimate chance to score for the next two and a half innings until Aaron Boone came to bat in the bottom half of the 11th, facing Wakefield. Boone wrote a memorable new chapter of the Yankees' legend when he lofted a home run down the left field line.

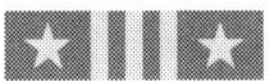

2003 World Series
New York Yankees (2) vs. Florida Marlins (4)

An almost anti-climactic Fall Classic was played after Florida survived the Bartman game in Wrigley Field and New York triumphed over Boston on a walk-off homer in extra innings. Though the Marlins were outscored, they emerged victorious in large part because of 23-year-old right-hander Josh Beckett, who allowed only two runs in 16[1]/3 innings and won both of his starts.

FLA (NL)

PLAYER, POS	G	AB	R	H	2B	3B	HR	RBI	BB	SO	SB	AVG	OBP	SLG
L.Castillo, 2b	6	26	1	4	0	0	0	1	0	7	1	.154	.154	.154
M.Cabrera, of	6	24	1	4	0	0	1	3	1	7	0	.167	.200	.167
D.Lee, 1b	6	24	2	5	0	0	0	2	1	7	0	.208	.240	.208
M.Lowell, 3b	6	23	1	5	1	0	0	2	2	3	0	.217	.280	.261
A.Gonzalez, ss	6	22	3	6	2	0	1	2	0	7	0	.273	.273	.364
I.Rodriguez, c	6	22	2	6	2	0	0	1	1	4	0	.273	.304	.364
J.Conine, of	6	21	4	7	1	0	0	0	3	2	0	.333	.417	.381
J.Pierre, of	6	21	2	7	2	0	0	3	5	2	1	.333	.462	.429
J.Encarnacion, of	6	11	1	2	0	0	0	1	1	5	0	.182	.250	.182
J.Beckett, p	2	2	0	0	0	0	0	0	0	2	0	.000	.000	.000
T.Hollandsworth, ph	2	2	0	0	0	0	0	0	0	1	0	.000	.000	.000
C.Pavano, p	2	2	0	0	0	0	0	0	0	1	0	.000	.000	.000
B.Penny, p	2	2	0	1	0	0	0	2	0	0	0	.500	.500	.500
M.Redmond, c	1	1	0	0	0	0	0	0	0	0	0	.000	.000	.000
Totals		203	17	47	8	0	2	17	14	48	2	.232	.284	.271

PITCHER	W	L	ERA	G	GS	SV	IP	H	BB	SO
J.Beckett	1	1	1.10	2	2	0	16.1	8	5	19
B.Penny	2	0	2.19	2	2	0	12.1	15	5	7
C.Pavano	0	0	1.00	2	1	0	9.0	8	1	6
B.Looper	1	0	9.82	4	0	0	3.2	6	0	4
D.Willis	0	0	0.00	3	0	0	3.2	4	2	3
C.Fox	0	0	6.00	3	0	0	3.0	4	4	4
U.Urbina	0	0	6.00	3	0	2	3.0	2	3	2
R.Helling	0	0	6.75	1	0	0	2.2	2	0	2
M.Redman	0	1	15.43	1	1	0	2.1	5	2	2
Totals	4	2	3.21	21	6	2	56.0	54	22	49

NY (AL)

PLAYER, POS	G	AB	R	H	2B	3B	HR	RBI	BB	SO	SB	AVG	OBP	SLG
D.Jeter, ss	6	26	5	9	3	0	0	2	1	7	0	.346	.370	.462
B.Williams, of	6	25	5	10	2	0	2	5	2	2	0	.400	.444	.480
H.Matsui, of	6	23	1	6	0	0	1	4	3	2	0	.261	.346	.261
A.Soriano, 2b-of	6	22	2	5	0	0	1	2	2	9	1	.227	.292	.227
A.Boone, 3b	6	21	1	3	0	0	1	2	0	6	0	.143	.143	.143
J.Posada, c	6	19	0	3	1	0	0	1	5	7	1	.158	.333	.211
J.Giambi, 1b	6	17	2	4	1	0	1	1	4	3	0	.235	.381	.294
N.Johnson, 1b	6	17	3	5	1	0	0	0	2	3	0	.294	.368	.353
K.Garcia, of	5	14	1	4	0	0	0	0	0	3	0	.286	.286	.286
J.Rivera, of	4	6	0	1	1	0	0	1	1	1	0	.167	.286	.333
R.Sierra, of	5	4	0	1	0	1	0	2	1	3	0	.250	.400	.750
E.Wilson, 2b-3b	2	4	0	2	1	0	0	1	1	0	0	.500	.600	.750
M.Mussina, p	1	3	0	0	0	0	0	0	0	3	0	.000	.000	.000
R.Clemens, p	1	2	0	1	0	0	0	0	0	0	0	.500	.500	.500
D.Dellucci, of	4	2	1	0	0	0	0	0	0	0	0	.000	.000	.000
J.Flaherty, c	1	2	0	0	0	0	0	0	0	0	0	.000	.000	.000
Totals		207	21	54	10	1	6	21	22	49	2	.261	.341	.319

PITCHER	W	L	ERA	G	GS	SV	IP	H	BB	SO
A.Pettitte	1	1	0.57	2	2	0	15.2	12	4	14
D.Wells	0	1	3.38	2	2	0	8.0	6	2	1
R.Clemens	0	0	3.86	1	1	0	7.0	8	0	5
M.Mussina	1	0	1.29	1	1	0	7.0	7	1	9
J.Contreras	0	1	5.68	4	0	0	6.1	5	5	10
J.Nelson	0	0	0.00	3	0	0	4.0	4	2	5
M.Rivera	0	0	0.00	2	0	1	4.0	2	0	4
C.Hammond	0	0	0.00	1	0	0	2.0	2	0	0
J.Weaver	0	1	9.00	1	0	0	1.0	1	0	0
Totals	2	4	2.13	17	6	1	55.0	47	14	48

GAME 1 / OCT. 18						
PENNY, WILLIS(6), URBINA(8) VS. WELLS, NELSON(8), CONTRERAS(9)						55,769
FLA	100	020	000	3	7	1
NY	001	001	000	2	9	0

Leadoff speedster Juan Pierre was part of all three Florida runs, helping the Marlins to an early lead by scoring in the first after singling, then driving in two runs with a base hit in the fifth. Dontrelle Willis and Ugueth Urbina both pitched out of late-inning jams to preserve the win.

GAME 2 / OCT. 19						
REDMAN, HELLING(3), FOX(6), PAVANO(7), LOOPER(8) VS. PETTITTE, CONTRERAS(9)						55,750
FLA	000	000	001	1	6	0
NY	310	200	00X	6	10	2

The Yankees roughed up Mark Redman and the Marlins for four runs in the first two innings as Andy Pettitte allowed just a single unearned run in 8 1/3 innings.

GAME 3 / OCT. 21

MUSSINA, RIVERA(8) VS. BECKETT, WILLIS(8), FOX(8), LOOPER(9)					65,731
NY	000 100 014	6	6	1	
FLA	100 000 000	1	8	0	

Ninth-inning homers by Aaron Boone and Bernie Williams, the latter a three-run blast, opened up what had been a tight game. Mariano Rivera pitched two innings to save the game for Mike Mussina, who struck out nine in seven frames.

GAME 4 / OCT. 22

CLEMENS, NELSON(8), CONTRERAS(9), WEAVER(12) VS. PAVANO, URBINA(9), FOX(10), LOOPER(11)					65,934
NY	010 000 002 000	3	12	0	
FLA	300 000 000 001	4	10	0	

Things looked dire for the Marlins, who blew a two-run lead in the ninth and came perilously close to falling behind 3-games-to-1 after the first two Yankees reached in the 11th. After a sac bunt put runners on second and third with one out, Braden Looper got two easy outs to keep the Marlins alive until Florida won it in the 12th on Alex Gonzalez' leadoff home run.

GAME 5 / OCT. 23

WELLS, CONTRERAS(2), HAMMOND(5), NELSON(7) VS. PENNY, WILLIS(8), LOOPER(9), URBINA(9)					65,975
NY	100 000 102	4	12	1	
FLA	030 120 00X	6	9	1	

After allowing an unearned run in the first, Brad Penny limited New York to six hits and a run over the next six innings. That allowed the Marlins to go up by five, making a late-inning rally by the Yankees moot.

GAME 6 / OCT. 25

BECKETT VS. PETTITTE, RIVERA(8)					55,773
FLA	000 011 000	2	7	0	
NY	000 000 000	0	5	1	

The concluding game belonged to young lion Beckett, masterfully tossing a five-hit shutout. The Marlins managed a tally in the fifth on three straight hits with two outs, adding an unearned run in the sixth after an error by Derek Jeter. Beckett completely dominated from that point, retiring eight of the final nine hitters and 14 of the last 15.

2004 AL Division Series
New York Yankees (3) vs. Minnesota Twins (1)

The Yankees eliminated the Twins in the opening round for the second straight year, though the 2004 series was much more competitive. Minnesota, which lost two one-run games in extra innings, proved they belonged in the postseason, even if they did win nine fewer games than the Yankees and six fewer than the Wild Card Red Sox.

NY (E)

PLAYER, POS	G	AB	R	H	2B	3B	HR	RBI	BB	SO	SB	AVG	OBP	SLG
D.Jeter, ss	4	19	3	6	1	0	1	4	1	4	1	.316	.350	.368
A.Rodriguez, 3b	4	19	3	8	3	0	1	3	2	1	2	.421	.476	.579
J.Posada, c	4	18	2	4	0	0	0	0	0	6	0	.222	.222	.222
G.Sheffield, of	4	18	2	4	1	0	1	2	3	1	0	.222	.333	.278
B.Williams, of	4	18	2	5	1	0	1	3	1	2	0	.278	.316	.333
H.Matsui, of	4	17	3	7	1	0	1	3	3	4	0	.412	.500	.471
M.Cairo, 2b	4	14	3	3	1	0	0	1	2	5	0	.214	.313	.286
J.Olerud, 1b	4	14	2	3	2	0	0	0	1	2	0	.214	.267	.357
R.Sierra, dh	3	12	1	2	0	0	1	3	2	3	1	.167	.286	.167
K.Lofton, dh	1	4	0	1	0	0	0	1	0	1	0	.250	.250	.250

NY (E) (CONT.)

PLAYER, POS	G	AB	R	H	2B	3B	HR	RBI	BB	SO	SB	AVG	OBP	SLG
A.Clark, 1b	1	1	0	0	0	0	0	0	0	1	0	.000	.000	.000
B.Crosby, of	2	0	0	0	0	0	0	0	0	0	0	.000	.000	.000
Totals		154	21	43	10	0	6	20	15	30	4	.279	.347	.344

PITCHER	W	L	ERA	G	GS	SV	IP	H	BB	SO
M.Mussina	0	1	2.57	1	1	0	7.0	7	1	7
J.Lieber	0	0	4.05	1	1	0	6.2	7	1	4
K.Brown	1	0	1.50	1	1	0	6.0	8	0	1
M.Rivera	1	0	0.00	4	0	0	5.2	2	0	2
J.Vazquez	0	0	9.00	1	1	0	5.0	7	2	6
T.Gordon	0	0	4.91	3	0	0	3.2	2	0	3
T.Sturtze	0	0	6.75	2	0	0	2.2	4	3	4
E.Loaiza	0	0	0.00	1	0	0	2.0	4	0	0
P.Quantrill	1	0	0.00	2	0	0	2.0	2	0	1
F.Heredia	0	0	54.00	1	0	0	0.1	0	0	0
Totals	3	1	3.73	17	4	0	41.0	43	7	28

MIN (W)

PLAYER, POS	G	AB	R	H	2B	3B	HR	RBI	BB	SO	SB	AVG	OBP	SLG
J.Jones, of	4	20	3	6	1	0	2	2	0	6	0	.300	.300	.350
S.Stewart, of-dh	4	20	1	4	0	0	0	2	0	2	0	.200	.200	.200
T.Hunter, of	4	17	5	6	1	0	1	2	1	1	2	.353	.389	.412
J.Morneau, 1b	4	17	1	4	2	0	0	2	0	3	0	.235	.235	.353
M.Cuddyer, 2b-1b	4	15	1	7	0	0	0	2	0	3	0	.467	.467	.467
C.Guzman, ss	4	15	2	5	0	0	0	0	2	3	1	.333	.412	.333
C.Koskie, 3b	4	13	2	4	1	0	0	2	3	2	0	.308	.421	.385
L.Ford, dh-of	3	11	1	3	1	0	0	2	0	2	1	.273	.273	.364
H.Blanco, c	4	8	1	2	0	0	1	2	0	2	0	.250	.250	.250
J.Kubel, dh	2	7	0	1	1	0	0	0	0	2	0	.143	.143	.286
M.LeCroy, c-1b	3	3	0	1	0	0	0	0	1	1	0	.333	.500	.333
J.Offerman, ph	3	3	0	0	0	0	0	1	0	0	0	.000	.000	.000
P.Borders, c	2	2	0	0	0	0	0	0	0	1	0	.000	.000	.000
L.Rivas, 2b	3	1	0	0	0	0	0	0	0	0	0	.000	.000	.000
Totals		152	17	43	7	0	4	17	7	28	4	.283	.327	.329

PITCHER	W	L	ERA	G	GS	SV	IP	H	BB	SO
J.Santana	1	0	0.75	2	2	0	12.0	14	4	12
B.Radke	0	0	7.11	1	1	0	6.1	8	3	0
J.Nathan	0	1	3.60	3	0	1	5.0	2	5	6
C.Silva	0	1	10.80	1	1	0	5.0	10	0	1
J.Rincon	0	0	10.80	3	0	0	3.1	4	2	5
T.Mulholland	0	0	3.00	1	0	0	3.0	3	0	0
G.Balfour	0	0	0.00	2	0	0	2.2	0	0	2
K.Lohse	0	1	4.50	1	0	0	2.0	1	0	3
J.Romero	0	0	9.00	2	0	0	1.0	0	1	1
J.Crain	0	0	0.00	1	0	0	0.1	1	0	0
Totals	1	3	4.65	17	4	1	40.2	43	15	30

GAME 1 / OCT. 5

SANTANA, RINCON(8), NATHAN(9) VS. MUSSINA, GORDON(8), RIVERA(9)					55,749
MIN	001 001 000	2	7	0	
NY	000 000 000	0	9	0	

Cy Young winner Johan Santana wasn't dominant, but worked around nine hits and a walk to hold the Yankees scoreless through seven. Ricardo Rincon and Joe Nathan each pitched a hitless inning of relief to save it.

GAME 2 / OCT. 6

RADKE, BALFOUR(7), RINCON(8), NATHAN(10), ROMERO(12) VS. LIEBER, GORDON(7), RIVERA(8), STURTZE(10), QUANTRILL(12)					56,354
MIN	120 000 020 001	6	12	0	
NY	102 010 100 002	7	9	0	

Minnesota had plenty of chances to take a commanding lead. A solo homer by Torii Hunter in the 12th gave them a brief lead, but the Yankees rallied for two in the bottom of the inning on a double by Alex Rodriguez and a sacrifice fly by Hideki Matsui.

GAME 3 / OCT. 8

BROWN, QUANTRILL(7), HEREDIA(8), STURTZE(9), RIVERA(9) VS. SILVA, ROMERO(6), CRAIN(6), MULHOLLAND(7)					54,803
NY	030 004 100	8	14	1	
MIN	100 000 003	4	12	1	

The Yankees routed Carlos Silva, rapping 10 hits and six runs off the Minnesota sinkerballer in five innings. They added two more and entered the ninth with a commanding 8–1 lead before a harmless Twins' rally.

GAME 4 / OCT. 9

VAZQUEZ, LOAIZA(6), GORDON(8), RIVERA(10) VS. SANTANA, BALFOUR(6), RINCON(8), NATHAN(8), LOHSE(10)					52,498
NY	001 000 040 01	6	11	0	
MIN	100 130 000 00	5	12	1	

The Yankees advanced to the ALCS on an inopportune wild pitch after knotting the game with four runs in the eighth, three on a long ball by Ruben Sierra. Rodriguez doubled with one out in the 11th, easily stole third, then scored when a rattled Kyle Lohse threw one in the dirt.

2004 AL Championship Series
New York Yankees (3) vs. Boston Red Sox (4)

With the Yankees up three games to none in the ALCS against the rival Red Sox, the remaining balance on the 84-year-old invoice for Babe Ruth finally came due. The Yankees outscored the Red Sox, 32–16, in the first three games, building an historically insurmountable 3-games-to-none lead. Thereafter, Boston stunned the baseball world by winning the last four games, outscoring New York, 22–9.

BOS (E)

PLAYER, POS	G	AB	R	H	2B	3B	HR	RBI	BB	SO	SB	AVG	OBP	SLG
J.Damon, of	7	35	5	6	0	0	2	7	2	8	2	.171	.216	.171
D.Ortiz, dh	7	31	6	12	0	1	3	11	4	7	0	.387	.457	.452
B.Mueller, 3b	7	30	4	8	1	0	0	1	2	1	0	.267	.313	.300
M.Ramirez, of	7	30	3	9	1	0	0	0	5	4	0	.300	.400	.333
O.Cabrera, ss	7	29	5	11	2	0	0	5	3	5	1	.379	.438	.448
T.Nixon, of	7	29	4	6	1	0	1	3	0	5	0	.207	.207	.241
J.Varitek, c	7	28	5	9	1	0	2	7	2	6	0	.321	.367	.357
M.Bellhorn, 2b	7	26	3	5	2	0	2	4	5	11	0	.192	.323	.269
K.Millar, 1b	7	24	4	6	3	0	0	2	5	4	0	.250	.379	.375
D.Mientkiewicz, 1b	4	4	0	2	1	0	0	0	0	1	0	.500	.500	.750
G.Kapler, of	2	3	0	1	0	0	0	0	0	0	0	.333	.333	.333
D.Mirabelli, c	1	1	0	0	0	0	0	0	0	0	0	.000	.000	.000
P.Reese, 2b	3	1	0	0	0	0	0	0	0	1	0	.000	.000	.000
D.Roberts, ph	2	0	2	0	0	0	0	0	0	0	1	.000	.000	.000
Totals		271	41	75	12	1	10	40	28	53	4	.277	.347	.328

PITCHER	W	L	ERA	G	GS	SV	IP	H	BB	SO
P.Martinez	0	1	6.23	3	2	0	13.0	14	9	14
D.Lowe	1	0	3.18	2	2	0	11.1	7	1	6
C.Schilling	1	1	6.30	2	2	0	10.0	10	2	5
T.Wakefield	1	0	8.59	3	0	0	7.1	9	3	6
K.Foulke	0	0	0.00	5	0	1	6.0	1	6	6
M.Timlin	0	0	4.76	5	0	0	5.2	10	5	2
A.Embree	0	0	3.86	6	0	0	4.2	9	1	2
B.Arroyo	0	0	15.75	3	1	0	4.0	8	2	3
C.Leskanic	1	0	10.13	3	0	0	2.2	3	3	2
M.Myers	0	0	7.71	3	0	0	2.1	5	1	4
R.Mendoza	0	1	4.50	2	0	0	2.0	2	0	1
Totals	4	3	5.87	37	7	1	69.0	78	33	51

NY (E)

PLAYER, POS	G	AB	R	H	2B	3B	HR	RBI	BB	SO	SB	AVG	OBP	SLG
B.Williams, of	7	36	4	11	3	0	2	10	0	5	0	.306	.306	.389
H.Matsui, of	7	34	9	14	6	1	2	10	2	4	0	.412	.444	.647
A.Rodriguez, 3b	7	31	8	8	2	0	2	5	4	6	0	.258	.343	.323
D.Jeter, ss	7	30	5	6	1	0	0	5	6	2	1	.200	.333	.233
G.Sheffield, of	7	30	7	10	3	0	1	5	6	8	0	.333	.444	.433
J.Posada, c	7	27	4	7	1	0	0	2	7	1	0	.259	.417	.296
M.Cairo, 2b	7	25	4	7	3	0	0	0	2	4	1	.280	.333	.400
T.Clark, 1b	5	21	0	3	1	0	0	1	0	9	0	.143	.143	.190
R.Sierra, dh	5	21	1	7	1	1	0	2	3	8	0	.333	.417	.476
J.Olerud, 1b	4	12	1	2	0	0	1	2	1	1	0	.167	.231	.167
K.Lofton, dh	3	10	1	3	0	0	1	2	2	3	1	.300	.417	.300
B.Crosby, of	1	0	1	0	0	0	0	0	0	0	0	.000	.000	.000
Totals		277	45	78	21	2	9	44	33	51	3	.282	.371	.372

PITCHER	W	L	ERA	G	GS	SV	IP	H	BB	SO
J.Lieber	1	1	3.14	2	2	0	14.1	12	1	5
M.Mussina	1	0	4.26	2	2	0	12.2	10	2	15
M.Rivera	0	0	1.29	5	0	2	7.0	6	2	6
T.Gordon	0	0	8.10	6	0	0	6.2	10	2	3
E.Loaiza	0	1	1.42	2	0	0	6.1	5	3	5
J.Vazquez	1	0	9.95	2	0	0	6.1	9	7	6
O.Hernandez	0	0	5.40	1	1	0	5.0	3	5	6
K.Brown	0	1	21.60	2	2	0	3.1	9	4	2
P.Quantrill	0	1	5.40	4	0	0	3.1	8	0	2
T.Sturtze	0	0	2.70	4	0	0	3.1	2	2	2
F.Heredia	0	0	0.00	3	0	0	1.1	1	0	1
Totals	3	4	5.17	33	7	2	69.2	75	28	53

GAME 1 / OCT. 12

SCHILLING, LESKANIC(4), MENDOZA(5), WAKEFIELD(6), EMBREE(7), TIMLIN(8), FOULKE(8) VS. MUSSINA, STURTZE(7), GORDON(8), RIVERA(8) — **56,135**

				R	H	E
BOS	000	000	520	7	10	0
NY	204	002	02X	10	14	0

The Red Sox fell behind 8–0 as the Yankees pounded injured Curt Schilling. Mike Mussina retired 19 straight Red Sox, but Boston exploded for five runs in the eighth—all with two outs—including a two-run home run by Jason Varitek. The Red Sox scored twice more in the top of the eighth on a David Ortiz drive that bounced off Hideki Matsui's glove, bringing in two runs to cut it to 8–7. Mariano Rivera came in and got the last out and pitched through trouble in the ninth—a two-run double by Bernie Williams provided a cushion—as the Yankees took the opener for the first time in three Yankees-Red Sox ALCS.

GAME 2 / OCT. 13

MARTINEZ, TIMLIN(7), EMBREE(7), FOULKE(8) VS. LIEBER, GORDON(8), RIVERA(8) — **56,136**

				R	H	E
BOS	000	000	010	1	5	0
NY	100	002	00X	3	7	0

Pedro Martinez allowed a run-scoring single to Gary Sheffield in the first inning and a two-run homer to John Olerud in the sixth, but Jon Lieber allowed just three hits in seven innings. The only run charged to him came in on a groundout in the eighth.

GAME 3 / OCT. 16

BROWN, VAZQUEZ(3), QUANTRILL(7), GORDON(9) VS. ARROYO, MENDOZA(3), LESKANIC(4), WAKEFIELD(4), EMBREE(7), MYERS(8) — **35,126**

				R	H	E
NY	303	520	402	19	22	1
BOS	042	000	200	8	15	0

After a rainout, the Yankees scored three times in the first inning before the Red Sox tied it in the second and went ahead on Derek Jeter's error. The lead lasted one batter. Alex Rodriguez homered, starting a barrage that saw the Yanks score 15 more times against a half-dozen pitchers. A-Rod, Gary Sheffield, Hideki Matsui, and Bernie Williams, batting consecutively, accounted for 16 hits, 15 runs (including a run by a pinch runner), and 15 RBIs. The Red Sox couldn't keep up the pace, although the teams combined for 37 hits in the highest-scoring postseason game in a best-of-seven series.

GAME 4 / OCT. 17

HERNANDEZ, STURTZE(6), RIVERA(8), GORDON(10), QUANTRILL(12) VS. LOWE, TIMLIN(6), FOULKE(7), EMBREE(10), MYERS(11), LESKANIC(11) — **34,826**

					R	H	E
NY	002	002	000	000	4	12	1
BOS	000	030	001	002	6	8	0

The Red Sox faced elimination as they batted in the ninth inning of Game 4 down by one run, facing the most successful reliever in postseason history. Mariano Rivera's leadoff walk to Kevin Millar, though, spurred hope. Pinch runner Dave Roberts stole second base by an eyelash, then scored the tying run on Bill Mueller's single. David Ortiz' two-run homer in the 12th won the game.

GAME 5 / OCT. 18

MUSSINA, STURTZE(7), GORDON(7), RIVERA(8), HEREDIA(10), QUANTRILL(10), LOAIZA(11) VS. MARTINEZ, TIMLIN(7), FOULKE(8), ARROYO(10), MYERS(11), EMBREE(11), WAKEFIELD(12) — **35,120**

						R	H	E
NY	010	003	000	000	00	4	12	1
BOS	200	000	020	000	01	5	13	1

Ortiz came through again at two crucial junctures. "Big Papi" homered off Tom Gordon in the eighth; Jason Varitek tied the game with a sacrifice fly off Rivera later in the inning. Then, some six innings and many breathless moments later, Ortiz ended the suspense by singling in Johnny Damon. The Yankees left 18 runners on base.

GAME 6 / OCT. 19

SCHILLING, ARROYO(8), FOULKE(9) VS. LIEBER, HEREDIA(8), QUANTRILL(8), STURTZE(9) — **56,128**

				R	H	E
BOS	000	400	000	4	11	0
NY	000	000	110	2	6	0

Curt Schilling started despite a ruptured ankle tendon that bloodied his sock, stymieing the Yankees. Boston scored all its runs in the third inning, three of them coming on Mark Bellhorn's home run after umpires changed their call. The umpires did another reversal in the eighth when Rodriguez slapped the ball out of Bronson Arroyo's hand near first base. The reversals netted the Sox two runs, took away one from the Yankees, and evened the series.

GAME 7 / OCT. 20

LOWE, MARTINEZ(7), TIMLIN(8), EMBREE(9) VS. BROWN, VAZQUEZ(2), LOAIZA(4), HEREDIA(7), GORDON(8), RIVERA(9) **56,129**

				R	H	E
BOS	240	200	011	10	13	0
NY	001	000	200	3	5	1

Series MVP Ortiz hit his third homer in four games to help the Red Sox go ahead in Game 7. Johnny Damon clubbed a grand slam in the second to knock out Kevin Brown, later adding another homer and finishing the game with six RBIs. Starter Derek Lowe was outstanding, allowing one hit and a single run.

2005 AL Division Series
New York Yankees (2) vs. Los Angeles Angels (3)

The Yankees repeated as division winners again only because they won a tiebreaker with the Red Sox, with whom they'd ended the season in a dead heat. It seemed important at the time, because it meant New York would face the Angels in the Division Series instead of the White Sox, who had the AL's best record. As it turned out, the White Sox steamrolled over everyone on their way to the world championship.

ALA (W)

PLAYER, POS	G	AB	R	H	2B	3B	HR	RBI	BB	SO	SB	AVG	OBP	SLG
O.Cabrera, ss	5	21	3	5	2	0	0	3	0	1	0	.238	.238	.333
C.Figgins, 3b-of	5	21	2	3	1	1	0	2	1	8	0	.143	.182	.286
D.Erstad, 1b	5	20	1	6	2	0	0	3	0	6	0	.300	.300	.400
G.Anderson, of	5	19	2	5	0	1	2	7	0	0	0	.263	.263	.368
V.Guerrero, of	5	18	5	6	0	0	0	0	2	2	1	.333	.400	.333
B.Molina, c	5	18	5	8	0	0	3	5	0	0	0	.444	.444	.444
A.Kennedy, 2b	5	17	0	4	0	1	0	2	0	3	0	.235	.235	.353
J.Rivera, dh	5	17	3	6	1	0	1	1	1	2	0	.353	.389	.412
S.Finley, of	5	11	2	1	1	0	0	1	1	4	0	.091	.167	.182
C.Kotchman, ph	2	2	0	0	0	0	0	0	0	0	0	.000	.000	.000
R.Quinlan, 3b	2	2	0	1	0	0	0	0	0	0	0	.500	.500	.500
J.Molina, c	1	1	1	1	0	0	0	1	0	0	0	1.000	1.000	1.000
J.Da Vanon, ph	1	0	1	0	0	0	0	0	0	0	0	.000	.000	.000
J.Paul, ph	1	0	0	0	0	0	0	0	0	0	0	.000	.000	.000
Totals		167	25	46	7	3	6	25	5	26	1	.275	.305	.353

PITCHER	W	L	ERA	G	GS	SV	IP	H	BB	SO
J.Lackey	0	0	2.38	2	2	0	11.1	7	9	9
B.Colon	0	1	4.50	2	2	0	8.0	10	1	7
K.Escobar	1	0	1.29	4	0	0	7.0	2	5	5
E.Santana	1	0	5.06	1	0	0	5.1	5	3	2
S.Shields	1	1	3.60	4	0	0	5.0	4	3	5
P.Byrd	0	0	9.82	1	1	0	3.2	7	2	2
F.Rodriguez	0	0	2.70	3	0	2	3.1	5	0	2
B.Donnelly	0	0	27.00	1	0	0	0.1	2	1	0
Totals	3	2	3.89	18	5	2	44.0	42	24	32

NY (E)

PLAYER, POS	G	AB	R	H	2B	3B	HR	RBI	BB	SO	SB	AVG	OBP	SLG
D.Jeter, ss	5	21	4	7	0	0	2	5	1	5	1	.333	.364	.333
G.Sheffield, of	5	21	1	6	0	0	0	2	1	2	0	.286	.318	.286
H.Matsui, of	5	20	4	4	1	0	1	1	2	3	0	.200	.273	.250
R.Cano, 2b	5	19	3	5	3	0	0	5	2	4	0	.263	.333	.421
J.Giambi, 1b-dh	5	19	1	8	3	0	0	2	3	4	0	.421	.500	.579
B.Williams, of-dh	5	19	2	4	2	0	0	1	1	3	0	.211	.250	.316
A.Rodriguez, 3b	5	15	2	2	1	0	0	0	6	5	1	.133	.381	.200
J.Posada, c	5	13	3	3	1	0	1	2	6	2	0	.231	.474	.308
B.Crosby, of	3	8	0	2	0	0	0	1	0	1	1	.250	.250	.250
T.Martinez, 1b	4	8	0	0	0	0	0	0	1	2	0	.000	.111	.000
R.Sierra, of	3	3	0	1	0	0	0	1	0	1	0	.333	.333	.333
M.Bellhorn, ph	1	0	0	0	0	0	0	0	0	0	0	.000	.000	.000
J.Flaherty, c	1	0	0	0	0	0	0	0	1	0	0	.000	1.000	.000
T.Womack, ph	2	0	0	0	0	0	0	0	0	0	0	.000	.000	.000
Totals		166	20	42	11	0	4	20	24	32	3	.253	.354	.319

NY (E) (cont.)

PITCHER	W	L	ERA	G	GS	SV	IP	H	BB	SO
M.Mussina	1	1	5.40	2	2	0	8.1	11	1	7
R.Johnson	0	0	6.14	2	1	0	7.1	12	1	4
C.Wang	0	1	1.35	1	1	0	6.2	6	0	1
S.Chacon	0	0	2.84	1	1	0	6.1	4	1	5
A.Leiter	1	0	7.36	4	0	0	3.2	2	1	2
M.Rivera	0	0	3.00	2	0	2	3.0	1	1	2
A.Small	0	1	6.75	1	0	0	2.2	4	0	2
T.Gordon	0	0	3.86	3	0	0	2.1	2	0	2
S.Proctor	0	0	0.00	2	0	0	2.0	3	0	1
T.Sturtze	0	0	13.50	2	0	0	0.2	1	0	0
Totals	2	3	4.40	20	5	2	43.0	46	5	26

GAME 1 / OCT. 4

MUSSINA, LEITER(6), STURTZE(7), GORDON(7), RIVERA(9) VS. COLON, SHIELDS(8) **45,142**

				R	H	E
NY	310	000	000	4	9	0
ALA	000	000	101	2	7	0

Robinson Cano's three-run double provided the Yankees with more than enough runs as Mike Mussina and four relievers combined to hold the Angels to seven hits and two runs.

GAME 2 / OCT. 5

WANG, LEITER(7), PROCTOR(8) VS. LACKEY, SHIELDS(6), ESCOBAR(7), RODRIGUEZ(9) **45,150**

				R	H	E
NY	010	010	001	3	6	2
ALA	000	011	21X	5	7	0

After falling behind by two early, the Angels scored five unanswered runs, with Juan Rivera and Bengie Molina both homering.

GAME 3 / OCT. 7

BYRD, DONNELLY(4), SHIELDS(5), ESCOBAR(7), RODRIGUEZ(9) VS. JOHNSON, SMALL(4), STURTZE(6), GORDON(7), LEITER(7), PROCTOR(8) **56,277**

				R	H	E
ALA	302	002	220	11	19	1
NY	000	420	010	7	12	1

Seven extra base hits—three doubles, two triples and two home runs—fueled the Angels comeback after they blew a 5–0 lead.

GAME 4 / OCT. 9

LACKEY, SHIELDS(6), ESCOBAR(7) VS. CHACON, LEITER(7), RIVERA(8) **56,226**

				R	H	E
ALA	000	002	000	2	4	0
NY	000	001	20X	3	4	1

The Yankees staved off elimination with two runs in the seventh on a single and a groundout. New York closer Mariano Rivera retired the side in order in both the eighth and ninth innings.

GAME 5 / OCT. 10

MUSSINA, JOHNSON(3), GORDON(8) VS. COLON, SANTANA(2), ESCOBAR(7), RODRIGUEZ(8) **45,133**

				R	H	E
NY	020	000	100	3	11	0
ALA	032	000	00X	5	9	0

Circumstances appeared dire for the Angels when starting pitcher Bartolo Colon was forced out with a sore shoulder after only one inning. But their offense scored five times in two innings, knocking out Mike Mussina in the third. Ervin Santana, a 22-year-old rookie, pitched admirably, allowing three runs in $5^1/_3$ innings of relief for the win.

2006 AL Division Series
New York Yankees (1) vs. Detroit Tigers (3)

After their late-season collapse, the Wild Card Tigers were given almost no chance of besting the mighty Yankees—winners of their ninth consecutive AL East title—in the Division Series. And, after the Bombers convincingly won the first game at the Stadium, few thought it was even necessary to play out the rest of the series. The Tigers, however, scratched out a win in Game 2, then returned to Detroit to stun the baseball world by thoroughly dominating New York.

DET (C)

PLAYER, POS	G	AB	R	H	2B	3B	HR	RBI	BB	SO	SB	AVG	OBP	SLG
S.Casey, 1b	4	17	1	6	3	0	0	4	0	0	0	.353	.353	.529
C.Granderson, of	4	17	3	5	0	1	2	5	0	1	1	.294	.294	.412
P.Polanco, 2b	4	17	3	7	1	0	0	2	1	1	0	.412	.444	.471
C.Monroe, of	4	16	3	3	1	0	2	3	0	3	0	.188	.188	.250
B.Inge, 3b	4	15	1	2	0	0	0	0	0	6	0	.133	.133	.133
M.Ordonez, of	4	15	3	4	1	0	1	2	1	2	0	.267	.313	.333
M.Thames, dh	4	15	2	5	2	0	0	1	1	5	0	.333	.375	.467
C.Guillen, ss	4	14	3	8	3	0	1	2	2	1	0	.571	.625	.786
I.Rodriguez, c	4	13	3	3	1	0	0	3	2	3	0	.231	.333	.308
Totals		139	22	43	12	1	6	22	7	22	1	.309	.342	.410

PITCHER	W	L	ERA	G	GS	SV	IP	H	BB	SO
J.Bonderman	1	0	2.16	1	1	0	8.1	5	1	4
K.Rogers	1	0	0.00	1	1	0	7.2	5	2	8
N.Robertson	0	1	11.12	1	1	0	5.2	12	0	1
J.Verlander	0	0	5.06	1	1	0	5.1	7	4	5
J.Walker	1	0	4.91	3	0	0	3.2	3	1	1
T.Jones	0	0	0.00	2	0	1	2.0	1	0	2
J.Zumaya	0	0	0.00	2	0	0	2.0	0	0	3
J.Grilli	0	0	0.00	1	0	0	0.1	0	0	0
Totals	3	1	3.60	12	4	1	35.0	33	8	24

NY (E)

PLAYER, POS	G	AB	R	H	2B	3B	HR	RBI	BB	SO	SB	AVG	OBP	SLG
J.Damon, of	4	17	3	4	0	0	1	3	1	2	0	.235	.278	.235
D.Jeter, ss	4	16	4	8	4	0	1	1	1	2	0	.500	.529	.750
H.Matsui, of-dh	4	16	1	4	1	0	0	1	0	2	0	.250	.250	.313
B.Abreu, of	4	15	2	5	1	0	0	4	2	2	0	.333	.412	.400
R.Cano, 2b	4	15	0	2	0	0	0	0	0	1	0	.133	.133	.133
J.Posada, c	4	14	2	7	1	0	1	2	2	2	0	.500	.563	.571
A.Rodriguez, 3b	4	14	0	1	0	0	0	0	0	4	0	.071	.071	.071
G.Sheffield, 1b	3	12	1	1	0	0	0	1	0	4	0	.083	.083	.083
J.Giambi, dh-1b	3	8	1	1	0	0	1	2	2	3	1	.125	.300	.125
M.Cabrera, of	2	3	0	0	0	0	0	0	0	0	0	.000	.000	.000
B.Williams, dh	1	3	0	0	0	0	0	0	0	2	0	.000	.000	.000
A.Phillips, 1b	1	1	0	0	0	0	0	0	0	0	0	.000	.000	.000
Totals		134	14	33	7	0	4	14	8	24	1	.246	.303	.299

PITCHER	W	L	ERA	G	GS	SV	IP	H	BB	SO
M.Mussina	0	1	5.14	1	1	0	7.0	8	0	5
C.Wang	1	0	4.05	1	1	0	6.2	8	1	4
R.Johnson	0	1	7.94	1	1	0	5.2	8	2	4
S.Proctor	0	0	2.25	3	0	0	4.0	5	1	1
B.Bruney	0	0	3.38	3	0	0	2.2	1	0	4
J.Wright	0	1	10.13	1	1	0	2.2	5	1	1
K.Farnsworth	0	0	0.00	2	0	0	2.0	1	1	1
C.Lidle	0	0	20.25	1	0	0	1.1	4	0	1
M.Rivera	0	0	0.00	1	0	0	1.0	1	0	0
R.Villone	0	0	0.00	1	0	0	1.0	1	1	1
M.Myers	0	0	INF	1	0	0	0.0	1	0	0
Totals	1	3	5.56	16	4	0	34.0	43	7	22

GAME 1 / OCT. 3

ROBERTSON, GRILLI(6), WALKER(7) VS. WANG, MYERS(7), PROCTOR(7), FARNSWORTH(8), RIVERA(9) — **56,291**

				R	H	E
DET	000	030	100	4	12	1
NY	005	002	01X	8	14	0

New York broke away with five runs in the third on six consecutive hits, including doubles by Derek Jeter and Bobby Abreu and a home run by Jason Giambi. The home team then coasted to the victory, as Abreu singled home two more in the sixth to finish off Nate Robertson.

GAME 2 / OCT. 5

VERLANDER, WALKER(6), ZUMAYA(7), JONES(9) VS. MUSSINA, PROCTOR(8), BRUNEY(9) — **56,252**

				R	H	E
DET	010	011	100	4	8	0
NY	000	300	000	3	8	1

Johnny Damon's three-run homer in the fourth gave the Yanks a 3–1 lead, but veteran warhorse Mike Mussina couldn't nail it down. The visitors tied the score on Carlos Guillen's home run in the sixth, then forged ahead on Curtis Granderson's triple in the seventh. The Detroit bullpen finished with $3^2/_3$ spotless innings, with flamethrower Joel Zumaya striking out three of the five hitters he faced.

GAME 3 / OCT. 6

JOHNSON, BRUNEY(6), VILLONE(8) VS. ROGERS, ZUMAYA(8), JONES(9) — **43,440**

				R	H	E
NY	000	000	000	0	5	0
DET	030	002	10X	6	10	0

Kenny Rogers pitched the game of his life against a club he seemingly never could beat, fanning eight in $7^2/_3$ scoreless innings.

GAME 4 / OCT. 7

WRIGHT, LIDLE(3), BRUNEY(5), PROCTOR(5), FARNSWORTH(8) VS. BONDERMAN, WALKER(9) — **43,126**

				R	H	E
NY	000	000	102	3	6	1
DET	031	031	00X	8	13	0

Joe Torre demoted 1-for-11 superstar Alex Rodriguez to the No. 8 slot in the order, but the shake-up didn't help as young righty Jeremy Bonderman baffled the Yankees for eight innings before tiring in the ninth. Underdog Detroit scored three in the second and three in the fifth on its way to its huge upset.

2007 AL Division Series
New York Yankees (1) vs. Cleveland Indians (3)

CLE (C)

PLAYER, POS	G	AB	R	H	2B	3B	HR	RBI	BB	SO	SB	AVG	OBP	SLG
C.Blake, 3b	4	17	1	2	1	0	0	2	0	5	0	.118	.118	.176
A.Cabrera, 2b	4	17	3	3	0	0	1	2	1	4	0	.176	.222	.176
V.Martinez, c-1b	4	17	2	6	1	0	1	4	1	3	0	.353	.389	.412
T.Hafner, dh	4	16	4	4	0	0	1	2	5	3	0	.250	.429	.250
K.Lofton, of	4	16	2	6	1	0	0	4	2	1	1	.375	.444	.438
G.Sizemore, of	4	16	3	6	0	1	1	1	4	4	1	.375	.500	.500
J.Peralta, ss	4	15	2	7	3	0	0	2	4	3	1	.467	.579	.667
R.Garko, 1b	3	11	3	4	0	0	1	3	1	1	0	.364	.417	.364
F.Gutierrez, of	4	10	2	2	0	0	0	0	2	5	0	.200	.333	.200
T.Nixon, of	1	4	1	2	1	0	1	2	0	1	0	.500	.500	.750
K.Shoppach, c	1	3	1	2	2	0	0	0	0	0	0	.667	.667	1.333
J.Michaels, of	1	1	0	1	1	0	0	0	0	0	0	1.000	1.000	2.000
Totals		143	24	45	10	1	6	22	20	30	3	.315	.417	.399

PITCHER	W	L	ERA	G	GS	SV	IP	H	BB	SO
F.Carmona	0	0	1.00	1	1	0	9.0	3	2	5
R.Perez	1	0	1.50	3	0	0	6.0	3	1	6
P.Byrd	1	0	3.60	1	1	0	5.0	8	2	2
C.Sabathia	1	0	5.40	1	1	0	5.0	4	6	5
J.Westbrook	0	1	10.80	1	1	0	5.0	9	0	1
R.Betancourt	0	0	0.00	2	0	0	2.0	1	0	3
J.Borowski	0	0	4.50	2	0	1	2.0	1	2	1
J.Lewis	0	0	0.00	2	0	0	2.0	0	0	4
A.Fultz	0	0	0.00	1	0	0	1.0	2	1	1
Totals	3	1	3.41	14	4	1	37.0	31	14	28

NY (E)

PLAYER, POS	G	AB	R	H	2B	3B	HR	RBI	BB	SO	SB	AVG	OBP	SLG
J.Damon, of	4	18	2	5	0	0	2	5	1	5	0	.278	.316	.278
D.Jeter, ss	4	17	0	3	0	0	0	1	0	4	0	.176	.176	.176
M.Cabrera, of	4	16	2	3	0	0	1	2	0	1	0	.188	.188	.188
B.Abreu, of	4	15	1	4	1	0	1	2	2	3	1	.267	.353	.333
R.Cano, 2b	4	15	3	5	1	0	2	3	1	1	0	.333	.375	.400
J.Posada, c	4	15	1	2	1	0	0	0	2	3	0	.133	.235	.200
A.Rodriguez, 3b	4	15	2	4	0	0	1	1	2	6	0	.267	.353	.267
H.Matsui, dh	4	11	4	2	0	0	0	0	5	2	0	.182	.438	.182
D.Mientkiewicz, 1b	4	6	0	0	0	0	0	0	1	0	0	.000	.143	.000
S.Duncan, 1b	3	4	1	2	0	0	0	0	0	1	0	.500	.500	.500
J.Giambi, 1b	3	4	0	1	0	0	0	0	0	2	0	.250	.250	.250
B.Sardinha, of	1	0	0	0	0	0	0	0	0	0	0	.000	.000	.000
Totals		136	16	31	3	0	7	14	14	28	1	.228	.300	.250

PITCHER	W	L	ERA	G	GS	SV	IP	H	BB	SO
A.Pettitte	0	0	0.00	1	1	0	6.1	7	2	5
P.Hughes	1	0	1.59	2	0	0	5.2	3	0	6
C.Wang	0	2	19.06	2	2	0	5.2	14	4	2
M.Mussina	0	0	3.86	1	0	0	4.2	4	4	3
M.Rivera	0	0	0.00	3	0	0	4.2	2	1	6
J.Chamberlain	0	0	4.91	2	0	0	3.2	3	3	4
R.Clemens	0	0	11.57	1	1	0	2.1	4	2	1
K.Farnsworth	0	0	0.00	1	0	0	1.0	1	0	2
R.Ohlendorf	0	0	27.00	1	0	0	1.0	4	1	0
J.Veras	0	0	0.00	2	0	0	0.2	1	1	1
L.Vizcaino	0	1	13.50	1	0	0	0.2	2	2	0
R.Villone	0	0	0.00	1	0	0	0.1	0	0	0
Totals	1	3	5.89	18	4	0	36.2	45	20	30

GAME 1 / OCT. 4

WANG, OHLENDORF(5), VERAS(6), HUGHES(7) VS. SABATHIA, PEREZ(6), LEWIS(8), BETANCOURT(9) — **44,608**

				R	H	E
NY	100	110	000	3	5	0
CLE	301	052	01X	12	14	0

Cleveland coasted to a lopsided win at the Jake after breaking the game open by posting a five-spot in the fifth as New York ace Chien-Ming Wang was pounded for eight runs, including two homers, in $4^2/_3$ innings. Three Tribe relievers nailed down the opening game by fanning six and allowing only one hit in four scoreless innings.

GAME 2 / OCT. 5

PETTITTE, CHAMBERLAIN(7), RIVERA(9), VIZCAINO(11) VS. CARMONA, PEREZ(10) 44,732

					R	H	E
NY	001	000	000	00	1	3	0
CLE	000	000	010	01	2	9	1

Fausto Carmona hurled nine frames of three-hit, one-run ball, setting the stage for an 11th-inning win. Travis Hafner singled in the winning run with the bases loaded off Luis Vizcaino after Mariano Rivera had pitched two scoreless innings in relief.

GAME 3 / OCT. 7

WESTBROOK, FULTZ(6), LEWIS(7), BOROWSKI(8) VS. CLEMENS, HUGHES(3), CHAMBERLAIN(7), RIVERA(9) 56,358

				R	H	E
CLE	111	000	010	4	9	1
NY	001	043	00X	8	11	1

Roger Clemens' (as well as the Yankees') bacon was saved by Phil Hughes, 24 years The Rocket's junior, as the 21-year-old phenom pitched 3²/₃ innings of scoreless relief. Johnny Damon's three-run home run in the fifth was the big event in the New York comeback, which saw them score seven times in the fifth and sixth.

GAME 4 / OCT. 8

BYRD, PEREZ(6), BETANCOURT(8), BOROWSKI(9) VS. WANG, MUSSINA(2), VILLONE(6), FARNSWORTH(7), VERAS(8), RIVERA(8) 56,315

				R	H	E
CLE	220	200	000	6	13	0
NY	010	001	101	4	12	0

Grady Sizemore set the tone by leading off the game with a home run off Yankees ace Wang, who barely lasted past the first inning while being roughed up for four runs. Meanwhile, soft-tossing Indians starter Paul Byrd hung on for five frames before the Cleveland bullpen took over. The Yanks made it interesting by hitting three solo homers. Nevertheless, for the third straight year, the Bombers exited the postseason early by failing to win the Division Series.

Postseason Batter Register

YEAR	G	AB	R	H	2B	3B	HR	RBI	BB	SO	SB	AVG	OPS	POS
BOB ABREU														
DS 2006	4	15	2	5	1	0	0	4	2	2	0	.333	.812	O
DS 2007	4	15	1	4	1	0	1	2	2	3	1	.267	.886	O
DS Total	8	30	3	9	2	0	1	6	4	5	1	.300	.849	
SPENCER ADAMS														
WS 1926	2	0	0	0	0	0	0	0	0	0	0	+	+	H
MIKE ALDRETE														
LC 1996	1	0	0	0	0	0	0	0	0	0	0	+	+	H
WS 1996	2	1	0	0	0	0	0	0	0	0	0	.000	.000	O-1
SANDY ALOMAR SR.														
LC 1976	2	1	0	0	0	0	0	0	0	0	0	.000	.000	D-1
FRANK BAKER														
WS 1921	4	8	0	2	0	0	0	0	1	0	0	.250	.583	3-2
WS 1922	1	1	0	0	0	0	0	0	0	0	0	.000	.000	H
WS Total	5	9	0	2	0	0	0	0	1	0	0	.222	.522	
HANK BAUER														
WS 1949	3	6	0	1	0	0	0	0	0	0	0	.167	.333	O
WS 1950	4	15	0	2	0	0	0	1	0	0	0	.133	.267	O
WS 1951	6	18	0	3	0	1	0	3	1	1	0	.167	.488	O
WS 1952	7	18	2	1	0	0	0	1	4	3	0	.056	.283	O
WS 1953	6	23	6	6	0	1	0	1	2	4	0	.261	.283	O
WS 1955	6	14	1	6	0	0	0	1	0	1	0	.429	.857	O-5
WS 1956	7	32	3	9	0	0	1	3	0	5	1	.281	.656	O
WS 1957	7	31	3	8	2	1	2	6	1	6	0	.258	.862	O
WS 1958	7	31	6	10	0	0	4	8	0	5	0	.323	1.032	O
WS Total	53	188	21	46	2	3	7	24	8	25	1	.245	.678	
MARK BELLHORN														
DS 2005	1	0	0	0	0	0	0	0	0	0	0	+	+	H
CLAY BELLINGER														
DS 1999	1	0	0	0	0	0	0	0	0	0	0	+	+	D
DS 2000	2	1	0	1	1	0	0	1	0	0	0	1.000	3.000	O
DS 2001	1	0	0	0	0	0	0	0	0	0	0	+	+	R
DS Total	4	1	0	1	1	0	0	1	0	0	0	1.000	3.000	
LC 1999	3	1	0	0	0	0	0	0	0	1	0	.000	.000	D-2,S-1
LC 2000	5	0	0	0	0	0	0	0	0	0	0	+	+	O
LC 2001	1	1	0	0	0	0	0	0	0	0	0	.000	.000	O
LC Total	9	2	0	0	0	0	0	0	0	1	0	.000	.000	
WS 2000	4	0	0	0	0	0	0	0	0	0	0	+	+	O
WS 2001	2	2	0	0	0	0	0	0	0	2	0	.000	.000	O
WS Total	6	2	0	0	0	0	0	0	0	2	0	.000	.000	
BENNY BENGOUGH														
WS 1927	2	4	1	0	0	0	0	0	1	0	0	.000	.200	C
WS 1928	4	13	1	3	0	0	0	1	1	1	0	.231	.516	C
WS Total	6	17	2	3	0	0	0	1	2	1	0	.176	.440	
YOGI BERRA														
WS 1947	6	19	2	3	0	0	1	2	1	2	0	.158	.516	C-4,O-2
WS 1949	4	16	2	1	0	0	0	1	1	3	0	.063	.180	C
WS 1950	4	15	2	3	0	0	1	2	2	1	0	.200	.694	C
WS 1951	6	23	4	6	1	0	0	0	2	1	0	.261	.624	C
WS 1952	7	28	2	6	1	0	2	3	2	4	0	.214	.731	C
WS 1953	6	21	3	9	1	0	1	4	3	3	0	.429	.731	C
WS 1955	7	24	5	10	1	0	1	2	3	1	0	.417	1.065	C

YEAR	G	AB	R	H	2B	3B	HR	RBI	BB	SO	SB	AVG	OPS	POS
WS 1956	7	25	5	9	2	0	3	10	4	1	0	.360	1.248	C
WS 1957	7	25	5	8	1	0	1	2	4	0	0	.320	.894	C
WS 1958	7	27	3	6	3	0	0	2	1	0	0	.222	.583	C
WS 1960	7	22	6	7	0	0	1	8	2	0	0	.318	.830	O-4,C-3
WS 1961	4	11	2	3	0	0	1	3	5	1	0	.273	1.045	O
WS 1962	2	2	0	0	0	0	0	0	2	0	0	.000	.500	C-1
WS 1963	1	1	0	0	0	0	0	0	0	0	0	.000	.000	H
WS Total	75	259	41	71	10	0	12	39	32	17	0	.274	.810	
PAUL BLAIR														
LC 1977	3	5	1	2	0	0	0	0	0	0	0	.400	.800	O
LC 1978	4	6	1	0	0	0	0	0	0	1	0	.000	.000	O-3,2-1
LC Total	7	11	2	2	0	0	0	0	0	1	0	.182	.364	
WS 1977	4	4	0	1	0	0	0	1	0	0	0	.250	.500	O-3
WS 1978	6	8	2	3	1	0	0	0	1	4	0	.375	.944	O
WS Total	10	12	2	4	1	0	0	1	1	4	0	.333	.801	
JOHNNY BLANCHARD														
WS 1960	5	11	2	5	2	0	0	2	0	0	0	.455	1.091	C-2
WS 1961	4	10	4	4	1	0	2	3	2	0	0	.400	1.600	O-2
WS 1962	1	1	0	0	0	0	0	0	0	1	0	.000	.000	H
WS 1963	1	3	0	0	0	0	0	0	0	0	0	.000	.000	O-1
WS 1964	4	4	0	1	1	0	0	0	0	1	0	.250	.750	H
WS Total	15	29	6	10	4	0	2	5	2	2	0	.345	1.077	
WADE BOGGS														
DS 1995	4	19	4	5	2	0	1	3	3	5	0	.263	.890	3
DS 1996	3	12	0	1	1	0	0	0	0	2	0	.083	.250	3
DS 1997	3	7	1	3	0	0	0	2	0	0	0	.429	.857	3-2
DS Total	10	38	5	9	3	0	1	5	3	7	0	.237	.687	
LC 1996	3	15	1	2	0	0	0	0	1	3	0	.133	.321	3
WS 1996	4	11	0	3	1	0	0	2	1	0	0	.273	.697	3
DON BOLLWEG														
WS 1953	3	2	0	0	0	0	0	0	0	2	0	.000	.000	1-1
AARON BOONE														
DS 2003	4	15	1	3	1	0	0	0	0	3	1	.200	.467	3
LC 2003	7	17	2	3	0	0	1	2	1	6	1	.176	.321	3
WS 2003	6	21	1	3	0	0	1	2	0	6	0	.143	.000	3
FRENCHY BORDAGARAY														
WS 1941	1	0	0	0	0	0	0	0	0	0	0	+	+	R
CLETE BOYER														
WS 1960	4	12	1	3	2	1	0	1	0	1	0	.250	.833	3-4,S-1
WS 1961	5	15	0	4	2	0	0	3	4	0	0	.267	.821	3
WS 1962	7	22	2	7	1	0	1	4	1	3	0	.318	.821	3
WS 1963	4	13	0	1	0	0	0	0	1	6	0	.077	.220	3
WS 1964	7	24	2	5	1	0	1	3	1	5	1	.208	.615	3
WS Total	27	86	5	20	6	1	2	11	7	15	1	.233	.683	
HARRY BRIGHT														
WS 1963	2	2	0	0	0	0	0	0	0	2	0	.000	.000	H
SCOTT BROSIUS														
DS 1998	3	10	1	4	0	0	1	3	0	3	0	.400	1.100	3
DS 1999	3	10	0	1	1	0	0	1	0	0	0	.100	.300	3
DS 2000	5	17	0	3	1	0	0	1	1	4	0	.176	.458	3
DS 2001	5	17	0	1	0	0	0	1	0	3	0	.059	.458	3
DS Total	16	54	1	9	2	0	1	6	1	10	0	.167	.456	

YEAR	G	AB	R	H	2B	3B	HR	RBI	BB	SO	SB	AVG	OPS	POS
LC 1998	6	20	2	6	1	0	1	6	2	4	0	.300	.321	3
LC 1999	5	18	3	4	0	1	2	3	1	4	0	.222	.930	3
LC 2000	6	18	2	4	0	0	0	0	2	3	0	.222	.522	3
LC 2001	5	16	3	3	2	0	0	2	0	6	0	.188	.500	3
LC Total	22	72	10	17	3	1	3	11	5	17	0	.236	.713	
WS 1998	4	17	3	8	0	0	2	6	0	4	0	.471	1.294	3
WS 1999	4	16	2	6	1	0	0	1	0	5	0	.375	.813	3
WS 2000	5	13	2	4	0	0	1	3	2	2	0	.308	.813	3
WS 2001	7	24	1	4	2	0	1	3	0	8	0	.167	.542	3
WS Total	20	70	8	22	3	0	4	13	2	19	0	.314	.862	

Bobby Brown

YEAR	G	AB	R	H	2B	3B	HR	RBI	BB	SO	SB	AVG	OPS	POS
WS 1947	4	3	2	3	2	0	0	3	1	0	0	1.000	2.667	H
WS 1949	4	12	4	6	1	2	0	5	2	2	0	.500	1.488	3-3
WS 1950	4	12	2	4	1	1	0	1	0	0	0	.333	.917	3
WS 1951	5	14	1	5	1	0	0	0	2	1	0	.357	.866	3-4
WS Total	17	41	9	18	5	3	0	9	5	3	0	.439	1.207	

Bobby Brown

YEAR	G	AB	R	H	2B	3B	HR	RBI	BB	SO	SB	AVG	OPS	POS
DS 1981	1	0	0	0	0	0	0	0	0	0	0	+	+	R
LC 1980	3	10	1	0	0	0	0	0	1	2	0	.000	.091	O
LC 1981	3	1	2	1	0	0	0	0	0	0	0	1.000	2.000	O-2
LC Total	6	11	3	1	0	0	0	0	1	2	0	.091	.258	
WS 1981	4	1	1	0	0	0	0	0	0	1	0	.000	.000	O-2

Homer Bush

YEAR	G	AB	R	H	2B	3B	HR	RBI	BB	SO	SB	AVG	OPS	POS
DS 1998	1	0	0	0	0	0	0	0	0	0	1	+	+	D
LC 1998	2	0	1	0	0	0	0	0	0	0	1	+	+	D-1
WS 1998	2	0	0	0	0	0	0	0	0	0	0	+	+	D-1

Sammy Byrd

YEAR	G	AB	R	H	2B	3B	HR	RBI	BB	SO	SB	AVG	OPS	POS
WS 1932	1	0	0	0	0	0	0	0	0	0	0	+	+	O

Melky Cabrera

YEAR	G	AB	R	H	2B	3B	HR	RBI	BB	SO	SB	AVG	OPS	POS
DS 2006	2	3	0	0	0	0	0	0	0	0	0	.000	.000	O-1
DS 2007	4	16	2	3	0	0	1	2	0	1	0	.188	.563	O
DS Total	6	19	2	3	0	0	1	2	0	1	0	.158	.474	

Miguel Cairo

YEAR	G	AB	R	H	2B	3B	HR	RBI	BB	SO	SB	AVG	OPS	POS
DS 2004	4	14	3	3	1	0	0	1	2	5	0	.214	.598	2
LC 2004	7	25	4	7	3	0	0	0	2	4	1	.280	.000	2

Robinson Cano

YEAR	G	AB	R	H	2B	3B	HR	RBI	BB	SO	SB	AVG	OPS	POS
DS 2005	5	19	3	5	3	0	0	5	2	4	0	.263	.754	2
DS 2006	4	15	0	2	0	0	0	0	0	1	0	.133	.267	2
DS 2007	4	15	3	5	1	0	2	3	1	1	0	.333	1.175	2
DS Total	13	49	6	12	4	0	2	8	3	6	0	.245	.737	

Jose Canseco

YEAR	G	AB	R	H	2B	3B	HR	RBI	BB	SO	SB	AVG	OPS	POS
WS 2000	1	1	0	0	0	0	0	0	0	1	0	.000	.000	H

Andy Carey

YEAR	G	AB	R	H	2B	3B	HR	RBI	BB	SO	SB	AVG	OPS	POS
WS 1955	2	2	0	1	0	1	0	1	0	0	0	.500	2.000	H
WS 1956	7	19	2	3	0	0	0	0	1	6	0	.158	.358	3
WS 1957	2	7	0	2	1	0	0	1	1	0	0	.286	.804	3
WS 1958	5	12	1	1	0	0	0	0	0	3	0	.083	.167	3
WS Total	16	40	3	7	1	1	0	2	2	9	0	.175	.464	

Tom Carroll

YEAR	G	AB	R	H	2B	3B	HR	RBI	BB	SO	SB	AVG	OPS	POS
WS 1955	2	0	0	0	0	0	0	0	0	0	0	+	+	R

Rick Cerone

YEAR	G	AB	R	H	2B	3B	HR	RBI	BB	SO	SB	AVG	OPS	POS
DS 1981	5	18	1	6	2	0	1	5	0	2	0	.333	.944	C
LC 1980	3	12	1	4	0	0	1	2	0	1	0	.333	.917	C
LC 1981	3	10	1	1	0	0	0	0	0	0	0	.100	.917	C
LC Total	6	22	2	5	0	0	1	2	0	1	0	.227	.625	
WS 1981	6	21	2	4	1	0	1	3	4	2	0	.190	.701	C

Bob Cerv

YEAR	G	AB	R	H	2B	3B	HR	RBI	BB	SO	SB	AVG	OPS	POS
WS 1955	5	16	1	2	0	0	1	1	0	4	0	.125	.438	O-4
WS 1956	1	1	0	1	0	0	0	0	0	0	0	1.000	2.000	H
WS 1960	4	14	1	5	0	0	0	0	0	3	0	.357	.714	O-3
WS Total	10	31	2	8	0	0	1	1	0	7	0	.258	.613	

Chris Chambliss

YEAR	G	AB	R	H	2B	3B	HR	RBI	BB	SO	SB	AVG	OPS	POS
LC 1976	5	21	5	11	1	1	2	8	0	1	2	.524	.625	1
LC 1977	5	17	0	1	0	0	0	0	3	4	0	.059	.259	1
LC 1978	4	15	1	6	0	0	0	2	0	4	0	.400	.800	1
LC Total	14	53	6	18	1	1	2	10	3	9	2	.340	.878	
WS 1976	4	16	1	5	1	0	0	1	0	2	0	.313	.613	1
WS 1977	6	24	4	7	2	0	1	4	0	2	0	.292	.792	1
WS 1978	3	11	1	2	0	0	0	0	1	1	0	.182	.432	1
WS Total	13	51	6	14	3	0	1	5	1	5	0	.275	.694	

Ben Chapman

YEAR	G	AB	R	H	2B	3B	HR	RBI	BB	SO	SB	AVG	OPS	POS
WS 1932	4	17	1	5	2	0	0	6	2	4	0	.294	.780	O

Allie Clark

YEAR	G	AB	R	H	2B	3B	HR	RBI	BB	SO	SB	AVG	OPS	POS
WS 1947	3	2	1	1	0	0	0	1	1	0	0	.500	1.167	O-1

Anthony Clark

YEAR	G	AB	R	H	2B	3B	HR	RBI	BB	SO	SB	AVG	OPS	POS
DS 2004	1	1	0	0	0	0	0	0	0	1	0	.000	.000	1

Tony Clark

YEAR	G	AB	R	H	2B	3B	HR	RBI	BB	SO	SB	AVG	OPS	POS
LC 2004	5	21	0	3	1	0	0	1	0	9	0	.143	.333	1

Jerry Coleman

YEAR	G	AB	R	H	2B	3B	HR	RBI	BB	SO	SB	AVG	OPS	POS
WS 1949	5	20	0	5	3	0	0	4	0	4	0	.250	.650	2
WS 1950	4	14	2	4	1	0	0	3	2	0	0	.286	.732	2
WS 1951	5	8	2	2	0	0	0	0	1	2	0	.250	.583	2
WS 1955	3	3	0	0	0	0	0	0	0	1	0	.000	.000	S
WS 1956	2	2	0	0	0	0	0	0	0	0	0	.000	.000	2
WS 1957	7	22	2	8	2	0	0	2	3	1	0	.364	.895	2
WS Total	26	69	6	19	6	0	0	9	6	8	0	.275	.696	

Joe Collins

YEAR	G	AB	R	H	2B	3B	HR	RBI	BB	SO	SB	AVG	OPS	POS
WS 1950	1	0	0	0	0	0	0	0	0	0	0	+	+	1
WS 1951	6	18	2	4	0	0	1	3	2	1	0	.222	.689	1-6,O-1
WS 1952	6	12	1	0	0	0	0	0	1	3	0	.000	.077	1
WS 1953	6	24	4	4	1	0	1	2	3	8	0	.167	.593	1
WS 1955	5	12	6	2	0	0	2	3	6	4	1	.167	1.111	1-5,O-1
WS 1956	6	21	2	5	2	0	0	2	2	3	0	.238	.638	1-5
WS 1957	6	5	0	0	0	0	0	0	0	3	0	.000	.000	1-5
WS Total	36	92	15	15	3	0	4	10	14	22	1	.163	.600	

Pat Collins

YEAR	G	AB	R	H	2B	3B	HR	RBI	BB	SO	SB	AVG	OPS	POS
WS 1926	3	2	0	0	0	0	0	0	0	1	0	.000	.000	C
WS 1927	2	5	0	3	1	0	0	0	3	0	0	.600	1.550	C
WS 1928	1	1	0	1	1	0	0	0	0	0	0	1.000	3.000	C
WS Total	6	8	0	4	2	0	0	0	3	1	0	.500	1.386	

Earle Combs

YEAR	G	AB	R	H	2B	3B	HR	RBI	BB	SO	SB	AVG	OPS	POS
WS 1926	7	28	3	10	2	0	0	2	5	2	0	.357	.883	O
WS 1927	4	16	6	5	0	0	0	2	1	2	0	.313	.883	O
WS 1928	1	0	0	0	0	0	0	1	0	0	0	+	+	H
WS 1932	4	16	8	6	1	0	1	4	4	3	0	.375	1.125	O
WS Total	16	60	17	21	3	0	1	9	10	7	0	.350	.901	

Ron Coomer

YEAR	G	AB	R	H	2B	3B	HR	RBI	BB	SO	SB	AVG	OPS	POS
DS 2002	1	2	0	1	0	0	0	0	0	0	0	.500	1.000	D

Bubba Crosby

YEAR	G	AB	R	H	2B	3B	HR	RBI	BB	SO	SB	AVG	OPS	POS
DS 2004	2	0	0	0	0	0	0	0	0	0	0	+	+	O-1
DS 2005	3	8	0	2	0	0	0	1	0	1	1	.250	.500	O
DS Total	5	8	0	2	0	0	0	1	0	1	1	.250	.500	
LC 2004	1	0	1	0	0	0	0	0	0	0	0	+	+	O

Frankie Crosetti

YEAR	G	AB	R	H	2B	3B	HR	RBI	BB	SO	SB	AVG	OPS	POS
WS 1932	4	15	2	2	1	0	0	0	2	3	0	.133	.435	S
WS 1936	6	26	5	7	2	0	0	3	3	5	0	.269	.691	S
WS 1937	5	21	2	1	0	0	0	0	3	2	0	.048	.214	S
WS 1938	4	16	1	4	2	1	1	6	2	4	0	.250	.214	S
WS 1939	4	16	2	1	0	0	0	1	2	2	0	.063	.229	S
WS 1942	1	3	0	0	0	0	0	0	0	1	0	.000	.000	3
WS 1943	5	18	4	5	0	0	0	1	2	3	1	.278	.628	S
WS Total	29	115	16	20	5	1	1	11	14	20	1	.174	.530	

Roy Cullenbine

YEAR	G	AB	R	H	2B	3B	HR	RBI	BB	SO	SB	AVG	OPS	POS
WS 1942	5	19	3	5	1	0	0	2	1	2	1	.263	.616	O

Chad Curtis

YEAR	G	AB	R	H	2B	3B	HR	RBI	BB	SO	SB	AVG	OPS	POS
DS 1997	4	6	0	1	0	0	0	0	3	1	0	.167	.611	O
DS 1998	3	3	1	2	1	0	0	0	1	1	1	.667	1.750	O
DS 1999	3	3	1	0	0	0	0	0	0	0	0	.000	.000	O
DS Total	10	12	2	3	1	0	0	0	4	2	1	.250	.771	
LC 1998	2	4	0	0	0	0	0	0	1	2	0	.000	.200	O
LC 1999	3	6	1	0	0	0	0	0	0	2	1	.000	.000	O-2,D-1
LC Total	5	10	1	0	0	0	0	0	1	4	1	.000	.091	
WS 1999	3	6	3	2	0	0	2	2	0	0	0	.333	1.667	O

Babe Dahlgren

YEAR	G	AB	R	H	2B	3B	HR	RBI	BB	SO	SB	AVG	OPS	POS
WS 1939	4	14	2	3	2	0	1	2	0	4	0	.214	.786	1

Johnny Damon

YEAR	G	AB	R	H	2B	3B	HR	RBI	BB	SO	SB	AVG	OPS	POS
DS 2006	4	17	3	4	0	0	1	3	1	2	0	.235	.690	O
DS 2007	4	18	2	5	0	0	2	5	1	5	0	.278	.927	O
DS Total	8	35	5	9	0	0	3	8	2	7	0	.257	.812	

Chili Davis

YEAR	G	AB	R	H	2B	3B	HR	RBI	BB	SO	SB	AVG	OPS	POS
DS 1998	2	6	0	1	0	0	0	0	0	2	0	.167	.333	D
DS 1999	1	3	0	1	0	0	0	0	0	2	0	.333	.667	D
DS Total	3	9	0	2	0	0	0	0	0	4	0	.222	.444	
LC 1998	5	14	2	4	1	0	1	5	2	3	0	.286	.091	D
LC 1999	5	11	0	1	0	0	0	1	3	4	0	.091	.377	D
LC Total	10	25	2	5	1	0	1	6	5	7	0	.200	.683	
WS 1998	3	7	3	2	0	0	0	2	3	2	0	.286	.786	D-2
WS 1999	1	4	0	0	0	0	0	0	0	2	0	.000	.000	D
WS Total	4	11	3	2	0	0	0	2	3	4	0	.182	.539	

Russ Davis

YEAR	G	AB	R	H	2B	3B	HR	RBI	BB	SO	SB	AVG	OPS	POS
DS 1995	2	5	0	1	0	0	0	0	0	2	0	.200	.400	3

David Dellucci

YEAR	G	AB	R	H	2B	3B	HR	RBI	BB	SO	SB	AVG	OPS	POS
DS 2003	1	0	0	0	0	0	0	0	0	0	0	+	+	H
LC 2003	3	3	2	1	0	0	0	0	0	1	1	.333	.683	O-1
WS 2003	4	2	1	0	0	0	0	0	0	0	0	.000	.000	O-2

Joe DeMaestri

YEAR	G	AB	R	H	2B	3B	HR	RBI	BB	SO	SB	AVG	OPS	POS
WS 1960	4	2	1	1	0	0	0	0	0	1	0	.500	1.000	S-3

Bucky Dent

YEAR	G	AB	R	H	2B	3B	HR	RBI	BB	SO	SB	AVG	OPS	POS
LC 1977	5	14	1	3	1	0	0	2	1	0	0	.214	.552	S
LC 1978	4	15	0	3	0	0	0	4	0	0	0	.200	.400	S
LC 1980	3	11	0	2	0	0	0	0	0	1	0	.182	.364	S

YEAR	G	AB	R	H	2B	3B	HR	RBI	BB	SO	SB	AVG	OPS	POS
LC Total	12	40	1	8	1	0	0	6	1	1	0	.200	.445	
WS 1977	6	19	0	5	0	0	0	2	2	1	0	.263	.596	S
WS 1978	6	24	3	10	1	0	0	7	1	2	0	.417	.898	S
WS Total	12	43	3	15	1	0	0	9	3	3	0	.349	.763	

Al DeVormer

YEAR	G	AB	R	H	2B	3B	HR	RBI	BB	SO	SB	AVG	OPS	POS
WS 1921	2	1	0	0	0	0	0	0	0	0	0	.000	.000	C-1

Bill Dickey

YEAR	G	AB	R	H	2B	3B	HR	RBI	BB	SO	SB	AVG	OPS	POS
WS 1932	4	16	2	7	0	0	0	4	2	1	0	.438	.000	C
WS 1936	6	25	5	3	0	0	1	5	0	4	0	.120	.454	C
WS 1937	5	19	3	4	0	1	0	3	2	2	0	.211	.602	C
WS 1938	4	15	2	6	0	0	1	2	1	0	1	.400	1.038	C
WS 1939	4	15	2	4	0	0	2	5	1	2	0	.267	.979	C
WS 1941	5	18	3	3	1	0	0	1	3	1	0	.167	.508	C
WS 1942	5	19	1	5	0	0	0	0	1	0	0	.263	.563	C
WS 1943	5	18	1	5	0	0	1	4	2	2	0	.278	.794	C
WS Total	38	145	19	37	1	1	5	24	15	12	1	.255	.709	

Joe DiMaggio

YEAR	G	AB	R	H	2B	3B	HR	RBI	BB	SO	SB	AVG	OPS	POS
WS 1936	6	26	3	9	3	0	0	3	1	3	0	.346	.832	O
WS 1937	5	22	2	6	0	0	1	4	0	3	0	.273	.682	O
WS 1938	4	15	4	4	0	0	1	2	1	1	0	.267	.779	O
WS 1939	4	16	3	5	0	0	1	3	1	1	0	.313	.853	O
WS 1941	5	19	1	5	0	0	0	1	2	2	0	.263	.590	O
WS 1942	5	21	3	7	0	0	0	3	0	1	0	.333	.667	O
WS 1947	7	26	4	6	0	0	2	5	6	2	0	.231	.837	O
WS 1949	5	18	2	2	0	0	1	2	3	5	0	.111	.516	O
WS 1950	4	13	2	4	1	0	1	2	3	1	0	.308	.516	O
WS 1951	6	23	3	6	2	0	1	5	2	4	0	.261	.798	O
WS Total	51	199	27	54	6	0	8	30	19	23	0	.271	.760	

Brian Doyle

YEAR	G	AB	R	H	2B	3B	HR	RBI	BB	SO	SB	AVG	OPS	POS
LC 1978	3	7	0	2	0	0	0	1	1	1	0	.286	.661	2
WS 1978	6	16	4	7	1	0	0	2	0	0	0	.438	.938	2

Joe Dugan

YEAR	G	AB	R	H	2B	3B	HR	RBI	BB	SO	SB	AVG	OPS	POS
WS 1922	5	20	4	5	1	0	0	0	0	1	0	.250	.938	3
WS 1923	6	25	5	7	2	1	1	5	3	0	0	.280	.917	3
WS 1926	7	24	2	8	1	0	0	2	1	1	0	.333	.735	3
WS 1927	4	15	2	3	0	0	0	0	0	0	0	.200	.400	3
WS 1928	3	6	0	1	0	0	0	1	0	0	0	.167	.333	3
WS Total	25	90	13	24	4	1	1	8	4	2	0	.267	.672	

Shelley Duncan

YEAR	G	AB	R	H	2B	3B	HR	RBI	BB	SO	SB	AVG	OPS	POS
DS 2007	3	4	1	2	0	0	0	0	0	1	0	.500	1.000	1

Mariano Duncan

YEAR	G	AB	R	H	2B	3B	HR	RBI	BB	SO	SB	AVG	OPS	POS
DS 1996	4	16	0	5	0	0	0	3	0	4	0	.313	1.000	2
LC 1996	4	15	0	3	2	0	0	0	0	3	0	.200	.661	2
WS 1996	6	19	1	1	0	0	0	0	0	4	1	.053	.105	2

Leo Durocher

YEAR	G	AB	R	H	2B	3B	HR	RBI	BB	SO	SB	AVG	OPS	POS
WS 1928	4	2	0	0	0	0	0	0	0	1	0	.000	.000	2

Cedric Durst

YEAR	G	AB	R	H	2B	3B	HR	RBI	BB	SO	SB	AVG	OPS	POS
WS 1927	1	1	0	0	0	0	0	0	0	0	0	.000	.000	H
WS 1928	4	8	3	3	0	0	1	2	0	1	0	.375	1.125	O
WS Total	5	9	3	3	0	0	1	2	0	1	0	.333	1.000	

Nick Etten

YEAR	G	AB	R	H	2B	3B	HR	RBI	BB	SO	SB	AVG	OPS	POS
WS 1943	5	19	0	2	0	0	0	2	1	2	0	.105	.255	1

Tony Fernandez

YEAR	G	AB	R	H	2B	3B	HR	RBI	BB	SO	SB	AVG	OPS	POS
DS 1995	5	21	0	5	2	0	0	0	2	2	0	.238	.638	S

Chick Fewster

YEAR	G	AB	R	H	2B	3B	HR	RBI	BB	SO	SB	AVG	OPS	POS
WS 1921	4	10	3	2	0	0	1	2	3	3	0	.200	.885	O

Cecil Fielder

YEAR	G	AB	R	H	2B	3B	HR	RBI	BB	SO	SB	AVG	OPS	POS
DS 1996	3	11	2	4	0	0	1	4	1	2	0	.364	1.053	D
DS 1997	2	8	0	1	0	0	0	1	0	3	0	.125	.250	D
DS Total	5	19	2	5	0	0	1	5	1	5	0	.263	.721	
LC 1996	5	18	3	3	0	0	2	8	4	5	0	.167	.818	D
WS 1996	6	23	1	9	2	0	0	2	2	2	0	.391	.918	1-3,D-3

John Flaherty

YEAR	G	AB	R	H	2B	3B	HR	RBI	BB	SO	SB	AVG	OPS	POS
DS 2005	1	0	0	0	0	0	0	0	1	0	0	+	1.000	C
WS 2003	1	2	0	0	0	0	0	0	0	0	0	.000	.000	C

Barry Foote

YEAR	G	AB	R	H	2B	3B	HR	RBI	BB	SO	SB	AVG	OPS	POS
DS 1981	1	0	0	0	0	0	0	0	0	0	0	+	+	H
LC 1981	2	1	0	1	0	0	0	0	0	0	0	1.000	2.000	C-1
WS 1981	1	1	0	0	0	0	0	0	0	1	0	.000	.000	H

Andy Fox

YEAR	G	AB	R	H	2B	3B	HR	RBI	BB	SO	SB	AVG	OPS	POS
DS 1996	2	0	0	0	0	0	0	0	0	0	0	+	+	D-1
DS 1997	2	0	0	0	0	0	0	0	0	0	0	+	+	2
DS Total	4	0	0	0	0	0	0	0	0	0	0	+	+	
LC 1996	2	0	0	0	0	0	0	0	0	0	0	+	+	D
WS 1996	4	0	1	0	0	0	0	0	0	0	0	+	+	2-1,3-1

Lonny Frey

YEAR	G	AB	R	H	2B	3B	HR	RBI	BB	SO	SB	AVG	OPS	POS
WS 1947	1	1	0	0	0	0	0	1	0	0	0	.000	.000	H

Oscar Gamble

YEAR	G	AB	R	H	2B	3B	HR	RBI	BB	SO	SB	AVG	OPS	POS
DS 1981	4	9	2	5	1	0	2	3	1	2	0	.556	1.933	D
LC 1976	3	8	1	2	1	0	0	1	1	1	0	.250	.708	O
LC 1980	2	5	1	1	0	0	0	0	1	1	0	.200	.533	O-1,D-1
LC 1981	3	6	2	1	0	0	0	1	5	3	0	.167	.533	D-2,O-1
LC Total	8	19	4	4	1	0	0	2	7	5	0	.211	.671	
WS 1976	3	8	0	1	0	0	0	1	0	0	0	.125	.250	O-2
WS 1981	3	6	1	2	0	0	0	1	1	0	0	.333	.762	O-2
WS Total	6	14	1	3	0	0	0	2	1	0	0	.214	.481	

Karim Garcia

YEAR	G	AB	R	H	2B	3B	HR	RBI	BB	SO	SB	AVG	OPS	POS
LC 2003	5	16	1	4	0	0	0	3	2	4	0	.250	.671	O
WS 2003	5	14	1	4	0	0	0	0	0	3	0	.286	.571	O

Billy Gardner

YEAR	G	AB	R	H	2B	3B	HR	RBI	BB	SO	SB	AVG	OPS	POS
WS 1961	1	1	0	0	0	0	0	0	0	0	0	.000	.000	H

Mike Gazella

YEAR	G	AB	R	H	2B	3B	HR	RBI	BB	SO	SB	AVG	OPS	POS
WS 1926	1	0	0	0	0	0	0	0	0	0	0	+	.000	3

Lou Gehrig

YEAR	G	AB	R	H	2B	3B	HR	RBI	BB	SO	SB	AVG	OPS	POS
WS 1926	7	23	1	8	2	0	0	4	5	4	0	.348	.899	1
WS 1927	4	13	2	4	2	2	0	4	3	3	0	.308	.899	1
WS 1928	4	11	5	6	1	0	4	9	6	0	0	.545	2.433	1
WS 1932	4	17	9	9	1	0	3	8	2	1	0	.529	1.697	1
WS 1936	6	24	5	7	1	0	2	7	3	2	0	.292	.954	1
WS 1937	5	17	4	5	1	1	1	3	5	4	0	.294	1.102	1
WS 1938	4	14	4	4	0	0	0	0	2	3	0	.286	.661	1
WS Total	34	119	30	43	8	3	10	35	26	17	0	.361	1.200	

Jason Giambi

YEAR	G	AB	R	H	2B	3B	HR	RBI	BB	SO	SB	AVG	OPS	POS
DS 2002	4	14	5	5	0	0	1	3	4	1	0	.357	1.933	1-3,D-1
DS 2003	4	16	1	4	2	0	0	2	2	5	0	.250	.708	D
DS 2005	5	19	1	8	3	0	0	2	3	4	0	.421	1.079	1-3,D-2
DS 2006	3	8	1	1	0	0	1	2	2	3	1	.125	.800	D-2,1-1
DS 2007	3	4	0	1	0	0	0	0	0	2	0	.250	.500	1-2
DS Total	19	61	8	19	5	0	2	9	11	15	1	.311	.916	
LC 2003	7	26	4	6	0	0	3	3	4	7	0	.231	.910	D
WS 2003	6	17	2	4	1	0	1	1	4	3	0	.235	1.200	1-2

Joe Girardi

YEAR	G	AB	R	H	2B	3B	HR	RBI	BB	SO	SB	AVG	OPS	POS
DS 1996	4	9	1	2	0	0	0	0	4	1	0	.222	.684	C
DS 1997	5	15	2	2	0	0	0	0	1	3	0	.133	.321	C
DS 1998	2	7	0	3	0	0	0	0	0	1	0	.429	.857	C
DS 1999	2	6	0	0	0	0	0	0	0	1	0	.000	.000	C
DS Total	13	37	3	7	0	0	0	0	5	6	0	.189	.475	
LC 1996	4	12	1	3	0	1	0	0	1	3	0	.250	.724	C
LC 1998	3	8	2	2	0	0	0	0	1	0	0	.250	.583	C
LC 1999	3	8	0	2	0	0	0	0	0	2	0	.250	.500	C
LC Total	10	28	3	7	0	1	0	0	2	5	0	.250	.621	
WS 1996	4	10	1	2	0	1	0	1	1	2	0	.200	.673	C
WS 1998	2	6	0	0	0	0	0	0	0	2	0	.000	.000	C
WS 1999	2	7	1	2	0	0	0	0	0	1	0	.286	.571	C
WS Total	8	23	2	4	0	1	0	1	1	5	0	.174	.469	

Pedro Gonzalez

YEAR	G	AB	R	H	2B	3B	HR	RBI	BB	SO	SB	AVG	OPS	POS
WS 1964	1	1	0	0	0	0	0	0	0	0	0	.000	.000	3

Joe Gordon

YEAR	G	AB	R	H	2B	3B	HR	RBI	BB	SO	SB	AVG	OPS	POS
WS 1938	4	15	3	6	2	0	1	6	1	3	1	.400	1.171	2
WS 1939	4	14	1	2	0	0	0	1	0	2	0	.143	.286	2
WS 1941	5	14	2	7	1	1	1	5	7	0	0	.500	1.595	2
WS 1942	5	21	1	2	1	0	0	0	0	7	0	.095	.238	2
WS 1943	5	17	2	4	1	0	1	2	3	3	0	.235	.821	2
WS Total	23	81	9	21	5	1	3	14	11	15	1	.259	.805	

Johnny Grabowski

YEAR	G	AB	R	H	2B	3B	HR	RBI	BB	SO	SB	AVG	OPS	POS
WS 1927	1	2	0	0	0	0	0	0	0	0	0	.000	.000	C

Eli Grba

YEAR	G	AB	R	H	2B	3B	HR	RBI	BB	SO	SB	AVG	OPS	POS
WS 1960	1	0	0	0	0	0	0	0	0	0	0	+	+	R

Todd Greene

YEAR	G	AB	R	H	2B	3B	HR	RBI	BB	SO	SB	AVG	OPS	POS
LC 2001	1	1	0	0	0	0	0	0	0	0	0	.000	.000	C
WS 2001	1	2	1	1	1	0	0	0	0	0	0	.500	1.500	C

Ron Guidry

YEAR	G	AB	R	H	2B	3B	HR	RBI	BB	SO	SB	AVG	OPS	POS
LC 1976	1	0	0	0	0	0	0	0	0	0	0	+	+	R
LC 1977	2	0	0	0	0	0	0	0	0	0	0	+	+	P
LC 1978	1	0	0	0	0	0	0	0	0	0	0	+	+	P
LC 1980	1	0	0	0	0	0	0	0	0	0	0	+	+	P
LC Total	5	0	0	0	0	0	0	0	0	0	0	+	+	

Hinkey Haines

YEAR	G	AB	R	H	2B	3B	HR	RBI	BB	SO	SB	AVG	OPS	POS
WS 1923	2	1	1	0	0	0	0	0	0	0	0	.000	.000	O

Buddy Hassett

YEAR	G	AB	R	H	2B	3B	HR	RBI	BB	SO	SB	AVG	OPS	POS
WS 1942	3	9	1	3	1	0	0	2	0	1	0	.333	.778	1

Charlie Hayes

YEAR	G	AB	R	H	2B	3B	HR	RBI	BB	SO	SB	AVG	OPS	POS
DS 1996	3	5	0	1	0	0	0	1	0	0	0	.200	.475	3-2
DS 1997	5	15	0	5	0	0	0	1	0	2	0	.333	.667	3-5,2-1
DS Total	8	20	0	6	0	0	0	2	0	2	0	.300	.586	
LC 1996	4	7	0	1	0	0	0	0	2	2	0	.143	.476	3-2,D-1
WS 1996	5	16	2	3	0	0	0	1	1	5	0	.188	.423	3-4,1-1

Mike Heath

YEAR	G	AB	R	H	2B	3B	HR	RBI	BB	SO	SB	AVG	OPS	POS
WS 1978	1	0	0	0	0	0	0	0	0	0	0	+	+	C

Mike Hegan

YEAR	G	AB	R	H	2B	3B	HR	RBI	BB	SO	SB	AVG	OPS	POS
WS 1964	3	1	1	0	0	0	0	0	1	1	0	.000	.500	H

YEAR	G	AB	R	H	2B	3B	HR	RBI	BB	SO	SB	AVG	OPS	POS
HARVEY HENDRICK														
WS 1923	1	1	0	0	0	0	0	0	0	0	0	.000	.000	H
ELLIE HENDRICKS														
LC 1976	1	1	0	1	0	0	0	0	0	0	0	1.000	2.000	H
WS 1976	2	2	0	0	0	0	0	0	0	0	0	.000	.000	H
TOMMY HENRICH														
WS 1938	4	16	3	4	1	0	1	1	0	1	0	.250	.750	O
WS 1941	5	18	4	3	1	0	1	1	3	3	0	.167	.750	O
WS 1947	7	31	2	10	2	0	1	5	2	3	0	.323	.848	O
WS 1949	5	19	4	5	0	0	1	1	3	0	0	.263	.785	1
WS Total	21	84	13	22	4	0	4	8	8	7	0	.262	.786	
GLENALLEN HILL														
DS 2000	4	12	1	1	0	0	0	2	1	5	0	.083	.237	D-3
LC 2000	2	2	0	0	0	0	0	0	0	2	0	.000	.000	H
WS 2000	3	3	0	0	0	0	0	0	0	0	0	.000	.000	D-1
MYRIL HOAG														
WS 1932	1	0	1	0	0	0	0	0	0	0	0	+	+	R
WS 1937	5	20	4	6	1	0	1	2	0	1	0	.300	.800	O
WS 1938	2	5	3	2	1	0	0	1	0	0	0	.400	1.000	O-1
WS Total	8	25	8	8	2	0	1	3	0	1	0	.320	.840	
FRED HOFMANN														
WS 1923	2	1	0	0	0	0	0	0	1	0	0	.000	.500	H
JOHNNY HOPP														
WS 1950	3	2	0	0	0	0	0	0	0	0	0	.000	.000	1
WS 1951	1	0	0	0	0	0	0	0	1	0	0	+	1.000	H
WS Total	4	2	0	0	0	0	0	0	1	0	0	.000	.333	
RALPH HOUK														
WS 1947	1	1	0	1	0	0	0	0	0	0	0	1.000	2.000	H
WS 1952	1	1	0	0	0	0	0	0	0	0	0	.000	.000	H
WS Total	2	2	0	1	0	0	0	0	0	0	0	.500	1.000	
ELSTON HOWARD														
WS 1955	7	26	3	5	0	0	1	3	1	8	0	.192	.530	O
WS 1956	1	5	1	2	1	0	1	1	0	0	0	.400	1.600	O
WS 1957	6	11	2	3	0	0	1	3	1	3	0	.273	.879	1-3
WS 1958	6	18	4	4	0	0	0	2	1	4	1	.222	.485	O
WS 1960	5	13	4	6	1	1	1	4	1	4	0	.462	.485	C-4
WS 1961	5	20	5	5	3	0	1	1	2	3	0	.250	.868	C
WS 1962	6	21	1	3	1	0	0	1	1	4	0	.143	.372	C
WS 1963	4	15	0	5	0	0	0	1	0	3	0	.333	.667	C
WS 1964	7	24	5	7	1	0	0	2	4	6	0	.292	.726	C
WS Total	47	153	25	40	7	1	5	18	11	35	1	.261	.733	
REGGIE JACKSON														
DS 1981	5	20	4	6	0	0	2	4	1	5	0	.300	.933	O
LC 1977	5	16	1	2	0	0	0	1	2	2	1	.125	.347	O-4,D-1
LC 1978	4	13	5	6	1	0	2	6	3	4	0	.462	.347	D-3,O-1
LC 1980	3	11	1	3	1	0	0	0	1	4	0	.273	.697	O
LC 1981	2	4	1	0	0	0	0	1	1	0	1	.000	.200	O
LC Total	14	44	8	11	2	0	2	8	7	10	2	.250	.778	
WS 1977	6	20	10	9	1	0	5	8	3	4	0	.450	.733	O
WS 1978	6	23	2	9	1	0	2	8	3	7	0	.391	1.157	D
WS 1981	3	12	3	4	1	0	1	1	2	3	0	.333	1.095	O
WS Total	15	55	15	22	3	0	8	17	8	14	0	.400	1.375	
DION JAMES														
DS 1995	4	12	0	1	0	0	0	0	1	1	0	.083	.237	O
JACKIE JENSEN														
WS 1950	1	0	0	0	0	0	0	0	0	0	0	+	+	R
DEREK JETER														
DS 1996	4	17	2	7	1	0	0	1	0	2	0	.412	.882	S
DS 1997	5	21	6	7	1	0	2	2	3	5	1	.333	1.083	S
DS 1998	3	9	0	1	0	0	0	0	2	2	0	.111	.384	S
DS 1999	3	11	3	5	1	1	0	0	2	3	0	.455	1.266	S
DS 2000	5	19	1	4	0	0	0	2	2	3	0	.211	1.266	S
DS 2001	5	18	2	8	1	0	0	1	1	0	0	.444	.974	S
DS 2002	4	16	6	8	0	0	2	3	2	3	0	.500	1.431	S
DS 2003	4	14	2	6	0	0	1	1	4	2	1	.429	1.198	S
DS 2004	4	19	3	6	1	0	1	4	1	4	1	.316	.876	S
DS 2005	5	21	4	7	0	0	2	5	1	5	1	.333	.983	S
DS 2006	4	16	4	8	4	0	1	1	1	2	0	.500	1.467	S
DS 2007	4	17	0	3	0	0	0	1	0	4	0	.176	.353	S
DS Total	50	198	33	70	9	1	9	21	19	35	4	.354	.958	
LC 1996	5	24	5	10	2	0	1	1	0	5	2	.417	1.042	S
LC 1998	6	25	3	5	1	1	0	2	2	5	3	.200	.579	S
LC 1999	5	20	3	7	1	0	1	3	2	3	0	.350	.959	S
LC 2000	6	22	6	7	0	0	2	5	6	7	1	.318	1.055	S
LC 2001	5	17	0	2	0	0	0	2	2	2	0	.118	1.055	S
LC 2003	7	30	3	7	2	0	1	2	2	4	1	.233	.681	S
LC 2004	7	30	5	6	1	0	0	5	6	2	1	.200	.567	S
LC Total	41	168	25	44	7	1	5	20	20	28	8	.262	.743	
WS 1996	6	20	5	5	0	0	0	1	4	6	1	.250	.000	S
WS 1998	4	17	4	6	0	0	0	1	3	3	0	.353	.803	S
WS 1999	4	17	4	6	1	0	0	1	1	3	3	.353	.801	S
WS 2000	5	22	6	9	2	1	2	2	3	8	0	.409	1.344	S
WS 2001	7	27	3	4	0	0	1	1	0	6	0	.148	.407	S
WS 2003	6	26	5	9	3	0	0	2	1	7	0	.346	.832	S
WS Total	32	129	27	39	6	1	3	8	12	33	4	.302	.800	

YEAR	G	AB	R	H	2B	3B	HR	RBI	BB	SO	SB	AVG	OPS	POS
CLIFF JOHNSON														
LC 1977	5	15	2	6	2	0	1	2	1	2	0	.400	1.171	D-4
LC 1978	1	1	0	0	0	0	0	0	0	0	0	.000	.000	H
LC Total	6	16	2	6	2	0	1	2	1	2	0	.375	1.099	
WS 1977	2	1	0	0	0	0	0	0	0	0	0	.000	.000	C-1
WS 1978	2	2	0	0	0	0	0	0	0	1	0	.000	.000	H
WS Total	4	3	0	0	0	0	0	0	0	1	0	.000	.000	
ERNIE JOHNSON														
WS 1923	2	0	1	0	0	0	0	0	0	0	0	+	+	S-1
NICK JOHNSON														
DS 2002	3	11	1	2	0	0	0	1	1	5	0	.182	.432	D-2,1-1
DS 2003	4	13	2	1	1	0	0	2	3	2	0	.077	.432	1
DS Total	7	24	3	3	1	0	0	3	4	7	0	.125	.443	
LC 2003	7	26	4	6	1	0	1	3	2	4	0	.231	.670	1
WS 2003	6	17	3	5	1	0	0	0	2	3	0	.294	.721	1-5
ROY JOHNSON														
WS 1936	2	1	0	0	0	0	0	0	0	1	0	.000	.000	H
BILLY JOHNSON														
WS 1943	5	20	3	6	1	1	0	3	0	3	0	.300	.750	3
WS 1947	7	26	8	7	0	3	0	2	3	4	0	.269	.750	3
WS 1949	2	7	0	1	0	0	0	0	0	2	1	.143	.286	3
WS 1950	4	6	0	0	0	0	0	0	0	3	0	.000	.000	3
WS Total	18	59	11	14	1	4	0	5	3	12	1	.237	.676	
JAY JOHNSTONE														
WS 1978	2	0	0	0	0	0	0	0	0	0	0	+	+	O
DAVID JUSTICE														
DS 2000	5	18	2	4	0	0	1	1	3	4	0	.222	.722	O
DS 2001	4	13	3	3	0	1	1	1	2	5	0	.231	.949	O-2,D-2
DS Total	9	31	5	7	0	1	2	2	5	9	0	.226	.817	
LC 2000	6	26	4	6	2	0	2	8	2	7	0	.231	.824	O
LC 2001	5	18	3	5	1	0	0	4	3	1	0	.278	.824	D
LC Total	11	44	7	11	3	0	2	12	5	8	0	.250	.795	
WS 2000	5	19	1	3	2	0	0	3	3	2	0	.158	.000	O
WS 2001	5	12	0	2	0	0	0	0	1	9	0	.167	.397	O-2,D-2
WS Total	10	31	1	5	2	0	0	3	4	11	0	.161	.523	
CHARLIE KELLER														
WS 1939	4	16	8	7	1	1	3	6	1	2	0	.438	1.658	O
WS 1941	5	18	5	7	2	0	0	5	3	1	0	.389	.976	O
WS 1942	5	20	2	4	0	0	2	5	1	3	0	.200	.738	O
WS 1943	5	18	3	4	0	1	0	2	2	5	1	.222	.633	O
WS Total	19	72	18	22	3	2	5	18	7	11	1	.306	.978	
PAT KELLY														
DS 1995	5	3	3	0	0	0	0	1	1	3	0	.000	.817	2-4
CHUCK KNOBLAUCH														
DS 1998	3	11	0	1	0	0	0	0	0	4	0	.091	.817	2
DS 1999	3	12	1	2	0	0	0	0	1	3	0	.167	.397	2
DS 2000	3	9	1	3	0	0	0	1	0	2	1	.333	.667	D-2
DS 2001	5	22	1	6	1	0	0	1	0	0	1	.273	.591	O
DS Total	14	54	3	12	1	0	0	2	1	9	2	.222	.491	
LC 1998	6	25	4	5	1	0	0	0	4	2	0	.200	.795	2
LC 1999	5	18	3	6	1	0	0	1	3	0	1	.333	.817	2
LC 2000	6	23	3	6	2	0	0	2	3	4	0	.261	.694	D
LC 2001	5	18	0	6	1	0	0	3	2	3	0	.333	.789	O
LC Total	22	84	10	23	5	0	0	6	12	9	1	.274	.704	
WS 1998	4	16	3	6	0	0	1	3	3	2	1	.375	.978	2
WS 1999	4	16	5	5	1	0	1	3	1	3	1	.313	.915	2
WS 2000	4	10	1	1	0	0	0	1	2	1	0	.100	.350	D-2
WS 2001	6	18	1	1	0	0	0	0	1	2	0	.056	.161	O-4,D-2
WS Total	18	60	10	13	1	0	2	7	7	8	2	.217	.642	
MARK KOENIG														
WS 1926	7	32	2	4	1	0	0	2	0	6	0	.125	.281	S
WS 1927	4	18	5	9	2	0	0	2	0	2	0	.500	1.111	S
WS 1928	4	19	1	3	0	0	0	0	0	1	0	.158	.316	S
WS Total	15	69	8	16	3	0	0	4	0	9	0	.232	.507	
TONY KUBEK														
WS 1957	7	28	4	8	0	0	2	4	0	4	0	.286	.786	O-5,3-2
WS 1958	7	21	0	1	0	0	0	1	1	7	0	.048	.786	S
WS 1960	7	30	6	10	1	0	0	3	2	2	0	.333	.742	S-7,O-2
WS 1961	5	22	3	5	0	0	0	1	1	4	0	.227	.488	S
WS 1962	7	29	2	8	1	0	0	1	1	3	0	.276	.610	S
WS 1963	4	16	1	3	0	0	0	0	0	3	0	.188	.375	S
WS Total	37	146	16	35	2	0	2	10	5	23	0	.240	.558	
TONY LAZZERI														
WS 1926	7	26	2	5	1	0	0	3	1	6	0	.192	.558	2
WS 1927	4	15	1	4	1	0	0	2	1	4	0	.267	.646	2
WS 1928	4	12	2	3	1	0	0	0	1	0	2	.250	.641	2
WS 1932	4	17	4	5	0	0	2	5	2	1	0	.294	1.015	2
WS 1936	6	20	4	5	0	0	1	7	4	4	0	.250	.775	2
WS 1937	5	15	3	6	0	1	1	2	3	3	0	.400	1.233	2
WS Total	30	105	16	28	3	1	4	19	12	18	2	.267	.765	
RICKY LEDEE														
DS 1999	3	11	1	3	2	0	0	2	1	5	0	.273	.788	O
LC 1998	3	5	0	0	0	0	0	0	0	0	0	.000	.000	O-2,D-1
LC 1999	3	8	2	2	0	0	1	4	1	4	0	.250	.958	O-2
LC Total	6	13	2	2	0	0	1	4	1	4	0	.154	.599	

YEAR	G	AB	R	H	2B	3B	HR	RBI	BB	SO	SB	AVG	OPS	POS
WS 1998	4	10	1	6	3	0	0	4	2	1	0	.600	.765	O
WS 1999	3	10	0	2	1	0	0	1	1	4	0	.200	.573	O
WS Total	7	20	1	8	4	0	0	5	3	5	0	.400	1.058	

Joe Lefebvre

YEAR	G	AB	R	H	2B	3B	HR	RBI	BB	SO	SB	AVG	OPS	POS
LC 1980	1	0	0	0	0	0	0	0	0	0	0	+	+	O

Jim Leyritz

YEAR	G	AB	R	H	2B	3B	HR	RBI	BB	SO	SB	AVG	OPS	POS
DS 1995	2	7	1	1	0	0	1	2	0	1	0	.143	.788	C
DS 1996	2	3	0	0	0	0	0	1	0	1	0	.000	.000	C-1
DS 1999	2	2	0	0	0	0	0	1	1	0	0	.000	.333	D
DS Total	6	12	1	1	0	0	1	4	1	2	0	.083	.548	
LC 1996	3	8	1	2	0	0	1	2	1	4	0	.250	.958	C-2,O-1
WS 1996	4	8	1	3	0	0	1	3	3	2	1	.375	1.295	C-3
WS 1999	2	1	1	1	0	0	1	2	1	0	0	1.000	5.000	D-1
WS Total	6	9	2	4	0	0	2	5	4	2	1	.444	1.726	

Johnny Lindell

YEAR	G	AB	R	H	2B	3B	HR	RBI	BB	SO	SB	AVG	OPS	POS
WS 1943	4	9	1	1	0	0	0	0	1	4	0	.111	.311	O
WS 1947	6	18	3	9	3	1	0	7	5	2	0	.500	.311	O
WS 1949	2	7	0	1	0	0	0	0	0	2	0	.143	.286	O
WS Total	12	34	4	11	3	1	0	7	6	8	0	.324	.910	

Phil Linz

YEAR	G	AB	R	H	2B	3B	HR	RBI	BB	SO	SB	AVG	OPS	POS
WS 1963	3	3	0	1	0	0	0	0	0	1	0	.333	.667	H
WS 1964	7	31	5	7	1	0	2	2	2	5	0	.226	.724	S
WS Total	10	34	5	8	1	0	2	2	2	6	0	.235	.719	

Kenny Lofton

YEAR	G	AB	R	H	2B	3B	HR	RBI	BB	SO	SB	AVG	OPS	POS
DS 2004	1	4	0	1	0	0	0	1	0	1	0	.250	.500	D
LC 2004	3	10	1	3	0	0	1	2	2	3	1	.300	1.017	D

Sherm Lollar

YEAR	G	AB	R	H	2B	3B	HR	RBI	BB	SO	SB	AVG	OPS	POS
WS 1947	2	4	3	3	2	0	0	1	0	0	0	.750	2.000	C

Dale Long

YEAR	G	AB	R	H	2B	3B	HR	RBI	BB	SO	SB	AVG	OPS	POS
WS 1960	3	3	0	1	0	0	0	0	0	0	0	.333	.667	H
WS 1962	2	5	0	1	0	0	0	1	0	1	0	.200	.400	1
WS Total	5	8	0	2	0	0	0	1	0	1	0	.250	.500	

Hector Lopez

YEAR	G	AB	R	H	2B	3B	HR	RBI	BB	SO	SB	AVG	OPS	POS
WS 1960	3	7	0	3	0	0	0	0	0	0	0	.429	.857	O-1
WS 1961	4	9	3	3	0	1	1	7	2	3	0	.333	1.343	O-3
WS 1962	2	2	0	0	0	0	0	0	0	0	0	.000	.000	H
WS 1963	3	8	1	2	2	0	0	0	0	1	0	.250	.750	O-2
WS 1964	3	2	0	0	0	0	0	0	0	2	0	.000	.000	O-1
WS Total	15	28	4	8	2	1	1	7	2	6	0	.286	.869	

Jerry Lumpe

YEAR	G	AB	R	H	2B	3B	HR	RBI	BB	SO	SB	AVG	OPS	POS
WS 1957	6	14	0	4	0	0	0	2	1	1	0	.286	.619	3-3
WS 1958	6	12	0	2	0	0	0	0	1	2	0	.167	.397	3-3,S-2
WS Total	12	26	0	6	0	0	0	2	2	3	0	.231	.516	

Elliott Maddox

YEAR	G	AB	R	H	2B	3B	HR	RBI	BB	SO	SB	AVG	OPS	POS
LC 1976	3	9	0	2	1	0	0	1	0	1	0	.222	.556	O
WS 1976	2	5	0	1	0	1	0	0	1	2	0	.200	.933	O-1,D-1

Mickey Mantle

YEAR	G	AB	R	H	2B	3B	HR	RBI	BB	SO	SB	AVG	OPS	POS
WS 1951	2	5	1	1	0	0	0	0	2	1	0	.200	.629	O
WS 1952	7	29	5	10	1	1	2	3	3	4	0	.345	1.061	O
WS 1953	6	24	3	5	0	0	2	7	3	8	0	.208	.755	O
WS 1955	3	10	1	2	0	0	1	1	0	2	0	.200	.700	O-2
WS 1956	7	24	6	6	1	0	3	4	6	5	1	.250	1.067	O
WS 1957	6	19	3	5	0	0	1	2	3	1	0	.263	.785	O-5
WS 1958	7	24	4	6	0	1	2	3	7	4	0	.250	1.003	O
WS 1960	7	25	8	10	1	0	3	11	8	9	0	.400	1.345	O
WS 1961	2	6	0	1	0	0	0	0	0	2	0	.167	.333	O
WS 1962	7	25	2	3	1	0	0	0	4	5	2	.120	.401	O
WS 1963	4	15	1	2	0	0	1	1	1	5	0	.133	.521	O
WS 1964	7	24	8	8	2	0	3	8	6	8	0	.333	1.258	O
WS Total	65	230	42	59	6	2	18	40	43	54	3	.257	.908	

Cliff Mapes

YEAR	G	AB	R	H	2B	3B	HR	RBI	BB	SO	SB	AVG	OPS	POS
WS 1949	4	10	3	1	1	0	0	2	2	4	0	.100	.450	O
WS 1950	1	4	0	0	0	0	0	0	0	1	0	.000	.000	O
WS Total	5	14	3	1	1	0	0	2	2	5	0	.071	.330	

Roger Maris

YEAR	G	AB	R	H	2B	3B	HR	RBI	BB	SO	SB	AVG	OPS	POS
WS 1960	7	30	6	8	1	0	2	2	2	4	0	.267	.813	O
WS 1961	5	19	4	2	1	0	1	2	4	6	0	.105	.577	O
WS 1962	7	23	4	4	1	0	1	5	5	2	0	.174	.669	O
WS 1963	2	5	0	0	0	0	0	0	0	1	0	.000	.000	O
WS 1964	7	30	4	6	0	0	1	1	1	4	0	.200	.526	O
WS Total	28	107	18	20	3	0	5	10	12	17	0	.187	.624	

Billy Martin

YEAR	G	AB	R	H	2B	3B	HR	RBI	BB	SO	SB	AVG	OPS	POS
WS 1951	1	0	1	0	0	0	0	0	0	0	0	+	+	R
WS 1952	7	23	2	5	0	0	1	4	2	2	0	.217	.000	2
WS 1953	6	24	5	12	1	2	2	8	1	2	1	.500	1.478	2
WS 1955	7	25	2	8	1	1	0	4	1	5	0	.320	.786	2
WS 1956	7	27	5	8	0	0	2	3	1	6	0	.296	.840	2-7,3-1
WS Total	28	99	15	33	2	3	5	19	5	15	1	.333	.937	

Tino Martinez

YEAR	G	AB	R	H	2B	3B	HR	RBI	BB	SO	SB	AVG	OPS	POS
DS 1996	4	15	3	4	2	0	0	0	3	1	0	.267	.789	1
DS 1997	5	18	1	4	1	0	1	4	2	4	0	.222	.789	1
DS 1998	3	11	1	3	2	0	0	0	0	2	0	.273	.727	1
DS 1999	3	11	2	2	0	0	0	0	2	2	0	.182	.490	1
DS 2000	5	19	2	8	2	0	0	4	1	3	0	.421	.976	1
DS 2001	5	18	1	2	0	0	1	2	1	6	0	.111	.436	1
DS 2005	4	8	0	0	0	0	0	0	1	2	0	.000	.111	1
DS Total	29	100	10	23	7	0	2	10	10	20	0	.230	.666	
LC 1996	5	22	3	4	1	0	0	0	0	2	0	.182	.556	1
LC 1998	6	19	1	2	1	0	0	1	6	8	2	.105	.478	1
LC 1999	5	19	3	5	1	0	1	3	2	4	0	.263	.807	1
LC 2000	6	25	5	8	2	0	1	1	2	4	0	.320	.890	1
LC 2001	5	20	3	5	1	0	1	3	0	4	0	.250	.700	1
LC Total	27	105	15	24	6	0	3	8	10	22	2	.229	.673	
WS 1996	6	11	0	1	0	0	0	0	2	5	0	.091	.322	1-5
WS 1998	4	13	4	5	0	0	1	4	4	2	0	.385	1.145	1
WS 1999	4	15	3	4	0	0	1	5	2	4	0	.267	.820	1
WS 2000	5	22	3	8	1	0	0	2	1	4	0	.364	.800	1
WS 2001	6	21	1	4	0	0	1	3	2	2	0	.190	.594	1
WS Total	25	82	11	22	1	0	3	14	11	17	0	.268	.745	

Jim Mason

YEAR	G	AB	R	H	2B	3B	HR	RBI	BB	SO	SB	AVG	OPS	POS
LC 1976	2	0	0	0	0	0	0	0	0	0	0	+	+	S
WS 1976	3	1	1	1	0	0	1	1	0	0	0	1.000	5.000	S

Hideki Matsui

YEAR	G	AB	R	H	2B	3B	HR	RBI	BB	SO	SB	AVG	OPS	POS
DS 2003	4	15	2	4	1	0	1	3	2	3	0	.267	.886	O
DS 2004	4	17	3	7	1	0	1	3	3	4	0	.412	.886	O
DS 2005	5	20	4	4	1	0	1	1	2	3	0	.200	.673	O
DS 2006	4	16	1	4	1	0	0	1	0	2	0	.250	.563	O-3,D-1
DS 2007	4	11	4	2	0	0	0	0	5	2	0	.182	.619	D
DS Total	21	79	14	21	4	0	3	8	12	14	0	.266	.789	
LC 2003	7	26	3	8	3	0	0	4	1	3	0	.308	.000	O
LC 2004	7	34	9	14	6	1	2	10	2	4	0	.412	1.268	O
LC Total	14	60	12	22	9	1	2	14	3	7	0	.367	1.041	
WS 2003	6	23	1	6	0	0	1	4	3	2	0	.261	5.000	O

Don Mattingly

YEAR	G	AB	R	H	2B	3B	HR	RBI	BB	SO	SB	AVG	OPS	POS
DS 1995	5	24	3	10	4	0	1	6	1	5	0	.417	1.148	1

Carlos May

YEAR	G	AB	R	H	2B	3B	HR	RBI	BB	SO	SB	AVG	OPS	POS
LC 1976	3	10	1	2	1	0	0	0	1	4	0	.200	.573	D
WS 1976	4	9	0	0	0	0	0	0	0	1	0	.000	.000	D

Gil McDougald

YEAR	G	AB	R	H	2B	3B	HR	RBI	BB	SO	SB	AVG	OPS	POS
WS 1951	6	23	2	6	1	0	1	7	2	2	0	.261	.755	3-5,2-4
WS 1952	7	25	5	5	0	0	1	3	5	2	1	.200	.653	3
WS 1953	6	24	2	4	0	1	2	4	1	3	0	.167	.653	3
WS 1955	7	27	2	7	0	0	1	1	2	6	0	.259	.681	3
WS 1956	7	21	0	3	0	0	0	1	3	6	0	.143	.393	S
WS 1957	7	24	3	6	0	0	0	2	3	3	1	.250	.583	S
WS 1958	7	28	5	9	2	0	2	4	2	4	0	.321	.974	2
WS 1960	6	18	4	5	1	0	0	2	2	3	0	.278	.683	3
WS Total	53	190	23	45	4	1	7	24	20	29	2	.237	.692	

Norm McMillan

YEAR	G	AB	R	H	2B	3B	HR	RBI	BB	SO	SB	AVG	OPS	POS
WS 1922	1	2	0	0	0	0	0	0	0	0	0	.000	.000	O

Mike McNally

YEAR	G	AB	R	H	2B	3B	HR	RBI	BB	SO	SB	AVG	OPS	POS
WS 1921	7	20	3	4	1	0	0	1	1	3	2	.200	.000	3
WS 1922	1	0	0	0	0	0	0	0	0	0	0	+	+	2
WS Total	8	20	3	4	1	0	0	1	1	3	2	.200	.523	

George McQuinn

YEAR	G	AB	R	H	2B	3B	HR	RBI	BB	SO	SB	AVG	OPS	POS
WS 1947	7	23	3	3	0	0	0	1	5	8	0	.130	.416	1

Bud Metheny

YEAR	G	AB	R	H	2B	3B	HR	RBI	BB	SO	SB	AVG	OPS	POS
WS 1943	2	8	0	1	0	0	0	0	0	2	0	.125	.250	O

Bob Meusel

YEAR	G	AB	R	H	2B	3B	HR	RBI	BB	SO	SB	AVG	OPS	POS
WS 1921	8	30	3	6	2	0	0	3	2	5	1	.200	.517	O
WS 1922	5	20	2	6	1	0	0	2	1	3	1	.300	.683	O
WS 1923	6	26	1	7	1	2	0	8	0	3	0	.269	.731	O
WS 1926	7	21	3	5	1	1	0	0	6	1	0	.238	.731	O
WS 1927	4	17	1	2	0	0	0	1	1	7	1	.118	.284	O
WS 1928	4	15	5	3	1	0	1	3	2	5	2	.200	.761	O
WS Total	34	129	15	29	6	3	1	17	12	24	5	.225	.630	

Douglas Mientkiewicz

YEAR	G	AB	R	H	2B	3B	HR	RBI	BB	SO	SB	AVG	OPS	POS
DS 2007	4	6	0	0	0	0	0	0	1	0	0	.000	.143	1

Larry Milbourne

YEAR	G	AB	R	H	2B	3B	HR	RBI	BB	SO	SB	AVG	OPS	POS
DS 1981	5	19	4	6	1	0	0	0	0	1	0	.316	.684	S
LC 1981	3	13	4	6	0	0	0	1	0	0	0	.462	.923	S
WS 1981	6	20	2	5	2	0	0	3	4	0	0	.250	.725	S

Elmer Miller

YEAR	G	AB	R	H	2B	3B	HR	RBI	BB	SO	SB	AVG	OPS	POS
WS 1921	8	31	3	5	1	0	0	2	2	5	0	.161	.725	O

Johnny Mize

YEAR	G	AB	R	H	2B	3B	HR	RBI	BB	SO	SB	AVG	OPS	POS
WS 1949	2	2	0	2	0	0	0	2	0	0	0	1.000	2.000	H
WS 1950	4	15	0	2	0	0	0	0	0	1	0	.133	.267	1
WS 1951	4	7	2	2	1	0	0	1	2	0	0	.286	.873	1-2
WS 1952	5	15	3	6	1	0	3	6	3	1	0	.400	1.567	1-4
WS 1953	3	3	0	0	0	0	0	0	0	1	0	.000	.000	H
WS Total	18	42	5	12	2	0	3	9	5	3	0	.286	.909	

Raul Mondesi

YEAR	G	AB	R	H	2B	3B	HR	RBI	BB	SO	SB	AVG	OPS	POS
DS 2002	4	12	1	3	0	0	0	1	3	1	0	.250	.684	O

YEAR	G	AB	R	H	2B	3B	HR	RBI	BB	SO	SB	AVG	OPS	POS
Jerry Mumphrey														
DS 1981	5	21	2	2	0	0	0	0	0	1	1	.095	.190	O
LC 1981	3	12	2	6	1	0	0	0	3	2	0	.500	1.183	O
WS 1981	5	15	2	3	0	0	0	0	3	2	1	.200	.533	O
Thurman Munson														
LC 1976	5	23	3	10	2	0	0	3	0	1	0	.435	.957	C
LC 1977	5	21	3	6	1	0	1	5	0	2	0	.286	.957	C
LC 1978	4	18	2	5	1	0	1	2	0	0	0	.278	.778	C
LC Total	14	62	8	21	4	0	2	10	0	3	0	.339	.833	
WS 1976	4	17	2	9	0	0	0	2	0	1	0	.529	1.059	C
WS 1977	6	25	4	8	2	0	1	3	2	8	0	.320	.890	C
WS 1978	6	25	5	8	3	0	0	7	3	7	1	.320	.833	C
WS Total	16	67	11	25	5	0	1	12	5	16	1	.373	.909	
Bobby Murcer														
DS 1981	2	1	0	0	0	0	0	0	1	0	0	.000	.500	H
LC 1980	1	4	0	0	0	0	0	0	0	2	0	.000	.000	D
LC 1981	1	3	0	1	0	0	0	0	1	1	0	.333	.833	D
LC Total	2	7	0	1	0	0	0	0	1	3	0	.143	.393	
WS 1981	4	3	0	0	0	0	0	0	0	0	0	.000	.000	H
Graig Nettles														
DS 1981	5	17	1	1	0	0	0	1	3	1	0	.059	.259	3
LC 1976	5	17	2	4	1	0	2	4	3	3	0	.235	.997	3
LC 1977	5	20	1	3	0	0	0	1	0	3	0	.150	.300	3
LC 1978	4	15	3	5	0	1	1	2	0	1	0	.333	1.000	3
LC 1980	2	6	1	1	0	0	1	1	0	1	0	.167	.833	3
LC 1981	3	12	2	6	2	0	1	9	1	0	0	.500	.833	3
LC Total	19	70	9	19	3	1	5	17	4	8	0	.271	.877	
WS 1976	4	12	0	3	0	0	0	2	3	1	0	.250	.000	3
WS 1977	6	21	1	4	1	0	0	2	2	3	0	.190	.499	3
WS 1978	6	25	2	4	0	0	0	1	0	6	0	.160	.320	3
WS 1981	3	10	1	4	1	0	0	0	1	1	0	.400	.955	3
WS Total	19	68	4	15	2	0	0	5	6	11	0	.221	.530	
Gus Niarhos														
WS 1949	1	0	0	0	0	0	0	0	0	0	0	+	+	C
Irv Noren														
WS 1952	4	10	0	3	0	0	0	1	1	3	0	.300	.664	O-3
WS 1953	2	1	0	0	0	0	0	0	1	0	0	.000	.500	H
WS 1955	5	16	0	1	0	0	0	1	1	1	0	.063	.180	O
WS Total	11	27	0	4	0	0	0	2	3	4	0	.148	.381	
John Olerud														
DS 2004	4	14	2	3	2	0	0	0	1	2	0	.214	.259	1
LC 2004	4	12	1	2	0	0	1	2	1	1	0	.167	.647	1
Paul O'Neill														
DS 1995	5	18	5	6	0	0	3	6	5	5	0	.333	.259	O
DS 1996	4	15	0	2	0	0	0	0	0	2	0	.133	.267	O
DS 1997	5	19	5	8	2	0	2	7	3	0	0	.421	1.342	O
DS 1998	3	11	1	4	2	0	1	1	1	1	0	.364	1.235	O
DS 1999	2	8	2	2	0	0	0	0	1	1	0	.250	.583	O
DS 2000	5	19	4	4	1	0	0	0	2	4	0	.211	.549	O
DS 2001	3	11	1	1	1	0	0	0	0	0	0	.091	.273	D-2,O-1
DS Total	27	101	18	27	6	0	6	14	12	13	0	.267	.847	
LC 1996	4	11	1	3	0	0	1	2	3	2	0	.273	.974	O
LC 1998	6	25	6	7	2	0	1	3	3	4	2	.280	.837	O
LC 1999	5	21	2	6	0	0	0	1	1	5	0	.286	.604	O
LC 2000	6	20	0	5	0	0	0	5	1	2	0	.250	.604	O
LC 2001	5	12	2	5	0	0	2	3	1	0	0	.417	1.378	O
LC Total	26	89	11	26	2	0	4	14	9	13	2	.292	.803	
WS 1996	5	12	1	2	2	0	0	0	3	2	0	.167	.667	O-4
WS 1998	4	19	3	4	1	0	0	0	1	2	0	.211	.513	O
WS 1999	4	15	0	3	0	0	0	4	2	2	0	.200	.494	O
WS 2000	5	19	2	9	2	2	0	2	3	4	0	.474	1.335	O
WS 2001	5	15	1	5	1	0	0	0	2	2	1	.333	.812	O
WS Total	23	80	7	23	6	2	0	6	11	12	1	.287	.786	
Ben Paschal														
WS 1926	5	4	0	1	0	0	0	1	1	2	0	.250	.650	H
WS 1928	3	10	0	2	0	0	0	1	1	0	0	.200	.473	O
WS Total	8	14	0	3	0	0	0	2	2	2	0	.214	.527	
Roger Peckinpaugh														
WS 1921	8	28	2	5	1	0	0	0	4	3	0	.179	.496	S
Joe Pepitone														
WS 1963	4	13	0	2	0	0	0	0	1	3	0	.154	.496	1
WS 1964	7	26	1	4	1	0	1	5	2	3	0	.154	.522	1
WS Total	11	39	1	6	1	0	1	5	3	6	0	.154	.489	
Andy Phillips														
DS 2006	1	1	0	0	0	0	0	0	0	0	0	.000	.000	1
Jack Phillips														
WS 1947	2	2	0	0	0	0	0	0	0	0	0	.000	.000	1-1
Lou Piniella														
DS 1981	4	10	1	2	1	0	1	3	0	0	0	.200	.800	D
LC 1976	4	11	1	3	1	0	0	0	0	1	0	.273	.636	D-3
LC 1977	5	21	1	7	3	0	0	2	0	1	0	.333	.810	O-4,D-1
LC 1978	4	17	2	4	0	0	0	0	0	3	0	.235	.471	O
LC 1980	2	5	1	1	0	0	1	1	2	1	0	.200	1.229	O
LC 1981	3	5	2	3	0	0	1	3	0	0	0	.600	1.800	D-2,O-1
LC Total	18	59	7	18	4	0	2	6	2	6	0	.305	.802	

YEAR	G	AB	R	H	2B	3B	HR	RBI	BB	SO	SB	AVG	OPS	POS
WS 1976	4	9	1	3	1	0	0	0	0	0	0	.333	.778	O-2,D-2
WS 1977	6	22	1	6	0	0	0	3	0	3	0	.273	.778	O
WS 1978	6	25	3	7	0	0	0	4	0	0	1	.280	.560	O
WS 1981	6	16	2	7	1	0	0	3	0	1	1	.438	.938	O-3
WS Total	22	72	7	23	2	0	0	10	0	4	2	.319	.672	
Wally Pipp														
WS 1921	8	26	1	4	1	0	0	2	2	3	1	.154	.407	1
WS 1922	5	21	0	6	1	0	0	3	0	2	1	.286	.619	1
WS 1923	6	20	2	5	0	0	0	2	4	1	0	.250	.619	1
WS Total	19	67	3	15	2	0	0	7	6	6	2	.224	.538	
Luis Polonia														
DS 2000	1	1	0	1	0	0	0	0	0	0	0	1.000	2.000	H
LC 2000	1	1	0	0	0	0	0	0	0	1	0	.000	.000	H
WS 2000	2	2	0	1	0	0	0	0	0	0	0	.500	1.000	H
Jorge Posada														
DS 1995	1	0	1	0	0	0	0	0	0	0	0	+	+	R
DS 1997	2	2	0	0	0	0	0	0	0	1	0	.000	.000	C
DS 1998	1	2	1	0	0	0	0	0	1	2	0	.000	.333	C
DS 1999	1	4	0	1	1	0	0	0	0	0	0	.250	.750	C
DS 2000	5	17	2	4	2	0	0	1	3	5	0	.235	.703	C
DS 2001	5	18	3	8	1	0	1	2	2	2	1	.444	1.167	C
DS 2002	4	17	2	4	0	0	1	3	0	3	0	.235	1.167	C
DS 2003	4	17	1	3	1	0	0	0	0	6	0	.176	.412	C
DS 2004	4	18	2	4	0	0	0	0	0	6	0	.222	.444	C
DS 2005	5	13	3	3	1	0	1	2	6	2	0	.231	1.012	C
DS 2006	4	14	2	7	1	0	1	2	2	2	0	.500	1.348	C
DS 2007	4	15	1	2	1	0	0	0	2	3	0	.133	.435	C
DS Total	40	137	18	36	8	0	4	10	16	32	1	.263	.746	
LC 1998	5	11	1	2	0	0	1	2	4	2	0	.182	.855	C
LC 1999	3	10	1	1	0	0	1	2	1	2	0	.100	.582	C
LC 2000	6	19	2	3	1	0	0	3	5	5	0	.158	.582	C
LC 2001	5	14	4	3	1	0	0	0	6	7	0	.214	.736	C
LC 2003	7	27	5	8	4	0	1	6	3	4	0	.296	.922	C
LC 2004	7	27	4	7	1	0	0	2	7	1	0	.259	.708	C
LC Total	33	108	17	24	7	0	3	15	26	21	0	.222	.748	
WS 1998	3	9	2	3	0	0	1	2	2	2	0	.333	1.121	C
WS 1999	2	8	0	2	1	0	0	1	0	3	0	.250	.625	C
WS 2000	5	18	2	4	1	0	0	1	5	4	0	.222	.669	C
WS 2001	7	23	2	4	1	0	1	1	3	8	0	.174	.617	C
WS 2003	6	19	0	3	1	0	0	1	5	7	1	.158	.544	C
WS Total	23	77	6	16	4	0	2	6	15	24	1	.208	.675	
Scott Pose														
DS 1997	1	0	0	0	0	0	0	0	0	0	0	+	+	R
Jake Powell														
WS 1936	6	22	8	10	1	0	1	5	4	4	1	.455	1.175	O
WS 1937	1	1	0	0	0	0	0	0	0	1	0	.000	.000	H
WS 1938	1	0	0	0	0	0	0	0	0	0	0	+	+	O
WS Total	8	23	8	10	1	0	1	5	4	5	1	.435	1.127	
Jerry Priddy														
WS 1942	3	10	0	1	1	0	0	1	1	0	0	.100	.382	1-3,3-1
Tim Raines Sr.														
DS 1996	4	16	3	4	0	0	0	0	3	1	0	.250	.618	O
DS 1997	5	19	4	4	0	0	1	3	3	1	2	.211	.618	O-3,D-2
DS 1998	2	4	1	1	1	0	0	0	1	1	0	.250	.900	D-1
DS Total	11	39	8	9	1	0	1	3	7	3	2	.231	.674	
LC 1996	5	15	2	4	1	0	0	0	1	1	0	.267	.646	O
LC 1998	3	10	0	1	0	0	0	1	2	5	0	.100	.350	D-2,O-1
LC Total	8	25	2	5	1	0	0	1	3	6	0	.200	.526	
WS 1996	4	14	2	3	0	0	0	0	2	1	0	.214	.527	O
Willie Randolph														
DS 1981	5	20	0	4	0	0	0	1	1	4	0	.200	.438	2
LC 1976	5	17	0	2	0	0	0	1	3	1	1	.118	.368	2
LC 1977	5	18	4	5	1	0	0	2	1	0	0	.278	.368	2
LC 1980	3	13	0	5	2	0	0	1	1	3	0	.385	.967	2
LC 1981	3	12	2	4	0	0	1	2	0	1	0	.333	.917	2
LC Total	16	60	6	16	3	0	1	6	5	5	1	.267	.685	
WS 1976	4	14	1	1	0	0	0	0	1	3	0	.071	.205	2
WS 1977	6	25	5	4	2	0	1	1	2	2	0	.160	.582	2
WS 1981	6	18	5	4	1	1	2	3	9	0	1	.222	.582	2
WS Total	16	57	11	9	3	1	3	4	12	5	1	.158	.704	
Jack Reed														
WS 1961	3	0	0	0	0	0	0	0	0	0	0	+	+	O
Dave Revering														
DS 1981	2	0	0	0	0	0	0	0	0	0	0	+	+	1
LC 1981	2	2	0	1	0	0	0	0	0	0	0	.500	1.000	1
Bobby Richardson														
WS 1957	2	0	0	0	0	0	0	0	0	0	0	+	+	2-1
WS 1958	4	5	0	0	0	0	0	0	0	0	0	.000	.000	3
WS 1960	7	30	8	11	2	2	1	12	1	1	0	.367	1.054	2
WS 1961	5	23	2	9	1	0	0	0	0	0	1	.391	.826	2
WS 1962	7	27	3	4	0	0	0	0	3	1	0	.148	.381	2
WS 1963	4	14	0	3	1	0	0	0	1	3	0	.214	.552	2
WS 1964	7	32	3	13	2	0	0	3	0	2	1	.406	.875	2
WS Total	36	131	16	40	6	2	1	15	5	7	2	.305	.735	
Juan Rivera														
DS 2002	4	12	2	3	0	0	0	3	1	3	0	.250	.558	O
DS 2003	4	12	2	4	0	0	0	0	1	0	0	.333	.718	O

YEAR	G	AB	R	H	2B	3B	HR	RBI	BB	SO	SB	AVG	OPS	POS
DS Total	8	24	4	7	0	0	0	3	2	3	0	.292	.638	
LC 2003	2	2	0	0	0	0	0	0	0	1	0	.000	.000	O
WS 2003	4	6	0	1	1	0	0	1	1	1	0	.167	.619	O-2
Ruben Rivera														
DS 1996	2	1	0	0	0	0	0	0	0	1	0	.000	.000	O
Mickey Rivers														
LC 1976	5	23	5	8	0	1	0	0	1	1	0	.348	.810	O
LC 1977	5	23	5	9	2	0	0	2	0	2	1	.391	.870	O
LC 1978	4	11	0	5	0	0	0	0	2	0	0	.455	.993	O
LC Total	14	57	10	22	2	1	0	2	3	3	1	.386	.873	
WS 1976	4	18	1	3	0	0	0	0	1	2	1	.167	.377	O
WS 1977	6	27	1	6	2	0	0	1	0	2	1	.222	.519	O
WS 1978	5	18	2	6	0	0	0	1	0	2	1	.333	.667	O-4
WS Total	15	63	4	15	2	0	0	2	1	6	3	.238	.520	
Phil Rizzuto														
WS 1941	5	18	0	2	0	0	0	0	3	1	1	.111	.349	S
WS 1942	5	21	2	8	0	0	1	1	2	1	2	.381	.959	S
WS 1947	7	26	3	8	1	0	0	2	4	0	2	.308	.746	S
WS 1949	5	18	2	3	0	0	0	1	3	1	1	.167	.452	S
WS 1950	4	14	1	2	0	0	0	0	3	0	1	.143	.437	S
WS 1951	6	25	5	8	0	0	1	3	2	3	0	.320	.437	S
WS 1952	7	27	2	4	1	0	0	0	5	2	0	.148	.466	S
WS 1953	6	19	4	6	1	0	0	0	3	2	1	.316	.778	S
WS 1955	7	15	2	4	0	0	0	1	5	1	2	.267	.717	S
WS Total	52	183	21	45	3	0	2	8	30	11	10	.246	.650	
Andre Robertson														
LC 1981	1	1	0	0	0	0	0	0	0	0	0	.000	.000	S
WS 1981	1	0	0	0	0	0	0	0	0	0	0	+	+	R
Gene Robertson														
WS 1928	3	8	1	1	0	0	0	2	1	0	0	.125	.347	3
Aaron Robinson														
WS 1947	3	10	2	2	0	0	0	1	2	1	0	.200	.533	C
Eddie Robinson														
WS 1955	4	3	0	2	0	0	0	1	2	1	0	.667	.533	1-1
Alex Rodriguez														
DS 2004	4	19	3	8	3	0	1	3	2	1	2	.421	1.213	3
DS 2005	5	15	2	2	1	0	0	0	6	5	1	.133	1.213	3
DS 2006	4	14	0	1	0	0	0	0	0	4	0	.071	.143	3
DS 2007	4	15	2	4	0	0	1	1	2	6	0	.267	.820	3
DS Total	17	63	7	15	4	0	2	4	10	16	3	.238	.757	
LC 2004	7	31	8	8	2	0	2	5	4	6	0	.258	.000	3
Aurelio Rodriguez														
LC 1980	2	6	0	2	1	0	0	0	0	0	0	.333	.833	3
LC 1981	1	0	0	0	0	0	0	0	0	0	0	+	+	3
LC Total	3	6	0	2	1	0	0	0	0	0	0	.333	.833	
WS 1981	4	12	1	5	0	0	0	0	1	2	0	.417	.878	3-3
Red Rolfe														
WS 1936	6	25	5	10	0	0	0	4	3	1	0	.400	.864	3
WS 1937	5	20	3	6	2	1	0	1	3	2	0	.300	.891	3
WS 1938	4	18	0	3	0	0	0	1	0	3	1	.167	.333	3
WS 1939	4	16	2	2	0	0	0	0	0	0	0	.125	.250	3
WS 1941	5	20	2	6	0	0	0	0	2	1	0	.300	.664	3
WS 1942	4	17	5	6	2	0	0	0	1	2	0	.353	.859	3
WS Total	28	116	17	33	4	1	0	6	9	9	1	.284	.672	
Buddy Rosar														
WS 1941	1	0	0	0	0	0	0	0	0	0	0	+	+	C
WS 1942	1	1	0	1	0	0	0	0	0	0	0	1.000	2.000	H
WS Total	2	1	0	1	0	0	0	0	0	0	0	1.000	2.000	
Babe Ruth														
WS 1921	6	16	3	5	0	0	1	4	5	8	2	.313	.976	O
WS 1922	5	17	1	2	1	0	0	1	2	3	0	.118	.976	O
WS 1923	6	19	8	7	1	1	3	3	8	6	0	.368	1.556	O-6,1-1
WS 1926	7	20	6	6	0	0	4	5	11	2	1	.300	1.448	O
WS 1927	4	15	4	6	0	0	2	7	2	2	1	.400	1.271	O
WS 1928	4	16	9	10	3	0	3	4	1	2	0	.625	2.022	O
WS 1932	4	15	6	5	0	0	2	6	4	3	0	.333	1.207	O
WS Total	36	118	37	41	5	1	15	30	33	26	4	.347	1.282	
Rey Sanchez														
DS 1997	5	15	1	3	1	0	0	1	1	2	0	.200	.517	2
Bronson Sardinha														
DS 2007	1	0	0	0	0	0	0	0	0	0	0	+	+	O
Wally Schang														
WS 1921	8	21	1	6	1	1	0	1	5	4	0	.286	.852	C
WS 1922	5	16	0	3	1	0	0	0	0	3	0	.188	.438	C
WS 1923	6	22	3	7	1	0	0	0	1	2	0	.318	.711	C
WS Total	19	59	4	16	3	1	0	1	6	9	0	.271	.694	
Everett Scott														
WS 1922	5	14	0	2	0	0	0	1	1	0	0	.143	.694	S
WS 1923	6	22	2	7	0	0	0	3	0	1	0	.318	.636	S
WS Total	11	36	2	9	0	0	0	4	1	1	0	.250	.513	

YEAR	G	AB	R	H	2B	3B	HR	RBI	BB	SO	SB	AVG	OPS	POS
Bob Seeds														
WS 1936	1	0	0	0	0	0	0	0	0	0	0	+	+	R
George Selkirk														
WS 1936	6	24	6	8	0	1	2	3	4	4	0	.333	1.095	O
WS 1937	5	19	5	5	1	0	0	6	2	0	0	.263	.649	O
WS 1938	3	10	0	2	0	0	0	1	2	1	0	.200	.533	O
WS 1939	4	12	0	2	1	0	0	0	3	2	0	.167	.583	O
WS 1941	2	2	0	1	0	0	0	0	0	0	0	.500	1.000	H
WS 1942	1	1	0	0	0	0	0	0	0	0	0	.000	.000	H
WS Total	21	68	11	18	2	1	2	10	11	7	0	.265	.779	
Hank Severeid														
WS 1926	7	22	1	6	1	0	0	1	1	2	0	.273	.623	C
Joe Sewell														
WS 1932	4	15	4	5	1	0	0	3	4	0	0	.333	.623	3
Gary Sheffield														
DS 2004	4	18	2	4	1	0	1	2	3	1	0	.222	.778	O
DS 2005	5	21	1	6	0	0	0	2	1	2	0	.286	.604	O
DS 2006	3	12	1	1	0	0	0	1	0	4	0	.083	.167	1
DS Total	12	51	4	11	1	0	1	5	4	7	0	.216	.567	
LC 2004	7	30	7	10	3	0	1	5	6	8	0	.333	.978	O
Norm Siebern														
WS 1956	1	1	0	0	0	0	0	0	0	0	0	.000	.000	H
WS 1958	3	8	1	1	0	0	0	0	3	2	0	.125	.489	O
WS Total	4	9	1	1	0	0	0	0	3	2	0	.111	.444	
Ruben Sierra														
DS 1995	5	23	2	4	2	0	2	5	2	7	0	.174	.567	D
DS 2003	1	2	0	0	0	0	0	0	0	0	0	.000	.000	O
DS 2004	3	12	1	2	0	0	1	3	2	3	1	.167	.702	D
DS 2005	3	3	0	1	0	0	0	1	0	1	0	.333	.667	O-1
DS Total	12	40	3	7	2	0	3	9	4	11	1	.175	.694	
LC 2003	3	2	1	1	0	0	1	1	1	0	0	.500	2.667	O-1
LC 2004	5	21	1	7	1	1	0	2	3	8	0	.333	.893	D-4
LC Total	8	23	2	8	1	1	1	3	4	8	0	.348	1.053	
WS 2003	5	4	0	1	0	1	0	2	1	3	0	.250	1.150	O-1
Charlie Silvera														
WS 1949	1	2	0	0	0	0	0	0	0	0	0	.000	.000	C
Harry Simpson														
WS 1957	5	12	0	1	0	0	0	1	0	4	0	.083	.167	1-4
Bill Skowron														
WS 1955	5	12	2	4	2	0	1	3	0	1	0	.333	1.083	1-3
WS 1956	3	10	1	1	0	0	1	4	0	3	0	.100	.500	1-2
WS 1957	2	4	0	0	0	0	0	0	0	0	0	.000	.000	1
WS 1958	7	27	3	7	0	0	2	7	1	4	0	.259	.767	1
WS 1960	7	32	7	12	2	0	2	6	0	6	0	.375	.767	1
WS 1961	5	17	3	6	0	0	1	5	3	4	0	.353	.979	1
WS 1962	6	18	1	4	0	1	0	1	1	5	0	.222	.596	1
WS Total	35	120	17	34	4	1	7	26	5	23	0	.283	.818	
Enos Slaughter														
WS 1956	6	20	6	7	0	0	1	4	4	0	0	.350	.818	O
WS 1957	5	12	2	3	1	0	0	0	3	2	0	.250	.733	O
WS 1958	4	3	1	0	0	0	0	0	1	1	0	.000	.250	H
WS Total	15	35	9	10	1	0	1	4	8	3	0	.286	.809	
Elmer Smith														
WS 1922	2	2	0	0	0	0	0	0	0	2	0	.000	.000	H
Eric Soderholm														
LC 1980	2	6	0	1	0	0	0	0	0	0	0	.167	.333	D
Luis Sojo														
DS 1996	2	0	0	0	0	0	0	0	0	0	0	+	+	2
DS 2000	5	16	2	3	2	0	0	5	2	1	0	.188	.000	2
DS Total	7	16	2	3	2	0	0	5	2	1	0	.188	.576	
LC 1996	3	5	0	1	0	0	0	0	0	1	0	.200	.400	2
LC 1998	1	0	0	0	0	0	0	0	0	0	0	+	+	1
LC 1999	2	1	0	0	0	0	0	0	0	0	0	.000	.000	2
LC 2000	6	23	1	6	1	0	0	2	2	3	0	.261	.624	2-6,3-2
LC 2001	1	1	0	0	0	0	0	0	0	0	0	.000	.000	1
LC Total	13	30	1	7	1	0	0	2	2	4	0	.233	.548	
WS 1996	5	5	0	3	1	0	0	1	0	0	0	.600	1.400	2-3
WS 1999	1	0	0	0	0	0	0	0	0	0	0	+	+	2
WS 2000	4	7	0	2	0	0	0	2	1	0	1	.286	.661	2-2,3-2
WS 2001	2	3	0	1	0	0	0	1	0	0	0	.333	.667	1-1
WS Total	12	15	0	6	1	0	0	4	1	0	1	.400	.904	
Alfonso Soriano														
DS 2001	5	18	2	4	0	0	0	3	1	5	2	.222	.485	2
DS 2002	4	17	2	2	1	0	1	2	1	4	1	.118	.485	2
DS 2003	4	19	2	7	1	0	0	4	0	6	2	.368	.789	2
DS Total	13	54	6	13	2	0	1	9	2	15	5	.241	.614	
LC 2001	5	15	5	6	0	0	1	2	3	3	2	.400	.548	2
LC 2003	7	30	0	4	1	0	0	3	1	11	2	.133	.328	2
LC Total	12	45	5	10	1	0	1	5	4	14	4	.222	.611	
WS 2001	7	25	1	6	0	0	1	2	0	7	0	.240	.600	2
WS 2003	6	22	2	5	0	0	1	2	2	9	1	.227	.655	2-5,O-1
WS Total	13	47	3	11	0	0	2	4	2	16	1	.234	.627	

YEAR	G	AB	R	H	2B	3B	HR	RBI	BB	SO	SB	AVG	OPS	POS
Jim Spencer														
LC 1980	1	1	0	0	0	0	0	0	0	0	0	.000	.000	H
WS 1978	4	12	3	2	0	0	0	0	2	4	0	.167	.452	1-3
Shane Spencer														
DS 1998	2	6	3	3	0	0	2	4	0	1	0	.500	2.000	O
DS 2001	3	8	1	2	1	0	0	0	1	4	0	.250	.708	O
DS 2002	1	0	0	0	0	0	0	0	0	0	0	+	+	O
DS Total	6	14	4	5	1	0	2	4	1	5	0	.357	1.257	
LC 1998	3	10	1	1	0	0	0	0	1	3	0	.100	.282	O
LC 1999	3	9	1	1	0	0	0	0	1	6	0	.111	.311	O
LC 2001	5	7	1	2	1	0	0	0	1	1	1	.286	.804	O
LC Total	11	26	3	4	1	0	0	0	3	10	1	.154	.434	
WS 1998	1	3	1	1	1	0	0	0	0	2	0	.333	1.000	O
WS 2001	7	20	1	4	0	0	1	2	2	6	0	.200	.623	O-6
WS Total	8	23	2	5	1	0	1	2	2	8	0	.217	.671	
Tuck Stainback														
WS 1942	2	0	0	0	0	0	0	0	0	0	0	+	+	R
WS 1943	5	17	0	3	0	0	0	0	0	2	0	.176	.353	O
WS Total	7	17	0	3	0	0	0	0	0	2	0	.176	.353	
Fred Stanley														
LC 1976	5	15	1	5	2	0	0	0	2	0	0	.333	.878	S
LC 1977	2	0	0	0	0	0	0	0	0	0	0	+	+	S
LC 1978	2	5	0	1	0	0	0	0	0	2	0	.200	.400	2
LC Total	9	20	1	6	2	0	0	0	2	2	0	.300	.764	
WS 1976	4	6	1	1	1	0	0	1	3	1	0	.167	.778	S
WS 1977	1	0	0	0	0	0	0	0	0	0	0	+	+	S
WS 1978	3	5	0	1	1	0	0	0	1	0	0	.200	.733	2
WS Total	8	11	1	2	2	0	0	1	4	1	0	.182	.764	
Mike Stanley														
DS 1995	4	16	2	5	0	0	1	3	2	1	0	.313	.889	C
DS 1997	2	4	1	3	1	0	0	1	0	1	0	.750	.889	D-1
DS Total	6	20	3	8	1	0	1	4	2	2	0	.400	1.078	
Snuffy Stirnweiss														
WS 1943	1	1	1	0	0	0	0	0	0	0	0	.000	.000	H
WS 1947	7	27	3	7	0	1	0	3	8	8	0	.259	.762	2
WS 1949	1	0	0	0	0	0	0	0	0	0	0	+	+	H
WS Total	9	28	4	7	0	1	0	3	8	8	0	.250	.738	
Darryl Strawberry														
DS 1995	2	2	0	0	0	0	0	0	0	1	0	.000	.000	H
DS 1996	2	5	0	0	0	0	0	0	0	2	0	.000	.000	D
DS 1999	2	6	2	2	0	0	1	3	1	0	0	.333	1.262	D
DS Total	6	13	2	2	0	0	1	3	1	3	0	.154	.599	
LC 1996	4	12	4	5	0	0	3	5	2	2	0	.417	1.667	O
LC 1999	3	6	1	2	0	0	1	1	1	2	0	.333	1.262	D
LC Total	7	18	5	7	0	0	4	6	3	4	0	.389	1.532	
WS 1996	5	16	0	3	0	0	0	1	4	6	0	.188	.538	O
WS 1999	2	3	0	1	0	0	0	0	1	2	0	.333	.833	D-1
WS Total	7	19	0	4	0	0	0	1	5	8	0	.211	.586	
Johnny Sturm														
WS 1941	5	21	0	6	0	0	0	2	0	2	1	.286	.586	1
Gary Thomasson														
LC 1978	3	1	0	0	0	0	0	0	0	0	0	.000	.000	O
WS 1978	3	4	0	1	0	0	0	0	0	1	0	.250	.500	O
Marv Throneberry														
WS 1958	1	1	0	0	0	0	0	0	0	1	0	.000	.000	H
Tom Tresh														
WS 1962	7	28	5	9	1	0	1	4	1	4	2	.321	.809	O
WS 1963	4	15	1	3	0	0	1	2	1	6	0	.200	.650	O
WS 1964	7	22	4	6	2	0	2	7	6	7	0	.273	.650	O
WS Total	18	65	10	18	3	0	4	13	8	17	2	.277	.859	
John Vander Wal														
DS 2002	2	2	0	0	0	0	0	0	0	1	0	.000	.000	O-1
Randy Velarde														
DS 1995	5	17	3	3	0	0	0	1	6	4	0	.176	.000	2-4,3-2,O-2
DS 2001	2	5	0	1	0	0	0	0	0	1	0	.200	.400	D
DS Total	7	22	3	4	0	0	0	1	6	5	0	.182	.561	
LC 2001	1	1	0	0	0	0	0	0	0	0	0	.000	.000	3
WS 2001	1	3	0	0	0	0	0	0	1	1	0	.000	.250	1
Otto Velez														
LC 1976	1	1	0	0	0	0	0	0	0	0	0	.000	.000	H
WS 1976	3	3	0	0	0	0	0	0	0	3	0	.000	.000	H
Robin Ventura														
DS 2002	4	14	1	4	2	0	0	4	1	2	0	.286	.561	3
Jose Vizcaino														
DS 2000	1	0	1	0	0	0	0	0	0	0	0	+	+	2
LC 2000	4	2	3	2	1	0	0	2	0	0	2	1.000	.000	2-3
WS 2000	4	17	0	4	0	0	0	1	0	5	0	.235	.471	2

YEAR	G	AB	R	H	2B	3B	HR	RBI	BB	SO	SB	AVG	OPS	POS
Aaron Ward														
WS 1921	8	26	1	6	0	0	0	4	2	6	0	.231	.471	2
WS 1922	5	13	3	2	0	0	2	3	3	3	0	.154	.928	2
WS 1923	6	24	4	10	0	0	1	2	1	3	1	.417	.982	2
WS Total	19	63	8	18	0	0	3	9	6	12	1	.286	.771	
Bob Watson														
DS 1981	5	16	2	7	0	0	0	1	1	1	0	.438	.908	1
LC 1980	3	12	0	6	3	1	0	0	0	0	0	.500	1.417	1
LC 1981	3	12	0	3	0	0	0	1	0	1	0	.250	.500	1
LC Total	6	24	0	9	3	1	0	1	0	1	0	.375	.958	
WS 1981	6	22	2	7	1	0	2	7	3	0	0	.318	.771	1
Roy Weatherly														
WS 1943	1	1	0	0	0	0	0	0	0	0	0	.000	.000	H
Rondell White														
DS 2002	1	3	1	1	0	0	1	1	0	0	0	.333	1.667	D
Roy White														
LC 1976	5	17	4	5	3	0	0	3	5	1	1	.294	.925	O
LC 1977	4	5	2	2	2	0	0	0	1	0	0	.400	1.300	O-1,D-1
LC 1978	4	16	5	5	1	0	1	1	1	2	0	.313	.915	O-3,D-1
LC Total	13	38	11	12	6	0	1	4	7	3	1	.316	.975	
WS 1976	4	15	0	2	0	0	0	0	3	0	0	.133	.411	O
WS 1977	2	2	0	0	0	0	0	0	0	0	0	.000	.000	H
WS 1978	6	24	9	8	0	0	1	4	4	5	2	.333	.887	O
WS Total	12	41	9	10	0	0	1	4	7	5	2	.244	.671	
Bernie Williams														
DS 1995	5	21	8	9	2	0	2	5	7	3	1	.429	1.381	O
DS 1996	4	15	5	7	0	0	3	5	2	1	1	.467	1.381	O
DS 1997	5	17	3	2	1	0	0	1	4	3	0	.118	.462	O
DS 1998	3	11	0	0	0	0	0	0	1	4	0	.000	.083	O
DS 1999	3	11	2	4	1	0	1	6	1	2	0	.364	1.144	O
DS 2000	5	20	3	5	3	0	0	1	1	4	0	.250	.686	O
DS 2001	5	18	4	4	3	0	0	5	3	3	0	.222	.722	O
DS 2002	4	15	4	5	1	0	1	3	3	2	0	.333	1.044	O
DS 2003	4	15	3	6	2	0	0	3	2	2	0	.400	1.004	O
DS 2004	4	18	2	5	1	0	1	3	1	2	0	.278	.816	O
DS 2005	5	19	2	4	2	0	0	1	1	3	0	.211	.566	O-3,D-2
DS 2006	1	3	0	0	0	0	0	0	0	2	0	.000	.000	D
DS Total	48	183	36	51	16	0	8	33	26	31	2	.279	.864	
LC 1996	5	19	6	9	3	0	2	6	5	4	1	.474	1.531	O
LC 1998	6	21	4	8	1	0	0	5	7	4	1	.381	.964	O
LC 1999	5	20	3	5	1	0	1	2	2	5	1	.250	.768	O
LC 2000	6	23	5	10	1	0	1	3	2	3	1	.435	.768	O
LC 2001	5	17	4	4	0	0	3	5	5	4	0	.235	1.174	O
LC 2003	7	26	5	5	1	0	0	2	4	3	0	.192	.531	O
LC 2004	7	36	4	11	3	0	2	10	0	5	0	.306	.861	O
LC Total	41	162	31	52	10	0	9	33	25	28	4	.321	.962	
WS 1996	6	24	3	4	0	0	1	4	3	6	1	.167	.551	O
WS 1998	4	16	2	1	0	0	1	3	2	5	0	.063	.417	O
WS 1999	4	13	2	3	0	0	0	0	4	2	1	.231	.643	O
WS 2000	5	18	2	2	0	0	1	1	5	5	0	.111	.582	O
WS 2001	7	24	2	5	1	0	0	1	4	6	0	.208	.571	O
WS 2003	6	25	5	10	2	0	2	5	2	2	0	.400	.571	O
WS Total	32	120	16	25	3	0	5	14	20	26	2	.208	.677	
Gerald Williams														
DS 1995	5	5	1	0	0	0	0	0	2	3	0	.000	.286	O
Enrique Wilson														
DS 2002	1	0	0	0	0	0	0	0	0	0	0	+	+	H
LC 2001	1	1	0	1	0	0	0	0	0	0	0	1.000	2.000	S
LC 2003	2	7	0	1	0	0	0	0	0	1	0	.143	.286	3
LC Total	3	8	0	2	0	0	0	0	0	1	0	.250	.500	
WS 2001	2	3	0	0	0	0	0	0	0	0	0	.000	.000	S-1
WS 2003	2	4	0	2	1	0	0	1	1	0	0	.500	1.350	2-1,3-1
WS Total	4	7	0	2	1	0	0	1	1	0	0	.286	.804	
George Wilson														
WS 1956	1	1	0	0	0	0	0	0	0	1	0	.000	.000	H
Dave Winfield														
DS 1981	5	20	2	7	3	0	0	0	1	5	0	.350	.881	O
LC 1981	3	13	2	2	1	0	0	2	2	2	1	.154	.497	O
WS 1981	6	22	0	1	0	0	0	1	5	4	1	.045	.268	O
Whitey Witt														
WS 1922	5	18	1	4	1	1	0	0	1	2	0	.222	.652	O
WS 1923	6	25	1	6	2	0	0	4	1	1	0	.240	.589	O
WS Total	11	43	2	10	3	1	0	4	2	3	0	.233	.616	
Tony Womack														
DS 2005	2	0	0	0	0	0	0	0	0	0	0	+	+	H
Gene Woodling														
WS 1949	3	10	4	4	3	0	0	0	3	0	0	.400	1.238	O
WS 1950	4	14	2	6	0	0	0	1	2	0	0	.429	.929	O
WS 1951	6	18	6	3	1	1	1	1	5	3	0	.167	.848	O-5
WS 1952	7	23	4	8	1	1	1	1	3	3	0	.348	1.032	O-6
WS 1953	6	20	5	6	0	0	1	3	6	2	0	.300	.912	O
WS Total	26	85	21	27	5	2	3	6	19	8	0	.318	.972	

Postseason Pitcher Register

YEAR	W	L	SV	ERA	G	GS	CG	SHO	IP	H	ER	BB	SO
DOYLE ALEXANDER													
WS 1976	0	1	0	7.50	1	1	0	0	6	9	5	2	1
JOHNNY ALLEN													
WS 1932	0	0	0	40.50	1	1	0	0	0.2	5	3	0	0
IVY ANDREWS													
WS 1937	0	0	0	3.18	1	0	0	0	5.2	6	2	4	1
LUIS ARROYO													
WS 1960	0	0	0	13.50	1	0	0	0	0.2	2	1	0	1
WS 1961	1	0	0	2.25	2	0	0	0	4	4	1	2	3
WS Total	1	0	0	3.86	3	0	0	0	4.2	6	2	2	4
JIM BEATTIE													
LC 1978	1	0	0	1.69	1	1	0	0	5.1	2	1	5	3
WS 1978	1	0	0	2.00	1	1	1	0	9	9	2	4	8
BILL BEVENS													
WS 1947	0	1	0	2.38	2	1	1	0	11.1	3	3	11	7
EWELL BLACKWELL													
WS 1952	0	0	0	7.20	1	1	0	0	5	4	4	3	4
BRIAN BOEHRINGER													
DS 1996	1	0	0	6.75	2	0	0	0	1.1	3	1	2	0
DS 1997	0	0	0	0.00	1	0	0	0	1.2	1	0	1	2
DS Total	1	0	0	3.00	3	0	0	0	3	4	1	3	2
WS 1996	0	0	0	5.40	2	0	0	0	5	5	3	0	5
TINY BONHAM													
WS 1941	1	0	0	1.00	1	1	1	0	9	4	1	2	2
WS 1942	0	1	0	4.09	2	1	1	0	11	9	5	3	3
WS 1943	0	1	0	4.50	1	1	0	0	8	6	4	3	9
WS Total	1	2	0	3.21	4	3	2	0	28	19	10	8	14
HANK BOROWY													
WS 1942	0	0	0	18.00	1	1	0	0	3	6	6	3	1
WS 1943	1	0	0	2.25	1	1	0	0	8	6	2	3	4
WS Total	1	0	0	6.55	2	2	0	0	11	12	8	6	5
JIM BOUTON													
WS 1963	0	1	0	1.29	1	1	0	0	7	4	1	5	4
WS 1964	2	0	0	1.56	2	2	1	0	17.1	15	3	5	7
WS Total	2	1	0	1.48	3	3	1	0	24.1	19	4	10	11
MARV BREUER													
WS 1941	0	0	0	0.00	1	0	0	0	3	3	0	1	2
WS 1942	0	0	0	+	1	0	0	0	0	2	0	0	0
WS Total	0	0	0	0.00	2	0	0	0	3	5	0	1	2
MARSHALL BRIDGES													
WS 1962	0	0	0	4.91	2	0	0	0	3.2	4	2	2	3
KEVIN BROWN													
DS 2004	1	0	0	1.50	1	1	0	0	6	8	1	0	1
LC 2004	0	1	0	21.60	2	2	0	0	3.1	9	8	4	2
BRIAN BRUNEY													
DS 2006	0	0	0	3.38	3	0	0	0	2.2	1	1	0	4
JOE BUSH													
WS 1922	0	2	0	4.80	2	2	1	0	15	21	8	5	6
WS 1923	1	1	0	1.08	3	1	1	0	16.2	7	2	4	5
WS Total	1	3	0	2.84	5	3	2	0	31.2	28	10	9	11
TOMMY BYRNE													
WS 1949	0	0	0	2.70	1	1	0	0	3.1	2	1	2	1
WS 1955	1	1	0	1.88	2	2	1	0	14.1	8	3	8	8
WS 1956	0	0	0	0.00	1	0	0	0	0.1	1	0	0	1
WS 1957	0	0	0	5.40	2	0	0	0	3.1	1	2	2	1
WS Total	1	1	0	2.53	6	3	1	0	21.1	12	6	12	11
SHAWN CHACON													
DS 2005	0	0	0	2.84	1	1	0	0	6.1	4	2	1	5
JOBA CHAMBERLAIN													
DS 2007	0	0	0	4.91	2	0	0	0	3.2	3	2	3	4
SPUD CHANDLER													
WS 1941	0	1	0	3.60	1	1	0	0	5	4	2	2	2
WS 1942	0	1	1	1.08	2	1	0	0	8.1	5	1	1	3
WS 1943	2	0	0	0.50	2	2	2	1	18	17	1	3	10
WS 1947	0	0	0	9.00	1	0	0	0	2	2	2	3	1
WS Total	2	2	1	1.62	6	4	2	1	33.1	28	6	9	16
RANDY CHOATE													
DS 2000	0	0	0	6.75	1	0	0	0	1.1	0	1	1	1
LC 2000	0	0	0	0.00	1	0	0	0	0.1	0	0	0	1
WS 2001	0	0	0	2.45	2	0	0	0	3.2	7	1	1	2

YEAR	W	L	SV	ERA	G	GS	CG	SHO	IP	H	ER	BB	SO
KEN CLAY													
LC 1978	0	0	1	0.00	1	0	0	0	3.2	0	0	3	2
WS 1977	0	0	0	2.45	2	0	0	0	3.2	2	1	1	0
WS 1978	0	0	0	11.57	1	0	0	0	2.1	4	3	2	2
WS Total	0	0	0	6.00	3	0	0	0	6	6	4	3	2
ROGER CLEMENS													
DS 1999	1	0	0	0.00	1	1	0	0	7	3	0	2	2
DS 2000	0	2	0	8.18	2	2	0	0	11	13	10	8	10
DS 2001	0	1	0	5.40	2	2	0	0	8.1	9	5	4	6
DS 2002	0	0	0	6.35	1	1	0	0	5.2	8	4	3	5
DS 2003	1	0	0	1.29	1	1	0	0	7	5	1	1	6
DS 2007	0	0	0	11.57	1	1	0	0	2.1	4	3	2	1
DS Total	2	3	0	5.01	8	8	0	0	41.1	42	23	20	30
LC 1999	0	1	0	22.50	1	1	0	0	2	6	5	2	2
LC 2000	1	0	0	0.00	1	1	1	1	9	1	0	2	15
LC 2001	0	0	0	0.00	1	1	0	0	5	1	0	4	7
LC 2003	1	0	0	5.00	2	2	0	0	9	11	5	2	8
LC Total	2	1	0	3.60	5	5	1	1	25	19	10	10	32
WS 1999	1	0	0	1.17	1	1	0	0	7.2	4	1	2	4
WS 2000	1	0	0	0.00	1	1	0	0	8	2	0	0	9
WS 2001	1	0	0	1.35	2	2	0	0	13.1	10	2	4	19
WS 2003	0	0	0	3.86	1	1	0	0	7	8	3	0	5
WS Total	3	0	0	1.50	5	5	0	0	36	24	6	6	37
JIM COATES													
WS 1960	0	0	0	5.68	3	0	0	0	6.1	6	4	1	3
WS 1961	0	0	1	0.00	1	0	0	0	4	1	0	1	2
WS 1962	0	1	0	6.75	2	0	0	0	2.2	1	2	1	3
WS Total	0	1	1	4.15	6	0	0	0	13	8	6	3	8
RIP COLEMAN													
WS 1955	0	0	0	9.00	1	0	0	0	1	5	1	0	1
RIP COLLINS													
WS 1921	0	0	0	54.00	1	0	0	0	0.2	4	4	1	0
DAVID CONE													
DS 1995	1	0	0	4.60	2	2	0	0	15.2	15	8	9	14
DS 1996	0	1	0	9.00	1	1	0	0	6	8	6	2	8
DS 1997	0	0	0	16.20	1	1	0	0	3.1	7	6	2	2
DS 1998	1	0	0	0.00	1	1	0	0	5.2	2	0	1	6
DS Total	2	1	0	5.87	5	5	0	0	30.2	32	20	14	30
LC 1996	0	0	0	3.00	1	1	0	0	6	5	2	5	5
LC 1998	1	0	0	4.15	2	2	0	0	13	12	6	6	13
LC 1999	1	0	0	2.57	1	1	0	0	7	7	2	3	9
LC 2000	0	0	0	0.00	1	0	0	0	1	0	0	0	0
LC Total	2	0	0	3.33	5	4	0	0	27	24	10	14	27
WS 1996	1	0	0	1.50	1	1	0	0	6	4	1	4	3
WS 1998	0	0	0	3.00	1	1	0	0	6	2	2	3	4
WS 1999	1	0	0	0.00	1	1	0	0	7	1	0	5	4
WS 2000	0	0	0	0.00	1	0	0	0	0.1	0	0	0	0
WS Total	2	0	0	1.40	4	3	0	0	19.1	7	3	12	11
JOSE CONTRERAS													
LC 2003	0	1	0	5.79	4	0	0	0	4.2	6	3	2	7
WS 2003	0	1	0	5.68	4	0	0	0	6.1	5	4	5	10
BUD DALEY													
WS 1961	1	0	0	0.00	2	0	0	0	7	5	0	0	3
WS 1962	0	0	0	0.00	1	0	0	0	1	1	0	1	0
WS Total	1	0	0	0.00	3	0	0	0	8	6	0	1	3
RON DAVIS													
DS 1981	1	0	0	0.00	3	0	0	0	6	1	0	2	6
LC 1980	0	0	0	2.25	1	0	0	0	4	3	1	1	3
LC 1981	0	0	0	0.00	2	0	0	0	3.1	0	0	2	4
LC Total	0	0	0	1.23	3	0	0	0	7.1	3	1	3	7
WS 1981	0	0	0	23.14	4	0	0	0	2.1	4	6	5	4
MURRY DICKSON													
WS 1958	0	0	0	4.50	2	0	0	0	4	4	2	0	1
ART DITMAR													
WS 1957	0	0	0	0.00	2	0	0	0	6	2	0	0	2
WS 1958	0	0	0	0.00	1	0	0	0	3.2	2	0	0	2
WS 1960	0	2	0	21.60	2	2	0	0	1.2	6	4	1	0
WS Total	0	2	0	3.18	5	2	0	0	11.1	10	4	1	4
ATLEY DONALD													
WS 1941	0	0	0	9.00	1	1	0	0	4	6	4	3	2
WS 1942	0	1	0	6.00	1	0	0	0	3	3	2	2	1
WS Total	0	1	0	7.71	2	1	0	0	7	9	6	5	3
AL DOWNING													
WS 1963	0	1	0	5.40	1	1	0	0	5	7	3	1	6
WS 1964	0	1	0	8.22	3	1	0	0	7.2	9	7	2	5
WS Total	0	2	0	7.11	4	2	0	0	12.2	16	10	3	11
KARL DREWS													
WS 1947	0	0	0	3.00	2	0	0	0	3	2	1	1	0

Postseason

YEAR	W	L	SV	ERA	G	GS	CG	SHO	IP	H	ER	BB	SO
Ryne Duren													
WS 1958	1	1	1	1.93	3	0	0	0	9.1	7	2	6	14
WS 1960	0	0	0	2.25	2	0	0	0	4	2	1	1	5
WS Total	1	1	1	2.03	5	0	0	0	13.1	9	3	7	19
Dock Ellis													
LC 1976	1	0	0	3.38	1	1	0	0	8	6	3	2	5
WS 1976	0	1	0	10.80	1	1	0	0	3.1	7	4	0	1
Kyle Farnsworth													
DS 2006	0	0	0	0.00	2	0	0	0	2	1	0	1	1
DS 2007	0	0	0	0.00	1	0	0	0	1	1	0	0	2
DS Total	0	0	0	0.00	3	0	0	0	3	2	0	1	3
Tom Ferrick													
WS 1950	1	0	0	0.00	1	0	0	0	1	1	0	1	0
Ed Figueroa													
LC 1976	0	1	0	5.84	2	2	0	0	12.1	14	8	2	5
LC 1977	0	0	0	10.80	1	1	0	0	3.1	5	4	2	3
LC 1978	0	1	0	27.00	1	1	0	0	1	5	3	0	0
LC Total	0	2	0	8.10	4	4	0	0	16.2	24	15	4	8
WS 1976	0	1	0	5.63	1	1	0	0	8	6	5	5	2
WS 1978	0	1	0	8.10	2	2	0	0	6.2	9	6	5	2
WS Total	0	2	0	6.75	3	3	0	0	14.2	15	11	10	4
Whitey Ford													
WS 1950	1	0	0	0.00	1	1	0	0	8.2	7	0	1	7
WS 1953	0	1	0	4.50	2	2	0	0	8	9	4	2	7
WS 1955	2	0	0	2.12	2	2	1	0	17	13	4	8	10
WS 1956	1	1	0	5.25	2	2	1	0	12	14	7	2	8
WS 1957	1	1	0	1.13	2	2	1	0	16	11	2	5	7
WS 1958	0	1	0	4.11	3	3	0	0	15.1	19	7	5	16
WS 1960	2	0	0	0.00	2	2	2	2	18	11	0	2	8
WS 1961	2	0	0	0.00	2	2	1	1	14	6	0	1	7
WS 1962	1	1	0	4.12	3	3	1	0	19.2	24	9	4	12
WS 1963	0	2	0	4.50	2	2	0	0	12	10	6	3	8
WS 1964	0	1	0	8.44	1	1	0	0	5.1	8	5	1	4
WS Total108		0	2.71	22	22	7	3	146	132	44	34	94	
George Frazier													
LC 1981	1	0	0	0.00	1	0	0	0	5.2	5	0	1	5
WS 1981	0	3	0	17.18	3	0	0	0	3.2	9	7	3	2
Lefty Gomez													
WS 1932	1	0	0	1.00	1	1	1	0	9	9	1	1	8
WS 1936	2	0	0	4.70	2	2	1	0	15.1	14	8	11	9
WS 1937	2	0	0	1.50	2	2	2	0	18	16	3	2	8
WS 1938	1	0	0	3.86	1	1	0	0	7	9	3	1	5
WS 1939	0	0	0	9.00	1	1	0	0	1	3	1	0	1
WS Total	6	0	0	2.86	7	7	4	0	50.1	51	16	15	31
Dwight Gooden													
DS 1997	0	0	0	1.59	1	1	0	0	5.2	5	1	3	5
DS 2000	0	0	0	21.60	1	0	0	0	1.2	4	4	1	1
DS Total	0	0	0	6.14	2	1	0	0	7.1	9	5	4	6
LC 2000	0	0	0	0.00	1	0	0	0	2.1	1	0	0	1
Tom Gordon													
DS 2004	0	0	0	4.91	3	0	0	0	3.2	2	2	0	3
DS 2005	0	0	0	3.86	3	0	0	0	2.1	2	1	0	2
DS Total	0	0	0	4.50	6	0	0	0	6	4	3	0	5
LC 2004	0	0	0	8.10	6	0	0	0	6.2	10	6	2	3
Tom Gorman													
WS 1952	0	0	0	0.00	1	0	0	0	0.2	1	0	0	0
WS 1953	0	0	0	3.00	1	0	0	0	3	4	1	0	1
WS Total	0	0	0	2.45	2	0	0	0	3.2	5	1	0	1
Rich Gossage													
DS 1981	0	0	3	0.00	3	0	0	0	6.2	3	0	2	8
LC 1978	1	0	1	4.50	2	0	0	0	4	3	2	0	3
LC 1980	0	1	0	54.00	1	0	0	0	0.1	3	2	0	0
LC 1981	0	0	1	0.00	2	0	0	0	2.2	1	0	0	2
LC Total	1	1	2	5.14	5	0	0	0	7	7	4	0	5
WS 1978	1	0	0	0.00	3	0	0	0	6	1	0	1	4
WS 1981	0	0	2	0.00	3	0	0	0	5	2	0	2	5
WS Total	1	0	2	0.00	6	0	0	0	11	3	0	3	9
Bob Grim													
WS 1955	0	1	1	4.15	3	1	0	0	8.2	8	4	5	8
WS 1957	0	1	0	7.71	2	0	0	0	2.1	3	2	0	2
WS Total	0	2	1	4.91	5	1	0	0	11	11	6	5	10
Jason Grimsley													
LC 2000	0	0	0	0.00	2	0	0	0	1	2	0	3	1
WS 1999	0	0	0	0.00	1	0	0	0	2.1	2	0	2	0
Ron Guidry													
DS 1981	0	0	0	5.40	2	2	0	0	8.1	11	5	3	8
LC 1977	1	0	0	3.97	2	2	1	0	11.1	9	5	3	8
LC 1978	1	0	0	1.13	1	1	0	0	8	7	1	1	7
LC 1980	0	1	0	12.00	1	1	0	0	3	5	4	4	2
LC Total	2	1	0	4.03	4	4	1	0	22.1	21	10	8	17
WS 1977	1	0	0	2.00	1	1	1	0	9	4	2	3	7
WS 1978	1	0	0	1.00	1	1	1	0	9	8	1	7	4
WS 1981	1	1	0	1.93	2	2	0	0	14	8	3	4	15
WS Total	3	1	0	1.69	4	4	2	0	32	20	6	14	26

YEAR	W	L	SV	ERA	G	GS	CG	SHO	IP	H	ER	BB	SO
Don Gullett													
LC 1977	0	1	0	18.00	1	1	0	0	2	4	4	2	0
WS 1977	0	1	0	6.39	2	2	0	0	12.2	13	9	7	10
Bump Hadley													
WS 1936	1	0	0	1.13	1	1	0	0	8	10	1	1	2
WS 1937	0	1	0	33.75	1	1	0	0	1.1	6	5	0	0
WS 1939	1	0	0	2.25	1	0	0	0	8	7	2	3	2
WS Total	2	1	0	4.15	3	2	0	0	17.1	23	8	4	4
Steve Hamilton													
WS 1963	0	0	0	0.00	1	0	0	0	1	0	0	0	1
WS 1964	0	0	1	4.50	2	0	0	0	2	3	1	0	2
WS Total	0	0	1	3.00	3	0	0	0	3	3	1	0	3
Chris Hammond													
WS 2003	0	0	0	0.00	1	0	0	0	2	2	0	0	0
Harry Harper													
WS 1921	0	0	0	20.25	1	1	0	0	1.1	3	3	2	1
Felix Heredia													
DS 2003	0	0	0	0.00	1	0	0	0	2	1	0	1	1
DS 2004	0	0	0	54.00	1	0	0	0	0.1	0	2	0	0
DS Total	0	0	0	7.71	2	0	0	0	2.1	1	2	1	1
LC 2003	0	0	0	3.38	5	0	0	0	2.2	0	1	3	3
LC 2004	0	0	0	0.00	3	0	0	0	1.1	1	0	0	1
LC Total	0	0	0	2.25	8	0	0	0	4	1	1	3	4
Orlando Hernandez													
DS 1999	1	0	0	0.00	1	1	0	0	8	2	0	6	4
DS 2000	1	0	0	2.45	2	1	0	0	7.1	5	2	5	5
DS 2001	1	0	0	3.18	1	1	0	0	5.2	8	2	2	5
DS 2002	0	1	0	2.84	2	0	0	0	6.1	5	2	0	7
DS Total	3	1	0	1.98	6	3	0	0	27.1	20	6	13	21
LC 1998	1	0	0	0.00	1	1	0	0	7	3	0	2	6
LC 1999	1	0	0	1.80	2	2	0	0	15	12	3	6	13
LC 2000	2	0	0	4.20	2	2	0	0	15	13	7	8	14
LC 2001	0	1	0	7.20	1	1	0	0	5	5	4	5	7
LC 2004	0	0	0	5.40	1	1	0	0	5	3	3	5	6
LC Total	4	1	0	3.26	7	7	0	0	47	36	17	26	46
WS 1998	1	0	0	1.29	1	1	0	0	7	6	1	3	7
WS 1999	1	0	0	1.29	1	1	0	0	7	1	1	2	10
WS 2000	0	1	0	4.91	1	1	0	0	7.1	9	4	3	12
WS 2001	0	0	0	1.42	1	1	0	0	6.1	4	1	4	5
WS Total	2	1	0	2.28	4	4	0	0	27.2	20	7	12	34
Oral Hildebrand													
WS 1939	0	0	0	0.00	1	1	0	0	4	2	0	0	3
Sterling Hitchcock													
DS 1995	0	0	0	5.40	2	0	0	0	1.2	2	1	2	1
DS 2001	0	0	0	6.00	1	0	0	0	3	5	2	0	2
DS Total	0	0	0	5.79	3	0	0	0	4.2	7	3	2	3
WS 2001	1	0	0	0.00	2	0	0	0	4	1	0	0	6
Bobby Hogue													
WS 1951	0	0	0	0.00	2	0	0	0	2.2	1	0	0	0
Steve Howe													
DS 1995	0	0	0	18.00	2	0	0	0	1	4	2	0	0
Waite Hoyt													
WS 1921	2	1	0	0.00	3	3	3	1	27	18	0	11	18
WS 1922	0	1	0	1.13	2	1	0	0	8	11	1	2	4
WS 1923	0	0	0	15.43	1	1	0	0	2.1	4	4	1	0
WS 1926	1	1	0	1.20	2	2	1	0	15	19	2	1	10
WS 1927	1	0	0	4.91	1	1	0	0	7.1	8	4	1	2
WS 1928	2	0	0	1.50	2	2	2	0	18	14	3	6	14
WS Total	6	3	0	1.62	11	10	6	1	77.2	74	14	22	48
Philip Hughes													
DS 2007	1	0	0	1.59	2	0	0	0	5.2	3	1	0	6
Catfish Hunter													
LC 1976	1	1	0	4.50	2	2	1	0	12	10	6	1	5
LC 1978	0	0	0	4.50	1	1	0	0	6	7	3	3	5
LC Total	1	1	0	4.50	3	3	1	0	18	17	9	4	10
WS 1976	0	1	0	3.12	1	1	1	0	8.2	10	3	4	5
WS 1977	0	1	0	10.38	2	1	0	0	4.1	6	5	0	1
WS 1978	1	1	0	4.15	2	2	0	0	13	13	6	1	5
WS Total	1	3	0	4.85	5	4	1	0	26	29	14	5	11
Hideki Irabu													
LC 1999	0	0	0	13.50	1	0	0	0	4.2	13	7	0	3
Grant Jackson													
LC 1976	0	0	0	8.10	2	0	0	0	3.1	4	3	1	3
WS 1976	0	0	0	4.91	1	0	0	0	3.2	4	2	0	3
Tommy John													
DS 1981	0	1	0	6.43	1	1	0	0	7	8	5	2	0
LC 1980	0	0	0	2.70	1	1	0	0	6.2	8	2	1	3
LC 1981	1	0	0	1.50	1	1	0	0	6	6	1	1	3
LC Total	1	0	0	2.13	2	2	0	0	12.2	14	3	2	6
WS 1981	1	0	0	0.69	3	2	0	0	13	11	1	0	8

YEAR	W	L	SV	ERA	G	GS	CG	SHO	IP	H	ER	BB	SO
RANDY JOHNSON													
DS 2005	0	0	0	6.14	2	1	0	0	7.1	12	5	1	4
DS 2006	0	1	0	7.94	1	1	0	0	5.2	8	5	2	4
DS Total	0	1	0	6.92	3	2	0	0	13	20	10	3	8
SAM JONES													
WS 1922	0	0	0	0.00	2	0	0	0	2	1	0	1	0
WS 1923	0	1	1	0.90	2	1	0	0	10	5	1	2	3
WS 1926	0	0	0	9.00	1	0	0	0	1	2	1	2	1
WS Total	0	1	1	1.38	5	1	0	0	13	8	2	5	4
SCOTT KAMIENIECKI													
DS 1995	0	0	0	7.20	1	1	0	0	5	9	4	4	4
STEVE KARSAY													
DS 2002	1	0	0	6.75	4	0	0	0	2.2	3	2	0	1
JIMMY KEY													
DS 1996	0	0	0	3.60	1	1	0	0	5	5	2	1	3
LC 1996	1	0	0	2.25	1	1	0	0	8	3	2	1	5
WS 1996	1	1	0	3.97	2	2	0	0	11.1	15	5	5	1
JOHNNY KUCKS													
WS 1955	0	0	0	6.00	2	0	0	0	3	4	2	1	1
WS 1956	1	0	0	0.82	3	1	1	1	11	6	1	3	2
WS 1957	0	0	0	0.00	1	0	0	0	0.2	1	0	1	1
WS 1958	0	0	0	2.08	2	0	0	0	4.1	4	1	1	0
WS Total	1	0	0	1.89	8	1	1	1	19	15	4	6	4
BOB KUZAVA													
WS 1951	0	0	1	0.00	1	0	0	0	1	0	0	0	0
WS 1952	0	0	1	0.00	1	0	0	0	2.2	0	0	0	2
WS 1953	0	0	0	13.50	1	0	0	0	0.2	2	1	0	1
WS Total	0	0	2	2.08	3	0	0	0	4.1	2	1	0	3
DAVE LAROCHE													
WS 1981	0	0	0	0.00	1	0	0	0	1	0	0	0	2
DON LARSEN													
WS 1955	0	1	0	11.25	1	1	0	0	4	5	5	2	2
WS 1956	1	0	0	0.00	2	2	1	1	10.2	1	0	4	7
WS 1957	1	1	0	3.72	2	1	0	0	9.2	8	4	5	6
WS 1958	1	0	0	0.96	2	2	0	0	9.1	9	1	6	9
WS Total	3	2	0	2.67	7	6	1	1	33.2	23	10	17	24
AL LEITER													
DS 2005	1	0	0	7.36	4	0	0	0	3.2	2	3	1	2
CORY LIDLE													
DS 2006	0	0	0	20.25	1	0	0	0	1.1	4	3	0	1
JON LIEBER													
DS 2004	0	0	0	4.05	1	1	0	0	6.2	7	3	1	4
LC 2004	1	1	0	3.14	2	2	0	0	14.1	12	5	1	5
PAUL LINDBLAD													
WS 1978	0	0	0	11.57	1	0	0	0	2.1	4	3	0	1
GRAEME LLOYD													
DS 1996	0	0	0	0.00	2	0	0	0	1	1	0	0	0
DS 1997	0	0	0	0.00	2	0	0	0	1.1	0	0	0	1
DS 1998	0	0	0	0.00	1	0	0	0	0.1	0	0	0	0
DS Total	0	0	0	0.00	5	0	0	0	2.2	1	0	0	1
LC 1996	0	0	0	0.00	2	0	0	0	1.2	0	0	0	1
LC 1998	0	0	0	0.00	1	0	0	0	0.2	1	0	0	0
LC Total	0	0	0	0.00	3	0	0	0	2.1	1	0	0	1
WS 1996	1	0	0	0.00	4	0	0	0	2.2	0	0	0	4
WS 1998	0	0	0	0.00	1	0	0	0	0.1	0	0	0	0
WS Total	1	0	0	0.00	5	0	0	0	3	0	0	0	4
ESTEBAN LOAIZA													
DS 2004	0	0	0	0.00	1	0	0	0	2	4	0	0	0
LC 2004	0	1	0	1.42	2	0	0	0	6.1	5	1	3	5
ED LOPAT													
WS 1949	1	0	0	6.35	1	1	0	0	5.2	9	4	1	4
WS 1950	0	0	0	2.25	1	1	0	0	8	9	2	0	5
WS 1951	2	0	0	0.50	2	2	2	0	18	10	1	3	4
WS 1952	0	1	0	4.76	2	2	0	0	11.1	14	6	4	3
WS 1953	1	0	0	2.00	1	1	1	0	9	9	2	4	3
WS Total	4	1	0	2.60	7	7	3	0	52	51	15	12	19
SPARKY LYLE													
LC 1976	0	0	1	0.00	1	0	0	0	1	0	0	1	0
LC 1977	2	0	0	0.96	4	0	0	0	9.1	7	1	0	3
LC 1978	0	0	0	13.50	1	0	0	0	1.1	3	2	0	0
LC Total	2	0	1	2.31	6	0	0	0	11.2	10	3	1	3
WS 1976	0	0	0	0.00	2	0	0	0	2.2	1	0	0	3
WS 1977	1	0	0	1.93	2	0	0	0	4.2	2	1	0	2
WS Total	1	0	0	1.23	4	0	0	0	7.1	3	1	0	5
DUKE MAAS													
WS 1958	0	0	0	81.00	1	0	0	0	0.1	2	3	1	0
WS 1960	0	0	0	4.50	1	0	0	0	2	2	1	0	1
WS Total	0	0	0	15.43	2	0	0	0	2.1	4	4	1	1
PAT MALONE													
WS 1936	0	1	1	1.80	2	0	0	0	5	2	1	1	2

YEAR	W	L	SV	ERA	G	GS	CG	SHO	IP	H	ER	BB	SO
RUDY MAY													
DS 1981	0	0	0	0.00	1	0	0	0	2	1	0	0	1
LC 1980	0	1	0	3.38	1	1	1	0	8	6	3	3	4
LC 1981	0	0	0	8.10	1	1	0	0	3.1	6	3	0	5
LC Total	0	1	0	4.76	2	2	1	0	11.1	12	6	3	9
WS 1981	0	0	0	2.84	3	0	0	0	6.1	5	2	1	5
CARL MAYS													
WS 1921	1	2	0	1.73	3	3	3	1	26	20	5	0	9
WS 1922	0	1	0	4.50	1	1	0	0	8	9	4	2	1
WS Total	1	3	0	2.38	4	4	3	1	34	29	9	2	10
MICKEY MCDERMOTT													
WS 1956	0	0	0	3.00	1	0	0	0	3	2	1	3	3
JIM MCDONALD													
WS 1953	1	0	0	5.87	1	1	0	0	7.2	12	5	0	3
JACK MCDOWELL													
DS 1995	0	2	0	9.00	2	1	0	0	7	8	7	4	6
RAMIRO MENDOZA													
DS 1997	1	1	0	2.45	2	0	0	0	3.2	3	1	0	2
DS 2001	0	0	0	0.00	3	0	0	0	4.1	2	0	1	5
DS 2002	0	0	0	13.50	2	0	0	0	1.1	5	2	0	0
DS Total	1	1	0	2.89	7	0	0	0	9.1	10	3	1	7
LC 1998	0	0	0	0.00	2	0	0	0	4.1	4	0	0	1
LC 1999	0	0	1	0.00	2	0	0	0	2.1	0	0	0	2
LC 2001	0	0	0	1.69	3	0	0	0	5.1	3	1	2	4
LC Total	0	0	1	0.75	7	0	0	0	12	7	1	2	7
WS 1998	1	0	0	9.00	1	0	0	0	1	2	1	0	1
WS 1999	0	0	0	10.80	1	0	0	0	1.2	3	2	1	0
WS 2001	0	0	0	0.00	2	0	0	0	2.2	1	0	0	1
WS Total	1	0	0	5.06	4	0	0	0	5.1	6	3	1	2
PETE MIKKELSEN													
WS 1964	0	1	0	5.79	4	0	0	0	4.2	4	3	2	4
ZACH MONROE													
WS 1958	0	0	0	27.00	1	0	0	0	1	3	3	1	1
WILCY MOORE													
WS 1927	1	0	1	0.84	2	1	1	0	10.2	11	1	2	2
WS 1932	1	0	0	0.00	1	0	0	0	5.1	2	0	0	1
WS Total	2	0	1	0.56	3	1	1	0	16	13	1	2	3
TOM MORGAN													
WS 1951	0	0	0	0.00	1	0	0	0	2	2	0	1	3
WS 1955	0	0	0	4.91	2	0	0	0	3.2	3	2	3	1
WS 1956	0	1	0	9.00	2	0	0	0	4	6	4	4	3
WS Total	0	1	0	5.59	5	0	0	0	9.2	11	6	8	7
JOHNNY MURPHY													
WS 1936	0	0	1	3.38	1	0	0	0	2.2	1	1	1	1
WS 1937	0	0	1	0.00	1	0	0	0	0.1	0	0	0	0
WS 1938	0	0	1	0.00	1	0	0	0	2	2	0	1	1
WS 1939	1	0	0	2.70	1	0	0	0	3.1	5	1	0	2
WS 1941	1	0	0	0.00	2	0	0	0	6	2	0	1	3
WS 1943	0	0	1	0.00	2	0	0	0	2	1	0	1	1
WS Total	2	0	4	1.10	8	0	0	0	16.1	11	2	4	8
MIKE MUSSINA													
DS 2001	1	0	0	0.00	1	1	0	0	7	4	0	1	4
DS 2002	0	0	0	9.00	1	1	0	0	4	6	4	0	2
DS 2003	0	1	0	3.86	1	1	0	0	7	7	3	3	6
DS 2004	0	1	0	2.57	1	1	0	0	7	7	2	1	7
DS 2005	1	1	0	5.40	2	2	0	0	8.1	11	5	1	7
DS 2006	0	1	0	5.14	1	1	0	0	7	8	4	0	5
DS 2007	0	0	0	3.86	1	0	0	0	4.2	4	2	4	3
DS Total	2	4	0	4.00	8	7	0	0	45	47	20	10	34
LC 2001	1	0	0	3.00	1	1	0	0	6	4	2	1	3
LC 2003	0	2	0	4.11	3	2	0	0	15.1	16	7	4	17
LC 2004	1	0	0	4.26	2	2	0	0	12.2	10	6	2	15
LC Total	2	2	0	3.97	6	5	0	0	34	30	15	7	35
WS 2001	0	1	0	4.09	2	2	0	0	11	11	5	4	14
WS 2003	1	0	0	1.29	1	1	0	0	7	7	1	1	9
WS Total	1	1	0	3.00	3	3	0	0	18	18	6	5	23
MIKE MYERS													
DS 2006	0	0	0	\	1	0	0	0	0	1	1	0	0
DENNY NEAGLE													
LC 2000	0	2	0	4.50	2	2	0	0	10	6	5	7	7
WS 2000	0	0	0	3.86	1	1	0	0	4.2	4	2	2	3
JEFF NELSON													
DS 1996	1	0	0	0.00	2	0	0	0	3.2	2	0	2	5
DS 1997	0	0	0	0.00	4	0	0	0	4	4	0	2	0
DS 1998	0	0	0	0.00	2	0	0	0	2.2	2	0	1	2
DS 1999	0	0	0	0.00	3	0	0	0	1.2	1	0	1	3
DS 2000	0	0	0	0.00	2	0	0	0	2	0	0	0	2
DS 2003	0	0	0	+	1	0	0	0	0	0	0	1	0
DS Total	1	0	0	0.00	14	0	0	0	14	9	0	7	12
LC 1996	0	1	0	11.57	2	0	0	0	2.1	5	3	0	2
LC 1998	0	1	0	20.25	3	0	0	0	1.1	3	3	1	3
LC 1999	0	0	0	0.00	2	0	0	0	0.2	0	0	0	0
LC 2000	0	0	0	9.00	3	0	0	0	3	5	3	0	6
LC 2003	0	0	0	6.00	4	0	0	0	3	4	2	0	3

Postseason

YEAR	W	L	SV	ERA	G	GS	CG	SHO	IP	H	ER	BB	SO
LC Total	0	2	0	9.58	14	0	0	0	10.1	17	11	1	14
WS 1996	0	0	0	0.00	3	0	0	0	4.1	1	0	1	5
WS 1998	0	0	0	0.00	3	0	0	0	2.1	2	0	1	4
WS 1999	0	0	0	0.00	4	0	0	0	2.2	2	0	1	3
WS 2000	1	0	0	10.13	3	0	0	0	2.2	5	3	1	1
WS 2003	0	0	0	0.00	3	0	0	0	4	4	0	2	5
WS Total	1	0	0	1.69	16	0	0	0	16	14	3	6	18
Bobo Newsom													
WS 1947	0	1	0	19.29	2	1	0	0	2.1	6	5	2	0
Ross Ohlendorf													
DS 2007	0	0	0	27.00	1	0	0	0	1	4	3	1	0
Joe Ostrowski													
WS 1951	0	0	0	0.00	1	0	0	0	2	1	0	0	1
Joe Page													
WS 1947	1	1	1	4.15	4	0	0	0	13	12	6	2	7
WS 1949	1	0	1	2.00	3	0	0	0	9	6	2	3	8
WS Total	2	1	2	3.27	7	0	0	0	22	18	8	5	15
Monte Pearson													
WS 1936	1	0	0	2.00	1	1	1	0	9	7	2	2	7
WS 1937	1	0	0	1.04	1	1	0	0	8.2	5	1	2	4
WS 1938	1	0	0	1.00	1	1	1	0	9	5	1	2	9
WS 1939	1	0	0	0.00	1	1	1	1	9	2	0	1	8
WS Total	4	0	0	1.01	4	4	3	1	35.2	19	4	7	28
Herb Pennock													
WS 1923	2	0	1	3.63	3	2	1	0	17.1	19	7	1	8
WS 1926	2	0	0	1.23	3	2	2	0	22	13	3	4	8
WS 1927	1	0	0	1.00	1	1	1	0	9	3	1	0	1
WS 1932	0	0	2	2.25	2	0	0	0	4	2	1	1	4
WS Total	5	0	3	2.06	9	5	4	0	52.1	37	12	6	21
Andy Pettitte													
DS 1995	0	0	0	5.14	1	1	0	0	7	9	4	3	0
DS 1996	0	0	0	5.68	1	1	0	0	6.1	4	4	6	3
DS 1997	0	2	0	8.49	2	2	0	0	11.2	15	11	1	5
DS 1998	1	0	0	1.29	1	1	0	0	7	3	1	0	8
DS 1999	1	0	0	1.23	1	1	0	0	7.1	7	1	0	5
DS 2000	1	0	0	3.97	2	2	0	0	11.1	15	5	3	7
DS 2001	0	1	0	1.42	1	1	0	0	6.1	7	1	2	4
DS 2002	0	0	0	12.00	1	1	0	0	3	8	4	0	1
DS 2003	1	0	0	1.29	1	1	0	0	7	4	1	3	10
DS 2007	0	0	0	0.00	1	1	0	0	6.1	7	0	2	5
DS Total	4	3	0	3.93	12	12	0	0	73.1	79	32	20	48
LC 1996	1	0	0	3.60	2	2	0	0	15	10	6	5	7
LC 1998	0	1	0	11.57	1	1	0	0	4.2	8	6	3	1
LC 1999	1	0	0	2.45	1	1	0	0	7.1	8	2	1	5
LC 2000	1	0	0	2.70	1	1	0	0	6.2	9	2	1	2
LC 2001	2	0	0	2.51	2	2	0	0	14.1	11	4	2	8
LC 2003	1	0	0	4.63	2	2	0	0	11.2	17	6	4	10
LC Total	6	1	0	3.92	9	9	0	0	59.2	63	26	16	33
WS 1996	1	1	0	5.91	2	2	0	0	10.2	11	7	4	5
WS 1998	1	0	0	0.00	1	1	0	0	7.1	5	0	3	4
WS 1999	0	0	0	12.27	1	1	0	0	3.2	10	5	1	1
WS 2000	0	0	0	1.98	2	2	0	0	13.2	16	3	4	9
WS 2001	0	2	0	10.00	2	2	0	0	9	12	10	2	9
WS 2003	1	1	0	0.57	2	2	0	0	15.2	12	1	4	14
WS Total	3	4	0	3.90	10	10	0	0	60	66	26	18	42
Bill Piercy													
WS 1921	0	0	0	0.00	1	0	0	0	1	2	0	0	2
George Pipgras													
WS 1927	1	0	0	2.00	1	1	1	0	9	7	2	1	2
WS 1928	1	0	0	2.00	1	1	1	0	9	4	2	4	8
WS 1932	1	0	0	4.50	1	1	0	0	8	9	4	3	1
WS Total	3	0	0	2.77	3	3	2	0	26	20	8	8	11
Scott Proctor													
DS 2005	0	0	0	0.00	2	0	0	0	2	3	0	0	1
DS 2006	0	0	0	2.25	3	0	0	0	4	5	1	1	1
DS Total	0	0	0	1.50	5	0	0	0	6	8	1	1	2
Paul Quantrill													
DS 2004	1	0	0	0.00	2	0	0	0	2	2	0	0	1
LC 2004	0	1	0	5.40	4	0	0	0	3.1	8	2	0	2
Jack Quinn													
WS 1921	0	1	0	9.82	1	0	0	0	3.2	8	4	2	2
Vic Raschi													
WS 1947	0	0	0	6.75	2	0	0	0	1.1	2	1	0	1
WS 1949	1	1	0	4.30	2	2	0	0	14.2	15	7	5	11
WS 1950	1	0	0	0.00	1	1	1	1	9	2	0	1	5
WS 1951	1	1	0	0.87	2	2	0	0	10.1	12	1	8	4
WS 1952	2	0	0	1.59	3	2	1	0	17	12	3	8	18
WS 1953	0	1	0	3.38	1	1	1	0	8	9	3	3	4
WS Total	5	3	0	2.24	11	8	3	1	60.1	52	15	25	43
Hal Reniff													
WS 1963	0	0	0	0.00	3	0	0	0	3	0	0	1	1
WS 1964	0	0	0	0.00	1	0	0	0	0.1	2	0	0	0
WS Total	0	0	0	0.00	4	0	0	0	3.1	2	0	1	1

YEAR	W	L	SV	ERA	G	GS	CG	SHO	IP	H	ER	BB	SO
Rick Reuschel													
DS 1981	0	1	0	3.00	1	1	0	0	6	4	2	1	3
WS 1981	0	0	0	4.91	2	1	0	0	3.2	7	2	3	2
Allie Reynolds													
WS 1947	1	0	0	4.76	2	2	1	0	11.1	15	6	3	6
WS 1949	1	0	1	0.00	2	1	1	1	12.1	2	0	4	14
WS 1950	1	0	1	0.87	2	1	1	0	10.1	7	1	4	7
WS 1951	1	1	0	4.20	2	2	1	0	15	16	7	11	8
WS 1952	2	1	1	1.77	4	2	1	1	20.1	12	4	6	18
WS 1953	1	0	1	6.75	3	1	0	0	8	9	6	4	9
WS Total	7	2	4	2.79	15	9	5	2	77.1	61	24	32	62
Dave Righetti													
DS 1981	2	0	0	1.00	2	1	0	0	9	8	1	3	13
LC 1981	1	0	0	0.00	1	1	0	0	6	4	0	2	4
WS 1981	0	0	0	13.50	1	1	0	0	2	5	3	2	1
Mariano Rivera													
DS 1995	1	0	0	0.00	3	0	0	0	5.1	3	0	1	8
DS 1996	0	0	0	0.00	2	0	0	0	4.2	0	0	1	1
DS 1997	0	0	1	4.50	2	0	0	0	2	2	1	0	1
DS 1998	0	0	2	0.00	3	0	0	0	3.1	1	0	1	2
DS 1999	0	0	2	0.00	2	0	0	0	3	1	0	0	3
DS 2000	0	0	3	0.00	3	0	0	0	5	2	0	0	2
DS 2001	0	0	2	0.00	3	0	0	0	5	4	0	0	4
DS 2002	0	0	1	0.00	1	0	0	0	1	1	0	0	0
DS 2003	0	0	2	0.00	2	0	0	0	4	0	0	0	4
DS 2004	1	0	0	0.00	4	0	0	0	5.2	2	0	0	2
DS 2005	0	0	2	3.00	2	0	0	0	3	1	1	1	2
DS 2006	0	0	0	0.00	1	0	0	0	1	1	0	0	0
DS 2007	0	0	0	0.00	3	0	0	0	4.2	2	0	1	6
DS Total	2	0	15	0.38	31	0	0	0	47.2	20	2	5	35
LC 1996	1	0	0	0.00	2	0	0	0	4	6	0	1	5
LC 1998	0	0	1	0.00	4	0	0	0	5.2	0	0	1	5
LC 1999	1	0	2	0.00	3	0	0	0	4.2	5	0	0	3
LC 2000	0	0	1	1.93	3	0	0	0	4.2	4	1	0	1
LC 2001	1	0	2	1.93	4	0	0	0	4.2	2	1	1	3
LC 2003	1	0	2	1.13	4	0	0	0	8	5	1	0	6
LC 2004	0	0	2	1.29	5	0	0	0	7	6	1	2	6
LC Total	4	0	10	0.93	25	0	0	0	38.2	28	4	5	29
WS 1996	0	0	0	1.59	4	0	0	0	5.2	4	1	3	4
WS 1998	0	0	3	0.00	3	0	0	0	4.1	5	0	0	4
WS 1999	1	0	2	0.00	3	0	0	0	4.2	3	0	1	3
WS 2000	0	0	2	3.00	4	0	0	0	6	4	2	1	7
WS 2001	1	1	1	1.42	4	0	0	0	6.1	6	1	1	7
WS 2003	0	0	1	0.00	2	0	0	0	4	2	0	0	4
WS Total	2	1	9	1.16	20	0	0	0	31	24	4	6	29
Kenny Rogers													
DS 1996	0	0	0	9.00	2	1	0	0	2	5	2	2	1
LC 1996	0	0	0	12.00	1	1	0	0	3	5	4	2	3
WS 1996	0	0	0	22.50	1	1	0	0	2	5	5	2	0
Tom Rogers													
WS 1921	0	0	0	6.75	1	0	0	0	1.1	3	1	0	1
Dutch Ruether													
WS 1926	0	1	0	4.15	1	1	0	0	4.1	7	2	2	1
Red Ruffing													
WS 1932	1	0	0	3.00	1	1	1	0	9	10	3	6	10
WS 1936	0	1	0	5.14	2	2	1	0	14	16	8	5	12
WS 1937	1	0	0	1.00	1	1	1	0	9	7	1	3	8
WS 1938	2	0	0	1.50	2	2	2	0	18	17	3	2	11
WS 1939	1	0	0	1.00	1	1	1	0	9	4	1	1	4
WS 1941	1	0	0	1.00	1	1	1	0	9	6	1	3	5
WS 1942	1	1	0	4.08	2	2	1	0	17.2	14	8	7	11
WS Total	7	2	0	2.63	10	10	8	0	85.2	74	25	27	61
Marius Russo													
WS 1941	1	0	0	1.00	1	1	1	0	9	4	1	2	5
WS 1943	1	0	0	0.00	1	1	1	0	9	7	0	1	2
WS Total	2	0	0	0.50	2	2	2	0	18	11	1	3	7
Johnny Sain													
WS 1951	0	0	0	9.00	1	0	0	0	2	4	2	2	2
WS 1952	0	1	0	3.00	1	0	0	0	6	6	2	3	3
WS 1953	1	0	0	4.76	2	0	0	0	5.2	8	3	1	1
WS Total	1	1	0	4.61	4	0	0	0	13.2	18	7	6	6
Ray Scarborough													
WS 1952	0	0	0	9.00	1	0	0	0	1	1	1	0	1
Art Schallock													
WS 1953	0	0	0	4.50	1	0	0	0	2	2	1	1	1
Bobby Shantz													
WS 1957	0	1	0	4.05	3	1	0	0	6.2	8	3	2	7
WS 1960	0	0	1	4.26	3	0	0	0	6.1	4	3	1	1
WS Total	0	1	1	4.15	6	1	0	0	13	12	6	3	8
Bob Shawkey													
WS 1921	0	1	0	7.00	2	1	0	0	9	13	7	6	5
WS 1922	0	0	0	2.70	1	1	1	0	10	8	3	2	4
WS 1923	1	0	0	3.52	1	1	0	0	7.2	12	3	4	2
WS 1926	0	1	0	5.40	3	1	0	0	10	8	6	2	7
WS Total	1	2	0	4.66	7	4	1	0	36.2	41	19	14	18

YEAR	W	L	SV	ERA	G	GS	CG	SHO	IP	H	ER	BB	SO
Spec Shea													
WS 1947	2	0	0	2.35	3	3	1	0	15.1	10	4	8	10
Rollie Sheldon													
WS 1964	0	0	0	0.00	2	0	0	0	2.2	0	0	2	2
Urban Shocker													
WS 1926	0	1	0	5.87	2	1	0	0	7.2	13	5	0	3
Aaron Small													
DS 2005	0	1	0	6.75	1	0	0	0	2.2	4	2	0	2
Bill Stafford													
WS 1960	0	0	0	1.50	2	0	0	0	6	5	1	1	2
WS 1961	0	0	0	2.70	1	1	0	0	6.2	7	2	2	5
WS 1962	1	0	0	2.00	1	1	1	0	9	4	2	2	5
WS Total	1	0	0	2.08	4	2	1	0	21.2	16	5	5	12
Mike Stanton													
DS 1997	0	0	0	0.00	3	0	0	0	1	1	0	1	3
DS 2000	1	0	0	2.08	3	0	0	0	4.1	5	1	1	3
DS 2001	1	0	0	0.00	3	0	0	0	4.2	3	0	0	1
DS 2002	0	1	0	10.13	3	0	0	0	2.2	6	3	1	1
DS Total	2	1	0	2.04	12	0	0	0	12.2	15	4	3	0
LC 1998	0	0	0	0.00	3	0	0	0	3.2	2	0	1	4
LC 1999	0	0	0	0.00	3	0	0	0	0.1	1	0	1	0
LC 2001	0	0	0	27.00	2	0	0	0	1	1	3	2	0
LC Total	0	0	0	5.40	8	0	0	0	5	4	3	4	4
WS 1998	0	0	0	27.00	1	0	0	0	0.2	3	2	0	1
WS 1999	0	0	0	0.00	1	0	0	0	0.1	0	0	0	1
WS 2000	2	0	0	0.00	4	0	0	0	4.1	0	0	0	7
WS 2001	0	0	0	3.18	5	0	0	0	5.2	3	2	1	3
WS Total	2	0	0	3.27	11	0	0	0	11	6	4	1	12
Mel Stottlemyre Sr.													
WS 1964	1	1	0	3.15	3	3	1	0	20	18	7	6	12
Tom Sturdivant													
WS 1955	0	0	0	6.00	2	0	0	0	3	5	2	2	0
WS 1956	1	0	0	2.79	2	1	1	0	9.2	8	3	8	9
WS 1957	0	0	0	6.00	2	1	0	0	6	6	4	1	2
WS Total	1	0	0	4.34	6	2	1	0	18.2	19	9	11	11
Tanyon Sturtze													
DS 2004	0	0	0	6.75	2	0	0	0	2.2	4	2	3	4
DS 2005	0	0	0	13.50	2	0	0	0	0.2	1	1	0	0
DS Total	0	0	0	8.10	4	0	0	0	3.1	5	3	3	4
LC 2004	0	0	0	2.70	4	0	0	0	3.1	2	1	2	2
Steve Sundra													
WS 1939	0	0	0	0.00	1	0	0	0	2.2	4	0	1	2
Ralph Terry													
WS 1960	0	2	0	5.40	2	1	0	0	6.2	7	4	1	5
WS 1961	0	1	0	4.82	2	2	0	0	9.1	12	5	2	7
WS 1962	2	1	0	1.80	3	3	2	1	25	17	5	2	16
WS 1963	0	0	0	3.00	1	0	0	0	3	3	1	1	0
WS 1964	0	0	0	0.00	1	0	0	0	2	2	0	0	3
WS Total	2	4	0	2.93	9	6	2	1	46	41	15	6	31
Myles Thomas													
WS 1926	0	0	0	3.00	2	0	0	0	3	3	1	0	0
Dick Tidrow													
LC 1976	1	0	0	3.68	3	0	0	0	7.1	6	3	4	0
LC 1977	0	0	0	3.86	2	0	0	0	7	6	3	3	3
LC 1978	0	0	0	4.76	1	0	0	0	5.2	8	3	2	1
LC Total	1	0	0	4.05	6	0	0	0	20	20	9	9	4
WS 1976	0	0	0	7.71	2	0	0	0	2.1	5	2	1	1
WS 1977	0	0	0	4.91	2	0	0	0	3.2	5	2	0	1
WS 1978	0	0	0	1.93	2	0	0	0	4.2	4	1	0	5
WS Total	0	0	0	4.22	6	0	0	0	10.2	14	5	1	7
Mike Torrez													
LC 1977	0	1	0	4.09	2	1	0	0	11	11	5	5	5
WS 1977	2	0	0	2.50	2	2	2	0	18	16	5	5	15
Bob Turley													
WS 1955	0	1	0	8.44	3	1	0	0	5.1	7	5	4	7
WS 1956	0	1	0	0.82	3	1	1	0	11	4	1	8	14
WS 1957	1	0	0	2.31	3	2	1	0	11.2	7	3	6	12
WS 1958	2	1	1	2.76	4	2	1	1	16.1	10	5	7	13
WS 1960	1	0	0	4.82	2	2	0	0	9.1	15	5	4	0
WS Total	4	3	1	3.19	15	8	3	1	53.2	43	19	29	46
Jim Turner													
WS 1942	0	0	0	0.00	1	0	0	0	1	0	0	1	0
Tom Underwood													
LC 1980	0	0	0	0.00	2	0	0	0	3	3	0	0	3
Javier Vazquez													
DS 2004	0	0	0	9.00	1	1	0	0	5	7	5	2	6
LC 2004	1	0	0	9.95	2	0	0	0	6.1	9	7	7	6
Jose Veras													
DS 2007	0	0	0	0.00	2	0	0	0	0.2	1	0	1	1
Ron Villone													
DS 2006	0	0	0	0.00	1	0	0	0	1	1	0	1	1
DS 2007	0	0	0	0.00	1	0	0	0	0.1	0	0	0	0
DS Total	0	0	0	0.00	2	0	0	0	1.1	1	0	1	1
Luis Vizcaino													
DS 2007	0	1	0	13.50	1	0	0	0	0.2	2	1	2	0
Chien-Ming Wang													
DS 2005	0	1	0	1.35	1	1	0	0	6.2	6	1	0	1
DS 2006	1	0	0	4.05	1	1	0	0	6.2	8	3	1	4
DS 2007	0	2	0	19.06	2	2	0	0	5.2	14	12	4	2
DS Total	1	3	0	7.58	4	4	0	0	19	28	16	5	7
Allen Watson													
LC 1999	0	0	0	0.00	3	0	0	0	1	2	0	2	1
Dave Weathers													
DS 1996	1	0	0	0.00	2	0	0	0	5	1	0	0	5
LC 1996	1	0	0	0.00	2	0	0	0	3	3	0	0	0
WS 1996	0	0	0	3.00	3	0	0	0	3	2	1	3	3
Jeff Weaver													
DS 2002	0	0	0	6.75	2	0	0	0	2.2	4	2	3	1
WS 2003	0	1	0	9.00	1	0	0	0	1	1	1	0	0
David Wells													
DS 1997	1	0	0	1.00	1	1	1	0	9	5	1	0	1
DS 1998	1	0	0	0.00	1	1	0	0	8	5	0	1	9
DS 2002	0	1	0	15.43	1	1	0	0	4.2	10	8	0	0
DS 2003	1	0	0	1.17	1	1	0	0	7.2	8	1	0	5
DS Total	3	1	0	3.07	4	4	1	0	29.1	28	10	1	15
LC 1998	2	0	0	2.87	2	2	0	0	15.2	12	5	2	18
LC 2003	1	0	0	2.35	2	1	0	0	7.2	5	2	2	5
LC Total	3	0	0	2.70	4	3	0	0	23.1	17	7	4	23
WS 1998	1	0	0	6.43	1	1	0	0	7	7	5	2	4
WS 2003	0	1	0	3.38	2	2	0	0	8	6	3	2	1
WS Total	1	1	0	4.80	3	3	0	0	15	13	8	4	5
Butch Wensloff													
WS 1947	0	0	0	0.00	1	0	0	0	2	0	0	0	0
John Wetteland													
DS 1995	0	1	0	14.54	3	0	0	0	4.1	8	7	2	5
DS 1996	0	0	2	0.00	3	0	0	0	4	2	0	4	4
DS Total	0	1	2	7.56	6	0	0	0	8.1	10	7	6	9
LC 1996	0	0	1	4.50	4	0	0	0	4	2	2	1	5
WS 1996	0	0	4	2.08	5	0	0	0	4.1	4	1	1	6
Gabe White													
DS 2003	0	0	0	0.00	1	0	0	0	1.1	1	0	0	1
LC 2003	0	0	0	4.50	2	0	0	0	2	4	1	0	1
Kemp Wicker													
WS 1937	0	0	0	0.00	1	0	0	0	1	0	0	0	0
Bob Wickman													
DS 1995	0	0	0	0.00	3	0	0	0	3	5	0	0	3
Stan Williams													
WS 1963	0	0	0	0.00	1	0	0	0	3	1	0	0	5
Jay Witasick													
DS 2001	0	0	0	13.50	1	0	0	0	0.2	1	1	1	0
LC 2001	0	0	0	9.00	1	0	0	0	3	6	3	0	2
WS 2001	0	0	0	54.00	1	0	0	0	1.1	10	8	0	4

World Series Leaders

MOST GAMES PLAYED

1	Yogi Berra	75
2	Mickey Mantle	65
3	Hank Bauer	53
	Gil McDougald	53
5	Phil Rizzuto	52
6	Joe DiMaggio	51
7	Elston Howard	47
8	Bill Dickey	38
9	Tony Kubek	37
10	Joe Collins	36
	Bobby Richardson	36
	Babe Ruth	36
13	Bill Skowron	35
14	Lou Gehrig	34
	Bob Meusel	34
16	Derek Jeter	32
	Bernie Williams	32
18	Tony Lazzeri	30
19	Frankie Crosetti	29
20	Roger Maris	28
	Billy Martin	28
	Red Rolfe	28

MOST AT BATS

Rank	Player	AB
1	Yogi Berra	259
2	Mickey Mantle	230
3	Joe DiMaggio	199
4	Gil McDougald	190
5	Hank Bauer	188
6	Phil Rizzuto	183
7	Elston Howard	153
8	Tony Kubek	146
9	Bill Dickey	145
10	Bobby Richardson	131
11	Derek Jeter	129
	Bob Meusel	129
13	Bill Skowron	120
	Bernie Williams	120
15	Lou Gehrig	119
16	Babe Ruth	118
17	Red Rolfe	116
18	Frankie Crosetti	115
19	Roger Maris	107
20	Tony Lazzeri	105

MOST RUNS

1	Mickey Mantle	42
2	Yogi Berra	41
3	Babe Ruth	37
4	Lou Gehrig	30
5	Joe DiMaggio	27
	Derek Jeter	27
7	Elston Howard	25
8	Gil McDougald	23
9	Hank Bauer	21
	Phil Rizzuto	21
	Gene Woodling	21
12	Bill Dickey	19
13	Charlie Keller	18
	Roger Maris	18
15	Earle Combs	17
	Red Rolfe	17
	Bill Skowron	17
18	Frankie Crosetti	16
	Tony Kubek	16
	Tony Lazzeri	16
	Bobby Richardson	16
	Bernie Williams	16

MOST HITS

Rank	Player	H
1	Yogi Berra	71
2	Mickey Mantle	59
3	Joe DiMaggio	54
4	Hank Bauer	46
5	Gil McDougald	45
	Phil Rizzuto	45
7	Lou Gehrig	43
8	Babe Ruth	41
9	Elston Howard	40
	Bobby Richardson	40
11	Derek Jeter	39
12	Bill Dickey	37
13	Tony Kubek	35
14	Bill Skowron	34
15	Billy Martin	33
	Red Rolfe	33
17	Bob Meusel	29
18	Tony Lazzeri	28
19	Gene Woodling	27
20	Thurman Munson	25
	Bernie Williams	25

MOST DOUBLES

Rank	Player	2B
1	Yogi Berra	10
2	Lou Gehrig	8
3	Elston Howard	7
4	Clete Boyer	6
	Jerry Coleman	6
	Joe DiMaggio	6
	Derek Jeter	6
	Mickey Mantle	6
	Bob Meusel	6
	Paul O'Neill	6
	Bobby Richardson	6
12	Bobby Brown	5
	Frankie Crosetti	5
	Joe Gordon	5
	Thurman Munson	5
	Babe Ruth	5
	Gene Woodling	5
18	Johnny Blanchard	4
	Joe Dugan	4
	Tommy Henrich	4
	Ricky Ledee	4
	Gil McDougald	4
	Jorge Posada	4
	Red Rolfe	4
	Bill Skowron	4

MOST TRIPLES

1	Billy Johnson	4
2	Hank Bauer	3
	Bobby Brown	3
	Lou Gehrig	3
	Billy Martin	3
	Bob Meusel	3
7	Charlie Keller	2
	Mickey Mantle	2
	Paul O'Neill	2
	Bobby Richardson	2
	Gene Woodling	2
12	Clete Boyer	1
	Andy Carey	1
	Frankie Crosetti	1
	Bill Dickey	1
	Joe Dugan	1
	Joe Girardi	1
	Joe Gordon	1
	Elston Howard	1
	Derek Jeter	1
	Tony Lazzeri	1
	Johnny Lindell	1
	Hector Lopez	1
	Elliott Maddox	1
	Gil McDougald	1
	Willie Randolph	1
	Red Rolfe	1
	Babe Ruth	1
	Wally Schang	1
	George Selkirk	1

MOST HOME RUNS

Rank	Player	HR
1	Mickey Mantle	18
2	Babe Ruth	15
3	Yogi Berra	12
4	Lou Gehrig	10
5	Joe DiMaggio	8
	Reggie Jackson	8
7	Hank Bauer	7
	Gil McDougald	7
	Bill Skowron	7
10	Bill Dickey	5
	Elston Howard	5
	Charlie Keller	5
	Roger Maris	5
	Billy Martin	5
	Bernie Williams	5
16	Scott Brosius	4
	Joe Collins	4
	Tommy Henrich	4
	Tony Lazzeri	4
	Tom Tresh	4

MOST RBIS

Rank	Player	RBI
1	Mickey Mantle	40
2	Yogi Berra	39
3	Lou Gehrig	35
4	Joe DiMaggio	30
	Babe Ruth	30
6	Bill Skowron	26
7	Hank Bauer	24
	Bill Dickey	24
	Gil McDougald	24
10	Tony Lazzeri	19
	Billy Martin	19
12	Elston Howard	18
	Charlie Keller	18
14	Reggie Jackson	17
	Bob Meusel	17
16	Bobby Richardson	15
17	Joe Gordon	14
	Tino Martinez	14
	Bernie Williams	14
20	Scott Brosius	13
	Tom Tresh	13

MOST WALKS

Rank	Player	BB
1	Mickey Mantle	43
2	Babe Ruth	33
3	Yogi Berra	32
4	Phil Rizzuto	30
5	Lou Gehrig	26
6	Gil McDougald	20
	Bernie Williams	20
8	Joe DiMaggio	19
	Gene Woodling	19
10	Bill Dickey	15
	Jorge Posada	15
12	Joe Collins	14
	Frankie Crosetti	14
14	Derek Jeter	12
	Tony Lazzeri	12
	Roger Maris	12
	Bob Meusel	12
	Willie Randolph	12
19	Joe Gordon	11
	Elston Howard	11
	Tino Martinez	11
	Paul O'Neill	11
	George Selkirk	11

MOST STRIKEOUTS

Rank	Player	SO
1	Mickey Mantle	54
2	Elston Howard	35
3	Derek Jeter	33
4	Gil McDougald	29
5	Babe Ruth	26
	Bernie Williams	26
7	Hank Bauer	25
8	Bob Meusel	24
	Jorge Posada	24
10	Joe DiMaggio	23
	Tony Kubek	23
	Bill Skowron	23
13	Joe Collins	22
14	Frankie Crosetti	20
15	Scott Brosius	19
16	Tony Lazzeri	18
17	Yogi Berra	17
	Lou Gehrig	17
	Roger Maris	17
	Tino Martinez	17
	Tom Tresh	17

MOST STOLEN BASES

Rank	Player	SB
1	Phil Rizzuto	10
2	Bob Meusel	5
3	Derek Jeter	4
	Babe Ruth	4
5	Mickey Mantle	3
	Mickey Rivers	3
7	Chuck Knoblauch	2
	Tony Lazzeri	2
	Gil McDougald	2
	Mike McNally	2
	Lou Piniella	2
	Wally Pipp	2
	Bobby Richardson	2
	Tom Tresh	2
	Roy White	2
	Bernie Williams	2
17	Hank Bauer	1
	Clete Boyer	1
	Joe Collins	1
	Frankie Crosetti	1
	Roy Cullenbine	1
	Bill Dickey	1
	Mariano Duncan	1
	Joe Gordon	1
	Elston Howard	1
	Billy Johnson	1
	Charlie Keller	1
	Jim Leyritz	1
	Billy Martin	1
	Jerry Mumphrey	1

HIGHEST AVERAGE (50 AT-BATS MINIMUM)

Rank	Player	AVG
1	Reggie Jackson	.400
2	Thurman Munson	.373
3	Lou Gehrig	.361
4	Earle Combs	.350
5	Babe Ruth	.348
6	Billy Martin	.333
7	Lou Piniella	.319
8	Gene Woodling	.318
9	Scott Brosius	.314
10	Charlie Keller	.306
11	Bobby Richardson	.305
12	Derek Jeter	.302
13	Paul O'Neill	.287
14	Aaron Ward	.286
15	Red Rolfe	.285
16	Bill Skowron	.283
17	Tom Tresh	.277
18	Jerry Coleman	.275
19	Chris Chambliss	.275
20	Yogi Berra	.274

HIGHEST SLUGGING AVERAGE (50 AT-BATS MINIMUM)

Rank	Player	SLG
1	Reggie Jackson	.891
2	Babe Ruth	.788
3	Lou Gehrig	.731
4	Charlie Keller	.611
5	Billy Martin	.566
6	Mickey Mantle	.535
7	Gene Woodling	.529
8	Scott Brosius	.529
9	Bill Skowron	.508
10	Tom Tresh	.508
11	Thurman Munson	.493
12	Joe Gordon	.457
13	Tommy Henrich	.452
14	Yogi Berra	.452
15	Earle Combs	.450
16	Derek Jeter	.434
17	Tony Lazzeri	.429
	Aaron Ward	.429
19	Joe DiMaggio	.422
20	Elston Howard	.418

HIGHEST ON-BASE PERCENTAGE (50 AT-BATS MINIMUM)

Rank	Player	OBP
1	Reggie Jackson	.500
2	Babe Ruth	.493
3	Lou Gehrig	.477
4	Earle Combs	.444
5	Gene Woodling	.442
6	Thurman Munson	.417
7	Derek Jeter	.375
8	Paul O'Neill	.374
	Mickey Mantle	.374
10	Billy Martin	.371
11	Charlie Keller	.367
	George Selkirk	.367
13	Yogi Berra	.359
14	Phil Rizzuto	.355
15	Tino Martinez	.355
16	Tom Tresh	.351
17	Joe Gordon	.348
18	Tony Lazzeri	.339
19	Wally Schang	.338
20	Aaron Ward	.338

HIGHEST OPS (50 AT-BATS MINIMUM)

Rank	Player	OPS
1	Reggie Jackson	1.391
2	Babe Ruth	1.282
3	Lou Gehrig	1.208
4	Charlie Keller	.978
5	Gene Woodling	.972
6	Billy Martin	.937
7	Thurman Munson	.909
8	Mickey Mantle	.908
9	Earle Combs	.894
10	Scott Brosius	.862
11	Tom Tresh	.859
12	Bill Skowron	.823
13	Yogi Berra	.811
14	Derek Jeter	.809
15	Joe Gordon	.805
16	Paul O'Neill	.786
17	Tommy Henrich	.786
18	George Selkirk	.779
19	Tony Lazzeri	.767
20	Aaron Ward	.767

MOST WINS

Rank	Player	W
1	Whitey Ford	10
2	Allie Reynolds	7
	Red Ruffing	7
4	Lefty Gomez	6
	Waite Hoyt	6
6	Herb Pennock	5
	Vic Raschi	5
8	Ed Lopat	4
	Monte Pearson	4
	Bob Turley	4
11	Roger Clemens	3
	Ron Guidry	3
	Don Larsen	3
	Andy Pettitte	3
	George Pipgras	3
16	Jim Bouton	2
	Spud Chandler	2
	David Cone	2
	Bump Hadley	2
	Orlando Hernandez	2
	Wilcy Moore	2
	Johnny Murphy	2
	Joe Page	2
	Mariano Rivera	2
	Marius Russo	2
	Spec Shea	2
	Mike Stanton	2
	Ralph Terry	2
	Mike Torrez	2

MOST SAVES

1	Mariano Rivera	9
2	Johnny Murphy	4
	Allie Reynolds	4
	John Wetteland	4
5	Herb Pennock	3
6	Rich Gossage	2
	Bob Kuzava	2
	Joe Page	2
9	Spud Chandler	1
	Jim Coates	1
	Ryne Duren	1
	Bob Grim	1
	Steve Hamilton	1
	Sam Jones	1
	Pat Malone	1
	Wilcy Moore	1
	Bobby Shantz	1
	Bob Turley	1

MOST INNINGS

Rank	Player	IP
1	Whitey Ford	146.0
2	Red Ruffing	85.2
3	Waite Hoyt	77.2
4	Allie Reynolds	77.1
5	Vic Raschi	60.1
6	Andy Pettitte	60.0
7	Bob Turley	53.2
8	Herb Pennock	52.1
9	Ed Lopat	52.0
10	Lefty Gomez	50.1
11	Ralph Terry	46.0
12	Bob Shawkey	36.2
13	Roger Clemens	36.0
14	Monte Pearson	35.2
15	Carl Mays	34.0
16	Don Larsen	33.2
17	Spud Chandler	33.1
18	Ron Guidry	32.0
19	Joe Bush	31.2
20	Mariano Rivera	31.0

MOST STRIKEOUTS

Rank	Player	SO
1	Whitey Ford	94
2	Allie Reynolds	62
3	Red Ruffing	61
4	Waite Hoyt	48
5	Bob Turley	46
6	Vic Raschi	43
7	Andy Pettitte	42
8	Roger Clemens	37
9	Orlando Hernandez	34
10	Lefty Gomez	31
	Ralph Terry	31
12	Mariano Rivera	29
13	Monte Pearson	28
14	Ron Guidry	26
15	Don Larsen	24
16	Mike Mussina	23
17	Herb Pennock	21
18	Ryne Duren	19
	Ed Lopat	19
20	Jeff Nelson	18
	Bob Shawkey	18

BEST ERA (30 INNINGS MINIMUM)

1	Monte Pearson	1.01
2	Mariano Rivera	1.16
3	Roger Clemens	1.50
4	Spud Chandler	1.62
5	Waite Hoyt	1.62
6	Ron Guidry	1.69
7	Herb Pennock	2.06
8	Vic Raschi	2.24
9	Carl Mays	2.38
10	Ed Lopat	2.60
11	Red Ruffing	2.63
12	Don Larsen	2.67
13	Whitey Ford	2.71
14	Allie Reynolds	2.79
15	Joe Bush	2.84
16	Lefty Gomez	2.86
17	Ralph Terry	2.93
18	Bob Turley	3.19
19	Andy Pettitte	3.90
20	Bob Shawkey	4.66

Postseason Leaders (Through 2007)

MOST GAMES PLAYED

1	Derek Jeter	123
2	Bernie Williams	121
3	Jorge Posada	96
4	Tino Martinez	81
5	Paul O'Neill	76
6	Yogi Berra	75
7	Mickey Mantle	65
8	Scott Brosius	58
9	Chuck Knoblauch	54
10	Hank Bauer	53
	Gil McDougald	53
12	Phil Rizzuto	52
13	Joe DiMaggio	51
14	Elston Howard	47
15	Lou Piniella	44
16	Graig Nettles	43
17	Hideki Matsui	41
18	Bill Dickey	38
	Alfonso Soriano	38
20	Tony Kubek	37
	Willie Randolph	37

MOST AT BATS

1	Derek Jeter	495
2	Bernie Williams	465
3	Jorge Posada	322
4	Tino Martinez	287
5	Paul O'Neill	270
6	Yogi Berra	259
7	Mickey Mantle	230
8	Joe DiMaggio	199
9	Chuck Knoblauch	198
10	Scott Brosius	196
11	Gil McDougald	190
12	Hank Bauer	188
13	Phil Rizzuto	183
14	Hideki Matsui	162
15	Graig Nettles	155
16	Elston Howard	153
17	Tony Kubek	146
	Alfonso Soriano	146
19	Bill Dickey	145
20	Lou Piniella	141

MOST RUNS

1	Derek Jeter	85
2	Bernie Williams	83
3	Mickey Mantle	42
4	Yogi Berra	41
	Jorge Posada	41
6	Babe Ruth	37
7	Tino Martinez	36
	Paul O'Neill	36
9	Lou Gehrig	30
10	Joe DiMaggio	27
	Reggie Jackson	27
	Hideki Matsui	27
13	Elston Howard	25
14	Chuck Knoblauch	23
	Gil McDougald	23
16	Hank Bauer	21
	Phil Rizzuto	21
	Gene Woodling	21
19	Roy White	20
20	Scott Brosius	19
	Bill Dickey	19
	Thurman Munson	19

MOST HITS

1	Derek Jeter	153
2	Bernie Williams	128
3	Paul O'Neill	76
	Jorge Posada	76
5	Yogi Berra	71
6	Tino Martinez	69
7	Mickey Mantle	59
8	Joe DiMaggio	54
9	Hideki Matsui	49
10	Scott Brosius	48
	Chuck Knoblauch	48
12	Hank Bauer	46
	Thurman Munson	46
14	Gil McDougald	45
	Phil Rizzuto	45
16	Lou Gehrig	43
	Lou Piniella	43
18	Babe Ruth	41
19	Elston Howard	40
	Bobby Richardson	40

MOST DOUBLES

1	Bernie Williams	29
2	Derek Jeter	22
3	Jorge Posada	19
4	Tino Martinez	14
	Paul O'Neill	14
6	Hideki Matsui	13
7	Yogi Berra	10
8	Thurman Munson	9
9	Scott Brosius	8
	Lou Gehrig	8
11	Elston Howard	7
	Chuck Knoblauch	7
	Lou Piniella	7
14	Clete Boyer	6
	Jerry Coleman	6
	Joe DiMaggio	6
	Jason Giambi	6
	Ricky Ledee	6
	Mickey Mantle	6
	Bob Meusel	6
	Willie Randolph	6
	Bobby Richardson	6
	Alex Rodriguez	6
	Roy White	6

MOST TRIPLES

1	Billy Johnson	4
2	Hank Bauer	3
	Bobby Brown	3
	Lou Gehrig	3
	Derek Jeter	3
	Billy Martin	3
	Bob Meusel	3
8	Joe Girardi	2
	Charlie Keller	2
	Mickey Mantle	2
	Paul O'Neill	2
	Bobby Richardson	2
	Ruben Sierra	2
	Gene Woodling	2
15	Clete Boyer	1
	Scott Brosius	1
	Andy Carey	1
	Chris Chambliss	1
	Frankie Crosetti	1
	Bill Dickey	1
	Joe Dugan	1
	Joe Gordon	1
	Elston Howard	1
	David Justice	1
	Tony Lazzeri	1
	Johnny Lindell	1
	Hector Lopez	1
	Hideki Matsui	1
	Gil McDougald	1
	Graig Nettles	1

MOST HOME RUNS

1	Bernie Williams	22
2	Mickey Mantle	18
3	Derek Jeter	17
4	Babe Ruth	15
5	Yogi Berra	12
	Reggie Jackson	12
7	Lou Gehrig	10
	Paul O'Neill	10
9	Jorge Posada	9
10	Scott Brosius	8
	Joe DiMaggio	8
	Tino Martinez	8
13	Hank Bauer	7
	Gil McDougald	7
	Bill Skowron	7
16	Jason Giambi	6
	Hideki Matsui	6
18	Bill Dickey	5
	Elston Howard	5
	Charlie Keller	5
	Roger Maris	5
	Billy Martin	5
	Graig Nettles	5
	Darryl Strawberry	5

MOST RBIS

1	Bernie Williams	80
2	Derek Jeter	49
3	Mickey Mantle	40
4	Yogi Berra	39
5	Lou Gehrig	35
6	Paul O'Neill	34
7	Tino Martinez	32
8	Jorge Posada	31
9	Scott Brosius	30
	Joe DiMaggio	30
	Babe Ruth	30
12	Reggie Jackson	29
13	Hideki Matsui	26
	Bill Skowron	26
15	Hank Bauer	24
	Bill Dickey	24
	Gil McDougald	24
18	Graig Nettles	23
19	Thurman Munson	22
20	Tony Lazzeri	19
	Billy Martin	19
	Lou Piniella	19

MOST WALKS

1	Bernie Williams	71
2	Jorge Posada	57
3	Derek Jeter	51
4	Mickey Mantle	43
5	Babe Ruth	33
6	Yogi Berra	32
	Paul O'Neill	32
8	Tino Martinez	31
9	Phil Rizzuto	30
10	Lou Gehrig	26
11	Chuck Knoblauch	20
	Gil McDougald	20
13	Joe DiMaggio	19
	Jason Giambi	19
	Gene Woodling	19
16	Hideki Matsui	18
	Willie Randolph	18
18	Reggie Jackson	16
19	Bill Dickey	15
20	Joe Collins	14
	Frankie Crosetti	14
	David Justice	14
	Alex Rodriguez	14
	Roy White	14

MOST STRIKEOUTS

1	Derek Jeter	96
2	Bernie Williams	85
3	Jorge Posada	77
4	Tino Martinez	59
5	Mickey Mantle	54
6	Scott Brosius	46
7	Alfonso Soriano	45
8	Paul O'Neill	38
9	Elston Howard	35
10	Reggie Jackson	29
	Gil McDougald	29
12	David Justice	28
13	Chuck Knoblauch	26
	Babe Ruth	26
15	Hank Bauer	25
	Jason Giambi	25
17	Bob Meusel	24
18	Joe DiMaggio	23
	Tony Kubek	23
	Hideki Matsui	23
	Bill Skowron	23
	Shane Spencer	23

MOST STOLEN BASES

1	Derek Jeter	16
2	Phil Rizzuto	10
	Alfonso Soriano	10
4	Bernie Williams	8
5	Chuck Knoblauch	5
	Bob Meusel	5
7	Mickey Rivers	4
	Babe Ruth	4
9	Mickey Mantle	3
	Paul O'Neill	3
	Alex Rodriguez	3
	Roy White	3
13	Aaron Boone	2
	Chris Chambliss	2
	Chad Curtis	2
	Reggie Jackson	2
	Tony Lazzeri	2
	Tino Martinez	2
	Gil McDougald	2
	Jerry Mumphrey	2
	Lou Piniella	2
	Wally Pipp	2
	Jorge Posada	2
	Tim Raines	2
	Willie Randolph	2
	Bobby Richardson	2
	Tom Tresh	2
	Dave Winfield	2

HIGHEST AVERAGE (50 AT-BATS MINIMUM)

1	Bob Watson	.371
2	Lou Gehrig	.361
3	Thurman Munson	.357
4	Earle Combs	.350
5	Babe Ruth	.348
6	Billy Martin	.333
7	Reggie Jackson	.328
8	Larry Milbourne	.327
9	Gene Woodling	.318
10	Derek Jeter	.309
11	Mickey Rivers	.308
12	Chris Chambliss	.308
13	Charlie Keller	.306
14	Bobby Richardson	.305
15	Lou Piniella	.305
16	Hideki Matsui	.303
17	Aaron Ward	.286
18	Red Rolfe	.285
19	Bill Skowron	.283
	Cecil Fielder	.283

HIGHEST SLUGGING AVERAGE (50 AT-BATS MINIMUM)

1	Babe Ruth	.788
2	Lou Gehrig	.731
3	Reggie Jackson	.672
4	Charlie Keller	.611
5	Billy Martin	.566
6	Bob Watson	.564
7	Darryl Strawberry	.560
8	Mickey Mantle	.535
9	Gene Woodling	.529
10	Ruben Sierra	.522
11	Jason Giambi	.510
12	Bill Skowron	.508
13	Tom Tresh	.508
14	Hideki Matsui	.506
15	Thurman Munson	.496
16	Bernie Williams	.480
17	Derek Jeter	.469
18	Cecil Fielder	.467
19	Paul O'Neill	.459
20	Joe Gordon	.457

HIGHEST ON-BASE PERCENTAGE (50 AT-BATS MINIMUM)

1	Babe Ruth	.493
2	Lou Gehrig	.477
3	Earle Combs	.444
4	Gene Woodling	.442
5	Reggie Jackson	.417
6	Jason Giambi	.403
7	Bob Watson	.403
8	Roy White	.387
9	Thurman Munson	.378
10	Derek Jeter	.377
11	Larry Milbourne	.375
12	Mickey Mantle	.374
13	Alex Rodriguez	.372
14	Hideki Matsui	.372
15	Billy Martin	.371
16	Bernie Williams	.371
17	Charlie Keller	.367
	George Selkirk	.367
19	Darryl Strawberry	.367
20	Yogi Berra	.359

HIGHEST OPS (50 AT-BATS MINIMUM)

1	Babe Ruth	1.282
2	Lou Gehrig	1.208
3	Reggie Jackson	1.089
4	Charlie Keller	.978
5	Gene Woodling	.972
6	Bob Watson	.967
7	Billy Martin	.937
8	Darryl Strawberry	.927
9	Jason Giambi	.913
10	Mickey Mantle	.908
11	Earle Combs	.894
12	Hideki Matsui	.878
13	Thurman Munson	.874
14	Tom Tresh	.859
15	Bernie Williams	.850
16	Derek Jeter	.845
17	Ruben Sierra	.839
18	Cecil Fielder	.825
19	Bill Skowron	.823
20	Roy White	.818

MOST WINS

1	Andy Pettitte	13
2	Whitey Ford	10
3	Orlando Hernandez	9
4	Mariano Rivera	8
5	Roger Clemens	7
	Allie Reynolds	7
	Red Ruffing	7
	David Wells	7
9	David Cone	6
	Lefty Gomez	6
	Waite Hoyt	6
12	Ron Guidry	5
	Mike Mussina	5
	Herb Pennock	5
	Vic Raschi	5
16	Ed Lopat	4
	Monte Pearson	4
	Mike Stanton	4
	Bob Turley	4
20	Don Larsen	3
	Sparky Lyle	3
	George Pipgras	3
	Dave Righetti	3

MOST SAVES

1	Mariano Rivera	34
2	Rich Gossage	7
	John Wetteland	7
4	Johnny Murphy	4
	Allie Reynolds	4
6	Herb Pennock	3
7	Joe Page	2
8	Spud Chandler	1
	Sparky Lyle	1
	Ramiro Mendoza	1
	Wilcy Moore	1
	Bob Turley	1

MOST INNINGS

1	Andy Pettitte	193.0
2	Whitey Ford	146.0
3	Mariano Rivera	117.1
4	Roger Clemens	102.1
5	Orlando Hernandez	102.0
6	Mike Mussina	97.0
7	Red Ruffing	85.2
8	Waite Hoyt	77.2
9	Allie Reynolds	77.1
10	David Cone	77.0
11	David Wells	67.2
12	Ron Guidry	62.2
13	Vic Raschi	60.1
14	Bob Turley	53.2
15	Herb Pennock	52.1
16	Ed Lopat	52.0
17	Lefty Gomez	50.1
18	Ralph Terry	46.0
19	Catfish Hunter	44.0
20	Jeff Nelson	40.1

MOST STRIKEOUTS

1	Andy Pettitte	123
2	Orlando Hernandez	101
3	Roger Clemens	99
4	Whitey Ford	94
5	Mariano Rivera	93
6	Mike Mussina	92
7	David Cone	68
8	Allie Reynolds	62
9	Red Ruffing	61
10	Ron Guidry	51
11	Waite Hoyt	48
12	Bob Turley	46
13	Jeff Nelson	44
14	Vic Raschi	43
	David Wells	43
16	Lefty Gomez	31
	Ralph Terry	31
18	Monte Pearson	28
19	Don Larsen	24
	Mike Stanton	24

BEST ERA (30 INNINGS MINIMUM)

1	Mariano Rivera	0.77
2	Monte Pearson	1.01
3	Spud Chandler	1.62
4	Waite Hoyt	1.62
5	Herb Pennock	2.06
6	Vic Raschi	2.24
7	Carl Mays	2.38
8	Tommy John	2.48
9	Ed Lopat	2.60
10	Red Ruffing	2.63
11	Orlando Hernandez	2.65
12	Don Larsen	2.67
13	Whitey Ford	2.71
14	Allie Reynolds	2.79
15	Joe Bush	2.84
16	Lefty Gomez	2.86
17	Ralph Terry	2.93
18	Ron Guidry	3.02
19	Jeff Nelson	3.12
20	Bob Turley	3.19

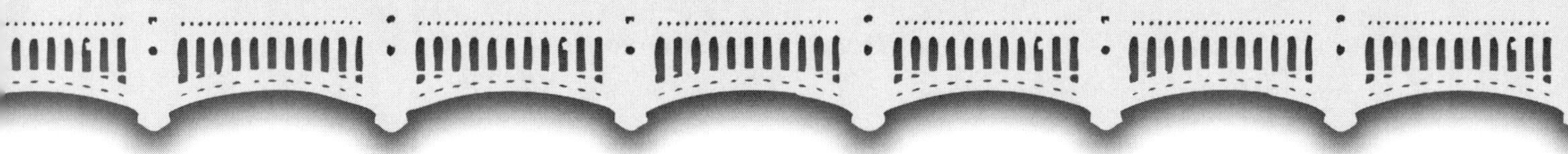

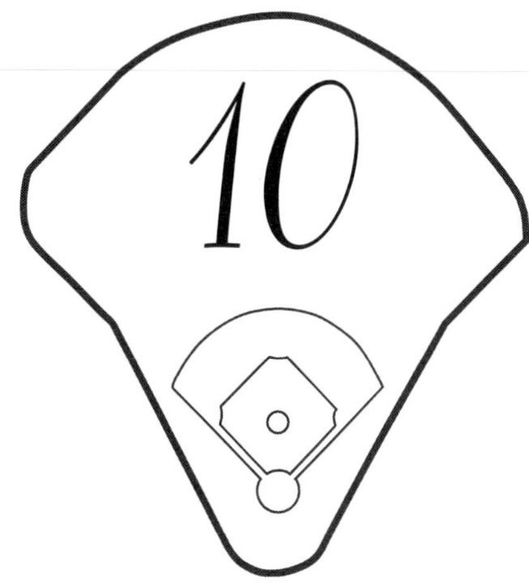

Yankees and the All-Star Game

Yankee Stadium will serve as the home of the 2008 All-Star Game after a 31-year gap between the third and fourth All-Star Games held in the Bronx (the Midsummer Classic was previously staged there in 1939, 1960, and 1977). It is entirely fitting for the game to return for the last year of Yankee Stadium since the franchise has played an integral role in the All-Star Game over its 75-year history.

The first All-Star pitch in history was thrown by Lefty Gomez in the inaugural game at Comiskey Park on July 6, 1933. He pitched the first three innings and was credited with the win. In fact, Gomez started the first three All-Star Games—and five of the first six—picking up wins in 1933, 1935, and 1937 and losing in 1938. Two other Yankees have won the All-Star Game—Spud Chandler in 1942 and Spec Shea in 1947—but the last nine times a Yankees' pitcher has received a decision in the game (starting with Red Ruffing in 1940 and extending to Tommy John in 1980), he has taken the loss. As the saying goes, though, "You have to be in it to win it."

The Yankees have dominated the All-Star Game from the bench as well, having eight different men manage the game a total of 34 times for the American League: Joe McCarthy, Bucky Harris, Casey Stengel, Ralph Houk, Billy Martin, Bob Lemon, Buck Showalter, and Joe Torre. Stengel managed the All-Star team 10 times, a major league record, going 4–6 at the AL helm.

Many Yankees hitters have excelled in the All-Star Game, starting with Babe Ruth, who hit the first home run in the game's history in support of Gomez in 1933. In the midst of his famous hitting streak eight years later, Joe DiMaggio (who had hit in his last 48 games) singled in that game in Detroit as well. He scored three times, including the winning run on Ted Williams's three-run blast in the bottom of the ninth. All-Star MVPs were first given out in 1962, but only one Yankee to date has won the award: Derek Jeter in 2000.

All Yankees players who have played in the Midsummer Classic or who have been named to the All-Star team are listed in this section. Positions are shown for where the player appeared in the game, even if that was not his regular position. **dnp** signifies that the player was chosen but did not play, **injured** means he was chosen but could not play, and **replacement** signifies he was named to the team after another player was injured. Box scores of the three games played at Yankee Stadium are also included, along with game summaries. (The box scores used were obtained free of charge from and are copyrighted by Retrosheet *www.retrosheet.org.*)

Finally, Yankees selected for *The Sporting News* All-Star Teams, which predate the major league All-Star Game by eight years, are listed as well.

Yankees Selected to the All-Star Game

1933
Chapman, of
Dickey, c (dnp)
Gehrig, 1b
Gomez, p
Lazzeri, 2b (dnp)
Ruth, of

1934
Chapman, of
Dickey, c
Gehrig, 1b
Gomez, p
Ruffing, p
Ruth, of

1935
Chapman, of
Gehrig, 1b
Gomez, p

1936
Crosetti, ph
Dickey, c
DiMaggio, of
Gehrig, 1b
Gomez, p (dnp)
Pearson, p (dnp)
Selkirk, ph

1937
Dickey, c
DiMaggio, of
Gehrig, 1b
Gomez, p
Murphy, p (dnp) (replacement)
Rolfe, 3b

1938
Dickey, c
DiMaggio, of
Gehrig, 1b
Gomez, p
Murphy, p (dnp) (replacement)
Rolfe, 3b (dnp)
Ruffing, p (dnp)

1939
Crosetti, ss (dnp)
Dickey, c
DiMaggio, of
Gehrig, 1b (honorary)
Gomez, p (dnp)
Gordon, 2b
Murphy, p (dnp) (replacement)
Rolfe, 3b
Ruffing, p
Selkirk, of

1940
Dickey, c
DiMaggio, of
Gordon, 2b
Keller, of
Pearson, p (dnp)
Rolfe, 3b (injured)
Ruffing, p

1941
Dickey, c
DiMaggio, of
Gordon, 2b
Keller, of
Ruffing, p (dnp)
Russo, p (dnp)

1942
Bonham, p (dnp)
Chandler, p
Dickey, c (injured)
DiMaggio, of
Gordon, 2b
Henrich, of
Rizzuto, ss (dnp)
Rosar, c (dnp)
Ruffing, p (dnp)

1943
Bonham, p (dnp)
Chandler, p (dnp)
Dickey, c (dnp)
Gordon, 2b (dnp)
Keller, of (injured)
Lindell, of (dnp)

1944
Borowy, p
Hemsley, c
Page, p (dnp)

1945 (NO GAME)
Borowy, p
Etten, 1b
Grimes, 3b
Stirnweiss, 2b

1946
Chandler, p (dnp)
Dickey, ph
DiMaggio, of (dnp)
Gordon, 2b
Keller, of
Stirnweiss, 2b

1947
Chandler, p (dnp)
DiMaggio, of
Henrich, of (replacement)
Johnson, 3b
Keller, of (injured)
McQuinn, 1b
Page, p
Robinson, c (dnp)
Shea, p

1948
Berra, c (dnp)
DiMaggio, ph
Henrich, of
McQuinn, 1b
Page, p (dnp)
Raschi, p

1949
Berra, c
DiMaggio, of
Henrich, of (dnp)
Raschi, p
Reynolds, p (dnp)

1950
Berra, c
Byrne, p (dnp)
Coleman, 2b
DiMaggio, of
Henrich, ph
Raschi, p
Reynolds, p
Rizzuto, ss

1951
Berra, c
DiMaggio, of (injured)
Lopat, p
Rizzuto, ss

1952
Bauer, of
Berra, c
Mantle, of (dnp)
McDougald, ph (replacement)
Raschi, p
Reynolds, p (dnp)
Rizzuto, ss

1953
Bauer, of
Berra, c
Mantle, of
Mize, ph
Reynolds, p
Rizzuto, ss
Sain, p (dnp)

1954
Bauer, of
Berra, c
Ford, p
Mantle, of
Noren, of (replacement)
Reynolds, p (injured)

1955
Berra, c
Ford, p
Mantle, of
Turley, p (dnp)

1956
Berra, c
Ford, p
Kucks, p (dnp)
Mantle, of
Martin, ph
McDougald, ss (dnp)

1957
Berra, c
Grim, p
Howard, c (dnp)
Mantle, of
McDougald, ss
Richardson, 2b (dnp)
Shantz, p (dnp)
Skowron, 1b

1958
Berra, c
Duren, p (dnp)
Ford, p (dnp)
Howard, of (dnp)
Kubek, ss (dnp)
Mantle, of
McDougald, ss
Skowron, 1b
Turley, p

1959 (G1)
Berra, c (dnp)
Duren, p
Ford, p
Mantle, of
McDougald, pr
Skowron, 1b

1959 (G2)
Berra, c
Duren, p (dnp)
Howard, c (dnp) (replacement)
Kubek, of (replacement)
Mantle, of
McDougald, ss (injured)
Richardson, 2b (dnp) (replacement)
Skowron, 1b (injured)

1960 (G1)
Berra, c
Coates, p
Ford, p (dnp)
Howard, c
Mantle, of
Maris, of
Skowron, 1b

1960 (G2)
Berra, c
Coates, p (dnp)
Ford, p
Howard, c (dnp)
Mantle, of
Maris, of
Skowron, 1b

1961 (G1)
Berra, c
Ford, p
Howard, c
Kubek, ss
Mantle, of
Maris, of

1961 (G2)
Arroyo, p (dnp)
Berra, c (dnp)
Ford, p (dnp)
Howard, c
Kubek, ss (injured)
Mantle, of
Maris, ph
Skowron, 1b (dnp) (added)

1962 (G1)
Howard, c (dnp)
Mantle, of
Maris, of
Richardson, 2b
Terry, p (dnp)
Tresh, ss (dnp)

1962 (G2)
Berra, ph (added)
Howard, c
Mantle, of (dnp)
Maris, of
Richardson, 2b
Terry, p (dnp)
Tresh, ss

1963
Bouton, p
Howard, c
Mantle, of (injured)
Pepitone, 1b
Richardson, 2b
Tresh, of

1964
Ford, p (dnp)
Howard, c
Mantle, of
Pepitone, 1b
Richardson, 2b

1965
Howard, c (dnp)
Mantle, of (injured)
Pepitone, ph (replacement)
Richardson, 2b
Stottlemyre, p (dnp)

1966
Richardson, 2b
Stottlemyre, p

1967
Downing, p
Mantle, ph

1968
Mantle, ph
Stottlemyre, p

1969
Stottlemyre, p
White, ph (replacement)

1970
Peterson, p
Stottlemyre, p
White, of (dnp)

1971
Munson, c
Murcer, of

1972
Murcer, of

1973
Lyle, p
Munson, c
Murcer, of

1974
Munson, c
Murcer, of

1975
Bonds, of
Hunter, p
Munson, c
Nettles, 3b

1976
Chambliss, ph
Hunter, p
Lyle, p (dnp)
Munson, c
Randolph, 2b (injured)
Rivers, of

1977
Jackson, of
Lyle, p
Munson, ph
Nettles, 3b
Randolph, 2b

1978
Gossage, p
Guidry, p
Jackson, of (injured)
Munson, c (injured)
Nettles, 3b

1979
Guidry, p
Jackson, of
John, p (dnp)
Nettles, 3b

1980
Dent, ss
Gossage, p
Jackson, of
John, p
Nettles, 3b
Randolph, 2b

1981
Davis, p (replacement)
Dent, ss
Gossage, p (injured)
Jackson, of
Randolph, 2b
Winfield, of

1982
Gossage, p (dnp)
Guidry, p (dnp)
Winfield, of

1983
Guidry, p (injured)
Winfield, of

1984
Mattingly, ph
Niekro, p (dnp)
Winfield, of

1985
Henderson, of
Mattingly, 1b
Winfield, of

1986
Henderson, of
Mattingly, 1b
Righetti, p
Winfield, of

1987
Henderson, of
Mattingly, 1b
Randolph, 2b
Righetti, p
Winfield, of

1988
Henderson, of
Mattingly, 1b
Winfield, of

1989
Mattingly, 1b
Sax, 2b

1990
Sax, 2b

1991
Sanderson, p (dnp)

1992
Kelly, of

1993
Boggs, 3b
Key, p

1994
Boggs, 3b
Key, p
O'Neill, ph

1995
Boggs, 3b
O'Neill, of
Stanley, c

1996
Boggs, 3b
Pettitte, p (dnp)
Wetteland, p (dnp)

1997
Cone, p
Martinez, 1b
O'Neill, of (replacement)
Rivera, p
Williams, of

1998
Brosius, 3b
Jeter, ss

O'Neill, of
Wells, p
Williams, of (injured)

1999

Cone, p
Jeter, ss
Rivera, p (declined)
Williams, of

2000

Jeter, ss
Posada, c
Rivera, p
Williams, of

2001

Clemens, p
Jeter, ss
Pettitte, p
Posada, c
Rivera, p (injured)
Stanton, p
Williams, of

2002

Giambi, 1b
Jeter, ph
Posada, c
Rivera, p
Soriano, 2b
Ventura, 3b

2003

Clemens, p (replacement)
Giambi, 1b (replacement)
Matsui, of
Posada, c
Soriano, 2b

2004

Giambi, 1b
Gordon, p
Jeter, ss
Matsui, of
Rivera, p
Rodriguez, 3b
Sheffield, of
Vazquez, p (replacement)

2005

Rivera, p
Rodriguez, 3b
Sheffield, of

2006

Cano, 2b (injured)
Jeter, ss
Rivera, p
Rodriguez, 3b

2007

Jeter, ss
Posada, c
Rodriguez, 3b

Yankees All-Star Batter Register

YEAR	POS	AVG	AB	R	H	2B	3B	HR	RBI	BB	SO	SB
Hank Bauer												
1952	of	.333	3	0	1	0	0	0	0	0	1	0
1953	of	.000	2	0	0	0	0	0	0	1	1	0
1954	of	.500	2	0	1	0	0	0	0	0	1	0
total	3	.286	7	0	2	0	0	0	0	1	3	0
Yogi Berra												
1948	c (dnp)											
1949	c	.000	3	0	0	0	0	0	0	0	0	0
1950	c	.000	2	0	0	0	0	0	0	0	0	0
1951	c	.250	4	1	1	0	0	0	0	0	0	0
1952	c	.000	2	0	0	0	0	0	0	0	0	0
1953	c	.000	4	0	0	0	0	0	0	0	0	0
1954	c	.500	4	2	2	0	0	0	0	1	0	0
1955	c	.167	6	1	1	0	0	0	0	0	0	0
1956	c	1.000	2	0	2	0	0	0	0	0	0	0
1957	c	.333	3	0	1	0	0	0	1	1	0	0
1958	c	.000	2	0	0	0	0	0	0	0	0	0
1959–1	c (dnp)											
1959–2	c	.333	3	1	1	0	0	1	2	0	2	0
1960–1	c	.000	2	0	0	0	0	0	0	0	0	0
1960–2	c	.000	2	0	0	0	0	0	0	0	1	0
1961–1	c	.000	1	0	0	0	0	0	0	0	0	0
1961–2	c (dnp)											
1962–2	ph	.000	1	0	0	0	0	0	0	0	0	0
total	15	.195	41	5	8	0	0	1	3	2	3	0
Wade Boggs												
1993	3b	.000	1	0	0	0	0	0	0	1	0	0
1994	3b	.333	3	1	1	0	0	0	0	0	2	0
1995	3b	.500	2	0	1	0	0	0	0	0	0	0
1996	3b	.000	3	0	0	0	0	0	0	0	0	0
total	4	.222	9	1	2	0	0	0	0	1	2	0
Bobby Bonds												
1975	of	.000	3	0	0	0	0	0	0	0	1	0
Scott Brosius												
1998	3b	.500	2	1	1	0	0	0	0	0	1	1
Robinson Cano												
2006	2b (injured)											
Chris Chambliss												
1976	ph	.000	1	0	0	0	0	0	0	0	0	0
Ben Chapman												
1933	of	.200	5	0	1	0	0	0	0	0	1	0
1934	of	.500	2	0	1	0	1	0	0	0	0	0
1935	of	.000	0	0	0	0	0	0	0	0	0	0
total	3	.286	7	0	2	0	1	0	0	0	1	0
Jerry Coleman												
1950	2b	.000	2	0	0	0	0	0	0	0	2	0
Frankie Crosetti												
1936	ph	.000	1	0	0	0	0	0	0	0	1	0
1939	ss (dnp)											
Bucky Dent												
1980	ss	.500	2	0	1	0	0	0	0	0	1	0
1981	ss	1.000	2	0	2	1	0	0	0	0	0	0
total	2	.750	4	0	3	1	0	0	0	0	1	0
Bill Dickey												
1933	c (dnp)											
1934	c	.500	2	1	1	0	0	0	0	2	1	0
1936	c	.000	2	0	0	0	0	0	0	0	0	0
1937	c	.667	3	1	2	1	0	0	1	1	0	0
1938	c	.250	4	0	1	1	0	0	0	0	0	0
1939	c	.000	3	1	0	0	0	0	0	1	0	0
1940	c	.000	1	0	0	0	0	0	0	0	0	0
1941	c	.333	3	0	1	0	0	0	0	0	0	0
1942	c (injured)											
1943	c (dnp)											
1946	ph	.000	1	0	0	0	0	0	0	0	1	0
total	8	.263	19	3	5	2	0	0	1	4	2	0
Joe DiMaggio												
1936	of	.000	5	0	0	0	0	0	0	0	0	0
1937	of	.250	4	1	1	0	0	0	0	1	2	0
1938	of	.250	4	1	1	0	0	0	0	0	1	1
1939	of	.250	4	1	1	0	0	1	1	0	0	0
1940	of	.000	4	0	0	0	0	0	0	0	0	0
1941	of	.250	4	3	1	1	0	0	1	1	0	0
1942	of	.500	4	0	2	0	0	0	0	0	0	0
1946	of (dnp)											
1947	of	.333	3	0	1	0	0	0	0	1	0	0
1948	ph	.000	1	0	0	0	0	0	1	0	0	0
1949	of	.500	4	1	2	1	0	0	3	0	0	0
1950	of	.000	3	0	0	0	0	0	0	0	0	0
1951	of (injured)											
total	11	.225	40	7	9	2	0	1	6	3	3	1
Nick Etten												
1945	1b (no game)											
Lou Gehrig												
1933	1b	.000	2	0	0	0	0	0	0	2	1	0
1934	1b	.000	4	1	0	0	0	0	0	1	3	0
1935	1b	.000	3	1	0	0	0	0	0	1	0	0
1936	1b	.500	2	1	1	0	0	1	1	2	0	0
1937	1b	.500	4	1	2	1	0	1	4	0	2	0
1938	1b	.333	3	0	1	0	0	0	0	0	0	0
1939	1b (honorary)											
total	6	.222	18	4	4	1	0	2	5	6	6	0
Jason Giambi												
2002	1b	.500	2	1	1	0	0	0	0	0	1	0
2003	1b	1.000	1	1	1	0	0	1	1	0	0	0
2004	1b	.500	2	1	1	0	0	0	0	0	0	0
total	3	.600	5	3	3	0	0	1	1	0	1	0
Joe Gordon												
1939	2b	.000	4	0	0	0	0	0	0	0	1	0
1940	2b	.000	2	0	0	0	0	0	0	0	2	0
1941	2b	.500	2	1	1	0	0	0	0	0	0	0
1942	2b	.000	4	0	0	0	0	0	0	0	3	0
1943	2b (dnp)											
1946	2b	.500	2	0	1	1	0	0	2	0	0	0
total	5	.143	14	1	2	1	0	0	2	0	6	0
Oscar Grimes												
1945	3b (no game)											
Rollie Hemsley												
1944	c	.000	2	0	0	0	0	0	0	0	0	0
Rickey Henderson												
1985	of	.333	3	1	1	0	0	0	0	0	1	1
1986	of	.000	3	0	0	0	0	0	0	0	1	0
1987	of	.333	3	0	1	0	0	0	0	0	0	0
1988	of	.500	2	0	1	0	0	0	0	1	0	0
total	4	.273	11	1	3	0	0	0	0	1	2	1
Tommy Henrich												
1942	of	.250	4	1	1	1	0	0	0	0	1	0
1947	of	.000	1	0	0	0	0	0	0	0	1	0
1948	of	.000	3	0	0	0	0	0	0	1	2	0
1949	of (dnp)											
1950	ph	.000	1	0	0	0	0	0	0	0	0	0
total	4	.111	9	1	1	1	0	0	0	1	4	0
Elston Howard												
1957	c (dnp)											
1958	of (dnp)											
1959–2	c (dnp)											
1960–1	c	.000	1	0	0	0	0	0	0	1	1	0
1960–2	c (dnp)											

YEAR	POS	AVG	AB	R	H	2B	3B	HR	RBI	BB	SO	SB
1961–1	c	.000	0	0	0	0	0	0	0	0	0	0
1961–2	c	.000	2	0	0	0	0	0	0	0	1	0
1962–1	c (dnp)											
1962–2	c	.000	2	0	0	0	0	0	0	0	2	0
1963	c	.000	1	0	0	0	0	0	0	0	1	0
1964	c	.000	3	1	0	0	0	0	0	0	2	0
1965	c (dnp)											
total	6	.000	9	1	0	0	0	0	0	1	7	0
Reggie Jackson												
1977	of	.500	2	0	1	0	0	0	0	0	1	0
1978	of (injured)											
1979	of	.000	1	0	0	0	0	0	0	1	0	0
1980	of	.500	2	0	1	0	0	0	0	1	1	0
1981	of	.000	1	0	0	0	0	0	0	0	0	0
total	4	.333	6	0	2	0	0	0	0	2	2	0
Derek Jeter												
1998	ss	.000	1	0	0	0	0	0	0	0	1	0
1999	ss	.000	1	0	0	0	0	0	0	0	1	0
2000	ss	1.000	3	1	3	1	0	0	2	0	0	0
2001	ss	1.000	1	1	1	0	0	1	1	0	0	0
2002	ph	.000	1	0	0	0	0	0	0	0	1	0
2004	ss	1.000	3	1	3	0	0	0	0	0	0	0
2006	ss	.000	3	0	0	0	0	0	0	0	2	0
2007	ss	.333	3	0	1	0	0	0	0	0	0	0
total	8	.500	16	3	8	1	0	1	3	0	5	0
Billy Johnson												
1947	3b	.000	0	0	0	0	0	0	0	0	0	0
Charlie Keller												
1940	of	.000	2	0	0	0	0	0	0	0	1	0
1941	of	.000	1	0	0	0	0	0	0	0	1	0
1943	of (injured)											
1946	of	.250	4	2	1	0	0	1	2	1	1	0
1947	of (injured)											
total	3	.143	7	2	1	0	0	1	2	1	3	0
Roberto Kelly												
1992	of	.500	2	0	1	1	0	0	2	0	1	0
Tony Kubek												
1958	ss (dnp)											
1959–2	of	.000	1	1	0	0	0	0	0	1	1	0
1961–1	ss	.000	4	0	0	0	0	0	0	0	1	0
1961–2	ss (injured)											
total	2	.000	5	1	0	0	0	0	0	1	2	0
Tony Lazzeri												
1933	2b (dnp)											
Johnny Lindell												
1943	of (dnp)											
Mickey Mantle												
1952	of (dnp)											
1953	of	.000	2	0	0	0	0	0	0	1	0	0
1954	of	.400	5	1	2	0	0	0	0	0	1	0
1955	of	.333	6	1	2	0	0	1	3	0	1	0
1956	of	.250	4	1	1	0	0	1	1	0	3	0
1957	of	.250	4	1	1	0	0	0	0	1	1	0
1958	of	.500	2	0	1	0	0	0	0	2	0	0
1959–1	of	.000	0	0	0	0	0	0	0	0	0	0
1959–2	of	.333	3	0	1	0	0	0	0	1	1	0
1960–1	of	.000	0	0	0	0	0	0	0	2	0	0
1960–2	of	.250	4	0	1	0	0	0	0	0	1	0
1961–1	of	.000	3	0	0	0	0	0	0	0	2	0
1961–2	of	.000	3	0	0	0	0	0	0	1	2	0
1962–1	of	.000	1	0	0	0	0	0	0	1	1	0
1962–2	of (dnp)											
1963	of (injured)											
1964	of	.250	4	1	1	0	0	0	0	0	2	0
1965	of (injured)											
1967	ph	.000	1	0	0	0	0	0	0	0	1	0
1968	ph	.000	1	0	0	0	0	0	0	0	1	0
total	16	.233	43	5	10	0	0	2	4	9	17	0
Roger Maris												
1960–1	of	.000	2	0	0	0	0	0	0	0	1	0
1960–2	of	.000	4	0	0	0	0	0	0	1	0	0
1961–1	of	.250	4	0	1	0	0	0	0	1	2	0
1961–2	ph	.000	1	0	0	0	0	0	0	0	0	0
1962–1	of	.000	2	0	0	0	0	0	1	0	1	0
1962–2	of	.250	4	2	1	1	0	0	1	1	0	0
total	6	.118	17	2	2	1	0	0	2	3	4	0
Billy Martin												
1956	ph	.000	1	0	0	0	0	0	0	0	0	0
Tino Martinez												
1997	1b	.000	2	0	0	0	0	0	0	0	0	0
Hideki Matsui												
2003	of	.500	2	0	1	0	0	0	0	0	0	0
2004	of	.000	1	0	0	0	0	0	0	0	1	0
total	2	.333	3	0	1	0	0	0	0	0	1	0

YEAR	POS	AVG	AB	R	H	2B	3B	HR	RBI	BB	SO	SB
Don Mattingly												
1984	ph	.000	1	0	0	0	0	0	0	0	0	0
1985	1b	.000	1	0	0	0	0	0	0	0	0	0
1986	1b	.000	3	0	0	0	0	0	0	0	2	0
1987	1b	.000	1	0	0	0	0	0	0	2	0	0
1988	1b	.000	2	0	0	0	0	0	0	0	0	0
1989	1b	1.000	1	0	1	1	0	0	0	0	0	0
total	6	.111	9	0	1	1	0	0	0	2	2	0
Gil McDougald												
1952	ph	.000	1	0	0	0	0	0	0	0	0	0
1956	ss (dnp)											
1957	ss	.000	2	1	0	0	0	0	0	0	0	0
1958	ss	1.000	1	0	1	0	0	0	1	0	0	0
1959–1	pr	.000	0	0	0	0	0	0	0	0	0	0
1959–2	ss (injured)											
total	4	.250	4	1	1	0	0	0	1	0	0	0
George McQuinn												
1947	1b	.000	4	0	0	0	0	0	0	0	1	0
1948	1b	.500	4	1	2	0	0	0	0	0	0	1
total	2	.250	8	1	2	0	0	0	0	0	1	1
Johnny Mize												
1953	ph	1.000	1	0	1	0	0	0	0	0	0	0
Thurman Munson												
1971	c	.000	0	0	0	0	0	0	0	0	0	0
1973	c	.000	2	0	0	0	0	0	0	0	1	0
1974	c	.333	3	1	1	1	0	0	0	1	0	0
1975	c	.500	2	0	1	0	0	0	0	0	0	0
1976	c	.000	2	0	0	0	0	0	0	0	0	0
1977	ph	.000	1	0	0	0	0	0	0	0	1	0
1978	c (injured)											
total	6	.200	10	1	2	1	0	0	0	1	2	0
Bobby Murcer												
1971	of	.333	3	0	1	0	0	0	0	0	1	0
1972	of	.000	3	0	0	0	0	0	0	0	0	0
1973	of	.000	3	0	0	0	0	0	0	1	0	0
1974	of	.000	2	0	0	0	0	0	0	0	0	0
total	4	.091	11	0	1	0	0	0	0	1	1	0
Graig Nettles												
1975	3b	.250	4	0	1	0	0	0	0	0	1	1
1977	3b	.000	2	0	0	0	0	0	0	0	1	0
1978	3b	.000	0	0	0	0	0	0	0	0	0	0
1979	3b	1.000	1	0	1	0	0	0	0	0	0	0
1980	3b	.000	2	0	0	0	0	0	0	0	0	0
total	5	.222	9	0	2	0	0	0	0	0	2	1
Irv Noren												
1954	of	.000	0	0	0	0	0	0	0	0	0	0
Paul O'Neill												
1994	ph	.000	1	0	0	0	0	0	0	0	0	0
1995	of	.000	1	0	0	0	0	0	0	0	0	0
1997	of	.000	2	0	0	0	0	0	0	0	1	0
1998	of	.000	2	0	0	0	0	0	0	0	0	0
total	4	.000	6	0	0	0	0	0	0	0	1	0
Joe Pepitone												
1963	1b	.000	4	0	0	0	0	0	0	0	2	0
1964	1b	.000	0	0	0	0	0	0	0	0	0	0
1965	ph	.000	1	0	0	0	0	0	0	0	1	0
total	3	.000	5	0	0	0	0	0	0	0	3	0
Jorge Posada												
2000	c	.000	2	0	0	0	0	0	0	0	1	0
2001	c	1.000	1	0	1	1	0	0	0	0	0	0
2002	c	.000	3	0	0	0	0	0	0	0	2	0
2003	c	.000	2	0	0	0	0	0	0	0	2	0
2007	c	.333	3	0	1	1	0	0	0	0	0	0
total	5	.182	11	0	2	2	0	0	0	0	5	0
Willie Randolph												
1976	2b (injured)											
1977	2b	.200	5	0	1	0	0	0	1	0	2	0
1980	2b	.500	4	0	2	0	0	0	0	0	0	0
1981	2b	.333	3	0	1	0	0	0	0	0	1	0
1987	2b	.000	1	0	0	0	0	0	0	0	0	0
total	4	.308	13	0	4	0	0	0	1	0	3	0
Bobby Richardson												
1957	2b (dnp)											
1959–2	2b (dnp)											
1962–1	2b	.000	1	0	0	0	0	0	0	0	0	0
1962–2	2b	.000	0	1	0	0	0	0	0	0	0	0
1963	2b	.000	2	0	0	0	0	0	0	0	0	0
1964	2b	.250	4	0	1	0	0	0	0	0	1	0
1965	2b	.000	2	0	0	0	0	0	0	0	0	0
1966	2b	.000	2	0	0	0	0	0	0	0	0	0
total	6	.091	11	1	1	0	0	0	0	0	1	0
Mickey Rivers												
1976	of	.500	2	0	1	0	0	0	0	0	1	0

YEAR	POS	AVG	AB	R	H	2B	3B	HR	RBI	BB	SO	SB
PHIL RIZZUTO												
1942	ss (dnp)											
1950	ss	.333	6	0	2	0	0	0	0	0	1	0
1951	ss	.000	1	0	0	0	0	0	0	0	0	0
1952	ss	.000	2	0	0	0	0	0	0	0	0	0
1953	ss	.000	0	0	0	0	0	0	0	0	0	0
total	4	.222	9	0	2	0	0	0	0	0	1	0
AARON ROBINSON												
1947	c (dnp)											
ALEX RODRIGUEZ												
2004	3b	.333	3	0	1	0	1	0	1	0	1	0
2005	3b	.500	2	1	1	0	0	0	0	1	0	0
2006	3b	.000	2	0	0	0	0	0	0	0	0	0
2007	3b	.333	3	0	1	0	0	0	0	0	0	1
total	4	.300	10	1	3	0	1	0	1	1	1	1
RED ROLFE												
1937	3b	.500	4	2	2	0	1	0	2	1	0	0
1938	3b (dnp)											
1939	3b	.250	4	0	1	0	0	0	0	0	0	0
1940	3b (injured)											
total	2	.375	8	2	3	0	1	0	2	1	0	0
BUDDY ROSAR												
1942	c (dnp)											
BABE RUTH												
1933	of	.500	4	1	2	0	0	1	2	0	2	0
1934	of	.000	2	1	0	0	0	0	0	2	1	0
total	2	.333	6	2	2	0	0	1	2	2	3	0
STEVE SAX												
1989	2b	.000	1	0	0	0	0	0	0	0	0	0
1990	2b	.000	1	0	0	0	0	0	0	1	0	1
total	2	.000	2	0	0	0	0	0	0	1	0	1
GEORGE SELKIRK												
1936	ph	.000	0	0	0	0	0	0	0	1	0	0
1939	of	.500	2	0	1	0	0	0	1	2	0	0
total	2	.500	2	0	1	0	0	0	1	3	0	0
GARY SHEFFIELD												
2004	of	.000	1	0	0	0	0	0	0	0	0	0
2005	of	.000	1	0	0	0	0	0	0	0	0	0
total	2	.000	2	0	0	0	0	0	0	0	0	0
BILL SKOWRON												
1957	1b	.667	3	1	2	1	0	0	0	0	0	0
1958	1b	.000	4	0	0	0	0	0	0	0	1	0
1959–1	1b	.667	3	0	2	0	0	0	0	0	0	0
1959–2	1b (injured)											
1960–1	1b	.333	3	0	1	0	0	0	0	0	2	0
1960–2	1b	1.000	1	0	1	0	0	0	0	1	0	0
1961–2	1b (dnp)											
total	5	.429	14	1	6	1	0	0	0	1	3	0
ALFONSO SORIANO												
2002	2b	.500	2	1	1	0	0	1	1	0	1	0
2003	2b	.000	3	0	0	0	0	0	0	0	1	0
total	2	.200	5	1	1	0	0	1	1	0	2	0
MIKE STANLEY												
1995	c	.000	1	0	0	0	0	0	0	0	0	0
SNUFFY STIRNWEISS												
1945	2b (no game)											
1946	2b	.333	3	1	1	0	0	0	0	0	1	0
TOM TRESH												
1962–1	ss (dnp)											
1962–2	ss	.500	2	0	1	1	0	0	1	0	0	0
1963	of	.000	0	0	0	0	0	0	0	0	0	0
total	2	.500	2	0	1	1	0	0	1	0	0	0
ROBIN VENTURA												
2002	3b	.000	1	0	0	0	0	0	0	0	1	0
ROY WHITE												
1969	ph	.000	1	0	0	0	0	0	0	0	1	0
1970	of (dnp)											
BERNIE WILLIAMS												
1997	of	.000	0	1	0	0	0	0	0	1	0	0
1998	of (injured)											
1999	of	.000	1	0	0	0	0	0	0	0	1	0
2000	of	.000	3	0	0	0	0	0	0	0	0	0
2001	of	.000	1	0	0	0	0	0	0	0	0	0
total	4	.000	5	1	0	0	0	0	0	1	1	0
DAVE WINFIELD												
1981	of	.000	4	0	0	0	0	0	0	1	0	0
1982	of	.500	2	0	1	0	0	0	0	0	0	0
1983	of	1.000	3	2	3	1	0	0	1	0	0	0
1984	of	.250	4	0	1	1	0	0	0	0	1	0
1985	of	.333	3	0	1	0	0	0	0	0	0	1
1986	of	1.000	1	1	1	1	0	0	0	0	0	0
1987	of	.200	5	0	1	1	0	0	0	1	0	0
1988	of	.333	3	1	1	1	0	0	0	0	0	0
total	8	.360	25	4	9	5	0	0	1	2	1	1

Yankees All-Star Pitcher Register

YEAR	W	L	ERA	GS	SV	IP	H	R	ER	HR	BB	SO
LUIS ARROYO												
1961–2 (dnp)												
TINY BONHAM												
1942 (dnp)												
1943 (dnp)												
HANK BOROWY												
1944	0	0	0.00	1	0	3.0	3	0	0	0	1	0
1945 (no game)												
JIM BOUTON												
1963	0	0	0.00	0	0	1.0	0	0	0	0	0	0
TOMMY BYRNE												
1950 (dnp)												
SPUD CHANDLER												
1942	1	0	0.00	1	0	4.0	2	0	0	0	0	2
1943 (dnp)												
1946 (dnp)												
1947 (dnp)												
ROGER CLEMENS												
2001	0	0	0.00	1	0	2.0	0	0	0	0	0	1
2003	0	0	0.00	0	0	1.0	0	0	0	0	0	2
total	0	0	0.00	1	0	3.0	0	0	0	0	0	3
JIM COATES												
1960–1	0	0	0.00	0	0	2.0	2	0	0	0	0	0
1960–2 (dnp)												
DAVID CONE												
1997	0	0	0.00	0	0	1.0	0	0	0	0	2	0
1999	0	0	4.50	0	0	2.0	4	1	1	0	1	3
total	0	0	3.00	0	0	3.0	4	1	1	0	3	3
RON DAVIS												
1981	0	0	9.00	0	0	1.0	1	1	1	0	0	1
AL DOWNING												
1967	0	0	0.00	0	0	2.0	2	0	0	0	0	2
RYNE DUREN												
1958 (dnp)												
1959–1	0	0	0.00	0	0	3.0	1	0	0	0	1	4
1959–2 (dnp)												
WHITEY FORD												
1954	0	0	0.00	1	0	3.0	1	0	0	0	1	0
1955	0	0	16.20	0	0	1.2	5	5	3	0	1	0
1956	0	0	18.00	0	0	1.0	3	2	2	0	1	2
1958 (dnp)												
1959–1	0	1	54.00	0	0	0.1	3	2	2	0	0	0
1960–1 (dnp)												
1960–2	0	1	9.00	1	0	3.0	5	3	3	0	0	1
1961–1	0	0	3.00	1	0	3.0	2	1	1	0	0	2
1961–2 (dnp)												
1964 (dnp)												
total	0	2	8.25	3	0	12.0	19	13	11	0	3	5
LEFTY GOMEZ												
1933	1	0	0.00	1	0	3.0	2	0	0	0	0	1
1934	0	0	12.00	1	0	3.0	3	4	4	0	1	3
1935	1	0	1.50	1	0	6.0	3	1	1	0	2	4
1936 (dnp)												
1937	1	0	0.00	1	0	3.0	1	0	0	0	0	0
1938	0	1	0.00	1	0	3.0	2	1	0	0	0	1
1939 (dnp)												
total	3	1	2.50	5	0	18.0	11	6	5	0	3	9
TOM GORDON												
2004	0	0	0.00	0	0	0.1	0	0	0	0	0	0

YEAR	W	L	ERA	GS	SV	IP	H	R	ER	HR	BB	SO
Rich Gossage												
1978	0	1	36.00	0	0	1.0	4	4	4	0	1	1
1980	0	0	0.00	0	0	1.0	1	0	0	0	0	0
1981 (injured)												
1982 (dnp)												
total	0	1	18.00	0	0	2.0	5	4	4	0	1	1
Bob Grim												
1957	0	0	0.00	0	1	0.1	0	0	0	0	0	0
Ron Guidry												
1978	0	0	0.00	0	0	0.1	0	0	0	0	0	0
1979	0	0	0.00	0	0	0.1	0	0	0	0	1	0
1982 (dnp)												
1983 (injured)												
total	0	0	0.00	0	0	0.2	0	0	0	0	1	0
Catfish Hunter												
1975	0	1	9.00	0	0	2.0	3	2	2	0	0	2
1976	0	0	9.00	0	0	2.0	2	2	2	0	0	3
total	0	1	9.00	0	0	4.0	5	4	4	0	0	5
Tommy John												
1979 (dnp)												
1980	0	1	11.57	0	0	2.1	4	3	3	0	0	1
Jimmy Key												
1993	0	0	9.00	0	0	1.0	2	1	1	0	0	1
1994	0	0	4.50	1	0	2.0	1	1	1	0	0	1
total	0	0	6.00	1	0	3.0	3	2	2	0	0	2
Johnny Kucks												
1956 (dnp)												
Ed Lopat												
1951	0	1	27.00	0	0	1.0	3	3	3	0	0	0
Sparky Lyle												
1973	0	0	0.00	0	0	1.0	1	0	0	0	0	1
1976 (dnp)												
1977	0	0	9.00	0	0	2.0	3	2	2	0	0	1
total	0	0	6.00	0	0	3.0	4	2	2	0	0	2
Johnny Murphy												
1937 (dnp)												
1938 (dnp)												
1939 (dnp)												
Phil Niekro												
1984 (dnp)												
Joe Page												
1944 (dnp)												
1947	0	0	0.00	0	1	1.1	1	0	0	0	1	0
1948 (dnp)												
Monte Pearson												
1936 (dnp)												
1940 (dnp)												
Fritz Peterson												
1970	0	0	0.00	0	0	0.0	1	0	0	0	0	0
Andy Pettitte												
1996 (dnp)												
2001	0	0	0.00	0	0	1.0	1	0	0	0	0	1
Vic Raschi												
1948	1	0	0.00	0	0	3.0	3	0	0	0	1	3
1949	0	0	0.00	0	1	3.0	1	0	0	0	3	1
1950	0	0	6.00	1	0	3.0	2	2	2	0	0	1
1952	0	0	4.50	1	0	2.0	1	1	1	0	0	3
total	1	0	2.45	2	1	11.0	7	3	3	0	4	8

YEAR	W	L	ERA	GS	SV	IP	H	R	ER	HR	BB	SO
Allie Reynolds												
1949 (dnp)												
1950	0	0	0.00	0	0	3.0	1	0	0	0	1	2
1952 (dnp)												
1953	0	1	9.00	0	0	2.0	2	2	2	0	1	0
1954 (injured)												
total	0	1	3.60	0	0	5.0	3	2	2	0	2	2
Dave Righetti												
1986	0	0	0.00	0	0	0.2	2	0	0	0	0	0
1987	0	0	0.00	0	0	0.1	1	0	0	0	0	0
total	0	0	0.00	0	0	1.0	3	0	0	0	0	0
Mariano Rivera												
1997	0	0	0.00	0	1	1.0	0	0	0	0	0	1
1999 (declined)												
2000	0	0	0.00	0	0	1.0	2	1	0	0	0	0
2001 (injured)												
2002	0	0	0.00	0	0	1.0	1	0	0	0	0	0
2004	0	0	0.00	0	0	1.0	0	0	0	0	0	0
2005	0	0	0.00	0	1	0.1	0	0	0	0	0	1
2006	0	0	0.00	0	1	1.0	0	0	0	0	0	0
total	0	0	0.00	0	3	5.1	3	1	0	0	0	2
Red Ruffing												
1934	0	0	27.00	0	0	1.0	4	3	3	0	1	0
1938 (dnp)												
1939	0	0	3.00	1	0	3.0	4	1	1	0	1	4
1940	0	1	9.00	1	0	3.0	5	3	3	0	0	2
1941 (dnp)												
1942 (dnp)												
total	0	1	9.00	2	0	7.0	13	7	7	0	2	6
Marius Russo												
1941 (dnp)												
Johnny Sain												
1953 (dnp)												
Scott Sanderson												
1991 (dnp)												
Bobby Shantz												
1957 (dnp)												
Spec Shea												
1947	1	0	3.00	0	0	3.0	3	1	1	0	2	2
Mike Stanton												
2001	0	0	0.00	0	0	0.2	0	0	0	0	0	0
Mel Stottlemyre												
1965 (dnp)												
1966	0	0	0.00	0	0	2.0	1	0	0	0	1	0
1968	0	0	0.00	0	0	0.1	0	0	0	0	0	1
1969	0	1	9.00	1	0	2.0	4	3	2	0	0	1
1970	0	0	0.00	0	0	1.2	0	0	0	0	0	2
total	0	1	3.00	1	0	6.0	5	3	2	0	1	4
Ralph Terry												
1962–1 (dnp)												
1962–2 (dnp)												
Bob Turley												
1955 (dnp)												
1958	0	0	16.20	1	0	1.2	3	3	3	0	2	0
Javier Vazquez												
2004	0	0	0.00	0	0	1.0	0	0	0	0	0	2
David Wells												
1998	0	0	0.00	1	0	2.0	0	0	0	0	1	1
John Wetteland												
1996 (dnp)												

All-Star Games at Yankee Stadium

1939 All-Star Game AL 3, NL 1

Tuesday, July 11, 1:55 PM Attendance: 62,892
Managers: Joe McCarthy (AL), Gabby Hartnett (NL)
Umpires: Cal Hubbard, Larry Goetz, Eddie Rommel, George Magerkurth

It was "home, sweet home" in the first All-Star Game at Yankee Stadium. Six Yankees started, including Red Ruffing on the mound. The seventh All-Star Game marked the sixth time a Yankees' hurler started the game (Lefty Gomez had already started five and was a reserve in '39). Ruffing allowed the first run of the game in the third inning when Lonnie Frey doubled in a run but, after an intentional walk to Ival Goodman loaded the bases, he retired Frank McCormick and Ernie Lombardi.

The American League countered in the fourth against Bill Lee when George Selkirk singled in the tying run and another scored on Arky Vaughn's error. Joe DiMaggio launched a homer in the fifth inning, the third homer by a Yankee in All-Star competition (Babe Ruth and Lou Gehrig had preceded him).

The lead was in immediate trouble when Tommy Bridges filled the bases with one out in the sixth. Bob Feller, 18, entered his first All-Star Game and promptly induced Vaughn to hit into a double play, then allowed just a hit and walk over the final three innings. The AL improved to 5–2 in All-Star competition, with Joe McCarthy, managing his fourth straight Classic, evening his record.

NL	001	000	000	1	7	1
AL	000	210	00X	3	6	1

NATIONAL LEAGUE	AB	R	H	RBI	BB	SO	PO	A
Hack 3b	4	0	1	0	1	3	1	1
Frey 2b	4	0	1	1	0	0	0	4
Goodman rf	1	0	0	0	1	0	0	0
Herman ph	1	0	0	0	0	1	0	0
Moore cf	1	0	0	0	0	0	0	0
McCormick 1b	4	0	0	0	0	1	7	1
Lombardi c	4	0	2	0	0	0	6	0
Medwick lf	4	0	0	0	0	1	1	0
Ott cf,rf	4	0	2	0	0	0	4	0
Vaughan ss	3	1	1	0	1	0	4	1
Derringer p	1	0	0	0	0	1	0	0
Camilli ph	1	0	0	0	0	1	0	0
Lee p	0	0	0	0	0	0	0	0
Phelps ph	1	0	0	0	0	0	0	0
Fette p	0	0	0	0	0	0	1	0
Mize ph	1	0	0	0	0	1	0	0
Totals	34	1	7	1	3	9	24	7

NATIONAL LEAGUE	IP	H	R	ER	BB	SO	HR
Derringer	3	2	0	0	0	1	0
Lee L(0–1)	3	3	3	2	3	4	1
Fette	2	1	0	0	1	1	0
Totals	8	6	3	2	4	6	1

FIELDING
E: Vaughan (1)

BATTING
2B: Frey (1,off Ruffing)
IBB: Goodman (1,by Ruffing)
Team LOB: 9.

PITCHING
IBB: Lee (1,Selkirk)

AMERICAN LEAGUE	AB	R	H	RBI	BB	SO	PO	A
Cramer rf	4	0	1	0	0	1	3	0
Rolfe 3b	4	0	1	0	0	0	1	0
DiMaggio cf	4	1	1	1	0	0	1	0
Dickey c	3	1	0	0	1	0	10	0
Greenberg 1b	3	1	1	0	1	0	7	1
Cronin ss	4	0	1	0	0	1	2	4
Selkirk lf	2	0	1	1	2	0	0	0
Gordon 2b	4	0	0	0	0	1	2	4
Ruffing p	0	0	0	0	0	0	0	0
Hoag ph	1	0	0	0	0	1	0	0
Bridges p	1	0	0	0	0	1	1	0
Feller p	1	0	0	0	0	1	0	0
Totals	31	3	6	2	4	6	27	9

AMERICAN LEAGUE	IP	H	R	ER	BB	SO	HR
Ruffing	3	4	1	1	1	4	0
Bridges W(1–0)	2.1	2	0	0	1	3	0
Feller SV(1)	3.2	1	0	0	1	2	0
Totals	9	7	1	1	3	9	0

FIELDING
DP: 1. Gordon-Cronin-Greenberg
E: Cronin (1)

BATTING
HR: DiMaggio (1,5th inning off Lee 0 on 2 out)
IBB: Selkirk (1,by Lee)
Team LOB: 8

PITCHING
IBB: Ruffing (1,Goodman)

1960 All-Star Game NL 6, AL 0

Wednesday, July 13, 2:42 PM Attendance: 38,362
Managers: Al Lopez (AL), Walter Alston (NL)
Umpires: Nestor Chylak, Dusty Boggess, Jim Honochick, Tom Gorman, Johnny Stevens, Vinnie Smith

The first All-Star Game at Yankee Stadium in 21 years was the second All-Star game in three days. Because the players were building a pension fund, two All-Star exhibitions were held each season from 1959–62. Like the previous contest in Kansas City on Monday, this was a National League win. Frank Lary and Gary Bell pitched in both games for the American League.

Whitey Ford, making the second of his three career All-Star starts, allowed hits to the first two batters at half-full Yankee Stadium. Though Ford got out of the jam by picking Willie Mays off third base with two outs, he wasn't so fortunate in the second inning when Joe Adcock led off with a single and Eddie Mathews followed with a home run. Ford also allowed a homer to Mays in the third.

The AL, meanwhile, did nothing against Vern Law and five other NL pitchers. The four Yankees in the starting lineup in the No. 3 through No. 6 spots—Roger Maris, Mickey Mantle, Bill Skowron, and Yogi Berra—went a combined 2-for-11. Orioles rookie Ron Hansen was the only AL player with multiple hits. Mays had three hits; NL third basemen Mathews and Ken Boyer each hit two-run homers; Stan Musial hit his sixth and final career All-Star home run.

NL	021	000	102	6	10	0
AL	000	000	000	0	8	0

NATIONAL LEAGUE	AB	R	H	RBI	BB	SO	PO	A
Mays cf	4	1	3	1	0	0	5	0
Pinson cf	0	0	0	0	1	0	0	0
Skinner lf	3	0	1	0	0	1	2	0
Cepeda lf	2	0	0	0	0	0	0	0
Aaron rf	3	0	0	0	0	0	1	0
Clemente ph,rf	0	0	0	0	1	0	0	0
Banks ss	3	0	1	0	0	0	2	3
Groat ph,ss	1	0	0	0	0	0	0	1
Adcock 1b	2	1	1	0	0	1	3	0
White 1b	1	0	0	0	0	0	2	0
Larker ph,1b	0	1	0	0	1	0	3	0
Mathews 3b	3	1	1	2	0	0	0	1
Boyer 3b	1	1	1	2	0	0	1	0
Mazeroski 2b	2	0	0	0	0	0	0	0
Neal 2b	1	0	0	0	0	0	1	2
Taylor 2b	1	0	1	0	0	0	2	1
Crandall c	2	0	0	0	0	0	3	0
Williams p	0	0	0	0	0	0	0	0
Musial ph	1	1	1	1	0	0	0	0
Bailey c	1	0	0	0	0	0	0	0
Law p	1	0	0	0	0	0	0	1
Podres p	0	0	0	0	0	0	0	1
Burgess ph,c	2	0	0	0	0	1	2	0
Jackson p	0	0	0	0	0	0	0	0
Henry p	0	0	0	0	0	0	0	0
McDaniel p	0	0	0	0	0	0	0	0
Totals	34	6	10	6	3	3	27	10

NATIONAL LEAGUE	IP	H	R	ER	BB	SO	HR
Law W(1–0)	2	1	0	0	0	1	0
Podres	2	1	0	0	3	1	0
Williams	2	2	0	0	1	2	0
Jackson	1	1	0	0	2	0	0
Henry	1	2	0	0	0	0	0
McDaniel SV(1)	1	1	0	0	0	0	0
Totals	9	8	0	0	6	4	0

FIELDING
DP: 2. Law-Banks-Adcock, Banks-Neal-White

BATTING
HR: Mathews (1,2nd inning off Ford 1 on 0 out); Mays (1,3rd inning off Ford 0 on 0 out); Musial (1,7th inning off Staley 0 on 2 out); Boyer (1,9th inning off Bell 1 on 0 out)
SH: Henry (1,off Bell)
Team LOB: 5.

BASERUNNING
SB: Mays (1,3rd base off Ford/Berra)
CS: Mays (1,Home by Ford/Berra)

AMERICAN LEAGUE	AB	R	H	RBI	BB	SO	PO	A
Minoso lf	2	0	0	0	1	1	1	0
Williams ph	1	0	1	0	0	0	0	0
Robinson pr,3b	1	0	0	0	0	0	0	0
Runnels 2b	2	0	0	0	1	1	0	1
Staley p	0	0	0	0	0	0	1	1
Kaline ph,lf	1	0	1	0	1	0	3	0
Maris rf	4	0	0	0	1	0	0	0
Mantle cf	4	0	1	0	0	1	3	0
Skowron 1b	1	0	1	0	1	0	6	0
Power 1b	2	0	0	0	0	0	5	1
Berra c	2	0	0	0	0	1	4	1
Lollar c	2	0	1	0	0	0	0	0
Malzone 3b	2	0	0	0	1	0	2	2
Lary p	0	0	0	0	0	0	0	0
Smith ph	1	0	0	0	0	0	0	0
Bell p	0	0	0	0	0	0	0	1
Hansen ss	4	0	2	0	0	0	2	4
Ford p	0	0	0	0	0	0	0	0
Kuenn ph	1	0	0	0	0	0	0	0
Wynn p	0	0	0	0	0	0	0	0
Fox ph,2b	3	0	1	0	0	0	0	1
Totals	33	0	8	0	6	4	27	12

AMERICAN LEAGUE	IP	H	R	ER	BB	SO	HR
Ford L(0–1)	3	5	3	3	0	1	2
Wynn	2	0	0	0	0	2	0
Staley	2	2	1	1	0	0	1
Lary	1	1	0	0	1	0	0
Bell	1	2	2	2	2	0	1
Totals	9	10	6	6	3	3	4

FIELDING
DP: 1. Fox-Hansen-Power

BATTING
2B: Lollar (1,off Henry)
Team LOB: 12

1977 All-Star Game NL 7, AL 5

Tuesday, July 19, 2:34 PM Attendance: 56,683
Managers: Billy Martin (AL), Sparky Anderson (NL)
Umpires: Bill Kunkel, Doug Harvey, Dave Phillips, Dick Stello, Frank Pulli, Joe Brinkman

Yankee Stadium, which had reopened in 1976 after two years of renovations, saw its first All-Star Game where fans picked the starting position players. Two Yankees—Willie Randolph and Reggie Jackson—were elected to the team, but for the first time in three All-Star Games in the Bronx, a Yankees pitcher did not start on the mound as New York manager Billy Martin chose Baltimore ace Jim Palmer. Joe Morgan led off the game with a home run. Palmer allowed a single to Dave Parker, an RBI-double to George Foster, and another home run to Greg Luzinski, then was knocked out in the third inning after Steve Garvey connected for the NL's third home run.

Don Sutton, who wound up as the game's MVP, fanned four in three innings while allowing just a hit and a walk. Randolph and Jackson each had a hit, while Yankees reserves Thurman Munson and Graig Nettles went hitless. Sparky Lyle had a rough opening inning, allowing three hits and two runs—both knocked in by San Diego's Dave Winfield—plus a hit batter and a wild pitch. Lyle retired the NL in order in his second frame of relief.

Tom Seaver, recently traded by the Mets, received a huge ovation when he entered the game in his Reds' uniform. He also allowed the AL to get on the board on Richie Zisk's two-run double. Rich Gossage, who would be wearing a Yankees cap at the next All-Star Game, was at his intimidating best for the Pirates, though George Scott took him deep for a two-run homer in the ninth that made it 7–5. Gossage got Randolph to ground out and fanned Munson to give the NL its 14th win in the last 15 All-Star Games.

				R	H	E
NL	401	000	020	7	9	1
AL	000	002	102	5	8	0

NATIONAL LEAGUE	AB	R	H	RBI	BB	SO	PO	A
Morgan 2b	4	1	1	1	0	1	1	0
Trillo 2b	1	0	0	0	0	1	0	1
Garvey 1b	3	1	1	1	0	2	1	0
Montanez 1b	2	0	0	0	0	1	6	1
Parker rf	3	1	1	0	0	1	2	0
Templeton ss	1	1	1	0	0	0	1	2
Foster cf	3	1	1	1	0	1	2	0
Morales cf	0	1	0	0	0	0	1	0
Luzinski lf	2	1	1	2	0	0	0	0
Winfield lf	2	0	2	2	0	0	1	0
Cey 3b	2	0	0	0	1	1	0	0
Seaver p	0	0	0	0	0	0	0	1
Smith ph	1	0	1	0	0	0	0	0
Schmidt pr	0	0	0	0	0	0	0	0
Reuschel p	0	0	0	0	0	0	0	0
Stearns c	0	0	0	0	0	0	2	0
Bench c	2	0	0	0	0	1	4	0
Lavelle p	0	0	0	0	0	0	0	0
Rose ph,3b	2	0	0	0	0	0	0	1
Concepcion ss	1	0	0	0	1	0	1	1
Valentine rf	1	0	0	0	1	0	0	0
Sutton p	0	0	0	0	0	0	0	1
Simmons c	3	0	0	0	0	0	5	0
Gossage p	0	0	0	0	0	0	0	0
Totals	33	7	9	7	3	9	27	8

NATIONAL LEAGUE	IP	H	R	ER	BB	SO	HR
Sutton W(1–0)	3	1	0	0	1	4	0
Lavelle	2	1	0	0	0	2	0
Seaver	2	4	3	2	1	2	0
Reuschel	1	1	0	0	0	0	0
Gossage	1	1	2	2	1	2	1
Totals	9	8	5	4	3	10	1

FIELDING
DP: 1. Montanez-Templeton-Montanez
E: Templeton (1)

BATTING
2B: Foster (1,off Palmer); Winfield (1,off LaRoche); Templeton (1,off Lyle)
HR: Morgan (1,1st inning off Palmer 0 on 0 out); Luzinski (1,1st inning off Palmer 1 on 1 out); Garvey (1,3rd inning off Palmer 0 on 0 out)
SH: Sutton (1,off Palmer)
HBP: Morales (1,by Lyle)
Team LOB: 4

BASERUNNING
CS: Concepcion (1,3rd base by Palmer/Fisk)

PITCHING
HBP: Reuschel (1, Singleton)

AMERICAN LEAGUE	AB	R	H	RBI	BB	SO	PO	A
Carew 1b	3	1	1	0	0	0	7	0
Scott 1b	2	1	1	2	0	0	4	0
Randolph 2b	5	0	1	1	0	2	2	6
Brett 3b	2	0	0	0	1	0	2	1
Campbell p	0	0	0	0	0	0	0	0
Fairly ph	1	0	0	0	0	1	0	0
Lyle p	0	0	0	0	0	0	0	0
Munson ph	1	0	0	0	0	1	0	0
Yastrzemski cf	2	0	0	0	0	1	0	0
Lynn cf	1	1	0	0	1	0	2	0
Zisk lf	3	0	2	2	0	1	0	0
Singleton rf	0	0	0	0	0	0	0	0
Jackson rf	2	0	1	0	0	1	0	0
Rice rf,lf	2	0	1	0	0	0	1	0
Fisk c	2	0	0	0	0	1	6	1
Wynegar c	2	1	1	0	0	0	3	0
Burleson ss	2	0	0	0	0	0	0	0
Campaneris ss	1	1	0	0	1	1	0	1
Palmer p	0	0	0	0	0	0	0	0
Kern p	0	0	0	0	0	0	0	0
Jones ph	1	0	0	0	0	0	0	0
Eckersley p	0	0	0	0	0	0	0	1
Hisle ph	1	0	0	0	0	0	0	0
LaRoche p	0	0	0	0	0	0	0	0
Nettles 3b	2	0	0	0	0	1	0	1
Totals	35	5	8	5	3	10	27	11

AMERICAN LEAGUE	IP	H	R	ER	BB	SO	HR
Palmer L(0–1)	2	5	5	5	1	3	3
Kern	1	0	0	0	0	2	0
Eckersley	2	0	0	0	0	1	0
LaRoche	1	1	0	0	1	0	0
Campbell	1	0	0	0	1	2	0
Lyle	2	3	2	2	0	1	0
Totals	9	9	7	7	3	9	3

FIELDING
DP: 1. Randolph-Scott

BATTING
2B: Zisk (1,off Seaver)
HR: Scott (1,9th inning off Gossage 1 on 1 out)
HBP: Singleton (1,by Reuschel)
Team LOB: 7

PITCHING
Palmer faced 1 batter in the 3rd inning
WP: Palmer (1), Lyle (1)
HBP: Lyle (1,Morales)

The Sporting News All-Stars

Almost a decade before baseball's All-Star Game was born, *The Sporting News* was selecting its own All-Star Team at the end of every major league season. From 1925 through 1960, *The Sporting News* named one All-Star Team covering both leagues. Since 1961, the first year the major leagues expanded, *The Sporting News* has named one All-Star Team for each league. The composition of the All- Star teams has varied little over the years, though the number of pitchers selected has fluctuated and a slot for the designated hitter was added to the AL team in 1974.

Following is a year-by-year list of the Yankees who were named by *The Sporting News* as All-Stars. (Years in which no Yankees were selected to the team are not shown.) Also shown is a ranking of how many times each Yankees player has been so honored; the career total in brackets includes years on other teams.

1926
P Herb Pennock
OF Babe Ruth

1927
1B Lou Gehrig
OF Babe Ruth

1928
P Waite Hoyt
1B Lou Gehrig
OF Babe Ruth

1929
OF Babe Ruth

1930
OF Babe Ruth

1931
1B Lou Gehrig
OF Babe Ruth

1932
C Bill Dickey
2B Tony Lazzeri

1933
C Bill Dickey

1934
P Lefty Gomez
1B Lou Gehrig

1936
C Bill Dickey
1B Lou Gehrig

1937
P Red Ruffing
1B Lou Gehrig
3B Red Rolfe
OF Joe DiMaggio

1938
P Lefty Gomez
P Red Ruffing
C Bill Dickey
3B Red Rolfe
OF Joe DiMaggio

1939
P Red Ruffing
C Bill Dickey
2B Joe Gordon
3B Red Rolfe
OF Joe DiMaggio

1940
2B Joe Gordon
OF Joe DiMaggio

1941
C Bill Dickey
2B Joe Gordon
OF Joe DiMaggio

1942
P Tiny Bonham
2B Joe Gordon
OF Joe DiMaggio

1943
P Spud Chandler
3B Billy Johnson

1946
C Aaron Robinson

1947
OF Joe DiMaggio

1948
OF Joe DiMaggio

1949
P Joe Page
1B Tommy Henrich
SS Phil Rizzuto

1950
P Vic Raschi
C Yogi Berra
SS Phil Rizzuto

1951
P Allie Reynolds
SS Phil Rizzuto

1952
P Allie Reynolds
C Yogi Berra
SS Phil Rizzuto
OF Mickey Mantle

1954
C Yogi Berra

1955
P Whitey Ford

1956
P Whitey Ford
C Yogi Berra
OF Mickey Mantle

1957
C Yogi Berra
SS Gil McDougald
OF Mickey Mantle

1958
P Bob Turley

1960
1B Bill Skowron
OF Roger Maris

1961
P Whitey Ford
C Elston Howard
2B Bobby Richardson
SS Tony Kubek
OF Mickey Mantle
OF Roger Maris

1962
P Ralph Terry
2B Bobby Richardson
SS Tom Tresh
OF Mickey Mantle

1963
P Whitey Ford
C Elston Howard
1B Joe Pepitone
2B Bobby Richardson

1964
C Elston Howard
2B Bobby Richardson
OF Mickey Mantle

1965
P Mel Stottlemyre
2B Bobby Richardson

1966
2B Bobby Richardson

1971
OF Bobby Murcer

1972
OF Bobby Murcer

1973
C Thurman Munson
OF Bobby Murcer

1974
C Thurman Munson

1975
C Thurman Munson
3B Graig Nettles

1976
C Thurman Munson
1B Chris Chambliss
OF Mickey Rivers

1977
2B Willie Randolph
3B Graig Nettles

1978
3B Graig Nettles
LHP Ron Guidry

1980
C Rick Cerone
2B Willie Randolph
OF Reggie Jackson*
DH Reggie Jackson*
LHP Tommy John

*Yes, Reggie won at both positions

1981
LHP Ron Guidry

1982
OF Dave Winfield

1983
OF Dave Winfield
LHP Ron Guidry

1984
1B Don Mattingly
OF Dave Winfield

1985
1B Don Mattingly
OF Rickey Henderson
DH Don Baylor
LHP Ron Guidry

1986
1B Don Mattingly

1987
1B Don Mattingly
2B Willie Randolph

1993
C Mike Stanley
LP Jimmy Key

1994
3B Wade Boggs
LP Jimmy Key

1996
P Andy Pettitte

1997
1B Tino Martinez

1998
3B Scott Brosius
LHP David Wells

2000
C Jorge Posada
OF Bernie Williams

2001
C Jorge Posada
RHP Roger Clemens

2002
C Jorge Posada
1B Jason Giambi
2B Alfonso Soriano
OF Bernie Williams

2003
P Andy Pettitte
C Jorge Posada

2005
3B Alex Rodriguez

2006
2B Robinson Cano
SS Derek Jeter

2007
C Jorge Posada
3B Alex Rodriguez
SS Derek Jeter

PLAYER	YEARS
Joe DiMaggio	8
Bill Dickey	6
Lou Gehrig	6
Mickey Mantle	6
Bobby Richardson	6
Babe Ruth	6
Yogi Berra	5
Jorge Posada	5
Joe Gordon	4 [6]
Whitey Ford	4
Ron Guidry	4
Don Mattingly	4
Thurman Munson	4
Phil Rizzuto	4
Dave Winfield	3 [4]
Elston Howard	3
Bobby Murcer	3
Graig Nettles	3
Willie Randolph	3
Red Rolfe	3
Red Ruffing	3
Alex Rodriguez	2 [8]
Reggie Jackson	2* [6]
Derek Jeter	2
Jimmy Key	2 [3]
Lefty Gomez	2
Roger Maris	2
Andy Pettitte	2
Allie Reynolds	2
Bernie Williams	2
Wade Boggs	1 [7]
Roger Clemens	1 [5]
Don Baylor	1 [3]
Rickey Henderson	1 [3]
Alfonso Soriano	1 [3]
David Wells	1 [2]
Tiny Bonham	1
Scott Brosius	1
Robinson Cano	1
Rick Cerone	1
Chris Chambliss	1
Spud Chandler	1
Jason Giambi	1
Tommy Henrich	1
Waite Hoyt	1
Tommy John	1
Billy Johnson	1
Tony Kubek	1
Tony Lazzeri	1
Tino Martinez	1
Gil McDougald	1
Joe Page	1
Herb Pennock	1
Joe Pepitone	1
Vic Raschi	1
Mickey Rivers	1
Aaron Robinson	1
Bill Skowron	1
Mike Stanley	1
Mel Stottlemyre	1
Ralph Terry	1
Tom Tresh	1
Bob Turley	1

All-Star Game

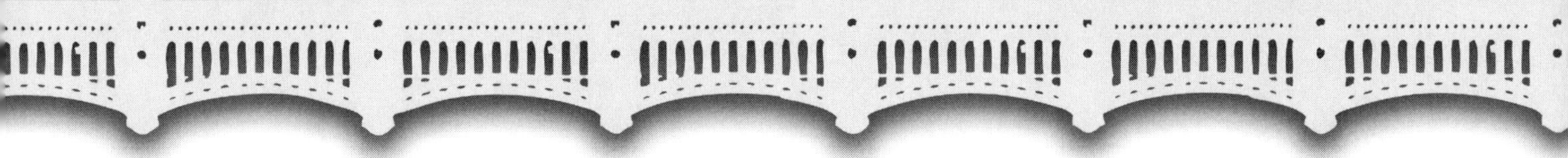

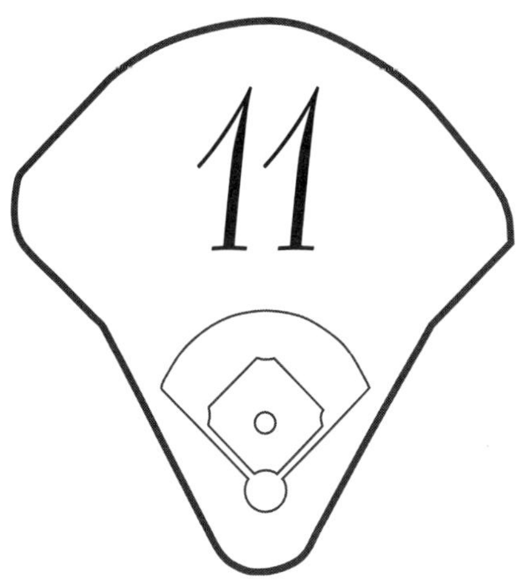

11

Yankees All-Time Team and Leaders

When you're looking at the greatest Yankees of all-time, where do you start? The Hall of Fame is just a starting point. Several of the first-team players could find their way on an all-time team for the history of the game: Babe Ruth, Lou Gehrig, Whitey Ford, Mariano Rivera—and don't forget the man who saw more World Series than anyone in history, Yogi Berra. Chosen by the editors of *The ESPN Baseball Encyclopedia*, this list provides a few surprising choices. The editors looked at longevity with club, club records, postseason achievements, and a heavy dose of historical importance.

The Leaders section that follows the All-Time Teams is based strictly on the numbers.

Yankees All-Time Team, First Team

Catcher Yogi Berra

While his Yogisims have made him famous around the world—as has Yoo Hoo soft drink and a cartoon bear noted for swiping "pic-a-nic" baskets—Berra was a conduit for manager Casey Stengel and the pitching staff. And man, could he hit.

Berra had 358 homers as a Yankee and drove in 1,430 while hitting .285 with .483 slugging (only three points lower than Bill Dickey). Berra played outfield for 260 of his 2,116 games as a Yankee (third-most in club history, and more than Babe Ruth or Joe DiMaggio). He was the kind of person who always seemed to be at the right place at the right time, and he usually came through. He played in a major league record 14 World Series and won 10. He is also the only man to win a pennant as manager of both the Mets and Yankees.

First Base Lou Gehrig

The tendency today is to solely associate Gehrig with his streak of 2,130 consecutive games, but he was an unparalleled slugger and first baseman. The Iron Horse wore No. 4 because of where he batted in the lineup when the Yanks first donned numbers in 1929. Having No. 3, Babe Ruth, in front of him gave him someone to constantly drive in, and Gehrig did just that. Gehrig's 2,721 hits, 163 triples, and 1,995 RBIs are tops in Yankees history. His 184 RBIs in 1931 remain the American League record. His .340 career average, .442 on-base percentage, and .632 slugging are second only to Ruth in club history. His 493 home runs place him third. He had one more extra-base hit than the Babe in pinstripes (1,190–1,189).

Gehrig was unstoppable in the World Series. His career .475 Series on-base percentage is still the best ever. His 35 RBIs in the World Series rank behind only Mickey Mantle and Yogi Berra. Gehrig's 43 World Series hits are ninth of all time, even though his 34 Series games don't even crack the top 25. He was the linchpin for both Ruth's powerhouse teams and the even more dominant late 1930s clubs with Joe DiMaggio.

There's no saying how much more Gehrig might have achieved had he not been stricken with Amyotrophic Lateral Sclerosis (ALS), a motor neuron disease that ended his career at age 35, and took his life at 37. His 1939 farewell speech is still one of the most significant moments in the history of Yankee Stadium.

Second Base Willie Randolph

Before the 1970s Yankees won any pennants, they stole a 20-year-old second baseman from the Pirates in the Dock–Doc trade of December 1975 (Dock Ellis, Ken Brett, and Randolph for Doc Medich). Randolph stayed in the Bronx for 13 seasons, six of them as an All-Star. Patient and fast, he was an ideal number two hitter and never flinched while turning a double play.

Randolph retired having stolen more bases than any Yankee except former teammate Rickey Henderson (Derek Jeter surpassed Randolph's 251 in 2007). His 1,005 walks are the fifth-most in club history, the only four-digit total by someone who wasn't a slugger (Randolph had 48 homers as a Yankee). He played in four pennant winners in New York and another in Oakland. Well-schooled in the "Yankee Way," the one-time team captain Randolph returned to coach in the Bronx for 11 years before finally getting a chance to manage with the Mets.

Shortstop Derek Jeter

Jeter is the quintessential Yankee, a captain who leads by example in the tradition of Lou Gehrig and Thurman Munson. It's no coincidence that Jeter's arrival in 1996 was the year the Yankees began their run of dominance, winning four world championships in his first five full years in the major leagues. After 12 seasons in the major leagues, he has still never been on a Yankees team that didn't reach the postseason.

For much of that time he has been the face of the franchise, his fist-clench at key moments a sign to all that the game has turned to his team's advantage. He has a knack for putting himself at the right place at the right time. His meander all the way to the foul line to corral a bad throw and flip it to Jorge Posada at the plate in Game 3 of the 2001 Division Series in Oakland helped rescue the Yankees from the verge of elimination. His game-winning home run in Game 4 of the World Series that year, at the witching hour of Halloween, christened him "Mr. November."

If one adds up all postseason totals, Jeter has played in more games, batted more often, collected more hits, and scored more runs than any player in history. (He has also struck out more often than anyone in those circumstances.) Jeter's face is plastered everywhere in New York and it is also part of numerous national ad campaigns, but where he can be found most often is in the Yankees lineup, climbing ever higher on the rolls of all-time Yankees elite.

Third Base Graig Nettles

Until recently, third base has been a spot where the Yankees have had steady if unspectacular contributors on championship clubs: Joe Dugan, Red Rolfe, Gil McDougald, and Clete Boyer, to name a few. One who broke that mold was an outspoken slugger with a superb glove named Graig Nettles.

Traded by both Minnesota and Cleveland, Nettles wound up in New York and in 1976 became the first Yankee to win a home run crown since Roger Maris. He led the club with 37 homers the next year, outhomering Reggie Jackson. Nettles earned ALCS MVP against former manager Billy Martin's A's in 1981. He won successive Gold Glove awards in 1977 and 1978, but that total seems paltry considering how his glove rescued the Yankees in the '78 World Series. His remarkable fielding display in Game 3 helped New York win after dropping the first tow games in Los Angeles. The Yankees did not lose again in the Series.

He is seventh on the Yankees all-time list with 250 home runs. An impressive feat made more so because he is the only one of the seven besides Joe DiMaggio not to have exceeded 2,000 games with the club. (Nettles played 1,535 games for New York, by far the most of any third baseman.) His combination of power, defense, and durability places him at the top of the list in his field.

Left Field Charlie Keller

Amid all the big names in Yankees history, King Kong Keller is sometimes overlooked, but he clearly belongs with the club's all-time greats. Among Yankees with more than 1,000 games, he is fourth of all-time with a .408 on-base percentage and fifth in slugging at .518. He is 12th in franchise history with 760 walks, even though everyone both in front of and behind him on the list had far more plate appearances. In 1940 Keller, Joe DiMaggio, and Tommy Henrich became the first American League outfield to each reach 30 homers.

He hit .306 with five home runs in four World Series for the Yankees. He knocked over Cincinnati catcher Ernie "Schnozz" Lombardi to score the go-ahead run in the 10th inning of Game 4 of the 1939 World Series, and Joe DiMaggio circled the bases as the catcher lay stunned at home plate in what became known as "Schnozz's Snooze." His double in the 1941 World Series—after Brooklyn catcher Mickey Owen couldn't handle what would have been the last pitch of Game 4—brought in the tying and go-ahead runs.

The left-handed swinging Keller was not the same player after the war, though he managed one more 30-homer, 100-RBI season in 1946. Back problems ended his career just after his 36th birthday.

Center Field Mickey Mantle

When looking at the various Yankees leaders in the club's illustrious history, three names come up repeatedly: Babe Ruth, Lou Gehrig, and Mickey Mantle. Mantle ranks first in games and at bats; second in home runs and walks; third in runs, hits, RBIs, total bases, and on-base percentage; and fourth in slugging. His 1,710 strikeouts stood as the all-time record until it was surpassed by a host of sluggers, only a handful of whom (Reggie Jackson, Mike Schmidt, and Sammy Sosa) ever passed Mantle on the all-time home run list. And none of them ever won a Triple Crown like Mantle did in 1956. He also earned three American League MVP Awards.

Mantle was speed and power personified from both sides of the plate. He was a fleet center fielder—converted from shortstop—whose knees were never the same after he tripped over a drainpipe at Yankee Stadium during the 1951 World Series. In World Series play he hit more home runs (18) scored more (42), and drove in more (40) than any player in history, with teammate Yogi Berra second in each category. Mantle walked more (43) and fanned more (54) than any player in Series history.

Mantle was as popular as any player in the game. Fans were much more at ease with him breaking Babe Ruth's single-season home run mark than Roger Maris. The teammates slugged it out throughout 1961, with Maris breaking the mark after illness ended Mantle's chase at 54 home runs in 153 games. Mantle was able to play just twice in the World Series, but the Yankees won anyway. He moved to first base in his last years, and was about the only drawing card after the dynasty collapsed. He retired in 1968, an All-Star 16 times in an 18-year career.

Right Field Babe Ruth

The Yankees were New York's second team before Babe Ruth. That all changed after he arrived from Boston. A few thousand fans for a ballgame was the norm until the Polo Grounds swelled to the point that the landlord, the Giants, pressed the Yankees to find a new home, what became known as the House That Ruth Built. Even eight decades after his greatest seasons, Babe Ruth still dominates the record books and remains a household name.

Many of his major league marks have been surpassed over time, but his Yankees records are mostly intact despite generations of great players who followed him. His career marks for home runs (659), total bases (5,131), walks (1,852), on-base percentage (.479), slugging (.711), and batting average (.349) are still unchallenged, and many of those numbers may never be topped.

What the Yankees wanted most of all was championships, and Ruth powered that cause. He helped Boston win three world championships as a pitcher and then slugged the Yankees to their first three titles (plus three Series defeats). Many of his Series marks were eclipsed by Mickey Mantle, but Ruth is the only player to twice hit three home runs in a Series game. His "called shot" in 1932 at Wrigley Field remains one of the most disputed moments in baseball history. He mesmerized fans with an unprecedented 54 home runs his first year as a Yankee in 1920 and then matched or exceeded that number three times, with his fabled 60 home runs in 1927. The gregarious Bambino put the Yankees on the map and kept baseball in the public eye after the 1919 Black Sox Scandal. While there can be discussions about the greatest players in major league history, there's a simple answer to the question of who was the greatest Yankee ever: The Babe.

Designated Hitter Reggie Jackson

Reggie wasn't a Yankee for long, but he transformed the team simply by being there. The 1976 club was a group of skilled professionals, Jackson was the new "Superduperstar" as *Sports Illustrated* dubbed him, or as he dubbed himself, "the straw that stirs the drink." One of the first major free agent signings in history, George Steinbrenner lured him to New York with a five-year, $2.96 million contract after the 1976 season. Turbulence between Jackson and manager Billy Martin nearly came to blows during a nationally-televised game at Fenway Park.

Jackson led the club with 110 RBIs in 1977, clubbing 32 home runs. He was second in the league in doubles and third in slugging. His three home runs in Game 6 of the World Series against the Dodgers secured his place among the game's postseason greats. His fourth world championship in six years—and second Series MVP—forever assigned him the name "Mr. October." He added a fifth title the following year.

He finished second to George Brett in the MVP voting in 1980, collecting 41 homers, 111 RBIs, and his lone .300 season as a Yankee. New York finished second to Brett's Royals in the ALCS. Jackson made it to the Series one more time in 1981, but for the only time in his career, his club wound up on the losing end of the Fall classic. Though he left for the Angels as a free agent and finished his career where it began with the A's, Jackson returned to the Yankees as a consultant. He finished with 563 home runs and set the all-time major league mark with 2,597 strikeouts.

Starting Pitchers Whitey Ford

"Chairman of the Board" was the most formidable ace in club history. He was nearly impossible to score on, much less beat, in the World Series. Ford went five starts without allowing a run in World Series competition. He won 10 times and struck out 94 in 146 World Series innings, all records.

He was pretty good at getting people out during the regular season as well. Ford's 236 wins remain the most in club history and his .690 winning percentage was the best of any major league pitcher in the 20th century. He was 25–4 in 1961 to pick up his only Cy Young Award and he went 24–7 two years later to place third in the MVP voting to his catcher, Elston Howard. (Ford might have won the Cy Young that year, but only one was given for both leagues and it went to Sandy Koufax of the Dodgers.) Ford holds the club standard in most categories, including shutouts (45), strikeouts (1,956), starts (438), innings (3,170.1), and a few less flattering categories as well.

Ford admitted to using his ring to doctor the ball in his final years before he was eventually forced to remove it. He had plenty of other rings. The Yankees won six world championships during his 16 years with the club; they lost five times.

Starting Pitchers Red Ruffing

A close second to Whitey Ford on the club's all-time list is Red Ruffing. He benefited greatly by playing for the powerhouse Yankees teams of Ruth, Gehrig, and DiMaggio, but he'd paid his dues by going 39–96 in Boston before Ed Barrow liberated him for $50,000 and Cedric Durst. Ruffing won 231 times with the Yankees and was part of six world champions. He topped off 20-win seasons with World Series titles each year between 1936 and 1939.

His 3.47 ERA with the Yankees doesn't sound impressive, but offense was all the rage in the 1930s. Ruffing was durable, starting and completing as many games as any American League pitcher in his era. His 261 complete games are by far the most in club history and his 40 shutouts are tied for second. It didn't hurt that Ruffing was a great hitter too. He hit at least one homer a year in each of his first 14 years as a Yankee and finished with 36 in his major league career.

Starting Pitchers Lefty Gomez

Gomez was the lefty component on those great teams with Red Ruffing. Gomez won five world championships, never playing on a loser or even losing a game. In seven Series starts he was 6–0 with a 2.76 ERA. Gomez also represented his league well, starting five of the first six All-Star Games and going 3–1 with a 2.50 ERA. Besides throwing the first pitch in All-Star history, he drove in the first-ever run with a single.

His best year was 1934 when he went 26–5 in 281.1 innings with 158 strikeouts, six shutouts, and a 2.33 ERA, all tops in the league. He completed 25 games and finished five more games in relief as he had his third 20-win season in four years. He won the pitching Triple Crown again in 1937.

The fun-loving Gomez was usually around to finish what he started, compiling 173 complete games as a Yankee to place second to Ruffing.

Starting Pitchers Ron Guidry

A small frame hid a hellacious left arm. "Louisiana Lightning" was and as pitching coach, still is—a crowd favorite. And why not. Guidry's 25–3, 1.74 ERA, 16 complete games, and nine shutouts in 1978 was the stuff of legend. After facing more batters in one year than he had in his entire career, Guidry still had enough left for the most important game of his career, the one-game playoff against the Red Sox. Guidry gave up a couple of early runs, but won the game at Fenway as the Yankees took the division. He took the Cy Young Award, as if that was ever in question.

Guidry had two more 20-win seasons and he was consistently well below the league average ERA and he had a 3-to-1 career strikeout to walk ratio. He never led the league in strikeouts, but his 18-K performance at Yankee Stadium on June 17, 1978 began the practice of fans cheering when a pitcher reaches two strikes. It's still the club record for K's in a game. He is second only to Whitey Ford with 1,778 strikeouts—his 226 homers allowed are just two behind Ford—and Guidry's 170 wins are fourth. Only three Yankees were called on to start more often than Guidry's 356 times.

Relief Pitchers Mariano Rivera

This decision is as effortless as Rivera protecting a three-run lead in the ninth. Not only is Rivera without a doubt the best reliever in Yankees history—and there have been quite a few great ones—but Rivera may be the best at his job in history. He is certainly the best ever when it comes to October.

Combining all postseason games into one category, Rivera has more than double the saves accrued by Dennis Eckersley, the man previously considered by many to be the best ever at this job. Rollie Fingers, another candidate for the title, also trails Rivera in Series saves. Rivera is the only reliever anywhere near the top 20 in postseason strikeouts.

As for getting to the postseason, Rivera's quite good in that category as well. He has the most regular-season appearances in Yankees history, along with the lowest ERA, and twice as many saves as the previous record holder, Dave Righetti. What speaks loudest is the respect given him by opponents. When he closes out the All-Star Game, something he's done flawlessly three times while never allowing a run in six appearances, his American League teammates look completely relaxed in the field. They know from experience that the game's over.

Relief Pitchers Rich Gossage

Gossage brought heat and racked up saves, and not just the begin-the-ninth-inning-with-nobody-on kind. New York already had the best reliever in the American League in Sparky Lyle when George Steinbrenner signed the best in the game, Gossage, who'd shown the world his heat while wearing a Pirates hat in the 1977 All-Star Game at Yankee Stadium.

Goose was critical to the Yankees' remarkable comeback in the summer of '78. He saved a league-best 27 games and threw 134.1 innings. He blew 10 saves, but he converted the biggest one of his career on October 2, 1978 at Fenway Park. He entered with two men on in the seventh, and pitched out of jams each inning, getting Carl Yastrzemski to pop up in the ninth to give the Yankees the division title. He was on the mound two weeks later when the Yanks won the World Series. Gossage compiled 151 saves in 319 appearances as a Yankee, giving up a couple of famous home runs to George Brett (the 1980 ALCS and the 1983 "Pine Tar Game"), but few others got good wood on him, as illustrated by his 512 K's in 533 innings as a Yankee.

Relief Pitchers Sparky Lyle

Lyle was stolen from the Red Sox and became a major weapon against Boston and the rest of the American League as the Yankees returned to dominance in the 1970s. Lyle won 57 and saved 141 in seven seasons with the Yankees. His stellar 1977 season—13 wins, 26 saves, 2.17 ERA, and career-high 137 innings—helped the Yankees hold off the Red Sox and Orioles for the division title. It also earned Lyle the first American League Cy Young Award given to a reliever.

Lyle enabled the Yankees to rally in the last two games of the ALCS in Kansas City. With the Yankees clinging to a 5–4 lead he came on to retire George Brett in the fourth inning and allowed two hits over the last five innings. He came back to stifle the Royals the next night as the Yankees rallied in the ninth for the pennant. He got the win in both games and earned another two nights later with a 3.2-inning effort in the World Series opener against the Dodgers. Then George Steinbrenner brought in Rich Gossage that winter and Lyle was relegated to second banana. He pitched 59 times in 1978, but he appeared just once in the postseason. Lyle was shipped to Texas in a 10-player deal that turned into another steal for a talented young lefty: Dave Righetti.

Yankees All-Time Team, Second Team

Catcher Bill Dickey

Dickey was one of the greatest hitting catchers in history and he also handled a staff that won seven World Series in eight tries. He made the All-Star team 11 out of 12 years after its institution. Like a lot of catchers, the amount of rest required by the position keeps him off the leader board for many counting stats, but his .313 batting average is tied for sixth in club history.

Dickey is second to Yogi Berra in nearly every statistical category for catchers in club history. Impossible to strike out, he walked three times for every whiff. Some would consider Thurman Munson a sentimental favorite as second to Yogi Berra in Yankees history, but Dickey, whom Berra followed, was a key figure on a truly dominating team and had a lethal left-handed bat.

First Base Don Mattingly

One of the most beloved Yankees ever, Mattingly had a run in the 1980s that looked like it had been lifted from the hard-hitting 1930s. He drove in 110 runs or more five times in six years, batting .303 or better each season and missing 20 homers just once between 1984 and 1989. He became the first Yankee to win a batting title in 28 years in 1984. He captured the AL MVP in '85, the first Yankee to win the award since Thurman Munson in 1976, and Mattingly finished second to Roger Clemens for the award the following year when he led the league in RBIs. His 238 hits in 1986 set the team mark.

"Donnie Baseball" set the major league record with six grand slams in 1987 and tied another mark that summer by homering in eight straight games. He made the All-Star team six times and gathered nine Gold Gloves. The lefty even played third base three times in 1986 when the Yankees were strapped for infielders. Back and wrist problems curtailed the Yankee captain's career and forced him to retire just as the Yankees were on the verge of becoming a powerhouse in 1995.

Second Base Tony Lazzeri

It's a tight call between Tony Lazzeri and Joe Gordon for the spot at second base. Lazzeri played 11 years as a Yankee to Gordon's seven; Lazzeri was on seven pennant winners, Gordon five. Gordon was the superior fielder and had more power; "Poosh 'Em Up" Tony knocked in 100 runs seven times (Gordon did it twice). Lazzeri was from northern California, Gordon was from southern California (that's not significant but what is worth noting is that World War II interrupted Gordon's career while epilepsy was a constant fear in Lazzeri's).

As a rookie Lazzeri helped the Yankees reach the World Series in 1926 with 114 RBIs, but he was forever branded—and even noted on Grover Cleveland Alexander's Hall of Fame plaque—for striking out against Alex the Great with the bases loaded in Game 7 of that year's World Series. Lazzeri got his own Hall of Fame plaque in 1991.

Shortstop Phil Rizzuto

People who grew up in the New York decades after his retirement may remember the recently deceased Rizzuto more for his mental meanderings as an announcer or "Money Store" commercials, but the Scooter was a very good ballplayer. An expert table-setter and bunter for the Yankees teams that scored early and often in the 1930s and 1940s, Rizzuto walked twice as often as he struck out and was a superb fielder.

His best year was 1950, when he had his only 200-hit season and had career bests across the board in walks (92), runs (125), and average (.324). He won the MVP with almost as much ease as the Yankees won the World Series, something they did seven times in nine tries during his 13-year career. Much politicking helped get him into the Hall of Fame via the Veterans Committee in 1994.

Third Base Alex Rodriguez

A-Rod, A-God, Stray-Rod, Lightning-Rod, call him any nickname you like, but his four years in New York are among the best the Yankees have seen. Given that this list includes Ruth, Gehrig, DiMaggio, and Mantle, to name four, that is high praise indeed for a player foolishly chided in some circles pre-2007 for not being a "true Yankee." The only thing keeping A-Rod on the second team of Yankees greats is his time in New York.

Disparaged for the drama that surrounds him and past postseason failures, Rodriguez answered his critics in 2007, surpassing 50 home runs for the third time in his career and reaching 100 RBIs for the 11th time in his first 12 full seasons. Granted they were from different eras, but A-Rod far exceeded Reggie Jackson's totals as a Yankee over about the same number of games, scoring an extra 100 times than a man whose number is retired in the Bronx and has an "NY" on his Hall of Fame plaque.

Left Field Dave Winfield

George Steinbrenner derided him as "Mr. May" because he felt Winfield was the antitheses of Reggie Jackson, "Mr. October." If the Boss had looked at the numbers, though, he would have seen that Winfield's .277 career average in May was far below the .295 he hit in April and June or his .500 slugging in October (though over just 144 at bats). His October numbers as a Yankee left something to be desired. In the 1981 World Series he hit just .045 (1-for-22) as New York lost to the Dodgers. That first year of his record 10-year, $23-million contract was the only time the Yankees made the postseason while Winfield was in the Bronx. (He later won the Babe Ruth Award for his World Series-winning hit as a Blue Jay.)

His 205 home runs as a Yankee are in the club's top 10 and his numbers in New York, including his .290 batting average—he narrowly missed the 1984 batting crown—along with his eight All-Star appearances and five Gold Gloves, trump anything he did in San Diego over a similar number of games. Yet when he went into the Hall of Fame in 2001, the hat on his plaque read "SD" instead of "NY."

Center Fielder Joe DiMaggio

Three years missed because of World War II and quitting while he was still near his peak puts Joe D. on the second team, but he is still without a doubt one of the greatest Yankees in history. Despite placing 10th on the list for games played as a Yankee—his successor in center, Mickey Mantle, appeared in 665 more games—DiMaggio remains third in RBI (1,537) and triples (131), and fourth in runs (1,390), home runs (361), total bases (3,948), on-base percentage (.398), and slugging (.579). He rarely swung and missed, fanning just 369 times in his career, and then there's that 56-game hitting streak he had everyone singing about in 1941 (and ever since).

Graceful and swift, he rarely threw to the wrong base or made a gaffe on the basepaths. He also hardly ever showed emotion on the field, except when he famously kicked the dirt after Al Gionfriddo's remarkable catch robbed him in the 1947 World Series. Until his final year in 1951, he had only one season in which he failed to drive in at least 95 runs. That was 1949, when a heel problem kept him out for most of the first half and he still wound up hitting .346 as the Yankees surged past the Red Sox on the final weekend of the year. DiMaggio had somewhat pedestrian numbers for the World Series given his other numerous achievements: .271 average with eight homers and 30 RBIs in 51 World Series games. The Yankees still went 9–1 with him roaming center in October. Joltin' Joe was a symbol for Italian-Americans and Yankees fans; many in both groups still revere the Yankee Clipper.

Right Field Tommy Henrich

Though Roger Maris certainly deserves consideration, Henrich had 500 more hits. While Maris obviously hit with a lot more power than Henrich, Henrich hit for a much higher average and played many more games in a Yankees uniform. Two of Henrich's most memorable moments came against Brooklyn in the World Series. In 1941 Hugh Casey struck him out, but Mickey Owen couldn't stop the ball and Henrich made it to first; he scored the tying run and the Yankees won. With the opener of 1949 a scoreless tie in the ninth, he homered to win the game against Don Newcombe. The Yankees won all four World Series he played in.

Freed from the Indians by Judge Landis in 1937 because he was being "covered up" in their farm system, Henrich signed with the Yankees and broke into their All-Star outfield. Henrich, a five-time All-Star, only knocked in 100 runs once, but scored 100 four times, including a league-leading 138 in '48. "Old Reliable" got his name from Mel Allen after a train in Alabama from the broadcaster's youth that was always on time; just like Henrich.

Designated Hitter Paul O'Neill

O'Neill was considered a "warrior" by both George Steinbrenner and fans alike for his ferocity and excellence in crucial situations. The Ohio native won a world championship in Cincinnati, and after he landed in New York—for Roberto Kelly in a steal—the Yankees won four world championships and just missed a fifth in what was his final game as a ballplayer.

The brooding, curly-haired O'Neill is one of just nine Yankees to hit .300 over 1,000 or more games. Only five major leaguers had more hits (85) and doubles (17) in postseason competition than O'Neill. Of his 38 postseason bases on balls, his leadoff walk in Game 1 of the 2000 World Series led to the tying run in the bottom of the ninth against the Mets. O'Neill never left a doubt that he wanted to win as much as—if not more than—anyone sitting in the stands.

Starting Pitchers Waite Hoyt

Spirited away from the Red Sox, Waite Hoyt came to New York and pitched in six World Series in nine-plus seasons. He won 157 times and completed 156 games as a Yankee, both top 10 numbers in club history. He even closed out wins for other pitchers when it wasn't his day to start.

When the Yankees were new at this postseason thing, Hoyt did everything possible to will the team past the Giants in their first World Series. Hoyt pitched three complete games with an ERA of 0.00 in the first all-New York World Series in 1921. He had two shutouts, but lost the Series-deciding start on an unearned run. He went 6–4 for the Yankees in the World Series, including wins in his last two Yankees postseason starts in 1928. Hoyt became the first player to go behind the microphone, and the Hall of Fame pitcher had no shortage of tales about Babe Ruth and the powerhouse Yankees

Starting Pitchers Eddie Lopat

He drove hitters crazy. His "junk" induced countless grounders and bats flung into the ground in frustration as the Yankees won five consecutive world championships between 1949 and 1953. Lopat went 80–36 in that span, including 21–9 with a 2.91 ERA and 20 complete games in 1951, plus two more wins in the World Series. He was 4–1 with a 2.70 ERA in Series competition.

A control artist, the lefty Lopat led the league in ERA (2.42), winning percentage (.800), and walks per nine innings (1.61) in 1953. Lopat went 113–59 with a 3.19 ERA as a Yankee and passed his secrets of the soft stuff onto a young lefty named Whitey Ford.

Starting Pitchers Herb Pennock

Like Red Ruffing, Waite Hoyt, and, of course, Babe Ruth, Herb Pennock came from the Red Sox and helped the Yankees become champions. The year he arrived, 1923, the Yankees won their first championship, with Pennock getting the win in the clinching game. He went 5–0 with a 1.95 ERA in World Series play.

Pennock didn't throw hard, but he made batters hit their way on. He stands in fourth place in club history in complete games (164), eighth in wins (162) and innings (2,203.1), and ninth in starts (268).

Starting Pitchers Andy Pettitte

The Yankees brought in many pitchers from other organizations, but the best arm in Joe Torre's rotation year in and year out belonged to their homegrown southpaw. Pettitte finished third in the Rookie of the Year Award in 1995 and then barely missed the Cy Young the following year. Pettitte went 21–10 with a 3.90 ERA in '96; he had the same record and almost the exact same ERA seven years later. That was his last year in pinstripes before leaving to play for his hometown Astros. He convinced Houston resident Roger Clemens to pitch there as well.

In 2007 both Pettitte and Clemens returned to New York. Pettitte won his 200th major league game and resumed his quest for most wins and innings in postseason history.

Relief Pitchers Johnny Murphy

Fordham Johnny was a full-fledged reliever at a time when relievers weren't a factor on most teams, but Murphy proved invaluable to six world champions in the 1930s and 1940s. He led relievers in wins seven times and though saves weren't official, he had more than anyone else four times. He only pitched eight times in the World Series, but he had a direct part in winning six of those games with a 1.10 postseason ERA. He got the win in the clinching game in 1939 and the "Mickey Owen Game" in 1941.

While his numbers are dwarfed compared to modern relievers—except for innings per appearance (2.5)—the only Yankees with fewer than 50 starts to surpass Murphy's 383 appearances are Mariano Rivera, Mike Stanton, and Sparky Lyle. Murphy jumped into the front office with the rival Red Sox and later joined the fledgling Mets. He was general manager of the Miracle Mets in 1969 and died shortly after their improbable world championship.

Relief Pitchers Allie Reynolds

Superchief was a hybrid. No, not because he was part Native American, but because of his ability to excel both as a starter and reliever. He edges out Carl Mays on the All-Time Team in this versatile category. Mays was a controversial and effective submariner, whose pitch killed Ray Chapman during a Yankee game at the Polo Grounds in 1920. Reynolds lasted longer and was more effective, not to mention more liked.

A six-time All-Star, Reynolds pitched in six World Series with the Yankees winning each time. Reynolds is second of all-time with Red Ruffing and Bob Gibson with seven World Series wins and is third with 62 strikeouts. He went 131–60 as a Yankee, never winning fewer than 13 games or losing more than 12, while compiling a 3.30 ERA. He was the first American League pitcher to have two no-hitters in the same season, doing it in just over two months in 1951.

Relief Pitchers* *Dave Righetti

Righetti became a dominant closer by way of the rotation. He was 1981 Rookie of the Year as a formidable 22-year-old southpaw starter. His July 4, 1983 no-hitter was the first by a Yankee since Don Larsen's perfect game in the 1956 World Series. And 76 of his first 80 appearances as a Yankee were as a starter. There was a need for relief, Rags stepped in, and he never started another game as a Yankee.

He won 17 and saved 60 over his first two years as closer. In 1986 he set the all-time saves mark with 46, a record that has since been surpassed several times, but not by a pitcher throwing 106⅔ innings like Rags. He finished fourth in the Cy Young voting and made the All-Star team. Righetti saved 25 or more games in each of his seven seasons as Yankees closer. Although Mariano Rivera has since passed his 522 games and 224 saves, Rags remains among the best in Yankees history.

Yankees All-Time Leaders

The Leaders section that follows is based strictly on fact. It looks at numbers two ways: for a single season and for a career.

The differences between the Deadball Era and the modern era are so great that several categories in this section are additionally sorted by era. Six eras are defined since the founding of the American League and the advent of modern baseball in 1901:

- 1901–20, covering the deadball game and World War I, the banning of the spitball, and the scandal of the Black Sox, ending when offensive numbers start to jump;
- 1921–42, from the start of the offensive explosion wrought by Babe Ruth until World War II created severe player shortages, this era was dominated by gaudy batting averages and high scoring;
- 1943–60, beginning with the peak war years, continuing through integration and the first franchise relocation in 50 years;
- 1961–72, featuring expansions of both leagues as well as the strike zone (plus its later reversion), the 162-game schedule, collapse of offense, and the onset of divisional play;
- 1973–87, beginning with the designated hitter and featuring the heyday of multipurpose stadiums and artificial turf. More people come to the games and witness more offense, but the first prolonged strike splits the 1981 season in two;
- 1988–present, featuring a new explosion of offense and home runs, smaller ballparks, bigger crowds, more expansion, the Wild Card, and interleague play.

Players are only eligible to be listed in one era. Regardless of whether their careers spanned more than one era, leaders are placed in the era in which they played the most games or pitched the most innings. Their lifetime totals, however, are used to rank them in that era.

Some areas require further explanation:

- Plate Appearances count every time a batter completes an at bat, including hits, outs, walks, sacrifices, hit-by-pitches, reaching on errors, etc.
- Strikeout Percentage divides strikeouts by at bats to indicate what percentage of the time a batter strikes out.
- At Bats per Strikeout indicates how infrequently a batter strikes out.
- Relative Batting Average is a player's batting average compared to the league's batting average (where the latter is 1.0).
- Home Runs per 500 At Bats is derived by dividing home runs by games played and multiplied by 150. While the regular season has been 162 games since 1961, for most of baseball history the schedule has been 154 games or less.
- Runs/150 Games and RBI 150/Games show a player's typical production in a full season.
- Total Chances consists of putouts plus assists plus errors.
- Relief Wins and Relief Losses are decisions for pitchers who did not start the game.
- Blown Saves and Save Percentage are from 1969 to the present only.

The minimums for Single-Season Leaders include these areas for pitchers, hitters, and fielders:

- Starting Pitchers (for rate statistics): 1 inning pitched per scheduled game;
- Relief Pitchers (for rate statistics): 0.5 innings pitched per scheduled game;
- Pitcher Winning Percentage: 15 wins;
- Save Percentage: 20 saves;
- Batters (for rate statistics): 3.1 plate appearances per scheduled game;
- Pinch-Hit Batting Average: 30 at bats;
- Pitcher Batting Average: 20 hits (does not count pitcher batting stats since 1973 because of the DH rule);
- Stolen Base Percentage: 20 steals
- Fielding Statistics: 0.66 games played per scheduled game. Exceptions are outfielders with a 1.000 fielding average must have a minimum of 250 total chances, and pitchers with a 1.000 fielding average must field a minimum of 50 total chances.
- Catcher Fielding Statistics: 0.5 games played per scheduled game.

The minimum for Career Leaders include these areas for pitchers, hitters, and fielders:

- Starting Pitchers (for rate statistics): 400 innings pitched;
- Relief Pitchers (for rate statistics): 200 innings pitched;
- Save Percentage: 25 saves;
- Batters (for rate statistics): 400 games;
- Pinch-Hit Batting Average: 15 pinch hits;
- Pitcher Batting Average: 20 hits;
- Stolen Base Percentage: 40 steals.

GAMES

1	Mickey Mantle	2401
2	Lou Gehrig	2164
3	Yogi Berra	2116
4	Babe Ruth	2084
5	Bernie Williams	2076
6	Roy White	1881
7	**Derek Jeter**	**1835**
8	Bill Dickey	1789
9	Don Mattingly	1785
10	Joe DiMaggio	1736
11	Willie Randolph	1694
12	Frankie Crosetti	1683
13	Phil Rizzuto	1661
14	Tony Lazzeri	1659
15	Graig Nettles	1535
16	Elston Howard	1492
17	Wally Pipp	1488
18	Earle Combs	1455
19	**Jorge Posada**	**1432**
20	Thurman Munson	1423
21	Bobby Richardson	1412
22	Hank Bauer	1406
23	Gil McDougald	1336
24	Bob Meusel	1294
25	Tommy Henrich	1284
26	Bobby Murcer	1256
27	Paul O'Neill	1254
28	Horace Clarke	1230
29	Roger Peckinpaugh	1219
30	Red Rolfe	1175
31	Dave Winfield	1172
32	Tom Tresh	1098
33	Tony Kubek	1092
34	Bill Skowron	1087
35	Clete Boyer	1068
36	Charlie Keller	1066
37	Hal Chase	1061
38	Tino Martinez	1054
39	Joe Pepitone	1051
40	Lou Piniella	1037
41	Joe Gordon	1000
42	Ben Chapman	910
43	Joe Collins	908
	Aaron Ward	908
45	Chris Chambliss	885
46	Snuffy Stirnweiss	884
47	Willie Keeler	873
48	Hector Lopez	864
49	Roger Maris	850
50	George Selkirk	846

PLATE APPEARANCES

1	Mickey Mantle	9909
2	Lou Gehrig	9660
3	Babe Ruth	9198
4	Bernie Williams	9053
5	**Derek Jeter**	**8425**
6	Yogi Berra	8355
7	Roy White	7735
8	Don Mattingly	7721
9	Joe DiMaggio	7671
10	Willie Randolph	7465
11	Frankie Crosetti	7273
12	Bill Dickey	7060
13	Tony Lazzeri	7058
14	Phil Rizzuto	6711
15	Earle Combs	6507
16	Wally Pipp	6341
17	Graig Nettles	6247
18	Thurman Munson	5903
19	Bobby Richardson	5783
20	**Jorge Posada**	**5679**
21	Bob Meusel	5544
22	Elston Howard	5485
23	Tommy Henrich	5409
24	Red Rolfe	5405
25	Gil McDougald	5395
26	Hank Bauer	5373
27	Paul O'Neill	5368
28	Roger Peckinpaugh	5269
29	Horace Clarke	5143
30	Dave Winfield	5021
31	Bobby Murcer	4997
32	Tom Tresh	4518
33	Tony Kubek	4494
34	Hal Chase	4466
	Charlie Keller	4466
36	Tino Martinez	4244
37	Joe Gordon	4216
38	Joe Pepitone	4116
39	Bill Skowron	4102
40	Clete Boyer	4035
41	Ben Chapman	4014
42	Snuffy Stirnweiss	3800
43	Willie Keeler	3792
44	Chris Chambliss	3633
45	Lou Piniella	3577
46	Aaron Ward	3565
47	Roger Maris	3475
48	Joe Dugan	3328
49	George Selkirk	3322
50	Wid Conroy	3300

AT BATS

1	Mickey Mantle	8102
2	Lou Gehrig	8001
3	Bernie Williams	7869
4	Yogi Berra	7546
5	**Derek Jeter**	**7429**
6	Babe Ruth	7217
7	Don Mattingly	7003
8	Joe DiMaggio	6821
9	Roy White	6650
10	Willie Randolph	6303
11	Bill Dickey	6300
12	Frankie Crosetti	6277
13	Tony Lazzeri	6094
14	Phil Rizzuto	5816
15	Earle Combs	5746
16	Wally Pipp	5594
17	Graig Nettles	5519
18	Bobby Richardson	5386
19	Thurman Munson	5344
20	Elston Howard	5044
21	Bob Meusel	5032
22	Red Rolfe	4827
23	**Jorge Posada**	**4814**
24	Hank Bauer	4784
25	Horace Clarke	4723
26	Paul O'Neill	4700
27	Gil McDougald	4676
28	Tommy Henrich	4603
29	Roger Peckinpaugh	4555
30	Dave Winfield	4485
31	Bobby Murcer	4428
32	Tony Kubek	4167
33	Hal Chase	4158
34	Tom Tresh	3920
35	Joe Pepitone	3841
36	Tino Martinez	3770
37	Bill Skowron	3748
38	Joe Gordon	3686
39	Charlie Keller	3677
40	Clete Boyer	3658
41	Ben Chapman	3539
42	Chris Chambliss	3383
43	Willie Keeler	3313
44	Lou Piniella	3291
45	Snuffy Stirnweiss	3281
46	Aaron Ward	3139
47	Joe Dugan	3043
48	Roger Maris	3007
49	Wid Conroy	3005
50	George Selkirk	2790

RUNS

1	Babe Ruth	1959
2	Lou Gehrig	1888
3	Mickey Mantle	1677
4	Joe DiMaggio	1390
5	**Derek Jeter**	**1379**
6	Bernie Williams	1366
7	Earle Combs	1186
8	Yogi Berra	1174
9	Willie Randolph	1027
10	Don Mattingly	1007
11	Frankie Crosetti	1006
12	Roy White	964
13	Tony Lazzeri	952
14	Red Rolfe	942
15	Bill Dickey	930
16	Tommy Henrich	901
17	Phil Rizzuto	877
18	Wally Pipp	820
19	Hank Bauer	792
20	Bob Meusel	764
21	Graig Nettles	750
22	**Jorge Posada**	**744**
23	Dave Winfield	722
24	Paul O'Neill	720
25	Charlie Keller	712
26	Gil McDougald	697
27	Thurman Munson	696
28	Roger Peckinpaugh	670
29	Bobby Richardson	643
30	Bobby Murcer	641
31	Ben Chapman	626
32	Joe Gordon	596
33	Elston Howard	588
34	Tino Martinez	566
35	Snuffy Stirnweiss	562
36	Hal Chase	551
37	Tom Tresh	549
38	Horace Clarke	543
39	Tony Kubek	522
40	Roger Maris	520
41	Bill Skowron	517
42	Rickey Henderson	513
43	George Selkirk	503
44	**Alex Rodriguez**	**492**
45	Willie Keeler	482
46	**Jason Giambi**	**447**
47	Joe Pepitone	435
48	Clete Boyer	434
49	**Hideki Matsui**	**431**
50	Joe Dugan	426

RUNS BY ERA

1988–2007

1	**Derek Jeter**	**1379**
2	Bernie Williams	1366
3	Don Mattingly	1007
4	**Jorge Posada**	**744**
5	Paul O'Neill	720
6	Tino Martinez	566
7	**Alex Rodriguez**	**492**

1973–87

1	Willie Randolph	1027
2	Graig Nettles	750
3	Dave Winfield	722
4	Thurman Munson	696
5	Rickey Henderson	513
6	Chris Chambliss	415
7	Lou Piniella	392

1961–72

1	Roy White	964
2	Bobby Richardson	643
3	Bobby Murcer	641
4	Elston Howard	588
5	Tom Tresh	549
6	Horace Clarke	543
7	Tony Kubek	522

1943–60

1	Mickey Mantle	1677
2	Yogi Berra	1174
3	Phil Rizzuto	877
4	Hank Bauer	792
5	Gil McDougald	697
6	Snuffy Stirnweiss	562
7	Bill Skowron	517

1921–42

1	Babe Ruth	1959
2	Lou Gehrig	1888
3	Joe DiMaggio	1390
4	Earle Combs	1186
5	Frankie Crosetti	1006
6	Tony Lazzeri	952
7	Red Rolfe	942

1901–20

1	Wally Pipp	820
2	Roger Peckinpaugh	670
3	Hal Chase	551
4	Willie Keeler	482
5	Wid Conroy	356
6	Birdie Cree	345
7	Kid Elberfeld	330

RUNS/150 GAMES BY ERA

1988–2007

1	**Alex Rodriguez**	**117.3**
2	**Derek Jeter**	**112.7**
3	Chuck Knoblauch	105.2
4	Bernie Williams	98.7
5	Alfonso Soriano	97.6
6	**Hideki Matsui**	**94.9**
7	**Jason Giambi**	**89.2**

1973–87

1	Rickey Henderson	129.1
2	Dave Winfield	92.4
3	Willie Randolph	90.9
4	Mickey Rivers	88.5
5	Reggie Jackson	87.3
6	Don Baylor	84.3
7	Ken Griffey	74.9

1961–72

1	Roger Maris	91.8
2	Roy White	76.9
3	Bobby Murcer	76.6
4	Tom Tresh	75.0
5	Tony Kubek	71.7
6	Bobby Richardson	68.3
7	Horace Clarke	66.2

1943–60

1	Mickey Mantle	104.8
2	Snuffy Stirnweiss	95.4
3	Hank Bauer	84.5
4	Yogi Berra	83.2
5	Phil Rizzuto	79.2
6	Gil McDougald	78.3
7	Gene Woodling	77.6

1921–42

1	Babe Ruth	141.0
2	Lou Gehrig	130.9
3	Earle Combs	122.3
4	Red Rolfe	120.3
5	Joe DiMaggio	120.1
6	Tommy Henrich	105.3
7	Ben Chapman	103.2

1901–20

1	Bert Daniels	87.7
2	Willie Keeler	82.8
3	Wally Pipp	82.7
4	Roger Peckinpaugh	82.4
5	Hal Chase	77.9
6	Del Pratt	77.9
7	Fritz Maisel	75.3

HITS

1	Lou Gehrig	2721
2	Babe Ruth	2518
3	Mickey Mantle	2415
4	**Derek Jeter**	**2356**
5	Bernie Williams	2336
6	Joe DiMaggio	2214
7	Don Mattingly	2153
8	Yogi Berra	2148
9	Bill Dickey	1969
10	Earle Combs	1866
11	Roy White	1803
12	Tony Lazzeri	1784
13	Willie Randolph	1731
14	Phil Rizzuto	1588
15	Wally Pipp	1577
16	Bob Meusel	1565
17	Thurman Munson	1558
18	Frankie Crosetti	1541
19	Bobby Richardson	1432
20	Paul O'Neill	1426
21	Elston Howard	1405
22	Graig Nettles	1396
23	Red Rolfe	1394
24	**Jorge Posada**	**1334**
25	Hank Bauer	1326
26	Dave Winfield	1300
27	Tommy Henrich	1297
28	Gil McDougald	1291
29	Bobby Murcer	1231
30	Horace Clarke	1213
31	Hal Chase	1182
32	Roger Peckinpaugh	1170
33	Tony Kubek	1109
34	Bill Skowron	1103
35	Ben Chapman	1079
36	Charlie Keller	1053
37	Tino Martinez	1039
38	Joe Gordon	1000
39	Willie Keeler	974
40	Lou Piniella	971
41	Joe Pepitone	967
	Tom Tresh	967
43	Chris Chambliss	954
44	Snuffy Stirnweiss	899
45	Clete Boyer	882
46	Joe Dugan	871
47	Aaron Ward	840
48	George Selkirk	810
49	Roger Maris	797
50	Birdie Cree	761

HITS BY ERA

1988–2007

1	**Derek Jeter**	**2356**
2	Bernie Williams	2336
3	Don Mattingly	2153
4	Paul O'Neill	1426
5	**Jorge Posada**	**1334**
6	Tino Martinez	1039
7	**Hideki Matsui**	**753**

1973–87

1	Willie Randolph	1731
2	Thurman Munson	1558
3	Graig Nettles	1396
4	Dave Winfield	1300
5	Lou Piniella	971
6	Chris Chambliss	954
7	Rickey Henderson	663

1961–72

1	Roy White	1803
2	Bobby Richardson	1432
3	Elston Howard	1405
4	Bobby Murcer	1231
5	Horace Clarke	1213
6	Tony Kubek	1109
7	Joe Pepitone	967
	Tom Tresh	967

1943–60

1	Mickey Mantle	2415
2	Yogi Berra	2148
3	Phil Rizzuto	1588
4	Hank Bauer	1326
5	Gil McDougald	1291
6	Bill Skowron	1103
7	Snuffy Stirnweiss	899

1921–42

1	Lou Gehrig	2721
2	Babe Ruth	2518
3	Joe DiMaggio	2214
4	Bill Dickey	1969
5	Earle Combs	1866
6	Tony Lazzeri	1784
7	Bob Meusel	1565

1901–20

1	Wally Pipp	1577
2	Hal Chase	1182
3	Roger Peckinpaugh	1170
4	Willie Keeler	974
5	Birdie Cree	761
6	Wid Conroy	750
7	Frank Baker	735

DOUBLES

1	Lou Gehrig	534
2	Bernie Williams	449
3	Don Mattingly	442
4	Babe Ruth	424
5	Joe DiMaggio	389
6	**Derek Jeter**	**386**
7	Mickey Mantle	344
8	Bill Dickey	343
9	Bob Meusel	338
10	Tony Lazzeri	327
11	Yogi Berra	321
12	Earle Combs	309
13	Paul O'Neill	304
	Jorge Posada	**304**
15	Roy White	300
16	Tommy Henrich	269
17	Frankie Crosetti	260
18	Wally Pipp	259
	Willie Randolph	259
20	Red Rolfe	257
21	Phil Rizzuto	239
22	Dave Winfield	236
23	Thurman Munson	229
24	Hank Bauer	211
	Elston Howard	211
26	Ben Chapman	209
27	Graig Nettles	202
28	Bobby Richardson	196
29	Bobby Murcer	192
30	Tino Martinez	189
31	Gil McDougald	187
32	Joe Gordon	186
33	Tony Kubek	178
	Lou Piniella	178
35	Roger Peckinpaugh	174
36	Bill Skowron	173
37	Chris Chambliss	171
38	Tom Tresh	166
39	Hal Chase	165
40	Charlie Keller	163
41	**Hideki Matsui**	**158**
42	Horace Clarke	149
43	Joe Dugan	147
44	Clete Boyer	140
	Snuffy Stirnweiss	140
46	Aaron Ward	133
47	George Selkirk	131
48	Alfonso Soriano	124
49	Jimmy Williams	123
50	Frank Baker	121

DOUBLES BY ERA

1988–2007

1	Bernie Williams	449
2	Don Mattingly	442
3	**Derek Jeter**	**386**
4	Paul O'Neill	304
	Jorge Posada	**304**
6	Tino Martinez	189
7	**Hideki Matsui**	**158**

1973–87

1	Willie Randolph	259
2	Dave Winfield	236
3	Thurman Munson	229
4	Graig Nettles	202
5	Lou Piniella	178
6	Chris Chambliss	171
7	Rickey Henderson	119

1961–72

1	Roy White	300
2	Elston Howard	211
3	Bobby Richardson	196
4	Bobby Murcer	192
5	Tony Kubek	178
6	Tom Tresh	166
7	Horace Clarke	149

1943–60

1	Mickey Mantle	344
2	Yogi Berra	321
3	Phil Rizzuto	239
4	Hank Bauer	211
5	Gil McDougald	187
6	Bill Skowron	173
7	Snuffy Stirnweiss	140

1921–42

1	Lou Gehrig	534
2	Babe Ruth	424
3	Joe DiMaggio	389
4	Bill Dickey	343
5	Bob Meusel	338
6	Tony Lazzeri	327
7	Earle Combs	309

1901–20

1	Wally Pipp	259
2	Roger Peckinpaugh	174
3	Hal Chase	165
4	Jimmy Williams	123
5	Frank Baker	121
6	Birdie Cree	117
7	Wid Conroy	111

Triples

1	Lou Gehrig	163
2	Earle Combs	154
3	Joe DiMaggio	131
4	Wally Pipp	121
5	Tony Lazzeri	115
6	Babe Ruth	106
7	Bob Meusel	87
8	Tommy Henrich	73
9	Bill Dickey	72
	Mickey Mantle	72
11	Charlie Keller	69
12	Red Rolfe	67
13	Snuffy Stirnweiss	66
14	Frankie Crosetti	65
15	Ben Chapman	64
16	Birdie Cree	62
	Phil Rizzuto	62
18	Wid Conroy	59
19	Willie Randolph	58
20	Hank Bauer	56
21	Bernie Williams	55
22	**Derek Jeter**	**54**
23	Roger Peckinpaugh	53
24	Gil McDougald	51
	Roy White	51
26	Hal Chase	50
	Elston Howard	50
28	Yogi Berra	49
29	Aaron Ward	46
30	Johnny Lindell	45
	Jimmy Williams	45
32	Bill Skowron	44
33	George Selkirk	41
34	Gene Woodling	40
35	Joe Gordon	38
36	Bobby Richardson	37
37	Mark Koenig	35
	Dave Winfield	35
39	Roy Hartzell	34
40	Bert Daniels	33
	Frank LaPorte	33
	Tom Tresh	33
43	Thurman Munson	32
44	Harry Wolter	31
45	Billy Johnson	30
	Willie Keeler	30
	Tony Kubek	30
48	Bobby Murcer	29
49	3 players tied	28

Triples by Era

	Player	
1988–2007		
1	Bernie Williams	55
2	**Derek Jeter**	**54**
3	Don Mattingly	20
4	Paul O'Neill	14
5	Chuck Knoblauch	13
6	**Robinson Cano**	**12**
	Roberto Kelly	12
1973–87		
1	Willie Randolph	58
2	Dave Winfield	35
3	Thurman Munson	32
4	Mickey Rivers	26
5	Chris Chambliss	25
6	Graig Nettles	20
	Lou Piniella	20
1961–72		
1	Roy White	51
2	Elston Howard	50
3	Bobby Richardson	37
4	Tom Tresh	33
5	Tony Kubek	30
6	Bobby Murcer	29
7	Clete Boyer	25
1943–60		
1	Mickey Mantle	72
2	Snuffy Stirnweiss	66
3	Phil Rizzuto	62
4	Hank Bauer	56
5	Gil McDougald	51
6	Yogi Berra	49
7	Johnny Lindell	45
1921–42		
1	Lou Gehrig	163
2	Earle Combs	154
3	Joe DiMaggio	131
4	Tony Lazzeri	115
5	Babe Ruth	106
6	Bob Meusel	87
7	Tommy Henrich	73
1901–20		
1	Wally Pipp	121
2	Birdie Cree	62
3	Wid Conroy	59
4	Roger Peckinpaugh	53
5	Hal Chase	50
6	Jimmy Williams	45
7	Roy Hartzell	34

Home Runs

1	Babe Ruth	659
2	Mickey Mantle	536
3	Lou Gehrig	493
4	Joe DiMaggio	361
5	Yogi Berra	358
6	Bernie Williams	287
7	Graig Nettles	250
8	Don Mattingly	222
9	**Jorge Posada**	**218**
10	Dave Winfield	205
11	Roger Maris	203
12	Bill Dickey	202
13	**Derek Jeter**	**195**
14	Tino Martinez	192
15	Paul O'Neill	185
16	Charlie Keller	184
17	Tommy Henrich	183
18	**Jason Giambi**	**177**
19	Bobby Murcer	175
20	**Alex Rodriguez**	**173**
21	Tony Lazzeri	169
22	Joe Pepitone	166
23	Bill Skowron	165
24	Elston Howard	161
25	Roy White	160
26	Hank Bauer	158
27	Joe Gordon	153
28	Bob Meusel	146
29	Reggie Jackson	144
30	Tom Tresh	140
31	Thurman Munson	113
32	Gil McDougald	112
33	George Selkirk	108
34	Mike Pagliarulo	105
35	**Hideki Matsui**	**103**
36	Frankie Crosetti	98
	Alfonso Soriano	98
38	Clete Boyer	95
39	Oscar Gamble	87
40	Joe Collins	86
41	Danny Tartabull	81
42	Wally Pipp	80
43	Chris Chambliss	79
44	Rickey Henderson	78
45	Gary Sheffield	76
46	Mike Stanley	72
47	Don Baylor	71
	Matt Nokes	71
49	Hector Lopez	69
	Red Rolfe	69

Home Runs by Era

1988–2007		
1	Bernie Williams	287
2	Don Mattingly	222
3	**Jorge Posada**	**218**
4	**Derek Jeter**	**195**
5	Tino Martinez	192
6	Paul O'Neill	185
7	**Jason Giambi**	**177**
1973–87		
1	Graig Nettles	250
2	Dave Winfield	205
3	Reggie Jackson	144
4	Thurman Munson	113
5	Mike Pagliarulo	105
6	Oscar Gamble	87
7	Chris Chambliss	79
1961–72		
1	Roger Maris	203
2	Bobby Murcer	175
3	Joe Pepitone	166
4	Elston Howard	161
5	Roy White	160
6	Tom Tresh	140
7	Clete Boyer	95
1943–60		
1	Mickey Mantle	536
2	Yogi Berra	358
3	Bill Skowron	165
4	Hank Bauer	158
5	Gil McDougald	112
6	Joe Collins	86
7	Nick Etten	63
	Johnny Lindell	63
1921–42		
1	Babe Ruth	659
2	Lou Gehrig	493
3	Joe DiMaggio	361
4	Bill Dickey	202
5	Charlie Keller	184
6	Tommy Henrich	183
7	Tony Lazzeri	169
1901–20		
1	Wally Pipp	80
2	Frank Baker	48
3	Roger Peckinpaugh	36
4	Hal Chase	20
5	Ping Bodie	16
	Jimmy Williams	16
7	Wid Conroy	12
	Elmer Miller	12

Home Runs/500 at Bats

1	Babe Ruth	45.7
2	**Alex Rodriguez**	**36.6**
3	**Jason Giambi**	**35.7**
4	Roger Maris	33.8
5	Mickey Mantle	33.1
6	Lou Gehrig	30.8
7	Reggie Jackson	30.7
8	Johnny Blanchard	30.1
9	Oscar Gamble	29.9
10	Danny Tartabull	26.6
11	Joe DiMaggio	26.5
12	Mike Stanley	26.2
13	Matt Nokes	25.8
14	Tino Martinez	25.5
15	Charlie Keller	25.0
16	Alfonso Soriano	24.4
17	Yogi Berra	23.7
18	Don Baylor	23.6
19	Mike Pagliarulo	23.1
20	Dave Winfield	22.9
21	Graig Nettles	22.6
22	**Jorge Posada**	**22.6**
23	Bill Skowron	22.0
24	Joe Pepitone	21.6
25	Joe Gordon	20.8
26	**Hideki Matsui**	**20.2**
27	Ron Blomberg	20.0
28	Tommy Henrich	19.9
29	Bobby Murcer	19.8
30	Paul O'Neill	19.7
31	George Selkirk	19.4
32	Joe Collins	18.5
33	Bernie Williams	18.2
34	Tom Tresh	17.9
35	Mel Hall	17.5
36	Jim Leyritz	17.2
37	Scott Brosius	17.1
38	Rickey Henderson	16.9
39	Hank Bauer	16.5
40	Bill Dickey	16.0
41	Elston Howard	16.0
42	Don Mattingly	15.9
43	Nick Etten	15.4
44	**Robinson Cano**	**14.8**
45	Bob Meusel	14.5
46	Tony Lazzeri	13.9
47	Hector Lopez	13.7
48	**Derek Jeter**	**13.1**
49	Clete Boyer	13.0
50	Ken Griffey	12.4

Home Runs/500 at Bats by Era

1988–2007		
1	**Alex Rodriguez**	**36.6**
2	**Jason Giambi**	**35.7**
3	Danny Tartabull	26.6
4	Mike Stanley	26.2
5	Matt Nokes	25.8
6	Tino Martinez	25.5
7	Alfonso Soriano	24.4
1973–87		
1	Reggie Jackson	30.7
2	Oscar Gamble	29.9
3	Don Baylor	23.6
4	Mike Pagliarulo	23.1
5	Dave Winfield	22.9
6	Graig Nettles	22.6
7	Ron Blomberg	20.0
1961–72		
1	Roger Maris	33.8
2	Johnny Blanchard	30.1
3	Joe Pepitone	21.6
4	Bobby Murcer	19.8
5	Tom Tresh	17.9
6	Elston Howard	16.0
7	Hector Lopez	13.7
1943–60		
1	Mickey Mantle	33.1
2	Yogi Berra	23.7
3	Bill Skowron	22.0
4	Joe Collins	18.5
5	Hank Bauer	16.5
6	Nick Etten	15.4
7	Johnny Lindell	12.3
1921–42		
1	Babe Ruth	45.7
2	Lou Gehrig	30.8
3	Joe DiMaggio	26.5
4	Charlie Keller	25.0
5	Joe Gordon	20.8
6	Tommy Henrich	19.9
7	George Selkirk	19.4
1901–20		
1	Frank Baker	9.4
2	Wally Pipp	7.2
3	Roger Peckinpaugh	4.0
4	Ray Caldwell	3.7
5	Del Pratt	3.2
6	Jimmy Williams	3.2
7	Hal Chase	2.4

Extra Base Hits

1	Lou Gehrig	1190
2	Babe Ruth	1189
3	Mickey Mantle	952
4	Joe DiMaggio	881
5	Bernie Williams	791
6	Yogi Berra	728
7	Don Mattingly	684
8	**Derek Jeter**	**635**
9	Bill Dickey	617
10	Tony Lazzeri	611
11	Bob Meusel	571
12	**Jorge Posada**	**530**
13	Tommy Henrich	525
14	Earle Combs	521
15	Roy White	511
16	Paul O'Neill	503
17	Dave Winfield	476
18	Graig Nettles	472
19	Wally Pipp	460
20	Hank Bauer	425
21	Frankie Crosetti	423
22	Elston Howard	422
23	Charlie Keller	416
24	Bobby Murcer	396
25	Red Rolfe	393
26	Tino Martinez	392
27	Bill Skowron	382
28	Joe Gordon	377
29	Thurman Munson	374
30	Willie Randolph	365
31	Gil McDougald	350
32	Phil Rizzuto	339
	Tom Tresh	339
34	Ben Chapman	333
35	Roger Maris	330
36	Joe Pepitone	303
37	**Jason Giambi**	**293**
38	**Alex Rodriguez**	**287**
39	George Selkirk	280
40	Chris Chambliss	275
41	Reggie Jackson	273
42	**Hideki Matsui**	**271**
43	Bobby Richardson	267
44	Tony Kubek	265
45	Roger Peckinpaugh	263
46	Clete Boyer	260
47	Lou Piniella	255
48	Hal Chase	235
49	Snuffy Stirnweiss	233
50	Alfonso Soriano	232

Total Bases

1	Babe Ruth	5131
2	Lou Gehrig	5060
3	Mickey Mantle	4511
4	Joe DiMaggio	3948
5	Bernie Williams	3756
6	Yogi Berra	3641
7	**Derek Jeter**	**3435**
8	Don Mattingly	3301
9	Bill Dickey	3062
10	Tony Lazzeri	2848
11	Roy White	2685
12	Earle Combs	2657
13	Bob Meusel	2515
14	Graig Nettles	2388
15	Wally Pipp	2318
16	Paul O'Neill	2313
17	**Jorge Posada**	**2308**
18	Tommy Henrich	2261
19	Willie Randolph	2250
20	Frankie Crosetti	2225
21	Dave Winfield	2221
22	Elston Howard	2199
23	Thurman Munson	2190
24	Hank Bauer	2123
25	Phil Rizzuto	2065
26	Bobby Murcer	2006
27	Red Rolfe	1992
28	Gil McDougald	1916
29	Charlie Keller	1906
30	Bill Skowron	1859
31	Tino Martinez	1826
32	Bobby Richardson	1804
33	Joe Gordon	1721
34	Joe Pepitone	1626
35	Tom Tresh	1619
36	Ben Chapman	1596
37	Roger Peckinpaugh	1558
38	Roger Maris	1550
39	Tony Kubek	1518
40	Hal Chase	1507
41	Horace Clarke	1489
42	Chris Chambliss	1412
43	Lou Piniella	1360
44	Clete Boyer	1357
45	**Alex Rodriguez**	**1352**
46	George Selkirk	1347
47	**Jason Giambi**	**1299**
48	Snuffy Stirnweiss	1252
49	**Hideki Matsui**	**1240**
50	Reggie Jackson	1236

Runs Batted In

1	Lou Gehrig	1995
2	Babe Ruth	1971
3	Joe DiMaggio	1537
4	Mickey Mantle	1509
5	Yogi Berra	1430
6	Bernie Williams	1257
7	Bill Dickey	1209
8	Tony Lazzeri	1154
9	Don Mattingly	1099
10	Bob Meusel	1005
11	**Derek Jeter**	**933**
12	**Jorge Posada**	**861**
13	Paul O'Neill	858
14	Graig Nettles	834
15	Wally Pipp	826
16	Dave Winfield	818
17	Tommy Henrich	795
18	Roy White	758
19	Tino Martinez	739
20	Elston Howard	733
21	Charlie Keller	723
22	Thurman Munson	701
23	Bobby Murcer	687
24	Bill Skowron	672
25	Hank Bauer	654
26	Frankie Crosetti	649
27	Earle Combs	632
28	Joe Gordon	617
29	Ben Chapman	589
30	Gil McDougald	576
	George Selkirk	576
32	Phil Rizzuto	563
33	Willie Randolph	549
34	Roger Maris	548
35	Joe Pepitone	541
36	**Alex Rodriguez**	**513**
37	**Jason Giambi**	**508**
38	Red Rolfe	497
39	Hal Chase	494
40	Tom Tresh	493
41	**Hideki Matsui**	**462**
42	Reggie Jackson	461
43	Chris Chambliss	454
44	Roger Peckinpaugh	427
45	Lou Piniella	417
46	Clete Boyer	393
47	Bobby Richardson	390
	Aaron Ward	390
49	Billy Johnson	388
50	Frank Baker	375

Runs Batted In by Era

1988–2007		
1	Bernie Williams	1257
2	Don Mattingly	1099
3	**Derek Jeter**	**933**
4	**Jorge Posada**	**861**
5	Paul O'Neill	858
6	Tino Martinez	739
7	**Alex Rodriguez**	**513**
1973–87		
1	Graig Nettles	834
2	Dave Winfield	818
3	Thurman Munson	701
4	Willie Randolph	549
5	Reggie Jackson	461
6	Chris Chambliss	454
7	Lou Piniella	417
1961–72		
1	Roy White	758
2	Elston Howard	733
3	Bobby Murcer	687
4	Roger Maris	548
5	Joe Pepitone	541
6	Tom Tresh	493
7	Clete Boyer	393
1943–60		
1	Mickey Mantle	1509
2	Yogi Berra	1430
3	Bill Skowron	672
4	Hank Bauer	654
5	Gil McDougald	576
6	Phil Rizzuto	563
7	Billy Johnson	388
1921–42		
1	Lou Gehrig	1995
2	Babe Ruth	1971
3	Joe DiMaggio	1537
4	Bill Dickey	1209
5	Tony Lazzeri	1154
6	Bob Meusel	1005
7	Tommy Henrich	795
1901–20		
1	Wally Pipp	826
2	Hal Chase	494
3	Roger Peckinpaugh	427
4	Frank Baker	375
5	Jimmy Williams	358
6	Birdie Cree	332
7	Wid Conroy	266
	Roy Hartzell	266

WALKS

1	Babe Ruth	1852
2	Mickey Mantle	1733
3	Lou Gehrig	1508
4	Bernie Williams	1069
5	Willie Randolph	1005
6	Roy White	934
7	Tony Lazzeri	830
8	Frankie Crosetti	792
9	Joe DiMaggio	790
10	**Jorge Posada**	**766**
11	**Derek Jeter**	**761**
12	Charlie Keller	760
13	Tommy Henrich	712
14	Yogi Berra	704
15	Bill Dickey	678
16	Earle Combs	670
17	Phil Rizzuto	651
18	Graig Nettles	627
19	Don Mattingly	588
20	Paul O'Neill	586
21	Gil McDougald	559
22	**Jason Giambi**	**543**
23	Red Rolfe	526
24	Tom Tresh	511
25	Roger Peckinpaugh	508
26	Hank Bauer	491
	Bobby Murcer	491
28	Wally Pipp	490
29	George Selkirk	486
30	Joe Gordon	481
31	Dave Winfield	477
32	Snuffy Stirnweiss	468
33	Thurman Munson	438
34	Roger Maris	413
35	Rickey Henderson	406
36	Tino Martinez	405
37	Ben Chapman	404
38	Gene Woodling	378
39	Horace Clarke	357
40	**Alex Rodriguez**	**356**
41	Bob Meusel	349
42	Elston Howard	342
43	Joe Collins	338
44	Roy Hartzell	328
45	Reggie Jackson	326
46	Wade Boggs	324
47	**Hideki Matsui**	**314**
48	Nick Etten	301
49	Clete Boyer	297
50	Danny Tartabull	294

WALK PERCENTAGE (BB/PA)

1	Babe Ruth	20.13
2	Mickey Mantle	17.49
3	**Jason Giambi**	**17.36**
4	Charlie Keller	17.02
5	Lou Gehrig	15.61
6	Rickey Henderson	14.84
7	George Selkirk	14.63
8	Gene Woodling	14.12
9	**Jorge Posada**	**13.49**
10	Willie Randolph	13.46
11	Tommy Henrich	13.16
12	Oscar Gamble	13.01
13	**Alex Rodriguez**	**12.74**
14	Nick Etten	12.69
15	Joe Collins	12.52
16	Wade Boggs	12.46
17	Snuffy Stirnweiss	12.32
18	Roy White	12.07
19	Reggie Jackson	12.04
20	Roger Maris	11.88
21	Bernie Williams	11.81
22	Tony Lazzeri	11.76
23	Roy Hartzell	11.69
24	Wally Schang	11.55
25	Bobby Brown	11.49
26	Joe Gordon	11.41
27	Sammy Byrd	11.36
28	Tom Tresh	11.31
29	Paul O'Neill	10.92
30	Frankie Crosetti	10.89
31	Jim Leyritz	10.89
32	**Hideki Matsui**	**10.78**
33	Chuck Knoblauch	10.61
34	Gil McDougald	10.36
35	Joe DiMaggio	10.30
36	Earle Combs	10.30
37	Fritz Maisel	10.21
38	Ben Chapman	10.06
39	Graig Nettles	10.04
40	Bobby Murcer	9.83
41	Red Rolfe	9.73
42	Jerry Coleman	9.73
43	Phil Rizzuto	9.70
44	Roger Peckinpaugh	9.64
45	Bill Dickey	9.60
46	Tino Martinez	9.54
47	Dave Winfield	9.50
48	Billy Johnson	9.40
49	Fred Stanley	9.33
50	Hank Bauer	9.14

STRIKEOUTS

1	Mickey Mantle	1710
2	**Derek Jeter**	**1291**
3	Bernie Williams	1212
4	**Jorge Posada**	**1139**
5	Babe Ruth	1122
6	Tony Lazzeri	821
7	Frankie Crosetti	799
8	Lou Gehrig	790
9	Graig Nettles	739
10	Elston Howard	717
11	Paul O'Neill	710
12	Roy White	708
13	Dave Winfield	652
14	Tom Tresh	651
15	Gil McDougald	623
16	Clete Boyer	608
17	**Jason Giambi**	**595**
18	Hank Bauer	594
19	Bill Skowron	588
20	Reggie Jackson	573
21	Thurman Munson	571
22	Bobby Murcer	564
23	Bob Meusel	556
24	Tino Martinez	546
25	**Alex Rodriguez**	**529**
26	Willie Randolph	512
27	Mike Pagliarulo	510
28	Joe Gordon	508
29	Wally Pipp	495
30	Charlie Keller	481
31	Roger Peckinpaugh	457
32	Roberto Kelly	446
33	Don Mattingly	444
34	Tony Kubek	441
35	Danny Tartabull	436
36	Alfonso Soriano	430
37	Roger Maris	417
38	Hector Lopez	415
39	Joe Pepitone	413
40	Yogi Berra	411
41	Aaron Ward	399
42	Phil Rizzuto	398
43	Randy Velarde	395
44	Tommy Henrich	383
45	Jim Leyritz	380
46	Jesse Barfield	379
47	Snuffy Stirnweiss	373
48	Joe DiMaggio	369
49	**Hideki Matsui**	**363**
50	Ben Chapman	362

AT BATS PER STRIKEOUT

1	Everett Scott	29.3
2	Frank Baker	22.4
3	Bobby Richardson	22.2
4	Bill Dickey	21.8
5	Mark Koenig	21.7
6	Del Pratt	21.3
7	Earle Combs	20.7
8	Whitey Witt	19.0
9	Joe DiMaggio	18.5
10	Bobby Brown	18.4
11	Yogi Berra	18.4
12	Nick Etten	17.3
13	Joe Dugan	16.6
14	Don Mattingly	15.8
15	Steve Sax	15.0
16	Bucky Dent	14.7
17	Phil Rizzuto	14.6
18	Red Rolfe	14.4
19	Horace Clarke	13.3
20	Gene Woodling	12.3
21	Willie Randolph	12.3
22	Tommy Henrich	12.0
23	Lou Piniella	11.9
24	Mickey Rivers	11.9

STRIKEOUT PERCENTAGE

1	Danny Tartabull	28.59
2	Reggie Jackson	24.39
3	**Jason Giambi**	**24.03**
4	**Jorge Posada**	**23.66**
5	Mike Stanley	22.89
6	Jim Leyritz	22.59
7	Mike Pagliarulo	22.43
8	**Alex Rodriguez**	**22.41**
9	Alfonso Soriano	21.39
10	Mickey Mantle	21.11
11	Pat Kelly	20.59
12	Bob Meacham	20.13
13	Randy Velarde	19.94
14	Roberto Kelly	19.37
15	**Derek Jeter**	**17.38**
16	Scott Brosius	17.20
17	Clete Boyer	16.62
18	Tom Tresh	16.61
19	Hector Lopez	16.53
20	Bill Skowron	15.69
21	Babe Ruth	15.55
22	Bernie Williams	15.40
23	Paul O'Neill	15.11
24	Gene Michael	14.80

BATTING AVERAGE

1	Babe Ruth	.349
2	Lou Gehrig	.340
3	Earle Combs	.325
4	Joe DiMaggio	.325
5	**Derek Jeter**	**.317**
6	**Robinson Cano**	**.314**
7	Wade Boggs	.313
8	Bill Dickey	.313
9	Bob Meusel	.311
10	Don Mattingly	.307
11	Ben Chapman	.305
12	Paul O'Neill	.303
13	**Alex Rodriguez**	**.303**
14	Ron Blomberg	.302
15	Whitey Witt	.300
16	Mickey Rivers	.299
17	Mickey Mantle	.298
18	Wally Schang	.297
19	Bernie Williams	.297
20	Lou Piniella	.295
21	**Hideki Matsui**	**.295**
22	Del Pratt	.295
23	Bill Skowron	.294
24	Willie Keeler	.294
25	Steve Sax	.294
26	Tony Lazzeri	.293
27	Birdie Cree	.292
28	Thurman Munson	.292
29	George Selkirk	.290
30	Dave Winfield	.290
31	Red Rolfe	.289
32	Frank Baker	.288
33	Rickey Henderson	.288
34	Charlie Keller	.286
35	Joe Dugan	.286
36	Gene Woodling	.285
37	Mike Stanley	.285
38	Mark Koenig	.285
39	Ken Griffey	.285
40	Yogi Berra	.285
41	Hal Chase	.284
42	Myril Hoag	.284
43	Alfonso Soriano	.284
44	Chris Chambliss	.282
45	Wally Pipp	.282
46	Tommy Henrich	.282
47	Reggie Jackson	.281
48	Sammy Byrd	.281
49	Bobby Brown	.279
50	Elston Howard	.279

BATTING AVERAGE BY ERA

1988–2007

1	**Derek Jeter**	**.317**
2	**Robinson Cano**	**.314**
3	Wade Boggs	.313
4	Don Mattingly	.307
5	Paul O'Neill	.303
6	**Alex Rodriguez**	**.303**
7	Bernie Williams	.297

1973–87

1	Ron Blomberg	.302
2	Mickey Rivers	.299
3	Lou Piniella	.295
4	Thurman Munson	.292
5	Dave Winfield	.290
6	Rickey Henderson	.288
7	Ken Griffey	.285

1961–72

1	Elston Howard	.279
2	Bobby Murcer	.278
3	Roy White	.271
4	Tony Kubek	.266
5	Bobby Richardson	.266
6	Roger Maris	.265
7	Hector Lopez	.262

1943–60

1	Mickey Mantle	.298
2	Bill Skowron	.294
3	Gene Woodling	.285
4	Yogi Berra	.285
5	Bobby Brown	.279
6	Hank Bauer	.277
7	Gil McDougald	.276

1921–42

1	Babe Ruth	.349
2	Lou Gehrig	.340
3	Earle Combs	.325
4	Joe DiMaggio	.325
5	Bill Dickey	.313
6	Bob Meusel	.311
7	Ben Chapman	.305

1901–20

1	Del Pratt	.295
2	Willie Keeler	.294
3	Birdie Cree	.292
4	Frank Baker	.288
5	Hal Chase	.284
6	Wally Pipp	.282
7	Frank LaPorte	.274

ON-BASE PERCENTAGE

1	Babe Ruth	.484
2	Lou Gehrig	.447
3	Mickey Mantle	.421
4	**Jason Giambi**	**.410**
	Charlie Keller	.410
6	**Alex Rodriguez**	**.403**
7	George Selkirk	.400
8	Joe DiMaggio	.398
9	Earle Combs	.397
10	Wade Boggs	.396
11	Rickey Henderson	.395
12	Wally Schang	.390
13	**Derek Jeter**	**.388**
	Gene Woodling	.388
15	Bill Dickey	.382
	Tommy Henrich	.382
17	**Jorge Posada**	**.381**
	Bernie Williams	.381
19	Ben Chapman	.379
	Tony Lazzeri	.379
21	Paul O'Neill	.377
	Mike Stanley	.377
23	Whitey Witt	.375
24	Willie Randolph	.374
25	Danny Tartabull	.372
26	Reggie Jackson	.371
	Hideki Matsui	**.371**
28	Ron Blomberg	.370
	Nick Etten	.370
30	Birdie Cree	.368
	Lyn Lary	.368
	Butch Wynegar	.368
33	Bobby Brown	.367
34	Sammy Byrd	.366
	Chuck Knoblauch	.366
36	Snuffy Stirnweiss	.365
37	Bert Daniels	.361
	Oscar Gamble	.361
39	Red Rolfe	.360
	Roy White	.360
41	Jim Leyritz	.359
42	Joe Gordon	.358
	Don Mattingly	.358
	Bob Meusel	.358
45	Roger Maris	.357
46	Gil McDougald	.356
	Dave Winfield	.356
48	Roy Hartzell	.355
49	Phil Rizzuto	.351
50	Joe Collins	.350

SLUGGING AVERAGE

1	Babe Ruth	.711
2	Lou Gehrig	.632
3	Joe DiMaggio	.579
4	**Alex Rodriguez**	**.573**
5	Mickey Mantle	.557
6	Reggie Jackson	.526
7	**Jason Giambi**	**.525**
8	Charlie Keller	.518
9	Roger Maris	.515
10	Mike Stanley	.504
11	Alfonso Soriano	.502
12	Bob Meusel	.500
13	Oscar Gamble	.496
14	Bill Skowron	.496
15	Dave Winfield	.495
16	Paul O'Neill	.492
17	Tommy Henrich	.491
18	**Robinson Cano**	**.489**
19	Bill Dickey	.486
20	Ron Blomberg	.486
21	**Hideki Matsui**	**.485**
22	Tino Martinez	.484
23	George Selkirk	.483
24	Yogi Berra	.483
25	**Jorge Posada**	**.479**
26	Bernie Williams	.477
27	Danny Tartabull	.473
28	Don Baylor	.472
29	Don Mattingly	.471
30	Tony Lazzeri	.467
31	Joe Gordon	.467
32	Earle Combs	.462
33	**Derek Jeter**	**.462**
34	Johnny Blanchard	.461
35	Rickey Henderson	.455
36	Bobby Murcer	.453
37	Ben Chapman	.451
38	Hank Bauer	.444
39	Matt Nokes	.437
40	Mel Hall	.437
41	Elston Howard	.436
42	Gene Woodling	.434
43	Graig Nettles	.433
44	Nick Etten	.429
45	Scott Brosius	.428
46	Johnny Lindell	.428
47	Mike Pagliarulo	.427
48	Joe Pepitone	.423
49	Mickey Rivers	.422
50	Sammy Byrd	.422

ON-BASE PLUS SLUGGING

1	Babe Ruth	1195
2	Lou Gehrig	1079
3	Mickey Mantle	978
4	Joe DiMaggio	977
5	**Alex Rodriguez**	**976**
6	**Jason Giambi**	**935**
7	Charlie Keller	928
8	Reggie Jackson	897
9	George Selkirk	883
10	Mike Stanley	881
11	Tommy Henrich	873
12	Roger Maris	872
13	Paul O'Neill	869
14	Bill Dickey	868
15	**Jorge Posada**	**860**
16	Earle Combs	859
17	Bob Meusel	858
	Bernie Williams	858
19	Oscar Gamble	857
20	Ron Blomberg	856
	Hideki Matsui	**856**
22	Dave Winfield	851
23	Rickey Henderson	850
	Derek Jeter	**850**
25	Tony Lazzeri	846
26	Danny Tartabull	845
27	Bill Skowron	842
28	**Robinson Cano**	**835**
29	Yogi Berra	831
	Tino Martinez	831
31	Ben Chapman	830
32	Don Mattingly	829
33	Joe Gordon	825
34	Alfonso Soriano	824
35	Gene Woodling	822
36	Don Baylor	816
37	Wade Boggs	803
38	Bobby Murcer	802
39	Nick Etten	799
40	Wally Schang	796
41	Hank Bauer	791
42	Sammy Byrd	788
43	Johnny Blanchard	786
44	Red Rolfe	773
45	Jim Leyritz	772
46	Joe Collins	771
	Johnny Lindell	771
48	Chuck Knoblauch	768
49	Birdie Cree	766
	Gil McDougald	766

ADJUSTED OPS

1	Babe Ruth	212
2	Lou Gehrig	182
3	Mickey Mantle	173
4	Joe DiMaggio	156
5	Charlie Keller	153
6	**Alex Rodriguez**	**152**
7	Ron Blomberg	149
8	Reggie Jackson	147
9	**Jason Giambi**	**145**
10	Roger Maris	141
11	Oscar Gamble	140
12	Mike Stanley	135
13	Rickey Henderson	134
	Dave Winfield	134
15	Tommy Henrich	132
16	Bill Skowron	131
17	Bobby Murcer	130
18	Danny Tartabull	129
19	Bill Dickey	128
	George Selkirk	128
21	Don Baylor	127
	Yogi Berra	127
	Earle Combs	127
	Nick Etten	127
	Don Mattingly	127
	Paul O'Neill	127
27	Bernie Williams	125
	Gene Woodling	125
29	Birdie Cree	124
	Hideki Matsui	**124**
	Jorge Posada	**124**
32	Tony Lazzeri	123
33	**Derek Jeter**	**122**
34	Ben Chapman	121
	Joe Gordon	121
	Bob Meusel	121
	Roy White	121
38	Hank Bauer	116
	Johnny Blanchard	116
	Robinson Cano	**116**
	Thurman Munson	116
42	Alfonso Soriano	115
43	Frank Baker	114
	Johnny Lindell	114
	Tino Martinez	114
	Graig Nettles	114
	Tom Tresh	114
48	Wade Boggs	113
49	Joe Collins	112
	Gil McDougald	112

GAMES

FIRST BASE

1 Lou Gehrig....2137
2 Don Mattingly....1634
3 Wally Pipp....1468
4 Tino Martinez....1026
5 Hal Chase....1016

SECOND BASE

1 Willie Randolph....1688
2 Tony Lazzeri....1441
3 Bobby Richardson....1339
4 Horace Clarke....1081
5 Joe Gordon....970

SHORTSTOP

1 Derek Jeter....1825
2 Phil Rizzuto....1647
3 Frankie Crosetti....1516
4 Roger Peckinpaugh....1214
5 Tony Kubek....882

THIRD BASE

1 Graig Nettles....1509
2 Red Rolfe....1084
3 Clete Boyer....909
4 Joe Dugan....774
5 Mike Pagliarulo....684

OUTFIELD

1 Babe Ruth....2045
2 Mickey Mantle....2019
3 Bernie Williams....1924
4 Joe DiMaggio....1721
5 Roy White....1625
6 Earle Combs....1387
7 Hank Bauer....1347
8 Paul O'Neill....1221
9 Bob Meusel....1192
10 Dave Winfield....1123

CATCHER

1 Bill Dickey....1708
2 Yogi Berra....1697
3 Jorge Posada....1360
4 Thurman Munson....1278
5 Elston Howard....1029

PITCHER

1 Mariano Rivera....787
2 Dave Righetti....522
3 Whitey Ford....498
4 Mike Stanton....456
5 Red Ruffing....426

FIELDING AVERAGE

FIRST BASE

1 Don Mattingly....996
2 Tino Martinez....994
3 Joe Pepitone....993
4 Chris Chambliss....993
5 Bill Skowron....992

SECOND BASE

1 Steve Sax....988
2 Gil McDougald....984
3 Horace Clarke....983
4 Robinson Cano....981
5 Billy Martin....981

SHORTSTOP

1 Bucky Dent....976
2 Derek Jeter....975
3 Alvaro Espinoza....972
4 Phil Rizzuto....968
5 Tony Kubek....967

THIRD BASE

1 Wade Boggs....973
2 Clete Boyer....965
3 Graig Nettles....962
4 Joe Dugan....961
5 Alex Rodriguez....960

OUTFIELD

1 Gene Woodling....991
2 Bernie Williams....990
3 Paul O'Neill....988
4 Roy White....988
5 Roger Maris....985
6 Dave Winfield....985
7 Roberto Kelly....985
8 Irv Noren....984
9 Bobby Murcer....983
10 Hideki Matsui....983

CATCHER

1 Elston Howard....992
2 Rick Cerone....992
3 Jorge Posada....992
4 Butch Wynegar....991
5 Yogi Berra....989

PITCHER

1 Scott Kamieniecki....992
2 Orlando Hernandez....989
3 Bill Stafford....987
4 Chien-Ming Wang....986
5 Hank Borowy....986

TOTAL CHANCES/GAME (INFIELD)

FIRST BASE

1 Wally Pipp....11.08
2 Hal Chase....10.82
3 Nick Etten....9.75
4 Lou Gehrig....9.73
5 Chris Chambliss....9.63
6 Joe Pepitone....9.47
7 Don Mattingly....9.38
8 Bill Skowron....8.90
9 Tino Martinez....8.57
10 Joe Collins....6.97

SECOND BASE

1 Del Pratt....5.90
2 Joe Gordon....5.87
3 Aaron Ward....5.66
4 Jimmy Williams....5.54
5 Tony Lazzeri....5.53
6 Snuffy Stirnweiss....5.50
7 Horace Clarke....5.44
8 Willie Randolph....5.43
9 Robinson Cano....5.07
10 Bobby Richardson....5.02

SHORTSTOP

1 Kid Elberfeld....5.91
2 Roger Peckinpaugh....5.64
3 Mark Koenig....5.38
4 Frankie Crosetti....5.25
5 Everett Scott....5.13
6 Gene Michael....5.09
7 Tony Kubek....5.02
8 Phil Rizzuto....4.95
9 Alvaro Espinoza....4.84
10 Bucky Dent....4.76

THIRD BASE

1 Wid Conroy....3.66
2 Frank Baker....3.56
3 Clete Boyer....3.56
4 Red Rolfe....3.24
5 Graig Nettles....3.19
6 Andy Carey....3.16
7 Billy Johnson....3.01
8 Joe Dugan....3.00
9 Gil McDougald....2.97
10 Scott Brosius....2.70

ASSISTS (INFIELD)

FIRST BASE

1 Don Mattingly....1104
2 Lou Gehrig....1087
3 Wally Pipp....950
4 Bill Skowron....639
5 Tino Martinez....623
6 Chris Chambliss....597
7 Hal Chase....594
8 Joe Pepitone....482
9 Joe Collins....376
10 Nick Etten....334

SECOND BASE

1 Willie Randolph....4996
2 Tony Lazzeri....4392
3 Bobby Richardson....3445
4 Horace Clarke....3132
5 Joe Gordon....3091
6 Aaron Ward....2108
7 Jimmy Williams....2040
8 Snuffy Stirnweiss....1996
9 Gil McDougald....1518
10 Jerry Coleman....1408

SHORTSTOP

1 Derek Jeter....4666
Phil Rizzuto....4666
3 Frankie Crosetti....4484
4 Roger Peckinpaugh....3963
5 Tony Kubek....2734
6 Gene Michael....2254
7 Bucky Dent....2170
8 Kid Elberfeld....1986
9 Mark Koenig....1473
10 Everett Scott....1452

THIRD BASE

1 Graig Nettles....3459
2 Clete Boyer....2162
3 Red Rolfe....2128
4 Joe Dugan....1415
5 Frank Baker....1376
6 Andy Carey....1316
7 Billy Johnson....1227
Mike Pagliarulo....1227
9 Alex Rodriguez....1063
10 Wade Boggs....1059

ASSISTS/GAME (INFIELD)

FIRST BASE

1 Chris Chambliss....0.70
2 Joe Pepitone....0.70
3 Don Mattingly....0.68
4 Wally Pipp....0.65
5 Bill Skowron....0.65
6 Nick Etten....0.62
7 Tino Martinez....0.61
8 Hal Chase....0.59
9 Joe Collins....0.53
10 Lou Gehrig....0.51

SECOND BASE

1 Del Pratt....3.32
2 Joe Gordon....3.19
3 Aaron Ward....3.16
4 Tony Lazzeri....3.05
5 Robinson Cano....3.00
6 Jimmy Williams....2.98
7 Willie Randolph....2.96
8 Steve Sax....2.96
9 Horace Clarke....2.90
10 Snuffy Stirnweiss....2.86

SHORTSTOP

1 Roger Peckinpaugh....3.27
2 Kid Elberfeld....3.24
3 Gene Michael....3.18
4 Bucky Dent....3.13
5 Tony Kubek....3.10
6 Alvaro Espinoza....3.06
7 Everett Scott....3.05
8 Mark Koenig....2.97
9 Frankie Crosetti....2.96
10 Phil Rizzuto....2.84

THIRD BASE

1 Clete Boyer....2.38
2 Graig Nettles....2.30
3 Frank Baker....2.12
4 Wid Conroy....2.02
5 Andy Carey....2.01
6 Red Rolfe....1.97
7 Wade Boggs....1.96
8 Gil McDougald....1.96
9 Scott Brosius....1.87
10 Joe Dugan....1.83
11 Billy Johnson....1.83

DOUBLE PLAYS

FIRST BASE

1 Lou Gehrig....1575
2 Don Mattingly....1500
3 Wally Pipp....989
4 Bill Skowron....922
5 Tino Martinez....750

SECOND BASE

1 Willie Randolph....1233
2 Bobby Richardson....963
3 Tony Lazzeri....798
4 Joe Gordon....761
5 Horace Clarke....689

SHORTSTOP

1 Phil Rizzuto....1217
2 Derek Jeter....989
3 Frankie Crosetti....944
4 Tony Kubek....569
5 Roger Peckinpaugh....532

THIRD BASE

1 Graig Nettles....293
2 Clete Boyer....219
3 Red Rolfe....184
4 Andy Carey....148
5 Gil McDougald....127

OUTFIELD

1 Babe Ruth....39
2 Bob Meusel....33
3 Joe DiMaggio....30
4 Tommy Henrich....27
Mickey Mantle....27
6 Willie Keeler....24
7 Earle Combs....23
8 Birdie Cree....20
9 Hank Bauer....19
10 George Selkirk....18
Bernie Williams....18

CATCHER

1 Yogi Berra....175
2 Bill Dickey....137
3 Thurman Munson....82
4 Elston Howard....79
5 Jorge Posada....72

PITCHER

1 Whitey Ford....49
2 Fritz Peterson....39
Red Ruffing....39
4 Mel Stottlemyre....38
5 Herb Pennock....32

PUTOUTS (OUTFIELD)

OUTFIELD

1 Bernie Williams....4710
2 Joe DiMaggio....4516
3 Mickey Mantle....4438
4 Babe Ruth....4062
5 Earle Combs....3449
6 Roy White....3356
7 Paul O'Neill....2325
8 Hank Bauer....2255
9 Dave Winfield....2243
10 Bobby Murcer....2214
11 Charlie Keller....2203
Bob Meusel....2203
13 Tommy Henrich....2008
14 Ben Chapman....1737
15 Johnny Lindell....1597
16 Roberto Kelly....1560
17 George Selkirk....1559
18 Rickey Henderson....1518
19 Roger Maris....1456
20 Tom Tresh....1360
21 Gene Woodling....1336
22 Lou Piniella....1331
23 Mickey Rivers....1318
24 Birdie Cree....1252
25 Hideki Matsui....1201
26 Willie Keeler....1148
27 Whitey Witt....1050
28 Hector Lopez....1014
29 Reggie Jackson....1007
30 Jesse Barfield....834
31 Bert Daniels....831
32 Ken Griffey....821
33 Irv Noren....789
34 Jerry Mumphrey....782
35 Ping Bodie....770
36 Sammy Byrd....735
37 Mel Hall....715
38 Elmer Miller....713
39 Hugh High....664
40 Joe Pepitone....659
41 Melky Cabrera....639
42 Myril Hoag....637
43 Roy Hartzell....631
44 Bud Metheny....615
45 Charlie Hemphill....614
46 Harry Wolter....609
47 Dave Fultz....602
48 Chad Curtis....572
49 Jake Powell....554
50 Gary Sheffield....549

PUTOUTS/GAME (OUTFIELD)

OUTFIELD

1 Rickey Henderson....2.73
2 Joe DiMaggio....2.63
3 Roberto Kelly....2.50
4 Earle Combs....2.49
5 Johnny Lindell....2.45
6 Bernie Williams....2.45
7 Ben Chapman....2.30
8 Charlie Keller....2.20
9 Mickey Mantle....2.20
10 Bobby Murcer....2.19
11 Roy White....2.07
12 Gene Woodling....2.04
13 George Selkirk....2.02
14 Dave Winfield....2.00
15 Babe Ruth....1.99
16 Tommy Henrich....1.98
17 Reggie Jackson....1.98
18 Hideki Matsui....1.98
19 Paul O'Neill....1.91
20 Tom Tresh....1.90
21 Bob Meusel....1.85
22 Birdie Cree....1.82
23 Roger Maris....1.81
24 Lou Piniella....1.81
25 Hank Bauer....1.68
26 Hector Lopez....1.62
27 Willie Keeler....1.36

FIELDING RUNS

1 Clete Boyer....159
2 Willie Randolph....140
3 Phil Rizzuto....117
4 Gil McDougald....106
5 Joe Gordon....101
6 Yogi Berra....92
7 Thurman Munson....84
8 Tony Kubek....77
9 Graig Nettles....67
Roger Peckinpaugh....67
11 Alvaro Espinoza....63
12 Horace Clarke....57
Bill Dickey....57
14 Gene Michael....56
15 Del Pratt....48
16 Jimmy Williams....45
17 Mike Gallego....43
18 Lute Boone....41
Jerry Kenney....41
Aaron Ward....41
21 Elston Howard....37
22 Ben Chapman....33
Bucky Dent....33
24 Snuffy Stirnweiss....32
25 Andy Carey....31
26 Wid Conroy....30
27 Joe Girardi....28
28 Wade Boggs....26
29 Benny Bengough....25
Leo Durocher....25
Kid Elberfeld....25
Rickey Henderson....25
33 Jesse Barfield....24
Billy Martin....24
35 Pat Kelly....23
36 Randy Velarde....22
37 Jerry Coleman....21
Wayne Tolleson....21
39 Roxy Walters....19
40 Willy Miranda....18
41 Jimmy Austin....16
Joe Collins....16
Jake Gibbs....16
Mike McNally....16
Ezra Midkiff....16
Everett Scott....16
Gene Woodling....16
48 Clyde Engle....15
49 3 players tied....14

FIELDING WINS

1 Clete Boyer....16.5
2 Willie Randolph....14.0
3 Phil Rizzuto....11.7
4 Gil McDougald....10.7
5 Joe Gordon....9.8
6 Yogi Berra....9.2
7 Thurman Munson....8.7
8 Tony Kubek....8.0
9 Roger Peckinpaugh....7.0
10 Graig Nettles....6.8
11 Alvaro Espinoza....6.4
12 Horace Clarke....6.2
13 Gene Michael....6.0
14 Bill Dickey....5.3
15 Del Pratt....4.9
16 Jimmy Williams....4.9
17 Lute Boone....4.5
18 Jerry Kenney....4.4
19 Mike Gallego....4.1
20 Aaron Ward....3.9
21 Elston Howard....3.8
22 Bucky Dent....3.3
23 Wid Conroy....3.3
24 Snuffy Stirnweiss....3.3
25 Andy Carey....3.1
26 Ben Chapman....3.0
27 Kid Elberfeld....2.7
28 Joe Girardi....2.6
29 Rickey Henderson....2.4
30 Wade Boggs....2.4
31 Jesse Barfield....2.4
32 Billy Martin....2.4
33 Leo Durocher....2.4
34 Benny Bengough....2.4
35 Pat Kelly....2.2
36 Randy Velarde....2.2
37 Roxy Walters....2.1
38 Wayne Tolleson....2.1
39 Jerry Coleman....2.1
40 Willy Miranda....1.8
41 Jimmy Austin....1.8
42 Jake Gibbs....1.8
43 Clyde Engle....1.7
44 Ezra Midkiff....1.7
45 Joe Collins....1.6
46 Gene Woodling....1.6
47 Everett Scott....1.6
48 Mike McNally....1.5
49 Charlie Silvera....1.4
50 Elliott Maddox....1.4

STOLEN BASES

1	Rickey Henderson	326
2	**Derek Jeter**	**264**
3	Willie Randolph	251
4	Hal Chase	248
5	Roy White	233
6	Ben Chapman	184
	Wid Conroy	184
8	Fritz Maisel	183
9	Mickey Mantle	153
10	Horace Clarke	151
	Roberto Kelly	151
12	Phil Rizzuto	149
13	Tony Lazzeri	147
	Bernie Williams	147
15	Bert Daniels	145
16	Roger Peckinpaugh	143
17	Bob Meusel	134
18	Birdie Cree	132
19	Snuffy Stirnweiss	130
20	Alfonso Soriano	121
21	Willie Keeler	118
22	Kid Elberfeld	117
	Steve Sax	117
24	Wally Pipp	114
25	Frankie Crosetti	113
26	Chuck Knoblauch	112
27	Babe Ruth	110
28	Lou Gehrig	102
29	Earle Combs	98
	Roy Hartzell	98
31	Mickey Rivers	93
32	Dave Fultz	90
33	**Alex Rodriguez**	**88**
34	Harry Wolter	85
35	Charlie Hemphill	80
	Paul O'Neill	80
37	Dave Winfield	76
38	Bobby Murcer	74
39	Bobby Richardson	73
40	Joe Gordon	68
41	Frank Baker	63
	John Knight	63
43	Danny Hoffman	62
	Ed Sweeney	62
45	Jerry Kenney	59
	Jimmy Williams	59
47	Bob Meacham	58
	George Moriarty	58
49	Doc Cook	56
	Pat Kelly	56

STOLEN BASE AVERAGE

1	Rickey Henderson	85.1
2	**Alex Rodriguez**	**83.0**
3	Mickey Mantle	80.1
4	**Johnny Damon**	**80.0**
5	**Derek Jeter**	**79.0**
6	Alfonso Soriano	77.1
7	Steve Sax	76.0
8	Roberto Kelly	75.9
9	Willie Randolph	75.4
10	Chuck Knoblauch	75.2
11	Mickey Rivers	73.8
12	Chad Curtis	73.2
13	Sandy Alomar	73.0
14	Horace Clarke	72.2
15	Phil Rizzuto	72.0
16	Snuffy Stirnweiss	71.4
17	Lyn Lary	71.2
18	Bob Meacham	70.7
19	Red Rolfe	68.8
20	Dave Winfield	67.9
21	Pat Kelly	67.5
22	Jerry Kenney	67.0
23	Paul O'Neill	66.7
	Luis Polonia	66.7

BASE STEALING WINS

Rank	Player	Wins
1	Rickey Henderson	5.1
2	**Derek Jeter**	**3.1**
3	Willie Randolph	2.6
4	Mickey Mantle	2.1
5	Roberto Kelly	1.7
6	Horace Clarke	1.4
7	Alfonso Soriano	1.3
8	Steve Sax	1.3
9	Phil Rizzuto	1.2
10	**Alex Rodriguez**	**1.2**
11	Chuck Knoblauch	1.1
12	Roy White	1.1
13	Snuffy Stirnweiss	1.1
14	Mickey Rivers	0.9
15	Ben Chapman	0.7
16	**Johnny Damon**	**0.7**
17	**Miguel Cairo**	**0.5**
18	Sandy Alomar	0.4
19	Tony Lazzeri	0.4
20	Bob Meacham	0.4
21	Claudell Washington	0.4
22	Dave Winfield	0.4
23	Tony Womack	0.4
24	**Bobby Abreu**	**0.4**

PITCHER BATTING AVERAGE BY ERA

1988–2007

1973–87

1961–72

1	Mel Stottlemyre	.160
2	Fritz Peterson	.159
3	Ralph Terry	.155

1943–60

1	Johnny Sain	.267
2	Don Larsen	.243
3	Tommy Byrne	.240
4	Joe Page	.205
5	Vic Raschi	.190
6	Art Ditmar	.185
7	Ed Lopat	.179

1921–42

1	Joe Bush	.313
2	Carl Mays	.279
3	Red Ruffing	.270
4	Ed Wells	.230
5	Monte Pearson	.224
6	Bob Shawkey	.222
7	Waite Hoyt	.210

1901–20

1	Al Orth	.266
2	Ray Caldwell	.241
3	Russ Ford	.218
4	Jack Chesbro	.201

PITCHER BATTING RUNS

1	Red Ruffing	125
2	Tommy Byrne	33
3	Joe Bush	29
4	Whitey Ford	27
5	Don Larsen	26
6	Ray Caldwell	25
7	Al Orth	20
	Mel Stottlemyre	20
9	Carl Mays	19
10	Spud Chandler	17
11	Johnny Sain	16
12	Monte Pearson	13
13	Ed Lopat	11
14	Urban Shocker	9
15	Sam Jones	8
	Fritz Peterson	8
	Marius Russo	8
18	Russ Ford	7
	Hank Johnson	7
20	Bobby Shantz	6
21	Joe Page	5
	Vic Raschi	5
	Allie Reynolds	5
	Bob Shawkey	5
	Spec Shea	5
	Fred Talbot	5
27	Vito Tamulis	4
28	Luis Arroyo	3
	Eli Grba	3
	Tom Morgan	3
	Dutch Ruether	3
	Tom Sturdivant	3
33	Art Ditmar	2
	George McConnell	2
	Bill Stafford	2
	Tom Zachary	2
37	Kevin Brown	1
	Jack Chesbro	1
	Roger Clemens	**1**
	David Cone	1
	Clark Griffith	1
	Jason Grimsley	1
	Sparky Lyle	1
	Sal Maglie	1
	Johnny Murphy	1
	Mike Mussina	**1**
	Andy Pettitte	**1**
	Butch Wensloff	1
	Dooley Womack	1

ADJUSTED BATTING RUNS

1	Babe Ruth	1281
2	Lou Gehrig	1028
3	Mickey Mantle	884
4	Joe DiMaggio	532
5	Bernie Williams	314
6	Charlie Keller	292
7	Don Mattingly	266
8	**Derek Jeter**	**259**
9	Bill Dickey	257
10	Yogi Berra	245
11	Earle Combs	240
12	Tommy Henrich	219
13	Roy White	214
14	Tony Lazzeri	209
15	Dave Winfield	208
16	Paul O'Neill	197
	Jorge Posada	**197**
18	**Jason Giambi**	**191**
19	**Alex Rodriguez**	**190**
20	Roger Maris	168
	Bobby Murcer	168
22	Reggie Jackson	154
23	Bill Skowron	141
24	Bob Meusel	130
	George Selkirk	130
26	Rickey Henderson	129
27	Ben Chapman	113
28	Thurman Munson	112
29	Red Ruffing	107
30	Joe Gordon	105
31	Graig Nettles	101
32	**Hideki Matsui**	**96**
33	Hank Bauer	93
	Willie Randolph	93
35	Gene Woodling	89
36	Oscar Gamble	83
	Tom Tresh	83
38	Birdie Cree	81
	Gil McDougald	81
40	Nick Etten	76
41	Mike Stanley	74
42	Ron Blomberg	73
43	Tino Martinez	72
44	Gary Sheffield	70
45	Danny Tartabull	68
46	Elston Howard	59
47	Wade Boggs	58
48	Don Baylor	57
49	Lou Piniella	47
50	Harry Wolter	43

ADJUSTED BATTING WINS

Rank	Player	Wins
1	Babe Ruth	117.6
2	Lou Gehrig	93.7
3	Mickey Mantle	89.4
4	Joe DiMaggio	50.2
5	Bernie Williams	29.5
6	Charlie Keller	28.7
7	Don Mattingly	26.1
8	Yogi Berra	24.4
9	**Derek Jeter**	**24.3**
10	Bill Dickey	24.0
11	Roy White	22.4
12	Earle Combs	22.4
13	Tommy Henrich	21.1
14	Dave Winfield	20.5
15	Tony Lazzeri	19.4
16	**Jorge Posada**	**18.5**
17	Paul O'Neill	18.3
18	**Jason Giambi**	**18.0**
19	**Alex Rodriguez**	**17.8**
20	Bobby Murcer	17.4
21	Roger Maris	17.1
22	Reggie Jackson	15.3
23	Bill Skowron	14.1
24	Rickey Henderson	12.6
25	Bob Meusel	12.3
26	George Selkirk	12.0
27	Thurman Munson	11.6
28	Ben Chapman	10.4
29	Graig Nettles	10.2
30	Joe Gordon	10.2
31	Red Ruffing	9.9
32	Hank Bauer	9.3
33	Willie Randolph	9.3
34	**Hideki Matsui**	**9.1**
35	Tom Tresh	8.8
36	Gene Woodling	8.8
37	Birdie Cree	8.6
38	Oscar Gamble	8.4
39	Gil McDougald	8.2
40	Nick Etten	8.0
41	Ron Blomberg	7.7
42	Mike Stanley	7.0
43	Tino Martinez	6.7
44	Gary Sheffield	6.6
45	Danny Tartabull	6.5
46	Elston Howard	6.1
47	Don Baylor	5.6
48	Wade Boggs	5.4
49	Lou Piniella	4.8
50	Harry Wolter	4.5

BATTER-FIELDER WINS BY ERA

1988–2007

Rank	Player	Wins
1	**Jorge Posada**	**27.0**
2	Bernie Williams	24.6
3	**Derek Jeter**	**17.3**
4	Don Mattingly	15.4
5	**Alex Rodriguez**	**15.3**
6	Paul O'Neill	12.1
7	**Jason Giambi**	**9.0**
8	Mike Stanley	8.2
9	Wade Boggs	7.9
10	**Hideki Matsui**	**6.5**
11	**Robinson Cano**	**6.4**
12	Mike Gallego	5.3
13	Gary Sheffield	4.8
14	Alfonso Soriano	4.2

1973–87

Rank	Player	Wins
1	Willie Randolph	34.4
2	Thurman Munson	25.0
3	Rickey Henderson	18.7
4	Graig Nettles	14.9
5	Dave Winfield	12.5
6	Reggie Jackson	11.1
7	Oscar Gamble	7.1
8	Ron Blomberg	4.7
9	Don Baylor	4.4
10	Bobby Bonds	3.8
11	Jerry Mumphrey	3.6
12	Elliott Maddox	3.5
13	Butch Wynegar	3.3
14	Mickey Rivers	2.2

1961–72

Rank	Player	Wins
1	Roy White	14.8
2	Elston Howard	12.3
3	Bobby Murcer	10.1
4	Clete Boyer	10.0
5	Tom Tresh	9.1
6	Roger Maris	8.8
7	Horace Clarke	4.8
8	Tony Kubek	4.5
9	Gene Michael	4.2
10	Frank Fernandez	3.1
11	Jerry Kenney	1.8

1943–60

Rank	Player	Wins
1	Mickey Mantle	71.8
2	Yogi Berra	40.2
3	Gil McDougald	24.2
4	Phil Rizzuto	18.7
5	Snuffy Stirnweiss	13.3
6	Bill Skowron	9.6
7	Gene Woodling	5.6
8	Aaron Robinson	4.1
9	Hank Bauer	2.8
10	Nick Etten	2.7
11	Joe Collins	2.5
12	Andy Carey	2.3
	Gus Niarhos	2.3
14	Oscar Grimes	2.0

1921–42

Rank	Player	Wins
1	Babe Ruth	101.9
2	Lou Gehrig	70.9
3	Joe DiMaggio	45.8
4	Bill Dickey	38.5
5	Joe Gordon	25.5
6	Charlie Keller	21.7
7	Tony Lazzeri	17.4
8	Tommy Henrich	15.0
9	Earle Combs	12.0
10	Ben Chapman	11.7
11	George Selkirk	8.1
12	Lyn Lary	4.7
13	Wally Schang	4.3
14	Pat Collins	3.5

1901–20

Rank	Player	Wins
1	Roger Peckinpaugh	12.4
2	Jimmy Williams	7.5
3	Frank Baker	7.4
	Kid Elberfeld	7.4
5	Del Pratt	6.7
6	Birdie Cree	2.9
7	Les Nunamaker	2.8
8	Clyde Engle	2.2
9	Harry Wolter	1.8
10	Walt Alexander	1.4
	Roxy Walters	1.4
12	Joe Yeager	1.3
13	John Ganzel	1.2

BATTER-FIELDER WINS

Rank	Player	Wins
1	Babe Ruth	101.9
2	Mickey Mantle	71.8
3	Lou Gehrig	70.9
4	Joe DiMaggio	45.8
5	Yogi Berra	40.2
6	Bill Dickey	38.5
7	Willie Randolph	34.4
8	**Jorge Posada**	**27.0**
9	Joe Gordon	25.5
10	Thurman Munson	25.0
11	Bernie Williams	24.6
12	Gil McDougald	24.2
13	Charlie Keller	21.7
14	Rickey Henderson	18.7
	Phil Rizzuto	18.7
16	Tony Lazzeri	17.4
17	**Derek Jeter**	**17.3**
18	Don Mattingly	15.4
19	**Alex Rodriguez**	**15.3**
20	Tommy Henrich	15.0
21	Graig Nettles	14.9
22	Roy White	14.8
23	Snuffy Stirnweiss	13.3
24	Dave Winfield	12.5
25	Roger Peckinpaugh	12.4
26	Elston Howard	12.3
27	Paul O'Neill	12.1
28	Earle Combs	12.0
29	Ben Chapman	11.7
30	Reggie Jackson	11.1
31	Bobby Murcer	10.1
32	Clete Boyer	10.0
33	Bill Skowron	9.6
34	Tom Tresh	9.1
35	**Jason Giambi**	**9.0**
36	Roger Maris	8.8
37	Mike Stanley	8.2
38	George Selkirk	8.1
39	Wade Boggs	7.9
40	Jimmy Williams	7.5
41	Frank Baker	7.4
	Kid Elberfeld	7.4
43	Oscar Gamble	7.1
44	Del Pratt	6.7
45	**Hideki Matsui**	**6.5**
46	**Robinson Cano**	**6.4**
47	Gene Woodling	5.6
48	Mike Gallego	5.3
49	Horace Clarke	4.8
	Gary Sheffield	4.8

PINCH HITS

1	Red Ruffing	46
2	Yogi Berra	44
3	Johnny Mize	42
4	Enos Slaughter	40
5	Bob Cerv	39
6	Elston Howard	38
	Lou Piniella	38
8	Ray Caldwell	34
9	Hector Lopez	32
10	2 players tied	27

PINCH HIT AVERAGE

1	Les Nunamaker	.462
2	Ron Blomberg	.375
3	Hank Bauer	.317
4	Bill Skowron	.316
5	Charley Smith	.314
6	Bob Cerv	.293
7	Ruben Sierra	.289
8	Dion James	.281
9	Johnny Mize	.280

PINCH HIT HOME RUNS

1	Yogi Berra	8
	Bob Cerv	8
3	Mickey Mantle	7
	Bobby Murcer	7
5	Johnny Blanchard	6
6	Elston Howard	5
	Matt Nokes	5
	Bill Skowron	5
	Johnny Mize	5
10	Many players tied	4

WINS

1 Whitey Ford 236
2 Red Ruffing 231
3 Lefty Gomez 189
4 Ron Guidry 170
5 Bob Shawkey 168
6 Andy Pettitte 164
Mel Stottlemyre 164
8 Herb Pennock 162
9 Waite Hoyt 157
10 Allie Reynolds 131
11 Jack Chesbro 128
12 Vic Raschi 120
13 Ed Lopat 113
14 Spud Chandler 109
Fritz Peterson 109
16 Mike Mussina 103
17 Ray Caldwell 96
18 Johnny Murphy 93
George Pipgras 93
20 Tommy John 91
21 Roger Clemens 83
22 Bob Turley 82
23 Jack Quinn 81
24 Carl Mays 80
25 Tiny Bonham 79
26 Ralph Terry 78
27 Ray Fisher 76
28 Dave Righetti 74
29 Russ Ford 73
30 Tommy Byrne 72
Al Downing 72
Al Orth 72
33 Jack Warhop 69
34 David Wells 68
35 Sam Jones 67
36 Atley Donald 65
37 David Cone 64
38 Catfish Hunter 63
Monte Pearson 63
40 Joe Bush 62
Ed Figueroa 62
Mariano Rivera 62
43 Orlando Hernandez 61
Urban Shocker 61
45 Sparky Lyle 57
Joe Page 57
47 Hank Borowy 56
48 Stan Bahnsen 55
Jim Bouton 55
50 2 players tied 54

WINS BY ERA

1988–2007

1 Andy Pettitte 164
2 Mike Mussina 103
3 Roger Clemens 83
4 David Wells 68
5 David Cone 64
6 Mariano Rivera 62
7 Orlando Hernandez 61

1973–87

1 Ron Guidry 170
2 Tommy John 91
3 Dave Righetti 74
4 Catfish Hunter 63
5 Ed Figueroa 62
6 Sparky Lyle 57
7 Rudy May 54

1961–72

1 Mel Stottlemyre 164
2 Fritz Peterson 109
3 Ralph Terry 78
4 Al Downing 72
5 Stan Bahnsen 55
Jim Bouton 55
7 Bill Stafford 43

1943–60

1 Whitey Ford 236
2 Allie Reynolds 131
3 Vic Raschi 120
4 Ed Lopat 113
5 Bob Turley 82
6 Tiny Bonham 79
7 Tommy Byrne 72

1921–42

1 Red Ruffing 231
2 Lefty Gomez 189
3 Bob Shawkey 168
4 Herb Pennock 162
5 Waite Hoyt 157
6 Spud Chandler 109
7 Johnny Murphy 93
George Pipgras 93

1901–20

1 Jack Chesbro 128
2 Ray Caldwell 96
3 Jack Quinn 81
4 Ray Fisher 76
5 Russ Ford 73
6 Al Orth 72
7 Jack Warhop 69

LOSSES

1 Mel Stottlemyre 139
2 Bob Shawkey 131
3 Red Ruffing 124
4 Whitey Ford 106
Fritz Peterson 106
6 Lefty Gomez 101
7 Ray Caldwell 99
8 Waite Hoyt 98
9 Jack Chesbro 93
10 Jack Warhop 92
11 Ron Guidry 91
12 Herb Pennock 90
13 Andy Pettitte 87
14 Ray Fisher 78
15 Al Orth 73
16 Jack Quinn 65
17 George Pipgras 64
18 Mike Mussina 63
19 Dave Righetti 61
20 Tommy John 60
Allie Reynolds 60
22 Ed Lopat 59
Ralph Terry 59
24 Al Downing 57
George Mogridge 57
26 Russ Ford 56
Sam Jones 56
28 Catfish Hunter 53
Johnny Murphy 53
30 Stan Bahnsen 52
Bob Turley 52
32 Jim Bouton 51
33 Tiny Bonham 50
Bill Hogg 50
Vic Raschi 50
36 Joe Page 49
37 Rudy May 46
38 Mariano Rivera 44
39 Spud Chandler 43
40 Roger Clemens 42
41 Tommy Byrne 40
David Cone 40
Orlando Hernandez 40
Ray Keating 40
Sparky Lyle 40
Doc Medich 40
47 Ed Figueroa 39
Scott Kamieniecki 39
Carl Mays 39
Melido Perez 39

WINNING PERCENTAGE

1 Johnny Allen .725
2 Chien-Ming Wang .719
3 Spud Chandler .717
4 Jim Coates .712
5 David Wells .708
6 Vic Raschi .706
7 Monte Pearson .700
8 Whitey Ford .690
9 Mike Stanton .689
Bob Wickman .689
11 Allie Reynolds .686
12 Jimmy Key .676
13 Carl Mays .672
14 Roger Clemens .664
15 Atley Donald .663
16 Ed Lopat .657
17 Andy Pettitte .653
18 Don Larsen .652
19 Lefty Gomez .652
20 Ron Guidry .651
21 Hank Borowy .651
22 Red Ruffing .651
23 Tommy Byrne .643
Herb Pennock .643
25 Randy Johnson .642
26 Johnny Murphy .637
27 Tom Morgan .633
28 Wilcy Moore .632
29 Steve Hamilton .630
30 Bobby Shantz .625
31 Johnny Sain .623
32 Urban Shocker .622
33 Mike Mussina .620
34 Joe Bush .620
35 Dennis Rasmussen .619
36 Waite Hoyt .616
37 David Cone .615
Phil Niekro .615
39 Ed Figueroa .614
40 Ramiro Mendoza .614
41 Bump Hadley .613
42 Tiny Bonham .612
43 Bob Turley .612
44 Orlando Hernandez .604
45 Tommy John .603
46 Rich Gossage .600
47 Johnny Broaca .597
48 Art Ditmar .595
49 George Pipgras .592
50 Tom Sturdivant .590

GAMES STARTED

1 Whitey Ford 438
2 Red Ruffing 391
3 Mel Stottlemyre 356
4 Ron Guidry 323
5 Lefty Gomez 319
6 Andy Pettitte 310
7 Waite Hoyt 276
8 Bob Shawkey 274
9 Herb Pennock 268
10 Fritz Peterson 265
11 Jack Chesbro 227
12 Mike Mussina 214
13 Allie Reynolds 209
14 Vic Raschi 207
15 Tommy John 203
16 Ed Lopat 202
17 Ray Caldwell 196
18 Spud Chandler 184
19 Al Downing 175
Bob Turley 175
21 Roger Clemens 174
22 George Pipgras 170
23 Ray Fisher 166
24 Ralph Terry 161
25 Jack Warhop 150
26 Al Orth 145
Jack Quinn 145
28 David Cone 144
29 Tiny Bonham 141
30 Stan Bahnsen 139
31 Orlando Hernandez 136
Catfish Hunter 136
33 Jim Bouton 131
34 Sam Jones 130
35 Russ Ford 129
36 Ed Figueroa 126
37 Carl Mays 124
38 David Wells 123
39 Tommy Byrne 118
40 Atley Donald 115
41 Monte Pearson 114
42 Urban Shocker 111
43 Doc Medich 108
44 George Mogridge 103
45 Rudy May 102
46 Hank Borowy 96
Dennis Rasmussen 96
Bill Stafford 96
49 3 players tied 94

GAMES STARTED BY ERA

1988–2007

1 Andy Pettitte 310
2 Mike Mussina 214
3 Roger Clemens 174
4 David Cone 144
5 Orlando Hernandez 136
6 David Wells 123
7 Scott Kamieniecki 94
Jimmy Key 94

1973–87

1 Ron Guidry 323
2 Tommy John 203
3 Catfish Hunter 136
4 Ed Figueroa 126
5 Doc Medich 108
6 Rudy May 102
7 Dennis Rasmussen 96

1961–72

1 Mel Stottlemyre 356
2 Fritz Peterson 265
3 Al Downing 175
4 Ralph Terry 161
5 Stan Bahnsen 139
6 Jim Bouton 131
7 Bill Stafford 96

1943–60

1 Whitey Ford 438
2 Allie Reynolds 209
3 Vic Raschi 207
4 Ed Lopat 202
5 Bob Turley 175
6 Tiny Bonham 141
7 Tommy Byrne 118

1921–42

1 Red Ruffing 391
2 Lefty Gomez 319
3 Waite Hoyt 276
4 Bob Shawkey 274
5 Herb Pennock 268
6 Spud Chandler 184
7 George Pipgras 170

1901–20

1 Jack Chesbro 227
2 Ray Caldwell 196
3 Ray Fisher 166
4 Jack Warhop 150
5 Al Orth 145
Jack Quinn 145
7 Russ Ford 129

COMPLETE GAMES

1 Red Ruffing 261
2 Lefty Gomez 173
3 Jack Chesbro 168
4 Herb Pennock 164
Bob Shawkey 164
6 Whitey Ford 156
Waite Hoyt 156
8 Mel Stottlemyre 152
9 Ray Caldwell 150
10 Spud Chandler 109
11 Jack Warhop 105
12 Al Orth 102
13 Russ Ford 100
14 Vic Raschi 99
15 Allie Reynolds 96
16 Ron Guidry 95
17 Tiny Bonham 91
Ed Lopat 91
Carl Mays 91
20 Ray Fisher 88
21 George Pipgras 84
22 Jack Quinn 83
23 Fritz Peterson 81
24 Sam Jones 66
25 Catfish Hunter 65
26 Joe Bush 61
George Mogridge 61
28 Bob Turley 58
29 Urban Shocker 57
30 Ralph Terry 56
31 Atley Donald 54
Monte Pearson 54
33 Hank Borowy 53
Tommy John 53
35 Jack Powell 51
36 Marius Russo 48
37 Bill Bevens 46
Al Downing 46
39 Bill Hogg 43
Doc Medich 43
41 Johnny Broaca 42
Tommy Byrne 42
Ed Figueroa 42
44 Ray Keating 41
45 Johnny Allen 39
46 Stan Bahnsen 36
47 Clark Griffith 35
Rube Manning 35
49 Steve Kline 33
50 Jim Bouton 32

COMPLETE GAMES BY ERA

1988–2007

1 Andy Pettitte 23
2 David Wells 19
3 Mike Mussina 12
Melido Perez 12
5 Tim Leary 9
Rick Rhoden 9
7 Orlando Hernandez 8
Scott Kamieniecki 8

1973–87

1 Ron Guidry 95
2 Catfish Hunter 65
3 Tommy John 53
4 Doc Medich 43
5 Ed Figueroa 42
6 Rudy May 30
7 Pat Dobson 25

1961–72

1 Mel Stottlemyre 152
2 Fritz Peterson 81
3 Ralph Terry 56
4 Al Downing 46
5 Stan Bahnsen 36
6 Steve Kline 33
7 Jim Bouton 32

1943–60

1 Whitey Ford 156
2 Vic Raschi 99
3 Allie Reynolds 96
4 Tiny Bonham 91
Ed Lopat 91
6 Bob Turley 58
7 Hank Borowy 53

1921–42

1 Red Ruffing 261
2 Lefty Gomez 173
3 Herb Pennock 164
Bob Shawkey 164
5 Waite Hoyt 156
6 Spud Chandler 109
7 Carl Mays 91

1901–20

1 Jack Chesbro 168
2 Ray Caldwell 150
3 Jack Warhop 105
4 Al Orth 102
5 Russ Ford 100
6 Ray Fisher 88
7 Jack Quinn 83

SHUTOUTS

1 Whitey Ford 45
2 Mel Stottlemyre 40
3 Red Ruffing 35
4 Spud Chandler 26
Ron Guidry 26
Bob Shawkey 26
7 Vic Raschi 24
8 Bob Turley 21
9 Ed Lopat 20
10 Jack Chesbro 18
Fritz Peterson 18
12 Ray Caldwell 17
13 Waite Hoyt 15
14 Al Orth 14
Herb Pennock 14
Allie Reynolds 14
Ralph Terry 14
18 Ray Fisher 13
19 Al Downing 12
Lefty Gomez 12
21 Tiny Bonham 11
Hank Borowy 11
Jim Bouton 11
Catfish Hunter 11
George Pipgras 11
26 Tommy Byrne 10
Russ Ford 10
28 Ed Figueroa 9
Doc Medich 9
30 Stan Bahnsen 8
Sam Jones 8
George Mogridge 8
Mike Mussina 8
Spec Shea 8
35 Don Larsen 7
Tom Morgan 7
37 Johnny Allen 6
Bill Bevens 6
Joe Bush 6
Atley Donald 6
Bill Hogg 6
Tommy John 6
Steve Kline 6
Johnny Kucks 6
Jack Quinn 6
Marius Russo 6
Bill Stafford 6
48 Clark Griffith 5
Rudy May 5
Urban Shocker 5

SAVES

1 Mariano Rivera 443
2 Dave Righetti 224
3 Rich Gossage 151
4 Sparky Lyle 141
5 Johnny Murphy 104
6 Steve Farr 78
7 Joe Page 76
8 John Wetteland 74
9 Lindy McDaniel 58
10 Luis Arroyo 43
11 Hal Reniff 41
Allie Reynolds 41
13 Pedro Ramos 40
14 Johnny Sain 39
15 Steve Hamilton 36
16 Wilcy Moore 35
17 Jack Aker 31
Steve Howe 31
19 Waite Hoyt 28
20 Tom Morgan 26
Bob Shawkey 26
22 Dooley Womack 24
23 Dick Tidrow 23
24 Ron Davis 22
Sam Jones 22
26 Lee Guetterman 21
Herb Pennock 21
28 Brian Fisher 20
29 Marshall Bridges 19
Bobby Shantz 19
Jim Turner 19
32 Ramiro Mendoza 16
33 Jim Coates 15
Jim Konstanty 15
Mike Stanton 15
36 Bob Kuzava 13
Pete Mikkelsen 13
Allan Russell 13
39 Tommy Byrne 12
George Frazier 12
Cecilio Guante 12
Steve Karsay 12
Bob Turley 12
44 Art Ditmar 11
Carl Mays 11
George Pipgras 11
Tim Stoddard 11
Bob Wickman 11
49 3 players tied 10

SAVES BY ERA

1988–2007

1	**Mariano Rivera**	**443**
2	Steve Farr	78
3	John Wetteland	74
4	Steve Howe	31
5	Lee Guetterman	21
6	Ramiro Mendoza	16
7	Mike Stanton	15

1973–87

1	Dave Righetti	224
2	Rich Gossage	151
3	Sparky Lyle	141
4	Dick Tidrow	23
5	Ron Davis	22
6	Brian Fisher	20
7	George Frazier	12

1961–72

1	Lindy McDaniel	58
2	Luis Arroyo	43
3	Hal Reniff	41
4	Pedro Ramos	40
5	Steve Hamilton	36
6	Jack Aker	31
7	Dooley Womack	24

1943–60

1	Joe Page	76
2	Allie Reynolds	41
3	Johnny Sain	39
4	Tom Morgan	26
5	Bobby Shantz	19
	Jim Turner	19
7	Jim Konstanty	15

1921–42

1	Johnny Murphy	104
2	Wilcy Moore	35
3	Waite Hoyt	28
4	Bob Shawkey	26
5	Sam Jones	22
6	Herb Pennock	21
7	Carl Mays	11
	George Pipgras	11

1901–20

1	Allan Russell	13
2	George Mogridge	8
3	Jack Warhop	7
4	Jack Quinn	6
5	Ray Fisher	5
6	Ray Caldwell	4
7	Russ Ford	3
	Clark Griffith	3
	George McConnell	3

SAVE PERCENTAGE

1	**Mariano Rivera**	**88.25**
2	John Wetteland	88.10
3	Steve Farr	81.25
4	Rich Gossage	78.24
5	Dave Righetti	78.05
6	Sparky Lyle	76.22
7	Steve Howe	75.61
8	Jack Aker	65.96

BLOWN SAVES

1	Dave Righetti	63
2	**Mariano Rivera**	**59**
3	Sparky Lyle	44
4	Rich Gossage	42
5	Lindy McDaniel	24
6	Bob Wickman	20
7	Mike Stanton	19
8	Steve Farr	18
	Jeff Nelson	18
10	Luis Arroyo	17
11	Jack Aker	16
12	Ramiro Mendoza	15
13	Ron Davis	14
	Steve Hamilton	14
15	Brian Fisher	13
	Tom Gordon	13
17	**Scott Proctor**	**11**
18	John Habyan	10
	Steve Howe	10
	Hal Reniff	10
	Dick Tidrow	10
	John Wetteland	10
23	Marshall Bridges	9
	Lee Guetterman	9

INNINGS PITCHED

1	Whitey Ford	3170.1
2	Red Ruffing	3168.2
3	Mel Stottlemyre	2661.1
4	Lefty Gomez	2498.1
5	Bob Shawkey	2488.2
6	Ron Guidry	2392.0
7	Waite Hoyt	2272.1
8	Herb Pennock	2203.1
9	**Andy Pettitte**	**2008.0**
10	Jack Chesbro	1952.0
11	Fritz Peterson	1857.1
12	Ray Caldwell	1718.1
13	Allie Reynolds	1700.0
14	Vic Raschi	1537.0
15	Ed Lopat	1497.1
16	Spud Chandler	1485.0
17	Jack Warhop	1412.2
18	Ray Fisher	1380.1
19	Tommy John	1367.0
20	**Mike Mussina**	**1352.2**
21	George Pipgras	1351.2
22	Jack Quinn	1270.0
23	Bob Turley	1269.0
24	Al Downing	1235.1
25	Ralph Terry	1198.0
26	Tiny Bonham	1176.2
27	Al Orth	1172.2
28	Dave Righetti	1136.2
29	Russ Ford	1112.2
30	**Roger Clemens**	**1103.0**
31	Carl Mays	1090.0
32	Sam Jones	1089.1
33	Jim Bouton	1013.2
34	Tommy Byrne	993.2
35	Catfish Hunter	993.0
36	Johnny Murphy	990.1
37	Stan Bahnsen	985.2
38	George Mogridge	965.2
39	**Mariano Rivera**	**953.0**
40	Atley Donald	932.1
41	Urban Shocker	932.0
42	David Cone	922.0
43	Ed Figueroa	911.2
44	Orlando Hernandez	876.1
45	David Wells	851.2
46	Rudy May	841.2
47	Monte Pearson	825.2
48	Doc Medich	787.0
49	Joe Bush	783.0
50	Hank Borowy	780.2

INNINGS PITCHED BY ERA

1988–2007

1	**Andy Pettitte**	**2008.0**
2	**Mike Mussina**	**1352.2**
3	**Roger Clemens**	**1103.0**
4	**Mariano Rivera**	**953.0**
5	David Cone	922.0
6	Orlando Hernandez	876.1
7	David Wells	851.2

1973–87

1	Ron Guidry	2392.0
2	Tommy John	1367.0
3	Dave Righetti	1136.2
4	Catfish Hunter	993.0
5	Ed Figueroa	911.2
6	Rudy May	841.2
7	Doc Medich	787.0

1961–72

1	Mel Stottlemyre	2661.1
2	Fritz Peterson	1857.1
3	Al Downing	1235.1
4	Ralph Terry	1198.0
5	Jim Bouton	1013.2
6	Stan Bahnsen	985.2
7	Bill Stafford	730.0

1943–60

1	Whitey Ford	3170.1
2	Allie Reynolds	1700.0
3	Vic Raschi	1537.0
4	Ed Lopat	1497.1
5	Bob Turley	1269.0
6	Tiny Bonham	1176.2
7	Tommy Byrne	993.2

1921–42

1	Red Ruffing	3168.2
2	Lefty Gomez	2498.1
3	Bob Shawkey	2488.2
4	Waite Hoyt	2272.1
5	Herb Pennock	2203.1
6	Spud Chandler	1485.0
7	George Pipgras	1351.2

1901–20

1	Jack Chesbro	1952.0
2	Ray Caldwell	1718.1
3	Jack Warhop	1412.2
4	Ray Fisher	1380.1
5	Jack Quinn	1270.0
6	Al Orth	1172.2
7	Russ Ford	1112.2

FEWEST HITS/9 INNINGS

1	Rich Gossage	6.59
2	Hal Reniff	7.16
3	**Mariano Rivera**	**7.17**
4	Steve Hamilton	7.20
5	Tommy Byrne	7.24
6	Bob Turley	7.27
7	Al Downing	7.39
8	Spec Shea	7.54
9	Don Larsen	7.54
10	Rudy May	7.65
11	Tom Sturdivant	7.71
12	Whitey Ford	7.85
13	Hank Borowy	7.87
14	Vic Raschi	7.89
15	Bobby Shantz	7.90
16	Dave Righetti	7.91
17	Allie Reynolds	7.94
18	Ray Caldwell	7.96
19	Johnny Allen	7.96
20	Catfish Hunter	7.97
21	Dennis Rasmussen	7.97
22	Orlando Hernandez	8.01
23	Allan Russell	8.02
24	Lindy McDaniel	8.03
25	Sparky Lyle	8.04
26	Spud Chandler	8.04
27	Bill Stafford	8.05
28	Jack Chesbro	8.08
29	David Cone	8.09
30	Jim Bouton	8.11
31	Russ Ford	8.17
32	Marius Russo	8.17
33	Joe Page	8.20
34	Stan Bahnsen	8.23
35	Mel Stottlemyre	8.23
36	Lefty Gomez	8.24
37	Art Ditmar	8.24
38	Ron Guidry	8.27
39	Clark Griffith	8.33
40	Ralph Terry	8.33
41	Bob Shawkey	8.33
42	Bill Hogg	8.35
43	Bill Bevens	8.38
44	Randy Johnson	8.38
45	Jim Coates	8.39
46	Melido Perez	8.40
47	Jack Powell	8.40
48	Al Orth	8.41
49	Steve Kline	8.43
50	Ray Keating	8.43

FEWEST HITS/9 INNINGS BY ERA

1988–2007

1	**Mariano Rivera**	**7.17**
2	Orlando Hernandez	8.01
3	David Cone	8.09
4	Randy Johnson	8.38
5	Melido Perez	8.40
6	**Roger Clemens**	**8.52**
7	Mike Stanton	8.63

1973–87

1	Rich Gossage	6.59
2	Rudy May	7.65
3	Dave Righetti	7.91
4	Catfish Hunter	7.97
5	Dennis Rasmussen	7.97
6	Sparky Lyle	8.04
7	Ron Guidry	8.27

1961–72

1	Hal Reniff	7.16
2	Steve Hamilton	7.20
3	Al Downing	7.39
4	Lindy McDaniel	8.03
5	Bill Stafford	8.05
6	Jim Bouton	8.11
7	Stan Bahnsen	8.23

1943–60

1	Tommy Byrne	7.24
2	Bob Turley	7.27
3	Spec Shea	7.54
4	Don Larsen	7.54
5	Tom Sturdivant	7.71
6	Whitey Ford	7.85
7	Hank Borowy	7.87

1921–42

1	Johnny Allen	7.96
2	Spud Chandler	8.04
3	Marius Russo	8.17
4	Lefty Gomez	8.24
5	Bob Shawkey	8.33
6	Red Ruffing	8.51
7	Johnny Murphy	8.58

1901–20

1	Ray Caldwell	7.96
2	Allan Russell	8.02
3	Jack Chesbro	8.08
4	Russ Ford	8.17
5	Clark Griffith	8.33
6	Bill Hogg	8.35
7	Jack Powell	8.40

HOME RUNS ALLOWED

1	Whitey Ford	228
2	Ron Guidry	226
3	Red Ruffing	200
4	Mel Stottlemyre	171
5	**Andy Pettitte**	**159**
6	**Mike Mussina**	**149**
7	Fritz Peterson	139
8	Lefty Gomez	138
9	Ralph Terry	133
10	Bob Turley	118
11	**Roger Clemens**	**116**
	Ed Lopat	116
13	Orlando Hernandez	114
14	Catfish Hunter	113
15	Allie Reynolds	111
16	Jim Bouton	105
	Bob Shawkey	105
18	Vic Raschi	104
19	David Cone	98
	David Wells	98
21	Al Downing	96
22	Waite Hoyt	93
23	Herb Pennock	91
24	Stan Bahnsen	88
25	Dennis Rasmussen	85
26	Tommy John	80
27	Bill Stafford	75
28	Tommy Byrne	74
	Art Ditmar	74
30	Tiny Bonham	71
31	Doc Medich	69
	Ramiro Mendoza	69
33	Hideki Irabu	68
34	Pat Dobson	66
	Atley Donald	66
36	Scott Kamieniecki	65
	Dave Righetti	65
38	Spud Chandler	64
	Melido Perez	64
40	Ed Figueroa	63
41	Dick Tidrow	62
42	Randy Johnson	60
	Jimmy Key	60
44	Johnny Kucks	59
45	Don Larsen	57
	George Pipgras	57
47	Hank Johnson	56
48	Bump Hadley	55
49	Sam Jones	53
50	2 players tied	51

HOME RUNS ALLOWED BY ERA

1988–2007

1	**Andy Pettitte**	**159**
2	**Mike Mussina**	**149**
3	**Roger Clemens**	**116**
4	Orlando Hernandez	114
5	David Cone	98
	David Wells	98
7	Ramiro Mendoza	69

1973–87

1	Ron Guidry	226
2	Catfish Hunter	113
3	Dennis Rasmussen	85
4	Tommy John	80
5	Doc Medich	69
6	Pat Dobson	66
7	Dave Righetti	65

1961–72

1	Mel Stottlemyre	171
2	Fritz Peterson	139
3	Ralph Terry	133
4	Jim Bouton	105
5	Al Downing	96
6	Stan Bahnsen	88
7	Bill Stafford	75

1943–60

1	Whitey Ford	228
2	Bob Turley	118
3	Ed Lopat	116
4	Allie Reynolds	111
5	Vic Raschi	104
6	Tommy Byrne	74
	Art Ditmar	74

1921–42

1	Red Ruffing	200
2	Lefty Gomez	138
3	Bob Shawkey	105
4	Waite Hoyt	93
5	Herb Pennock	91
6	Atley Donald	66
7	Spud Chandler	64

1901–20

1	Ray Caldwell	41
2	Jack Warhop	28
3	Russ Ford	27
	Jack Quinn	27
5	Jack Chesbro	26
6	Ray Fisher	24
	George Mogridge	24

WALKS

1	Lefty Gomez	1090
2	Whitey Ford	1086
3	Red Ruffing	1066
4	Bob Shawkey	855
5	Allie Reynolds	819
6	Mel Stottlemyre	809
7	Tommy Byrne	763
8	Bob Turley	761
9	**Andy Pettitte**	**648**
10	Ron Guidry	633
11	Waite Hoyt	631
12	Vic Raschi	620
13	Ray Caldwell	576
14	George Pipgras	545
15	Al Downing	526
16	Dave Righetti	473
17	Herb Pennock	471
18	Spud Chandler	463
19	Jack Chesbro	434
20	Monte Pearson	426
21	Johnny Murphy	416
22	Joe Page	414
23	Sam Jones	405
	Ed Lopat	405
25	Hank Johnson	403
26	Jack Warhop	400
27	**Roger Clemens**	**398**
	David Cone	398
29	Ray Fisher	393
30	Bump Hadley	375
31	Atley Donald	369
32	Don Larsen	362
33	Fritz Peterson	332
34	Jim Bouton	331
35	Tommy John	324
36	Bill Hogg	319
37	Stan Bahnsen	312
38	Joe Bush	311
39	Ed Figueroa	305
40	Orlando Hernandez	304
41	Jack Quinn	291
42	Russ Ford	287
	Mike Mussina	**287**
44	Hank Borowy	284
45	Scott Kamieniecki	282
46	Rudy May	281
47	Carl Mays	279
48	Mike Kekich	276
49	Ralph Terry	270
50	Spec Shea	269

FEWEST WALKS/9 INNINGS

1988–2007

1	David Wells	1.47
2	**Mike Mussina**	**1.91**
3	Ramiro Mendoza	1.98
4	Scott Sanderson	2.09
5	Randy Johnson	2.24
6	**Mariano Rivera**	**2.25**
7	Jimmy Key	2.37

1973–87

1	Tommy John	2.13
2	Ron Guidry	2.38
3	Catfish Hunter	2.42
4	Dick Tidrow	2.61
5	Doc Medich	2.73
6	Pat Dobson	2.74
7	Sparky Lyle	2.82

1961–72

1	Fritz Peterson	1.61
2	Steve Kline	1.93
3	Ralph Terry	2.03
4	Lindy McDaniel	2.58
5	Mel Stottlemyre	2.74
6	Steve Hamilton	2.78
7	Stan Bahnsen	2.85

1943–60

1	Tiny Bonham	1.58
2	Johnny Sain	2.11
3	Art Ditmar	2.43
4	Ed Lopat	2.43
5	Bobby Shantz	2.58
6	Tom Morgan	2.85
7	Johnny Kucks	2.98

1921–42

1	Herb Pennock	1.92
2	Carl Mays	2.30
3	Urban Shocker	2.39
4	Waite Hoyt	2.50
5	Spud Chandler	2.81
6	Wilcy Moore	2.88
7	Red Ruffing	3.03

1901–20

1	Clark Griffith	1.58
2	Al Orth	1.77
3	Jack Chesbro	2.00
4	George Mogridge	2.05
5	Jack Quinn	2.06
6	Jack Powell	2.26
7	Russ Ford	2.32

STRIKEOUTS

1	Whitey Ford	1956
2	Ron Guidry	1778
3	Red Ruffing	1526
4	Lefty Gomez	1468
5	**Andy Pettitte**	**1416**
6	Mel Stottlemyre	1257
7	Bob Shawkey	1163
8	**Mike Mussina**	**1128**
9	Al Downing	1028
10	**Roger Clemens**	**1014**
11	Allie Reynolds	967
12	Dave Righetti	940
13	Jack Chesbro	913
14	Bob Turley	909
15	Fritz Peterson	893
16	David Cone	888
17	**Mariano Rivera**	**857**
18	Vic Raschi	832
19	Ray Caldwell	803
20	Waite Hoyt	713
21	Orlando Hernandez	703
22	Herb Pennock	700
23	George Pipgras	656
24	Ralph Terry	615
25	Spud Chandler	614
26	Tommy Byrne	592
27	Rudy May	586
28	Ray Fisher	583
29	Jim Bouton	561
30	David Wells	557
31	Russ Ford	553
32	Stan Bahnsen	534
33	Melido Perez	519
34	Joe Page	515
35	Rich Gossage	512
36	Ed Lopat	502
37	Catfish Hunter	492
38	Tommy John	483
39	Jack Quinn	478
40	Jack Warhop	463
41	Sparky Lyle	454
42	Doc Medich	431
43	Ramiro Mendoza	414
44	Bill Stafford	408
45	Hank Johnson	407
	Mike Stanton	407
47	Monte Pearson	406
48	Al Orth	402
49	Jimmy Key	400
50	Johnny Allen	395

STRIKEOUTS/9 INNINGS

1	David Cone	8.67
2	Rich Gossage	8.65
3	**Roger Clemens**	**8.27**
4	Mike Stanton	8.17
5	**Mariano Rivera**	**8.09**
6	Randy Johnson	8.00
7	**Mike Mussina**	**7.51**
8	Al Downing	7.49
9	Dave Righetti	7.44
10	Melido Perez	7.40
11	Orlando Hernandez	7.22
12	Steve Hamilton	7.20
13	Ron Guidry	6.69
14	Greg Cadaret	6.64
15	Bob Turley	6.45
16	Sterling Hitchcock	6.38
17	**Andy Pettitte**	**6.35**
18	Rudy May	6.27
19	Hal Reniff	6.16
20	Lindy McDaniel	6.00
21	Jimmy Key	5.96
22	Joe Page	5.94
23	Dennis Rasmussen	5.92
24	Phil Niekro	5.89
25	David Wells	5.89
26	Johnny Allen	5.78
27	Tom Sturdivant	5.72
28	Bob Wickman	5.56
29	Whitey Ford	5.55
30	Sparky Lyle	5.48
31	Tim Leary	5.39
32	Tommy Byrne	5.36
33	Ramiro Mendoza	5.33
34	Bobby Shantz	5.31
35	Lefty Gomez	5.29
36	Scott Sanderson	5.25
37	Shane Rawley	5.25
38	Hank Johnson	5.14
39	Allie Reynolds	5.12
40	Pat Dobson	5.08
41	Bill Stafford	5.03
42	Jim Coates	5.01
43	Jim Bouton	4.98
44	Doc Medich	4.93
45	Don Larsen	4.89
46	Stan Bahnsen	4.88
47	Vic Raschi	4.87
48	Mike Kekich	4.85
49	Allan Russell	4.78
50	Scott Kamieniecki	4.63

EARNED RUN AVERAGE

1	Rich Gossage	2.14
2	**Mariano Rivera**	**2.35**
3	Sparky Lyle	2.41
4	Russ Ford	2.54
5	Jack Chesbro	2.58
6	Clark Griffith	2.66
7	Al Orth	2.72
8	Tiny Bonham	2.73
	George Mogridge	2.73
	Bobby Shantz	2.73
11	Hank Borowy	2.74
12	Whitey Ford	2.75
13	Steve Hamilton	2.78
14	Jack Powell	2.81
15	Spud Chandler	2.84
16	Lindy McDaniel	2.89
17	Ray Fisher	2.91
18	Steve Kline	2.96
19	Mel Stottlemyre	2.97
20	Ray Caldwell	3.00
21	Allan Russell	3.05
22	Bill Hogg	3.06
23	Bill Bevens	3.08
24	Stan Bahnsen	3.10
	Fritz Peterson	3.10
26	Dave Righetti	3.11
27	Rudy May	3.12
	Bob Shawkey	3.12
	Jack Warhop	3.12
30	Marius Russo	3.13
31	Rube Manning	3.14
	Urban Shocker	3.14
33	Jack Quinn	3.15
34	Ed Lopat	3.19
	Tom Sturdivant	3.19
36	Al Downing	3.23
37	Art Ditmar	3.24
38	Carl Mays	3.25
39	Hal Reniff	3.26
40	Ron Guidry	3.29
41	Allie Reynolds	3.30
42	Wilcy Moore	3.31
	Johnny Sain	3.31
44	Lefty Gomez	3.34
45	Jim Bouton	3.36
	Ray Keating	3.36
47	Doc Medich	3.40
48	Joe Bush	3.44
	Joe Page	3.44
	Ralph Terry	3.44

OPPONENT BATTING AVERAGE

1	Rich Gossage	.207
2	**Mariano Rivera**	**.216**
3	Hal Reniff	.221
4	Tommy Byrne	.222
	Steve Hamilton	.222
6	Bob Turley	.223
7	Al Downing	.224
8	Don Larsen	.227
9	Spec Shea	.229
10	Rudy May	.231
11	Tom Sturdivant	.232
12	Hank Borowy	.234
13	Johnny Allen	.235
	Whitey Ford	.235
15	Orlando Hernandez	.236
	Vic Raschi	.236
	Dave Righetti	.236
18	Catfish Hunter	.238
	Allie Reynolds	.238
	Bobby Shantz	.238
21	Dennis Rasmussen	.239
	Bill Stafford	.239
23	Spud Chandler	.240
	David Cone	.240
	Lindy McDaniel	.240
26	Jim Bouton	.241
	Lefty Gomez	.241
28	Jack Chesbro	.242
	Marius Russo	.242
30	Art Ditmar	.243
	Sparky Lyle	.243
32	Stan Bahnsen	.244
	Ray Caldwell	.244
	Ron Guidry	.244
35	Russ Ford	.245
	Joe Page	.245
	Allan Russell	.245
	Mel Stottlemyre	.245
	Ralph Terry	.245
40	Randy Johnson	.246
41	Jim Coates	.247
	Clark Griffith	.247
	Steve Kline	.247
	Melido Perez	.247
45	Tiny Bonham	.248
	Bill Hogg	.248
	Jack Powell	.248
	Red Ruffing	.248
49	**Roger Clemens**	**.249**
50	2 players tied	.250

OPPONENT ON-BASE PCT.

1	**Mariano Rivera**	**.271**
2	Rich Gossage	.277
3	Tiny Bonham	.282
4	Steve Hamilton	.284
5	Clark Griffith	.286
6	Ralph Terry	.288
7	Catfish Hunter	.289
	Steve Kline	.289
	Fritz Peterson	.289
10	Jack Chesbro	.290
	Al Orth	.290
12	Ron Guidry	.292
	Lindy McDaniel	.292
14	Bobby Shantz	.294
15	Rudy May	.295
16	Art Ditmar	.296
17	David Wells	.297
18	Russ Ford	.298
19	Whitey Ford	.300
	Randy Johnson	.300
	Jack Powell	.300
22	Spud Chandler	.301
	Mike Mussina	**.301**
24	Stan Bahnsen	.302
	Sparky Lyle	.302
26	Hank Borowy	.303
	Jim Bouton	.303
	Johnny Sain	.303
	Mel Stottlemyre	.303
30	Al Downing	.304
31	Bill Stafford	.305
32	Orlando Hernandez	.306
33	George Mogridge	.308
34	Jimmy Key	.310
	Red Ruffing	.310
	Scott Sanderson	.310
37	Doc Medich	.311
	Dennis Rasmussen	.311
39	Marius Russo	.312
40	Ray Caldwell	.313
	Vic Raschi	.313
	Dave Righetti	.313
	Tom Sturdivant	.313
44	Johnny Allen	.314
45	Ed Lopat	.316
46	Pat Dobson	.317
47	Bill Bevens	.318
	Roger Clemens	**.318**
	Bob Shawkey	.318
	Urban Shocker	.318

ADJUSTED PITCHING RUNS

1	Don Gullett	369
2	Whitey Ford	324
3	Red Ruffing	250
4	Lefty Gomez	244
5	**Mariano Rivera**	**240**
6	Rudy May	236
7	Steve Karsay	195
8	Ron Guidry	192
9	Melido Perez	190
10	Allen Watson	188
11	**Carl Pavano**	**172**
12	Mike Witt	168
13	Randy Keisler	166
14	Bob Shawkey	156
15	Spud Chandler	148
16	Waite Hoyt	139
17	**Andy Pettitte**	**129**
18	Joe Verbanic	125
19	Mel Stottlemyre	116
20	Tiny Bonham	112
21	Herb Pennock	110
22	Ed Lopat	107
23	Dave Righetti	106
24	Rich Gossage	101
	Allie Reynolds	101
26	Sparky Lyle	94
27	Carl Mays	81
28	**Mike Mussina**	**80**
29	Vic Raschi	77
30	David Cone	72
31	Russ Ford	69
32	Johnny Murphy	68
33	Monte Pearson	67
34	**Roger Clemens**	**66**
	Orlando Hernandez	66
36	Tommy John	62
37	Urban Shocker	61
38	Jimmy Key	60
39	Marius Russo	59
40	Hank Borowy	55
41	Joe Bush	53
42	David Wells	52
43	**Chien-Ming Wang**	**48**
44	Jack Chesbro	44
45	Bobby Shantz	43
46	Tom Gordon	40
	Jeff Nelson	40
	Fritz Peterson	40
	Mike Stanton	40
50	Lindy McDaniel	37

GAMES

1	**Mariano Rivera**	**787**
2	Dave Righetti	522
3	Whitey Ford	498
4	Mike Stanton	456
5	Red Ruffing	426
6	Sparky Lyle	420
7	Bob Shawkey	415
8	Johnny Murphy	383
9	Ron Guidry	368
10	Lefty Gomez	367
11	Waite Hoyt	365
12	Mel Stottlemyre	360
13	Herb Pennock	346
14	Jeff Nelson	331
15	Rich Gossage	319
	Andy Pettitte	**319**
17	Steve Hamilton	311
18	Allie Reynolds	295
19	Fritz Peterson	288
20	Ramiro Mendoza	278
	Joe Page	278
22	Jack Chesbro	269
23	Lindy McDaniel	265
24	Ray Caldwell	248
25	George Pipgras	247
	Hal Reniff	247
27	Bob Turley	234
28	Lee Guetterman	233
29	Steve Howe	229
30	Jack Quinn	228
31	Bob Wickman	223
32	Tommy Byrne	221
	Jack Warhop	221
34	Ray Fisher	219
35	Vic Raschi	218
36	Ed Lopat	217
37	**Mike Mussina**	**215**
38	Tommy John	214
39	Spud Chandler	211
	Dick Tidrow	211
41	Ralph Terry	210
42	Al Downing	208
43	Sam Jones	202
44	Jim Bouton	197
45	**Scott Proctor**	**190**
46	Greg Cadaret	188
47	Rudy May	184
48	**Roger Clemens**	**175**
49	George Mogridge	171
	Wilcy Moore	171

RELIEF WINS

1	Johnny Murphy	73
2	**Mariano Rivera**	**59**
3	Sparky Lyle	57
4	Rich Gossage	42
5	Joe Page	41
	Dave Righetti	41
7	Lindy McDaniel	38
8	Ramiro Mendoza	33
9	Steve Hamilton	31
	Mike Stanton	31
11	Wilcy Moore	28
	Bob Shawkey	28
13	Ron Davis	27
14	Bob Grim	26
15	Jeff Nelson	23
16	Luis Arroyo	22
17	Lee Guetterman	21
18	Dick Tidrow	19
19	Waite Hoyt	18
	Steve Howe	18
	Hal Reniff	18
22	4 players tied	17

RELIEF LOSSES

1	Johnny Murphy	43
2	**Mariano Rivera**	**41**
3	Sparky Lyle	40
4	Dave Righetti	38
5	Joe Page	34
6	Rich Gossage	28
7	Lindy McDaniel	27
8	Hal Reniff	20
9	Steve Hamilton	19
	Jeff Nelson	19
	Bob Shawkey	19
12	Lee Guetterman	17
	Ramiro Mendoza	17
14	Wilcy Moore	16
15	Ryne Duren	15
	Dooley Womack	15
17	Mike Stanton	14
	Dick Tidrow	14
19	Pedro Ramos	13
20	Bob Grim	12
21	Tom Morgan	11
	Rudy May	11
23	5 players tied	10

RELIEF GAMES

1	**Mariano Rivera**	**777**
2	Mike Stanton	455
3	Dave Righetti	446
4	Sparky Lyle	420
5	Johnny Murphy	343
6	Jeff Nelson	331
7	Rich Gossage	319
8	Steve Hamilton	304
9	Lindy McDaniel	262
10	Hal Reniff	247
11	Joe Page	233
12	Lee Guetterman	231
13	Steve Howe	229
14	Ramiro Mendoza	221
15	Bob Wickman	195
16	**Scott Proctor**	**189**
17	John Habyan	164
18	Steve Farr	159
	Tom Gordon	159
20	Wilcy Moore	156
21	Greg Cadaret	153
22	Dick Tidrow	152
23	Dooley Womack	151
24	Ron Davis	144

RELIEF INNINGS PITCHED

Rank	Player	IP
1	**Mariano Rivera**	**903.0**
2	Sparky Lyle	745.2
3	Johnny Murphy	709.1
4	Dave Righetti	627.1
5	Rich Gossage	533.0
6	Lindy McDaniel	523.0
7	Joe Page	500.2
8	Mike Stanton	444.1
9	Steve Hamilton	443.0
10	Hal Reniff	428.1
11	Ramiro Mendoza	372.0
12	Bob Shawkey	351.2
13	Lee Guetterman	340.2
14	Dick Tidrow	332.1
15	Wilcy Moore	316.0
16	Jeff Nelson	311.0
17	Ron Davis	291.2
18	Bob Shirley	257.2
19	Bob Wickman	255.1
20	George Frazier	254.2
21	Bob Grim	244.1
22	Greg Cadaret	235.1
23	Rich Monteleone	232.2
24	Dooley Womack	230.2

ADJUSTED RELIEVER RUNS

1	**Mariano Rivera**	**247**
2	Rich Gossage	105
3	Sparky Lyle	99
4	Dave Righetti	79
5	Johnny Murphy	64
6	Ramiro Mendoza	48
7	Gerry Staley	44
8	Jeff Nelson	42
9	Joe Page	42
10	Waite Hoyt	40
11	Tom Gordon	40
12	Lindy McDaniel	36
13	Mike Stanton	34
14	Ron Davis	33
15	Bob Shawkey	32
16	Johnny Sain	30
17	Steve Hamilton	29
18	Steve Farr	29
19	Jack Aker	28
20	John Wetteland	27
21	Fred Beene	26
22	Bob Grim	24
23	Bob Wickman	22
24	John Habyan	22

RELIEF RANKING

1	**Mariano Rivera**	**443**
2	Rich Gossage	187
3	Sparky Lyle	159
4	Dave Righetti	142
5	Johnny Murphy	107
6	Joe Page	67
7	Waite Hoyt	62
8	Ramiro Mendoza	60
9	Jeff Nelson	58
10	John Wetteland	52
11	Steve Farr	50
12	Tom Gordon	50
13	Ron Davis	47
14	Bob Shawkey	46
15	Gerry Staley	46
16	Jack Aker	44
17	Mike Stanton	40
18	Johnny Sain	39
19	Lindy McDaniel	37
20	Bob Grim	34
21	Steve Hamilton	32
22	Luis Arroyo	29
23	Ryne Duren	27
24	Jim Konstanty	24

ADJUSTED EARNED RUN AVERAGE

1	**Mariano Rivera**	**194**
2	Rich Gossage	181
3	Sparky Lyle	148
4	Whitey Ford	133
5	Spud Chandler	132
6	Bobby Shantz	131
7	Tiny Bonham	129
8	Dave Righetti	128
9	Russ Ford	126
10	Lefty Gomez	125
11	Hank Borowy	124
	Marius Russo	124
13	Jimmy Key	123
14	Steve Hamilton	121
	Ed Lopat	121
	Carl Mays	121
17	Ron Guidry	120
	Rudy May	120
	Chien-Ming Wang	**120**
20	Lindy McDaniel	119
	Red Ruffing	119
	Mike Stanton	119
23	David Cone	118
	Urban Shocker	118
25	Joe Bush	117
	Wilcy Moore	117
	Monte Pearson	117
	Bob Shawkey	117
29	Johnny Murphy	116
	Andy Pettitte	**116**
	Tom Sturdivant	116
32	Orlando Hernandez	115
	Waite Hoyt	115
	Allie Reynolds	115
35	Bill Bevens	113
	Roger Clemens	**113**
	Tommy John	113
	Mike Mussina	**113**
	Herb Pennock	113
	Mel Stottlemyre	113
	David Wells	113
42	Clark Griffith	112
43	Art Ditmar	111
	Steve Kline	111
	Ramiro Mendoza	111
	Vic Raschi	111
47	George Mogridge	110
	Phil Niekro	110
49	Jack Chesbro	109
	Joe Page	109

ADJUSTED ERA BY ERA

1988–2007

1	**Mariano Rivera**	**194**
2	Jimmy Key	123
3	**Chien-Ming Wang**	**120**
4	Mike Stanton	119
5	David Cone	118
6	**Andy Pettitte**	**116**
7	Orlando Hernandez	115

1973–87

1	Rich Gossage	181
2	Sparky Lyle	148
3	Dave Righetti	128
4	Ron Guidry	120
	Rudy May	120
6	Tommy John	113
7	Phil Niekro	110

1961–72

1	Steve Hamilton	121
2	Lindy McDaniel	119
3	Mel Stottlemyre	113
4	Steve Kline	111
5	Stan Bahnsen	107
	Fritz Peterson	107
7	Hal Reniff	106
	Ralph Terry	106

1943–60

1	Whitey Ford	133
2	Bobby Shantz	131
3	Tiny Bonham	129
4	Hank Borowy	124
5	Ed Lopat	121
6	Tom Sturdivant	116
7	Allie Reynolds	115

1921–42

1	Spud Chandler	132
2	Lefty Gomez	125
3	Marius Russo	124
4	Carl Mays	121
5	Red Ruffing	119
6	Urban Shocker	118
7	Joe Bush	117
	Wilcy Moore	117
	Monte Pearson	117
	Bob Shawkey	117

1901–20

1	Russ Ford	126
2	Clark Griffith	112
3	George Mogridge	110
4	Jack Chesbro	109
5	Jack Quinn	106
6	Al Orth	104
7	Ray Fisher	103

PITCHER WINS BY ERA

1988–2007

Rank	Player	Wins
1	**Mariano Rivera**	**43.2**
2	**Andy Pettitte**	**14.2**
3	**Mike Mussina**	**8.8**
4	David Cone	7.2
5	**Roger Clemens**	**6.8**
6	Orlando Hernandez	6.7
7	Jimmy Key	6.4

1973–87

Rank	Player	Wins
1	Ron Guidry	20.5
2	Rich Gossage	18.3
3	Dave Righetti	16.7
4	Sparky Lyle	16.0
5	Tommy John	6.9
6	Rudy May	5.6
7	Ron Davis	5.0

1961–72

Rank	Player	Wins
1	Mel Stottlemyre	16.7
2	Fritz Peterson	6.4
3	Lindy McDaniel	4.8
4	Jack Aker	4.4
5	Steve Hamilton	4.0
6	Luis Arroyo	3.3
7	Dooley Womack	2.4

1943–60

Rank	Player	Wins
1	Whitey Ford	37.2
2	Ed Lopat	12.8
3	Allie Reynolds	10.9
4	Tiny Bonham	10.8
5	Vic Raschi	7.6
6	Bobby Shantz	6.1
7	Hank Borowy	6.0

1921–42

Rank	Player	Wins
1	Red Ruffing	34.7
2	Lefty Gomez	20.4
3	Spud Chandler	19.1
4	Bob Shawkey	17.9
5	Waite Hoyt	13.5
6	Carl Mays	11.5
7	Johnny Murphy	10.0
	Herb Pennock	10.0

1901–20

Rank	Player	Wins
1	Russ Ford	8.4
2	Ray Caldwell	7.1
3	Jack Chesbro	6.6
4	Al Orth	4.7
5	Jack Quinn	3.9
6	George Mogridge	2.6
7	Clark Griffith	2.2

PITCHER WINS

Rank	Player	Wins
1	**Mariano Rivera**	**43.2**
2	Whitey Ford	37.2
3	Red Ruffing	34.7
4	Ron Guidry	20.5
5	Lefty Gomez	20.4
6	Spud Chandler	19.1
7	Rich Gossage	18.3
8	Bob Shawkey	17.9
9	Dave Righetti	16.7
	Mel Stottlemyre	16.7
11	Sparky Lyle	16.0
12	**Andy Pettitte**	**14.2**
13	Waite Hoyt	13.5
14	Ed Lopat	12.8
15	Carl Mays	11.5
16	Allie Reynolds	10.9
17	Tiny Bonham	10.8
18	Johnny Murphy	10.0
	Herb Pennock	10.0
20	Joe Bush	9.0
21	**Mike Mussina**	**8.8**
22	Russ Ford	8.4
23	Vic Raschi	7.6
24	Monte Pearson	7.4
25	David Cone	7.2
26	Ray Caldwell	7.1
27	Tommy John	6.9
28	**Roger Clemens**	**6.8**
29	Orlando Hernandez	6.7
30	Jack Chesbro	6.6
	Urban Shocker	6.6
32	Jimmy Key	6.4
	Fritz Peterson	6.4
34	Marius Russo	6.3
35	Bobby Shantz	6.1
36	Hank Borowy	6.0
37	Rudy May	5.6
	Chien-Ming Wang	**5.6**
39	Steve Farr	5.4
40	Jeff Nelson	5.2
41	Ron Davis	5.0
	Tom Gordon	5.0
	David Wells	5.0
44	Lindy McDaniel	4.8
45	Al Orth	4.7
46	Joe Page	4.6
47	John Wetteland	4.5
48	Jack Aker	4.4
49	Don Larsen	4.3
	Mike Stanton	4.3

PLAYER OVERALL WINS BY ERA

1988–2007

Rank	Player	Wins
1	**Mariano Rivera**	**43.2**
2	**Jorge Posada**	**27.0**
3	Bernie Williams	24.6
4	**Derek Jeter**	**17.3**
5	Don Mattingly	15.4
6	**Alex Rodriguez**	**15.3**
7	**Andy Pettitte**	**14.2**
8	Paul O'Neill	12.1
9	**Jason Giambi**	**9.0**
10	**Mike Mussina**	**8.8**
11	Mike Stanley	8.2
12	Wade Boggs	7.9
13	David Cone	7.2
14	**Roger Clemens**	**6.8**

1973–87

Rank	Player	Wins
1	Willie Randolph	34.4
2	Thurman Munson	25.0
3	Ron Guidry	20.5
4	Rickey Henderson	18.7
5	Rich Gossage	18.3
6	Dave Righetti	16.7
7	Sparky Lyle	16.0
8	Graig Nettles	14.9
9	Dave Winfield	12.5
10	Reggie Jackson	11.1
11	Oscar Gamble	7.1
12	Tommy John	6.9
13	Rudy May	5.6
14	Ron Davis	5.0

1961–72

Rank	Player	Wins
1	Mel Stottlemyre	16.7
2	Roy White	14.8
3	Elston Howard	12.3
4	Bobby Murcer	10.1
5	Clete Boyer	10.0
6	Tom Tresh	9.1
7	Roger Maris	8.8
8	Fritz Peterson	6.4
9	Lindy McDaniel	4.8
	Horace Clarke	4.8
11	Tony Kubek	4.5
12	Jack Aker	4.4
13	Gene Michael	4.1
14	Steve Hamilton	4.0

1943–60

Rank	Player	Wins
1	Mickey Mantle	71.8
2	Yogi Berra	40.2
3	Whitey Ford	37.2
4	Gil McDougald	24.2
5	Phil Rizzuto	18.7
6	Snuffy Stirnweiss	13.3
7	Ed Lopat	12.8
8	Allie Reynolds	10.9
9	Tiny Bonham	10.8
10	Bill Skowron	9.6
11	Vic Raschi	7.6
12	Bobby Shantz	6.1
13	Hank Borowy	6.0
14	Gene Woodling	5.6

1921–42

Rank	Player	Wins
1	Babe Ruth	101.5
2	Lou Gehrig	70.9
3	Joe DiMaggio	45.8
4	Bill Dickey	38.5
5	Red Ruffing	34.7
6	Joe Gordon	25.5
7	Charlie Keller	21.7
8	Lefty Gomez	20.4
9	Spud Chandler	19.1
10	Bob Shawkey	17.9
11	Tony Lazzeri	17.4
12	Tommy Henrich	15.0
13	Waite Hoyt	13.5
14	Earle Combs	12.0

1901–20

Rank	Player	Wins
1	Roger Peckinpaugh	12.4
2	Russ Ford	8.4
3	Jimmy Williams	7.5
4	Frank Baker	7.4
	Kid Elberfeld	7.4
6	Ray Caldwell	7.1
7	Del Pratt	6.7
8	Jack Chesbro	6.6
9	Al Orth	4.6
10	Jack Quinn	3.9
11	Birdie Cree	2.9
12	Les Nunamaker	2.8
13	George Mogridge	2.6
14	Clark Griffith	2.2
	Clyde Engle	2.2

PLAYER OVERALL WINS

Rank	Player	Wins
1	Babe Ruth	101.5
2	Mickey Mantle	71.8
3	Lou Gehrig	70.9
4	Joe DiMaggio	45.8
5	**Mariano Rivera**	**43.2**
6	Yogi Berra	40.2
7	Bill Dickey	38.5
8	Whitey Ford	37.2
9	Red Ruffing	34.7
10	Willie Randolph	34.4
11	**Jorge Posada**	**27.0**
12	Joe Gordon	25.5
13	Thurman Munson	25.0
14	Bernie Williams	24.6
15	Gil McDougald	24.2
16	Charlie Keller	21.7
17	Ron Guidry	20.5
18	Lefty Gomez	20.4
19	Spud Chandler	19.1
20	Rickey Henderson	18.7
	Phil Rizzuto	18.7
22	Rich Gossage	18.3
23	Bob Shawkey	17.9
24	Tony Lazzeri	17.4
25	**Derek Jeter**	**17.3**
26	Dave Righetti	16.7
	Mel Stottlemyre	16.7
28	Sparky Lyle	16.0
29	Don Mattingly	15.4
30	**Alex Rodriguez**	**15.3**
31	Tommy Henrich	15.0
32	Graig Nettles	14.9
33	Roy White	14.8
34	**Andy Pettitte**	**14.2**
35	Waite Hoyt	13.5
36	Snuffy Stirnweiss	13.3
37	Ed Lopat	12.8
38	Dave Winfield	12.5
39	Roger Peckinpaugh	12.4
40	Elston Howard	12.3
41	Paul O'Neill	12.1
42	Earle Combs	12.0
43	Ben Chapman	11.7
44	Carl Mays	11.5
45	Reggie Jackson	11.1
46	Allie Reynolds	10.9
47	Tiny Bonham	10.8
48	Bobby Murcer	10.1
49	Johnny Murphy	10.0
	Herb Pennock	10.0
	Clete Boyer	10.0
52	Bill Skowron	9.6
53	Tom Tresh	9.1
54	Joe Bush	9.0
	Jason Giambi	**9.0**
56	**Mike Mussina**	**8.8**
	Roger Maris	8.8
58	Russ Ford	8.4
59	Mike Stanley	8.2
60	George Selkirk	8.1
61	Wade Boggs	7.9
62	Vic Raschi	7.6
63	Jimmy Williams	7.5
64	Monte Pearson	7.4
	Frank Baker	7.4
	Kid Elberfeld	7.4
67	David Cone	7.2
68	Ray Caldwell	7.1
	Oscar Gamble	7.1
70	Tommy John	6.9
71	**Roger Clemens**	**6.8**
72	Orlando Hernandez	6.7
	Del Pratt	6.7
74	Jack Chesbro	6.6
	Urban Shocker	6.6
76	**Hideki Matsui**	**6.5**
77	Jimmy Key	6.4
	Fritz Peterson	6.4
	Robinson Cano	**6.4**
80	Marius Russo	6.3
81	Bobby Shantz	6.1
82	Hank Borowy	6.0
83	Rudy May	5.6
	Chien-Ming Wang	**5.6**
	Gene Woodling	5.6
86	Steve Farr	5.4
87	Mike Gallego	5.3
88	Jeff Nelson	5.2
89	Ron Davis	5.0
	Tom Gordon	5.0
	David Wells	5.0
92	Lindy McDaniel	4.8
	Horace Clarke	4.8
	Gary Sheffield	4.8
95	Ron Blomberg	4.7
	Lyn Lary	4.7
97	Al Orth	4.6
	Joe Page	4.6
99	John Wetteland	4.5
	Tony Kubek	4.5

PLAYER OVERALL WINS (CONT.)

Rank	Player	Wins
101	Jack Aker	4.4
	Don Baylor	4.4
103	Don Larsen	4.3
	Mike Stanton	4.3
	Wally Schang	4.3
106	Alfonso Soriano	4.2
107	Gene Michael	4.1
	Aaron Robinson	4.1
	Danny Tartabull	4.1
110	Steve Hamilton	4.0
111	Jack Quinn	3.9
	Tom Sturdivant	3.9
113	Ramiro Mendoza	3.8
	Bobby Bonds	3.8
115	Johnny Sain	3.6
	Jerry Mumphrey	3.6
117	Tommy Byrne	3.5
	Jesse Barfield	3.5
	Pat Collins	3.5
	Elliott Maddox	3.5
121	Luis Arroyo	3.3
	Butch Wynegar	3.3
123	Frank Fernandez	3.1
124	Birdie Cree	2.9
125	Hank Bauer	2.8
	Les Nunamaker	2.8
	Randy Velarde	2.8
128	Art Ditmar	2.7
	Doc Medich	2.7
	Alvaro Espinoza	2.7
	Nick Etten	2.7
132	George Mogridge	2.6
133	Ed Figueroa	2.5
	Joe Collins	2.5
	Robin Ventura	2.5
136	Lee Guetterman	2.4
	Steve Howe	2.4
	Dooley Womack	2.4
139	Stan Bahnsen	2.3
	Al Downing	2.3
	Oral Hildebrand	2.3
	Andy Carey	2.3
	Gus Niarhos	2.3
144	Clark Griffith	2.2
	Steve Kline	2.2
	Bobby Abreu	**2.2**
	Clyde Engle	2.2
	Roberto Kelly	2.2
	Mickey Rivers	2.2
150	Johnny Allen	2.1
	Steve Sax	2.1
152	Jim Konstanty	2.0
	Oscar Grimes	2.0
154	Butch Wensloff	1.9
	Jack Clark	1.9
	Bucky Dent	1.9
157	Ivy Andrews	1.8
	Catfish Hunter	1.8
	David Justice	1.8
	Jerry Kenney	1.8
	Bob Meusel	1.8
	Harry Wolter	1.8
163	Tom Morgan	1.7
	Phil Niekro	1.7
	Ron Hassey	1.7
	Billy Martin	1.7
167	Fred Beene	1.6
	Bill Bevens	1.6
	Ray Fisher	1.6
	John Habyan	1.6
	Buddy Rosar	1.6
172	Bump Hadley	1.5
	Pascual Perez	1.5
	Bob Turley	1.5
	Andy Stankiewicz	1.5
176	George Frazier	1.4
	Steve Karsay	1.4
	George McConnell	1.4
	Hal Reniff	1.4
	Spec Shea	1.4
	Walt Alexander	1.4
	Bob Cerv	1.4
	Ken Griffey	1.4
	Hersh Martin	1.4
	Willy Miranda	1.4
	Red Rolfe	1.4
	Charlie Silvera	1.4
	Roxy Walters	1.4
189	Dutch Ruether	1.3
	George McQuinn	1.3
	Bob Watson	1.3
	Joe Yeager	1.3
193	Charles Hudson	1.2
	Bob Kuzava	1.2
	Sammy Byrd	1.2
	John Ganzel	1.2
	Johnny Lindell	1.2
	Ben Paschal	1.2
	Joe Sewell	1.2
	Jim Spencer	1.2

PLATE APPEARANCES

1 Frankie Crosetti, 1938....757
2 Bobby Richardson, 1962.......754
3 Derek Jeter, 2005..........752
4 Derek Jeter, 1997..........748
5 Frankie Crosetti, 1939....743
6 Don Mattingly, 1986........742
7 Alfonso Soriano, 2002....741
8 Frankie Crosetti, 1936....740
Red Rolfe, 1937.............740
10 Derek Jeter, 1999..........739
11 Lou Gehrig, 1931............738
12 Phil Rizzuto, 1950..........735
13 Alfonso Soriano, 2003....734
14 Horace Clarke, 1970......732
15 Red Rolfe, 1939.............731
16 Derek Jeter, 2002..........730
17 Bobby Richardson, 1964........728
Roy White, 1976.............728
19 Don Mattingly, 1985........727
20 Earle Combs, 1927.........724
21 Snuffy Stirnweiss, 1944............723
Roy White, 1973.............723
23 Frankie Crosetti, 1937....721
Derek Jeter, 2004..........721
25 Lou Gehrig, 1936............719
26 Lou Gehrig, 1927............717
Snuffy Stirnweiss, 1945............717
Steve Sax, 1989.............717
29 Chuck Knoblauch, 1999........715
Alex Rodriguez, 2005...715
Derek Jeter, 2006..........715
32 Red Rolfe, 1938.............714
Derek Jeter, 2007..........714
34 Bobby Richardson, 1965.......713
35 Lyn Lary, 1931................712
Phil Rizzuto, 1949..........712
Tom Tresh, 1962.............712
Roy White, 1970.............712
39 Earle Combs, 1928.........709
40 Lou Gehrig, 1932............708
Alex Rodriguez, 2007...708
42 Steve Sax, 1991.............707
43 Red Rolfe, 1935.............706
Bobby Richardson, 1961.......706
Chuck Knoblauch, 1998.........706
46 Lou Gehrig, 1930............703
Hideki Matsui, 2005......703
48 Rickey Henderson, 1986.......701
49 Lou Gehrig, 1937............700
50 4 players tied.................699

AT BATS

1 Alfonso Soriano, 2002....696
2 Bobby Richardson, 1962.......692
3 Horace Clarke, 1970......686
4 Alfonso Soriano, 2003....682
5 Bobby Richardson, 1964.......679
6 Don Mattingly, 1986........677
7 Bobby Richardson, 1965.......664
8 Bobby Richardson, 1961.......662
9 Frankie Crosetti, 1939....656
10 Derek Jeter, 1997..........654
Derek Jeter, 2005..........654
12 Don Mattingly, 1985........652
Steve Sax, 1991.............652
14 Steve Sax, 1989.............651
15 Earle Combs, 1927.........648
Red Rolfe, 1937.............648
Red Rolfe, 1939.............648
18 Joe Dugan, 1923............644
Derek Jeter, 2002..........644
20 Snuffy Stirnweiss, 1944............643
Derek Jeter, 2004..........643
22 Horace Clarke, 1969.......641
Chris Chambliss, 1976...641
Roberto Kelly, 1990.........641
25 Don Mattingly, 1992........640
26 Red Rolfe, 1935.............639
Roy White, 1973.............639
Derek Jeter, 2007..........639
29 Joe DiMaggio, 1936.......637
30 Dave Winfield, 1985........633
31 Frankie Crosetti, 1936....632
Snuffy Stirnweiss, 1945............632
33 Red Rolfe, 1938.............631
Frankie Crosetti, 1938....631
Don Mattingly, 1989........631
36 Bobby Richardson, 1963.......630
37 Hideki Matsui, 2005......629
38 Derek Jeter, 1999..........627
39 Earle Combs, 1928.........626
Roy White, 1976.............626
Derek Jeter, 1998..........626
42 Horace Clarke, 1971.......625
Chris Chambliss, 1978...625
44 Bob Meusel, 1925..........624
45 Hideki Matsui, 2003......623
Derek Jeter, 2006..........623
47 Tom Tresh, 1962.............622
48 Joe DiMaggio, 1937.......621
49 Lou Gehrig, 1931............619
50 5 players tied.................617

RUNS

1 Babe Ruth, 1921............177
2 Lou Gehrig, 1936............167
3 Babe Ruth, 1928............163
Lou Gehrig, 1931............163
5 Babe Ruth, 1920............158
Babe Ruth, 1927............158
7 Babe Ruth, 1923............151
Joe DiMaggio, 1937.......151
9 Babe Ruth, 1930............150
10 Lou Gehrig, 1927............149
Babe Ruth, 1931............149
12 Rickey Henderson, 1985.......146
13 Babe Ruth, 1924............143
Lou Gehrig, 1930............143
Earle Combs, 1932.........143
Red Rolfe, 1937.............143
Alex Rodriguez, 2007...143
18 Babe Ruth, 1926............139
Lou Gehrig, 1928............139
Red Rolfe, 1939.............139
21 Lou Gehrig, 1932............138
Lou Gehrig, 1933............138
Lou Gehrig, 1937............138
Tommy Henrich, 1948....138
25 Earle Combs, 1927.........137
Frankie Crosetti, 1936....137
27 Lou Gehrig, 1926............135
28 Derek Jeter, 1999..........134
29 Joe DiMaggio, 1936.......132
Red Rolfe, 1938.............132
Mickey Mantle, 1956.......132
Mickey Mantle, 1961.......132
Roger Maris, 1961..........132
34 Rickey Henderson, 1986.......130
35 Earle Combs, 1930.........129
Joe DiMaggio, 1938.......129
Mickey Mantle, 1954.......129
38 Roger Peckinpaugh, 1921........128
Lou Gehrig, 1934............128
Alfonso Soriano, 2002....128
41 Lou Gehrig, 1929............127
Frankie Crosetti, 1937....127
Mickey Mantle, 1958.......127
Derek Jeter, 1998..........127
45 Lou Gehrig, 1935............125
Snuffy Stirnweiss, 1944............125
Phil Rizzuto, 1950..........125
48 Derek Jeter, 2002..........124
Alex Rodriguez, 2005...124
50 2 players tied.................123

RUNS BY ERA

1988–2007

1 Alex Rodriguez, 2007...143
2 Derek Jeter, 1999..........134
3 Alfonso Soriano, 2002....128
4 Derek Jeter, 1998..........127
5 Derek Jeter, 2002..........124
Alex Rodriguez, 2005...124
7 Bobby Abreu, 2007.......123

1973–87

1 Rickey Henderson, 1985.......146
2 Rickey Henderson, 1986.......130
3 Don Mattingly, 1986........117
4 Don Mattingly, 1985........107
5 Dave Winfield, 1984........106
6 Dave Winfield, 1985........105
7 Roy White, 1976.............104

1961–72

1 Mickey Mantle, 1961.......132
Roger Maris, 1961..........132
3 Roy White, 1970.............109
4 Bobby Murcer, 1972........102
5 Bobby Richardson, 1962..99
6 Mickey Mantle, 1962.........96
7 Bobby Murcer, 1970.........95

1943–60

1 Tommy Henrich, 1948....138
2 Mickey Mantle, 1956.......132
3 Mickey Mantle, 1954.......129
4 Mickey Mantle, 1958.......127
5 Snuffy Stirnweiss, 1944..........125
Phil Rizzuto, 1950..........125
7 Mickey Mantle, 1955.......121
Mickey Mantle, 1957.......121

1921–42

1 Babe Ruth, 1921............177
2 Lou Gehrig, 1936............167
3 Babe Ruth, 1928............163
Lou Gehrig, 1931............163
5 Babe Ruth, 1927............158
6 Babe Ruth, 1923............151
Joe DiMaggio, 1937.......151

1901–20

1 Babe Ruth, 1920............158
2 Wally Pipp, 1920............109
Roger Peckinpaugh, 1920........109
4 Willie Keeler, 1906...........96
5 Willie Keeler, 1903...........95
6 Birdie Cree, 1911..............90
7 Roger Peckinpaugh, 1919..........89

HITS

1 Don Mattingly, 1986........238
2 Earle Combs, 1927.........231
3 Lou Gehrig, 1930............220
4 Derek Jeter, 1999..........219
5 Lou Gehrig, 1927............218
6 Joe DiMaggio, 1937.......215
7 Derek Jeter, 2006..........214
8 Red Rolfe, 1939.............213
9 Lou Gehrig, 1931............211
Don Mattingly, 1985........211
11 Lou Gehrig, 1928............210
Lou Gehrig, 1934............210
13 Bobby Richardson, 1962.......209
Alfonso Soriano, 2002....209
15 Lou Gehrig, 1932............208
16 Don Mattingly, 1984........207
17 Joe DiMaggio, 1936.......206
Derek Jeter, 2007..........206
19 Babe Ruth, 1923............205
Lou Gehrig, 1936............205
Snuffy Stirnweiss, 1944...........205
Steve Sax, 1989.............205
23 Babe Ruth, 1921............204
Bernie Williams, 2002.....204
25 Earle Combs, 1925.........203
Derek Jeter, 1998..........203
27 Earle Combs, 1929.........202
Bernie Williams, 1999.....202
Derek Jeter, 2005..........202
30 Derek Jeter, 2000..........201
31 Babe Ruth, 1924............200
Lou Gehrig, 1937............200
Phil Rizzuto, 1950..........200
34 Babe Ruth, 1931............199
35 Lou Gehrig, 1933............198
Steve Sax, 1991.............198
Alfonso Soriano, 2003....198
38 Red Rolfe, 1938.............196
39 Snuffy Stirnweiss, 1945...........195
40 Earle Combs, 1928.........194
Joe DiMaggio, 1938.......194
Alex Rodriguez, 2005...194
43 Hal Chase, 1906.............193
Tony Lazzeri, 1929.........193
Joe DiMaggio, 1941.......193
Dave Winfield, 1984.......193
47 Babe Ruth, 1927............192
Red Rolfe, 1935.............192
Yogi Berra, 1950............192
Hideki Matsui, 2005......192

HITS BY ERA

1988–2007

1 Derek Jeter, 1999..........219
2 Derek Jeter, 2006..........214
3 Alfonso Soriano, 2002....209
4 Derek Jeter, 2007..........206
5 Steve Sax, 1989.............205
6 Bernie Williams, 2002.....204
7 Derek Jeter, 1998..........203

1973–87

1 Don Mattingly, 1986........238
2 Don Mattingly, 1985........211
3 Don Mattingly, 1984........207
4 Dave Winfield, 1984........193
5 Thurman Munson, 1975........190
6 Chris Chambliss, 1976...188
7 Bobby Murcer, 1973.......187

1961–72

1 Bobby Richardson, 1962.......209
2 Horace Clarke, 1969.......183
3 Bobby Richardson, 1964.......181
4 Roy White, 1970.............180
5 Tom Tresh, 1962.............178
6 Danny Cater, 1970.........175
Bobby Murcer, 1971.......175

1943–60

1 Snuffy Stirnweiss, 1944...........205
2 Phil Rizzuto, 1950..........200
3 Snuffy Stirnweiss, 1945...........195
4 Yogi Berra, 1950............192
5 Joe DiMaggio, 1948.......190
6 Mickey Mantle, 1956.......188
7 Tommy Henrich, 1948....181

1921–42

1 Earle Combs, 1927.........231
2 Lou Gehrig, 1930............220
3 Lou Gehrig, 1927............218
4 Joe DiMaggio, 1937.......215
5 Red Rolfe, 1939.............213
6 Lou Gehrig, 1931............211
7 Lou Gehrig, 1928............210
Lou Gehrig, 1934............210

1901–20

1 Hal Chase, 1906.............193
2 Willie Keeler, 1904..........186
3 Birdie Cree, 1911............181
4 Willie Keeler, 1906..........180
Del Pratt, 1920...............180
6 Babe Ruth, 1920............172
7 Wally Pipp, 1920............171

DOUBLES

1 Don Mattingly, 1986.........53
2 Lou Gehrig, 1927.............52
3 Alfonso Soriano, 2002......51
4 Don Mattingly, 1985.........48
5 Lou Gehrig, 1926.............47
Bob Meusel, 1927............47
Lou Gehrig, 1928.............47
8 Red Rolfe, 1939...............46
9 Babe Ruth, 1923..............45
Bob Meusel, 1928............45
Hideki Matsui, 2005........45
12 Babe Ruth, 1921..............44
Joe DiMaggio, 1936.........44
Don Mattingly, 1984.........44
Derek Jeter, 2004............44
16 Joe DiMaggio, 1941.........43
17 Lou Gehrig, 1930.............42
Lou Gehrig, 1932.............42
Tommy Henrich, 1948......42
Paul O'Neill, 1997............42
Hideki Matsui, 2003........42
Jorge Posada, 2007........42
23 Ben Chapman, 1932........41
Lou Gehrig, 1933.............41
Robinson Cano, 2006.....41
Robinson Cano, 2007.....41
27 Bob Meusel, 1920............40
Bob Meusel, 1921............40
Bob Meusel, 1924............40
Lou Gehrig, 1934.............40
Don Mattingly, 1992.........40
Paul O'Neill, 1998............40
Jorge Posada, 2002........40
Bobby Abreu, 2007.........40
35 Babe Ruth, 1924..............39
Red Rolfe, 1936...............39
Reggie Jackson, 1977......39
Paul O'Neill, 1999............39
Derek Jeter, 2006............39
Derek Jeter, 2007............39
41 Ben Chapman, 1935........38
Tony Kubek, 1961............38
Bobby Richardson, 1962..38
Chris Chambliss, 1975.....38
Don Mattingly, 1987.........38
Steve Sax, 1991...............38
Bernie Williams, 2001.......38
48 Many players tied.............37

DOUBLES BY ERA

1988–2007

1 Alfonso Soriano, 2002......51
2 Hideki Matsui, 2005........45
3 Derek Jeter, 2004............44
4 Paul O'Neill, 1997............42
Hideki Matsui, 2003........42
Jorge Posada, 2007........42
7 Robinson Cano, 2006.....41
Robinson Cano, 2007.....41

1973–87

1 Don Mattingly, 1986.........53
2 Don Mattingly, 1985.........48
3 Don Mattingly, 1984.........44
4 Reggie Jackson, 1977......39
5 Chris Chambliss, 1975.....38
Don Mattingly, 1987.........38
7 Lou Piniella, 1978............34
Dave Winfield, 1984.........34
Dave Winfield, 1985.........34

1961–72

1 Tony Kubek, 1961............38
Bobby Richardson, 1962..38
3 Roger Maris, 1962............34
4 Roy White, 1969...............30
Roy White, 1970...............30
Bobby Murcer, 1972.........30
7 Tom Tresh, 1965...............29
Roy White, 1972...............29

1943–60

1 Tommy Henrich, 1948......42
2 Mickey Mantle, 1952........37
3 Phil Rizzuto, 1950............36
4 Nick Etten, 1943...............35
Snuffy Stirnweiss, 1944...............35
Tommy Henrich, 1947......35
7 Bill Skowron, 1960............34

1921–42

1 Lou Gehrig, 1927.............52
2 Lou Gehrig, 1926.............47
Bob Meusel, 1927............47
Lou Gehrig, 1928.............47
5 Red Rolfe, 1939...............46
6 Babe Ruth, 1923..............45
Bob Meusel, 1928............45

1901–20

1 Bob Meusel, 1920............40
2 Del Pratt, 1920.................37
3 Babe Ruth, 1920..............36
4 Hal Chase, 1911...............32
5 Jimmy Williams, 1904.......31
6 Jimmy Williams, 1903.......30
Birdie Cree, 1911..............30
Wally Pipp, 1920..............30

TRIPLES

1 Earle Combs, 1927...........23
2 Birdie Cree, 1911..............22
Earle Combs, 1930...........22
Snuffy Stirnweiss, 1945.............22
5 Earle Combs, 1928...........21
6 Lou Gehrig, 1926.............20
7 Wally Pipp, 1924..............19
8 Lou Gehrig, 1927.............18
9 Lou Gehrig, 1930.............17
10 Birdie Cree, 1910.............16
Babe Ruth, 1921..............16
Bob Meusel, 1921............16
Tony Lazzeri, 1932..........16
Earle Combs, 1933...........16
Snuffy Stirnweiss, 1944.............16
Johnny Lindell, 1944........16
17 Harry Wolter, 1911...........15
Earle Combs, 1929...........15
Tony Lazzeri, 1930..........15
Lou Gehrig, 1931.............15
Ben Chapman, 1932........15
Joe DiMaggio, 1936.........15
Red Rolfe, 1936...............15
Joe DiMaggio, 1937.........15
Charlie Keller, 1940..........15
26 Wally Pipp, 1916..............14
Wally Pipp, 1920..............14
Tony Lazzeri, 1926...........14
Tommy Henrich, 1948......14
30 Wally Pipp, 1915..............13
Babe Ruth, 1923..............13
Earle Combs, 1925...........13
Lou Gehrig, 1928.............13
Earle Combs, 1931...........13
Ben Chapman, 1934........13
Joe DiMaggio, 1938.........13
Joe DiMaggio, 1942.........13
Tommy Henrich, 1947......13
Willie Randolph, 1979......13
40 Many players tied.............12

TRIPLES BY ERA

1988–2007

1 Bernie Williams, 1995.........9
Derek Jeter, 1999..............9
3 Derek Jeter, 1998..............8
Melky Cabrera, 2007.........8
5 Bernie Williams, 1996.........7
Derek Jeter, 1997..............7
Kenny Lofton, 2004............7
Robinson Cano, 2007.......7

1973–87

1 Willie Randolph, 1979......13
2 Willie Randolph, 1977......11
3 Jerry Mumphrey, 1982......10
4 Roy White, 1974.................8
Mickey Rivers, 1976...........8
Mickey Rivers, 1978...........8
Dave Winfield, 1982...........8
Dave Winfield, 1983...........8

1961–72

1 Bill Robinson, 1968............7
Roy White, 1968.................7
Horace Clarke, 1969...........7
Jerry Kenney, 1970............7
Horace Clarke, 1971...........7
Roy White, 1971.................7
Bobby Murcer, 1972...........7

1943–60

1 Snuffy Stirnweiss, 1945.............22
2 Snuffy Stirnweiss, 1944.............16
Johnny Lindell, 1944........16
4 Tommy Henrich, 1948......14
5 Tommy Henrich, 1947......13
6 Johnny Lindell, 1943........12
Mickey Mantle, 1954........12

1921–42

1 Earle Combs, 1927...........23
2 Earle Combs, 1930...........22
3 Earle Combs, 1928...........21
4 Lou Gehrig, 1926.............20
5 Wally Pipp, 1924..............19
6 Lou Gehrig, 1927.............18
7 Lou Gehrig, 1930.............17

1901–20

1 Birdie Cree, 1911..............22
2 Birdie Cree, 1910..............16
3 Harry Wolter, 1911...........15
4 Wally Pipp, 1916..............14
Wally Pipp, 1920..............14
6 Wally Pipp, 1915..............13
7 Jimmy Williams, 1903.......12
Wid Conroy, 1903.............12
Wid Conroy, 1904.............12
John Anderson, 1904........12
Ray Demmitt, 1909...........12
Wally Pipp, 1917..............12
Ping Bodie, 1920..............12

HOME RUNS

1	Roger Maris, 1961	61
2	Babe Ruth, 1927	60
3	Babe Ruth, 1921	59
4	Babe Ruth, 1920	54
	Babe Ruth, 1928	54
	Mickey Mantle, 1961	54
	Alex Rodriguez, 2007	**54**
8	Mickey Mantle, 1956	52
9	Babe Ruth, 1930	49
	Lou Gehrig, 1934	49
	Lou Gehrig, 1936	49
12	**Alex Rodriguez, 2005**	**48**
13	Babe Ruth, 1926	47
	Lou Gehrig, 1927	47
15	Babe Ruth, 1924	46
	Babe Ruth, 1929	46
	Babe Ruth, 1931	46
	Lou Gehrig, 1931	46
	Joe DiMaggio, 1937	46
20	Tino Martinez, 1997	44
21	Mickey Mantle, 1958	42
22	Babe Ruth, 1923	41
	Lou Gehrig, 1930	41
	Babe Ruth, 1932	41
	Reggie Jackson, 1980	41
	Jason Giambi, 2002	**41**
	Jason Giambi, 2003	**41**
28	Mickey Mantle, 1960	40
29	Joe DiMaggio, 1948	39
	Roger Maris, 1960	39
	Alfonso Soriano, 2002	39
32	Alfonso Soriano, 2003	38
33	Lou Gehrig, 1937	37
	Mickey Mantle, 1955	37
	Graig Nettles, 1977	37
	Dave Winfield, 1982	37
	Jason Giambi, 2006	**37**
38	**Alex Rodriguez, 2004**	**36**
	Gary Sheffield, 2004	36
40	Babe Ruth, 1922	35
	Lou Gehrig, 1929	35
	Mickey Mantle, 1964	35
	Don Mattingly, 1985	35
	Alex Rodriguez, 2006	**35**
45	Lou Gehrig, 1932	34
	Babe Ruth, 1933	34
	Mickey Mantle, 1957	34
	Tino Martinez, 2001	34
	Gary Sheffield, 2005	34
50	4 players tied	33

HOME RUNS BY ERA

	1988–2007	
1	**Alex Rodriguez, 2007**	**54**
2	**Alex Rodriguez, 2005**	**48**
3	Tino Martinez, 1997	44
4	**Jason Giambi, 2002**	**41**
	Jason Giambi, 2003	**41**
6	Alfonso Soriano, 2002	39
7	Alfonso Soriano, 2003	38
	1973–87	
1	Reggie Jackson, 1980	41
2	Graig Nettles, 1977	37
	Dave Winfield, 1982	37
4	Don Mattingly, 1985	35
5	Bobby Bonds, 1975	32
	Graig Nettles, 1976	32
	Reggie Jackson, 1977	32
	Dave Winfield, 1983	32
	Mike Pagliarulo, 1987	32
	1961–72	
1	Roger Maris, 1961	61
2	Mickey Mantle, 1961	54
3	Mickey Mantle, 1964	35
4	Roger Maris, 1962	33
	Bobby Murcer, 1972	33
6	Joe Pepitone, 1966	31
7	Mickey Mantle, 1962	30
	1943–60	
1	Mickey Mantle, 1956	52
2	Mickey Mantle, 1958	42
3	Mickey Mantle, 1960	40
4	Joe DiMaggio, 1948	39
	Roger Maris, 1960	39
6	Mickey Mantle, 1955	37
7	Mickey Mantle, 1957	34
	1921–42	
1	Babe Ruth, 1927	60
2	Babe Ruth, 1921	59
3	Babe Ruth, 1928	54
4	Babe Ruth, 1930	49
	Lou Gehrig, 1934	49
	Lou Gehrig, 1936	49
7	Babe Ruth, 1926	47
	Lou Gehrig, 1927	47
	1901–20	
1	Babe Ruth, 1920	54
2	Wally Pipp, 1916	12
3	Bob Meusel, 1920	11
	Wally Pipp, 1920	11
	Aaron Ward, 1920	11
6	Frank Baker, 1916	10
	Frank Baker, 1919	10

HOME RUNS/500 AT BATS

1	Babe Ruth, 1920	59.0
2	Babe Ruth, 1927	55.6
3	Babe Ruth, 1921	54.6
4	Mickey Mantle, 1961	52.5
5	Roger Maris, 1961	51.7
6	Babe Ruth, 1928	50.4
7	Mickey Mantle, 1956	48.8
8	Babe Ruth, 1926	47.5
9	Babe Ruth, 1930	47.3
10	**Alex Rodriguez, 2007**	**46.3**
11	Babe Ruth, 1929	46.1
12	Babe Ruth, 1932	44.9
13	Babe Ruth, 1924	43.5
14	Babe Ruth, 1922	43.1
15	Babe Ruth, 1931	43.1
16	Lou Gehrig, 1934	42.3
	Lou Gehrig, 1936	42.3
18	**Jason Giambi, 2006**	**41.5**
19	Mickey Mantle, 1958	40.5
20	Lou Gehrig, 1927	40.2
21	Reggie Jackson, 1980	39.9
22	Mickey Mantle, 1962	39.8
23	**Alex Rodriguez, 2005**	**39.7**
24	Babe Ruth, 1923	39.3
25	Roger Maris, 1960	39.1
26	**Jason Giambi, 2005**	**38.4**
27	**Jason Giambi, 2003**	**38.3**
28	Mickey Mantle, 1960	38.0
29	Mickey Mantle, 1964	37.6
30	Lou Gehrig, 1931	37.2
31	Babe Ruth, 1933	37.0
	Joe DiMaggio, 1937	37.0
	Tino Martinez, 1997	37.0
34	**Jason Giambi, 2002**	**36.6**
35	Mickey Mantle, 1957	35.9
36	Mickey Mantle, 1955	35.8
37	Lou Gehrig, 1930	35.3
38	Dave Winfield, 1982	34.3
39	Joe DiMaggio, 1948	32.8
40	Charlie Keller, 1941	32.5
41	Lou Gehrig, 1937	32.5
42	Joe DiMaggio, 1939	32.5
43	Lou Gehrig, 1929	31.6
44	Gary Sheffield, 2004	31.4
45	Graig Nettles, 1977	31.4
46	**Jorge Posada, 2003**	**31.2**
47	Reggie Jackson, 1979	31.2
48	Mike Pagliarulo, 1987	30.7
49	**Alex Rodriguez, 2006**	**30.6**
50	Joe DiMaggio, 1940	30.5

HOME RUNS/500 AT BATS BY ERA

	1988–2007	
1	**Alex Rodriguez, 2007**	**46.3**
2	**Jason Giambi, 2006**	**41.5**
3	**Alex Rodriguez, 2005**	**39.7**
4	**Jason Giambi, 2005**	**38.4**
5	**Jason Giambi, 2003**	**38.3**
6	Tino Martinez, 1997	37.0
7	**Jason Giambi, 2002**	**36.6**
	1973–87	
1	Reggie Jackson, 1980	39.9
2	Dave Winfield, 1982	34.3
3	Graig Nettles, 1977	31.4
4	Reggie Jackson, 1979	31.2
5	Mike Pagliarulo, 1987	30.7
6	Reggie Jackson, 1977	30.5
7	Bobby Bonds, 1975	30.2
	1961–72	
1	Mickey Mantle, 1961	52.5
2	Roger Maris, 1961	51.7
3	Mickey Mantle, 1962	39.8
4	Mickey Mantle, 1964	37.6
5	Elston Howard, 1963	28.7
6	Bobby Murcer, 1972	28.2
7	Roger Maris, 1962	28.0
	1943–60	
1	Mickey Mantle, 1956	48.8
2	Mickey Mantle, 1958	40.5
3	Roger Maris, 1960	39.1
4	Mickey Mantle, 1960	38.0
5	Mickey Mantle, 1957	35.9
6	Mickey Mantle, 1955	35.8
7	Joe DiMaggio, 1948	32.8
	1921–42	
1	Babe Ruth, 1927	55.6
2	Babe Ruth, 1921	54.6
3	Babe Ruth, 1928	50.4
4	Babe Ruth, 1926	47.5
5	Babe Ruth, 1930	47.3
6	Babe Ruth, 1929	46.1
7	Babe Ruth, 1932	44.9
	1901–20	
1	Babe Ruth, 1920	59.0
2	Bob Meusel, 1920	12.0
3	Aaron Ward, 1920	11.1
4	Wally Pipp, 1916	11.0
5	Wally Pipp, 1920	9.0
6	Frank Baker, 1919	8.8
7	Roger Peckinpaugh, 1919	7.7

EXTRA BASE HITS

1	Babe Ruth, 1921	119
2	Lou Gehrig, 1927	117
3	Lou Gehrig, 1930	100
4	Babe Ruth, 1920	99
	Babe Ruth, 1923	99
6	Babe Ruth, 1927	97
7	Joe DiMaggio, 1937	96
8	Lou Gehrig, 1934	95
9	Lou Gehrig, 1936	93
10	Babe Ruth, 1924	92
	Lou Gehrig, 1931	92
	Alfonso Soriano, 2002	92
13	Babe Ruth, 1928	91
14	Joe DiMaggio, 1936	88
15	Lou Gehrig, 1928	87
16	Babe Ruth, 1930	86
	Don Mattingly, 1985	86
	Don Mattingly, 1986	86
19	Lou Gehrig, 1932	85
	Lou Gehrig, 1933	85
	Alex Rodriguez, 2007	**85**
22	Joe DiMaggio, 1941	84
23	Lou Gehrig, 1926	83
	Lou Gehrig, 1937	83
25	Babe Ruth, 1926	82
26	Tommy Henrich, 1948	81
	Roger Maris, 1961	81
28	Bob Meusel, 1921	80
	Babe Ruth, 1931	80
30	Bob Meusel, 1925	79
	Mickey Mantle, 1956	79
	Alfonso Soriano, 2003	79
33	Babe Ruth, 1929	78
	Alex Rodriguez, 2005	**78**
35	Lou Gehrig, 1929	77
	Joe DiMaggio, 1938	77
	Tino Martinez, 1997	77
38	Joe DiMaggio, 1948	76
	Mickey Mantle, 1961	76
	Jason Giambi, 2002	**76**
41	Joe DiMaggio, 1950	75
42	Mickey Mantle, 1955	73
	Reggie Jackson, 1977	73
	Bernie Williams, 2000	73
45	Joe Gordon, 1940	72
46	**Hideki Matsui, 2005**	**71**
47	Red Rolfe, 1939	70
	Bobby Murcer, 1972	70
	Don Mattingly, 1987	70
	Derek Jeter, 1999	**70**

TOTAL BASES

1	Babe Ruth, 1921	457
2	Lou Gehrig, 1927	447
3	Lou Gehrig, 1930	419
4	Joe DiMaggio, 1937	418
5	Babe Ruth, 1927	417
6	Lou Gehrig, 1931	410
7	Lou Gehrig, 1934	409
8	Lou Gehrig, 1936	403
9	Babe Ruth, 1923	399
10	Babe Ruth, 1924	391
11	Babe Ruth, 1920	388
	Don Mattingly, 1986	388
13	Alfonso Soriano, 2002	381
14	Babe Ruth, 1928	380
15	Babe Ruth, 1930	379
16	Mickey Mantle, 1956	376
	Alex Rodriguez, 2007	**376**
18	Babe Ruth, 1931	374
19	Lou Gehrig, 1932	370
	Don Mattingly, 1985	370
21	**Alex Rodriguez, 2005**	**369**
22	Joe DiMaggio, 1936	367
23	Lou Gehrig, 1937	366
	Roger Maris, 1961	366
25	Babe Ruth, 1926	365
26	Lou Gehrig, 1928	364
27	Lou Gehrig, 1933	359
28	Alfonso Soriano, 2003	358
29	Joe DiMaggio, 1948	355
30	Mickey Mantle, 1961	353
31	Babe Ruth, 1929	348
	Joe DiMaggio, 1938	348
	Joe DiMaggio, 1941	348
34	**Derek Jeter, 1999**	**346**
35	Tino Martinez, 1997	343
36	Bob Meusel, 1925	338
37	**Jason Giambi, 2002**	**335**
38	Bob Meusel, 1921	334
39	Earle Combs, 1927	331
40	Tommy Henrich, 1948	326
41	Don Mattingly, 1984	324
42	Lou Gehrig, 1929	323
43	Red Rolfe, 1939	321
44	Joe DiMaggio, 1940	318
	Yogi Berra, 1950	318
	Don Mattingly, 1987	318
47	Bernie Williams, 1999	317
48	Mickey Mantle, 1955	316
49	Joe Gordon, 1940	315
	Mickey Mantle, 1957	315

RUNS BATTED IN

1	Lou Gehrig, 1931	184
2	Lou Gehrig, 1927	175
3	Lou Gehrig, 1930	174
4	Babe Ruth, 1921	171
5	Joe DiMaggio, 1937	167
6	Lou Gehrig, 1934	165
7	Babe Ruth, 1927	164
8	Babe Ruth, 1931	163
9	Lou Gehrig, 1937	159
10	**Alex Rodriguez, 2007**	**156**
11	Joe DiMaggio, 1940	155
12	Babe Ruth, 1929	154
13	Babe Ruth, 1930	153
14	Lou Gehrig, 1936	152
15	Lou Gehrig, 1932	151
16	Babe Ruth, 1926	146
17	Don Mattingly, 1985	145
18	Lou Gehrig, 1928	142
	Babe Ruth, 1928	142
	Roger Maris, 1961	142
21	Tino Martinez, 1997	141
22	Joe DiMaggio, 1938	140
23	Lou Gehrig, 1933	139
24	Bob Meusel, 1925	138
25	Babe Ruth, 1920	137
	Babe Ruth, 1932	137
27	Bob Meusel, 1921	135
28	Bill Dickey, 1937	133
	Joe DiMaggio, 1940	133
30	Babe Ruth, 1923	131
31	Mickey Mantle, 1956	130
	Alex Rodriguez, 2005	**130**
33	Mickey Mantle, 1961	128
34	Lou Gehrig, 1929	126
	Joe DiMaggio, 1939	126
36	Joe DiMaggio, 1936	125
	Joe DiMaggio, 1941	125
	Yogi Berra, 1954	125
39	Yogi Berra, 1950	124
40	Tino Martinez, 1998	123
	Gary Sheffield, 2005	123
42	Ben Chapman, 1931	122
	Charlie Keller, 1941	122
	Joe DiMaggio, 1950	122
	Jason Giambi, 2002	**122**
46	Babe Ruth, 1924	121
	Tony Lazzeri, 1930	121
	Bernie Williams, 2000	121
	Gary Sheffield, 2004	121
	Alex Rodriguez, 2006	**121**

RUNS BATTED IN BY ERA

	1988–2007	
1	**Alex Rodriguez, 2007**	**156**
2	Tino Martinez, 1997	141
3	**Alex Rodriguez, 2005**	**130**
4	Tino Martinez, 1998	123
	Gary Sheffield, 2005	123
6	**Jason Giambi, 2002**	**122**
7	Bernie Williams, 2000	121
	Gary Sheffield, 2004	121
	Alex Rodriguez, 2006	**121**
	1973–87	
1	Don Mattingly, 1985	145
2	Dave Winfield, 1983	116
3	Don Mattingly, 1987	115
4	Dave Winfield, 1985	114
5	Don Mattingly, 1986	113
6	Reggie Jackson, 1980	111
7	Reggie Jackson, 1977	110
	Don Mattingly, 1984	110
	1961–72	
1	Roger Maris, 1961	142
2	Mickey Mantle, 1961	128
3	Mickey Mantle, 1964	111
4	Roger Maris, 1962	100
	Joe Pepitone, 1964	100
6	Bobby Murcer, 1972	96
7	Roy White, 1970	94
	Bobby Murcer, 1971	94
	1943–60	
1	Joe DiMaggio, 1948	155
2	Mickey Mantle, 1956	130
3	Yogi Berra, 1954	125
4	Yogi Berra, 1950	124
5	Joe DiMaggio, 1950	122
6	Roger Maris, 1960	112
7	Nick Etten, 1945	111
	1921–42	
1	Lou Gehrig, 1931	184
2	Lou Gehrig, 1927	175
3	Lou Gehrig, 1930	174
4	Babe Ruth, 1921	171
5	Joe DiMaggio, 1937	167
6	Lou Gehrig, 1934	165
7	Babe Ruth, 1927	164
	1901–20	
1	Babe Ruth, 1920	137
2	Del Pratt, 1920	97
3	Wally Pipp, 1916	93
4	Roy Hartzell, 1911	91
5	Duffy Lewis, 1919	89
6	Birdie Cree, 1911	88
7	Frank Baker, 1919	83
	Bob Meusel, 1920	83

WALKS

1	Babe Ruth, 1923	170
2	Babe Ruth, 1920	150
3	Mickey Mantle, 1957	146
4	Babe Ruth, 1921	145
5	Babe Ruth, 1926	144
6	Babe Ruth, 1924	142
7	Babe Ruth, 1927	137
	Babe Ruth, 1928	137
9	Babe Ruth, 1930	136
10	Lou Gehrig, 1935	132
11	Babe Ruth, 1932	130
	Lou Gehrig, 1936	130
13	Mickey Mantle, 1958	129
	Jason Giambi, 2003	**129**
15	Babe Ruth, 1931	128
16	Lou Gehrig, 1937	127
17	Mickey Mantle, 1961	126
18	Lou Gehrig, 1929	122
	Mickey Mantle, 1962	122
20	Willie Randolph, 1980	119
21	Lou Gehrig, 1931	117
22	Babe Ruth, 1933	114
	Charlie Keller, 1942	114
24	Charlie Keller, 1946	113
	Mickey Mantle, 1955	113
	Jack Clark, 1988	113
27	Mickey Mantle, 1956	112
28	Mickey Mantle, 1960	111
29	**Jason Giambi, 2006**	**110**
30	Lou Gehrig, 1927	109
	Lou Gehrig, 1934	109
	Jason Giambi, 2002	**109**
33	Lou Gehrig, 1932	108
	Jason Giambi, 2005	**108**
35	Lou Gehrig, 1938	107
	Mickey Mantle, 1967	107
	Jorge Posada, 2000	**107**
38	Frankie Crosetti, 1938	106
	Charlie Keller, 1940	106
	Charlie Keller, 1943	106
	Mickey Mantle, 1968	106
42	Lou Gehrig, 1926	105
43	Babe Ruth, 1934	104
44	George Selkirk, 1939	103
	Danny Tartabull, 1992	103
46	Charlie Keller, 1941	102
	Mickey Mantle, 1954	102
	Paul O'Neill, 1996	102
49	Lou Gehrig, 1930	101
50	Bernie Williams, 1999	100

WALK PERCENTAGE (BB/PA)

1	Babe Ruth, 1920	24.35
2	Babe Ruth, 1923	24.32
3	Mickey Mantle, 1962	24.30
4	Mickey Mantle, 1957	23.43
5	Babe Ruth, 1926	22.09
6	Babe Ruth, 1932	22.07
7	Babe Ruth, 1921	20.92
8	Babe Ruth, 1924	20.85
9	Babe Ruth, 1930	20.12
10	Babe Ruth, 1928	20.03
11	Babe Ruth, 1927	19.83
12	Babe Ruth, 1933	19.83
13	**Jason Giambi, 2005**	**19.82**
14	Mickey Mantle, 1958	19.72
15	Lou Gehrig, 1935	19.64
16	Danny Tartabull, 1992	19.58
17	Mickey Mantle, 1961	19.50
18	Mickey Mantle, 1968	19.38
19	Mickey Mantle, 1967	19.35
20	Babe Ruth, 1931	19.31
21	George Selkirk, 1939	19.18
22	**Jason Giambi, 2006**	**19.00**
23	**Jason Giambi, 2003**	**18.70**
24	Willie Randolph, 1980	18.54
25	Jack Clark, 1988	18.34
26	Lou Gehrig, 1937	18.14
27	Lou Gehrig, 1936	18.08
28	Mickey Mantle, 1955	17.71
29	Lou Gehrig, 1929	17.63
30	Mickey Mantle, 1964	17.46
31	Charlie Keller, 1940	17.41
32	Charlie Keller, 1946	17.25
33	Charlie Keller, 1942	17.25
34	Mickey Mantle, 1960	17.24
35	Mickey Mantle, 1956	17.18
36	**Jorge Posada, 2000**	**17.15**
37	Tommy Henrich, 1949	17.13
38	Charlie Keller, 1943	17.10
39	Gene Woodling, 1953	17.01
40	Babe Ruth, 1922	16.97
41	Charlie Keller, 1941	16.72
42	Charlie Keller, 1939	16.53
43	Oscar Grimes, 1945	16.30
44	Paul O'Neill, 1994	16.25
45	**Jorge Posada, 2004**	**16.09**
46	Robin Ventura, 2002	16.01
47	Tommy Henrich, 1938	16.00
48	George Selkirk, 1936	15.88
49	Lou Gehrig, 1931	15.85
50	**Jason Giambi, 2002**	**15.82**

STRIKEOUTS

1	Alfonso Soriano, 2002	157
2	Danny Tartabull, 1993	156
3	**Jorge Posada, 2000**	**151**
4	Jesse Barfield, 1990	150
5	Roberto Kelly, 1990	148
6	**Jorge Posada, 2002**	**143**
7	Jack Clark, 1988	141
8	**Jason Giambi, 2003**	**140**
9	**Alex Rodriguez, 2005**	**139**
	Alex Rodriguez, 2006	**139**
11	Bobby Bonds, 1975	137
12	Reggie Jackson, 1978	133
13	**Jorge Posada, 2001**	**132**
14	**Alex Rodriguez, 2004**	**131**
15	Alfonso Soriano, 2003	130
16	Reggie Jackson, 1977	129
17	Kevin Maas, 1991	128
18	Mickey Mantle, 1959	126
19	Mickey Mantle, 1960	125
	Derek Jeter, 1997	**125**
	Alfonso Soriano, 2001	125
22	Reggie Jackson, 1980	122
23	Mickey Mantle, 1958	120
	Mike Pagliarulo, 1986	120
	Alex Rodriguez, 2007	**120**
26	**Derek Jeter, 1998**	**119**
27	**Derek Jeter, 2005**	**117**
28	**Derek Jeter, 1999**	**116**
29	Danny Tartabull, 1992	115
	Bobby Abreu, 2007	**115**
31	**Derek Jeter, 2002**	**114**
32	Mickey Mantle, 1967	113
33	Mickey Mantle, 1961	112
	Jason Giambi, 2002	**112**
35	Mickey Mantle, 1952	111
	Mike Pagliarulo, 1987	111
	Danny Tartabull, 1994	111
38	Tom Tresh, 1964	110
	Charley Smith, 1967	110
	Jorge Posada, 2003	**110**
41	**Jason Giambi, 2005**	**109**
42	Bill Skowron, 1961	108
43	Mickey Mantle, 1954	107
	Reggie Jackson, 1979	107
45	Clete Boyer, 1962	106
	Dave Winfield, 1986	106
	Bernie Williams, 1993	106
	Mike Stanley, 1995	106
	Jason Giambi, 2006	**106**
50	Frankie Crosetti, 1937	105

STRIKEOUT PERCENTAGE

	1988–2007	
1	Jesse Barfield, 1990	31.51
2	Danny Tartabull, 1993	30.41
3	**Jorge Posada, 2000**	**29.90**
4	Jack Clark, 1988	28.43
5	**Jorge Posada, 2002**	**27.98**
6	Danny Tartabull, 1994	27.82
7	Danny Tartabull, 1992	27.32
	1973–87	
1	Reggie Jackson, 1978	26.03
2	Bobby Bonds, 1975	25.90
3	Reggie Jackson, 1977	24.57
4	Reggie Jackson, 1981	24.55
5	Mike Pagliarulo, 1986	23.81
6	Reggie Jackson, 1980	23.74
7	Reggie Jackson, 1979	23.01
	1961–72	
1	Mickey Mantle, 1967	25.68
2	Mickey Mantle, 1968	22.30
3	Mickey Mantle, 1964	21.94
4	Mickey Mantle, 1961	21.79
5	Bill Skowron, 1962	20.71
6	Mickey Mantle, 1962	20.69
7	Tom Tresh, 1964	20.64
	1943–60	
1	Mickey Mantle, 1960	23.72
2	Mickey Mantle, 1959	23.29
3	Mickey Mantle, 1958	23.12
4	Mickey Mantle, 1952	20.22
5	Mickey Mantle, 1954	19.71
6	Mickey Mantle, 1953	19.52
7	Norm Siebern, 1958	18.91
	1921–42	
1	Babe Ruth, 1922	19.70
2	Babe Ruth, 1933	19.61
3	Babe Ruth, 1923	17.82
4	Joe Gordon, 1942	17.66
5	Frankie Crosetti, 1937	17.18
6	Tony Lazzeri, 1937	17.04
7	Tony Lazzeri, 1931	16.53
	1901–20	
1	Babe Ruth, 1920	17.47
2	Aaron Ward, 1920	16.94
3	Wally Pipp, 1915	16.91
4	Bob Meusel, 1920	15.65
5	Wally Pipp, 1916	15.05
6	Joe Gedeon, 1916	14.02
7	Sammy Vick, 1919	13.51

BATTING AVERAGE

1	Babe Ruth, 1923	.393
2	Joe DiMaggio, 1939	.381
3	Lou Gehrig, 1930	.379
4	Babe Ruth, 1924	.378
5	Babe Ruth, 1921	.378
6	Babe Ruth, 1920	.376
7	Lou Gehrig, 1928	.374
8	Lou Gehrig, 1927	.373
9	Babe Ruth, 1931	.373
10	Babe Ruth, 1926	.372
11	Mickey Mantle, 1957	.365
12	Lou Gehrig, 1934	.363
13	Babe Ruth, 1930	.359
14	Paul O'Neill, 1994	.359
15	Joe DiMaggio, 1941	.357
16	Earle Combs, 1927	.356
17	Babe Ruth, 1927	.356
18	Tony Lazzeri, 1929	.354
19	Lou Gehrig, 1936	.354
20	Mickey Mantle, 1956	.353
21	Joe DiMaggio, 1940	.352
22	Don Mattingly, 1986	.352
23	Lou Gehrig, 1937	.351
24	**Derek Jeter, 1999**	**.349**
25	Lou Gehrig, 1932	.349
26	Birdie Cree, 1911	.348
27	Joe DiMaggio, 1937	.346
28	Earle Combs, 1929	.345
29	Babe Ruth, 1929	.345
30	Earle Combs, 1930	.344
31	**Derek Jeter, 2006**	**.343**
32	Don Mattingly, 1984	.343
33	Willie Keeler, 1904	.343
34	Earle Combs, 1925	.342
35	**Robinson Cano, 2006**	**.342**
36	Bernie Williams, 1999	.342
37	Wade Boggs, 1994	.342
38	Babe Ruth, 1932	.341
39	Lou Gehrig, 1931	.341
40	Dave Winfield, 1984	.340
41	**Derek Jeter, 2000**	**.339**
42	Bernie Williams, 1998	.339
43	**Jorge Posada, 2007**	**.338**
44	Bob Meusel, 1927	.337
45	Charlie Keller, 1939	.334
46	Lou Gehrig, 1933	.334
47	Bernie Williams, 2002	.333
48	Bill Dickey, 1937	.332
49	Bobby Murcer, 1971	.331
50	Wally Pipp, 1922	.329

BATTING AVERAGE BY ERA

	1988–2007	
1	Paul O'Neill, 1994	.359
2	**Derek Jeter, 1999**	**.349**
3	**Derek Jeter, 2006**	**.343**
4	**Robinson Cano, 2006**	**.342**
5	Bernie Williams, 1999	.342
6	Wade Boggs, 1994	.342
7	**Derek Jeter, 2000**	**.339**
	1973–87	
1	Don Mattingly, 1986	.352
2	Don Mattingly, 1984	.343
3	Dave Winfield, 1984	.340
4	Don Mattingly, 1987	.327
5	Mickey Rivers, 1977	.326
6	Don Mattingly, 1985	.324
7	Thurman Munson, 1975	.318
	1961–72	
1	Bobby Murcer, 1971	.331
2	Mickey Mantle, 1962	.321
3	Mickey Mantle, 1961	.317
4	Elston Howard, 1964	.313
5	Mickey Mantle, 1964	.303
6	Thurman Munson, 1970	.302
7	Bobby Richardson, 1962	.302
	1943–60	
1	Mickey Mantle, 1957	.365
2	Mickey Mantle, 1956	.353
3	Phil Rizzuto, 1950	.324
4	Yogi Berra, 1950	.322
5	Joe DiMaggio, 1948	.320
6	Irv Noren, 1954	.319
7	Snuffy Stirnweiss, 1944	.319
	1921–42	
1	Babe Ruth, 1923	.393
2	Joe DiMaggio, 1939	.381
3	Lou Gehrig, 1930	.379
4	Babe Ruth, 1924	.378
5	Babe Ruth, 1921	.378
6	Lou Gehrig, 1928	.374
7	Lou Gehrig, 1927	.373
	1901–20	
1	Babe Ruth, 1920	.376
2	Birdie Cree, 1911	.348
3	Willie Keeler, 1904	.343
4	Bob Meusel, 1920	.328
5	Hal Chase, 1906	.323
6	Hal Chase, 1911	.315
7	Del Pratt, 1920	.314

ON-BASE PERCENTAGE

1	Babe Ruth, 1923	.545
2	Babe Ruth, 1920	.532
3	Babe Ruth, 1926	.516
4	Babe Ruth, 1924	.513
5	Babe Ruth, 1921	.512
6	Mickey Mantle, 1957	.512
7	Babe Ruth, 1931	.495
8	Babe Ruth, 1930	.493
9	Babe Ruth, 1932	.489
10	Mickey Mantle, 1962	.486
11	Babe Ruth, 1927	.486
12	Lou Gehrig, 1936	.478
13	Lou Gehrig, 1927	.474
14	Lou Gehrig, 1930	.473
15	Lou Gehrig, 1937	.473
16	Lou Gehrig, 1928	.467
17	Lou Gehrig, 1935	.466
18	Lou Gehrig, 1934	.465
19	Mickey Mantle, 1956	.464
20	Babe Ruth, 1928	.463
21	Paul O'Neill, 1994	.460
22	George Selkirk, 1939	.452
23	Lou Gehrig, 1932	.451
24	Mickey Mantle, 1961	.448
25	Joe DiMaggio, 1939	.448
26	Charlie Keller, 1939	.447
27	Lou Gehrig, 1931	.446
28	Mickey Mantle, 1958	.443
29	Babe Ruth, 1933	.442
30	**Jason Giambi, 2005**	**.440**
31	Joe DiMaggio, 1941	.440
32	**Derek Jeter, 1999**	**.438**
33	**Jason Giambi, 2002**	**.435**
34	Bernie Williams, 1999	.435
35	Babe Ruth, 1922	.434
36	Wade Boggs, 1994	.433
37	Lou Gehrig, 1929	.431
38	Mickey Mantle, 1955	.431
39	Babe Ruth, 1929	.430
40	Tony Lazzeri, 1929	.429
41	Gene Woodling, 1953	.429
42	Wally Schang, 1921	.428
43	Willie Randolph, 1980	.427
44	Bobby Murcer, 1971	.427
45	**Jorge Posada, 2007**	**.426**
46	Joe DiMaggio, 1940	.425
47	Lou Gehrig, 1933	.424
48	Earle Combs, 1930	.424
49	Mickey Mantle, 1964	.423
50	**Alex Rodriguez, 2007**	**.422**

ON-BASE PERCENTAGE BY ERA

	1988–2007	
1	Paul O'Neill, 1994	.464
2	**Jason Giambi, 2005**	**.441**
3	**Derek Jeter, 1999**	**.441**
4	**Jason Giambi, 2002**	**.439**
5	Bernie Williams, 1999	.438
6	Wade Boggs, 1994	.437
7	**Jorge Posada, 2007**	**.428**
	1973–87	
1	Willie Randolph, 1980	.429
2	Rickey Henderson, 1985	.422
3	Willie Randolph, 1987	.415
4	Don Mattingly, 1986	.399
5	Reggie Jackson, 1980	.399
6	Elliott Maddox, 1974	.397
7	Dave Winfield, 1984	.397
	1961–72	
1	Mickey Mantle, 1962	.488
2	Mickey Mantle, 1961	.452
3	Bobby Murcer, 1971	.429
4	Mickey Mantle, 1964	.426
5	Roy White, 1969	.400
6	Roy White, 1971	.399
7	Mickey Mantle, 1967	.394
	1943–60	
1	Mickey Mantle, 1957	.515
2	Mickey Mantle, 1956	.467
3	Mickey Mantle, 1958	.445
4	Mickey Mantle, 1955	.433
5	Gene Woodling, 1953	.429
6	Phil Rizzuto, 1950	.418
7	Tommy Henrich, 1949	.416
	1921–42	
1	Babe Ruth, 1923	.545
2	Babe Ruth, 1926	.516
3	Babe Ruth, 1924	.513
4	Babe Ruth, 1921	.512
5	Babe Ruth, 1931	.495
6	Babe Ruth, 1930	.493
7	Babe Ruth, 1932	.489
	1901–20	
1	Babe Ruth, 1920	.532
2	Birdie Cree, 1911	.415
3	Harry Wolter, 1911	.396
4	Willie Keeler, 1904	.390
5	Roger Peckinpaugh, 1919	.390
6	Harry Wolter, 1913	.377
7	Roy Hartzell, 1911	.375

SLUGGING AVERAGE

1	Babe Ruth, 1920	.847
2	Babe Ruth, 1921	.846
3	Babe Ruth, 1927	.772
4	Lou Gehrig, 1927	.765
5	Babe Ruth, 1923	.764
6	Babe Ruth, 1924	.739
7	Babe Ruth, 1926	.737
8	Babe Ruth, 1930	.732
9	Lou Gehrig, 1930	.721
10	Babe Ruth, 1928	.709
11	Lou Gehrig, 1934	.706
12	Mickey Mantle, 1956	.705
13	Babe Ruth, 1931	.700
14	Babe Ruth, 1929	.697
15	Lou Gehrig, 1936	.696
16	Mickey Mantle, 1961	.687
17	Joe DiMaggio, 1937	.673
18	Babe Ruth, 1922	.672
19	Joe DiMaggio, 1939	.671
20	Mickey Mantle, 1957	.665
21	Lou Gehrig, 1931	.662
22	Babe Ruth, 1932	.661
23	Lou Gehrig, 1928	.648
24	**Alex Rodriguez, 2007**	**.645**
25	Joe DiMaggio, 1941	.643
26	Lou Gehrig, 1937	.643
27	Joe DiMaggio, 1940	.626
28	Lou Gehrig, 1932	.621
29	Roger Maris, 1961	.620
30	Mickey Mantle, 1955	.611
31	**Alex Rodriguez, 2005**	**.610**
32	Lou Gehrig, 1933	.605
33	Mickey Mantle, 1962	.605
34	Paul O'Neill, 1994	.603
35	**Jason Giambi, 2002**	**.598**
36	Joe DiMaggio, 1948	.598
37	Reggie Jackson, 1980	.597
38	Mickey Mantle, 1958	.592
39	Mickey Mantle, 1964	.591
40	Joe DiMaggio, 1950	.585
41	Lou Gehrig, 1929	.584
42	Lou Gehrig, 1935	.583
43	Babe Ruth, 1933	.582
44	Roger Maris, 1960	.581
45	Joe DiMaggio, 1938	.581
46	Charlie Keller, 1941	.580
47	Tino Martinez, 1997	.577
48	Joe DiMaggio, 1936	.576
49	Bernie Williams, 1998	.575
50	Don Mattingly, 1986	.573

SLUGGING AVERAGE BY ERA

	1988–2007	
1	**Alex Rodriguez, 2007**	**.645**
2	**Alex Rodriguez, 2005**	**.610**
3	Paul O'Neill, 1994	.603
4	**Jason Giambi, 2002**	**.598**
5	Tino Martinez, 1997	.577
6	Bernie Williams, 1998	.575
7	Bernie Williams, 2000	.566
	1973–87	
1	Reggie Jackson, 1980	.597
2	Don Mattingly, 1986	.573
3	Don Mattingly, 1985	.567
4	Dave Winfield, 1982	.560
5	Don Mattingly, 1987	.559
6	Reggie Jackson, 1977	.550
7	Reggie Jackson, 1979	.544
	1961–72	
1	Mickey Mantle, 1961	.687
2	Roger Maris, 1961	.620
3	Mickey Mantle, 1962	.605
4	Mickey Mantle, 1964	.591
5	Bobby Murcer, 1971	.543
6	Bobby Murcer, 1972	.537
7	Elston Howard, 1963	.528
	1943–60	
1	Mickey Mantle, 1956	.705
2	Mickey Mantle, 1957	.665
3	Mickey Mantle, 1955	.611
4	Joe DiMaggio, 1948	.598
5	Mickey Mantle, 1958	.592
6	Joe DiMaggio, 1950	.585
7	Roger Maris, 1960	.581
	1921–42	
1	Babe Ruth, 1921	.846
2	Babe Ruth, 1927	.772
3	Lou Gehrig, 1927	.765
4	Babe Ruth, 1923	.764
5	Babe Ruth, 1924	.739
6	Babe Ruth, 1926	.737
7	Babe Ruth, 1930	.732
	1901–20	
1	Babe Ruth, 1920	.847
2	Bob Meusel, 1920	.517
3	Birdie Cree, 1911	.513
4	Ping Bodie, 1920	.446
5	Harry Wolter, 1911	.440
6	Wally Pipp, 1920	.430
7	Del Pratt, 1920	.427

ON-BASE PLUS SLUGGING

1	Babe Ruth, 1920	1379
2	Babe Ruth, 1921	1359
3	Babe Ruth, 1923	1309
4	Babe Ruth, 1927	1258
5	Babe Ruth, 1926	1253
6	Babe Ruth, 1924	1252
7	Lou Gehrig, 1927	1240
8	Babe Ruth, 1930	1225
9	Babe Ruth, 1931	1195
10	Lou Gehrig, 1930	1194
11	Mickey Mantle, 1957	1177
12	Lou Gehrig, 1936	1174
13	Babe Ruth, 1928	1172
14	Lou Gehrig, 1934	1172
15	Mickey Mantle, 1956	1169
16	Babe Ruth, 1932	1150
17	Mickey Mantle, 1961	1135
18	Babe Ruth, 1929	1128
19	Joe DiMaggio, 1939	1119
20	Lou Gehrig, 1937	1116
21	Lou Gehrig, 1928	1115
22	Lou Gehrig, 1931	1108
23	Babe Ruth, 1922	1106
24	Mickey Mantle, 1962	1091
25	Joe DiMaggio, 1937	1085
26	Joe DiMaggio, 1941	1083
27	Lou Gehrig, 1932	1072
28	**Alex Rodriguez, 2007**	**1067**
29	Paul O'Neill, 1994	1064
30	Joe DiMaggio, 1940	1051
31	Lou Gehrig, 1935	1049
32	Mickey Mantle, 1955	1042
33	Mickey Mantle, 1958	1035
34	**Jason Giambi, 2002**	**1034**
35	**Alex Rodriguez, 2005**	**1031**
36	Lou Gehrig, 1933	1030
37	Babe Ruth, 1933	1023
38	Lou Gehrig, 1929	1015
39	Mickey Mantle, 1964	1015
40	Bernie Williams, 1998	997
41	Charlie Keller, 1941	996
42	Reggie Jackson, 1980	995
43	Joe DiMaggio, 1948	994
44	Roger Maris, 1961	993
45	Tony Lazzeri, 1929	991
46	**Derek Jeter, 1999**	**989**
47	Bill Dickey, 1937	987
48	Bill Dickey, 1938	981
49	Joe DiMaggio, 1950	979
50	**Jason Giambi, 2005**	**975**

ON-BASE PLUS SLUGGING BY ERA

	1988–2007	
1	**Alex Rodriguez, 2007**	**1067**
2	Paul O'Neill, 1994	1064
3	**Jason Giambi, 2002**	**1034**
4	**Alex Rodriguez, 2005**	**1031**
5	Bernie Williams, 1998	997
6	**Derek Jeter, 1999**	**989**
7	**Jason Giambi, 2005**	**975**
	1973–87	
1	Reggie Jackson, 1980	995
2	Don Mattingly, 1986	967
3	Don Mattingly, 1985	939
4	Don Mattingly, 1987	937
5	Rickey Henderson, 1985	934
6	Reggie Jackson, 1979	926
7	Reggie Jackson, 1977	925
	1961–72	
1	Mickey Mantle, 1961	1135
2	Mickey Mantle, 1962	1091
3	Mickey Mantle, 1964	1015
4	Roger Maris, 1961	993
5	Bobby Murcer, 1971	969
6	Bobby Murcer, 1972	898
7	Elston Howard, 1963	869
	1943–60	
1	Mickey Mantle, 1957	1177
2	Mickey Mantle, 1956	1169
3	Mickey Mantle, 1955	1042
4	Mickey Mantle, 1958	1035
5	Joe DiMaggio, 1948	994
6	Joe DiMaggio, 1950	979
7	Mickey Mantle, 1960	957
	1921–42	
1	Babe Ruth, 1921	1359
2	Babe Ruth, 1923	1309
3	Babe Ruth, 1927	1258
4	Babe Ruth, 1926	1253
5	Babe Ruth, 1924	1252
6	Lou Gehrig, 1927	1240
7	Babe Ruth, 1930	1225
	1901–20	
1	Babe Ruth, 1920	1379
2	Birdie Cree, 1911	928
3	Bob Meusel, 1920	876
4	Harry Wolter, 1911	836
5	Willie Keeler, 1904	799
6	Del Pratt, 1920	798
7	Ping Bodie, 1920	796

ADJUSTED OPS
1 Babe Ruth, 1920 252
2 Babe Ruth, 1923 238
3 Babe Ruth, 1921 236
4 Babe Ruth, 1927 229
5 Babe Ruth, 1926 228
6 Lou Gehrig, 1927............224
7 Babe Ruth, 1931 223
8 Mickey Mantle, 1957 223
9 Babe Ruth, 1924 221
10 Babe Ruth, 1930 216
11 Lou Gehrig, 1934............213
12 Mickey Mantle, 1956 213
13 Babe Ruth, 1928 211
14 Mickey Mantle, 1961 210
15 Lou Gehrig, 1930............207
16 Babe Ruth, 1932 206
17 Lou Gehrig, 1931............199
18 Babe Ruth, 1929 199
19 Mickey Mantle, 1962 198
20 Lou Gehrig, 1928............197
21 Lou Gehrig, 1936............193
22 Mickey Mantle, 1958 189
23 Joe DiMaggio, 1941 186
24 Joe DiMaggio, 1939 185
25 Lou Gehrig, 1932............184
26 Bobby Murcer, 1971 182
27 Mickey Mantle, 1955 181
28 Lou Gehrig, 1933............181
29 Babe Ruth, 1922 181
30 Babe Ruth, 1933 180
31 Lou Gehrig, 1935............180
32 Paul O'Neill, 1994...........179
33 Lou Gehrig, 1937............177
34 Mickey Mantle, 1964 177
35 Joe DiMaggio, 1940 176
36 Alex Rodriguez, 2007 ...175
37 Jason Giambi, 2002......173
38 Reggie Jackson, 1980....172
39 Alex Rodriguez, 2005 ...171
40 Roger Maris, 1961 170
41 Lou Gehrig, 1929............170
42 Bobby Murcer, 1972 169
43 Joe DiMaggio, 1937 168
44 Charlie Keller, 1943........167
45 Mickey Mantle, 1960 166
46 Mickey Mantle, 1952 166
47 Charlie Keller, 1942........164
48 Tony Lazzeri, 1929.........164
49 Bernie Williams, 1998.....164
50 Joe DiMaggio, 1948 164

ADJUSTED BATTING WINS
1 Babe Ruth, 1923 ....11.1
2 Babe Ruth, 1921 ....10.6
3 Babe Ruth, 1920 ....10.2
4 Lou Gehrig, 1927...........10.0
5 Babe Ruth, 1927 ....9.9
6 Babe Ruth, 1926 ....9.6
7 Babe Ruth, 1924 ....9.5
8 Babe Ruth, 1931 ....9.4
9 Mickey Mantle, 1957 ....9.4
10 Lou Gehrig, 1934.............9.0
11 Babe Ruth, 1930 ....8.8
12 Lou Gehrig, 1930.............8.7
13 Babe Ruth, 1928 ....8.6
14 Mickey Mantle, 1956 ....8.5
15 Mickey Mantle, 1961 ....8.3
16 Lou Gehrig, 1931.............8.2
17 Lou Gehrig, 1936.............7.8
18 Lou Gehrig, 1928.............7.8
19 Babe Ruth, 1932 ....7.3
20 Mickey Mantle, 1958 ....7.1
21 Lou Gehrig, 1932.............7.1
22 Lou Gehrig, 1937.............6.6
23 Babe Ruth, 1929 ....6.6
24 Lou Gehrig, 1935.............6.6
25 Lou Gehrig, 1933.............6.5
26 Joe DiMaggio, 1941 ....6.4
27 Bobby Murcer, 1971 ....6.4
28 Alex Rodriguez, 2005....6.3
29 Alex Rodriguez, 2007....6.3
30 Jason Giambi, 2002.......6.2
31 Mickey Mantle, 1962 ....6.2
32 Mickey Mantle, 1955 ....6.1
33 Lou Gehrig, 1929.............5.8
34 Don Mattingly, 1986.........5.6
35 Roger Maris, 1961 ....5.5
36 Babe Ruth, 1933 ....5.5
37 Mickey Mantle, 1964 ....5.5
38 Joe DiMaggio, 1937 ....5.4
39 Bobby Murcer, 1972 ....5.3
40 Joe DiMaggio, 1939 ....5.3
41 Joe DiMaggio, 1940 ....5.2
42 Derek Jeter, 1999...........5.1
43 Reggie Jackson, 1980.......5.1
44 Mickey Mantle, 1960 ....5.1
45 Charlie Keller, 1942.........5.0
46 Tony Lazzeri, 1929...........5.0
47 Don Mattingly, 1985.........5.0
48 Mickey Mantle, 1952 ....4.9
49 Charlie Keller, 1943.........4.8
50 Joe DiMaggio, 1948 ....4.8

STOLEN BASES
1 Rickey Henderson, 1988..93
2 Rickey Henderson, 1986..87
3 Rickey Henderson, 1985..80
4 Fritz Maisel, 1914.............74
5 Ben Chapman, 1931 61
6 Snuffy Stirnweiss, 1944 55
7 Fritz Maisel, 1915.............51
8 Birdie Cree, 1911..............48
9 Dave Fultz, 1905 44
10 Mickey Rivers, 1976.........43
Steve Sax, 1989 43
Steve Sax, 1990 43
Alfonso Soriano, 2001 43
14 Charlie Hemphill, 1908 42
Roberto Kelly, 1990 42
16 Wid Conroy, 1907 41
Bert Daniels, 1910 41
Rickey Henderson, 1987 ..41
Alfonso Soriano, 2002 41
20 Hal Chase, 1910...............40
Bert Daniels, 1911 40
22 Harry Wolter, 1910 39
23 Roger Peckinpaugh, 1914 38
Ben Chapman, 1932 38
Chuck Knoblauch, 2001 38
26 Bert Daniels, 1912............37
Willie Randolph, 1976 37
28 Hal Chase, 1911...............36
Willie Randolph, 1978 36
30 Roberto Kelly, 1989..........35
Alfonso Soriano, 2003 35
32 Derek Jeter, 2006............34
33 Wid Conroy, 1903.............33
Hal Chase, 1912...............33
Snuffy Stirnweiss, 1945 33
Horace Clarke, 1969 33
Willie Randolph, 1979 33
38 Wid Conroy, 1906.............32
Hal Chase, 1907...............32
Neal Ball, 1908..................32
Roberto Kelly, 1991 32
Derek Jeter, 2002............32
43 Roy White, 1976...............31
Steve Sax, 1991 31
Chuck Knoblauch, 1998 31
46 Many players tied 30

STOLEN BASE AVERAGE
1 Derek Jeter, 2002.........91.4
2 Derek Jeter, 2001.........90.0
Johnny Damon, 2007 ..90.0
4 Rickey Henderson, 1985.......88.9
5 Paul O'Neill, 2001...........88.0
6 Rickey Henderson, 1988.......87.7
7 Mickey Mantle, 1959 .....87.5
Alex Rodriguez, 2004..87.5
9 Derek Jeter, 2006.........87.2
10 Mickey Rivers, 1976.......86.0
11 Willie Randolph, 1980 ....85.7
Alex Rodriguez, 2007..85.7
13 Derek Jeter, 2004.........85.2
14 Roberto Kelly, 1992.......84.8
15 Derek Jeter, 2000.........84.6
16 Tony Womack, 2005.......84.4
17 Horace Clarke, 1967 .....84.0
18 Willie Randolph, 1978 ....83.7
19 Rickey Henderson, 1987.......83.7
20 Snuffy Stirnweiss, 1944...........83.3
Mickey Rivers, 1978.......83.3
Derek Jeter, 1998.........83.3
23 Rickey Henderson, 1986.......82.9
24 Steve Sax, 1990.............82.7

BASE STEALING WINS
1 Rickey Henderson, 1988.........1.6
2 Rickey Henderson, 1985.........1.4
3 Rickey Henderson, 1986.........1.3
4 Fritz Maisel, 1914.............1.1
5 Snuffy Stirnweiss, 1944 ....0.9
6 Fritz Maisel, 1915.............0.7
7 Mickey Rivers, 1976.........0.7
8 Steve Sax, 1990 ....0.6
9 Rickey Henderson, 1987.0.6
10 Derek Jeter, 2002...........0.6
11 Willie Randolph, 1978 ......0.6
12 Derek Jeter, 2006...........0.5
13 Chuck Knoblauch, 2001 ..0.5
14 Ben Chapman, 1931 ....0.5
15 Willie Randolph, 1980 .....0.5
16 Johnny Damon, 2007 ....0.5
17 Alfonso Soriano, 2003.....0.5
18 Derek Jeter, 2001...........0.5
19 Roberto Kelly, 1992.........0.4
20 Alex Rodriguez, 2004.....0.4
21 Alfonso Soriano, 2001 .....0.4
22 Alfonso Soriano, 2002.....0.4
23 Derek Jeter, 1998...........0.4
24 Sandy Alomar, 1975 ....0.4

PITCHER BATTING AVERAGE BY ERA
1988–2007

1973–87

1961–72
1 Fritz Peterson, 1972.......232
2 Ralph Terry, 1961 227
3 Fritz Peterson, 1966.......224
4 Fritz Peterson, 1970 ....[illegible]
5 Bill Stafford, 1962...........218
6 Mel Stottlemyre, 1972 200
7 Ralph Terry, 1962 189

1943–60
1 Tom Sturdivant, 1956 313
2 Al Gettel, 1945................281
3 Monk Dubiel, 1945 276
4 Tommy Byrne, 1950 272
5 Whitey Ford, 1953..........267
6 Ed Lopat, 1949...............263
7 Spud Chandler, 1943......258

1921–42
1 Red Ruffing, 1930 374
2 Carl Mays, 1921 ....[illegible]
3 Red Ruffing, 1935 339
4 Joe Bush, 1924 339
5 Red Ruffing, 1931 330
6 Joe Bush, 1922 326
7 Bob Shawkey, 1924........319

1901–20
1 Al Orth, 1907 324
2 George McConnell, 1912.......297
3 Russ Ford, 1912..............286
4 Lew Brockett, 1909.........283
5 Ray Fisher, 1913 278
6 Al Orth, 1906 274
7 Ray Caldwell, 1911.........272

PITCHER BATTING RUNS
1 Red Ruffing, 1930 ....16.4
2 Red Ruffing, 1936 ....14.3
3 Red Ruffing, 1932 ....13.2
4 Joe Bush, 1924 ....13.1
5 Red Ruffing, 1935 ....12.9
6 Red Ruffing, 1941 ....10.9
7 Carl Mays, 1921 ....10.7
8 Red Ruffing, 1931 ....10.0
9 Red Ruffing, 1938 ....8.9
10 Mel Stottlemyre, 1970 .....8.5
11 Ray Caldwell, 1915 ....8.1
12 Red Ruffing, 1939 ....7.9
13 Joe Bush, 1922 ....7.8
14 Red Ruffing, 1933 ....7.8
15 Bob Shawkey, 1924.........7.3
16 Ed Lopat, 1950................7.2
17 Sam Jones, 1922 ....7.1
18 Al Orth, 1907 ....7.0
19 Joe Bush, 1923 ....6.8
20 Whitey Ford, 1959...........6.7
21 Tommy Byrne, 1950 ....6.7
22 Ed Lopat, 1949................6.5
23 Spud Chandler, 1943.......6.4
24 Red Ruffing, 1934 ....6.2
25 Red Ruffing, 1942 ....6.1
26 Al Orth, 1906 ....5.7
27 Monte Pearson, 1936.......5.7
28 Jack Chesbro, 1904 ....5.6
29 Don Larsen, 1956............5.6
30 Ray Caldwell, 1917 ....5.5
31 Russ Ford, 1912...............5.4
32 Waite Hoyt, 1925.............5.3
33 Whitey Ford, 1953...........5.3
34 Fritz Peterson, 1970.........5.1
35 Allie Reynolds, 1949........5.0
36 Mel Stottlemyre, 1969 ......4.8
37 Dutch Ruether, 1927 ....4.6
38 Hank Johnson, 1930 ....4.6
39 Urban Shocker, 1925........4.5
40 Jesse Tannehill, 1903.......4.5
41 Ray Caldwell, 1918 ....4.5
42 Russ Ford, 1910...............4.2
43 Johnny Sain, 1953............4.1
44 Fritz Peterson, 1966.........3.8
45 Ray Caldwell, 1911...........3.7
46 Bob Shawkey, 1921..........3.6
47 Jack Quinn, 1910 ....3.5
48 Fritz Peterson, 1972.........3.4
49 Ray Fisher, 1913 ....3.4
50 Spud Chandler, 1942........3.3

FIELDING AVERAGE
FIRST BASE
1 Don Mattingly, 1994........998
2 Don Mattingly, 1993........998
3 Chris Chambliss, 1978 ...997
4 Joe Pepitone, 1965 997
5 Don Mattingly, 1992........997

SECOND BASE
1 Snuffy Stirnweiss, 1948 993
2 Steve Sax, 1991 ....[illegible]
3 Horace Clarke, 1967 990
4 Willie Randolph, 1988 988
5 Miguel Cairo, 2004 987

SHORTSTOP
1 Derek Jeter, 1998..........986
2 Fred Stanley, 1976 983
3 Bucky Dent, 1980 982
4 Phil Rizzuto, 1950 982
5 Bucky Dent, 1978 981

THIRD BASE
1 Wade Boggs, 1995.........981
2 Graig Nettles, 1978 975
3 Joe Sewell, 1932............974
4 Joe Dugan, 1920............974
5 Graig Nettles, 1977 974

OUTFIELD (250 CHANCES ACCEPTED)
1 Roy White, 1971.......... 1.000
Paul O'Neill, 1996........ 1.000
Bernie Williams, 2000.. 1.000
Rondell White, 2002 .... 1.000
5 Joe DiMaggio, 1947 997
6 Roy White, 1968 997
7 Bernie Williams, 2003.....997
8 Tom Tresh, 1964............996
9 Roger Maris, 1964..........996
10 Gene Woodling, 1952.....996

CATCHER
1 Yogi Berra, 1958.......... 1.000
2 Thurman Munson, 1971 993
3 Rick Cerone, 1987..........998
4 Elston Howard, 1964 998
5 Yogi Berra, 1959.............997

PITCHER (90 CHANCES ACCEPTED)
1 Carl Mays, 1920 992
2 Wilcy Moore, 1927..........991
3 Mel Stottlemyre, 1965 990
4 George Mogridge, 1918 989
5 Jack Chesbro, 1903 983

TOTAL CHANCES/GAME (INFIELD)
FIRST BASE
1 Wally Pipp, 1922 .... 11.63
2 John Ganzel, 1903 ...... 11.60
3 Wally Pipp, 1919 .... 11.57
4 Wally Pipp, 1920 .... 11.53
5 Lou Gehrig, 1927......... 11.39
6 Wally Pipp, 1921 .... 11.30
7 Hal Chase, 1910.......... 11.28
8 John Ganzel, 1904 ...... 11.20
9 Wally Pipp, 1917 .... 11.19
10 Wally Pipp, 1915 .... 11.14

SECOND BASE
1 Snuffy Stirnweiss, 1945 ....6.27
2 Joe Gordon, 1938...........6.12
3 Joe Gordon, 1943...........6.09
4 Snuffy Stirnweiss, 1944 ....6.05
5 Willie Randolph, 1976 ....5.98
6 Joe Gordon, 1946...........5.96
7 Del Pratt, 1918 ....5.94
8 Del Pratt, 1919 ....5.94

SHORTSTOP
1 Kid Elberfeld, 1907 ....6.33
2 Roger Peckinpaugh, 1919.......6.18
3 Neal Ball, 1908...............6.05
4 Mark Koenig, 1927 ....6.00
5 Roger Peckinpaugh, 1918.......5.96
6 Kid Elberfeld, 1904 ....5.88
7 Frankie Crosetti, 1938 ...5.76
8 Kid Elberfeld, 1905 ....5.72
9 Roger Peckinpaugh, 1914.......5.70
10 Roger Peckinpaugh, 1915.......5.68

THIRD BASE
1 Jimmy Austin, 1909 ....4.00
2 Aaron Ward, 1920 ....3.96
3 Jimmy Austin, 1910 ....3.89
4 Clete Boyer, 1962..........3.85
5 Wid Conroy, 1908...........3.83
6 Andy Carey, 1954...........3.77
7 Frank Baker, 1917..........3.75
8 Frank Baker, 1918..........3.73
9 Clete Boyer, 1961..........3.70
10 Wid Conroy, 1903...........3.60

ASSISTS (INFIELD)
FIRST BASE
1 Don Mattingly, 1984........124
2 Joe Pepitone, 1964 121
3 Buddy Hassett, 1942...... 118
4 Don Mattingly, 1992........ 116
5 Bill Skowron, 1960.......... 115

SECOND BASE
1 Del Pratt, 1920 515
2 Joe Gordon, 1940...........505
3 Robinson Cano, 2007...497
4 Aaron Ward, 1923 493
5 Snuffy Stirnweiss, 1945 492
6 Del Pratt, 1919 491
7 Joe Gordon, 1943...........490
8 Aaron Ward, 1922 489
9 Snuffy Stirnweiss, 1944 481
10 Horace Clarke, 1970 478
Willie Randolph, 1979 478

SHORTSTOP
1 Everett Scott, 1922.........538
2 Bucky Dent, 1979...........512
3 Frankie Crosetti, 1938....506
4 Roger Peckinpaugh, 1914........500
5 Bucky Dent, 1980...........489
6 Lyn Lary, 1931 484
7 Gene Michael, 1971 474
8 Alvaro Espinoza, 1989 ...471
9 Roger Peckinpaugh, 1915........468
Roger Peckinpaugh, 1916........468

THIRD BASE
1 Graig Nettles, 1973 410
2 Clete Boyer, 1962...........396
3 Graig Nettles, 1976 383
4 Graig Nettles, 1975 379
5 Graig Nettles, 1974 377
6 Clete Boyer, 1965...........354
7 Clete Boyer, 1961...........353
8 Graig Nettles, 1979 339
9 Billy Johnson, 1943 326
Graig Nettles, 1978 326

ASSISTS/GAME (INFIELD)
FIRST BASE
1 Don Mattingly, 1984.......0.93
2 Buddy Hassett, 1942.....0.89
3 Don Mattingly, 1992.......0.81
4 Bill Skowron, 1960.........0.81
5 Joe Pepitone, 1964 ....0.78
6 Joe Pepitone, 1966 ....0.77

SECOND BASE
1 Joe Gordon, 1938..........3.57
2 Tony Lazzeri, 1927 ....3.52
3 Del Pratt, 1919 ....3.51
4 Lute Boone, 1915..........3.41
5 Willie Randolph, 1976 ...3.35
6 Del Pratt, 1920 ....3.34
7 Aaron Ward, 1921 ....3.32
8 Jimmy Williams, 1903....3.32
9 Joe Gordon, 1940..........3.26
10 Aaron Ward, 1923 ....3.24

SHORTSTOP
1 Bucky Dent, 1979..........3.63
2 Gene Michael, 1972 ....3.61
3 Roger Peckinpaugh, 1918........3.60
4 Roger Peckinpaugh, 1919........3.59
5 Kid Elberfeld, 1904.........3.54
6 Everett Scott, 1922.........3.49
7 Gene Michael, 1971 ....3.49
8 Bucky Dent, 1980...........3.47
9 Mark Koenig, 1927 ....3.47
10 Tom Tresh, 1968............3.44

THIRD BASE
1 Aaron Ward, 1920 ....2.66
2 Graig Nettles, 1973 ....2.61
3 Clete Boyer, 1962..........2.52
4 Clete Boyer, 1961..........2.50
5 Charley Smith, 1967.......2.46
6 Graig Nettles, 1974 ....2.45
7 Graig Nettles, 1976 ....2.42
8 Graig Nettles, 1975 ....2.41
9 Clete Boyer, 1965..........2.41
10 Andy Carey, 1954..........2.36

DOUBLE PLAYS

FIRST BASE

1	Lou Gehrig, 1938	157
2	Don Mattingly, 1985	154
3	Nick Etten, 1945	149
4	Nick Etten, 1943	148
5	Bill Skowron, 1961	146

SECOND BASE

1	Jerry Coleman, 1950	137
2	Bobby Richardson, 1961	136
	Robinson Cano, 2007	**136**
4	Willie Randolph, 1979	128
5	Joe Gordon, 1942	121
	Billy Martin, 1953	121
	Bobby Richardson, 1965	121

SHORTSTOP

1	Phil Rizzuto, 1950	123
2	Frankie Crosetti, 1938	120
3	Frankie Crosetti, 1939	118
	Phil Rizzuto, 1949	118
5	Phil Rizzuto, 1952	116

THIRD BASE

1	Clete Boyer, 1965	46
2	Clete Boyer, 1962	41
3	Graig Nettles, 1973	39
4	Gil McDougald, 1952	38
5	Andy Carey, 1955	37

OUTFIELD

1	Harry Wolter, 1911	8
	Frank Gilhooley, 1918	8
	Bob Meusel, 1921	8
4	Willie Keeler, 1904	7
	Ray Demmitt, 1909	7
	Earle Combs, 1928	7
	Ben Chapman, 1935	7
8	10 players tied	6

CATCHER

1	Yogi Berra, 1951	25
2	Yogi Berra, 1949	18
3	Truck Hannah, 1918	16
	Yogi Berra, 1950	16
5	Bill Dickey, 1933	15
	Yogi Berra, 1956	15

PITCHER

1	Monte Pearson, 1938	8
	Spud Chandler, 1942	8
	Bobby Shantz, 1957	8
4	Jack Chesbro, 1904	7
	Marius Russo, 1941	7
	Spud Chandler, 1946	7
	Fritz Peterson, 1970	7
	Fritz Peterson, 1971	7
	Mel Stottlemyre, 1972	7

PUTOUTS (OUTFIELD)

OUTFIELD

1	Johnny Lindell, 1944	468
2	Joe DiMaggio, 1948	441
3	Rickey Henderson, 1985	439
4	Bernie Williams, 1995	432
5	Rickey Henderson, 1986	426
6	Earle Combs, 1928	424
7	Roberto Kelly, 1990	420
8	Joe DiMaggio, 1937	413
9	Earle Combs, 1927	411
10	Joe DiMaggio, 1942	409
11	Mickey Rivers, 1976	407
12	Earle Combs, 1925	401
13	Roberto Kelly, 1992	389
14	Joe DiMaggio, 1941	385
	Melky Cabrera, 2007	**385**
16	Mickey Rivers, 1978	384
17	Bobby Murcer, 1972	382
18	Bernie Williams, 1999	381
19	Bobby Murcer, 1973	380
	Roy White, 1976	380
	Mickey Rivers, 1977	380
22	Babe Ruth, 1923	378
23	Earle Combs, 1926	375
	Bobby Murcer, 1970	375
25	Ben Chapman, 1935	372
	Mickey Mantle, 1955	372
27	Mickey Mantle, 1956	370
28	Ben Chapman, 1934	368
29	Joe DiMaggio, 1938	366
	Mickey Mantle, 1959	366
	Bernie Williams, 1993	366
32	Joe DiMaggio, 1950	363
33	Whitey Witt, 1924	362
34	Joe DiMaggio, 1940	359
35	Earle Combs, 1929	358
36	Whitey Witt, 1923	357
37	Roberto Kelly, 1989	353
	Bernie Williams, 2000	353
39	Mickey Mantle, 1961	351
40	Bernie Williams, 2002	350
41	Babe Ruth, 1921	348
	Bernie Williams, 2001	348
43	Mickey Mantle, 1952	347
44	Earle Combs, 1932	343
45	Babe Ruth, 1924	340
46	Joe DiMaggio, 1936	339
	Roy White, 1973	339
48	Charlie Keller, 1943	338
49	Jerry Mumphrey, 1982	336
50	Earle Combs, 1931	335

PUTOUTS/GAME (OUTFIELD)

OUTFIELD

1	Johnny Lindell, 1944	3.14
2	Rickey Henderson, 1985	3.11
3	Bernie Williams, 1995	3.00
4	Mickey Rivers, 1976	2.99
5	Rickey Henderson, 1986	2.92
6	Joe DiMaggio, 1948	2.90
7	Earle Combs, 1928	2.85
8	Joe DiMaggio, 1939	2.80
9	Mickey Rivers, 1977	2.79
10	Mickey Rivers, 1978	2.78
11	Jerry Mumphrey, 1981	2.77
12	Joe DiMaggio, 1941	2.77
13	Joe DiMaggio, 1940	2.76
14	Joe DiMaggio, 1937	2.75
15	Jerry Mumphrey, 1982	2.73
16	Earle Combs, 1927	2.70
17	Ben Chapman, 1935	2.70
18	Earle Combs, 1925	2.67
19	Roberto Kelly, 1992	2.66
20	Mickey Mantle, 1953	2.66
21	Joe DiMaggio, 1942	2.66
22	Joe DiMaggio, 1950	2.65
23	Claudell Washington, 1988	2.64
24	Bernie Williams, 1993	2.63
25	Roberto Kelly, 1990	2.63
26	**Melky Cabrera, 2007**	**2.62**
27	Johnny Lindell, 1947	2.61
28	Earle Combs, 1931	2.60
29	Bernie Williams, 1994	2.59
30	Earle Combs, 1926	2.59
31	Roberto Kelly, 1989	2.58
	Bernie Williams, 2000	2.58
33	Mickey Mantle, 1956	2.57
34	Mickey Mantle, 1955	2.57
35	Mickey Mantle, 1959	2.56
36	Babe Ruth, 1923	2.55
37	Joe DiMaggio, 1951	2.55
38	Earle Combs, 1929	2.54
39	Bobby Murcer, 1972	2.53
40	Joe DiMaggio, 1938	2.52
41	Bernie Williams, 2003	2.52
42	Whitey Witt, 1924	2.51
43	Whitey Witt, 1923	2.48
44	Elliott Maddox, 1974	2.47
45	Ben Chapman, 1934	2.47
46	Earle Combs, 1932	2.47
47	Mickey Mantle, 1952	2.46
48	Bernie Williams, 1999	2.46
49	Joe DiMaggio, 1936	2.46
50	Roy White, 1976	2.44

FIELDING RUNS

FIRST BASE

1	Don Mattingly, 1984	15
2	Buddy Hassett, 1942	11

SECOND BASE

1	Horace Clarke, 1968	29
2	Snuffy Stirnweiss, 1945	25
3	Lute Boone, 1915	25
4	Joe Gordon, 1943	25
5	Del Pratt, 1919	25

SHORTSTOP

1	Bucky Dent, 1979	32
2	Phil Rizzuto, 1942	30
3	Roger Peckinpaugh, 1919	25
4	Gene Michael, 1971	25
5	Gene Michael, 1972	24

THIRD BASE

1	Clete Boyer, 1962	34
2	Graig Nettles, 1973	33
3	Clete Boyer, 1961	29
4	Clete Boyer, 1965	21
5	Wade Boggs, 1993	21

OUTFIELD

1	Clyde Engle, 1909	15
2	Ben Chapman, 1933	14
3	Ben Chapman, 1935	13
4	Gene Woodling, 1950	12
5	Tom Tresh, 1966	11
6	Elliott Maddox, 1974	10
7	Rickey Henderson, 1985	10

CATCHER

1	Thurman Munson, 1975	19
2	Rick Cerone, 1980	18
3	Thurman Munson, 1973	16
4	Bill Dickey, 1937	16
5	Thurman Munson, 1970	14

PITCHER

1	Wilcy Moore, 1927	8
2	Mel Stottlemyre, 1969	8
3	Jack Quinn, 1910	7
4	Bobby Shantz, 1957	7
5	Carl Mays, 1920	6

FIELDING AVERAGE

FIRST BASE

1	Don Mattingly, 1994	.998
2	Don Mattingly, 1993	.998
3	Chris Chambliss, 1978	.997
4	Joe Pepitone, 1965	.997
5	Don Mattingly, 1992	.997

SECOND BASE

1	Snuffy Stirnweiss, 1948	.993
2	Steve Sax, 1991	.990
3	Horace Clarke, 1967	.990
4	Willie Randolph, 1988	.988
5	Miguel Cairo, 2004	.987

SHORTSTOP

1	**Derek Jeter, 1998**	**.986**
2	Fred Stanley, 1976	.983
3	Bucky Dent, 1980	.982
4	Phil Rizzuto, 1950	.982
5	Bucky Dent, 1978	.981

THIRD BASE

1	Wade Boggs, 1995	.981
2	Graig Nettles, 1978	.975
3	Joe Sewell, 1932	.974
4	Joe Dugan, 1923	.974
5	Graig Nettles, 1977	.974

OUTFIELD (250 CHANCES ACCEPTED)

1	Roy White, 1971	1.000
	Paul O'Neill, 1996	1.000
	Bernie Williams, 2000	1.000
	Rondell White, 2002	1.000
5	Joe DiMaggio, 1947	.997
6	Roy White, 1968	.997
7	Bernie Williams, 2003	.997
8	Tom Tresh, 1964	.996
9	Roger Maris, 1964	.996
10	Gene Woodling, 1952	.996

CATCHER

1	Yogi Berra, 1958	1.000
2	Thurman Munson, 1971	.998
3	Rick Cerone, 1987	.998
4	Elston Howard, 1964	.998
5	Yogi Berra, 1959	.997

PITCHER (90 CHANCES ACCEPTED)

1	Carl Mays, 1920	.992
2	Wilcy Moore, 1927	.991
3	Mel Stottlemyre, 1965	.990
4	George Mogridge, 1918	.989
5	Jack Chesbro, 1903	.983

RELATIVE BATTING AVERAGE

1	Mickey Mantle, 1957	1.388
2	Willie Keeler, 1904	1.365
3	Babe Ruth, 1923	1.354
4	Don Mattingly, 1986	1.344
5	Joe DiMaggio, 1939	1.330
6	Mickey Mantle, 1956	1.320
7	Paul O'Neill, 1994	1.316
8	Don Mattingly, 1984	1.302
9	Babe Ruth, 1931	1.300
10	Bobby Murcer, 1971	1.298
11	Lou Gehrig, 1928	1.295
12	Joe DiMaggio, 1941	1.294
13	Dave Winfield, 1984	1.291
14	Babe Ruth, 1920	1.289
15	Lou Gehrig, 1930	1.284
16	Babe Ruth, 1926	1.282
17	Lou Gehrig, 1927	1.274
18	**Derek Jeter, 1999**	**1.270**
19	Babe Ruth, 1924	1.269
20	Hal Chase, 1906	1.264
21	Joe DiMaggio, 1940	1.262
22	Bernie Williams, 2002	1.262
23	Babe Ruth, 1921	1.261
24	Lou Gehrig, 1934	1.259
25	Wade Boggs, 1994	1.253
26	**Derek Jeter, 2006**	**1.248**
27	**Jorge Posada, 2007**	**1.247**
28	Bernie Williams, 1998	1.246
29	**Robinson Cano, 2006**	**1.243**
30	Bernie Williams, 1999	1.243
31	Dave Winfield, 1988	1.242
32	Don Mattingly, 1985	1.239
33	Birdie Cree, 1911	1.239
34	Thurman Munson, 1975	1.234
35	Don Mattingly, 1987	1.234
36	**Derek Jeter, 2000**	**1.227**
37	Lou Gehrig, 1932	1.224
38	Elston Howard, 1964	1.224
39	Mickey Rivers, 1977	1.223
40	Mickey Mantle, 1962	1.220
41	Willie Keeler, 1905	1.218
42	Mickey Rivers, 1976	1.218
43	Babe Ruth, 1930	1.217
44	Earle Combs, 1927	1.217
45	Tony Lazzeri, 1929	1.214
46	Babe Ruth, 1927	1.214
47	Lou Gehrig, 1937	1.213
48	Joe Gordon, 1942	1.210
49	Bernie Williams, 1997	1.210
50	**Derek Jeter, 2003**	**1.209**

BATTER-FIELDER WINS BY ERA

1988–2007

1	**Alex Rodriguez, 2005**	**6.0**
2	**Alex Rodriguez, 2007**	**5.2**
3	**Jorge Posada, 2003**	**5.1**
4	**Jason Giambi, 2002**	**4.5**
	Derek Jeter, 2005	**4.5**
6	Bernie Williams, 1999	4.3
	Jorge Posada, 2000	**4.3**
8	**Jorge Posada, 2007**	**4.1**
9	Paul O'Neill, 1994	4.0
	Bernie Williams, 1998	4.0
11	Rickey Henderson, 1988	3.8
	Mike Gallego, 1993	3.8
13	Alfonso Soriano, 2003	3.5
14	**Derek Jeter, 1999**	**3.4**

1973–87

1	Rickey Henderson, 1985	6.9
2	Don Mattingly, 1984	5.3
3	Willie Randolph, 1980	5.0
4	Thurman Munson, 1973	4.9
5	Thurman Munson, 1975	4.5
	Don Mattingly, 1986	4.5
7	Graig Nettles, 1976	4.2
8	Reggie Jackson, 1980	4.0
9	Willie Randolph, 1984	3.9
10	Bobby Bonds, 1975	3.8
11	Graig Nettles, 1973	3.7
12	Rickey Henderson, 1986	3.6
13	Dave Winfield, 1984	3.4
	Rickey Henderson, 1987	3.4
	Willie Randolph, 1987	3.4

1961–72

1	Mickey Mantle, 1961	7.5
2	Mickey Mantle, 1962	5.0
3	Elston Howard, 1961	4.5
	Bobby Murcer, 1971	4.5
5	Bobby Murcer, 1972	4.3
6	Elston Howard, 1964	4.2
	Tom Tresh, 1966	4.2
8	Thurman Munson, 1970	3.9
9	Roy White, 1971	3.8
10	Clete Boyer, 1962	3.6
11	Elston Howard, 1963	3.4
	Mickey Mantle, 1964	3.4
13	Mickey Mantle, 1967	3.3
14	Roger Maris, 1961	3.1
	Roy White, 1970	3.1

1943–60

1	Mickey Mantle, 1956	8.1
2	Mickey Mantle, 1957	8.0
3	Snuffy Stirnweiss, 1945	7.2
4	Snuffy Stirnweiss, 1944	6.8
5	Joe Gordon, 1943	5.6
6	Mickey Mantle, 1955	5.5
	Mickey Mantle, 1958	5.5
8	Gil McDougald, 1957	5.3
9	Joe DiMaggio, 1948	4.5
10	Yogi Berra, 1954	4.4
11	Yogi Berra, 1956	4.3
12	Charlie Keller, 1943	4.0
	Phil Rizzuto, 1950	4.0
14	Mickey Mantle, 1952	3.9

1921–42

1	Babe Ruth, 1923	10.1
2	Babe Ruth, 1921	9.4
3	Babe Ruth, 1927	8.8
4	Babe Ruth, 1926	8.5
5	Babe Ruth, 1924	8.4
	Lou Gehrig, 1927	8.4
7	Babe Ruth, 1931	8.1
8	Lou Gehrig, 1934	7.9
9	Lou Gehrig, 1930	7.7
10	Babe Ruth, 1930	7.6
11	Babe Ruth, 1928	7.1
12	Lou Gehrig, 1936	6.6
	Joe DiMaggio, 1941	6.6
14	Babe Ruth, 1932	6.5

1901–20

1	Babe Ruth, 1920	9.3
2	Roger Peckinpaugh, 1919	5.1
3	Del Pratt, 1919	3.1
4	Frank Baker, 1918	2.9

BATTER-FIELDER WINS

1	Babe Ruth, 1923	10.1
2	Babe Ruth, 1921	9.4
3	Babe Ruth, 1920	9.3
4	Babe Ruth, 1927	8.8
5	Babe Ruth, 1926	8.5
6	Babe Ruth, 1924	8.4
	Lou Gehrig, 1927	8.4
8	Babe Ruth, 1931	8.1
	Mickey Mantle, 1956	8.1
10	Mickey Mantle, 1957	8.0
11	Lou Gehrig, 1934	7.9
12	Lou Gehrig, 1930	7.7
13	Babe Ruth, 1930	7.6
14	Mickey Mantle, 1961	7.5
15	Snuffy Stirnweiss, 1945	7.2
16	Babe Ruth, 1928	7.1
17	Rickey Henderson, 1985	6.9
18	Snuffy Stirnweiss, 1944	6.8
19	Lou Gehrig, 1936	6.6
	Joe DiMaggio, 1941	6.6
21	Babe Ruth, 1932	6.5
22	Lou Gehrig, 1931	6.0
	Alex Rodriguez, 2005	**6.0**
24	Lou Gehrig, 1928	5.9
25	Joe Gordon, 1942	5.8
26	Joe DiMaggio, 1937	5.7
27	Bill Dickey, 1937	5.6
	Joe Gordon, 1943	5.6
29	Joe DiMaggio, 1939	5.5
	Mickey Mantle, 1955	5.5
	Mickey Mantle, 1958	5.5
32	Babe Ruth, 1929	5.4
33	Lou Gehrig, 1935	5.3
	Gil McDougald, 1957	5.3
	Don Mattingly, 1984	5.3
36	Tony Lazzeri, 1929	5.2
	Alex Rodriguez, 2007	**5.2**
38	Roger Peckinpaugh, 1919	5.1
	Lou Gehrig, 1932	5.1
	Jorge Posada, 2003	**5.1**
41	Mickey Mantle, 1962	5.0
	Willie Randolph, 1980	5.0
43	Thurman Munson, 1973	4.9
44	Lou Gehrig, 1937	4.8
45	Lou Gehrig, 1933	4.7
	Babe Ruth, 1933	4.7
47	Phil Rizzuto, 1942	4.6
48	Many players tied	4.5

PINCH HITS

1	Johnny Mize, 1953	19
2	Eddie Robinson, 1954	15
3	Enos Slaughter, 1958	13
4	Enos Slaughter, 1954	11
	Bob Cerv, 1955	11
	Ray Barker, 1965	11
7	5 players tied	10

PINCH HIT AVERAGE

1	Ron Hassey, 1986	.667
2	Ken Phelps, 1989	.545
3	Kevin Maas, 1992	.500
4	Don Baylor, 1985	.455
5	Norm Siebern, 1959	.450
6	Phil Linz, 1962	.438
7	Gil McDougald, 1960	.429
	Lou Clinton, 1966	.429
	Lou Piniella, 1982	.429
	Roy Smalley, 1984	.429

PINCH HIT HOME RUNS

1	Johnny Blanchard, 1961	4
2	Tommy Henrich, 1950	3
	Bob Cerv, 1961	3
	Ray Barker, 1965	3
	Dan Pasqua, 1987	3
6	Many players tied	2

WINS

1 Jack Chesbro, 1904 ... 41
2 Al Orth, 1906 ... 27
Carl Mays, 1921 ... 27
4 Russ Ford, 1910 ... 26
Carl Mays, 1920 ... 26
Joe Bush, 1922 ... 26
Lefty Gomez, 1934 ... 26
8 Whitey Ford, 1961 ... 25
Ron Guidry, 1978 ... 25
10 Bob Shawkey, 1916 ... 24
George Pipgras, 1928 ... 24
Lefty Gomez, 1932 ... 24
Whitey Ford, 1963 ... 24
14 Jack Powell, 1904 ... 23
Jack Chesbro, 1906 ... 23
Herb Pennock, 1926 ... 23
Waite Hoyt, 1928 ... 23
Ralph Terry, 1962 ... 23
Catfish Hunter, 1975 ... 23
20 Russ Ford, 1911 ... 22
Waite Hoyt, 1927 ... 22
Tommy John, 1980 ... 22
Ron Guidry, 1985 ... 22
24 Jack Chesbro, 1903 ... 21
Sam Jones, 1923 ... 21
Herb Pennock, 1924 ... 21
Lefty Gomez, 1931 ... 21
Lefty Gomez, 1937 ... 21
Red Ruffing, 1938 ... 21
Red Ruffing, 1939 ... 21
Tiny Bonham, 1942 ... 21
Vic Raschi, 1949 ... 21
Vic Raschi, 1950 ... 21
Ed Lopat, 1951 ... 21
Vic Raschi, 1951 ... 21
Bob Turley, 1958 ... 21
Jim Bouton, 1963 ... 21
Mel Stottlemyre, 1968 ... 21
Tommy John, 1979 ... 21
Ron Guidry, 1983 ... 21
Andy Pettitte, 1996 ... 21
Andy Pettitte, 2003 ... 21
43 Many players tied ... 20

WINS BY ERA

1988–2007

1 **Andy Pettitte, 1996 ... 21**
Andy Pettitte, 2003 ... 21
3 David Cone, 1998 ... 20
Roger Clemens, 2001 ... 20
5 **Andy Pettitte, 2000 ... 19**
David Wells, 2002 ... 19
Chien-Ming Wang, 2006 ... 19
Chien-Ming Wang, 2007 ... 19

1973–87

1 Ron Guidry, 1978 ... 25
2 Catfish Hunter, 1975 ... 23
3 Tommy John, 1980 ... 22
Ron Guidry, 1985 ... 22
5 Tommy John, 1979 ... 21
Ron Guidry, 1983 ... 21
7 Ed Figueroa, 1978 ... 20

1961–72

1 Whitey Ford, 1961 ... 25
2 Whitey Ford, 1963 ... 24
3 Ralph Terry, 1962 ... 23
4 Jim Bouton, 1963 ... 21
Mel Stottlemyre, 1968 ... 21
6 Mel Stottlemyre, 1965 ... 20
Mel Stottlemyre, 1969 ... 20
Fritz Peterson, 1970 ... 20

1943–60

1 Vic Raschi, 1949 ... 21
Vic Raschi, 1950 ... 21
Ed Lopat, 1951 ... 21
Vic Raschi, 1951 ... 21
Bob Turley, 1958 ... 21
6 Spud Chandler, 1943 ... 20
Spud Chandler, 1946 ... 20
Allie Reynolds, 1952 ... 20
Bob Grim, 1954 ... 20

1921–42

1 Carl Mays, 1921 ... 27
2 Joe Bush, 1922 ... 26
Lefty Gomez, 1934 ... 26
4 George Pipgras, 1928 ... 24
Lefty Gomez, 1932 ... 24
6 Herb Pennock, 1926 ... 23
Waite Hoyt, 1928 ... 23

1901–20

1 Jack Chesbro, 1904 ... 41
2 Al Orth, 1906 ... 27
3 Russ Ford, 1910 ... 26
Carl Mays, 1920 ... 26
5 Bob Shawkey, 1916 ... 24
6 Jack Powell, 1904 ... 23
Jack Chesbro, 1906 ... 23

LOSSES

1 Joe Lake, 1908 ... 22
2 Al Orth, 1907 ... 21
Russ Ford, 1912 ... 21
Sam Jones, 1925 ... 21
5 Jack Chesbro, 1908 ... 20
Mel Stottlemyre, 1966 ... 20
7 Jack Powell, 1904 ... 19
Jack Warhop, 1912 ... 19
Tim Leary, 1990 ... 19
10 Russ Ford, 1913 ... 18
Mel Stottlemyre, 1972 ... 18
12 Al Orth, 1906 ... 17
Jack Chesbro, 1906 ... 17
Herb Pennock, 1925 ... 17
15 Al Orth, 1905 ... 16
Rube Manning, 1908 ... 16
Bill Hogg, 1908 ... 16
Ray Caldwell, 1912 ... 16
Ray Fisher, 1913 ... 16
Marty McHale, 1914 ... 16
Ray Caldwell, 1915 ... 16
Ray Caldwell, 1917 ... 16
Joe Bush, 1924 ... 16
Stan Bahnsen, 1969 ... 16
Fritz Peterson, 1969 ... 16
Mel Stottlemyre, 1973 ... 16
Doc Medich, 1975 ... 16
Melido Perez, 1992 ... 16
29 Jack Chesbro, 1903 ... 15
Jesse Tannehill, 1903 ... 15
Jack Chesbro, 1905 ... 15
Jack Warhop, 1909 ... 15
George McConnell, 1913 ... 15
Jack Warhop, 1914 ... 15
Bob Shawkey, 1917 ... 15
Joe Bush, 1923 ... 15
George Pipgras, 1930 ... 15
Lefty Gomez, 1935 ... 15
Ralph Terry, 1963 ... 15
Jim Bouton, 1965 ... 15
Mel Stottlemyre, 1967 ... 15
Fritz Peterson, 1972 ... 15
Fritz Peterson, 1973 ... 15
Pat Dobson, 1974 ... 15
Doc Medich, 1974 ... 15
Catfish Hunter, 1976 ... 15
Andy Hawkins, 1989 ... 15
48 Many players tied ... 14

WINNING PERCENTAGE

1 Ron Guidry, 1978 ... .893
2 **Roger Clemens, 2001 ... .870**
3 Whitey Ford, 1961 ... .862
4 Ralph Terry, 1961 ... .842
5 Lefty Gomez, 1934 ... .839
6 Spud Chandler, 1943 ... .833
7 David Wells, 1998 ... .818
8 Russ Ford, 1910 ... .813
9 Johnny Allen, 1932 ... .810
Jimmy Key, 1994 ... .810
11 Tiny Bonham, 1942 ... .808
12 Ed Lopat, 1953 ... .800
13 Hank Borowy, 1942 ... .789
14 Joe Bush, 1922 ... .788
15 Ron Guidry, 1985 ... .786
16 Lefty Gomez, 1932 ... .774
Whitey Ford, 1963 ... .774
18 Jack Chesbro, 1904 ... .774
19 Bob Grim, 1954 ... .769
20 Waite Hoyt, 1928 ... .767
21 Spud Chandler, 1942 ... .762
Tommy Byrne, 1955 ... .762
23 Herb Pennock, 1923 ... .760
Whitey Ford, 1956 ... .760
Chien-Ming Wang, 2006 ... .760
26 Waite Hoyt, 1927 ... .759
27 Carl Mays, 1921 ... .750
Urban Shocker, 1927 ... .750
Red Ruffing, 1938 ... .750
Red Ruffing, 1939 ... .750
Lefty Gomez, 1941 ... .750
Whitey Ford, 1953 ... .750
Bob Turley, 1958 ... .750
Luis Arroyo, 1961 ... .750
Jim Bouton, 1963 ... .750
Rudy May, 1980 ... .750
Dennis Rasmussen, 1986 ... .750
Jimmy Key, 1993 ... .750
39 Red Ruffing, 1937 ... .741
David Cone, 1998 ... .741
41 Herb Pennock, 1928 ... .739
Allie Reynolds, 1949 ... .739
Whitey Ford, 1964 ... .739
44 Wilcy Moore, 1927 ... .731
Monte Pearson, 1936 ... .731
David Wells, 2002 ... .731
Chien-Ming Wang, 2007 ... .731
48 Vic Raschi, 1952 ... .727
Tom Sturdivant, 1957 ... .727
50 4 players tied ... .724

GAMES

1 Paul Quantrill, 2004 ... 86
2 Scott Proctor, 2006 ... 83
3 Tom Gordon, 2004 ... 80
4 Mike Stanton, 2002 ... 79
Tom Gordon, 2005 ... 79
6 Steve Karsay, 2002 ... 78
7 Jeff Nelson, 1997 ... 77
Luis Vizcaino, 2007 ... 77
9 Mike Stanton, 2001 ... 76
10 Dave Righetti, 1985 ... 74
Dave Righetti, 1986 ... 74
Mariano Rivera, 2004 ... 74
13 Jeff Nelson, 1996 ... 73
Mike Stanton, 1999 ... 73
Jeff Nelson, 2000 ... 73
16 Sparky Lyle, 1977 ... 72
Kyle Farnsworth, 2006 ... 72
18 **Mariano Rivera, 2001 ... 71**
Mariano Rivera, 2005 ... 71
20 Lee Guetterman, 1989 ... 70
Ron Villone, 2006 ... 70
22 Mike Stanton, 2000 ... 69
23 Greg Cadaret, 1991 ... 68
24 Mike Stanton, 1998 ... 67
Mariano Rivera, 2007 ... 67
26 Sparky Lyle, 1974 ... 66
John Habyan, 1991 ... 66
Mariano Rivera, 1997 ... 66
Mariano Rivera, 1999 ... 66
Mariano Rivera, 2000 ... 66
31 Luis Arroyo, 1961 ... 65
Pedro Ramos, 1965 ... 65
Dooley Womack, 1967 ... 65
34 Sparky Lyle, 1976 ... 64
Rich Gossage, 1980 ... 64
Dave Righetti, 1984 ... 64
Lee Guetterman, 1990 ... 64
Lee Guetterman, 1991 ... 64
Mike Stanton, 1997 ... 64
Mariano Rivera, 2003 ... 64
Tanyon Sturtze, 2005 ... 64
Kyle Farnsworth, 2007 ... 64
43 Rich Gossage, 1978 ... 63
George Frazier, 1982 ... 63
Bob Wickman, 1995 ... 63
Jason Grimsley, 2000 ... 63
Mariano Rivera, 2006 ... 63
48 5 players tied ... 62

GAMES BY ERA

1988–2007

1 Paul Quantrill, 2004 ... 86
2 Scott Proctor, 2006 ... 83
3 Tom Gordon, 2004 ... 80
4 Mike Stanton, 2002 ... 79
Tom Gordon, 2005 ... 79
6 Steve Karsay, 2002 ... 78
7 Jeff Nelson, 1997 ... 77
Luis Vizcaino, 2007 ... 77

1973–87

1 Dave Righetti, 1985 ... 74
Dave Righetti, 1986 ... 74
3 Sparky Lyle, 1977 ... 72
4 Sparky Lyle, 1974 ... 66
5 Sparky Lyle, 1976 ... 64
Rich Gossage, 1980 ... 64
Dave Righetti, 1984 ... 64

1961–72

1 Luis Arroyo, 1961 ... 65
Pedro Ramos, 1965 ... 65
Dooley Womack, 1967 ... 65
4 Lindy McDaniel, 1970 ... 62
5 Sparky Lyle, 1972 ... 59
6 Hal Reniff, 1966 ... 56
7 Marshall Bridges, 1962 ... 52
Pedro Ramos, 1966 ... 52

1943–60

1 Joe Page, 1949 ... 60
2 Joe Page, 1947 ... 56
3 Joe Page, 1948 ... 55
4 Art Ditmar, 1957 ... 46
Bob Grim, 1957 ... 46
6 Johnny Sain, 1954 ... 45
Jim Konstanty, 1955 ... 45

1921–42

1 Wilcy Moore, 1927 ... 50
2 Carl Mays, 1921 ... 49
3 Herb Pennock, 1925 ... 47
4 Waite Hoyt, 1924 ... 46
Waite Hoyt, 1925 ... 46
George Pipgras, 1928 ... 46
7 Sam Jones, 1922 ... 45

1901–20

1 Jack Chesbro, 1904 ... 55
2 Bob Shawkey, 1916 ... 53
3 Jack Chesbro, 1906 ... 49
4 Jack Powell, 1904 ... 47
5 Al Orth, 1906 ... 45
Jack Chesbro, 1908 ... 45
George Mogridge, 1918 ... 45
Carl Mays, 1920 ... 45

GAMES STARTED

1 Jack Chesbro, 1904 ... 51
2 Jack Powell, 1904 ... 45
3 Jack Chesbro, 1906 ... 42
4 Al Orth, 1906 ... 39
Whitey Ford, 1961 ... 39
Ralph Terry, 1962 ... 39
Mel Stottlemyre, 1969 ... 39
Pat Dobson, 1974 ... 39
Catfish Hunter, 1975 ... 39
10 Jack Chesbro, 1905 ... 38
Carl Mays, 1921 ... 38
George Pipgras, 1928 ... 38
Mel Stottlemyre, 1973 ... 38
Doc Medich, 1974 ... 38
15 Al Orth, 1905 ... 37
Carl Mays, 1920 ... 37
Vic Raschi, 1949 ... 37
Whitey Ford, 1962 ... 37
Whitey Ford, 1963 ... 37
Ralph Terry, 1963 ... 37
Jim Bouton, 1964 ... 37
Mel Stottlemyre, 1965 ... 37
Fritz Peterson, 1969 ... 37
Fritz Peterson, 1970 ... 37
Mel Stottlemyre, 1970 ... 37
Doc Medich, 1975 ... 37
27 Jack Chesbro, 1903 ... 36
Whitey Ford, 1964 ... 36
Whitey Ford, 1965 ... 36
Mel Stottlemyre, 1967 ... 36
Mel Stottlemyre, 1968 ... 36
Mel Stottlemyre, 1972 ... 36
Catfish Hunter, 1976 ... 36
Tommy John, 1979 ... 36
Tommy John, 1980 ... 36
36 Russ Ford, 1912 ... 35
Ray Caldwell, 1915 ... 35
Al Downing, 1964 ... 35
Mel Stottlemyre, 1966 ... 35
Stan Bahnsen, 1970 ... 35
Fritz Peterson, 1971 ... 35
Mel Stottlemyre, 1971 ... 35
Fritz Peterson, 1972 ... 35
Ed Figueroa, 1978 ... 35
Ron Guidry, 1978 ... 35
Andy Pettitte, 1997 ... 35
47 Many players tied ... 34

GAMES STARTED BY ERA

1988–2007

1 **Andy Pettitte, 1997 ... 35**
2 Andy Hawkins, 1989 ... 34
Scott Sanderson, 1991 ... 34
Jimmy Key, 1993 ... 34
Andy Pettitte, 1996 ... 34
Mike Mussina, 2001 ... 34
Randy Johnson, 2005 ... 34
Andy Pettitte, 2007 ... 34

1973–87

1 Pat Dobson, 1974 ... 39
Catfish Hunter, 1975 ... 39
3 Mel Stottlemyre, 1973 ... 38
Doc Medich, 1974 ... 38
5 Doc Medich, 1975 ... 37
6 Catfish Hunter, 1976 ... 36
Tommy John, 1979 ... 36
Tommy John, 1980 ... 36

1961–72

1 Whitey Ford, 1961 ... 39
Ralph Terry, 1962 ... 39
Mel Stottlemyre, 1969 ... 39
4 Whitey Ford, 1962 ... 37
Whitey Ford, 1963 ... 37
Ralph Terry, 1963 ... 37
Jim Bouton, 1964 ... 37
Mel Stottlemyre, 1965 ... 37
Fritz Peterson, 1969 ... 37
Fritz Peterson, 1970 ... 37
Mel Stottlemyre, 1970 ... 37

1943–60

1 Vic Raschi, 1949 ... 37
2 Vic Raschi, 1951 ... 34
Bob Turley, 1955 ... 34
4 Whitey Ford, 1955 ... 33
5 Spud Chandler, 1946 ... 32
Ed Lopat, 1950 ... 32
Vic Raschi, 1950 ... 32

1921–42

1 Carl Mays, 1921 ... 38
George Pipgras, 1928 ... 38
3 Bob Shawkey, 1922 ... 34
Herb Pennock, 1924 ... 34
Lefty Gomez, 1937 ... 34
6 Herb Pennock, 1926 ... 33
George Pipgras, 1929 ... 33
Lefty Gomez, 1934 ... 33
Red Ruffing, 1936 ... 33

1901–20

1 Jack Chesbro, 1904 ... 51
2 Jack Powell, 1904 ... 45
3 Jack Chesbro, 1906 ... 42
4 Al Orth, 1906 ... 39
5 Jack Chesbro, 1905 ... 38
6 Al Orth, 1905 ... 37
Carl Mays, 1920 ... 37

HOME RUNS ALLOWED BY ERA

1988–2007

1 Orlando Hernandez, 2000 ... 34
2 Javier Vazquez, 2004 ... 33
3 Randy Johnson, 2005 ... 32
4 David Wells, 1998 ... 29
5 Scott Sanderson, 1992 ... 28
Randy Johnson, 2006 ... 28
7 Richard Dotson, 1988 ... 27
Hideki Irabu, 1998 ... 27
Mike Mussina, 2002 ... 27

1973–87

1 Dennis Rasmussen, 1987 ... 31
2 Catfish Hunter, 1977 ... 29
Joe Cowley, 1985 ... 29
Phil Niekro, 1985 ... 29
5 Catfish Hunter, 1976 ... 28
Ron Guidry, 1985 ... 28
Ron Guidry, 1986 ... 28
Dennis Rasmussen, 1986 ... 28

1961–72

1 Ralph Terry, 1962 ... 40
2 Jim Bouton, 1964 ... 32
3 Ralph Terry, 1963 ... 29
4 Stan Bahnsen, 1969 ... 28
5 Whitey Ford, 1963 ... 26
6 Fritz Peterson, 1971 ... 25
7 Fritz Peterson, 1970 ... 24

1943–60

1 Art Ditmar, 1960 ... 25
2 Bob Turley, 1958 ... 24
3 Allie Reynolds, 1947 ... 23
Tommy Byrne, 1950 ... 23
5 Vic Raschi, 1951 ... 20
Whitey Ford, 1955 ... 20
7 5 players tied ... 19

1921–42

1 Red Ruffing, 1940 ... 24
2 Lefty Gomez, 1932 ... 23
3 Red Ruffing, 1936 ... 22
4 Marv Breuer, 1940 ... 20
5 Ed Wells, 1929 ... 19
6 Red Ruffing, 1934 ... 18
Lefty Gomez, 1935 ... 18

1901–20

1 Jack Powell, 1904 ... 15
2 Carl Mays, 1920 ... 13
3 Russ Ford, 1912 ... 11
4 Hank Thormahlen, 1919 ... 10
Bob Shawkey, 1920 ... 10
6 Russ Ford, 1913 ... 9
7 6 players tied ... 8

COMPLETE GAMES BY ERA

1988–2007

1 Melido Perez, 1992 ... 10
2 Jack McDowell, 1995 ... 8
David Wells, 1998 ... 8
4 John Candelaria, 1988 ... 6
Tim Leary, 1990 ... 6
6 4 players tied ... **5**

1973–87

1 Catfish Hunter, 1975 ... 30
2 Catfish Hunter, 1976 ... 21
Ron Guidry, 1983 ... 21
4 Mel Stottlemyre, 1973 ... 19
5 Doc Medich, 1974 ... 17
Tommy John, 1979 ... 17
7 Ron Guidry, 1978 ... 16
Tommy John, 1980 ... 16

1961–72

1 Mel Stottlemyre, 1969 ... 24
2 Mel Stottlemyre, 1968 ... 19
Mel Stottlemyre, 1971 ... 19
4 Ralph Terry, 1963 ... 18
Mel Stottlemyre, 1965 ... 18
6 Fritz Peterson, 1969 ... 16
Fritz Peterson, 1971 ... 16

1943–60

1 Allie Reynolds, 1952 ... 24
2 Vic Raschi, 1949 ... 21
3 Spud Chandler, 1943 ... 20
Spud Chandler, 1946 ... 20
Ed Lopat, 1951 ... 20
6 Hank Borowy, 1944 ... 19
Monk Dubiel, 1944 ... 19
Bob Turley, 1958 ... 19

1921–42

1 Carl Mays, 1921 ... 30
2 Herb Pennock, 1924 ... 25
Lefty Gomez, 1934 ... 25
Red Ruffing, 1936 ... 25
Lefty Gomez, 1937 ... 25
6 Waite Hoyt, 1927 ... 23
7 8 players tied ... 22

1901–20

1 Jack Chesbro, 1904 ... 48
2 Jack Powell, 1904 ... 38
3 Al Orth, 1906 ... 36
4 Jack Chesbro, 1903 ... 33
5 Ray Caldwell, 1915 ... 31
6 Russ Ford, 1912 ... 30
7 Russ Ford, 1910 ... 29

SHUTOUTS

1	Ron Guidry, 1978	9
2	Russ Ford, 1910	8
	Whitey Ford, 1964	8
4	Allie Reynolds, 1951	7
	Whitey Ford, 1958	7
	Mel Stottlemyre, 1971	7
	Mel Stottlemyre, 1972	7
	Catfish Hunter, 1975	7
9	Jack Chesbro, 1904	6
	Al Orth, 1905	6
	Carl Mays, 1920	6
	Lefty Gomez, 1934	6
	Lefty Gomez, 1937	6
	Tiny Bonham, 1942	6
	Spud Chandler, 1946	6
	Vic Raschi, 1948	6
	Allie Reynolds, 1952	6
	Bob Turley, 1955	6
	Bob Turley, 1958	6
	Jim Bouton, 1963	6
	Mel Stottlemyre, 1968	6
	Tommy John, 1980	6
23	Hippo Vaughn, 1910	5
	Ray Caldwell, 1914	5
	Bob Shawkey, 1920	5
	Herb Pennock, 1928	5
	Red Ruffing, 1934	5
	Red Ruffing, 1939	5
	Spud Chandler, 1943	5
	Whitey Ford, 1955	5
	Ron Guidry, 1977	5
	David Wells, 1998	5
33	Many players tied	4

SAVES

1	**Mariano Rivera, 2004**	**53**
2	**Mariano Rivera, 2001**	**50**
3	Dave Righetti, 1986	46
4	**Mariano Rivera, 1999**	**45**
5	John Wetteland, 1996	43
	Mariano Rivera, 1997	**43**
	Mariano Rivera, 2005	**43**
8	**Mariano Rivera, 2003**	**40**
9	Dave Righetti, 1990	36
	Mariano Rivera, 1998	**36**
	Mariano Rivera, 2000	**36**
12	Sparky Lyle, 1972	35
13	**Mariano Rivera, 2006**	**34**
14	Rich Gossage, 1980	33
15	Dave Righetti, 1984	31
	Dave Righetti, 1987	31
	John Wetteland, 1995	31
18	Rich Gossage, 1982	30
	Steve Farr, 1992	30
	Mariano Rivera, 2007	**30**
21	Luis Arroyo, 1961	29
	Lindy McDaniel, 1970	29
	Dave Righetti, 1985	29
24	**Mariano Rivera, 2002**	**28**
25	Joe Page, 1949	27
	Sparky Lyle, 1973	27
	Rich Gossage, 1978	27
28	Sparky Lyle, 1977	26
29	Dave Righetti, 1988	25
	Dave Righetti, 1989	25
	Steve Farr, 1993	25
32	Sparky Lyle, 1976	23
	Steve Farr, 1991	23
34	Johnny Sain, 1954	22
	Rich Gossage, 1983	22
36	Ryne Duren, 1958	20
	Rich Gossage, 1981	20
38	Johnny Murphy, 1939	19
	Bob Grim, 1957	19
	Pedro Ramos, 1965	19
41	Marshall Bridges, 1962	18
	Hal Reniff, 1963	18
	Dooley Womack, 1967	18
	Rich Gossage, 1979	18
45	Joe Page, 1947	17
46	Joe Page, 1948	16
	Jack Aker, 1970	16
48	Johnny Murphy, 1941	15
	Sparky Lyle, 1974	15
	Steve Howe, 1994	15

SAVES BY ERA

1988–2007		
1	**Mariano Rivera, 2004**	**53**
2	**Mariano Rivera, 2001**	**50**
3	**Mariano Rivera, 1999**	**45**
4	John Wetteland, 1996	43
	Mariano Rivera, 1997	**43**
	Mariano Rivera, 2005	**43**
7	**Mariano Rivera, 2003**	**40**
1973–87		
1	Dave Righetti, 1986	46
2	Rich Gossage, 1980	33
3	Dave Righetti, 1984	31
	Dave Righetti, 1987	31
5	Rich Gossage, 1982	30
6	Dave Righetti, 1985	29
7	Sparky Lyle, 1973	27
	Rich Gossage, 1978	27
1961–72		
1	Sparky Lyle, 1972	35
2	Luis Arroyo, 1961	29
	Lindy McDaniel, 1970	29
4	Pedro Ramos, 1965	19
5	Marshall Bridges, 1962	18
	Hal Reniff, 1963	18
	Dooley Womack, 1967	18
1943–60		
1	Joe Page, 1949	27
2	Johnny Sain, 1954	22
3	Ryne Duren, 1958	20
4	Bob Grim, 1957	19
5	Joe Page, 1947	17
6	Joe Page, 1948	16
7	Ryne Duren, 1959	14
1921–42		
1	Johnny Murphy, 1939	19
2	Johnny Murphy, 1941	15
3	Wilcy Moore, 1927	13
4	Johnny Murphy, 1938	11
	Johnny Murphy, 1942	11
6	Johnny Murphy, 1937	10
7	Pat Malone, 1936	9
	Johnny Murphy, 1940	9
1901–20		
1	Bob Shawkey, 1916	8
2	George Mogridge, 1918	7
3	Allan Russell, 1916	6
4	Bob Shawkey, 1919	5
5	Allan Russell, 1918	4
6	Jack Warhop, 1912	3
	George McConnell, 1913	3
	Jack Quinn, 1920	3

SAVE PERCENTAGE

Rank	Player	PCT
1	**Mariano Rivera, 2004**	**93.0**
2	Dave Righetti, 1990	92.3
3	**Mariano Rivera, 2006**	**91.9**
4	**Mariano Rivera, 1999**	**91.8**
5	John Wetteland, 1996	91.5
	Mariano Rivera, 2005	**91.5**
7	Pedro Ramos, 1965	90.5
8	Dooley Womack, 1967	90.0
9	Rich Gossage, 1980	89.2
10	**Mariano Rivera, 2007**	**88.2**
11	**Mariano Rivera, 1998**	**87.8**
	Mariano Rivera, 2000	**87.8**
13	**Mariano Rivera, 2001**	**87.7**
14	**Mariano Rivera, 2002**	**87.5**
15	Ryne Duren, 1958	87.0
	Rich Gossage, 1981	87.0
	Mariano Rivera, 2003	**87.0**
18	Rich Gossage, 1979	85.7
19	John Wetteland, 1995	83.8
20	Sparky Lyle, 1972	83.3
	Steve Farr, 1992	83.3
22	Lindy McDaniel, 1970	82.9
23	**Mariano Rivera, 1997**	**82.7**
24	Dave Righetti, 1986	82.1

BLOWN SAVES

Rank	Player	BS
1	Rich Gossage, 1983	13
	Dave Righetti, 1987	13
3	Luis Arroyo, 1961	10
	Rich Gossage, 1978	10
	Ron Davis, 1979	10
	Dave Righetti, 1985	10
	Dave Righetti, 1986	10
8	Rich Gossage, 1982	9
	Dave Righetti, 1984	9
	Brian Fisher, 1986	9
	Dave Righetti, 1988	9
	Dave Righetti, 1989	9
	Bob Wickman, 1995	9
	Mariano Rivera, 1997	**9**
15	Marshall Bridges, 1962	8
	Jack Aker, 1971	8
	Sparky Lyle, 1976	8
	Sparky Lyle, 1977	8
19	Many players tied	7

HOME RUNS ALLOWED

1	Ralph Terry, 1962	40
2	Orlando Hernandez, 2000	34
3	Javier Vazquez, 2004	33
4	Jim Bouton, 1964	32
	Randy Johnson, 2005	32
6	Dennis Rasmussen, 1987	31
7	Ralph Terry, 1963	29
	Catfish Hunter, 1977	29
	Joe Cowley, 1985	29
	Phil Niekro, 1985	29
	David Wells, 1998	29
12	Stan Bahnsen, 1969	28
	Catfish Hunter, 1976	28
	Ron Guidry, 1985	28
	Ron Guidry, 1986	28
	Dennis Rasmussen, 1986	28
	Scott Sanderson, 1992	28
	Randy Johnson, 2006	28
19	Richard Dotson, 1988	27
	Hideki Irabu, 1998	27
	Mike Mussina, 2002	**27**
22	Whitey Ford, 1963	26
	Ron Guidry, 1983	26
	Jimmy Key, 1993	26
	Hideki Irabu, 1999	26
	Roger Clemens, 2000	**26**
27	Art Ditmar, 1960	25
	Fritz Peterson, 1971	25
	Catfish Hunter, 1975	25
	Doc Medich, 1975	25
	Jack McDowell, 1995	25
	David Cone, 2000	25
33	Red Ruffing, 1940	24
	Bob Turley, 1958	24
	Fritz Peterson, 1970	24
	Doc Medich, 1974	24
	Ron Guidry, 1984	24
	Jim Abbott, 1994	24
	Terry Mulholland, 1994	24
	David Wells, 1997	24
	Orlando Hernandez, 1999	24
	Roger Clemens, 2003	**24**
	David Wells, 2003	24
44	Many players tied	23

BY ERA

Rank	Player	HR/9
1988–2007		
1	**Andy Pettitte, 1997**	**0.26**
2	**Chien-Ming Wang, 2007**	**0.41**
3	**Chien-Ming Wang, 2006**	**0.50**
4	Jimmy Key, 1994	0.54
5	Tommy John, 1988	0.56
6	Melido Perez, 1992	0.58
7	Scott Kamieniecki, 1992	0.62
1973–87		
1	Tommy John, 1979	0.29
2	Rudy May, 1975	0.38
3	Ray Fontenot, 1984	0.43
4	Ron Guidry, 1978	0.43
5	Mel Stottlemyre, 1973	0.43
6	Tommy John, 1980	0.44
7	Ed Figueroa, 1976	0.46
1961–72		
1	Al Downing, 1963	0.36
2	Whitey Ford, 1964	0.37
3	Steve Kline, 1972	0.42
4	Mel Stottlemyre, 1972	0.45
5	Stan Bahnsen, 1968	0.47
6	Fritz Peterson, 1969	0.50
7	Mel Stottlemyre, 1971	0.53
1943–60		
1	Spud Chandler, 1943	0.18
2	Spud Chandler, 1946	0.24
3	Butch Wensloff, 1943	0.28
4	Allie Reynolds, 1952	0.37
5	Bill Bevens, 1946	0.40
6	Bob Grim, 1954	0.41
7	Whitey Ford, 1954	0.43
1921–42		
1	Herb Pennock, 1928	0.09
2	Waite Hoyt, 1921	0.10
3	George Pipgras, 1927	0.11
4	George Pipgras, 1928	0.12
5	Wilcy Moore, 1927	0.13
6	Waite Hoyt, 1926	0.17
7	Herb Pennock, 1927	0.21
1901–20		
1	Jack Chesbro, 1907	0.00
2	Jack Warhop, 1910	0.04
3	Hippo Vaughn, 1910	0.04
4	Ray Keating, 1914	0.04
5	Bill Hogg, 1905	0.04
6	Ray Caldwell, 1912	0.05
7	Al Orth, 1906	0.05

INNINGS PITCHED

Rank	Player	IP
1	Jack Chesbro, 1904	454.2
2	Jack Powell, 1904	390.1
3	Al Orth, 1906	338.2
4	Carl Mays, 1921	336.2
5	Catfish Hunter, 1975	328.0
6	Jack Chesbro, 1906	325.0
7	Jack Chesbro, 1903	324.2
8	Carl Mays, 1920	312.0
9	Al Orth, 1905	305.1
10	Ray Caldwell, 1915	305.0
11	Jack Chesbro, 1905	303.1
12	Mel Stottlemyre, 1969	303.0
13	George Pipgras, 1928	300.2
14	Russ Ford, 1910	299.2
	Bob Shawkey, 1922	299.2
16	Ralph Terry, 1962	298.2
	Catfish Hunter, 1976	298.2
18	Russ Ford, 1912	291.2
19	Mel Stottlemyre, 1965	291.0
20	Jack Chesbro, 1908	288.2
21	Herb Pennock, 1924	286.1
22	Whitey Ford, 1961	283.0
23	Waite Hoyt, 1921	282.1
24	Lefty Gomez, 1934	281.2
25	Russ Ford, 1911	281.1
26	Pat Dobson, 1974	281.0
27	Doc Medich, 1974	279.2
28	Mel Stottlemyre, 1968	278.2
29	Lefty Gomez, 1937	278.1
30	Herb Pennock, 1925	277.0
31	Bob Shawkey, 1916	276.2
32	Tommy John, 1979	276.1
33	Joe Bush, 1923	275.2
34	Vic Raschi, 1949	274.2
35	Fritz Peterson, 1971	274.0
36	Ron Guidry, 1978	273.2
37	Waite Hoyt, 1928	273.0
	Mel Stottlemyre, 1973	273.0
39	Doc Medich, 1975	272.1
40	Fritz Peterson, 1969	272.0
41	Jim Bouton, 1964	271.1
42	Red Ruffing, 1936	271.0
	Mel Stottlemyre, 1970	271.0
44	Mel Stottlemyre, 1971	269.2
45	Joe Lake, 1908	269.1
	Whitey Ford, 1963	269.1
47	Ralph Terry, 1963	268.0
48	Bob Shawkey, 1920	267.2
49	Stan Bahnsen, 1968	267.1
50	Herb Pennock, 1926	266.1

INNINGS PITCHED BY ERA

Rank	Player	IP
1988–2007		
1	Melido Perez, 1992	247.2
2	**Andy Pettitte, 1997**	**240.1**
3	Jimmy Key, 1993	236.2
4	**Mike Mussina, 2001**	**228.2**
5	Randy Johnson, 2005	225.2
6	**Andy Pettitte, 1996**	**221.0**
7	**Roger Clemens, 2001**	**220.1**
1973–87		
1	Catfish Hunter, 1975	328.0
2	Catfish Hunter, 1976	298.2
3	Pat Dobson, 1974	281.0
4	Doc Medich, 1974	279.2
5	Tommy John, 1979	276.1
6	Ron Guidry, 1978	273.2
7	Mel Stottlemyre, 1973	273.0
1961–72		
1	Mel Stottlemyre, 1969	303.0
2	Ralph Terry, 1962	298.2
3	Mel Stottlemyre, 1965	291.0
4	Whitey Ford, 1961	283.0
5	Mel Stottlemyre, 1968	278.2
6	Fritz Peterson, 1971	274.0
7	Fritz Peterson, 1969	272.0
1943–60		
1	Vic Raschi, 1949	274.2
2	Vic Raschi, 1951	258.1
3	Spud Chandler, 1946	257.1
4	Vic Raschi, 1950	256.2
5	Whitey Ford, 1955	253.2
6	Spud Chandler, 1943	253.0
7	Hank Borowy, 1944	252.2
1921–42		
1	Carl Mays, 1921	336.2
2	George Pipgras, 1928	300.2
3	Bob Shawkey, 1922	299.2
4	Herb Pennock, 1924	286.1
5	Waite Hoyt, 1921	282.1
6	Lefty Gomez, 1934	281.2
7	Lefty Gomez, 1937	278.1
1901–20		
1	Jack Chesbro, 1904	454.2
2	Jack Powell, 1904	390.1
3	Al Orth, 1906	338.2
4	Jack Chesbro, 1906	325.0
5	Jack Chesbro, 1903	324.2
6	Carl Mays, 1920	312.0
7	Al Orth, 1905	305.1

FEWEST HITS/9 INNINGS

1	Tommy Byrne, 1949	5.74
2	Russ Ford, 1910	5.83
3	Al Downing, 1963	5.84
4	Bob Turley, 1957	6.12
5	Bob Turley, 1955	6.13
6	Ron Guidry, 1978	6.15
7	Spec Shea, 1947	6.40
8	Ray Caldwell, 1914	6.46
9	Bob Turley, 1958	6.53
10	Bob Shawkey, 1916	6.64
11	Don Larsen, 1956	6.66
12	Whitey Ford, 1955	6.67
13	Jack Chesbro, 1904	6.69
14	Spec Shea, 1948	6.76
15	Catfish Hunter, 1975	6.80
16	Jim Bouton, 1963	6.89
17	Art Ditmar, 1959	6.95
18	Allie Reynolds, 1951	6.96
19	Spud Chandler, 1946	6.99
20	Spud Chandler, 1943	7.01
21	Vic Raschi, 1952	7.02
22	Al Downing, 1967	7.05
23	Ron Guidry, 1981	7.09
24	Lefty Gomez, 1934	7.13
25	Dennis Rasmussen, 1986	7.13
26	Whitey Ford, 1958	7.14
27	Allie Reynolds, 1952	7.15
28	David Cone, 1997	7.15
29	Bob Turley, 1960	7.17
30	Ray Caldwell, 1913	7.17
31	Butch Wensloff, 1943	7.21
32	Allan Russell, 1916	7.25
33	Whitey Ford, 1954	7.26
34	Stan Bahnsen, 1968	7.27
35	Jack Warhop, 1909	7.29
36	Rudy May, 1980	7.39
37	Hank Thormahlen, 1919	7.39
38	Al Downing, 1964	7.41
39	Ron Guidry, 1977	7.43
40	Whitey Ford, 1956	7.46
41	Vic Raschi, 1953	7.46
42	Bill Hogg, 1906	7.47
43	Bob Shawkey, 1919	7.51
44	Joe Lake, 1909	7.52
45	Jim Bouton, 1964	7.53
46	Lefty Gomez, 1937	7.53
47	Fritz Peterson, 1969	7.54
48	Jack Warhop, 1914	7.56
49	Tom Sturdivant, 1957	7.59
50	Ray Caldwell, 1917	7.59

FEWEST HITS/9 INNINGS BY ERA

1988–2007		
1	David Cone, 1997	7.15
2	David Cone, 1999	7.63
3	Hideki Irabu, 1998	7.70
4	Melido Perez, 1992	7.70
5	Orlando Hernandez, 1999	7.85
6	**Mike Mussina, 2001**	**7.95**
7	Melido Perez, 1994	7.97
1973–87		
1	Ron Guidry, 1978	6.15
2	Catfish Hunter, 1975	6.80
3	Ron Guidry, 1981	7.09
4	Dennis Rasmussen, 1986	7.13
5	Rudy May, 1980	7.39
6	Ron Guidry, 1977	7.43
7	Rudy May, 1975	7.60
1961–72		
1	Al Downing, 1963	5.84
2	Jim Bouton, 1963	6.89
3	Al Downing, 1967	7.05
4	Stan Bahnsen, 1968	7.27
5	Al Downing, 1964	7.41
6	Jim Bouton, 1964	7.53
7	Fritz Peterson, 1969	7.54
1943–60		
1	Tommy Byrne, 1949	5.74
2	Bob Turley, 1957	6.12
3	Bob Turley, 1955	6.13
4	Spec Shea, 1947	6.40
5	Bob Turley, 1958	6.53
6	Don Larsen, 1956	6.66
7	Whitey Ford, 1955	6.67
1921–42		
1	Lefty Gomez, 1934	7.13
2	Lefty Gomez, 1937	7.53
3	Johnny Allen, 1932	7.59
4	Red Ruffing, 1932	7.61
5	Lefty Gomez, 1931	7.63
6	Monte Pearson, 1936	7.71
7	Bump Hadley, 1939	7.71
1901–20		
1	Russ Ford, 1910	5.83
2	Ray Caldwell, 1914	6.46
3	Bob Shawkey, 1916	6.64
4	Jack Chesbro, 1904	6.69
5	Ray Caldwell, 1913	7.17
6	Allan Russell, 1916	7.25
7	Jack Warhop, 1909	7.29

WALKS

1 Tommy Byrne, 1949 179
2 Bob Turley, 1955 177
3 Tommy Byrne, 1950 160
4 Vic Raschi, 1949 138
Allie Reynolds, 1950 138
6 Monte Pearson, 1936 135
7 Bob Turley, 1958 128
8 Allie Reynolds, 1947 123
Allie Reynolds, 1949 123
10 Lefty Gomez, 1936 122
11 Al Downing, 1964 120
Phil Niekro, 1985 120
13 Joe Bush, 1923 117
14 Slim Love, 1918 116
Vic Raschi, 1950 116
16 Red Ruffing, 1932 115
17 Monte Pearson, 1938 113
Whitey Ford, 1955 113
19 Allie Reynolds, 1948 111
20 Whitey Ford, 1953 110
21 Joe Bush, 1924 109
22 Dave Righetti, 1982 108
23 Ray Caldwell, 1915 107
24 Lefty Gomez, 1933 106
25 Lefty Gomez, 1932 105
Al Downing, 1965 105
27 Sam Jones, 1925 104
Hank Johnson, 1928 104
Hank Johnson, 1930 104
Red Ruffing, 1934 104
31 George Pipgras, 1928 103
Lefty Gomez, 1941 103
Vic Raschi, 1951 103
Bob Turley, 1956 103
35 Bob Shawkey, 1923 102
Hank Johnson, 1931 102
Bill Burbach, 1969 102
38 Bill Hogg, 1905 101
Tommy Byrne, 1948 101
Whitey Ford, 1954 101
41 Allie Reynolds, 1951 100
42 Lefty Gomez, 1938 99
Rudy May, 1975 99
44 Bob Shawkey, 1922 98
45 Allie Reynolds, 1952 97
Mel Stottlemyre, 1969 97
47 Lefty Gomez, 1934 96
Don Larsen, 1956 96
49 George Pipgras, 1929 95
50 Ed Figueroa, 1976 94

FEWEST WALKS/9 INNINGS

1 David Wells, 2003 .... 0.85
2 Jon Lieber, 2004 .... 0.92
3 Tiny Bonham, 1942 .... 0.96
4 Tiny Bonham, 1945 .... 1.10
5 Herb Pennock, 1930 .... 1.15
6 David Wells, 1998 .... 1.22
7 Fritz Peterson, 1968 .... 1.23
8 Scott Sanderson, 1991 .... 1.25
9 Jesse Tannehill, 1903 .... 1.28
10 Ralph Terry, 1963 .... 1.31
11 Fritz Peterson, 1971 .... 1.38
12 Fritz Peterson, 1970 .... 1.38
13 Clark Griffith, 1903 .... 1.39
14 Fritz Peterson, 1969 .... 1.42
15 Herb Pennock, 1931 .... 1.43
16 Herb Pennock, 1926 .... 1.45
17 Ron Guidry, 1985 .... 1.46
18 Steve Kline, 1971 .... 1.50
19 Marty McHale, 1914 .... 1.55
20 Barney Wolfe, 1903 .... 1.58
21 Fritz Peterson, 1972 .... 1.58
22 **Mike Mussina, 2006 .... 1.60**
23 Herb Pennock, 1929 .... 1.60
24 Ed Lopat, 1953 .... 1.61
25 George Mogridge, 1918 .... 1.62
26 Jimmy Key, 1993 .... 1.64
27 **Mike Mussina, 2001 .... 1.65**
28 Fritz Peterson, 1966 .... 1.67
29 Steve Kline, 1972 .... 1.68
30 **Mike Mussina, 2003 .... 1.68**
31 Jack Quinn, 1920 .... 1.71
32 Herb Pennock, 1928 .... 1.71
33 Ralph Terry, 1962 .... 1.72
34 Nick Cullop, 1916 .... 1.72
35 Tiny Bonham, 1944 .... 1.73
36 Jack Chesbro, 1904 .... 1.74
37 Ed Lopat, 1954 .... 1.75
38 Al Orth, 1906 .... 1.75
39 Ron Guidry, 1986 .... 1.78
40 George Mogridge, 1917 .... 1.79
41 Al Orth, 1905 .... 1.80
42 Jack Warhop, 1914 .... 1.83
43 **Andy Pettitte, 2001 .... 1.84**
44 Whitey Ford, 1965 .... 1.84
45 Ron Guidry, 1981 .... 1.84
46 Urban Shocker, 1927 .... 1.85
47 David Wells, 1997 .... 1.86
48 Whitey Ford, 1963 .... 1.87
49 Randy Johnson, 2005 .... 1.87
50 Carl Mays, 1922 .... 1.88

STRIKEOUTS

1 Ron Guidry, 1978 248
2 Jack Chesbro, 1904 239
3 David Cone, 1997 222
4 Melido Perez, 1992 218
5 Al Downing, 1964 217
6 **Mike Mussina, 2001 .... 214**
7 **Roger Clemens, 2001 .... 213**
8 Randy Johnson, 2005 211
9 Bob Turley, 1955 210
10 Russ Ford, 1910 209
Whitey Ford, 1961 209
David Cone, 1998 209
13 Jack Powell, 1904 202
14 Ron Guidry, 1979 201
15 **Mike Mussina, 2003 .... 195**
16 Lefty Gomez, 1937 194
17 **Roger Clemens, 2002 .... 192**
18 Red Ruffing, 1932 190
Roger Clemens, 2003 190
20 Whitey Ford, 1963 189
21 **Roger Clemens, 2000 .... 188**
22 **Mike Mussina, 2002 .... 182**
23 **Andy Pettitte, 2003 .... 180**
24 Al Downing, 1965 179
25 Catfish Hunter, 1975 177
David Cone, 1999 177
27 Lefty Gomez, 1932 176
Ralph Terry, 1962 176
Ron Guidry, 1977 176
30 Catfish Hunter, 1976 173
Jimmy Key, 1993 173
32 Whitey Ford, 1964 172
Randy Johnson, 2006 172
Mike Mussina, 2006 172
35 Al Downing, 1963 171
Al Downing, 1967 171
37 Dave Righetti, 1983 169
38 Bob Turley, 1958 168
39 Ron Guidry, 1980 166
Andy Pettitte, 1997 166
41 Vic Raschi, 1951 164
Andy Pettitte, 2001 164
43 Lefty Gomez, 1933 163
Dave Righetti, 1982 163
David Wells, 1998 163
Roger Clemens, 1999 163
47 Whitey Ford, 1965 162
Stan Bahnsen, 1968 162
Ron Guidry, 1982 162
Andy Pettitte, 1996 162

STRIKEOUTS/9 INNINGS

1 David Cone, 1997 .... 10.25
2 **Roger Clemens, 2002 .... 9.60**
3 David Cone, 1998 .... 9.06
4 Al Downing, 1963 .... 8.76
5 **Roger Clemens, 2001 .... 8.70**
6 **Mike Mussina, 2001 .... 8.42**
7 Randy Johnson, 2005 .... 8.42
8 **Roger Clemens, 2000 .... 8.28**
9 David Cone, 1999 .... 8.24
10 **Mike Mussina, 2003 .... 8.18**
11 Melido Perez, 1993 .... 8.17
12 Ron Guidry, 1978 .... 8.16
13 **Roger Clemens, 2003 .... 8.08**
14 Dave Righetti, 1982 .... 8.02
15 Al Downing, 1964 .... 8.00
16 Melido Perez, 1992 .... 7.92
17 **Mike Mussina, 2006 .... 7.84**
18 **Roger Clemens, 1999 .... 7.82**
19 **Andy Pettitte, 2003 .... 7.78**
20 Bob Turley, 1957 .... 7.76
21 Bob Turley, 1955 .... 7.66
22 Ron Guidry, 1979 .... 7.65
23 Al Downing, 1967 .... 7.63
24 Al Downing, 1965 .... 7.60
25 **Mike Mussina, 2002 .... 7.60**
26 Randy Johnson, 2006 .... 7.55
27 Ron Guidry, 1977 .... 7.52
28 Ron Guidry, 1981 .... 7.37
29 **Andy Pettitte, 2001 .... 7.36**
30 **Mike Mussina, 2004 .... 7.21**
31 **Mike Mussina, 2005 .... 7.11**
32 Hideki Irabu, 1999 .... 7.07
33 Dave Righetti, 1983 .... 7.01
34 David Wells, 1998 .... 6.84
35 Al Downing, 1966 .... 6.84
36 Rudy May, 1980 .... 6.83
37 Javier Vazquez, 2004 .... 6.82
38 Ron Guidry, 1980 .... 6.80
39 Whitey Ford, 1961 .... 6.65
40 Doc Gooden, 1996 .... 6.64
41 Red Ruffing, 1932 .... 6.60
42 **Andy Pettitte, 1996 .... 6.60**
43 Orlando Hernandez, 1999 .... 6.59
44 Jimmy Key, 1993 .... 6.58
45 Ron Guidry, 1982 .... 6.57
46 Hideki Irabu, 1998 .... 6.55
47 Ron Guidry, 1986 .... 6.55
48 Jack McDowell, 1995 .... 6.49
49 Orlando Hernandez, 2000 .... 6.49
50 Melido Perez, 1994 .... 6.48

EARNED RUN AVERAGE

1 Spud Chandler, 1943 .... 1.64
2 Russ Ford, 1910 .... 1.65
3 Ron Guidry, 1978 .... 1.74
4 Jack Chesbro, 1904 .... 1.82
5 Hippo Vaughn, 1910 .... 1.83
6 Joe Lake, 1909 .... 1.88
7 Ray Caldwell, 1914 .... 1.94
8 Whitey Ford, 1958 .... 2.01
9 Nick Cullop, 1916 .... 2.05
10 Stan Bahnsen, 1968 .... 2.05
11 Allie Reynolds, 1952 .... 2.06
12 Spud Chandler, 1946 .... 2.10
13 Ray Fisher, 1915 .... 2.11
14 Lew Brockett, 1909 .... 2.12
15 Whitey Ford, 1964 .... 2.13
16 George Mogridge, 1918 .... 2.18
17 Jack Chesbro, 1905 .... 2.20
18 Bob Shawkey, 1916 .... 2.21
19 Bill Bevens, 1946 .... 2.23
20 Tiny Bonham, 1942 .... 2.27
21 Russ Ford, 1911 .... 2.27
22 Tiny Bonham, 1943 .... 2.27
23 Wilcy Moore, 1927 .... 2.28
24 Ray Fisher, 1914 .... 2.28
25 George Mogridge, 1916 .... 2.31
26 Lefty Gomez, 1937 .... 2.33
27 Lefty Gomez, 1934 .... 2.33
28 Al Orth, 1906 .... 2.34
29 Jack Warhop, 1914 .... 2.37
30 Jack Quinn, 1910 .... 2.37
31 Spud Chandler, 1942 .... 2.38
32 Steve Kline, 1972 .... 2.40
33 Jack Warhop, 1909 .... 2.40
34 Ray Caldwell, 1913 .... 2.41
35 Ed Lopat, 1953 .... 2.42
36 Bob Shawkey, 1917 .... 2.44
37 Jack Powell, 1904 .... 2.44
38 Bobby Shantz, 1957 .... 2.45
39 Bob Shawkey, 1920 .... 2.45
Mel Stottlemyre, 1968 .... 2.45
41 Rudy May, 1980 .... 2.46
42 Whitey Ford, 1956 .... 2.47
43 Hank Borowy, 1942 .... 2.52
44 Jim Bouton, 1963 .... 2.53
45 Jack Chesbro, 1907 .... 2.53
46 Butch Wensloff, 1943 .... 2.54
47 Tom Sturdivant, 1957 .... 2.54
48 Fritz Peterson, 1969 .... 2.55
49 Herb Pennock, 1928 .... 2.56
50 Al Downing, 1963 .... 2.56

EARNED RUN AVERAGE BY ERA

1988–2007

1 David Cone, 1997 .... 2.82
2 Melido Perez, 1992 .... 2.87
3 **Andy Pettitte, 1997 .... 2.88**
4 Jimmy Key, 1993 .... 3.00
5 **Mike Mussina, 2001 .... 3.15**
6 Jimmy Key, 1994 .... 3.27
7 **Mike Mussina, 2003 .... 3.40**

1973–87

1 Ron Guidry, 1978 .... 1.74
2 Rudy May, 1980 .... 2.46
3 Catfish Hunter, 1975 .... 2.58
4 Tommy John, 1981 .... 2.63
5 Ron Guidry, 1981 .... 2.76
6 Ron Guidry, 1979 .... 2.78
7 Ron Guidry, 1977 .... 2.82

1961–72

1 Stan Bahnsen, 1968 .... 2.05
2 Whitey Ford, 1964 .... 2.13
3 Steve Kline, 1972 .... 2.40
4 Mel Stottlemyre, 1968 .... 2.45
5 Jim Bouton, 1963 .... 2.53
6 Fritz Peterson, 1969 .... 2.55
7 Al Downing, 1963 .... 2.56

1943–60

1 Spud Chandler, 1943 .... 1.64
2 Whitey Ford, 1958 .... 2.01
3 Allie Reynolds, 1952 .... 2.06
4 Spud Chandler, 1946 .... 2.10
5 Bill Bevens, 1946 .... 2.23
6 Tiny Bonham, 1943 .... 2.27
7 Ed Lopat, 1953 .... 2.42

1921–42

1 Tiny Bonham, 1942 .... 2.27
2 Wilcy Moore, 1927 .... 2.28
3 Lefty Gomez, 1937 .... 2.33
4 Lefty Gomez, 1934 .... 2.33
5 Spud Chandler, 1942 .... 2.38
6 Hank Borowy, 1942 .... 2.52
7 Herb Pennock, 1928 .... 2.56

1901–20

1 Russ Ford, 1910 .... 1.65
2 Jack Chesbro, 1904 .... 1.82
3 Hippo Vaughn, 1910 .... 1.83
4 Joe Lake, 1909 .... 1.88
5 Ray Caldwell, 1914 .... 1.94
6 Nick Cullop, 1916 .... 2.05
7 Ray Fisher, 1915 .... 2.11

ADJUSTED EARNED RUN AVERAGE

1 Ron Guidry, 1978 210
2 Spud Chandler, 1943 197
3 Lefty Gomez, 1937 191
4 Whitey Ford, 1958 176
5 Lefty Gomez, 1934 174
6 Whitey Ford, 1964 170
7 Wilcy Moore, 1927 169
8 Spud Chandler, 1946 164
9 Allie Reynolds, 1952 .... [illegible]
10 Russ Ford, 1910 161
11 Rudy May, 1980 161
12 Russ Ford, 1911 158
13 David Cone, 1997 158
14 Whitey Ford, 1956 156
15 Bob Shawkey, 1920 156
16 **Andy Pettitte, 1997 .... 154**
17 Bill Bevens, 1946 154
18 Ed Lopat, 1953 152
19 Tiny Bonham, 1942 152
20 Red Ruffing, 1937 149
21 Jack Chesbro, 1904 149
22 Lefty Gomez, 1931 149
23 Red Ruffing, 1939 149
24 Ron Guidry, 1979 148
25 Herb Pennock, 1924 147
26 Herb Pennock, 1928 147
27 Bobby Shantz, 1957 147
28 Waite Hoyt, 1927 146
29 Bump Hadley, 1939 146
30 Hippo Vaughn, 1910 145
31 Spud Chandler, 1942 145
32 Herb Pennock, 1925 144
33 Catfish Hunter, 1975 144
34 Whitey Ford, 1955 143
35 Ray Caldwell, 1914 142
36 Stan Bahnsen, 1968 142
37 Tiny Bonham, 1943 142
38 Nick Cullop, 1916 141
39 **Mike Mussina, 2001 .... 141**
40 Tom Sturdivant, 1957 141
41 Jimmy Key, 1994 141
42 Ron Guidry, 1977 141
43 Jimmy Key, 1993 139
44 Ray Fisher, 1915 139
45 Jim Bouton, 1963 139
46 Tommy John, 1979 139
47 Carl Mays, 1921 139
48 Bill Stafford, 1961 139
49 Fritz Peterson, 1969 138
50 Melido Perez, 1992 138

ADJUSTED PITCHING WINS

1 Lefty Gomez, 1937 .... 7.0
2 Ron Guidry, 1978 .... 6.4
3 Lefty Gomez, 1934 .... 5.9
4 Jack Chesbro, 1904 .... 5.1
5 Wilcy Moore, 1927 .... 4.8
6 Bob Shawkey, 1920 .... 4.7
7 Catfish Hunter, 1975 .... 4.7
8 Spud Chandler, 1943 .... 4.3
9 Spud Chandler, 1946 .... 4.3
10 Carl Mays, 1921 .... 4.2
11 Allie Reynolds, 1952 .... 4.2
12 Herb Pennock, 1924 .... 4.2
13 Red Ruffing, 1939 .... 4.0
14 Whitey Ford, 1956 .... 4.0
15 Red Ruffing, 1937 .... 4.0
16 Bill Bevens, 1946 .... 4.0
17 Lefty Gomez, 1931 .... 4.0
18 **Andy Pettitte, 1997 .... 4.0**
19 Waite Hoyt, 1927 .... 3.9
20 Russ Ford, 1910 .... 3.9
21 Herb Pennock, 1925 .... 3.8
22 Whitey Ford, 1964 .... 3.7
23 **Mike Mussina, 2001 .... 3.7**
24 Bob Shawkey, 1922 .... 3.7
25 Ron Guidry, 1979 .... 3.7
26 Whitey Ford, 1958 .... 3.6
27 Red Ruffing, 1938 .... 3.6
28 Bob Shawkey, 1916 .... 3.6
29 Waite Hoyt, 1921 .... 3.6
30 Tiny Bonham, 1942 .... 3.5
31 Lefty Gomez, 1938 .... 3.3
32 Russ Ford, 1911 .... 3.3
33 Whitey Ford, 1955 .... 3.2
34 Fritz Peterson, 1969 .... 3.2
35 Herb Pennock, 1928 .... 3.2
36 Rudy May, 1980 .... 3.2
37 Tommy John, 1979 .... 3.2
38 Jimmy Key, 1993 .... 3.1
39 Ed Lopat, 1951 .... 3.1
40 Stan Bahnsen, 1968 .... 3.1
41 David Cone, 1997 .... 3.0
42 Carl Mays, 1920 .... 3.0
43 Jim Bouton, 1963 .... 3.0
44 Melido Perez, 1992 .... 2.9
45 Ron Guidry, 1977 .... 2.9
46 Red Ruffing, 1935 .... 2.9
47 Tiny Bonham, 1940 .... 2.9
48 Mel Stottlemyre, 1969 .... 2.9
49 Al Orth, 1906 .... 2.8
50 **Andy Pettitte, 1996 .... 2.8**

OPPONENT BATTING AVERAGE

1 Tommy Byrne, 1949 .... .183
2 Al Downing, 1963 .... .184
3 Russ Ford, 1910 .... .188
4 Bob Turley, 1955 .... .193
5 Ron Guidry, 1978 .... .193
6 Bob Turley, 1957 .... .194
7 Spec Shea, 1947 .... .200
8 Don Larsen, 1956 .... .204
9 Ray Caldwell, 1914 .... .205
10 Bob Turley, 1958 .... .206
11 Whitey Ford, 1955 .... .208
12 Jack Chesbro, 1904 .... .208
13 Spec Shea, 1948 .... .208
14 Catfish Hunter, 1975 .... .208
15 Bob Shawkey, 1916 .... .209
16 Art Ditmar, 1959 .... .211
17 Jim Bouton, 1963 .... .212
18 Allie Reynolds, 1951 .... .213
19 Ron Guidry, 1981 .... .214
20 Spud Chandler, 1943 .... .215
21 Lefty Gomez, 1934 .... .215
22 Vic Raschi, 1952 .... .216
23 Al Downing, 1967 .... .217
24 Dennis Rasmussen, 1986 .... .217
25 Whitey Ford, 1958 .... .217
26 Spud Chandler, 1946 .... .218
27 Allie Reynolds, 1952 .... .218
28 David Cone, 1997 .... .218
29 Butch Wensloff, 1943 .... .219
30 Stan Bahnsen, 1968 .... .221
31 Ray Caldwell, 1913 .... .221
32 Bob Turley, 1960 .... .222
33 Al Downing, 1964 .... .223
34 Lefty Gomez, 1937 .... .223
35 Vic Raschi, 1953 .... .224
36 Ron Guidry, 1977 .... .224
37 Rudy May, 1980 .... .224
38 Tom Sturdivant, 1956 .... .224
39 Jim Bouton, 1964 .... .225
40 Joe Lake, 1909 .... .225
41 Lefty Gomez, 1931 .... .226
42 Red Ruffing, 1932 .... .226
43 Whitey Ford, 1954 .... .227
44 Allie Reynolds, 1947 .... .227
45 Johnny Allen, 1932 .... .228
46 Hank Thormahlen, 1919 .... .228
47 Whitey Ford, 1956 .... .228
48 Fritz Peterson, 1969 .... .229
49 Bill Hogg, 1906 .... .229
50 Dave Righetti, 1982 .... .229

OPPONENT ON-BASE PCT.

1 Russ Ford, 1910 .... .245
2 Ron Guidry, 1978 .... .250
3 Jack Chesbro, 1904 .... .252
4 Ron Guidry, 1981 .... .257
5 Tiny Bonham, 1942 .... .259
6 Ray Caldwell, 1914 .... .260
7 Spud Chandler, 1943 .... .261
8 Fritz Peterson, 1969 .... .263
9 Catfish Hunter, 1975 .... .263
10 David Wells, 1998 .... .266
11 Rudy May, 1980 .... .268
12 Art Ditmar, 1959 .... .270
13 Ralph Terry, 1962 .... .270
14 Fritz Peterson, 1968 .... .272
15 Stan Bahnsen, 1968 .... .273
16 Ralph Terry, 1963 .... .273
17 Jim Bouton, 1964 .... .273
18 Bob Shawkey, 1916 .... .273
19 Whitey Ford, 1958 .... .276
20 Steve Kline, 1971 .... .276
21 **Mike Mussina, 2001 .... .276**
22 Whitey Ford, 1964 .... .276
23 **Mike Mussina, 2003 .... .276**
24 Ralph Terry, 1961 .... .277
25 Al Downing, 1963 .... .277
26 Ron Guidry, 1985 .... .279
27 Fritz Peterson, 1966 .... .279
28 **Mike Mussina, 2006 .... .279**
29 Fritz Peterson, 1970 .... .280
30 Scott Sanderson, 1991 .... .281
31 Steve Kline, 1972 .... .281
32 Mel Stottlemyre, 1968 .... .281
33 Butch Wensloff, 1943 .... .282
34 Tiny Bonham, 1943 .... .282
35 Jimmy Key, 1993 .... .282
36 Lefty Gomez, 1934 .... .282
37 Whitey Ford, 1963 .... .283
38 Joe Lake, 1909 .... .283
39 Al Downing, 1967 .... .283
40 Clark Griffith, 1903 .... .283
41 Vic Raschi, 1953 .... .283
42 Nick Cullop, 1916 .... .284
43 Jim Bouton, 1963 .... .284
44 Ron Guidry, 1977 .... .284
45 Al Orth, 1905 .... .284
46 Jack Chesbro, 1905 .... .284
47 Mel Stottlemyre, 1971 .... .285
48 Jack Warhop, 1914 .... .286
49 Jack Powell, 1904 .... .286
50 Catfish Hunter, 1976 .... .286

RELIEF WINS
1 Luis Arroyo, 1961 15
2 Joe Page, 1947 14
Ron Davis, 1979................14
4 Joe Page, 1949 13
Sparky Lyle, 1977.............13
Rich Gossage, 1983.........13
7 Johnny Murphy, 1937.......12
Johnny Murphy, 1943.......12
Bob Grim, 1957 12
Lindy McDaniel, 1973.......12
Dave Righetti, 1985..........12
12 Lee Guetterman, 1990 11
13 Rich Gossage, 1978.........10
14 Lindy McDaniel, 1970..........9
Sparky Lyle, 1972..............9
Sparky Lyle, 1974..............9
Sparky Lyle, 1978..............9
Ron Davis, 1980.................9
Brian Fisher, 1986..............9
Mike Stanton, 2001 9
Tom Gordon, 2004.............9
22 Many players tied 8

RELIEF LOSSES
1 Rich Gossage, 1978......... 11
2 Johnny Murphy, 1942.......10
Lindy McDaniel, 1971.......10
4 Sparky Lyle, 1973...............9
5 Joe Page, 1948 8
Joe Page, 1949 8
Bob Grim, 1957 8
Pedro Ramos, 1966 8
Sparky Lyle, 1976...............8
Dave Righetti, 1986............8
11 Joe Page, 1947 7
Joe Page, 1950 7
Tom Morgan, 1956 7
Hal Reniff, 1966..................7
Dooley Womack, 1968 7
Sparky Lyle, 1975...............7
Rich Bordi, 1985.................7
Dave Righetti, 1985............7
Lee Guetterman, 1990 7
Jeff Nelson, 1997 7
21 Many players tied 6

RELIEF GAMES
1 Paul Quantrill, 2004..........86
2 Scott Proctor, 2006...........83
3 Tom Gordon, 2004.............80
4 Mike Stanton, 2002 79
Tom Gordon, 2005.............79
6 Steve Karsay, 2002 78
7 Jeff Nelson, 1997 77
Luis Vizcaino, 2007 77
9 Mike Stanton, 2001 76
10 Dave Righetti, 1985..........74
Dave Righetti, 1986..........74
Mariano Rivera, 2004......74
13 Jeff Nelson, 1996 73
Jeff Nelson, 2000 73
15 Sparky Lyle, 1977.............72
Mike Stanton, 1999 72
Kyle Farnsworth, 2006.............72
18 Mariano Rivera, 2001......71
Mariano Rivera, 2005......71
20 Lee Guetterman, 1989 70
Ron Villone, 2006............70
22 Mike Stanton, 2000 69
23 Mike Stanton, 1998 67
Mariano Rivera, 2007......67

RELIEF INNINGS PITCHED
1 Lindy McDaniel, 1973.. 138.1
2 Sparky Lyle, 1977......... 137.0
3 Joe Page, 1949.......... 135.1
4 Rich Gossage, 1978...... 134.1
5 Joe Page, 1947 .... 134.0
6 Ron Davis, 1980.......... 131.0
7 Luis Arroyo, 1961 .... 119.0
8 George Frazier, 1983 .. 115.1
9 Sparky Lyle, 1974........ 114.0
10 Lindy McDaniel, 1970.. 112.0
11 Sparky Lyle, 1978........ 111.2
George Frazier, 1982 .. 111.2
13 Sparky Lyle, 1972......... 107.2
Mariano Rivera, 1996....... 107.2
15 Dave Righetti, 1985...... 107.0
Neil Allen, 1988 .... 107.0
17 Dave Righetti, 1986..... 106.2
18 Dick Tidrow, 1977........ 104.1
19 Sparky Lyle, 1976......... 103.2
20 Lee Guetterman, 1989....... 103.0
21 Scott Proctor, 2006...... 102.1
22 Joe Page, 1948 .... 102.0
23 Rich Gossage, 1980...... 99.0
24 Jay Howell, 1984........... 98.2

ADJUSTED RELIEVER RUNS
1 Mariano Rivera, 1996... 34.6
2 Sparky Lyle, 1977.......... 28.1
3 Mariano Rivera, 2005... 25.8
4 Rich Gossage, 1978...... 25.4
5 Sparky Lyle, 1974.......... 24.5
6 Tom Gordon, 2004......... 24.0
7 Mariano Rivera, 2004... 23.4
8 Mariano Rivera, 2006... 23.2
9 Mariano Rivera, 1999... 22.9
10 Joe Page, 1949 .... 22.7
11 Mariano Rivera, 2003... 22.2
12 Luis Arroyo, 1961 .... 21.8
13 Joe Page, 1947 .... 21.6
14 Mariano Rivera, 1997... 21.0
15 Lindy McDaniel, 1970.... 20.2
Dave Righetti, 1986........ 20.2
17 Rich Gossage, 1980...... 19.0
Mariano Rivera, 2001... 19.0
19 Rich Gossage, 1982...... 18.9
20 Brian Fisher, 1985......... 18.7
21 Fred Beene, 1973........... 18.6
22 Jeff Nelson, 2000 .... 18.5
23 John Habyan, 1991 .... 18.4
24 Mariano Rivera, 1998... 17.9

RELIEF RANKING
1 Mariano Rivera, 2005... 51.6
2 Rich Gossage, 1978...... 47.2
3 Mariano Rivera, 2006... 46.4
4 Mariano Rivera, 2004... 46.2
5 Mariano Rivera, 1999... 45.8
6 Sparky Lyle, 1977.......... 45.3
7 Luis Arroyo, 1961 .... 43.6
8 Mariano Rivera, 2003... 43.3
9 Mariano Rivera, 1997... 42.0
10 Joe Page, 1949 .... 41.8
11 Dave Righetti, 1986....... 40.5
12 Mariano Rivera, 2001... 38.0
13 Joe Page, 1947 .... 36.7
14 Mariano Rivera, 1996... 34.8
15 Rich Gossage, 1983....... 33.7
16 Tom Gordon, 2004......... 33.4
17 Mariano Rivera, 2000... 33.3
18 Lindy McDaniel, 1970.... 32.6
19 Dave Righetti, 1985........ 31.0
20 Sparky Lyle, 1974.......... 30.4
21 Johnny Murphy, 1941 .... 30.4
22 John Wetteland, 1996 .... 30.2
23 Rich Gossage, 1982....... 29.9
24 Jeff Nelson, 2000 .... 28.7

PITCHER WINS
1 Lefty Gomez, 1937.......... 6.8
2 Ron Guidry, 1978 .... 6.4
3 Jack Chesbro, 1904 .... 6.1
4 Lefty Gomez, 1934......... 5.5
5 Carl Mays, 1921 .... 5.4
6 Spud Chandler, 1943....... 5.3
7 Mariano Rivera, 2004..... 4.9
Mariano Rivera, 2005..... 4.9
9 Red Ruffing, 1939 .... 4.8
10 Mariano Rivera, 2006..... 4.7
11 Bob Shawkey, 1920......... 4.6
Whitey Ford, 1956 .... 4.6
13 Wilcy Moore, 1927........... 4.5
Red Ruffing, 1938 .... 4.5
Spud Chandler, 1946........ 4.5
Mariano Rivera, 1999..... 4.5
17 Luis Arroyo, 1961 .... 4.4
Catfish Hunter, 1975........ 4.4
19 Sparky Lyle, 1977............ 4.3
Rich Gossage, 1978......... 4.3
Mariano Rivera, 2003..... 4.3
22 Russ Ford, 1910.............. 4.2
Red Ruffing, 1935 .... 4.2
Dave Righetti, 1986.......... 4.2
25 Allie Reynolds, 1952........ 4.1
Andy Pettitte, 1997 .... 4.1
Mariano Rivera, 1997..... 4.1
28 Red Ruffing, 1932 .... 4.0
Red Ruffing, 1937 .... 4.0
Joe Page, 1949 .... 4.0
31 Red Ruffing, 1936 .... 3.9
Whitey Ford, 1958 .... 3.9
Whitey Ford, 1964 .... 3.9
34 Herb Pennock, 1924......... 3.8
Waite Hoyt, 1927 .... 3.8
Mel Stottlemyre, 1969 ..... 3.8
Mariano Rivera, 2001..... 3.8
38 Mike Mussina, 2001 .... 3.7
39 Lefty Gomez, 1931 .... 3.6
Ron Guidry, 1979 .... 3.6
41 Carl Mays, 1920 .... 3.5
Lindy McDaniel, 1970....... 3.5
43 Al Orth, 1906 .... 3.4
Bob Shawkey, 1916.......... 3.4
Whitey Ford, 1955 .... 3.4
Fritz Peterson, 1969 .... 3.4
47 Many players tied 3.3

PITCHER WINS BY ERA

1988–2007
1 Mariano Rivera, 2004..... 4.9
Mariano Rivera, 2005..... 4.9
3 Mariano Rivera, 2006..... 4.7
4 Mariano Rivera, 1999..... 4.5
5 Mariano Rivera, 2003..... 4.3
6 Andy Pettitte, 1997 .... 4.1
Mariano Rivera, 1997..... 4.1
8 Mariano Rivera, 2001..... 3.8
9 Mike Mussina, 2001 .... 3.7
10 Mariano Rivera, 1996..... 3.3
Tom Gordon, 2004........... 3.3
12 Mariano Rivera, 2000..... 3.2
13 Jimmy Key, 1993 .... 3.1
14 Steve Farr, 1991 .... 2.9
Melido Perez, 1992 .... 2.9
Jimmy Key, 1994 .... 2.9
David Cone, 1997............ 2.9

1973–87
1 Ron Guidry, 1978 .... 6.4
2 Catfish Hunter, 1975........ 4.4
3 Sparky Lyle, 1977............ 4.3
Rich Gossage, 1978......... 4.3
5 Dave Righetti, 1986.......... 4.2
6 Ron Guidry, 1979 .... 3.6
7 Tommy John, 1979.......... 3.3
8 Rudy May, 1980 .... 3.2
Rich Gossage, 1982......... 3.2
Dave Righetti, 1985.......... 3.2
11 Rich Gossage, 1983......... 3.1
12 Rich Gossage, 1981......... 3.0
13 Sparky Lyle, 1974............ 2.9
Ron Guidry, 1977 .... 2.9

1961–72
1 Luis Arroyo, 1961 .... 4.4
2 Whitey Ford, 1964 .... 3.9
3 Mel Stottlemyre, 1969 ..... 3.8
4 Lindy McDaniel, 1970....... 3.5
5 Fritz Peterson, 1969......... 3.4
6 Sparky Lyle, 1972............ 3.1
7 Bill Stafford, 1961 .... 2.8
Mel Stottlemyre, 1965 ..... 2.8
Fritz Peterson, 1970......... 2.8
10 Whitey Ford, 1962 .... 2.7

1943–60
1 Spud Chandler, 1943....... 5.3
2 Whitey Ford, 1956 .... 4.6
3 Spud Chandler, 1946........ 4.5
4 Allie Reynolds, 1952........ 4.1
5 Joe Page, 1949 .... 4.0
6 Whitey Ford, 1958 .... 3.9
7 Whitey Ford, 1955 .... 3.4
8 Joe Page, 1947 .... 3.3
Ed Lopat, 1951 .... 3.3
10 Bill Bevens, 1946............. 3.2
11 Ed Lopat, 1953 .... 2.9
12 Bobby Shantz, 1957 .... 2.7
13 Ed Lopat, 1949 .... 2.6
Tom Sturdivant, 1957 .... 2.6
Ryne Duren, 1958 .... 2.6
Whitey Ford, 1959 .... 2.6

1921–42
1 Lefty Gomez, 1937.......... 6.8
2 Lefty Gomez, 1934.......... 5.5
3 Carl Mays, 1921 .... 5.4
4 Red Ruffing, 1939 .... 4.8
5 Wilcy Moore, 1927........... 4.5
Red Ruffing, 1938 .... 4.5
7 Red Ruffing, 1935 .... 4.2
8 Red Ruffing, 1932 .... 4.0
Red Ruffing, 1937 .... 4.0
10 Red Ruffing, 1936 .... 3.9
11 Herb Pennock, 1924......... 3.8
Waite Hoyt, 1927 .... 3.8
13 Lefty Gomez, 1931 .... 3.6
14 Waite Hoyt, 1921 .... 3.3
Bob Shawkey, 1922.......... 3.3
Herb Pennock, 1925......... 3.3
Monte Pearson, 1936 .... 3.3

1901–20
1 Jack Chesbro, 1904 .... 6.1
2 Bob Shawkey, 1920......... 4.6
3 Russ Ford, 1910.............. 4.2
4 Carl Mays, 1920 .... 3.5
5 Al Orth, 1906 .... 3.4
Bob Shawkey, 1916.......... 3.4
7 Russ Ford, 1911 .... 3.0
Ray Caldwell, 1914 .... 3.0

PLAYER OVERALL WINS BY ERA

1988–2007
1 Alex Rodriguez, 2005 .... 6.0
2 Alex Rodriguez, 2007 .... 5.2
3 Jorge Posada, 2003....... 5.1
4 Mariano Rivera, 2004..... 4.9
Mariano Rivera, 2005..... 4.9
6 Mariano Rivera, 2006..... 4.7
7 Mariano Rivera, 1999..... 4.5
Jason Giambi, 2002........ 4.5
Derek Jeter, 2005........... 4.5
10 Mariano Rivera, 2003..... 4.3
Bernie Williams, 1999...... 4.3
Jorge Posada, 2000........ 4.3
13 Andy Pettitte, 1997 .... 4.1
Mariano Rivera, 1997..... 4.1
Jorge Posada, 2007........ 4.1

1973–87
1 Rickey Henderson, 1985 .... 6.9
2 Ron Guidry, 1978 .... 6.4
3 Don Mattingly, 1984.......... 5.3
4 Willie Randolph, 1980 ..... 5.0
5 Thurman Munson, 1973 .. 4.9
6 Thurman Munson, 1975 .. 4.5
Don Mattingly, 1986.......... 4.5
8 Catfish Hunter, 1975........ 4.4
9 Sparky Lyle, 1977............ 4.3
Rich Gossage, 1978......... 4.3
11 Dave Righetti, 1986.......... 4.2
Graig Nettles, 1976 .... 4.2
13 Reggie Jackson, 1980..... 4.0
14 Willie Randolph, 1984 ..... 3.9

1961–72
1 Mickey Mantle, 1961 .... 7.5
2 Mickey Mantle, 1962 .... 5.0
3 Elston Howard, 1961 .... 4.5
Bobby Murcer, 1971 .... 4.5
5 Luis Arroyo, 1961 .... 4.4
6 Bobby Murcer, 1972 .... 4.3
7 Elston Howard, 1964 .... 4.2
Tom Tresh, 1966.............. 4.2
9 Whitey Ford, 1964 .... 3.9
Thurman Munson, 1970 .. 3.9
11 Mel Stottlemyre, 1969 ..... 3.8
Roy White, 1971 .... 3.8
13 Clete Boyer, 1962............ 3.6
14 Lindy McDaniel, 1970....... 3.5

1943–60
1 Mickey Mantle, 1956 .... 8.1
2 Mickey Mantle, 1957 .... 8.0
3 Snuffy Stirnweiss, 1945 .... 7.2
4 Snuffy Stirnweiss, 1944 .... 6.8
5 Joe Gordon, 1943............ 5.6
6 Mickey Mantle, 1955 .... 5.5
Mickey Mantle, 1958 .... 5.5
8 Spud Chandler, 1943....... 5.3
Gil McDougald, 1957........ 5.3
10 Whitey Ford, 1956 .... 4.6
11 Spud Chandler, 1946........ 4.5
Joe DiMaggio, 1948 .... 4.5
13 Yogi Berra, 1954.............. 4.4
14 Yogi Berra, 1956.............. 4.3

1921–42
1 Babe Ruth, 1923 .... 10.1
2 Babe Ruth, 1921 .... 9.4
3 Babe Ruth, 1927 .... 8.8
4 Babe Ruth, 1926 .... 8.5
5 Babe Ruth, 1924 .... 8.4
Lou Gehrig, 1927.............. 8.4
7 Babe Ruth, 1931 .... 8.1
8 Lou Gehrig, 1934............. 7.9
9 Lou Gehrig, 1930............. 7.7
10 Babe Ruth, 1930 .... 7.6
11 Babe Ruth, 1928 .... 7.1
12 Lefty Gomez, 1937.......... 6.8
13 Lou Gehrig, 1936............. 6.6
Joe DiMaggio, 1941 .... 6.6

1901–20
1 Babe Ruth, 1920 .... 9.3
2 Jack Chesbro, 1904 .... 6.1
3 Roger Peckinpaugh, 1919 .... 5.1
4 Bob Shawkey, 1920......... 4.6
5 Russ Ford, 1910.............. 4.2
6 Carl Mays, 1920 .... 3.5
7 Al Orth, 1906 .... 3.4
Bob Shawkey, 1916.......... 3.4
9 Del Pratt, 1919 .... 3.1
10 Russ Ford, 1911 .... 3.0
Ray Caldwell, 1914 .... 3.0
12 Frank Baker, 1918........... 2.9

PLAYER OVERALL WINS
1 Babe Ruth, 1923 .... 10.1
2 Babe Ruth, 1921 .... 9.4
3 Babe Ruth, 1920 .... 9.3
4 Babe Ruth, 1927 .... 8.8
5 Babe Ruth, 1926 .... 8.5
6 Babe Ruth, 1924 .... 8.4
Lou Gehrig, 1927.............. 8.4
8 Babe Ruth, 1931 .... 8.1
Mickey Mantle, 1956 .... 8.1
10 Mickey Mantle, 1957 .... 8.0
11 Lou Gehrig, 1934............. 7.9
12 Lou Gehrig, 1930............. 7.7
13 Babe Ruth, 1930 .... 7.6
14 Mickey Mantle, 1961 .... 7.5
15 Snuffy Stirnweiss, 1945 .... 7.2
16 Babe Ruth, 1928 .... 7.1
17 Rickey Henderson, 1985 .... 6.9
18 Lefty Gomez, 1937.......... 6.8
Snuffy Stirnweiss, 1944 .... 6.8
20 Lou Gehrig, 1936............. 6.6
Joe DiMaggio, 1941 .... 6.6
22 Babe Ruth, 1932 .... 6.5
23 Ron Guidry, 1978 .... 6.4
24 Jack Chesbro, 1904 .... 6.1
25 Lou Gehrig, 1931............. 6.0
Alex Rodriguez, 2005 .... 6.0
27 Lou Gehrig, 1928............. 5.9
28 Joe Gordon, 1942............ 5.8
29 Joe DiMaggio, 1937 .... 5.7
30 Bill Dickey, 1937.............. 5.6
Joe Gordon, 1943............ 5.6
32 Lefty Gomez, 1934.......... 5.5
Joe DiMaggio, 1939 .... 5.5
Mickey Mantle, 1955 .... 5.5
Mickey Mantle, 1958 .... 5.5
36 Carl Mays, 1921 .... 5.4
Babe Ruth, 1929 .... 5.4
38 Spud Chandler, 1943....... 5.3
Lou Gehrig, 1935............. 5.3
Gil McDougald, 1957........ 5.3
Don Mattingly, 1984.......... 5.3
42 Tony Lazzeri, 1929 .... 5.2
Alex Rodriguez, 2007 .... 5.2
44 Roger Peckinpaugh, 1919 .... 5.1
Lou Gehrig, 1932............. 5.1
Jorge Posada, 2003....... 5.1
47 Mickey Mantle, 1962 .... 5.0
Willie Randolph, 1980 ..... 5.0
49 Mariano Rivera, 2004..... 4.9
Mariano Rivera, 2005..... 4.9
Thurman Munson, 1973 .. 4.9
52 Red Ruffing, 1939 .... 4.8
Lou Gehrig, 1937............. 4.8
54 Mariano Rivera, 2006..... 4.7
Lou Gehrig, 1933............. 4.7
Babe Ruth, 1933 .... 4.7
57 Bob Shawkey, 1920......... 4.6
Whitey Ford, 1956 .... 4.6
Phil Rizzuto, 1942 .... 4.6
60 Wilcy Moore, 1927........... 4.5
Red Ruffing, 1938 .... 4.5
Spud Chandler, 1946........ 4.5
Mariano Rivera, 1999..... 4.5
Lou Gehrig, 1929.............. 4.5
Bill Dickey, 1939.............. 4.5
Joe DiMaggio, 1940 .... 4.5
Joe DiMaggio, 1948 .... 4.5
Elston Howard, 1961 .... 4.5
Bobby Murcer, 1971 .... 4.5
Thurman Munson, 1975 .. 4.5
Don Mattingly, 1986.......... 4.5
Jason Giambi, 2002........ 4.5
Derek Jeter, 2005........... 4.5
74 Luis Arroyo, 1961 .... 4.4
Catfish Hunter, 1975........ 4.4
Yogi Berra, 1954.............. 4.4
77 Sparky Lyle, 1977............ 4.3
Rich Gossage, 1978......... 4.3
Mariano Rivera, 2003..... 4.3
Yogi Berra, 1956.............. 4.3
Bobby Murcer, 1972 .... 4.3
Bernie Williams, 1999...... 4.3
Jorge Posada, 2000........ 4.3
84 Russ Ford, 1910.............. 4.2
Red Ruffing, 1935 .... 4.2
Dave Righetti, 1986.......... 4.2
Bill Dickey, 1936.............. 4.2
Charlie Keller, 1942.......... 4.2
Elston Howard, 1964 .... 4.2
Tom Tresh, 1966.............. 4.2
Graig Nettles, 1976 .... 4.2
92 Allie Reynolds, 1952........ 4.1
Andy Pettitte, 1997 .... 4.1
Mariano Rivera, 1997..... 4.1
Bill Dickey, 1938.............. 4.1
Jorge Posada, 2007........ 4.1
97 Many players tied 4.0

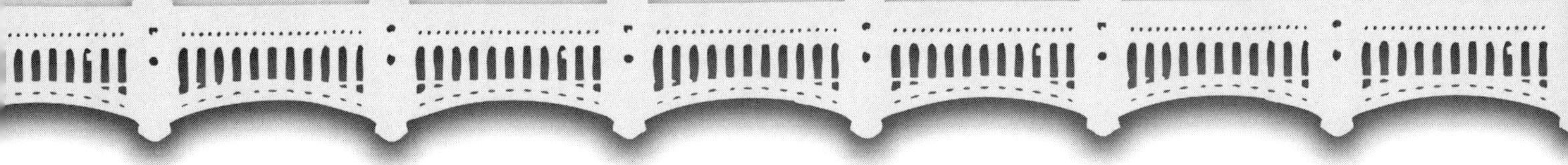

Yankees Rosters

Too many reference books ignore the *team* element of the game, focusing on player statistics and giving cursory, at best, details of the teams themselves. This section shows the regular players at every position for each Yankees team from 1903–2007, including the starting rotation and bullpen. Every other player who appeared in a game for that year is also shown. Moreover, these rosters provide much more complete information than typical rosters about how each team was put together and how players were utilized in a given season. This is especially true in the past two decades, when teams have become much more reluctant to let young pitchers learn the ropes or to let struggling players work their way out of slumps. The increasing frequency of serious injuries has also resulted in less stable lineups. The enormous amount of money at stake is also a major factor in the decreasing amount of patience exhibited by teams at every level.

Big-league teams, managers, and players have lived under the microscope of the media throughout baseball history, but now the media broadcasts high definition, full-color video accompanied by unabashedly critical commentary, 24–7. This intense pressure has resulted in numerous lineups and fewer set positions than in the past. This roster-coding scheme may seem complex, but it gives a much more detailed understanding of each team.

Simpler rosters that showed pitching staffs composed simply of **SP**s and **RP**s would be far less useful than rosters showing that many pitchers spent part of the season in the rotation as well as the bullpen. Rosters that showed position players only by their primary positions, or that labeled all reserves simply as utility players, would also omit much useful information. The most common combination codes are, not surprisingly, **RS** and **SR**, followed by several codes for utility players. Two-position combination codes normally show up only a few times for each team.

From top to bottom, rosters list starting pitchers first, then relief pitchers, then regular position players, and then reserves. Non-playing managers are shown last.

Pitchers

There are more than just starters and relievers. The versatile pitcher who fills several roles is listed by the role he occupied most. Pitcher codes are:

SP starting pitcher;
RP relief pitcher;
SR starter-reliever;
RS reliever-starter;
CL closer.

Pitchers are assigned codes according to the following rules:

- If a starting pitcher has 0–9 games in relief, he is labeled as **SP**.
- If a pitcher has 10 or more games in relief, and if at least one third of his appearances are games started, then he is labeled as **SR**.
- If the pitcher has started at least 5 games and has 10 or more games in relief, he is labeled as **RS**—provided he started less than one third of the time.
- If a relief pitcher has from 0–4 games started, he is labeled as **RP**.
- If a relief pitcher's saves total is equal to at least one third of his relief appearances, then he is labeled as **CL**.

Position Players

All position players are listed by the position they played most, even if that position was "utility." Position players who played in fewer than 60 percent of their team's games are marked by a dash after their position code.

Regular players are always listed in the order shown below. If a player appeared in at least 75 percent of his team's games at one position, he is shown as the regular with the following codes:

C catcher
1B first base (**1** when combined with other positions)
2B second base (**2** when combined)
3B third base (**3** when combined)
SS shortstop (**S** when combined)
LF left fielder (**L** when combined)
CF center fielder (**M** when combined)
RF right fielder (**R** when combined)
DH designated hitter (**D** when combined)

If no one played at least 75 percent of a team's games at one position, the regular shown will be the player who played the most games at that position—unless a player happened to have played the most games at two positions. If so, that player will be shown where he played the most, and the player with the second-most games at the other position will be shown as the regular.

In the overwhelming majority of circumstances, the regular at each position will have the standard position code or a combination code that starts with the first letter of that position (e.g., **3S** for third base/shortstop; **L1** for left field/first base). However, when a team has several players shifting among different positions during the season, the regular shown at a particular position might not have the expected code. (This usually happens on bad teams that have no set lineup.)

In these rare circumstances, the "regular" third baseman might be someone who played only 40 games there, but who still played a third more than anyone else on that team who wasn't a regular at another position.

Aside from the position codes shown above, four other codes are used for players who have played less than 75 percent of their games at one position. Details on these codes are found below:

OF outfield (**O** when used in combination);
IF infield (**I** when used in combination);
UT utility player (**U** when used in combination);
P Pitcher (when used in combination with position codes).

Combination Position Codes

Most of the rules in this section apply only to a small fraction of the players and pitchers listed in the team rosters. Most of the remaining players are shown with two-position codes. But these exceptions require some explanation.

If a player played between 50 percent and 75 percent of his games at one position, his primary position will be signified by the *first* letter of the above codes. (Exception: To avoid confusion with catcher, we have revived the old newspaper box score code **M**—for "middle outfielder"—to indicate center field.)

Players with at least half their games at one position, but less than three quarters of their games at that position, are also given a secondary position code. The secondary code assigned depends on how many games they played at other positions, of course, as well as the number of other positions they played. The rules for secondary position codes are:

- If a player played at least 25 percent of his other games at a position other than his primary position, the secondary position will be shown as the second letter of his position code.
- If the player did not play 25 percent of his other games at any single position, but he did play at least 25 percent of his additional (i.e., non-primary position) games in the infield, the second letter of his position code will be **I**.
- If the player did not play 25 percent of his other games at a single position, but he did play at least 25 percent of his additional games in the outfield, the second letter of his position code will be **O**. If a player's games are scattered among so many positions that none of these conditions apply, his secondary code will be **U**.
- If the player's secondary position was pitcher and he pitched in at least 10 games, his second letter will be **P**. Only a few position players since 1901—the most famous being Babe Ruth, of course—have pitched in 10 games in one year while also playing in half their team's games.

Utility Codes

No two-letter coding scheme can account for all the ways that managers can use players during a season. Therefore, a few utility codes are used to cover versatile players who didn't play 50 percent of their games at any position. (Of course, complete data on games at position for every player can be found in the Player Register.) Utility codes indicating specific positions are used only for catchers. Otherwise, utility codes are assigned by the following rules:

- If the player played all three outfield positions but never played the infield, he will be labeled **UO** (utility outfielder).
- If the player played two outfield positions but never played the infield, he will be labeled **OF** (outfield).
- If the player played three or four infield positions but never played the outfield, he will be labeled as **UI** (utility infielder).
- If the player played two infield positions but never played the outfield, he will be labeled as **IF** (infielder).
- If the player played two or more outfield positions as well as at least one infield position, and he played more games in the outfield than in the infield, he will be labeled as **OI** (outfielder-infielder).
- If the player played two or more infield positions and at least one outfield position, and he played more games in the infield than in the outfield, he will be labeled as **IO** (infielder-outfielder).
- If a player's first or second position (in terms of number of games) is catcher, but he played less than 50 percent of his games there or at any other position, he will be labeled as **IC** (infielder/catcher) or **OC** (outfielder/catcher) depending on whether he played primarily in the infield or the outfield. If he played more games at catcher than elsewhere, and he did not play another defensive position in most of his other games (i.e., he was a **DH** or a pinch hitter), he will be labeled as **UC** (utility catcher).
- If a player doesn't fit into any of these categories, he will be labeled as **UT** (utility).

Managers

Managers are indicated by the code **M**; see the Manager Register introduction for an explanation of who qualifies as a manager. If a team had multiple managers in a season, the order in which these managers served is shown by the number after the **M** (i.e., the first manager will be **M1**, the second **M2**, etc.). Managers' names are *italicized* in the rosters. Player/managers are shown with standard position code(s) and located as a player; their italicization indicates managerial status. Non-playing managers are shown at the end of the team roster.

Rosters

1903
SP J Chesbro
SP J Tannehill
SP C Griffith
SR H Howell
SP B Wolfe
SP J Deering
SP- S Wiltse
SP- A Puttmann
SP- D Adkins
SP- E Bliss
SP- E Quick
C M Beville
1B J Ganzel
2B J Williams
SS K Elberfeld
3B W Conroy
LF L Davis
ML H McFarland
RF W Keeler
SS- E Courtney
CF- D Fultz
3S- P Greene
1B- F Holmes
1B- T Jordan
SS- H Long
C- P McCauley
C- J O'Connor
C- J Zalusky

1904
SP J Chesbro
SP J Powell
SP A Orth
SP T Hughes
SP C Griffith
SP W Clarkson
SP A Puttmann
SP- B Wolfe
SP- N Garvin
C D McGuire
1B J Ganzel
2B J Williams
SS K Elberfeld
3B W Conroy
LF P Dougherty
OI J Anderson
RF W Keeler
CF D Fultz
IC- M Beville
RF- E Bliss
CF- O Collins
C- R Kleinow
C- F McManus
3S- C Osteen
3M- J Thoney
3U- B Unglaub

1905
SP A Orth
SP J Chesbro
SR B Hogg
SR J Powell
SP A Puttmann
SP D Newton
SP W Clarkson
SP- L LeRoy
SP- W Good
SP- A Goodwin
RS C Griffith
C- R Kleinow
1B H Chase
2B J Williams
SS K Elberfeld
3B J Yeager
LF P Dougherty
CF D Fultz
RF W Keeler
UT W Conroy
MU- J Anderson
3B- J Cockman
C- J Connor
3B- P Cooney
1B- F Curtis
1L- F Delahanty
1B- J Doyle
SS- C Fallon
UO- E Hahn
C- F Jacklitsch
2B- F LaPorte
C- J McCarthy
C- D McGuire
SS- R Oldring
1C- D Powers

1906
SP A Orth
SP J Chesbro
SP B Hogg
SR W Clarkson
SP D Newton
SP- L LeRoy
SP- S Doyle
SP- N Hahn
SP- T Hughes
SP- C Barger
RP C Griffith
C R Kleinow
1B H Chase
2B J Williams
SS K Elberfeld
3B F LaPorte
UT W Conroy
CF D Hoffman
RF W Keeler
LF- F Delahanty
LF- P Dougherty
OF- E Hahn
C- D McGuire
3U- G Moriarty
C- I Thomas
UI- J Yeager

1907
SP A Orth
SP J Chesbro
SP S Doyle
SP B Hogg
SP D Newton
SP E Moore
SP F Kitson
SP T Neuer
SP L Brockett
SP- T Hughes
SP- R Tift
SP- W Clarkson
SP- R Castleton
SP- R Manning
SP- C Griffith
SP- C Barger
RP B Keefe
C- R Kleinow
1B H Chase
2B J Williams
SS K Elberfeld
3U G Moriarty
LS W Conroy
CF D Hoffman
RF W Keeler
UT F LaPorte
S2- N Ball
LR- R Bell
C- W Blair
3B- B Louden
C- D McGuire
OC- B Rickey
C- I Thomas

1908
SR J Chesbro
SR J Lake
SR R Manning
SP B Hogg
SP A Orth
SR D Newton
SP S Doyle
SP- P Wilson
SP- J Warhop
SP- F Glade
SP- H Billiard
SP- A O'Connor
SP- H Vaughn
C R Kleinow
1B H Chase
2B H Niles
SS N Ball
3B W Conroy
LF- J Stahl
CF C Hemphill
RF- W Keeler
13 G Moriarty
C- W Blair
CF- B Cree
LF- F Delahanty
3B- M Donovan
SS- K Elberfeld
2B- E Gardner
2O- F LaPorte
RL- I McIlveen
IO- Q O'Rourke
C- E Sweeney
M1 C Griffith

1909
SR J Warhop
SP J Lake
SP R Manning
SP L Brockett
SP S Doyle
SP T Hughes
SR J Quinn
SP P Wilson
SP J Chesbro
SP- D Newton
SP- D Carroll
SP- B Schmidt
SP- R Ford
C- R Kleinow
1B H Chase
2B- F LaPorte
SI J Knight
3B J Austin
LF C Engle
MR R Demmitt
RF W Keeler
UT B Cree
S3 K Elberfeld
2B- N Ball
C- W Blair
2B- E Gardner
OF- C Hemphill
1B- G McConnell
1B- I McIlveen
IP- A Orth
C- E Sweeney
1B- E Tiemeyer
2B- B Vaughn
SU- J Wanner
2B- J Ward
M G Stallings

1910
SP R Ford
SR J Warhop
SP J Quinn
SP H Vaughn
SP T Hughes
SR R Fisher
SP R Manning
SP J Frill
SP- R Caldwell
SP- S Doyle
C- E Sweeney
1B H Chase
2U F LaPorte
SI J Knight
3B J Austin
ML B Cree
MR C Hemphill
RF H Wolter
LF B Daniels
C- W Blair
LF- L Channell
C- L Criger
LU- C Engle
SU- E Foster
2B- E Gardner
C- R Kleinow
2B- T Madden
LF- L McClure
C- F Mitchell
SS- R Roach
C- J Walsh
M1 G Stallings

1911
SP R Ford
SR R Caldwell
SP J Warhop
SR J Quinn
SP R Fisher
SP H Vaughn
SP L Brockett
SP- C Hoff
SP- A Coakley
SP- H Ables
SP- E Klepfer
C- W Blair
1B H Chase
2B E Gardner
SI J Knight
3B R Hartzell
LF B Cree
MO B Daniels
RF H Wolter
U2- B Bailey
2B- J Curry
3B- C Dolan
UT- G Elliott
LU- J Fitzgerald
OF- M Handiboe
MU- C Hemphill
SI- O Johnson
IF- S Magner
23- J Priest
S2- R Roach
C- E Sweeney
C- J Walsh
UT- E Wilkinson
C- B Williams
UO- G Zinn

1912
SP R Ford
SR J Warhop
SP R Caldwell
SP G McConnell
SP J Quinn
SP R Fisher
SP H Vaughn
SP G Davis
SP- R Keating
SP- T Thompson
SP- A Schulz
SP- C Hoff
SP- G Shears
C E Sweeney
1B H Chase
2B H Simmons
SS- J Martin
UT R Hartzell
LR B Daniels
UT- D Sterrett
RM G Zinn
2B- G Batten
3B- C Coleman
LF- B Cree
3B- C Dolan
SS- J Dowd
C- G Fisher
2B- E Gardner
CF- B Kauff
CF- J Lelivelt
CF- J Little
CF- P Maloney
SS- T McMillan
3B- E Midkiff
CF- B Otis
3B- D Paddock
3B- J Priest
MR- K Smith
C- G Street
SI- B Stumpf
C- H Thompson
C- B Williams
OF- H Wolter
US- H Wolverton

1913
SR R Fisher
SP R Ford
SR A Schulz
SR G McConnell
SR R Caldwell
SP R Keating
SP J Warhop
SP M McHale
SP- E Klepfer
SP- C Pieh
SP- J Hanley
SP- C Hoff
RP- G Clark
C E Sweeney
12- J Knight
2U R Hartzell
SS R Peckinpaugh
3B- E Midkiff
LF B Cree
CF H Wolter
RF B Daniels
SU- L Boone
1B- B Borton
1U- F Chance
1U- H Chase
MR- D Cook
CF- D Costello
SU- C Derrick
RF- F Gilhooley
C- D Gossett
C- H Hanson
CF- B Holden
U1- J Lelivelt
3B- F Maisel
2U- B McKechnie
C- B Reynolds
C- J Smith
IC- D Sterrett
S2- B Stumpf
UO- G Whiteman
1B- H Williams
C- B Williams
SS- R Young
UI- R Zeider

1914
SR J Warhop
SP R Caldwell
SR R Fisher
SP R Keating
SP M McHale
SR K Cole
SP B Brown
SP- A Schulz
SP- G Cooper
RP C Pieh
C- E Sweeney
1B- C Mullen
2B L Boone
SS R Peckinpaugh
3B F Maisel
LO R Hartzell
CF- B Cree
RF D Cook
US- A Aragon
CF- A Burr
1B- F Chance
1B- L Channell
OF- T Daley
RF- F Gilhooley
C- D Gossett
1L- J Harris
MU- B Holden
UM- H Kingman
MR- C Meara
C- L Nunamaker
UC- B Reynolds
C- J Rogers
C- P Schwert
2B- F Truesdale
LF- J Walsh
1B- H Williams

1915
SP R Caldwell
SP R Fisher
SP J Warhop
SP B Brown
SR C Pieh
SP B Shawkey
SP R Keating
SP M McHale
SP K Cole
SP- G Mogridge
SP- B Donovan
SP- D Vance
SP- A Russell
SP- C Markle
SP- E Cottrell
SP- D Tipple
SP- N Brady
C- L Nunamaker
1B W Pipp
2B L Boone
SS R Peckinpaugh
3B F Maisel
LF R Hartzell
ML H High
RF D Cook
C- W Alexander
ML- E Barney
23- P Baumann
MU- B Cree
OF- T Daley
RF- F Gilhooley
CF- T Hendryx
C- E Krueger
MU- G Layden
CF- E Miller
1U- C Mullen
C- P Schwert
CF- S Shelton
C- E Sweeney
C- R Walters

1916
SR B Shawkey
SP G Mogridge
SR R Fisher
SR A Russell
SP N Cullop
SP R Caldwell
SP R Keating
SP U Shocker
SP- C Markle
SP- J Buckles
SP- M Cantwell
SP- B Donovan
RP S Love
C- L Nunamaker
1B W Pipp
2B J Gedeon
SS R Peckinpaugh
3B F Baker
LF H High
CF L Magee
RF- F Gilhooley
C- W Alexander
3U- A Aragon
UT- P Baumann
3S- L Boone
RF- D Cook
UO- R Hartzell
RF- T Hendryx
CF- S Hofman
UT- F Maisel
UO- E Miller
UT- C Mullen
RF- R Oldring
1B- G Schaefer
C- R Walters

1917
SP B Shawkey
SP R Caldwell
SP G Mogridge
SR N Cullop
SR U Shocker
SP R Fisher
SR A Russell
SP- E Monroe
SP- B McGraw
SP- N Brady
SP- B Piercy
SP- H Thormahlen
SP- J Enright
SP- W Smallwood
RS S Love
C L Nunamaker
1B W Pipp
2B F Maisel
SS R Peckinpaugh
3B F Baker
LF H High
UO E Miller
RU T Hendryx
C- W Alexander
UT- A Aragon
UT- P Baumann
CF- H Camp
2B- C Fewster
2B- J Gedeon
RF- F Gilhooley
LF- B Lamar
CF- L Magee
CF- A Marsans
C- M Ruel
RF- S Vick
C- R Walters
SS- A Ward
M B Donovan

1918
SR G Mogridge
SP S Love
SP R Caldwell
SP A Russell
SR H Finneran
SP H Thormahlen
SP H Robinson
SP R Keating
SP- R Sanders
SP- B Shawkey
SP- D Vance
SP- E Monroe
SP- A Ferguson
SP- W Bernhardt
SP- B McGraw
C T Hannah
1B W Pipp
2B D Pratt
SS R Peckinpaugh
3B F Baker
LF P Bodie
CF- E Miller
RF F Gilhooley
IF- Z Beck
UR- C Fewster
1B- J Fournier
UO- H High
UT- J Hummel
OI- H Hyatt
ML- B Lamar
CF- A Marsans
C- P O'Connor
CU- M Ruel
RU- S Vick
C- R Walters
SU- A Ward
M M Huggins

1919
SP J Quinn
SR B Shawkey
SP H Thormahlen
SR G Mogridge
SP C Mays
SP E Shore
SR A Russell
SP- P Schneider
SP- L Nelson
SP- W Smallwood
SP- B McGraw
SP- L O'Doul
C- M Ruel
1B W Pipp
2B D Pratt
SS R Peckinpaugh
3B F Baker
LF D Lewis
CF P Bodie
RF S Vick
UT- C Fewster
LU- F Gleich
OF- G Halas
C- T Hannah
C- F Hofmann
C- F Kane
OI- B Lamar
RF- C Walker
UI- A Ward
RU- A Wickland
M M Huggins

1920
SP C Mays
SP B Shawkey
SP J Quinn
SR R Collins
SR H Thormahlen
SR G Mogridge
SP- E Shore
SP- L O'Doul
RP- B McGraw
C- M Ruel
1B W Pipp
2B D Pratt
SS R Peckinpaugh
3B A Ward
LF D Lewis
CF P Bodie
RL B Ruth
UT B Meusel
CF- T Connelly
IF- C Fewster
SU- R French
UO- F Gleich
C- T Hannah
C- F Hofmann
IF- J Lucey
RU- S Vick
M M Huggins

1921
SR C Mays
SR W Hoyt
SP B Shawkey
SR R Collins
SR J Quinn
SP B Piercy
SP H Harper
SP- T Rogers
RP A Ferguson
RP- T Sheehan
C W Schang
1B W Pipp
2B A Ward
SS R Peckinpaugh
3B F Baker
LF B Ruth
CF- E Miller
RF B Meusel
MU- P Bodie
RM- T Connelly
C- A DeVormer
MU- C Fewster
OF- C Hawks
C- F Hofmann
3U- M McNally
S2- J Mitchell
UO- B Roth
M M Huggins

1922
SP B Shawkey
SR S Jones
SP W Hoyt
SR J Bush
SP C Mays
SP- L O'Doul
SP- C Llewellyn
RP G Murray
C W Schang
1B W Pipp
2B A Ward
SS E Scott
3B- J Dugan
LR B Ruth
CF W Witt
RL B Meusel
3B- F Baker
CU- A DeVormer
LF- C Fewster
C- F Hofmann
OI- N McMillan
3I- M McNally
CF- E Miller
SS- J Mitchell
OF- C Skinner
OF- E Smith
M M Huggins

1923
SP J Bush
SP B Shawkey
SR S Jones
SP H Pennock
SP W Hoyt
SP- G Pipgras
SP- O Roettger
RS C Mays
C- W Schang
1B W Pipp
2B A Ward
SS E Scott
3B J Dugan
LR B Meusel
CF W Witt
OI B Ruth
C- B Bengough
S2- M Gazella
1U- L Gehrig
UO- H Haines
OF- H Hendrick
C- F Hofmann
SS- E Johnson
UI- M McNally
RU- E Smith
M M Huggins

1924
SP H Pennock
SP J Bush
SR W Hoyt
SR B Shawkey
SR S Jones
SP- W Beall
SP- C Markle
SP- G Pipgras
SP- B Shields
SP- O Roettger
RP M Gaston
RP- A Mamaux
C W Schang
1B W Pipp
2B A Ward
SS E Scott
3B J Dugan
LR B Meusel
CF W Witt
RL B Ruth
C- C Autry
C- B Bengough
UO- E Combs
UT- L Gehrig
OF- H Hendrick
2B- M Hillis
C- F Hofmann
UO- S Horan
UI- E Johnson
23- M McNally
CF- B Paschal
M M Huggins

1925
SR H Pennock
SR W Hoyt
SR S Jones
SR U Shocker
SR B Shawkey
SP- B Shields
SP- G Braxton
SP- W Beall
SP- J Marquis
SP- R Francis
SP- C Caldwell
RP H Johnson
RS A Ferguson
C B Bengough
1B L Gehrig
2B A Ward
SS P Wanninger
3B J Dugan
LR B Meusel
CF E Combs
RL B Ruth
3B- L Durocher
UC- F Hofmann
UI- E Johnson
SS- M Koenig
C- R Luebbe
1U- F Merkle
3B- H Odom
C- S O'Neill
UO- B Paschal
1B- W Pipp
C- W Schang
SS- E Scott

UT- H Shanks
RU- B Veach
OF- W Witt
M M Huggins

1926
SP H Pennock
SP U Shocker
SR W Hoyt
SR S Jones
SR M Thomas
SR B Shawkey
SR W Beall
SP- D Ruether
SP- H Johnson
RP G Braxton
RP- H McQuaid
C P Collins
1B L Gehrig
2B T Lazzeri
SS M Koenig
3B J Dugan
LR B Meusel
CF E Combs
LR B Ruth
UO B Paschal
IF- S Adams
C- H Barnes
C- B Bengough
UR- R Carlyle
CF- N Cullop
RF- K Davis
3U- M Gazella
1B- F Merkle
C- H Severeid
C- B Skiff
IF- A Ward
M M Huggins

1927
SP W Hoyt
SP H Pennock
SP U Shocker
SP D Ruether
SP G Pipgras
SR M Thomas
SP- W Beall
RS W Moore
RP B Shawkey
RP- J Giard
C- P Collins
1B L Gehrig
2I T Lazzeri
SS M Koenig
3B J Dugan
LR B Meusel
CF E Combs
RL B Ruth
C- B Bengough
OI- C Durst
3B- M Gazella
C- J Grabowski
2U- R Morehart
UO- B Paschal
3U- J Wera
M M Huggins

1928
SP G Pipgras
SR W Hoyt
SP H Pennock
SP H Johnson
SR A Shealy
SP F Heimach
SP S Coveleski
SP T Zachary
SP- R Ryan
SP- U Shocker
RP W Moore
RP- M Thomas
RP- A Campbell
C- J Grabowski
1B L Gehrig
2B T Lazzeri
SS M Koenig
3B J Dugan
LR B Meusel
CF E Combs
RL B Ruth
2S L Durocher
C- B Bengough
1U- G Burns
C- P Collins
CU- B Dickey
OI- C Durst
3U- M Gazella
UO- B Paschal
3B- G Robertson
M M Huggins

1929
SP G Pipgras
SP W Hoyt
SP E Wells
SP H Pennock
SR R Sherid
SR T Zachary
SP- H Johnson
SP- G Rhodes
SP- B Nekola
SP- M Thomas
RS F Heimach
RP W Moore
C B Dickey
1B L Gehrig
2B T Lazzeri
SS L Durocher
3B- G Robertson
LR B Meusel
CF E Combs
RL B Ruth
S3 M Koenig
C- B Bengough
C- G Burns
RM- S Byrd
LO- C Durst
LF- L Funk
C- J Grabowski
C- A Jorgens
3U- L Lary
UO- B Paschal
3B- J Wera
M1 M Huggins
M2 A Fletcher

1930
SR G Pipgras
SP R Ruffing
SR R Sherid
SR H Johnson
SP H Pennock
SP E Wells
SP L Gomez
SP W Hoyt
SP- O Carroll
SP- T Zachary
SP- F Barnes
SP- B Henderson
SP- S Gibson
SP- G Rhodes
SP- F Edwards
RP L McEvoy
RP- K Holloway
C B Dickey
1B L Gehrig
23 T Lazzeri
SS L Lary
32 B Chapman
UO E Combs
CF H Rice
RL B Ruth
C- B Bengough
LR- S Byrd
UO- D Cooke
LF- C Durst
C- B Hargrave
C- A Jorgens
LU- B Karlon
SS- M Koenig
2U- J Reese
SS- B Werber
SS- Y Wuestling
M B Shawkey

1931
SR L Gomez
SP R Ruffing
SR H Johnson
SP H Pennock
SR G Pipgras
SR E Wells
SP G Rhodes
SP R Sherid
SP- I Andrews
SP- L McEvoy
RS J Weaver
RP- L Weinert
C B Dickey
1B L Gehrig
23 T Lazzeri
SS L Lary
3B J Sewell
LR B Chapman
CF E Combs
RL B Ruth
UO S Byrd
OF- D Cooke
OI- M Hoag
C- A Jorgens
C- C Perkins
2B- J Reese
SS- R Rolfe
LR- D Walker
M J McCarthy

1932
SP L Gomez
SP R Ruffing
SP G Pipgras
SR J Allen
SP H Pennock
SP D Mac Fayden
SP- H Johnson
SP- W Moore
SP- I Andrews
SP- G Rhodes
SP- C Devens
SP- J Murphy
RP J Brown
RP- E Wells
C B Dickey
1B L Gehrig
2B T Lazzeri
S3 F Crosetti
3B J Sewell
RL B Chapman
CF E Combs
RL B Ruth
MU S Byrd
CF- D Cooke
2I- D Farrell
C- J Glenn
LU- M Hoag
C- A Jorgens
SS- L Lary
C- E Phillips
2B- J Saltzgaver
2B- R Schalk
M J McCarthy

1933
SP R Ruffing
SP L Gomez
SP J Allen
SR R Van Atta
SP D Brennan
SR J Brown
SP C Devens
SP G Uhle
SP- G Pipgras
SP- P Appleton
RS D Mac Fayden
RP W Moore
RS H Pennock
C B Dickey
1B L Gehrig
2B T Lazzeri
SS F Crosetti
3B J Sewell
RL B Chapman
MU E Combs
RL B Ruth
MU D Walker
UO- S Byrd
S2- D Farrell
C- J Glenn
C- A Jorgens
3S- L Lary
C- T Rensa
UM- B Werber
M J McCarthy

1934
SP L Gomez
SP R Ruffing
SR J Murphy
SP J Broaca
SR J DeShong
SR D Mac Fayden
SP J Allen
SP- G Uhle
SP- H Smythe
SP- C Devens
SP- V Tamulis
SP- F Newkirk
RS R Van Atta
RP- B Grimes
C B Dickey
1B L Gehrig
2U T Lazzeri
SS F Crosetti
3B J Saltzgaver
RL M Hoag
ML B Chapman
RL B Ruth
RL S Byrd
CF- E Combs
2B- D Heffner
C- A Jorgens
1B- L Lary
S3- R Rolfe
LF- G Selkirk
C- Z Taylor
UR- D Walker
M J McCarthy

1935
SP L Gomez
SP R Ruffing
SP J Broaca
SP J Allen
SR V Tamulis
SR J Brown
SP- R Van Atta
RS J Murphy
RP J DeShong
RP P Malone
C B Dickey
1B L Gehrig
2B T Lazzeri
SS- F Crosetti
3B R Rolfe
LF J Hill
CF B Chapman
RF G Selkirk
LU- E Combs
C- J Glenn
2B- D Heffner
RU- M Hoag
C- A Jorgens
SS- N Richardson
SS- B Ryan
UI- J Saltzgaver
UR- D Walker
M J McCarthy

1936
SP R Ruffing
SP M Pearson
SR J Broaca
SP L Gomez
SR B Hadley
SP- K Wicker
SP- S Sundra
RS P Malone
RS J Murphy
RP J Brown
RP- T Kleinhans
C B Dickey
1B L Gehrig
2B T Lazzeri
SS F Crosetti
3B R Rolfe
UO J DiMaggio
OF- J Powell
RF G Selkirk
CF- B Chapman
C- J Glenn
UI- D Heffner
MR- M Hoag
OF- R Johnson
C- A Jorgens
UI- J Saltzgaver
RU- B Seeds
CF- D Walker
M J McCarthy

1937
SP L Gomez
SP R Ruffing
SP B Hadley
SP M Pearson
SP K Wicker
SP S Chandler
SP I Andrews
SP- J Broaca
SP- J Vance
RP J Murphy
RS P Malone
RP F Makosky
C B Dickey
1B L Gehrig
2B T Lazzeri
SS F Crosetti
3B R Rolfe
LF J Powell
CF J DiMaggio
RO M Hoag
SS- B Dahlgren
C- J Glenn
2I- D Heffner
OF- T Henrich
LF- R Johnson
C- A Jorgens
UR- J Saltzgaver
RF- G Selkirk
M J McCarthy

1938
SP R Ruffing
SP L Gomez
SP M Pearson
SP S Chandler
SR B Hadley
SP J Beggs
SP- W Ferrell
SP- A Donald
SP- J Vance
SP- L Stine
SP- K Wicker
RP J Murphy
RS S Sundra
RP I Andrews
C B Dickey
1B L Gehrig
2B J Gordon
SS F Crosetti
3B R Rolfe
LF G Selkirk
CF J DiMaggio
RF T Henrich
IF- B Dahlgren
C- J Glenn
UO- M Hoag
C- A Jorgens
2U- B Knickerbocker
LF- J Powell
M J McCarthy

1939
SP R Ruffing
SP L Gomez
SP B Hadley
SP A Donald
SP M Pearson
SP O Hildebrand
SR S Sundra
SR M Russo
SP- W Ferrell
SP- M Breuer
RP J Murphy
RP- S Chandler
C B Dickey
1B B Dahlgren
2B J Gordon
SS F Crosetti
3B R Rolfe
LR G Selkirk
CF J DiMaggio
RL C Keller
RM T Henrich
RF- J Gallagher
1B- L Gehrig
CU- A Jorgens
IF- B Knickerbocker
LU- J Powell
C- B Rosar
M J McCarthy

1940
SP R Ruffing
SP M Russo
SP S Chandler
SP M Breuer
SR A Donald
SP M Pearson
SP T Bonham
SP- L Gomez
SP- L Grissom
RS S Sundra
RP B Hadley
RP J Murphy
RP- O Hildebrand
C B Dickey
1B B Dahlgren
2B J Gordon
SS F Crosetti
3B R Rolfe
LR G Selkirk
CF J DiMaggio
RL C Keller
UL- M Chartak
RM- T Henrich
IF- B Knickerbocker
OF- B Mills
UO- J Powell
C- B Rosar
M J McCarthy

1941
SP M Russo
SP R Ruffing
SP S Chandler
SP A Donald
SP L Gomez
SP M Breuer
SP T Bonham
SP S Peek
SP- G Washburn
RP J Murphy
RP N Branch
RP C Stanceu
C B Dickey
1B J Sturm
2B J Gordon
SS P Rizzuto
3B R Rolfe
LF C Keller
CF J DiMaggio
RF T Henrich
OF- F Bordagaray
S3- F Crosetti
LF- J Lindell
23- J Priddy
C- B Rosar
OF- G Selkirk
C- K Silvestri
M J McCarthy

1942
SP T Bonham
SP S Chandler
SP R Ruffing
SP H Borowy
SP M Breuer
SP A Donald
SP L Gomez
SP- M Russo
SP- J Turner
SP- M Queen
RP J Murphy
RP J Lindell
RP- N Branch
C- B Dickey
1B B Hassett
2B J Gordon
SS P Rizzuto
3B- F Crosetti
LF C Keller
CF J DiMaggio
RF T Henrich
1B- M Chartak
RF- R Cullenbine
C- R Hemsley
C- E Kearse
1B- E Levy
3I- J Priddy
3B- R Rolfe
C- B Rosar
U3- G Selkirk
OF- T Stainback
M J McCarthy

1943
SP S Chandler
SP T Bonham
SP B Wensloff
SP H Borowy
SP B Zuber
SP A Donald
SR M Russo
SP- T Byrne
SP- M Breuer
RP J Murphy
RP- J Turner
C- B Dickey
1B N Etten
2B J Gordon
SS F Crosetti
3B B Johnson
LF C Keller
RM J Lindell
RF B Metheny
IF- O Grimes
C- R Hemsley
RF- A Robinson
C- K Sears
MU- T Stainback
SS- S Stirnweiss
CF- R Weatherly
M J McCarthy

1944
SP H Borowy
SP M Dubiel
SP T Bonham
SR A Donald
SP B Zuber
SP J Page
SR S Roser
SP M Queen
SP- B Bevens
SP- S Chandler
RP J Turner
RP- A Lyons
RP- J Johnson
C- M Garbark
1B N Etten
2B S Stirnweiss
SS M Milosevich
3B O Grimes
LF- H Martin
CF J Lindell
RF B Metheny
C- R Collins
UM J Cooney
SS- F Crosetti
OF- R Derry
UC- B Drescher
C- R Hemsley
LF- E Levy
UO- L Rosenthal
3B- D Savage
RO- T Stainback
2B- P Waner
M J McCarthy

1945
SP B Bevens
SP T Bonham
SR A Gettel
SP M Dubiel
SP H Borowy
SP B Zuber
SR J Page
SP R Ruffing
SP A Donald
SP- S Chandler
SP- P Schreiber
RP J Turner
RP K Holcombe
RP- S Roser
C- M Garbark
1B N Etten
2B S Stirnweiss
SS F Crosetti
3B O Grimes
LF H Martin
CF T Stainback
RF B Metheny
UR- J Buzas
C- H Crompton
MO- R Derry
CU- B Drescher
LF- C Keller
CF- J Lindell
SU- M Milosevich
C- A Robinson
UT- D Savage
2B- P Waner
M J McCarthy

1946
SP S Chandler
SP B Bevens
SR J Page
SR R Gumpert
SP T Bonham
SR A Gettel
SR C Marshall
SP R Ruffing
SP- M Russo
SP- V Raschi
SP- F Hiller
SP- T Byrne
SP- A Lyons
SP- K Drews
SP- B Zuber
SP- C Stanceu
SP- S Roser
SP- H Karpel
RP J Murphy
RP- B Wight
RP- J Wade
RP- M Queen
C A Robinson
1B N Etten
2B J Gordon
SS P Rizzuto
32 S Stirnweiss
LF C Keller
CF J DiMaggio
R1 T Henrich
OI J Lindell
C- Y Berra
3B- E Bockman
S3- B Brown
RF- F Colman
SS- F Crosetti
CU- B Dickey
CU- B Drescher
S2- O Grimes
3B- B Johnson
UR- H Majeski
3M- B Metheny
C- G Niarhos
C- K Silvestri
U3- S Souchock
3B- R Weatherly
M1 J McCarthy
M3 J Neun

1947
SP A Reynolds
SP S Shea
SP B Bevens
SP S Chandler
SP B Newsom
SP V Raschi
SP D Johnson
SP B Wensloff
SP- D Starr
SP- A Lyons
SP- B Wight
SP- M Queen
SP- T Byrne
SP- R Ardizoia
RP J Page
RP K Drews
RS R Gumpert
C- A Robinson
1B G McQuinn
2B S Stirnweiss
SS P Rizzuto
3B B Johnson
LF J Lindell
CF J DiMaggio
RF T Henrich
CO- Y Berra
UT- B Brown
OF- A Clark
UC- F Colman
IF- F Crosetti
UC- L Frey
C- R Houk
LF- C Keller
C- S Lollar
UC- J Lucadello
2B- R Mack
1U- J Phillips
C- T Sepkowski
C- K Silvestri
M B Harris

1948
SP A Reynolds
SP E Lopat
SP V Raschi
SP S Shea
SR T Byrne
SP B Porterfield
SR R Embree
SP- D Starr
SP- C Marshall
RP J Page
RS F Hiller
RP- K Drews
RP- R Gumpert
C- G Niarhos
1B G McQuinn
2B S Stirnweiss
SS P Rizzuto
3B B Johnson
LF- J Lindell
CF J DiMaggio
R1 T Henrich
CR Y Berra
UT B Brown
OF- H Bauer
3B- J Collins
IF- F Crosetti
CF- L Frey
C- R Houk
LF- C Keller
UC- S Lollar
UO- C Mapes
1B- J Phillips
C- C Silvera
1U- S Souchock
1B- B Stewart
M B Harris

1949
SP V Raschi
SP E Lopat
SP A Reynolds
SP T Byrne
SR F Sanford
SP B Porterfield
SP- D Pillette
SP- F Hiller
SP- H Casey
SP- W Hood
RP J Page

RP S Shea
RP C Marshall
RP- R Buxton
C Y Berra
R1 T Henrich
2B J Coleman
SS P Rizzuto
3B B Brown
LU G Woodling
MR C Mapes
RO H Bauer
3U B Johnson
1U- J Collins
MU- J Delsing
CF- J DiMaggio
C- R Houk
OF- C Keller
1B- D Kryhoski
LF- J Lindell
UM- J Mize
1B- F Mole
C- G Niarhos
1B- J Phillips
C- C Silvera
2U- S Stirnweiss
2B- M Witek
M C Stengel

1950

SP V Raschi
SP A Reynolds
SP E Lopat
SP T Byrne
SP W Ford
SR F Sanford
SP- B Porterfield
SP- D Johnson
SP- D Pillette
SP- E Nevel
SP- D Madison
SP- L Burdette
RP J Page
RP T Ferrick
RP J Ostrowski
C Y Berra
1B J Collins
2B J Coleman
SS P Rizzuto
3B B Johnson
LF G Woodling
CF J DiMaggio
RL H Bauer
3B B Brown
RU C Mapes
1B- J Delsing
UR- T Henrich
1L- J Hopp
C- R Houk
OF- J Jensen
LF- J Lindell
2U- B Martin
1B- J Mize
1B- G Niarhos
C- C Silvera
2U- S Stirnweiss
2B- D Wakefield
1U- H Workman
M C Stengel

1951

SP V Raschi
SP E Lopat
SR A Reynolds
SR T Morgan
SR S Shea
SR B Kuzava
SP- A Schallock
SP- J Sain
SP- F Sanford
SP- T Byrne
SP- T Ferrick
SP- B Wiesler
SP- B Hogue
SP- E Nevel
SP- B Muncrief
SP- B Porterfield
RP J Ostrowski
RP- S Overmire
RP- J Kramer
C Y Berra
1B J Collins
2B J Coleman
SS P Rizzuto
3B B Brown
LF G Woodling
CF J DiMaggio
RL H Bauer
RF M Mantle
32 G McDougald
1B J Mize
SS- J Brideweser
RF- B Cerv
C- C Courtney
1U- J Hopp
C- R Houk
UO- J Jensen
3B- B Johnson
RU- C Mapes
IO- B Martin
C- C Silvera
RU- A Wilson
M C Stengel

1952

SP A Reynolds
SP V Raschi
SR J Sain
SP E Lopat
SR B Kuzava
SP T Morgan
SP B Miller
SP T Gorman
SP- R Scarborough
SP- E Blackwell
SP- H Schaeffer
SP- J Schmitz
SP- A Schallock
RS J McDonald
RP B Hogue
RP- J Ostrowski
C Y Berra
1B J Collins
2B B Martin
SS P Rizzuto
3B G McDougald
LF G Woodling
CF M Mantle
RF H Bauer
3B- L Babe
SU- J Brideweser
3B- B Brown
3B- A Carey
OF- B Cerv
2B- J Coleman
1B- J Hopp
C- R Houk
MU- J Jensen
LU- C Keller
UL- J Mize
OI I Noren
2B- K Segrist
C- C Silvera
C- A Wilson
M C Stengel

1953

SP W Ford
SR J Sain
SP V Raschi
SP E Lopat
SR A Reynolds
SP J McDonald
SP- S Kraly
SP- A Schallock
SP- E Blackwell
SP- J Schmitz
RS B Kuzava
RP T Gorman
RP R Scarborough
RP- B Miller
C Y Berra
1B J Collins
2B B Martin
SS P Rizzuto
3B G McDougald
LF G Woodling
CF M Mantle
RF H Bauer
UO I Noren
3B- L Babe
1U- D Bollweg
U1- J Brideweser
3B- A Carey
3B- B Cerv
2B- J Coleman
C- R Houk
SS- W Miranda
U1- J Mize
LU- B Renna
SS- A Schult
C- C Silvera
1C- G Triandos
SS- F Verdi
M C Stengel

1954

SP W Ford
SR B Grim
SP E Lopat
SR A Reynolds
SR T Morgan
SP H Byrd
SP J McDonald
SP- T Byrne
SP- B Wiesler
SP- J Konstanty
SP- A Schallock
SP- R Branca
SP- B Miller
RP J Sain
RP- B Kuzava
RP- T Gorman
RP- M Stuart
C Y Berra
1B J Collins
23 G McDougald
SS P Rizzuto
3B A Carey
OI I Noren
CF M Mantle
RF H Bauer
2S J Coleman
LF G Woodling
CU- L Berberet
3U- B Brown
U3- B Cerv
SS- W Held
SS- R Houk
1U- F Leja
SS- W Miranda
U2- E Robinson
C- C Silvera
1U- B Skowron
OF- E Slaughter
CU- G Triandos
M C Stengel

1955

SP W Ford
SP B Turley
SP T Byrne
SR J Kucks
SP D Larsen
SR B Grim
SP E Lopat
SP B Wiesler
SP- R Coleman
SP- J Sain
SP- T Gray
SP- A Schallock
SP- G Staley
RP J Konstanty
RP T Morgan
RP T Sturdivant
C Y Berra
1U B Skowron
2B G McDougald
SS B Hunter
3B A Carey
LF I Noren
CF M Mantle
RF H Bauer
1R J Collins
LU E Howard
CU- L Berberet
C- J Blanchard
UC- T Carroll
UO- B Cerv
S2- J Coleman
UL- F Leja
2B- B Martin
2S- B Richardson
SS- P Rizzuto
1U- E Robinson
C- C Silvera
1B- E Slaughter
LF- D Tettelbach
1B- M Throneberry
M C Stengel

1956

SP W Ford
SP J Kucks
SR D Larsen
SR T Sturdivant
SP B Turley
SR M McDermott
SP- R Terry
SP- J Konstanty
SP- S Dixon
SP- J Coates
SP- G Staley
RS T Byrne
RS R Coleman
RP T Morgan
RS B Grim
C Y Berra
1B B Skowron
2B B Martin
SS G McDougald
3B A Carey
LC E Howard
CF M Mantle
RF H Bauer
OI J Collins
IF- T Carroll
LM- B Cerv
2S- J Coleman
SS- B Hunter
SS- J Lumpe
OI- I Noren
2B- B Richardson
SS- P Rizzuto
1U- E Robinson
LF- N Siebern
C- C Silvera
C- L Skizas
LU- E Slaughter
OF- G Wilson
M C Stengel

1957

SP T Sturdivant
SR J Kucks
SP B Turley
SP B Shantz
SP D Larsen
SP W Ford
SP- S Maglie
SP- R Terry
RS A Ditmar
RP B Grim
RP T Byrne
RP A Cicotte
C Y Berra
1B B Skowron
2B B Richardson
SS G McDougald
3B- A Carey
LC E Howard
CF M Mantle
RF H Bauer
UT T Kubek
LU E Slaughter
RU- Z Bella
23- J Coleman
UT- J Collins
CF- B Del Greco
CF- W Held
C- D Johnson
3B- J Lumpe
23- B Martin
OI- H Simpson
M C Stengel

1958

SP B Turley
SP W Ford
SR A Ditmar
SR J Kucks
SR B Shantz
SP D Larsen
SP D Maas
SP T Sturdivant
SP- S Maglie
SP- M Dickson
SP- J James
RP R Duren
RS Z Monroe
RP- V Trucks
RP- B Grim
CU Y Berra
1B B Skowron
2B G McDougald
SS T Kubek
3B A Carey
LF N Siebern
CF M Mantle
RF H Bauer
CU E Howard
2B- F Brickell
LF- B Del Greco
C- D Johnson
3B- J Lumpe
2U- B Richardson
OF- H Simpson
OF- E Slaughter
1U- M Throneberry
M C Stengel

1959

SP W Ford
SR A Ditmar
SR B Turley
SR D Maas
SP R Terry
SP D Larsen
SP- T Sturdivant
SP- J Gabler
SP- J Kucks
SP- M Freeman
SP- Z Monroe
RP J Coates
RP B Shantz
RP R Duren
RS E Grba
RP- J Bronstad
RP- G Blaylock
C Y Berra
1B- B Skowron
2B B Richardson
SO T Kubek
3L H Lopez
LU N Siebern
CF M Mantle
RF H Bauer
IC E Howard
UI G McDougald
OC- J Blanchard
S3- C Boyer
SS- F Brickell
3B- A Carey
RF- K Hunt
3I- J Lumpe
LO- J Pisoni
OF- E Slaughter
1U- M Throneberry
LU- G Windhorn
M C Stengel

1960

SP A Ditmar
SP W Ford
SR B Turley
SR R Terry
SR J Coates
SR E Grba
SP B Stafford
SP B Short
SP- F Kipp
SP- H Stowe
RP B Shantz
RP D Maas
RP R Duren
RP J Gabler
RP L Arroyo
RP- J James
C E Howard
1B B Skowron
2B B Richardson
SS T Kubek
3B C Boyer
LU H Lopez
CF M Mantle
RF R Maris
CO Y Berra
32 G McDougald
CU- J Blanchard
3L- A Carey
LU- B Cerv
IF- J DeMaestri
UC- J Gonder
UL- K Hadley
LO- K Hunt
3B- D Johnson
UL- D Long
LM- J Pisoni
C- B Shantz
UL- E Valo
M C Stengel

1961

SP W Ford
SR B Stafford
SP R Terry
SR R Sheldon
SP B Daley
SP B Turley
SP A Ditmar
SP- D McDevitt
SP- A Downing
SP- R Duren
SP- J James
SP- D Maas
RP L Arroyo
RS J Coates
RP- H Reniff
RP- T Clevenger
C E Howard
1B B Skowron
2B B Richardson
SS T Kubek
3B C Boyer
LU Y Berra
CF M Mantle
RF R Maris
CU- J Blanchard
OI- B Cerv
SI- J DeMaestri
3B- B Gardner
3B- J Gonder
US- B Hale
3U- D Johnson
LU- H Lopez
ML- J Reed
1B- L Thomas
UM- E Torgeson
UM- T Tresh
M R Houk

1962

SP R Terry
SP W Ford
SP B Stafford
SR J Bouton
SR R Sheldon
SP- H Brown
SP- J Cullen
SP- H Reniff
SP- A Downing
RS J Coates
RS B Daley
RP M Bridges
RS B Turley
RP- L Arroyo
RP- T Clevenger
C E Howard
1B B Skowron
2B B Richardson
SL T Tresh
3B C Boyer
LU H Lopez
CF M Mantle
RM R Maris
OC- Y Berra
OC- J Blanchard
OF- B Cerv
IF- B Gardner
3U- J Gibbs
SS- T Kubek
IO- P Linz
1B- D Long
OI- J Pepitone
UO- J Reed
M R Houk

1963

SP W Ford
SP R Terry
SR J Bouton
SP A Downing
SP S Williams
SR B Stafford
SP- T Metcalf
SP- L Arroyo
SP- B Daley
RP H Reniff
RP S Hamilton
RP- B Kunkel
RP- M Bridges
C E Howard
1B J Pepitone
2B B Richardson
SS T Kubek
3B C Boyer
LF H Lopez
ML T Tresh
UO J Reed
CU- Y Berra
RL- J Blanchard
1U- H Bright
UC- J Gibbs
2U- P Gonzalez
UT- P Linz
U2- D Long
CF- M Mantle
RF- R Maris
M R Houk

1964

SP J Bouton
SP A Downing
SP W Ford
SR R Terry
SP R Sheldon
SP M Stottlemyre
SR S Williams
SP- B Meyer
RP P Mikkelsen
RP H Reniff
RP B Stafford
RP S Hamilton
RP- B Daley
RP- P Ramos
C E Howard
1B J Pepitone
2B B Richardson
SS T Kubek
3B C Boyer
LM T Tresh
MU M Mantle
RU R Maris
UT P Linz
LO H Lopez
OC- J Blanchard
1U- H Bright
CU- J Gibbs
UT- P Gonzalez
UC- M Hegan
LF- E Jimenez
OI- A Moore
RF- R Repoz
M Y Berra

1965

SP M Stottlemyre
SP W Ford
SP A Downing
SP J Bouton
SP B Stafford
SP J Cullen
SP- R Beck
SP- R Sheldon
SP- J Brenneman
SP- M Jurewicz
RP P Ramos
RP H Reniff
RP P Mikkelsen
RP S Hamilton
RP- B Tiefenauer
RP- G Blanco
C E Howard
1B J Pepitone
2B B Richardson
SS T Kubek
3B C Boyer
LF M Mantle
ML T Tresh
OI H Lopez
1U R Barker
SU P Linz
C- J Blanchard
U1- D Carmel
UI- H Clarke
C- D Edwards
CU- J Gibbs
C- P Gonzalez
OF- A Lopez
RF- R Maris
RU- A Moore
MR- R Moschitto
SS- B Murcer
CF- R Repoz
C- B Schmidt
RU- R White
M J Keane

1966

SP M Stottlemyre
SP F Peterson
SP A Downing
SP F Talbot
SP J Bouton
SR W Ford
SP- B Friend
SP- S Bahnsen
SP- J Cullen
SP- B Henry
RP H Reniff
RP P Ramos
RP S Hamilton
RP D Womack
C E Howard
1B J Pepitone
2B B Richardson
SU H Clarke
3S C Boyer
OI T Tresh
CF M Mantle
RF R Maris
LU R White
SS- R Amaro
1B- R Barker
CU- B Bryan
RU- L Clinton
3B- M Ferraro
C- J Gibbs
1B- M Hegan
OF- H Lopez
1L- J Miller
SS- B Murcer
CF- R Repoz
SS- D Schofield
MR- S Whitaker
M1 J Keane
M2 R Houk

1967

SP M Stottlemyre
SP A Downing
SP F Peterson
SP F Talbot
SP S Barber
SP- W Ford
SP- C Perkins
SP- D Roberts
RS B Monbouquette
RP D Womack
RS T Tillotson
RS J Verbanic
RP S Hamilton
RP- J Bouton
RP- H Reniff
C J Gibbs
1B M Mantle
2B H Clarke
SS R Amaro
3B C Smith
LF T Tresh
CF J Pepitone
RO S Whitaker
UO B Robinson
1B- R Barker
UC- B Bryan
UL- L Clinton
C- F Fernandez
1B- M Hegan
CU- E Howard
UI- D Howser
UI- J Kennedy
SS- J Kenney
UO- R Moschitto
RF- C Sands
LF- T Shopay
UC- F Tepedino
CU- B Tillman
OI- R White
M R Houk

1968

SP M Stottlemyre
SP S Bahnsen
SP F Peterson
SP S Barber
SR F Talbot
SP B Monbouquette
SP A Downing
SP- J Bouton
SP- T Tillotson
SP- J Wyatt
SP- J Cumberland
RS J Verbanic
RP D Womack
RP S Hamilton
RP L McDaniel
C J Gibbs
1B M Mantle
2B H Clarke
SS T Tresh
3B B Cox
LU R White
UO B Robinson
RU A Kosco
CF J Pepitone
IF- R Amaro
RU- R Colavito
C- F Fernandez
3B- M Ferraro
UI- D Howser
SU- G Michael
C- E Rodriguez
US- C Smith
1B- T Solaita
UO- S Whitaker
M R Houk

1969

SP M Stottlemyre
SP F Peterson
SP S Bahnsen
SP B Burbach
SR A Downing
SR M Kekich
SP- R Klimkowski
SP- F Talbot
SP- D Nottebart
SP- J Cumberland
RP L McDaniel
RP J Aker
RP S Hamilton
RP- K Johnson
C- J Gibbs

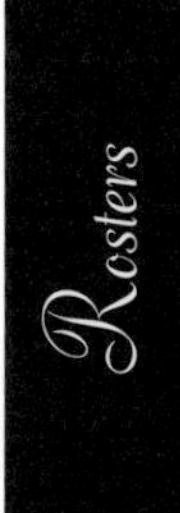

1B J Pepitone
2B H Clarke
SS G Michael
3U J Kenney
LF R White
CF- R Woods
RU B Murcer
LU- R Blomberg
UI- L Boehmer
UO- B Cowan
3U- B Cox
CU J Ellis
CU- F Fernandez
OI- J Hall
CF- J Lyttle
1B- D McDonald
C- T Munson
RF- N Oliver
OI- B Robinson
OF- T Shopay
LM- D Simpson
RF- F Tepedino
SS- T Tresh
M R Houk

1970

SP M Stottlemyre
SP F Peterson
SP S Bahnsen
SP S Kline
SR M Kekich
SP J Cumberland
SP- M McCormick
SP- B Burbach
SP- J Verbanic
SP- R Gardner
SP- L Colson
SP- G Jones
RP L McDaniel
RP R Klimkowski
RP J Aker
RS G Waslewski
RP- S Hamilton
C T Munson
1B D Cater
2B H Clarke
SS G Michael
3B J Kenney
LF R White
CF B Murcer
RF C Blefary
SS- F Baker
1U- J Ellis
C- J Gibbs
UI- R Hansen
RU- J Lyttle
RU- B Mitchell
UT- F Tepedino
UR- P Ward
RU- R Woods
M R Houk

1971

SP F Peterson
SP M Stottlemyre
SP S Bahnsen
SP S Kline
SR M Kekich
SP- J Hardin
SP- T Ley
SP- B Burbach
SP- R Gardner
RP L McDaniel
RP J Aker
RP- G Waslewski
RP- R Hambright
RP- A Closter
RP- G Jones
C T Munson
13 D Cater
2B H Clarke
SS G Michael
3B J Kenney
LF R White
CF B Murcer
OI F Alou
SS- F Baker
UT- C Blefary
RF- R Blomberg
UR- L Boehmer
1B- J Ellis
CU- J Gibbs
UI- R Hansen
UO- J Lyttle
RU- R Swoboda
UR- F Tepedino
OF- R Torres
RU- D Walton
OF- R Woods
M R Houk

1972

SP M Stottlemyre
SP F Peterson
SP S Kline
SP M Kekich
SP R Gardner
SP- R Hinton
SP- C Cox
SP- L Gowell
SP- J Aker
SP- S Blateric
SP- A Closter
SP- D Medich
RP S Lyle
RP L McDaniel
RP F Beene
RP- R Klimkowski
RP- J Roland
RP- W Blasingame
C T Munson
1B R Blomberg
2B H Clarke
SS G Michael
3B- C Sanchez
LF R White
CF B Murcer
RF- J Callison
1B F Alou
3U- B Allen
IC- J Ellis
SS- J Kenney
3B- H Lanier
3B- R McKinney
RU- C Spikes
RU- R Swoboda
RF- F Tepedino
RF- R Torres
M R Houk

1973

SP M Stottlemyre
SP D Medich
SP F Peterson
SP P Dobson
SP S McDowell
SP S Kline
SP- J Magnuson
SP- T Buskey
SP- W Granger
SP- M Kekich
SP- D Pagan
SP- C Cox
RP L McDaniel
RP S Lyle
RP F Beene
C T Munson
1U- F Alou
2B H Clarke
SS G Michael
3B G Nettles
LF R White
CF B Murcer
R1 M Alou
DH J Hart
D1 R Blomberg
2B- B Allen
RU- J Callison
C- R Dempsey
1B- M Hegan
SI- H Lanier
C- J Moses
IO- C Sanchez
DC- D Sims
SS- F Stanley
OF- R Swoboda
RF- O Velez
M R Houk

1974

SP P Dobson
SP D Medich
SP D Tidrow
SP R May
SP M Stottlemyre
SP L Gura
SR D Pagan
SP- S McDowell
SP- D Woodson
SP- S Kline
SP- F Beene
SP- F Peterson
SP- T Buskey
SP- K Wright
SP- R Sawyer
RP S Lyle
RP C Upshaw
RP M Wallace
RP- T Martinez
C T Munson
1B C Chambliss
2B- S Alomar
SS J Mason
3B G Nettles
LU L Piniella
CF E Maddox
RM B Murcer
DU- R Blomberg
UT R White
2B- H Clarke
C- J Deidel
CU R Dempsey
2B- F Gonzalez
UC- J Hart
1B- M Hegan
UT- A Johnson
2S- G Michael
UO- L Murray
DU- D Sims
S2- F Stanley
IF- B Sudakis
1B- O Velez
MU- T Whitfield
OF- W Williams
M B Virdon

1975

SP C Hunter
SP D Medich
SP R May
SP P Dobson
SP L Gura
SP- R Guidry
SP- R Sawyer
SP- M Wallace
RP S Lyle
RP D Tidrow
RP- T Martinez
RP- D Pagan
C T Munson
1B C Chambliss
2B S Alomar
SS- J Mason
3B G Nettles
LF R White
CF- E Maddox
RM B Bonds
UC- E Herrmann
S2 F Stanley
RF- D Bergman
CF- R Bladt
DH- R Blomberg
SS- E Brinkman
UO- R Coggins
OC- R Dempsey
CF- K Dineen
DU- A Johnson
SS- E Leon
UO- L Murray
IF- B Oliver
OF- L Piniella
UT- O Velez
RF- T Whitfield
OI- W Williams
M1 B Virdon
M2 B Martin

1976

SP C Hunter
SP E Figueroa
SP D Ellis
SP K Holtzman
SP D Alexander
SP R May
SP- D Pagan
SP- R Guidry
SP- J York
SP- K Brett
RP S Lyle
RP D Tidrow
RP G Jackson
RP- T Martinez
C T Munson
1B C Chambliss
2B W Randolph
SS F Stanley
3B G Nettles
LF R White
CF M Rivers
RF O Gamble
DH- C May
OF L Piniella
2U- S Alomar
OI- J Bernhardt
H- R Blomberg
OF- R Coggins
OC- R Dempsey
MR- K Dineen
CU- F Healy
CU- E Hendricks
SS- M Klutts
UT- G Locklear
OF- E Maddox
SS- J Mason
CF- L Murray
DH- C Tovar
UT- O Velez
LF- T Whitfield
M B Martin

1977

SP E Figueroa
SP M Torrez
SP R Guidry
SP D Gullett
SP C Hunter
SP K Holtzman
SP- G Patterson
SP- D Ellis
SP- L McCall
SP- S Thomas
RP S Lyle
RS D Tidrow
RP K Clay
C T Munson
1B C Chambliss
2B W Randolph
SS B Dent
3B G Nettles
LF R White
CF M Rivers
RF R Jackson
DH- C May
OI L Piniella
UT- D Alston
OI- D Bergman
MR- P Blair
C- F Healy
CU- E Hendricks
UC- C Johnson
H- D Kingman
3B- M Klutts
LF- G Locklear
3B- M Perez
SS- F Stanley
DO- J Wynn
2B- G Zeber
M B Martin

1978

SP R Guidry
SP E Figueroa
SP D Tidrow
SP J Beattie
SP C Hunter
SP D Gullett
SP- R Eastwick
SP- B Kammeyer
SP- A Messersmith
SP- K Holtzman
SP- P Lindblad
SP- L McCall
SP- D Rajsich
SP- R Davis
RP R Gossage
RP S Lyle
RS K Clay
C T Munson
1B C Chambliss
2B W Randolph
SS B Dent
3B G Nettles
LU L Piniella
CF M Rivers
RD R Jackson
DC- C Johnson
LU R White
2B- D Alston
MU- P Blair
2I- B Doyle
2B- D Garcia
C- F Healy
C- M Heath
OF- J Johnstone
3B- M Klutts
SS- D Ramos
3D- D Sherrill
UT- J Spencer
SS- F Stanley
UO- G Thomasson
UL- G Zeber
M1 B Martin
M2 D Howser
M3 B Lemon

1979

SP T John
SP R Guidry
SP L Tiant
SP E Figueroa
SP C Hunter
SP J Beattie
SP- D Righetti
SP- P Mirabella
SP- M Griffin
SP- R Anderson
SP- R Slagle
SP- B Kammeyer
RP R Davis
RS K Clay
RP R Gossage
RS D Hood
RP J Kaat
RP- R Burris
RP- D Tidrow
C T Munson
1B C Chambliss
2B W Randolph
SS B Dent
3B G Nettles
LU L Piniella
CF- B Murcer
RF R Jackson
DU J Spencer
ML- J Beniquez
MR- P Blair
MU- B Brown
23- B Doyle
LU- O Gamble
SS- D Garcia
C- B Gulden
DH- C Johnson
LU- J Johnstone
DH- D Jones
C- J Narron
OF- L Randle
CF- M Rivers
C- B Robinson
DH- G Scott
3B- R Staiger
S3- F Stanley
US- D Werth
UT- R White
M1 B Lemon
M2 B Martin

1980

SP T John
SP R Guidry
SR T Underwood
SR R May
SP L Tiant
SP E Figueroa
SP M Griffin
SP G Perry
SP- J Kaat
RP R Davis
RP R Gossage
RP D Bird
RP- T Lollar
C R Cerone
1B B Watson
2B W Randolph
SS B Dent
3B- G Nettles
LF L Piniella
MO B Brown
RD R Jackson
D3- E Soderholm
OF B Murcer
1B- J Spencer
LR- P Blair
1D- M Brant
2S- B Doyle
OF- O Gamble
C- B Gulden
2B- R Holt
CF- R Jones
RL- J Lefebvre
C- J Oates
C- B Robinson
3B- A Rodriguez
S2- D Sherrill
UI- F Stanley
UT- D Werth
UO- T Wilborn
M D Howser

1981

SP R May
SP T John
SP R Guidry
SP D Righetti
SP R Reuschel
SP G Nelson
SP T Underwood
SP- A McGaffigan
SP- D Wehrmeister
SP- M Griffin
RP R Davis
RP R Gossage
RP D Bird
RP D LaRoche
RP- G Frazier
RP- B Castro
C R Cerone
1B- B Watson
2B W Randolph
SS B Dent
3B G Nettles
RP R Gossage
LF D Winfield
CF J Mumphrey
RD R Jackson
DU- B Murcer
OF O Gamble
2U- T Ashford
1B- S Balboni
UO- B Brown
C- B Foote
SI- L Milbourne
C- J Oates
LF- M Patterson
OF- L Piniella
1B- D Revering
SS- A Robertson
3U- A Rodriguez
1B- J Spencer
1U- D Werth
M1 G Michael
M2 B Lemon

1982

SP R Guidry
SP T John
SP D Righetti
SR S Rawley
SP M Morgan
SP R Erickson
SP D Alexander
SP- J Howell
SP- J Pacella
SP- C Kaufman
SP- L McGlothen
SP- S Wever
SP- J Lewis
RP R Gossage
RP G Frazier
RS R May
RP D LaRoche
C- R Cerone
1B- J Mayberry
2B W Randolph
S3 R Smalley
3B G Nettles
LF D Winfield
CF J Mumphrey
RF K Griffey
DR O Gamble
OI D Collins
DR L Piniella
1B- S Balboni
SS- B Dent
C- J Espino
UI- B Evans
C- B Foote
D1- B Hobson
LU- D Mattingly
1U- L Mazzilli
SI- L Milbourne
DU- B Murcer
MU- M Patterson
C- B Ramos
1B- D Revering
S2- A Robertson
2B- E Rodriguez
S2- R Scott
HU- D Stegman
1B- B Watson
C- B Wynegar
M1 B Lemon
M2 G Michael
M3 C King

1983

SP R Guidry
SP S Rawley
SP D Righetti
SP B Shirley
SP R Fontenot
SP J Howell
SP M Keough
SP- J Montefusco
SP- D Alexander
SP- R Erickson
SP- C Kaufman
SP- D LaRoche
RP G Frazier
RP R Gossage
RP D Murray
RP- R May
C- B Wynegar
1B K Griffey
2B W Randolph
SI R Smalley
3B G Nettles
LF D Winfield
CF- J Mumphrey
RF S Kemp
DH D Baylor
SS A Robertson
1U- S Balboni
23- B Campaneris
C- R Cerone
LF- B Dayett
C- J Espino
OF- O Gamble
UT- D Mattingly
SS- B Meacham
2I- L Milbourne
CF- O Moreno
HU- B Murcer
OF- O Nixon
CF- R Office
RL- L Piniella
M B Martin

1984

SP P Niekro
SP R Guidry
SR R Fontenot
SP D Rasmussen
SP J Cowley
SP J Montefusco
SP- S Rawley
SP- M Bystrom
SP- J Deshaies
RP D Righetti
RS B Shirley
RP J Howell
RP J Rijo
RS M Armstrong
RP- C Christiansen
RP- D Murray
RP- C Brown
C B Wynegar
1B D Mattingly
2B W Randolph
SS B Meacham
3B- T Harrah
OI K Griffey
CF O Moreno
RF D Winfield
DH D Baylor
LC- S Bradley
C- R Cerone
LF- B Dayett
UI- T Foli
DU- O Gamble
2B- R Hudler
OF- S Javier
LF- S Kemp
MR- V Mata
C- M O'Berry
3B- M Pagliarulo
LR- L Piniella
SS- A Robertson
3I- R Smalley
SS- K Smith
M Y Berra

1985

SP R Guidry
SP P Niekro
SP J Cowley
SP E Whitson
SP D Rasmussen
SP- M Bystrom
SP- M Armstrong
SP- R Scurry
SP- J Niekro
SP- D Cooper
SP- J Montefusco
SP- D Murray
RP D Righetti
RP B Fisher
RS B Shirley
RP R Bordi
RP- N Allen
C B Wynegar
1B D Mattingly
2B W Randolph
SS B Meacham
3B M Pagliarulo
LF K Griffey
CF R Henderson
RF D Winfield
DH D Baylor
3B- D Berra
2B- J Bonilla
UC- S Bradley
ML- H Cotto
C- J Espino
C- R Hassey
2B- R Hudler
UO- V Mata
MU- O Moreno
LU- D Pasqua
3S- A Robertson
LF- B Sample
SS- K Smith
M1 Y Berra
M2 B Martin

1986

SP D Rasmussen
SP R Guidry
SP D Drabek
SP B Tewksbury
SP J Niekro
SP T John
SP S Nielsen
SP- A Pulido
SP- J Montefusco
SP- M Armstrong
SP- B Arnsberg
RP D Righetti
RS B Shirley
RP B Fisher
RP T Stoddard
RP- A Holland
RP- R Scurry
RP- E Whitson
C- B Wynegar
1B D Mattingly
2B W Randolph
SS- W Tolleson
3B M Pagliarulo
LU D Pasqua
CF R Henderson
RF D Winfield
DH M Easler
IF- D Berra
ML- H Cotto
SS- I DeJesus
C- J Espino
S2- M Fischlin
LF- K Griffey
C- R Hassey
3B- L Hernandez
DH- R Kittle
2B- B Little
OC- P Lombardi
SS- B Meacham
UT- G Roenicke
C- J Skinner
UO- C Washington
SS- P Zuvella
M L Piniella

1987

SP T John
SP R Rhoden
SR C Hudson
SP D Rasmussen
SP R Guidry
SP J Niekro
SP- B Gullickson
SP- S Trout
SP- B Tewksbury
SP- N Allen
SP- A Leiter
SP- P Filson
SP- B Arnsberg
SP- A Holland
SP- B Fulton
RP D Righetti
RP T Stoddard
RP P Clements
RP- C Guante
RP- B Shirley
RP- R Bordi
C R Cerone
1B D Mattingly
2B W Randolph
SS W Tolleson
3B M Pagliarulo
OI G Ward
MU C Washington
RF D Winfield
LU D Pasqua
2B- J Bonilla
UO- J Buhner
MO- H Cotto
UT- O Destrade
OF- M Easler
OF- R Henderson
CF- K Hughes
MU- R Kelly
DH- R Kittle
CU- P Lombardi
S2- B Meacham

Rosters

UT- J Moronko
3U- J Royster
32- L Sakata
C- M Salas
C- J Skinner
SS- R Velarde
2S- P Zuvella
M L Piniella

1988

SP R Rhoden
SP T John
SP R Dotson
SP J Candelaria
SR C Hudson
SP A Leiter
SP R Guidry
SP- S Nielsen
SP- D Eiland
SP- P Clements
RP N Allen
RP D Righetti
RP C Guante
RP S Shields
RP T Stoddard
RP- L Guetterman
RP- D Mohorcic
RP- H Pena
C D Slaught
1B D Mattingly
2B W Randolph
SS R Santana
3B M Pagliarulo
LF R Henderson
CF C Washington
RF D Winfield
DU J Clark
32- L Aguayo
MU- J Buhner
CF- C Chambliss
OF- J Cruz
2S- A Espinoza
C- B Geren
MU- R Kelly
S2- B Meacham
OF- H Morris
DU- K Phelps
C- J Skinner
23- W Tolleson
2S- R Velarde
UT- G Ward
M1 B Martin
M2 L Piniella

1989

SP A Hawkins
SP C Parker
SP D LaPoint
SR C Cary
SP G Cadaret
SP W Terrell
SP T John
SP R Dotson
SP J Candelaria
SP J Jones
SP- D Eiland
SP- A Leiter
SP- D Schulze
SP- K Mmahat
SP- B Davidson
SP- S Nielsen
RP L Guetterman
RP D Righetti
RP L McCullers
RS E Plunk
RP D Mohorcic
RP- R Gossage
C D Slaught
1B D Mattingly
2B S Sax
SS A Espinoza
3B- M Pagliarulo
OF M Hall
CF R Kelly
RF J Barfield
DU S Balboni
3B- M Blowers
3B- T Brookens
RM- B Brower
C- B Dorsett
C- B Geren
LF- R Henderson
RU- S Jefferson
3B- S Kiefer
LU- M Lawton
3B- H Meulens
OI- H Morris
DU- K Phelps
LF- L Polonia
IC- J Quirk
CF- D Sanders
UI- W Tolleson
3B- R Velarde
RF- G Ward
M1 D Green
M2 B Dent

1990

SP T Leary
SP A Hawkins
SP D LaPoint
SP C Cary
SP M Witt
SR J Jones
SP- D Eiland
SP- M Leiter
SP- S Adkins
SP- C Parker
SP- P Perez
SP- J Habyan
SP- R Monteleone
RS G Cadaret
RP L Guetterman
RP D Righetti
RP J Robinson
RP E Plunk
RP- A Mills
RP- L McCullers
C B Geren
1B D Mattingly
2B S Sax
SS A Espinoza
3B- R Velarde
LU- O Azocar
CF R Kelly
RF J Barfield
DU S Balboni
OF M Hall
3B- M Blowers
CU- R Cerone
CD- B Dorsett
3B- J Leyritz
1U- K Maas
LF- H Meulens
CD- M Nokes
UC- L Polonia
LM- D Sanders
SU- W Tolleson
UI- J Walewander
LU- C Washington
LD- D Winfield
M1 B Dent
M2 S Merrill

1991

SP S Sanderson
SP J Johnson
SR T Leary
SP W Taylor
SP P Perez
SP D Eiland
SP S Kamieniecki
SP C Cary
SP- A Mills
SP- A Hawkins
SP- D Chapin
SP- M Witt
RS G Cadaret
RS E Plunk
RP L Guetterman
RP S Farr
RP J Habyan
RP S Howe
RP- R Monteleone
C M Nokes
1B D Mattingly
2B S Sax
SS A Espinoza
3B- P Kelly
ML R Kelly
CF- B Williams
UO M Hall
DU K Maas
RF- J Barfield
3B- M Blowers
C- B Geren
OI- M Humphreys
3U- J Leyritz
3B- T Lovullo
OF- S Lusader
LU- H Meulens
CD- J Ramos
SU- C Rodriguez
UO- P Sheridan
3S- R Velarde
M S Merrill

1992

SP M Perez
SP S Sanderson
SP S Kamieniecki
SP T Leary
SR S Hillegas
SP S Militello
SP J Johnson
SP B Wickman
SP- C Young
SP- S Hitchcock
RS G Cadaret
RP R Monteleone
RP S Farr
RP J Habyan
RP- T Burke
RP- S Howe
RP- L Guetterman
RP- J Nielsen
RP- R Springer
C M Nokes
1B D Mattingly
2B P Kelly
S2 A Stankiewicz
3B C Hayes
LU M Hall
ML R Kelly
RD D Tartabull
DU K Maas
SU R Velarde
RF- J Barfield
2B- M Gallego
LD- M Humphreys
UO- D James
UC- J Leyritz
3B- H Meulens
SS- D Silvestri
1B- J Snow
C- M Stanley
CF- B Williams
RF- G Williams
M B Showalter

1993

SP J Key
SP J Abbott
SP M Perez
SR S Kamieniecki
SR B Wickman
SP- M Witt
SP- D Jean
SP- S Hitchcock
SP- M Hutton
SP- F Tanana
SP- L Smith
SP- S Militello
SP- A Cook
SP- J Johnson
RP R Monteleone
RP S Farr
RP S Howe
RP- B Munoz
RP- J Habyan
RP- P Gibson
RP- N Heaton
RP- P Assenmacher
C M Stanley
1B D Mattingly
2B P Kelly
SS S Owen
3B W Boggs
LF D James
CF B Williams
RL P O'Neill
DR D Tartabull
UI M Gallego
UO- M Humphreys
UT- J Leyritz
D1- K Maas
LU- H Meulens
CU- M Nokes
S3- D Silvestri
UI- A Stankiewicz
LS- R Velarde
UO- G Williams
M B Showalter

1994

SP J Key
SP J Abbott
SP M Perez
SP T Mulholland
SP S Kamieniecki
SP- G Harris
SP- M Hutton
SP- B Ojeda
SP- R Murphy
RP B Wickman
RP S Howe
RS S Hitchcock
RP X Hernandez
RP D Pall
RP- P Gibson
RP- J Ausanio
RP- J Reardon
C M Stanley
1B D Mattingly
2B P Kelly
SS M Gallego
3B W Boggs
LF L Polonia
CF B Williams
RF P O'Neill
DH D Tartabull
IC J Leyritz
S3 R Velarde
UO- D Boston
3B- R Davis
SS- R Eenhoorn
SS- K Elster
IC- B Melvin
CU- M Nokes
2B- D Silvestri
UO- G Williams
M B Showalter

1995

SP J McDowell
SP A Pettitte
SP S Hitchcock
SP D Cone
SP S Kamieniecki
SP M Perez
SP M Rivera
SP- J Key
SP- B Boehringer
SP- D Eiland
SP- D Pavlas
SP- J Patterson
SP- R Honeycutt
RP J Wetteland
RP B Wickman
RP S Howe
RP R Mac Donald
RP- J Ausanio
RP- S Bankhead
RP- J Manzanillo
C M Stanley
1B D Mattingly
2B P Kelly
SS T Fernandez
3B W Boggs
LR G Williams
CF B Williams
RF P O'Neill
DH- R Sierra
2S R Velarde
3B- R Davis
2S- R Eenhoorn
SS- K Elster
OI- D James
SS- D Jeter
CU- J Leyritz
LF- L Polonia
C- J Posada
LF- R Rivera
UI- D Silvestri
OF- D Strawberry
DR- D Tartabull
M B Showalter

1996

SP A Pettitte
SP K Rogers
SP D Gooden
SP J Key
SP D Cone
SP R Mendoza
SP- S Kamieniecki
SP- D Weathers
SP- W Whitehurst
SP- R Bones
SP- B Brewer
SP- P Gibson
RP M Rivera
RP J Wetteland
RP B Wickman
RP J Nelson
RP- B Boehringer
RP- J Mecir
RP- M Hutton
RP- D Pavlas
RP- D Polley
RP- S Howe
RP- G Lloyd
C J Girardi
1B T Martinez
2B M Duncan
SS D Jeter
3B W Boggs
LU G Williams
CF B Williams
RF P O'Neill
DL- R Sierra
23 A Fox
OI- M Aldrete
2B- R Eenhoorn
DH- C Fielder
3B- C Hayes
2B- M Howard
LU- D James
2B- P Kelly
CU- J Leyritz
R- M Luke
IC- T McIntosh
CD- J Posada
LF- T Raines
UO- R Rivera
2B- L Sojo
OF- D Strawberry
M J Torre

1997

SP A Pettitte
SP D Wells
SP D Cone
SP K Rogers
SR R Mendoza
SP D Gooden
SP H Irabu
SP- W Banks
SP- J Borowski
SP- D Rios
RP M Rivera
RP J Nelson
RP M Stanton
RP G Lloyd
RP- B Boehringer
RP- J Mecir
RP- D Weathers
C J Girardi
1B T Martinez
2B- L Sojo
SS D Jeter
3B C Hayes
LM- C Curtis
CF B Williams
RF P O'Neill
DH C Fielder
3U W Boggs
2B- H Bush
UT- I Cruz
2B- M Duncan
CD- M Figga
3I- A Fox
H- P Incaviglia
2U- P Kelly
C- J Posada
LR- S Pose
LF- T Raines
2B- R Sanchez
D1- M Stanley
UT- D Strawberry
LU- M Whiten
M J Torre

1998

SP A Pettitte
SP D Wells
SP D Cone
SP H Irabu
SP O Hernandez
SR R Mendoza
SP- W Banks
SP- R Bradley
SP- J Borowski
SP- J Bruske
SP- J Tessmer
SP- M Jerzembeck
SP- T Erdos
RP M Rivera
RP M Stanton
RP D Holmes
RP- J Nelson
RP- M Buddie
RP- G Lloyd
C J Posada
1B T Martinez
2B C Knoblauch
SS D Jeter
3B S Brosius
LM C Curtis
CF B Williams
RF P O'Neill
DH D Strawberry
DL T Raines
2D- H Bush
DH- C Davis
C- M Figga
C- J Girardi
LF- R Ledee
3B- M Lowell
UI- L Sojo
RL- S Spencer
1U- D Sveum
M J Torre

1999

SP O Hernandez
SP D Cone
SP A Pettitte
SP R Clemens
SP H Irabu
SP- E Yarnall
SP- T Erdos
SP- J Tessmer
SP- J Juden
SP- M Buddie
SP- T Fossas
RS R Mendoza
RP M Rivera
RP J Grimsley
RP M Stanton
RP D Naulty
RP- A Watson
RP- J Nelson
C J Posada
1B T Martinez
2B C Knoblauch
SS D Jeter
3B S Brosius
LF- C Curtis
CF B Williams
RF P O'Neill
DH C Davis
31- C Bellinger
C- M Figga
C- J Girardi
3B- D Jimenez
LF- R Ledee
IF- J Leyritz
1U- J Manto
UI- L Sojo
DU- A Soriano
LR- S Spencer
DU- D Strawberry
LR- T Tarasco
M1 D Zimmer
M2 J Torre

2000

SP A Pettitte
SP R Clemens
SP O Hernandez
SP D Cone
SP D Neagle
SP R Mendoza
SP- B Ford
SP- R Keisler
SP- T Lilly
SP- J Tessmer
SP- J Westbrook
SP- E Yarnall
RP M Rivera
RP J Grimsley
RP J Nelson
RP M Stanton
RS D Gooden
RP- T Erdos
RP- A Watson
RP- R Choate
RP- D Einertson
RP- C Dingman
C J Posada
1B T Martinez
2B C Knoblauch
SS D Jeter
3B S Brosius
LR- D Justice
CF B Williams
RF P O'Neill
OF- S Spencer
UT C Bellinger
DU- J Canseco
UI- W Delgado
DL- G Hill
OF- L Johnson
OF- F Jose
LM- R Kelly
LU- R Ledee
DU- J Leyritz
LU- L Polonia
23- L Sojo
UI- A Soriano
LM- R Thompson
C- C Turner
2B- J Vizcaino
M J Torre

2001

SP M Mussina
SP R Clemens
SP A Pettitte
SP T Lilly
SP O Hernandez
SP S Hitchcock
SP R Keisler
SP- A Hernandez
SP- B Knight
SP- C Parker
SP- B Jodie
RP M Rivera
RP R Mendoza
RP M Stanton
RP- R Choate
RP- J Witasick
RP- B Boehringer
RP- M Wohlers
RP- T Williams
RP- C Almanzar
C J Posada
1B T Martinez
2B A Soriano
SS D Jeter
3B S Brosius
LF C Knoblauch
CF B Williams
RF P O'Neill
DH D Justice
SD- E Almonte
UT- C Bellinger
RU- D Bragg
MD- M Coleman
C- B Estalella
C- T Greene
1D- N Johnson
OF- D McDonald
C- J Oliver
MR- R Perez
RM- J Rivera
UR- H Rodriguez
H- S Seabol
UI- L Sojo
LR- S Spencer
UT- R Velarde
UO- G Williams
UI- E Wilson
M J Torre

2002

SP M Mussina
SP D Wells
SP R Clemens
SP O Hernandez
SP A Pettitte
SP J Weaver
SP T Lilly
SP- B Knight
SP- A Hernandez
SP- J Tessmer
RP S Karsay
RP R Mendoza
RP M Stanton
RP M Rivera
RP- S Hitchcock
RP- M Thurman
RP- R Choate
C J Posada
1D N Johnson
2B A Soriano
SS D Jeter
3B R Ventura
LF R White
CF B Williams
RL- S Spencer
1D J Giambi
3U- A Arias
C- A Castillo
RF- R Coomer
LR- K Garcia
HU- D Henson
RF- R Mondesi
LR- J Rivera
RL- M Thames
RU- J Vander Wal
C- C Widger
RO- G Williams
IO- E Wilson
M J Torre

2003

SP M Mussina
SP D Wells
SP R Clemens
SP A Pettitte
SP J Weaver
SP J Contreras
SP- J DePaula
SP- A Benitez
SP- B Claussen
SP- D Miceli
SP- R Choate
SP- B Prinz
RP M Rivera
RP C Hammond
RP A Osuna
RP S Hitchcock
RP- J Acevedo
RP- J Anderson
RP- J Nelson
RP- A Reyes
RP- F Heredia
RP- G White
RP- J Orosco
C J Posada
1D- N Johnson
2B A Soriano
SS D Jeter
3B- R Ventura
LM H Matsui
CF B Williams
RF R Mondesi
1D J Giambi
SS- E Almonte
3B- A Boone
RF- D Dellucci
C- J Flaherty
RL- K Garcia
UT- C Gipson
3U- D Henson
C- M Hernandez
OF- C Latham
RL- C Pride
LR- J Rivera
1U- F Seguignol
DO- R Sierra
IF- L Sojo
DU- B Trammell
S3- E Wilson
IF- T Zeile
M J Torre

2004

SP J Vazquez
SP J Lieber
SP M Mussina
SP K Brown
SP J Contreras
SP O Hernandez
SP- E Loaiza
SP- B Halsey
SP- D Osborne
SP- J Padilla
SP- J DePaula
SP- S Karsay
SP- A Graman
SP- S Marsonek
RP M Rivera
RP P Quantrill
RP T Gordon
RP T Sturtze
RP- F Heredia
RP- B Prinz
RP- S Proctor
RP- G White
RP- C Nitkowski
C J Posada
1B T Clark
2B M Cairo
SS D Jeter
3B A Rodriguez
LF H Matsui
MD B Williams
RF G Sheffield
DO R Sierra
UT- H Bush
UO- B Crosby
SS- F Escalona
C- J Flaherty
1D- J Giambi
1B- T Lee
CF- K Lofton
C- D Navarro
1B- J Olerud
3B- A Phillips
2B- E Wilson
M J Torre

2005

SP R Johnson
SP M Mussina
SP C Wang
SP C Pavano
SP S Chacon
SP A Small
SP K Brown
SP J Wright
SP A Leiter
SP- S Henn
SP- J DePaula
SP- D May
SP- J Anderson
SP- S Karsay

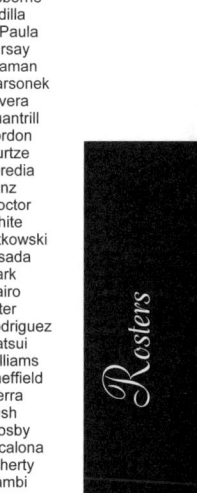

SP- C Bean
SP- A Graman
SP- R Mendoza
SP- T Redding
RP M Rivera
RP T Gordon
RP T Sturtze
RP- S Proctor
RP- P Quantrill
RP- F Rodriguez
RP- B Groom
RP- A Embree
RP- M Stanton
RP- W Franklin
C J Posada
1B T Martinez
2B R Cano
SS D Jeter
3B A Rodriguez
LU H Matsui
CF B Williams
RF G Sheffield
1D J Giambi
OI T Womack
UI- M Bellhorn
CF- M Cabrera
MR- B Crosby
S3- F Escalona
C- J Flaherty
IO- R Johnson
RL- M Lawton
C- W Nieves
1U- A Phillips
LM- K Reese
UI- R Sanchez
OF- R Sierra
RF- M Vento
M J Torre

2006

SP C Wang
SP R Johnson
SP M Mussina
SP J Wright
SP S Chacon
SP- C Lidle
SP- J Karstens
SP- A Small
SP- D Rasner
SP- S Ponson
SP- S Erickson
SP- S Henn
SP- K Wilson
SP- C Bean
RP M Rivera
RP S Proctor
RP R Villone
RP K Farnsworth
RP- M Myers
RP- B Bruney
RP- T Beam
RP- M Smith
RP- J Veras
RP T Sturtze
RP- O Dotel
C J Posada
1B A Phillips
2B R Cano
SS D Jeter
3B A Rodriguez
LF M Cabrera
CF J Damon
UO B Williams
D1 J Giambi
RF- B Abreu
2I- M Cairo
SS- A Cannizaro
UO- B Crosby
C- S Fasano
UI- N Green
OI- A Guiel
RO- T Long
LD- H Matsui
C- W Nieves
OF- K Reese
RU- G Sheffield
C- K Stinnett
RO- K Thompson
1B- C Wilson
M J Torre

2007

SP A Pettitte
SP C Wang
SP M Mussina
SP R Clemens
SP P Hughes
SP K Igawa
SP- M DeSalvo
SP- T Clippard
SP- D Rasner
SP- I Kennedy
SP- J Karstens
SP- C Pavano
SP- J Veras
SP- C Wright
SP- R Ohlendorf
SP- C Bean
SP- J Brower
CL M Rivera
RP L Vizcaino
RP K Farnsworth
RP S Proctor
RP B Bruney
RP- R Villone
RP- M Myers
RP- S Henn
RP- J Chamberlain
RP- E Ramirez
RP- C Britton
C J Posada
1B- D Mientkiewicz
2B R Cano
SS D Jeter
3B A Rodriguez
LF H Matsui
CF M Cabrera
RF B Abreu
DU- J Giambi
OI J Damon
3U- C Basak
IO- W Betemit
IO- M Cairo
OI- S Duncan
SS- A Gonzalez
C- J Molina
C- W Nieves
1B- J Phelps
1B- A Phillips
OI- B Sardinha
UO- K Thompson
M J Torre

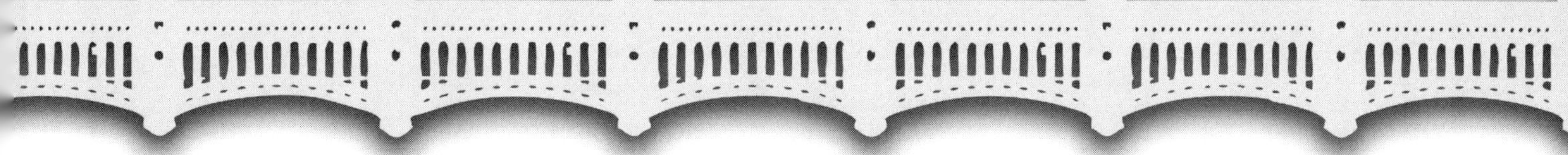

Yankees Farm System

From Mickey Mantle to Thurman Munson to Mariano Rivera, the Yankees have enjoyed the benefits of great homegrown players. Finding and nurturing talent, though, can be a risky proposition. Plenty of hot prospects have turned to dust upon their promotion to the big leagues, or faded away before they ever got close. The minor leagues have long been the proving ground of whether a prospect is a building block for the future, trade bait, or an expendable commodity. Most minor leaguers invariably fall into the latter category.

The structure of the minor leagues has changed greatly since the practice of farm clubs became widespread in the early 1930s. Before then, minor leagues operated independently of the major leagues—a few still do—and sold players to the majors on an individual basis. Branch Rickey's system, begun with the St. Louis Cardinals, of tracking a player's progress through several levels of its own system soon became the way that all teams worked. The players are always changing, and so are the places they play.

The Yankees have switched affiliates many times over and leagues have come and gone and merged. The Yankees started with five farm clubs in 1932, all on the East Coast. By 1939 the Yankees had 16 teams all over the country, including two different Newarks (New Jersey and Ohio). World War II brought that number down to five, but it hit a franchise-high of 24 in 1948. The deep system not only churned out stars, it also kept plenty of major league caliber players waiting in the minor leagues. Fans liked to say that the Yankees' farm club in Newark (New Jersey) could beat half the teams in the American League. With the Yankees winning regularly in the majors and the minors, it was hard to argue.

By 1959 the Yankees had less than 10 minor league teams and it dropped all the way to four in the mid-1970s, fewer teams than during World War II and the lowest number since 1933. Since 1993 the Yankees have held at six clubs, including a rookie team in the Gulf Coast League.

With more and more players coming from the Dominican Republic, the Yankees have at least shared one Dominican Summer League team since the late 1980s. In some years they have had two teams and in others they have shared a club. The Yankees had a presence in Venezuela, sharing a team there from 1998 to 2001. Players from these leagues, who usually turn professional at age 16, usually stay in their home country at facilities owned by the major league club. The better players from these teams advance to the club's affiliates in the U.S. Even after players get to one of the six affiliates on U.S. soil, there is still a long way to go to New York.

Since 1963, the minor leagues have been divided into three different classes: A, AA, and AAA. Currently there are two levels of Class A: short-season A and full-season A. Virtually every major league team, however, still effectively promotes players through three levels of Class A baseball: short-season A, full-season A, and A+ (usually referred to as High A). The Yankees' teams in 2007 included Staten Island in the New York–Penn League (short season, beginning in June), Charleston in the South Atlantic League (long season, starting in April), and Tampa of the Florida State League (the A+ club and also the home of the Yankees' spring training facility). Even if they skip a few stops, most Yankees farmhands ticketed for the Bronx wind up in Tampa at some point in their development.

There was a time leagues were classified by letters of the alphabet other than A. In 1963, after a decade during which the minor leagues shrunk dramatically as a result of the rising popularity of watching television instead of seeing prospects in person, the structure of the minor leagues was overhauled. In most cases, Class D baseball leagues turned into short-season Class A leagues, Class C baseball leagues became full-season Class A or Low A leagues, and Class B teams emerged as Class A+ or High A leagues. But not all leagues emerged from the transition in the same slot they were in before; the Florida State League, for example, transformed from a Class D league into a High A league. That is the reason the charts in this section have been broken down into groups through 1962 and from 1963 to present.

The current structure for minor league clubs differs in other ways from how it was in the first half of the 20th century. What was considered Class AA before World War II has been the equivalent of Class AAA baseball since 1946. During its 10 years of existence, A1 was considered higher than A yet lower than AA. A1 was, however, equivalent to what the Class AA level is today. That's a mouthful of the alphabet, but it can be summarized somewhat simply:

- A (1902–11) = AA (1912–45) = AAA (1946–present)
- A1 (1936–45) = AA (1946–present)
- A (1912–62) = AA (1963–present)
- Class B, C, D (through 1962) = Class A (1963–present)

Rookie Leagues were a new classification as of 1963. While some Class D leagues may have been essentially for players just starting professional baseball, the Rookie Leagues started in 1963 were new in that they were designed for this specific purpose. Today, the Appalachian League and the Pioneer League are considered more advanced Rookie Leagues than the Gulf Coast League and Arizona League, both of which play their games at spring training complexes and do not try to attract fans to their games.

And there were always plenty of leagues. Below are abbreviations for many of the minor leagues affiliated by the major leagues.

ABBR.	LEAGUE
AFL	Alabama Florida League
APL	Appalachian League
AASN	American Association
AML	Arkansas-Missouri League
ARL	Arkansas State League
ASL	Alabama State League
ATL	Arizona Texas League
AZL	Arizona League
BIS	Bi-State League
BL	Border League
BRL	Blue Ridge League
BSL	Big State League
CAL	Canadian American League
CCL	Cape Breton Colliery League
CCR	Cocoa Rookie League
CL	California League
CNL	Colonial League
CPL	Coastal Plain League
CRL	Carolina League
CSL	Cotton States League
CTA	Central Association
CTL	Central League
DL	Dixie League
DSL	Dominican Summer League
EDL	East Dixie League
EL	Eastern League
EL	Eastern League
ESL	Eastern Shore League
ETL	East Texas League
EVL	Evangeline League
FRL	Florida Rookie League
FSL	Florida State League

ABBR.	LEAGUE
FWL	Far West League
GAL	Georgia Alabama League
GCL	Gulf Coast League
GFL	Georgia Florida League
GSL	Georgia State League
GSL	Gulf States League
III	Three I League
IL	International League
ISL	Illinois State League
ITL	Interstate League
KIT	Kentucky-Illinois-Tennessee League
KOM	Kansas-Oklahoma-Missouri League
LHL	Longhorn League
LSL	Lone Star League
MAL	Middle Atlantic League
MOL	Mississippi-Ohio Valley League
MSL	Michigan State League
MTL	Mountain State League
MWL	Midwest League
NAL	North Atlantic League
NAR	Northeast Arkansas League
NCL	North Carolina State League
NEL	New England League
NEN	Northeastern League
NRL	Northern League
NSL	Nebraska State League
NWL	Northwest League
NYP	New York-Penn League
OIL	Ohio-Indiana League
OSL	Ohio State League
PCL	Pacific Coast League
PML	Piedmont League

ABBR.	LEAGUE
PNL	Pioneer League
PONY	Pennsylvania-Ontario-New York League
PSA	Pennsylvania State Association
PVL	Provincial League
QPL	Quebec Provincial League
RGV	Rio Grande Valley League
SA	Southern Association
SAL	South Atlantic League
SEL	Southeastern League
SIL	Southwest International League
SL	Southern League
SML	Sophomore League
SRL	Sarasota Rookie League
SSL	Sooner State League
SUNS	Sunset League
SWL	Southwestern League
THL	Tar Heel League
TL	Texas League
TML	West Texas-New Mexico League
TPL	Twin Ports League
TRL	Tri-State League
TSL	Tobacco State League
TVL	Texas Valley League
VL	Virginia League
VSL	Venezuelan Summer League
WA	Western Association
WCL	Western Carolina League
WDL	West Dixie League
WIL	Western International League
WL	Western League
WSL	Wisconsin State League
WTNM	West Texas-New Mexico League

Notes

Yankees farm teams that have changed classes over time include:

- Augusta: B to A
- Binghamton: B to A
- Butler, PA: D to C
- Denver: A to AAA

Yankees farm teams that have changed leagues over time include:

- Binghamton: New York-Penn League 1932–37, Eastern League 1938–62
- Denver: Western League to American Association

Bisbee of the Arizona-Texas League in 1947 became Bisbee-Douglas in 1948.

The original South Atlantic League ceased operating after 1963; a new South Atlantic League at a lower classification started up in 1980.

YEAR	CLASS AAA	CLASS AA	CLASS A	CLASS A	CLASS A	CLASS A	CLASS A	ROOKIE	DOMINICAN	VENEZUELA
2007	Scranton-Wilkes Barre (IL)	Trenton (EL)	Tampa (FSL)		Charleston (SAL)	Staten Island (NYP)		Gulf Coast (GCL)	DSL (2)	
2006	Columbus (IL)	Trenton (EL)	Tampa (FSL)		Charleston (SAL)	Staten Island (NYP)		Gulf Coast (GCL)	DSL (2)	
2005	Columbus (IL)	Trenton (EL)	Tampa (FSL)		Charleston (SAL)	Staten Island (NYP)		Gulf Coast (GCL)	DSL (2)	
2004	Columbus (IL)	Trenton (EL)	Tampa (FSL)		Battle Creek (MWL)	Staten Island (NYP)		Gulf Coast (GCL)	DSL (2)	
2003	Columbus (IL)	Trenton (EL)	Tampa (FSL)		Battle Creek (MWL)	Staten Island (NYP)		Gulf Coast (GCL)	DSL (2)	
2002	Columbus (IL)	Norwich (EL)	Tampa (FSL)		Greensboro (SAL)	Staten Island (NYP)		Gulf Coast (GCL)	DSL (2)	
2001	Columbus (IL)	Norwich (EL)	Tampa (FSL)		Greensboro (SAL)	Staten Island (NYP)		Gulf Coast (GCL)	DSL	Shared
2000	Columbus (IL)	Norwich (EL)	Tampa (FSL)		Greensboro (SAL)	Staten Island (NYP)		Gulf Coast (GCL)	DSL	Shared
1999	Columbus (IL)	Norwich (EL)	Tampa (FSL)		Greensboro (SAL)	Staten Island (NYP)		Gulf Coast (GCL)	DSL	Shared
1998	Columbus (IL)	Norwich (EL)	Tampa (FSL)		Greensboro (SAL)	Oneonta (NYP)		Gulf Coast (GCL)	DSL	Shared
1997	Columbus (IL)	Norwich (EL)	Tampa (FSL)		Greensboro (SAL)	Oneonta (NYP)		Gulf Coast (GCL)	DSL	
1996	Columbus (IL)	Norwich (EL)	Tampa (FSL)		Greensboro (SAL)	Oneonta (NYP)		Gulf Coast (GCL)	DSL	
1995	Columbus (IL)	Norwich (EL)	Tampa (FSL)		Greensboro (SAL)	Oneonta (NYP)		Gulf Coast (GCL)	DSL	
1994	Columbus (IL)	Albany-Colonie (EL)	Tampa (FSL)		Greensboro (SAL)	Oneonta (NYP)		Gulf Coast (GCL)	DSL	
1993	Columbus (IL)	Albany-Colonie (EL)	Prince William, VA (CL)		Greensboro (SAL)	Oneonta (NYP)		Gulf Coast (GCL)	Shared	
1992	Columbus (IL)	Albany-Colonie (EL)	Prince William, VA (CL)	Ft. Lauderdale (FSL)	Greensboro (SAL)	Oneonta (NYP)		Gulf Coast (GCL)	Shared	
1991	Columbus (IL)	Albany-Colonie (EL)	Prince William, VA (CL)	Ft. Lauderdale (FSL)	Greensboro (SAL)	Oneonta (NYP)		Gulf Coast (GCL)	Shared	
1990	Columbus (IL)	Albany-Colonie (EL)	Prince William, VA (CL)	Ft. Lauderdale (FSL)	Greensboro (SAL)	Oneonta (NYP)		Gulf Coast (GCL)	DSL	
1989	Columbus (IL)	Albany-Colonie (EL)	Prince William, VA (CL)	Ft. Lauderdale (FSL)		Oneonta (NYP)		Gulf Coast (GCL)	DSL	
1988	Columbus (IL)	Albany-Colonie (EL)	Prince William, VA (CL)	Ft. Lauderdale (FSL)		Oneonta (NYP)		Gulf Coast (GCL)		
1987	Columbus (IL)	Albany-Colonie (EL)	Prince William, VA (CL)	Ft. Lauderdale (FSL)		Oneonta (NYP)		Gulf Coast (GCL)		
1986	Columbus (IL)	Albany-Colonie (EL)		Ft. Lauderdale (FSL)		Oneonta (NYP)		Gulf Coast (GCL)		
1985	Columbus (IL)	Albany-Colonie (EL)		Ft. Lauderdale (FSL)		Oneonta (NYP)		Gulf Coast (GCL)		
1984	Columbus (IL)	Nashville (SL)		Ft. Lauderdale (FSL)	Greensboro (SAL)	Oneonta (NYP)		Gulf Coast (GCL)		
1983	Columbus (IL)	Nashville (SL)		Ft. Lauderdale (FSL)	Greensboro (SAL)	Oneonta (NYP)				
1982	Columbus (IL)	Nashville (SL)		Ft. Lauderdale (FSL)	Greensboro (SAL)	Oneonta (NYP)	Paintsville, KY (APL)	Gulf Coast (GCL)		
1981	Columbus (IL)	Nashville (SL)		Ft. Lauderdale (FSL)	Greensboro (SAL)	Oneonta (NYP)	Paintsville, KY (APL)	Gulf Coast (GCL)		
1980	Columbus (IL)	Nashville (SL)		Ft. Lauderdale (FSL)	Greensboro (SAL)	Oneonta (NYP)	Paintsville, KY (APL)	Gulf Coast (GCL)		
1979	Columbus (IL)	West Haven (EL)		Ft. Lauderdale (FSL)		Oneonta (NYP)	Paintsville, KY (APL)			
1978	Tacoma (PCL)	West Haven (EL)		Ft. Lauderdale (FSL)		Oneonta (NYP)				
1977	Syracuse (IL)	West Haven (EL)		Ft. Lauderdale (FSL)		Oneonta (NYP)				
1976	Syracuse (IL)	West Haven (EL)		Ft. Lauderdale (FSL)		Oneonta (NYP)				
1975	Syracuse (IL)	West Haven (EL)		Ft. Lauderdale (FSL)		Oneonta (NYP)				
1974	Syracuse (IL)	West Haven (EL)		Ft. Lauderdale (FSL)		Oneonta (NYP)	Johnson City, TN (APL)			
1973	Syracuse (IL)	West Haven (EL)		Ft. Lauderdale (FSL)		Oneonta (NYP)	Johnson City, TN (APL)			
1972	Syracuse (IL)	West Haven (EL)	Kinston, NC (CL)	Ft. Lauderdale (FSL)		Oneonta (NYP)	Johnson City, TN (APL)			
1971	Syracuse (IL)	Manchester (EL)	Kinston, NC (CL)	Ft. Lauderdale (FSL)		Oneonta (NYP)	Johnson City, TN (APL)			
1970	Syracuse (IL)	Manchester (EL)	Kinston, NC (CL)	Ft. Lauderdale (FSL)		Oneonta (NYP)	Johnson City, TN (APL)			
1969	Syracuse (IL)	Manchester (EL)	Kinston, NC (CL)	Ft. Lauderdale (FSL)		Oneonta (NYP)	Johnson City, TN (APL)			
1968	Syracuse (IL)	Binghamton (EL)	Kinston, NC (CL)	Ft. Lauderdale (FSL)		Oneonta (NYP)	Johnson City, TN (APL)			
1967	Syracuse (IL)	Binghamton (EL)	Greensboro (CL)	Ft. Lauderdale (FSL)		Oneonta (NYP)	Johnson City, TN (APL)			
1966	Toledo (IL)	Columbus, GA (SL)	Greensboro (CL)	Ft. Lauderdale (FSL)		Binghamton (NYP)	Johnson City, TN (APL)	Gulf Coast (GCL)		
1965	Toledo (IL)	Columbus, GA (SL)	Greensboro (CL)	Ft. Lauderdale (FSL)		Binghamton (NYP)	Johnson City, TN (APL)	Florida (FRL))		
1964	Richmond (IL)	Columbus, GA (SL)	Greensboro (CL)	Ft. Lauderdale (FSL)		Shelby, NC (WCL)	Johnson City, TN (APL)	Sarasota (SRL)		
1963	Richmond (IL)	Augusta (SAL)	Greensboro (CL)	Ft. Lauderdale (FSL)		Shelby, NC (WCL)	Harlan, KY (APL)	Idaho Falls (PNL)		

BEFORE 1963	SECOND TEAM	THIRD TEAM	FOURTH TEAM
Class AAA			
Richmond 1956–62 (IL)			
Denver 1955–58 (AASN)			
Kansas City, MO 1946–54 (AASN)	Syracuse 1953 (IL)		
	San Francisco 1951–52 (PCL)		
	Newark, NJ 1946–1949 (IL)		
Class AA			
Amarillo 1960–62 (TL)			
Binghamton, NY 1946-61 (EL)			
New Orleans 1957–58 (SA)			
Birminghamm, AL 1953–56 (SA)			
Beaumont, TX 1946–52 (TL)			
Newark, NJ 1932–45 (IL)	Oakland 1935–37 (PCL)		
Kansas City, MO 1937–45 (AASN)			
Mission, CA (PCL) 1936			
Class A			
Augusta, GA 1946–49, 1962 (SAL)	Denver 1947 (WL)		
Muskegon, MI 1950–51 (CTL)			
Binghamton, NY 1933–37 (NYP), 1938–45 (EL)			
Springfield, MA 1932 (EL)			
Class B			
Greensboro 1958–62 (CRL)			
Peoria 1957 (III)			
Quincy, IL 1946–56 (III)	Winston-Salem 1955–56 (CRL)		
Norfolk 1934–55 (PML)	Manchester, NH 1948–49 (NEL)		
Augusta, GA 1937–40 (SAL)			
Victoria, British Columbia 1946–49 (WIL)	Sunbury, PA 1946–47 (ITL)		
Wenatchee, WA 1938–40 (WIL)			
Jackson, MS 1937–38 (SEL)			
Durham 1933 (PML)			
Erie, PA 1932 (CTL)			
Binghamton 1932 (NYP)			
Class C			
Idaho Falls 1940–41, 1962 (PNL)			
Modesto 1954–61(CL)	Fargo-Moorhead 1958–60 (NRL)	Alexandria, LA 1957 (EVL)	
Monroe, LA 1955–56 (EVL)			
St. Joseph, MO 1954 (WA)			
Boise 1952–53 (PL)			
Joplin, MO 1935–42, 1946–53 (WA)			
Amsterdam, NY 1938–42, 1946–51 (CAL)	Twins Falls, ID 1946–51 (PL)		
Grand Forks, ND 1948–50 (NRL)	Ventura, CA 1947–49 (CL)		
Butler, PA 1946–48 (MAL)	Longview, TX 1948 (LSL)	Bisbee, AZ 1947 (ATL)	
Akron, OH 1935–41 (MAL)		Bisbee-Douglas, AZ 1948 (ATL)	
Bartlesville, OK 1937 (WA)	Smiths Falls, Ontario 1937 (CAL)		
Wheeling 1933–34 (MAL)			
Cumberland, MD 1932 (MAL)			
Class D			
Fort Lauderdale 1962 (FSL)	Harlan, KY 1961–62 (APL)		
St. Petersburg 1957–61 (FSL)	Auburn, NY 1958–61 (NYPL)	Greenville, TX 1957 (SSL)	
Kearney, NE 1956–59 (NSL)	Bradford, Ontario 1956 (PONY)		
McAlester, OK 1948–56(SSL)	Owensboro, KY 1953–55 (KIT)	Bristol, VA 1954–55 (APL)	Olean, NY 1952–53 (PONY)
Fon du Lac, WI 1946–52 (WSL)	Independence, KS 1947–50 (KOM)	Newark, OH 1948–51 (OIL)	
LaGrange, GA 1948–51 (GAL)	Belleville, IL 1949 (MOL)		
Easton, MD 1939–41, 1946–49 (ESL)	Blackstone, VA 1948 (VL)	Stroudsburg, PA 1947 (NAL)	
Wellsville, NY 1942–46 (PONY)			
Norfolk, NE 1937–41 (NSL)			
Neosho, KS 1938–40(AML)	Big Spring, TX 1939 (WTNM)	El Paso 1939 (ATL)	Newport, TN 1939 (APL)
Butler, PA 1936–42 (PSA)	Palatka, FL 1937 (FSL)		
Washington, PA 1934–35 (MAL)			

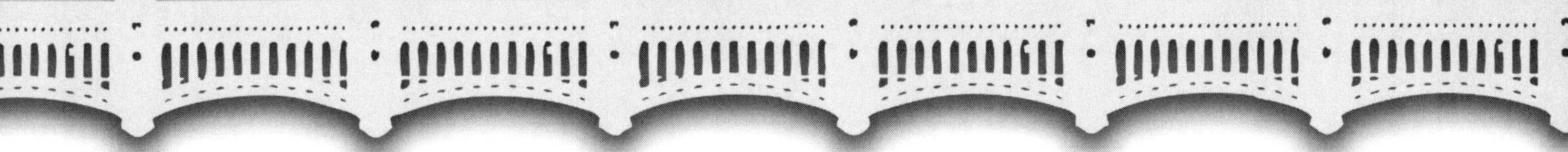

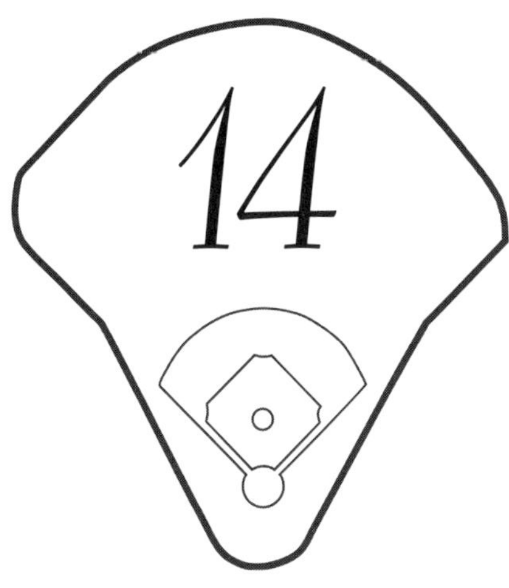

Yankees Trades & Free Agents

The blueprint for building dynasties has been a little different for the Yankees each time they've won multiple championships. In the 1920s and 1930s, it involved using a lot of available parts from Boston and watching them transform into winners in New York, courtesy of former Red Sox manager Ed Barrow running the show for the Yanks. In the 1940s and 1950s, scouted talent came to the fore, always supplemented with small transactions that turned blockbuster with the passage of time. By the 1950s and 1960s, it was a farm system bursting with future stars with a few scrupulous trades thrown in that made the most dominant team in the game.

The club that won five division titles, four pennants, and two World Series over a six-season span between 1976 and 1981 was the first to utilize major league talent that didn't require sending a player back in return directly. Free agency was an important factor, but trades glued together the Yankees lineup, not to mention homegrown stars like Ron Guidry and Thurman Munson. When the Yankees emerged in the 1990s, it was a similar mix. The dynasty that could conquer all in a three-tier postseason was a confluence of players from trades—Paul O'Neill, Tino Martinez, Jeff Nelson, and David Cone, among a host of others—and prospects: Bernie Williams, Andy Pettitte, Derek Jeter, Jorge Posada, and Mariano Rivera. Add in the right number of free agents like Joe Girardi, David Wells, and Mike Stanton, plus the burgeoning international free agent route that enabled the Yankees to import Orlando Hernandez and Hideki Matsui, and the Yankees managed a postseason streak that lasted a club-record 13 consecutive seasons.

This section looks at the best and worst trades from the arrival of American League baseball in New York in 1903 to the pinstripe mania that sees the Yankees with their own TV network, sophisticated international scouting, and erecting a new stadium. Free agents are taken into account from 1974, when Catfish Hunter got a little early start because of a technicality. (This special case didn't make the star-studded list that follows, but he acted like a neon sign for future free agents to come to the Bronx.)

The Yankees have always had the resources to spend freely, but they have spent wisely, for the most part. And even when they haven't, the Yankees have been able to cover up their mistakes or pass them off on another unsuspecting team. The Yankees' accumulated wealth has enabled them to continue winning to keep their demanding fan base happy. That part of the formula has remained unchanged since Babe Ruth arrived in town in 1920.

Best Yankees Trades

1. January 3, 1920 Purchased Babe Ruth from the Boston Red Sox for $100,000

Trading $100,000 for the Babe turned out to be the smartest move in the history of baseball, but the deal was not seen as such an obviously grand move at the time. While Ruth's talents were obvious to everyone after his record-breaking 1919, so were his behavioral issues, and those certainly didn't go away after he became a Yankee. Nobody in the Red Sox organization mourned the loss of Ruth until after they saw what he did as a Yankee. And Boston ended up better off than they would have if they had taken the other offer they had for Ruth: Joe Jackson straight up (after Jackson took part in the 1919 World Series fix and before he was banned). No one on either side of the most significant Yankees–Red Sox deal could have foreseen how Ruth would proceed to revolutionize baseball and serve as the cornerstone for the building of baseball's dominant franchise.

2. December 11, 1975 Traded Doc Medich to the Pittsburgh Pirates for Willie Randolph, Ken Brett, and Dock Ellis

The Yankees had already gotten the best three years of Doc Medich's career when they traded him for two veteran pitchers and a young second baseman with only 30 major league games to his credit. Medich managed to hang on in the majors for another seven years, mostly as a journeyman starter, but the young second baseman would end up as a six-time All-Star and the Yankees all-time leader in games played at second base. While Randolph would never make the noise that Yankees with gaudier offensive stats generated, his solid all-around play on both offense and defense would be a significant factor in the team having the best record in baseball during his time with the Bronx Bombers.

3. May 6, 1930 Traded Cedric Durst and $50,000 to the Boston Red Sox for Red Ruffing

The last of a series of deals with which the Yankees plundered virtually every Red Sox starting pitcher of talent, New York got a bit more out of Ruffing than the other Sox pitchers acquired over the previous dozen years. In Boston, Ruffing had been less than impressive, but the Red Sox teams of the time were so horrendous it was almost impossible to attain any level of success with them. Ruffing showed immediate improvement upon becoming a Yankee, though he didn't reach his peak as a pitcher until several years later. What made Ruffing unique wasn't his pitching, but his hitting—he ranks as the second best hitting pitcher of all time behind Wes Ferrell. While the Yankees also obtained Hall of Fame hurlers Waite Hoyt and Herb Pennock from Boston, Ruffing pitched longer and won more often than any pitcher ever acquired by the Yankees.

4. March 22, 1972 Traded a player to be named later (Mario Guerrero on June 30, 1972) and Danny Cater to the Boston Red Sox for Sparky Lyle

In what may be the most inexplicable trade on the list, the Yankees obtained a successful young reliever for a utility player/pinch hitter clearly on the downside of his career. Lyle proceeded to spend seven seasons as New York's bullpen ace and was a major factor in the Yankees' three straight pennants from 1976 to 1978. Cater proceeded to live on as the answer to a trivia question.

5. November 10, 1978 Traded Domingo Ramos, Mike Heath, Sparky Lyle, Larry McCall, Dave Rajsich, and cash to the Texas Rangers for Dave Righetti, Juan Beniquez, Mike Griffin, Paul Mirabella, and Greg Jemison

In 1978 the Yankees signed Rich Gossage to use in the bullpen alongside Sparky Lyle. But in the long run, the Yankees couldn't have two closers. After that season, Lyle, who was clearly starting to show some wear and tear, was traded to Texas in a 10-player deal that brought the Yankees the pitcher who in many ways would be Lyle's successor as a left-handed closer for New York. It took three years—plus a July 4 no-hitter at Yankee Stadium—before the Yankees decided that Righetti would be a reliever, but he ended up giving New York 10 successful seasons, never once posting an ERA above league average. Lyle had one good year in Texas before fading. A number of other players in the deal managed to stay around the majors over the next decade, but none made a significant impact.

6. January 30, 1923 Traded Camp Skinner, Norm McMillan, George Murray, and $50,000 to the Boston Red Sox for Herb Pennock

(See discussion below.)

7. December 15, 1920 Traded Muddy Ruel, Del Pratt, Sammy Vick, and Hank Thormahlen to the Boston Red Sox for Waite Hoyt, Harry Harper, Wally Schang, and Mike McNally

Two more trades for Red Sox pitching; two more Hall of Fame pitchers for the Yankees. Pennock had been a league average starter for Boston, but immediately was more successful as a Yankee and proceeded to roll out six great seasons before losing effectiveness in 1929. Hoyt came to the Yankees at a much younger age than Pennock, and managed to pitch eight effective (though far more variable) seasons for the Yankees before he also started to fade in 1929. Hoyt, unlike Pennock, was quickly exiled (to Detroit) once he was no longer performing up to the Yankees' standards. Neither pitcher would be in the Hall of Fame if they hadn't pitched for such a great team, but both were excellent pitchers who made major contributions to the first Yankees dynasty.

8. November 27, 1972 Traded John Ellis, Jerry Kenney, Charlie Spikes, and Rusty Torres to the Cleveland Indians for Graig Nettles and Jerry Moses

The Yankees picked up their best third baseman of the 20th century in this deal in which they gave up . . . well, not much. Nettles's power and spectacular glove kept him as a fixture at the hot corner for 11 seasons with the Yankees. Combined with the seven-player deal with Cleveland in April 1974 that brought Chris Chambliss and Dick Tidrow to New York, the 1970s Yankees owe a lot to the Tribe because they certainly didn't give them much at the time.

9. November 3, 1992 Traded Roberto Kelly to the Cincinnati Reds for Paul O'Neill and Joe DeBerry

This deal looked pretty even at the time; the Yankees gave up a center fielder (traded to make room for Bernie Williams) with many tools for a solid corner outfielder. Kelly never lived up to his early promise and ended up playing for seven different teams over the next seven years. O'Neill, meanwhile, stopped being helpless against left-handed pitching and became a .300 hitter with significant power, playing a key role in the Yankees' winning four World Series titles.

10. December 11, 1959 Traded Don Larsen, Hank Bauer, Norm Siebern, and Marv Throneberry to the Kansas City Athletics for Roger Maris, Joe DeMaestri, and Kent Hadley

It may be surprising that this trade isn't higher on this list, or that it is the only representative of the infamous deals with the Kansas City Athletics, who served, more or less, as a major league feeder team for the Yankees from the mid-1950s to the early 1960s. But while the Yankees did get a lot of talent from the Kansas City-to-the-Bronx shuttle, no one deal stands out that much. Even the Maris deal is not one-sided as people remember. In Norm Siebern the Yankees actually gave up a quality player who performed quite well for the A's and other teams over the following seven seasons. And while Roger Maris was spectacular in 1960 and 1961, the contributions he made during the rest of his time in New York were rather minimal, primarily because he couldn't stay healthy. None of that means that it wasn't a great trade for the Yankees, just that it wasn't as great in reality as it has become in legend.

Worst Yankees Trades

1. December 9, 1982 Traded Dave Collins, Fred McGriff, Mike Morgan, and cash to the Toronto Blue Jays for Dale Murray and Tom Dodd

After the Yankees failed to get to the World Series for the first time in four years in 1979, owner George Steinbrenner pressed for quick fixes. These quick fixes generally involved sending away the Yankees' best young talent for some veteran who was either overrated or near the end of his career. In this case, the Yankees traded away a future 493-home-run hitter for a so-so relief pitcher who had 121 major league innings left in his arm. Mike Morgan, though not a star, was popular with movers and realtors alike, making 12 stops during his 141-win, 2,700-inning career.

2. April 30, 1989 Traded Al Leiter to the Toronto Blue Jays for Jesse Barfield

Jesse Barfield was a terrific player in his prime, but his hitting ability had already faded significantly by the time the Yankees dealt wild-but-talented Al Leiter for him. It took several more years for Leiter to stick in the big leagues, but once he did he put together a 2,000-inning career that lasted through 2005. He twice finished in the top 10 in Cy Young voting and was an ace on the other side of New York. Barfield wasn't bad but managed less than 1,200 at bats with the Yankees before he retired.

3. November 26, 1986 Traded Doug Drabek, Brian Fisher, and Logan Easley to the Pittsburgh Pirates for Rick Rhoden, Cecilio Guante, and Pat Clements

Another great young talent—this time a 24-year-old pitcher with 21 starts in 1986—traded away for veteran pitching. Doug Drabek would win the NL Cy Young in 1992 and finish in the top five in voting two other years. In 13 major-league seasons he logged more than 2,500 innings. The three pitchers the Yankees received were all major league pitchers, but aside from one solid year from Rick Rhoden (and a memorable start as the designated hitter) they did not make any significant contributions the rest of their careers.

4. December 13, 1948 Traded Sherm Lollar, Red Embree, Dick Starr, and $100,000 to the St. Louis Browns for Roy Partee and Fred Sanford

Few baseball fans today have heard of Sherm Lollar, but this catcher, traded at the age of 24 by the Yankees to the St. Louis Browns, ended up having a 19-year major league career and was named to the All-Star team seven times. The large sum paid to the Browns on top of it adds insult to injury.

5. May 3, 1952 Traded Jackie Jensen, Spec Shea, Jerry Snyder, and Archie Wilson to the Washington Senators for Irv Noren and Tom Upton

Jackie Jensen was a college football star with baseball talent, but the Yankees, with no shortage of outfielders at the height of their dominance in the 1950s sent Jensen and three others, including 1947 World Series pitching hero Spec Shea, to the Senators. Shea had a couple of good seasons for woeful Washington, but Jensen was dealt after one All-Star season to the Red Sox, where he batted behind Ted Williams and became an MVP. Noren had one All-Star season with the Yankees, but only had one year he played a position regularly.

6. December 9, 1941 Traded Tommy Holmes to the Boston Braves in exchange for players to be named later (Buddy Hassett on December 16, 1941 and Gene Moore on February 5, 1942)

Two days after Pearl Harbor, the Yankees sent the Boston Braves a 24-year-old outfielder who eventually wound up in two All-Star Games and was named on MVP ballots four times. The players who were later sent back were clearly afterthoughts.

7. February 1, 1999 Traded Mike Lowell to the Florida Marlins for Mark J. Johnson, Ed Yarnall, and Todd Noel

The only truly bad trade of general manager Brian Cashman's reign so far, Lowell was dealt because the Yankees decided they were happy with Scott Brosius at third base and felt that Lowell could be used to replenish the Yankees' farm system with pitching prospects. Yarnall was a highly regarded prospect and both Noel and Johnson were former first-round draft picks, so the deal was well received at the time. But none of the pitchers became effective major leaguers. Lowell survived testicular cancer and endured some up-and-down years, but he has had a very successful major league career with the Marlins and later the Red Sox.

8. July 21, 1988 Traded Jay Buhner, Rich Balabon, and a player to be named later (Troy Evers on October 12, 1988) for Ken Phelps

Mark down another tragic trade of young for old in the 1980s. Ken Phelps seemed like a reasonable acquisition at the time, but his swing turned out not to work at Yankee Stadium and he had much less left in the tank than anyone realized at the time. Buhner ended up with a 15-year career during which he hit more than 300 home runs and helped make the Mariners cool in Seattle.

9. October 21, 1981 Traded Willie McGee to the St. Louis Cardinals for Bob Sykes

Sykes never played in another major league game, while McGee was a hero in the World Series less than a year later. McGee had 18 up-and-down years in the majors and played in the postseason six times. He finished his career with 2,254 hits, three Gold Gloves, two batting titles, and an NL MVP.

10. July 13, 1987 Traded Bob Tewksbury, Rich Scheid, and Dean Wilkins to the Chicago Cubs for Steve Trout

Unlike the other young players traded away for veterans in the deals listed here, Bob Tewksbury never became a star. His pinpoint control, though, kept him in the majors for 13 seasons and over 1,800 innings. Trout, who'd had a solid career for both Chicago teams, turned out to be one of those pitchers who became nothing more than a punch line in New York. Neither his career nor his control ever recovered from being dealt to the Yanks.

Best Yankees Free Agent Signings

1. November 22, 1977 Rich Gossage signed for six years, $3.6 million

Despite being awarded what was an incredibly rich contract at the time, Gossage still managed to exceed expectations. His performance over the next six seasons ranged from great to awesome. The highest ERA he posted in those years was 2.62. He led the team in saves every year, reaching a high of 33 in 1980. (At the time the single-season record was 38.) In each of the last four seasons of his contract, he struck out more batters than innings pitched. He threw fewer than 87 innings only twice during his six years in New York.

2. November 29, 1976 Reggie Jackson signed for five years, $2.9 million

Most free agents who sign with the Yankees do so for the money or in the hope that they'll make it to the World Series; they view the attention they'll get indifferently at best. Reggie, however, was attracted to the spotlight of New York. And while most of his greatest seasons—and three Oakland world championships—were already behind him, he still had plenty left. Jackson ended his first season with the Yankees with one of the most memorable performances in baseball history, hitting three home runs in the clinching game of the World Series. He got his own candy bar in 1978 and slumped a bit while continuing his feud with manager Bill Martin, yet Reggie still contributed to a championship team (under Bob Lemon). He came back strong in 1979 and 1980, finishing second in MVP voting in the latter year. Only the final season of his contract was a disappointment, ending with a World Series loss to the Dodgers. The Yankees let him leave for California as a free agent. But George Steinbrenner would forever be on the lookout for a free agent to make the same impact as Reggie.

3. November 21, 1978 Tommy John signed for three years, $1.4 million

This deal turned out to be one of the few bargains in free agency for the Yankees. John's 1978 season with the Dodgers was solid but not great, and he was only three years removed from what has become known as "Tommy John surgery." No one was sure how long an arm—even one that threw as softly as his—could hold up after such surgery, so John didn't get as large a contract as other pitchers of his ilk did in the late 1970s. But his performance with the Yankees was more than worthy. He won 21 and then 22 games in the first two years of the contract while finishing second and then fourth in the Cy Young voting. In 1981 he posted his lowest ERA, 2.63, since the strike zone had shrunk in 1969. After his option was picked up for a fourth year, John wasn't as strong and he was traded to the Angels for Dennis Rasmussen before the end of the 1982 season. He later returned to the Yankees, signing four different one-year contracts through age 45, showing the world how long a Tommy John arm might last.

4. December 15, 1980 Dave Winfield signed for 10 years, $24 million

Steinbrenner was all smiles the day he signed the powerful Padre; he didn't stay smiling for long. Evidently, "The Boss" thought the contract was worth significantly less than it was, because he didn't quite seem to get the importance of the compounding interest it promised. So the long marriage between Winfield and Steinbrenner went downhill rather quickly. Owner and star battled for years, both in the public arena and in court. Eventually, Steinbrenner's obsession with Winfield led to his self-banishment from the Yankees and baseball for much of the early 1990s. But while Steinbrenner famously tagged

Winfield with the label "Mr. May," after Winfield failed to produce at all in the 1981 World Series, the Yankees wound up getting a lot out of the multi-talented Winfield when all was said and done (especially compared to the terrible deals they made during this span). Winfield remained productive in New York until he missed the 1989 season with a back injury. Winfield was able to return to form offensively, though the Yankees traded him too early in 1990 to see those results. No, Winfield wasn't Reggie, and the Yankees didn't win a World Series with Winfield, but the Yankees did get half of a fine Hall of Fame career, making him more than worth his contract. And in the end, the Yankees might not have won any titles later in the 1990s if Steinbrenner's obsession with getting dirt on Winfield hadn't led to George pushing his way out of baseball long enough for the unconstrained farm system to produce the main building blocks for a new run of world championships.

5. December 10, 1992 Jimmy Key signed by the Yankees for four years, $17 million

Key performed spectacularly in his first two years with the Bombers, placing fourth and then second in the Cy Young voting. The southpaw was important in making the Yankees a competitive team again in the 1990s after a disastrous start to the decade. Injuries cost Key almost all of 1995, and while he didn't return to form in 1996, he pitched above-average baseball that season and played a major role in the Yankees winning their first pennant since 1981. His last victory in pinstripes was the clincher in the 1996 World Series.

Worst Yankees Free Agent Signings

1. December 9, 1982 Steve Kemp signed for five year, $5.45 million

In today's baseball dollars, this would be a $15 million per year contract. The Yankees made Kemp their second-highest paid player confident in the fact that he would be the left-handed cleanup hitter the team needed. Steinbrenner praised his new outfielder by commenting, "Steve is the supreme hustler. He'll turn New York on." Kemp himself expressed his hope "that some years from now, George can look back and say, 'Steve Kemp was one of the best acquisitions I made.' " Nobody seemed to notice at the time that Kemp was already on the downside of a career that was not all that impressive in its prime. Kemp proved to be a complete bust, lasting only two mediocre seasons with the Yankees, not even playing well enough to remain a full-time player. The Yankees have overpaid a lot of free agents over the last three decades, but Kemp remains their ultimate bad signing.

2. December 20, 2004 Carl Pavano signed for four years, $40 million

(See discussion below.)

3. December 28, 2004 Jaret Wright signed for three years, $21 million

Merry Christmas and Happy New Year! Pavano and Wright had both enjoyed excellent years in 2004, but neither had enjoyed spectacular careers. Pavano had first made it to the major leagues in 1998 (after being traded for Pedro Martinez), but injuries had sharply limited his early development. He had never thrown 150 innings in a season before 2003. There's no question that Pavano's 2004 success was real, but he had not proven himself over the long term. Wright's 2004 success, on the other hand, may very well have been a mirage, or at least a gift from Braves pitching coach Leo Mazzone. While familiar to Yankees fans who recalled him knocking out New York in the 1997 Division Series for Cleveland, a lot had gone wrong for Wright in the five years before he emerged in Atlanta in '04. His suitors, especially the Yankees, were not discouraged. There was competition for both—the Red Sox, among others, were especially interested in Pavano—but in the end the Yankees' overwhelming generosity brought them both to New York eight days apart. It quickly became evident that the signings were major mistakes. Pavano started having arm problems, and Wright reverted to his pre-2004 form. The Yankees were able to foist the last year of Wright's contract on the Orioles in 2007, but they still had to pay $4 million to Baltimore for the privilege.

4. December 27, 1984 Ed Whitson signed for five years, $4.4 million

The Yankees' expectations for Whitson weren't particularly high; they knew he wasn't going to be the ace of the staff, but they thought, based on his pitching in San Diego, that he could be a reliable middle-of-the-rotation starter. Whitson's first year as a Yankee was a disappointment, but it wasn't all that dissimilar from some of his poorer past seasons in the National League. Just before the end of that first season, however, on September 22, 1985, Whitson's stint in New York took a dramatic turn for the worse when he broke manager Billy Martin's arm in a bar fight. Fans had already taken a disliking to Whitson due to his on-field performance compared to his (for the time) massive contract. After the fight and Martin's subsequent dismissal, Whitson became even a bigger target. Boos and jeers unmercifully rained down upon Whitson every time he pitched at Yankee Stadium in 1986. Whitson was unable to ignore the hostility, and his ERA soared. He spent the first half begging to be traded, and his wish was finally granted when he was sent back to the Padres on July 9, 1986. To this day, Whitson refuses to sign any pictures with him wearing a Yankees uniform. And also to this day, the Yankees try to take careful measure that every player they bring to New York doesn't turn out to be "another Ed Whitson."

5. December 8, 1988 Andy Hawkins signed for three years, $3.6 million

What is it with these December signings? The Yankees offered Hawkins far more money than any other team; the best offer by anyone else was two years, $2 million from the

Padres. The Yankees expected more out of Hawkins than was reasonable, and Hawkins delivered less than should have been expected. His poor performance in the first season was somewhat masked by strong run support, and he finished at 15–15. But his luck ran out in 1990. On July 1 Hawkins pitched the game that he is most remembered for: no hits in eight innings but a 4–0 loss to the White Sox at Comiskey Park. Officially, it was a no-hitter back then, but Major League Baseball changed the technical definition of a no-hitter the next season and deleted his effort from their official list. It was a loss—and a mortifying one—under any ruling. After posting a 9.95 ERA the first month of the following season, Hawkins was released by the Yankees on May 9. A brief stint in Oakland ended with Hawkins being released for the second time that season—and final time in his career—on August 20.

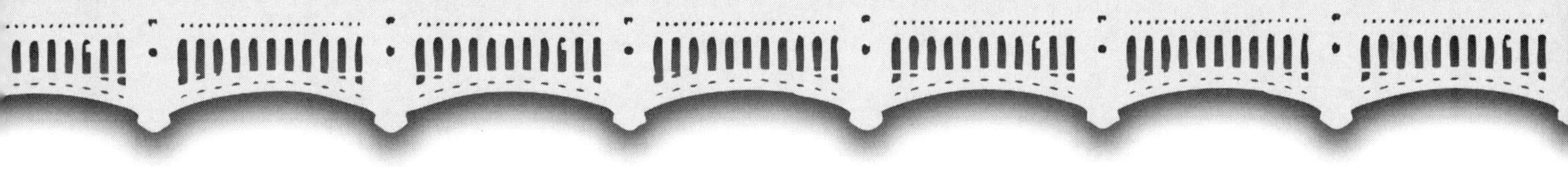

The Awards

The league's Most Valuable Player has long been the game's most prestigious award. It was first awarded in 1911 under the name Chalmers Award because the automotive manufacturer gave the winner in each league a car. No Yankee drove away with anything, but they had a lot more luck with the MVP when it was given out starting in 1922. Babe Ruth won it in '23 and Lou Gehrig in '27 and each would probably have more if there hadn't been the stipulation that a player couldn't win the award more than once. This rule and several others that voters found restrictive and downright foolish, led to the MVP being voted out of existence after 1928. It returned three years later with the rules we recognize today.

Gehrig became the first Yankee to be named MVP more than once when he took it in 1936. From there he was joined by Joe DiMaggio, Yogi Berra, and Mickey Mantle, who won it three times apiece. Mantle and Roger Maris are the only Yankees to be named MVP in successive years.

There are plenty of other awards that garner serious attention each year. The Cy Young Award has gone to five Yankees since it was added in 1956. Bob Turley (1958) was the first Yankee and first American League pitcher to win it (until 1967 one award covered both leagues). Eight Yankees have been named Rookie of the Year, starting with Gil McDougald in 1951. The Yankees have received 53 Gloves for fielding excellence since they were first awarded in 1957. Silver Sluggers have been awarded to the top hitters at each position since 1980, with the Yankees taking the award 29 times.

Their awards keep coming. Some are distributed by a newspaper (*The Sporting News*) and one is even doled out by an antacid manufacturer (Rolaids). There are awards for perseverance and managing excellence that have found their way into the hands of deserving Yankees. Whoever is giving an award, Yankees are sure to be in the running, even if the final vote says something different.

Finalists for the MVP, Cy Young, and Rookie of the Year are listed by their places in the voting (with their place in parentheses). An asterisk is used when there is a tie in the voting. No year is listed if a Yankee did not finish in the top 10 for MVP and top five for the Cy Young, Rookie of the Year, or Manager of the Year.

Most Valuable Player Award

Yankee Top 10 Finishes by Year

YEAR	PLAYER (RANK)
2006	Derek Jeter (2)
2005	Alex Rodriguez (1), Gary Sheffield (8), Mariano Rivera (9), Derek Jeter (10)
2004	Gary Sheffield (2), Mariano Rivera (9)
2003	Jorge Posada (3)
2002	Jason Giambi (5), Bernie Williams (10)

YEAR	PLAYER (RANK)
2001	Roger Clemens (8), Derek Jeter (10)
2000	Derek Jeter (10)
1999	Derek Jeter (6)
1998	Derek Jeter (3), Bernie Williams (7)
1997	Tino Martinez (2)
1994	Paul O'Neill (5), Jimmy Key (6)
1988	Dave Winfield (4)

Yankee Top 10 Finishes by Year (cont.)

YEAR	PLAYER (RANK)
1987	Don Mattingly (7)
1986	Don Mattingly (2), Dave Righetti (10)
1985	Don Mattingly (1), Rickey Henderson (3)
1984	Don Mattingly (5), Dave Winfield (8)
1983	Dave Winfield (7)
1981	Dave Winfield (7), Rich Gossage (9)

YEAR	PLAYER (RANK)
1980	Reggie Jackson (2), Rich Gossage (3), Rick Cerone (7)
1978	Ron Guidry (2), Graig Nettles (6)
1977	Graig Nettles (5), Sparky Lyle (6), Thurman Munson (7), Reggie Jackson (8T)

Yankee Top 10 Finishes by Year (cont.)

YEAR	PLAYER (RANK)
1976	Thurman Munson (1), Mickey Rivers (3), Chris Chambliss (5)
1975	Thurman Munson (7)
1974	Elliot Maddox (8)
1973	Bobby Murcer (9)
1972	Sparky Lyle (3), Bobby Murcer (5)
1971	Bobby Murcer (7)
1968	Mel Stottlemyre (10)
1965	Tom Tresh (9)
1964	Mickey Mantle (2), Elston Howard (3)
1963	Elston Howard (1), Whitey Ford (3), Bobby Richardson (10)
1962	Mickey Mantle (1), Bobby Richardson (2)
1961	Roger Maris (1), Mickey Mantle (2), Whitey Ford (5), Luis Arroyo (6), Elston Howard (10)
1960	Roger Maris (1), Mickey Mantle (2), Bill Skowron (9)
1958	Bob Turley (2), Mickey Mantle (5)
1957	Mickey Mantle (1), Gil McDougald (5)
1956	Mickey Mantle (1), Yogi Berra (2), Gil McDougald (7)
1955	Yogi Berra (1), Mickey Mantle (5), Hank Bauer (8)
1954	Yogi Berra (1)
1953	Yogi Berra (2), Phil Rizzuto (6)
1952	Allie Reynolds (2), Mickey Mantle (3), Yogi Berra (4)
1951	Yogi Berra (1), Allie Reynolds (3), Vic Raschi (8), Gil McDougald (9)
1950	Phil Rizzuto (1), Yogi Berra (3), Vic Raschi (7), Joe DiMaggio (9)
1949	Phil Rizzuto (2), Joe Page (3), Tommy Henrich (6)
1948	Joe DiMaggio (2), Tommy Henrich (6)
1947	Joe DiMaggio (2), Joe Page (4), George McQuinn (6)
1945	Snuffy Stirnweiss (3)
1944	Snuffy Stirnweiss (4)
1943	Spud Chandler (1), Billy Johnson (4), Nick Etten (7), Bill Dickey (8)
1942	Joe Gordon (1), Tiny Bonham (5), Joe DiMaggio (7)
1941	Joe DiMaggio (1), Charlie Keller (5), Joe Gordon (7)
1940	Joe DiMaggio (3)
1939	Joe DiMaggio (1), Red Ruffing (5), Bill Dickey (6), Joe Gordon (9)
1938	Bill Dickey (2), Red Ruffing (4), Joe DiMaggio (6)
1937	Joe DiMaggio (2), Lou Gehrig (4), Bill Dickey (5T), Red Ruffing (8), Lefty Gomez (9)
1936	Lou Gehrig (1), Bill Dickey (5), Joe DiMaggio (8)
1935	Lou Gehrig (5)
1934	Lefty Gomez (3), Lou Gehrig (5)
1933	Lou Gehrig (4)
1932	Lou Gehrig (2), Lefty Gomez (5), Babe Ruth (6T), Tony Lazzeri (8)
1931	Lou Gehrig (2), Babe Ruth (5)
1928	Tony Lazzeri (3T), Earle Combs (6), Waite Hoyt (10)
1927	Lou Gehrig (1)
1926	Herb Pennock (3), Lou Gehrig (10)
1924	Herb Pennock (4)
1923	Babe Ruth (1)
1922	Joe Bush (4), Wally Pipp (8)
1911	Birdie Cree (6T)

Yankee Top 10 Finishes by Player, Alphabetical

PLAYER	YEARS (RANK)
Luis Arroyo	1961 (6)
Hank Bauer	1955 (8)
Yogi Berra	1950 (3), 1951 (1), 1952 (4), 1953 (2), 1954 (1), 1955 (1), 1956 (2)
Tiny Bonham	1942 (5)
Joe Bush	1922 (4)
Rick Cerone	1980 (7)
Chris Chambliss	1976 (5)
Spud Chandler	1943 (1)
Roger Clemens	2001 (8)
Earle Combs	1928 (6)
Birdie Cree	1911 (6T)
Bill Dickey	1936 (5), 1937 (5), 1938 (2), 1939 (6), 1943 (8)
Joe DiMaggio	1936 (8), 1937 (2), 1938 (6), 1939 (1), 1940 (3), 1941 (1), 1942 (7), 1947 (1), 1948 (2), 1950 (9)
Nick Etten	1943 (7)
Whitey Ford	1961 (5), 1963 (3)
Lou Gehrig	1927 (1), 1931 (2), 1932 (2), 1933 (4), 1934 (5), 1935 (5), 1936 (1), 1937 (4)
Jason Giambi	2002 (5)
Lefty Gomez	1932 (5), 1934 (3), 1937 (9)
Joe Gordon	1939 (9), 1941 (7), 1942 (1)
Rich Gossage	1980 (3), 1981 (9)

Yankee Top 10 Finishes by Player, Alphabetical (cont.)

PLAYER	YEARS (RANK)
Ron Guidry	1978 (2)
Tommy Henrich	1948 (6), 1949 (6)
Rickey Henderson	1985 (3)
Elston Howard	1961 (10), 1963 (1), 1964 (3)
Waite Hoyt	1928 (10)
Reggie Jackson	1977 (8), 1980 (2)
Derek Jeter	1998 (3), 1999 (6), 2000 (10), 2001 (10), 2005 (10), 2006 (2)
Billy Johnson	1943 (4)
Charlie Keller	1941 (5)
Jimmy Key	1994 (6)
Tony Lazzeri	1926 (10), 1928 (3), 1932 (8)
Sparky Lyle	1972 (3), 1977 (6)
Elliot Maddox	1974 (8)
Mickey Mantle	1952 (3), 1955 (5), 1956 (1), 1957 (1), 1958 (5), 1960 (2), 1961 (2), 1962 (1), 1964 (2)
Roger Maris	1960 (1), 1961 (1)
Tino Martinez	1997 (2)
Don Mattingly	1984 (5), 1985 (1), 1986 (2), 1987 (7)
Gil McDougald	1951 (9), 1956 (7), 1957 (5)
George McQuinn	1947 (6)
Thurman Munson	1975 (7), 1976 (1), 1977 (7)
Bobby Murcer	1971 (7), 1972 (5), 1973 (9)
Graig Nettles	1977 (5), 1978 (6)
Paul O'Neill	1994 (5)
Joe Page	1947 (4), 1949 (3)
Herb Pennock	1924 (4), 1926 (3)
Wally Pipp	1922 (8)
Jorge Posada	2003 (3)
Vic Raschi	1950 (7), 1958 (8)
Allie Reynolds	1951 (3), 1952 (2)
Bobby Richardson	1962 (2), 1963 (10)
Dave Righetti	1986 (10)
Mariano Rivera	2004 (9), 2005 (9)
Mickey Rivers	1976 (3)
Phil Rizzuto	1949 (2), 1950 (1), 1953 (6)
Alex Rodriguez	2005 (1)
Red Ruffing	1932 (8), 1933 (4), 1934 (5)
Babe Ruth	1923 (1), 1931 (5), 1932 (6)
Gary Sheffield	2004 (2), 2005 (8)
Bill Skowron	1960 (9)
Snuffy Stirnweiss	1944 (4), 1945 (3)
Mel Stottlemyre	1968 (10)
Tom Tresh	1965 (9)
Bob Turley	1958 (2)
Bernie Williams	1998 (7), 2002 (10)
Dave Winfield	1981 (7), 1983 (7), 1984 (8), 1988 (4)

Yankee Top 10 Finishes, Total

PLAYER	TOTAL	PLAYER	TOTAL
Joe DiMaggio	10	Bernie Williams	2
Mickey Mantle	9	Luis Arroyo	1
Lou Gehrig	8	Hank Bauer	1
Yogi Berra	7	Tiny Bonham	1
Bill Dickey	5	Joe Bush	1
Don Mattingly	4	Rick Cerone	1
Dave Winfield	4	Chris Chambliss	1
Lefty Gomez	3	Spud Chandler	1
Joe Gordon	3	Roger Clemens	1
Elston Howard	3	Earle Combs	1
Tony Lazzeri	3	Birdie Cree	1
Gil McDougald	3	Nick Etten	1
Thurman Munson	3	Jason Giambi	1
Bobby Murcer	3	Ron Guidry	1
Phil Rizzuto	3	Rickey Henderson	1
Red Ruffing	3	Waite Hoyt	1
Babe Ruth	3	Billy Johnson	1
Whitey Ford	2	Charlie Keller	1
Rich Gossage	2	Jimmy Key	1
Tommy Henrich	2	Elliot Maddox	1
Sparky Lyle	2	Tino Martinez	1
Roger Maris	2	George McQuinn	1
Graig Nettles	2	Paul O'Neill	1
Joe Page	2	Wally Pipp	1
Herb Pennock	2	Jorge Posada	1
Vic Raschi	2	Mickey Rivers	1
Allie Reynolds	2	Alex Rodriguez	1
Bobby Richardson	2	Bill Skowron	1
Mariano Rivera	2	Mel Stottlemyre	1
Gary Sheffield	2	Tom Tresh	1
Snuffy Stirnweiss	2	Bob Turley	1

Cy Young Award

Yankee Top 5 Finishes by Year

YEAR	PLAYER (RANK)
2006	Chien-Ming Wang (2)
2005	Mariano Rivera (2)
2004	Mariano Rivera (3)
2001	Roger Clemens (1), Mike Mussina (5)
2000	Andy Pettitte (4)
1999	Mariano Rivera (3)
1998	David Wells (3), David Cone (4)
1997	Andy Pettitte (5)
1996	Andy Pettitte (2), Mariano Rivera (3)
1995	Jimmy Key (2)
1994	Jimmy Key (4)
1986	Dave Righetti (4)
1985	Ron Guidry (2)
1983	Ron Guidry (5)
1981	Rich Gossage (5)
1980	Rich Gossage (3), Tommy John (4)
1979	Tommy John (2), Ron Guidry (3)
1978	Ron Guidry (1), Rich Gossage (5)
1977	Sparky Lyle (1)
1976	Ed Figueroa (4)
1975	Catfish Hunter (2)
1961	Whitey Ford (1)
1958	Bob Turley (1)
1956	Whitey Ford (3)

Yankee Top 5 Finishes, Total

PLAYER	TOTAL
Ron Guidry	4
Rich Gossage	3
Andy Pettitte	3
Mariano Rivera	3
Whitey Ford	2
Tommy John	2
Jimmy Key	2
Roger Clemens	1
David Cone	1
Ed Figueroa	1
Catfish Hunter	1
Sparky Lyle	1
Mike Mussina	1
Dave Righetti	1
Bob Turley	1
Chien-Ming Wang	1
David Wells	1

Yankee Top 5 Finishes by Pitcher, Alphabetical

PLAYER	YEARS (RANK)
Roger Clemens	2001 (1)
David Cone	1998 (4)
Ed Figueroa	1976 (4)
Whitey Ford	1956 (3), 1961 (1)
Rich Gossage	1978 (5), 1980 (3), 1981 (5)
Ron Guidry	1978 (1), 1979 (3), 1983 (5), 1985 (2)
Catfish Hunter	1975 (2)
Tommy John	1979 (3), 1980 (4)
Jimmy Key	1994 (4), 1995 (2)
Sparky Lyle	1977 (1)
Mike Mussina	2001 (5)
Andy Pettitte	1996 (2), 1997 (5), 2000 (4)
Dave Righetti	1986 (4)
Mariano Rivera	1996 (3), 1999 (3), 2004 (3), 2005 (2)
Bob Turley	1958 (1)
Chien-Ming Wang	2006 (2)
David Wells	1998 (3)

Rookie of the Year Award

Yankee Top 5 Finishes by Year

YEAR	PLAYER (RANK)
2005	Robinson Cano (2)
2003	Hideki Matsui (2)
2001	Alfonso Soriano (3)
1998	Orlando Hernandez (4)
1996	Derek Jeter (1)
1995	Andy Pettitte (3)
1990	Kevin Maas (2)
1981	Dave Righetti (1)
1979	Ron Davis (4T)
1973	Doc Medich (3T)
1970	Thurman Munson (1)
1968	Stan Bahnsen (1)
1962	Tom Tresh (1)
1958	Ryne Duren (2)
1956	Tony Kubek (1)
1954	Bob Grim (1)
1951	Gil McDougald (1)
1950	Whitey Ford (2)
1949	Jerry Coleman (3)
1947	Spec Shea (3)

Manager of the Year Award

Yankee Top 5 Finishes by Year

YEAR	PLAYER (RANK)
2006	Joe Torre (4)
2005	Joe Torre (3)
2004	Joe Torre (4)
2003	Joe Torre (5)
2002	Joe Torre (4)
2001	Joe Torre (5)
2000	Joe Torre (5)
1999	Joe Torre (3)
1998	Joe Torre (1)
1996	Joe Torre (2)
1995	Buck Showalter (4)
1994	Buck Showalter (1)
1993	Buck Showalter (2)
1987	Lou Piniella (5T)
1986	Lou Piniella (5)
1985	Billy Martin (4)

Yankee Top Five Finishes, Total

PLAYER	TOTAL
Joe Torre	10
Buck Showalter	3
Lou Piniella	2
Billy Martin	1

Yankee Top Five Finishes by Manager, Alphabetical

PLAYER	YEARS (RANK)
Lou Piniella	1986 (5), 1987 (5T)
Billy Martin	1984 (4)
Buck Showalter	1993 (2), 1994 (1), 1995 (4)
Joe Torre	1996 (2), 1998 (1), 1999 (3), 2000 (5), 2001 (5), 2002 (4), 2003 (5), 2004 (4), 2005 (3), 2006 (4)

Silver Slugger Award

Yankee Silver Slugger Winners, Alphabetical

PLAYER	POS	YEARS
Don Baylor	DH	1983, 1985
Wade Boggs	3B	1993–94
Robinson Cano	2B	2006
Jason Giambi	1B	2002
Rickey Henderson	OF	1985
Reggie Jackson	OF	1980
Derek Jeter	SS	2006
Tino Martinez	1B	1997
Don Mattingly	1B	1985–87
Jorge Posada	C	2000–03
Willie Randolph	2B	1980
Alex Rodriguez	3B	2005
Gary Sheffield	OF	2004–05
Alfonso Soriano	2B	2002
Mike Stanley	C	1993
Bernie Williams	OF	2002
Dave Winfield	OF	1981–85

Yankee Silver Slugger Winners by Times Won

PLAYER	TOTAL
Dave Winfield	6
Jorge Posada	4
Don Mattingly	3
Gary Sheffield	2
Don Baylor	2
Wade Boggs	2
Robinson Cano	1
Jason Giambi	1
Rickey Henderson	1
Reggie Jackson	1
Derek Jeter	1
Tino Martinez	1
Willie Randolph	1
Alex Rodriguez	1
Alfonso Soriano	1
Mike Stanley	1
Bernie Williams	1

Golden Glove Award

Yankee Gold Glove Winners, Alphabetical

PLAYER	POS	YEARS
Wade Boggs	3B	1994–95
Scott Brosius	3B	1999
Ron Guidry	P	1982–86
Elston Howard	C	1963–64
Derek Jeter	SS	2004–06
Mickey Mantle	OF	1962
Roger Maris	OF	1960
Don Mattingly	1B	1985–89, 1991–94
Thurman Munson	C	1973–75
Mike Mussina	P	2003
Graig Nettles	3B	1977–78
Joe Pepitone	1B	1965–66, 1969
Bobby Richardson	2B	1961–65
Bobby Shantz	P	1957–60
Norm Siebern	OF	1958
Tom Tresh	OF	1964
Bernie Williams	OF	1997–2000
Dave Winfield	OF	1982–85, 1987

Yankee Gold Glove Winners by Position and Times Won

POS	PLAYER	TOTAL
Catcher (2)	Thurman Munson	3
	Elston Howard	2
First Base (2)	Don Mattingly	9
	Joe Pepitone	3
Second Base (1)	Bobby Richardson	5
Third Base (3)	Wade Boggs	2
	Graig Nettles	2
	Scott Brosius	1
Shortstop (1)	Derek Jeter	3
Outfield (6)	Dave Winfield	5
	Bernie Williams	4
	Mickey Mantle	1
	Roger Maris	1
	Norm Sieburn	1
	Tom Tresh	1
Pitcher (3)	Ron Guidry	5
	Bobby Shantz	4
	Mike Mussina	1

The Sporting News Awards

The Sporting News *AL Player of the Year*

YEAR	PLAYER
1986	Don Mattingly
1985	Don Mattingly
1984	Don Mattingly
1976	Thurman Munson
1962	Mickey Mantle
1961	Roger Maris
1960	Roger Maris
1956	Mickey Mantle
1950	Phil Rizzuto
1942	Joe Gordon
1941	Joe DiMaggio
1939	Joe DiMaggio
1936	Lou Gehrig
1934	Lou Gehrig
1931	Lou Gehrig

The Sporting News *MLB Player of the Year*

YEAR	PLAYER
2007	Alex Rodriguez
1985	Don Mattingly
1978	Ron Guidry
1958	Bob Turley
1956	Mickey Mantle
1950	Phil Rizzuto
1943	Spud Chandler
1939	Joe DiMaggio

The Sporting News *AL Pitcher of the Year*

YEAR	PLAYER
2001	Roger Clemens
1994	Jimmy Key
1978	Ron Guidry
1963	Whitey Ford
1961	Whitey Ford
1958	Bob Turley
1955	Whitey Ford
1943	Spud Chandler

The Sporting News *Rookie Player of the Year*

YEAR	PLAYER
1996	Derek Jeter

The Sporting News *Rookie Pitcher of the Year*

YEAR	PLAYER
1981	Dave Righetti
1968	Stan Bahnsen
1958	Ryne Duren
1954	Bob Grim
1950	Whitey Ford

The Sporting News *Major League Manager of the Year (1936–1985) and AL Manager of the Year (1986–Present)*

YEAR	PLAYER
1936	Joe McCarthy
1938	Joe McCarthy
1943	Joe McCarthy
1947	Bucky Harris
1949	Casey Stengel
1953	Casey Stengel
1958	Casey Stengel
1961	Ralph Houk
1974	Bill Virdon
1994	Buck Showalter
1998	Joe Torre

The Sporting News *AL Comeback Player of the Year*

YEAR	PLAYER
2005	Jason Giambi
1976	Dock Ellis

The Sporting News *AL Fireman/Reliever of the Year*

YEAR	PLAYER
2005	Mariano Rivera (T)
2004	Mariano Rivera
2001	Mariano Rivera
1999	Mariano Rivera
1997	Mariano Rivera
1996	John Wetteland
1987	Dave Righetti (T)
1986	Dave Righetti
1978	Rich Gossage
1972	Sparky Lyle
1961	Luis Arroyo

The Sporting News *Major League Executive of the Year*

YEAR	PLAYER
1974	Gabe Paul
1961	Dan Topping
1960	George Weiss
1952	George Weiss
1951	George Weiss
1950	George Weiss
1941	Ed Barrow
1937	Ed Barrow

Other Awards

Rolaids Relief Man of the Year Award

YEAR	PLAYER
2005	Mariano Rivera
2004	Mariano Rivera
2001	Mariano Rivera
1999	Mariano Rivera
1996	John Wetteland
1987	Dave Righetti
1986	Dave Righetti
1978	Rich Gossage

The Roberto Clemente Award

YEAR	PLAYER
1985	Ron Guidry
1984	Don Baylor

The Fred Hutchinson Memorial Award

YEAR	PLAYER
1965	Mickey Mantle

The Lou Gehrig Memorial Award

YEAR	PLAYER
1993	Don Mattingly
1981	Tommy John
1963	Bobby Richardson
1958	Gil McDougald

Retired Numbers

YANKEE	NUMBER	YEAR RETIRED
Billy Martin (Manager)	1	1986
Babe Ruth	3	1948
Lou Gehrig	4	1939
Joe DiMaggio	5	1952
Mickey Mantle	7	1969
Bill Dickey	8	1972
Yogi Berra	8	1972
Roger Maris	9	1984
Phil Rizzuto	10	1985
Thurman Munson	15	1979
Whitey Ford	16	1974
Don Mattingly	23	1997
Elston Howard	32	1984
Casey Stengel (Manager)	37	1970
Reggie Jackson	44	1993
Ron Guidry	49	2003

Monument Park features monuments to 4 of these players—Lou Gehrig, Babe Ruth, Mickey Mantle, and Joe DiMaggio. There are also monuments to former Yankee manager Miller Huggins (the first Yankee to be so honored) and to 9/11's heroes and victims. The 21 plaques in Monument Park recognize Jacob Ruppert, Edward Barrow, Joe McCarthy, Casey Stengel, Thurman Munson, Elston Howard, Roger Maris, Phil Rizzuto, Billy Martin, Lefty Gomez, Whitey Ford, Yogi Berra, Bill Dickey, Allie Reynolds, Mel Allen, Bob Sheppard, Reggie Jackson, Red Ruffing, Jackie Robinson, and the visits of Pope Paul VI and Pope John Paul II. Only three Yankee players (and no managers) and one other major league player have been honored in Monument Park without having their number retired—Lefty Gomez (11), Allie Reynolds (22), Red Ruffing (15, which has been retired for Thurman Munson), and Jackie Robinson (whose number 42 will be retired by the Yankees in honor of Robinson and almost certainly also in honor of current wearer Mariano Rivera after Rivera retires).

Yankees in the Hall of Fame in Cooperstown

A total of 40 former members of the Yankees' organization have been inducted into the National Baseball Hall of Fame since its inception in 1936. Seven of those 40—Yogi Berra, Bill Dickey, Joe DiMaggio, Whitey Ford, Lou Gehrig, Mickey Mantle, and Phil Rizzuto—spent their entire players careers with the Yankees. Sixteen Yankees players and managers have been enshrined in the Hall with a Yankees cap on their plaques. A total of 21 plaques in Cooperstown belong to men who spent at least 30 percent of their career with the Yankees.

This section contains the voting for every Yankee who has ever received at least one vote in Hall of Fame balloting, players, managers, and executives are listed in alphabetical order. After each name is the percentage of that individual's career spent with the Yankees. When balloting was conducted by an organization other than the Baseball Writers Association of America, it is noted as following:

V	Veteran's Election of 1936;
O/T Com.	Old-Timers Committee, 1939 to 1949; and
Vet. Com.	Veterans Committee, 1953 to present.

Other abbreviations used include **N**, which indicates the 1946 Nominating Committee vote (from which no one was directly elected), and **RO**, which indicates a run-off election. Run-offs were held twice during the 1960s after an initial round of balloting but the writers failed to elect anyone.

PLAYER (YEARS PLAYED)	POS	YEAR
Frank Baker (1916–1922)	Third Base	1955
Ed Barrow (1920–1945)	**Manager**	**1953**
Yogi Berra (1946–1965, 1984–1985)	**Catcher**	**1972**
Wade Boggs (1993–1997)	Third Base	2005
Frank Chance (1913–1914)	First Base	1946
Jack Chesbro (1903–1909)	**Pitcher**	**1946**
Earle Combs (1924–1935)	***Outfield***	***1970***
Stan Coveleski (1928)	Pitcher	1969
Bill Dickey (1928–1943, 1946)	***Catcher***	***1954***
Joe DiMaggio (1936–1942, 1946–1951)	***Outfield***	***1955***
Leo Durocher (1925, 1928–1929)	Manager*	1994
Whitey Ford (1950–1967)	***Pitcher***	***1974***
Lou Gehrig (1923–1939)	***First Base***	***1939***
Lefty Gomez (1920–1942)	***Pitcher***	***1972***
Clark Griffith (1903–1908)	Manager	1946
Burleigh Grimes (1934)	Pitcher	1964
Bucky Harris (1947–1948)	Manager	1975
Waite Hoyt (1921–1930)	***Pitcher***	***1969***
Miller Huggins (1918–1929)	***Manager***	***1964***
Catfish Hunter (1975–1979)	Pitcher	1987
Reggie Jackson (1977–1981)	*Outfield*	*1993*
Willie Keeler (1903–1909)	**Outfield**	**1939**
Tony Lazzeri (1926–1937)	***Shortstop***	***1991***
Bob Lemon (1978–1979, 1981–1982)	Pitcher*	1976
Larry MacPhail (1945–1947)	General Manager	1978
Lee MacPhail (1967–1974)	General Manager	1998
Mickey Mantle (1951–1968)	***Outfield***	***1974***
Joe McCarthy (1931–1946)	***Manager***	***1957***

PLAYER (YEARS PLAYED)	POS	YEAR
Bill McKechnie (1913)	Manager*	1962
Johnny Mize (1949–1953)	First Base	1981
Phil Niekro (1984–1985)	Pitcher	1997
Herb Pennock (1923–1933)	**Pitcher**	**1948**
Gaylord Perry (1980)	Pitcher	1991
Branch Rickey (1907)	General Manager*	1967
Phil Rizzuto (1941–1942, 1946–1956)	***Shortstop***	***1994***
Red Ruffing (1930–1941, 1945–1946)	*Pitcher*	*1967*
Babe Ruth (1920–1934)	***Outfield***	***1936***
Joe Sewell (1931–1933)	Shortstop	1977
Enos Slaughter (1954–1959)	Outfield	1985
Casey Stengel (1949–1960)	***Manager***	***1966***
Dazzy Vance (1915, 1918)	Pitcher	1955
Paul Waner (1944–1945)	Outfield	1952
George Weiss (1947–1960)	**General Manager**	**1971**
Dave Winfield (1981–1988, 1990)	**Outfield**	**2001**

Players in **bold** spent more years with the Yankees than any other team.
Players in *italics* are enshrined wearing a Yankees cap.

JIM ABBOTT (21.3)
2005 ... 13

JOHNNY ALLEN (26.7)
1955 ... 1

FELIPE ALOU (16.5)
1980 ... 3

MATTY ALOU (7.4)
1980 ... 5

JIMMY AUSTIN (17.0)
1958 ... 1

FRANK BAKER (42.9)
INDUCTED IN 1955
1936 ... 1
1937 ... 13
1938 ... 32
1939 ... 30
1942 ... 39
1945 ... 26
1946 NOM ... 39
1946 ... 36
1947 ... 49
1948 ... 4
1950 ... 4
1951 ... 8
1955 Vet. Com.

ED BARROW (93.3)
INDUCTED IN 1953 EXECUTIVE
1953 Vet. Com.

DON BAYLOR (18.3)
1994 ... 12
1995 ... 12

HANK BAUER (91.1)
1967 ... 23
1967 RO ... 9

YOGI BERRA (99.8)
INDUCTED IN 1972
1971 ... 242
1972 ... 339

EWELL BLACKWELL (5.5)
1968 ... 5
1969 ... 11
1970 ... 14

PAUL BLAIR (8.8)
1986 ... 8

WADE BOGGS (24.7)
INDUCTED IN 2005
2005 ... 474

BOBBY BONDS (7.8)
1987 ... 24
1988 ... 27
1989 ... 29
1990 ... 30
1991 ... 39
1992 ... 40
1993 ... 45
1994 ... 37
1995 ... 35
1996 ... 24
1997 ... 20

CLETE BOYER (61.9)
1978 ... 1
1979 ... 3

JAY BUHNER (2.1)
2007 ... 1

LEW BURDETTE (0.3)
1973 ... 12
1974 ... 7
1975 ... 11
1976 ... 21
1977 ... 85
1978 ... 76
1979 ... 53
1980 ... 66
1981 ... 48
1982 ... 43
1983 ... 43
1984 ... 97
1985 ... 82
1986 ... 96
1987 ... 96

JOE BUSH (23.5)
1958 ... 5

JOHNNY CALLISON (7.3)
1979 ... 1

BERT CAMPANERIS (2.6)
1989 ... 14

JOHN CANDELARIA (5.8)
1999 ... 1

FRANK CHANCE (1.0)
INDUCTED IN 1946
1936 ... 5
1937 ... 49
1938 ... 133
1939 ... 158
1942 ... 136
1945 ... 179
1946 NOM ... 144
1946 ... 150
1946 O/T Com.

SPUD CHANDLER (100.0)
1950 ... 2
1951 ... 1
1956 ... 1
1962 ... 2
1964 ... 6

BEN CHAPMAN (53.0)
1949 ... 1
1952 ... 1

HAL CHASE (55.3)
1936 ... 11
1937 ... 18

JACK CHESBRO (68.6)
INDUCTED IN 1946
1937 ... 1
1938 ... 2
1939 ... 6
1946 NOM ... 1
1946 O/T Com.

JACK CLARK (7.5)
1998 ... 7

ROCKY COLAVITO (2.1)
1974 ... 2
1975 ... 1

EARLE COMBS (100.0)
INDUCTED IN 1970
1937 ... 4
1938 ... 7
1939 ... 3
1945 ... 1
1948 ... 6
1949 ... 6
1950 ... 3
1952 ... 1
1953 ... 3
1955 ... 1
1956 ... 14
1958 ... 34
1960 ... 43
1962 ... 6
1970 Vet. Com.

WID CONROY (57.9)
1945 ... 1

CLINT COURTNEY (0.1)
1967 ... 1

STAN COVELESKI (2.7)
INDUCTED IN 1969
1938 ... 1
1948 ... 2
1949 ... 3
1950 ... 1
1958 ... 34
1969 Vet. Com.

LOU CRIGER (2.7)
1936 V ... 1
1936 ... 7
1937 ... 16
1938 ... 11
1939 ... 2
1946 NOM ... 6

JOSE CRUZ (1.6)
1994 ... 2

CHILI DAVIS (7.4)
2005 ... 3

RICK DEMPSEY (8.0)
1998 ... 1

BUCKY DENT (49.9)
1990 ... 3

JIM DESHAIES (0.8)
2001 ... 1

BILL DICKEY (100.0)
INDUCTED IN 1954
1945 ... 17
1946 NOM ... 40
1946 ... 32
1948 ... 39
1949 ... 65
1949 RO ... 39
1950 ... 78
1951 ... 118
1952 ... 139
1953 ... 179
1954 ... 202

JOE DIMAGGIO (100.0)
INDUCTED IN 1955
1945 ... 1
1953 ... 117
1954 ... 175
1955 ... 223

BILL DONOVAN (2.4)
1937 ... 3
1938 ... 1
1939 ... 2
1945 ... 3
1946 NOM ... 4

JACK DOYLE (0.1)
1936 V ... 1

DOUG DRABEK (6.8)
2004 ... 2

JOE DUGAN (54.3)
1937 ... 1
1938 ... 1
1948 ... 3
1949 ... 2
1956 ... 1
1958 ... 5
1960 ... 8

KID ELBERFELD (51.6)
1936 ... 1
1937 ... 1
1938 ... 2
1942 ... 1
1945 ... 2

DOCK ELLIS (10.1)
1985 ... 1

TONY FERNANDEZ (5.0)
1990 ... 4

WES FERRELL (1.5)
1948 ... 1
1949 ... 1
1956 ... 7
1960 ... 8
1962 ... 1

CECIL FIELDER (10.3)
2004 ... 1

WHITEY FORD (100.0)
INDUCTED IN 1974
1973 ... 255
1974 ... 284

EDDIE FOSTER (2.0)
1938 ... 2

LOU GEHRIG (100.0)
INDUCTED IN 1939
1936 ... 51
1939 Spec. El.

LEFTY GOMEZ (99.7)
INDUCTED IN 1972
1945 ... 7
1946 NOM ... 4
1947 ... 1
1948 ... 16
1949 ... 17
1950 ... 18
1951 ... 23
1952 ... 29
1953 ... 35
1954 ... 38
1955 ... 71
1956 ... 89
1958 ... 76
1960 ... 51
1962 ... 20
1972 Vet. Com.

JOE GORDON (63.9)
1945 ... 1
1955 ... 1
1956 ... 4
1958 ... 11
1960 ... 11
1962 ... 4
1964 ... 30
1964 RO ... 1
1966 ... 31
1967 ... 66
1967 RO ... 13
1968 ... 77
1969 ... 97
1970 ... 79

RICH GOSSAGE (31.8)
2000 ... 166
2001 ... 228
2002 ... 203
2003 ... 209
2004 ... 206
2005 ... 285
2006 ... 336
2007 ... 388

KEN GRIFFEY SR. (26.3)
1997 ... 22

CLARK GRIFFITH (19.2)
INDUCTED IN 1946 EXECUTIVE
1937 ... 4
1938 ... 10
1939 ... 20
1942 ... 71
1945 ... 108
1946 NOM ... 73
1946 ... 82
1946 O/T Com.

BURLEIGH GRIMES (1.6)
INDUCTED IN 1964
1937 ... 1
1938 ... 1
1939 ... 1
1948 ... 7
1949 ... 8
1950 ... 6
1951 ... 5
1952 ... 9
1953 ... 9
1955 ... 3
1956 ... 25
1958 ... 71
1960 ... 92
1962 ... 43
1964 Vet. Com.

RON GUIDRY (100.0)
1994 ... 24
1995 ... 25
1996 ... 37
1997 ... 31
1998 ... 37
1999 ... 31
2000 ... 44
2001 ... 27
2002 ... 23

BILL GULLICKSON (2.0)
2000 ... 1

BUBBLES HARGRAVE (5.3)
1947 ... 1
1958 ... 1
1960 ... 1

TOBY HARRAH (4.1)
1992 ... 1

BUCKY HARRIS (6.9)
INDUCTED IN 1975 MANAGER
1938 ... 1
1939 ... 1
1948 ... 3
1949 ... 11
1950 ... 4
1951 ... 9
1952 ... 12
1953 ... 21
1958 ... 45
1960 ... 31
1975 Vet. Com.

TOMMY HENRICH (100.0)
1952 ... 4
1953 ... 10
1956 ... 2
1958 ... 11
1960 ... 10
1962 ... 3
1964 ... 13
1968 ... 22
1969 ... 50
1970 ... 62

KEN HOLTZMAN (9.8)
1985 ... 4
1986 ... 5

RICK HONEYCUTT (0.4)
2003 ... 2

ELSTON HOWARD (93.0)
1974 ... 19
1975 ... 23
1976 ... 55
1977 ... 43
1978 ... 41
1979 ... 30
1980 ... 29
1981 ... 83
1982 ... 40
1983 ... 32
1984 ... 45
1985 ... 54
1986 ... 51
1987 ... 44
1988 ... 53

WAITE HOYT (54.2)
INDUCTED IN 1969
1939 ... 1
1942 ... 1
1946 NOM ... 1
1948 ... 7
1949 ... 7
1950 ... 11
1951 ... 13
1952 ... 12
1953 ... 14
1954 ... 14
1955 ... 33
1956 ... 37
1958 ... 37
1960 ... 29
1962 ... 18
1969 Vet. Com.

MILLER HUGGINS (64.7)
INDUCTED IN 1964 MANAGER
1937 ... 5
1938 ... 48
1939 ... 97
1942 ... 111
1945 ... 133
1946 NOM ... 129
1946 ... 106
1948 ... 4
1950 ... 2
1964 Vet. Com.

CATFISH HUNTER (27.4)
INDUCTED IN 1987
1985 ... 212
1986 ... 289
1987 ... 315

REGGIE JACKSON (23.2)
INDUCTED IN 1993
1993 ... 396

JACKIE JENSEN (7.5)
1967 ... 3
1968 ... 3
1969 ... 1
1970 ... 1
1971 ... 2
1972 ... 1

TOMMY JOHN (28.2)
1995 ... 98
1996 ... 102
1997 ... 97
1998 ... 129
1999 ... 93
2000 ... 135
2001 ... 146
2002 ... 127
2003 ... 116

2004............111
2005............123
2006............154
2007............125

SAM JONES (31.2)
1939............1
1955............1
1956............1

JIM KAAT (4.9)
1989............87
1990............79
1991............62
1992............114
1993............125
1994............98
1995............100
1996............91
1997............107
1998............129
1999............100
2000............125
2001............139
2002............109
2003............130

WILLIE KEELER (41.1)
INDUCTED IN 1939
1936 V............33
1936............40
1937............115
1938............177
1939............207

CHARLIE KELLER (91.1)
1953............1
1956............2
1958............9
1960............7
1962............1
1964............12
1968............11
1969............14
1970............7
1971............14
1972............24

JIMMY KEY (20.0)
2004............3

DAVE KINGMAN (0.4)
1992............3

BOB KUZAVA (48.8)
1964............1

HAL LANIER (7.9)
1979............1

DON LARSEN (31.1)
1974............29
1975............23
1976............47
1977............39
1978............32
1979............53
1980............31
1981............33
1982............32
1983............22
1984............25
1985............32
1986............33
1987............30
1988............31

TONY LAZZERI (95.3)
INDUCTED IN 1991
1945............1
1947............1
1948............21
1949............20
1949 RO............6
1950............21
1951............27
1952............29
1953............28
1954............30
1955............66
1956............64
1958............80
1960............59
1962............8
1991 Vet. Com.

DUFFY LEWIS (17.0)
1937............3
1938............5
1939............6
1945............1
1951............2
1952............11
1953............20
1954............20
1955............34

HERMAN LONG (1.2)
1936 V............16
1937............1
1938............1
1939............1
1945............1
1946 NOM............1

ED LOPAT (63.8)
1968............2
1969............2
1970............1
1971............4
1972............2

SPARKY LYLE (46.7)
1988............56
1989............25
1990............25
1991............15

LARRY MACPHAIL (12.0)
INDUCTED IN 1978
EXECUTIVE
1978 Vet. Com.

LEE MACPHAIL (29.6)
INDUCTED IN 1998
EXECUTIVE
1998 Vet. Com.

SAL MAGLIE (4.3)
1964............13
1968............11

MICKEY MANTLE (100.0)
INDUCTED IN 1974
1974............322

ROGER MARIS (58.1)
1974............78
1975............70
1976............87
1977............72
1978............83
1979............127
1980............111
1981............94
1982............69
1983............69
1984............107
1985............128
1986............177
1987............176
1988............184

BILLY MARTIN (51.6)
1967............1

DON MATTINGLY (100.0)
2001............145
2002............96
2003............68
2004............65
2005............59
2006............64
2007............54

CARL MAYS (33.5)
1958............6

JOE MCCARTHY (66.7)
INDUCTED IN 1957
MANAGER
1939............3
1947............2
1951............1
1953............1
1958............2
1957 Vet. Com.

LINDY MCDANIEL (26.8)
1981............1
1982............3

GIL MCDOUGALD (100.0)
1966............5
1967............4
1968............4
1969............3
1970............1
1971............4
1972............4
1973............2
1974............3

JACK MCDOWELL (10.8)
2005............4

ANDY MESSERSMITH (1.7)
1985............3
1986............3

BOB MEUSEL (92.0)
1937............1
1938............1
1945............1
1948............6
1949............3
1950............2
1952............1
1955............2
1956............1
1958............5
1960............10

JOHNNY MIZE (19.9)
INDUCTED IN 1981
1960............45
1962............14
1964............54
1964 RO............12
1966............81
1967............89
1967 RO............14
1968............103
1969............116
1970............126
1971............157
1972............157
1973............157
1981 Vet. Com.

HAL MORRIS (2.4)
2006............5

THURMAN MUNSON (100.0)
1981............62
1982............26
1983............18
1984............29
1985............32
1986............35
1987............28
1988............32
1989............31
1990............33
1991............28
1992............32
1993............40
1994............31
1995............30

BOBBY MURCER (65.8)
1989............3

GRAIG NETTLES (56.9)
1994............38
1995............28
1996............37
1997............22

BOBO NEWSOM (2.8)
1960............6
1962............3
1964............17
1964 RO............1
1966............25
1967............19
1967 RO............6
1968............22
1969............32
1970............12
1971............17
1972............31
1973............33

JOE NIEKRO (5.1)
1994............6

PHIL NIEKRO (7.5)
INDUCTED IN 1997
1993............278
1994............273
1995............286
1996............321
1997............380

LEFTY O'DOUL (4.1)
1948............4
1949............4
1950............9
1951............13
1952............19
1953............11
1956............5
1958............27
1960............45
1962............13

PAUL O'NEILL (61.1)
2007............12

STEVE O'NEILL (2.2)
1948............2
1949............6
1950............1
1951............3
1952............10
1953............13
1958............10

MONTE PEARSON (54.0)
1958............1

HERB PENNOCK (56.1)
INDUCTED IN 1948
1937............15
1938............37
1939............40
1942............72
1945............45
1946 NOM............41
1946............16
1947............86
1948............94

CY PERKINS (1.4)
1958............2

GAYLORD PERRY (1.3)
INDUCTED IN 1991
1989............304
1990............320
1991............342

LOU PINIELLA (59.4)
1990............2

WALLY PIPP (79.5)
1958............1

BOB PORTERFIELD (12.6)
1966............1

JACK QUINN (30.2)
1948............2
1958............9
1960............2

WILLIE RANDOLPH (76.9)
1998............5

VIC RASCHI (81.0)
1962............1
1964............8
1968............1
1969............3
1971............2
1972............4
1973............7
1974............3
1975............37

JEFF REARDON (1.3)
2000............24

RICK REUSCHEL (2.2)
1997............2

ALLIE REYNOLDS (68.0)
1956............1
1960............24
1962............15
1964............35
1964 RO............6
1966............60
1967............77
1967 RO............19
1968............95
1969............98
1970............89
1971............110
1972............105
1973............93
1974............101

BOBBY RICHARDSON (100.0)
1972............8
1973............2
1974............5

DAVE RIGHETTI (72.7)
2001............2

JOSE RIJO (6.4)
2001............1

MICKEY RIVERS (33.4)
1990............2

PHIL RIZZUTO (100.0)
INDUCTED IN 1994
1956............1
1962............44
1964............45
1964 RO............11
1966............54
1967............71
1967 RO............14
1968............74
1969............78
1970............79
1971............92
1972............103
1973............111
1974............111
1975............117
1976............149
1994 Vet. Com.

RED ROLFE (100.0)
1950............7
1951............6
1952............4
1953............5
1956............3
1958............13
1960............10
1962............1

MUDDY RUEL (11.6)
1946 NOM............1
1950............4
1951............1
1952............1
1953............8
1954............5
1955............11
1956............16
1958............10
1960............9

RED RUFFING (68.3)
INDUCTED IN 1967
1948............4
1949............22
1949 RO............4
1950............12
1951............9
1952............10
1953............24
1954............29
1955............60
1956............97
1958............99
1960............86
1962............72
1964............141
1964 RO............184
1966............208
1967............212
1967 RO............266

BABE RUTH (83.3)
INDUCTED IN 1936
1936............215

JOHNNY SAIN (31.6)
1962............1
1964............3
1968............7
1969............8
1970............9
1971............11
1972............21
1973............47
1974............51
1975............123

STEVE SAX (26.6)
2000............2

GERMANY SCHAEFER (0.1)
1942............1
1953............1

WALLY SCHANG (28.7)
1948............1
1950............1
1956............1
1958............8
1960............11

EVERETT SCOTT (29.1)
1937............2
1938............2
1939............1
1942............1
1947............1
1948............3
1949............3
1950............3
1951............2
1952............4
1953............5
1954............4
1955............8
1956............1

GEORGE SCOTT (0.8)
1986............1

HANK SEVEREID (2.9)
1948............1

JOE SEWELL (20.5)
INDUCTED IN 1977
1937............1
1948............1
1954............1
1955............1
1956............3
1958............1
1960............23
1977 Vet. Com.

BOBBY SHANTZ (25.7)
1970............7
1971............5
1972............9
1973............5
1974............3

URBAN SHOCKER (36.9)
1938............1
1939............1
1948............1
1949............2
1958............4

ENOS SLAUGHTER (14.7)
INDUCTED IN 1985
1966............100
1967............123
1967 RO............48
1968............129
1969............128
1970............133
1971............165
1972............149
1973............145
1974............145
1975............177
1976............197
1977............222
1978............261
1979............297
1985 Vet. Com.

LEE SMITH (0.8)
2003............210
2004............185

2005......200
2006......234
2007......217

CASEY STENGEL (48.0)
INDUCTED IN 1966 MANAGER

1938......2
1939......6
1945......2
1948......1
1949......3
1950......3
1951......8
1952......27
1953......61
1966 Vet. Com.

MEL STOTTLEMYRE (100.0)

1980......3

DANNY TARTABULL (30.2)

2003......1

IRA THOMAS (25.6)

1938......1

LUIS TIANT (9.6)

1988......132
1989......47
1990......42
1991......32
1992......50
1993......62
1994......42
1995......45
1996......64
1997......53
1998......62
1999......53
2000......86
2001......63
2002......85

EARL TORGESON (1.3)

1967......2

MIKE TORREZ (6.3)

1990......1

VIRGIL TRUCKS (4.8)

1964......4

GEORGE UHLE (3.0)

1956......1
1958......4
1960......4

ELMER VALO (0.4)

1967......2

DAZZY VANCE (2.3)
INDUCTED IN 1955

1936......1
1937......10
1938......10
1939......15
1942......37
1945......18
1946 NOM......31
1947......50
1948......23
1949......33
1949 RO......15
1950......52
1951......70
1952......105
1953......150
1954......158
1955......205

BOBBY VEACH (3.1)

1937......1

DIXIE WALKER (6.9)

1962......1
1964......6
1968......6
1969......9

PAUL WANER (0.4)
INDUCTED IN 1952

1946 NOM......4
1948......51
1949......73
1949 RO......63
1950......95
1951......162
1952......195

BOB WATSON (10.7)

1990......3

GEORGE WEISS (82.9)
INDUCTED IN 1971 EXECUTIVE

1971 Vet. Com.

BILLY WERBER (0.5)

1949......1
1950......1
1952......1
1958......3

JOHN WETTELAND (19.7)

2006......4

DAVE WINFIELD (39.4)
INDUCTED IN 2001

2001......435

WHITEY WITT (40.7)

1949......1

TOM ZACHARY (6.8)

1958......1
1960......1

Note
Bob Lemon was elected to the Hall of Fame as a pitcher. Since he managed but never pitched for New York, he is not shown on this list. Three former Yankees players—Leo Durocher, Bill McKechnie, and Branch Rickey—were inducted into Cooperstown for their accomplishments after their playing careers as managers or general managers. Because they were not elected as players, they are not shown on this list.

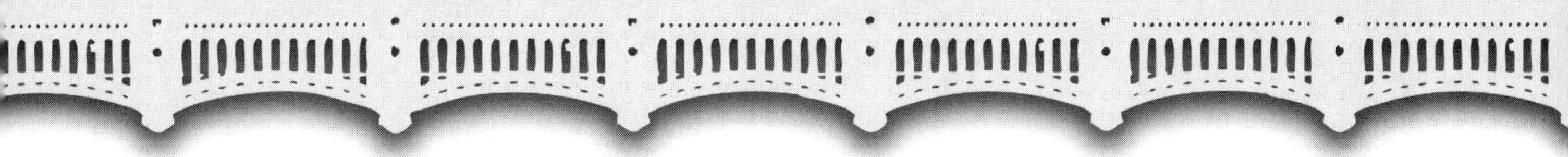

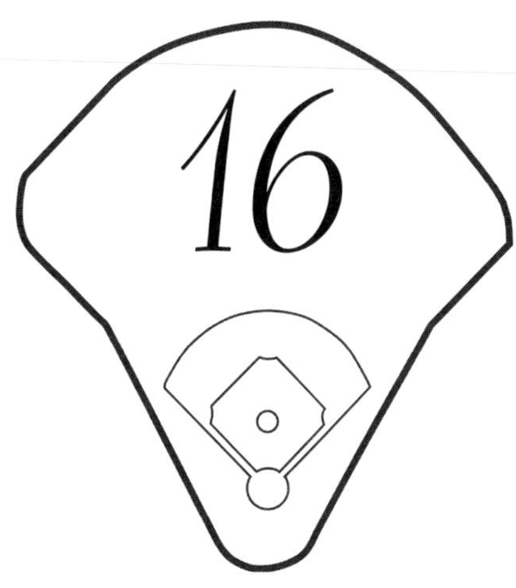

Great Performances

THE YANKEES ARE RENOWNED FOR their success as a team, but they've also enjoyed some of the most outstanding individual performances in the game's history. This chapter focuses on the great numbers and memorable feats. Lists cover everything from league leaders to great games to remarkable moments, with breakdowns of selected events.

The section begins with lists of Yankees who have finished at the top of American League statistical categories. These lists are set up by most recent seasons, so Alex Rodriguez's prodigious slugging in 2007 leads things off. Few franchises can boast a history with as many greats as the Yankees, as is well illustrated in the pages that follow. An asterisk signifies a tie for the league lead.

League Leaders

Yankees American League Home Run Champions

YEAR	PLAYER	HR
2007	Alex Rodriguez	54
2005	Alex Rodriguez	48
1980	Reggie Jackson	41
1976	Graig Nettles	32
1961	Roger Maris	61
1960	Mickey Mantle	40
1958	Mickey Mantle	42
1956	Mickey Mantle	52
1955	Mickey Mantle	37
1948	Joe DiMaggio	39
1944	Nick Etten	22
1937	Joe DiMaggio	46
1936	Lou Gehrig	49
1934	Lou Gehrig	49
1931	Babe Ruth	46
	Lou Gehrig*	46
1930	Babe Ruth	49
1929	Babe Ruth	46
1928	Babe Ruth	54
1927	Babe Ruth	60
1926	Babe Ruth	47
1925	Bob Meusel	33
1924	Babe Ruth	46
1923	Babe Ruth	41
1921	Babe Ruth	59
1920	Babe Ruth	54
1917	Wally Pipp	9
1916	Wally Pipp	12

Yankees American League RBI Leaders

YEAR	PLAYER	RBIS
2007	Alex Rodriguez	156
1985	Don Mattingly	145
1961	Roger Maris	142
1960	Roger Maris	112
1956	Mickey Mantle	130
1948	Joe DiMaggio	155
1945	Nick Etten	111
1941	Joe DiMaggio	125
1934	Lou Gehrig	165
1931	Lou Gehrig	184
1930	Lou Gehrig	174
1928	Lou Gehrig	142
	Babe Ruth*	142
1927	Lou Gehrig	175
1926	Babe Ruth	145
1925	Bob Meusel	138
1923	Babe Ruth	131
1921	Babe Ruth	171
1920	Babe Ruth	137

Yankees American League Batting Champions

YEAR	PLAYER	AVG
1998	Bernie Williams	.339
1994	Paul O'Neill	.359
1984	Don Mattingly	.343

Yankees American League Batting Champions (cont.)

YEAR	PLAYER	AVG
1956	Mickey Mantle	.353
1945	Snuffy Stirnweiss	.309
1940	Joe DiMaggio	.352
1939	Joe DiMaggio	.381
1934	Lou Gehrig	.363
1924	Babe Ruth	.378

Yankees American League Runs Leaders

YEAR	PLAYER	RUNS
2007	Alex Rodriguez	143
1998	Derek Jeter	127
1986	Rickey Henderson	130
1985	Rickey Henderson	146
1976	Roy White	104
1972	Bobby Murcer	102
1960	Mickey Mantle	119
1958	Mickey Mantle	127
1957	Mickey Mantle	121
1956	Mickey Mantle	132
1954	Mickey Mantle	129
1948	Tommy Henrich	138
1945	Snuffy Stirnweiss	107
1944	Snuffy Stirnweiss	125
1939	Red Rolfe	139
1937	Joe DiMaggio	151
1936	Lou Gehrig	167
1934	Lou Gehrig	128
1933	Lou Gehrig	138
1931	Lou Gehrig	163
1928	Babe Ruth	163
1927	Babe Ruth	158
1926	Babe Ruth	139
1924	Babe Ruth	143
1923	Babe Ruth	151
1921	Babe Ruth	177
1920	Babe Ruth	158
1904	Patsy Dougherty	80

Yankees American League Hits Leaders

YEAR	PLAYER	HITS
1999	Derek Jeter	219
1986	Don Mattingly	238
1984	Don Mattingly	207
1962	Bobby Richardson	209
1945	Snuffy Stirnweiss	195
1944	Snuffy Stirnweiss	205
1939	Red Rolfe	213
1931	Lou Gehrig	211
1927	Earle Combs	231

Yankees American League On-Base Percentage Leaders

YEAR	PLAYER	AVG
2005	Jason Giambi	.440
1964	Mickey Mantle	.423
1962	Mickey Mantle	.486
1955	Mickey Mantle	.431
1953	Gene Woodling	.429
1937	Lou Gehrig	.473
1936	Lou Gehrig	.478
1935	Lou Gehrig	.466
1934	Lou Gehrig	.465
1932	Babe Ruth	.489
1931	Babe Ruth	.495
1930	Babe Ruth	.493
1928	Lou Gehrig	.467
1927	Babe Ruth	.486
1926	Babe Ruth	.516
1924	Babe Ruth	.513
1923	Babe Ruth	.545
1921	Babe Ruth	.512
1920	Babe Ruth	.533

Yankees American League Slugging Percentage Leaders

YEAR	PLAYER	AVG
2007	Alex Rodriguez	.645
2005	Alex Rodriguez	.610
1986	Don Mattingly	.573
1962	Mickey Mantle	.605
1961	Mickey Mantle	.687
1960	Roger Maris	.581
1956	Mickey Mantle	.705

Yankees American League Slugging Percentage Leaders (cont.)

YEAR	PLAYER	AVG
1955	Mickey Mantle	.611
1950	Joe DiMaggio	.585
1945	Snuffy Stirnweiss	.476
1937	Joe DiMaggio	.673
1936	Lou Gehrig	.696
1934	Lou Gehrig	.706
1931	Babe Ruth	.700
1930	Babe Ruth	.732
1929	Babe Ruth	.697
1928	Babe Ruth	.709
1927	Babe Ruth	.772
1926	Babe Ruth	.737
1924	Babe Ruth	.739
1923	Babe Ruth	.764
1922	Babe Ruth	.672
1921	Babe Ruth	.846
1920	Babe Ruth	.849

Yankees American League Wins Leaders

YEAR	PLAYER	WINS
1998	David Cone	20
1996	Andy Pettite	21
1994	Jimmy Key	17
1985	Ron Guidry	22
1978	Ron Guidry	25
1962	Ralph Terry	23
1961	Whitey Ford	25
1958	Bob Turley	21
1943	Spud Chandler	20
1938	Red Ruffing	21
1937	Lefty Gomez	21
1934	Lefty Gomez	26
1928	George Pipgras	24
1927	Waite Hoyt	22
1921	Carl Mays	27
1904	Jack Chesbro	41

Yankees American League ERA Leaders

YEAR	PLAYER	ERA
1980	Rudy May	2.47
1979	Ron Guidry	2.78
1978	Ron Guidry	1.74
1958	Whitey Ford	2.01
1957	Bobby Shantz	2.45
1956	Whitey Ford	2.47
1953	Eddie Lopat	2.43
1952	Allie Reynolds	2.07
1943	Spud Chandler	1.64
1937	Lefty Gomez	2.33
1934	Lefty Gomez	2.33
1927	Wilcy Moore	2.28
1920	Bob Shawkey	2.45

Yankees American League Strikeout Leaders

YEAR	PLAYER	SO
1964	Al Downing	217
1952	Allie Reynolds	160
1951	Vic Raschi	164
1937	Lefty Gomez	194
1934	Lefty Gomez	158
1933	Lefty Gomez	163
1932	Red Ruffing	190

Yankees American League Innings Pitched Leaders

YEAR	PLAYER	IP
1975	Catfish Hunter	328.0
1962	Ralph Terry	298.2
1961	Whitey Ford	283.0
1934	Lefty Gomez	281.2
1925	Herb Pennock	277.0
1921	Carl Mays	336.2
1906	Al Orth	338.2
1904	Jack Chesbro	454.2

Yankees American League Triple Crown Winners

YEAR	PLAYER	AVG	HR	RBI
1934	Lou Gehrig	.363	49	165
1956	Mickey Mantle	.353	52	130

YEAR	PLAYER	WINS	SO	ERA
1934	Lefty Gomez	26	158	2.33
1937	Lefty Gomez	21	194	2.33

Highs & Lows

Yankees Single Season Highs, Individual Batters

RECORD	PLAYER	STAT
Most Games	Hideki Matsui (2003)	163
Most At-Bats	Alfonso Soriano (2002)	696
Most Hits	Don Mattingly (1986)	238
Most Runs	Babe Ruth (1921)	177
Most Singles	Steve Sax (1989)	171
Most Doubles	Don Mattingly (1986)	53
Most Triples	Earle Combs (1927)	23
Most Home Runs	Roger Maris (1961)	61
Most Home Runs, Right-handed Batter	Alex Rodriguez (2007)	54
Most Grand Slam Home Runs	Don Mattingly (1987)	6
Most RBI	Lou Gehrig (1931)	184
Most Extra-Base Hits	Babe Ruth (1921)	119
Most Total Bases	Babe Ruth (1921)	457
Most Strikeouts	Alfonso Soriano (2002)	157
Most Walks	Babe Ruth (1923)	148
Most Intentional Walks	Mickey Mantle (1957)	23
Most Sacrifice Hits	Willie Keeler (1905)	42
Most Sacrifice Flies	Roy White (1971)	17
Most Stolen Bases	Rickey Henderson (1988)	93
Most Times Caught Stealing	Doc Cook (1914)	32
Most Times Hit by Pitch	Don Baylor (1985)	24
Most Times Grounded into Double Play	Dave Winfield (1983)	30
Highest Batting Average	Babe Ruth (1923)	.393
Highest Batting Average, Right-handed Batter	Joe DiMaggio (1939)	.381
Highest On-Base Percentage	Babe Ruth (1923)	.545
Highest Slugging Average	Babe Ruth (1920)	.847

Yankees Single Season Lows, Individual Batters

RECORD	PLAYER	STAT
Fewest Strikeouts	Joe Sewell (1932)	3
Lowest Batting Average	Frankie Crosetti (1940)	.194
Lowest On-Base Percentage	Pee-Wee Wanniger (1925)	.256
Lowest Slugging Average	Horace Clark (1968)	.254

Yankees Single Game Highs, Individual Batters

RECORD	PLAYER	STAT
Most At-Bats	Bobby Richardson (June 24, 1962 vs. Det)	11
Most Hits, 9 Inning Game	Myril Hoag (June 6, 1934 vs. Bos)	6
Most Singles	Myril Hoag (June 6, 1934 vs. Bos)	6
Most Doubles	Johnny Lindell (August 8, 1944 vs. Cle)	4
	Jim Mason (July 8, 1974 vs. Tex)	4
Most Triples	Hal Chase (August 30, 1906 vs. Was)	3
	Earle Combs (September 22, 1927 vs. Det)	3
	Joe DiMaggio (August 27, 1938 vs. Cle G1)	3
Most Home Runs	Lou Gehrig (June 3, 1932 vs. Phi)	4
Most Grand Slams	Tony Lazzeri (May 24, 1936 vs. Phi)	2
Most Total Bases	Lou Gehrig (June 3, 1932 vs. Phi)	16
Most RBI	Tony Lazzeri (May 24, 1936 vs. Phi)	11

Yankees Single-Inning Highs, Individual Batters

RECORD	PLAYER	STAT
Most Home Runs	Joe DiMaggio (June 3, 1936 vs. Chi)	2
	Joe Pepitone (May 23, 1962 vs. KC)	2
	Cliff Johnson (June 30, 1977 at Tor)	2

Yankees Season-Highs, Individual Pitchers

RECORD	PLAYER	STAT
Most Wins	Jack Chesbro (1904)	41
Most Losses	Joe Lake (1908)	22
Most Shutouts	Ron Guidry (1978)	9
Most Complete Games	Jack Chesbro (1904)	48
Most Innings Pitched	Jack Chesbro (1904)	454

Yankees Season-Highs, Individual Pitchers (cont.)

RECORD	PLAYER	STAT
Most Games	Paul Quantrill (2004)	86
Most Saves	Mariano Rivera (2004)	51
Most Strikeouts	Ron Guidry (1978)	248
Most Strikeouts Per 9 Innings	David Cone (1997)	10.25
Most Walks	Bob Turley (1955)	177
Most Walks Per 9 Innings	Tommy Byrne (1949)	8.22
Most Hits Allowed	Jack Chesbro (1904)	337
Most Hits Allowed Per 9 Innings	Herb Pennock (1931)	11.74
Most Runs Allowed	Russ Ford (1912)	127
Most Home Runs Allowed	Ralph Terry (1962)	40
Most Home Runs Allowed Per 9 Innings	Orlando Hernandez (2000)	1.56
Most Hit Batsmen	Jack Warhop (1909)	26
Most Wild Pitches	Tim Leary (1990)	23
Most Balks	Rick Rhoden (1988)	6
	Vic Raschi (1950)	6
Highest SO/BB Ratio	Jon Lieber (2004)	5.67
Highest Winning Percentage	Ron Guidry (1978)	.893
Highest ERA	Bump Hadley (1937)	5.30

Yankees Single-Season Lows, Individual Pitchers

RECORD	PLAYER	STAT
Fewest Home Runs Allowed	Jack Chesbro (1907)	0
Fewest Walks Per 9 Innings	David Wells (2003)	0.85
Fewest Hits Per 9 Innings	Tommy Byrne (1949)	5.74
Fewest Strikeouts Per 9 Innings	Carl Mays (1922)	1.54
Lowest ERA	Spud Chandler (1943)	1.64
Lowest Winning Percentage	George McConnell (1913)	.211

Yankees Single-Game Highs, Individual Pitchers

RECORD	PLAYER	STAT
Hits Allowed	Jack Quinn (June 29, 1912)	21
Runs Allowed	Jack Warhop (July 31, 1911 vs. Chi)	13
	Ray Caldwell (October 3, 1913 vs. Phi)	13
	Carl Mays (July 17, 1923 vs. Cle)	13
Home Runs Allowed	Joe Ostrowski (June 22, 1950 vs. Cle)	5
	John Cumberland (May 24, 1970 vs. Cle)	5
	Ron Guidry (September 17, 1985 vs. Det)	5
	Jeff Weaver (July 21, 2002 vs. Bos)	5
	David Wells (July 4, 2003 vs. Bos)	5
Most Strikeouts	Ron Guidry (June 17, 1978 vs. Cal)	18
Most Strikeouts in Relief	Ron Davis (May 4, 1981 vs. Cal)	8
Most Walks	Tommy Byrne (June 8, 1949 vs. Det)	13
Most Balks	Vic Raschi (May 3, 1950 vs. Chi)	4

Yankees Single-Inning Highs, Individual Pitchers

RECORD	PLAYER	STAT
Home Runs Allowed	Catfish Hunter (June 17, 1977 vs. Bos)	4
	Scott Sanderson (May 5, 1992 vs. Min)	4
	Randy Johnson (August 21, 2005 vs. Chi)	4

Yankees Single-Season Team Records

RECORD	YEAR	STAT
Most Wins	1998	114
Most Home Wins	1961	65
Most Road Wins	1939	54
Most Losses	1908	103
Most Home Losses	1908	47
	1913	47
Most Road Losses	1912	58
Most Times Shutout	1914	17
Most Games	1964	164
	1968	164
Most Players Used	2005	51
Most Pitchers Used	2005	28

Yankees Single-Season Team Highs, Offense

RECORD	YEAR	STAT
Most At-Bats	1997	5,710
Most Runs	1931	1,067
Most Hits	1930	1,638
Most Singles	1988	1,237
Most Doubles	2006	327
Most Triples	1930	110
Most Home Runs	2004	242
Most Grand Slams	1987	10
Most Total Bases	1936	2,703
Most RBI	1936	995
Most Walks	1932	766
Most Times Hit By Pitch	2003	81
Most Stolen Bases	1910	289
Most Times Caught Stealing	1920	82
Most Strikeouts	2002	1,171
Most Times GIDP	1996	153
Highest Batting Average	1930	.309
Highest On-Base Percentage	1930	.384
Highest Slugging Average	1927	.489

Yankees Team Record Streaks

RECORD	YEAR	STAT
Most Consecutive Wins	1947	19
Most Consecutive Home Wins	1942	18
Most Consecutive Road Wins	1953	15
Most Consecutive Losses	1913	13
Most Consecutive Home Losses	1913	17
Most Consecutive Road Losses	1908	12
Most Consecutive Shutout Innings	1932	40
Most Consecutive Games Scoring in Double Digits	June 12, 1930– June 17, 1930	5
Most Consecutive Errorless Games	1977	10
	1993	10
	1995	10

Yankees Single-Season Team Highs, Pitching

RECORD	YEAR	STAT
Most Innings Pitched	1964	1506.2
Most Complete Games	1904	123
Most Shutouts	1951	24
Most Saves	2004	59
Most Hits Allowed	1930	1566
Most Home Runs Allowed	2004	182
Most Grand Slam Home Runs Allowed	2000	9
Most Runs Allowed	1930	898
Most Walks Allowed	1949	812
Most Strikeouts	2001	1266
Highest ERA	1904	4.88

Yankees Single-Season Team Lows, Pitching

RECORD	YEAR	STAT
Fewest Walks	1903	245
Fewest Home Runs Allowed	1907	113
Fewest Shutouts	1994	2
Lowest ERA	1904	2.57

Yankees Single-Season Team Highs, Fielding

RECORD	YEAR	STAT
Most Errors	1912	386
Most Double Plays	1956	214

Yankees Single-Season Team Highs, Fielding (cont.)

RECORD	YEAR	STAT
Most Passed Balls	1913	32
Most Assists	1904	2086
Highest Fielding Percentage	1995	.986

Yankees Single-Season Team Lows, Fielding

RECORD	YEAR	STAT
Fewest Errors	1996	91
Fewest Double Plays	1912	81
Fewest Passed Balls	1931	0
Fewest Assists	2000	1487
Lowest Fielding Percentage	1912	.939

Yankees Single Game Team Highs, Offense

RECORD	GAME	STAT
Most Runs, 9 Inning Game	May 24, 1936 vs. Phi	25
Most Runs, 9 Inning Home Game	July 26, 1931 vs. Chi (G2)	22
Most Runs, Both Teams	May 3, 1912 vs. Phi	33
	May 22, 1930 vs. Phi (G2)	33
	June 3, 1932 vs. Phi	33
Most Hits, 9 Inning Game	September 28, 1923 vs. Bos	30
Most Singles	August 12, 1953 vs. Was	22
Most Doubles	April 12, 1988 vs. Tor	10
	June 5, 2003 vs. Cin	10
Most Triples	May 1, 1934 vs. Was	5
Most Home Runs	June 28, 1939 vs. Phi (G1)	8
Most Walks	June 23, 1915 vs. Phi	16
Most Strikeouts	September 10, 1999 vs. Bos	17
Most Stolen Bases	September 28, 1911 vs. StL	15

Yankees Single-Inning Team Highs, Offense

RECORD	GAME	STAT
Most Runs	July 6, 1920 vs. Was	14
Most Home Runs	June 30, 1977 vs. Tor	4
	June 21, 2005 vs. TB	4

Yankees Single-Game Team Highs, Pitching

RECORD	GAME	STAT
Most Hits Allowed	September 29, 1928 vs. Det	24
Most Runs Allowed	July 29, 1928 vs. Cle	24
Most Home Runs Allowed	July 4, 2003 vs. Bos	7
Most Strikeouts	June 17, 1978 vs. Cal	18
Most Walks Allowed	September 11, 1949 vs. Was	17

Yankees Single-Inning Team Highs, Pitching

RECORD	GAME	STAT
Most Runs Allowed	July 17, 1925 vs. Cle	13
Most Home Runs Allowed	June 17, 2077 vs. Bos	4
	May 2, 1992 vs. Min	4
	August 21, 2005 vs. Chi	4
Most Walks Allowed	September 11, 1949 vs. Was	11

No Hitters & Major Hitters

Yankees No-Hitters

PLAYER	TEAM	DATE
George Mogridge	*Boston Red Sox*	*April 24, 1917*
Sad Sam Jones	*Philadelphia Athletics*	*September 4, 1923*
Monte Pearson	Cleveland Indians	August 27, 1928 (G2)
Allie Reynolds	*Cleveland Indians*	*July 12, 1951*
Allie Reynolds	Boston Red Sox	September 28, 1951 (G1)
Don Larsen	**Brooklyn Dodgers**	**October 8, 1956**
Dave Righetti	Boston Red Sox	July 4, 1983
Jim Abbott	Cleveland Indians	September 4, 1993
Dwight Gooden	Seattle Mariners	May 14, 1996
David Wells	**Minnesota Twins**	**May 17, 1998**
David Cone	**Montreal Expos**	**July 18, 1999**

italics = road game; **bold** = perfect game

The Iron Horse

From June 1, 1925 to April 30, 1939, Lou Gehrig played 2,130 consecutive major league games. He broke the previous record, which, at 1,307 games, belonged to Everett Scott. A teammate of Gehrig's on the Yankees, Scott's streak ended less than a month before Gehrig made his major league debut, on August 16, 1923. Gehrig's record streak, ended tragically by a fatal disease, remained unbroken until Baltimore's Cal Ripken Jr. broke it on September 6, 1995. Ripken played in an era when the American League had nearly twice as many opponents as Gehrig faced (and also had the luxury of airplane travel as opposed to trains). The Iron Horse's streak consisted of the following number of games against these seven teams:

TEAM	GAMES	TEAM	GAMES
Boston Red Sox	300	Philadelphia Athletics	301
Chicago White Sox	303	St. Louis Browns	307
Cleveland Indians	304	Washington Senators	308
Detroit Tigers	307		

Improbable DiMaggio

The late paleontologist Stephen Jay Gould once wrote that Joe DiMaggio's 56-game hitting streak in 1941 is "the most extraordinary thing that has ever happened in American sport." Gould explained that the streak had defied the laws of probability and simply should not have been able to occur. Nevertheless it did happen. (DiMaggio even got a hit in the All-Star Game in Detroit during the streak, bringing the National League under his spell, albeit unofficially.) DiMaggio's record in all 56 games against the AL is included below. His streak ended in Cleveland on July 17 against Al Smith and Jim Bagby, thanks to two spectacular plays by third baseman Ken Keltner. Then he hit in his next 16 games.

GAME	DATE	PITCHER	TEAM	AB	R	H	2B	3B	HR	RBI
1	May 15	Eddie Smith	Chi	4	0	1	0	0	0	1
2	May 16	Thornton Lee	Chi	4	2	2	0	1	1	1
3	May 17	Johnny Rigney	Chi	3	1	1	0	0	0	0
4	May 18	Bob Harris	StL	3	3	3	1	0	0	1
		Johnny Niggeling								
5	May 19	Denny Galehouse	StL	3	0	1	1	0	0	0
6	May 20	Elden Auker	StL	5	1	1	0	0	0	1
7	May 21	Schoolboy Rowe	Det	5	0	2	0	0	0	1
		Al Benton								
8	May 22	Archie McKain	Det	4	0	1	0	0	0	2
9	May 23	Dick Newsome	Bos	5	0	1	0	0	0	2
10	May 24	Earl Johnson	Bos	4	2	1	0	0	0	2
11	May 25	Lefty Grove	Bos	4	0	1	0	0	0	0
12	May 27	Ken Chase	Was	5	3	4	0	0	1	3
		Red Anderson								
		Alex Carrasquel								
13	May 28	Sid Hudson	Was	4	1	1	0	1	0	0
14	May 29	Steve Sundra	Was	3	1	1	0	0	0	0
15	May 30	Earl Johnson	Bos	2	1	1	0	0	0	0
16	May 30	Mickey Harris	Bos	3	0	1	1	0	0	0
17	June 1	Al Milnar	Cle	4	1	1	0	0	0	0
18	June 1	Mel Harder	Cle	4	0	1	0	0	0	0
19	June 2	Bob Feller	Cle	4	2	2	1	0	0	0
20	June 3	Dizzy Trout	Det	4	1	1	0	0	1	1
21	June 5	Hal Newhouser	Det	5	1	1	0	1	0	1
22	June 7	Bob Muncrief	StL	5	2	3	0	0	0	1
		Johnny Allen								
		George Caster								
23	June 8	Elden Auker	StL	4	3	2	0	0	2	4
24	June 8	George Caster	StL	4	1	2	1	0	1	3
		Jack Kramer								
25	June 10	Johnny Rigney	Chi	5	1	1	0	0	0	0
26	June 12	Thornton Lee	Chi	4	1	2	0	0	1	1
27	June 14	Bob Feller	Cle	2	0	1	1	0	0	1
28	June 15	Jim Bagby	Cle	3	1	1	0	0	1	1
29	June 16	Al Milnar	Cle	5	0	1	1	0	0	0
30	June 17	Johnny Rigney	Chi	4	1	1	0	0	0	0
31	June 18	Thornton Lee	Chi	3	0	1	0	0	0	0
32	June 19	Eddie Smith	Chi	3	2	3	0	0	1	2
		Buck Ross								
33	June 20	Bobo Newsome	Det	5	3	4	1	0	0	1
		Archie McKain								
34	June 21	Dizzy Trout	Det	4	0	1	0	0	0	1
35	June 22	Hal Newhouser	Det	5	1	2	1	0	1	2
		Bobo Newsom								
36	June 24	Bob Muncrief	StL	4	1	1	0	0	0	0
37	June 25	Denny Galehouse	StL	4	1	1	0	0	1	3
38	June 26	Elden Auker	StL	4	0	1	1	0	0	1
39	June 27	Chubby Dean	Phi	3	1	2	0	0	1	2
40	June 28	Johnny Babich	Phi	5	1	2	1	0	0	0
		Lum Harris								
41	June 29	Dutch Leonard	Was	4	1	1	1	0	0	0
42	June 29	Red Anderson	Was	5	1	1	0	0	0	1
43	July 1	Mickey Harris	Bos	4	0	2	0	0	0	1
		Mike Ryba								
44	July 1	Jack Wilson	Bos	3	1	1	0	0	0	1
45	July 2	Dick Newsome	Bos	5	1	1	0	0	1	3
46	July 5	Phil Marchildon	Phi	4	2	1	0	0	1	2
47	July 6	Johnny Babich	Phi	5	2	4	1	0	0	2
		Bump Hadley								
48	July 6	Jack Knott	Phi	4	0	2	0	1	0	2
49	July 10	Johnny Niggeling	StL	2	0	1	0	0	0	0
50	July 11	Bob Harris	StL	5	1	4	0	0	1	2
		Jack Kramer								
51	July 12	Elden Auker	StL	5	1	2	1	0	0	1
		Bob Muncrief								

Improbable DiMaggio (cont.)

GAME	DATE	PITCHER	TEAM	AB	R	H	2B	3B	HR	RBI
52	July 13	Ted Lyons	Chi	4	2	3	0	0	0	0
		Jack Hallett								
53	July 13	Thornton Lee	Chi	4	0	1	0	0	0	0
54	July 14	Johnny Rigney	Chi	3	0	1	0	0	0	0
55	July 15	Eddie Smith	Chi	4	1	2	1	0	0	2
56	July 16	Al Milnar	Cle	4	3	3	1	0	0	0
		Joe Krakauskas								

Yankees with Three Home Runs in a Single Game

PLAYER	DATE	TEAM
Tony Lazzeri	June 8, 1927	White Sox
	May 24, 1936	Athletics
Lou Gehrig	June 23, 1927	Red Sox
	May 4, 1929	White Sox
	May 22, 1930	Athletics
	June 3, 1932	Athletics (Four Home Runs)
Babe Ruth	May 21, 1930	Athletics
Ben Chapman	July 6, 1932	Tigers
Joe DiMaggio	June 13, 1937	Browns
	May 23, 1948	Indians
	September 10, 1950	Senators
Bill Dickey	July 26, 1939	Browns
Charlie Keller	July 28, 1940	White Sox
Johnny Mize	September 15, 1950	Tigers
Mickey Mantle	May 13, 1955	Tigers
Tom Tresh	June 6, 1965	White Sox
Bobby Murcer	June 24, 1970	Indians
	July 13, 1973	Royals
Cliff Johnson	June 30, 1977	Blue Jays
Mike Stanley	August 10, 1995	Indians
Paul O'Neill	August 31, 1995	Angels
Darryl Strawberry	August 6, 1996	White Sox
Tino Martinez	April 2, 1997	Mariners
Tony Clark	August 28, 2004	Blue Jays
Alex Rodriguez	April 26, 2005	Angels

Yankees Hitting for the Cycle

PLAYER	DATE	TEAM
Bert Daniels	July 25, 1912	White Sox
Bob Meusel	May 7, 1921	Senators
	July 3, 1922	Athletics
	July 26, 1928	Tigers
Tony Lazzeri	June 3, 1932	Athletics
Lou Gehrig	June 25, 1934	White Sox
Joe DiMaggio	July 9, 1937	Senators
Lou Gehrig	August 1, 1937	Browns
Buddy Rosar	July 19, 1940	Indians
Joe Gordon	September 8, 1940	Red Sox
Joe DiMaggio	May 20, 1948	White Sox
Mickey Mantle	July 23, 1957	White Sox
Bobby Murcer	August 29, 1972	Rangers
Tony Fernandez	September 3, 1995	Athletics

All-Time Yankees Grand Slam Leaders

PLAYER	GS
Lou Gehrig	23
Joe DiMaggio	13
Babe Ruth	12 (16 Career)
Bernie Williams	11

The Sultan of September

Babe Ruth was already having a remarkable season in 1927 when the calendar reached August 31. His team was in first place by 17 games with a .706 winning percentage (89–37) and he had 43 home runs. The Babe and the Yankees had a remarkable September. The Yanks won 20 times (in 27 games) to finish with 110 wins and a club-best .714 winning percentage. At the same time, the Babe launched a club-record 17 home runs for the magical sum of 60. Ruth had reached 59 in 1921, but even he was impressed with his new total that seemed more, well, Ruthian.

Roger Maris began his pursuit of 61 home runs slowly. He had just one at the end of April and 12 at the end of May. June was his month. He hit 14 in June—one of three straight months he reached double digits—to get in position to pass the Babe for both the single-season and club record. He hit nine in September, but the one he hit on October 1 put him ahead of the Babe. Ruth played in 151 of the Yankees' 155 games, while Maris wound up playing in 161 of his team's 163. Both seasons included a tie that was replayed. Below are the details of each home run Ruth and Maris hit in their historic record-setting months and seasons. (G1 and G2 stand for first and second games of doubleheaders, respectively; *italics* indicate road games.)

Babe Ruth, 60 Home Runs

HR	G	DATE	PITCHER	TEAM
1	4	April 15, 1927	Howard Ehmke	Athletics
2	*11*	*April 23, 1927*	*Rube Walberg*	*Athletics*
3	*12*	*April 24, 1927*	*Sloppy Thurston*	*Senators*
4	*14*	*April 29, 1927*	*Slim Harriss*	*Red Sox*
5	16	May 1, 1927	Jack Quinn	Athletics
6	16	May 1, 1927	Rube Walberg	Athletics
7	*24*	*May 10, 1927*	*Milt Gaston*	*Browns*
8	*25*	*May 11, 1927*	*Ernie Nevers*	*Browns*
9	*29*	*May 17, 1927*	*Rip Collins*	*Tigers*
10	*33*	*May 22, 1927*	*Ben Karr*	*Indians*
11	*34*	*May 23, 1927*	*Sloppy Thurston*	*Senators*
12	37	May 28, 1927	Sloppy Thurston	Senators
13	39	May 29, 1927	Danny MacFayden	Red Sox
14	*40*	*May 30, 1927*	*Rube Walberg*	*Athletics*
15	*42*	*May 31, 1927*	*Jack Quinn*	*Athletics*
16	*43*	*May 31, 1927*	*Howard Ehmke*	*Athletics*
17	47	June 5, 1927	Earl Whitehill	Tigers
18	48	June 7, 1927	Tommy Thomas	White Sox
19	52	June 11, 1927	Garland Buckeye	Indians
20	52	June 11, 1927	Garland Buckeye	Indians
21	53	June 12, 1927	George Uhle	Indians
22	55	June 16, 1927	Tom Zachary	Browns
23	*60*	*June 22, 1927*	*Hal Wiltse*	*Red Sox*
24	*60*	*June 22, 1927*	*Hal Wiltse*	*Red Sox*
25	70	June 30, 1927	Slim Harriss	Red Sox
26	*73*	*July 3, 1927*	*Hod Lisenbee*	*Senators*
27	*78*	*July 8, 1927*	*Don Hankins*	*Tigers*
28	*79*	*July 9, 1927*	*Ken Holloway*	*Tigers*
29	*79*	*July 9, 1927*	*Ken Holloway*	*Tigers*
30	*83*	*July 12, 1927*	*Joe Shaute*	*Indians*
31	*94*	*July 24, 1927*	*Tommy Thomas*	*White Sox*
32	95	July 26, 1927	Milt Gaston	Browns
33	95	July 26, 1927	Milt Gaston	Browns
34	98	July 28, 1927	Lefty Stewart	Browns
35	106	August 5, 1927	George S. Smith	Tigers
36	*110*	*August 10, 1927*	*Tom Zachary*	*Senators*
37	*114*	*August 16, 1927*	*Tommy Thomas*	*White Sox*
38	*115*	*August 17, 1927*	*Sarge Connally*	*White Sox*
39	*118*	*August 20, 1927*	*Jake Miller*	*Indians*
40	*120*	*August 22, 1927*	*Joe Shaute*	*Indians*
41	*124*	*August 27, 1927*	*Ernie Nevers*	*Browns*
42	*125*	*August 28, 1927*	*Ernie Wingard*	*Browns*
43	127	August 31, 1927	Tony Welzer	Red Sox
44	*128*	*September 2, 1927*	*Rube Walberg*	*Athletics*
45	*132*	*September 6, 1927*	*Tony Welzer*	*Red Sox*
46	*132*	*September 6, 1927*	*Tony Welzer*	*Red Sox*
47	*133*	*September 6, 1927*	*Jack Russell*	*Red Sox*
48	*134*	*September 7, 1927*	*Danny MacFayden*	*Red Sox*
49	*134*	*September 7, 1927*	*Slim Harriss*	*Red Sox*
50	138	September 11, 1927	Milt Gaston	Browns
51	139	September 13, 1927	Willis Hudlin	Indians
52	140	September 13, 1927	Joe Shaute	Indians
53	143	September 16, 1927	Ted Blankenship	White Sox
54	147	September 18, 1927	Ted Lyons	White Sox
55	148	September 21, 1927	Sam Gibson	Tigers
56	149	September 22, 1927	Ken Holloway	Tigers
57	152	September 27, 1927	Lefty Grove	Athletics

Babe Ruth, 60 Home Runs (cont.)

HR	G	DATE	PITCHER	TEAM
58	153	September 29, 1927	Hod Lisenbee	Senators
59	153	September 29, 1927	Paul Hopkins	Senators
60	154	September 30, 1927	Tom Zachary	Senators

Roger Maris, 61 Home Runs

HR	G	DATE	PITCHER	TEAM
1	*11*	*April 26, 1961*	*Paul Foytack*	*Tigers*
2	*17*	*May 3, 1961*	*Pedro Ramos*	*Twins*
3	*20*	*May 6, 1961*	*Eli Grba*	*Angels*
4	29	May 17, 1961	Pete Burnside	Senators
5	*30*	*May 19, 1961*	*Jim Perry*	*Indians*
6	*31*	*May 20, 1961*	*Gary Bell*	*Indians*
7	32	May 21, 1961	Chuck Estrada	Orioles
8	35	May 24, 1961	Gene Conley	Red Sox
9	38	May 28, 1961	Cal McLish	White Sox
10	*40*	*May 30, 1961*	*Gene Conley*	*Red Sox*
11	*40*	*May 30, 1961*	*Mike Fornieles*	*Red Sox*
12	*41*	*May 31, 1961*	*Billy Muffett*	*Red Sox*
13	*43*	*June 2, 1961*	*Cal McLish*	*White Sox*
14	*44*	*June 3, 1961*	*Bob Shaw*	*White Sox*
15	*45*	*June 4, 1961*	*Russ Kemmerer*	*White Sox*
16	48	June 6, 1961	Ed Palmquist	Twins
17	49	June 7, 1961	Pedro Ramos	Twins
18	52	June 9, 1961	Ray Herbert	Athletics
19	55	June 11, 1961	Eli Grba	Angels
20	55	June 11, 1961	Johnny James	Angels
21	*57*	*June 13, 1961*	*Jim Perry*	*Indians*
22	*58*	*June 14, 1961*	*Gary Bell*	*Indians*
23	*61*	*June 17, 1961*	*Don Mossi*	*Tigers*
24	*62*	*June 18, 1961*	*Jerry Casale*	*Tigers*
25	*63*	*June 19, 1961*	*Jim Archer*	*Athletics*
26	*64*	*June 20, 1961*	*Joe Nuxhall*	*Athletics*
27	*66*	*June 22, 1961*	*Norm Bass*	*Athletics*
28	74	July 1, 1961	Dave Sisler	Senators
29	75	July 2, 1961	Pete Burnside	Senators
30	75	July 2, 1961	Johnny Klippstein	Senators
31	77	July 4, 1961	Frank Lary	Tigers
32	78	July 5, 1961	Frank Funk	Indians
33	82	July 9, 1961	Bill Monbouquette	Red Sox
34	*84*	*July 13, 1961*	*Early Wynn*	*White Sox*
35	*86*	*July 15, 1961*	*Ray Herbert*	*White Sox*
36	*92*	*July 21, 1961*	*Bill Monbouquette*	*Red Sox*
37	95	July 25, 1961	Frank Baumann	White Sox
38	95	July 25, 1961	Don Larsen	White Sox
39	96	July 25, 1961	Russ Kemmerer	White Sox
40	96	July 25, 1961	Warren Hacker	White Sox
41	106	August 4, 1961	Camilo Pascual	Twins
42	*114*	*August 11, 1961*	*Pete Burnside*	*Senators*
43	*115*	*August 12, 1961*	*Dick Donovan*	*Senators*
44	*116*	*August 13, 1961*	*Bennie Daniels*	*Senators*
45	*117*	*August 13, 1961*	*Marty Kutyna*	*Senators*
46	118	August 15, 1961	Juan Pizarro	White Sox
47	119	August 16, 1961	Billy Pierce	White Sox
48	119	August 16, 1961	Billy Pierce	White Sox
49	*124*	*August 20, 1961*	*Jim Perry*	*Indians*
50	*125*	*August 22, 1961*	*Ken McBride*	*Angels*
51	*129*	*August 26, 1961*	*Jerry Walker*	*Athletics*
52	135	September 2, 1961	Frank Lary	Tigers
53	135	September 2, 1961	Hank Aguirre	Tigers
54	140	September 6, 1961	Tom Cheney	Senators
55	141	September 7, 1961	Dick Stigman	Indians
56	143	September 9, 1961	Mudcat Grant	Indians
57	*151*	*September 16, 1961*	*Frank Lary*	*Tigers*
58	*152*	*September 17, 1961*	*Terry Fox*	*Tigers*
59	*155*	*September 20, 1961*	*Milt Pappas*	*Orioles*
60	*159*	*September 26, 1961*	*Jack Fisher*	*Orioles*
61	163	October 1, 1961	Tracy Stallard	Red Sox

Postseason Performances

Not surprisingly, Yankees players own most World Series career records. Three players from the Yankees' 1950s and 1960s teams—Yogi Berra, Mickey Mantle, and Whitey Ford—dominate the list of the club's World Series record holders.

Hitting Records, World Series

RECORD	PLAYER	STAT
Most Series	Yogi Berra	14
Most Series, Winning Team	Yogi Berra	10
Most Series, Losing Team	Elston Howard*†	6
Most Games	Yogi Berra	75
Most At-Bats	Yogi Berra	259

Hitting Records, World Series (cont.)

RECORD	PLAYER	STAT
Most Runs	Mickey Mantle	40
Most Hits	Yogi Berra	71
Most Extra-Base Hits	Mickey Mantle	26
Most Total Bases	Mickey Mantle	123
Most Singles	Yogi Berra	49
Most Doubles	Yogi Berra*	10
Most Home Runs	Mickey Mantle	18
Most Consecutive Games with Home Runs	Lou Gehrig	4
	Reggie Jackson	4
Most RBI	Mickey Mantle	40
Most Walks	Mickey Mantle	43
Most Times Hit by Pitch	Yogi Berra†	3
	Elston Howard†	3

Hitting Records, World Series (cont.)

RECORD	PLAYER	STAT
Most Times Hit by Pitch *(cont.)*	Reggie Jackson†	3
	Derek Jeter†	3
Most Strikeouts	Mickey Mantle	54
Most Steals of Home	Bob Meusel	2
Most Positions Played	Babe Ruth*†	6
	Tony Kubek	6
	Elston Howard*†	6
Most Series, .300 or Higher Batter Average	Babe Ruth*	6
Highest Slugging Average	Reggie Jackson*	.755

Pitching Records, World Series

RECORD	PLAYER	STAT
Most Series	Whitey Ford	11
Most Series, Relief Pitchers	Johnny Murphy	6
	Mariano Rivera	6
Most Games	Whitey Ford	22
Most Games, Relief Pitchers	Mike Stanton*	20
	Mariano Rivera	20
Most Innings Pitched	Whitey Ford	146
Most Games Started	Whitey Ford	22
Most Wins	Whitey Ford	10
Most Losses	Whitey Ford	8
Most Saves	Mariano Rivera	9
Most Runs Allowed	Whitey Ford	51
Most Hits Allowed	Whitey Ford	132
Most Home Runs Allowed	Catfish Hunter*	9
Most Walks	Whitey Ford	34
Most Strikeouts	Whitey Ford	94

Ford Tough (to Score On)

Whitey Ford's record of 33 consecutive scoreless innings in World Series play has now stood longer than the previous record Babe Ruth established in 1918. Ford's record consisted primarily of five games between the 1960 and 1962 World Series. When San Francisco's Jose Pagan's two-out bunt scored Willie Mays in the second inning of Game 1 of the 1962 World Series, it was the first World Series run off Ford since he'd been knocked out of Game 6 of the 1958 World Series in the second inning. That game in San Francisco also turned out to be the last of his major league record 10 World Series wins. Here's how Ford and the Yankees fared during his streak.

DATE	GAME	TEAM	IP	H	R	ER	BB	SO	DEC
October 8, 1960	3	Pit	9	4	0	0	1	3	W, 10–0
October 12, 1960	6	Pit	9	7	0	0	1	6	W, 12–0
October 4, 1961	1	Cin	9	2	0	0	1	6	W, 2–0
October 8, 1961	4	Cin	5	4	0	0	0	1	W, 7–0
October 4, 1962	9	SF	9	10	2	2	2	6	W, 6–2

Yankees with Three Home Runs in a World Series Game

PLAYER	DATE	TEAM
Babe Ruth	October 10, 1926	St. Louis Cardinals
	October 9, 1928	St. Louis Cardinals
Reggie Jackson	October 18, 1977	Los Angeles Dodgers

The Bambino's Series Clouts

Before he became a fulltime outfielder, Babe Ruth set a long-standing mark of 29 consecutive innings without allowing a run in the World Series as a pitcher for the Red Sox. So when he started slugging full-time, it was only fitting that he continue to break new ground on baseball's big stage. Before 1923, when Ruth swatted three home runs in the seven-game World Series against the New York Giants to help the Yankees claim their first world championship, no one had ever hit more than two home runs in a World Series. In his next Series in 1926, he tied his own mark in one afternoon.

In Game 4 at Sportsman's Park, the Yankees trailed two games to one when Ruth stepped up against St. Louis hurler Flint Rhem in the first inning. The Babe slammed the first pitch over the right-field roof. He homered there again in the third inning. In the sixth he belted one with a man on to the bleachers in center against Hi Bell. Ruth came up in the eighth with a chance for his fourth home run, but Wild Bill Hallahan proved wise and walked him on four pitches, Ruth's second walk of the game. Although the Babe also homered in Game 7 at Yankee Stadium, he is better remembered for being thrown out stealing to end the Series and give the Cardinals their first world championship.

Two years and 211 New York wins later, the Yankees and Cardinals met again in the World Series. This time there was no fiddling around. The Yankees took the first three games in routine fashion yet trailed 2–1 after six innings of Game 4 at Sportsman's Park. Ruth, who'd accounted for the only run with a home run over the right-field pavilion, blasted another to the same spot to tie the game. Lou Gehrig, overshadowed by the man in front of him, followed with his fourth homer of the Series to drive in his ninth run (a Series first). In the eighth Ruth hit another on top of the pavilion, giving him a new record with nine runs and the club a new mark with nine homers in the Series. Sweeter still, it came off Grover Cleveland Alexander, the hero of the St. Louis' 1926 Series win over New York.

Ruth's consecutive scoreless innings string and his record of 15 World Series home runs would both last into the 1960s. Yankees Whitey Ford and Mantle would pass them, but no one has ever surpassed the Babe for flair.

Reggie! Reggie! Reggie!

Reggie Jackson's three home runs on three consecutive pitches against the Dodgers in Game 6 of the World Series on October 18, 1977, forever earned him the title of Mr. October. His last at bat in Game 5 in Los Angeles had also produced a home run. So, having walked on four straight balls in his first plate appearance of Game 6, Jackson actually hit home runs with four consecutive swings. Here are the details of the three home runs that have earned Reggie baseball immortality.

INNING	SITUATION	PITCHER	PITCH	LANDED
4	1 on, 0 out	Burt Hooton	Fastball	Right field
5	1 on, 2 out	Elias Sosa	Fastball	Right field
8	Leadoff	Charlie Hough	Knuckleball	Center field

Walk Away

Through 2006, there have been 14 game-ending or "walk off" home runs in World Series history. The Yankees have been involved in half of them. Four have come off their bats, and three have been the result of their pitches. When you play in 39 World Series, there's a lot that can happen in that last inning.

Tommy Henrich had the first such home run in the opener of the 1949 World Series against Brooklyn. While Bill Mazeroski's Series-clinching blast for Pittsburgh in 1960 is one of the most famous moments in baseball history, the most memorable from a Yankees point of view came off the bat of Derek Jeter against Arizona in Game 4 of the 2001 World Series. The home run was struck just after midnight on Halloween night (the Series was postponed a week as a result of the attack on the World Trade Center several weeks earlier). Jeter was immediately christened "Mr. November," but Tino Martinez's blast with two outs in the bottom of the ninth against Byung-Hyun Kim had set the stage for Jeter's deed. The next night Scott Brosius hit a game-tying homer in the ninth off Kim and the Yankees won in 12. That Series saw three games won in the last at bat, with the Diamondbacks getting last licks.

What follows is a list of the walk-off home runs in Yankees World Series history, the good and the bad.

YEAR	GAME	BATTER	PITCHER	SCORE	PLACE
1949	1	Tommy Henrich (NYY)	Don Newcombe (Bro)	1–0	Bronx
1957	4	Eddie Mathews (Mil)	Bob Grim (NYY)	7–5	Milwaukee
1960	7	Bill Mazeroski (Pit)	Ralph Terry (NYY)	10–9	Brooklyn
1964	3	Mickey Mantle (NYY)	Barney Schultz (StL)	2–1	Bronx
1999	3	Chad Curtis (NYY)	Mike Remlinger (Atl)	6–5	Bronx
2001	4	Derek Jeter (NYY)	Byung-Hyun Kim (Ari)	4–3	Bronx
2003	4	Alex Gonzalez (Fla)	Jeff Weaver (NYY)	4–3	Florida

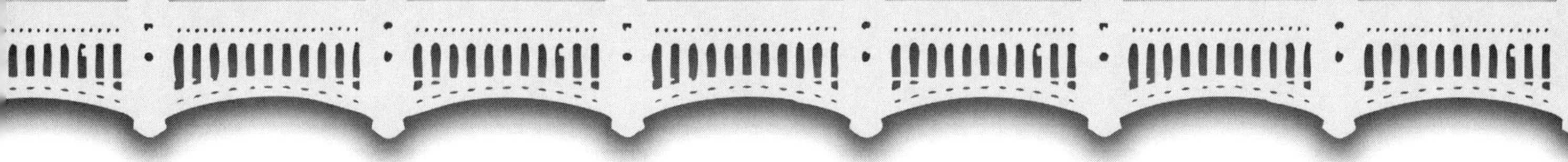

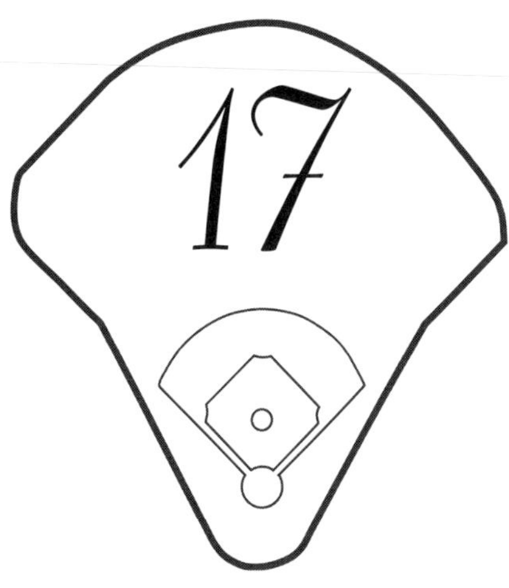

Yankee Stadium

The History of the Stadium in the Bronx

When Yankees owner Jacob Ruppert decided in 1920 that the time was right for the Yankees to build their own ballpark, his main instruction to the architects was that the stadium should be built like the city that would be its home: *big*. Ruppert knew that, for the Yankees to achieve the level of success he expected, the team had to take full advantage of its location in New York, the nation's most populous city.

The location selected for Yankee Stadium, in the Bronx just across the river from the Polo Grounds, was easily accessible to much of the city's population by way of a recently built subway line. Unlike most other big-league ballparks of the time, the Yankees' new home was not designed to be intimate. As the first three-tiered sports facility built in this country, it would not have been appropriate to name the place Yankee Field or Yankee Park; it could only be called Yankee *Stadium*.

When it opened, the new stadium seated 58,000, though many more people were sometimes crammed in for big games until stricter fire codes were enforced after World War II. No crowd anywhere near that size had ever attended a baseball game when the Stadium was being built, and many were skeptical that the Yankees could fill their new home. Yet the Yankees had already started outdrawing their landlords, the very popular New York Giants, and Ruppert was confident that his team would have enough drawing power to justify the enormous capacity. The reported crowd on Opening Day at Yankee Stadium—74,217—shattered all records. That figure may have been a little juiced, but the record-setting throngs of fans that showed up were quite real.

The field of Yankee Stadium was designed to enhance the new kind of baseball that Babe Ruth and his teammates had been demonstrating to the league. While Yankee Stadium today remains widely known by the nickname that writer Fred Lieb gave it, "The House that Ruth Built," wags have claimed from the beginning that a more appropriate nickname would be "The House that was Built for Ruth." Indeed, Yankee Stadium's right field corner was built to be a reachable target for Ruth at only 295 feet from home plate. Over Ruth's career, however, Yankee Stadium didn't help Ruth so much as it hurt right-handed power hitters and the teams that relied upon them: during Ruth's years with the Yankees at the Stadium, he hit 259 home runs at home and 252 on the road.

Yankee Stadium received its first round of renovations just after Ruth left when the second and third decks were extended further into right field and concrete bleachers replaced the old wooden bleachers. After Larry MacPhail took over the club in 1945, the stadium was further spruced up. Lights were added, greener grass was installed, the stadium was repainted, and a huge bar was constructed inside the stadium.

After MacPhail drank himself out of his job, Yankees co-owners Del Webb and Dan Topping decided that Yankee Stadium could serve another purpose besides hosting ballgames. As a result, the Stadium and the land it sat on became involved in a series of complicated financial dealings that enriched Webb and Topping even more. Thus, in 1953, the club sold Yankee Stadium to Arnold E. Johnson and leased it back. Two years later, Johnson was ready to purchase the Philadelphia Athletics and move them to Kansas City, and owning Yankee Stadium was a conflict of interest that threatened league approval of his purchase. So Johnson announced deals to sell the land on which Yankee Stadium resides to the Knights of Columbus, and then sell the Stadium itself to John Cox. Johnson was later questioned by Congress about the sale of the stadium to Cox, and the Kansas City Athletics owner told Congress that there was no contract written up for the sale because the deal was made on a handshake between two gentlemen.

Many observers were quite suspicious of Johnson's dealings, which was appropriate. The deals made between Johnson, the Yankees' owners, and others were often not what they were represented to be. Johnson's decade as the Athletics' owner has become best known for the way in which the corrupt A's served the dynastic Yankees as something like an unofficial Quadruple-A farm club.

John Cox proceeded to donate his ownership rights to Yankee Stadium to Rice University so, when CBS bought the Yankees from Topping and Webb in 1964, neither the Stadium nor the land came as part of the deal. Despite not owning the land or stadium, CBS did spend $1.5 million after the 1966 season on repainting and new seats. In general, though, ownership had not worked to keep up the physical plant in good condition since Larry MacPhail left, and CBS was not interested in spending any more money on a stadium it didn't own in a deteriorating neighborhood.

That dynamic ultimately changed for several reasons. New York City had already seen two baseball clubs leave town, and no mayor wanted to be held responsible for another team leaving. In addition, CBS was able to point out the benefits of coming to the aid of the network's team. New York City was in deep trouble financially, but it nevertheless committed to solving the Yankees' stadium problems. In early 1971, Mayor John Lindsay obligated the city to spend $24 million on the acquisition and renovation of Yankee Stadium. As a first step, the city used eminent domain to acquire ownership of the Stadium and the land beneath it from Rice University and the Knights of Columbus, reportedly paying the two entities a combined $3.5 million. The city then proceeded to launch an aggressive plan, not only to renovate but also to partially reconstruct Yankee Stadium. The Yankees played in Shea Stadium for two seasons while construction crews worked on the unprecedented rebuilding.

The most important goal of the project was to remove all 118 columns in the stadium in order to improve the views from seats that had always been partially obstructed. Because of that, much of the grandstand and concourses had to be rebuilt to compensate for the loss of those support columns. The extensive renovations brought many other changes to the historic ballpark as well. The distinctive frieze on top of the stadium was removed, the size of fair territory was reduced, Monument Park was moved outside the playing field, and as much as half the bleacher seating was eliminated. Every seat was replaced, elevators were installed, and a new parking garage was built across the street to make suburban ticket holders feel more comfortable when coming to the Stadium by car.

The exact cost of the rebuilding of Yankee Stadium is unknown. Nevertheless, it's safe to say that the city and state ended up spending far, far more than the $24 million that was originally proposed, perhaps as much as six times that amount. While the structure of the stadium was successfully rebuilt, though, the new Yankee Stadium did not have the impact that the city and the Yankees had hoped for. By the mid-1980s, George Steinbrenner was threatening to move the Yankees to New Jersey. Steinbrenner continued the complaints of previous owners, that the South Bronx neighborhood around the Stadium kept too many fans away from games. The reality that the heavy police presence on game nights probably made the area the safest place in the city didn't prevent Steinbrenner from scaring fans away with his complaints.

In 1993, the Yankees stepped up their lobbying for a new ballpark. Three years later, New York City Mayor Rudolph Giuliani, a devoted Yankees fan, proposed building a new domed stadium for the Yankees on the West Side of Manhattan. Despite Giuliani's support, New York City politicians were unwilling to build a new home for the Yankees free of charge on the West Side, or anywhere else. Eventually, the Yankees realized that their future was in the Bronx and, in July 2004, announced a proposal for a new Yankee Stadium adjacent to the current one.

In June 2005, a complicated deal was reached with the city for a new Yankee Stadium. While the Yankees are bearing most of the billion-dollar-plus costs, the city is pitching in by paying for expensive new infrastructure such as a new commuter rail station near Yankee Stadium—something that the Yankees have been lobbying for since the historic Stadium opened in 1923.

The "Yankee Stadium"—in reality, two different structures on the same site—that fans have known since 1923 will be torn down after the 2008 season, having hosted 74 seasons of big-league baseball.

The Original Yankee Stadium in Brief

Owned by: New York Yankees (1923–1953); Arnold M. Johnson (Land 1953, Stadium 1953–1955); Knights of Columbus (Land 1953–1971); John W. Cox (Stadium 1955–1962); Rice University (Stadium 1962–1971); New York City (1971–1973)

Designed by: Osborn Engineering

Cost to Build: $2.5 million

Paid for: by Yankees

Opening Capacity: 58,000

Highest Capacity: 71,699

Final Capacity: 65,010

Original Outfield Dimensions: 281–395–460–490–429–370–295

Final Outfield Dimensions: 301–402–457–463–407–344–296

Fence Heights: 3.92′–7.83′/13.83′/7.83′–3.75′

Distance to Backstop: 82 ft. (as of 1942)

Altitude: 20 ft.

Home Opener: April 18, 1923 (Yankees 4, Red Sox 1)

Final Game: September 30, 1973 (Tigers 8, Yankees 5)

Major Renovations: In 1928, the second and third decks were extended into left field. In 1937, permanent concrete bleachers were constructed while the second and third decks were stretched into right field. Lights were installed on May 28, 1946.

Unique Features: First triple-decked stadium in the major leagues. The copper frieze on the stadium's roof was the stadium's most distinctive feature, while the short right-field porch was probably the stadium's most talked about feature.

Other Tenants: NFL New York Yankees (1927–1928); NFL New York Yanks (1950–1951); NFL New York Giants (1956–1973); AAFC New York Yankees (1946–1949); USA New York Skyliners (1967); NPSL New York Generals (1967); NASL New York Generals (1968), New York Cosmos (1971)

Other Events: Whitney M. Young Urban League Classic (1971–1973); New York University, Army, Notre Dame, Fordham, and Grambling College football; Professional soccer; Boxing (including 29 championship fights); Religious Gatherings (Jehovah's Witnesses Conventions and services led by Cardinal Spellman, Pope Paul VI, and Billy Graham)

Historic Moments: September 24, 1925: With the Yankees down by three in the bottom of the 10th inning, Babe Ruth hits a grand slam to win the ballgame; November 12, 1928: Coach Knute Rockne coaxes his Army football team to "win one for the Gipper" against Notre Dame; July 4, 1939: Lou Gehrig bids farewell to the Yankees and their fans, explaining to a packed Yankee Stadium that "Today, I consider myself the luckiest man on the face of the earth"; July 2, 1941: Joe DiMaggio hits a three-run homer to extend his hitting streak to 45 games, breaking Wee Willie Keeler's record; April 27, 1949: On Babe Ruth Day, Ruth hoarsely tells fans that "the only real game in the world is baseball"; October 5, 1947: Al Gionfriddo goes "back, back, back, back, back, back" and "makes a one-handed catch against the bullpen!" saving the Game 6 of the World Series for the Dodgers; August 17–18, 1951: More than 100,000 people come to see Babe Ruth's body in the days after his death; September 28, 1951: Allie Reynolds pitches his second no-hitter of the season on the same day that Joe DiMaggio hits the final home run of his career; August 25, 1952: Virgil Trucks pitches his second no-hitter of the season for the Tigers, but only after shortstop Johnny Pesky convinces the official scorer that an earlier hit should be ruled an error on Pesky; June 21, 1955: Mickey Mantle becomes the first player to ever reach the center field bleachers with a home run; December 28, 1958: After eight minutes of sudden death overtime, Alan Ameche rushes into the end zone for the winning touchdown as the Colts win the NFL Championship over the Giants in front of a riveted national television audience; October 1, 1961: Roger Maris hits his 61st home run of the season off Tracy Stallard, thus breaking Babe Ruth's single season record; May 14, 1967: Mickey Mantle launches home run No. 500 off Orioles pitcher Stu Miller.

World Series Hosted: 1923, 1926, 1927, 1928, 1932, 1936, 1937, 1938, 1939, 1941, 1942, 1943, 1947, 1949, 1950, 1951, 1952, 1953, 1954, 1955, 1956, 1957, 1958, 1960, 1961, 1962, 1963, and 1964, 1976, 1977, 1978, 1981, 1996, 1998, 1999, 2000, 2001, and 2003

All-Star Games Hosted: 1939, 1960 (G2), and 1977

Lowest Season Attendance: 618,330 (1943)

Highest Season Attendance: 2,373,901 (1948)

Largest Crowd: 81,841 (doubleheader against Boston on May 30, 1938)

Public Address Announcers: Jack Lenz, George Levy, Arthur 'Red' Patterson, Bob Sheppard (1951–1973)

Perfect Game: October 10, 1956 (Don Larsen of the Yankees against the Dodgers during the World Series)

Last Regular Season No-Hitter: August 25, 1952 (Virgil Trucks of the Tigers)

Longest Game, Innings: August 29, 1967 (G2) vs. Red Sox (20 innings)

Most Home Runs by a Player, Career: 266 (Mickey Mantle)

Retired Numbers: No. 1 (Billy Martin), No. 3 (Babe Ruth), No. 4 (Lou Gehrig), No 5 (Joe DiMaggio), No. 7 (Mickey Mantle), Nos. 8 (Bill Dickey and Yogi Berra)

Average Ticket Prices, 1950: $1.69

Average Ticket Price, 1960: $2.12

Average Ticket Price, 1970: $2.42

The Current Yankee Stadium in Brief

Owned by: New York City
Renovated Stadium Designed by: Prager-Kavanaugh-Waterbury
Cost of Renovations: $160 Million
Renovations Paid for: by New York City
Original Capacity: 54, 028
Current Capacity: 57,478
Original Outfield Dimensions: 312–387–430–417–385–353–310
Current Outfield Dimensions 318–379–399–408–385–353–314
Original Fence Heights: 8′–8′/7′/7′–10′
Current Fence Heights: 8′–7.5′/7.33′/7.33′–9′
Current Distance to Backstop: 84 ft.
Altitude: 20 ft.
Home Opener: April 15, 1976 (Yankees 11, Twins 4)
Other Tenants: NASL New York Cosmos (1976)

Other Events: Whitney M. Young Urban League Classic (1976–1987); New York University and Grambling College football; Ali vs. Norton Heavyweight Championship Bout; Religious Gatherings (Jehovah's Witnesses Conventions and a mass said by Pope John Paul II); Youth World Assembly Day; Concerts (Isley Brothers, Billy Joel, U2, Pink Floyd); Nelson Mandela visit; 1994 Unity Games closing ceremonies; and A Prayer For America service for 9/11 victims

Historic Moments: October 18, 1977: Reggie Jackson blasts a towering 475-foot home run off Dodgers pitcher Charlie Hough into the black center field seats for his third home run in Game 6 of the World Series; June 24, 1983: Umpire Tim McClelland disallows George Brett's go-ahead home run in the ninth inning because of excessive pine tar on Brett's bat, triggering one of the most celebrated controversies in baseball history; August 18, 1983: the "Pine Tar Game" resumes, thanks to AL President Lee MacPhail overruling McClelland, as Kansas City quickly finished off the Yankees for the victory; August 4, 1985: Tom Seaver leads the White Sox to a 4–1 win over the Yankees for his 300th career victory; September 17, 1993: Lee Smith pitches the final inning of a 5–4 Yankees victory over the Red Sox and becomes the fifth pitcher ever to earn 300 saves; June 13, 2003: Roger Clemens posts win No. 300 by pitching the Yankees to a 5–2 victory over the Cardinals; July 17, 2006: Mariano Rivera shuts down the White Sox for the last two innings of a 6–4 Yankees victory and becomes the fourth pitcher ever to earn 400 saves.

World Series Hosted: 1976, 1977, 1978, 1981, 1996, 1998, 1999, 2000, 2001, and 2003

Other Postseason Series (type) Hosted: 1976 (LCS), 1977 (LCS), 1978 (LCS), 1980 (LCS), 1981 (Divisional playoffs, LCS), 1996 (DS, LCS), 1997 (DS), 1998 (DS, LCS), 1999 (DS, LCS), 2000 (DS, LCS), 2001 (DS, LCS), 2002 (DS), 2003 (DS, LCS), 2004 (DS, LCS), 2005 (DS), 2006 (DS), 2007 (DS)

All-Star Games Hosted: 1977 and 2008 (scheduled)
Lowest Season Attendance: 1,748,733 (1992)
Highest Season Attendance: 4,243,780 (2006)
Largest Crowd, Regular Season: April 10, 1998, 56,717
Largest Crowd, Postseason: October 7, 1999 vs. Texas (Game 2 of 1999 ALDS), 57,485
Smallest Crowd: 413 (September 22, 1966 vs. Red Sox)
Public Address Announcer: Bob Sheppard (1976-Present)
Perfect Games: May 17, 1998 (David Wells against the Twins); July 18, 1999 (David Cone against the Expos; Don Larsen threw out the first pitch)
Last No-Hitter: July 18, 1999 (David Cone against the Expos)
Most Home Runs by a Player, Career: 143 (Bernie Williams)
Longest 9-Inning Game, Time: August 18, 2006 vs. Boston (4:46)
Longest Game, Innings: August 25, 1976 vs. Twins (19 Innings)

Retired Numbers: No. 1 (Billy Martin), No. 3 (Babe Ruth), No. 4 (Lou Gehrig), No. 5 (Joe DiMaggio), No. 7 (Mickey Mantle), Nos. 8 (Bill Dickey and Yogi Berra), No. 9 (Roger Maris), No. 10 (Phil Rizzuto), No. 15 (Thurman Munson), No 16 (Whitey Ford), No. 23 (Don Mattingly), No. 32 (Elston Howard), No. 37 (Casey Stengel), No. 44 (Reggie Jackson), No. 49 (Ron Guidry)

Average Ticket Price, 1980: $6.17
Average Ticket Price, 1991: $10.54
Average Ticket Price, 2002: $24.26

Yankees Home Park Effects

The table below shows park factors for all years for the Yankees. The (pre-Yankees) Highlanders played in Hilltop Park, a notorious bandbox, from 1903–12. Because the club wasn't very good back then, no one paid much attention to the park and its existence has been largely forgotten by Yankees fans. The Yankees moved to the Polo Grounds in 1913, but were evicted when Babe Ruth and pennant-winning clubs meant they started to outdraw their landlords, the New York Giants. The Polo Grounds was a good park for hitting home runs, showing about double the league average. However, it was only about average for scoring, since any ball that did not go into the stands near the foul lines was liable to be caught.

Yankee Stadium was opened in 1923 and remodeled in 1974–75. The Yanks moved across town to Shea Stadium for two years while the Stadium in the Bronx was being rebuilt, so the 1974–75 factors represent the Yankees playing at Shea. The original Yankee Stadium was somewhat more pitcher-friendly than the new version.

Categories shown here are games, wins, losses, ties, runs and opponent runs, and home runs and opponents' home runs. All are shown for the Yankees' home park, for away games, and are also totaled. Then a number of ratings are created, all normalized to 100. For batters, a rating above 100 indicates better-than-average hitting. For pitchers, a rating below 100 (i.e., less scoring) shows above-average pitching.

The ratings abbreviations and explanations are:

HRF is the park's Home Run Factor;
HRB is the team Batting Home Run rating, taking into account the home-run factor;
HRP is the team Pitching Home Run rating, taking into account the home-run factor;
RF is the park Run Factor;
RB is the team Batting Run rating, after compensating for the home park;
RP is the team Pitching Run rating, after compensating for the home park;
BPF is the Batting Park Factor, adjusted for the team's Run ratings and allowing for the fact that half their games are played at home; and
PPF is the Pitching Park Factor, adjusted for the team's Run ratings and allowing for the fact that half their games are played at home.

All of these factors compensate for the team's batters and pitchers not having to face each other, so the pitching staff of a high-scoring team actually ends up with a slightly below-average level for the remaining teams. Each decade also has an average HRF, RF, BPF, and PPF shown.

For example, the 1939 Yankees, one of the greatest teams of all-time, actually outperformed the famous 1927 bunch. Who knows what they would have done if Lou Gehrig hadn't become ill? After compensating for their 75 park factor (25% below the norm, which is very hostile to hitters), the '39 Bombers' batters were rated at 133. The '39 Yankees' pitchers ended up at 84. That means their batters were 33% above average and the pitchers 16% better; the team outscored its opponents by an unbelievable 411 runs. In 1927, the comparable factors were 128 for the batters and 94 for the pitchers, with an enormous run differential of 376.

	HOME								ROAD								TOTAL															
YEAR	G	W	L	T	R	OR	HR	OHR	G	W	L	T	R	OR	HR	OHR	G	W	L	T	R	OR	HR	OHR	HRF	HRB	HRP	RF	RB	RP	BPF	PPF
1903	67	41	26	0	301	269	10	6	69	31	36	2	278	304	8	13	136	72	62	2	579	573	18	19	81	88	87	101	104	103	100	100
1904	75	46	29	0	321	288	22	25	80	46	30	4	277	238	5	4	155	92	59	4	598	526	27	29	357	63	61	124	97	87	112	111
1905	75	40	35	0	316	303	15	16	77	31	43	3	270	319	8	10	152	71	78	3	586	622	23	26	161	94	107	107	103	109	102	103
1906	76	53	23	0	398	294	14	8	79	37	38	4	246	249	3	13	155	90	61	4	644	543	17	21	137	79	108	139	94	82	120	118
1907	75	33	40	2	331	372	10	7	77	37	38	2	274	293	5	6	152	70	78	4	605	665	15	13	147	93	86	123	100	109	109	110
1908	77	30	47	0	234	352	11	16	78	21	56	1	225	361	2	10	155	51	103	1	459	713	13	26	194	57	126	100	90	132	95	101
1909	77	41	35	1	338	263	11	9	76	33	42	1	252	324	5	12	153	74	77	2	590	587	16	21	114	118	154	103	113	113	99	99
1910	77	49	25	3	343	284	13	7	79	39	38	2	283	273	7	9	156	88	63	5	626	557	20	16	125	94	81	114	103	93	107	106
1911	77	36	40	1	365	422	14	14	76	40	36	0	319	302	11	12	153	76	76	1	684	724	25	26	117	94	97	121	88	92	111	111
																									159			115			106	107
1912	76	31	44	1	352	423	14	16	77	19	58	0	278	419	4	12	153	50	102	1	630	842	18	28	168	67	111	109	91	118	101	105
1913	75	27	47	1	265	339	5	20	78	30	47	1	264	329	3	11	153	57	94	2	529	668	8	31	166	32	109	104	87	107	101	104
1914	78	36	40	2	278	259	8	24	79	34	44	1	259	291	4	6	157	70	84	3	537	550	12	30	252	42	83	99	94	96	100	100
1915	82	37	43	2	306	303	28	32	72	32	40	0	278	285	3	9	154	69	83	2	584	588	31	41	307	64	105	95	98	98	98	98
1916	79	46	31	2	306	277	22	22	77	34	43	0	271	284	13	15	156	80	74	2	577	561	35	37	144	183	194	102	99	97	101	101
1917	75	35	40	0	269	292	19	24	80	36	42	2	255	266	8	4	155	71	82	2	524	558	27	28	282	97	81	112	87	92	107	107
1918	67	37	29	1	251	237	10	22	59	23	34	2	242	238	10	3	126	60	63	3	493	475	20	25	189	148	130	91	114	110	94	94
1919	73	46	25	2	326	255	33	30	68	34	34	0	252	251	12	17	141	80	59	2	578	506	45	47	180	107	118	107	94	85	106	104
																									211			102			101	102
1920	77	49	28	0	424	308	71	36	77	46	31	0	414	321	44	12	154	95	59	0	838	629	115	48	173	189	83	101	112	87	102	99
1921	78	53	25	0	500	355	83	34	75	45	30	0	448	353	51	17	153	98	55	0	948	708	134	51	155	176	75	104	118	91	103	99
1922	77	50	27	0	387	291	53	48	77	44	33	0	371	327	42	25	154	94	60	0	758	618	95	73	143	123	95	99	102	85	101	99
1923	76	46	30	0	407	329	62	50	76	52	24	0	416	293	43	18	152	98	54	0	823	622	105	68	168	152	97	105	109	85	104	101
1924	78	45	32	1	397	324	57	46	75	44	31	0	401	343	41	13	153	89	63	1	798	667	98	59	167	158	91	95	106	90	99	97
1925	79	42	36	1	354	356	54	56	77	27	49	1	352	418	56	22	156	69	85	2	706	774	110	78	131	149	104	91	91	98	96	97
1926	75	50	25	0	417	326	58	33	80	41	38	1	430	387	63	23	155	91	63	1	847	713	121	56	112	222	117	98	116	100	99	97
1927	77	57	19	1	479	267	83	30	78	53	25	0	496	332	75	12	155	110	44	1	975	599	158	42	129	251	79	94	128	84	100	94
1928	77	52	25	0	400	301	69	36	77	49	28	0	494	384	64	23	154	101	53	0	894	685	133	59	119	205	103	83	133	105	92	89
1929	77	49	28	0	463	362	69	55	77	39	38	0	436	413	73	28	154	88	66	0	899	775	142	83	120	180	111	98	118	104	99	97
																									142			97			100	97
1930	76	47	29	0	471	390	69	54	78	39	39	0	591	508	83	39	154	86	68	0	1062	898	152	93	104	184	122	83	142	123	90	87
1931	77	51	25	1	545	337	84	39	78	43	34	1	522	423	71	28	155	94	59	2	1067	760	155	67	123	194	95	96	137	102	98	93
1932	77	62	15	0	482	300	81	44	79	45	32	2	520	424	79	49	156	107	47	2	1002	724	160	93	102	180	115	88	129	97	95	91
1933	75	51	23	1	421	324	79	26	77	40	36	1	506	444	65	40	152	91	59	2	927	768	144	66	103	186	96	83	134	114	91	88
1934	77	53	24	0	416	275	75	34	77	41	36	0	426	394	60	37	154	94	60	0	842	669	135	71	112	145	84	87	112	91	96	93
1935	74	41	33	0	341	294	60	51	75	48	27	0	477	338	44	40	149	89	60	0	818	632	104	91	130	114	102	82	115	93	93	90
1936	77	56	21	0	492	311	82	41	78	46	30	2	573	420	100	43	155	102	51	2	1065	731	182	84	90	201	106	85	128	92	95	90
1937	79	57	20	2	520	298	94	41	78	45	32	1	459	373	80	51	157	102	52	3	979	671	174	92	103	168	98	99	117	84	102	97
1938	79	55	22	2	524	342	112	43	78	44	31	3	442	368	62	42	157	99	53	5	966	710	174	85	141	125	70	106	109	83	105	102

	HOME								ROAD								TOTAL															
YEAR	G	W	L	T	R	OR	HR	OHR	G	W	L	T	R	OR	HR	OHR	G	W	L	T	R	OR	HR	OHR	HRF	HRB	HRP	RF	RB	RP	BPF	PPF
1939	77	52	25	0	382	261	84	48	75	54	20	1	585	295	82	37	152	106	45	1	967	556	166	85	109	160	90	75	133	84	91	85
																									112			88			96	92
1940	76	52	24	0	414	284	83	63	79	36	42	1	403	387	72	56	155	88	66	1	817	671	155	119	117	132	105	93	108	90	99	96
1941	78	51	26	1	396	295	76	44	78	50	27	1	434	336	75	37	156	101	53	2	830	631	151	81	108	157	92	92	114	90	98	95
1942	77	58	19	0	394	226	62	39	77	45	32	0	407	281	46	32	154	103	51	0	801	507	108	71	127	144	101	93	123	82	99	94
1943	77	54	23	0	321	241	60	33	78	44	33	1	348	301	40	27	155	98	56	1	669	542	100	60	136	144	94	90	115	96	96	94
1944	78	47	31	0	388	307	58	45	76	36	40	0	286	310	38	37	154	83	71	0	674	617	96	82	129	156	139	112	100	94	106	105
1945	76	48	28	0	395	297	65	51	76	33	43	0	281	309	28	15	152	81	71	0	676	606	93	66	220	111	70	113	106	97	107	106
1946	77	47	30	0	342	262	68	34	77	40	37	0	342	285	68	32	154	87	67	0	684	547	136	66	102	163	88	97	109	90	100	98
1947	77	55	22	0	392	242	54	49	78	42	35	1	402	326	61	46	155	97	57	1	794	568	115	95	99	140	119	91	128	95	97	92
1948	77	50	27	0	413	315	70	54	77	44	33	0	444	318	69	40	154	94	60	0	857	633	139	94	113	151	107	97	118	90	100	96
1949	78	54	23	1	419	304	72	53	77	43	34	0	410	333	43	45	155	97	57	1	829	637	115	98	135	100	89	98	114	91	100	97
																									129			98			100	97
1950	77	53	24	0	440	333	78	51	78	45	32	1	474	358	81	67	155	98	56	1	914	691	159	118	91	138	106	96	118	92	99	96
1951	78	56	22	0	366	258	72	43	76	42	34	0	432	363	68	49	154	98	56	0	798	621	140	92	98	134	93	80	123	98	91	88
1952	77	49	28	0	345	264	64	48	77	46	31	0	382	293	65	46	154	95	59	0	727	557	129	94	102	130	99	92	115	91	98	95
1953	77	50	27	0	347	255	64	39	74	49	25	0	454	292	75	55	151	99	52	0	801	547	139	94	80	143	101	81	128	93	93	88
1954	78	54	23	1	388	274	68	42	77	49	28	0	417	289	65	44	155	103	51	1	805	563	133	86	101	126	86	95	125	92	99	94
1955	77	52	25	0	378	248	89	44	77	44	33	0	384	321	86	64	154	96	58	0	762	569	175	108	91	153	100	91	114	88	98	94
1956	77	49	28	0	412	303	88	48	77	48	29	0	445	328	102	66	154	97	57	0	857	631	190	114	84	152	98	95	121	93	99	95
1957	77	48	29	0	316	241	60	51	77	50	27	0	407	293	85	59	154	98	56	0	723	534	145	110	80	123	98	83	118	91	94	90
1958	78	44	33	1	362	318	78	62	77	48	29	0	397	259	86	54	155	92	62	1	759	577	164	116	100	122	91	103	114	90	103	99
1959	77	40	37	0	293	305	63	45	78	39	38	1	394	342	90	75	155	79	75	1	687	647	153	120	69	131	104	84	109	104	93	92
																									90			90			97	93
1960	77	55	22	0	350	273	92	52	78	42	35	1	396	354	101	71	155	97	57	1	746	627	193	123	88	150	102	87	116	100	94	92
1961	81	65	16	0	411	251	112	59	82	44	37	1	416	361	128	78	163	109	53	1	827	612	240	137	87	166	101	89	117	88	96	93
1962	80	50	30	0	369	306	92	67	82	46	36	0	448	374	107	79	162	96	66	0	817	680	199	146	90	135	102	86	121	103	94	92
1963	80	58	22	0	367	246	88	55	81	46	35	0	347	301	100	60	161	104	57	0	714	547	188	115	93	128	83	98	108	85	101	98
1964	81	50	31	0	363	290	69	56	83	49	32	2	367	287	93	73	164	99	63	2	730	577	162	129	80	113	92	103	106	86	103	101
1965	83	40	43	0	320	306	77	63	79	37	42	0	291	298	72	63	162	77	85	0	611	604	149	126	99	109	93	101	95	94	101	101
1966	82	35	46	1	302	280	74	63	78	35	43	0	309	332	88	61	160	70	89	1	611	612	162	124	88	126	100	87	105	105	94	94
1967	82	43	38	1	268	271	60	47	81	29	52	0	254	350	40	63	163	72	90	1	522	621	100	110	102	81	89	89	92	107	94	96
1968	82	39	42	1	268	268	56	50	82	44	37	1	268	263	53	49	164	83	79	2	536	531	109	99	104	95	87	101	95	94	101	101
1969	80	48	32	0	284	245	44	51	82	32	49	1	278	342	50	67	162	80	81	1	562	587	94	118	84	73	90	88	89	92	95	96
																									92			93			97	96
1970	81	53	28	0	317	257	60	40	82	40	41	1	363	355	51	90	163	93	69	1	680	612	111	130	74	89	96	83	109	98	92	91
1971	81	44	37	0	327	297	39	61	81	38	43	0	321	344	58	65	162	82	80	0	648	641	97	126	83	85	109	94	107	106	97	97
1972	77	46	31	0	270	219	53	37	78	33	45	0	287	308	50	50	155	79	76	0	557	527	103	87	92	109	92	85	113	106	92	92
1973	81	50	31	0	359	263	74	42	81	30	51	0	282	347	57	67	162	80	82	0	641	610	131	109	94	103	86	99	92	88	101	100
1974	81	47	34	0	315	295	42	50	81	42	39	0	356	328	59	54	162	89	73	0	671	623	101	104	83	95	99	90	106	99	96	95
1975	78	43	35	0	331	283	50	56	82	40	42	0	350	305	60	48	160	83	77	0	681	588	110	104	103	88	83	99	98	86	101	100
1976	80	45	35	0	349	294	67	51	79	52	27	0	381	281	53	46	159	97	62	0	730	575	120	97	117	120	100	97	115	93	99	97
1977	81	55	26	0	412	305	84	63	81	45	36	0	419	346	100	76	162	100	62	0	831	651	184	139	86	137	106	95	115	92	98	97
1978	81	55	26	0	358	275	68	59	82	45	37	0	377	307	57	52	163	100	63	0	735	582	125	111	118	94	84	95	109	87	99	97
1979	81	51	30	0	360	308	77	59	79	38	41	0	374	364	73	64	160	89	71	0	734	672	150	123	98	106	88	90	103	95	96	95
																									95			93			97	96
1980	81	53	28	0	409	315	91	47	81	50	31	0	411	347	98	55	162	103	59	0	820	662	189	102	92	147	83	97	113	93	99	98
1981	51	32	19	0	203	154	47	24	56	27	29	0	218	189	53	40	107	59	48	0	421	343	100	64	85	142	92	97	96	79	100	99
1982	81	42	39	0	346	338	73	55	81	37	44	0	363	378	88	58	162	79	83	0	709	716	161	113	88	113	81	93	101	102	96	97
1983	81	51	30	0	398	323	67	55	81	40	41	0	372	380	86	61	162	91	71	0	770	703	153	116	85	120	94	97	108	99	99	98
1984	81	51	30	0	372	292	62	49	81	36	45	0	386	387	68	71	162	87	75	0	758	679	130	120	81	101	92	87	113	101	94	93
1985	80	58	22	0	411	288	92	67	81	39	42	0	428	372	84	90	161	97	64	0	839	660	176	157	94	118	105	90	120	95	96	94
1986	80	41	39	0	384	396	93	96	82	49	33	0	413	342	95	79	162	90	72	0	797	738	188	175	111	110	102	106	104	96	103	103
1987	81	51	30	0	401	346	98	88	81	38	43	0	387	412	98	91	162	89	73	0	788	758	196	179	99	104	96	94	102	98	98	97
1988	80	46	34	0	378	345	77	75	81	39	42	0	394	403	71	82	161	85	76	0	772	748	148	157	101	110	116	93	115	111	96	95
1989	81	41	40	0	373	419	64	88	80	33	47	0	325	373	66	62	161	74	87	0	698	792	130	150	115	101	114	111	97	109	104	105
																									95			97			99	98
1990	81	37	44	0	296	361	64	78	81	30	51	0	307	388	83	66	162	67	95	0	603	749	147	144	95	119	117	94	90	110	97	98
1991	81	39	42	0	356	380	82	84	81	32	49	0	318	397	65	68	162	71	91	0	674	777	147	152	122	95	99	102	92	105	101	102
1992	81	41	40	0	385	387	88	70	81	35	46	0	348	359	75	59	162	76	86	0	733	746	163	129	116	119	96	108	101	103	104	104
1993	81	50	31	0	389	342	88	85	81	38	43	0	432	419	90	85	162	88	74	0	821	761	178	170	99	122	117	87	115	107	94	93
1994	57	33	24	0	291	260	63	62	56	37	19	0	379	274	76	58	113	70	43	0	670	534	139	120	93	114	100	85	121	99	93	92
1995	73	46	26	1	411	323	69	76	72	33	39	0	338	365	53	83	145	79	65	1	749	688	122	159	105	76	98	103	100	93	102	102
1996	80	49	31	0	448	374	76	76	82	43	39	0	423	413	86	67	162	92	70	0	871	787	162	143	102	80	71	101	98	89	101	101
1997	80	47	33	0	399	333	75	71	82	49	33	0	492	355	86	73	162	96	66	0	891	688	161	144	95	92	83	90	116	91	96	94
1998	81	62	19	0	472	314	97	74	81	52	29	0	493	342	110	82	162	114	48	0	965	656	207	156	92	120	93	97	119	83	100	97
1999	81	48	33	0	411	323	84	74	81	50	31	0	489	408	109	84	162	98	64	0	900	731	193	158	84	110	92	84	115	95	93	91
																									100			95			98	97
2000	80	44	36	0	454	412	117	92	81	43	38	0	417	402	88	85	161	87	74	0	871	814	205	177	121	96	85	107	99	93	104	103
2001	80	51	28	1	423	331	116	82	81	44	37	0	381	382	87	76	161	95	65	1	804	713	203	158	122	102	82	101	102	91	101	100
2002	80	52	28	0	434	339	108	78	81	51	30	0	463	358	115	66	161	103	58	0	897	697	223	144	105	123	82	97	117	93	99	97
2003	82	50	32	0	401	368	106	76	81	51	29	1	476	348	124	69	163	101	61	1	877	716	230	145	95	130	85	94	113	94	98	96
2004	81	57	24	0	446	372	126	89	81	44	37	0	451	436	116	93	162	101	61	0	897	808	242	182	104	128	98	94	114	104	97	96
2005	81	53	28	0	477	381	126	80	81	42	39	0	409	408	103	84	162	95	67	0	886	789	229	164	110	125	93	106	113	102	102	102
2006	81	50	31	0	450	354	111	85	81	47	34	0	480	413	99	85	162	97	65	0	930	767	210	170	107	112	92	92	122	102	96	95
2007	81	52	29	0	520	382	107	81	81	42	39	0	448	395	94	69	162	94	68	0	968	777	201	150	115	116	88	107	118	97	104	102
																									110			100			100	99

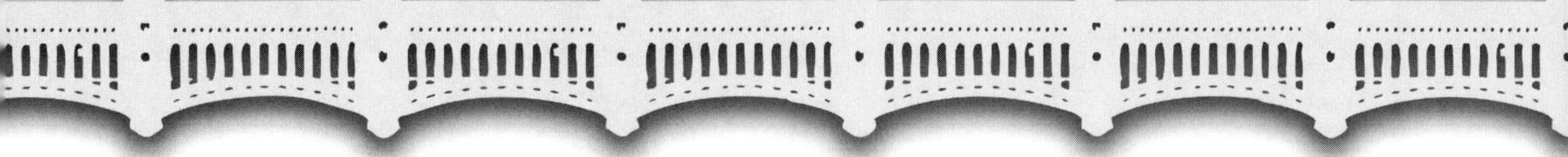

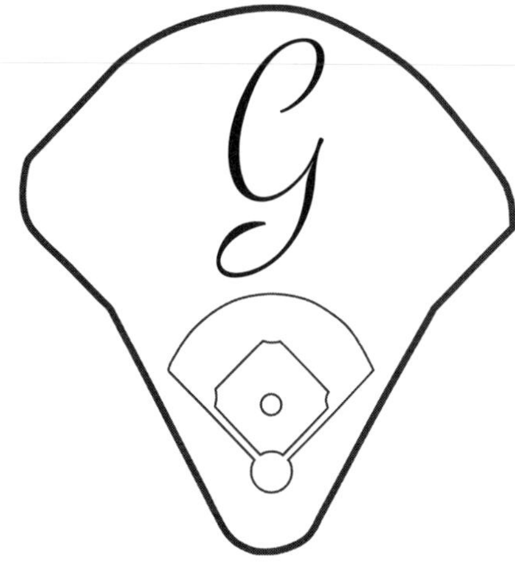

Glossary

Average Value The analytical statistics in this book almost always use the league average as a baseline. The use of this baseline, which in this book is always set to equal zero, enables readers to quickly see whether the performance being measured is above-average, below-average, and how much above or below. Above-average players are needed to win pennants; below-average players can only make limited contributions to their teams because their efforts, by definition, lead teams to losing. Examples: Zero (0) means average, *+10* would be 10% above average, and *–20* would be 20 percent below average. Note that, for batters, league averages do not include pitcher batting.

Basestealing Runs The basic formula for BSR is (.22 times Stolen Bases) minus (.35 times Caught Stealings).

Basestealing Wins Basestealing Runs divided by Runs per Win, which varies by year but is usually in the neighborhood of 10. The actual number is equal to 10 times the square root of the combined number of runs scored by both teams per inning, which is usually around 1.

Batter-Fielder Wins The sum of a player's Batting Wins, Basestealing Wins, and Fielding Wins.

Batting Runs The basic formula for BR is .33 times (BB plus HBP), plus (.47 times Hits), plus (.38 times Doubles), plus (.55 times Triples), plus (.93 times Home Runs), minus *x* times (At-Bats –Hits), where *x* is a factor to make the league average come out at zero (normally around .25 to .30).

Batting Wins Batting Runs divided by Runs per Win, which varies by year but is usually about 10.

Blown Saves The number of Save Opportunities not converted by the relief pitcher into Saves because he allowed the tying run to score. This statistic has only been compiled back to 1969, when the modern save was first defined.

Caught Stealing This statistic is not available for any year prior to 1914 and is not always available for the years 1914–1951.

Differential The measure of the difference between how many games the team was projected to win (based on its hitting, pitching, fielding, and baserunning performances), and how many games the team actually won. It is shown the same way as teams measure how many games they are behind in the standings.

Earned Run Average The number of earned runs allowed per 9 innings pitched. The formula for its calculation is (Earned Runs times 9) divided by Innings Pitched. The formula for Adjusted ERA is (League ERA times Park Factor) divided by ERA.

Fielding Runs Fielding Runs are an estimate of the number of runs saved by a fielder compared to an average player at his position. There is a different formula for every position.

Fielding Wins Fielding Runs divided by Runs per Win.

Games Behind (or Ahead) The number of games one team is behind (or ahead) of another team in the standings. In this volume, it is usually used when referring to how far a team is out of first place or how far a team in first place is ahead of its rival or rivals. If the Red Sox are 83–66, the Yankees are 72–76, and the Devil Rays are 60–89, the Red Sox are 10½ games in front of the Yankees and 23 games ahead of the Devil Rays, the

Yankees are 10½ games behind the Red Sox and 12½ games ahead of the Devil Rays, and the Devil Rays are 23 games behind the Red Sox and 12½ games behind the Yankees.

Normalizing Most baseball statistics need to be placed in context to be properly understood. A .467 slugging average in Yankee Stadium in 1965 means something very different than a .467 slugging average in Fenway Park in 2005—the former is a far more impressive performance than the latter. By normalizing a statistic and setting the baseline to zero, readers can easily compare players across leagues and eras simply by comparing the percentage by which players over- or underperformed their peers.

On-Base Percentage OBP is currently defined as (Hits plus Bases on Balls plus Hit-by-Pitches) divided by (At Bats plus Bases on Balls plus Hit-by-Pitches plus Sacrifice Flies). This volume uses that definition from 1954 on, but sacrifice fly data is not available in previous years, so it is not used in calculating the statistic in earlier years.

OPS The sum of on-base percentage and slugging average was first introduced in the 1984 book *The Hidden Game of Baseball.* Its popularity has increased greatly in recent years because it is easy to calculate when OBP and SLG are available and because it provides an easy-to-understand raw measurement of offensive production. Adjusted OPS measures the percentage by which a player's offensive production is better or worse than that of his peers. The formula for AOPS is 100 times (Player OBP divided by League OBP) plus (Player SLG divided by League SLG)) – 200. Thus a player with OBP and SLG equal to the league average will have a rating of 0 (100 x 2 – 200).

Park Factor This measure of how the team's home park affects hitters and pitchers is used to adjust performance to take into account the context of the team's home park. Separate park factors are used for batting and pitching in order to adjust for the fact that pitchers and hitters never get to face their own teammates.

Pitching Runs The number of runs a pitcher saves or allows compared to a league average pitcher. The basic formula for Pitching Runs is (League ERA times Innings Pitched) minus Earned Runs. The Pitching Runs calculations in this book include an additional factor that takes Unearned Runs into account.

Pitcher Wins The total number of wins a pitcher is worth to his team compared to the average pitcher, including his pitching, his fielding, and his batting and basestealing (if any).

Pitching Wins The wins a pitcher achieves for his team above and below that of a league average pitcher *while pitching.* It is calculated by dividing Adjusted Pitcher Runs by Runs per Win and then adjusting the result for the impact of his innings (since the innings of relief pitchers can have more impact on team wins and losses than the same number of innings from starters).

Positional Adjustment Value in baseball is determined by the scarcity of talent: it is a lot harder to find a shortstop who can hit 20 home runs per year than a first baseman that can hit 20 homers. Therefore, when calculating the overall value of a player, he is compared to other players at his position.

Quality Relief A QR is a relief appearance in which a pitcher allows less than one run for every two innings pitched. Inherited runners are counted only in excess of their expected rates of scoring, based on the bases occupied and number of outs, while runners left for the next pitcher are counted at the expected scoring rates, regardless of what actually happens. Note that the QR statistic was developed because the most commonly used stat to evaluate setup pitchers, the Hold, only applies when a reliever is brought into the game in a Save Situation. Thus, it inappropriately applies a measurement designed for closers to middle relievers, who don't get many chances to finish the game and earn the Save. For more information on the research behind QR, see *MapleStreetPress.com.*

Quality Starts A QS is any start in which a pitcher throws at least six innings and does not allow more than three earned runs.

Run Support Run support is calculated by adding up all the runs scored in a pitcher's starts, dividing that total by his games started, adjusting that result for the context of his league and home park, and then setting the baseline to zero. The reason to count all runs scored by a pitcher's team is that a pitcher's won-lost record can obviously be affected by runs scored long after he leaves the game. (Note that this definition is different than most published run support numbers, which simply take the number of runs scored by a pitcher's team while he was in the game and normalize to nine innings pitched.)

Save The Save rule has been changed several times since it was first instituted in 1969. The current definition was adopted in 1975; it awards a Save if a relief pitcher finishes off a victory—and is not the winning pitcher—in three different situations:

1) He enters with a lead of no more than three runs and pitches at least one inning;
2) He enters with the tying run at bat, on-base, or on-deck; or
3) He pitches at least three innings effectively.

For the years before the Save became an official statistic, the original 1969 rule was retroactively applied. That simpler and much easier standard awarded a Save to any pitcher who finished off a win and did not get credit for the victory.

Stolen Bases The current definition of a Stolen Base has been used since 1955. Previously, the rules specifying when a Stolen Base was credited to a baserunner had been changed numerous times.

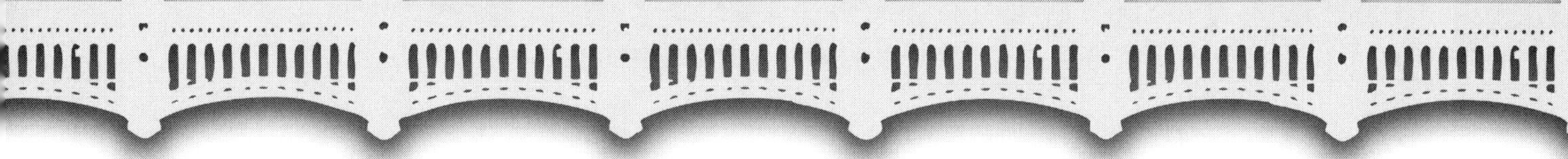

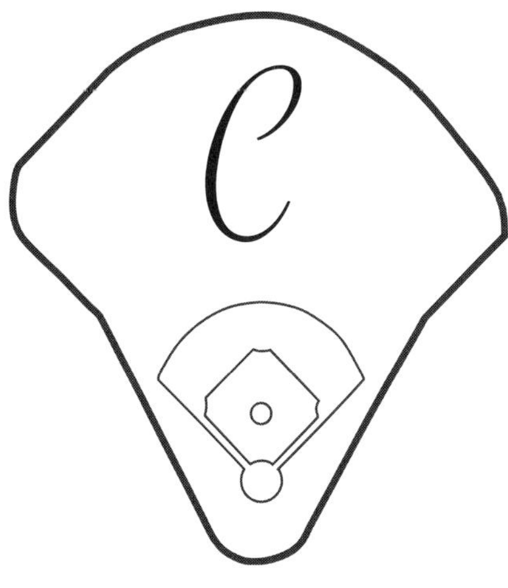

Contributors

Gary Gillette is the co-editor and the creative force behind two groundbreaking sports encyclopedias: *The ESPN Baseball Encyclopedia*—the fifth edition of which will be published in 2008—and the *ESPN Pro Football Encyclopedia*, now in its second edition. A nationally known baseball author and analyst, he has authored, edited, or contributed to dozens of baseball books and periodicals. Gillette is president of 24–7 Baseball, L.L.C. and co-chair of the Society for American Baseball Research's Business of Baseball Committee.

Gillette's recent projects include editing *Tigers Corner 2007*, a new annual from Maple Street Press that was published in March. He is working on a new Tigers encyclopedia for Maple Street called *The Ultimate Tigers Companion* as well as on a history of big-league ballparks, entitled *Diamonds in the Grass*, which will be published by Sterling in 2008. Gillette was also a baseball columnist for *ESPN.com*'s MLB Insider in 2005–06.

A member of the board of directors of the Old Tiger Stadium Conservancy, Gillette is actively involved in the effort to save and redevelop the historic ballpark structure and the site at Michigan and Trumbull in Detroit. He is also a member of the Sports Panel Council (electors) of the National Polish-American Sports Hall of Fame. Gillette lives in the Indian Village neighborhood on the East Side of Detroit with Vicki, his wife of 33 seasons, and their two children, Karolina and Kamil.

Pete Palmer is the co-editor of *The ESPN Baseball Encyclopedia* and *The ESPN Pro Football Encyclopedia*. Palmer also co-authored *The Hidden Game of Baseball*, co-edited *Total Baseball* (editions one through seven) and *Who's Who in Baseball*, and is a contributor to *The Sporting News MLB Fact Book* and *The Sporting News Record Book*. Inventor of on-base plus slugging, now universally used as a good measure of batting strength, he also discovered the concept of 10 runs per win (i.e., an increase of 10 runs scored or a decrease of 10 runs allowed results is about one extra win). Palmer developed other seminal analytical concepts, linear weights and player and pitcher wins. He was a member of the board of directors of Project Scoresheet, a grass roots organization set up to collect play-by-play information for current games, and is a contributor to Retrosheet.

Palmer has been a member of SABR since 1973 and was chairman of the Statistical Analysis Committee for 15 years (1974–88). He was given the Bob Davids Award, SABR's highest honor, in 1989. He was editor of the original *Barnes Official Encyclopedia of Baseball* from 1975–79; served as a consultant to Sports Information Center, the official statisticians for the American League from 1976–87; and introduced on-base percentage as an official AL stat in 1979.

Lucky enough to be in attendance at Fenway Park at Ted Williams' last game in Boston on September 28, 1960, Palmer has been blessed by his marriage to Beth Statz, the grand-niece of 1920 Red Sox outfielder Jigger Statz—regarded as the best player in Pacific Coast League history. They live in Hollis, New Hampshire, and Highland Beach, Florida, with their three children: Emily, Daniel, and Stephen.

Stuart Shea is the editor of Maple Street Press' annual Chicago Cubs preview *Wrigley Season Ticket*. He is an associate editor of *The ESPN Baseball Encyclopedia*, published by Sterling. Shea is the author of four books, including *Fab Four FAQ: Everything Left to Know About the Beatles . . . and More!* and *Wrigley Field: The Unauthorized Biography*. Shea and Gary Gillette have also co-authored three baseball annuals.

Along with best-selling author James Finn Garner, Shea is co-founder of Bardball, an online, reader-driven site collecting baseball poetry and doggerel at *Bardball.com*. A music aficionado, freelance editor, guitarist, record collector, and disc jockey, Shea lives in Chicago with his wife Cecila Garibay. He can be found in cyberspace at *www.stuartshea.blogspot.com*.

Matthew Silverman is author of *Mets Essential* for Triumph Books in 2007, and is co-author with Jon Springer for the forthcoming *Mets by the Numbers* with Skyhorse Publishing and co-editor with Greg Spira for *Meet the Mets* by Maple Street Press. He is the managing editor of *The ESPN Pro Football Encyclopedia* and has been an associate editor for *The ESPN Baseball Encyclopedia* since 2004.

As associate publisher at Total Sports Publishing, he served as principal editor for *Baseball: The Biographical Encyclopedia*. He was also managing editor for the sixth and seventh editions of *Total Baseball* and the second edition of *Total Football*. He has edited several other books, including *Total Packers, Total Cowboys, Total Super Bowl*, and two versions of *Total Mets*. He was managing editor for *The Ultimate Red Sox Companion* for Maple Street Press in 2007. This is the first book he has worked on about Yankees history—although he did play for a team by that name at Iona Grammar School in New Rochelle, New York, and he was at Yankee Stadium for the clinching game of the 1999 World Series. He resides in High Falls, New York, with his wife, Debbie, daughter, Jan, and son, Tyler.

Greg Spira is a writer, editor, and researcher residing in Kingston, N.Y. He has served as an associate editor on all five editions of *The ESPN Baseball Encyclopedia* and the two editions of *The ESPN Pro Football Encyclopedia*. He also co-edited the *USA Today Sports Weekly's Best Baseball Writing 2005*. Spira has contributed articles about baseball to a variety of books, including *Baseball Prospectus* and *Wrigley Season Ticket 2007*.

Along with Matthew Silverman—with whom Spira has collaborated on both Maple Street Press' *Ultimate Red Sox Companion* and this volume—Spira will co-edit Maple Street Press' upcoming book, *Meet the Mets*. Earlier, Spira worked as an editor for Total Sports Publishing and served as an associate editor on the seventh edition of *Total Baseball* while also contributing to books such as *Baseball: The Biographical Encyclopedia* and *Total Basketball*. Spira has been a member of the Society for Baseball Research for more than 15 years. As an Internet denizen since the early 1990s, he has contributed to many web sites both editorially and conceptually. *BaseballBooks.net*, a web site he maintains, focuses on sports books. Spira grew up in Whitestone, New York, and graduated with a degree in history from Harvard College.

Cecilia Tan is the editor of Maple Street Press' *Bombers Broadside*, an annual look at the New York Yankees, as well as the author of *The 50 Greatest Yankee Games*. She is a Senior Writer for *Gotham Baseball* magazine and writes weekly about the Yankees for the web site *GothamBaseball.com*. Her contributions have appeared in *Yankees Magazine, Baseball Ink, Baseball Savvy, Mudville*, and elsewhere.

Tan has co-edited and contributed to several books on the Red Sox, including *The Fenway Project, '75: The Red Sox Team that Saved Baseball*, and *The Impossible Dream 1967 Red Sox*. She was the co-author of *The 50 Greatest Red Sox Games*. Tan is a member of the Society for American Baseball Research (SABR) and the Association for Women in Sports Media (AWSM).

Doug White is a college baseball umpire and an associate editor of *The ESPN Baseball Encyclopedia* who has been writing about baseball since 1996. He has contributed to many publications, including *The Great American Baseball Stat Book, The Scouting Report*, and *The USA Today Baseball Weekly Insider*. A contributing editor to *Total Baseball Daily*, he now covers the Reds for *MLB.com*. He also writes for John Benson's annual *Rotisserie League Baseball* scouting book and *Rotisserie Baseball Annual*. White umpires college and semi-pro baseball. He and his wife, Anita, live in Muncie, Indiana, with their children Aaron, Sarah, and Katherine.